D1372106

The Dictionary of Art · volume thirteen

The Dictionary of Art

EDITOR Jane Turner

13

Goodnough

TO

Habsburg, §I: Austrian branch

GROVE

An imprint of Oxford University Press

Oxford University Press

Oxford New York
Auckland Bangkok Buenos Aires Cape Town Chennai
Dar es Salaam Delhi Hong Kong Istanbul Karachi Kolkata
Kuala Lumpur Madrid Melbourne Mexico City Mumbai Nairobi
São Paulo Shanghai Taipei Tokyo Toronto

Published by Oxford University Press, Inc.
198 Madison Avenue, New York, New York 10016
www.oup-usa.org

ISBN 0-19-517068-7

The Dictionary of Art, edited by JANE TURNER, was published in thirty-four volumes
in 1996 by Macmillan Publishers Limited

Text keyboarded by Wearset Limited, Sunderland, England
Database management by Pindar plc, York, England
Imagesetting by William Clowes Limited, Suffolk, England
Printed and bound by China Translation and Printing Services Ltd. , Hong Kong

Contents

General Abbreviations vi

A Note on the Use of *The Dictionary* xii

The Dictionary, volume thirteen:
Goodnough–Habsburg, §I: Austrian branch 1

Illustration Acknowledgements 923

General Abbreviations

The abbreviations employed throughout this dictionary, most of which are listed below, do not vary, except for capitalization, regardless of the context in which they are used, including bibliographical citations and for locations of works of art. The principle used to arrive at these abbreviations is that their full form should be easily deducible, and for this reason acronyms have generally been avoided (e.g. Los Angeles Co. Mus. A. instead of LACMA). The same abbreviation is adopted for cognate forms in foreign languages and in most cases for plural and adjectival forms (e.g. A.= Art, Arts, Arte, Arti etc). Not all related forms are listed below. Occasionally, if a name, for instance of an artists' group or exhibiting society, is repeated within the text of one article, it is cited in an abbreviated form after its first mention in full (e.g. The Pre-Raphaelite Brotherhood (PRB) was founded...); the same is true of archaeological periods and eras, which are abbreviated to initial letters in small capitals (e.g. In the Early Minoan (EM) period...). Such abbreviations do not appear in this list. For the reader's convenience, separate full lists of abbreviations for locations, periodical titles and standard reference books and series are included as Appendices A–C in vol. 33.

A.	Art, Arts
A.C.	Arts Council
Acad.	Academy
AD	Anno Domini
Add.	Additional, Addendum
addn	addition
Admin.	Administration
Adv.	Advances, Advanced
Aesth.	Aesthetic(s)
Afr.	African
Afrik.	Afrikaans, Afrikaner
A.G.	Art Gallery
Agrar.	Agrarian
Agric.	Agriculture
Agron.	Agronomy
Agy	Agency
AH	Anno Hegirae
A. Inst.	Art Institute
AK	Alaska (USA)
AL	Alabama (USA)
Alb.	Albanian
Alg.	Algerian
Alta	Alberta (Canada)
Altern.	Alternative
a.m.	ante meridiem [before noon]
Amat.	Amateur
Amer.	American
An.	Annals
Anatol.	Anatolian
Anc.	Ancient
Annu.	Annual
Anon.	Anonymous(ly)
Ant.	Antique
Anthol.	Anthology
Anthropol.	Anthropology
Antiqua.	Antiquarian, Antiquaries
app.	appendix
approx.	approximately
AR	Arkansas (USA)
ARA	Associate of the Royal Academy
Arab.	Arabic
Archaeol.	Archaeology
Archit.	Architecture, Architectural
Archv, Archvs	Archive(s)
Arg.	Argentine
ARHA	Associate of the Royal Hibernian Academy
ARIBA	Associate of the Royal Institute of British Architects
Armen.	Armenian
ARSA	Associate of the Royal Scottish Academy
Asiat.	Asiatic
Assist.	Assistance
Assoc.	Association
Astron.	Astronomy
AT&T	American Telephone & Telegraph Company
attrib.	attribution, attributed to
Aug	August
Aust.	Austrian
Austral.	Australian
Auth.	Author(s)
Auton.	Autonomous
Aux.	Auxiliary
Ave.	Avenue
AZ	Arizona (USA)
Azerbaij.	Azerbaijani
B.	Bartsch [catalogue of Old Master prints]
b	born
BA	Bachelor of Arts
Balt.	Baltic
bapt	baptized
BArch	Bachelor of Architecture
Bart	Baronet
Bask.	Basketry
BBC	British Broadcasting Corporation
BC	Before Christ
BC	British Columbia (Canada)
BE	Buddhist era
Beds	Bedfordshire (GB)
Behav.	Behavioural
Belarus.	Belarusian
Belg.	Belgian
Berks	Berkshire (GB)
Berwicks	Berwickshire (GB; old)
BFA	Bachelor of Fine Arts
Bibl.	Bible, Biblical
Bibliog.	Bibliography, Bibliographical
Biblioph.	Bibliophile
Biog.	Biography, Biographical
Biol.	Biology, Biological
bk, bks	book(s)
Bkbinder	Bookbinder
Bklore	Booklore
Bkshop	Bookshop
BL	British Library
Bld	Build
Bldg	Building

Bldr	Builder
BLitt	Bachelor of Letters/Literature
BM	British Museum
Boh.	Bohemian
Boliv.	Bolivian
Botan.	Botany, Botanical
BP	Before present (1950)
Braz.	Brazilian
BRD	Bundesrepublik Deutschland [Federal Republic of Germany (West Germany)]
Brecons	Breconshire (GB; old)
Brez.	Brezonek [lang. of Brittany]
Brit.	British
Bros	Brothers
BSc	Bachelor of Science
Bucks	Buckinghamshire (GB)
Bulg.	Bulgarian
Bull.	Bulletin
bur	buried
Burm.	Burmese
Byz.	Byzantine
C	Celsius
C.	Century
c.	*circa* [about]
CA	California
Cab.	Cabinet
Caerns	Caernarvonshire (GB; old)
C.A.G.	City Art Gallery
Cal.	Calendar
Callig.	Calligraphy
Cam.	Camera
Cambs	Cambridgeshire (GB)
can	canonized
Can.	Canadian
Cant.	Canton(s), Cantonal
Capt.	Captain
Cards	Cardiganshire (GB; old)
Carib.	Caribbean
Carms	Carmarthenshire (GB; old)
Cartog.	Cartography
Cat.	Catalan
cat.	catalogue
Cath.	Catholic
CBE	Commander of the Order of the British Empire
Celeb.	Celebration
Celt.	Celtic
Cent.	Centre, Central
Centen.	Centennial
Cer.	Ceramic
cf.	confer [compare]
Chap., Chaps	Chapter(s)
Chem.	Chemistry
Ches	Cheshire (GB)
Chil.	Chilean
Chin.	Chinese
Christ.	Christian, Christianity
Chron.	Chronicle
Cie	Compagnie [French]
Cinema.	Cinematography
Circ.	Circle
Civ.	Civil, Civic
Civiliz.	Civilization(s)
Class.	Classic, Classical
Clin.	Clinical
CO	Colorado (USA)
Co.	Company; County
Cod.	Codex, Codices
Col., Cols	Collection(s); Column(s)
Coll.	College
collab.	in collaboration with, collaborated, collaborative
Collct.	Collecting
Colloq.	Colloquies
Colomb.	Colombian
Colon.	Colonies, Colonial
Colr	Collector
Comm.	Commission; Community
Commerc.	Commercial
Communic.	Communications
Comp.	Comparative; compiled by, compiler
Concent.	Concentration
Concr.	Concrete
Confed.	Confederation
Confer.	Conference
Congol.	Congolese
Congr.	Congress
Conserv.	Conservation; Conservatory
Constr.	Construction(al)
cont.	continued
Contemp.	Contemporary
Contrib.	Contributions, Contributor(s)
Convalesc.	Convalescence
Convent.	Convention
Coop.	Cooperation
Coord.	Coordination
Copt.	Coptic
Corp.	Corporation, Corpus
Corr.	Correspondence
Cors.	Corsican
Cost.	Costume
Cret.	Cretan
Crim.	Criminal
Crit.	Critical, Criticism
Croat.	Croatian
CT	Connecticut (USA)
Cttee	Committee
Cub.	Cuban
Cult.	Cultural, Culture
Cumb.	Cumberland (GB; old)
Cur.	Curator, Curatorial, Curatorship
Curr.	Current(s)
CVO	Commander of the [Royal] Victorian Order
Cyclad.	Cycladic
Cyp.	Cypriot
Czech.	Czechoslovak
$	dollars
d	died
d.	denarius, denarii [penny, pence]
Dalmat.	Dalmatian
Dan.	Danish
DBE	Dame Commander of the Order of the British Empire
DC	District of Columbia (USA)
DDR	Deutsche Demokratische Republik [German Democratic Republic (East Germany)]
DE	Delaware (USA)
Dec	December
Dec.	Decorative
ded.	dedication, dedicated to
Democ.	Democracy, Democratic
Demog.	Demography, Demographic
Denbs	Denbighshire (GB; old)
dep.	deposited at
Dept	Department
Dept.	Departmental, Departments
Derbys	Derbyshire (GB)
Des.	Design
destr.	destroyed
Dev.	Development
Devon	Devonshire (GB)
Dial.	Dialogue
diam.	diameter
Diff.	Diffusion
Dig.	Digest
Dip. Eng.	Diploma in Engineering
Dir.	Direction, Directed
Directrt	Directorate
Disc.	Discussion
diss.	dissertation
Distr.	District
Div.	Division
DLitt	Doctor of Letters/Literature
DM	Deutsche Mark
Doc.	Document(s)
Doss.	Dossier
DPhil	Doctor of Philosophy
Dr	Doctor
Drg, Drgs	Drawing(s)
DSc	Doctor of Science/Historical Sciences
Dut.	Dutch
Dwell.	Dwelling
E.	East(ern)

EC European (Economic) Community
Eccles. Ecclesiastical
Econ. Economic, Economies
Ecuad. Ecuadorean
ed. editor, edited (by)
edn edition
eds editors
Educ. Education
e.g. *exempli gratia* [for example]
Egyp. Egyptian
Elem. Element(s), Elementary
Emp. Empirical
Emul. Emulation
Enc. Encyclopedia
Encour. Encouragement
Eng. English
Engin. Engineer, Engineering
Engr., Engrs Engraving(s)
Envmt Environment
Epig. Epigraphy
Episc. Episcopal
Esp. Especially
Ess. Essays
est. established
etc *etcetera* [and so on]
Ethnog. Ethnography
Ethnol. Ethnology
Etrus. Etruscan
Eur. European
Evangel. Evangelical
Exam. Examination
Excav. Excavation, Excavated
Exch. Exchange
Excurs. Excursion
exh. exhibition
Exp. Exposition
Expermntl Experimental
Explor. Exploration
Expn Expansion
Ext. External
Extn Extension
f, ff following page, following pages
F.A. Fine Art(s)
Fac. Faculty
facs. facsimile
Fam. Family
fasc. fascicle
fd feastday (of a saint)
Feb February
Fed. Federation, Federal
Fem. Feminist
Fest. Festival
fig. figure (illustration)
Fig. Figurative
figs figures
Filip. Filipina(s), Filipino(s)
Fin. Finnish
FL Florida (USA)
fl *floruit* [he/she flourished]
Flem. Flemish
Flints Flintshire (GB; old)
Flk Folk
Flklore Folklore
fol., fols folio(s)
Found. Foundation
Fr. French
frag. fragment
Fri. Friday
FRIBA Fellow of the Royal Institute of British Architects
FRS Fellow of the Royal Society, London
ft foot, feet
Furn. Furniture
Futur. Futurist, Futurism
g gram(s)
GA Georgia (USA)
Gael. Gaelic
Gal., Gals Gallery, Galleries
Gaz. Gazette
GB Great Britain
Gdn, Gdns Garden(s)
Gdnr(s) Gardener(s)
Gen. General
Geneal. Genealogy, Genealogist
Gent. Gentleman, Gentlemen
Geog. Geography
Geol. Geology
Geom. Geometry
Georg. Georgian
Geosci. Geoscience
Ger. German, Germanic
G.I. Government/General Issue (USA)
Glams Glamorganshire (GB; old)
Glos Gloucestershire (GB)
Govt Government
Gr. Greek
Grad. Graduate
Graph. Graphic
Green. Greenlandic
Gr.-Roman Greco-Roman
Gt Great
Gtr Greater
Guat. Guatemalan
Gym. Gymnasium
h. height
ha hectare
Hait. Haitian
Hants Hampshire (GB)
Hb. Handbook
Heb. Hebrew
Hell. Hellenic
Her. Heritage
Herald. Heraldry, Heraldic
Hereford & Worcs Hereford & Worcester (GB)
Herts Hertfordshire (GB)
HI Hawaii (USA)
Hib. Hibernia
Hisp. Hispanic
Hist. History, Historical
HMS His/Her Majesty's Ship
Hon. Honorary, Honourable
Horiz. Horizon
Hort. Horticulture
Hosp. Hospital(s)
HRH His/Her Royal Highness
Human. Humanities, Humanism
Hung. Hungarian
Hunts Huntingdonshire (GB; old)
IA Iowa
ibid. *ibidem* [in the same place]
ICA Institute of Contemporary Arts
Ice. Icelandic
Iconog. Iconography
Iconol. Iconology
ID Idaho (USA)
i.e. *id est* [that is]
IL Illinois (USA)
Illum. Illumination
illus. illustrated, illustration
Imp. Imperial
IN Indiana (USA)
in., ins inch(es)
Inc. Incorporated
inc. incomplete
incl. includes, including, inclusive
Incorp. Incorporation
Ind. Indian
Indep. Independent
Indig. Indigenous
Indol. Indology
Indon. Indonesian
Indust. Industrial
Inf. Information
Inq. Inquiry
Inscr. Inscribed, Inscription
Inst. Institute(s)
Inst. A. Institute of Art
Instr. Instrument, Instrumental
Int. International
Intell. Intelligence
Inter. Interior(s), Internal
Interdiscip. Interdisciplinary
intro. introduced by, introduction
inv. inventory

Inven.	Invention
Invest.	Investigation(s)
Iran.	Iranian
irreg.	irregular(ly)
Islam.	Islamic
Isr.	Israeli
It.	Italian
J.	Journal
Jam.	Jamaican
Jan	January
Jap.	Japanese
Jav.	Javanese
Jew.	Jewish
Jewel.	Jewellery
Jord.	Jordanian
jr	junior
Juris.	Jurisdiction
KBE	Knight Commander of the Order of the British Empire
KCVO	Knight Commander of the Royal Victorian Order
kg	kilogram(s)
kHz	kilohertz
km	kilometre(s)
Knowl.	Knowledge
Kor.	Korean
KS	Kansas (USA)
KY	Kentucky (USA)
Kyrgyz.	Kyrgyzstani
£	libra, librae [pound, pounds sterling]
l.	length
LA	Louisiana (USA)
Lab.	Laboratory
Lancs	Lancashire (GB)
Lang.	Language(s)
Lat.	Latin
Latv.	Latvian
lb, lbs	pound(s) weight
Leb.	Lebanese
Lect.	Lecture
Legis.	Legislative
Leics	Leicestershire (GB)
Lex.	Lexicon
Lg.	Large
Lib., Libs	Library, Libraries
Liber.	Liberian
Libsp	Librarianship
Lincs	Lincolnshire (GB)
Lit.	Literature
Lith.	Lithuanian
Liturg.	Liturgical
LLB	Bachelor of Laws
LLD	Doctor of Laws
Lt	Lieutenant
Lt-Col.	Lieutenant-Colonel
Ltd	Limited
m	metre(s)
m.	married
M.	Monsieur
MA	Master of Arts; Massachusetts (USA)
Mag.	Magazine
Maint.	Maintenance
Malay.	Malaysian
Man.	Manitoba (Canada); Manual
Manuf.	Manufactures
Mar.	Marine, Maritime
Mason.	Masonic
Mat.	Material(s)
Math.	Mathematic
MBE	Member of the Order of the British Empire
MD	Doctor of Medicine; Maryland (USA)
ME	Maine (USA)
Mech.	Mechanical
Med.	Medieval; Medium, Media
Medic.	Medical, Medicine
Medit.	Mediterranean
Mem.	Memorial(s); Memoir(s)
Merions	Merionethshire (GB; old)
Meso-Amer.	Meso-American
Mesop.	Mesopotamian
Met.	Metropolitan
Metal.	Metallurgy
Mex.	Mexican
MFA	Master of Fine Arts
mg	milligram(s)
Mgmt	Management
Mgr	Monsignor
MI	Michigan
Microne s.	Micronesian
Mid. Amer.	Middle American
Middx	Middlesex (GB; old)
Mid. E.	Middle Eastern
Mid. Eng.	Middle English
Mid Glam.	Mid Glamorgan (GB)
Mil.	Military
Mill.	Millennium
Min.	Ministry; Minutes
Misc.	Miscellaneous
Miss.	Mission(s)
Mlle	Mademoiselle
mm	millimetre(s)
Mme	Madame
MN	Minnesota
Mnmt, Mnmts	Monument(s)
Mnmtl	Monumental
MO	Missouri (USA)
Mod.	Modern, Modernist
Moldav.	Moldavian
Moldov.	Moldovan
MOMA	Museum of Modern Art
Mon.	Monday
Mongol.	Mongolian
Mons	Monmouthshire (GB; old)
Montgoms	Montgomeryshire (GB; old)
Mor.	Moral
Morav.	Moravian
Moroc.	Moroccan
Movt	Movement
MP	Member of Parliament
MPhil	Master of Philosophy
MS	Mississippi (USA)
MS., MSS	manuscript(s)
MSc	Master of Science
MT	Montana (USA)
Mt	Mount
Mthly	Monthly
Mun.	Municipal
Mus.	Museum(s)
Mus. A.	Museum of Art
Mus. F.A.	Museum of Fine Art(s)
Music.	Musicology
N.	North(ern); National
n	refractive index of a medium
n.	note
N.A.G.	National Art Gallery
Nat.	Natural, Nature
Naut.	Nautical
NB	New Brunswick (Canada)
NC	North Carolina (USA)
ND	North Dakota (USA)
n.d.	no date
NE	Nebraska; Northeast(ern)
Neth.	Netherlandish
Newslett.	Newsletter
Nfld	Newfoundland (Canada)
N.G.	National Gallery
N.G.A.	National Gallery of Art
NH	New Hampshire (USA)
Niger.	Nigerian
NJ	New Jersey (USA)
NM	New Mexico (USA)
nm	nanometre (10^{-9} metre)
nn.	notes
no., nos	number(s)
Nord.	Nordic
Norm.	Normal
Northants	Northamptonshire (GB)
Northumb.	Northumberland (GB)
Norw.	Norwegian
Notts	Nottinghamshire (GB)
Nov	November
n.p.	no place (of publication)
N.P.G.	National Portrait Gallery
nr	near

Nr E.	Near Eastern
NS	New Style; Nova Scotia (Canada)
n. s.	new series
NSW	New South Wales (Australia)
NT	National Trust
Ntbk	Notebook
Numi.	Numismatic(s)
NV	Nevada (USA)
NW	Northwest(ern)
NWT	Northwest Territories (Canada)
NY	New York (USA)
NZ	New Zealand
OBE	Officer of the Order of the British Empire
Obj.	Object(s), Objective
Occas.	Occasional
Occident.	Occidental
Ocean.	Oceania
Oct	October
8vo	octavo
OFM	Order of Friars Minor
OH	Ohio (USA)
OK	Oklahoma (USA)
Olymp.	Olympic
OM	Order of Merit
Ont.	Ontario (Canada)
op.	opus
opp.	opposite; opera [pl. of opus]
OR	Oregon (USA)
Org.	Organization
Orient.	Oriental
Orthdx	Orthodox
OSB	Order of St Benedict
Ott.	Ottoman
Oxon	Oxfordshire (GB)
oz.	ounce(s)
p	pence
p., pp.	page(s)
PA	Pennsylvania (USA)
p.a.	per annum
Pak.	Pakistani
Palaeontol.	Palaeontology, Palaeontological
Palest.	Palestinian
Pap.	Paper(s)
para.	paragraph
Parag.	Paraguayan
Parl.	Parliament
Paroch.	Parochial
Patriarch.	Patriarchate
Patriot.	Patriotic
Patrm.	Patrimony
Pav.	Pavilion
PEI	Prince Edward Island (Canada)
Pembs	Pembrokeshire (GB; old)
Per.	Period
Percep.	Perceptions
Perf.	Performance, Performing, Performed
Period.	Periodical(s)
Pers.	Persian
Persp.	Perspectives
Peru.	Peruvian
PhD	Doctor of Philosophy
Philol.	Philology
Philos.	Philosophy
Phoen.	Phoenician
Phot.	Photograph, Photography, Photographic
Phys.	Physician(s), Physics, Physique, Physical
Physiog.	Physiognomy
Physiol.	Physiology
Pict.	Picture(s), Pictorial
pl.	plate; plural
Plan.	Planning
Planet.	Planetarium
Plast.	Plastic
pls	plates
p.m.	post meridiem [after noon]
Polit.	Political
Poly.	Polytechnic
Polynes.	Polynesian
Pop.	Popular
Port.	Portuguese
Port.	Portfolio
Posth.	Posthumous(ly)
Pott.	Pottery
POW	prisoner of war
PRA	President of the Royal Academy
Pract.	Practical
Prefect.	Prefecture, Prefectural
Preserv.	Preservation
prev.	previous(ly)
priv.	private
PRO	Public Record Office
Prob.	Problem(s)
Proc.	Proceedings
Prod.	Production
Prog.	Progress
Proj.	Project(s)
Promot.	Promotion
Prop.	Property, Properties
Prov.	Province(s), Provincial
Proven.	Provenance
Prt, Prts	Print(s)
Prtg	Printing
pseud.	pseudonym
Psych.	Psychiatry, Psychiatric
Psychol.	Psychology, Psychological
pt	part
Ptg(s)	Painting(s)
Pub.	Public
pubd	published
Publ.	Publicity
pubn(s)	publication(s)
PVA	polyvinyl acetate
PVC	polyvinyl chloride
Q.	quarterly
4to	quarto
Qué.	Québec (Canada)
R	reprint
r	*recto*
RA	Royal Academician
Radnors	Radnorshire (GB; old)
RAF	Royal Air Force
Rec.	Record(s)
red.	reduction, reduced for
Ref.	Reference
Refurb.	Refurbishment
reg	*regit* [ruled]
Reg.	Regional
Relig.	Religion, Religious
remod.	remodelled
Ren.	Renaissance
Rep.	Report(s)
repr.	reprint(ed); reproduced, reproduction
Represent.	Representation, Representative
Res.	Research
rest.	restored, restoration
Retro.	Retrospective
rev.	revision, revised (by/for)
Rev.	Reverend; Review
RHA	Royal Hibernian Academician
RI	Rhode Island (USA)
RIBA	Royal Institute of British Architects
RJ	Rio de Janeiro State
Rlwy	Railway
RSA	Royal Scottish Academy
RSFSR	Russian Soviet Federated Socialist Republic
Rt Hon.	Right Honourable
Rur.	Rural
Rus.	Russian
S	San, Santa, Santo, Sant', São [Saint]
S.	South(ern)
s.	solidus, solidi [shilling(s)]
Sask.	Saskatchewan (Canada)
Sat.	Saturday
SC	South Carolina (USA)
Scand.	Scandinavian
Sch.	School
Sci.	Science(s), Scientific
Scot.	Scottish
Sculp.	Sculpture

SD	South Dakota (USA)
SE	Southeast(ern)
Sect.	Section
Sel.	Selected
Semin.	Seminar(s), Seminary
Semiot.	Semiotic
Semit.	Semitic
Sept	September
Ser.	Series
Serb.	Serbian
Serv.	Service(s)
Sess.	Session, Sessional
Settmt(s)	Settlement(s)
S. Glam.	South Glamorgan (GB)
Siber.	Siberian
Sig.	Signature
Sil.	Silesian
Sin.	Singhala
sing.	singular
SJ	Societas Jesu [Society of Jesus]
Skt	Sanskrit
Slav.	Slavic, Slavonic
Slov.	Slovene, Slovenian
Soc.	Society
Social.	Socialism, Socialist
Sociol.	Sociology
Sov.	Soviet
SP	São Paulo State
Sp.	Spanish
sq.	square
sr	senior
Sri L.	Sri Lankan
SS	Saints, Santi, Santissima, Santissimo, Santissimi; Steam ship
SSR	Soviet Socialist Republic
St	Saint, Sankt, Sint, Szent
Staffs	Staffordshire (GB)
Ste	Sainte
Stud.	Study, Studies
Subalp.	Subalpine
Sum.	Sumerian
Sun.	Sunday
Sup.	Superior
suppl., suppls	supplement(s), supplementary
Surv.	Survey
SW	Southwest(ern)
Swed.	Swedish
Swi.	Swiss
Symp.	Symposium
Syr.	Syrian
Tap.	Tapestry
Tas.	Tasmanian
Tech.	Technical, Technique
Technol.	Technology
Territ.	Territory
Theat.	Theatre
Theol.	Theology, Theological
Theor.	Theory, Theoretical
Thurs.	Thursday
Tib.	Tibetan
TN	Tennessee (USA)
Top.	Topography
Trad.	Tradition(s), Traditional
trans.	translation, translated by; transactions
Transafr.	Transafrican
Transatlant.	Transatlantic
Transcarpath.	Transcarpathian
transcr.	transcribed by/for
Triq.	Triquarterly
Tropic.	Tropical
Tues.	Tuesday
Turk.	Turkish
Turkmen.	Turkmenistani
TV	Television
TX	Texas (USA)
U.	University
UK	United Kingdom of Great Britain and Northern Ireland
Ukrain.	Ukrainian
Un.	Union
Underwtr	Underwater
UNESCO	United Nations Educational, Scientific and Cultural Organization
Univl	Universal
unpubd	unpublished
Urb.	Urban
Urug.	Uruguayan
US	United States
USA	United States of America
USSR	Union of Soviet Socialist Republics
UT	Utah
v	*verso*
VA	Virginia (USA)
V&A	Victoria and Albert Museum
Var.	Various
Venez.	Venezuelan
Vern.	Vernacular
Vict.	Victorian
Vid.	Video
Viet.	Vietnamese
viz.	*videlicet* [namely]
vol., vols	volume(s)
vs.	versus
VT	Vermont (USA)
Vulg.	Vulgarisation
W.	West(ern)
w.	width
WA	Washington (USA)
Warwicks	Warwickshire (GB)
Wed.	Wednesday
W. Glam.	West Glamorgan (GB)
WI	Wisconsin (USA)
Wilts	Wiltshire (GB)
Wkly	Weekly
W. Midlands	West Midlands (GB)
Worcs	Worcestershire (GB; old)
Wtrcol.	Watercolour
WV	West Virginia (USA)
WY	Wyoming (USA)
Yb., Y.-b.	Yearbook, Year-book
Yem.	Yemeni
Yorks	Yorkshire (GB; old)
Yug.	Yugoslavian
Zamb.	Zambian
Zimb.	Zimbabwean

A Note on the Use of the Dictionary

This note is intended as a short guide to the basic editorial conventions adopted in this dictionary. For a fuller explanation, please refer to the Introduction, vol. 1, pp. xiii–xx.

Abbreviations in general use in the dictionary are listed on pp. vi–xi; those used in bibliographies and for locations of works of art or exhibition venues are listed in the Appendices in vol. 33.

Alphabetization of headings, which are distinguished in bold typeface, is letter by letter up to the first comma (ignoring spaces, hyphens, accents and any parenthesized or bracketed matter); the same principle applies thereafter. Abbreviations of 'Saint' and its foreign equivalents are alphabetized as if spelt out, and headings with the prefix 'Mc' appear under 'Mac'.

Authors' signatures appear at the end of the article or sequence of articles that the authors have contributed; in multipartite articles, any section that is unsigned is by the author of the next signed section. Where the article was compiled by the editors or in the few cases where an author has wished to remain anonymous, this is indicated by a square box (□) instead of a signature.

Bibliographies are arranged chronologically (within section, where divided) by order of year of first publication and, within years, alphabetically by authors' names. Abbreviations have been used for some standard reference books; these are cited in full in Appendix C in vol. 33, as are abbreviations of periodical titles (Appendix B). Abbreviated references to alphabetically arranged dictionaries and encyclopedias appear at the beginning of the bibliography (or section).

Biographical dates when cited in parentheses in running text at the first mention of a personal name indicate that the individual does not have an entry in the dictionary. The presence of parenthesized regnal dates for rulers and popes, however, does not necessarily indicate the lack of a biography of that person. Where no dates are provided for an artist or patron, the reader may assume that there is a biography of that individual in the dictionary (or, more rarely, that the person is so obscure that dates are not readily available).

Cross-references are distinguished by the use of small capital letters, with a large capital to indicate the initial letter of the entry to which the reader is directed; for example, 'He commissioned LEONARDO DA VINCI . . .' means that the entry is alphabetized under 'L'.

G

[continued]

Goodnough, Robert (*b* Cortland, NY, 23 Oct 1917). American painter. From 1936 to 1940 he studied at Syracuse University, NY, and he was then drafted into the army. On being discharged he settled in New York in 1946 and attended the Amédée Ozenfant School of Fine Arts. The following year he studied with Hans Hofmann, meeting painters such as Larry Rivers and Alfred Leslie (*b* 1927), as well as Clement Greenberg. From 1947 to 1950 he studied for an MA in art education at New York University and from 1948 to 1949 was one of a number of abstract artists who formed the core of Abstract Expressionism. In 1952 he had his first one-man show at the Tibor de Nagy Galleries in Los Angeles. His work of the early 1950s was abstract and spontaneous in appearance, though sometimes with a figurative base, as in *Pegasus* (1952; Mr and Mrs B. F. Friedman priv. col., see Guest and Friedman, p. 9). From 1952 he began to experiment with collage and also began a series of constructions of dinosaurs, birds and humans.

In the later 1950s, rebelling against the formlessness of Abstract Expressionism, Goodnough was influenced by Cubism and produced works such as *Seated Figure with Grey* (1956; New York, Whitney). As part of his fascination for dynamic art, in the early 1960s he painted a number of works based on Rubens's paintings. The *Abduction* series, for example, was based on Rubens's *Rape of the Daughters of Leucippus* and included such near-abstract works as *Abduction X* (1961; Chicago, IL, A. Inst.). He returned to full abstraction, the paintings of the late 1960s resembling his collages of that period, as in *Anghiari II* (1968; Houston, TX, Mus. F.A.). After the 1970s his paintings consisted of large areas of pale colour with small clusters of geometric shapes, as in *Slate Grey Statement* (1972; Boston, MA, Mus. F.A.).

BIBLIOGRAPHY

R. Guest and B. H. Friedman: *Goodnough* (Paris, 1970)

M. H. Bush and K. Moffett: *Goodnough* (Wichita, 1973)

Robert Goodnough (exh. cat. by J. Harithas, New York, Emmerich Gal., 1974)

□

Goodrich, Lloyd (*b* Nutley, NJ, 10 July 1897; *d* New York, 27 March 1987). American museum administrator, critic and art historian. He first intended to follow a career as an artist, studying at both the Art Students League and the National Academy of Design, New York. From 1923 to 1925 he worked for the Macmillan publishing house. In 1925 he began an association with the magazine *The Arts*, as associate editor (1925–7), European editor (1927–8) and contributing editor (1929–31). In 1931 he joined the Whitney Museum of American Art as a writer and researcher, from 1935 working there as a research curator and subsequently as an associate curator (1947), associate director (1948) and director (from 1958 until his retirement in 1968); he was Director Emeritus at the time of his death. His role at the Whitney was never merely administrative, and he was credited both with building the core collection of work by living American artists and with guiding the Whitney from being a private collection to a major public cultural institution; he also strove to bring greater attention to American art.

In addition to the many boards and artistic advisory groups on which he served, Goodrich was a member of the New York Regional Committee of the Public Work of Art Project from 1933 to 1934 and was director of the American Art Research Council from 1942 to 1949. He also acted as a leading member of the editorial board of the *Magazine of Art* from 1942 to 1950. Most of his writing and exhibition organizing was devoted to living American artists, and he always tried to ensure that proper recognition and financial awards were given to the artists themselves.

WRITINGS

Thomas Eakins (New York, 1933)

Contemporary American Landscape (Pittsburgh, 1939)

Y. Kuniyoshi (New York, 1948)

Georgia O'Keeffe (New York, 1970)

Edward Hopper (New York, 1971)

Reginald Marsh (New York, 1972)

Thomas Eakins (Cambridge, MA, and London, 1982)

with W. I. Homer: *Albert Pinkham Ryder: Painter of Dreams* (New York, 1989)

BIBLIOGRAPHY

Obituary, *NY Times* (28 March 1987)

'Remembering Lloyd Goodrich', *Amer. A. J.*, xx/2 (1988), pp. 6–19

DAVID M. SOKOL

Goodwin, Albert (*b* Maidstone, Kent, 17 Jan 1845; *d* London, 10 April 1932). English painter. During the early 1860s Goodwin studied with Arthur Hughes and Ford Madox Brown, who predicted that his pupil would become 'one of the greatest landscape painters of the age'. Hughes and Brown impressed on Goodwin the Pre-Raphaelite principles of high finish, vivid colour and working directly from nature that inform his early landscape style, and from which he later struggled to free himself.

In 1871 he worked for John Ruskin at Abingdon, near Oxford, and the following year he accompanied Ruskin and another of Ruskin's protégés, Arthur Severn (1842–1931), to Italy. Goodwin credited Ruskin with instilling in him a love of form and an appreciation of the importance of drawing.

Goodwin worked chiefly in watercolour and was elected an associate of the Society of Painters in Water-Colours in 1871, becoming a full member in 1881. He also worked in oils, but in 1876 Ruskin dissuaded him from pursuing a career as an oil painter. There are biblical as well as literary subjects in his work, but throughout his life he remained predominantly a painter of places. He travelled widely in Europe, the Middle East, India and North America, all of which he turned to account in his art, for example in *Engelburg* (1911; London, BM).

By the 1880s the Pre-Raphaelite influence in his work had waned. Precise naturalism was replaced by consciously poetic and resolutely ethereal effects. His distinctive combination of vaporous colour and defining pen-work undoubtedly derived from the late watercolour technique of J. M. W. Turner, of whom Goodwin considered himself the spiritual heir.

BIBLIOGRAPHY

H. Smith: *Albert Goodwin, RWS, 1845–1932* (Leigh-on-Sea, 1977)

Albert Goodwin, 1845–1932 (exh. cat., ed. E. M. M. Hancock; Bolton, Mus. & A.G., 1981)

Albert Goodwin, RWS, 1845–1932 (exh. cat., ed. C. Beetles; London, Chris Beetles, 1986)

SCOTT WILCOX

Goodwin [née Roodish]**, Betty** (*b* Montreal, 19 March 1923). Canadian printmaker and draughtswoman. Following a short but decisive training in printmaking in 1968 and 1969 with Yves Gaucher at the Sir George Williams University, Montreal (now Concordia University), she opted for a figurative aesthetic that was almost abstract. A highly expressive figurative style centred around considerations of the human condition: the fragility of people in their own identity and their relation to the world.

Goodwin's mature work is marked by a number of major breakthroughs, notably the series of etchings and assemblages *Vest* (1969–74), *Tarpaulin* (1975–6), the large-format drawings *Swimmer* (1982–3) and the series *Carbon* (1986–7). The latter began with a mural of the same title (275×975 mm) executed on panels of honeycomb galvanized aluminium (see 1987 exh. cat., no. 76).

BIBLIOGRAPHY

Betty Goodwin (exh. cat., text A. Parent; Montreal, Mus. A. Contemp., 1976)

Betty Goodwin: Passages (exh. cat., text G. Bogardi; Montreal, Concordia U., Williams A. Gals, 1986)

Betty Goodwin: Oeuvres de 1971 à 1987 (exh. cat., text Y. Racine and R. Storr; Montreal, Mus. F.A., 1987)

J. Bentley-Mays: 'The Prime of Betty Goodwin', *The Globe & Mail* (9 May 1987), p. C6

YOLANDE RACINE

Goody [née Edelman]**, Joan Edelman** (*b* New York, 1 Dec 1935). American architect, teacher and writer. She studied architecture at Cornell University, Ithaca, NY (BA, 1956), and Harvard University, Cambridge, MA (March, 1960). In 1960 she married the architect Marvin E. Goody (*d* 1980) and they became partners in the firm of Goody, Clancy and Associates, Boston, engaged in the design of residential, academic and commercial buildings. She began her teaching career at the Boston Architectural Center (1961–6) and subsequently taught at Harvard (1973–80; 1985). One of Goody's primary design considerations was the context of buildings: their setting and surroundings, as well as the particular functions of the brief. In such residential projects as the housing complex for the elderly (1978), Stockbridge, MA, for example, traditional New England architectural forms and materials were integrated with the surrounding landscape; the functional effectiveness of the complex is characterized by the design of each unit with two exposed sides, thus ensuring an efficient natural ventilation system. Context was also an important consideration in Goody's renovation projects, as at the Hemenway Gymnasium (1982), Radcliffe College, Cambridge, MA, a building originally designed in 1902 by McKim, Mead & White, with a tall, beautifully articulated interior space. Rather than inserting several new storeys into this space, as some suggested, Goody insisted on maintaining its original configuration, while other parts of the building, such as the basement, were totally reworked. The Paine Webber Building (1984), 265 Franklin Street, Boston, reveals a concern for the historical urban context. At 20 storeys it mediates between the skyscrapers of the financial district and the low-rise buildings of the adjacent preservation area; its lower storeys are clad in roughly textured red granite, relating to the older brick buildings, while the polished pink granite and glass cladding of the tower relates to the colours and forms of the financial district.

WRITINGS

New Architecture in Boston (Cambridge, MA, 1965)

BIBLIOGRAPHY

Contemp. Architects

B. Diamonstein: *American Architecture Now*, ii (New York, 1985)

WALTER SMITH

Gool, Jan [Johan] **van** (*b* The Hague, 1687; *d* The Hague, 1763). Dutch writer and painter. He trained as an artist with Simon van der Does (1653–1718) and painted landscapes with cattle in the tradition of Paulus Potter and Adriaen van de Velde (e.g. *Milking Time*; Amsterdam, Rijksmus.); van Gool's chief adversary, Gerard Hoet (ii) (*see* HOET, (2)), described his paintings as stiff, dry and over-detailed. Van Gool was more important, however, as a writer, renowned for his two volumes of artists' biographies. The *Nieuwe schouburg* was written as a sequel to Arnold Houbraken's *Groote schouburgh* and dovetails into the last, unfinished book of the latter. The *Nieuwe schouburg* (which was illustrated by Jacobus Houbraken) covers Dutch art of the late 17th century and the first half of the 18th and is the most valuable source available for this period. It is more reliable than Houbraken's work, on which it was closely modelled, since van Gool relied less on published sources and more on his personal memories, interviews and correspondence with artists and their relatives; he even undertook archival research. Little art theory is included, but much attention is given to social status and financial success, which are linked directly to the quality of the artists' work. The painters' personalities are also considered in relation to their social and artistic success or failure.

Works of art are discussed separately from the biographies. Van Gool may be ranked among the first published Dutch art critics: his eye for quality was acute and his approbation was not exclusively directed towards one style or group of artists. His remarks about 'natuurlijkheid' indicate that he advocated emulation of 17th-century Dutch art, which he admired for its naturalness, but felt that its cruder elements should be avoided: he strongly attacked such Leiden 'Fine' painters as Willem van Mieris and his imitators, preferring a freer and more spirited use of the brush. Van Gool considered the Dutch art of his time to be in decline and his book was written to stimulate both young artists and prospective collectors to reinvigorate the tradition. However, by decline, van Gool meant quantity not quality. He noted that a number of the different kinds of subject painting developed in the previous century were no longer practised, and that only The Hague and Amsterdam survived as worthwhile centres of artistic activity. Furthermore, he observed that it had become impossible for painters to survive without the protection of a patron. Although he occasionally alluded to the country's economic problems, van Gool saw the fashion for wall hangings (gilded leather, painted canvas or woven fabrics) as one of the main causes of the decline in demand for contemporary paintings. Even more serious was the growing interest of collectors in the art of the past. Van Gool dated the onset of this decline to 1710–20, thus including Gerard de Lairesse, Adriaen van der Werff, Godfried Schalcken, Caspar Netscher and Jan Weenix as part of the 'golden age'. His views were not received favourably in all quarters, and Gerard Hoet (ii) attacked both the author and the book in two sharply critical pamphlets.

WRITINGS

De nieuwe schouburg der Nederlantsche kunstschilders en schilderessen [The new theatre of Dutch painters], 2 vols (The Hague, 1750–51/*R* Soest, 1971)

Antwoordt op den zoo genaemden brief aen een vrient [Reply to the so-called 'letter to a friend'] (The Hague, 1752/3)

BIBLIOGRAPHY

G. Hoet: *Brief aan een vrient* [Letter to a friend] (The Hague, 1751)

——: *Catalogus of naamlyst van schilderyen* (The Hague, 1752/*R* Soest, 1976), i, pp. vii-xii

——: *Aanmerkingen op het eerste en tweede deel des 'Nieuwen schouburgs'* [Comments on the first and second volumes of the 'New Theatre'] ([The Hague], [?1753])

Lo de Vries: *Diamante gedenkzuilen en leerzaeme voorbeelden: Een bespreking van Johan van Gools 'Nieuwe schouburg'* [Diamond commemorative columns and instructive examples: a discussion of Jo van Gools 'Nieuwe schouburg'] (Groningen, 1990) [incl. facs. of pamphlets exchanged between Hoet and Gool]

LYCKLE DE VRIES

Gopagiri. *See* GWALIOR.

Gopas, Rudolf (*b* Šilutė, Lithuania, 13 Dec 1913; *d* Christchurch, NZ, 23 July 1983). New Zealand painter of Lithuanian birth. Trained in a Lithuanian art school, he arrived in New Zealand as a refugee in 1949. He first produced realistic landscapes but by the mid-1950s the expressionist style for which he is best known was established in works such as *Landscape* (1960; Christchurch, NZ, Canterbury Lib.). He was an important teacher, lecturing in painting at the University of Canterbury for 18 years from 1959. He was a fundamental influence on what became seen as a school of expressionist artists based in Christchurch, including Philip Clairmont (1949–84), Tony Fomison and Philip Trusttum (*b* 1940).

By the end of the 1960s Gopas's intense interest in astronomy surfaced in his painting. He was fascinated by how the infinities of space could be represented in art, in his *Galactic Paintings* such as *Nebula* (1969; Auckland, C.A.G.) and then by his series *Paintings for the Sun* in 1975 and 1976. However, faced with incomprehension, he sent most of these paintings to Ehrwald, a small town in Austria where he had lived as a refugee, where they are displayed in the Zugspitze Hall. His last works were hand-coloured photocopies, combining text and images, denouncing the possible atomic destruction of the earth.

BIBLIOGRAPHY

Rudolf Gopas (exh. cat. by J. Barr and M. Barr, New Plymouth, NZ, Govett-Brewster A.G., 1982)

M. Dunn: 'Rudolf Gopas: A Teacher and Painter in Retrospect', *A. NZ*, 27 (1983), pp. 28–33

JIM BARR, MARY BARR

Gopura [Skt: 'cow gate'; Tamil *gopuram*]. Temple gateway commonly found in south India. Low reliefs from BHARHUT, SANCHI and elsewhere show that barrel-vaulted gateways with thatched roofs and horseshoe-arch gables were built all over India at an early date. As in the later *gopuras* of south India, these timber gates had a rectangular plan with the entrance passage running through the long side. By the 3rd century AD reliefs show a smaller form of gateway consisting of a simple opening sheltered by a roll-cornice (Skt *kapota*) and crowned by a barrel-vaulted pavilion (*sālā*). This form is depicted in the *c.* 6th-century wall paintings at AJANTA and is built in stone to form entrances to temples of the Pallava and Chola periods in Tamil Nadu: for example, the early 8th-century Kailasanatha at KANCHIPURAM and the late 10th-century Nilakantheshvara at Laddigam. This one-storey, *sālā*-topped type is essentially one of the forms of the southern (*draviḍa*) minor shrine (*alpa vimāna*), but with a passageway instead of a sanctuary.

When, from the beginning of the 11th century, more monumental *gopuras* developed, these followed the compositional principles of more complex shrine types. Thus the *sālā*-topped minor shrine became the uppermost storey of a tiered pyramid, each storey (*tala*) surrounded by a chain of shrine-images crowned by domed, usually square pavilions (*kūṭas*), horseshoe-arched pavilions (*pañjaras*) and the barrel-vaulted *sālās*. Projections running up the middle of the two wider faces were introduced above the lintel-spanned passage, culminating at the central horseshoe-arched pavilions on the sides of the giant crowning *sālā*. These projections contained openings lighting the various internal floors. The shrine-like character of *gopuras* was such that they were even provided with vestibules opening off the two sides of the passageway, suggesting a sanctuary split in half, often with vestigial ambulatory. An interpretation in terms of splitting is supported by the split pilasters that frame the openings: a device long familiar in

Outer eastern *gopura* at Arunachaleshvara Temple, Tiruvannamalai, North Arcot District, Tamil Nadu, 1572

wall niches, conveying the idea that a pilaster has divided into two as the enshrined image emerges from within.

Monumental *gopuras* became well established during the later Chola period (11th–13th century), the first examples being built at the Rajarajeshvara Temple, THANJAVUR (*c.* 1010). These set the norm of using stone for the first storey and brick for the superstructure. From the 12th century *gopuras* were added to existing temples. The gateways typically formed part of a succession of enclosures built one after the other around an established temple. *Gopuras* became the most prominent elements of the complex, as, for example, at CHIDAMBARAM. The *gopuras* of the Vijayanagara and Nayaka periods (14th–17th century), often with slightly concave profiles, are notable for their great scale; striking examples include those at MADURAI and TIRUVANNAMALAI (see fig.). Modern *gopuras*, found as far apart as Ujjain and Singapore, are generally of brick, with their surface details in thick cement, brightly painted. They follow the 17th-century trend of covering the exterior with a swarm of figures that almost obscure the architectural framework.

BIBLIOGRAPHY

J. C. Harle: *Temple Gateways in South India: The Architecture and Iconography of the Cidambaram Gopuras* (Oxford, 1963)

S. Huntington: *The Art of Ancient India: Buddhist, Hindu, Jain* (New York and Tokyo, 1985)

ADAM HARDY

Goravsky, Apollinary (Gilyaryevich). *See* HARAŬSKI, APALINARY.

Gorbunovo peat-bog [Gorbunovsky Torfyanik]. Peat-bog near the town of Nizhny Tagil, *c.* 120 km north of Yekaterinburg, Russia. In 1908 the remains of a settlement dating from the Neolithic period to the Bronze Age (third millennium BC–10th–9th centuries BC) were discovered there. A large number of everyday artefacts were found, suggesting that this may have been a place of sacrifice. Among the finds were wood-carvings, mainly in the round: spoons and ladles with carefully polished surfaces are in the shape of waterfowl such as swans and geese, with handles in the form of a head on a smoothly curving neck. Two alder vessels in the form of elk with a cavity in the body (Nizhny Tagil, Reg. Mus.; Moscow, Hist. Mus.) retain traces of notches on the surface; the heads are disproportionately large, the lines of the mouth and the nostrils are marked out and the pupils of the eyes clearly had incrustations of some sort, while the legs are schematic. Of coarser execution are individual heads of waterfowl (untraced) and a writhing snake cut from a board (Moscow, Hist. Mus.). An unusual piece is the idol or human figure with schematically rendered trunk (the arms are missing) and legs and a distinctive treatment of the face: the cheeks and eye sockets are on one plane beneath a strongly projecting forehead (Nizhny Tagil, Reg. Mus.). Also extant is a poorly preserved head from another idol (Moscow, Hist. Mus.). The wooden carvings from Gorbunovo peat-bog form a specific group, along with a stylistically related series of finds from Shigir' peat-bog (Shigirsky Torfyanik) near Nev'yansk in the same region, which includes a scoop with the head of an elk and an idol (Yekaterinburg, Reg. Mus.). This wood-carving tradition influenced the whole development of art in the Urals and western Siberia (*see* UST'-POLUY).

BIBLIOGRAPHY

D. N. Eding: 'Reznaya skul'ptura Urala' [Carved sculpture from the Urals], *Trudy Gosudarstvennogo Istor. Muz.*, x (1940)

V. I. Moshinskaya: *Drevnyaya skul'ptura Urala i Zapadnoy Sibiri* [Ancient sculpture of the Urals and western Siberia] (Moscow, 1976)

V. YA. PETRUKHIN

Gordeyev, Fyodor (Gordeyevich) (*b* ?Tsarskoye Selo [now Pushkin], 1744; *d* St Petersburg, 23 Jan 1810). Russian sculptor. The son of a cowherd from Tsarskoye Selo, he studied (1759–67) at the Academy of Arts in St Petersburg under Nicolas-François Gillet, and he completed his education in Paris (1767–9) under Jean-Baptiste Lemoyne (ii) and in Rome (1769–72). The only surviving example of Gordeyev's work from this period is a statue of *Prometheus* (plaster, 1769; Moscow, Tret'yakov Gal.), which shows his classical orientation. He returned to Russia in 1772 and soon began teaching at the Academy of Arts. From 1777 he was in charge of the sculpture class there, and he was a professor from 1782.

At the end of the 1770s, after the departure of Etienne-Maurice Falconet from Russia, Gordeyev finished the monument to *Peter the Great* on Senate (now Decembrists') Square in St Petersburg. He was responsible for the decorative plaster reliefs on the façade of the Academy of Arts (1784) and the façade of the old Hermitage (1786) and also for the interior of the palace at Ostankino (1794). Gordeyev made models for numerous bronze copies of famous antique and modern statues, including *Venus Callipyga* (1780), the *Apollo Belvedere* (1782), *Thalia* (1792; all St Petersburg, Pavlovsk Park), the Farnese *Hercules* (1786) and the Farnese *Flora* (1787; both Pushkin, Cameron Gal.). He also executed the relief (1801) on the bronze pedestal of the monument to *General Aleksandr Vasilyevich Suvorov* in Marsovo Pole (now on Suvorov Square) in St Petersburg.

Gordeyev's most successful works are the three classical tombstones for *N. M. Golitsyna* (marble, 1780; Moscow, Don Monastery), *A. M. Golitsyn* (marble, 1788; St Petersburg, Mus. City Sculp.) and *D. M. Golitsyn* (marble, 1799; Moscow, Don Monastery). These tombstones laid the foundations for the tradition of Russian memorial sculpture, which was continued by the following generation of sculptors. Gordeyev was an important teacher, whose pupils included a number of major artists, such as Ivan Prokof'yev.

BIBLIOGRAPHY

V. M. Rogachevsky: *Fyodor Gordeyevich Gordeyev, 1744–1810* (Leningrad and Moscow, 1960)

SERGEY ANDROSSOV

Gordillo, Luis (*b* Seville, 24 Aug 1934). Spanish painter. He studied painting privately with Santiago del Campo while studying law at Seville University, and then at the Escuela de Bellas Artes in Seville from 1956 to 1958. He spent summer 1958 in Paris, where he came under the influence of contemporary painters such as Wols, Jean Fautrier and Jean Dubuffet and produced abstract paintings in which he used newspapers as collage elements. Until 1963 he was dedicated solely to abstraction, almost always working on paper and incorporating numerous changes as a way of stressing the process.

From summer 1959 to 1961 Gordillo was again in Paris, earning his living from various jobs unrelated to painting and studying French at the Sorbonne. Sensing that *Art informel* held fewer and fewer possibilities for him, he visited London in summer 1962 and studied Pop art at first hand, which on his return to Spain encouraged him to introduce figurative elements in an obsessive and feverish series of drawings produced in Madrid in 1963. This new idiom took a more personal form in the *Heads* series of 1963 to 1965. In 1963 Gordillo also began an eight-year period of psychoanalysis, which he claimed was a key influence on the development of his art. His meeting in 1964 with the young critic and painter Juan Antonio

Luis Gordillo: *Second Red Series*, acrylic on cardboard and wood, three panels each 1.56×1.07 m, 1982 (Madrid, Museo Español de Arte Contemporáneo)

Aguirre, who played an important part in the art life of Spain during the 1960s and 1970s, brought him into contact with younger painters such as José Luis Alexanco. In 1968 he exhibited groups of paintings entitled, for example, *Motorists in the Landscape* (1968; Madrid, Mus. A. Contemp.), *Motorists* and *Pedestrians*, in which he sought to give form to dynamic beings that expressed what he termed 'paralytic movement' and that, according to his own psychological interpretation, were symbols of anxiety.

The rise of conceptual art precipitated a second period of crisis in Gordillo's work, for he felt himself to have been displaced by the new artistic vanguard. By the time he participated in the Venice Biennale in 1970, however, he had a secure critical reputation, and his influence on younger painters such as Carlos Alcolea (*b* 1949), Carlos Franco (*b* 1951), Rafael Pérez-Mínguez (*b* 1949) and Guillermo Pérez Villalta (*b* 1948) was so extensive, particularly in Madrid, as to become a style referred to as 'Gordillism'. Between 1971 and 1973 Gordillo collaborated with these artists on group exhibitions and on portfolios of screenprints. In works such as *Bather 'en plein soleil'*, *The Bathtub* and *The Family*, all shown at his important first exhibition at the Galería Vandrés, Madrid, in 1971, he displayed a new sense of colour and irony. The recurring image of a swimming pool in these works represented for Gordillo an enclosure of nothingness, 'an antidote against death'. His later works, such as *Second Red Series* (1982; Madrid, Mus. A. Contemp.; see fig.), continued to demonstrate the legacy of the contrasting tendencies to which Gordillo had addressed himself, including Expressionism, *Art informel*, geometric abstraction and Pop art, in what he referred to as the 'aesthetics of combat'.

BIBLIOGRAPHY

Gordillo, 1958–1974 (exh. cat. by S. Marchán Fiz, Seville, Cent. A. M-11, 1974) [first retrospective]

F. Calvo Serraller: *Luis Gordillo* (Madrid, 1981)

Luis Gordillo (exh. cat. by F. Calvo Serraller, Bilbao, Mus. B.A., 1981)

Luis Gordillo: Premio Nacional de Artes Plásticas (exh. cat. by J. A. Aguirre, Madrid, Mus. A. Contemp., 1981)

F. Calvo Serraller: *Dibujos de Luis Gordillo: La memoria como collage* (Madrid, 1982)

——: *Luis Gordillo* (Madrid, 1986)

M. DOLORES JIMÉNEZ-BLANCO

Gordion [Gordium; now Yassıhöyük]. Site in Turkey, *c.* 100 km south-west of Ankara. The site of Gordion, the capital of the Iron-Age kingdom of Phrygia, *c.* 900–695 BC, is a flat mound on the right bank of the River Sangarios. It contains earlier settlements dating back to the beginning of the 3rd millennium BC, but Gordion attained its greatest prominence in the period of the PHRYGIANS. About 70 Phrygian burial mounds (tumuli) lie on higher ground to the east of the mound. The site is associated in Greek mythology with King Midas, whose wealth was proverbial and whose father, Gordios, allegedly tied the Gordian knot, which was cut by Alexander the Great. King Midas is to be identified with the historical Mita of Mushki (*reg* *c.* 735–695 BC), who was known to the Assyrians.

In 1900 G. Körte and A. Körte excavated five tumuli and probed the city mound. Major excavations were conducted from 1950 to 1974 by Rodney S. Young, working through Hellenistic levels to expose at least three stages of a large Phrygian citadel, of which the second is of the Midas period. Some 20 Phrygian tumuli were also excavated, among them the presumed burial mound of King Midas. The objects from Young's excavations are in the Museum of Anatolian Civilizations in Ankara. Finds from the campaign of 1900 are in Istanbul (Archaeol. Mus.) and in Berlin (Schloss Charlottenburg).

1. Citadel. 2. Tumuli. 3. Phrygian and Greek artefacts.

1. CITADEL. The mound had fortifications built of limestone masonry of fairly regular appearance. A monumental gateway of the Midas period has come to light on the east side. Its flanking towers with sloping outer faces

are preserved to a height of 9 m. A wide entrance ramp enters the citadel at an oblique angle, bordered in the inner part of the entrance court (23 m long) by wide ledges. Its technique and design, as also in the underlying earlier Phrygian citadel, follow the old west Anatolian traditions best known from Troy VI (*c.* 1600 BC).

The interior of the citadel is subdivided by cross-walls into a series of courts with controlled entrances. In these courts stand the major buildings of the Midas period, which are parallel, rectangular structures of the megaron type, consisting of a large main room with a shallow entrance room or porch on the short side. These buildings were gabled, as is proved by the shape of a voluted limestone acroterion and by sketches incised on the masonry of Megaron 2. These Phrygian megara are related to 3rd- and possibly early 4th-millennium BC predecessors known from Troy I–II, to the megara of Mycenaean palaces of *c.* 1400–*c.* 1200 BC and to Greek temples, which continued the pedimental roofing system. The megara were built of mud-brick and timber on stone foundations. Megaron 3, the largest, had a main room of *c.* 19×15 m. Inside, two rows of wooden posts flanked the walls and supported the roof. It may be surmised that galleries formed the second floor of this palatial building. Megaron 2 had a floor of pebble mosaic; its patterns, in white, dark red and dark blue, are irregular in orientation as if imitating scattered rugs with individual designs of chequer-work, diamonds, swastikas and filled circles. Round hearths lay in the centre of most rooms (see fig. 1). The incised sketches of lions, birds of prey and megaron façades complete with acroteria on the exterior of Megaron 2 are graffiti of the 8th century BC. They may hint at the special character of Megaron 2 as a temple of the goddess Kybele, who was associated in Phrygia with hawks and lions.

There is some limestone sculpture of the 8th century BC. Two *protomes* of roaring lions, carved in a linear, patterned style, must have projected from the façade of a building. Fragmentary orthostats are decorated with reliefs of humans and animals and are based on the Neo-Hittite sculptural tradition (*see* HITTITE). The pieces from Gordion are too battered for reconstruction of complete designs, but a typical Phrygian trait is seen in the frontal, three-dimensional head of a lion facing the spectator as it turns out of the relief slab, again with linear stylization and striation.

The citadel of the Midas period, especially the megara on the west side of the main courts and the storage buildings set on a terrace behind them, was burnt down after looting by Cimmerian invaders *c.* 695 BC. The raiders took away the precious objects (paradoxically no gold or silver was found in the so-called Midas Tomb), but traces of carved wooden furniture, some ivory inlays and geometric-patterned rugs give a glimpse of Phrygian decorative arts. Pottery was abundantly represented. The citadel was rebuilt and enlarged after the Cimmerian destruction. The plan remained basically the same, but the new buildings were set on enormous terraces of clay and rubble. The reconstruction was completed under Lydian auspices in the 7th century BC and early 6th, and little was altered in the days of Persian control after 546 BC. Pebble mosaics of chequer-work design decorated the floors of what may have been a Persian governor's mansion. By the Hellenistic period the citadel had lost its monumental appearance.

1. Gordion, Megaron 2, cella seen from north-east showing mosaic floor, 8th century BC

2. TUMULI. The Phrygians introduced the custom of burying chieftains in timber chambers and covering these with piles of stone and mounds of earth. A tumulus was meant to be a landmark, a visible monument to the person buried. Special markers may have stood on the lower slope or even on top, as Plato ironically hints (*Phaedrus* 264e), but all the earth mounds have suffered from erosion. The Gordion chambers were simple timber-lined rectangular pits with flat roofs. They measure up to *c.* 4.5×3.5 m in size but are not deep enough to imitate living rooms. Only in the case of the largest tumulus, the presumed tomb of Midas, did the builders enlarge the chamber to make it resemble a wooden gabled house of Phrygian type, finished carefully on the inside only. The roof was supported by three triangular gables, one in the middle and one at each end. The measurements were 6.20×5.55 m, with a height of 3.25 m (3.86 m to the top of the gable). There was no door. Body and paraphernalia were, as always, lowered into the tomb chamber before the roof was put on.

Midas' tomb was a symbolic living room equipped with special furniture, textiles, personal belongings, and a large number of metal vessels provided for a permanent funeral meal for the 65-year-old king, whose body lay in an open log coffin. The inventory of the tomb illustrates Phrygian art in several categories. Two boxwood stands for bronze vessels had fronts made as screens inlaid with juniper in geometric patterns (see fig. 2). Meander swastikas are set in a field of small triangles and diamonds, leaving room in the lower part for a relief roundel with curvilinear patterns and curved pendants ending in ribbed bolsters at the lower corners. The craftsmanship is as admirable as the total effect of dense linear texture with formalized central symbols. A tripod table, known as the Pagoda Table, had an openwork supporting frame with richly inlaid struts and panels. This furniture is unlike any known from the Ancient Near East; it reveals an art that the craftsmen of Midas may well have inherited from generations of predecessors.

Samples of patterned woven fabric have also survived. Simple meander bands, squares with meander hooks and

2. Gordion, serving stands with geometric screens, boxwood with juniper inlay, h. 950 mm, found in the Midas Tomb, early 7th century BC (Ankara, Museum of Anatolian Civilizations)

multi-coloured composite lozenges can be recognized. Fragments from the burnt ruins on the citadel match these pieces. In Tumulus P the walls had textile hangings attached to rows of pegs. Weaving of patterned clothing was a famous Phrygian craft. Midas' ally King Warpalawas had himself represented dressed in a Phrygian robe with meander panels on his relief at Ivriz (*see* ANATOLIA, ANCIENT, fig. 5).

Phrygians excelled in the manufacture of large and small bronze vessels. Three large cauldrons stood against the east wall of the Midas Tomb. They had carrying rings and figural attachments, bulls' heads made locally and winged human *protomes* imported from east Anatolia. The small cauldrons that stood on the carved serving stands are good functional vessels, as are large and small trefoil jugs, bowls with ring handles and petalled omphalos bowls. Although blossom bowls are eastern in origin, the Phrygian omphalos bowl transforms their floral ornament into an abstract radiating or lobed pattern around the central boss, which may be set off by multiple rings. Two situlae—bucket-handled dippers in the shape of a lion's and ram's head respectively—are examples of exotic imports, Neo-Hittite or Assyrian. A typical adjunct of Phrygian costume was the bronze fibula, a sturdy safety pin that could be embellished by mouldings, studding and beading. Metal belts have similar decoration, and those from Tumulus P present a pattern book of Phrygian ornament in fine geometric engraving.

Gordion pottery is usually monochrome dark ware, as is evident from vessels in all the tumuli and in the burnt buildings on the mound. The dark-on-light wares have painted geometric or wavy line decoration (*see* ANATOLIA, ANCIENT, fig. 11c). The finest decorated ware is evident in Tumulus P, which had a child's burial and a less severe ceramic inventory. A figural style on jugs has animal panels set in what look like textile bands: bulls, lions, stags, birds and a sphinx are patterned with stripes and stippling. A jug from Tumulus W, with an extravagant long and fragile trough-spout, is a fine example of the abstract style of Phrygian vase painting.

3. PHRYGIAN AND GREEK ARTEFACTS. Phrygian art, as found in 8th-century BC Gordion, generally shows a preference for abstract patterning on functional objects and media. The origin of this decorative art is often explained with reference to the geometric phase of Greek art. Gordion shows that the matter is not so simple, for there are no Greek imports among the tumulus inventory or from stratified contexts on the citadel mound. The craftsmen who made the Midas furniture, textiles and the mosaics from Megaron 2 were working in local traditions and media.

Representational art was incipient at the time of the Midas dynasty, as in the orthostats of the mound, which attempted to imitate Neo-Hittite sculpture. In the minor arts animal figures decorate some of the metalwork and pottery. Tumulus P had a collection of small wooden sculptures of mixed stylistic parentage. Orientalizing lions and a lion–bull group are influenced by the Near Eastern tradition, in spite of Phrygian linear mannerisms. Other figures, such as a griffin eating a fish and a tubular long-snouted deer, are bold native carvings, related to small ivory relief plaques from furniture burnt in the citadel. In this case there is also a rare human figure, a horseman, hidden by his shield and Phrygian helmet, on a spindly-legged horse. Horsemen also appear in a burnt wooden panel with carvings of 'windblown' horned animals in a stance better known from stags painted on pottery from Alişar in central Anatolia. Samples of such pots reached Gordion. These carvings belong to a very un-Greek world.

Greek art appeared under Lydian auspices in the 7th and 6th centuries BC. In architecture, terracotta revetments replaced wood-carving as ornament on exterior wall surfaces and cornices. The decoration is partly copied from traditional Phrygian meander and lozenge patterns and partly representational, with scenes of Theseus and the Minotaur, as at Sardis in Lydia. Eastern Greek iconography and style are most strikingly represented in fragments of wall paintings that decorated a small structure set between two megara of the 7th–6th century BC. These paintings date from the period of Persian rule at Gordion (the last quarter of the 6th century BC) and show the strength of the eastern Greek pictorial tradition in Lydian and Phrygian Anatolia. Most of the architecture, metalwork and pottery continued in the Phrygian tradition. Changes occurred in the Hellenistic period, but by then Gordion had become a follower instead of a leader.

BIBLIOGRAPHY

G. Körte and A. Körte: *Gordion: Ergebnisse der Ausgrabung im Jahre 1900* (Berlin, 1904)

Amer. J. Archaeol., lix (1955), pp. 1–18; lx (1956), pp. 249–66; lxi (1957), pp. 319–31; lxii (1958), pp. 139–54; lxiv (1960), pp. 227–43; lxvi (1962), pp. 153–68; lxviii (1964), pp. 279–92; lxx (1966), pp. 267–78; lxii (1968), pp. 231–41 [excavation reports from Gordion by R. S. Young]

G. R. Edwards: 'Gordion: Preliminary Report', *Amer. J. Archaeol.*, lxiii (1959), pp. 263–68

G. K. Sams: 'Phrygian Painted Animals: Anatolian Orientalizing Art', *Anatol. Stud.*, xxiv (1974), pp. 169–96

R. S. Young: *Gordion: A Guide to the Excavations and Museum* (Ankara, 1975)

From Athens to Gordion: The Papers of a Memorial Symposium for Rodney S. Young (Philadelphia, 1980)

R. S. Young: *The Gordion Excavations: Final Reports, I: Three Great Early Tumuli* (Philadelphia, 1981) [pubd posthumously]

E. Simpson: 'Reconstructing an Ancient Table', *Expedition*, xxv/4 (1983), pp. 11–26

——: 'Royal Wooden Furniture from Gordion', *Archaeology*, xxxix/6 (1986), pp. 40–45

M. J. MELLINK

Gordon, Arturo (*b* Valparaíso, 7 Aug 1883; *d* Valparaíso, 27 Oct 1944). Chilean painter. He entered the Academia de Bellas Artes in Santiago in 1903, studying drawing under Cosme San Martín and painting under Pedro Lira, Juan Francisco González and later with the Spanish painter Fernando Alvarez de Sotomayor (1875–1960). Under the influence of Alvarez de Sotomayor and especially of González, Gordon and other like-minded Chilean painters such as Pedro Luna and Agustín Abarca (1882–1953), who became known as the Generación del Trece, began to free themselves from the academic naturalism that dominated Chilean art at that time. Gordon was one of the most prominent members of the group because of the innovations that he introduced in his treatment of light, which he regarded as an independent element in its own right, and his use of bright colours. The partial disintegration of forms in his pictures, his use of coloured shadows and his emphasis on the luminosity of atmosphere link his work to French Impressionism. His choice of subject-matter was also novel in Chilean painting, since he addressed himself not only to landscapes but also to the activities of the poor and deprived, painting scenes of everyday life and religious subjects as well as festivals and popular dances, as in *Evening Party* (Santiago, Mus. N. B.A.).

Gordon also produced some murals, notably a series for the Biblioteca Nacional in Santiago in 1926, and in 1928 he travelled to Seville with another Chilean painter, Laureano Guevara, to decorate the Chilean pavilion at the Exposición Internacional taking place there. From 1936 to 1944 he taught painting at the Escuela de Bellas Artes in Viña del Mar.

BIBLIOGRAPHY

Arturo Gordon y su obra (exh. cat. by A. Romera and R. Bindis, Santiago, Sala Capilla, 1974)

MILAN IVELIĆ

Gore, Spencer (Frederick) (*b* Epsom, Surrey, 26 May 1878; *d* Richmond, Surrey, 27 March 1914). English painter. He studied at the Slade School of Fine Art, London (1896–9), where he met Harold Gilman, who became a close friend. In 1902 he visited Spain with another Slade contemporary, Wyndham Lewis, and two years later he visited Sickert in Dieppe. From that time on his work was influenced by French art, and Gore learnt much about Degas's paintings through Sickert's teaching. After Sickert's return to London in 1905 Gore frequently accompanied him to music halls and made them the subject of several paintings, for example *The Mad Pierrot Ballet, the Alhambra* (*c*. 1905; London, Anthony d'Offay Gal.).

As a founder-member of the Fitzroy Street Group, Gore came into contact with Lucien Pissarro, whose Impressionist method he adopted in his garden scenes and in the *Cricket Match* (*c*. 1908–9; Wakefield, A.G.). With Gilman and others he helped found the Allied Artists' Association and was also involved in the formation of the CAMDEN TOWN GROUP in 1911. After seeing Roger Fry's Post-Impressionist exhibitions of 1910 and 1912, he was one of the first Camden Town artists to switch from an Impressionist-based technique to one that comes closer in appearance to stained glass. It is first seen in landscapes he painted at Letchworth in summer 1912, for instance in the insistent pattern-making in *The Beanfield* (London, Tate); he later gave way to the influence of Cézanne, employing a more complex orchestration of form following his move from Camden Town to Richmond, Surrey, in 1913. His early death was caused by pneumonia.

BIBLIOGRAPHY

Spencer Frederick Gore, 1878–1914 (exh. cat.; ACGB, 1955)
Spencer Frederick Gore (exh. cat.; London, Anthony d'Offay Gal., 1983)

For further bibliography *see* CAMDEN TOWN GROUP.

FRANCES SPALDING

Gorge. *See* SCOTIA.

Gorgon Painter. *See* VASE PAINTERS, §II.

Gorham. American silverware firm formed in 1831 by Jabez Gorham (*b* Providence, RI, 18 Feb 1792; *d* Providence, 24 March 1869). When he was fourteen Gorham began a seven-year apprenticeship with Nehemiah Dodge (*fl* 1794–1807), a Providence silversmith. He completed his training in 1813 and in the same year opened a jewellery business known as 'The Firm' that lasted until 1818, when economic hardships led to its dissolution. Jabez continued in business in Providence throughout the 1820s, and in 1831 he expanded his production to include the manufacture of coin-silver spoons with Henry Webster (1808–65). In 1837 William G. Price (*d* 1839) also became a partner in what became known as Gorham, Webster & Price, and in 1841 Gorham brought his son, John Gorham (1820–98), into the business under the name J. Gorham & Son. They expanded their line of flatware to include forks, tongs, thimbles, nursing tubes, toiletries and other small articles, sold mainly through the shop and a network of travelling peddlers. By 1847 John Gorham's ambitious plans for the company included the acquisition of larger working space and steam-powered machinery. Jabez Gorham retired in 1848. In 1850 John Gorham made his cousin, Gorham Thurber (1825–88), partner, and the company became known as Gorham & Thurber, producing hollow-ware and flatware using machines and new technology. In 1865 the firm was incorporated as the Gorham Manufacturing Co., and in the same year electroplating was introduced. In 1868 the English silversmith Thomas Joseph Pairpoint (*fl* 1860–80) joined the company and designed wares in a high-Victorian style (e.g. Furber Service, 1873; Providence, RI, Gorham Col.). Gorham went bankrupt in 1877 and was forced to resign, but the company continued to produce wares in Revival styles. During the 1890s Art Nouveau wares were produced and the Martelé (hammered) line of silverware and jewellery was introduced. In 1925 the Danish designer Erik Magnussen (1884–1961) became the company director and introduced Art Deco style wares. During World War II production was reduced, but normal production was resumed in the 1950s. In 1967 the firm was merged with the Textron Corporation of Providence. In 1974–5 a table service in the King Charles pattern was made for the White House, Washington, DC.

BIBLIOGRAPHY

D. T. Rainwater: *Encyclopedia of American Silver Manufacturers* (West Chester, 1966, rev. 3/1986)

H. N. Flynt and M. G. Fales: *The Heritage Foundation Collection of Silver, with Biographical Sketches of New England Silversmiths, 1625–1825* (Old Deerfield, 1968), p. 230

C. H. Carpenter jr: *Gorham Silver, 1831–1981* (New York, 1982)

GERALD W. R. WARD

Gori, Antonio Francesco (*b* Florence, 9 Dec 1691; *d* Florence, 21 Jan 1757). Italian theologian and writer. He was prior of S Giovanni in Florence, where he also taught history at the university and founded the Accademia Columbaria (1735). He wrote books on theology and translated Greek writers but is remembered chiefly for his studies of Etruscan antiquities and inscriptions. These remain of value and, together with the work of Bernard de Montfaucon and the Comte de Caylus, made important contributions to the 18th-century re-evaluation of Etruscan history (*see* ETRUSCAN, §VIII). He was also a leading student of gems, his publication on the collection of Anton Maria Zanetti (i) being especially well known to other scholars of the period.

WRITINGS

Museum Florentinum, exhibens insigniora vetustatis monumenta quae Florentiae sunt, 6 vols (Florence, 1731–66)

Museum Etruscum exhibens insignia veterum Etruscorum monumenta, 3 vols (Florence, 1737–43)

'Gemmae antiquae A. M. Zanetti . . . notis Latinis', *Dactyliotheca zanettiana* (Venice, 1750)

BIBLIOGRAPHY

P. Berghaus, ed.: *Der Archäologe: Graphische Bildnisse aus dem Porträtarchiv Diepenbrock* (Münster, 1983)

M. Cristofani: *La scoperta degli etruschi: Archaeologia e antiquaria nel '700* (Rome, 1983)

DAVID CAST

Gori Gandellini, Giovanni (*b* Siena, March 1703; *d* Rome, 15 Dec 1769). Italian businessman, collector and writer. He initially trained for the priesthood but rejected this career and instead married Vittoria Gandellini, the daughter of a merchant whose name and business he subsequently inherited. Business links with Germany, and especially with Augsburg, gave him the opportunity to pursue his interest in engraving. Over the years he acquired a notable collection and became a fine connoisseur of prints. He read extensively on the history of printmaking, including the writings of the 17th-century German artist and writer Joachim von Sandrart, and amassed much material on the lives of engravers. After his death his sons, Francesco and Pietro, decided that his notes should be published. *Notizie istoriche degl' intagliatori* thus appeared in 1771. Gori Gandellini was not always a critical reader, and his work was less comprehensive and less reliable than the *Dictionnaire des graveurs* (Paris, 1767) by his French contemporary P. F. Basan, but both books marked an important step in the recognition of engraving as an art form with its own distinct history.

WRITINGS

Notizie istoriche degl' intagliatori, 3 vols (Siena, 1771); rev. and enlarged by L. de Angelis, 15 vols (Siena, 1808–16)

BIBLIOGRAPHY

E. de Tipaldo, ed.: *Biografia degli italiani illustri nelle scienze, lettere ed arti del secolo XVIII, e de' contemporanei*, 10 vols (Venice, 1838), vi, pp. 149–53 [biog. by L. de Angelis]

JANET SOUTHORN

Gorin, (Albert) Jean (*b* Saint-Emilion-de-Blain, Loire-Atlantique, 2 Dec 1899; *d* Niort, 29 March 1981). French painter and sculptor. He studied at the Académie de la Grande Chaumière in Paris from 1914 to 1916 and at the Ecole des Beaux-Arts in Nantes from 1919 to 1922. Initially influenced by Matisse, van Gogh and Cézanne, he discovered Cubism in Paris in 1923 and was particularly impressed by Albert Gleizes's book *Du Cubisme* (Paris, 1921). After a brief flirtation with Purism, he continued to move towards abstraction, especially after encountering Mondrian's Neo-plasticism in 1926. Almost immediately, and permanently, he was converted to this aesthetic, creating works such as *Composition No. 5* (1926; Paris, Pompidou). Gorin first exhibited his work in April 1928 at Lille with the group S.T.U.C.A. (Sciences, Techniques, Urbanisme, Confort, Art), alongside Mondrian, César Domela and others, in a show organized by Félix del Marle, founder of the review *Vouloir*.

Gorin continued working as a Neo-plasticist and from 1926 produced constructions, such as *Plastic Construction No. 97* (1930–37; Nantes, Mus. B.-A.), which led in 1929 to plane relief constructions, for example *Composition No. 4* (1931; The Hague, Gemeentemus.). In 1930 he exhibited with Cercle et Carré, though rarely attending the meetings. Two years later he helped found Abstraction-Création with Jean Hélion, Auguste Herbin and others. He exhibited at the important *Art Concret* exhibition in Paris in 1945 and in the same year began his 'mounted plane' compositions, using multiple layered plane constructions. From its foundation in 1946 until 1966, he exhibited at the Salon des Réalités Nouvelles. Moving away from the original forms of Neo-plasticism, though not its spirit, he superimposed circles on to his works of 1958 to 1962.

BIBLIOGRAPHY

M. Lemoine: 'Jean Gorin', *Rev. A.* [Paris], 5 (1969), pp. 100–02

Jean Gorin (exh. cat. by M. Allendy, Paris, Cent. N. A. Contemp., 1969)

M. Le Pommeré: *The Works of Jean Gorin* (Zurich, 1985)

□

Goris [Gorys], **Gerard** (*fl* 1438–42). South Netherlandish wood-carver. He entered the Leuven guild of sculptors in 1434. In 1438 he was commissioned to restore the organ case in St Pieterskerk, Leuven, and in 1439, with the Brussels carver Claes de Bruyn (*fl* 1439–42), he began work on the choir-stalls for which he received final payment in 1442. The respective roles of Goris and de Bruyn in the production of the stalls are not specified, but only de Bruyn was given the title 'Master', perhaps suggesting seniority, and it was he who was asked to carve a cult image of the Virgin (untraced) for the church in 1440. Originally there were two rows of stalls set against the wainscot panelling that lined the walls of the choir. Many were destroyed in 1803, leaving only the 30, relatively simple in structure, that formed the back row. The themes of the surviving misericord carvings are secular and include fools, dragons, demons and animals, some taken from bestiaries and fables. The technique is bold and vigorous, with a firm grasp of structure and space and a startlingly naturalistic style. A head of a woman of oriental appearance is deeply incised, simplified and strongly characterized without being exaggerated; the angular folds of the neck-cloth and turban are convincingly portrayed.

BIBLIOGRAPHY
E. van Even: *Louvain monumental* (Leuven, 1860), pp. 179, 200
J. Borchgrave d'Altena: 'Notes pour servir a l'étude des stalles en Belgique', *An. Soc. Royale Archéol. Bruxelles*, xli (1937), pp. 238–40, figs 11–35
T. Müller: *Sculpture in the Netherlands, Germany, France and Spain, 1400–1500*, Pelican Hist. A. (Harmondsworth, 1966), p. 63, pl. 71

KIM W. WOODS

Gor'ky. *See* NIZHNY NOVGOROD.

Gorky, Arshile [Adoian, Vosdanig Manoog] (*b* Dzov, Turkish Armenia, 15 April 1904; *d* Sherman, CT, 21 July 1948). American painter of Armenian birth. One of the most illustrious artists of the post-war New York School, he began his life in possibly the most obscure circumstances of any international modern master. His father emigrated to the USA to avoid conscription into the Turkish Army in World War I; in the Turkish persecution of the Armenians, Gorky's mother died in her son's arms after a 120-mile march. With his sister (who later figured prominently in his paintings) Gorky made his way to the coast and then, by ship, to the USA, arriving at New York in April 1920.

1. Early work. 2. First success and evolution of style. 3. Personal crisis.

1. EARLY WORK. Gorky settled into a community of Armenians in New England and attempted a reconciliation with his father, but when that failed he moved from Massachusetts to New York City (*c.* 1925). There he assumed his pseudonym, claiming to be a cousin of the Russian writer, Maksim Gor'ky whose name, however, was a *nom de plume.* In the late 1920s New York was full of White Russian immigrants of various degrees of nobility, and the implausibility of Gorky's claim was not noticed at the time. He quickly moved from the status of student to teacher at the Grand Central School of Art.

Gorky at first set himself the task of documenting his family and worked on a portrait of himself and his mother (based on a photograph taken in 1912 in Armenia). The style combined something of an icon's oriental flavour, with the bravura painting of Baroque masters such as Titian and Velázquez and the tonality of Picasso's Blue Period. These works occupied him from the mid-1920s until the 1940s, some of them repeatedly were repainted throughout that period. The best of these works, *Portrait of the Artist and his Mother* (1926–9; New York, Whitney; see fig. 1; *see also* ABSTRACT EXPRESSIONISM, §1), is a masterpiece in which the surface (shaved with a razor as each layer of paint dried) has the lustrous smoothness of ivory. This was a formative period: these protracted enterprises laid the foundations of an art characterized by a personal subject-matter (however abstracted in subsequent years) and techniques borrowed from the Old Masters.

Almost totally self-taught, Gorky set himself a programme in which he would recreate the evolution of modern art. At first (even before coming to New York), he painted in the manner of the French Impressionists, rendering views of his surroundings in a *plein-air* style with high-value colours. In the 1930s he began painting in the style of Cézanne, producing landscapes in prismatic colours with saturated hues and still-lifes of intense colour.

1. Arshile Gorky: *Portrait of the Artist and his Mother*, oil on canvas, 1.5×1.25 m, 1926–9 (New York, Whitney Museum of American Art)

Having experimented with Picasso's early style, he then explored Synthetic Cubism and related work by Léger.

Gorky executed endless drawings and a small series of pictures entitled *Night-time, Enigma, and Nostalgia* (whose composition was based on works by De Chirico and Vaello), in which the initial abstract appearance masks what seem to be lingering references to his domestic circumstances. It was with this style that he first came to public prominence with a set of large murals produced under the auspices of the Works Progress Administration's Federal Arts Project for Newark airport, NJ: *Aviation: Evolution of Forms under Aerodynamic Limitations* (1935–8). These were among the earliest abstract murals to appear anywhere in the USA. In fact, as was true for so much of Gorky's later works, the apparently non-referential design of these murals was still based on a firm transcription of reality. Gorky's ability to disguise the appearance of things suggested to him that he should support the war effort (he was too old to be conscripted in World War II) by teaching camouflage; he prepared a short descriptive prospectus, but the proposed course never materialized.

By the end of the 1930s Gorky had abandoned teaching in institutions and began to support himself through occasional sales and a handful of private students. Without a regular source of income he subsisted on a meagre diet, the veiled charity of friends, and his magnetic, if difficult, personality. His enormous frame and striking appearance contributed to the development of a celebrity cult surrounding him in the New York art world. His affectation of 'Russian' manners (which in his mind allowed him eccentric and unpredictable exhortations), and his pretensions to Old Master status may have appeared slightly ridiculous, but the brilliance of his work and pronouncements on art were nevertheless viewed with great seriousness. Gorky's experience as a mural painter, including his work on two large murals, one for the World's Fair of 1939 and the other for the Riviera nightclub (destr.), distinguished him from his contemporaries. Unintimidated by large surfaces, he was able to design over an extended composition. The confidence that he gained from the experience encouraged him to enlarge the scale of his easel paintings, which in turn influenced the preference for the larger format among the Abstract Expressionists.

2. First success and evolution of style. Gorky was first allied with the Russian immigrants such as Moses Soyer and Raphael Soyer, David Burliuk, Ilya Bolotowsky and John Graham. Subsequently he had a great effect on a group of artists, including Stuart Davis, Jacob Kainen (*b* 1909) and particularly Willem de Kooning, who in turn were of great influence. De Kooning, a virtual disciple, repeatedly stated his debt to Gorky. Nevertheless, in spite of his evident mastery, he was without a clearly identifiable style. He saw himself as the disciple of the entire modernist tradition of art and considered that, in order to extend this tradition, it was necessary to subjugate himself to his models: he did not hold originality in high regard. Yet his skill as a draughtsman, which he practised obsessively, was widely admired, even by artists as different from him as Jackson Pollock.

Gorky was an incorrigible plagiarist, borrowing not only his name but also material for his private letters, public pronouncements and paintings. However inauthentic his personality, his authenticity as an artist was never disputed. His style continued to evolve through successive periods of modern art as he 'apprenticed' himself to the absent, or long-dead, masters of painting. His paint-handling loosened as he mastered the most complex and advanced treatment of surfaces. Despite his own growing accomplishment and his place at the head of the New York school, as late as 1942 he still maintained that he had been a student of Kandinsky's, when queried by MOMA concerning its acquisition of his work.

By the early 1940s Gorky had emulated the paint-handling of Picasso and something of Miró's composition. As he tended towards the imagism of the Surrealists he began to part with John Graham, previously one of his closest colleagues, who found the Surrealists intolerable for their 'play' and lack of ultimate responsibility for the image. Gorky's own use of Surrealism was highly idiosyncratic and limited to the special purposes to which he put their styles. By this time the Surrealists were arriving in New York, driven from Europe before the onslaught of the Fascists.

Guided by his dealer, Julien Levy, who had been the first to show the Surrealists in the USA, Gorky met Roberto Matta; soon Gorky was drawing and painting

2. Arshile Gorky: *The Liver Is the Cock's Comb*, oil on canvas, 1.86×2.48 m, 1944 (Buffalo, Albright–Knox Art Gallery)

with the swift line and biomorphic shapes that were Matta's hallmark. In 1944 Gorky met André Breton, the 'Pope' of Surrealism, who recognized in Gorky's sweeping black lines and glowing washes of colour, an achievement unmatched by any of the European Surrealists (see fig. 2). His admiration for Gorky was attested by the catalogue introduction he wrote for one of his shows. The synthesis wrought by Gorky in paintings such as *One Year the Milkweed* (1944; Washington, DC, N.G.A.) was complex, mixing advanced artistic theory and personal need. His talent as a painter can best be understood by comparing some of his (often full-scale) preparatory drawings with the innumerable small sketches with which he began. These careful sketches, in oils, pen and ink and crayon, always preceded his seemingly 'spontaneous' works. He essayed his ideas for compositions beginning with rough notes on small pieces of paper, which he then developed in a manner worthy of a Renaissance master. Once Gorky arrived at a design for a subject he did not alter it, but, over time, reused the composition in a series of works, perhaps altering the colour scheme or the paint handling. Beneath the dextrous washes of oil paint Gorky displayed the underlying drawing, which remained of structural importance but which was virtually invisible to uninitiated spectators, who believed they were seeing 'abstract' works—unedited and unpremeditated, from the artist's unconscious. This idea, then fashionable, that art should be made without external reference, would not have accommodated Gorky's personal need for depiction.

Gorky's supportive drawings defined the space and the characters portrayed in his mature paintings. Colour cues refer back to the original subjects, sometimes as mere touches of hue, at other times as opaque blocks, but it can be argued that the colours in his mature (and apparently most non-objective works) derive from naturalistic representations. By 1943 he had begun to form his mature style, a rich amalgam of all his previous work. He continued to oblige his audience by implying that his pictures were formed casually and spontaneously but he did not practise automatism, instead carefully planning his imagery. Similarly he claimed that his titles came to him in the manner of automatic writing, but they were just as consciously considered.

3. Personal crisis. During this period of rising recognition for his art, Gorky did not enjoy either financial success or personal stability. He had been married once in the 1930s, but divorced and married again, becoming the father of two girls in the mid-1940s. Still impoverished, he lived in a rented house in Sherman, CT. The family that he had craved since his own had been murdered or scattered in Armenia was now forming around him, but life in the New World was not as stable as he would have liked. He was in command of his painting style and had moved to the very forefront of advanced artistic production, but he was once again struck by tragedy.

In 1946 drawings and dozens of his heavily worked paintings were destroyed in a fire at his studio. He was diagnosed as suffering from throat cancer, and was obliged to give his doctor two paintings because of his inability to pay for treatment. His marriage disintegrated, and he lost the long-sought company of his wife and children. He descended into a profound depression, surrounded by his art but haunted by the numerous shams that he himself had erected. Demoralized not only by his poor health but by his lack of general appreciation and by his estrangement from his family, he hanged himself. Within only a few years of his death his reputation was securely established as one of the founding figures of postwar American art.

BIBLIOGRAPHY

A. Breton: 'The Eye-spring: Arshile Gorky', *Le Surréalisme et la peinture* (Paris, 1945), pp. 196–9

Arshile Gorky (exh. cat., foreword A. Gottlieb; New York, Kootz Gal., 1950)

J. I. H. Baur: *Revolution and Tradition in Modern American Art* (Cambridge, MA, 1951)

Arshile Gorky Memorial Exhibition (exh. cat., ed. E. Schwabacher; New York, Whitney; Minneapolis, MN, Walker A. Cent.; San Francisco, CA, Mus. A.; 1951)

W. C. Seitz: *Arshile Gorkey: Paintings, Drawings, Studies*, foreword J. Levy (New York, 1962)

Arshile Gorky: Drawings (exh. cat. by F. O'Hara, ACGB, 1964)

Arshile Gorky: Paintings and Drawings (exh. cat. by R. Melville, London, Tate, 1965)

J. Levy: *Arshile Gorky* (New York, 1966)

A. Mag., 1/7 (1976) [special issue on Gorky]

H. Rand: *Arshile Gorky: The Implications of Symbols* (Montclair, NJ, 1981, rev. 1982/*R* Berkeley, 1991) [incl. comprehensive bibliog.]

J. Jordan: *The Paintings of Arshile Gorky: A Critical Catalogue* (New York, 1982)

Arshile Gorky, 1904–1948 (exh. cat., essays by J. Golding, R. Storr, M. Spender and L. Corrin; Madrid, Fund. Caja Pensiones; London, Whitechapel A.G., 1989)

HARRY RAND

Gor'ky, Maksim [Gorky, Maxim; Peshkov, Aleksey (Maksimovich)] (*b* Nizhny Novgorod, 28 March 1868; *d* Moscow, 18 June 1936). Russian writer and critic. Early in his career he worked as an art critic for the *Nizhegorodskiy Listok* and published several articles (May–Sept, 1896) on the All-Russian Industrial and Art Exhibition in Nizhny Novgorod in 1896. His aesthetic principles were very significantly influenced by the 'philosophy of life' of Friedrich Nietzsche, but on the other hand he borrowed heavily from the 'revolutionary democratic aesthetics' proposed by V. G. Belinsky, N. A. Dobroliubov and N. G. Chernyshevsky. He regarded as great art academic-style paintings that were intelligible to the people, and he opposed the 'decadent' and 'antisocial', which he saw in much new art, not least the work of Mikhail Vrubel'. Gor'ky's interest in politics was evident in both his writing (e.g. the novel *Mat'* ['Mother'], 1906) and his fund-raising for the Bolsheviks. However, in his defence of artistic monuments (*Revolution and Culture*, 1918), he protested that the recent revolution was anti-cultural and in an attempt to oppose the destruction of Russian culture he founded the Culture and Freedom Society, which published a bulletin and collection of articles emphasizing the ideas that the material (outer) culture directly affects the spiritual (inner) one; that culture is non-party; and that the cultural heritage must be preserved. As a realist and a friend of Il'ya Repin he came into conflict not only with formalist critics such as Victor Shklovsky but also those Symbolists, Futurists and other avant-garde artists who felt that the revolution should build a distinctly Soviet culture using new artistic methods and approaches. From May 1917 to July 1918 Gor'ky published articles in which he combined the idea of Fyodor Dostoyevsky about the supreme power of beauty with Aleksandr Bogdanov's notions of a new proletarian culture. Accordingly, he regarded the aim of culture as the development of man's social conscience, attainable through Realism. However, his unwillingness to embrace a new culture brought criticism from Vladimir Mayakovsky and others, who saw in him the old revolutionary lacking the courage to give up his old comforts. Gor'ky, however, was able to appreciate the talents and, to some extent, the significance of the avant-garde. In the early 1930s, having been declared a classic author of proletarian literature by the State, he actively participated in the establishment of SOCIALIST REALISM.

WRITINGS

'Beglyye zametki' [Passing remarks], *Nizhegorodskiy Listok* (21 May–10 Sept 1896)

'Nesvoyevremennyye mysli' [Untimely thoughts], *Novaya zhizn'* (1 May 1917–16 July 1918); repr. in *Nesvoyevremennyye mysli: Zametki o revolyutsii i kul'ture* [Untimely thoughts: notes on revolution and culture] (Petrograd, 1918); Eng. trans. as *Notes on Revolution, Culture and the Bolsheviks, 1917–1918* (New York, 1968)

Revolyutsiya i kul'tura: Stat'i [Revolution and culture: articles] (Berlin, 1918)

Sobraniye sochineniy [Collected works], 30 vols (Moscow, 1949–55)

Polnoye sobraniye sochineniy [Complete collected works] (Moscow, 1974–)

BIBLIOGRAPHY

Gor'kiy i khudozhniki (sbornik vospominaniy) [Gorky and artists (collection of reminiscences)] (Moscow, 1963)

N. I. Zholtova: *Maksim Gor'kiy i izobrazitel'noye iskusstvo* [Maksim Gor'ky and fine art] (Moscow, 1965)

I. Weil: *Gorky: His Literary Development and Influence on Soviet Intellectual Life* (New York, 1966)

E. Clowes: *Maksim Gorky: A Reference Guide* (Boston, 1987)

SERGEY KUZNETSOV

Gorman, Rudolph Carl (*b* Chinle, AZ, 26 July 1932). Native American Navajo painter, printmaker and sculptor. After attending Northern Arizona University in Flagstaff, where he majored in literature and minored in art, he received a scholarship in 1958 from the Navajo Tribal Council to study art at Mexico City College. He also studied at San Francisco State University and at other California institutions. The style that he developed stemmed from his experiences in Mexico and reveals the influence of his teachers as well as that of the Mexican muralists. He maintained a studio and gallery for his own works and those of other Native American artists in Taos, NM. While Gorman has handled such subject-matter as interpretations of Navajo rugs and pottery designs, his most successful and best-received works have been his studies of Navajo women. He portrayed them as archetypes; as monumental, nurturing 'earth mothers'. He grouped women in conventional poses or engaged in domestic pursuits, ranging from stolid affirmations to revelations of inner beauty and grace. He used various media, sometimes painting and drawing in acrylics, pastels and pencil in the same work. He worked out personal technical processes and used these with great effectiveness. His style is well-suited to lithographs, which he has produced in great number. He has also produced sculptures.

Gorodets, carved wooden house shutter, detail showing lion, 19th century–early 20th

BIBLIOGRAPHY

D. Monthan: *R. C. Gorman: The Lithographs* (Flagstaff, 1978)

T. Hurst: *R. C. Gorman: The Posters* (Flagstaff, 1980)

C. Henningsen and S. Parks: *R. C. Gorman: A Portrait* (Bulfinch, 1983)

R. C. Gorman, Chinle to Taos (exh. cat. by V. Dooley, Taos, NM, Navajo Gal., 1988)

ARTHUR SILBERMAN

Gormaz, García de San Esteban y. *See* SAN ESTEBAN Y GORMAZ, GARCÍA DE.

Gornea. *See* GARNI.

Gorno-Altay region. *See under* RUSSIA, §XII, 4.

Goro. *See* BIAGIO DI GORO GHEZZI.

Gorodets. Russian town, 70 km north-west of Nizhny Novgorod (formerly Gor'ky). It is one of the oldest settlements on the River Volga and was founded in 1152 by Prince Yuri Dolgoruky (*reg* 1149–57). The earthen rampart that fortified the ancient kremlin is partly preserved. Gorodets is principally known for its wood-carving and painting. The rich openwork carving on pediments and platbands gives a particular originality to the old residential buildings, most of which were built in the 19th and early 20th centuries. Houses of this period were also decorated with 'Nizhny Novgorod wild carving', which is characterized by high relief on a flat ground (see fig.). The technique's alternative name of 'ship's carving' is derived from its use by local carpenters in the decoration of Volga boats. After the 1890s the carved designs spread to other towns in Central Russia. In the mid-19th century the Gorodets style of painting developed as a particular form of folk art. It is characterized by simple, brightly coloured pictures, which were used to decorate distaffs, furniture, shutters, doors and wooden utensils. Genre scenes, flower designs and such ancient motifs as mounted figures by the Tree of Life were all executed in broad, free brushstrokes and graphically outlined in black and white, thus stressing the lively play of rhythms. Although this folk art declined in the early 20th century it was revived with the foundation in 1936 of a cooperative, which by 1960 had developed into a factory producing souvenirs in the local style.

BIBLIOGRAPHY

D. V. Prokop'yev: *Khudozhestvennyye promysly Gor'kovskogo Kraya* [Artistic crafts of the Gor'ky region] (Gor'ky, 1939)

T. Mavrina, ed.: *Gorodetskaya Zhivopis'* [Gorodets painting] (Leningrad, 1970)

M. A. Nekrasova: 'Istoki Gorodetskoy rospisi i yeyo khudozhestvennyy stil'' [Sources of Gorodets painting and its artistic style], *Russkoye iskusstvo XVIIIv* [Russian art of the 18th century] (Moscow, 1973)

——: *Narodnoye iskusstvo kak chast' kul'tury* [Folk art as part of culture] (Moscow, 1983), pp. 198–234

MARIYA A. NEKRASOVA

Goro di Gregorio (*fl* 1300–34). Italian sculptor and goldsmith. He is documented in Siena, Massa Marittima and Messina. He was the son of Goro di Guccio Ciuti (*d* before 1311), a Florentine sculptor who, with Lapo and Donato, assistants of Nicola Pisano, was granted citizenship in Siena in 1271. Goro di Guccio Ciuti's sons Neri and Ambrogio, of whom nothing further is known, followed in their father's footsteps, as did Goro.

Goro's earliest works are probably the monumental busts on the interior of the north portal of the main façade of the cathedral in Siena, dating from around 1300. One of the two lions on the interior of the main portal also dates from around this time. Goro must have made the sculptural figures, chased in silver, on the shepherd's staff in the Museo Capitolare in Città di Castello during the first decade of the 14th century. He probably made a statue of a *Prophet* (sold London, Sotheby's, 20–27 June 1978) between 1310 and 1315. A tomb in San Gimignano and three large statues of *Apostles* for the cathedral in Siena (Siena, Cripta delle Statue) date from 1315 to 1320. Three half-figures of Christ, an Apostle and an angel holding a pall (San Gimignano, Mus. A. Sacra and Mus. Civ.), have survived from the tomb. Goro is mentioned for the first time in 1320 in connection with an unspecified payment as a *maestro di pietra*; he was then living in Siena in the Vallepiatta di sotto contrada. He signed and dated the urn known as the Arca di S Cerbone in Massa Marittima Cathedral in 1324, and in 1329 he received payment in Siena for work he had done at the fortress of Sassoforte in Maremma.

The reliefs on the Arca di S Cerbone show that Goro was one of the finest sculptors in Siena in the 1320s. The figures are graceful and fully modelled, creating a lively alternation of light and shade, which emphasizes the rhythmic flow of the draperies; the architectural features are finely elaborated, and the backgrounds are decorated with a richness reminiscent of goldsmiths' work. Two silver figures of the *Virgin* and *St John* on the reliquary of the cross in the cathedral in Padua can be dated to 1324. Goro built the tomb of the lawyer *Guglielmo di Ciliano* (Siena, University), who died in 1324, in the following few years. A statue of the *Virgin* (Florence, priv. col.) and a statue of the *Annunciation* (Boston, MA, Mus. F. A.) show the direction of Goro's artistic development around 1330 in the swaying movement of the forms, the litheness of the figures and the flowing of the drapery. His latest known works are the tomb of *Archbishop Guidotto de' Tabiati* (*d* 1333) in the cathedral in Messina, signed and dated 1334, and the *Madonna degli Storpi* (Messina, Mus. Reg.).

BIBLIOGRAPHY

G. Della Valle: *Lettere sanesi*, ii (Rome, 1785), pp. 121–36

G. Milanesi: *Documenti per la storia dell'arte senese*, i (Siena, 1854), pp. 153–4

E. Carli: *Goro di Gregorio* (Florence, 1946)

Il gotico a Siena (exh. cat. by E. Cioni Liserani and D. Cinelli, Siena, Pal. Pub., 1982), pp. 104–8, 201–5

R. Bartalini: 'Goro di Gregorio e la tomba del giurista Guglielmo di Ciliano', *Prospettiva*, xli (1985), pp. 21–38

——: 'Du nouveau sur Goro di Gregorio', *Rev. A.*, 87 (1990), pp. 42–51

G. Kreytenberg: 'Goro di Gregorio vor 1324', *Stadel-Jb.*, 13 (1991)

G. KREYTENBERG

Görres, Johann Joseph von (*b* Koblenz, 25 Jan 1776; *d* Munich, 29 Jan 1848). German writer, philosopher and teacher. As a youth he was a radical, seeking to reconcile liberal French Revolutionary ideas with his Rhenish nationalist impulses. From 1797 he was active in the Koblenz Patriotic Club, which promoted the idea of an independent 'Cis-Rhenish Republic' under French protection, but after a visit to Paris in 1799 as the representative of Koblenz, he became disillusioned with politics and took up teaching at his old school, the Koblenz Gymnasium.

In his first book, *Aphorismen über die Kunst* (1802), Görres tried to create a rational framework by which all art and science could be described as a system of opposites. He postulated a philosophical system based on dualities: colour and line, harmony and melody, the sentimental and the naive. It was in the reconciling of these opposites that he saw the process by which art is created. Despite its immaturity, the *Aphorismen* marked the beginning of Görres's appreciation of the art of the Middle Ages in preference to the 'malaise of this present century', and it heralded his growing disenchantment with the Enlightenment and his interest in Romanticism. This interest was reinforced when he was appointed to teach at Heidelberg University (1806) and became interested in German folk culture, publishing collections of German folk songs and poetry (1807 and 1817). In 1808 he returned to the Koblenz Gymnasium, and during the Napoleonic Wars he became an increasingly influential spokesman for German nationalism, chiefly through his controversial newspaper, the *Rhenischer Merkur* (1814–16). In an article in 1815 he demanded the return of all art and scientific objects plundered during the French occupation, creating the notion of art works as the permanent cultural property of a nation. This insistence on the intimate connection between art and nationalism became a hallmark of his later writings.

During the French occupation, Görres became fascinated by medieval architecture. In 1814 he took up the cause of architecture, arguing for the completion of Cologne Cathedral, left unfinished since the Middle Ages, as the most appropriate monument to the defeat of Napoleon and the independence of Germany. He regarded its ruinous incompletion as an image of Germany and therefore a symbol of the new empire he wished to see built. His manifesto was the most important statement of the Germanic character of Gothic architecture since Johann Wolfgang von Goethe's paean on Strasbourg Cathedral (*Von Deutscher Baukunst*, 1772) and brought him national renown.

After 1815, however, Görres gradually became disillusioned with pan-German nationalism and became a champion of liberal regionalism. He offended the Prussian authorities by collecting signatures for constitutional reform in Koblenz, in 1815 absorbed into Prussia. When he published his political manifesto *Teutschland und die Revolution* (1819), his arrest was ordered and he fled into exile, first to Strasbourg and then to Munich. Having renounced the Roman Catholic Church in his youth, he now became reconciled to it in exile. At the same time, his appreciation of Gothic architecture developed, particularly through his friendship with Sulpiz Boisserée, author of a monumental treatise on Cologne Cathedral, the editorship of which Görres declined, protesting his layman's status.

From 1827 until his death, Görres refined his philosophy of history while teaching as professor of 'general and literary history' at Munich University. Eventually his longstanding anthropological and political interests came to stamp his understanding of art. Rather than looking at art in isolation, he became increasingly interested in the way in which the structure and organization of society affected culture. In 1828 he commemorated Gothic art as the expression of the free society of the Middle Ages, 'pious in belief but bold and free in life', a belief that had implications for the present. Chastened by recent historical events, Görres was suspicious of Hegel's doctrine of the historical mission of the nation state and warned of the concentration of power in that state. As an alternative model for Germany, he upheld the feudal decentralization of political power.

In his later years Görres devoted most of his energies to Church–State relations. His book *Athanasius* (1838), a defence of the Archbishop of Cologne who had been arrested (1837) by the Prussian authorities for enforcing Church teachings on inter-denominational marriages, and his contributions to the journal *Historisch-politische Blätter*, which he co-founded, helped initiate the political Catholicism that played so important a role in German public life in the second half of the 19th century. In 1842 Görres's monograph on Cologne and Strasbourg cathedrals presented his most mature work on Gothic architecture. This was no longer strictly nationalist, although he still insisted on the Germanic origin of the Gothic; it also depicted Gothic architecture as a rational and orderly geometric system, reflecting the latest discoveries of Friedrich Hoffstadt (1802–46).

Görres was one of Germany's most important political philosophers, his writings forming a response to the upheavals of modernism confronting Germany at the beginning of the 19th century. He brought into the political arena many of the ideas and concerns of German Romanticism, such as the glorification of medieval society, a reverence for folk culture, the national importance of art and a sense of the importance of religion in modern life. He was influential in the debate about the future shape of a unified, national Germany and offered a compelling vision of a variegated German nation, which reconciled the conflicting goals of national unity, religious freedom and regional autonomy by distributing political power among interlocking and counterpoised institutions. Characteristic of his thought was the political importance of art and architecture. By making Gothic art a symbol, first of German nationhood, then of a healthy and robust medieval society, Görres helped create the political and theoretical background for the German Gothic Revival.

WRITINGS

Aphorismen über die Kunst (Koblenz, 1802, 2/1804)
Die teutschen Volksbücher (Heidelberg, 1807)
Altteutsche Volks- und Meisterlieder aus den Handschriften der Heidelberger Bibliothek (Frankfurt am Main, 1817)
Teutschland und die Revolution (Koblenz, 1819; Fr. trans., Paris, 1819; Eng. trans., London, 1820)
Die christliche Mystik, 4 vols (Regensburg, 1836–42, 2/1879–80)
Athanasius (Regensburg, 1838, rev. 4/1838; Fr. trans., Paris, 1838; It. trans., Turin, 1839)
Der Dom von Cöln und das Münster von Strassburg (Munich, 1842)

BIBLIOGRAPHY

NDB
F. Schultz: *Joseph Görres als Herausgeber, Literarhistoriker, Kritiker im zusammenhang mit der jüngeren Romantik* (Berlin, 1902)
G. Kallen: *Joseph Görres und der deutsche Idealismus* (Münster, 1926)
H. Kapfinger: *Der Eoskreis, 1828 bis 1832* (Munich, 1928)
R. Saitschick: *Joseph Görres und die abendländische Kultur* (Olten, 1953)
R. Habel: *Joseph Görres: Studien über den Zusammenhang von Natur, Geschichte und Mythos in seinen Schriften* (Wiesbaden, 1960)

MICHAEL J. LEWIS

Gortázar, Fernando González. *See* GONZÁLEZ GORTÁZAR, FERNANDO.

Gortyn. Site of a city on the northern edge of the Mesara Plain in southern Crete, *c.* 6 km north-east of Moíres, which flourished *c.* 700 BC–AD 670. The westernmost of the hills enclosing it to the north served as its acropolis, where, following Neolithic occupation, there was a Bronze Age settlement after the 13th century BC. The acropolis is separated from the hills to the east by the River Mitropolianos, the course of which also divided the Greco-Roman and Byzantine city into two unequal parts. Excavations were begun by Federico Halbherr in 1884 and were continued by the Italian Archaeological Mission in Crete and from 1912 onwards by the Italian Archaeological School in Athens.

1. ANCIENT. The most significant late Bronze Age (*c.* 1580–*c.* 1100 BC) remains from the area derive from the rural villa of Kannia, to the south-west of modern Mitropolis, which comprised 30 rooms, including at least four small domestic shrines distinguished by benches and by statuettes and ex-votos of the Minoan goddess. The 50 or so large storage pithoi that were found in many of the rooms and that attest to the villa's connection with agriculture date from Late Minoan (LM) IB (*c.* 1480–*c.* 1425 BC), but the latest statuettes from the shrines show that, after its destruction *c.* 1425 BC, the villa was partially reoccupied in LM IIIB (*c.* 1335–*c.* 1190 BC).

The main architectural remains of the Geometric period (*c.* 900–*c.* 700 BC) are a late 9th- or early 8th-century BC temple and an associated altar (perhaps of later date) on the acropolis and a roughly contemporary tholos tomb on flat ground at its foot. It is possible that the temple's layout is derived from north Syrian prototypes: almost square, it consists of two sections, the one at the southern end subdivided into small cells with a central offering pit. Some of the hundreds of terracottas discovered in a votive repository by the altar show that the building was dedicated to Athena as protectress of the city. The layout of the temple on the acropolis recurred in a more highly developed form in the Pythion (the Temple of Apollo Pythios; 7th century BC), Gortyn's most revered sacred building, which lies to the south-east on the other side of the Mitropolianos. During Hellenistic times (323–27 BC) a pronaos was added and wooden posts forming the internal partition were replaced by stone supports. These were in turn replaced in Roman times in the late 1st and late 2nd centuries AD by two rows of four Corinthian columns of marble, and a concrete apse was built into the centre of the west wall.

Architectural remains of the Classical (*c.* 525/480–323 BC) and Hellenistic periods are confined to stone blocks inscribed with the very significant law code (early 5th century BC; now displayed near the foot of the acropolis), and important fortifications extending over the hills to the north of the city, which were built in two stages. The sections with walls 3.8–4.5 m thick at the foundations date from the late 3rd century BC, and those with walls 1–2 m thick equipped with square external towers date from the beginning of the 1st century BC. They were being restored when they were destroyed by an earthquake around 30 BC.

Gortyn was the capital of the Roman province of Crete and Cyrenaica from 27 BC until the reforms of Diocletian (*reg* AD 284–305) and was the main seat of the proconsul until at least the first half of the 2nd century AD. The Cretan monuments of the Roman period were initially built of stone, later of brick and cement, and finally of small stone blocks. Among the most important is the praetorium (1st century AD), 100 m east of the Pythion, which originally consisted of the proconsul's residence and a temple probably dedicated to the imperial cult. At the beginning of the 2nd century AD the proconsul's residence was replaced by monumental baths, flanked to the west by a basilica. Near by was the nymphaeum (2nd century AD), with niches in the centres of its wings and its long façade fronted by eight Ionic columns. (Under the Byzantine emperor Heraklios (*reg* AD 610–41) its broad pool was transformed into a large vaulted cistern and the nymphaeum itself became a monumental fountain.) Also of interest is the odeion (later 1st century BC; rebuilt AD 100; see fig.), situated near where the law code is now displayed, which has unusual vaults made from large stone blocks. Gortyn also had three theatres. The smallest, from the 2nd century AD, was linked to the Pythion; another, possibly a rebuilt Classical theatre, stood on the lowest south-eastern outcrop of the acropolis; and the third, constructed almost entirely of concrete but with a magnificent marble entablature, was built near the eastern boundary of the Roman city under Antoninus Pius (*reg* AD 138–61) and his successors and was once believed to be a rare example of an amphitheatre–theatre, though it is actually a typical Roman theatre with a stage on two levels. A true amphitheatre was identified beneath the village of Hagi Deka in 1984, but little of it remains. To its south lay a large circus or stadium. Significant remains of late 6th-century AD aqueducts are also visible. The principal structure crossed the city centre on broad arches from north to south.

Gortyn's importance in the development of early Greek sculpture is shown by the Daedalic terracottas from the votive repository in the temple on the acropolis and by the tradition that Dipoinos and Skyllis, the sons of Daidalos, were natives of the city. Hellenistic capitals, sculptures and sarcophagi produced at Gortyn were influenced chiefly by Attic models, but Roman specimens resemble those from Asia Minor.

BIBLIOGRAPHY

D. Levi: 'Gortina', *Boll. A.*, xliv (1959), pp. 273–5

G. Rizza and V. Santa Maria Scrinari: *Il santuario sull'acropoli di Gortina*, i (Rome, 1968)

Gortyn, aerial view from the south, showing the odeion at the top and the basilica of Hagios Titos at the bottom

L. Beschi: 'Antichità cretesi a Venezia', *Annu. Scu. Archeol. Atene & Miss. It. Oriente*, l–li (1972–3), pp. 479–502

A. Di Vita: 'I terremoti a Gortina in età Romana e proto-bizantina: Una nota', *Annu. Scu. Archeol. Atene & Miss. It. Oriente*, lvii–lviii (1979–80), pp. 435–507

I. F. Sanders: *Roman Crete* (Warminster, 1982), pp. 61–7, 71–80

F. Ghedini: 'Sculture dal ninfeo e dal pretorio di Gortina', *Annu. Scu. Archeol. Atene & Miss. It. Oriente*, lxii (1984)

E. Ghisellini: 'Sarcofagi romani di Gortyna', *Annu. Scu. Archeol. Atene & Miss. It. Oriente*, lxii (1984), pp. 249–335

M. A. Rizzo: 'Capitelli corinzio-italici da Creta', *Annu. Scu. Archeol. Atene & Miss. It. Oriente*, lxii (1984), pp. 151–76

A. Di Vita in *Creta antica* (Rome, 1985), pp. 69–116

M. Ricciardi: 'Il tempio di Apollo Pizio a Gortina', *Annu. Scu. Archaeol. Atene & Miss. It. Oriente*, lxiv–lxv (1986–7), pp. 7–130

A. Di Vita: 'L'anfiteatro ed il grande teatro romano di Gortina', *Annu. Scu. Archaeol. Atene & Miss. It. Oriente*, lxiv–lxv (1986–7), pp. 327–47

A. Di Vita, ed.: *Gortina*, i (Rome, 1988)

ANTONINO DI VITA

2. EARLY CHRISTIAN. Under Constantine the Great, Crete became a separate province with Gortyn as its capital. The 6th-century AD *Synekdemos* of Hierokles places 'Gortyn metropolis' at the head of Crete's 22 cities, which

were governed by a *consularis*. As the province's administrative, financial, religious and cultural centre, Gortyn was endowed with numerous monuments and public buildings, the remains of which, together with the many inscriptions that have been recovered from the city and the surrounding villages, provide valuable information for the history of Early Christian Gortyn.

In the 4th and 5th centuries the city probably reached its greatest extent (*c*. 150 ha), covering an area between the acropolis hill to the north and the cemeteries on the other three sides. The ancient temple on the acropolis probably remained in use until the 4th century, when a simple Christian basilica was built on top of it (rest. 6th century). In the late 7th century the acropolis was fortified. Although many ancient buildings in the city proper, such as two of the theatres, the odeion, the nymphaeum and the baths, remained in use for some time, most of them, with the notable exception of the praetorium, either changed function or were gradually abandoned after the triumph of Christianity. The Temple of Apollo Pythios, for example, was converted into a three-aisled Christian basilica. The church of Hagios Titos, built *c*. 600 in the forum area, is a three-aisled basilica of large limestone blocks (see fig.). There is a narthex to the west and a triconch chancel flanked by two *pastophoria* to the east. In the nave the cross-arms were probably barrel-vaulted; both the north and south arms ended in an apse. Numerous carved architectural fragments have survived (*in situ* and Herakleion, Archaeol. Mus.), including columns, capitals and parts of the screen and ambo, some of which reflect the influence of sculptural models from Constantinople. The church survived the Arab invasion of 827–8 and remained in use during the Middle Byzantine period. A second basilica was built on the site of an earlier temple, now known as Mauropapa; two more basilicas have been uncovered to the south of the city, as well as a 5th-century triconch, possibly a martyrium, and a five-aisled basilica (*c*. 560s) near the village of Mitropolis. The latter was paved with mosaics and marble slabs, and it originally had galleries above the aisles. It was destroyed by an earthquake *c*. 618, rebuilt with the same layout and finally destroyed *c*. 670. It has been suggested that this church, rather than Hagios Titos, served as the cathedral.

During the city's last period of prosperity in the early 7th century the aqueducts were restored and numerous fountains built with decorative brick niches. Other finds include many Christian tombs from the three cemeteries and a distinctive style of 6th-century pottery overpainted with geometric designs. Severe earthquakes, the Arab raids and the ruralization of city life contributed to Gortyn's dramatic decline from *c*. 650. Although it ceased to be the capital of Crete after the Arab conquest, it remained the episcopal see until long after the Byzantine reconquest of 961.

BIBLIOGRAPHY

D. Stiernon and L. Stiernon: 'Gortyn', *Dictionnaire d'histoire et de géographie ecclésiastique*, ed. A. Baudrillat and others, xxi (Paris, 1986), cols 786–811

D. Tsougarakis: *Byzantine Crete: From the Fifth Century to the Venetian Conquest* (Athens, 1988)

A. Di Vita: 'I ricenti scavi della SAIA a Gortina', *XXXVIII Corso di cultura sull'arte ravennate a Bizantina: Ravenna, 1991*, pp. 159–83

DIMITRIS TSOUGARAKIS

Gortys. *See under* MEGALOPOLIS.

Görtz, Sebastian. *See* GÖTZ, SEBASTIAN.

Gorze, Order of. Benedictine monastic reform movement of the 10th century that took its name from the monastery near Metz, France. The monastery was established in AD 754 by St Chrodegag (*d* 766) as a model episcopal monastic community and was very influential over the next four centuries. In 934 a reform of Benedictine monasticism, begun at Gorze in 933 and based on the rule of St Benedict of Aniane (*d* 821), was introduced into St Maximin at Trier and spread quickly throughout Lotharingia. During the next century it swept into the Benedictine houses of adjoining regions to the north, east and south-east, countered only on the west by the stricter Cluniac reform. In England St Dunstan incorporated many of the *consuetudines Gorziensis* into his *Regularis concordia* (957–65), while during the 11th century, variants of the Gorze customs arose on the Continent.

Gorze's reforms were organized by region. Each sub-centre organized a network of affiliated religious houses, usually by reciprocal consent. Exchanges were made over these networks that contributed significantly to the development of early Romanesque art and architecture. Reformed houses included St Maximin at Trier, St Willibrord at Echternach, St Emmeram at Regensburg, St Michael at Hildesheim, St Nazarius at Lorsch, Stavelot-Malmedy, Fulda, Hersfeld, Corvey, Reichenau-Mittelzell, Einsiedeln and St Gall.

The *Ordo Gorziensis* was supported by powerful secular authorities, as shown for example at Cologne. Bruno, younger brother of the Emperor Otto I, became Archbishop after studies at St Maximin in Trier and established model monasteries at St Pantaleon in Cologne and St Patroclus at Soest; Gero, another monk of St Maximin, became Abbot of the reformed Mönchen-Gladbach community in 975 and later Archbishop; and Archbishop Heribert of Cologne, founder of the Benedictine monastery at Deutz in 1002, was educated at Gorze. The Gorze–Trier reform and its later variants extended beyond monastic precincts to include cathedral chapters and imperial chanceries as its supporters were elevated to important sees throughout the Holy Roman Empire. With such important sponsorship, artistic production in the workshops of the reform abbeys was greatly encouraged.

The 'Reichenau' style of manuscript illumination, as practised at the Gorze–Trier reformed monastery of Reichenau-Mittelzell in Germany, was apparently also followed at St Maximin of Trier and at Echternach. The Reichenau 'school' seems to have spread among the outstanding workshops of Gorze–Trier establishments. Variations of the style appeared in works attributed to other reformed monasteries such as Fulda, while distinctive new modes developed from the Reichenau manner in, for example, 11th-century Echternach and Cologne. Other styles of painting were developed by the 11th century at St Maximin, Trier (where the Master of the Registrum Gregorii, the anonymous illuminator and restorer of ancient volumes, was active), and independently at St Emmeram at Regensburg (see fig.) and St Michael at Hildesheim, both Trier filiations.

Important changes in early Romanesque architecture that reflected liturgical innovations took place among houses affiliated to the Order of Gorze. The diminution of the Carolingian westwork, the great centralized, towered and galleried structure at the west end of the church, occurred as the number of outer crypts extending beyond the east choir of the reformed monastic churches increased. At the same time, the outer crypt replaced the westwork as the setting for the cult of the Saviour. As the outer crypt increased in importance and symbolic meaning at such reformed churches as St Maximin (952), St Emmeram at Regensburg (980), Saint-Amand (1040), Stavelot (1046) and Saint-Riquier (1056), the westwork became the special place for the cult of the Archangel Michael.

Serious Cluniac inroads began in the 11th century, and by the late 12th century the *Ordo Gorziensis* was practically eradicated. The final fragments of the early medieval abbey were destroyed in 1609, and only a Late Romanesque parish church remains to mark the site of the once great and proud Benedictine monastery.

BIBLIOGRAPHY

K. Hallinger: *Gorze-Kluny. Studien zu den monastischen Lebensformen und Gegensätzen im Hochmittelalter*, Studia Anslemiana, 2 vols (Rome, 1950)

C. R. Dodwell and D. H. Turner: *Reichenau Reconsidered: A Re-assessment of the Place of Reichenau in Ottonian Art*, Warb. Inst. Surv., ii (London, 1965)

K. B. Powell: 'Observations on a Number of Liuthas Manuscripts', *J. Warb. & Court. Inst.*, xxxiv (1971), pp. 1–11

W. Sanderson: 'Monastic Reform in Lorraine and the Architecture of the Outer Crypt, 950–1100', *Trans. Amer. Philos. Soc.*, lxi/6 (1971), pp. 1–36

R. Fuchs and D. Oltrogge: 'Kerald und Heribert: Zur Entstehungsgeschichte des Widmungsbildes im Codex Egberti', *Kurtrie. Jb.* (1989), pp. 65–86

WARREN SANDERSON

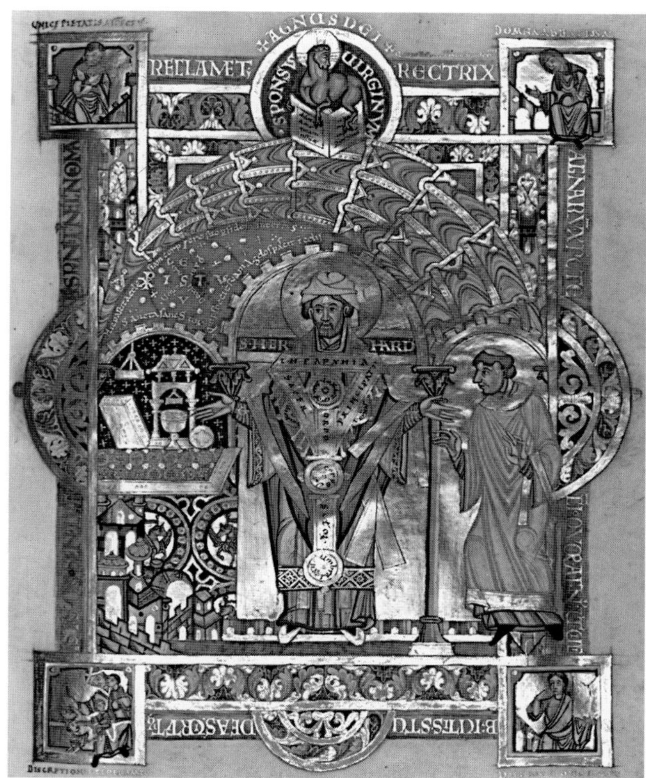

St Erhard at the Altar, illumination from the Pericopes of Abbess Uta, from Regensburg, *c.* 1025 (Munich, Bayerische Staatsbibliothek, Cod. Clm 13601, fol. 4*r*)

Goscombe John, Sir **William.** *See* JOHN, WILLIAM GOSCOMBE.

Goshun. *See* MATSUMURA GOSHUN.

Goslar Palace. Imperial palace in Lower Saxony, Germany, *c.* 40 km south of Brunswick. Goslar, an Imperial Diet town whose wealth was derived from the lead- and silver-mines of the Harz Mountains, was the favourite residence of the Salian emperors (*reg* 1024–1125). The imperial hall was originally built under Henry III (*reg* 1039-56), but it had to be repaired after a fire in 1065 and a partial collapse in 1132. The palace received much attention from late 19th-century patriots and revivalists: in its present form it mostly dates from a restoration of 1873–9, which gave it a 12th-century character. A vast cycle of frescoes by Hermann Wislicenus (1825–99), celebrating its days as an imperial residence, was added to the upper hall between 1879 and 1897.

The imperial hall stands at the top of an eastward-facing slope, which was used for large official assemblies, and at the bottom of which the royal chapel (later the cathedral; destr. 1819) was built by Henry III. The elongated plan of the palace, with the hall flanked to north and south by residential blocks with chapels, is similar to the Bishop's Palace at Bamberg in Bavaria, where royalty also stayed, although it is uncertain which building is the earlier. The northern residential block, including a two-storey Lady chapel built *c.* 1035 by Conrad II (*reg* 1024–39), was the first to be constructed, although the present structure dates from the restoration. Details from the imperial apartments (destr.) and the chapel of St Ulrich at the south end suggest a date in the first quarter of the 12th century. The plan of the chapel, which contains the tomb of Henry III, is in the form of a Greek cross, changing to an octagon above.

The hall itself (47×15 m) has two storeys: the enclosed ground floor could be heated by a hypocaust, while central piers support the vast upper storey, which has two aisles and a wooden roof and was originally open to the assembly area below through windows with triple arches (now glazed). A central transept opening to a balcony marks the position of the imperial throne, midway along the building. The central arch dates from 1090–97. The windows were continually altered: under Henry IV (*reg* 1056–1106) they were probably divided into three arches of equal height; the present arrangement, with the central arch of each group *c.* 300 mm higher, probably originated in the 13th century.

The staircase porch at the southern end of the hall is built over a passage at ground level, with stairways at either side. On the upper level of the main façade are two arches, each subdivided into three sub-arches, and to either side are moulded doorways. The unusually richly ornamented column shafts and capitals indicate a late date. Their similarity to the Neuwerk abbey church in Goslar (ded. 1186) has been emphasized, and it suggests a late 12th-century date for the staircase building, although it has also been dated 1225.

BIBLIOGRAPHY

U. Hoelscher: *Die Kaiserpfalz Goslar* (Berlin, 1927)

H. Reuther: 'Studien zur Goslarer Pfalzkapelle St. Ulrich', *Niedersächs. Beitr. Kstgesch.*, vii (1968), pp. 65–84

FRITZ ARENS

Gospel book. Book containing the four canonical Gospels of Matthew, Mark, Luke and John. The illustration of these manuscripts was an important art form during the early medieval period in western Europe and at all times in the history of the Eastern Church. The oldest extant decorated Gospel books are of the 6th century AD and show considerable diversity in their illustrations. They suggest that the inclusion of New Testament narrative cycles was a widespread practice at that period, although the cycles might be arranged according to quite varied formats. For example, the ROSSANO GOSPELS (Rossano, Mus. Dioc.), written in Greek, include some ten narrative illustrations and seem originally to have contained four portraits of the Evangelists (*see* AUTHOR PORTRAIT) and ornamented canon tables (*see* CANON TABLE); the latter two features came, in the following centuries, to be the most consistently repeated features of Gospel book design. In the RABBULA GOSPELS (Florence, Bib. Medicea-Laurenziana, MS. Plut. 1. 56), written in Syriac, the text is preceded by 19 pages of canon tables, bordered by small paintings of scenes from the *Life of Christ*, and a few full-page paintings of further Christological subjects. A Latin Gospel book, the ST AUGUSTINE GOSPELS (Cambridge, Corpus Christi Coll., MS. 286), contains, in its present fragmentary state, two painted pages, each with small scenes from the *Life of Christ*; it has been estimated from this that it may originally have had as many as 100 Christological illustrations.

Gospel books have a leading place among the manuscripts made in Irish and Northumbrian monasteries during the late 7th century and throughout the 8th, but, in contrast to 6th-century manuscripts, Insular Gospel books contain very little narrative illustration. Their typical design includes decorated canon-table pages, a portrait of the Evangelist and/or his symbol preceding each Gospel, a full page of elaborately patterned ornament facing the first page of each Gospel, and greatly enlarged, richly decorated letters marking the opening of each Gospel text (for illustration *see* LINDISFARNE GOSPELS). The aesthetic emphasis is on abstract ornament, with extensive use of Hiberno-Saxon motifs.

Many Gospel books were produced in early Carolingian times, during the late 8th century; the large number of these manuscripts stands in sharp contrast to the rarity of such works among preceding Frankish manuscripts of the Merovingian period. This suggests the possibility of significant Insular influence on the first Carolingian Gospel books, even though they are ornamented in a much more classicizing style (*see* INSULAR ART, §3). A series of Gospel books was produced by the Court School of Charlemagne, known as the Ada group. In addition to Evangelist portraits and other typical decorations, a few of these manuscripts make sparing use of very small-scale New Testament illustrations (e.g. the Harley Golden Gospels; see fig.). Gospel books are among the most famous Carolingian works of art, notably the Coronation Gospels of Charlemagne (Vienna, Schatzkam.; *see* CAROLINGIAN ART, fig. 7) and that of EBBO, Archbishop of Reims (Épernay, Bib. Mun., MS. 1). While many of them are of a high artistic order, their iconographic content tends to be restrained, seldom involving much illustration beyond the four Evangelist portraits.

Among the revivals of manuscript art across north-west Europe in the late 10th century and the 11th, Gospel books were particularly significant in Ottonian Germany, where they included lengthy pictorial narratives of the life of Christ, as in the magnificent GOSPELS OF OTTO III, dated *c.* 1000 (Munich, Bayer. Staatsbib., Clm. 4453; *see* OTTONIAN ART, fig. 4), which has 29 full-page Christological paintings. It is difficult to establish whether this sudden iconographical expansion was due principally to the inspiration of Early Christian manuscripts, or to the large illustrative cycles in contemporary Byzantine manuscripts, or to sources in other media. During the same period many Gospel books were also produced at monastic centres in England, northern France and the Meuse region. These manuscripts, painted in a wide variety of local styles, are not illustrated with such extensive narrative cycles as Ottonian Gospel books and tend to adhere to restrictive Carolinigian precedents.

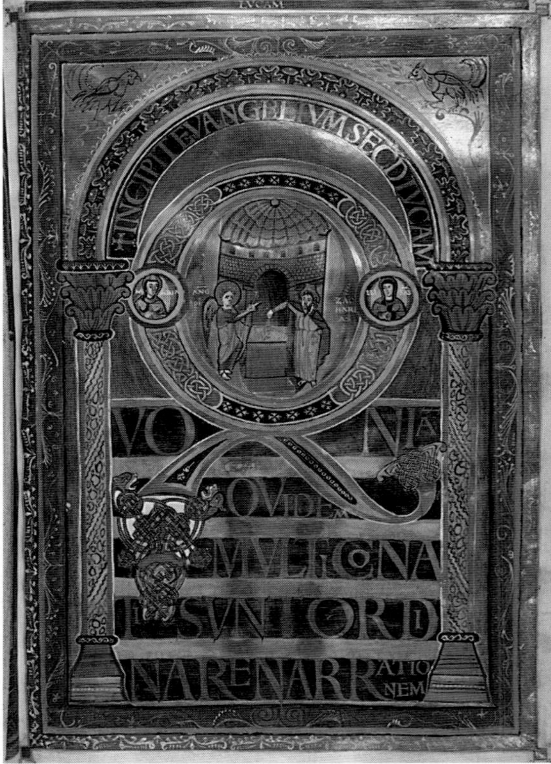

Harley Golden Gospels, *Annunciation to Zacharias*, historiated initial, *c.* AD 790–800 (London, British Library, Harley MS. 2788, fol. 109*r*)

In the 12th century the making of luxury Gospel books decreased and thereafter such manuscripts were of relatively little importance in the art of western Europe, presumably because of the increasing practice of incorporating liturgical Gospel readings into Missals. There are, however, several very fine 12th-century Gospel books, such as the Averbode Gospels (U. Liège, Bib. Gén., MS. 363), a Mosan manuscript with typological illustrations; or the fragmentarily preserved Gospel book of Abbot Wedric of Liessies (Avesnes-sur-Helpe, Mus. Soc. Archéol.). An unusually sumptuous German example is the Gospels of Henry the Lion, Duke of Saxony (Wolfenbüttel, Herzog August Bib., Cod. Guelf. 105 noviss. 2; for illustration *see* WOLFENBÜTTEL), which has 17 elaborate canon-table pages and 20 full pages of Christological illustration.

In the Byzantine Empire and elsewhere in the Eastern Church, Gospel books and Lectionaries remained important to liturgical practice and consequently were produced in significant quantities throughout the history of manuscript production in those areas (*see also* EARLY CHRISTIAN AND BYZANTINE ART, §V, 2(ii)). As in the West, decorated canon tables and Evangelist portraits were the most frequently used illustrations, although many of the manuscripts also include narrative scenes. The early history of Byzantine Gospel books is little understood because of the lack of preserved manuscripts; it is therefore difficult to establish to what extent the New Testament picture cycles that appeared after the Iconoclasm of the 10th and 11th centuries repeat pre-Iconoclastic models or use new iconography, perhaps related to post-Iconoclastic theology. One typical scheme places small, unframed narrative scenes in horizontal strips interrupting the pages of text; an important example of this is an 11th-century Gospel book in Paris (Bib. N., MS. gr. 74), which contains over 350 illustrations. A more formal design allows for full-page images or full pages divided into several scenes, as exemplified by an 11th-century manuscript in Parma (Bib. Palatina, MS. Pal. 5).

The decoration of Byzantine Gospel books was influential throughout the Eastern Christian world, many regions of which continued their production long after the fall of the Byzantine Empire. In Slavonic Europe, where there was little indigenous artistic tradition, the influence of Byzantine art was particularly strong; a 14th-century Bulgarian Gospel book (London, BL, Add. MS. 39627) contains a vast narrative cycle that closely matches the 11th-century example in Paris (Bib. N., MS. gr. 74). Gospel books influenced by Byzantine manuscripts were also made in Russia, Georgia and in the Near East. They hold a dominant place in the long history of manuscript production in Armenia. There, as in Syria, the influence of Byzantine art blends with native artistic styles to produce Gospel books with a perceptible Islamic accent. Numerous Gospel books of a markedly colourful, provincial character were also made in Coptic Egypt: one of the more richly decorated is a 12th-century example in Paris (Bib. N., MS. copt. 13).

BIBLIOGRAPHY

RBA; *RDK*

H. Omont: *Evangiles avec peintures byzantines du XIe siècle* (Paris, n.d.) [on Paris, Bib. N., MS. gr. 74]

C. R. Dodwell: *Painting in Europe, 800–1200*, Pelican Hist. A. (Harmondsworth, 1971)

K. Weitzmann: *Late Antique and Early Christian Book Illumination* (New York, 1977)

E. M. Korkhmazian: *Armenian Miniatures* (Leningrad, 1984)

G. Henderson: *From Durrow to Kells: The Insular Gospel-books, 650–800* (London, 1987)

DON DENNY

Gospels of Otto III. The manuscript (Munich, Bayer. Staatsbib., Clm. 4453) comprises 276 pages measuring 334×242 mm; it has been preserved with its original front cover, in the centre of which is a 10th-century Byzantine ivory representing the *Dormition of the Virgin*. It was produced on the island of Reichenau *c*. 1000. The text is embellished with 12 canon tables magnificently arranged in arcades (fols 11*v*–22*r*), a double-page picture of the *Emperor* (fols 23*v*–24*r*), portraits of the *Four Evangelists*, paired with incipit pages (fols 25*v*–26*r*, 94*v*–95*r*, 139*v*–140*r*, 206*v*–207*r*) and 29 full-page miniatures illustrating scenes from the New Testament, which are interspersed throughout the text. The *Emperor* is shown enthroned amid the secular and spiritual representatives of his realm; figures of the four provinces, *Roma*, *Gallia*, *Germania* and *Sclavinia*, approach from the left with gifts to offer their allegiance (*see* OTTONIAN ART, fig. 4). The subject-matter suggests that the Emperor should be identified as Otto III in his final years when Rome was central to his policy, a dating that accords with the style of the painting. Described as 'Visionary Evangelists', the portraits of the *Four Evangelists* are iconographically significant: above their heads are images of clouds thronged with angels and figures from the Old Testament, alongside the symbols of the Evangelists. The New Testament illustrations, which continue the pictorial tradition of New Testament cycles at Reichenau, are notable in that the chronological sequence of events is preserved, and a more or less equal number of pictures is used for each Gospel. The scope and planning of the book give it the foremost position among Reichenau manuscripts; its quality and style make it a superb example of the Liuthard group (*see* OTTONIAN ART, §IV, 2). The manuscript passed with Otto III's heritage to his successor Emperor Henry II who donated it to Bamberg Cathedral. When secularization was introduced in 1803 it went to Munich.

BIBLIOGRAPHY

Das Evangeliar Ottos III. Clm. 4453 der Bayerischen Staatsbibliothek München (Frankfurt am Main, 1978) [facs. with contrib. by F. Dressler, F. Mütherich and H. Beumann; extensive bibliog.]

P. E. Schramm: *Die deutschen Kaiser und Könige in Bildern ihrer Zeit, 751–1190*, ed. F. Mütherich (Munich, 1983), pp. 205–7

FLORENTINE MÜTHERICH

Gospels of Queen Mlk‘e. Armenian Gospel book (350×295 mm; Venice, Abbey of S Lazzaro degli Armeni, Bib., MS. 1144/86) written in double columns in large Mesropian uncials on parchment, and comprising 466 folios in 58 gatherings of 8 leaves. There are two colophonic inscriptions, indicating two possible dates of production, AD 851 and 862. The date of 851 was proposed by Sargisian, while that of 862 was put forward by Adontz. Janashian, on the other hand, has suggested that the manuscript may have been copied in 851, and rebound in 862. Queen Mlk‘e, wife of King Gagik I (*reg* 990–1020), was the third owner of the manuscript, and gave it to the monastery of Varag in the kingdom of Vaspurakan. Between 1208 and 1830, when Grigor Nersisian presented it to the monastery library of S Lazzaro, the manuscript had several owners at different locations.

The illustrations include the decorative borders of the Letter of Eusebios to Karpianos (fols 1*r*–2*r*) and of the canon tables (fols 2*v*–3*v*), as well as *Evangelist Portraits* (fols 8*v*, 9*r* and *v*, 10*r*) and a narrative miniature of the *Ascension* (fol. 8*r*). The iconography, the impressionistic application of colour and the subjects illustrated are reminiscent of those in the 6th-century Syriac RABBULA GOSPELS, thus indicating the antiquity of the models on which the Armenian illustrations are based. It has been suggested that the *Crocodile Hunt* on the tympanum of the arcade framing the Letter of Eusebios is derived from some early Alexandrian model, and that the *Evangelist Portraits*, two of whom are shown seated and two standing, are based on those in the Rabbula Gospels. The classicizing architectural background in one of these portraits has also been identified as a *scaenae frons* of a Roman theatre. Although the animated group of Apostles, the attitude of the Virgin and the flight of the angels carrying the aureole in the *Ascension* reflect Classical influences, the hieratic pose of Christ and of the Archangels, in imperial costume, indicate that both scribe and artist were Armenians belonging to the same milieu and period.

BIBLIOGRAPHY

B. Sargisian: *Grand Catalogue of the Armenian Manuscripts in the Library of the Mekhitarist Fathers of Venice* (Venice, 1914)

N. Adontz: ‘MlkB±Re awetarani grutB±Rean tarin’ [The date for the copying of the Queen MlkB±Re Gospels], *Sion*, ix (1936), pp. 274–5

M. Janashian: *Armenian Miniature Paintings* (Venice, 1966), pp. 45–72

Armenian Miniature Paintings of the Monastic Library at San Lazzaro, i (Venice, 1966), pp. 16–23

VREJ NERSESSIAN

Goss, William Henry (*b* London, ?July 1833; *d* ?Hanley, Staffs, 4 Jan 1906). English potter and manufacturer. He studied art and design in London and in 1857 was employed as a modeller by W. T. Copeland & Sons Ltd, Stoke-on-Trent, Staffs. In 1858 he set up a factory in partnership with a Mr Peake, producing a variety of high-quality parian porcelain: jugs, vases, lidded jars, portrait busts and ‘jewelled’ porcelain. He had observed that the ‘jewelled’ pieces made at the Sèvres porcelain factory were often lacking their enamel ‘stones’ and he developed a method of securely counter-sinking these into the clay. He modelled many of the prototypes himself, and the factory made pierced and coloured floral jewellery, crosses, scent bottles and other small luxury items. He also invented a light, lustrous ware called ‘ivory porcelain’, which was adopted by the Belleek factory in Co. Fermanagh, N. Ireland, and experimented with commercial glazes to produce brilliantly coloured pieces. In 1870 Goss established his own factory, the Falcon Works, at Hanley, Stoke-on-Trent, where, from the 1880s until 1914, porcelain heraldic wares were manufactured: a multitude of such pieces as figures, urns, lighthouses and horseshoes were transfer-printed with the coats of arms of a British town or county. The heraldic porcelains were an overwhelming success, selling as keepsakes or souvenirs by the thousand (examples in Stoke-on-Trent, City Mus. & A.G.), and a Goss collectors’ club was founded *c*. 1904. During World War I the factory made models of tanks and zeppelins and pots bearing regimental badges. Production dwindled in the 1930s; the Goss works were absorbed by the Cauldon Potteries Ltd, Hanley, and closed down in 1940.

BIBLIOGRAPHY

D. Rees and M. G. Cawley: *A Pictorial Encyclopaedia of Goss China* (Newport, 1970)

□

Gossart [Gossaert; van Henegouwe; de Waele], **Jan** [Iennin; Janin; Jennyn] [Mabuse] (*b* ?Maubeuge, *c*. 1478; *d* ?Antwerp, 1 Oct 1532). South Netherlandish painter, draughtsman and printmaker. During the first decade of the 16th century he was one of the earliest exponents of ANTWERP MANNERISM. Following his trip to Italy in 1508–9 in the entourage of the humanist sea admiral Philip of Burgundy, later Bishop of Utrecht, Gossart played an important role in the Netherlands in effecting the transition between Late Gothic and ‘Romanism’, a northern style based on antique and Italian Renaissance models. He was also the first Netherlandish artist to paint classically inspired, mythological nudes.

1. Life and work. 2. Working methods and technique. 3. Critical reception and posthumous reputation.

1. LIFE AND WORK.

(i) Early years in the southern Netherlands, to 1507. (ii) Trip to Rome, 1508–9. (iii) Return to the Netherlands, 1509–16. (iv) Affirmation of Italian Renaissance ideals, 1516–32.

(i) Early years in the southern Netherlands, to 1507. Signatures found on a number of his paintings, *Iennin Gossart de Mabu*[se] and later *Ioannes Malbodius*, suggest that he was born in or near Maubeuge in the province of Hainaut (now in France). His date of birth is deduced from the usual age of accession to the status of master and from the inscription on a portrait dated 1528 (untraced; recorded by Arnhout van Buchell in 1623), which stated that Gossart was then aged 50.

Certain stylistic features in Gossart’s work led Weisz (1913) and Winkler (1921) to suppose that he trained in Bruges, perhaps with Gerard David. Duverger (1968), however, inclined towards an apprenticeship in Antwerp, where Gossart, under the name ‘Jennyn van Henegouwe’ (Jan of Hainaut), became a master in the Guild of St Luke in 1503. The Antwerp guild records do not mention Gossart before 1503, but they are incomplete around 1500. Gossart established a workshop in Antwerp and remained there at least until 1507. During this period he took on two pupils: in 1505 ‘Hennen Mertens’ (who may be identical to Jan Mertens) and in 1507 ‘Machiel in’t Swaenken’ (who has not been identified).

No known works can be dated with certainty to Gossart’s period in Antwerp. Two signed pen-and-ink drawings, the *Mystic Marriage of St Catherine* (Copenhagen, Stat. Mus. Kst) and the *Vision of the Emperor Augustus* (Berlin, Kupferstichkab.), are usually assigned to these years because of their Late Gothic character. Yet there is a perceptible development between the typically Gothic style of the first, with its excessive pen hatching and fussy drapery folds, and the controlled mannerism and coherent spatial construction of the second. Depending on whether these drawings are dated *c.* 1505 (Winkler, 1921; Friedländer, 1931; 1986–7 exh. cat.) or as late as 1520 (von der Osten), Gossart emerges either as a principal initiator of Antwerp Mannerism or merely as a later participant in the movement. The small triptych of the *Holy Family with SS Catherine and Barbara* (Lisbon, Mus. N. A. Ant.), only partially attributed to Gossart by von der Osten (who dates it *c.* 1510–15) and totally rejected by Gibson, is nevertheless characteristic both of Gossart's Mannerist phase and of the influence of Gerard David.

(ii) Trip to Rome, 1508–9. After 1507 Gossart's name disappears from the Antwerp archives. By then he seems to have been engaged by Philip of Burgundy, Admiral of Zeeland and illegitimate son of Philip the Good, Duke of Burgundy; however, according to the testimony in 1529 of Gerard Geldenhauer (1482–1542), Chaplain and Secretary to Philip of Burgundy, the Admiral did not actually secure the services of Gossart before the end of 1515. Whether or not he was officially employed, Gossart undoubtedly accompanied the Admiral when he left Mechelen on 26 October 1508 with an embassy sent by Margaret of Austria, Regent and Governess of the Netherlands, to Pope Julius II. The delegation arrived in Rome on 14 January 1509. Geldenhauer (1529) recorded that 'nothing pleased him [Philip] better in Rome than the sacred testimonies of its Antiquity, which he had reproduced for himself by the very famous painter and Apelles of our century, Jan Gossart of Maubeuge'. Four of Gossart's copies of Roman antiquities, all pen-and-ink drawings, have been identified: the *Colosseum* (Berlin, Kupferstichkab.); the *Apollo* (Venice, Accad.), after the *Apollo Kitharoedos* (Naples, Mus. Archeol. N.); the *Hercules* (London, heirs of Lord Wharton priv. col., see 1986–7 exh. cat., p. 185, fig. 2) after the Capitoline *Hercules* (Rome, Mus. Conserv.); and the *Spinario and other Studies* (Leiden, Rijksuniv., Prentenkab.) showing the famous statue (Rome, Mus. Conserv.) in the middle of the sheet. Gossart reproduced these Classical models as a northern artist still rooted in the Late Gothic tradition: the proportions are elongated, the muscles treated in a highly detailed and ornamental way and the drapery broken down into decorative, angular folds. His discovery of antique art appears to have been too sudden to allow him to assimilate immediately all of its principles, but the experience of seeing Classical sculpture in vivid relief in the strong southern light resulted in an increased sense of volume in his drawings.

Gossart also came into contact with 15th- and early 16th-century Italian painting during the embassy's journey through Trento, Verona, Mantua and Florence on the way to Rome, where Michelangelo had just begun work on the frescoes in the Sistine Chapel and Raphael on those in the Vatican Stanze. Gossart may have had access to their workshops, or to certain cartoons, as testified by what is presumed to be a lost painting of *Adam and Eve*, the composition of which is known through what is either a late drawing or possibly a copy (Providence, RI Sch. Des., Mus. A.), which reflects Michelangelo's *Creation of Adam*. The embassy returned to the southern Netherlands at the end of June 1509, but Gossart was still active in Rome in July of that year.

(iii) Return to the Netherlands, 1509–16. On his return from Rome, Gossart seems to have settled in Zeeland, for at the end of 1509 a 'Janin de Waele' (Jan the Walloon) was registered in the confraternity of Onze-Lieve-Vrouw at Middelburg. It is difficult to determine exactly where he was established, since he received commissions from a wide range of sources between 1509 and 1516. If, as Geldenhauer claimed, he was not yet in the service of Philip of Burgundy, this would explain why there is so little of Classical inspiration reflected in the work of this period. Gossart's commissions were for religious rather than secular works, and this doubtless meant that he had less scope to exploit what he had learnt in Rome. At this time there was apparently neither a demand nor a market for classicizing compositions in the Netherlands, where, outside of the courts, secular humanism penetrated only slowly.

No dated works from this phase of Gossart's career are known, but it can be partially reconstructed on the basis of a few chronological reference points and an analysis of his stylistic development. Although he was limited by the conventional nature of his subject-matter, it was for him a period of intense maturation and experimentation. The concentration on religious themes must have facilitated his reintegration in his native Netherlandish school, but he enriched this local tradition with the new breadth of vision he had gained through contact with a world previously unknown to him. He returned to the Netherlands with knowledge and appreciation not only of Italian and Classical art but also of the graphic art of such contemporaries as Albrecht Dürer and Jacopo de' Barbari (whose name was linked with Gossart's in 1529 by Geldenhauer, who compared them both with Zeuxis and Apelles).

Far from abandoning his Netherlandish artistic heritage, Gossart actually participated in the archaizing trend then current in the Low Countries. He developed its traditional oil-painting technique and even took inspiration from well-known south Netherlandish compositions, as demonstrated, for example, by his *Christ between the Virgin and St John the Baptist* (Madrid, Prado), a relatively faithful copy of the three principal figures in Jan van Eyck's Ghent Altarpiece (Ghent, Cathedral of St Bavo). The *Adoration of the Magi* (London, N.G.; see fig. 1), painted *c.* 1510–12 for the Benedictine Abbey of Geraardsbergen (Grammont) and signed twice IENNI[N]/GOSSART/DEMABV[SE] and IENNIN/GOS[SART], refers back to the work of Hugo van der Goes and Gerard David, but its mastery of perspective and sense of grandeur also testify to Gossart's familiarity with Quattrocento painting. In the small *Virgin and Child with SS Catherine and Barbara*, known as the Malvagna Triptych (Palermo, Gal. Reg. Sicilia), such features as the brilliant colour, exuberant Late Gothic architectural setting, and figures and landscape inspired by Gerard David reflect Netherlandish sources, whereas the music-making putti were inspired by Italian Renaissance art. The Malvagna Triptych can be dated after 1511, the publication date of Dürer's *Small Woodcut Passion* series, from which one of the plates, the *Fall of Man*, has been copied in reverse on an outer wing of the triptych.

Gossart copied van Eyck's tiny painting of the *Virgin in the Church* (Berlin, Gemäldegal.) on the left wing of a

1. Jan Gossart: *Adoration of the Magi*, oil on panel, 1.77×1.61 m, *c.* 1510–12 (London, National Gallery)

diptych (Rome, Pal. Doria-Pamphili), which has a portrait of *Antonio Siciliano with St Anthony* on the right wing. The diptych, the attribution of which has been contested by Weisz and von der Osten (except for the portrait), was probably commissioned by Siciliano, Chamberlain of Maximilian Sforza, Duke of Milan, at the time of the Duke's diplomatic visit to Margaret of Austria in Mechelen in 1513. On this occasion Siciliano probably acquired the Grimani Breviary (Venice, Bib. N. Marziana, MS. Lat. I, 99), which includes an illumination, the *Dispute of St Barbara*, signed GOS[S]ART and MABVS[E]; Gossart would have been responsible for the architectural setting, while the figures would have been left to Simon Bening or his workshop.

Gossart's drawings of the period, such as the black chalk *Virgin and Child with SS Barbara and Catherine* (*c.* 1511; Amsterdam, Rijksmus.), show that he was still strongly influenced by Antwerp Mannerism, although he tempered the style by introducing Classical architectural elements. He departed still further from Netherlandish tradition in a triptych, of which only the central panel depicting the *Agony in the Garden* (Berlin, Gemäldegal.)

and the two grisaille outer wings showing the *Penitent St Jerome before the Crucifix* (Washington, DC, N.G.A.) survive. In the central panel Christ is shown kneeling in a rocky, moonlit landscape; the rigorous draughtsmanship and peculiar striated rock formations reveal Gossart's debt to both Dürer and Andrea Mantegna (cf. his version of the same subject, London, N.G.). With its intense chiaroscuro, Gossart's picture is also one of the first examples of a coherent nocturnal scene in northern painting.

Perhaps between 1509 and 1516 Gossart painted what van Mander described as an exceptionally large altarpiece with double wings, which was commissioned by Abbot Maximilian of Burgundy (*d* 1524), nephew of Philip of Burgundy, for the high altar of the Abbey of Middelburg. According to tradition, the work (destr. by lightning 1568) depicted Christ's descent from the Cross, but Dhanens (1985) has suggested instead that it represented a Mass of St Gregory, a subject better suited to the eucharistic theme of the altar's embroidered antependium (Brussels, Mus. Royaux A. & Hist.), which she has identified. The altarpiece was completed before December 1520, when Dürer visited the abbey during his trip to the Netherlands to admire it. (Dürer preferred the painting technique to the composition: 'nit so gut im Hauptstreichen als in Gemäl'.)

Gossart's most important work of this period, the large signed altarpiece of *St Luke Drawing the Virgin* (Vienna, Ksthist.; see fig. 2), was executed for the altar of the painters' guild in Mechelen Cathedral. Probably finished as early as 1513–14 (Monballieu), it combines Gothic characteristics, such as a profusion of drapery folds, and elaborate symbolism (de Jongh) within a classicizing architectural setting with several references to Roman sculpture. The altarpiece's admirable system of linear perspective, then highly unusual in the Netherlands, was also derived from Italian Renaissance art.

2. Jan Gossart: *St Luke Drawing the Virgin*, oil on panel, 2.30×2.05 m, 1513–14 (Vienna, Kunsthistorisches Museum)

(iv) Affirmation of Italian Renaissance ideals, 1516–32. Towards the end of 1515 Philip of Burgundy commissioned Gossart and Jacopo de' Barbari to decorate his castle of Suytburg (now Souburg, Walcheren Island), which he intended to make a Renaissance centre in the north. Philip, passionately fond of Classical art and literature and familiar with the writings of Vitruvius, wanted a palace in the Italian manner. He is even said to have inspired the decorative programme himself. Gossart's involvement in the undertaking turned him into a true Renaissance painter. Philip's desire to surround himself with scenes from Classical mythology led Gossart to explore methods of painting the nude human body in movement. Curiously, rather than refer directly to the poses of the antique models he had copied in Rome, he drew inspiration from the interpretive nude studies of such contemporaries as Dürer, Marcantonio Raimondi and the German sculptor Conrat Meit, whom he met in both Mechelen and Suytburg. More important, however, seems to have been the frequent contact he had at both these courts with Jacopo de' Barbari, whose theories of human proportion profoundly influenced his style.

The only surviving picture that seems likely to have formed part of the decoration of Suytburg is the *Neptune and Amphitrite* (1516; Berlin, Bodemus.; see fig. 3). These two secular, life-size nude figures were unprecedented in Netherlandish painting but were never copied or imitated. The picture bears what is ostensibly Gossart's first latinized signature, IOANNES+MALBODIVS+PINGEBAT+1516, written in Roman capitals. A tribute to the humanist tastes of Philip of Burgundy, whose name and motto it carries, this panel is a genuine manifesto of a new style, corroborating Guicciardini's claim that Gossart was 'the first to bring from Italy to these lands [the northern and southern Netherlands] the art of painting historical and poetical subjects with nude figures'. In it Gossart succeeded in fusing diverse sources into a personal and well-balanced composition: he combined the ideals of Classical architecture, which he had seen in Rome but which he refined through study of Vitruvian theory; scientific perspective, drawn primarily from the prints of Dürer and Jacopo de' Barbari; the pose of the male figure in Dürer's famous engraving of *Adam and Eve* (1504; B. 1), which Gossart adapted for the figure of Neptune; and Pausanias' description of Phidias' statue of Zeus at Olympia, published in his *Description of Greece* (Venice, 1516), which may have influenced Gossart's arrangement of the figures in the temple. The monumental figures of Neptune and Amphitrite reverberate in a profusion of light and reflected light, recalling the modelling of Gossart's Roman drawings.

During this period Philip of Burgundy apparently allowed Gossart to accept other commissions, such as that for the designs for a hearse with *all'antica* decoration for the funeral in Brussels in 1516 of Ferdinand the Catholic, King of Aragon. Gossart also painted a number of portraits, including two of Eleanor of Austria (1498–1558) for her brother Charles V (one in a priv. col., see 1987

3. Jan Gossart: *Neptune and Amphitrite*, oil on panel, 1.88×1.24 m, 1516 (Berlin, Bodemuseum)

exh. cat., no. 208; the other untraced), and one of *Jean Carondelet* (1517; Paris, Louvre), a member of the Privy Council in Mechelen. The portrait of Carondelet, which forms a diptych with a panel of the *Virgin and Child*, placed Gossart in the ranks of the best portrait painters of the northern Renaissance. Like all his portraits, it is distinguished by the immediacy of the sitter, the analytical rigour and the subtlety of the modelling.

In 1517 Philip of Burgundy was named Bishop of Utrecht and installed himself in the castle of Wijk-bij-Duurstede, some 30 km south of Utrecht. Philip undertook to decorate the castle with large mythological paintings, probably painted by Gossart (Sterk). Several small-scale panels from this period depicting groups of two or three mythological figures could be reduced versions of paintings either from the castle of Suytburg or from that of Wijk-bij-Duurstede: *Hercules and Deianeira* (1517; U. Birmingham, Barber Inst.), *Venus* (Rovigo, Accad. Concordi) and *Hermaphroditus and Salmacis* (Rotterdam, Boymans–van Beuningen), which was presented by Philip of Burgundy to Margaret of Austria.

In 1520 Gossart was commissioned, probably by his patron the Bishop of Utrecht, to design choir stalls for Utrecht Cathedral, which were never built. Around the same time he painted a second version of *St Luke Drawing the Virgin* (Vienna, Ksthist. Mus.). It is the most Italianate of all Gossart's work, with a Raphaelesque Virgin in Glory and grotesque architectural ornamentation inspired by frescoes by Filippino Lippi (Rome, S Maria Sopra Minerva). The painting demonstrates both Gossart's technical virtuosity and the evolution of his style towards a more self-contained space, enclosed by solid architecture (which counterbalances the over-abundant ornamentation), a more vivid light defining the volumes, and clearer colours that harmonize with the stone decoration.

Gossart's few attempts at printmaking date from the 1520s, following Dürer's visit in 1520 to the Low Countries and the increased diffusion of his prints. Gossart made two engravings of the *Virgin and Child* (one dated 1522, B. 1; the other undated, B. 2) and one etching, the *Man of Sorrows* (Hollstein, no. 1), while two woodcuts, *Cain Killing Abel* (Hollstein, no. 4) and *Hercules and Deianeira* (B. 3), were done either by him or after his designs. Around 1520–25 he also produced several representations of Adam and Eve: four pen-and-ink drawings (e.g. Vienna, Albertina) and three panel paintings (e.g. London, Hampton Court, Royal Col.) of extraordinary power and originality. The nudes are shown in somewhat unstable proto-Baroque poses and express a sense of eroticism never before seen with this biblical theme.

In 1523 Margaret of Austria employed Gossart to restore several oil paintings in her collection at Mechelen. The following year, after the death of Philip of Burgundy, Gossart returned to Zeeland, where he worked for Philip's great-nephew Adolph of Burgundy, Admiral of Zeeland and later Marquis de Veere (1489–1540). He presumably did not work exclusively for Adolph, for his fame attracted numerous commissions from other patrons for both portraits and religious paintings. The number of copies of his smaller compositions suggests that he opened a workshop in Middelburg to satisfy the demand for his work.

Gossart's late portraits differ from earlier ones, which tend to have plain coloured backgrounds (e.g. *Elderly Couple*, London, N.G.); the sitters in portraits executed after 1525 are set against a slab of reddish-brown, purple or green marble which is bordered by a *trompe-l'oeil* frame. This formula, apparently of Italian inspiration, confers on the sitters an impressive sculptural vigour, as in the *Man with a Rosary* (*c.* 1527; London, N.G.) and the *Children of Christian II of Denmark* (*c.* 1526; London, Hampton Court, Royal Col.), one of the first secular group portraits. Gossart did a pen-and-ink portrait of *Christian II, King of Denmark* (Paris, Fond. Custodia, Inst. Néerl.; see fig. 4), who was deposed in 1523 and took refuge with Adolph of Burgundy. The drawing, one of the most masterly portraits of the northern Renaissance, was engraved by Jakob Binck. Clearly influenced by Dürer's engraved portraits, Gossart's graphic style is bold, even aggressive, and he recorded with comparable skill a variety of surface textures and densely packed decorative and heraldic detail. Christian II also commissioned designs from Gossart for the tomb and epitaph of his wife, Isabella of Austria (1501–26).

Gossart's many paintings of the Virgin and Child, mostly late in date and sometimes known only through copies, evince an inexhaustible richness of invention, both in their poses, some of them inspired by Raphael, and in their settings. As with the portraits, the background is either plain (e.g. Münster, Westfäl. Landesmus.) or formed of a

4. Jan Gossart: *Christian II, King of Denmark*, pen and two shades of brown ink, 268×215 mm, *c.* 1525 (Paris, Fondation Custodia, Institut Néerlandais)

marble slab surrounded by mouldings (e.g. Berlin, Gemäldegal.). His last certain dated work is another *Virgin and Child* (1531; Cleveland, OH, Mus. A.), an innovative composition that includes a distant landscape in the background instead of the usual plain or marble setting.

During the last months of his life, and perhaps as early as 1530, Gossart enjoyed the patronage of Mencia de Mendoza, third wife of Henry III, Count of Nassau-Breda, whose portrait he also painted (Fort Worth, TX, Kimbell A. Mus.). She assigned him a pension of 100 guilders a year, the last receipt for which was dated 12 September 1532; on 13 October Gossart's widow received a gratuity from his patroness. About 1600 Theodore Galle specified Gossart's place and date of death in the fourth edition of Lampsonius' *Illustrium quos Belgium habuit pictorum effigies* and that he was buried in Antwerp Cathedral. Jan Gossart's brother Nicasius (*d* 1537) was probably an architect; he was commissioned in 1529 to provide models and plans for the old and new port of Middelburg. Of Jan's three children, one son, Pierre (*c.* 1521–after 1578), was a painter in Middelburg.

2. WORKING METHODS AND TECHNIQUE. In his search for the most appropriate means of expression to convey his own acute powers of observation and powerful originality, Gossart turned to the works of the great masters. At a time when some of Gossart's Netherlandish contemporaries were adopting a less painstaking method of oil painting, Gossart looked back to the work of Jan van Eyck, whose subtle technique, based on the application of thin, translucent paint layers, he assimilated and refined. For his drawings Gossart was inspired above all by Dürer, whose strong and rigorous draughtsmanship proved a constant stimulus throughout his career.

(i) Drawings. Gossart's earliest drawings, with their profusion of pen strokes, are still firmly rooted in the flamboyant and decorative style of Late Gothic Mannerism. However, his draughtsmanship soon developed into an elegant and firm style (e.g. in the *Vision of the Emperor Augustus*; Berlin, Kupferstichkab.), which finally reached maturity in his copies of Roman antiquities. Gossart's nude figures after Classical statues are modelled by long, supple strokes, with volume conveyed by contrasting areas of light and finely hatched shading. This process subsequently characterized the rendering of all his nudes, whether drawn or painted. This supple and refined technique is also present in the black chalk drawing of the *Virgin and Child with SS Barbara and Catherine* (Amsterdam, Rijksmus.), a rare example of a drawing from his post-Roman period. The cross-hatching technique combined with long contour lines, enabled the artist to achieve a remarkable flexibility of expression in later nude studies, especially in the drawings of Adam and Eve made in the early 1520s: areas of light provided by the blank white paper stand out against a network of closely hatched shadows (e.g. *Adam and Eve*, Vienna, Albertina) or, working in reverse, a combination of pen hatching and white heightening are superimposed on a neutral prepared ground (e.g. *Adam and Eve*, Chatsworth, Derbys). In some drawings, for instance the *Women's Bath* (London, BM), the shading is more delicate and the artist used long, vigorous contour lines to define the volumes.

Other drawings by Gossart are more highly finished, for example the portrait of *Christian II, King of Denmark*, the technique of which is no doubt determined by its function as a preparatory study for an engraving. The head is modelled in a darker shade of brown ink, suggesting that it was drawn from life, the costume and architectural setting having been completed by him earlier in the studio. Function also seems to have affected the choice of media and technique for other studies. A few drawings, apparently preliminary studies for paintings, are much less linear and graphic: for these the artist used graphite and stumping or pen and wash (e.g. *Hercules Slaying the Centaur Eurytion*; Amsterdam, Rijksmus.).

(ii) Paintings. Few of Gossart's paintings have been examined scientifically, but the principal characteristics of his painting technique can be identified by the naked eye. His earlier panels, including those done shortly after his trip to Italy (e.g. the Malvagna Triptych), are painted in densely applied, pure saturated colours; the forms are modelled by visible brushstrokes. However, his technique was more polished, notably in the flesh tones, in large-scale works, such as the *Adoration of the Magi* (London, N.G.).

In later works Gossart's palette became cooler, favouring blues, greys and madder lakes, and the desaturated colours are covered with a rich, crystalline glaze, producing an enamel-like surface. Facial features were modelled by short, parallel brushstrokes, and although the decorative ornament and highlights were still applied in slight impasto, on the whole the paint layer became thinner and more fluid, sometimes revealing the underdrawing. For the underdrawing the artist most often used a brush and paint to sketch in the main forms and figures, which are shaded with long parallel hatching; he then apparently employed black chalk to create a network of zigzag lines indicating the drapery folds. The painted nude figures are modelled using a *sfumato* technique, in which the ambient light is reflected back repeatedly from the shadows. For the carefully blended shading the painter used either a light grey scumble or a background colour mixed into the shadows; a thin, clear zone, often emphasized by a dark outline, skirts the shadows as in his drawings.

3. CRITICAL RECEPTION AND POSTHUMOUS REPUTATION. Gossart's art was perhaps too innovative in terms of subject-matter and aesthetics to exert a profound influence on artists of his own generation, with the possible exception of Dirck Vellert, who from the 1520s absorbed much of Gossart's formal vocabulary. However, the following generation of painters sought inspiration from the prestigious older artist, who had seen and copied the art of the Antique. Jan van Scorel, who came to study with Gossart in Utrecht *c.* 1517, may have been encouraged shortly thereafter by Gossart to travel to Italy, a journey that had profound consequences on the art of the northern Netherlands. Scorel's pupil, Maarten van Heemskerck, was also strongly influenced by Gossart's work. About 1526–7 Lucas van Leyden came to see Gossart in Middelburg, before setting out with him on a tour visiting painters in Ghent, Mechelen and Antwerp; Lucas's late engravings clearly reflect the consequences of this encounter. The Liège artist Lambert Lombard is also supposed to have worked with Gossart in Middelburg *c.* 1525, but for how long is not known. In the southern Netherlands the artists most profoundly influenced by his style were Pieter Coecke van Aelst and Jan van Hemessen: Coecke imitated his compositions, modelling and figure types in several works, van Hemessen his bold foreshortening, and both his enamel-like painting technique and cool palette. Coecke's son Pauwels Coecke van Aelst (*b c.* 1530) was an able copyist of works by Gossart.

Gossart's renown was widespread even after his death, beginning in the Romanist period when early Italian writers (Guicciardini, 1567; Vasari, 1568) credited him with being the first artist to introduce 'the true art of painting historical and poetical subjects with nude figures' in the Netherlands. Flemish historians (Van Vaernewijck, 1566; Molanus, 1582) also praised him as a famous painter. Early sources especially admired his large, double-winged altarpiece in the Abbey of Middelburg, described as 'the principal and most glorious of his creations' (van Mander, 1604), even after it had perished in flames in 1568. Throughout the 17th and 18th centuries the artist's triptych commissioned by Pedro de Salamanca for the Augustinian church in Bruges (central panel, *Descent from the Cross*, St Petersburg, Hermitage; wings, *St John the Baptist* and *St Peter*, both Toledo, OH, Mus. A.) captured the interest and attention of historians and travel writers. Since then, despite fluctuations in taste, the fame and importance of this inventive artist, whose technical mastery allowed him the freedom of expression to pursue his formal and stylistic innovations, has never faltered.

BIBLIOGRAPHY

Hollstein: *Dut. & Flem.*; *NBW*: 'Gossaert (genaamed Mabuse), Jan'; Thieme–Becker

EARLY SOURCES

G. Geldenhauer: *Vita clarissimi principis Philippi a Burgundia* (Strasbourg, 1529); ed. J. Prinsen: 'Collectanea van Gerardus Geldenhauer Noviomagus', *Kron. Hist. Genoot. Utrecht*, iii (1901), pp. 223–48 (232–3, 235)

M. van Vaernewijck: *Van de beroerlicke tijden in de Nederlanden en voornamelijk in Ghendt* (Ghent, 1566–8); ed. F. Vanderhaegen in *Maatschapp. Vl. Biblioph.*, i/4 (1872–81), p. 148

L. Guicciardini: *Descrittione de' tutti i Paesi Bassi* (Antwerp, 1567), p. 98

G. Vasari: *Vite* (2/1568); ed. G. Milanesi (1878–85), vii, p. 584

J. Molanus: *Historiae Lovaniensium libri XIV*, chap. xxxiv (1582); ed. P. F. X. de Ram: *Les Quatorze Livres sur l'histoire de la ville de Louvain . . . de Jean Molanus* (Brussels, 1861), i, p. 611

A. van Buchell: *'Res pictoriae': Aantekeningen over kunstenaars en kunstwerken . . .* (1583–1639); eds G. J. Hoogewerff and J. Q. van Regteren Altena (The Hague, 1928), pp. 22–3, 43

K. van Mander: *Schilder-boeck* ([1603]–1604), pp. 225–6

GENERAL

A. von Bartsch: *Le Peintre-graveur* (1803–21), vii, p. 546 [B.]

M. J. Friedländer: *Die altniederländische Malerei* (Berlin, 1927–37); Eng. trans. as *Early Netherlandish Painting* (Leiden, 1967–76), viii; ix, pp. 44–6

J. Sterk: *Philips van Bourgondië (1465–1524), bisschop van Utrecht* (Zutphen, 1980), pp. 136–7

P. Philippot: *La Peinture dans les anciens Pays-Bas: XVe–XVe siècles* (Paris, 1994), pp. 125–34

MONOGRAPHS AND EXHIBITION CATALOGUES

M. Gossart: *Un des peintres peu connus de l'école flamande de transition, Jean Gossart de Maubeuge: Sa vie et son oeuvre, d'après les dernières recherches et des documents inédits* (Lille, 1902)

E. Weisz: *Jan Gossart gen. Mabuse: Sein Leben und seine Werke* (Parchim, 1913)

Jan Gossaert dit Mabuse (exh. cat. by H. Pauwels, H. R. Hoetinck and S. Herzog, Rotterdam, Boymans–van Beuningen; Bruges, Groeningemus.; 1965) [sources, bibliog., numerous pls]; reviewed by J. Bruyn in *Burl. Mag.*, cvii (1965), pp. 462–7

Kunst voor de beeldenstorm (exh. cat., eds J. P. Filedt Kok, W. Halsema-Kubes and W. T. Kloek; Amsterdam, Rijksmus., 1986), i, pp. 11–13, 40, 50; ii, pp. 92–3, 119–26, 143

The Age of Bruegel: Netherlandish Drawings in the Sixteenth Century (exh. cat. by J. O. Hand and others, Washington, DC, N.G.A.; New York, Pierpont Morgan Lib.; 1986–7), pp. 176–88, cat. nos 63–8

De Habsburger en Mechelen (exh. cat., Mechelen, Stadsmus. Hof van Busleyden, 1987), p. 101, no. 208, repr. p. 41

SPECIALIST STUDIES

F. Winkler: 'Die Anfänge Jan Gossarts', *Jb. Kön.-Preuss. Kstsamml.*, xlii (1921), pp. 5–19 (14)

J. Duverger: 'Jacopo de Barbari en Jan Gossart bij Filips van Burgondië te Souburg (1515)', *Mélanges Hulin de Loo* (Brussels, 1931), pp. 142–53 (147–8)

M. J. Friedländer: Über die Frühzeit Jan Gossarts', *Mélanges Hulin de Loo* (Brussels, 1931), pp. 182–6 (185)

J. Folie: 'Les Dessins de Jean Gossart dit Mabuse', *Gaz. B.-A.*, xxxviii/1 (1951; pubd 1960), pp. 77–98

G. von der Osten: 'Studien zu Jan Gossart', *Essays in Honor of Erwin Panofsky* (New York, 1961), pp. 454–75 (458, 460–62)

J. Duverger: 'Jan Gossaert te Antwerpen', *Bull. Mus. Boymans*, xix (1968), pp. 16–24 (17)

S. Herzog: 'Tradition and Innovation in Gossart's *Neptune and Amphitrite* and *Danae*', ibid., pp. 25–41 (34)

E. de Jongh: 'Speculaties over Jan Gossaerts Lucas Madonna te Praag', ibid., pp. 43–61

H. Pauwels: 'Jan Gossaert en Van Eyck', ibid., pp. 4–15 (15)

A. Monballieu: 'Bij de interpretatie en de datering van J. Gossaerts *Lucas en de Madonna* uit Mechelen', *Miscellanea Jozef Duverger* (Ghent, 1968), pp. 125–38 (134–5)

R. W. Scheller: 'Jan Gossaerts Triomfwagen', *Essays in Northern European Art Presented to Egbert Haverkamp-Begemann* (Doornspijk, 1983), pp. 228–36

E. Dhanens: 'Het graf van rooms-koning Willem II en de rol van Jan Gossart in de wederuitrusting van de koorkerk te Middelburg in Zeeland' [The tomb of the Roman Catholic King William II and the role of Jan Gossart in the refitting of the chancel of the Abbey at Middelburg in Zeeland], *Acad. Anlct.*, xlvi (1985), pp. 61–136 (121–2)

L. Silver: ' "Figure nude, historie, e poesie": Gossart and the Renaissance Nude in the Netherlands', *Ned. Ksthist. Jb.*, xxxvii (1986), pp. 1–40
J. R. Judson: 'Jan Gossaert and the New Aesthetic', *The Age of Bruegel: Netherlandish Drawings in the Sixteenth Century* (exh. cat. by J. O. Hand and others, Washington, DC, N.G.A.; New York, Pierpont Morgan Lib.; 1986–7), pp. 13–24
W. S. Gibson: 'Jan Gossart: The Lisbon Triptych Reconsidered', *Simiolus*, xvii/2–3 (1987), pp. 79–89
J. R. Judson: 'Jan Gossaert North of the Rivers' *Ned. Ksthist. Jb.*, xxxviii (1987), pp. 128–35
L. Silver: 'The "Gothic" Gossaert: Native and Traditional Elements in a Mabuse Madonna', *Pantheon*, xlv (1987), pp. 58–69

JACQUELINE FOLIE

Gosse, Sir **Edmund (William)** (*b* London, 3 May 1849; *d* London, 16 May 1928). English writer and art critic. Although best known for his autobiographical work *Father and Son* (London, 1907), Gosse enjoyed a considerable reputation as a poet and as a critic of literature and art. His articles on art, usually unsigned, date mainly from the period 1879–95 and appeared in such journals as the *Saturday Review*, the *Cornhill Magazine*, the *Magazine of Art* and the *Pall Mall Gazette.* Through his friendship with Hamo Thornycroft, one of the foremost artists of the New Sculpture movement, Gosse developed a wide interest in sculpture, reviewing the summer exhibitions at the Royal Academy, writing profiles of contemporary British sculptors and trying to interest the public in looking at and collecting sculpture. Gosse was the first important critic to recognize the significance of the stylistic changes that English sculpture was undergoing in the late 19th century. He coined the term 'New Sculpture' in his 1894 essay of that title for the *Art Journal*; it long remained the definitive account of this movement.

The principal characteristic of the New Sculpture, for Gosse, was a close and reverent observation of nature, transcribed by careful and sensitive modelling. While still valid, this definition takes little account of other characteristics of the sculpture of prominent artists associated with the movement, such as the non-naturalistic symbolism of George Frampton and the decorative fantasy of Alfred Gilbert. Gosse also seemed indifferent to the relationship between the New Sculpture and the Arts and Crafts Movement, as manifested in the contemporary revival of interest in architectural sculpture. Gosse's daughter Sylvia Gosse (1881–1965) was a talented painter and etcher, who produced work in the style of her teacher Walter Sickert.

WRITINGS

'Living English Sculptors', *C. Ill.*, n.s. xxvi (1883), pp. 162–85; n.s. xxvi (1886), pp. 39–50
'The New Sculpture 1879–84', *A.J.* [London] (1894), pp. 138–42, 199–203, 277–82, 306–11
Regular contributions (1879–95) to *Sat. Rev.*, *Cornhill Mag.*, *Mag. A.*, *Pall Mall Gaz.*

BIBLIOGRAPHY

Sickert Women and Sickert Girls (exh. cat., intro. W. Baron; London, Michael Parkin Gal., 1974)
S. Beattie: *The New Sculpture* (New Haven and London, 1983)
A. Thwaite: *Edmund Gosse: A Literary Landscape, 1849–1928* (London, 1984/*R* 1985)
M. Stocker: 'Edmund Gosse on Sculpture', *U. Leeds Rev.*, xxviii (1985–6), pp. 283–310

MARK STOCKER

Gosset, Isaac (*b* St Helier, Jersey, 2 May 1713; *d* London, 28 Nov 1799). English wood-carver and wax-modeller. He was the sixth son of Jean Gosset, a Huguenot from Normandy who had settled in Jersey, and he trained in London as a frame-carver and wax-modeller with his uncle Matthew Gosset (1683–1744) of Poland Street, Soho. He developed an ability to produce a startling likeness in wax of a sitter's profile in as little as half an hour. His original models cost four guineas and were used to produce casts from which replicas were made and sold in oval frames for a guinea each. They were much copied and reproduced by James Tassie and Josiah Wedgwood.

Gosset's works include wax portrait reliefs of *Frederick and Augusta, Prince and Princess of Wales*, *William Augustus, Duke of Cumberland*, *George III as Prince of Wales* (all Windsor Castle, Berks, Royal Col.) and a group of portraits of nine members of the Murray and Stanhope families (Chevening, Kent), modelled to commemorate a wedding in 1745. He also produced a series of ancient and modern worthies that included the *Twelve Roman Emperors* and both Classical and British writers. He exhibited with the Society of Artists until 1778. Gosset carved frames for his artist friends William Hogarth, Allan Ramsay and Thomas Gainsborough. No such frame is known to survive, however. In 1799 the anonymous author of his obituary in the *Gentleman's Magazine* declared: 'In the line of his art he may be said to have been unique'.

BIBLIOGRAPHY

Gunnis
M. H. Gosset: 'A Family of Modellers in Wax', *Proc. Huguenot Soc. London*, iii (1888–91), p. 547
E. J. Pyke: *A Biographical Dictionary of Wax Modellers* (Oxford, 1973)
The Quiet Conquest: The Huguenots 1685–1985 (exh. cat., ed. T. Murdoch; London, Mus. London, 1985)
'Courtiers and Classics: The Gosset Family', *Country Life*, clxxvii (9 May 1985), pp. 1282–3

TESSA MURDOCH

Gosset de Guines, Louis-Alexandre. *See* GILL, ANDRÉ.

Gostomski, Zbigniew (*b* Bydgoszcz, Pomerania, 14 Nov 1932). Polish conceptual artist. He studied at the Academy of Fine Arts, Warsaw, in 1953–9. His earliest work draws on his experience of Minimalism and Op art. The series *Optical Objects* (1958–65), for example, geometrical reliefs modelled according to mathematical calculations and painted in a range of tones from white to grey to black, exploits both natural and artificial effects of light and shade. *Environment* (1968), an assembly of solid three-dimensional forms, could be seen simultaneously as a unified structure and as a collection of individual 'works', and it was on the periphery of architecture, sculpture and painting.

In 1970 Gostomski conceived the piece *It Begins in Wrocław*, an 'impossible' project, in which three arbitrarily selected forms, beginning in a defined point in the centre of Wrocław, were to spread out in an equally arbitrary manner through the city, the continent, the globe, and eventually into galactic infinity. In *Pascal's Triangle* (1973), a familiar mathematical law is 'altered' by means of an inverted graphic inscription, given a literary analogy by means of an appropriate citation from James Joyce's *Ulysses* and a visual one by means of a photograph of conical piles of coal. In the work *From 1 to 10* (1974), the visual effect of eight mixed pigments and one separated one is repeated in all in nine combinations, and each combination is then repeated in the numerical inscription 1–9. Similarly in *To John Cage's Lecture on Nothing* (1976), the original text is inscribed in a manner that gives it a geometric and a musical rhythmic order. Works from the 1980s consist of 'empty' models of representational or abstract paintings, whose topographical perspective is negated by means of deformed elements of the frame and an illusionistic imposition of planes or free-standing shapes on the canvas.

BIBLIOGRAPHY

A. Kępińska: *Nowa sztuka polska w latach 1945–1973* [New Polish art from the years 1945–1973] (Warsaw, 1981)

Présences polonaises (exh. cat., ed. D. Bozo and R. Stanisławski; Paris, Pompidou, 1983), pp. 73–4

Z. Taranienko: Rozmowy o malarstwie [Conversations about painting] (Warsaw, 1987), pp. 202–13 [interview with the artist]

EWA MIKINA

Got, Bertrand du. *See* CLEMENT V.

Gotch, Thomas Cooper (*b* Kettering, 10 Dec 1854; *d* Newlyn, 1 May 1931). English painter. He studied at Heatherleys in London (1876–7), at the Koninklijke Academie voor Schone Kunsten in Antwerp (1877–8) and with Alphonse Legros at the Slade (1878–80). At the Slade, Gotch became close friends with Henry Scott Tuke and Caroline Yates (fl 1880–96), whom he married in 1881. While studying in Paris in the early 1880s Gotch began to practise the *plein-air* approach later associated with the NEWLYN SCHOOL. *Mental Arithmetic* (1883; Melbourne, N.G. Victoria), painted in Newlyn, exemplifies the Newlyn painters' concern with light conditions and traditional rural themes.

Gotch settled in Newlyn in 1887, but he continued to experiment with subjects, styles and media. Many oils and watercolours are indebted to the tonal and compositional innovations of his friend James McNeill Whistler. Portrait painting (e.g. *Sir William Drake in the Morning Room*, 1885; priv. col.) remained Gotch's primary source of income throughout his life. He sought a new focus for his work in Florence between 1891 and 1892, and in a series of paintings resulting from this visit, beginning with *My Crown and Sceptre* (1892; Sydney, A.G. NSW), he returned to allegorical genre painting. His new combination of symbolic female figures, decorative Italian textiles and the static order of early Renaissance art finally brought him recognition. *Alleluia* (1896; London, Tate) was purchased by the Chantrey Bequest trustees. Gotch was active in the Royal Society of British Artists and the Royal Institution. He was a founding member of the New English Art Club and the Royal British Colonial Society of Artists, serving as president between 1913–28.

BIBLIOGRAPHY

A. L. Baldry: 'The Work of T. C. Gotch', *The Studio*, xiii (March 1898), pp. 73–82

Artists of the Newlyn School, 1880–1900 (exh. cat. by C. Fox and F. Greenacre, Newlyn, Orion Gals, 1979), pp. 172–85

B. Cogger Rezelman: *The Newlyn Artists and their Place in Late-Victorian Art* (diss., Bloomington, IN U., 1984)

Painting in Newlyn, 1880–1930 (exh. cat. by C. Fox and F. Greenacre, London, Barbican A.G., 1985), pp. 75–7, 105–6, 121–3

BETSY COGGER REZELMAN

Göteborg [Gothenburg]. City on the west coast of Sweden, situated on a hilly site at the mouth of the River Göta. The second largest Swedish city and the most important port in Scandinavia, it has flourished since the 18th century, its buildings reflecting every significant architectural movement in Sweden. It is now a business and industrial centre, with a population of *c.* 450,000.

Göteborg was founded in 1619 by King Gustav II Adolf (*reg* 1611–32) at a strategically important position for defence against Denmark and Norway. With the assistance of Dutch engineers, the city was laid out with a regular network of streets, canals and a moat. Its fortifications were considerable, comprising the island fortress of New Älvsborg and two forts by Erik Dahlbergh, The Lion (1689) and The Crown (1700; now the Military Museum), situated on elevated bastions outside the former city wall. Among prominent 17th-century buildings are the red-brick artillery depot (now part of the City Museum), built in 1643–53 and the oldest surviving building in the city, the cathedral, which was rebuilt in 1808–15 to plans by Carl Wilhelm Carlberg (1745–1814), the Kristine Church (rebuilt 1746–80), the Governor's Residence and the Town Hall (1672; rebuilt 1814–17; enlarged 1935–7 by Gunnar Asplund).

Owing to the success of the East India Company, Göteborg enjoyed immense importance as a harbour and market during the 18th century. Scottish and English merchants used it for trade with Canton: collections of imported china are housed in the former office and warehouse of the Company (1750–62; now the Museum of History), designed by Bengt Wilhelm Carlberg (1696–1778), at the Stora Hamnkanal quay.

Between 1717 and 1814 architecture in Göteborg was dominated by the classical style of three members of the Carlberg family, some idea of which survives in such streets as Södra Hamngatan. Johan Eberhard Carlberg (1683–1773) became the first City Engineer in 1717. He was succeeded in 1727 by his brother Bengt Wilhelm Carlberg, whose son Carl Wilhelm Carlberg took over in 1775. Under their building regulations, the town centre was uniformly built of two- or three-storey houses with façades of yellow brick or plaster. Well-preserved examples of Carl Wilhelm Carlberg's Neo-classical style include the cathedral, the house of William Chalmers (1807) at Södra Hamngatan and a timber villa, Gunnebo (1784), a few miles outside the city.

During the first decade of the 19th century the city walls were demolished and the area beyond the moat was landscaped. The historicist movement is reflected in such buildings as the former Sahlgren Hospital (1852) and the Fish Hall (1874), both by Victor von Gegerfelt (1817–1915); the Grand Theatre (1856–9) by Bror Carl Malmberg (1818–77); the Werner Villa (1889) by Adrian Petterson (1835–1912); the synagogue (1845) by August Krüger; and the neo-Gothic church (1856–9) at Haga and the central railway station (1858), both by Adolf Wilhelm Edelsvärd. The Market Hall (Saluhallen), the Palm House (1878) and the largest city park, Slottskogen, belong to the same period. Owing to a strong tradition of local patronage, there has always been a close link between the commercial and cultural life of the city, symbolized by the Exchange (1849) by Pehr Johan Ekman (1816–84).

Trade and industry expanded in the later 19th century, the rapid growth of the city causing major housing problems. One of the main purposes of the city plan of 1866, which was based on a grid pattern, was to provide new residential areas. The so-called Governor's House (*landshövdingehus*), with a stone ground-floor and two timber upper storeys, has since been a unique feature of Göteborg. On either side of the Aveny, more fashionable blocks of flats were built with richly decorated, plastered, neo-Renaissance façades.

Hans Hedlund (*b* 1855) introduced the ideas of H. H. Richardson with the Dickson Library, the City Archives and other buildings around the turn of the 20th century. National Romanticism is represented by such impressive buildings as the Masthuggskyrkan (1910–14) by SIGFRID ERICSON and the Röhsska Museum (1910–14; now the Arts and Crafts Museum) by Carl Westman (1866–1936). These heavy, red-brick buildings have several equivalents in contemporary schools and apartment blocks. By this time the grid plan had been abandoned by the town planner Albert Lilienberg, who created new areas under the influence of the ideas of Camillo Sitte.

In the 1920s painting began to flourish in Göteborg through the work of such artists as Tor Bjurström (*b* 1888), Ivan Ivarson (1900–39), Inge Schiöler (*b* 1908), Åke Göransson (1902–42) and Ragnar Sandberg (*b* 1902), often called the Göteborgskolorister (Göteborg Colourists). Architectural classicism continued in the 1920s with terraces of delicate timber houses and the yellow-brick Carl Johan School (1924) by Gunnar Asplund. The Göteborg Jubilee Exhibition of 1923 initiated one of the most grandiose urban planning projects in Sweden: the Götaplats, with the Konstmuseum and Exhibition Hall by Arvid Bjerke (1880–1952) and Sigfrid Ericson, and the Poseidon Fountain (1927–30) by Carl Milles. The Götaplats was completed by the addition of the Civic Theatre (1935) by CARL BERGSTEN and the acoustically distinguished Concert Hall (1935) by NILS EINAR ERIKSSON. As head of the City Planning Office (1932–43), the radical modernist Uno Åhrén played an important role, including the design of the residential district of Upper Johanneberg.

Swedish Functionalism of the 1950s and 1960s is clearly reflected in several new residential areas, planned as prefabricated units for rapid construction. At this time, too, parts of the city centre were demolished: Östra Nordstaden shopping mall is an example of new development in the 1970s. Göteborg became the subject of post-modern experiments in the 1980s, with threats to its low-rise skyline. The most striking example of a new high-rise building is the bright red-and-white Skanska office building (1989) by Ralph Erskine. The closure of most of the former shipyards has enabled much of the northern riverfront to be redeveloped.

BIBLIOGRAPHY

A. F. Baeckström: *Studier i Göteborgs byggnadshistoria före 1814: Ett bidrag till svensk stadsbyggnadshistoria* [Studies in Göteborg's architectural history before 1814: a contribution to the architectural history of Swedish towns] (Stockholm, 1923)

H. Almquist: *Göteborgs historia: Grundläggningen och de första hundra åren* [The history of Göteborg: the foundation and first hundred years], 2 vols (Göteborg, 1929–35)

G. Munthe and K. W. Gullers: *Gothenburg: Sweden's Gateway to the West* (Stockholm, 1948)

O. Thulin, ed.: *Göteborg* (Göteborg, 1948)

C. Caldenby, ed.: *Byggnader i Göteborg* [Buildings in Göteborg] (Göteborg, 1979)

H. Bjur: *Stadsplanering kring 1900* [Town planning around 1900] (Göteborg, 1984)

Göteborg: Årsbok 1988 (Stockholm, 1988)

G. Schönbeck: *Victor von Gegerfelt: Arkitekt i Göteborg* (Göteborg, 1991)

GUNILLA LINDE

Gothart Nithart, Mathis. *See* GRÜNEWALD, MATTHIAS.

Göthe, Erik Gustav (*b* Stockholm, 26 July 1779; *d* Stockholm, 26 Nov 1838). Swedish sculptor. In 1795 he entered the Konstakademi in Stockholm where he studied under Johan Tobias Sergel and produced numerous portrait busts. In 1803 he left Stockholm and travelled to Rome via Paris. In Rome he worked with Antonio Canova and under his influence and that of his own studies of Classical sculpture developed a fairly undistinguished Neo-classical style, to which he remained constant for the rest of his career. Among the works he produced in Rome was a seated marble statue of *Bacchus* (1808; Stockholm, Nmus.). In 1810 he returned to Stockholm where he concentrated on portrait busts and statues of Swedish royalty. One of the most notable of these is the bronze statue of *Karl XIII* set up in the Royal Gardens in Stockholm in 1821. Between 1822 and 1826 Göthe spent much time in St Petersburg where he produced, among other works, a seated statue of *Catherine the Great* (1823; St Petersburg, Hermitage) and mythological sculptures such as *Venus and Cupid* (1823; terracotta model, Stockholm, Nmus.). In 1827 Göthe was appointed professor at the Konstakademi in Stockholm. Thereafter he devoted himself primarily to portrait works and among his later sculptures is a portrait medallion of *R. R. Stokoe* (1831; Stockholm, Nmus.).

BIBLIOGRAPHY

SBL

G. Nordensvan: *Svensk konst i nittonde århundradet* [Swedish art in the 19th century] (Stockholm, 1892), pp. 184–5, 333–4

□

Göthe, Johann Friedrich Eosander. *See* EOSANDER, JOHANN FRIEDRICH.

Gothic. Term used to denote, since the 15th century, the architecture and, from the 19th, all the visual arts of Europe during a period extending by convention from about 1120 to *c.* 1400 in central Italy, and until the late 15th century and even well into the 16th in northern Europe and the Iberian Peninsula. The Early Gothic style overlapped chronologically with ROMANESQUE and flourished after the onset of RENAISSANCE art in Italy and elsewhere. Scholarly preoccupations with the nature of the Gothic style (*see* §I below) have been centred almost exclusively on architecture, and the term has never been satisfactory for the figural arts, especially painting (*see* §IV below); but the 19th-century tradition of classification has proved so enduring that it continues to be used for figural styles.

I. Introduction. II. Architecture. III. Sculpture. IV. Painting. V. Metalwork. VI. Enamels. VII. Ivories. VIII. Stained glass. IX. Textiles.

DETAILED TABLE OF CONTENTS

I. Introduction 33

II. Architecture 35

1. *c.* 1120–the late 13th century 35

(i) Introduction 35

(ii) France 36
(a) First manifestations of a new vision, *c.* 1120–50 36
(b) The first synthesis and the quest for height, 1150–90 38
(c) Maturation and experiment, 1190–1230 39
(d) Rayonnant architecture, 1230–1300 41
(iii) British Isles 43
(a) The reception of Gothic, *c.* 1150–85 43
(b) From Canterbury to Westminster, 1185–1245 45
(c) Westminster Abbey and its impact, 1245–1300 46
(iv) Holy Roman Empire 47
(a) Isolated experiences, *c.* 1170–1230 47
(b) German architectural modernism, 1230–1300 48
(v) Scandinavia 50
(vi) Spain 50
(vii) Italy 51
2. Late 13th century–the 16th 53
(i) Introduction 53
(ii) British Isles 53
(iii) Holy Roman Empire, Scandinavia and Eastern Europe 56
(a) *Backsteingotik* and Rhenish Rayonnant 56
(b) The Parler legacy 57
(iv) France 59
(v) Low Countries 61
(vi) Italy 63
(a) Introduction 63
(b) The south, the Veneto and Lombardy 63
(c) Tuscany and its influence 65
(vii) Spain 66
(a) Catalonia, to *c.* 1450 67
(b) Castile, Aragon and Andalusia, to *c.* 1570 68
(c) Hispano-Flemish style and the last Gothic cathedrals, *c.* 1475–1593 69
(viii) Portugal 70

III. Sculpture 71
1. Stone 72
(i) France 72
(a) Introduction 72
(b) 12th and 13th centuries 72
– The revival of stone sculpture in the north 72
– The Early Gothic phase 73
– Laon and Chartres 73
– Amiens, Paris and Reims 74
(c) 14th century 75
– Patronage and the court 76
– The influence of Paris 77
(d) 15th century 77
– Burgundy 77
– Berry and Bourbonnais 78
– Loire Valley 79
– Languedoc 79
– Lorraine and Champagne 79
– Paris and the north 79
(ii) British Isles 80
(a) Introduction 80
(b) Late 12th century and the 13th 80
(c) 14th century 82
(d) 15th century 84
(iii) Holy Roman Empire 85
(a) Introduction 85
(b) 13th century 86
– Stylistic developments 86
– Iconography 87
(c) 14th and 15th centuries 87
– *c.* 1300–*c.* 1350 88
– *c.* 1350–*c.* 1420 88
– *c.* 1420–*c.* 1500 90
(iv) Italy 93
(a) Introduction 93
(b) Tuscany 93
(c) Lombardy 94
(d) Veneto 95
(e) Emilia-Romagna 95
(f) Umbria 96
(g) Lazio 97
(h) Campania 98
(v) Low Countries 98
(a) 1250–1300 98
(b) 1300–1350 99
(c) 1350–1430 99
(d) 1430–1530 100
(vi) Portugal 101
(vii) Scandinavia 101
(viii) Spain 103
(a) 13th and 14th centuries 103
– Castile and León 103
– Navarre 105
– Aragon 105
(b) Early 15th century 106
– Castile 106
– Aragon 106
– Navarre 107
(c) Later 15th century and the early 16th 107
– Castile 107
– Andalusia 108
2. Wood 109
(i) Introduction 109
(ii) Low Countries 109
(a) 1240–1300 109
(b) 1300–1350 110
(c) 1350–1430 110
(d) 1430–1530 111
– Brabant 111
– Tournai and Hainault 112
– Flanders 113
– Meuse Valley 113
– North Netherlands 114
(iii) Holy Roman Empire 115
(a) Introduction 115
(b) 1300–1420 116
(c) 1420–1500 117
(iv) Scandinavia 118
(a) 13th century 118
(b) 14th century 120
(c) 15th century and the early 16th 120
(v) British Isles 121
(vi) Spain 122
(vii) Italy 123
(viii) Portugal 124
(ix) France 125
(a) 14th century 125
(b) 15th century 125

IV. Painting 126
1. Introduction 126
(i) Ecclesiastical patronage and subject-matter 127
(ii) Lay patronage and subject-matter 127
(iii) Representation and response 128
2. Forms 129
(i) Manuscript 129
(ii) Panel 130

(iii) Stained glass 132
(iv) Wall 132
3. Working practices 132
4. Techniques 133
(i) Fresco, secco and panel 133
(ii) Colour 135
(iii) Illumination, modelling and treatment of surface 137
5. Stylistic and regional development 139
(i) Transitional style, *c.* 1180–*c.* 1250 139
(ii) Parisian and related styles, *c.* 1240–*c.* 1320 140
(iii) Holy Roman Empire, *c.* 1230–*c.* 1300 142
(iv) Scandinavia and the Iberian Peninsula, *c.* 1230–*c.* 1340 143
(v) Italy, *c.* 1265–*c.* 1320 144
(vi) England and France, *c.* 1300–*c.*1350 147
(a) England 147
(b) France 148
(vii) Italy, Spain and papal Avignon, *c.* 1320–*c.* 1400 149
(viii) Holy Roman Empire, *c.* 1300–*c.* 1400 151
(ix) England, *c.* 1350–*c.* 1410 152
(x) France, *c.* 1350–*c.* 1410 153
(xi) International Gothic style, *c.* 1380–*c.* 1440 155
V. Metalwork 157
1. Introduction 157
2. France 158
3. Low Countries 159
4. Holy Roman Empire 160
5. Eastern Europe 161
6. Italy 163
7. British Isles 163
8. Spain 165
9. Portugal 166
10. Scandinavia 166
VI. Enamels 167
1. Champlevé 167
(i) Limoges 167
(ii) Tuscany 168
(iii) Upper Rhineland 168
2. *Email de plique* 168
3. *Basse-taille* 168
4. Filigree 170
5. *En ronde bosse* 170
6. *Plique à jour* 170
7. Painted 170
VII. Ivories 171
1. Craft organization 171
2. Chronological survey 172
(i) First half of the 13th century 172
(ii) The 'Soissons' group 172
(iii) Parisian style in the middle and second half of the 13th century 172
(iv) First half of the 14th century 174
(v) Parisian style in the second half of the 14th century 175
(vi) Non-Parisian workshops 175
(a) England 176
(b) Italy 176
(c) Rhineland and Meuse region 176
VIII. Stained glass 178
1. Introduction 178
2. France 178
3. Low Countries 181
4. British Isles 183
(i) Before *c.* 1380 183
(ii) *c.* 1380–*c.* 1550 183
5. Holy Roman Empire 185
(i) *c.* 1220–1340 185
(ii) After 1340 187
6. Eastern Europe 189
7. Scandinavia 190
8. Spain 191
9. Portugal 192
10. Italy 192
IX. Textiles 194
1. Introduction 194
2. Tapestry and embroidery 194
(i) Production 194
(ii) Use 196
3. Silk fabrics 197

I. Introduction.

The people who produced what has since come to be known as Gothic art needed no name to distinguish what they were doing from other styles. They were aware of differences of appearance between the churches they built and buildings of earlier periods, but if these had any significance for them, it was mainly iconographical. As the defining characteristics of Gothic are always more conspicuous in ecclesiastical than in secular art, they no doubt considered its primary function to be in the service of the Church. Otherwise they seem to have been unaware that their arts had a history. It needed the comprehensive changes of taste associated with the Renaissance to introduce the notion of Gothic into the vocabulary of art. During the 15th century educated Italians such as Alberti and Lorenzo Valla (1407–57), who were attuned to the superior decorum of all things Classical, began to use the adjective 'Gothic' to convey their sense of contemporary architecture as rough, rustic or crude, by comparison with that of ancient Rome. The word was overtly pejorative, being derived from the barbarian Goths who sacked Rome in AD 410 and again in 455. It also came to designate the architecture of the Germans or northern Europe generally, and this purely descriptive use outlasted its role as an epithet of derision. When 16th-century Italians tried to explain the phenomenon of Gothic, they supposed that the pointed arch, the most notable of Gothic solecisms, would come naturally to the minds of men whose original habitat had been the northern forests. Despite its manifest absurdity, this theory has recurred from time to time among believers in *Menschheitpsychologie*, following the writings of Wilhelm Worringer.

Gothic was rehabilitated in the religious revival that followed the French Revolution, and for much of the 19th century the historicist GOTHIC REVIVAL was in vogue all over the world as the approved style for new churches; it was also used for public buildings and even domestic design. The reunion of Gothic with the practice of architecture was anticipated by, and to some extent rooted in, a better understanding of the medieval buildings from which the style derived its prestige. By the second half of the 18th century, the science of mechanics was sufficiently developed to demonstrate that pointed arches could be more efficient than semicircular arches as load-bearing structures, and that far from being inept, Gothic architects had been superb structural engineers. The re-evaluation entailed by these discoveries culminated in the definition of Gothic by EUGENE-EMMANUEL VIOLLET-LE-DUC as the conjunction of pointed arches, ribbed vaults and flying buttresses. Until German shells in World War I contrived to demonstrate that Gothic structures did not always behave as theory prescribed (*see* VAULT: RIB), Viollet-le-Duc's technological interpretation of the style was accepted by architectural historians as the undoubted truth, and the demise of the theory after 1918 proved epoch-making (*see* MASONRY, §III).

The second major step towards a sharper definition of Gothic was the achievement of a precise chronology. When it was realized, by the late 17th century, that pointed arches, the *sine qua non* of Gothic, did not appear until *c.* 1100, the proper understanding of the 700 years between then and late antiquity, and their relation to the three Gothic centuries, became a serious problem. Wren complicated matters by noting that pointed arches had been used by Muslim architects long before they appeared in Christian churches (*see* ARCH, §§2 and 3(iii)), and he proposed that the pointed style be renamed Saracenic. The revision proved too much for Goethe and the generation after Winckelmann, for whom it remained axiomatic that Gothic was German. Eventually attention was shifted from pointed arches to ribbed vaults as the defining characteristic, and Gothic became *le style ogival*. Few early 19th-century antiquaries pursued documentary research, which probably helped them to side-step the hazards presented by the actual chronology of ribbed vaults. It was largely a matter of luck that they came up with the right answer. Once the date of 1144 for the choir of Saint-Denis Abbey was firmly established, it was conceded on all sides, although to everyone's surprise, that Gothic had originated in northern France in the second quarter of the 12th century (*see* §II, 1(i) below).

The detailed examination of Gothic buildings (the perception of what went with what, and the classification of these clusters of forms into a sequence of substyles) began in earnest during the first quarter of the 19th century. The pioneer was Thomas Rickman in England (*see* EARLY ENGLISH; DECORATED STYLE; PERPENDICULAR STYLE), followed soon after by Arcisse de Caumont in France. Much of the subsequent discussion has been about where the lines of demarcation should be drawn between the several phases, and what causal mechanisms presided over the changes. Nineteenth-century architects and antiquaries, who knew a lot about buildings but not much history, tended to think about style as though it was a living organism, on the analogy of the dominant science of the day, biology. Styles thus evolved from tentative beginnings (*see* EARLY GOTHIC) to a brief maturity, known variously as HIGH GOTHIC, RAYONNANT STYLE or Early English, after which they went into decline, as seen in FLAMBOYANT STYLE, LATE GOTHIC, Decorated, Perpendicular, SONDERGOTIK and *Reduktionsgotik*.

Such a hypothesis carried an inherent criterion of quality. The best buildings belonged to the 'best periods'. Early buildings could show promise; but anything that was late was almost irretrievably damned to decadence. This suited the French well enough. Their High Gothic cathedrals have never ceased to bask in the good fortune of coinciding with the apex of the Gothic cycle; and they have never had much of an opinion of their Late Gothic (Flamboyant). The Germans, who had next to no High Gothic and more than their fair share of the late style, sought to correct this imbalance by reappraising all so-called late styles. The notion of style notably promulgated by Alois Riegl and Heinrich Wölfflin was pruned of most of its biological overtones, and transformed into an extremely subtle instrument for detecting nuances and shifts of expressive intention. For architecture, what now turned buildings into works of art was how their designers handled the shaping of space (*Raumform*); and the leitmotif of Gothic was spatial fusion (*Raumverschmelzung*; *see* SCHMARSOW, AUGUST), which achieved its most extreme manifestations in German Late Gothic hall churches. Early and High Gothic, however, were equally amenable to spatial analysis, and when the modulation of spatial effects by means of light, colour and pattern were taken into account, together with the paring away of superfluous structures, the art historians' aesthetic insights could be substituted for Viollet-le-Duc's theories as soon as the latter were disproved.

Yet the distinctive task of the 20th century has been not so much to appreciate the artistry of Gothic, as to place individual Gothic buildings in their proper historical setting, following the lead given for Renaissance works by Aby Warburg, who saw style ideally as an exact equation between form and content. To understand the content, vast learning and intensive research were often required, but for Gothic churches the contextual material was not easy to find, and the reconstruction of the specific occasions difficult to accomplish. It therefore took several decades before the results began to show. Here Erwin Panofsky's *Abbot Suger on the Abbey Church of Saint-Denis and its Art Treasures* (Princeton, 1946) played a decisive role.

The historical approach brought with it shifts of emphasis that have both extended and diluted the meaning of Gothic. It introduced the notion of function: the expectations and purposes of the patrons and users of Gothic churches. Attention was now paid to practical requirements of the cult, as these affected both clergy and laity. Beyond that, however, much of the imaginative effort that went into the design process made sense as the presentation of the Church as allegory. The building came to be seen as a comprehensive religious symbol in which the architecture was no longer just an evocative shape, but a frame with specific iconographical associations of its own (e.g. the Heavenly Jerusalem) and inhabited by appropriate images rendered in stone and wood or else painted in stained glass and on walls. All the arts worked in conjunction with one another and towards the same end (Sedlmayr). The invention of Gothic architecture in the 12th century had its precise counterpart in the transformation of the human figure from the stylized abstractions of Romanesque into a naturalism that could be called Gothic by association. In due course these major art forms were joined by a repertory of Gothic ornament, and rather belatedly it has been recognized that Gothic art was never exclusively religious, but that it spilled over into the pageantry of public and domestic life throughout Europe. There was hardly any category of artefact made during the last three medieval centuries that was not in some measure affected by the style. Ruskin's vision of the honest medieval craftsman may have been tinged by Utopian socialism, but his sense of an all-pervasive craftsmanship was not entirely wishful thinking.

BIBLIOGRAPHY

S. Wren, ed.: *Parentalia; or, Memoirs of the Family of the Wrens* (London, 1750/*R* 1965), p. 306

J. W. von Goethe: *Von deutscher Baukunst* (Frankfurt am Main, 1772)

T. Rickman: *An Attempt to Discriminate the Styles of English Architecture from the Conquest to the Reformation* (Liverpool, 1817, rev. 7/1888)

E.-E. Viollet-le-Duc: *Dictionnaire raisonné de l'architecture française du XIe au XVIe siècle*, 10 vols (Paris, 1854–68)

A. Riegl: *Die spätrömische Kunstindustrie* (Vienna, 1901, rev. 2/1927/*R* 1973)

W. R. Worringer: *Formprobleme der Gotik* (Munich, 1911; Eng. trans., London, 1957)

H. Sedlmayr: *Die Entstehung der Kathedrale* (Zurich and Freiburg im Breisgau, 1950)

P. Frankl: *The Gothic: Literary Sources and Interpretations through Eight Centuries* (Princeton, 1960) [complete bibliog. with commentary, up to *c.* 1950]

J. Białostocki: 'Late Gothic: Disagreements about the Concept', *J. Brit. Archaeol. Assoc.*, 3rd ser., xxix (1966), pp. 76–105

W. Sauerländer: 'Style or Transition? The Fallacies of Classification Discussed in the Light of German Architecture, 1190–1260', *Archit. Hist.*, xxx (1987), pp. 1–30

II. Architecture.

The success of Gothic as an architectural style is reflected both in the length of time that it flourished, from early in the 12th century to very late in the 16th, and in its geographical extent. Gothic buildings can be found from Ireland and Scandinavia in north-western Europe, to Cyprus and the Levant. Manuals of architectural history once emphasized contrasts between Gothic and the architecture of Classical antiquity and the Renaissance, but, as art historians have become better historians, the sharp distinction has been blurred and diminished. If only because it was the architecture that corresponded to the 12th century Renaissance, it is unlikely that Gothic, alone among the arts and sciences of the time, was completely divorced from the inheritance from antiquity (*see* VITRUVIUS, §3(i)). Below the level of visual dissimilarities, continuities of method can be detected, from which it may be inferred that, far from being a fresh start, Gothic only marks the stage where medieval architects emancipated themselves from the restraints of precedents. Henceforth they felt free to construct whatever forms they or their patrons wanted, subject only to the reservation that they conformed to the perennial principles of good architecture, which they believed (with good reason) had been handed down to them from the ancients.

The stylistic development of Gothic architecture is discussed in the article below. For analysis of Gothic structure *see also* MASONRY, III; for Gothic design techniques *see* MASON (i).

PETER KIDSON

1. *c.* 1120–the late 13th century. 2. Late 13th century–the 16th.

1. *c.* 1120–THE LATE 13TH CENTURY.

(i) Introduction. (ii) France. (iii) British Isles. (iv) Holy Roman Empire. (v) Scandinavia. (vi) Spain. (vii) Italy.

(i) Introduction. Between 1120 and 1300 European architecture enjoyed one of its most brilliantly creative periods. The art of building was transformed by a series of new structural features, and major edifices achieved a previously unparalleled size, lightness and visual complexity. Contemporaries referred to this architecture as the *opus francigenum* (or later *maniera tedesca*), but most often it was simply described as 'new'. Since it first appeared and was developed in northern France, there has been a tendency to view Gothic architecture in terms of French features and to evaluate building in other countries by its resemblance to French models. Specific structural elements, such as ribbed vaults, pointed arches, the flying buttress, large windows and bar tracery, and a general emphasis on verticality and lightness have been identified as the defining components of the style. Increasingly, however, emphasis is being placed on the diversity of 12th- and 13th-century construction. Buildings outside France are seen less as timid, conservative or failed attempts to emulate French architecture, than as independent creations resulting from their local histories, functions and patrons. A crucial distinction must be made between the absorption of French structural principles that made possible breathtaking spaciousness, overwhelming size and lightness, and the adoption of Gothic ornament, such as bar tracery or crocket capitals, which combined with local building traditions to create an image of stylistic modernity.

Down to the end of the 13th century, France, as the centre of the most intense, sustained activity, dominated developments. Yet French architecture did not provide the sole standard of evaluation for the rest of Europe; and Gothic architecture cannot be circumscribed by an exclusive set of forms or criteria. In addition, the history of Gothic building cannot be told only in terms of the great church. The deliberately simplified architecture of the Cistercians (*see* §(ii)(a) below), Dominicans and Franciscans (*see* §(vii)(a) below), formulated as an alternative to the rich cathedral Gothic, had in some ways a greater impact on building than the small number of élite structures. In England, Germany, Spain and Italy, the Cistercians seem to have been the agents of such proto-Gothic forms as ribbed vaults and pointed arches, and established contacts with France. Further, there existed a dynamic interaction between structures of different classes, types and size. It cannot be presumed that the modest monastic and parish churches inevitably mirrored cathedral models.

In spite of the importance of civil construction, this article will concentrate on ecclesiastical architecture. While there was certainly interchange between ecclesiastic and secular building, the fundamental concerns of the castle-builder lay not with arranging corridors of circulation or with the representational issues, but with pragmatic problems of defence and living (*see* CASTLE, §I). It was in ecclesiastical architecture that the most salient structural innovations took place and the most complex visual effects were achieved.

BIBLIOGRAPHY

A. Dimier: *Recueil de plans d'églises cisterciennes*, 2 vols (Paris, 1949)

H. Hahn: *Die frühe Kirchenbaukunst der Zisterzienser* (Berlin, 1957)

F. Bucher: 'Cistercian Architectural Purism', *Comp. Stud. Soc. & Hist.*, iii (1960), pp. 89–105

R. Branner: *Gothic Architecture* (New York, 1961)

P. Frankl: *Gothic Architecture*, Pelican Hist. A. (Harmondsworth, 1962)

F. Bucher: 'Micro-architecture as the "Idea" of Gothic Theory and Style', *Gesta*, xv (1976), pp. 71–89

L. Grodecki: *L'Architecture gothique* (Paris, 1976; Eng. trans., New York, 1977)
R. Mark: *Experiments in Gothic Structure* (Cambridge, MA, 1982)
W. Sauerländer: *Le Siècle des cathédrales, 1140–1260* (Paris, 1989)
C. Wilson: *The Gothic Cathedral: The Architecture of the Great Church, 1130–1530* (London, 1990)

(ii) France.

(a) First manifestations of a new vision, *c.* 1120–50. (b) The first synthesis and the quest for height, 1150–90. (c) Maturation and experiment, 1190–1230. (d) Rayonnant architecture, 1230–1300.

(a) First manifestations of a new vision, c. *1120–50.* By *c.* 1120 French builders, like their peers from Lombardy to northern England, had integrated the ribbed vault and pointed arch into their constructional repertory (*see* ROMANESQUE, §II). The use of such masonry vaults necessitated complex systems of support, while the introduction of ribs produced a more intimate coordination of the vault with elevations that were articulated with networks of columnar shafts and mouldings (*see* MASONRY, §III, 3(iii)). The pointed arch, which may have offered slight structural advantages relative to the semicircular arch, visually underscored verticality, and when combined with the ribbed vault, as at Durham Cathedral (1093–1133; *see* DURHAM, fig. 2), created new potential for spatial expansion and integration.

Similarly, in plan design from the late 11th century onwards spatial complication and unification, especially in the choir had begun to be explored. The plan of an ambulatory and radiating chapels was adapted at Fécamp Abbey (ded. 1093) and Avranches Cathedral (ded. 1121; destr. 1794), but by multiplying and setting the chapels contiguously a series of uniform interior spaces enclosed by a continuous exterior wall was created. Apses in echelon, originating with the secondary abbey church (begun *c.* 955; destr.) at Cluny and elaborated at Saint-Sever Abbey (*c.* 1100), provided a corridor of circulation around the main liturgical space and produced a unified envelope of tangential chapels (*see* CHURCH, §II, 3(i)).

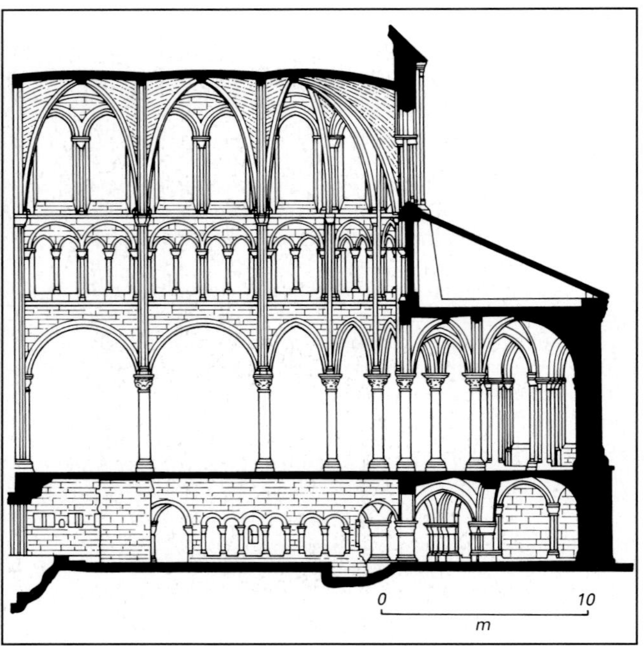

1. France, Saint-Denis Abbey, choir elevation, 1140–44; reconstruction drawing

Early 12th-century French architecture, however, was structurally and visually diverse, and the progressive edifices of the Ile-de-France were conceived within a context of experimentation and historical reverence. During the second quarter of the 12th century, Paris was established definitively as the royal capital, a vital commercial hub and Europe's leading intellectual centre. Vigorous architectural activity accompanied this efflorescence as the monarchy promoted projects that enhanced its image and the cult of its patron, St Denis. The abbey church of Saint-Denis (*see* SAINT-DENIS ABBEY, §I, 2) was the most spectacular manifestation of a wave of building that also included an expansion of the royal palace on the Ile-de-la-Cité and the rebuilding of the churches of St Pierre-de-Montmartre, St Magloire and St Germain-des-Prés (see below). The absence of an entrenched building tradition in the Paris region may also have contributed to an atmosphere conducive to architectural innovation.

The west façade (*c.* 1137–40) of Saint-Denis (*see* SAINT-DENIS ABBEY, fig. 2) was indebted most immediately to recent works in Normandy, such as the late 11th-century abbeys of St Etienne and La Trinité in Caen. It articulated more emphatically the contrast between an assertive supporting frame of aggressively projecting buttresses, strong piers and arches enclosed by thin walls and ample, glazed openings. The choir, built in the second campaign (1140–44; see fig. 1) is noted for its two rings of slender columns defining a double-ambulatory scheme in which the outer aisle is integrated with a continuous series of shallow chapels. The exterior wall is composed largely of expansive glass windows stretched between isolated masonry salients. Vestigial mural mass is dissimulated behind groups of applied shafts that are coordinated rigorously with ribs and arches of the vaults above.

The master mason's ability to perfect a combination of existing architectural forms that produced an essentially new whole displayed genius. In the plan, he pursued the implications of previous experiments in spatial expansion. Ambulatories with a continuous corona of chapels appeared in Paris at the abbey of St Magloire (before ?1138; destr.) and in an awkward double-ambulatory variant in the Cluniac house of St Martin-des-Champs (*c.* 1130–40). Both churches were at least partially rib vaulted, a technology that had appeared in the Ile-de-France possibly in the late 11th century at St Etienne (rebuilt after 1180), Beauvais, and found currency in numerous structures in the region, such as Notre-Dame (*c.* 1130) at Morienval. The Saint-Denis master's system of ribbed vaults of uniform curvature and pointed arches achieved a disciplined regularity of texturally consistent, integrated spaces and lent itself to an efficient workshop production of standardized parts.

The determinants of the structure were Abbot Suger's demand for capacious windows (for a discussion of the place of light metaphysics at Saint-Denis *see* SUGER) and columnar supports. Not only did the latter's cylindrical form enhance the spatial fluidity of the interior, but their slender dimensions required the builder to realize an exceptionally light superstructure, characteristic of such contemporary Parisian churches (all 1130s) as Ste Geneviève, St Pierre-de-Montmartre and the circular nave of the Temple (destr.) Nevertheless, the columns of Saint-Denis also reflected their surviving 8th-century analogues in the nave, in some cases supporting reused capitals, satisfying Suger's concern to join harmoniously the new work with the old. The columns and the west façade, with its echoes of Roman triumphal arches and Carolingian and Ottonian westworks, set up associations with both the medieval past and the Early Christian structures of Rome, demonstrating St Denis's status as a disciple of St Peter and apostle to Gaul.

Although the Saint-Denis choir was widely known, an accurate assessment of its influence is hampered by uncertainties in the dating of other structures. The choir plans of Noyon Cathedral and the abbey church of Saint-Germer-de-Fly, for example, are often classed as members of a 'school of Saint-Denis' and dated in the 1150s. However, their plans with tangential chapels may have been laid out in the 1130s and derived from such nearby models as Thérouanne Cathedral (*c.* 1133; destr.). Thus, they may be parallels to rather than followers of the royal abbey. The choir of St Germain-des-Prés Abbey, Paris, however, was rebuilt *c.* 1145–63. Like Saint-Denis, this Benedictine house, which sheltered the tombs of the Merovingian rulers, was important in the Capetians' effort to establish their pedigree. The three-storey elevation, a columnar arcade surmounted by a false triforium of biforate openings and an ample clerestory, offers the closest extant reflection of Suger's choir; the single ambulatory, the handling of ribs and arches and the orientation of capitals defined interior spaces more crisply, however.

Within the Ile-de-France, Senlis Cathedral (begun *c.* 1151; *see* SENLIS, §1), located in another centre of Capetian power, adopted shallow chapels, monolithic columns and shafts *en délit*, large windows, and base, abacus and rib profiles from Saint-Denis; but it also synthesized elements culled from Normandy and around Beauvais: rectangular stair-towers placed east of the projecting transept, a central vessel covered with sexpartite vaults carried on alternating piers and columns, and a spacious gallery set between the arcade and clerestory. Saint-Denis should, therefore, be seen neither as a miraculous apparition nor as the progenitor of all Gothic churches. For all its precocity, it was part of an energetic regional movement inaugurated around 1130 and developed in both major projects fostered by the crown and allied ecclesiastical magnates and in such relatively modest buildings as the parish church of St Maclou (choir and transepts 1140–65), Pontoise. The inimitable character of Saint-Denis resulted from its triple function as monastery, pilgrimage centre and royal church, and from the talents of its masons.

Sens Cathedral brings into focus the complex filiations of the earliest buildings to bear the label 'Gothic' (*see* SENS, §2(i)). Begun in a local Burgundian Romanesque style, with a plan common to a broad area south of Paris, most notably Chartres Cathedral (after 1020; rebuilt) as erected by Bishop Fulbert (*reg* 1006–28), its final appearance was the fortuitous accident of the rapid architectural changes *c.* 1140. The voluminous central vessel offered a distinct alternative to the lateral expansiveness of Saint-Denis's interior. Its pattern of broad cubic units echoed in the nave of Le Mans Cathedral (*c.* 1145–58; *see* LE MANS, fig. 1), recalls such German imperial buildings as Speyer Cathedral (*see* SPEYER, §1) and may have its ultimate source in Lombard architecture. Around 1145, however, the central vessel was redesigned as a structure of thin mural planes articulated by a taut armature of shafts and mouldings as seen in the Ile-de-France. The alternation of piers and twin columns that carry sexpartite vaults parallels that of Senlis Cathedral, while the original configuration of the upper two storeys (rebuilt 13th century) repeated that at St Germain-des-Prés and Saint-Denis. The stability of the enormous ribbed vaults was ensured by a system of vertical piers that launched exposed arches over the aisle to abut the light clerestory wall (see fig. 2).

In south-west France well-established Romanesque approaches were recast using the new structural techniques, but the influence of Paris in planning or elevation design is not discernible. Ribbed vaults and pointed arches, possibly derived from Normandy, were employed in the single nave of Angers Cathedral (*c.* 1150) to transform the compartmentalized interior typical of the region's domed churches into a unified space bounded by walls that are treated as perforated tympana. Similarly, Poitiers Cathedral (*c.* 1160) influenced the design of the local hall churches, leading to the elegant vaulted canopies (*c.* 1210) of St Serge, Angers (*see* ANGERS, §2(iii)).

Cistercian architecture also acted as a foil to contemporary developments in the Ile-de-France, and as a prelude

2. France, Sens Cathedral, interior of the nave looking east, *c.* 1145

to the Order's role as a primary conduit for the transmission of French ideas throughout Europe (*see* CISTERCIAN ORDER, §III, 1). At Cîteaux II, Clairvaux, Fontenay and Pontigny in the 1130s and 1140s, the Cistercians drew largely on Burgundian Romanesque forms and traditions (*see* ROMANESQUE, §II, 5(i)), but they expertly incorporated the ribbed vault into their conventual buildings. The Order's later detailed architectural legislation, which forbade stained-glass windows, excessive height and width, towers and sculptural embellishment, seems a conscious rejection of the elaborate spatial and light effects at the heart of the new architecture.

Ironically, Cistercian design was infiltrated by recent developments almost immediately after the death of Bernard of Clairvaux in 1153. The new choir of Clairvaux III (*c.* 1154–74; destr. 1812–19), with its ambulatory, radiating chapels and clerestoried apse, was a simplified version of the royal necropoleis of Saint-Denis and St Germain-des-Prés, intended presumably as an appropriately grand setting for Bernard's tomb (*see* CLAIRVAUX ABBEY). Cîteaux III (rebuilt by 1190) introduced a variant scheme with a rectangular ambulatory bordered by contiguous chapels (*see* CÎTEAUX ABBEY). While the 'Bernardine' cruciform plan was repeated in France (e.g. Le Thoronet Abbey, Languedoc) and abroad into the 13th century, more ambitious choir plans, usually with rib-vaulted, two-storey elevations of an arcade and clerestory, characterized such larger houses as the abbeys at Pontigny (1180s; *see* PONTIGNY ABBEY, fig. 2) and Vaucelles (late 12th century).

Between 1120 and 1150, then, French architecture, far from being a homogeneous movement emanating from Paris, showed a striking variety in its approaches to structure and space. The use of ribbed vaults, the interest in large windows and the taste for columns were not induced by pragmatic or liturgical considerations. Although its underlying motivations are not fully understood and probably varied according to place and patron, the new architecture of the Ile-de-France coincided with the effective reassertion of royal power and the appearance of a conscious modernity in the élite intellectual circles of Paris.

(b) The first synthesis and the quest for height, 1150–90. Architecture between 1150 and 1190 was dominated by large-scale ecclesiastical projects in the burgeoning urban centres of northern France. A series of cathedrals and abbeys was begun *c.* 1150 that explored greater height as they retained the lightness introduced during the previous decades. A four-storey elevation, composed of arcade, gallery, triforium passage or decorated wall zone and clerestory, generally combined with sexpartite vaults, was favoured in the cathedrals of Cambrai (*c.* 1150; destr.), Arras (*c.* 1160; destr. 1804), Laon (*c.* 1155–60; *see* LAON, §1(i) and fig. 2), Paris (*c.* 1160), Soissons (south transept begun *c.* 1176), Rouen (nave after 1200; *see* ROUEN, §IV, 1(i)(b) and fig. 5) and Meaux (*c.* 1200), the abbeys of Notre-Dame-la-Grande (after 1171; destr.) in Valenciennes, Notre-Dame-en-Vaux (*c.* 1157–*c.* 1180) at Châlons-sur-Marne, the choirs of St Remi (*c.* 1170–90; see fig. 3), Reims, and Montier-en-Der Abbey (*c.* 1190–1200), and

3. France, Reims, St Remi, interior of the choir, *c.* 1170–90

the parish church (*c.* 1190) at Chars. Although the four-storey design with ribbed vaults may have appeared in the Ile-de-France during the 1130s at Saint-Germer-de-Fly and slightly later at Noyon Cathedral (1150), probably under the influence of St Lucien (1095–1140; destr. 1791–1819), Beauvais, the sources of this elevation lay in Rhenish architecture, for example the nave of Essen Minster (mid-11th century; destr. 1275), and is implied in the palatine chapel (*c.* 790–805) at Aachen. The concentration of this scheme in northern France and the contemporary construction in a Romanesque idiom of the transepts of Tournai Cathedral (*see* TOURNAI, fig. 3) and St Donatien (destr. 1799) in Bruges underscores the variety of interpretations possible in a given regional building type.

Four-storey elevations were set over quite different ground-plans, cruciform at Laon (*see* LAON, fig. 1) and Arras, but with apsidal transepts at Cambrai, Valenciennes, Soissons and Noyon, based on the trefoil plans of such major Romanesque buildings as St Lucien, Beauvais, Tournai Cathedral or St Maria im Kapitol (consecrated 1065) in Cologne. The five-aisled plan of Notre-Dame, Paris, with a non-projecting transept (*see* PARIS, fig. 30) seems to have realized the projected form of Suger's Saint-Denis, but may have been inspired equally by its Merovingian predecessor. The location of the transept towards the middle of the plan produced a significantly deeper choir, which separated the clerical and congregational spaces.

Within the French examples, master masons' handling of walls, approaches to support and choices of form were borrowed freely from Normandy, Paris and Picardy. At Laon, for example, an essentially thick-wall elevation was adopted, as at St Remi, Reims, which included a gallery and triforium passage on the interior and an exterior walkway at clerestory level (*see* THICK-WALL STRUCTURE). Both edifices have cylindrical piers, while at Arras the choir structure was carried on piers and twin columns and the Cambrai transepts rose on composite piers. Laon's multiplicity of towers, two each on the transept and west façades, and a crossing lantern (*see* LAON, fig. 1), continued a Romanesque theme also found at Tournai. At Notre-Dame in Paris, on the other hand, towers were restricted to the public entrance of the west façade.

The builders of Arras Cathedral, Notre-Dame-en-Vaux, Châlons-sur-Marne, and St Remi, Reims, experimented simultaneously with new approaches to unity and the effects of disalignment, with results that were more complex visually than at Saint-Denis and Sens. In the former churches, the clerestory window mouldings were continued downward into the triforium, linking the two levels. At the same time, the different pattern of openings in the front and back walls of the gallery and the use of free-standing columns across the mouths of the chapels created an ambiguous play of light through arcaded screens set one before the other. In a brilliantly unorthodox solution, the master of the Noyon transepts (*c*. 1170–80) reversed the second and third storeys of the four-storey choir elevation to concentrate two glazed levels in the upper half of the wall. Constructed of three superposed passages and pierced by three zones of glazing, the Noyon transepts achieved a nuanced luminosity and diaphanous fragility unsurpassed in 12th-century architecture.

At Notre-Dame, Paris, begun *c*. 1160, four-storey elevation was combined with the characteristically local thin-wall structure and columnar piers; but its most remarkable aspect was its height, nearly 33 m, surpassing even the largest Romanesque churches and fully one-third taller than Noyon or Laon. According to Clark and Mark a two-tiered arrangement of flying buttresses (rest.) stayed the gallery and clerestory and resisted the substantial wind forces against the steeply pitched roof (*see* BUTTRESS). While the presence of such a system in the choir and the primacy of the cathedral in the development of the flying buttress remain unresolved, there is little doubt that Notre-Dame's soaring, light structure set a new standard for emulation. In his condemnation of sumptuous church building (*c*. 1180), Peter the Chanter (*d* 1197) captured the pride and spirit of competition that informed the architecture of leading ecclesiastics: 'Men sin even in building churches; for their heads should be more lowly than their bodies . . . Today on the contrary, the choirs of churches are built higher and higher.' (*Verbum abbreviatum*; ed. in *PL*, ccv (1855), col. 258).

Although the four-storey elevation dominated large-scale church architecture during the third quarter of the 12th century, the three-storey composition continued to appear widely. Some smaller churches were conceived as reduced versions of four-storey models: in the vicinity of Paris, for example, the cathedral's structure of flat walls and flying buttresses was adopted at Notre-Dame, Mantes-la-Jolie, and St Martin, Champeaux; Mantes has a gallery while Champeaux has oculi in the middle level. In and around the capital, the parish churches of St Hermeland, Bagneux, St Denis, Arceuil, and Ferrières-en-Brie all contain extensive reflections of Notre-Dame, and the two-storey pilgrimage church of St Mathurin, Larchant, has been attributed to a cathedral master. North of Paris, the Benedictine abbey of St Vincent (*c*. 1175; destr.) at Laon and the Premonstratensian St Yved (*c*. 1176–1208), Braine, show the local response to Laon Cathedral. Orbais Abbey (*c*. 1165–1200) clearly derived its columnar supports and triforium–clerestory linkage from St Remi, Reims. Their shared three-storey composition with a band triforium passage of uniform arches set between balanced arcade and clerestory zones was to be profoundly influential on the next generation of Gothic architects. The scheme seems to have developed less in reaction against the four-storey type than as a variant appropriate to the liturgical needs and modest scale of monastic and parish churches.

Finally, the influence of the first generation of French Gothic structures continued to the end of the century. Sens Cathedral was particularly significant within its immediate area, as shown at St Quiriace (1157–85), Provins, and the priory of St Martin (late 12th century), Chablis. The choir (second half of the 12th century) of the Cluniac priory church of St Nicolas at Saint-Leu-d'Esserent was indebted mostly to nearby Senlis Cathedral. The rebuilding of the choir (*c*. 1180–1200) of Ste Madeleine at Vézelay on a plan and elevation design stemming from Sens and probably from Saint-Denis is a reminder that the three-storey elevation was not relegated to secondary edifices, but appeared at even the most important cult sites.

(*c*) *Maturation and experiment, 1190–1230.* Around 1195 the image of the great church was altered at the cathedrals of Bourges, Chartres and Soissons, where the potential of the flying buttress to increase the height of a building was dramatically developed. Rather than achieving subtle effects in depth, their masons erected thin flat walls framing enormous openings and articulated by a legible framework of shafts and mouldings. As the solutions formulated at this time persisted in élite European architecture for the next three centuries, this moment of French building has been labelled HIGH GOTHIC and seen as a period of maturity after the diverse experiments of the preceding half century. In reality, while acknowledging the critical role that these structures played for future builders, the architectural activity between 1190 and 1230 was as intensely speculative and heterogeneous as in the 1130s and 1140s.

The elevation of Chartres Cathedral, reconstructed after a fire in 1194, has often been seen as the classic configuration, formed by a three-storey central vessel, with a triforium passage, towering over flanking aisles (see fig. 4; *see also* CHARTRES, fig. 1), that was passed on to the cathedrals of Soissons, Reims, Amiens and Beauvais. It is probably more accurate to see Chartres and the choir (begun *c*. 1200) of Soissons as closely related but simultaneous creations from common sources. Both were indebted fundamentally to architecture emanating from the Laon area and the three-storey elevations found at St

is wide, with an arcade that rises to half the total height. The AA elevation sets up a series of unifying lateral views into the aisles and squeezes space emphatically upward. The nave was ordered with consummate rigour and clarity:

of avant-garde edifices.

(*d*) *Rayonnant architecture, 1230–1300.* The linearity and preciosity made possible by bar tracery established in

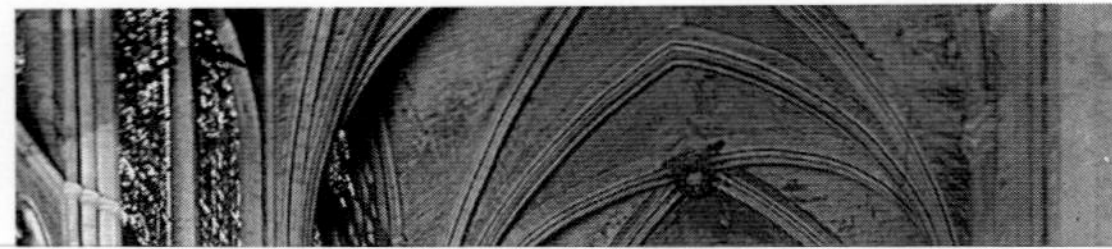

vast bulk of Chartres in *c.* 25 years bears witness both to diocesan prosperity, which sustained continuous building, and to their workshops' efficient methods of construction.

In seeking to integrate the supports more closely with the structure above, builders of the 1190s followed the

France a general theme with countless local variations and references to earlier Gothic and even Romanesque works (*see* RAYONNANT STYLE). The career of Gautier de Varinfroy (*fl c.* 1240–75) demonstrates the ability of a master mason to tailor his work to the physical and stylistic parameters of each particular project. He remodelled the four-storey elevation of Meaux Cathedral, built the upper half of the nave of Evreux Cathedral over a Romanesque arcade, perhaps repaired the western bays of Sens Cathedral after the south tower collapsed in 1268, and constructed the triforium and clerestory of the choir at St Pierre, Chartres.

Paris was apparently the crucible for the assimilation of developments of local origin and derived from other centres such as Amiens. Royal patronage under Blanche of Castile and Louis IX (*see* CAPET, (1) and (2)) realized a series of ambitious projects that defined the *opus francigenum* and created monuments that were to be widely imitated throughout Europe. The reconstructed nave of Saint-Denis (begun *c.* 1231; *see* SAINT-DENIS ABBEY, fig. 4) shows, despite the constraints imposed by the preservation of much of Suger's building, the combination of influences from Normandy, Burgundy and Reims that produced a new stylistic synthesis. The articulation of mouldings, the recession of aisle windows behind a Remois passage, and the planar recession of the clerestory marked the final step in the dissolution of the solid wall of the three-storey elevation. The building's contrasts of surface and depth, of physical and optical means of unification, animated a wide variety of experiments during the remaining years of the century. The Saint-Denis master may also have been responsible for the glazed triforium and clerestory of Troyes Cathedral (after 1228; *see* TROYES, fig. 2) and the royal chapel (*c.* 1230) at Saint-Germain-en-Laye. Saint-Denis also influenced the chapels (1235–40) added to the nave of Notre-Dame, Paris, and penetrated into provinces far from the capital, best seen in Clermont-Ferrand Cathedral (1248–80).

In the Sainte-Chapelle, Paris, built *c.* 1241–8 to house relics of the Passion of Christ acquired by Louis IX, the minimalist structural members created an unobtrusive scaffolding for a multimedia covering of sculpture, stained glass, painting and glass inlay that present the sacral character of French kingship and the nation as the chosen of God (*see* PARIS, §V, 2(i) and fig. 34). Its most salient features, perforated gables above the upper windows and florid pinnacles crowning the buttresses, combine with the huge traceried windows to impart a character reminiscent of metalwork to the architecture that conveys its character as a monumental reliquary (see fig. 6). The imitation of so-called micro-architecture (Bucher, 1976) can be recognized in the delicate sculpted piers of the south transept porch of Chartres (*c.* 1220–30) or the quatrefoil reliefs of the Amiens façade dado, but, before the Sainte-Chapelle, never had an entire edifice been conceived in an aesthetic so close to metalwork.

Following the Sainte-Chapelle, chapels of special status, such as the Virgin Chapel (1259–67) at Saint-Germer-de-Fly, and commemorative churches, notably St Urbain (1262–*c.* 1280; *see* TROYES, fig. 3), Troyes, and St Louis (begun 1298), Poissy, were built in the image of shrines through exteriors decorated with gables and tracery. From

6. France, Paris, Sainte-Chapelle, view from the south, *c.* 1241–8

about 1250 the decoration of gables became increasingly important in the ornamental work applied to prestigious buildings. New choirs at the cathedrals of Cambrai (*c.* 1250), Tournai (begun 1245; *see* TOURNAI, fig. 4) and Limoges (*c.* 1265) were festooned with gables, perhaps to emphasize the sacred connotations of the eastern arm. Even interior arcades at Sées Cathedral (1278–94; for illustration *see* CROCKET) and the triforia of Clermont-Ferrand Cathedral and the Amiens choir were enriched by applied gables.

Façades erected in the mid-13th century were treated with an especially intense ornamentality. Now conceived as flat closing walls coordinated with the interior elevation, for example at Reims for St Nicaise (*c.* 1242/5–*c.* 1256; destr. 1798–1819) and the cathedral (after 1252; *see* REIMS, fig. 4) and for the transepts (*c.* 1250–67) of Notre-Dame, Paris, screens of sharp, openwork gables were deployed across the portal zone while enormous rose windows, the patterns of which gave the Rayonnant period its name, dematerialized the upper levels. The transept façades of Notre-Dame (for illustration *see* RAYONNANT STYLE), although differing in the handling of ornament, were both based on the Saint-Denis transepts. They influenced a whole series of cathedral transepts in the later 13th century and the early 14th, including the north arm at Tours, the south transept at Meaux and both façades at Rouen, Clermont-Ferrand and Bordeaux.

At St Urbain, Troyes, elision, the elimination of capitals and the introduction of continuous and 'dying' mouldings (*see* MOULDING, §III, 3(ii)) began to destroy the clear definition and distinction of parts. Southern France, in the cathedrals of Narbonne (begun 1272; *see* NARBONNE, §1(i) and fig. 2), Toulouse (choir 1272–86), Carcassonne (now St Nazaire; 1269–1330; *see* CARCASSONNE, fig. 2), and Bordeaux (begun *c.* 1280), as well as the Dominican chapel at Toulouse (now Jacobin church, begun 1230–50; *see* TOULOUSE, fig. 1), emerged as an area of particular importance at the end of the 13th century. Employing northern French thin walls and bar tracery, their emphasis on height and luminosity broke with the indigenous southern tradition of mural mass and unified breadth, doubtless as an affirmation of their bishops' royal allegiances and their sees as centres of orthodoxy in a region still afflicted with rebellion and heresy. Nevertheless, the interior spaciousness and the reassertion of wall surfaces in these structures may look to local sensibility, exemplified by the single nave (vaulted 1211–13) of Toulouse Cathedral and later continued at Albi Cathedral (begun *c.* 1277; for illustration *see* ALBI).

The columnar pier, most recently a feature of Cistercian and mendicant architecture alone, was adopted at Narbonne, Toulouse and Carcassonne, perhaps as a sign of sobriety intended to counter criticism of architectural materialism. Simplified pier forms combined with complex mouldings of vaults, arches and window tracery produced a spare network of linear elements that replaced the logic of perfect linkage. At Narbonne, for example, the ribs and arches of the ambulatory vaults arise from a single frail shaft attached to the apse pier, while the arcade mouldings merge into the pier core well above the level of the simple moulded capital.

Thus, the Rayonnant style of Paris, embodied by Saint-Denis and the Sainte-Chapelle, retained a particular currency in aristocratic projects through the first half of the 14th century, but it was complemented by ideas emanating from other centres, such as Troyes and Narbonne. It was taken up by masters at such diverse cathedrals as Gloucester, Girona and Prague, whose approaches to space and redefinition of articulation in many ways set the stage for the developments of the Late Gothic era (*see* §2 below).

BIBLIOGRAPHY

L. Serbat: 'Quelques Eglises anciennement détruites du nord de la France', *Bull. Mnmtl*, lxxxviii (1929), pp. 367–435

C. Seymour: *Notre-Dame of Noyon in the Twelfth Century: A Study in the Early Development of Gothic Architecture* (New Haven, 1939, rev. New York, 1968)

M. Aubert: *L'Architecture cistercienne en France*, 2 vols (Paris, 1943, 2/1947)

E. Panofsky: *Gothic Architecture and Scholasticism* (Latrobe, PA, 1951)

O. von Simson: *The Gothic Cathedral: The Origins of Gothic Architecture and the Medieval Concept of Order* (New York, 1956)

J. Bony: 'Resistance to Chartres in Early Thirteenth-century Architecture', *J. Brit. Archaeol. Assoc.*, 3rd ser., xx–xxi (1957–8), pp. 35–52

P. Héliot: 'Les Oeuvres capitales du gothique français primitif et l'influence de l'architecture anglaise', *Wallraf-Richartz Jb.*, xx (1958), pp. 85–114

R. Branner: *Burgundian Gothic Architecture* (London, 1960)

——: *La Cathédrale de Saint-Etienne de Bourges* (Bourges, 1961); Eng. trans.; rev. S. Prager-Branner as *The Cathedral of Bourges and its Place in Gothic Architecture* (New York, 1989)

——: 'Gothic Architecture, 1160–1180, and its Romanesque Sources', *Acts of the XX International Congress of the History of Art. Studies in Western Art: New York, 1961*, i, pp. 92–104

A. Mussat: *Le Style gothique de l'ouest de la France, XIIe–XIIIe siècles* (Paris, 1963)

R. Branner: *Saint Louis and the Court Style in Gothic Architecture* (London, 1965)

P. Héliot: *La Basilique de Saint-Quentin* (Paris, 1967)

F. Salet: 'Le Premier Colloque international de la Société française d'archéologie: Chronologie de la cathédrale de Reims', *Bull. Mnmtl*, cxxv (1967), pp. 347–94

P. Kurmann: *La Cathédrale Saint-Etienne de Meaux* (Paris, 1971)

M. Durliat: 'L'Architecture gothique méridionale au XIIIe siècle', *Ecole Ant. Nîmes*, viii–ix (1973–4), pp. 63–132

A. Prache: 'Les Arcs-boutants au XIIe siècle', *Gesta*, xv (1976), pp. 31–42

A. Erlande-Brandenburg: 'Le Septième Colloque international de la Société française d'archéologie: La Façade de la cathédrale d'Amiens', *Bull. Mnmtl*, cxxxv (1977), pp. 253–93

P. Kurmann and D. von Winterfeld: 'Gautier de Varinfroy, ein "Denkmalpfleger" im 13. Jahrhundert', *Festschrift für Otto von Simson zum 65. Geburtstag* (Berlin, 1977), pp. 101–59

N. Bongartz: *Die frühen Bauteile der Kathedrale in Troyes: Architekturgeschichtliche Monographie* (Stuttgart, 1979)

R. Pestell: 'The Design Sources for the Cathedrals of Chartres and Soissons', *A. Hist.*, iv (1981), pp. 1–13

J. Bony: *French Gothic Architecture of the 12th and 13th Centuries* (Berkeley, 1983)

M. Caviness: 'Saint-Yved of Braine: The Primary Sources for Dating the Gothic Church', *Speculum*, lix/3 (1984), pp. 524–48

W. Clark and R. Mark: 'The First Flying Buttresses: A New Reconstruction of the Nave of Notre-Dame de Paris', *A. Bull.*, lxvi (1984), pp. 47–65

D. Kimpel and R. Suckale: *Die gotische Architektur in Frankreich, 1130–1270* (Munich, 1985)

S. Gardner: 'The Theory of Centripetal Implosion and the Birth of Gothic Architecture', *Acts of the XXVI International Congress of the History of Art. World Art: Themes of Unity in Diversity: Washington, DC, 1986*, i, pp. 111–16

M. Bideault and C. Lautier: *Les Eglises de la vallée de l'Oise et du Beauvaisis* (1987), i of *Ile-de-France gothique* (Paris, 1987–)

P. Kidson: 'Panofsky, Suger and Saint-Denis', *J. Warb. & Court. Inst.*, l (1987), pp. 1–9

D. Vermand: *La Cathédrale Notre-Dame de Senlis au XIIe siècle* (Senlis, 1987)

(iii) British Isles. Until *c.* 1300 architecture in the British Isles developed differently from that in France. Although in England there was a comparable burst of prosperity and population growth, the concentration of wealth in the hands of the bishops and the persistent strength of regional barons meant that the crown was relatively less influential in establishing a coherent formal vocabulary that was passed on to provincial centres. The history of Gothic architecture in the British Isles has frequently been written in terms of regional schools, but Cistercian buildings and certain key edifices, such as Canterbury and Lincoln cathedrals or Westminster Abbey, override such localism. Rather than a consistently paced, methodical evolution, there was a succession of pivotal moments in which the impact of external influences redirected architectural thinking in unanticipated directions.

(a) The reception of Gothic, *c.* 1150–85. (b) From Canterbury to Westminster, 1185–1245. (c) Westminster Abbey and its impact, 1245–1300.

(a) The reception of Gothic, c. *1150–85.* The first intimations of French Gothic forms in England appeared in the second generation of buildings by the Cistercians in the north, notably Kirkstall (W. Yorks), Furness II (Cumbria) and Roche (S. Yorks). Kirkstall (1152) was articulated by ribbed vaults and compact clustered piers, and the terminal wall of the south transept even included a triforium passage. Furness II (*c.* 1160) and Roche (*c.* 1170), however, introduced a more conscious strain of French architecture that can be termed Early Gothic. Furness was the first Cistercian church to have a three-storey elevation in its main vessel, possibly to demonstrate its prominence

and wealth, intended to rival episcopal structures. Its Gothic character essentially resided in the overall effect of wall surfaces, pierced by large openings and framed by shafts and mouldings, that resembled churches in the Soissons–Laon region, such as St Omer, Lillers, and Nouvion-le-Vineux. Roche, with its three-storey elevation, sharply pointed arches and ribbed vaults rising above uninterrupted wall shafts, looked to more advanced models from the Ile-de-France. As at Furness, however, connections were made not with French cathedral Gothic, but with such relatively modest churches as St Hildevert, Gournay-en-Bray, and at Notre-Dame d'Acey Abbey, Vitreux (Jura), in a style acceptable to the Cistercians. The architectural link between northern England and north-east France followed a pattern of close ecclesiastical relations within the Order.

The ambitious projects of Roger Pont L'Evêque, Archbishop of York (*reg* 1154–81) at York Minster (*see* YORK, §III, 1(i)), Ripon Cathedral and the Cistercian church at Byland Abbey (both N. Yorks) were important in the development of early English Gothic. The exact relation of these three churches is controversial. The Byland and York choirs were laid out with flat east walls and rectangular ambulatories connecting a succession of chapels. This may represent a chain of influence from such continental structures as St Bavo (destr. 1540) in Ghent and St Bartholomew (*c.* 1140–50; destr.) in Liège, through Evesham Abbey (Hereford & Worcs; destr.) and the cathedral (consecrated 1092; destr.) at Old Sarum, near Salisbury, then to Byland via York. Equally it may indicate the minster's appropriation of a Cistercian plan transmitted from Morimond to Byland. This arrangement was widely adopted, at, for example, Wells Cathedral (begun *c.* 1185), GLASTONBURY ABBEY (1185), Lichfield Cathedral (*c.* 1215; Staffs) and Salisbury Cathedral.

The treatment of the structure at Byland, Ripon and York was similarly complex in its filiations and no less important in the formulation of a distinctive English style. The French-derived Furness elevation was joined with the Anglo-Norman thick-wall. The remains of Byland and the surviving upper levels of Ripon, as well as reflections of the scheme at Hexham Priory (early 13th century; Northumb.), indicate that clustered piers, elaborate moulding profiles and an overlay of blind arcading created a veneer that masked and fractured solid mural mass. The constantly shifting patterns of openings produced a surface animation both reminiscent of Anglo-Norman decoration and parallel to the experiments in syncopated screens at Arras and St Remi, Reims (*see* §(ii)(b) above). The wooden vaults and the truncated shaft responds in the arcade spandrels above the piers emphasized the horizontality of three superposed zones.

In the west of England, the Romanesque thick-wall elevation was retained in the nave (after 1175) of Worcester Cathedral, although the application of attenuated shafts and mouldings may betray awareness of Parisian architecture. The banded elevation of the Byland type found its most inventive sequel in the nave of Wells Cathedral, where vertical divisions were assiduously avoided (*see* WELLS, §1(i) and fig. 1). Like York, Wells underscores the difficulties of satisfactorily defining English Gothic when the terms of analysis move away from French-based criteria. While it may be argued that the Romanesque thick-wall structure merely changed its decorative clothing by adopting a mantle of sharper, finely scaled forms, the increased luminosity, emphasis on sharply moulded surfaces, consistent use of pointed arches and shedding of all references to classical forms demonstrate the formulation of a Gothic architecture, in the sense of a non-historicizing style that was even more fully realized than in France.

French Early Gothic architecture was most directly influential in the choir of Canterbury Cathedral, rebuilt after the fire of 1174 (see fig. 7; *see also* CANTERBURY, §III, 1 (iv) and fig. 8). Within the constraints imposed by the retention of the Romanesque crypt and outer walls, Canterbury represented the transplantation of an architecture derived from north-east France and the area of Valenciennes. The columnar arcade, false triforium and clerestory recessed behind a continuous passage were crowned by sexpartite vaults, linked to alternating triple and single colonnette responds. The clerestory passage, although an Anglo-Norman feature, links Canterbury to the architectural current that ran from Switzerland (e.g. Geneva and Lausanne) to the south Netherlands (*see* §(ii)(c) above).

The clerestory passage at Canterbury demonstrates the fundamental compatibility of continental and English architecture in the later 12th century and the ability of masons to inflect structure and design to meet the requirements and taste of a given region or set of patrons. This is true also of the use at Canterbury of dark marble shafts attached to piers and walls, employing colouristic accents that enjoyed a modest vogue at Valenciennes and Tournai.

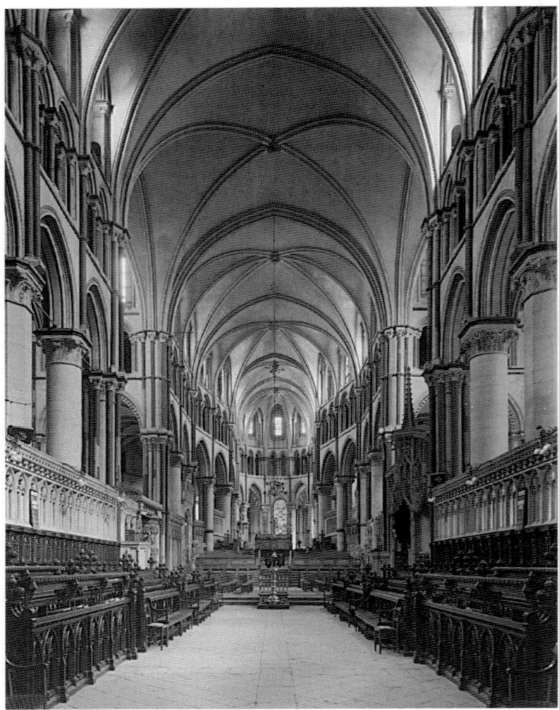

7. England, Canterbury Cathedral, interior of the choir and Trinity Chapel, after 1174

This may perhaps be connected with the reference by Gervase that WILLIAM OF SENS imported stone 'from across the sea'. The extraordinary popularity of marble shafts in 13th-century England, at Lincoln, Salisbury and Westminster, exemplifies the insular tendency to appropriate and develop isolated elements rather than entire systems from French sources.

William the Englishman, master mason of the Trinity Chapel and Corona, effected subtle but significant structural changes by introducing a true passage into the triforium and reinforcing the thin clerestory wall with low flying buttresses. While the model for the flyers remains elusive, they point to an awareness of recent French structural innovations at Sens, Paris and Cambrai. In the Trinity Chapel, the setting for Becket's shrine, the architectural richness increases: the arcade columns are ringed by changing configurations of two, four and eight shafts; the twin hemicycle columns, as at Arras or Sens, are themselves coloured polished marble. Together with the incomparable stained glass and wall paintings, the Canterbury choir seems to be an almost literal representation of the Heavenly City (Revelations 21).

(b) From Canterbury to Westminster, 1185–1245. The importance of the Canterbury choir lay not in generating a series of copies, but in directing English architecture towards new effects of lightness and linearity (*see* EARLY ENGLISH). This was best captured at Lincoln Cathedral in a sequence of building campaigns (1192–*c.* 1250: St Hugh's choir, the two transepts and the nave; *see* LINCOLN, §2(i)(b)). At Lincoln, however, the design was driven by considerations of space and light rather than structural logic. Following the Canterbury type of elevation, disalignment and syncopated layering were raised to the status of guiding principles. The dark Purbeck 'marble' shaft of the vault respond is cut off above the level of the arcade capital and meets the rib at a seemingly arbitrary level in the triforium spandrel, destroying the visual relationship of the vault to the piers. Truncated vault shafts had previously been used at Byland and the similarity of triforium designs would also seem to confirm Lincoln's connection to the north.

The most unusual feature of St Hugh's choir, the so-called 'crazy vaults' comprising groups of three ribs that converge on two centres at the crown (see fig. 8), marked the first appearance of tiercerons, ribs that arc from wall to keystone, a form that was to trigger myriad inventive variations in English vault design (*see* VAULT). By multiplying the number of ribs and introducing two keystones tied by a longitudinal ridge rib, the Lincoln vaults further broke down the centralized focus and integrity of the individual bay and intensified the effects of horizontality. These vaults were not, however, the product of capricious design by a perverse master mason, but an ingenious solution that permitted an expansion of the windows in the choir to include three broad openings per bay. In this regard the architect of St Hugh's choir was the heir to William the Englishman's explorations of luminosity in the upper levels of the Canterbury presbytery and Trinity Chapel. The vault of St Hugh's choir was further refined in the nave (*c.* 1220–*c.* 1237), the solution of which was to be repeated in ever more elaborate variations throughout

8. England, Lincoln Cathedral, interior of St Hugh's choir looking west, begun 1192

the 13th century, as in the Ely presbytery (*c.* 1234–52; *see* ELY CATHEDRAL, §1(i)(c) and fig. 3) and the rebuilding of Exeter Cathedral (from *c.* 1279).

The multiplication of linear elements and layered arcaded walls used at Lincoln was explored, together with other influences, in the east end (*c.* 1225–50) of Beverly Minster, the Worcester Cathedral choir and presbytery (completed 1231) and the Glasgow Cathedral choir (*c.* 1240; *see* GLASGOW, §3). Worcester and other West Country buildings influenced the designs of the first Gothic buildings in Ireland, all begun in the 13th century, the cathedrals of Waterford and Christ Church and St Patrick in Dublin (*see* DUBLIN, §IV, 1 and 2). At the same time, a current of greater restraint and sobriety informed Salisbury (1220–66), rebuilt on a rectilinear double-transept plan that seems to reflect the requirements of the newly devised liturgical Use of Sarum (*see* SALISBURY, §2(i)). Rather than the variety at Canterbury and Lincoln, a form of *pilier cantonné* and quadripartite vaults are consistently applied at Salisbury, yet the potential of the former to unify the elevation vertically was ignored. The attached Purbeck shafts, set against the light stone of the cylindrical core, would have worked with the stained glass to create a sparkling, coloured interior, as at Canterbury, and the truncation of vault shafts in the manner of Wells maintained the English emphasis on horizontality.

The expansive triplet windows of the Salisbury clerestory and especially the elegant eastern Lady chapel reveal the English interest in spaciousness and luminosity. In its hall-church format, the Lady chapel resembles a miniaturized version of St Serge, Angers. The open interior and reduction of supports to attenuated bundles of shafts throws primary emphasis on the almost continuous glazing of the exterior wall. This multiplication of windows, the most conspicuous example being the Five Sisters in the north transept (*c.* 1220–55) of York Minster, set the stage for the architectural developments following the reception of bar tracery at Westminster Abbey (*see* §(c) below).

Salisbury and Wells also demonstrate the English taste for screen façades, developed in some Anglo-Norman buildings, with the concomitant reduction in the size and importance of the western towers. At Salisbury tiers of sculpture-filled niches and passages that featured in liturgical performances dissolve the solidity and coherence of the wall. Wells Cathedral presents the most spectacular west façade of its age. Although the portals remained characteristically small, the expansive wall and square flanking towers became the stage for the display of figures set in delicate tabernacles. Wells, no less than the Sainte-Chapelle in Paris, monumentalized the effects of metalwork to lend a transcendent image to the church structure.

(c) Westminster Abbey and its impact, 1245–1300. The king emerged as a major patron and influence on church architecture only with the rebuilding of Westminster Abbey (from 1246) by Henry III. As a royal abbey, the king's burial-church, place of coronation, shrine of St Edward the Confessor and reliquary for such sacred treasures as the Holy Blood, Westminster thus looked to the analogous churches in France at Reims, Royaumont Abbey (1227–36), Saint-Denis and the Sainte-Chapelle (*see* LONDON, §V, 2(i)). Precise models were identified and their combination was meant as an assertion of English parity with the French.

Superficially the plan and elevation (see fig. 9) are strikingly French. The plan, including an ambulatory with polygonal chapels and an aisled transept, the aisle window passage, the *piliers cantonnés*, the main vessel tracery and the two-tiered flying buttresses can all be found at Reims. The pattern of the triforium and the slight restriction of the windows resemble Royaumont. Richly coloured materials and the painted and gilded diaperwork of the wall surfaces (for illustration *see* DIAPER) imparted a splendour to the building that must have been inspired by the Sainte-Chapelle. Finally, the narrow proportion of the main vessel in relation to its width and the treatment of the wall as a flat, perforated plane broke decisively with current English practice. Structurally and in detail, however, the building is English. The contrast between the spindly piers and the thick, moulded arcades they support counters the unifying tendency of the ascending vault respond. With the absence of linkage of the triforium, which in fact masks a deep, vaulted tribune, and the clerestory, the liberal use of Purbeck 'marble' shafting and a prominent longitudinal ridge rib, Henry of Reyns (*d c.* 1253) systematically tempered the elevation's verticality with an insistent horizontal sub-theme.

The introduction of bar tracery at Westminster and the treatment of the wall as a panelled framework were the basis of essential elements in the succeeding styles (*see* §2 below; DECORATED STYLE; PERPENDICULAR STYLE), but the building's spatial and structural premises had little influence. The French type of plan reappeared only at the royal abbeys of Hailes (1246–51; destr.; Glos), sponsored by Henry III's brother, Richard, Earl of Cornwall (1209–72), and Battle (destr.; E. Sussex). Work directly influenced by Westminster, such as the north transept (*c.* 1255) of Hereford Cathedral or the Lichfield Cathedral nave (*c.* 1265), has to be carefully distinguished from its more general stimulus in furnishing a fresh catalogue of forms that led to the adoption of Rayonnant elements in other projects.

9. England, London, Westminster Abbey, interior of the choir looking east, from 1246

The new choir (begun 1258) of Old St Paul's Cathedral (destr. after 1666; *see* LONDON, §V, 1(i)(b) and fig. 24), which was probably built to rival Westminster, featured flying buttresses and large traceried windows in patterns that can be found in the most modern Parisian works of the 1250s. The rose-in-square above a glazed passage in the flat east wall was clearly based on the transept façades of Notre-Dame. The rose may mark the first appearance of the OGEE curve that was to form a leitmotif of the Decorated style over the next century. Moreover, the vertical buttresses and tracery mullions and horizontal transom articulate the east wall in a proto-Perpendicular grid. The premises inherent in St Paul's were taken further in St Stephen's Chapel in the Palace of Westminster (*see* LONDON, §V, 3(i)(a)). Begun under Edward I in 1292 and destroyed by fire in 1834, St Stephen's incorporated the latest Rayonnant tracery patterns in an elaborate rectilinear network that framed dynamic, ogee-headed forms.

In the Angel choir (1256–80) of Lincoln Cathedral, bar tracery, sculpture, Purbeck 'marble' and stained glass were, as at Westminster, assembled as a sumptuous setting for a shrine, but the flat east wall with its huge eight-lancet window and the low, boxy section of the building were thoroughly English, repeating the disposition of the presbytery and nave, and possibly reflecting a patronal demand for interior harmony (*see* LINCOLN, §2(i)(c)). Tracery patterns, most immediately derived from Westminster Abbey and its chapter house, were laid on to this traditional thick-wall frame in a felicitous blending of intense rippling surfaces and three-dimensional wall zones.

The building that came closest to Rayonnant was the nave (begun 1291) of York Minster, which included such up-to-date elements as composite piers with unbroken vertical vaults and a gabled triforium linked with the flat clerestory windows (*see* YORK, fig. 6). Stylistic elements have been connected variously to Saint-Denis Abbey and the cathedrals of Troyes, Clermont-Ferrand and, most recently, Cologne (begun 1248), but York can best be appreciated as an original work composed of ideas derived both directly and indirectly from French sources, shaped to fit with the existing sections of the minster and seasoned by an English sensibility for dense linear textures. That French architecture was not copied slavishly at York is demonstrated by the chapter house (begun *c.* 1280). Huge traceried windows, following on those of Westminster Abbey or Salisbury chapter houses, combine with a deep dado arcade and wooden tierceron vault hung from a hidden roof structure to produce an interior in which the space and walls achieve a full, three-dimensional unity. Tracery patterns and individual ornamental motifs may have derived from France (compelling parallels have been drawn between the York chapter house vestibule and St Urbain, Troyes), but their assembly and context reveal, as much as Lincoln or Wells, England's architectural independence.

BIBLIOGRAPHY

J. Bilson: 'The Architecture of the Cistercians with Special Reference to Some of their Earlier Churches in England', *Archaeol. J.*, lxvi (1909), pp. 185–280

J. Bony: 'French Influences on the Origins of English Gothic Architecture', *J. Warb. & Court. Inst.*, xii (1949), pp. 1–15

F. Nordstrom: 'Peterborough, Lincoln, and the Science of Robert Grosseteste: A Study in Thirteenth-century Architecture and Iconography', *A. Bull.*, xxxvii (1955), pp. 241–72

G. Webb: *Architecture in Britain: The Middle Ages*, Pelican Hist. A. (Harmondsworth, 1956)

P. Brieger: *English Art, 1216–1307* (Oxford, 1957, rev. 1967)

R. Branner: 'Westminster Abbey and the French Court Style', *J. Soc. Archit. Historians*, xxiii (1964), pp. 3–18

P. Kidson, P. Murray and P. Thomson: *A History of English Architecture* (Harmondsworth, 1965, rev. 1979)

J. Bony: *The English Decorated Style: Gothic Architecture Transformed, 1250–1350* (Oxford, 1979)

M. Dean: 'The Angel Choir and its Local Influence', *British Archaeological Association Conference Transactions. Medieval Art and Architecture at Lincoln Cathedral: Lincoln, 1982*, pp. 90–101

M. Hearn: 'Ripon Minster and the Beginning of the Gothic Style in England', *Trans. Amer. Philos. Soc.*, lxxiii/6 (1983), pp. 1–196

P. Fergusson: *Architecture of Solitude: Cistercian Abbeys in Twelfth-century England* (Princeton, 1984)

N. Pevsner and P. Metcalf: *The Cathedrals of England*, 2 vols (Harmondsworth, 1985)

P. Draper: 'Recherches récentes sur l'architecture dans les Iles britanniques à la fin de l'époque romane et au début du gothique', *Bull. Mnmtl*, cxliv (1986), pp. 305–28

C. Wilson: 'The Cistercians as "Missionaries of Gothic" in Northern England', *Cistercian Art and Architecture in the British Isles*, ed. C. Norton and D. Park (Cambridge, 1986), pp. 86–116

(iv) Holy Roman Empire. The following section is limited to the core of the Empire, covering present-day Germany and Austria.

(a) Isolated experiences, c. *1170–1230.* German architecture was characterized by a strongly entrenched tradition closely associated with imperial court patronage. Before *c.* 1230 Gothic elements, drawn from a variety of external sources, were essentially added to a Romanesque base (*see* ROMANESQUE, §II, 2(iii)). The western choir (after 1171) at Worms Cathedral continued the double-ended plan, the structure of heavy walls decorated with pilasters, dwarf galleries, corbel tables and grouped towers of Ottonian and, ultimately, Carolingian origin (*see* WORMS, §1). Contemporary architecture was acknowledged in such details as window forms, but did not significantly alter the building's Romanesque demeanour. Ribbed vaults may have appeared in the Mainz Cathedral nave and east chancel by 1137 (rebuilt *c.* 1200) but derived probably from Lombardy rather than France.

The Cistercians were again instrumental in creating simplified, understated architecture that offered an alternative to the majestic secular cathedrals, yet could be assimilated with German practices. Around 1200 a series of churches began to marry Cistercian traits with both the indigenous Romanesque and a variety of approaches that indicates a broad spectrum of external connections. The three-storey elevation of Bonn Minster, for example, includes a triforium and screened clerestory passages inside that most plausibly looked to neighbouring Switzerland or Burgundy for inspiration. Despite more light from the larger window area, the vertical accents of the continuous vault respond of the clustered piers, and the coherence of

10. Germany, Bamberg Cathedral, interior of the nave and choir looking east, after 1211, completed 1237

its armature of shafts and ribs, the consistent use of round arches, broad interior volumes and general heaviness of detail at Bonn produce a palpably Romanesque air.

Bamberg and Münster cathedrals also emphasized cubic bays using rather different elevations. Although Münster (*c.* 1225–64) has sometimes been linked to Angevin sources, its primary features of domical vaults with ridge ribs and triplet windows seem to have originated around Cologne. At Bamberg (after 1211, completed 1237; see fig. 10) Cistercian architecture was adapted to imperial expression, with 'Gothic' elements limited to such details as pointed arches and ribbed vaults (*see* BAMBERG, §2(i)), but its superficially French appearance was not a deliberately symbolic emulation of French models. German ecclesiastical architecture at the turn of the century was otherwise notable for its strongly defined personality that accepted, but was not fundamentally altered by, external influences. More consciously French forms appeared at Limburg an der Lahn Cathedral (begun *c.* 1190–1200), which combined a four-storey elevation, often associated with Laon Cathedral, with an exterior that remained Romanesque in appearance despite the incorporation of flying buttresses. The decagon (1219–27) at St Gereon, Cologne, also adopted a four-storey elevation (*see* COLOGNE, §IV, 2(i)) and influence from Laon has been thought responsible for the transformation of Bamberg's towers from closed boxes at the east to open aediculae at the west.

The most striking demonstration that imperial German architecture was not a static or closed system was offered by Magdeburg Cathedral (begun 1209; *see* MAGDEBURG, §1(i) and fig. 1), on which work continued through the first half of the 13th century. Its design displays a balance between a preservationist sensibility and the search for a modern aristocratic language. Architectural relics from the mid-10th-century cathedral were incorporated into the new fabric to establish a tangible link with the Ottonian past. The unmoulded arcades and gallery not only recall the palatine chapel at Aachen but may also indicate the survival of Carolingian imperial ritual practices. Despite the radiating chapels around the rib-vaulted ambulatory, the exterior remains a collection of massive independent blocks akin to Basle Minster (*c.* 1185–*c.* 1200). Conversely, the narrow central vessel of the choir and the tall clerestory windows are apparently French in inspiration, recalling 12th-century structures in the Ile-de-France, such as at Senlis and Mantes, although it is possible that the remodelled Notre-Dame, Paris, influenced this royal cathedral at the eastern edge of the Empire.

11. Germany, Cologne Cathedral, interior of the nave looking east, begun 1248

(b) German architectural modernism, 1230–1300. In the 1230s German builders, perhaps stimulated by new demands from their patrons, began to adopt not only the superficial formal vocabulary of French Gothic, but its linearity and lightness as well. In the centralized Liebfrauenkirche (*c.* 1235–60) at Trier diagonally turned chapels, like those at St Yved, Braine, or St Nicaise, Reims, were set between the main vessels' cruciform arms (*see* TRIER, fig. 3) to produce a complex polygonal plan. The slim columnar supports and the adoption of the *pilier cantonné* and bar tracery from Reims formed a skeletal frame closed by membranes of glass rather than masonry.

At the cathedrals of Strasbourg and Cologne an even greater intimacy with French architecture was achieved, for in many ways these edifices were full participants in progressive developments rather than followers. The Strasbourg nave (*c.* 1240–75) was conceived as a fully Rayonnant work, essentially based on the new work at Saint-Denis Abbey (*see* STRASBOURG, §III, 1 and fig. 3). The façade, inaugurated in 1275 and evolved through a sequence of design stages of which some elevation drawings survive (Strasbourg, Mus. Oeuvre Notre-Dame; *see* ARCHITECTURAL DRAWING, fig. 1), was a virtuoso performance in bar tracery as a trellis of openwork gables and free-standing mullions was slipped over the actual structure of the portals and towers (*see* STRASBOURG, fig. 4). While the metalwork-like character of the architecture points ultimately to the Paris transept façades and the brittle cages of tracery parallel St Urbain in Troyes, Strasbourg attained a level of true originality in the composition of individual patterns and in the use of tracery to unify and dematerialize the façade.

Cologne Cathedral was the most elaborate realization of Gothic architecture in 13th-century Germany (*see* COLOGNE, §IV, 1(i)). Begun in 1248, the choir (h. 47.5 m; see fig. 11) was the project of Konrad von Hochstaden (*reg* 1238–61), the ambitious Archbishop and imperial Elector. The design of the first master mason, Gerhard, and his successor, Arnold, has been discussed frequently as a direct transplantation to German soil of French architecture, as embodied by Amiens and Beauvais cathedrals; this explanation in terms of French sources alone, however, ignores Cologne's individual nuances and, more importantly, the reasons behind the adoption of French style.

Cologne incorporated the full range of modern forms: tracery akin to Amiens, a glazed triforium like the Amiens or Beauvais choirs, statuary attached to the interior chevet piers and an exterior bristling with gables and pinnacles (*see* COLOGNE, fig. 7) in the manner of the Sainte-Chapelle, Paris. Its builders, however, were not content merely to ape French models, for the innovative oval cores of its piers were to appear in France only in the 1260s at St Urbain, Troyes. The relentlessly consistent use of gables, tracery and pointed-arch windows on the west front, designed *c.* 1300 by Master Michael, achieved perhaps the most harmonious façade composition of its time (*see* ARCHITECTURAL DRAWING, fig. 2). The three-storey elevation's ABA scheme has led to speculation that Cologne, along with Orléans Cathedral (begun 1287; destr. 1568; rebuilt 1601), represented something of a 'revival' of the dignified High Gothic elevation of Chartres or Reims (Kurmann). In spite of the thorough awareness of contemporary French forms, Cologne was fabricated according to local Rhenish stone-cutting methods that had changed little since the Romanesque period.

Cologne, like the nearby Cistercian house of Altenberg (*c.* 1255–80), which drew heavily on the French royal abbeys of Saint-Denis and Royaumont, was not created by a francophile patron. Contemporary writers made German antipathy towards the French abundantly clear and Archbishop Konrad consistently opposed candidates backed by Louis IX during the struggle for the imperial throne after the death of Emperor Frederick II in 1250. While elaborate tracery, sculpture and high, light space may have embodied the *opus francigenum* to the clerical patrons at SS Peter und Paul (1269), Wimpfen-im-Thal, the abbey church at Altenberg, and Cologne and Strasbourg cathedrals also reveal that the German nobility and bishops recognized the Rayonnant style as an international language of royal grandeur and spiritual transcendence.

Apart from these few exceptional aristocratic structures, German churches of the mid- to late 13th century tended towards a characteristic interior spaciousness and ornamental restraint. The two-storey elevations of Freiburg im Breisgau Cathedral (nave begun *c.* 1250), Halberstadt Cathedral (nave *c.* 1260), and the Marienkirche (chancel *c.* 1260–90), Lübeck, represent variants of the three-storey basilica adopted by middle-class patrons and in smaller dioceses that find close parallels in monastic architecture. Recent Cistercian buildings, such as Ourscamp (*c.* 1245; Oise) or Chorin (begun 1270–72; for illustration *see* CHORIN ABBEY), and the new mendicant foundations, for example the Franciscan Ste Marie-Madeleine (*c.* 1255–62; destr.) in Paris or the Dominican St Paul (after 1233) at Esslingen, eliminated the triforium, perhaps as a sign of humility, but these houses offered easily imitated and economic prototypes couched in light, linear structural terms.

The HALL CHURCH, formed by three vessels of equal height, assumed a particular importance in 13th-century Germany. The Elisabethkirche (begun 1235) at Marburg was the most notable early example (*see* MARBURG, ELISABETHKIRCHE, §1). The details of the nave resemble those of the Liebfrauenkirche at Trier and the individual elements of the structure have obvious French sources, but the elegant simplicity of both the structure and spatial handling had no counterpart in the great churches of northern France. Although Angevin sources have been proposed for the German hall churches, the mechanism of transmission is not clear. It is more likely that the hall church was developed from the simplified elevations of monastic architecture. The Marburg scheme was to cut across ecclesiastical divisions and appeared in the Cistercian foundations of Haina (begun 1228) and Heiligenkreuz (choir consecrated 1295; *see* §2(iii) below), the Severikirche (1278–1330) at Erfurt and the cathedrals of Minden (*c.* 1270; see fig. 12), Verden an der Aller (1274–1313) and the choir (1304–40) of the Stephansdom, Vienna (*see* VIENNA, §V, 1(i)).

12. Germany, Minden Cathedral, interior of the choir and nave looking west, *c.* 1270

German architecture of the later 12th century and the 13th, if evaluated according to French criteria, appears conservative and (until Strasbourg and Cologne) indecisive in its assimilation of the Gothic style. Viewed on its own terms, however, German building was conditioned by its own charged historical tradition and the accommodation of Gothic form operated on distinctly different levels depending on the edifice and the patrons' aims. Nevertheless, the period of greatest inventiveness was yet to occur: by the series of Expertises in Milan at the end of the 14th century (*see* MASON (i), §IV, 3(iii)) architectural modernity was epitomized by the *maniera tedesca* not the *opus francigenum*.

BIBLIOGRAPHY

R. Hamann and K. Wilhelm-Kästner: *Die Elisabethkirche zu Marburg und ihre künstlerische Nachfolge*, 2 vols (Marburg, 1924–9)

R. Krautheimer: *Die Kirchen der Bettelordern in Deutschland* (Cologne, 1925)

H. Eydoux: *L'Architecture des églises cisterciennes d'Allemagne* (Paris, 1952)

H.-J. Kunst: 'Die Entstehung des Hallenumgangeschores der Domchor zu Verden an der Aller und seine Stellung in der gotischen Architektur', *Marburg, Jb. Kstwiss.*, xviii (1969), pp. 1–104
L. Grodecki: 'Les Arcs-boutants de la cathédrale de Strasbourg et leur origine', *Gesta*, xv (1976), pp. 43–51
U. Schröder: 'Royaumont oder Köln? Zum Problem der Ableitung der gotischen Zisterzienser-Abteikirche Altenberg', *Köln. Dombl.*, xlii (1977), pp. 209–42
P. Kurmann: 'Köln und Orléans', *Köln. Dombl.*, xliv–xlv (1979–80), pp. 255–76
M. Davis: 'The Abbey of Altenberg: Cistercian Simplicity and Aristocratic Iconography', *Studies in Cistercian Art and Architecture*, ed. M. Lillich (Kalamazoo, 1984), i, pp. 130–60
R. Nussbaum: *Deutsche Kirchenbaukunst der Gotik: Entwicklung und Bauformen* (Cologne, 1985)
D. von Winterfeld: 'Zum Stande der Baugeschichtsforschung', *Der Dom zu Limburg*, ed. W. Nicol (Mainz, 1985), pp. 41–84
W. Sauerländer: 'Style or Transition: The Fallacies of Classification Discussed in the Light of German Architecture, 1190–1220', *Archit. Hist.*, xxx (1987), pp. 1–13

(v) Scandinavia. The Gothic style in Denmark, Norway and Sweden appeared primarily in monastic foundations and cathedral architecture. Unlike in England or Germany, Scandinavian architecture did not develop a strongly defined personality through sustained experiment. The Cistercians were again foremost in importing new ideas that established an alternative to indigenous traditions and their finely cut stone buildings offered technical models to an area where wooden churches were built into the 12th century. Alvastra (ruined), Nydala (both 1143) and Roma (1164; ruined; Gotland) carried Bernardine formulae of planning and structure into Sweden. In Denmark, square quadripartite vaults set on massive walls at Sorø (1165–1240) and Holme (1180–1250), near Arhus, reflect continental examples represented by Bebenhausen (Tübingen) and Marienfeld, and seem to indicate German influence. Varnhem (*c.* 1200–50; Västergötland) was laid out with a circular ambulatory that appears to be distantly related to the new choirs of Clairvaux III and Pontigny II. Finally, the two-storey elevation at Løgum (*c.* 1200–70), which may derive from the Cistercian mother houses, is an early example of the type discussed in connection with Freiburg im Breisgau (*see* §(iv)(b) above). That the Scandinavians kept abreast of developments in France was partly due to the annual general chapter meetings, which served as forums for the exchange of architectural ideas.

The stylistic choices in Scandinavian cathedral-building were heterogeneous and connected to lines established by trade and through ecclesiastical and educational contacts. Trondheim Cathedral was begun after 1140 in an Anglo-Norman style (*see* TRONDHEIM, §2(i)). After Archbishop Eystein (*reg* 1157–88) returned from England in 1183 plans were changed to reflect the impact of contemporary projects. The vast octagonal choir chapel (*c.* 1190–1200) sheltering the tomb of St Olaf was possibly inspired by the Corona of Canterbury Cathedral or the octagon of Lincoln Cathedral. Roskilde Cathedral was built during the tenure of bishops who had studied in Paris (for further discussion and illustration *see* ROSKILDE, §1). Its plan, with an ambulatory (*c.* 1175) and the apse elevation with vaulted tribunes and triplet openings (*c.* 1200), suggests that these prelates sought to emulate the architecture of northern France. A strong German flavour informs the cathedrals of Linköping (begun *c.* 1230; *see* LINKÖPING, §1), Strängnäs (consecrated 1291) and St Maria, Visby. These were all hall churches, but instead of the light, vaulted canopies of Marburg, these churches' domical quadripartite vaults separated by heavy arches and supported by severe, square piers recall the early 13th-century German examples of Bamberg or Münster.

French influence, apart from the Cistercians, was not altogether absent from Scandinavia, for in 1287 the Parisian master ETIENNE DE BONNEUIL was hired by the Uppsala chapter to head the cathedral workshop. The Swedish ecclesiastical élite would have had direct knowledge of architecture in Paris through the presence of scholars at the university, but the act of hiring a Parisian master also testifies to the prestige that French architecture and its builders enjoyed on an international level. Work on the cathedral had started *c.* 1280 and the extent of Etienne's work is unknown, but Uppsala has a taut, two-storey structure and a plan composed of an ambulatory, a continuous suite of pentagonal chapels and a projecting transept (for further discussion and illustration *see* UPPSALA, §2). While the plan shares some features with Reims Cathedral, the elevation is characteristic of later 13th-century Germany. Uppsala closely resembles the Marienkirche, Lübeck, and underscores the importance of the Hanseatic city as a centre of architectural influence in the Baltic region.

BIBLIOGRAPHY

J. Roosval: *Die Kirchen Gotlands: Ein Beitrag zur mittelalterlichen Kunstgeschichte Schwedens* (Leipzig, 1912)
T. Paulsson: *Scandinavian Architecture* (London, 1958)
P. Héliot: 'La Cathédrale de Roskilde et l'influence de l'architecture française en Danemark vers 1150–1220', *Bull. Mnmtl*, cxxii (1964), pp. 233–59
I. Swartling: *Nydala Abbey: An Outline of its Architecture from Foundation to Dissolution* (Stockholm, 1967)
——: *Alvastra Abbey: The First Cistercian Settlement in Sweden* (Stockholm, 1969)

(vi) Spain. Until the late 13th century and the formation of a Catalan school, seen in the churches of Barcelona and later at Girona Cathedral (east end begun 1312), Gothic architectural styles were imported to Spain variously from south-west France, Burgundy and the Ile-de-France. These external influences were transmitted along the pilgrimage routes, through the architectural activity of the Cistercians as they established foundations throughout the Christianized parts of the peninsula, and by royal imitations of prestigious French models. A number of currents coexisted by the last third of the 12th century, but none engendered a school of building.

In Cistercian circles, the monastery of Santes Creus (*c.* 1174) continued the Bernardine plan of Fontenay, while the second church (begun *c.* 1170) at POBLET ABBEY, S María la Real, Fitero, and S María, Moreruela (both *c.* 1170–90), adopted a Clairvaux III configuration and were at least partially rib vaulted. Cistercian influences probably lay behind the two-storey elevations of the cathedrals at Ciudad Rodrigo (begun *c.* 1170; *see* CIUDAD RODRIGO, §2) and Lleida (begun 1203; *see* LLEIDA, SEU VELLA), while their domical ribbed vaults recall Angevin structures (*see* §(ii)(a) above). Ávila Cathedral (begun *c.* 1175; *see* ÁVILA, §2(i)(a) and fig. 1) adopted a plan and elevation derived from Suger's Saint-Denis Abbey, Ste Madeleine, Vézelay, and Angers Cathedral. Finally, the Pórtico de la Gloria and crypt (from 1168) of Santiago de Compostela Cathedral mingled mouldings, capital types and semicircular diagonal ribs characteristic of Burgundy with such northern French motifs as rose windows. Despite the acceptance of certain French plan types and technical features or the insertion of northern ornament, these edifices ignored the overall image of expansive spaciousness and glazed walls. Instead they retained the heavy interior structure with small windows, to reveal the continuing strength of Romanesque traditions.

The decisive victory over the Almohads at Las Navas de Tolosa in 1212, which dramatically extended Christian control in southern Spain, seems to have inaugurated a new building phase. Castile was the primary beneficiary and direct connections with France were established through the marriage of Blanche of Castile to Louis VIII (*reg* 1223–6). Every aspect of the French Gothic structural system was adopted at the cathedrals of Toledo, Burgos and León, together with the associations of the Church Militant and Triumphant. Given the indigenous taste for broad interior spaces and compact plans, it is not surprising that the influence of Bourges Cathedral should be felt, most clearly in the five-vessel plan, pyramidal massing, pier and window designs of Toledo Cathedral (begun *c.* 1220; *see* TOLEDO, figs 5 and 6). Yet the inclusion at Toledo of a non-projecting transept and Y-shaped flying buttresses betray an apparent awareness of Notre-Dame in Paris; the three-storey choir aisle with a lit triforium and clerestory oculi drew on the inner aisle (1225–32) of the Beauvais transepts and ambulatory. Decorative elements of Islamic and *Mudéjar* heritage were added, such as the interlaced arches of the triforium.

Burgos Cathedral (begun 1221; *see* BURGOS, fig. 2) also looked to Bourges, although its three-aisled plan eliminated the possibility of measured, stepped elevation, and Paris was the probable source of the traceried gallery of kings on the north transept façade (*c.* 1240). León Cathedral (begun *c.* 1255) embodied the most purely French work of the 13th century in Spain. It was based on churches intimately associated with the French monarchy, setting a 13th-century Saint-Denis superstructure, composed of composite piers with continuous vault responds, a glazed triforium and bar-traceried clerestory, over a Reims-type plan (*see* LEÓN, §II, 1(i) and fig. 1). The example of León was not followed, however, and, apart from an abortive project for the enlargement of the chevet (1258–76) at Santiago de Compostela, French influence remained the exception rather than the rule in Spanish architecture. León Cathedral, like Westminster Abbey in London, represented a deliberate break with existing traditions and a selection of new royal models to underscore the prestige of its aristocratic patron.

BIBLIOGRAPHY

E. Lambert: *L'Art gothique en Espagne aux XIIe et XIIIe siècles* (Paris, 1931)

L. Torres Balbás: *Arquitectura gótica*, A. Hisp., vii (Madrid, 1952)

R. Branner: 'The Movements of Gothic Architects between France and Spain in the Early Thirteenth Century', *Acts of the XIX International Congress of the History of Art: Paris, 1958*, pp. 44–8

J. Puente Migeuz: 'La catedral gótica de Santiago de Compostela: Un proyecto frustrado de D. Juan Arias, 1238–1266', *Compostellanum*, xxx (1985), pp. 245–75

(vii) Italy. Italy is perhaps the most problematic area for the discussion of Gothic architecture. The absence of a powerful aristocracy and centralized monarchy, the prominence of the monastic orders and the political fragmentation, with the lead in building within the individual city-states assumed by the secular governments, led to a strikingly different pattern of development from the rest of Europe (*see* ITALY, §II, 2). Italian builders and patrons generally showed little interest in the structural complexities or ornamental elaboration that animated French and English building in particular. Integrated into an approach that maintained its Early Christian and Romanesque identity, Gothic features were limited to window designs and pointed arches that produced a slightly more linear and vertical emphasis. Italian communes were indeed motivated by intense rivalry in the creation of impressive structures, but they tended to manufacture their images in terms of civic monuments and the Roman past rather than the royal models of the north.

The spread of the Cistercians into Italy during the 12th century introduced the Order's familiar architectural formulae. Fossanova Abbey (1187–1208; *see* CISTERCIAN ORDER, fig. 1), with cruciform piers, a two-storey elevation and groin vaults, reproduces features from mid-12th-century French Cistercian churches, such as the nave at Pontigny. Chiaravalle Milanese (completed by 1196) and Casamari (1203–17) are exclusively rib vaulted, but their structures remain Romanesque in character. S Andrea (1219–25) at Vercelli, although it has French-style crocket capitals, perpetuates the local rib-vaulted Romanesque traditions of northern Italy into which Cistercian elements were easily assimilated.

Italian architecture was transformed in the 1220s by the mendicant orders' structural repertory of ribbed vaults and pointed arches that produced a truly Gothic spaciousness in which the interior is suffused with light and walls are reduced to taut membranes (*see* DOMINICAN ORDER, §III; FRANCISCAN ORDER, §III). Yet the Dominican and Franciscan churches continued Cistercian methods of planning and were laid out to simple plans on a geometry of square units. The mendicants' architectural legislation strengthened many of the Cistercians' restrictions, seeking a monumental poverty that was the antithesis of northern cathedral complexity and continued the spirit of understatement of the Early Christian tradition.

Yet, unlike the Cistercians and despite the extensive building prescriptions, neither the Franciscans nor the Dominicans developed an identifiable style of their own, apart from the provision of an open congregational space suited to preaching, and a shared tone of restraint. Few churches were based on S Francesco (1228–53), Assisi, the most important church of the Franciscan Order. The continuous responds supporting quadripartite vaults, the wall passage, bar tracery, west rose window and crocket capitals have led scholars to propose connections with Burgundian Gothic and the cathedrals of Reims and Angers. The two-level structure (*see* ASSISI, fig. 1) even recalls the long-standing tradition of aristocratic chapels, which, together with the traceried and glazed windows and elaborate wall painting cycles, creates a 'mendicant Sainte-Chapelle' intended to display St Francis's tomb. The squat, rather heavy proportions, however, and the balanced tranquillity of its hall-like interior reveal the translation of these northern features into a dialect that spoke directly with the Roman past.

The diversity of Franciscan architecture is demonstrated in examples with distinctly different plans and elevations. S Francesco (1236–50), Bologna, has a two-storey basilican format over a plan with an ambulatory and radiating chapels. The similar arrangement in the choir (1270–90) of S Lorenzo, Naples (*see* NAPLES, §IV, 2 and fig. 8), surely reflects the French-inspired patronage of the Angevin court. Il Santo (begun 1230s) at Padua has a suite of Venetian domed compartments (*see* PADUA, §4(i) and fig. 3), while S Francesco (begun by 1239) in Gubbio and S Fortunato (begun 1292) in Todi (see fig. 13) were built as hall churches. The Dominicans were no less energetic builders throughout the 13th century, producing such important edifices as S Maria Novella, Florence (nave and transepts begun *c.* 1277; *see* FLORENCE, §IV, 6 and fig. 20), and S Maria sopra Minerva (*c.* 1279), Rome. In both of these a minimalist structure, consisting only of slim piers that support wide, rounded arches, square, domical ribbed vaults and pointed transverse arches, achieved a maximal spatial expansion.

Episcopal edifices in 13th-century Italy remained conservative, even retrospective. Within the basilican framework, buildings incorporated such features as ribbed vaults and pointed arches, already present in Romanesque architecture, and added bar tracery and gables as isolated 'modern' details. Each cathedral seems to be the result of a conscious search for a distinctive individualism that would set it apart from those in other cities. Siena Cathedral, completed in the early 1270s, can be seen as a vaulted version of Pisa Cathedral (begun 1063), its interior dominated by the crossing lantern, its piers and walls faced with alternating bands of white, pink and dark green marble (*see* SIENA, §III, 1(i) and fig. 5). The façade, the lower level of which is attributed to Giovanni Pisano and was partially built from 1284 to 1297, may reflect the impact of such French designs as Reims Cathedral or the Paris transepts in the emphasis on portal gables and the display of a populous sculptural programme (*see* SIENA, fig. 6). The screen-like character of the Siena façade, however, as at Orvieto Cathedral (begun 1290; *see* ORVIETO, §2(ii)(a)), departed decisively from French models. The simplicity of Arezzo Cathedral (begun 1277–8), apart from its slightly larger windows and more elaborate tracery patterns, is hardly distinguishable from mendicant architecture (see above). The structure and elevation of the central vessel are nearly identical to those of S Maria Novella in Florence.

13. Italy, Todi, S Fortunato, interior of the nave looking north-east, begun 1292

The independent character of Italian ecclesiastical architecture at the end of the 13th century and the importance of both imperial Roman and Early Christian architecture are best seen at Orvieto and Florence. While Orvieto Cathedral was a slightly medievalized version of an unvaulted basilica (*see* ORVIETO, fig. 2), the cathedral of S Maria del Fiore (*see* FLORENCE, §IV, 1(i)(a)) was an original hybrid. The initial scheme (begun after 1294), which has usually been attributed to Arnolfo di Cambio, appears already to have envisaged a timber-roofed nave with a dome above the crossing of a triconch choir, which would have surpassed those at Pisa and Siena and produced an impressive antique image that compensated for the city's lack of an important Roman past (*see* §2(vi) below).

BIBLIOGRAPHY

J. White: *Art and Architecture in Italy, 1250–1400*, Pelican Hist. A. (Harmondsworth, 1965)

A. Busignani and R. Bencini: *Le chiese di Firenze* (Florence, 1982)

J. Krüger: *S. Lorenzo Maggiore in Neapel: Ein Franziskanerkirche zwischen Ordensideal und Herrschaftsarchitektur* (Werl, 1986)

D. Gillerman: 'S Fortunato in Todi: Why the Hall Church', *J. Soc. Archit. Historians*, xlviii (1989), pp. 158–71

C. Bruzelius: '*Ad modum Franciae*: Charles of Anjou and Gothic Architecture in the Kingdom of Sicily', *J. Soc. Archit. Historians*, l (1991), pp. 402–20

M. Trachtenberg: 'Gothic/Italian "Gothic": Toward a Redefinition', *J. Soc. Archit. Historians*, l (1991), pp. 22–37

MICHAEL T. DAVIS

2. LATE 13TH CENTURY–THE 16TH.

(i) Introduction. (ii) British Isles. (iii) Holy Roman Empire, Scandinavia and Eastern Europe. (iv) France. (v) Low Countries. (vi) Italy. (vii) Spain. (viii) Portugal.

(i) Introduction. Most aspects of Gothic architecture after *c*. 1300 can be defined as either a radical refashioning or a fundamental rejection of the essential character of French Rayonnant: its systematic and ubiquitous application of bar tracery. These responses correspond to a broad north–south divide, Italy, southern France and eastern Spain tending to favour mural simplicity and enlarged interior spaciousness, while in the north Rayonnant underwent a series of subtle but radical modifications, starting in England and spreading to Germany and France itself, to the Low Countries and then to central and southern Spain, and to Portugal. The *de luxe* character of Rayonnant was intensified, its tracery and decorative nichework extended to all aspects of the structure.

These two broad strands often overlapped, and equally they contained within them divisions and alignments in the geography of style. Around 1300 various social and religious trends emerged that affected all the arts and influenced architecture in ways that transcended the boundaries just described. There was a shift in the balance of authority away from the Church towards secular rulers, with the declining moral force of the Papacy (exiled in Avignon 1308–78 and weakened by the Schism 1378–1429), and the rise of royal and aristocratic court cultures not only in such centralized kingdoms as France and England but in Lisbon, Naples, Florence, Prague, Kraków and Malbork—places that, once on the fringe of both Europe and the Gothic style, now became politically and artistically central. The cult of the secular ruler was embodied in the new palace-castles that now enjoyed the stylistic priority once given to churches, with secular influence accordingly becoming manifest in ecclesiastical buildings. The type of palace chapel based on the Sainte-Chapelle, Paris, became an important model for church choirs of all ranks, although the only new genre of church building in this later period was the light, open structure developed by the mendicant orders. Mendicant influence was such a strong unifying factor in Late Gothic, however, that it underlay church designs, especially in towns, right across Europe.

Planning and church interiors were also affected by new forms of lay piety: the new doctrine of Transubstantiation and the feast of Corpus Christi, with their emphasis on the altar and on the real presence of Christ, encouraged the development of exquisitely ornate sacrament houses and other liturgical furnishings, the micro-architectural forms of which were reflected not only in the monumental architecture but also in the votive and funerary chantry chapels and side chapels that now clustered in and around the church building proper, and in the elaborate screens that increasingly separated the liturgical spaces and the clergy from the laity.

These, then, were among the factors unifying the architecture that developed as Paris declined as the architectural centre of Europe. Yet the emergence of 'nation states' in England, France and the Iberian Peninsula encouraged the growth of autonomous regional or national styles, many of them generated by royal patronage based in new, fixed centres of government. To set out the history of Late Gothic architecture under national headings reflects a genuine shift in artistic power from northern France to its immediate neighbours at the turn of the 13th and 14th centuries.

BIBLIOGRAPHY

W. Gross: *Die abendländische Architektur um 1300* (Stuttgart, 1948)

W. Swaan: *The Late Middle Ages: Art and Architecture from 1350 to the Advent of the Renaissance* (London, 1977)

M. Untermann: *Der Zentralbau im Mittelalter* (Darmstadt, 1989)

For further bibliography *see* §1(i) above.

(ii) British Isles. English royal patronage made a more significant contribution to the formation of Late Gothic than that of any other European monarchy. The three enterprises begun under Edward I in the 1290s did much to promote the language of Late Gothic ornament (*see* PLANTAGENET, (3)). All three were clearly intended to surpass their French models: the Eleanor Crosses (the *montjoies* of St Louis; *see* CROSS, §II, 2 and 3), the tombs of *Edmund Crouchback, Earl of Lancaster* (*d* 1296) and his wife *Aveline* in Westminster Abbey (the royal tombs in Royaumont and Saint-Denis abbeys), and St Stephen's Chapel (the Sainte-Chapelle); in addition to their unprecedentedly rich surface finishes, however, they undermined the fundamental aesthetic principles of French Rayonnant with a new repertory of decorative effects, handled with a hitherto unknown freedom. In particular, the two-storey St Stephen's Chapel (begun 1292; *see* LONDON, §V, 3(i)(a)) embodied radical innovations: in the upper chapel (destr. 1334) a dominant horizontal crenellated cornice, a quotation from contemporary carpentry (perhaps screens or tournament podia), which ran above the main windows and severed the elevation from the vault, denied the fundamental French principle of the self-sufficient bay unit; in the lower chapel the integrity of the bay was also

compromised by the first known English appearance of lierne ribs, the linear patterning of which conceals the vault structure.

The second main tenet of French Rayonnant, the extension of clear geometric tracery over all adjacent surfaces to become the organizing principle of the interior (*see* TRACERY, §2(ii)), was partly subverted by the use of sinuous ogee arches in the window tracery (the first examples of curvilinear tracery in Europe); here, however, it was fundamentally undermined by the use of a miniature, tracery-backed canopy, hitherto confined to French portals and buttresses (although a version had appeared in the chapter house at York Minster in the 1280s) in a way quite consistent with the traditional English preference for treating walls in depth, as the major component in the elevation. Released from the systematic discipline of Rayonnant tracery, the repetition at different heights of such decorative elements as the cornice, the niche and tracery grids re-established all-over unity by sheer accumulation.

The splendour and originality of Edward's chapel made it a fountainhead of the later phase of the English DECORATED STYLE (*c.* 1250–*c.* 1360). The influence of St Stephen's was felt most strongly in the north and east of England, in the flame-like tracery windows (1330s) of York and Beverley minsters, and in the niche-encrusted interior of the Lady Chapel (1321–49) at Ely Cathedral (see fig. 14); and bulbous ogee arches and seaweedy foliage appeared in a series of elaborate interior furnishings, for example at Lincoln Cathedral, Beverley Minster, Southwell Minster, All Saints, Hawton, St Andrew, Heckington (for illustration *see* EASTER SEPULCHRE), and Exeter Cathedral. In the West of England, where architects showed a comparable interest in disguising structure (e.g. Bristol, St Mary Redcliffe, north porch; *c.* 1325), the search for the exotic and the unexpected took a more spatial turn. The choir (begun 1298) of St Augustine's, Bristol, is a stone version of contemporary wooden-roofed secular halls, combined with an array of lierne and net vaults clearly elaborated from St Stephen's.

From *c.* 1320 the remodelling of the east end of Wells Cathedral (*see* WELLS, §1(i)) relaxed the traditional rigidities of English ground-plans with a sequence of distinct spaces, each covered with vaults of almost Islamic elaboration, and each tailored to its separate functions and associations: an octagonal Lady chapel, which evokes the traditional connection between the Virgin and centralized buildings; a low retrochoir in the shape of a hall crypt (*see* WELLS, fig. 2), and a taller, net-vaulted choir. The latter's chapel-like forms, containing clear quotations from St Stephen's, underscore the self-contained, collegiate character of the space. This ingenious adaptation to the exigencies of a local liturgy occurred also at Ely Cathedral, where the monks' choir was rebuilt from 1322 with a programme of images in all media celebrating the monastery's Anglo-Saxon benefactors and the cult of its patron, St Etheldreda (*see* ELY CATHEDRAL, §1(iv)). The crossing itself was appropriately conceived as a vast martyrium-like octagon crowned by the unique wooden vault and lantern,

14. England, Ely Cathedral, Lady Chapel, interior, 1321–49

possibly by William of Hurley, which confirms the ancient status of the cathedral priory in the most spectacular fashion.

Even while Decorated ornament was still flourishing, the Rayonnant notion of tracery as the organizing principle of the interior was restated in the remodelling of the south transept and choir (1331–67) of Gloucester Cathedral (*see* GLOUCESTER, §1). This adumbration of the PERPENDICULAR STYLE, which was to dominate English architecture for the following two hundred years, rejected the lavish particularity of Decorated in favour of a comprehensive visual unity based on the constant repetition of similar tracery panels. The remodelling of the nave of Winchester Cathedral by William Wynford after 1394 consisted of similar tracery panels disguising a Romanesque core (*see* WINCHESTER, §III, 1(ii)). The nave (1378–1405) of Canterbury Cathedral by the king's chief architect, Henry Yevele (*see* CANTERBURY, fig. 9), showed how successfully the suave recessions and delicate gradations of Perpendicular moulded stonework could be applied to a type of basilican structure, rare in English great church architecture, with such tall side aisles and arcades that it approximates to the hall-like interiors of contemporary friars' and parish churches (see below).

It is an indication of the decorative conservatism of Perpendicular that the elevations of Gloucester and Canterbury served as the models for the royal chapels at Windsor, Cambridge and Westminster Abbey that were the crowning architectural achievements of the 15th century. The basilican St George's Chapel (1475–1506; *see* WINDSOR CASTLE, §2; *see also* ENGLAND, fig. 3), founded by Edward IV, is little more than a ceremonious amalgam of Canterbury's piers and Gloucester's tracery panels, while Henry VII's Chapel (*c.* 1503–9) in Westminster Abbey (*see* LONDON, §V, 2(i)) and, particularly, the box-like King's College Chapel (1448–1515; *see* CAMBRIDGE (i), §2(i)) recall, behind their Tudor decorative pomp, the grid-like homogeneity of Gloucester. What separates the latter two from their distant prototype is the adoption of large-scale fan vaults. This feature was unique to England and perhaps the single most original component of Perpendicular, extending the old Rayonnant identity of masonry and window tracery to its logical conclusion. Each rib cone, decorated with regular spokes of bifurcating tracery, exactly resembles in plan a bisected rose window.

Their expense and structural indeterminacy confined fans at first to such small enterprises as porches, towers, cloister walks (the earliest extant examples are in the east cloister walk (*c.* 1351–64 at Gloucester) and small micro-architectural chantry chapels. The earliest surviving examples in a high vault are at Sherborne Abbey (begun *c.* 1425), Dorset, before their belated royal adoption in the side aisles (*c.* 1480) at Windsor, and their monumental deployment at King's and Westminster. The King's vaults, by John Wastell, articulate a monumental vista (*see* CAMBRIDGE (i), fig. 4), while those at Westminster, of unsurpassed technical brilliance, combine fan vaults with pendant bosses to suggest not only the masonic equivalent of wooden pendant roofs but a fantastically enlarged version of the 'toy' vaults of chantry chapels.

More austere variants of Perpendicular were found principally in secular and utilitarian structures, and most

15. England, Long Melford, Holy Trinity, view from south, *c.* 1460

obviously in parish churches. The spacious town and parish churches of the later Middle Ages, of simple rectangular plan, with slender pillars supporting wooden roofs, owed nothing to great churches except perhaps their window tracery and their scale.

The inspiration of secular halls cannot be discounted, although the real catalyst in the change seems to have been the architecture of the friars, particularly the great London churches (first half of the 14th century) of the Augustinian friars (destr. 1940; rebuilt) and Franciscans (destr.), which set the pattern for the grandest friars' churches (most destr.) outside the capital and in turn became the ultimate model for the great 'wool' churches of East Anglia (e.g. SS Peter and Paul, Lavenham; Holy Trinity, Long Melford; see fig. 15) and the Cotswolds (e.g. St Mary, Fairford; SS Peter and Paul, Northleach). Architecturally their interiors were treated as showcases for elaborate furnishings and scaffoldings for the support of bright new clerestories and ornate and expensive timber roofs (e.g. St Wendreda, March; St John the Baptist, Needham Market).

Many of these churches were dominated by single western towers. The later Middle Ages was the age of great steeples, which were applied to parish churches in an ingenious variety of forms, such as the regional groups that can be isolated in Somerset, Yorkshire and East Anglia. By the end of the 14th century, however, spires had mostly been abandoned in favour of the characteristically English flat-topped, battlemented silhouette. In great churches the steeple became a compelling ideal with the construction at Salisbury Cathedral of the central tower and spire (begun *c.* 1300; *see* SALISBURY, fig. 3), certainly a monument to institutional pride and architectural extravagance, but also, like all steeples, a symbol of heaven. The unpopularity of the French two-tower west façade in England meant that most of the greatest cathedral steeples rise over the crossing, and all of them give to the prevailing horizontality of the church a contrasting vertical élan. Salisbury was followed quickly by Lincoln, Hereford and Wells, and the series extended into the Perpendicular period at Worcester, York, Durham and Gloucester, finishing with John Wastell's majestic Bell Harry (completed by 1509) at Canterbury. Although sometimes conceived with a cavalier disregard for structural soundness, these great steeples belatedly brought into the open an unexpected audacity, a talent for structural improvization, lacking in the churches they crowned.

Owing to different historical and political circumstances, Late Gothic did not become an established tradition in Scotland and Ireland (*see* SCOTLAND, §II and IRELAND, §II). The abbey church at Melrose, rebuilt in the 15th century, displays a striking mixture of influences from 14th-century Yorkshire, French Flamboyant detailing, a star vault and Perpendicular windows; in Lothian a more coherent design appears at the richly ornamented ROSLIN CHAPEL. In Ireland, Late Gothic motifs appeared in the 15th-century Franciscan convents, where curvilinear tracery was used in both tomb gables and windows, for example at Rosserk Abbey (1440s), Co. Mayo.

BIBLIOGRAPHY

H. M. Colvin, ed.: *The Middle Ages* (1963), i–ii of *The History of the King's Works*, 6 vols (London, 1963–82)

J. Harvey: *The Perpendicular Style, 1330–1485* (London, 1978)

J. Bony: *The English Decorated Style: Gothic Architecture Transformed, 1250–1350* (Oxford, 1979)

W. C. Leedy: *Fan Vaulting: A Study of Form, Technology and Meaning* (Berkeley, 1980)

C. Platt: *The Castle in Medieval England and Wales* (London, 1982)

F. Woodman: *The Architectural History of King's College Chapel and its Place in the Development of Late Gothic Architecture in England and France* (London, 1986)

N. Coldstream: 'Le "Decorated Style": Recherches récentes', *Bull. Mnmtl*, cxlvii (1989), pp. 55–80

(iii) Holy Roman Empire, Scandinavia and Eastern Europe. German architectural patronage reflected the politically fragmented nature of the Empire. The intense rivalries of small courts, powerful Elector–archbishops and virtually autonomous Free Imperial Cities (*Reichstädte*; the most powerful artistic patrons in later medieval Germany) discouraged the growth of dominant architectural language and promoted a stylistic diversity without parallel in Europe. This thriving multiplicity contrasted with the large and relatively homogeneous territories in the east: the territory of the Teutonic Knights, the kingdom of Bohemia and the Habsburg duchy of Austria. Further east lay the emerging nation-states of Poland and Hungary. Some of the most original experiments in Late Gothic architecture were made in these eastern principalities in the 14th century, generating new currents of influence, westwards, across the older sections of the Empire.

(a) *Backsteingotik* and Rhenish Rayonnant. (b) The Parler legacy.

(a) Backsteingotik *and Rhenish Rayonnant.* A division that cuts across this political and artistic patchwork is that between the stone building areas of the south and the brick architecture (*Backsteingotik*) of the north German plain and the Baltic coastal cities (*see* BRICK, §II, 3(i)(b)). Brick Gothic provided unique opportunities for architectural colour, not only in its gaudy interior finishes (e.g. Lübeck, Marienkirche; *c.* 1260–91), but in the vivid constructional polychromy of its exteriors (e.g. Brandenburg, St Katharinen; *c.* 1401–34; for illustration *see* BRANDENBURG). It owed its finest achievements to the patronage of the Baltic Hansa, with its capital at Lübeck and its networks extending as far east as Estonia. The internationalist ambitions of *Backsteingotik* and its civic pretensions were set out in the Marienkirche (*see* LÜBECK, §2), a colossal brick version of an up-to-date Franco-Flemish cathedral, dwarfing the city's own cathedral. It was followed by a series of close imitations, all in brick, many of them in the coastal cities founded from Lübeck (e.g. St Nikolai, Stralsund; Marienkirche, Rostock; St Marien, Wismar), but some extending into Sweden (e.g. Malmö, St Peter; *c.* 1300) and Denmark (e.g. Vor Frue Kirke, Copenhagen; destr. 1728). The model was also accepted outside the areas of Hansa patronage, for example for the abbey church (1291–1336) at Doberan and for Schwerin Cathedral.

Early 14th-century Rhenish architecture continued to be dominated by the cathedrals of Strasbourg and Cologne, and in particular by the aesthetic problems posed by new types of towers and façades (*see* §1(iv)(b) above). The great west façades of Strasbourg and Cologne (1275 and *c.* 1300, respectively) mark, like Edward I's enterprises in England, the emancipation from French Rayonnant, with tracery in eccentric and dynamic forms (propellers, panels, mouchettes) extended to every surface of the façade, standing in front of it like harp-strings. In Cologne, perhaps for the first time, the solid faces of the spire are dissolved into geometrical openwork. The French notion of the harmonized façade gave way to an overwhelming concentration on enlarged towers, reducing the residual façade element between them to a narrow connecting panel; at Cologne, indeed, the traditional rose was abandoned in favour of an upright window like those in the adjoining towers. The accumulation of attenuated tracery motifs, particularly the repetitive gables that overlap all the horizontals, magnifies the vertiginous height of the steeples and generates throughout an overpowering verticality.

Almost inevitably the followers of Cologne and Strasbourg separated altogether the idea of the tower and the façade. The show façade on the south side of the nave of the Katharinenkirche (begun 1317) at Oppenheim was transformed into a three-tiered display of the latest Rhenish tracery patterns (see fig. 16). At Freiburg im Breisgau Cathedral the single western spire (1300) in the old German Romanesque tradition was so brilliantly dissolved into tracery that it quickly became the archetype for all the great steeples of southern Germany.

German 14th-century architecture offers many instances of the incorporation of Rhenish Rayonnant tracery into simpler and more distinctly local forms. Most paradoxical was the use of giant screens of 'harp-string' tracery to decorate the great east gables of mid-14th-century hall churches in Mecklenburg (Marienkirche, Prenzlau; St Marien, Neubrandenburg), all executed in the unlikely material of coloured brick. The high side aisle walls of hall churches, the most popular of German 'local' structures, provided perfect surfaces for tracery displays. Almost simultaneously, in Westphalia and Lower Austria, where the HALL CHURCH had appeared early, large halls, with open interiors, subdivided by slender and widely spaced pillars, were enclosed in diaphanous skins of tracery, for example at HEILIGENKREUZ ABBEY (consecrated 1295) and St Maria zur Wiese (begun 1313) in Soest (*see* SOEST, fig. 1).

The churches of the friars and the Cistercians, orders whose architectural contribution was stronger in Germany than anywhere in Europe outside Italy, show a greater

16. Germany, Oppenheim, Katharinenkirche, south façade, begun 1317

tendency to reduce and simplify Rayonnant. The mendicant development of the 'long choir' (the Sainte-Chapellian chancel with attenuated windows), particularly under Habsburg encouragement in Austria, as shown in the Dominican Neukloster at Wiener Neustadt, and by the Carmelites (Zu den neun Engelschören; 1386–1403) and Augustinian friars (1330–38) in Vienna, profoundly influenced the design of mendicant and parish church choirs in Bohemia, Silesia and southern Poland, and ensured its popularity even at the cathedrals of Erfurt (*c.* 1350) and Passau (begun 1405). Mendicant naves were equally influential. The Dominicans' double-nave hall church at Imbach (*c.* 1270; now Mariae Geburt), Lower Austria, triggered a lasting fascination in eastern Europe for axially placed pillars, drawing on the double-nave format or its variants for some of the most ingenious examples of spatial manipulation in Austrian, Bohemian and Polish Late Gothic. The mendicant basilica, with much blank walling between arcades and clerestory (e.g. Erfurt, Franciscan church; 14th century), provided a starting point for a host of parish churches and a few less ambitious great churches (e.g. the choir of Freiburg im Breisgau Cathedral); while the slender columns without capitals in the naves of a group of early 14th-century mendicant halls in the Upper Rhine, including the Dominican churches at Guebwiller and Colmar, prepared the way for similar columns in the 15th-century hall churches of Lower Bavaria (e.g. Heiliggeistkirche, Landshut).

Contemporary Cistercian churches in southern Germany, such as those at Sedlec (begun *c.* 1280), Salem (begun 1299) and Zlatá Koruna (rebuilt 1663), adopted the same spare and elegant language, although their inclusion of fashionable Rhenish tracery patterns (Salem) and their grand scale made them the obvious models for the modest cathedral architecture of 14th-century Poland (e.g. Gniezno; Kraków; the nave at Wrocław), and for the great basilican churches in Lower Silesia, including SS Stanislas and Wenceslas, Świdnica, SS Peter and Paul, Strzegom, and, in Wrocław, St Mary Magdalene and St Elizabeth. What gave these Cistercian churches a more than provincial importance was their very early use (1330s) of decorative vaults, such as in the chapter house at Maulbronn (*see* MAULBRONN ABBEY, fig. 2), at Salem and in the summer refectory (1335) at Bebenhausen, exactly when similar star and umbrella-shaped vaults were proliferating in the territory of the Teutonic Order. The inspiration there, particularly in the earliest vaults, such as those in the brick Cistercian church of Pelplin (begun 1276; for illustration *see* PELPLIN ABBEY) and in the chapter house and Great Refectory (*c.* 1320–40) at Malbork Castle, may have come from Lincoln and Lübeck; but by the third quarter of the century large areas of Eastern Europe, from Prussia through Silesia and Poland to southern Bohemia, had begun to experiment with decorative vault patterns. In some cases they were the main indicators of a regional style, as in the jumping vaults (*see* VAULT: RIB) of Lower Silesian hall churches, for example in Wrocław (St Mary-on-the-Sands and Holy Cross) or the ingenious series of double-nave hall churches erected by Kasimir III in Little Poland, including St Mary, Wiślica (for discussion and illustration *see* WIŚLICA, §1; *see also* PIAST, (1)). From 1356 they were to become the characteristic feature of Late Gothic architecture in Prague.

(b) The Parler legacy. Many of these strands were brought together by Peter Parler (*see* PARLER, (3)), whose artistic partnership with Charles IV (*see* LUXEMBOURG, (3)) in the reconstruction of Prague was the closest Germany came to the centralized and metropolitan patronage of contemporary French and English architecture. Peter's completion of the choir (1356–85) of Prague Cathedral amounted to a transformation of German Rayonnant, as exemplified at Cologne, in a spirit of radical and empirical freedom comparable only to the work at St Stephen's, Westminster. At Prague the rigidities of Cologne were softened and invigorated, with some of the earliest examples of dynamic curvilinear tracery on the Continent; and the verticality and flatness of the Cologne elevation was undermined by the strongly longitudinal triforium balustrade, the strange zigzagging depth of the triforium and clerestory, and by the net-like barrel vault that subverted the bay structure.

Whether this assault on Rayonnant orthodoxy owed its inspiration to the decorative vaults and set-back clerestories of English Decorated architecture (*see* §(i) above), to Peter Parler's deft synthesis of more local traditions or even to the Emperor's Italo-Byzantine taste, it was executed with such inventive bravura that Prague Cathedral became the source of German Late Gothic styles. The dynasty of Parler architects and sculptors, still acknowledged reverently in late 15th-century architects' manuals as the '*Junkers* of Prague', worked in an area extending from the Rhine to Vienna, Košice and Milan, and Peter's influence was felt beyond their circle, even in the Parlerian details introduced by HINRICH BRUNSBERG in the gabled frontispiece of St Katharinen, Brandenburg. Peter's decorative inventiveness, all especially evident in the south transept and south tower of Prague Cathedral (*see* PRAGUE, fig. 14), was most ingeniously developed in the tracery-encrusted giant steeples that dominate much of German Late Gothic: at the Stephansdom (only properly under way *c.* 1400; *see* VIENNA, fig. 13), at Frankfurt am Main Cathedral (begun 1415; *see* GERTHENER, MADERN) and in the prodigious spires of Ulm (1392) and Strasbourg (1399; *see* ENSINGEN, (1)), although structurally, as single steeples, they all followed Freiburg im Breisgau.

The more spatial aspects of Peter Parler's legacy—the play with decorative vaulting and the unorthodox manipulation of apsidal polygons, for example at St Bartholomew, Kolín (*see also* KUTNA HORA, §1; SCHWÄBISCH GMÜND, CATHEDRAL OF THE HOLY CROSS, §1(ii))—were taken up in the Lower Bavarian hall churches of HANS VON BURGHAUSEN and their Swabian offshoots (for discussion and illustration *see* DINKELSBÜHL and NÖRDLINGEN, §1). These mid-15th-century halls, with their closed, cubic exteriors surmounted by vast roofs, and their smoothly flowing interiors crowned with variations on net and star vaults, are the equivalents of the contemporary 'Soft' style in the figural arts.

A new dynamism and angularity was introduced in the late 15th century by ARNOLD VON WESTFALEN and BENEDIKT RIED, whose seminal works are the 'representative' interiors of large palaces. Arnold's idiosyncratic interiors in the Albrechtsburg (begun 1471) at Meissen fragmented both the linear and the spatial language of German Late Gothic (see fig. 17). By drawing buttresses into the interior he obscured the real limits of the space and its light sources; by discontinuing ribs halfway across the vault he made their terminations arbitrary, and separated them visually and conceptually from the vault surface. His adoption of a form of cellular vault pushed the free shaping of the vault structure to the limits of fantasy. The decorative dissonances of the Meissen lodge had a wide following in Eastern Europe: their portal designs reappeared in Kraków and Transylvania, and cellular vaults spread into Bohemia and as far north as Gdańsk and Lithuania.

17. Germany, Meissen, Albrechtsburg, Grosser Saal, by Arnold von Westfalen, begun 1471

Ried's contribution also centred around vaulting, through the structurally audacious application of curving ribs across wide or unorthodox spaces to create a sense of unlimited spatial extension, and of weightless and supercharged energy, as in the Vladislav Hall (completed 1502) in Hradčany, Prague, and the galleried nave of St Barbara, KUTNÁ HORA (vault designed 1512). Similar petal vaults were constructed in Upper Austria at the turn of the 16th century (e.g. Mariä Himmelfahrt, Königswiesen; St Stephan, Weistracht), possibly under the influence of Anton Pilgram, but it was Ried's achievement that caught the imagination of George, Duke of Saxony (1471–1539), and his architects, and triggered the invention of the last and most monumental series of German hall churches, in Upper Saxony and northern Bohemia. At the Annenkirche, ANNABERG (begun 1499), and the parish church of the Assumption (begun 1511; moved 1975) at Most, the combination of Prague-like curving vaults and Meissen's internal buttresses defines a vibrant and luminous space, where the celestial and the organic are merged in seamless movement.

BIBLIOGRAPHY

A. Lindblom: *Sveriges konsthistoria från förtid til nutid* [Swedish art history from early times to the present day], i (Stockholm, 1944)
M. Meyer: *Schweizerische Münster und Kathedralen des Mittelalters* (Zurich, 1945)
K. H. Clasen: *Deutsche Gewölbe der Spätgotik* (Berlin, 1958)
T. Paulsson: *Scandinavian Architecture* (London, 1958)
G. Fehr: *Benedikt Ried: Ein deutscher Baumeister zwischen Gotik und Renaissance* (Munich, 1961)
K. M. Swoboda, ed.: *Gotik in Böhmen* (Munich, 1969)
L. Gerevich: *The Art of Buda and Pest in the Middle Ages* (Budapest, 1971)
R. Recht: *L'Alsace gothique de 1300–1365* (Colmar, 1974)
G. Entz: *Gotische Baukunst in Ungarn* (Budapest, 1976)
Die Parler und der Schöne Stil, 1350–1400: Europäische Kunst unter den Luxemburgern (exh. cat., ed. A. Legner; Cologne, Schnütgen-Mus., 1978)
W. Braunfels: *Die Kunst im Heiligen Römischen Reich*, 6 vols (Munich, 1979–89)
T. Mroczko: *Architektura Gotycka na ziemi Chelminskiej* [Gothic architecture in the Chelmno region] (Warsaw, 1980)
N. von Holst: *Der deutsche Ritterorden und seine Bauten* (Berlin, 1981)
E. Ullmann, ed.: *Geschichte der deutschen Kunst, 1350–1470* (Leipzig, 1981)
C. Meckseper: *Kleine Kunstgeschichte der deutschen Stadt im Mittelalter* (Darmstadt, 1982)
E. Ullmann, ed.: *Geschichte der deutschen Kunst, 1470–1550* (Leipzig, 1984)
P. Crossley: *Gothic Architecture in the Reign of Kasimir the Great: Church Architecture in Lesser Poland, 1320–1380* (Kraków, 1985)
N. Nussbaum: *Deutsche Kirchenbaukunst der Gotik: Entwicklung und Bauformen* (Cologne, 1985)
H. J. Böker: *Die mittelalterliche Backsteinarchitektur Norddeutschlands* (Darmstadt, 1988)
F. Möbius and H. Sciurie, eds: *Geschichte der deutschen Kunst, 1200–1350* (Leipzig, 1989)
G. Brucher: *Gotische Baukunst in Österreich* (Salzburg and Vienna, 1990)
W. Krassowski: *Dzieje budownictwa i architektury na ziemiach Polski* [History of architecture and building in Poland], ii and iii (Warsaw, 1990)

(iv) France. French patrons were naturally reluctant to abandon the elegance and logic of Rayonnant, as is shown by Philip IV's foundation (1298) of Poissy priory church in a style of mid-13th-century Parisian Rayonnant. In the second half of the 14th century the French kings and the royal dukes devoted most effort and inventiveness to palace architecture, and signs of the last phase of Gothic in France, the FLAMBOYANT STYLE, first appeared in royal palaces. Initial efforts consisted of deploying curvilinear tracery, seen in Guy de Dammartin's work for Jean, Duc de Berry, in his castle chapel (1382) at Riom and the fireplace in the great chamber (1390s) of the ducal palace at Poitiers, and in the La Grange chapels (*c.* 1375) at Amiens Cathedral, where the sculpture-framed windows may reflect the façades of contemporary loggia staircases in the royal castles at Saumur and, perhaps, the Louvre, Paris. The Dammartin tracery suggests English inspiration, a connection quite consistent with his patron's imprisonment in England (1360–67); but the Amiens tracery looks more Parlerian (*see* §(iii)(b) above).

The flickering mouchettes and soufflets that gave rise to the term were not the only characteristics of the Flamboyant style, which was as much a reinterpretation of Rayonnant as the experiments a century or so earlier in England and Germany. Tracery-dominated surfaces were sometimes replaced by an almost pre-Gothic murality and simplicity, or developed to an unprecedented intricacy and richness. The continuity of Rayonnant surfaces was broken with effects of depth, plasticity and movement; the orthogonal regularity of Rayonnant ground-plans was undermined with new kinds of polygonal chevets and porches; ambiguous elisions were made between hitherto separate forms. Capitals were often omitted so that arch mouldings thread together, or die into walls and piers, and for the first time in French Gothic decorative vaults enjoyed widespread popularity. These changes extended throughout the regions, beyond the Capetian circles based on Paris.

The Valois kings encouraged with tax concessions the completion of the great churches at Reims, Senlis and Troyes, and endowed masterpieces of the style, from Charles VII's foundations at Cléry-Saint-André (1449–85) and St Aignan (1439–1509; part destr. 1568), Orléans, to Margaret of Austria's at Brou (1513–32), near Bourg-en-Besse (*see* BROU, PRIORY CHURCH). Their impoverishment in the Hundred Years' War, however, and their reluctance to carry out their officially acknowledged duties as patrons of church architecture restored much architectural initiative to the provinces and the higher clergy. Like Rayonnant, however, Flamboyant was historically conservative: nostalgia for the great church played a crucial part in the continued dominance of the basilican format in France to the end of the Middle Ages, although in some cases this reflected the need to complete older basilicas in a properly sympathetic style. The Flamboyant naves of the cathedrals of Auxerre (*see* AUXERRE, §1(i)), Troyes (*see* TROYES, fig. 2), Orléans (rebuilt from 1601) and Metz, or St Ouen at Rouen (*see* ROUEN, fig. 7), maintained the proportions of their earlier choirs, revealing their period only in details of tracery and mouldings. Yet throughout the northern half of France—in Normandy, (Nantes Cathedral, begun early 15th century), Lorraine (Saint-Nicolas-de-Port) and southern Champagne (the ultra-conservative elevation of Notre-Dame-de-l'Epine, begun *c.* 1410)—the basilican plan was commonly retained.

Many of these trends emerged intermittently in 14th-century Valois palace architecture. Their conservative chapels were all paraphrases of the Sainte-chapelle form, but many of the royal palaces adopted features—simplified wall surfaces, intersecting shafts with bases—hitherto associated with low-status architecture (cellars, undercrofts etc). These were assumed into the realm of the high art at the Salle des Gens d'Armes beneath Philip the Fair's Grand Salle in the Palais de la Cité (1299–1323), Paris, and the ground-floor interior of the Tour Maubergeon (*c.* 1390) of the ducal palace in Poitiers. Such features could easily be transferred from here to an ecclesiastical context. The Flamboyant juxtaposition of bare wall and intricate passages of tracery was anticipated in Guy de Dammartin's synthesis of an austere military substructure and an ethereal Rayonnant superstructure at Mehun-sur-Yèvre Castle (begun 1367; ruined).

From these tentative intimations, mature Flamboyant eventually emerged in the 1430s and 1440s along the Loire

18. France, Cléry-Saint-André, Notre-Dame, interior looking east, 1449–85

and the lower Seine. Notre-Dame, Cléry (see fig. 18), and St Aignan, Orléans, highlighted the aesthetic possibilities of juxtaposing sharply linear elements (English-looking flowing tracery and richly profiled arcade arches) with plain wall surfaces (polygonal piers and much blank walling between arcade and clerestory), and then allowing them to interpenetrate by removing all capitals. The result, an interior of understated elegance enlivened by piquant contrasts, was to inspire such Parisian churches as St Séverin, St Gervais-St Protais and St Germain-l'Auxerrois at the end of the century. More conservative, but no less influential, was the elevation of the choir (begun 1436) of St Maclou, Rouen, the steep, three-storey interior of which, with a typically Norman 'grill' triforium and capital-less, deeply moulded arcades (*see* ROUEN, §IV, 3), may have inspired a distinguished sequence of Norman and Vexin basilicas, including the south transept (?first third of the 15th century) of Notre-Dame, Le Grand Andely; Notre-Dame (*c.* 1430–40), Vernon; and, with simple columns, the choir (1450–87) of Notre-Dame, Caudebec-en-Caux; Notre-Dame (begun 1477), Alençon; and St Michel, Pont-l'Evêque.

Some of the details at St Maclou were seemingly borrowed from Germany. Although some German influence might be expected in the border territories of Alsace and Lorraine, such as the star vaults of Saint-Nicolas-de-Port (begun 1481) and the west façade (begun 1460) of Toul Cathedral, which may reflect knowledge of the two-towered plan for the façade (*c.* 1410) of Regensburg Cathedral, nothing in Rouen, apart from the Parler-like pendant bosses in the late 14th-century south porch of St Ouen, anticipates the Parlerian placing of the eastern choir pillar on the axis of the church at St Maclou and the consequent diagonality of the apse and its disalignment with the chapels behind it. This inspired the axial choir pillars of St Paul, Le Neubourg, Notre-Dame, Caudebec-en-Caux, and St Pierre, Caen, and a general loosening of chevet plans from the 15th century, by pulling the western half of the Lady chapel into the ambulatory, as at St Etienne (begun 1505), Bar-sur-Seine, and La Madeleine (1498–1501), Troyes, or pushing the apse eastwards into it, as in Martin Chambiges's St Etienne (from *c.* 1502) at Beauvais. St Maclou's façades may also be German-inspired. The earliest precedents for the tiers of diagonal-facing, ogee-topped niches and clusters of tapering and rotated pinnacles on the transepts are the steeples of Prague, Vienna and Ulm; for the projecting, three-sided west porch, Maria am Gestade in Vienna, St Martin at Landshut, and the triangular west porch of Regensburg Cathedral. This again prefigured a group of late 15th-century projecting porches in Normandy at Notre-Dame, Alençon, La Trinité, Falaise, Notre-Dame, Louviers (see fig. 19), and St Vincent, Rouen.

The reconciliation of a three-dimensional and essentially miniaturistic vocabulary of pinnacles and niches with the

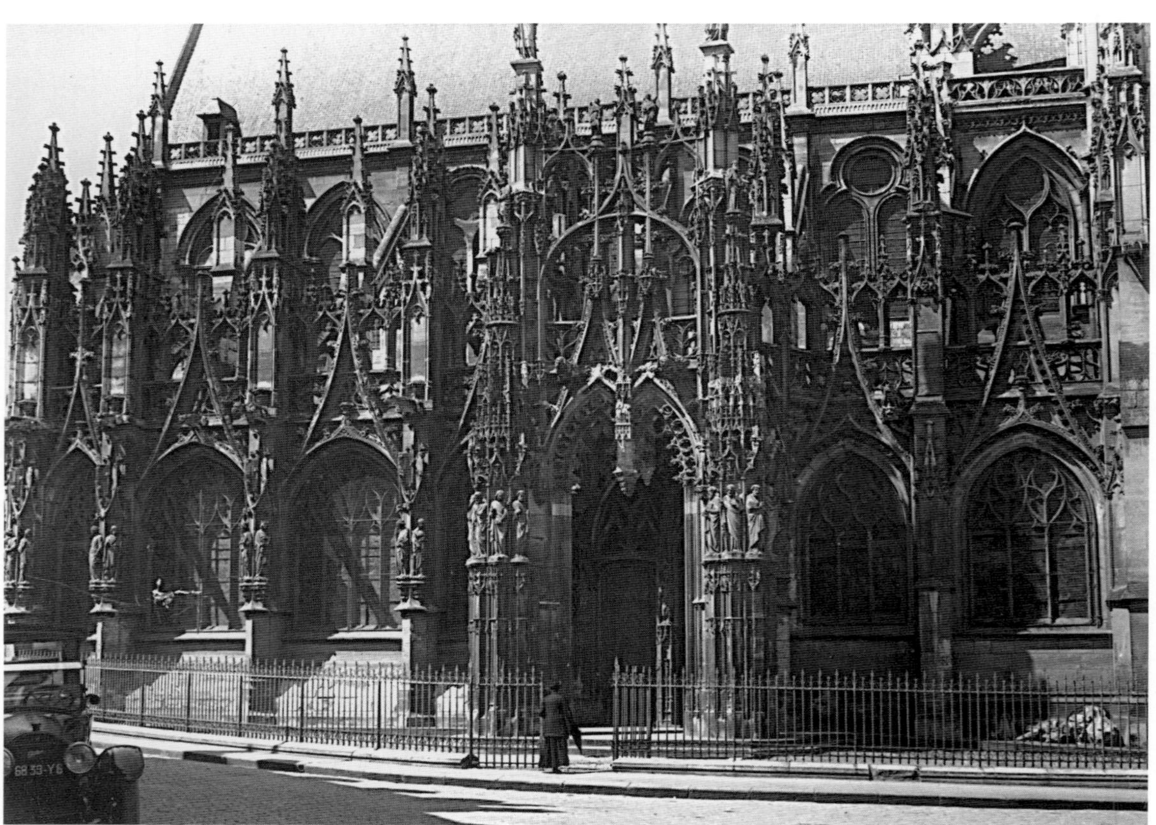

19. France, Louviers, Notre-Dame, south façade, late 15th century

flat and monumental character of the traditional great church façade was one of the principal achievements of Martin Chambiges (*see* CHAMBIGES, (1)), the most prolific French architect between *c.* 1480 and *c.* 1530, when economic recovery led to the late revival of the Flamboyant. Chambiges endowed his façades for the cathedrals of Sens, Beauvais and Troyes (*see* TROYES, §3(i)(a)) with micro-architectural elements to create a new mobility and depth. The portal zone spreads outwards by extending its niches into the flanking buttresses, which at Beauvais (for illustration *see* CHAMBIGES, (1)) and Troyes take the form of staircase turrets, their polygonal sides splayed back towards the portals and the rose window. The transformation of the portal buttress into a niche-encrusted polygon was taken up by Jacques Le Roux and Roulland Le Roux in the central portal of the west façade (begun 1508) of Rouen Cathedral and in the north transept façade of Evreux Cathedral, with staircase turrets based on those by Chambiges. The increasing diagonality and mobility of the façade was most fully developed in the design for the uncompleted west façade (*c.* 1500–20; destr. 1845) of St Ouen, Rouen. To enlarge the miniature forms of altarpieces and screens to the scale of a High Gothic façade was prohibitively expensive: the cheaper stone-cutting needed for the new Renaissance aesthetic and its antique-based ornament, as in the grotesquely inflated details of Pierre Chambiges's south transept façade (1530–38) of Senlis Cathedral, was among its many advantages.

BIBLIOGRAPHY

L. Schürenberg: *Die kirchliche Baukunst in Frankreich zwischen 1270 und 1380* (Berlin, 1934)
M. M. Tamir: 'The English Origin of the Flamboyant Style', *Gaz. B.-A.*, 6th ser., xxix (1946), pp. 257–68
R. Sanfaçon: *L'Architecture flamboyante en France* (Quebec, 1971)
A. Villes: *La Cathédrale de Toul: Histoire et architecture* (Toul, 1983)
U. Albrecht: *Von der Burg zum Schloss: Französische Schlossbaukunst im Spätmittelalter* (Worms, 1986)
M. Bideault and others: *Ile-de-France gothique*, Monuments de la France Gothique, 2 vols (Paris, 1987–8)
M.-C. Burnand: *Lorraine gothique*, Monuments de la France Gothique (Paris, 1989)
A. Erlande-Brandenburg: *La Cathédrale* (Fayard, 1989)
J. Gardelles: *Aquitaine gothique*, Monuments de la France Gothique (Paris, 1992)

(v) Low Countries. The architectural history of the late medieval Low Countries reflects less its position between Burgundy and the Empire than traditional ties and local allegiances. The real benefactors of church and civic architecture were the towns, in particular the newly rich towns of Brabant and the coastal cities of Zeeland and Holland rather than the giant Flemish metropolises of Ghent, Bruges and Ypres. Flanders was to play no formative role in the creation of Netherlandish Late Gothic.

As in northern Germany, distinctions of patronal wealth were registered in the broad division between the hall church and the basilica, the latter reserved only for the ambitions of the urban patriciate. Hall churches figure most prominently in the coastal areas of Flanders and in the eastern provinces bordering on German lands. The Flemish group are all in brick, usually with three parallel wooden roofs (e.g. Onze Lieve Vrouwekerk, Damme; *c.* 1300; partly destr. 1725), while the 'eastern' halls are usually vaulted, and by the early 15th century the St

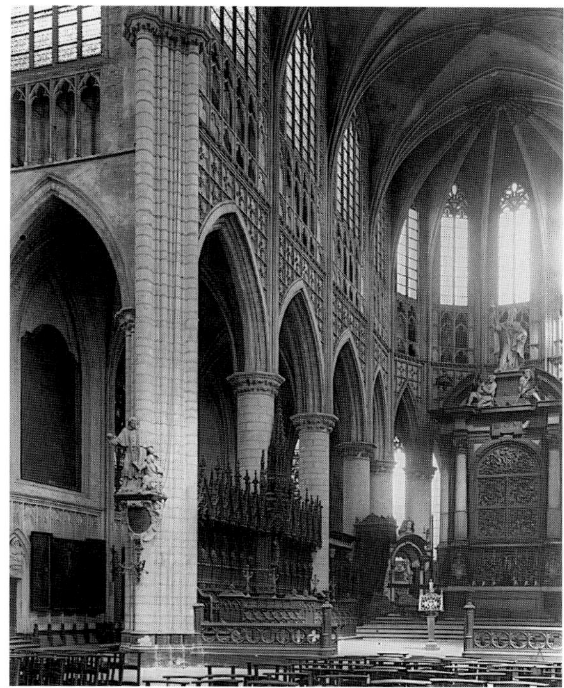

20. Low Countries, Mechelen, St Rombouts, interior of choir looking east, begun *c.* 1342

Jacobikerk, Utrecht, St Michaelskerk, Zwolle, and particularly St Martinus, Venlo, had achieved a spacious elegance comparable to the later Westphalian hall churches (*see* §(iii) above).

In contrast, the collective achievement of Netherlandish great churches forms a noteworthy episode in European Late Gothic architecture. The series opened with three colossal choirs, all begun within a generation (*c.* 1340–70), at St Rombouts, Mechelen, Antwerp Cathedral and St Janskerk, 's Hertogenbosch (*see* 'S HERTOGENBOSCH, §2). The last in the line was the colossal chevet (uncomplete) at Antwerp Cathedral, begun in 1521. At a time when great church building in northern Europe had almost ceased, towns in the Netherlands, mainly in Brabant and what is now southern Holland, which previously had little or no experience of Gothic architecture, produced more than 30 great churches, many of cathedral scale. The initiative sprang from the ideal of 'cathedral Gothic' as the highest expression of civic virtue, although other inducements included civic rivalry, phenomenal industrial and commercial wealth and the promotion of many town parish churches to collegiate status with the consequent need to extend or rebuild choirs.

Netherlandish Late Gothic began in Brabant with the foundation of the choir (begun ?1342) of St Rombouts, Mechelen (see fig. 20), and Antwerp Cathedral (begun 1352; *see* ANTWERP, §IV, 1). Their slim, elegant, tracery-clad elevations introduced the refinements of northern French late Rayonnant, although Antwerp's two-storey elevation, with its interior clerestory passage and elaborately moulded, almost capital-less, arcades, was to have a less immediate impact than Mechelen's three-storey format with simple arcade columns and tall 'grill' triforium. The latter, reminiscent of the most sophisticated Norman Rayonnant (e.g. Rouen Cathedral, nave clerestory), was part of the fashionable repertory that made Mechelen's Picard architect, Jean d'Oisy, and his principal successors, the brothers Jacob van Tienen (*fl* 1377–1405) and Hendrik van Tienen, so successful in Brabant in the second half of the 14th century. Jean d'Oisy's Onze Lieve Vrouw ten Poel (1358–75) at Tienen has a chapel choir in a Netherlandish tradition that goes back to Notre-Dame (1311–77) at Huy, but its Sainte-Chapelle-like delicacy must have encouraged the continuation of the format in Brabant and the Meuse Valley into the early 16th century, for example at Onze Lieve Vrouwe, Tongeren, Notre-Dame du Sablon, Brussels, and St Martin, Liège. Similarly the set-piece essays in Rayonnant decoration by the van Tienen brothers, separately or in partnership, at St Sulpitius, Diest, Brussels Cathedral, the choir clerestory of St Janskerk, 's Hertogenbosch, or the portal to the old belfry of Brussels Hôtel de Ville, show the extent of their infiltration into the leading Brabant workshops.

The choir of Mechelen inspired a prolific series of Brabant great churches, extending into the early 16th century, and modifying the Mechelen elevation format only in details: St Janskerk (begun *c.* 1370), 's Hertogenbosch, Onze Lieve Vrouwekerk (begun *c.* 1400), Breda, St Pieterskerk (begun 1409–10), Leuven, which has some of the earliest flowing tracery in the Low Countries, Ste Waudru (begun 1450), Mons (Hainault), and St Gummarus (choir complete in 1515) in Lier. The conservatism of these churches is made explicit in the documented deliberations over the design of Ste Waudru (Mons, Archvs Etat), when prospective local architects were sent by the nuns to visit and report not only on the churches of Leuven and Mechelen but also the much older cathedrals at Tournai and Brussels (Philipp).

The spread of the Mechelen type outside Brabant was paralleled by its rapid assimilation in the 15th century into southern Holland, at St Bavo, Haarlem (*see* HAARLEM, §3), the Grote Kerk, Dordrecht, the Nieuwe Kerk, Delft, the Oude Kerk, Amsterdam (*see* AMSTERDAM, fig. 7), and the Pieterskerk, Leiden. These giants were all built in brick with a few stone dressings, on cruciform ground-plans of 'cathedral' amplitude, but with a reduced Antwerp-type elevation of two storeys, with an arcade of round columns, and a small balustrade running in front of a tall clerestory passage. A number of the most important churches were directed by Antwerp architects as well as those based at Mechelen: Evert Spoorwater (*d* 1474) and Herman de Waghemakere, both from Antwerp, worked variously at Haarlem, Dordrecht, St Willibrordusbasiliek, Hulst, and St Gertrudiskerk, Bergen op Zoom.

Despite its stylistic introspection, Netherlandish great church architecture was occasionally sensitive to the achievements of its neighbours. The choirs of St Nicolaaskerk (begun 1369), Kampen, and NOTRE-DAME-DE-HAL (1399–1409) owe their drum-like exteriors to the simplified chevets by Peter Parler. The vaults (?1440s) in the transepts of St Janskerk, 's Hertogenbosch, are Parlerian nets and the south porch displays the motif of large, crossed ogee arches modelled on those that crown the octagonal storey of the Strasbourg Cathedral spire. Yet these German influences were wholly isolated. This separation is all the more surprising since Germany and the Low Countries were the only areas to develop a consistent Late Gothic tradition of very elaborate prodigy towers.

As in Germany, single western towers were consistent with both Romanesque traditions and civic hubris. The great sequence of Netherlandish steeples, among them some of the most impressive *tours de force* of Late Gothic architecture, began with the single axial tower (1321–82) of Utrecht Cathedral (see fig. 21). With its two clearly defined storeys and short crowning octagon, it established the general format of all Netherlandish steeples, although its block-line silhouette was followed only at St Janskerk, Maastricht (almost a pastiche), Onze Lieve Vrouwe (all but tower destr. 1787), Amersfoort, and the Martinikerk, Groningen. A more sophisticated design, with smoother transitions and more complex surface effects, appeared simultaneously in the north tower of Antwerp Cathedral (*see* ANTWERP, fig. 8) and the west tower of St Rombouts, Mechelen (both extended above the square stage in the 1480s); the intended design of the latter's spire (unexecuted) is preserved in an accurate mid-16th-century drawing (Brussels, Bib. Royale Albert 1er, B.R. 11 1354 (6453)). It is an indication of the priority given in the Netherlands to civic architecture that the novel feature of both these towers—their sophisticated transition between square lower storeys and a delicately buttressed polygonal lantern and spire—was anticipated by Jan van Ruysbroeck's great steeple (1449–55) for Brussels Hôtel de Ville (*see* BRUSSELS, fig. 10).

21. Low Countries, Utrecht Cathedral, view from east; tower built 1321–82

Many of the tower designs that followed Antwerp and Mechelen were by the KELDERMANS, such as St Lieven, Zierikzee, St Jacobskerk (begun 1525), Antwerp, St Gertrudiskerk (most destr. 1747), Bergen op Zoom, and St Katharinakerk, Hoogstraten; only the latter was completed, probably because it was in the cheaper material of brick. The colossal, three-spired westwork (begun 1507; destr. 1612–30) for St Pieterskerk, Leuven, built by Joost Massys (1463–1530), suffered both demolition and collapse; but the original three-towered design by MATHEUS DE LAYENS is echoed in the tabernacle (*c.* 1450; h. 12.2 m) in the church itself and in the three-towered gable façades of Leuven Stadhuis (1448–63). In the Netherlands flamboyant steeple ornament was applied, with no sense of indecorum, to the façades of some of the finest town halls of the early 16th century, such as those designed by the Keldermans or the Antwerp cathedral architects at Middelburg, Ghent (*see* GHENT, fig. 5) and the first design for Mechelen. It is perhaps fitting that the urban patriciate, who funded so many unfinished towers, ensured that their ornamental splendours should at least survive in the centres of civic government.

BIBLIOGRAPHY

D. Roggen and J. Withof: 'Grondleggers en grootmeesters der Brabantse Gothiek', *Gent. Bijdr. Kstgesch.*, x (1944), pp. 83–209

M. D. Ozinga and R. Meischke: *Gothische kerkelijke bouwkunst* (Amsterdam, 1953)

H. E. van Gelder and J. Duverger, eds: *Kunstgeschiedenis der Nederlanden*, i (Utrecht, 1954)

E. Haslinghuis and C. Peeters: *De dom van Utrecht* (The Hague, 1965)

R. Hootz, ed.: *Kunstdenkmäler in den Niederlanden: Ein Bildhandbuch* (Berlin, 1971)

A. J. L. van der Walle: *Gothic Art in Belgium* (Brussels, 1971)

J. H. van Mosselveld, ed.: *Keldermans: Een architectonisch netwerk in de Nederlanden* (The Hague, 1987)

K. J. Philipp: 'Sainte-Waudru in Mons (Bergen, Hennegau): Die Planungsgeschichte einer Stiftskirche, 1449–1450', *Z. Kstgesch.*, li/3 (1988), pp. 372–413

(vi) Italy.

(a) Introduction. (b) The south, the Veneto and Lombardy. (c) Tuscany and its influence.

(a) Introduction. Late medieval architecture in Italy responded flexibly to the diverse cultural influences (Byzantine, Moslem, northern Gothic and Classical) and the country's developing patchwork of conflicting political systems: the tyrannical governments of Lombardy, Emilia and Piedmont in the north; the largely republican city-states of Tuscany and Umbria; the Angevin kings of Apulia and Naples in the south; and the maritime republics of Genoa and Venice. After 1308 the Papacy ceased to be a source of architectural patronage. Internal rivalries guaranteed further diversity, particularly among the city-states of central Italy. Even in a single city the stylistic contrasts between the fortress-like Palazzo Vecchio, the choir of Santa Croce, influenced by the Sainte-Chapelle in Paris, and the marble-encrusted exterior of Florence Cathedral, all associated with ARNOLFO DI CAMBIO, testify to the differing needs of distinct, often competing, urban institutions (*see* §(c) below).

The results of this fragmentation are obvious in the eclecticism of Italian Gothic, which was compounded in the 15th century by the more fundamental antagonism between a flourishing Late Gothic in Lombardy and the Veneto, and the revival of antique forms in Tuscany. Any common factors in Italian later Gothic (except in Angevin architecture) can be found in a distrust of modernity. The Italians were profoundly historicist, proud of their inheritance as the guardians of the Classical past. Gothic was identified as something essentially alien, and even at the height of its brief popularity in the 14th century the Early Christian traditions of polychromatic stone cladding, free-standing bell-towers and spacious wooden-roofed basilicas were never wholly abandoned. The rediscovery of antiquity in 15th-century Florence may be considered only the most systematic and successful of a long series of attempts to recover a style that the Italians could call their own. Continuity with the Roman past centred principally on wealthy towns and developed civic life. The 14th century was the golden age of the Italian city-state, especially in Tuscany, where inter-civic architectural rivalries and the growth of communal urbanism flourished within the precepts of Roman *civitas.*

In contrast, the proliferation and relative poverty of the Italian bishoprics, and the transfer of much of their architectural power, including the construction and upkeep of cathedrals, to civic governments, meant that there are fewer great churches in Italy than in France, Spain or England: cathedrals and their construction, especially in central Italy, were revered as the heart of a city's religious and communal life. As a corollary to this civic pre-eminence, the architectural power of the friars, the urban leaders of Italian spirituality, was greater throughout Italy than elsewhere. In the 13th century they had been the principal missionaries of Gothic in the Italian peninsula (*see* §1(vii) above) and they continued to create the most refined syntheses between local Romanesque traditions and northern Gothic.

(b) The south, the Veneto and Lombardy. The Angevin kings showed the same fashionable generosity towards the mendicants as their royal contemporaries in France and England (*see* §§(ii) and (iv) above), and imported French architects to Naples as part of a pro-Papal and anti-Imperial policy. The pattern of Neapolitan mendicant, and mendicant-influenced, architecture had been set at S Lorenzo (*see* §1(vii) above) *c.* 1270. The modification of the contrast between its Rayonnant chevet and its wooden-roofed *nef unique* of Romanesque simplicity became the main theme of several early 14th-century Neapolitan friars' churches: the naves of S Pietro a Maiella and S Domenico Maggiore (1283–1324), for example, resemble a 12th-century Apulian basilica, while the Sainte-Chapelle-like choir of S Maria Donnaregina (founded 1307) is the purest transplant of French Rayonnant anywhere in 14th-century Italy. Only in S Chiara (founded 1310) was the choir's identity finally absorbed into a barn-like nave, wooden-roofed, single-aisled and articulated by the Romanesque and Cistercian device of in-drawn buttresses between low side chapels.

The mendicants in Venice and the Veneto in the first half of the 14th century also developed a refined but simplified synthesis of local Romanesque and northern Gothic. The gradual transformation of a traditional Lombard brick basilica, with cylindrical columns and exterior pilasters and corbel tables, into a Rayonnant system of

22. Italy, Venice, Ca' d'Oro, façade, 1422–40

sharply delineated vertical spaces, terminated in transepts and choir by brilliantly glazed polygonal apses, was marked in an impressive sequence that had led from S Lorenzo (founded 1280), Vicenza, developing through S Anastasia (begun *c.* 1290), Verona, and S Nicolò (early 14th century), Treviso, to maturity in Venice in the Dominican SS Giovanni e Paolo (*see* VENICE, fig. 22) and the Franciscan S Maria Gloriosa dei Frari (both begun 1330s). Yet the product was still local in character, especially the high, polylobed, wooden roof of S Nicolò, Treviso, an example of the ingenious roof carpentry that constituted one of the Veneto's main contributions to Italian 14th-century architecture.

It is indicative of the shift in interest towards secular architecture that the largest single-span roof in medieval Europe was built, like a vast upturned hull (*c.* 1306; destr. 1420; rebuilt 1756), over the Palazzo della Ragione in Padua. The Doge's Palace (begun 1340; *see* VENICE, §IV, 6(i)) is a traditional north Italian palazzo comunale with ground-floor arcaded loggias and a main council-chamber above, but it is made typically Venetian by the delicacy of its marble arcades, the flat textile-like polychromy of its upper walls, its Islamic cresting and the general emphasis on light, colour and movement. The structurally subversive idea of a palace façade composed largely of open tiers of delicate Gothic arcading dominated Venetian architecture to the end of the Middle Ages, for example in the Ca' d'Oro (1422–40; see fig. 22) and the Ca' Foscari (1452).

Outside the Veneto, the initiative in secular architecture lay with such increasingly powerful local families as the della Scala and Visconti, who secured their positions through conventional land-based or town castles and also through a new type of urban fortress. The Castello Visconteo (*c.* 1360; part destr. 1527) in Pavia, for example, blends the town palace with the monastic cloister, within the town fortifications but planned as an isolated and moated symmetrical block round a courtyard reinforced by four corner towers (*see* VISCONTI (i), (3)).

The Cistercian and Early Gothic tradition of Piedmont, Emilia and Lombardy was reworked in the 14th century. Wide, low proportions were retained for a group of Lombard hall churches, headed by S Lorenzo in Mortara, but the only hall church to reflect any interest in the attenuated spaciousness of contemporary German halls was Asti Cathedral (1323–48) in Piedmont. The screen façades of Crema (*c.* 1341) and Cremona (*c.* 1350) cathedrals might, but for a few decorative details, belong to the early 12th century. Even the ambitious S Maria del Carmine (begun 1370) in Pavia has an archaic Cistercian plan, a Romanesque screen façade and a Lombardic double-bay system. The short-lived creativity of Lombard architecture around 1300 was concentrated on brick bell-towers, for example at the Cistercian abbey of Chiaravalle Milanese, the Torrazzo of Cremona Cathedral and the elegant fusion of Lombardic multiple arcading and Gothic verticality at S Gottardo (1336) in Milan.

Only at the end of the 14th century did Lombard architecture look beyond the Po Valley. Milan Cathedral (founded 1385) was the most ambitious attempt to come to terms with northern Late Gothic (*see* MILAN, §IV, 1(i)(a) and VISCONTI (i), (4)). French and German masons were imported to work alongside Italians, provoking inevitable conflicts regarding taste and building practice (*see* MASON (i), §IV, 3(iii)), and Milan became the principal channel for northern Gothic influence in Italy until the end of the 15th century. The structure, however, remains Lombardic, especially its five-aisled nave, which recalls S Tecla (4th century AD) in Milan, the three-aisled transepts with projecting end chapels (e.g. Piacenza and Parma cathedrals), the domed crossing (Como Cathedral) and the contrast between an exceptionally dark nave and a choir accentuated by enormous windows. Over this cautiously traditional framework, the stability of which caused much unjustified northern misgiving, was laid a fancy dress of the latest northern details that echoed and even anticipated some of the liveliest caprices of French and German Late Gothic, but was to have no lasting influence.

(c) Tuscany and its influence. North of the Papal states, northern Rayonnant was radically accepted and understood only in Tuscany and Umbria. Civic oligarchies ensured that experiments in the new style were concentrated on towers and façades to which were applied combinations of Rayonnant tracery ornament and monumental statue cycles with traditional Tuscan polychromatic marble incrustation and mosaic decoration. The design (Siena, Mus. Opera Duomo) attributed to Giotto for the campanile of Florence Cathedral presents a typically Florentine format of cubic body and progressively increasing fenestration, incongruously crowned by an octagonal openwork spire (unexecuted; *see* FLORENCE, §IV, 1(iii)(a)) modelled directly on Freiburg im Breisgau Cathedral. The executed west façade (begun 1310) of Orvieto Cathedral and its preparatory drawings (*see* ORVIETO, §2(ii)(a) and fig. 3) show experimental adjustments of mosaic and sculpture to linear and geometric motifs borrowed from the west front of Reims Cathedral and the south transept façade of Notre-Dame, Paris. The common factor in this synthesis may have been metalwork, for the Orvieto façade resembles an enlarged version of the cathedral's reliquary of the Holy Corporal (1337–8; for discussion and illustration *see* UGOLINO DI VIERI) and betrays close knowledge of Plan B for the façade of Strasbourg Cathedral (*see* §1(iii)(a) above). Tuscan infatuation with German Rayonnant may also have owed much to Sienese goldsmiths' work, for a goldsmith, Lando di Pietro (*d* 1340), was appointed *capomaestro* of Siena Cathedral in 1339, and the façade of the baptistery (begun 1316) is both a Tuscan paraphrase of Plan B and the closest approach in Italy to a northern Rayonnant façade.

Throughout the 14th century shrine buildings, furnishings, reliquaries and portals were decorated with extravagant displays of Rayonnant ornament combined with coloured marbles and inlays, for example at S Maria della Spina (after 1333), Pisa, the tabernacle (begun 1352) in Orsanmichele (*see* CIONE, (1) and FLORENCE, fig. 16) and Simone Talenti's marble nave portals for Florence Cathedral. Yet the main body of the church remained dependent on Romanesque and Early Christian traditions, as in the continued use of striped polychromatic cladding. Early Christian pretensions were given a new Roman authority in Florence from the 1290s by the arrival of Arnolfo di Cambio. At Santa Croce (begun *c.* 1292; *see* FLORENCE, §IV, 4 and fig. 18) a Cistercian and local mendicant system of raised choir and eastern chapel arches (e.g. S Francesco, Cortona) was combined with a lightweight wooden-roofed nave derived from Orvieto, but on a scale that emulated the largest Early Christian basilicas of Rome. Not surprisingly, the project for the new cathedral in Florence, begun in 1294 and only partly realized, had the same gravitas, with a façade reminiscent of a Roman theatre's *scaenae frons* and an unvaulted nave in the style of Santa Croce. This contrasted with the enormous trefoil-plan east end, slightly smaller than the present choir, radiating from a domed octagonal crossing, which spanned the whole breadth of the nave and aisles. Perhaps intended to outclass the earlier dome at Siena, Florence's main municipal adversary, the Florence cupola, which was based on the octagonal plan of the Baptistery, slightly enlarged in the later 14th-century and triumphantly realized by Brunelleschi (*see* DOME, §1), became the model for the centralized churches of the Renaissance (*see* FLORENCE, §IV, 1(i) and fig. 12).

The sheer scale of Arnolfo's projects in Florence initiated a Tuscan taste for gigantism that frequently exceeded its architects' structural knowledge and experience, especially when some were primarily painters or goldsmiths. The walls of the campanile of Florence Cathedral, which Giotto had designed as only 1.5 m thick to support a shaft more than 100 m tall, were hastily thickened after his death. The extensions of Siena Cathedral (begun 1339; abandoned 1348; *see* SIENA, §III, 1(i)) were designed to outshine Orvieto (*see* §1(vii) above) and Florence by combining their 'Early Christian' size and lightweight spaciousness with more up-to-date rib vaults. At Florence work on the nave restarted in 1357 to a new design by Francesco Talenti that was more successful in supporting colossal rib vaults over a gigantic space (only 4 m lower than the choir of Beauvais Cathedral), but only after tie-bars had been introduced to remedy alarming cracks. The design combined elements from the masterpieces of Florentine church architecture (see fig. 23): the piers from Orsanmichele, the corbelled balustrade from Santa Croce, the oculi and square-vaulted bays from S Maria Novella. Its impact in Tuscany, however, was limited to the Loggia dei Lanzi (from 1376) in Florence and the reconstruction of Lucca Cathedral (from 1372).

By the end of the 14th century the great church enterprises and the civic, communal independence that had financed them were everywhere in decline. Paradoxically the growing power of absolutism and single-family oligarchies in 15th-century Lombardy, just when Florence was abandoning its Gothic past, inspired a spectacular afterglow to the achievements of 14th-century Tuscany. The façade of Monza Cathedral (completed 1396), for example, is clearly Tuscan. In Bologna Matteo Gattapone introduced Florentine forms in the Collegio di Spagna

23. Italy, Florence Cathedral, nave by Francesco Talenti, interior looking west, from 1357

(1365–70), while Antonio di Vincenzo's S Petronio, begun in 1390 but never finished, is Lombardy's culminating tribute to 14th-century Tuscan architectural sophistication. The quotations from Florence Cathedral seem only fitting for the leading church of the commune: the form of its pillars, its vast spaciousness and the (unrealized) dome over a prominent crossing (*see* BOLOGNA, fig. 5). A typically Lombard gigantism was added to this, however, in the shape of a brick-built corpus with five aisles (the outer in the form of chapels), staggered in height and clearly derived from Milan Cathedral, which was intended to outstrip Milan and Florence in both length and height. The many disparate strands of Italian Gothic were finally drawn together at S Petronio with elegant clarity and soaring spaciousness.

BIBLIOGRAPHY

A. M. Romanini: *L'architettura gotica in Lombardia*, 2 vols (Milan, 1964)
H. Dellwing: 'Studien zur Baukunst der Bettelorden im Veneto', *Kstwiss. Stud.*, xliii (1970)
E. Arslan: *Gothic Architecture in Venice* (London, 1972)
W. Braunfels: *Mittelalterliche Stadtbaukunst in der Toskana* (Berlin, 1979)
G. Lorenzoni: 'L'architettura', *La Basilica di San Petronio in Bologna*, ed. L. Bellosi and others (Bologna, 1983), i, pp. 53–124
J. White: *Art and Architecture in Italy, 1250–1400*, Pelican Hist. A. (Harmondsworth, 1987)

(vii) Spain. By 1300 the pilgrimage to Santiago de Compostela, which had linked Spanish culture to the achievements of northern Europe, was no longer an effective channel of French influence; while the sensitivity to Parisian-based culture shown by the 13th-century rulers of Castile had been replaced by introversion and stagnation. The Spanish climate favoured cool, dark interiors; it encouraged a characteristically flat exterior silhouette by allowing vaults to be covered by flat roofs and it rendered obsolete the tall, gabled frontispieces of northern Gothic façades. Liturgically, the 12th-century practice of giving over the whole of the eastern arm of the church to the sanctuary (capilla mayor), and removing the choir (*coro*) into the eastern bays of the nave, separating the two spaces by a prominent crossing, sometimes dramatically crowned by a lantern tower (*cimborio*), became the standard arrangement for ambitious Spanish churches to the end of the Middle Ages. More than any other French-inspired cathedral of the 13th century, Toledo exercised a continuing

fascination for Late Gothic architects, partly owing to its metropolitan status, and partly because its slow building progress made it a continuously prestigious foyer for architectural talent well into the 15th century (*see* §1(vi) above; TOLEDO, §IV, 1).

(a) Catalonia, to *c*. 1450. (b) Castile, Aragon and Andalusia, to *c*. 1570. (c) Hispano-Flemish style and the last Gothic cathedrals, *c*. 1475–1593.

(a) Catalonia, to c. *1450.* It was in the coastal cities of Catalonia and Levante that a new Gothic—at once civic, royal and distinctly Spanish—first emerged in the early 14th century. Catalonia was the commercial heartland of the kingdom of Aragon and the headquarters of a maritime empire stretching from the Balearic islands to Naples and Athens. As in Hanseatic Germany, central Italy and the other leading centres of late medieval urban patronage, architects in Catalonia fashioned a distinctive regional style by fusing mendicant simplicity with French 'cathedral Gothic', which produced a style not dissimilar to *Backsteingotik* or Italian civic architecture, in which unarticulated wall surfaces were combined with bold handling of vast interior spaces.

This Catalan version, however, owed much to royal intervention. The formative buildings, the Dominican and Franciscan churches of Barcelona (both mid-13th century; destr.), were sponsored by James I (*reg* 1213–76). The design, a luminous choir opening directly on to a darker, very wide, single-aisled nave, the vaults of which were buttressed by the internal walls of cellular chapels, proved remarkably flexible for both secular and ecclesiastical purposes. The unvaulted version of the scheme, in which the wooden roof rested on large diaphragm arches, a system already common in local Cistercian dormitories at POBLET ABBEY and Santes Creus, was preferred by the Carmelites and taken up by James II (*reg* 1291–1327) in his palace chapel of S Agata (1302–6) in Barcelona. It was then adapted for the giant halls of a series of ambitious Catalan civic and royal buildings, notably in Barcelona, of a grandeur and richness without parallel in Spain: the main chamber (Saló dels Cent; begun 1369) of the town hall, the hospital of Santa Creu (begun 1401) and the grandiose reception hall (Saló del Tinell; 1359–70) in the Palau Reial Major. In a royal context the vaulted type could be combined with exquisite and judiciously placed Rayonnant tracery, as in the Clarissan church at Pedralbes (founded 1326–7), Barcelona, or its choir could be embellished with a ring of radiating chapels, as in Palma de Mallorca at S Francesc (begun 1314) and S Jaume (begun *c*. 1320). On the grandest scale, for example at S María del Pi (begun *c*. 1322; *see* BARCELONA, §IV, 3), the format acquired a particular dignity.

No great church in Catalonia could escape the legacy of this royal-sponsored and largely mendicant architecture. Barcelona Cathedral was begun in 1298: its cellular side chapels, attenuated transept and the prominence of its main transverse arches, resembling diaphragm arches, all echo local mendicant patterns (*see* BARCELONA, §IV, 1 and fig. 5). These are ingeniously interwoven with 'cathedral Gothic' references, some derived from the southern French cathedrals associated with Jean Deschamps (the chevet is based on Narbonne, the clustered piers on Clermont-Ferrand and Limoges), but most still followed Bourges and Toledo. In particular, the Bourges principle of spatially bringing together the separate elevation systems of the inner aisles and main vessel was used to mingle the largely 'cathedral' references in the central space with the 'mendicant' character of the side elevations.

The spatial, and specifically Catalan, aspects of this accomplished synthesis were highly influential, but its concessions to French Rayonnant attracted few followers: an exception was the almost identical chevet (1312–47) of Girona Cathedral. Similarly the quotations from Toledo Cathedral found little favour, although the device of vaulting a chevet in alternating square and triangular bays was adopted in the choir chapels of Tortosa Cathedral (begun 1346) and the ambulatory of S María de la Seu (begun 1328), Manresa. In most Catalan great churches, however, French decorative veneers were discarded in an effort to distill the cathedral's spatial and structural power. In Barcelona, for example, S María del Mar (begun 1329; *see* BARCELONA, §IV, 2) borrowed the cathedral's plan and stepped section, but otherwise developed Catalan mendicant traditions in its provision for 33 cellular chapels and in the interior's austerity and structural audacity, with the vast central vault seeming to float over wafer-thin walls and attenuated columns.

The last and most ambitious Catalan churches seem to have been intended to push the structural system of Gothic architecture to its physical limits. The nave of Palma de Mallorca Cathedral (revised *c*. 1350; see fig. 24) has a prodigious series of stepped-up spaces, rivalling the dimensions of the largest Gothic churches, such as those

24. Spain, Palma de Mallorca Cathedral, interior looking east, begun 1306

with similar five-part sections at Bourges, Milan, Cologne and Beauvais, and it exceeds them all in void-to-masonry ratio, for its walls were built thin, and its bare, octagonal piers are the most attenuated supports in any Gothic basilica. This astonishing sense of weightlessness is matched by a luminosity unprecedented in Catalonia. Although Palma was never completed, its visionary fusion of light and space may have influenced the deliberations in 1416 over the nave design of Girona Cathedral (*see* MASON (i), §IV, 3(ii)). The single span (w. 22.25 m) that was approved required the construction of the widest of all Gothic vaults. It also guaranteed greater luminosity, for many of the advisers insisted on large rose windows in the eastern gable wall.

The austerity of much Catalan Late Gothic was often relieved by concentrating elaborate Rayonnant and Flamboyant decoration on the portals, cloisters and towers. The Portal del Mirador (1390s) at Palma de Mallorca Cathedral displays some of the earliest Flamboyant tracery in Catalonia. In secular architecture, the façade (from 1399) of Barcelona Town Hall dramatically contrasts stretches of unadorned wall with lavish portals and window tracery in a manner later adapted in 15th-century Castilian churches. The luxuries of ecclesiastical Gothic spilled over into the most characteristic of Catalan civic spaces, the Llotja (market-exchange): at Barcelona (1380–92) the hall-like arcades resemble those of the cathedral and at Palma (begun 1425) Guillem Sagrera combined spiral columns and exquisite Flamboyant window tracery.

In particular, cloisters provided an opportunity for virtuoso tracery design, which might be of a conventionally French Rayonnant cast (e.g. Pamplona Cathedral, north walk; 1317–55; *see* PAMPLONA, §2), geometrically more intricate and capricious (e.g. Vic Cathedral; 1324–1400; rebuilt 1806), reflective of the latest trends in English curvilinear tracery (e.g. Santes Creus Abbey; 1332–51) or on a scale worthy of the general Catalan taste for gigantism (*see* LLEIDA, SEU VELLA). Towers were often unadorned prismatic shafts, for example at S Feliú (1368–92), Girona, and in Barcelona at Pedralbes and S María del Pi, but they could also sport the most elaborate and advanced tracery. At Valencia Cathedral, for example, the crossing *cimborio* (*c*. 1330–60) displays tracery of Rhenish complexity, while the architect of its free-standing, richly traceried belfry (El Miguelete; begun 1381) was sent to Narbonne, Lleida and elsewhere to learn from their towers.

(b) Castile, Aragon and Andalusia, to c. *1570.* The audacity and openness of 14th-century Catalan architecture contrasts sharply with the artistic stagnation of Castile. The friars never played a formative role in Castilian architecture, and the completion of its great 13th-century cathedrals kept alive a certain conservatism, for example at Palencia Cathedral (begun 1321) and S María, Castro-Urdiales. Many later 14th-century churches reverted to the old Cistercian-based elevation of heavy arcades and a short, dark clerestory separated by large stretches of bare wall, such as at the old cathedral (now S María) of Plasencia and S María la Antígua, Valladolid. The former sensitivity of northern Spain to French culture was regained only under Charles III, King of Navarre (*reg* 1387–1425). French artists were brought to work on the imposing OLITE CASTLE (begun 1399) and the ingeniously planned chevet of Pamplona Cathedral (begun 1397), which shows the influence of Bayonne Cathedral, the collegiate church at Uzeste and even St Maclou, Rouen.

Elsewhere in northern and central Spain, especially under the Trastamara kings of Castile (1369–1474), there was a flourishing tradition of MUDÉJAR craftsmanship. Gothic was either wholly suppressed or transformed into an Islamic brick vernacular of extraordinary decorative complexity, for example in the cloister (1402–12) of the Hieronymite monastery at GUADALUPE (*see also* BRICK, §V, 3(i)(h)). Nearly all architecture in Aragon was in brick and *Mudéjar* dominated to the virtual exclusion of Gothic, such as in the ribbons and bows of geometrical *laceria* patterns on the portal and apse of S Domingo, Calatayud, in ribs and keystones carved with stalactite ornament, and in repetitive brickwork trellis patterns (*ajaracas*). *Mudéjar* appears most prominently in the numerous detached, minaret-like, brick belfries, which at first were square in plan (e.g. Teruel Cathedral) and later, under the influence of the stone bell-towers of Catalonia and Valencia, octagonal, for example the Torre Nueva (1504; destr. 1894) in Saragossa.

Seville Cathedral (begun 1402; *see* SEVILLE, §IV, 1) was to have a great impact on the extraordinary revival of great church architecture in central Spain in the early 16th century (see below). From the first its design was coloured by the triumphalist megalomania that usually inspired the most ambitious Gothic churches, especially those, such as the cathedrals of Cologne, Prague and Milan, built in a style that had been imported into a traditional and potentially resistant cultural context. It was intended to be, and is, the largest of all medieval cathedrals: a colossal rectangle (11,020 sq. m) formed by five aisles and two rows of outer cellular chapels, which resembles the generous breadth of Toledo Cathedral rather than the low mosque that it replaced. Its cross-section, however, ignores the precedent of Toledo in favour of double side aisles of equal height, more closely resembling the tallest Gothic structures, such as the choirs of Reims, Beauvais, Amiens and Cologne, and Heinrich von Gmünd's suggested cross-section for Milan (*see* MASON (i), §IV, 3(iii)), all of which are distinguished from the Bourges group by their giant clerestories. Seville's disappointingly low clerestory, and the consequent awkward flattening of the trajectories of its flyers, suggests that originally a much taller central vessel was intended, topped by the highest vaults in Christendom.

The employment at Seville of Norman and Breton craftsmen in the 1440s and 1450s tallies with the very early appearance in Spain of north-west French Flamboyant mannerisms, including overshooting mouldings in the piers and a balustrade beneath the clerestory. A similar influx of foreign craftsmen, largely from northern France, the Low Countries and the Rhineland, revived Castilian architecture and sculpture from the mid-15th century, particularly in the cathedral workshops at Palencia, León, Burgos and Toledo, which provided long-term employment. Although these churches offered little opportunity for structural innovation, there was scope for the application of flowing tracery and decorative vaults to steeples, cloisters and the characteristically Iberian mausoleum chapel, a large, semi-independent, centralized structure that opened loosely off the aisles and ambulatory, and joined with other chapels to form a cluttered and picturesque fringe around the body of the church.

German, Flemish and north French architects and sculptors set the tone for this new Castilian Flamboyant at Toledo and Burgos cathedrals. Flowing tracery had appeared sporadically in Spain since the mid-14th century (e.g. Santes Creus Abbey), and had flourished in Catalonia, for example on the high altar (1425–33) of Tarragona Cathedral and on Marc Safont's façade for the chapel of S Jordi (completed 1434) in the Palau de la Diputació General, Barcelona. In Castile it was first used lavishly by Hanequin de Bruselas in completing the funeral chapel of Alvaro de Luna (1440s) in Toledo Cathedral (*see* EGAS, (1)), which influenced many other memorial chapels in Castile, ultimately Burgundian in their lavish heraldic and tracery decoration, but traditionally Spanish in their vaulting and ground-plans. The chapel's triradial vault, its straight sides made polygonal by squinch-like triangular bays, connects it to the most inventive aspect of Castilian 13th- and 14th-century architecture, perhaps inspired by the ingenuities of Islamic vaulting, the distinguished series of centralized and star-vaulted chapter houses (e.g. Burgos, Palencia and Salamanca) and chapels (e.g. Barbazana Chapel, Pamplona Cathedral; S Ildefonso Chapel, Toledo Cathedral).

Lierne vaults, however, seem to have been introduced in the Visitation Chapel (1440–42) at Burgos, built by the German Juan de Colonia, whose Rhenish origins are plain in the openwork western spires (1442–58) of Burgos Cathedral. More consistent with local usage was his *cimborio* (1457–95; destr. 1539; replaced 1540–68) over the crossing, which was much praised for its delicacy and scale, and triggered a splendid series of crossing lanterns, in which Muslim-influenced vaults merged perfectly with the Spanish fascination for tall, luminous and semi-independent centralized spaces; examples include those of S Juan de los Reyes (by Juan Guas; see below) in Toledo, Orense Cathedral (1505; by Rodrigo de Badajoz), Saragossa Cathedral (1520) and the replacement lantern at Burgos itself (*see* BURGOS, §2(i)(a)).

(c) Hispano-Flemish style and the last Gothic cathedrals, c. *1475–1593.* The creative dominance of the Toledan and Burgalese workshops, their preference for florid surface ornament, elaborate vaulting and well-lit polygonal spaces continued into the later 15th century to shape the most inventive period of Spanish Late Gothic, the HISPANO-FLEMISH STYLE that flourished under Ferdinand II of Aragon and Isabella of Castile, and the higher nobility and prelates of their household. Decoratively, it contrived to reconcile Gothic and *Mudéjar*-Muslim forms; structurally, it added nothing to older conventions of space and planning. Its masterpieces are often façades, cloisters and centralized mausolea. It was devised to promote a rampant and predominantly sculptural decoration, combining figural carving, ostentatious heraldry and flamboyant Gothic tracery with clear references to Islamic ornament, sometimes to specific *Mudéjar* patterns, but often to the general Islamic preference for counter-curving arches and repetitive, small-scale motifs.

The focal point of this ornamental and devotional aesthetic was the gigantic wooden *retablo mayor*, a Spanish peculiarity of an unprecedented size that was bound to have a unique influence on the surrounding architecture (*see* RETABLE, §1). It made any ambulatory invisible, and at Seville, Astorga and Plasencia cathedrals the traditional chevet plan was rejected in favour of a simple, polygonal capilla mayor. The choirs of Zamora and Tuy cathedrals, for example, were remodelled in the late 15th century to accommodate the *retablo*, while the new cathedral at Salamanca (see below) had a flat east end. Unlike contemporary Netherlandish and German altarpieces, the *retablos* were not free-standing, but structurally and visually part of the architecture, devised with the closest cooperation between architect and sculptor (sometimes the same individual). The aesthetic and liturgical possibilities of transferring their profuse figure-carving and lavish micro-architecture to other symbolically distinctive parts of the church, particularly its thresholds, were dramatically exploited by Alonso de Burgos, Bishop of Palencia (*reg* 1485–99) and Queen Isabella's confessor. In both form and position the *trascoro* (completed 1519) at Palencia Cathedral, perhaps by Simón de Colonia, is halfway between a *retablo* and a façade (see fig. 25). The façade of the Colegio de S Gregorio (1487–96) in Valladolid is a reredos in stone (for illustration *see* VALLADOLID), across which the achievements of the Catholic monarchs are trumpeted by woodwoses, proto-Renaissance putti and an ostentatious heraldry.

Hispano-Flemish Gothic is best exemplified in the work of its two leading exponents, Simón de Colonia (*see*

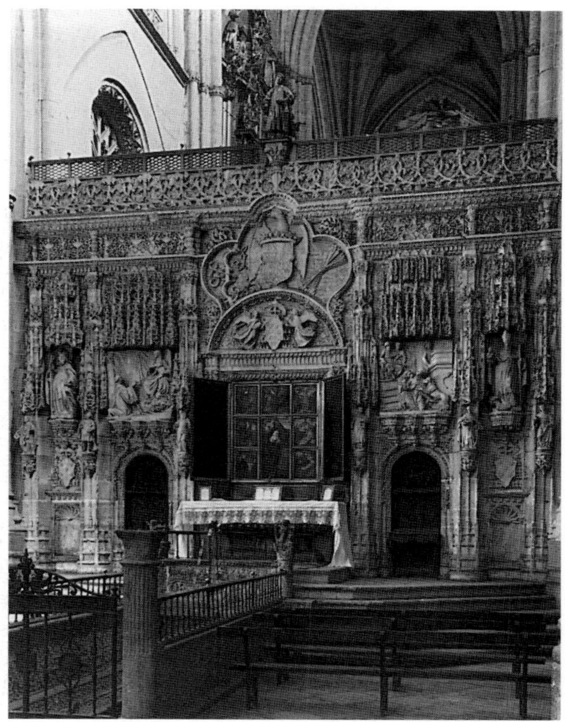

25. Spain, Palencia Cathedral, *trascoro*, complete by 1519

COLONIA, (2)) representing the Burgalese origins of the style, and JUAN GUAS, representing the Toledan. Guas's masterpiece was S Juan de los Reyes (founded 1476) in Toledo. Its expansive east end, reminiscent of an enlarged, centralized mausoleum chapel, is encrusted with an indescribably rich blend of heraldic sculpture, Flamboyant tracery and *Mudéjar* decoration, including stalactite capitals, broken ogees framed by *alfices*, and an Islamic net vault over the *cimborio* (see fig. 26). Like the Muslim chains hung as trophies around the exterior, the Islamic quotations inside the church celebrate the appropriation of a conquered culture. No other Spanish Gothic interior surpassed this profligate richness, although Juan also used similar idiosyncratic details in other commissions: broken ogees, which became almost his trademark, dominate the upper arcades of the cloister of S Juan (*see* TOLEDO, fig. 3); distinctive lierne vaults were deployed in Segovia at Santa Cruz (begun 1482) and El Parral (eastern parts *c.* 1480). His secular flirtations with a *Mudéjar* vernacular (*see* GUADALAJARA, PALACIO DEL INFANTADO) also employed diamond-studded walls, stalactite corbels and *artesonado* ceilings. Significantly, Enrique Egas's design for the Capilla Real (1506–21) at Granada used a simplified version of the plan of S Juan, and ornament was restricted to a lavish exterior portal (*see* GRANADA, fig. 1) and lierne vaults with curving ribs.

26. Spain, Toledo, S Juan de los Reyes, by Juan Guas, interior looking east, founded 1476

The restrained elegance and preference for contrasts of bare wall and intricate surface ornament in Egas's work set the tone for the 16th-century cathedrals of Spain, the last cathedrals of the Middle Ages. The ideal of the Gothic great church persisted in Spain when it had ceased to have any real value elsewhere, and Gothic continued to be thought appropriate even after secular architecture had adopted *Mudéjar* forms and the PLATERESQUE STYLE. This can be explained only by the higher clergy's continuing dominance over Spanish life, coupled, perhaps, with an implicit feeling that Gothic embodied an essential Spanishness and evoked a glorious past that had been lost after the kingdom's incorporation into the Habsburg Empire in 1516. The earliest, Plasencia Cathedral (1497–1578; unfinished; *see* PLASENCIA), is also the most impressive. Egas laid out the choir as a vastly enlarged forerunner of the Capilla Real, but the driving force behind the cathedral's final form was probably JUAN DE ALAVA, who, in the closest approach in Spain to the intricate vistas devised by Benedikt Ried and his followers (*see* §(iii) above), conceived the transepts, crossing and (unfinished) nave as an extraordinarily wide hall church, with slender, finely moulded piers from which a delicate net of curving ribs spins out across a space as wide as Notre-Dame, Paris.

The more conventional system of Seville Cathedral was reverted to at Salamanca and Segovia cathedrals, with cellular chapels and an elevation marked by very strongly scanned bays, articulated by tall and bulky compound piers, supporting a low, balustraded clerestory. At Salamanca (begun 1513), however, various proposals were suggested before the final design was fixed, including lower side aisles than at present and, more surprisingly, a hall church. This solution had never been popular in Spain, but now it was chosen for the new cathedrals of Plasencia and Saragossa. The latter's seven-part section and short nave (1540s–50s) is the most extreme example of the Spanish preference for lateral extension. The basilican final form of Salamanca was rescued from ponderousness by the fantasy of the curving vaults devised by Juan Gil de Hontañón (i) (*see* GIL DE HONTAÑÓN, (1)), who also designed the last of the Spanish cathedrals, Segovia (begun 1522; *see* SEGOVIA, §2(i)). This is a slightly refined version of Salamanca, but with the significant addition of a *capilla mayor* with a proper radiating chevet, instead of Salamanca's unsatisfactory flat east end. The completion of the choir (1563–93) marked the end of almost three centuries of Late Gothic ingenuity.

For bibliography *see* §(viii) below.

(viii) Portugal. No single dynasty played such a decisive role in the formation of a country's Late Gothic architecture as the Aviz kings of Portugal. Between the accession of John I (*reg* 1385–1433) and the death of Manuel I in 1521 (*see* AVIZ, (6)), all the most creative strands of secular and ecclesiastical architecture in Portugal owed their lavish decor, ambitious scale and symbolic power, not to episcopal or middle-class patronage, but to the monarchy's fierce nationalism and ostentatious display of new riches. The rich upper bourgeoisie of Portugal's coastal towns, despite their comparable maritime economies and colonial

ambitions, were not prepared to divert their resources into the cathedral-like town churches that distinguished the coastal cities of Holland, Catalonia and the southern Baltic. Whereas the Spanish episcopacy remained the leader of great church architecture until well into the 16th century, in Portugal the bishops preserved most of their 12th-century cathedrals (e.g. Coimbra, ÉVORA and Oporto; *see also* PORTUGAL, §II, 1), and only exceptionally, and then under the pressure of Spanish fashions, rebuilt the choirs in an advanced Gothic idiom, for example at Lisbon (before 1345) and Braga (under construction 1511). On the rare occasions when a complete rebuilding was undertaken, for example at Guarda Cathedral (1504–17), the results were modest when set beside the lavishness of contemporary royal foundations, particularly those by Diogo Boitac (see below).

Like their Spanish counterparts, the Portuguese bishops encouraged the late 15th-century influx of predominantly German and Flemish craftsmen into the Iberian Peninsula, but most were metalworkers and sculptors, not architects, and the influence of their micro-architectural extravagances (*see* PORTUGAL, §IX) on masonry construction is difficult to elucidate. As nearly all important buildings were royal commissions, Portuguese Gothic was an extravagant but superficial phenomenon—a number of brilliant *tours de force* that were fuelled by a short-lived prosperity and that stood out against a background of thinly spread and unpretentious Muslim- and Romanesque-influenced buildings.

Portuguese Late Gothic found its first distinctive idiom in the royal necropolis at BATALHA, begun for the Dominicans in 1388 by John I. HUGUET, who completed most of the monastery and church with a structural audacity and decorative eclecticism that characterized Portuguese architecture to the end of the Middle Ages. The English-looking tracery that enlivens the chapter house, west façade and adjoining Founder's Chapel suggests a specific knowledge of the work of William Ramsey and of late Decorated and early Perpendicular decoration in East Anglia (*see* §(ii) above), perhaps derived through John's wife Philippa (1360–1415), daughter of John of Gaunt, Duke of Lancaster (1340–99). Huguet's structural imagination also rose to the challenges of centralized planning. The Capelas Imperfeitas, the colossal octagonal mausoleum (for illustration *see* BATALHA) laid out to the east of the church by King Edward (*reg* 1433–8), ranks with the most ambitious centralized buildings of the Gothic period, such as St Marien (1476–92) at Ettal Abbey and the Karlov Church (1351–77) in Prague, and is the most impressive Gothic version of the archetypal mausoleum of Christendom, the church of the Holy Sepulchre, Jerusalem.

Architecture in the reign of Manuel I reflected Portugal's colonial expansion and its prodigious increase in prosperity, celebrated in architecture of ostentatious vitality known, appropriately, as the MANUELINE STYLE. Its exuberance was partly derived from its eclectic mixture of Spanish Late Gothic (both Hispano-Flemish and Plateresque), Flamboyant motifs from France and the Low Countries, dense carpet-like ornament (vaguely but suggestively reminiscent of Indian decoration) and, perhaps most significantly, naturalistic ornament (shells, corals, fish, rope etc), which amounted to an iconography of Portugal's maritime achievement, and armillary spheres and heraldry that symbolized her world domination.

The earliest indications of the new style appeared simultaneously in the work of MATEUS FERNANDES I at Batalha and in one of Boitac's earliest projects, the Franciscan monastery of Jesus (*c.* 1494–8) at Setúbal. The dynamic rope-like quality of the ribs, twisted corbels and plaited spiral piers at the latter (for illustration *see* BOITAC, DIOGO) established much of the vocabulary of the Manueline style for the next quarter of a century. The style appeared in buildings of varied symbolic significance: Belém Abbey (begun 1502) and its military counterpart, the Tower of Belém (1515–20), built by Francisco de Arruda at the approaches to Lisbon as both a military bastion and a symbolic overture to Portugal's maritime glory (for discussion and illustration *see* BELÉM (i)); and the church of the Order of Christ at Tomar, which celebrated the Portuguese union of empire and chivalry (*see* TOMAR ABBEY). In the west façade at Tomar (for illustration *see* ARRUDA, (1); *see also* MANUELINE STYLE), the heraldic and naturalistic strains of European Late Gothic are carried to a sensational extreme. The cross of the Order of Christ, armillary spheres, the royal arms and even an enormous buckled garter are woven into an iconography of oceanic adventure: stone carved to resemble seaweed, algae and barnacles; string courses masquerading as ropes, chains and corks; windows dripping and oozing with voluptuous aquatic ornament. Like the contemporary branchwork of German Late Gothic, all these dissolutions of Gothic architecture's conventional and specific vocabulary into the generalized and universal language of nature seem to be associated with ideas of nationhood, history and myth. The Italian Renaissance was to find a new artistic language to embody these constructions of national mythology.

BIBLIOGRAPHY

G. E. Street: *Some Account of Gothic Architecture in Spain* (London, 1865, rev. 2/1869/*R* 1912)

P. Lavedan: *L'Architecture religieuse en Catalogne, Valence, et Baléares* (Paris, 1935)

M. T. Chico: *Historia da arte em Portugal* (Oporto, 1948)

R. dos Santos: *O estilo Manuelino* (Lisbon, 1952)

L. Torres Balbás: *Arquitectura gótica*, A. Hisp., vii (Madrid, 1952)

J. Harvey: *The Cathedrals of Spain* (London, 1957)

J. M. Azcárate: *La arquitectura gótica toledana del siglo XV* (Madrid, 1958)

M. Durliat: *L'Art dans le royaume de Majorque: Les Débuts de l'art gothique en Roussillon, en Cerdagne et aux Baléares* (Toulouse, 1962)

R. C. Smith: *The Art of Portugal, 1500–1800* (London, 1968)

P. Dias: *Historia da arte em Portugal*, ii (Lisbon, 1986)

E. Cooper: *Castillos Señoriales en La Coruña de Castilla*, 4 vols (León, 1992)

PAUL CROSSLEY

III. Sculpture.

Whether architectural, monumental or free-standing, sculpture played a central role in Gothic art. The article below discusses sculpture mainly in stone and wood (*see also* ALABASTER, §1). Chronologically, Gothic sculpture is defined conterminously with the architecture, and is held to begin in the 1130s and extend into the 15th century or the 16th, depending on location. Stylistically, the term is arbitrary. The definition depends closely on French developments, which provide a standard by which other areas may be assessed. As in architecture, however, in most regions outside France, French influence was one among many, with strong local traditions and developments. Styles in general were close to the figurative arts in other media, and the direction of influence is not always clear. The Romanesque style continued alongside Gothic for up to a century or even longer (*see* ROMANESQUE, §III), with closely related iconography and even aspects of style: over the earliest phase, division between them reflects scholarly perceptions rather than any genuine distinction.

1. Stone. 2. Wood.

1. STONE. Stone sculpture was used copiously, as architectural ornament both inside and outside buildings, on tombs and liturgical furnishings, and for statues. It was often painted: figures in particular were given naturalistic colouring (*see* POLYCHROMY, colour pl. V, fig. 2), and were often embellished with such metal or wood attachments as crowns, swords or censers; draperies could be studded with gemstones. The sculptor, as a craftsman distinct from other workers in stone, appears in the records from the late 13th century (earlier in Italy), when forms of employment such as tomb-making became an established alternative to great church workshops. In the geographical and chronological stylistic survey that follows, France, where the style developed and remained dominant until the 14th century, is discussed first. Discussion of the rest of Europe includes both the relation of each region to France and local and indigenous developments. □

(i) France. (ii) British Isles. (iii) Holy Roman Empire. (iv) Italy. (v) Low Countries. (vi) Portugal. (vii) Scandinavia. (viii) Spain.

(i) France.

(a) Introduction. (b) 12th and 13th centuries. (c) 14th century. (d) 15th century.

(a) Introduction. In the last four centuries of the Middle Ages sculpture was a major art form in France, from the great church portals of the 12th and 13th centuries to the dramatic free-standing Entombment groups of the 15th. Increased lay patronage also ensured that it appeared frequently in secular contexts. Architectural sculpture continued to predominate, but it became less obviously a substitute for the architectural members, while at the same time the architecture became more of a setting for sculpture. With the gradual acceptance of naturalistic modes of expression, forms went through various phases of idealization. From the 13th century Paris dominated both production and styles, but following the political, military and economic disturbances that shook the capital in the 15th century, centres of production became widespread across the country. While these still felt the influence of former Parisian art, it was not until Italian influences arrived in the 16th century that styles once again became more homogeneous.

See also FRANCE, §IV, 1.

BIBLIOGRAPHY

M. Aubert: *La Sculpture française du moyen âge* (Paris, 1947)
R. Jullian: *La Sculpture gothique* (Paris, 1965)

DANY SANDRON

(b) 12th and 13th centuries. The displays of statuary that adorn the portals of the great French cathedrals of the 13th century arguably represent the apogee of medieval stone sculpture. The expense and ambition reflected by the west doorways of Chartres, Amiens and Reims were seldom matched throughout the medieval period, yet much of northern France had been an artistic backwater only a century before. Few new churches were being built and few local masons were adept in the art of stone sculpture. This situation began to change during the 1120s and 1130s, as the power and prestige of the Capetian dynasty increased. New wealthy patrons emerged, now based in the cathedrals rather than the monasteries, and skilled architects, masons and sculptors were attracted to the area by the prospect of fresh commissions.

Most surviving French Gothic sculpture was carved for church doorways, but on the great cathedrals this was often extended to buttresses and the upper façades. Internal sculpture, with the exception of capitals, was less common. Figural capitals were eschewed in favour of foliate designs, with crockets giving way to naturalistic foliage at Reims in the mid-13th century. The figural panels on the inner west wall of Reims Cathedral (*c.* 1250–60; *see* REIMS, §IV, 1(ii)) and the *Apostles* (1241–8) of the Sainte-Chapelle (*see* PARIS, §V, 2(ii) and fig. 35) are both unusual, if not unique, ensembles. Surviving cloister carvings date mainly from the 12th century and include a small column statue (*c.* 1145) and a lavabo (*c.* 1200) from Saint-Denis Abbey, fragments from Châlons-sur-Marne (*c.* 1175–80; *see* CHÂLONS-SUR-MARNE, NOTRE-DAME-EN-VAUX) and the chapter house façade (*c.* 1160–65) of the former abbey church of St Georges at Saint-Martin-de-Boscherville.

Most non-architectural sculpture was also produced in an ecclesiastical context. Many church furnishings were destroyed during the late 18th century, but fragments of choir-screens are preserved at Chartres (*c.* 1230–40) and Bourges (*c.* 1260; *see* BOURGES, §II, 1(ii)(c)). More funerary sculpture survives, including the idealized effigies on the tombs of *Henry II, Eleanor of Aquitaine* and *Richard I* (early 13th century; *see* FONTEVRAULT ABBEY) and *Robert the Pious* and *Constance of Arles* (*c.* 1264; Saint-Denis Abbey). Surviving tomb-chests are usually carved with weepers or funeral processions (*see* WEEPER). Tomb recesses include that of *c.* 1180 reset in the north transept of Reims Cathedral.

French sculptors in the 12th and 13th centuries were anonymous, itinerant laymen. They would have designed iconographic programmes with the help of pattern books, none of which survives, and through consultation with their patrons. Elements of doorways were carved separately in workshops and then assembled as the building progressed, the sculptor always working ahead of the builders. Although few traces survive, it is probable that all carvings were painted and gilded while the scaffolding was still in position.

The revival of stone sculpture in the north. The new churches built in and around Paris in the mid-12th century are regarded as the first manifestations of Gothic architecture (*see* §II, 1(ii)(a) above) and their carved decoration can be viewed similarly as the embodiment of a new aesthetic. As in Romanesque buildings, it was concentrated on the main doorways, but the first Gothic doorways neither slavishly imitated those produced by the well-established regional schools of Burgundy and south-west France (*see* ROMANESQUE, §III, 1(ii)(f) and (g)), nor did they break completely free from the past. Instead they borrowed elements from diverse sources and presented them in innovative combinations.

This is illustrated clearly at Saint-Denis in the central of the three west portals (*c.* 1130–35; *see* SAINT-DENIS ABBEY, §II, 1(i) and fig. 6). An established theme, the *Last Judgement*, was selected for the tympanum, but the supernatural energy of Romanesque representations such as those at Conques (*see* CONQUES, STE FOY, §1 and fig. 2) and Autun Cathedral (*see* AUTUN, §2(ii) and fig. 2), was subdued. Heaven and Hell were relegated to the inner archivolt, while the three outer archivolts were carved with the 24 *Elders of the Apocalypse*, now arranged tangentially rather than radially. Sculptors in Burgundy and western France had experimented rather awkwardly with tangential voussoir figures, for example at Anzy-le-Duc Priory and Angoulême Cathedral, but at Saint-Denis the form was adopted with a new assurance. Not every feature of the Saint-Denis doorways was necessarily derived from Burgundy, Languedoc or western France. There are close parallels in Italy for the decoration of the doorjambs and the sculptural style has been compared with Mosan metalwork. The column statues at Saint-Denis, however, may have been the first such use on portal embrasures (*see* SAINT-DENIS ABBEY, fig. 5).

In a sense the COLUMN STATUE was merely the last and most successful in a series of experiments from *c.* 1125 into the application of large-scale sculpture to the jambs of doorways (*see* MOISSAC, ST PIERRE, §2; VEZELAY, STE MADELEINE, §2(ii)). It was to become the most distinctive element of French Gothic portal sculpture and the most liberated from its architectural context. Together, column statues and tangential voussoir figures created continuous carved bands that visually unified portal compositions. Their potential to carry figures and themes that elucidated the important central image on the tympanum was to be explored throughout the following century.

The Early Gothic phase. The Saint-Denis portals must have made a great impression on visiting dignitaries and certainly contained intimations of future developments, yet their direct influence cannot be detected in surviving monuments. The Royal Portal (*c.* 1145) of Chartres Cathedral, on the other hand, is the supreme example of a formula that proved extremely popular throughout the royal domain (*see* CHARTRES, §I, 2(i)). While the three Saint-Denis doorways had separate identities, those of Chartres were unified by horizontal bands of sculpture, which ran across the embrasures and over the slender buttresses that defined each bay. At Chartres the aesthetic impact of the pointed arch on doorways is evident for the first time: a comparison between the tympanum compositions of Saint-Denis and Chartres draws attention to the former's horizontality and the latter's verticality, enhanced by the division of the tympanum area into registers.

No triple portal scheme survives from the decades immediately after the Royal Portal, but many single doorways betray its influence. The *Christ in Majesty* (*Maiestas*) of its central doorway, an abbreviated version of the Apocalyptic vision that first became common on portals in Burgundy in the early 12th century, proved especially popular. The choice of subsidiary themes varied: *Elders of the Apocalypse* at the cathedrals of Angers (*c.* 1155; *see* ANGERS, §2(i)(b) and fig. 2) and Bourges (1160s; *see* BOURGES, §II, 1(ii)(a)), as at Chartres; saints at Le Mans Cathedral (before 1158; *see* LE MANS, §1(ii) and fig. 2) and Saint-Loup-de-Naud (1167); and scenes from the *Last Judgement* at Ivry-la-Bataille Abbey and St Ayoul (*c.* 1160), Provins.

The enthroned *Virgin and Child* adored by angels on the south doorway of Chartres revealed a new interest in Marian iconography, appropriate to the foremost shrine of the Virgin in France. A further development in the iconography of the Virgin occurred *c.* 1165 at Senlis Cathedral, north of Paris. The *Coronation of the Virgin* on the tympanum of the west doorway is accompanied by the *Tree of Jesse* on the archivolts, the *Death* and *Assumption of the Virgin* on the lintel, and Old Testament figures on the embrasures bearing attributes that enable them to be identified (*see* SENLIS, §1). After Senlis, Marian iconography grew in popularity, while the *Maiestas* was largely abandoned.

Twisted poses and convoluted draperies lend a restless energy to the figures at Senlis, particularly those on the archivolts. This lively style, ultimately derived from Mosan metalwork (*see* ROMANESQUE, §VI, 3), can be seen in a modified form at Châlons-sur-Marne (see above) and on the central west doorway (*c.* 1175–80) of NOTRE-DAME, MANTES. More popular towards the end of the 12th century was a restrained classicizing style characterized by soft draperies, which can be seen on the doorways (*c.* 1185–1200) of Sens Cathedral (*see* SENS, §1(ii) and fig. 3), the *Virgin and Child* (*c.* 1180) reset over the north transept doorway at Reims Cathedral and the Saint-Denis lavabo. Portal embrasures underwent certain structural changes around this time. At Senlis, and to a greater degree at Sens, plinths were now treated as a suitable field for low-relief sculpture. A further modification was introduced at Sens by replacing the stepped recession of embrasures with a smooth, sloping wall surface. This encouraged a more three-dimensional treatment of column statues, which now occupied a less rigidly defined space: at Chartres column statues had been surmounted by separate architectural canopies and capitals, but at Sens these elements were integrated.

Laon and Chartres. The west doorways (*c.* 1195–1205) of Laon Cathedral are more expansive than any previous example and are integrated within the overall façade design to a hitherto unparalleled degree (*see* LAON, §1(ii) and fig. 3). They are preceded by intercommunicating porches bearing figural scenes in their gables, thus challenging the supremacy of the tympana. Sculpture extends on to the upper storeys of the façade, including cycles of the *Creation* and the *Liberal Arts* around the two lancet windows and, on the aediculae of the towers, sixteen oxen. Much of the surviving figure sculpture reveals a more intimate knowledge of antique sculpture than earlier monuments, with fine drapery sensitively delineating rounded limbs. Two of the doorways are devoted to the Virgin, with the *Coronation of the Virgin* in the centre and the *Adoration of the Magi*

27. *Visitation*, column statues, north transept, east portal, Chartres Cathedral, France, *c.* 1220

on the north, while the *Last Judgement* is depicted on the south. The *Adoration of the Magi* is accompanied by the *Virtues* and *Vices*, and prefigurations of Mary's virginity.

The main themes of Laon reappeared on the six transept portals (1205–10) of Chartres Cathedral, but were augmented by numerous subsidiary scenes. On the *Last Judgement* doorway, in the centre of the south transept, the *Apostles* were removed from the tympanum on to the embrasures, where they carry the instruments of their martyrdom. This increased the importance of the intercessors, the *Virgin* and *St John*, on the tympanum; the warnings of 12th-century representations were replaced by a more hopeful message. The archivolts were carved with choirs of angels and the programme was expanded by flanking doorways dedicated to martyrs and confessors. The two *Virgin* portals on the north transept were accompanied by a third, carved with *Old Testament* scenes. On the *Adoration* doorway the *Annunciation* and *Visitation* (see fig. 27) were enacted by column statues. Sculptors from Laon seem to have been employed at Chartres, but the relaxed poses of the Laon figures had now stiffened and draperies thickened. The sheer scale of the programmes may have necessitated different working methods at Chartres, and stylistic uniformity crept in.

Amiens, Paris and Reims. A new figural style that appeared *c.* 1220 on the west doorways of Notre-Dame, Paris, is characterized by voluminous drapery, which falls in broad folds and conceals the limbs (see fig. 28; *see also* PARIS, §V, 1(ii)). The figural pose is no longer described by the drapery and attempts at *contrapposto* are more superficial. This style was favoured by the workshop responsible for the west portals (*c.* 1220–35) of Amiens Cathedral, where it became increasingly mechanical, suggesting mass production (*see* AMIENS, §1(ii) and fig. 3). It can be seen in its simplest form on the column statues of the prophets *Zephanaiah* and *Habakkuk*. The doorways were conceived on a massive scale. The distinction between the portals and their porches was blurred, as the embrasure sculpture flowed on to the sides of the gabled porches and over the buttresses. Higher up the façade was a gallery of kings, a feature perhaps inspired by the aediculae of the Chartres porches and also adopted at Paris. Contrasting with the vast proportions of the architecture, the portal sculpture of Amiens appears precious rather than monumental. The steeply pointed tympana were subdivided into horizontal bands, leaving relatively little room for the focal images of the programmes. Archivolts and voussoir figures were multiplied and, by continuing the embrasures laterally, it became possible to introduce extra column statues.

The High Gothic style of Paris and Amiens spread rapidly and can be found on provincial monuments, such as the doorways of Notre-Dame (*c.* 1240), Villeneuve-l'Archevêque and Rampillon (*c.* 1245). In Paris in the 1240s this was developed into a more elegant so-called court style, which spread to all artistic media (*see also* §IV, 5(ii) below). The *Apostles* (1241–8) inside the Sainte-Chapelle are more attenuated than the Amiens column statues and demonstrate a renewed interest in movement and posture, overlaid by weighty, angular draperies. This can also be seen at Notre-Dame, on the north transept portal (*c.* 1250), the Rayonnant south transept portal (*c.* 1260) and the Porte Rouge (*c.* 1260; *see* PARIS, §V, 1(ii)(b) and fig. 33). At Reims Cathedral it appears side by side with strongly classicizing figures (*c.* 1245–55). This can be seen most clearly on the right embrasure of the central doorway of the west façade, where the 'Court' style

28. Tympanum showing the *Death* and *Coronation of the Virgin*, Coronation Portal, west façade, Notre-Dame, Paris, France, *c.* 1225–30

Annunciation (*see* MASTERS, ANONYMOUS, AND MONOGRAMMISTS, §I: JOSEPH MASTER) contrasts sharply with the 'antique' style of the *Visitation.*

The vast amount of sculpture carved for Reims Cathedral in the mid-13th century represents the culmination of High Gothic sculpture. The design of the west doorways developed tendencies implicit in those of Laon, Chartres and Amiens, but took them to the boldest of conclusions. The previously separate entities of portal and porch become totally fused in a composition that seems to stand proud of the façade itself. The tympana, still supported by lintels and trumeaux, are glazed and traceried, and the focal images of the programmes now occupy gables over the archivolts. The logical relationship between the tympanum image, the surrounding archivolt and the embrasure sculpture has been disrupted, and the impact of the main scenes (*Coronation of the Virgin*, *Last Judgement* and *Crucifixion*), now distanced from the viewer, has been drastically reduced.

Glazed tympana were not taken up elsewhere and there was soon a return to stone tympana, which might be divided into numerous horizontal registers, for example on the south transept portal (*c.* 1260–79) of Amiens Cathedral and the west portal (*c.* 1260) of Auxerre Cathedral, or compartmentalized by tracery, as on the west portal (after 1268) of Sens Cathedral. In the mid-12th century the format of Amiens spread beyond northern France and High Gothic portals were produced at the cathedrals of Bourges (1240–60; *see* BOURGES, §II, 1(ii)(b)), Poitiers (*c.* 1250; *see* POITIERS, §2(i)(a)), Bazas (*c.* 1250), DAX (1250–75) and elsewhere. This phenomenon was partly due to a decline in lucrative commissions in the royal domain, where every major cathedral had recently been rebuilt, and an increase elsewhere. Regional versions of High Gothic, for example *c.* 1250 at St Seurin, Bordeaux, were often of such a high quality that sculptors trained in northern France must have been directly involved.

BIBLIOGRAPHY

W. Vöge: *Die Anfänge des monumentalen Stils im Mittelalter* (Strasbourg, 1894)

E. Mâle: *L'Art religieux du XIIIe siècle en France* (Paris, 1898, rev. 6/1925; Eng. trans., London, 1913)

A. Lapeyre: *Des Façades occidentales de Saint-Denis et de Chartres aux portails de Laon: Etudes sur la sculpture monumentale dans l'Ile-de-France et les régions voisines au XIIe siècle* ([Paris], 1960)

W. Sauerländer: *Gotische Skulptur in Frankreich, 1140–1270* (Munich, 1970; Eng. trans., London, 1972)

W. S. Stoddard: *Sculptors of the West Portals of Chartres Cathedral* (New York, 1987)

KATHRYN MORRISON

(c) 14th century. In the 14th century sculpture emerged as an art form in its own right, and was less subordinate to architecture. Apart from some portals at the cathedrals of Rouen and Auxerre (*see* AUXERRE, §1(ii)), the era of encyclopedic sculptural programmes was over: no 14th-century façade can rival the scale of those at the cathedrals of Reims and Amiens (*see* §(b) above). Instead sculptors

tackled new genres or those that hitherto had been poorly represented, for the production of works that were portable, carved in the round or secular in purpose. The sculpture of recognizable likenesses was also rediscovered. The names of a few artists have been recorded; they and others explored the new possibilities arising from a growing interest in individualism.

Religious sculpture was still dominant, but no longer monopolized the output. There was a decline in monumental religious sculpture, although the upper levels of façades and naves and the springers of the vaults provided a setting for architectural sculpture that was more welcoming and less restraining than before. An increasing freedom in statuary is shown in such works as the *Martyrdom of St Stephen* in Limoges Cathedral and the Apostolic colleges that peopled the chancels of many churches, including St Jacques-de-l'Hôpital, Paris (figures now in Paris, Mus. Cluny). The same tendencies appear in the interior decoration (fragments in Toulouse, Mus. Augustins) commissioned between 1333 and 1344 by Jean Tissendier, Bishop of Toulouse, for a chapel in the chevet of the Franciscan church (destr. 1871), Toulouse. This avoids the academicism that afflicted sculptural programmes of the first third of the 14th century in southern France, including those in Bordeaux and Carcassonne cathedrals, which were confined merely to reproducing the previous century's formulae for monumental sculpture. This liberation of form may also be seen in the decoration of vault bosses and consoles, for example in the Sainte-Chapelle in the château of Vincennes. The relief sculpture on liturgical furnishings, including altarpieces, became more narrative in tone. The triumph of sculpture as an art in its own right, however, may be seen most clearly in the development of sculpture in the round for devotional statues of saints and, especially, the Virgin and Child, of which more than a thousand examples survive.

Patronage and the court. One of the most important innovations of the 14th century was the increasing diversity of lay patronage. The resulting demand for secular statuary developed alongside the production of higher quality religious sculpture. The example was set from above, since the initiatives of Philip IV (*reg* 1285–1314) and Charles V (*reg* 1364–80) were decisive as each sought to promote the French monarchy and the person of the king. Philip, for example, commissioned a life-size, painted series for the Gallery of the Kings in the Grand' Salle of his palace on the Ile-de-la-Cité, Paris (*see* EVRARD D'ORLÉANS), and the representations of *Louis IX*, *Margaret of Provence* and their children (now in Poissy, Notre-Dame) for the collegiate church of St Louis at Poissy (*see* CAPET, (3)). Charles V almost systematized this expression of political will half a century later, ensuring that he was represented on every major project with which he was connected. The portals of churches that he founded, such as the church of the Célestins (destr. 1770s), Paris, or enlarged, including the Augustinian church (destr.), Paris, were decorated with the figure of the King, while in the Louvre his statue also formed the focus of the series of figures on the staircase built by Raymond du Temple (*see* VALOIS, (2); *see also* JEAN DE LIÈGE (i)). Royal tombs were also made for the King's body (1364, by André Beauneveu) at Saint-Denis Abbey, his entrails (1374; now Paris, Louvre) at Maubuisson Abbey and his heart (1368, by Jean de Liège; destr.) in Rouen Cathedral.

The royal promotion of sculpture could not fail to influence other patrons' commissions. Enguerrand de Marigny (*d* 1315), Superintendent of Finances to Philip IV, placed life-size figures of himself and his wife (both destr.) in the portal of NOTRE-DAME, ECOUIS, shown presenting the church to the Virgin. Mahaut, Countess of Artois, commissioned a gallery of sculpted portraits of her ancestors for her château (destr. 1553) at Hesdin (Artois). Charles V's brothers followed his example during the second half of the 14th century, notably Jean, Duc de Berry, who had himself portrayed above the monumental chimney (*Belle cheminée*; *c.* 1380) in the great chamber of his palace (now the Palais de Justice) at Poitiers, alongside his nephew *Charles VI* (see fig. 29) and their wives (*see also* HALL, fig. 1). A sculpture of Philip the Bold, Duke of Burgundy, appears on the embrasures of the portal at the

29. *Charles VI*, from the chimney of the great chamber, Palais de Justice, Poitiers, France, *c.* 1380

Charterhouse of Champmol (*see* DIJON, §IV, 1(ii) and fig. 4; *see also* SLUTER, CLAUS, §1). Cardinal Jean de La Grange commissioned the so-called *Beau pilier* on the north side of Amiens Cathedral, on which are represented *Charles V*, his two sons and his most prominent counsellors, one of whom was naturally the Cardinal himself (*see* AMIENS, §1(ii)).

In the 14th century artistic production was directly associated with the king and his immediate followers. Princes, lay and ecclesiastical aristocracy and the king's counsellors were all active patrons, favouring materials and styles that reflected their wealth. The taste for fine materials, such as black and white marble and alabaster, the refined use of polychromy and gilding, the elegance of the figures' characteristic *déhanchement* posture, with the weight shifted slightly to one side, and the play of the draperies, with superimposed cascades of scrolling folds, created a mannered effect that was very different from the idealizing styles of the previous century. Yet the paths it followed were diverse. Some works, for example the *Virgin and Child* (early 14th century) in the parish church at Mainneville, Eure, appear almost classical in the balance between the overall composition of the figure and the handling of ornament. The realism present in others, however, betrays an anxiety that belies a definition of 14th-century art as mannered; the latter may be applied only to those works that repeat the elaborate formulae of the beginning of the century, pushing ever further the penchant for detail.

Most significant of all was the rediscovery of sculpted likenesses, which had not been made since antiquity. A comparison between the reclining figures in Saint-Denis Abbey of *Philip III* (*d* 1285; *see* JEAN D'ARRAS) and *Charles V* (1364; *see* BEAUNEVEU, ANDRÉ) illustrates well the development from the former's idealized features to the latter's prematurely aged, but still alert, expression. The figure of *Charles V* was made during his lifetime and may be considered more as a portrait from life, yet funerary sculpture was still subject to formal conventions and the weight of tradition. The psychological dimension that is the true mark of the portrait is more discernible in the statue of *Charles V* as donor (Paris, Louvre) and that of *Charles VI* in Poitiers (see fig. 29 above), in which the early stages of his madness may be sensed in a strange, lascivious melancholy. There is a startling contrast between the King's expression and the seductive frivolity seen in the accompanying statue of his wife, *Isabeau of Bavaria*.

The influence of Paris. These changes benefited from the matchless creativity arising from conditions in Paris. While the French monarchy prospered, the capital attracted artists from far afield, such as Evrard d'Orléans and JEAN PÉPIN DE HUY during the reigns of Philip IV and his sons, or Jean de Liège and André Beauneveu under Charles V. The city was in a perpetual state of agitation and commissions tailed away during crises, forcing artists to emigrate to provincial courts and centres of production at Avignon, Dijon, Bourges and Poitiers, or abroad to Prague and Cologne, all of which show strong Parisian influence. Many of the finest works are unattributed, and will probably remain so, but the few artists known by name and the sculptures associated with them are an eloquent testimony to the continual cross-fertilization of styles at the French court.

Almost every great sculptor passed through Paris. This phenomenon is typified by Beauneveu, who worked in Paris for Charles V from 1364 to 1366 (see above). From at least 1374 he was active in the south Netherlands, where his patrons included Louis de Mâle, Count of Flanders, while from 1386 he was in the service of Jean, Duc de Berry, at Bourges and Mehun-sur-Yèvre. Beauneveu benefited from the high regard in which artists were held and was given flattering titles, such as *ymagier* (figure sculptor) to the King, anticipating the cult of the individual artist that appeared in Renaissance Italy. This phenomenon can also be observed in the parallel career of CLAUS SLUTER, whose trenchant and visionary style was to fascinate sculptors in the early 15th century. His work at Dijon, for example on the Well of Moses (begun *c.* 1396; *see* RENAISSANCE, fig. 3), the portal (1390–93) of the Charterhouse of Champmol and the tomb of *Philip the Bold* (Dijon, Mus. B.-A.), has a refinement and elegance that appear to constitute a homage to French art and its diffusion into secular art, and was to offer a real alternative to the Soft style that prevailed throughout Europe at the end of the century (*see* §(iii)(c) below).

DANY SANDRON

(d) 15th century. The sculptural themes of the previous century (*see* §(c) above) were taken over with a few modifications in the 15th, but scarcely any new ones were developed. The tombs of royalty and the nobility display an even greater determination to impress. Such common themes of the Passion as Christ Carrying the Cross, the Agony in the Garden, the Man of Sorrows, crucifixes, Pietàs, the Virgin and Child, Apostles, prophets and saints were all represented in monumental form and on altarpieces. A characteristic new development was that of the Entombment with numerous fully rounded, barely life-size figures placed in a chapel-like area. Increasingly sculptors began to set up their own workshops in the towns, supplanting the dominance of the great building works. More artists are known by name from various documentary sources, but it is often difficult to assign the surviving works. The international trend represented by the Soft style (*see* §(iii)(c) below) persisted into the middle of the century, although a gradual hardening and dissolution of the unified form may be seen from the second quarter of the century. Some sculptors adopted Renaissance forms towards the end of the 15th century, but medieval attitudes may often be detected until well into the 16th. It is often difficult to distinguish precisely between individual, regional and period styles, since important artists sometimes worked in several areas, but a regional approach provides the clearest indication of the varying influences and developments throughout the century.

Burgundy. Until the second quarter of the century, when power shifted to Flanders, Dijon was the seat of the duchy of Burgundy and an important artistic centre. Claus Sluter was succeeded as *tailleur d'ymages et varlet de chambre* by CLAUS DE WERVE, who had collaborated with his uncle since 1396. The appointment of the younger man by Duke John the Fearless was intended to ensure the completion

30. Guillaume Chandelier (attrib.): tomb of *Philippe Pot*, from Cîteaux Abbey, France, *c.* 1480–83 (Paris, Musée du Louvre)

(by 1411) of the marble and alabaster tomb of *Philip the Bold* (Dijon, Mus. B.-A.). By Sluter's death little more than the rough form of the tomb had been completed. Most of the finely polished alabaster figures (*see* WEEPER) and the recumbent figure of the Duke (destr. 1793) were by the younger sculptor, who had assimilated Sluter's pathetic, expressive style to such an extent that it is difficult to determine the contributions of the two artists and their various collaborators. A large seated *Virgin and Child* (New York, Met.), formerly in the church of the Poor Clares in Poligny (Jura), retains its original rich polychromy and should be attributed to Claus de Werve. The Virgin's majestic regularity is lacking in the figure of *Jean Chousat* (*c.* 1420; Poligny, St Hippolyte) and other items made for the same church, and this raises the question of the role played by workshop assistants.

Claus de Werve's successor, JUAN DE LA HUERTA (*see also* §(viii) below), who is first mentioned in Dijon in 1431, may already have worked as one of Claus's assistants at Baume-les-Messieurs Abbey, not far south of Poligny. In 1443 Juan was commissioned by Philip the Good to complete the tomb of *John the Fearless and Margaret of Bavaria* (Dijon, Mus. B.-A.); the contract stated that the work was to be 'equal to or better than' the earlier ducal tomb at the Charterhouse of Champmol. Juan, however, left Dijon in 1456 before completing the project. His work tends to be somewhat conservative, although some very beautiful figures of the Virgin and Child have been attributed to him, including that made for Cardinal Jean Rolin II (now in Autun, Mus. Rolin) and others in Notre-Dame, Auxonne, and the parish churches at Saint-Jean-de-Losne, Rouvres-en-Plaine and Chalon-sur-Saône. The tomb was completed in 1470 with the two recumbent figures and some of the weepers by ANTOINE LE MOITURIER, a nephew and pupil of Jacques Morel (see below). Other sculptors of varying significance active in Burgundy have been identified by Camp. The tomb of *Philippe Pot* (*c.* 1480–83; Paris, Louvre; see fig. 30), which originally stood in Cîteaux Abbey and can be attributed to Guillaume Chandelier (*d* before 1502), may be regarded as a further development of the early Burgundian type of tomb represented by those at Champmol.

Berry and Bourbonnais. There were several important centres of production in this region. André Beauneveu and JEAN DE CAMBRAI, both of whom originally came from the south Netherlands, had been active in Bourges and its surroundings from 1386–7, working mainly for Jean, Duc de Berry. Although they lacked Sluter's innovative greatness, both may be described as individual and original. Some attributions, however, remain controversial. The only authenticated work of Jean de Cambrai is his collaboration on the tomb of *Jean, Duc de Berry* (1422–38; Bourges Cathedral), which was based on that of *Philip the Bold.* A *Virgin and Child* in Marcoussis Church has been identified as that made *c.* 1408 as a gift from the

Duke to the Celestine monastery near by; the linear flow of the vertical, parallel folds in low relief and the figure's unified outline would appear to be typical of Jean de Cambrai. Soon after he also worked on the tomb of *Louis II of Bourbon* (*d* 1410) and *Anne of Auvergne* (Souvigny, St Pierre).

Sculpture in Bourges seems to have declined perceptibly after Jean de Berry's death in 1416. Unfortunately very little has survived of the work commissioned by Jacques Coeur. Three prophet consoles and three reliefs on the façade of the Palais Jacques-Coeur (1443–51), Bourges, are reminiscent of the forms used by Beauneveu. Three remarkable sculptures of *St John the Baptist*, a courtier and the *Virgin and Child* (second quarter of the 15th century; Morogues Church), which are believed to have come from the Sainte-Chapelle in Bourges (*see* BOURGES, §II, 2), differ markedly from the formal severity of Beauneveu and Jean de Cambrai. In his work on the tomb of *Charles I, Duke of Bourbon, and Agnes of Burgundy* (1448–53; Souvigny, St Pierre), Jacques Morel (*see* MOREL, (2)) countered Burgundian verism with a new ideal of relaxed beauty. Michel Colombe, who was possibly born in Bourges and has been termed the 'last Gothic' French sculptor (Pradel), worked at the court of the dukes of Bourbon from 1484 (*see* COLOMBE, (1)).

Loire Valley. The most important centres in the Loire region were Tours, Loches and Angers. Jean de Cambrai's influence may be detected in Tours in the first half of the century. Some writers have attributed the tomb of *Agnès Sorel* (*d* 1450; Loches Castle) to Morel. Nine sculptors are documented as working for René I, Duke of Anjou (*see* ANJOU, II(4)). Morel, Jean Poncet (*d* 1452) and his son Pons Poncet (*fl* 1450–60), for example, were employed to make the wall tomb of *René I* and his first wife *Isabella of Lorraine* (begun 1450; Angers Cathedral; destr. French Revolution), which was in the Angevin and Italian tradition (*see* §(iv)(h) below; *see also* DELF, COPPIN) rather than that of the dukes of Burgundy and Berry. Early Renaissance motifs were introduced by Francesco Laurana and Pietro di Martino da Milano, who were in the Duke's service from 1461. Michel Colombe lived in Tours from at least 1496 until his death in 1514; his many disciples were active until the mid-16th century.

Languedoc. The important centres of production were Avignon, Rodez, Toulouse and Albi. Only fragments have survived of three monumental tombs to cardinals *Guillaume II d'Aigrefeuille*, *Jean de La Grange* and *Nicolas de Brancas*, which were installed in St Martial, Avignon, around 1400. The second of these (*see* LA GRANGE, JEAN DE) was originally at least 15 m high. The interplay of the wide, undulating, feather-edged folds indicate links with Champmol. The Belcastel workshop, which has been named after the crude and stocky figures on the tomb of *Alzias de Saunhac* (*d* 1418; Belcastel Church), was also responsible for reliefs of the *Entombment* (Rodez Cathedral) and the *Pietà* (Grand-Vabre Church). During the second quarter of the century Morel worked successively in Avignon, Rodez and Toulouse: at Notre-Dame-de-Grasse, a seated *Virgin and Child* (Toulouse, Mus. Augustins) from a *Presentation* group, has an appealing delicacy that was long influential. His workshop also worked on the south portal of Rodez Cathedral, in which town Pierre Viguier's workshop was active in the second half of the century. The superb Flamboyant rood screen made for Albi Cathedral during the first decade of the episcopacy of Bishop Louis I of Ambroise (*reg* 1474–1503), complete with a parclose screen featuring a cycle of apostles and prophets, carries echoes of the realism of such sculptors as Sluter and marks the final resistance to Renaissance ideas (*see* ALBI, §1).

Lorraine and Champagne. Sculptors in Lorraine and Champagne were open to influences from Burgundy and the Rhineland. Some 70 items, especially reliefs for altarpieces and tombs, statuettes and architectural sculpture, such as keystones, are known from a workshop active in the region of Joinville and Vignory during the first half of the 15th century, for example at St Etienne, Vignory. Their graceful outlines and stereotyped faces are indicative of the long survival of the Soft style until about the middle of the century. The *Entombment* (*c.* 1420) in St Martin, Pont-à-Mousson, is one of the earliest treatments of the theme. Towards the end of the century Troyes developed into an important centre of production in southern Champagne, with artists from the Colas, Jubert, Gailde-Halins and BACHOT families (*see* TROYES, §2). The progressive acceptance of Renaissance forms may be seen in later works, such as the choir-screen (*c.* 1508–15) in the Madeleine, Troyes, by JEAN GAILDE.

Paris and the north. The artistic decline of Paris (*see* §(c) above) was fully evident by *c.* 1420. The tomb of *Anne of Burgundy, Duchess of Bedford* (*d* 1432; Paris, Louvre), carved by GUILLAUME VLUTEN for the monastery church of the Célestins, is one of the few examples made for Parisian churches and is striking more for the detailed reproduction of the clothing than for the facial expression. The most outstanding work made in northern France (probably Lille) in the early 15th century is the alabaster *Crucifixion* altar (*c.* 1430; Frankfurt am Main, Liebieghaus), formerly in S Maria delle Grazie, Rimini (*see* MASTERS, ANONYMOUS, AND MONOGRAMMISTS, §I: MASTER OF RIMINI). Northern sculptors were sometimes strongly influenced by contemporary painters. The Master of Rimini, for example, shows the influence of the Master of Flémalle, while the hard, broken folds of the *Virgin and Child* (mid-15th century; Lille, Mus. B.-A.) originally in St Sauveur, Lille, are reminiscent of Rogier van der Weyden.

Epitaphs in relief that are particularly notable for their content include those of *Guille Lefrançois* (1446; Arras, Mus. B.-A.), *Canon Jean Lamelin* (*d* 1470; Tournai Cathedral) and *Guillaume Dufay* (*d* 1474; Lille, Mus. B.-A.), formerly in Cambrai Cathedral. Entombment groups in Normandy (e.g. Notre-Dame et St Laurent, Eu; Notre-Dame, Louviers; La Madeleine, Verneuil-sur-Avre) mainly date from the beginning of the 16th century. The most characteristic sculptural type in Brittany comprises large wayside shrines representing Calvary. One of the finest early examples (*c.* 1450–70) is at Notre-Dame-de-Tronoën, near Pont l'Abbé; it is of granite and has two registers carved with scenes from the *Infancy of Christ* and the *Passion.*

BIBLIOGRAPHY

M. de Bévotte: *La Sculpture à la fin de la période gothique dans la région de Toulouse, d'Albi et de Rodez, 1400–1520* (Paris, 1936)
G. Troescher: *Die burgundische Plastik des ausgehenden Mittelalters und ihre Wirkungen auf die europäische Kunst*, 2 vols (Frankfurt am Main, 1940)
P. Pradel: *Michel Colombe: Le Dernier Imagier gothique* (Paris, 1953)
P. Quarré: 'La Collégiale Saint-Hippolyte de Poligny et ses statues', *Congr. Archéol. France*, cxviii (1960), pp. 209–24
H. D. Hofmann: *Die lothringische Skulptur der Spätgotik* (Saarbrücken, 1962)
Statuaire autunoise de la fin du moyen âge (exh. cat., ed. P. Quarré; Autun, Mus. Rolin, 1968)
H. D. Hofmann: 'L'Atelier de sculpture de Joinville-Vignory, 1393–1442', *Bull. Mnmtl*, cxxvii (1969), pp. 209–22
W. H. Forsyth: *The Entombment of Christ: French Sculptures of the Fifteenth and Sixteenth Centuries* (Cambridge, MA, 1970)
G. Bou: *Sculpture gothique en Rouergue* (Rodez, 1971)
S. K. Scher: 'Un Problème de la sculpture en Berry: Les Statues de Morogues', *Rev. A.*, xiii (1971), pp. 11–24
G. Bou: *Sculpture gothique albigeoise* (Rodez, 1972)
J. Boccador: *Statuaire médiévale en France de 1400 à 1530*, 2 vols (Zug, 1974)
La Sculpture bourguignonne à la fin du XVe siècle (exh. cat., ed. P. Quarré; Dijon, Mus. B.-A., 1974)
P. Quarré: *La Sculpture en Bourgogne à la fin du moyen âge* (Fribourg, 1978) [Fr., Eng. and Ger. text]
F. Baron: 'Collèges apostoliques et couronnement de la Vierge dans la sculpture avignonnaise des XIVe et XVe siècles, *Rev. Louvre*, xxix (1979), pp. 169–86
M. de Bévotte: *La 'Nostre Dame de Grasse' du Musée des Augustins de Toulouse et le rayonnement de son art dans les régions voisines à la fin de l'ère gothique* (Rodez, 1982)
J.-L. Biget, Y. Carbonell-Lamothe and M. Pradalier-Schlumberger: 'Le Choeur de la cathédrale d'Albi', *Congr. Archéol. France* (1982), pp. 63–91
F. Robin: *La Cour d'Anjou-Provence: La Vie artistique sous le règne de René* (Paris, 1985)
J. Baudoin: *La Sculpture flamboyante en Champagne-Lorraine* (Nonette, 1990)
P. Camp: *Les Imageurs bourguignons de la fin du moyen âge*, Cah. Vieux-Dijon, 17–18 (Dijon, 1990)
J. Baudoin: *La Sculpture flamboyante en Normandie et Ile-de-France* (Nonette, 1992)
M. Beaulieu and V. Beyer: *Dictionnaire des sculpteurs français du moyen âge* (Paris, 1992)

ANDREAS BRÄM

(ii) British Isles.

(a) Introduction. (b) Late 12th century and the 13th. (c) 14th century. (d) 15th century.

(a) Introduction. Most Gothic sculpture in Britain is found in England, and little was produced in Scotland or Wales. Much destruction has been wrought by time and iconoclasm, but the surviving evidence indicates that, while the French type of portal programme as such was never popular, sculpture was deployed in profusion across both interiors and exteriors. Interior sculpture included large- and small-scale figure sculpture, foliage and ornamental work. The main foreign influences were from the Ile-de-France area and the Low Countries, the latter especially in the 15th century.

BIBLIOGRAPHY

E. S. Prior and A. Gardner: *An Account of Medieval Figure-sculpture in England* (Cambridge, 1912)
A. Gardner: *English Medieval Sculpture* (Cambridge, 1951, rev. New York, 1973)
L. Stone: *Sculpture in Britain: The Middle Ages*, Pelican Hist. A. (Harmondsworth, 1955, rev. 2/1972)

(b) Late 12th century and the 13th. English figure sculpture between 1190 and 1300 is characterized by a diversity despite the relative scarcity of surviving examples. Classicizing influences present in Mosan metalwork during the 12th century, especially in the work of Nicholas of Verdun from *c.* 1180, had transformed French figure sculpture by the end of the century (*see* §(i)(b) above). These aesthetic impulses were slower to affect English sculpture and, when received, were translated into recognizably English statements. The new French style was characterized by idealized faces and proportions, controlled animation of the body, and classicizing drapery flowing in closely repeated folds over the well-expressed body beneath. In England these concepts first appeared in ten life-size column figures from a *Christophores* cycle (*c.* 1200 or later; York, Yorks Mus.) intended for a portal (destr.) in St Mary's Abbey that was also formally and iconographically indebted to France (*see* YORK, §III, 2). The statues appear stiffer and more heavily proportioned than French versions, with weightier drapery in active patterns formed by deeply channelled, parallel and catenary folds.

Other English sculptors continued to draw upon earlier conventions. The figures, for example, in the wine harvest and other secular scenes on the capitals in the south transept (*c.* 1200) of Wells Cathedral retain Romanesque proportions, with short, flexible legs and squat bodies that are too small for their large heads. The emphasis on facial expression, which verges on caricature or reflects a preoccupation with likeness, gathered momentum throughout the century, for example on a limestone head (*c.* 1240; Salisbury, Salisbury & S. Wilts Mus.) from Clarendon Palace, and on corbel heads from Salisbury Cathedral and its chapter house (1220–80) and the transepts (*c.* 1250–58) of Westminster Abbey. In contrast, the relatively unrestored secular and biblical scenes in the spandrels of the blind arcades in the south-east transept (*c.* 1220) of Worcester Cathedral used a different Romanesque vocabulary. Diminutive, agile, often spidery figures with summary faces gesture broadly as they climb, stride, tiptoe or balance on the springing arches. Draperies patterned to emphasize movements are formed by close parallel folds that terminate in stiff, brittle hemlines.

The French Gothic aesthetic took root in England by 1229 with the formation of a large workshop to execute the vast sculptural programme in white lias across the west façade and towers of Wells Cathedral (*see* WELLS, §1(ii) and fig. 4). The dominant figure style of two outstanding masters supplied the main directions. The style of the first master is characterized by finely pleated V-shaped and parallel folds evoking the fluid movement of thin fabrics, although in lesser hands such folds became monotonous and the figures excessively elongated and rigid. This artist was responsible for the *Old Testament* scenes and many angels in quatrefoils, the *Virgin and Child* in the central tympanum and monumental figures in aedicules, notably several queens on the north tower. The work of the other major master is best exemplified by the central *Coronation of the Virgin* and the *New Testament* scenes, where draperies formed by broader sweeping folds and torsion in the upper body animate the figures. A more refined version of the first of these two styles is found at Winchester Cathedral in the so-called *Synagoga* (*c.* 1235–40; see fig. 31). A billowing mantle frames her swaying torso and her gown, belted tightly at the waist, falls in

31. *Synagoga*, Doulting stone, h. 1.28 m, Winchester Cathedral, England, *c.* 1235–40

many folds until it spills generously over and around her feet. This English masterpiece compares with such examples of French figure sculpture of *c.* 1220–30 as *St Modesta* on the north transept porch of Chartres Cathedral.

An intermediate stage in the transmission of the Wells style is represented by the greater interplay of sweeping curves on the drapery, concentric V-shaped folds, closely pleated cascades, mannered gestures and stances, evident in the *Annunciation* group (1253), associated with a payment to William Yxwerth, in the chapter house of Westminster Abbey (*see* LONDON, §V, 2(ii)(a); ENGLAND, fig. 25). Within the Abbey, the two censing angels in the triforium spandrels of the south transept (*see* LONDON, fig. 29) and the elegant bosses of the muniment room depart from the Wells tradition. The angel in the south-east spandrel exemplifies the changes with such distinctive characteristics as his delicate facial features, rippling drapery fluttering from his outstretched arm, and the torsion and sway of his body, lightly veiled by drapery forming folds with ridges flattened into shallow bands. This new so-called court style is reflected slightly later at Salisbury Cathedral in the choir-screen (*c.* 1260; now in the north-east transept).

The style derived from Wells can also be detected on the sculpture on the Judgement Portal (*c.* 1270s) of Lincoln Cathedral (*see* LINCOLN, §2(ii)(b) and fig. 5). It would appear that the master who carved the *Annunciation* figures in the Westminster chapter house may also have been responsible for the figures of *Church* and *Synagogue* that flank the Lincoln portal. He achieved effects through intensifying the interplay of highlight and shadow, but insistent verticals still balance the curving folds. Compared with the *Coronation* figure at Wells, the tympanum *Christ* has become stiffer, more elongated and the drapery folds flattened, sharp-edged and increasingly calligraphic. The slightly earlier angels in the triforium spandrels of the Angel choir reflect French influences of the 1240s for the first time, including the smile of the annunciate angel at Reims Cathedral. Here sculpture executed in the Wells tradition postdates ponderous, seated figures of the Angel choir with their heavy drapery rendered as broad, smooth surfaces interrupted by deep, crumpled folds.

The influence of a Parisian style of the 1260s and 1270s, which may have been introduced through portable objects, such as ivory-carvings, can be seen in the *Old Testament* scenes in the chapter house of Salisbury Cathedral (*see* SALISBURY, §2(ii)(b) and fig. 5). The figures in the spandrels, which were carved by two masters, became increasingly attenuated and mannered, and the simplified draperies more angular and linear in the work of the second master. The figures turn, twist and assume elegant poses that, in typically English fashion, dramatize the narrative. The severely weathered monumental statues (*c.* 1290–1300; *see* SALISBURY, §2(ii)(a)) in aedicules on the screen façade are stylistically unrelated to the chapter house carvings. Their fully realized three-dimensional forms are swathed in voluminous, naturalistically rendered drapery. Together with the sculpture of the Eleanor Crosses, they introduced a style that would continue into the 14th century, typified by the *contrapposto* stance with the figures leaning back slightly and the head turned and bowed; it is possible that they are the work of William of Ireland, who carved some figures for the Eleanor Cross (1291–4) at Hardingstone, Northants. The mantle, like a chasuble, is draped across the body to form cascading clusters of deeply undercut, tubular folds at the side, with hemlines breaking into crumpled folds around the feet. During the 14th century these characteristics were to become more exaggerated, losing the earlier pronounced stability and monumentality. The contemporary statues of *Queen Eleanor* (on loan to London, V&A) by Alexander of Abingdon from the Waltham Eleanor Cross perpetuated the restraint and elegance of the earlier French court style. Only the cascades of tubular folds formed on both sides of the figures' mantles reflected the stylistic conceits that enlivened drapery towards the end of the century.

See also ENGLAND, §IV, 1.

BIBLIOGRAPHY

W. St J. Hope and W. R. Lethaby: 'The Imagery and Sculptures on the West Front of Wells Cathedral Church', *Archaeologia*, lix (1905), pp. 125–204
A. Gardner: *Lincoln Angels*, Lincoln Minster Pamphlets, 6 (Lincoln, 1952, rev. 2/1960)
P. Brieger: *English Art, 1216–1307* (Oxford, 1957/*R* 1968)
W. Sauerländer: 'Sens and York: An Enquiry into the Sculpture from St Mary's, York', *J. Brit. Archaeol. Assoc.*, 3rd ser., xxii (1959), pp. 53–69
G. Zarnecki: 'The Transition from Romanesque to Gothic in English Sculpture', *Studies in Western Art* (Princeton, 1963), pp. 152–8
The Year 1200 (exh. cat., ed. K. Hoffmann; New York, Met., 1970)
P. Tudor-Craig: *One Half of our Noblest Art: A Study of the Sculptures of Wells West Front* (Wells, 1976)
——: 'Wells Sculpture', *Wells Cathedral: A History*, ed. L. S. Colchester (Shepton Mallet, 1982), pp. 102–31
Age of Chivalry: Art in Plantagenet England, 1200–1400 (exh. cat., ed. J. Alexander and P. Binski; London, Hayward Gal., 1987)

PAMELA Z. BLUM

(c) 14th century. During the 14th century sculpture was used in English churches to give aesthetic emphasis to the main façade and doorways, entrances to chapels, the chancel, altars and other significant parts of the building. This embellishment to heighten the beauty of God's House did not represent a great change in function from earlier periods, but fashion, especially in the first half of the century, was characterized by a taste for significantly more complex ornament than had been customary earlier. There was also a distinct increase in pedagogy, in maximizing the potential for figures in the round to communicate aspects of the Church's teachings.

Sculpture was used extensively for ornamentation around altars, particularly in the chancel and on the liturgical furnishings of the high altar. Before the middle of the century, lavishly carved stone altar and chancel furnishings were provided at the cathedrals of Exeter (*see* EXETER, §1(ii)), St David's, Lincoln, Old St Paul's (destr.) in London and Peterborough, at Beverley (*see* BEVERLEY MINSTER, §2) and at Southwell Minster, and in many parish churches, for example St Andrew, Heckington, St Peter, Navenby (Lincs) and All Saints, Hawton (Notts). These included stone altar screens and pulpita, *piscinae* and sedilia, and special shrine-like furnishings, such as the Easter sepulchres or Tombs of Christ in Lincoln Cathedral, Navenby, Hawton and Heckington (*see* EASTER SEPULCHRE). In addition to this decoration enhancing the central worship of God and of Christ, devotion to the Virgin and the saints was made manifest by vividly carved, painted, gilded and bejewelled images near altars. The cult of saints was further promoted by the elaborate settings for their shrines, many of which were placed on carved stone bases (Coldstream, 1976), including those of St Alban (*c.* 1302–8; rest.; St Albans Cathedral), St Werburgh (*c.* 1340; rest.; Chester Cathedral) and St William of York (remains York, Yorks Mus.).

The role of sculpture in bringing spiritual matter to lifelike intensity was of paramount importance. Figure sculpture had an immediate and powerful impact in popular religious instruction, which involved teaching by example and easily comprehensible anecdote. The Yorkshire canon Walter Hilton (*d* 1396), for example, realized its potential to act as an inspiration to the mass of the populace: 'they judge of divine things from the analogy of corporeal things' (Owst). This means of instruction is reflected in the increased predominance of carved figures in 14th-century church decoration. As well as the figures around altars, shrines and screens, numerous exterior decorative schemes in greater and lesser churches involved carved, life-size figures ranked within niches, for example on the west fronts of Lichfield Cathedral (*c.* 1290–*c.* 1320), York Minster (*c.* 1330) and Exeter Cathedral (*c.* 1350–80), the outer north porch (*c.* 1325) of St Mary Redcliffe, Bristol, the east front (*c.* 1330) of Howden Abbey and the exterior (*c.* 1320–35) of St Andrew, Heckington. Indeed, if a single feature were to be isolated as characteristic of the period, it would be the figure set within a niche, not because the form was invented in the 14th century, but because it was the main component of nearly all decorative schemes and treated with increased flamboyance and pedagogic intent. It was to the 14th century what the historiated capital was to the 12th.

Whereas in the previous century the niche was a restrained frame with plainly moulded, pointed head and carved foliage capitals, for example on the west front of Wells Cathedral (*see* WELLS, fig. 4), in the 14th century it was treated much more as miniature architecture and became a vehicle for great sculptural virtuosity, thus more overtly designating its purpose as an appropriate tabernacle for a holy scene or figure. By 1320 the typical form had a projecting ('nodding') cusped ogee head, decorated above with frilly leafed crockets and surmounted by a foliate pinnacle (*see* DECORATED STYLE). In more developed examples, including those in St Mary Redcliffe, Bristol, and the Lady Chapel (*c.* 1321–49) of Ely Cathedral, it would be set beneath a triangular-headed gable, similarly ornamented. Fictive pinnacled and lavishly crocketed buttresses separated series of niches, ornamented typically at the level of the springing of the niche head with gablets supported by tiny animal or grimacing human heads. Every part of the niche afforded scope for decorative enrichment and sometimes for carved figures illustrating stories or legends for didactic purposes. This is well exemplified in the Lady Chapel at Ely, where the spandrels of the vast series of ground-level niches form the framework for extensive narrative scenes on the *Life and Miracles of the Virgin* (*see* ELY CATHEDRAL, §1(iv)).

After the middle of the century, although niches were still a major decorative feature, stylistically their execution became less inventive and more formulaic. Canopywork became more angular and nodding ogees flattened, with more rounded cusps and sub-cusps terminating in pendant bosses. On the Neville screen (*c.* 1375) in Durham Cathedral, for example, pinnacles became more attenuated, decorated with foliate crockets that were much smaller and stiffer than was the custom at the beginning of the century. Sometimes, as at Westminster Hall (as rebuilt *c.* 1385) and Winchester College (*c.* 1390), heads of niches were heightened to reveal miniature vaults framing the heads of the figures.

The notable uniformity of figure style during the first half of the 14th century extended to the representations of ecclesiastics and wealthy mortals shown on their tombs, images of the saints and even of Christ and the Virgin. All were represented as idealized 'counterfeits', identified by appropriate clothing or attributes of status, occupation or life history. All figures, whether male or female, were represented with the weight slightly to one side, giving them an appearance of leaning in a slightly curved posture, allowing loose garments to fall in elegant drapes (*déhanchement*). Whereas 'counterfeit' representation remained the norm throughout the century, after *c.* 1350 figures were much less ethereal in appearance. This was partly a result of changing fashion, but may also have reflected an increasing familiarity with the idea of the image as an earthly representative of a spiritual being. *Déhanchement* became less marked, particularly in those figures that conformed to the current courtly preference for tight clothing and plate armour. The consequent constriction of movement was represented variously by the stylized angularity evident in the seated *Kings* on the west front (*c.* 1380) of Lincoln Cathedral or as fleshy solidity, of which the most extreme example, albeit carved by a sculptor from Brabant (*see* JEAN DE LIÈGE (i)), and that closest to portraiture, is the tomb of *Philippa of Hainault* (1367; London, Westminster Abbey). Even more traditionally and voluminously draped figures, such as the *Kings* (*c.* 1385–8) in Westminster Hall and the saints of the upper storeys (*c.* 1380) of Exeter Cathedral, have a substantial and stocky presence.

Contrasting with the sober images of saints and deceased mortals are peripheral figures such as niche supporters, roof or vault corbels or gargoyles, which are often deliberately grotesque, deformed, unruly creatures intended to illustrate episodes from the moral teachings of the Church. Particularly extensive series of this genre, which is closely related to a similar phenomenon in the borders of early 14th-century manuscripts (*see also* BORDER, MANUSCRIPT), are found at St Mary Redcliffe, Bristol, and a number of parish churches (before *c.* 1350) in the region around Sleaford (Lincs). The English delight in semi-hidden imagery in the church is also evident in the fashion for carved roof bosses (see fig. 32), which expanded in popularity as vault designs became increasingly elaborate. As with other forms of sculptural enrichment, roof bosses not only added to the beauty of the space, often carved purely decoratively as faces or foliage, but appropriate subject-matter was also used to signal especially holy parts of the church, such as the positions of important altars, shrines or the dedication of chapels.

Although there was a broad consistency of style at any single time, indicating that any skilled mason knew the current fashion and was capable of carving in it, distinct regional schools may be discerned each with their own stylistic variations and specialities, notably in eastern England, Yorkshire, the Midlands and the West Country. Studies of regional workshops (e.g. Coldstream, 1980; Dawton; Sekules) have shown that generally masons seem to have moved about within a restricted area, attached to lodges on site, unless they were 'impressed' by the sheriff for the King's works, in which case they could travel long distances (Sekules; Knoop and Jones; Colvin). There also seem to have been specialist image workshops sending finished work, notably tomb effigies, over a wider area (Gittos and Gittos). Innovation was probably only permissible within strict limitations, and the mason who carved had not necessarily devised the scheme. Masons sometimes worked collaboratively on particularly large or elaborate monuments. In such cases it is not clear whether one of the masons, a supervisory master mason, the proprietor of an image workshop, the patron or a combination of all of these was responsible for control of overall design.

32. Carved stone boss showing *Pentecost*, surrounded by the *Symbols of the Evangelists*, in the nave of Tewkesbury Abbey, Gloucestershire, England, *c.* 1345–55

BIBLIOGRAPHY

D. Knoop and G. P. Jones: *The Medieval Mason* (Manchester, 1933)

G. R. Owst: *Literature and Pulpit in Medieval England* (Oxford, 1933/*R* 1961)

H. M. Colvin, ed.: *The Middle Ages* (1963), i–ii of *The History of the King's Works* (London, 1963–82)

N. Coldstream: 'English Decorated Shrine Bases', *J. Brit. Archaeol. Assoc.*, 3rd ser., xxxix (1976), pp. 15–34

——: 'York Minster and the Decorated Style in Yorkshire: Architectural Reaction to York in the First Half of the Fourteenth Century', *Yorks Archaeol. J.*, lii (1980), pp. 89–110

N. Dawton: 'The Percy Tomb Workshop', *Medieval Art and Architecture in the East Riding of Yorkshire. British Archaeological Association Conference Transactions: Cottingham, 1983*, pp. 121–32

B. Gittos and M. Gittos: 'A Survey of East Riding Sepulchral Monuments before 1500', *Medieval Art and Architecture in the East Riding of Yorkshire. British Archaeological Association Conference Transactions: Cottingham, 1983*, pp. 91–108

V. Sekules: 'A Group of Masons in Early Fourteenth-century Lincolnshire', *Studies in Medieval Sculpture*, ed. F. H. Thompson, Society of Antiquaries Occasional Paper, n. s., iii (London, 1983), pp. 151–64

V. SEKULES

(d) 15th century. The highly realistic sculpture of the late Middle Ages, with its emphasis on Eucharistic themes, pietistic narratives and the intercession of saints, aroused the strong antagonism of reformers in the mid-16th century and during the Commonwealth and suffered widespread destruction. At Oxford, for example, all the original imagery was removed from the great reredoses in the chapels of All Souls (*c.* 1438–42) and Magdalen College (*c.* 1474–80), which followed the format of that in New College (*c.* 1380–86). The statuary on the Great Screens of St Albans Abbey (now Cathedral; 1476–84) and Winchester Cathedral (*c.* 1470–90; *see* WINCHESTER, §III, 3) was also removed. Most of the period's chantry chapels, the other major location of interior figure-sculpture, lost their sculpted images even when the tomb effigy itself survived, for example in the chantry of Bishop William Waynflete (*reg* 1447–86; *see* WINCHESTER, fig. 5).

Against these losses should be set the nearly intact survival of the imagery from Henry V's chantry chapel in Westminster Abbey, London (see below; *see also* LONDON, §V, 2(ii)(a)), and the partial survival of that in the chapel of Richard Beauchamp, Earl of Warwick (begun 1442–3), St Mary, Warwick, as well as isolated images from the chapels of Humphrey, Duke of Gloucester (after 1440) in St Albans Cathedral and Bishop Alcock (1488–1500) in Ely Cathedral (*see* ELY CATHEDRAL, §1(i)(e)). These, and the numerous scattered fragments from Winchester Cathedral, St Cuthbert's, Wells, and other locations make it possible to develop a chronological typology.

The stylistic difficulties of providing such a framework have been highlighted by Stone ('firmly dated figures on the screenwork of the Divinity School at Oxford, of 1481, show little advance on statues in the east window at Warwick of 1443–7'). The problems of classification have been aggravated by the redating to *c.* 1450–60 of both the six *Kings* on the Canterbury Cathedral pulpitum (conventionally ascribed to 1390–1411; Woodman) and the *Kings* on the choir-screen of York Minster (Harvey). The latter, which are often dated to the late 15th century or the early 16th, are individually characterized within the stylistic boundaries permitted by their coils of curly hair, furrowed brows and lively expressions. A more extreme redating is the head of an ecclesiastic from Glastonbury Abbey from the late 15th century to the mid-13th (1987 exh. cat., no. 296).

33. *Anointing at the King's Coronation*, detail of the lateral panel of the chantry chapel of Henry V, Westminster Abbey, London, England, mid-15th century

It has been widely accepted that the 15th century was a period of aesthetic retrogression. In brass memorials, however, the decline from the level achieved in the brass of *Thomas, Lord Camoys* (*d* 1419) and his wife (Trotton, St George; *see* BRASSES, MONUMENTAL) may reflect the changing status of brass memorials in the late 15th century, rather than any wider malaise in English sculpture. The finest alabaster tombs, such as those of *Ralph Greene and Katherine Mallory* (1418; Lowick, St Peter; *see* PRENTYS, THOMAS) and *Henry IV and Joan of Navarre* (Canterbury Cathedral; ascribed by Stone to a London workshop) were produced in the first half of the century, yet standards were later maintained in the Fitzherbert family tombs (*c.* 1470–85) in St Mary, Norbury (Derbys), and the tomb of *Alice, Duchess of Suffolk* (*c.* 1470–80; Ewelme, St Mary), which includes a cadaver that is also carved from alabaster. Later monuments tend to display a highly developed sense of modelling rather than concentrate on surface embellishment.

There was a considerable market in England and on the Continent for mass-produced tombs and alabaster panels, which might be intended as single items for devotional use, such as the 'St John's Head' (e.g. London, V&A; Stone), or grouped together in large reredoses. As early as 1382 English alabaster images were being exported to Rome, while in 1408 Thomas Colyn, Thomas Holewell and Thomas Poppehowe were commissioned to make the tomb of *John IV, Duke of Brittany* (destr.) for a church in Nantes. Three main centres for the manufacture of alabaster tombs have been identified at London, Chellaston/Nottingham and York. Although it has generally been alleged that the tomb-sculptors were entirely separate from those responsible for the alabaster panels, this appears unlikely.

The influence of foreign sculpture has been difficult to assess. The pre-restoration state of the Westminster Hall *Kings* (1385–7; *see* §(c) above), as seen in Carter's engravings, do not suggest direct European influence. Imported works of art, manuscripts and foreign travel by patrons probably account for continental influence, particularly Flemish and Burgundian, in mid-fifteenth century sculpture. There is also considerable evidence that continental artists were active in England, especially Netherlandish and German; the former may have been prominent among those responsible for the imagery of the Great Screen of Winchester Cathedral and for Henry VII's Chapel (*c.* 1503–9; London, Westminster Abbey).

Woodman's dating of the Canterbury screen is supported by the stylistic similarity between the weathered figures of *Henry IV* and *Archbishop Chichele* from All Souls College, Oxford, where John Massingham was documented in 1438–42, and the six *Kings* on the Canterbury pulpitum (*see* MASSINGHAM, (1)). He was also active at the Beauchamp Chapel in St Mary, Warwick, although his precise involvement is unclear. The original reredos has been destroyed and all images have been removed from the twelve niches on the side walls, the two large niches at the east end of the chapel and the four above the door to the vestry, but the sculptural programme around the east window remains intact. The jambs and mullions feature the nine orders of angels, *SS Barbara, Catherine, Mary Magdalene* and *Margaret*, censing angels, half-length angels bearing shields and, at the apex, *God the Father* in a radiating aureole. The Purbeck marble tomb-chest, carved in Dorset by John Bourd, is surmounted by a gilt-bronze effigy of the Earl and the side niches contain gilt-bronze weepers, with enamelled shields beneath, and angels holding scrolls (*see* ENGLAND, fig. 26). Materials for the construction of the other great mid-century chantry chapel, that of Henry V in Westminster Abbey, were assembled from 1438. Considering its extraordinarily elaborate design, with imagery encrusting the twin turrets that provide access, and statuary and reliefs on the lateral and western screens, it is not surprising that work was still under way in 1450. The reredos (see fig. 33) has lost its central image of the *Trinity*, but the flanking *Annunciation, SS Edward the Confessor and Edmund* and *SS Denis and George* survive.

In 1471 a contract was signed with John Stowell (*fl* 1457–71) for the *Tree of Jesse* reredos in the south transept of St Cuthbert, Wells. It remains controversial, however, whether the damaged imagery from that church, with precisely articulated heads and bodies, and considerable surviving polychromy, should be associated with this or the undocumented north transept reredos. Some of the finest English late medieval sculpture is found among the highly realistic, life-size heads at Winchester Cathedral. It is probable that many of these fragments came from the Great Screen; they are matched in quality by the smaller, damaged, *Virgin and Child* and the head of *God the Father*. One sculptural scheme that does survive *in situ*, albeit with some losses, appears in the Divinity School, Oxford, the statuary of which was installed in 1481. *Saints* and *Evangelists* were grouped around a *Crucifixion* (destr.) at the east door, and there is a *Virgin and Child* at the west end. The schematic and jagged-edged folds of the draperies, the boneless quality of some of the figures and their odd proportions are much less elevated in quality than the Winchester images, which seem to prefigure the imagery of Henry VII's Chapel.

BIBLIOGRAPHY

J. Carter: *Specimens of Ancient Sculpture and Painting*, 2 vols (London, 1780–87, 2/1838)

W. H. St J. Hope: 'On the Early Working of Alabaster in England', *Archaeol. J.*, lxi (1904), pp. 221–40

E. S. Prior and A. Gardner: *An Account of Medieval Figure-sculpture in England* (Cambridge, 1912)

F. H. Crossley: *English Church Monuments, AD 1150–1550* (London, 1921/*R* 1933)

A. Gardner: *Alabaster Tombs of the Pre-Reformation Period in England* (Cambridge, 1940)

L. Stone: *Sculpture in Britain: The Middle Ages*, Pelican Hist. A. (Harmondsworth, 1955, 2/1972)

P. Tudor-Craig: *Richard III* (London, 1973), pp. 9–10

J. H. Harvey: 'Architectural History from 1291–1558', *A History of York Minster*, ed. G. E. Aylmer and R. Cant (Oxford, 1977), pp. 181–6

F. Woodman: *The Architectural History of Canterbury Cathedral* (London, 1981), pp. 188–98

F. Cheetham: *English Medieval Alabasters: With a Catalogue of the Collection in the Victoria and Albert Museum* (Oxford, 1984)

Age of Chivalry: Art in Plantagenet England, 1200–1400 (exh. cat., ed. J. Alexander and P. Binski; London, RA, 1987)

PHILLIP LINDLEY

(iii) Holy Roman Empire.

(a) Introduction. (b) 13th century. (c) 14th and 15th centuries.

(a) Introduction. Throughout the geographical area represented by the Holy Roman Empire, the term Gothic is applied to sculpture created between 1220 and 1500. Sculptors in the 13th and 14th centuries mainly worked in the great building workshops, to provide decoration for cathedrals and urban churches. As well as local varieties of stone, the materials used were alabaster, stucco and, from the end of the 14th century, sometimes reconstituted stone. Gothic sculpture, like the architecture of the period, tended to be very much an urban art, centred in towns that had grown rich through trade and in episcopal seats, such as Strasbourg, Freiburg im Breisgau, Bamberg, Ulm, Cologne, Magdeburg, Nuremberg, Prague, Lübeck and Danzig (now Gdańsk), to some extent building on earlier traditions.

The origin and characteristics of Gothic stone sculpture in the Empire were associated with exposure to a great variety of artistic influences about 1200, especially those derived from antique and Byzantine art; at the same time there was a revival of local Carolingian and Ottonian traditions. Between 1220 and 1280 this phase produced within the Empire a vocabulary of form characterized by a high degree of naturalism in the representation of the human figure, which was particularly reflected in the expression of states of mind and feelings. With the onset of the 14th century a new stylization and abstraction conveying heightened expressivity became prevalent, especially in cult and devotional pictures, on which artistic production tended increasingly to be concentrated as work on the great churches began to tail off. The most impressive examples of such statues, poised between the monumental and the small-scale, are the *Schöne Madonnen* (beautiful Madonnas), which are masterpieces of a stylistic trend based on beauty of line and elegance that affected all centres of European art *c.* 1400.

In the 15th century, under the influence of Netherlandish painting, sculpture, too, was derived from an interest in the precise, detailed representation of earthly things. Newly emerging pictorial themes, such as the portrait, were in line with this development, as was the increasing social recognition accorded to leading artists, who, as elsewhere, often enhanced their wealth and status by running large workshop-based businesses.

BIBLIOGRAPHY

H. Huth: *Künstler und Werkstatt der Spätgotik* (Augsburg, 1923)

W. Pinder: *Die Kunst der ersten Bürgerzeit bis zur Mitte des 15. Jahrhunderts* (Leipzig, 1937)

W. Paatz: 'Prolegomena zu einer Geschichte der deutschen spätgotischen Skulptur im 15. Jahrhundert', *Abh. Heidelberg. Akad. Wiss., Phil.-Hist. Klasse*, ii/21 (1956)

E. Panofsky: *Renaissance and Renascences in Western Art* (Stockholm, 1960)

L'Europe gothique, XIIe–XIVe siècles (exh. cat., Paris, Louvre, 1968)
K. M. Swoboda, ed.: *Gotik in Böhmen* (Munich, 1969)
J. Białostocki: *Spätmittelalter und beginnende Neuzeit*, Propyläen-Kstgesch., vii (Berlin, 1972)
A. Kutal: *Gothic Art in Bohemia and Moravia* (London, 1972)
O. von Simson: *Das Mittelalter, II: Das hohe Mittelalter*, Propyläen-Kstgesch., vi (Berlin, 1972)
W. Swaan: *The Late Middle Ages* (London, 1977)
A. Legner: *Deutsche Kunst der Romanik* (Munich, 1982)
A. Erlande-Brandenburg: *L'Art gothique*, L'Art et les Grandes Civilisations, 13 (Paris, 1983)
A. von Ulmann: *Bildhauertechnik des Spätmittelalters und der Frührenaissance* (Darmstadt, 1984)
F. Möbius and H. Sciurie, eds: *Geschichte der deutschen Kunst, 1200–1350* (Leipzig, 1989)

ULRICH HENZE

(b) 13th century. About 1280 Burchard of Hall recorded recent changes to the abbey church of SS Peter und Paul at Wimpfen im Tal, stating that in 1259 Deacon Richard had called a master from Paris to rebuild the choir and transept in the French style (*opus francigenum*; *see* §II, 1(i) above). Traditional scholarship has retained Burchard's methodological standpoint and viewed 13th-century German sculpture as a 'Germanization' of French works. The chronological priority of the French models has contributed to their perceived primacy, with a consequent secondary status for those works outside Capetian territory. More recent studies of German monuments, however, have suggested that stylistic influences may have travelled both ways (*see* BAMBERG, §2(ii)), that iconography was chosen in response to a political situation inherently different from that in France, and that biblical and theological subjects were presented in quite a distinct fashion.

34. *St Martin and the Beggar*, sandstone relief, h. 1143 mm, from Mainz Cathedral, Germany, *c.* 1240 (Bassenheim, St Martin)

Stylistic developments. The earliest works in Germany in which Gothic influences may be traced belong to an international idiom variously known as the 'style of 1200', Late Romanesque or late Hohenstaufen. During the 1210s and 1220s liturgical furnishings in wood, stucco and metal gave way to larger figures in stone, which were incorporated into the fabric of the building itself, on exterior portals and buttresses and inside on choir piers. These developments are well illustrated in Saxony. At Halberstadt Cathedral, for example, the various influences of the local painting tradition (*Zackenstil*), Byzantine elements and French sculpture, especially that from the transepts of Chartres Cathedral (*see* CHARTRES, §I, 2(ii)), are evident in the stucco reliefs of the choir-screen (*c.* 1200) and the five figures of the wooden triumphal cross group (1215–20; *see also* ROMANESQUE, §III, 2(vi)). The same influences are also apparent in the region's earliest Gothic architectural sculpture at the cathedrals of Magdeburg (*see* MAGDEBURG, §1(ii)) and Freiberg (*see* FREIBERG, §1). Along the Empire's western border there were more direct connections with France: sculptors responsible for the north transept at Chartres, for example, also executed the south transept sculpture (*c.* 1230) at Strasbourg Cathedral (*see* STRASBOURG, §III, 2(ii) and figs 5 and 6).

Stylistic developments at Reims Cathedral were particularly influential in Germany from *c.* 1230 to 1260. The work of the younger workshop at Bamberg Cathedral suggests knowledge of several groups of sculptures of the 1230s at Reims (*see* MASTERS, ANONYMOUS, AND MONOGRAMMISTS, §I: BAMBERG MASTER). Acceptance of Winterfeld's amended date for the Prince's Portal at Bamberg would move this workshop's activity from 1225–35 to the mid-1220s, which would necessitate a revision of the sculptural chronology at Reims and a re-evaluation of the direction of influences. A further development in this style may be seen at Magdeburg Cathedral in the *Foolish Virgins* (1240s or 1260s; *see* MAGDEBURG, fig. 2), which were intended for the choir-screen and installed in the north portal *c.* 1300.

The direct influence of Reims is also apparent at Mainz, Naumburg and Meissen. At Mainz Cathedral, for example, the soft folds and lively poses on the west choir-screen reliefs (*c.* 1239; destr. 1682; fragments in Mainz, Bischöf. Dom- & Diözmus.; *see* MAINZ, §2(i)(b) and fig. 2) draw on the side portal lintels on the west front at Reims. The same qualities are evident on the relief of *St Martin and the Beggar* (*c.* 1240; Bassenheim, St Martin; see fig. 34), which may come from Mainz Cathedral. At Naumburg Cathedral the sculpture of the choir-screen and the 12 life-size figures (1240s or 1250s) in the west apse is highly expressive and individualized (*see* NAUMBURG, §1(ii) and fig. 1; *see also* DRESS, fig. 15). A member of the Naumburg workshop later executed seven figures in the 1250s for Meissen Cathedral (*see* MEISSEN, §2). The work of the JOSEPH MASTER, who was responsible for the final sculptures (*c.* 1245–55) on the west front at Reims (*see* MASTERS, ANONYMOUS, AND MONOGRAMMISTS, §I: JOSEPH MASTER; REIMS, fig. 5), is echoed in the *Prophets* on the central portal of the west façade (begun 1277) at Strasbourg Cathedral.

A later influence on German sculptors was the south transept tympanum (first half of the 1260s) of Notre-Dame, Paris, which appears to have been known by both the ERMINOLD MASTER (*see* MASTERS, ANONYMOUS, AND MONOGRAMMISTS, §I), who worked at Basle Minster (*c.* 1270) and Regensburg Cathedral (1280s), and the sculptor of the jamb figures on the right portal at Strasbourg Cathedral. In these German works dramatic effects were heightened and the expressive character increased through the coordination of drapery, gesture and facial expression.

Iconography. The west façade of Strasbourg Cathedral was the first example in Germany to adopt the French type with three portals. Until then German sculptors did not have the space to develop the complex iconographic programmes possible in France and sought different solutions. The earliest Gothic figural portal to have survived in Germany, the Golden Portal (*c.* 1225–40) of Freiberg Cathedral, combines within a single portal the *Adoration of the Magi with the Coronation of the Virgin and the Last Judgement.* Similar thematic compression can be seen in the south portals at SS Peter und Paul, Wimpfen im Tal (1280s), and Worms Cathedral (1280s; remodelled *c.* 1300; *see* WORMS, §1(ii)), and the west portal and narthex (1290s) at Freiburg im Breisgau Cathedral (*see* FREIBURG IM BREISGAU, §2(ii)). There was a simultaneous adoption of elaborate narrative programmes. The tympanum and lintel reliefs of the south transept portal at Strasbourg recounted the *Death, Funeral Procession, Assumption* and *Coronation of the Virgin*, while the west rood screen at Naumburg Cathedral comprises a detailed sequence of scenes from the *Passion.* This tendency recurs in the lengthy *Infancy of Christ, Passion* and *Last Judgement* narratives on the multi-banded tympana of the west front at Strasbourg.

The prominence given to certain themes that had been of lesser importance on French portals suggests that there was a preference in Germany for literal and moralizing readings of biblical texts rather than subtle theological interpretation. A notable example at Strasbourg is that of the *Wise and Foolish Virgins* on the embrasures of the south portal. Here the cycle is completed with the Bridegroom leading the Wise Virgins into the church and a non-textual counterpart, the Tempter, luring their foolish companions away from the door (*see* STRASBOURG, fig. 7). The associated theme of *Virtues* trampling on *Vices* appears on the jambs of the north portal. The west façade at Basle Minster was similarly decorated with *Wise and Foolish Virgins*, while both themes recur in the porch at Freiburg im Breisgau.

Statues of founders and donors were sometimes placed within a context that emphasized an institution's prestigious origins and important rights. At Bamberg Cathedral, for example, *Henry II* and *Kunigunde* appear alongside the cathedral's patron saints on the tympanum of the Portal of Grace (Gnadenportal; *c.* 1220) and opposite *Adam and Eve* on the jambs of the Adam's Portal. The presence of the latter figures is surprising, but may be compared with the large-scale portrayals at Strasbourg of such anti-models as *Synagogue* and the *Foolish Virgins.* As earthly rulers redeemed by Christ, *Adam and Eve* also served as antetypes for the canonized Ottonians. Within a church the area associated with a particular liturgy might be defined by single figures attached to supports. Apostles and local saints installed in the choir of Magdeburg Cathedral in the 1230s, for example, recall the church's foundation, its missionary role and the archbishop's judicial rights conferred by the Emperor and exercised in the choir. Local concerns may have been similarly expressed in the cycle of 11th-century benefactors at Naumburg Cathedral (see above), the founders and local saints (1250s) that may have been intended for a portal but are now installed in the choir of Meissen Cathedral, and the founders of the major monastic orders (1270s) at Wimpfen im Tal. Only the latest of such groups were derived iconographically from French models: the idea of the Apostles as the supports of the Church, as represented at the Sainte-Chapelle (*see* PARIS, fig. 35), reappears in the nave (1270s) at Freiburg im Breisgau and the choirs (1290s) of Xanten and Cologne cathedrals (*see* §(c) below).

It is believed that the *Rider* figures at Bamberg (1230–37; *see* BAMBERG, fig. 3) and Magdeburg (1230s; original in Magdeburg, Kulthist. Mus.), both of which may represent Emperor Frederick II, were designed to legitimize conveyed rights. The Magdeburg figure was originally installed on the Alter Markt, where judicial proceedings were held. The south transept of Strasbourg Cathedral was also used for legal purposes, as is reflected in the iconographic selection of *Evangelists* and angels blowing trumpets beneath *Christ the Judge* on the Judgement Pillar (*c.* 1230). The figures of the *Three Marys*, the guards and the angel within the dodecagon of the Tomb of Christ (1260s or 1280s) in the Mauritiuskapelle of Konstanz Cathedral were also intended to give visible form to ritual settings (*see* EASTER SEPULCHRE). The direct relationship between the sculpture and devotional practice anticipated the role of the *Andachtsbilder* that became popular later in the century.

BIBLIOGRAPHY

E. Panofsky: *Die deutsche Plastik des 11. bis 13. Jahrhunderts* (Munich, 1924)

H. Jantzen: *Deutsche Bildhauer des 13. Jahrhunderts* (Leipzig, 1925)

W. Valentiner: *The Bamberg Rider: Studies of Medieval German Sculpture* (Los Angeles, 1956)

W. Grzimek: *Deutsche Stuckplastik, 800–1300* (Berlin, 1974)

D. Schubert: *Von Halberstadt nach Meissen: Bildwerke des 13. Jahrhunderts in Thüringen, Sachsen und Anhalt* (Cologne, 1974)

D. von Winterfeld: 'Zur Baugeschichte des Bamberger Fürstenportales', *Z. Kstgesch.*, xxxix (1976), pp. 147–66

W. Sauerländer: 'Reims und Bamberg: Zu Art und Umfang der Übernahmen', *Z. Kstgesch.*, xxxix (1976), pp. 167–92

——: 'Spätstaufische Skulptur in Sachsen und Thüringen: Überlegungen zum Stand der Forschung', *Z. Kstgesch.*, xli (1978), pp. 181–216

A. Legner: *Deutsche Kunst der Romanik* (Munich, 1982)

E. Schubert: 'Zur Naumburg-Forschung der letzten Jahrzehnte', *Wien. Jb. Kstgesch.*, xxxv (1982), pp. 121–38

F. Möbius and H. Sciurie, eds: *Geschichte der deutschen Kunst, 1200–1350* (Leipzig, 1989)

V. R. Kaufmann: 'The Magdeburg Rider: An Aspect of the Reception of Frederick II's Roman Revival North of the Alps', *Intellectual Life at the Court of Frederick II Hohenstaufen*, ed. W. Tronzo, Stud. Hist. A., xxiv (Washington, DC, 1994), pp. 62–88

JOAN A. HOLLADAY

(c) 14th and 15th centuries. Stone sculpture within this period may be divided into three phases. The first, which was concentrated in the large towns on the Upper and

Lower Rhine (Strasbourg, Freiburg im Breisgau and Cologne) and in south Germany, is mainly characterized by a linear, planar style. A clear change may be seen from the mid-14th century, initiated by the work associated with the many branches of the PARLER family. Their powerful idiom was developed especially in the Bohemian capital of Prague and played a direct role in shaping the Late Gothic style about 1400. The true Late Gothic phase of stone sculpture developed in the second quarter of the 15th century, not least under the influence of Netherlandish painting. Sculptors now produced mainly altarpieces, tombs, epitaphs and individualized single works. It was not until the end of the century that increasing receptivity to the new Italian idioms led to a decisive move away from the Gothic tradition.

c. *1300*–c. *1350.* The figures made *c.* 1290–1300 by the workshop of Cologne Cathedral to be attached to the piers in the chancel (consecrated 1322) mark a new stage of sculptural development. The cycle comprises *Christ*, the *Virgin* (*see* COLOGNE, fig. 8) and *Twelve Apostles*, the latter of which stand beneath canopies bearing music-making angels. The elegant animation and delicate, slender build of these figures and the masterful treatment of the drapery placed them foremost among late 13th-century European sculptures. Their stylistic sources have not been identified satisfactorily. There are certainly links with French art, especially that of Paris, and the influence is apparent of Upper Rhenish sculpture of *c.* 1280, for example the west portals of Strasbourg Cathedral (*see* STRASBOURG, §III, 2(iv) and fig. 7) and the narthex of Freiburg im Breisgau Cathedral (*see* FREIBURG IM BREISGAU, §2(ii)). There may also be stylistic links with 13th-century English sculpture. The polychromy of the figures, which were restored to their original state in 1840–42, gives a good idea of the original painted appearance of High Gothic sculpture.

The capricious style of the chancel figures was imitated elsewhere in the Rhineland, especially in wood-carving (*see* §2(iii)(b) below), manuscript illumination, panel- and glass-painting. The Cologne workshops, which had long maintained links with artistic centres on the Meuse and the Moselle, adapted Lotharingian metalworking techniques to the demands of stone sculpture. Accordingly the sumptuous, sparingly gilded statuettes on the cathedral's high altar (*c.* 1320; fragments in Cologne, Schnütgen-Mus.) display the somewhat broad build that was to become a typical component of Cologne art in the 14th century. The unbroken tradition of delicate work in precious materials is apparent in the exquisite combination of the light-coloured, partly gilded figures and the black marble of the altar table.

The idiom developed *c.* 1280 in Strasbourg and Freiburg im Breisgau was further elaborated and consolidated in south Germany during the first half of the 14th century. In Freiburg itself this is seen in the Tomb of Christ (*c.* 1330–40) built into a chapel on the south side of the nave. The elongated proportions and the unbroken contours of the *Three Marys* show that stylistically these are late descendants of the Strasbourg *Prophets.* The rich treatment of the latter's garments, however, has given way to a very planar style that, owing to its reduced plasticity,

35. *Annunciation* and *Adoration of the Magi*, north portal, Kapellenkirche Unserer Lieben Frau, Rottweil, Germany, *c.* 1330–50

emphasizes the incorporeality of the subject. The four figures of about the same time in the St Catherine Chapel of Strasbourg Cathedral show similar stylistic characteristics.

The tympanum (1340s) above the south-east portal of the Frauenkirche, Esslingen, which was begun in 1320, indicates how this tradition was also continued in relief work. The three scenes from the *Life of the Virgin* directly adopt and further elaborate the ascetic style of the Freiburg figures. Extensive sculpture (some now in Rottweil, Lorenzkapelle) covered the three portals (see fig. 35) and the two lower storeys of the unusually sumptuous west tower of the Kapellenkirche Unserer Lieben Frau (1330–50) at Rottweil, which was also used as a courtroom and town archive. The sharply drawn, lean, reserved faces of the *Prophets* (*c.* 1340) directly recall the figures on the west façade at Strasbourg, although they share the completely two-dimensional nature of the *Three Marys* on the Freiburg Tomb of Christ. Their bodily presence is only hinted at behind the shallow folds of their thin, insubstantial garments.

c. *1350*–c. *1420.* The basic tendencies of the new sense of form that began to be felt rather suddenly about 1350, again in south-west Germany, were to remain effective until the beginning of the 15th century. The new style stood in stark contrast to the tenor of sculpture in the previous half century. The elongated proportions and incorporeal presence of the attenuated, shallow figures were displaced by vigorously modelled bodies that display strong moulding and strikingly vivid facial expressions and movements. The first evidence of the new style appears without any discernible predecessors in the two youngest *Prophets* from the south porch at Schwäbisch Gmünd (*see* SCHWÄBISCH GMÜND, CATHEDRAL OF THE HOLY CROSS, §2). These figures, produced soon after the middle of the century, display a sculptural treatment quite unlike that of the Rottweil sculptures, which had been made only about 10 years before. Thickset and squat, they stand solidly on the ground and their three-dimensionality is emphasized by horizontal folds and the positioning of their arms. The large, powerfully modelled heads move organically and unfold the figures in their space in a manner quite foreign to the verticality of the Rottweil *Prophets.* The earliest documented member of the Parler clan, Heinrich of Cologne, was Master of the Works in charge of rebuilding the church of the Holy Cross (*see* PARLER, (1)) and may have designed, and even executed, the sculptures.

The new style was taken further most notably by Heinrich's son Peter Parler and the latter's nephew Heinrich von Gmünd (*see* PARLER, (3) and (7)) and represented one of the foremost contributions to European art in the 14th century. The centre of the 'Parler style' was Prague, to which Peter Parler was summoned by Emperor Charles IV in 1356 to take over direction of the rebuilding of the cathedral of St Vitus. Peter's extraordinary talent is attested by the Emperor's willingness to entrust a relatively young artist with such responsibilities. His style suggests that he was trained at various sites in south Germany as well as at Schwäbisch Gmünd. These are likely to have included the alterations to Augsburg Cathedral (*see* AUGSBURG, §4(i)), the chancel of Freiburg Cathedral (rebuilt from 1356; *see* PARLER, (3)) and the Frauenkirche (1355–8) in Nuremberg, where Heinrich was also Master of the Works.

The imperial commission for the building and decoration of Prague Cathedral held a position in the later 14th century comparable to that of the Rhine Valley cathedrals of the high Middle Ages and of Saint-Denis Abbey and Reims Cathedral in the 12th and 13th centuries, respectively. The sculptural programme, for which Peter Parler was responsible, was correspondingly ambitious and expensive (*see* PRAGUE, §IV, 2(ii)). A particularly important aspect was the erection of six new tombs (1376–7) for Charles's Přemyslid forebears, which were arranged in pairs in the ambulatory chapels in the most solemn part of the cathedral as a demonstration of the Emperor's legitimate authority over Bohemia (*see also* CZECH REPUBLIC, §IV). Peter was personally responsible for one of the finest, the reclining representation of *Přemysl Ottakar I* on the tomb slab (completed 1377). Although the work is slightly damaged, the vitality and dignity of the king are shown with particular poignancy in the powerful treatment of the garments and the parts of the body, especially through the slightly asymmetrical placing of the figure on the cover. The tomb of *Ottakar II*, which can also be attributed to Peter Parler, shares similar qualities. The other four reclining figures were by other masters, who probably included Heinrich von Gmünd.

Peter Parler must also have been responsible for the design and planning of the cycle of 21 busts in the triforium, above the former openings between the gallery piers, which was produced in parallel with the tombs in the ambulatory. Apart from members of the Přemyslid–Luxemburg dynasty, the busts include the first three archbishops of Prague, the two Masters of the Works, *Mathias of Arras* and *Peter Parler* (*see* PARLER, (3), fig. 2), and the five Clerks of the Works. Iconographically the cycle, which was executed by several members of the workshop, brings together people from different estates who had variously contributed to the welfare of the see of Prague. The bust of *Charles IV* occupies the most prominent position in the eastern part of the triforium, exactly above the sarcophagus of *Borzhivoi I*, the founder of Přemyslid rule. The position also corresponds to that of the head of *Christ* belonging to a cycle of saints that runs around the exterior of the apse. The features of the triforium busts are sometimes strongly individualized, as if resembling a portrait, and bear witness to the new interest in reality that the 'Parler style' brought to later 14th-century sculpture. The bust motif was probably also part of Peter's design, although there was a long tradition of mounting carved heads in churches, especially in England, for example the heads adorning the interior of Salisbury Cathedral.

Heinrich von Gmünd, the second important sculptor from the Parler family, began his career at Prague, where the statue of *St Wenceslas* (*c.* 1373) in the saint's chapel is probably by him (*see* PRAGUE, fig. 16). From about 1380 he undertook several commissions in Cologne, including archivolt figures in the St Peter's portal of the cathedral and a female corbel-head inscribed with the Parler hook (Cologne, Schnütgen-Mus.).

Parler influence was felt in many parts of Europe and was apparently not confined to purely stylistic characteristics. The general rejection of schematic, stylized formulae and the adoption of a realistic, individualized image of man were accompanied by changes in iconography. 'Portrait' sculpture had been restricted previously to biblical figures, saints and the idealized representation of donors. The statues of *Rudolf IV* (*see* VIENNA, fig. 7) and his wife *Catherine of Bohemia* on the Singertor (completed *c.* 1361), the south portal of the Stephansdom, mark a new departure from accepted forms (*see* VIENNA, §§III, 1; V, 1(ii)). Another 'topical' sculptural programme appears above the porch of the south transept at St Maria, Mühlhausen, where stone figures of *Charles IV*, his wife and two attendants peer down from a balcony (*see* MÜHLHAUSEN, §1). This unusual ensemble (*c.* 1380), the figures of which are linked stylistically to those of the Stephansdom workshop, was possibly intended to commemorate the Emperor's visit in 1375 and represents visually the ruler's permanent presence in the town.

Towards the end of the 14th century the Parlers' powerful sculptural approach merged with the general European phenomenon of Late Gothic referred to as the Beautiful style (Ger. *schöner Stil*) or the Soft style (Ger. *weicher Stil*). Common to artistic centres between Paris, London and Prague was a new stylistic sensibility not only in sculpture but also in painting and goldsmiths' work, characterized by elegant lines and a predilection for costliness in colour and materials. The Parler style was an important catalyst of this refined style at the borders of the Empire, so it is not surprising that Bohemia and the Prague workshops made a decisive contribution to the spread of the most significant Central European artistic phenomenon of *c.* 1400, the type of statue of the Virgin and Child known as the *Schöne Madonna.* Those produced between 1390 and 1420 are distinguished by a multiplicity of common features in both motifs and style, but the hypothesis, often advanced, that a single sculptor was responsible for creating the finest examples is untenable.

One of the most significant of such figures, and one of the earliest (*c.* 1390; Altenmarkt im Pongau, Unserer Lieben Frau; see fig. 36), was made in Bohemia; the dating is based on a letter of indulgence issued for the statue in Prague in 1393. The use of Bohemian ragstone, the under life-size format and the octagonal plinth that became characteristic of the type are all present.

More significant, however, are the stylistic and expressive features. The sculpture is animated by an inner movement filled with tension without being capricious. The drapery, with large dished folds and flat areas alternating with intricate cascades, is organized to reinforce the movement of the torso. The material enfolds the figure in soft abundance without sharp edges or angular corners. Everything in the figure's arrangement aims at harmony and a perfect balance of forms. This is reflected in the Virgin's noble features and the playful gestures of the naked child Jesus, whom the Virgin supports on her left hip. The way in which her fingers sink gently into the child's soft body shows an exact observation of nature and the artist's feeling for the skin's yielding texture. Although the figure was repainted in the 17th century after considerable damage and restoration, some of the original polychromy survives.

36. *Virgin and Child* (*Schöne Madonna* type), limestone, h. 860 mm, from Bohemia, *c.* 1390 (Altenmarkt im Pongau, Unserer Lieben Frau)

Many of the finest *Schöne Madonnen*, for example the Krumau *Madonna and Child* (*c.* 1400; Vienna, Ksthist. Mus.), which came from Český Krumlov, appear to have been made in Bohemia, probably Prague. Their small size made it possible to export them economically throughout Germany (e.g. Bonn, Rhein. Landesmus.), Austria, Poland (for example that formerly in St Elizabeth, Wrocław, now in Warsaw, N. Mus.; *see also* POLAND, §IV, 2 and fig. 11) and even to Venice (now in Düsseldorf, Kstmus.). The peculiarities of the style were not confined to statues of the Virgin and Child, although the intimate, charming idiom of the Soft style seems to have found its most suited expression in subjects devoted to the veneration of the Virgin. This is also illustrated in contemporary groups of the *Pietà* (*see* AUSTRIA, fig. 19), in which the Virgin's grief over her dead son is shown with a dignified restraint: one of the finest examples (*c.* 1400; Munich, Bayer. Nmus.) was originally in Seeon Abbey.

c. *1420–*c. *1500.* The course of Gothic sculpture in the 15th century was closely tied to the decline of the traditional associations of church builders and craftsmen and the growing importance of wood-carving. Work was largely abandoned on the new cathedrals at Prague and Cologne and there were fewer commissions to produce whole cycles of figures for porches or to decorate the complete interior of a church. Instead greater attention was paid to the creation of isolated works, such as statues, tombs and altarpieces. Economic and social conditions changed as sculptors and masons, some of whom ran large workshops based in a particular location, organized themselves into urban guilds. This fostered the development of local styles, although the constant spread of different ideas, which were often introduced through a sculptor's other activities as wood-carver, panel-painter and in painting wood-carvings, ensured that these remained receptive to outside influences.

The period between 1420 and 1500 may be seen as the last phase of Gothic sculpture north of the Alps. Sculpture in the Empire largely clung to traditional forms, although these were developed with bold virtuosity to the highest pitch of perfection. The first moves away from the refined idiom of the Soft style may be seen in the work of the Lower Saxon master CONRAD VON EINBECK, who was probably trained at the workshop of Prague Cathedral and was in charge of the new church of St Moritz at Halle an der Saale from 1388. His sculpture there, notably a

Mourning Virgin from a *Crucifixion* group (1430s), which has a worldly quality characterized by an astringent naturalism, is far removed from the beauty of line and delicate feeling manifested in the *Schöne Madonnen.*

Although no other artists followed Conrad's style, his works show the changing perception of reality and form that was emerging in the 1420s. In stone sculpture this was accompanied by an increasing adaptation of the styles developed by André Beauneveu and Claus Sluter in Burgundy and the south Netherlands (*see* §(i)(c) above and §(v) below). The advances in panel painting made by Robert Campin and Jan van Eyck were of particular importance and the first German sculptor to adapt these to a sculptural idiom was HANS MULTSCHER, who was probably trained in the Netherlands and was admitted as a freeman of Ulm in 1427. Even his earliest works in Ulm, for example the group of figures (*c.* 1427–30; Ulm, Ulm Mus.) made for the east side of the Rathaus and the *Man of Sorrows* (1429; see fig. 37) beside the west portal of Ulm Minster, show a spontaneous and arresting freshness of treatment and an ability to grasp the momentary effect. The latter particularly demonstrates the artist's concern for anatomical exactitude in reproducing the human body. The delicate slenderness prevalent about 1400 has given way to a naturalistic approach, which is also expressed in the muted animation and the deliberate gestures. These tendencies emerge even more clearly if the *Man of Sorrows* is compared with a slightly earlier statue on the west portal of *St Martin* (*c.* 1420; *see* HARTMANN, MEISTER; ULM, §2(i)(b) and fig. 3), in which the features, posture and treatment of the drapery remain entirely within the Soft style, which here threatens to become a rigid formula.

The outstanding sculptor in the Empire during the second third of the 15th century was Nicolaus Gerhaert, who was also strongly influenced by Netherlandish artists. His most mature surviving works include two heads of red sandstone (Frankfurt am Main, Liebieghaus; *see* NICOLAUS GERHAERT, fig. 1; Strasbourg, Mus. Oeuvre Notre-Dame), which came from the portal (*c.* 1465–7; destr. French Revolution) of the New Chancellery at Strasbourg. A bust (Strasbourg, Mus. Oeuvre Notre-Dame), which probably came from the same context and is usually referred to as a self-portrait, is remarkable for its twisted posture, which seems to encompass the surrounding space, and its meditative expression. Other works that were to be influential include a monumental sandstone Crucifix (signed and dated 1467; Baden-Baden, SS Peter und Paul) and the tomb slab of *Frederick III* (Vienna, Stephansdom), on which Gerhaert worked from 1467 until *c.* 1473.

The representation of the everyday world that was a notable feature of Netherlandish painting was soon absorbed into stone sculpture throughout the Empire. After *c.* 1430 closer attention was paid to reproducing the contents of a room or the details of a landscape within the context of late medieval themes. Much of the sculpture showing Netherlandish influence was made on the Lower Rhine in the western part of the Empire, where the workshops sometimes specialized in making sculpture for export. The demand shown by the less wealthy classes for devotional images and artefacts was so great that items were often mass-produced from cheap materials. Such 'sculpture bakers', much of whose work comprised small

37. Hans Multscher: *Man of Sorrows*, sandstone, h. 1.68 m, west portal, Ulm Minster, Germany, 1429

clay figures made in series, were especially active in Cologne and the region around the border between Westphalia and the Netherlands. Workshops on the Lower Rhine, in Cologne, Cleve, Xanten and Wesel, were also influential in spreading Gerhaert's innovations: the Lower Rhenish variety of Gerhaert's style is particularly well demonstrated by the group with *Christ* and the *Virgin* (*c.* 1466) in St Maria im Kapitol, Cologne.

The works of TILMAN RIEMENSCHNEIDER and VEIT STOSS, the two most influential sculptors of the second half of the 15th century, both of whom worked in wood and stone, mark the transition to 16th-century German art. Riemenschneider was trained in various towns in southern Germany, including Strasbourg and Ulm, which introduced him to Swabian sculpture and Gerhaert's style, and he settled in Würzburg in 1483. Although best known for the production of costly wooden altarpieces (*see* §2(iii) below), his work on the tomb of *Henry II and Kunigunde* (1499–1513; Bamberg Cathedral) demonstrates that he was also the leading Franconian sculptor in stone. The slightly over life-size figures in light sandstone of *Adam* and *Eve* (1491–3; Würzburg, Mainfränk. Mus.; see fig. 38 and *see* TILMAN RIEMENSCHNEIDER, fig. 1), which the Würzburg city council commissioned to be placed either side of the south portal of the Marienkapelle, are his earliest documented works in the city. Although these could be considered as architectural decoration that would have been visible from a distance, they are conceived as independent sculptures that create space around them through their playful mobility. The masterful use of stone is seen most clearly in the execution of the highly differentiated faces: the characterization of *Adam* as a beardless youth, chosen at the artist's instigation, was a new departure that was permitted only after a resolution by the city council in 1492.

38. Tilman Riemenschneider: *Adam*, sandstone, h. 1.89 m, from the Marienkapelle, Würzburg, Germany, 1491–3 (Würzburg, Mainfränkisches Museum)

The work of Veit Stoss comes at the end of the Late Gothic tradition, and his last works can scarcely be encompassed within the definition. It is probable that he also encountered the work of Gerhaert while training on the Upper Rhine, although too little is known of his career to identify the precise sources of his style. In his use of the most diverse materials, carving wood and stone, painting panels and statues, and engraving, he was a typical representative of the late medieval artists who attempted to draw together all the various genres into a single homogeneous entity. For many years he was counted among the leading artists in Nuremberg, together with ADAM KRAFT and members of the VISCHER family. Between 1477 and 1492 he was in Kraków, where his work culminated in the canopied tomb of *Kasimir IV* (signed and dated 1492; Kraków, Wawel Cathedral). The sumptuous garments of the King's reclining figure, in mottled red marble, are in stark contrast to his features, which are marked by decay and the agony of death. The tomb represents the most mature and moving expression of the central themes of late medieval iconography, death and redemption.

BIBLIOGRAPHY

O. Schmitt: *Gotische Skulpturen des Strassburger Münsters* (Frankfurt am Main, 1924)

W. Pinder: *Die deutsche Plastik des 14. Jahrhunderts* (Munich, 1925)

O. Schmitt: *Gotische Skulpturen des Freiburger Münsters*, 2 vols (Frankfurt am Main, 1926)

J. Baum: *Die Bildwerke der Rottweiler Lorenzkapelle* (Augsburg, 1929)

H. Wilm: *Gotische Tonplastik in Deutschland* (Augsburg, 1929)

Europäische Kunst um 1400 (exh. cat., Vienna, Ksthist. Mus., 1962)

Schöne Madonnen, 1350–1450 (exh. cat., ed. D. Grossmann; Salzburg, 1965)

K. Gerstenberg: *Die deutsche Baumeisterbildnisse des Mittelalters* (Berlin, 1966)

T. Müller: *Sculpture in the Netherlands, Germany, France and Spain, 1400–1500*, Pelican Hist. A. (Harmondsworth, 1966)

A. Legner: 'Die Hochaltarmensa des Kölner Doms und ihr Skulpturenschmuck', *Rhein und Maas: Kunst und Kultur, 800–1400* (exh. cat., Cologne, Ksthalle; Brussels, Musées Royaux A. & Hist., 1972), i, pp. 371–4

K.-H. Clasen: *Der Meister der Schönen Madonnen: Herkunft, Entfaltung und Umkreis* (Berlin, 1974)

W. Hart: *Die Skulpturen des Freiburger Münsters* (Freiburg im Breisgau, 1975)

K. Bauch: *Das mittelalterliche Grabbild: Figürliche Grabmäler des 11. bis 15. Jahrhunderts in Europa* (Berlin, 1976)

Die Parler und der Schöne Stil, 1350–1400: Europäische Kunst unter den Luxemburgern, 3 vols (exh. cat., ed. A. Legner; Cologne, Schnütgen-Mus., 1978)

R. Suckale: 'Die Kölner Domchorstatuen: Kölner und Pariser Skulptur in der zweiten Hälfte des 13. Jahrhunderts', *Köln. Dombl.*, xliv–xlv (1979–80), pp. 223–54

R. Didier and R. Recht: 'Paris, Prague, Cologne et la sculpture de la seconde moitié du XIVe siècle: A propos de l'exposition des Parler à Cologne', *Bull. Mnmtl.*, cxxxviii (1980), pp. 173–219

E. Ullmann, ed.: *Geschichte der deutschen Kunst, 1350–1470* (Leipzig, 1981)

J. M. Liebmann: *Deutsche Plastik, 1350–1550* (Leipzig, 1982)

D. L. Ehresmann: *Middle Rhenish Sculpture, 1380–1440* (Ann Arbor, 1984)
P. Havel: *Schöne Madonnen: Meisterwerke gotischer Kunst* (Würzburg, 1984)
E. Ullmann: *Deutsche Architektur und Plastik, 1470–1550* (Gütersloh, 1984)
Verschwundenes Inventarium: Der Skulpturenfund im Kölner Domchor (exh. cat., ed. U. Bergmann; Cologne, Schnütgen-Mus., 1984)
Gothic and Renaissance Art in Nuremberg, 1300–1550 (exh. cat., ed. J. P. O'Neill; New York, Met.; Nuremberg, Ger. Nmus.; 1986)
N. Jopek: *Studien zur deutschen Alabasterplastik des 15. Jahrhunderts* (Worms, 1988)

ULRICH HENZE

(iv) Italy.

(a) Introduction. (b) Tuscany. (c) Lombardy. (d) Veneto. (e) Emilia-Romagna. (f) Umbria. (g) Lazio. (h) Campania.

(a) Introduction. Owing to the strength of the antique and Byzantine traditions in the Italian peninsula, the penetration of French ideas and styles tended to be limited and specific. Sculpture was deployed on façades, although generally not on great portal programmes; but it was more commonly used on capitals and such church furnishings as pulpits, ciboria, shrines and tombs. In contrast to northern Europe many individual sculptors are documented from early on, but although the leading craftsmen were employed over a wide area the political divisions ensured that styles remained strongly regional. For these reasons this section is treated on a regional, rather than a chronological, basis.

□

(b) Tuscany. Gothic stone sculpture was produced in Tuscany during a relatively brief period (*c.* 1250–1400) and was mainly concentrated on Pisa, Siena and Florence. The movement away from Romanesque in both Siena and Pisa during the mid-13th century (*see* ROMANESQUE, §III, 1(vi)(e)) coincided with Nicola Pisano's arrival from southern Italy, where a synthesis of the Romanesque tradition, an appreciation of antiquity and the influence of French Gothic had developed (*see* §(a) above); the latter element became increasingly evident in his later works (*see* PISANO (i), (1)). More recent French influences may be found in the work of Giovanni Pisano, who was active from the 1270s and developed a dramatic form of personal expression, rich in contrasts, in such works as the statues on the façade of Siena Cathedral (1284–97; see fig. 39; *see also* SIENA, §III, 1(ii) and fig. 7). The reliefs on the pulpits in S Andrea, Pistoia (*see* PISANO (i), (2), fig. 1), and Pisa Cathedral (1302; *see* PULPIT, §1 and fig. 1), however, were still based on those of antique sarcophagi.

An original style that developed in Siena, even while Giovanni was working there, was inspired by the city's own painting tradition (*see* §IV, 5(v) below) and French Gothic sculpture. Examples may be found in Siena Cathedral on the upper sections of the façade (1300–17) and the Duomo Nuovo (1340–48), in Arezzo, Cortona, Massa Marittima and Grosseto, and beyond Tuscany in Orvieto (*see* §(f) below), Naples (*see* §(h) below) and even Messina in Sicily. Among the foremost exponents were GANO DI FAZIO, LORENZO MAITANI, TINO DI CAMAINO, GORO DI GREGORIO, AGOSTINO DI GIOVANNI and Lando di Pietro (*d* 1340). The production of marble sculpture in Siena ended abruptly at the Black Death in 1348.

39. Giovanni Pisano: *Isaiah*, h. 1.9 m, from the façade of Siena Cathedral, Italy, 1284–97 (Siena, Museo dell'Opera del Duomo)

Sculpture in Pisa was strongly influenced by Giovanni Pisano until his death, probably in 1314, and Tino di Camaino was active there until 1315. During the following decades of provincial stagnation Giovanni di Balduccio, Giovanni's only notable Pisan pupil, was active mainly in Sarzana, Florence and northern Italy and did hardly any work in Pisa itself. Sculpture regained its former status after Andrea Pisano returned from Florence, probably in 1341. While his figures draw on Classical ideals, his sons Nino Pisano and Tommaso Pisano continued to adhere to Gothic forms (*see* PISANO (ii)). About 1370, however, there was a remarkable move, already discernible in Tommaso's work, away from marble as the preferred material to painted wood, which resulted in a more naturalistic figure style.

The first significant Gothic sculpture in Florence was that associated with the cathedral's richly sculptured façade (begun after 1294; *see* ARNOLFO DI CAMBIO, fig. 3; FLORENCE, §IV, 1(i)(b)). Tino di Camaino was active there from 1318 to 1323/4 on groups of statues for the Baptistery and the city's first monumental tombs (*see* TINO DI CAMAINO, fig. 2), and Giovanni di Balduccio was present from 1330 to 1334. Andrea Pisano was engaged as a goldsmith in 1330 to execute the first bronze door for the Baptistery (*see* FLORENCE, fig. 14), but from about 1334 he produced marble sculpture of a truly monumental quality (originals now in Florence, Mus. Opera Duomo) that was strongly influenced by Giotto. The tabernacle that Andrea di Cione made for Orsanmichele from 1352 bears a vast array of statues and reliefs that rely on various illusionistic effects (*see* CIONE, (1), §2).

The strength of Florentine sculpture between 1350 and 1380 is evident in the work of Francesco Talenti, ALBERTO ARNOLDI, Francesco Sellaio (*fl* 1354–83), Simone Talenti (*see* TALENTI, (3)), Giovanni Fetti (*fl* 1350–86) and Zanobi di Bartolo (*fl* 1377). A new generation of sculptors from about 1380 included Jacopo di Piero Guidi (*fl* 1379–1405), GIOVANNI D'AMBROGIO, Piero di Giovanni Tedesco (*fl* 1386–1402) and Niccolò di Piero Lamberti (*see* LAMBERTI, (1)), all of whom worked on the Porta della Mandorla (1391–*c*. 1423) of Florence Cathedral during the 1390s. Their works demonstrate an intensive study of antiquities that places them on the threshold of the Renaissance.

BIBLIOGRAPHY

M. Wundram: 'Toskanische Plastik von 1250 bis 1400', *Z. Kstgesch.*, xxi (1958), pp. 243–70
——: 'Jacopo di Piero Guidi', *Mitt. Ksthist. Inst. Florenz*, xiii (1968), pp. 195–222
A. Garzelli: *Sculture toscane nel duecento e nel trecento* (Florence, 1969)
M. Seidel: 'Studien zu Giovanni di Balduccio und Tino di Camaino: Die Rezeption des Spätwerks von Giovanni Pisano', *Städel-Jb.*, v (1975), pp. 37–84
G. Kreytenberg: 'Tre cicli di apostoli dell'antica facciata del duomo fiorentino', *Ant. Viva*, 16 (1977), pp. 13–29
E. Carli: *Gli scultori senesi* (Milan, 1980)
G. Previtali: 'Alcune opere "fuori contesto": Il caso di Marco Romano', *Boll. A.*, xxii (1983), pp. 43–68
G. Kreytenberg: *Andrea Pisano und die toskanische Skulptur des 14. Jahrhunderts* (Munich, 1984)
A. Middeldorf Kosegarten: *Sienesische Bildhauer am Duomo vecchio: Studien zur Skulptur in Siena, 1250–1330* (Munich, 1984)
R. Bartalini: *Una bottega di scultori senesi del trecento: Agostino di Giovanni e i figli Giovanni e Domenico* (diss., U. Siena, 1986)
G. Kreytenberg: *Tino di Camaino* (Florence, 1986)

G. KREYTENBERG

(c) Lombardy. Lombard sculpture in the earlier 14th century showed no awareness of the innovations introduced by Nicola and Giovanni Pisano in Tuscany (*see* §(b) above). Carved tombs in Milan, Brescia and Bergamo were still dominated by the region's vigorous Romanesque traditions (*see* ROMANESQUE, §III, 1(vi)(b)). The sculpture of GIOVANNI DI BALDUCCIO, who introduced the new concepts to the region and was active in Milan from 1334, is marked by the use of Pisan forms, narrative quality and considerable technical ability. A major product of his workshop was the elaborate polychromed marble shrine of St Peter Martyr (signed and dated 1339; Milan, S Eustorgio; see fig. 40), which has a sarcophagus carved with scenes from the *Life of St Peter Martyr*, supported on caryatids representing the *Vices* and *Virtues*, with a tabernacle above. Other signed works include the tomb of *Guarniero degli Antelminelli* (*c*. 1327–8; Sarzana, S Francesco), the pulpit in S Maria del Prato, San Casciano in Val di Pesa, and the doorway (1347; destr. 1808; fragments in Milan, Castello Sforzesco) from S Maria di Brera, Milan; these, however, incorporate an increasing amount of local Lombard elements.

Balduccio's influence can be recognized in the work of Giovanni da Campione (*see* CAMPIONESI, §2), whose workshop was involved in the decoration of the baptistery

40. Giovanni di Balduccio: shrine of St Peter Martyr, polychromed marble, S Eustorgio, Milan, Italy, 1339

at Bergamo, signed by him in 1340, and who carved elongated, angular figures of *Virtues* in Veronese marble for the external niches. The concept of the figures is related to the caryatids of the shrine of St Peter Martyr, but they are interpreted in a more Romanesque manner. Elements of Giovanni Pisano's style may be recognized on panels with scenes from the *Life of Christ* inside the baptistery. The free-standing figures that Campione carved for the north portal (*c*. 1353) of S Maria Maggiore, Bergamo, include an equestrian *St Alexander*.

The characteristic format of an armoured rider, of which there are many examples in Lombardy, was originally adopted from German Romanesque and Gothic sculpture (*see* §(iii)(b) above), but a more immediate source would have been the series of equestrian statues surmounting the della Scala tombs outside S Maria Antica, Verona (*see* VERONA, §3(iii) and fig. 5). Tomb sculpture became increasingly ornate, showing the influence of goldsmiths' work: large tombs were set against church exteriors, making public statements on the status and role of the individual or family commemorated in the changing political organization of the city-states. Among Bonino da Campione's funerary monuments was an equestrian statue of *Bernabò Visconti* (1363; Milan, Castello Sforzesco), originally cased in gold and silver, set on a sarcophagus (1380–85) supported on columns. The elaborate tomb of *Cansignorio della Scala* (*d* 1375; Verona, S Maria Antica; for illustration *see* SCALA, DELLA), surmounted by a conventional equestrian figure, is a complex gabled structure, originally polychrome, that echoes contemporary metalwork (*see* §V, 6 below) and is characteristic of the free-standing tabernacle type.

Much sculpture in Lombardy in the late 14th century and the 15th was carved by French and German craftsmen, rather than in a specifically local style. The late 14th-century marble sculpture of Milan Cathedral, for example, represents a collaboration between imported and Lombard artists (*see* MILAN, §IV, 1(ii)), but a more local style can be recognized in 15th-century work in the cathedral, particularly that by Alberto II da Campione (*fl* 1404).

BIBLIOGRAPHY

C. Baroni: *Scultura gotica lombarda* (Milan, 1944)

F. De Maffei: *Le arche scaligere di Verona* (Verona, 1955)

F. Russoli: *Arte lombarda dai Visconti agli Sforza* (Milan, 1958)

□

(d) Veneto. From as early as *c.* 1175–80 elements from the Early Gothic sculpture of Champagne were apparently introduced to the Veneto in the dismantled portal to the sacristy anteroom at S Giustina, Padua (Zuliani), but generally the local production remained faithful to the Byzantine–Romanesque tradition (*see* ROMANESQUE, §III, 1(vi)(d)). The influence of any French works that may have been present in the area, and of Mosan goldsmiths' work in the so-called 'style of 1200', remains problematic. In Venice developments towards Gothic appeared first in the sculptural decoration of the main portal at S Marco (*c.* 1240), although its relationship to the transept portals at Chartres seems to be indirect.

Tuscan artists introduced mature Gothic elements in the 14th century, for example in Giovanni Pisano's *Virgin and Child between Two Angels* (1305–6) for the Arena Chapel, Padua. The only certain work of MARCO ROMANO is the *St Simeon* (1318) in S Simeone Grande, Venice, which displays Sienese traits (Previtali). The *Virgin and Child* over the tomb of *Doge Marco Cornaro* (*d* 1368; Venice, SS Giovanni e Paolo) was signed by Nino Pisano. The dating and attribution of the capitals (most of which are in storage) at the Doge's Palace are controversial, as also is the rich civic iconography on the corner reliefs (*see* VENICE, §IV, 6(i)). Part of the palace was built from 1341 by FILIPPO CALENDARIO and Pietro Basegio, and further work was executed after 1424 under Doge Francesco Foscari. Wolters's convincing attribution of some of the palace's sculptures to the earlier campaign makes them exceptionally modern for their time. The most significant artist of the mid-14th century, although not a revolutionary one, was ANDRIOLO DE' SANTI, who is known mainly for tombs in the Eremitani church and the Santo, Padua. Late Gothic forms were introduced towards the end of the 14th century by northern artists present in the area and also by Jacobello dalle Masegne and Pierpaolo dalle Masegne (*see* MASEGNE, DALLE).

Lombard sculptors from the Milan Cathedral workshop, such as MATTEO RAVERTI, are documented in Venice in the first quarter of the 15th century working on the Ca' d'Oro (Paoletti; see fig. 22 above), as well as indigenous artists, including Giovanni Buon and Bartolomeo Buon (*see* BUON (i)). Other Tuscan sculptors in the Veneto, some of whom had been pupils of Ghiberti, were Niccolò di Pietro, Piero di Niccolò Lamberti (*see* LAMBERTI, (2)), Giovanni di Martino da Fiesole (*fl* 1423), NANNI DI BARTOLO and MICHELE DA FIRENZE. Renaissance elements are evident in the work of the MASTER OF THE MASCOLI ALTAR, whose identity has been disputed (*see* MASTERS, ANONYMOUS, AND MONOGRAMMISTS, §I). The finest work of this period appears on the Porta della Carta (1438–42) of the Doge's Palace; although this was a joint project it was signed by Bartolomeo Buon alone. One of his pupils was possibly responsible for the tomb of *Doge Francesco Foscari* (*c.* 1460; *see* BREGNO, (2)) in S Maria Gloriosa dei Frari, Venice.

Some examples of 14th-century sculpture influenced by Venetian models appear in Istria and the Greek islands, but it was not until the first half of the 15th century, when the inland cities of the Veneto, Friuli and Lombardy and the regions along the Adriatic coasts came under Venetian control, that the city's Gothic sculpture began to influence the surrounding regions.

BIBLIOGRAPHY

P. Paoletti: *L'architettura e la scultura del rinascimento a Venezia* (Venice, 1893)

G. Mariacher: 'Appunti per un profilo della scultura gotica veneziana', *Atti Ist. Ven. Sci., Lett. & A.*, cxiii (1950–51), pp. 225–46

W. Wolters: *La scultura veneziana gotica, 1300–1460*, 2 vols (Venice, 1976)

A. Markham Schulz: *Niccolò di Giovanni Fiorentino and Venetian Sculpture of the Early Renaissance* (New York, 1978)

F. Zuliani: 'Il portale maggiore della basilica romanica', *Benedettini a Padova e nel territorio padovano attraverso i secoli* (exh. cat. by P. Fassera and others, Padua, S Giustina, 1980)

G. Previtali: 'Alcune opere "fuori contesto": Il caso di Marco Romano', *Boll. A.*, xxii (1983), pp. 43–68

G. Tigler: 'Il portale maggiore di San Marco a Venezia: Aspetti iconografici e stilistici dei rilievi duecenteschi', *Mem. Ist. Ven. Sci., Lett. & A.* (Venice, 1994)

GUIDO TIGLER

(e) Emilia-Romagna. Apart from a few unconnected examples in Modena, Imola, Bagnacavallo, Cesena and Ravenna, the contexts of which cannot be reconstructed precisely, Gothic stone sculpture in Emilia-Romagna is largely confined to Bologna. Much was produced for its churches and civic buildings, although there were some long gaps in the continuity. A characteristic type of funerary sculpture, although not confined to Bologna, is that of the master of the Studio (the University) shown lecturing to his students. These wall tombs were intended to affirm the master's prestige and are related stylistically to the expressive vivacity and strong facial characteristics of local painting and manuscript illumination (*see* BOLOGNA, §II, 1). They also, however, show strong links with the sculpture of the Po Valley, particularly that of Lombardy and Verona (*see* §(c) above). This complexity is evident in the monuments to *Bartoluzzo de' Preti* (1318), *Michele da Bertalia* (1328; both Bologna, S Francesco), *Pietro Cerniti* (1333), *Bonifacio Galluzzi* (1346) and, especially, the vivid tomb of *Giovanni di Andrea* (1348; see fig. 41; all Bologna, Mus. Civ. Med.), which Vasari attributed to one Jacopo Lanfrani.

41. Tomb of *Giovanni di Andrea*, marble, from Bologna, Italy, 1348 (Bologna, Museo Civico Medioevale e del Rinascimento)

Tombstones and other types became more common during the mid-14th century: that of the knight *Colaccio Beccadelli* (1341; Imola, S Domenico), for example, signed by Bettino, the only Bolognese stone-carver who has been identified. A few other sculptors are documented, some of Lombard or Venetian extraction. The presence of Tuscan masters is confirmed by the Pisan Giovanni di Balduccio who carved a marble polyptych (destr.; fragments in Bologna, Mus. S Stefano; Bologna, Mus. Civ. Med.; Faenza, Pin. Com.), formerly in S Domenico, Bologna.

The strong revival of sculpture that followed the long depression caused by the effects of the Black Death was mainly linked to the presence of Jacobello dalle Masegne and Pierpaolo dalle Masegne, both of whom signed the monument of *Giovanni da Legnano* (*d* 1383; fragments in Bologna, Mus. Civ. Med.; Rocchetta Mattei; *see* MASEGNE, DALLE). With a larger group of assistants, Pierpaolo later worked on the high altar (1388–92) of S Francesco. Antonio di Vincenzo, who has been variously connected with the dalle Masegne, gave sculpture considerable importance in the buildings he designed in Bologna, including the Foro dei Mercanti (1391) and the lower levels of S Petronio (1393–1400). The Venetian Paolo di Bonaiuto played an especially important role at the latter, where reliefs of saints and biblical figures show a clear movement towards a style that may have been influenced by Claus Sluter in Burgundy (*see* §(i)(c) above).

By the end of the 14th century tomb stones, such as that of *Andrea Manfredi* (1396; Bologna, S Maria dei Servi), were frequent, although perhaps more typical were those of *Lorenzo Pini* (1398) and the large sarcophagus of *Bartolomeo da Saliceto* (1412; both Bologna, Mus. Civ. Med.), which was signed by ANDREA DA FIESOLE, a Tuscan who was long active in Bologna. Among the works executed by Jacopo della Quercia, another Tuscan, was the monumental Porta Magna of S Petronio (*see* JACOPO DELLA QUERCIA, §1(iii) and fig. 4), which was commissioned by Cardinal Lodovico Alemanno in 1425.

BIBLIOGRAPHY

R. Grandi: *I monumenti dei dottori e la scultura a Bologna, 1267–1348* (Bologna, 1982)

——: 'Cantiere e maestranze agli inizi della scultura petroniana', *La Basilica di S Petronio in Bologna*, i (Milan, 1983), pp. 125–62

——: 'Dottori, scultori, pittori: Ancora sui monumenti bolognesi', *Skulptur und Grabmal des Spätmittelalters in Rom und Italien. Akten des Kongresses Scultura e monumento sepolcrale del tardo medioevo a Roma e in Italia: Roma, 1985*, pp. 353–65

——: 'La scultura tardogotica: Dai dalle Masegne a Jacopo della Quercia', *Il tramonto del medioevo a Bologna: Il cantiere di S Petronio* (exh. cat., ed. R. D'Amico and R. Grandi; Bologna, Pin. N., 1987), pp. 127–59

R. GRANDI

(f) Umbria. The presence of Nicola Pisano, Giovanni Pisano and Arnolfo di Cambio in Umbria during the 1270s was to have a lasting influence on the region's sculpture. The first major Gothic sculpture in Umbria appears on the rich decoration by Nicola and Giovanni Pisano on the Great Fountain (1277–8) at Perugia (*see* FOUNTAIN, §IV, 1 and fig. 1; PISANO, (1), §4). Between 1277 and 1281 Arnolfo di Cambio was working in Perugia on a smaller fountain (destr. by 1301). Two writers and three thirsting figures (all Perugia, G.N. Umbria) are notable for the reintroduction of a three-dimensional Cistercian rendering of space and demonstrate a familiarity with contemporary Parisian sculpture and the use of antique models that Arnolfo learnt from Nicola Pisano. For the tomb of *Cardinal Guillaume de Braye* (*d* 1282; see fig. 42; fragments also in Orvieto, Mus. Opera Duomo) in S Domenico, Orvieto, Arnolfo collaborated with Roman sculptors (*see* §(g) below), who also worked elsewhere in Umbria.

The figured capitals of Todi Cathedral, which was rebuilt in the second half of the 13th century, show French influence, but the later statues on the façade (especially the *Virgin*) clearly reveal the teaching of Nicola Pisano. Arnolfo's influence appears on several statues, for example that of *St Prosper* (Perugia, S Prospero) and *St Peter* on the exterior of the Palazzo dei Priori, Perugia. Giovanni Pisano's influence can be seen on fragmentary works at Spoleto and Perugia. The tomb of *Benedict XI* (*d* 1304; Perugia, S Domenico) shows an easy mastery of modern Gothic forms. The sculptor's origins are disputed, although it is usually accepted that he also worked at Orvieto Cathedral. He, or perhaps a pupil, may also have been responsible for the three saints later set in the lunette over the main portal of the Palazzo dei Priori, Perugia. These are usually dated after the 1320s, although they may be as early as *c.* 1315, and demonstrate the movement of Umbrian sculpture towards a more definitely Gothic phase, usually known as 'Orvietan' or 'Sienese'.

The cosmopolitan and French-orientated workshop of Orvieto Cathedral was active throughout the 14th century. Its finest work, conceived as a unitary plan, appears on the bas-relief carving on the west façade pilasters (*see* ORVIETO, §2(ii)(b) and fig. 4), which shows links with France but remains within the Italian tradition owing to the greater flatness of the design. Many names, including Lorenzo Maitani, have been suggested for the two main

42. Arnolfo di Cambio: tomb of *Cardinal Guillaume de Braye*, marble and marble inlay, S Domenico, Orvieto, Italy, *c.* 1282

masters: the work of the first seems to proceed from Nicola Pisano's plasticism while the second, whose style has a more definite Gothic character, worked in a more narrative and poetic manner and may have carved the *Virgin and Child* over the main portal. Much has been made of the 'Sienese' character of these sculptures and it has been suggested that there was a specifically Umbrian school (Previtali).

The decoration of the basilica of S Francesco, Assisi, brought together the various influences on Umbrian Gothic sculpture. The architectural sculpture of the Upper Church and the portal, for example, demonstrate close links with the cathedrals of the Ile-de-France, especially Reims. The Umbrian Romanesque tradition was not rejected, but mixed with foreign ideas and some Cistercian influence (*see* §(g) below). Roman marble-workers produced opulent decoration for the liturgical furnishings, and the work of sculptors from Todi has been recognized in the tomb of a member of the Cerchi family.

BIBLIOGRAPHY

U. Tarchi: *L'arte medievale nell'Umbria e nella Sabina*, iii–iv (Milan, 1938–40)

M. Guardabassi and F. Santi: *Il Portale Maggiore del Palazzo dei Priori a Perugia* (Perugia, 1953)

A. Bertini Calosso: 'La scultura del '200 in Umbria', *L'Umbria nella storia, nella letteratura e nell'arte* (Bologna, 1954), pp. 273–92

V. Martinelli: 'Arnolfo a Perugia', *Storia e arte in Umbria nell'età comunale. Atti del VI convegno di studi umbri: Gubbio, 1968*, i, pp. 113–30

A. Garzelli: *Scultura toscana nel '200 e nel '300* (Florence, 1969), pp. 207–11

F. Santi: 'Le tre arti dal medioevo all'ottocento', *Umbria* (Venice, [1970]), pp. 213–406

A. Prandi and M. Righetti: *Il Duomo di Todi* (Perugia, 1975)

Roma anno 1300. Atti della IV settimana di studi di storia dell'arte medievale dell'Università di Roma 'La Sapienza': Roma, 1980, pp. 27–72, 141–62

Skulptur und Grabmal des Spätmittelalters in Rom und Italien. Akten des Kongresses Scultura e monumento sepolcrale del tardo medioevo a Roma e in Italia: Roma, 1985, pp. 107–28, 257–64

M. Semff: 'Textiler Festschmuck in Stein? Überlegungen zu den Orvietaner Fassadereliefs', *Münchn. Jb. Bild. Kst*, xxxviii (1987), pp. 83–106

G. Previtali: *Studi sulla scultura gotica in Italia: Storia e geografia* (Turin, 1991)

(g) Lazio. Apart from the localized influence of the Cistercians (see below), the artistic life of Lazio in the 13th and 14th centuries was dominated by Rome, where several diverse influences converged. The Roman tradition of the marble-workers (*see* COSMATI; ROMANESQUE, §III, 1(vi)(f)) remained strong, although some examples demonstrate a closer study of both nature and Classical models that parallels developments in France. Some works indeed, such as the corbel heads in S Maria in Aracoeli (rebuit from 1250), Rome, and the pulpit in S Maria la Rosa, San Vittore del Lazio, may be likened to the 'Frederician' sculpture produced by the imperial workshops in Campania (*see* §(h) below).

Arnolfo di Cambio arrived in Rome *c.* 1270 and created a personal style, through his combination of French Gothic influences and Classical forms, in which a continuous development can be seen. Among Arnolfo's collaborators there were also Roman marble-workers. One of these may have been PIETRO DI ODERISIO who may be identified with the *Socio Petro* who signed the ciborium of S Paolo fuori le Mura (*see* ARNOLFO DI CAMBIO, fig. 2). Pietro di Oderisio also designed the tomb of *Clement IV* (*c.* 1270; Viterbo, S Francesco), the first canopied tomb with a reclining figure in Italy, an innovation that Arnolfo developed and spread to other areas.

Deodatus Cosmati and Johannes Cosmati (*see* COSMATUS) were among the few local sculptors to take an interest in modern ideas, perhaps because papal commissions remained very conservative. The Roman tradition died out during the Avignonese captivity after 1309 as some artists left Rome while others arrived from elsewhere. The most important commission of this period, for example, the ciborium (1370) of S Giovanni in Laterano, is by the Sienese Giovanni di Stefano (*fl* 1366–91). Even after Gregory XI (*reg* 1370–78) returned, Gothic sculpture was mainly limited to tombs, such as the heavily ornamented double tomb of *Francesco Anguillara* (*d* 1406) *and Nicolò Anguillara* (*d* 1408; Capranica, S Francesco), which was made by local artists but nonetheless shows the influence of Tuscan art. Elsewhere in Lazio Gothic sculpture is found in church furnishing, fountains and architectural decoration.

Cistercian abbeys, which were numerous in the region from the 13th century, introduced another tradition of architectural sculpture concentrated on keystones and capitals, which were often carved with images of monastic life. At Fossanova Abbey (1187–1208) there appears to have beeen a collaboration between an architectural tradition drawn from Burgundy and Roman craftsmen, as demonstrated by the 'Classical' portal and some of the capitals. Similarly local elements are evident in the capitals, the lunettes over the portals and seven panels that formed part of a choir enclosure at Casamari Abbey (1208–17). The Cistercian style spread to the cities, notably Ferentino, where the influence of the Casamari workshop appears in S Maria Maggiore, S Lucia, S Ippolito and S Pancrazio. At VITERBO the nearby abbey of S Martino al Cimino appears to have been influential in the cloister (1266–8) of the Dominican church of S Maria in Gradi, the rich ornamentation of which shows evidence of the 'realism', favoured by the Dominicans, that became typical of sculpture in Viterbo, for example on the exterior of the Casa Poscia (early 14th century).

BIBLIOGRAPHY

L. Ciaccio: 'L'ultimo periodo della scultura gotica a Roma', *Ausonia*, i (1906), pp. 68–92

L. Filippini: *La scultura del trecento in Roma* (Rome, 1908)

G. Matthiae: 'Fulcro unificante della civiltà occidentale', *Lazio* (Milan, [1975]), pp. 237–492 (277–331)

I Cistercensi e il Lazio. Atti delle giornate di studio dell'Istituto di storia dell'arte dell'Università di Roma: Roma, 1978

Federico II e l'arte del duecento italiano. Atti della III settimana di studi di storia dell'arte medievale dell'Università di Roma 'La Sapienza': Roma, 1978

C. Zannella: 'Ferentino', *Inchieste su centri minori*, ed. F. Zeri, Storia dell'arte italiana, iii/1 (Turin, 1980)

A. Cadei: 'Immagini e segni nella scultura architettonica cistercense', *Presenza benedettina nel Piacentino. Atti delle giornate di studio: Bobbio and Chiaravalle della Colomba, 1981*

M. Righetti Tosti-Croce: *La Sabina medievale* (Cinisello-Balsamo, 1985)

Skulptur und Grabmal des Spätmittelalters in Rom und Italien. Akten des Kongresses Scultura e monumento sepolcrale del tardo medioevo a Roma e in Italia: Roma, 1985

P. C. Claussen: *Magistri doctissimi Romani: Die römischen Marmorkünstler der Mittelalters* (Stuttgart,1987)

A. M. D'Achille: 'La scultura', *Roma nel duecento: L'arte dei papi da Innocenzo III a Bonifacio VIII* (Turin, 1991), pp. 146–235

A. M. Romanini: 'Arnolfo di Cambio', *Enciclopedia dell'arte medievale*, ii (Rome, 1991), pp. 504–14

S. Fabiano: 'I capitelli tardo-duecenteschi di S Maria di Gradi a Viterbo', *A. Med.*, vi/2 (1992), pp. 113–35

J. Gardner: *The Tomb and the Tiara: Curial Tomb Sculpture in Rome and Avignon in the Later Middle Ages* (Oxford, 1992)

ANNA MARIA D'ACHILLE

(h) Campania. Gothic sculpture in Campania developed over two centuries, but there were many gaps in continuity. The new style, which drew on an interest in Classical models and knowledge of developments in France, as well as local Romanesque traditions, spread rapidly across southern Italy in the first half of the 13th century under the influence of Emperor Frederick II, whose antiquarian interests were most prominently demonstrated in the decorative sculpture of the town gate of CAPUA (1234–40; destr. 1557; sculpture in Capua, Mus. Prov. Campano; for illustration *see* HOHENSTAUFEN, (2)). Further examples of this 'Frederician' sculpture may be found in the abbey of the Trinità di Cava and to the north in Lazio (*see* §(g) above). The imperial workshops trained some of the most important sculptors of the second half of the 13th century, including NICOLA DI BARTOLOMEO DA FOGGIA, who made the pulpit (1272) in Ravello Cathedral, Melchiorre da Montalbano, creator of the portal (1279) and pulpit of Teggiano Cathedral, PEREGRINO DA SALERNO and probably Nicola Pisano himself.

There was a massive injection of the latest French Gothic trends after the Angevin dynasty established itself in 1266 (*see* NAPLES, §II, 1). Among the artists who came from north of the Alps were Teodorico and Giletto 'de Alemania', who were documented there in 1309 and carved the tomb of *Charles II* for Naples Cathedral (fragments only *in situ*). Among the few surviving works from this period are a beautiful royal head (Naples, Capodimonte) and three reclining statues of the Lagonissa family, including *Caterina Extendarda Lagonissa* (*c.* 1304) in Montevergine Abbey.

Until the early 14th century French influence ran parallel to that of the Romanesque tradition and Arnolfo di Cambio. This combination is evident in the tomb of *Archbishop Filippo Minutolo* (*d* 1301; Naples Cathedral) and in the work of Nicola da Monteforte, for example the *St Bartholomew* on the façade of Benevento Cathedral. Relations with central Italy grew more intense from the second decade, culminating in the arrival of the Sienese sculptor Tino di Camaino, who remained in Naples from 1324 until his death in 1337 (*see* TINO DI CAMAINO, §3) and established a well-organized workshop that monopolized all the most important commissions from the court and its circle. This brought a strong Sienese current into Neapolitan sculpture, while two Tuscan followers of Andrea Pisano, Pacio and Giovanni Bertini, were later commissioned to build the tomb of *Robert I* (1343–5; Naples, S Chiara).

Throughout the second half of the 14th century an army of local craftsmen followed, although not always with equal stylistic rigour, the formal models and monumental projects of Tino di Camaino and the Bertini. The Lazio sculptor Antonio Baboccio da Piperno (1351–*c.* 1435), who is documented in Naples from 1407, when he carved the portal (rebuilt) of Naples Cathedral, to 1421 (the tomb of *Ludovico Aldomorisco* in S Lorenzo Maggiore), introduced the French Flamboyant style from Milan, but this marked the end of Gothic sculpture in Naples, for it soon yielded to the progressive spread of the Tuscan Renaissance.

BIBLIOGRAPHY

O. Morisani: *Tino di Camaino a Napoli* (Naples, 1945)

——: 'L'arte di Napoli nell'età angioina', *Stor. Napoli*, iii (Naples, 1969), pp. 577–90, 620–33

F. Negri Arnoldi: 'Pietro di Oderisio, Nicola da Monteforte e la scultura campana del primo trecento', *Commentari*, xxiii (1972), pp. 12–30

F. Abbate: 'Percorso di Antonio Baboccio da Piperno', *Il monumento della regina Margherita di Durazzo* (Salerno, 1988), pp. 13–23 [with bibliog.]

F. Bologna: 'La Porta di Capua', *Fridericiana*, i/2 (1990–91), pp. 129–53 [with bibliog.]

FRANCESCO ACETO

(v) Low Countries.

(a) 1250–1300. Although the influence of northern French cathedral sculpture appeared sporadically in the Netherlands in the first half of the 13th century, for example on the Bergportaal (*c.* 1230) of St Servatius, Maastricht, the new style became pervasive only after 1250. The initial phase (*c.* 1250–80) appears on several abbreviated and provincial adaptations of French schemes, including the baptistery portal of Notre-Dame, Dinant,

and the *Last Judgement* portal of St Niklaas, Veurne. The best-preserved is the portal of St Jans Hospitaal (*c.* 1270–80), Bruges, in which elements of French Coronation and Last Judgement programmes are combined in a single tympanum. A Mosan *Virgin and Child* (*c.* 1280; Namur, Mus. Dioc.) from Bourseigne-Vieille is closely based on a Parisian formal type and shows greater maturity. A regional, probably Tournaisian style is represented by the monumental *Virgin and Child* (*c.* 1280–1300) in the De Potterie hospital chapel, Bruges, and a series of historiated rib consoles in the choir of St Walburga, Veurne. The workshops of Tournai and the Mosan region (*see* ROMANESQUE, §III, 1(viii)) continued to specialize in fonts and funerary monuments in blue-grey limestone, such as for the tomb of *Thiery d'Houffalize* (*d* 1282; Houffalize, Ste Catherine).

(b) 1300–1350. The greater autonomy of Netherlandish sculpture in the first half of the 14th century is shown in the appearance of regional schools, of which the most fully studied is that of the Meuse valley. Statues of the Virgin and Child (*c.* 1330–50; e.g. Antwerp Cathedral, see fig. 43; New York, Met.) by the Master of the Marble Madonnas, who was probably active in Liège, are among the finest examples of the mannered elegance and decorative linear complexity then favoured across Europe. White marble, associated with the adoption of grisaille techniques, was used by Gilles de Liège for the impressive black and white marble tombs of Archbishops *Walram von Jülich* (*d* 1349) and *Wilhelm von Gennep* (*d* 1362; both Cologne Cathedral). Their Mosan origin is suggested by comparison with the Porte de Bethléem (mid-14th century) of Notre-Dame, Huy, and the south portal (*c.* 1330–40) of Notre-Dame, Dinant. The latter is particularly important for an understanding of this regional school's origins: the *Coronation of the Virgin* in the gable is based directly on the reliefs on the exterior of the chevet chapels (*c.* 1320) of Notre-Dame, Paris, while figures in the archivolt surrounding the tympanum appear to be local variants on French formal types.

The *Virgin and Child* (*c.* 1310–20) on the west façade of Tournai Cathedral was an important influence on the Scheldt region for more than a century. Among the finest known examples of the Tournai school is the bluestone tomb effigy of a female figure (?Mahaut, Countess of Artois) in the abbey church of Saint-Denis. This work occupies a transitional position stylistically, combining the elongated, triangular facial type of *c.* 1300 with the planar and linear drapery, arranged in thin, sharply pointed vertical folds, that became characteristic of Tournai *c.* 1320–50. The tomb of *Jacques Castaigne* (*d* 1327; Tournai, St Jacques) and a female *gisant* (*c.* 1330–40) in the former abbey church of Cambron-Casteau illustrate the development towards a more graphic surface treatment.

Although the duchy of Brabant remained open to neighbouring influences, its indigenous tradition is apparent in the architectural sculpture, probably made by a single workshop, of the Lakenhal (begun 1317), Leuven, and in the south transept and aisle of St Genoveva, Oplinter. The hair and beards of the male heads have the abundant corkscrew curls that appear in later Brabantine works, such as several corbels in the tower vault (*c.* 1341–

43. Master of the Marble Madonnas: *Virgin and Child*, marble, from ?Liège, Low Countries, *c.* 1330–50 (Antwerp Cathedral)

50) of Notre-Dame-de-Hal and the three huge *Kings* decorating the north tower of the west façade of Reims Cathedral (Schmidt).

(c) 1350–1430. The tendency towards simpler, more monumental forms and an increasingly realistic treatment

44. *Entombment* group, stone, from the Low Countries, *c.* 1440–50 (Soignies, St Vincent)

of detail soon after the mid-14th century culminated in André Beauneveu's life-size alabaster *St Catherine* (1374–7; Kortrijk, Onze Lieve Vrouwkerk; for illustration *see* BEAUNEVEU, ANDRÉ). His style, which offers the best point of reference for the local development of Late Gothic sculpture, was rooted in the Scheldt regional tradition (e.g. a statuette of *St Catherine*, *c.* 1320; Lille, Mus. B.-A.). Beauneveu was active in the Netherlands and France (*see also* §(i)(c) above) and his influence extended to the end of the century, for example on various figures of the *Virgin and Child* of Tournai origin, including those on the south-west (*c.* 1380) and north (*c.* 1400) portals of Notre-Dame-de-Hal, and in Burgundy at St Just, Arbois; it can also be seen in Tournaisian 'picture epitaphs' of the early 15th century. From the early 1370s, however, it was gradually superseded by a Soft style tendency characterized by the more ample, expansive draperies and a deeper commitment to realism apparent in the *Coronation of the Virgin* (1390–1400) at St Jacques, Liège, and the historiated consoles (*c.* 1379; destr. 1792) from the façade of Bruges Stadhuis (*see* JEAN DE VALENCIENNES).

Stone sculpture in Brabant at this time was associated with a renewal of the lodge tradition led by Jean d'Oisy and his followers, as demonstrated on the west façade portals (?1360) of Onze Lieve Vrouw ten Poel, Tienen, and the sculpture in the choir of St Rombouts, Mechelen (*see* §II, 2(v) and fig. 20 above). Brussels was increasingly important by the early 15th century, partly owing to the activity of the MASTER OF HAKENDOVER (*see* MASTERS, ANONYMOUS, AND MONOGRAMMISTS, §I) on the sculpture (*c.* 1404–5; Brussels, Mus. Com.) for the belfry portal of Brussels Hôtel de Ville and the *Apostles* and wall tabernacle (*c.* 1408–9) in Notre-Dame-de-Hal. Although this sculptor's realistic style has been associated traditionally with the influence of Claus Sluter, it is more closely dependent on Beauneveu's late manner. Parallel Soft style tendencies are also encountered in the Tournai *Entombment* group (*c.* 1400–10; Ath, Mus. Athois) from Mainvault, which is possibly the earliest such ensemble in European sculpture, and the *St Anthony* (*c.* 1408) in the chapel of St Antoine-en-Barbefosse, near Mons.

The stylistic transition of the 1420s is exemplified by the monumental *Virgin and Child* (1422) in the abbey church at Tongerlo, which exhibits an amplitude of form and drapery motifs that anticipate the GRISAILLE techniques on the Ghent Altarpiece (*c.* 1423–32; Ghent, St Bavo; for illustration *see* EYCK, VAN, (1)). Important examples of small-scale architectural sculpture from this period in the northern Netherlands include figural consoles (early 15th century) in the choir of St Jan, Maastricht, and historiated bosses (*c.* 1412–20), possibly by a Brabantine workshop, in the choir of the Pieterskerk, Leiden.

(d) 1430–1530. Brussels became the artistic capital of the Netherlands during the Late Gothic period and its influence was to extend eventually to most of Europe. The first indications, however, of a new style appear in the work of JEAN DELEMER, whose *Annunciation* (completed 1428; Tournai Cathedral) introduced an eminently spatial narrative presentation enlivened by sharply defined, abruptly angular drapery. The new formal vocabulary emerged a few years later in Brabant, for example on the funerary relief of *Ditmar de Brême* (*d* 1439; Anderlecht, collegiate church of SS Pierre et Guidon), which is animated by a rhythmic play of lines. These tendencies culminated in the incisive Late Gothic 'Hard style' of surface treatment and facial expression found in the *Entombment* (*c.* 1440; Soignies, St Vincent; see fig. 44). Later works became less intense, showing an expressive linearity disciplined and modified by an elegance similar to that in the paintings of Rogier van der Weyden. About 1500 this style yielded to one displaying greater breadth and ample volumes.

Although portal sculpture declined in importance, Netherlandish workshops specialized in embellishing church interiors with extraordinarily rich sculptural programmes. These sometimes shared the pictorial and anecdotal themes of contemporary wooden altarpieces (*see also* §2(v) below), either as direct copies or in a parallel development as, for example, on the historiated consoles (*c.* 1440–50) on the exterior of Leuven Stadhuis, or on the narrative groups of the choir-screen at Onze Lieve Vrouwkerk, Aarschot. Monumental stone sculpture remained important, but much has been destroyed: notable survivals include an impressive *St Adrian* (*c.* 1460; Brussels, Musées Royaux A. & Hist.), sometimes attributed to Nicolaus Gerhaert, three *Apostles* (*c.* 1470–80; ex-Ste Gertrude, Nivelles; Nivelles, Mus. Com. Archéol.) and *Entombment* groups in the chapel of St André, Binche, and Onze Lieve Vrouwhospitaal, Kortrijk. Work executed elsewhere by Netherlandish sculptors, such as the rich decoration of the priory church at Brou (*see* MEIT, CONRAT), helps to provide a more complete impression of their output.

The transition to Late Gothic in the northern Netherlands may be studied in the remarkable spandrel series that decorates the south portal (*c.* 1430) of St Janskerk, 's Hertogenbosch; their discontinuous, although still fluid, surfaces may be compared with the contemporary *Apostles* in the choir of Aachen Cathedral. A head of *St Peter* (*c.* 1440–50; Arnhem, Gemeentemus.) shows how the forms became more rigid and austerely linear. Between *c.* 1430 and 1450 Utrecht developed into a leading sculptural centre with a distinctive regional style typified by the limestone *Saints* (*c.* 1455; Utrecht, Cent. Mus.) from the cathedral, now attributed to Jan Nude. Few examples in stone survive, the most notable being a series of 'picture epitaphs' and damaged altarpieces; these, however, are of consistently high quality and originality.

BIBLIOGRAPHY

J. Duverger: *De Brusselsche steenbickeleren der XIVe en XVe eeuw: Klaas Sluter en zijn Brusselsche medewerkers te Dijon* (Ghent, 1933)

R. Bergius: *Französische und belgische Konsol- und Zwickelplastik im 14. und 15. Jahrhundert* (Munich, 1936)

J. Steppe: *Het koordoksaal in de Nederlanden* (Brussels, 1952)

D. Roggen: 'Prae-Sluteriaanse, Sluteriaanse, post-Sluteriaanse Nederlandse sculptuur', *Gent. Bijdr. Kstgesch. & Oudhdknd.*, xvi (1956), pp. 111–87

R. Didier, M. Henss and J. A. Schmoll gen. Eisenwerth: 'Une Vierge tournaisienne à Arbois (Jura) et le problème des Vierges de Hal: Contribution à la chronologie et à la typologie', *Bull. Mnmtl*, cxxviii/2 (1970), pp. 93–113

G. Schmidt: 'Bemerkungen zur Königsgalerie der Kathedrale von Reims', *Wien. Jb. Kstgesch.*, xxv (1972), pp. 96–106

Rhein und Maas: Kunst und Kultur, 800–1400 (exh. cat., Cologne, Ksthalle; Brussels, Musées Royaux A. & Hist.; 1972)

R. Didier: 'Skulpturen des Maasgebiets aus Jahren 1330–1360', *Westfalen*, lv (1977), pp. 8–29

K. Morand: 'Claus Sluter: The Early Years', *Liber amicorum Herman Libaers*, ed. F. Vanwijngaerden and others (Brussels, 1984), pp. 561–84

R. Didier: *La Sculpture mosane du XIVe siècle* (Namur, 1993)

J. STEYAERT

(vi) Portugal. Gothic sculpture did not appear in Portugal until the mid-13th century. Development was slow, and until the 14th century its quality lagged behind that in the main centres of France and Germany. The principal centre of production was Coimbra, which was then the main royal residence. The patronage of the court was augmented by that of the bishops and the city's many monasteries and collegiate churches, which were influential throughout the country. Good quality Ançã stone was readily available and there were excellent facilities for river transport. Although much fine work was also produced after 1340 in association with the court circle of Lisbon, for example the tomb of *Lobo Fernandes Pacheco* (Lisbon Cathedral), and under the patronage of Bishop Pedro of Évora, including the west portal, the cloisters and the Bishop's tomb in Évora Cathedral, it has been estimated that nearly three quarters of Portuguese Gothic sculpture was made in Coimbra. Most sculpture was for tombs and single figures. Altarpieces were few and small, and Portuguese taste did not extend to large figured portals: the west façade (*c.* 1400–*c.* 1420) of Batalha Abbey, although probably made by a workshop from Coimbra, may owe much to the possible origins of its designer, Huguet, on the Mediterranean coast of Spain.

The figures on the earliest Gothic tombs, such as those of Bishops *Tiburcio* (*d* 1246), *Egas Fafes* (1286; both

45. Tomb of *Peter I, King of Portugal*, limestone, Alcobaça Abbey, Portugal, commissioned 1355

Coimbra, Sé Velha) and the *Infante Rodrigo Sanches* (Grijó, monastery of S Salvador), are more stiffly portrayed than those of the preceding Romanesque style. Greater naturalism, however, was gradually introduced, notably in the historiated capitals in the cloister of the monastery of Celas, Coimbra. Portuguese sculpture in the early 14th century was revolutionized by the arrival of the Aragonese MESTRE PÊRO, who was responsible for the tombs of *St Isabel* (*d* 1336; Coimbra, convent of S Clara), *Archbishop Gonçalo Pereira* (Braga Cathedral) and the Greek princess *Vetaça* (Coimbra, Sé Velha). The output of his busy workshop, for example the tomb of *Dona Leonor* (Santarém, S Clara) and sculpture in Oporto, Lamego (Lamego, Mus. Reg.), and the parish church at Oliveira do Hospital, became steadily more graceful and accomplished. It is difficult to ascribe to any single workshop the limestone tombs of *Peter I* and *Inês de Castro* (commissioned 1355) in Alcobaça Abbey (*see* ALCOBAÇA ABBEY, §1), the highest achievements of Portuguese Gothic sculpture (see fig. 45). The influence of the best French workshops cannot be excluded, but the basic tradition is that of Coimbra, raised to a peak by the King's wish to surpass all previous memorials.

From the 14th century tombs in northern Portugal were occasionally executed in granite and decorated with hunting scenes along the sides of the sarcophagus; the most outstanding example is the enormous tomb of *Pedro, Count of Barcelos* (*d* 1354) in the former Cistercian abbey church at São João da Tarouca. During the early 15th century individual statues, including figures of the Virgin and Child (e.g. Coimbra, Mus. N. Machado de Castro), display the Burgundian influence that was then current in Spain. The final phase of Gothic sculpture in Portugal was represented by the intricately entwined architectural decoration characteristic of the MANUELINE STYLE (*see also* §II, 2(viii) above).

BIBLIOGRAPHY

V. Correia: *Três túmulos* (Lisbon, 1924)

——: 'A escultura em Portugal nos séculos XII, XIII e XIV', *Biblos* (Coimbra, 1929)

R. dos Santos: *A escultura em Portugal*, 2 vols (Lisbon, 1950–51)

A. Nogueira Conçalves: *Estudos de história da arte medieval* (Coimbra, 1978)

P. Dias: *O gótico* (1986), iv of *História da arte em Portugal* (Lisbon, 1986)

PEDRO DIAS

(vii) Scandinavia. Stone sculpture was much less widespread in Scandinavia than it had been in the preceding centuries (*see* ROMANESQUE, §III, 1(xi)). This partly reflected the changing iconography of baptismal fonts, which usually were no longer decorated with biblical scenes. Of greater importance, however, was the increasing use of brick as a building material for Gothic churches in Denmark, Skåne and the region of Mälardalen, west of Stockholm. Accordingly there was little demand for architectural sculpture in stone throughout much of Scandinavia and building in cut stone, which was mainly executed by specially imported workshops, continued only where suitable material was easily accessible, for example in Norway and central Sweden. Unlike many of their Romanesque predecessors, Gothic sculptors did not sign their work.

Soft soapstone continued to be worked in Norway, notably at Trondheim Cathedral, which was the main centre for stone sculpture in the 13th century (*see* TRONDHEIM, §2(ii)). The most expressive examples are the large statues of *Christ*, the *Apostles* and various saints (1260s–1270s) on the west façade, which were carved in a mature French Gothic style of swelling draperies, corkscrew curls and well-balanced *contrapposto*. With this important exception, Norwegian sculpture was dominated by English influences. The new choir (1272–1303) of Stavanger Cathedral, for example, was decorated with many corbel heads representing the king, duke and bishop. Similarly lively and well-characterized heads (1280s; Oslo, Hist. Mus.) have survived from Oslo Cathedral (destr.). The portal of the church at Eidsberg, decorated with an enthroned *St Olav* and two atlantids, is a rare example of Gothic stone sculpture in a parish church.

In Sweden sandstone was employed in Västergötland. The development from Early Gothic around the mid-13th century to High Gothic at the end of the century may be traced on portals, corbel heads and two princely tombs in the Cistercian abbey churches at Varnhem and Gudhem, and at Skara Cathedral. English influence may be discerned in the green men, rulers and founders on the corbel heads, some of which resemble portraiture, and on the capitals in the choir of the Nikolaikyrkan, Örebro. About 1320 the blind arcades at the west end of the nave at Linköping Cathedral were richly embellished with sculptural decoration (*see* LINKÖPING, §1). The figures represented include two wrestlers, someone pulling out a thorn and an elderly half-naked couple, who are shown defecating. These contrast with the courteous expressions, wavy hair and detailed costumes, including chain mail and a veil, that characterize the protruding male and female heads leaning towards each other from the spandrels in five of the arches. Exuberant foliage on the arcade in the Decorated style and contemporary English coins found underneath point to the presence of English artists; the closest parallel to the heads appears in the arch of the blind arcade of the choir screen at Southwell Minster. The same sculptor also carved green men on the roof bosses in the nave vaults, which are by turns frighteningly distorted or sadly beautiful. He was succeeded by a German who set his mark on refined tympanum reliefs of scenes from the *Nativity* and *Passion* (*c.* 1330), which were arranged in several registers, in the German fashion, above the south portal (fragments now inside the church).

In 1287 stone-carvers from Paris under the leadership of ETIENNE DE BONNEUIL were summoned to Uppsala Cathedral. Only two of the limestone column statues they made for the portals have survived. There are, however, 24 seated *Apostles* and *Prophets* in soapstone on the double archivolt of the south portal and 6 reliefs (some restored) of the *Creation* on the lintel. All are in elegant French style of well-balanced, harmonizing forms. Construction had originally been in limestone, but the German workshop that took over in the early 1300s worked in brick. Its stone architectural sculpture for a sequence of 12 dramatic corbel reliefs includes *Jacob Wrestling with the Angel*, the *Death of the Virgin* and two unusual subjects, the *Jewish Sow* (an anti-Semitic motif of mainly German origin) and the Swedish tale of *Staffan the Stableboy*, shown watering his horses under the star of Bethlehem.

Conditions were very different on Gotland, where more than 50 parish churches were decorated with limestone sculpture, especially during the first half of the 14th century. Production was dominated by a large workshop known as Egypticus, which decorated portals with reliefs, churchtowers with imaginative gargoyles and put large masks on interior capitals and corbels. The workshop's lively narrative style was influenced by the German-inspired reliefs of Linköping and Uppsala cathedrals. The figures are proportionately small with large heads, and hems are represented by a double-lined border. Scenes from the Life of Christ, especially the Infancy of Christ, are most frequently presented, often including elements reflecting daily life on Gotland, for example on the south portal of Stånga Church. One of the finest cycles was carved by Fabulator, the leading sculptor of the Egypticus workshop, on the three portals of Martebo church, one of which contains the *Nativity*, *Presentation in the Temple* and the *Flight into Egypt* (see fig. 46).

The only important centre for Gothic sculpture during the later 15th century was Linköping Cathedral, where the choir was completed in two campaigns (*c*. 1408–20 and 1487–1500), for the second of which sculptors were summoned from Cologne. One known as the Mimic Master decorated corbels and two tabernacles with animatedly grimacing and gesticulating figures. ADAM VAN DÜREN, who executed some 16 heraldic bosses in the choir, entered the service of the Danish king in the late 1490s; many of his reliefs bear his mark.

BIBLIOGRAPHY

H. Fett: *Billedhuggerkunsten i Norge under Sverraetten* [The art of sculpture in Norway at the time of the Sverre dynasty] (Kristiania, 1908)

G. Boëthius and A. Romdahl: *Uppsala domkyrka, 1258–1435* (Uppsala, 1935)

F. Nordström: *Virtues and Vices on the 14th-century Corbels in the Choir of Uppsala Cathedral*, Acta U. Upsaliensis: Figura, vii (1956)

G. Fischer: *Domkirken i Stavanger* (Oslo, 1964) [Eng. summary]

——: *Kirkebygget i middelalderen* [Church building in the Middle Ages] (1965), i of *Domkirken i Trondheim* (Oslo, 1965)

E. Lagerlöf: *Gotländsk stenskulptur från gotiken: En stenhuggarverkstad på 1300-talet* [Gothic stone sculpture from Gotland: a stone-carving workshop from the 1300s] (Stockholm, 1975)

B. Cnattingius: *Studier i Linköpings domkyrkas byggnadshistoria* [Studies in the building history of Linköping Cathedral] (Stockholm, 1977)

R. Edenheim and I. Rosell: *Varnhems klosterkyrka*, Sveriges Kyrkor, Konsthistoriskt Inventarium, cxc (Stockholm, 1982)

B. Cnattingius and others: *Linköpings domkyrka*, Sveriges Kyrkor, Konsthistoriskt Inventarium, cc–cci (Stockholm, 1987) [Eng. summary and captions]

J. Svanberg: *Furstebilder från Folkungatid* [Portraits of princes from the time of the Folkungs] (Skara, 1987)

Age of Chivalry: Art in Plantagenet England, 1200–1400 (exh. cat., ed. J. Alexander and P. Binski; London, RA, 1987), pp. 324–7

JAN SVANBERG

(viii) Spain. Scholars have devised various terms to describe the new trends that developed in Spanish sculpture in the late 12th century: Yarza, for example, referred to the period as marking the 'dissolution of the Romanesque'. The Pórtico de la Gloría (*c*. 1188) carved by MATEO at Santiago de Compostela Cathedral (*see* SANTIAGO DE COMPOSTELA, §1(ii) and fig. 3) belongs to a series of works from the last third of the 12th century in which the sculptors drew on elements imported from south-west France, Burgundy and the Ile-de-France, without abandoning Romanesque traditions (*see also* §II, 1(vi) above).

46. Fabulator: *Presentation in the Temple* and *Flight into Egypt*, relief from the choir portal, Martebo Church, Gotland, Sweden, *c*. 1340

The resulting style has been termed 'proto-Gothic' (Azcárate) or 'Early Gothic' (Ara).

(a) 13th and 14th centuries. (b) Early 15th century. (c) Later 15th century and the early 16th.

(a) 13th and 14th centuries.

Castile and León. The evolution towards both a free and elegant form and the idealizing naturalism evident at Santiago was more fully developed by the arrival of craftsmen from northern France early in the 13th century. The earliest examples of Gothic sculpture in Spain appear on the west façade portal (*c*. 1218–36) of Túy Cathedral in Galicia (*see* TÚY, §1). Two sculptors have been identified, working in a style that draws inspiration from the cathedrals at Laon, Sens and Chartres. To the south in León, the west portal of Ciudad Rodrigo Cathedral has been dated after 1224 by Gómez Moreno (*see* CIUDAD RODRIGO, §2). The figures of *Abraham*, the *Queen of Sheba*, *Solomon*, *Moses* and *David* are related to earlier examples at Chartres.

The cathedrals of Burgos, León and Toledo provide the finest collections of Spanish High Gothic sculpture, reflecting the rivalries between their respective provinces of Old Castile, León and New Castile. The earliest, Burgos Cathedral (*see* BURGOS, §2(i)(b)), was built after 1221 with a donation by Ferdinand III (*reg* 1217–52), who had combined the crowns of Castile and León and wished to make Burgos his royal city in opposition to León. Since Bishop Maurice (*reg* 1217–38) had travelled in France and was aware of the latest artistic changes in the neighbouring country, it is not surprising that artists were summoned from France. The Puerta del Sarmental (*c*. 1235–40; see fig. 47) in the south transept, for example, shows the influence of the master responsible for the trumeau *Christ* (*'Beau Dieu'*) at Amiens (*see* AMIENS, §1(ii)). Whereas for emblematic reasons the representation of the apocalyptic *Christ* surrounded by tetramorph, Apostles and the elders of the Apocalypse employs archaic iconography that had been typical of Romanesque sculpture but had been obsolete in France from *c*. 1170, the *Last Judgement* on the north transept's Puerta de los Apóstolores (or de la Coronería; *c*. 1240) draws on the account by St Matthew (24:29–51) and has direct links with work at Chartres. The cloister portal (after 1260) is a harmonious work extolling the coming of Christ as God and Messiah; the figures to the side have sometimes been identified as *Ferdinand II*

47. *Christ with Symbols of the Evangelists*, tympanum detail, Puerta del Sarmental, Burgos Cathedral, Spain, *c.* 1235–40

and *Beatrice of Hohenzollern* (*see* BURGOS, fig. 3). Although the three portals of the west façade, dedicated to the Virgin, were destroyed in the 18th century, much of the interior sculpture and the narrative scenes carved on the corbels and capitals of the cloisters has survived.

León Cathedral (begun *c.* 1255) is a synthesis of various French churches. As work continued throughout the second half of the 13th century, its sculpture varied widely in quality and style (Franco Mata; *see* LEÓN, §II, 1(ii)). Its architect, Master Enrique, was also Master of the Works at Burgos Cathedral, from where he copied the design of the south transept portal, although the León example is of notably inferior quality. The diaphanous west portals imitate those of the transepts of Chartres Cathedral. Sculptors from Burgos included the so-called Master of La Virgen Blanca, who carved the central figure of the *Virgin and Child* (see fig. 48). Above this are particularly fine figures of the *Blessed* by the Master of the Last Judgement, who followed French models (*see* LEÓN, fig. 2). The importance of funerary sculpture in León, of which sculptors from the cathedral workshop produced such outstanding examples as the tomb of *Bishop Martín Fernández* (*reg* 1254–89; León Cathedral), has been insufficiently recognized.

The innovations at Burgos and León spread to the neighbouring regions. The portals at S María la Real, Sasamón, and S Estéban (late 13th century), near Castrojeriz, for example, were both influenced by sculpture at Burgos, and the south transept portal of El Burgo de Osma Cathedral, which was begun in 1232 but remained unfinished until the following century, shows the influence specifically of the Puerta del Sarmental. The figures on the doorjambs, however, are inspired by such Leonese sculpture as the north portal (late 13th century) of Ávila Cathedral (*see* ÁVILA, §2(i)(b)).

The sculptural decoration of the cloisters at Burgos Cathedral served as a model for others in Castile and León, including those of Oviedo Cathedral (late 13th century–mid-15th). The cloisters of León Cathedral were also begun towards the end of the 13th century and construction continued until the 16th. The decoration includes biblical scenes, Apostles and saints, fables and legends, scenes from daily life, Virtues and Vices, real and fantastic animals, heraldic devices and vegetation.

Similar influences were also exported to the province of Palencia. The so-called Master of the Jambs was responsible for the portal of the Templars' church of S María la Blanca at Villalcázar de Sirga, which also contains the tombs of *Felipe* (*d* 1274), brother of Alfonso X, King of Castile, and his wife. A number of sculptors are documented in Palencia, Valladolid and León, including Pedro Pintor, who carved the tomb of *Alvar Fernández Podestat* (*d* 1262; Carrión de los Condes, Convento de S Zoilo), and Roi Martínez de Burueva, who was responsible for the tomb of *Rodrigo Gonzáles Girón* in the monastery of Nuestra Señora de Benavides, near León. Between 1230 and the early 14th century many tombs were commissioned by members of the Castañeda, Villalobos, Beni-Gómez,

48. Master of La Virgen Blanca: *Virgin and Child*, detail, west portal, León Cathedral, Spain, after *c.* 1255

Téllez de Meseses and other noble families. The west Puerta de la Majestad (late 13th century) of the collegiate church of S María la Mayor, Toro, combines within its original iconographic programme the influences of the Puerta de la Coronería at Burgos and the León Master of the Last Judgement.

The dense iconographic programme of sculpture, which covers the three archivolts, the tympanum, lintel and jambs of the Puerta del Reloj (1280–1300) at Toledo Cathedral is connected to the Mozarabic liturgy; it includes scenes of the *Infancy and Ministry of Christ* and others of the *Life and Martyrdom of St Ildefonsus* (Pérez Higuera). Italian influence, although less extensive in Toledo than in Aragon (see below), became important in the 14th century and may be seen in the treatment of the *Deposition*. Toledo's importance in the 14th century is reflected in the funerary chapels and tombs of *Cardinal Gil de Albornoz* (*d* 1367) and *Archbishop Pedro Tenorio* (*d* 1399, by Fernán González). The city's pluralist religious nature is well displayed on the 57 reliefs of scenes from *Genesis* and *Exodus* placed on the outer panels of the choir-screens. These correspond to the 12 prophesies that appear in the Easter Vigil readings. Medieval legends were also inserted. Adam, in the *Creation of Adam*, is shown without a navel, a tradition drawn from Jewish texts that indicates a clear connection with the iconography of haggadot, especially the Sarajevo Haggadah (14th century; Sarajevo, N. Mus.)

Although there are fine examples of 'proto-Gothic' sculpture in the province of Alava, including those at S Andrés (begun *c.* 1181), Armentia, and S María (early 13th century), Estíbaliz, it was not until the 14th century that Vitoria became an important political centre. This was accompanied by a frenzied building campaign and the formation of a sculptural workshop of exceptional originality, in spite of the influence of Burgos, Navarre and other nearby workshops. Its work may be seen, for example, in S María (now the cathedral) on the portal of St Anne, which lies west of the transept on the Epistle side, and the scenes from the *Life of the Virgin* on the more monumental west portal. The exaltation of the Virgin is also the theme of the magnificent portal (late 14th century) of S María de los Reyes, Laguardia, which was then under the control of Navarre.

Navarre. During the 14th century a splendid artistic tradition developed in the kingdom of Navarre, which had close dynastic contacts with France. This was based on an eclectic stylistic combination of French, Castilian, German and English influences and mainly centred around Pamplona. Bishop Arnaldo de Barbazán (*reg* 1318–55) was an enthusiastic patron whose commissions included the north and east walks of the cloisters and their associated buildings at Pamplona Cathedral, which constitutes one of the most accomplished ensembles in Spanish sculpture (*see* PAMPLONA, §2). The Puerta Preciosa in the cloisters is an extraordinary work decorated with scenes of the *Death* and *Coronation of the Virgin* taken from apocryphal texts. Other sculpture includes that on the portal of Nuestra Señora del Amparo and on the pulpit, corbels and bosses in the refectory, which is believed to date from before 1330, while the tombs of *Bishop Barbazán*, *Miguel Sánchez de Asiaín* (*d* 1364) and a princess, perhaps *Blanca* (*c.* 1370), the daughter of Charles I, King of Navarre (*reg* 1349–87), are notable examples of funerary art. Elsewhere in Navarre, the doorway (third quarter of the 14th century) of S María, Ujué, displays a rich sculptural array.

Aragon. Although French influence was not absent from Catalonia in the 13th century, the distinctively eclectic forms of Catalan Gothic did not develop until the reign of James II, King of Aragon (*reg* 1291–1327), as a result of cultural and political relations with southern France (Durliat) and southern Italy (Franco; *see also* §II, 2(vii)(a) above). Trading relations with Liguria and Tuscany also encouraged artistic contact with those regions. Funerary art was especially sensitive to Italian trends: the royal tombs in Palermo Cathedral, for example, inspired the series in the abbey church at Santes Creus, including those of *Peter III* (1291, by MASTER BARTOMEU), *James II* and his first wife *Blanche of Anjou* (*d* 1310). The tomb of *Archbishop Juan de Aragón* (*d* 1334; Tarragona Cathedral) is closely related to Tuscan sculpture, especially that of Tino di Camaino, Andrea Pisano and Nino Pisano. Pisan influences associated with Giovanni Pisano (Franco, 1988) are apparent in the reliefs of scenes from the saint's life on the alabaster sarcophagus of *St Eulalia* (1327; Barcelona Cathedral); the first stage of these was carried out by a pupil of Giovanni Pisano named Lupo di Francesco.

Lleida was also sensitive to the influence of Italian sculpture, generally blended with ideas from southern

France, or drawing on the Italianizing Gothic forms that were developing in Catalonia. Italian influence is also evident in such outstanding products of the Girona workshop, which developed in the second half of the 14th century (*see* GIRONA, §1(ii)), as the alabaster retable dedicated to the White Virgin and the tomb of the *Blessed Miró* in the collegiate church of San Joan de les Abadesses. The influence of English sculpture, alongside that of Italian, may be seen at Huesca and Valencia in the first half of the century. The Puerta de los Apóstoles in Valencia Cathedral, for example, contains Anglo-French elements and has been associated with Nicolás de Antona (or Southampton; *fl* 1304). It served as the model for the portals at S María la Mayor, Morella, and S María, Sagunto.

Stone retables were characteristic of Catalonia in the 14th and 15th centuries: more than 50 survive, spread throughout the region. They are usually large, dedicated to the Virgin or to saints, and the decoration is strongly narrative in tone. One of the most beautiful examples is the alabaster retable of the Virgin (*c.* 1345) in S María, Cornellà del Conflent, signed by JAUME CASCALLS, who was perhaps the foremost sculptor in Catalonia in the 14th century. He was one of several artists, including Master Aloi (*fl* 1351), Pedro Guines and, after 1363, Jordi de Deu (*fl c.* 1361–1418), who were commissioned by Peter IV (*reg* 1336–87) to work on the royal tombs (fragments *in situ*) at Poblet Abbey. Various influences may be discerned in Cascalls's style, including that of his father-in-law, Ferrer Bassa, the most Italianate painter in the region. Cascalls was also Master of the Works at the Seu Vella, Lleida, and collaborated on the retable of St Ursula in S Llorenç, Lleida. The retable (1376) by Bartomeu Robio in Lleida Cathedral is a further demonstration of how Catalan artists in the second half of the century had assimilated foreign influences and developed a personal style.

The sculptor and goldsmith PERE MORAGUES, who was documented in Barcelona from 1358 and lived in Saragossa from 1379 to 1385, executed several works for Peter IV. The tomb of *Archbishop Lope Fernández de Luna* (1379–*c.* 1382) in the 'Parroquieta' (parish chapel) of Saragossa Cathedral is a beautiful example of 14th-century Catalan funerary art, with the *Apostles* on the front of the sarcophagus and the *Entombment* and saints set below. The tomb of *Juan Fernández de Heredia* in the collegiate church at Caspe (Saragossa) is also attributed to him.

(b) Early 15th century. The export of wool to the south Netherlands from the reign of John I, King of Castile (*reg* 1379–90), enriched many aristocratic families. In the absence of strong royal government, their rivalry sometimes manifested itself in ostentatious displays of wealth. John II (*reg* 1406–54), for example, left control to the all-powerful Álvaro de Luna (*d* 1453), who built his imposing castle–palace at Escalona from 1435 and funerary chapel (1440s) in Toledo Cathedral, both of which have lavish heraldic decoration (*see* LUNA (ii)). Even before the end of the 14th century the work of PERE ÇA ANGLADA displays signs of the Netherlandish influence, introduced from the duchy of Burgundy (*see* §§(i)(d) and (v) above), that was to be the dominant stylistic trend in Castile, Aragon and Navarre for most of the first half of the 15th century. Features of the style include a characteristic fusing of pathos and melancholy, and the arrangement of heavy folds of thick drapery to produce chiaroscuro effects.

Castile. The new influences were soon incorporated into funerary sculpture. One of the most representative examples is the tomb of *Bishop Alonso Carrillo de Albornóz* (*d* 1439; see fig. 49) in the presbytery of Sigüenza Cathedral. The recumbent figure, shown as if asleep with the head and body turned slightly to one side, and the singing angels that keep vigil at the head and feet are dominated by a sense of movement and naturalness. The biblical figures arranged beneath the arcosolium are elegantly dressed and have individualized expressions. Across the front of the sarcophagus are three narrative reliefs, dated by inscription to 1426, which run together to form a frieze of the *Life of St Eustace.*

Around Valladolid, Burgundian influence is evident in the tombs of *María de Molina* (*c.* 1410–*c.* 1430; Valladolid, convent of Las Huelgas) and *Doña Juana Enriquez* (1444; Torrelobatón, SS María y Pedro). The Founder's Chapel (1430–35) in the convent of S Clara, Tordesillas, is one of the purest examples of the style and contains monumental statues of the *Apostles* and the tombs of *Fernán López de Saldaña*, his wife *Elvira de Acebedo*, their family and *Elvira de Portocarrero*, the first wife of Don Alvaro de Luna. The alabaster effigies of *Gómez de Manrique and Sancha de Rojas* (second quarter of the 15th century; Burgos, Mus. Arqueol. Prov.), which were originally placed in their funerary chapel in the Hieronymite monastery of Fresdeval, show French influence, although they are more realistic in approach. The tomb in the church of the Hospital of Simon Ruiz, Medina del Campo, of *Fray Lope de Barrientos*, Bishop of Segovia (*d* 1454), is notable for the original manner in which the deceased is shown kneeling at prayer. This pose may have been taken from the statues intended for the tomb of *Álvaro de Luna and Doña Juana de Pimentel* (*c.* 1440; destr.; fragments in Toledo Cathedral). The Bishop's tomb is the first stone example of the type, which became widespread by the end of the century (*see* §(c) below), for example for the tomb of *Peter the Cruel* (*c.* 1450; Madrid, Mus. Arqueol. N.).

Aragon. There is abundant documentary evidence of connections between Catalan and Mallorcan artists and the south Netherlands, and of northern masters working in Aragon. Pere Ça Anglada's assistants in the execution of the upper choir-stalls (1394–9) of Barcelona Cathedral included ANTONI CANET, PERE OLLER and the Picardian Pere de Sant Joan, who was later Master of the Works at the cathedrals of Gerona and Palma de Mallorca. Canet's alabaster tomb of *Bishop Ramon d'Escales* (1409; Barcelona Cathedral) incorporates a frieze of weepers that shows close familiarity with Franco-Flemish models derived from the work of Claus Sluter. The presence of JUAN DE LA HUERTA in Dijon from the 1430s provides evidence that artistic exchange was not limited to one direction. Another representative, and well-travelled, artist during the first phase of Franco-Flemish influence was GUILLEM SAGRERA, who was active in Perpignan and Naples as well as Barcelona and Palma de Mallorca, where he carved the magnificent *St Peter* (1422) on the Portal del Mirador of the cathedral, and probably also *SS Paul* and *John.*

49. Tomb of *Bishop Alonso Carrillo de Albornóz*, Sigüenza Cathedral, Spain, second quarter of the 15th century

Pere Johan (*d* after 1458), the son of Jordi de Deu, provides a link to the Catalan artists of the previous generation who were influenced by Italian sculpture. This continuing tradition, which was further demonstrated by the 12 marble reliefs of scenes from the *Old Testament* and *New Testament* (1418–24) carved by Giuliano Fiorentino for the rood screen in the old choir of Valencia Cathedral, is evident in Pere's roundel of *St George* (1418) on the balustrade of the Palau de la Generalitat, Barcelona. He executed notably expressive reliefs of scenes from the *Life of St Thecla* for the *retablo mayor* (1426–33) of Tarragona Cathedral (*see* TARRAGONA, §2). From 1444 until 1450, when he went to Naples, he worked on the retable of Saragossa Cathedral; this was completed (1477–80) by Hans von Gmünd.

Navarre. Navarre's close links with France ensured that Sluter's influence, as introduced through Avignon (*see* §(i)(d) above) and Toulouse, was soon evident in the kingdom. There were also direct connections with Burgundy, since JEHAN LOME lived in Dijon from 1405 to 1410 and is documented in Navarre from the following year. The hooded weepers and lamenting ladies of the court set in niches along the tomb-chest of his finest work, the marble and alabaster tomb of *Charles III and Eleonor of Castile* (1413–19; Pamplona Cathedral), are influenced by those processing around the tomb of *Philip the Bold* (Dijon, Mus. B.-A.; for illustration *see* WEEPER).

(c) Later 15th century and the early 16th. The most expressive reflection of the realism introduced through the influence of Netherlandish painting towards the mid-15th century is the tomb of *Bishop Bernat de Pau* (*d* 1457; Girona Cathedral), the recumbent figure of which recalls that of *Cardinal Juan de Cervantes* (*d* 1453; Seville Cathedral) by Lorenzo Mercadante (see below). The former is one of the period's few important examples of stone sculpture in eastern Spain, since patronage had shifted towards Castile and Andalusia.

Castile. The gradual evolution from Castilian Flamboyant towards the last manifestation of Gothic in Spain, the HISPANO-FLEMISH STYLE (*see also* §II, 2(vii)(b) and (c) above), was led not by Spanish artists but by those who had come from Germany, the south Netherlands and northern France, attracted by the possibility of work or at the request of a prelate: Juan de Colonia, for example, was probably summoned by Alonso de Cartagena, Bishop of Burgos (*reg* 1415–56). Just as Jorge Inglés introduced the latest trends in Flemish painting to the Castilian court, and as Hanequin de Bruselas brought the most modern architectural styles to Toledo, so Mercadante, Egas Cueman and JUAN ALEMÁN adapted northern sculptural techniques to the requirements of Spanish patrons for retables, tombs and religious images, rather than architectural sculpture. Egas Cueman, for example, adopted the recently developed wall-tomb type with a kneeling effigy for the tomb of *Alonso de Velasco* and his wife (1467–80; Monastery of Guadalupe; *see* EGAS, (1)) but decorated it with a wealth of south Netherlandish detail.

50. Sebastián de Toledo: tomb of *Álvaro de Luna and Doña Juana de Pimentel*, marble, Toledo Cathedral, Spain, 1489

The artists of the next generation integrated these northern Gothic elements with the native *Mudéjar* decoration to create the exuberance of Hispano-Flemish. In Toledo the surprising results of this combination may be seen in the rich exterior decoration of the apse and the abundant interior statuary at S Juan de los Reyes (founded 1476; see fig. 26 above), designed by JUAN GUAS. The sculptural tradition that developed in Toledo is particularly well illustrated by the double tomb of *Álvaro de Luna and Doña Juana de Pimentel* (1489; Toledo Cathedral; see fig. 50) by SEBASTIÁN DE TOLEDO.

Burgos was the second important artistic centre during the second half of the 15th century (*see* BURGOS, §2). Members of the DE COLONIA family and their extensive workshop were active here for more than six decades after Juan de Colonia's arrival *c.* 1442. The increasingly Spanish nature of their later output, such as the decoration devised in Valladolid for the façades of the Colegio of S Gregorio (1487–96; for illustration *see* VALLADOLID) and of S Pablo (*c.* 1492), demonstrates the evolution away from their Lower Rhenish origins to the Hispano-Flemish style. For the last two decades of the 15th century the Colonia workshop's dominance, now overseen by Simón de Colonia (*see* COLONIA, DE, (2)), was rivalled by that of Gil de Siloe. His tombs in the charterhouse of Miraflores, near Burgos, include the alabaster double tomb of *John II and Isabella of Portugal* (1489–93; for illustration *see* SILOE, (1)) and the wall tomb of the *Infante Alfonso* (1489–93). The latter is of the type showing the prince at prayer, as is that of *Juan de Padilla* (*c.* 1500–03; ex-Fresdeval Monastery; Burgos, Mus. Arqueol. Prov.), in which early traces of French Renaissance influence are discernible, perhaps owing to the presence in Burgos of Felipe Vigarny after 1498.

Andalusia. Córdoba and Seville had passed to Castilian control in the 13th century and until the mid-15th century Andalusian sculpture was closely linked to that of Castile, with an important workshop at Seville Cathedral. From 1454 the Breton LORENZO MERCADANTE was active there, working in the most highly developed, austere, Netherlandish–Burgundian style. One of his first works for Seville Cathedral must have been the alabaster tomb of *Cardinal Juan de Cervantes* (*d* 1453) and he was to show his versatility as a modeller in the outstanding decoration of the Puerta del Nacimiento on the west façade, most of which was executed in coloured terracotta between 1464 and 1467. This technique imbues the figures with a profound emotional impact. Mercadante was followed in the use of terracotta by PEDRO MILLÁN who was active in Seville from 1487 to 1507. His sculpture displays an eclectic combination of Hispanic iconography and south Netherlandish influence, while his later work, for example the tondo of *SS Cosmas and Damian* (1504) for the portal of S Paula, Seville, incorporates ideas from Renaissance art.

BIBLIOGRAPHY

A. Durán i Sanpere: *Els retaules de pedra*, Monumenta Cataloniae, 2 vols (Barcelona, 1932–4)

B. G. Proske: *Castilian Sculpture: Gothic to Renaissance* (New York, 1951)
M. Durliat: 'Sculpteurs français en Catalogne dans la première moitié du XIVe siècle', *Pallas*, viii (1959) pp. 91–103
M. Gómez Moreno: *Provincia de Salamanca*, Catálogo Monumental de España, 2 vols (Madrid, 1967)
J. M. de Azcárate: *El protogótico hispánico* (Madrid, 1974)
S. Moralejo: *Escultura gótica en Galicia, 1200–1350* (Santiago de Compostela, 1975)
A. Franco Mata: *La escultura gótica en León* (León, 1976)
C. J. Ara Gil: *Escultura gótica en Valladolid y su provincia* (Valladolid, 1977)
R. S. Janke: *Jehan Lomme y la escultura gótica posterior en Navarra* (Pamplona, 1977)
J. Yarza: *Arte y arquitectura en España, 500–1250* (Madrid, 1979), pp. 249–309
A. Franco: *Escultura gótica española en el siglo XIV y sus relaciones con la Italia trecentista* (Madrid, 1984)
T. Pérez Higuera: *La Puerta del Reloj en la catedral de Toledo* (Toledo, 1987)
A. Franco: 'Relaciones hispano-italianas de la escultura funeraria del siglo XIV', *La idea y el sentimiento de la muerte en la historia y en el arte: Santiago de Compostela, 1988*, pp. 99–125
J. Yarza Luaces: 'La capilla funeraria hispana en torno a 1400', *La idea y el sentimiento de la muerte en la historia y en el arte: Santiago de Compostela, 1988*, pp. 67–91
J. M. de Azcárate: *Arte gótico en España* (Madrid, 1990)
J. Ara: 'Un grupo de sepulcros palentinos del siglo XIII: Los primeros talleres de Carrión de los Condes, Pedro Pintor y Roi Martínez de Burueva', *II curso de cultura medieval 'Alfonso VIII y su época': Aguilar de Campoo, 1992*, pp. 21–52

ANGELA FRANCO MATA

2. Wood.

(i) Introduction. (ii) Low Countries. (iii) Holy Roman Empire. (iv) Scandinavia. (v) British Isles. (vi) Spain. (vii) Italy. (viii) Portugal. (ix) France.

(i) Introduction. Throughout much of western Europe the surviving Gothic wood sculpture gives little indication of its original distribution and the quantities that were produced. In many regions nearly all has been destroyed owing to fire, damage by insects and fungi, iconoclasm or changing tastes: even the mightiest of carved altarpieces in Germany, for example, were sometimes broken up since they appeared to have no place in Baroque church interiors. Wood was used for cult statues, crucifixes, groups such as the Entombment or Calvary, and liturgical furnishings—bench ends, screens and choir-stalls—as well as large altarpieces. Stylistically, the carvers worked in close relation to craftsmen in other media.

Later engravings of sculptors at work and the evidence of some surviving sculptures, for example a *Virgin and Child* (*c.* 1220–40; Oslo, U. Oldsaksaml.) from Enebakk Church in Norway, show that the block of wood was supported by clamps or cylindrical shafts at the ends and the sculpture roughed out with an axe or adze. Various chisels and drills, which are represented on a misericord of 1383–92 at All Hallows, Wellingborough, England, were then used to carve the figure, and the surface was smoothed as much as possible to receive a gesso ground, pigment, gilding and even incrustations, in a technique similar to that used in panel painting. In order to prevent the wood splitting as it dried, the backs were often hollowed out.

Wood sculpture was always painted until the 15th century, and the surviving works give little idea of its original appearance. Wood was regarded as inferior to precious metals, ivory, marble, alabaster and other stones, which were themselves never painted all over. It was not until about 1400 that wood achieved the same status as other media, and the change came about partly as a result of advances in wood-carving techniques. The carver and the painter were often the same person. In France, for instance, the term *imagier* can refer to both carving and painting sculptures. Yet the two altarpieces (installed 1399; Dijon, Mus. B.-A.; see fig. 51) commissioned by Philip the Bold, Duke of Burgundy, from Jacques de Baerze for the Charterhouse of Champmol were expressly required to be painted by Melchior Broederlam. Like sculptors in stone, specialist wood-sculptors seem to have emerged towards the end of the 13th century: if the *Livres des Métiers* of Etienne Boileau can be trusted, it was at this time that figure sculptors were being distinguished from general carpenters, although the latter continued to produce works that modern scholars would unhesitatingly classify as sculpture.

PETA EVELYN, ULRICH HENZE, DANY SANDRON

(ii) Low Countries.

(a) 1240–1300. (b) 1300–1350. (c) 1350–1430. (d) 1430–1530.

(a) 1240–1300. Studies have shown the assimilation of French Gothic influence in the Meuse region during the

51. Jacques de Baerze: *Crucifixion* altarpiece, wood with gilt and polychromy, h. 1.67 m, from the Charterhouse of Champmol, Dijon, France, begun 1390 (Dijon, Musée des Beaux-Arts)

13th century. The hieratic expression formerly apparent in statues of the Virgin and Child Enthroned was gradually replaced by a greater naturalism, for example in that of *c.* 1240 in St Leonardus, Zoutleeuw. The fluid, rounded folds characteristic of the 'style of 1200' were simplified (e.g. Hamont Church) and then rigidified into angular, sharply broken drapery forms (e.g. *c.* 1240–50; Huy, St Mort). The earliest local standing *Virgin and Child* (*c.* 1240; oak; Tongeren, Onze Lieve Vrouwebasiliek) is somewhat provincial, but later examples (e.g. *c.* 1260–70; Rotselaar, St Pieter), probably under the influence of French ivories, are closer to French models in style and execution; by the end of the century this type had largely superseded that of the *sedes sapientiae*. Other figures (e.g. Brussels, Musées Royaux A. & Hist.; Buenos Aires, priv. col.) until *c.* 1300 were based on the Rotselaar *Virgin*. Crucifixes show a parallel change, with Christ now represented as the suffering saviour rather than in triumph. In Calvary groups the transition towards hard, more jagged drapery is evident in the example (soon after 1250) in Westerlo Church, while that of *c.* 1280 in Lauw Church displays a return to more compact, simpler forms and more contemplative expressions characteristic of some Mosan works from about 1300.

It is more difficult to trace the emergence of the style in the Scheldt region. The robustly natural, smiling faces of the *Virgin and Child* (*c.* 1270–80) in Stambruges Church display a heightened treatment of the rarefied courtly Parisian style. A youthful king, possibly a *Magus* (*c.* 1280–1300; New York, Cloisters), from the St Elisabeth Begijnhof, Ghent, is stylistically related but more tempered in expression. The same regional character appears in decorative sculpture, notably in Ghent on the beam ends of the house 'De Zwarte Moor' and on a vault boss with a foliate head from the Dominican church. The finest examples of the style were the head corbels in the Lakenhalle (*c.* 1300; destr. World War I) at Ypres. This regional style was probably centred on Tournai, from where it spread to Flanders, Hainault and Brabant.

(b) 1300–1350. The Mosan region again provides the most complete picture of a return to abstract stylization and Gothic lightness in the first half of the 14th century, with a preference for planar compositions and linear surface treatment. Comparison between a statue of *St Mark* (early 14th century; Liège, Mus. Relig. A. & Mosan), the drapery of which introduces a characteristically local formulation, and the tall, sinuous *Virgin* from a *Calvary* group (*c.* 1330) in Notre-Dame, La Gleize, indicates progress towards a mannered style derived from northern France, for example on the *Assumption* relief from the chevet exterior of Notre-Dame, Paris. The sculptor of the La Gleize *Virgin*, who was active in Liège and appears to have directed an influential workshop, has been associated with several statuettes (e.g. London, V&A; Münster, Westfäl. Landesmus.) that belonged to the earliest known Netherlandish wooden altarpiece. This originally included a central *Coronation of the Virgin* flanked by enthroned saints (another *Coronation* of *c.* 1330–40 by the same workshop is in the Metropolitan Museum of Art, New York), which was to remain typical of Gothic altarpieces in the region. A *Calvary* ensemble (*c.* 1320–30) in Notre-Dame, Louviers (Normandy), is similar stylistically: Christ on the Cross, the soldiers and a swooning Virgin group may have belonged to a monumental altarpiece, now dismantled.

There is documentary evidence that altarpieces were produced in Tournai from at least the 1320s, but its wood sculpture has been little studied. The attenuated forms and graphic drapery of a *Virgin and Child Enthroned* known as 'Notre Dame d'Heureux Trépas' (Tournai, St Nicolas) suggest a date close to 1320. The transition to more elongated proportions and decorative linearity in Hainault is represented by statues of the *Virgin and Child* from Hautrage (*c.* 1300; priv. col.) and in Lecelles Church (*c.* 1320–30), the latter of which was influenced by the stone *Virgin and Child* (*c.* 1310–20) on the west façade of Tournai Cathedral.

The half life-size *Apostles* and bosses (*c.* 1300–20) in Onze Lieve Vrouwekerk, Damme, which form the most extensive cycle of wood sculpture from this time in Flanders, may be attributed to sculptors from Bruges, where several closely related works survive, for example the monumental *Virgin and Child* in the Begijnhof. In Ghent the naturalism current *c.* 1300 was transformed into a harsh and sombre expressive stylization most clearly evident in decorative architectural sculpture, for example on vault bosses with heads of *Christ* and the *Apostles* (*c.* 1320–40; ex-Leugemete Chapel, Ghent). The sculptor of the bosses and consoles in the south aisle and transept of St Genoveva, Oplinter, was probably also responsible for an impressive *Virgin and Child* (*c.* 1300–20) formerly in a museum at Neder-over-Heembeek, near Brussels. A regional Brabantine style apparent in a later Crucifix (*c.* 1340; Orp-le-Grand Church) may also be seen in local stone sculpture, for example on the consoles in the apse of Vilvoorde Church.

(c) 1350–1430. The influence of André Beauneveu is evident throughout the Low Countries in the second half of the 14th century, for example on a *Virgin with Writing Christ Child* (Bruges, St Janshospitaal) and on figures of the *Virgin and Child* from Brabant (e.g. Lier, Begijnhof) and the Meuse region (e.g. Sint Truiden, Onze Lieve Vrouwekerk). A few examples of the *Schöne Madonna* type known from the early 15th century may have been imported (e.g. Maastricht, St Servatius) or, as in a *Virgin and Child* (Utrecht, Cent. Mus.) from Ankeveen, adapted locally from German models. *Pietà* groups appeared in great numbers: the *Pietà* (1365; Leuven, Mus. Vander Kelen-Mertens), originally from Onze Lieve Vrouw van Ginderbuiten, Leuven, is the region's earliest dated example of a *Calvary Pietà* type, derived from Italian painting. Rhenish influece may be traced through several typologically similar, simplified versions (e.g. Aachen, Suermondt-Ludwig-Mus.; Leuven, Mus. Vander Kelen-Mertens) of the 'Beautiful *Pietà*' (*c.* 1420–30) in Gräfrath Church, near Cologne.

The earliest wooden altarpieces of Netherlandish origin to have survived intact were made towards the end of the 14th century. These include the two altarpieces (Dijon, Mus. B.-A.; see fig. 51 above) by JACQUES DE BAERZE ordered in 1390 for the Charterhouse of Champmol,

52. Master of Hakendover: *St Catherine*, wood, h. 440 mm, from Brussels, Low Countries, *c*. 1400–04 (Hakendover, St Salvator)

Dijon, in which anecdotal narrative is enlivened by genre elements in a manner that became common in later altarpieces. The altarpiece in St Salvator, Hakendover, which was made in a leading Brussels workshop soon after 1400, is more advanced in its use of space, since the figures (see fig. 52) and scenes were no longer arranged in flat planes. The most important of the many examples elsewhere in Europe, notably in Germany, Spain and Portugal, is the *Calvary* altarpiece (*c*. 1415–20; Dortmund, Reinoldikirche) by the MASTER OF HAKENDOVER (*see* MASTERS, ANONYMOUS, AND MONOGRAMMISTS, §I). This introduced a characteristic Late Gothic format of a rectilinear triptych with a salient central section, shutters painted on both sides and, inside, a miniature chapel-like space created by vaulted canopies and tracery that provided settings for the narrative. It has been more difficult to localize others of Netherlandish origin, although it has been suggested that several closely related altarpieces in the Sankt-Annen-Museum, Lübeck, St Nikolai, Lüneburg, and the chapel at Santo Antão da Faniqueira (Portugal) may be attributed to a Bruges workshop.

(d) 1430–1530. The Late Gothic style represents a highpoint in the artistic development of the Low Countries. Netherlandish iconographic and formal solutions, marked by the close interaction between painting and sculpture, proliferating detail and narrative elaboration, were spread across Europe through the emigration of artists and the export of works of art, especially altarpieces. Brussels was the predominant centre and its influence extended to all other Netherlandish schools from *c*. 1450. Wood sculpture was used to enrich church interiors with narrative and devotional images. Several themes that became popular at this time, such as the Trinity Pietà (*see* ANDACHTSBILD), would appear to be of local origin (e.g. Lille, Mus. Dioc. A. Relig.). A fine example of *Christ Seated before his Crucifixion* made in Brussels *c*. 1450–60 and preserved in the Grand' Salle of the Hôtel-Dieu, Beaune, may be one of the prototypes of this type, which became very common in the Netherlands by *c*. 1500.

Brabant. The earliest documented Brussels altarpiece was made by the sculptor Michiel for the high altar of St Bavo, Haarlem, in 1412. The transition from the Soft style to Late Gothic is illustrated in two fragments from a *Nativity* altarpiece (*c*. 1420–25; Ramerupt Church, Champagne) by an anonymous sculptor whose work parallels the paintings of the Master of Flémalle and appears to have been very influential in the Brussels school. His direct impact may be seen in the output of the prolific workshop of the Master of the Rieden Retable (*c*. 1430–50; Stuttgart, Württemberg. Landesmus.) and of Willem Ards, who made the *Passion* altarpiece (*c*. 1450) in St Katharina, Schwäbisch Hall. The emphasis on breadth and volume in these works was gradually superseded by the so-called Style of the Long Lines, which was developed in Tournai and transplanted to Brussels during the 1430s by JEAN DELEMER and Rogier van der Weyden; an important example is an altarpiece dedicated to the Virgin (*c*. 1440; Laredo, Nuestra Señora de la Asunción).

Van der Weyden's influence appears in altarpiece sculpture from the second half of the century. The outstanding Brussels sculptor of the Arenberg *Lamentation* (*c*. 1460–70; Detroit, MI, Inst. A.; see fig. 53) translated the painter's design in a spirit of trenchant poignancy and austere beauty. The central *Calvary* of the altarpiece (Vienna, Votivkirche) originally made for Pfalzel Abbey and the

53. Arenberg *Lamentation* (detail), wood, 0.88×1.40 m, from Brussels, Low Countries, *c.* 1460–70 (Detroit, MI, Institute of Arts)

Passion altarpiece of Claudio de Villa (soon after 1470; Brussels, Musées Royaux A. & Hist.) display a more popular treatment of the same style. Jan Borman II was the dominant artist at the turn of the century and his altarpiece of *St George* (1492; Brussels, Musée Royaux A. & Hist.; for illustration *see* BORMAN) introduces ample forms, more aerated spatial groupings and highly differentiated characterizations ranging from youthful idealization to a near bestial ugliness. His many followers in the early 16th century included his son Passier Borman, who made the altarpiece of *SS Crispin and Crispinian* in St Waldetrudis, Herentals, and Jan Borman III, who was responsible for the *Passion* altarpiece (1522) in Güstrow Parish Church.

It is more difficult to resolve the chronology of the many free-standing wood sculptures of Brussels origin, which were particularly varied and influential in the mid-15th century. Later developments in north Netherlandish sculpture, for example, may be traced in the refined idealization and elegance of a Brussels *Virgin and Child* (*c.* 1440–50; Brussels, Mus. Com.) that resembles a Late Gothic 'Beautiful Madonna', while the combination of emotional intensity and a decorative treatment of detail in a Crucifix (*c.* 1450–70) in the convent of Sacré-Coeur, Mons, suggests the origins of the style of the Lower Rhenish sculptor Master Arnt (see below). The transition from more ample and painterly forms to a crisp and sharpened expression is further illustrated by exported figures of the Virgin and Child, including a walnut statue (1443) in the abbey church at Vadstena, Sweden, and the figure known as 'Nuestra Señora de la Antigua' (*c.* 1480–90) in Granada Cathedral. A *Virgin and Child Enthroned* in the Augustinian convent at Hérent, near Leuven, is representative of the quality and virtuosity achieved by the Brussels workshops *c.* 1500, although their extraordinarily numerous statues are often retrospective in character. Two outstanding works attributed to Jan Bormann II are a youthful and serene *St Mary Magdalene* (Paris, Mus. Cluny) and a *St Hubert* (Leuven, St Jacob) with realistically moulded, craggy features. In their tempered realism and quiet restraint, these works and their many Brabantine derivatives represent a tendency towards harmonious restraint characteristic of most early 16th-century Brussels sculpture.

Other Brabantine centres were influenced by Brussels, notably Antwerp, where important sculptural workshops were active throughout the 15th century. The earliest altarpieces that may be attributed to Antwerp workshops, such as the *Passion* altarpieces in the monastery church (*c.* 1450–60) of S Antonio el Real, Segovia, and in St Michael, Schwäbisch Hall (*c.* 1470), differ from Brussels examples in their preference for multi-figured, panoramically rendered *Calvary* scenes, often incorporating continuous narrative groups. Several altarpieces that carry the Antwerp townmarks, for example in the former church (*c.* 1480) of the Augustinian canons at Klausen and in the Votivkirche, Vienna (*c.* 1473–80), display a similar approach. Many altarpieces were exported in the first three decades of the 16th century, although their quasi-industrial production often relied on stereotyped formulae. The more creative among the later sculptors included one responsible for figures of *Joseph and Nicodemus* (*c.* 1500–10; Beauvais, Mus. Dépt. Oise) and another (*fl c.* 1520) who is known from an altarpiece in Botkyrka, near Stockholm, whose masterpiece is a figure from a *Martyrdom of St Stephen* (Baltimore, MD, Walters A.G.). The striking realism and expressive intensity of these figures, which distinguishes them from the more restrained sculpture from Brussels, is also found in statues of *Christ Seated* (e.g. Binche, cemetery chapel of St André; Burgos Cathedral), which carry Antwerp townmarks.

From the late 15th century workshops in Mechelen specialized in charming statuettes of the Virgin and Child (*'poupées de Malines'*) with saints, which were often incorporated in small domestic altarpieces or symbolic 'enclosed garden' ensembles. The earliest and finest of these (e.g. *c.* 1500; Antwerp, Mus. Mayer van den Burgh) are easily confused with their Brussels models, but later examples, including the *Virgin and Child with St Anne* (*c.* 1510–20; New York, Met.) and *St Margaret* (*c.* 1520; Aachen, Suermondt-Ludwig-Mus.), are more local in character. The plentiful sculpture produced in Leuven, the most fully studied of the lesser Brabantine centres, adheres closely to Brussels models, although motifs and expressive nuances were sometimes varied, for example in a fragmentary half-length *Virgin and Child* (early 16th century; Paris, Louvre).

Tournai and Hainault. Although wood sculpture has been less studied in Tournai than painting or stone sculpture (*see* §1(v) above), and much in Tournai itself was destroyed in 1566, enough free-standing figures survive in north-west Hainault and the southern tip of Flanders to illustrate local developments. The transition to Late Gothic is evident in various artistic solutions, including simpler, more compact figures, such as those of *St John the Evangelist* (*c.* 1410–20; Tournai, St Jean) and a *Virgin and St John* from a *Calvary* group (*c.* 1430–40; ex-Wallez Chapel, Maulde). Traditional types, such as the Virgin and Child, were adapted to the emerging styles (e.g. *c.* 1430–40; Ath, chapel of Notre-Dame-de-Loreto). A more important trend may be associated with Jean Delemer, whose energetic, linear manner is reflected in a *Trinity* group (*c.* 1430–50; Lille, Mus. Dioc. A. Relig.) and a *St Michael* (*c.* 1425; Ellezelles Church). Both of these, and perhaps also a *Virgin and Child Enthroned* (*c.* 1430–40; Houtaing Church), were probably based on prototypes made by Delemer before he went to Brussels (see above). The influence of such formal types may be seen throughout Late Gothic art: the complex, dance-like, corkscrew pose of the Lille *Christ*, for example, had a great impact on German art, while the diagonally thrusting movement of the *St Michael* was similarly influential. These works display a significant relation between sculpture and painting. The Houtaing *Virgin* resembles the work of the Master of Flémalle, and a comparison may be made between the expressive head of *God the Father* in the Lille *Trinity* and the *Joseph of Arimathea* in Rogier van der Weyden's *Deposition* (*c.* 1435; Madrid, Prado).

While Delemer and van der Weyden introduced this Tournaisian style to Brussels, from where it spread throughout Europe, Tournai itself lost some of its significance, although it remained of regional importance. Later developments still followed Delemer's legacy: two corbels with a high relief *Annunciation* (Montreuil-au-Bois Church), for example, which may be dated *c.* 1450–75 by the more consistent use of incisive triangular and zigzag folds, are a smaller variant on his monumental stone *Annunciation* (1428; Tournai, Ste Marie-Madeleine). This tendency was developed further in two beam ends with shield-bearing angels (1483 or soon after) in the former Hôpital de la Planque, Tournai, where the draperies are completely dissolved by parallel and criss-cross folds. This mannered version of the 'Style of the Long Lines' was dominant in Tournai *c.* 1500, for example on a *Calvary* group in the parish church at Rebaix. Many sculptors, however, looked back to the second quarter of the 15th century, as in a figure of *St Fiacre* (Wannebecq Church), to the earlier Soft style, for example an *Entombment* (Arc, St Martin), or show the influence of Brabant, such as on a *St Nicholas Enthroned* (ex-Théodore priv. col., Lille) from Péruwelz.

Many influences were exerted on Hainault. The distribution of Calvary groups (e.g. Chièvres, St Martin) shows the paramount influence of Tournai in the north-west. Brabantine influence appeared elsewhere, especially after 1450, in imported altarpieces (e.g. Renlies Church) and statues, such as a *Virgin and Child* (Soignies, St Vincent) and *Christ Seated* (Binche, cemetery chapel of St André; see above). Most works, however, are clearly of local origin. There is documentary evidence for workshops in Mons, Valenciennes and other cities. The most easily identifiable group consists of several early 16th-century altarpieces, including those of the *Virgin* in Boussu-lez-Mons and La Flamengrie, and of related statues, for example of *SS John and Andrew* (Rance Church) and of *SS Peter and Paul* (Avesnelles Church). These are closely based on Brussels models, but their local origin is confirmed by their nervous, curvilinear drapery and extreme facial expressions, and by their stylistic similarity to such local stone-carving as the altarpiece in the church at Horrues.

Flanders. Although much Late Gothic sculpture has survived in Bruges, it has been little studied. The heads of two *Angels with the Instruments of the Passion* (*c.* 1425–35; Madrid, Prado), signed by Tideman Maes (*fl c.* 1429–52), closely resemble those in the Ghent Altarpiece (*c.* 1423–32; Ghent, St Bavo; *see* EYCK, VAN, (1)). The drapery style of a *Virgin and Child* (*c.* 1440; Meetkerke Church) is related stylistically but is slightly later. Although there may have been Tournaisian antecedents for this work, the rather earthy, jovial faces and pronounced features are perhaps typical of Bruges work. The most progressive carvings among the extensive misericord narrative scenes, prophets and saints on the choir-stalls (*c.* 1440) of St Salvator, Bruges, such as the hand-rest figures of *SS Mary Magdalene and Paul*, show the distinctively flattened wedge and forked folds characteristic of the Bruges school. These formulae were later sharpened into more brittle, splinter-like forms, as in a *St Nicholas Enthroned* (?*c.* 1450) and a *Virgin and Child with a Pear* (*c.* 1440–60; both Bruges, Gruuthusemus.).

A particularly happy fusion of a Brussels formal type with Bruges sensibility towards 1500 appears in a *Virgin and Child with an Open Book* (Bruges, Gruuthusemus.). One of Bruges's leading artists during the early 16th century adopted a similar style for a Crucifix (Sint-Kruis, monastery of St Truiden); his workshop also produced a half-length *Daniel in the Lions' Den* (Bruges, St Salvator) and a *Calvary* group (Bruges, St Janshospitaal). Altarpiece production in Bruges is recorded but remains largely unstudied, although a few indigenous fragments can be identified, including a *Pentecost* group in St Salvator and a *Nativity* (Bruges, Gruuthusemus.).

Few sculptures have survived elsewhere in Flanders, largely owing to the ravages of iconoclasm. The handful of works remaining in Ghent, however, including a graceful *St Michael* (based on Delemer's early style) that appears among a stylistically diverse series of saints decorating beam brackets in Het Toreken (Tanners' House; 1451–2), suggest that at first traditional links were maintained with Tournai. Four similar brackets with the *Fathers of the Church* (*c.* 1450–60) in the Music Conservatory ('Achtersickel') are more advanced stylistically, with drapery represented by crisply cut, triangular and nested V-folds that appear to be characteristic of Ghent. Other works that exhibit similarly fractured drapery may also have been made locally, including a *God the Father Enthroned* (*c.* 1440–60; Ghent, Mus. S. Kst.). The only complete altarpiece traditionally associated with Ghent is one with the *Death of the Virgin* (London, V&A) said to have come from St Bavo. It is, however, probably of Hainault origin rather than Flemish, and a more plausible case for local manufacture may be made for an *Entombment* group (Ghent, Mus. Sierkst.) from a *Passion* altarpiece.

Meuse Valley. The emergence of Late Gothic in the Mosan region is illustrated by an altarpiece with the *Virgin and Child with Saints* and the *Coronation of the Virgin* (*c.* 1430–40; Brussels, Musées Royaux A. & Hist.) from the Begijnhof, Tongeren. Its statuettes combine local traditions, such as the broad, lateral tufts of hair on the female heads, which represent an updated version of types encountered in early Mosan painting influenced by Jan van Eyck, and more progressive tendencies probably drawing on Brussels. Although rather indifferent in quality, these have allowed other finer works from Liège to be identified, notably a *St Barbara* (*c.* 1425–30; Lives-sur-Meuse Church), which may be seen as a Mosan counterpart to Delemer's Tournai *Virgin Annunciate*, and a Late Gothic 'Beautiful *Madonna*' (*c.* 1440; Huy, St Mort). The stern features of a *St Leonard* (*c.* 1420; Holsbeek Church) that can be associated with this school are characteristic of an emergent 'Hard style' aesthetic.

The greater variety in Mosan sculpture of the later 15th century and the early 16th undoubtedly resulted from outside influences and the development of smaller centres. The impact of Brussels is evident in Mosan altarpieces and free-standing sculpture, for example on *Christ Carrying the Cross* (*c.* 1430–40; Namur, Mus. A. Anc.) from a *Calvary* altarpiece and on a *Calvary* group (early 16th century; Liège, St Nicolas), although their local character is never in doubt. Sometimes, for example on a *Calvary* group (early 16th century; Fise-le-Marsal Church), this resulted in a curiously hybrid format. During the early 16th century workshops proliferated in secondary centres, including Dinant, Huy, Marche-en-Famenne and Luxembourg (Didier).

North Netherlands. Owing to extensive destruction very little sculpture has survived from before *c.* 1450. The choir-stalls of *c.* 1430–60 in St Janskerk, 's Hertogenbosch, and of *c.* 1440 in Onze Lieve Vrouwekerk, Breda, show direct south Netherlandish influence, combined with an indigenous emphasis on breadth and an impressive monumentality, for example on prophets and saints from the bench-end reliefs in St Janskerk. The creative assimilation of southern influences is especially clear after the mid-century, for example in a self-assured *Virgin and Child* (*c.* 1460–65; Paris, Louvre), attributed to Jan Nude, and, to a lesser extent, in another (*c.* 1470–80; Arnhem, Martinikerk), by the Master of Soeterbeeck, both of which are derived from Brussels models, such as the Vadstena *Virgin and Child* (see above).

The emergence of Utrecht as the principal north Netherlandish centre of wood sculpture is closely associated with ADRIAEN VAN WESEL. The surviving fragments (1475–7; e.g. Amsterdam, Rijksmus.; Berlin, Bodemus; see fig. 54) from the altarpiece that was commissioned by the Confraternity of Our Lady for its chapel in St Janskerk, 's Hertogenbosch, suggest that he was fully aware of Brussels sculpture of the 1440s, for example the standing *Virgin and Child* (Brussels, Mus. Com.; see above). The highly personal style that he developed from this, however, was suited to intimate genre groups, courtly elegance or a deeply felt but restrained sense of pathos. Other Utrecht works of these years display the same stylistic trends, notably graceful and statuesque figures of *SS Agnes and Catherine* (*c.* 1470; Emmerich, St Aldegundis).

54. Adriaen van Wesel: *St Joseph and Musicmaking Angels*, oak, 445×375 mm, from the altarpiece in the chapel of the Confraternity of Our Lady, St Janskerk, 's Hertogenbosch, Low Countries, 1475–7 (Amsterdam, Rijksmuseum)

The stylized features of a *Virgin and Child* (*c.* 1500; priv. col.) from IJsselstein, near Utrecht, with an ovoid, fleshy face, a high, convex forehead, 'squinting' eyes and a haughty expression, indicate the renewed influence of the Brussels tradition. This recurs in the work of the so-called Master of the Utrecht Stone Female Head (*fl* 1500–50; see fig. 55), whose prolific workshop produced five altarpieces exported to Norway (e.g. Grip Church; Leka Church). These comprise the largest surviving ensemble from the north Netherlands, but their small size and relatively simple compositions give little indication of local accomplishments. Evidence that elaborate narrative altarpieces were produced that were comparable with southern examples is provided by the original architectural framework surrounding two of van Wesel's shutters in St Janskerk, 's Hertogenbosch, and some other small fragments, including the remains of a *Passion* altarpiece (late 15th century; Amsterdam, Rijksmus.) from Soest.

The outstanding sculptor active in Holland at this time has been named after an altarpiece group of the *Meeting of Joachim and Anna* (*c.* 1460–70; Amsterdam, Rijksmus.). The small group of works that may be attributed to the Master of Joachim and Anna display a direct and profoundly human treatment of religious subjects, presented with a formal economy and a rigorous sense of abstraction. This contrasts with the restless, expressive art of the eastern Netherlands, which was linked artistically to the German Lower Rhine. The rhythmic, neo-courtly art of the south Netherlands was introduced by MASTER ARNT and modified by more incisive detail, more complex poses and heightened emotional intensity, for example on the choir-stalls (1474) of the former Franciscan church at

55. Master of the Utrecht Stone Female Head: *St Ursula*, polychromed wood, h. 1 m, from Utrecht, Low Countries, *c.* 1520–30 (Amsterdam, Rijksmuseum)

Cleve. This style was elaborated by his numerous successors, such as the Master of Elsloo (*fl c.* 1500–45), who carved the *Virgin and Child with St Anne* in Elsloo Parish Church, into a linear movement of fully fledged Late Gothic mannerism.

BIBLIOGRAPHY

J. Destrée: 'Etude sur la sculpture brabançonne au moyen âge', *An. Soc. Royale Archéol. Bruxelles*, viii (1894), pp. 7–113; ix (1895), pp. 363–405; xiii (1899), pp. 273–330

J. Roosval: *Schnitzaltäre in schwedischen Kirchen und Museen aus der Werkstatt des Jan Borman* (Strasbourg, 1903)

J. de Bosschère: *La Sculpture anversoise aux XVe et XVIe siècles* (Brussels, 1909)

M. Devigne: *La Sculpture mosane du XIIe au XVIe siècle: Contribution à l'étude de l'art dans la région de la Meuse Moyenne* (Paris and Brussels, 1932)

J. Roosval: 'Retables d'origine néerlandaise dans les pays nordiques', *Rev. Belge*, iii (1933), pp. 136–58

J. de Borchgrave d'Altena: *Les Retables brabançons* (Brussels, 1942)

——: *Les Retables brabançons conservés en Suède* (Brussels, 1948)

——: *Notes pour servir à l'étude des retables anversois* (Brussels, 1957–8)

Middeleeuwse kunst der noordelijke Nederlanden (exh. cat., Amsterdam, Rijksmus., 1958), pp. 188–226

Flanders in the Fifteenth Century: Art and Civilization (exh. cat., Detroit, MI, Inst. A., 1961)

T. Müller: *Sculpture in the Netherlands, Germany, France, Spain, 1400–1500*, Pelican Hist. A. (Harmondsworth, 1966)

W. Paatz: *Verflechtungen in der Kunst der Spätgotik zwischen 1360 und 1530: Einwirkungen aus den westlichen Nachbarländern auf Westdeutschland längs der Rheinlinie und deutsch-rheinische Einwirkungen auf diese Länder* (Heidelberg, 1967)

G. van der Osten and H. Vey: *Painting and Sculpture in Germany and the Netherlands, 1500–1600*, Pelican Hist. A. (Harmondsworth, 1969)

H. Meurer: *Das Klever Chorgestühl und Arnt Beeldesnider* (Düsseldorf, 1970)

J. J. M. Timmers: *De gotiek en de renaissance* (1971), ii of *De kunst van het Maasland* (Assen, 1971) [Eng., Fr. and Ger. summaries]

Aspekten van de laatgotiek in Brabant (exh. cat., Leuven, Mus. Vander Kelen-Mertens, 1971)

Gent: Duizend jaar kunst en cultuur (exh. cat. by G. Milis-Proost and others, Ghent, Cent. Kst. & Cult., 1975), pp. 431–70

Sint-Janshosp., Brugge, 1188–1976 (exh. cat., Bruges, St Janshospitaal, 1976), pp. 444–81

R. Didier: 'La Sculpture gothique', *La Wallonie: Le Pays et les hommes: Lettres—arts—culture* (Brussels, 1977), i, pp. 317–28, 385–404, 441–5

J. Duverger: 'De middeleeuwen, de beeldhouwkunst', *Kunst en wetenschap* (1978), ix of *Twintig eeuwen Vlaanderen* (Hasselt, 1972), pp. 94–117

Die Parler und der Schöne Stil, 1350–1400: Europäische Kunst unter den Luxemburgern, i (exh. cat., ed. A. Legner; Cologne, Schnütgen-Mus., 1978)

Adriaen van Wesel, ca. 1417–ca. 1490: Een Utrechtse beeldhouwer uit de late middeleeuwen (exh. cat. by W. Halsema-Kubes, G. Lemmens and G. de Ward, Amsterdam, Rijksmus., 1980–81) [Eng. summaries]

R. Didier: 'Christs et calvaires mosans du XIIIe siècle', *Millénaire de la collégiale Saint-Jean de Liège: Exposition d'art et d'histoire: Liège, 1982*, pp. 141–72

——: 'Sculptures mosanes des années 1400–1450', *Clio et son regard: Mélanges d'histoire de l'art et d'archéologie J. Stiennon* (Liège, 1982), pp. 143–73

——: 'La Vierge assise à l'enfant (Sedes sapientiae)', *Millénaire de la collégiale Saint-Jean de Liège: Exposition d'art et d'histoire: Liège, 1982*, pp. 123–38

——: 'Sculptures des années 1400–1450 en Hainaut', *Recueil d'études d'histoire hainuyère offertes à Maurice A. Arnould* (Mons, 1983), pp. 361–400

——: 'De H. Cornelius van het Sint-Janshospitaal en de Brugse beeldhouwkunst omstreeks 1400', *Rond de restauratie van het XIVde eeuwse Corneliusbeeld* (Bruges, 1984), pp. 19–52

L. Jacobs: *Aspects of Netherlandish Carved Altarpieces, 1380–1530* (diss., New York U., Ann Arbor, 1986)

J. Zeigler: *Sculpture of Compassion: The Pietà and the Beguines in the Southern Low Countries,* c. *1300–*c. *1600* (Brussels and Rome, 1992)

J. Steyaert: *Late Gothic Sculpture: The Burgundian Netherlands* (Ghent, 1994)

J. STEYAERT

(iii) Holy Roman Empire.

(a) Introduction. (b) 1300–1420. (c) 1420–1500.

(a) Introduction. In many respects the Gothic wood sculpture of the Holy Roman Empire is richer and more varied than stone sculpture in the region. Wood-carving flourished during the 14th century and, especially, the 15th, partly owing to the gradual decline of the stonemasons' workshops (*see* §1(iii) above). Increasingly wood was used for the sculptural decoration of church interiors, notably for expensive, monumental altarpieces. Many of the wooden figures that have survived originally came from such ensembles, which sometimes comprised extensive cycles. Stylistically the sculpture may be divided into that produced during the 14th century and the early 15th, including that under the influence of the Soft style, and Late Gothic sculpture from after *c.* 1420. Gothic figure style and ornamentation were superseded by Italianate influences *c.* 1500.

More important than the changes introduced by stylistic developments, however, was the evolution of new pictorial themes and the creation of new functional contexts for sculpture that often broke with established traditions. The iconography of 14th-century wood sculpture was marked by the development and rapid dissemination of *Andachtsbilder* (Ger. 'devotional images'), which drew mainly on themes relating to the Passion, intended to arouse pity in the faithful (*see* ANDACHTSBILD). These powerful, sensitive and sometimes graphic representations of the sufferings of Christ and the Virgin, as shown in such themes as St John resting his head on Christ's shoulder, the Pietà and the Man of Sorrows, are a visual expression of the emotional and religious fervour that permeated 14th-century society and displayed itself in a mystical emphasis on Christ the Redeemer.

Apart from free-standing individual statues and groups, however, especially standing figures of the Virgin and Child, which were often placed on altars as cult images, the primary purpose of wood sculpture was for the decoration of large altarpieces. During the 14th century the winged altarpiece (*Flügelaltar*) evolved into the most important functional frame for wooden sculpture (*see* ALTARPIECE, §2(ii)). This complex structure combined carved miniature architecture with the format of an iconostasis to create a precious shrine that was to become the dominant artistic and liturgical feature within the church. There was a close relationship between sculpture and painting: altarpieces often contain both panel paintings and carved figures, which at first were always painted, and painters therefore had a decisive influence on a sculpture's final appearance. It was not until *c.* 1400 that wood was sometimes left unpainted, making the work's impact entirely dependent on the wood-carver's skills.

(b) 1300–1420. Wood sculpture was well equipped to convey both the stylization of court ideals and the pessimism in the face of natural and social disaster that moulded the intellectual tendencies of the 14th century. This ambivalent mood is illustrated by two impressive and nearly contemporary sculptures in Cologne, which also illustrate the changing preferences in iconographic types. The so-called Milanese *Madonna* (*c.* 1300; Cologne Cathedral) is one of the finest examples of the standing Virgin and Child figures that evolved during the 13th century into a characteristic Gothic type and supplanted the majestic *sedes sapientiae* of Romanesque wood sculpture. This reflected the influence of French cathedral sculpture, and there was a conscious reference to the traditional Byzantine variant. The statue is linked stylistically with the figures that the cathedral workshop made *c.* 1290–1300 for the piers in the chancel and demonstrates the close collaboration between the workshop's wood-carvers and stone-sculptors (*see* §1(iii)(c) above). The refined and elegant manner in which the majestic, dignified Virgin holds out the Christ Child on her left arm, while he gives a blessing, indicates knowledge of 13th-century Parisian art. The appearance, however, of the impressive *Gabelkruzifix* (Y-shaped Crucifix; 1304) in St Maria im Kapitol presents a complete contrast. It is one of the earliest examples of the type disseminated widely in the 14th century as the *Pestkreuz* (*see* CRUCIFIX, §3(i)). Christ is shown with torn flesh and devoid of all nobility and dignity. This is not the crucified king, but a human being tortured to death, his head sunk lifelessly on to his breast and his emaciated body displaying the ugly marks of the torments he has endured.

The *Andachtsbilder* demonstrate similar divergences of style and expression. The liturgical function of these intimate, meditation-inducing images, generally small in size, has not been clearly defined. Wood sculpture using these themes first emerged about 1320, especially in the Upper Rhine region and Swabia, and soon achieved widespread popularity. Its dissemination apparently owed much to the courtly love of God cultivated within religious houses as part of the period's emotionalized piety. Most of the *Andachtsbild* types may be traced to two-dimensional sources, especially to the extensive thematic range displayed in richly illustrated French manuscripts of the *Bibles moralisées*, originating in the first half of the 13th century, and to the image veneration associated with Italo-Byzantine art. One of the finest examples represents *St John Resting his Head on Christ's Shoulder* (*c.* 1330; Berlin, Skulpgal.). This was made in south Germany by a wood-carver and painter whose spare but highly sensitive idiom beautifully expresses faith and trust in Christ's redemption. The so-called Roettgen *Pietà* (*c.* 1325; Bonn, Rhein. Landesmus.; *see* PIETÀ, §3(i)) presents a stark contrast. Christ's body is cruelly disfigured, his head is bent sharply back and outsize drops of blood are shed as a sign of his suffering for the redemption of man.

The creation of wooden altarpieces became increasingly important in the 14th century. These were often monumental in scale and were usually conceived as folding shrines, which could be variously arranged to suit different liturgical requirements. Wooden sculptures and painted panels, usually mounted on the wings, were often combined to create smaller versions of the stone iconostases found mainly on the façades, rood and chancel screens of 13th-century churches. Altarpieces also often served as receptacles for precious relics, the significance of which was generally reflected in the decorative programme. One of the earliest surviving examples (*c.* 1320), in which the characteristics of a high and Late Gothic reliquary altarpiece are already fully developed, is found in the former Benedictine abbey church at Cismar (*see* ALTARPIECE, fig. 3). Its three-winged structure is enclosed by an architectural frame decorated with pinnacles and triangular gables. Inside, arranged in several registers, are reliefs of *Passion* scenes that allude to the relics owned by the monastery. Later winged altarpieces, such as the *St Ursula* altar (*c.* 1325) in the Cistercian abbey church at Marienstatt and the high altar (*c.* 1330) of Unserer Lieben Frau, Oberwesel, represent an advanced stage in which the miniature architecture is more richly detailed and forms niches for single three-dimensional sculptures or reliefs. The lower register of the Marienstatt altar also has 12 reliquary busts of a type that was made mainly in Cologne during the 14th century. The Grabow Altarpiece (1383; Hamburg, Ksthalle), which was made by the painter and wood-carver Master Bertram for the Petrikirche, Hamburg, represents an impressive combination of wood sculpture and painting (*see* BERTRAM, MASTER, §2(ii)).

Against this background of near-serial production of small reliquary statues and extensive cycles for altarpieces, it is not surprising that few individual works of stylistic significance were created at this time. Between roughly 1380 and 1420 wood sculpture, together with most artistic genres, shows the influence of the Soft style. Although the most commonly chosen themes remained constant, changes may be found in the artistic idiom and expressive content. This process is displayed especially clearly in crucifixes, on which the exaggerated, expressive rendering of the dead Christ on the Cross gives way to Christ the Redeemer, who is devoid of all harshness and horror (e.g. *c.* 1425; Gdańsk, St Mary). A similar development may be seen in a *Pietà* (1380; Münster, Westfäl. Landesmus.), made in a workshop on the Middle Rhine, which concentrates on the Virgin's quietly intense affection and emotive grieving for her dead son rather than on a frightening representation of the cruelly tortured Christ. This is emphasized by the formal structure and the extensive gilding.

In some respects the period around 1400 may be seen as a turning-point in the development of wood sculpture in the Empire. Small, expensively painted and highly intimate statuettes for private devotion, such as the so-called *Virgin in the Sun* (Cologne, Schnütgen-Mus.), became an increasingly important aspect of the wood-carvers' output, rivalling the public commissions. There are also the first signs of a new evaluation of wood's ability to bear the emotional weight of the subject without concealing its individual qualities behind illusionistic polychromy. This, however, was dependent on the development of advanced wood-carving skills to elaborate the details that previously had been the responsibility of the painter. The large figure of the *Virgin and Child* (*c.* 1410–20) in St Foillan, Aachen, is possibly one of the oldest surviving, unpainted, monumental wooden figures of the late Middle Ages.

(c) 1420–1500. During the early 15th century wood sculpture in the German-speaking lands, especially altarpieces, increasingly displays the influence of south Netherlandish artists, such as the MASTER OF HAKENDOVER (*see* §(II)(c) above; *see also* MASTERS, ANONYMOUS, AND MONOGRAMMISTS, §I). One of the first sculptors in the Empire consciously to incorporate south Netherlandish elements was Hans Multscher, who lived in Ulm from 1427. His extensive knowledge of Burgundian sculpture, especially that made by the circle of Claus Sluter and his successors, shaped not only his stone sculptures (*see* §1(iii)(c) above) but also the wood-carvings produced by his workshop, such as an impressive, life-size standing *Virgin and Child* (*c.* 1435; Landsberg am Lech, St Mariä Himmelfahrt; *see* MULTSCHER, HANS, fig. 2), which probably belonged originally to a large winged altarpiece. The statuesque figure, conceived with extraordinary realism, is a far departure from the flowing lines and gentle folds of the Soft style.

Unlike south Netherlandish compositions, which are usually assembled from many small components, Multscher's work shows a tendency towards monumentality that was to be the dominant feature of south German altarpiece production in the 15th century. His most important work in wood was the high altar (1456–9; destr. 1779; fragments in Basle, priv. col.; Innsbruck, Tirol. Landesmus.; Munich, Bayer. Nmus.; Vipiteno, Mus. Muellscher) made for the parish church of Unserer Lieben Frau, Sterzing (now Vipiteno). The destruction of most of this altarpiece entailed the loss of what must have been an important stage in the development of wood-carving and altar construction in south Germany and the Tyrol during the second half of the 15th century and the early 16th (*see* SCHNITZALTAR). Similarly, whereas the stone sculpture of NICOLAUS GERHAERT, who worked mainly in the Upper Rhine region and Austria, is relatively well preserved, many of his principal works in wood have not survived, notably the very influential altarpiece (1465–7; destr. *c.* 1530) for the high altar of Konstanz Cathedral.

By the 1470s the characteristic features of the south German *Schnitzaltar* were already present in the altarpiece (1471–81) made by Michael Pacher's workshop in Bruneck (now Brunico) and assembled in the parish church of St Wolfgang in the Salzkammergut (*see* PACHER, MICHAEL, §2 and figs 1–3). This monumental (h. 11.1 m overall; w. 6.5 m overall) winged altarpiece is one of the best-preserved and most mature works of its genre, in which carved figures in the central *Corpus*, either side of the shrine and in the architectural superstructure above, are combined with panel paintings fitted to the inner and outer wings, which may be opened or closed to reveal different scenes. Whereas the sculpture is still clearly indebted to Multscher and Gerhaert, the paintings demonstrate Pacher's familiarity with north Italian art, especially that of Padua. The subject-matter includes scenes from the *Life of Christ* and various saints, some of local significance. There is, however, a particular emphasis on the Virgin as the Mother of God, culminating in the central *Coronation of the Virgin*, in which God the Father and the Virgin, flanked by SS Wolfgang and Benedict, appear beneath an elaborate ciborium of tracery and pinnacles. Pacher's mastery as a wood-carver is demonstrated by his use of gilding, rather than polychromy. Various compositional techniques are used to create an extraordinarily dynamic setting for the celestial event, notably the spatially offset arrangement of God the Father and the Virgin, which creates a tension between them. The whole scene is given a circling motion by the placing of angels holding the Virgin's cloak below and spreading a chalice veil behind and above the main figures. The flanking figures, however, function rather as static spectators.

The principal centres of wood sculpture in south Germany, other than the workshops of the Tyrol, were in Ulm, Nuremberg and Würzburg. The most important wood-carvers in Ulm during the second half of the 15th century were Michel Erhart (*see* ERHART, (1)) and Jörg Syrlin the elder (*see* SYRLIN, (1)), both of whom were involved in the construction of the choir-stalls (1469–74) of Ulm Minster. The busts of *Prophets*, *Sibyls* (see fig. 56), *Apostles* and *Martyrs* carved on the stall-ends and backs display a striking naturalism that places them among the most impressive of the city's Late Gothic wood-carvings. The main surviving work attributed to Erhart's workshop is the high altar (*c.* 1493–4) in the former abbey church of Blaubeuren (for illustration *see* SCHNITZALTAR), in which the picturesquely arranged reliefs of the *Nativity* and the *Adoration of the Magi* on the inner wings contrast with the static structure of the central shrine, which contains individual figures of the *Virgin and Child* with *SS Benedict, John the Baptist, John the Evangelist* and *Scholastica.*

One of the foremost masters in Nuremberg was VEIT STOSS, although no works that might be securely attributed to him have survived from before 1477, when he travelled to Poland. The high altar (1477–9) that he made for St Mary, Kraków, is the largest example to have survived

56. Michel Erhart (attrib.): *Libyan Sibyl*, oak, h. *c.* 450 mm, choir-stall from Ulm Minster, Germany, *c.* 1469–74

from the 15th century: the almost fully rounded figures in the central shrine's *Death of the Virgin* (above which is the *Assumption of the Virgin*) are up to 2.8 m high. Their features and gestures suggest the direct influence of the painting of Rogier van der Weyden. The wings are decorated with reliefs of scenes from the *Life of the Virgin* and the *Passion* (from the *Annunciation* to *Pentecost*), which are presented in an austere narrative style that indicates Netherlandish influence, probably mediated through Stoss's knowledge of Gerhaert's sculpture.

The wooden altarpieces of TILMAN RIEMENSCHNEIDER of Würzburg stand in contrast to the heavy monumentality of Stoss's work in Kraków. A representative example is the Altar of the Holy Blood (1499–1505; Rothenburg ob der Tauber, Jakobskirche), in which the perforated predella and finely carved superstructure create a floating lightness that is carried over into the *Last Supper* represented in the central shrine. The clarity of the strictly symmetrical composition is underlined by Riemenschneider's avoidance of the dramatic effects usually achieved with polychromy, relying solely on the sensitively carved faces and hands and the crystalline folds of the drapery to bring the figures to life.

The standards achieved by south German wood-carvers were rarely matched by those in the north, where the demand for wood sculpture was often met by north and south Netherlandish imports. There were, however, prolific workshops in the Baltic towns, notably Lübeck, and the lands of the Teutonic Order, which exported many works to Scandinavia (*see* §(iv)(c) below). The most prominent sculptor in Lübeck was Bernt Notke, whose creative power is demonstrated in his idiosyncratic and materially lavish triumphal cross (*c.* 1475) for Lübeck Cathedral and the *St George* group (1489; Stockholm, Storkyrkan; *see* NOTKE, BERNT, §2 and fig. 2).

BIBLIOGRAPHY

RDK: 'Altarretabel'

H. Wilm: *Die gotische Holzfigur: Ihre Wesen und ihre Technik* (Leipzig, 1923)

C. T. Müller: *Mittelalterliche Plastik Tirols: Von der Frühzeit bis zur Zeit Michael Pachers* (Berlin, 1935)

H. Wentzel: *Die Christus-Johannes-Gruppen des 14. Jahrhunderts* (Stuttgart, 1960)

Europäische Kunst um 1400 (exh. cat., Vienna, Ksthist. Mus., 1962)

W. Paatz: *Süddeutsche Schnitzaltäre der Spätgotik* (Heidelberg, 1963)

H. Sachs: *Mittelalterliches Chorgestühl* (Leipzig, 1964)

P. Bloch: *Kölner Madonnen: Die Muttergottes in der Kölner Bildnerei des Mittelalters* (Mönchengladbach, 1967)

Spätgotik am Oberrhein: Meisterwerke der Plastik und des Kunsthandwerks, 1450–1530 (exh. cat., Karlsruhe, Bad. Landesmus., 1970)

R. Haussherr: 'Über Christus-Johannes-Gruppen: Zum Problem "Andachtsbilder" und deutsche Mystik', *Beiträge zur Kunst des Mittelalters: Festschrift für Hans Wentzel* (Berlin, 1975), pp. 79–103

M. von Alemann-Schwarz: *Cruzifixus dolorosus: Beiträge zur Polychromie und Ikonographie rheinischer Gabelkruzifixe* (diss., Bonn, Rhein. Friedrich-Wilhelms-U., 1976)

K. Stoll, E. M. Vetter and E. Oellermann: *Triumphkreuz im Dom zu Lübeck: Ein Meisterwerk Bernt Notkes* (Wiesbaden, 1977)

J. Bier: *Tilman Riemenschneider: Die späten Werke in Holz* (Vienna, 1978)

H. Schindler: *Der Schnitzaltar: Meisterwerke und Meister in Süddeutschland, Österreich und Südtirol* (Regensburg, 1978)

P. Skubiszewski: 'Der Stil des Veit Stoss: Die Quellen und die Krakauer Periode', *Z. Kstgesch.*, xli (1978), pp. 93–133

J. Taubert: *Farbige Skulpturen: Studien zu ihrer Bedeutung, Fassung und ihrer Gestaltung* (Munich, 1978)

Die Parler und der Schöne Stil, 1350–1400: Europäische Kunst unter den Luxemburgern (exh. cat., ed. A. Legner; Cologne, Schnütgen-Mus., 1978)

M. Baxandall: *The Limewood Sculpture of Renaissance Germany* (New Haven, 1980)

D. L. Ehresmann: *Middle Rhenish Sculpture, 1380–1440* (Ann Arbor, 1984)

E. König: 'Gesellschaft, Material, Kunst: Neue Bücher zur deutschen Skulptur um 1500', *Z. Kstgesch.*, xlvii (1984), pp. 535–58

Gothic and Renaissance Art in Germany (exh. cat., ed. J. P. O'Neill; New York, Met.; Nuremberg, Ger. Nmus.; 1986)

U. Bergmann: *Das Chorgestühl des Kölner Doms*, 2 vols (Neuss, 1987)

——: *Schnütgen-Museum: Die Holzskulpturen des Mittelalters, 1000–1400*, ed. A. Legner (Cologne, 1989)

ULRICH HENZE

(iv) Scandinavia.

(a) 13th century. (b) 14th century. (c) 15th century and the early 16th.

(a) 13th century. The first wood sculpture in Scandinavia to show the pronounced influence of northern French Gothic appeared *c.* 1225–50, although no directly imported French work has been identified. Much 13th-century sculpture has survived in Denmark and some examples, such as the triumphal cross group (Lund U., Hist. Mus.) from Gualöv, Skåne, which then belonged to Denmark, and the *Three Marys at the Tomb* (Copenhagen, Nmus.) from the Roskilde Cathedral triumphal cross, are of outstanding quality and clearly connected with French work. The distribution of Danish sculpture beyond the kingdom is demonstrated by the triumphal cross group (beech; Visby, Gotlands Fornsal) from Bro Church on Gotland and the fine crucifixes on the Swedish mainland in the former abbey church of Skokloster and at Ununge.

The Danish school also influenced production in southern Sweden and eastern Norway. An oak *Apostle* (h. 1.89m; Skara, Skaraborgs Länsmus.) from Norra Vånga Church, for example, shows a pronounced French style but it is not certain that it was imported. The wealth of Gotland, its substantial German population and lively contacts with the Continent ensured its continuing importance (*see also* ROMANESQUE, §III, 2(vii)), and French influences were introduced via Saxony and Westphalia. The enormous triumphal oak crosses at Lau Church and from Hablingbo (Visby, Gotlands Fornsal), and figures of the *Virgin and Child* (oak, h. 1.51m; Visby, Gotlands Fornsal) from Hejnum, Tingstäde and St Maria, Visby, all show the clear influence of Saxony: the Hejnum *Virgin*, for example, resembles that on the Golden Portal (*c.* 1225–40) of Freiberg Cathedral. A number of works have been attributed by af Ugglas and Roosval to the masters (*fl* *c.* 1230–60) identified by their figures at Hejnum and Tingstäde. There are several examples in wood of the ring cross type on Gotland, including an outstanding triumphal cross group (*c.* 1270–80; h. *c.* 4.2 m; Öja Church) in which the cross is surrounded by small figural groups and a ring decorated with roses.

Wood sculpture in Norway includes some particularly distinguished figures, which often retain their original bright polychromy in an astounding state of preservation. Although French traits may be identified, English influences are even more evident, combined with distinctly Norwegian woodworking techniques. Regional schools have been identified centred on Oslo in the east, Bergen in the west, which produced the Hove *Virgin and Child* (U. Bergen, Hist. Mus.), and Trondheim in northern Norway. Many works made in the mid-13th century have been attributed to the so-called Balke Master, who has been named after an oak *Calvary* group (Oslo, U. Oldsaksaml.) from Balke Church. A particularly well-preserved figure in this style is the *St Paul* (late 13th century; Stockholm, Nordiska Mus., on dep. Oslo, U. Oldsaksaml.; see fig. 57) from Vestre Gausdal (*see also* POLYCHROMY, §2). An earlier seated figure of *St Olaf* (h. *c.* 1.55 m; Stockholm, Nordiska Mus., on dep. Oslo, U. Oldsaksaml.) from Fresvik has individualistic features that, unusually, resemble portraiture. Connections with English art are clearly evident in sculpture from the region of Trondheim, notably the Mosvik *St Michael* (*c.* 1250–60; U. Trondheim, Mus.; see fig. 58 below).

Work in the Anglo-Norwegian style was exported to Sweden or imitated there, for example in a pinewood *St Michael* (h. *c.* 1.4 m; Östersund, Jämtlands Läns Mus.) from Näskott and a pinewood *Virgin and Child* at Lillhärdal. It is believed that a small *Virgin and Child* (Stockholm, Stat. Hist. Mus.) in the English style from Västra Skrukeby was imported. The introduction of direct French influence in the 1280s, for example in a monumental *St Olaf* or *St Erik* (h. 2.33m) at Roslagsbro and a seated *Virgin and Child* (h. 1.19m; Uppsala, U. Kstsamml.) of unknown provenance, is associated with Uppsala, where the cathedral workshop was headed by Etienne de Bonneuil from 1287 (*see* §1(vii) above).

Throughout the Middle Ages statues were often placed on a plinth within a wooden shrine with a canopy or ciborium and fitted with carved doors. The backs of the doors have tiers of architectural niches in which are set small figures cut in relief. Most Gothic examples are known from Sweden, such as those at Östra Vram (Skåne) and from Fröskog (Stockholm, Stat. Hist. Mus.), both of

57. *St Paul*, oak and polychromy, h. 1.81 m, from Vestre Gausdal, Norway, late 13th century (Stockholm, Nordiska Museum, on deposit at Oslo, Universitetets Oldsaksamlingen)

which preserve their carved doors; others have survived in Norway, including a pinewood shrine (h. *c.* 870 mm; Oslo, U. Oldsaksaml.) from Dal, which has lost its doors; in Finland, for example at Urdiala (now Helsinki, N. Mus.) and Kumlinge; and in Iceland at Mule (now Copenhagen, Nmus.). A variant, mostly found on Gotland, has the devotional figure set directly against the backpiece and covered by a gabled canopy; originally this type did not have doors.

(b) 14th century. Whereas numerous sculptures have been preserved in Sweden from the first half of the 14th century, when production on Gotland was particularly prolific, little from the second half of the century has survived anywhere in Scandinavia. Works attributed to the Bunge Master (*fl c.* 1310–50), named after a seated figure of *St Olaf* (Stockholm, Stat. Hist. Mus.) from Bunge Church, are particularly notable. Sculpture was exported from Gotland to the Swedish mainland and Finland, such as the figures of the *Virgin and Child* at Överselö, on Lake Mälaren, Sweden, and in Nousianinen Cathedral (*see* FINLAND, §IV, 1). About 15 fixed altarpieces on Gotland also date from this period. Some, including that (Visby, Gotlands Fornsal) from Ala, show links with French or Rhenish art, but even these were certainly made on Gotland. Most have the Coronation of the Virgin or the Crucifixion in a large architectural frame flanked by figures, mainly Apostles (h. *c.* 400–450 mm), set in an arcade of niches. It is believed that the altarpiece at Skattunge (Dalarna) is the only surviving example made on the Swedish mainland. Figures from lost altarpieces at Hubbo Church and from By (*c.* 1340s; Stockholm, Stat. Hist. Mus.), which show Rhenish influence, were probably imported. The existence of larger figures (h. *c.* 700–750 mm), for example at Sigtuna in Sweden, suggests that other forms of altar decoration were also current in the mid-14th century.

The earliest complete winged altarpieces in Scandinavia (mid-14th century) are found on Gotland. At Endre Church, for example, the shutters may be closed but the exterior panels are not painted, a feature that was to appear later in the century at Gammelgarn. The north German style typified by Master Bertram's Grabow Altarpiece (*c.* 1380; Hamburg, Ksthalle; *see* §(iii)(b) above) appears in Skåne at Lund Cathedral and in the altarpiece (Lund U., Hist. Mus.) from St Peter, Ystad. Both were made in the 1390s by the same workshop, but it remains uncertain whether this was in Lübeck, Doberan or in Skåne. The central *Corpus* of these and the contemporary Swedish altarpieces at Munktorp and Evertsberg represents the Coronation of the Virgin or the Pietà.

(c) 15th century and the early 16th. Production of wooden altarpieces, shrines and sculpture for the whole of Scandinavia was dominated by Lübeck. Altarpieces from *c.* 1430 in the diocese of Linköping are comparatively small (h. *c.* 1–1.75 m) and the *Corpus* is often divided into two registers, the main scene of which is the Coronation of the Virgin or the Crucifixion. From the mid-15th century until the Reformation (1527 in Sweden, 1536 in Denmark) nearly every church in Scandinavia acquired a winged altarpiece. Some of these are of considerable size: Bernt Notke's altarpiece (1479) in Århus Cathedral, for example, is 12 m high overall, while the *Corpus* of the early 16th-century altarpiece at Köping is 2.59 m high.

Works were commissioned from renowned Lübeck craftsmen, most notably Notke's tremendous *St George* group (1489; Stockholm, Storkyrkan; *see* NOTKE, BERNT, §2 and fig. 2). Other Lübeck commissions include the altarpiece at Bälinge, near Uppsala, signed by JOHANNES STENRAT OF LÜBECK, in 1471 and an altarpiece by HENNING VON DER HEIDE. The altarpiece (*c.* 1517–22; Odense Cathedral) originally made for the Franciscan church in Odense is the most important work by CLAUS BERG, who is documented in Denmark from 1507. In Norway an altarpiece (Oslo, U. Oldsaksaml.) from Kvefjord is attributed to another Lübeck master, Benedikt Dreyer (*c.* 1485–after 1555).

Lübeck was not the sole source, however, for work was also imported from other German Baltic towns. Sculpture preserved in Finland, on Gotland and on the Swedish mainland, for example, was carved in the lands of the Teutonic Order during the first half of the 15th century. It has generally been accepted that the large triumphal cross (*c.* 1420–30) in Vadstena Abbey was made in Lübeck, but more recent research, especially into the choice of walnut, suggests a more easterly origin, perhaps in the Order's territories. Altarpieces imported from Antwerp and Brussels (*see* §(ii)(d) above) towards the end of the Middle Ages mostly survive in Sweden. The largest and most important of these (its *Corpus* measures 2.59×3.44 m) was made in Brussels and forms the high altar (*c.* 1480) of Strängnäs Cathedral. Five altarpieces (e.g. Leka Church) were imported into Norway from the north Netherlands in the early 16th century.

As well as these imported works, wood sculpture was produced throughout Scandinavia during the 15th century and especially between *c.* 1500 and the Reformation. Some important sculptors are known by name, notably the prolific Haaken Gulleson (*fl c.* 1500–30) in Hälsingland; examples of his work, such as a shrine of *St Anne* (1520) in the Old Church at Enånger, are spread across northern Sweden. These local masters were influenced by continental trends, especially German, but still developed a colourful independent style.

BIBLIOGRAPHY

H. Fett: *Billedhuggerkunsten i Norge under Sverreætten* [The art of sculpture in Norway at the time of Sverre] (Kristiania, 1908)

C. R. af Ugglas: *Gotlands medeltida träskulptur till och med höggotikens inbrott* [Medieval wood sculpture in Gotland up to and including the beginning of the High Gothic era] (Stockholm, 1915)

J. Roosval: *Medeltida skulptur i Gotlands Fornsal* [Medieval sculpture in the Fornsal, Gotland] (Stockholm, 1925)

E. S. Engelstad: *Senmiddelalderens kunst i Norge, cirka 1400–1535* [Late medieval art in Norway, *c.* 1400–1535] (Oslo, 1936)

A. Andersson: *English Influence in Norwegian and Swedish Figure Sculpture in Wood, 1220–1270* (Stockholm, 1949/*R* 1950)

V. Thorlacius-Ussing, ed.: *Danmarks billedhuggerkunst* [Sculpture of Denmark] (Copenhagen, 1950)

M. Blindheim: *Main Trends of East Norwegian Wooden Sculpture in the Second Half of the Thirteenth Century* (Oslo, 1952)

Medieval Wooden Sculpture in Sweden, Stockholm, Stat. Hist. Mus. cat., 5 vols (Stockholm, 1964–80)

C. A. Nordman: 'Medeltida skulptur i Finland', *Fin. Fornminnesfören. Tidskr./Suomen Muinmuist. Aikak.*, 62 (1965)

E Lassen: *Dansk Kunsthistorie: Fra nunesten til altertavle, c. 900–1500* (Copenhagen, 1972)

R. Norberg: *Nordisk medeltid* (1974), i of *Bildkonsten i Norden* (Stockholm, 1974)
H. von Aachen: 'Sengotiske altarskabe i Hordaland: Studier i senmiddelalderens kunstmiljø', *Foreningen til Norske Fortidsminnesmerkers bevaring* (Oslo, 1981)
P. Tångeberg: *Mittelalterliche Holzskulpturen und Altarschreine in Schweden: Studien zu Form, Material und Technik* (Stockholm, 1986)

PETER TÅNGEBERG

(v) British Isles. Cult images, altarpieces and rood screens must have been produced in the British Isles in large numbers between the 13th century and the early 16th, particularly for pilgrimage churches, which would have housed several altars. Even the most humble parish church needed a crucifix, and wood was both comparatively cheap and readily available. Oak was the most popular wood in England, but boxwood and walnut were also used. All wood sculpture was painted, although much has been lost through wear or stripped by later collectors and dealers. The destruction of devotional imagery in the British Isles during the Reformation and under the Commonwealth in the mid-17th century was particularly severe. Larger objects, however, and those that formed part of the church fabric, have survived in greater numbers throughout England. These include tomb effigies, for example those of *Robert Curthose, Duke of Normandy* (*c.* 1250; Gloucester Cathedral) and *Sir Robert du Bois* (*c.* 1340; Fersfield, St Andrew), choir-stalls (*see* CHOIR-STALLS, §3(i) and fig. 1; *see also* MISERICORD) and roof bosses.

Although itinerant lay craftsmen were more in evidence towards the end of the period, at first medieval woodcarvers and painters frequently belonged to monastic orders, such as the monk shown painting a statuette of the Virgin and Child on the frontispiece of the Lambeth Apocalypse (*c.* 1260–70; London, Lambeth Pal. Lib., MS. 209). Matthew Paris mentions works created *c.* 1214–35 at St Albans Abbey by Master Walter of Colchester ('an incomparable painter and sculptor'), although unfortunately all of these have been lost, including the large rood over the altar dedicated to the Virgin and 'a most elegant figure of Our Lady'.

The style of a painted oak altar figure of the *Virgin and Child* (*c.* 1200–20; h. 475 mm; London, V&A) from St Mary, Langham (Essex), a rare example of small-scale sculpture, is similar to that of the Westminster Psalter (*c.* 1200; London, BL, Royal MS. 2.A.XXII). The survival in Scandinavia of several related Virgin and Child sculptures (e.g. mid-13th century; Rimbo Church) supports the theory that a workshop of English sculptors was active in Norway in the 13th century and that many similar figures may have been produced at this time (*see* §(iv) above). There is also documentary evidence, for example the small figures of the Virgin and saints in the chapel of St Peter ad Vincula in the Tower of London that are mentioned in the Liberate Rolls for 1240. Later examples that have survived include six figures in oak of *Christ* and the *Virgin* (together forming a *Glorification of the Virgin*) with *St Peter*, *St Paul*, *St Matthew* and *St John the Evangelist* (*c.* 1350–1400; h. *c.* 320 mm; London, V&A), which have been stripped of their polychromy, although close comparisons can be made with contemporary continental sculpture, most notably Mosan examples. Originally these would have been attached to an altarpiece that probably resembled the surviving, later examples in Sweden, such as an oak altarpiece (*c.* 1435; Stockholm, Stat. Hist. Mus.) from Tjällmo, Östergötland.

Andersson (1949) has demonstrated that Late Romanesque and Gothic wood sculpture was extensively exported to Scandinavia from England, for example a *St Michael* (*c.* 1250–60; see fig. 58) from Mosvik and the Austråt *Virgin and Child* (*c.* 1255; both in U. Trondheim, Mus.). The size of the *St Michael* (h. 1.65 m) suggests that it did

58. *St Michael*, polychromed oak, h. 1.65 m, from Mosvik, Norway, *c.* 1250–60 (Trondheim, Universitet i Trondheim, Museet)

not belong to an altarpiece but was placed against a wall or pier in the same manner as surviving German examples, for example in St Michaelis, Jena. Its origins are confirmed by its close stylistic similarity to the *Annunciation* group (*c.* 1250) in the chapter house at Westminster Abbey (*see* §1(ii)(b) above). The well-preserved polychromy demonstrates the range of colours employed, including gold, silver, red, pink, orange, brown–red, black, azure blue and green; in addition the green and red mantle is scattered with gold fleurs-de-lis.

All the examples cited above are no longer in their original setting. It is possible that an *Annunciation* group (*c.* 1363) against the east wall of the hall of the Vicars' Choral at Wells Cathedral is in its original position, although it is more likely that it was set within elaborate wooden arcading. Stylistic affiliations have been recognized with Mosan sculpture, such as a *Virgin* (*c.* 1330; La Gleize, Notre-Dame) from an *Annunciation* or *Calvary* group (*see* §(ii)(b) above), as well as with English brasses and manuscript illumination. This cross-fertilization is not surprising, since medieval craftsmen often worked in various media.

BIBLIOGRAPHY

W. H. Stevenson and J. B. W. Chapman, eds: *Calendar of the Liberate Rolls Preserved in the Public Record Office of the Reign of Henry III*, ii (London, 1930)

A. Andersson: *English Influence in Norwegian and Swedish Figure Sculpture in Wood, 1220–1270* (Stockholm, 1949/*R* 1950)

Die Zeit der Staufer: Geschichte–Kunst–Kultur (exh. cat., ed. R. Haussherr; Stuttgart, Württemberg. Landesmus., 1977), i, no. 459

R. Vaughan, ed.: *Chronicles of Matthew Paris: Monastic Life in the Thirteenth Century* (Gloucester, 1984/*R* 1986)

Age of Chivalry: Art in Plantagenet England 1200–1400 (exh. cat., ed. J. Alexander and P. Binski; London, RA, 1987–8)

P. Williamson with P. Evelyn: *Northern Gothic Sculpture, 1200–1450*, London, V&A cat. (London, 1988)

P. Williamson: *Gothic Sculpture 1140–1300*, Pelican Hist. A. (London, 1995)

PETA EVELYN

(vi) Spain. The quantity and variety of Gothic woodcarving in Spain is much greater than its stone sculpture. Between the 13th century and the early 16th its principal uses varied according to developing liturgical practices. As well as three-dimensional devotional images, which might be free-standing or placed against a support, funerary effigies and altarpieces, Gothic decoration may be found on liturgical furniture, notably choir-stalls, pulpits and ceremonial chairs.

During the 13th century figural sculpture may be seen as a continuation of the Romanesque tradition (*see* ROMANESQUE, §III, 2(ii)), although more life and a sense of idealistic naturalism was gradually introduced. Spanish crucifixes display great typological variety, and nine variants have been identified. Except for a few early examples with four nails, Gothic crucifixes are of the three-nail type. Christ is usually represented as dead, at first wearing a royal crown, as in Romanesque examples, but this was later replaced by the crown of thorns. This change is linked to the growing emphasis on suffering and pain in contemporary mystical literature. The term *Crucifijo gótico doloroso* (or *Crucifijo patético* in Castile) has been applied to a series of crucifixes that developed during the 14th century (see fig. 59), in which Christ's sufferings are graphically conveyed in his contorted posture, the agony evident in his expression and the blood that flows from

59. Crucifix, polychromed wood, from Spain *c.* 1330–60 (Sanlucar la Mayor, S María)

his brow and body. This is emphasized by the polychromy or by the stylized carved drops of blood that sometimes cover Christ's body (e.g. *c.* 1315–20; Campos de Fonollosa, Parish Church, destr. 1936). In the 15th century crucifixes imported from northern Europe were characterized by a strong torso and a short *perizonium*, and this became the predominant type.

Calvary groups, comprising Christ, the Virgin and St John, are found throughout Spain, especially in Castile. The most spectacular Deposition groups, however, are found in Catalonia, such as the example of *c.* 1250 in the collegiate church at San Joan de les Abadesses. In Castile the influence of liturgical drama is evident in a beautiful group in the choir of the monastery of Las Huelgas at Burgos. The Pietà became immensely popular during the 15th century. Annunciation groups are distributed widely throughout León, Castile, Navarre and Galicia, in the last of which there are stylistic links with Portugal (*see* §(viii) below). Devotion to the Virgin and Child was particularly strong in Castile from the reign of Alfonso VIII (*reg* 1158–1214). The most common iconographic type during the 13th century was that of the *sedes sapientiae.* Although some standing figures of the Virgin and Child were made at this time, it was not until the 14th century that this became an important theme. The Virgin was usually represented dressed in the height of fashion (Bernis

Madrazo). Among other Marian themes, the Immaculate Conception was sometimes represented through groups of the Virgin and Child with St Anne, notably during the 15th century.

The relatively scarce and crude 13th-century statues of saints display a rigidity inherited from Romanesque sculpture. In the 14th century, however, the *Golden Legend* of Jacopo de Voragine inspired more richly varied devotions, and statues of patron saints were placed prominently in churches. Burgundian influence in the first half of the 15th century and south Netherlandish in the second half (*see also* §1(viii) above) resulted not only in stylistic changes but also in the introduction of new cults from northern Europe, such as St Adelelmus, who was venerated in Burgos as St Lesmes.

Only a few wooden altar frontals, a Romanesque legacy, were made in the 13th century, for example that in S María la Real, Mave (Palencia). These were gradually replaced in use by altarpieces, which initially were decorated with Christ in Majesty surrounded by the Symbols of the Evangelists, or sometimes by the Virgin and Child Enthroned. A more narrative tone was introduced in the 14th century, for example in the *Nativity* and *Passion* scenes that decorate a rectangular, landscape-format, altarpiece (Burgos, Mus. Arqueol. Prov.) formerly in the convent of S Pablo, Burgos. The same iconographic programme is present in the monumental altarpiece (1351) of Tortosa Cathedral (Tarragona). The varying dimensions of surviving altarpieces reflect the proportions of the chapels for which they were made. From the 14th century those intended for the *capilla mayor* of an important cathedral grew progressively larger until they reached the colossal heights of those in Seville (from 1482, designed by Pieter Dancart), Toledo (from 1498) and Oviedo (1525). Examples commissioned for funerary chapels are more restrained.

Although funerary sculpture was not often carved from wood, some splendid examples have survived from the late 13th century or the early 14th, such as those from Villasandino, the church of the Benedictine monastery at Palacios de Benaver and from S María de Real, Vileña (all now Burgos, Mus. Arqueol. Prov.). These comprise a recumbent figure set on a sarcophagus, the sides of which are decorated with scenes of the *Entombment*. The tomb of *Doña Urraca* from Vileña, for example, is beautifully carved and retains its original polychromy.

Most of the furniture that has been preserved was intended for liturgical use. Early examples are characterized by elements of the *Mudéjar* style, which may be traced in the 13th-century choir-stalls in the monastery of S María, Gradefes, and in those of the 14th century at S Clara, Astudillo, and S Clara, Moguer. Secular furniture displays similar traits. The choir-stalls of Barcelona Cathedral, which were begun by PERE ÇA ANGLADA in 1394, are carved in the purest Gothic style and draw on an exceptionally varied range of secular themes. The iconographic programme, often on moralizing subjects combined with simple decoration generally based on tracery forms, was to provide the basis for many of the large ensembles that were carved in the last decades of the 15th century. These include the choir-stalls, now in the collegiate church at Belmonte, that Egas Cueman finished *c.* 1460 for Cuenca Cathedral and those in the cathedrals at León (*c.* 1463–8 and Seville (completed ?1478). The choir-stalls of the charterhouse of Miraflores, near Burgos, much of which was carved by Martín Sánchez in 1486–9, provide an exceptional example of the style. Some of the most important ensembles of the late 15th century may be associated with RODRIGO ALEMÁN, including those at the cathedrals of Zamora (1505–07; (*see* CHOIR-STALLS, fig. 3), Plasencia (1497–1503) and Ciudad Rodrigo (1498). Pulpits and ceremonial chairs were generally decorated with tracery and *Mudéjar* elements.

BIBLIOGRAPHY

A. Durán Sanpere and J. Ainaud de Lasarte: *Escultura gótica*, A. Hisp., viii (Madrid, 1956)
C. Bernis Madrazo: 'La moda y las imágenes españolas de la Virgen: Claves para su fechación', *Archv Esp. A.*, xliii (1970), pp. 193–215
E. Junyent: *El monestir de Santi Joan de les Abadesses* (San Joan de les Abadesses, 1976)
I. Mateo Gómez: *Temas profanos en la escultura gótica española: Las sillerías de coro* (Madrid, 1979)
A. J. Pitarch and N. de Dalmases Balaña: *L'art gotic s. XIV–XV* (1983), iii of *Història de l'art català* (Barcelona, 1983–7)
D. Kraus and H. Kraus: *The Gothic Choirstalls of Spain* (London, 1986)
R. Terés Tomás: 'Maciá Bonafé y el coro de la catedral de Barcelona: Nuevas consideraciones en torno a su intervención', *Bol. Mus. & Inst. 'Camón Aznar'*, xxiv (1986), pp. 65–85
A. Franco Mata: *Museo Arqueológico Nacional: Catálogo de la escultura gótica* (Madrid, 1993)
——: 'L'Influence germanique sur le crucifix douloureux espagnol du XIVe siècle', *Figur und Raum* (Berlin, 1994), pp. 53–69

ANGELA FRANCO MATA

(vii) Italy. In the early 13th century wood-carving in Italy remained a fairly independent form, but from the end of the century it closely reflected the evolving styles of stone sculpture and metalwork. There were several major regional schools and much awareness of contemporary French and German Gothic styles. Crucifixes, either for processional use or placed in a permanent position, normally above the altar, were important. By the late 13th century the Crucifixion was being interpreted in an increasingly naturalistic manner, as in wall and panel painting. The cross was often shown as the *lignum vitae* (living tree; representing the Tree of Knowledge), and the living Christ of Byzantine tradition, triumphing over death, was increasingly supplanted by the dead Christ, with drooping head and contorted body. The crown of thorns, graphically piercing the skin, was common from the mid-13th century.

Several crucifixes have been attributed to Giovanni Pisano, whose workshop covered Pisa, Siena and Pistoia (*see* PISANO (i), (2)). The close connection between his wood and stone sculpture is demonstrated by the sense of movement, emotion and technical skill evident in these crucifixes, which created models for subsequent work. The *contrapposto* of Christ's body set against the Y-shaped *lignum vitae* cross of a heavily repainted Crucifix (Siena, Mus. Opera Duomo; see fig. 60), contemporary with his work from 1284 on the cathedral façade, creates a graceful outline. The style of the wooden Crucifix in S Andrea, Pistoia, echoes the plasticity of his pulpit there (signed and dated 1301). The cross is of the conventional form, but the arms of the dead Christ are extended upwards, with blood shown dripping from the crown of thorns. In Pisa Cathedral there is a stylistic similarity between Giovanni's pulpit (1302–10) and the living Christ on the tree cross later placed above the tomb of *Archbishop Elci*

60. Giovanni Pisano (attrib.): Crucifix, polychromed wood, from Tuscany, Italy, *c.* 1300 (Siena, Museo dell'Opera del Duomo)

(*d* 1742). Giovanni may also have worked on the *Crucifix* in S Nicola, Pisa.

The elegant linearity of Sienese painting and the graceful style of the sculpture of Orvieto Cathedral may be recognized in two Crucifixes there and one in S Francesco, Orvieto, all of which date from the 1320s and have been attributed to LORENZO MAITANI. Christ expresses serenity rather than anguish and the drapery is treated ornamentally rather than suggesting the underlying form. The living *Christ* in SS Annunziata, Arezzo, is treated in a highly ornamental fashion, with the drops of blood on the forehead forming patterns and the loincloth shown as overlapping, angular folds. A head of the crucified *Christ* (1320s; Siena, Osservanza) may be attributed firmly to the architect and metalworker Lando di Pietro (*d* 1340). In Florence, Giovanni di Balduccio's Crucifix (1333) in the Baptistery has stylized ribs and musculature, blood flowing vigorously from the wound in Christ's side, an ornamentally knotted loincloth and exaggerated hair patterns. That in Orsanmichele has been attributed to Andrea di Cione, who carved the church's tabernacle from 1352. Andrea Pisano or his workshop may also have made wooden Crucifixes (1340s; e.g. Florence, Pitti; Monticelli, S Pietro).

Nino Pisano's work in silver, marble and wood during the 1350s and 1360s inspired a group of *Annunciation* carvings (e.g. London, V&A; Paris, Louvre; Pisa, Mus. N. S Matteo) that combine delicacy with a sophisticated simplicity and show considerable awareness of French Gothic, particularly of ivories. Maitani and his followers also carved Annunciation scenes, marked by elongated bodies, elaborate hair and drapery. The subject became very popular in the second half of the 14th century; the vividly coloured, rigid and less sophisticated examples made in remoter areas contrast with those from the advanced northern workshops. Statues of the Virgin and Child remained popular devotional images, which might be presented as formally enthroned and crowned or, more tenderly, standing in graceful *contrapposto* (once more reflecting French influence). An iconographic innovation in the 14th century was the standing infant Jesus, with chubby face, arms, neck and tightly curled hair, making the gesture of blessing. There were also groups of the Nativity and the Adoration of the Magi, and individual saints.

Relief-carving was sometimes combined with panel painting: the *Virgin and Child Enthroned*, for example, on an altarpiece (late 13th century; Florence, S Maria Maggiore) attributed to Coppo di Marcovaldo has fully modelled faces, haloes and hands, which add realism to the brightly painted scene (*see* COPPO DI MARCOVALDO, §2). The central panel of a triptych in S Maria, Fossa, is a relief of the *Virgin and Child*, while the two wings are painted. Panels carved in relief were also used for decoration. The choir-stalls (*c.* 1331–40) of Orvieto Cathedral, for example, which combine the forms of stone-carving with the delicacy achieved in gold and ivory, are carved with foliage designs in low relief that contrast with the deep relief half-length saints in the trefoil-arched niches above each stall. In the gable of the canopy above the bishop's throne there is a copy in intarsia wood inlay (original in Orvieto, Mus. Opera Duomo) of the *Coronation of the Virgin* mosaic on the cathedral façade; this use of inlay was to become characteristic of the 15th century. Other examples of panel carving appear on an altarpiece by the Moranzone family workshop in Atri Cathedral, showing *Old and New Testament* scenes, and on an arcaded altarpiece with scenes from the *Life of Christ* (late 14th century; Turin, Mus. Civ.) made by another Venetian workshop.

Although increasing realism may be recognized in Italian wood sculpture from the later part of the 14th century, laying the foundations of early Renaissance carving, the established Gothic formulae were maintained until well into the 15th.

BIBLIOGRAPHY

E. Carli: *La scultura lignea senese* (Milan and Florence, 1951)
G. Marchetti and G. Nicoletti: *La scultura lignea nel Friuli* (Milan, 1956)
E. Carli: *La scultura lignea italiana dal XII al XVI secolo* (Milan, 1960)
G. Mariacher: *Scultura lignea nel mondo latino* (Milan, 1966)
J. White: *Art and Architecture in Italy, 1250–1400*, Pelican Hist. A. (Harmondsworth, 1966)
M. Lisner: *Holzkruzifixe in Florenz und in der Toskana von der Zeit um 1300 bis zum frühen Cinquecento* (Munich, 1970)
P. Biavati and G. Marchetti: *Antiche sculture lignee in Bologna dal XII al XIX secolo* (Bologna, 1974)
G. Previtali: *Studi sulla scultura gotica in Italia* (Turin, 1991)

CAROLA HICKS

(viii) Portugal. The relative unimportance of Gothic wood-carving in Portugal was largely due to the scale and

dominance of the Coimbra stone-carving workshops (*see* §1(vi) above). Wood was used only occasionally, chiefly in northern Portugal and to exploit the material's particular strengths for figures of Christ on the Cross. Skilled wood-carving was not practised until towards the end of the Middle Ages (especially in the early 16th century), when it was encouraged by the presence and influence of Netherlandish and German sculptors.

Romanesque elements are still unmistakable in crude statues of the *Virgin*, *St Peter* and *St Paul* (14th century; Lamego, Mus. Reg.). More developed skills are apparent in some other 14th-century figures, including a *Virgin and Child Enthroned* (Viseu, Mus. Grão Vasco), others of the same subject in the parish churches at Gestosa (nr Carrazeda de Ansiães) and Torre de Vilela (nr Coimbra), a *Bishop* (Viseu, Mus. Grão Vasco) and a large *Christ* in the Bernardine convent church of S Maria at Almoster. The most striking 14th-century wooden sculpture in Portugal is the so-called Cristo Negro (Coimbra, Mus. N. Machado de Castro), originally in the convent of Santa Cruz, Coimbra, which is unequalled in its vigorous plasticity, dramatic urgency and avoidance of caricature. Many fine 15th-century figures of Christ on the Cross have been preserved (e.g. Aveiro, Mus. Reg.; Oporto, Góis Church; Pombal, Convento de S Francisco).

The status and quality of Portuguese wood sculpture were transformed at the very end of the 15th century, chiefly through the work of OLIVIER OF GHENT. The great retable (1500–02) that he carved, together with Jean d'Ypres (*fl* 1498–1510), for the Sé Velha at Coimbra introduced vigorous, deeply carved and brightly coloured forms. His carvings for S Francisco, Évora, have been destroyed, but the rich collection of his statues in the rotunda at the convent of Christ, Tomar, includes a beautiful group of the *Virgin and St John* and two angels bearing the arms of Portugal (*see also* MUÑOZ, FERNÃO), which are clearly south Netherlandish in style. These were influential stylistically, but most local sculptors continued to work in stone rather than wood and nearly all Portuguese Late Gothic wood-carving was executed by artists from northern Europe. In Santa Cruz, Coimbra, for example, the important figural compositions on the impressive choir-stalls are by Master Machim, and the *Deposition* group (*c.* 1520) that formed part of the high altar was executed by João Alemão. After *c.* 1520 this Late Gothic tradition continued alongside the first traces of Renaissance influences, introduced by Portuguese and French artists (*see* LORETE, FRANCISCO).

BIBLIOGRAPHY

R. dos Santos: *A escultura em Portugal*, 2 vols (Lisbon, 1950–51)

P. Dias: *O gótico* (1986), iv of *História da arte em Portugal* (Lisbon, 1986)

PEDRO DIAS

(ix) France.

(a) 14th century. Studies of French 14th-century wood sculpture have often been inhibited by a belief that the material is less 'noble' than marble or stone, and that wood sculpture is essentially popular. This view, however, is contradicted by a few surviving masterpieces. Wood, most commonly walnut or oak, was chosen for precise purposes. Some of the work produced by craftsmen whom Etienne de Boileau classed as 'carpenters', for example the choir-stalls of Evreux Cathedral and the extraordinary church-warden's pew in Morogues Church, which was originally in the Sainte-Chapelle (destr.) at Bourges, is of such quality that modern scholarship classes it as sculpture.

The term '*imagier*', which occurs in references to wood sculpture, can refer to the painting of the sculpture (*see* §(i) above). The application of colour on a plaster ground, often enhanced by gilding and encrustations, reinforces a figure's expression in a manner comparable to that sometimes achieved through the application of goldsmiths' work to the wooden core of reliquaries. An example of the latter technique is the reliquary-bust of *St Aredius* (New York, Met.), formerly in the monastery at Saint-Yrieix-la-Perche, which was made by a leading sculptor. Almost all the surviving wood sculpture has been falsified by the disappearance of the original polychromy or by later repainting. It is thus necessary to imagine the difference that it would have made to statuary, such as the Calvary groups that were placed on rood beams in churches, for example at Savins, near Provins, or to the cult statues of the Virgin and Child and saints that were placed in niches or on altars next to the narrative scenes carved on altarpieces, as are preserved in the church at Saint-Thibault-en-Auxois (Burgundy). In addition, the widespread destruction of fragile wood sculpture, whether deliberate or through neglect and decay, has prevented the reconstruction of its stylistic evolution in the 14th century. Yet it is not certain that its scarcity in France is solely the result of loss: Sterling's theory concerning contemporary panel painting might appear to suggest equally that there was comparatively little interest in wood-carving, in contrast to the extensive quantities that were produced in, for example, the Empire and Italy.

BIBLIOGRAPHY

R. de Lespinasse and F. Bonnardot, eds: *Les Métiers et corporations de la ville de Paris, XIIIe siècle: Le Livre des métiers d'E. Boileau* (Paris, 1879)

C. Sterling: *La Peinture mediévale à Paris, 1300–1500*, 2 vols (Paris, 1987–90)

DANY SANDRON

(b) 15th century. Far fewer examples of 15th-century wood sculpture have been preserved in France than in Germany and the Low Countries, partly owing to the preference of both artists and patrons for stone and alabaster and to the systematic destruction of works in less durable wood. It would appear that the greatest influence on its stylistic development was sculpture in stone.

Many churches in the 15th century were adorned with a Calvary group placed on the rood beam at the entrance to the sanctuary. Notable concentrations of examples have been preserved in churches in the regions of Auxerre, Tonnerre and near Montargis in the Gatinais, and also in northern France (e.g. Cambrai, Mus. Mun.). Monumental Entombment groups, such as those from Monthureux-sur-Saône and Moncheux (now in Berlin, Bodemus.), were also sometimes made in wood. The example in the abbey church of St Pierre at Moissac originally comprised 12 figures (see fig. 61). It was made for the tomb of *Abbot Pierre de Carmaing* (*d* 1485), whose arms, together with those of the town and the abbey, appear on the sarcophagus. Pietàs and crucifixes formed part of the furnishings

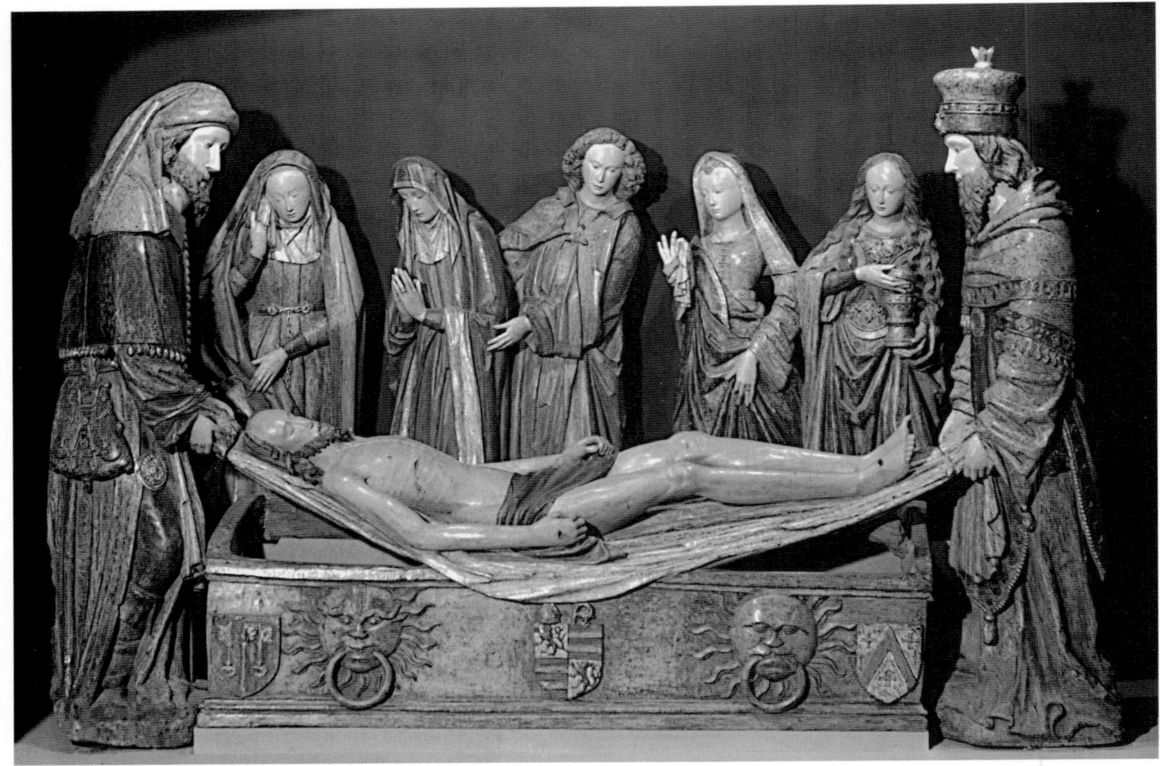

61. *Entombment*, polychromed wood, h. *c.* 2 m, from Moissac, France, *c.* 1485 (Moissac, St Pierre)

of most churches. Free-standing statues of the Virgin and Child and various saints have been preserved in fairly large numbers, but these rarely attain the quality evident in the flowing, spontaneous drapery of a *Virgin Suckling the Infant Christ* (early 15th century) in Villiers-en-Désoeuvre Church, near Ivry-la-Bataille.

The elaborate decoration often lavished on choir-stalls puts them somewhere between wood-carving and joinery. Notable Late Gothic examples in France include those made *c.* 1400 by Jean de Liège for the Charterhouse of Champmol (now in Dijon, Mus. B.-A., *see* JEAN DE LIÈGE, (ii)), the choir-stalls in the abbey church at Saint-Benoît-sur-Loire (completed 1413), Rouen Cathedral (completed 1469) and Amiens Cathedral (1508–22), and the set originally made for Jumièges Abbey (after 1501; now in New York, Cloisters). A group known as the Savoyard choir-stalls is remarkably unified stylistically and in the iconographic programmes adopted, with alternating Apostles and Prophets carved on the backs. This comprises more than a dozen examples in Savoy and western Switzerland, including those in Saint-Claude Cathedral (1449–65; south side destr. 1983), which were completed by Jehan de Vitry, and Fribourg Cathedral (1462–4, by Antoine Peney).

BIBLIOGRAPHY

M. B. Freeman: 'Panneaux de bois sculpté d'origine normande', *Jumièges. Congrès scientifique du 130e centenaire: Rouen, 1954*, pp. 551–6

P. Quarré: 'Un dossier de chaire de la Chartreuse de Champmol, oeuvre de Jean de Liège, *Miscellanea: Prof. Dr D. Roggen*, ed. E. J. Hoebeke (Antwerp, 1957), pp. 219–28

D. Kraus and H. Kraus: *Le Monde caché des miséricordes* (Paris, 1986)

A propos des stalles de Saint-Claude. Actes du colloque de Saint-Claude et Lons-le-Saunier: 1990

Stalles de la Savoie médiévale (exh. cat., ed. C. Lapaire and S. Aballéa; Geneva, Mus. A. & Hist., 1991)

For further bibliography *see also* §1(i)(d) above.

ANDREAS BRÄM

IV. Painting.

The term Gothic is applied to western European painting of the 13th century to the early 15th. Unlike Gothic architecture (*see* §§I and II above), it is distinguished more by developments in style and function than in technique, and even in these areas there is considerable national and regional diversity. The applicability of the term to Italian painting is debated, as is its usefulness in accounting for developments in Netherlandish painting from the early 15th century. Contact with Byzantine art was close in the early 13th century, but after *c.* 1250 survived principally in the Holy Roman Empire and Italy.

1. Introduction. 2. Forms. 3. Working practices. 4. Techniques. 5. Stylistic and regional development.

1. INTRODUCTION. Manuscript illumination, wall and panel painting, stained glass, architectural and sculptural polychromy all retained their importance in the later Middle Ages. However, with changes in clerical patronage, the development of the medieval urban economy and the rise of the laity as patrons in the course of the 12th and 13th centuries, the market for painting of all types widened and diversified. Late Romanesque and Gothic painting

was associated both with changes in the production of painting, which profoundly affected style and function, and with changes in the content and purpose of figurative art in general. Widely heterogeneous in its forms and functions, techniques and development, the Gothic style was essentially one attuned to new methods of communication, particularly of psychological states. It was thus especially closely associated with religious imagery that emphasized the humanity of Christ and a more subjective, empathetic spirituality.

(i) Ecclesiastical patronage and subject-matter. (ii) Lay patronage and subject-matter. (iii) Representation and response.

(i) Ecclesiastical patronage and subject-matter. The development of Gothic painting in the 13th century coincided with the widespread consolidation and institutionalization of intellectual and spiritual currents that had first emerged in western Europe in 11th- and 12th-century monastic writing associated with such figures as St Anselm, Bernard of Clairvaux and the Victorines; these ideas are sometimes related to the so-called 12th-century Renaissance. Romanesque art, formulated within the milieu of monastic reform and with frequent reference to patristic and later theological exposition, was pre-eminently an art of intellectual analysis and synthesis. In contrast, Gothic art was associated with new, less inherently scholarly genres: greater attention was paid to the imagery of the Virgin Mary, the Passion of Christ, and the saints, and to the reformulation of this imagery in terms of its emotional content. In painting, as in the other figurative arts, this led to the introduction of a new physical presence, often, if somewhat misleadingly, described as 'naturalism' (for further discussion *see* §(iii) below). The 13th-century mendicant orders of Franciscans and Dominicans exemplified and, to a large extent, created new patterns of devotion that became influential on art (*see* FRANCISCAN ORDER, §II and DOMINICAN ORDER, §II). St Francis's stigmatization symbolized the imaginative identification with the physical facts of Christ's Passion typical of some 13th- and 14th-century painting, and generally the friars helped cultivate a new religious outlook among the laity. With the establishment of new religious orders, especially in urban centres, clerical patronage was revitalized.

From the early 13th century further attempts to codify Christian belief had an indirect but widespread influence on the subject-matter and character of painting. The doctrine of Transubstantiation, which held that at Mass the bread and wine were converted by the priest's consecration into the actual flesh and blood of Christ, was promulgated at the Fourth Lateran Council of 1215. This may have lent authority to the new upgrading of altar decorations, and from then onwards the altarpiece became extremely important as a focus for innovation in painting (*see also* §2(ii) below). The doctrine contributed to the broader artistic trend towards the pictorial emphasis of Christ's incarnation and suffering, features that were already apparent in Byzantine panel painting. The inauguration of the feast of *Corpus Christi* in 1264 was part of the same doctrinal focus. The Fourth Lateran Council's decree *Omnis utriusque sexus* also required the laity to make confession and take communion each year, indirectly stimulating the production of a new penitential literature and imagery for lay spiritual edification.

In addition to changes in sacramental theology, the gradual, but never fully coherent, development of the doctrine of Purgatory led to the granting of partial remission of penance due for sin in return for prayer to an image. An early example of this is the Roman image–relic of the Veronica, which was given an indulgence in 1216 by Pope Innocent III. Increasingly, images gained the power to confer spiritual benefits that was formerly attributed to the relics of saints. In the 12th and, especially, the 13th century the enrichment of ecclesiastical liturgies, for example those related to the cult of the Virgin Mary, had numerous consequences for the visual arts. In the 14th and 15th centuries images increasingly corresponded with audience expectations as developed in such mystical and devotional literature as the 15th-century *Devotio moderna* from the Netherlands.

(ii) Lay patronage and subject-matter. Several broad patterns of lay patronage emerged during this period: their organization through religious fraternities or civic corporations, which sponsored votive wall and panel painting serving specific joint interests; the related growth of commercial sponsorship in towns, reflected in the range of donors of stained glass in such great churches as Chartres Cathedral and York Minster; and the increasing occurrence of family-based patronage sponsoring private decorated chapels or chantry spaces.

There was a tendency for the late medieval Church to marginalize the laity in liturgical issues, for example through the systematic withholding of the chalice from the laity at Mass, and the emphasis on the altar as the place of consecration of the Host by and for the priest. As physical participation by the laity in communion dwindled, grace conferred by the sight of the Host was stressed, and from this, eucharistic visions, devotion to the Holy Sacrament and Grail legends began to appear. New means of structuring lay experience were also developed, particularly through the Book of Hours (for further discussion *see* §2(i) below) and such vernacular instruction manuals as the 12th-century *Lay Folk's Mass Book* (e.g. Paris, Bib. N., MS. fr. 13342), which indicated what to do and think during Mass.

The consummation of this late medieval outlook is the painted rood screen (*see* SCREEN (i), §3), a pierced timber division between clergy and people, decorated with angels, Apostles and Fathers of the Church. Such screens permitted sight of the altar and sacrament, while establishing around it a boundary decorated, in effect, with a protective but exclusive litany of saints and angels. The diversification of votive, narrative and liturgical art in churches and the increasing fragmentation or 'privatization' of public space was often from the 13th century onwards emphasized by the construction of a variety of screens and partitions.

One reflection of the importance of purely domestic painting in the late Middle Ages is the increasingly widespread documentation of painters in cities and at courts. This occurred at all levels of lay patronage. Royal and aristocratic patronage, in particular, burgeoned in the 13th and 14th centuries as governmental institutions became increasingly identified with specific locations associated

62. Wall paintings showing didactic imagery (*c.* 1330), Great Chamber, Longthorpe Tower, Cambridgeshire, England

with royal or imperial palaces, for example in Paris, London and Prague. There was an attendant formation of styles associated with court patronage, usually, in view of the concentration of government in cities, urban and heterogeneous in its nature; expanding urban and court cultures interrelated closely. Studies of manuscript illumination in Paris in the 13th century have shown that 'court' styles in painting, illumination and architecture were only one facet of the sophistication and eclecticism of contemporary metropolitan culture (Branner). The relationship between court patronage and specific styles, however, remains unelucidated.

Experimentation and diversity were hallmarks of the new genres of domestic interior decoration. The exemplary Bible narratives that were chosen for some schemes, for example in the Painted Chamber (destr. 1834; *see* LONDON, §V, 3(i)(b)) at Westminster Palace, correspond to the Augustinian understanding of history already evident in Carolingian court art. Other forms of subject-matter expressed an increasingly dynastic outlook, inaugurating biographical painting in the early 14th century: in 1320, Mahaut, Countess of Artois, had her father's crusading exploits painted in her castle at Conflans; in 1324 Edward II, King of England, adorned the Palace of Westminster with a pictorial life of his father, Edward I; the Holy Roman Emperor Charles IV had dynastic genealogical cycles (after 1355; destr.) painted at Karlštejn Castle (*see* §5(viii) below). Didactic imagery, a form of 'spiritual encyclopedia', was typical of more modest secular schemes such as that (*c.* 1330) at Longthorpe Tower (Cambs; see fig. 62), while decorations of a heraldic and military nature became almost universal. Pastoral themes also appeared: Henry III, King of England, and Louis IX, King of France, had 'green chambers'; the Palais des Papes at Avignon contains a mid-14th-century Chambre du Cerf depicting greenery and outdoor pastimes (*see* §5(vii) below; *see also* AVIGNON, fig. 3). Narrative themes were drawn from romances such as the Arthurian cycle, from the military parts of the Bible or from Classical history. Themes increasingly crossed from religious to secular contexts: in the 14th century, scenes from the *Apocalypse* were chosen for the chapel of the Virgin at Karlštejn Castle, for the chapter house at Westminster Abbey and for the series of tapestries made for Louis I, Duke of Anjou.

Civic patronage also expanded in the 14th century. In Italy, civic government commissioned frescoes for the Palazzo Pubblico in Siena depicting politically acute, quasi-allegorical subjects drawn from pre-humanistic political theory, presided over by the heavenly court of the Virgin and defended by local military heroes (*see* SIENA, §III, 3(ii) and figs 10–12; *see also* WALL PAINTING, colour pl. II, fig. 2). Criminals or enemies of the state were shown hanging in effigy at the Bargello in Florence. Likewise in the north, at Ghent around 1350, the armed militia of the corporation was painted (destr.) in the hospice of SS Peter and Paul. Formal mural schemes that expounded religious doctrine in the 12th century expounded the themes of dynasty and secular authority in the 14th.

(iii) Representation and response. Gothic painting is often described as being more 'naturalistic' than Romanesque, and it is generally agreed that mimesis was an increasingly prominent concern of late medieval artists from about the mid-13th century, beginning in north-western Europe; there was, however, no uniform or consistent development of mimetic idioms. The founding fathers of art-historical scholarship accounted for the tendency towards a more imitative art between the early 13th century and the 15th in several ways: most commonly this was either in terms of the reconciliation of symbolic pictorial sensibilities (associated with northern painting) and aesthetic ones (associated with Italian painting) or as a consequence of the relative influence of Neo-Platonic ideas and Aristotelian natural philosophy. Such dialectical argumentation has been abandoned in favour of interpreting naturalism as the product of an autonomous artistic process and stressing the relationship between art and spectator. Gothic representation, therefore, is seen to be determined to some extent by its spectator's requirements.

In religious painting, conventional narrative material concerning Christ's Passion was supplemented to provide more complex focuses of devotion. From the 13th century there was a straightforward expansion of the figurative content of religious representations. For example 12th- and 13th-century scenes of the Crucifixion showing the dead Christ on the Cross were transformed into dramatically scenic narratives by a process of augmentation with motifs such as the Virgin swooning before the Cross (see fig. 63). In this period the illustrated hagiographic *libellus* was also amplified into an elaborate pictorial biography, and the same process was behind the contemporary proliferation of apocryphal elements in the lives of Christ and the Virgin. A popular source for the interpretation of the apocryphal Gospels was the *Golden Legend* (1255–66), a compendium of saints' lives, by the Dominican JACOPO DE VORAGINE. Apocryphal detail—of the sort in the copiously illustrated English Holkham Bible Picture Book

63. Duccio: *Crucifixion*, tempera on panel, *c.* 1.00×0.76 m, detail from the *Maestà* altarpiece, from Siena Cathedral, Italy, completed 1311 (Siena, Museo dell'Opera del Duomo)

(*c.* 1320–30; London, BL, Add. MS. 47682)—further stimulated the spiritual imagination and devotional attention.

This expanded information had to be selected and re-encoded in terms of new priorities in order to result in 'naturalism'. Accordingly, in 13th-century western Europe narrative material, especially from the Gospels, was concentrated into affective tableaux, a process influenced by two factors: the importation of Byzantine icons with their developed language of mimetic, empathetic, figurative representation and new icon-types (*see* EARLY CHRISTIAN AND BYZANTINE ART, §VI, 1); and meditative literature of the sort associated with St Edmund Rich, the Pseudo-Bonaventura, Mechthild of Magdeburg, St Bridget of Sweden and Heinrich Suso. For example in the late 13th-century Solger Hours (Nuremberg, Stadtbib., MS. Solger, 4°, 4), produced in Paris for a lay patron, the normal sequence of Gospel events is dislocated to juxtapose the events of Christ's Passion with the liturgical Hours, to accord with a contemplative procedure that is associated with the writings of St Edmund Rich and the Pseudo-Bonaventura; this became standard practice for images in Books of Hours.

Other elements were isolated from the narrative as new themes located midway between *historia* and cult image, and these manipulated the attention of the devout by means of a summary, rapidly assimilable, compassionate image. By the 14th century such images, in panel painting and manuscript illumination, reached a high degree of pictorial complexity. In keeping with icon prototypes, they often took the form of 'close ups', impressing the spectator by a strikingly expressive language of facial expression and gesture. Such images as the Man of Sorrows (*see also* §2(ii) below), precisely because of the reference to several stages of a narrative, were universally valid, suited to a diversity of taste and function. These images were not only thematic, but emblematic, illustrating the infinite nuances of categorization in late medieval religious thinking and the tendency to multiply focuses of devotion. Their role in the development of corporate identity is also notable: in the later Gothic period, churches, guilds and confraternities were formed in association with specific images, and there emerged *Andachtsthemen*, that is dedications to a devotional preoccupation such as the Holy Blood or *Corpus Christi*. Thus potentially autonomous images evolved that functioned outside the constraints of conventional religious narrative or public liturgy, but within an expanded (and in a sense more versatile) sense of spiritual introspection and contemplation.

The connection between this new form of attention and the production of mimetic art is apparent. The intention behind much of later Gothic painting is to transmit symbolic information and to persuade its audience by an emotive, expressive language, thereby catering to the 'need to see'. The 'objective' symbolic content is retained and enhanced by the use of 'subjective' imagery, inviting a corresponding response from the viewer. The difference between a Romanesque and a Gothic image is analogous to the difference between intransitive and transitive verbs in language: Romanesque images are intransitively 'expressive', but Gothic ones can be transitively expressive of something, typically grief or happiness. The emphasis of the mature 14th- and especially 15th-century painted image is adverbial and anecdotal. The concern is commonly as much with a mental state (e.g. the Man of Sorrows or Joys of the Virgin) as with a specific historical moment.

For general bibliography *see* §2 below.

2. FORMS.

(i) Manuscript. (ii) Panel. (iii) Stained glass. (iv) Wall.

(i) Manuscript. During the Gothic period there was an expansion in both the quantity and the diversity of illuminated books, while existing types of book were adapted to suit the needs of new patrons and users (*see also* MANUSCRIPT, §II, 1). The illustration of traditional Christian subject-matter was continued for religious books. Innovation occurred for the most part by the selective editing and recombination of older themes. In narrative art, older stocks of iconography, most often based on a literal interpretation of the Bible, were continually drawn on: miniatures by William de Brailes, the mid-13th-century Oxford book illuminator, share iconographic features found in Anglo-Saxon Bibles; earlier Western and Byzantine picture cycles influenced extensive programmes of Bible illustration independent of the text, such as that in the mid-13th-century French Maciejowski Bible (New York, Pierpont Morgan Lib., MS. M. 638). In the 13th century the Bible and Psalter remained the staple focus of artistic activity. The PSALTER, in particular, was enlarged with textual and illustrative elements that reflected new

64. William de Brailes: scenes from the *Crucifixion*; miniature from a Book of Hours, 150×123 mm, from Oxford, England, *c.* 1240 (London, British Library, Add. MS. 49999, fol. 47*v*)

devotional preoccupations. Demand for decorated liturgical books, including Breviaries, Missals, Graduals, Antiphonaries and Pontificals, increased in order to cater for the widespread liturgical upgrading typical of churches of all ranks in the 13th century.

Existing types of illustrated book, such as Apocalypses, chronicles, saints' lives, bestiaries and spiritual didactic texts, were produced in greater numbers and often translated into the vernacular to serve the interests of a more diverse audience, notably the increasingly powerful landholding classes. At the same time new genres, for example illustrated romances, became established (*see* ROMANCE, MANUSCRIPT, §1). Most were commissioned by secular patrons and were part of the vast increase in the illustration of vernacular texts that resulted from changes in patronage and readership. The rise of the universities in the 13th century also affected the production of books, bringing about a well-organized and regulated book trade to satisfy the requirements of students: a new type of small-scale, single-volume illuminated Bible was developed and produced in greater numbers, especially in Paris (*see* BIBLE, §I, 1); Bolognese book producers specialized in glossed canon and civil law texts, some being exported unilluminated and unbound for completion to local taste (*see* BOLOGNA, §II, 1); and biblical commentaries such as the *Glossa ordinaria* and Peter Lombard's *Sentences* became standard texts.

With the rise of production methods geared to an ever-widening market, both lay and ecclesiastical, there was a complementary shift from monastic workshops to lay, commercial ones, commonly based in urban centres. In the same period, private reading became more common, leading to a drastic reduction in book sizes; during the 13th and 14th centuries Bibles and Books of Hours were produced that were no larger than a pocket diary. Compression of size brought about corresponding adjustments to the scale and technique of illumination, the *multum in parvo* miniaturization of much Gothic illumination, whereby the tendency was towards the development of pictorial techniques suited, but not specific, to small-scale work. The pictorial language of Gothic miniatures is often deft and summary, its sometimes routine quality a reflection of the greater number of works produced.

These changes are exemplified by the emergence and widespread popularity of the Book of Hours (*see* BOOK OF HOURS, §1). Based on the text of the Divine Office in monastic and secular Breviaries, the Book of Hours gradually displaced the Psalter to become the primary text of private lay devotion between the 13th and 14th centuries. The first extant illustrated example was painted in the mid-13th century by William de Brailes (*c.* 1240; London, BL, Add. MS. 49999; see fig. 64). Because it provided a new devotional focus, then relatively unconstrained by tradition and open to new material, the Book of Hours is a fertile source for evidence of late medieval religious preoccupations. Ultimately, in the 15th century, such texts were also printed; this was the period of transition to mass-produced texts and images.

(ii) Panel. Painted panels had been produced in western Europe during the Romanesque period, but they did not yet have the authority of icons in Byzantine culture. Related to this were two developments that changed the status of the painted panel: the evolution of the altarpiece and the impact of Byzantine icons on the West. Painted altarpieces were developed from the 12th century and based on the rectangular form and decoration of the altar frontal. According to some authorities (e.g. Van Os), the use of the altarpiece accelerated after the promulgation of the doctrine of Transubstantiation (1215), but it is probable that the reasons are more complex (*see* ALTARPIECE, §2). Throughout Europe in the second half of the 13th century, altarpieces, like the altars themselves, expanded in size, often resembling the Byzantine iconostasis, though with a very different function. In Italy composite formats consisting of numerous icon-like figurative representations surrounding a larger principal subject, usually the titular saint of the altar, were adopted. By *c.* 1300 in central Italy the main features of the multiform altarpiece, or POLYPTYCH, were established. These developments culminated in the so-called painted 'walls of wood' such as Duccio's *Maestà* (completed 1311; Siena, Mus. Opera Duomo; *see* DUCCIO, fig. 3) for Siena Cathedral. In Italy especially, the altarpiece became a major expression of the corporate civic outlook of the city state and of the devotional requirements of the religious orders and confraternities, exemplifying the pre-eminent role of urban patronage in pictorial innovation in this period.

In northern Europe the pattern was somewhat different. Painted altarpieces commonly retained the rectangular form of the frontal, and the massing of images over altars occurred more through painted statuary set in niches

65. Matthew Paris: *Virgin and Child, Veronica Head and Man of Sorrows*, tinted drawing from the *Chronica maiora*, *c.* 362×244 mm, from ?St Albans, England, 1235–59 (Cambridge, Corpus Christi College, MS. 26, fol. vii)

forming a screen behind the altar. Panel painting was nonetheless practised in such centres as London, Paris, Bergen, Cologne, Hamburg and Prague, and in Brabant and Flanders. Although much has been lost, the surviving works by Melchior Broederlam and Jean Malouel, and the remarkable range of 14th-century German painted altarpieces, show that panel painting was not necessarily less important in the north than manuscript painting. Indeed scholars have increasingly stressed the importance of panel painting for the antecedents of early Netherlandish art, hitherto mostly traced in smaller-scale manuscript illumination (*see* NETHERLANDS, THE, §III, 2).

A second factor in the increased demand for panel painting may have been the impact of Byzantine icons reaching Western Europe after the sack of Constantinople in 1204 (Belting, 1981). Icons were influential in several spheres: the Italian composite altarpiece, the imagery of the painted cross and, no less widespread, the popularization of Western versions of icons of Byzantine type, notably the *Imago pietatis* or Man of Sorrows. The earliest occurrence of this subject in north-western Europe appears *c.* 1250 in the manuscript painting of the Benedictine illuminator Matthew Paris (Cambridge, Corpus Christi Coll., MS. 26; see fig. 65). Icons were the principal locus of notions of both authentic representation and spiritual power and retained their hold throughout the later Middle Ages: such Early Christian icons as the Aracoeli *Virgin* were reproduced in Bohemian painting as late as 1400 (e.g. Prague, N.G., convent of St George), and even later in 15th-century Germany.

Panel paintings are thought to be symptomatic of a more private devotional religious culture in the late Middle Ages and, further, of a more image-centred culture than had been the case in the Latin West before the 12th century. Modest devotional panel paintings became, like Books of Hours, a common occurrence in lay households, and the subject-matter of much 15th-century panel painting, particularly in early Netherlandish art, implies a domestic audience. The last inventory (1416) of an outstanding bibliophile, Jean, Duc de Berry, includes over 20 paintings on wood.

The genre of portraiture developed in the wake of the proliferation of panel paintings with their increasing emphasis on imitation and the representation of holy faces. The earliest recorded discrete panel portrait is that of Petrarch's *Laura* (untraced), painted, according to Petrarch, by Simone Martini in 1336. Portraits emerged

66. Girard d'Orléans (attrib.): *John II*, tempera on panel, 910×410 mm, from ?Paris, France, *c.* 1350–60 (Paris, Musée du Louvre)

especially as an expression of family history and self-awareness; the 14th-century panel paintings of *John II* (Paris, Louvre; see fig. 66), and of *Rudolf IV*, Duke of Austria (Vienna, Dom- & Diözmus.), probably belonged to more extended 'galleries' showing only the heads of figures in full or half profile. By this means confusion with full-frontal religious icons was avoided.

(iii) Stained glass. In north-western Europe during the 12th and 13th centuries stained glass was employed in ever larger quantities in religious buildings of all types (for further discussion *see* §VIII below). It proved, however, to be a less efficient medium of indoctrination and devotion than wall painting, since in the late Middle Ages it ceased to convey solely the symbolic and narrative images (e.g. the Tree of Jesse) for which it had been employed in the 12th century. The immense expansion in window sizes in the 13th century, apparent first in the clerestory of Chartres Cathedral (designed 1190s), undoubtedly reflected the decorative glamour of the medium and introduced important changes in glazed window design. With the advent of tall, glazed clerestories, stained-glass compositions became increasingly dominated by single standing figures and architectural motifs. The simultaneous widening and lightening of the palette from the mid-13th century arose principally as a response to the demand for better illumination, especially for the celebration of Mass.

(iv) Wall. There is little truth in the idea that Gothic architecture in northern Europe deprived mural painters of wall surfaces and so contributed to a decline in the medium. Most Gothic churches are not of the structurally radical type that characterize great Gothic church design, and in the wake of the doctrinal and educational pronouncements of the Fourth Lateran Council wall painting proliferated in smaller churches as the major medium of religious instruction. The changes marking the transition from Romanesque to Gothic wall painting were thus primarily the result of changes in style, technique, content and audience, rather than status. Abstract painted polychromy on walls and surfaces also retained a major role in elucidating structure in larger interiors, such as at Chartres Cathedral (early 13th-century interior paintwork), and in enhancing religious experience in smaller interiors, for example in the Sainte-Chapelle (1240s), Paris, which was explicitly praised for the religious effect of its coloration and decoration by Jean de Jandun (*fl c.* 1323) in the 1320s.

In its content, northern wall painting of this period reflected neither the formality of Romanesque wall painting, with its sustained narrative histories and impressive hieratic compositions, nor the clear exposition of religious themes typical of contemporary sculpture, especially portal sculpture. This was a consequence of the assumption and fragmentation of patronage by an increasingly wide range of patrons intent on a more individualistic piety.

In Italy by the late 13th century and the early 14th, although stained glass was adopted for some decorative schemes (S Francesco, Assisi; Santa Croce, Florence), the initiative lay increasingly with fresco painters. Fresco, commonly combined with secco painting, had existed in the Romanesque period, but underwent a revival in Rome and central Italy in the later 13th century in the workshops of Cavallini, Cimabue, Giotto and the masters employed at Assisi. Wall painting in Italy flourished within a tradition that, since the Early Christian period, had favoured large-scale, formally arranged narrative display. Such displays were revived in the late 13th century, especially under the aegis of Franciscan and papal patronage. A major example of this, the frescoes of the *St Francis Legend* (*c.* 1300) in the Upper Church of S Francesco at Assisi, the contents of which were transmitted in the form of large-scale copies to other Franciscan churches, indicates that frescoes also created canonical picture cycles in this period (for further discussion *see* §5(v) below).

GENERAL BIBLIOGRAPHY

J. Burckhardt: *Die Kultur der Renaissance in Italien* (Basle, 1860; Eng. trans., London, 1878)

J. von Schlosser: 'Ein veronesisches Bilderbuch und die höfische Kunst des XIV. Jahrhunderts', *Jb. Ksthist. Samml. Allhöch. Ksrhaus.*, xvi (1895), pp. 144–230

L. Courajod: *Origines de la Renaissance* (1901), ii of *Leçons professées à l'Ecole du Louvre* (Paris, 1899–1903)

J. Braun: *Der christliche Altar in seiner geschichtlichen Entwicklung*, 2 vols (Munich, 1924)

J. Huizinga: *The Waning of the Middle Ages* (London, 1924, rev. 1955)

E. Panofsky: 'Imago pietatis', *Festschrift für Max J. Friedlander zum 60. Geburtstage* (Leipzig, 1927)

H. Focillon: *Art âccidental: Le moyen age Roman et Gothique* (Paris, 1938; Eng. trans., London, 1963)

G. Haseloff: *Die Psalterillustration im 13. Jahrhundert: Studien zur Buchmalerei in England, Frankreich und den Niederlanden* (Kiel, 1938)

M. Meiss: *Painting in Florence and Siena after the Black Death* (Princeton, 1951)

J. Dupont and C. Gnudi: *La Peinture gothique* (Geneva, 1954; Eng. trans., London, 1979)

R. Berliner: 'Arma Christi', *Münchn. Jb. Bild. Kst*, n.s. 2, vi (1955), pp. 35–152

E. Panofsky: *Renaissance and Renascences in Western Art* (Stockholm, 1960)

I. Ragusa and R. B. Green, eds: *Meditations on the Life of Christ: An Illustrated Manuscript of the Fourteenth Century* (Princeton, 1961)

P. Verdier: *The International Style* (Baltimore, 1962)

Europäische Kunst um 1400 (exh. cat., Vienna, Ksthist. Mus., 1962)

S. Ringbom: *Icon to Narrative* (Åbo, 1965, rev. Doornspijk, 2/1983)

F. Deuchler, ed: *The Year 1200: A Background Survey* (New York, 1970)

The Year 1200 (exh. cat., ed. K. Hoffmann; New York, Met., 1970)

Art and the Courts: France and England from 1259 to 1328, 2 vols (exh. cat. by P. Brieger and others, Ottawa, N.G., 1972)

The Year 1200. A Symposium: New York, 1975

R. Branner: *Manuscript Painting in Paris during the Reign of Saint Louis* (Berkeley, 1977)

J. Marrow: *Passion Iconography in Northern European Art of the Late Middle Ages and Early Renaissance* (1979)

H. Belting: *Das Bild und sein Publikum im Mittelalter* (Berlin, 1981)

F. O. Büttner: *Imitatio pietatis: Motive der christlichen Ikonographie als Modelle zur Verähnlichung* (Berlin, 1983)

H. Van Os: *Sienese Altarpieces, 1215–1460: Form, Content, Function*, i (Groningen, 1984)

L. Grodecki and C. Brisac: *Gothic Stained Glass, 1200–1300* (London, 1985)

R. S. Wieck: *Time Sanctified: The Book of Hours in Medieval Art and Life* (Baltimore, 1988)

M. Camille: *The Gothic Idol* (Cambridge, 1989)

J. Wirth: *L'Image mediévale: Naissance et dévelopement, VI–XVe siècle* (Paris, 1989)

H. Belting: *Bild und Kult: Eine Geschichte des Bildes vor dem Zeitalter der Kunst* (Munich, 1990)

3. WORKING PRACTICES. With the shift from oral to written culture between the 12th and 14th centuries, the quantity of written information about working practices and about artists increased. Formal contracts, painters'

manuals and administrative records concerning the execution of paintings became more common in the course of the 13th century; wills and other archival records supply evidence for the social status of painters in a way not possible before the 12th century. Such documents indicate broad patterns of change. While painting and illuminating continued to be practised in religious communities, notably monasteries, by the 13th century the crafts tended to be concentrated in towns and were predominantly practised by specialized lay professionals. Consequently they were documented by the new urban administrations. Thus, for example, by the mid-14th century the records of the painters' corporation of Ghent show that it could provide over 40 men for the town militia; such large reserves of painters present in many 14th-century cities were probably the result of a high demand for ordinary residential painting.

Parisian tax documents of the 1290s reveal that the division of painting and illuminating, not envisaged explicitly in Theophilus' 12th-century treatise *De diversis artibus*, had become normal practice. By the 14th century, with the formation of painters' and illuminators' guilds, the two crafts had acquired different religious emblems, St Luke being the patron of painters, St John the Baptist of illuminators. Painters had higher taxable income than illuminators, who themselves were concentrating into distinct professional quarters, living in close proximity to one another, a pattern replicated in other university cities such as Oxford.

Painting and illuminating required separate training; according to the 14th-century ordinances of the Tournai Corporation of St Luke, illuminators received a shorter training than painters: two years, not four. The 1391 statutes of the Parisian Confraternity of St Luke, to which painters and sculptors belonged, make no mention of illuminators, and by the 15th century the distinction appears to have become entrenched in south Netherlandish centres such as Bruges, where the movements of artists and materials were much regulated (*see* BRUGES, §II). In Italy there seems to have been less of a division between large- and small-scale painting: for example the six choir-books at Padua Cathedral made around 1306 have historiated initials closely related to Giotto's contemporary work in the Arena Chapel, Padua, and the prefatory miniature in the manuscript known as Petrarch's *Virgil* (Milan, Bib. Ambrosiana, MS. A. 49 inf.) is attributed to the painter Simone Martini. There is further evidence, especially in the 14th century, of painters and illuminators executing work in or for other media: the Parisian illuminator Jean Pucelle designed seals, the painter Orcagna was associated with sculpture, Giotto was in charge of the construction of the campanile of Florence Cathedral, the sculptor André Beauneveu is linked with the execution of some miniatures for Jean, Duc de Berry, and the Netherlandish painter Melchior Broederlam with a wide range of artistic activities. The ambiguity of the French term *imagier*, applied to both painters and sculptors, indicates that adaptable skills were still regarded as normal in the best artists.

Relations between painters and clients were increasingly formalized. Between *c.* 1250 and *c.* 1420 the basically informal arrangements whereby painters working at court were employed for specific commissions, without necessarily occupying a court position, tended to be replaced by the more formalized appointment of an artist to an office, either 'King's Painter' or some nominal household post such as *valet de chambre* at the French court. Such offices may have acted as retainers in order to fend off competition from other well-placed patrons. Similarly, the language of written contracts of the type associated from the late 13th century in Italy with the production of large altarpieces (e.g. that for Duccio's *Maestà*) tended to become more formalized, displacing any oral component in a commission. This process was complete by the 15th century and apparent, for example, in Spanish altarpiece contracts (Sobré).

Painters' manuals in this period, while continuing to offer practical instruction in the tradition of 12th-century works, also provide evidence about the position and role of artists. Cennino Cennini's late 14th-century *Il libro dell'arte*, which records workshop practices stemming from Giotto and Taddeo Gaddi, is both technical and theoretical (*see* CENNINI, CENNINO). The text describes the increasing specialization of late medieval craft practice; painters differ from illuminators and glaziers and are presumed to work on altarpiece panels constructed by joiners in separate workshops. Cennini attributed a wide range of skills to painters but considered their superiority to lie in their mastery of design (*disegno*), manner of study and social status. He anticipated the 15th-century humanist attempt to elevate painting to the status of a liberal art and to remove it from the preserve of the purely manual, mechanical arts represented by guild organization. His stress on 'design' also demonstrates a late-medieval re-evaluation of prototype designs. While architectural drawing flourished from the mid-13th century onwards, there is little sign that artists' designs were valued in themselves until around 1400, when (in the case of a dispute between Jacquemart de Hesdin, one of Jean, Duc de Berry's painters, and one Jan van Holland) there is evidence of the theft of designs and so, in effect, of the notion of design copyright. By the 15th century, Italian painters were described as 'learned', for example in Ghiberti's *Commentarii*, indicating a pretention to an intellectual stature possessed in northern Europe mostly by master masons.

BIBLIOGRAPHY

V. W. Egbert: *The Mediaeval Artist at Work* (Princeton, 1967)

A. Martindale: *The Rise of the Artist in the Middle Ages and Early Renaissance* (London, 1972)

P. Binski: *Painters*, Medieval Craftsmen (London, 1991)

S. Brown and D. O'Connor: *Glass-painters*, Medieval Craftsmen (London, 1991)

C. de Hamel: *Scribes and Illuminators*, Medieval Craftsmen (London, 1992)

For further bibliography *see* §4 below.

4. TECHNIQUES.

(i) Fresco, secco and panel. (ii) Colour. (iii) Illumination, modelling and treatment of surface.

(i) Fresco, secco and panel. The technique of true (or *buon*) fresco was common in Romanesque wall painting (*see* FRESCO), but in the course of the 13th and 14th centuries secco painting (*see* SECCO), also anticipated in the Romanesque period, became increasingly important north of the Alps (*see also* WALL PAINTING, §I). Fresco persisted, however, in some more conservative traditions, notably

67. *Charles IV and Anne of Swidnica with the Reliquary Cross*, wall painting, west wall, chapel of St Catherine, Karlštejn Castle, Bohemia

the 13th-century German *Zackenstil*, and was also often used in the preparatory stages of wall painting (e.g. St Cäcilien, Cologne). Secco painting usually involved pigments suspended in lime water (*see* LIME SECCO), but tempera and even oil (*see* OIL PAINTING) are also common, and more evidence for the use of oil media and varnishes in Gothic wall painting is emerging. For example oil was purchased for wall paintings at the Palace of Westminster in the 13th century, Ely Cathedral, and at the castle of the Counts of Artois at Conflans in the 14th. Depending on the medium used, secco painting can produce either matt or gloss effects, but most Gothic wall painting schemes have a matt finish. This is produced by the rapid application of thin water- or tempera-based paint layers over preliminary designs drawn in red earth (*sinopia*) or incised into the plaster ground. Another feature of Gothic wall painting is the transition away from the dark underpainting for flesh tones that was customary in Romanesque painting, which occurred in the period 1180–1300, depending on the region.

Indicative of new trends in wall painting are the medallions in the dado arcade of the upper chapel of the Sainte-Chapelle in Paris, executed in the 1240s. Some of these compositions, painted in transparent pastel-hued pigments on a white ground, are set off against glazed metal leaf reflective grounds; painting is here seen as a counterpart to such light-producing surfaces as stained glass. This 'aristocratic' tradition of wall painting, inaugurated in the 13th century, is of fundamental importance in understanding the realignment of media characteristic of the late 13th century and the 14th throughout Europe. By the mid-14th century the wall paintings in another royal chapel, St Stephen's in Westminster Palace, were executed in an oil technique comparable to panel painting, again adorned with gilt encrustation; and the same applies to the interior decorations at Karlštejn Castle in Bohemia, with their dazzling quasi-Romanesque array of encrusted, roughly cut hardstones (see fig. 67). There is no reason to doubt that the rise of translucent paint surfaces in northern European painting was associated with the power of stained glass to transmit light, and in the 14th century with the taste for *basse taille* or translucent enamels (*see* §VI, 3 below). This movement towards translucency, with its attendant media of oil and varnishes, substantially predates 15th-century Netherlandish painting; Jan van Eyck did not invent oil painting, but rather refined a traditional, northern Gothic procedure.

In the north, therefore, the tendency was for panel and wall painting to draw closer together, both in the media used and in the way paint was applied; the pictorial arts became an area of technical experiment. This may partly explain why mosaic decoration failed so utterly north of the Alps. It was certainly known if not practised: Theophilus referred to the salvaging of glass tesserae from pagan (i.e. Roman) remains, for the manufacture of enamel. By the 1140s, however, it was regarded as archaic. Abbot Suger employed the technique for the north tympanum (destr.) of the west portal at Saint-Denis Abbey (and also for floors within the basilica), acknowledging that this was contrary to contemporary fashion: the choice illustrates some of the more conservative elements in his scheme. Around 1370 Venetian mosaic was again used externally for the south façade of Prague Cathedral (*see* PRAGUE, §IV, 2(iii)), again in a milieu, that of Emperor Charles IV, at once modern and backward-looking and with a taste for large-scale displays of inlaid hardstones.

The primary reasons for the absence of mosaic in the north are clear: there was no tradition of such work outside the Mediterranean region, and mosaic could not accommodate the smooth tonal transitions and detail so fundamental to High Gothic painting.

By the late 13th century northern European panel painting was invariably executed in oil (usually linseed or walnut) or tempera on chalk or gypsum (gesso) grounds. Supports were usually oak or pine. Oil and tempera were sometimes combined within a single work, as in some Norwegian altar frontals executed in the late 13th century (e.g. Frontal no. 1 from Tingelstad; Oslo, U. Oldsaksaml.). It was common for media to vary according to the pigments used, but such external considerations as the substantial growth in demand for altarpieces around 1300 may explain the adoption of rapid single-layer painting in Norway and Germany, and the gradual disappearance of the earlier laborious, and therefore expensive, multilayered oil and tempera painting executed on silvered grounds.

Cennini described painting in oil on wall or panel as a technique the Germans (i.e. northerners) were much given to (*Il libro dell'arte*, 89). The technique was certainly practised in Italy and Spain, often without success, but in Italy, on the whole, greater, if not exclusive, stress was laid on fresco painting. In the later Middle Ages in the West, true fresco painting was concentrated almost wholly within Italy and its sphere of influence: southern France (e.g. Béziers Cathedral; Avignon) and Catalonia in the 14th century. It is generally agreed that fresco painting underwent a significant revival in late 13th-century Rome in the circles of Cimabue and Cavallini, rapidly spreading to Tuscany and Umbria. This probably reflected a new interest in the ancient, Early Christian and Byzantine heritage of fresco painting. Experiments in pictorial space (i.e. the revival of strongly foreshortened viewpoints of objects), inaugurated, for instance, in the Upper Church of S Francesco in Assisi in the years around 1300, were probably informed by survivals of Roman wall painting. In technique, however, 14th-century fresco differed from that of Roman painting, which was executed in lime secco (i.e. the pigments were mixed in lime, rather than pure water); 14th-century fresco is thus clearer and lighter than its ancient prototypes. The revival of monumental mosaic decoration in late 13th-century Rome may also have influenced the interest in fresco, since there are close similarities between the preparatory stages of both techniques. Major artisans associated with fresco around 1300, such as Cavallini, Cimabue, Torriti and Giotto, were also associated with mosaic work.

Because some pigments are incompatible with fresco technique, secco painting was commonly an adjunct to fresco in Roman and Tuscan painting: thus Giotto added pigments in tempera over fresco in the Arena Chapel (*c.* 1305), Padua, and Simone Martini employed secco in his *Maestà* (*c.* 1315) in the Palazzo Pubblico in Siena (*see* WALL PAINTING, colour pl. II, fig. 2). The 'frescoes' by Giotto's workshop in the Peruzzi Chapel in Santa Croce, Florence, are in fact largely secco in technique. Secco painting retained a major role in Italy where panels painted in tempera (usually on poplar) were produced in huge quantities, becoming more important in the later Middle Ages.

(ii) Colour. Stained glass shows the broader changes in colour aesthetic that occurred in Gothic painting (*see* STAINED GLASS, §II, 1). The workshop arrangements prescribed by Theophilus in the 12th century implicitly connect the manufacture of stained glass and precious metalwork, and the coloration and design of 12th-century glass produced in France and Germany, as well as Mosan manuscript painting, certainly borrowed extensively from metalwork. During the first half of the 13th century these Late Romanesque standards of coloration and layout prevailed in most stained glass executed in northern Europe. Coloration was thus predominantly drawn from a palette of saturated reds and blues, and compositional formulae were, on the whole, derived from precious media. For example, multiform medallion frames to articulate small figurative compositions, typical of metalwork, remained in vogue between the glazing of the Trinity Chapel in Canterbury Cathedral (see fig. 68) in the first decades of the 13th century, and the glass of the 1240s in the Sainte-Chapelle, Paris (*see* STAINED GLASS, colour pl. I). The restoration of glass and the study of its saturated coloration have resulted in the revision of former conceptions about the importance of luminosity in Early Gothic glass. The mystical theology embodied in Christian Neo-Platonic philosophy, once seen as the source for the explanation of the increased emphasis on luminosity, has

68. *Miracles of Thomas Becket*, stained glass, north aisle, Trinity Chapel, Canterbury Cathedral, England, *c.* 1200–20

69. Band glazing, apse, St Urbain, Troyes, France, *c.* 1270

been recognized to be of questionable applicability. Thus the tendency to stress the comparative darkness of 12th-century glazing can be overplayed, as has been revealed by the cleaning, and consequent lightening, of the west windows of Chartres Cathedral.

From the mid-13th century, however, there were distinct developments in stained glass. Its palette began to change, becoming lighter and including a wider range of colours. The commonly stated view that this was due to a desire for more light in buildings is almost certainly correct: in the 13th and 14th centuries there is some textual evidence that older buildings were thought too dark and that good illumination was necessary for high altars (e.g. the visitation records, diocese of Worcester). Furthermore, fundamental changes in window construction were accompanied by a reorientation in the use of glazed colour. In France by the later 13th century (e.g. Tours Cathedral; St Urbain, Troyes; see fig. 69) the coloured glass used for figurative subjects was concentrated in a new sort of composition, the band window, in which coloured compositions were set in large rectangular fields within larger areas of bright grisaille glass.

Clear glass, much the hardest to make and accordingly the most costly, became more common, and from the mid-13th century there was also a more general use of grisaille glass—clear glass shaded with grey or green in abstract patterns (*see* GRISAILLE). This had originally been adopted by the Cistercians in the 12th century but found favour, especially in England, within a tradition of architectural design which concentrated on the tonal values of building materials themselves (e.g. the use of coloured Purbeck marble), in a way not usual in France. When set with fields of darker glass, as with band glazing, such windows set up a strong and typically late medieval rhythm of simple contrasting and alternating tonalities (*see* STAINED GLASS, colour pl. VI, fig. 1). By about 1300 red and blue were joined by a wide variety of browns, emeralds, violets and yellows, a change in the palette of glass that accelerated in the early 1300s with the adoption of silver-stain, a method of firing glass coated with silver nitrate to produce a warm golden hue. This was one of the few true technical innovations of the period.

A wider palette is generally typical of later 13th- and 14th-century painting throughout Europe. Secondary hues such as violet, lime green, pink, orange and grey occurred increasingly in the 14th century in Italian and northern wall, panel and manuscript painting: for example strong yellows appear in the frescoes of Taddeo Gaddi in Florence, and the use of violet is recommended in the 14th-century Neapolitan text *De arte illuminandi*. Such colours allowed daring changes of iridescent hue on one surface: Simone Martini shaded rose-coloured garments with a lurid green, and similar coloration characterizes some mid-14th-century Parisian illumination. As painting increasingly aimed at sophistication and subtlety of surface effect, so methods of coloration gained in complexity.

Little fundamental technical change took place in Gothic manuscript painting (*see also* MANUSCRIPT, §III, 3). Full-colour opaque painting on parchment, of the sort brought to technical perfection in the 12th century, was the staple technique at the beginning of this period. There was, however, a gradual shift in the medium with which pigments were mixed, from glair (egg white) to gum, which produced a lighter, brighter effect. For the most part, such formal illuminated religious manuscripts as Bibles, Psalters and liturgical texts tended to be painted in a restricted range of colours, typically a dull red and blue, combined with burnished and incised gold grounds; hence the characterization of much 13th-century French book painting as the *Style au fonds d'or*. In keeping with general tendencies towards lighter, wider palettes and subtler textures, full-colour painting in, for example, Paris tended to lighten in tonality after *c.* 1260.

Other techniques were derived from scribal practice, especially the use of coloured penwork or flourished letters; this was widespread throughout northern Europe, but was particularly developed in late 13th-century England, for instance in such manuscripts as the Windmill Psalter (New York, Pierpont Morgan Lib., MS. M. 102). In accordance with older Anglo-Saxon tradition, drawing techniques, occasionally combined with gilding, were common in 13th-century England for some types of illustrated book, typically narrative pictures of the Apocalypse and saints' lives; and in the 14th century for popular didactic illustration, as in the *Biblia pauperum* and the *Speculum humanae salvationis*. It also occurred in northern France, for instance in the St Eligius rotulus (*c.* 1250; Paris, Carnavalet, no. D 7075) and the *Liber floridus* of Lambert

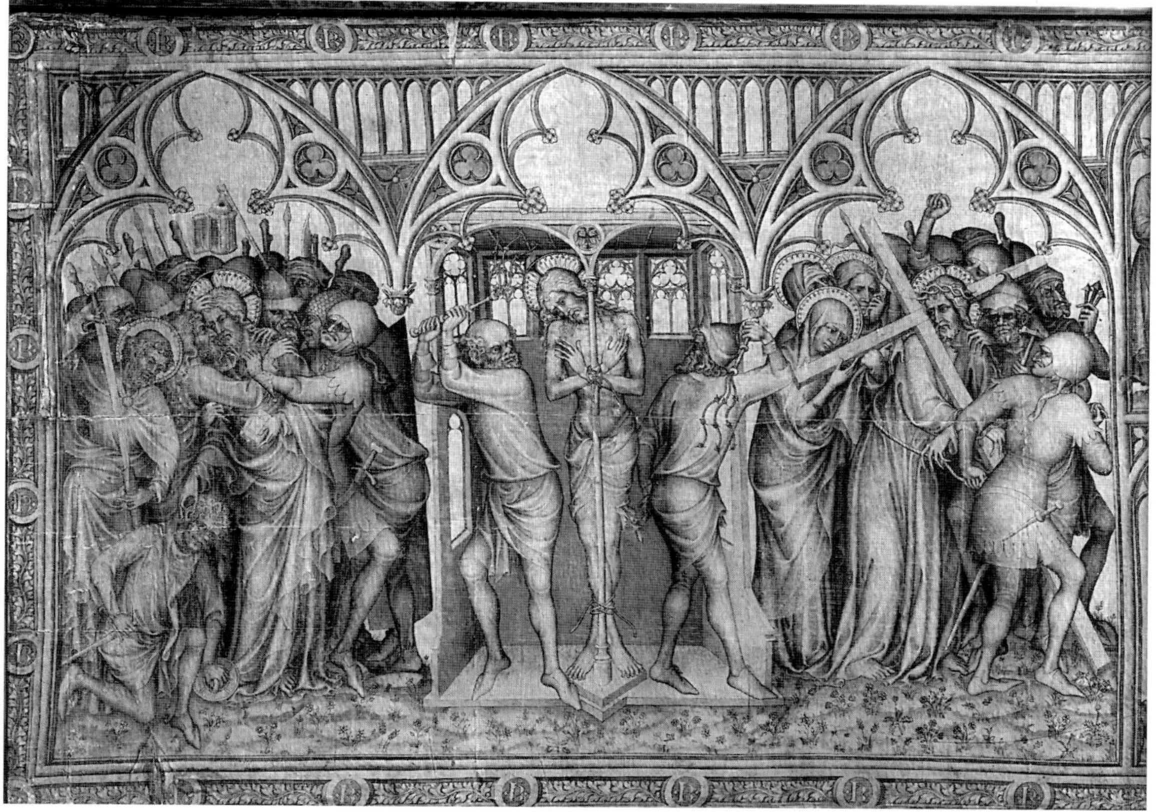

70. Master of the Parement de Narbonne: *Betrayal of Christ, Flagellation and Christ Carrying the Cross*, monochrome ink drawing on silk, detail from the *Parement de Narbonne*, from France, *c.* 1375–80 (Paris, Musée du Louvre)

of Saint-Omer, and surfaced again in German, Bohemian and Italian 14th-century illumination.

Occasionally techniques analogous to pen and wash were practised in English wall painting, for instance the fragmentary cloister murals at Windsor Castle, produced under English royal patronage *c.* 1250. The use of figurative grisaille in the 14th century, both in manuscripts and on painted cloth, for example the monochrome drawing in ink, the *Parement de Narbonne* (*c.* 1375–80; Paris, Louvre; see fig. 70) made for Charles V, King of France, illustrates the sophistication of relationships of tone as well as hue that some Gothic painters began to seek in their work.

In Gothic book decoration a hierarchy of coloration and ornamentation was often employed to clarify the text. In calendars, for example, black, red and gold lettering, though often merely decorative, may also indicate the differing status of saints' feasts (*see* CALENDAR), while painted initials of various sizes and colours in the main text of the manuscript herald its various divisions (*see* BORDER, MANUSCRIPT). The most concise embodiment of this emphasis on colour as a means of organization and enrichment rather than imitation is found in the formal prescriptions concerning colour in heraldry, a sign system that emerged in the West in the 12th century (*see* HERALDRY, §II, 1). The descriptive language of heraldry (blazon) indicates how this system could be reduced to a code of etiquette, whereby certain colour or material combinations were acceptable but others were not. These distinctions could thus generate symbolic meaning when colour etiquette was deliberately breached, and especially when used with appropriate symbols or charges (Pastoureau, 1979, 1982).

Throughout the later Middle Ages, in accordance with this understanding of colour as possessing an objective status and hierarchy, it was customary for the patron to require the use of the most expensive pigments, typically ultramarine, in panel and wall paintings. This may be regarded both as the assertion of a materialist attitude towards colour symbolism (colours through their materials embodying symbolic qualities and so enhancing the content of an image) and as an expression of the patron's and painter's concern with high-quality and stable materials. Such concerns are reflected closely in medieval painters' guild regulations on the use of materials; painters were expected to understand the origins and classifications of materials, as contemporary manuals testify, primarily as a guarantee of quality.

(iii) Illumination, modelling and treatment of surface. In a famous passage Dante alluded to the 'art which in Paris is called illuminating' (*Purgatorio*, XI, 80–81), and the term illuminate is generally used of manuscript decoration. One

reason behind this was the notion that illumination was associated metaphorically with the Word of God and so with intellectual and spiritual enlightenment, largely the preserve of the book: St Thomas Aquinas, described by Pope John XXII as 'illuminating' the church by his work, is sometimes shown holding his *Summa contra gentiles* with the text open and radiating light (e.g. the S Caterina Polyptych; before 1319; Pisa, Mus. N. S Matteo). Theophilus, however, appeared to use the term '*luminae*' to describe highlights in monumental painting, and although the exact range of this word's usage is still unknown, it appears that to illuminate something meant, at first, either to model in highlights or, more strictly, to highlight by means of crosshatching in white paint. This technique, found in such English mid-13th-century work as the Sarum Missal of Henry of Chichester (Manchester, John Rylands U. Lib., MS. lat. 24) and in some German *Zackenstil* products, was of Byzantine origin. An analogous method is found in Byzantine and from the mid-13th century in Italian, especially Sienese, painting; here, the hatched highlights take the form of fine lines of gold.

Methods of paint application varied and are usually considerably more complex than contemporary technical manuals would suggest. One of the most common was the application of single laying-in colours over preparatory drawings. Final articulation was provided by black outlines that reproduce the preliminary drawing. This flat compartmentalized coloration occurs in much manuscript painting of the 13th century, and also in panel and wall painting. A second widespread method was two-stage coloration, whereby a relief effect was produced by the addition of a darker shading hue to the laying-in colour. This process was known as *incidere* (literally to incise, as in engraving or metalwork) in the textual tradition of the *Mappae clavicula* and, especially, the treatise *De coloribus et mixtionibus*. Two-stage coloration is again very common and found in extremely sophisticated illumination, such as the Windmill Psalter, already noted for its penwork (*see* §(ii) above). Wash or bistre is aesthetically related to two-stage coloration, the exposed parchment acting as the background colour, the washes as shadows. In three-stage coloration, highlights are added to the laying-in and shading colours in a process called *matizare* in the *De coloribus*. These highlights are usually composed of the laying-in tone mixed with white and give a surface sheen to continuously modelled surfaces. Modelling is thus attained by working both up and down from the laying-in hue.

Three-stage coloration underwent radical changes in the last decades of the 13th century, both in northern Europe and in Italy, and is a sign of a profound and general transformation in figurative painting whereby growing emphasis was laid on plasticity of form, volume and continuity of surface. The technique can be traced in manuscript painting in France and England from at least the 1260s. Some of the artists working on the Parisian St Louis Psalter (Paris, Bib. N., MS. lat. 10525) employed true wet-in-wet highlighting, and this technique was no less common in English work of the period, such as the Gulbenkian Apocalypse (1260s; Lisbon, Mus. Gulbenkian, MS. LA 139). It is clear from the most accomplished panel painting of the period, for instance the Westminster Retable (London, Westminster Abbey; see fig. 71), that the technique was used in oil and tempera work in England, and possibly also in France, in the period 1260–90 (*see also* LONDON, §V, 2(iii)). In late 13th-century Parisian illumination loosely associated with Master Honoré, the method is fully developed, and by the 14th century it had become commonplace.

In Italy, however, highlighting was understood in a fundamentally different way. In northern Europe before the late 14th century, highlighting was an attribute of surface, the illumination of figures consisting of intrinsic changes in surface, tonality and hue. Experiments in showing extrinsic directional lighting, where light and shade indicate a distinct point of view, separate late 13th- and early 14th-century Roman, Tuscan and Umbrian monumental painting by Cavallini, Giotto and Taddeo Gaddi from northern painting. Even in Italy mimesis itself was not a constant; experiments with cast light dwindled in the course of the 14th century, and frequently the portrayal of light effects was inconsistent. Pietro Lorenzetti's work (*c.* 1319) in the Lower Church at Assisi demonstrates the first assertive use of cast shadows, hitherto avoided in 14th-century painting. Mimesis was also adjusted to the theological status of the subjects represented. Cennini recommended that shot (i.e. unnaturally modulated) colours should be kept for the draperies of appropriate figures such as angels. There was inevitably some difficulty in construing the relationship between supernatural light (e.g. haloes, glories) and mundane cast light, but it was not an inhibiting one. In 14th-century Italy

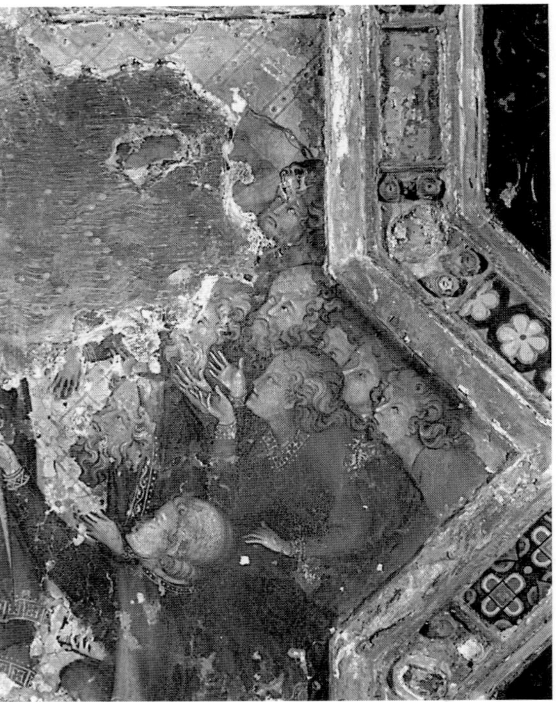

71. *Miracle of the Loaves and Fishes* (detail), oil and tempera on panel, from the Westminster Retable, 0.95×3.33 m, from England, *c.* 1270–80, (London, Westminster Abbey)

alone there coexisted two visual outlooks, one rationally mimetic and optically substitutive, the other often fantastically abstract and decorative. In some fields this coexistence survived the conceptual shift of Alberti's recommendation that painters should evoke the effect of gold in pictures rather than actually using gold itself.

Despite the development of illusionistic techniques, and the imitative substitution in paint of effects previously created by the use of real materials added to the surface of pictures, Italian and northern European 14th-century painters continued to dress wall paintings and panels with an elaborate array of decorative adjuncts that served to stress the objectively material, surface nature of their work. Three techniques of surface enrichment, all noted by Cennini, were particularly important in the Gothic painter's workshop: incised and (eventually) punched patterns in the gilt grounds (*see* GILDING, colour pl. III, fig. 1), particularly developed in the Sienese circle of Simone Martini and the Lorenzetti brothers; modelled or cast gesso or pastiglia, again to produce pattern in relief, common in Florentine and Neapolitan work of the early 14th century; and sgraffito, by which designs were scratched into the layer of paint. To these effects should be added the inlaying of glass or gilt tin to otherwise painted surfaces; tin is mentioned in wall-painting accounts for Westminster Palace as early as the 1290s. *Verre eglomisé* was another distinct class of work used, for example, by Paolo di Giovanni Fei, whereby painted panels had inserts of glass, backed with gold that was scratched away to show figurative designs. Effulgent light, resulting from the breaking up of luminous surfaces by reflective material and by fine gilt textures, remained central to the surface aesthetic of Italian painting, particularly in Siena; Simone, for instance, kept his punchwork small and fine in order not to interfere with the smooth grain of his paintwork, stressing the intimate relationship between his decorative and representational outlook.

The widespread use of these techniques—decorated gesso was used in Italian and Byzantine work in the 13th century and was common in German, Bohemian, English, Netherlandish and Spanish work throughout the 14th—illustrates the general principle that while significant changes in the technology of representation occurred in this period, painting remained a craft allied aesthetically to the decorative arts, whether goldsmiths' work or textiles (Hills). The polyptych forms of Tuscan painting in the 14th century employ a hybrid Gothic micro-architectural language inspired by smaller precious artefacts. The textured gilt grounds of English late medieval panel paintings such as the Despencer Retable (*c.* 1390; Norwich Cathedral) or the 15th-century rood screen at St Edmund, Southwold (Suffolk) resemble expensive brocades, and so the art form is aligned with secular taste in a way similar to earlier Sienese work. Decorative pastiglia was commonly applied to the drapery of painted statuary to enhance its lifelikeness.

Painting in the 14th and 15th centuries is an art of high artifice. Surface embellishment in monumental painting, however, was also a Late Romanesque practice. Just as glass inserts had been used to make wall paintings tinsillate at Berzé-la-Ville in 12th-century Burgundy, so the technique was revived in the crypt of Canterbury Cathedral in the 14th century; raised gesso is also found in Catalan and Sienese panel painting in the early 13th century and in the later German *Zackenstil* in Carinthia, for example in the wall painting at Gurk Cathedral. The Gothic 'aristocratic' tradition of glazed paintings represented by the interior of the Sainte-Chapelle and the Westminster Retable was inseparable from the use of relief adornment and glass decoration, and it is in the light of this self-conscious *varietas* that the pictorial and craftsmanlike language of painters from Simone Martini to Gentile da Fabriano, in the so-called International Gothic period, should be seen.

BIBLIOGRAPHY

C. Cennini: *Il libro dell'arte* (MS., Padua, 1390s); ed. and trans. D. V. Thompson, 2 vols (New Haven, 1932–3); Eng. trans. also as *The Craftsman's Handbook* (New York and London, 1954)

M. T. Engels: *Zur Problematik der mittelalterlichen Glasmalerei* (Berlin, 1937)

E. W. Bulatkin: 'The Spanish Word "Matiz": Its Origin and Semantic Evolution in the Technical Vocabulary of Medieval Painters', *Traditio*, x (1954), pp. 459–527

J. Marette: *Connaissance des primitifs par l'étude du bois du XIIe au XVIe siècle* (Paris, 1961)

E. Frodl-Kraft: *Die Glasmalerei: Entwicklung, Technik, Eigenart* (Vienna and Zurich, 1970)

L. E. Plahter, E. Skaug and U. Plahter: *Gothic Painted Altar Frontals from the Church of Tingelstad: Materials, Technique, Restoration* (Oslo, 1974)

E. Frodl-Kraft: 'Die Farbsprache der gotischen Malerei', *Wien. Jb. Kstgesch.*, xxx–xxxi (1977–8), pp. 89–178

M. Pastoureau: *Traité d'héraldique* (Paris, 1979)

J. Gage: 'Gothic Glass: Two Aspects of a Dionysian Aesthetic', *A. Hist.*, v (1982), pp. 36–58

M. Pastoureau: *L'Hermine et le sinople: Etudes d'héraldique médiévale* (Paris, 1982)

M. H. Caviness and E. R. Staudinger: *Stained Glass before 1540: Annotated Bibliography* (Boston, 1983)

N. Morgan: 'Aspects of Colour in English and French Manuscript Painting of the Late Thirteenth Century', *Akten des XXV. Internationalen Kongresses für Kunstgeschichte: Wien, 1983*, vi, pp. 111–16 [bibliog.]

P. Mora, L. Mora and P. Philippot: *Conservation of Wall Paintings* (London, 1984)

P. Hills: *The Light of Early Italian Painting* (New Haven and London, 1987)

Art in the Making: Italian Painting before 1400 (exh. cat. by D. Bomford and others, London, N.G., 1989–90) [bibliog.]

J. Gage: 'Color in Western Art: An Issue?', *A. Bull.*, lxxii/4 (1990), pp. 518–41

For further bibliography *see* §3 above.

5. STYLISTIC AND REGIONAL DEVELOPMENT.

(i) Transitional style, *c.* 1180–*c.* 1250. (ii) Parisian and related styles, *c.* 1240–*c.* 1320. (iii) Holy Roman Empire, *c.* 1230–*c.* 1300. (iv) Scandinavia and the Iberian Peninsula, *c.* 1230–*c.* 1340. (v) Italy, *c.* 1265–*c.* 1320. (vi) England and France, *c.* 1300–*c.* 1350. (vii) Italy, Spain and papal Avignon, *c.* 1320–*c.* 1400. (viii) Holy Roman Empire, *c.* 1300–*c.* 1400. (ix) England, *c.* 1350–*c.* 1410. (x) France, *c.* 1350–*c.* 1410. (xi) International Gothic style, *c.* 1380–*c.* 1440.

(i) Transitional style, c. *1180–1250.* Gothic painting developed from stylistic tendencies already apparent in Late Romanesque art, and these continued to provide an underlying source of diversity throughout the 13th century (*see* ROMANESQUE, §IV, 2(vi)(g)). It is generally agreed that they first appear in what has been termed the TRANSITIONAL STYLE or 'style of *c.* 1200', which is often regarded, like the so-called International Gothic style (*see* §(xi) below), as an entity in its own right. In the 14th century and the early 15th, in the works of such literati as Dante and Christine de Pisan, Paris was recognized as the centre of high art production in the new Gothic style. Even as early as the mid-13th century a Bolognese law

professor wrote of a father complaining of his son wasting money in Paris on books that 'prattled' with gold letters. It is, however, increasingly clear that Paris acted primarily as a catalyst rather than as the sole innovator for much of the Gothic period and that regional developments should receive equal attention.

Gothic painting originated within the triangle of territory between the Rhine, central France and southern England between *c.* 1180 and *c.* 1240. Two strands of development from *c.* 1180 are of particular importance. One grew out of the tendency in Late Romanesque art, influenced technically and stylistically by Byzantine painting and by a classicizing approach typical of Mosan metalwork, to produce a monumental figure style, with a broad quasi-Roman gravitas. English examples of this idiom are found in the late work (*c.* 1180) on the WINCHESTER BIBLE (Winchester, Cathedral Lib.), in work of *c.* 1200 in the Westminster Psalter (London, BL, MS. Royal 2. A. xxii) and the Munich Psalter (Munich, Bayer. Staatsbib., MS. Clm. 835) and in the last copy of the Utrecht Psalter made at Canterbury (*c.* 1190–1200; Paris, Bib. N., MS. lat. 8846).

In northern France, notably in the Ingeborg Psalter (*c.* 1195; Chantilly, Mus. Condé, MS. 9/1695; *see* ROMANESQUE, fig. 70), this style resembled the Mosan MULDENFALTENSTIL metalwork of Nicholas of Verdun (*see* NICHOLAS OF VERDUN, fig. 2). It occurred in French wall painting (e.g. Chamalières-sur-Loire) and Parisian miniature painting of the 1220s and 1230s, as in the *Bibles moralisées* (e.g. fragment, New York, Pierpont Morgan Lib., MS. M. 240; see fig. 72), and was generally a style attuned to the taste for increasingly fully modelled surfaces characteristic of French painting in the following decades. It lacks, however, the latter's most important feature: the tendency to flatten and simplify surfaces. On the contrary, this was a style that inclined towards muscular, rounded physiques, classicizing head types and softly corrugated surfaces. In sculpture this style culminated in the powerful plasticity of the north portal figures at Reims Cathedral of *c.* 1225–30, which resemble, to some degree, the appearance of the Carolingian antique style practised in painting at Reims four centuries earlier. The Reims-influenced drawings of VILLARD DE HONNECOURT (*c.* 1220–40; Paris, Bib. N., MS. fr. 19093) are among its last occurrences.

An opposing, but contemporary tendency, again anticipated in Romanesque painting, was marked by a preference for slender and elastic forms. It is present in an English bestiary of *c.* 1200 (Cambridge, U. Lib., MS. Ii.4.26) and characterizes stained-glass production in northern France and southern England, as in the *Miracles of St Thomas Becket* at Canterbury Cathedral, probably *c.* 1200–20 (Caviness). This light, slender figure style prevailed in England well into the second half of the 13th century, extending from such works as a Psalter made in London (*c.* 1230; Cambridge, Trinity College, MS. B.11.4) and the tinted drawing technique of such mid-13th-century artists as MATTHEW PARIS at St Albans (e.g. his *Life of St Alban*, *c.* 1245–52; Dublin, Trinity Coll. Lib., MS. 177) to fully painted work typical of the group of manuscripts produced *c.* 1250 in the region of Salisbury (e.g. the Missal of Henry of Chichester; Manchester, John Rylands U. Lib., MS. lat. 24). In drawn form, the style embodies the lightness of touch of pre-Conquest Anglo-Saxon painting.

72. *Figures of a King, Queen, Scribe and Iconographer*; miniature from a *Bible moralisée*, 375×265 mm, from Paris, *c.* 1230 (New York, Pierpont Morgan Library, MS. M. 240, fol. 8*r*)

The style was associated with a general transformation of decorative motifs; light, elastic foliate forms composed of coils or tendrils, terminating in small trefoil pads, replaced the fleshy, overblown forms of Late Romanesque foliage. In the Beatus page of the early 13th-century English Huntingfield Psalter (New York, Pierpont Morgan Lib., MS. M. 43), for example, the slim, coiling foliage anticipates the taste in French Gothic building for slender, taut bar tracery, inaugurated at Reims after 1211. The characteristic framing motif of this phase is that of the medallion, whether round or quadrilobe. Medallion formats occur in stained glass (*c.* 1180–90; Canterbury Cathedral), manuscript painting (from *c.* 1220; the Parisian *Bibles moralisées*) as well as in other media, for example sculpture (Amiens Cathedral, west façade dado) and metalwork.

(ii) Parisian and related styles, c. *1240–*c. *1320.* The spry, thin figurative style was also characteristic of much stained glass produced in northern France, including the region of Paris, up to the 1240s; it has been identified as a 'Channel style', and as such it was not the last example of formative artistic relations between southern England, Paris and northern France in the Gothic period (Caviness). This phenomenon is matched by the close links between Canterbury and such northern French centres as Reims, Laon, Arras and Valenciennes in ecclesiastical architecture. In the glass of the Sainte-Chapelle of *c.* 1245 (*see* PARIS, fig. 35) the narratives still comprise restless compositions

similar to the scenes of martyrdom in the painted wall medallions beneath, but with one important exception: the garment forms in the murals are distinctly flatter and crisper. This is the result of the influence of a new monumental sculptural style that arose in the Ile-de-France and surrounding territories in the 1230s and 1240s.

This style departed radically from the classicizing Transitional idiom in its approach to surfaces and textures, producing figures of greater physical presence: garment forms began to fill out and flatten, and anatomies to reduce and gain in elasticity. Physiognomies are sharper, the eyes narrowed and mobile, gestures more pointed and silhouettes harder and more angular. The style is typical of the sculptures of *Apostles* placed around the Sainte-Chapelle's interior, and its introduction into painting is notable in the later Parisian *Bible moralisée* styles *c.* 1240–46 (e.g. London, BL, Harley MS. 1527; *see* BIBLE, §I, 3(i) and fig. 8) and in the narrative biblical illustrations in the contemporary northern French Maciejowski Bible (*c.* 1250; New York, Pierpont Morgan Lib., MS. M. 638). Typical of this phase is the effetely quickened, choreographed narrative style of the St Louis Psalter (Paris, Bib. N., MS. lat. 10525) executed in Paris *c.* 1260–70. Its miniatures feature up-to-date aedicular decoration in the spirit of contemporary Parisian architecture and a simplified surface treatment achieved through a three-stage wet-in-wet coloration. By the 1260s and 1270s, at Amiens, Troyes and Beauvais, this idiom was also influencing stained glass in tandem with the spread of aedicular formats, band glazing and lightened palettes.

The appeal of this new, sharper idiom may be measured by its rapid adoption in areas outside Paris and northern France. By *c.* 1260–70 there are unambiguous signs of contact between English and French painters working in southern England and the Midlands, as in the Bible of William of Devon (London, BL, MS. Royal 1.D.I; *see* BORDER, MANUSCRIPT, fig. 1). In England the sharp style took on an exceptionally exaggerated guise, for example in the Lambeth Apocalypse (London, Lambeth Pal. Lib. MS. 209), reminiscent less of Parisian work, than of the drawn illustrations in the St Eligius rotulus (Paris, Carnavalet, no. D 7075) probably made in the 1250s in the region of Noyon. English metropolitan and especially court-related patronage, however, produced the most interesting works in this style. In the 1260s the light, slim anatomies of London painting became clothed in the sharper, simplified garment forms of northern France, and there was a gradual tendency to fill out anatomical forms and increase their weight. With this new weightiness came the fleshy, somewhat grotesque, but superbly accomplished style typical of the Douce Apocalypse (*c.* 1270; Oxford, Bodleian Lib., MS. Douce 180; see fig. 73), made for Edward I, panel painting such as the Westminster Retable (London, Westminster Abbey; see fig. 71 above) and the wall paintings (destr. 1834) in the Painted Chamber at Westminster. The mannerism of this style—for example the taste for extremely contrived postures, hidden profiles and back-turned figures—has been traced to Parisian art of *c.* 1270, but it seems to have been prevalent throughout the territories that first produced Gothic painting in this period.

73. *Angel with the Millstone*; miniature from the Douce Apocalypse, 312×215 mm, from ?London, England, *c.* 1270 (Oxford, Bodleian Library, MS. Douce 180, fol. 51*r*)

In the period 1240–1320 painting in the region between Paris and Cologne, including the Mosan heartlands and the dioceses of Cambrai, Verdun, Tournai and Liège, exhibits a growing orientation towards the new northern French style; in the Mosan region, especially, older Germanic elements were abandoned. There is a close relationship with English painting; fundamentally similar work to that in the Douce Apocalypse is found, for example, in a picture-book of saints (Paris, Bib. N., MS. nouv. acq. fr. 16251) produced perhaps in Hainault in the 1280s.

It is also characteristic of this period that in illuminated manuscripts the areas outside the text, the page margins, received unprecedented attention (*see also* BORDER, MANUSCRIPT). In the mid-13th century the characteristic repertory of Gothic foliate ornament, developed from fully painted, decorated initials, exploded into life with birds, beasts and humans, creating a new realm of pictorial interest and diversion. The first signs of this trend are *c.* 1250 in English illumination, in the work of the remarkably innovative Oxford illuminator WILLIAM DE BRAILES (e.g. Oxford, New Coll., MS. 322) and in the Rutland Psalter (London, BL, Add. MS. 62925). Such decorative features are peculiarly characteristic of English painting, but by 1300 they were more widely spread, to the extent that it is not always easy to discriminate by decoration alone between southern English and northern French work. The mannered but delicate borders of the English Alphonso Psalter (*c.* 1284; London, BL, MS. Add. 24686; *see* HERALDRY, fig. 20) are extremely similar to slightly later French-allied works such as the Bar Breviary (London, BL, Yates Thompson MS. 8; see fig. 74). Up to the years *c.* 1300, therefore, a second, more purely Gothic 'Channel style' emerged, which echoed the geographical patterns of its forerunner *c.* 1200 but extended southwards into north-eastern France and Lotharingia.

In Paris, trends of the 1280s and 1290s, in which something of the thin and dry qualities of the period 1240–70 disappear, are anticipated in the Martyrology of St Germain-des-Prés (1270s; Paris, Bib. N., MS. lat. 12834):

74. Beatus page from the Bar Breviary, from northern France, *c.* 1300 (London, British Library, Yates Thompson MS. 8, fol. 7*r*)

figures tended to be squatter, with drapery folds more rounded and less angular and hairstyles fuller and more richly convoluted; foliate ornament was reduced to cobweb delicacy; while the technique and palette used was softer. It was in this period—*c.* 1270–1300—that the 'S-bend' stance of figures was developed, as in, for example, the Parisian Nuremberg Hours (Nuremberg, Stadtbib., MS. Solger 4°, 4). The culmination of this new, rounded and soft style is often identified, although on controversial documentary grounds, with the career of Master Honoré, an illuminator recorded in Parisian tax records of the 1290s. He provides an example of a Picard illuminator working in Paris, again raising the question as to the extent of the purely Parisian, as opposed to north-eastern French, Lotharingian and even English genesis of such works as the *Somme le roi* (1290s; London, BL, Add. MS. 54180) and the Breviary of Philip the Fair (?before 1296; Paris, Bib. N., MS. lat. 1023; for illustration *see* HONORÉ, MASTER). Honoré's illuminator son-in-law Richard of Verdun, for example, was probably from eastern France. Similar patterns of exchange are apparent in late 14th-century northern France (*see* §(x) below). It is this late 13th-century style, elegant in manner and sophisticated in its tonal relations, that points forward to the work in the 1320s of Jean Pucelle, another Parisian artist of obscure origins, but wide stylistic resources (*see* §(vi)(b) below).

These formal characteristics were equally typical of wall painting and stained glass. The new, softly decorative style associated with the increased use of architectural frames and *rinceaux* grounds prevailed in stained glass throughout the northern French and English milieux between 1260 and 1310, for example at St Pierre, Chartres; Merton College, Oxford; York Minster; and Strasbourg Cathedral. It occurs in wall painting at Westminster Abbey around 1300 and probably characterized the mural commissions of Mahaut, Countess of Artois, a few years later. A Franco-German variant of the style is also apparent in the first glazing campaigns at S Francesco at Assisi of the mid-to-late 13th century (*see* ASSISI, §II, 3).

A distinctive development in the *mise-en-scène* of painting in this period is the increasing preference for the architectural aedicula as a means of framing compositions. As the compositional methods and colouristic techniques typical of metalwork were gradually abandoned, shallow gabled constructions dominated many compositional types from the late 13th century onwards, with motifs often drawn from the repertory of French High Gothic architecture. This is especially true of stained glass (e.g. 1250s or 1260s, Strasbourg Cathedral; see fig. 75) but was typical also of wall painting, for example the *St Maurille* murals (1280s) at Angers Cathedral and the Painted Chamber (1290s) at Westminster. This rise of architectural formats coincided with the establishment of a stable grammar of Rayonnant design, sleek and graphic in nature, which also emerged in the early examples of architectural drawing of the period, for example the Reims Palimpsest (*c.* 1240; Reims, Archvs Ville) and, particularly, later 13th-century instances such as the façade design of Strasbourg Cathedral (*c.* 1275; Strasbourg, Mus. Oeuvre Notre-Dame; *see* ARCHITECTURAL DRAWING, fig. 1).

(iii) Holy Roman Empire, c. *1230–*c. *1300.* The Holy Roman Empire was largely unaffected by the first wave of the new French idiom. Although some buildings, notably the Liebfrauenkirche at Trier (begun 1235) and Cologne Cathedral (begun 1248), exhibit a clear understanding of the principles of French Gothic architecture, German painting, especially in the Rhineland, Saxony and Thuringia, remained firmly wedded to Late Romanesque, indeed Byzantine, techniques and style. Strong shot colours, massive decorative motifs, hard geometric medallion forms and exaggeratedly angular drapery folds all typify the ZACKENSTIL, a regional interpretation of Byzantine art roughly parallel to the new, sharper styles of the French milieu, but particularly closely related to some late 12th-century Sicilian mosaics, and thus a reflection of the close relationship between Germany and Mediterranean culture. This brittle, but often technically accomplished, style is characteristic of works of the period 1230–80: for example the illumination of the Besançon Psalter (Besançon, Bib. Mun., MS. 54) and the Aschaffenburg Golden Gospels (Aschaffenburg, Schloss Johannisburg, Hof- & Stiftsbib., MS. 13; for illustration *see* ZACKENSTIL); panel paintings such as the Thurgau *Crucifix* and the Soest Antependium (Berlin, Bodemus.); and stained glass as at Mönchengladbach (*c.* 1265) and Heiligenkreuz Abbey (1290s).

The combination of essentially Gothic iconographic types and High Romanesque decorative features, characteristic of this idiom, is evident in the large painted *Tree of Jesse* ceiling at St Michael's, Hildesheim. In manuscripts

75. Stained glass, north aisle, Strasbourg Cathedral detail showing architectural canopies, France, *c.* 1250–60

monumental compositions are also characteristic, and with them religious tableaux reflecting the impact of Franciscan spirituality. In wall painting, the persistence of Late Romanesque genres such as the *Throne of Solomon* (*c.* 1260–70; *see* AUSTRIA, fig. 12) at Gurk Cathedral (Carinthia), indicates a further conservatism of outlook, at least by French standards, although there is a progressive softening of style. The extent of resistance to French ideas may be measured by the absence in painting of any counterparts to the correspondences between the sculpture at Reims and that at Bamberg, and the stylistic discrepancy between the Champenois-like sculptures in the choir at Naumburg Cathedral and its *Zackenstil* glazing in the period *c.* 1250–60. German works of the period thus lack the single-minded formal outlook of *opus francigenum.* The response of German painting to French taste is, therefore, characteristically different from that of England in this period, since German painting is generally marked by a strident emotionalism out of keeping with the slim and sweet styles of English art and the elegant reserve of the French.

(iv) Scandinavia and the Iberian Peninsula, c. *1230–*c. *1340.* Scandinavian painting exhibits a much more strongly Gothicizing tendency in the period, and in Norway and Iceland, particularly, the strongest links in the 13th century appear to be with England, northern France and Flanders (Fett; Lindblom). The most significant work in Scandinavia is found in polychrome wood sculpture, decorated wooden church interiors, for example that at Aal (*c.* 1250–1300; Oslo, U. Oldsaksaml.), and Norwegian painted altarpieces, usually altar frontals, about 30 of which survive. Among the earliest panels, one (Oslo, U. Oldsaksaml.) from an altar tabernacle at Faaberg in Norway corresponds closely to the drawing style of Matthew Paris, especially the *Virgin and Child* in the *Historia anglorum* (*c.* 1250–55; London, BL, Royal MS. 14. C. VII, fol.6*r*). This pattern of English influence is followed by the frontals from Ulvik and Kinsarvik (U. Bergen, Hist. Mus.). The Tingelstad series of frontals (e.g. Frontal no.1; Oslo, U. Oldsaksaml.; see fig. 76) are evidence of the new, sharp styles emerging in the period 1260–90. A frontal from Odda (U. Bergen, Hist. Mus.) resembles the earlier work in the English Psalter of Robert de Lisle (London, BL, Arundel MS. 83, pt II) and the painted sedilia at Westminster Abbey, both of *c.* 1310. Some panels, such as that from Nes (U. Bergen, Hist. Mus.), indicate contact with late 13th-century miniature painting in north-eastern France (e.g. Paris, Bib. N., MS. fr. 95). By the second quarter of the 14th century, however, English influences were displaced by those from Germany.

The reception of Anglo-French styles in the Iberian Peninsula is broadly comparable until the 1330s. Until well into the 13th century, late Romanesque features prevailed in panel painting, and it is notable that some areas (e.g. the wall paintings at Sigena, Aragon) were open to Siculo-Norman Byzantinism from the late 12th century. By the

76. *Virgin and Child* with scenes from the *Infancy of Christ*, tempera and oil on panel, altar frontal from Tingelstad, Norway, late 13th century (Oslo, Universitetets Oldsaksamlingen)

third quarter of the 13th century some Spanish illumination was taking on French features, and decisive signs of northern French influence (paralleled in monumental sculpture at León and Burgos) emerge in manuscript painting for Alfonso X, King of Castile and León (e.g. *Las cantigas*; Madrid, Escorial, Bib. Monasterio S Lorenzo, MSS B.I.2 and T.I.1), and in Catalan and Valencian panel painting (e.g. the *St Perpetua* frontal; Barcelona, Mus. Dioc.). These works are not wholly French in idiom, but betray a deep-seated Mozarabic taste, the impact of which was felt throughout the southern Moorish sector of Spain and Toledo, in particular. In Aragon a style related to the northern French Maciejowski Bible is apparent in the murals on the tomb of *Eximino de Foces* (S Miguel de Foces); an English or French style characterizes the *St Peter* frontal (Brussels, Musées Royaux A. & Hist.). Similar trends characterize Navarre panel painting well into the 14th century (e.g. the *St Peter* frontal; Barcelona, Plandiura priv. col.). The provincial flavour of much of this work anticipates the displacement of northern sytles by those of Tuscan, which became apparent in south-eastern Spain by the 1340s.

(v) Italy, c. *1265–*c. *1320.* The first intersection of Italian painting with the new Gothic movement occurs in the late 13th century in the wall paintings of the north (right) transept of the Upper Church at S Francesco in Assisi (*see* ASSISI, §II, 2). The earliest decorations (*c.* 1265–80) in the Upper Church were begun by northern painters from either England, France or, more probably (in view of the style of the basilica's stained glass), Germany, in cooperation with Italian artists associated with Cimabue and Jacopo Torriti. Their contribution, however, was short-lived since the style of Cimabue prevails in the remainder of the liturgical east end of the church (*see* CIMABUE, fig. 1). The occurrence of northern artists working in a building, itself designed on French models, would not be remarkable, were it not for Assisi's role as a showcase of the new narrative style of painting associated with papal and Franciscan patronage, a style unaffected by northern Gothic example. The critical phase in the decorations at Assisi was inaugurated in the late 1280s by Pope Nicholas IV, former Master-General of the Franciscan Order. Between *c.* 1280 and *c.* 1310 the diversity of styles at the liturgical east end of the Upper Church gave way, via the work of the Isaac Master and his companions, to the style of the *St Francis Legend* on the lower walls of the nave (*see* MASTERS, ANONYMOUS, AND MONOGRAMMISTS, §I: MASTER OF THE LEGEND OF ST FRANCIS).

This gradual narrowing of stylistic range at Assisi is instructive. Cennini attributed to Giotto the restoration of what he called 'Roman' as against 'Greek' painting, a theme familiar in later Renaissance art history. Cennini's position may represent a hardening of opinion in the wake of success and undoubtedly underestimated the extent of Byzantine influence on late 13th-century schemes such as that at Assisi (there are signs, for instance, that mosaics were planned for the church); but it does suggest that Italian innovation, especially in fresco, was associated with a revival of *romanitas*, particularly during the pontificate (1277–80) of Nicholas III (Belting). The motivating forces operating in late 13th-century Italian painting were thus diametrically opposed to those in contemporary France, where features of the Antique were disappearing from the figurative arts. This regalvanizing is striking in view of Rome's relatively unimportant artistic role for the greater part of the 13th century, but it reflects the complex culture of central Italy at a time of growing French political hegemony in the region. Paradoxically, French influence may have had its effect not via the Gothic style, but rather in the creation of a set of political circumstances (for example a French-dominated papacy) against which Italian, and especially Roman, patrons reacted by reasserting local traditions.

Numerous elements in the iconography of the biblical narrative at Assisi relate in format and content to contemporary Roman art. Cimabue, Cavallini and Giotto were all associated with Rome at various points in their careers; Cimabue from as early as 1272, Cavallini from *c.* 1273 and Giotto is held to have been there for the 1300 Jubilee. The undertaking of the repainting of Early Christian mural schemes at Old St Peter's, S Lorenzo and S Paulo fuori le Mura (all destr.), at a particularly conservative phase of the papacy's development (1270s and 1280s), was a sign of renewed interest in Rome's Late Antique heritage. Nicholas IV's redecoration of the basilica of S Maria Maggiore is a characteristic example. Its mosaics by Torriti (apse and triumphal arch; for illustration *see* TORRITI, JACOPO), Filippo Rusuti (façade) and a painter working in secco (left transept) and allied with the Isaac Master at Assisi, fall into a fairly tight chronological sequence with Cavallini's mosaics of the 1290s at S Maria in Trastevere and his frescoes (1290s–early 1300s) at S Cecilia in Trastevere and S Maria in Aracoeli, Rome (*see* CAVALLINI, PIETRO, figs 1 and 2). Thus Roman monumental painting possessed a range of styles and activity similar to Assisi in the 1290s.

The distinctly new features of painting in Rome, Umbria and Tuscany include a preference for fresco technique, bulkiness of forms, strong external lighting and modelling, the emphatic use of oblique, volumetric constructions and an expressive pictorial rhetoric. The *giornata* technique of fresco preparation was more extensively used. Important to this style was the imitation of materials (notably fictive Cosmati mosaic) and optical effects in pigment. In some respects the gravitas of this style corresponds to the broader modelled forms emerging in Anglo-French work of the last decades of the century, although the Italian phenomenon seems to have drawn inspiration from specifically local sources. Thus the impressionistic and illusionistic techniques of Late Antique mosaics such as those (5th century AD) at S Maria Maggiore were now revived; and the tendency towards the fully modelled classicizing forms of central Italian sculpture, represented by the Pisano family, was absorbed. Some decorative elements were drawn from contemporary architectural features as used by artists in the circle of Arnolfo di Cambio, but others may have been derived from survivals of ancient Roman domestic decoration close to the Pompeian Second Style. The first wholehearted essay in the synthesis of these elements, the undated *St Francis Legend* cycle (see fig. 77; *see also* MASTERS, ANONYMOUS, AND MONOGRAMMISTS, §I: MASTER OF THE LEGEND OF ST FRANCIS) at Assisi, perhaps begun in the late 1290s, also indicates an interest in creating optimum spectator viewpoints by illusionistic

77. Master of the Legend of St Francis: *Vision of the Chariot* (*c.* 1290–1300), fresco, Upper Church, S Francesco, Assisi, Italy

framing devices, especially Roman-style dentil cornices. These bring the paintings and their physical support into a coherent visual relationship in a way that was alien to the Gothic movement north of the Alps throughout the later Middle Ages.

It was certainly in this period that the formal basis was laid for the work of such artists as the ST CECILIA MASTER (*see* MASTERS, ANONYMOUS, AND MONOGRAMMISTS, §I), who collaborated at Assisi, and for Giotto's Paduan style of the early 1300s; this is also true of numerous works associated with Florence. The debate over Giotto's contribution at Assisi is unresolved, but no proof has been offered of his presence there before his work in the Arena Chapel, Padua, of 1303–1306, which is usually taken as the definitive statement of the new narrative idiom (*see* GIOTTO, figs. 1–5; PADUA, §4(ii)). His autograph style at Padua differs decidedly from those of the later masters of the Upper Church at Assisi; it is more technically assured than the *St Francis Legend* cycle and employs tighter, fuller compositions, more coherent perspectival constructions and subtler textures. However, it is not for these reasons necessarily more advanced. The main period of Giottesque influence at Assisi was in the early decades of the 14th century in the Lower Church and in the hands of an atelier rather than an individual. The new style seems to have been adopted by a range of artists with fluid regional connections, of which Giotto's workshop is traditionally, and probably correctly, regarded as the most important representative. Such considerations render the assessment of the chronological relationship of seminal works such as Assisi and Padua highly problematic.

An alternative idiom to the grave Roman style was developed in Sienese circles between the 1280s and *c.* 1310 on significantly different bases: it was initially associated almost exclusively with tempera panel painting; Byzantine physiognomies and narrative models were followed more closely; lighter, slimmer anatomies were employed; greater emphasis was placed on small descriptive details; and it was associated with a wider range of colour and decorative ornamentation, especially punched ornament. The principal agent in the transformation of late 13th-century Sienese painting was DUCCIO. He was the first of a comparatively large group of Sienese panel painters (including Segna di Bonaventura and Ugolino di Nerio) to develop a specifically new idiom, which was transferred to radically enlarged altarpieces, most notably Duccio's double-fronted *Maestà* (completed 1311) for Siena Cathedral (see fig. 63 above; *see also* CONSERVATION AND RESTORATION, colour pl. X). This process had begun with Cimabue, whose softly modulated but striking style extended both to fresco and large panels (e.g. the Santa Trìnita *Virgin and Child*; Florence, Uffizi) and established the basis for Duccio's Rucellai *Madonna* (late 1280s; Florence, Uffizi). Exactly the same process—the massive expansion of the painted altarpiece—was occurring in Rome and Florence in this period.

Sienese painting, while distinctive, was more inherently eclectic and by about 1300 less keenly local in inspiration than its Roman counterpart, and contacts with transalpine painting were a more formative influence. The Gothicism of Duccio is, of course, mostly piecemeal and to a great extent lies in the world of period fashion rather than in the fundamental tenets of Sienese art. Suggestions that he is named in Parisian tax documents of the 1290s are unconvincing (Stubblebine); but some such link to northern Gothic is rendered virtually certain by the presence on the front of the *Maestà* and on such related works as a triptych (*c.* 1300; London, N.G.; *see* DUCCIO, fig. 4) of postures and garment formations developed in northern French and southern English painting *c.* 1270–90. In this respect, Sienese art of the turn of the 14th century is comparable to the northern work in the north transept at Assisi. The significance of Duccio's art lies not in whether he was selfconsciously reconciling Sienese traditions with advanced northern tendencies, but in the tendency to marry softly modelled surfaces with delicate surface ornamentation. Early documents record Duccio as a painter of book covers, and thus he is associated with painting on a small scale. In contrast with Assisi and Padua, these tendencies correspond much more closely with contemporary northern patterns of change, best represented, though not literally, by such panels as the Westminster Retable; this 'miniaturist' tendency in Sienese and northern painting of the 14th century, however, should not be overstressed.

The reconciliation of styles apparent *c.* 1300 in Siena was developed further by the workshop of SIMONE MARTINI. His large *St Louis of Toulouse* altarpiece (1317; Naples, Capodimonte; see fig. 78)—one of a group of his works celebrating the themes of secular authority—is a vivid hybrid, combining surface ornateness and visual adventurousness, its predella having small narrative scenes in the manner of Duccio's *Maestà*, with foreshortened settings disposed around a single vanishing-point. Simone was the first Italian painter to produce a convincing synthesis of lavish planar ornamentation and supple, rounded painting. This blend is no less characteristic of his wall painting in the Palazzo Pubblico, Siena, notably his *Maestà* of *c.* 1315, which absorbs purely northern tracery forms for the Virgin's throne, while filling out figural forms with a soft bulk and fluidity typical of Duccio. In this way Sienese art between about 1290 and 1320 adumbrated many of the important features of the so-called International Gothic style of the later 14th century and the 15th.

78. Simone Martini: *St Louis of Toulouse*, tempera on panel, 2.5×1.8 m, from ?Naples, Italy, 1317 (Naples, Museo e Gallerie Nazionali di Capodimonte)

From *c.* 1305 two broad developments contributed to a new complexity of change in Italy. First, Roman patronage declined with the move in 1308 of the papacy from Rome to Avignon, and with it the coherence of regional patterns began to loosen. By 1308 Cavallini is documented in the service of Charles II of Anjou, King of Naples and Sicily; wall paintings (*c.* 1320) in Cavallini's style survive at S Maria Donna Regina, Naples. In 1317 Simone, like Giotto after him, was also attracted to the Angevin court at Naples; he worked for the Dominicans in Pisa, and later went to Avignon (*c.* 1335). Second, Roman and Sienese artists increasingly cooperated, influencing one another to create a more supple version of Giotto's Paduan style and collaborating on the decoration of the Lower Church of S Francesco, Assisi, in the first decades of the century. Here, around 1317–22, Simone collaborated with Giottesque artists and perhaps under their influence pressed his own distinct idiom further, notably in his *St Martin* frescoes in the Montefiore Chapel of S Martino (*see* ASSISI, fig. 6 and MARTINI, SIMONE, fig. 1) in which the style he established in the Palazzo Pubblico in Siena is continued.

(vi) England and France, c. *1300–*c. *1350.* North of the Alps the impact of Italian painting was limited and socially restricted. Until the mid-14th century, surviving examples of direct influence are few, despite the appearance of a French papacy and an active Angevin dynasty in southern Italy (*see* §(vii) below). Where it did have an effect, Italian painting was important in providing northern painters with a new repertory of painting effects and in encouraging an eclecticism of approach already apparent in late 13th-century painting in the Anglo-French court milieu. Early occurrences in the north of contact with Italian art are aristocratic: in 1298 Philip IV, King of France, sent a royal painter, Etienne d'Auxerre (*fl c.* 1292–1301), to Rome on some unspecified business. This was perhaps connected with the arrival of the Roman painters and mosaicists of the Rusuti clan at the French court in the following decade. As Painters to the King, the Rusuti were active at Poitiers and probably Paris from 1304/5 to 1317. In the early 1300s painters working in the style of Cavallini were at Béziers Cathedral (also related to court circle patronage) in southern France, before the Avignonese papacy (1308–77). By 1328 Mahaut of Artois was obtaining Roman-style panel painting in Paris. Clearly, then, the movement of artists and works of art was compelling, but how influential it was in practice is not measurable.

(a) England. The English response to Italian art was extremely restricted and is on the whole irrelevant to an understanding of the period *c.* 1300–*c.* 1350. Manuscript, wall, panel and glass painting tended instead towards regionalism, developed out of the late 13th-century mixture of styles typical of southern England and northern France (*see* §(ii) above). This in part reflected the growing concentration of wealth in eastern England. In manuscripts commissioned by East Anglian patrons, especially such showy Psalters as the Peterborough Psalter (*c.* 1300–before 1318; Brussels, Bib. Royale Albert 1er, MSS 9961–2) with its developed language of border ornament, a complex network of exchanges is apparent with English metropolitan painting and with that in north-eastern France. These are best represented by the dissemination throughout eastern England in the period 1310–30 of the idiom employed in the metropolitan workshop responsible for the QUEEN MARY PSALTER (London, BL, Royal MS. 2. B. VII); this was essentially French in derivation but executed with a characteristically English deftness and sweetness of demeanour, as well as with a native taste for narrative and marginalia.

The rise of regional styles deserves note, since Italian features, when they occur, are documented first in those areas with only recently established local traditions. Norwich in the 1320s and 1330s was especially important, since, in works connected to this area, signs of Sienese influence are manifest in the contributions of later artists to works that were begun in indigenous styles, but executed over a protracted period; this is particularly true of the luxury Gorleston Psalter (*c.* 1310–20 and *c.* 1330–40; London, BL, Add. MS. 49622) and Ormesby Psalter (early 14th century and *c.* 1330–40; Oxford, Bodleian Lib., MS. Douce 366). The added *Crucifixion* leaf (fol. 7*r*, see fig. 79) in the Gorleston Psalter is the best example of the impact of the type of Tuscan panel paintings known to have been imported into England in this period. Two of the most important of these are mentioned in metropolitan contexts, in the records of the estate of Edward II's Queen Isabel (*d* 1358) and in the will of a court painter, Hugh of St Albans (*d* 1361). Termed *opera lombardorum,* such imports indicate the facility with which Italian notions could spread, and it is in these and in patrons with long-standing Avignonese contacts such as John Grandisson, Bishop of Exeter (1327–69), that the explanation of the increasingly eclectic pattern of stylistic development in England (probably begun in the 1320s) should be sought.

On the whole, English painting in the first half of the 14th century demonstrates the extremely haphazard way in which Italian forms were assimilated. The phase of literal influence apparent in the Gorleston Psalter was brief, and in the 1330s and 1340s English painting was becoming more eclectic in its sources and exhibiting closer

79. *Crucifixion*, *c.* 1330–40; miniture inserted in the Gorleston Psalter, 374×235 mm, from East Anglia, England, *c.* 1310–20 (London, British Library, Add. MS. 49622, fol. 7*r*)

ties with the southern Netherlands, as for example in the LUTTRELL PSALTER (*c.* 1330–40; London, BL, Add. MS. 42130). English painting of this period has sometimes been unjustly described as decadent; in fact, the deployment of lavish ornament and spry figure styles closely matches patterns of change in regions bordering the North Sea throughout this period.

(b) France. Regional developments in France are still less well understood. It is partly for this reason that the figure of JEAN PUCELLE, supposedly a Parisian master active *c.* 1319–34, whose workshop was patronized by aristocratic patrons, enjoys such prominence, even though the precise extent of his oeuvre is still unknown. His exact role apart, Pucelle's idiom was practised within a workshop context that survived his death, and it is likely that one illuminator in particular—JEAN LE NOIR (alias the Passion Master)—continued to work in this style, serving members of the royal house of France, well into the second half of the century. To Pucelle's circle has been attributed a small number of manuscripts dating to the mid-1320s that conclusively demonstrate contact with contemporary Italian painting: the BELLEVILLE BREVIARY (Paris, Bib. N., MSS lat. 10483–4), the Byllyng Bible (Paris, Bib. N., MS. lat. 11935) and a tiny Book of Hours, known as the Hours of Jeanne d'Evreux (New York, Cloisters, MS. 54. 1. 2).

The Book of Hours indicates access, direct or indirect, to Duccio's *Maestà*, or something extremely similar to it, since specifically Ducciesque iconographic features and handling of pictorial space are used, although Duccio's facial types are adapted to existing French traditions. Familiarity with Giovanni Pisano's sculpted pulpit in S Andrea, Pistoia, has also been mooted. Sienese spatial formulations, however, did not transform the bulk of the pictures in the manuscript; where they occur, as in the *Annunciation* of the Hours (fol. 16*r*; *see* PUCELLE, JEAN, fig. 2), they appear to have been incorporated as part of the iconography, but certainly never unintelligently. In general, the *mises-en-scène* relate to earlier Parisian illumination such as the *Life of St Denis* (before 1317; Paris, Bib. N., MSS fr. 2090–92). Unlike the Belleville Breviary and the Bylling Bible, the Hours of Jeanne d'Evreux (see fig. 80) is distinctive in the use of a grisaille technique. This should be seen primarily in the context of French taste: first the emphasis on purely tonal relations in the modelled work of Master Honoré's circle of the 1290s and first decades of the 14th century (*see* §(ii) above); second, the persistent use of white marble funerary sculpture, typical of the French court. Italy may also have been influential: grisaille was employed by Giotto in the Arena Chapel, Padua, and this type of tonality is also apparent in the work of Taddeo Gaddi.

Whether Italian ideas permeated northern culture primarily through such miniatures is debatable. Pucelle's works, however remarkable, are unlikely in the absence of

80. Jean Pucelle: *Queen Jeanne d'Evreux at the Tomb of St Louis* and the *Education of St Louis*; grisaille illustrations from the Hours of Jeanne d'Evreux, page size 90×60 mm, from northern France, 1325–8 (New York, The Cloisters, MS. 54. 1. 2, fols 102*v*–103*r*)

corresponding, but now lost, monumental counterparts to have introduced Italian ideas into French art, and earlier French royal patronage of Roman artists, continuing into the 1320s, is of equal importance. The evidence of contemporary stained glass indicates that these manuscripts—and with them Pucelle's work—formed part of a more general current of change in the Ile-de-France and Normandy in the 1320s and 1330s. Isolated Italianate motifs—shallow perspectival constructions and Florentine physiognomies not unlike the glazing style of Maso di Banco of the 1330s—occur in the immense glazing programme inaugurated at St Ouen in Rouen around 1317 and completed by 1339, and reflect familiarity with the range of styles characteristic of the Lower Church of Assisi in this period.

Jean Pucelle's workshop was also unquestionably influential. Its influence lay not so much in its receptivity to Italian ideas as in providing iconographic motifs that proved paradigmatic for later French illumination and in developing a new figure style: poised, supple, fleshy and rounded, painted with a wide range of colours, which through its widespread dissemination revitalized the northern Gothic movement. This style is typical of much French illumination of the 1330s and 1340s, for instance the Hours of Joanna of Navarre (Paris, Bib. N., MS. nouv. acq. lat. 3145). It influenced a late campaign (before 1339) on the English Psalter of Robert de Lisle (London, BL, Arundel MS. 83, pt II) and together with models drawn ultimately from Duccio, the stained glass of the west nave windows of York Minster (*c.* 1339). Henceforth its manifestations can also be traced much more widely in northern Europe, to the east in Germany and Bohemia, and to some extent in Italy. Gothic painting was, in effect, being reinvigorated by a third wave of influence that transcended regions; French-based, its scope was now broader, and the role of Italy, although mostly latent, was increasingly perceptible.

(vii) Italy, Spain and papal Avignon, c. *1320–*c. *1400.* The impact of the Black Death (principally 1348–9) on western European art has been emphasized by some authorities (notably Meiss, 1951). Although the extent to which the plague had an effect on painting has been disputed, there is no doubt that many urban painters, among whom may be counted the brothers Pietro and Ambrogio Lorenzetti, perished in the plague: in this sense its effect was simply to interrupt production and training. Between *c.* 1320 and *c.* 1350 Italian painting continued to develop along the lines established in Tuscany around the turn of the century, though regional variations were considerable. The tradition of Giottesque fresco painting was continued in Tuscany by Taddeo Gaddi, by the prolific Bernardo Daddi and by Maso di Banco. During the period there were seminal developments that can be attributed to a small group of primarily Sienese masters, especially Simone Martini and the Lorenzetti brothers. Their work, delving constantly into the themes of Giottesque and Ducciesque painting, established a repertory of painting effects and devices that formed a backdrop for developments not only throughout the Italian peninsula (including Riminese, Bolognese, Neapolitan, Pisan and Venetian painting) but also north of the Alps.

From *c.* 1350 the established Sienese fresco tradition flourished in the hands of Barna (e.g. San Gimignano, Collegiata; *see* ITALY, fig. 28), Lippo Vanni and Bartolo di Fredi Cini and, via a host of minor masters including Niccolò di Sér Sozzo, Paolo di Giovanni Fei and Taddeo di Bartolo, continued into the 15th century in a strikingly consistent fashion, notably in the work of Giovanni di Paolo. Giottesque painting continued to be practised in a somewhat more supple and increasingly prettified fashion, with variations on themes inaugurated in the early 14th century by Agnolo Gaddi, Niccolò di Pietro Gerini, Lorenzo Monaco and Spinello Aretino. The most profound deviations in this period, however, are to be seen in another circle of painters associated with the decoration (1330s) of the Camposanto, Pisa (*see* MASTERS, ANONYMOUS, AND MONOGRAMMISTS, §I: MASTER OF THE TRIUMPH OF DEATH and fig.), and with Orcagna in Florence (active between the 1340s and 1360s). In this sphere there appear markedly different iconographic formulations, and a tendency towards the abandonment of the 'naturalistic' endeavours of earlier 14th-century Tuscany. In painting of the 1350s by Orcagna (e.g. the Strozzi Altarpiece; Florence, S Maria Novella; *see* CIONE, ANDREA DI, fig. 1) and in the work of Nardo and Jacopo di Cione and Giovanni del Biondo there is a pronounced shift to a grandiose, theological austerity, which Meiss cited as evidence of the impact of the plague (*see* CIONE, (1)).

Major initiatives were increasingly taken in northern Italy in the second half of the 14th century. There was a resurgence in Paduan painting at the end of the century under Giusto de' Menabuoi and Altichiero. With the building of a new and vast cathedral and the influence of the Visconti courts, Milan became established as a centre of artistic production; the manuscripts commissioned in this sphere, culminating in the delicately empirical studies of Giovannino de Grassi (*see* GRASSI, (1)) in the last decades of the century, for example in the Bergamo Sketchbook (Bergamo, Bib. Civ. A. Mai, MS. delta. vii. 14) and in the Visconti Hours (Florence, Bib. N. Cent., MSS Banco Rari 397 and Landau Finaly 22), are among the most lavish and attractive of the period. Earlier in the century, Bologna had emerged as a significant university centre of manuscript production with wider European connections and had retained its importance in monumental art, especially through the work of Tomaso da Modena in the 1350s (e.g. S. Nicolò, Treviso; for illustration *see* TOMASO DA MODENA). Tomaso's links with Bohemia, the absorption of French decorative forms in Lombard manuscripts and the reuse of Italian motifs by the Limbourgs, all underline the reciprocal relationship between this region and the north towards 1410.

If the French and English response to Italian painting was characteristically selective, developments in the Iberian Peninsula and in papal Avignon in southern France can be regarded more as direct offshoots of the central Italian milieu. In monumental painting, the position in Spain around 1330 is well represented by the Navarrese paintings signed by Juan Oliver in the refectory at Pamplona Cathedral, dated 1330 (see fig. 81), which resemble closely Anglo-French work of the early 14th century, especially the English Ormesby Psalter (*see* §(vi) above). This type of orientation is typical of work associated with

81. Juan Oliver: scenes from the *Passion and Resurrection*, wall painting, 6.15×3.76 m, from the refectory, Pamplona Cathedral, Spain, 1330 (Pamplona, Museo de Navarra)

Salamanca, Toledo and Catalonia (e.g. Lleida Cathedral; S Domingo in Puigcerda, Girona). From *c.* 1335, however, centres in Catalonia—especially Barcelona and Valencia—were associated with a sub-Tuscan style of fresco and panel painting. The work of Ferrer Bassa in fresco (1346) in the S Miguel Chapel at the convent of Pedralbes, Barcelona, and on panel the *Coronation of the Virgin* (destr.) at Bellpuig, are in a soft Sienese manner comparable to contemporary work at Urbino. This type of work, continued by the Master of S Marco, Lluís Borrassà and eventually Alvaro Portugallo, set the pattern for Valencian and Catalan work for some generations.

A parallel phenomenon occurred in southern France at the Palais des Papes, Avignon, during the pontificate of Clement VI (*reg* 1342–52). Simone Martini's activity at Avignon has already been noted, and the stamp of his Sienese idiom is fully apparent in paintings for the Carthusian monastery at Villeneuve and in the frescoes commissioned by Clement for the chapels and audience chambers in the papal residence at Avignon, mostly executed by the atelier of the papal painter MATTEO GIOVANETTI, in service 1343–68. Matteo's style is a Franco-Italian hybrid, but its basis in Tuscan practice is clear enough, and it should be remembered that in this period Avignon was also acting as a clearing-house of Italian panel painting (Meiss, 1951); Florentine-looking paintings are also found at St Didier, Avignon. In his residential chambers, and especially the Chambre du Cerf, the French pope Clement VI was evidently striving towards a synthesis of native and Italian elements; the room's fresco decoration (*c.* 1343–55) depicts a panoramic woodland filled with hunting scenes, birds and humans, alluding at once to the northern tradition of green chambers and also to something akin to Pompeian garden painting (*see* AVIGNON, §3(ii)(b) and fig. 3). The wall paintings commissioned in the 1360s by Charles V for the Hôtel St Pol in Paris revived Clement's theme of fruit-picking children present in the Chambre du Cerf. This is unlikely to have been the first of such royal contacts, since John II, King of France, had visited Clement's curia in 1342, and Charles IV, Holy Roman Emperor, sought contacts in this sphere too.

Avignon sustained its influence for some time and provided one port of entry for Italian painting into northern Europe. So, indirectly, did Angevin Naples, especially under Robert, King of Naples and Jerusalem, a patron of Cavallini, Simone and Giotto in a centre that cultivated, in the work of Montano d'Arezzo (*d* 1313) and the Minutolo Master, its own interpretation of Tuscan painting (Bologna, 1969). Simone and Giotto were both effectively involved in the execution of works embodying a Guelph–Angevin political programme, beginning with Simone's *St Louis of Toulouse* panel (1317; *see* §(v) and fig. 17 above) and continuing until Giotto's execution of the *Nine Worthies* (destr.) at the palace at Naples in 1328–33. Giotto's elevation to the Arte de Medici e Speziali in Florence at this time may have given him some diplomatic weight on Florence's behalf while working for the Angevins and also later for Azzo Visconti at Milan. Indeed the careers of Simone and Giotto symbolize the importance of new dynastic alignments in the formation and spread of an international Gothic idiom.

(viii) Holy Roman Empire, c. *1300–*c. *1400.* In the period *c.* 1300–60 German painting began to show signs of influence from the Norman–Parisian idiom associated with Pucelle, and to some extent its path of development was related to the course of events in England where this influence became evident in the 1330s. From *c.* 1300 the earliest contacts appear to have been with north-eastern French art, probably through the mediation of Mosan work; manuscript and panel painting in the Cologne region reveals a decisive shift towards the new pliant French style. This is apparent in such manuscripts as the Aarau Gradual (Aarau, Aargau. Kantbib., MS. Bibl. Wett fol. Max.3) and the Graduals illuminated by Johannes von Valkenburg (both 1299; Bonn, UBib., MS. 384, and Cologne, Erzbischöf. Diöz.- & Dombib., MS. 1b) and also further south in manuscripts associated with the Austrian abbey of St Florian (Schmidt, 1962; *see* ST FLORIAN ABBEY, §2). Slightly later larger-scale Cologne painting, notably the wall paintings over the choir-stalls in Cologne Cathedral, is connected more closely to the Pucellian style and to the wall painting at Saint-Dié (Vosges) and also demonstrates the sort of latent Italianism apparent in the glazing of St Ouen at Rouen.

This style occurs also to the south: it is found in the Swiss Manasse Codex (1320s; Heidelberg, Ubib., MS. Pal. germ. 848), a work linked to Norman illumination of the sort in the contemporary Cloisters Apocalypse (New York, Cloisters); in a number of *Biblia pauperum* manuscripts (e.g. *c.* 1310; Markt St Florian, Stiftsbib., MS. III. 207; *see* BIBLE, §I, 3(ii) and fig. 9); and most especially in Austrian stained glass and panel panting. An outstanding example executed around 1331 is the set of panels (see fig. 82) backing the 12th-century enamel pulpit of Nicholas of Verdun now forming an altarpiece at Klosterneuburg Abbey, near Vienna. These depict events from the *Passion* in a fashion distantly reminiscent of Pucelle, but substantially harder in technique; an Italian orientation is apparent in the use of Tuscan oblique architectural settings, found also in contemporary work from Munich. Similar styles characterize stained glass, notably at Königsfelden in Switzerland and in the cloister at Klosterneuburg, *c.* 1330.

From *c.* 1350–60 the tendency in the extensive survivals of panel painting from Cologne (e.g. the Klaren Altar in Cologne Cathedral), Westphalia, Soest and Lübeck was towards a stiffer, more mannered style frequently accompanied by elaborate architectural settings, as found, for example, in the Königsfelden Altar Frontal (Berne, Hist. Mus.). This corresponds closely to contemporary developments in English painting. A decorative popular style is also associated in this period with Nuremberg. By the 1370s and 1380s this style gave way yet again to a more characteristically Hanseatic idiom—a 'town' style—of broad, plain physical types, typical of MASTER BERTRAM of Hamburg, as represented by his Grabow Altarpiece (completed 1383; Hamburg, Ksthalle; *see* GERMANY, fig. 15) and the *Apocalypse* triptych (London, V&A) attributed to a follower. These paintings illustrate the growing links with Bohemian art in the late 14th century.

82. *Coronation of the Virgin*, tempera on panel, Leopoldskapelle, Klosterneuburg Abbey, near Vienna, Austria

The heterogeneity of German painting towards 1360 (Stange, 1934–61) corresponds approximately to the situation in the Czech territories, although there, as evinced by panel painting in particular, the range of reference was somewhat different. Until *c.* 1350 Bohemian painting followed closely the precedent set in southern Germany, both in such manuscripts as the Passional of Abbess Kunhuta (*c.* 1313–21; Prague, Libs Facs & Insts Charles U., MS. XIV. A. 17) and the Velislav Bible (Prague, Libs Facs & Ints Charles U., MS. XXIII. C. 124) and in wall painting, for example at the commandery of St John at Strakonice. Around 1350 there appeared a distinctive new idiom combining Germanic, Sienese and Venetian elements, especially apparent in the Cistercian Vyšší Brod Altarpiece (*c.* 1350; Prague, N.G., Convent of St. George; *see* MASTERS, ANONYMOUS, AND MONOGRAMMISTS, §I: MASTER OF THE VYŠŠÍ BROD ALTAR), the Kosatky *Death of the Virgin* (Boston, MA, Mus. F.A.) and the outstanding Glatz *Madonna* (Berlin, Gemäldegal.), which are painted in a rich range of colours with pretty detail, oblique spatial settings and an Italianate sense of pathos. Shortly after 1360, however, new impetus in manuscript illumination appears to have come from north Germany, Flanders, Tuscany, Avignon and conceivably Paris; coloration and draughtsmanship became noticeably softer and the figure types broader, as in the *Liber viaticus* of Jan of Středa (before 1364; Prague, N. Mus. Lib., MS. XIII. A. 12) and a Gospel Book (Vienna, Österreich. Nbib., Cod. 1182).

These tendencies culminated in the hybrid styles of the wall paintings at Karlštejn Castle and the related work at the Emmaus Monastery (cloister extant) in Prague itself,

83. Master Theodoric: *Saint* (completed *c.* 1367), tempera on panel, Chapel of the Holy Cross, Karlštejn Castle, near Prague, Czech Republic

commissioned in the later 1350s by the Holy Roman Emperor, Charles IV (*see* LUXEMBOURG, (3)). It was under Charles in the 1350s that Prague emerged as the third major centre after Avignon and Naples, and here that there occurred another set of artistic realignments, this time between Italy, Germany and the Netherlands (*see* PRAGUE, §II, 1). Charles's artistic contacts seem to have been unusually wide-ranging, since he had access to French and possibly English-trained architects for the construction of Prague Cathedral, and both Italy and the older imperial territories provided sources for his painting as well as for the Venetian mosaics at the cathedral.

At Karlštejn, Charles called on the services of an Italian, Tomaso da Modena, and also employed northern painters steeped in Tuscan practices. The most important of these, MASTER THEODORIC, decorated the chapel of the Holy Cross (consecrated 1365) with an extended series of wall-mounted framed panels (completed *c.* 1367) depicting key Bohemian and other saints (see fig. 83). A related style is found in the *Laus Mariae* of Konrad von Heimburg (Prague, N. Mus. Lib., Cod. XVI. D. 13). Theodoric's style, based partly on that of Simone Martini, is nevertheless northern in type, possessing the broad proportions, the soft, baggy garments and the bulbous-featured physiognomies that were at this time appearing in painting especially in the Low Countries and northern Germany, and specifically in the somewhat later work of Master Bertram of Hamburg. The more striking elements in Theodoric's technique are also of northern derivation, notably his extensive use of textured gilt pastiglia, which although clearly influenced by Sienese painting was perhaps inspired more directly by Netherlandish and Rhenish work of *c.* 1360 as represented by the *Crucifixion* of Hendrik van Rijn (1363; Antwerp, Kon. Mus. S. Kst.) and by the Cologne Klaren Altar. Although more refined, the Bohemian Soft style of the last two decades of the 14th century found in the Třeboň or Wittingau Altarpiece (after 1380; three panels in Prague, N.G., Convent of St George; *see* PRAGUE, fig. 7) exemplifies precisely the same northern orientation.

(ix) England, c. *1350–*c. *1410.* Parallel to developments in Bohemia under Charles IV and his successor Václav IV, in English painting from the reign of Edward III (*reg* 1327–77) there was a significant increase in influence from the region between Cologne and Paris, and also from Tuscany; with the marriage of Richard II Plantagenet and Anne of Bohemia in 1382, artistic connections between the two dynasties may also have strengthened, although this is disputed (Simpson).

After *c.* 1340–50 French influence, apparent to some extent in English stained glass, waned considerably with the rise of a new hybrid idiom owing more to the south Netherlands and Italy. In the period *c.* 1360 the vigorous native styles associated with East Anglia and the Midlands reached their logical conclusion in the stained glass of the east window of Gloucester Cathedral (see fig. 105 below), where grisaille figures set on coloured grounds identical in taste (but not style) to such French work as the Psalter of Bonne of Luxembourg (*c.* 1345–50; New York, Cloisters, MS. 69.88) were employed; the same process occurs in the mid-century glazing at York Minster, which reveals incidental contacts with Jean le Noir's Parisian work. A new departure in monumental painting was inaugurated by Edward III in the decorations (mostly destr. 1800) of St Stephen's Chapel in Westminster Palace (*see* LONDON, §V, 3(i)(b)). The glazing and painting was undertaken *c.* 1350–63 by craftsmen employed from a wide geographical area, including the southern Netherlands. The fragmentary remains of this scheme (London, BM) indicate an eclecticism not unlike that found at Charles IV's Karlštejn Castle, since Italian sources were clearly called on for the style of the small Old Testament narratives and for the pictures on the east wall showing the royal family and the *Infancy of Christ,* with the entire scheme using embossed pastiglia extensively; the range of reference includes Avignonese, Netherlandish and Bohemian painting, combined with a restrained reception of Italianate decorative themes.

Royal or metropolitan commissions such as the tester of the tomb of *Edward, the Black Prince* (*d* 1376) at Canterbury and the *Last Judgement* wall paintings (1372–1404) in the chapter house at Westminster Abbey are also strongly Italianate, drawing on works from the circle of Simone Martini and the Lorenzetti brothers. The situation in manuscript illumination is, however, more complex. A dry Giottesque (perhaps Florentine or Neapolitan) style occurs *c.* 1350–60 in the Egerton Genesis (London, BL, Egerton MS. 1894) at the same time as the emergence of an eclectic style reminiscent of south Netherlandish and

German (Westphalian) work in the Fitzwarin Psalter (Paris, Bib. N., MS. lat. 765) (Pächt). In the same period (late 1340s to 1380s) another hybrid idiom, related to manuscripts produced for Louis II de Mâle, Count of Flanders and Duke of Brabant (e.g. Brussels, Bib. Royale Albert 1er, MSS 9217 and 9427), appears in the so-called BOHUN manuscripts made for the Earls of Hereford, Essex and Northampton, and best represented by a Psalter in Vienna (begun *c.* 1350–60; Österreich. Nbib., Cod. 1826*). These works contain extremely small figurative compositions and thin border ornament, which is ultimately related to such south Netherlandish work of the 1340s as the illustrated *Romance of Alexander* (Oxford, Bodleian Lib., MS. Bodley 264); in moving away from later 'East Anglian' styles, the Bohun manuscripts effectively coordinate Anglo-Netherlandish motifs inaugurated somewhat before the Black Death.

By the 1380s and 1390s the hybrid style of the Bohun group gave way to influences drawn more firmly from the Holy Roman Empire. The central example of this is the *Liber regalis* of *c.* 1390–1400 (London, Westminster Abbey, Muniment Room & Lib., MS. 38), which reflects contacts with Bohemian illumination and panel painting not of the period before 1380, but rather *c.* 1400: for instance the Golden Bull of Charles IV (Vienna, Österreich. Nbib., Cod. 338) and the Hasenburk Missal dated 1409 (Vienna, Österreich. Nbib., Cod. 1844). The panel portrait of *Richard II* (*c.* 1390–1400; London, Westminster Abbey) is less closely related to Bohemian painting. Less ambiguous are the German, probably Hamburg-related, *Apocalypse* wall paintings (*c.* 1400) in the Westminster Chapter House, executed by a painter in the circle of Master Bertram, which indicate the breakdown of the specifically local traditions that were evident at Westminster in the early 14th century.

By the end of the 14th century there is firm documentary evidence for the importation of German panel painting into England, and it is in this light that the fragmentary wall paintings in the Byward Tower in the Tower of London (*c.* 1390–1400) should be seen. Contact with north Netherlandish painting is implied in the Carmelite Missal (London, BL, Add. MSS 29704–5). The outstanding artistic monument of Richard's reign is the enigmatic Wilton Diptych (London, N.G.), which though wholly void of Bohemian influence has similarities with features in French, Italian and perhaps Netherlandish painting of the period 1390–1410. Similar traits mark the Sherborne Missal (*c.* 1396–1407; London, BL, Loan MS. 83, on loan from Alnwick Castle, Northumb.) and the Beaufort–Beauchamp Hours (London, BL, Royal MS. 2. A. XVIII).

(x) France, c. *1350*–c. *1410.* Interest in French painting in this period has focused on the aristocratic patronage of the family of Charles V (*see* VALOIS, (2)), and has thus been primarily concerned with Paris, Burgundy and Berry, largely to the exclusion of regional painting. Charles, along with his brothers Louis I, King of Naples, Philip the Bold, Duke of Burgundy and Jean, Duc de Berry, was the centre of a network of patronage notable for the relatively new phenomenon of the documentation of art collecting, particularly through detailed inventories. Large private libraries now appeared. Philip's collection numbered about 200 manuscripts, Jean de Berry's 300 by *c.* 1413, and Charles V's 900. This development is remarkable in its own right; but these patrons also signed their books and often had themselves depicted within them, so exemplifying the personalization of the book that had become increasingly apparent from the 13th century. This development may also explain some aspects of the nature of French royal art in this period. A library that contained illuminated manuscripts executed over many generations was a formidable pictorial resource that could influence, if not determine, new work: Charles, for example, lent out an Apocalypse manuscript (Paris, Bib. N., MS. fr. 403) on which Louis's Angers tapestries were based. Continuity with earlier French royal patronage of the time of Charles's father, John II, and earlier was assured by the preservation and study of works by Pucelle. These patrons also shared their artists: Philip retained two of the Limbourg brothers in his service before Jean, Duc de Berry, employed them, while such Netherlanders as André Beauneveu and Jean Malouel worked in France for several of these patrons.

The interrelationship of French painting in this period with south Netherlandish, Italian and indigenous elements is similar to the situation in later 14th-century England, although the two took distinctly different paths. Ties with

84. *Love Introducing his Children to the Poet*; miniature from from the Paris region, France, Guillaume de Machaut: *Le Remède de fortune*, 300×210 mm, *c.* 1350 (Paris, Bibliothèque Nationale, MS. fr. 1586, fol. 51*r*)

the southern Netherlands had begun in the Paris region towards 1350, notably in the case of the Missal of St Denis (London, V&A, MS. 1346–1891), a superb illustrated copy of Guillaume de Machaut's *Le Remède de fortune* (Paris, Bib. N., MS. fr. 1586; see fig. 84), and the *Bible moralisée* (Paris, Bib. N., MS. fr. 167) of John II, King of France. This type of work, although in a sturdier guise, occurs in the oeuvre of the so-called MASTER OF THE BOQUETAUX (*see* MASTERS, ANONYMOUS, AND MONOGRAMMISTS, §I) of the 1350s and 1360s, for example the Bible of Jean de Sy (Paris, Bib. N., MS. fr. 15397) begun in 1355. This illuminator's career spanned the reign of Charles V, for whom he frequently worked. Among his latest and certainly most accomplished miniatures are the pair added *c.* 1377 to the works of Guillaume de Machaut (MS. fr. 1586). These show Nature and Love introducing their children to the poet against detailed landscape backgrounds (fols D–E).

A succession of major artists from territories to the north-east of Paris, whose influence from the 1370s was formative, reiterated the geographical pattern found in the late 13th century in this region. One south Netherlandish painter, JAN BOUDOLF, was active in Paris between the late 1360s and 1380s, most notably in the service of Charles V. Boudolf continued work on the Pucellian Savoy Hours (New Haven, CT, Yale U., Beinecke Lib., MS. 390), but his most refined work is the dedication miniature in the *Bible historiale* (The Hague, Rijksmus. Meermanno-Westreenianum, MS. 10. B. 23, fol. 2*r*) made for Charles and signed in 1371. He is also known to have made designs (before *c.* 1377; untraced) for the *Apocalypse* tapestries (Angers, Château, Col. Tap., *see* ANGERS, fig. 4) made for Louis I, Duke of Anjou. Despite his Parisian context, Boudolf's style is monumental, sturdy and soft, akin to the styles evolving in German, Bohemian and Netherlandish painting in this period.

This is also true to a lesser extent of ANDRÉ BEAUNEVEU, a sculptor and painter who emerged from Valenciennes in the same years in the service of Charles V, Louis II de Mâle of Flanders and eventually Jean, Duc de Berry. Beauneveu executed for the Duc a series of grisaille prophets and apostles in a Psalter (1380s; Paris, Bib. N., MS. fr. 13091). A similar monumentality of style, combined with new attention to Italianate elements drawn from the Lorenzetti and followers such as Barna, is also apparent in the work of the so-called MASTER OF THE PAREMENT DE NARBONNE (*see* MASTERS, ANONYMOUS, AND MONOGRAMMISTS, §I) named after the *Parement de Narbonne*, made for Charles V (*c.* 1375–80; Paris, Louvre; see fig. 70 above); this master was also responsible for miniatures in the first campaign of decoration (*c.* 1380) in the Très Belles Heures de Notre-Dame of Jean, Duc de Berry (Paris, Bib. N., MS. nouv. acq. lat. 3093).

JACQUEMART DE HESDIN was also probably a northerner. His career, documented largely at Bourges in the service of the Duc de Berry between 1384 and 1413 may have included work as a painter and designer of glass, but he was certainly an illuminator. The Duc's inventories associate miniatures in two Books of Hours with him: the Très Belles Heures or Brussels Hours (*c.* 1390–95; Brussels, Bib. Royale Albert 1er, MSS 11060–61) and the Grandes Heures (before 1409; Paris, Bib. N., MS. lat. 919), the sole surviving scene by Jacquemart, now detached, the *Road to Calvary* (Paris, Louvre). He is also thought to have worked on another, the Petites Heures (*c.* 1375–90; Paris, Bib. N., MS. lat. 18014). This group of works represents a critical phase in the history of northern Gothic painting, perhaps the most important since Pucelle's generation, to which Jacquemart's collaborators (who may have included Jean le Noir) notably deferred in numerous compositions.

The influence of Pucelle's work is evinced by a dramatic resurgence of Italianate themes, present first in the Petites Heures, which exhibits familiarity with the elaborate ecclesiastical interior settings, sombre backgrounds and lamentation rituals in products from the circles of Simone Martini and Ambrogio Lorenzetti. Even more significant in this respect are the Hours in Brussels, in which the dedication images of Jean de Berry recommended to the Virgin by his patron saints show striking resemblance to the English Wilton Diptych. The full-page miniatures indicate a study of the works of Simone and the Lorenzetti, which transformed both the iconography and presentation of the material; here for the first time in northern painting religious subject-matter is presented with the scenic landscape setting of 14th-century Italian art. This style was further developed in the 1390s by Melchior Broederlam of Ypres, a major court artist in the employ of the Dukes of Burgundy, and exemplified in his altarpiece for the

85. Boucicaut Master: *Annunciation*; miniature from the Boucicaut Hours, 275×190 mm, from Paris, France, after 1401 (Paris, Musée Jacquemart-André, MS. 2, fol. 53*v*)

charterhouse at Dijon (1393–9; Dijon, Mus. B.-A.; for illustration *see* BROEDERLAM, MELCHIOR).

The final stage in this process is marked by the early 15th-century BOUCICAUT MASTER (*see* MASTERS, ANONYMOUS, AND MONOGRAMMISTS, §I), named after the Hours commissioned by Jean II le Meingre de Boucicaut (after 1401; Paris, Mus. Jacquemart-André, MS. 2; see fig. 85; *see also* MANUSCRIPT, colour pl. IV), and by the work of the Limbourg brothers, Pol, Herman and Jean. The Boucicaut Master produced a scenically and emblematically richer version of the style of Jacquemart, to some extent anticipating the work of the first Netherlandish panel painters. The work of the Limbourg brothers, for example in the TRÈS RICHES HEURES of Jean, Duc de Berry (*c.* 1411/13–16; Chantilly, Mus. Condé, MS. 65), was more specialized (*see* LIMBOURG, DE). Originating from Guelders but associated with Paris and the patronage of the Duke of Burgundy, the Limbourgs continued recent practices in employing a circumstantially detailed, hyper-refined manner and an enlarged stock of Italian motifs recorded in model-books. These include references to Florentine fresco painting (Taddeo Gaddi) and Italian medals in the Duc's collection. It is for this reason that their work has come to epitomize the highpoint of the so-called International Gothic style (*see* §(xi) below.

(xi) International Gothic style, c. *1380–*c. *1440.* The expressions 'Courant international' and 'Gothicité international' were first employed by Courajod with reference to analogies between French and Italian sculpture of the period around 1400. He intended to demonstrate Franco-Netherlandish impulses for the Renaissance and to establish the existence of a universal late medieval Gothic style. Von Schlosser (1895) also described the formation of a European-wide 'höfische Kunst' marked by widespread occurrences of the same subject-matter, notably in the more mobile medium of tapestry. What became known as the International Gothic style (or International Style) was seen as the product of courtly patronage and eclectic, supra-regional, stylistic and iconographic preferences. Many of its formal qualities were held to persist well into the 15th century in Spain, Germany, the Netherlands, Poland, Bohemia and Italy. The term has been applied to such artists as Giovannino dei Grassi and the Limbourg brothers and has been used freely within the period *c.* 1380–*c.* 1440 in reference to, among others, Pisanello, Gentile da Fabriano and Master Francke.

The term has functioned both to describe an entire culture, including poetry, and an artistic style. Its cultural and aesthetic background was formulated by such historians as Huizinga, Focillon and Panofsky (1953) who, following Burckhardt, accepted the notion that later medieval culture in northern Europe, especially France and Burgundy, was one of selfconscious aestheticism, with a collective tendency to retrospection and, ultimately, morbidity. This was contrasted with the cultural optimism and individualism of the Renaissance in Italy. As a result, the definition of the formal qualities of the International Style followed from a broader historical presupposition about the relationship between medieval and Renaissance art. Panofsky gave more explicit substance to the stylistic definition: painting of the period was lyrical in mood, exhibited close attention to detail, employed model-books extensively and was, above all, mannered, refined and extravagant. He regarded this extravagance as a sign of new social anxieties and, following the sociologist Sombart, ascribed its formal character to 'conspicuous waste'. Contemporary iconography was seen as reformulating the image of social classes to express notions of difference, especially between peasants and aristocrats (as for example in the calendar pages of the Très Riches Heures; for illustration *see* VALOIS, (3)); the depiction of Joseph as an archetypal peasant in contemporary Nativity scenes was regarded as a classic instance of this reformulation. The style was thus initially viewed as aristocratic and as a means of re-establishing older social hierarchies threatened by a rising bourgeoisie; but as a result of social competition, the style was imitated and spread by the new classes. Its dissemination was attributed by Panofsky to the breakdown of regionalizing ecclesiastical patronage and to the lack, at that point, of a strong local guild system.

These processes, however, had long existed, and their consequences are in any case unclear. Ecclesiastical patronage, in monastic circles especially, was probably one of the most powerfully internationalizing forces in art and architecture in the late Middle Ages. The rise of art collections and libraries in late 14th-century France and Burgundy, and the phenomenon of inter-dynastic alliance, also represented the intensification of much older practices. Many of the salient features of the style as traditionally described are anticipated in the work of Simone Martini, which provided a fertile source of reference well into the 15th century. Similarly, the guild structure that prevailed in the 15th century in many European cities was responsible for perpetuating and further developing most of the features attributed to the International Gothic style. The dramatic and truly international exchanges between the northern Gothic movement and 14th-century Italy, which laid the foundations for most 15th-century Gothic styles, were largely complete by 1400.

The term has unfairly come to denote a certain conservatism by the standards of the 'progressive' contemporary Renaissance art; it is customarily identified with Huizinga's 'waning' of the Middle Ages. This position is founded in part on a false opposition of the art of the 'progressive' Masaccio and the 'conservative' Gentile da Fabriano, and also on the inbred retrospective quality of late 14th-century French royal illuminated manuscripts. Its central premise, however, that painting throughout Europe was no longer distinguishable by nationality, has been disputed; the premise arose from a desire to lend coherence and stability to descriptions of late medieval art, based on the collective models of cultural history, without adequate national studies of the type advocated by Delaissé and others. Thus refinement of the term—for example the introduction of the regional German and Bohemian Soft style (Ger. *weicher Stil*) and Beautiful style (Ger. *schöner Stil*)—has been necessary.

The expression 'International' is also of dubious value, since at this time comparatively few nation states (in the early modern sense of the term) existed. There are no grounds, therefore, for supposing that earlier medieval styles were selfconsciously national in their formation.

Thus the term, which presupposes an implicitly nationalistic outlook, reflects its 19th-century formulation. Western Europe was divided either into a complex agglomeration of small principalities, often with geographically irrational dynastic interconnections, proto-modern nation states (England) or symbolically important, but ethnically diverse entities (the Holy Roman Empire). The most representative of these is certainly the empire established under the Dukes of Burgundy between 1384 and 1467, in which leading centres of art production (Ghent, Bruges, Ypres, Dijon, Brabant, Holland and Guelders) were encompassed. Such masters as Claus Sluter, Melchior Broederlam, Jean Malouel, Henri Bellechose and Jan van Eyck, as well as the host of minor pre-Eyckian masters employed in the ancient heartland of Gothic art, the Meuse region, were active here. This sphere remained in contact with the older centres of the Gothic movement of the previous two centuries, notably Paris. The products from this period, far from representing a single 'Late Gothic' style, were of considerable heterogeneity and varied greatly in their local manifestations, as for example in the work of Master Francke, Stefan Lochner and later Cologne masters, and in 15th-century Spain. As yet there is no satisfactory general formulation to cover 15th-century painting, and it seems unjustified to describe events in the southern Netherlands (with particular reference to pre-Eyckian art), England, Spain, Bohemia, Poland and Scandinavia as merely interpretations of a unified late medieval manner.

BIBLIOGRAPHY

ENGLAND

W. R. Lethaby: 'English Primitives', *Burl. Mag.*, xxix (1916), pp. 189–98, 281–8, 351–6; xxxiii (1918), pp. 3–7, 169–71

T. Borenius and E. W. Tristram: *English Medieval Painting* (Florence, 1927)

O. Pächt: 'A Giottesque Episode in English Mediaeval Art', *J. Warb. & Court. Inst.*, vi (1943), pp. 51–70

E. W. Tristram: *English Medieval Wall Painting: The Thirteenth Century*, 2 vols (Oxford, 1950)

M. Rickert: *Painting in Britain: The Middle Ages*, Pelican Hist. A. (Harmondsworth, 1954)

E. W. Tristram: *English Wall Painting of the Fourteenth Century* (London, 1955)

G. Henderson: 'Studies in English Manuscript Illumination', *J. Warb. & Court. Inst.*, xxx (1967), pp. 71–137; xxxi (1968), pp. 103–47

M. H. Caviness: *The Early Stained Glass of Canterbury Cathedral* (Princeton, 1977)

S. M. Newton: *Fashion in the Age of the Black Prince: A Study of the Years 1340–1365* (Woodbridge, 1980)

R. Marks and N. J. Morgan: *The Golden Age of English Manuscript Painting, 1200–1500* (London, 1981)

N. J. Morgan: *Early Gothic Manuscripts, 1190–1285*, 2 vols (1982–8), iv of *A Survey of Manuscripts Illuminated in the British Isles*, ed. J. J. G. Alexander (London, 1975–)

P. Binski: *The Painted Chamber at Westminster* (London, 1986)

L. Freeman Sandler: *Gothic Manuscripts, 1285–1385*, 2 vols (1986), v of *A Survey of Manuscripts Illuminated in the British Isles*, ed. J. J. G. Alexander (London, 1975–)

Age of Chivalry: Art in Plantagenet England, 1200–1400 (exh. cat., ed. J. J. G. Alexander and P. Binski; London, RA, 1987–8)

J. Stratford: *The Bedford Inventories: The Worldly Goods of John, Duke of Bedford, Regent of France (1389–1435)* (London, 1993)

FRANCE

G. Vitzthum: *Die Pariser Miniaturmalerei von der Zeit des hl. Ludwig bis zu Philipp von Valois und ihr Verhältnis zur Malerei in Nordwesteuropa* (Leipzig, 1907)

A. de Laborde: *La Bible moralisée illustrée conservée à Oxford, Paris et Londres*, 5 vols (Paris, 1911–27)

R. André-Michel: *Avignon, les fresques du Palais des Papes* (Paris, 1920, rev. 2/1926)

H. M. R. Martin: *La Miniature française du XIIIe au XVe siècle* (Paris, 1923)

V. Leroquais: *Les Livres d'heures manuscrits de la Bibliothèque nationale*, 3 vols (Paris, 1927); suppl. (1943)

H. R. Hahnloser: *Villard de Honnecourt* (Vienna, 1935, rev. Graz, 1972)

J. Adhémar: *Influences antiques dans l'art du moyen âge français* (London, 1939)

C. Sterling: *Les Peintres du moyen-âge* (Paris, 1941)

E. Panofsky, ed.: *Abbot Suger on the Abbey Church of St-Denis and its Art Treasures* (Princeton, 1946)

L. Lefrançois-Pillon and J. Lafond: *L'Art du XIVe siècle en France* (Paris, 1954), pp. 185–238

M. Aubert: *Le Vitrail français* (Paris, 1958)

M. Aubert and others: *Les Vitraux de Notre-Dame et de la Sainte-Chapelle de Paris*, Corp. Vitrearum Med. Aevi: France, i (Paris, 1959)

E. Millar: *The Parisian Miniaturist Honoré* (London, 1959)

J. Porcher: *L'Enluminure française* (Paris, 1959)

M. Laclotte: *L'Ecole d'Avignon* (Paris, 1960)

P. Deschamps and M. Thibout: *La Peinture murale en France au début de l'époque gothique* (Paris, 1963)

F. Deuchler: *Der Ingerborgpsalter* (Berlin, 1967)

M. Meiss: *French Painting in the Time of Jean de Berry*, 3 vols (London and New York, 1967–74)

R. Branner: 'The Painted Medallions in the Sainte-Chapelle in Paris', *Trans. Amer. Philos. Soc.*, n.s., lviii/2 (1968), pp. 1–42

C. R. Sherman: *The Portraits of Charles V of France (1338–1380)* (New York, 1969)

R. Branner: *Manuscript Painting in Paris during the Reign of Saint Louis* (Berkeley, 1977)

F. Avril: *Manuscript Painting at the Court of France: The Fourteenth Century (1310–1380)* (London, 1978)

E. Beer: 'Pariser Buchmalerei in der Zeit Ludwigs des Heiligen und im letzten Viertel des 13. Jahrhunderts', *Z. Kstgesch.*, xliv/1 (1981), pp. 62–91

Les Fastes du Gothique: Le Siècle de Charles V (exh. cat. by J. Favier and others, Paris, Grand Pal., 1981–2)

P. M. de Winter: *La Bibliothèque de Philippe le Hardi, duc de Bourgogne (1364–1404): Etudes sur les manuscrits à peintures d'une collection princière à l'époque du 'Style Gothique International'* (Paris, 1985)

HOLY ROMAN EMPIRE

C. Aldenhoven: *Geschichte der Kölner Malerschule* (Lübeck, 1902)

A. Goldschmidt: *German Illumination* (Florence and New York, 1921)

H. Brockmann: *Die Spätzeit der Kölner Malerschule* (Bonn and Leipzig, 1924)

G. Gläser: *Die altdeutsche Malerei* (Munich, 1924)

P. Clemen: *Die gotischen Monumentalmalereien der Rheinlande*, 2 vols (Düsseldorf, 1930)

A. Stange: *Deutsche Malerei der Gotik*, 11 vols (Berlin, 1934–61)

O. H. Forster: *Stefan Lochner: Ein Maler zu Köln* (Frankfurt am Main, 1938)

A. Matějček and J. Pesina: *La Peinture gothique tchèque, 1350–1450* (Prague, 1955)

A. Friedl: *Master Theodoric* (Prague, 1956)

G. Schmidt: *Die Armenbibeln des XIV. Jahrhunderts* (Graz and Cologne, 1959)

——: *Die Malerschule von St Florian* (Graz and Cologne, 1962)

V. Dvořáková and others: *Gothic Mural Painting in Bohemia and Moravia, 1300–1378* (London, 1964)

R. Becksmann: *Die architektonische Rahmung des hochgotischen Bildfensters: Untersuchungen zur oberrheinischen Glasmalerei von 1250 bis zum 1350* (Berlin, 1967)

A. Stange, ed.: *Kritisches Verzeichnis der deutschen Tafelbilder vor Dürer*, i of *Beiträge zur Kunstwissenschaft* (Munich, 1967–78)

Meister Francke und die Kunst um 1400 (exh. cat., Hamburg, Ksthalle, 1969)

Vor Stefan Lochner: Die Kölner Maler von 1300–1430 (exh. cat., Cologne, Wallraf-Richartz-Mus., 1974)

E. Bachman, ed.: *Gothic Art in Bohemia* (Oxford, 1977)

H. Belting: 'Zwischen Gotik und Byzanz: Gedanken zur Geschichte der sächsischen Buchmalerei im 13. Jahrhundert', *Z. Kstgesch.*, xli (1978), pp. 217–57

Kaiser Karl IV: Staatsman und Mäzen (exh. cat. by F. Seibt, Munich, 1978)

A. Simpson: *The Connections between English and Bohemian Painting during the Second Half of the Fourteenth Century* (New York, 1984)

ITALY

R. van Marle: *The Development of the Italian Schools of Painting*, 18 vols (The Hague, 1923–36)
P. d'Ancona: *La Miniature italienne du Xe au XVIe siècle* (Paris, 1925)
R. Offner and K. Steinweg: *Corpus* (1930–79); rev. M. Boskovits (1986–)
F. Antal: *Florentine Painting and its Social Background* (London, 1948, dated 1947/*R* Cambridge, MA, and London, 1986)
E. B. Garrison: *Italian Romanesque Panel Painting* (Florence, 1949)
M. Meiss: *Painting in Florence and Siena after the Black Death* (Princeton, 1951)
P. Toesca: *Il Trecento* (Turin, 1951/*R* 1971)
R. Oertel: *Die Frühzeit der italienischen Malerei* (Stuttgart, 1953)
M. Salmi: *La miniatura italiana* (Milan, 1955)
J. White: *The Birth and Rebirth of Pictorial Space* (London, 1957, rev. 3/1987)
E. Borsook: *The Mural Painters of Tuscany* (Oxford, 1960, rev. 1980)
M. Meiss: *Giotto and Assisi* (New York, 1960)
F. Bologna: *La pittura italiana delle origini* (Rome and Dresden, 1962)
H. Hager: *Die Anfänge des italienischen Altarbildes* (Munich, 1962)
J. White: *Art and Architecture in Italy, 1250–1400*, Pelican Hist. A. (Harmondsworth, 1966, rev. 2/1987) [bibliog.]
B. Degenhart and A. Schmitt: *Corpus der italienischen Zeichnungen, 1300–1450* (Berlin, 1968–)
F. Bologna: *I pittori alla corte angioina di Napoli, 1266–1400*, 2 vols (Rome, 1969)
J. Gardner: 'The Stefaneschi Altarpiece: A Reconsideration', *J. Warb. & Court. Inst.*, xxxvii (1974), pp. 57–103
R. Fremantle: *Florentine Gothic Painters from Giotto to Masaccio: A Guide to Painting in and near Florence* (London, 1975)
H. Belting: *Die Oberkirche von San Francesco in Assisi* (Berlin, 1977)
A. Smart: *The Dawn of Italian Painting, 1250–1400* (Oxford, 1978)
J. H. Stubblebine: *Duccio di Buoninsegna and his School*, 2 vols (Princeton, 1979)
J. White: *Duccio, Tuscan Art and the Medieval Workshop* (London, 1979)
A. Conti: *La miniatura bolognese: Scuole e botteghe, 1270–1340* (Bologna, 1981)
H. Van Os: 'The Black Death and Sienese Painting: A Problem of Interpretation', *A. Hist.*, 4 (1981), pp. 237–49
R. Gibbs: 'Recent Developments in the Study of Bolognese and Trecento Illustration', *Burl. Mag.*, cxxvi (1984), pp. 638–41
——: *Tomaso da Modena* (Cambridge, 1989)

THE NETHERLANDS

P. Durrieu: *La Miniature flamande* (Brussels, 1921)
E. Panofsky: *Early Netherlandish Painting: Its Origins and Character* (Cambridge, MA, 1953)
L. M. J. Delaissé: *La Miniature flamande: Le mécénat de Philippe le Bon* (Brussels, 1959)
——: *A Century of Dutch Manuscript Illumination* (Berkeley, 1968)
S. Hindman: *Text and Image in Fifteenth-century Illustrated Dutch Bibles* (Leiden, 1977)
The Golden Age of Dutch Manuscript Painting (exh. cat. by H. L. M. Defoer, C. M. Wüstefeld and C. M. Wilhelmina, with intro. by J. H. Marrow, New York, Pierpont Morgan Lib., 1990)

SCANDINAVIA

H. Fett: *Miniatyrer fra islandske haandskrifter* [Miniatures from Icelandic manuscripts] (Bergen, 1910)
A. Lindblom: *La Peinture gothique en Suède et en Norvège* (Stockholm, 1916)
H. Fett: *Norges Malerkunst i middelalderen* [Norwegian painting in the middle ages] (Kristiania, 1917)

SPAIN

C. R. Post: *A History of Spanish Painting*, 8 vols (Cambridge, MA, 1930–41)
J. Gudiol Ricart: *Pintura gótica*, A. Hisp., ix (Madrid, 1955)
J. Guerrero Lovilo: *Miniatura gótica castellana, siglos XIII y XIV* (Madrid, 1956)
J. B. Sobré: *Behind the Altar Table: The Development of the Painted Retable in Spain, 1350–1500* (Columbia, MO, 1988)

For further bibliography *see also* §§1–4 above.

PAUL BINSKI

V. Metalwork.

Gothic metalwork is characterized by fantastic architectural forms; naturalistically modelled figures and animals, which are frequently framed within a pointed arch; a wider range of reliquaries than in the Romanesque period, including bust, arm and multiple reliquaries (*see* RELIQUARY, §I, 3); and new types of statue, such as the Virgin enthroned (or *sedes sapientiae*) and figures of saints. Other innovations included small devotional altarpieces and monstrances, the latter used in the Corpus Christi processions that originated *c.* 1260. Two styles of lettering on metalwork occur: Lombardic, used until *c.* 1400, and black letter (*textura*), used from *c.* 1350 until *c.* 1500 (later in northern Europe).

1. Introduction. 2. France. 3. Low Countries. 4. Holy Roman Empire. 5. Eastern Europe. 6. Italy. 7. British Isles. 8. Spain. 9. Portugal. 10. Scandinavia.

1. Introduction.

The evidence of the relatively few surviving objects in metalwork from the period suggest that metalworkers were slow to adopt the Gothic idiom. Development during the 13th and 14th centuries was led by France. In most of Europe distinctively national stylistic characteristics appeared from *c.* 1300, flourished throughout the 15th century, and from *c.* 1530 gave way to Renaissance features. The exception is Italy, where Gothic motifs were superseded *c.* 1450.

Surviving objects give an unbalanced view: while the majority of surviving gold and silver items and many pewter ones are liturgical (*see* CHALICE; CIBORIUM (i); CROSIER; CROSS, §III, 1(ii); and PATEN), the production of secular plate and jewellery in these metals was probably far greater from *c.* 1350. Items produced in brass and bronze included funerary monuments, lecterns, fonts (also made of lead), fountains, bells, door-knockers, censers and ewers. Iron was used for door fittings and ornamentation, chests and their fittings, grilles and screens, candelabra and other light-holders. Aside from the destructive vagaries of fashion and of war, all metals were valuable and readily recyclable, and the modern picture of stylistic development is probably too episodic to be flawless.

Techniques changed little, although fashions in decoration varied. The principal techniques were casting (including the lost-wax method), forging, embossing, repoussé, engraving, enamelling (*see* §VI below), niello, gilding and setting with gems or pastes (*see* GOLD, §2; METAL, §§I and V). By at least the 13th century, metalworkers were grouped into guilds regulated by rules determining the quality of the workmanship and the metal (for example, the lead content in pewter) and working hours. Marks indicating quality control were introduced in the 14th and 15th centuries, particularly in France, England and Spain, but took a long time to become established practice. Since tools and moulds were often handed down from father to son, style is an unreliable indicator of date.

BIBLIOGRAPHY

J. Braun: *Das christliche Altargerät* (Munich, 1932)
——: *Die Reliquiäre des christlichen Kultes* (Freiburg im Breisgau, 1940/*R* 1971)
Europäische Kunst um 1400 (exh. cat., ed. V. Oberhammer; Vienna, Ksthist. Mus., 1962)
L'Europe gothique (exh. cat., ed. P. Pradel; Paris, Louvre, 1968)
Rhein und Maas: Kunst und Kultur, 800–1400 (exh. cat., Cologne, Kunsthalle; Brussels, Musées Royaux A. & Hist., 1972)
P. Boucaud and C. Frégnac: *Les Etains des origines au début du XIXe siècle* (Fribourg, 1978)
H. Lockner: *Messing* (Munich, 1982)

E. Taburet-Delahaye: *L'Orfèvrerie gothique au Musée de Cluny* (Paris, 1987)
P. Benoit and D. Cailleaux, eds: *Hommes et travail du métal dans les villes médiévales* (Paris, 1988)
P. Hornsby: *Copper and Brass* (London, 1991)
R. W. Lightbown: *Medieval European Jewellery, with a Catalogue of the Collection in the Victoria and Albert Museum* (London, 1992)

MARIAN CAMPBELL

2. FRANCE. Much metalwork in France did not survive the Revolution, but what did shows that the north played an important part in the development of the 'style of 1200', which is particularly exemplified in the reliquaries of the True Cross decorated with filigree and niello that came from the Cistercian abbeys of Clairmarais (Saint-Omer, Mus. Hôtel Sandelin), Paraclet (Amiens, Trésor de la Cathédrale Notre-Dame) and Bonnefontaine (Blanchefosse Church). The style also spread through central and southern France, as is evident from several reliquaries (Varzy, Mus. Mun.) and a considerable number of copper-gilt reliefs and champlevé enamel plaques executed between 1200 and 1240 in Limoges.

New stylistic currents in Parisian metalwork appeared towards the mid-13th century, particularly in two Evangeliary covers (*c.* 1240–50 and *c.* 1260–70; both Paris, Bib. N.) and the Reliquary of SS Lucian, Julian and Maximian (1261; Paris, Mus. Cluny), which was executed for the Sainte-Chapelle. These tendencies spread outwards from the Ile-de-France, as is seen in the shrines of St Taurin of Evreux (1240–55; Evreux, St Taurin), and St Romain of Rouen (*c.* 1260–80; Rouen Cathedral) and also in the shrines of Souillac (*c.* 1250–1300; ex-Grandselve Abbey; Tarn et Garonne; untraced) in the south-west. During the reign of Philip IV (*reg* 1285–1314), metalwork became richer and more refined, as demonstrated by the Reliquary of St Louis (Bologna, Mus. S Domenico), donated by the King to the Dominicans of Bologna. This new trend was characterized by the vogue for *plique-à-jour* enamels (*see* §VI, 6 below) such as were used to decorate the reliquary bust of *St Louis* (destr.) made by GUILLAUME JULIEN for the treasury of the Sainte-Chapelle.

During the 14th century royal patronage became increasingly important. The inventories of Clementia of Hungary (*d* 1328) and Joanna of Burgundy (*d* 1348), dated 1328 and 1349, give some indication of the wealth of the collections amassed by the queens of France at this time. A silver-gilt *Virgin and Child* (Paris, Louvre; see fig. 86) was donated by Joanna of Evreux (1310–71) to the treasury of Saint-Denis Abbey in 1339. Its base is decorated with *basse-taille* (translucent) enamel. The use of the Parisian fleur-de-lis hallmark had been made obligatory in 1275 by Philip III (*reg* 1270–85) but spread only gradually through Paris and the provinces during the 14th century. The master craftsman's hallmark was made obligatory by John II in 1355 but again did not come into use immediately.

During the last few decades of the 14th century royal and princely patronage took on even greater dimensions. Only a few items remain from the great collections amassed by Charles V and his brother Louis, Duke of Anjou (1339–84), notably the sceptre of Charles V (Paris, Louvre), possibly executed by Jean du Vivier (*fl* 1378–1401); the Royal Gold Cup or Cup of St Agnes (*c.* 1380–90; London, BM; *see* ENAMEL, colour pl. III, fig. 1), decorated with translucent enamels, including *rouge cler*, and doubtless executed for Charles V; the mirror panels (Paris, Louvre) in enamelled gold, described in the inventory (1379) of Louis of Anjou; and the *Libretto* (Florence, Mus. Opera Duomo) donated by Charles V to his brother Louis.

86. *Virgin and Child*, silver gilt, enamel and jewels, h. 690 mm, from Paris, France, 1339 (Paris, Musée du Louvre)

Opaque enamelling on sculpture in the round, the use of diamonds and the cutting of precious stones to create facets, all mentioned in inventories from the second half of the 14th century, became widespread in the 15th. Several pieces of jewellery in enamelled gold dating from the beginning of the century are the finest examples of the luxurious taste and affectation of this period: they include the *Calvary* (1402; Esztergom, Cathedral Treasury), a New Year's gift from Margaret of Flanders (1350–1405) to her husband Philip the Bold, and the Little Gold Horse (or Goldenes Rössl, Altötting, SS Philipp & Jakob, Schatzkam.), given to Charles VI by Isabeau of Bavaria as a New Year's gift in 1404 (*see* §VI below). The cross of the Oath of the Order of the Golden Fleece (before 1400; Vienna, Schatzkam.), with its regular decoration in square-cut stones, the *Virgin and Child* (before 1402; Toledo, Mus. Catedralicio) and the Reliquary of the Holy Thorn (London, BM), decorated with opaque enamels on gold sculpture in the round, were all executed for Jean, Duc de Berry, who was probably also the donor of the ivory and jet *Virgin* seated on a gilt throne (Burgos, Mus. Dioc.–Catedralicio). The richly mounted Burgundy Goblet (1453–67; Vienna, Schatzkam.), executed for Philip the Good, combines diamonds with other precious stones in its setting. The Reliquary of the Veil of St Aldegonde (after 1469; Maubeuge, Mus.-Trésor Eglise), stamped with a Valenciennes pattern, and the ex-voto of Charles the Bold by Gerard Loyet (1467; Liège Cathedral) both gave expression to the flamboyant forms and the realist tendencies of Late Gothic art.

For further discussion of secular metalwork *see* FRANCE, §§IX, 2 and X, 3.

BIBLIOGRAPHY

Trésors des églises de France (exh. cat., ed. J. Dupont; Paris, Mus. A. Déc., 1965)

La France de Saint Louis (exh. cat., ed. P. Pradel; Paris, Pal. Justice, Salle Gens-d'arme, 1970–71)

F. Salet: 'La Croix du Serment de l'Ordre de la Toison d'or', *J. Sav.* (1974), pp. 73–94

E. Kovacs: 'Problèmes de style autour de 1400', *Rev. A.* [Paris], xxviii (1975), pp. 25–33

R. W. Lightbown: *Secular Goldsmiths' Work in Medieval France: A History* (London, 1978)

D. Gaborit-Chopin and E. Taburet: *Objets d'art du Moyen Age*, Ecole du Louvre, Notices d'histoire de l'art, 4 (Paris, 1981)

Les Fastes du Gothique: Le Siècle de Charles V (exh. cat., ed. F. Baron; Paris, Grand Pal., 1981–2)

J. Taralon: 'La Châsse de Saint-Taurin d'Evreux', *Bull. Mnmtl*, cxl/1 (1982), pp. 41–56

D. Gaborit-Chopin: 'La Croix d'Anjou', *Cah. Archéol.*, xxxiii (1985), pp. 157–78

——: 'Les Collections d'orfèvrerie des princes français au milieu du XIVe siècle d'après les comptes et inventaires', *Hommage à Hubert Landais: Art, objets d'art, collections* (Paris, 1987), pp. 46–52

J. Stratford: *The Bedford Inventories: The Worldly Goods of John, Duke of Bedford, Regent of France, 1389–1435* (London, 1993)

ELIZABETH TABURET-DELAHAYE

3. LOW COUNTRIES. The transitional style of HUGO D'OIGNIES can be considered a watershed in the development from Romanesque to Gothic in Netherlandish metalwork, as is illustrated by his three surviving signed works (all Namur, Trésor Hugo d'Oignies; see fig. 87). During the Gothic period the identity of individual metalworkers, like that of other craftsmen, becomes easier to ascertain. Leading silversmiths can sometimes be identified from their masters' marks. The portrait of the gold- and silversmith *Jan de Leeuw* of Bruges (1436; Vienna, Ksthist. Mus.; *see* BRUGES, fig. 3) by Jan van Eyck ensured his fame, although none of his works can be identified. On the other hand, the work of one important master, Elias Scerpswert of Utrecht is identifiable, for example the reliquary bust of *Bishop Frederick* (1362; Amsterdam, Rijksmus.). Many high-quality gold and silver pieces, are, however, anonymous. Among these are the arm reliquary of St Thomas (*c.* 1450), made in Maastricht, and the small reliquary busts of *St John the Baptist* and *St Livinus* (*c.* 1400) from the southern Netherlands (all Maastricht,

87. Engraved book cover by Hugo d'Oignies showing *Christ in Majesty*, parcel gilt and jewels, h. 325 mm, from the Low Countries, *c.* 1230 (Namur, Trésor Hugo d'Oignies Institut des Soeurs de Notre Dame)

Schatkamer St-Servaasbasiliek). Eight chased and originally partially gilded and polychrome silver reliefs (Hamburg, Mus. Kst & Gew.) are from the pedestal of the lost bust of *St Servatius* (*c.* 1400) from Maastricht. Other High Gothic objects that have long been located in the Netherlands may actually be French or Rhenish; examples include the silver-gilt crosier (second quarter of 14th century; Haarlem, Bishop's Pal.) with *basse-taille* enamel of the abbot of Egmond, and the silver-gilt and enamel chalice (early 15th century; Gouda, Stedel. Mus. Catharina Gasthuis) of Jacoba van Beieren, Countess of Holland (1401–36).

High-quality work in brass and bronze was concentrated in the Meuse region. The tradition of the animal-shaped ewer was continued there, and repoussé bowls were also made. The centre of the trade was Dinant (*see also* BRASS, §II), where, in the second half of the 14th century, the earliest Gothic lectern (Tongeren, Onze Lieve Vrouwe) was made by Johan Josès (*fl* 1360–78). After the city was destroyed by Charles the Bold in 1466, metalworkers settled elsewhere, leading to the new importance of Mechelen, Brussels, Bruges and Middelburg for bronze- and brass-casting. Metalworkers had in any case already spread beyond the Meuse region. Hainault, especially Tournai, was another important centre. JACQUES DE GÉRINES achieved a prominent position in Brussels. Nothing survives of his work, but it is reflected in ten brass statuettes (1476; Amsterdam, Rijksmus.), probably from the tomb of *Isabel of Bourbon* (*d* 1465; Antwerp Cathedral), which were cast by a follower of Gérines, presumably Renier van Thienen (*see* THIENEN, VAN, (2)), who made the monumental paschal candelabrum of 1483 at St Leonarduskerk, Zoutleeuw, and, perhaps with Jan Borman, the tomb of *Mary of Burgundy* (1491; Bruges, Onze-Lieve-Vrouw-ter-Potterie). Late in the 15th century Aert van Tricht was producing large-scale cast work in Maastricht. Families of bell-founders, who also cast mortars and cannon, were often itinerant. Other bronze and brass objects made included tomb slabs, fonts and chandeliers.

Works in iron were mostly utilitarian or military, and few have survived. The colourfully painted lever of the font-cover in St Janskerk, 's Hertogenbosch, was made in 1492 by a local ironsmith. In St Walburgskerk, Zutphen, is a 15th-century chandelier, the lower rim of which has figural decoration, while in the Kluizekerk, Lier, is the wrought-iron monument known as the 'Tree of St Gummarus' (1479), which commemorates the first miracle performed by the local saint. The richly decorated wrought-iron superstructure of the well on the Handschoenmarkt in Antwerp is attributed to Quinten Metsys.

BIBLIOGRAPHY

A. Peltzer: 'Geschichte der Messingindustrie und der künstlerischen Arbeiten in Messing (Dinanderien) in Aachen und den Ländern zwischen Maas und Rhein von der Römerzeit bis zur Gegenwart', *Z. Aachen. Geschver.*, xxx (1909), pp. 235–463

J. T. Perry: *Dinanderie* (London, 1910)

S. Collon-Gevaert: *Histoire des arts du métal en Belgique* (Brussels, 1951)

J. M. Fritz: *Goldschmiedekunst der Gotik in Mitteleuropa* (Munich, 1982)

E. G. Grimme: *Bronzebildwerke des Mittelalters* (Darmstadt, 1985)

Zilver uit 's-Hertogenbosch: Van bourgondisch tot biedermeier (exh. cat., ed. A. M. Koldeweij; 's-Hertogenbosch, Noordbrabants Mus., 1985)

Zilver uit de Gouden Eeuw van Antwerpen (exh. cat., ed. P. Baudouin and A. M. Claessens-Peré; Antwerp, Rockoxhuis, 1988)

L. E. van den Bergh-Hoogterp: *Goud- en zilversmeden te Utrecht in de late middeleeuwen* (The Hague and Maarssen, 1990)

A. M. KOLDEWEIJ

4. HOLY ROMAN EMPIRE. The main centres of bronze and brass production in the Empire were north Germany, the Rhineland and South Germany (*see* NUREMBERG, §III, 2). The principal work of free-standing sculpture is the equestrian monument of *St George* (1373; Prague, N.G., Convent of St George) by the brothers MARTIN AND GEORGE OF KOLOZSVÁR. The reliquary bust of *St Catherine of Siena* (*c.* 1455–60; New York, Frick) is probably by Hans Multscher. Another expressive work is the 'Hansel' (Nuremberg, Ger. Nmus.; see fig. 88), a 1.22 m flute-playing fountain figure cast in Nuremberg *c.* 1380. Many small figural sculptures from tombs, shrines or candlesticks have also survived. Lecterns have an architectural support or a round central shaft, surmounted by an eagle or a pelican with outspread wings to support a book.

The earliest reclining metal tomb effigy of the period is *Bishop Wolfart of Rot* (*d* 1302; Augsburg Cathedral). This was followed by the tombs of *Bishop Heinrich of Bokholt* (*d* 1341; Lübeck Cathedral), *Archbishop Friedrich von Saarwerden* (*d* 1414; Cologne Cathedral), *Elector Frederick the Warlike of Saxony* (*d* 1428; Meissen Cathedral), *Archbishop Ernst von Sachsen* (*d* 1513; Magdeburg Cathedral) and *Count Otto IV of Henneberg* (*d* 1502; Römhild, parish church). In the 15th century the Vischer family in Nuremberg became the most important suppliers of central

88. Bronze fountain figure known as 'Hansel', h. 1.22 m, from Nuremberg, Germany, *c.* 1380 (Nuremberg, Germanisches Nationalmuseum)

German, east German, Franconian and Polish tombs. The finest is the tomb of *St Sebaldus* (*c.* 1507–19; Nuremberg, St Sebalduskirche), which has a three-level rectangular casing of pier buttresses, decorated with a rich programme of figures in relief and full-round sculpture: at the bottom are *St Sebaldus* and four scenes from his legend, personifications of the Virtues, ancient gods, heroes, fabulous creatures and a portrait of *Peter Vischer*; in the middle are the *Apostles*; and at the top *Prophets* (*see* VISCHER and fig. 4). Although the overall impression is Late Gothic, many details indicate Renaissance influence. The full-length figures (Meissen Cathedral) of the Saxon electors *Frederick II* ('the Mild'; *d* 1464), *Ernest* (*d* 1484) and *Duke Albert* (*d* 1500), said to be based on a design by Dürer, are of high quality.

At the end of the 13th century a new, chalice-like form of font with a central shaft emerged (e.g. Godehardskirche, Brandenburg). Fonts of the 14th century are more elegant, with relief figures under arcades on the sides. A number of Mecklenburg fonts are inscribed with the makers' names, for example that (1342) in Wittenburg by Master Wilkin (*fl* 1312–42) or that (1365) in the Marienkirche, Parchim, by Master Hermann (*fl c.* 1350–73). Hans Apengeter (*fl* 1332–42/4) cast among other works the font in the Marienkirche, Lübeck, in 1337, that in the Nikolaikirche, Kiel, in 1344 and a seven-armed candelabrum in Kolberg Cathedral in 1327.

The most important bronze tabernacle is the slender tower in the Marienkirche, Lübeck, almost 10 m high, cast in 1476–9 by Klaus Grude (*d* after 1493). Among other works are fountains. One in Goslar (*c.* 1300) consists of three basins joined by a central shaft with an eagle, and another in Brunswick of 1408 has three lead basins and a baldacchino with figures at the top. Chandeliers generally consist of a central shaft, often with a figure of the Virgin (e.g. Amsterdam, Rijksmus.), and foliate curved arms in a stellar formation on as many as three levels. This type was also used in domestic settings. Variants with casket-shaped middle sections are found in Lübeck Cathedral (the 'Müllerkrone') and in the Rathaus at Goslar (both 15th century). Many large standing candelabra with three to seven arms and round feet were produced for churches.

From 1400 animal-shaped ewers (aquamanilia) and repoussé bowls with Christian figural scenes in relief at the centre were cast in Nuremberg. These were also produced in other regions of Germany, as were round-bellied pots with animal spouts and other receptacles, bells and mortars. Lion-head door handles (e.g. Marburg, Elisabethkirche) continued to be produced. In the 14th century they were sometimes surrounded by perforated *rinceaux* incorporating biblical figures (e.g. Petrikirche, Hamburg). The superbly modelled handle (*c.* 1400) of the Lübeck Rathaus shows the German Emperor surrounded by the seven electors.

Iron was generally forged. The most important works are chandeliers, such as the wheel-shaped example (1489) by Gert Bulsinck in St Felicitas, Vreden. Smiths also made lattices to separate rooms and for windows, door fittings, including hinges elaborated into foliate branches (e.g. *c.* 1475; Munich, Rathaus), and heart-shaped hinged knocker rings (e.g. 15th century; Dinkelsbühl, St Georg).

Coppersmiths produced works with repoussé decoration. Among the surviving examples is a fire-gilt censer (15th century; London, V&A). The 5 m figure of *St Michael* for the tower of the Brussels Hôtel de Ville was completed by Martin van Rode in 1454. Numerous vessels and other items were made of pewter, although many were later melted down and recast. The pitcher had many regional variants. The pewter baptismal basins of the 14th century (e.g. Mainz Cathedral) resemble those in bronze. In Bohemia numerous fonts with three long, splayed legs were produced in the 15th century (e.g. Týn Church, Prague).

BIBLIOGRAPHY

LK; *RDK*

F. Schottmüller: *Bronze Statuetten und Geräte* (Berlin, 1921)

E. Hintze: *Die deutschen Zinngiesser und ihre Marken*, i–vii (Leipzig, 1921–31)

A. Feulner: *Peter Vischers Sebaldusgrab* (Munich, 1924)

F. Stuttmann: *Deutsche Schmiedeeisenkunst*, i–v (Munich, 1927–30)

F. Tischer: *Böhmisches Zinn und seine Marken* (Leipzig, 1928)

H. T. Bossert, ed.: *Geschichte des Kunstgewerbes aller Zeiten und Völker*, v (Berlin, 1932)

O. von Falke and E. Meyer: 'Romanische Leuchter und Gefässe, Giessgefässe der Gotik', *Bronzegeräte des Mittelalters*, i (Berlin, 1935)

W. Holzhausen: *Geschichte des deutschen Kunsthandwerks* (Munich, 1955)

H.-U. Haedeke: *Metalwork* (London, 1970)

V. Baur: 'Kerzenleuchter aus Metall', *Geschichte, Form und Technik* (Munich, 1973)

J. M. Fritz: *Goldschmiedekunst der Gotik in Mitteleuropa* (Munich, 1982)

E. Turner: *Brass* (London, 1982)

Gothic and Renaissance Art in Nuremberg, 1300–1550 (exh. cat., ed. E. Schultz; New York, Met.; Nuremberg, Ger. Nmus.; 1986)

G. REINHECKEL

5. EASTERN EUROPE. Metalwork in this region is principally restricted to Hungary, its northern highlands (now Slovakia) and its Transylvanian territories, and to Poland. The Soft style of Bohemian art emerges as a link between Germany, Poland and 14th-century Hungary. Court art flourished under several great rulers: in Hungary, Charles Robert (*reg* 1309–43) and Louis I (*reg* 1342–82; *see* ANJOU, §I(2) and (3)); in Poland Kasimir III (*reg* 1333–70; *see* PIAST, (1)).

Metalwork under the Anjou dynasty was profoundly influenced by Italy (*see* §6 below) and, through Austria, by Germany and France. It is not possible to identify a specific national style, except perhaps for the Hungarian cloisonné (see below). Only a few objects survived centuries of destruction and war and 150 years of Turkish rule (*see* HUNGARY, §VIII); these can be attributed to specific masters and workshops only with difficulty. The work of Hungarian, Bohemian and Polish artists deeply influenced the German masters who had settled in Eastern Europe and who gradually developed an independent style in the Hungarian uplands and the Saxon towns of Transylvania.

The leading metalsmiths worked in the royal workshops, making seals and, in the 14th century, coins; they also made liturgical and secular objects for royal gifts. By the 14th century, however, metalwork was being produced in the developing towns for the aristocracy and the wealthy bourgeoisie as well as the king. In this period, also, guilds began to be established. As Hungary was a producer of precious metals, metalworking centres developed in many new mining towns. Besides silver and gold, gilt bronze and copper were used for liturgical items. The higher church dignitaries wore cope clasps decorated with holy figures, engraved rings set with gemstones, and chains.

The favoured decorative form was engraving, primarily copied from German pattern books. Moulded elements appeared in the 15th century: these included floral ornament, figurines, fleur-de-lis chalice mouldings and rosettes. Patterns were rarely chased, the most popular decoration being enamel (*see* §VI below), particularly *basse-taille* from Italy and a form of cloisonné, which, with its characteristic colours and varied flower forms, became known throughout Europe as 'Hungarian enamel'. Just after 1400 the earliest known cloisonné treasure, a bust reliquary (Győr Cathedral), was made for the skull of the Hungarian king, St Ladislas (*reg* 1077–95).

In the 14th century chalices were mainly decorated with engraved pictures of saints and fleurs-de-lis. Louis I's Zadar Chalice (Zadar, St Simeon) is among the most decorative. Characteristic of the Anjou period is the pyx-shaped ciborium on a high plinth: that of Szepeskortvélyesi (Bésán Collection) is an example. The sides are engraved with biblical scenes and Latin inscriptions. In 1367 Louis I sent reliquaries of Hungarian saints, candlesticks, chalices, enamelled prayer books and framed icons to the palatine chapel at Aachen (now Aachen, Domschatzkam.).

The 15th century is much richer than the 14th in surviving Hungarian goldsmiths' work. The Torna Chalice, engraved with saints in cusped niches, was probably a gift from Sigismund's wife Queen Barbara (?1390–1451). The most beautiful chalices were made in the second half of the century and are in cloisonné: the Suky Chalice (Esztergom, Cathedral Treasury; see fig. 89); the Nyári family chalice, covered in cloisonné and engraved depictions of saints; and the Barbara Telegdy Chalice (Győr, Cathedral Treasury) with its lavish multicoloured enamelled flowers. From the northern highlands the Nyitra (now Nitra, Slovakia) and Pozsony (now Bratislava, Slovakia) cloisonné chalices survive; in Transylvania most churches preserve at least one cloisonné chalice, and it was there, primarily in Kolozsvár (now Cluj-Napoca, Romania), that this technique flourished (*see also* ROMANIA, §VI). Monstrances had sculptural ornament. On one example (ex-Szendrő; Budapest, N. Mus.), Hungarian saints were engraved on the base; on another from Óbuda Parish Church are *SS Peter and Paul*; and on that of Kecskemét Parish Church is *St Michael*. Crosses in the churches of Poprád and Szepesszombat (now Poprad and Spišska Sobota, Slovakia) in the northern highlands have engraved *Symbols of the Evangelists* and are identical in decoration and form to the crosses in St Mary, Kraków.

89. Suky Chalice, gold, ornamented with filigree and embossed designs, from Hungary, *c.* 1500 (Esztergom, Cathedral Treasury)

Most surviving secular objects were recovered in excavations. Fine 14th-century jewellery was found with silver plates in the castle garden at Körmend, while similar rosettes, rings and bracelets were excavated at Kelébia. Bronze dies used in their making are in the National Museum, Budapest. There is also a belt (beginning of 15th century) from Nagytálya, engraved with a female falconer. The Budapest findings include Late Gothic rings and clasps engraved with lovers, flowers and animals.

Numerous Polish masters active in the court workshop at Kraków had studied in Hungary (*see* POLAND, §IX). Many others worked in Danzig (now Gdánsk), Boroszló and Posen (now Poznań), along with German masters. Among Kasimir III's commissions were two chalices (1351 and 1363; Trzemeszno and Kalisz churches) and a similar fleur-de-lis example given to Louis I. By the 15th century Hungarian cloisonné had been introduced into Poland; at the end of the 15th century and in the early 16th several cloisonné chalices were produced in the Kraków workshop. The finest Polish Gothic monstrance (Częstochowa, monastery of Jasna Góra Treasury, Sacristy & Mus.) was made in 1433 in Kraków and is decorated with richly engraved biblical scenes and figures of saints. Engraved monstrances in St John, Poznań and in the cathedral there are enriched with sculptures of saints. The reliquary of St Barbara (end of 15th century; Gniezno Cathedral) has moulded figures of saints on the side. A similar hexagonal reliquary made in 1510, by the Poznań goldsmith Jan Gelhor (*fl* 1507–14), for the relics of St Sabina survives in the cathedral at Poznań. In 1507 Peter Gelhor (*fl c.* 1500–33) from Poznań made the hand reliquary of St Adalbert (Trzemeszno, abbey church). The cloisonné head reliquary of St Dorothy (Warsaw), decorated in *c.* 1430, was probably made in Buda.

BIBLIOGRAPHY

D. Dercsényi: *The Age of Lajos the Great* (Budapest, n.d.)
S. Mihalik: 'Denkmäler und Schulen des ungarischen Drahtemails', *Acta Hist. A. Acad. Sci, Hung.*, V/1–2 (1958)
A. Bochnak and J. Pagaczewski: *Polskie rzemioslo artystyczne wiekow srednich* [Polish craft work in the Middle Ages] (Kraków, 1959)
J. Balogh: *Art in King Matthias's Court* (Budapest, 1966)
E. A. Grimme: 'Der Aachener Domschatz', *Aachen. Kstbl.*, xlii (1972), pp. 1–401
J. Kolba and A. Németh: *Goldsmith's Work* (Budapest, 1973)
C. Nicolescu: *Die Edelschmiedekunst in Rumänien* (Bucharest, 1973)
E. Toranova: *Zlatnictvo na Slovensku* [Slovak goldsmiths' work] (Bratislava, 1975)
J. Kolba: *Gothic Chalices in the Treasury of Győr* (Arrabon, 1977–8)
T. Guć-Jednaszewska: 'Europejskie Dziedzictwo Rozproszone: Gdańsk, 1992', *Ochrona Zabytków*, xlvi (1993), pp. 194–8
——: 'Przegląd prac konserwatorskich przy najcenniejszych zespołach dzieł sztuki gdańskiej' [Review of conservation works in the most important cooperatives of Gdańsk art], *Ochrona Zabytków*, xlvi/2 (1993), pp. 109–25

JUDIT KOLBA

6. ITALY. As in other artistic fields, the Gothic style of goldsmithing in Italy lasted for fewer years than in most other European countries. The penetration of Gothic forms was limited to the 13th century, because of the powerful roots in Roman and Byzantine traditions, while in the 15th century in some centres at least, Gothic forms were replaced by Renaissance ones. This short period was nevertheless one of the most brilliant in the history of Italian goldsmithing.

In the 13th century, Venice was a particularly active and flourishing centre. During the first half of the century Venetian goldsmiths produced works ornamented with filigree inspired by similar works in France and the Rhine–Moselle area. They were of such quality that the term *opus veneticum* was adopted in records to describe this kind of work. Several hardstone vases in the treasury of S Marco, Venice (e.g. a cruet in Sardinian onyx and a crystal vase) were given a mounting of this kind of silver-gilt filigree after the fire there in 1230/31, probably some time during the second half of the century (*see* VENICE, §IV, 1(iv)). Other Venetian works are preserved outside Venice: for example the reliquary and chandeliers (Bari, Mus. S Nicola) given to S Nicola, Bari, in 1296 by Charles II of Anjou were also classified at the time of the donation as 'de opere veneciarum'. The filigree decoration is also found on works from other regions, notably Tuscany, in the second half and at the very end of the 13th century: examples are the cross of Castiglion Fiorentino (Pin. Com.), the chalice of St Atto (Pistoia, Mus. Cap.) and the head reliquary of St Galgano (Siena, Mus. Opera Duomo).

Basse-taille (translucent) enamel appeared in Siena by the end of the 13th century. This new process enabled the goldsmith to endow his works with greater appearance of relief, as well as with pure and particularly appealing effects of colour. The earliest surviving dated example of the technique is on the silver-gilt chalice (Assisi, Tesoro Mus. Basilica S Francesco) made by GUCCIO DI MANNAIA and given *c.* 1290 to S Francesco, Assisi, by Pope Nicholas IV (see fig. 90; *see also* §VI, 3 below). The technique was rapidly perfected and propagated, and the reliquary of the Holy Corporal of Bolsena (1337–8; Orvieto Cathedral), by UGOLINO DI VIERI and his associates, constitutes the acme of this development.

Numerous Italian centres of production adopted the technique and often also the style of Sienese works (*see* SIENA, §II); in this category are Florence, as is shown by the reliquary bust of *St Zenobius* (1330–31; Florence Cathedral) by ANDREA ARDITI, and Pistoia, as exemplified by the workshop responsible for the silver altar in the cathedral (*see* ANDREA DI JACOPO D'OGNABENE and LEONARDO DI SER GIOVANNI). In certain towns the Sienese influence was combined with others. In Naples it was coupled with that of goldsmiths from France; the arm reliquaries (1337–8) of St Luke (Paris, Louvre) and St Louis of Toulouse made for Queen Sancha (*d* 1345) show this. In Venice it mingled with vigorous local traditions: translucent enamels, in a style very distinct from that of Tuscan work, occupy only a very modest place on the mounting of the serpentine chalice in the treasury of S Marco, but on the other hand form the main ornament of the arm reliquary of St George in the same treasury, where Sienese influence is in this case indisputable. In the second half of the 14th century and the first decades of the 15th, most Italian centres of production continued, often in simplified form, to use the techniques and styles established in the first half of the century.

90. Chalice base showing *Pope Nicholas IV*, by Guccio di Mannaia, silver gilt and *basse-taille* enamel, h. 224 mm, from Siena, Italy, *c.* 1290 (Assisi, Tesoro Museo della Basilica di San Francesco)

BIBLIOGRAPHY

F. Rossi: *Capolavori di oreficeria italiana* (Milan, 1956)
H. R. Hahnloser: *Il tesoro di San Marco: Il tesoro e il museo* (Florence, 1971)
M. Ciardi Dupré dal Poggetto, ed.: *Il tesoro della basilica di San Francesco ad Assisi* (Assisi and Florence, 1980)
I. Hueck: 'Pace di Valentino und die Entwicklung des Kelches im Duecento', *Mitt. Ksthist. Inst. Florenz*, xxvi/3 (1982), pp. 259–78
Il Gotico a Siena (exh. cat., Siena, Pal. Pub., 1982)
E. Taburet-Delahaye: 'Sienne et Florence: A propos de quelques oeuvres d'orfèvrerie émaillée', *Communication au colloque Sienne et l'Europe: Avignon 1983*
L'Art gothique siennois (exh. cat. by M. Laclotte and others, Avignon, Mus. Petit Pal., 1983)
L. Gai: *L'altare argenteo di San Jacopo nel Duomo di Pistoia* (Turin, 1984)
An. Scu. Norm. Sup. Pisa, Lett., Stor. Filos., 3rd ser., xiv (1984); xviii/1 (1988); xxi/1 (1991) [whole issues on Italian metalwork]
The Treasury of San Marco, Venice (exh. cat., New York, Met., 1984)
D. Gaborit-Chopin: 'Le Bras-reliquaire de Saint Luc au Musée du Louvre', *Mélanges Verlet: Antologia de Belle Arti*, xxvii–xxviii (1985), pp. 5–18
Le Trésor de Saint Marc de Venise (exh. cat., Paris, Grand Pal., 1988)
C. Baracchini: *Oreficeria sacra a Lucca dal XIII al XV secolo* (Florence, 1993)

ELIZABETH TABURET-DELAHAYE

7. BRITISH ISLES. Isolated pieces are all that remain as evidence of the art of the British metalworker in this period, although contemporary records testify to the splendour and quantity of precious metal plate and jewellery. During the Reformation, England and Scotland experienced the comprehensive destruction of their shrines and of many liturgical vessels, although some have survived through accidental loss, concealment or burial. Secular metalwork fared much worse, for it was prized as

much for its intrinsic value as for its craftsmanship, and was often melted down. The surviving secular pieces are largely to be found in the ancient corporations, universities or the Livery Companies of the City of London.

For many types of ecclesiastical object no examples survive in precious metal, although their style may sometimes be judged by base metal survivals. The most costly and ambitious commissions, the shrines (*see* SHRINE (i), §I), have vanished, although descriptions and illustrations of some are known. Also gone are the large altarpieces, candlesticks, holy water vessels and sacring bells. The most numerous ecclesiastical pieces to survive are chalices and patens, about 200 in all, dating from between *c.* 1200 and 1530, mostly of silver, with a few in copper gilt. Over thirty 15th-century processional and altar crosses in brass and just one in silver (Dublin, N. Mus.), from Ballylongford, Ireland, are known; all are of markedly similar design. Only a few paxes, pyxides, chrismatories and censers, mostly in brass, have been preserved. Numerous monumental brasses survive from *c.* 1300 onwards. The late 15th-century gold and enamel Langdale Rosary (London, V&A; for illustration *see* ROSARY) is the oldest known example of its kind in Britain. Predominant among secular items are drinking vessels, spoons, rings and brooches in precious metal; badges and dishes in pewter; and lecterns, bells and ewers in brass and bronze. More pieces survived from the affluent 15th century, notably the distinctively English hour-glass-shaped salts and silver-mounted mazers.

The scale of the losses hampers any assessment of the relative popularity of different metals and of the evolution of style and ornament. England was producing significant quantities of lead and tin and lesser amounts of iron and silver; Ireland and Scotland had reserves of copper and gold. All metals were available from recycling, supplemented by such imports as brass from the Low Countries and iron from Spain and Sweden. In the 15th century, reversing the pattern of the previous two centuries, gold appears to have been more commonly used than silver for jewellery; the use of pewter for table vessels and copper alloys for the kitchen seems to have grown from *c.* 1300, while iron, used sparingly in the 13th century for door fittings and locks, was by the 15th being used for ambitiously designed wrought screens and grilles, aping stone or wood, and was beginning to be cast into grave-slabs and firebacks. Despite the regulations imposed by London's metalworking guilds, little extant Gothic metalwork (except for some pewter dishes and silver spoons) bears any stamps or marks, doubtless a reflection of law evasion as well as of the fact that a customer's own melted-down metal did not require marking when refashioned.

The marked classicism, rooted in Mosan tradition, of much work of *c.* 1100–1250 (*see* ROMANESQUE, §VI, 6) gave way to the growing naturalism that dominated the 13th century. This is evident in the figures and foliage on a silver-gilt buckle (*c.* 1220; Stockholm, Stat. Hist. Mus.) found in Gotland. More lushly naturalistic leaves and fruit are embossed, engraved or cast on several great silver-gilt Anglo-Norwegian chalices of *c.* 1250 (e.g. Cardiff, N. Mus.). Similar motifs are stamped all over the iron grille in Westminster Abbey made for the effigy of *Eleanor of Castile* in 1294 by Thomas de Leghtune [de Leightone], a rare instance in metalwork of a surviving object where maker, price (£12) and date are known. Eleanor's effigy itself, and that of *Henry III*, are the earliest extant bronze effigies in England, cast life-size by the goldsmith WILLIAM TOREL in 1292–3.

The dominance of architectural forms and motifs throughout the 14th century is best exemplified by the Canterbury Cathedral iron choir-screens of *c.* 1300, where simple intersecting notched bars make up a rich diaper of sexfoils and trefoils; by the silver-gilt Ramsey Abbey Censer of *c.* 1325 (London, V&A; see fig. 91), its polygonal form reminiscent of a miniature chapter house; and by the silver-gilt and enamel cup of *c.* 1340 (King's Lynn, Guildhall of the Holy Trinity; *see* ENGLAND, fig. 73), its body, foot and stem sinuously cast with vegetal forms, cusps and mouchettes. Typical of the style of *c.* 1400 is the gold and gem-set crown (Munich, Residenzmus.) of Princess Blanche (daughter of Henry IV), which has been claimed as English, French or Bohemian work. The silver-gilt and enamel crosier of William of Wykeham, bequeathed by him in 1402 to New College, Oxford, has a knop with heavily coruscating tiers of distinctively English

91. Ramsey Abbey Censer, silver gilt, h. 108 mm, diam. 53 mm, from ?Ramsey Abbey, England, *c.* 1325 (London, Victoria and Albert Museum)

architectural forms derived from the styles of the previous 50 years. (*See also* ENGLAND, §IX, 1, (i).)

Scotland and Ireland shared a common Celtic artistic heritage, at this period overlaid by the influence of imported Gothic models (*see* SCOTLAND, §IX, 1 and 2; IRELAND, §IX, 1). Although they are splendid, there is nothing distinctively Scottish in style about the Bute Mazer of *c.* 1320 (on loan to Edinburgh, Mus. Ant.) or the 15th-century mace of the Canon Law faculty of St Andrews University (*in situ*); nor is there anything distinctively Irish about the silver-gilt crosier and mitre of 1418 (Limerick Cathedral) signed by Thomas O'Carryd, or the unique silver cross of 1479 from Ballylongford. Characteristic of both countries was a Gaelic cultural revival in the later Middle Ages, which led to the restoration of such ancient relics as St Fillan's Crosier (Edinburgh, Royal Mus. Scotland) and the Domnach Airgid Shrine (Dublin, N. Mus.).

BIBLIOGRAPHY

J. Hunt: *The Limerick Mitre and Crozier* (Dublin, n. d.)

C. J. Jackson: *A History of English Plate* (London, 1911)

G. C. Druce: 'Lead Fonts in England', *J. Brit. Archaeol. Assoc.*, n. s., xxxix (1934), pp. 289–329

J. Buckley: *Some Irish Altar Plate* (Dublin, 1943)

G. E. P. How and J. How: *English and Scottish Silver Spoons and Pre-Elizabethan Hall-Marks* (London, 1952–7)

C. Oman: *English Church Plate* (Oxford, 1957)

H. Hamilton: *The English Brass and Copper Industries to 1500* (London, 1973)

J. Hatcher: *English Tin Production and Trade before 1500* (Oxford, 1973)

J. Hatcher and T. C. Barker: *A History of British Pewter* (London, 1974)

M. L. Campbell: 'Exhibits at Ballots: The Standing Pyx', *Antiqua. J.*, lxv/2 (1985), pp. 465–7

J. Blair and N. Ramsay, eds: *English Medieval Industries, Craftsmen, Techniques, Products* (London, 1991)

For further bibliography *see* JEWELLERY, §1.

MARIAN CAMPBELL

8. SPAIN. Among the items typically produced during the Gothic period, the monstrance was especially frequent in Spanish goldsmiths' work, and the processional kind often had architectural features. Liturgical objects were made both from precious metals and from such base metals as brass (e.g. the 15th-century silver-lined pyx, Madrid, Mus. Arqueol. N.) and pewter. Lead was also used to make decorative plaques (e.g. Calahorra, Mus. Tesoro Catedralicio & Dioc.) and brass for domestic items.

Crosses, which were almost always the Latin type, had fleur-de-lis terminals (e.g. Girona, Mus. Catedralicio; Vic, Mus. Episc.). One example from Vilabertrán (first quarter of 14th century; Vilabertrán, Colegiata S Maria) is decorated with quatrefoil medallions in repoussé, engraving and stamping, with filigree, enamels, cabochon gems and Classical cameos. Among processional and altar crosses is a silver-gilt example (*c.* 1357–60; Girona, Mus. Catedralicio) attributed to Pere Bernès (Pedro Berneč; *fl c.* 1358), decorated with repoussé, engraving and enamels; the outer edge has crenellations. Patriarchal, or double crosses (e.g. *c.* 1400; London, V&A) were also made.

In Catalonia, the centres for goldsmithing were Girona, Barcelona (*see* BARCELONA, §III) and, to a lesser extent, Tarragona. In Aragon it was not until the 15th century that, in spite of lingering Catalan influence, a distinctive character emerged, in Saragossa and Daroca. In 1384 Peter IV (*reg* 1336–87) commissioned for Daroca a silver-gilt monstrance (Daroca, Mus. Santísimo Misterio) from PERE MORAGUES. Its outline and repoussé follow the style of Bernès, while the figures are slimmer and more elegant. The wide engraved and enamelled foot opens into a double fleur-de-lis, and the hexagonal central body rests on a shrine-shaped knop and has two reliefs under festooned round arches. In Navarre, following the death of Sancho VII (*reg* 1194–1234), a succession of French monarchs (1234–1425) resulted in the importation of work and craftsmen. This had some impact on local work. Navarrese statues of the Virgin Enthroned include an example (Roncevalles, Real Colegiata) from the second half of the 14th century, showing French influence. Goldsmithing in Castile was relatively conservative, although marking was more thorough than in Aragon and included three marks, of the maker, assayer and town.

Burgos produced crosses of three main types: one with a horizontal arm to hold statues of the Virgin and St John (see fig. 92); one with an undulating design on the arms, enclosing tulip-like flowers; and one with convex tracery on the arms and quatrefoil terminals. Monstrances were composed of two hexagonal vessels, the lower one open. Valladolid (*see* VALLADOLID, §2) produced a distinctive type of chalice with a calyx of large, fleshy, overlapping leaves, an architectural knop and lower body, and a lobed foot with naturalistic foliage decoration. One example (Valladolid, Mus. Dioc. & Catedrálicio) is by Pedro de

92. Processional cross from S Martín, Vega de Poja, Pola de Siero, Asturias, Spain, first third of the 15th century (Madrid, Museo Arqueológico Nacional)

Ribadeo (*fl* 1497–1518). A profoundly influential goldsmith of the same period was Enrique de Arfe (*see* ARFE, (1)).

Toledan workmanship (*see* TOLEDO, §III) is seen in a chalice and paten (*c.* 1300; Toledo, Mus. Catedralicio) showing a synthesis of Romanesque tradition (*see* ROMANESQUE, §VI) with new Gothic ideas. The wide bowl has a spherical knop with the *Symbols of the Evangelists*; the paten, retaining the traditional lobed shape, has a *Crucifixion* instead of the *Paschal Lamb*. The cross (second half of 14th century) at San Martín de Valdeiglesias, near Madrid, is an outstanding example of Toledan workmanship.

Gothic architectural ironwork reached its peak in the 15th century with a series of crested grilles made in three panels, with a central two-leaved gate. From the 14th century the bars were sometimes twisted or split to form hearts, lozenges or lobate shapes. A master from Morella forged the magnificent presbytery grille (6×16 m; 1443) of Tarragona Cathedral, and Master Bujil made the grilles for the reliquary chapel in Burgos Cathedral. Ironwork also included many types of light holder and chests with fittings that became progressively larger and more decorative, sometimes ornamented with religious or secular scenes. A notable iron-bound chest is the late 13th-century Arca del Tesoro in the Alcázar, Segovia.

BIBLIOGRAPHY

J. Catalina: 'Crismeras de plomo historiado', *Bol. Soc. Esp. Excurs.*, iii (1895–6), pp. 38–41

A. Gascón de Gotor: *El Corpus Christi y las custodias procesionales en España* (Barcelona, 1916)

E. Tormo: 'Orfebrería valenciana de fines del siglo XIV: Las cruces procesionales de Játiva y Onteniente', *Bol. Soc. Esp. Excurs.*, xxviii (1920), pp. 103–204

I. Ceballos Escalera: 'La cruz de Vilabertrán', *Bol. Soc. Esp. Excurs.*, lviii (1950), pp. 167–81

J. Subías Galter: 'El retablo de plata de la Seo de Gerona', *An. Inst. Estud. Gerund.*, viii (1953), pp. 218–29

C. Oman: *The Golden Age of Hispanic Silver, 1400–1665* (London, 1968)

J. C. Brasas Egido: *La platería vallisoletana y su difusión* (Valladolid, 1980)

F. Olaguer-Feliú: *Las rejas de la catedral de Toledo* (Toledo, 1980)

J. M. Cruz Valdovinos: *Museo Arqueológico Nacional: Catálogo de la platería* (Madrid, 1982)

P. Freixas i Camps: *L'art gòtic a Girona, segles XIII–XV: L'orfebrería* (Barcelona, 1983), pp. 231–47

N. Dalmases: *Orfebrería catalana medieval: Barcelona, 1300–1500 (Aproximació al seu estudi)*, 4 vols (diss. U. Barcelona, 1984)

9. PORTUGAL. During the 14th and 15th centuries foreign goldsmiths, principally Jews, worked in Portugal for noble and royal patrons. Few secular commissions survive (the following examples are all in Coimbra, Mus. N. Machado de Castro). Fragments remain of a necklace in gold, precious stones and pearls which belonged to Isabella (1271–1336), wife of King Diniz (*reg* 1279–1325). Queen Isabella also had a silver reliquary statue of the *Virgin and Child* (first quarter of 14th century), which is remarkable for the engraving of the drapery and clasp. A casket in the form of a sarcophagus with a double-pitched roof is Portuguese work. The graceful reliquary of the True Cross (early 14th century) in gilt, coral and enamel that Queen Isabella gave to the convent of S Clara-a-Velha bears the Aragonese arms and, in the centre, a *Calvary*.

The period covering the second half of the 14th century and the 15th was one of particular splendour in Portuguese goldsmiths' work. Most surviving pieces are salvers and aquamanilia, the former generally in silver gilt with naturalistic foliage decoration—thistles, artichokes, acorns (e.g. Oporto, Casa–Mus. Guerra Junqueiro). The 'wild man' motif appears on several examples (Lisbon, Fund. Ricardo Espirito S Silva; London, V&A; New York, Met.). Reliquaries, processional crosses and monstrances combine silver gilt with rock crystal (e.g. Coimbra, Mus. N. Machado de Castro; Lisbon, Mus. N. A. Ant.; Setúbal, Mus. Setúbal). The silver gilt cross from Alcobaça Abbey (Lisbon, Mus. N. A. Ant.) has fleur-de-lis terminals and is lavishly decorated with interlace surrounding *Christ* and the *Symbols of the Evangelists*. Some reliquaries are casket-shaped: one from Guimarães (1457; Guimarães, Mus. Alberto Sampaio) has a hipped roof, while the roof of another from Aveiro (Lisbon, Mus. N. A. Ant.) is semicylindrical and is supported by four small figures of angels. Reliquaries in the form of a church include a 15th-century cylindrical example (Coimbra, Mus. N. Machado de Castro) with a gable crowned by a *Calvary* and two with supported roofs (15th-century; Lisbon, Mus. N. A. Ant.). Chalices (e.g. Lisbon, Mus. N. A. Ant.) have shallow bowls, knops decorated with rhombuses or shields, and feet of varied outline. The largest piece of goldsmiths' work is the triptych of the *Nativity* (Guimarães, Mus. Alberto Sampaio), in silver gilt on cedar wood, which shows the *Nativity* flanked by the *Annunciation*, the *Annunciation to the Shepherds*, the *Epiphany* and the *Presentation in the Temple*. Although an artist familiar with English alabasters has been proposed, the style suggests the influence of 14th-century Catalan goldsmiths' work.

Works in copper include a 14th-century crosier with cabochon and enamel incrustations (Coimbra, Mus. N. Machado de Castro). The upper part has a foliage scroll enclosing a frame that originally contained a religious scene. It is a local work influenced by Limoges. Ironwork included 15th-century boxes for Books of Hours and prayerbooks (e.g. Lisbon, Mus. N. A. Ant.; Viana do Castelo, Mus. Mun.).

BIBLIOGRAPHY

Les Trésors de l'orfèvrerie du Portugal (exh. cat., Paris, Mus. A. Déc., 1954–5)

Portuguese Art, 800–1800 (exh. cat., London, RA, 1955–6)

J. Couto and A. M. Gonçalves: *A ourivesaria em Portugal* (Lisbon, 1960)

N. C. Guedes: *Museu Nacional de Arte Antiga: Roteiro de Ourivesaria* (Lisbon, 1975)

A. N. Gonçalves: *O teosuro de D. Isabel de Aragao, Rainha de Portugal* (Coimbra, 1983)

Ourivesaria do norte de Portugal (exh. cat., Oporto, Arquiv. Hist. Mun. Porto, 1984)

Os móveis e o seu tempo: Mobiliario artístico português do Museu Nacional de Arte Antiga (exh. cat., Lisbon, Mus. N. A. Ant., 1985)

P. Dias: 'O Gótico', *História da arte em Portugal*, iv (Lisbon, 1986)

Le Langage des orfèvres de Portugal/A linguagem dos nossos ourives (exh. cat., Luxembourg; Lisbon; 1988)

Arte y cultura en torno a 1492 (exh. cat. by R. Rispa and C. A. Aquaza, Seville, 1992)

Portugal en el Medievo: De los monasterios a la monarquia (exh. cat., Madrid, Fund. Banco Cent. Hispamer., 1992)

ANGELA FRANCO MATA

10. SCANDINAVIA. By the time Gothic reached central Scandinavia, Romanesque motifs and patterns had already supplanted the distinctive Nordic features. The Nordic countries were well integrated into the Roman Catholic Church by then and the prototypes were brought over from the Continent; Germany later became the most

important source. German silversmiths, bronze and pewter founders, through the Hansa, settled in the new Nordic towns; surviving names substantiate the dominating German stylistic influences. The high quality of the many communion vessels preserved from the 14th century in Sweden, especially in the area around Mälaren, is directly owed to German influence. Surviving objects and documentary sources are evidence that there were many bronze and pewter foundries in the 14th and 15th centuries, the products of which were also derived from northern German prototypes. It is hard to distinguish between imported works and those that were made in Scandinavia, even though some researchers seem to detect a rustic style in the latter.

As in the Romanesque era, ironwork was important. The German influence is evident in individual motifs and features of Danish ironwork, whereas the Norwegian and Swedish material retained its own forms; this was mostly because the local village forges in the 14th century lost contact with developments in Europe. No ironwork has survived from the many town and monastic churches built during the Early Gothic period, and except for Gotland there was very little activity in the rural areas. With the renewed building activity of the 15th century the forges in many areas lacked reference to any contemporary prototypes and were forced to repeat ancient basic compositions. Although the details were Gothic, the overall appearance remained Romanesque in style (*see* ROMANESQUE, §VI, 10). The same unmodelled silhouettes found on doors from *c.* 1200 are repeated on the latticework at Strängnäs. A French Cistercian motif was introduced to Gotland by monasteries during the early 13th century and this dominated developments for the next 150 years, while it was adapted to the simpler proportions that were prevalent in the local parish churches on Gotland. The patterns had a significantly more robust character without losing any of the basic principles. During the decades around 1500, a large and unique group of doors was created on the island of Fyn in Denmark. They had long inscriptions made up of individually forged letters which in many cases cover the whole surface of the door.

BIBLIOGRAPHY

F. Uldall: *Danmarks midderalderlige Kirkeklokker* [The medieval church clocks of Denmark] (Copenhagen, 1906)

T. Kielland: *Norsk gullsmedkunst i middelaldern* [The Norwegian goldsmith's art in the Middle Ages] (Oslo, 1927)

C. R. af Ugglas: *Bidrag till den medeltida guldsmedskonstens historia* [Contribution to the history of the art of the medieval goldsmith] (Stockholm, 1941)

——: *Senmedeltida profant silversmide i Sverige* [Late medieval silversmithing in Sweden] (Stockholm, 1942)

A. Andersson: *Silberne Abendmahlgeräte in Schweden aus dem XIV. Jahrhundert* (Stockholm, 1956)

M. Åmark: *Sveriges medeltida kyrkklockor* [The medieval church clocks of Sweden] (Uppsala, 1960)

A. Oldeberg: *Metallteknik under vikingatid och medeltid* [Metalwork techniques in Viking and medieval times] (Stockholm, 1966)

C. A. Nordman: *Finlands medeltida konsthantverk* [Medieval crafts in Finland] (Helsinki, 1980)

L. Karlsson: *Medieval Ironwork in Sweden* (Stockholm, 1988)

LENNART KARLSSON

VI. Enamels.

From *c.* 1220 to *c.* 1500, enamels produced in western Europe can be classified as 'Gothic', for they share an aesthetic commonly defined as such where it appears in other media. The history of enamelling is inextricably linked to that of goldsmithing (for further discussion *see* §V, 1 above). In general, Gothic enamels were produced by lay goldsmiths working in urban centres, often maintaining the workshops through several generations of a family. Documents for individual artists working with enamel and their workshop practices are greater than for the earlier Middle Ages, thanks to tax records and guild regulations, yet knowledge is incomplete, and there has been too great a tendency in the literature to assign important surviving enamels to known masters.

Over the course of the period, the preferred materials and techniques of enamelling changed; each technique produced its own distinct artistic effect. Gaining an overall view of Gothic enamel production is complicated by the later destruction of innumerable examples. Works done on copper survive in greater numbers than those that use precious metals. This is not, however, a barometer of their original numbers, since during this time precious metal was increasingly used for the base plate. Inventories allow a fuller view of the many types of enamelling employed. Each of the principal techniques is discussed below, with examples both of surviving and destroyed works.

For further discussion *see* ENAMEL.

1. Champlevé. 2. *Email de plique.* 3. *Basse-taille.* 4. Filigree. 5. *En ronde bosse.* 6. *Plique à jour.* 7. Painted.

1. CHAMPLEVÉ.

A technique in which pulverized, coloured glass is fired into troughs that have been cut into a metal plate, usually made of copper. Gothic enamels of this type were produced in the 13th and 14th centuries, chiefly in Limoges and in the regions of Tuscany and the Upper Rhine.

(i) Limoges. The greatest number of later medieval champlevé enamels were produced in Limoges, and from the 12th century the name of the city became synonymous with its renowned enamels, which are commonly referred to in inventories as *opus lemovicense* (*see* LIMOGES, §1). Made of relatively thick copper, which was both sturdy and less likely to be melted down than gold or silver, many of these enamels survive. Since the enamel is securely held in deep channels, most are well preserved. Limoges enamels display a dominant blue palette, with characteristic colour bands in single fields, often red/green/yellow or blue/white. From about 1220, carpet-like fields of enamelled floral design were frequently used in combination with copper-gilt relief sculpture.

Limoges enamellers created a full range of altar equipment. The quality of surviving examples varies widely as does the type, from objects appropriate to use in any church to specially commissioned altar furniture. Pyxides with conical roofs survive by the hundred; they are decorated with simple floral designs, sometimes coarsely enamelled, or with easily legible Christograms inscribed in gilt discs that suggest the form of the Host. Also for Eucharistic reservation, but representing a masterpiece of Limoges work, is the tabernacle (*c.* 1220; New York, Met.; see fig. 93) excavated at Cherves: the scrolling enamel ground is finely engraved, apparently with the aid of compasses; its figural scenes stress devotion to the physical

93. Cherves Tabernacle, champlevé enamel and silver gilt, 838×502×260 mm, from Limoges, France, *c.* 1220 (New York, Metropolitan Museum of Art)

body of Christ. Thematic parallels between such scenes as the *Noli me tangere* and the *Incredulity of Thomas* are visually emphasized by the use of similar compositions. Contemporary with the tabernacle is a copper-gilt plaque with the *Annunciation to the Shepherds* (Paris, Louvre). A fragment from an unidentified ensemble that probably set shimmering copper-gilt reliefs against a rich blue field, it is characterized by a narrative lyricism that recalls Gothic manuscript illumination and is unequalled in other Limoges work. Limoges enamels of this quality for liturgical use are few in the second half of the 13th century and the early 14th, although a notable example is the reliquary bust of *St Ferreolus* made for and preserved in the parish church at Nexon (Haute-Vienne), signed by the Limousin artist Aymeric Chrétien and dated 1346.

From the mid-13th century the attention of Limousin enamellers returned to funerary monuments (*see* ROMANESQUE, §VII). Their activity in England and France is well documented, both in archives and in a series of drawings made by Roger de Gaignières. Effigies of *John* and *Marie of France* (both *d* 1247), commissioned by their father Louis IX for the royal necropolis at Royaumont Abbey, are preserved at Saint-Denis Abbey, while the effigy of *William de Valence* (*d* 1296) is at Westminster Abbey. Possibly associated with the latter's family is the casket (*c.* 1305–12; London, V&A) bearing coats of arms including those of Valence. For this and other pieces, it remains uncertain whether the enamels were made in the Limousin, by Limousin artists resident in other cities, or by local artists imitating a Limousin style. A surviving contract indicates that the enamel tomb of *Walter de Merton, Bishop of Rochester* (1276; destr. *c.* 1550) was to be made by John of Limoges. Limoges enamellers continued to enjoy the favour of the French court in the first half of the 14th century; in 1307 Philip IV ordered a shaffron of Limoges work to be presented to the King of Lesser Armenia.

(ii) Tuscany. In Tuscan champlevé enamels of the late 13th century and the 14th the figural decoration is either applied in relief or reserved and engraved on the copper plate, while the background is enamelled in a repeating floral or geometric pattern with a reduced palette of blue and red. Most commonly produced were liturgical implements, such as incense boats, and altar furniture, for example the frieze of enamel made in 1313 for the altar of the Baptistery in Florence. Its iconic representation of the *Virgin* recalls Byzantinizing Italian painted images of her. The goldsmith, Andrea Pucci Sardi, is identified in an inscription on the altar.

(iii) Upper Rhineland. Soon after a fire in 1322, plaques were added to the pulpit (now altar) at Klosterneuburg Abbey, made in the late 12th century by NICHOLAS OF VERDUN. This prompted the suggestion in earlier literature that Austria was a centre for champlevé enamelling in the 14th century, but the region of the Upper Rhine, centering on Konstanz, is now generally believed to have been the locus for workshops that produced these and related enamels. Figures are reserved in copper gilt against a deep blue ground, often punctuated with rosettes of reserved metal and deep red enamel. The drapery of the figures is accented with enamel, as in the roundel of the *Visitation* (Stuttgart, Württemberg. Landesmus.).

2. EMAIL DE PLIQUE. The term, commonly found in French princely and ecclesiastical inventories by the first half of the 13th century and up to the early 15th, refers to cloisonné enamels on gold. The technique seems first to be recorded in use on the cross of Philip II Augustus (destr.). The enamels are characterized by brilliant translucent colour, predominantly green and blue, with accents of yellow, and opaque red and white. The cloisons are typically set in delicate floral patterns. Such enamels often decorated precious table-objects; the hanap cover of *c.* 1297 at All Souls College, Oxford, is one of the few surviving secular examples (*see* HERALDRY, fig. 10). In liturgical contexts, quatrefoils, lozenges or circles of *émail de plique* were set in combination with jewels, as on the bust reliquaries of *St Denis* (destr.), made for his titular abbey *c.* 1280, and of *St Louis* (destr. 1791), made for the Sainte-Chapelle in Paris and completed by the translation of the relic of his skull in 1306. Most surviving *émaux de plique* have been associated with GUILLAUME JULIEN, but he was only one of a number of Parisian goldsmiths proficient in this technique.

3. BASSE-TAILLE. Sometimes referred to as translucent enamel, *basse-taille* features clear, thin glazes laid over an engraved silver or gold plate, the glass secured only by the irregularities in the surface of the metal plate created by the design. Subtle tones and shading could be produced by varying the depth of the engraving. The extensive palette and use of coloured glazes over a shimmering metal surface create an effect that is similar to Gothic stained glass and panel painting. It is not known where it first developed, but translucent enamelling rapidly became a favoured technique in a number of important centres of goldsmithing, only some of which can be reviewed here (references to additional centres of production are given in the bibliography).

The earliest dated example to survive is the chalice (*c.* 1290; Assisi, Tesoro Mus. Basilica S Francesco; see fig. 90 above) made at the order of the Franciscan pope Nicholas IV and signed by the Sienese artist GUCCIO DI MANNAIA. Lozenges of translucent enamel adorn the cup base, knop and foot of the chalice, with the polylobe foot richly worked in repoussé and the tulip-shaped bowl being hallmarks of Tuscan Gothic chalices. A number of translucent enamel chalices have specifically Franciscan iconography, with inscriptions on the knop naming the artist or patron. Among large-scale commissions, the most ambitious is the reliquary of the Holy Corporal of Bolsena (1337–8), signed by UGOLINO DI VIERI. Preserved in Orvieto Cathedral, it mimics the building's architectural forms and presents rectangular narrative panels with all the perspectival interest, compositional complexity and jewel-like palette of contemporary Italian panel painting. Sienese enamellers also worked for the papal court at Avignon and Rome. Among the most important commissions were the bust reliquaries of *SS Peter and Paul* (1369–72; destr. 1799), produced by Giovanni di Bartolo and Giovanni di Marco for S Giovanni in Laterano, Rome, which are known only through engravings by Giuseppe Maria Soresini.

The premier Parisian example of the combination of translucent enamel with Gothic sculpture in precious metal is the image of the *Virgin and Child* (Paris, Louvre; see fig. 86 above) made at the order of Queen Joanna of Evreux (1310–71). A gift to Saint-Denis Abbey in 1339, it shows scenes of the *Life of Christ* around its base. The approximation of the effects of stained glass that could be achieved with translucent enamel is patently clear in such works as the reliquary of Elizabeth of Hungary (*c.* 1340–50; New York, Cloisters; see fig. 94), attributed to the Parisian goldsmith Jean de Touyl, where the enamels are set in a miniature Gothic chapel of silver gilt framing the central image of the *Virgin and Child* flanked by angels. The Royal Gold Cup (*c.* 1380–90; London, BM) is enamelled with scenes of the *Life of St Agnes* and is noteworthy for its accomplished painting style and rich palette, especially the use of translucent red enamel (*see* ENAMEL, colour pl. III, fig.1). From inventory records it can be seen that the translucent red (*rouge cler*) found on the cup and associated with surviving enamels from the end of the century was already in use by the mid-14th century. Translucent enamels were not only produced in Paris. Rouen was the most important north French city for goldsmithing after Paris, while in the south, Montpellier and Toulouse were dominant. A number of south French pieces entered the collection of Louis I, Duke of Anjou (*reg* 1356–84), owing to his position as governor of the Languedoc.

As elsewhere in Europe, enamellers active in Spain in the 14th century adopted professional standards under which they agreed to work. The registered names of some are indicative of the degree of international exchange among these artists: for example the Italian John of Pisa and the German Consolí Blanc at Barcelona. No less than in other centres, they enjoyed the favour of the court, fulfilling such duties as the making of royal inventories. Spanish translucent enamels are epitomized by the heavy engraving of the metal plate under the enamel and by the rich decoration of unenamelled metal surfaces. A chalice (New York, Cloisters) offers a particularly fine example of this combination, with delicate stippled decoration of the silver-gilt surface and a richly varied enamel palette set over a deeply cut engraved plate. Girona Cathedral preserves the enamelled retable and ciborium made for its high altar. The principal part was made by Bartomeu of Girona from 1320; additions were made from the mid-14th century by Pere Bernès (*fl* after 1355) of Valencia and Andreu (*fl* 1357). The enamels, with their highly varied palette, are subordinated to the narrative repoussé reliefs.

94. Reliquary of Elizabeth of Hungary, attributed to Jean de Touyl, *basse-taille* enamel and silver gilt, 250×165 mm, from Paris, France, *c.* 1340–50 (New York, The Cloisters)

As it had been for champlevé enamel at the beginning of the 14th century, Konstanz also became a centre for translucent enamelling: a crosier (London, V&A) bears an inscription indicating that it was made in 1351 for Master Eberhard of Brandis, Abbot of Reichenau (1343–79). Translucent enamelling was clearly favoured in the Rhineland, especially in the Cologne area. The most ambitious examples are the works produced for the treasury at Aachen. Like the Parisian shrine of St Elizabeth of Hungary, the bust reliquary of *Charlemagne* and the Three Tower Reliquary (*c.* 1350; both Aachen, Domschatzkam.; *see* RELIQUARY, §I, 3) derive their form from the vocabulary of Gothic architecture. In the Aachen pieces, however, the translucent enamels are clearly secondary in importance, serving much more as decorative enhancement than as primary narrative elements.

The technique appeared early in England: in 1317 Edward II presented to Pope John XXII a ewer and basin with translucent enamel, bought from a London goldsmith. Surviving translucent enamels attributed to England mostly assume the form of precious jewellery or devotional objects (e.g. jewel reliquary of the Holy Thorn, *c.* 1340; London, BM; *see* RELIQUARY, fig. 5), the most celebrated recently discovered example being the Middleham Pendant (York, Yorks Mus.). With only traces of enamel surviving, it demonstrates the accomplished engraving that was required for this technique.

4. FILIGREE. In filigree enamel, glass flux is used as a purely decorative surface colorant. It is laid on the metal ground to fill in the design created by soldered rope-like wire, usually set in patterns of flowers or grape decoration. Utilized in Venice and Naples, filigree enamel became very popular on the Dalmatian coast and in Hungary. Numerous chalices are to be found both there and in Poland. Opaque green and blue dominate the palette of these enamels, with accents of red and white. Inscriptions and coats of arms indicate that they were gifts of local churchmen and of merchants, who maintained strong contacts with Italy.

5. EN RONDE BOSSE. In this technique, precious sculptural gold figures were covered first with white enamel and then coloured where necessary. It is seen in more than 40 surviving complete and fragmentary objects dating to the early 15th century, although it was already practised by the mid-14th during the reign (1350–64) of John II, King of France. The inventories of Charles VI and of his uncle, Jean, Duc de Berry, describe diverse enamels of this type. The Dunstable Swan Jewel (London, BM; *see* ENAMEL, fig. 1), a gold swan with feathers tipped in white opaque enamel, was made *c.* 1400, probably by a London goldsmith. The most important surviving example of the technique is the Goldenes Rössl (1403–4; Altötting, SS Philipp & Jakob, Schatzkam.; see fig. 95). In a stage-like setting, *Charles VI*, to whom it was given in 1404 as a New Year's gift from his wife, Isabeau of Bavaria, kneels before the enthroned *Virgin and Child*, while his page and horse wait below.

6. PLIQUE À JOUR. With this technique cloisons of translucent enamel were suspended in a network of gold strips, without backing metal, to give the effect of stained glass. Particularly associated with the courts of France and Burgundy from the late 14th century, the only surviving medieval example is the Mérode Cup (*c.* 1430; London, V&A).

7. PAINTED. In painted enamel, both sides of a piece of metal are covered with fired glass. This technique appears first to have been adopted for use in luxury secular objects at the courts of Burgundy and France. Whereas most medieval enamelling was undertaken to achieve colour, these early painted enamels are primarily grisaille, as in the Monkey Beaker (1425–50; New York, Cloisters).

At the end of the 15th century Limoges re-emerged as a principal centre for painted enamelling, championing the technique that once again used a copper plate as a support. By first coating the reverse of the plate with enamel, the artist could sketch the design on the front and then literally paint with glass on the front, enhancing the highly polished surface with 'gems' (*paillons*) of glass and gold paint. Commonly these works took the form of triptychs, with the enamels set in thin gilt frames. A central scene such as the Nativity or Crucifixion would often be flanked by single standing saints in the wings. Compositions are frequently indebted to contemporary engravings and printed books. Deep blues and purples dominate the palette. Both their subject-matter and their preciousness suggest that, like Books of Hours, these enamel triptychs were privately owned, devotional objects. Indeed, a Book of Hours in the Art Institute of Chicago from the collection of a Limousin family appears to be by the same artist, known as the Master of the Orleans Triptych, who created a number of painted enamels. The technique of the earliest examples appears to have been still in experimental stages, for many dating before about 1410 now show crizzling of the surface.

95. Goldenes Rössl, enamel *en ronde bosse* and silver gilt, h. 620 mm, from Paris, France, 1403–4 (Altötting, SS Philipp und Jakob, Schatzkammer)

BIBLIOGRAPHY

J. M. Soresinus: *De capitibus sanctorum Apostolorum Petri et Pauli in sacrosancto Lateranensi ecclesia Romae* (Rome, 1673)

T. Stapelton: 'A Brief Summary of the Wardrobe Accounts of the Tenth, Eleventh and Fourteenth Years of Edward the Second', *Archaeologia*, xxvi (1836), pp. 318–45

E. Rupin: *L'Oeuvre de Limoges* (Paris, 1890)

J.-J. Marquet de Vasselot: *Emaux limousins de la fin du XVe siècle et de la première partie du XVIe* (Paris, 1921)

C. Enlart: 'L'Emaillerie cloisonnée à Paris sous Philippe le Bel', *Mnmts Piot*, xxix (1927–8), pp. 1–97
V. Juaristi: *Esmaltes: Con especial mención de los españoles* (Barcelona, 1933)
M. C. Ross: 'Basse-taille Enamelling at Montpellier', *A. Q.* [Detroit], iv/1 (1941), pp. 32–9
A. M. Johnson: *Hispanic Silverwork* (New York, 1944)
I. Schroth: *Mittelalterliche Goldschmiedekunst am Oberrhein* (Freiburg im Breisgau, 1948)
M.-M. Gauthier: *Emaux limousins du XIIe au XIVe siècle* (Paris, 1950)
K. Guth-Dreyfus: *Transluzides Email in der ersten Hälfte des 14. Jahrhunderts am Ober-, Mittel- und Niederrhein*, Basl. Stud. Kstgesch., ix (Basle, 1954)
T. Müller and E. Steingräber: 'Die französische Goldemailplastik um 1400', *Münchn. Jb. Bild. Kst*, 3rd ser., iv (1954), pp. 29–79
A. Andersson: *Silberne Abendsmahlgeräte in Schweden aus dem XIV. Jahrhundert* (Stockholm, 1956)
E. G. Grimme: *Aachener Goldschmiedekunst im Mittelalter, von Karl dem Grossen bis zu Karl V* (Cologne, 1957)
U. Middeldorf: 'On the Origins of *émail sur ronde-bosse*', *Gaz. B.-A.*, 6th ser., lv (1960), pp. 233–44
S. Mihalik: *Old Hungarian Enamels* (Budapest, 1961)
E. Steingräber: 'Beiträge zur gotischen Goldschmiedekunst Frankreichs', *Pantheon*, xx (1962), pp. 156–66
——: 'Venezianische Goldschmiedekunst des 15. Jahrhunderts', *Mitt. Ksthist. Inst. Florenz*, x (1963), pp. 147–92
P. Michaels: 'Technical Observations on Early Painted Enamels of Limoges: Their Materials, Structure, Technique and Deterioration', *J. Walters A.G.*, xxvii–xxviii (1964–5), pp. 21–43
Enamels: The XII to the XVI Century (exh. cat. by D. F. Rowe, Chicago, IL, Loyola U., D'Arcy Gal., 1970)
M.-M. Gauthier: *Emaux du moyen âge occidental* (Fribourg, 1972)
J. Adhémar: 'Les Tombeaux de la collection Gaignières: Dessins d'archéologie du XVIIe siècle', *Gaz. B.-A.*, lxxxiv (1974), pp. 3–192; lxxxviii (1976), pp. 3–88
Les Fastes du Gothique: Le Siècle de Charles V (exh. cat., Paris, Grand Pal., 1981–2), pp. 220–24
C. Blair and M. Campbell: 'The Little Golden Horse of Altötting', *Conn. A.*, xxvii (April 1982), pp. 34–45
J. M. Fritz: *Goldschmiedekunst der Gotik in Mitteleuropa* (Munich, 1982)
M. Campbell: *An Introduction to Medieval Enamels* (London, 1983)
D. Gaborit-Chopin: 'Les Collections d'orfèvrerie des princes français au milieu du XVIe siècle d'après les comptes et inventaires', *Hommage à Hubert Landais: Art, objets d'art, collections* (Paris, 1987), pp. 46–52
'Oreficerie e smalti translucidi nel secolo XIV e XV', *Boll. A.*, xliii [suppl.] (1987)
J. Cherry: 'Heraldry as Decoration in the Thirteenth Century', *England in the Thirteenth Century*, ed. W. M. Ormrod, Harlaxton Medieval Studies, i (Stamford, 1991), pp. 123–34
D. Gaborit-Chopin: 'The Reliquary of Elizabeth of Hungary at The Cloisters', *The Cloisters: Studies in Honor of the Fiftieth Anniversary* (New York, 1992), pp. 326–53
J. Stratford: *The Bedford Inventories: The Worldly Goods of John, Duke of Bedford, Regent of France (1389–1425)* (London, 1993)

BARBARA DRAKE BOEHM

VII. Ivories.

In the 13th and 14th centuries there was a profound change in ivory-carving, the result of both stylistic developments common to all the arts and of significant changes in the working conditions of ivory-carvers. From the 13th century elephant ivory, which had been difficult to obtain in the 11th and 12th centuries, and remained very precious, came to the West in larger quantities, mainly through the Atlantic coastal ports (*see also* IVORY, §1). There could now be abundant production of both religious and secular pieces; and some of the numerous free-standing statuettes were of large size, for example the Herlufsholm *Christ* (h. 720 mm; Næstved, Herlufsholm Skole; see fig. 96) and the *Virgin* by Giovanni Pisano (h. 530 mm; Pisa, Mus. Opera Duomo).

Scholarly interest in Gothic ivories is a fairly recent phenomenon, and despite numerous specialized studies, the fundamental work remains that of Raymond Koechlin (1924). His catalogue is the standard reference work (here indicated by K followed by a number).

96. Herlufsholm *Christ*, ivory Crucifix figure, h. 720 mm, from Denmark, *c.* 1220–30 (Næstved, Herlufsholm Skole)

1. Craft organization. 2. Chronological survey.

1. CRAFT ORGANIZATION. The craft of ivory-carving began to be properly organized from the 13th century when stalls and shops collected around St-Germain-l'Auxerrois and the Rue Saint-Denis. About 1260–70, the *Livre des métiers* of ÉTIENNE BOILEAU mentioned, among the craftsmen who were allowed to work in ivory, the makers of combs ('peingniers') and lanterns ('lanterniers'), of writing tablets ('tabletiers'), of dice, draughts and chess pieces ('déciers'), of knife handles, buttons, buckles and paternoster beads ('patenostriers'), and also haberdashers ('merciers') and especially painters and 'tailleurs d'ymages', who carved wood, stone, bone, horn, ivory and 'toute matière de peinture', and 'ymagiers tailleurs' and 'ceux qui taillent crucefis', who were also authorized to carve bone, ivory, wood etc.

References in accounts and inventories of princely or ecclesiastical treasuries indicate that most surviving Gothic ivories (statuettes of the Virgin, Christ or the saints, tabernacles, diptychs, triptychs, mirror-cases, caskets etc) were made by the painters' and carvers' guilds, even though documents are very rare for the 13th century and give only an incomplete view. Among the principal suppliers of ivories can be noted: Renault the goldsmith, the haberdashers Jehan le Frizon and Jehan le Scelleur, the goldsmith Jehan le Braelier, the carver Jehan Aubert and the 'tabletier' and 'pinguier' Jean Girost, who in 1377 sold

26 livres of ivory for one of the Duke of Burgundy's sculptors, Jean de Marville. It would, however, be wrong to reduce Gothic ivories to a branch of monumental sculpture: although they are certainly linked with it, ivories have their own pattern of evolution, iconography, canons and even style. Even though the large ivory statuettes of the second half of the 13th century were probably carved by the best sculptors, or at least in their circle, they are never reduced versions of sculpture in stone or marble. Also influenced by painting, they were enhanced by delicate colouring, which, when it was not brutally cleaned or restored in the 19th and 20th centuries, has usually left only traces. It is also known through inventory descriptions that the mounting on ivory of jewelled or enamelled examples of the goldsmith's craft was considered one of the precious arts.

2. CHRONOLOGICAL SURVEY. In the Romanesque period there had been centres of ivory-carving all over Europe, and in the 13th and 14th centuries production no doubt continued in the main ones. From the mid-13th century, however, Paris became predominant, and Parisian styles were so much imitated that it is difficult to identify 'non-Parisian' ivories. The pre-eminence of Paris was encouraged by the accessibility of the material through the Channel ports and a cultural milieu in which monumental sculpture, illumination and goldsmiths' work all flourished. Further impetus was provided by commissions from the royal entourage, some members of which were great enthusiasts for precious objects, especially in the 14th century.

(i) First half of the 13th century. (ii) The 'Soissons' group. (iii) Parisian style in the middle and second half of the 13th century. (iv) First half of the 14th century. (v) Parisian style in the second half of the 14th century. (vi) Non-Parisian workshops.

*(i) First half of the 13th century.*The first manifestations of a Gothic style appear in Late Romanesque ivories of contested date and provenance, such as the *Corpus* (Oslo, Kstindustmus.), which is sometimes associated with the cross (New York, Cloisters), possibly from Bury St Edmunds, *c.* 1140, or the small relief of the *Rest on the Flight into Egypt* (New York, Met.), attributed to England but with undeniable affiliations to the monumental sculpture of the Ile-de-France *c.* 1170–90. Yet the first works clearly dependent on the MULDENFALTENSTIL (trough style) originated in northern Europe. The Herlufsholm *Christ* (K 15) is the uncontested masterpiece of this tendency. This crucifix figure (see fig. 96) is of Danish origin, belonging to a group all of the same provenance (Horne Book cover; *Adoration of the Magi*; both Copenhagen, Nmus.), but it also shows affinities to French sculpture of the first half of the 13th century (Chartres Cathedral, transept portals; *Christ* from Cérisiers, Sens Cathedral).

Several statuettes of the enthroned Virgin and Child testify to the growth of Marian worship during this period and are variously adapted, from the iconographic type of the *sedes sapientiae* (Throne of Wisdom) to that of the *Vierge de tendresse*: for example a *Virgin and Child* (*c.* 1230; Hamburg, Mus. Kst & Gew., K 5) from the Meuse region or England, the *Virgin of Ourscamp* (Paris, Petit Pal., K 7) and a *Virgin and Child* (Paris, Mus. Cluny, K 8), probably a little later and closer to mid-century Gothic. A parallel tendency, the 'Block-style', characterized by very elaborate geometricization, is represented by figures of the Virgin in the Art Institute of Chicago, the Walters Art Gallery, Baltimore, and to a lesser degree in a type of Virgin like that in the Louvre (Paris, Louvre, K 22), perhaps from the workshops of northern France or the northern Ile-de-France. The *Virgin of Aulne* (Namur, Trésor Hugo d'Oignies, K 4), connected to this geometric tendency but slighter and more subtle, should also be compared to the so-called 'Soissons' group (*see* §(ii) below), which developed in the second half of the 13th century.

(ii) The 'Soissons' group. Most of the diptychs and triptychs dated to the 13th century or the beginning of the 14th are gathered together under this name, around a diptych originating from St-Jean-des-Vignes in Soissons (London, V&A, K 38). The group is heterogeneous, the production of many workshops: the workshop of the Soissons Diptych and Baltimore Diptych (Baltimore, MD, Walters A.G., K 40); that of the Berlin Diptych (Berlin, ex-Kaiser-Friedrich Mus., K 39); and the workshop of two diptychs (St Petersburg, Hermitage, K 34; Rome, Vatican, Mus. Sacro, K 37), the Salting Leaf (London, V&A, K 36), the Lyon Triptych (Lyon, Mus. B.-A., K 55) and the knop of a crosier (Antwerp, Mus. Mayer van den Bergh) from the treasury of Beauvais Cathedral. These ivories are mainly devoted to representations, in niches with turrets and gables pierced by oculi, of animated scenes of the Infancy of Christ and the Passion, most often with tall, slender figures, whose simply draped mantles are treated with broad surfaces.

The style appears to be related both to manuscript illumination and goldsmiths' work from northern France, and to the Paris milieu. The higher-quality members of the group can be dated between 1250 and 1280, but some pieces, such as the Berlin Diptych, could have been carved at the end of the century. The *Liberal Arts* cup (K 1243) in the treasury of Milan Cathedral, whose reliefs evoke monumental Bolognese sculpture from the first half of the 14th century, should no longer be regarded as part of the Soissons group.

(iii) Parisian style in the middle and second half of the 13th century. This was the period when Parisian ivory work became predominant, and it coincided with the full development of the Gothic style in all media. The main characteristics of the figure style were the elegant poses, exuberant 'beak-fold' drapery and sharply delineated, smiling faces that were first established in monumental sculpture. The bulk of ivory production was devoted to statuettes, which were sometimes very large (taking into account the limitations of the material), and they were closely related to manuscript illumination and monumental sculpture. Despite attempts to limit their dating between 1240 and 1270, is seems clear that, as in monumental sculpture, this stylistic trend persisted up to the reign of Philip IV (*reg* 1285–1314).

Although 'tailleurs de crucifix' were authorized to carve ivory, very few figures of the crucified Christ survive. The very softly modelled figure in the Metropolitan Museum, New York, could be dated *c.* 1250, but it remains fairly isolated. Those in Nuremberg (Nuremberg, Ger. Nmus.)

and Florence (Florence, Bargello), with a more broken outline and taller proportions, are later: the Florence *Christ*, a sorrowful figure of impressive quality, is still fixed to its metallic cross, dated by its decoration *c.* 1270–80.

Statuettes of the Virgin and Child, standing or seated, are by far the most numerous. The *Virgin and Child* of Zwettl Abbey in Austria (*in situ*, K 62), accompanied by appliqué figures, probably once fixed to the wings of the wooden tabernacle that enclosed it, is one of the rare dated pieces: it was brought back to Zwettl *de partibus superioris Franciae* by Abbot Bohuslaw (*reg* 1248–59). Unfortunately, however, the heads of the *Virgin* and *Christ Child* have been remade. The Sainte-Chapelle *Virgin and Child* (Paris, Louvre, K 95; see fig. 97) belongs to the same stylistic current as that of Zwettl. It is mentioned in an inventory of the treasury of the Sainte-Chapelle in Paris, written between 1265 and 1279. Its elegant proportions and authoritative pose, the charming triangular face with a slightly ironic smile, and the power and harmony of the large 'beak' folds of its mantle, animated by a lightly turning pose, seem to have occasioned immediate admiration. A work of exceptional quality, destined for the chapel of the royal palace, it appears to have been a kind of model, to which a whole group of Virgin and Child statuettes of the second half of the 13th century (e.g. Orléans, Mus. Hist. & Archéol. Orléanais, K 73; New York, Met., K 74; Amsterdam, Rijksmus., K 98; Paris, Louvre, K 96; Kortrijk, Jesuit Church) refers more or less faithfully. Despite their reduced dimensions, they reflect the smiling ease and subtlety of the Sainte-Chapelle *Virgin* and the turning movement of her mantle. Other statuettes, however, are more clearly dissociated from this prestigious model: the large *Virgin and Child* in the treasury of Toledo Cathedral (K 107) is in a more geometric style, and around 1250–70 the workshop of a *Nativity* plaque (Paris, Louvre, K 33) and of figures of the *Virgin and Child* (Paris, Louvre, K 79; Paris, Mus. Cluny, K 80; Caen, Mus. B.-A., K 67) was strongly influenced by the style of the reliefs on the north portal of Notre-Dame, Paris.

Some statuettes with round, smiling faces framed by long locks of tightly curled hair, and slightly sharp drapery (figures of the *Virgin and Child*, New York, Met., K 109; Raleigh, NC, Mus. A.; Paris, Louvre, K 623; torso of a *Virgin*, Baltimore, MD, Walters A.G.) form a coherent group datable to the last quarter of the century, and show the influence of eastern France. This is even more apparent in the *Virgin* from the former Mège collection (Paris, Louvre, K 100), which demonstrates that a provincial, but nevertheless very conscientious, version of the Sainte-Chapelle type of Virgin could still be produced at the end of the 13th century or beginning of the 14th.

While some of these statuettes could have been set off by adornments in precious metal (e.g. the Sainte-Chapelle *Virgin*) or integrated into tabernacles (e.g. the Zwettl *Virgin*, Tournai Cathedral *Virgin*), others were members of figure groups, probably set in an architectural frame. Thus the *Virgin and Child* from Saint-Denis Abbey (Cincinnati, OH, Taft Mus., K 97) was formerly flanked by two angels carrying candlesticks (Rouen Cathedral Treasury, K 718) and crowned by a small angel. Some of these large ivory ensembles survive, at least in part

97. *Virgin and Child*, ivory, h. 410 mm, from the Sainte-Chapelle, Paris, *c.* 1250–70 (Paris, Musée du Louvre)

(*Annunciation* figures, *Coronation of the Virgin*, Paris, Louvre, K 20, 16), the most remarkable being that of the *Descent from the Cross*, which still includes three principal statuettes, to which should be added the figures of *Ecclesia* and a *Nicodemus* (transformed into a prophet by restoration; Paris, Louvre, K 19, 19 bis, 18). Giovanni Pisano's Pisa *Virgin and Child* (Pisa, Mus. Opera Duomo) was also part of a group.

Apart from the large 'Soissons' group (*see* §(ii) above), bas-reliefs dating before 1300 are rare: for example the diptych of *Christ the Judge* (New York, Cloisters), by the workshop of the Baltimore–London Diptych (Baltimore, MD, Walters A.G., and London, Wallace, K 235); and *Christ the Judge* (Paris, Louvre, K 775). In the last decades of the century or *c.* 1300, the triptych from Saint-Sulpice-du-Tarn (Paris, Mus. Cluny, K 203) is a significant transitional piece, uniting the qualities of the 'Soissons' group bas-reliefs with those of statuettes of the third quarter of the 13th century. The centre panel of the triptych, with the *Crucifixion* and *Virgin in Glory*, is carved in very high relief while the wings are carved with *New Testament* scenes in flatter relief. Although certain aspects of the work are still very close to contemporary or earlier sculpture (e.g. proportions of the figures, exuberant 'beak-fold' drapery), there are also stylistic novelties, such as apron-like cross folds, flattened draperies, the use of sinuous lines and volutes, and facial types, that anticipate 14th-century developments. Only the central part of a triptych representing the *Crucifixion* (London, Wallace, K 229) can rival that of the Saint-Sulpice-du-Tarn Triptych or even surpass it, but other transitional triptychs and tabernacles survive from the last decades of the 13th century, their more conservative centre panels contrasting with the style of their wings. The style clearly shows links with diptychs of the first half of the 14th century (e.g. tabernacles in London, V&A, K 154; St Petersburg, Hermitage, K 172; Toledo, OH, Mus. A., K 165).

One of the most charming expressions of ivory work during the reigns of Philip IV and his sons was provided by secular ivories: mirror-cases illustrated among other themes scenes of courtly life, such as the *Crowning of a Lover* (London, V&A, K 1002), chess games perhaps alluding to the *Roman de Tristan et Yseult* (Paris, Louvre, K 1053; London, V&A, K 1046), and a royal family evoking Solomon and the Queen of Sheba (Paris, Mus. Cluny, K 1057). Several 'composite' caskets group scenes from different romances, especially from the *Romans de la Table Ronde* (e.g. Baltimore, MD, Walters A.G., K 1281; London, V&A, K 1282; New York, Met., K 1284). The smiling figures, with round cheeks and delicate features, dressed in long, ample gowns, are worked in a soft, delicate style, which reflects both contemporary monumental sculpture and the illumination of Master Honoré.

98. Ivory triptych showing the *Virgin in Glory*, h. 330 mm, from France, *c.* 1320–30 (Angers, Hôtel Pincé)

(iv) First half of the 14th century. Although it has been assumed that the fashion for large statuettes declined in the 14th century, examples still exist. Several free-standing figures of the *Virgin and Child*, standing or seated, can be dated between *c.* 1300 and *c.* 1330. Deeply grooved 'beak folds' persisted, but were now associated with a general flattening of volumes; and slightly heavy faces with pointed noses and prominent chins became characteristic. In seated figures of the Virgin the torso was extremely elongated (e.g. Baltimore, MD, Walters A.G.; New York, Met.; London, V&A), a characteristic shared by the Villeneuve-lès-Avignon *Virgin and Child* (Villeneuve-lès-Avignon, Collégiale, Treasury, K 103), whose round, serene face nevertheless suggests a different workshop. This large statuette (h. 450 mm), which retains many traces of superb polychromy, is thought to have been given to the former collegiate church of Notre-Dame by Cardinal Arnaud de Via (*d* 1335).

Sharper-featured and more at ease than the Virgin figures mentioned above, the *Virgin in Glory* (Virgin and Child between two angels) of the Angers Triptych (Angers, Hôtel Pincé, K 117; see fig. 98) belongs to this trend, although the influence of the type of the Saint-Sulpice-du-Tarn Triptych is still apparent. On the other hand, with the tabernacle (Paris, Louvre, K 156), whose wing reliefs are strongly comparable to those of the tabernacles mentioned above (*see* §(iii) above), the head of the *Virgin* on the central panel is free-standing, with a well-delineated nose and chin. The short mantle is draped crosswise and the Virgin's silhouette is framed in the swirling cascades of her garments, a trait characteristic of French work in the second quarter of the 14th century.

The quality of workmanship and the technique of openwork ivory give the appliqué scenes of the Passion a special place in ivory production of the first third of the 14th century. In addition to figures of *Christ* and a *Tormenter* (Paris, Louvre, K 224, 225) from a *Flagellation* scene, five reliefs or fragments of reliefs are known: *Arrest of Christ* (Paris, Louvre, K 223); *Mocking of Christ* (Antwerp, Mus. Mayer van den Bergh, K 226); *Descent from the Cross* (New York, Met., K 227); *Descent from the Cross* (Oslo, Kstindustmus., K 227 bis); *Holy Women at the Tomb* (London, V&A, K 228). These appliqué fragments in high relief, intended to be fixed on a backing of contrasting colour or of precious metal, are the remains of altarpieces designed like contemporary examples in marble or stone. The style of some of the figures derives from the broad, flatter manner of the wings of the Saint-Sulpice-du-Tarn Triptych, but the elegance, and the graceful drapery, of the *Arrest of Christ*, the *Mocking of Christ* or even the Oslo *Descent from the Cross* suggest a relationship to the illumination of Jean Pucelle. The large appliqué *Christ* from the former Homberg collection (Paris, Louvre, K 736), which comes from a book cover, is close to this series, although the *Tormenter* and the *Flagellation* figures and the reliefs of the New York *Descent from the Cross* and the London *Holy Women* (the latter treated in a heavier style) are from different workshops.

Heavy production of Parisian ivories continued through the second quarter of the century. The style of several workshops can be distinguished despite their strong attachment to formulae perfected a generation before and their stereotyped iconography. These include the workshop of the triptych formerly in the Martin Le Roy collection (K 210); the triptych (K 211) and the *Passion* diptych (K 240; both Amiens, Bib. Mun.); the Baltimore Diptych (Baltimore, MD, Walters A.G., K 569); and the diptych with rows of arcades (Paris, Louvre, K 292). The Master of the Mège Diptych (*c.* 1340–50; Paris, Louvre, K 537), who endowed his figures with dignified, well-structured faces and sinuous outlines clothed in supple drapery, was one of the most interesting personalities of this period (ivories in Paris, Louvre; Baltimore, MD, Walters A.G.; London, Wallace).

Free-standing figures, more carefully worked and more elaborate, dominate Parisian production: the dreamy *Virgin and Child* (Assisi, Tesoro Mus. Basilica S Francesco), mentioned in an inventory in 1370, is dated by her cape-like mantle, broadened outline and thinner profile to *c.* 1320–40. The same characteristics appear in the *Virgin and Child* of Noyon (Paris, Louvre, K 630), while the *St Margaret* issuing from the dragon's back (London, BM, K 709) adopts the iconography used in enamelled goldsmiths' work. A masterpiece of grace and tenderness, the *Virgin and Child* of the dukes of Tuscany (Florence, Bargello, K 633) can be compared to the finest monumental statues of the second quarter of the century or to the silver gilt *Virgin* (Paris, Louvre; see fig. 86 above) offered to Saint-Denis Abbey in 1339 by Joanna of Evreux, Queen of France; however, the skilful simplicity of its back drapery and the elasticity of the skin of her face could indicate a later date, *c.* 1370–80, in the sphere of André Beauneveu.

Probably carved in the same workshops as religious ivories, secular ivories diversified their traditional themes and introduced new ones: for example mirror-cases with courtly scenes and the assault of the Castle of Love; 'composite' caskets (e.g. Kraków, Cathedral Mus., K 1285; Florence, Bargello, K 1286), which are related to the workshop of the diptych with rows of arcades (K 292); caskets illustrating a single romance, such as those of the *Châtelaine de Vergy*; as well as other practical objects, including gravers, writing tablets and knife handles.

(v) Parisian style in the second half of the 14th century. It was in these secular works that the distinct change in fashions of dress, which occurred around the middle of the 14th century, appeared: long, flowing robes were replaced by tight-fitting gowns with split sleeves, fitted cloaks or short tunics held at the hips by a belt (e.g. the writing tablet with games of *hautes coquilles* and *la grenouille*, Paris, Louvre, K 1173). The religious ivories datable between 1350 and 1380, however, remained faithful to traditional types, although the style was modified: outlines were broadened by large, swirling falls of drapery, as in the group of the Bologna Diptych (Bologna, Mus. Civ., K 539), and iconography was developed, with the multiplication of scenes and figures under rows of small arches, as in the sizable group of 'large Passion diptychs', probably contemporary with Charles V (*reg* 1364–80). There, close, dense drapery folds, still in the tradition of the second quarter of the century, contrast with the attempt to individualize faces that characterized the second half of the century. This 'naturalistic' tendency, though rarely employed in ivories, is evident in the plaques illustrating the *Lives of Saints* (Paris, Mus. Cluny, K 344, 345), which share the thin silhouettes and bony faces that also appear in manuscript illumination made for Charles V (*see* §IV, 5(x) above).

Although ivories were frequently mentioned in the inventories of the collections of Charles V and his brother Jean, Duc de Berry, few of those pieces can be identified, but some statuettes give an idea of the ivories that made up these fabulous treasuries: the *Angel* (New York, Met., K 852); *St Catherine* (Paris, Louvre, K 847); a Burgundian *Trinity* (Houston, TX, Mus. F.A., Strauss Col.); an ivory and jet *Virgin* (Burgos, Cathedral Treasury of Condestable Chapel); later *Virgin* (Baltimore, MD, Walters A.G., K 982). Fewer works of the second half of the 14th century are now attributable to Parisian workshops than of the first half, and the civil wars in France, especially during the reign of Charles VI (*reg* 1380–1422), and the disturbances that ravaged Paris at this time brought about the dispersal or disappearance of Parisian ivory workshops. The principal source of the little-known ivory work from well on in the 15th century was no longer the Ile-de-France but the Loire Valley, Flanders, Burgundy, Italy or the Germanic lands.

(vi) Non-Parisian workshops. Owing to the perceived dominance of Paris in the production of Gothic ivories, scholars have been hesitant to identify 'non-Parisian' ivories, and this perception explains the uncertainties involved in the attribution of some works, for example the pieces belonging to the 'Soissons' group, certain 'followers' of the Sainte-Chapelle *Virgin* or some 14th-century secular ivories. On the other hand, from the mid-14th century, the presence in Parisian court circles of numerous artists from the Netherlands or the Rhineland introduced many outside influences, so that, for example,

the origins of the *Virgin in Glory* triptych (Berlin, Altes Mus., K 120), one of the most beautiful creations of the 14th century, in which the type of Virgin anticipates that of the *Schönen Madonnen*, can be placed either in France under strong German influence, or in a Rhenish milieu with knowledge of French style.

(a) England. Some secular ivories have been recognized as English. These include several chess pieces (New York, Met.; Compiègne, Mus. Mun. Vivenel; Oxford, Ashmolean; London, V&A) and a mirror-case (Oxford, Ashmolean, K 990). Moreover, one of the finest 13th-century figures of *Christ* (*c.* 1270–80; London, V&A, K 738 bis) can be taken as English, despite its closeness to French models, as can several enthroned Virgin figures with tiered drapery (e.g. New Haven, CT, Yale U. A.G.; New York, Cloisters), which are comparable to carved limestone figures at Glastonbury Abbey (Glastonbury Abbey Mus.). But the most incontestable examples of English ivories are the Salting Diptych (London, V&A, K 113 B) and the triptychs and (?)polyptych (London, BM, K 272 A) executed *c.* 1330–40 for John Grandisson, Bishop of Exeter (*reg* 1328–69), the latter also showing knowledge of contemporary Sienese art.

(b) Italy. The Pisa *Virgin and Child* (Pisa, Mus. Opera Duomo) is a dated statuette of assured provenance, carved by Giovanni Pisano *c.* 1298. The contracts for the work and the cathedral inventories indicate that it was part of an ensemble. Very close in style to Pisano's monumental figures, it nonetheless shows the surprising influence of Parisian Gothic (e.g. the type of Virgin on the north portal of Notre-Dame and ivory statuettes). Two other ivory statuettes of the crucified *Christ* (London, V&A; see fig. 99; priv. col.) and, to a lesser degree, the figure of an *Apostle* (Baltimore, MD, Walters A.G., K 717) have been linked with Pisano or his workshop, confirming the importance of ivory work in Tuscany.

Traditionally used for the so-called 'siculo-arabic' crosiers in the 12th and 13th centuries, ivory was joined in the 14th century by bone for making large crosiers with architectural knops and great palmette volutes, set off with gilding, painting and inscriptions. Most of the surviving examples (London, V&A; Florence, Bargello; Siena, Mus. Opera Duomo) were intended for churches in central Italy. From this tradition issued the output of the EMBRIACHI workshop in Genoa, Florence and then Venice from the end of the 14th century until 1433, which specialized in large ensembles of wooden inlay, enclosing panels composed of small plaques of bone carved in low relief with coloured highlights. Some of these ensembles could be of impressive size such as the altarpieces in the charterhouse of Pavia, donated by Giangaleazzo Visconti, and that from Poissy Abbey, made for Jean, Duc de Berry (now Paris, Louvre). The success of the Embriachi inspired many imitations, including a group of state saddles which, from their inscriptions in Latin, Italian or German, seem to have come from northern Italy or the Tyrol, some perhaps from Hungary. They are covered with small plaques, engraved or in very low relief.

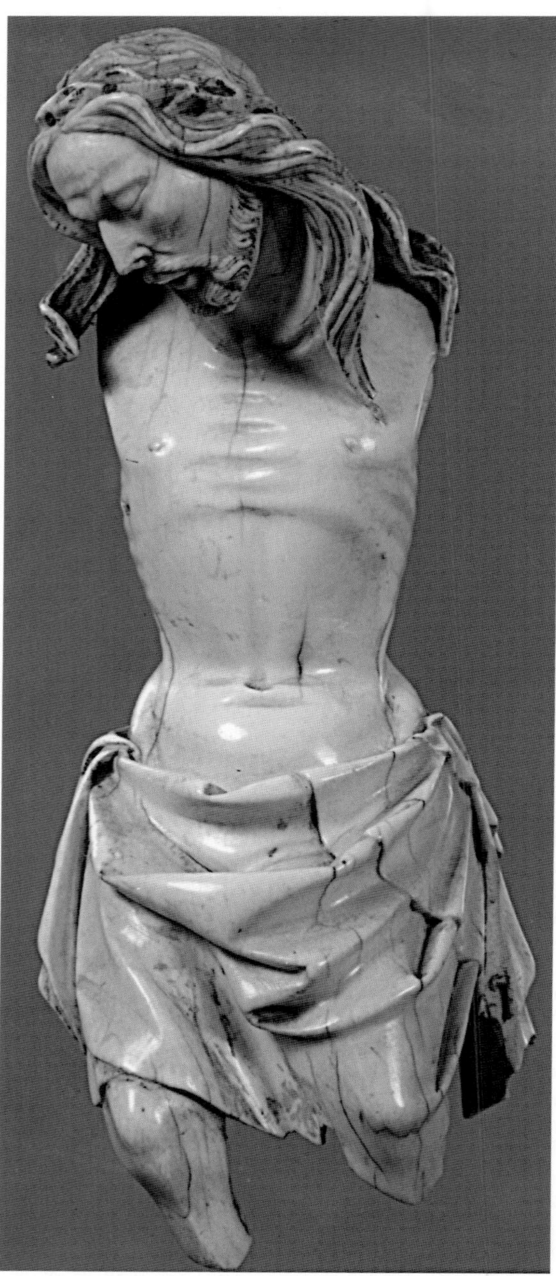

99. Giovanni Pisano (attrib.): *Christ*, ivory Crucifix figure, h. 152 mm, from Tuscany, Italy, *c.* 1300 (London, Victoria and Albert Museum)

(c) Rhineland and Meuse region. The attribution of ivories to the Meuse region or the Rhineland remains more subject to caution. A Mosan (or possibly English) origin has been suggested for the Hamburg *Virgin* (*see* §(i) above). A series of 14th-century Virgin and Child statuettes is clearly distinguishable from Parisian production: generally of great size and fairly static, the figures have the same solid and impassive face (e.g. Cologne, Wallraf-

Richartz-Mus., K 658; Munich, Bayer. Nmus., K 659; Amsterdam, Hist. Mus., K 667; Copenhagen, Nmus., K 696). The iconography of one example (New York, Met., K 701), where the *Virgin* holds a cradle on her knees, links them to the Rhineland or the south Netherlands, regions where worship of the cradle of the Christ Child was widespread.

A group of diptychs close to that of the *Adoration of the Magi* (Paris, Louvre, K 488 bis), treated in a carefully worked and very refined style, is probably Mosan. It differs from the attractive Cologne Gothic in which French influence is more marked, one of the best examples of which is provided by the small *St Martin* diptych (Cleveland, OH, Mus. A.): the three bishops represented on one of its leaves can be associated with Cologne sculpture of the 1340s. The very closely related ivory booklet (London, V&A) is decorated with scenes painted by a north German illuminator. Although Morey (1936) suggested that in the Crucifixion scenes of certain diptychs the stream of blood or the sword springing from Christ's side to touch the heart of the Virgin shows some Rhenish or Italian influence, this iconography was already known in the Parisian milieu in the first quarter of the 14th century, and it does not in itself affirm the German origin of an ivory.

A group of very high-quality secular ivories of the first decades of the 14th century could be linked to Rhenish Gothic. It includes a series of mirror-cases (London, V&A, K 1018, 1034, 1044; Florence, Bargello, K 993; Naples, Mus. N. S Martino, K 994) and a small plaque (ex-Kaiser-Friedrich Mus., Berlin, K 1187) decorated with courtly scenes and, above all, the beautiful casket with amorous couples in the treasury of St Ursula, Cologne: graceful figures dressed in long, supple robes, their hair held by bands encrusted with precious stones (the group with jewelled headbands) could be Parisian, but the emphasis on their hair and smiles and the preciousness of their poses have more parallels in the contemporary art of Cologne.

All the same, there is some doubt over the Parisian origin of many works of the second half or end of the 14th century, which are characterized by broad draperies, an unaccustomed fullness of form and very full faces, as found in a series of figures of the *Virgin and Child* (Dijon, Mus. B.-A., K 676; Prague Cathedral Treasury, K 627; Kraków, Czartoryski Col., K 698; Florence, Bargello, K 699). The same elements are found in a coherent series of *Virgin and Child* figures (Baltimore, MD, Walters A.G.; Berlin, Altes Mus., K 844; Toledo, OH, Mus. A.; London, V&A; Langenhorst, Augustinian Convent; Compiègne, Mus. Mun. Vivenel; St Petersburg, Hermitage), with complicated and fragmented, but very elegant, draperies, and chubby faces with fine features, which are delicately cut using a drill.

These statuettes are close to the 'Kremsmünster workshop', a very prolific but perhaps heterogeneous shop named after the diptych of the *Crucifixion* and *Adoration of the Magi* (K 824) preserved in the Kremsmünster Abbey Treasury since at least the 18th century. These ivories (see fig. 100) have dense compositions of chubby-faced figures in theatrical poses, their fine features delineated with a drill. The figures are clothed in garments with complex folds, with long, agitated surfaces and jagged falls of twisting drapery. The architectural elements include rows of arches, 'masonry' walls, rosette friezes, billet work and pierced quatrefoils. The iconography frequently breaks with tradition. This very distinct style appears to represent a reaction to certain tendencies in French art of *c.* 1400, as in the *Virgin* of the Goldenes Rössl (Paris, 1403; Altötting, SS Philip & Jakob, Schatzkam.; *see* §VI, 5 above). Affinities with the style of Madern Gerthener in the Commemoration Portal of Mainz Cathedral (*c.* 1425) give some idea of a possible origin.

100. *The Passion*, detail from an ivory diptych, h. 220 mm, from ?the Rhineland, early 15th century (Berlin, Dahlem, Skulpturensammlung)

BIBLIOGRAPHY

GENERAL

R. Koechlin: *Les Ivoires gothiques français*, 3 vols (Paris, 1924) [K]

H. Schnitzler, P. Bloch and W. F. Volbach: *Skulpturen Elfenbein, Perlmutter, Stein, Holz: Europäisches Mittelalter: Sammlung E. und M. Kofler-Truniger Luzern*, i (Lucerne, 1964)

D. Gaborit-Chopin: *Ivoires du moyen âge occidental* (Fribourg, 1978)

P. Williamson: *An Introduction to Medieval Ivory Carvings* (London, 1982)

R. H. Randall jr: *Masterpieces of Ivory from the Walters Art Gallery* (Baltimore, 1985)

Musée du Louvre: Nouvelles acquisitions du Département des objets d'art, 1980–1984 (exh. cat., Paris, Louvre, 1985)

Songs of Glory: Medieval Art from 900 to 1500 (exh. cat., Oklahoma City, OK, Mus. A., 1985)

P. Williamson: *The Thyssen-Bornemisza Collection: Medieval Sculpture and Works of Art* (London, 1987), pp. 110–41

L. Martini and C. Rizzardi: *Avori bizantini e medievali nel Museo Nazionale di Ravenna* (Ravenna, 1990)

Musée du Louvre: Nouvelles acquisitions du Département des objets d'art, 1985–1989 (exh. cat., Paris, Louvre, 1990)

R. H. Randall jr: *The Golden Age of Ivory: Gothic Carvings in North American Collections* (New York, 1993)

SPECIALIST STUDIES

C. R. Morey: 'A Group of Gothic Ivories in the Walters Art Gallery', *A. Bull.*, xviii (1936), pp. 199–212

B. de Montesquiou-Fezensac: 'Le Reliquaire de Saint-Romain', *Mnmts Hist. France*, n. s., ii (1956), pp. 137–41

P. B. Cott: *Siculo-Arabic Ivories* (Princeton, NJ, 1959)

F. Deuchler, ed.: *The New Year 1200: A Background Survey* (New York, 1970)

The Year 1200 (exh. cat., ed. K. Hoffman; New York, Met., 1970)

A. Andersson: 'The Holy Rood of Skokloster and the Scandinavian Early Gothic', *Burl. Mag.*, cxii (1970), pp. 132–40

J. Pope-Hennessy: *An Ivory by Giovanni Pisano* (London, 1971)

R. Suckale: *Studien zu Stilbildung und Stilwandel der Madonnestatuen der Ile-de-France, zwischen 1230 und 1300* (diss., U. Munich, 1971)

D. Gaborit-Chopin: 'La Vierge à l'Enfant d'ivoire de la Sainte-Chapelle', *Bull. Mnmtl*, cxxx (1972), pp. 213–24

M. Seidel: 'Die Elfenbeinmadonna im Domschatz zu Pisa', *Mitt. Ksthist. Inst. Florenz*, xvi (1972), pp. 1–50

W. D. Wixom: 'Twelve Additions to the Medieval Treasury', *Bull. Cleveland Mus. A.* (April 1972), pp. 95–101

L'Art et la cour/Art and the Courts: France and England from 1259 to 1328 (exh. cat., Ottawa, N.G., 1972)

R. H. Randall jr: 'A Monumental Ivory', *Gatherings in Honor of Dorothy E. Miner* (Baltimore, 1974), pp. 283–300

P. Verdier: 'La Trinité debout de Champmol', *Etudes d'art français offertes à Charles Sterling* (Paris, 1975), pp. 65–90

The Year 1200. A Symposium: New York, 1975

Avori gotici francesi (exh. cat., Milan, Mus. Poldi Pezzoli, 1976)

J. Eisler: 'Zu den Fragen der Beinsättel des ungarischen Nationalmuseums', *Fol. Archaeol.*, xxviii (1977), pp. 189–209; xxx (1979), pp. 205–44

W. H. Monroe: 'An Early Gothic French Ivory of the Virgin and Child', *Mus. Stud.*, ix (1978), pp. 7–29

C. T. Little: 'Ivoire et art gothique français', *Rev. A.*, xlvi (1979), pp. 58–67

R. H. Randall jr: 'A Parisian Ivory Carver', *J. Walters A.G.*, xxxviii (1980), pp. 60–9

Les Fastes du Gothique: Le Siècle de Charles V (exh. cat., Paris, Grand Pal., 1981)

P. Verdier: 'Le Triptyque d'ivoire à volets peints au Musée des beaux-arts de Lyon', *Bul. Mus. & Mnmts Lyon.*, vii/2 (1982), pp. 17–30

D. Gaborit-Chopin: 'Une Vierge d'ivoire du XIIIe siècle', *Rev. Louvre* (1983), pp. 270–9

N. Stratford: 'Glastonbury and Two Gothic Ivories', *Studies in Medieval Sculpture*, ed. F. H. Thompson, Soc. Antiqua. London, Occas. Pap., n. s., iii (1983), pp. 208–16

M. Seidel: '*Opus Heburneum*: Die Entdeckung einer Elfenbeinskulptur von Giovanni Pisano', *Pantheon*, xlii (1984), pp. 219–29

The Age of Chivalry: Art in Plantagenet England, 1200–1400 (exh. cat., ed. J. Alexander and P. Binski; London, RA, 1987); review by W. Sauerländer in *Burl. Mag.*, cxxx/2 (1988), pp. 149–50

Le Trésor de Saint-Denis (exh. cat., ed. D. Gaborit-Chopin; Paris, Louvre, 1991)

M. Gibson: *The Liverpool Ivories* (Liverpool, 1994)

DANIELLE GABORIT-CHOPIN

VIII. Stained glass.

Stained glass was a primary decorative medium in the later Middle Ages. The increased size of windows and the invention of bar tracery (*see* §II, 1 above and TRACERY, §2(ii)) allowed greater expanses to be glazed, and stained glass achieved the status of wall painting and manuscript illumination, although its didactic function was perhaps less significant (*see* §IV, 2(iii) above). Owing to the passage of time and the adverse effects of war and iconoclasm much Gothic stained glass has been destroyed. The largest quantity survives in France, but it was a major art form in north-western Europe and those parts of Spain that came under French influence. It was less fashionable in Italy.

1. Introduction. 2. France. 3. Low Countries. 4. British Isles. 5. Holy Roman Empire. 6. Eastern Europe. 7. Scandinavia. 8. Spain. 9. Portugal. 10. Italy.

1. INTRODUCTION. Stained glass occurred in both secular and ecclesiastical buildings, but nearly all the surviving glass is in churches. Techniques of glass making were much the same as in the Romanesque period (*see* ROMANESQUE, §IX): pot-metal glass (in which the metallic oxides were added to the glass in clay pots) remained predominant, and the main technical innovation was silver-stain (also known as yellow-stain), by which a solution of silver compounds was painted on to the exterior surface of the glass and fired, to turn white glass yellow or blue glass green. This was known in France and England by the late 13th century or the early 14th, but exact dates and priorities are uncertain. The technique enabled two colours to appear on a single piece of glass and thus reduced the amount of leading required (*see* STAINED GLASS, §I).

With the increased size of windows came developments in armature and the arrangement of subject-matter. The medallion window, with an armature of circles or foiled shapes set against an ornamental, patterned ground, which first appeared in the transitional period from Romanesque around 1200 (*see* ROMANESQUE, fig. 84), was dominant until *c.* 1270, when the band window was introduced in France. Here a band of coloured figures or scenes was set against a white or grisaille ground, greatly increasing luminosity. Grisaille itself remained popular throughout the period.

Subject-matter also continued from the earlier period, with emphasis on biblical scenes and saints' lives (*see* STAINED GLASS, §III, 1). TYPOLOGICAL CYCLES, juxtaposing New Testament scenes with their Old Testament antitypes, were significant, and in the later period there were new iconographical sources, such as the *Biblia pauperum* (*see* BIBLE, §I, 3(ii)). Such fashions from manuscript illumination as marginalia were adopted for background ornament. The increasing occurrence of donors in the glazing (see fig. 104 below) reflects the widening base of patronage, to include merchants, burgesses, gentry and the lesser clergy. Many of these developments are best observed in French stained glass, which can provide the context for studying the less well-preserved glass elsewhere.

BIBLIOGRAPHY

E. Frodl-Kraft: *Die Glasmalerei: Entwicklung, Technik, Eigenart* (Vienna and Munich, 1970)

L. Lee, G. Seddon and F. Stephens: *Stained Glass* (London, 1976)

D. Evans: *A Bibliography of Stained Glass* (Woodbridge, 1982)

L. Grodecki and C. Brisac: *Le Vitrail gothique au XIIIe siècle* (Fribourg, 1984; Eng. trans., London, 1985)

S. Brown and D. O'Connor: *Glass-painters*, Medieval Craftsmen (London, 1991)

2. FRANCE. Virtually every medieval church in France contains some vestige of its glazing programme, and much, in addition, is documented of glass lost in social and military conflict. General conclusions can thus be drawn about both window composition and iconography, which can also be applied to other countries where the evidence is more scarce. The typical French early 13th-century window is the medallion window, multi-sectioned, with an average of about 36 scenes in 12 registers, with a surface

pattern formed by configurations of various geometric shapes: a system of wheels (Bourges Cathedral, windows of the *Relics of St Stephen* and *New Alliance*, 1200–14), petals (Sens Cathedral, window of *St Eustace*, 1207–13; see fig. 101), canted squares (Sens Cathedral, *Good Samaritan* window, 1207–13; Chartres Cathedral, window of *St James the Great*, 1220–25) and ornate foliate and mosaic grounds. Within each scene the designer has simplified pictorial space by silhouetting dramatic actions against uniform red or blue backgrounds.

Reflecting contemporary hagiographic conventions, similar iconographic motifs characterize similar actions. Healing the sick, the resurrection of the dead, curing the possessed and martyrdom appear regularly. The viewer did not 'read' the story so much as identify a number of key images most frequently associated with specific saints. Catherine's wheel, Margaret's dragon or Andrew's X-shaped cross immediately marked the subject of the story. The iconography often followed a typological format, especially in the correspondence of clerestory windows, where apostles and prophets were paired across the choir or nave, as at the cathedrals of Bourges and Reims. Old and New Testament themes, however, were not invariably combined for typological reasons. The rise of narrative in contemporary Romance literature may well have inspired designers to elaborate familiar biblical and hagiographical stories, such as Joseph (Auxerre Cathedral, Bourges Cathedral, Rouen Cathedral), the Prodigal Son (the cathedrals of Bourges and Sens; *see* SENS, fig. 4), St Thomas Becket (Sens Cathedral), St Martin (Bourges Cathedral), St Margaret or St Catherine (Chartres Cathedral).

Similarities between glass and manuscript painting are clear. The classicizing tendencies in the draftsmanship of the Ingeborg Psalter (Chantilly, Mus. Condé, MS. 1695; *see* TRANSITIONAL STYLE, fig. 2) appear in a number of glazing programmes in northern France around 1200, and are often cited in discussions of the glass in the cathedrals of Soissons and Laon (*see* LAON, §1(iii)) and in the former collegiate church of St Quentin, Saint-Quentin (Deuchler). Both the medallion format and the painting style of the *Bibles moralisées* (e.g. Paris, Bib. N., MS lat. 11560) have been associated with glazing traditions in the Ile-de-France, for example in the windows of St Vincent, St-Germain-lès-Corbeil. The insistent architectural framework and clear relationships of figure to ground in the Psalter of St Louis (Paris, Bib. N., MS. lat. 10525) are features found in mid-13th century Parisian glass painting, especially in the Sainte-Chapelle (1243–8; *see* PARIS, §V, 2(iii); *see* STAINED GLASS, colour pl. I).

An overview of French Gothic glass is difficult, despite efforts to define regional styles and workshops. Mâle, at the beginning of the 20th century, attempted to designate schools by iconographic analysis. Grodecki (1948) documented workshop development, tracing an atelier originating in Poitiers to Bourges (*see* BOURGES, §II, 1(iii)), and later back to Poitiers. He analysed medallion formats, armature patterns, decorative motifs, and the formulaic rendering of the figure in space. His study of the glazing of the Sainte Chapelle, Paris, partitioned the work among a number of masters and their assistants. Raguin has defined travelling glazing workshops originating in the Paris area and active also in Burgundy; and Caviness

101. *St Eustace* window (*c.* 1207–13), stained glass, Sens Cathedral, France

102. *Passion* window (*c.* 1210; detail), stained glass, Laon Cathedral, France

(1977, 1990) has isolated a workshop travelling with its own contingent of glass blowers, responsible for windows at St Yved, Braine, St Remi, Reims (and, outside France, at Canterbury Cathedral). Lillich has traced a late 13th-century regional style of western France at St Pierre, Chartres, the church of the Trinity, Vendôme, Notre-Dame-de-l'Epine, Evron, Sées Cathedral, the former cathedral of St Samson, Dol-de-Bretagne, and Ste Radegonde, Poitiers.

Much of the dating in glass studies has been associated with stylistic development within regions similar to those evolved for Gothic sculpture (*see* §III, 1(i) above). Some regional characteristics can be discerned despite the consistent evidence of travelling workshops. In northern France *c.* 1200, programmes at the cathedrals of Laon (see fig. 102) and Soissons; at St Yved, Braine; at Saint-Quentin; at St Remi, Reims; and at the former abbey church, Orbais, and in the castle chapel at Baye, both in Champagne, display monumental compositions and classicizing modelling, which appear also in the contemporary sculpture, manuscripts and metalwork of the area.

These qualities, however, do not appear to have been confined to the north. Workshops, or individual artists, must have moved beyond this region since windows showing strong connections to the northern style have been identified in the cathedrals of Chartres, Troyes (*see* TROYES, §2), Lyon and Bourges. In Anjou and Poitou 12th-century traditions were continued in glass painting as in architecture. Windows in the cathedrals at Le Mans, Angers and Poitiers (*see* POITIERS, §2(i)(b)) show a vigorous, almost brutal drafting style, sharp angular drapery folds, variable body proportions, dramatic facial expressions, and an emphasis on ornament. Eastern France, which is considered still to be Romanesque until the late 13th century, is linked artistically to the Rhineland, as is shown by similarities between the glass of Alsace (Strasbourg; Niederhaslach Abbey) and such German monuments as Freiburg im Breisgau Cathedral (*see* FREIBURG IM BREISGAU, §2(iii)). The Paris area was particularly important during the second quarter of the 13th century: its style appears to combine influences from such areas as Amiens, Beauvais and Chartres with earlier local traditions. Artists trained in the Paris area then worked elsewhere after 1250 (for example, the cathedrals of Tours, Le Mans, Auxerre and Soissons; *see* STAINED GLASS, colour pl. VI, fig. 1).

The evolution of styles, however, is best understood as an interaction of patron, monument and workshop. This is exemplified by the development of the Chartrain style (*see* CHARTRES, §I, 3) which is the product not of any one region, but of intense interaction of diverse artists in a well-funded project. The dominance of the Parisian style during the second quarter of the 13th century is hardly a triumph of a regional expression: the vast glazing programmes in one of the first great urban centres of Europe

103. *Annunciation* window (*c.* 1450), stained glass, Bourges Cathedral, France

produced a large number of trained artists who inevitably moved out of the capital to seek commissions. The increasingly regional nature of styles after 1300 is linked to the general decline in economic strength of the country and the diminished ability of the capital to provide continuous employment.

Attention to creating a systematic progression of style has, in recent scholarly literature, increasingly given way to studies of differences in patronage, location of a window within the edifice, and the juxtaposition of the glazing with pre-existing works within the building such as mosaics, wall paintings, metalwork or manuscripts, which may all have modified the format of a window. It is evident, for example, that the axial lancets, whether of the choir or ambulatory, were often reserved for the most significant donor, the reigning monarch (e.g. the cathedrals of Soissons and Poitiers) or presiding bishop (Le Mans Cathedral; *see* LE MANS, §1(iii)). The subject-matter could determine the style of presentation: a theme such as the Tree of Jesse, established and widely used in the 12th century, could, when used in 13th-century programmes, as at Beauvais Cathedral (*see* BEAUVAIS, §1(ii)), show more retardataire stylistic tendencies. Artists modified styles to accommodate distance from the viewer, reserving bolder, more simplified drawing for the large figures of the clerestory and more complex, varied expressions for the small-scale work of the medallion windows lower down, as seen in the cathedrals of Chartres and Auxerre. There were progressive modifications in pattern and colour as windows were installed during the construction of the choir of St Remi, Reims (Caviness, 1990; *see* REIMS, §IV, 3(iii)).

The evolution of French Gothic window design is, therefore, problematic, but basic changes can be identified. During the first half of the 13th century, windows were predominantly of medallion patterns of deeply coloured glass, most often a scheme of blues and reds. Grisaille and plain glazing, however, had never been abandoned, as is testified by many monuments with more intact programmes (the abbey church of Orbais; St Jean, Saint Jean-aux-Bois). Often only eastern openings were provided with narrative windows, and the side windows were plain glazed to provide more light (Virgin Chapel, Auxerre Cathedral). Deeply coloured programmes enjoyed temporary popularity after the Sainte-Chapelle, Paris, but with the glazing of Tours Cathedral, after 1259, the formula of the band window declared its eminent practicality. In the band window grisaille frames bands of coloured figural glass, and at St Urbain, Troyes, *c.* 1270 (see fig. 69 above), a band window system appeared even for narrative scenes in both upper and lower windows. By the early 14th century, the band window was the preferred form for many programmes, for example St Pierre, Chartres, and St Ouen, Rouen.

The development of glazing systems in the 14th and 15th century, despite many local differences, was characterized by interplay between the real architecture of the building and the fictive architecture of the painted formats. The medallion window with its interacting episodes was replaced by a sequential format reading as a book and often accompanied by vernacular inscriptions. In many programmes the selected images from the hagiographic or biblical stories occupied an entire lancet. Large, volumetric figures in three-dimensional settings appeared under increasingly realistic architectural canopies (e.g. the cathedrals of Evreux and Bourges; St Séverin, Paris). The *Annunciation* window of Bourges Cathedral (*c.* 1450; see fig. 103), donated by Jacques Coeur, demonstrates, in its golden-haired saints, damask robes, jewelled hems, gold-trimmed sculpture and painted vaults, renderings of spatial recession and texture that parallel the art of Jan van Eyck (e.g. the *Virgin and Child with Canon George van der Paele*, *c.* 1436, Bruges, Groeningemus.).

Painting on glass, the most public of all forms of monumental painting, underwent the same stylistic evolution as the art of panels and manuscripts. Around 1500 workshops began to incorporate Italian concepts of pictorial space and focused dramatic narrative. Compositions extended across entire windows, ignoring the division of the mullions (e.g. *Martyrdom of St Eustace*, 1543, from Rouen Cathedral, now Detroit, MI, Inst. A.). Increasingly naturalistic and detailed narratives filled vast bays with dramatic and legible texts (e.g. the *Creation* window, St Florentin, 1525). The richness of the colours, balanced by broad expanses of painted and silver-stained grisaille, opened up new forms of expression in the art, seen for instance at St Patrice, St Vincent and St Godard in Rouen, St Etienne and the cathedral of Beauvais, and Ste Foy, Conches-en-Ouche.

BIBLIOGRAPHY

E. Mâle: *L'Art religieux du XIIIe siècle en France* (Paris, 1913; Eng. trans. London, 1961)

Y. Delaport and E. Houvet: *Les Vitraux de la cathédrale de Chartres*, 4 vols (Chartres, 1926)

G. Ritter: *Les Vitraux de la cathédrale de Rouen* (Cognac, 1926)

L. Grodecki: 'A Stained Glass "atelier" of the XIIIth Century: A Study of the Windows in the Cathedrals of Bourges, Chartres and Poitiers', *J. Warb. & Court. Inst.*, xi (1948), pp. 87–111

M. Aubert and others: *Le Vitrail français* (Paris, 1958)

France, Corp. Vitrearum. Med. Aevi (1959–)

Les Vitraux de Notre-Dame et de la Sainte-Chapelle de Paris, Corp. Vitrearum Med. Aevi, i (Paris, 1959)

F. Deuchler: *Der Ingeborgpsalter* (Berlin, 1967), pp. 155–60

W. Sauerländer: *Gotische Skulptur in Frankreich, 1140–1270* (Munich, 1970; Eng. trans. London, 1972)

M. Caviness: *The Early Stained Glass of Canterbury Cathedral* (Princeton, 1977)

L. Grodecki: 'Les Problèmes de l'origine de la peinture gothique et le "maître de Saint Chéron" de la cathédrale de Chartres', *Rev. A.*, xl–xli (1978), pp. 43–64

M. Lillich: *The Stained Glass of Saint-Père-de-Chartres* (Middletown, CT, 1978)

V. Raguin: *Stained Glass in Thirteenth-century Burgundy* (Princeton, 1982)

M. Caviness: *Sumptuous Arts at the Royal Abbeys in Reims and Braine: Ornatus elegantiae varietate stupendis* (Princeton, 1990)

M. Lillich: *Rainbow Like an Emerald: Stained Glass in Lorraine in the Thirteenth and Early Fourteenth Centuries* (University Park, PA, 1991)

For further bibliography *see* §1 above

VIRGINIA CHIEFFO RAGUIN

3. LOW COUNTRIES. Before the Gothic period, the existence of stained glass in the Low Countries is testified only by excavated glass (Eime, 11th century; Stavelot, mid-12th century) and documentary evidence. Almost no stained glass survives from the 13th century, and as a result of the 16th-century religious wars and later destructions, almost all the Gothic stained glass has been lost in the south Netherlands and nothing has survived in the

north Netherlands. Information about stained-glass production, glaziers and their social organization is more plentiful for the 13th to 15th centuries than for earlier periods. Archival sources reveal that in the 13th century glaziers were active in numerous locations in the south Netherlands, including Brussels, Leuven, Mechelen, Liège, Tournai and Waulsort. The only glass surviving from this period consists of fragments found in the triforium oculi of Brussels Cathedral, at the Cistercian abbey of Ter Duinen, Koksijde, and other pieces discovered at the Dominican friary in Ghent featuring musicians and hybrid figures in quatrefoils, very similar to the marginal grotesques of late 13th-century and early 14th-century manuscripts (*see* §IV, 5(vi) above).

In the 14th century glaziers are mentioned in guild registers or in connection with work for abbeys, churches and public monuments under the patronage of princes, noblemen, civil and church dignitaries and municipal or commercial patrons. Some artists moved from town to town and others went abroad to work in such places as Dijon and Milan. The few examples that have been preserved from the 14th century show predominantly French influence and, later, that of the Holy Roman Empire. Among these are two panels (mid-14th century; Brussels, Musées Royaux A. & Hist.) representing a nobleman and his wife kneeling under architectural canopies (see fig. 104), which show the importance that the donor had acquired. They exhibit a treatment of architecture that is still limited in scope combined with a great delicacy of design in the patterns, clothes and faces. At Zichem Church, in a window (1387–98) depicting the *Crucifixion*, the canopies have acquired greater importance through their larger size and more three-dimensional style. The similarities between the Zichem window, a panel (late 14th century; London, V&A) from Winchester College and a *Calvary* (early 15th century; Cologne, Schnütgen-Mus.) demonstrate the probable circulation of models and the undeniable influence of the Holy Roman Empire in the Low Countries at this period.

The angels (early 15th century; Bruges, Gruuthuse-mus.), presumably originating from Bruges Stadhuis and possibly attributable to Christian Van de Voorde (*fl* 1385–1404), are characterized by their prettiness and their pointed noses, rounded cheeks and clothes curling around their bodies. They recall the altarpiece (1399; Dijon, Mus. B.-A.) by Melchior Broederlam for the charterhouse of Champmol in Dijon. The same style is again perceptible in the prettiness and elegance of the stained glass showing the *Creation* in Onze Lieve Vrouwbasiliek at Halle (Brabant) and the *Calvary* in Sensenruth Church (province of Luxembourg), both of the first half of the 15th century.

Gradually, however, the stylistic influence of such artists as Rogier van der Weyden, Dieric Bouts and Hugo van der Goes began to appear, and it is quite clear in the late 15th-century windows of St Gummaruskerk, Lier, SS Pierre et Guidon, Anderlecht, Brussels, and in the beautiful *Pietà* (*c.* 1476; cartoon attrib. Vrancke van der Stockt, Antwerp, Mus. Mayer van dem Bergh) at the château of Loppem. Many more glaziers are known from the 15th century than the 14th, especially from the second half of the century, and references to their works in both major

104. Stained-glass panel showing a donor, 560×460 mm, from the Low Countries, *c.* 1350 (Brussels, Musées Royaux d'Art et d'Histoire)

cities and lesser towns and villages are numerous. Commissions came from the dukes of Burgundy and other great families, as well as from abbeys and cathedral chapters, town councils and guilds. There were whole dynasties of glaziers. Some glaziers exported their designs or went to work in such countries as Italy and Britain (*see* §4 below).

Many 15th-century windows, for example at the St Gummaruskerk, Lier, depict patrons or saints under huge canopies of white painted glass. In windows (end of 15th century) in the chapel of the Holy Blood, Bruges, members of the Burgundy family with their coats of arms were set beneath smaller canopies (panels, London, V&A). In other designs such as the *Coronation of the Virgin* (third quarter of 15th century; St Gummaruskerk, Lier), an innovative approach whereby a picture filled the window without taking account of the mullions was adopted, and in other cases a narrative sequence would occupy several windows, as in the scheme (*c.* 1500; Tournai Cathedral) by ARNOULT DE NIMÈGUE depicting scenes from the history of the diocese. Although the transition at the end of the 15th century from Gothic to Renaissance styles is discernible in the work of such artists as Arnoult de Nimègue and NICOLAS ROMBOUTS (who worked at Leuven and Brussels), Gothic styles persisted in many windows of the first quarter of the 16th century, for example those in the collegiate church of Diest and at St Waudru, Mons.

BIBLIOGRAPHY

J. Helbig: *De Glasschilderkunst in België: Repertorium en documenten* (Antwerp, 1943–51)

Belgique, Corp. Vitrearum Med. Aevi (1961–)

Moyen Age (exh. cat., ed. Y. Vanden Bemden; Brussels, Gal. CGER, 1986), pp. 21–53

C. Fontaine-Hodiamont, L. Maes and Y. Vanden Bemden: 'Un vitrail de la *Pietà* (XVe siècle) au château de Loppem: Etude et restauration', *Bull. Inst. Royal Patrm. A.*, xxiii (1990–91), pp. 5–32

L.-F. Genicot and T. Coomans: 'Grisailles du triforium du choeur de la cathédrale de Bruxelles (XIIIe siècle)', *Rev. Archéologues & Historiens A. Louvain*, xxiv (1991), pp. 9–19

YVETTE VANDEN BEMDEN

4. BRITISH ISLES. Gothic stained glass in the British Isles is found not only in the large cathedral and collegiate buildings but also extensively in parish churches. The glass in parish churches provides the main evidence for certain developments in style and iconography, particularly from 1350 onwards (*see also* STAINED GLASS, §III, 1). The majority of the extant material is found in England, with a small quantity in north Wales but hardly anything in Scotland. As a result of destruction, mainly at the Reformation and during the Civil War, regional survival is unbalanced, very little Gothic stained glass surviving from the churches of the religious orders or from secular buildings.

(i) Before *c.* 1380. (ii) *c.* 1380–*c.* 1550.

(i) Before c. *1380.* As hardly any Romanesque stained glass survives in England the background to the earliest works of the Early Gothic period is difficult to assess. The fact that more glass of this period has survived in France has resulted in a view of the English material as being dependent on developments in France, but this was not necessarily the case. The first major works of the Early Gothic period, dating *c.* 1180–1280, are in the cathedrals of Canterbury, Lincoln and Salisbury (*see* CANTERBURY, §III, 3; LINCOLN, §2(iii) and SALISBURY, §2(iii)) and at Westminster Abbey. These are medallion windows (see fig. 68 above), with the circles or foiled shapes set against an ornamental patterned ground, the whole being framed by wide borders containing foliage patterns. Blue glass is predominant, and red, green and yellow are extensively used, with some white, resulting in strong, dark colour effects. Windows at Lincoln (before *c.* 1235) and Salisbury (*c.* 1235–50) are good examples of GRISAILLE; glass (*c.* 1260) of the same type is found in the Five Sisters Window in the north transept of York Minster (*see* YORK, §III, 1(iii)).

In the later 13th century a form of the band window was introduced. Figures and scenes are placed under architectural canopies and flanked by narrow borders incorporating heraldic motifs, foliage and patterned ornament. The coloured glass of the figure panels is sometimes set against grisaille glass, creating a contrast between the brightly coloured panel and the white grisaille with its foliage or geometrical pattern. Blue glass is no longer as prominent as it was earlier in the century, and there is a balanced tonality of colour. Work of this period (*c.* 1290) is to be found in the chapter house vestibule at York Minster, in the side windows (*c.* 1289–96) of the chapel of Merton College, Oxford, and in the east window (*c.* 1299–1307) of St Mary's, Selling (Kent). The patrons of such glazing schemes were increasingly represented as kneeling donors, their arms displayed in shields or in motifs in the borders of the windows (*see* HERALDRY, §II, 4 and fig. 19).

These tendencies are more pronounced in works of the first few decades of the 14th century. The use of architectural frames for the figural and narrative panels is more elaborate, as also is border decoration. The borders contain a wide range of decorative forms, including the grotesque creatures that also populate the borders of contemporary manuscripts. In works of the second decade of the century the effect of newly invented silver-stain is evident in the more liberal use of white and yellow in figural and ornamental work. Green glass is used more extensively, while blue and red are much less prominent than in the 13th century (*see also* §IV, 4(ii) above). These tendencies are best seen in the windows of the nave aisles and chapter house at York Minster, the choir of Exeter Cathedral (*see* EXETER, §1(iii)), the choir aisles at Wells Cathedral (*see* WELLS, §1(iii)) and in parish churches, for example the two east lancets at SS Peter and Paul, Upper Hardres (Kent), and the windows at St Michael, Eaton Bishop (Hereford & Worcs).

During the second quarter of the 14th century there was some influence from France and Italy. An elegant figure style, characterized by very tall, elongated forms and delicate faces with small eyes and mouths, was derived from France, perhaps from such churches in Normandy as St Ouen (*c.* 1317–39) at Rouen and EVREUX CATHEDRAL. Fragments (Ely Cathedral, Stained Glass Mus.) from the Lady chapel at Ely Cathedral were influenced by French glass. An interest in the portrayal of pictorial space and three-dimensional form came from Italy, perhaps via France, and is best seen in glass now located in the east windows and choir windows of York Minster. As in the earlier years of the century, works of this period exhibit a balanced combination of green, yellow and red glass, with relatively little blue. Towards 1350 the use of white glass increased, and in some windows an extensive use of white glass and silver-stain led to a preponderance of white and yellow over other colours. Alternatively, as in the east window (*c.* 1350–60) of Gloucester Cathedral, white glass was combined with red and blue with much emphasis on the white canopies (see fig. 105; *see also* §IV, 5(ix) above), a form of design that achieved great popularity in the 15th century. The period 1350-80 continued in a similar vein and is best represented by work in St Michael's, Heydour (Lincs), and at Edington Priory (Wilts). The sense of three-dimensional form in the canopies and the faces of the figures may derive from south Netherlandish work, perhaps through the influence of such imported monumental brasses as the Walsokne and Braunche brasses (*c.* 1350–70; King's Lynn, St Margaret's Church).

(ii) c. *1380–*c. *1550.* In the final two decades of the 14th century new attitudes to style, colour and design developed. These changes are much associated with Thomas of Oxford, who worked *c.* 1380–94 for WILLIAM OF WYKEHAM at his foundations of New College, Oxford (*see* OXFORD, §3(ii)), and Winchester College (*see also* WINCHESTER, §III, 4). Most of the glass from Winchester and much of that from New College has been lost or removed

105. *Coronation of the Virgin* flanked by *Saints* (*c.* 1350–60), stained glass, central section of the great east window, entire window 24×11.69 m, Gloucester Cathedral, England

to other locations, including the south choir aisle of York Minster and the Victoria and Albert Museum, London. Thomas's figures have softly modelled draperies, strong facial expressions and bulky forms, features that came to characterize Late Gothic in England. He also introduced new types of architectural canopy with strongly three-dimensional arches surmounted by pinnacles and crocketed gables. These had a lasting influence in England in the 15th century. The sources of his innovations were perhaps eastern France (Metz) or the north Rhineland around Cologne, but exact parallels are difficult to find.

John Thornton of Coventry (*fl* 1405–33) was the leading glazier in the generation following Thomas of Oxford. His major surviving work is the great east window (1405–8) of York Minster, which depicts a number of *Old Testament* scenes and a series of scenes of the *Apocalypse*. His style derives in part from that of Thomas of Oxford but differs in the greater elegance of the figures and in the use of colour, red, blue and white glass being predominant. The *St William of York* window (*c.* 1423) in the north-east transept of York Minster is also by John Thornton, and the *St Cuthbert* window (*c.* 1440) in the south-east transept reflects his style. These works show a characteristic Late Gothic elegance of figure forms and sweetness of facial expression, and this manner is also seen in the east window (*c.* 1440) of Great Malvern Priory (Hereford & Worcs).

Towards the mid-15th century these sinuous, elegant forms gave way to sturdier poses and crisply drawn facial features with stern or blank expressions. These figures have a sculptural solidity and bulkiness. Evidence of this change is seen in the glass made *c.* 1441–7 by John Glazier for the chapel of All Souls College, Oxford, and also in the glass (*c.* 1447–50) by the King's Glazier John Prudde (*fl* 1440–73) in the Beauchamp Chapel, St Mary's, Warwick. This style was further developed in the choir windows (*c.* 1445–70) of Great Malvern Priory, and certain well-defined regional schools show distinctive variants of it. The one from which most material survives is the Norwich School of glass painters working in Norfolk and Suffolk. An early work of the school is the east window (*c.* 1440–60) of St Peter Mancroft, Norwich (*see* NORWICH, §3(ii)). A slightly later example of the Norwich school's work is the east window of the church of SS Peter and Paul, East Harling (Norfolk). Similar regional groups occur in Somerset and Devon, north Wales and the West Midlands. The large quantity of surviving glass of the last few decades of the 15th century has received relatively little study.

Towards the end of the 15th century and in the early 16th glaziers began to follow the continental example of carrying a single design across several lights. In this they were led by Netherlandish glaziers, the most important of whom were Barnard Flower (*fl c.* 1505–17) and Galyon Hone (*fl c.* 1517–51). They introduced the Netherlandish Renaissance style with its Mannerist tendencies and associated classicizing ornament and architectural forms. Their work is seen in the scheme (*c.* 1495–1505) at St Mary's, Fairford (Glos); in the glazing (*c.* 1523) at the chapel of The Vyne (Hants); in the work (*c.* 1536-7) at Withcote Chapel (Leics); in the windows (1500-06) at St George's Chapel, Windsor; and, in its fullest form, in Cambridge at King's College Chapel (1515–17 and 1526–46; *see* CAMBRIDGE (i), §2(ii) and fig. 5). DIRK VELLERT was apparently a major source for the designs used. In parish churches of this late 15th- and early 16th-century period there is usually a continuation of the purely English styles of the second half of the 15th century, although often not very distinguished in quality. The Reformation in the 1530s brought in general a decline in the making of figure glass, but stained glass continued to be made for secular buildings, heraldic glass being particularly popular (*see also* STAINED GLASS, §II, 1).

BIBLIOGRAPHY

P. Nelson: *Ancient Painted Glass in England, 1170–1500* (London, 1913)
J. D. Le Couteur: *English Medieval Painted Glass* (London, 1926)
H. Read: *English Stained Glass* (London, 1926)
C. Woodforde: *Stained Glass in Somerset, 1250–1830* (Oxford, 1946/R Bath, 1970)
——: *English Stained and Painted Glass* (Oxford, 1954)
J. Baker: *English Stained Glass* (London, 1960)
M. Lewis: *Stained Glass in North Wales up to 1850* (Altrincham, 1970)
M. H. Caviness: *The Early Stained Glass of Canterbury Cathedral, c. 1175–1220* (Princeton, 1977)
Great Britain, Corp. Vitrearum Med. Aevi (1979–)
M. H. Caviness: *Stained Glass before 1540: An Annotated Bibliography* (Boston, 1983), pp. 85–124
P. Cowen: *A Guide to Stained Glass in Britain* (London, 1985)
S. Crewe: *Stained Glass in England, 1180–1540* (London, 1987)
R. Marks: 'Stained Glass *c.* 1200–1400', *Age of Chivalry* (exh. cat., ed. J. Alexander and P. Binski; London, RA, 1987), pp. 137–47
R. Marks: *Stained Glass in England during the Middle Ages* (London, 1993)

NIGEL J. MORGAN

5. HOLY ROMAN EMPIRE. Only a fraction of the stained glass produced during the Gothic period in the Holy Roman Empire has survived. The completely intact tracery and glazing of the Dominican Heiligkreuz Church (1360s) in Regensburg, for example, is a rarity. Thus particular caution is needed when assessing its quality or style. Factors of major importance in the development of a new style were the indigenous Romanesque tradition and the assimilation of French glazing ideas.

(i) *c.* 1220–1340. (ii) After 1340.

(i) c. *1220–1340.* In the large cycle of windows (*c.* 1220–30) at St Kunibert, Cologne, there is a distinct manifestation of the 'style of 1200'. The most prominent example is the *Tree of Jesse* window which features prophets with scrolls, saints, angels and donors. Figures are elongated and their dress reflects contemporary court fashion. The style suggests knowledge of French Gothic column statues and classicizing tendencies. The rounded arches and complicated ornamental bands, as in the *St Cecilia* window

106. *St Cecilia* window (*c.* 1230), stained glass, St Kunibert, Cologne, Germany

(see fig. 106) are, however, reminiscent of Romanesque style.

The glass paintings (*c.* 1235–49) of the Elisabethkirche, Marburg, rank among the finest and most famous examples of 13th-century German glass. The nobility and beauty of the standing figures of *Church* and *Synagogue* are similar to the slender verticality of the figures on the south transept of Strasbourg Cathedral. The carpet patterns behind the scenes enhance this concept. Yet the framing ornament, the horizontal accent of the folds in the drapery and the direction of the action counteract the verticality of the figures. This results in what has been termed a 'mixed style' (Wentzel) reflecting various sources of inspiration, such as local influence from Saxony–Thuringia and a dependence on Sicilian mosaics, which are in turn indebted to the Byzantine tradition. The influence of this 'mixed style' was far-reaching, with examples surviving from the Lutheran church at Breitenfelde (Schleswig-Holstein) and the Protestant church at Endre (Gotland, Sweden) and as far afield as the windows (*c.* 1253–60) of the choir in the Upper Church of S Francesco, Assisi (*see* §10 below).

The apparent presence of innovative French-inspired aspects blended with traditional regional elements is most typically exemplified in the Barfüsserkirche, Erfurt. The surviving 18 panels combine fragments (after 1228) from

107. *Baptism*, stained glass, detail of the Bible window from the Dominican church, Wimpfen im Tal, Germany, late 13th century (Darmstadt, Hessisches Landesmuseum)

the windows depicting the *Tree of Jesse*, the *Miracles of Christ*, and the *Life of St Francis*, among others. Pronounced waves of drapery with pointed fold lines are characteristic of this style. Certain patterns in the backgrounds and on clothing are identical with examples from the Elisabethkirche, Marburg (Bierschenk), thus testifying to the proximity of these two examples of glass painting.

The stained glass (*c.* 1250–60) in the west choir of Naumburg Cathedral marks a highpoint of Gothic style and is comparable with the glass of the Three Kings Chapel at Cologne Cathedral (*see* COLOGNE, §IV, 1(iii)). Narrow, ornamental carpet grounds contain elongated multilobed panels displaying such figures as saints, bishops, virtues and vices. Draperies are rendered with the hard, jagged folds of the ZACKENSTIL conjoined with diagonally placed attributes. The spatial concept of these windows, the courtly postures and the self-confidence in the facial expressions link the glass with the adjacent stone sculptures (*c.* 1240–60) of the Naumburg donors and with such other leading centres of architecture and art as Bamberg Cathedral.

Shortly after 1250 the finest Rhenish glaziers were executing the commission for the upper nave of Strasbourg Cathedral (*see* STRASBOURG, §III, 2 and 3); 13 of the original 14 windows remain. Made up of four lancets, each window is in perfect harmony with the surrounding architecture. Figures are placed on ornamented pedestals, framed by highly imaginative borders and surmounted by fantastic tabernacles (see fig. 75 above). The iconography and style of the glass are particularly close to contemporary French art in other media, notably sculpture from the west façade of the cathedral. Both glass and sculpture employ increasingly slim, elongated figures that exhibit emotions such as anxiety. Strasbourg influenced workshops west of the Rhine at Brandenburg (*c.* 1295); Wimpfen im Tal (Bad Wimpfen) in Baden Württemberg (1290–1310; see fig. 107); Freiburg im Breisgau (early 14th century; *see* FREIBURG IM BREISGAU, §2(iii)); Esslingen (1320–30); and Wienhausen in Lower Saxony (*c.* 1320), among others. In addition, this influence spread from north Germany, with notable glass workshops in Lübeck (although almost no glass has survived, 14th-century wall paintings imitating glass designs are to be seen in Marienkirche) and Lüneburg, as far as Scandinavia (*see* §7 below). Typical features are 'S-curved' figures, supple drapery and vegetal background ornament. An increasing emphasis on a calligraphic rhythm of contours and vivid colours may also be noted.

Further east, in what later became Austria, the most important stained glass of this period (1290s and 1300–20 respectively) is preserved in the two former Cistercian abbeys of Heiligenkreuz and Klosterneuburg. At Klosterneuburg typological, multilobed medallions, inspired by the pulpit (1181; Klosterneuburg Abbey) by Nicholas of Verdun, display elegant figures. The complex interrelationships between images and surrounding texts make these works masterpieces. The influence on this glass of the illumination of the *Biblia pauperum* (*see* BIBLE, §I, 3(ii)) has been repeatedly noted.

By 1315 a style reminiscent of the art of the imperial court had manifested itself in Cologne, for example in panels preserved in St Gereon. Figures of saints are executed in silver-stain (some of the earliest examples of its use in glass painting) and in delicate pastel colours—a result of including grisaille grounds—which were to remain popular through to the end of the 15th century. This can also be seen in the clerestory glass (*c.* 1304–32) of the choir of Cologne Cathedral, which features Old Testament kings and prophets and was presumably commissioned *c.* 1320 by the archbishop. There are striking formal and stylistic similarities with contemporary Cologne panel painting. The influence of regional and English book illumination on these works has been pointed out (Grodecki and Brisac). Cologne was one of the most powerful centres of the Empire, and its glass workshops were to exert enormous influence across the Rhineland.

The choir windows of Regensburg Cathedral, glazed *c.* 1325 under Bishop Nicholas von Ybbs, depict Christological and hagiographical subjects, some of which were inspired by Franciscan thought. Though they adhered to formal traditions, the glass painters were surprisingly inventive in the realm of ornamental carpet patterns. Large quantities of white glass were used. Once developed, this style remained popular in Regensburg throughout the 15th century. The choir of the former Franciscan abbey church at Königsfelden near Zurich may be called one of the pinnacles of Gothic stained glass. The programme of the 11 windows (*c.* 1325) emphasizes Franciscan spirituality, combined with references to the Habsburgs, who had founded the convent in 1301. The style is closely linked to upper Rhenish and Alsatian workshops, for it copies certain ornamental details and combines others in unprecedented ways. Its calligraphic drawing style has been linked to book illumination from the Lake Constance area (Grodecki and Brisac).

Two important windows (1320–40) depicting the *Throne of Solomon* are preserved in the cathedrals of Freiburg im Breisgau and Augsburg. Owing to a lack of comparative material the imposing window in Augsburg which spans seven lancets (the throne alone extends over three lancets), remains an 'erratic block', although the colour composition is reminiscent of Königsfelden (Beckmann). The glass in Freiburg was commissioned and donated by the silversmiths' guild. Stylistically it resembles contemporary book illumination from Basle. The gable of the middle portal at Strasbourg Cathedral is an iconographic parallel.

(ii) After 1340. The very few examples of Bohemian glass that survived the Hussite upheavals, the Thirty Years' War and the 18th-century unrest and are still *in situ* include the *Apostles* cycle (before 1380) at St Procopius, Nadslav, and the *Crucifixion* (*c.* 1370) in St Catherine's Oratory at Karlštejn Castle. Other surviving glass is from St Bartholomeus, Kolín, showing scenes from the *Life of the Virgin* (Prague, Mus. Dec. A.), from Žebnice (*c.* 1330; Prague, N. Mus.), from Slivenec (last quarter of 14th century; Prague, Mus. Dec. A.), and from St Mary's, Chełmno (ex-chapel of Malbork Castle; Toruń, Distr. Mus.). The compact and careful composition of these examples gives some idea of the probable high quality of the lost Bohemian stained glass (*see also* §6 below). The short, heavy, stern figures of some panels reflect sculpture by the PARLER family. Peter Parler is thought to have designed glass (destr.) at St Vitus's Cathedral, Prague (*see also* CZECH REPUBLIC, §II), thus indicating that there were close ties between Nuremberg, Prague, Vienna and points further east.

One of the centres of Late Gothic glass was Erfurt Cathedral (*see* ERFURT, §2(ii)), where glazing took place 1349–72 and was completed by a second generation of artists after 1400. Unprecedented in size, 640 panels are distributed over four lancet windows. The cycle includes the important *Genesis* window (*c.* 1370). A shift from blue and ruby-red to such brighter colours as yellow and green can be noted. Each window is filled with scenes arranged in numerous horizontal bands. Increasingly plastic figures are placed under tabernacles that enhance the vertical aspects of the compositions. The mostly monochrome backgrounds are covered with ornamental scrolls, which offer an appropriately neutral setting for the imposing architecture. This glass has stylistic parallels with contemporary Parler architecture (e.g. the portals of Holy Cross Church, Schwäbish Gmünd or of Ulm Minster) and constitutes the most extensive narrative cycle of the period in the Empire. The influence of the Erfurt workshop can be noted in remaining glass in such places as Wismar and the parish church at Kirchstück (Mecklenburg-Vorpommern).

Another workshop associated with the Parler style was active *c.* 1400 at St Martha and St Sebaldus, Nuremberg. Many windows were commissioned by aristocrats, among them the notable Schürstab window (1392–8; Nuremberg, St Sebaldus) which was donated and executed by Anton Schürstab. Whereas the figure style is coarser than at Erfurt, the German inscriptions are an innovative element. This reflects the introduction of German as the official written language at the court chancery under Charles IV.

Based on the Erfurt and Nuremberg models, the oldest remaining glass (1380–1400) in Ulm Minster, possibly executed by Jakob Acker, features more elongated, elegant figures with finely delineated features, composed into coherent colour schemes. Most of the other glass, however, is stylistically close, in the stoutness of the figures to the Parler style. The characteristics of the so-called Soft (Ger. *weicher Stil*) style—a more charming, friendlier rendering of features and a more painterly approach—may be noted in, for example, the panels devoted to the *Joys of the Virgin*. Of significance for Swabian–Bavarian glass painting are the *Old Testament* and *New Testament* panels (*c.* 1400) in the Jakobskirche, Rothenburg ob der Tauber. They afford an early example of the use of brightly coloured glass. Rendered in a fluid drawing style in *Schwarzlot* (black enamel), the lines are sketchy and executed with the most vivid brushstrokes.

The glass of the *Weicher* style tends to be bright and diverse in style *c.* 1400. A parallel with drawing is discernible. Examples survive in Lübeck (most destr. 1942) where the most important window, dedicated to Mary Magdalene, was donated in 1406. The Lübeck workshop gave its name to the Lübeck style and had an international reputation which in 1436 led the senate of Florence to seek its services. The *Helden* ('Heroes') window (*c.* 1410) in Lüneburg Rathaus was produced by the Lübeck workshop. It represents the earliest surviving large-scale secular glass painting in the Empire. The 'heroes' iconography first appeared in French literature of the early 14th century. By 1360 a heroes cycle decorated the Hansasaal of Cologne Rathaus, making an association between heroes and exemplary jurisdiction. The Lüneburg workshop influenced the glazing (*c.* 1410) at nearby Ebstorf Abbey. Of the initial 90 panels, 67 survive, depicting the *Speculum humanae salvationis.* The glazing (1412) of the Leprosenkapelle at St Viti, Uelzen, was also inspired by this workshop. A closeness to Conrad von Soest's style has been noted.

Over 1000 panels of the original glass survive in Stendal Cathedral. Begun *c.* 1420, the glazing continued until the 1470s. It was the most ambitious project yet undertaken in the Empire. Stylistically, the glass shows the influence of both Erfurt and Lübeck. Characterized by the slender figures, the scenes are framed by multilobed borders with loose contours, linked by soft scrolls and vines. The programme (not preserved in its original format) is dedicated to the sacrificial deaths of Christ and the martyrs for the salvation of mankind. There are similarities with surviving contemporary glass at Havelberg, Halberstadt, Werben an der Elbe and Wilsnack.

Commissioned *c.* 1420 by the patrician Heinrich Besserer, the scheme of the Besserer Chapel in Ulm Minster was executed by an anonymous master (contemporary with Lukas Moser, Hans Multscher and Konrad Witz who have themselves also been suggested as possible makers). The cycle comprises scenes ranging from the *Creation* to the *Death of the Virgin.* For formal and stylistic reasons a Bruges source (possibly an illuminated Bible) had been

108. Peter Hemmel von Andlau: *St Catherine*, stained glass, from the Nonnbergkirche, Salzburg, Austria, 1480 (Darmstadt, Hessisches Landesmuseum)

suggested, linking this glass with the most distinguished contemporary illuminators' workshops, yet without precluding the theory that they were executed in an Ulm workshop. Late 14th-century book illumination from Bohemia has also been suggested as a source of inspiration (Becksmann). This early example of realistic glass painting is notable for its painterly qualities.

The *Passion* window (1440–41) in Berne Minster is well documented: consisting of 56 panels, it was produced by 'master Hansen von Ulm' and cost 157 florins. Under a vast arch that spans four lancets, Christ is depicted among the citizens of Berne, with angels holding coats of arms. A stylistic proximity to the Besserer Chapel has been emphasized, and Hans von Ulm has been identified with HANS ACKER, although the evidence is not conclusive. While open to formal, colouristic and technical innovation, Hans von Ulm remained indebted to the traditions of monumental glass painting (Becksmann).

PETER HEMMEL VON ANDLAU made Strasbourg a leading centre for stained glass: surviving commissions in Frankfurt am Main Cathedral (1474), Nonnbergkirche, Salzburg (1480; see fig. 108), Stadtkirche, Oberehnheim in Alsace (1474 and 1485), Maria Himmelfahrtskirche, Thaur in the Tyrol (1501) and Freiburg im Breisgau Cathedral (1480s; *see* FREIBURG IM BREISGAU §2(iii)), among others, are evidence of his fame and popularity. This artist's relationship with contemporaries is of particular interest: one of his designs at the Nonnbergkirche (*see* STAINED GLASS, colour pl. IV), for example, features a free adaptation of a print by Martin Schongauer; thus he was absorbing a style inspired by early Netherlandish painting. The masterful renderings of faces and drapery are so delicate and accomplished that they constitute a highpoint of 15th-century glass painting. Hemmel's Volckamer window (1488) made for Peter Volckamer at St Lorenz, Nuremberg, is a radiantly coloured depiction of the *Tree of Jesse*. Closely related to his Kramer window (1479–80) at Ulm Minster, it exemplifies the great number of works exported from the Hemmel workshop. It is considered to be largely by the artist himself and exerted a strong influence on stylistic development throughout Albrecht Dürer's time in Nuremberg.

The transition to Renaissance glass painting was manifested technically in increasingly large windows filled with thinner glass and with a more differentiated colour scheme (as a result of an increasingly refined knowledge of chemical compositions and the melting conditions of glass). This led to an eventual reduction of lead fillets and opened up the possibility of the *Kabinettmalerei* (a window of colourless glass painted with enamel and silver stain), which remained popular throughout the 17th century. With the adoption of the latest artistic innovations, such as linear perspective, and the participation of leading artists in supplying designs and cartoons, stained glass was beginning to display all the characteristics of the Renaissance. In the early 16th century numerous famous masters, including Albrecht Dürer, HANS SÜSS VON KULMBACH, Jörg Breu (i) and others, were associated with important commissions, primarily in the south-west German area. (*See also* STAINED GLASS, §II, 1 and fig. 10.)

BIBLIOGRAPHY

H. Schmitz: *Die Glasgemälde des Königlichen Kunstgewerbemuseums zu Berlin*, 2 vols (Berlin, 1913)

F. Kieslinger: *Gotische Glasmalerei in Österreich bis 1450* (Vienna, 1920)

H. Wentzel: *Meisterwerke der Glasmalerei* (Berlin, 1951)

A. Matějček and P. Jaroslav: *Gotische Malerei in Böhmen, 1350–1450* (Prague, 1955)

Deutschland, Corp. Vitrearum Med. Aevi (1958–)

Österreich, Corp. Vitrearum Med. Aevi (1962–)

E. Frodl-Kraft: *Die Glasmalerei: Entwicklung, Technik, Eigenart* (Vienna and Munich, 1970)

Tschechoslowakei, Corp. Vitrearum Med. Aevi (1975)

Deutsche Demokratische Republik, Corp. Vitrearum Med. Aevi (1976–)

E. Drachenberg, K.-J. Maercker and C. Richter: *Mittelalterliche Glasmalerei in der Deutschen Demokratischen Republik* (Berlin, 1979)

L. Grodecki and C. Brisac: *Le Vitrail gothique au XIIIe siècle* (Fribourg, 1984; Eng. trans., London, 1985)

France, Bas-Rhin, Corp. Vitrearum Med. Aevi (1986–)

R. Kahsnitz: 'Stained Glass in Nuremberg', *Gothic and Renaissance Art in Nuremberg, 1300–1550* (exh. cat., New York, Met., 1986)

R. Becksmann: *Deutsche Glasmalerei des Mittelalters: Eine exemplarische Auswahl* (Stuttgart, 1988)

M. Bierschenk: *Glasmalereien der Elisabethkirche in Marburg: Die figürlichen Fenster um 1240* (Berlin, 1991)

H. Scholz: *Entwurf und Ausführung: Werkstattpraxis in der Nürnberger Glasmalerei der Dürerzeit* (Berlin, 1991)

DANIEL KLETKE

6. Eastern Europe. The original extent of the stained glass in Eastern Europe cannot easily be ascertained. Much has been lost, and too few sources have been preserved. Surviving examples indicate that medieval stained glass existed only in countries such as Poland, Bohemia (*see* §5 above) and perhaps Transylvania that had particularly close links with Western Europe.

In Poland there are about 283 surviving panels, of which the most important group (219) are located in Kraków. The earliest of these come from the former Dominican monastery. There are three panels (Kraków, N. Mus.) with upper sections consisting of large standing figures: *St Augustine* (1288; see fig. 109), *St Stanislas* (1288) and the *Virgin and Child* (*c*. 1320). The two saints have stylistic links with Austrian stained glass, while the *Virgin and Child* is apparently based on Italian models (Kalinowski). The three choir windows of St Mary's, Kraków, are adorned by panels originally from nine or eleven stained-glass windows. The grandly conceived iconographic programme contained biblical subjects, including scenes from *Genesis*, the *Life of Christ* and the *Life of the Virgin*, dating from the second half of the 14th century, most possibly 1350–75. The 15th-century scenes from the *Passion* and figures of saints in Corpus Christi Church, Kraków, may originally have come from nine windows but have been combined in one. They are remarkable for their white-blue colouring, despite the presence of red, yellow and green glass, and for the confinement of figures and scenes to individual panels without any architectural frame. The panel at Iwkowa, near Kraków, may be by the same workshop.

The oldest surviving glass (second half of the 13th to the mid-14th century) in Toruń is in the tracery of the west window in St John's Church. Most other panels from this area, including those from the Dominican church of St Nicholas (*c*. 1320; destr. 1832), the former 15th-century Franciscan church of St Mary and St Mary's, Chełmno (*c*. 1380), are now in Toruń District Museum. Those in St Nicholas depict prophets and scenes from the *Life of Christ*. An image of the *Mater Dolorosa* and other fragments came from St Mary's, Toruń, and panels depicting scenes from the *Infancy of Christ* and the *Passion*, the apostles and the prophets are from St Mary's, Chełmno. While the stylistic characteristics of the panels from St Nicholas suggest a dependence on south Germany and Austria, those from Chełmno reveal a Bohemian influence, in particular that of Master Theodoric. Glaziers from Toruń may also have worked for or in Włocławek around the mid-14th century. The medallions in the cathedral, six Christological scenes and sixteen *Prophets*, bear many similarities to the panels from St Nicholas.

In Romania a few fragments (14th–15th century) in the parish churches of Biertan, Crit, Atel, Mośna, Richis and Sighisoara, all in Transylvania, indicate that originally there used to be coloured windows there. The explanation for the isolated occurrence of medieval stained glass in that region is that this area was colonized by Germans, who had strong links with Western European traditions. Although relatively few examples of Eastern European Gothic stained glass have been preserved, those of high artistic quality and technical excellence suggest that leaded stained-glass windows were an established and integral part of the furnishing and iconographical programme of the churches in Poland and perhaps Transylvania.

109. *St Augustine* (detail), stained glass, from the former Dominican monastery, Kraków, Poland, 1288 (Kraków, National Museum)

BIBLIOGRAPHY

K. Jung: *Katedra Włocławska* (Włocławek, 1900)

F. Kopera: 'Alte polnische Glasmalerei', *Z. Alte & Neue Glasmal.* (1913), pp. 97–9

R. Heuer: 'Werke der bildenden Kunst und des Kunstgewerbes in Thorn bis zum Ende des Mittelalters', *Mitt. Copernicus-Ver. Wiss. & Kst Thorn*, xxiv (1916), pp. 1–90

W. Stromer: 'O Witrażu średnowiecznym w katedrze Włocławskiej' [The medieval stained glass in Włocławek Cathedral], *Prace sekcji historii sztuki i kultury Tow. Nauk w Lwowie* [Transactions of the history of art and culture section of the Lwow Society of Learning] (1929), pp. 71–92

G. Chmarzyński: 'Srednowieczny witraż Toruński' [Medieval stained glass in Toruń], *Biul. Hist. Sztuki & Kult.*, ii/1 (1933)

V. Roth, ed.: *Die deutsche Kunst in Siebenbürgen* (Berlin, 1934)

H. Niedermeier: 'Alte polnische Glasmalerei', *Belvedere*, xiii (1938–43), pp. 204–5

E. Kwiatkowski: 'Witraże średniowieczne Torunia i Chełmna w kaplicy malborskiej' [Medieval stained glass from Toruń and Chełmno in Malbork Chapel], *Dokumentacja Konserwatorska: Akta PKZ* (Toruń, 1956–9)

——: 'Witraże Gotyckie z Torunia i Chełmna w zbiorach muzeum w Toruniu' [Gothic stained glass from Toruń and Chełmno in the collections of Toruń Museum], *Roc. Muz. Toruniu*, i/3 (1963), pp. 98–133

E. Drachenberg: *Die mittelalterliche Glasmalerei im Erfurter Dom*, Corp. Vitrearum Med. Aevi, 2 vols (Berlin, 1980–83)

L. Kalinowski: 'Die ältesten Glasgemälde der Dominikanerkirche in Krakau', *Bau- und Bildkunst im Spiegel internationaler Forschung* (Berlin, 1989), pp. 113–24

ERHARD DRACHENBERG

7. SCANDINAVIA. The Gothic stained glass of Scandinavia is very unevenly distributed. Most is found in Sweden, with a particular concentration on the island of Gotland. There are no surviving complete windows in Norway but only fragments with ornamental motifs dating from the 13th and 14th centuries. Denmark has a few more examples, with mid-13th-century figures that are still Late Romanesque in style at Roager Church and St Martin's, Bjerreby (Tåsinge), 14th-century fragments from Roskilde Cathedral and 15th-century panels from Holmstrup. The earliest glass in Finland is a group of mid-13th-century fragments from Jomala Church. Later windows show the influence of German glass; panels (Helsinki, N. Mus.) from churches in the south-west include an early 14th-century *St Martin* from Raisio, Finland, in the Lübeck style (*see* §VIII, 5 above); this style is also found in Gotland and on 15th-century figures from Nagu and Vehmaa in Finland.

The reasons for this imbalance lie in the nature of Scandinavian Gothic. It is not possible to define a regional glass painting style, since, as in other media, although there were local craftsmen, the models always came from elsewhere. Gotland, however, was a wealthy island, and many churches were built during the period and new windows were added to existing buildings. Stained glass was first installed *c.* 1220 when a German glass painter founded a workshop in VISBY to glaze St Maria's Cathedral. Both glass and buildings remained under Germanic influence until the later part of the century when French and English styles also became evident and continued into the 14th century. Various local schools were based on the cathedrals and great churches of the region, each working in its own manner.

110. *Annunciation*, stained glass, 610×470 mm, from Gotland, Sweden, first half of the 13th century (Mora, Zornmuseet)

Although the earliest Gotlandic glass dates from the 13th century, it shows the survival of late 12th-century features that were still popular in parts of the Holy Roman Empire. A group of churches have glazing schemes of some variety but all broadly in the Late Romanesque–Byzantine style of north German glass. The iconography is generally derived from the New Testament, with scenes from the Nativity to the Resurrection carried out in a vivid narrative style and strong colours, red, blue and green being predominant. The ornamental backgrounds are fairly simple and consist mainly of stereotyped scrolls. At Endre Church there is glass of high quality and lively design with strong, glowing colours, showing scenes from the *Life of Christ* in a combination of rectangular panels and round medallions set in foliage, which are not otherwise typical of Gotland glass. These date from the mid-13th century. Similar well-designed panels (mid-13th century) of the *Passion* and a figure of *St Margaret* survive at Dalhem Church; this particular workshop provided glass for several local churches and it is possible to distinguish various hands. The churches at Sjonhem and Rone have very similar New Testament groups (*c.* 1240), marked by simple backgrounds and borders. Other windows of the first half of the 13th century, with rather more muted colours, come from Lojsta Church, and there is an *Annunciation* panel of unknown provenance in a particularly delicate Byzantine manner (Mora, Zornmus.; see fig. 110). Vesica-shaped medallions from the later part of the 13th century are found at Alskog, where the three narrow lancets in the choir have a *Passion* cycle; there are also simple canopies, and the borders and backgrounds show the influence of manuscript design. The main colours are red and light green.

German influence, especially from the workshops of Lübeck in Lower Saxony, continued to be felt during the 14th century. The local craftsmen did not generally achieve the more delicate qualities of mature Gothic glass elsewhere, but there is some fine work at Lye Church where the east window of *c.* 1330 has scenes from the *Life of Christ* framed by saints and bishops under canopies with foliage and grisaille. The central panels are in a beautifully restrained style with elegant figures and simple backgrounds. The same, Visby-based, workshop probably made windows for several other churches in the area between 1320 and 1350. French influence can be recognized in the *Passion* cycle at Etelham, now in rather poor condition, and also at Hörsne in a panel of *St Bartholomew*. Later 14th-century windows were installed at Grötlingbo and the Pfarrkirche, Heijde, where the subjects are from the Old Testament and include scenes from the story of *Adam and Eve*.

After the mid-14th century the combined effects of the Black Death and the Danish occupation of the island led to a decline in prosperity and the cessation of the programme of church building. On the mainland there was some revival in the 15th century. The more detailed glass painting of a *Crucifixion* (late 15th century) and a heraldic panel (*c.* 1480) at Vika in Dalarna illustrates the continuing influence of the Lübeck school. A further range of panels from Gotland and elsewhere (Stockholm, Nmus.; Stockholm, Stat. Hist. Mus.) again shows that, of the Scandinavian countries, Sweden had by far the widest range of glass.

BIBLIOGRAPHY

J. Roosval: 'Medieval Schools of Stained Glass Painting on Gotland', *Gaz. B.-A.*, lxxxvii (1945), pp. 193–204

Skandinavien, Corp. Vitrearum Med. Aevi (1964)

L. Grodecki: *Le Vitrail roman* (Fribourg, 1977)

8. SPAIN. The earliest Gothic stained glass in Spain dates from the 13th century and is in a fully French style, Gothic architecture having been introduced from the Ile-de-France. It did not at first become a major Spanish art but in the 14th century continued to employ foreign, mainly south Netherlandish glaziers. In the 15th century a period of expansion resulted in glass made by glaziers from the Low Countries, France, Germany and Italy becoming an integral part of the major cathedrals. This process of fusion eventually led to the development of a distinctively Spanish style which continued until it was superseded by Renaissance styles in the 16th century.

Stained glass remained a marginal art form during the 13th century. The great 13th-century cathedrals of León, Burgos (*see* LEÓN, §II, 1(iii) and BURGOS, §2(i)(c)) and Toledo were essentially French-style buildings on Spanish soil; the extent of their intended glazing schemes can be compared with that of the scheme at Chartres Cathedral, but it is only in León that a rather archaic French style survives. Rose windows did not immediately develop into the elaborate traceried structures of the northern cathedrals but remained relatively small, frequently without mullions, until a later flowering in the 15th century.

During the 14th century the craft, mainly undertaken by south Netherlandish glaziers, began to spread throughout the regions. In Catalonia work included the glazing of the apse and nave in the monastery of S Maria de Pedralbes and scenes from the *Life of Christ* in the monastery of Santes Creus, dating from the 1340s. Windows were made for the cathedrals of Viç and Girona (*see* GIRONA, §1(iii)), and a great glazing programme was begun (main scheme from 1418) at Toledo (*see* TOLEDO, §IV, 3), where brightly coloured *Saints* and *Prophets* stand under canopies and the rose window in the north transept displays a central *Crucifixion* surrounded by tiers of figures. South Netherlandish influence remained strong throughout the century because of Spain's relationship with its provinces.

In the early 15th century many workshops of foreign glaziers were established. The programme at Toledo continued under Juan Dolfin, a French glazier, who made the choir, transept clerestory and some apse windows (1418–27). The delicate west rose window dates from the first half of the century and incorporates south Netherlandish glass. Work was continued on the cathedral by French, south Netherlandish and German glaziers, including Pedro Bonifacio (*fl* 1459), who is known also to have worked on Barcelona Cathedral. A major figure in the 1480s was

111. Enrique Aleman: *Four Prophets* (1478), stained glass, 7.8×3.2 m, nave, Seville Cathedral, Spain

the German Enrique Aleman (*fl* 1485; *d* before *c.* 1492), who made the windows of the nave clerestory and aisles at Toledo, the south in vivid colours and the north in more muted tones. He used mainly imported glass and worked in the monumental and expressive style of German painting of this date. Some of his designs for Toledo were reused from his earlier work (1478–84) at Seville Cathedral (see fig. 111). There his *Saints*, *Evangelists* and Old Testament *Prophets* provided the nave with a unified design; they were painted with almost the realism of Jan van Eyck, combined with a strong sense of colour. The programme at Seville was to continue into the 16th century with processions of saints in the nave aisles and the *Life of Christ* in the crossing, painted by Arnao de Flandes (*fl* 1525–38; *d* 1557) in the new Renaissance style that combined south Netherlandish and Italian influences. Seville remained an important centre, particularly for the work of south Netherlandish craftsmen in the region.

Barcelona was the home of many foreign glaziers, known both from documents and from their windows, including the scheme for S Eulalia Cathedral and the rose window in S María del Mar, a *Coronation of the Virgin* (*c.* 1460), made by Antonio Llonye, who had also worked at Piedmont and Toulouse. From this cosmopolitan atmosphere, especially following the defeat of the Moors and the unification, a markedly Spanish style emerged. This style was determined partly by the climate, with the strong sunlight necessitating fewer and smaller openings rather than great walls of glass. Rich colours, particularly red, were used. The abstract geometric patterns of Moorish art and the expressionist nature of Mozarabic art were important elements, producing a powerful and stylized idiom.

During the 16th century the developing Spanish style underwent a transition towards the more international features of the Renaissance, including modelling, perspective, landscapes and detailed enamel painting. At Segovia and Astorga cathedrals brightly coloured *New Testament* scenes perpetuated the 15th-century tradition; south Netherlandish influences were still present at Salamanca Cathedral; and Nicolás Vergara the elder (*see* VERGARA, (1)), the glazier of Segovia Cathedral, installed a rose window (after 1542) in the south transept at Toledo Cathedral. Renaissance windows (1520–22) made by Alberto de Holanda, a north Netherlandish glazier who had worked at Burgos, are found on the north side of Ávila Cathedral, contrasting with the Late Gothic ones on the south side.

BIBLIOGRAPHY

C. H. Sherrill: *Stained Glass Tours in Spain and Flanders* (London, 1924)
J. A. de Lasarte: 'Vidrieras', *A. Hisp.*, x (1952), pp. 374–97
V. N. Alcaide: 'El maestro Enrique Aleman: Vidriero de las catedrales de Sevilla y Toledo', *Archv Esp. A.*, clvii (1967), pp. 55–82
España, Corp. Vitrearum Med. Aevi (1969–)

For further bibliography *see* §1 above.

9. PORTUGAL. Portugal possesses few examples of medieval stained glass. Although glazing schemes were perhaps not a major element, there is no reason to suppose that Portuguese buildings had none, as there are many documentary references to glaziers as well as 19th-century descriptions of glass that is now missing. South Netherlandish glaziers were known from the early 15th century, while in the 16th both south Netherlandish and Portuguese glaziers were contributing to the exuberant MANUELINE STYLE. Destruction and theft may be partly to blame for the loss of glass: in the 19th century the monks of Batalha Abbey were reported to be giving away pieces of glass to visitors. With the craft in decline there was no way of repairing the surviving remains.

BATALHA Abbey church is the only building with an important range of glass. Dating from the early 15th century to the late 16th, it was in such poor condition by the 1840s that emergency restorations on the nave and chapels were undertaken, with further extensive work in the 1930s on the chapter house. The earliest glass (*c.* 1400–20), which is in the south Netherlandish style and was reset in the north and south nave, is an elaborate programme of scenes from the *Life of Christ.* Later 15th-century glass, including a *Last Judgement*, is to be seen in the Founder's Chapel and the main façade. It can perhaps be attributed to the south Netherlandish Master Guilhelme (*fl* 1477) and the German glazier Luis, referred to in 1446. There are also references to Portuguese glaziers at this time. Another south Netherlandish craftsman, Master João (*fl* 1489; *d* 1528), may have created the *Passion* (1514) in the chapter house in collaboration with Francisco Henriques. Several different hands worked on the chancel windows in a detailed Renaissance style, and their works include the *Annunciation*, the *Visitation* and the *Resurrection*, all early 16th century and now heavily restored. In the second half of the 16th century two generations of the Portuguese Taca family (both named Antonio; *fl* 1532–6 and 1569–96) were responsible for the glazing at Batalha Abbey, and their workshops also provided glass for other churches, including Tomar Abbey and the chapel of the Hospital Real de Todos-os-Santos, Lisbon.

Other surviving glass includes a 15th-century heraldic panel (Oporto, Mus. N. Soares dos Reis), formerly in the convent of S Clara, Vila do Conde; an early 16th-century figure of *St Peter*, now reset as two windows in the church at Viana do Alentejo and possibly by FRANCISCO HENRIQUES, who also designed windows in Évora, Sintra and Batalha; and a fragment (1539; Setúbal, Mus. Setúbal) which came from the monastery of Jesus at Setubal.

BIBLIOGRAPHY

J. M. Neale: 'Batalha', *The Ecclesiologist*, xv (1854), pp. 223–36
Portugal, Corp. Vitrearum Med. Aevi (1983)

10. ITALY. Stained glass developed relatively late in Italy, flourished only in the northern half of the country and was never fully integrated architecturally. This was because of the survival of the Classical tradition and the advances in Italian painting; glass remained a painter's art rather than a glazier's craft. Its distinctive character arose from its pictorial nature and rich colours, suitable for the strong sunlight.

The earliest windows (*c.* 1253–60) are in the Upper Church of S Francesco, Assisi (*see* ASSISI, §II, 1 and 3), in the apse (a typological sequence of biblical scenes) and nave, made by German and French workshops. Other early work is in Siena, and the first influence of painting on window design is seen in the Byzantine-type *Virgin and Child* (*c.* 1280; Siena, Madonna della Grotta Oratory) and in the rose window (*c.* 1290; see fig. 112), formerly attributed to Duccio, in the choir of Siena Cathedral. During the 13th century eye (*occhi*) and wheel windows developed from the small round openings of Romanesque buildings and were to remain typical.

By the 14th century foreign influence had ceased and designs were showing an increasing awareness of modelling and perspective. At S Francesco, Assisi, early 14th-century windows in the Lower Church reflect the styles of Giotto and Cimabue; the windows in St Martin's Chapel may have been designed by Simone Martini, who had painted the frescoes *c.* 1317 (*see* MARTINI, SIMONE, fig. 1), while mural artists from Umbria provided designs for windows in the Upper Church. Glass in S Maria Novella, Santa Croce, and Orsanmichele, in Florence, shows the

112. *Death, Assumption and Coronation of the Virgin with Saints and the Evangelists* (*c.* 1290), stained glass, choir rose window, Siena Cathedral, Italy

direct influence of contemporary paintings, and it was not unusual for well-known painters also to design stained glass.

In Perugia however the apse windows (1410) in S Domenico were based on the Gothic formula of saints under canopies and display the first example in Italy of silver-stain, a century later than its appearance in France. Yet other windows, designed by Renaissance painters and sculptors, show naturalistic and three-dimensional qualities. Among these are the *Virgin and Child* (1450s) in Prato Cathedral designed by Fra Filippo Lippi and the Old Testament figures (*c.* 1460) in Pisa Cathedral, by Alesso Baldovinetti. In Florence are Domenico Ghirlandaio's apse windows in S Maria Novella (where he painted the Tornabuoni frescoes, 1485–90) and Pietro Perugino's eye window of the *Descent of the Holy Spirit* (*c.* 1487) in Santo Spirito; the Gesuati (Jesuit) workshops specialized in providing painters' designs for windows, frequently modified and reused. Workshops also flourished in Bologna and Milan, the latter cathedral having been glazed by several schools, combining Germanic and Lombardic styles; its side windows were donated by guilds in the 1470s to honour their patron saints. By the mid-16th century, however, the craft had virtually ceased.

BIBLIOGRAPHY

C. H. Sherrill: *A Stained Glass Tour in Italy* (London, 1913)
G. Marchini: *Italian Stained Glass Windows* (London, 1957)
Italia, Corp. Vitrearum Med. Aevi (1973–)

For further bibliography *see* §1 above.

CAROLA HICKS

113. *Presentation in the Temple*, embroidery, detail from the Bologna Cope, from England, *c.* 1315–35 (Bologna, Museo Civico Medioevale e del Rinascimento)

IX. Textiles.

Most extant Gothic textiles are chance survivors. They do not constitute a fair representation of their art form, nor do they necessarily show the very best of what was produced. For a fairer assessment of these matters much attention must be given to the surviving documentary evidence, of which there is fortunately a great amount. Taken together, extant works and documents can well establish the importance in the history of art of Gothic textiles, particularly tapestry and embroidery, as objects of great iconographical interest and stylistic influence.

1. Introduction. 2. Tapestry and embroidery. 3. Silk fabrics.

1. INTRODUCTION. All Gothic textiles were made to be used, and the likely requirements and consequences of use were considered in their making. Strength was sought in the places and instances where it was thought necessary, and stability of colour thought essential for at least as long as was required for satisfactory use. Made mostly from thread of animal fibre, textiles necessarily deteriorate. Moreover, misuse, abuse and indifference greatly accelerate this process. Thus the vast majority of Gothic textiles have disappeared forever, their existence known only from contemporary or later records. Changes in taste and artistic style caused many to be thought outmoded or superfluous to changing needs and to be replaced by contemporary textiles or other more popular media. Retiral from former prominence often led not to forgotten preservation, but to harsher and more unsuited uses, perhaps sold down the social scale, bequeathed to less style-conscious religious establishments or merely put to other use (one tapestry was found in France in the 19th century covering a cart of apples). Many more textiles were easy objects of destruction during social and religious turmoil and war.

In the Middle Ages, when material possessions were fewer and more prized than at present, the making and possession of any textile was necessarily of great significance, particularly those produced to satisfy the desire for display and to communicate aspirations, whether religious or secular, personal or corporate. Moreover, of those that consequently required such skills, materials and time as could not be justified on purely utilitarian grounds, the most highly prized were textiles that reflected also the subtle workings of the human imagination from conception to execution.

2. TAPESTRY AND EMBROIDERY. Foremost among the patterned textiles during this period were embroideries and tapestries. As luxury and artistic goods many share certain common features: they were made with the highest quality of materials and skills, were costly to produce, market and buy, were designed by the most imaginative artists and communicated significant ideas and aspirations. Iconographically and stylistically they parallel developments in the other arts, such as painting and ivories (see fig. 113, and figs 80 and 97 above). The methods of their production, however, differed as did their functions and formats, both forms contributing individually to medieval art.

(i) Production. (ii) Use.

(i) Production. Tapestry is a type of weaving, embroidery a type of needlework (for their techniques *see* TAPESTRY, §I; EMBROIDERY, §I). For both embroidery and tapestry, materials were limited. Most tapestries consisted mainly of woollen thread offset by varying amounts of silk thread. Sometimes linen thread replaced the wool, particularly in the warp threads, as in the majority of German and Swiss tapestries. Most embroideries consisted mainly of silk thread for the stitching and undyed linen cloth for the 'ground', sometimes replaced by dyed silk cloth or velvet. In both techniques textiles of a higher quality often included thread of precious metal that generally took the form of silver or gold thread wound round silk thread, and some more precious embroideries had added coloured beads, enamels, plates of gold, pearls, precious stones and gems. Vegetable dyes, such as weld, madder and woad for yellow, red and blue, were mostly derived locally. Other dyes, such as indigo and kermes, were imported for occasional use. After boiling the thread with mordants, such as alum, further boiling with the dye substance secured a textile with a relatively narrow, but stable range of colours. Most colours have even now faded relatively little and only a few dark tones, such as black, have disappeared owing to the particularly corrosive effects of the metallic mordant.

Both tapestries and embroideries are strictly secondary forms of art. The visible textile design does not begin at the point of weaving or embroidering but at an earlier stage in the drawing or painting of that design. In this respect both textiles are similar in their creation to most other forms of art produced in the Gothic period, including wall and panel painting. Yet the two processes were often entirely separate activities, and the craftsmen were from distinct groups. The painters seem to have been particularly keen to keep the activities separate and establish a monopoly in designing such textiles. Thus very many of them, including some now more famous for their panel and wall painting, such as Cosimo Tura and Jacques Daret, worked on textile designs. Antonio Pollaiuolo (*see* POLLAIUOLO, (1)), for example, designed the embroideries (*c.* 1469–80) of the *Life of St John the Baptist* (Florence, Mus. Opera Duomo). A monopoly was not, however, sustainable, especially one generally dependent on ad hoc cooperation. In-house designs and specialists became particularly important as production expanded and accelerated into a manufacturing process. Inevitably, standards fell, and earlier designs were reused in part or in unsuitable combinations.

Many tapestries came into being only after the creation of both a small and a full-size cartoon, each often by different painters, the first by the more able artist. For the *Story of Herkinbald* tapestry (Brussels, Musées Royaux A. & Hist.), for example, made in 1513 for the Confraternity of the Holy Sacrament in Leuven, the small cartoons were made by JAN VAN ROOME and the large ones by 'Philippe le paintre'. Only then could the design be marked up on the warp threads and transposed by the weavers on to the tapestry. Comparison of pieces woven from the same cartoons suggests that the large cartoon left very little scope for innovation of design at the loom. This is shown by two surviving tapestries (Zamora Cathedral Treasury, on loan to Zamora, Mus. Cat.; New York, Met.) of the *Arming of Hector* from the *Trojan War* set, which was sold by the Grenier family of Tournai in the 1470s and 1480s (*see* GRENIER, PASQUIER, and TOURNAI, §3(i)(a); *see also* TAPESTRY, colour pl. I, fig. 2). More direct, perhaps, were embroideries where the design could be drawn or painted on the ground textile before embroidering began. Occasionally, because of damage, omission or deliberate intention this design can still be seen, as in the Pienza Cope (early 14th century; Pienza, Mus. Cattedrale).

Most embroideries and tapestries of significance were produced professionally. Organized into local guilds, both tapestry-weavers and embroiderers sought to sustain and protect their craft through long apprenticeships and strict codes of practice. In addition, such local municipal authorities as London, Brussels and Tournai sought by sanctioning the craft regulations to encourage and maintain high standards of work in order to establish and sustain their town's reputation for high-quality goods. Regular inspection of workshops and the application of the seal of approval was also required and executed by the authorities. More dynamic was the progressively greater role played by merchants, for example Nicolas Bataille and the Grenier family for tapestry and Adam of Basing, Mayor of London in 1251, for embroidery. They could afford the often high costs of materials and arrange for their importation. They could offer the craftsmen more secure financial backing for expensive and risky projects, bring together into cooperation several workshops for larger projects and sell what they produced. By the end of this period it was such men as Pasquier Grenier and his family who were in control, often to the detriment of the guild system and to the quality of the goods.

114. *King Arthur*, detail from the *Nine Worthies* tapestry, probably by Nicolas Bataille, whole tapestry 3.05×4.13 m, from Paris, France, *c.* 1385 (New York, The Cloisters)

Also of vital importance to the development of the production of fine embroidery and tapestry was the proximity of a prosperous and active court, such as that of Charles V, King of France, and his family (see fig. 114). Here were to be found most of those who could afford the high prices of such luxury goods and here too were those with the right needs and preferences. Already drawn to such centres was the necessary commercial and mercantile activity. Thus, for example, much of the finest English embroidery was produced in London, and French and Netherlandish tapestry in Paris and close to the court of the Burgundian dukes. Tapestry-weavers and embroiderers, therefore, came to share the fortunes and mirror in their products the preferences of these courts. Indeed, several had salaried court appointments.

From *c.* 1250–*c.* 1350 embroidery made in England, then known across Europe as OPUS ANGLICANUM, reached a peak of excellence that was rarely matched. During the same period, however, high-quality embroidery was produced in several of the principal towns of Italy (e.g. Milan and Florence), Spain and also, much influenced stylistically by England and Italy, France. Other European centres were of less significance, except that of the

Burgundian Netherlands in the second half of the 15th century. In general, therefore, embroidery developed along similar lines to many other arts of this period.

Tapestry, on the other hand, had a rather different development (*see* TAPESTRY, §II, 1). High-quality production was generally limited throughout this period to the north of France and the Burgundian Netherlands, and steady growth in the production of figurative tapestry production was established only around the middle of the 14th century. Thus the name Arras (fin fil d'Arras) became widely synonymous for the best type of tapestry. Other centres of high-quality tapestry production included parts of Germany and Switzerland, such as Nuremberg, Alsace and Basle. Surviving examples, however, although made with very rich materials, do not match the grand scale of Arras. Although further centres, such as Siena, were established during the 15th century, often through the importation of weavers from the major centres of the north, few could match the northern products, even by the end of the century. The much later emergence of Arras was the result of its close dependence on economic and social factors. In particular, growth in mercantile activity and in the power and wealth of the secular courts did much to facilitate the trade in such a luxury item. Furthermore, its emergence and the decline of *opus anglicanum* coincided with a general shift of the centres of artistic activity away from England to the north of France and the Burgundian Netherlands. Artistic influence then began to work in the opposite direction across the Channel, and English art was regarded progressively as for local consumption and on the margins of the mainstream of European artistic development. Thus by the second half of the 15th century the highest quality embroidery needed to be imported into England from the Netherlands.

Both types of textile often travelled far from their place of production. *Opus anglicanum* and Arras in particular were acquired by clerics and nobility throughout Europe and beyond. Unifying factors, such as the Church, political and dynastic ties and established trading routes, greatly facilitated this dissemination. Gifts of embroideries and tapestries from those in whose lands production prospered were much prized by their recipients, and their proud possession in distant lands often influenced the preferences of other inhabitants. Thus the popes at Rome and Avignon came to possess a very large number of English embroideries (Molimir; Hoberg), despite the ready availability of fine Italian ones, and successive English monarchs, their relatives and courtiers displayed tapestries consisting mainly of English wool, but woven by French or Netherlandish weavers in their lands across the Channel (e.g. the *Millefleurs* tapestry with the arms of John, Lord Dinham, *d* 1501; New York, Cloisters; *see also* HERALDRY, colour pl. III, fig.2). Moreover, so strong was the unity of taste across Europe that even many Renaissance patrons were proud owners of northern tapestries: six tapestries (untraced) of the *Triumphs* were made for Giovanni de' Medici by Pierre de Los of Lille in 1453–5; Federigo II Montefeltro, Duke of Urbino, bought a set of eleven pieces of the *Trojan War* from Pasquier Grenier in 1476; and Matthias Corvinus, King of Hungary, is known from a description by Antonio Bonifini of festivities in Buda in 1495 to have owned a similar set of the *Trojan War* (Souchal).

(ii) Use. Surviving examples of embroideries give a distorted view of the balance between those intended for secular use and those for religious use. The implication that most, if not all, were for the latter purpose is not confirmed by the documentary evidence. Secular use offered many opportunities for the finest embroidery in court and ceremonial clothes and fantastically decorated furnishings, for example, the two red velvet fragments (*c.* 1338; Paris, Mus. Cluny; *see* HERALDRY, fig. 21) embroidered with the royal leopards of England, associated with Edward III (*reg* 1327–77) and thought to have been a horse trapper. Surviving tapestries, on the other hand, provide at least a sample of works intended for secular use. They do not, however, adequately reflect the great range and variety of works recorded in the major princely European collections, particularly those dating from before 1450. Inevitably such a fortunate survival as the *Apocalypse* tapestries (Angers, Château, Col. Tap.; *see* ANGERS, §3) distorts by its present uniqueness perceptions of this matter, and it needs to be offset by contemporary records of works of equally grand proportions that depicted secular subjects.

Given its production during this period as a relatively inflexible textile, tapestry was generally unsuitable for clothing. Its most obvious uses were therefore as large furnishings for both the church and castle. Among these were wall hangings, bed furnishings and altar frontals. Individual rooms could be furnished by one set of tapestry furnishings and larger halls by the combination of different pieces, sometimes in more than one layer along the walls. Embroidery, although more suited to clothing, was also employed for similar furnishings. Embroidered wall hangings, bed furnishings and altar frontals were all regularly made and sought-after. In addition smaller embroideries were produced for ecclesiastical and secular uses. Common examples were embroidered purses, burses and seal bags: two seal bags (London, Guildhall, Corp. London Rec. Office) with the English royal arms and those of the City of London are attached to two charters dated 1319; two mid-14th-century French purses (Hamburg, Mus. Kst. & Gew.; Sens Cathedral Treasury) are embroidered with pairs of lovers. The most numerous survivors, however, are embroidered items of clothing, principally religious vestments (*see* EMBROIDERY, colour pl. II, fig. 2). Vestments that attracted some of the finest work were the cope (e.g. the English copes at Pienza (*see* §(i) above) and Bologna, *c.* 1315–35; Bologna, Mus. Civ.), the mantle (e.g. the mid-15th-century Netherlandish Mantle of the Order of the Golden Fleece; Vienna, Schatzkam.) and chasuble (e.g. the Chichester–Constable Chasuble, second quarter of the 14th century; New York, Met.). The latter often had orphreys of such outstanding quality that they alone were preserved and reused on later chasubles, as on the Westminster Chasuble (Wardour Castle, Wilts) or on altar frontals, for example the orphreys of the first half of the 15th century attached to a 17th-century satin frontal (London, V&A).

The shape of both embroideries and tapestries was largely determined by their intended function or purpose.

Long thin strips were produced for hanging above choir-stalls or above wainscotting in a chapter house. Even thinner strips formed valences for beds. Size also reflected purpose, a large size, as in the Angers *Apocalypse* series, giving full opportunity for the clear and bold communication of a particular narrative or set of ideas, while providing onlookers with the general impression of wealth and power. Placement of such textiles also reflected their purpose. The use of particular images in a bed-of-state or on an altar frontal are two instances. More generally, the particular attention paid to the orphreys on a chasuble issues from the position of the priest celebrating mass: as he faced the altar his back was turned to the people, and so too were the images of the Life of Christ worked in splendid embroidery, as on the Wokyndon Cross-orphrey (first half of the 14th century; London, V&A). Many such textiles were reserved for special occasions. Religious feast days brought out the most splendid possessions of many cathedrals. Indeed, until very recent times, Easter provided the sole annual opportunity to see the vast collections of textiles collected by such cathedrals in Spain as Toledo and Saragossa. The peripatetic secular courts also reserved many of their textiles to impress onlookers at births, marriages (e.g. that of Charles the Bold, Duke of Burgundy, to Margaret of York in 1468), funerals, state visits and triumphal entries.

3. SILK FABRICS. Western manufacture of silk fabrics began in Italy early in the 13th century. Here, the main centres of production became Venice, Genoa, Milan, Florence and Siena. Sicily, long considered one of the earliest and most active centres, has been shown to be of much less importance, and, although silk fabrics were also made in Spain, principally in the Muslim cities of the south, north Italy continued to be the main Western centre for the rest of the period. Here the techniques of weaving plain dyed silk fabrics steadily developed under the influence of the East, and by the 15th century the production of the most luxurious varieties, samite, satin, damask and velvet, had attained a rare peak of perfection.

For most of the 13th century silk design was highly dependent on Byzantine and Islamic practices: compositions based on repeated patterns were generally static and symmetrical. Around the end of the 13th century, however, there was a significant change. At this point there emerged the so-called free or wild style, the hallmarks of which are asymmetry and movement. Real and imaginary animals began to twist and turn freely in sinuous movements, and plants sprouted, often entangling the animals. The opening of trade with the East after the Mongol conquests and the consequent importation of Chinese textiles appear to have been the principal cause of the adoption of this freer style in the Italian silk-producing centres. In the 15th century silk design returned to fewer and much more uniform styles. By far the most common among extant examples is the so-called pomegranate, the shape of which bears more resemblance to a pine-cone or pineapple. In general, movement and animal life were no longer considered as suitable motifs; plant forms were much enlarged and became the dominant or sole feature of designs.

Production of both plain and patterned silk fabrics soon became a very important commercial activity involving

115. Fragment of a chasuble, silk, from Italy, 14th century (Cleveland, OH, Museum of Art)

many persons and requiring much organization and capital investment. At the highest level very skilled weavers were needed to execute complicated designs. The spinning and dyeing needed to be of very high quality. As was the case for tapestries and embroideries, merchants and the secular courts greatly promoted the growth of such luxury goods. Silk fabrics were much used for clothing, especially court dress and ecclesiastical vestments (see fig. 115). Plain and patterned fabrics, sometimes wholly or partly woven in silk thread wound round with gold thread, were also often used as furnishings in both ecclesiastical and secular settings. At the richest courts and churches such silk hangings frequently accompanied embroideries and tapestries in displays of wealth and splendour.

BIBLIOGRAPHY

GENERAL

J. J. Marquet de Vasselot and R. A. Weigert: *Bibliographie de la tapisserie, des tapis et de la broderie en France* (Paris, 1935)

R. A. Weigert: *La Tapisserie et le tapis* (Paris, 1964) [suppl. to 1935 bibliog.]

Raiment for the Lord's Service: A Thousand Years of Western Vestments (exh. cat. by C. C. Mayer, Chicago, IL, A. Inst., 1975)

B. Schmedding: *Mittelalterliche Textilien in Kirchen und Klöstern der Schweiz* (Berne, 1978)

A. Geijer: *Ur textillconstens historia* (Stockholm, 1979; Eng. trans., London, 1979)

Textiles in Daily Life in the Middle Ages (exh. cat., ed. R. Martin; Cleveland, OH, Mus. A., 1985)

D. King: 'Embroidery and Textiles', *Age of Chivalry: Art in Plantagenet England, 1200–1400* (exh. cat., ed. J. J. G. Alexander and P. Binski; London, RA, 1987), pp. 157–61
——: *European Textiles in the Keir Collection, 400 BC to 1800 AD* (London, 1990)
J. Stratford: *The Bedford Inventories: The Worldly Goods of John, Duke of Bedford, Regent of France (1389–1435)* (London, 1993)

TAPESTRY

J. J. Guiffrey, E. Müntz and A. Pinchart: *Histoire générale de la tapisserie*, 3 vols (Paris, 1878–85)
W. G. Thomson: *A History of Tapestry* (London, 1906, rev. Wakefield, 3/1973)
H. Göbel: *Wandteppiche*, 3 vols (Leipzig, 1923–34; Eng. trans., vol. i, New York, 1924)
G.-J. Demotte: *Tapisserie gothique*, 2 vols (Paris, 1924–6)
R. A. Weigert: *La Tapisserie française* (Paris, 1956; Eng. trans., 1962)
G. Souchal: 'Charles VIII et la tenture de la Guerre de Troie', *Rev. Belge Archéol. & Hist. A./Belge Tijdschr. Oudhdknde & Kstgesch.*, xxxix (1970), p. 187
J. Lestocquoy: *Deux Siècles de l'histoire de la tapisserie, 1300–1500* (Arras, 1978)

EMBROIDERY

E. Molimir: 'Inventoire du Trésor du Saint Siège sous Boniface VIII (1295)', *Bib. Ecole Chartes*, xliii (1882), pp. 276–310, 626–46; xlv (1884), pp. 31–57; xlvi (1885), pp. 16–44; xlvii (1886), pp. 646–67; xlix (1888), pp. 226–37
L. de Farcy: *La Broderie du XIe siècle jusqu'à nos jours d'après des spécimens authentiques et les inventaires*, 4 vols (Angers, 1890–1919)
A. G. I. Christie: *English Medieval Embroidery* (London, 1938)
H. Hoberg, ed.: *Die Inventore des päpstlichen Schatzes in Avignon, 1314–1376*, Studi e testi, iii (Rome, 1944), pp. 401–64
M. Schuette and S. Müller-Christensen: *The Art of Embroidery* (London, 1963)
Opus Anglicanum: English Medieval Embroidery (exh. cat., ed. D. King; London, ACGB, 1963)
D. King: 'A Venetian Embroidered Altar Frontal', *V&A Mus. Bull.*, i/4 (1965), pp. 14–25; rev., V&A Mus. Bull. Reprints, 12 (London, 1970)
K. Staniland: *Embroiderers*, Medieval Craftsmen (London, 1991)

SILK FABRICS

G. Migeon: *Les Arts du tissu* (Paris, 1909, rev. 2/1929)
F. L. May: *Silk Textiles of Spain, Eighth to Fifteenth Century* (New York, 1957)
B. Klesse: *Seidenstoffe in der italienische Malerei des 14. Jahrhunderts* (Berne, 1967)
D. Devoti: *L'arte del tessuto in Europa* (Milan, 1974)
B. Markowsky: *Europäische Seidengewebe des 13–18. Jahrhunderts* (Cologne, 1976)

SCOT MCKENDRICK

Gothick. Term used in a more or less discriminatory way to identify the 18th-century works of the GOTHIC REVIVAL in British architecture and interior design. Some historians use the term as a convenient shorthand for the 18th-century phase of the Revival; others intend it to highlight the ways in which the 'Gothick' of the 18th century—the fanciful and thinly decorative architecture associated with dilettanti and antiquaries—is manifestly distinct from the more historicist works of the 19th-century 'Gothic Revival', whose architects not only drew upon different forms or styles of medieval Gothic but were motivated by liturgical, religious and social concerns rather than by 18th-century Associationist aesthetics. Both spellings were used in the 18th century, but during the 19th century 'Gothick' became obsolete: Eastlake (1872) wrote only of 'Gothic' and Clark (1928) followed his example. That preference has been maintained by such historians as Macaulay (1975) and McCarthy (1987), while others, notably Crook (1983), have sought to revive the obsolete form and with it the distinctions between the architecture of the 18th century and that of the 19th. In the introduction to his edition (1970) of Eastlake's study Crook proposed a further subdivision: 'Rococo Gothick' for the early to mid-18th century and 'Picturesque Gothick' for the later. Other labels were introduced by Davis (1974), whose 'Georgian Gothick' incorporates the whole of the 18th century, and Harris (1983), who identified as 'Kentian Gothick' the innovative style of the influential 18th-century architect WILLIAM KENT. Whatever merit such coinages may have, research on the origins of the Gothic Revival has established that historicism and asymmetry—acknowledged features of its 19th-century phase—were already significant characteristics during the 18th century, for instance at Horace Walpole's remodelled home, Strawberry Hill (1750s), Twickenham, London (*see* WALPOLE, (2), fig. 3).

See also ENGLAND, §I, 2(iv) and (v).

BIBLIOGRAPHY

C. L. Eastlake: *A History of the Gothic Revival* (London, 1872); ed. J. M. Crook (Leicester, 1970)
K. Clark: *The Gothic Revival: An Essay in the History of Taste* (London, 1928, rev. 1950)
P. Breman, ed.: *The Gothic of Gothick: English Church Building in Nineteenth Century Theory and Practice*, B. Weinreb, Architecture Catalogue, 14 (London, 1966)
T. Davis: *The Gothick Taste* (London, 1974)
J. Macaulay: *The Gothic Revival, 1745–1845* (Glasgow, 1975)
Gothick, 1720–1840 (exh. cat., ed. D. Simpson; Brighton, A.G. & Mus., 1975)
J. M. Crook, ed.: *A Gothick Symposium* (London, 1983) [incl. J. Harris: 'William Kent's Gothick']
M. McCarthy: *The Origins of the Gothic Revival* (London, 1987)
G. Worsley: 'The Origins of the Gothic Revival: A Re-appraisal', *Trans. Royal Hist. Soc.*, 6th ser., iii (1993), pp. 105–51
M. Aldrich: *Gothic Revival* (London, 1994)

MICHAEL MCCARTHY

Gothic Revival. Term applied to a style of architecture and the decorative arts inspired by the Gothic architecture of medieval Europe. It has been particularly widely applied to churches but has also been used to describe castellated mansions, collegiate buildings and houses. The Gothic Revival has also been described by many scholars as a movement, rather than style, for in the mid-19th century it was associated with and propagated by religious and political faith. From a hesitant start in the mid-18th century in England and Scotland, in the 19th century it became one of the principal styles of building throughout the world and continued in some huge projects until well into the 20th century (e.g. Episcopal Cathedral, Washington, DC, 1908–90; by G. F. BODLEY and others). 'Gothic Revival' became the standard English term when Charles Locke Eastlake published *A History of the Gothic Revival* (1872). The word 'Gothic' had by then definitely mutated from a depreciatory ephithet into the denomination of a style or period of medieval architecture. To distinguish medieval Gothic from modern Gothic, most European languages used the prefix 'neo-' (e.g. Dut. *neogotiek*; Fr. *néo-gothique*; It. *neogotico*; Ger. *Neogotik*, *Neugotik*). Thus the term 'neo-Gothic' is sometimes used in English translations of texts in other languages or when dealing with Gothic Revival architecture outside the UK.

Art historians have subdivided the successive manifestations of the Gothic style roughly into 'Gothic' (*c.* 1120–*c.* 1550), Gothic Survival (*c.* 1550–*c.* 1750) and Gothic Revival (from *c.* 1750). Although the Gothic Revival spread throughout the world, this article concentrates on the history and development of the style in Europe and North America.

See also GOTHIC, §I.

I. Architecture. II. Decorative arts.

I. Architecture.

1. History. 2. Literature.

1. HISTORY.

(i) Transition from 'Survival' to 'Revival'. (ii) Early development. (iii) Growth, theory and alliance with nationalism. (iv) Later developments.

(i) Transition from 'Survival' to 'Revival'. During the 16th and 17th centuries Gothic style was slowly reduced to a series of such features or elements as the pointed arch, tracery window, battlement, fan and rib vault, buttress and pinnacle. The result of this reduction, which varied from country to country, is generally referred to as GOTHIC SURVIVAL. There was, however, an intermediate stage between Survival and Revival, when medieval buildings, mainly large churches, were restored or completed, for example Westminster Abbey by Christopher Wren (repairs, 1698–1722) and later Nicholas Hawksmoor (west gable and towers, 1734–45); Orléans Cathedral (early 17th century to 1793) by Pierre-Adrien Pâris and others; the abbey church of Corbie, near Amiens, by a gifted but anonymous architect; and Milan Cathedral by Luigi Vanvitelli (designs, 1745; unexecuted) and other architects. All these architects continued designing and building in an obsolete style in order to render their work consistent with existing parts and to guarantee the harmony of the whole edifice. In so doing, they followed the time-honoured device of conformity. Most of the gothicizing work of GIOVANNI SANTINI, too, was reshaping of medieval Gothic churches, such as Kladruby (1712–26), though in a much more 'baroque' manner than Wren, with whom Santini may have been acquainted, since he had travelled in England.

The rebuilding of colleges in conformity with surviving medieval parts required (or at least allowed) a more synthetic style. Wren justified his 'Gothic' Tom Tower at Christ Church, Oxford, in a letter of 1681 (V. Fürst: *The Architecture of Sir Christopher Wren*, London,1956, p. 51): 'I resolued it ought to be Gothic to agree with the Founders worke.' It was for the same reason that Hawksmoor chose the 'Gothick' for the design of the north quadrangle (1715–56) of All Souls College, Oxford. The Codrington Library wing has a central feature comprising twin towers in the manner of a cathedral front, and the opposite wing is interrupted by a gateway (1734) surmounted by a cupola that Hawksmoor described as being in 'ye Monastick manner' (K. Downes: *Hawksmoor*, London, 1969, p. 162), an expression that seems to have been coined to express associative rather than formal qualities.

(ii) Early development. The Gothic Revival proper began when buildings were erected inspired by Gothic for its own sake, rather than being modelled on Gothic to conform to earlier examples. These included garden buildings in particular. In Nymphenburg, near Munich, in the grounds of the summer residence of the Bavarian Electors, the French-trained architect Joseph Effner built the Magdalenenklause (1725–80), a hermitage that exhibits elements of a sham ruin and a grotto containing a fairly 'Gothic' chapel, decorated with shellwork and frescoes and consecrated by the Archbishop of Cologne. The first English 'Gothick' garden pavilions are of a 'political' or 'patriotic' nature: the Gothic Temple (after 1717), Shotover, Oxon, attributed to William Townesend, a vaulted arcade of three bays erected for James Tyrell to celebrate the Whig triumph over arbitrary government; and Alfred's Hall (1721–32), Cirencester Park, Glos, a battlemented two-storey lodge with two round towers built for the 1st Earl of Bathurst, a Tory. Other examples of Gothick garden buildings include the Temple to the Liberty of our Ancestors or Gothic Temple (1741–7), Stowe, Bucks, built by JAMES GIBBS for Richard Temple, 1st Viscount Cobham, a leading Whig; the Cuttle Mill (*c.* 1740), Rousham, Oxon, by William Kent (*see* KENT, WILLIAM, §2(ii)); and Edgehill Castle Tower (1745–7), Radway, Warwicks, built for himself by SANDERSON MILLER, an amateur architect whose buildings included several sham castles and other Gothick works. Kent was also responsible for Esher Place, Surrey, a late 15th-century gatehouse that he enlarged and transformed by the addition of wings (1729–33; destr.) into a Rococo–Gothic villa. The early phase of the Gothic Revival that is linked with the Rococo is often distinguished from the 19th-century 'archaeological' Gothic Revival (in England, at least) by being called GOTHICK.

The best documented (and therefore sometimes perhaps overrated) Early Gothic Revival villa is Strawberry Hill, on the River Thames at Twickenham, Middx. It was originally a small, two-storey, undistinguished house but was reshaped from 1730 by its owner, Horace Walpole, into a model for domestic architecture (*see* WALPOLE, (2), fig. 3). Walpole was helped in his undertaking by the amateur architect JOHN CHUTE, the illustrator Richard Bentley (1708–82) and also Johann Heinrich Müntz, possibly the most gifted designer among them. When finished in 1776, Strawberry Hill was as much a picture gallery as a villa, for Walpole excelled not only as the author of the first Gothic novel (*The Castle of Otranto*, 1764) and of a history of English art but also as a collector. The major innovation that he produced at Strawberry Hill was the asymmetry of its plan. He was also ahead of his time in stressing its archaeological accuracy or at least dependence on medieval models, even if transformed in reuse (e.g. ceiling in the Round Room, 1766–7, by Robert Adam, based on a window in Old St Paul's Cathedral, London).

The earliest Gothic Revival work outside Great Britain is the Gotische Haus (1773; later extensions), Wörlitz, by Georg Christoph Hesekiel (1732–1818), the first of a series of buildings in this style around Dessau. The house is a two-storey art gallery and incorporates much Swiss and German 16th- and 17th-century stained glass. The Kanalfront or main façade was modelled on that of S Maria dell'Orto, Venice. The landscape garden at Wörlitz, commissioned by the most enlightened German prince of his day, Francis, Prince of Anhalt-Dessau, owes much to English models; the Prince visited the British Isles four times (1763–4, 1766, 1775, 1785). By the time of its construction, the English style of garden design was being accepted across Europe, as were 'Gothic' garden buildings, though to a lesser extent. The French painter Hubert Robert, for example, designed the garden of Betz (Oise) in 1780 with a ruined Gothic tower and with a small Gothic chapel (both extant). As with the Gothic Survival, the Gothic features of many Gothic Revival buildings were reduced to crenellations or battlements. As early as 1707, John Vanbrugh proposed to the 4th Earl of Manchester to give his seat at Kimbolton, Hants, 'Something of the Castle Air, tho' at the Same time to make it regular', an intention that he eventually realized by dismissing columns and pilasters and by using battlements instead of a classical cornice (*see* VANBRUGH, JOHN, §2(iii)). At his own house at Greenwich (1718–19), London, the turrets and the battlements justify its name, Vanbrugh Castle. Around 1720 he designed a scheme for Inveraray, Argyll, in the same style. Vanbrugh never, however, crossed the dividing line between 'castellated' and 'Gothic', for he never used pointed arches or other borrowings from ecclesiastical architecture, and his Gothic effects were achieved more by massing than by detail.

It is a significant comment on the change of taste in the second quarter of the 18th century that Inveraray Castle, although loosely modelled on Vanbrugh's castellated design, was eventually built (from 1745) in full Gothic Revival form by Roger Morris (*see* MORRIS, (1)). It is a stern, rectangular building with an elevated central hall and four round corner towers, all regularly pierced by tracery windows and, of course, battlemented. As the first large Gothic Revival building in Europe it deserves special attention. It may justly be argued that, as the highland residence of Archibald Campbell (1682–1761; from 1743 3rd Duke of Argyll), an eminent Whig politician and later the chief of the most powerful of all Scottish clans, Inveraray Castle was simultaneously intended to be, and understood as, the model of a fashionable country seat and the traditional symbol of a landowner's authority.

The first battlemented building of the 18th century in Germany was the Nauener Tor (1755; altered), Potsdam, a city gate erected after the medievalizing rather than Gothic Revival design of Frederick the Great. None of the castellated Gothic buildings of the 18th century in present-day Germany and Austria was intended to be a residence, not even the two largest ones: the Löwenburg (1793–1801), Wilhelmshöhe, Kassel, by HEINRICH CHRISTOPH JUSSOW; and the Franzensburg (1798–1801), Laxenburg, near Vienna, by Franz Jäger (1743–1809). The climax of 18th-century secular Gothic Revival was the huge and ephemeral Fonthill Abbey (1796–1817), Wilts, by James Wyatt (*see* WYATT, (2), fig. 2). It was ruined by the collapse (1825) of its 84-m high tower, so that today it is known mainly through literary and visual records. It was built for WILLIAM BECKFORD, who originally wanted no more than a pleasure house 'in the shape of an abbey'; whereas many English country seats were labelled 'Priory' or 'Abbey' after a pre-existing monastery on the estate, Fonthill was probably the first to be so named purely due to the whim of its proprietor. Beckford retained its character and name, however, after it grew into a full-sized mansion, housing a spectacular art collection. With its windmill-like plan and slender central tower, Fonthill resembled stage scenery rather than either a medieval abbey or a comfortable dwelling.

The churches of the early, 18th-century phase of the Gothic Revival are few, and far from being conspicuous. From *c.* 1720 the gothicizing completion of medieval churches was more and more seconded by Gothick furnishings, such as Giovanni Santini's reredos in Kladruby church, Bohemia, and William Kent's screen (1741; destr.) in Gloucester Cathedral (*see also* §II below). A completely new church was St Mary's (1753–8; ruined), Hartwell, Bucks, by Henry Keene for Sir William Lee, of octagonal form with fan vault. Parallel to the secular development of the style, English ecclesiastical architecture was affected by the archaeological spirit. JAMES ESSEX, who carried out scholarly restorations of Ely Cathedral (1757–62) and Lincoln Cathedral (1762–5) was the first practising architect to take an antiquarian interest in medieval architecture, and his knowledge of Gothic construction methods was unique until the 19th century.

Early Gothic Revival churches in Germany were the result of princely whims, for example Löwenburg church (1795–6), near Kassel, by Jussow; Hohenheim church (1797; re-erected at Monrepos, Ludwigsburg, 1803; ruined since 1940s) by Nikolaus Friedrich von Thouret (see

1. Gothic Revival church built originally at Hohenheim by Nikolaus Friedrich von Thouret, 1797; re-erected at Monrepos, Ludwigsburg, 1803

fig. 1); and Paretz church (1797), Ketzin, Potsdam, by Friedrich Gilly.

(iii) Growth, theory and alliance with nationalism. Gothic Revival theory emerged from, and tried to influence, the 19th-century society and public opinion of Britain and her counterparts on the European and American continents. Never before, and perhaps never since, have architectural competitions and judgements been discussed as extensively and relentlessly as they were in this period. Hence a great deal of architectural writing is concerned with controversy and criticism rather than with aesthetics. It should also be borne in mind how many prolific architectural writers on the Gothic Revival movement were politicians. No wonder that Gothic Revival theory was closely related, as we shall see, to the topics of the day: national identity, industrialization, demography, religious controversy and the preservation of national monuments. This theory may be defined as the system of ideas, topics, principles and arguments underlying the whole writing of the Gothic Revival movement's protagonists and competing with the theories of other movements, factions and schools of 19th-century architecture.

The politicians interested in the Gothic Revival and in propagating it by polemical writing included: in England, A. J. B. Hope (*see* HOPE, (2)), son of the Neo-classicist Thomas Hope and a Conservative Member of Parliament, President of the Ecclesiological Society and later of the Royal Institute of British Architects, and author of *The English Cathedral of the Nineteenth Century* (1861); in France, CHARLES FORBES RENÉ DE MONTALAMBERT, a Roman Catholic Liberal, member of the Chambre des Pairs, and author of an article in the *Revue de deux mondes* (1833) entitled 'Du Vandalisme en France', in which he called for the preservation and imitation of medieval architectural monuments; and in Germany, AUGUST VON REICHENSPERGER, a lawyer and member of the parliament in Frankfurt am Main, later deputy of the Reichstag, founder of the Roman Catholic Zentrumspartei and editor of the *Kölner Domblatt* for many years. He was also a friend of A. W. N. Pugin, Montalambert and Hope, but remarkably he ignored the critic John Ruskin, despite sharing many of his ideas, especially concerning traditional crafts (*see* RUSKIN, JOHN, §2).

If the Gothic Revival of the mid-19th century was an international movement, one may then question how it was possible to ascertain, as its theorists did, that the Gothic was the only proper and national style or, at least, the necessary precondition for the emergence of a new national style, regardless of building type. Nationalism based itself upon civilization, language and history. After the end of the Napoleonic Wars in 1815 there was a general tendency to idealize the Middle Ages. They were considered as the epoch when the modern languages supplanted Latin, when the civilization of Western Europe equalled those of Classical Antiquity, when builders created the Gothic style, the antipode of the Greek, and when the history of the northern nations began.

The Gothic was by then conceived as a series of national idioms and sometimes named accordingly: 'Early English', '*le style Philippe-Auguste*', or '*deutsche Baukunst*'. Some nomenclature also emphasized the common religious background: 'Christian architecture', '*christlich-germanische Baukunst*'. The 18th-century Gothic Revival in the British Isles may be seen as the stylistic continuation or at least an imitation of the Late Gothic of the 15th and early 16th centuries. Contemporary European architects often copied English models and pattern books. The Neo-classical ideals of simplicity and grandeur, however, harmonized better with the Gothic of the 13th and 14th centuries than with the later Flamboyant or Tudor Gothic, and for a short time *c.* 1845 the theorists of the Gothic Revival movement advocated a return to the style of *c.* 1250 and, of course, also to 'national' models. Very soon, however, earlier models took the lead, the taste for 'early' periods and 'primitivism' being a common bias of the critics ready to approve of early Florentine art and architecture or early Netherlandish painting. In the 1850s it was hoped that a new style would develop from the very roots of the Gothic.

The Gothic Revival could not fulfil its role as the alternative to the classical styles until it was applicable to every building type. No one expressed this better than George Gilbert I Scott (ii), arguably one of the style's most prolific exponents (*see* SCOTT (ii), (1)). In his *Remarks on Secular and Domestic Architecture, Present and Future* (1857), dedicated to A. J. B. Hope, Scott pointed out what he called 'the absurdity of the theory that one style is suited to churches and another to houses, and of the consequent divorce between ecclesiastical and secular architecture'. He went on to show that he aimed 'at developing upon the basis of the indigenous architecture of our own country, a style which will be pre-eminently that of our own age'. As the number of good models for civic architecture proved to be too small, Scott included foreign and Late Gothic buildings, for example English colleges, as well as Flemish and Italian town halls.

During the 19th century the Gothic Revival became the standard style for a wide range of building types, its acceptability encouraged by religious and moral considerations. In the first years of the century ecclesiastical authorities and conservative Christians reclaimed their positions held before 1789 and associated themselves with the genius of the Middle Ages: in 1802 FRANÇOIS-RENÉ CHÂTEAUBRIAND published his major book *Le Génie du Christianisme.* In 1804 Charles Percier and Pierre-François-Léonard Fontaine chose Gothic Revival decoration for Napoleon's coronation in Notre-Dame, Paris. In 1805 Benjamin Henry Latrobe submitted alternative designs for the Roman Catholic Cathedral in Baltimore, MD, one 'Gothic' (rejected), the other 'Greek' (built 1804–14). In 1815 KARL FRIEDRICH SCHINKEL proposed the construction of a 'Gothic' cathedral in Berlin (unexecuted), intended to be a monument to the Napoleonic Wars, the sepulchre of the Prussian kings and a Protestant church. From 1814 German writers postulated the completion of Cologne Cathedral as a national monument (*see* COLOGNE, §IV, 1), initiating one of the greatest enterprises of the Gothic Revival (completed 1842–80; by ERNST FRIEDRICH ZWIRNER and RICHARD VOIGTEL; *see* COLOGNE, fig. 7). In contrast, however, the National Monument (begun 1824; incomplete) at Calton Hill, Edinburgh, by William Henry Playfair and C. R. Cockerell, and the Walhalla

(1830–42), near Regensburg, by Leo von Klenze, a Pantheon of 'Germanic' heroes of different eras, social classes and public virtues (*see* GREEK REVIVAL, fig. 3), followed the model of the Parthenon, with Periclean Athens providing an alternative ideal for public life and order.

The increase in populations and growth of urban areas caused by industrialization necessitated church-building programmes, virtually all over the Christian world. In London the population rose from 1 million in 1801 to over 3.8 million in 1871, and the built-up area expanded from a radius of 8 miles to 13 miles. Other large towns in Britain spread no less dramatically. Migration created new communities of various denominations, the most conspicuous being the Roman Catholic community in England and Anglican groups in colonies abroad of both commercial and tourist origin (e.g. Stuttgart and Rome). The British way of countering revolutionary fervour was by strengthening the established Church of England. New manufacturing centres frequently had no churches within easy reach. In 1818 Parliament passed a Church Building Act enabling a special commission (hence the name 'Commissioners' churches') to subsidize the building of *c.* 600 churches in the first half of the century. The Commissioners' most prolific architect was THOMAS RICKMAN, who could design with equal facility in Gothic or classical style, but who invented the terminology for the comparative classification of Gothic architecture. An important contemporary of Rickman's in this early archaeological phase of the Gothic Revival was ANTHONY SALVIN. In Ireland a vast church-building programme for the Protestant Church of Ireland began (slowly) in the late 18th century but peaked in the 1820s and 1830s (*see* IRELAND, §II). Almost all the churches built during the British programme were in Gothic Revival style, even those abroad, as if to compensate for the feeling of homelessness of life outside Britain. The best known is All Saints (1880–85), Rome, by G. E. Street, inspired by Italian models.

In the USA and Canada towns were also supplied with countless Gothic Revival churches. An early example is St John's Protestant Episcopal Cathedral (1809–10; later enlarged), at Providence, RI, still in the Batty Langley manner, by John Holden Greene. An early 19th-century Gothic Revival Canadian church is the Roman Catholic Notre-Dame at Montreal (1823–9; later enlargements and alterations) by James O'Donnell (1774–1830), an Irish Protestant converted to Roman Catholicism.

Many European churches of interest at this period owe their Gothic Revival style to patronage. These include the abbey church of Hautecombe, Savoie, France, remodelled (1824–43) in the Gothic Revival style by ERNESTO MELANO as the sepulchre of the Sardinian royal family; the Friedrichwerdersche-Kirche (1824–30; now the Schinkelmuseum), Berlin, by Schinkel (*see* SCHINKEL, KARL FRIEDRICH, fig. 2), the style suggested by the Crown Prince Frederick William; the Mariahilfkirche (1831–9), Auvorstadt, near Munich, by DANIEL OHLMÜLLER for King Ludwig I; the church of Notre-Dame-de-Laeken (begun 1852), Brussels, by Joseph Poelaert for King Leopold I; and the Votivkirche (1856–79), Vienna, by Heinrich von Ferstel under the patronage of the Emperor's brother Ferdinand Max (for further discussion and illustration *see* FERSTEL, HEINRICH VON).

For associational reasons in a difficult post-Napoleonic world, the Gothic Revival also became fashionable for royal and imperial residences, including Windsor Castle (*see* WINDSOR CASTLE, §3), remodelled (1824–40) by Jeffry Wyatville (*see* WYATT, (3)); the English Tudor style Schloss Babelsberg (1833–48), near Potsdam, by Schinkel and Ludwig Persius for Prince William of Prussia, later Emperor William I; Schloss Hohenschwangau (1833–7), near Füssen, Bavaria, by Domenico Quaglio (*see* QUAGLIO, (3)) and Ohlmüller for Prince Maximilian, later King Maximilian II (*reg* 1848–64); Schloss Stolzenfels (1836–42), near Koblenz, by Schinkel for the Crown Prince, later King Frederick William IV of Prussia; the château of Pierrefonds (1858–70), near Compiègne, by Viollet-le-Duc for Emperor Napoleon III (*see* VIOLLET-LE-DUC, EUGÈNE-EMMANUEL, fig. 2); and Schloss Marienburg (1858–67), near Hannover, by CONRAD WILHELM HASE for Mary, Queen of Hannover.

Royal residences had by then partly lost their public character, whereas parliaments and administrations required new settings, shaped on, or at least evoking the image of, older building types, such as late medieval castles, mansions, town halls and guild halls. The Gothic Revival style was thus especially in demand. The winning competition design (1835) by CHARLES BARRY for the

2. Gothic Revival church of Notre-Dame-de-Bonsecours, Blosseville, Rouen, by Jacques-Eugène Barthélemy, 1840–44

Houses of Parliament (built 1840–65; *see* ENGLAND, fig. 9) had a modern and logical plan but was 'Perpendicular Gothic' in detail, thus following the stipulation 'that the style of the building be either Gothic or Elizabethan' (*see also* LONDON, §V, 3(iii)). American, French and many other parliaments after 1789 looked to classical precedents, and they were housed accordingly in Neo-classical buildings, whereas the British Parliament vindicated time-honoured continuity, which was expressed on the one hand by a national style, on the other hand by preserving some of the medieval remains of the old Palace of Westminster, including the Lower Chapel of St Stephen's Chapel and Westminster Hall. At least two other parliamentary buildings followed the Westminster precedent: the Canadian Parliament House (1861–7), Ottawa, by Thomas Fuller and Chilion Jones (1835–1912) with administrative blocks by Augustus Laver (1834–98) and Thomas Stent (1822–1912); and the Hungarian Parliament House (1884–1904), Budapest, by IMRE STEINDL (*see* HUNGARY, fig. 4).

Little mention has been made hitherto of the Gothic Revival in France and Italy. France, which could claim to be the birthplace of Gothic architecture, was a latecomer in its revival, partly due to the Beaux-Arts tradition in French architectural education and the centralism of the French government (*see* FRANCE, §II, 4(iii), and VIOLLET-LE-DUC, EUGÈNE-EMMANUEL). The restored Bourbon dynasty had a preference for a spindly form of Gothic Revival called the Troubadour style, but it was not until 1842 that the first French Gothic Revival building reached completion: the church of Notre-Dame-de-Bonsecours (1840–44), Blosseville, Rouen, by JACQUES-EUGÈNE BARTHÉLEMY (see fig. 2). In Italy, of course, the revival of her own medieval vocabulary was preferred.

Supported by members of the national parliaments and by influential institutions, such as the Roman Catholic and the Anglican Churches, a considerable number of architects specialized in the Gothic Revival style, especially between the 1840s and the 1860s. They dominated church building, college building and the restoration of medieval monuments. They all considered the Gothic of the 13th and 14th centuries as the best style to be imitated first and then to be adapted and developed into an appropriate expression of modern life. This marked the evolution from the imitative revival to eclecticism and the passion for overall design. The prototype of a universal designer was A. W. N. Pugin (*see* PUGIN, (2)), in many respects the central figure of the Gothic Revival, responsible for the internal decoration of the Houses of Parliament (*see* LONDON, fig. 38) as well as a series of Roman Catholic churches, such as St Mary's Cathedral (1842–1912), Killarney (*see* IRELAND, §II, 3). He was followed by other versatile architects, such as WILLIAM BURGES, the architect of St Finbar's Cathedral (1865–79), Cork, and the restorer of Castel Coch (1875–91) for the Marquess of Bute (*see* STUART, (2)); Eugène-Emmanuel Viollet-le-Duc in France; and in Germany GEORG GOTTLOB UNGEWITTER and AUGUST OTTMAR VON ESSENWEIN, the Director of the Germanisches Nationalmuseum, Nuremberg. Contemporary critics recognized William Butterfield as the most inventive architects of the Gothic Revival movement. He moved rapidly from the picturesqueness of his Vicarage (1845) at Coalpit Heath, Glos (see fig. 3), to the highly sophisticated 'ugliness' of All Saints' (1850–59), Margaret Street, London (*see* BUTTERFIELD, WILLIAM, fig. 1); G. E. Street, who began as a church builder but crowned his career with the construction of the Law Courts (1874–82) in The Strand, London; P. J. H. Cuypers (*see* CUYPERS, (1)), better known for his Northern-Renaissance Revival Rijksmuseum, Amsterdam, than for the restorations and Roman Catholic church buildings that dominated his work, such as the church of Onze Lieve Vrouwe Onbevlekt Ontvangen (1860–63; 'Posthoorn' church), Amsterdam; FRIEDRICH VON SCHMIDT, who trained under Zwirner in Cologne and became a major church builder, whose principal civic works, the Akademisches Gymnasium (1863–6; see fig. 4) and the Rathaus (1872–83), are both in Vienna; and, in France, JEAN-BAPTISTE LASSUS, whose enthusiasm for the Gothic of Chartres Cathedral reached its most complete expression in the church of the Sacré-Coeur (1849–81), Moulins.

3. Gothic Revival house by William Butterfield: The Vicarage, Coalpit Heath, Gloucestershire, 1845

If the North American architecture of the 1840s still followed the English taste, its achievements also began to keep abreast of the foremost buildings of Great Britain. The prominent architects of the Gothic Revival in the USA distinguished themselves as designers of Protestant Episcopal churches; they included Richard Upjohn, (1), architect of Trinity Church (1839–46), New York (*see* UPJOHN, (1), fig. 1), and St Mary's (1846–54), Burlington, NJ; and JOHN NOTMAN, who designed St Mark's (1847–52), Philadelphia, PA, with unplastered walls of hammer-dressed stone and a dark, open timber roof. It was not until James Renwick designed the Roman Catholic cathedral of St Patrick (1858–79; twin spires completed 1888), New York (*see* RENWICK, JAMES, fig. 2), that French models, both medieval and modern, were introduced to American church building. English architects had by then also turned to continental models, especially for competitions outside the British Isles. The first to do so was

4. Gothic Revival school building by Friedrich von Schmidt: entry hall of the Akademisches Gymnasium, Vienna, 1863–6

George Gilbert Scott. With his competition design for the Nikolaikirche (1846–63; destr. 1943, except tower), Hamburg, he eclipsed his German rival Gottfried Semper. Scott's most popular works in London are the Albert Memorial (1863–72) and the St Pancras Station Hotel (1868–74).

By around the last quarter of the 19th century younger architects, such as Street's pupils PHILIP WEBB and RICHARD NORMAN SHAW, when they designed domestic architecture, had begun to turn from 'Gothic' to 'vernacular', from 'revival' to 'tradition'. Every style of architectural history was by then 'available' and seemed worthy of imitation, especially transitional styles, which were understood as models of, or starting-points for, syntheses, such as Late Romanesque used for H. H. Richardson's Trinity Church (1874–7), Boston (*see* RICHARDSON, H. H., fig. 1) or Alfred Waterhouse's National History Museum (1872–81), London (for illustration *see* WATERHOUSE, ALFRED).

(iv) Later developments. Until World War II most church buildings of all denominations remained openly, allusively or secretly 'Gothic', from the Sagrada Familia, Barcelona (taken over by Antoni Gaudí in 1883, partially completed; *see* GAUDÍ, ANTONI, fig. 2), to Notre-Dame-du-Raincy (1922–3), Paris, by Auguste Perret (*see* PERRET and fig. 1), and the Roman Catholic church of St John the Baptist (1922–7), Neu-Ulm, by Dominikus Böhm (*see* BÖHM, (1)). Many post-1918 secular buildings of North America have Gothic Revival characteristics, even including two skyscrapers, the *Chicago Tribune* Building (1922–5; *see* COMPETITION, fig. 3) by JOHN MEAD HOWELLS and Raymond Hood, and the Cathedral of Learning (1926–7), University of Pittsburgh, by Charles Z. Klauder (1872–1938), designed in the deeply rooted collegiate Gothic style. Monumental brick architecture of the 20th century often has Gothic overtones, for example the Beursgebouw (1896–1903), Amsterdam, by H. P. BERLAGE, the Town Hall (1911–22), Stockholm, by RAGNAR ÖSTBERG, and the Museum of National Art (1912–38; now Romanian Peasant Museum), Bucharest, by NICOLAE GHIKA-BUDEȘTI.

2. LITERATURE. In some ways comparable to the Greek Revival, the Gothic Revival was in many respects dependent on historical and archaeological accounts of buildings illustrated by measured drawings. The works of James Cavanah Murphy (1760–1814) on BATALHA PRIORY, Portugal (1792–5), and of Sulpiz BOISSERÉE on Cologne Cathedral (1821–32) tried to eclipse James Stuart and Nicholas Revett's standard work on Greek architecture, *Antiquities of Athens* (1762–1816). Pattern books modelled on the works of Sebastiano Serlio or Jacopo Vignola or HANS BLUM, such as Batty Langley's *Ancient Architecture Restored, and Improved* (1742), or the *Gothisches A-B-C-Buch* (1840) by Friedrich Hoffstadt (1802–46), had at first a big impact as well but were then replaced by collections of medieval details such as VINCENZ STATZ and Georg Gottlob Ungewitter's *Gothisches Musterbuch* (1856–61). Modern Gothic schemes, whether executed or not, appeared in separate works such as *A Collection of Designs for Rural Retreats, as Villas, principally in the Gothic and Castle Styles of Architecture* (1802) by James Malton (*d* 1803) and in the rapidly growing number of illustrated periodicals such as *The Builder* (from 1843) on the one hand or the High-Church *The Ecclesiologist* (from 1841) on the other. Like *The Builder*, the French *Revue générale de l'architecture* (from 1840) and the Viennese *Allgemeine Bauzeitung mit Abbildungen* (from 1836) were by no means exclusive publicists of the Gothic Revival, but nevertheless they published perhaps more, and more important, Gothic Revival designs than the *Annales archéologiques* (from 1844) and the *Organ für christliche Kunst* (from 1851), which were biased towards genuine medieval aspects of the Gothic.

Stage-coaches and railways facilitated architectural tours, so that gradually every facet of medieval Gothic was recorded. One could copy details from topographical works such as *The Architectural Antiquities of Great Britain* (1807–26) by JOHN BRITTON, architectural compositions from sketchbooks like that of the widely travelled Rev. John Louis Petit (1810–68), *Remarks on Church Architecture* (1841), technical hints from the structural analysis of Eugène-Emmanuel Viollet-le-Duc's *Dictionnaire raisonné de l'architecture française du XIe au XVIe siècle* (1854–68) and add further ideas from one's own drawings.

Besides architectural history, which was about to organize the accumulated knowledge of Gothic architecture, there emerged an architectural theory regularizing the design and execution of modern Gothic. Horace Walpole thus justified the Gothicism of Strawberry Hill and succeeded in making it fashionable through *A Description of the Villa of Mr Horace Walpole at Strawberry-Hill* (1784). A. W. N. Pugin developed a theory based, as he thought, on principles (*The True Principles of Pointed or Christian*

Architecture, 1841). August Reichensperger followed his lead (*Die christlich-germanische Baukunst*, 1845). Finally, John Ruskin's major book on the nature and social impact of medieval Gothic architecture (*The Seven Lamps of Architecture*, 1849) and his criticism of 19th-century building attracted an ever-growing bourgeois public.

Charles Locke Eastlake's *History of the Gothic Revival* (1872) appeared shortly after the movement had reached its peak. Naturally enough, Eastlake eulogistically treated the movement as a continuous process. Two generations later Kenneth Clark published what has become a standard work on the subject, *The Gothic Revival: An Essay in the History of Taste* (1928).

BIBLIOGRAPHY

EARLY SOURCES

B. Langley: *Ancient Architecture Restored, and Improved* (London, 1742); rev. as *Gothic Architecture, Improved by Rules and Proportions* (London, 1747)

H. Walpole: *A Description of the Villa of Mr Horace Walpole at Strawberry-Hill* (Strawberry Hill, 1784)

J. C. Murphy: *Plans, Elevations, Sections, and Views of the Church of Batalha in the Province of Estremadura in Portugal* (London, 1792–5)

F. R. de Chateaubriand: *Le Génie du Christianisme* (Paris, 1802)

J. Malton: *A Collection of Designs for Rural Retreats, as Villas, Principally in the Gothic and Castle Styles of Architecture* (London, 1802)

J. Britton: *The Architectural Antiquities of Great Britain*, 5 vols (London, 1807–26)

S. Boisserée: *Geschichte und Beschreibung des Doms von Köln, nebst Untersuchungen über die alte Kirchenbaukunst, als Text zu den Ansichten, Rissen und einzelnen Theilen des Doms von Köln*, 2 vols (Stuttgart and Paris, 1823–32) [pls pubd 1821–32]

C.-R. de Montalambert: 'Du Vandalisme en France', *Rev. Deux Mondes* (1 March 1833); also repr. in *Œuvres*, vi (Paris, 1861), pp. 7–75

F. Hoffstadt: *Gothisches A-B-C-Buch*, 2 vols (Frankfurt am Main, 1840)

J. L. Petit: *Remarks on Church Architecture*, 2 vols (London, 1841)

A. W. N. Pugin: *The True Principles of Pointed or Christian Architecture* (London, 1841)

A. von Reichensperger: *Die christlich-germanische Baukunst* (Trier, 1845)

J. Ruskin: *The Seven Lamps of Architecture* (London, 1849)

E. E. Viollet-le-Duc: *Dictionnaire raisonné de l'architecture française du XIe au XVIe siècle*, 10 vols (Paris, 1854–68)

V. Statz and G. G. Ungewitter: *Gotisches Musterbuch*, 2 vols (Leipzig, 1856–61)

G. G. Scott: *Remarks on Secular and Domestic Architecture, Present and Future* (London, 1857)

A. Beresford-Hope: *The English Cathedral of the Nineteenth Century* (London, 1861)

C. L. Eastlake: *A History of the Gothic Revival* (London, 1872)

PERIODICALS

Allg. Bauztg Abbild. (1836–)

Rev. Gén. Archit. (1840–)

The Ecclesiologist (1841–)

The Builder (1843–)

Köln. Dombl. (1843–)

An. Archéol. (1844–)

Organ Christ. Kst. (1851–)

Rev. A. Chrét. (1857–)

GENERAL

K. Clark: *The Gothic Revival: An Essay in the History of Taste* (London, 1928)

P. Collins: *Changing Ideals in Modern Architecture, 1750–1950* (London, 1965)

G. Germann: *Gothic Revival in Europe and Britain: Sources, Influences and Ideas* (London, 1972, rev. and Ger. trans., Stuttgart, 1974)

N. Pevsner: *Some Architectural Writers of the Nineteenth Century* (Oxford, 1972)

R. Wagner-Rieger and W. Krause, eds: *Historismus und Schlossbau* (Munich, 1975)

C. Baur: *Neugotik* (Munich, 1981)

C. Mignot: *L'Architecture au XIXe siècle* (Fribourg, 1983)

L. J. Sutthof: *Gotik im Barock: Zur Frage der Kontinuität des Stiles ausserhalb seiner Epoche* (Münster, 1990)

NATIONAL STUDIES

Austria

R. Wagner-Rieger: *Wiens Architektur im 19. Jahrhundert* (Vienna, 1970)

Belgium

C. van Gerwen: *De neogotische beeldhouwkunst in de Onze-Lieve-Vrouwekathedraal van Antwerpen* (Antwerp, 1977)

P. Colman: 'L'Architecture néo-gothique en Wallonie et à Bruxelles: Conflits d'hier, d'aujourd'hui et de demain', *Bull. Cl. B.-A. Acad. Royale Sci. Lett. & B.-A. Belgique*, n. s. 4, lxviii (1986), pp. 18–35

J. de Maeyer, ed.: *De Sint-Lucasscholen en de neogotiek, 1862–1914* (Leuven, 1988) [Eng. and Fr. summaries]

Czech Republic

V. Kotrba: *Česká barokní gotika: Dílo Jana Santiniho-Aichla* [The Baroque Gothic in Bohemia: the work of Giovanni Santini-Aichl] (Prague, 1976)

France

P. Lavedan: 'Eglises néo-gothiques', *Archvs A. Fr.*, n. s., xxv (1978), pp. 351–9

Viollet-le-Duc: Architect, Artist, Master of Historic Preservation (exh. cat. by F. Bercé and B. Foucart, Washington, DC, Trust Mus. Exh., 1988)

J. -M. Leniand: *Viollet-le-Duc ou les délires du système* (Paris, 1994)

Germany

A. Neumeyer: 'Die Erweckung der Gotik in der deutschen Kunst des späten 18. Jahrhunderts: Ein Beitrag zur Vorgeschichte der Romantik', *Repert. Kstwiss.*, xlix (1928), pp. 75–123, 159–85

P. Korneli: 'Die Anfänge der Neugotik in Anhalt, Sachsen und Thüringen', *Sächs. Heimatbl.*, x (1964), pp. 37–53, 323–40; xi (1965), pp. 70–84

W. D. Robson-Scott: *The Literary Background of the Gothic Revival in Germany: A Chapter in the History of Taste* (Oxford, 1965)

S. Muthesius: *Das englische Vorbild: Eine Studie zu den deutschen Reformbewegungen in Architektur, Wohnbau und Kunstgewerbe im späteren 19. Jahrhundert* (Munich, 1974)

H. J. Giersberg: 'Zur neugotischen Architektur in Berlin und Potsdam um 1800', *Studien zur deutschen Kunst um 1800*, ed. P. Betthausen (Dresden, 1981), pp. 210–32

O. Dann, ed.: *Religion—Kunst—Vaterland: Der Kölner Dom im 19. Jahrhundert* (Cologne, 1983)

H. Mai: *Kirchen in Sachsen: Vom Klassizismus bis zum Jugendstil* (Berlin and Leipzig, 1992)

M. J. Lewis: *The Politics of the German Gothic Revival: August Reichensperger* (Cambridge, MA, and London, 1993)

Hungary

D. Komárik: 'A gótizáló romantika építészete Magyar-országon' [Gothic Romantic architecture in Hungary], *Építés- & Építészettudomány*, xiv (1982), pp. 275–319

J. Sisa: 'Steindl, Schulek und Schulcz: Drei ungarische Schüler des Wiener Dombaumeisters Friedrich von Schmidt', *Mitt. Ges. Vergl. Kstforsch. Wien*, xxxvii/3 (1985), pp. 1–8

A. Hung., xv/1 (1987) [special issue on Historicism, with contributions by I. Bibó, D. Komárik and J. Sisa; Ger. summaries]

Italy

C. L. V. Meeks: *Italian Architecture, 1750–1914* (New Haven and London, 1966)

R. Wittkower: *Gothic versus Classic: Architectural Projects in Seventeenth Century Italy* (London, 1974)

Cultura figurativa e architettonica negli stati del re di Sardegna (1773–1861) (exh. cat. by E. Castelnuovo and M. Rosci, Turin, Pal. Reale, Pal. Madama and Promot. B.A., 1980)

Gotico, neogotico, ipergotico: Architettura e arti decorative a Piacenza, 1856–1915 (exh. cat., Piacenza, 1984)

Netherlands

H. P. R. Rosenberg: *De 19de-eeuwse kerkelijke bouwkunst in Nederland* (The Hague, 1972)

P. A. M. Geurts and others, eds: *J. A. Alberdingk Thijm (1820–1889), Erflater van de negentiende eeuw* (Nijmegen, 1992)

Poland

T. S. Jaroszewski: *O siedzibach neogotyckich w Polsce* [On neo-Gothic country houses in Poland] (Warsaw, 1981) [Eng. summary]

P. Krakowski: 'Architektura neogotycke w Krakowie' [Neo-gothic architecture in Kraków], *Fol. Hist. A.*, xx (1984), pp. 137–81 [Fr. summary]

M. Kühn, ed.: *Karl Friedrich Schinkels Lebenswerk: Ausland, Bauten und Entwürfe* (Munich, 1989)

Romania

G. Ionescu: *Arhitectura pe teritoriul României de-a lungul veacurilor* [Architecture on Romanian territory over the centuries] (Bucharest, 1982) [Eng. summary]

Sweden

K. Malmström: *Centralkyrkor: Inom svenska kyrkan, 1820–1920. Med en byggnadsantikvarisk inventering* [The principal churches within the Swedish Church, 1820–1920. With a historic buildings inventory] (Stockholm, 1990) [Eng. abstract, Ger. summary]

Switzerland

A. Meyer: *Neugotik und Neuromantik in der Schweiz: Die Kirchenarchitektur des 19. Jahrhunderts* (Zurich, 1973)

P. Bissegger: *Le Moyen Age romantique au Pays de Vaud, 1825–1850: Premier Épanouissement d'une architecture néo-médiévale* (Lausanne, 1985)

United Kingdom

C. L. Eastlake: *A History of the Gothic Revival: An Attempt to Show How the Taste for Mediaeval Architecture which Lingered in England during the Two Last Centuries Has since Been Encouraged and Developed* (London, 1872/*R* Leicester and New York, 1970 [with 209 additional pages containing intro., updated bibliog. etc. by J. M. Crook])

H.-R. Hitchcock: *Early Victorian Architecture in Britain*, 2 vols (New Haven, 1954)

P. Breman: 'The Gothic of Gothick: English Church Building in Nineteenth Century Theory and Practice', *B. Weinreb, Architecture, Catalogue 14* (London, 1966)

Victorian Church Art (exh. cat., London, V&A, 1971)

G. L. Hersey: *High Victorian Gothic: A Study in Associationism* (Baltimore and London, 1972)

S. Muthesius: *The High Victorian Movement in Architecture, 1850–1870* (London and Boston, 1972)

J. Macaulay: *The Gothic Revival, 1745–1845* (Glasgow, 1975)

R. Dixon and S. Muthesius: *Victorian Architecture* (London, 1978)

H. Wischermann: *Fonthill Abbey: Studien zur profanen Neugotik Englands im 18. Jahrhundert* (Freiburg im Breisgau, 1979)

N. Miller: *Strawberry Hill: Horace Walpole und die Ästhetik der schönen Unregelmässigkeit* (Munich and Vienna, 1986)

J. M. Crook: *The Dilemma of Style: Architectural Ideas from the Picturesque to the Post-Modern* (London, 1987)

M. McCarthy: *The Origins of the Gothic Revival* (New Haven and London, 1987)

P. Fontaney, ed.: *Le Renouveau gothique en Angleterre: Idéologie et architecture: Introduction, anthologie bilingue, notes* (Bordeaux, 1989)

P. Atterbury and C. Wainwright, eds: *Pugin: A Gothic Passion* (New Haven and London, 1994)

P. Spencer-Silver: *Pugin's Builder: The Life and Work of George Myers* (Hull, 1994)

USA

P. B. Stanton: *The Gothic Revival and American Church Architecture: An Episode in Taste, 1840–1856* (Baltimore, 1968)

W. Andrews: *American Gothic: Its Origins, its Trials, its Triumph* (New York, 1975)

C. Loth and J. T. Sadler jr: *The Only Proper Style: Gothic Architecture in America* (Boston, 1975)

D. Shand-Tucci: *Ralph Adams Cram: American Medievalist* (Boston, 1975)

W. H. Pierson jr: *Technology and the Picturesque, the Corporate and Early Gothic Styles*, ii of *American Buildings and their Architects* (Garden City, NY, 1978)

GEORG GERMANN

II. Decorative Arts.

Alongside architectural developments, the Gothic Revival was adopted as a suitable style for interior design and then extended to all forms of the applied arts. In the 18th century the applied arts had figured alongside architecture most famously in England in the furnishings designed for Strawberry Hill (from 1753; *see* WALPOLE, (2), fig. 2), and William Beckford's Fonthill Abbey (from 1796), which were both characterized by a picturesque interpretation of Gothic motifs. In the 19th century, when the Gothic Revival was at its most significant as an intellectual, moral and artistic phenomenon, the concept of the integrated interior and the crucial design role of architects meant that architecture and the decorative arts were closely entwined. England remained at the forefront of the movement, influencing developments in Europe and North America as a more archaeological and historically correct approach gained momentum. A decorative vocabulary that drew upon Gothic architectural features—pointed arches, lancets, tracery, crockets, quatrefoils and trefoils, and naturalistic foliage—was applied to furniture, metalwork (including silver, ironwork and jewellery), ceramics (including porcelain and earthenware), glass and stained glass, textiles and wallpapers. These objects were often designed to complement a contemporary architectural shell. The use of colour was also important. The Gothic Revival, however, meant more than purely surface decoration. In some cases, for example for furniture and metalwork, the reintroduction of medieval structures and techniques, as far as they were known, became part of the philosophy of the movement. Scholarship and collecting added impetus and helped to fuel the academic debate that played a key role in determining the course of the Revival; literature, embodied by Sir Walter Scott's novel *Waverley* (1814), contributed to the popularity of the style. There was a general romantic interest in the medieval period, characterized by the Eglington Tournament of 1839. During the 19th century the burgeoning wealth of the middle class put the Gothic interior within reach of a greater number of people.

The chronology of the Revival falls into several distinct phases. In England the early part of the 19th century was characterized by a greater degree of exploration of medieval forms. The architect LEWIS NOCKALLS COTTINGHAM, who established a private collection of medieval architectural fragments, published *Working Drawings of Gothic Ornaments, etc., with a Design for a Gothic Mansion* (London, [1824]), one of the most powerful documents of Gothic Revival ornament. He also designed a wide range of Gothic furniture, often incorporating original, medieval fragments. A. C. Pugin also developed a specialized knowledge of Gothic style in a series of important sourcebooks. His furniture designs also appeared in Rudolph Ackermann's influential *Repository of Arts* (1809–28) from 1825 (see fig. 5).

In the same period the Gothic Revival was gaining pace in continental Europe. In northern Europe nationalist and religious regeneration helped create a climate in which the Gothic Revival could thrive. In France Gothic was being identified as a 'national' style, partly as a rejection of Napoleon's espousal of Neo-classicism as his court style. The TROUBADOUR STYLE or 'Style cathédrale', a romantic evocation of medieval chivalric and courtly life that extended to the decorative arts, was the main expression of this interest. In 1823 the Sèvres Porcelain Factory embarked on the ambitious 'Service de la Chevalerie', and such patrons as the Duchesse de Berry ordered furniture and porcelain in the 'style gothique'. Gothic was also being reevaluated as the national style in Germany, with the encouragement of such literary figures as Johann Wolfgang von Goethe, as part of the surge of nationalism after the Prussian War of Liberation of 1813. A symbol of this was the National Monument to the Liberation known as the

Kreuzberg for the Tempelhofer Berg, Berlin, designed as a massive pinnacled cross in 1817–18 (completed 1821) and forged in cast iron by the architect and designer Karl Friedrich Schinkel. Schinkel also produced Gothic designs for furniture, for example for Prince William of Prussia, at Schloss Babelsburg, Potsdam, from 1833, and for silver, manufactured by the Berlin goldsmith George Hossauer, in particular the three presentation cups made for the medieval tournament festival the 'Magic Spell of the White Rose' in 1830. Although decorated with Gothic ornament, the basic shape of the cups is classical, a contradiction then still considered perfectly acceptable. This eclectic attitude was overturned in England in the second phase of the Revival, from the late 1830s to 1850s, which was dominated by A. W. N. Pugin (*see* PUGIN, (2)). Pugin's contribution to the Revival was fundamental in terms of design (*see* §I above). As a result, the religious emphasis of the Revival became more pronounced, particularly after Pugin's conversion to Roman Catholicism in 1835. During the 19th century there was a boom in the building of churches needed for the growing industrial centres. Owing to Pugin's influence the majority of these were in the Gothic style. One of Pugin's main concerns was honesty—that objects should reflect their medieval prototypes in design and structure, which should not be disguised, hence his approval of the 'X'-frame construction for chairs, and his opinion that pattern should be bold, colourful and appropriate to the context—for example that flat objects should have two-dimensional patterns. These views were elaborated in his publications *Gothic Furniture in the Style of the 15th Century Designed and Etched by A. W. N. Pugin* (London, 1835), *Designs for Gold and Silversmiths* and *Designs for Iron and Brass Work in the Style of the XV and XVI Centuries Drawn and Etched by A. W. N. Pugin* (both London, 1836). His influence spread: the Belgian architect and designer Jean-Baptiste Charles François Bethune absorbed the ideology, and furniture designs were copied in Germany and the USA.

Pugin used a circle of craftsmen to execute his designs: the firm of John Hardman of Birmingham made secular and ecclesiastical plate including chalices and candlesticks, jewellery and monumental brasses from 1838. Ceramics, including tableware and medieval-style encaustic tiles, were provided by Herbert Minton from 1840. Stained glass was made by Thomas Willement (1786–1871) and John Hardman Powell (1827–95), and furniture by several firms including John Webb and John Gregory Crace (*see* CRACE, (1)), for whom Pugin also designed wallpaper, textiles and carpets. Other manufacturers capitalized on the growing popularity of the Gothic Revival. For example, the Staffordshire potteries produced such stoneware jugs with relief figures in Gothic niches as the Minster Jug (1842; London, V&A) by Charles Meigh of Hanley.

Among Pugin's many commissions for Gothic interiors, the New Palace of Westminster, for which he designed the furnishings and decoration, stands out as a symbol of the Revival. The other major monument to Pugin's influence was his arrangement of the Medieval Court at the Great Exhibition in London in 1851, which acted as a showcase for manufacturers of Gothic Revival decorative arts and received widespread acclaim. The *London Illustrated News* commented that it demonstrated 'the applicability of Mediaeval art in all its richness and variety to the uses of the present day'. The Great Exhibition also highlighted continental developments. The firm Carl Leistler & Son in Vienna showed an immense architectural bookcase (London, V&A) that, along with an oak cabinet (London, V&A) by Pugin, was thought to be the most important piece of Gothic Revival furniture.

5. *Pugin's Gothic Furniture* by A. C. Pugin, from Rudolph Ackermann's *Repository of Arts*, x (London, 1827), pl. 23

From 1841 the Ecclesiological Society (formerly the Cambridge Camden Society), founded out of concerns for the preservation of church fabric and fittings, made influential pronouncements in its magazine *The Ecclesiologist.* It also produced a design series for church metalwork and furniture called *Instrumenta Ecclesiastica* (1844–7 and 1850–52/1856). This was edited by William Butterfield, who provided all of the designs for the first series, and the society later employed first G. E. Street and then William Burges as official metalwork designers. The same role was

6. Gothic Revival interior of the church of the Nativity of SS Mary and Philip, Vive-Kapelle, near Bruges, by Jean-Baptiste Charles François Bethune, 1860–69

performed in Germany by the *Kölner Domblatt* and in France by the periodical *Annales archéologiques*. The creation of the Musée de Cluny, in the 15th-century Hôtel des Abbés de Cluny, Paris, by ALEXANDRE DU SOMMERARD in 1832 provided medieval models for designers and was symptomatic of a growing interest in antiquarianism. Jean-Baptiste Lassus, architect and designer in a scholarly medieval style, encouraged craftsmen, among them the metalworker Achillé Legost, to rediscover such medieval techniques as champlevé enamelling. As in England, the church was a major patron of Gothic Revival decorative arts, supplied by such goldsmiths as Placide Poussielgue-Rusand (1824–89) in Paris and Thomas-Joseph Armand-Calliat (*fl c.* 1862–81) in Lyon. François-Désiré Froment-Meurice (1802–55) produced fine metalwork and jewellery, winning a medal at the Great Exhibition of 1851. Like many manufacturers, he did not work exclusively in the Gothic manner, and his style was not particularly archaeological (*see* FRANCE, §IX, 1(iv)).

The influence of EUGÈNE-EMMANUEL VIOLLET-LE-DUC was a key factor in the credibility of the Revival. His publications, notably the *Dictionnaire du mobilier* (6 vols, Paris, 1858–75), illustrated his commitment to French 13th-century Gothic and proved indispensable to designers. He designed for a range of materials, including stained glass for the Sèvres Porcelain Factory, and the prestige of some of his commissions, notably the château of Pierrefonds (from 1858) for Emperor Napoleon III, raised the profile of the Gothic style. A similar role was played in Germany by GEORG GOTTLOB UNGEWITTER, an architect and designer who propagated the Gothic Revival through teaching at the Höhere Gewerbeschule in Kassel. He published furniture designs in *Entwürfe zu gothischen Möbel* (1851), some of which were based on original models. This was followed by the *Gothisches Musterbuch* (1856–61), which included designs for metalwork and stained glass. In Belgium, where A. W. N. Pugin's influence was particularly strong, there were some notable examples of buildings both domestic and religious with complete interiors all in the Gothic Revival style. Examples include the Loppem Castle (design, 1856), near Bruges, by E. W. Pugin and Bethune and the Roman Catholic complex SS Mary and Philip with the church of the Nativity of Vive-Kapelle (1860–69; see fig. 6), also by Bethune.

In the USA the Gothic Revival took longer to take hold. The first published evidence of the style was the sideboard used as a frontispiece to Robert Conner's *The Cabinet Maker's Assistant* (New York, 1842), although developments in Europe had already been absorbed by the architect and designer ALEXANDER JACKSON DAVIS. Davis designed a number of houses in the Gothic taste for wealthy patrons, including Lyndhurst (originally 'Knoll'; from 1838) at Tarrytown for General William Paulding, the Mayor of New York. Davis also designed the furniture for the mansion, including beds, which lent themselves to the application of Gothic ornament. Although inspired by Pugin, he was an advocate of 'carpenter's Gothic', or decoration of furniture not necessarily

Gothic in form by Gothic mouldings and ornament. Considerable quantities of Gothic Revival furniture were made in the 1840s and 1850s by such firms as John and Joseph W. Meeks. The aesthete and landscape architect A. J. Downing, a prolific author on taste, also propagated the style. In *The Architecture of Country Houses* (1850), he debated the suitability of Gothic for domestic interiors, concluding that it was appropriate for libraries, halls and bedrooms. Very little Gothic Revival silver was produced in the USA. The Boston & Sandwich Glass Co. (est. 1825) in Sandwich, MA, did, however, produce pressed and moulded jugs, decanters and dishes incorporating arcading and tracery patterns (*see* UNITED STATES OF AMERICA, fig. 45).

During the 1860s there was a further change in the direction of the Gothic Revival with the introduction in England of 'Reformed Gothic' under the influence of such architects and designers as William Butterfield, G. E. Street, Richard Norman Shaw and, most importantly, William Burges. The stress was still on honesty, but using 13th-century French models to design new forms appropriate to the needs of the 19th century, rather than the pure 14th-century sources advocated by Pugin. Examples of the style were first seen at the Medieval Court at the 1862 International Exhibition in London. The architect George Gilbert I Scott (ii), who designed extensive fittings for churches, displayed a polychromed wrought-iron chancel screen (London, V&A) for Hereford Cathedral made by the silversmith Francis Skidmore's Art Manufactures Co. in Coventry. The interiors designed by Burges for Cardiff Castle from 1868 are among the finest expressions of the style (*see* BURGES, WILLIAM, fig. 1). Such pattern books as Bruce J. Talbert's *Gothic Forms Applied to Furniture, Metal Work and Decoration for Domestic Purposes* (Dundee, 1867) and Owen Jones's *The Grammar of Ornament* (London, 1856) provided a readily available corpus of decoration. Charles Locke Eastlake's *Hints on Household Taste in Furniture, Upholstery and Other Details* (London, 1868) was a popular manual of decoration based on the work of such designers as Street and J. P. Seddon, advocating honesty of construction and materials. It had a dramatic impact in the USA.

By the 1870s the use of the Gothic Revival for domestic interiors was waning, although it remained important for ecclesiastical buildings and fittings until well into the 20th century. In England, WILLIAM MORRIS, whose roots were firmly in the Gothic style, had already established Morris, Marshall, Faulkner and Co. (from 1875 Morris & Co.), the genesis of the ARTS AND CRAFTS MOVEMENT. By the early 1880s the Aesthetic Movement was under way. In Germany the Munich Exhibition of 1876 indicated a revival of German Renaissance styles. There were exceptions. Schloss Neuschwanstein, near Füssen, built between 1868 and 1886 for Ludwig II, King of Bavaria, was provided with elaborate Gothic interiors by Julius Hoffmann. Hermann Robert Bichweiler designed Gothic interiors for the furniture manufacturer H. C. Wolbrandt from 1872 and set up a highly successful art factory in Altona in 1878, which included Gothic patterns among its output. A further variant was the *Alte deutsche* style that developed in the last quarter of the century, manifested in the work of such goldsmiths as Gabriel Hermeling of Cologne and Alexander Schönauer of Hamburg, who produced replicas of Late Gothic lobed beakers, and was part of a surge in interest in medieval collecting that led to the production of many interesting fakes. By the 1890s revivalist styles in general were outmoded, as indicated by the emergence of the Art Nouveau and *Jugendstil*.

BIBLIOGRAPHY

The Industry of All Nations, 1851: The Art Journal Illustrated Catalogue (exh. cat., London, Great Exhibition, 1851)
T. S. R. Boase: *English Art, 1800–1870* (Oxford, 1959)
J. B. Waring: *Masterpieces of Industrial Art and Sculpture at the International Exhibition, 1862*, 3 vols (London, 1963)
Nineteenth-century America: Furniture and Other Decorative Arts (exh. cat., ed. B. B. Tracy; New York, Met., 1970)
M. Girouard: *The Victorian Country House* (Oxford, 1971)
Victorian Church Art (exh. cat., London, V&A, 1971)
G. Germann: *Gothic Revival in Europe and Britain: Sources, Influences and Ideas* (London, 1972)
Victorian and Edwardian Decorative Art: The Handley-Read Collection (exh. cat., London, RA, 1972)
High Victorian Design (exh. cat., ed. S. Jervis; Ottawa, N. Museums, 1974)
The Gothic Revival Style in America, 1830–1879 (exh. cat. by K. S. Howe and D. B. Warren, Houston, TX, Mus. F.A., 1976)
Historismus in Hamburg und Norddeutschland: Höhe Kunst zwischen Biedermeier und Jugendstil (exh. cat., ed. H. Jedding; Hamburg, Mus. Kst & Gew., 1977)
L'Art en France sous le Second Empire (exh. cat., Paris, Grand Pal., 1979)
Le 'Gothique' retrouvé avant Viollet-le-Duc (exh. cat., Paris, Hôtel de Sully, 1979)
B. Mundt: *Historismus: Kunstgewerbe zwischen Biedermeier und Jugendstil* (Munich, 1981)
S. Jervis: *The Penguin Dictionary of Design and Designers* (Harmondsworth, 1984)
L. de Gröer: *Les Arts décoratifs de 1790 à 1850* (Fribourg, 1985); Eng. trans. as *Decorative Arts in Europe, 1790–1850* (Fribourg, 1986)
Art and Design in Europe and America, 1800–1900, London, V&A cat. (London, 1987)
C. Wainwright: *The Romantic Interior: The British Collector at Home, 1750–1850* (New Haven and London, 1989)
Of Knights and Spires: Gothic Revival in France and Germany (exh. cat. by P. Hunter-Stiebel, New York, Rosenberg & Stiebel Inc., 1989)
M. Aldrich, ed.: *The Craces: Royal Decorators, 1768–1899* (Brighton, 1990)
Un Age d'or des arts décoratifs, 1814–1848 (exh. cat., Paris, Grand Pal., 1991)
M. J. Lewis: *The Politics of the German Gothic Revival: August Riechensperger* (Cambridge, MA, 1993)
P. Atterbury and C. Wainwright, eds: *Pugin: A Gothic Passion* (New Haven and London, 1994)

PIPPA SHIRLEY

Gothic survival. Term used to describe the survival of Gothic architecture in western Europe, a phenomenon that was more widespread and more prolonged than is generally recognized. Interested in the first manifestations of a new style rather than the last recurrences of an old one, architectural historians have tended to pay too little attention to the persistence of Gothic forms alongside those introduced in the Renaissance. What are often seen as isolated anachronisms prove on investigation to be so numerous and so widespread as to represent an alternative tradition that cannot be dismissed as of no significance. In any case, in northern Europe the assimilation of the Renaissance was a long-drawn-out process that was not fully accomplished until the latter part of the 17th century. Until then much new building, especially in rural areas, was basically medieval in form, though often with classical details added, such as doorways and altarpieces. Each country clung to some different feature from the past that had become too deeply embedded in its architectural consciousness (or sub-consciousness) to be easily dispensed with: in France it was the high-pitched roof sustained by an intricate mass of carpentry; in northern Germany the stepped gable; in England the battlemented parapet; in Scotland the fortified tower-house; in Spain the frenetic elaboration of decoration that, when classicized, became the Plateresque.

1. BACKGROUND AND CHARACTERISTICS. Much of this Late Gothic architecture was due simply to conservatism: peasant farmers and country clergy have rarely been prone to artistic innovation, and the masons they employed were slow to assimilate classical ideas. But an informed architectural conservatism could also be found in some more sophisticated circles. The most striking instance of this is the Jesuit Order, which built a number of Gothic churches during the 17th century in northern France, western Germany and the Netherlands. This must have been a conscious choice, for Jacopo Vignola's Il Gesù in Rome (begun 1565) was one of the most celebrated classical churches of the Counter-Reformation and the first Jesuit church in the Low Countries (at Douai, 1591) had also been built in the classical style. It was only in subsequent years that the decision was made to build Gothic churches at Arras, Lille, Luxembourg, Tournai, Valenciennes and elsewhere. What led the Jesuits to favour the Gothic style is not clear, but elsewhere it was, paradoxically, a humanist principle that often lay behind the desire to build in Gothic. All over Europe there were major churches begun in the later Middle Ages that were still incomplete when they were overtaken by new ideas in the Renaissance. They came to be seen as outdated in style, but the doctrine of harmony and consistency that was basic to the Renaissance theory of design required their completion in the same manner. So here the Gothic style was deliberately (if sometimes reluctantly) adhered to for aesthetic reasons. Thus in Italy in the late 15th century, such outstanding designers as Leonardo da Vinci and Bramante favoured a Gothic format for the central tower of Milan Cathedral, and when the design for its façade was under consideration in the mid-17th century, no less a person than Bernini commended a solution that was Gothic in detail, though classical in organization. At Bologna, in the same way, a whole series of Gothic designs for the façade of S Petronio was made during the 16th century by architects as distinguished as Baldassare Peruzzi and Vignola in an attempt to build it in a manner that would conform to the style of the 15th-century nave. In France, not only were there cathedrals still incomplete but there were others severely damaged in the Wars of Religion that had to be rebuilt.

No other type of building presented quite the same problem of stylistic consistency as churches. Palaces often retained an ancient core within a complex of buildings of various styles and dates, but most major churches of the late Middle Ages represented a single conception that did not lend itself easily to stylistic modification. Hence, in the 16th and 17th centuries, great Gothic churches could still be seen slowly progressing towards completion on the lines laid down in the 14th or 15th centuries. It was no doubt partly for this reason that Gothic came to be seen as a style especially appropriate for churches, if for no other purpose. Thus in France it is noticeable that when monasteries were rebuilt after destruction by the Huguenots, their churches were Gothic, but the refectories, chapter houses and other conventual buildings were classical in style. This link between Gothic and church-building was implicit in the minds of the fellows of St John's College, Cambridge, when they resolved in 1623 to adopt 'the old fashion of church window' for their new library, and it is noticeable that in early 17th-century England, symbolic representations of 'the Church' invariably show the figure of 'Ecclesia' accompanied by a Gothic church.

A different, but equally sophisticated, attitude to Gothic architecture is represented by some buildings in which Gothic and classical elements were mixed in a way that was obviously deliberate. Examples of this include the church of St Etienne-du-Mont (1610), Paris, Heriot's Hospital (begun 1628), Edinburgh, and the chapel and library (begun 1656) of Brasenose College, Oxford. In such buildings as these the Renaissance ideal of harmony was flouted by architects who evidently saw in the stylistic clash a new opportunity to achieve Mannerist effects. It is perhaps to this category that the churches built by Bishop Julius Echter von Mespelbrunn of Würzburg, such as Dettelbach (1610–13), should be assigned. Gothic forms are also to be found among the engravings in that most Mannerist of pattern books, Wendel Dietterlin's *Architectura* (1598).

In 16th- and 17th-century Europe there was no lack of technical ability to build in the Gothic style. In France the tradition of expertise in vaulting was manifested at Orléans, Saint-Maixent and elsewhere and continued to be exploited in such 18th-century churches as St Vaast (begun *c.* 1750), Arras, that are wholly classical in vocabulary. In England as late as *c.* 1640 a London mason was able to build the spectacular fan-vault over the staircase at Christ Church, Oxford, which rivalled, in the elegant exiguity of its support, the most daring achievements of the past. But in general, although 16th- and 17th-century masons were capable of continuing incomplete buildings or reinstating damaged ones in a variety of Gothic manners (and occasionally even in Romanesque), their work rarely shows any evidence of new invention. It is difficult to point to any stylistic development that can be regarded as generally characteristic of Late Gothic. Motifs from the past were often used in a way that was historically 'incorrect'. In England church towers sometimes have Perpendicular windows at ground level and Decorated ones above (e.g. Dalham, Suffolk, 1635). In France, Flamboyant tracery may be found in combination with mouldings of earlier or later character (e.g. St Eustache, Paris). There was, of course, no possibility of a more consciously accurate historicism, because no one had yet worked out that sequence of architectural forms that ARCISSE DE CAUMONT in France and THOMAS RICKMAN in England established only in the 19th century. Until then Gothic (a term first employed in the early 17th century) was seen as an old way of building, embracing many varieties of moulding and tracery that could be combined at will. The result was a retrospective Gothic whose practitioners had none of the missionary zeal of the Gothic Revivalists of the 19th century and whose products were later to be either mistaken for genuine medieval work or else despised as 'debased' perversions of it. Only now can the phenomenon of Gothic survival be seen dispassionately as a characteristic feature of European architecture in the 16th and 17th centuries.

2. GEOGRAPHICAL EXTENT. In England the Dissolution of monasteries and chantries in the 1530s and 1540s removed a major source of architectural patronage, while Lichfield, Staffs, was the only cathedral that needed major repair after the Civil War in the 1640s. Late Gothic in England is therefore represented chiefly by parish churches and, in Oxford and Cambridge, by college buildings such as halls and chapels. Few completely new churches were built. Low Ham (1620), Somerset, St Katherine Cree (completed 1630), London, Staunton Harold (1653), Leics, and Charles Church (1665), Plymouth, are examples. But many church towers were rebuilt, either to replace ones that had collapsed, or to render them capable of standing up to stresses caused by the new fashion for change-ringing. A representative selection might include Cullompton (1548), Devon; St Mary's (1594–1624), Reading; St John's (1612), Peterborough; Godmanchester (1623), Hunts; Christow (1630), Devon; Calne (1639–50), Wilts; Barholme (1648), Lincs; Deddington (1683–5), Oxon; and Dursley (1708–12), Glos. In France important churches completed or reconstructed in the Gothic style in the 16th and 17th centuries include the cathedrals of Auch (tower completed 1678), Blois (1680–1730), Luçon (façade *c.* 1700), Mende (partly reconstructed 1599–1620), Montpellier (1634), Nantes (completed 1660), Orléans (1601–1829) and Tours (completed 1547). Others include the abbey churches of Celles-sur-Belle (1668–76; see fig.), Poitou; Corbie (1701–32), Somme; Evaux (*c.* 1660), Creuse; Figeac (1636 on), Guyenne; and Saint-Maixent (1670–82), Poitou; the collegiate church of Aire-sur-la-Lys (nave completed *c.* 1600), Pas de Calais; the parish church of Mézières (1499–1615), Ardennes; and many other churches in various parts of the country, especially in Roussillon. In Artois and Picardy, the Beauvaisis and the Valois, many towers and spires were built or rebuilt, notably that of Beauvais Cathedral, 153 m high and Flamboyant in style, which collapsed in 1573, only a few years after its completion. More representative examples, usually following the pattern of the medieval steeple of Senlis Cathedral, were Béthisy-Saint Pierre (1520), Hadrancourt-le-Haut-Clocher, Montagny-Sainte-Félicité and Versigny.

In Germany the outstanding examples of Late Gothic (*Nachgotik*) are the Jesuit churches of Mariä Himmelfahrt (1618–*c.* 1630), Cologne, St Georg (1614–18), Molsheim, and Unsere Liebe Frau at Halle (begun 1529). In the Low Countries, in addition to the Jesuit churches already mentioned, there are examples of Late Gothic at Antwerp in St Just's Chapel of the Virgin (1642–6), in parts of St Bavo's Cathedral and of St Peter's Abbey at Ghent, the church of St Hubert (1525–67) in the Ardennes and the hall-church at the former abbey of Lobbes (1550–1624). In Scotland the tradition of fortified domestic architecture continued well into the 17th century, and such castles as Crathes and Craigievar (both Grampian; for illustration of Craigievar *see* TOWER HOUSE) represent the

Poitou, abbey church of Celles-sur-Belle, nave looking east, 1668–76

survival and indeed vigorous development of late medieval architectural forms better than the few Gothic churches. The latter, however, include the north-west steeple of Dunfermline Abbey Church (*c.* 1590), the apsidal east end of Terregles Church (1585), Dumfries & Galloway, and the churches of Dairsie (1621) and Fordell Castle (1650), both in Fife, the latter with Flamboyant tracery. In Spain the great series of late medieval cathedrals continued into the 16th century with Salamanca (begun 1512), Almería (1524–73), Segovia (1525–*c.* 1570), Saragossa, La Seo (nave 1546–59) and Gerona (nave completed 1598). At Gerona the external west front was classical, but at Salamanca a decision was made in 1588 to complete the façade in Gothic rather than in the classical style.

BIBLIOGRAPHY

ENGLAND

J. H. Parker: 'On the Late, or Debased, Gothic Buildings of Oxford', *ABC of Gothic Architecture* (Oxford, 1881), pp. 219–56

H. M. Colvin: 'Gothic Survival and Gothick Revival', *Archit. Rev.* [London], ciii (1948), pp. 91–8

A. W. Clapham: 'The Survival of Gothic in Seventeenth-century England', *Archaeol. J.*, cvi (1952), pp. 4–9

A. Woodger: 'Post-Reformation Mixed Gothic in Huntingdonshire Church Towers and its Campanological Associations', *Archaeol. J.*, cxli (1984), pp. 269–308

G. W. Bernard: 'The Dating of Church Towers: Huntingdon Re-examined', *Archaeol. J.*, cxlix (1992), pp. 344–50

FRANCE

G. Durand: 'Clochers picards, avec flèches gothiques des XVII et XVIII siècles', *Congr. Archéol. France*, lxxii (1906), pp. 623–36

E. Lefèvre-Pontalis: 'Les Clochers du XIIIe et du XVIe siècles dans le Beauvaisis et le Valois', *Congr. Archéol. France*, lxxii (1906), pp. 592–622

Canon Chenesseau: 'Cathédrale d'Orléans', *Congr. Archéol. France*, xciii (1931), pp. 11–51
L. Hautecoeur: *Architecture classique* (1943–57), i/1, pp. 2–96
P. Héliot: 'La Fin de l'architecture gothique en France durant les XVII et XVIII siècles', *Gaz. B.-A.*, n. s. 6, xxxiii (1951), pp. 111–27
——: 'L'Héritage médiéval dans l'architecture de l'Anjou et de l'Aquitaine aux XVII et XVIII siècles', *An. Midi*, lxvii (1955), pp. 143–59
J. Guerot: 'Eglises gothiques des XVII et XVIII siècles en Roussillon', *Bull. Mnmtl*, cxxi (1963), pp. 93–5
G. Giordanengo: 'La Reconstruction des églises paroissiales dans le diocèse d'Embrun, XVe siècle–milieu du XVI siècle', *Congr. Archéol. France*, cxxx (1974), pp. 162–81

GERMANY

J. Braun: *Die Kirchenbau der deutschen Jesuiten* (Freiburg im Breisgau, 1908–10)
W. Buchowiecki: *Die gotischen Kirchen Österreichs* (Vienna, 1952), pp. 403–9
H. R. Hitchcock: *German Renaissance Architecture* (Princeton, 1981)

ITALY

R. Wittkower: *Gothic Versus Classic: Architectural Projects in Seventeenth-century Italy* (London, 1974)

LOW COUNTRIES

L. Serbat: 'L'Architecture gothique des Jésuites au XVII siècle', *Bull. Mnmtl*, lxvi (1902), pp. 315–70; lxvii (1903), pp. 84–134
J. Braun: *Die belgischen Jesuitkirchen* (Freiburg im Breisgau, 1907)
S. Brigorde: *Les Eglises gothiques de Belgique* (Brussels, 1947)

SCOTLAND

D. MacGibbon and T. Ross: *The Castellated and Domestic Architecture of Scotland*, 5 vols (Edinburgh, 1887–92)
G. Hay: *The Architecture of Scottish Post-Reformation Churches* (Oxford, 1957)

SPAIN

L. T. Balbás: 'Arquitectura gotica', *A. Hisp.*, vii (1952), pp. 369–84
J. Harvey: *The Cathedrals of Spain* (London, 1957)

HOWARD COLVIN

Gotlib, Henryk (*b* Kraków, 1890; *d* Godstone, Surrey, 30 Dec 1966). Polish painter, draughtsman, printmaker and writer, active in England. He came from a middle-class Jewish family in Kraków. From 1908 to 1910 he studied at the Academy of Fine Arts in Kraków and, due to pressure from his parents, read law at the university there. He continued both his art and law studies in Vienna (1911–13) and later became a pupil of Angelo Jank at the Akademie der Bildenden Künste, Munich (1913–14). At the end of World War I he joined the Society of Polish Artists, who organized his first one-man show in Warsaw (1918). The following year he returned to Kraków and became a leading member of the avant-garde Formist movement. From 1923 to 1929 he lived and worked in France, participating in exhibitions at the Salon d'Automne, the Salon des Tuileries and the Salon des Indépendants. In 1930 he returned to Poland and joined the Group of Ten. From 1933 to 1935 he again lived abroad, spending long periods in Italy, Greece and Spain, though he continued to exhibit regularly in his native country. During a visit to London in 1938, he met his wife, who was a native of Scotland, and the following year, with the outbreak of World War II, he settled in England, where he remained for the rest of his life (except for a year spent teaching in Poland in 1949–50). In 1940 he was invited to join the London Group, which then had no other foreign members. From the 1940s onwards Gotlib exhibited extensively in Britain, where his works are well represented in public collections.

The rediscovery in 1978 of a cache of drawings by Gotlib from the period 1906–30 (dispersed), found in the attic of his former home in Kraków, shed new light on his early development: these show his youthful experiments with styles such as that of Vuillard and late Cubism. Typical of his later oil paintings are generalized depictions of nudes, dark and grainy in tone and painted with a heavy impasto (e.g. *Nude by the Garden Door*, 1942; Edinburgh, N.G. Mod. A.). His palette was usually vibrant and intense. Like his thickly contoured charcoal drawings, his paintings fall broadly within the tradition of German Expressionism: the portrait of *John Nowell* (1959; London, priv. col., see 1988 exh. cat., no. 16), for instance, reveals the influence of the late works of Lovis Corinth and the early works of Oskar Kokoschka. Gotlib's technical debt to Rembrandt, whose richly impastoed handling of paint and darkly glowing colours he so much admired, was openly acknowledged in his semi-autobiographical painting *Rembrandt in Heaven* (1950–60; London, Tate). As a figurative artist, Gotlib and his work fell out of favour during the 1950s, when abstract art came into fashion. He was also a prolific and talented writer, with contributions to several newspapers and magazines. His only book, *Travels of a Painter* (*c.* 1938–9), was commissioned by a Warsaw publisher. Gotlib's original illustrations for it were destroyed during the war, and the published edition, which appeared in Polish only in 1947, contained Old Master drawings instead.

UNPUBLISHED SOURCES

London, Boundary Gal. [photocopy of MS. cat. rai. of Gotlib's work by his widow, J. Gotlib]

WRITINGS

Wedrówti malarza [Travels of a painter] (Warsaw, 1947); Eng. trans. of last chapter, 'W kraju właśniej wizii' [The land of my own vision], *Studio Int.* (May 1970)

BIBLIOGRAPHY

Henryk Gotlib: Paintings and Drawings (exh. cat., Edinburgh, N.G. Mod. A.; Southampton, C.A.G.; Cardiff, N. Mus.; 1970)
Henryk Gotlib (1890–1966) (exh. cat., Warsaw, N. Mus., 1980)
British Landscape Painting, 1850–1950 (exh. cat., London, Hayward Gal.; Bristol, Mus. & A.G.; Stoke-on-Trent, City Mus. & A.G.; Sheffield, Mappin A.G.; 1983)
Homage to Henryk Gotlib (exh. cat., Leicester, Mus. & A.G., 1983)
Henryk Gotlib (1890–1966): A European Master (exh. cat., foreword by C. M. Kauffmann and essays by J. Russell Taylor and M. Bohm-Duchen, London, Boundary Gal., 1988)

LOLEK HOLZER

GoToba (*b* Heiankyō [now Kyoto], 1180; *reg* 1183–98; *d* Naka no shima, Oki Islands [now in Shimane Prefect.], 1239). Emperor of Japan during the Kamakura period (1185–1333), patron, scholar and poet. The dual-polity government that prevailed in Japan just before GoToba's reign in the late 12th century rested uneasily on a complex political relationship between the shogunate (*bakufu*) under the Hōjō family in the eastern capital of Kamakura and the emperor in the capital at Heian (now Kyoto). At the age of 18 GoToba ceded the throne to his son, and during his ascendancy as the 'abdicated' or 'cloistered' emperor (*in*) he sought to challenge Kamakura authority. In 1221 he declared war on the Hōjō; this action was known as the Jōkyū Disturbance (Jōkyū no Ran). Within a month, however, GoToba's armies were easily defeated by *bakufu* forces, and he and his followers were immediately exiled from the capital; GoToba spent the rest of his life on the Oki Islands in the Sea of Japan. Ironically the outcome was that even more political power accrued to the Hōjō. Despite the waning political authority of the court during his life, however, GoToba and other members of the aristocracy continued to be the arbiters of cultural taste.

GoToba is also known as the inspiration for an important collection of Japanese poetry, the *Shinkokinshū* (or *Shinkokinwakashū*; 'New collection of ancient and modern times'; 1205), compiled by Fujiwara no Teika (*see* FUJIWARA (ii), (7)) and a group of other high-ranking courtiers, but in which the Emperor himself invested much energy and interest and to which he contributed 34 of his own poems. GoToba is also known to have sponsored both the rebuilding of 18 imperial residences and paintings executed in indigenous Japanese styles and was a patron of the artist Fujiwara no Nobuzane (*see* FUJIWARA (ii), (8)), who developed the Japanese form of portraiture known as *nisee* ('likeness pictures'; *see* JAPAN, §VI, 3(iii) and 4(ii)).

BIBLIOGRAPHY

Kyōto Shi: Kyōto no rekishi [History of Kyoto], 9 vols (Kyoto, 1968–76)
J. W. Hall and J. P. Mass: *Medieval Japan: Essays in Institutional History* (Stanford, 1974)
J. P. Mass: *The Development of Kamakura Rule, 1180–1250: A History with Documents* (Stanford, 1979)
J. P. Mass, ed.: *Court and Bakufu: Essays in Kamakura History* (New Haven and London, 1982)

NICOLE FABRICAND-PERSON

Gott, Joseph (*b* Leeds, 1786; *d* Rome, 8 January 1860). English sculptor. He trained in London between 1798 and 1802 under John Flaxman, and from 1805 at the Royal Academy Schools. In 1822 he moved permanently to Rome, and in 1826 it was reported that he and John Gibson were 'getting for themselves and their country a high reputation'. Gott made frequent visits to England to obtain commissions from both the aristocracy and the industrial magnates of the North and exhibited regularly at the Royal Academy between 1820 and 1848. He made many terracotta and plaster maquettes but finished works were always carved in marble. In 1823 William Spencer Cavendish, 6th Duke of Devonshire, purchased *Greyhound with her Two Puppies Suckling* (Chatsworth House, Derbys); Gott was henceforth called the 'Landseer of marble'. His range of subject matter was perhaps more varied than that of any other sculptor in Europe at that time, as a representative list suggests: *Metobus and Camilla* (1828–30; Leeds, C.A.G.), after *The Aeneid*; *Venus Dissuading Adonis from the Chase* (1822–4; Leeds, C.A.G.); the *Death of Spartacus* (1820; London, Soane Mus.); *Ruth* (n.d.; York, C.A.G.); *Hindu Girl Placing her Lamp upon the Ganges* (n.d.; priv. col., see 1972 exh. cat., no. 48, pl. 35), from Thomas Moore's *Lalla Rookh*; *Titania and the Changeling Boy* (untraced), after Shakespeare; portrait busts, medallions and statues (e.g. Leeds, C.A.G.); as well as children at play and church monuments. Gott was never attracted by the austere neo-Greek style practised by Gibson and Richard James Wyatt: his sculpture is unheroic, pastoral, romantic. The period 1822 to 1837 was his most fertile; thereafter his work became less distinguished and received hostile criticism.

BIBLIOGRAPHY

Gunnis
Joseph Gott, 1786–1860, Sculptor (exh. cat. by T. Friedman and T. Stevens, Leeds, C.A.G.; Liverpool, Walker A.G.; 1972)

TERRY FRIEDMAN

Gottardi (Folin), Roberto (*b* Venice, 30 Jan 1927). Italian architect and stage designer, active in Cuba. He graduated from the Istituto Superiore d'Archittetura in Venice in 1952, where he was a pupil of Carlo Scarpa, Franco Albini and Luigi Piccinato (*b* 1899). He began his professional career in BBPR Architectural Studio in Milan. In 1957 he went to Venezuela to work in a local studio and in 1960 was invited to join a Cuban programme. Thereafter he trained architectural students in the problems of creativity and plasticity as professor of Basic Design of the Faculty of Architecture in Havana. In 1961 he took part with Ricardo Porro and Vittorio Garatti in designing the Escuelas Nacionales de Arte at Cubanacán, Havana, his particular role being the designing of the Escuela de Artes Dramáticas. In this building he combined the compact volumetric tradition of brick walls and the irregular urban spaces of medieval Italian cities with the internal courtyards of Spanish colonial tradition. The work was broken off in 1965 but the project was resumed in 1980, when he combined High Tech components with pre-existing elements. In the Menocal Command Post in the province of Havana (1967) he adapted prefabricated structural elements to form an organic-looking structure that develops down from the top of a hill. His later stage designs introduced a meaningful connection between architecture, painting and scenic arts in Cuban culture. Examples include *Girón* (1981) and *Dédalo* (1989), designed for the Conjunto de Danza Contemporánea de Cuba.

BIBLIOGRAPHY

H. Consuegra: 'Las escuelas nacionales de arte', *Arquitectura/Cuba*, 335 (1965), pp. 14–25
R. Segre: *Cuba: Architettura della rivoluzione* (Padua, 1970)
G. Fiorese: *Architettura e istruzione a Cuba* (Milan, 1980)
R. Segre: *Arquitectura y urbanismo de la revolución cubana* (Havana, 1989)

ROBERTO SEGRE

Gottardo de Scottis [Scotti] (*b* Piacenza; *fl* Milan, 1454–85). Italian painter. He is first documented in 1454 as a native of Piacenza. Between 1456 and 1470 he appears frequently in the account-books of Milan Cathedral working on commissions from various members of the Sforza court. He is also recorded working for the Borromeo family during the same period. His work seems to have consisted of minor tasks, such as the gilding of statues and the design of processional banners and embroidered altarcloths.

In 1472 Gottardo and the painter Giacomo Vismara (*fl* 1470s) estimated Zanetto Bugatto's frescoes in S Maria delle Grazie outside Vigevano. He may have been at work on Duke Galeazzo Maria Sforza's chapel in the Castello Sforzesco, Milan, in 1473 and was part of the team that painted the ducal chapel in Pavia in 1474. In 1475 he was commissioned to paint a *Maestà* (untraced) for the high altar in Milan Cathedral and was listed as a member of the Milanese painters' guild in 1481. In 1485 he was referred to as painter to the cathedral. Only two pictures can reasonably be ascribed to the artist. The first, a triptych of the *Madonna of Mercy* (Milan, Mus. Poldi Pezzoli), is signed *Gotardu[s] [de] [S]cotis de Mello Pinsit* ('Mello' is probably an abbreviation for Milan). It is a competent work showing the influence of Vincenzo Foppa in its heavy figures and detailed architectural forms. Similar characteristics can be seen in four small panels of the *Annunciation*, *Nativity*, *Massacre of the Innocents* and *Christ among the Doctors* (Milan, Cologna priv. col.), which have been convincingly attributed to Gottardo.

BIBLIOGRAPHY

F. Malaguzzi-Valeri: *Pittori lombardi del quattrocento* (Milan, 1902)
G. Biscaro: 'Note di storia dell'arte e della cultura a Milano dai libri mastri Borromeo, 1427–1478', *Archv Stor. Lombardo*, xvi (1914), pp. 72–108
M. Salmi: 'Bernardino Butinone', *Dedalo*, x (1929–30), p. 401
M. Natale: *Museo Poldi Pezzoli: Dipinti* (Milan, 1982), pp. 72–4

E. SAMUELS WELCH

Götting, Gottfried (*b* Düsseldorf, 20 Feb 1830; *d* Aachen, May 1879). German sculptor. He may have been taught by his father, Johann Peter Götting (1795–1865), a painter and sculptor with whom he is often confused. In 1858 he settled in Aachen, where the restoration of the cathedral provided plenty of work for sculptors. He produced several series of sandstone statues for the exterior of the building, modelling his style closely on that of the cathedral's surviving medieval sculptures. The figures of the twelve *Apostles* and four *Evangelists* in the Matthiaskapelle were completed in 1865, the *Ancestors of Christ* for the Annakapelle in 1871 and the 29 statues on the flying buttresses of the choir in 1873. He also provided the figures for the Karlskapelle and the Hubertuskapelle.

In 1872 Götting was appointed to a teaching position at the Rheinisch-Westfälische Technische Hochschule in Aachen. He executed sculptural decorations for the façade of the college building, as well as marble portrait busts of King Frederick William IV and Crown Prince William. In 1877 he made sculptures for the Marienbrunnen on Münsterplatz in Aachen. In recognition of his extensive work for the minster he was appointed cathedral sculptor in 1877. A relief representing the *Adoration of the Three Wise Men* above the Dreikönigen-Portal of the Rathaus in Aachen is believed to have been his last work.

BIBLIOGRAPHY

E. Stephany: *Der Dom zu Aachen* (Mönchengladbach, 1958)
H. P. Schmitz and R. Cremer: 'Erbauer der Technischen Hochschule und Restaurator des Münsters zu Aachen', *Aachen. Beitr. Baugesch. & Heimatkst*, 5 (1969), pp. 55–63
P. Bloch: *Skulpturen des 19. Jahrhunderts im Rheinland* (Düsseldorf, 1975)
H. P. Hilger: 'Altäre und Ausstattungen rheinischer Kirchen', *Kunst des 19. Jahrhunderts im Rheinland*, ed. E. Trier and W. Weyres, iv (Düsseldorf, 1980), pp. 135–6
E. Trier: 'Die religiösen Denkmäler', ibid., pp. 182, 189 (fig. 16)

INGE ZACHER

Gottlieb, Adolph (*b* New York, 14 March 1903; *d* Easthampton, NY, 4 March 1974). American painter and sculptor. He was one of the few members of the New York School born in New York, and he studied at the Art Students League under Robert Henri and John Sloan in 1920–21. He spent the following year travelling through France and Germany and studying at the Académie de la Grande Chaumière, Paris. On his return to New York in 1923, he attended the Parsons School of Design and Cooper Union Institute. He was the best travelled of the New York painters (rivalled only by Franz Kline), having been to Paris, Munich and Berlin before even beginning advanced formal studies, and the breadth of his training and art-historical knowledge served him well in his teaching, which was his principal means of support during the mid-1930s. His first one-man exhibition was in 1930, and he showed regularly thereafter as a member of the emerging New York School respected by his contemporaries for his learned and earnest approach to painting.

In 1935, with Mark Rothko, Lee Gatch, William Baziotes and Ilya Bolotowsky among others, Gottlieb founded the Ten, a group that exhibited until 1940. His early paintings of American scenes, such as *Sun Deck* (1936; College Park, U. MD A.G.), were influenced by the simplified representational idiom of Milton Avery. In 1936 he worked in the Works Progress Administration Federal Art Project's easel painting division and from 1937 to 1939 lived in the Arizona desert. There he painted representational images of cacti and barren scenery; these images gradually metamorphosed into Surrealist-inspired paintings, for example *The Sea Chest* (1942; New York, Guggenheim), in which mysterious incongruities were injected into otherwise uniform landscapes. Together, these varied experiences informed the grand spaces characteristic of his mature monumental painting. Whereas Pollock had found the Atlantic to be a visual equivalent to the wide open spaces of his native West, ironically Gottlieb, whose hobby was sailing, rejected the insubstantiality of sky and sea and adopted the great western deserts as images of space. This sense of space expressed itself only in his later pictures.

In a letter that Gottlieb and Rothko wrote to the *New York Times* in June 1943, they (and Barnett Newman in a subsequent letter) laid the theoretical foundations for ABSTRACT EXPRESSIONISM. 'We favor the simple expression of the complex thought. We are for the large shape because it has the impact of the unequivocal. We wish to reassert the picture plane. We are for flat forms because they destroy illusion and reveal truth.' During World War II, the exiled European Surrealists with whom Gottlieb came into contact in New York contributed to his belief that a truly evocative art has its roots in the artist's subconscious and led him to experiment with essential or archetypal motifs.

Gottlieb had begun using primitive, timeless images in the *Pictographs* initiated in 1941 after his return to New York. These paintings, for instance *Voyager's Return* (1946; New York, MOMA), in which apparently archaic signs, actually invented symbols, were set into a compartmented surface, reflected his investigations into early cultures, mainly those of North America, but also those of the Ancient Near East. Whenever Gottlieb discovered that one of his signs had an actual precedent in a past culture, he dropped it from his painting vocabulary, thereby rendering his work 'mute'. This was his gesture towards a universal grammar, or principle of order common to all humanity. Gottlieb hoped that by calling attention to the fundamental properties of language, he would involve spectators in a universal experience.

By the early 1950s his *Pictographs* had been superseded by a series of *Imaginary Landscapes* (e.g. *Frozen Sounds II*, 1952; Buffalo, NY, Albright–Knox A.G.). These works maintained the parallel with written language but also invoked the object-field relationships of deep space. This was not a question of representing a particular landscape, but of suggesting a general sense of foreground and background.

The *Burst* series that followed presented a radically simplified image. They usually consisted of two shapes, a red disc above a writhing black mass near the bottom of the picture (e.g. *Blast I*, 1957; New York, MOMA; see fig.). Together these forms, in various combinations, continued to play out not only the relationship of object to ground in landscape painting, but also an almost theatrical confrontation of two protagonists as in history painting. He experimented with similar shapes in sculptures such as *Petaloid* (cor-ten steel, 1967; New York, E. Gottlieb priv. col., see H. Geldzahler: *New York Painting and Sculpture, 1940–1970*, London, 1969, p. 168). Gottlieb distilled the most fundamental relationships out of a complex of sensations re-created with the utmost economy.

Adolph Gottlieb: *Blast I*, oil on canvas, 2.28×1.14 m, 1957 (New York, Museum of Modern Art)

BIBLIOGRAPHY

M. Friedman: *Adolph Gottlieb* (Minneapolis, 1963)
H. Rand: 'Adolph Gottlieb in Context', *Artmagazine*, li/6 (1977), pp. 112–35
I. Sandler: 'Adolph Gottlieb', *A. Int.*, xxi/3 (1977), pp. 35–8
K. Wilkin: 'Adolph Gottlieb: The Pictographs', *A. Int.*, xxi/6 (1977), pp. 27–33 [on the exhibition at Edmonton, Alta, A.G.]
Adolph Gottlieb: Pictographs (exh. cat. by K. Wilkin, Edmonton, Alta, A.G.; Toronto, A.G. Ont.; 1977–8)

HARRY RAND

Gottlieb, Maurycy [Moritz] **(Moses)** (*b* Drohobycz, Galicia, 21/28 Feb 1856; *d* Kraków, 17 July 1879). Polish painter. He was the elder brother of the painters Filip Gottlieb (*b c.* 1870), Marceli Gottlieb, Marcin Gottlieb (1867–1936) and Leopold Gottlieb (1879/83–1934). He came from a wealthy, orthodox Jewish family and his artistic talent manifested itself very early in his life. From 1869 he studied drawing with Michał Goldewski the elder (1799–1875), an amateur painter in Lwów (now Lviv, Ukraine). In October 1871 he travelled to Vienna, where in 1872 he studied under Karl Mayer (1810–76), and subsequently under Karl von Blaas at the Akademie der Bildenden Künste. In 1873–4 he studied with Jan Matejko at the School of Fine Arts, Kraków, but soon returned to Vienna to study historical composition under Carl Wurzinger (1817–83). He painted a number of works in Kraków, partly completing them in Vienna in 1875. These include a *Self-portrait* in the magnificent costume of a Polish nobleman (ex-J. Felsen priv. col., Vienna, see Rogoyska, p. 5) as well as unsuccessful historical compositions, for example the *Investiture of Albert of Brandenburg by Sigismund I* (Kraków, L. Reich priv. col.). In 1875 he left Vienna, staying briefly in Kraków and Drohobycz; towards the end of the year, with a letter of recommendation from Jan Matejko, he studied under Karl von Piloty at the Munich Akademie der Bildenden Künste. In Munich he painted one of his most outstanding early works, *Shylock and Jessica* (Warsaw, Zofia Tabecka priv. col., see Rogoyska, p. 9), after Shakespeare's *Merchant of Venice.* This painting was highly praised both in Poland and abroad, and brought fame to the young artist. Filip Gottlieb (in 1886) and Marcin Gottlieb (in 1887) both produced copies of the painting. In 1875 Gottlieb also painted a *Self-portrait as Ahasuerus* (Kraków, N. Mus.). In 1876 he was again in Drohobycz, where he made a number of sketches for his *Jewish Wedding-feast.* At the end of 1876 he returned to Vienna, to study under Heinrich von Angeli in the Akademie. Through this teacher he came under the influence of Hans Makart, as may be seen in his lyrical costume-composition of 1877, *Uriel and Judith* (ex-Hipolit Wawelberg priv. col., Warsaw; ?Mexico City, Holzer priv. col., see 1991 exh. cat., no. 15), after Karl Gutzkow's *Uriel Acosta.* The *Self-portrait in Arab Costume* (ex-Governor Hurka priv. col.; ?destr.), copied by his brother Marcin (Warsaw, Jew. Hist. Inst., see 1991 exh. cat., no. 7), belongs to this period, as do the *Shulamite Woman* (Bytom, Mus. Upper Silesia) and the *Slave-girls' Market in Cairo* (?New York, priv. col., see 1991 exh. cat., no. 33), copied by his brother Filip, and a number of portraits of men, women and children. In 1878 Gottlieb painted the portrait of *Ignacy Kuranda* (Kraków, N. Mus.), leader of the Jewish community in Vienna, and in the same year he travelled to St Petersburg and Munich in order to work on illustrations for Lessing's *Nathan der Weise*, commissioned by the publisher Bruckmann. Here he painted the religious composition *Jews Praying on the Day of Atonement* (Tel Aviv, Mus. A.). In the second half of 1878 he left Munich and, with a grant from the Fanni Jejtteles Foundation, travelled to Italy. There he met Matejko, and, at his prompting, he returned to the School of Fine Arts in Kraków to study composition. In Kraków in 1879 he painted a striking portrait of a *Jewish Woman* (Warsaw, N. Mus.), and he also worked on the painting *Christ Preaching at Capharnum* (Warsaw, N. Mus.), which he never finished. In his early youth Gottlieb had had little contact with Polish society, but later on he was torn between his attachment to the Jewish people and his Polish patriotism.

BIBLIOGRAPHY

PSB; *SAP*
M. Waldman: *Maurycy Gottlieb 1856–1879* (Kraków, 1932)
M. Rogoyska: 'Maurycy Gottlieb', *Przegląd A.* (1954), no. 3, pp. 5–15
Polnische Malerei von 1830 bis 1914 (exh. cat., Kiel, Ksthalle; Stuttgart, Württemberg. Kstver.; Wuppertal, von der Heydt-Mus.; 1978–9)
La Peinture polonaise du XVIe au début du XXe siècle, Warsaw, N. Mus. cat. (Warsaw, 1979)
In the Flower of Youth: Maurycy Gottlieb, 1856–1879 (exh. cat. by N. Guralnik, Tel Aviv, Mus. A., 1991)

WANDA MAŁASZEWSKA

Gottlob, Kaj (*b* Copenhagen, 9 Nov 1887; *d* Copenhagen, 12 May 1976). Danish architect, designer and teacher. He studied at the Academy of Arts School of Architecture, Copenhagen (1907–14), and then became an assistant to Hack Kampmann in Copenhagen. He made an early reputation in housing projects and also designed furniture and silverware, exhibiting at the Exposition Internationale des Arts Décoratifs et Industriels Modernes, Paris (1925). Gottlob belonged to the generation of architects who gave Danish classicism of the 1920s a distinctive elegance and strength. His chief works during this period were the church of St Lucas, Århus, won in competition in 1918 and completed in 1926 (with Anton Frederiksen); the Law Court (1922), Frederiksberg; and the Danish Students' Hostel (1930) at the Cité Universitaire, Paris, also won in competition. His classicist works sometimes show a tendency to Mannerism and exaggerated proportions, especially evident in the church of St Lucas. From 1924 to 1938 he held a chair at the Academy of Arts School of Architecture in Copenhagen. After 1930 Gottlob was influenced by the ideals of modernism, although he retained a classicist approach to architectonic articulation. In his modernist works he took full advantage of the expressive potential of new materials and construction techniques, seen in such buildings in Copenhagen as the reinforced-concrete office block Ørstedshus (1934), with Art-Deco designs in the lobby and stairway; the bridge at Knippelsbro (1937); and the School on the Sound (1937), with an open-air section reminiscent of the Ecole en Plein Air (1934), Suresnes, France, by Eugène Beaudouin and Marcel Lods. From the late 1930s he was involved in the development of the new university park at Nørre Fælled, Copenhagen, designing the Pharmaceutical College (1939–41; altered 1964–7), the Odontological College (1939–41; altered 1967), the Anatomical Institute (1940–42) and the Egmont H. Petersen Hall of Residence (1950–59). He also carried out sensitive restoration projects on historic buildings and worked on the recording and preservation of the Danish architectural heritage.

BIBLIOGRAPHY

S. E. Rasmussen: *Nordische Baukunst* (Copenhagen and Berlin, 1940), pp. 114–15, 151–4
Nordisk klassicism/Nordic Classicism, 1910–30 (exh. cat., ed. S. Paavilainen; Helsinki, Mus. Fin. Archit., 1982), p. 61

JØRGEN SESTOFT

Gottschalk, Albert (*b* Stege, Møn, 3 July 1866; *d* Copenhagen, 13 Feb 1906). Danish painter. From 1883 to 1884 he received his first artistic education from the critic, writer and painter Karl Madsen (1855–1938), who introduced him to the work of Corot, and the painter Karl Jensen (1851–1933). From 1884 to 1888 he attended the Free Art School in Copenhagen, set up in reaction to the Akademi by a group of artists that included P. S. Kroyer. Thereafter Gottschalk was dedicated to *plein-air* landscape painting. His works originated from numerous excursions made in Denmark, even to the most remote parts. *Spring, Glostrup* (1887; Copenhagen, Stat. Mus. Kst) combines a daring diagonal composition with a sensitive rendering of colour and light. He also visited Paris and Germany and spent several months in Rome in 1904.

Gottschalk's work has been seen as a continuation of the 'Golden Age' of Danish painting in the 1830s and 1840s, related in its use of colour to the work of Christen Købke. His ideas, however, were rooted in the realist approach to nature that came to the fore in Europe during the 1870s and 1880s. Over the years the improvised, expressive side of Gottschalk's work became increasingly dominant, as can be seen in his painting *View of Kronborg* (1904; Copenhagen, Stat. Mus. Kst.), in which the castle at Elsinore, seen from a dramatic angle, emerges as a dominant vertical structure, while the hastily painted skyscape underlines the Expressionist aspect of the work. This becomes all-pervasive in *From Tisvilde* (1905; Silkeborg, Kstmus.), in which fleeting and jagged brushstrokes convey the transitory aspect of nature. This quality led to his work being condemned as 'mere sketches, though talented'.

Gottschalk's devotion to the open country and the outskirts of the towns corresponded with the emotions and forms of expression of contemporary Danish poetry. His work served as a source of inspiration for several generations of Danish painters, and its dramatic style and concept of nature seem today more related to early Expressionism than to the mid-19th-century tradition.

BIBLIOGRAPHY

P. Uttenreiter: *Albert Gottschalk* (Copenhagen, 1943)
T. Andersen: *Albert Gottschalk* (Copenhagen, 1977)

TROELS ANDERSEN

Gottsched, Johann Christoph (*b* Königsberg, 2 Feb 1700; *d* Leipzig, 12 Dec 1766). German philosopher. He was the first of the philosophers influenced by Johann Christian von Wolff (1679–1754) to establish a place in Wolff's system for the fine arts. He attended the universities of Königsberg and Leipzig in the early 1720s, where he wrote theses on Wolffian topics. In 1730 he published his enormously influential *Versuch einer critischen Dichtkunst*. This essay brings together traditional poetics, the theory of taste and Wolffian philosophy. Although he employed the traditional framework of commenting on Horace's *Ars poetica*, Gottsched focused on the relation between taste and perfection: perfection is rational, the unity of a manifold, but may be 'obscurely perceived' by taste. His relaxation of the stern rationalism of Wolff was insufficient for the Zurich critics Bodmer and Breitinger, generating a controversy that rumbled on into the 1750s. It was also unacceptable to the later generation of romantic aestheticians, notably Goethe, who found his compromise between the rules of art and the demands of taste still too restrictive.

WRITINGS

Versuch einer critischen Dichtkunst (Halle, 1730), vi of *Johann Christoph Gottsched Ausgewählte Schriften*, ed. J. Birke and B. Birke (Berlin and New York, 1973)

BIBLIOGRAPHY

A. Baumler: *Das Irrationalitätsproblem in der Ästhetik und Logik des 18. Jahrhunderts bis zur Kritik der Urteilskraft* (Halle, 1923; *R* Darmstadt, 1967)
A. Nivelle: *Kunst und Dichtungstheorien zwischen Aufklärung und Klassik* (Berlin, 1960)
J. Birke: 'Gottscheds Neuorientierung der deutschen Poetik auf der Philosophie Wolffs', *Z. Dt. Philol.*, lxxxv (1966), pp. 560–75
H. Freier: *Kritische Poetik: Legitimation und Kritik der Poesie in 'Gottscheds Dichtkunst'* (Stuttgart, 1973)

HOWARD CAYGILL

Götz, Gottfried Bernhard. *See* GÖZ, GOTTFRIED BERNHARD.

Götz, Joseph Matthias (*b* Bamberg, 1696; *d* Munich, Aug 1760). German sculptor. He probably learnt the sculptor's craft from his father, Johann Georg Götz (*fl* 1695). In 1713 he became an apprentice in the workshop of Joseph Hartmann (*c.* 1674–1734) in Passau. In 1715 he took over the sculpture workshop of the Augustinian collegiate foundation of St Nikola, near Passau. He worked chiefly in wood. Among works attributed to Götz or attested as his by documentary evidence are the pulpit and side altars (1715) for St Nikola (now Vilshofen, parish church); the high altar and probably the two side altars nearest the front (1723–8) in the abbey church at Aldersbach, near Passau; and the carved wood tabernacle group of the *Creation*, as well as alabaster figures and other small sculptures and reliefs in wood and marble (1720–40), for the altars of the Pfarr-und Wallfahrtskirche at Stadl-Paura, near Lambach, Upper Austria. In collaboration with the architect Joseph Munggenast, Götz made the organ case and high altar (1731) in the collegiate church at Zwettl, Lower Austria. He also made the high altar (1735–9) of the Wallfahrtskirche at Maria Taferl, near Melk; the columned altar in the parish church at Krems; the pulpit and choir-stalls (1732–6) and the side altars and high altar (1740–41) of the Karmelitenkirche at Straubing; and the stone *Trinity* column (1738) at Krems. Influenced by the Italian Baroque tradition, Götz created sculpture of high quality. His elegant and virtuoso figures are not subordinate to the surrounding architecture but stand out in front of it. Götz was a master at composing large, animated figural scenes, and in his free-standing, columned tabernacle altars he achieved admirable ensemble effects, not least by making the windows and light play their part.

In the years following 1738 Götz worked chiefly as an architect and engineer. In 1739 he was entrusted with the building of the Cistercian church of Mariae Himmelfahrt at Fürstenzell, near Passau, but proved unequal to the task, which was handed over to Johann Michael Fischer. In 1742, during the War of the Austrian Succession, Götz left St Nikola to serve in the Bavarian army as surveyor and Chief Engineer.

BIBLIOGRAPHY

R. Guby: 'Passauer Bildhauer des 18. Jahrhunderts: Joseph Matthias Götz', *Niederbayer. Mschr.*, 6 (1917), pp. 53, 59, 84–9, 122–34; 7 (1918), pp. 20–26, 65–83; 8 (1919), pp. 21–33, 85–92, 120–28
H. Schindler: *Grosse bayerische Kunstgeschichte*, ii (Munich, 1976), pp. 350–52
——: *Bayerische Bildhauer: Manierismus, Barock, Rokoko in altbayerischen Unterland* (Munich, 1985), pp. 147–52

BARBARA DAENTLER

Götz, Karl-Otto (*b* Aachen, 22 Feb 1914). German painter, photographer, film maker, draughtsman, printmaker, writer and teacher. From 1932 to 1933 he attended the Webe- und Kunstgewerbeschule in Aachen. Inspired by Picasso, Gris, Klee and the Expressionists, Götz reduced the figures in his painting to minimal linear outlines from 1933, as a result of which he was prohibited from painting and exhibiting from 1935 to 1936. During his military service from 1936 to 1938 he experimented with spray painting, overpainted photograms (of his wife), photograms (produced by laying objects on photographic paper exposed to light) and abstract cine-films. In 1938 he settled in Wurzen, Saxony, and from 1938 to 1939 attended the Kunstakademie in Dresden where he began to concentrate on abstract works, using a mixture of organic and geometric elements. In 1940 he moved to Dresden, where his friends included Will Grohmann and Otto Dix. He served in the German army in Norway from 1941 to 1945. During this period he studied Surrealism, corresponded with Willi Baumeister and composed his *Fakturenfibel* ('Introductory primer'; 1945; artist's col., see 1984 exh. cat., p. 143), which presents, in ink sketches, a systematic alphabet of forms compiled of individual elements and their compound variations; after World War II he produced accompanying woodcuts (1943–5; artist's col., see 1984 exh. cat., p. 143).

Alongside works in tempera and gouache, Götz made particular use of monotype from 1946. In the same year he began experimenting with solarization, a procedure related to photograms, in which the image is exposed to light during processing to give a halo effect. Following his first one-man shows in 1947–8, he was associated with a number of groups, including Cobra, which he joined in 1948, QUADRIGA, which he co-founded in 1952, and Zen 49, with whom he made a guest appearance in 1955. From 1952 he became a leading figure in German *Art informel* and exhibited widely, for example in the Venice Biennale of 1958 and the *Documenta 2* exhibition in Kassel in 1959. Götz wrote under the pseudonym of André Tamm, edited the journal *Meta* from 1948 to 1953, studied information theory intensively for over ten years, published scientific articles and conducted empirical investigations into colour perception.

During this period Götz developed his own technique of gestural painting. Having applied his paint to a wet ground, he would then add or scrape off paint in rapid movements using a number of different tools (e.g. *Picture from 8.2*, 1953; Saarbrücken, Saarland-Mus.). Götz combined clear compositional elements such as those analysed in his *Fakturenfibel* with a rapid manner of execution that permitted chance variations and that was influenced by Surrealist theories of automatism. In most of his work, including the gouaches, he created a powerful impression of spatial depth by strong contrasts of black and one or two other colours, such as red, yellow or blue, on a white ground. In the second half of the 1950s Götz executed several series of variations on a particular basic structure: the *Spiral Pictures* from 1956, featuring two crossing diagonals, with curving brushstrokes and horizontals running in opposite directions; the so-called *Submarine Pictures* from 1957, in which the canvas is ruled by a dominant horizontal and a vertical descending from above; and the *Waterfall Pictures*, whose surface is dissected by parallel diagonals, as in *Tulva* (1957; Münster, Westfäl. Landesmus.). In 1959 he began teaching at the Kunstakademie Düsseldorf, Hochschule für Bildende Künste, which he continued to do for the next 20 years.

In the mid-1960s Götz started to produce works executed in three parts, each part painted in a day and then covered up while the next was completed. The dimensions of these rectangular works, which included *Födsel* (1.74×4.39 m, 1964; Bonn, Rhein. Landesmus.), increased over a period of several years. At this time Götz refined his formal vocabulary into more fluid, spiralling figurations, employing powerful spatial illusionism; in many works of the 1960s and 1970s he used only black and white (e.g. *Kelesin*, 1975; artist's col., see 1984 exh. cat., pl. 89). In the 1980s his colours became brighter, and his brushstrokes smaller and more intricate.

WRITINGS

with K. Götz: *Probleme der Bildästhetik: Eine Einführung in die Grundlagen des anschaulichen Denkens* (Düsseldorf, 1972)

Erinnerungen und Werk, 2 vols (Düsseldorf, 1983)

BIBLIOGRAPHY

Deutsches Informel. Symposium Informel (exh. cat., ed. G. W. Költzsch; Saarbrücken, Saarland-Mus., 1983) [exh. and conference]

K. O. Götz: Monotypien, Gemälde, Gouachen, 1935–1983 (exh. cat., ed. J. Harten; Düsseldorf, Städt. Ksthalle; Saarbrücken, Saarland-Mus.; Esslingen, Gal. Stadt.; 1984)

U. Geiger: *Die Maler der Quadriga: Otto Greis—Karl Otto Götz—Bernard Schulze—Heinz Kreutz und ihre Stellung im Informel* (Nuremberg, 1987)

CLAUDIA BÜTTNER

Götz [Görtz; Grottes]**, Sebastian** (*b* Zizers, nr Chur, *c.* 1575; *d* after 1621). German sculptor of Swiss birth. In 1589 he was commissioned by the ducal court in Munich to work on the Jesuit church of St Michael and the building known as the Wilhelminische Feste (destr. 1944). At that time he compiled a collection of sketches that he submitted when applying in 1604 for employment at the court of the Elector Palatine at Heidelberg. Johann Schoch, the master builder of the new Friedrichbau, recommended Götz to the Elector Frederick IV, who granted him the responsibility for the sculpture of the façades of the Friedrichbau; this comprised 16 statues of Electors, as well as escutcheons, decorative panels, and heads of lions and humans. The statues were to represent, among others, the ancestors of the House of Wittelsbach, beginning with *Charlemagne* and including *Ludwig IV of Bavaria*, *Elector Rupert III* (founder of Heidelberg University), *Elector Otto Henry* and *Frederick IV* himself. The court painter, Friedrich von Hammel (*fl c.* 1600), began gilding the statues in May 1607, so Götz's extensive task must have been largely finished by then, having taken him and his assistants less than four years. In all probability, however, Götz did not come unprepared to the work; in negotiating the contract, he claimed that he had already helped to make statues of princes in Munich. The Heidelberg statues were made of grey Heilbronn sandstone, contrasting with the red sandstone façade of the building. The execution of the figures was technically highly accomplished, details of the armour, crowns and robes being rendered with astonishing assurance and delicacy. For his models, Götz used portraits of the princes of Bavaria engraved by Jost Ammann. As monumental, characterized figures, these sculptures were unique in their time in south-west Germany; indeed, they anticipate the Baroque in their combination of emotional power with decorative corporeal reality.

After 1607 Götz worked in Aschaffenburg, probably collaborating in the decoration of the Schloss Johannisburg, which was completed in 1614; in that year he was back in Heidelberg, this time under the Elector Frederick V. Götz executed for him a tomb for *Frederick IV* in red and black marble (destr. 1693). The full extent of his involvement in the elaboration and erection of the 'Elisabethentor' in the gardens of the Heidelberg Schloss (1615) is not certain, but the statues of *Ludwig V* and *Frederick V* (1619) are his work. Götz is last mentioned in the archives of Heidelberg in April 1621, after which all trace of him vanishes.

BIBLIOGRAPHY

Thieme–Becker

Die Renaissance im deutschen Südwesten (exh. cat., Heidelberg, Schloss, 1986), pp. 91, 934

A. von Oechelhäuser: *Das Heidelberger Schloss* (Heidelberg, 1987), pp. 43, 65–7, 75, 86, 112

KAI BUDDE

Götzenberger, Jakob (*b* Heidelberg, 4 Nov 1802; *d* Darmstadt, 6 Oct 1866). German painter. He studied from 1820 at the Kunstakademie in Düsseldorf and was then employed by his teacher, Peter Cornelius, as an assistant in producing paintings for the Glyptothek in Munich (destr.; cartoons, Berlin, Alte N.G.). He also worked on the fresco *Theology* for the main hall of the University of Bonn, where in 1825 he was commissioned to design and execute three further frescoes: *Philosophy* (1828; destr.; cartoon, Karlsruhe, Staatl. Ksthalle), *Jurisprudence* and *Medicine* (1832–4; destr.; lithographs, see Hinz, figs 6–8). In 1834 he became court painter to Leopold, Grand Duke of Baden, as well as curator of the palace collections in Mannheim. During this period he painted religious frescoes for the chapel of the von Dalberg-Herdingschen Schloss in Nierstein, including the *Adoration of the Christ-child* (*in situ*), in which, as in the Bonn frescoes, Raphael's influence is clear.

Götzenberger painted 14 monumental frescoes for the Neue Trinkhalle in Baden-Baden in 1840, depicting legends from the Schwarzwald (*in situ*). In these works he overcame the Nazarene concentration on line by including landscapes, which, however, are not always seamlessly combined with the figure compositions. In 1847, after the loss of his post in Mannheim, he went to London, where he undertook portrait and fresco commissions. He painted a series of frescoes for Francis Egerton, Earl of Ellesmere, *Scenes from the History of the House of Bridgewater* (*in situ*; cartoons, Heidelberg, Kurpfälz. Mus.), with accompanying paintings on themes from John Milton's *Comus*. The Bridgewater series is in his Nazarene style, with some scenes in medieval dress, some in 17th century. His last work was four large cartoons, begun *c.* 1863, inspired by the traditional English ballad of 'Lord Percy', for a room in Northumberland House in London, in a style reminiscent of his earlier Nazarene work.

BIBLIOGRAPHY

O. Moser, ed.: *Die Fresken der neuen Trinkhalle zu Baden von J. Götzenberger* (Baden-Baden, 1876)
A. von Schneider: 'Badische Malerei des 19. Jahrhunderts', *Forschungen zur deutschen Kunstgeschichte*, xi (Berlin, 1935, rev. Karlsruhe, 2/1968)
B. Hinz: 'Friede der Fakultäten: Zur Programmatik des Verhältnisses von Kunst und Wissenschaft zwischen Aufklärung und Vormärz: Die Fakultätenbilder in Bonn', *'Geschichte allein ist zeitgemäss': Historismus in Deutschland*, eds M. Brix and M. Steinhauser (Lahn-Giessen, 1978)

JÖRN BAHNS

Gouache [bodycolour]. Commercially manufactured opaque watercolour paint popular with designers, illustrators and airbrush artists. The term also, and more correctly, refers to the use of opaque watercolours in a loosely defined area of technique and the materials and effects associated with such painting. Gouache, also called bodycolour, is simply water-based paint rendered opaque by the addition of white paint or pigment (e.g. Chinese white) or a white substance, such as chalk or even marble dust. It is an evolved form of TEMPERA paint, descended from distemper. The application of the term gouache is often imprecise, but it is most often associated with colours bound in glue-size or gum. The commercial product varies considerably. It is usually bound with gum arabic or dextrin. An inferior version is known as poster colour or poster paint. Gouache produces flat, matt, even colour, and, being thinned with water for use, it is a convenient and quick medium to employ, hence its continuing popularity with designers and illustrators.

The history and evolution of gouache are vague, as its characteristics are common to several types and traditions of painting. Ancient Egyptian wall paintings and Indian miniatures, for example, answer to its general description. Although in Western art it is associated at first with tempera painting and manuscript illumination, it is reasonable to assume a wider use, perhaps of considerable antiquity. Raphael's tapestry cartoons of the *Lives of SS Peter and Paul* (1515–16; British Royal Col., on loan to the V&A, London), can quite reasonably be described as gouache paintings, as can Dürer's watercolour studies of the *Young Hare* (1502) and *Large Piece of Turf* (1503; both Vienna, Albertina). From the 16th to the 18th century gouache is represented by the bodycolour of the limner or miniature painter and by the decorative use of distemper. It then emerged as a rediscovered medium, perhaps associated in some way with the development of pastels and transparent watercolours during the 18th century. It was certainly combined with these materials from that point onwards. In the 20th century it has been used by Matisse (e.g. *The Snail*, 1953; London, Tate).

See also WATERCOLOUR.

BIBLIOGRAPHY

M. B. Cohn: *'Wash + Gouache': A Study of the Development of Materials of Watercolour* (1939/*R* Cambridge, MA, 1977)
J. Stephenson: *The Materials and Techniques of Painting* (London, 1989)

JONATHAN STEPHENSON

Gouache manner [Fr. *gravure en teinte aux outils*]. Type of copperplate-engraving process that attempts to imitate a gouache or watercolour drawing. It unites detailed tool work on the copper (creating a very tight network of dots and short strokes) with colour printing using four or more plates. The tints of the original drawing are reproduced by printing primary colours in superimposed layers, and shading is created by having a background delicately worked with a battery of tools. The technique was allegedly begun by Jean-François Janinet in 1771, but in fact he merely synthesized the inventions of others (*see* §2 below).

1. MATERIALS AND TECHNIQUES. The main contours of the subject to be reproduced are etched on an initial plate. From this first plate proofs are pulled that will be used as counterproofs on the other plates to ensure exact superimposition. Three other plates similarly prepared are then engraved or, less often, etched according to the colour they will carry. The copper is left intact in the parts in which colour is not to appear and hollowed out to a greater or lesser depth according to the desired shade. When a pure colour is to appear in the final print, the copper is worked more.

The tools used are those employed for the CRAYON MANNER: chasing tools; mattoirs with points that are generally sharper than those used in crayon manner, and called mushrooms; mattoirs with roller wheels; and also more traditional instruments (burins, engraving needles, scrapers, burr-cutters, burnishers). (The engraver Laurent Guyot's inventory after his death in 1808 included 157 mushrooms and 23 roulettes of various sizes.) The aim is to create a network of dots and shading traditionally obtained by mezzotint, and from the 1760s by aquatint, with very dense work executed directly on to the copper. Although a longer process, it has the advantage of responding more precisely to the needs of the engraver, who can, in reworking the copper, blend tones, join them together, take up preliminary sketches, increase their liveliness by further hollowing out the dots or decrease it by using a burnisher.

The plates worked in this way are coated with coloured inks and then pulled, one after the other, fixed in place by a pin in the traditional order: yellow, red and blue; a supplementary plate for carmine or white highlights can also be used. The inks must be relatively transparent in order to blend when superimposed. However, all the gradations of tone, the shadows and highlights, are given by the fourth plate pulled in black ink. Usually it is the first plate on which the contours have been engraved that is reworked using the same tools. The plate pulled in black is the basis of the engraving; in the rare places in which the colour has to remain pure, it is left intact, the half-tones marked by less deeply cut and finer dots, the darker tones by more concentrated work applied to the shadows on the brown made up of the three superimposed primary colours.

In relation to other techniques of multiple-plate engraving, mezzotint or aquatint, the use of tools for gouache-manner engravings allows the engraver to master his gradations of tone better and above all to take advantage of good proofs, since copper worked in this way wears out less quickly. Long and meticulous work is, however, needed, which some methods can accelerate. Numerous engravers use resin aquatint, at least to prepare their plates before finishing the work with their tools. It is not always easy in the final proof to distinguish the respective parts played by chemical and mechanical processes, and as intermediate stages have not been preserved, specialists freely debate the technique used. Likewise, to reduce the number of plates to be engraved, some artists use the ink-and-dauber method (also known as *à la poupée*). This consists of arranging the colours on a single plate with a small rag, called 'doll' (or dauber) by French publishers. The print is then printed in a single pull. The difficulties posed by superimposing primary colours, arranged on several plates, each engraved in relation to the others, are therefore eliminated, but the quality of the print henceforth depends on the printer and not on the engraver. Inking with a dauber is often linked to a more simple use of engraving with tools: stipple (*see* STIPPLE (i), §1). To gain time, some engravers use multiple-plate printing in conjunction with the dauber.

2. HISTORY. Colour printing with three or four plates had been discovered at the beginning of the 18th century by Jacob Christoph Le Blon who had sought to apply the colour theory of Isaac Newton (1642–1727) to the field of engraving. After commercial failure in Britain, he travelled to France in 1734 and on 12 November 1737 obtained an exclusive privilege from Louis XV, King of France, lasting 20 years, to publish colour prints. He used four plates (although he only admitted to using three) engraved in mezzotint and aspired to imitate oil painting. After his death, his privilege passed to Jacques-Fabien Gautier-Dagoty, who used it only to engrave a few anatomical plates. The process had only limited success, aroused more by curiosity than by admiration. The exclusive privilege of Le Blon, and then of Gautier-Dagoty, theoretically forbade any other engraver to publish his prints using their method until 1757; furthermore, its basis was mezzotint, generally scorned in France for its lack of vitality and for the small number of proofs that could be pulled. Few engravers were therefore in a position to use it, owing to lack of experience.

Interest in work with tools on copper, designed to create a dense network of irregular dots, had been aroused through the discovery in 1757 of crayon-manner engraving. Jean-Charles François, the inventor of this technique, tried as early as 1758 to reproduce the effect of wash with aquatint, to which he added finishing touches with the tools used for crayon manner: roulettes and mattoirs. These investigations had been taken up by Louis Marin Bonnet, who had added to working on copper with tools the use of multiple-plate printing, notably in his pastel-manner engravings. However, he sought more to juxtapose than superimpose his colours and coated some of his plates with different-coloured inks manually, with a dauber. Jean-François Janinet worked in Bonnet's studio in 1771, the date at which the latter brought out two small unsigned colour prints imitating watercolour after Clément-Pierre Marillier, *The Procurator* and *The Tailor* (Hérold, nos 35.2, 35.3), printed with four plates. Janinet was probably the author, and in 1772 under his own name he brought out two prints, *The Operator* and *The Meeting* (*Inventaire du fonds français*, nos 1, 2), after Peter-Paul Benazech (*c.* 1730–after 1783), in the margin of which he declared himself the inventor of engraving 'imitating coloured wash'. Relegating his roulettes to second place, he had made some finer-grained mattoirs, also known as mushrooms, but he virtually never used chemical aquatint. Like Bonnet, and in contrast to Gautier-Dagoty and Le Blon, he would leave the plate inked in black to be pulled last. He was also astute enough to demand of multiple-plate engraving that it should try to render the effect not of paintings but of gouache drawings or, with a finer web and more transparent inks, watercolours. He specialized in the 'gallant' subjects that Pierre-Antoine Baudouin had made fashionable and that Niclas Lafrensen gave him, and the landscapes drawn by Pierre Antoine de Machy and Hubert Robert. The general vogue for this type of engraving encouraged many artists. In Paris the most famous were Charles-Melchior Descourtis, a pupil of Janinet, Laurent Guyot and above all Philibert-Louis Debucourt.

In Britain coloured stipple engravings were occasionally produced with several plates, more often inked with a dauber. The fame of such artists as William Wynne Ryland and Francesco Bartolozzi quickly spread to France, where their prints after Angelica Kauffman were immediately snatched up. Louis Marin Bonnet attempted to exploit their popularity; from 1777 he published 'English prints' in colour, stipple engraved, with titles and inscriptions in English (and sometimes false signatures of these masters), but printed with several plates and not with a dauber. From 1778, while continuing his imitations, he also published several gouache-manner prints. In 1775–85, in a desire to take advantage of the vogue for colour prints, Jacques-Fabien Gautier-Dagoty and his sons also published several reproductions of paintings engraved in mezzotint and printed in four colours, according to Le Blon's method; they had little success, however, for the public was used to seeing gouaches rather than oil paintings reproduced in colour.

It was not until Philibert-Louis Debucourt that the number of engraving techniques successfully increased. He had no doubt learnt from Laurent Guyot, between 1782 and 1785, the technique of engraving with tools. As a painter and draughtsman he engraved mainly from his own compositions and felt the need to vary his technique in order to reach a more exact equivalence between his originals and his prints. Through using more delicate instruments, he developed engraving in the wash manner, but above all he did not hesitate to take up mezzotint (e.g. *Broken Jug*, 1787; *Inventaire du fonds français*, no. 8), aquatint engraving with resin (e.g. *Crossing*, 1792; *Inventaire du fonds français*, no. 23), swiftly completed by working with tools (e.g. *Public Promenade*, 1792; *Inventaire du fonds français*, no. 26; see fig.). In this last type of engraving,

Gouache-manner engraving by Philibert-Louis Debucourt: *Public Promenade*, 1792 (Paris, Bibliothèque Nationale)

aquatint allowed him to lay in the main areas of the composition, and tools then served to soften, accentuate or vary the tones.

With the French Revolution (1789–95), scenes of gallantry, the topic most often reproduced in engravings, passed out of fashion; moreover, the market diminished for lack of custom, and finally the predominance of drawing over work in colour was once more reaffirmed. Engravers therefore sought to simplify their work, and more of them adopted inking with daubers, which required only one engraved plate. The British techniques did, however, develop, better adapted to this type of inking: mezzotint and stipple engraving. Sometimes there was even a reversion to the traditional use of manuscript illumination of a simple etched line. Engravers still faithful to multiple plates tended, following Debucourt, to prepare their plate with chemical aquatint. Genre scenes and even portraits continued to be engraved, but increasingly colour printing was reserved for illustrating scientific works, such as the flower books by Pierre-Joseph Redouté, *Liliaceae* (Paris, 1802–16) and *Roses* (Paris, 1817–24). Gouache-manner engraving survived during the first third of the 19th century without recovering the status it had enjoyed at the end of the Ancien Régime. It disappeared only after the invention of colour lithography by Godefroy Engelmann in 1837.

BIBLIOGRAPHY

J. Frankau: *Eighteenth-century Colour Prints* (London, 1900)

Les Procédés de gravure: Exposition Debucourt (exh. cat. by A. Vuaflard and J. Hérold, Paris, Mus. A. Déc., 1920), pp. 65–124

J. Hérold: *Louis Marin Bonnet (1756–1793): Catalogue de l'oeuvre gravé* (Paris, 1935)

Inventaire du fonds français: Graveurs du dix-huitième siècle, vi (Paris, 1949), xii (Paris, 1973)

V. Carlson, J. W. Ittman and others: *Regency to Empire, French Printmaking, 1715–1814* (Baltimore, 1984)

O. M. Lilien: *Jacob Christoph Le Blon, 1667–1741: Inventor of Three- and Four-colour Printing* (Stuttgart, 1985)

A. Griffiths: 'Notes on Early Aquatint in England and France', *Prt Q.*, iv (1987), pp. 255–70

CHRISTIAN MICHEL

Goubau [Goubeau]**, Antoni** [Antoine]**, I** (*b* Antwerp, 27 May 1616; *d* Antwerp, 11 March 1698). Flemish painter, active in Italy. He was the son of Antoine Cornet and Livine Cornet. In 1629 he was apprenticed to Jan Farius (*fl* 1622) and seven years later became a master in the Antwerp Guild of St Luke. He lived in Rome from *c.* 1644 until 1650. He is known primarily as a painter of market scenes situated in Roman or Mediterranean settings and often decorated with many tiny figures. His journey to Italy and his introduction to the work of such masters as Paul Bril, Jan Miel, Michiel Sweerts and Johannes Lingelbach were of decisive importance for his development. On his return to Antwerp, he painted Italianate landscapes in the style of Bartholomeus Breenbergh and Jan Both. Rather than rendering exact topographical views, he wanted to evoke a Roman atmosphere. His earliest dated work, the *Market Scene near the Triumphal Arch of Titus* (1658; Karlsruhe, Staatl. Ksthalle), illustrates this clearly. Actual architectural features, such as the Arch of Titus and the ruins of the Temple of Saturn in the Forum Romanum, are combined with imaginary structures or buildings from elsewhere. The artist wanted to give a kind of synthesis of what could be seen in Rome. Other works, however, such as the *View of the Piazza Navona* (1680; Antwerp, Kon. Mus. S. Kst.), reveal a more specific topographical interest. Apart from townscapes, he also made a number of religious compositions, mostly intended for churches in Antwerp.

Between 1652 and 1694 Goubau took on 12 pupils, the most important being Nicolas de Largillierre and Jan Frans van Bloemen. In 1662 the guild wanted to appoint him dean, but he managed to buy himself out by offering it a painting, the *Study of Art in Rome* (1662; Antwerp, Kon. Mus. S. Kst.; *see* ROME, fig. 14), which shows several members of the Schildersbent, the association of Netherlandish artists in Rome, set in a landscape dominated by Roman ruins.

BIBLIOGRAPHY

F. J. van den Branden: *Geschiedenis der Antwerpsche schilderschool* (Antwerp, 1883), pp. 1010–13

D. Bodart: *Les Peintres des Pays-Bas méridionaux et de la principauté de Liège au XVIIe siècle* (Brussels, 1970), i, pp. 432–40; ii, pls 243–7

D. Coeckelbergs: 'Contribution à l'étude du paysage italianisant flamand et hollandais au XVIIe siècle: Oeuvres inédites de A. Goubeau, L. de Vadder, J. Both', *Rev. Archéologues & Historiens A. Louvain*, viii (1975), pp. 106–9

G. Briganti, L. Trezzani and L. Laureati: *I Bamboccianti: Pittori della vita quotidiana a Roma nel seicento* (Rome, 1983), pp. 295–9

T. Kren: 'Some Bamboccianti by Antoine Goubau', *Essays in Northern European Paintings Presented to E. Haverkamp Begemann* (Doornspijk, 1983), pp. 123–6

HANS DEVISSCHER

Gouda. City in the Netherlands, situated near the confluence of the rivers Gouwe and Hollandse IJssel *c.* 20 km north-east of Rotterdam. A dam, later a lock, was built across the Gouwe in the medieval period, as well as a stronghold for the levy of tolls. The later castle was owned from 1305 by the Counts of Holland and demolished by the citizens in 1577. With the reclamation of the surrounding fen country from the 12th century onwards, Gouda flourished and was granted its first charter by Count Floris V (*reg* 1256–96). The city was walled in the 14th century and reached the height of its prosperity in the 15th and 16th centuries. Gouda is a typical Dutch polder city, and, although the ramparts have been levelled, the original plan is well preserved. It is centred on a large triangular marketplace, on which is the Late Gothic Stadhuis (town hall; 1448–59) and the main parish church of St Jan (*see* §1 below). The classical Waag (cheese weigh-house) was built in 1668 by Pieter Post.

1. ST JANSKERK. The Late Gothic basilica, with transepts and double aisles, dates mostly from after a fire of 1552, which destroyed everything but the 14th-century tower, the early 15th-century west bays and the choir (1485–1510). Although 11 choir windows dating from *c.* 1530–50 survived the fire, the church is noted particularly for its collection of 62 Renaissance stained-glass windows that date from the rebuilding. They are divided into two groups: the windows given before the Reformation of 1573 and those given after. The earlier group was mostly given by leading ecclesiastics and lay people, including King Philip II of Spain. The subject-matter comprises scenes from the lives of Christ, John the Baptist and their Old Testament forerunners. The windows donated after 1573 were mainly the gift of cities and state institutions in the province of Holland, and their themes concentrate on metaphors of freedom of conscience, the liberation of cities and some biblical scenes. The windows were designed and executed by various artists, among them Dirck Crabeth and Wouter Crabeth (i) (*see* CRABETH, (1) and (2)); between 1555 and 1571 Dirck made nine windows and Wouter four. All 62 windows display a highly distinctive colour scheme (abundant white and shades of grey) and new techniques (life-size cartoons and larger pieces of glass). Many of the original cartoons have survived and are kept in the church.

BIBLIOGRAPHY

Beschrijving van de kunstig geschilderde glazen binnen de St Janskerk te Gouda (Gouda, *c.* 1920)

Kunstreisboek voor Nederland, Rijksdienst voor de Monumentenzorg (Amsterdam and Antwerp, 1977)

C. Coebergh-Surie: *De Goudse glazen* (diss., Rijksuniv. Utrecht, 1985)

A. Steegh: *Monumentenatlas van Nederland* (Zutphen, 1985)

J. A. VAN DER HOEVE

Goudt, Hendrik (*b* The Hague, 1583; *d* Utrecht, 1648). Dutch engraver, draughtsman and painter. He was the illegitimate son of Arend Goudt and Anneken Cool. On 10 January 1604 the marriage—and hence the son—was legitimized. Hendrik's mother suffered from hysteria, which may account for his later insanity. He possibly trained in The Hague under Simon Frisius but modelled his style on Jacques de Gheyn II, who was in The Hague from 1598, and Hendrick Goltzius, whose engraved figures Goudt adapted. It is likely that Goudt's skill in calligraphy—shown in the elaborate inscriptions on his engravings—was learnt from Jan van de Velde II, who dedicated one of the pages of the *Spieghel der schrijftkonst* (1605) to Goudt. The only authenticated works from this period appear to be such drawings as the *Mocking of Christ* (Berlin, Kupferstichkab.), a possibly signed *Female Nude* (sold London, Christie's, 7 April 1981, lot 122) and a signed copy (Amsterdam, Rijksmus.) after Lucas van Leyden's engraving *Virgilius the Magician in a Basket* (B. 136). What Goudt produced between these works and his better-known engravings of 1608 remains a mystery.

In 1604 Goudt went to Rome and, according to census records, lived in the household of Adam Elsheimer from 1607. In 1609 he is recorded in a house of a neighbouring street. Early sources seem to imply that he was both Elsheimer's pupil and patron, subsidizing the family and accepting works by Elsheimer in lieu, and finally consigning him to the debtors' prison, where he caught his fatal illness. Whether this is true or not, Goudt did at least one great service to Elsheimer, through the seven engravings he made after some of his works; these were widely disseminated throughout Europe and helped to spread Elsheimer's fame. The quality of the engravings is something of a miracle, as no previous works by Goudt anticipate such masterpieces, which with their strong sense of chiaroscuro foreshadow the technique of mezzotint. Two of the plates were made in Rome during Elsheimer's lifetime and bear his name as *inventor* (designer): *Tobias and the Angel* (the '*Small Tobias*', 1608; Hollstein, no. 1, drawing in Paris, Mus. Petit Pal.) and the *Mocking of Ceres* (1610; Hollstein, no. 5). The remainder were done in 1612 and 1613, after Goudt returned to the northern Netherlands, and have Elsheimer's name suppressed. Hence it is likely that Goudt actually possessed the original paintings, which he also showed to Sandrart when he visited him in Utrecht in 1625 and 1626. These later prints were another version of *Tobias and the Angel* (the '*Large Tobias*', 1613;

Hendrik Goudt: *Tobias and the Angel* (the '*Large Tobias*'), engraving, 256×269 mm, 1613 (London, British Museum)

Hollstein, no. 2; see fig.; signed drawing in New York, Pierpont Morgan Lib.); *Aurora* (1613; Hollstein, no. 7); *Philemon and Baucis* (1612; Hollstein, no. 6); *Flight into Egypt* (1612; Hollstein, no. 3); and the little *Beheading of St John* (Hollstein, no. 4)—the only print without a date.

Goudt's drawing style was (deliberately or not) based on that of Elsheimer, so that many of his drawings have been ascribed to his master: for example all the sheets in the *Klebeband* (Frankfurt am Main, Städel. Kstinst. & Städt. Gal.) are now accepted as being by Goudt. His style, with its broad ink-strokes, is undisciplined and his compositions lack originality, relying on those of other artists. (Drost's idea (1957) that some of the drawings show the hands of both Elsheimer and Goudt cannot be accepted.) In the Utrecht Guild of St Luke Goudt was registered as an engraver (1611), but Italian sources refer to him as a painter. However, the only painting that can be attributed to him is *Philemon and Baucis* (Vånas, Wachmeister Col.), for which a drawing exists in the *Klebeband* album. Goudt was inordinately proud of receiving the Papal Order ('Palatinus comes et aurea militiae eques'), which, in fact, was freely distributed at the time and could even have been conveyed by a patron such as Cardinal Scipione Borghese, to whom the engraving of the *Mocking of Ceres* was dedicated. Drawings by Goudt are listed in the inventory of Jan van de Cappelle (1680).

BIBLIOGRAPHY

Hollstein: *Dut. & Flem.*

J. von Sandrart: *Teutsche Academie* (1675–9); ed. A. R. Peltzer (1925), p. 180

H. Weizsäcker: 'Hendrik Goudt', *Oud-Holland*, xlv (1928), pp. 110–22

W. Drost: 'Hendrik Goudt', *Adam Elsheimer und sein Kreis* (Potsdam, 1933), pp. 165–70

H. Weizsäcker: 'Das Rätsel des Hendrik Goudt', *Adam Elsheimer: Der Maler von Frankfurt* (Berlin, 1936), i, pp. 272–87

——: 'Ein Gemälde von Hendrik Goudt', *Oud-Holland*, lvi (1939), pp. 185–92

J. J. ten Hove [D. Hoek]: *Het raadsel van Arend en Hendrik Goudt* (Amsterdam, 1944)

M. Eger: *Der Stil der Handzeichnungen des Hendrik Goudt* (diss., U. Erlangen, 1952)

W. Drost: *Adam Elsheimer als Zeichner: Goudts Nachahmungen Weiterleben bei Rembrandt* (Stuttgart, 1957)

H. Möhle: 'Das Problem "Elsheimer oder Goudt?"', *Die Zeichnungen Adam Elsheimers* (Berlin, 1966), pp. 52–107

D. Hoek: 'Biografische bijzonderheden over Hendrik Goudt', *Oud-Holland*, lxxxv (1970), pp. 54–5

K. Andrews: *Adam Elsheimer* (Oxford, 1977), p. 38

F. Stampfle: 'Goudt's Drawings of *Tobias and the Angel*', *Essays in Northern European Art Presented to Egbert Haverkamp-Begemann* (Doornspijk, 1983), pp. 257–60

KEITH ANDREWS

Goudy, Frederic William (*b* Bloomington, IL, 8 March 1865; *d* Marlboro-on-Hudson, NY, 11 May 1947). American typographer, printer and graphic designer. He demonstrated his interest in letter forms when a child, cutting out 3000 in paper. While working as a clerk in Boston, he discovered the Kelmscott Press. In 1895 Goudy founded the Booklet Press, a small printing shop, later renamed the Camelot Press. In 1896 he designed his first type, called Camelot, and in 1899 set up as a freelance designer, producing book designs and advertising lettering. His Village Press printed two books before 1904 when he moved to Hingham, MA, where a further nine books were produced over the next two years. The establishment of the press in New York was followed by a fire (January 1908) in which all Goudy's property was lost. From this point he abandoned general printing in favour of type design. A trip to Europe in 1909 enabled him to study inscriptions. His first two types to achieve serious recognition and success were Kennerley and Forum, an inscriptional titling letter. Between 1916 and 1924 Goudy taught lettering at the Art Students League in New York. He also founded the periodical *Ars typographica* and wrote books on type design and production. In 1923 he moved to Marlboro-on-Hudson, where he worked at the Village Letter Foundry until it too burnt down in January 1939. He received numerous awards for his work as a type designer. His output was prolific: 122 different types are discussed in his autobiography, many of which were widely used and highly successful in his lifetime (for one of his typefaces *see* TYPOGRAPHY, fig. 4). The Grolier Club of New York and the American Institute for Graphic Art devoted exhibitions to his work (1923, 1933).

WRITINGS

The Alphabet (New York, 1918)/*R* with *The Elements of Lettering* (Berkeley and London, 1942)
The Elements of Lettering (New York and London, 1922)
Typologia (Berkeley, 1940)
A Half-century of Type Design and Typography, 1895–1945 (New York, 1946)

BIBLIOGRAPHY

V. Orton: *Goudy, Master of Letters* (Chicago, 1939)
P. Beilenson: *The Story of Frederic W. Goudy* (New York, 1965)
E. H. Emmons: *Goudy in Rhyme* (Pittsburgh, 1967)

LAURA SUFFIELD

Gouffier. French family of patrons. They originally came from Poitou and, for the best part of a century, were one of the foremost families in France. The Gouffier ascendancy began under Charles VII with Guillaume Gouffier (i) (*b c.* 1420; *d* Amboise, 23 May 1495), to whom the King awarded the seigneuries of Oiron (1449), Poitou, and Boisy (1456), near Roanne. By the beginning of the reign of Francis I, Guillaume's sons were occupying eminent positions: the eldest, Artus Gouffier (*b c.* 1475; *d* Montpellier, May 1519), was a Grand Maître; Guillaume Gouffier (ii) (*b c.* 1488; *d* 24 Feb 1525), the Seigneur de Bonnivet, was Amiral de France; and Adrien Gouffier (*d* 24 July 1523) was a cardinal and papal legate. Artus's son Claude Gouffier (*b* Dec 1501/2; *d* 1570) became Grand Ecuyer (chief equerry) in 1546 and continued to enjoy the favour of Henry II and of Charles IX (*reg* 1560–74), who made him Duc de Roannez (Roannais) in 1566. After his death the family fortunes began to decline. In 1631 Louis Gouffier (*b* 25 Nov 1575; *d* 16 Dec 1642) was exiled to Oiron by Richelieu. The last of the family, Charlotte Gouffier (*b* 15 April 1633; *d* 13 Feb 1683), married in 1667 François d'Aubusson de La Feuillade (1625–91), who became Seigneur d'Oiron and Duc de Roannez.

The two great châteaux built by the Gouffier family were both situated in Poitou: the château of Oiron, near Thouars, and the château of Bonnivet, near Poitiers. The first château of Oiron, built *c.* 1470 on the orders of Guillaume Gouffier (i), probably resembled that of Le Plessis-Bourré (1468–73), Maine-et-Loire, which is built around a rectangular courtyard, with round towers at the corners. Oiron was partially modified by Artus, who began the aisle of the gallery (*c.* 1515), and by Claude, who finished the gallery and added the great staircase (*c.* 1540–45). It was later completely altered (1620–42) by Louis Gouffier, whose work was completed by La Feuillade (*c.* 1670), giving it the appearance it has today. The collegiate church of St Maurice, in which the family vaults were situated, was built beside the château; it was started by Artus and completed by Claude. The gallery that Claude built contained some exceptionally fine decorative painting, the most important outside Fontainebleau to have survived; it is the sole known work of Noël Jallier, who may have trained in Rome and at Fontainebleau. Between 1546 and 1549 he painted on the gallery walls the story of the *Trojan War*, as well as three scenes from the *Aeneid*. The work was executed in fresco secco, which accounts for its poor condition, and it consists of 14 large compositions framed in *trompe l'oeil* devices; the style incorporated an original combination of elements borrowed from Italy, from Fontainebleau and from the Netherlands.

A number of other works that bear witness to Claude Gouffier's artistic tastes include the great terminal figures in terracotta that adorned the exterior wall of the gallery, one of which is in the Louvre, Paris; a number of illuminated manuscripts (Paris, Bib. N., and New York, Pierpont Morgan Lib.); a collection of portraits (among them that of *John the Good*, now Paris, Louvre); and the marble tombs in the collegiate church, which were the last works to be executed by the Giusti family. Claude had Raphael's *St John* (Paris, Louvre), with his coat of arms painted on it, placed on an altar facing his own tomb in the same church. He also owned a *Holy Family* (Paris, Louvre) by the same artist: at that time, these were the only works by Raphael in France outside the royal collection.

The château of Bonnivet was a building of different character, the Renaissance elements being more imposing. From 1516 its construction proceeded without interruption under the orders of Guillaume (ii); it was left unfinished on his death. Bonnivet was only slightly modified subsequently. Shortly before the French Revolution its last owner sold it for demolition. It was, next to the château of Chambord, the most ambitious architectural undertaking of the early Renaissance in France: its principal building, including the towers, was 100 m long. Its centre was occupied by a great spiral staircase, open to the air, which had arcades opening both on to the internal courtyard and on to the exterior façade: in this respect it was the only one of its kind in France, and Rabelais alluded to it in his description in *Gargantua* of the abbey of Thélème. Some fragments of Bonnivet's decorative sculpture, which was of extremely high quality, escaped destruction; most of these are now in the Musée des Beaux-Arts, Poitiers.

BIBLIOGRAPHY

M. Dumolin: *Le Château d'Oiron* (Paris, 1931)
J. Guillaume: *L'Architecture de la première renaissance en Poitou* (doctoral thesis, U. Paris IV, 1981)
T. Crepin-Leblond: *Les Trésors du Grand Ecuyer* (exh. cat., Paris, Château d'Ecouen, 1994)
J. Guillaume: *La Galerie du Grand Ecuyer: L'Histoire de Troie au château d'Oiron* (Niort, 1996)

JEAN GUILLAUME

Gough, Piers (*b* Brighton, 24 April 1946). English exhibition designer, architect and teacher. He studied from 1965 to 1971 at the Architectural Association, London, and then in 1975 he formed the partnership CZWG, with Nick Campbell (*b* 1947), Roger Zogolovitch (*b* 1947) and Rex Wilkinson (*b* 1947), initially producing straightforwardly commercial projects. In 1982 he received the Architectural Design Award Bronze Medal for an exhibition on Lutyens at the Hayward Gallery, London, in the design of which Gough echoed many elements of Lutyens's own style. This technique was repeated in an exhibition (1985) on Alfred Gilbert at the Royal Academy, London. In the same year Gough was invited to submit a design proposal for the extension to the National Gallery, London. His plan, consisting of a high Basilica-style gallery, was short-listed and then rejected, but it initiated a phase of large-scale projects, including the residential China Wharf Building and Cascades Building (both 1988) and the Wolfe Crescent flats and housing development (1989), all in the Docklands, London. Smaller-scale projects include the Street-Porter House (1987), London, which reflects his experiments with conventional building materials and the effects of colour and texture. Gough's eclectic style can be seen to embrace elements of the Arts and Crafts movement and of classicism. The latter is evident in the National Gallery plan and at Howe Green Manor House (1990), Herts.

BIBLIOGRAPHY

C. Amery: 'The Gough Mixture', *Interiors*, cxli/10 (1982), pp. 157–65
D. Sudjic: 'Piers Gough: Architecture's B Movie Hero', *Blueprint*, xxvi (1986), pp. 16–20
D. Sudjic, P. Cook and J. Meades: *English Extremists: The Architecture of CZWG* (London, 1988)
J. M. Robinson: 'Classical Quartet: New Country Houses', *Country Life*, clxxxiv/35 (30 Aug 1990), pp. 74–7

□

Gough, Richard (*b* London, 21 Oct 1735; *d* ?Enfield, Middx, 20 Feb 1809). English antiquary, topographer and writer. He was born into an enterprising family (at the age of 11, his father, Harry, had gone to China with his uncle, the explorer Sir Richard Gough) and displayed prodigious talents, learning Latin from Samuel Dyer, a friend of Dr Samuel Johnson, and at 11 himself began a *History of the Bible Translated from the French*, printed privately by James Waugh in 1747. On his father's death in 1751 he inherited the family estates in Hertfordshire. From 1752 to 1756 he attended Corpus Christi College, Cambridge, where he was a conscientious, if solitary, student, but left without a degree. He then began the first of his extensive tours around England, and his notes and descriptions from these journeys formed most of his writings. In 1762 he was elected a Fellow of the Society of Antiquaries and served as Director, from 1771 to 1776. He was a Fellow of the Royal Society between 1775 and 1795. He was also a regular correspondent of the *Gentleman's Magazine*. In 1808 his works were destroyed in a fire at the printing shop of John Nicholls, his friend, biographer and travelling companion. He had suffered ill-health for some time, but the loss threatened his reason, and he died soon afterwards.

Among Gough's numerous contributions to antiquarian literature three works stand out: *Anecdotes of British Topography* (1768); *Sepulchral Monuments of Great Britain* (1786–96), which holds a special place among English books owing to the number and beauty of its plates by James Basire (i); and his greatly enlarged and augmented edition of William Camden's *Britannia* (1789). This was seven years in translation and nine in printing, and Gough was unsparing in his efforts towards it. The third edition, on the presses and almost completed, was destroyed in the 1808 fire. Most of his books and manuscripts were bequeathed to the University of Oxford; a partial catalogue of his bequests to the Bodleian Library was published by Dr Bulkely Bandinel in 1814.

WRITINGS

Anecdotes of British Topography (London, 1768); rev. as *British Topography, or an Historical Account of What Has Been Done for Illustrating the Topographical Antiquities of Great Britain and Ireland*, 2 vols (London, 1780)
Sepulchral Monuments of Great Britain Applied to Illustrate the History of Families, Manners, Habits and Arts from the Norman Conquest, 3 vols (London, 1786–96)
ed. and trans.: W. Camden: *Britannia* (London, 1586, rev. 6/1607) as *Camden's Britannia: Translated from the Edition Published by the Author MDCVII: Enlarged by the Latest Discoveries*, 3 vols (London, 1789, rev. 2/1806)

BIBLIOGRAPHY

DNB
B. Bandinel: *A Catalogue of the Books, Relating to British Topography, and Saxon and Northern Literature, Bequeathed to the Bodleian Library in MDCCXCIX, by Richard Gough* (Oxford, 1814)
J. Nicholls: *Literary Anecdotes of the Eighteenth Century*, vi (London, 1815), pp. 262–343
W. Y. Fletcher: *English Book Collectors* (London, 1902), pp. 238–40
S. de Ricci: *English Collectors of Books and Manuscripts* (Cambridge, 1930), pp. 53, 65–8

JACQUELINE COLLISS HARVEY

Goujon, Jean (*b c.* 1510; *d* ?Bologna, *c.* 1565). French sculptor, illustrator and architect. He was one of the great masters of relief sculpture. Through his collaboration with the architect Pierre Lescot he was involved in many major building projects, and in his refined relief sculptures, such as the carved panels for the Fountain of the Innocents, Paris (see fig. 1), he achieved a highly personal synthesis between the mannered style of the FONTAINEBLEAU SCHOOL and a classicism derived from his study of antique sculpture. He illustrated with skilful and lively wood-engravings Jean Baptiste Martin I's first complete French translation (Paris, 1547) of Vitruvius, *De architectura: Architecture ou art de bien bastir*, an edition that was to have considerable influence on the revival of the classical style in France.

1. ORIGINS AND EARLY WORKS, TO 1544. Goujon was possibly of Norman origin, and the knowledge of the sculpture and architecture of anti-quity and the Italian Renaissance displayed in his works suggests that he spent time in Italy. He is first recorded at Rouen in 1541, in the accounts of the church of St Maclou where he executed the organ loft, a modest piece of architectural and decorative work whose columns and capitals demonstrate a perfect assimilation of the rules laid down by Vitruvius. Goujon has been associated with works at Rouen Cathedral, but the extent of his responsibility remains unclear. Records referring to the marble praying effigy of *Cardinal Georges II d'Amboise* on the Amboise tomb are not explicit, while the marble sculptures on the tomb (1544) of *Louis de Brézé*, husband of Diane de Poitiers, do not correspond to Goujon's style in execution; it is possible that he provided only the design for this remarkable two-storey classical structure, which has Corinthian columns on the

lower tier and pairs of caryatids articulating the upper register.

2. Paris, 1544–62.

(i) Work at St Germain-l'Auxerrois and the château of Ecouen. In 1544 Goujon was in Paris, working on the rood screen designed by Pierre Lescot at St Germain-l'Auxerrois, a work that began the long collaboration between the sculptor and the architect. The sculptural decoration had been started in 1542 by two image-carvers ('*imagiers*'), Simon Le Roy (*fl* mid-16th century) and Lorenzo Naldini, both of whom had worked at Fontainebleau. The screen was in the form of a triumphal arch; five marble bas-reliefs (Paris, Louvre) survived its demolition in 1745. Of these, the principal panel, the *Deposition*, has compositional borrowings from an engraving by Parmigianino (B. 5) and from Rosso Fiorentino's *Pietà* from the chapel of the château of Ecouen (Paris, Louvre). It is executed with a sensitivity and delicacy of touch that amply demonstrate Goujon's mastery of relief sculpture. The elegant and supple forms of the figures and the fluid grace of the finely pleated draperies recall Florentine sculpture of the 15th century as well as the antique statue of *Ariadne* (Rome, Vatican, Mus. Pio-Clementino), of which there was a cast at the château of Fontainebleau. The special technique of bas-relief contributed to Goujon's linear style, and almost all his subsequent work was founded on it. The subsidiary panels representing the *Four Evangelists* seated seem to be derived from engravings by Antonio Veneziano after Marcantonio Raimondi (B. 92–5). Although Beaulieu has suggested that they may be from the hands of Goujon's collaborators Naldini and Le Roy, there seems little reason to doubt they are by Goujon. In using works by Parmigianino and Rosso as sources for the *Deposition*, Goujon transformed the rhetorical emphasis of the former and the feverish agitation of the latter into a vision of confident serenity that can only be described as classical.

1. Jean Goujon: stone reliefs of two nymphs, detail from the Fountain of the Innocents, 1547–9 (Paris, Place des Innocents)

In 1545 Goujon worked for the Constable of France, Anne, Duc de Montmorency, at the château of Ecouen, where, according to the dedication of Martin's edition of Vitruvius, he was active as an architect and as a sculptor. The building history of the château is obscure and controversial, and it is not clear exactly what Goujon's contribution was. It is possible that he was responsible for the sinuous figures of *Fame* that appear in the corner spandrels of the triumphal arch in the manner of classical genii. These figures reappeared in more graceful forms at the Louvre, Paris. The frenzied relief of *Fame* on the polychrome chimney-piece of the Grand Salle is close to his stone *Fame Blowing a Trumpet* on the pavilion of Henry II at the Louvre, Paris, and is doubtless based on his specification. It also seems likely that the sculptural decoration of the chapel, including the altar reliefs of the *Sacrifice of Abraham*, the *Four Evangelists* and *Four Virtues* (all marble, 1544–8; Chantilly, Mus. Condé), is by assistants or collaborators working to his designs.

(ii) Royal commissions. With the accession of Henry II in 1547, Goujon passed into royal service. In 1549 he collaborated with Jean Cousin (i) in organizing the ceremonial entry of Henry II into Paris, an event that allowed the new generation of classicizing artists to display their skills. Goujon's most famous work, the Fountain of the Innocents, the architecture of which was probably by Lescot, was originally built as a monument for this occasion. It was, until 1787, a rectangular structure on a corner, presenting two arched bays to the Rue aux Fers and one to the Rue Saint-Denis. The bays were articulated by fluted composite pilasters, between which were narrow vertical relief panels of nymphs holding urns (see fig. 1). Horizontal relief panels of tritons and nymphs were placed above and below each bay, and the spandrels of the arches were filled by winged personifications of Fame. The present appearance of the monument, as a free-standing, four-sided structure, is the result of a late 18th-century rebuilding for which Augustin Pajou provided extra sculpture in an able pastiche of Goujon's style (*see* Fountain, fig. 4). The vertical relief panels remain *in situ*, but the horizontal ones were removed around 1810 (now Paris, Louvre). All these reliefs, with their undulating contours, light, transparent draperies and finesse of execution, exude a pagan gaiety. Goujon transformed his sources in engravings after Rosso and antique sculpture to create a masterpiece of grace and harmony in which an echo of Hellenistic art can be caught.

From 1547 Goujon was principally occupied with the sculptural decoration of Lescot's new buildings at the Louvre (*see* PARIS, §V, 6(ii)), where the rich, allegorical system of decoration evolved for the interior of the château of Fontainebleau (*see* FONTAINEBLEAU, §1) was for the first time extended to the full height of a façade. Apart from repetitive architectural decoration, the principal embellishments are the magnificent female allegorical relief figures that surround the oeil-de-boeuf windows above the three doors of the south-west wing of the Cour Carrée: *War*, *Peace*, *Fame*, *History*, *Victory* and the *Glory of the King* (stone, 1547–50; *in situ* but restored). Although in part inspired by details from Trajan's Column in Rome (casts of which had been brought to France by Francesco Primaticcio in 1540), these figures, with their delicately carved and insubstantial drapery, have the movement and exuberance of the Mannerist style. In the same way, Goujon's four caryatids supporting the gallery of the Salle des Caryatides in the Louvre (stone, 1550–51; *in situ* but restored; see fig. 2), though derived from those of the Erechtheion, Athens, have a supple and voluptuous grace typical of French 16th-century taste. They are his only documented sculptures in the round. In all these works Goujon rejected the classicizing 'purity' of the Fountain of the Innocents, following instead the example of the school of Fontainebleau.

The numerous allegorical high-reliefs on the projecting bays of the attic storey of Lescot's wing of the Cour Carrée (stone, 1552–5; *in situ* but restored) have also disconcerted those critics who preferred to see in Goujon a purist in love with classicism. With their ample figures projecting well beyond the architectural framework, and carved in high relief, their compositions recall Rosso and Giulio Romano and demonstrate a sophisticated understanding both of Mannerist contrapposto and of the foreshortening necessary for decorative sculpture mounted high on a building. However, it is clear that by this stage in his career Goujon was increasingly helped by sculptors from his workshop, among them Etienne Carmoy (*fl* 1540–68), Martin Lefort (*fl* mid-16th century), Pierre Nanyn (*fl* 1562–8) and the brothers François Lheureux and Pierre Lheureux (both *fl* mid-16th century). It was no doubt with the same team of craftsmen that he carried out the rich sculptural decoration of the staircase of Henry II during the years 1555–6.

3. FINAL YEARS, 1562 AND AFTER, AND POSTHUMOUS REPUTATION. In 1562 Goujon was forced to flee France because of his Protestantism, and his workshop was left with the task of completing the sculptures of the south wing of the Louvre (stone, 1559–68; destr. early 19th century; fragments Paris, Louvre and Ecole N. Sup. B.-A.). However, records of payments to Goujon until 1562 indicate that he was still active there up to the time of his flight. He was last recorded in Bologna in 1563 as one of a group of Huguenot refugees.

Goujon's style has wrongly been seen as a slow but continuous progression from a Mannerism influenced by Parmigianino to a classicism influenced by antique models. It has also been common to attribute indiscriminately to him any elegant female figure of the period, most notably the famous marble group of *Diana with a Stag* (Paris, Louvre) from the château of Anet, Eure-et-Loire; this work is more likely to be by Germain Pilon, who dominated French sculpture in the second half of the 16th century. Despite his large workshop, Goujon had no real successor. From the 19th century he was extolled as the great sculptor of the Renaissance in France and made the champion of triumphant paganism.

2. Jean Goujon: stone caryatids (1550–51), Salle des Caryatides, Musée du Louvre, Paris

BIBLIOGRAPHY

A. von Bartsch: *Le Peintre-graveur* (1803–21) [B.]
R. Lister: *Jean Goujon: His Life and Work* (London, 1903)
——: 'Jean Goujon', *L'Art et les artistes* (London, 1907), pp. 292–3
P. Vitry: *Jean Goujon* (Paris, [1908])
P. du Colombier: *Jean Goujon* (Paris, 1949) [the standard text and catalogue of works, but with over-generous attributions]
A. Blunt: *Art and Architecture in France, 1500–1700*, Pelican Hist. A. (Harmondsworth, 1953, rev. 3/1970) [contains the best stylistic analysis of Goujon's work and rejects the attribution to him of *Diana with a Stag*]
C. Delvoye: 'La Sculpture en France au XVIe siècle et l'art antique', *Rev. U. Libre Bruxelles*, vii (1955–6), pp. 254–80
L'Ecole de Fontainebleau (exh. cat., ed. S. Béguin, B. Jestaz and J. Thirion; Paris, Grand Pal., 1972)
N. Miller: *French Renaissance Fountains* (New York, 1977), pp. 121–47
M. Beaulieu: *Renaissance française*, ii of *Description raisonnée des sculptures du Musée du Louvre* (Paris, 1978), pp. 92–103
G. Bresc-Bautier: 'La Sculpture de l'Attique du Louvre par l'atelier de Jean Goujon', *Rev. Louvre*, xxxix (1989), pp. 97–111
J. Thirion: 'La Fontaine des nymphes', *Les Saints innocents* (Paris, 1990), pp. 121–43

JACQUES THIRION

Gounaropoulos, Giorgos (*b* Sozopolis [now Sozopol, Bulgaria], 22 March 1890; *d* 1977). Greek painter. In 1906 he enrolled at the Higher School of Fine Arts in Athens. He graduated in 1912, but for the next seven years saw war service in the Balkan Wars and in World War I. In

1919 he won a scholarship to Paris. There he studied at the Académie Julien (until 1924) and at the Grande Chaumière, and exhibited at the Salon d'Automne and the Salon des Indépendants. His first one-man exhibition was at the Galerie Vavin-Raspail, Paris (1926). His first one-man show in Athens, however, at the Galerie Strategopoulos in 1929, gave rise to controversy, for its parallels with Parisian Surrealism made it seem a protest against the outdated academicism and chromatically subdued Impressionism that characterized Greek art at the time. Despite this, Gounaropoulos returned to Greece in 1931 and settled in Athens, where he was successful in winning a number of important commissions, such as that for the decoration of the council chamber of the town hall in 1939.

The post-war years brought Gounaropoulos further success. He was one of the founder-members of the Stathmi group in 1949, and exhibited frequently in Athens and abroad. In 1957 a retrospective exhibition was organized by the Institut Français, Athens. A second retrospective exhibition was organized at the National Picture Gallery, Athens, in 1975. Most of Gounaropoulos's works are to be found in private collections in Greece or in his studio, which after his death was transformed into a museum. In terms of subject-matter, his works are characterized by the use mainly of female figures, treated idealistically as nereids or nymphs, set in imaginary aquatic landscapes.

BIBLIOGRAPHY

D. Papastamos: *Painting, 1930–40: The Artistic and Aesthetic Vision of the Decade* (Athens, 1986), pp. 78–81

FANI-MARIA TSIGAKOU

Goupil, (Jean-Michel-)Adolphe (*b* 7 March 1806 or 1809; *d* May 1893). French print publisher and dealer. He was a descendant on his mother's side of the Drouais family of painters. At the age of 21 he set up as a printseller in association with JOHN ARROWSMITH, and in 1829 registered officially as a printseller in partnership with J. H. Rittner (1802–40), who had gone to Paris from Dresden with the intention of dealing in German prints. The critic Feuillet de Conches drew Goupil's attention to Paul Delaroche, and prints after this artist's work began to appear with some frequency. By 1840 the firm had made a name as publisher of copperplate engravings executed by the most famous engravers of the day, Luigi Calamatta and Louis-Pierre Henriquel-Dupont. Delaroche was the favourite of the firm. In 1841, following the death of Rittner, the firm was dissolved and re-established in partnership with Théodore Vibert, also a publisher of engravings. The firm published for an international market; Goupil opened a branch in London in 1841 and one in New York in 1845. In 1849 he was associated with an enterprise that aimed to support American artists in Paris and also to sell the works of living French artists in America. By 1862 there was a branch of Goupil in Berlin followed by ones in Vienna in 1865 and in Brussels in 1866. In 1861, together with Léon Boussod (*see* BOUSSOD, VALADON & CIE), he had gone into partnership with the firm of Van Gogh at the Hague, owned by the uncle of the painter Vincent van Gogh, who himself was to work for them for a time in 1869 and later in London from 1873–4. By this period the main premises of Goupil were at 9 Rue Chaptal in Paris, with a branch at 19 Boulevard Montmartre.

The first evidence of Goupil's activity as a dealer in paintings was his purchase, on the opening day of the 1844 Salon, of Charles Landelle's pendants *Idyll* and *Elegy* (untraced). He bought them together with the engraving rights and almost immediately drew up a contract with the artist. From then on he increasingly bought paintings he intended to reproduce. The very large-scale sale of prints and later of photographs helped to extend the popularity of the artists Goupil supported: Charles Gleyre, for example, although famous after the success of *Lost Illusions* (Paris, Louvre) at the Salon of 1843, received little financial gain until Goupil bought his Neo-Greek painting *Hercules and Omphale* (1863; Neuchâtel, Mus. A. & Hist.) for 18,000 francs. As a result of dealing with Goupil, Gleyre thereafter received large sums for his paintings. In 1859, three years after Delaroche's death, Goupil commissioned his former pupil Jean-Léon Gérôme to paint the *Death of Caesar* (completed 1867; Baltimore, MD, Walters A.G.) as a pendant to Delaroche's *Assassination of the Duc de Guise* (1834; Chantilly, Mus. Condé), in order to sell the pair as photographs. Gérôme sold almost everything he painted via Goupil to America.

As well as the Neo-Greek style associated with the firm there was another strain—of picturesque sentiment—represented by the work of Landelle and Charles Jalabert, and later by that of William-Adolphe Bouguereau and Hugues Merle (1823–81). Between 1861 and 1875 over 300 pictures by the latter artists appeared in Goupil's stock books. Almost all were for export. As a result of Goupil's connection with Holland, Elbert van Wisselingh arrived in Paris as a trainee manager in the late 1860s. From then on some Barbizon pictures and works by the modern Dutch landscape school came into the gallery. This prepared the ground for the direction the firm was to take after Goupil's retirement, when it was run by Boussod and his son-in-law René Valadon. Theo van Gogh (*d* 1891), the painter's brother, began to introduce Impressionist paintings at the Boulevard Montmartre, while Boussod's son Etienne continued from new premises at the Place de l'Opéra.

BIBLIOGRAPHY

DBF

E. Saglio: 'Exposition de tableaux modernes dans la Galerie Goupil', *Gaz. B.-A.*, vii (1860), pp. 46–52

B. Gould: *Two van Gogh Contacts: E. J. Van Wisselingh, Art Dealer; Daniel Cottier, Glass Painter and Decorator* (London, 1969)

J. Rewald: 'Theo van Gogh, Goupil and the Impressionists', *Gaz. B.-A.*, n. s. 5, lxxxi (1973), pp. 1–108

M. Nonne: 'Les Marchands de van Gogh', *Van Gogh à Paris* (exh. cat., Paris, Mus. d'Orsay, 1988), pp. 330–45

LINDA WHITELEY

Goupy, Joseph (*b* Nièvre, 1686; *d* London, before 3 April 1770). English painter, printmaker, collector and curator of French birth. A nephew of the French-born portrait painter Louis Goupy (*c.* 1674–1747), he visited Malta early in his career, producing four panoramic views of the port of *Valletta* (Melbourne Hall, Derbys), later engraved by Antoine Benoist. In 1711 he was among the first subscribers to Godfrey Kneller's Academy in London. Goupy's speciality from then on appears to have been the production of small copies in pastel or gouache of Old Master paintings; they were widely admired and initially fetched high prices. Through his acquaintance with Marco Ricci, Goupy painted sets for productions by the Royal Academy of Music during the 1720s. These included several operas by George Frideric Handel, with whom he developed a close friendship; it ended with the publication of the *True Representation and Character of the Charming Brute* (1730), the print made after Goupy's savage caricature (gouache; Cambridge, Fitzwilliam) of the composer as a bewigged hog playing the organ.

Goupy's elevated status in the art world of 18th-century London is demonstrated by Gawen Hamilton's inclusion of him in his group portrait *A Conversation of Virtuosi at the King's Armes* (1735; London, N.P.G.; *see* LONDON, fig. 18). Goupy was employed by George I to restore Andrea Mantegna's *Triumphs of Caesar* (London, Hampton Court, Royal Col.), and in 1736 Frederick, Prince of Wales, appointed him his 'cabinet painter', which involved assembling and maintaining Frederick's collection and instructing his family in drawing. He maintained his links with the royal family throughout his career. An example of his work as a copyist in pastels is *Belisarius* (Brit. Royal Col.), the original of which was then attributed to Anthony van Dyck, while Goupy's small gouache of his friend *Brook Taylor* (London, N.P.G.) is typical of his portrait style. Goupy's own art collection was sold posthumously in London (3 April 1770).

BIBLIOGRAPHY

C. R. Grundy: 'Documents Relating to an Action Brought against Joseph Goupy in 1738', *Walpole Soc.*, ix (1921), pp. 77–87

F. Lugt: *Marques* (1921)

E. Croft-Murray: *Decorative Painting in England, 1537–1837*, ii (London, 1970), pp. 211–12

Handel (exh. cat., ed. J. Simon; London, N.P.G., 1985)

RICHARD JEFFREE

Gourdaine, Jan Piotr Norblin de la. *See* NORBLIN DE LA GOURDAINE, JAN PIOTR

Gourd. Large and diverse group of plants of the Cucurbitaceae family, related to pumpkins and squash. Gourds occur in a wide variety of sizes, shapes and colours. Although grown for their ornamental fruit, the hand-shelled varieties of gourds are often used for bottles, drinking cups, musical instruments etc. Their hard rind provides an ideal surface for decoration.

1. AMERICAS. Gourds are available throughout the Americas and were domesticated *c.* 11,000 BC in the Andes and by *c.* 7500 BC in Mesoamerica. By Pre-Ceramic phase VI (*c.* 2500 BC–*c.* 1800 BC), gourds were being decorated at the central Andean site of Huaca Prieta by incising and, to a limited extent, excising designs depicting highly geometricized feline, avian and reptilian motifs (*see* SOUTH AMERICA, PRE-COLUMBIAN, fig. 22). Gourds continued in use into ceramic-using periods and are found at Ancón, Paracas and Nazca. They were decorated by means of incision, excision and burning (possibly done using acids to create various colours in the decorated areas), painting, dyeing and inlaying with mother-of-pearl, shells and hardstones. Designs range from simple feline figures, birds or fish, in both positive and negative styles, to complicated, stylized, incised figures.

New uses and shapes were developed in the Colonial and Republican periods, particularly in southern Peru and northern Argentina, and development continues in the central highlands of Peru (see fig.). The artists of Mayocc and Cochas Grande, for example, produce finely incised gourds with narrative decorations. Designs from Cochas Grande are less detailed and are filled in with colours burnt on using various plant dyes. From the late 1970s, probably in response to increasing tourism, new art forms and styles developed, such as gourds containing *retablos* (nativity scenes), scenes with figures and shops, or gourds dyed a single colour and incised with extremely fine lines. Collections of Pre-Columbian and contemporary carved gourds are located in the Museo de la Cultura, the Museo de la Nación, the Museo Nacional de Antropología y Arqueología, the Colección Luza, all in Lima, and the Museo Nacional de Antropología, Mexico City.

BIBLIOGRAPHY

J. B. Bird: 'Pre-ceramic Art from Huaca Prieta, Chicama Valley', *Ñawpa Pacha*, i (1963), pp. 29–34

J.-C. Spahni: *Mates decorados del Perú* (Lima, 1969)

V. Toneyama: *The Popular Arts of Mexico* (New York, 1974)

E. Menzie: *Hand-carved and Decorated Gourds of Peru* (Santa Monica, 1976)

C. Sayer: *Crafts of Mexico* (London, 1977), pp. 60–75, 88–91

W. IAIN MACKAY

2. CHINA. The gourd's importance in China dates to the Neolithic period (*c.* 6500–*c.* 1600 BC), when it was cultivated as food and used to make containers, utensils and musical instruments. Reverence for the gourd is evident in Chinese mythology: several minority groups in southern China believed that humanity was born from a gourd, while the Han Chinese pictured paradise hidden inside its bulbous form. Gourds were associated with the immortals, being symbols of the unity of heaven (the upper lobe) and earth (the lower lobe). Because of its many seeds the gourd was also a fertility symbol.

Gourds have appeared in Chinese art for more than 2000 years. Artisans in the Zhou period (*c.* 1050–256 BC) cast gourd-shaped *hu*, bronze ritual wine vessels. In the Song period (960–1279), renewed interest in the gourd as a vessel led to the production of elegant green-glazed, gourd-shaped ceramic bottles, vases and ewers for secular use. The zenith of the ceramic gourd-form was reached in the reign of the Jiajing emperor (*reg* 1522–66), who was obsessed with finding a Daoist elixir of immortality and used gourd-shaped vessels because of their magical associations. In the 16th century a form of ceramic vase in polychrome (*wucai*) or blue-and-white decoration and shaped like a gourd with a flat back for hanging on the wall was created. The upper lobe was often painted with such heavenly creatures as phoenixes and cranes, and the lower with terrestrial images of deer and peonies, alluding to the gourd as a cosmic symbol.

BIBLIOGRAPHY

J. Rawson, ed.: *The British Museum Book of Chinese Art* (London, 1992), p. 208

W. Shixang: *The Charms of the Gourd*, trans. by Hu Shiping (Hong Kong, 1993)

JAN STUART

'Carved' gourd by David Saldaña García and his brother, 370×240 mm, from Cochas Chico, Peru, *c.* 1992 (London, British Museum)

Gourlier, Charles-Pierre (*b* Paris, 15 May 1786; *d* Paris, 16 Feb 1857). French architect, writer and engraver. He was a pupil of Jean-Antoine Alavoine and Jean-Nicolas Huyot at the Ecole des Beaux-Arts, Paris, and began his career as a vérificateur (1811–15) in the Direction des Travaux Publics from its creation in 1811, subsequently becoming Chef de la Révision (1815–19). He was sous-inspecteur for the restoration (1819–20) of the Porte St Martin, Paris, and then inspecteur of the Bourse (1821–6) and architect of the reserve granary (1827–31). At the same time he worked (1819–33) for the Conseil des Bâtiments Civils, serving as its secretary from 1824 to 1831. In 1835 he was involved in important work on several cathedrals on behalf of the Ministère des Cultes, including the choir at Nantes and rebuilding the nave roof at Chartres, following a fire in 1836. Gourlier was also an engraver and exhibited at the Salon many architectural designs, which were published in 1825–50 as *Choix d'édifices publics, projetés et construits en France depuis le commencement du XIXe siècle*, a work that established his reputation, forming a perfect summary of the architectural philosophy of the Conseil des Bâtiments Civils. His interest in workers' housing, baths and wash-houses was reflected in his Salon exhibits of 1853 and 1855.

UNPUBLISHED SOURCES

Paris, Archvs N., MS. F21.909

WRITINGS

Choix d'édifices publics, projetés et construits en France depuis le commencement du XIXe siècle, 3 vols (Paris, 1825–50)

Voies publiques et des habitations particulières (Paris, 1852)

BIBLIOGRAPHY

Bauchal; Bellier de La Chavignerie–Auvray

JEAN-MICHEL LENIAUD

Gourmont, de. French family of artists.

(1) Jean de Gourmont (i) (*b* Carquebut, Manche, *c*. 1483; *d c*. 1551). Engraver, draughtsman, painter and possible goldsmith. He was the most distinguished member of the family. He worked in Paris (*c*. 1508–20) together with his brothers Robert and Gilles de Gourmont; subsequently he was in Lyon (1522–6). His engravings have been identified with those of the monogrammist JG; this is confirmed by the portrait of *Cardinal Charles de Bourbon* (*c*. 1551, see Linzeler and Adhémar, no. 26), where this monogram is followed by the inscription *ourmont fe*, completing his name. Three of his plates bear the word *Alion*. His engraved work, executed with very fine and close lines, comprises *c*. 30 pieces, two of which, *St Barbara* and *St Sebastian* (LA 10, 11), are copies after Marcantonio Raimondi. There is also a portrait of *Charles, Cardinal de Guise-Lorraine* (1575, LA 27) and several arabesque strips (LA 28), which may be part of a collection published by the Gourmont family in Paris in 1546: *Le Livre des moresques*, intended for goldsmiths, engravers, painters and embroiderers.

Gourmont's other engravings represent a variety of subjects, always superimposed on grandiose architectural backgrounds, in which complicated perspective effects and luminous zones contrasting with long shadows are employed to render each composition theatrical and unreal, for example in the *Mystic Marriage of St Catherine* (LA 8) and the *Massacre of the Innocents* (LA 3). His allusions

Jean de Gourmont (i): *St John the Baptist as a Child*, engraving, diam. 115 mm, (Paris, Bibliothèque Nationale, Cabinet des Estampes)

to antiquity are fantastical, as in *Laokoon* (after 1520, LA 20) and *St John the Baptist as a Child* (LA 9; see fig.). These works bring to mind the Venetian scenography of Paris Bordone, or the works of Jean Cousin (i) or Jacques Androuet Du Cerceau (i), but the artist to whom Gourmont is closest is Master C. C., who also worked in Lyon. Between these two engravers there exists a clear community of spirit and invention.

Jean de Gourmont may also have been a painter. During the 18th century the collector Pierre-Jean Mariette drew a comparison (Mariette, ii, pp. 326–7) between Gourmont's engravings and the painting of the *Adoration of the Shepherds* (*c*. 1525; Paris, Louvre) from the chapel of the château of Ecouen, Val d'Oise. This attribution is still considered valid. More recently Gourmont has been credited with the painting *The Cave* (1537; Frankfurt am Main, Städel Kstinst). It was again Mariette who suggested that the artist might have been a goldsmith, because his technique was so precise and meticulous, and because he depicted this craft on three occasions: *St Eligius and King Dagobert* (LA 12); *St Eligius* (LA 13); and the *Combat of Goldsmiths* (LA 21). Three pen-and-wash drawings have been attributed to him: the *Massacre of the Innocents* (Paris, Bib. N.) and the *Flagellation* and the *Holy Family* (both New York, Pierpont Morgan Lib.), although the Paris example, in the scale of its architecture, brings to mind the Master C.C.

(2) Jean de Gourmont (ii) (*b c*. 1537; *d* before 21 July 1598). Printmaker, bookseller and print publisher, great-nephew of (1) Jean de Gourmont (i). He became a master bookseller in 1581 but from 1559 was associated as a wood-engraver with two Parisian illustrators, Jean Pignot and Geoffroi Ballin. Gourmont made almost 130 plates after Ballin's drawings illustrating *Reynaert de Vos* (1566) and the works of Nicander (1567–8), published by Christophe Plantin (*c*. 1520–89) in Antwerp. His own engravings, sometimes signed IDG, are usually copies or interpretations of prints by other artists. Their quality is inconsistent, except for some decorative prints. He owned and published the copperplates of René Boyvin, notably the portrait of *Henri IV*, a reworking of Boyvin's portrait of *Henri II*, with the head replaced.

Together with his brother François de Gourmont (*b c.* 1540; *d* before 21 July 1598), Jean de Gourmont (ii) ran the family publishing house in Rue St Jean-de-Latran, Paris, at the sign of L'Arbre sec. François, who had been a bookseller since 1587, was also a copperplate- and wood-engraver. The only known work to bear his name is a wood-engraving of fine quality representing *Salvator mundi and the Holy Virgin Praying*.

BIBLIOGRAPHY

Mariette; Thieme–Becker

A. P. F. Robert-Dumesnil: *Le Peintre-graveur français* (Paris, 1835–71), vii, pp. 18–27, and xi, pp. 204–6

A. Linzeler and J. Adhémar: *Inventaire du fonds français: Graveurs du seizième siècle*, Paris, Bib. N., Cab. Est. cat., Paris, i (1932), pp. 437–46, ii (1938), pp. 335–9 [LA]

De Clouet à Matisse: Dessins français des collections américaines (exh. cat., Paris, Mus. Orangerie, 1958)

Le XVIe Siècle européen: Gravures et dessins du Cabinet Edmond de Rothschild (exh. cat., Paris, Louvre, 1965)

Le XVIe Siècle européen: Peintures et dessins dans les collections publiques françaises (exh. cat., Paris, Petit Pal., 1965)

C. L. Ragghianti: 'Pertinenze francesi nel cinquecento', *Crit. A.*, 122 (1972), pp. 22–41

C. Grodecki: *Documents du Minutier central des notaires de Paris: Histoire de l'art au XVIe siècle, 1540–1600*, ii (Paris, 1986), no. 861

M. Préaud, P. Casselle, M. Grivel and C. Le Bitouzé: *Dictionnaire des éditeurs d'estampes à Paris sous l'ancien régime* (Paris, 1987)

PHILIPPE ROUILLARD

Gourmont, Remy de (*b* Bazoches-en-Houlme, Orne, 4 April 1858; *d* Paris, 27 Sept 1915). French writer and draughtsman. He came from a family that had, in the 15th and 16th centuries, produced many notable painters, engravers and publishers, including Jean de Gourmont the elder and the younger. Though he had from an early age wanted to become a writer, he entered the university at Caen in 1876 to study law. He graduated in 1879 and in 1881 started working at the Bibliothèque Nationale in Paris, where he published many articles, populist books and a novel, *Merlette* (Paris, 1886). At the Bibliothèque Nationale he met the writer Villiers de l'Isle Adam, who became a close friend and introduced him to Joris-Karl Huysman in 1889. The poet Stéphane Mallarmé was another of his associates at this time. In 1890 he was one of the co-founders of the journal *Mercure de France* together with Albert Aurier, Jules Renard (1864–1910) and others. He was a regular contributor and his article 'Le Joujou patriotisme' (April 1890), calling for a rapprochement between France and Germany, was considered to be so outrageous that he lost his job at the Bibliothèque Nationale.

By this time Gourmont was in contact with most of the members of the literary Symbolist movement, and it was as a Symbolist critic and aesthetician that he was most influential in art. In 1893 his book *L'Idéalisme* was published with a frontispiece by Charles Filiger, an artist whom he had 'discovered'. Idealism was the philosophy that, more or less explicitly, underpinned all Symbolist thought, and Gourmont opened the book with a brief survey of its more recent philosophical exponents: Kant, Schopenhauer and Hegel. In the section entitled 'Le Symbolisme' he expressed the common Symbolist desire to find an absolute reality beneath personal experience (p. 27): 'The Absolute itself is truly unknowable and beyond being formulated in symbols; it is therefore only to the relative absolute that Symbolism aims, to show what is eternal in the personal.'

In 1894 Gourmont co-founded the periodical *L'Ymagier* with the writer Alfred Jarry. The first issue appeared in October 1894 and the eighth and last in December 1896. Gourmont was the real driving force behind this intriguing periodical, which consisted largely of woodcuts, as well as a few metal engravings and lithographs, together with verses, music for popular songs and brief articles. The images ranged from the 14th century onwards, with work by such early artists as Dürer, Martin Schongauer and Lucas Cranach, and by such contemporary artists as Gauguin, Georges d'Espagnat, Filiger, Emile Bernard and Whistler. The images were often violent or grotesque, depicting Christian scenes of demons, persecutions and the crucifixion, with mystical and legendary subjects being well represented. The second issue published Henri Rousseau's full-page woodcut *War*, Rousseau being another of Gourmont's 'finds'.

Gourmont wrote several collections of essays, one of which, *La Culture des idées* (Paris, 1900), includes a section entitled 'Le Paganisme éternel' in which, in an essay entitled 'Une Religion d'art', he documents, in reference to Huysman's book *La Cathédrale* (Paris, 1898), the absorption of Classical pagan iconography into Christian art. *Le Problème du style* (Paris, 1902) includes the typically Symbolist essay 'L'Art et le peuple' in which Gourmont rejects both Tolstoy's view that all art should be accessible and also the view that there are two sorts of art, one for an élite and one that has popular appeal. He asserted that all art 'is, in its essence, absolutely unintelligible to the people' and that art should rightly be judged by its manner of execution, not, as was always the case, by the mistaken criterion of content. This formalist approach justifies his conclusion (p. 194): 'The public is not made for art, nor art for the public. The public has no taste for the exception and, I maintain, art is a perpetual exception.' As well as writing about art, Gourmont occasionally produced illustrations himself, for example those for his novel *Phocas* (Paris, 1895).

WRITINGS

L'Idéalisme (Paris, 1893)

La Culture des idées (Paris, 1900)

Le Problème du style (Paris, 1902)

Pensées inédites (Paris, 1920) [preface by Guillaume Apollinaire and illustrations by Raoul Dufy]

Dernières Pensées inédites (Paris, 1924)

La Fin de l'art (Paris, 1925)

BIBLIOGRAPHY

P. de Querlon: *Remy de Gourmont* (Paris, 1903)

P. Delior: *Remy de Gourmont et son oeuvre* (Paris, 1909)

J. de Gourmont: *Souvenirs sur Remy* (Paris, 1924)

P. E. Jacob: *Remy de Gourmont* (Urbana, 1931)

F. Amery, ed.: *The Angels of Perversity* (Sawtry, Cambs, 1992)

□

Gournia. Site in eastern Crete, near the northern end of the Ierapetra Isthmus. Set on a low spur overlooking the Bay of Mirabello, it was occupied from Early Minoan (EM)

II till Late Minoan (LM) I (*c.* 2900/2600–*c.* 1425 BC) and was resettled in LM IIIA:2 and IIIB (*c.* 1360–*c.* 1190 BC). Following the work of HARRIET BOYD (later Hawes) in 1901–4, it is the most completely excavated Minoan town in Crete, with a well-preserved system of streets and residential blocks. Finds from Gournia include a clay goddess with upraised arms (LM IIIB, *c.* 1335–*c.* 1190 BC; Herakleion, Archaeol. Mus.), a bronze figurine of a male worshipper (LM I, *c.* 1600–*c.* 1425 BC; Herakleion, Archaeol. Mus.) with hand on chest and hair tresses comparable to those of the '*Boxing Boys*' fresco from Akrotiri on Thera (*see* THERA, §1), Marine style pottery (LM IB, *c.* 1480–*c.* 1425 BC) and a Red Lustrous ware spindle bottle (Herakleion, Archaeol. Mus.) imported from Cyprus or Syria. There is also a rich collection of objects of daily use, including a cache of carpenters' tools buried before the town's destruction by fire *c.* 1425 BC.

The settlement (*c.* 185×*c.* 135 m) contains no buildings of EM II and EM III, but the contents of a pottery dump in the 'North Trench' have established the characteristics of the EM III white-on-dark ware (*see* MINOAN, §III, 3(iii)). It was probably in the Proto-Palatial (Middle Minoan (MM) IB–II, *c.* 1900–1675 BC) 'Early Gournia' phase of its existence that the town's street and block system was begun. The North Spur cemetery, with its built dwelling-like 'house tombs', was also in use at this time, and a thick (?defensive) wall at the north end of the settlement may be of this period too. The MM pottery suggests that Gournia fell within a cultural sphere centred on MALLIA but extending around the Lasithi Mountains to MYRTOS on the south side of eastern Crete. A silver lobed kantharos (Herakleion, Archaeol. Mus.) from the house tombs is the sole MM vessel of precious metal to have survived in Crete (*see* MINOAN, fig. 4 and §IX, 1(ii)).

Gournia was especially prosperous in LM I, when an official house ('Palace') was built at the top of the town. Many features of the building, which was probably the local seat of government, are based on those of the palaces at Knossos and elsewhere (*see* MINOAN, §II). Its one unusual element is a tower. The town's houses, which mostly survive only to basement level, are divided into blocks by streets that follow the contours of the ridge and run up it. Buildings dating from the resettlement of the site in LM IIIA:2 may include House He, built with ashlar masonry. The small shrine (bench sanctuary) a little to the north of the 'Palace' contained various objects, all probably of LM IIIB date. In addition to the clay goddess mentioned above, and fragments of similar figurines, these included clay tubular stands (sometimes known as 'snake-tubes') for bowls or baskets of offerings. To the north of the main site, at the nearby harbour of Sphoungaras, is a small Late Neolithic (*c.* 4500–*c.* 3800 BC) settlement and an EM II–LM I cemetery. Across the valley to the east are the excavated remains of the LM I Hill House.

BIBLIOGRAPHY

H. B. Hawes: *Gournia, Vasiliki, and Other Prehistoric Sites on the Isthmus of Hierapetra, Crete* (Philadelphia, 1908)
E. H. Hall: *Excavations in Eastern Crete: Sphoungaras* (Philadelphia, 1912)
J. S. Soles: 'The Early Gournia Town', *Amer. J. Archaeol.*, lxxxiii (1979), pp. 149–67
Proceedings of the Temple University Aegean Symposium: Philadelphia, 1979
P. P. Betancourt: *Minoan Objects Excavated from Vasilike, Pseira, Sphoungaras, Priniatikos Pyrgos, and Other Sites* (Philadelphia, 1983), pp. 43–51
S. Damiani Indelicato: 'Gournia, cité minoenne', *Aux origines de l'hellénisme: La Crète et la Grèce. Hommage à Henri van Effenterre* (Paris, 1984), pp. 47–54
G. C. Gesell: *Town, Palace, and House Cult in Minoan Crete*, Stud. Medit. Archaeol., lxvii (Göteborg, 1985), pp. 43, 70–73, 145, 147–9
B. Rutkowski: *The Cult Places of the Aegean* (New Haven and London, 1986), pp. 161–2, 168
M. S. F. Hood: 'A Baetyl at Gournia?', *Ariadne*, v (1989), pp. 17–21 [*Aphieroma ston Styrliano Alexiou*]
P. P. Betancourt and J. S. Silverman: *Pottery from Gournia* (Philadelphia, 1991)
J. S. Soles: 'The Gournia Palace', *Amer. J. Archaeol.*, xcv (1991), pp. 17–78
G. Cadogan: 'Gournia', *The Aerial Atlas of Ancient Crete*, ed. J. W. Myers, E. E. Myers and G. Cadogan (Berkeley, 1992), pp. 104–111
J. S. Soles: 'The Prepalatial Cemeteries at Mochlos and Gournia and the House Tombs of Bronze Age Crete', *Hesperia*, suppl. xxiv (1992)
V. Fotou: 'New Light on Gournia. Unknown Documents of the Excavation at Gournia and Other Sites on the Isthmus of Ierapetra by Harriet Ann Boyd', *Aegaeum* [Liège], ix (1993)

GERALD CADOGAN

Goût grec. Stylistic term for the first phase of French Neo-classicism. Contemporary usage was loose as regards both the objects referred to (even coffee and hair lotion were advertised as 'à la grecque') and their style (which might only have the faintest classicizing flavour). It is correctly applied only to those examples of French decorative arts and architecture dating from the mid-1750s to the late 1760s that are severely rectilinear, with chunky classical details, such as Vitruvian scrolls, Greek-key frets and geometrical garlands. The style was effectively inaugurated by a set of furniture, comprising a combined writing-table and cabinet (for illustration *see* LOUIS XVI STYLE) and a clock (Chantilly, Mus. Condé), made for the Parisan financier Ange-Laurent de La Live de Jully from designs (1756–8) by the painter and amateur architect Louis-Joseph Le Lorrain. The monumental and unfrivolous style of these pieces, executed in ebony-veneered oak with heavy gilt bronze mounts, was quite different from the current Rococo idiom. The Comte de Caylus, Europe's foremost antiquary and Le Lorrain's influential mentor, praised the furniture extravagantly. Another key role in the creation and dissemination of the *goût grec* was played by the engravings of the architect Jean-François de Neufforge, a member of Caylus's circle and a collaborator with Le Lorrain on the publication of Julien-David Le Roy's *Les Ruines des plus beaux monuments de la Grèce* (Paris, 1758). This early, extreme phase of Neo-classicism was attacked by Charles-Nicolas Cochin *le fils* and Jacques-François Blondel and was parodied in Ennemond-Alexandre Petitot's *Mascarade à la grecque* (Parma, 1771). The brief but intense flowering of the *goût grec* soon gave way to the less rigorous Louis XVI style.

BIBLIOGRAPHY

S. Eriksen: 'La Live de Jully's Furniture "à la Grecque"', *Burl. Mag.*, ciii (1961), pp. 340–47
——: *Early Neo-classicism in France* (London, 1974)

RICHARD JOHN

Gouthière, Pierre (*b* Bar-sur-Aube, *bapt* 13 Jan 1732; *d* Paris, 8 June 1813). French bronze-caster and gilder. He became a master gilder and chaser in Paris on 14 April 1758 and took over the establishment and married the widow of his employer, François Ceriset, a modest craftsman. He then worked under the sign of the 'Boucle d'Or'. On 7 November 1767 he received the warrant of 'Doreur Seul Ordinaire des Menus Plaisirs du Roi', signed by the Duc d'Aumont (*d* 1782), one of his most important patrons. His reputation as the most eminent bronzeworker and gilder in the reign of Louis XVI was established during his lifetime. Many of the bronze pieces produced during this period were thought to have been made by Gouthière, but some of the most important works have been reattributed to Pierre-Philippe Thomire and François Rémond on the basis of documentary evidence. Louis XVI acquired for his private museum 20 of the 34 pieces by Gouthière that were in the Aumont collection, while three of them were bought by Marie-Antoinette. His other clients consisted of the leading connoisseurs of his day, including the Comte d'Artois, the Comtesse Du Barry, the Duc de Duras, the Duchesse de Villeroy, Princess Kinsky, the Marquis de Marigny and the financiers Paul Randon de Boisset, Baudart de Saint-James and Thélusson. At the same time the administrators of the Menus Plaisirs and of the Bâtiments du Roi competed for the right to provide Gouthière with commissions.

It is difficult to describe the style of Gouthière's work, as he rejected the most austere aspects of Neo-classicism early in his career. His earliest known works (*c.* 1765) are classical mounts for imitation porphyry vases (Warsaw, Royal Castle), which were commissioned by the goldsmith François-Thomas Germain. These were closely followed by candlesticks with lions' heads, a design copied by Matthew Boulton, and by small classical statues of graceful, nude female figures. Gouthière was the most eloquent exponent of the arabesque phase of Neo-classicism in French bronzework, as illustrated by the mounts for a pair of celadon porcelain vases (Paris, Louvre) for the Duc d'Aumont, the mounts for a jasper perfume-burner (London, Wallace) made for the same patron and later bewitching Marie-Antoinette, and the door-knobs (Paris, Mus. A. Déc.) for Madame Du Barry's Pavillon de Louveciennes.

Gouthière was an incomparable gilder and invented the technique of matt-finish gilding. He was also extremely skilled in chasing and modelling. He was inundated with commissions during his period of success in the early 1770s, and at that time he managed a large number of subcontractors, whose work he painstakingly supervised, sometimes under the guidance of such architects as Charles de Wailly, Claude-Nicolas Ledoux and François-Joseph Bélanger, or such sculptors as Louis-Simon Boizot and Jean-Joseph Foucou, whose designs he executed.

Gouthière also made many types of furnishing objects, including table legs made entirely of bronze, ornaments for mantelpieces, pedestals, stoves and even coaches, as well as mounts for porcelain, marble or ivory vases. The Avignon Clock (London, Wallace; *see* FRANCE, fig. 82), made in 1771, the year in which Ledoux entrusted production of all the bronzes for the Pavillon de Louveciennes to Gouthière, shows the level of technical perfection achieved by him. He then executed a number of high-quality objects in imaginative designs, among them a lyre-shaped candelabrum (Malibu, CA, Getty Mus.) decorated with a head of Apollo, candelabra with symbols of Mercury (Paris, Louvre), fire-dogs decorated with camels (Paris, Louvre) and fire-dogs decorated with eagles (Paris, Mobilier N.). A number of chimney-pieces by Gouthière are extant and provide fascinating examples of the development of his work. They are in the Salon Ovale (1771) at Louveciennes, the Bibliothèque du Roi (1774), the Chambre des Bains du Roi (1785), Cabinet de la Méridienne (1781), Salon des Nobles and Cabinet Intérieur de la Reine (1785), all at the château of Versailles, and in Marie-Antoinette's Boudoir Turc at the château of Fontainebleau (1777), the Pavillon de Bagatelle (1777) in the Bois de Boulogne and the Duchesse de Mazarin's reception room (1780; New York, Met.).

From 1776 Gouthière's affairs descended into disorder, due to an ambitious property business, financial speculation and uncertain management of his workshop. All this, together with the deaths of his two main patrons, the Duchesse de Mazarin (1781) and the Duc d'Aumont, led to his bankruptcy in 1787. He nevertheless continued to work on a small scale, and his final official commission, completed in 1801, was for the Palais du Corps Législatif, Paris.

BIBLIOGRAPHY

J. Robiquet: *Vie et oeuvre de Pierre Gouthière* (Paris, 1920)

C. Baulez: 'Pierre Gouthière (1732–1813)', *Vergoldete Bronzen*, ii (Munich, 1986), pp. 561–642

JEAN-DOMINIQUE AUGARDE

Govaerts [Goevaerts; Gouvaert; Goyvaert], **Abraham** (*bapt* Antwerp, 30 Aug 1589; *d* Antwerp, 9 Sept 1626). Flemish painter. He was the son of Elisabeth Yselstein and Willem Govaerts, a dealer in second-hand clothes and paintings. He was admitted as a master to the Antwerp Guild of St Luke in 1607–8. In 1609 he bought two houses on the St Jansstraat next to his parents' home. On 9 February 1622 he married Isabella Gillis; they had two daughters. He trained a number of painters: Hans Groenrijs (1617), Andries van den Bogaerde (1619–20), Niclaes Aertsen, Gysbrecht van den Berch and Frans Snyders (the last three from 1623 to 1624).

Govaerts painted mainly wooded landscapes, and his early works reveal stylistic affinities with the work of Gillis van Coninxloo. His *Wooded Landscape* (1612; The Hague, Mauritshuis), with a vista into the distance on the left and a screen of foliage on the right, is similar in construction and composition to van Coninxloo's *Landscape with a View of a Castle* (Strasbourg, Mus. B.-A.). Other works, such as his *Mountainous Landscape* (1614; Antwerp, Mus. Mayer van den Bergh), owe more to Josse de Momper II. Around 1620 the archaisms in his colouring, which included an exaggeration of the brown foreground and the blue tones in the foliage, disappeared, and his work became more like that of Jan Breughel the elder. This can be seen particularly in the pure and brilliant colours applied in light stippling and in the juxtaposition of different colours to represent gradual shading and gentle transitions. Govaerts's works typically also employ dynamic details, such as the splintered and contorted tree trunks in the foreground, and powerful light–dark effects.

BIBLIOGRAPHY

F. J. Van den Branden: *Geschiedenis der Antwerpsche schilderschool* (Antwerp, 1883), pp. 460–62

Y. Thiery: 'L'Auberge d'Abraham Govaerts', *Mus. Royaux B.-A. Belgique: Bull.*, i (1952), pp. 135–8

——: *Le Paysage flamand du XVIIe siècle* (Brussels, 1953), pp. 76–7

——: *Les Peintres flamands de paysage au XVIIe siècle: Des précurseurs à Rubens* (Brussels, 1986), pp. 217–23

HANS DEVISSCHER

Govardhan [Govardhana] (*fl c.* 1596–1640). Indian miniature painter. The son of Bhavani Das, a minor painter in the Mughal imperial atelier, Govardhan began his career during the reign of Akbar (*reg* 1556–1605), developed into a mature master painter under Jahangir (*reg* 1605–27) and continued to produce outstanding paintings well into the reign of Shah Jahan (*reg* 1628–58). He is known mainly for his many depictions of Indian ascetics.

Among the earliest known works by Govardhan are five illustrations in an *Akbarnāma* (1596–7; London, BL, Or. MS. 12988; and Dublin, Chester Beatty Lib., MS. 3; alternatively dated *c.* 1604). Two of these employ the grey and brown tones that Govardhan favoured throughout his long career. Such lightly coloured drawings gained popularity at the Mughal court in the late 16th century, but Govardhan continued to work in this muted style long after it had passed from fashion. A double-page scene of Abu'l-Fazl presenting the text of the *Akbarnāma* to the Emperor (Dublin, Chester Beatty Lib., MS. 3, fols 176–7) includes two facial types that became standard in Govardhan's work: one, a plump-cheeked, boxy countenance with a slight double chin, pointed nose and high, thin eyes, and another, also in three-quarter view, with an irregular profile created by protruding cheekbones and brow.

Two dated folios of an album compiled by Jahangir (Berlin, Staatsbib. Preuss. Kultbes., MS. A.117) bear inscriptions naming Govardhan as the artist. On the first (fol. 25*v*), dated AH 1018 (1609–10), Govardhan is credited with the border decorations, including a series of sensitively drawn figures; the second (fol. 23*r*), a portrait of *Rao Bharah*, is identified in Jahangir's own hand and is dated AH 1027 (1617–18). The remainder of Govardhan's work is dated by external evidence, primarily by reference to the broad stylistic developments of Mughal painting in the 1620s and 1630s.

Although Govardhan is not mentioned in the memoirs of Jahangir, his greatest patron, his many paintings of Indian ascetics have brought him modern acclaim. Unfettered by contemporary conventions of the formal *darbār* or court portrait, Govardhan's paintings of spiritual seekers appeal to the modern taste for innovation and psychological insight. Like Basawan, considered by some to be the younger painter's mentor, Govardhan has been credited with an elaborate artistic personality. His exotic subjects have led some scholars to perceive him as a spiritualist whose special sympathy for sages is revealed in his sensitive characterizations and painterly style.

Images such as *A Rustic Concert* (Dublin, Chester Beatty Lib.) and *Hindu Holy Men* (priv. col., see Welch, 1978, pl. 24) draw much of their power from Govardhan's distinctive formal vocabulary. His muted palette, granular modelling and predilection for long, curling fingers and heavy-lidded eyes cast in distant gazes are ideally suited to depictions of holy men with weathered skin and unusual physiognomies. Yet the artist also employed these same features to depict royal and non-religious personages, adapting his style to these more worldly subjects only in a slightly greater use of gold and bright colours. In *Princely Gathering in a Garden* (Dublin, Chester Beatty Lib.; see fig.), from the dispersed Minto Album, the sole accents of strong colour are the scarlet bolster in the centre and the orange robe of the prince to the left. With colour relegated to a minor role, the painting is dominated by Govardhan's superb modelling of faces and form. Strong contours bind profiles and shoulders; light sketchy lines lend a tactile quality to skin, hair and cloth. Drapery clings tightly to the figures' voluminous bodies and gathers about their forearms in thick folds highlighted with daubs of white. Despite their luxurious clothing and tranquil garden setting, several members of the princely entourage are no less individualized or carefully observed than their ascetic counterparts, a point that underscores the evenhandedness of Govardhan's treatment of figures of all social positions.

Although formal and iconographic elements of European art were a regular feature of Mughal painting by the 1620s, Govardhan stands out as an artist who fully assimilated European devices for rendering volume, the nude human figure, and space. His modelling skilfully describes the rounded forms of huddled figures clad in coarse robes or diaphanous garments. His subtle transitions are even more apparent in the curving forms of the nude or nearly nude figures of such paintings as *An Astrologer* (Paris, Mus. Guimet) or *Hindu Holy Men*. Their poses seem drawn not from specific models, but from

Govardhan: *Princely Gathering in a Garden*, opaque colour on paper, 209×119 mm, *c.* 1630 (Dublin, Chester Beatty Library and Gallery of Oriental Art, MS. 7:8)

extensive experience with European art. Similarly, he applies the principles of diminution and atmospheric perspective to indigenous and European-type genre scenes set in the background of such paintings as *Four Mullas* (Los Angeles, CA, Co. Mus. A.). Such techniques are used to maximum effect in Govardhan's intimate, humanistic scenes of the 1620s and 1630s.

Govardhan also worked in a more conventional style using brighter colours, as, for example, in *Timur Handing his Imperial Crown to Babar* (London, V&A) from the Minto Album. His late work includes a folio from a manuscript of the *Gulistān* ('Rose garden') of Sa'di (priv. col., see Welch, 1985, pl. 158a) which had six illustrations substituted for damaged paintings in the 1640s. Only one illustration (fol. 133*r*) in the great *Pādshāhnāma* ('History of the Emperor'; Windsor Castle, Royal Lib., MS. HB.149), which recounts the events of Shah Jahan's reign, can be attributed to Govardhan. Possibly his age precluded a greater contribution.

See also INDIAN SUBCONTINENT, §V, 4(i)(b)–(d).

BIBLIOGRAPHY

E. Kühnel and H. Goetz: *Indian Book Painting from Jahangir's Album in the State Library, Berlin* (London, 1926)

T. W. Arnold and J. V. S. Wilkinson: *The Library of A. Chester Beatty: A Catalogue of Indian Miniatures*, 3 vols (London, 1936)

S. C. Welch: *Imperial Mughal Painting* (New York, 1978)

The Grand Mogul: Imperial Painting in India, 1600–1660 (exh. cat. by M. C. Beach, Williamstown, MA, Clark A. Inst.; Baltimore, MD, Walters A.G.; Boston, MA, Mus. F.A.; New York, Asia House Gals; 1978–9)

India: Art and Culture, 1300–1900 (exh. cat. by S. C. Welch, New York, Met., 1985)

L. Leach: *Indian Miniature Paintings and Drawings: The Cleveland Museum* (Cleveland, OH, 1986)

S. C. Welch and others: *The Emperors' Album* (New York, 1987)

JOHN SEYLLER

Government building. Building designed for the exercise of state power. A tradition of such buildings in the West can be traced back to the assembly places of Classical times. However, in modern democratic states the constitutional division of powers has led to the emergence of five principal forms of government building: the parliament or legislature; the official seat of the head of government; ministries and offices of the executive; law courts; and, at a municipal level, the town hall, which in the 19th and 20th centuries has served a combination of legislative, executive and administrative functions. For the last two of these forms a distinct architectural typology can be said to have emerged, and these are thus discussed separately (*see* LAW COURT and TOWN HALL). The other forms of government buildings constitute a less clearly defined architectural type, but all forms tend to be characterized by an appearance of sobriety and grandeur.

1. Before 1900. 2. 1900 and after.

1. BEFORE 1900. In terms of their function, modern government buildings form part of a tradition of state assembly places going back to Greek and Roman antiquity. This tradition has been constantly referred to in deciding institutional and architectural questions, with the Athenian BOULEUTERION and STOA, for example, serving to define notions of public space and acting as forerunners of modern civic buildings (*see* GREECE, ANCIENT, §II, 1(i)(b)). In the Middle Ages political meetings or public assemblies for the administration of justice took place primarily in the open air, in a fenced-in area (Lat. *brolium*), but also in any kind of space suited to the purpose (churches, church porches, by town gates and so on). From Carolingian times, however, a special type of building for assemblies emerged: the rectangular two-storey hall, the upper floor of which was taken up by a single chamber reached by an external staircase. This was the *pallas* of the palace of the king or emperor, the feudal prince or bishop. The medieval town hall was also based on this building type. The presiding dignitary (king, bishop or mayor) sat halfway along the long wall, with the other members of the assembly seated in rows facing him to either side. Below, markets and other forms of commercial activity took place, as well as political and legal business, in open or closed halls. In the post-medieval period new types of building emerged that tried to unite in a single place the larger number of rooms required by an increasingly complex set of public institutions. The result was such palatial buildings as the town halls of Augsburg (1615–20; *see* AUGSBURG, fig. 2) and Amsterdam (1648–55; now the Royal Palace; *see* AMSTERDAM, §V, 2; *see also* TOWN HALL, fig. 3). In other cases separate buildings were erected for individual functions (especially justice and administration). These were not always derived from the two-storey hall structure (e.g. the Palais de Justice, Rouen, 1499–1526; *see* ROUEN, fig. 2; or the Uffizi in Florence, built from 1560 as an administrative building; *see* FLORENCE, §IV, 10). In the absolutist state the prince's palace usually accommodated all political functions, with a large throne room or audience chamber forming the core of the building in a continuation of the medieval tradition.

With the evolution of the modern democratic state as a constitutional monarchy or parliamentary democracy, founded on the division of powers, distinct types of government building began to develop and gradually displaced the palace as the most prestigious secular building type. The fact that there was no established typological tradition for each of the distinct forms of government building made it difficult to find appropriate architectural forms. The efforts of such revolutionary architects as Etienne-Louis Boullée and Jean-Nicolas-Louis Durand to create new architectural types for the new functions formed a kind of experimental phase. Boullée was particularly concerned with the symbolic significance of the building's shape, while Durand was more interested in the rational, functional arrangement of the plan and superstructure. Gradually, however, architects reverted to the traditional visual features of prestigious architecture—projecting bays, porticos and especially domes—while the design of the plan tended to be derived from examples of palace architecture. Corridors with rows of separate rooms led from the centrally situated main rooms and staircase. This gave rise to structures of varying size, from the single-wing building through the four-wing arrangement with an internal courtyard to the four-wing structure with inscribed cruciform wings surrounding four or more courtyards. These patterns could be used for the most diverse functions.

Eventually a more or less standardized internal arrangement was developed for each type of government building, although the choice of architectural style remained an open and sometimes controversial question. The functional core of the modern parliament building, for example, is formed by the assembly hall or halls. In addition there are a large lobby or vestibule, rooms for ministers, deputies, the press, restaurant(s), library and cloakrooms. In the assembly hall the rows of deputies' seats are usually arranged in a semicircle before the raised podium with a lectern and government bench. This type, adopted from existing theatres and lecture halls, was used for a parliament for the first time in the Chambre des Députés (1799; altered 1828–33) in the Palais Bourbon, Paris, which was based on the Ecole de Chirurgie (1771–86; by Jacques Gondoin), also in Paris. One exception is the Houses of Parliament in London, where—in the tradition of medieval palaces and town halls—the members' benches are arranged parallel and facing each other with the Speaker at one end. The assembly rooms and side rooms generally came to be arranged symmetrically to the left and right of the central lobby, following the example of the first true new parliament building, the Federal Capitol in Washington, DC (begun 1793; *see* WASHINGTON, DC, §III, 1). Later examples include the parliament buildings in London (from 1834; by Charles Barry and A. W. N. Pugin; *see* LONDON, §V, 3(iii)), Vienna (1873–83; by Theophilus Hansen) and Budapest (1884–1904; by Imre Steindl). By contrast, there was only one chamber in the centre behind the lobby in the Reichstag building (1884–94; by Paul Wallot) in Berlin.

Stylistically, however, there was great variety in the design of parliament buildings in the 18th and 19th centuries. The parliament in Dublin (from 1729; by Edward Lovett Pearce), for example, shows the influence of the Palladian style and is modelled on the typical palace, with a *cour d'honneur* (*see* DUBLIN, fig. 3). A symmetrical palace design, extending laterally from a central domed area, was first used by William Kent in his unexecuted plan of 1735 for the parliament in London and then by William Thornton at the Federal Capitol in Washington. The structural type established at the Federal Capitol by Thornton, Benjamin Latrobe and Charles Bulfinch was used as a model for a number of American state capitols (e.g. Ohio State Capitol, Columbus, 1838–57; by Henry Walters), replacing earlier projects based on the Roman temple (e.g. Virginia State Capitol, Richmond, 1785–90; by Thomas Jefferson). However, while a classicism looking towards antiquity or English Palladianism persisted in the USA throughout the 19th century (e.g. the extension and new dome of the Federal Capitol in Washington, DC, 1851–65; by Thomas U. Walter), elsewhere there was greater stylistic diversity in the design of parliament buildings. The Palais Bourbon in Paris has a Roman peristyle (1804–7; by Bernard Poyet). For Barry's and Pugin's new Houses of Parliament in London (*see* ENGLAND, fig. 9) the Perpendicular style was chosen for its specifically English character. This in turn influenced the design of the parliament in Ottawa, Canada (1859–67; by Thomas Fuller; *see* OTTAWA, §2). At the Parlament in

1. Government building by Charles Barry: Treasury Building, London, 1845–7

Vienna, Theophilus Hansen used a mixture of Neo-classical and Renaissance stylistic elements, though with allusions to Classical Greek features in the interior as a reminder of Athenian democracy; to emphasize the classical form he did without a prestigious dome. The neo-Gothic style of the parliament in Budapest was modelled on the Houses of Parliament in London and the Rathaus in Vienna. In both competitions (1872 and 1882) for the Reichstag building in Berlin, designs using a highly decorative Baroque idiom were predominant. The design executed, by Paul Wallot, is in a monumental style based on the Roman High Baroque, with the modern addition of an angular dome in iron and glass (*see* GERMANY, fig. 10).

In the European monarchies the seat of the head of state continued to be the PALACE. In the republics, buildings that had formerly served as royal or other palaces were generally also used as the seat of the head of state or government. Examples include the Palais de l'Elysée in Paris, which became the seat of the French president in 1849, or the Hôtel de Matignon, the seat of the French prime minister from 1873. The official residence of the British prime minister at 10 Downing Street, London, was an originally fairly modest 17th-century house, enlarged in the 18th century. The most significant new building to be designed as the official residence of a state president during this period was in the archetypal modern republic, the USA. The White House in Washington (*see* WASHINGTON, DC, fig. 6), begun in 1792, was altered and enlarged in the type of a Palladian mansion by Benjamin Henry Latrobe and others in 1829. Official residences were also built in much of Africa, Asia and Australasia for the representatives there of the colonial governments. In addition to serving as administrative centres, these tended to provide a social focus for the colonial community and were often instrumental in introducing Western architectural ideals.

2. Government building by Wallace K. Harrison and others: United Nations Headquarters, New York, 1947–53

For ministries, no specific building types evolved. In many cases existing buildings, such as former nobles' palaces, were adapted in the 19th century, but the largest new ministry building was the Admiralty in St Petersburg (1806–12; by ANDREYAN ZAKHAROV). The most prestigious new ministry buildings were erected in Paris—for example, the Foreign Ministry (1845–56) on the Quai d'Orsay—and London—for example the Treasury Building (1845–7; see fig. 1) by Charles Barry, or the Foreign Office (1863–8) by George Gilbert Scott I. In both capitals the new ministries tended to be modelled on Italian High Renaissance or Baroque palaces. Often several ministries were housed in one building, as at Somerset House (1898–1912), London, or the Gesamtministerium of Saxony (1899–1904) in Dresden.

2. 1900 AND AFTER. In the established states there was little need for new government buildings in the 20th century. Those that were built, mainly in the capitals of new states, continued to be in the prestigious styles that had dominated the 19th century. In Washington, DC, until the mid-20th century ministries and other state buildings were still erected in the classical style. Elsewhere, too, in the period before World War II there was great diffidence towards new styles, with Modernism not being perceived as a means of projecting a suitable image. In Geneva, for example, the palace of the League of Nations was built in 1930 in a conventional classicist palatial idiom, instead of using Le Corbusier's prize-winning competition entry. The totalitarian states in particular fell back on a conventional classical idiom, using colonnades to achieve an imposing effect. The new Reichskanzlei in Berlin, designed by Albert Speer for Hitler in 1938–9, contained a monumental suite of rooms intended to impress foreign diplomats. In 1942, for the planned expansion of Berlin after the anticipated victory in World War II, Speer and others designed a monumental programme of government buildings along a new street axis, with eclectic motifs and allusions to a variety of historical styles. This was to culminate in a gigantic domed structure modelled on the dome of St Peter's, Rome, intended to be the largest building in the world. In the USSR, Boris Iofan planned a Palace of the Soviets (1933–41; unexecuted) as the seat of parliament; this was in the form of a stepped round tower, crowned by a gigantic statue of Lenin.

The most important government building of the immediate post-war years was the United Nations Headquarters in New York (1947–53; see fig. 2), planned and designed by an international committee under the chairmanship of Wallace K. Harrison. Here the conventional architectural approach was discarded for the first time. The building consists of a tall, thin office block and a low chamber. The high-rise administrative tower, indistinguishable from the tall commercial office building or even the residential blocks, became the accepted form for government buildings and town halls, for example in the Civic Center and Federal Center in Chicago (from 1964). In the new government buildings of Brasília (1958–60; by OSCAR NIEMEYER) and CHANDIGARH (1950–64; by Le Corbusier), significant new visual forms were derived from modern art: large-scale forms showing affinities to Minimalism in Brasília and sculptural forms in concrete in

Chandigarh. In the government buildings of Dhaka (1962–74), Louis Kahn created distinctive new types with an archaizing, timeless character. The most successful attempts at modernist designs for government buildings, however, are to be found in designs for town and city halls, especially in Boston (1962–70; by Kallmann, McKinnell & Knowles) and Toronto (1958–64; by VILJO REVELL), where two narrow, curved high-rise sections enclose the circular assembly hall. In the last decade of the 20th century, after unification, German architects were given a new opportunity to design government buildings in Berlin.

BIBLIOGRAPHY

G. Brown: *History of the United States Capitol* (Washington, DC, 1900–02)

T. Hamlin: *Greek Revival Architecture in America* (Oxford, 1944)

A. Briggs: *Victorian Cities* (London, 1963)

J. Paul: *Die mittelalterlichen Kommunalpalaste in Italien* (PhD diss., U. Freiburg im Breisgau, 1963)

J.-M. Pérouse de Montclos: *Etienne-Louis Boullée, 1728–1799: De l'architecture classique à l'architecture révolutionnaire* (Paris, 1969)

J. H. Price and P. Price: *Executive Mansions and Capitols of America* (New York, 1969)

N. Pevsner: *A History of Building Types* (London, 1976)

E. Mai, J. Paul and S. Waetzoldt, eds: *Das Rathaus im Kaiserreich, Kunst und Kultur im deutschen Kaiserreich* (Berlin, 1982)

JÜRGEN PAUL, with STEPHAN ALBRECHT

Gowan, James (*b* Glasgow, 18 Oct 1923). Scottish architect and teacher. He trained at the Glasgow School of Art (1940–42) and at Kingston School of Art (1946–8). On leaving Kingston he first joined the firm of Powell and Moya, then Stevenage New Town Corporation and finally he worked for Lyons, Israel and Ellis. At this office he met JAMES STIRLING with whom he entered into partnership in 1956. This collaboration lasted until 1964 and created some of the most important and influential post-war buildings in Britain. Their low-rise flats (1957) at Ham Common, Richmond, London, started a widespread trend of using brick and exposed concrete elements in public housing. The last project they worked on together was the Engineering School (1959–63) at Leicester University, a dramatic design with large areas of sawtooth greenhouse glazing and red brick or tile elements; it is often hailed as the building to have changed the course of British architecture away from the dominant International Style and towards a new and expressive use of materials. After 1964 Gowan worked on a number of smaller projects that received much less publicity than his earlier work. Much of his work was concerned with housing, both private and public, for example the very simple brick housing at Creek Road (1967), Greenwich, London, which is reminiscent of work by W. M. Dudok, or Trafalgar Road (1968), London. His use of elemental geometrical forms combined with meticulous detailing is exemplified in the cylindrical weekend house (1967) at St Davids, as well as the later pedimented Schreiber House (1980) at Chester. He also taught architecture, notably at the Architectural Association and Royal College of Art as well as lecturing abroad.

BIBLIOGRAPHY

D. Dunster, ed.: *James Gowan*, Architectural Monographs (London, 1978)

□

Gower, George (*b c.* 1540; *bur* London, 30 Aug 1596). English painter. Four portraits, inscribed and dated 1573, show that he was by then an accomplished artist, established in London and commanding the patronage of wealthy and well-connected sitters. *Sir Thomas Kytson* and *Lady Kytson* (see fig.; both London, Tate) are in oil on panel, and *Sir Francis Willoughby* and *Lady Willoughby* (both Lord Middleton priv. col.) on canvas; both ladies are elaborately dressed. The respective family accounts show that both pairs of portraits were paid for in September 1573 and both couples seem to have sat for Gower in London. In 1576–7 he seems to have been painting Edward Manners, 3rd Earl of Rutland.

Gower was unusual among artists of the day in being of the gentry, bearing arms as grandson of Sir John of Stettenham in Yorkshire. In his *Self-portrait* of 1579 (Milton Park, Cambs) is a pair of scales with his arms outweighed by dividers, the instrument of the painter's craft; in doggerel verse at top right he says that 'yovthfull wayes me did intyse [entice], from armes and uertewe [virtue] yet thankt be God for his god gift, w[hi]ch long did rest as slepe', meaning presumably that he had neglected his talent in early youth. But 'Now skill reuyues [revives] with gayne . . . by pensils [brushes] trade'—his profession is profitable. It is also honourable: arms display his birth, and 'what Parents bare by iust renowne, my skill mayntenes [maintains] the prayes [praise]'.

The artist's work is recognizable by its bold, clear-cut style and warmth of palette, the strongly modelled features and prominent eyes of the sitters, and plain backgrounds

George Gower: *Lady Kytson*, oil on panel, 683×521 mm, 1573 (London, Tate Gallery)

often enriched with coats of arms; in later portraits the face becomes an expressionless mask, a motif in the overall design. Gower probably painted Lady Kytson's father, *Sir Thomas Cornwallis* of Brome Hall in Suffolk, in 1577 (Audley End, Hon. R. H. C. Neville priv. col.), her sister *Mary Cornwallis c.* 1580–85 (Manchester, C.A.G.), and her daughters *Margaret, Lady Cavendish* in 1580 and *Mary, Lady Darcy* in 1583 (both ex-G. C. Golding priv. col; see Strong, 1969, pp. 176–7). Family ties linked the Kytsons, Cornwallises and Bourchiers, Earls of Bath, which may strengthen the stylistic attributions. The portrait of Sir Philip Sidney's friend *Sir Thomas Coningsby* (1572; London, N.P.G.) is in the Gower style, as is that of his wife *Dame Phillipa Coningsby* (1578; Indianapolis, IN, Herron Sch. A.). Among other plausible attributions are *Anne, Lady Fitzwilliam* (1577; Milton Park, Cambs), *Lettice, Countess of Leicester* (*c.* 1585; Longleat House, Wilts) and *Elizabeth I* (*c.* 1588; Woburn Abbey, Beds), the celebrated 'Armada' portrait (*see* ENGLAND, fig. 16). Here the theme is one of imperial triumph, and the bejewelled Queen rests her right hand on a globe; to the left and right of her head are Drake's fire-ships sailing out to meet the advancing Spanish fleet, and its ultimate shipwreck. The horizontal shape for a life-size picture of Elizabeth I is unprecedented in the history of the representation of the Queen and suggests that there had been a new sitting and format to mark the great event.

Gower was presumably highly thought of by the Queen, and there is evidence that, for a time at least, he lived at court. By patent of 5 July 1581 he had been appointed Serjeant Painter, with the customary annuity of £10 (*see* SERJEANT PAINTER). No holder of the office before Gower had been a 'painter' in the modern sense. His responsibilities ranged from decorative painting in palaces and courts of law to painting and gilding the wooden 'Queen's beasts' in the privy garden at Whitehall. In 1588–9, at Whitehall, he and his men cleaned and restored a painting of the 'discourse' of Henry VIII's coronation and his 'goinge to Bulleyne [Boulogne]' and also a 'greate table' [picture] of the King and his children Edward, Mary and Elizabeth; this is thought to be the important painting, now at Hampton Court, London, which dates from the period immediately after Holbein's death. Gower's team treated the 'discourse' and 'table' with a special varnish 'made with out sente [scent]' and in the following year, at Greenwich, painted 32 pillars with blue bice tempered with size made of rose-water 'to avoyde smell'—a reminder of the Queen's well-known dislike of strong or disagreeable odours. In 1584 Gower and Nicholas Hilliard had made an apparently concerted, but unsuccessful, attempt to secure a monopoly of royal portraiture 'in great' and 'in small compasse' respectively; however, in 1596 Gower was entrusted by the Privy Council with oversight of all portraits of the Queen. He died intestate and was buried at St Clement Danes, London.

BIBLIOGRAPHY

J. W. Goodison: 'George Gower, Serjeant Painter to Queen Elizabeth', *Burl. Mag.*, xc (1948), pp. 261–5
E. K. Waterhouse: 'A Note on George Gower's Self-portrait at Milton Park', *Burl. Mag.*, xc (1948), p. 267
E. Auerbach: *Tudor Artists* (London, 1954), pp. 52, 107–11, 113–15, 118, 130, 142, 147
R. Strong: *The English Icon: Elizabethan and Jacobean Portraiture* (London, 1969), pp. 15–16, 167–84
M. Edmond: 'Limners and Picturemakers', *Walpole Soc.*, xlvii (1980), pp. 178–82, 212, n. 541
R. Strong: *Gloriana: The Portraits of Queen Elizabeth I* (London, 1987), pp. 14–16, 74, 89, 95, 131–3

MARY EDMOND

Gower, Henry de. *See* HENRY DE GOWER.

Gower, Lord **Ronald.** *See* LEVESON-GOWER, (2).

Gowin, Emmet (*b* Danville, WV, 22 Dec 1941). American photographer. He was a student of fine arts at Richmond Professional Institute, VA, from 1961 to 1965 and at the Rhode Island School of Design, where he studied with Harry Callahan from 1965 to 1967. From the late 1960s he was also influenced by Frederick Sommer. Gowin's deeply religious upbringing played an important role in his work. Most of his photographs from the mid-1960s until the early 1980s focus upon his wife and her family in Danville, VA, transforming them into universal symbols of ritual and family relationships. Many of these are deeply personal and almost religious in the powerful symbols they evoke; in *Edith, Danville, Virginia, 1971* (see Gowin, 1976, p. 51) his wife is seen, as if clandestinely, in the privacy of a dark bedroom. His occasional use of a lens that vignettes the image into a circle also evoked ideas of a microcosm of the earth or of tourist photographs taken with an early Kodak camera.

More recent landscapes taken throughout the USA and Europe play upon symbolic and iconic places, exploring rocky and volcanic formations that suggest the earth's beginnings. A meticulous printer of his photographs, Gowin often used many techniques to manipulate delicate tonal variations.

PHOTOGRAPHIC PUBLICATIONS

Emmet Gowin: Photographs (New York, 1976)
Petra: In the Hashemite Kingdom of Jordan (New York, 1986)

BIBLIOGRAPHY

Private Realities: Recent American Photographs by Emmet Gowin (exh. cat., ed. C. Ackley; Boston, MA, Mus. F.A., 1974)
Mirrors and Windows: American Photography since 1960 (exh. cat., ed. J. Szarkowski; New York, MOMA, 1978)
A. D. Coleman: *Light Readings: A Photography Critic's Writings, 1968–1978* (New York, 1979) [essay first published in *New York Times* (30 Dec 1973)]
Photographs, 1966–1983 (exh. cat., Tempe, AZ State U., Northlight Gal., 1983)

MARY CHRISTIAN

Goya (y Lucientes), Francisco (José) de (*b* Fuendetodos, 30 March 1746; *d* Bordeaux, 16 April 1828). Spanish painter, draughtsman and printmaker. The most important Spanish artist of the last quarter of the 18th and first quarter of the 19th centuries, he served three generations of Spanish kings. Stylistically his work spans the period from the late Rococo to Romanticism and, at the last, presages Impressionism. During his six active decades he produced some 700 paintings, 900 drawings and almost 300 prints, which reflect his rapidly changing world: the Bourbon Spain of Charles III and the reign of Charles IV, the Enlightenment, the French occupation, the turmoil of the Peninsular War, the despotic reign of Ferdinand VII (and the Inquisition) and Spain's few years of constitutional government. Appreciation of his prints by non-Spaniards even during his lifetime soon ensured his reputation abroad. Known by 1801 as the 'Apelles of Spain', he has been regarded since as a major master of international stature and as the first 'modern' artist.

I. Life and work. II. Working methods and technique. III. Character and personality. IV. Critical reception and posthumous reputation.

I. Life and work.

1. Early years: Saragossa, Rome and Madrid, to 1774. 2. Goya at the Madrid court, 1774–92. 3. The mature Goya, 1793–1819. 4. Late years in Madrid, 1819–24. 5. Final years: Madrid and Bordeaux, 1824–8.

1. EARLY YEARS: SARAGOSSA, ROME AND MADRID, TO 1774. Goya moved with his parents to Saragossa, where he occasionally assisted his father, a master gilder. His education began in the school of the Piarist Father Joaquín; his fellow pupil Martín Zapater y Clavería (1752–1803) became a close friend, and Goya's later correspondence with him (1775–99) remains important source material. In his teens Goya studied in Saragossa with José Luzán Martínez (1710–85), who had painted in Naples when it was under the rule of the future King Charles III of Spain. Luzán's pupils included Francisco and Ramón Bayeu, Goya's future colleagues and brothers-in-law. Goya remembered his four years with Luzán as largely spent in copying prints, then a common practice designed to develop mastery in drawing. His earliest known work in oils, variously dated from 1758 to 1769, was the painting of a small reliquary cabinet in his baptismal church at Fuendetodos (destr. 1936; see GW, no. 1).

In January 1764 and again in 1766 Goya entered the competitions of the Real Academia de Bellas Artes de S Fernando in Madrid but failed in both attempts; he then went to Rome. While studying what he later called Rome's 'celebrated' paintings, he perhaps observed as Taddäus Kuntz painted in oils, tempera and fresco. In 1771, declaring himself a pupil of Francisco Bayeu, Goya submitted from Rome to the annual Parma Accademia competition his *Victorious Hannibal Seeing Italy for the First Time from the Alps* (Cudillero, Selgas-Fagalde Found.), following the stipulated theme. It came second, despite favourable votes and commendations. He was once more in Saragossa by June 1771, having asked for his *Hannibal* to be sent to him in Spain.

Of paintings attributed to Goya's early years, a *Sacrifice to Pan* reflects 18th-century classical compositions by, among others, Jacob de Wit, and a *Sacrifice to Vesta* of 1771 (both Barcelona, J. Gudiol Ricart priv. col., see GW no. 22) recalls a sacrifice scene etched by Giovanni Battista Tiepolo *c.* 1757–62 for his *Scherzi di fantasia* (see H. D. Russell: *Rare Etchings by G. B. and G. D. Tiepolo*, Washington, DC, 1972, nos 50–51). Goya's early historical and biblical compositions resemble works by Sebastiano Conca, whose paintings were known at the Spanish court.

Saints and religious scenes painted in oils on the walls of the chapel of the Casa de Sobradiel, Saragossa (1770–72; dispersed), are based on prints after Simon Vouet (*Burial of Christ*, Madrid, Mus. Lázaro Galdiano), Carlo Maratti (*St Joseph's Dream*, Saragossa, Mus. Zaragoza, based on an etching by Maratti after one of his own paintings) and Correggio. The volumetrically conceived figures, concern for light and shade and Goya's colouring, settings and techniques also reflect the art of Antonio González Velázquez, active in Madrid and Saragossa, as well as that of González's master, Corrado Giaquinto. Their influence is discernible in Goya's earliest Saragossa fresco commission, the *Adoration of the Name of God*, completed by June 1772 on a vault ceiling in the Cathedral of Nuestra Señora del Pilar (*in situ*).

Goya's major early religious series, the *Life of the Virgin*, was painted in oils high up on the walls of the Carthusians' monastery church of Aula Dei (*in situ*), near Saragossa, and completed in 1774. Obeying the requirements of perspective and lighting, the huge, framed scenes with their monumental, classically inspired figures convincingly offer a 'view into the heavens'. His earliest etching, *Flight into Egypt* (*c.* 1774–5; GW no. 52), similarly concerned with modelling and chiaroscuro, was perhaps associated with the Aula Dei project.

2. GOYA AT THE MADRID COURT, 1774–92. In July 1773 Goya had married Josefa Bayeu in Madrid but had continued to work in Saragossa; late in 1774, however, he was called to Madrid to paint for the Real Fábrica de Tapices de Santa Bárbara. Under Francisco Bayeu's direction, he produced large oil-on-canvas cartoons from which tapestries destined for the royal palaces could be made. Between 1774 and June 1792 Goya submitted 63 cartoons. Nine hunting scenes completed in 1775 for the dining-room of the Princes of Asturias at the Escorial adhere to the required format and fashion and are distinguishable from Ramón Bayeu's cartoons primarily through documentation; Goya's few preparatory figure drawings (Madrid, Bib. N., Inst. Valencia Don Juan, Prado; Boston, MA, Mus. F.A.) do not disclose any individuality either. However, as his son (Francisco) Javier Goya y Bayeu (1784–1854) reported in 1832 (see Canellas López, 1981), Goya's early 'extraordinary' facility in painting tapestry cartoons astonished the Neo-classical painter Anton Raphael Mengs. Goya exercised greater compositional invention and showed increasing confidence in design and colour in the genre scenes he painted from 1776 for the Palacio del Pardo tapestries, for example the *Picnic* (Madrid, Prado). The cartoons of 1786–8 depict seasonal and current activities; the *Pradera de San Isidro* (1788; Madrid, Prado), a wide landscape oil sketch (which he admitted in a letter of 31 May to Zapater (AS, p. 182) that he found difficult), charmingly shows crowds of people enjoying their patron saint's feast day near the Hermitage of St Isidore across the river from Madrid, whose buildings shimmer in the sunlit distance. Goya's final cartoons, of 1791–2, are the rural and humorous scenes that Charles IV had requested for his Escorial office, though a new mood approaching the satirical is intimated in the *Wedding* and *Blanket-tossing* (both 1791–2; Madrid, Prado).

A cartoon of 1778, the *Blind Guitarist* (Madrid, Prado), inspired Goya's largest etching (see GW, no. 87), the composition of which is simpler than the cartoon version. As prints after paintings (especially those in royal collections) were in demand, in 1778 he began to offer for sale his etchings after paintings by Diego Velázquez. Apart from *Bacchus* (after Velázquez's *Feast of Bacchus*, 1629;

Madrid, Prado; see J. Brown, *Velázquez*, London, 1986, pl. 69), his 19 prints present royal and court portraits, including *Las meninas* (after Velazquez's painting, 1656; Madrid, Prado; B pl. 10). Around this time Goya also etched the *Garroted Man* (late 1770s; GW no. 122), a powerful and original image that resembles the work of Tiepolo in its etching technique.

In May 1780 Goya was elected to the Real Academia de Bellas Artes de S Fernando in Madrid. His painting of the *Crucifixion* (1780; Madrid, Prado), presented with his application for membership, reflects the academicism of Mengs. Goya's growing independence was asserted, however, in another commission for the Cathedral of Nuestra Señora del Pilar, Saragossa, where he painted the cupola frescoes of the *Virgin, Queen of Martyrs* (1780–81; *in situ*). His initial sketches for the pendentive designs, *Faith, Patience, Fortitude* and *Charity* (Saragossa, Mus. Catedral), displeased the cathedral authorities, and he was forced to submit revisions to Francisco Bayeu. Goya's reaction to this experience is well documented (*see* §III below).

During this period, however, Goya triumphed over competing artists (including Francisco Bayeu) with his altarpiece of *St Bernardino of Siena Preaching before Alfonso V of Aragon* (1781–3; Madrid, S Francisco el Grande). In this well-received painting, whose composition recalls Michel-Ange Houasse's *St Francis Regis Preaching* (Madrid, Prado), Goya proudly included himself among the saint's audience. He was commissioned to paint the *Death of St Joseph, SS Bernard and Robert* and *St Lutgard* for the convent church of S Anna, Valladolid (1787; *in situ*), and *St Francis Borgia and the Dying Impenitent* and *St Francis Borgia Taking Leave of his Family* for the St Francis Borgia chapel in Valencia Cathedral (both 1788; *in situ*). The Valladolid paintings are quietly classical in form and mood and are appropriate for the new church's Neo-classical architecture, while those at Valencia, commissioned by the 9th Duque de Osuna for the family chapel, include Goya's first depictions of netherworld monsters in a dramatic scene of exorcism.

By the 1780s Goya was becoming increasingly successful as a portrait painter. He again included himself in two paintings of 1783, though now as an artist and in proximity to major figures: presenting a sketch to the *Conde de Floridablanca* (Madrid, Banco Urquijo, see GW, no. 203); and seated at his canvas before the candle-lit portrayal, a large though intimate conversation piece, of the *Infante Don Luis and his Family* (1783; Parma, Corte Mamiano Found., see GW, no. 208). During this decade Goya masterfully portrayed other members of the court, including children, in such works as *María Teresa de Borbón* (1784; Washington, DC, N.G.A.) and *Manuel Osorio de Zúñiga* (1788; New York, Met.). The Osuna family became increasingly important as patrons (*Duque de Osuna*, 1785; England, priv. col., see GW no. 219; *Condesa-Duquesa de Benavente*, 1785; Madrid, Bartolomé March priv. col., see GW, no. 220; the *Family of the Duque de Osuna*, 1788; Madrid, Prado); among his other aristocratic portraits are the *Marquesa de Pontejos* (1786; Washington, DC, N.G.A.) and the *Condesa de Altamira with her Daughter María Agustina* (1787–8; New York, Met.). He also portrayed professionals and scholars, for instance the architect *Ventura Rodríguez* (1784; Stockholm, Nmus.) and the writer and collector *Juan Agustín Ceán Bermúdez* (*c*. 1785; Madrid, Conde de Cienfuegos priv. col., see GW no. 222). For Ceán Bermúdez's *Diccionario histórico de los más ilustres profesores de las bellas artes en España* (Madrid, 1800), which was published without illustrations, Goya prepared several portrait drawings (GW nos 697–707).

From 1785 Goya was deputy director of painting in the Real Academia, and in July 1786 he was appointed Pintor del Rey; in May 1787 he was granted an amanuensis and a colour-grinder. Among his royal portraits is a sympathetic depiction of *Charles III Dressed as a Hunter* (*c*. 1788; Madrid, Duquesa de Arco priv. col., see GW, no. 230), depicting the King as ruddy-faced, affable and homely. He was now extremely busy, and he wrote to Zapater in July 1788 (AS p. 184) that he would prefer some tranquillity and time for things of his own taste. With Charles III's death, however, and the accession of Charles IV and his Queen, María Luisa, early in 1789, Goya was immediately asked for portraits of the new monarchs, and in April 1789 they appointed him Primer Pintor de Cámara.

Goya continued to work on tapestry cartoons despite a reluctance shared by his co-worker Ramón Bayeu. Both perhaps suspected a health hazard in the work, and both became ill during the winter of 1792–3. Ramón Bayeu died at Aranjuez in March, and Goya went to Cádiz to spend several months with the collector Sebastián Martínez Pérez, whose portrait he painted (1792; New York, Met.). He slowly recuperated but with total loss of hearing.

3. THE MATURE GOYA, 1793–1819.

(i) 1793–1800. (ii) 1801–12. (iii) 1813–18.

(i) 1793–1800. Goya returned to Madrid weakened and deaf in 1793. He asserted that he was unable to resume work on the large tapestry cartoons, and he turned to more manageable and more personal projects, perhaps inspired by works from abroad that he had seen while in Cádiz. His small 'cabinet' pictures of 1793–4 introduce a new vein in his art, and it was now that his individual genius began to emerge. In January 1794 he sent to the Real Academia 14 small paintings on tinplate (designated as for the Marqués de Villaverde) with a note stating that they had been painted in part to recompense costs incurred while he was ill but also to occupy his mind, blunted by sickness. He said that in them he had been able to make 'observations' not usually possible in commissioned works, which did not allow invention or caprice (CL p. 34). Many of the scenes depict entertainments: bullfighting, outdoor theatre and local genre. Such other subjects as *The Deluge* (1793–4; Madrid, Plácido Arango Arias priv. col., see GW, no. 328), *The Madhouse* (1794; Dallas TX, S. Methodist U., Meadows Mus. & Gal.) and a dramatic *Fire at Night* (1793–4; San Sebastián, J. Varez priv. col., see GW no. 329) show an alertness to themes popular abroad in Romantic art and literature. These cabinet pictures were succeeded *c*. 1798 by six painted for the Duquesa de Osuna to decorate the Alameda of Osuna, near Madrid, including the *Witches' Sabbath* (Madrid, Mus. Lázaro Galdiano), its dark and dramatic though humorous scenes drawn from tales of witchcraft and from theatre presentations.

Goya wrote to Zapater in April 1794 that he experienced alternating periods of hyperactivity and of tranquillity

(AS p. 218). In a *Self-portrait* of *c.* 1790–95 (Madrid, Real Acad. S Fernando, Mus.) he depicted himself standing at his easel against the white light of a window wearing the candle-rimmed hat that he used when daylight had faded. His return to full-scale portraiture of court figures resulted in such works as the *Duque and Duquesa de Alba* (1795; Madrid, Real Acad. S Fernando, Mus.), *Mariana Waldstein, Marquesa de Santa Cruz* (1797–8; Paris, Louvre) and the *Marqués de Bondad Real* (1799; New York, Hisp. Soc. America). Other portraits of this period reflect Spain in the context of the Enlightenment, liberalism, revolution and war, such as his depictions of statesmen and military officials, for example the Minister *Gaspar Melchor de Jovellanos* (1798; Madrid, Prado), the French Ambassador *Ferdinand Guillemardet* (1799; Paris, Louvre) and *General Don José de Urrutia* (*c.* 1798; Madrid, Prado). Similar concerns are also reflected in his portraits of the Spanish intellectuals *Bernardo de Iriarte* (1797; Strasbourg, Mus. B.-A.), *Juan Meléndez Valdés* (*c.* 1797; Barnard Castle, Bowes Mus.) and *Leandro Fernández de Moratín* (1799; Madrid, Real Acad. S Fernando, Mus.) as well as the painter *Ascensió Juliá* (1798; Lugano, Col. Thyssen-Bornemisza) and several bullfighters.

From May 1796 until April 1797 Goya was in Andalusia, and by July 1796 he was staying at the Alba estate in Sanlúcar de Barrameda. This provided the setting for one of his most important portraits, that of the *Duquesa de Alba* (1797; New York, Hisp. Soc. America; for illustration *see* ALBA). She had been widowed in June 1796 and is seen in black *maja* dress. The names 'Goya' and 'Alba' on her rings and the words 'Solo Goya' traced in the sand at her feet testify to a close relationship between the artist and Madrid's reigning beauty. He retained this portrait until giving it to his son in 1812. The Sanlúcar visit also resulted in Goya's sketchbook, Album A or the Sanlúcar Album (1796–7; dispersed), in which with brush and grey wash he recorded intimate moments observed, as in the *Duquesa de Alba Holding María de la Luz* (ink and wash; Madrid, Prado). He developed these homely themes in a second, larger sketchbook continued in Madrid, Album B or the Madrid Album (1796–7; dispersed). At about midpoint, however, he turned to satire, caricature and social commentary, which he elaborated with brief but cogent penned inscriptions, for instance in *Happy Caricature* (ink and wash; Madrid, Prado). The two sketchbooks were Goya's source for the *Caprichos* prints, published in February 1799. This masterfully executed series, satirizing the follies of contemporary Spanish society in terms that are universally understandable and applicable, brought him international attention. It was his expressed hope that his 80 captioned *Caprichos* would help to remove harmful beliefs: he aimed to perpetuate a testimony of truth by censuring, through ridicule, human errors, extravagances and vices (see fig. 1). The frontispiece to the *Caprichos* is a *Self-portrait* in which Goya depicted himself in profile, as if in the role of observer and interpreter. In plate 43, however, a different self appears: a man, menaced by looming demons and burying his head in his arms, droops over a desk that bears the warning *The Sleep of Reason Produces Monsters* (*see* AQUATINT, fig. 2). This image was initially planned to introduce the series, but instead it marks a shift of focus in the volume towards scenes of witchcraft and madness. These disturbing visions are open to various interpretations, though the moralizing quality of Goya's intentions is clear (*see also* §III below).

1. Francisco de Goya: *Because She Was Susceptible*, aquatint, 215×150 mm, pl. 32 of the *Caprichos*, 1799

While in Andalusia Goya also executed three large semicircular paintings of scenes from the *Life of Christ* for placement high on the walls of the Oratory of S Cueva, Cádiz (1796–7; *in situ*). The simplicity of the compositions, the poses of the figures and the primary colours in the *Last Supper* recall Nicolas Poussin's *Eucharist* (1647; Duke of Sutherland priv. col., on dep. Edinburgh, N.G.), though Goya's more earthy figure types prevail, most noticeably in the *Miracle of the Loaves and Fishes.* The third scene represents the *Parable of the Guest without a Wedding Garment.*

Goya's next major religious project was the dramatic and brilliantly coloured frescoes (1798; *in situ*) in the Hermitage church of S Antonio de la Florida, Madrid. A preparatory sketch (oil on canvas, Madrid, priv. col., see GW, no. 718) for the circular cupola fresco also survives. On the ceiling of the cupola he depicted the *Miracle of St Anthony of Padua* in the form of a circular *trompe l'oeil* scene in which the participants, actively engaged in the event, are contemporary Madrilenian figures; angels on the walls below are shown as robust, theatrically lit women who look up towards the miracle. It is a very personal and inspired interpretation, but Goya's reversal of the positions of the heavenly and earthly zones and the transposition of the miracle into his own time brought criticism. The *Betrayal of Christ* (1798; Toledo Cathedral, Sacristy) nonetheless won the praise of fellow Academicians and of Jovellanos, who had helped Goya obtain the S Antonio commission. Figures and settings of a contemporary character also appear in Goya's allegorical paintings of these years, as in the circular *Industry*, *Agriculture* and *Commerce* (1797–1800; all Madrid, Prado), which were painted for Manuel Godoy's palace in Madrid, and as in *Poetry* and *Truth, Time and History* (both *c*. 1797–1800; Stockholm, Nmus.).

The *Naked Maja* was certainly owned by Godoy by 1800, as was (by 1808 at the least) its companion *Clothed Maja* (both 1797–1805; Madrid, Prado; see fig. 2). The reclining pose of the young Spanish woman in both pictures is simultaneously inviting yet matter-of-fact; it reflects an 18th-century licentiousness as seen, for example, in Gabriel-Jacques de Saint-Aubin's *L'Académie particulière* print (see *La Peinture dans la peinture*, exh. cat., Dijon, Mus. B.A., 1983, p. 197, no. 349) that shows a similarly posed female. In May 1815 Goya was summoned before the Tribunal of the Inquisition, which proscribed depiction of the female nude and which was aware of those from Godoy's collection (including the *Maja*); however, Goya escaped penalty.

Goya's portrait of Godoy's wife, *Dona María Teresa de Borbón y Vallabriga, Condesa de Chinchón* (1800; Madrid, Duke of Sueca priv. col., see GW no. 793), brilliantly captures her sadness and fragility during pregnancy. A connection with Godoy is implicit in the large and important *Family of Charles IV* (1800; Madrid, Prado; see fig. 3), in which the lighting and her central position focus attention on the most powerful person in the family, Queen María Luisa, whose close relationship with Godoy became notorious. Goya spent the spring of 1800 in Aranjuez making oil sketches (Madrid, Prado) for this awesome official family portrait, in which the dozen royal personages stand in glittering dress looking outwards; Goya is seen in the shadow at the left standing before a large easel, evoking Velázquez's self-portrait in the less formal *Las meninas*, which Goya had copied and etched in 1778. Goya's merciless characterization of the Queen and King affirmed his respect for truth and for nature, which he believed consisted not only of that which was visable but also that which the mind understood.

(ii) 1801–12. During the opening years of the 19th century Spain was ruled by the infamous unholy 'Trinity' (Charles IV, María Luisa and Godoy); the period of Napoleonic occupation from 1808 was followed by the Peninsular War. Goya remained active primarily as a portrait painter. His depiction of *Manuel Godoy, Príncipe de la Paz* (1801; Madrid, Real Acad. S Fernando, Mus.) shows the bloated officer relaxing pensively in military dress while encamped after the victory over Portugal.

Goya also portrayed other distinguished sitters in fine portraits: for example the *Conde de Fernán Núñez* and *Condesa de Fernán Núñez* (1803; Madrid, Fernán Núñez priv. col., see GW, nos 807–8) and the *Marquesa de Villafranca* (1804; Madrid, Prado); the last-mentioned is depicted painting a portrait of her husband. *Joaquina Téllez Girón, Marquesa de Santa Cruz* (1805; Madrid, Prado) is shown as a high-spirited Euterpe reclining with her lyre in a pose that recalls Classical art discovered not long before at Herculaneum. Soldiers also sat for him, as did the actor *Isidoro Máiquez* (1807; Madrid, Prado) and the singer *Pedro Mocarte* (*c*. 1805–6; New York, Hisp. Soc. America).

In 1805 the marriage of Goya's son Javier to Gumersinda Goicoechea prompted a group of personal family portraits: four small drawings, including *Javier Goya* (1805; Madrid, Marqués de Casa Torres priv. col., see GW,

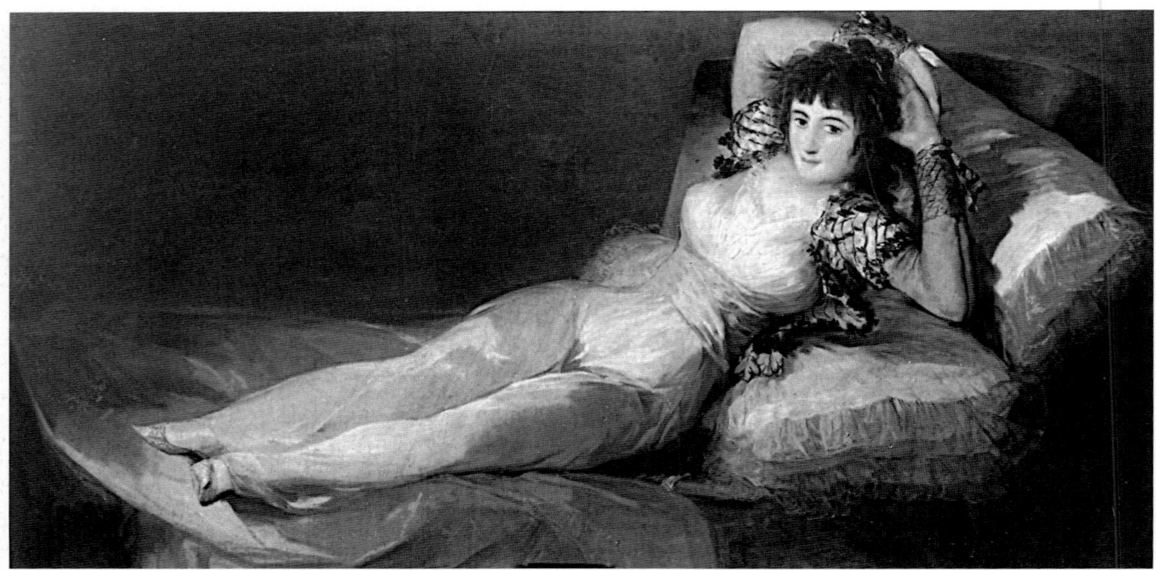

2. Francisco de Goya: *Clothed Maja*, oil on canvas, 0.94×1.90 m, 1797–1805 (Madrid, Museo del Prado)

3. Francisco de Goya: *Family of Charles IV*, oil on canvas, 2.80×3.36 m, 1800 (Madrid, Museo del Prado)

no. 843), and some seven circular miniatures painted in oils, for example *Gerónima Goicoechea* (1805; Providence, RI, Sch. Des., Mus. A.). All are of exceptional charm, intimacy and freedom of line and brushwork.

Following Charles IV's abdication in March 1808 the Real Academia de Bellas Artes de S Fernando in Madrid commissioned from Goya a portrait of Charles's son, *Ferdinand VII on Horseback* (1808; Madrid, Real Acad. S. Fernando, Mus.). Then in late December 1809 the city asked him for a portrait of Joseph Bonaparte, the brother Napoleon had installed on the Spanish throne. Within two months Goya completed his large *Allegory of Madrid* (1810; Madrid, Mus. Mun.), portraying Joseph in an oval medallion towards which the allegorical female figure of Madrid calmly points. But when constitutional government triumphed in 1812 the word 'Constitution' replaced Joseph's portrait. Reinstated by Felipe Abas (a Goya pupil; *see* §IV below) when Joseph returned to the throne, it was again replaced by 'Constitution' in 1813; and when Ferdinand reassumed the throne in 1814, his portrait replaced 'Constitution'. Finally in 1872 the words '2nd of May' were inscribed in the medallion.

In 1810 Goya portrayed the French general *Nicholas Guye* (1810; Richmond, VA, Mus. F.A.). Then, following the entry of Arthur Wellesley, 1st Duke of Wellington, into Madrid in August 1812, Goya painted his equestrian portrait (1812; London, Apsley House), which was exhibited in September in the Real Academia.

Goya's unofficial works of this period include such etchings as *Landscape with Waterfall* (1800–06; Madrid, Bib. N.) and such drawings as a *Balloon-launching Scene* (black chalk, 1800–08; Hamburg, Ksthalle). He also produced an architectural design (brush and India ink, *c*. 1802–3; Madrid, Berganza de Martin priv. col., see GW no. 759) for the tomb of his beloved Duquesa de Alba (*d* 1802). On six small panels he serialized in oils the *Capture of El Maragato by Friar Pedro* (1806–7; Chicago, IL, A. Inst.). Other small paintings dramatically present acts of primitive savagery as well as murky prison and hospital scenes, such as *Plague Hospital* (1808–12; Madrid, Marqués de la Romana priv. col., see GW, no. 919). This recalls John Flaxman's *Vale of Disease*, an illustration for Dante's *Inferno* (H. F. Carey, trans.: *The Vision; or Hell, Purgatory and Paradise of Dante Alighieri*, London, 1819, i, facing

p. 225); among Goya's drawings of 1800–08 are six after other Flaxman prints (Madrid, Bib. N.; Madrid, Prado) including *Religious Submission* (brush and India ink; Paris, priv. col., see GW no. 764).

During the Peninsular War Goya was called to a besieged Saragossa in October 1808 to paint its citizens' 'glorious deeds' against the French armies. He recorded the atrocities and horrors he saw in drawings and small paintings, and these formed the basis for his print series, *Disasters of War*, begun by 1810.

In June 1812 Goya's wife, Josefa, died. Their estate was divided that October between husband and son; Javier received all the paintings and prints, possibly because Goya planned to flee to a 'free' country if the French returned (as they did early in November). Many of the paintings numbered and listed by title or subject in the division agreement are identifiable, thus establishing their pre-1812 dates. Until then Goya retained several portraits, notably the aforementioned one of the *Duquesa de Alba* (1797). Others included *Celestina and her Daughter* (*c*. 1808–12; Madrid, Bertolomé March priv. col., see GW, no. 958); such genre scenes as *The Water-carrier* and *The Knife-grinder* (both *c*. 1808–12; Budapest, Mus. F.A.); small paintings of banditry and war; paintings of saints; a dozen still-lifes of food, among them *Dead Turkey* (1808–12; Madrid, Prado); and allegorical paintings, including one entitled 'giant' (probably the *Colossus*, *c*. 1808–12; Madrid, Prado), and *Time and the Old Women* (*c*. 1810–12; Lille, Mus. B.-A.), in which the main figure of an aged hag is a thinly veiled portrait of Queen María Luisa.

(iii) 1813–18. With Ferdinand's return to the throne in 1814, Goya again fulfilled royal commissions (e.g. *Ferdinand VII in a Royal Cape*, 1814–15; Madrid, Prado). That year he was challenged about his sympathies during the French occupation, and in March he astutely requested official permission to immortalize Spain's 'glorious insurrection' against Napoleon, the 'tyrant' of Europe. Six years after the events he painted two large canvases, the *Second of May 1808* and the *Third of May 1808* (both 1814; Madrid, Prado). In the former, which depicts an event he may have witnessed and which predates by a decade Eugène Delacroix's similar paintings of combat, he vividly portrayed the maelstrom of colour and violent action erupting as knife-wielding Spaniards on foot attacked Mameluke horsemen brandishing swords in the Puerta del Sol in the centre of Madrid. The terrifyingly stark *Third of May* (see fig. 4) illustrates the execution of captured Spaniards by firing squad that took place the following night on the Príncipe Pío hill, then on the outskirts of the city. Though the composition recalls prints by others (including one by Miguel Gamborino published in 1813),

4. Francisco de Goya: *Third of May 1808*, oil on canvas, 2.66×3.45 m, 1814 (Madrid, Museo del Prado)

Goya's *Third of May* creates a potent image in which the group is dramatically lit within the overwhelming dark of night, contrasting the terror of the victims with the facelessness of the executioners, an image which was to inspire several later artists including Edouard Manet.

Goya's 82 *Disasters of War* prints, on which he worked from 1810 until 1820, were etched from red chalk preparatory drawings. They record moments during the Peninsular War and its aftermath while compellingly projecting universally appalling horrors. The initial scenes illustrate the death and destruction Goya witnessed when called to Saragossa in October 1808, each print bearing a succinct comment: *This I Saw* (pl. 44), *All This and More* (pl. 7), *Bury Them and Keep Quiet* (pl. 16) and, simply, *Why?* (pl. 49). With plate 48 (*The Same*) there appear less violent scenes of devastation and death that he observed during the famine of 1811–12 in Madrid. Plates 65 to 77 present bitterly satirical and anti-clerical 'emphatic caprices', such as *This Is the Worst of All* (pl. 74). The personification of Truth as an innocent young woman (the *Death of Truth* and *Will She Arise Again?*, pls 79–80) culminates in the final plate (*This Is the Truth*, pl. 82), in which she is standing before an aureole of light in a peaceful countryside accompanied by a bearded, bent farmer and a lamb. This scene might be considered an affirmation of Voltaire's conclusion to *Candide* ('we must cultivate our garden') and, by extension, an affirmation of the belief that Adam's neglect in cultivating the gardens of Paradise led to the suffering from which humanity could be redeemed only through Christ, son of the Virgin, here evoked in Goya's figure of Truth.

With the resurrection of Truth and allied implications of peace inherent in the series, the *Disasters* could hardly be published while Ferdinand and the Inquisition ruled; they remained unpublished until 1863. Three additional small etchings (GW 986, 988, 920), made *c.* 1810–20, presenting ragged prisoners chained and manacled, were also associated with the series.

Goya said he had no funds in 1814 when he proposed painting the *Second of May* and *Third of May* and was reported to be impoverished in 1815. In October 1816 he announced the sale of his *Tauromaquia* ('Art of Bullfighting') prints. His draughtsmanship, and his focus on essentials in illustrating historical and contemporary events in Spanish bullfighting, created a series that is exceptional in seeming to record a series of instants in the action, drama and excitement of the bullfight. One of the boldest compositions is *Charles II Spearing a Bull in the Ring at Valladolid* (pl. 10), notable for its thrusting movement. The *Tauromaquia* was soon followed by the *Disparates* ('Absurdities', or 'Follies'), 22 prints made between 1816 and 1824. The title is derived from the first word of the brief inscriptions Goya penned on some proofs. Etched on English copperplates identical in size with those of the *Tauromaquia*, one print of men flying that is usually associated with the *Disparates* (as pl. 13) is found bound at the conclusion of at least one *Tauromaquia* set (as pl. 34). Never completed, as unetched red chalk and wash drawings attest, the *Disparates* evidently proved as unviable as the *Disasters*. They were eventually published in 1864 as the *Proverbios*, as their subjects were by then associated with Spanish proverbs. In the absence of explanatory texts they are Goya's most enigmatic prints, presenting complex, mystifying, often stage-like scenes that resist interpretation and understanding, such as *Poor Folly* (pl. 11) and *Carnival Folly* (pl. 14).

Goya's many drawings of these years, spontaneously rendering the life he saw and that of his imagination, were essentially brushed in black and sepia wash in several sketchbooks, or 'albums', none of which is dated securely. The 133 drawings of Album C (1808–20; 120 in Madrid, Prado) show one or a few figures illustrating the captions he inscribed on each sheet, such as *Do Not Open your Eyes* (ink and sepia, 1823; Madrid, Prado). This album begins with depictions of common human traits, faults and foibles that stimulate thought; then follow caricature-like images (e.g. *Comic Vision*, India ink wash; Madrid, Prado), scenes and figures from daily life and of witchcraft in more intense chiaroscuro and scenes of the persecution, imprisonment and torture inflicted by the Inquisition. In the final pages, reflecting constitutional victory, the welcome arrival of Divine Liberty, Light, Justice and Reason (e.g. *Light of Justice*, India ink wash; Madrid, Prado) is followed by drawings of nuns and priests discarding their clerical dress in order to re-enter secular life.

The 18 known Album D drawings (1812–20; dispersed) that also bear Goya's captions repeat some of the themes of Album C along with burlesque and satirical compositions, although the figures become more isolated on the page (e.g. *Wicked Woman*, ink and grey wash; Paris, Louvre), a characteristic continued in the carefully composed black-bordered drawings (also captioned) of Album E (1814–24; dispersed). Consisting of more than 50 drawings, possibly the finest Goya ever made, this album reveals him again choosing aspects of the world and of his imagination to comment on and illustrate moral observations. A symbolic image of great beauty is seen in *Resignation* (ink and wash, 1814–24; Boston, MA, Mus. F.A.).

The more than 90 known sepia-wash drawings of Album F (1817–24; dispersed, some in Madrid, Prado) lack captions and vary widely in subject. They include religious compositions and scenes of witchcraft, prisons, torture, savagery and misery (e.g. *Poverty*, Madrid, Prado) as well as duelling, hunting and more prosaic daily occupations; there is one drawing of a young female figure, *Truth Beset by Dark Spirits* (no. 45; New York, Met.), that is perhaps related to plates 79 and 80 of the *Disasters of War*.

During the period 1815–19 Goya's portraits were mostly bust and half-length. Among his subjects were members of the court and distinguished secular and clerical personalities. He also depicted the engraver *Rafael Esteve y Vilella* (1815; Valencia, Mus. B.A.), his young grandson *Mariano Goya* (1813–14; Madrid, Duke of Alburquerque priv. col., see GW, no. 1553), shown as a charming figure in a high hat before a sheet of music, and himself aged 69 (1815; versions in Madrid, Real Acad. S Fernando, Mus.; Madrid, Prado, see fig. 5). Some portraits of court figures were perhaps associated with his huge canvas the *Meeting of the Company of the Philippines* (1815; Castres, Mus. Goya), in which he endowed what might otherwise have been a routine, static scene with considerable force, colour and drama. This is seen in the implied vastness of the setting,

5. Francisco de Goya: *Self-portrait*, oil on canvas, 460×350 mm, 1815 (Madrid, Museo del Prado)

its perspectival depth leading to the small, centrally placed figure of Ferdinand VII presiding in the distance and in the way the light falls across the floor from lateral windows, touching only those seated at the sides of the room.

Although commissions for religious paintings diminished, in 1816–17 Goya painted in tempera for the royal apartments of Isabel of Braganza, second wife of Ferdinand VII, a relief-like, theatrically lit scene in grisaille, *St Elizabeth of Hungary Tending a Sick Woman* (1816–17; Madrid, Pal. Real). In 1817, encouraged by Ceán Bermúdez, he painted for Seville Cathedral a large, oil-on-canvas *SS Justa and Rufina* (Sacristy). While it might evoke comparison with Bartolomé Esteban Murillo's treatment of the same subject (*c.* 1665–6; Seville, Mus. B.A.), which Goya had seen in the Cathedral with Ceán, it is clearly of its own time in the use of colour and in the upward-glancing, contemporary faces of the two young women who portray the saints.

4. Late years in Madrid, 1819–24. Early in 1819 Goya experimented with lithography, then newly introduced in Madrid. Initially he produced only a few proofs: an *Old Woman Spinning* (dated February), a duelling scene repeating an Album F drawing, two scenes of couples fighting, two multi-figured compositions on the theme of the Inferno perhaps associated with his *Disparates* project, and possibly the genre groups, *Monk* and another *Duel*, often assigned to his years in Bordeaux. In late February 1819 he bought the suburban Madrid property already called the Quinta del Sordo ('Deaf man's country house').

In May 1819 Goya was commissioned by the Escolapian Order (teaching Piarists) to paint the *Last Communion of St Joseph Calasanz* for a chapel in the church of S Antón (*in situ*), Madrid. He imbued the scene with deep religious pathos; and he returned much of his fee out of respect for St Joseph, founder of the Order. He also gave the Piarists (who helped to teach the deaf to speak) a small *Agony in the Garden* (1819; Madrid, S Antón), which he said would be the last picture he would 'make' in Madrid. Late in 1819, as many Spaniards contracted the *peste* (apparently yellow fever), Goya was seriously ill. The ex-voto-like painting *Goya and his Doctor, Don Eugenio Garcia Arrieta* (1820; Minneapolis, MN, Inst. A.) documents his bedridden condition; its inscription pragmatically renders his gratitude to the physician who effected his recovery.

Goya was recuperating at a time when the liberals' victory of January 1820 forced Ferdinand VII to accept the Constitution. Goya's response to constitutional freedom is witnessed in the 14 *'Black Paintings'* (1820–23;

6. Francisco de Goya: *'Saturn'*, mural painting transferred to canvas, 1460×830 mm, 1820–23 (Madrid, Museo del Prado)

Madrid, Prado) that he executed on the walls of two rooms in his country house, the Quinta del Sordo. Dark in tone, mood and subject, these sometimes horrifying yet edifying scenes (transferred to canvas and restored in the 1870s) include *Witches' Sabbath*, the *Holy Office* (of the Inquisition), *The Fates*, *Old Woman and Skeletal Figure Eating*, *Judith and Holofernes* and *'Saturn'* (see fig. 6). Then, as the return of Ferdinand and the Inquisition became imminent in September 1823, Goya gave the house, with its paintings, to his grandson Mariano Goya y Goicoechea (1806–74).

5. FINAL YEARS: MADRID AND BORDEAUX, 1824–8. From 1824 Goya painted only some 20 oils on canvas, mostly easel-size and more than half portraits. In Madrid he struggled with the likeness of *José Duaso y Latre* (1824; Seville, Mus. B.A.); he and others found refuge with Duaso during the winter and spring of 1824, and Goya also portrayed two of Duaso's nephews, one in a miniature-like pencil drawing, *Francisco Otín* (Madrid, J. Rodríguez Babé priv. col., see GW no. 634). The black chalk portrait of his son *Javier Goya* (New York, Lehman col., see GW no. 1636), and an ink and sepia circular *Self-portrait* (Madrid, Prado), thought to have been penned in Paris some months later, are also miniatures; such portraits were easily carried remembrances.

Following Ferdinand's declaration of an amnesty for constitutionalist sympathizers, Goya was granted permission to leave for France, ostensibly for health reasons. Arriving in Bordeaux late in June 1824, he departed for Paris three days later. He remained there with relatives throughout August, visiting other Spanish émigrés; he portrayed *Manuela Álvarez Coiñas de Ferrer* and *Joaquín María Ferrer*, bibliophile and publisher, and in July painted *Bullfighting Scene* for them (all 1824; Rome, Marchioness de la Gándara priv. col., see GW nos 1660, 1659 and 1672). On his return to Bordeaux, he painted another portrait of the writer *Leandro Fernández de Moratín* (1824; Bilbao, Mus. B.A.) and other friends. The undiminished intensity of his vision culminated in the unfinished *José Pío de Molina, Mayor of Madrid under Joseph* (1828; Winterthur, Samml. Oskar Reinhart) which, like the light-struck *Milkmaid of Bordeaux* (*c.* 1827; Madrid, Prado), foreshadows Impressionism in approach, brushwork and use of colour.

Encouraged to reissue his *Caprichos*, ten of which were, in fact, published in copies in Paris in 1825, Goya instead proposed a new series based on 'better ideas'. Using black chalk in two sketchbooks, he drew more than 100 figures and scenes viewed and remembered or developed in his imagination. The captioned Bordeaux Album G drawings (dispersed) illustrate and satirize humanity and its weaknesses (e.g. *Madmen*, black chalk, *c.* 1824–8; London, BM), while also, as in the untitled Bordeaux Album H drawings (1824–8; dispersed), presenting street and circus-like figures as well as allegorical, mythological and historical subjects. Six or seven small, late prints (the attribution of one is disputed) include several repeating Album H figures: a standing *maja*, a cape-wrapped 'smuggler' and an old person on a swing.

During the winter of 1824–5 Goya painted some 40 miniatures on ivory in an innovative technique that, he claimed, resembled more the brushwork of Velázquez than that of Mengs. His 20 known miniatures reflect types and subjects explored earlier, while a painting of *Susanna and the Elders* (1824; London, S. Sebba priv. col., see GW no. 1682) invokes Rembrandt. Though again ill in the spring of 1825, by December Goya completed his four large lithographs of bullfighting scenes, known as the *Bulls of Bordeaux* (GW 1707–10). These were printed in Bordeaux by C.-C.-M.-N. Gaulon, of whom Goya made an impressive lithograph (1824–5; Middletown, CT, Wesleyan U., Davison A. Cent.).

Goya returned twice to Spain: in May 1826, when, still a powerful figure, his portrait was painted in Madrid by Vicente López y Portaña (1826; Madrid, Casón Buen Retiro); and in 1827, when he perhaps painted the direct, almost Romantic portrait of his grandson *Mariano Goya* (1827; Lausanne, Georges A. Embiricos priv. col., see GW, no. 1664), before returning to France on 19 September 1827. When Goya died in Bordeaux at his bedside were José Pío de Molina (Goya's portrait of whom remained unfinished) and Antonio Brugada Vila (?1804–1863), a young Spanish painter who often accompanied him in Bordeaux and later listed his belongings.

II. Working methods and technique.

1. PAINTINGS.

(i) Oil. Goya's oil paintings range in size from portrait miniatures some 80 mm in diameter to wall paintings 3 m high and 10 m wide. He painted on canvas, wood, metal and on the plaster of walls, working with a brush, occasionally a palette knife and the small cane or bamboo knives of his own making, and even with his fingers. There are relatively few preparatory drawings for his paintings, though for several paintings Goya referred to the small sketchbook he had begun in Italy (Madrid, Prado). Among drawings for commissioned paintings are two red chalk female head studies (Madrid, Prado; Madrid, Carderera priv. col.) for his Saragossa fresco of 1772, the *Adoration of the Name of God*; several sketches, most in black chalk, of figures in tapestry cartoons of the 1770s (e.g. *Man Beating Time*, black chalk with white, 1777, for *Dance on the Banks of the Manzanares*; both Madrid, Prado); white chalk sketches on blue-grey paper for religious and historical compositions of 1780–90 (e.g. *St Francis Borgia Taking Leave of his Family*; 1788; Madrid, Prado); a red chalk and a wash sketch (both Madrid, Prado) and an oil sketch (Boston, MA, Mus. F.A.) associated with *Truth, Time and History* (1797–1800; Stockholm, Nmus.); a sepia pen and wash drawing (Madrid, Prado) for the *Burial of the Sardine* (*c.* 1812–19; Madrid, Real Acad. S Fernando, Mus.); chalk and pencil studies of *Ferdinand VII* (1808; Madrid, Bib. N.) and *Arthur Wellesley, 1st Duke of Wellington* (1812; London, BM); and pencil and sepia brush (and wash) drawings (1799–1801; London, BM; Madrid, Prado) for an equestrian portrait of *Charles IV and María Luisa* and a standing *Duque de Osuna* (*c.* 1785; Madrid, Prado). Album drawings were a basis for *The Water-seller* (1808–12; Budapest, Mus. F.A.; drawing, Album C, Malibu, CA, Getty Mus.) and *The Forge* (*c.* 1808–12; New York, Frick; drawing, Album F, New York, Met.).

For his earliest oils, such as the series of the *Life of the Virgin* for the Aula Dei monastery, as well as on many canvases painted throughout his career, Goya used a red bole primer applied over a ground of plaster (on walls) or gesso (on canvas), often allowing the bole to come through his surface colours to yield a nuanced, rosy hue. When he wanted light and cooler colours, he painted directly on a light-toned primer. Some canvases, including those for the tapestry cartoons, were delivered to Goya on (reusable) stretchers, requiring little additional preparation, though for the cartoons he was assigned a colour-grinder who also assisted in priming canvases. Microscopic analysis of his paintings verifies his continuing use of irregularly hand-ground pigments, though commercially ground pigments of a finer texture were sold in Madrid before he left for France in 1824.

When without proper canvases Goya reused others, painting over whatever lay upon them, as when portraying *Don Alberto Foraster* (1804; New York, Hisp. Soc. America). Shortage of other materials could frustrate him as well. Writing to General Palafox in December 1814 concerning the equestrian portrait of him (1814; Madrid, Prado), Goya lamented the scarcity of colours and complained of adulterated oils that delayed the drying process, mentioning the 'estracto de saturno' (lead extract) he had used as a drying agent.

Goya's brushstrokes varied; they were freer and more expansive in large compositions than in smaller works intended to be seen at close hand. Nonetheless, some small sketches, such as the *Betrayal of Christ* (1798; Madrid, Prado), give evidence of a heavy impasto and show considerably more freedom than some 'finished' paintings of equal size.

Goya's son Javier reported that the pictures his father most favoured and which he kept for himself were done with palette knife instead of brush, producing an admirable effect when viewed from a proper distance. Javier also reported that Goya's best portraits, those of friends, were accomplished in a single session, sometimes lasting ten hours. The fact that he often worked at night is known not only from Javier but from the candle-rimmed hat in Goya's *Self-portrait c.* 1790–95; candlelight was best for producing the highlights that reinforced qualities of chiaroscuro.

(ii) Fresco. The judgement of the Saragossa authorities, who in 1780–81 found Goya's work on the Cathedral frescoes deficient in taste and care, is indicative of his daring. The great area of wall and ceiling to be frescoed and the demands of the technique, in which the pigments had to be applied before the plaster dried, necessitated painting broadly and quickly. Conservators of his frescoes at Saragossa Cathedral and at S Antonio de la Florida, Madrid, discovered that he often painted on plaster which he had striated deeply to provide a grip for his colours, disregarding the incised lines of his underdrawing and with an impasto as rich as that of his wall paintings in oils.

Goya's approach and technique for wall paintings in either fresco or oils were very similar and defy precise description. His son knew the S Antonio paintings to be fresco, but others thought them to be tempera or some 'original' mixed medium. Until the late 1860s his Quinta del Sordo wall paintings (the *'Black Paintings'* of 1820–23) were known as frescoes, though they had been modified with dark, glistening retouched areas, visible in early photographs and perhaps caused by the use of 'printers' black' (*negro de imprenta*), a substance which in 1835 was known to have caused crude and excessive blackening in his late paintings. Since they were transferred to canvas, restored and varnished, despite analysis of their many layers, they can only be regarded as oils.

(iii) Miniature. In contrast to the fine detail achieved by miniature painters in dotting colour on ivory, Goya evolved a method in Bordeaux during the winter of 1824–5 of shaping images by working the water-thinned blacks he had applied to the small ivory plaques; he manipulated drops of water to produce lighter, more translucent areas. It was a process not unlike that developed in England by Alexander Cozens in his 'accidental' ink-wash or ink-blot drawings, investigated by John Constable by 1800 and subsequently practised by Eugenio Lucas Velázquez and Jenaro Pérez Villaamil. Goya further defined his forms with touches of painted black line, white line achieved by scratching through dark areas and thin washes of colour. He asserted that his rapidly and freely executed ivory miniatures were quite original and unlike any others he had seen.

2. DRAWINGS. For most of his drawings, mainly done in sketchbooks and usually on laid paper, Goya chose black, red and, occasionally, white chalk; he also used dark brown, sepia or black ink applied with pen or brush, often adding washes of like colour, as well as graphite or lead pencil and, during his late years, lithographic crayon and tusche. He drew more ephemeral caricatures in sand poured from inkstands. Detail was as successfully achieved with chalk as with ink, and the chiaroscuro with broad sweeps of sanguine or blackish-brown ink. Occasionally he used white chalk on toned paper to produce highlighted dark or nocturnal scenes.

Drawings relating to Goya's *Caprichos* prints of 1799 (Albums A and B; *see* §I, 3(i) above) include careful pen and brush sketches as well as broadly brushed compositions. His red chalk drawings for the later *Disasters of War* (*c.* 1810–20) and *Tauromaquia* (1816) prints embrace a descriptive mastery that in the *Tauromaquia* drawings becomes increasingly less deliberate and in the sanguine drawings for the *Disparates* (1816–23) remarkably free (*see* §I, 3(iii) above). Black chalk alone incisively defines and underlines subject and character in his late Bordeaux Albums G and H (1824–8; *see* §I, 5 above).

3. PRINTS. Goya's prints reveal an artist–printmaker's concern for conveying imagery in chiaroscuro. To his earliest prints of etched line he introduced aquatint in those he made in 1778 after Velázquez's paintings. The *Caprichos* (1799) includes his print in aquatint alone, *Because She Was Susceptible* (pl. 32; see fig. 1 above). In his *Disparates* series (1816–23) Goya worked from drawings he prepared in ink or chalk, often with added wash. He rolled both drawing and grounded plate through the press to transfer the drawing and then worked the traces that remained on the plate with etcher's needle and, if desired, with burin, burnisher, lavis and/or aquatint. His working

proofs illustrate this procedure, one that gave painterly depth, light and shade to etched-line images.

With Goya's *Bulls of Bordeaux* lithographs (1825) his painter's vision found maximum expression. Placing the lithograph stone on his easel like a canvas he drew vigorously (and corrected) directly on it. With hatching strokes made by lithographic crayon he shaped darker areas that he could then scrape or scratch through to reveal the whites of the underlying stone.

III. Character and personality.

Goya's personal and professional life, his thoughts on art and, less often, his religious and political leanings emerge from correspondence and other documentation. Early independence is hinted at by the jury report of the Parma competition of 1771 commending his brushwork, figural tones and attitudes but faulting his compositional accommodation and truthfulness of colour. His letters to Martín Zapater in Saragossa, some with informal, caricature-like pen drawings, tell of his daily concerns, disappointments and triumphs, of his passions (hunting, chocolate, sausage), familial preoccupations (Josefa's several childbirths, financial arrangements), investments and illnesses. In response to the Saragossa Cathedral authorities' request that he should submit to Francisco Bayeu's 'corrections' in his work on the *Faith*, *Patience*, *Fortitude* and *Charity* pendentives (*see* §I, 2 above), Goya expressed his outrage in a letter of March 1781 (CL pp. 227–34). He contended that a painter was sustained by his most delicate honour, and it was his reputation that gave him sustenance; he asserted that although Bayeu might accuse him of pride, wilfulness and arrogance, he could not, as an accredited Academician, submit to another's directions without damaging his honour. It was the power of the imagination that produced not merely a routine artist but an original one. Noting that he was already favoured at court and no mere executor of Bayeu's designs, Goya asked that an impartial fellow Academician judge his work; yet he also expressed regret for having failed to please and agreed to provide new sketches painted in accordance with Bayeu. He wrote to Zapater in July 1781 (AS pp. 63–4) of 'burning alive' on recalling the criticism.

In October 1792, replying to a request from the Real Academia, Goya stated his thoughts on the study of art (CL pp. 310–12). Art academies, he felt, must not be private; they should not fix prerequisites and should do no more than freely assist those wishing to study in them. Invoking Annibale Carracci's liberality in permitting students to follow their own inclinations and thus help to reverse the decline that painting had suffered since Raphael's time, Goya urged that free rein be given to the genius of those studying art. Nor, he wrote, should academy regulations emasculate an art so liberal and noble as painting. For Goya there could be no rules in painting, an art closer to the divine than any other since it represents that which God has created. In painting, as in the other arts, he believed that great works can result only from the imitation of divine Nature. To study from casts after antique Greek statues—then common studio practice—and to undervalue nature, or truth, was scandalous; for statues were copies of divine nature and by man's 'miserable' hands, not by those of God. In concluding he wrote that if his reply might seem too impassioned, it was because he had devoted his entire life to striving to attain the fruit of precisely such beliefs.

Truth, as revealed by the artistic imagination, was uppermost in Goya's mind when he announced the sale of his *Caprichos* prints in 1799 (CL pp. 323, 327–8). While the imitation of nature was as difficult as it was admirable, he was now purposefully departing from this pursuit; the only reality in his *Caprichos* was that of his imagination. Though a disclaimer for any possible references to known persons and events, his recourse to imagination enabled him to convey universal truths. In departing from nature, painting—like poetry (or the written word)—could unite elements that in nature are found in diverse individuals, the artist selecting whatever is most appropriate for his purpose; and the artist who wisely and ingeniously tries to attain the universal through synthesizing specific elements is an inventor or creator and no mere copyist. Goya now assumed the role of moralist, stressing that his art could censure society's common vices and errors even more forcefully than could eloquence and poetry, since it exposed to the eye thoughts and attitudes previously hidden in impassioned, confused and unenlightened minds.

In January 1801 Goya supplied the Real Academia with an astute analysis of painting restoration, admitting that his 'frank' nature was 'animated' by his feelings (CL pp 331–2). Requested to examine a restorer's work, methods and materials, he found dissonance between original and retouched areas; he considered the force of the original artist's brushwork to be lost and the mastery of delicate, knowing touches to be destroyed. Goya remarked that the more paintings are retouched under the pretext of conservation, the more they are destroyed; not even the original artist could perfectly retouch the tones of a painting that had altered with the passage of time.

As his son wrote in a brief biography of 1831 (CL pp. 516–19), Goya knew the magic (*magia*, a word he favoured) generated by the ambience of a painting. Although Velázquez and Rembrandt were the artists Goya most esteemed, nature was the master he studied most; when success eluded him he would say he had 'forgotten how to paint'.

A lack of religious feeling in Goya may seem to be implied in Ceán Bermúdez's letter of September 1817 (CL pp. 495–6), telling of his efforts to inspire in Goya, while he painted his *SS Justa and Rufina* (1817), such qualities opposed to his character as correctness (*decoro*), modesty, devotion and worthiness of action, as well as dignified, sensitive composition and religious attitude. However, Goya's wish to ensure that this painting would equal the excellence of the older masterpieces in Seville Cathedral showed great respect, as does his *Last Communion of St Joseph Calasanz* (1819).

Letters from Goya's close friend in Bordeaux, Leandro Fernández de Moratín, to a mutual friend in Madrid (R. Andioc, ed.: *Epistolario de Leandro Fernández de Moratín*, Madrid, 1973) tell of the aging artist's character and objectives from 1824 onwards: his urgency to go to Paris; his wish once again to portray *Moratín* (1799,

Madrid, Real Acad. S Fernando, Mus.; 1824, Bilbao, Mus. B.A.); his domestic and financial concerns; and his fierce independence in travelling alone to Madrid. In June 1825 Moratín wrote that Goya, again having recovered from illness, was in high spirits, painting vigorously though with no desire to correct anything he painted. In December Goya wrote to Joaquín María Ferrer in Paris of his bullfight lithographs, his projected 'new' *Caprichos* and his innovative miniatures on ivory (Sayre, 1966, pp. 112–14).

Goya's political convictions, not known to have been formally expressed, were evidently those of a socially conscious, independently minded though cautious individual who observed but did not often overtly react to his complex, rapidly changing surroundings. If he was an *afrancesado* (one sympathetic to French thinking and action) and/or a liberal, as were many in the Madrid court and in Spanish intellectual circles before and during the French occupation, he denied such inclinations following the return of the monarchy. When in 1820 the Constitution supplanted the monarchy he was referred to in print in April 1820 as 'such a patriot' that it was proposed he be asked to immortalize in paint or in drawing the evils of the Inquisition, and it was understood that he would do so with his usual fairness. His move to France when the monarchy was reinstated, as well as such works as the concluding plates of the *Disasters of War* (1815–20) and the *'Black Paintings'* (1820–23), now understandable as projecting evils of the past at a time when truth and reason ruled, provide further evidence that if not formally a 'liberal', Goya believed in constitutional government and the freedoms it ensured.

Although he could visit Spain while living in France, Goya felt obliged to remain abroad, as he asserted, for health reasons; for on 24 December 1824 he wrote to his son that although he liked Bordeaux this was not a sufficient reason to leave one's country (CL p. 388). In May 1826 Goya travelled to Madrid where, on 17 May, Ferdinand VII granted his retirement and pension requests, in this way acknowledging the 53 years he had served the royal family with the greatest effort, taste and intelligence.

IV. Critical reception and posthumous reputation.

Goya had few pupils or collaborators, so his immediate influence was limited. From the early 1780s Agustín Esteve y Marques was under Goya's influence, and from 1789 to 1808 he collaborated in painting replicas of royal portraits. Other painters whose portraits were sometimes confused with those of Goya include Joaquín Inza and Antonio Carnicero. Ascensió Juliá has long been considered a pupil of Goya, who portrayed his 'friend, Asensi' (*c.* 1798, Lugano, Col. Thyssen-Bornemisza; 1814, Williamstown, MA, Clark A. Inst.) and in 1806 directed him in a painting project; Juliá in turn painted copies of *Goya and his Doctor, Don Eugenio Garcia Arrieta* (1820; Madrid, priv. col.) and reflected some subjects after Goya types in his drawings and paintings.

Goya's few documented pupils are less well known. Luís Gil Ranc (1787–1867) went to Madrid to study with Goya in 1803 and in 1808 accompanied him to Aragon. Goya referred to Felipe Abas (1777–1813/14) as a pupil (*discípulo*) in a letter of January 1813 (CL pp. 367–8) regarding Abas's reinstatement of the Joseph Bonaparte portrayal within Goya's *Allegory of Madrid* (1810; *see* §I, 3(ii) above). Felipe Arrojo (Valdés) (*c.* 1801–70) is noted as a pupil in an inscription on the recto of a sheet of Goya drawings entitled *Head of a Dying Man* (1818; Madrid, Prado), which Goya gave to Arrojo. Goya's son Javier was directed in art studies by his father, as was noted in 1803 when Goya, in exchange for giving his *Caprichos* plates to the King, requested funds to enable his son to travel abroad and study painting (CL, p. 477). During his final years in Bordeaux Goya taught María del Rosario Weiss (1814–43), daughter of his companion Leocadia Weiss; she went on to teach drawing to Queen Isabel II in Madrid. A sketchbook attributed to María's years with Goya survives (New York, Hisp. Soc. America).

The taste for Goya's art in Spain lessened during his two final decades; many preferred the portraiture of Vicente López y Portaña and the academic classicism of José de Madrazo, Federico de Madrazo y Kuntz and their school. Some romanticist and *costumbrista* artists, however, continued to reflect elements of Goya's art. In the 1840s Leonardo Alenza y Nieto produced Goya-like *Caprichos* drawings, some later issued as prints, but these lack the impact of Goya's work.

Others copied (and some falsified) Goya paintings. In the late 1860s Eduardo Gimeno (1838–68) painted copies of Goya's *'Black Paintings'*, then still at the Quinta del Sordo, to aid him in producing prints illustrating the paintings for publication. Eugenio Lucas Velázquez, who owned several plates from the *Disparates*, and was one of three to appraise the *'Black Paintings'* in the 1850s, was Goya's most successful and prolific imitator. Attributions have fluctuated for certain problematic works, for example *City on a Rock* (New York, Met.).

Abroad, Goya's prints, especially the *Caprichos*—valued, as he knew in 1803, by 'foreigners' (CL, p. 360)—first earned him the respect of artists and collectors. In France Delacroix made drawings after the *Caprichos* by the mid-1820s; late in December 1824 Charles Motte (1785–1836) registered ten lithographed 'Spanish caricatures after Goya' copying some of Goya's *Caprichos*; and by 1835 Goya was known in Spain to have had an impact on the 'new, Romantic' French painters (see Harris, 1969). The first catalogue of Goya's prints (by Eugène Piot, friend of Théophile Gauthier, who had written of Goya; see Glendinning, 1977, pp. 71, 198, 259, 327 n.1) was published in Paris in 1842; and in 1856 a Spaniard in Paris bought 80 small copies of the *Caprichos* painted on canvas. Most of Goya's paintings, however, remained in Spain. From 1838 to 1848 the Spanish paintings exhibited in Louis-Philippe's Galerie Espagnole in the Louvre in Paris included eight by Goya and created an interest in Spanish art. Later in the century many artists went to Spain to study other works by Spanish painters, and only then could Goya's painting be fully appreciated. Manet, who had already been stimulated in Paris by Goya's prints and paintings, studied Goya's colour in Spain in 1865 and two years later evoked the *Third of May 1808* in his painting of the *Execution of the Emperor Maximilian* (1867; Mannheim, Städt. Ksthalle). Other artists in France impressed by Goya's works include Nicolas-François Regnault, Auguste Renoir,

Paul Cézanne, Vincent van Gogh, Henri de Toulouse-Lautrec and Jean-Louis Forain.

By the outset of the 19th century admirers in Madrid referred to Goya as famed and unrivalled and as one sought out by visitors from abroad. A liberal, in 1804, poetically praising his daring, grace and harmony in painting, wrote presciently that non-Spaniards one day would bow in ecstasy on hearing his name (see Glendinning, 1977, p. 53). While his inventiveness, daring and individuality, his mastery of colour and chiaroscuro, of drawing and printmaking to create illusion, suspense and life-like truthfulness were esteemed by some contemporaries, the more academically minded then and later faulted his sketchiness, the lack of 'finish' or 'polish'. In 1818 this led him to be described as leader of a school of painting that sacrificed all to effect (Glendinning, 1977, pp. 53–4). Critics associated such perceived faults with impatience, a lack of discipline and a disregard for the rules of art, fine draughtsmanship and technical refinement.

After Goya's death the objectives of his socio-politically inspired art were submerged and forgotten in post-Constitutional Spain. Not until after the 1868 revolution could this 'celebrated' painter again be claimed in print as a patriot and as a victim of Ferdinand VII's despotic reign. His motivations in creating such apparent 'horrors' as the *'Black Paintings'* were no longer understood; many in Spain and abroad viewed such works merely as repugnant and ugly (though, as Baudelaire realized in 1857, Goya obtained beauty from ugliness), and they were even seen as the products of a 'diseased' mind.

The Impressionists and their sympathizers, however, appreciated Goya's painting in their own terms, seeing his colour, movement, boldness and disregard for detail as modern. Having been considered the last of Spain's Old Masters around 1830, in the 1890s he was heralded as revolutionary, free and modern; and he has since been considered the first 'modern' artist. Symbolist, Expressionist, Surrealist and contemporary artists have found inspiration in his work. In achieving the universal that he constantly sought to attain in his art, Goya created an oeuvre that can be appreciated by all people, in all times.

WRITINGS

A. Canellas López, ed.: *Francisco de Goya, diplomatario* (Saragossa, 1981) [incl. biographical note of 1832 by Goya's son] [CL]

M. Agueda and X. de Salas, eds: *Cartas a Martín Zapater* (Madrid, 1982) [Goya's letters to Zapater, 1775–99] [AS]

BIBLIOGRAPHY

GENERAL

Ceán Bermúdez

L'Art européen à la cour d'Espagne au XVIIIe siècle (exh. cat., Bordeaux, Gal. B.-A.; Paris, Grand Pal.; Madrid, Prado; 1979–80)

De Greco à Picasso (exh. cat., Paris, Petit Pal., 1987–8)

DOCUMENTARY MATERIAL

F. J. Sánchez Cantón: 'Como vivía Goya', *Archv Esp. A.*, xviii (1946), pp. 73–109

M. del Saltillo: *Miscelánea madrileña, histórica y artística . . . : 'Goya en Madrid: Su familia y allegados' (1746–1856)* (Madrid, 1952)

J.-R. Bosquet Fajardo, ed.: *La Cartuja de Aula Dei de Zaragoza (ventanas al cielo)* (Saragossa, 1986) [with excellent colour plates]

EXHIBITION CATALOGUES

Goya (exh. cat., ed. J. Baticle and A. B. de Vries; The Hague, Mauritshuis, 1970) [in Dut., Eng., Fr. and Ger.]

The Changing Image: Prints by Francisco Goya (exh. cat., ed. E. A. Sayre; Boston, MA, Mus. F.A., 1974)

Goya, 1746–1828: Peintures–dessins–gravures (exh. cat., ed. J. Guillaud and M. Guillaud; Paris, Cent. Cult. Marais, 1979)

Goya: Das Zeitalter der Revolutionen, 1789–1830 (exh. cat., ed. W. Hofmann; Hamburg, Ksthalle, 1980–81)

Goya: Zeichnungen und Druckgraphik (exh. cat., ed. M. Stuffmann; Frankfurt am Main, Städel. Kstinst., 1981)

Goya dans les collections suisses (exh. cat., ed. P. Gassier; Martigny, Fond. Pierre Gianadda, 1982)

Goya y la constitución de 1819 (exh. cat., ed. M. Agulló y Cobo; Madrid, Mus. Mun., 1982–3)

Goya en las colecciones madrileñas (exh. cat., ed. E. Lafuente Ferrari; Madrid, Prado, 1983)

Goya: Europalia 85 España (exh. cat. by J. Gallego and A. E. Pérez Sánchez, Brussels, Musées Royaux B.-A., 1985)

Goya in spanischen Privatsammlungen (exh. cat., ed. M. Victor Chico; Lugano, Col. Thyssen-Bornemisza, 1986) [in Ger. and Eng.]

Goya joven (1746–1776) y su entorno (exh. cat., ed. R. Buendía; Saragossa, Mus. Camón Aznar, 1986)

Goya y el espíritu de la ilustración (exh. cat. by A. E. Pérez Sánchez and others, Madrid, Prado, 1988); Eng. edn as *Goya and the Spirit of the Enlightenment* (Boston, MA, Mus. F.A.; New York, Met.; 1989)

Goya, 1746–1828 (exh. cat. by J. Gallego and others, Venice, Ca' Pesaro, 1989)

Goya, toros y toreros (exh. cat., ed. Pierre Gassier; Arles, Espace Van Gogh, 1990) [colour and black-and-white illus.]

Goya and the Satirical Print in England and on the Continent, 1730–1850 (exh. cat. by R. Wolf; Boston, MA, Boston College Museum of Art; New York, Spanish Institute; 1991)

Goya (exh. cat., Saragossa, Lonja, 1992)

Goya, la década de los Caprichos, dibujos y aguafuertes (exh. cat., ed. J. Wilson-Bareau; Madrid, Real Acad. S Fernando, 1992) [colour illus.]

Goya, la década de los Caprichos, retratos 1792–1804 (exh. cat., ed. N. Glendinning; Madrid, Real Acad. S Fernando, 1992) [colour illus.]

Goya/Rembrandt, la mémoire de l'oeil (exh. cat., ed. I. Rose-de Viejo; Geneva, Cab. Est. Mus. A. & Hist., 1993) [black-and-white illus.]

Goya, el capricho y la invención, cuadros de gabinete, bocetos y miniaturas (exh. cat., eds. J. Wilson-Bareau and M. B. Mena Marqués; Madrid, Prado; London, RA; Chicago, IL, A. Inst.; 1993–4) [colour and black-and-white illus.; Eng. trans. as *Goya, Truth and Fantasy: The Small Paintings*]

El cuaderno italiano, 1770–1786, los orígenes del arte de Goya (Madrid, Prado, 1994) [exh. cat. and facs. ed. of Goya's It. sketchbook]

MONOGRAPHS, CATALOGUES AND ESSAYS

General

C. Baudelaire: 'Quelques Caricaturistes français: Goya', *Le Présent* (1857)

L. Mathéron: *Goya* (Paris, 1858)

V. Carderera: 'François Goya: Sa vie, ses dessins et ses eaux-fortes', *Gaz. B.-A.*, vii (1860), pp. 215–27

C. Yriarte: *Goya: Sa biographie, les fresques, les toiles, les tapisseries, les eaux-fortes et le catalogue de l'oeuvre* (Paris, 1867) [with cat. of paintings]

P. A. Lefort: *Francisco Goya: Etude biographique et critique suivie de l'essai d'un catalogue raisonné de son oeuvre gravé et lithographié* (Paris, 1877)

C. de la Viñaza: *Goya: Su tiempo, su vida, sus obras* (Madrid, 1887) [with cat. of paintings and prints]

V. von Loga: *Francisco de Goya* (Berlin, 1903) [with cat. of works]

A. F. Calvert: *Goya* (London, 1908) [with cat. of paintings and of series of prints]

A. L. Mayer: *Francisco de Goya* (Munich, 1923); Eng. trans. (London, 1924) [with cat. of works]

Colección de cuatrocientos cuarenta y nueve reproducciones de cuadros, dibujos y aguafuertes de don Francisco de Goya: Precedidos de un epistolario . . . y . . . noticias biográficas publicadas por don Francisco Zapater y Gómez en 1860 (Madrid, 1924)

E. Lafuente Ferrari: *Antecedentes, coincidencias y influencias del arte de Goya* (Madrid, 1947/*R* 1987)

F. D. Klingender: *Goya in the Democratic Tradition* (London, 1948)

A. Malraux: *Saturne* (Paris, 1950); Eng. trans. as *Saturn: An Essay on Goya* (London, 1957)

F. J. Sánchez Cantón: *Vida y obras de Goya* (Madrid, 1951); rev. Eng. trans. (Madrid, 1964)

M. S. Soria: *Agustín Esteve y Goya* (Valencia, 1957)

F. Nordström: *Goya, Saturn and Melancholy* (Stockholm, 1962)

J. Gudiol: *Goya* (New York, 1964)

R. Schickel: *The World of Goya, 1746–1828* (New York, 1968)

E. Harris: *Goya* (London, 1969)

J. Gudiol: *Goya, 1746–1828: Biografía, estudio analítico y catálogo de sus pinturas*, 4 vols (Barcelona, 1970); Eng. trans., 2 vols (Barcelona, 1985) [cat. numbering differs]
P. Gassier and J. Wilson: *The Life and Complete Works of Francisco Goya* (Fribourg, 1971); Eng. trans. (New York, 1971) [with full bibliog. and illus. cat. of works in all media] [GW]
F. Licht: *Goya in Perspective* (Englewood Cliffs, 1973)
N. Glendinning: *Goya and his Critics* (London, 1977)
S. Symmons: *Goya* (London, 1977)
X. de Salas: *Goya* (Milan, 1978); Eng. trans. (London, 1979) [with cat. of paintings]
J. Fauque and R. Villanueva Etcheverria: *Goya y Burdeos, 1824–1828* (Saragossa, 1982) [in Eng., Fr. and Sp.]
J. M. Arnaiz: *Francisco de Goya, cartones y tapices* (Madrid, 1987) [black-and-white and some colour illus.]
Goya, nuevas visiones: Homenaje a Enrique Lafuente Ferrari (Madrid, 1987)
S. Symmons: *Goya in Pursuit of Patronage* (London, 1988)
J. A. Tomlinson: *Francisco Goya: The Tapestry Cartoons and Early Career at the Court of Madrid* (Cambridge, 1989) [black-and-white illus.]
——: *Goya in the Twilight of the Enlightenment* (New Haven and London, 1992)
——: *Francisco Goya y Lucientes* (London, 1994)

Paintings

A. de Beruete y Moret: *Goya: Pintor de retratos* (Madrid, 1916)
X. Desparmet Fitz-Gerald: *L'Oeuvre peint de Goya*, 4 vols (Paris, 1928–50)
E. M. Aguilera: *Las pinturas negras de Goya* (Madrid, 1935)
X. de Salas: *Goya: La familia de Carlos IV* (Barcelona, 1944)
V. de Sambricio: *Tapices de Goya* (Madrid, 1946)
E. du Gué Trapier: *Goya: A Study of his Portraits, 1797–99* (New York, 1955)
E. Lafuente Ferrari: *Goya: The Frescoes in San Antonio de la Florida* (Geneva, 1955) [incl. appx by R. Stolz on Goya's fresco technique]
F. J. Sánchez Cantón and X. de Salas: *Le pitture nere di Goya alla Quinta del Sordo* (Milan, 1963); Eng. trans. as *Goya and the Black Paintings* (London, 1964)
E. du Gué Trapier: *Goya and his Sitters* (New York, 1964)
E. A. Sayre: 'Goya's Bordeaux Miniatures', *Boston Mus. Bull.*, lxiv (1966), pp. 84–123
H. Thomas: *Goya: The Third of May 1808* (New York, 1972)
J. Gantner: 'Goya's "Black" Paintings from the Quinta del Sordo, Madrid', *Sandoz Bulletin*, xxx (1973) [whole issue]
R. de Angelis: *L'opera pittorica completa di Goya* (Milan, 1974)
B. Heuken: *Francisco Goya: Las pinturas negras* (Bonn, 1974)
E. Torra and others: *Regina martirum-Goya* (Saragossa, 1982)
M. del C. Garrido: 'Algunas consideraciones sobre la técnica de las pinturas negras de Goya', *Bol. Mus. Prado*, v/13 (1984), pp. 4–40
P. E. Muller: *Goya's 'Black' Paintings: Truth and Reason in Light and Liberty* (New York, 1984)

Prints and drawings

P. Lafond: *Nouveaux Caprices de Goya: Suite de trente-huit dessins inédits* (Paris, 1907)
L. Delteil: *Francisco Goya* (1922), xiv–xv of *Le Peintre-graveur illustré* (Paris, 1906–30) [cat. rai.]
F. J. Sánchez Cantón: *Los Caprichos de Goya y sus dibujos preparatorios* (Barcelona, 1949)
J. Camón Aznar: *'Los Disparates' de Goya y sus dibujos preparatorios* (Barcelona, 1951)
E. Lafuente Ferrari: *Los Desastres de la Guerra de Goya y sus dibujos preparatorios* (Barcelona, 1952)
J. López-Rey: *Goya's Caprichos: Beauty, Reason and Caricature*, 2 vols (Princeton, 1953)
F. J. Sánchez Cantón: *Museo del Prado: Los dibujos de Goya* (Madrid, 1954)
J. López-Rey: *A Cycle of Goya's Drawings* (London, 1956)
E. Lafuente Ferrari: *Goya: Gravures et lithographies, oeuvre complète* (Paris, 1961); Eng. trans. (London, 1962)
E. F. Helman: *Trasmundo de Goya* (Madrid, 1963, rev. 1983)
T. Harris: *Goya: Engravings and Lithographs*, 2 vols (Oxford, 1964) [with cat. rai.]
H. Holländer: *Goya: Los Disparates (Los Proverbios de Goya)* (Tübingen, 1968)
E. F. Helman: *Los Caprichos de Goya* (Madrid, 1971)
P. Gassier: *Francisco Goya: Drawings: The Complete Albums* (New York, 1973) [cat. rai.]
——: *The Drawings of Goya: The Sketches, Studies and Individual Drawings* (New York, 1975) [cat. rai.]
E. Lafuente Ferrari: *Los Caprichos de Goya* (Barcelona, 1978)
——: *Goya: Dibujos* (Madrid, 1980) [Prado drawings]
J. W. Bareau: *Goya's Prints: The Tomás Harris Collection in the British Museum* (London, 1981) [B]
Francisco de Goya, 'Los Caprichos', N.G. Stogdon Inc. and Artemis Fine Arts Ltd (New York and London, 1987) [new census of working and trial proofs]
Francisco de Goya: Grabador. Instantáneas. Caprichos (Madrid, 1992) [illus. of Goya's pls]
Francisco de Goya: Grabador. Instantáneas. Desastres de la Guerra (Madrid, 1992) [illus. of Goya's pls]
Francisco de Goya: Grabador. Instantáneas. Tauromaquia (Madrid, 1992) [illus. of Goya's pls]

PRISCILLA E. MULLER

Goybault [Grymbault]**, Paoul** (*b* Parthenay, Deux-Sèvres, ?1430–35; *d* Parthenay, after 1497). French painter, illuminator and priest. He was dean of the chapter of the collegiate church of Ste Croix, Parthenay, and one of the few French ecclesiastics who was also a painter. The form 'Grymbault' derives from an erroneous reading of his name in some of the documents. He worked for the Connétable, Arthur de Richemont (1393–1458), until the latter's death, and then for Jean de Dunois, Bâtard d'Orléans (*d* Nov 1468), in whose castle chapel at Châteaudun he painted 'several things'. He stayed at Châteaudun for at least a year, but between 1462 and 1464 he was 'chaplain and illuminator' to René of Anjou, King of Naples, at Bar-sur-Aube. He was also involved in the construction of the organ in St Hilaire, Poitiers. None of these works is known to have survived.

Jean Lemaire's journal of his travels in south-west France in 1513 recorded that the church of Ste Croix contained 'several rich paintings and images of "Duc Arthus de Bretaigne, connestable de France" [i.e. Arthur de Richemont], and again his face from life by a great painter and companion of Fouquet master Paoul'. A 16th-century crayon drawing of Arthur de Richemont (Paris, Bib. N., OA 14, fol. 48) by François-Roger de Gaignières may have been executed after a portrait by Goybault. The much restored wall painting of the *Last Judgement* (5×4 m) in the castle chapel at Châteaudun is controversial. Sterling attributed it to Goybault (mistakenly calling him 'Grymbault'), believing it to have been executed before the death of Jean de Dunois in 1468, but Demezil argued that it was partly painted on a wall built after 1493 and suggested a later date, which had already been proposed on iconographic grounds by Abbé Thiercelin. The *Last Judgement* should probably be attributed instead to Piètre André, who worked for both Jean de Dunois and his son François, Duc de Longueville.

BIBLIOGRAPHY

Abbé Thiercelin: 'Fresque du Jugement dernier dans la chapelle du château de Châteaudun', *Bull. Soc. Dunoise* (1926), pp. 23–40 [issue for 1913–15]
C. Sterling: 'Paoul Grymbault, éminent peintre français du XVe siècle', *Rev. A.*, viii (1970), pp. 17–32
M. M. Demezil: 'La Sainte-Chapelle du château de Châteaudun', *Bull. Mnmtl*, cxxx (1972), pp. 113–28
P. Gasnault: 'Paul Goybault, peintre français de la seconde moitié du XVe siècle', *Bull. Soc. N. Antiqua. France* (1977), pp. 124–8
C. Schaefer: 'Lemaire de Belges, Fouquet et maître Paoul Goybault: La Peinture murale du Jugement dernier de la Sainte-Chapelle de Châteaudun', *Bull. Soc. N. Antiqua. France* (1985), pp. 249–64

CLAUDE SCHAEFER

Goyen, Jan (Josephsz.) van (*b* Leiden, 13 Jan 1596; *d* The Hague, 27 April 1656). Dutch painter and draughtsman. He ranks as one of the leading and most prolific Dutch 17th-century landscape artists.

1. Life. 2. Work. 3. Influence and reputation.

1. LIFE. His father, Joseph (Jansz.) van Goyen (*d* 1625), was a cobbler. The Leiden chronicler J. J. Orlers reported that Jan was only ten when he was apprenticed first to the painter Coenraet A. van Schilperoort (*c.* 1577–1635/6), then to Isaac van Swanenburgh, Jan (Arentsz.) de Man (*fl* 1587) and Hendrick Clock in Leiden before spending two years with Willem Gerritsz. (*fl* 1587) in Hoorn. After a year spent travelling through France (1615–16), he trained for a year (1617–18) in Haarlem with Esaias van de Velde (i), who was six years older. On his return to Leiden, he married Anna Willemsdr. van Raelst (5 Aug 1618) and lived in the Zonneveldsteeg. In 1632 he moved to the capital, The Hague, where he settled and in 1634 acquired rights of citizenship. In 1638 and 1640 he was head of the Guild of St Luke there. From 1639 he lived in his own house on the Singelgracht (now Dunne Bierkade 16) next door to the painter Johannes Schoeff (1608–66). From 1649 to 1652 he let the adjoining house to Paulus Potter. Of van Goyen's three daughters, Maria married the still-life painter Jacques de Claeuw (*fl* 1642–76) in 1649 and in the same year Margaretha married the genre painter Jan Steen. Around 1652–3 Gerard ter Borch (ii) painted a portrait of van Goyen (Vaduz, Samml. Liechtenstein).

An important feature of van Goyen's life was his ambitious striving for prosperity and recognition. Artistic work was generally poorly paid and he was therefore also intermittently active as an art dealer and collector, auctioneer, estate agent and picture valuer. In 1637 he lost a lot of money speculating in tulips. Despite producing more than 1200 paintings and 800 drawings, he was unable to cover his debts. In 1652 and 1654 he had to sell his possessions at public auction. He then moved to the Wagenstraat, but so many debts remained after his death that his widow (*d* 1672) had to auction all his remaining assets, including the house.

2. WORK.

(i) Paintings. Van Goyen's early landscapes, produced between 1620 and 1626, clearly show the influence of Esaias van de Velde. Following Flemish examples, he painted some in circular format as pendants (e.g. *Summer* and *Winter*, both 1625; Amsterdam, Rijksmus.). For other landscapes he adopted an elongated rectangular format (e.g. *Village Street with Soldiers in De Bilt*, 1623; Brunswick, Herzog Anton Ulrich-Mus.), which offered a broader setting for the narrative content. These village or beach scenes (e.g. *Round Tower on the Beach*, 1625; Poznań, N. Mus.) are full of bustling activity, with numerous figures set under a cloudy, blue-white sky. In keeping with the warlike times, soldiers are often included, but unlike van de Velde and Pieter de Neyn, van Goyen did not depict raids or cavalry skirmishes. He enlivened summer and winter scenes alike with bright local colour. The viewer's eye is drawn into the depth of the painting by gradations of perspective—for example by means of a tall tree dividing the composition down the middle or serving as a screen to one side with farms in the middle distance (e.g. *River*, 1625; Bremen, Ksthalle). The backgrounds typically consist of buildings, brush and dunes.

Around 1626 van Goyen's art changed, going well beyond van de Velde's example. The change is closely linked to contemporary Haarlem artists' creation of a specifically Dutch style of landscape painting that emphasized tonality and realism. Pieter Molijn, Salomon van Ruysdael and Pieter Dircksz. van Santvoort (1603/4–35) were the other principal exponents of this new development, which used native subject-matter and more natural colours. This phenomenon is known by modern art historians as the 'tonal phase'. Jan Porcellis (known to van Goyen in Leiden), also experimented with tonality in his marine pictures. From 1629 and through the 1630s van Goyen produced simple landscapes showing dunes and rivers in brown and green tones, which achieve an impression of depth with the help of diagonals. He sometimes softened the effects of this compositional device by moving the tallest tree from the edge towards the centre, as in *Angler on a Small Wooden Bridge* (1634; Pretoria, A. Mus.). The scarcity and small size of the figures in these 'tonal' pictures add to the desolation and bleakness of the dune scenery. In slightly later paintings (e.g. *Recreation on the Ice by the Ruin of the Huis te Merwede*, 1638; Leiden, Stedel. Mus. Lakenhal), travellers and carriages or fishermen on land and in boats restored an element of animation, and van Goyen began to open up the background by means of a misty horizon.

In 1637 there was a pause in van Goyen's creative activity, perhaps due to his speculation in tulips. Then, at the end of the 1630s, he began a period of classical harmony that unified picture and paint, producing works in which an idealized overall impression outweighs local colour. Until about 1638 a subtly differentiated silvery-grey tone predominated (e.g. *Two Fishermen*, 1638; London, N.G.) but in the 1640s this gave way to austerely monochromatic paintings in yellowy golden-brown, with a tonal range that, though unrealistic, used colour attractively. He gradually abandoned this style from 1643 and in 1650–51, especially in his paintings on paper (e.g. *Ferry with Two Cows and Five Passengers*, 1651; Dresden, Kupferstichkab.), employed a distinctly brown monochrome, finally returning, towards the end of his life, to a more natural colour range.

In the 1640s van Goyen tended to adopt a horizontal format, especially in his distant views (e.g. *Extensive Panorama*, (1646; New York, Met.), though he still produced landscapes with a disguised diagonal structure (e.g. *Old Tall Tower*, 1646; New York, Met.). Buildings assume an important role, from churches, castles, ruins, gates and towers to monumental town views, such as the *View of Dordrecht* (1644; Washington, DC, N.G.A.; see fig. 1). Seascapes in vertical format, such as *Old Watch-tower in a River Delta* (1646; The Hague, Dienst Versp. Rijkscol.), in which a high, cloudy sky contrasts with flat terrain, and distant panoramic views in oblong format, such as *Flat Landscape with a Windmill* (1641; Schwerin, Staatl. Mus.), are impressive pictorial achievements. Clouds cast shadows over the earth or lakes (van Goyen never painted the open sea, only inland waters such as the Haarlemer Meer)

1. Jan van Goyen: *View of Dordrecht*, oil on panel, 647×959 mm, 1644 (Washington, DC, National Gallery of Art)

and display the contrasting effects of light. Sailing boats occupy an important place in his compositions: in works of the early 1630s they appear in the background of quiet river scenes; by the 1640s they occupy an increasingly prominent foreground position as the river banks were made to recede (e.g. *Two Large Sailboats*, 1647; Paris, Louvre). In seascapes with level banks in the background, such as *Fishing Boats in an Estuary* (1655; Hamburg, Ksthalle), they are essential to the illusion of perspective.

In keeping with van Goyen's inventive and experimental temperament, he made several seascapes that include dramatic natural events, such as an approaching thunderstorm and lightning flashing across a pale yellow horizon (e.g. *Storm over the Sea*, 1647; Karlsruhe, Staatl. Ksthalle). In his freely composed seascapes of the 1650s he reached the apex of his creative work, producing paintings of striking perfection. A calm sea in the still of the evening (e.g. *Fishing Boats on a Wide Inland Lake*, 1656; Frankfurt am Main, Städel. Kstinst.) and a distant frigate firing a salute anticipate works by Willem II van de Velde (ii), the great master of Dutch marine painting. At the end of his life, van Goyen painted seascapes in silvery grey with grey-blue shadows and touches of local colour in the figures of fishermen, the sails and the flags on the boats.

In van Goyen's paintings his signature, often followed by a date, usually stands out boldly in the landscape or on a beam. He signed his early works I.V. GOIEN, which, from 1630, he changed to VGOYEN, and sometimes, on large works, to J. VGOYEN (in each case linking the letters VG). Usually, however, he adopted the monogram VG, first used in 1628. Dendrochronological research has shown that, unlike his contemporaries, van Goyen preferred to paint on wood panels made from freshly felled trees.

(ii) Drawings. Van Goyen is as important as a draughtsman as he is for his paintings. His output began in 1624 with small-scale drawings in brown ink: summer landscapes (e.g. *Ferry with Cart*, 1624; Hamburg, Ksthalle) and seascapes. At the same time he produced humorous genre scenes of everyday life, executed in brush and coloured washes (e.g. *Mussel Seller*, 1625; Leiden, Rijksuniv.). From 1626 he found black chalk the ideal medium to suit his fluent technique; he often brushed over the chalk outlines with grey wash, although in 1651 he used brown tones. He animated the scenes with wittily drawn figures, whose outlines capture their restless vivacity.

Van Goyen travelled the length and breadth of the Netherlands recording details of landscape and topography in chalk sketches, and his studies filled many sketchbooks (e.g. Dresden, Kupferstichkab.; others dispersed). In 1648 he ventured further afield, via the mouth of the River Scheldt to Antwerp and Brussels. In 1650 he was in Cleve and Arnhem and in 1651 in Haarlem and Amsterdam, where he drew the devastation resulting from the collapse of the St Anthonis Dike. Once home, he used the results of his travel sketches to create paintings and drawings. Time and again these works demonstrate how van Goyen was able to combine different actual motifs into imaginary landscape compositions. He was not attempting to depict accurate views but rather landscapes in which topographical elements happened to feature. Drawings survive for every year of van Goyen's creative life; in

1631, 1647, 1649 and 1651–3 he was particularly prolific. Especially popular with collectors are winter, beach and market scenes, an example of the last being *Market-day near a Canal* (1651; Chicago, IL, A. Inst.; see fig. 2). His preferred paper sizes were approximately 110×190 mm and approximately 170×270 mm, and he used fine white paper; he sketched on somewhat coarser paper with different watermarks (from which dates, where missing on the drawings, can be established).

3. Influence and reputation. According to Houbraken, van Goyen's pupils were Jan Steen (his son-in-law), Nicolaes Berchem and Adriaen van der Cabel. Several of Steen's early landscape paintings reveal the effects of van Goyen's tuition. Some of Berchem's early chalk drawings also show the influence of his teacher. Many other artists were inspired by van Goyen's compositions, painting style and draughtsmanship. A. J. van der Croos (1606/07–1663), Jacob Moscher (*fl* 1635–55) and C. S. van der Schalcke (1611–71) drew in a similarly relaxed manner. The etched landscapes of Simon de Vlieger and Anthoni Waterlo owe a debt to him. Etchings of landscapes, signed *Jan van Groye* and previously attributed to van Goyen (e.g. Hollstein, nos 3–7) have since been attributed to Jan van de Cappelle. In the medium of oil paint his influence can be seen in the early landscapes of Aelbert Cuyp, which adhere closely to van Goyen's muted palette and modest, simple subject-matter. Other successors, including Jan Coelenbier (1610–77), Frans de Hulst, Maerten Fransz. van der Hulft, Wouter Knijff, Willem Kool (1608/09–66), Pieter de Neyn and Johannes Schoeff (1608/9–62/6), developed their own recognizable painting style, while many anonymous artists merely imitated him.

In common with the art of many of his contemporaries, the low prices van Goyen's works commanded during his lifetime and for several generations thereafter make it difficult to assess earlier opinions of his artistic standing. He appears to have received commissions only occasionally, such as for the large *View of the Valkhof at Nijmegen* (1641; Nijmegen, Stadhuis) or *Huis Rouwkoop on the Vliet* (1642; Heemskerk, Gevers van Marquette priv. col.; see Beck, G488). Around 1651 he received two public commissions: he was paid 650 guilders for a large *Panoramic Landscape with View of The Hague* (The Hague, Gemeentemus.) for the Burgomaster's room in the Town Hall, and for the royal palace Honselaersdijk he produced a landscape depicting one of the royal estates in Burgundy. Not until Charles Sedelmeier's exhibitions in Vienna (1873) and later in Paris did he achieve international recognition; after the first van Goyen exhibition in Amsterdam, held by Frederik Muller & Cie (1903), his works began to enter public collections.

BIBLIOGRAPHY

J. J. Orlers: *Beschrijvinge der stadt Leyden...* (Leiden, 1641), pt i, pp. 373–4
A. Houbraken: *De groote schouburgh* (1718–21), i, pp. 170–71
P. Mantz: 'Jan van Goyen', *Gaz. B.-A.*, xii (1875), pp. 138–51, 298–311
H. U. Beck: *Jan van Goyen: 1596–1656: Ein Oeuvreverzeichnis*, i and ii (Amsterdam, 1972–3); iii (Doornspijk, 1987)
C. Wright: 'Van Groyen: A History of British Taste', *Jan van Goyen, 1596–1656: Poet of the Dutch Landscape* (exh. cat., London, Alan Jacobs Gal., 1977)
M. L. Wurfbain: 'Van Goyen: The Leyden Years', *Jan van Goyen, 1596–1656: Conquest of Space* (exh. cat., Amsterdam, Ksthandel K. & V. Waterman, 1981)

2. Jan van Goyen: *Market-day near a Canal*, black chalk and brown and grey wash, 170×274 mm, 1651 (Chicago, IL, Art Institute of Chicago)

Dutch Landscape: The Early Years, Haarlem and Amsterdam, 1590–1650 (exh. cat. by C. Brown, London, N.G., 1986), pp. 146–50
Masters of 17th-century Dutch Landscape Painting (exh. cat. by P. C. Sutton and others, Amsterdam, Rijksmus.; Boston, MA, Mus. F.A.; Philadelphia, PA, Mus. A.; 1987–8), pp. 317–32
H.-U. Beck: *Künstler um van Groyen* (Doornspijk, 1991)

H.-U. BECK

Go(o)yer, Salomon van de. *See* RUYSDAEL, SALOMON VAN.

Goyri, Roberto González. *See* GONZÁLEZ GOYRI, ROBERTO.

Göz [Goez; Götz]**, Gottfried Bernhard** (*b* Velehrad, Moravia, 10 Aug 1708; *d* Augsburg, 23 Nov 1774). Moravian painter and engraver, active in southern Germany. After studies at a Jesuit school, from 1726–7 he was apprenticed in Brünn [Brno] to Franz Gregor Ignaz Eckstein, whose frescoes transmitted to him some of the ideas of Annibale Carracci, Giovanni Lanfranco and Andrea Pozzo. In 1729–30 Göz worked with Johann Georg Bergmüller, and from 1730 he continued his training with Johann Georg Rothbletz (*fl* 1719–33), finally qualifying as a painter in 1733.

After relatively small-scale frescoes (1739; Augsburg, Köpf-Haus), at the Hofkapelle in Meersburg (1741), the audience chamber of the Benediktinerabtei at Weingarten (1742), the Klosterkirche in Habsthal (1748), and the Dompropstei (deanery) in Konstanz (1749), Göz's first major work was ceiling paintings for the Wallfahrtskirche at Birnau (*c.* 1749). These paintings on Marian themes, including Mary *gravida*, Mary as the *sedes sapentiae*, as the mother of piety, knowledge and hope, and also as the *Gnadenbild* of Birnau, are no longer conceived as extensions of church space, but are deliberately intended as 'picture areas in their own right above the architecture' (Bauer, p. 25). Göz was responsible for other fairly large works at Schloss Leitheim in 1751 and in the Salesianerinnenkirche in Amberg in 1758.

Göz sought out opportunities for pictures involving a large number of figures—a technique not fully mastered as regards composition and foreshortening in his *St John Nepomuk* of *c.* 1739 (priv. col., Isphording, no. 2). Thus his 1745 proposal to the abbot of Admont (Austria) for a cycle of church teachers talked of 'many figures', which would have to be 'ingeniously' presented. The results here (1745–7; *in situ*) are well disciplined as compositions; colour and light are used with skilful emphasis, and even unwieldy objects are incorporated harmoniously into the overall picture. The bright colouring and the free yet sure placing of the figures in *Duns Scotus before the Virgin and the Holy Trinity* (1754; Überlingen, Franziskanerkirche) show Göz's capabilities as a mature painter.

Göz's graphic work must have included over 500 engravings; about 450 are known today. His colour engravings have a stipple effect created by a burin, and were then printed in an elaborate process from a coloured and treated copperplate. Only a few of these have survived. He also produced some 250 outstanding stipple engravings, again using only the burin. In them, each individual dot is created deliberately, an extremely laborious process. Though there has been a basic knowledge of such techniques, there have been no other comparable achievements as regards both quality and quantity in the history of engraving. His book illustrations, generally to prayer texts such as the *Christliche Tages-zeit* (Augsburg, 1766; Wildmoser, nos 1–521–001f) and the *Heilige Communion- und Buss-Spiegel* (Augsburg, 1766; Wildmoser, 1–521–001f), account for much of his activity as an engraver. Besides this, from 1733–4 Göz independently developed pictures with no frame, which he put down on paper, as he himself expressed it, in a 'free manner'.

Göz's letters show him as very aware of the status of his works as an 'imperial court painter, engraver and art publisher', a post held from 1744. He took legal action on several occasions to protect his interests. The signature 'Göz Cath[olicus]', sometimes found on his engravings, is a clear reference to his clerical clientele. His pupils included Franz Ignaz Oefele (1721–97) and Franz Anton Zeiller (1716–93).

BIBLIOGRAPHY

E. Rüber: *Der Augsburger Maler und Kupferstecher Gottfried Bernhard Göz* (diss., U. Würzburg, 1923)
H. Bauer: 'Der Inhalt der Fresken von Birnau', *Das Münster*, xiv (1961), pp. 324–33
K.-A. Wirth: 'Sapientia aedificavit sibi domum, excidit columnas septem. Prov. 9.v.l.', *Jb. Ver. Augsburg. Bistumsgesch.* xiii (1979), p. 213
E. Isphording: *Gottfried Bernhard Göz 1708–1774. Ölgemälde und Zeichnungen*, 2 vols (Weissenhorn, 1982, 1984)
R. Wildmoser: 'Gottfried Bernhard Göz, (1708–1774) als ausführender Kupferstecher. Untersuchung und Katalog der Werke', *Jb. Ver. Augsburg. Bistumsgesch.*, xviii (1984), pp. 257–340; xix (1985), pp. 140–396

RUDOLF WILDMOSER

Gozzi, Gasparo (*b* Venice, 4 Dec 1713; *d* Padua, 26 Dec 1786). Italian writer. The brother of the playwright Carlo Gozzi, and the husband of the poet Luisa Bergalli, he was a theatrical impresario, an essayist, novelist and short story writer and the editor of *La Gazzetta veneta* and *L'Osservatore veneto*, journals in the new style of the Enlightenment. His most successful works were short stories, rich in pungent dialogue and sharp observations of contemporary society and morals. At a time when admiration for French culture and political thought had a strong influence on opinion in Italy, he recognized the greatness of Dante's poetry, appreciated the originality of Carlo Goldoni's plays, and translated many European literary texts into Italian. He was interested in the moral implications of painting, which he believed should be concerned with the significant moments of everyday life and express the advanced social ideals of the Enlightenment. He disliked the Baroque, and two essays he wrote for *La Gazzetta veneta* (13.8.1760) and *L'Osservatore veneto* (14.2.1761) convey his admiration for the art of Pietro Longhi, whose realistic genre scenes are claimed as equal to the history paintings of Giambattista Tiepolo.

WRITINGS

Favole esopiane (Venice, 1748)
Lettere diverse, 2 vols (Venice, 1750–52)
Difesa di Dante (Venice, 1758)
Opere in versi e in prosa (Venice, 1794)
N. Mangini, ed.: *Scritti scelti* (Turin, 1960) [with introd. essay]

BIBLIOGRAPHY

DBI
A. Zardo: *G. Gozzi nella letteratura del suo tempo in Venezia* (Bologna, 1923)
A. Zardo, ed.: *La Gazetta veneta* (Florence, 1957), pp. 242–6

F. Haskell: *Patrons and Painters* (London, 1963, rev. New Haven and London, 1980)

FRANCO BERNABEI

Gozzoli, Benozzo [Benozzo di Lese] (*b* Florence, *c*. 1420–22; *d* Pistoia, 4 Oct 1497). Italian painter. He was one of the most prolific fresco painters of his generation. Active principally in Tuscany, but also in Umbria and Rome, he had a facility for satisfying current tastes that secured him a steady stream of commissions throughout his career.

1. Life and work. 2. Working methods and technique.

1. LIFE AND WORK. The origin of the name Gozzoli is unclear. Vasari first appended it to Benozzo in the second edition (1568) of the *Vita* without explanation.

Benozzo may have trained as a painter with Fra Angelico, and his hand has been identified in some of the cell frescoes (*c*. 1440–45) in S Marco, Florence. On 24 January 1445 he signed a contract with Lorenzo Ghiberti and Vittorio Ghiberti I to work for three years on the east doors of the Florentine Baptistery. Although in the contract he is described as a painter, he appears to have assisted with the chasing of the cast panels and decorative borders of the doors. In 1447 Benozzo broke his contract with the Ghiberti workshop and went to Rome to join Fra Angelico as his chief assistant on the decoration of the chapels of S Pietro (destr.) and Pope Nicholas V in the Vatican palace. In summer 1448 he assisted Fra Angelico on the chapel of S Brizio in Orvieto Cathedral. He was unsuccessful in his application to continue the S Brizio frescoes when he returned to Orvieto in 1449, but he did receive some private commissions in that town. A panel of *St Ursula* (Washington, DC, N.G.A.) probably dates from this time.

Benozzo's earliest signed and dated work is the fresco of the *Virgin and Child Enthroned* (1450; partially destr.) in S Fortunato near Montefalco, Umbria. In the same

1. Benozzo Gozzoli: *Virgin and Child Enthroned with Saints and Angels*, tempera on panel, 1.62×1.70 m, 1461 (London, National Gallery)

church he painted frescoes of *St Fortunatus Enthroned* (above the altar) and of the *Virgin and Child with Saints* (in a lunette above the entrance). He also painted an altarpiece of the *Virgin Presenting a Girdle to St Thomas* (Rome, Pin. Vaticana). Although its five predella scenes of the *Life of the Virgin* are conventional in iconography and narrative organization, their compositional coherence illustrates a grasp of formal design that was developed in later, larger works.

While still in Montefalco Benozzo completed, in 1452, two fresco cycles in S Francesco: in the chapel of St Jerome (partially destr.), which appears to be largely the work of assistants; and in the choir, where he painted 12 scenes from the *Life of St Francis*. In the latter he achieved a balance between formal and iconographic demands in the sequence of episodes and organization of scenes, which were selected to emphasize the parallel between the life of Christ and that of St Francis. Although Benozzo did not use pictorial space for narrative ends in as complex a way as Paolo Uccello or Piero della Francesca, he was conscious of its dramatic potential. The scene of *St Francis Receiving the Stigmata* is divided between lunettes so that the divine rays from the seraph, in the lunette above the single window of the central wall, appear to cut across the corner of the vault to St Francis kneeling in the lunette on the right. The visual impact is heightened by the lighting of the scene, which corresponds with the fall of natural light.

In 1453 Benozzo painted a fresco cycle (destr. 1632) in the Franciscan church of S Rosa, Viterbo. Watercolours exist (Viterbo, Mus. Civ.) that show densely crowded compositions and architecture that is overtly antique in character. An altarpiece completed three years later for the company of St Jerome, Perugia (1456; Perugia, G.N. Umbria), may have been painted in Rome, where Benozzo was employed before 1458 on a fresco cycle (destr.) of the *Life of St Anthony of Padua* in the Albertini family chapel, S Maria in Aracoeli. The frescoed altarpiece of *St Anthony with Donors* survives.

In 1459 Benozzo began work in Florence on frescoes in the private chapel of the Palazzo Medici; they were probably finished in 1461. The *Journey of the Magi* covers three walls of the chapel, while in the sanctuary ranks of angels look towards the altarpiece of the *Virgin Adoring the Christ Child*. Three separate processions wind across rocky terrain and fertile valleys. The high horizon level of the frescoes, the compact groups of figures and the decorative pageantry recall tapestries. The cycle further differs from other frescoes executed by the artist in the extensive use of rich colours such as azure, vermilion and gold, reflecting the taste of the patron Piero de' Medici. Benozzo frequently introduced portraits into his work, for contemporary interest and variety. Here, members of the Medici family have been identified in the young king's procession, which includes a self-portrait of the artist; the words *Opus Benotii* are on the border of his red cap. The treatment of their features, and of other portrait heads in the retinues, distinguishes them from the standardized faces of the kings and pages. Benozzo wrote three letters to Piero de' Medici about this commission, acknowledging Piero's criticism of cherubim, informing him of his progress and requesting money to buy more materials.

In 1461 Benozzo was commissioned to paint an altarpiece, the *Virgin and Child Enthroned with Saints and Angels* (London, N.G.; see fig. 1), for the Confraternity of the Purification, affiliated to S Marco, Florence. The contract stipulated that the composition of the main panel was to be based on Fra Angelico's high altarpiece in S Marco. In contrast to the main panel, the predella scenes (London, N.G.; Berlin, Gemäldegal.; Washington, DC, N.G.A.; Milan, Brera.; Philadelphia, PA, Mus. A.), with stories of the attendant saints, are more inventive and anecdotal.

Two years later Benozzo was commissioned by Domenico Strambi, a distinguished Augustinian theologian, to paint a cycle of 17 scenes from the *Life of St Augustine* (1463–5; for illustration *see* AUGUSTINIAN HERMITS) in the choir of S Agostino, San Gimignano. The two most important events in the saint's life, his *Conversion to Christianity* and his *Baptism* (April 1464), occupy the central register of the altar wall. In *Augustine Teaching Rhetoric in Rome* (see fig. 2), the students are arranged around the central seated figure of Augustine. Their symmetrical grouping is emphasized by the antique architecture, but the solemnity is relieved by the animated facial features of the figures and by the small dog in the foreground. Despite an interruption of the work by an outbreak of plague in the town in 1464, Benozzo was able to complete, in addition to the Augustinian cycle, two frescoed, votive images of *St Sebastian*, in S Agostino and in the Collegiata.

In 1465 Benozzo served on a committee with Alesso Baldovinetti and Neri di Bicci to evaluate a fresco of Dante by Domenico di Michelino in Florence Cathedral. The following year he was contracted to work in the Palazzo Comunale, San Gimignano, on, among other projects, the restoration of Lippo Memmi's *Maestà* (1317; *in situ*). The frescoed tabernacles in the Tuscan towns of Monteoliveto, Certaldo and Castelfiorentino of this date are substantially the work of assistants, two of whom are recorded by name: Andrea di Giusto and Pier Francesco Fiorentino.

Benozzo's most ambitious undertaking was the completion of the 14th-century fresco decoration in the Camposanto, Pisa, which, according to Vasari, would have daunted a 'legion of painters'. Benozzo's trial piece, the *Drunkenness of Noah*, was approved in 1468, and he was commissioned to paint a further 24 scenes from the Old Testament. In the use of anecdotal detail, the scenes relate closely to the contemporary frescoes of Domenico Ghirlandaio and Cosimo Rosselli in the Sistine Chapel. Benozzo continued to work on the cycle until at least 1484. The frescoes suffered severe damage in 1944 but have been recorded in 19th-century engravings and photographs (Pisa, Camposanto).

While in Pisa, Benozzo also painted a fresco cycle (destr.), an altarpiece (Pisa, Mus. N. S Matteo) for the nuns of S Benedetto, and a panel of the *Triumph of St Thomas Aquinas* (Paris, Louvre), originally placed behind the Bishop's throne in the cathedral. Dating from the same period are frescoed tabernacles in the north Tuscan towns of Legoli and Castelnovo d'Elsa, and a fresco of the *Journey of the Magi* in the chapel of the Addolorata, Volterra

2. Benozzo Gozzoli: *Augustine Teaching Rhetoric in Rome* (1463–5), fresco, S Agostino, San Gimignano

Cathedral. The artist relied increasingly on assistants in his later works.

Benozzo's last years were divided between Pisa, Florence and Pistoia. In 1497 he evaluated frescoes by Alesso Baldovinetti in Santa Trìnita, Florence, together with Cosimo Rosselli, Pietro Perugino and Filippino Lippi. Two late works, a *Resurrection of Lazarus* (Washington, DC, N.G.A.) and a *Crucifixion* (Florence, Mus. Horne), were painted in Pistoia just before he died. He was buried in the cloister of the church of S Domenico.

Although Benozzo enjoyed considerable popularity among contemporaries, his influence on succeeding generations was limited. His style was assimilated by minor artists who may have worked as his assistants on projects outside Florence. It was not until the 19th century, when Carlo Lasinio's engravings of the frescoes in the Camposanto were published, that interest in Benozzo's work was renewed.

2. Working methods and technique. Benozzo followed the traditional Florentine practice of working out ideas in small drawings that were then scaled up. He sometimes used cartoons to transfer drawings onto walls or panels, and there are traces of pouncing on some frescoes. The underdrawings of his frescoes vary from simple contours, which establish the scale and general configuration of the scene, to more precise shading and perspectival grids; these were often modified as the work progressed. Benozzo usually worked in true fresco (*buon fresco*), reserving the dry technique (*fresco a secco*) for such details as faces and architectural ornament.

Most of Benozzo's panel paintings were executed in egg tempera, but at least two of his last works from Pistoia, the *Resurrection of Lazarus* and the *Crucifixion*, are in oil. Compositions are based on standard formulae and rarely display the energy and inventiveness of the artist's narrative frescoes. Contours are sharply defined, and a lack of aerial perspective gives a hardness to the imagery.

Over 100 sheets of drawings have been attributed to Benozzo and his workshop. Some are related directly to specific projects; others may have been used as general reference material. Most were made on coloured grounds in silverpoint or pen and ink heightened with white. They are inconsistent in quality but at their finest have a confidence and sensitivity of handling seen, for example, in the preliminary studies of angels for the chapel in the Palazzo Medici (Harewood House, W. Yorks).

Benozzo tended to use well-tried solutions for his figures, often reusing drawings or repeating or reversing cartoons, which sometimes reduced his figures to stereotypes; he was not adventurous in his portrayal of emotional interaction. In his early work he subdivided scenes so that each narrative episode was confined to the limits of its setting. In his later cycles, at San Gimignano and Pisa, he extended the narrative field, allowing figure groups within a scene to share a common foreground. His scenes are sometimes overcrowded, and the scale of figures can be exaggerated in proportion to their setting. However, he achieved a visual harmony through his use of colour and design. The polychrome buildings of his paintings and their increasingly elaborate ornament, inspired by contemporary *sgraffito* and stucco decoration, complement the colourful costumes of the figures they frame. A palette of whites, light greens and pinks characterizes the Franciscan scenes at Montefalco, while bold maroons and blues dominate the Augustinian cycle at San Gimignano.

BIBLIOGRAPHY

G. Vasari: *Vite* (1550, rev. 2/1568); ed. G. Milanesi (1878–85), pp. 45–63

C. Lasinio: *Pitture a fresco del Camposanto di Pisa disegnate e incise* (Florence, 1812)

G. Gaye: *Carteggio inedito di artisti*, 8 vols (Florence, 1840), i, pp. 191, 209, 271

L. Pecori: *Storia di San Gimignano* (Florence, 1853/*R* Rome, 1975)

E. Müntz: *Les Arts à la cour des papes* (Paris, 1878)

——: *Les Arts à la cour des papes, nouvelles recherches* (Paris, 1884)

L. Fumi: *Il duomo di Orvieto* (Rome, 1891)

M. Wingenroth: *Die Jugendwerke des Benozzo Gozzoli* (Heidelberg, 1897)

E. Contaldi: *Benozzo Gozzoli* (Milan, 1928)

G. Hoogewerff: *Benozzo Gozzoli* (Paris, 1930)

M. Lagaisse: *Benozzo Gozzoli: Les Traditions trécentistes et les tendances nouvelles chez un peintre florentin du '400* (Paris, 1934)

P. Bargellini: *La fiaba pittorica di Benozzo Gozzoli* (Florence, 1946)

P. Pouncey: 'A Drawing by Benozzo Gozzoli for his Fresco Cycle at Viterbo', *Burl. Mag.*, lxxix (1947), pp. 9–13, 98

R. G. Mather: 'Documents Mostly New Relating to Florentine Painters and Sculptors of the Fifteenth Century', *A. Bull.*, xxx (1948), p. 40

E. Borsook: *The Mural Painters of Tuscany from Cimabue to Andrea del Sarto* (London, 1960, rev. Oxford, 2/1980), pp. x, xxxi, xliii–xliv, xlvi, l, 47, 107, 110–11

M. Bucci and L. Bertolini: *Camposanto monumentale di Pisa* (Pisa, 1960)

A. Boschetto: *Gli affreschi di Benozzo Gozzoli nella chiesa di San Francesco a Montefalco* (Milan, 1961) [excellent pls]

A. Grote: 'A Hitherto Unpublished Letter on Benozzo Gozzoli's Frescoes in the Palazzo Medici-Riccardi', *J. Warb. & Court. Inst.*, xxvii (1964), pp. 321–2

E. Gombrich: 'The Early Medici as Patrons of Art', *Norm and Form: Studies in the Art of the Renaissance*, i (London, 1966, rev. Oxford, 4/1985), pp. 35–57

P. Scarpellini: *Benozzo Gozzoli* (Milan, 1966)

B. Degenhart and A. Schmitt: *Corpus der italienischen Zeichnungen, 1300–1450*, 4 vols (Berlin, 1968), i, pp. ii–iv

E. Berti Toesca: *Benozzo Gozzoli: Gli affreschi della Cappella Medicea* (Milan, 1970) [excellent pls]

M. Meiss: *The Great Age of Fresco* (London, 1970), pp. 13, 56–7, 162, 228

A. Padoa Rizzo: *Benozzo Gozzoli: Pittore fiorentino* (Florence, 1972)

A. Caleca, G. Nencini and G. Piancastelli: *Pisa: Museo delle sinopie* (Pisa, 1979)

K. Christiansen: 'Early Renaissance Narrative Painting in Italy', *Met. Mus. J.* (1982), pp. 3–56

F. Ames-Lewis and J. Wright: *Drawing in the Italian Renaissance Workshop* (London, 1983)

S. Pasti: 'Lo scomparso ciclo di affreschi di S Rosa da Viterbo di Benozzo Gozzoli e la sua influenza nel Viterbese: Gli affreschi dell'Isola Bisentina', *Il '400 a Roma e nel Lazio: Il quattrocento a Viterbo* (Rome, 1983), pp. 159–78

D. Cole Ahl: 'Benozzo Gozzoli's Frescoes of the *Life of St Augustine* in San Gimignano: Their Meaning in Context', *Artibus & Hist.* (1986)

C. Acidini Luchinot, ed.: *Benozzi Gozzoli: La Capella dei Magi* (Milan, 1993); Eng. trans. as *The Chapel of the Magi: Benozzo Gozzoli's Frescoes in the Palazzo Medici-Riccardi, Florence* (London and New York, 1994)

AILSA TURNER

Graat, Barent [Barend] (*b* Amsterdam, 21 Sept 1628; *d* Amsterdam, 4 Nov 1709). Dutch painter and draughtsman. At the age of 16 he was apprenticed to his uncle 'Master Hans', an animal painter, with whom he studied for six to seven years. He spent his entire career in Amsterdam. At first he painted landscapes with cattle in the style of Pieter van Laer, but his best works are either domestic interiors or history paintings with figures, or full-length group portraits set in a landscape or interior. These small paintings (e.g. *Family in a Landscape*, Amsterdam, Rijksmus.) required considerable technical dexterity. Despite the fact that Graat's work is of an excellent standard, he received little recognition. Consequently, his paintings have been sold under the name of better-known artists such as Gerard ter Borch (ii), with whose work his own has much in common.

Graat was also a good draughtsman, who made preliminary figure studies for both portraits and historical subjects (e.g. *Seated Man*, black and white chalk, Paris, Fond. Custodia, Inst. Néer.; for the *Portrait of a Married Couple in a Garden*, 1660; Vienna, Gemäldegal. Akad. Bild. Kst.). For 15 years he ran a 'Training College in the manner of the Royal Academy' (Houbraken), where artists could make life drawings. Among his pupils was Johann Heinrich Roos.

In 1708 Graat's daughter Geertruyd married the engraver Mathijs Pool (1670–1732), who produced engravings after Graat's paintings. Graat transferred his belongings, including his collection of drawings and prints, to his daughter as a wedding gift on the condition that for the rest of his life—which turned out to be only a few months—the couple would provide for him. The collection was sold in 1710, after his death.

BIBLIOGRAPHY

A. Houbraken: *De groote schouburgh* (1718–21), ii, p. 203

J. Immerzeel jr: *De levens en werken der Hollandsche en Vlaamsche kunstschilders, beeldhouwers, graveurs en bouwmeesters* (Amsterdam, 1842–3, 2/1855, rev. 1974), i, pp. 290–91

A. Bredius: *Künstler-Inventare: Urkunden zur Geschichte der holländischen Kunst des XVIten, XVIIten und XVIIIten Jahrhunderts* (The Hague, 1915–22), iv, pp. 1319–32

Dutch Figure Drawings from the Seventeenth Century (exh. cat. by P. Schatborn, Amsterdam, Rijksmus.; Washington, DC, N.G.A.; 1981–2), pp. 96–7, 137

B. Haak: *The Golden Age: Dutch Painters of the Seventeenth Century* (London, 1984), p. 491

TRUDY VAN ZADELHOFF

Grabar, André (*b* Kiev, 26 July 1896; *d* Paris, 5 Oct 1990). French art historian and archaeologist of Ukrainian birth. One of the most important and prolific scholars of Late Antique and medieval art, he studied at the universities of Kiev and Petrograd. He was Professor of the History of Art at Strasbourg and at the Ecole des Hautes Etudes (Paris) and held the chair of Early Christian and Byzantine Archaeology of the Collège de France from 1946 to 1966. He was a member of the British Academy, as well as of the academies of several European countries, and was awarded honorary doctorates at the universities of Princeton, Uppsala and Edinburgh.

Over his long career Grabar contributed a large body of writing to Byzantine scholarship, but his most important work was broadly concerned with the functions of objects within their theological, historical and liturgical contexts.

For example, as an extension of the cult of relics (*Martyrium*, 1943), religious images were invested by the Christian faithful with great potency, which was the focus of attention during Iconoclasm (*Iconoclasme byzantin*, 1957). In Late Antiquity function was often the only indication that a work of art was intended to be Christian rather than pagan (*Christian Iconography*, 1968). Grabar founded the periodical *Cahiers Archéologiques* (Paris), to which he was a regular contributor, and he also wrote for a general audience, including such books as *Byzance* and *Le Premier Art chrétien.*

WRITINGS

La Peinture religieuse en Bulgarie (Paris, 1928)
L'Empereur dans l'art byzantin (Paris, 1936)
Martyrium, 2 vols (Paris, 1943/*R* 1946)
La Peinture byzantine (Geneva, 1953)
Le Haut Moyen Age (Geneva, 1957; Eng. trans., Lausanne, 1957)
Iconoclasme byzantin (Paris, 1957)
Les Ampoules de Terre Sainte (Paris, 1958)
La Peinture romane (Geneva, 1958; Eng. trans., Lausanne, 1958)
L'Art byzantin du Moyen Age (Paris, 1963; Eng. trans., London, 1966)
Sculptures byzantines de Constantinople (Paris, 1963)
L'Age d'or de Justinien, Univers des Formes (Paris, 1966)
Le Premier Art chrétien, Univers des Formes (Paris, 1966)
L'Art de la fin de l'antiquité et du Moyen Age, 3 vols (Paris, 1968) [bibliog. to 1967, pp. 1215–23]
Christian Iconography: A Study of its Origins (Princeton, 1968)
A. Grabar, ed.: *Synthronon* (Paris, 1968)
Les Manuscrits grecs enluminés de provenance italienne (Paris, 1972)
Les Revêtements en or et en argent des icônes byzantines du Moyen Age (Venice, 1975)
Sculptures byzantines du Moyen Age (Paris, 1976)
Les Voies de la création en iconographie chrétienne (Paris, 1979)

BIBLIOGRAPHY

Who's Who in France, 1963/4, 1975/6, 1988/9
Répertoire international des médiévistes (Poitiers), 1965, 1971, 1979, 1987
Obituary, *The Independent*, 9 Oct 1990, p. 14; *Dumbarton Oaks Pap.*, xlv (1991), pp. xiii-xv

□

Grabar', Igor' (Emmanuilovich) (*b* Budapest, 13 March 1871; *d* Moscow, 16 May 1960). Russian painter, writer and museum director of Hungarian birth. He studied law at the University of St Petersburg before enrolling at the Academy of Arts there in 1894. He moved in 1896 to Munich, where he took lessons from Anton Ažbe (1861–1905). He remained in Germany until 1901, assimilating the principles of *Jugendstil*, a strong influence on his early painting and graphic work, as in *Lady at the Piano* (1899; Moscow, priv. col., see Podobedova, p. 55), which is reminiscent, in its Art Nouveau treatment of the *femme fatale*, of Léon Bakst's *Supper* (1902; St Petersburg, Rus. Mus.).

Back in St Petersburg, Grabar' became closely involved with the World of Art group, contributing to its journal and exhibitions, but in 1903 he joined the Union of Russian Artists, which reflected his interest in Impressionist landscape. This is evident from his lovely winter scenes of the early 1900s, such as *September: Snow* (1903), *White Winter: Rooks' Nests* (1904) and *February: Azure* (1904; all Moscow, Tret'yakov Gal.). Such paintings express Grabar''s developed perception of colour and texture and his acute sensibility to the effects of light. Until the Revolution he travelled widely in Russia and abroad, and many of his paintings record the places he visited, especially old Russian towns such as Vologda.

In 1913 Grabar' became a professor at the Academy of Arts, St Petersburg, and director of the Tret'yakov Gallery, Moscow (until 1925). During his tenure he did much to preserve, restore and reassess old Russian icons, and he can be regarded as the initiator of the successful school of restorers of Russian architecture, painting and the applied arts. After the Revolution Grabar' worked as a professor of art history at Moscow State University (until 1946), as Director of the State Central Restoration Studios in Moscow and as Director of the Scientific Research Institute of Art History at the Academy of Sciences (1944–60).

In his painting Grabar' sometimes adjusted his style to more overtly political ends, as in *Lenin on the Wire* (also called *Lenin Receiving a Cable*, 1927–33; Moscow, Cent. Lenin Mus.). During the 1930s and 1940s, however, he continued to paint simple landscapes and still-lifes (e.g. *Morning Tea: Snowdrops*, 1939–45; Tashkent, Mus. A. Uzbekistan), and he paid particular attention to portraiture, both of his immediate family and of luminaries such as the Academician *Sergey Chaplygin* (1935; Abramtsevo, Mus.–Estate), shown at the Exposition Universelle in Paris in 1937. Grabar' continued to paint and write until shortly before his death, and his books and articles on various aspects of Russian art and architecture—especially his editorship of the multi-volume *Istoriya russkogo iskusstva* ('History of Russian art', 1910–15, Soviet version and continuation, 1953–69)—still serve as important sources of information and criticism.

WRITINGS

Moya zhizn: Avtomonografiya [My life: an automonograph] (Moscow, 1937)
T. Kazhdan and others, eds: *Igor' Grabar': Pis'ma* [Igor' Grabar': letters], 3 vols (Moscow, 1974–83)

BIBLIOGRAPHY

O. Podobedova: *Igor' Emmanuilovich Grabar'* (Moscow, 1964)
V. Azarkovich, ed.: *Igor' Grabar'* (Leningrad, 1977)

JOHN E. BOWLT

Grabuloski-Grabul, Jordan (*b* Prilep, 19 March 1925; *d* Skopje, 28 May 1986). Macedonian sculptor. He was apprenticed to a local stonecutter in Prilep from *c.* 1940, and from 1945 he attended the class of Dimo Todorovski (1907–83), founder of modern Macedonian sculpture, at the School of Applied Arts in Skopje. Grabuloski graduated from the Academy of Arts in Belgrade in 1952, having studied under Lojze Dolinar (1893–1970) and Sreten Stojanović (1898–1960). He returned to Skopje and in 1953 founded the Denes group. In the following years he attempted to embody in his work the group's programme for a synthesis of the arts and architecture. Between 1968 and 1974 he came closest to achieving that aim when he created the huge spherical Monument of Ilinden at Kruševo, central Macedonia, with eight mine-like, radial protrusions arranged on two levels. Comparable in spirit to this monumental project were the 'ambient sculptures' that he displayed at his one-man exhibition in the Museum of Contemporary Art in Skopje (1970). These he made from brightly coloured chipboard and hardboard, giving them swinging contours. He took part in several group exhibitions in London (1970), Vienna (1975), Athens (1977 and 1987) and Zagreb (1983). From the mid-1960s he referred to his works as 'objects' rather than sculptures, and he eventually became interested in environmental art and installations.

BIBLIOGRAPHY

Jordan Grabul—Objekti [Jordan Grabul—objects] (exh. cat. by B. Petkovski, Skopje, Mus. Contemp. A., 1970)

S. Abadjieva Dimitrova: *Jordan Grabuloski Grabul* (Skopje, 1988) [with Eng. summary]

BOJAN IVANOV

Grabuset, Thomas (*b* Auxonne; *fl* 1453; *d* ?1483). Burgundian painter. He was the son of Jean Grabuset, a painter of Besançon, and his brothers and nephew were also painters; like him, they settled in Provence. He may have been trained in the workshop of Guillaume Dombet, as he is first mentioned as a witness for him in Avignon in 1453. Thomas Grabuset settled in Beaucaire in 1456 and was evidently esteemed in the Avignon region, for he worked for such wealthy patrons as King René I of Naples, the Duke of Anjou, the executors of Cardinal Pierre de Foix and the magistrates of Avignon. His activity was varied: he painted sculpture and supplied stained glass, decorations and altarpieces. He produced altarpieces for Ste Marthe (1456) and for the Franciscan church (1457), both in Tarascon; he completed an altarpiece begun by Aubry Dombet for Arnaud de Montjoie (1465); and he delivered panels for an inhabitant of Baux-de-Provence (1466), for the Dominican church in Arles (1470) and for the church of Caromb (1481). None of these can be identified, although it has been suggested that an equestrian *St George* (1.35×0.65 m) in Caromb Church, Vaucluse, formed part of the last work. Other attributions to Grabuset are purely hypothetical: the *Pietà of Tarascon* (*c*. 1456–7; Paris, Mus. Cluny) and *SS John the Baptist and Francis with Two Donors Contemplating the Bare Cross*, the so-called Pérussis Altarpiece (1480; New York, Met.).

BIBLIOGRAPHY

L. H. Labande: *Les Primitifs français: Peintres et peintres-verriers de la Provence occidentale* (Marseille, 1932), pp. 87, 254

P. Pansier: *Les Peintres d'Avignon aux XIVe et XVe siècles: Biographies et documents* (Avignon, 1934), pp. 132–42

H. Chobaut: 'Documents inédits sur les peintres et peintres-verriers d'Avignon, du Comtat et de la Provence occidentale de la fin du XIVe siècle au premier tiers du XVIe siècle', *Mém. Acad. Vaucluse*, iv (1939), pp. 83–145

C. Sterling: 'La Pietà de Tarascon', *Rev. A.*, v/1 (1955), pp. 25–46

——: 'La Pietà de Tarascon et les peintres Dombet', *Rev. Louvre*, xvi/1 (1966), pp. 13–26

M. Laclotte and D. Thiébaut: *L'Ecole d'Avignon* (Paris, 1983), p. 248

DOMINIQUE THIÉBAUT

Gračanica. Byzantine monastery in the Kosovo region between Montenegro and Macedonia, 8 km south of Priština. It was founded by the Serbian king Stephen Uroš II Milutin (*reg* 1282–1321). The church of the Dormition (originally Annunciation; 1311–21; see fig.) is all that survives and is one of the outstanding achievements of Late Byzantine architecture (*see* EARLY CHRISTIAN AND BYZANTINE ART, §II, 2(iv)(c)). It was built on the site of two earlier churches. The dismantling of the second church—a small single-aisled 13th-century structure—is described in the monastery's charter, as recorded on the west wall of the south chapel, and has been confirmed by excavations. Gračanica also served as the seat of the bishops of Lipljan, the probable heirs to the bishopric of Ulpiana, a Roman and Early Christian city *c*. 1 km to the west. Milutin may also have intended Gračanica's church as his mausoleum.

Gračanica was a product of the political and cultural circumstances that prevailed in Serbia following Milutin's marriage in 1299 to Simonis, the daughter of the Byzantine emperor Andronikos II (*reg* 1282–1328). Milutin's relative political and economic strength enabled him to attract the best Byzantine architects and painters to Serbia (*see* EARLY CHRISTIAN AND BYZANTINE ART, §III, 5; and SERBIA, §III, 1(i)(b)). The head architect was probably from Thessaloniki, while one of his collaborators was in all likelihood from Epiros. Such conclusions are based on careful analysis of the plan and architecture of the building, which reveal a degree of sophistication and maturity unsurpassed among contemporary Byzantine monuments.

The church has a cross-in-square naos, enveloped by an east sanctuary with lateral chapels, north and south ambulatories, and an inner narthex. The attenuated domes, consisting of a large one in the centre and four smaller ones at the corners, give the church a carefully balanced exterior form. This is further distinguished by the restrained and highly sophisticated articulation of the cloisonné masonry of the outer walls.

The interior walls and vaults of Gračanica are covered with wall paintings that depict an unusually large number of individual scenes and figures, organized in seven horizontal zones and grouped in several distinct cycles. They have been successfully integrated with the architecture, from the point of view of both their liturgical disposition and their relationship to various structural elements. This complex decorative programme also reflects the influence of the higher clergy and the royal patron.

The paintings follow the iconography of Byzantine churches, with *Christ Pantokrator* in the centre of the main dome, the standing figures of *Prophets* around the drum, and the four *Evangelists* on the four pendentives. The *Twelve Feasts* appear in the uppermost zones and on

Gračanica, church of the Dormition, from the north-west, 1311–21

the vaults of the naos. The most prominent among these are the *Descent into Limbo* on the east wall, and the *Dormition* on the west wall, directly above the main entrance. In the main apse is a large *Virgin Orans*. Below her are the *Last Supper* and the *Liturgy of SS Basil and John Chrysotomos*. The walls of the sanctuary contain several Old Testament scenes (e.g. *Abraham and the Three Angels*, the *Sacrifice of Isaac*, the *Ark of the Covenant*). These scenes, together with an extensive *Life of the Virgin*, stress the themes of prefiguration, incarnation and salvation, and they reveal the subtle links between the dogma, the liturgy and church history that characterize much Late Byzantine painting.

The entire west wall of the inner narthex is occupied by an enormous *Last Judgement* and its subsidiary scenes. On the east wall are representations of Serbian historical figures including Milutin's deceased parents depicted as a monk and a nun, and the earliest representation of the *Nemanjić Family Tree*, which originally provided the setting for a baptismal font that stood directly in front of it. This composition and the donor portraits of *Milutin* and *Simonis*, who are shown being crowned by Christ on the sides of a large archway leading into the naos, reveal the strong influence of Byzantine imperial art. The portrait of *Milutin* depicts him as a very old man and was probably painted shortly before his death. The paintings were by an anonymous group of skilled artists, which may have included ASTRAPAS and Eutychios.

The outer narthex, along with open arcades and a belfry, was added to the church, probably in the 1340s. The narthex was apparently damaged and rebuilt in 1383. After further damage in 1570, the openings were blocked up and the interior repainted. The restorations undertaken in the 1950s and 1960s do not correspond to the structure's historical phases, although some elements have been preserved.

BIBLIOGRAPHY

S. Ćurčić: *Gračanica: King Milutin's Church and its Place in Late Byzantine Architecture* (University Park and London, 1979)

——: *Gračanica: Istorija i arhitektura* [Gračanica: history and architecture] (Belgrade and Priština, 1988)

B. Todić: *Gračanica: Slikarstvo* [Gračanica: painting] (Belgrade and Priština, 1988)

SLOBODAN ĆURČIĆ

Gradistea Muncelului. *See under* SARMIZEGETHUSA.

Grado. Town in Friuli, northern Italy. Situated on a lagoon island in the north Adriatic, it succeeded the harbour of Aquileia when this silted up in the 4th and 5th centuries AD. The new town was protected by a fort, traceable to the time of Bishop Augustinus of Aquileia (*reg* ?413–31) but soon extended, that still determines the plan of the old town today; an impressive remnant is the polygonal tower on Campo Porta Nuova. In AD 452 the population of Aquileia fled to Grado when the Huns destroyed their city, and at the time of the Lombard invasion in 468 Bishop Paulinus moved his see to Grado, which was still in Byzantine territory. Under Patriarch Elias (*reg* 571–86) Grado was at the centre of the Three Chapters controversy, the upheavals of which led to the splitting of the patriarchate into two politically opposed branches at Aquileia and Grado in 607. Grado became increasingly orientated towards Venice, where the patriarch resided from 1156 until 1451, when his office was abolished to make way for the new patriarchate of Venice.

The cathedral of S Eufemia, built of brick, still largely preserves the form it received under Patriarch Elias in 579. It is an aisled basilica (45.5×19.6 m) with an eastern apse, round on the inside but polygonal outside, and no transept. The ten pairs of marble columns and their capitals (without imposts) are possibly all spolia. Above every second column a pilaster rises to the ceiling, giving a sense of rhythm to the nave. Many of the fine mosaic floors also date from Elias's time, late examples of the Aquileian mosaic tradition, and some reused fragments survive of the old presbytery decoration. An annexe along the south wall, the so-called *salutatorium* ('reception room') of Elias, may go back to an earlier bishop's palace. Later additions include a Late Romanesque pulpit with reliefs of the Evangelist Symbols and a Venetian silver antependium of 1372; the Treasury houses some important examples of early metalwork. The ivory reliefs (7th/8th centuries) scattered in various museums and said to come from the 'cathedra of Grado' have no recorded connection with the city.

Excavations and restoration work at the cathedral (including the removal of Baroque decorations) undertaken since 1915 have enabled much of its early building history to be clarified. A hall-shaped cemetery building with an altar (14.7×6.7 m) was built in a necropolis in the second half of the 4th century; later an apse was added, with cathedra and *synthronon*, and the mosaic-decorated tomb of Petrus, a converted Jew, was erected. The cemetery was disused after the fort was enlarged, and the church, by now a cathedral, was replaced by a much larger building, the walls of which survive in the present church: it is described in a mosaic inscription of Elias as 'darkened by age' and is usually dated to the second half of the 5th century. This is probably also the date of the octagonal baptistery (diam. 12 m) to the north of the cathedral; there is no evidence, however, that its eastern apse was an addition of Elias's time.

S Maria delle Grazie, also built of brick, stands in the oldest nucleus of the fort next to the cathedral. It is an aisled basilica without transepts (18.9×11.2 m excluding the apse); a passage around the outside of the apse (see fig.) links the flanking *pastophoria*, unlike the comparable Syrian building type. The church, which was remodelled in the late 6th century under Patriarch Elias, retains the walls of an earlier building that has been linked with that built in the *castrum* and dedicated to the Virgin by Bishop Chromatius (*reg* 392–413). Remains of its floor have been exposed in the south aisle, while apse excavations show the original orientation of its presbytery. During the alterations carried out under Patriarch Elias, the number of pairs of columns was reduced from six to five. The articulation of the clerestory by pilasters rising above the second and fourth pair of columns and the concentration of its lighting in the middle of the nave are examples of the originality of his building. There are remains of a mosaic floor from Elias's time in the north aisle. The building was restored from 1920 to 1927, as far as possible to its state under Elias.

The remains of S Giovanni Evangelista at the south end of the enlarged fort were excavated from 1902 to

Grado, S Maria delle Grazie, interior of apse, *c.* AD 580

1962. The first church (22.9×10.1 m), without aisles but with a 'Syrian' apse (i.e. apse and *pastophoria* enclosed by rectangular walls), cathedra and *synthronon*, was built in the early 5th century, with a baptistery (diam. 8.2 m) near by. Its function, possibly an Arian cathedral, is controversial. The replacement of this church by an aisled basilica (40.5×19.22 m), also decorated with mosaics and with a 'Syrian' east end, evidently took place under Bishop Macedonius (*reg* 534–57). It was repaired in the early 9th century by Patriarch Fortunatus (reg 803–4 and 810–26), but shortly afterwards it seems to have fallen into ruin.

BIBLIOGRAPHY

G. Brusin and P. L. Zovatto: *Monumenti paleocristiani di Aquileia e di Grado* (Udine, 1957)

L. Bertacchi: 'La cappella con la tomba del vescovo Marciano nel duomo di Grado', *Aquileia Nostra*, xxxvii (1966), cols 89–104

M. Mirabella Roberti: 'La più antica basilica di Grado', *Arte in Europa: Scritti di storia dell'arte in onore di Edoardo Arslan*, i (Milan, 1966), pp. 105–12

G. Cuscito: 'Il nucleo antico della città di Grado', *Aquileia Nostra*, xl (1969), cols 143–82

L. Bertacchi: 'Le origini del duomo di Grado', *Aquileia Nostra*, xlii (1971), cols 65–70

M. Pozzetto: 'Appunti sul problema della configurazione spaziale delle basiliche eliane di Grado', *Felix Ravenna*, ciii–civ (1972), pp. 235–61

G. Bovini: *Grado paleocristiana* (Bologna, 1973)

M. Mirabella Roberti: 'Il mausoleo di Elia nel duomo di Grado', *Atti del III congresso di archeologia cristiana*, Antichità Altoadriat., vi (Trieste, 1974), pp. 107–17

——: 'Il castrum di Grado', *Aquileia Nostra*, xlv–xlvi (1974–5), cols 565–74

G. Cuscito: *Cristianesimo antico ad Aquileia e in Istria*, Fonti e studi per la storia della Venezia Giulia, II, iii (Trieste, 1977)

S. Tavano: 'Il territorio di Aquileia nell'alto medio evo: Note urbanistiche', *Il territorio di Aquileia nell'antichità*, ii, Antichità Altoadriat., xv (Udine, 1979), pp. 627–66 (646–54)

M. Mirabella Roberti, ed.: *Grado nella storia e nell'arte*, 2 vols, Antichità Altoadriat., xvii (Udine, 1980)

S. Tavano: *Aquileia e Grado: Storia, arte, cultura* (Trieste, 1986)

F. Castellan: *La selezione dei beni culturali: Archeologia e restauro nelle basiliche di Aquileia e di Grado*, Quaderni del dipartimento di conservazione delle risorse architettoniche e ambientali, ii (Milan, 1988)

PETER DIEMER

Gradual. *See under* CHOIR-BOOK.

Graeff, Cornelis de, Lord of Zuid-Polsbroek, Purmerland and Ilpendam (*b* Amsterdam, 15 Oct 1599; *d* 4 May 1664). Dutch diplomat, government official and patron. He belonged to one of the richest and most powerful families in Amsterdam. In 1636 he became a director of the East India Company; three years later he was captain of the archers' militia company. He was appointed Burgomaster of Amsterdam first in 1643, and after the unsuccessful attack on Amsterdam by the Stadholder William II, the centre of power switched from the Bicker family to de Graeff: he became Burgomaster-magnificus in 1651 and remained in that office, exercising virtually unlimited power (with breaks in 1657 and 1660), until 1663. De Graeff was renowned as a great diplomat who steered a moderate course between the States party and the Orangists. He actively supported the appointment and policies of the Secretary of State, Johann de Witt.

De Graeff commissioned the Amsterdam Stadhuis (now Royal Palace; *see* AMSTERDAM, §V, 3) from Jacob van Campen. In 1648 he had the former St Cornelis or Baptist chapel in the Oude Kerk in Amsterdam converted into his family tomb by the sculptor Artus Quellinus I. The same sculptor executed two profile portraits of *de Graeff* and his wife *Catharina Hooft* (both marble relief, 1660; Amsterdam, Rijksmus.). De Graeff's portrait as captain of the archers' company was painted by Jacob Backer (Amsterdam, Rijksmus.), and Nicolaes Eliasz. Pickenoy painted two pendants of de Graeff and his wife (both Berlin, Bodemus.). A portrait by Govaert Flinck (untraced) was included in the auction of the Ilpenstein collection in Amsterdam (3 December 1872, lot 8) and again in a sale by Lempertz in Cologne (11–12 March 1938, lot 122).

BIBLIOGRAPHY

NNBW

F. Lugt: *Ventes*, i (1938), p. 734

P. J. J. van Thiel and others: *All the Paintings of the Rijksmuseum in Amsterdam* (Amsterdam en Maarsen, 1976), p. 93

I. Geismeier: *Holländische und flämische Gemälde des siebzehnten Jahrhunderts im Bode-Museum* (Berlin, 1976), pp. 31–2

FEMY HORSCH

Graeser, Camille (*b* Geneva, 27 Feb 1892; *d* Wald, Zurich, 21 Feb 1980). Swiss painter. After studying under Adolf Hölzel at the academy in Stuttgart, he stayed on in Germany and practised both as an interior designer (collaborating on projects with Ludwig Mies van der Rohe, for instance at the Weissenhofsiedlung exhibitions in Stuttgart in 1927) and as a painter, influenced initially by Cubo-Futurism. As early as 1922 his work was non-figurative, using geometric forms; by the end of the 1930s he was seeking to justify the use of pictorial elements in his paintings. He left Germany and returned to Switzerland in 1933, and, becoming integrated into the Swiss modern art milieu, he joined the Allianz group in 1937 and participated in all the important events that marked the development of CONCRETE ART in Zurich. After 1945, he principally studied problems of surface and quantity, which he resolved by the use of a systematic process. The two dimensional surface of a painting is structured by means of a simple horizontal and vertical framework within which squares and rectangles are arranged. These elementary shapes, coloured in such a way that their surface cannot be separated from their colour, can be shifted by means of rotation, translation or permutation, for example a square taken out of line and teetering at 45°. It was one of Graeser's most beautifully poetic inventions and is shown in *Equivalence on the Horizontals* (1957–8; Winterthur, Kstmus.). Problems of quantity were approached from the viewpoint of balance and equality; neither horizontal nor vertical elements were allowed to dominate, creating compositions in equilibrium, with shape and colour used in equal quantities. Graeser's drawings, executed throughout his career, use lines and figures drawn with a ruler, set square and pair of compasses to present the same subject-matter as his paintings.

BIBLIOGRAPHY

W. Rotzler: *Camille Graeser* (Zurich, 1979)
Camille Graeser (exh. cat., ed. E. Billeter; Zurich, Ksthaus; Ludwigshafen, Hack-Mus. & Städt. Kstsamml.; 1979)
D. Schwarz: *Camille Graeser: Zeichnungen* (Zurich, 1986)
Camille Graeser (exh. cat., ed. R. Koella; Winterthur, Kstmus., 1992)

SERGE LEMOINE

Graevenitz, Gerhard von (*b* Schilde, Mark Brandenburg, 19 Sept 1934; *d* Switzerland, 25 Aug 1983). German painter, sculptor and kinetic artist. He first studied economics in Frankfurt am Main but then attended Ernst Geitlinger's painting class at the Akademie der Bildenden Künste in Munich (1956–61). He was interested in the teachings of the Bauhaus masters. Early exposure to the work of Jackson Pollock was also important. His first works of the 1950s were white structures and reliefs, such as *White Structure, 3 Fields* (1960; Leverkusen, Schloss Morsbroich). In his works the artist was not concerned with composition as such but rather with the problem of organizing an image. Graevenitz produced the journal *Nota* with Jürgen Morschel (1959–60) and ran the gallery of the same name in Munich (1960–61), becoming involved with artists such as Otto Piene and Heinz Mack. In the 1960s the non-hierarchical homogeneous structures became kinetic, being additionally moved by motors, resulting in constantly new regular and irregular arrangements in individual modules, sometimes further agitated by light-reflecting material (e.g. *Light Object*, 1963; Kassel, Neue Gal.).

From 1970 Graevenitz lived in Amsterdam. In the 1970s he produced many of these kinetic objects, but with a smaller number of individual moving parts, for example *Kinetic Object: 5 Black Rectangles on White* (1973; London, Tate). During this period he also produced environments, for example *Kinetic Object* (1977) in the Stedelijk Museum, Amsterdam, comprising 20 horizontal and vertical white beams spread over the walls of the gallery space. In 1968 he had joined *Nouvelle tendance*, and he helped to set up the International Art Committee in 1976. As an exhibition organizer he was particularly known for his concept for the *Pier and Ocean* exhibition (1980), held at the Hayward Gallery, London, and the Rijksmuseum Kröller-Müller, Otterlo. He was killed in an aeroplane crash.

BIBLIOGRAPHY

Gerhard von Graevenitz (exh. cat., Essen, Flkwang Mus., 1968)
Gerhard von Graevenitz (exh. cat., Kiel, Kstver., 1974)
Gerhard von Graevenitz (exh. cat., Eindhoven, Stedel. Van Abbemus., 1979)
Gerhard von Graevenitz (exh. cat., Otterlo, Kröller-Müller, 1984)

EVA MEYER-HERMANN

Graf, Urs (*b* Solothurn, *c.* 1485; *d* ?Basle, 1527–9). Swiss draughtsman, goldsmith, die-cutter, engraver, woodcut and stained-glass designer, painter and glass painter. He was the most original and gifted artist of the early Renaissance in German-speaking Switzerland. His highly imaginative drawings, created as independent works of art, are works of exceptional quality, vitality, expressiveness and often humour. For northern European art, Graf played an important role in the liberation of drawing from its traditionally subsidiary status as preparatory study for works of art in other media.

1. LIFE AND WORK. Graf was trained as a goldsmith by his father, Hug Graf (*d* 1527–30), and remained active in this profession throughout his career. Although almost none of his goldsmith work is preserved, examples such as the silver engraved plates (1519; London, BM; Zurich, Schweizer. Landesmus.) from a reliquary bust executed for a monastery in the canton of Lucerne are of a high quality. He received additional training (1507–8) from the goldsmith Lienhart Triblin (*fl* 1491–1507) in Zurich, but by 1503 was designing woodcut book illustrations for the printer Johann Knobloch (*fl* 1500–28) in Strasbourg and in 1508 for Hans Am Wasen (also known as Rüegger; *fl* 1503–17) in Zurich. In 1511 he was being trained as a stained-glass painter by Hans Heinrich Wolleb (*fl* 1490–1527) in Basle. He purchased citizenship in Basle in 1512 and joined the city's goldsmiths' guild, in which he held various offices until 1524. He was gaoled several times for wife-beating and public consorting with prostitutes, and an attempted homicide in 1518 forced him to flee to Solothurn. In 1519 the Basle city council invited him back to become die-cutter for the local mint, and the additional income from this prestigious position allowed him to purchase a house.

Graf's early work was influenced by Martin Schongauer, whose engravings he copied and adapted. He was the most sought-after book illustrator among Basle's printers until in 1515 Ambrosius Holbein and Hans Holbein (ii) moved to Basle and began to receive the majority of such commissions. Graf's prints encompass over 450 woodcuts, 8 engravings, 16 nielli and what is considered to be the earliest extant dated etching, *A Girl Washing her Feet* (1513; Hollstein, no. 834). He seems to have painted only rarely: an inventory of his possessions (1518) lists two small panels, but it is not certain they were his own work. No signed paintings have survived but the small *Wild Horde* panel (Basle, Kstmus.) has a convincing, very early attribution by Basilius Amerbach. Amerbach's collection, assembled in the later 16th century, forms the nucleus of the finest group of Graf's work, now in Basle, including *c.* 130 of *c.* 200 extant drawings.

Graf fully exploited the potential of the drawing medium for personal expression. Unorthodox in his treatment of traditional themes in art, innovative in his pictorial means and often satirical in tone, he addressed both personal and public issues. His work seems to have suffered none of the inherent limitations imposed on Renaissance art by function and patronage: he did not concern himself with the learned themes or dynastic allegories, religious pictures or portraits, commissioned by humanist or princely patrons. Instead he chose subjects from the life around him, the political climate, social conditions and popular culture of early 16th-century Basle. As a group these drawings constitute the most revealing visual commentary on an artist and his times that has survived from the Renaissance in northern Europe. Graf, attracted more by vice than by virtue, held up a mirror to the folly and foibles of his contemporaries. His drawings reveal which prejudices were most deeply entrenched in his generation, as in *Two Prostitutes Beating a Monk* (1521; Basle, Kstmus.; see fig.); which political issues were most vigorously debated, as in *Recruiting in a Guild Hall* (1521; Basle, Kstmus.); and what kinds of social conduct provoked scorn or ridicule. Many have erotic subjects. His political caricatures are unique in their time. Compared with the work of his contemporaries, Graf's seems astonishingly modern.

As one of the Swiss mercenaries who played a pivotal role in European politics and warfare *c.* 1500, Graf repeatedly abandoned his workshop and family in Basle to participate in military campaigns in hopes of adventure and booty. His experiences on the battlefields of Italy and Burgundy are the subject of some of his most memorable and poignant images. After the Swiss defeat at Marignano in 1515, a battle in which he participated, his images of exhilarated, victorious Swiss mercenaries gave way to more critical depictions of the vicissitudes of warfare; for example, a late drawing (1525; Basle, Kstmus.), juxtaposing a hanged mercenary, robbed of his possessions and dangling from a tree, with a richly attired, pregnant camp-follower or prostitute. When and where he died are unknown: his wife remarried in October 1528 but an autograph drawing is dated 1529.

Urs Graf: *Two Prostitutes Beating a Monk*, pen and ink and remnants of chalk on paper, 207×255 mm, 1521 (Basle, Kunstmuseum)

2. Working methods and technique. Most of Graf's drawings are executed in pen and black ink, the earlier ones often over a chalk preparatory sketch, which is sometimes still faintly visible. Simple black lines are the ideal medium for his decidedly decorative, highly calligraphic line. Around 1513 he became familiar with the chiaroscuro drawings of Hans Baldung, who was then working near Basle, in Freiburg im Breisgau. Graf rapidly developed a mastery in this technique, as his *Striding Standard-bearer* (1514; Basle, Kstmus.) attests. He also worked very skilfully with the point of the brush, as in a series of colourful working drawings (1521; Basle, Kstmus.) for round stained glass, and also in silverpoint in a magnificent series of sketches of standard-bearers (*c.* 1520; all Basle, Kstmus.). Too little of his painted oeuvre has survived for any analysis of its technique.

BIBLIOGRAPHY

Hollstein: *Ger.*

E. Major: 'Urs Graf: Ein Beitrag zur Geschichte der Goldschmiedekunst im 16. Jahrhundert', *Stud. Dt. Kstgesch.*, lxxvii (1907)

K. T. Parker: 'Die verstreuten Handzeichnungen Urs Grafs', *Anz. Schweiz. Altertkund.*, n. s., xxiii (1921), pp. 207–19

H. Koegler: *Beschreibendes Verzeichnis der Basler Handzeichnungen des Urs Graf* (Basle, 1926) [inc. exh. cat.; Basle, Öff. Kstsamml., 1926 (pp. 89–99)]

E. Major and E. Gradmann: *Urs Graf* (Basle, 1941)

H. Koegler: *Hundert Tafeln aus dem Gesamtwerk des Urs Graf* (Basle, 1947)

F. Bächtiger: 'Andreaskreuz und Schweizerkreuz: Zur Feindschaft zwischen Landsknechten und Eidgenossen', *Jb. Bern. Hist. Mus.*, li–lii (1971–2), pp. 205–70

C. Andersson: *Dirnen, Krieger, Narren: Ausgewählte Zeichnungen von Urs Graf* (Basle, 1978)

——: 'Jungfrau, Dirne, Fortuna: Das Bild der Frau in den Zeichnungen von Urs Graf', *Krit. Ber.*, xvi (1988), pp. 26–35

——: *Die Zeichnungen von Urs Graf*, xv of Werkkataloge Schweizer Künstler (in preparation)

CHRISTIANE ANDERSSON

Graff, Anton (*b* Winterthur, 18 Nov 1736; *d* Dresden, 22 June 1813). Swiss painter, active in Germany. He was a pupil of Johann Ulrich Schellenburg (1709–95) in Winterthur and continued his training with Johann Jakob Haid in Augsburg between 1756 and 1765. He worked for the court painter Leonhard Schneider (1716–62) in Ansbach from 1757 to 1759, producing large numbers of copies of a portrait of *Frederick the Great* (probably by Antoine Pesne). This was an important step in furthering his career, as were the months he spent in Regensburg (1764–5) painting miniatures of clerics and town councillors. He was court painter to the Elector Frederick-Christian of Saxe-Weimar in Dresden from 1766 and taught at the

Hochschule der Bildende Künste there. In 1771 he travelled to Berlin, where he painted portraits of *Jakob Mendelssohn*, *Gotthold Ephraim Lessing* and *J. G. Sulzer*. Sulzer introduced him at court, which resulted in many commissions. He was invited several times to teach at the Akademie der Künste in Berlin, but he remained in Dresden. He often travelled to Leipzig, and in summer he frequently went to Teplitz (now Teplice, Czech Republic) and Karlsbad (now Karlovy Vary, Czech Republic); he also worked in Berlin on several occasions and returned to Switzerland for visits.

Graff's prolific output includes more than 2000 paintings and drawings, over 100 of which are self-portraits, for example *Self-portrait* (1771; Winterthur, Mus. Lindengut). Most of Graff's work consisted of portraits: he painted the aristocracy of Saxony and Prussia and the socially ambitious middle classes of Augsburg, Regensburg, Dresden, Leipzig and Berlin. Graff left a pictorial record of this group, for example *Burgomaster of Leipzig* (1769; Winterthur, Kstmus.) and *Philip Erasmus Reich* (Leipzig, Ubib.; *see* LEIPZIG, fig. 2), which included merchants, doctors, scholars, clerics, actors, musicians and painters, together with their wives and children, amounting to *c.* 750 named sitters. He painted every style of portrait, although he was always mainly interested in the faces of his sitters. There are a few untypical three-quarter-length and full-length portraits, in which Graff was influenced by English painting and the sitters are shown against a landscape background. These paintings include some of his best works, such as *Prince Henry XIV* (1789; Berlin, Gemäldegal.).

Graff was the leading exponent of the middle-class portrait in Germany in the late 18th century and the early 19th, and he was the main portrait painter of German poets between the Enlightenment and the early Romantic periods. Johann Friedrich Bause (1738–1814), who was a friend of Graff's, reproduced more than 40 of these portraits as copper engravings, thereby increasing Graff's fame. Examples, such as *Salomon Gessner* (Berne, Kstmus.), are in many public collections. Graff played an important role in the early Romantic movement in Dresden: as well as painting portraits of its representatives, including *Heinrich von Kleist* (1808; Dresden, Gemäldegal. Neue Meister), he contributed to the development of Romantic landscape painting. His pure landscapes, painted *c.* 1800 (e.g. *Morning*, 1800; Dresden, Gemäldegal. Neue Meister), influenced both Philipp Otto Runge and Caspar David Friedrich. Although his creative activity was eventually restricted by eye trouble, Graff's power and capacity to change hardly diminished with age; his later portraits have a sparkling intensity derived from a use of impasto, which might almost be described as 'early Impressionist'.

BIBLIOGRAPHY

E. Berckenhagen: *Anton Graff: Leben und Werk* (Berlin, 1967)

M. Prause: *Bibliographie zur Kunstgeschichte des 19. Jahrhunderts* (Munich, 1984), p. 564

E. Berckenhagen: 'Nachträge zum Oeuvre Anton Graffs', *Z. Kstwiss.*, xliii (1989), pp. 7–20

EKHART BERCKENHAGEN

Graffiti. Term applied to an arrangement of institutionally illicit marks in which there has been an attempt to establish some sort of coherent composition; such marks are made by an individual or individuals (not generally professional artists) on a wall or other surface that is usually visually accessible to the public. The term 'graffiti' derives from the Greek *graphein* ('to write'). Graffiti (sing. graffito) or SGRAFFITO, meaning a drawing or scribbling on a flat surface, originally referred to those marks found on ancient Roman architecture. Although examples of graffiti have been found at such sites as Pompeii, the Domus Aurea of Emperor Nero (*reg* AD 54–68) in Rome, Hadrian's Villa at Tivoli and the Maya site of Tikal in Mesoamerica, they are usually associated with 20th-century urban environments. They may range from a few simple marks to compositions that are complex and colourful. Motives for the production of such marks may include a desire for recognition that is public in nature, and/or the need to appropriate a public space or someone else's private space for group or individual purposes. Graffiti are recognized as a way of dealing with problems of identification in overcrowded or self-denying environments, and are an outlet through which people may choose to publish their thoughts, philosophies or poems. Illegitimate counterparts to the paid, legitimate advertisements on billboards or signs, graffiti utilize the walls of garages, public toilets and gaol cells for their clandestine messages.

Because of the illicit nature of graffiti, a tin of paint and a brush are impractical, while spatial considerations may make a pen or pencil ineffective. To accommodate the need for size, visibility, speed and convenience, the ideal vehicle is the spray-can, which combines medium and applicator into one relatively small parcel that is easily concealed, transportable, easy to use; spray-paint may be applied to most surfaces. Different-sized nozzles are used to achieve various effects, for example a thin line as opposed to a wide band of paint. Almost anything may, however, serve as a substitute: the aforementioned pen, pencil, paint and brush, as well as chisels, knives, felt-tip markers, blood or even a finger on a dirty wall or window.

Since it is impossible to limit or regulate the resources that are available, graffiti as an art form and expressive medium are expandable, flexible and difficult to control. The graffiti medium constitutes an open channel for its users to manipulate and mould to suit their needs. It represents a type of discontinuous communicative strategy in which people can engage in a visual dialogue that does not rely on face-to-face interaction or on necessary knowledge or the writers' identities.

Communities that produce graffiti (as opposed to the individual 'scribbler') may target cryptic messages towards their own closed community, producing a seemingly confusing and unreadable product. The writers may not sign their real names; they instead employ the use of nicknames, codes and symbols within stylized aesthetic systems. This type of graffiti is geared towards people who already understand the messages and may act to enhance group solidarity. Such graffiti may easily be elevated to the category of art, because the cryptic codes, generalized content and stylistic features of community-based graffiti usually outlast the duration of an individual's membership within the community. If a community's ideological focus is geared towards the larger society or the politics of the larger state, the messages that graffiti project are usually

Graffiti art 'piece' in Santa Monica, California, by Mez: rendering of a skull surrounded by miscellaneous tags (PSK, TAK, MISK, FINK) and Chicano gang graffiti, *c.* 1.8×3.1 m, 1990

easier to read, lacking in cryptic encoding and generally not as stylized.

An example of this cross-culturally prevalent genre of graffiti, political graffiti may combine with other artistic and expressive forms such as poster and comic book production, mural painting, newspaper and pamphlet production and political art exhibitions. The marks may represent the work of unrecognized or underground political groups, radical student movements or simply dissatisfied individuals. Political graffiti may also arise from sudden emergency situations (e.g. riots) or in response to concurrent political legislation and party politics. Although concerned with the larger politics of the State, the groups that produce this type of graffiti generally comprise some 'subcultural' elements and may make wide use of symbols to further internally relevant quests for power and solidarity.

A second genre of graffiti, gang graffiti, is used as a marker by gangs usually active in urban areas. The content and form of their graffiti consist of cryptic codes and initials rigidly styled with specialized calligraphies. Gang members use graffiti to indicate group membership, to distinguish enemies and allies and, most generally, to mark boundaries that are both territorial and ideological. In this case, graffiti may merge with other art forms, like tattoo and clothing styles, to create a bounded system, the concerns of which may incorporate illegitimate economic and social practices that branch far beyond the reaches of the actual graffiti.

A third genre of graffiti, graffiti art, is commonly called 'hip-hop' or 'New York style' graffiti and derives from a tradition of subway graffiti that originated in New York in the 1970s. This type of graffiti has spread to large urban centres around the USA and the rest of the world, especially in Europe. Where subway cars like those in New York are unavailable, walls, rocks, road signs, billboards, train carriages and even motor vehicles are considered suitable 'canvases'. Graffiti artists may or may not belong to 'crews', which are groups of artists at differing levels of proficiency. Their work ranges from simple monochrome 'tags' (the artist's 'name tag' often represented in an exaggerated cursive style) to elaborate, multicoloured works called 'pieces' (derived from the word 'masterpiece'), which are considered in some circles to be of museum quality (see fig.).

As graffiti have begun to find their way from their original urban locations to the walls of galleries and museums, the question of vandalism and graffiti as an art form has provoked endless controversy, raising such questions as whether vandalism can be considered art or whether graffiti can be considered graffiti if they are made legally. The simplified imagery of graffiti has also become attractive to certain professional fine artists—the work of Keith Haring in particular became 'legitimized' as it moved from New York's subway walls to the walls of galleries and private collectors in the USA. It is in part the rapid movement lacuna hip-hop graffiti art and its concomitant controversies that have spurred the development of scholarly interest surrounding people's use of graffiti in all their aspects.

Graffiti are cross-cultural phenomena common to every literate society. Within the variable contexts of their production, graffiti personalize depersonalized space, construct landscapes of identity, make public space into private space and act as promoters of ethnic unity as well as diversity. In this way, graffiti can be understood as concrete manifestations of personal and communal ideologies that are visually striking, insistent and provocative; as such, they are worthy of the continued attention of art historians, social scientists and policy-makers alike.

BIBLIOGRAPHY

R. Reisner: *Graffiti: Two Thousand Years of Wall Writing* (New York, 1971)

R. Cybriwsky and D. Ley: 'Urban Graffiti as Territorial Markers', *An. Assoc. Amer. Geog.*, lxiv (1974), pp. 491–505

J. Romotsky and S. Romotsky: *Los Angeles Barrio Calligraphy* (Los Angeles, 1976)

E. Di Nallo: *Indiani in città* (Bologna, 1977)

C. Castleman: *Getting Up: Subway Graffiti in New York City* (Cambridge, MA, 1982)

M. Cooper and H. Chalfant: *Subway Art* (New York, 1984)

L. G. Chaffee: 'Political Graffiti and Wall Painting in Greater Buenos Aires: An Alternative Communication System', *Stud. Lat. Amer. Pop. Cult.*, viii (1987), pp. 37–60

A. Silva: *Punto de vista ciudadano: Focalización visual y puesta en escena del graffiti*, Series Minor (Bogotá, 1987)

R. Lachmann: 'Graffiti as Career and Ideology', *Amer. J. Sociol.*, xciv (1988), pp. 229–50

E. H. Spitz: 'An Insubstantial Pageant Faded', *A. Crit.*, iv/3 (1988), pp. 50–63

J. Bushnell: *Moscow Graffiti: Language and Subculture* (Boston, 1990)

High & Low: Modern Art, Popular Culture (exh. cat. by K. Varnedoe and A. Gopuik, New York, MOMA, 1990), pp. 68–99

R. Huchison: 'Blazon nouveau: Gang Graffiti in the Barrios of Chicago and Los Angeles', *Gangs: The Origins and Impact of Contemporary Youth Gangs in the United States*, ed. S. Cummings and D. J. Monti (New York, 1993), pp. 137–71

M. Cooper and J. Sciorra: *R.I.P.: New York Spraycan Memorials* (London, 1994)

SUSAN A. PHILLIPS

Graham, Anderson, Probst & White. American firm of architects. It was founded in 1912 (as Graham, Burnham & Co.) as a successor to D. H. Burnham & Co. by the practice's surviving partner Ernest Graham (*b* Lowell, MI, 22 Aug 1866; *d* Chicago, IL, 22 Nov 1936) and Burnham's sons Hubert Burnham and Daniel Burnham jr (*see* BURNHAM, DANIEL H.). In 1917 the Burnhams left to form Burnham Brothers, and Graham and the others, (William) Peirce Anderson (*b* Oswego, NY, 1870; *d* Chicago, 1924), Edward Probst (*b* Chicago, 1870; *d* Chicago 1942) and Howard Judson White (*b* Chicago, 21 Feb 1870; *d* Chicago, 18 Dec 1936), formed the current firm.

Graham was the son of a small general contractor and learnt building as an apprentice by doing carpentry, masonry and other jobs for his father. He never had formal training in an architectural school. Around 1886 he moved to Chicago and worked for Holabird & Roche on the Tacoma Building, before leaving to join Burnham as Assistant Chief of Construction for the World's Columbian Exposition of 1893, Chicago. In frequent contact with the nation's best-known architects through the exposition, Graham gained confidence in handling large-scale projects where the job demanded a highly developed, skilled architectural administrator.

Anderson studied at Harvard University, Cambridge, MA, until 1892 and studied electrical engineering at Johns Hopkins University, Baltimore, MD. He then studied at the Ecole des Beaux-Arts, Paris, receiving his diploma in 1899; he finished his education with a grand tour. On joining Burnham's office in 1900 he became chief designer almost immediately and a partner in 1908. His skill as a planner was especially noteworthy in his design for Union station (1903–7) in Washington, DC, the Cleveland Terminal Group (1919–29) and Union station (1924) in Chicago. Probst joined Burnham's office in 1893 and assumed responsibility for the supervision of the working drawings in 1908. He continued in this capacity until Graham's death when he became head of the firm, and he was in turn succeeded by his son Marvin G. Probst (*b* 1896; *d* 1970). White joined Burnham's office in 1898 as a draughtsman. In 1905 he became Graham's assistant in charge of letting contracts and supervising construction in the field.

Graham, Anderson, Probst & White designed buildings and plans for many cities, and the number of structures that evolved from their commissions for railway stations and the surrounding environs determined the urban character of large sections of Chicago and Cleveland, OH, and to some extent of Philadelphia, PA. In addition to railway stations, the practice of the firm focused on civic and cultural buildings, offices, department stores, banks and warehouses. At first the design practices were set by a series of architects trained at the Ecole des Beaux-Arts in Paris and reflected classical planning in their symmetrical, axial organization, with ceremonial public spaces, ornament, fine materials, the incorporation of sculpture and painting, clear composition and orderly arrangement. A notable example is the John G. Shedd Aquarium (1930), Chicago, built at the end of a long breakwater into Lake Michigan, which had appeared in Burnham's plan for Chicago (1909); it is a felicitous combination of site and building form. The simple hemisphere of its dome is supported by a base storey in marble. The Wrigley Building (1919–24), Chicago, is a Beaux-Arts adaptation of the Spanish Baroque to the requirements of a high-rise. From 1925 to 1932 the firm produced some examples of the Art Deco style, notably the Koppers Building (1927–9), Pittsburgh, and the Field Building (1929–34), Chicago.

BIBLIOGRAPHY

Architectural Works of Graham, Anderson, Probst and White, 2 vols (London, 1933) [privately printed]

C. W. Condit: *The Chicago School of Architecture: A History of Commercial and Public Building in the Chicago Area, 1875–1925* (Chicago, 1964)

——: *Chicago, 1910–1929: Building, Planning and Urban Technology* (Chicago, 1973)

S. A. Kitt Chappell: 'As If the Lights Were Always Shining', *Chicago Architecture, 1872–1922: Birth of a Metropolis*, ed. J. Zukowsky (Munich, 1988), pp. 291–301

——: 'Urban Ideals and the Design of Railroad Stations', *Technol. & Cult.*, xxx/2 (Jan 1989), pp. 354–75

——: *Architecture and Planning of Graham, Anderson, Probst and White, 1912–36: Transforming Tradition* (Chicago, 1991)

SALLY A. KITT CHAPPELL

Graham, Bruce (John). *See under* SKIDMORE, OWINGS & MERRILL.

Graham, Dan(iel Harry) (*b* Urbana, IL, 31 Mar 1942). American performance artist, video artist and writer. He founded the Daniels Gallery in New York and was director of it from 1964 to 1965; there he came into contact with Minimalist artists such as Carl André, Sol LeWitt and

Donald Judd. This led him to question the gallery structure and the art displayed and to experiment with conceptual art. From 1965 to 1969 he produced a series of works published in magazines, such as *Schema* (1966; Brussels, Daled priv. col., see 1988 exh. cat., p. 9). This series consisted merely of a descriptive list of its own contents, including the number of words, and so referred to nothing beyond itself, unlike Minimalist art that he believed referred to the surrounding display space. Furthermore, the magazine was, unlike a gallery, clearly related to time and change through its regular appearance and topicality.

From 1969 to 1978 Graham was primarily involved with performance, film and video. His first performance took place at the Loeb Student Center at New York University in May 1969. He stood in front of the audience repeating the word 'relax' to himself through a microphone while controlling his breathing; simultaneously the sound of a girl saying 'lax' and breathing was played until the two became synchronized. The performance was designed to make the audience monitor their own breathing and thus to consider the psychological and social distance between individuals. In 1974 he constructed eight Time Delay Rooms, such as *Present Continuous Past(s)* (1974; Paris, Pompidou). This work consisted of a mirrored room with a video camera and monitor, the monitor relaying the video image after a delay of eight seconds, the mirrored reflections producing a series of infinitely repeated and delayed images. Graham also produced a number of outdoor pavilions and sculptures using mirrored walls, such as *Two Adjacent Pavilions* (1978–81; Otterlo, Kröller-Müller), but continued to work with video and wrote extensively about his work.

WRITINGS

B. H. D. Buchloch, ed.: *Dan Graham: Video-Architecture-Television: Writings on Video and Video Works, 1970–8* (New York, 1979)

BIBLIOGRAPHY

Dan Graham (exh. cat. by J. Wall, Perth, A.G. W. Australia, 1985)
Dan Graham: Pavilions (exh. cat. by A. Rorimer, Munich, Kstver., 1988)

□

Graham, Fred (*b* Arapuni, NZ, 1928). Maori sculptor. His tribal affiliation is Ngati Koroki, Ngati Raukawa. Graham studied art at Ardmore and Dunedin Teachers' College, subsequently becoming one of the young Maori artists who worked under Pine Taiapa. He began carving in 1962, stimulated by the belief that Maori artists needed to retain traditional skills and techniques and understand the symbolic meaning within carvings. However, as a result of working with a group of artists who were increasingly interested in new materials and styles, he chose to move away from traditional carving, to enable him to use a far wider range of materials, including stone, stainless steel and copper, as well as native and exotic woods: this versatility reinforced his insistence that he was a sculptor rather than a carver. After his first exhibition in 1966, Graham showed his work extensively, contributing to many exhibitions throughout New Zealand and in other countries. His works, many of which take the form of large commissions, focus on a wide range of issues, including the Treaty of Waitangi (1840), Maori protest at the loss of land, and historical themes of interest to Maori people.

BIBLIOGRAPHY

D. Nicholas: *Seven Maori Artists* (Wellington, 1986), p. 21
Maori Art Today (exh. cat., Auckland, Inst. & Mus., 1987)
Kohia ko taikaka anake: Artists Construct New Directions. New Zealand's Largest Exhibition of Contemporary Maori Art (exh. cat., Wellington, NZ, N.A.G., 1990–91)

MEGAN TAMATI-QUENNELL

Graham, James Gillespie. *See* GILLESPIE GRAHAM, JAMES.

Graham, John [Dambrowsky, Ivan] (*b* Kiev, 1881; *d* London, 1961). Polish theorist and painter, active in the USA. His family were minor Polish aristocrats long resident in Russia. He studied law at the University of Kiev, before becoming a Tsarist cavalry officer, to fight the Revolution. He was captured by the Bolsheviks but escaped to western Europe and by 1920 had arrived in the USA. He changed his name to Graham, believing that this was similar to the Cyrillic orthography of Dambrowsky. In New York Graham studied in 1921 under John Sloan at the Art Students League, and he also seems to have had contacts with several Russian artists including Mikhail Larionov and David Burlyuk. In the 1920s he was active as an artist and corresponded with the American collector Duncan Phillips. Graham was acquainted with Picasso (an influence he eventually rejected) and in the late 1920s had one-man exhibitions in both the USA and Paris. In New York he became prominent as the principal link between modernist artists in New York and Paris.

As a theorist Graham used the term 'minimalism' to describe the irreducible part of a work that remained after repeated analyses of the forms, and his paintings, either pale or dark, demonstrated his ideas. His *System and Dialectics of Art* (1937) codified them further in question-and-answer form. Apart from his own work, in which he borrowed heavily from the Old Masters, Graham was very influential in promoting modern art in the USA; he introduced David Smith to the welded sculpture of Julio González. A friend of Arshile Gorky, Willem de Kooning and Jacob Kainen (*b* 1909), Graham also introduced Jackson Pollock to Lee Krasner when he exhibited their art together in 1941.

WRITINGS

System and Dialectics of Art (Paris and New York, 1937)

BIBLIOGRAPHY

C. Goldstein: 'John Graham during the 1920s: His Introduction to Modernism', *A. Mag.*, li/7 (1977), pp. 98–9

HARRY RAND

Graham, Maria. *See* CALCOTT, (2).

Graham, William (*b* Glasgow, Aug 1817; *d* Oakdene, nr Guildford, Surrey, 16 July 1885). Scottish merchant, politician, patron and collector. Suspicious of connoisseurship but open to the advice of Edward Burne-Jones, from the 1860s he assembled a large collection of early Italian paintings, often bought cheaply on his frequent trips to Italy. Among his more important pictures were Giotto's *Salvator Mundi* from the Rimini Crucifix (Surrey, priv. col.), Carlo Crivelli's *Virgin and Child Enthroned* (New York, Met.) and Pesellino's *Virgin and Child with St John* (Toledo, OH, Mus. A.). He was fond of unusual mythological subjects (e.g. Piero di Cosimo's *Discovery of*

Vulcan; Hartford, CT, Wadsworth Atheneum) and late 15th- and early 16th-century Venetian works, particularly from the circle of Giovanni Bellini. He readily bought minor pieces that appealed to his deep religious faith (he was a Presbyterian), but showed no interest in collecting drawings and little in non-Italian Old Masters; Claude Lorrain's *Landscape with Parnassus* (Boston, MA, Mus. F.A.) is a notable exception. A generous lender to the South Kensington Museum and the Royal Academy winter exhibitions, he was appointed a trustee of the National Gallery in 1884 by W. E. Gladstone, under whom he had served as Liberal MP for Glasgow from 1865 to 1874.

With F. R. Leyland, he was the most important patron of Dante Gabriel Rossetti's later work, particularly between 1868 and 1873. He owned the *Girlhood of the Virgin Mary* (1849) and *Ecce Ancilla Domini!* (1850; both London, Tate) and, unhappy with the gloomy colour and mood of Rossetti's late style, encouraged him without success to revert to a lighter key. The most important work Graham commissioned from Rossetti was *Dante's Dream* (1871; Liverpool, Walker A.G.). Disputes over money and unfinished pictures somewhat soured their later dealings.

Graham's relationship with Burne-Jones, however, was closer and more productive. Graham began buying his watercolours in 1865, and in the 1870s he commissioned the oil versions of *Chant d'amour* (1868–77; New York, Met.) and *Laus Veneris* (1873–8; Newcastle upon Tyne, Laing A.G.), whose warm tones reflect Graham's taste for Venetian colour and the paintings by the Old Masters that he frequently lent to the artist. Graham fostered Burne-Jones's talent for design with his commission of 1879 for the 'Graham' piano (Somerset, priv. col., see *Burne-Jones*, exh. cat., ACGB, 1975, no. 208) and did much to establish the financial security of Burne-Jones's later career, negotiating the sale in 1885 of the large *Briar Rose* series (Buscot Park, Oxon, NT).

Graham's letters to Burne-Jones (priv. col.) and Rossetti reveal him as an understanding patron, eager to encourage and alive to the difficulties of artistic creation. His collection was auctioned at Christie's on 2–3 and 8–10 April 1886.

UNPUBLISHED SOURCES

Vancouver, U. BC Lib. [letters to Rossetti]

BIBLIOGRAPHY

O. Garnett: 'William Graham e altri committenti di Burne-Jones', *Burne-Jones* (exh. cat., Rome, G.N.A. Mod., 1986), pp. 86–92

OLIVER GARNETT

Graham-Gilbert [Graham]**, John** (*b* Glasgow, April 1794; *d* Glasgow, 4 June 1866). Scottish painter and collector. The son of David Graham, a Glasgow merchant, he was a student at the Royal Academy Schools, London, from 1818 to 1821. He obtained both silver and gold medals there and exhibited at the Royal Academy from 1820 to 1823, before going to Italy for two years. In 1827 he settled in Edinburgh as a portrait painter and became an Academician of the Royal Scottish Academy in 1830. He exhibited regularly at the Glasgow Dilettante Society and at the Royal Scottish Academy exhibitions in Edinburgh. Returning to Glasgow, in 1834 he married the niece of Andrew Gilbert of Yorkhill, near Glasgow. In 1838 Mrs Graham inherited her uncle's estate, and Graham assumed the name of Graham-Gilbert; from then he lived and worked at Yorkhill. He no longer needed to paint to earn a living and had sufficient wealth to amass an extremely fine collection of Old Master paintings including works by Rubens and Rembrandt. Graham-Gilbert was interested in promoting local art in Glasgow: he became President of the West of Scotland Academy and helped to found the Glasgow Fine Arts Institute. In 1864 he failed by one vote to be elected President of the Royal Scottish Academy.

Graham-Gilbert painted some fancy pictures, but concentrated mainly on portraits. Although the male portraits suggest Raeburn's influence, his works are generally deliberately painted and highly finished, displaying a strong awareness of the Old Masters, especially the 16th-century Venetians. His female portraits were the most successful, being notable for good draughtsmanship and beauty and lucidity of colour. He bequeathed many of his own paintings and much of his collection of Old Masters to the Glasgow Art Gallery and Museum.

BIBLIOGRAPHY

R. Brydall: *Art in Scotland: Its Origin and Progress* (Edinburgh, 1889), p. 238

D. Irwin and F. Irwin: *Scottish Painters at Home and Abroad* (London, 1975)

CATHERINE WILLS

Grahor, Janko (Nikola) (*b* Petrinja, 6 Dec 1827; *d* Zagreb, 22 Nov 1906). Croatian architect. After completing his studies at the Building Crafts School in Frankfurt am Main in 1848, he spent a year at the Technische Hochschule in Vienna before returning first to Nova Gradiška and then to Zagreb. There he entered local authority employment and was appointed City Surveyor in 1861. In 1868, however, he established the independent firm of Grahor & Klein with the architect Franjo Klein (1828–1890), whose Viennese training had absorbed the influences of August Siccard von Siccardsburg and Theophilus Hansen. The partnership lasted until 1886, after which Grahor continued in practice with his sons, most notably Janko Josip Grahor (1855–1918), who had studied under Friedrich von Schmidt in Vienna. Although Grahor was primarily active in Zagreb as a building contractor, his firm also designed and built independently. Many commissions were for urban housing blocks, generally of two or three storeys and designed in a Viennese Renaissance Revival style with occasional Mannerist or Baroque Revival motifs. The Buratti Palace (1877), Zrinjevac 3, reminiscent of Hansen's Heinrichshof in Vienna, is a particularly grand example. Of his public buildings, the Croatian Musical Institute (1875), the Croatian Economic Association (1878) and the Croatian Savings Bank (1880) are the most notable.

BIBLIOGRAPHY

I. Maroević: *Graditeljska Obitelj Grahor* [The Grahor family of architect builders] (Zagreb, 1968)

FRANK ARNEIL WALKER

Graillon, Pierre-Adrien (*b* Dieppe, 19 Sept 1807; *d* Dieppe, 14 Dec 1872). French sculptor and painter. Employed in infancy in chalk-quarries and subsequently as a cobbler in Rouen and Paris, he returned to his native town in 1827, where he married and attended drawing-school while earning a living in local ivory and alabaster workshops. In 1836 he went to work in the Paris studio of Pierre-Jean David d'Angers. After his return to Dieppe in 1838, his reputation steadily increased as a sculptor in ivory, unbaked clay, terracotta, wood and alabaster. His small reliefs, figures and groups representing sailors, fisher-folk, vagrants and scenes from local life were appreciated by his more unassuming compatriots and acquired by tourists. Graillon retained the manner of a man of the people, and in his sculpture and paintings a deliberate roughness of treatment is allied to a strong formal sense and an instinct for natural grouping. He generally avoided the historical and exotic subjects that were the mainstay of the 19th-century statuette industry and was exceptional among contemporary sculptors in his preference for the ordinary local theme. A strain of romantic 'misérabilisme' in his work finds allegorical expression in the group *Misery* (terracotta, 1854; Dieppe, Château-Mus.), and there are echoes of earlier genre painters like David Teniers II, particularly noticeable in the relief of *Card-players* (terracotta, 1849; Rennes, Mus. B.-A. & Archéol.). Remarkably (in that they are little more than seaside souvenirs), Graillon's works anticipate the subjects and treatment of the Realists. He felt occasional dissatisfaction with his modest status. According to David d'Angers, this was exacerbated by a visit paid to him in 1858 by Napoleon III. In the following year, Graillon executed a life-size statue of *Abraham Duquesne* (bronze, Dieppe, Château-Mus.). After his death, his two sons, César (1831–?*c.* 1900) and Félix (1833–1893), continued to work in their father's idiom.

BIBLIOGRAPHY

Lami

A. Bruel, ed.: *Les Carnets de David d'Angers* (Paris, 1958)

P.-A. Graillon (exh. cat., Dieppe, Château-Mus., 1969)

PHILIP WARD-JACKSON

Grain, Jean le. *See* ZIARNKO, JAN.

Grain elevator [silo]. Building used for the storage of grain or other cereal, generally found with attached loading and distribution machinery in large agricultural areas, warehouses and ports. The giant grain elevators of the 20th century developed as a result of the massive expansion of agriculture in the late 19th century in South America, Russia and, above all, North America. During the 19th century industrialized countries in Europe experienced huge population increases, but agricultural output shrank, and most ceased to be self-sufficient in their food production; large-scale importation of grain thus became the norm. The use of pesticides and more efficient agricultural machinery led to increased agricultural productivity, and North America was in the forefront of this development, with its industrial design seen as a model for Europe. The latest structural developments were used in grain elevators, an innovative design being the iron-framed example (1860–61) built by George H. Johnson for the United States Warehousing Corp., Brooklyn, NY. The spandrel girders of the frame carried the panels of the traditional brick wall, thus removing its structural purpose. From the end of the 19th century concrete, cylindrical grain elevators were built in the USA. The Great Northern Railway's elevator (1909) at Superior, WI, is a typical early example of the use of concrete for this building type and is remarkable for its exploitation of the plasticity and strength of curved concrete forms; although it is 33.5 m tall, the walls are only 18 cm thick. By the early 20th century many avant-garde artists were embracing the concept of an ideal American culture of technology. Walter Gropius particularly admired the American utilitarian design and architecture, and he especially praised American grain elevators. Illustrations of giant silos formed part of his photographic collection, and in the 1913 yearbook of the Deutsche Werkbund Gropius put their monumentality on a par with that of the buildings of ancient Egypt. Architectural publications of the 1920s and 1930s also paid tribute to these structures, and Walter Müller-Wulkow (1886–1964) illustrated silos in his *Blue Books* (1929), showing examples with cylindrical concrete piers, following American models. The cylindrical form continued to be used at the end of the 20th century, although problems of humidity control and ventilation had replaced questions of design and the machine aesthetic.

BIBLIOGRAPHY

W. Gropius: 'Entwicklung moderner Industriebaukunst', *Die Kunst in Industrie und Handel*, Jahrbuch des deutschen Werkbundes (Berlin, 1913), pp. 17–22

W. Müller-Wulkow: *Bauten der Arbeit und des Verkehrs* (Königsstein/Taunus, 1929); repr. in *Architektur der Zwanziger Jahre in Deutschland* (Königsstein/Taunus, 1975)

L. Benevolo: *History of Modern Architecture* (London, 1971)

□

Grajeda Mena, Guillermo (*b* Guatemala City, 1 Oct 1918). Guatemalan sculptor, painter, draughtsman and printmaker. He studied at the Academia Nacional de Bellas Artes (1936–40) and at the Escuela de Artes Aplicadas in Santiago, Chile (1945–8), where he specialized in direct carving in hard stone and in bronze casting. From 1949 to 1962 he was professor of sculpture at the Escuela Nacional de Artes Plásticas, and from 1948 to 1986 he organized exhibitions at the Instituto de Antropología e Historia, both in Guatemala City.

Grajeda Mena's work is distinguished by its forceful draughtsmanship and strong expressive sense. His outstanding sculptures include *Maternity* (450×410×320 mm, 1947), directly carved in volcanic stone, *Archaic Christ* (wood, h 2.85 m, 1953–4; both Guatemala City, Mus. N. A. Mod.) and *The Conquest* (reinforced concrete relief, 6×10 m; Guatemala City, Pal. Mun.). As a painter he was noted for his colour sense and enthusiasm for experimenting with new materials. His most important murals include *Olmec Culture* (1972; Escuintla, Mus. Democ.) and *National History* (1981; Guatemala City, Acad. Geog. & Hist.). He also made a reputation as a caricaturist.

BIBLIOGRAPHY

Guillermo Grajeda Mena, datos biográficos (Guatemala City, 1975)

Exposición retrospectiva Guillermo Grajeda Mena (exh. cat., Guatemala City, 1986) [retrospective]

JORGE LUJÁN MUÑOZ

Grajera y Herboso, José (*b* Laredo, Santander, 24 Aug 1818; *d* Oviedo, 31 May 1897). Spanish sculptor. He studied first at the Sociedad Económica de Amigos del País, Oviedo. In 1841 he settled in Madrid, attending classes at the Real Academia de Bellas Artes de S Fernando under sculptors such as Elias Vallejo and José Piquer y Duart. He also worked in the studio of José Tomás (1795–1848). He competed in the exhibition organized by the Academia de S Fernando in 1850, submitting three figurines. Other early works include a number of ornamental pieces made for the gardens of La Granja de S Ildefonso, Madrid.

Grajera y Herboso failed to secure a grant to study abroad and had no official backing. From 1851 to 1857 he worked in the Prado as a sculpture restorer and conservator. During this period he won the competition for a monumental statue in memory of the poet and statesman *Juan Álvarez y Mendizábal* (1790–1853) in the Plaza del Progresso (now Tirso de Molina), in Madrid. Under his supervision the statue, depicting its subject wrapped in the Spanish cape, was cast in bronze in the Eck and Durand workshops in Paris between 1856 and 1857. The work was not, however, unveiled until 6 June 1869, after the success of the Revolution of 1868; it was removed 60 years later and melted down. Grajera y Herboso also executed a monument to the naturalist *Simón de Rojas Clemente* (destr.) for the Botanical Gardens, Madrid; it too depicted the subject wearing a Spanish cape. In the Exposición Nacional of 1866 he exhibited busts of *José de Uria y Terrero, Doña Obdulia CH. de C* and *Mendizábal*. For that of 1876 he submitted busts of the *Marqués de Barzanallana* (Madrid, Pal. de las Cortes), *Laureano Figuerola, Gabriel Rodriguez Villalonga* and a grandiose bust of the architect *Juan de Villanueva*, all executed for the collection of portraits of Spanish and Italian artists intended for the Prado, of which he was Assistant Director from 1866 until his retirement in 1889. In 1878 he carved the bust of *Alfonso XII* (Oviedo, Mus. B.A.).

One of Grajera y Herboso's most important works was the marble statue of the poet and statesman *Gaspar Melchor de Jovellanos* (1887; Madrid, Pal. de las Cortes), who is depicted wearing a lawyer's toga. It was made shortly before the sculptor moved back to Oviedo in 1889, following his retirement from the Prado. There he executed another important late monument, incorporating a full-length sculpture of *José Posada Herrera*, erected in Llanes in 1893 (destr.; model, Oviedo, Mus. B.A.). His work shows the influence of the Romantic movement, as well as the naturalistic tendencies inherent in the prevailing classicism of 19th-century Spanish sculpture.

BIBLIOGRAPHY

M. Ossorio y Bernard: *Galería biográfica de artistas españoles del siglo XIX* (Madrid, 1883–4), p. 315

E. Pardo Canalís: *Vida y arte de José Grajera* (Madrid, 1954)

J. A. Gaya Nuño: *Arte del siglo XIX*, A. Hisp. (Madrid, 1966), pp. 180–82

J. Marin Medina: *La escultura española contemporanea, 1800–1978: Historia y evolución crítica* (Madrid, 1972)

WIFREDO RINCÓN GARCÍA

Gramatica [Grammatica; della Grammatica], **Antiveduto** (*b* ?Rome, 1571; *d* Rome, 13 Jan 1626). Italian painter. He was from a Sienese family. According to Baglione, his parents were journeying from Siena to Rome when his mother went into labour and gave birth to him at an inn, an inconvenience that had been foreseen ('antiveduto') by his father and led to his unusual name. For a brief period he was a pupil of Giandomenico Angelini (*fl* 1550–1600), under whom he painted small-scale works, mainly on copper. His prolific production of devotional paintings, portraits and copies of portraits won him swift success; in 1593 he became a member of the Accademia di S Luca and in 1604 of the Congregazione dei Virtuosi. His early portraits have not been identified; they included highly popular copies of a series of *Famous Men* then at the Villa Medici, works that Caravaggio probably also copied when he worked for some months in his studio on his arrival in Rome in 1592 (Calvesi). Gramatica attracted the support of powerful patrons of Caravaggio, Cardinal Francesco Maria del Monte and Marchese Vincenzo Giustiniani.

Gramatica's earliest known religious works were the high altar (consecrated 1591) of S Stanislao dei Polacchi, Rome, showing the *Saviour in Glory between SS Stanislaus and Adalbert*, and *St Hyacinth Praying* (both *in situ*) and the perhaps slightly later *Presentation in the Temple* (*c*. 1600; Viterbo, Mus. Civ.). These works reflect the late 16th-century style of the Sienese Francesco Vanni and Ventura Salimbeni, artists working in Rome who had been influenced by Federico Barocci, and the style of Cristoforo Roncalli.

Gramatica's development from 1600 to 1620 is unclear, and several attributions have been proposed (Papi, Riedl and Schleier). He contributed an oval painting, the *Family of Darius before Alexander* (*c*. 1610; untraced, see Volpe, fig. 2), to an important cycle of pictures commissioned by Cardinal Alessandro Montalto. A keener rendering of objects and clarity of light from *c*. 1605 reflects the deepening influence of Caravaggesque naturalism. Paintings of this phase, which are also Caravaggesque in their composition, include *Salome with the Head of St John the Baptist* (Aschaffenburg, Schloss Johannisburg, Staatsgal.), *St Cecilia and Two Angels* (Lisbon, Mus. N. A. Ant.; see fig.), and the *Lute Player* (Turin, Gal. Sabauda).

Around 1619 the Camaldolese monks commissioned from Gramatica an altarpiece, the *Dream of St Romuald* (Frascati, Eremo dei Camaldoli), which remains his best-known work; Papi has attributed it to Giovanni Serodine. Between 1619 and 1621 he was in Naples where he painted, again for the Camaldolesi and probably with assistants, a cycle comprising four main canvases: the *Death of St Romuald*, and *Last Judgement*, *Hell* and *Paradise*, and smaller pictures, both full- and half-length, of saints and martyrs of the Camaldolese Order (Naples, S Maria Scala Coeli). In these canvases the abstract rendering of space is combined with a sharp, naturalistic light that tends to simplify the image, bestowing on it the character of an icon. Mancini, writing *c*. 1620, mentioned that Gramatica worked for private clients in Rome and sent many pictures to Spain; one such work is a *Flight into Egypt* (*c*. 1623–4; Toledo Cathedral, Sacristy).

In 1624 Gramatica was briefly Principe of the Accademia di S Luca in Rome, but lost the post when Mao Salini (1575–1625) opposed his attempt to sell off Raphael's *St Luke Painting the Virgin* (SS Luca e Martina). A fresco cycle in S Caterina (1625–6) has been destroyed. Works that have been ascribed to his late years include an *Adoration of the Shepherds* (*c*. 1622; Rome, S Giacomo in Augusta) and a *Nativity* (Rome, Gal. Doria-Pamphili), as

Antiveduto Gramatica: *St Cecilia and Two Angels*, *c.* 1605 (Lisbon, Museu Nacional de Arte Antiga)

well as some genre subjects, including the *Fortune-teller* (Florence, Pitti). In these works his Caravaggesque realism has become more deeply felt. The *Adoration of the Shepherds* and the *Nativity* concentrate on the grave and tender relationship between humble figures, naturalistically rendered, and on the careful observation of simple still-life detail.

BIBLIOGRAPHY

G. Mancini: *Considerazioni sulla pittura* (*c.* 1617–21); ed. A. Marucci and L. Salemo, 2 vols (Rome, 1956–7), i, p. 245; ii, p. 146
G. Baglione: *Vite* (1642); ed. V. Mariani (1935), pp. 292–4
R. Longhi: 'Quesiti caravaggeschi: I. Registro dei tempi', *Pinacotheca*, i (1928), pp. 17–33 (19–20)
——: 'Ultimi studi su Caravaggio e la sua cerchia', *Proporzioni*, i (1943), pp. 5–63
A. Marino: 'Un caravaggesco tra Controriforma e Barocco: Antiveduto Gramatica', *L'Arte*, iii–iv (1968), pp. 47–82
E. Borea: *Caravaggio e caravaggeschi nelle gallerie di Firenze* (Florence, 1970), pp. 41–2
C. Volpe: 'Altre notizie per le "Storie di Alessandro" del Cardinal Montalto', *Paragone*, xxviii/333 (1977), pp. 3–7
J. Rivera: 'Un inedito di Antiveduto Grammatica', *Bol. Sem. Estud. A. & Arqueol.*, xlvi, pp. 513–15
M. Calvesi: 'La realtà del Caravaggio: Seconda parte. I dipinti', *Stor. A.*, lv (1985), pp. 227–87 (228–9)
G. Papi: 'Note al Gramatica e al suo ambiente', *Paradigma*, ix (1990), pp. 107–27
A. Negro: 'Antiveduto Gramatica', *L'arte per i papi e per i principi nella Campagna Romana: Grande pittura del '600 e del '700* (exh. cat., ed. M. G. Bernardini; Rome, Pal. Venezia, 1990), pp. 49–50; review by G. Papi in *Paragone*, xli/485 (1990), pp. 73–88
H. P. Riedl and E. Schleier: 'Ein unbekanntes Hochaltarbild Antiveduto della Gramatica in Todi und weitere Neuzuweisungen', *Pantheon*, l (1992), pp. 61–73

ELENA FUMAGALLI

Gramcko, Elsa (*b* Puerto Cabello, 9 April 1925). Venezuelan painter and sculptor. She was essentially self-taught. Gramcko first exhibited geometrically abstract works, continuing to work in this style until the mid-1950s, when she turned to *Art informel* interpretations based on the exploration of different materials. She represented Venezuela in the fifth São Paulo Biennale in Brazil in 1959 and in the Venice Biennale in 1964. In 1968 she was awarded the Premio Nacional de Escultura at the 29th Salón Oficial Anual de Arte Venezolano. From then on she took part in numerous one-woman and group exhibitions at a national level. Her work is held in various collections throughout the Americas.

BIBLIOGRAPHY

Gramcko (exh. cat., Washington, DC, Pan Amer. Un., 1959)
M. Hernandez Serrano, ed.: *Diccionario de artes visuales en Venezuela*, 2 vols (Caracas, 1982)

ELIDA SALAZAR

Gramiccia, Lorenzo (*b* Cave, nr Rome, *fl* 1745–71). Italian painter. He studied in Rome with the Emilian painter Bonaventura Lamberti and was present in the Palazzo Farnese workshop until 1745. His works are documented only from 1749, when he worked for the oblates of S Maria Liberatrice in Rome and collaborated with Sebastiano Ceccarini in painting frescoes showing *God the Father with St Michael and Music-making Angels* in the choir of the monastery of Tor de' Specchi (*in situ*). In 1753 he painted the notable cycle of canvases in the church of S Carlo at Cave, with scenes from the *Life of St Joseph of Copertino.* His *Vision of St Anthony of Padua* (1756; Rome, S Dorotea) reveals the influence of his Bolognese classicist training, enriched by a Roman grace, resulting in a style that falls between Agostino Masucci and Carlo Costanzi. In 1756 he also painted an *Assumption of the Virgin*, for the church of the Palazzo di Valmontone, commissioned by the Princess Olimpia Caffarelli Pamphili; this work is courtly in style, reminiscent of Annibale Carracci and Carlo Maratti. There followed, in 1759, an interesting *Allegory of the Reign of Charles III of Spain* (Rome, Lemme priv. col.), influenced by Lamberti's teaching.

In 1765–6, after a short stay in Bologna, Gramiccia moved to Venice, where he alternated religious works that maintain the classicist tradition of his early training with genre paintings influenced by Pietro Longhi (ii). To the former group belong the *Virgin of the Rosary* (1768) in SS Giovanni e Paolo, which characteristically rejects the Rococo style, *Elijah and the Angel* (Venice, Accad.) and the *Virgin of the Seven Sorrows and Angels* (1770; Venice, S Giacomo dell'Orio). There is also the strikingly archaic *Holy Family* (1771; Quebec, Mus. Sémin.), which reflects the tradition of Raphael and Domenichino. An important work among his genre paintings is the *Family Gathering* (Udine, Mus. Civ.), around which may be grouped a number of works stylistically indebted to Longhi (Pignatti).

BIBLIOGRAPHY

Il settecento a Roma (exh. cat., ed. E. Lavagnino; Rome, Pal. Espos., 1959), pp. 121–2

T. Pignatti: *Pietro Longhi* (Venice, 1968), pp. 30, 119, 122–3

S. Rudolph: *La pittura del '700 a Roma* (Milan, 1983)

F. Pansecchi: 'Ceccarini e Gramiccia a Tor de' Specchi: Vicende di Lorenzo Gramiccia', *Boll. A.*, lxxi/37–8 (1986), pp. 129–36

UGO RUGGERI

Grammont [Flem. Geraardsbergen]. Belgian town in East Flanders. Situated in the approximate middle of the triangle created by OUDENAARDE, ENGHIEN and Aalst, the town was a centre of tapestry production in the 16th century, although little is known about the industry there. It has been conjectured that at the end of the 15th century Cornelis van Bomberghen (*fl* 1492–1508), an important Antwerp dealer, had in his stock six tapestry cushions made in Grammont that were decorated with fruit. In the oldest census documents or other records of the period, weavers are not mentioned. Most of them were probably employed in the countryside outside the city gates. They made fallacious use of various city marks, including those of Oudenaarde and Enghien. The general ordinance of 1544 concerning the tapestry industry in Flanders did not mention Grammont. Production did, however, exist: between *c.* 1540 and 1550 Peter Borremans headed a large workshop in Grammont, although there were complaints about the quality of his work. Between 1554 and 1564 the guild had numerous members and led an independent existence. Soon afterwards, however, decline set in. In 1617 and 1618 Jean Divy of Valenciennes and Rafaël Plasschaert respectively were willing, in exchange for numerous considerations, to settle in the city to teach the craft to young apprentices, which suggests that the tapestry industry in Grammont was by this time virtually non-existent.

Production in the town usually consisted of cushion covers and large-leaved *verdures* (e.g. second half of the 16th century; Hamburg, Mus. Kst & Gew.). The town mark is a cross on three steps, which can also be seen in the arms of the town. The town's mark appears on a few tapestries in such museums as the Museum für Kunst und Gewerbe, Hamburg, and the Kunsthistorisches Museum, Vienna, as well as on a *verdure* (Ghent, Provgebouw) depicting a rhinoceros—after an engraving by Dürer—and other wild animals. On the basis of this rather coarsely worked tapestry, with flowers, vases and fruit in bright colours surrounded by broad sculptural borders, it may be possible to attribute other *verdures* to Grammont.

BIBLIOGRAPHY

H. Göbel: *Wandteppiche I: Die Niederlande*, 2 vols (Leipzig, 1923–34); Eng. trans. of vol i (New York, 1924)

E. Roobaert: 'Het legwerkersbedrijf in het land van Aalst, vooral te Geraardsbergen van ca 1554 tot ca 1564' [The laidworkers' activity in the land of Aalst, especially in Geraardsbergen between *c.* 1554 and *c.* 1564], *A. Textiles*, iv (1957–8), pp. 39–53

R. A. d'Hulst: *Tapisseries flamandes du XIVe au XVIIIe siècle* (Brussels, 1960; Eng. trans., 1967)

J. P. Asselberghs: 'De tapijtkunst te Geraardsbergen' [The art of tapestry weaving in Geraardsbergen], *Geraardsbergen 1068–1968* (exh. cat., 1968)

ERIK DUVERGER

Gran. *See* ESZTERGOM.

Gran, Daniel (*bapt* Vienna, 22 May 1694; *d* St Pölten, 16 April 1757). Austrian painter. The son of an imperial court cook, he first studied with the landscape and genre painter Adam Pankraz Ferg (1651–1729) and then with the decorative and history painter Georg Werle (1668–1727). Werle trained Gran to paint frescoes and introduced him to his first employer and patron, Prince Adam Franz von Schwarzenberg (*d* 1732). Werle himself worked for the Prince between 1715 and 1719 on frescoes at Ohrada Hunting Lodge, near Frauenberg in Bohemia (now Hluboká, Czech Republic), where he was partly influenced by such Venetian painters as Gregorio Lazzarini and Sebastiano Ricci, as well as by Jacob van Schuppen (1670–1751), a director of the Akademie der Bildenden Künste in Vienna, and his mentors of the French Baroque classical movement; all were artists who later influenced Gran. Schwarzenberg lent Gran money to enable him to travel to Italy to perfect his painting skills. From 1719 he studied mainly with Francesco Solimena and Ricci, the leading masters of the Neapolitan and Venetian schools respectively. Their styles had a strong influence on Gran's subsequent work. He also studied painters of the Italian Renaissance and 17th century; those who influenced him most were Annibale Carracci and Agostino Carracci, Domenichino, Guido Reni, Nicolas Poussin, Andrea Sacchi and Carlo Maratti. In Venice he met Davide Antonio Fossati, who became his first pupil and assistant, and the

Daniel Gran: ceiling fresco (1726–30) in the dome of the grand hall (Redoutensaal side) of the Hofbibliothek (now Österreichische Nationalbibliothek), Vienna

two artists returned to Vienna together before Easter 1723. In the same year he married Anna Maria Barbara Werle, the daughter of his former teacher.

Until 1735 Gran worked in the service of the Schwarzenbergs (although Prince Adam Franz died in 1732), with administrative as well as artistic responsibilities. His first commission was for a dome fresco in the Gartenpalais on the Rennweg in Vienna, an allegory of *Dawn* (destr. 1945; oil sketches 1723; Vienna, Belvedere). The work was completed in 1724 and established Gran's reputation. He returned frequently in his later work to the theme of sunlight driving away the night, an idea vividly depicted in the earlier iconography of Cesare Ripa and others. Gran's fresco was notable for its atmospherically subdued colouring and its sense of space, in which spirits and deities of light and darkness floated freely. The slender figures in the sketches reveal Ricci's influence, and the composition as a whole suggests motifs from Solimena's ceiling painting *Aurora and Cephalus* (destr. 1950) for the Goldkabinett in the Upper Belvedere, Martino Altomonte's ceiling fresco of the *Apotheosis of Prince Eugene* in the Lower Belvedere (1716; *in situ*) and frescoes by Carlo Innocenzo Carlone (ii) of *Dawn* in the Upper Belvedere (1722; *in situ*). Carlone's ability to convey a sense of physical enjoyment also inspired Gran in his later works, especially those with a pagan theme. In the partially preserved frescoes in the apses of the domed room of the Gartenpalais (1724) and those in the marble room, including *Parnassus* (1726), Gran achieved the measured style to which he subsequently adhered, with warm, brightly glowing colours and less emphasis on atmospheric transfiguration. The changes in Gran's work were marked by his adoption of Veronese's approach to colour and an increasing use of Solimena's style of composition based on diagonals and the rhombus; the latter, however, was offset by the suggestion of weight in Gran's figures. The influence of Italian and French Baroque classicism is also evident, especially the work of Charles Le Brun. Other clear influences include Rubens, whose engravings he collected, and Johann Michael Rottmayr.

The Austrian Emperor's admiration of Gran's dome fresco at the Palais Schwarzenberg led to his commission to provide frescoes for the grand hall of the Hofbibliothek (now Österreichische Nationalbibliothek) in Vienna (see fig.). The frescoes were executed between 1726 and 1730 and remain Gran's most celebrated, extensive and artistically complex work. The paintings glorify the founder of the library, Emperor Charles VI, his virtues as a ruler and the blossoming of art and science. They were reproduced as engravings by Salomon Kleiner and Jeremias Jacob Sedelmayr (1706–61) and published in Vienna in 1737 as *Dilucida rapraesentatio magnificae et sumptuosae Bibliothecae*

Caesareae. Conrad Adolph von Albrecht, a court scholar, had worked out the extensive programme with its mythological and religious themes and matched it intelligently to Johann Bernhard Fischer von Erlach's structure: the central oval dome between two rectangular barrel-vaulted wings, the 'Peace Wing' to the north and the 'War Wing' to the south. The dome fresco itself shows an 'allegory of the imperial library'. In his own notes and plans for the scheme (Markt St Florian, Stiftsbib.) Gran called the scenes around the lower rim of the dome *The School of Athens*, borrowing freely from Raphael's Vatican fresco of that name. The figures shown towards the centre of the scene on the circling banks of cloud appear to be sinking rather than surging upwards; Gran's restraint here is significant in view of his repeated references to Rubens. It is above all the treatment of light and air, depicted in warmer tones than those used by Rottmayr or Paul Troger, that make this work one of the most outstanding fresco schemes of the 18th century.

In 1732 Gran frescoed a ceiling in the former imperial hunting lodge at Eckartsau on the Danube to the east of Vienna. The work, a *Glorification of Diana*, is similar in effect to that at the Hofbibliothek and is especially notable for its achievements in colour. The influence of Ricci can again be detected in the figures, while the composition recalls Werle's frescoes in Ohrada. Gran's frescoes in the following decades include those for the ceiling in the old manor house at Brünn (now Brno, Czech Republic; 1734–5), the cathedral at St Pölten (1740), the Wallfahrtskirche at Sonntagberg (1738–43), the pleasure palaces of Schönbrunn and Hetzendorf (both 1744), the Annakirche in Vienna (1747) and the abbey church at Herzogenburg (1748–9; all *in situ*). These clearly draw their inspiration from Solimena in their frequent and emphatic use of rhomboid forms of composition but are considerably stricter and grander; in colouring too, with richer tones predominating, Gran tends towards the style of Solimena. Often the feeling of depth is diminished to give greater clarity to the figures. His work at Jakob Prandtauer's Wallfahrtskirche at Sonntagberg is his most important church fresco cycle. It illustrates the story of salvation through the workings of the Holy Trinity and the Archangel Michael, and, as in the Hofbibliothek, painting and architecture work together. Gran's role in devising the fresco programme had been considerable; he was often engaged in a purely advisory capacity for fresco programmes, as in 1746 for the library and chapter house at St Florian, where they were then carried out by Bartolomeo Altomonte.

In his later frescoes Gran's style was increasingly simplified, with greater concentration on figures and action. The fresco (1749) in the cupola of the marble room at Klosterneuburg Abbey, on the theme of the *Glory of the Austrian Royal Family*, followed a programme of his own design. By isolating groups and scenes, some of them constructed as triangular compositions, and by making the figures even more monumental, he took a step towards true classicism, although this remained an isolated example in Austria for some time. In 1755 he worked at Schloss Friedau, near St Pölten, where he decorated a ceiling with an *Aurora Musis Benigna*, a subject taken from Ripa, and a secular counterpart to Gran's fresco at Klosterneuburg. In 1756 he painted his last fresco, the *Redemption of the World through the Coming of Christ*, in the dome of the Kapuzinerkirche at Und, near Stein an der Donau. This work may be seen to contain the essence of his mature style: the dynamism of the Baroque seems to permeate the stable coherence of form and content. Unlike his predecessors in fresco painting who followed Andrea Pozzo and other exponents of *quadratura* painting designed to give an illusion of greater space, and equally unlike Rottmayr and Franz Anton Maulbertsch, Gran allowed architecture to dominate decoration; his paintings complete the structure but do not overwhelm it, thus enriching their value through the quality of the architecture.

Of the altarpieces painted by Gran, which remain firmly within the Italian Renaissance and Baroque tradition, the most important are *St Elizabeth Distributing Alms* in the right transept of the Karlskirche in Vienna (1736–7; *in situ*) and the *Assumption of the Virgin* on the high altar of the abbey church at Lilienfeld (1745; *in situ*). In the former there are links with Maratti and Altomonte, while the swirling movement recalls Rubens; the bright warmth of Gran's colouring can well stand comparison with Ricci's *Assumption* in the chapel opposite. Ricci's painting, his last work, was a source of inspiration to Gran in the composition of his subsequent high-altar panel at Lilienfeld. He also drew on versions of the *Assumption of the Virgin* by Martino Altomonte and Bartolomeo Altomonte, but in carrying out the final work he applied a strict formality in the composition, which went beyond such models and is a distinguishing feature of his later work.

Most of Gran's surviving drawings are in the Graphische Sammlung Albertina in Vienna. Except for the more carefully executed examples intended as compositional models or as the basis of a contract, they are characterized by a Baroque turbulence and are constructed with a view to the overall effect, as in the drawings of Ricci or Solimena and most masters of the Baroque. He tended to produce a hastily dashed-off pencil sketch and follow it with a similarly rapid ink drawing, generally with little regard for the first sketch but giving a more developed, firmer concept of the subject. The single figure tends to emerge out of the overall composition in Gran's work. His strong, clearly defined strokes reveal a decisive and wilful character, attributes that kept his impulsive ideas under control in his search for a definitive personal style. It is clear, however, that the restraint in his work, and even his later classicism, were rooted in a highly temperamental Baroque sensibility. In 1751 he was offered the post of rector at the Akademie der Bildenden Künste in Vienna, but he declined it because of the low salary and relative insecurity of such a position. In 1755 he evolved a plan to establish an art academy in Hungary, but this came to nothing. His last years were clouded by poverty, illness and sadness following the death of his wife in 1754.

BIBLIOGRAPHY

A. Ilg: 'Zur Charakteristik des Malers Daniel Gran', *Österreich.–Ung. Kstchron.* (1879), pp. 57ff

K. L. Schwartz: *Daniel Gran* (diss., U. Vienna, 1932)

——: 'Zum ästhetischen Problem des Programms und der Symbolik und Allegorik in der barocken Malerei', *Wien. Jb. Kstgesch.*, xi (1937), pp. 87ff

E. Knab: 'Daniel Gran als Zeichner', *Wien. Jb. Kstgesch.*, xv (1953), pp. 145–72
Daniel Gran (exh. cat., ed. E. Knab; Vienna, Albertina, 1957)
E. Knab: *Daniel Gran* (Vienna, 1977)
E. Baum: *Katalog des Österreichischen Barockmuseums in Unteren Belvedere in Wien*, i (Vienna, 1980), pp. 194–206

ECKHART KNAB

Granacci, Francesco (*b* Villamagna, 1469; *d* Florence, 30 Nov 1543). Italian painter and draughtsman. A contemporary of Michelangelo and Fra Bartolommeo, he trained in Florence, with Michelangelo, in the workshop of Domenico Ghirlandaio, and the two then studied sculpture in the Medici garden at S Marco (*see* FLORENCE, §V, 2) under the supervision of Bertoldo di Giovanni. After Ghirlandaio's death in 1492, Granacci completed the altarpiece of *St Vincent Ferrer* (Rimini, Pin. Com. & Mus. Civ.), probably executing the figure of St Roch. His first documented works date from *c*. 1515, but the paintings identified with his earlier period are executed in a competent, inexpressive version of Ghirlandaio's style. These include the *Holy Family* (Honolulu, HI, Acad. A.), which is awkwardly composed for the tondo format, and a conventional *Virgin and Child Enthroned with St John the Baptist and the Archangel Michael* (Berlin, Bodemus.). Ambitions for a more monumental style are apparent in the *Rest on the Flight into Egypt* (*c*. 1494; Dublin, N.G.), which is notable for its charming exotic setting and luminous colour. The sculptural emphasis and compact figure grouping in this painting may reflect Michelangelo's influence, although the suggestion that he supplied a sketch for the composition is no longer generally accepted. Four lively narrative scenes from the *Life of St John the Baptist* (Cleveland, OH, Mus. A.; Liverpool, Walker A.G.; New York, Met.), not entirely autograph, also probably date from this period. In 1508 Granacci went to Rome to assist Michelangelo in painting the ceiling of the Sistine Chapel in the Vatican but was dismissed after only a brief stay.

The paintings Granacci executed after his return to Florence increasingly reflected the contemporary Florentine classical style, particularly the works of Fra Bartolommeo. This is evident in two versions of the *Madonna della Cintola* (ex-Earl of Warwick priv. col., see Holst, 1974, fig. 36; Sarasota, FL, Ringling Mus.), in which he attempted with only partial success a compositional type derived from Bartolommeo. In another painting of this period, of the *Virgin and Child Enthroned with Saints* (Florence, Accad.), the figures are more broadly modelled and again there are echoes of Bartolommeo, particularly in the upswept drapery in the background. A *Portrait of a Man in Armour* (London, N.G.), with a window view of Florence, is thought to date from this period. According to Vasari, Granacci was often employed by the Medici to design scenery and festive decorations, including for the

Francesco Granacci: *Arrest of Joseph*, oil on panel, 0.96×1.30 m. *c*. 1515 (Florence, Palazzo Davanzati)

visit to Florence of Pope Leo X in 1515. His earliest documented works were painted soon after 1515, two scenes from the *Life of Joseph* from a series for the bedroom of PIERFRANCESCO BORGHERINI, to which Andrea del Sarto, Bachiacca and Pontormo also contributed. Granacci's scenes, *Joseph Presenting his Father to Pharaoh* (Florence, Uffizi) and the *Arrest of Joseph* (*c.* 1515; Florence, Pal. Davanzati; see fig.), are sparely populated with small figures in precisely drawn architectural settings. Although the treatment is essentially conservative, recalling cassone decorations of the 15th century, the attenuation of the figures and their mannered poses, particularly in the *Arrest*, suggest influence from Pontormo. No hint of Mannerism appears in his painting of the *Trinity* (Berlin, Bodemus.) surrounded by sentimentally pretty putti, also painted for the Borgherini bedroom. A major altarpiece of this period, the *Virgin and Child with SS Francis and Zenobius* (Florence, Accad.), executed for the convent of S Gallo, again evokes the classicism of Bartolommeo, here with increased ease and coherence and more subtle modelling of the figures. This greater assurance is also apparent in the *Holy Family* (Duke of Buccleuch priv. col.), one of a number of compositions based on the Dublin *Rest on the Flight* (e.g. Greenville, SC, Bob Jones U. Gal. Sacred A.).

Around 1517 Granacci was again in contact with Michelangelo, who, according to Vasari, provided him with the design for the central panel (untraced) of his high altarpiece for the convent of S Apollonia in Florence. Four side panels for this altarpiece survive, half-length figures of *St Apollonia*, *St Jerome*, *St John the Baptist* and *Mary Magdalene* (all Munich, Alte Pin.), as well as an *Annunciation* (Corsham Court, Wilts) and predella panels showing scenes of martyrdom (Florence, Accad. and I Tatti). The fuller figure types on the four panels of saints and their elaborate drapery support Vasari's account of Michelangelo's involvement. In the predella panels the figures are treated with greater freedom, and their tapering limbs and small heads are clearly indebted to Pontormo, although they lack his expressive intensity. Such slender tapered figures also appear in Granacci's painting of the *Entry of Charles VIII into Florence* (Florence, Uffizi), possibly commissioned in connection with the wedding in 1518 of Lorenzo de' Medici. Unlike Pontormo and other younger artists, Granacci confined his use of Mannerist elements mainly to small-scale works and continued to follow conventional formulae in his major paintings, notably in the *Virgin and Child with Four Saints* (Montemurlo, Pieve), commissioned in 1521. A delicately drawn *Sacra conversazione* (London, BM) shows a composition similar to the Montemurlo Altarpiece. In the *Pietà with SS Peter and Stephen* (*c.* 1525; Fiesole, S Pietro a Quintole), the ungainly central group recalls northern European examples rather than Michelangelo's supple sculpted version (Rome, St Peter's). An appealing lunette of the *Adoration of the Shepherds* (Florence, SS Annunziata) includes figures repeated from his fresco of the subject (Monte Acuto, Villa Blasi Foglietti), notably the wistful St Joseph leaning on his staff. Perhaps the most impressive work of his maturity is the *Virgin in Glory with Saints* (Florence, Accad.), painted for the high altar of S Giorgio dello Spirito Santo, Florence, a graceful, balanced version of the Bartolommeo composition he had attempted earlier. Among his later works is a depiction of a mass crucifixion, the *Martyrdom of the Ten Thousand* (Florence, S Simone).

In Vasari's account of his life, Granacci is described as an easygoing character who avoided undue thought or effort. This view seems to be borne out by the derivative nature of much of his work and by his frequent repetition of compositions. His drawings, particularly those in chalk (Florence, Uffizi), and some of his small-scale works show a liveliness lacking in his larger paintings. Although there are indications in his work that he was attentive to the innovations of younger painters, his response was superficial, an adoption of detail rather than substance, and never seriously challenged his allegiance to the tradition in which he was trained.

BIBLIOGRAPHY

Thieme–Becker

G. Vasari: *Vite* (1550, rev. 2/1568); ed. G. Milanesi (1878–85), v, pp. 339–45

J. A. Crowe and G. B. Cavalcaselle: *A New History of Painting in Italy* (London, 1866), iii, pp. 534–41

S. Freedberg: *Painting of the High Renaissance in Rome and Florence* (Cambridge, MA, 1961), pp. 75–6, 211–12, 490–95

F. Zeri: 'Eccentrici fiorentini', *Boll. A.*, 2nd ser., xlvii/1 (1962), pp. 227–36

C. von Holst: 'Three Panels of a Renaissance Room Decoration at Liverpool and a New Work by Granacci', *Annu. Rep. & Bull., Walker A.G., Liverpool*, i (1970–71), pp. 32–7

——: *Francesco Granacci* (Munich, 1974) [full bibliog.]

A. Braham: 'The Bed of Pier Francesco Borgherini', *Burl. Mag.*, cxxi (1979), pp. 754–65

Il primato del disegno (exh. cat., ed. L. Berti; Florence, Pal. Strozzi, 1980), pp. 124–5

G. Briganti, ed.: *La pittura in Italia: Il cinquecento* (Milan, 1987, rev. 1988), pp. 303, 736–7

Making and Meaning: The Young Michelangelo (exh. cat. by M. Hirst and J. Dunkerton, London, N.G., 1994)

LUCINDA HAWKINS COLLINGE

Granada [Arab. Gharnāṭa]. Spanish city at the foot of the Sierra Nevada and at the confluence of the Darro and Genil rivers, with a population of more than a quarter of a million. Now the capital of Granada province, it was the capital of the NASRID dynasty (*reg* 1230–1492), who built the Alhambra palaces there (*see* §III below). Bronze, ceramics (*see* §II below), inlay, wood, leather and silk have all been produced in the city.

I. History and urban development. II. Art life. III. Alhambra.

I. History and urban development.

1. Before 1492. 2. 1492–*c.* 1600. 3. *c.* 1600 and after.

1. BEFORE 1492. Remnants of fortifications on Albaycín Hill attest to Iberian, Roman and early Christian settlements in the area. The city was conquered by Muslim troops *c.* 713 and a population of Christians, Muslims and Jews lived there until the 11th century. Early remains include the enclosure walls and rectangular towers of the old citadel (Arab. *al-qaṣaba al-qadīma*) on Albaycín Hill, and parts of a stone bridge over the Genil. In the 11th century the ZIRID dynasty (*reg* 1012–90) enlarged the northern section of the citadel with towers (two of them semicircular) and the Puerta Monaita and Puerta Nueva, both with right-angled bends in the entrance passages. They also linked the citadel to two small fortresses on the Alhambra and Mauror hills and built the Puerta de los

Tableros, which controlled access to the city at the Darro; it had polygonal towers flanking a horseshoe arch. Near it stands the Bañuelo (rest.), a typical bath of the Zirid period; it has a changing-room and a central pool preceding three vaulted rooms (a transverse *frigidarium*, a *tepidarium* with arcades on three sides and a transverse *caldarium* resting on hypocausts). An 11th-century minaret now forms the detached tower of the Mudéjar church of S José (1525).

Under the Almoravids (*reg* 1056–1147), who conquered the city in 1090, Granada flourished, to judge from carved wooden corbels and plaster fragments (Granada; Mus. Alhambra) found to the south of the Alhambra on Mauror Hill, some friezes with kufic inscriptions, and several bronze lamps, candlesticks and incense burners (Granada, Mus. Alhambra). It declined under the Almohad dynasty (*reg* 1147–1269), who took the city in 1166, as is suggested by the relatively low quality of some white marble and serpentine capitals (Granada, Mus. Alhambra).

In 1238, when the first Nasrid sultan, Muhammad I (*reg* 1230–72), founded the Alhambra city, he added several multi-storey towers to the Alcazaba and made it his dynastic seat. Many Muslim refugees came to Granada from territory reconquered by the Christians. In the 13th and 14th centuries the Albaycín Quarter was enclosed with a new north wall extending from the Darro on the east to the Puerta Monaita and the new Bab Ilbirah (now Puerta de Elvira) on the west, and two new city gates, the Bab al-Ramlà (moved in the 1930s to the Alhambra woods) and the Bab al-Tawwabin (destr.), were added. Thirteenth-century remains include the galleried courtyard of the Albaycín Mosque, a minaret (now used as the tower of S Juan de los Reyes, *c*. 1520) and, near the Genil, the hermitage of S Sebastián, which has a plaster vault of intersecting arches. The Casa de los Girones retains carved and painted stucco, part of the courtyard, the western and part of the northern wing, and a broad, cross-vaulted staircase. The Cuarto Real de S Domingo, the royal palace known as the Dar al-Manjara al-Kubra built under Muhammad II (*reg* 1272–1302), preserves its great throne room with three bays in the back wall and lateral rectangular alcoves (*see* ISLAMIC ART, §II, 6(iv)(a)). The Alcázar Genil (1319), built beside the river by Isma'il I (*reg* 1313–25), survives only as a square lantern-room with side chambers.

The house of Zafra (late 13th century; rest. 14th and 15th centuries; now convent of S Catalina de Zafra), has a rectangular courtyard with a pool; galleries at either end lead into rooms with alcoves. The Dar al-Hurra Palace (probably 15th century) has a similar layout, but its north wing has a two-storey gallery with a long transverse room with end alcoves and a projecting belvedere on each level; it recalls the Mirador de Lindaraja at the Alhambra. In 1349 Yusuf I (*reg* 1333–54) inaugurated the Yusufiyya Madrasa, of which only the oratory (rest.) remains next to the congregational mosque at the edge of the Alcaicería (*al-gayṣariyya*), a prosperous commercial district. The Corral del Carbón (14th century), originally the New Inn (*al-funduq al-jadīda*), has a monumental projecting portal deriving from an Oriental iwan (the Yusufiyya Madrasa had a similar portal) and a central courtyard surrounded by three levels of galleries supported on pillars. The Maristan, or hospital (1367; destr.), built by Muhammad V (*reg* 1354–9, 1362–91), had a rectangular plan: its court was surrounded by two storeys of galleries resting on pillars preceding the rooms. Waterspouts issuing from two large seated stone lions fed the pool in the centre of the court.

BIBLIOGRAPHY

Enc. Islam/2: 'Gharnāṭa'; 'Naṣrids'
M. Gómez-Moreno: *Guía de Granada* (Granada, 1892/facs. 1982, 1994)
L. Torres Balbás: 'La Alhambra de Granada antes del siglo XIII', *Al-Andalus*, v (1940)
——: 'El alminar de la iglesia de S Jose y las construcciones de los Ziries granadinos', *Al-Andalus*, vi (1941)
——: 'El Maristan de Granada', *Al-Andalus*, ix (1944), pp. 481–98
——: 'Las alhóndigas hispanomusulmanas y el Corral del Carbón de Granada', *Al-Andalus*, xi (1946), pp. 447–80
——: 'La supuesta puerta de los panderos y los puentes de la Granada musulmana', *Al-Andalus*, xiv (1949)
M. Gómez-Moreno: *El arte árabe español hasta los Almohades: Arte mozárabe*, A. Hisp. (Madrid, 1951)
L. Torres Balbás: 'Esquema demográfico de la ciudad de Granada', *Al-Andalus*, xxi (1956), pp. 131–46

ANTONIO FERNÁNDEZ-PUERTAS

2. 1492–*c*. 1600. In January 1492, as a result of the Nasrid capitulation, Granada became a Christian city. It was the last city in Spain to fall during the *Reconquista*. However, the presence of different ethnic groups created social tensions that affected urban development. The Alhambra, the Albaycín district and the lower city remained unchanged until developments during the 16th century superimposed new structures on the Nasrid city. Nevertheless, the city generally retained its earlier plan, with very narrow streets, many of them dead ends, with covered passages, overhanging buildings and *ajimeces* (Sp.:

1. Granada, portal leading into the Capilla Real, 1505–21

2. Granada, façade of the palace of Charles V, begun 1527

'twin-windows'), and gates that marked different districts and points of access. The new regime took over key institutions and areas. The *medina* ('city centre'), which was centred on the area in front of the Great Mosque, was most affected. The mosque, the adjacent baths and neighbouring buildings were demolished to make way for the royal funerary chapel, the Capilla Real (1505–21; see fig. 1), the cathedral (begun 1521; both by Enrique Egas), the Lonja (1522) and other religious and administrative buildings. Monuments in the Capilla Real include the tombs (1514–17) of *Ferdinand II* and *Isabella* by DOMENICO FANCELLI, and of *Joanna and Philip I* (from 1519) by BARTOLOMÉ ORDÓÑEZ. Some of Isabella's art collection remains in the Capilla Real (for further details and an illustration of her tomb *see* ARAGON, (6)). The madrasa was donated by Ferdinand II and Isabella to serve as the Casa de Cabildo Antiguo and the Alcaicería was retained for high-rental commercial use.

In 1501 the city was divided by Cardinal Pedro González de Mendoza into 23 parishes, and most were allocated smaller mosques to be consecrated for Christian use. This course of action reveals the intention to turn Granada into a Gothic city, as had happened in other reconquered Peninsular cities. The new churches were consistent to the point of uniformity and used a traditional conventual structure with *mudéjar* elements: a single nave with a timber-roofed chancel. Exceptionally, a Latin-cross plan was used, as at the church (1530; rest.) of La Merced (now Gobierno Militar), or a nave and two aisles (e.g. S Juan de los Reyes, *c.* 1520). At the same time, the court aristocracy initiated a series of Renaissance buildings. Under Charles V, Enrique Egas and Juan García de Pradas built the Hospital Real (founded 1504; built 1511–1640; now part of the university), which comprised a complex of hospitals with a Renaissance façade, Plateresque windows and a Baroque portal. Charles remodelled the buildings and gave its openings and patios classical ornamentation; Juan de Marquina (*fl* 1510–39), García de Pradas and Martín de Bolivar worked on the project. The Capilla Real was similarly decorated. The parish churches were provided with Renaissance portals, designed by the highly influential Diego de Siloé and his circle.

A second phase of Charles V's programme began in 1526. An ambitious plan was developed to make Granada the centre of an empire; Gothic was rejected in favour of a new vocabulary based on Greco-Roman antiquity. This was the justification for abandoning Enrique Egas's Gothic-style plan for Granada Cathedral and adopting a Renaissance-style one (1528) by Diego de Siloé (*see* SILOÉ, (2) and fig.): the cathedral's new imperial status required a style recalling that of Imperial Rome. After Siloé's death (1563) Juan de Maeda (*fl* 1563–82) continued the work. The Emperor's decision to locate within the Alhambra his residence, the palace of Charles V (see fig. 2), was a symbolic appropriation of a traditionally royal site (*see* §III, 1(v) below). The Tribunal de la Justicia, which was instituted in 1505, functioned precariously until 1526, when Charles V installed it in its own palace. The centralizing policy of Philip II worked to the detriment of Granada. Nevertheless, the prestige of the Tribunal was emphasized in 1587 by its new building (now Audiencia), with its magnificent façade built by Francisco del Castillo. As a manifestation of royal power it made a great impression on contemporaries and became a much imitated model. Large commemorative works commissioned by the court began to give way to Counter-Reformation constructions that were impressive but smaller in scale.

3. *c.* 1600 AND AFTER. Two very significant works mark the transition to the 17th century: the church of S María de la Alhambra (1581–1618), begun by Juan de Orea (*d* 1583) to designs by Juan de Herrera, and the abbey of Sacro Monte (1610; later enlarged). During the first quarter of the 17th century the combined activity of the municipal authorities, the Church and the religious orders transformed the city. These were years of feverish construction in every district. The Carrera de la Puerta de Guadix was rearranged to create a *paseo* centred on a fountain. At the other side of the city a series of houses was built near the Rastro. Ecclesiastical commissions included hermitages, oratories, crosses and statues by such artists as Alonso de Mena (*see* MENA, DE, (1)). Together, these works constituted a religious, celebratory programme. Above all, the conventual and monastic buildings completed the process of institutionalization begun after the *Reconquista* and characterized the 17th-century refashioning of the city as predominantly ecclesiastical. The convents of La Gracia, the Augustinian canons, the Capuchins and S Basilio were founded, and such older institutions as S Antonio Abad (1656; dome 1747) and the Discalced Carmelites (founded 1582) were remodelled. In the second half of the 17th century ALONSO CANO designed the Angel Custodio church and convent (*c.* 1652–3; destr. 1810), the interior of which became a model for later Baroque decoration, and the triumphant façade of the cathedral (1667; *see* SPAIN, §II, 3). He also produced paintings and sculptures to decorate the interior of the cathedral. His work was influential, and ideas from Italy were also used in the city.

In the 18th century Granada's appearance was not substantially altered. Existing projects continued, chiefly in the areas of expansion in the new districts (Magdalena, Angustias, Duquesa), and Counter-Reformation programmes were completed. Few entirely new buildings were planned, and architectural work was mainly confined to such sanctuaries as those of the Cartuja monastery (founded 1506; *sagrario* 1702–20) and the cathedral (1704–5), both by FRANCISCO HURTADO IZQUIERDO, and the *camarines* (Sp.: 'room behind the altar') of the Rosario and Angustias churches; their design was determined by municipal plans and the policies of the great Orders. The Cartuja's sacristy (authorized 1713; executed 1730–42) has been attributed to Hurtado Izquierdo; it was built by Luis de Arévalo and Fray José Vázquez. The only large building of this period was the church (1738–59) of the Hospital de S Juan de Dios. The DE MORA (ii) family and JOSÉ RISUEÑO contributed to the decoration of the city's churches.

During the French occupation (1808–13) some modernization was carried out. The Paseos del Salón and de la Bomba were laid out along the Genil with avenues and trees, and the Campillo district took shape. After the military occupation modernization and conservation were neglected, and disused churches and monastic buildings rapidly fell into disrepair. The principal urban centres remained unchanged under Ferdinand VII (*reg* 1808, 1813–33). Urban planning began during a period of political stability (1840–60). In 1842 the municipality set up a technical commission; its remit was to implement projects for widening and straightening streets, to identify derelict buildings and to follow through other measures concerning highways and lighting. A series of projects was initiated, which was completed after the Restoration in 1874, including the reorganization of the area around the Plaza Bibarrambla; the urbanization of the Plaza de Mariana Pineda; and, after the fire of 1843, the restoration of the Alcaicería.

In 1842 the idea of covering the Darro from the Plaza Nueva to the Puerta Real was proposed; it was carried out in the Calle de los Reyes Católicos between 1854 and 1884, a little later in Embovedado, and then, during the Second Republic (1931–9), it was completed as far as the confluence. Uniquely, there was no disagreement in intellectual circles concerning this project. The chief piece of 19th-century replanning was, however, the opening of the Gran Vía de Colón, a municipal project that dated from 1851, and which was made possible only by the economic boom resulting from the cultivation and industrial exploitation of sugar-beet in the fertile Vega (plain) to the west of Granada. The construction of the Gran Vía caused the destruction of important remains of the Arab and Christian city. Work started in 1895 and the necessary demolition work was concluded at the end of the century; the first new building was erected in 1901 and the last *c.* 1918. The project brought about the installation of the wealthy middle class in the heart of the city. Consequently, the bourgeoisie set out to reclaim the city centre and took action to create its own exclusive environment. Buildings with 20th-century façades and Art Nouveau or historicist ornamentation from foreign models were erected. The areas behind the new axis were neglected, especially the Calle Elvira.

Before the Civil War (1936–9) the city's growth took the form of several garden-city-type estates, for example Barrio de Figares, Hotelitos de Belén and Casas Azules. After the Civil War public building increased, the developments under Mayor Gallego y Burín (1938–51) being particularly important. Replanning within the city created the Calle Ganivet and the Ciudad Universitaria. The plan of 1951 determined the development of the city; its encroachment on to the Vega was limited by the Camino de Ronda, although building was permitted on both sides of the road, which inevitably led to a continuation of the spread. Dormitory suburbs developed for the working class on less expensive sites. A later plan (1972) regulated developments by establishing zones. Areas of historic interest, including the Gran Vía, were threatened, and the private occupation of historic and public areas was permitted, despite opposition from private citizens, neighbourhood associations and political parties. New plans governing the Alhambra and Albaycín came into force in the 1990s, and large-scale developments included a bypass to supersede the Camino de Ronda, creating a new ring-road system that destroys the Vega while failing to resolve the traffic problem.

BIBLIOGRAPHY

F. Henríquez de Jorquera: *Anales de Granada* (Granada, 1934/*R* 1987)
J. Bosque Maurel: *Geografía urbana de Granada* (Saragossa, 1962/*R* Granada, 1988)
I. Henares Cuellar: *Libro de Granada* (Granada, 1981)
J. Juste: *Arquitectura de postguerra* (Granada, 1981)
J. L. Orozco Pardo: *Christianópolis: Urbanismo y contrarreforma en la Granada del seiscientos* (Granada, 1985)
M. Martin: *La Gran Vía de Granada: Cambio económico y reforma interior urbana en la España de la restauración* (Granada, 1986)
R. López Guzmán: *Tradición y clasicismo en la Granada del siglo XVI: Arquitectura civil y urbanismo* (Granada, 1987)
C. Viñez Millet: *Historia urbana de Granada: Su evolución hasta fines del siglo XIX* (Granada, 1987)

RAFAEL LÓPEZ GUZMÁN

II. Art life.

As the seat of the Nasrid dynasty (*reg* 1230–1492), the kingdom of Granada was the centre for many of the luxury arts associated with Nasrid patronage. Fine ceramics were produced at several centres, including Málaga (*see* MÁLAGA, §2) and Granada, alongside everyday pottery and tiles (*see* ISLAMIC ART, §V, 4(iv)). The identification of wares produced in each centre, such as the enormous 'Alhambra' vases, is still a matter of much conjecture. After the Christian conquest (1492) the potteries in the Puerta de Fajalavza (Albaycín) district of Granada continued to produce traditional wares with blue floral designs and birds on a white ground.

The removal of Islamic manuscripts from Spain means that most of the evidence for the art of the book in Granada has been destroyed. A Koran manuscript on vellum (1303; Paris, Bib. N.; MS. arab. 385) has complex interlaced decoration similar to that found at the Alhambra. Its attribution to Granada has led other manuscripts (e.g. a dispersed 60-volume copy and Istanbul, Mus. Turk. & Islam. A., T.360) and fragments to be assigned there. Several astrolabes are known to have been made in the city, including one (Point Lookout, NY, Linton priv. col.; see *Al-Andalus*, no. 123) made in 1304–5 by the astrolabist Ahmad ibn Husayn ibn Basu, a member of an important family of timekeepers in the congregational mosque. Many fine silks are also thought to have been woven in the city or its environs (*see* ISLAMIC ART, §VI, 2(ii)(a) and TEXTILE, colour pl. VII, fig. 1). Granada was also a centre of fine woodworking, judging from a magnificent pair of incrusted cupboard doors (14th century; Granada, Mus. N. A. Hispmus.) from a private house, and a large rectangular casket (Madrid, Mus. Arqueol. N.; *see* MARQUETRY, colour pl. VIII, fig. 3) decorated with interlaced star patterns in stained ivory and various woods.

BIBLIOGRAPHY

P. M. de Artiñano: 'Cerámica hispano-morisca', *Bol. Soc. Esp. Excurs.*, xxv (1917), pp. 153–68
M. L. Sánchez Hernández: 'Cerámica de Andalucía Oriental', *Antiquaria*, vii (1984), pp. 46–53
S. S. Kenesson: 'Nasrid Luster Pottery: The Alhambra Vases', *Muqarnas*, ix (1992), pp. 93–115
Al-Andalus: The Art of Islamic Spain (exh. cat., ed. J. D. Dodds; Granada, Alhambra; New York, Met.; 1992)

M. LETICIA SÁNCHEZ HERNÁNDEZ

III. Alhambra.

The palaces of the Alhambra and Generalife form the most important architectural ensemble to survive from the Nasrid period (1232–1492). Art created under the NASRID dynasty in the Iberian Peninsula (*see* ISLAMIC ART, §II, 6(iv)(e)) provided the spark of originality for art in the neighbouring Christian kingdoms and for Marinid and Abd al-Wādid art in Morocco and Algeria. By the 9th century the citadel on the Sabīka spur of the Sierra Nevada overlooking Granada was called *al-ḥamrā'* (Arab.: 'the red') because its aging white stuccoed walls, probably belonging to a Visigothic fortress, were already stained red with ferruginous dust. In the 11th century the Zirids built defensive walls that linked this fortress with Albaycín Hill to the north and Torres Bermejas to the south. In 1238 the first Nasrid sultan, Muhammad I, organized the supply of water by canal, which allowed the building of a royal city on the Sabīka from the 13th to the 15th century. Enlarged and embellished by his descendants, the walled Alhambra city comprised the Alcazaba (*alqaṣaba*: 'fortress'), palaces, mansions, two mosques, baths (*ḥammāms*), an industrial zone with tanneries, a mint, kilns, workshops, and some adjacent royal estates such as the Generalife (see fig. 3).

After Granada was reconquered by the Christians in 1492, Charles V (*reg* 1516–56) attached a large Renaissance palace to the Nasrid palace of Comares. In the 19th century, Romantic travellers rediscovered the Alhambra, largely through the texts and illustrations of Joseph-Philibert Girault de Prangey, DAVID ROBERTS and OWEN JONES. Some names by which the parts of the Alhambra are known today are tags from this Romantic period. Later in the 19th century the Contreras family began restoring the palaces, and this work continued in the 20th century under MANUEL GÓMEZ MORENO and his pupils with meticulous historical accuracy.

1. Architecture. 2. Gardens.

1. ARCHITECTURE.

(i) Alcazaba, Generalife and Partal. (ii) The Salón de Comares, the Qalahurra of Yusuf I and the great gates. (iii) Sala de la Barca, patio and façade of the Palacio de Comares, and the Riyāḍ Palace (Palacio de los Leones). (iv) The Qalahurra of Muhammad VII. (v) The Christian period: the palace of Charles V.

(i) Alcazaba, Generalife and Partal. The first Nasrid stylistic period covers the sultanates of Muhammad I, Muhammad II, Muhammad III and Nasr. The Alcazaba (3(i)) has an 11th-century trapezoidal Zirid core with small solid towers. The Nasrids added a 13th-century outer enclosure and vaulted towers (Vela, Armas, Homenaje and Adarguero) under Muhammad I. The Alcazaba contains military quarters, a cistern, *ḥammām*, houses, storerooms and dungeons. A third northern enclosure was initiated with the great Puerta de las Armas (3(ii)), which controlled access from Granada. The Quebrada Tower on the east side of the fortress was probably rebuilt in the 14th century under Yusuf I.

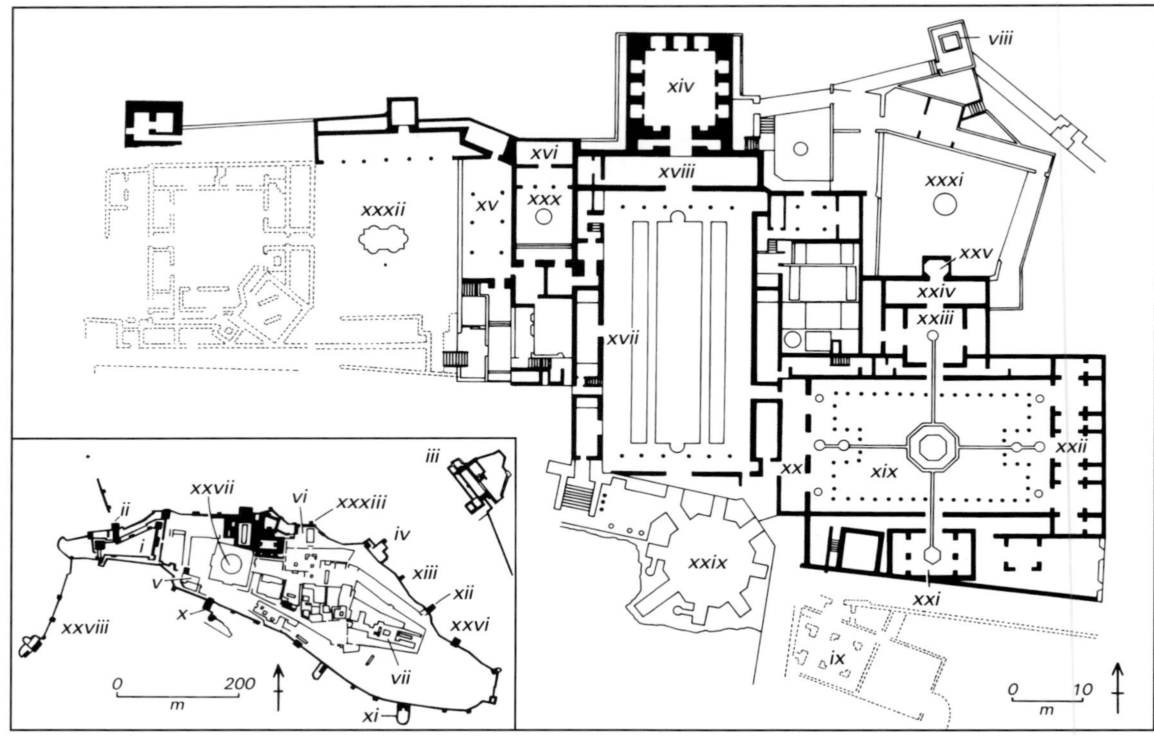

3. Granada, plan of the Alhambra: (i) Alcazaba; (ii) Puerta de las Armas; (iii) Generalife; (iv) Puerta de Hierro; (v) Puerta del Vino; (vi) Palacio del Partal; (vii) S Francisco; (viii) Torre del Peinador; (ix) Rawda (royal pantheon); (x) Bāb al-Sharʿia (esplanade gate); (xi) Bāb al-Ghudur (Puerta de las Albercas); (xii) Qalahurra of Yusuf I (Torre de la Cautiva); (xiii) Torre Cadí; (xiv) Salón de Comares; (xv) Sala del Mexuar; (xvi) Cuarto Dorado; (xvii) Patio de Comares; (xviii) Sala de la Barca; (xix) Patio de los Leones; (xx) Sala de los Mocárabes; (xxi) Sala de los Abencerrajes; (xxii) Sala de los Reyes; (xxiii) Qubba Mayor (Sala de las Dos Hermanas); (xxiv) Sala de los Ajimeces; (xxv) Mirador de Lindaraja (or de Daraxa); (xxvi) Qalahurra of Muhammad VII (Torre de las Infantas); (xxvii) palace of Charles V; (xxviii) Puerta de las Granádas; (xxix) chapel of the palace of Charles V; (xxx) Patio del Cuarto Dorado; (xxxi) Patio de Lindaraja; (xxxii) Patio de Machuca; (xxxiii) Torre de las Damas

The early Upper Partal and Abencerrajes palaces, which survive only in plan, belong to the time of Muhammad II as does the Generalife (3(iii)), built on ascending terraces. The sovereign reached the Generalife's royal mansion, the Dār al-Mamlaka al-Saʿīda ('royal house of felicity'), from the Alhambra's Puerta de Hierro (3(iv)), also built by Muhammad II. He ascended through orchards, crossed a first courtyard and entered the second through a guarded south portico, to ascend to a vestibule with a structural bench and up a steep staircase to the Patio de la Acequia. The mansion's south-east wing has storerooms and dwellings for servants. Its large upper-storey room has alcoves and a belvedere (restored and enlarged in the 1920s) overlooking the patio. In Nasrid times the patio's south-west flank was enclosed by a high wall (later pierced by Ferdinand the Catholic and Isabella the Catholic to form an open gallery), with a central belvedere kiosk given plaster decorations by Muhammad II, which were covered over in 1319 by his grandson Ismaʿil I with a later pattern. The north-east wing contains two dwellings and two staircases that probably led to the *ḥammām* and to the upper gardens, where a water staircase, alternating sections of stair with rounded landings, has channelled water coursing down steps and hand-rails; it probably ascended to an oratory. The mansion's north-west wing has a five-arched gallery, with its wider central arch framing optically the tripartite entrance portico to the palace's main, transverse room. Ismaʿil I remodelled this room and added the north-west tower, with stairs in it. The upper storey was reconstructed under Ferdinand and Isabella; the top gallery is entirely Christian work.

Muhammad III built the Alhambra mosque (its foundations lie partially under the church of S Maria). Only foundations survive of buildings on the spacious esplanade now occupied by the palace of Charles V extended to the Puerta del Vino (3(v)); the stone west façade also dates from the time of Muhammad III. The Palacio del Partal (3(vi)), with its exceptionally wide pool, was Muhammad III's crowning achievement. Its open gallery originally rested on pillars, mistakenly replaced in 1964 by modern columns. The palace's delicate decoration includes plaster arches with foliate patterns, a frieze of kufic cartouches, an upper geometric band below the flat wooden roof, and ceramic dados in cold colours made by the masterly school of artists who had built the earlier Dār al-Manjara (Cuarto Real de S Domingo) in Granada. A staircase and dwelling were added to the Partal palace under Muhammad III. The Partal pattern of six-pointed stars also appears in another early Alhambra royal mansion, which became the convent of S Francisco (the first burial place of Ferdinand and Isabella; 3(vii)) and is now a hotel; its central garden and canal are an earlier version of the Generalife's Dār al-Mamlaka al-Saʿīda.

Nasr introduced the lantern-room (previously used in *ḥammāms*) into palatine architecture, whereby a central square structure with overhead lighting is supported on pillars or columns and surrounded by outer rectangular areas, sometimes with lower windows. Nasr built the lantern-tower of the Peinador (3(viii)), although its inscription was altered by Yusuf I; Muhammad V replaced its pillars by columns and added the entrance; and its floor and decoration belong to Muhammad VII.

(ii) The Salón de Comares, the Qalahurra of Yusuf I and the great gates. The second stylistic period of Nasrid architecture is monumental. Ismaʿil I built the huge Puerta de las Armas and Rawḍa (royal pantheon; 3(ix)) and initiated the official palace called the sultan's palace, now known as Comares. In 1348 his son, Yusuf I, built the monumental Bāb al-Sharīʿa (esplanade gate; mistakenly called Justice Gate; 3(x)) that gives access from the south through a four-bend entrance. Its arched marble façade is set between large cubic projections and has a foundational inscription and decorative ceramic panel. Yusuf also built the Bāb al-Ghudur (Puerta de las Albercas; 3(xi)) and the palatial, military Qalahurra (Torre de la Cautiva; 3(xii)) which has a bent entrance, staircase and small central patio with a gallery supported on pillars. This leads to the main square room which has large window areas on three sides, and a geometric ceramic dado with unique purple pieces of lustre, bearing the Nasrid coat of arms. The plaster walls have decorative *sebka* (rhomboid patterns). In the four corners of the room above the dados, four poems by Ibn al-Jayyāb frame a kufic frieze that resembles a textile band. Yusuf I also built the oratory next to the Partal; it has open windows on either side, as does his Madraza oratory in Granada itself. The decoration of the Torre Cadí (3(xiii)), and the dwelling in the Partal with wall paintings, probably belong to the period of Yusuf I.

In his last years, Yusuf I enlarged his father's Palacio de Comares and built its huge tower containing a magnificent throne room (Salón de Comares), with original ceramic paving and patterned dados that crowned the masterly school of Dār al-Manjara in Granada. The throne room (3(xiv)) has three alcoves in each of its east, north and west walls, overlooking the city; the uniquely decorated central north alcove contains a poem (perhaps by the vizier Ibn al-Khaṭīb) stating it to be the throne alcove. The plaster decorations round the huge room are arranged in wide horizontal bands resembling subtly coloured fabrics. The great wooden ceiling symbolises the seven heavens of the Islamic paradise and the throne of God, and when fully coloured would have appeared golden. The hall is the culmination of Nasrid official architecture. The Comares *ḥammām* (built by Ismaʿil I, completed by Yusuf I) has a high and low apodyterium (lantern-room), and vaults cover the small frigidarium, tepidarium, caldarium, wood store and furnaces.

(iii) Sala de la Barca, patio and façade of the Palacio de Comares and the Riyāḍ Palace (Palacio de los Leones). Muhammad V initiated the third, highly complex stylistic period of Nasrid art. First he completed the Palacio de Comares. Its west area, mostly in ruins, was the Mexuar, or administrative area. The main west entrance from the square facing the Alcazaba led to a first courtyard that has the foundations of a small mosque and minaret. The second courtyard has a rectangular pool with semicircles in its sides and retains its Nasrid north gallery and an older pavilion (built by Yusuf I) overlooking the city. A double-bend stairway ascended from the south-east corner of this courtyard to the Private Council Room and thence to a tiny courtyard in front of the Mexuar façade. The Sala del Mexuar (3(xv)), with its lost central lantern supported on four marble columns, was reconstructed and decorated by Muhammad V with rich decorative panels that rise from the capitals. To the north of this room, a small Nasrid court communicated through a narrow arch on its eastern side with the triple-arched portico of the Cuarto Dorado (3(xvi)), which served as a waiting chamber when the sultan gave audience on the far (southern) side of the courtyard in front of the inner façade of his palace. This great façade is carefully proportioned to the width of the courtyard, and protected by large overhanging eaves like an awning. The plaster decoration resembles a huge hanging tapestry, with small lateral columns and corbels simulating gathered side curtains. From its upper windows women could watch public ceremonies unobserved. The façade has two identical entrances: the right-hand door was the private and service entrance; the left-hand door gave official access, through a guarded vestibule and ascending bent passage, to the Patio de Comares (3(xvii)) at the centre of the palace. The patio has a long central pool bordered by low hedges with two fountains and a seven-arched portico at each end, with a wider central arch. Friezes with floral decorative arches and verses adorn the end walls. The central *mocárabes* arch of the north portico has spandrels decorated with trees, and leads into the Sala de la Barca (3(xviii)), the sultan's bedroom and sitting room; at each end are alcoves crowned by magnificent *mocárabes* arches. The transverse passageway between this room and the throne room has a small oratory, and a staircase ascends to the upper winter quarters and roof.

The longitudinal naves of the Patio de Comares contain four dwellings, the official and service entrances, and access to the *ḥammām*. The south portico has a mezzanine floor and upper gallery with a wide central lintelled aperture. The beauty of this patio so impressed Pedro Machuca, architect of Charles V's palace, that he interrupted the Renaissance façade to preserve the Nasrid south gallery, each floor of which originally was thought to give on to a transverse room.

After completing the Palacio de Comares, Muhammad V built the Riyāḍ Palace (known since the Reconquest as the Palacio de los Leones). Constructed on sloping land in the palace garden (*riyāḍ* means 'garden'), the site was first made level on the north side by the construction of basement vaults. The entrance from the street at the south-west corner of the palace led to two guard rooms arranged in elbow bend (one survives) and thence to the cruciform Patio de los Leones (see figs 3(xix) and 4) at the heart of

4. Granada, Alhambra, Patio de los Leones, 1370s

the palace, which has a central fountain with twelve contemporary stylized standing lions, carved in white marble to fit exactly the proportions of the patio; the lions support a polygonal basin inscribed with a poem by Ibn Zamrak, a pupil of Ibn al-Khaṭīb.

The patio is surrounded by galleries with a projecting central kiosk at either end and an upper central belvedere on the longer sides. An older lantern-kiosk with a gadroon vault was incorporated into the south-east corner of the palace. The patio has magnificent rooms on all four sides. On its west side, the Sala de los Mocárabes (3(xx) above) is named for its original *mocárabes* ceiling (severely damaged in the 16th century, partially replaced in the 17th). On the south side, the Sala de los Abencerrajes lies below the level of the cobbled street that ran east to west to the south of the Comares and Riyāḍ palaces, separating them from the higher ground and the Rawḍa; the Sala de los Abencerrajes (3(xxi)) has a square ground-plan, which ascends by means of squinches to form a star-shaped drum supporting a supremely beautiful star-shaped *mocárabes* vault. On the east side, the Sala de los Reyes (3(xxii)) is sectioned into complex compartments surrounded by alcoves: three square spaces alternate with two rectangular ones; they are separated by elaborate *mocárabes* arches and enclosed on three sides by alternating rectangular chambers and vaulted cubicles. Three alcoves have vaults painted with Gothic–Muslim scenes; those on the lateral vaults show a Muslim knight and a Christian knight competing in hunting and for the love of a maiden; the Muslim wins, killing his adversary. The central vault shows a meeting of ten high-ranking Nasrids seated in council inside a tent. The other alcoves have exquisite *mocárabes* vaults.

The most successful Nasrid palatine complex lies on the patio's north side: the Qubba Mayor (Sala de las Dos Hermanas; 3(xxiii)). Its transverse entrance aisle has a latrine and stairs to the upper storey. The large square lantern-hall has side alcoves on both levels and ascends by means of *mocárabes* squinches to form an octagon at the upper level, where high windows illuminate its magnificent *mocárabes* vault. Constructed on a geometric pattern of eight-pointed stars, this ravishing vault creates an impression of floating spaces suspended above the room. Above the geometrically patterned dado runs a frieze resembling a textile band, containing the finest epigraphic composition in the Alhambra: a 24-verse poem by Ibn Zamrak, placed in lobed circles and rectangular cartouches. An arched entrance leads north to the transverse Sala de los Ajimeces (3(xxiv)) with another fine *mocárabes* vault, and thence to the intimate Mirador de Lindaraja (3(xxv)), where the decoration displays the culmination of Hispano-Muslim kufic patterning. The frames of the windows have a poem by Ibn Zamrak in fine cursive calligraphy, while the decorative glass ceiling on a wooden frame envelops the Mirador in coloured light.

(iv) The Qalahurra of Muhammad VII. The fourth stylistic period of Nasrid art survives in Muhammad VII's military and palatial Qalahurra (Torre de las Infantas; 3(xxvi) above). It follows the general plan of the Riyāḍ's Qubba Mayor, compressed to fit the tower: a bent entrance, with stairway to the upper floor and terrace, leads to a gallery surrounding the central lantern-hall, whose lintelled lower and upper galleries give on to other rooms. The main room has alcoves and a shallow belvedere reduced to the thickness of the wall. The decorative work shows marked stylistic decline. Fine large decorative lustre panels, and smaller ones in relief, survive from modifications made by Yusuf III to an older palace of Muhammad II in the Upper Partal.

(v) The Christian period: the palace of Charles V. The large Renaissance palace of Charles V (1526–50; 3(xxvii) above) adjoining the Patio de Comares was designed by PEDRO MACHUCA. He built the Puerta de las Granádas (*c.* 1546; 3(xxviii)) as a formal Renaissance entrance to the Alhambra precinct. The construction of the palace began in 1533; the design was revised by JUAN DE HERRERA, and work continued for over a century, but the palace was never completed. Perhaps the finest Renaissance palace in Spain, it has a square plan and a circular courtyard, the lower storey of which has an arcade of Doric columns; the upper level has Ionic pilasters between the windows. The octagonal chapel (3(xxix)) in the eastern corner of the palace was intended to have a dome, but this was never built.

BIBLIOGRAPHY

Enc. Islam/2: 'Gharnāṭa', 'Mukarbaṣ', 'Naṣrids'

L. Torres Balbás: 'La Alhambra de Granada antes del siglo XIII', *Al-Andalus*, v (1940)

——: *Arte Almohade, arte Nazarí, arte Mudéjar* (Madrid, 1949), iv of *Ars Hispaniae* (Madrid, 1947–77)

——: *La Alhambra y el Generalife* (Madrid, 1950)

R. Arié: 'Quelques remarques sur la costume des musulmans d'Espagne au temps des Naṣrides', *Arabica*, xii (1965)

M. Gómez Moreno: 'Granada en el siglo XIII', *Cuad. Alhambra*, ii (1966)

E. García Gómez and J. Bermúdez Pareja: *The Alhambra: The Royal Palace* (Granada, 1966)

A. Fernández-Puertas: 'Un paño decorativo de la torre de las Damas', *Cuad. Alhambra*, ix (1973)

——: *La escritura cúfica en los palacios de Comares y Leones* (Granada, 1974 and 1981)

A. Fernández-Puertas and D. Cabanelas: 'Inscripciones poéticas del Partal y de la fachada de Comares', *Cuad. Alhambra*, x–xi (1974–5)

A. Fernández-Puertas: 'El lazo de ocho occidental o andaluz', *Al-Andalus*., xl (1975)

B. Pavón Maldonado: *Estudios sobre la Alhambra*, 2 vols, of *Anejos de Cuadernos de la Alhambra* (Granada, 1975–6)
A. Fernández-Puertas: 'En torno a la cronología de la torre de Abū l-Hajjāj', *XXIII Congreso Internacional de Historia del Arte: Granada, 1977*
A. Fernández-Puertas and D. Cabanelas: 'El poema de la fuente de los Leones, Cuadernos de la Alhambra', *Cuad. Alhambra*, xv–xvi (1979–81)
A. Fernández-Puertas: *La fachada del palacio de Comares*, I (Granada, 1980)
——: 'Las puertas chapadas hispanomusulmanas', *Misc. Estud. Arab. & Heb.*, xxix–xxx (1980–81)
——: 'Memoria de excavación realizada en el sector N. del Mexuar del palacio de Comares', *Cuad. Alhambra*, xviii (1982)
——: 'El trazado de dos pórticos protnazariés: el del exconvento de San Francisco y el del patio de la Acequia del Generalife', *Misc. Estud. Arab. & Heb.*, xxxi (1982)
A. Fernández-Puertas and D. Cabanelas: 'Los poemas de las tacas del arco de acceso a la sala de la Barca', *Cuad. Alhambra*, xix–xx (1983–4)
P. Marinetto: *El capitel en el palacio de los Leones: génesis, evolución, estudio y catálogo* (Granada, 1984)
E. Garcia Gómez: *Poemas árabes en los muros y fuentes de la Alhambra* (Madrid, 1985)
——: *Foco de antigua luz sobre la Alhambra* (Madrid, 1988)
P. Marinetto: *Los capiteles del palacio de los Leones en la Alhambra: ejemplo para el estudio del capitel hispanomusulmán y su trascendencia arquitectónica* (Granada, 1995)
A. Fernández-Puertas: 'Alhambra: urbanismo del barrio castrense de la Alcazaba and 'casa en la Alhambra', *Casa y palacios de al-Andalus (siglos XII y XIII)* (Granada, 1995), pp. 255–86
——: *The Alhambra: Plans, Elevations, Sections and Drawings*, 2 vols., pls by Owen Jones (London, 1996)

ANTONIO FERNÁNDEZ-PUERTAS

2. GARDENS. During the medieval period Granada was an agriculturally rich region with two rivers providing abundant water for its famous farm estates, gardens and orchards, which produced, among other crops, excellent figs. According to the historian Ibn al-Khatib (1313–75), the Alhambra palace complex, like Granada, was densely planted with so many verdant gardens that the light-coloured stone of the towers and belvederes of the palace appeared like bright stars in an evening sky of dark vegetation.

In the gardens of the Alhambra there is a constant play between openness and closure. While enclosed spaces are defined and contained by architecture, they are also juxtaposed with miradors offering multi-levelled views on to the palace gardens situated on the lower slopes of the Alhambra, looking beyond to the Albaycín Hill and surrounding countryside, and views from the Generalife across the ravine to the Alhambra with the Sierra Nevada in the distance. Such cultivated vistas are often framed by arched polylobed windows, as in the Salón de Comares (see fig. 3(xiv) above) or the elegant Cuarto Dorado (fig. 3(xvi)). From the latter the view is north to the hills and streams of the 'natural', exterior landscape or in the opposite direction into an enclosed paved courtyard in which the only reference to nature is a fluted water basin in the centre. The all-encompassing, sweeping vistas of garden and landscape at the Alhambra and Generalife belie the traditional concept of the Islamic garden as a self-contained, private space organized according to a simple, rigid geometry; instead, they show that different kinds of landscape experience were incorporated into garden design by manipulating the direction and distance of the gaze.

The poetry inscribed on the walls and fountains of the Alhambra refers to the gardens and landscape. In the Patio de los Leones (fig. 3(xix) above), for example, Ibn Zamrak's verses refer to the watercourses and vegetation, the architecture and space surrounding the garden and the view on to the surrounding countryside, as well as to Muhammad V, the patron for whom the garden was built. The belvederes and pavilions in the middle of each of the galleried sides contain small water jets or rivulets that flow toward the Lion Fountain and create an axial organization that suggests a miniature, four-fold garden (Pers. *chahār bāgh*). A visitor in 1602 observed six orange trees in each quadrant; thus the garden in the Patio de los Leones was probably planted with orange trees, vegetation and flowers, the surface of the soil a half metre or more below the level of the pavement.

Several gardens in the Alhambra were refashioned after the Christian conquest of 1492. The Patio de Lindaraja (fig. 3(xxxi) above) in its original state was an open Islamic garden with an overlook provided by the projecting Mirador de Lindaraja (or de Daraxa; 3(xxv); Arab. *'ayn dār 'ā'isha*: 'Eye of the 'A'isha's Palace'), which was subsequently enclosed when converted into private apartments for Emperor Charles V. The Torre de las Damas (fig. 3(xxxiii)) in the Palacio del Partal is also of the Nasrid period, functioning as a mirador with ground-floor windows and a tower on the left side providing expansive views toward the Albaycín Hill; the gardens of the Partal, however, are 20th-century restorations with modern designs and types of plants.

When the Patio de la Acequia was excavated and restored in 1959 following a fire, a 13th-century quadripartite, Islamic garden was discovered. The original soil level was half a metre below the surrounding pavements, and the original irrigation system was intact, although neither was retained in the restoration. Two tall pavilions mark the ends of the garden, which is organized along a central axial watercourse, the water for which is supplied from the mountains via the same aqueduct that supplies the Alhambra. The water-channel is bordered by planted beds and intersected by a short, narrow walkway. Although the garden is enclosed on four sides, the west wall is pierced by arches and a projecting mirador, which looks over the lower gardens (rest.) and across to the Alhambra. Above and to the north-east are other water-channels, pools and gardens, redesigned in later centuries after the Christian conquest. The highest is reached via a stairway ascending through verdant vegetation; the coping of the low walls of the stairs is hollowed to conduct refreshing and decorative trickles of water while water jets adorn each landing. Elsewhere the 18th-century avenue of cypress trees leads to the modern entrance of the Generalife.

See also GARDEN, §V, 3.

BIBLIOGRAPHY

L. Torres Balbás: 'Patios de crucero', *Al-Andalus*, xxiii (1958), pp. 171–92
J. Bermúdez Pareja: 'El Generalife después del incendio de 1958', *Cuad. Alhambra*, i (1965), pp. 9–39
A. Fernández-Puertas: 'Los jardines hispanomusulmanes del Generalife según la poesía', *Les Jardins de l'Islam: Compte rendu [du] 2ème colloque international sur la protection et la restauration des jardins historiques: Granada, 1973*, pp. 196–201
F. Prieto Moreno: 'El jardín nazarí', *Les Jardins de l'Islam: Compte rendu [du] 2ème colloque international sur la protection et la restauration des jardins historiques: Granada, 1973*, pp. 170–75

——: *Los jardines de Granada* (Madrid, 1973)
J. Dickie [Y. Zaki]: 'The Islamic Garden in Spain', *The Islamic Garden*, ed. E. B. Macdougall and R. Ettinghausen (Washington, DC, 1976), pp. 87–105
D. Fairchild Ruggles: 'The Gardens of the Alhambra and the Concept of the Garden in Islamic Spain', *Al-Andalus: The Art of Islamic Spain* (exh. cat., ed. J. D. Dodds; Granada, Alhambra; New York, Met.; 1992), pp. 162–71

D. FAIRCHILD RUGGLES

Gran Chiriquí. Pre-Columbian culture of the Isthmian region of Latin America (classed archaeologically as part of the Intermediate area; *see* SOUTH AMERICA, PRE-COLUMBIAN, §II). Due to the paucity of archaeological investigation, the full geographic extent of Chiriquí material culture is not known. Chiriquí materials have been found in western Panama in Chiriquí Province and part of Bocas del Toro Province, and in south-eastern Costa Rica in the Pacific coastal region of Diquís and parts of Puntarenas and San José provinces. Thus the northern extent may be defined by the Talamanca and central mountain ranges of Costa Rica and Panama. The western and eastern boundaries are uncertain: Chiriquí-like materials have been found almost as far west as Quepos in south-central Costa Rica and as far east as the Veraguas River (Río Tabasara) in central Panama. The territory thus defined is extremely varied, having jagged coastlines with peninsulas, gulfs, bays and deltas, and mountain ranges up to 4000 m high. A range of wet and dry tropical and temperate climates provided numerous ecological niches in which cultures developed. The Spanish entered the region in the mid-16th century. By the 19th century large collections of Pre-Columbian pottery, carved stonework and metalwork had been made, including the McNiel Collection at the Smithsonian Institution, Washington, DC; the Minor C. Keith Collection at the American Museum of Natural History, New York, and in the Brooklyn Museum, New York. Objects excavated by Samuel Lothrop in Diquís in the 1960s are in the Peabody Museum of Archaeology and Ethnology, Harvard University, Cambridge, MA; and numerous other objects are in the Peabody Museum of Natural History, Yale University, New Haven, CT, and in the Museo del Hombre Panameño, Panama City.

1. POTTERY. The early ceramic phases of Chiriquí culture resemble those of most of Costa Rica and Panama (*see also* COCLÉ; EASTERN AND CENTRAL COSTA RICA, PRE-COLUMBIAN; and VERAGUAS). Decorative styles known as Aguas Buenas and Concepción seem to represent cultural spreads from central Costa Rica and Panama. Concepción ware belongs to the scarified tradition, with multiple-line incising on unslipped or unpainted buff or brown clay. Typical vessels are chimney-shaped or conical with tall, solid tripods or animal-shaped feet. Aguas Buenas ware features red and buff monochrome and bichrome vessels, often with lug handles and tripod supports in the form of slab feet. Shapes include small plates, bowls and globular jars with incurved rims, sometimes with small modelled human or animal figurines attached to the upper portion of the vessel.

As is true for the other cultural zones of Costa Rica and Panama, pottery made in the Gran Chiriquí region underwent drastic change around AD 600–800. The 'classic Chiriquí' ceramic inventory expanded and changed: Wolfgang Haberland identified 14 types based on decoration, including monochrome, bichrome, polychrome and negative-resist painted types as well as those with modelled and incised decoration. Tall, hollow tripod supports shaped like fish, crocodiles or other zoomorphic motifs (often with slits), modelled appliquéd decoration and clay pellets were other new features. The major vessel shapes were globular jars with short vertical necks and shallow, open-mouthed, oval bowls with tripod supports. There were several regional variations. One of the most elegant types is Biscuit ware (sometimes called Armadillo ware) which consists of polished but unpainted, thin-walled vessels, primarily tall (h. *c.* 180 mm), globular jars with constricted necks, and also of zoomorphic effigies with delicate silhouettes, including tiny appliquéd armadillo figures, frogs, monkeys and humans. A polychrome type, known as the Alligator group, comprises globular vessels with short, wide necks, sometimes supported on short tripod legs, with pale yellow or cream slips and stylized red and black alligator motifs applied in circles, bands, narrow zones or panels.

2. SCULPTURE. Chiriquí ceremonial stone-carvings are abundant, but are limited in distribution to the Diquís and Sierpe river deltas and to a few sites along the rivers. Figural images are rare except in the Diquís region of southern Costa Rica. The figures from BARRILES (*see* SOUTH AMERICA, PRE-COLUMBIAN, fig. 14), in Panama, and the few other examples of stone images from Chiriquí greatly resemble those from Diquís. Otherwise, the figure sculpture from Diquís is unique. It bears no relationship to the few pieces from GRAN NICOYA cultures and has only slight similarities to pieces from the Atlantic watershed and central highlands of Costa Rica and Panama. (In contrast, the carved ceremonial stone objects from the Atlantic watershed–central highlands and Gran Chiriquí are often indistinguishable.)

The Diquís–Chiriquí sculptured images fall into two groups. In one group, the images are sculpted on boulder-like granitic stones, whose general shape seems to have been modified only slightly. In the other the images are nearly flat figures carved from sandstone slabs. These sculptures range in size from a few centimetres to over life-size and include both male and female images. Regardless of size or shape, most of the Diquís sculptures have peg bases for insertion into the ground. The Barriles sculptures, a group of large oval grinding stones, may be imports into Chiriquí. Boulder figures were carved according to a strict pattern, although some deviate from the norm, having turned heads and arm variations. Most stand, squat or sit, and have arms flexed at their sides, asymmetrically placed on the torso or crossed over the chest or abdomen with hands free and fingers extended or holding a staff. While many are too eroded to decipher, others have broad faces with geometrically shaped features. Heads are large in proportion to bodies and frequently rest directly on the shoulders, increasing the boulder-like quality. Most are nude males while some have no indication of sex. The backs of the sculptures are flattened, with rectangular patterns representing shoulder-blades and buttocks.

Most of the figures from Lothrop's excavations in the Diquís delta (see Lothrop, 1963) are slab-like. They include human figures, deities and anthropomorphic images. All are standing figures with rounded peg bases. They stand and face frontally, with arms and legs represented; although the backs are usually carved, none are fully realistic. Most have a vertical slit between the legs, and many also have slits between the arms and the torso. Some appear to be masked human figures; others have animalistic faces with elongated, curved mouths and fierce feline or reptilian teeth, N-shaped canines or single or double serpent-tongues. Lothrop concludes that such anthropomorphic figures represented a local deity. Some hold trophy heads, and many represent warriors; others have arms drawn back and tied like prisoners. Animal images are also found among the Diquís sculptures but are not as common as human figures. Among these are jaguars, armadillos, deer or dogs, crocodiles and birds. While only a few have peg bases, all are rounded boulder-like forms related to both groups of human sculptures. Another, even more singular sub-group of stone sculptures from this region are spheres measuring as much as 2 m in diameter and weighing up to 16 tonnes. Most have been found on the surface in or near cemeteries or ritual centres, aligned in groups and sometimes placed on platforms. The Diquís images have close Northern Andean affiliations, their stylistic and iconographic features especially resembling those on Colombian metalwork (*see* SOUTH AMERICA, PRE-COLUMBIAN, §VIII, 5) and SAN AGUSTÍN stone sculpture. This may be attributed to northward migration of South American peoples or ideas into the Isthmian region between *c.* AD 500 and 800, and would date the development of the Diquís figure style after *c.* AD 800.

3. METALWORK. Gran Chiriquí cultures are also known for their goldwork, which comes mostly from tombs dated *c.* AD 1000–*c.* 1550. Since 1860 hundreds of gold and *tumbaga* (an alloy of gold and copper) artefacts have been found, and the greatest quantity and diversity of all Pre-Columbian goldwork have come from the Diquís region. One tomb in the delta region contained 88 cast and hammered gold and *tumbaga* artefacts. Judging by the quantities of objects and the few tombs from which they came, it seems likely that these were élite burials and that the artefacts served as symbols of rank or status. Most Chiriquí metal objects were manufactured by the lost-wax process; others were hammered from thin sheets of gold; still others appear to combine these techniques, plus soldering. Though often referred to as gold, the cast pieces range from nearly pure gold to pure copper, and most are *tumbaga.* Most were probably originally gilded and burnished on the surface.

The types of object and subject-matter are varied. Many are functional items, such as tweezers, buttons, fish-hooks and needles; others are items of personal adornment, including earrings, diadems, collars, beads, plaques, breastplates and pendants. Most items of jewellery represent forms in nature but few are realistically presented. Human, quadruped, avian and reptilian images are represented, frequently as composite or highly stylized creatures: musicians with drums, rattles, flutes or snakes; figures with human bodies and animal heads, including jaguar, eagle, alligator or bat; long-beaked birds with spread wings and tails; and sharks, monkeys, frogs, reptiles, spiders, scorpions, crabs and lobsters. Examples range in size from 20 to 100 mm. Among the largest, most naturalistic and elaborate are those representing frogs, cast as pendants, shown seated dorsal side up with rear legs bent and large flattened rectangular hind feet (see fig.). The animals represented, all somewhat dangerous, are the same types as those represented on stone and bone objects, and thus are probably part of a complex symbolic and perhaps religious system. Many of the cast anthropomorphic images are suggestive of fantastic creatures or supernatural beings. The largest collections of Chiriquí metalwork are in the Banco Nacional and in the Museo Nacional de Costa Rica, both in San José. Other collections are in the Smithsonian Institution, Washington, DC; in the Peabody Museum of Natural History, Yale University, New Haven, CT; in the Museum of the American Indian, Heye Foundation and in the American Museum of Natural History, both New York.

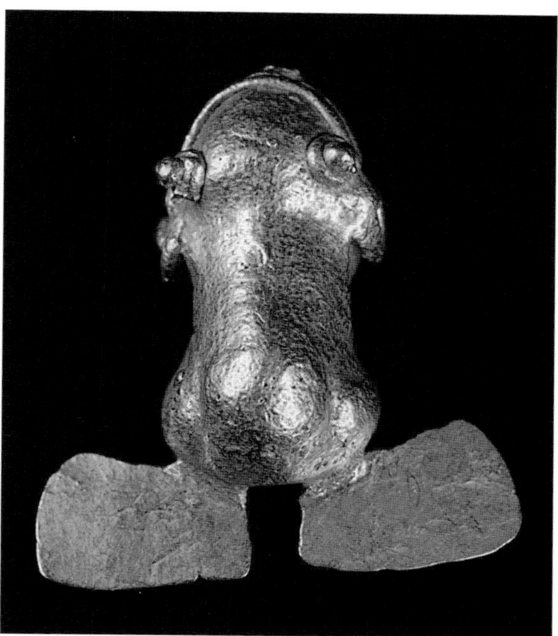

Gran Chiriquí metalwork, pendant in the shape of a frog, cast gold, h. 106 mm, ?from Puerto González Viquez, 11th–mid-16th century AD (New York, Jan Mitchell priv. col.)

BIBLIOGRAPHY

W. H. Holmes: 'Ancient Art of the Province of Chiriquí', *Bureau of American Ethnology 6th Annual Report, 1884–1885* (Washington, DC, 1888), pp. 12–186

G. G. MacCurdy: *A Study of Chiriquian Antiquities,* Memoirs of the Connecticut Academy of Arts and Sciences, iii (New Haven, 1911)

J. A. Mason: 'Costa Rican Stonework: The Minor C. Keith Collection', *Anthropol. Pap. Amer. Mus. Nat. Hist.,* xxxix/3 (1945) [whole issue]

S. K. Lothrop: *Archaeology of the Diquís Delta, Costa Rica,* Pap. Peabody Mus. Archaeol. & Ethnol., li (Cambridge, MA, 1963)

W. Haberland: 'On Stone Sculpture from Southern Central America', *The Iconography of Middle American Sculpture,* New York, Met. cat. (New York, 1973), pp. 134–53

E. P. Benson, ed.: *Between Continents, between Seas: Precolumbian Art of Costa Rica* (New York, 1981) [esp. W. Bray: 'Goldwork', pp. 153–66]

J. Jones: *The Art of Precolumbian Gold: The Jan Mitchell Collection* (New York, 1985)

JOAN K. LINGEN

Grancourt, Jacques-Onésyme Bergeret de. *See* BERGERET DE GRANCOURT, JACQUES-ONÉSYME.

Grande, Antonio del (*b* Rome, 1610–20; *d* Rome, ?1671). Italian architect. It is likely that he was self-taught. Surviving documents indicate that he worked in Rome from 1647 until December 1671 (see Pollak, 1909). In 1647 he restructured the Palazzo Monaldeschi (later Palazzo di Spagna) to serve as the Spanish embassy in Rome. He was responsible for the façade, the entrance vestibule and the fountain in the courtyard. The façade is conventional: a rusticated ground level supports a *piano nobile* articulated by windows with alternating pediments, and a modest mezzanine completes the exterior. The austere treatment of the façade is restated in the two rooms of the vestibule; subdivided by unadorned supports in three equal bays covered by shallow vaults, it provides a scenic approach to the staircase.

In 1650 del Grande became architect to the Colonna family. His major work for them was the Galleria (begun 1654; *see* DISPLAY OF ART, fig. 1) of the Palazzo Colonna in Piazza dei SS Apostoli, Rome. The salon is a long rectangular hall (the largest in a palace in Rome) covered with a cloister vault, and with screening columns defining the spatial boundaries. Del Grande's architecture and the later pictorial decoration (1675–8) by Giovanni Coli and Filippo Gherardi combine to create an exuberant Baroque space. The salon was much admired and may have influenced Johann Bernhard Fischer von Erlach's Hofbibliothek in Vienna. In 1652–5 del Grande built the Carceri Nuove on the Via Giulia on the initiative of Pope Innocent X. The Pope's intention was to gain control of the city's penal system and to improve the appalling prison conditions. His friend and adviser Virgilio Spada was consulted on the planning, and from the collaboration between Spada and del Grande came the innovative use of the modern system of individual cells, which had a significant impact on later prison design. Del Grande's building consists of two blocks connected by a loggia, rising in four storeys. Decoration of the flat façade is limited to the portal, the rectangular window surrounds and the double-curved cornice moulding.

In 1657 del Grande became architect to the Pamphili family, first serving as a member of the committee to evaluate the status of the church of S Agnese in Piazza Navona (*see* BORROMINI, FRANCESCO, §I, 7). When work was renewed under Carlo Rainaldi, del Grande served as an assistant, and for a time in the late 1660s he assumed direction of the project. His major commission for the Pamphili was the Palazzo Doria-Pamphili. Work began in September 1659, and the façade of the 15-bay wing on the Piazza del Collegio Romano was completed in 1661. A five-bay wing perpendicular to it was constructed in 1666–75, regularizing the piazza before the palace, a development authorized in 1659 by Pope Alexander VII. The façade displays nothing new: the quoining at ground level, the thin pilasters on the upper two storeys and the rusticated portal recall the decorative vocabulary of Mannerism. More interesting than the façade, however, is the entrance vestibule. It is rectangular, opened to either side by hemicycles. The powerful arcades, severe Tuscan supports and shallow vaults are typical of del Grande's work. Together, the vestibule and the staircase create a dramatic vista.

Del Grande's minor activities included the supervision of the construction from 1641 of Francesco Borromini's church of S Maria dei Sette Dolori and the completion of S Giuseppe del Falegnami (consecrated 1663), with Giovanni Battista Soria. He also worked outside Rome, at the Colonna palaces of Genazzano and Paliano (*c.* 1665), and at Marino, Rocca di Papa, Nettuno, Alatri and Valmontone. He worked in the shadow of the leading masters of the Roman Baroque, but he served some of the most important patrons of the time. The exteriors of his buildings, most of which were domestic, present a sober monumentality; his interiors, especially the vestibules and the Colonna Galleria, are moulded by means of mass and light. Del Grande was a conservative architect, fusing simplified Mannerist decoration with Baroque sculptural handling of space. This classicizing style was later echoed in the work of such architects as Carlo Fontana (iv).

BIBLIOGRAPHY

Thieme–Becker
O. Pollak: 'Antonio del Grande: Ein unbekannter römischer Architekt des XVII. Jahrhunderts', *Kstgesch. Jb. Ksr.-Kön. Zent.-Komm. Erforsch. & Erhaltung Kst- & Hist. Dkml.*, iii (1909), pp. 133–61
——: 'Italienische Künstlerbriefe aus der Barockzeit', *Jb. Kön.-Preuss. Kstsamml.*, xxxiv (1913), pp. 17–19
R. Wittkower: *Art and Architecture in Italy, 1600–1750*, Pelican Hist. A. (Harmondsworth, 1966, rev. 3/1973), pp. 141, 188
P. Portoghesi: *Roma Barocca: The History of an Architectonic Culture* (Cambridge, MA, 1970), pp. 283–4
G. Carandente: *Il Palazzo Doria-Pamphili* (Milan, 1975)
S. Jacob: *Italienische Zeichnungen der Kunstbibliothek Berlin: Architektur und Dekoration, 16. bis 18. Jahrhundert* (Berlin, 1975), pp. 78–9
L. Salerno, L. Spezzaferro and M. Tafuri: *Via Giulia: Una utopia urbanistica del 500* (Rome, 1975)
Marino e i Colonna, 1500–1800 (exh. cat., ed. F. Calabrese; Marino, Pal. Colonna, 1981), pp. 29–31
A. Blunt: *Guide to Baroque Rome* (London, 1982), pp. 110–11, 174–5, 197–8

CHRISTINE CHALLINGSWORTH

Grandi. Italian family of sculptors and bronze-casters from Vicenza, active there and elsewhere in the Veneto *c.* 1507–*c.* 1570. Lorenzo Grandi and his son the stone-cutter Gian Matteo Grandi (*d* 1545) both probably helped to train Lorenzo's younger son, Vincenzo (di Lorenzo) Grandi (*b* Vicenza, before 1500; *d* Padua, before 2 Aug 1578). Vincenzo would later work with Gian Matteo's son, Gian [Giovanni] Girolamo Grandi (*b* ?Vicenza, 1508; *d* Padua, 23 March 1560). By 1507 Vincenzo was in Padua, where he is recorded working on architectural ornament for a house belonging to Francesco dei Candi. In 1521, together with Gian Matteo, he completed the architectural elements of the monument to *Bishop Antonio Trombetta* (Padua, Il Santo), its bronze bust being executed by Andrea Riccio. The double cornucopia-like console supporting the niches of the monument is strongly reminiscent of the ornament used in the Lombardo family's architecture. In 1527 Vincenzo was paid for a *Lion of St Mark* for the Loggia del Consiglio, Padua.

From the late 1520s Vincenzo collaborated increasingly with his nephew, Gian Girolamo, and in 1532 they executed a fireplace for the Sala Grande of the newly restored Trent Castle, the residence of the Prince-Bishop Bernardo Cles (1485–1539). The following year several Paduan sculptors were summoned to Trent and a workshop set up: the marble workers were under Vincenzo's direction, the bronze workers under Gian Girolamo. Several projects for architectural decoration in the Castle were executed by the workshop, including the portal of S Virgilio. During this period the Grandi were also commissioned by Giovanni Antonio Zurletta to produce one of their most successful works, the marble Cantoria for S Maria Maggiore, on which they worked until 1542. The richly carved marble foliage of the architecture, narratives, putti and niche figures of the *Sibyls*, as well as Gian Girolamo's assured classical bronze portrait medallions on the underside of the Cantoria, attest to the sculptors' familiarity with the sculpture recently executed by Tullio Lombardo among others in the Cappella del Santo in Padua. Gian Girolamo's bronze-casting during his period in Trent included a number of domestic objects, such as a small bucket and a doorknocker, both with the arms of Cardinal Cles (both Trent, Mus. Prov. A.), as well as handbells and book cover decorations.

By 1542 Vincenzo and Gian Girolamo had returned to Padua, where they were assigned the final relief for the Cappella del Santo. The commission was never fulfilled, however, and the relief was eventually re-assigned in 1554 to Paolo Pelucca (*fl* 1554), a minor Florentine sculptor, although Gian Girolamo did complete a classicizing pilaster for the same chapel in 1542. Evidence of a bronze workshop in Padua is provided by the commission in 1544 from the Chapter of Padua Cathedral for a tabernacle (destr.) in bronze and marble. The next year the Grandi were active on the monument to *G. Antonio de' Rossi* (Padua, Chiostro del Noviziato al Santo, ex-S Giovanni di Verdara). Its architectural design by Vincenzo relates to their earlier *Trombetta* monument; the portrait bust of de' Rossi was executed by Gian Girolamo. The monument to *Simone Ardeo* (1548; Padua, Il Santo) has also been attributed, without documentation, to the Grandi; it was designed to emulate the nearby *Trombetta* monument, although its more sophisticated classicism suggests that it was designed by Gian Girolamo alone. His signed and dated monument to *Fra Girolamo Confalonieri* for the former Chiesa dei Crociferi, Padua (1549; moved to S Maria Maddalena; destr.), was highly praised (Petrucci, p. 142 and Rossetti, p. 250). After his nephew's death in 1562, Vincenzo was unsuccessful in securing Danese Cattaneo's uncompleted commission in the Santo, but may have been responsible for the tomb of *Isabella Alidosio* (1571) and the tomb of *Ippolito da Porto* (1572; both Vicenza, S Lorenzo).

BIBLIOGRAPHY

G. B. Rossetti: *Descrizione delle pitture, scultore ed architetture di Padova*, 2 vols (Padua, 1765)

N. Petrucci: *Biografie degli artisti Padovani* (Padua, 1858)

F. Cessi: *Vincenzo e Gian Girolamo Grandi, scultori (secolo XVI)* (Trent, 1967) [for earlier bibliog.]

S. Blake Wilk: 'La decorazione cinquecentesca della Cappella dell'Arca di S. Antonio', *Le sculture del Santo di Padova*, ed. G. Lorenzoni (Vicenza, 1984), pp. 109–72

Il 'Magno Palazzo' di Bernardo Cles, Principe Vescovo di Trento (exh. cat. by E. Chini and F. de Grammatica, Trent, Pal. Magno, 1985), pp. 32, 68

Bernardo Cles e l'arte del rinascimento nel Trentino (exh. cat., ed. E. Chini; Trent, Castello Buonconsiglio, 1985–6), pp. 142, 148–9, 182

ANTONIA BOSTRÖM

Grandi, Ercole (*b* Ferrara, *c.* 1463; *d* Ferrara, before 1 Nov 1525). Italian architect and painter. Vasari confused him with Ercole de' Roberti, a mistake that was corrected only in the early 20th century (Venturi, 1914). He is recorded as a master in 1489 at the Este Court in Ferrara. In 1495 he prepared the drawings for the façade, the interior and the marble decoration of S Maria in Vado, Ferrara, executed by Biagio Rossetti and Bartolomeo Tristano (*d* 1519), with Antonio di Gregorio (*d* 1503). The church was later radically altered, however. Also in 1495 Grandi produced a design (see Zaccarini, fig. 1) for a bronze equestrian statue of Ercole I d'Este, of which only the pedestal was made (untraced). He has also been credited with the design for the Porta dei Leoni at the Palazzo Castelli and the pilaster decoration on the Palazzo dei Diamanti, both in Ferrara (Venturi, 1888).

Grandi's activities as a painter are difficult to identify, as no work ascribed to him is supported by documentary evidence or an inscription. A painting of *St George* (Rome, Pal. Corsini), with Grandi's monogram inscribed on the

Ercole Grandi: *Martyrdom of St Sebastian* (Ferrara, Pinacoteca Nazionale)

horse's saddle, has long been accepted as being a youthful work by Francesco Francia. According to Vasari Grandi painted a predella (untraced) for the altarpiece by Lorenzo Costa (i) in S Petronio, Bologna. Venturi (1888) suggested that he was in Bologna working with Francia and Costa between 1489 and 1495, when he painted a *Crucifixion* (ex-Gal. Santini, Ferrara). One work that has been convincingly attributed to him is the *Assumption of Mary Magdalene* (Ferrara, Pin. N.) made for S Maria in Vado, where Grandi also worked as an architect. Grandi has been credited (Berenson) with an interesting sequence of eight tempera scenes from the Old Testament (*c.* 1500), which show the influence of Costa (some untraced; examples in Bergamo, Accad. Carrara B.A. and London, N.G.).

Grandi's major surviving works are the ceiling frescoes at the Palazzo Costabili (formerly Scrofa-Calcagnini) in Ferrara dating from the early 16th century. These are modelled on Andrea Mantegna's frescoes in the Camera degli Sposi in Mantua (1465–74; Pal. Ducale), one of the first attempts to create the illusion of open sky. The *Martyrdom of St Sebastian* (Ferrara, Pin. N.; see fig.), which Grandi painted for S Paolo in Ferrara, showing finely drawn portraits of the Mori family, can be classed as a late work.

BIBLIOGRAPHY

Thieme–Becker
G. Vasari: *Vite* (1550, rev. 2/1568); ed. G. Milanesi (1878–85), iii, pp. 141–8
A. Venturi: 'Ercole Grandi', *Archv Stor. A.*, i (1888), pp. 193–201
B. Berenson: *North Italian Painters of the Renaissance* (New York, 1907), p. 211
F. Filippini: 'Ercole Grandi, pittore ed architetto', *Atti & Mem. Regia Deput. Stor. Patria Prov. Romagna*, iv (1914), pp. 414–49
A. Venturi: *Storia*, vii (1914)
F. Filippini: 'Ercole da Ferrara ed Ercole da Bologna', *Boll. A.: Min. Pub. Istruzione*, xi (1917), pp. 49–63
D. Zaccarini: 'Il disegno di Ercole Grandi per il monumento ad Ercole I D'Este', *L'Arte*, xx (1917), pp. 159–67

SUSANNE KIEFHABER

Grandi, Ercole (di Giulio Cesare) de'. *See* ROBERTI, ERCOLE DE'.

Grandi, Giuseppe (*b* Ganna, nr Varese, 17 Oct 1843; *d* Ganna, 1 Dec 1894). Italian sculptor and etcher. He studied at the Accademia di Belle Arti di Brera, Milan, where he exhibited a sculpture of *Ulysses* (Milan, Gal. A. Mod.) in 1866; the work won a prize, but Grandi was accused of using a cast from life. In 1867 he moved to the Accademia Albertina di Belle Arti in Turin, where one of his teachers, Odoardo Tabacchi, also from Ganna, invited him to work in his studio. In 1869 he was again in Milan, where he joined GLI SCAPIGLIATI. The group favoured an impressionistic, 'pictorial' approach to sculpture, in which the sculptural masses seem about to dissolve into the atmosphere. Grandi produced, in the *scapigliatura* style, a sculpture of *St Thecla* (1869) for Milan Cathedral, which contrasted sharply with Tabacchi's *St Mary of Egypt* (1863/7), also for the cathedral. This was followed in 1871 by the statue of *Cesare Beccaria* (Milan, Pal. Giustizia): although this work was apparently traditional in its pose and costume, the artist moved away from academic realism with his relaxed, disjointed treatment of the subject.

After *Cesare Beccaria*, Grandi's work became increasingly more radical, concentrating on small- and medium-sized pieces. In 1873–4 he also experimented with etching, producing *c.* 12 plates in which, apart from the innovation of etchings produced in single editions, he showed a new affinity with the paintings of Daniele Ranzoni. These prints also express his desire to capture atmospheric values and the play of light and shadow on forms, for example the portraits of *Antonio Billia* (1874) and *Carlo Borghi* (1886; both Milan, Gal. A. Mod.), in which the faces of the subjects are barely perceptible against the dark background. In 1873 he exhibited at the Brera in Milan the *Page of Lara* (bronze version; Milan, Gal. A. Mod.), which caused a public scandal because, while its inspiration was literary, it went against the taste of Gli Scapigliati with certain colouristic effects in the refined, detailed working of the material. Such portraits as that of *Giuseppe Cremona* (1873–80; Milan, Gal. A. Mod.) went beyond naturalism, exemplifying Grandi's new conception of sculpture; in the small bronze of *Marshal Ney* (1875–8; Milan, Gal. A. Mod.), the unusual modelling, which dissolves the form with light, reveals Grandi already to be completely free from academic and romantic traditions. From 1875 Grandi produced works that were undoubtedly studied by Leonardo Bistolfi, for example *The Ivy* (1878; Milan, Gal. A. Mod.), the subject and style of which are similar to those of Tranquillo Cremona's paintings and which anticipated the work of Medardo Rosso.

Grandi's large commemorative sculptures show, if with less expressive force, the same pictorial approach and impressionistic effects as his plaster models and small bronze pieces. The monuments, which were free of both

Giuseppe Grandi: monument commemorating the Milanese anti-Austrian uprising of the Cinque Giornate in 1848, designed 1881, executed posthumously 1894–5, Piazza Cinque Giornati, Milan

complex architectural forms and naturalistic representation, created varied effects in different kinds of light and from different points of view, for example the model (*c.* 1881; Milan, Gal. A. Mod.) for a monument to *Dante* in Trent. In 1881 the city of Milan held a competition for a monument commemorating the Milanese anti-Austrian uprisings of the Cinque Giornate (1848). Grandi's plaster model, together with the two symbolic statues of the *Exhortation at the Barricades* and the *Grief for the Fallen*, won the contest. However, the actual monument (Milan, Piazza Cinque Giornate; see fig.) was not executed until 1894–5, after the artist's death: it is notable for its enormous scale and sense of movement.

BIBLIOGRAPHY

Thieme–Becker
E. Lavagnino: *L'arte moderna*, ii (Turin, 1956), pp. 647–50
E. Piceni and M. Cinotti: 'La scultura a Milano dal 1815 al 1915', *Storia di Milano*, xv (Milan, 1962), pp. 601–5
M. de Micheli: *La scultura del novecento* (Turin, 1981), pp. 14–15
L. Caramel: 'Un nuovo Maresciallo Ney di Giuseppe Grandi', *A. Crist.*, lxxvii/731 (March–April 1989), pp. 145–50
F. Tedeschi: *Le vicende storiche del monumento alle Cinque Giornate di Milano di Giuseppe Grandi*, Rendiconto delle classe di lettere e scienze morali e storiche, cxxiii (Milan, 1990)
M. de Micheli: *La scultura dell'ottocento* (Turin, 1992), pp. 153–62

VALERIO TERRAROLI

Grandjean, Jean (*b* Amsterdam, ?5 Feb 1752; *d* Rome, 12 Nov 1781). Dutch painter and draughtsman. In 1777 he was an assistant in the wallpaper workshop of Jurriaan Andriessen in Amsterdam. In the same year he enrolled in the Amsterdamse Stadstekenacademie and was one of the founder-members of the Félix Meritis Society for the promotion of art. The collectors Jan Tersteeg and Dirk Versteeg financed Grandjean's visit in 1779 to Italy, where he came into contact with a circle of artists centred on the sculptor Alexander Trippel, who gave lessons in drawing from the model in his Trippelsche Academie. Grandjean's Italian drawings (e.g. *Temple of the Sibyl at Tivoli*, 1779; Leiden, Rijksuniv., Prentenkab.) show that he was decisively influenced in his artistic development by his encounter with great Italian art, as well as by his contact with the German artists' circle. In both his landscapes and his figure studies, he changed from a typical Dutch wallpaper style to a type of international classicism. Grandjean would undoubtedly have been Holland's most important Neo-classical artist if his early death had not cut short his career.

BIBLIOGRAPHY

Dutch Masterpieces from the Eighteenth Century: Paintings and Drawings, 1700–1800 (exh. cat. by E. R. Mandle and J. W. Niemeijer, Minneapolis, MN, Inst. A.; Toledo, OH, Mus. A.; Philadelphia, PA, Mus. A.; 1971–2), pp. 46–7
J. W. Niemeijer: 'Academies and Other Figure Studies from Jean Grandjean's Roman Period', *Master Drgs*, xii (1974), pp. 351–8
Edele eenvoud: Neo-classicisme in Nederland, 1765–1800 [Noble simplicity: Neo-classicism in the Netherlands] (exh. cat. by F. Grijzenhout and C. van Tuyll van Serooskerken, Haarlem, Frans Halsmus. and Teylers Mus., 1989), pp. 218–20
Hollandse aquarellen uit de 18de eeuw (exh. cat. by J. W. Niemeijer, Amsterdam, Rijksmus., 1990–91), pp. 56–7

TON GEERTS

Grandjean de Montigny, Auguste-Henri-Victor (*b* Paris, 15 July 1776; *d* Rio de Janeiro, 1 March 1850). French architect and urban planner. He studied at the Ecole des Beaux-Arts in Paris with Charles Percier and Pierre Fontaine and won the Prix de Rome in 1799 with a scheme for a necropolis. In 1801 he moved to Italy to complete his studies at the French Academy of Fine Arts in Rome. There he restored (1803) the early imperial tomb of *Caecilia Metella* on the Via Appia and laid out the gardens of the Villa Medici, which was acquired by the French government in 1804. He travelled throughout Italy, studying, sketching and executing various designs, among them one for a theatre at Naples. In conjunction with Auguste Famin (1776–1859) he wrote *L'Architecture de la Toscane* (1815), which was widely read at the time by architects in search of details of early Renaissance buildings. In 1810 he was summoned by Jerome Bonaparte, King of Westphalia (*reg* 1807–13), to work on projects in Kassel. Notable among these are the salons of Simon Louis Du Ry's Schloss Wilhelmshöhe, the monument to Napoleon I in Opera Square, a triumphal arch and the design of the royal palace of Bellevue, which he did not complete because of the fall from power of Jerome Bonaparte in 1813.

Grandjean returned to Paris, where he was invited by Joachim Le Breton to join the French artistic mission that was to offer its services at the Portuguese court in Brazil. The mission, which made a profound impression on the arts in Brazil, was composed of the painters Jean-Baptiste Debret (1768–1848) and Nicolas-Antoine Taunay (1755–1830), the printmaker Charles-Simon Pradier (1786–1848), the sculptor Auguste-Marie Taunay (1768–1824), the engineer François Ovide and the secretary of the mission, Pierre Dillon. The artistic mission arrived in Rio de Janeiro in March 1816, with, among other items, a collection of 54 paintings that Le Breton had purchased in France. These formed the original nucleus of the Museu Nacional de Belas Artes. During the first few years the artists of the mission encountered great difficulties of adaptation and of gaining a sympathetic audience for teaching. The death of Le Breton in 1819 represented a severe setback for the mission and its position at the Portuguese court. Pradier and Nicolas-Antoine Taunay returned to Paris, while Auguste-Marie Taunay died in Rio in 1824. Debret and Grandjean were thus left with the responsibility for the training of local artists, although the situation improved with the arrival of the brothers Marc Ferrez (1788–1850) and Zephirin Ferrez (1797–1851) as assistants in sculpture and printmaking. The creation in 1820 of the Royal Academy of Design, Painting, Sculpture and Architecture did not have great impetus, however, because of the return to Portugal the following year of King John VI and his court. In 1826 it became the Academy of Fine Arts and was installed in an Empire-style building designed by Grandjean de Montigny, who succeeded Henrique José da Silva (1772–1834) as acting director in 1834. Among the more significant pupils in his architecture classes were Manuel de Araujo Porto Alegre (1806–79), Joaquín Bethencourt da Silva, Jacinto Rebelo and Antonio Baptista de Rocha.

Among Grandjean de Montigny's other projects in Brazil were official commissions for the Royal School of Arts and Trades, the adaptation of the Seminary of San Joaquín as the Colegio Pedro II (1838) and, most notably, the Merchants' Exchange (1819–20), Custom House (1820), the church of Maceio (1838), the Senado Palace

Auguste-Henri-Victor Grandjean de Montigny: Museum of the Pontificia Universidade Católica, Río de Janeiro, *c.* 1826

(1848) and Imperial Palace (1848). He also designed many ephemeral works for the royal court in Brazil: triumphal arches, catafalques, funeral pyres, obelisks and decorations. Most of his work, however, was for private patrons, for example the fine Plaza de Comercio (1820) and many residences, such as the House of Souza e Meneses and those at 22, Rua Catete and 81, Dutra. His own residence in the district of Gavea in Rio de Janeiro (*c.* 1826; now the Museum of the Pontificia Universidade Católica; see fig.) is striking for the way it sits in the landscape, a success repeated in the Casa de Campo at Catumbi.

Grandjean de Montigny was also active as an urban planner, advising on the layout of new streets, boulevards and squares and submitting designs for a water-supply system for gardens. The popularization of the Neo-classical style, which characterized Brazilian architecture in the second half of the 19th century, owed much to his designs and built works. The transition from popular Baroque, which had achieved its greatest successes in Minas Gerais and Bahia, to a more strictly classical style would not have been possible without the transformation of official taste by the French art mission and particularly the work of Grandjean de Montigny.

WRITINGS

Recueil des plus beaux tombeaux executés en Italie pendant les XVe et XVIe siècles (Paris, 1813)

L'Architecture de la Toscane (Paris, 1815)

BIBLIOGRAPHY

A. Morales de los Rios: *Grandjean de Montigny e a evolucão da arte brasileira* (Rio de Janeiro, 1941)

A. A. de Taunay: *A missão artistica de 1816* (Rio de Janeiro, 1956)

I. Arestizabal and others: *Uma cidade en questão. Grandjean de Montigny e o Rio de Janeiro* (Rio de Janeiro, 1979)

RAMÓN GUTIÉRREZ

Grandma Moses. *See* MOSES, GRANDMA.

Grand Manner [Great Style]. Term given to the imposing style of history painting advocated by the teaching academies throughout Europe from the late 17th century onwards, based on the art of Raphael, Poussin and the Carracci. The idea of an elevated style of writing, deriving from Classical rhetoric, was applied to visual art by late Renaissance theorists, especially Giovanni Pietro Bellori, who in 1664 urged 'noble' artists to form in their minds 'an example of superior beauty and, reflecting on it, improve upon nature until it is without fault'. He made it clear that this was an élite style, appreciated only by 'higher spirits' and not understood by the populace, who 'praise things painted naturalistically' and 'approve of novelty'.

As such, the Grand Manner formed the basis for the official aristocratic style of the French Académie Royale de Peinture et de Sculpture under the directorship of Charles Le Brun, and in England it was recommended by Anthony Ashley Cooper, 3rd Earl of Shaftesbury (1713), and Jonathan Richardson the elder (1715). However, the most lucid exposition of its aims and means was given by Joshua Reynolds in his *Discourses*, especially the 3rd (1770) and 4th (1771). Reynolds called it the 'Great Style' and defined it as the pursuit of perfect form, as opposed to the realistic imitation of particulars, in composition, expression, colouring and drapery. The subject must be 'generally interesting . . . There must be something either in the action, or in the object, in which men are universally concerned, and which powerfully strikes upon the publick sympathy'. In practice this meant incidents from ancient history or the Bible. A composition should include only a few figures, preferably but not necessarily life size, their poses and proportions adapted from Classical sculpture. Expression should be achieved mainly through gesture, and facial movements should be restrained (consistent with Renaissance ideals of gentlemanly conduct): Reynolds criticized Gianlorenzo Bernini's *David* (Rome, Gal. Borghese) for biting his lip in an undignified way. The aim is absolute clarity in story-telling, but within the limits of strict decorum, which Shaftesbury called 'decency of manners'. Colours should be strong, with a preference for primaries, disposed in broad, undifferentiated masses. Drapery should fall in large, simple folds, as in Classical sculpture, and the depiction of specific textures (e.g. fur, silk) should be avoided.

In Britain the Grand Manner was followed, up to a point, by Reynolds himself, George Romney, Gavin Hamilton, James Barry and Benjamin Robert Haydon; it was strongly revived by the Victorian Neo-classicists, such as G. F. Watts, Alfred Stevens and Frederic Leighton. In Italy it left intermittent traces on the work of Carlo Maratti and Pompeo Girolamo Batoni. But the supreme master, combining perfect form with intense feeling, was the French Neo-classical painter Jacques-Louis David. This was recognized by Diderot, who said of his *Belisarius* (Salon 1781): 'That young man shows great style (grande manière) in his handling of the work. He has sensibility. His heads have expression without affectation. His attitudes are noble and natural.'

See also REALISM.

BIBLIOGRAPHY

G. P. Bellori: *Vite* (1672); ed. E. Borea (1976)
A. A. Cooper, 3rd Earl of Shaftesbury: 'Notion of the Historical Draft or Tablature of the Judgment of Hercules', *Characteristics of Men, Manners, Opinions and Times*, 3 vols (London, 1711, rev. 1714)
J. Richardson: *An Essay on the Theory of Painting* (London, 1715)
E. G. Holt: *A Documentary History of Art*, ii (New York, 1958), pp. 243–59 [reprints Shaftesbury's essay]
J. Reynolds: *Discourses on Art*, ed. R. R. Wark (San Marino, 1959/*R* New Haven and London, 1975)
D. Diderot: *Salons*, ed. J. Seznec and J. Adhémar, iv (Oxford, 1967), p. 377

DAVID MANNINGS

Grand Rapids. American city in western Michigan, noted for its furniture production. Its situation at the rapids of the Grand River provided ease of river transportation and proximity to timber from Michigan's great pine and hardwood forests. The furniture industry began in Grand Rapids when the city's first cabinetmaker, William 'Deacon' Haldane (1807–98), established a shop there in 1836. By 1851 E. M. Ball of Powers & Ball was boasting that he could toss 'whole trees into the hopper and grind out chairs ready for use' to fill an order for 10,000 chairs in Chicago (Ransom, p. 5). In the 1870s Grand Rapids became a major factor in the American furniture market. Such companies as Berkey & Gay, Widdicomb, Phoenix and Nelson-Matter built large factories and hired Dutch and other European immigrants to operate them. While most of these manufacturers produced complete lines of bedroom, parlour and dining-room suites, some, like the Grand Rapids Chair Co. (established 1872), became large concerns by concentrating on a single product. To support these firms, smaller enterprises sprang up to produce such speciality items as castors, glue, finishes, veneer, carved ornaments, tools and packing materials.

After the Panic of 1873 almost half the firms in the city went bankrupt; it took several years for expansion to return. Grand Rapids manufacturers gained national recognition for high-quality furniture at the Centennial International Exhibition of 1876 in Philadelphia, where three firms won awards. To showcase new lines, Grand Rapids manufacturers came up with the innovative idea of semi-annual furniture exhibitions. Beginning in the 1870s, these fairs attracted salesmen and exhibitors from all over the country. By 1880 Grand Rapids had developed a nationwide reputation for quality and shipped furniture all over the world. Between 1880 and 1890 the value of furniture produced grew rapidly, and the city moved from seventh to third behind only New York and Chicago.

In the forefront of furniture design, Grand Rapids manufacturers responded quickly to changes in public taste. After the Civil War, high-quality Renaissance Revival styles competed with the Rococo Revival lines popular before the war. By the 1870s factories began making the Eastlake or Modern Gothic line. In the 1890s production of 18th-century style English, French and American Colonial Revival furniture predominated. Before World War I the Stickley Bros Co. produced oak Mission furniture.

In the 1920s only a much larger Chicago produced a greater value of furniture than Grand Rapids. By the 1930s the Modern style had gained a substantial following, although the Depression devastated the furniture industry. The city's furniture output plummeted by about 83%, and 25 of the city's 72 firms went bankrupt. Their high-quality lines were unable to compete with the medium- and low-priced furniture produced in the south. Prosperity returned after World War II, but the advantages that had made the city a leader in furniture production were also enjoyed by southern manufacturers, where there was the added benefit of lower labour costs. Grand Rapids companies continued to produce high-quality traditional and modern furniture, but the halcyon days when the city was the 'Furniture Capital of America' were over.

BIBLIOGRAPHY

F. E. Ransom: *The City Built on Wood: A History of the Furniture Industry in Grand Rapids, Michigan, 1850–1950* (Ann Arbor, 1955)
K. L. Ames: 'Grand Rapids Furniture at the Time of the Centennial', *Winterthur Port.*, x (1975), pp. 25–50

OSCAR P. FITZGERALD

Grand Tour. Journey usually through France and then Italy. It was made by the classically educated male members of the northern European ruling class to complete their education, to acquire manners and languages and to attain an understanding of the politics of other countries, their economies, geography and history. Especially from the 17th century onwards, it was undertaken to admire (or pretend to admire) the remains of the Classical past and to collect art and antiquities. The tour originated in the late 16th century and the early 17th, and the term 'Grand Tour' was first used in print by Richard Lassels, who in his *Voyage of Italy* (1670) wrote that no one could understand Livy and Caesar if they had not performed 'exactly' the 'Grand Tour of France and the Giro of Italy'. A Grand Tour might take one or two years, or as much as six to eight years if a lengthy period of study in France or Italy were included. Encouraged by the publication of the *Grand Tour* (1749) by Thomas Nugent (?1700–72), the practice flourished throughout the 18th century. It was interrupted by the French Revolution and by the Napoleonic Wars, but after 1815 travellers again flocked to Italy, many of them prepared through reading *A Classical Tour through Italy* (1813) by John Chetwode Eustace (?1762–1815).

The Grand Tour, a social and socializing practice of travel, was threatened by Romanticism, which developed a concept of travel as self-discovery; its end was finally brought about by the growth of the middle classes, and the development of modern tourism and of family travel. The Grand Tour did not have a fixed itinerary, but it did involve a journey across the boundaries that divided northern Europe from the Mediterranean, and it included some fixed points of reference. Paris was essential, while a lengthy period in Rome formed the climax not only to the Italian tour, which also embraced Florence, Naples and Venice, but to the entire Grand Tour. The route from France to Italy lay from Paris to Lyon, then over the Alps, usually across the Mont Cenis Pass to Susa, or by sea from Marseille to Livorno or Genoa. A common variant was to travel eastwards through the Low Countries and then to Germany and eastern Europe, with an emphasis on visits to Berlin, Dresden, Prague and Vienna, before proceeding to Italy. From the 1770s southern Italy, Sicily and Greece, whose attraction stemmed from the powerful fascination of Rome, became part of the Grand Tour, but whether travels beyond Europe, to countries such as Russia and Turkey, may be considered to form part of it is debatable. The British played a major role in its development, but it was popular in most European countries and was also called the *peregrinatio academica* and the *Kavaliersreise.* Recent studies, such as that by A. Frank-van Westrienen (1983), however, have attempted to minimize the role of the British; this article, however, concentrates primarily on British travellers and on the importance of the Grand Tour for art, collecting, patronage and taste.

I. Origins and precursors, *c.* 1550–*c.* 1630. II. Early development, *c.* 1630–*c.* 1700. III. The 'Classic ground', *c.* 1700–62. IV. The climax, 1763–97. V. Decline.

I. Origins and precursors, c. *1550–*c. *1630.*

'The diplomat, the courtier, the poet, the artist and the physician needed to know something of Italy, or suffer the handicap of ignorance' (Stoye, p. 72). This concept of travel, as the extension and completion of a political or academic education, or of a professional training, was held throughout Renaissance Europe: Polish noblemen, for example, 'flocked in their thousands to the universities of Padua, Paris and Bologna in the sixteenth century, returning home filled with the ideals of the Renaissance' (Davies, p. 321).

A first phase of British travel on the Continent, undertaken at leisure, and in a humanist spirit of inquiry, is best represented by Sir Thomas Hoby (1530–66) in the journal he made of his Italian tour in 1549–50, a pioneering landmark in travel literature; Hoby was also the translator (1561) of Baldassare Castiglione's *Il libro del cortegiano* (1528). However, the war with Spain, the consolidation of the English Reformation and the terrors of the Inquisition made European travel increasingly dangerous for the Elizabethans; the areas around Milan and Naples were inaccessible; Rome was excluded from the travel licences issued by the Privy Council, and only the brave, often disguised, ventured there. Elizabethan and early Jacobean travellers stayed longer in northern Italy, where three cities—Venice, Padua and Vicenza—were particularly favoured, and in Tuscany; by 1595 the Pope, Clement VIII, was complaining of the large number of English Protestants in Venice. Padua was much visited as the only Italian university to accept English Protestants; Sir Henry Unton (?1557–96), the Elizabethan diplomat, completed his legal training there, and in a memorial painting (*c.* 1596; London, N.P.G.) by an unknown artist he is shown having traversed 'ye Alpes' and riding with a parasol under the Italian sun. Yet the educational value of travel was hotly debated, and Roger Ascham (1515/16–68), who travelled on the Continent in 1550–53, expressed an English fear of the moral dangers presented by Italy in *The Scholemaster* (1570). Sir Philip Sidney spent three years in Europe (1572–5), where in 1574 he sat to Paolo Veronese for his portrait (untraced) in Venice; his interest in the visual arts, unusual in England at this period, is evident in his *Arcadia* (*c.* 1583, pubd 1590). The architect and painter John Shute was sent to Italy by his patron, John Dudley, 1st Duke of Northumberland, and in 1563 published the first Classical architectural treatise in English, *The First and Chief Groundes of Architecture.* Gardeners, too, sought new ideas and plants in Europe and were sent even from remote areas like Gwent to study in France and Italy. John TRADESCANT, for example, travelled to France and the Low Countries in 1611 to collect plant specimens for Robert Cecil, 1st Earl of Salisbury.

In the era after the Spanish Armada (1588), the peace treaties of 1598 and 1604 made it easier for English Protestants to visit Europe, and to travel more widely in Italy. A considerable number began to visit Rome, albeit hastily, and to venture hurriedly south to Naples. Early travel accounts, whose publication reflects this slackening of tension, include *A View of France* (London, 1606) by Robert Dallington and *Itinerary* (1617) by Fynes Moryson (1566–1630), both based on travel in the 1590s. *The Relation of a Journey begun An. Dom. 1610* (1615) by George Sandys (1578–1644) contains the first detailed account of the legendary landscape of the Phlegraean Fields, which, with Vesuvius, continued to be major Grand Tour attractions. In the late 16th century and early 17th Venice remained the greatest attraction in Italy, admired for its constitution and for its architectural splendour. The Venetian ambassador Sir HENRY WOTTON and the eccentric traveller THOMAS CORYATE were instrumental in establishing the art collections of Venice and the buildings of Andrea Palladio in Venice, Vicenza and along the banks of the Brenta Canal as an essential element of the Grand Tour, along with Venice's opera houses, brothels and ceremonies. Coryate, who devoted 130 pages of the *Crudities* (London, 1611) to Venice, gave an extremely detailed account of many buildings by Palladio (including the influential Villa Rotonda; *see* PALLADIO, ANDREA, fig. 6) and praised the 'many sumptuous and magnificent Palaces', the beauty of the Piazzo S Marco, and the new bridge at the Rialto. Wotton was the first Englishman to collect Palladian drawings, and, in the *Elements of Architecture* (London, 1624), to praise Palladian harmony and to denounce the Gothic as barbarous. He also collected Venetian paintings, both for himself and for English clients, such as Robert Cecil, 1st Earl of Salisbury, and George Villiers, 1st Duke of Buckingham. Wotton's agent, Daniel Nys, acquired the Gonzaga collection at Mantua for Charles I, thus whetting more aristocratic appetites for travel to Italy, and for collecting there.

The European journeys of Thomas Howard, 2nd Earl of Arundel and Surrey (*see* HOWARD (i), (1)), were the most significant undertaken by any 17th-century Englishman. His most celebrated Italian journey was that of 1613, with Inigo Jones as his companion; they wintered in Rome, despite the continuing difficulties for English travellers in the Papal States, and Arundel was given permission to excavate for antiquities. He began the first collection of Classical sculpture in Britain (Inigo Jones built a two-storey gallery on to Arundel House in the Strand, London, in which to display it), and through him this practice became another ingredient of a Grand Tour. (For a portrait of *Thomas Howard* by Daniel Mijtens I, showing the Arundel House sculpture gallery in the background, *see* LONDON, fig. 16.) He also began the first collection of Old Master drawings in Britain, and collected gems, painted chairs in the Italian style (*sgabello*), incunabula, manuscripts and coins and medals. In 1636 Arundel met WENCESLAUS HOLLAR in Germany, who accompanied him on this journey, making drawings on the way. Subsequently many artists were to accompany noble Grand Tourists; Hollar later came to England, where he introduced etching. He also founded a tradition of topographical art and of recording art collections.

II. Early development, c. *1630–*c. *1700.*

In the 1630s there was an increasingly relaxed relationship with the papal court (the Barberini family lavished hospitality on English nobles), and more Englishmen visited Rome. This development continued throughout the years of the Civil War (1642–8) in England, when many Englishmen, some exiled, travelled to avoid the disturbances at home. It was in this period that Rome assumed its central position, and that the isolated and spasmodic journeys made in the late 16th and early 17th century developed into a circular tour, linking the countries and cities of Europe, with particular emphasis on Italy. As Edward Chaney has written (1985): 'if one includes Rome and Naples as essential ingredients in a Grand Tour itinerary, as one certainly should according to the eighteenth-century definition of the term, then it was during this decade [the 1630s] that the Grand Tour can be said to have taken shape'.

Among such travellers were the exile John Bargrave (*c.* 1610–80) of Canterbury who made four journeys to Italy; the diarist John Evelyn; the gentleman amateur architect Sir Roger Pratt who toured in 1643–9 to avoid both debts and civil war; and many poets and writers, such as John Milton (1608–74), Thomas Killigrew (1612–83), Richard Lovelace (1618–58) and Edmund Waller (1606–87). English books and translations encouraged an interest in travel on the Continent. *Il Mercurio Italico, or an Itinerary Contayning a Voyage Made through Italy in the Yeare 1646 and 1647* (1648), the 'first comprehensive English guidebook to Italy' (Chaney, 1985), was published under the name of John Raymond, Bargrave's nephew; more influential was the *Voyage of Italy* (1670) by RICHARD LASSELS, which introduced the English to the new pleasures of connoisseurship and of Renaissance and Baroque art. In 1637–8 Lassels visited the workshops of both Bernini and François Du Quesnoy; Nicholas Stone II and Henry Stone, sons of the sculptor Nicholas Stone I, were in Rome (1638–42) collecting plaster casts and copies for their father; they too met Bernini.

The travels of JOHN EVELYN are perhaps the most famous and typical, from the middle years of the 17th century. Evelyn represents the 17th-century virtuoso, a type whom Anthony Ashley Cooper, 3rd Earl of Shaftesbury, later defined as 'real fine gentlemen . . . lovers of art and ingenuity'. Evelyn travelled in the Low Countries, where he marvelled at the variety of landscape and genre paintings, and of natural and scientific curiosities; his account (in his *Diary*), and that of Sir William Brereton (1604–61), are the best known regarding 17th-century travel in this region. In Italy, Evelyn studied the relics of the ancient world, but also admired the Renaissance ideals of town planning that characterized Genoa and the Rome of Sixtus V; he toured the great 16th-century Roman palaces and churches; he was especially observant of gardens, and admired the Renaissance and Mannerist gardens of France and Italy. Yet he was also fascinated by ingenuity, by scientific curiosities, natural wonders and intricate workmanship, marvelling at Italian cabinets of curiosity, such as that owned by Signor Rugini in Venice. In Florence, a medieval and therefore less attractive city, he and other English travellers tended to concentrate on a variety of rare and curious treasures. Some of Bargrave's Museum, which suggests a similar delight in the curious and includes Italian medals and Classical souvenirs from Rome, can be seen in the crypt of Canterbury Cathedral. Sir ROGER PRATT shared Evelyn's admiration for the palaces of Rome, Venice and Genoa, and the houses that he designed on his return (e.g. Coleshill, Berks; destr.) were prototypes for many others in the classical style.

In the later years of the 17th century English travellers began to acquire collections of contemporary Italian painting and to commission works from contemporary painters. Carlo Maratti became a particular favourite with British Grand Tourists. He painted the portrait of *John Cecil, 5th Earl of Exeter* (Burghley House, Cambs). John Cecil (*see* CECIL, (3)) was an energetic collector, who acquired works by Carlo Dolci, Luca Giordano and others on at least four trips to Italy, and commissioned contemporary Italian painting on an unprecedented scale. Maratti also painted a portrait of *Sir Thomas Isham* (*c.* 1677; Lamport Hall, Northants), who spent 10 months of his 17-month tour (1676–7) in and around Rome, acquiring furniture, copies after Raphael and paintings by Guido Reni, Guercino, Nicolas Poussin, Pietro da Cortona and Sebastiano Ricci (most of these are still at Lamport Hall). Other British travellers were painted by Carlo Dolci, Francesco Trevisani and Giuseppe Nogari.

III. The 'Classic ground', c. *1700–62.*

In the early years of the 18th century the aims of the Grand Tour, by now securely established as a social convention, subtly shifted. Art took precedence over science and ingenuity, and knowledge of those arts that best conveyed the nobility of man assumed a kind of moral and civic virtue. This concept was encouraged by the 3rd Earl of Shaftesbury's *Characteristicks of Men, Manners, Opinions and Times* (1711, rev. 1714), in which he stated, 'the science of virtuosos, and that of Virtue itself, became, in a manner, one and the same'. To be a virtuoso you had to make the Grand Tour, above all to Italy, the fount of the established canon of art and architecture. Jonathan Richardson's *An Account of Some of the Statues, Bas-reliefs, Drawings and Pictures in Italy, France etc.* (London, 1722) builds on Shaftesbury, and became one of the most influential Grand Tour guidebooks. Richardson believed that a study of the works of the best masters would result in 'nobler ideas, more moral virtue . . . he shall be a more ingenious and a better man' (Richardson, p. 56). Seventeenth-century travellers had been interested in the monuments of ancient Rome, but in the 18th century the British sought yet more passionately the sources of that broader Classical culture in which they had been steeped, and whose glories they sought to recreate. Joseph Addison crystallized the concept of Italy as the 'classic ground'. In his *Remarks upon Several Parts of Italy* (1705), he described the country as a shrine to Classical antiquity, seen through a haze of Classical associations and analogies, and took intense pleasure in seeking sites and objects described in ancient literature and comparing them with present reality; he delighted in Classical sculpture as a means of elucidating obscure passages in Classical history. Gothic architecture did not appeal, and Addison described Siena Cathedral (*see* SIENA, fig. 6) as barbarous. His book remained immensely influential until the end of the century, and 18th-century Grand Tourists journeyed muttering the words of Cicero, Virgil, Horace and Martial and with the great journeys of Odysseus, Aeneas and Horace in their minds. Places celebrated by ancient authors, such as Narni (famous for the Augustan Bridge described by Martial), the Temple of Clitumnus and the Falls of Terni in Umbria (both associated with Virgil), held a particular appeal for the Augustan traveller. Many young nobles toured Italy with tutors, referred to as bear-leaders, who were themselves Classical scholars. They were often clergymen but could also have been of the calibre of Thomas Hobbes (1588–1679) or John Locke (1632–1704) the philosophers, Joseph Addison the man of letters, Joseph Spence (1699–1768), Professor of Poetry at Oxford, or Adam Smith (1723–90), the economist. Travelling as a tutor was often the only way that scholars could afford to visit Europe. The aspirations of the young noble to acquire the taste or vertu of the connoisseur formed a popular subject for satire, and both nobles and their tutors were frequently caricatured. Pier Leone Ghezzi specialized in caricatures of Roman celebrities and Grand Tourists, such as *Dr James Hay as Bear-leader, and One of his Charges* (1737; London, BM; see fig. 1), with his charge shown as a young bear cub. Etchings (1737–42) by Arthur Pond after Ghezzi and Annibale Carracci popularized caricature in England. Later Joshua Reynolds and Thomas Patch painted caricature group paintings, such as Patch's the *Golden Asses* (1761; New Haven, CT, Yale U., Lewis Walpole Lib.); this was the nickname Italians used for British Grand Tourists.

A series of Grand Tours, undertaken by the most elevated of the British aristocracy, made a significant contribution to the development of the Palladian movement in British architecture. Richard Boyle, 3rd Earl of Burlington and 4th Earl of Cork (*see* BOYLE, (2)), THOMAS COKE, 1st Earl of Leicester, and HENRY HERBERT, 9th Earl of Pembroke, who all made the Grand Tour when very young, were among those who took an enormous practical interest in architecture. The effect of seeing such a variety and concentration of Classical and Renaissance

1. Pier Leone Ghezzi: *Dr James Hay as Bear-leader, and One of his Charges*, pen and brown ink, 362 × 245 mm, 1737 (London, British Museum)

architecture at an impressionable age was to engender a lifelong obsession. Burlington made two Grand Tours (1714, 1719), and on the second, his enthusiasm aroused by the first volume (1715) of *Vitruvius Brittanicus* by COLEN CAMPBELL, he visited Roman ruins and the buildings of Palladio, and bought some Palladio drawings (on dep. London, RIBA). He brought back with him 878 pieces of luggage and also WILLIAM KENT, who had acted as guide and dealer in Rome for other English milords, including Thomas Coke, with whom he built Holkham Hall, Norfolk. Coke spent six years on the Continent (1712–18), developing a taste for architecture, for collecting Classical sculpture, rare books and manuscripts, including Byzantine manuscripts, a Leonardo notebook (ex-Codex Hammer; presum. Seattle, Bill Gates' priv. col.), Renaissance and Baroque Italian paintings and drawings. Henry Herbert built up a distinguished collection of Classical sculpture, and in 1722 founded the Society of Roman Knights. In 1722 Palladianism was introduced to Ireland with the building of Castletown, Co. Kildare, to designs by Alessandro Galilei, with detailing by Sir EDWARD LOVETT PEARCE, an Irish architect who travelled in Italy (1723–4). Architecture remained a dominant interest among the next generation of British travellers. Robert Adam (*see* ADAM, (3)) made a Grand Tour between 1754 and 1758, taking care to appear as a gentleman; he met Giovanni Battista Piranesi in Rome, and was strongly influenced by him. His tour extended to the Palace of Diocletian at Spoleto (Split) in Dalmatia, his study of which was published in 1764. While Adam was in Italy so were at least 16 other British architects, including James Wyatt and William Chambers.

Jonathan Richardson, in his *Discourse on the Dignity, Certainty, Pleasure and Advantage of the Science of a Connoisseur* (London, 1715), wrote of the moral virtue and financial profit that could be derived from cultivating a love of painting and the science of connoisseurship. A study of prints was also encouraged, and Roger de Piles wrote in *L'Art de peinture* (Paris, 1668, 2/1673), 'nothing is more necessary than good prints' for anyone aspiring to be 'more gentlemanlike' for they 'may fill their memory with the most curious things of all times and all countries and . . . learn the several manners of painting'. Young men making the circuit of the Grand Tour wished to acquire a knowledge of paintings, and perhaps to form their own collection. Most adhered to an accepted canon of taste, admiring above all Italian painting of the 16th and 17th centuries. History painting was the most esteemed form of art, and Raphael, Michelangelo, Titian and Correggio were considered the most perfect painters. Seventeenth-century Bolognese artists, the heirs to Raphael, were also deeply admired, and Horace Walpole's comment in *Aedes Walpolianae* (London, 1747) that 'all the qualities of a perfect painter never met but in Raphael, Guido [Reni] and Carracci' is characteristic of this period. In Venice tourists admired Titian, especially the *Presentation of the Virgin* (Venice, Accad.), and Veronese, especially the *Marriage at Cana* (Paris, Louvre); in Bologna Raphael's *St Cecilia* (Bologna, Pin. N.) and works by Guido Reni and Guercino; in Parma the Correggios, and in Rome the most famous pictures were Daniele da Volterra's *Descent from the Cross* (Rome, Santa Trìnita dei Monti), Domenichino's *Last Communion of St Jerome* (*see* DOMENICHINO, fig. 1) and Raphael's *Transfiguration* (both Rome, Pin. Vaticana; *see* RAPHAEL, fig. 6). Tobias Smollett, in his caustic *Travels through France and Italy* (1766), was being characteristically provocative when he suggested that this last painting would look better cut in half. Works outside Italy were also praised, particularly the works of Rubens in the cathedrals of Antwerp and Ghent, and pictures in Paris and in the picture gallery at Düsseldorf. Most purchases were made in Italy, where English aristocrats and their agents, such as Robert Strange, scoured private collections and churches for possible prizes. An example of such a prize, which typifies the taste of the period, was Domenichino's *Madonna della Rosa* (Chatsworth, Derbys), bought by Burlington from the church of S Maria della Vittoria in Rome, where it had long been celebrated, for 1500 crowns. Burlington also had bronzes commissioned from Massimiliano Soldani, paintings by Maratti and Pietro da Cortona, and miniatures by Rosalba Carriera. The collection of Henry Somerset, 3rd Duke of Beaufort (*d* 1749), who travelled in Italy in the late 1720s, contained works by, or attributed to, Veronese, Raphael, Domenichino, Guido Reni and Salvator Rosa, and is similarly characteristic of this phase of Grand Tour collecting. Prints of paintings and drawings made many royal and aristocratic collections well known throughout Europe (e.g. the Earl of Arundel's; the Royal Collection in Brussels through *Le Théâtre des peintures*, 1660; and the collection of Pierre Crozat through the *Cabinet de Crozat*, 1729–42), stimulating emulation among travellers. Their demands were sometimes catered for by British printmakers working in Italy for British patrons, among them JOHN BAPTIST JACKSON in Venice, who was notable for his chiaroscuro woodcuts after Venetian paintings, and Alexander Cozens in Rome.

Travellers in Europe were generally less interested in contemporary painting, with the exception of portraiture and view painting. In Paris tourists sat to François-Hubert Drouais, Alexander Roslin or Maurice-Quentin de La Tour; in Venice to Rosalba Carriera, whose portraits of Grand Tourists include those of *Charles Sackville*, later 2nd Duke of Dorset (1737; Knole, Kent, NT), in Venetian carnival costume; and *Horace Walpole* (1741; Houghton Hall, Norfolk); and in Rome to Agostino Masucci and Francesco Trevisani. Theresia Concordia Mengs specialized in miniatures (e.g. the *5th Earl of Stamford* and *Sir Henry Mainwaring*, both *c.* 1762; Dunham Massey, Cheshire, NT). Coke met Francesco Solimena in Naples, and commissioned two pictures from him. View paintings (*see* VEDUTA) were also brought back by English aristocrats as souvenirs of the Grand Tour, among them views of Venice by Canaletto—the 21 views of Venice by Canaletto now at Woburn Abbey were probably bought by John, 4th Duke of Bedford (1710–71), during his Grand Tour (1731–2); scenes of Rome by Giovanni Battista Busiri (e.g. Felbrigg Hall, Norfolk, NT) and Gaspar van Wittel; Roman capriccios by Giovanni Paolo Panini, collected, for example, by Henry Howard (ii), 4th Earl of Carlisle, at Castle Howard; and Neapolitan coastal scenes by Claude-Joseph Vernet and Antonio Joli. Most influential, on both British artists and patrons, was Giovanni Battista Piranesi, who provided etched views of Rome for the Grand Tourist.

The 18th-century British traveller, seeking the 'classic ground', admired the landscapes of Gaspard Dughet and of Claude Lorrain, which seemed to enshrine the splendours of a lost Classical world. They contrasted the pastoral vision of these artists with the landscapes of 'savage' Salvator Rosa, whose name sprang instantly to mind as the traveller braved the terrors of the Alps; as Horace Walpole wrote in 1739, 'Precipices, mountains, torrents, wolves, rumblings—Salvator Rosa'. In the middle years of the 18th century British artists began to paint the sites around Rome, which were celebrated both by ancient Roman poets and by Claude and Dughet. Richard Wilson was in Rome from 1752 to 1755, and his Italian landscapes, such as the *Villa of Maecenas* (1752; Dublin, N.G.) and *Rome and the Ponte Molle* (Cardiff, N. Mus.), painted for English and Irish aristocrats, show sites famous since antiquity. They allude to the landscapes of Claude, and yet are gloomier and more evocative of the destructive power of time. Jonathan Skelton, one of the earliest British watercolourists to depict *Lake Albano and Castel Gandolfo* (1758; Manchester, Whitworth A.G.), arrived in Tivoli in 1758, and observed that Tivoli 'has been ye only school where our two most celebrated landscape painters Claude and Gaspar studied' (Clarke, p. 60).

As well as bulky art collections shipped back from Livorno, Grand Tourists brought back velvets and damasks from Genoa (still to be seen at Holkham and Houghton), fans and dress material. The Badminton Cabinet (USA, Barbara Johnson priv. col.), inlaid with Florentine pietra dura, then immensely fashionable, is one of the most celebrated pieces of furniture associated with the Grand Tour. Tourists also bought DOCCIA dinner services and *lattimo* glass plates (*see* VENICE, §III, 3), perhaps with views of Venice. Three sets each of twenty-four plates were made at Murano for Horace Walpole, JOHN CHUTE and Henry Fiennes Clinton (1720–84), 9th Earl of Lincoln and 2nd Duke of Newcastle-under-Lyme.

IV. The climax, 1763–97.

In this period, circumscribed by the Treaty of Paris (1763), which concluded the Seven Years War, and the war that followed the French Revolution, the Tour flourished as never before. A desire for novelty and the impact of the rediscovery of Herculaneum (*see* HERCULANEUM, §VI) and Pompeii (*see* POMPEII, §VI; and see fig. 2) led to the exploration of new areas, such as southern Italy and Sicily, Greece and Corsica. A new interest in wild nature, nourished by aesthetic theories of THE SUBLIME, led to a new pleasure in the Swiss Alps, and, within Italy, of the Appenines, the haunt of the *banditti* associated with the sinister landscapes of Rosa and of mounts Vesuvius and Etna. Outside Italy, the Low Countries and Germany became increasingly popular. Dutch and Flemish paintings were admired in England, and Johan Zoffany's *Sir Lawrence Dundas and his Grandson* (1769; Aske Hall, N. Yorks) shows an 18th-century cabinet devoted to 17th-century Dutch pictures, with, on the mantelshelf, a display of small bronze copies of celebrated antique sculptures. It vividly suggests the acquisitions made by the English squire in Italy and in the Low Countries, as he returned from his tour. In Germany the most aristocratic tourists were attracted by the delights of court life, and many visited the gallery at Dresden, where they admired Correggio's *Notte* and the Sistine *Madonna* of Raphael (both Dresden, Gemäldegal. Alte Meister). Antique and Renaissance art continued to be the major attraction, but the 1770s and 1780s were marked by the beginnings of a response to Gothic and Early Italian art. This was pioneered by the collector William Young Ottley, and is evident in John Flaxman's admiration for French Gothic sculpture and

2. Pietro Fabris: *Rediscovery of the Temple of Isis at Pompeii, 1765*; engraving from Sir William Hamilton: *Campi Phlegraei: Observations on the Volcanoes of the Two Sicilies*, 2 vols (London, 1776) (London, British Library)

Italian art of the 14th and 15th centuries, Thomas Patch's engravings after Giotto, Ghiberti and Masaccio, and Ignazio Hugford's collection of early Italian art. A wider range of travellers made the Tour; Americans, such as John Singleton Copley, began to play a significant role; women began to travel more widely, and Lady Anne Millar (1741–81), Hesther Thrale (1741–1821) and Mariana Starke (?1762–1838) published accounts of their journeys.

In this period the British passion for studying, admiring and collecting Classical antiquities reached its culmination. In France the tourist visited those sites famed for their ancient monuments: Orange, Nîmes and the Pont du Gard. A canon of antique sculptures, which to the Augustan represented a standard for all that was excellent in art, had by this date been established, and these works were enthusiastically, and repetitively, admired by the traveller. Many were in the Medici collection in Florence, and Johan Zoffany's the *Tribuna of the Uffizi* (1772; Windsor Castle, Berks, Royal Col.; *see* DISPLAY OF ART, fig. 3) is a vivid portrayal of famous Grand Tour personalities (among them Horace Mann and George Nassau Clavering-Cowper, 3rd Earl Cowper) admiring the most celebrated antique sculptures, the revered VENUS DE' MEDICI, the *Dancing Faun* and *The Wrestlers* (all Florence, Uffizi) in the Tribuna, the most celebrated room in the Uffizi. In Rome travellers admired the collections of ancient sculpture in the Vatican, in the Capitoline Museum, in the Palazzo Farnese and in the collection of Cardinal Alessandro Albani; they studied the collections of casts after the Antique in the Palazzo Mancini, the headquarters of the Académie de France in Rome. Most celebrated were the APOLLO BELVEDERE, the LAOKOON, the BELVEDERE TORSO (all Rome, Vatican, Mus. Pio-Clementino) and the FARNESE HERCULES (Naples, Mus. Archeol. N.). An increasingly subjective and aesthetic response to these works was encouraged by the great celebratory set-pieces, echoed in many travel accounts, that appeared in Johann Joachim Winckelmann's *Geschichte der Kunst des Altertums* (1764). The tourist avid for knowledge employed a cicerone to take him round the Classical sites. Most famous was JAMES BYRES, whose pricey courses could last up to six weeks, and whose most distinguished client was Edward Gibbon. Many Englishmen, such as CHARLES TOWNLEY, WILLIAM WEDDELL and HENRY BLUNDELL, formed collections of antique sculpture, profiting from the excavations made by GAVIN HAMILTON at Hadrian's Villa (1769–71) and Pantanello (1770–71), from the services of the dealer THOMAS JENKINS, who dominated the Roman art market, and of the restorer BARTOLOMEO CAVACEPPI. The gentleman traveller of more modest means was attracted by the small bronze copies of ancient sculptures made by Francesco Righetti and Giacomo Zoffoli.

The conventions of the Grand Tour portrait, anticipated in such works as Maratti's portrait of *Sir Thomas Isham* (1677; Lamport Hall, Northants) and Trevisani's portrait of *Thomas William Coke*, were brilliantly perfected by POMPEO BATONI. He showed the gilded youth of England and Scotland elegantly posed before the most celebrated statues and monuments of ancient Rome. Most extraordinary is his 'swagger portrait' of *Colonel William Gordon* (1766; Fyvie Castle, Grampian, NT Scotland). Clad in a kind of tartan toga, and posed as if a Classical hero, Gordon struts on a stage in front of the Colosseum, with Batoni's usual range of classical props. If Batoni were too expensive or not available, there were several other artists: the biographer James Boswell (1740–95) had his portrait painted in Rome in the Batoni manner by the Scottish student George Willison (1741–97), and Nathaniel Dance-Holland painted more modest works—Grand Tour conversation pieces, such as that of the *2nd Duke of Northumberland and Mr Lippyat* (1762; London, Syon House), which shows the duke with his tutor in front of the Colosseum. Frederick Augustus Hervey, 4th Earl of Bristol, sat for Elisabeth-Louise Vigée Le Brun against a background showing Mount Vesuvius (1790; Ickworth, Suffolk, NT); Wilhelm Tischbein's *Goethe in the Roman Campagna* (1786; Frankfurt am Main, Goethemus.) is a moving record of Goethe's passion for antiquity and influenced François-Xavier Fabre's *Allen Smith Seated above the Arno* (1797; Cambridge, Fitzwilliam).

The attraction of the Antique also drew tourists to Naples and its environs, which offered not only the rediscovered cities of Pompeii and Herculaneum but, in the Phlegraean Fields to the west of the city, an area that combined natural beauty and curiosity with a wealth of Classical associations. After visiting the legendary 'Virgil's Tomb' the traveller entered the Phlegraean Fields through the Grotta di Posillipo, and on to the Grotta del Cane, the Solfatara, Baia (once the pleasure resort of ancient Rome), Lake Avernus, where Aeneas made his descent to Hell, and Cuma, home of the Sibyl. Many ascended Mount Vesuvius, whose terrors satisfied a yearning for the Sublime. In Naples both tourists and artists enjoyed the hospitality of one of the most celebrated of Grand Tour personalities, the ambassador Sir WILLIAM HAMILTON (i), a distinguished collector of antiquities, and the husband of Emma Hamilton (*c.* 1765–1815), herself a Grand Tourist attraction, whose *Attitudes* (London, 1807) were admired by such luminaries as Goethe.

In the 1770s and 1780s more adventurous travellers, encouraged by the bear-leader Patrick Brydone (?1741–1818) and his popular *Tour through Sicily and Malta* (1773) and by *Travels in the Two Sicilies* (1783–5) by Henry Swinburne (1743–1803), began to extend the tour south of Naples. The Doric temples at Paestum, rediscovered in the middle of the 18th century, became popular, and the Classical sites of Sicily attracted, among others, GEORGE BERKELEY, JOHANN WOLFGANG VON GOETHE and RICHARD PAYNE KNIGHT. Sir Colt Hoare (*see* HOARE (i), (2)) made an extended tour from 1785 until 1791, retracing Horace's journey along the Appian Way and pioneering an interest (shared by James Byres) in Etruscan remains in Italy; his travels were recorded by CARLO LABRUZZI. Greece was a logical continuation of the Tour, and though famous and influential journeys had been made there earlier in the century, such as that of JAMES STUART and NICHOLAS REVETT in 1751–4, it became more fashionable in this period. J. B. S. Morritt (1771–1843), the owner of Rokeby Park on Teeside, set off in 1794 on a Grand Tour to Austria, Hungary, Asia Minor, Greece and Italy, commenting: 'No one is now accounted a traveller who has not . . . tasted the olives of Attica' (Morritt, 1985, vi). He was especially keen to explore the site of Troy, and attempted to acquire part of the Parthenon frieze in Athens. The SOCIETY OF DILETTANTI, founded in 1732 as a dining club for gentlemen who had undertaken the Grand Tour, began in this period to equip expeditions to Asia Minor and Greece and to publish the results in folio volumes.

Many artists of this period travelled in the entourage of noble tourists, recording their journeys, while others—particularly after the founding of the Royal Academy in 1768—themselves became Grand Tourists, travelling to Italy to seek a perfect landscape, to study Renaissance and ancient art, or to seek patronage in the Grand Tourist market. In his *Memoirs* the Welsh artist THOMAS JONES described a group of watercolour artists working for Grand Tourists in Rome and Naples; Jones was a pupil of Richard Wilson, and for him 'Every scene seemed anticipated in some dream—it appeared a Magick Land' (*Memoirs*, Dec 1776). His contemporaries in Italy included Francis Towne, William Pars, John 'Warwick' Smith and John Robert Cozens, who came to Rome in 1776–9 with Sir Richard Payne Knight and then travelled with WILLIAM BECKFORD in 1782–3. The watercolours of Pars, Towne and Cozens convey, for the first time, a sense of the sublime beauty of the Alps. Cozens also painted characteristic Grand Tourist sites (*see* COZENS, (2), figs 1 and 2) as well as views of Tivoli, Paestum, Elba, Lake Nemi and Naples. The Swiss artist Louis Ducros arrived in Rome in 1772 and was patronized by Sir Richard Colt Hoare, Frederick Augustus Hervey, 4th Earl of Bristol and Bishop of Derry, and visiting Swedish Grand Tourists. His many watercolours perfectly convey the atmosphere of the Grand Tour, recording such celebrated tourist sites as the Falls of Terni (also a speciality of the Scottish artist JACOB MORE), the Villa of Maecenas at Tivoli, both appreciated for their literary and Classical associations, Virgil's Tomb at Posillipo and the temples at Paestum; he also accompanied visiting Dutch antiquaries to Sicily and Malta in 1778. Idyllic views of Naples, such as those by PIETRO FABRIS, were popular, as were pictures of Vesuvius erupting, such as those by Joseph Wright of Derby, who also painted Virgil's Tomb, and Pierre-Jacques Volaire, who specialized in such images. The German landscape artist Philipp Hackert (*see* HACKERT, (1)) was in Rome from 1768, then Naples and Florence, and Sicily in 1777 as draughtsman to Payne Knight; the amateur watercolourist Charles Gore (1729–1807) also took part in this expedition to Sicily. In the 1780s Giovanni Battista Lusieri (*d* 1821) was a popular watercolourist in the Naples area, patronized by Sir William Hamilton, who recommended him to the 7th Earl of Elgin as a draughtsman (*see* BRUCE, THOMAS).

V. Decline.

In the Napoleonic wars (1793–1815) that followed the French Revolution, European travel, particularly to Italy, again became dangerous. The Revolutionary and Napoleonic period fundamentally altered the Italy that the Grand Tourist had known. Venice lost its independence in 1797, and the British colony in Rome dispersed in the 1790s. Collectors such as William Young Ottley and the Hungarian aristocrat Miklós Esterházy II took advantage of the Napoleonic upheavals to acquire from several major collections, the latter in his travels in Italy, France and England. Some travellers were tempted abroad by the illusory Peace of Amiens (1801), and *Remarks on Antiquities, Arts and Letters during an Excursion in Italy in the Years 1802 and 1803* (1813) by Joseph Forsyth (1763–1815) is one of the most attractive accounts of this period. After the establishment of a lasting peace in 1815, however, travellers again flocked to Italy. The publication of travel and guidebooks increased greatly in this period, reaching a climax in the 1820s. Among them was *Italy* (1818) by William Sotheby (1757–1833) and *Italy* (1822–8) by Samuel Rogers. Initially the values of the classical Grand Tour persisted. The most popular guidebook was John Chetwode Eustace's *A Classical Tour through Italy* (1813), which approached Italy in very much the way that Addison had done. The poet Percy Bysshe Shelley (1792–1822) visited Bologna to admire paintings by Reni, the Uffizi in Florence to look at the Classical sculpture, and commented in Rome that only Raphael, Reni and Rosa could bear comparison with antiquity. Yet slowly, as new kinds of middle-class traveller descended on Italy, taste began to change; Ingres's pencil drawings of family groups provided an individual form of portrait for this new class of tourist. By the mid-19th century early Italian painting had become popular, a taste encouraged by such writers as Alexander Lindsay, 25th Earl of Crawford and 8th Earl of Balcarres, and Anna Brownell Jameson; by 1818 John Keats could decry the mawkishness of Guido Reni, and with John Ruskin the reputation of the entire Bolognese school was destroyed. Romanticism encouraged a sensuous delight in the paradisial beauty of such landscapes as the lakes and bays of Italy, and fostered the myth of the Italian peasant as the innocent inhabitant of an Arcadian world. Many amateur artists painted Italian peasant scenes, leading to Thomas Uwins's complaint 'what a shoal of amateur artists we have got here' (Clarke, p. 119). New guidebooks were written for the traveller in a hurry, and Mariana Starke's *Letters from Italy* (1800) graded painters in Italy by exclamation marks. In 1836 John III Murray published the first of his Handbooks, and Karl Baedeker the first of his guides (*see* GUIDEBOOK). From 1840 the coach came to be replaced by the train and Thomas Cook organized his first tour of Italy in 1864. Byron's poem *Childe Harold's Pilgrimage* (1812; 1816; 1818) deeply influenced European travel, yet in a sense, with its long celebrations of Venice and of such antique sculptures as the *Dying Gaul* (Rome, Mus. Capitolino) and the *Venus de' Medici* (Florence, Uffizi), of the Temple of Clitumnus and the Falls of Terni, it is the swan song of the aristocratic Grand Tour.

BIBLIOGRAPHY

SOURCES

T. Hoby: *The Travaile and Lief of me Thomas Hoby* (written 1549–50; London, 1902)

R. Dallington: *A View of France* (London, ?1605)

T. Coryate: *Crudities Hastily Gobled up in Five Moneths Travells in France, Savoy, Italy, Rhetia, Helvetia . . . Some Parts of Germany and the Netherlands* (London, 1611/*R* 2 vols, 1905)

G. Sandys: *The Relation of a Journey begun An. Dom. 1610* (London, 1615)

F. Moryson: *Itinerary*, 4 vols (1617; Glasgow, 1907–8)

J. Evelyn: *The Diary of John Evelyn* (written 1640–1706); ed. E. S. de Beer, 6 vols (Oxford, 1955)

J. Raymond: *Il Mercurio Italico or an Itinerary Contayning a Voyage Made through Italy in the Yeare 1646 and 1647* (London, 1648)

The Memoirs and Travels of Sir John Reresby Bart. (written 1650s; London, 1813) [a Yorkshireman in France, Switzerland and Italy]
R. Lassels: *Voyage of Italy* (Paris, 1670, rev. London, 1670)
J. Addison: *Remarks upon Several Parts of Italy* (London, 1705)
A. A. Cooper, 3rd Earl of Shaftesbury: *Characteristicks of Men, Manners, Opinions and Times* (London, 1711, rev. 1714)
J. Richardson: *An Account of Some of the Statues, Bas-reliefs, Drawings and Pictures in Italy, France etc.* (London, 1722)
T. Nugent: *Grand Tour* (London, 1749)
C.-N. Cochin the younger: *Voyage d'Italie* (Paris, 1758); ed. C. Michel (Rome, 1991)
J. Boswell: *Account of Corsica* (London, 1768)
P. Brydone: *Tour through Sicily and Malta* (London, 1773)
R. Chandler: *Travels in Asia Minor* (London, 1775); abridged and with commentary on Pars's watercolours by A. Wilton (London, 1971)
H. Thrale: *French Journals of Mrs Thrale and Dr Johnson* (written 1775); ed. M. Tyson and H. Guppy (Manchester, 1932)
W. Beckford: *The Travel Diaries of William Beckford of Fonthill* (written 1782–3); ed. G. Chapman (London, 1928)
H. Swinburne: *Travels in the Two Sicilies*, 2 vols (London, 1783–5)
H. Thrale: *Observations and Reflections made in the Course of a Journey through France, Italy and Germany* (London, 1789); ed. H. Barrows (Ann Arbor, 1967)
E. Gibbon: *Memoirs of my Life* (London, 1796); ed. G. Bonnard (London, 1966)
M. Starke: *Letters from Italy between the Years 1792 and 1798* (London, 1800)
T. Hope: *Household Furniture and Interior Decoration* (London, 1807) [written after his travels in Italy, Greece and Egypt]
F.-R. Chateaubriand: *L'Itinéraire de Paris à Jérusalem* (Paris, 1811)
J. C. Eustace: *A Classical Tour through Italy* (London, 1813)
J. Forsyth: *Remarks on Antiquities, Arts and Letters during an Excursion to Italy in the Years 1802 and 1803* (London, 1813)
J. W. von Goethe: *Die italienische Reise* (Berlin, 1816–17; Eng. trans., Harmondsworth, 1970)
C. Hoare: *A Classical Tour through Sicily and Italy*, 2 vols (London, 1819)
M. Starke: *Information and Direction for Travellers on the Continent* (London, 1820, 8/1833)
W. Brereton: *Diary* (Manchester, 1844)
A. P. Oppé: 'The Memoirs of Thomas Jones', *Walpole Soc.*, xxxii (1946–8) [whole issue]
F. A. Pottle, ed.: *Boswell on the Grand Tour*, 2 vols (London, 1953–5)
B. Ford: 'The Letters of John Skelton Written from Rome and Tivoli in 1758', *Walpole Soc.*, xxxvi (1960)
The Letters of John B. S. Morritt of Rokeby, Descriptive of Journeys in Europe and Asia Minor in the Years 1794–1796. A Grand Tour, Letters and Journeys, 1794–96, ed. G. E. Marindin (London, 1985)

GENERAL

F. Saxl and R. Wittkower: *British Art and the Mediterranean* (Oxford, 1948/*R* 1969)
F. Haskell: *Patrons and Painters: Art and Society in Baroque Italy* (London, 1963, rev. New Haven and London, 1980)
The Age of the Grand Tour, intro. A. Burgess and F. Haskell (London, 1967) [unwieldy book with excellent anthology of source material]
C. Hibbert: *The Grand Tour* (London, 1969, rev. 1987) [the best general intro.; helpful bibliography; well-illustrated]
F. Herrmann: *The English as Collectors: A Documentary Chrestomathy* (London, 1972) [excellent anthology of sources]
R. S. Pine-Coffin: *Bibliography of British and American Travel in Italy to 1860* (Florence, 1974)
M. Clarke: *The Tempting Prospect: A Social History of English Watercolours* (London, 1981)
F. Haskell and N. Penny: *Taste and the Antique* (London, 1981)
A. Frank-van Westrienen: *De groote tour* (Amsterdam, 1983)
D. Constantine: *Early Greek Travellers and the Hellenic Ideal* (Cambridge, 1984)
N. Davies: *Heart of Europe: A Short History of Poland* (Oxford, 1984, rev. 1989)
R. Stoneman: *A Literary Companion to Travel in Greece* (London, 1984)
L. Stone and J. C. Fawtier Stone: *An Open Elite? England, 1540–1880* (Oxford, 1984, abridged 1986)
J. Black: *The British and the Grand Tour* (London, 1985)
E. Chaney: *The Grand Tour and the Great Rebellion* (Geneva, 1985)
British Landscape Watercolours, 1600–1850 (exh. cat. by L. Stainton and C. White, London, BM, 1985)
J. V. Beckett: *The Aristocracy in England, 1660–1914* (Oxford, 1986)
E. P. de G. Chaney: 'British and American Travellers in Southern Italy', intro. essay in the *Blue Guide to Southern Italy* (London and New York, 1986)
M. Coulson: *Southward to Geneva: 200 Years of English Travellers* (Gloucester, 1988)
L. Stainton: *Nature into Art: English Landscape Watercolours* (London, 1991)
The Great Age of British Watercolours, 1750–1880 (exh. cat. by A. Wilton and A. Lyles, London, RA, 1992)
E. Chaney: *The Evolution of the Grand Tour* (London, 1996)

16TH CENTURY

C. Howard: *English Travellers of the Renaissance* (London, 1914)
J. R. Hale: *England and the Italian Renaissance* (London, 1954)
R. Strong: 'Sir Henry Unton and his Portrait', *Archaeologia*, xcix (1965), pp. 53–76
The Age of the Marvelous (exh. cat., Hanover, NH, Dartmouth Coll., Hood Mus. A.; Raleigh, NC Mus. A.; Atlanta, GA, High Mus. A.; 1991) [the start of modern collecting in the 16th–17th centuries; European interest in science, botanical gardens, the non-European world]

17TH CENTURY

E. S. Bates: *Touring in 1600* (London, 1911/*R* 1987) [range of references in several languages]
J. W. Stoye: *English Travellers Abroad, 1604–1667* (London, 1952, rev. 1989)
A. L. Sells: *The Paradise of Travellers: The Italian Influence on Englishmen in the Seventeenth Century* (London, 1964)
J. Summerson: *Inigo Jones* (Harmondsworth, 1966)
Master Drawings of the Roman Baroque from the Kunstmuseum, Düsseldorf (exh. cat. by D. Graf, London, V&A; Edinburgh, N.G.A.; 1973)
D. E. L. Haynes: *The Arundel Marbles* (Oxford, 1975)
A. Radcliffe and P. Thornton: 'John Evelyn's Cabinet', *Connoisseur* (April 1978), pp. 260–62 [the cabinet is in the V&A, London]
M. Beal: *A Study of Richard Symonds: His Italian Notebooks and their Relevance to 17th-century Painting Techniques* (New York, 1984) [the MSS of the notebooks are in London, BL, and Oxford, Bodleian]
N. Silcox-Crowe: 'Sir Roger Pratt, 1620–1685: The Ingenious Gentleman Architect', *The Architectural Outsiders*, ed. R. Brown (London, 1984)
D. Howarth: *Lord Arundel and his Circle* (New Haven, 1985)
Thomas Howard, Earl of Arundel (exh. cat. by D. Howarth, Oxford, Ashmolean, 1985)

18TH CENTURY

T. Hodgkinson: 'Christopher Hewetson: An Irish Sculptor in Rome', *Walpole Soc.*, xxxiv (1958)
L. Lewis: *Connoisseurs and Secret Agents in Eighteenth Century Rome* (London, 1961)
A. Bury: *Francis Towne: Lone Star of Water Colour Painting* (London, 1962)
J. Fleming: *Robert Adam and his Circle in Edinburgh and Rome* (Edinburgh, 1962)
J. Lees-Milne: *Earls of Creation* (London, 1962/*R* 1988) [on Lords Burlington, Leicester, Pembroke]
B. Skinner: *The Scots in Italy in the 18th Century* (London, 1966)
Apollo of the Arts: Lord Burlington and his Circle (exh. cat. by J. Wilton-Ely, Nottingham, A.G., 1973)
B. Fothergill: *The Mitred Earl* (London, 1974) [on the 4th Earl of Bristol]
R. Wittkower: *Palladio and English Palladianism* (London, 1974) [on Shaftesbury]
British Artists in Rome, 1700–1800 (exh. cat., London, Kenwood House, 1974)
R. Trevelyan: *The Shadow of Vesuvius* (London, 1976) [discoveries at Herculaneum and Pompeii]
J. G. Links: *Canaletto and his Patrons* (London, 1977)
French Landscape Drawings and Sketches of the 18th Century (exh. cat. by R. Bacou, London, BM, 1977)
J. Wilton-Ely: *The Mind and Art of G. B. Piranesi* (London, 1978)
R. Morris: *HMS Colossus: The Story of the Salvage of the Hamilton Treasures* (London, 1979)
J. Harris: *The Palladians* (London, 1981)
M. Clarke and N. Penny, eds: *The Arrogant Connoisseur: Richard Payne Knight, 1751–1824* (Manchester, 1982)
Pompeo Batoni and his British Patrons (exh. cat., London, Kenwood House, 1982)
L. Stainton: 'Hayward's List: British Visitors to Rome, 1753–1775', *Walpole Soc.*, xlix (1983)
W. B. Stanford and E. J. Finopolos, eds: *The Travels of Lord Charlemont in Greece and Turkey, 1749* (London, 1984)

Images of the Grand Tour: Louis Ducros, 1748–1810 (exh. cat., London, Kenwood House, 1985)
Norfolk and the Grand Tour (exh. cat. by A. Moore, Norwich, Castle Mus., 1985)
Reynolds (exh. cat., ed. N. Penny; London, RA, 1986)
Sussex and the Grand Tour (exh. cat., Billingshurst, Summers Place, 1986)
Travels in Italy, 1776–1783 (exh. cat., ed. F. Hawcroft; U. Manchester, Whitworth A.G., 1988) [featuring the work of Thomas Jones; extensive bibliog.]
R. Tavernor: *Palladio and Palladianism* (London, 1991)
Drawings by Guercino from British Collections (exh. cat. by N. Turner and C. Plazzotta, London, BM, 1991) [intro. discusses British collectors]
Guercino in Britain: Paintings from British Collections, suppl. to *Burl. Mag.*, cxxxiii/1060 (1991)
J. Black: *The British Abroad: The Grand Tour in the 18th Century* (Gloucester, 1992)
The Swagger Portrait (exh. cat. by A. Wilton, London, Tate, 1992)
Anton Raphael Mengs, 1728–1779, and his British Patrons (exh. cat. by S. Roettgen, London, Kenwood House, 1993)
J. Ingamells, ed.: *The Brinsley Ford Dictionary of British Visitors to Italy in the 18th Century* (in preparation)

RESULTS

A. Michaelis: *Ancient Marbles in Great Britain* (London, 1882)
J. Summerson: *Architecture in Britain, 1530–1830* (Harmondsworth, 1953)
F. Hawcroft: 'The Cabinet at Felbrigg', *Connoisseur* (May 1958)
——: 'The Grand Tour and the Norfolk Museum', *Connoisseur* (May 1958)
R. B. Charleston: 'Souvenirs of the Grand Tour', *J. Glass Stud.*, vii (1959), pp. 63–81
M. Hadfield: *A History of British Gardening* (London, 1969/*R* 1979)
P. Willis: 'Lord Burlington and Landscape Design', *Apollo of the Arts* (exh. cat., ed. J. Wilton-Ely; Nottingham, A.G., 1973)
M. Girouard: *Life in the English Country House* (New Haven, 1978)
G. Jackson-Stops: *Petworth House*, NT Guidebk (London, 1978, rev. 1984)
Souvenirs of the Grand Tour (exh. cat., London, Wildenstein's, 1982)
Treasure Houses of Britain (exh. cat., ed. G. Jackson-Stops; Washington, DC, N.G.A., 1985) [essays by Millar, Haskell, Ford esp. useful]
J. M. Robinson: *Shugborough* (London, 1989)
'The Badminton Cabinet', *Burl. Mag.*, cxxxiii/1056 (1991), editorial and fig. 98
G. Jackson-Stops: *Ickworth House* (London, 1992)
C. M. Sicca: 'Holkham Hall, Norfolk', *18th-century Britain*, ed. B. Ford (Cambridge, 1992)
M. Symes: 'The English Taste in Gardening', *18th-century Britain*, ed. B. Ford (Cambridge, 1992)

JOHN REEVE

Grand Trianon. *See under* VERSAILLES.

Grandville, J(ean-)J(acques) [bapt. Gérard, Jean-Ignace-Isidore] (*b* Nancy, 15 Sept 1803; *d* Vanves, 17 March 1847). French caricaturist and illustrator. He was the son of the miniaturist Jean-Baptiste Gérard (1766–1854), and his paternal grandparents were actors known as 'Gérard de Grandville', the source of his pseudonym. He began to draw when very young and published his first lithograph, the *Cherry Seller*, in Nancy in 1825. From the start he copied the style of the little satirical scenes that had been popularized by the English and French satirical magazines of the period such as the *Nain jaune*. He went to Paris in 1825 and worked initially for the lithographer Mansion [pseud. of Léon-André Larue] (1785–1834) and with Hippolyte Lecomte on *Costumes* (1826). He published further series of *Theatre* colour lithographs in the English manner, *Sundays of a Paris Bourgeois* (1826) and *Every Age Has its Pleasures* (1827), for Langlumé. He had considerable success in 1829 with his album *Today's Metamorphoses* for the publisher Bulla, in which animals appeared dressed as humans: his penchant for fantasy was already obvious. A new series for Bulla in 1830, *Journey for Eternity*, was not as successful and was cut short after nine plates had been published.

In 1829 Grandville went to work for the satirical journal *La Silhouette*, where he met Charles Philipon. Deeply committed to the Republican movement, he published caricatures attacking Charles X and is said to have taken an active part in the Revolution of 1830. Grandville became one of the main illustrators for *La Caricature*, the satirical magazine launched by Philipon on 4 November 1830. In 1832 the paper crowned him 'roi de la caricature'. In order to pay legal costs arising from government attempts to suppress *La Caricature*, Philipon decided to sell large and violently political lithographs under the title the *Monthly Association* (1832). Grandville was responsible for 17 of the 24 prints published in this series. When Philipon founded the first illustrated daily paper, *Le Charivari*, in 1832, Grandville contributed *c.* 100 designs, but after press censorship was reintroduced in 1835 and political subjects were forbidden, his contributions to *Le Charivari* became scarce. Of the team of illustrators at *La Caricature* and *Le Charivari*, he was, with Honoré Daumier and Joseph Traviès, the most politically committed, and his prints, which intermingle realism and fantasy for the sake of caricature, are among the most powerful published at that time, especially in defence of freedom of the press. In the *Resurrection of Censorship: 'And on the Third Day it rose again'* (1832) the Comte d'Argout, the government censor and a frequent victim of Grandville's attacks, is depicted ascending, like the risen Christ, from the tomb, clutching an enormous pair of scissors, while various newspaper editors sleep on unconcerned. Grandville's venom and fertile imagination were more distinctive than the style of his lithographs; he was more a draughtsman than a lithographer and preferred to have his drawings transferred on to stone by the specialized lithographers employed by Philipon such as Auguste Desperet (*d* 1865), Marie-Alexandre Menut-Alophe (1812–83), Joseph Traviès and Jacques Guiaud (1811–76). The largest collection of Grandville's original drawings is in the Musée des Beaux-Arts, Nancy.

After 1835 Grandville preferred to concentrate on book illustration, on which he had a profound effect; not only did he extend its repertory of subjects to include dream-like, imaginary scenes, but he also gave precedence to image over text, which became no more than an accessory or accompaniment. His later designs were usually reproduced in wood-engravings. In 1842 he published *Scènes de la vie privée et publique des animaux*, with a text by Balzac, and in the same year *Petites Misères de la vie humaine.* In the former he satirized contemporary society through portraits of its leading figures and types lightly disguised as animals and set in appropriate, if bizarre, contexts. Published in instalments from 1843 and together in 1844, his most important work is *Un Autre Monde*, a series of fantastic compositions around which his friend the *Charivari* journalist Taxile Delord (1815–77) wove an appropriate text, drawn up along lines indicated by Grandville himself. In this original and disturbing book Grandville abandoned the logic of the conscious mind to depict the world of dreams, in which perspective, viewpoint, shape

J. J. Grandville: *Battle of the Cards*, wood-engraving, 1844; from T. Delord: *Un Autre Monde* (Paris, 1844), pl. opposite p. 247

and size undergo peculiar metamorphosis and distortion (see fig.).

Grandville was also able to produce a more conventional style of illustration, for example for *Jérôme Paturot* (Paris, 1846) or in his *Don Quichotte de la Manche*, which was published in Tours in 1848 after his death. He was involved in illustrating *c.* 50 works, many of them literary classics by such authors as La Fontaine (Paris, 1838), Daniel Defoe (Paris, 1840), Jean de La Bruyère (Paris, 1845) and Boccaccio (Paris, 1846). He returned to word and image games with the series *Animated Flowers* (1846–7) and *The Stars* (1849), a posthumous publication. A few days before his death he sent *Magasin pittoresque* two particularly fantastic and dream-like drawings, which were published in July 1847 and which well encapsulate the boldness of a visual imagination that anticipated the Surrealists. The writers André Breton and Georges Bataille saw him as a prophetic artist, and, although he shares something with the nonsense worlds of his contemporaries Edward Lear and Lewis Carroll, he really belongs to a later, post-Freudian age.

BIBLIOGRAPHY

J. Adhémar and J. Lethève: *Inventaire du fonds français après 1800*, ix, Paris, Bib. N., Cab. Est. (Paris, 1955), pp. 326–43

P. Kaenel: 'Autour de J. J. Grandville: Les Conditions de production socio-professionnelles du livre illustré "romantique"', *Romantisme*, xliii (1984), pp. 45–61

A. Renonciat: *La Vie et l'oeuvre de J. J. Grandville* (Paris, 1985)

P. Kaenel: 'Le Buffon de l'humanité: La Zoologie politique de J. J. Grandville (1803–1847)', *Rev. A.* [Paris], lxxiv (1986), pp. 21–8

Grandville: Dessins originaux (exh. cat. by C. F. Getty and S. Guillaume; Nancy, Mus. B.-A.; Paris, Carnavalet; 1986–8)

The Charged Image: French Lithographic Caricature, 1816–1848 (exh. cat. by B. Farwell, Santa Barbara, Mus. A., CA, 1989)

MICHEL MELOT

Granello [Granelo], **Nicolás** [Niccola] (*b* Genoa, *c.* 1550; *d* the Escorial, nr Madrid, 30 Nov 1593). Italian painter, active in Spain. He was the son of the painter Niccolosio Granello, a former pupil of Ottavio Semino. After his father's death, his mother Margherita married the architect and painter Giovanni Battista Castello (i), and his half-brother Fabrizio Castello (*see* CASTELLO (i), (2)) was born of this marriage. In 1566 or 1567 the family moved to Madrid, where Giovanni Battista Castello worked for the Spanish court, and when he died in 1569, Granello became Fabrizio Castello's guardian and taught him to paint. Granello himself probably studied under his stepfather and was one of the group of painters who worked with him in Spain. He assisted him with the decorations (destr.) in the Alcázar (destr.) in Madrid and was nominated Pintor del Rey to Philip II on 1 April 1571. His only surviving work is in the monastery of the Escorial, where, with his half-brother, he frescoed the vaults of the chapter rooms and the sacristy (1581–4). From 1585 to 1591 he and Castello, assisted by Lazzaro Tavarone and Orazio Cambiaso (*d* 1585), executed their most significant work: the decoration of the walls of the large Galería or Sala de Batallas in the state rooms of the Queen at the Escorial. They depicted the *Battle of San Quintín* and the *Battle of Higueruela* (the latter copied from a 15th-century wall hanging), as well as scenes of Spanish naval victories against Portugal in the Terceras (now Azores) in 1580–84. These paintings are rendered in a simple, descriptive and draughtsmanlike style suited to this type of narrative theme. The scenes are rigid and uniform, schematically decorated and are dominated by a concern for achieving historical fidelity so as to intensify the didactic nature of the ensemble.

BIBLIOGRAPHY

Ceán Bermúdez

J. Zarco Cuevas: *Pintores italianos en San Lorenzo el Real de El Escorial, 1575–1613* (Madrid, 1932), pp. 29–113

TRINIDAD DE ANTONIO SAÉNZ

Grañen, Blasco de [Master of Lanaja] (*fl* 1422–59). Spanish painter. He has been identified as the Master of Lanaja, the traditional name given to a painter who executed a series of altarpieces in Aragon. He is documented in Huesca, Saragossa and Teruel between 1422 and 1459 and evidently achieved considerable contemporary popularity. His altarpieces in the parish churches at Lanaja and Ontiñena (Huesca) disappeared in the Civil War of 1936–9 but are known from photographs. The most striking of Grañen's surviving works are the altarpieces in the parish churches at Anento and Tosos (Saragossa); that of *St John the Evangelist* in S Pedro, Siresa (Huesca); the *Cycle of the Passion* in the retable of S Salvador, Ejea de los Caballeros (1438–54; Saragossa); the *Virgin and Child with Music-making Angels* (1437; 1.6×1.05 m; Saragossa, Mus. Prov. B.A.) from the archbishop's palace of the Albalate, Teruel; and panels depicting *Scenes from the Life of Christ* (1439) from the former high altar retable of Tarazona Cathedral (Saragossa), now in the Town Hall of the city. Grañen's style is characterized by unusual compositions in which the small figures are luxuriously dressed in contemporary fashions, perhaps influenced by Franco-Flemish manuscript illuminations.

In his larger works the figures have a certain monumentality, reinforced by precise drawing and brilliant colours, with abundant use of gold.

BIBLIOGRAPHY

M. C. Lacarra Ducay: *La pintura gótica en la Corona de Aragon* (exh. cat., Saragossa, Inst. Mus. Camon Aznar, 1980), pp. 106–7
——: entries in *Gran enciclopedia aragonesa* (Saragossa, 1981), viii, pp. 2001–2; ix, pp. 2523–4
——: 'Retablo de San Salvador, ejea de los caballeros (Zaragoza)', *Joyas de mi patrimonio* (Saragossa, 1990), pp. 75–84

M. C. LACARRA DUCAY

Granet, François-Marius (*b* Aix-en-Provence, 17 Dec 1775; *d* Malvalat, 21 Nov 1849). French painter and museum official. The son of a master mason, he revealed an early talent for drawing in his copies of his father's collection of prints after François Boucher and Joseph Vernet. After studying with an unidentified Italian landscape painter, he became a pupil of J.-A. Constantin at the free drawing academy in Aix-en-Provence. One of his fellow pupils was Auguste de Forbin, the painter and future Director-General of the Musées Royaux. In 1793 Granet left Aix with the local Société Populaire to assist in the siege of Toulon. He worked as a draughtsman with the artillery battery; his autobiography provides a vivid account of his experiences during the siege and destruction of the town. On a subsequent tour of duty he was employed to paint republican motifs on ships in the naval base at Toulon.

Granet made his first journey to Paris in 1796. He studied in the Louvre, where he was encouraged by Fragonard, and in his memoirs he recorded his admiration for works of the Dutch and Flemish schools, mentioning in particular how he copied the *Prodigal Son* by Teniers (1644; Paris, Louvre). He made some money by painting mural decorations, most notably in the apartments belonging to the Marquis de Senneval and, on a visit to Provence in 1797, in the Château de la Barben, which belonged to Forbin's brother. On his return to Paris in 1798 he joined Forbin as a pupil of Jacques-Louis David, but he was soon forced to leave the studio because of lack of money. David's encouraging remarks to the young Provençal artist were recorded by Delécluze: 'This one will be a colourist; he likes chiaroscuro and beautiful effects of light'. Delécluze also noted that Granet associated with the 'aristocratic' group of painters from southern France in David's studio, including Fleury Richard and Pierre-Henri Révoil. Whereas the classical doctrines of David made little impact on Granet's work, his contact with these fellow pupils was crucial to his development; he shared their Catholic faith as well as their enthusiasm for medieval and royalist subjects.

Granet's first Salon success, the *Little Cloister of the Feuillants* (1799; untraced), an interior of a monastery in the Rue Saint-Honoré, Paris, marked the emergence of a theme that was to dominate his work. According to Delécluze, Granet had been working for several years in the Capuchin monastery in the Rue de la Paix, with Gros, Ingres, Bartolini and Girodet painting in neighbouring cells. Granet observed that it was the study of Flemish art that had opened his eyes to the potential of his subject, although he was probably also influenced by the dramatic displays of medieval and Renaissance sculpture in Alexandre Lenoir's Musée des Monuments Français in the Petits-Augustins convent.

In 1802 Granet set out for Rome with Forbin, visiting Pisa, Siena and Florence en route. The French chargé d'affaires, François Cacault, introduced him to Cardinal Fesch, who became his patron, but during his first years in Rome he made a living selling picturesque views of ancient monuments. His sketchbooks (Aix-en-Provence, Mus. Granet) contain numerous views of ruins and cloisters, and his first important canvas from Rome was the *Crypt of S Martino in Monte* (1802; Montpellier, Mus. Fabre). Granet remained in Rome until 1824, and during this time his working method became firmly established. The essential starting point was an awe-inspiring architectural motif, usually the interior of a church or monastery. A historical, literary or religious subject was then grafted on to his experience of the atmosphere and light effects of a particular site. Describing this process in his autobiography, Granet recalled how the *Painter Stella in Prison* (exh. Salon 1810; Moscow, Pushkin Mus. F.A.) was inspired by a visit to the former prisons of the Capitol, which reminded him of a passage in Félibien's *Entretiens* about the false imprisonment of the painter Jacques Stella. Granet was able to gain access to the prisons, and the picture was produced on the spot with models posing for the main figures.

Granet's work is often described as repetitious, yet, although he tended to re-use certain compositional formulae, his feeling for dramatic chiaroscuro and his skilful articulation of massive architectural forms relieve his work from the anecdotal features associated with many other exponents of the TROUBADOUR STYLE. These qualities are particularly apparent in the painting that sealed his official success, the *Choir of the Capuchin Church in Rome* (1814; New York, Met.; see fig.). Dominated by the elaborate perspective view of the vault, the monks are silhouetted against a strong central light source; through his sensitive depiction of light, Granet achieved a convincing harmony between figures and setting. Admired by Pius VII and Charles IV, the picture was bought off the easel by Caroline Murat, the Queen of Naples, who ceded it to her brother, Louis Bonaparte. Granet exhibited a larger version of this subject at the Salon of 1819 (probably the version in Cardiff, N. Mus.). The demand for this particular painting led Granet to produce at least 13 further variants (e.g. Buckingham Palace, Royal Col.), and his success earned him the Cross of the Légion d'honneur (1819) and the ribbon of the Order of St Michael (1822). The compositional format of the *Choir of the Capuchin Church in Rome* formed the basis for another major work, the *Lower Church of the Basilica of S Francesco at Assisi* (exh. Salon 1822; Paris, Louvre). This was followed by a succession of paintings developing his melancholy monastic themes, which were exhibited regularly at the Salon. He also painted events in the lives of famous artists, including *Domenichino at the Villa of Cardinal Aldobrandini* (exh. Salon 1822; untraced) and *Poussin on his Deathbed Receives the Blessing of Cardinal Massimo* (exh. Salon 1834; first version, Aix-en-Provence, Mus. Granet).

A rigorous study of nature remained the basis for Granet's work. Throughout his career he produced a large

François-Marius Granet: *Choir of the Capuchin Church in Rome*, oil on canvas, 1.97×1.48 m, *c.* 1814 (New York, Metropolitan Museum of Art)

number of landscape sketches; many of these were painted on his travels through Italy (he was particularly attracted to Assisi and the Roman Campagna) and, after 1824, in the Ile de France and the countryside around Aix (e.g. *Montagne Sainte-Victoire*; Aix-en-Provence, Mus. Granet). Working in oils or watercolour on paper he developed an accomplished and fluid style, simplifying the forms of the landscape and capturing subtle effects of outdoor light. These landscapes are among his most successful achievements.

In 1826 Forbin offered Granet a post as a curator at the Louvre. He was elected to the Institut in 1830 and in 1833 was appointed curator of Louis-Philippe's newly established Musée Historique at Versailles. For this museum, Granet was commissioned to paint a number of works depicting contemporary events, including *Louis-Philippe Bestowing the Biretta to Cardinal de Cheverus in the Chapel of the Tuileries, 10 March 1836* (exh. Salon 1837; Versailles, Château). In spite of his continued official recognition in the 1830s, Granet's work was no longer fashionable and his Salon submissions attracted little attention. He became an isolated figure, cutting himself off from all but his closest friends; he later observed that his pictures had a 'sad character which repels the men of our era'. Following the death of his wife in 1847 Granet returned to his property, 'Le Malvallat', at Malvalat near Aix. He decided to retire there after the Revolution of 1848, and he died the following year. Granet had been nominated an honorary Director of the Musée d'Aix in 1844 and, apart from 199 drawings that were bequeathed to the Louvre, he left his studio and collection, totalling more than 500 works, to this museum, since known as the Musée Granet.

WRITINGS

'Vie de Granet', *Le Temps* (28 Sept–28 Oct 1872) [posth. pubd autobiography; MS., Aix-en-Provence, Mus. Arbaud; Eng. trans. in 1988–9 exh. cat.]

BIBLIOGRAPHY

A. de la Fizelière: *Granet* (Paris, n.d.)
E.-J. Delécluze: *Louis David: Son école & son temps* (Paris, 1855)
H. Gibert: *Catalogue du Musée d'Aix* (Aix-en-Provence, 1862)
H. Pontier: *Musée d'Aix comprenant le Musée Granet* (Aix-en-Provence, 1900)
E. Ripert: *François-Marius Granet, 1775–1849: Peintre d'Aix et d'Assise* (Paris, 1937)
François-Marius Granet (exh. cat., Nice, Gal. Ponchettes, 1970)
De David à Delacroix: La Peinture française de 1775 à 1830 (exh. cat., Paris, Grand Pal., 1974), pp. 454–6
Granet: Paysages de l'Ile de France, aquarelles et dessins dans les collections du Musée Granet (exh. cat., Aix-en-Provence, Mus. Granet, 1984)
F. Pupil: *Le Style Troubadour ou la nostalgie du bon vieux temps* (Nancy, 1985)
Granet: Paysages de Provence (exh. cat., Aix-en-Provence, Mus. Granet, 1988)
François-Marius Granet: Watercolours from the Musée Granet at Aix-en-Provence (exh. cat., New York, Frick, 1988–9)
I. N. Daguerre and D. Coutagne: *Granet, peintre de Rome* (Aix-en-Provence, 1992)

JOHN LEIGHTON

Grangerize. Term applied in its strictest sense to the practice that became fashionable in England towards the end of the 18th century of collecting portrait prints and adding them as extra illustrations to a text. It began after the Rev. James Granger published the *Biographical History of England from Egbert the Great to the Revolution. . .Adapted to a Methodical Catalogue of Engraved British Heads* (1769; suppl. 1774). The term is also sometimes associated with any album (no matter what subject) that has been extra-illustrated.

BIBLIOGRAPHY

M. Pointon: *Hanging the Head: Portraiture and Social Formation in Eighteenth-century England* (New Haven and London, 1993), pp. 53–78

□

Granges, David des (*b* London, 1611; *d* after 1670). English painter and engraver. He came from a Guernsey family and was baptized in London both at the French church, Threadneedle Street, and at St Anne's, Blackfriars, in 1611. In 1636 he married Judith Hoskins, presumably a relative of the miniature painter John Hoskins (i). Des Granges is recorded in 1628 as the engraver of Raphael's *St George and the Dragon* (1506; Washington, DC, N.G.). He was a prolific miniature painter, with a reticent style that shows the influence of Hoskins, whose works he often copied. His use of dark grey or light brown backgrounds was unusual and he frequently signed his works with the initials *D.D.G.* arranged in a triangle. His earliest dated miniature is of *Catherine Manners, Duchess of Buckingham* (1639; Windsor Castle, Berks, Royal Col.). In 1640 he made a miniature copy, now at Ham House, Surrey, of Titian's *Allegory of Alfonso d'Avalos, Marchese del Vasto* (*c.* 1532; Paris, Louvre), then in the collection of Charles I. Des Granges took the royalist side during the English Civil War and Commonwealth period; he followed Charles II to Scotland and produced many miniatures of his royal patron. The earlier versions were copied from the portrait (*c.* 1648; see Murdoch, pl. 7e) by Adriaen Hannemann, but des Granges evolved a novel contribution to the iconography of Charles II in his portraits of the King *c.* 1651 (e.g. ex-Newdegate col., see Murdoch, pl. 155). In 1671, disabled and unable to support his family, he had to plead for the payment owed for 13 of these Civil War miniatures. He is believed to have died shortly after this.

Des Granges's oil paintings are less well known than his miniatures. The *Saltonstall Family* (1636–7; *see* LACE, fig. 3) is attributed to him on the basis of his other signed portraits. Despite its naive composition it has a sensitivity and intimacy that is exceptional in Stuart painting.

BIBLIOGRAPHY

E. Einberg: *Illustrated Catalogue of Acquisitions*, London, Tate cat. (London, 1974–6), pp. 22–3

M. Edmond: 'Limners and Picturemakers', *Walpole Soc.*, xlvii (1978–80), pp. 123–4

J. Murdoch and others: *The English Miniature* (London, 1981), pp. 135–9

GRAHAM REYNOLDS

Granja, La. *See* SAN ILDEFONSO.

Gran Nicoya. Pre-Columbian culture of the Isthmian region of Latin America (classed archaeologically as part of the Intermediate area; *see* SOUTH AMERICA, PRE-COLUMBIAN, §II). It flourished in the north-western portion of modern Costa Rica and the south-western part of Nicaragua, bordered to the north by the Gulf of Fonseca and the Honduran border, to the south by the Gulf of Nicoya, to the east by Lake Managua, Lake Nicaragua and the Costa Rican Cordillera Volcanica, and to the west by the Pacific Ocean. In the past the region was tropical dry forest land but is now mostly low hills and flatlands around lakes Managua and Nicaragua. Despite marked seasonality, there is little annual rainfall, and thus few permanent rivers. Gran Nicoya culture is defined principally by artefacts from the sites of Nacascolo, Papagayo, Ruiz, Las Haldas, Vidor, and Ometepe and Zapatera islands in Lake Nicaragua. The cultural uniformity of the region was recognized and defined by Samuel K. Lothrop; his assumption that the region had more connections with MAYA culture to the north has also been shown to be true.

1. Pottery. 2. Sculpture. 3. Lapidary arts.

1. POTTERY. Lothrop's analysis of Nicaraguan and Costa Rican pottery was based on museum and private collections, including monochrome, bichrome and polychrome ceramics. Among the earlier wares, up to *c.* AD 500, are bichromes similar to those found throughout the Atlantic watershed and central highlands region to the south-east (*see* EASTERN AND CENTRAL COSTA RICA, PRE-COLUMBIAN): red decorations on buff, brown or black pottery, often with incised lines, rocker stamping or appliqué. Forms include bowls, jars and globular vessels, and modelled human and animal effigy whistles and ocarinas. There are similarities with contemporary early incised ceramics from throughout Costa Rica and with ceramics from southern Mesoamerica.

About AD 500 the pottery of the Isthmian region began to take on more distinctive traits, and in the Gran Nicoya this was the beginning of a polychrome tradition. Such early styles as Carillo Polychrome and Galo Polychrome wares display geometric and zoomorphic designs in black, cream and red on brown or buff backgrounds. Motifs of serpents, jaguars, monkeys, alligators, and bats were executed in paint and as modelled forms. Galo ware, in particular, shows strong stylistic associations with Maya Ulúa Polychrome from Honduras and El Salvador. In both Carillo and Galo wares the painted decoration usually appears within horizontal bands encircling the vessels. Besides bowls and cylindrical and globular jars, there are tripod slab-footed forms, effigy-head vessels and full-bodied figurines with elaborate and complex body designs. The numerous design elements of these early incised and polychrome styles are closely related to those on carved volcanic stone objects. Among the most common are the guilloche, various rectangular interlace patterns and the equal-armed Kan cross, Mayan symbol for water and day sign in the calendrical system. Modelled Alligator ware was also developed early: these are large hemispherical vessels with lids, usually topped by a complex modelled anthropomorphic alligator or crocodile seated at the ventilation holes. Much of the vessel surface and effigy figure is covered with rough pellets, perhaps indicative of alligator scutes as in Curridabat ware from the Atlantic watershed–central highlands region.

The most characteristic polychromes of north-western Costa Rica are later cream- or white-slipped styles, such as Papagayo, Vallejo, Pataky and Luna wares. Of these, Papagayo Polychrome ware is the most easily recognized. Backgrounds are decorated in red, orange and black paint with designs derived from Mesoamerica, such as the serpent, which may represent the Mesoamerican deities Quetzalcóatl and Ehecatl (the plumed serpent, a creator god; god of learning and wind god). Vessel shapes include shallow bowls with effigy-tripod legs, gourd-shaped jars with ring bases and zoomorphic effigies. A Mesoamerican affiliation is also represented on Pataky ware, the most elaborate and distinct pottery from this region. Most Pataky vessels are large (up to 350 mm high) pear or gourd-shaped tripod jars with modelled jaguar heads and legs (see fig. 1). The realistic modelling of the effigies is combined with small intricate patterns in red and black, often covering the appendages and vessel neck bands. Luna ware, found mainly in the Nicaraguan lake region, was probably the most recent style. Its association with iron artefacts and glass beads in burials shows that it was still being manufactured at the time of the Spanish Conquest in the mid-16th century. The most common forms are relatively small, rounded, legless bowls or bowls with tripod effigy-head supports. Their cream-slipped surfaces are decorated with 'busy' black and red fine-line patterns of humans, simians, jaguars and serpents, showing similarities with both contemporary Mesoamerican and continental South American ceramic designs.

2. SCULPTURE. The volcanic stone sculptures of Gran Nicoya, with few exceptions, are distinct from those of the Atlantic watershed–central highlands and Diquís regions. Only the simplest, functional *metates* (grinding stones) bear any resemblance to those of the other areas. The only large collection of *metates* from Gran Nicoya comes from Las Huacas cemetery (Pittsburgh, PA, Carnegie Mus. Nat. Hist.). After his excavations there, Carl

1. Gran Nicoya, feline effigy pottery vessel, Pataky ware, h. 325 mm, *c.* AD 1200–1400 (San José, Instituto Nacional de Seguros)

Hartman estimated that the cemetery contained at one time over 200 *metates*. The associated ceramics give an occupation date of *c.* AD 100–500, and the chronology of the burials indicates a gradual stylistic development of *metate* carving from simple to complex, plain to elaborate. At the same time, low-relief carving developed from extremely naturalistic renderings of animals to highly stylized forms. Such decorated *metates* may have continued to be produced for up to 200 years more at other sites.

At Las Huacas, Hartman recovered 52 *metates* with tripod supports and dished, rimless grinding plates. On the decorated examples the plates are thin and rectangular, and the supports are slightly tapered, divergent and cylindrical. Decoration ranges from those with plain undersides to those carved in relief with an image of a monkey, crocodile, alligator, winged bird or human. Some figures are surrounded by carved bands of interlaced design; others simply have frames of geometric bands or parallel ridges on the edges of the underside of the plate. A few have a carved band on the top, consisting of the same motifs as the bottom frames, and still others have top bands, and geometric designs on the undersides surrounding central figures resembling the figures on small Nicoya gold ornaments or the images on polychrome ceramics. Another sub-group has three flattened triangular-shaped legs supporting a curved, rectangular plate. Some are effigies with avian, feline, canine or reptilian heads. Low-relief ornamentation is completely non-representational and consists primarily of interlaced bands, narrow friezes or all-over patterns. The carvings on the underside are generally all-over designs, such as basketwork or matting, while upper surface designs are interlaced or plaited horizontal and vertical bands. Legs are either solid or carved openwork motifs.

Tripod effigy *metates* range from simplified to elaborate examples. Among the least complex are those representing birds: some are obviously parrots or macaws; some have harpy eagle tufted heads; others have long beaks like toucans. Most Gran Nicoya effigy *metates*, however, like those from the neighbouring Atlantic watershed–central highlands region, are feline representations. Those from Nicoya are angular and highly stylized. Heads are unusually large, with open jaws exposing sharp fierce teeth. The undersides of grinding plates are also elaborately carved, and the complex legs often represent inverted human or simian motifs. Larger and still more complex are *metates* representing coyotes or other canine animals. Many of these have hollow appendages carved like latticework.

Large-scale free-standing stone statues were also carved, and examples were first published in the 19th century by Ephraim Squier (1852) and by Carl Bovallius (1886). The most spectacular sculptures come from the Nicaraguan lake region and fall into at least two groups. The Chontales style consists of columnar, low-relief sculptures measuring *c.* 2.0–4.8 m high. They appear to represent males carrying weapons and wearing belts, loincloths and headdresses, and in some cases necklaces with pendants. The second group, known as *'alter ego'* statues, shows considerable variation, ranging in size from 1 to 4 m. Most represent males, with perhaps some females, associated with an animal form, often clinging to the back and shoulders. Others are animals, which appear as headdresses or have a human emerging from the animal's jaws. Wolfgang Haberland identifies the animals as crocodiles, birds of prey, jaguars and deer. Associated pottery gives a date of production between *c.* AD 800 and *c.* 1000.

3. LAPIDARY ARTS. Jade was a valuable material in much of the Pre-Columbian world, and both carved and uncarved pieces have been recovered in Costa Rica; however, as no source of jade or jadeite has been found in Costa Rica, it seems likely that it was imported from Mesoamerican sources, such as that in the Motágua River valley, Guatemala. Upwards of a thousand jade objects are known from Gran Nicoya, the Atlantic watershed–central highlands region and Gran Chiriquí. In Gran Nicoya, as in the other regions, the use of jade, based on the associated ceramics, is dated between *c.* 100 BC and *c.* AD 500, much later than the Mesoamerican use of jade by the Olmec, as early as *c.* 800 BC (*see* MESOAMERICA, PRE-COLUMBIAN, §VIII). Among the typical forms from Gran Nicoya is the axe god pendant, a celt-like oval blade, between 80 and 200 mm long, with a carved human, animal or composite being at one end (see fig. 2). Judging by their inclusion in rich burials and the rarity of the material itself, jades were high-status items and may have had some ritual function. The figure is usually carved only from the waist up, with arms crossed over the body. While naturalistic traits appear, most are rigidly posed, symmetrically carved and highly stylized. Analysis of more than 175 examples representing harpy eagles and quetzal parrots from the Las Huacas area by Oscar Fonseca Zamora and Robert

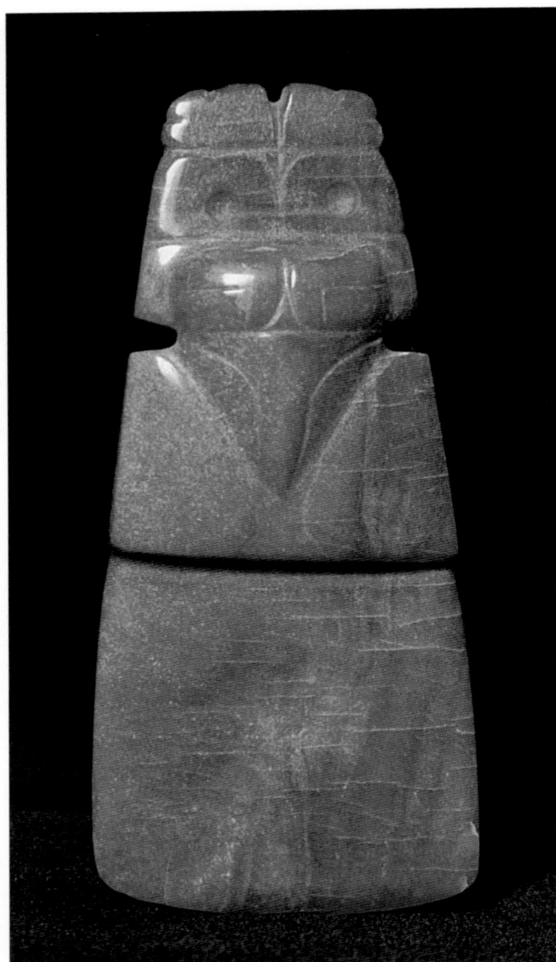

2. Gran Nicoya, axe god pendant in avian form, jade, h. 110 mm, *c.* 300 BC–AD 500 (San José, Instituto Nacional de Seguros)

Scaglion showed a seriated change in style from realistic to stylized, elaborate to simple. Other pendants represent bats, turtles, felines, humans, alligators, crabs and monkeys, and range from flat, silhouette images to fully three-dimensional forms. Most are well carved by drilling, sawing, burnishing and polishing. In addition to jade, other stones capable of taking a high polish were used, ranging in colour from almost white, through blue-green, to almost black.

BIBLIOGRAPHY

E. G. Squier: *Nicaragua: Its People, Scenery, Monuments*, 2 vols (New York and London, 1852)

C. Bovallius: *Nicaraguan Antiquities* (Stockholm, 1886)

C. V. Hartman: 'Archaeological Researches on the Pacific Coast of Costa Rica', *Mem. Carnegie Mus.*, iii/1 (1907) [whole issue]

S. K. Lothrop: 'Pottery of Costa Rica and Nicaragua', 2 vols, *Mem. Mus. Amer. Ind.*, viii (1926)

W. Haberland: 'On Stone Sculpture from Southern Central America', *The Iconography of Middle American Sculpture*, New York, Met. cat. (New York, 1973), pp. 134–53

O. Fonseca Zamora and R. Scaglion: 'Stylistic Analysis of Stone Pendants from the Las Huacas Burial Ground, Northwestern Costa Rica', *An. Carnegie Mus.*, xlvii (1978), pp. 210–98

E. K. Easby: 'Jade', *Between Continents, between Seas: Precolumbian Art of Costa Rica*, ed. E. P. Benson (New York, 1981), pp. 135–51

JOAN K. LINGEN

Gran Pajatén [Abiseo]. Pre-Columbian site in Río Abiseo National Park, Peru, occupied *c.* 450 BC–AD 1532. Gran Pajatén sits at 2850 m above sea-level in a highland rain-forest setting often compared to that of MACHU PICCHU. The site is a complex of stone terraces, stairways, platforms and circular buildings extending over approximately 1 ha along a crescent-shaped ridgetop above the Montecristo River, a tributary of the Abiseo and Huallaga rivers. Ceramic evidence and radiocarbon dates of *c.* 420 BC and *c.* 250 BC (Church, 1994) place Gran Pajatén among the oldest known sites of the Andean highland rain-forest. The architectural style, however, may not pre-date the Late Intermediate period (*c.* AD 1000–1476).

Stone cornices divide virtually all of the 26 known circular buildings into two levels. Tenoned heads and an unusual variety of stone friezes featuring anthropomorphic, zoomorphic and geomorphic motifs structurally incorporated into the tabular slate masonry distinguish Gran Pajatén from similar highland rain-forest sites near CHACHAPOYAS, to the north. The upper levels of three prominent buildings (nos 1, 7 and 8) were reached by broad external staircases, flanked at ground level by twin panels of anthropomorphic figures with headdresses and tenoned heads naturalistically carved in sandstone. A repeating stepped fret-and-scroll motif runs approximately halfway round the outside of the upper levels. Two bird friezes distinguish Building 2, while the upper levels of some other buildings are decorated with zigzag stone friezes. It is probable that all the buildings at Gran Pajatén originally had conical straw roofs internally supported by central wooden posts.

BIBLIOGRAPHY

P. Rojas Ponce: 'The Ruins of Pajatén', *Archaeology*, xx (1967), pp. 9–17

D. Bonavia: *Las Ruinas del Abiseo* (Lima, 1968)

G. Savoy: *Antisuyo: The Search for the Lost Cities of the Amazon* (New York, 1970)

T. J. Lennon, W. B. Church and M. Cornejo G.: 'Investigaciones arqueológicas en el Parque Nacional Río Abiseo, San Martín', *Bol. Lima*, lxii (1989), pp. 43–56

W. Church: 'Early Occupations at Gran Pajetén', *Andean Past*, iv (1994), pp. 281–318

WARREN B. CHURCH

Granpré Molière, Marinus Jan (*b* Oudenbosch, 13 Oct 1883; *d* Wassenaar, 13 Feb 1972). Dutch architect, urban planner, theorist and teacher. He received his training (1902–8) at the Technische Hogeschool, Delft. He is best known for his part in designing Vreewijk (1913–21), an urban extension of Rotterdam based on garden-city principles, and for his leading role in the Delft school (*see* DELFT SCHOOL (ii)). Although usually considered a traditionalist, there is little evidence of conservatism in either his writings or his designs. Granpré Molière was the first to investigate the possibility of urban renewal on the basis of garden-city principles on a large scale. The project at Vreewijk, which brought him international fame, was always intended as the urban expression of Ebenezer Howard's essentially anti-urban ideology of the garden city and was intended from the first to be an extension of Rotterdam. In the first phase, based on the street plan

(1913) by H. P. Berlage, Granpré Molière developed a housing typology based on the relationship between urbanism, architecture and planning. This resulted in the second phase of Vreewijk, the extension plan (1920) by Granpré Molière, Verhagen & Kok commissioned by the Eerste Rotterdamsche Tuindorp NV. A private initiative, it was nevertheless based on the belief that urbanism has not only to do with planning but also with expressing contemporary cultural and artistic ambitions, and that therefore it cannot be the result of a single person's intentions nor those of isolated parts of society, be they the state or private initiatives. Close cooperation with local government also led to the design (unexecuted) in 1923, developed from an initial project of 1921, of an extension plan for the left bank of the River Maas at Rotterdam and the regional plan for IJsselmonde, which was the first Dutch regional plan.

As a consequence of these activities Granpré Molière became one of the main influences on contemporary urbanism in the Netherlands and in the Netherlands Instituut voor Volkshuisvesting en Stedebouw, becoming chairman of its committee for urbanism in Amsterdam in the first half of the 1920s. In 1924 he lectured on the notion of the 'modern city' being a contradiction in terms, and in the same year his career underwent a major change when he accepted a professorial chair at the Technische Hogeschool at Delft. From then on he focused on the theoretical aspects of architecture, intending to find a fixed base for architectural design. His well-developed thinking on technical aspects led him to reject them as a basis for contemporary architecture. It also made him very critical of the Modern Movement after the founding of CIAM in 1928. He favoured a more complex approach including revitalization of traditional forms and typology of form, exemplified by his Delft school period of the 1930s. The more dominant position he accorded domestic architecture was due to the priority he gave to living conditions, which is exemplified both at Vreewijk and in the rich variety of his plans.

UNPUBLISHED SOURCES

Rotterdam, Nederlands Archit. Inst. [archvs of M. J. Granpré Molière]

WRITINGS

'Tweespalt in de hedendaagse kunst', *Wendingen*, iv (1918), pp. 7–10
'Kunst en publiek', *Wendingen*, ix (1918), pp. 6–9
'Ter inleiding van het eerste stedebouwkundige nummer', *Tijdschr. Vlkshuisvest. Stedebouw* (1921) [special issue]
De moderne bouwkunst en hare beloften (Delft, 1924)
'De moderne stad', *Tijdschr. Vlkshuisvest. Stedebouw*, viii (1924) [with bibliog.]
Woorden en werken (Heemstede, 1949)

BIBLIOGRAPHY

E. J. Hoogenberk: *Het idee van de hollandse stad* (Delft, 1980)
M. Steinman: 'Arbeit als Wissenschaft und Arbeit als Bild: Zur Tradition der gewöhnlichen Architektur', *Das Abenteuer der Ideen: Architektur und Philosophie seit der industriellen Revolution*, ed. C. Baldus (Berlin, 1984)
M. Tafuri: 'Realismus und Architektur: Zur Konstruktion volksbezogener Sprachen', ibid.
C. Wagenaar: *Tussen grandezza en schavot: De ontwerpen van Granpré Molière voor de wederopbouw van Groningen* (Groningen, 1991)
K. Bosma: *Ruimte voor een nieuwe tijd: De vormgeving van Nederlandse gewesten 1900–1945* [Planning a new era: the design of the Dutch regions 1900–1945] (diss., Groningen, Rijksuniv., 1993)

SJETTIE BRUINS

Grant, Duncan (James Corrowr) (*b* Rothiemurchus, Inverness, 21 Jan 1885; *d* Aldermaston, Berks, 9 May 1978). English painter and designer. From 1887 to 1894 he was in India and Burma, where his father was serving as a soldier. After attending a preparatory school in Rugby, he was sent to St Paul's School, London (1899–1901), where it was intended that he should be educated for the army. As he showed no interest in this he was allowed to move in 1902 to Westminster School of Art in London, where he remained for over two years. While there he was encouraged by Simon Bussy (1870–1954), a French painter who knew Matisse, and who was engaged to Grant's cousin Dorothy Strachey. In the winter of 1904–5 Grant visited Italy, where he copied the frescoes by Masaccio and Masolino in the Brancacci Chapel, S Maria del Carmine, Florence, and was also much impressed by the work of Piero della Francesca. In 1906–7 he studied at La Palette art school in Paris under Jacques-Emile Blanche, before visiting Italy again. His early work of this period reflects his study of works in the Louvre, as in *Still-life on Table* (1906; priv. col., see 1959 exh. cat., pl. 2), which shows the influence of Chardin. He also spent two terms at the Slade School of Fine Art, London (1907–8).

Back in Paris in 1909 Grant saw the works by Picasso and Matisse owned by Leo Stein and Gertrude Stein; in the same year he visited Matisse's studio and made the first of several visits (continuing until 1912) to Picasso's. In 1910, with his lifelong companion VANESSA BELL, he began painting a series of male and female figures as decoration for a room at Webb's Court, King's College, Cambridge (then occupied by John Maynard Keynes; completed 1922). Besides numerous other decorative projects, executed with Bell and Roger Fry or on his own, he provided the décor for various stage works, such as Jacques Copeau's production of Shakespeare's *Twelfth Night* at the Vieux Colombier in Paris in 1913. He visited Greece and Constantinople (now Istanbul) in 1910 and, with Keynes, travelled to Tunis and Sicily in 1911. *Football* and *Bathing* (both 1911; London, Tate), painted for the dining-room of Borough Polytechnic (destr.), London, have dynamic, highly stylized forms and muted colours. He exhibited as a member of the CAMDEN TOWN GROUP in 1911. That year he moved with Keynes to 38 Brunswick Square, the house of Adrian and Virginia Stephen (later Woolf), so becoming part of the BLOOMSBURY GROUP, whose members he had known for some years.

As with many English artists, Grant was strongly influenced by Fry's exhibition of *Manet and the Post-Impressionists*, held at the Grafton Galleries in London in 1910–11; this is evident in such works as the *Queen of Sheba* (1912; London, Tate), a pointillist sketch for a decorative project (unrealized) for Newnham College, Cambridge University. He contributed six works to Fry's *Second Post-Impressionist Exhibition* of 1912–13. In 1913 he became a co-director of the OMEGA WORKSHOPS in London, with which he remained associated until its closure in 1919. During this period he designed and decorated various objects such as a sewing-box (*c*. 1913–14; London, V&A) and a rug (1913; U. London, Courtauld Inst. Gals); these emphasize his interest in form rather than the literary or narrative aspects of art. Like Bell, Grant experimented with abstraction in 1914–15. One of the most original products of this period is the *Abstract Kinetic Collage Painting* (1914; London, Tate), a long roll of paper covered with abstract designs and collage elements; it was intended to be viewed in motion through a small rectangular aperture while listening to a piece of music by J. S. Bach. In 1915 he was invited to exhibit with the Vorticists as a non-member. In 1916 he moved with Bell and David Garnett to Charleston, a farmhouse near Firle, E. Sussex, where he spent much of his life thereafter, painting such works as *Vanessa Bell at Charleston* (*c*. 1917, London, N.P.G.; for illustration *see* BLOOMSBURY GROUP). As a conscientious objector during World War I, he was forced to do agricultural work.

In 1919 Grant became a member of the LONDON GROUP and the following year he had his first one-man show at the Carfax Gallery in London. A trip to the south of France with Bell in 1921–2 led to such works as *Landscape near St Tropez* (1922; London, Tate), which is characteristic of his work of the 1920s in its concern with solid forms, an influence probably absorbed from Cézanne and Derain. Between 1927 and 1938 he made regular trips to Cassis, near Marseille. He continued to paint a variety of still-lifes, interior scenes and landscapes in a broadly Post-Impressionist style, using loose brushstrokes and Fauve-influenced colour, as in *Figure in a Glass Case* (1938; Birmingham, Mus. & A.G.) and the sunlit *Hayrick* (1940; London, Tate).

In 1940 Grant was appointed an Official War Artist. With Bell he also carried out decorations (1940–43) for the parish church at Berwick, near Charleston, contributing the *Crucifixion* on the west wall and the *Four Seasons* on the chancel screen. One of his most notable canvases of these years is the magisterial portrait of *Vanessa Bell* (1942; London, Tate). In 1959 a series of large decorative panels by Grant was installed in the Russell Chantry in Lincoln Cathedral, including *Women with Child*, *Dockers* and the *Good Shepherd* (*in situ*). He remained active into the 1970s, his style largely unchanged and his subject-matter often derived from his travels, as in *Towards Cadiz* (1962; see 1964 exh. cat., pl. 18).

BIBLIOGRAPHY

R. Fry: *Duncan Grant* (London, 1923)
R. Mortimer: *Duncan Grant* (Harmondsworth, 1944)
Duncan Grant: A Retrospective Exhibition (exh. cat. by A. Clutton-Brock, London, Tate, 1959)
Duncan Grant and his World (exh. cat. by D. Sutton, London, Wildenstein's, 1964)
Duncan Grant: A 90th Birthday Exhibition of Paintings (exh. cat. by D. Brown, Edinburgh, N.G. Mod. A.; Oxford, MOMA; 1975)
Duncan Grant: Designer (exh. cat. by R. Shone and J. Collins, Liverpool, Bluecoat Gal.; Brighton, A.G. & Museums; 1980)
Duncan Grant (1885–1978): Works on Paper (exh. cat. by A. Garnett, London, Anthony d'Offay Gal., 1981)
S. Watney: *Duncan Grant* (London, 1990)

□

Grant, Sir **Francis** (*b* Edinburgh, 18 Jan 1803; *d* Melton Mowbray, Leics, 5 Oct 1878). Scottish painter. Following the death of his Perthshire landowner father in 1818, he spent his inheritance on foxhunting and collecting paintings and decided to restore his fortune by painting. Although he may briefly have been a pupil of Alexander Nasmyth, encouraged by Sir Walter Scott and the Earl of Elgin, he was largely self-taught and frequented the studios of Edinburgh artists. He was a friend and collaborator of John Ferneley in Leicestershire and his early paintings include small hunting pictures in Ferneley's style. He married his second wife, a niece of the 5th Duke of Rutland, in 1829.

Grant achieved recognition with the *Melton Breakfast* (1834; Jersey, Earl of Cromer priv. col.) and further enhanced his reputation with *Queen Victoria Riding Out* (1840; Windsor Castle, Royal Col.). He became fashionable in London for obtaining good likenesses and portraying animals well; he painted many equestrian portraits. Grant's sitters included Prince Albert, Sir Walter Scott, Macaulay, Palmerston and Disraeli. He obtained a gold medal at the 1855 Exposition Universelle in Paris, where his *Ascot Hunt* was greatly admired. Early works are generally small-scale, decoratively coloured and highly finished. His work gradually increased in size, freedom of technique and directness of approach, and the often huge late works are notable for broad paintwork, sober colouring and lack of flattery.

Grant became an ARA in 1842, RA in 1851 and in 1866 succeeded Sir Charles Eastlake as President, despite royal opposition. An effective, conscientious and popular President, his social connections with the government enabled him to obtain Burlington House for the Royal Academy on advantageous terms.

BIBLIOGRAPHY

J. Steegman: 'Sir Francis Grant PRA: The Artist in High Society', *Apollo*, lxxix (1964), pp. 479–85
D. Irwin and F. Irwin: *Scottish Painters at Home and Abroad* (London, 1975)

CATHERINE WILLS

Grantham, 2nd Baron. *See* ROBINSON, THOMAS.

Grão Vasco. *See* FERNANDES, VASCO.

Grapaldo [Grapaldi], **Francesco Maria** (*b* Parma, 3 Jan 1460; *d* Parma, Oct/Nov 1515). Italian scholar and writer. He studied for a time with the Bolognese humanist scholar Filippo Beroaldo I (1453–1505), and he then qualified as a notary. From 1486 he was a lecturer in humanities at the Studio (later University) of Parma. He held various public offices in the city, including the chancellorship of the Commune in 1497, and he was often entrusted with diplomatic missions. His most important written work was *De partibus aedium* (1494), which gives the correct Latin names of the various parts and contents of the house. Dividing the house into two—the ground floor (atrium, courtyard, cellars and kitchen garden) and the upper floors (living quarters)—Grapaldo offers a definition and an etymological explanation of the different parts of the house and of the objects within it, enriching his text with references to Classical and other authors. A valuable source of information on contemporary antiquarian scholarship, the book also offers an insight into domestic life and building in late 15th-century Parma, including the use of private chapels, which Grapaldo recommends should be decorated with devotional images by local artists. Conceived and completed in ten months, *De partibus aedium* was widely admired and went through many editions. Grapaldo's scholarship and ability as a teacher were also displayed in *De verborum explicatione (explanatione)* (1511), a dictionary offering definitions of particularly obscure Latin words. Other works included commentaries on the plays of Plautus and collections of poetry.

WRITINGS

De partibus aedium (Parma, 1494, rev. 1516/*R* 1517)
Salmi penitenziali (Parma, 1505)
De verborum explicatione (explanatione) (Parma, 1511)

BIBLIOGRAPHY

G. Tiraboschi: *Storia della letteratura italiana*, vii (Modena, 1792), p. 868
M. Corrado Cervi: 'Brevi note sui dati biografici di Francesco Maria Grapaldo, 1460–1515', *Aurea Parma*, xxxvii (1953), pp. 116–19
F. Rizzi: 'Francesco Maria Grapaldo', *Archv Stor. Prov. Parm.*, v (1953), pp. 135–69
V. Marchi: 'Note in margine al Grapaldo', *Aurea Parma*, xxxix (1955), pp. 147–54
F. da Maretto, ed.: *Bibliografia generale delle antiche provincie parmensi*, ii (Parma, 1974), pp. 552–3

JANET SOUTHORN

Graphite [black lead; plumbago]. Crystalline allotropic form of carbon, used primarily as a drawing material, in the form of a PENCIL. It is a friable substance, composed of flat, flaky grains, which are transferred to the surface of the support (usually paper) as the artist draws and impart a delicate sheen to the strokes. Synthetic graphite, which has been produced commercially since 1897, is obtained from carborundum.

Graphite was first excavated in Bavaria in the early 13th century, but its potential as an artists' medium remained unexploited until the discovery in the mid-16th century of pure graphite at Borrowdale in Cumbria, England. The Borrowdale mine was in full operation by the 1580s, when native graphite was taken from the mine, sawn into sheets and then into slender square rods forming the 'lead' and then encased in wood to form the pencil. Graphite seems to have been used first for underdrawing in the 16th century, supplanting the leadpoint stylus from which the term 'lead' pencil probably derived. Graphite does not seem to have been commonly used for drawing until well into the 17th century, and even though it was gaining popularity, black chalk and charcoal were still favoured for either preliminary sketches or finished drawings up to the 18th century. Graphite became widespread only in the 18th century, with the increasing difficulty of obtaining good-quality natural chalks and the simultaneous production of a fine range of graphite pencils. The medium still remains very popular today.

BIBLIOGRAPHY

A. P. Laurie: *The Painter's Methods and Materials* (Philadelphia, 1926/*R* New York, 1967)
R. J. Gettens and G. L. Stout: *Painting Materials: A Short Encyclopaedia* (New York, 1942, rev. 1966)
J. Watrous: *The Craft of Old-Master Drawings* (Madison, 1957)
M. Lefebure: *Cumberland Heritage* (London, 1970)
H. Petroski: *The Pencil: A History* (London, 1990)

SHIRLEY MILLIDGE

Grapp, Wendling. *See* DIETTERLIN, WENDEL.

Gras, Caspar (*b* Bad Mergentheim, nr Würzburg, 1585; *d* Schwaz, nr Innsbruck, 3 Dec 1674). Austrian sculptor of German birth. After training with his father, a goldsmith, and from 1600 to 1602 as an apprentice embosser at the court of Archduke Maximilian III in Bad Mergentheim, he followed his patron and teacher, Hubert Gerhard, to Innsbruck, where he remained a member of Gerhard's workshop until 1606. By 1610 Gras had obtained the post of Court Embosser and, after Gerhard's departure for Munich in 1613, he received most of the court's commissions, including the bronze memorial of *Maximilian III* (1615–19; Innsbruck Cathedral). The life-size kneeling statue of *Maximilian III* and the standing *St George*, together with the elaborate naturalistic decorations of the baldachino-like base, were designed by Gras and cast by his frequent collaborator, Heinrich Reinhart (*c.* 1570–1629). Gras's finest project was the monumental Leopold Fountain (1623–30) in the Rennweg, Innsbruck. It is surmounted by the equestrian statue of *Archduke Leopold V* (*d* 1632), the first Baroque statue of this kind in Austria, while various river deities and allegorical figures are set around the base and bowl.

Gras created many collector's or *Kunstkammer* pieces, including an elaborate mortar for Hans Taurnhauser of Schwaz (1617; Munich, Bayer. Nmus.). The small *St Eustace* (*c.* 1620; Hamburg, Mus. Kst. & Gew.) and *St George* (1620s; Vienna, Ksthist. Mus.) are probably by Gras. He was the leading bronze sculptor in the Tyrol during the first half of the 17th century, but with the death of Leopold V in 1632 and the financial depression prompted by the Thirty Years War, his career suffered considerably. His principal work of the 1630s and one of his few non-Austrian commissions was the large *Virgin and Child* designed in 1631 for the cathedral chapter of Konstanz. This group, cast in 1632 by Valentin Algeyer and initially intended for a sacramental altar, was later placed on a tall column at the cathedral's west door. On the basis of the Leopold Fountain and other documented works, several small-scale bronze equestrian statues of the late 1640s and 1650s, including *Emperor Ferdinand III* and other Habsburg princes (Vienna, Ksthist. Mus.), are ascribed to Gras. Apart from these, and also the Pegasus Fountain (1661) in Salzburg, little can be ascribed to his later years.

BIBLIOGRAPHY

E. Egg: 'Caspar Gras und der Tiroler Bronzegüss des 17. Jahrhunderts', *Veröff. Mus. Ferdinandeum Innsbruck*, xl (1960), pp. 5–57
H. R. Weihrauch: 'Die verlorengeglaubte Konstanzer Madonna des Kaspar Gras', *Pantheon*, xx (1962), pp. 227–34
L. L. Möller: 'Eine Innsbrucker Bronzegruppe "St Eustachius" aus dem frühen 17. Jahrhundert', *Z. Dt. Ver. Kstwiss.*, xxi (1967), pp. 165–73
H. Noflatscher: 'Archivalische Notizen zu Hubert Gerhard und Kaspar Gras', *Innsbruck. Hist. Stud.*, i (1978), pp. 221–6
Barock in Innsbruck (exh. cat. by E. Egg and G. Ammann, Innsbruck, Tirol. Landesmus., 1980), pp. 111–13
M. Leithe-Jasper: *Renaissance Master Bronzes from the Collection of the Kunsthistorisches Museum, Vienna* (London, 1986), pp. 246–60
S. Jacobs: 'Ein Amor in Braunschweig: Bemerkungen zum Werk Caspar Gras', *Z. Dt. Ver. Kstwiss.*, xliii (1989), pp. 7–29

JEFFREY CHIPPS SMITH

Grass and Earth Society [Sōdosha]. Japanese group of Western-style (*Yōga*) painters, active between *c.* 1915 and 1922 in Tokyo. Its principal member was the painter Ryūsei Kishida, who was said to have thought up the group's name when he saw grass growing by the roadside as he walked along a Tokyo street. Other founder-members were Kazumasa Nakagawa (1893–1991) and Shōhachi Kimura (1893–1958). Although Kishida was interested in the realistic depiction of nature, the group did not have a uniform style and concentrated on organizing exhibitions. In October 1915 the group held its first exhibition, sponsored by the Society of Contemporary Art, at the premises of the *Yomiuri* newspaper in Tokyo. The show comprised 172 works by 23 artists including the group's founders. In the second exhibition in 1916 were 118 works shown by 13 artists, including Kishida's *Sketch of a Road Cut Through a Hill* (1915; Tokyo, N. Mus. Mod. A.). A total of nine exhibitions were organized by the group, the last being held in 1922.

BIBLIOGRAPHY

Shirakaba to Taishōki no bijutsu [Art of the Shirakaba and Taishō period] (exh. cat., essay by T. Mushanokōji; Tokyo, Met. A. Mus., 1977)

Kishida Ryūsei to Sōdosha [Ryūsei Kishida and the Sōdosha] (exh. cat., essay by S. Hamamoto; Shimonoseki, Mun. Mus. A., 1985)

YASUYOSHI SAITO

Grasser, Erasmus (*b* Schmidmühlen, Upper Palatinate *c.* 1445–50; *d* Munich between 8 April and 1 June 1518). German sculptor, architect and hydraulic engineer. He worked mainly in Munich and was one of the most important south German sculptors in wood and stone around the turn of the 15th century. His sculptural oeuvre ranged from small pieces to large carved altars. Grasser probably spent his years as apprentice and travelling journeyman in the Upper Rhine and Swabia. He arrived in Munich about 1473, and was mentioned in documents in 1475; a letter of complaint from the local guild opposes the admission of the wood-carver as a master—Grasser had confidently applied to the guild while at the same time claiming exemption from taxes and defence levies. By this time he was probably already married to Dorothea Kaltenprunner, who came from a prosperous Munich family. Despite these initial difficulties, Grasser soon achieved considerable social and economic success. He was one of the four directors of the guild several times between 1480 and 1504, and from 1512–18 he was a member of the council. The taxation records of Munich after 1482 show him to be one of its richest citizens.

His first recorded contract was from Munich council. In 1477 he supplied 11 coats of arms (9 remaining; Munich, Stadtmus.) for the wooden ceiling of the Tanzsaal in the Altes Rathaus (destr. 1944–5) and depictions of the sun and moon (Munich, Stadtmus.). Also for the Tanzsaal, in 1480, for a fee of 172 florins, he produced the *Morris Dancers* (see fig.), 16 exquisitely carved lime-wood figures (h. *c.* 650 mm), of which 10 survive (rest.; Munich, Stadtmus.). Their vigorous characterization, graceful physicality and dynamic, spatial quality place the figures among the most significant achievements of Late Gothic secular sculpture. The epitaph of *Ulrich Aresinger* (1482; Munich, St Peterskirche) in mottled, red marble is the only work signed by Grasser himself. At the end of the 1480s Grasser worked for the cathedral chapter at Freising. In 1483 he had supplied the raw material for ten stone figures to be erected in Freising Cathedral, and in 1489 he was paid 328 florins for producing a tabernacle (destr. 1723–4) for the Late Gothic redecoration of the cathedral choir. In 1492 Grasser sent a sandstone monumental *Lamentation* group to Freising Cathedral; he did not charge for his labour but was paid only for the materials and costs of transport. A 'panel', probably an altar shrine, for which Grasser was

Erasmus Grasser: *Morris Dancer*, lime-wood, h. *c.* 650 mm, 1480 (Munich, Stadtmuseum)

paid by the monastery at Tegernsee (Upper Bavaria) in 1489, has not been preserved. Receipts from 1502–5 confirm that Grasser worked on a high altar in St Leonhard, Reichersdorf (Upper Bavaria), of which three shrine figures survive: a *Virgin and Child*, *St Leonard* and *St Eligius* (all *in situ*). In view of the qualitative differences between these and other securely attributed works, they must be seen as workshop products. Between 1503 and 1506 Grasser's workshop installed another Late Gothic winged retable on the smaller altar of St Achatius in St Leonhard; the retable (*in situ*) is documented in the Reichersdorf archives.

Other sculptures can be attributed to Grasser on stylistic grounds. Between 1470 and 1473 he produced figures of *St Mary* and *St John the Evangelist* for a *Crucifixion* group in St Leonhard, Traidendorf (Upper Palatinate; *in situ*); their sense of movement, the treatment of the faces and the carving of the hair are already characteristic. Bearing in mind his later architectural work, it is conceivable that *c.* 1473 he collaborated in the sculptural ornamentation of the Munich Frauenkirche, notably the corbel figures in the vaulting. Grasser produced the *Holy Cross* altar *c.* 1482 for St Maria, Ramersdorf (Munich); complex movements in its multi-figured *Crucifixion* scene recall the *Morris Dancers*. It is directly connected with a small monstrance altar in Munich (Bayer. Nmus.). The *Holy Spirit* altar in the Nonnberg convent in Salzburg, Austria, and lime-wood figures of a *Mater dolorosa* (rest.) and *St John the*

Evangelist (both h. 1.22 m) for a *Crucifixion* group (*c.* 1485–90; Munich, Bayer. Nmus.) from St Wolfgang, Pipping, are regarded as Grasser's. Together with Jan Polack he built the high altar of St Peterskirche, Munich; only the over life-size enthroned figure of *St Peter* (*c.* 1490) survives *in situ*. A half-length sculpture of *Daniel* (Berlin, Skulpgal.) probably also comes from this altar. Between 1495 and 1502 Grasser and his productive workshop produced the oak choir-stalls (some still *in situ*) for the Frauenkirche, Munich. This large contract included carved half-length figures of the apostles, prophets and saints. Following the destruction during World War II parts of the figural decoration were dispersed between the Frauenkirche and various collections; since the church's restoration in 1994 most parts have been returned and placed in the newly installed choir-stalls.

As an architect, Grasser is first mentioned submitting designs for the new monastery (begun 1487) of Mariaberg near Rorschach (Switzerland). In 1510, 1511 and 1515 he issued receipts for payments. A letter dated 1492 from Emperor Maximilian I names Grasser as the master mason at Unserer Lieben Frau Church in Schwaz (N. Tyrol), where he is recorded in the account books in 1503. Grasser acquired his reputation as a hydraulics expert in the 1490s. In 1494, at the request of the city of Munich, he inspected a saline spring near the abbey of Weyarn in Upper Bavaria. From 1498 he was a member of a special commission responsible for the reorganization of the ducal salt-works at Reichenhall and was appointed chief master builder there in 1507. In 1501 he advised the Munich authorities on bridge construction. In 1517, a year before his death, Grasser was staying in Beuerberg (Eurasburg, Upper Bavaria) 'on account of the water' at the wish of Philipp, Pfalzgraf bei Rhein, the Bishop of Freising (*reg* 1499–1541).

Grasser set new standards in Munich in the 1470s and 1480s. His travels in the Upper Rhine and Swabia, and the influence of Nicolaus Gerhaert shaped his work and are expressed in his adoption of the principle of 'interlocking movement' (Pinder). From the 1490s the emphasis in Grasser's wood-carvings on the volume of figures and on calm, gliding lines and curves draws on a south German tradition going back to Hans Multscher.

BIBLIOGRAPHY

NDB

P. M. Halm: *Erasmus Grasser*, Studien zur süddeutschen Plastik, iii (Augsburg, 1928)

W. Pinder: *Die deutsche Plastik der Hochrenaissance*, Handbuch der Kunstwissenschaft (Wildpark and Potsdam, 1929), pp. 378–81

M. Hasse: 'Der Salzburger Altar des Erasmus Grasser', *Jb. Preuss. Kstsamml.*, lx (1939), pp. 47–56

P. Frankl: *The Early Works of Erasmus Grasser*, *A. Q.* [Detroit] v (1942), pp. 242–58

H. Ramisch: 'Funde und Bemerkungen zu Erasmus Grasser und seinem Kreis', *Bayerisches Landesamt für Denkmalpflege*, xxvi (Munich, 1967), pp. 83–95

J. Müller: *Studien zum Frühwerk des Bildhauers Erasmus Grasser: Die Arbeiten für das Münchner Rathaus und Altarskulptur* (diss., U. Munich, 1970)

M. Baxandall: *The Limewood Sculptors of Renaissance Germany* (New Haven and London, 1980)

V. Liedke: 'Die Sitzfigur eines hl. Emmeram in Kleinhelfendorf: Ein bislang unbekanntes Hauptwerk des Münchner Bildschnitzers Erasmus Grasser', *A. Bavar.*, xxv/xxvi (1982), pp. 15–30

J. Müller-Meiningen: *Die Moriskentänzer und andere Arbeiten des Erasmus Grasser für das Alte Rathaus in München* (Munich and Zurich, 1984)

J. Rohmeder: 'Die Wirksamkeit Erasmus Grassers beim Bau von Mariaberg in Rorschach', *Ulrich Rösch, St. Galler Fürstabt und Landesherr*, ed. W. Vogeler (St Gall, 1987), pp. 343–62

Vera Icon: 1200 Jahre Christusbilder zwischen Alpen und Donau (exh. cat., ed. F. Fahr, H. Ramisch and P. B. Steiner; Freising, Diözmus., 1987), pp. 91–5

K. Otto: 'Erasmus Grasser und der Meister des Blutenburger Apostelzyklus: Studien zur Münchner Plastik des späten 15. Jahrhunderts', *Misc. Bavar. Monacensia*, cl (1988) [whole issue]

——: 'Das Chorgestühl der Frauenkirche im Wandel der Zeit', *Monachium sacrum: Festschrift zur 500-Jahr-Feier der Metropolitankirche zu Unserer Lieben Frau in München*, ed. H. Ramisch, ii (Munich and Berlin, 1994), pp. 303–76

FRANZ BISCHOFF

Grasset, Eugène(-Samuel) (*b* Lausanne, 25 May 1841; *d* Paris, 23 Oct 1917). French illustrator, decorative artist and printmaker of Swiss birth. Before arriving in Paris in the autumn of 1871, Grasset had been apprenticed to an architect, attended the Polytechnic in Zurich and travelled to Egypt. In Paris he found employment as a fabric designer and graphic ornamentalist, which culminated in his first important project, the illustrations for *Histoire des quatre fils Aymon* (1883). Grasset worked in collaboration with Charles Gillot, the inventor of photo-relief printing and an influential collector of Oriental and decorative arts, in the production of this major work of Art Nouveau book design and of colour photomechanical illustration. Grasset used a combination of medieval and Near Eastern decorative motifs to frame and embellish his illustrations, but most importantly he integrated text and imagery in an innovative manner which has had a lasting influence on book illustration.

In 1881 he was commissioned by Rodolphe Salis to design furnishing in a medieval style for the latter's new Chat Noir cabaret in Montmartre. This project brought him in direct contact with Montmartre avant-garde artists such as Adolphe Willette, Théophile-Alexandre Steinlen, Henri Rivière and Henri de Toulouse-Lautrec. Grasset's numerous posters include *Librairie romantique* (1887), *L'Encre Marquet* (1892), *Grafton Gallery, London* (1893) and the series of ten decorative panels produced in 1897 in which he combined his concern for design with the dramatic representation of women, a preoccupation characteristic of the 1890s. Most notable among Grasset's graphic achievements are the lithographs *La Vitrioleuse* (1894) for the album *L'Estampe originale* (1893–5) and *La Morphinomane* (1897), both of which are dramatic and frightening images of women, whose bold, decorative treatment is derived from Japanese prints. By the end of the century Grasset's reputation as a leading figure in the development of Art Nouveau poster design was well established; an article by Frederick Lees (*Mag. A.*, xxiii, 1899, p. 275) brackets him with Alphonse Mucha and Jules Chéret.

During the 1890s Grasset applied the same method of design that he had used in *Histoire des quatre fils Aymon* to his compositions for posters, ceramics, stained glass and tapestries. He enclosed areas of local colour within strong outlines in the manner of leaded stained glass. Grasset's form of Cloisonnism was reinforced by the theories of the Nabis, and he was one among several artists who created designs for Tiffany stained-glass windows that were included in the opening exhibition of Siegfried Bing's Salon de l'Art Nouveau in December 1895.

Grasset was an important figure in the Arts and Crafts movement in France. He acted as professor of decorative arts at the Ecole Normale d'Enseignement du Dessin, Paris, established by M. A. Guérin in 1881, and was on the editorial board of *Art et décoration*, founded in 1897. His two-volume *La Plante et ses applications ornementales* (1897–1900) is a graphic summation of his teaching on the subject during the previous two decades. Around 1900 he created the Grasset roman and italic typeface for Peignot Frères: this was followed in 1905 by *Méthode de composition ornementale*, which graphically explained basic design components valid for all media. His theories and designs were ideologically and stylistically compatible with those of the Vienna Secessionists, founded in 1897, and he was one of the few artists invited by the group to contribute to its magazine *Ver Sacrum*. At the Exposition Universelle, Paris, in 1900 Grasset was represented by tapestry, ceramics, stained glass and enamelled jewellery, while his students exhibited 150 wallpaper designs. Grasset's series of brooches and buckles for the exhibition were designed for the firm of Henri Vever and include such dramatic symbolist images as *Apparitions*, in which the haunting heads of two women are superimposed, as well as highly decorative floral designs based on tenets expressed in *La Plante et ses applications ornementales.*

In 1901 Grasset joined Hector Guimard, Eugène Gaillard and Albert-Louis Dammouse in organizing the Société des Artistes-Décorateurs. While the group never developed substantial projects or programmes of its own, it did inspire the organization of the Exposition Internationale des Arts Décoratifs et Industriels Modernes (Paris, 1925), which promoted the new theories of the Art Deco style. In 1909 Grasset was a founder-member of the Société d'Art Décoratif Français.

WRITINGS

La Plante et ses applications ornementales, 2 vols (Paris, 1897–1900)
Méthode de composition ornementale, 2 vols (Paris, 1905)
Ouvrages de ferronnerie moderne (Paris, 1906)

BIBLIOGRAPHY

La Plume, 122 (1894); 261 (1901) [special edn ded. to Grasset]
A. Alexandre: *Eugène Grasset et son oeuvre* (Paris, 1901)
V. Arwas: *Berthon & Grasset* (London, 1978)
Y. Plantin: *Eugène Grasset* (Paris, 1980)

PHILLIP DENNIS CATE

Grassi, de. Italian family of artists. Three members of the family are documented as working for the administrative body responsible for building the new cathedral in Milan between 1389 and 1400.

(1) Giovannino [Johannino] **de Grassi** (*fl* from 1380s; *d* 5 July 1398). Draughtsman, painter and architect. In contrast to his documented career, Giovannino's 20th-century reputation is as one of the most innovative and inventive of manuscript illuminators, despite the fact that his only documented illumination is 'tabulla una a grammatichi' (a grammar table/tablet; 1395), made for the seven-year-old son of Gian Galeazzo Visconti, 1st Duke of Milan. His reputation rests instead on the inscription '*Johininus de grassis designavit*' on a folio of wash drawings of animals in a sketchbook (Bergamo, Bib. Civ. A. Mai, MS. delta vii. 14, fol. 4*v*). Some of the late 14th-century drawings in this sketchbook are closely related to those of the Psalter–Hours begun for Gian Galeazzo (Florence, Bib. N. Cent., MS. Banco Rari 397 and MS. Landau Finaly 22; *see* MILAN, fig. 9) and completed some decades later for his son Filippo Maria. A change in the type of subsidiary decoration and variations in style show that the illumination for Giangaleazzo was undertaken in two campaigns. The two styles, however, are closely related, and a precise division between them is difficult to make. The earliest work on the manuscript, the first volume and the opening folios of the second volume, is generally attributed to Giovannino and was probably painted in the late 1380s, before he joined the payroll of the Milan Cathedral works. The light, bright colours, richly gilded with liquid and burnished gold, give the pages a scintillating appearance. Each border is of an individual design; in addition to conventional foliage, some include birds or animals and many have a resourceful incorporation of the emblems, arms, mottoes and even portraits of the owner.

In the two years from 5 May 1389 a Johannino de Grassi, 'painter', is recorded several times in the registers of the works of Milan Cathedral. He provided materials, furnished unspecified designs and painted a picture of *St Gall* placed on the high altar on the saint's feast day and two *Maestàs* (all untraced), used for collecting donations for the building works. On 12 July 1391 he was appointed as '*inzignerius*' and remained a salaried employee of the works until his death. His responsibilities were extremely varied: he painted such images as the portrait of *Boniface IX* on a banner for the jubilee (1391) and a *Mappamundi* (1396), provided designs, for example for a golden altar in which to set jewels from a ring presented by the Duchess of Milan, gilded and painted sculpture and provided a measured transverse section (1394) of the church and its sacristies. He even worked in stone; in June 1391 he was at work on a piece of marble and in August was paid for carving a *Christ and the Woman of Samaria*, to be placed in the right-hand sacristy (*in situ*). Primarily, however, his role seems to have been as a designer of architectural elements. He made models and templates for stonecutters, and his models, for example of capitals (1396), were put before the council of the works and considered for adoption. After his death his wooden model (untraced) of the church was to be preserved as an exemplum for the completion of the cathedral.

Giovannino was often responsible for the distribution of material to other workmen, and with Marco da Carona (*d* 8 July 1405), another *inzignerius*, he hired stonecutters and instructed them on preparing marble for colonnettes, window tracery and tabernacles. He often collaborated with Giacomo da Campione, and in 1392 their expertise prevailed when northern artists disputed the stability of the building. In August 1396 Giovannino, Marco and Giacomo went to Pavia to advise on the Certosa to be built there for Gian Galeazzo. Whereas it is likely that the distinctive form of the columns of Milan Cathedral (with capitals containing sculpted figures in tabernacles), and probably also the windows of the apse, can be attributed to Giovannino, it is impossible to isolate his probably considerable contribution to the overall appearance of the cathedral, since little of his documented work survives.

Connections can also be made between designs in the sketchbook and frescoes at Campomorto that have been attributed to Giovannino.

(2) Porrino de Grassi (*fl* 1395–9). Painter and illuminator, brother of (1) Giovannino de Grassi. He was paid by the works of Milan Cathedral in February 1395 for painting three small images of the *Virgin and Child* on panels 'for giving the Peace' to those who gave oblations and in March for a *Maestà* to be placed on the box on the high altar for collecting donations. In October 1395, in order to free himself to work on designs for the windows and capitals, Giovannino took on his brother Porrino, who was 'skilful in such work', to ornament in gold and azure the sculpture of the doorway of the sacristy. His final work for the works was apparently in April 1399, when he was paid for illuminating a Bull of Indulgence (untraced) conceded by Boniface IX. No certain work by him survives, but his collaboration in the manuscripts attributed to his brother and nephew (3) Salomone de Grassi is often suggested.

(3) Salomone de Grassi (*fl* 1397–1400). Illuminator, painter and designer, son of (1) Giovannino de Grassi. He was first employed by the works of Milan Cathedral as an illuminator during his father's lifetime. A record of payment of 16 October 1397 for gold, ultramarine and other colours specifies that Salomone had been appointed to illuminate the new copy of the book called 'Beroldus' (see below). He was paid for its illumination on 13 August 1398. The following month he was appointed to the salaried staff of the works for two years, and in November he was elected as '*designatore*'. The tasks he undertook included the painting of sculpture, a *confanonum* (standard) to be sent to the Podestà of Verona and a banner to be hung on the campanile. In June 1399 his salary was to be reduced by a quarter because he was also working for the Duke. In February 1400 Salomone showed Giangaleazzo his design for the tomb of his father, *Galeazzo II Visconti*. In December his pay was adjusted because from February to June he had been working for the Duchess 'on some books'.

The Beroldus manuscript survives (Milan, Castello Sforzesco, MS. 2262; see fig.), and its illumination is recognizably by the same artist as some folios of the Visconti Psalter–Hours, for example the series of *Creation* illustrations (Florence, Bib. N. Cent., MS. Landau Finaly 22, fols 19, 26, 30, 51 and 54). It is likely that Salomone was responsible for the second campaign of work on the manuscript. His exuberant borders and initials often include complex Gothic architectural forms. These may reflect Giovannino's designs for the cathedral, a collection of which was in Salomone's possession in January 1400. Illumination by Salomone is found in two other manuscripts: the first three volumes of a four-volume Bible (Milan, Bib. N. Braidense, MSS AE XIV 24–27) made for the Certosa di Pavia, and the *Historia plantarum* (Rome, Bib. Casanatense, MS. 459), which was subsequently owned by Matthias Corvinus, King of Hungary.

Salomone de Grassi: *St Ambrose Baptizing St Augustine* and *David and Goliath*; historiated initial and marginal illustration from the Beroldus manuscript, 395×275 mm, 1397–8 (Milan, Castello Sforzesco, Biblioteca Trivulziano, MS. lat. 2262, fol. 1*r*)

BIBLIOGRAPHY

Annali della Fabbrica del duomo di Milano dall'origine fino al presente (Milan, 1877–85), i and app. 1

P. Toesca: *La pittura e la miniatura nella Lombardia dei più antichi monumenti alla metà del quattrocento* (Milan, 1912/*R* Turin, 1966)

'Giovannino de Grassi, tacuino di disegni: Codice della Biblioteca di Bergamo', *Mnmt Bergomensia*, v (Milan, 1961) [whole issue]

A. Cadei: 'Giovannino de Grassi nel tacuino di Bergamo', *Crit. A.*, xvii (1970), pp. 17–36

M. Meiss and E. Kirsch: *The Visconti Hours* (New York and London, 1972)

A. Cadei: *Studi di miniatura Lombarda: Giovannino de Grassi, Belbello da Pavia* (Rome, 1984)

M. Bollati: 'Giovannino e Salomone de Grassi', *A. Crist.*, lxxv (1987), pp. 211–24

K. Sutton: 'Codici di lusso a Milano: Gli esordi', *Il millennio Ambrosiano: La nuova città dal comune alla signoria*, ed. C. Bertelli (Milan, 1989), pp. 110–39

M. T. Mazzilli Savini: 'Un inedito ciclo di affreschi tardogotici a Campomorto', *A. Lombarda*, 96–7 (1991–2), pp. 77–84

M. Rossi: 'Un contributo a Giovannino de Grassi pittore', *A. Lombarda*, 96–7 (1991–2), pp. 85–91

J. Shell: 'Giovannino de Grassi Takes an Apprentice', *A. Lombarda*, 96–7 (1991–2), pp. 131–2

M. Rossi: 'Novità su Giovannino de Grassi', *A. Lombarda*, 1–2 (1994)

E. Welch: *Art and Authority in Renaissance Milan* (in preparation)

KAY SUTTON

Grassi, Józef (*b* Vienna, 22 April 1757; *d* Dresden, 8 Jan 1838). Austrian painter. He was the son of a craftsman from Udine and the brother of the sculptor Anton Grassi (1755–1807). In 1768 he started as a student at the Akademie der Bildenden Künste in Vienna, to which he owed his entire education. His ambitious nature soon ensured that he entered aristocratic circles, where he became a favoured portrait painter, particularly of women, whom he painted in oils and in miniature. His most frequent type was the half-length portrait of young women, generally portrayed with hands crossed on their breast. With pale tones and a liberal use of highlights he achieved a velvety softness of texture and a sentimental atmosphere of dreaminess. The earliest dated work is a miniature of *Princess Helena Radziwiłł* (1784; untraced) known from copies (e.g. Warsaw, N. Mus.) and engravings to be one of the artist's most accomplished miniatures. As a rule, however, Grassi left his works unsigned; most of them remained in the collections of the sitters' families and were frequently copied or repeated by the artist himself. As a result Grassi's oeuvre can only partially be established, and information regarding individual works is often uncertain.

Grassi's style was established by the 1780s, and it remained unchanged for the rest of his working life. This style derived from that of English portraiture known through engravings. From the work of Sir Joshua Reynolds Grassi took the compositional format of women depicted in a garden setting (e.g. *Anna, Countess Krasińska*, *c.* 1795; Warsaw, N. Mus.). In a letter to Prince Michał Radziwiłł, Grassi wrote: 'in itself a portrait can bore the spectator, unless it is presented against a landscape background'. From English mezzotints he derived a soft and warm velvet-like surface, a blurred outline and a modelling dependent on tone rather than on line. From his earliest works he made use of engravings in planning portrait compositions in elaborate settings. In 1787 or 1788, for example, he painted *Prince Józef Poniatowski* (Kraków, N. Mus.; Poznań, N. Mus.) as an elegant youth, leaning against a white horse, an arrangement closely following John Raphael Smith's 1783 mezzotint after Thomas Gainsborough's portrait of the *Prince of Wales* (later George IV). Grassi made several copies of his portrait, which was also imitated by other painters.

Frequent contacts with Poles resident in Vienna, and, after 1783, the loss of clientele due to the popularity of the portrait painter Friedrich Heinrich Füger, led Grassi to consider moving from Vienna to Poland. After signing a contract with the Polish envoy in Vienna, he soon established himself as a leading portrait painter in Warsaw. About a hundred portraits of Polish sitters are attributed to Grassi, although not all of them were executed in Warsaw. His output consisted largely of half- and quarter-lengths, for which he charged 50 ducats, although full-lengths and even group compositions also figured in his work more frequently than before. He carefully selected poses and gestures, aiming for naturalness and animation in portraits both of young women and of national heroes, such as the portrait of the military leader *Tadeusz Kościuszko* (1792; Poznań, N. Mus.) symbolically wiping clean his blood-stained sword. Grassi moved in progressive, patriotic circles in Warsaw, and it was from these that his sitters generally came. His paintings, as well as his drawings, acquired a notable popularity and influenced the work of several Polish painters. During the years leading up to Kościuszko's insurrection of 1794, Grassi lost the substantial fortune he had built up in Poland. During the insurrection itself he left Warsaw for Karlsbad (now Karlovy Vary, Czech Republic) and then moved to Vienna.

Grassi's Warsaw period was the most fruitful in his career; but he was unable to re-establish himself in Vienna in the years 1795–9. Anna Biron (1761–1821), Princess of Kurland, whom he had known in Warsaw, came to his assistance, and he travelled to Sagan to paint her portrait (*c.* 1798; Warsaw, N. Mus.). In 1800, through her agency, he was appointed Professor of Fine Arts in Dresden, settling there for the rest of his life. Granted a sabbatical year in 1804, he spent the time in Gotha at the invitation of Prince Emile-Leopold-August Saxe-Gotha, for whom he executed seven large paintings of a decorative character, representing scenes from fables written by the Prince. In Gotha he also received numerous commissions for allegorical and more intimate portraits, historical scenes, and even copies of older Italian paintings. The princes of Gotha ensured Grassi long-lasting support, also enabling him to spend the years 1816–20 in Rome as Director of Studies for Saxon Artists. He achieved neither reputation nor success in Rome, however, with his emulation of classical and Neo-classical form and attempts at religious compositions and altarpieces. From 1721 until his death Grassi remained in Dresden, forgotten and in ill-health.

BIBLIOGRAPHY

SAP; Thieme–Becker

ANDRZEJ RYSZKIEWICZ

Grassi, Orazio (*b* Savona, 1 May 1583; *d* Rome, 23 July 1654). Italian priest, architect and mathematician. He was born into an established Savonese noble family but joined the Jesuit Order in Rome at the age of 17, taking his vows in 1618. As early as 1616 he was appointed professor of mathematics at the Collegio Romano, a position he held with interruptions until 1627. Although he soon earned the highest respect and engaged in discussions with Galileo Galilei on his theories about the nature of comets, he is best known for his achievements in the field of architecture. He may be considered the most important Jesuit architect of the first half of the 17th century.

Grassi seems to have come to the profession by way of architectural theory: in 1612 he was instructed by his Order to establish an academy to train Jesuit architects. This institution seems to have been short-lived, if it existed at all. From 1617 to 1624 and again from 1627 to 1628 Grassi held the office of Consiliarius Aedificiorum—building adviser and planning supervisor to the Jesuit general curia.

In 1624 Grassi worked at the Jesuit college in Florence, and in 1627 he produced plans (unexecuted) for the cathedral at Ronciglione, near Viterbo. His first major work is S Vigilio, Siena, begun for the Jesuits in 1625. It is a flat-ceilinged hall church with delicate wall treatment; its academic and understated formality seems indebted to the architecture of the late 16th century, particularly that of Francesco da Volterra and Giacomo della Porta. From October 1626 Grassi was entrusted with the planning of

S Ignazio, Rome, the largest ecclesiastical building realized *ex novo* in 17th-century Rome. The project was founded by Cardinal Ludovico Ludovisi and also involved Carlo Maderno, Paolo Maruscelli, Domenichino and Francesco Borromini, whose ideas were reflected in Grassi's final dome-model. The general conception is based on Il Gesù (*see* ROME, §V, 16), but the congregational space is divided into a distinct nave and two aisles, separated by a three-bay arcade, enriched by the insertion of a lower order of Ionic columns in the form of Serlianas. This attractive feature has often been imitated, as at the Jesuit church in Syracuse (begun in the late 17th century). It seems to have derived, however, not from Grassi but from Domenichino and is recorded in a sketched proposal (Windsor Castle, Royal Lib.). Grassi's ideas for the treatment of the exterior (drawings, Rome, Vatican, Bib. Apostolica) were unusual: he envisaged a broad, rectangular façade without pediments and with a uniform balustrade surmounting the entire building, the roofs being invisible behind it. Mistakes in the execution by the Jesuit master builder Antonio Sasso (1587–1649), however, and subsequent changes of plan (in which Giovanni Battista Soria was involved, as well as Maruscelli in 1642 and Girolamo Rainaldi in 1645) gave rise to a more conventional appearance in line with established Roman tradition. In 1651 the changed proportions necessitated a redesigned dome, for which Grassi proposed a highly original monumental solution suggestive of the work of Borromini. Although begun, it was never completed, and the crossing was later covered with a false perspective dome, painted by Andrea Pozzo in 1684–5.

Grassi devoted himself to numerous other buildings for the Jesuit Order. Between 1628 and 1631 he produced the project for S Ignazio in Ajaccio, which reveals his typical functional use of space and ability to harmonize form with purpose. Around 1629 he designed the north wing of the Collegio Romano and in 1632 produced designs for Jesuit colleges at Montepulciano (Paris, Bib. N., Hd-4a, 32), Terni and Viterbo. From 1633 he worked predominantly in Liguria, where Soprani attributed to him the completion of the interior of Savona Cathedral. About 1635–42 he planned the extension of the choir chapels at the Gesù in Genoa, including that of St Francis Xavier (Paris, Bib. N., Hd. 46, 52). He contributed to the planning and execution of the large Jesuit college founded by the Balbi family in the same city, adapting designs by Bartolomeo Bianco to the ideas of the Order while respecting the donor's desire for ostentation. Grassi's last design, in 1654, was for an imposing college building at Parma.

BIBLIOGRAPHY

R. Soprani: *Vite* (1674); enlarged, ed. C. G. Ratti (1768–9), pp. 9–11

C. Bricarelli: 'Il P. Orazio Grassi, architetto della chiesa di S Ignazio in Roma', *Civiltà Catt.*, lxxiii/2 (1922), pp. 13–25

D. Frey: 'Beiträge zur Geschichte der römischen Barockarchitektur', *Jb. Österreich. Bundesdkml.*, iii (1924), pp. 11–43

L. Montalto: 'Il problema della cupola di S Ignazio da P. Orazio Grassi e Fratel Pozzo ad oggi', *Boll. Cent. Stud. Stor. Archit.*, xi (1957), pp. 33–62

J. Vallery-Radot: *Le Recueil de plans d'édifices de la Compagnie de Jésus conservé à la Bibliothèque nationale de Paris* (Rome, 1960)

A. di Raimondo and L. Müller Profumo: *Bartolomeo Bianco e Genova: La controversa paternità dell'opera architettonica tra '500 e '600* (Genoa, 1982), pp. 81–107

L. Müller Profumo: 'Orazio Grassi e il collegio dei Gesuiti a Genova', *Studi in onore di R. Cataluccio* (Genoa, 1984), pp. 393–405

R. Bösel: *Die Baudenkmäler der römischen und der neapolitanischen Ordensprovinz* (1985), i of *Jesuitenarchitektur in Italien, 1540–1773*, 5 vols (Vienna, 1985–)

RICHARD BÖSEL

Grass-roots art. *See* ART BRUT.

Gratama, Jan (*b* Groningen, 16 Aug 1877; *d* Amsterdam, 1947). Dutch architect and writer. His most important service to Dutch architecture was his work on the councils of the main Dutch architectural associations. After studying at the Technische Hogeschool in Delft (1896–1903), he became general secretary of the Maatschappij tot Bevordering der Bouwkunst (Society for the Promotion of Architecture) and editor of the journals *Bouwkundig weekblad* and *Bouwkunst*. In 1917 as chairman, helped by Hendrik T. Wijdeveld and J. F. Staal, he reorganized the Architectura en Amicitia society into a platform for AMSTERDAM SCHOOL architects. From 1917 Gratama developed into a classicist among Amsterdam school architects, as in the country house (1918) in Bennebroek and the Incassobank (1929) at Enschede. The picturesque layout of the Transvaal district (1916–19) in Amsterdam and a single country house are exceptions. Although he was a great champion of new construction methods and the flat roof combined with traditional materials, innovative building was never the point of departure in his designs; for example in those for the garden suburb Watergraafsmeer (1922) in Amsterdam, which are mainly concrete houses. An important source of inspiration for Gratama was the balanced classicism of K. P. C. de Bazel. In his loveliest work, the plan for Amsterdam's stadium district (1922–8), he showed himself to be a careful pupil of H. P. Berlage. From 1930 his designs displayed increasing references to classical Dutch brick architecture of the 18th century, especially the competition design (1945; unexecuted) for the Stadhuis at Ede. Political activities during the German occupation brought an end to his career in 1945.

WRITINGS

'Enkele beschouwingen over de ontwikkeling der moderne bouwkunst in Nederland', *Architectura* [Amsterdam], xxii/2 (1914), pp. 86–8, 90–92

'Beschouwing over de "Nieuwe Zakelijkheid"', *Moderne bouwkunst in Nederland*, ed. H. P. Berlage (Rotterdam, 1932–5), i, pp. 37–91

BIBLIOGRAPHY

Nederland bouwt in baksteen, 1800–1940 (exh. cat., ed. D. Hannema; Rotterdam, Mus. Boymans, 1941)

M. Kuipers: *Bouwen in beton: Experimenten in de volkshuisvesting, 1900–1940* (The Hague, 1987)

JOUKE VAN DER WERF

Grate. *See under* FIREPLACE FURNISHINGS.

Grate, Eric (*b* Stockholm, 14 Aug 1896; *d* Stockholm, 3 Aug 1983). Swedish sculptor, painter and stage designer. After studying at the Akademi för de Fria Konsterna in Stockholm and travelling in Germany, Italy and Greece (1922–4), he lived in Paris until 1933. At that time his art developed in two directions, one more traditional, at times classical, the other modernist. Grate largely relinquished his modernist work in the alien cultural climate on his return to Sweden. His more traditional style was inspired by ancient Greek and Renaissance sculpture, and influenced by Aristide Maillol and Charles Despiau, among others. A series of female and male figures culminated in the *Four Seasons* (1937–44; entrance hall of the Kanslihus, Stockholm) and the powerfully simplified form of *Goddess at the Hyperborean Sea* (1949–56; in front of Gävle Stadshus), while a more complex, fanciful and narrative style led to the rich granite architecture of the *Fountain of Transformations* (1943–56; Sundbyberg, Marabou Park). By the time of the last two commissions Grate had resumed his modernist style. He was stimulated in particular by non-Western art, Kandinsky, Klee and later Surrealism. Although he never considered himself a Surrealist, many of his works are related to Surrealism, for example *Les Atlantides pleurent leurs Pâques perdues* (1932; Stockholm, Martin Olsson AB). His work metamorphoses human beings, animals, insects, fish, plants, trees, stones, jetsam and so on, combining them in ingenious and magical constellations. *Silvatica* (1958–60; Upplands Väsby, Marabou Park) and *The Columbines* (1959–60; Norrköping, Kstmus.), for example, are among those derived from vegetable forms, and the *Esox* series is derived from fishbones (e.g. *Esox Sorceta*; Linköping, County Council). The most controversial of his public monuments, *Entomological Rape* (1958; outside Karolinska Institutet, Stockholm), is a reworked version of reliefs from the early 1930s, in which studies of insects are combined with experiences from Parisian side-shows. It is mainly thanks to this modernist production that Grate became the most important Swedish sculptor of the generations following Carl Milles. Grate taught at the Akademi för de Fria Konsterna (1941–51). During his early period in Munich (1922–3) he also produced paintings and watercolours, in which Cubist and African tribal elements mingle with influences from Klee and Kandinsky (e.g. *Garden of Delights*, Norrköping, Kstmus.). Grate made stage designs (e.g. for Sartre's *Les Mouches*, Stockholm, Dramatiska Teatern, 1945), which show his interest in archaic and primitive art.

BIBLIOGRAPHY

R. von Holten, ed.: *Eric Grate* (Malmö, 1963)
Eric Grate: Sculpteur suédois (exh. cat. by K. Romare, Paris, Mus. N. A. Mod., 1963)
P. Grate and R. von Holten: *Eric Grate* (Stockholm, 1978)

PONTUS GRATE

Gratianopolis. *See* GRENOBLE.

Grattage. Technique for creating textures and patterns by simultaneously rubbing and scraping off layers of paint. □

Gratzen. *See* NOVÉ HRADY.

Grau, Enrique (*b* Cartagena, 1920). Colombian painter, sculptor, printmaker, film maker and stage designer. He studied at the Art Students League in New York from 1941 to 1943 and subsequently visited Italy, where he studied fresco and etching techniques before settling again in Colombia. Consistently devoted to the human form, he initially depicted figures with angular heads and striped tunics in a strong light, with symbolic objects such as eggs, masks or cages.

In such later paintings as *Boy with Umbrella* (1964; Washington, DC, Mus. Mod. A. Latin America) Grau's figures were transformed into plump, fleshy and voluptuous beings, richly arrayed with lace, feathers, hats and fans, like characters taken from the theatre or from popular turn-of-the-century postcards. His scenes were gradually filled with anecdotal details and numerous objects, including cupboards, easels, boxes, masks and flowers, through which he suggested emotionally charged atmospheres. Grau also produced murals, prints, stage sets, films and especially sculptures. The first of these were assemblages of antique and industrial objects, but he subsequently made cast-bronze sculptures that convey a sensuousness, mystery and nostalgia similar to that evoked by his paintings.

WRITINGS

El pequeño viaje del Barón von Humboldt (Bogotá, 1977)

BIBLIOGRAPHY

Cien años de arte colombiano (exh. cat. by E. Serrano, Bogotá, Mus. A. Mod., 1985)

EDUARDO SERRANO

Grau, Ricardo (*b* Bordeaux, France, 13 Sept 1907; *d* Lima, 4 June 1970). Peruvian painter, teacher and photographer. He studied at the Escuela Nacional de Bellas Artes, Lima, under José Sabogal from 1920 before attending the Académie Royale des Beaux-Arts, Brussels, in 1924. In 1925 he left to study under Fernand Léger, André Lhôte and Othon Friesz, among others, and he took part in various salons in Paris during the 1930s. His work at this time was influenced particularly by that of Cézanne, Matisse and Braque. In 1937 Grau returned to Peru, becoming one of the first representatives in Latin America of modern European painting, which stood in contrast with the Indigenist style then prevalent in Peru. Grau taught at the Universidad Nacional Mayor de San Marcos in Lima (1942) and was Director of the Escuela Nacional de Bellas Artes from 1945 to 1949. During this period his palette brightened, and by the 1950s he was showing considerable interest in Surrealism and in the art of such Pre-Columbian cultures as the Nazca and Chimú and particularly the Vicús (of which he had a substantial collection of artefacts). He returned to abstract art in the 1960s, using colour as an independent means of expression. In 1967, however, he took up photography (largely due to failing eyesight and adverse reactions to the chemicals in paints), and was successful notably for his portraiture.

BIBLIOGRAPHY

J. A. de Lavalle and W. Lang: *Pintura contemporánea*, Colección arte y tesoros del Perú, ii (Lima, 1976), pp. 78–85
Eduardo Moll: *Ricardo Grau, 1907–1970* (Lima, 1989)

W. IAIN MACKAY

Graubner, Gotthard (*b* Erlbach, Saxony, 13 June 1930). German painter. After studying at the Staatliche Hochschule für Bildende Künste in Berlin (1947–8) and at the Staatliche Kunstakademie in Dresden (1948–9 and 1951) under Wilhelm Rudolph (*b* 1889), he moved to Düsseldorf, where he studied at the Kunstakademie under Otto Pankok until 1959, when he exhibited for the first time with ZERO. Graubner's painting concentrated on allowing pure colour to appear in the most immaterial possible way. About 1960, the date of his first one-man exhibition, at Alfred Schmela's gallery in Düsseldorf, he produced panel paintings whose surface is built up of a differentiated nebulous colour formation. These paintings are essentially flat, but the application of colour in layers of varying degrees of transparency opens up the picture surface, producing a colour formation of indefinite depth comparable to the works of Rothko, as in *Colour Space: Pink Space I* (1.1×1.4 m, 1961; priv. col.). From 1963 Graubner experimented with 'cushion paintings'. At various points under the canvas he placed cushions of synthetic material, thus turning the painting into a three-dimensional body. In the early 1970s he began to produce 'colour-space bodies', with the objective of transcending the traditional categories of surface and frame in cushion-shaped, padded panel paintings such as *Bhutan* (2.8×1.8 m, 1976; Düsseldorf, Kstmus.). The canvas was lined underneath with synthetic cotton wool and other absorbent materials, which soaked up the paint and allowed it to spread. The structure of the painting is soft both in volume and outline, a theme Graubner continued to use in later works such as *Colour is Round* (1984–5; Lenz Schönberg priv. col., see 1987 exh. cat., p. 21).

BIBLIOGRAPHY

Gotthard Graubner: Farbräume, Farbraumkörper, Arbeiten auf Papier (exh. cat. by J. Harten and others, Düsseldorf, Städt.Ksthalle, 1977)

Gotthard Graubner: Zeichnung-Aquarell, 1946–1986 (exh. cat. by B. Growe and K. Schmidt, Bonn, Städt. Kstmus., 1986)

Gotthard Graubner: Malerei aus den Jahren 1984 bis 1986 (exh. cat. by M. Imdahl and J. Merkert, Düsseldorf, Kstsamml. Nordrhein-Westfalen, 1987)

Gotthard Graubner: Malerei auf Papier (exh. cat. by S. Salzmann, U. Lehmann and B. Growe, Bremen, Ksthalle; Brunswick, Kstver.; Esslingen, Gal. Stadt; 1989–90)

LUCIUS GRISEBACH

GRAV. *See* GROUPE DE RECHERCHE D'ART VISUEL.

Grave, Jean (*b* Le Breuil-sur-Couze, Puy-de-Dôme, 16 Oct 1854; *d* Vienne-en-Val, Loiret, 8 Dec 1939). French writer. Almost completely self-educated, he involved himself in political activity, becoming the leading anarchist writer and theoretician in France. In 1881 he attended the anarchist congress in London and launched the periodical *Bullétin des groupes anarchistes.* Two years later he moved to Geneva to collaborate with Prince Pyotr Kropotkin on the journal *La Révolté*, founded by the latter in 1879. He transferred *La Révolté* to Paris in 1885 and in 1887 changed it to *La Révolte.* During this period anarchism was widely supported by French intellectuals, especially by the Symbolist poets and writers and by the Neo-Impressionist artists. *La Révolte* acquired a wide readership among these groups, and its subscribers included such figures as Stéphane Mallarmé, Joris-Karl Huysmans, Paul Signac, Camille Pissarro and Maximilien Luce. In 1889 Pissarro produced *Turpitudes Sociales* (Berne, Bib. N.), a series of 78 drawings for his English nieces Alice and Esther Isaacson, which castigated French society and were mostly supplemented by quotations from *La Révolte.*

More than any of his fellow anarchists, Grave laid great importance on the power of art as an instrument for social change. In *La Société mourante et l'anarchie* (1892) he wrote that 'each should be able to procure those intellectual gratifications which the needs of his brain create'. *La Révolte*, which ran till 1894, had a literary supplement with regular contributions from Emile Zola and Octave Mirbeau; however, Grave's attention to the visual arts did not begin until he was prompted by the example of Emile Pouget's anarchist weekly *Père Peinard*, which was illustrated by Félix Vallotton, Luce, Lucien Pissarro and others. In 1896 he asked his painter friends to provide him with lithographs for the *Temps nouveaux*, the successor of *La Révolte*; he exercised no editorial control over their content. The contributors included Luce, Camille Pissarro, Signac, Charles Angrand, Henri Edmond Cross, Vallotton and Théophile-Alexandre Steinlen, the first two being Grave's closest supporters. The resulting lithographs were used in many ways; some appeared as frontispieces for the *Supplément littéraire*, some were available for purchase through the *Temps nouveaux*, and others were used to illustrate anarchist works published by Grave or were sold in lotteries to support various enterprises. Camille Pissarro (*see* PISSARRO, (1)), for example, produced a work entitled *The Homeless*, depicting a vagrant couple and child, for the 1895–1900 series of the *Temps nouveaux* (see Herbert, p. 476). Cross's work *The Wanderer* (see Herbert, p. 476), for the same series, reflects two characteristic anarchist themes: the depiction of social outcasts and the glorification of rural peasant life.

The *Temps nouveaux* came to an end in 1914, when Grave moved to England for the duration of World War I. Grave's political activity continued until the end of his life, invariably bringing him into trouble with the authorities, and he continued writing a steady stream of anarchist works. He was an important focus for the political aspirations of many artists who matured in the late 19th century.

WRITINGS

La Révolte (Paris, 1885–94)

La Societé mourante et l'anarchie (Paris, 1892)

Les Temps nouveaux (Paris, 1895–1914)

Quarante ans de propagande anarchiste (Paris, 1973)

BIBLIOGRAPHY

DBF

R. L. Herbert and E. W. Herbert: 'Artists and Anarchism: Unpublished Letters of Pissarro, Signac and others—I', *Burl. Mag.*, cii/692 (1960), pp. 473–82

R. E. Shikes and P. Harper: *Pissarro: His Life and Work* (New York, 1980)

R. Thomson: 'Camille Pissarro: "Turpitudes Sociales" and the Universal Exhibition of 1889', *A. Mag.*, lvi (1982), pp. 82–8

C. Lloyd, ed.: *Studies on Camille Pissarro* (London, 1986)

□

Grave, Josua de (*b* Amsterdam, 1643; *d* The Hague, 1712). Dutch draughtsman and painter. By 1648 his family was in Haarlem, where he entered the Guild of St Luke at the age of 16. He went to Paris in the mid-1660s, returning via Maastricht where he made drawings in 1669–71. Between 1672 and 1676 he was employed as an engineering officer with the army of the Dutch States-General under the Stadholder Prince William III of Orange Nassau. The drawings made during these years are of places in the southern Netherlands, and some include scenes of military activity, but never battles. De Grave settled in The Hague after 1678 and was employed again in the army in 1711.

De Grave's drawings reflect their topographical function and stylistically have little in common with earlier 17th-century Dutch landscapes. He worked quickly, drawing from life with loopy calligraphic strokes of pen and brown ink, supplemented with dabs of grey and sometimes brown wash. Most of the sheets measure *c*. 100×150 mm and are inscribed with the precise date and location; many are signed. Unsigned drawings are easily confused with those of Valentijn Klotz, who, with Constantijn Huygens (ii), also travelled with the army between 1672 and 1676. On occasion all three made drawings of the same place within a few days, for example of Thieusies, in Belgium, in late August 1675: de Grave's is in Paris (Ecole N. Sup. B.-A.; another version in Stockholm, Perman priv. col.); Klotz's is in Brussels (Mus. A. Anc.) and Huygens's in Paris (priv. col., see 1982 exh. cat., p. 121, no. 61). Some capriccio landscape drawings by de Grave are known, also usually signed and precisely dated, for example the *Landscape with a Fountain* (dated 31 Dec 1685; Paris, Ecole N. Sup. B.-A.). He also painted a few capriccio landscapes in the 1680s. De Grave's drawing style evolved little after the intense activity of the 1670s, although his later drawings are slightly freer, with sparing use of the pen and more wash.

BIBLIOGRAPHY

R. J. van Hasselt: 'Drie tekenaars van topografie van Roosendaal in de 16/17e eeuw', *Oudhdknd. Jb.*, xxv (1965), pp. 145–92

M. H. Breitbarth-Van der Stok: 'Josua de Grave, Valentinus Klotz en Barnardus Klotz', *Bull. Kon. Ned. Oudhdknd. Bond*, lxviii (1968), pp. 93–115

Met Huygen op Reis (exh. cat., ed. J. F. Heijbroek; Amsterdam, Rijksmus., 1982)

GEORGE GORDON

Gravelot [Bourguignon, Hubert-François] (*b* Paris, 26 March 1699; *d* Paris, 20 April 1773). French illustrator, engraver, painter and draughtsman.

1. LIFE AND WORK. He was born Hubert-François Bourguignon, son of a Parisian tailor. As a young man he took the name Gravelot, the surname of his godfather. Together with his elder brother, who later became the well-known geographer Jean-Baptiste Bourguignon d'Anville, Gravelot attended the Collège des Quatre Nations, Paris, but neglected his studies in favour of drawing. Under the patronage of Louis d'Aubusson, Duc de la Feuillade (1673–1725), Gravelot undertook a trip to Rome to study art, but when he reached Lyon his money ran out, and he was forced to return to Paris. Several years later Gravelot's father sent him to Santo Domingo (now the Dominican Republic) with the Chevalier de la Rochalard, Governor-General of the island. There Gravelot apparently tried to establish himself in the business of overseas trade, but an early loss of an expensive shipment of merchandise caused him to abandon the project. By *c*. 1729 Gravelot had returned penniless to Paris; all he had produced in Santo Domingo was a map of the island.

Gravelot then settled down to the serious study of art, first under Jean Restout II and then in François Boucher's studio. In 1732 or 1733 he travelled to London, having been invited by the engraver Claude Du Bosc (*fl c*. 1711–40), who was publishing an English translation (London, 1733–9) of Bernard Picart's *Cérémonies et coutumes religieuses de tous les peuples et de tous les temps* (Amsterdam, 1725–43) and needed assistance with the engraving. Gravelot's skill as an engraver and draughtsman brought him immediate success in England. He was soon in great demand as a book illustrator, also producing designs for goldsmiths; he is thought to have produced designs for furniture as well. He became friendly with a circle of English artists that included William Hogarth and Francis Hayman, and he taught at the St Martin's Lane Academy, where he helped to train a new generation of artists including Thomas Major, Charles Grignion and Thomas Gainsborough. Gravelot worked with Hayman on the designs for paintings to decorate the supper-boxes at Vauxhall Gardens, the popular pleasure gardens south of the Thames. He also produced several paintings of his own, the best known of which is *Le Lecteur* (or the *Judicious Lover*) (versions in London, Marble Hill House, see fig.; York, C.A.G.), which shows a young man reading passages from Ovid to his lady. Gravelot's importance to the development of art in England during this period cannot be overstated. He played a major role in introducing the contemporary French Rococo style into England, both through his teaching of and collaboration with English artists and through his book illustrations. He illustrated over 50 works during his 12 years in London; these include John Gay's *Fables* (1738), Samuel Richardson's *Pamela* (1742), and Thomas Hanmer's edition of Shakespeare (1743–4), on which he collaborated with Hayman.

In 1745, after the Battle of Fontenoy, Gravelot returned to Paris. English feeling against the French was running high, and he is said to have been made uncomfortable by the accusations and suspicions of some of his adopted countrymen. Gravelot's reputation as an outstanding illustrator travelled with him to Paris, and his work was immediately in demand. His best-known works from these later years include Boccaccio's *Decameron* (1757), Rousseau's *La Nouvelle Héloïse* (1761), the edition by Voltaire

Gravelot: *Le Lecteur* (or the *Judicious Lover*), oil on canvas, 311×234 mm, *c*. 1745 (London, Marble Hill House)

of Corneille's *Oeuvres* (1764), Marmontel's *Contes moraux* (1765), Ovid's *Metamorphoses* (1767–71), Luneau de Boisjermain's edition of Racine's *Oeuvres* (1768), Voltaire's own *Collection complette des oeuvres* (1768–74) and Tasso's *Gerusalemme liberata* (1771).

Gravelot's book illustrations, most of which are in a fairly small format, are characterized by an extreme precision of composition, a delicacy of line and an ability gracefully to animate his tiny figures in a variety of attitudes. His decorative sense is unerring; his scenes are often set in sumptuous Régence, Rococo or Georgian interiors, and his characterization of contemporary dress is meticulous. Critics have often differed in their preference for either Gravelot's English or French illustrations. Salomons, for example, complained of a certain stiffness and lack of feeling in the English work, while the Goncourt brothers and Portalis were more appreciative of the earlier illustrations.

2. WORKING METHODS AND TECHNIQUE. Gravelot's methods as an illustrator can be established fairly easily, thanks to the huge number of his drawings that survive. Suites of drawings for nearly all his major works are extant; over 1000 of these drawings were contained in a portfolio retained by the artist until his death and owned successively by the Marquis de Fourquevaulx, Emmanuel Bocher, Louis Roederer and Léon Olry-Roederer. In 1922 A. S. W. Rosenbach bought the portfolio and sold the contents to various American museums, collectors and libraries.

In his early sketches for an illustration, Gravelot usually concentrated on hastily sketched groups of figures, in chalk, pen and ink, or graphite, which are often unclothed. He refined the composition and the relationships between figures in further sketches, adding costumes and architectural background thereafter. Final drawings are of two types: detailed line drawings with no indications of modelling or shadows, and equally detailed wash drawings. Both types of drawing may have been sent to the engraver, one to indicate lines and the other to indicate tones. It has also been suggested that the wash drawings, more finished in appearance than the final line drawings, may have been produced after the engravings for sale or presentation to collectors. In preparing his compositions, Gravelot sketched from a set of fully articulated lay figures, each *c.* 380 mm high, made for him in England. He also collected various costumes for these models, ranging from Roman-style togas to contemporary dress.

In England, where skilled engravers were relatively few, Gravelot often engraved his own designs for book illustrations. He seems to have ceased this practice when he returned to France. Nevertheless, his intimate knowledge of the engraver's art ensured that the designs he submitted to the engravers would offer adequate guidance; this is perhaps why his work, even though engraved by a variety of artists, is of such consistently high quality.

BIBLIOGRAPHY

J.-B. Bourguignon d'Anville: 'Eloge de Monsieur Gravelot', *Le Nécrologe des hommes célèbres de France* (Paris, 1774), pp. 131–45

J. de Goncourt and E. de Goncourt: 'Gravelot', *Gaz. B.-A.*, xxiv/2 (1868), pp. 152–68

R. Portalis: *Les Dessinateurs d'illustrations au dix-huitième siècle* (Paris, 1877)

R. Portalis and H. Beraldi: *Les Graveurs du dix-huitième siècle*, 3 vols (Paris, 1880–82/*R* 1970)

V. Salomons: *Gravelot* (London, 1911)

H. Cohen: *Guide de l'amateur de livres à gravures du XVIIIe siècle* (Paris, 1912)

L. Réau: *La Gravure en France au XVIIIe siècle: La Gravure d'illustration* (Paris and Brussels, 1928)

P. Hofer: 'Preliminary Sketches for Gravelot's Corneille', *Harvard Lib. Bull.*, v (1951), pp. 197–208

O. E. Holloway: *French Rococo Book Illustration* (London, 1969)

H. Hammelmann and T. S. R. Boase: *Book Illustrators in Eighteenth-century England* (New Haven and London, 1975)

R. S. Kramer: 'Drawings by Gravelot in the Morgan Library', *Master Drgs*, xx/1 (1982), pp. 3–21

G. N. Ray: *The Art of the French Illustrated Book, 1700–1914*, i (New York, 1982), pp. 36–50

Rococo: Art and Design in Hogarth's England (exh. cat., London, V&A, 1984)

K. Rorschach: *Eighteenth-century French Book Illustration: Drawings by Fragonard and Gravelot from the Rosenbach Museum and Library* (Philadelphia, 1985)

Manners and Morals: Hogarth and British Painting, 1700–1760 (exh. cat., London, Tate, 1987–8)

KIMERLY RORSCHACH

Graver. *See* BURIN.

Graves, Michael (*b* Indianapolis, IN, 9 July 1934). American architect, teacher, painter and designer. He studied architecture at the University of Cincinnati, OH (1954–8), and Harvard University, New Haven, CT (MA 1959), and was a scholar at the American Academy in Rome (1960–62). He began a long teaching career at Princeton University, NJ, in 1962 and established a private practice in Princeton in 1964. Graves participated in a number of unexecuted projects and competition entries (1963–5) with Peter Eisenman and then built the first of several private houses of the 1960s and 1970s, the Hanselman House (1965), Fort Wayne, IN, based on a pristine white double cube with three layered façades. This was followed by the addition to the Benacerraf House (1969), Princeton, with geometric planes, coloured struts, free-form spatial effects and curves echoing elements of Le Corbusier's rationalist 'white' villas of the 1920s and 1930s. Both were included in the NEW YORK FIVE exhibition at MOMA, New York, in 1969. Colour was increasingly used in Graves's early houses, however, culminating in the Snyderman House (1972), Fort Wayne, a light, open, geometric composition whose elements were all painted different colours following the design logic and referring to the heavily wooded context.

Painting and drawing were important components of Graves's work, and he carried out several large murals in the 1970s. Painting also provided inspiration for architectural form. His approach borrowed much from Cubist art, particularly the layering and synchrony of imagery, structure and symbolism. His early work makes direct reference not only to Le Corbusier but also to such Cubist masters as Juan Gris, compounding fragments with overlays and superimposing perspective and structural grids contrasted with curves. In this historical interest in Modernism can be found the origins of Graves's later POST-MODERNISM. After the mid-1970s his work drew on a wide range of earlier sources for its imagery, including Ledoux, Boullée, Ingres, Poussin and Classical Greece and Rome, integrating representational forms and images into abstract, painterly collages with an increasingly Byzantine complexity in the multiple layering of imagery so that the architecture only gives the illusion of making direct historical references. His buildings also became increasingly colourful mosaics that reflected metaphorical associations with nature.

The Plocek House (1977), Warren, NJ, recalls an Italian palazzo but with abstracted columns and a missing keystone that reappears as the study pavilion in the garden. The Fargo-Moorhead Cultural Center (1977–8; see fig.) bridging the river between Fargo, ND, and Moorhead, MN, drew on Ledoux's project for a sluice-house over the River Loue with its semicircular arch, symbolic, slipped keystone and image of sluice. Other well-known buildings include the Portland Public Services Building (1978–82; *see* UNITED STATES OF AMERICA, fig. 11), Portland, OR, whose façade echoes the classical division of base, middle and top, with a portico as a central motif; the Humana Corporation headquarters (1983), Louisville, KY, a 27-storey steel-framed office building clad in coloured granite that has a gigantic columned and pedimented 'loggia' to the street frontage; and the addition to the Whitney Museum of American Art, New York, designed in 1985 but revised in 1988 to a more abstract scheme in response to Marcel Breuer's original building. His Disney hotels in Florida—the Swan (1988–9) and Dolphin (1988–90) at Lake Buena Vista—provided a rich canvas for a thematic approach, including giant sculptures and murals of waves and tropical vegetation.

The pictorial character of Graves's architecture is consistent with his approach to drawing. He rejected the abstract, minimal geometry of Modernism, believing it led to a sense of alienation from architecture, in favour of figurative elements thought to be derived from classical analogies of man and nature. His architecture also takes the form of a literary art in its attempt to create a new vocabulary of semiological, syntactic analogies that appeal to the collective memory. By re-establishing architecture as a mythic and symbolic representation of culture, he sought to increase its communication with the culture at large. His buildings represent these arguments in a series of provocative, sometimes puzzling and often amusing metaphors that are, above all, decorative. Graves's work, which was widely exhibited in the USA and Europe and won many awards, also included interior, industrial and furniture design (*see* UNITED STATES OF AMERICA, fig. 38); he designed showrooms for Sunar Furniture throughout the USA and also worked for Steuben Glass, Alessi and Memphis Furniture, both in Milan, and for Baldinger Architectural Lighting.

Michael Graves: Fargo-Moorhead Cultural Center, south elevation, 1977–8; pencil and prismacolor on yellow tracing paper, 314×314 mm (New York, Museum of Modern Art)

WRITINGS

'The Necessity for Drawing: Tangible Speculation', *Archit. Des.*, xlvii/6 (1977), pp. 384–94

BIBLIOGRAPHY

K. Frampton and C. Rowe: *Five Architects: Eisenman, Graves, Gwathmey, Hejduk, Meier* (New York, 1972)
M. Gandelsonas: 'On Reading Architecture: Eisenman and Graves: An Analysis', *Prog. Archit.*, liii/3 (1972), pp. 68–87
A. Colquhoun and others: *Michael Graves* (London, 1979)
K. V. Wheeler, P. Arnell and T. Bickford, eds: *Michael Graves: Buildings and Projects, 1966–1981* (New York, 1982)
Henry Hornbostel, Michael Graves: An Exhibition of Architectural Drawings, Photographs and Models (exh. cat. by C. V. Poling, Atlanta, GA, Emory U. Mus. A. & Archaeol., 1985)
K. V. Nichols, P. J. Burke and C. Hancock, eds: *Michael Graves: Buildings and Projects, 1982–1989* (New York, 1990)

MALCOLM QUANTRILL

Graves, Morris (Cole) (*b* Fox Valley, OR, 28 Aug 1910). American painter. A self-taught artist of great sensitivity, he absorbed influences from different cultures, initially seeking to capture the spirit of the American Northwest by depicting its birds, vegetation and primitive agricultural utensils using earth colours and a heavy impasto. *Moor Swan* (1933; Seattle, WA, A. Mus.) is a good example of this phase, but his work underwent a radical change in the 1930s following several trips to the Far East as a seaman from 1928 to 1931, through which he was exposed to oriental art and culture. He became fascinated by Buddhism, Daoism and Zen and began to experiment in works such as *Snake and Moon* (1938–9; New York, MOMA) with different techniques in order to translate the philosophical ideas into a pictorial language, particularly after meeting Mark Tobey and John Cage in the mid-1930s. Although he continued to use birds as symbols of spirituality and of a sense of oneness with the universe, as in *Little-known Bird of the Inner Eye* (1941; New York, MOMA), he became increasingly involved in works with the calligraphic marks and methods of all-over composition practised by Tobey. He drew ever closer to oriental art, particularly while working as an instructor from 1940 to 1942 at the Seattle Art Museum, with its exceptionally rich collection of oriental art.

Graves was awarded a Guggenheim fellowship in 1946 to study in Japan but was forbidden to go there because of the military occupation. Instead he travelled to Hawaii, where he spent a year studying the oriental art collection of the Honolulu Academy of Arts. In striking contrast to the dark mood of that period, he created works imbued with splendid sunlight and warmth. During the 1970s he produced realistic still-lifes, for example *Summer Flowers for Denise* (1978; Seattle, WA, A. Mus.). Although he afterwards turned again to more purely abstract works, this time using dynamic lines and curves to reflect the turmoil of modern life, he continued to incorporate bird-like shapes as reminders of the landscape in which his vision as an artist was first formed in his youth.

BIBLIOGRAPHY

J. T. Soby: *Contemporary Painters* (New York, 1948), pp. 40–50
K. Rethroth: 'The Visionary Painting of Morris Graves', *Persp. USA*, 10 (winter 1955), pp. 58–66
S. Rodman: *Conversations with Artists*, intro. A. Eliot (New York, 1957), pp. 8–14 [interview]
K. Kuh: *The Artist's Voice* (New York, 1962), pp. 105–17 [interview]
I. E. Rubin, ed.: *The Drawings of Morris Graves*, preface D. Daniels (Boston, 1974) [with comments by Graves]
Morris Graves: Vision of the Inner Eye (exh. cat., ed. R. Kass; Washington, DC, Phillips Col., 1983)

ALBERTO CERNUSCHI

Graves, Nancy (*b* Pittsfield, MA, 23 Dec 1940). American conceptual artist. While studying English literature at Vassar College, Poughkeepsie, NY, she received a fellowship in painting to the Yale–Norfolk Summer School. From 1961 to 1964 she studied fine art at Yale University, New Haven, CT, and in 1964 received a Fulbright–Hayes grant in painting to study in Paris. In 1966 she moved to New York, where she established a studio. Her first solo exhibition was in 1968 at the Graham Gallery, and later she became the first woman artist to have a solo retrospective at the Whitney Museum of American Art. Her work is founded on 20th-century conceptual discourses on art and draws on a wide range of sciences, including anatomy, palaeontology, anthropology, computer mapping, psychology and perception. Her curiosity for many subjects has been a consistent feature in works that include drawings, paintings, installations, sculptures and film. She is renowned for her first figurative pieces, for example *Camel VIII*, *Camel VI* and *Camel VII* (1969; all Ottawa, N.G.). These life-size, highly defined, handmade sculptures of wood, steel, burlap, polyurethane, skin, wax and oil, placed casually as if striding across the gallery floor, appear more camel-like than real camels and draw attention to perceptual problems of illusion and reality as well as to questions regarding the status and context of objects. In these and later figurative and non-figurative works (examples of which are held in the Wallraf-Richartz-Museum, Cologne, the Museum of Fine Arts, Dallas, and the Neue Galerie, Aachen), Graves has been open in her approach and exploration of the artistic process and conceptual boundaries in art. She lives and works in New York.

BIBLIOGRAPHY

Nancy Graves: A Survey, 1969–80 (exh. cat. by L. L. Cathcart, Buffalo, NY, Albright–Knox A.G., and elsewhere, 1980)
The Sculpture of Nancy Graves: A Catalogue Raisonné (New York, 1987)

□

Graves, Robert (*b* London, 7 Nov 1798; *d* London, 28 Feb 1873). English engraver. In 1812 he was apprenticed to John Romney (?1786–1863) and he first exhibited at the inaugural exhibition of the Society of British Artists, London, in 1824. Most of his book work was published before 1836, when he was elected Associate Engraver of the Royal Academy on the death of James Fittler (1758–1835). He did plates for J. Caulfield's *Portraits, Memoirs and Characters of Remarkable Persons* (London, 1819–20), Dove's *English Classics*, some portraits for J. P. Neale's *History of the Abbey Church of Westminster* (London, 1818–23), plates for such annuals as *Amulet*, *Forget-Me-Not*, *Iris*, *Literary Souvenir* and *Keepsake Français*, John Bunyan's *Pilgrim's Progress* (London, 1839), Sir Walter Scott's 'Waverley' novels (Edinburgh, 1871), John Milton's *Poetical Works* (London, 1841) and G. Burnet's *History of the Reformation* (London, 1838). He contributed eight plates to the *Art Journal* between 1850 and 1872. After 1836 he worked mainly for print publishers, including his brother Henry Graves. Most of his important engravings were exhibited regularly at the Royal Academy from 1836 until his death, commencing with *The Abbotsford Family* (1817; Edinburgh, N.P.G.), after Sir David Wilkie. *An Illicit Whisky Still in the Highlands* (1826–9; London, V&A), after Edwin Henry Landseer, first published by the Art Union of London in 1842, was considered to be his best plate. His last completed work was a portrait of *Charles Dickens* after William Powell Frith for the second volume of John Forster's *The Life of Dickens* (London, 1872–4). He left a portrait of *Lady Feversham* after Thomas Gainsborough unfinished at his death; the work was completed by James Stephenson (1808–86). His only pupil was John Richardson Jackson (1819–77).

BIBLIOGRAPHY

DNB
W. Sandby: *History of the Royal Academy* (London, 1862), p. 222
A. J. [London] (1873), p. 125
Illus. London News, lxii (1873), p. 247

BASIL HUNNISETT

Gravesande, Arent Arentsz. van 's. *See* ARENTSZ., (1).

Gravesande, Carel Nicolaas Storm van 's. *See* STORM VAN 'S-GRAVESANDE, CAREL NICOLAAS.

Gray, Basil (*b* 21 July 1904; *d* 10 July 1989). British museum curator and art historian. After taking a degree at Oxford, he spent a season in Istanbul with David Talbot-Rice at the British Academy excavations of the Great Palace of the Byzantine emperors. In 1928 he joined the staff of the Department of Printed Books at the British Museum; in 1930 he moved to the subdepartment of Oriental Prints and Drawings, then headed by LAURENCE BINYON, who encouraged his enthusiasm for the arts of Asia. Gray's involvement in the great 1931 Exhibition of Persian Art at the Royal Academy led to the publication with Binyon and J. V. S. Wilkinson of the monumental *Persian Miniature Painting*, and his relations with Binyon were strengthened by his marriage to Binyon's daughter Nicolète in 1933. He took charge of the Department of Oriental Antiquities in 1938 on the retirement of R. L. Hobson and was named Keeper in 1946, an office that he held until his retirement in 1969. During his tenure the Department's important but small holdings of Islamic and Far Eastern art were transformed into an outstanding collection of international renown. In 1966 he was elected a Fellow of the British Academy, and in 1968 he was named Acting Director and Principal Librarian of the

British Museum. After his retirement he continued work with international societies and congresses devoted to Near Eastern and Asian studies and received numerous international honours.

Gray's career was devoted to studying the history and nature of cultural relations between the Near and Far East. As a member of the governing council of the British Institute of Persian Studies, he suggested the excavation of SIRAF on the Persian Gulf, which revealed aspects of medieval trade between China and the Middle East. His major work, *Persian Painting*, delineated the development of Persian manuscript illustration and focused on the 14th and 15th centuries, when, under the rule of the Ilkhanid and Timurid dynasties, the impact of Chinese art was most forceful. In addition to writing on many aspects of Asian art, he also studied Tang and Song exports to the Middle East, the Mongols in Persia, Ming China and the expansion of the porcelain trade, and the relations of the courts of Western and Central Asia in the 14th and 15th centuries with the Ming emperors.

WRITINGS

with L. Binyon and J. V. S. Wilkinson: *Persian Miniature Painting* (Oxford, 1932)
Persian Painting from Miniatures of the XIII–XVI Centuries (London, 1947)
Treasures of Indian Miniatures in the Bikaner Palace Collection (Oxford, 1951/*R* 1955)
Early Chinese Pottery and Porcelain (London, 1953)
Japanese Screen Painting (London, 1955)
with A. Godard: *Iran: Persian Miniatures—Imperial Library* (New York, 1956)
Japanese Woodcuts (Oxford, 1957)
Buddhist Cave-Paintings at Tun-Huang (London, 1959)
Persian Painting (Geneva, 1961)
with D. Barrett: *Painting of India* (Geneva, 1963/*R* 1977)
ed.: D. Talbot-Rice: *The Illustrations to the 'World History' of Rashīd al-Dīn* (Edinburgh, 1976)
The 'World History' of Rashid al-Din: A Study of the Royal Asiatic Society Manuscript (London and Boston, 1978)
ed.: *The Arts of the Book in Central Asia* (New York, 1979)

BIBLIOGRAPHY

J. M. Rogers: 'Basil Gray', *Iran*, xvii (1979), pp. 3–9 [with bibliog. of his writings to 1977]

□

Gray, Eileen (*b* Enniscorthy, Co. Wexford, 9 Aug 1879; *d* Paris, 28 Nov 1976). Irish furniture designer and architect, active in France. In 1898 she entered the Slade School of Art, London, with additional instruction in oriental lacquer technique in D. Charles's shop in Soho. She moved to Paris in 1902, where she continued her training with the Japanese lacquer master Seizo Sugawara. Her first lacquered furniture, including decorative panels, folding screens, small tables and other large pieces, appeared in 1910 and reflected a unique stylistic pastiche of Far Eastern and French influences. At the Salon des Artistes Décorateurs in 1913 her pioneering modern furniture designs attracted the attention of Jacques Doucet. He commissioned three *pièces uniques*, two chairs and the lacquered screen Le Destin (1914). The screen, with Symbolist-inspired figures on one side and a starkly abstract design on a red-lacquered ground on the other, places Gray among the earliest 20th-century designers using geometric abstraction. She designed a theatrical interior in 1919 for the Paris milliner Suzanne Talbot, which, despite its African-inspired boat-shaped *chaise longue* and draped animal skins, revealed a greater tendency towards architectural shapes.

In 1922 Gray opened the Galerie Jean Désert in the Faubourg Saint-Honoré, where she displayed her own designs in furniture, carpets and lacquerware in addition to sculpture by Ossip Zadkine and engravings by Chana Orloff. Only the carpets attracted buyers, however, and the gallery closed in 1930. A white lacquer bedroom–boudoir, severely criticized when it was shown at the Salon des Artistes Décorateurs of 1923, was championed by J. J. P. Oud, who influenced the dedication of the entire issue of 1924 of the Dutch journal *Wendingen* to her work. She rejected the stylized revival designs of Art Deco and from 1925 began integrating contemporary materials and modern functionalism in her furniture. Tubular steel, aluminium and glass gradually replaced lacquer and rare woods as her primary materials. In 1927, encouraged by the Romanian architect Jean Badovici, she designed and built a villa for herself, 'E-1027', at Roquebrune on the Mediterranean coast. The house reflected a global conception of the habitat, emphasizing the organization of space and a sense of comfort. In 1930–31 she designed the Paris studio/apartment of Badovici and, in 1934, another villa for herself at Castellar, near Menton, where she lived until the mid-1950s. In 1937 her design for a cultural centre was shown by Le Corbusier at the Pavillon des Temps Nouveaux at the Exposition Internationale des Arts et Techniques dans la Vie Moderne in Paris. An active early member of the Union des Artistes Modernes, she returned to Paris in 1945. Shortly before her death she was working with new forms of plastic.

BIBLIOGRAPHY

Wendingen, 6 (1924) [issue dedicated to Gray]
Eileen Gray: Designer, 1879–1976 (exh. cat., London, V&A; New York, MOMA; 1979)

CHARLOTTE MOSER

Gray, William, Bishop of Ely (*b* before 1416; *d* Downham, 4 Aug 1478). Ecclesiastic, patron and collector. He was the third son of Sir Thomas Gray of Heton, Northumberland, and of Alice Neville. Educated at Balliol College, Oxford, from *c*. 1430, he had begun collecting books there by the time he became Chancellor of the University (1441–2). In 1431 his uncle William Gray, then Bishop of London, had given him a canonry of St Paul's, London, and numerous other benefices followed, all resigned on his election to Ely (see below). In 1442 Gray left Oxford to study in Cologne, *c*. 1442–4. He continued on to Italy, first to Florence, where he ordered manuscripts from Vespasiano da Bisticci; then to Padua, graduating in September 1444. By 1445 he was in Ferrara, studying with Guarino of Verona; here he took into his household the young humanist, Niccolò Perotti. He was in Rome *c*. 1446–54, as King's Proctor to the papal Curia, where he promoted canonization of St Oswald and came to know such humanists as Poggio Bracciolini, Lorenzo Valla, Pope Nicholas V and probably Biondo Flavio. Pope Nicholas nominated Gray first (1450) to the see of Lincoln, unsuccessfully, and then to Ely in June 1454. Gray then returned to England to attend to his diocese and took only an occasional part in public affairs: for example as High Treasurer of England 1469–70 and Commissioner to treat peace with the Scots, 1471–3. He was buried in Ely Cathedral and bequeathed his large library to Balliol College. The surviving books (over 180) show that he acquired manuscripts, many of them newly commissioned, in Oxford, both before and after 1442, in Cologne, Florence, Padua and Rome, and in Cambridge after his return to England. The texts are mostly theological but there are also interesting Classical and humanistic texts, some of which were copied in Oxford from the manuscripts of Humfrey, Duke of Gloucester. There is also one printed book: a Josephus text printed on parchment (Lübeck, before 1475).

BIBLIOGRAPHY

Vespasiano da Bisticci: *Vite di uomini illustri* (MS; 1480s); ed. A. Greco (Florence, 1970); Eng. trans. by W. G. Waters and E. Waters as *Renaissance Princes, Popes and Prelates: The Vespasiano Memoirs* (London, 1926/*R* New York, 1963), pp. 184–6

R. A. B. Mynors: 'William Gray and his Books', *Catalogue of the Manuscripts of Balliol College, Oxford* (Oxford, 1963), pp. xxiv–xlv [with further bibliog.]

A. C. DE LA MARE

Graz. Capital city of the region of Styria, Austria, and the country's second largest city (population *c.* 243,000). It stretches on both sides of the River Mur and is dominated by the Schlossberg, a Dolomite outcrop rising to 478 m; the centre of the Altstadt formed a crescent to the south-west of this. Graz probably takes its name from the small castle (Slav. *gradec*) erected by Alpine Slavonic settlers on the Schlossberg. The site was settled in prehistoric times. Occupation under the Romans can be demonstrated only outside the city centre. The Sporgasse, the old travellers' route from the east that crossed the Mur and joined the Roman road on the western edge of the Grazerfeld, was important at that time. When Roman rule ended, the territory of Graz was owned by the Alpine Slavs and later by the Bavarians and the Franks. The settlement was first documented under the Traungau princes in 1115 and 1128–9. By 1147 a street market was established between the Mur and the Schlossberg and *c.* 1160 the trapezoid site of the Hauptplatz was laid out. Under the Babenberg dukes of Styria (*reg* 1192–1246) the Teutonic Order settled in Graz and rebuilt the Leechkirche (1250–73). With its 105 surviving stained-glass panels (late 13th century–*c.* 1330) and its architecture influenced by the Sainte-Chapelle, Paris, the Leechkirche is one of the most important Gothic churches in Austria.

The Habsburg rule of Styria from 1276 was significant for the town's development. By the Treaty of Neuberg (1379) Graz became the residency of Duke Leopold II (*reg* 1358–86), and thereafter the seat of the Leopoldine line of the Habsburgs. From 1438 under Frederick V, later Emperor Frederick III, the Burg was built as the imperial residence and St Ägidius (cathedral from 1786) was rebuilt; an arcaded walkway linked the buildings. The cathedral is a type of hall church (*Staffelkirche*; Ger.: 'staggered church'), built probably by Hans Niesenberger from 1438 to 1462. Of its medieval furnishings the panel painting of the *Crucifixion* (1457; Graz, Diözmus.) by Conrad Laib, such remnants of frescoes as the votive image of plague (1480) and a *St Christopher* with the features of Frederick III survive. The Corpus Christi Chapel (*c.* 1440; partly destr.), probably built by a Graz stonemasons' workshop, the Bürgerspitalkirche zum Heiligen Geist (1461–3) and the Haupt- und Stadtpfarrkirche zum Heiligen Blut (1480–1519) are stylistically dependent on the cathedral. Frederick built the main living-quarters (destr. 1853–4) of the Burg; a stone double spiral staircase (1499–1500) was later incorporated under Maximilian I.

With the threat of Turkish invasion, Graz became the principal stronghold of middle Austria from 1543. The plans for the fortification of the Schlossberg and the city with bastions and curtain walls were probably by Lazarus Schwendi and executed by Domenico Allio I, among others; Allio also built the main wing (1557–65) of the Landhaus, seat of the provincial government, in the style of a northern Italian palace. In 1564, under Charles, Archduke of Austria and Duke of Styria (*reg* 1564–90), Graz again became the residency of Inner Austria. The Archduke and his wife, Maria of Bavaria, enlarged the Burg and established court there. The pro-Counter-Reformation policies of Charles and his wife led to the arrival of the Jesuit Order in Graz in 1572 and the founding of the university in 1585. The Jesuit College (from 1572) by Vinzenz de Verda was formerly linked to the cathedral by an arch. In 1607–9 the Old University (now the university library) adjoining the Jesuit College was built to a design by Pietro Valnegro (*fl* 1589; *d* 1639). The most important artist at the Inner Austrian court was PIETRO DE POMIS.

Graz, mausoleum of Ferdinand II by Pietro de Pomis, 1614–38

His main architectural work was the mausoleum of Ferdinand II (1614–38; see fig.). He also designed the Maria-Hilf-Kirche façade in 1611 and Schloss Eggenberg (*c.* 1623; rest.; now a museum) for Prince Hans Ulrich von Eggenberg. The Schloss, influenced by the Escorial, is noted for the symbolism of its architectural distribution (e.g. 365 windows, 52 windows in the ceremonial rooms) and that of the painted ceilings in the ceremonial rooms. The state armoury, or Zeughaus (1643–5), by Antonio Solar, also shows an early Baroque repertory of forms in its façade design. It contains *c.* 29,000 16th- and 17th-century artefacts.

After the defeat of the Turks the Baroque style spread, and an intensive building campaign was begun in Graz, decisively shaping its appearance: between 1660 and 1720 the finest palaces in the city were built, for example Welsersheimb Palace (1689–94) by Johann Joachim Carlone, Wildenstein Palace (*c.* 1700–05) by Andreas Stengg (*d* 1741) and Attems Palace (1705–10), possibly by Stengg. Johann Bernhard Fischer von Erlach, who was born in Graz, designed the stuccowork (1687) on the burial chapel of the mausoleum of Ferdinand II and the *St Catherine* altar, which was set up there in 1697. His influence is seen in the Meerscheinschlössl (*c.* 1706–8). The master builders Andreas Stengg, his son Johann Georg Stengg (*d* 1753), and Josef Hueber (who arrived from Vienna in 1740) worked on several churches, including the pilgrimage church of Maria Trost (1714–35; by Andreas and Johann Georg Stengg), the Barmherzigenkirche (1735–8; by Johann Georg Stengg) and the façade with twin towers (1742–4; by Josef Hueber) of the Maria-Hilf-Kirche. After the demolition of the fortifications by Emperor Joseph II (*reg* 1765–90), from 1782 the city began to expand. Such important squares as Jakominiplatz (1797) and Franzensplatz (from 1824) were laid out. After the unsuccessful siege of the Schlossberg by the French in 1809, the Schlossberg fortifications were razed; the clock-tower (1561) and the bell-tower (1588) survived. In 1839 the Schlossberg was grassed over by Freiherr von Welden, and from 1869 to 1872 the Stadtpark was laid out on the site of the glacis. Impressive Neo-classical and Biedermeier works include the Schauspielhaus (1825; by Peter von Nobile), the former Torwachhaus (1835–6; by Franz Xaver Aichinger) of the Burg and the Meran (1841–3) and Kees (1842) palaces by Georg von Hauberisser the elder.

In the late 19th century and the early 20th large-scale development of the city halted. New streets (e.g. Joanneumring), monumental churches and municipal and residential buildings were carved out of the Altstadt, for example the Gothic Revival Herz-Jesu-Kirche (1881–91) by Georg von Hauberisser the younger, the Rathaus (1888–93) by Alexander Wielemans (1843–1911) and Theodor Reuter (1837–1902), the Landesmuseum Joanneum (1890–94; now the Steiermärkisches Landesmuseum Joanneum) by August Gunolt, and the opera house (1898–9) by Ferdinand Fellner and Hermann Helmer (1849–1919). In 1908 Marcel Kammerer (*b* 1878), a pupil of Otto Wagner, built the Secessionist Hotel Wiesler with a mosaic (1905) in the dining-room by Leopold Forstner. In 1930–35 the Grazer Stadtwerke AG, designed by Rambald von Steinbüchel-Rheinwall, was the city's first high-rise building. In 1938 the suburbs were incorporated into the city and 16 (subsequently 17) municipal districts were created. The bombing of the city in 1944–5 destroyed 16% of the housing. In 1974 a law enforcing the preservation of the Altstadt was passed. In the late 20th century the Graz school brought new architectural influences to the city, evident, for example, in the work of the architectural partnership SZYSZKOWITZ-KOWALSKI.

BIBLIOGRAPHY

F. Popelka: *Die Geschichte der Stadt Graz*, 2 vols (Graz, 1929–35)

H. Ebner: *Steiermarks Burgen und Schlösser*, iii (Graz, 1967)

H. Schweigert: *Graz*, Dehio Handbuch: Die Kunstdenkmäler Österreichs (Vienna, 1979)

A. Sztatecsny, E. Schmölzer and I. Dorn: *Die Kunstdenkmäler der Stadt Graz: Die Profanbauten des IV. und V. Bezirkes*, Österreichische Kunsttopographie, xlvi (Vienna, 1984)

HORST SCHWEIGERT

Graziani, Ercole, II (*b* Bologna, 14 Aug 1688; *d* Bologna, 17 Dec 1765). Italian painter. He was the son of Ercole Graziani I (1651–1726). He studied first with Lodovico Mattioli and later with Donato Creti in the house of Conte Alessandro di Fava, where he made copies after his master and after his illustrious Bolognese predecessors, the Carracci, Guido Reni and Simone Cantarini. His earliest works, such as the *Virgin and Child with St Irene* (?1720; Brussels, Mus. A. Anc.), show the influence of Creti, but the grace of pose and warmth of colouring are Graziani's own. His first securely datable work is the *Ascension*, completed in 1728 (Cento, Pin. Civ.), for the oratory of the Purità, Bologna, in which the luminous colours show how far the Bolognese school had developed from the sombre palette of the 17th century. Graziani acquired a considerable reputation in the late 1720s and enjoyed official success at the Accademia Clementina, becoming director in 1727 and serving as principal in 1730. He made a number of large altarpieces for churches in Bologna and the surrounding area, but in them his colours lose something of their charm and freshness and his approach is somewhat pedestrian. Such works as the *Death of St Francis Regis* (6×4 m, 1732; Bologna, S Maria della Pietà) and especially the *Martyrdom of SS George and Catherine of Alexandria*, commissioned by Cardinal Tommaso Ruffo for the cathedral at Ferrara and unveiled in 1735 (*in situ*), are impressive mainly for their size. They were nonetheless held in high esteem by contemporaries, and in 1737 Pope Benedict XIV ordered a replica of the *St Peter Consecrating St Apollinaris as Bishop* (Bologna Cathedral) to be placed in the church of S Apollinaris in Rome.

It was in his smaller religious paintings and mythological works that Graziani was able to profit most from the lessons of contemporary Venetian colourists such as Sebastiano Ricci and Giovanni Battista Pittoni, and to temper Bolognese academicism with fresh colours and overtly graceful forms. However, such works as the *Diana and Endymion* and the *Rinaldo and Armida* (both *c.* 1737; Bologna, priv. col., see Roli, 1963, figs 68a–b) do not maintain the promise of the much earlier *Rape of Proserpina* and *Rape of Europa* (both *c.* 1720; Bologna, priv. col., see Roli, 1971, figs 2–3), indicating the decadence that afflicted Graziani and the whole Bolognese school in the mid-18th century.

BIBLIOGRAPHY

R. Roli: 'Ercole Graziani (1688–1765)', *A. Ant. & Mod.*, iii (1963), pp. 166–74

——: 'Nouvelles remarques sur Ercole Graziani', *Rev. A.* [Paris], xiii (1971), pp. 80–86
——: *Pittura bolognese, 1650–1800: Dal Cignani ai Gandolfi* (Bologna, 1977), pp. 119–20

□

Grazioli da Salò. *See* SALÒ, DA.

Great Coxwell Barn. Former Cistercian grange in Oxfordshire, England. The manor of Great Coxwell was given to Beaulieu Abbey, Hants, at the Abbey's foundation in 1204. The oak timbers of the barn (see fig.) have been dated by dendrochronology to *c.* 1300; this corresponds to the date proposed by Horn and Born in 1979, which is 50 years later than that suggested in 1970 (see Berger). The barn is particularly valuable for the history of vernacular architecture because virtually all the original timberwork remains in a good state of preservation.

The barn is 46.37 m long, 13.4 m wide and 14.6 m to the roof ridge. The main axis runs north to south. The portals of the end gables are modern, and in the Middle Ages the primary entrances were the gabled porches on the east and west flanks. The masonry walls and gables are constructed of Cotswold rubble reinforced by ashlar-faced buttresses.

The barn is divided internally into seven square bays by six principal aisle frames, buttressed at each bay. These main frames alternate with intermediate frames with short curved principals that spring from deep housings in the side walls and rise to arcade plate level. In addition to this combination of aisle and cruck-like framing, the main frames are connected longitudinally by a ridge-piece and trapped through-purlins (i.e. continuous through the length of the structure, as opposed to butt-purlins) as well as square-set arcade plates. All the frames are securely anchored to the masonry; the internal bracing and the integration of masonry and carpentry at Great Coxwell are particularly well designed for stability.

Great Coxwell Barn, Oxfordshire, interior, *c.* 1300

The slender principal posts rest on tall stone bases (*c.* 2 m high) and are linked transversely by tie-beams (*c.* 9 m from the ground). From these aisle posts, pairs of light-sectioned, straight braces extend diagonally in three directions, thereby adding support to the tie-beam as well as to the arcade plates. By forming triangles between the angles of the posts and the main transverse and longitudinal members, the frame is stiffened both along its length and crosswise at the tie-beam. Since the tie-beam carries the large arcade plate, this arrangement is distinguished as 'reversed assembly' in contrast to the normal (and later) method of framing the plates into the posts. The tie also supports the foot of a secondary rafter that extends to a collar in the upper section of the frame. Bent struts on each side of the tie rise to brace the secondary rafter at its mid-point, where a purlin is clasped between the inner and outer rafters. In the uppermost part of the principal frame there are also trapped purlins at the ends of the upper collar, and a king strut rises to support a yoke for the ridge-purlin.

The carpentry of the side aisles containing tie-beams and secondary rafters is similar to the central portion of the roof. Each aisle tie extends across two wall plates joined by a sole-piece and is supported by a curved brace springing from a wall post. These posts are carried on stone corbels with distinctive keeled profiles. In the intermediate bays the lower framing consists simply of the cruck-like blades set into the masonry with the lower purlins intersecting just above the mid-section. At the ends of the barn, the posts of the gable trusses rest on substantial masonry corbels.

The intermediate frames that bisect the large square bays are composed of raised principal blades set into the masonry midway down the outer wall. Each half-bay principal rises to the square-set arcade plate. Above this plate an extended sole-piece, or as Horn suggested (1965) a 'germinal form of hammer-beam construction', projects inwards and carries the secondary rafter on its inner end. As in the principal frames, the intermediate construction contains diagonal bracing and trapped purlins.

The timber framing of the Great Coxwell barn exhibits considerable skill in the integration of carpentry and masonry as well as efficiency in erecting a large-scale functional building. The unique alternation of lofty aisled principals and cruck-like blades not only creates a spacious interior but also reduces the number of long timbers required. The barn has been restored twice: in 1868 four of the tie-beams were reinforced, and between 1960 and 1962 the National Trust repaired the entire structure.

BIBLIOGRAPHY

W. Horn and E. Born: *The Barns of the Abbey of Beaulieu at its Granges of Great Coxwell and Beaulieu St Leonards* (Berkeley, 1965)
R. Berger, ed.: *Scientific Methods in Medieval Archaeology* (Berkeley, 1970)
J. T. Smith: 'Early Development of Timber Buildings: The Passing Brace and Reversed Assembly', *Archaeol. J.*, cxxxi (1974), pp. 238–63
W. Horn and E. Born: *The Plan of St Gall*, ii (Berkeley, 1979)
J. M. Fletcher and M. C. Tapper: 'Medieval Artefacts and Structures Dated by Dendrochronology', *Med. Archaeol.*, xviii (1984), pp. 112–32

LYNN T. COURTENAY

Great Gallery, Barrier Canyon, Utah, prehistoric pictographic panel

Great Gallery, Barrier Canyon. Prehistoric rock art site in North America, in the steep-walled sandstone canyon country of south-eastern Utah. The Great Gallery is the principal site in the canyon and features one of the finest painted pictograph panels in North America. It is dominated by dozens of large anthropomorphic figures (some nearly 2 m), best representative and definitive of the Barrier Canyon Style as described by Schaafsma (1971 and 1980). Anthropomorphs and accompanying zoomorphic images are painted on prepared red sandstone surfaces on the canyon walls with dark red pigments using both the fingers and spatter-painting techniques (see fig.). The figures are characterized by large, square-shouldered torsos, many with inverted bucket-shaped heads and 'crowns' of white dots. Arms and legs are rudimentary or non-existent. Torsos feature fine detail in painting and incising, including horizontal and vertical bands of colour, fine line and striping (sometimes white). Heads sometimes have large, round eyes, often giving them a skull-like appearance and the overall figures a ghostly quality. Small birds and mammals often occur on or near the figures, especially at the shoulders, suggesting to some that the groups represent shamans with tutelaries. Other sites featuring figures of this style are in a relatively circumscribed area along the Green and Colorado rivers in eastern Utah (Castleton, 1978–9). Figures and motifs show interesting parallels with those at Archaic period sites (*c.* 6000 BC–*c.* AD 500) in the Pecos River region of Texas, a considerable distance away. Based on these parallels, and the lack of specific resemblances to local Utah Fremont culture (*c.* AD 500–*c.* 1200) rock art, the Barrier Canyon and related art is suggested to be of Archaic date as well, perhaps as early as 5500 BC, but at least as early as *c.* 500 BC–AD 500.

BIBLIOGRAPHY

P. Schaafsma: *The Rock Art of Utah: A Study from the Donald Scott Collection, Peabody Museum, Harvard University*, Pap. Peabody Mus. Archaeol. & Ethnol., lxv (Cambridge, MA, 1971)

K. Castleton: *Petroglyphs and Pictographs of Utah*, 2 vols (Salt Lake City, 1978–9)

P. Schaafsma: *Indian Rock Art of the Southwest* (Albuquerque, 1980)

——: 'Rock Art', *Hb. N. Amer. Ind.*, xi (1986), pp. 215–26

CATHERINE S. FOWLER

Great Plains painting. Term applied to Hungarian late 19th- and 20th-century painting associated with the Great Plains, a large expanse of land in the Carpathian Basin, mainly in Hungary. The sparsely populated area contains numerous small farming communities loosely scattered around urban centres. Up to the end of World War II these communities probably represented the poorest stratum of Hungarian society; the unfavourable climate with its frequent droughts made their life especially difficult. The landscape and ethnic population of the area appeared occasionally in the work of certain Hungarian painters in the 19th century, but it was not until the Austrian painter August von Pettenkofen regularly visited the area that the depiction of the landscape and life style of the Great Plains became more widespread. From 1851 he returned annually to paint near Szolnok, bringing with him other Austrian, German and Hungarian painters from Paris (*see* SZOLNOK COLONY). The depiction of the Great Plains gradually became a romanticized image representing Hungary as a whole.

Apart from Szolnok, the most significant artistic centre in the area was Hódmezővásárhely, where artists created an artistic community under the leadership of JÁNOS TORNYAI (the museum there is named after him). Their association was free from institutional constraints, and they were united by their ideas and approach. They collected and inspired others to collect folk artefacts, set up scholarships, founded art and literary societies (1910), published the magazine *Jövendő* ('The Future'; 1910–12) and built a cultural centre. Tornyai, Gyula Rudnay (1878–1957) and Béla Endre (1870–1928) were the most outstanding representatives of this community. Their work displays a characteristic naturalism, especially in the depiction of social detail. Folk art had no effect on their painting style, which was rather influenced by the peasant genres of Mihály von Munkácsy, to which they added the expression of nationalist sentiments. In Tornyai's work the romanticized image of Hungary assumed symbolic power (e.g. *Woeful Hungarian Fate*, *c.* 1910; Budapest, N.G.). Rudnay's work, which employs dramatic chiaroscuro, evokes the atmosphere of Hungarian history, while Endre's paintings are generally more peaceful in tone with brighter colours and a lyrical atmosphere. Hódmezővásárhely remained one of the most important cultural centres of the Great Plains between the Wars. The career of Menyhért Tóth (1904–80) can be linked with its art life from the end of the 1930s, even though his work is visionary and surrealist.

After World War II a number of artists decided to establish themselves in Hódmezővásárhely or in the southern region of the Great Plains, including György Kohán (1910–1966), István D. Kurucz (*b* 1914), Ferenc Szalay (*b* 1931) and József Németh (*b* 1928). Their work, with its striving for monumentality and decorative realism, represents a well-defined trend in 20th-century Hungarian art. Great Plains painting can also be associated with groups of artists in Szeged and Debrecen, where, in the absence of established artists' colonies, the painters generally relied upon municipal scholarships or individuals in organizing study-trips abroad. Notable among the painters who started their careers there were István Bosznay (1868–1944), Sándor Nyilasy (1873–1934), Lajos Károlyi (1877–1927), József Szöri (1878–1914) and László Holló (1887–1976). Their work generally developed towards a nostalgic evocation of the past and a detailed depiction of everyday provincial life. The two solitary painters of life on the Great Plains were József Koszta and István Nagy. Koszta worked alone on an isolated farm near Szentes. His style is individual and passionate but still continues Munkácsy's heritage. Nagy spent a short but intensive period on the Great Plains during the 1920s; his work there idiosyncratically combined Expressionism and Constructivism. Another artistic centre in the area, the Kecskemét colony, was at the turn of the century more responsive to modernist tendencies and can be related to the Great Plains only geographically rather than stylistically.

BIBLIOGRAPHY

P. Bánszky: 'Látomások az Alföldről' [Visions of the Great Plains], *Művészet* [Art], xix/12 (1978), pp. 4–7

G. Rideg: 'Kinek a szemlélete az alföldi szemlélet?' [Whose perspective is the Great Plains perspective?], *Művészet* [Art], xix/12 (1978), pp. 2–4

G. Theisler: 'Támpontok és kételyek: Az alföldi festészet klasszikusairól' [The classic figures of Great Plains painting: basic facts and unanswered questions], *Művészet* [Art], xix/12 (1978), pp. 7–10

M. Egri and N. Aradi: 'Az Alföld képzőművészeti centrumai' [Art centres of the Great Plains], *Magyar Művészet 1890–1919* [Hungarian art 1890–1919], ed. L. Németh (Budapest, 1981), pp. 228–50

P. Kovács: 'Az alföldi festészet' [Painting of the Great Plains], *Magyar Művészet 1919–1945* [Hungarian art 1919–1945], ed. S. Kontha (Budapest, 1985), pp. 282–97

MÁRIA SZOBOR-BERNÁTH

Great Style. *See* GRAND MANNER.

Great Wall of China. Wall stretching across northern China from Hebei Province in the north-east through Shanxi, Shaanxi and Ningxia provinces to Gansu Province in the west. Running through inhospitable mountains and deserts, with numerous offshoots and parallel structures, it is one of the most spectacular feats of engineering in the history of the world. Although it was built primarily as a defence against the Central Asian nomads, it also provided a relatively efficient thoroughfare for the movement of troops, horses and supplies across difficult terrain. According to the traditional Chinese view, the wall also created a spiritual and physical barrier between the 'superior' and sedentary culture of China and the 'inferior' culture of its nomadic neighbours.

Defensive walls, such as that measuring 7 km at Zhengzhou, Henan, were a feature of Chinese cities from at least the Shang period (*c.* 1600–*c.* 1050 BC). Such building skills were extended to much grander projects; construction of the Great Wall may have been started in the 7th century BC, but its true origins lie in the walls erected by some states as protection against each other after the collapse of central power exercised by the Zhou dynasty (*c.* 1050–256 BC) during the period of the Warring States (403–221 BC). In particular, the powerful northern states of Yan, Zhao and Qin sought protection both from each other and from the Xiongnu nomads; walls provided more or less effective barriers against the horses on which the nomads relied for conquest. When the independent kingdoms were unified in 221 BC under Qin Shi Huangdi, the first emperor of China, a general, Meng Tian (*d* 209 BC), was appointed to organize an extensive building programme. Tens of thousands of peasants and political prisoners were commandeered from throughout the empire and set to work for ten years to establish a single, continuous structure. This probably ran across the Liaodong Peninsula (modern Liaoning Province) in the east, further north than the surviving Great Wall, to Gansu in the west. The structure followed the route dictated by the existing walls, as it would continue to do throughout its history. According to tradition, those who died during its construction were interred within the structure. Only small portions of the wall dating to this period remain, for example in Lintao County, Gansu.

The wall was further extended to modern Xinjiang Province and reinforced during the succeeding Han period (206 BC–AD 220). It continued to be restored and maintained under the Northern Wei (AD 386–534), Northern Qi (550–77), Sui (581–618) and Jin (1115–1234) dynasties. However, it was ultimately unsuccessful as protection against the Mongol invaders who ruled China as the Yuan dynasty (1279–1368). Following the restoration of an indigenous dynasty, the Ming (1368–1644), its first emperor, Hongwu (Zhu Yuanzhang; *reg* 1368–99), ordered a marshal, Xu Da (1329–83), to initiate a 100-year programme of extensive restoration and repair. During this time the wall reached its final length, from the Tianxia diyiguan ('First pass in the world') near Shanhaiguan, in Hebei, to Jiayuguan ('Jade Gate') in the Qilian Mountains, Gansu. This Ming construction was larger, more solid and more sophisticated than any of the earlier work; this section has been partially repaired and remains in the best condition.

From the earliest times, because of transport problems, it was necessary to use local building materials, and so construction methods differ from one area to another. Tamped earth (*hangtu*), stone, timber and tiles were used in pre-Ming construction, and rubble faced with stone on the vertical walls and paved along the top with a triple layer of bricks to form a thoroughfare, during the Ming. Dimensions also vary according to the terrain. The average height is 7.8 m. Pitched walls create an average base width of 6.6 m and an average width of 5.8 m on the top. The latter permitted horsemen to ride five abreast or soldiers to march ten abreast in wartime. At other times, commercial vehicles were able to travel relatively easily. Access was achieved through internal gateways built at intervals on the inner, or Chinese, side. The outer crenellated battlements were constructed 2 m high above the roadway. Drainage was provided by gutters and downspouts. Square watch-towers, both solid and hollow and originally constructed independently of the wall, rose at intervals of 140 m. They served as sentry-posts and living-quarters as well as a means of communication through a warning system of smoke and fire signals.

Gates in the wall gave access to the great trade routes and oases of Central Asia that connected China with the West. It is not known exactly how many openings have existed, as the number and names frequently changed. They ranged from simple openings to richly decorated superstructures with double, tiled roofs, such as the 15th-century Yanmenguan. Ornamentation was concentrated in the areas around such gates. Lokapala, the Buddhist Guardian Kings of the Four Quarters, were frequently portrayed in reliefs at strategic points and passes. More elaborate compositions were focused at the major gate constructions. They resembled those on the Yun tai ('Cloud terrace'), a 14th-century marble gate complex at Juyongguan, a structure that is not integral to the wall. It was originally the base of a tower spanning the road. The opening is vaulted with semi-hexagonal flat planes adorned with inscriptions in Chinese, Sanskrit, Uyghur, Tibetan and Tangut, and reliefs of the Lokapala. Other reliefs cover the interior of the passageway. Another gate, probably constructed about 1345, near Nankou, in Hebei, is similar in form. It contains some of the few extant examples of Yuan-period Tantric Buddhist sculpture with inscriptions in Chinese, Manchurian, Mongolian, Arabic and Jurchen. Other inscriptions include a calligraphic piece of 1472 by the scholar Xiao Xian, as well as those written at intervals recording the dates of completion of various sections of the wall and the names of workmen.

BIBLIOGRAPHY

R. Silverberg: *The Great Wall of China* (Philadelphia, 1965)
J. Gernet: *Le Monde chinois* (Paris, 1972)
Liu Dunzhen: *Zhongguo gudai jianzhu shi* [History of ancient Chinese architecture] (Beijing, 1980), pp. 58–63, 301–9
Luo Zhewen and others: *The Great Wall* (Maidenhead, 1981)
A. Waldron: *The Great Wall of China: From History to Myth* (New York and Melbourne, 1990)

MARY S. LAWTON

Great Zimbabwe. Complex of dry-stone walls among the hills on the south-eastern edge of the plateau *c.* 250 km south of Harare in Zimbabwe. It was built and occupied between the 11th and 15th centuries AD as the capital of a state of the Bantu-speaking peoples now known as the SHONA, for whom *zimbabwe* means 'ruler's court'. It is by far the largest of *c.* 200 similar stone buildings between the Zambezi and Limpopo rivers and is also probably the largest pre-Colonial construction in Sub-Saharan Africa, comprising one of the earliest, most powerful and longest-surviving indigenous states to develop in the African interior.

1. Discovery and excavation. 2. History. 3. Architecture. 4. Sculpture and other artefacts.

1. DISCOVERY AND EXCAVATION. The earliest surviving written description of Great Zimbabwe appears in João de Barros's account of the Portuguese conquests of south-east Africa, *Da Asia*, published in 1552 in Lisbon. This description, derived from reports of Swahili traders on the coast, reveals that Great Zimbabwe was believed to be a former palace of the Mutapa dynasty, which at the time ruled a state further north in the Zambezi Valley and its immediate hinterland. Although the Mutapa king no longer lived there, his kin and courtiers were said to do so. Portuguese relations with the Mutapa state were sustained over centuries, but no Portuguese traveller was ever allowed to visit Great Zimbabwe, although, during the 16th century, a few stayed in the stone-walled *zimbabwes* of lesser rulers and described these.

From the start, speculation was widespread that the buildings were not African but were associated with the biblical gold and wealth of Ophir, Phoenicia, King Solomon and the Queen of Sheba. Rumours of the great ruined city of the interior persisted in Europe, and, as white settlement spread northwards during the 19th century, expeditions were planned to visit the site.

Adam Render and Carl Mauch were the first outsiders reluctantly allowed by the local chief to pay brief visits to the enclosures between 1868 and 1871. They found Great Zimbabwe abandoned and overgrown, with parts of it used as a cattle pen by nearby villagers, themselves comparatively recent immigrants to the area with no knowledge of the city's history. The region's population movements and resultant internecine strife of the 18th and 19th centuries, along with the establishment of new local ruling dynasties as the earlier states declined and fragmented, ensured that despite the broad ethnic and cultural continuity linking Great Zimbabwe to the Shona people, no oral accounts of its history are recoverable.

With the occupation of the territory by British colonists in 1890, Great Zimbabwe became the subject of intense speculation and propaganda. Its size and majesty suggested that much gold might be found, and its supposed foreign origins provided a precedent and justification for colonization. In 1891, J. Theodore Bent, an antiquarian who had travelled in the Near East, was sponsored to investigate the ruins. On the evidence of a few dubious and generalized parallels, he pronounced it 'ancient' and 'Semitic'. The first official curator, Richard Hall, employed specifically as a publicist for its ancient origins, had no experience or understanding of archaeology. Expressly forbidden to excavate, he nevertheless indulged in such extensive 'clearance work' in and around the main walls that a wealth of archaeological material was destroyed without record.

In 1905 the first systematic archaeological excavations were conducted by David Randall-MacIver, a student of Flinders Petrie. Although MacIver found little datable material, which in those days meant foreign imported ceramics in securely stratified deposits, he was still able to show, with 'moral certainty' if not with 'absolute proof', that Great Zimbabwe was built by an indigenous African people within the last few centuries. His conclusions were rejected by Hall and by almost all the colonists. In 1929 Gertrude Caton-Thompson, another of Petrie's students, was invited to investigate the ruins and settle the controversy. She chose to excavate completely a minor enclosure, whose fine coursed walls were believed by the proponents of the theory of ancient and exotic origins to be characteristic of the work of the earliest foreign builders. By stripping the site and analysing completely all her finds she was able to distinguish two groups of ceramics: one preceding the building of the walls and the other associated with the occupation of the enclosure. She also demonstrated that all the ceramics and metalwork were so similar to traditional African artefacts that there could be no doubt of their African origins. In excavations through the deepest deposits at the site she recovered a series of glass beads, the only foreign imports found in the ruins in any quantity. Comparisons with similar beads made in India suggested a foundation date late in the 1st millennium AD; the beads are, however, so simple that it is difficult to establish with any precision either their origin or the dates of their manufacture.

In 1958 Keith Robinson and Roger Summers excavated a limited area of deep, undisturbed deposits within the main enclosure on the hill. Trenches were also laid across the Great Enclosure, the largest, and latest, important building on the site, where vestiges of occupation had escaped the 'clearance' of 50 years before. The successive stratified occupation and building levels enabled typological sequences of pottery and imported glass beads to be established, which could be correlated with developments in building techniques and architectural style. Most importantly, even though the necessary samples were few and the results lacked precision, radiocarbon analyses at last confirmed that the site was built and occupied in the 2nd millennium AD. Subsequent excavations, limited to small areas in danger of erosion and damage, have produced a consistent series of radiocarbon dates that confirm the sequence of settlement.

2. HISTORY. The earliest settlements at Great Zimbabwe probably date from the first centuries AD, although these have not been located. The first known permanent settlement was established on the hill around the 11th century, while the state that had its royal capital and palaces at Great Zimbabwe reached maturity during the 13th century. During the 14th century settlement expanded and building techniques and design were refined, leading to the construction of the latest and finest stone walls in the first half of the 15th century. From then on Great Zimbabwe declined.

During the 9th and 10th centuries AD, Botswana began to be settled by Bantu-speaking peoples from the north, and this led to a marked increase in cattle-keeping and to the emergence of hilltop towns with dependent villages and homesteads. During the 12th century, on the Shashi and Limpopo rivers to the east, the introduction of foreign trade, involving the exchange of ivory, gold and probably hides for glass beads and presumably cloth, gave rise to a ruling class living in considerable luxury on hilltops, defended by rough stone walls. Their wealth may be deduced from gold ornaments recovered from burials at Mapungubwe. Great Zimbabwe is best understood as part of the same widespread process, and in the succeeding centuries it achieved far greater centralized economic and political control than any other part of the Zimbabwean plateau. Despite this, claims about the extent of Great Zimbabwe's influence have been exaggerated, for while it was the first and largest capital of a south-east African state, it was not alone. There were at least seven important and independent capitals, spaced regularly *c.* 150 km apart around the edge of the plateau. It is probable that the cultural hegemony of Great Zimbabwe was strong, for the ruling class of other Shona states of the time sought to imitate its architecture, ceramics and lifestyle. Nevertheless, there is no evidence to support the popular view of the city as the capital of an empire that stretched from the Kalahari Desert to the Indian Ocean with subservient colonies settled and exploited by it, although other states may, intermittently, have been tributaries.

The city is estimated to have had a population in excess of 10,000, of whom only perhaps 200 or 300 lived in the stone enclosures. Given the light soils of the area, this large and permanent population cannot have depended solely on traditional extensive agriculture. Studies of the agriculture of Manekweni, a *zimbabwe* in Mozambique, have revealed a system of cattle management that provided the court with a meat diet. Studies of the bone food debris at Great Zimbabwe suggests that the economy and the political systems were based on the control of what became the 'royal cattle herds'. Foreign trade contributed to the economy but, judging by the rarity of imports, was subsidiary.

Great Zimbabwe's decline has been attributed to environmental degradation resulting from the size and permanency of the population. This is not entirely satisfactory, since the state managed to thrive for over two centuries. As the decline of Great Zimbabwe coincided with the rise of two other Shona states—Mutapa in the north and Khami in the west—and with the decline of the East African trading cities, it may be that the delicate balance of the new state systems were such that crisis in any one part of the system could have affected the entire system and led to Great Zimbabwe's irreversible decline.

3. ARCHITECTURE. The site may be divided into the Hill Ruin, set on a narrow ridge of granite to the north, and a series of structures, including the Elliptical Building, found on a low granite shelf on the opposite side of the

1. Great Zimbabwe, interior of the Elliptical Building, 11th–15th centuries; view from the top of the Outer Wall, looking towards the Hill Ruin (visible in the background)

valley (see fig. 1). Stone walls formed a system of enclosures and courtyards between and around groups of huts, which had thatched roofs supported by wooden posts and thick, low clay walls with a smooth, moulded and decorated finish, much of which was once painted. Interior furnishings—hearths, seats, pot-stands and sleeping platforms—were of the same finely moulded, decorated and painted clay.

As the stone walls were built neither to support roofs nor to serve a defensive function, and their role in giving shelter and privacy was hardly commensurate with their size, it seems likely that they were built primarily to display the prestige of the rulers and to demonstrate the power and authority of the state through its ability to raise and control a large labour force and develop awesome skills in architecture and masonry. Following Great Zimbabwe's example, stone walls became a symbol of ruling groups and were used across the whole plateau to surround the ruler, his kin and court.

The walls are built of blocks collected from the exposed granite slopes of the surrounding hills where the rock exfoliates naturally in parallel-sided slabs (*c.* 100–200 mm thick) that are easily cracked into manageable sizes for carrying and laying and which lend themselves to coursing without mortar. In the earliest walls the courses were short, undulating and irregular, often incorporating boulders *in situ*, and the blocks were ill-matched and not dressed. Later blocks were carefully matched and closely fitted, and their faces knapped to produce horizontal courses of an astonishing regularity. There were no foundations, but each course was set back from that beneath it to give a slight inward slope to the wall faces, and the cores were filled with loosely piled slabs. The faces were not bonded either together or to the core, nor were adjoining walls bonded together. Drains were laid through the walls. The finest and latest walls were more than 11 m high and 5.5 m thick.

A series of distinctive architectural features can be associated with the developing masonry techniques. At first doorways had square sides, while later they were rounded. Inside the later doorways were low, semicircular buttresses. Often both buttresses had a single vertical groove facing each other across the doorway. Small, solid turrets were built along the tops of many walls. Low, circular platforms of stone, once covered in clay, formed shrines or altars in many courtyards. Other platforms were built in a series of steps in the angles of enclosure walls to serve as seats or stands for the display of objects. Upright posts of granite and dolerite (and doubtless carved posts of soapstone and wood, although few of stone and none of wood survive) were set along the tops of walls, on the turrets and platforms and in the grooves of the doorway buttresses. Steps leading through doorways were built within the thicknesses of the walls in an idiosyncratic system of triple curves of progressively decreasing radius. The stone walls have little decoration. Blocks were laid in a long chevron pattern near the top of the largest wall of the Elliptical Building. Short lengths of herringbone and dentelle patterns and inlaid lines of darker ironstone blocks survive elsewhere. Later *zimbabwes* in the south-west of the plateau, the palaces of the successor state known as Khami, show a profusion of such designs.

4. SCULPTURE AND OTHER ARTEFACTS. Although an impressive range of artefacts has been recovered, almost all objects from Great Zimbabwe were found by the early investigators, whose lack of archaeological expertise obscured both context and association. Finds include tools used to smelt and work iron, copper and gold; instruments used to draw the two latter metals into fine wire jewellery and ornaments; copper ceremonial weapons and bracelets; a great hoard of iron hoes and blanks, found in a small stone-walled enclosure in the valley and forming part of the ruler's tribute payment; copper and gold beads; gold sheets used to cover wooden carvings; large carved stone platters; numerous small stone figurines; and discs cut from potsherds, which are generally interpreted as spindle-whorls and hence as evidence of a cotton-spinning and cotton-weaving industry. The scale and organization of the various forms of technology, the degree of specialization and the extent of royal patronage remain unknown.

BIBLIOGRAPHY

J. T. Bent: *The Ruined Cities of Mashonaland* (London, 1893)
R. N. Hall: *Great Zimbabwe* (London, 1905)
D. Randall-MacIver: *Mediaeval Rhodesia* (London, 1906)
G. Caton-Thompson: *The Zimbabwe Culture* (Oxford, 1931, rev. London, 2/1971)
K. R. Robinson and R. Summers: 'Zimbabwe Excavations, 1958', *Occas. Pap.: N. Mus. S. Rhodesia*, n.s. 2, xxiii/1 (1961) [whole issue]
P. S. Garlake: 'The Value of Imported Ceramics in the Dating and Interpretation of the Rhodesian Iron Age', *J. Afr. Hist.*, ix/1 (1968), pp. 1–33
——: *Great Zimbabwe* (London, 1973)
G. Barker: 'Economic Models for the Manekweni *zimbabwe*', *Azania*, xxiii (1975), pp. 71–100
P. S. Garlake: 'Pastoralism and *zimbabwe*', *J. Afr. Hist.*, xix (1978), pp. 479–93
——: *Great Zimbabwe Described and Explained* (Harare, 1982)
——: 'Prehistory and Ideology in Zimbabwe', *Africa*, lii/1 (1982), pp. 1–19
T. Huffman: 'Archaeology and Ethnohistory of the African Iron Age', *Annu. Rev. Anthropol.*, xi (1982), pp. 133–50

P. S. GARLAKE

Greaves, Walter (*b* London, 4 July 1846; *d* London, 28 Nov 1930). English painter and etcher. His father was a Chelsea boat-builder who had been J. M. W. Turner's boatman. Greaves and one of his brothers, Henry Greaves (1844–1904), met Whistler in 1863, introducing him to the delights of the Thames, becoming his studio assistants, pupils and close friends for over 20 years. Such early works as *Hammersmith Bridge on Boat-race Day* (*c.* 1862; London, Tate) and *Old Battersea Bridge* (*c.* 1863; priv. col., see 1984 sale cat., no. 2) show Greaves as a master of primitive art, but his later nocturnes, drawings and etchings demonstrate his absorption of Whistler's teachings. Much of his work also provides a fascinating record of 19th-century Chelsea (e.g. *Duke Street, Old Chelsea* etching, ?1860–73; London, BM). During the late 1870s Whistler began to gather a more sophisticated group of friends, including Walter Sickert and Mortimer Menpes. Excluded from this circle, Greaves suffered years of neglect, misfortune and poverty before his discovery by William Marchant, proprietor of the Goupil Galleries, who exhibited Greaves's work in his London Gallery in 1911. Greaves's new-found glory was shortlived, however: three weeks after the exhibition opened, Whistler's self-appointed biographers, Joseph and Elizabeth Pennell, sullied his reputation by claiming that he had plagiarized Whistler's work. Despite the admiration of a few fellow painters Greaves again fell into obscurity and spent his last eight years as a Poor Brother of the Charterhouse.

BIBLIOGRAPHY

E. R. Pennell and J. Pennell: *The Life of James McNeill Whistler*, 2 vols (Philadelphia and London, 1908, rev. 6/1920), vol. i, *passim*

E. R Pennell and J. Pennell, eds: *The Whistler Journal* (Philadelphia, 1921), pp. 114–45

R. R. Tatlock: 'Walter Greaves', *Burl. Mag.*, lviii (1931), pp. 261–2

Walter Greaves, 1846–1930 (exh. cat. by T. Pocock, London, Leighton House A.G. & Mus., 1967)

J. Ingamells: 'Greaves and Whistler', *Apollo*, lxxxix (1969), pp. 224–5

T. Pocock: *Chelsea Reach: The Brutal Friendship of Whistler and Walter Greaves* (London, 1970)

Walter Greaves & the Goupil Gallery (sale cat., London, Parkin Gal., 1984)

MICHAEL PARKIN

Grebber, Pieter (Fransz.) de (*b* Haarlem, *c.* 1600; *d* Haarlem, 1652–4). Dutch painter. Together with Salomon de Bray, he was a pioneer among the Haarlem Classicists—a group of artists who have often been unjustly overshadowed by other history painters, notably Rembrandt and his school, who are regarded as more indigenously Dutch. De Grebber was the son of the Haarlem painter and art dealer Frans Pietersz. de Grebber (1573–1643), who, among his other activities, served as Rubens's agent with the English Ambassador to The Hague, Sir Dudley Carleton. Pieter studied with his father, who painted militia company portraits and history subjects. The young de Grebber travelled to Antwerp with his father in 1618; there he may have met Rubens, whose art was a factor in the formation of his early style. Pieter also studied with the local Haarlem artist Hendrick Goltzius, whose history paintings probably had a formative effect on several of the Haarlem Classicists. De Grebber's earliest dated work is a *Portrait of a Woman* (1621; Delft, Klaeuwshofje). A *Caritas* (Houston, TX, Mus. F.A.) and a *Mother and Child* (Haarlem, Frans Halsmus.) both date from 1622, and the following year he executed a life-sized *Musical Company* (Washington, DC, priv. col.), a genre scene in the tradition of the Utrecht Caravaggisti. However, most of his paintings are religious scenes, and by 1625 these were executed in his own version of international Baroque Classicism (e.g. *Adoration of the Magi*, 1632; Turin, Gal. Sabauda). He also produced numerous portraits of Roman Catholic priests, nuns or beguins. He joined the Haarlem Guild of St Luke in 1632, and two years later he bought a house in the Beguinhof; throughout his life he remained closely allied to the Catholic community in the Netherlands, producing altarpieces for local recusant churches as well as for Catholic churches in Flanders and elsewhere (e.g. the *Annunciation*, 1633; Hannover, Amir Palczad priv. col., see 1980–81 exh. cat., p. 195). Despite his faith, he was elected dean of the Haarlem Guild of St Luke in 1642, was praised by the authors Samuel Ampzing (1628), Philips Angel (1642) and Petrus Schrevelius (1648), and received the official patronage of the Haarlem city fathers, Stadholder Frederick Henry (for whom he produced paintings for Honselaarsdijk Palace (destr.) in 1638) and the latter's widow, Amalia von Solms (who commissioned decorations for the Oranjezaal in the Huis ten Bosch, The Hague, 1648–50). De Grebber published his theory of art in 11 rules, printed on a single broadsheet in 1649. He was also active as an amateur poet and composer.

BIBLIOGRAPHY

P. Dirkse: 'Pieter de Grebber: Haarlems schilder tussen begijnen, kloppen en pastoors', *Jb. Haarlem* (1978), pp. 109–27

R. Hazelegger: *Pieter Fransz. de Grebber, schilder tot Haarlem* (diss., Rijksuniv. Utrecht, 1979)

Gods, Saints and Heroes: Dutch Painting in the Age of Rembrandt (exh. cat. by A. Blankert, Washington, DC, N.G.A.; Detroit, MI, Inst. A.; Amsterdam, Rijksmus.; 1980–81), pp. 192–5

PETER C. SUTTON

Gréber, Jacques (*b* Paris, 10 Sept 1882; *d* Paris, 5 June 1962). French architect and urban planner. He trained at the studio of Gaston Redon (1853–1921) in the Ecole des Beaux-Arts in Paris and obtained his diploma in architecture in 1908. He travelled in 1910 to the USA and to Canada where he designed several gardens for private residential properties including White Marsh Hall at Chestnut Hill, PA. He worked on the Fairmount Parkway and the Rodin Museum in Philadelphia (with Paul Cret). On his return he executed designs for a number of American cemeteries, and in 1920 he published *L'Architecture aux Etats-Unis*, in which he emphasized the influence of French ideas while at the same time advocating that French architects involved in reconstruction work adopt in their turn the American practice of using standardized units.

Gréber was a prizewinner in the competition of 1919 to submit designs for the planned expansion of Paris, with his suggestion for a continuous green belt following the line of the ancient city wall. In 1921 he began to teach at the Institut d'Urbanisme of the University of Paris. Although he designed a number of large houses, he was chiefly involved in designing urban planning schemes for several major French cities including Rouen, the Lille conurbation of Roubaix and Tourcoing and, above all, Marseille, where he developed plans for rebuilding the city centre while protecting the surrounding natural landscapes. Most of these schemes were implemented. For the Exposition Coloniale Internationale of 1931 in Paris, he executed plans for the reconstruction of George Washington's house and garden at Mount Vernon. Also in the

1930s he designed the garden of the Casa de Serralves at Oporto. In 1937 Gréber was chief architect for the Exposition Internationale des Arts et Techniques dans la Vie Moderne in Paris and then consultant architect for the World's Fair in New York in 1939. After World War II he took charge of the reconstruction work in Rouen and in a number of sectors of the outer ring of Paris, although the final period of his career was dominated by work on the planning and development of Ottawa, for which he executed the layout of 1951 (*see* OTTAWA, §1). In both cases Gréber maintained close links between the overall composition and the texture given by the layout of the parks and green spaces.

WRITINGS

L'Architecture aux Etats-Unis (Paris, 1920)

Jardins modernes (Paris, 1938)

BIBLIOGRAPHY

A. Lortie: *Jacques Gréber* (thesis, U. Paris XII, 1989)

JEAN-LOUIS COHEN

Greca, della. Italian family of architects. Vincenzo della Greca (*b* Palermo; *d* Rome, before 1663) was living in Rome by 1615. He was appointed architect at the Castel Sant'Angelo and from 1631 to 1644 was surveyor of works at the papal establishments of Castel Sant'Angelo, Civitavecchia and Castelfranco. Under Urban VIII he collaborated with Francesco Paparelli on the church of S Caio (1631–7; destr. 1885), a Barberini foundation built on the site of an Early Christian church in the Via Pia. In 1647 his project for rebuilding S Giovanni in Laterano was rejected in favour of a design by Francesco Borromini. Between 1654 and 1660 Vincenzo worked at SS Domenico e Sisto, where he designed a grand staircase in two curved flights.

Vincenzo's son, Felice della Greca (*b* Rome, *c.* 1626; *d* Rome, 1677), wrote a treatise on architecture (MS. in Stockholm) that emphasized the role of the orders, entrances, staircases and adjacent gardens. In 1649 he killed a man and was exiled from Rome. He returned under a papal pardon in 1656 and rose to become the house architect of Alexander VII. By 1663 he had completed the restructuring of the Palazzo Chigi in Piazza Colonna and had drafted a project for the Palazzo Chigi-Odescalchi (not executed), which was subsequently built (1664–6) by Gianlorenzo Bernini. In 1661 he was called in (as 'l'architetto più celebre della corte') to restore the roof of the Palazzo Venezia, and in 1662 he subscribed to the demolition of the Arco di Portogallo (early 2nd century AD) beside the Palazzo Fiano on the Via del Corso. In 1665 he is recorded in the service of the papal authorities and was also the architect in charge of maintaining the Acqua Felice water supply system. He submitted a project for the façade of S Giovanni in Laterano, which was not executed (Rome, Vatican, Bib. Apostolica, MS. Chigi P VII 9, pl. 1). He was elected a member of the Accademia di S Luca in 1676.

BIBLIOGRAPHY

A. Bertolotti: *Alcuni artisti siciliani a Roma nei secoli XVI e XVII* (Palermo, 1879), pp. 28–33

G. Gorrini: 'Lorenzo Bernini e le arti di Roma seicentesca nel guidizio dei diplomatici contemporanei', *Atti del III congresso nazionale di studi romani: Bologna, 1935*, ii, pp. 307–320

R. Lefevre: 'Schede su due architetti siciliani a Roma nel '600: I della Greca', *Stud. Merid.*, iv (1971), pp. 387–405

G. Curcio: 'La *Breve Relatione* inedita di Felice Della Greca a la trattatistica funzionale fra il cinquecento e il seicento', *Ric. Stor. A.*, viii (1978/9), pp. 99–118

JOSEPH CONNORS

Greche, Domenico dalle (*fl* Venice, 1543–58). Italian painter, wood-engraver and publisher. No paintings by him are known. In August 1546, on his return from a pilgrimage to the Holy Land, he requested from the Venetian Senate a licence to publish a series of drawings executed during his journey. This privilege being granted, the work was published under the title *Particularis et vera descriptio plateae sancti sepulcri . . . diligentia Dominici Dalle Greche Venet. Pict. descripta MDXLI . . .* (the date is clearly incorrect). He later provided illustrations for the *Pellegrinaggio di Ulrich von Wilkanaus* (Prague, 1547). He also provided the botanical illustrations for the codices by the naturalist Pietro Antonio Michiel (Venice, Bib. N. Marciana, MSS Marc. It. II. 26-30/4860–4). Apart from some maps, some of which are lost, his most notable undertaking is the 1549 edition of Titian's 12-block wood-engraving of the *Submersion of Pharaoh's Army in the Red Sea.* On the Pharaoh's scroll ornament is the inscription *La crudel persecutione del ostinato Re, contro il popolo tanto da Dio / amato, Con la sommersione di esso Pharaone, goloso dil inocente / sangue. Disegnata per mano dil grande, et immortal Titiano. In venetia p domeneco dalle greche depentore Venitiano. / M. DXLIX.* An attempt has been made to prove the existence of an earlier printing edited by Bernardino Benalius following a licence of 1515, but the evidence is inconclusive. Only with difficulty could Domenico, an artist of modest skill, have engraved a work of such quality; the inscription indicates only the publisher, and the date does not refer to Titian's involvement, so it is possible that Domenico could have acquired the blocks from Benalius's workshop. Two other engravings by Domenico dalle Greche are known, again after works by Titian, the *Lamentation* and *Christ Shown to the People.*

BIBLIOGRAPHY

L. Olivato: 'La Submersione di Pharaone', *Tiziano e Venezia: Convegno internazionale di studi: Venezia, 1976*, pp. 529–37 [incl. bibliog.]

M. A. Chiari: *Incisioni da Tiziano: Catalogo del fondo grafico a stampa del Museo Correr* (Venice, 1982), pp. 37–9

L. Olivato: 'La *Sommersione del Faraone nel Mar Rosso*', *Tiziano* (exh. cat., ed. S. Biadene; Venice, Doge's Pal., 1990), pp. 164–7

F. Benvenuti: 'Tiziano nella lente delle stampe', *Eidos*, vi (1992), pp. 8, 14, no. 26

T. Pignatti: 'Riflessione sulla *Sommersione del Faraone* di Tiziano', *Per Giuseppe Mazzariol* (Rome, 1992), pp. 195–7

K. Oberhuber: 'Tiziano: Le Passage de la Mer Rouge', *Le Siècle de Titien* (exh. cat., Paris, Grand Pal., 1993), pp. 448, 474, no. 132

FELICIANO BENVENUTI

Grechetto [Greco], **il (i).** *See* CESATI, ALESSANDRO.

Grechetto, il (ii). *See* CASTIGLIONE, (1).

Grechin, Olisey. *See* OLISEY GRECHIN.

Greco, Alberto (*b* Buenos Aires, 14 Jan 1915; *d* Barcelona, Spain, 14 Oct 1965). Argentine painter, sculptor, performance artist, conceptual artist, poet and illustrator. After studying in Buenos Aires at the Escuela Nacional de Bellas Artes and with Cecilia Marcovich and Tomás Maldonado, he quickly established a reputation for his scandalous views, attracting extreme disapproval and equally strong support. After delivering a lecture at the Juan Cristóbal bookshop, Buenos Aires, entitled 'Alberto Greco y los pájaros' he was briefly imprisoned for his 'Communism and subversive acts'. On his release in the same year he travelled to Paris on a French government grant, selling drawings and watercolours in the cafés and studying painting with Fernand Léger and printmaking with Johnny Friedlaender. Between 1956 and 1958 he lived in São Paulo, where he became aware of *Art informel*; he painted in this style in the late 1950s and early 1960s (Glusberg, pp. 284–5).

As early as 1959, when he had returned from São Paulo to Buenos Aires, Greco had expressed his corrosive vision of society through the form of his work. In his shows he exhibited tree trunks and rags for cleaning window gratings or floors. He moved again to Paris in 1961 and in March 1962 inaugurated an art form that he called 'Living Art', exhibiting white mice in a glass box with a black background. He explained that: 'Living Art seeks out the object, but once the object is found it leaves it in its place, it does not transform it, does not improve on it, does not take it into an art gallery' (quoted in Glusberg, p. 286). His sculptural installations and live events, like those of Yves Klein, whom he admired, contained elements that could be labelled retrospectively as conceptual art and performance art. He discovered his characters in the street, drawing chalk circles around them and adding his signature; he published recipes for Informalist cuisine in the supplement to the Buenos Aires newspaper *La Nación*; and in the centre of Buenos Aires he displayed posters announcing 'Greco, qué grande sos' ('Greco, how great you are!'). Greco turned against painting on the grounds that it had lost the eternity to which he aspired, claiming that the medium had completed its cycle with Klein's blue monochrome paintings. He committed suicide with barbiturates in a room bursting with sanitary appliances. On his left hand he wrote 'Fin' ('the end'). As death approached, he noted down his final sensations in scrawled handwriting.

BIBLIOGRAPHY

H. Safons: 'Del pañal a la cruz', *Periscopio*, 50 (1970), pp. 56–8

Alberto Greco a cinco años de su muerte (exh. cat. by L. F. Noé, Buenos Aires, Gal. Carmen Waugh, 1970)

J. Glusberg: *Del Pop-art a la Nueva Imagen* (Buenos Aires, 1985), pp. 283–8

HORACIO SAFONS

Greco, El [Theotokopoulos, Domenikos [Dominico; Dominikos; Menegos]] (*b* Candia [now Herakleion], Crete, *c.* 1541; *d* Toledo, 7 April 1614). Greek painter, designer and engraver, active in Italy and Spain. One of the most original and interesting painters of 16th-century Europe, he transformed the Byzantine style of his early paintings into another, wholly Western manner. He was active in his native Crete, in Venice and Rome, and, during the second half of his life, in Toledo. He was renowned in his lifetime for his originality and extravagance and provides one of the most curious examples of the oscillations of taste in the evaluation of a painter, and of the changes of interpretation to which an artist's work can be submitted.

1. Life and work. 2. Workshop organization. 3. Character and personality. 4. Critical reception and posthumous reputation.

1. LIFE AND WORK.

(i) Early work in Crete and Venice, before late 1570. (ii) Rome, late 1570–1577. (iii) Toledo, 1577–1614.

(i) Early work in Crete and Venice, before late 1570. El Greco appears to have belonged to a Catholic Greek family of officials who worked for the Venetian colonial service; his father was a tax-collector, and an elder brother combined this activity with that of trader and privateer. It is not known with whom El Greco trained, although Ioannes Gripiotes (*fl* 1516–69) has been suggested; by 1563, however, El Greco was a master painter. His presence in Crete is documented until December 1566, when Georgios Klontzas (*fl* 1540–1608) and another painter valued a painting by him that was to be sold in a lottery. He was in Venice by August 1568, when he gave a series of cartographic drawings to Manolis Dassypris (of Cyprus). He remained there until late 1570, perhaps studying and working in Titian's studio or perhaps only visiting it.

It is difficult to determine which among all the Madonnas attributed to El Greco belong to this period, and still less easy to establish which were painted in Candia and which in Venice. Probable Cretan works are the small tempera panels of *St Luke Painting the Virgin* (*c.* 1567; Athens, Benaki Mus.) and the signed *Dormition of the Virgin* (*c.* 1567; Syros, church of the Koimesis). The technique, iconography and style of these panels are Post-Byzantine; but the tendency to break up symmetry and frontality, the interest in foreshortening, movement and space, the corporeality of the figures despite the linear style, the richness of colour and the isolated but precise borrowings from Western art through Italian prints are all new. This deliberate use of Western motifs becomes more frequent in such works as the *Adoration of the Magi* (Athens, Benaki Mus.) and the so-called Modena Triptych (*c.* 1569; Modena, Gal. & Mus. Estense), which has on its verso a *View of Mt Sinai* after an engraving (1569) by Giovanni Battista Fontana. Despite the apparent hesitancy of his approach to Western stylistic sources, El Greco introduced an extreme use of colour, with Titianesque orange tones, and of light—clearly evident in the religious landscape—which combine to produce an effect of ghostly unity. There is a different feeling in other works of the 1560s, for instance the *Last Supper* (Bologna, Pin. N.), the *Flight into Egypt* (Basle, Hirsch col., see Wethey, fig. 2), the *Stigmatization of St Francis* (Naples, Capodimonte), the *Annunciation* (Madrid, Prado) and the *Adoration of the Shepherds* (Kettering, priv. col., see Wethey, 1962, fig. 7); these show his desire to master the depiction of the natural and organic movement of the human body and its place in space, and his tendency to employ a more naturalistic lighting, which culminated in the nocturnal scene of the *Adoration.*

The discovery of the signed Syros icon and the date proposed for the Modena Triptych have further confused the chronology of El Greco's early work and an understanding of the process—apparently very swift and late—of his conversion into a fundamentally Western painter.

If, as has been claimed, his *Christ Driving the Money-changers from the Temple* (tempera; Washington, DC, N.G.A.) and *Christ Healing the Blind Man* (mixed technique; Dresden, Gemäldegal. Alte Meister) were executed during his Venetian visit—as is implied by the multiple short brushstrokes, the definition of volume through light rather than shade, the one-point perspective (still incorrect) and the Venetian colouring—they must have been painted just before his move to Rome.

(ii) Rome, late 1570–1577. El Greco reached Rome at the end of 1570, having visited Verona, Parma and Florence on the way, with an introduction—perhaps through Titian—from the Croatian miniaturist Giulio Clovio to Cardinal Alessandro Farnese, who gave him lodging in his palace in Rome. On 18 September 1572 El Greco was admitted to the Accademia di S Luca as a painter, not as a miniaturist as has been conjectured; by the end of the year he had opened a workshop in which he was assisted by the Sienese Lattanzio Bonastri da Lucignano (*c.* 1550–*c.* 1590). Information on this period is limited, but there is evidence of enmity between El Greco and Pirro Ligorio and probably Giorgio Vasari, among other painters, and of his criticizing Michelangelo's *Last Judgement* in the Sistine Chapel, which probably caused his later departure for Spain. On the other hand, his stay in Rome and his friendships in the Farnese circle with Clovio and Fulvio Orsini provided the artist with a particular cultural and intellectual milieu and aroused his interest in humanist and philosophical questions, of which he was later proud. It was in this context that El Greco formed his artistic creed as a colourist in the Venetian tradition, critical of the Vasarian authorities Michelangelo and Raphael for their limitations as colourists, their excessive *disegno*, their rejection of the direct imitation of nature and their reverence for the Antique. El Greco preferred the dynamism of Correggio and the elegance of Parmigianino, and he considered the colour and light of the Venetians as the only possible means of imitating nature, thereby reinforcing the beauty of reality through art.

El Greco's second *Christ Driving the Money-changers from the Temple* (*c.* 1570; Minneapolis, MN, Inst. A.; see fig. 1), the two new variations of *Christ Healing the Blind Man* (New York, priv. col.; Parma, G.N.) and an *Annunciation* (Florence, Pitti) probably belong to his Roman period, if only because of the portrait in the first representing Giulio Clovio, together with Titian, Michelangelo and, perhaps, El Greco himself. His work here also included some portraits—he was introduced by Clovio as a 'rare portraitist'—and such landscapes as the version of the *View of Mt Sinai* (late 1570; Herakleion, Art Institute,

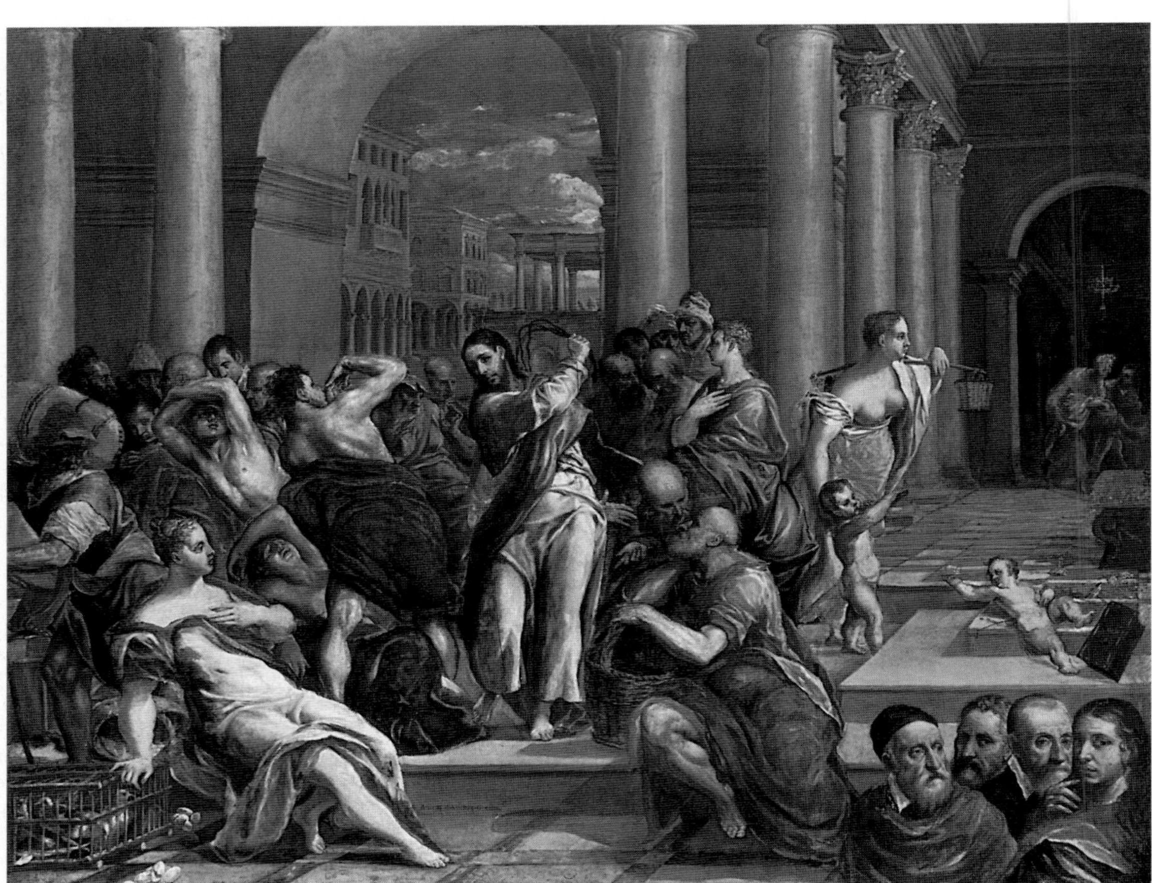

1. El Greco: *Christ Driving the Money-changers from the Temple*, oil on canvas, *c.* 1570 (Minneapolis, MN, Institute of Art)

see 1989 exh. cat., no. 11), probably painted for Fulvio Orsini, and an *ekphrasis* of the *Boy Lighting a Candle* (*'The Informer'*, Naples, Capodimonte)—a radical luminist and colourist realization of a lost picture by Antiphilus, described by Pliny. Of the portraits, the *Self-portrait* that amazed the Roman painters and the small paintings on copper of the Orsini collection are lost, but outstanding are those of his friends *Giulio Clovio* (Naples, Capodimonte) and *Vincenzo Anastagi* (*c.* 1575; New York, Frick). Already they clearly show the characteristics of dense impasto and great vivacity achieved through his sense of colour and movement that were to make El Greco a renowned portraitist in Spain.

(iii) Toledo, 1577–1614. Possibly because of his lack of public commissions in Rome, or perhaps attracted by the work being done on the decoration of the Escorial monastery and the possibility of royal patronage, El Greco left Italy in 1577, and after a short stay in Madrid he was in Toledo by 2 July of that year.

(a) Religious paintings. (b) Portraits, mythological and landscape paintings. (c) Sculptural and architectural designs.

(a) Religious paintings.

Public commissions. Thanks to his friendship with the Spanish ecclesiastic Diego de Castilla, who frequented the Farnese circle in Toledo, El Greco received his first institutional commissions, the canvas of *El Espolio* (*Disrobing of Christ*, 1577–9; Toledo Cathedral, Sacristy) and three retables (1577–9) for the monastery of S Domingo el Antiguo. The first—the composition of which resulted in his first clash with local clients—shows Venetian colouring combined with Roman monumentality, as well as the artist's flexibility in using colour to define form, volume and space. In the S Domingo el Antiguo retables, the *Adoration of the Shepherds* (Santander, Col. Emilio Botín Sanz; see 1989 exh. cat., p. 121, fig. 55) and the *Resurrection* (*in situ*), the importance of light, both artificial and natural, is accentuated through colour and through El Greco's ability to handle complex and dynamic compositions in which his debt to the print progressively diminished. The principal retable, representing the *Assumption of the Virgin* (Chicago, IL, A. Inst.) and the *Trinity* (Madrid, Prado), shows his tendency to combine the legacies of Titian and Michelangelo in an original way.

By this time El Greco had completed one commission for Philip II, the *Glory of Philip II* (or *Allegory of the Holy League*, *c.* 1577; Madrid, Escorial; modello on panel, London, N.G.), and was to embark on a second, the *Martyrdom of St Maurice* (1580–83; Madrid, Escorial). The latter is strongly dependent on contemporary Roman painting, with the martyrdom scene placed in the middle distance. The work did not please Philip and the Hieronymite congregation, however, and it was removed (though it remained in the King's collection). At this point, in his forties and with a son born in 1578, the artist decided to settle in Toledo and dedicate himself to a largely local clientele. In the 1580s he tended to give his paintings more clearly sculptural characteristics, closer to Spanish taste, using the portrayal of the mundane to create greater immediacy, and exaggerating features in the representation of divine and supernatural elements. An outstanding example of this is his magnificent *Burial of the Count of Orgaz* (1586–8; Toledo, S Tomé; see fig. 2). The scene of the miracle, SS Stephen and Augustine assisting at the burial of the 14th-century nobleman Gonzalo Ruiz de Toledo, Count of Orgaz, is crowned by a fantastic *Gloria*, with a frieze-like group of naturalistic portraits of contemporary Toledans below.

At the end of the century El Greco began receiving important commissions again, such as those from the Colegio de Doña María de Aragón in Madrid (1596–1600), the chapel of S José in Toledo (1597–9), the Colegio de S Bernardino, Toledo (1603), and the Hospital de la Caridad at Illescas (1603–5). The style of these works, although executed in the same period, varies greatly. The tendency towards a spectral treatment of lighting, and its effect on human forms within vertiginous compositions where mass and space merge, is found particularly in the canvases for the retable at the Colegio de Doña María de Aragón: the *Annunciation* and *Baptism* (Madrid, Prado), the *Adoration of the Shepherds* (Bucharest, N. Mus. A.), and perhaps also the *Crucifixion*, *Resurrection* and *Pentecost* (Madrid, Prado). In these he achieved an extraordinary sense of the miraculous, possibly deriving from the mystical thinking of the preacher Alfonso de Orozco (1500–91) or perhaps from El Greco's personal vision of the immanence of the divine. In the works for the hospital at Illescas, the immediacy of the *Virgin of Charity* (*in situ*) and the visual control of the tondi are particularly impressive.

These many directions and interests, together with a development towards a freer, sketchy style, reappear in his last works: the retables (1607–14) for the Ovalle Chapel of S Vicente Mártir, Toledo, representing the *Immaculate Conception* (Toledo, Mus. Santa Cruz) and the *Visitation* (Washington, DC, Dumbarton Oaks); the unfinished retables (1608–14) for the Hospital Tavera, Toledo, with scenes of the *Baptism* (*in situ*); the *Vision of St John* (New York, Met.); and, finally, the *Adoration of the Shepherds* (1612–14; Madrid, Prado; see fig. 3), intended by the artist for his own funerary monument in S Domingo el Antiguo. These works have been interpreted as late and extreme witnesses to El Greco's mystic and spontaneous expressionism; but they may alternatively be the result of his deliberate manipulation of form, using colour and movement to convey the effects of light, mass and space. Characteristics that are supposedly visionary, which are often accentuated in the nocturnal subjects, are perhaps only visual conventions.

Private commissions. From the beginning of his activity in Toledo, El Greco also specialized in religious paintings, sold from his workshop to private clients. His first paintings of single saints date from his early years there, when his search for beauty is evident: for instance the *St Sebastian* (*c.* 1577–8; Palencia Cathedral) and the *Mary Magdalene* (Budapest, Mus. F.A.). This devotional genre was one in which he specialized until his death, producing an enormous number of originals and workshop copies, gradually accentuating the superficial emotional expressions and the freedom of his brushwork. Outstanding among his half-length saints are *St Veronica* (tempera, *c.* 1577–8; Madrid, priv. col., see 1989 exh. cat., p. 229, fig. 109) and *St Lawrence* (*c.* 1578–80; Monforte de Lemos,

2. El Greco: *Burial of the Count of Orgaz*, oil on canvas, 4.6×3.6 m, 1586–8 (Toledo, S Tomé)

3. El Greco: *Adoration of the Shepherds*, oil on canvas, 3.19×1.8 m, 1612–14 (Madrid, Museo del Prado)

Colegio Cardinal). Figures become more sculptural in works of the 1580s, for example the *St Francis* (Omaha, NE, Joslyn A. Mus.), *Mary Magdalene in Penitence* (1585–90; Sitges, Mus. Cau Ferrat) and *St Dominic* (Toledo Cathedral). In the 1590s and early years of the 17th century, the canvases of the *Repentance of St Peter* (Toledo, Hosp. Tavera), *St Jerome as Cardinal* (1600–10; two versions: New York, Frick; New York, Met.) and the final series of *Apostles* (Toledo Cathedral and Toledo, Casa & Mus. El Greco) show a greater fluency.

Also for private customers were various versions of religious narrative scenes, for example *Christ Taking Leave of his Mother* (Toledo, Mus. Santa Cruz), the *Agony in the Garden* (1590–95; Toledo, OH, Mus. A.), *Christ Carrying the Cross* (New York, Brooklyn Mus.), *St Francis and Brother Leo* (*c.* 1600–05; Ottawa, N.G.) and the scenes of the *Holy Family* (1580–95; Toledo, Mus. Santa Cruz and Hosp. Tavera). Also very successful, although less devotional in character, were his full-length saints—portrayed singly, as in *St Peter* and *St Ildefonsus* (both *c.* 1610–14; Madrid, Escorial), or in pairs, as in *SS Andrew and Francis* (*c.* 1590–95; Madrid, Prado)—and his *Crucifixion with Two Donors* (*c.* 1580; Paris, Louvre) and *Crucifixion* (Cleveland, OH, Mus. A.).

For further illustration *see* CHRISTIANITY, fig. 5.

(b) Portraits, mythological and landscape paintings. El Greco was unanimously acclaimed by his contemporaries as a portraitist. A large number of his portraits survive, including a supposed *Self-portrait* (*c.* 1590; New York, Met.) and the portrait of his son, *Jorge Manuel Theotokopoulos* (*c.* 1600; Seville, Mus. B.A.). Most are of members of his immediate circle, from the sculptor *Pompeo Leoni* (*c.* 1577; untraced) to such friends and liberal professionals as the physician *Rodrigo de la Fuente* (*c.* 1585; Madrid, Prado), the scholar *Antonio de Covarrubias* (*c.* 1600; Paris, Louvre), the historian *Francisco de Pisa* (*c.* 1600; Fort Worth, TX, Kimbell A. Mus.), the preacher and poet *Fray Hortensio de Paravicino* (*c.* 1610; Boston, MA, Mus. F.A.), and the lawyer *Jerónimo de Ceballos* (*c.* 1610, Madrid, Prado). There is another group of unidentified Castilian gentlemen, such as the *Man with his Hand on his Breast* (1577–9) and the *Old Man* (*c.* 1580; both Madrid, Prado), and other titled noblemen. Portraits of more eminent figures such as *Cardinal Fernando Niño de Guevara* (*c.* 1600; New York, Met.; see fig. 4) are rare; the portrait

4. El Greco: *Cardinal Fernando Niño de Guevara*, oil on canvas, 1.71×1.08 m, *c.* 1600 (New York, Metropolitan Museum of Art)

5. El Greco: *View of Toledo*, oil on canvas, 1.21×1.08 m, *c.* 1610 (New York, Metropolitan Museum of Art)

of a *Woman with a Fur Wrap* (Glasgow, Pollok House), depicting a supposed princess or noblewoman, has been mistakenly attributed to El Greco.

All El Greco's portraits, austere and on a neutral ground except for the Titianesque, colouristic and naturalistic portrait of *Cardinal Niño de Guevara*, show his ability to render psychological and physical traits. These are conveyed through the impression of vitality and dynamism, in action or repose, of the sitter, who is thereby brought to life for the viewer. In contrast to the portraiture of the court painters of the time of Philip II, El Greco brought a new spirit to a genre not often practised in Spain and provided Spanish painting with an example of spontaneity, from which Velázquez was to learn.

El Greco cultivated other genres more rarely. Three versions of his *Allegory*, a fuller version of his previous *'Informers'*, belong to his Spanish period (the last, *c.* 1585; Edinburgh, N.G.). Only one other mythological painting is known, a version (*c.* 1610; Washington, DC, N.G.A.) of the Classical sculpture group, the *Laokoon* (Rome, Vatican, Mus. Pio-Clementino), which he would have seen in Rome, in which the compositional change from the sculptured group is of central interest. His two landscapes, *View of Toledo* (*c.* 1610; New York, Met.; see fig. 5) and *View and Plan of Toledo* (Toledo, Casa & Mus. El Greco), are also late works of *c.* 1610. In these El Greco is preoccupied with the means of representing what is perceived as well as an emblematic sense of the urban landscape and a zenithal projection of the city, a combination that was advanced in the representation of urban topography. It is possible that in Toledo and Madrid these works influenced interest in still-life and in landscape, genres that had, almost exclusively, been orientated towards a naturalistic type of formal structure.

(c) Sculptural and architectural designs. While El Greco's basic activity was as a painter, he also designed sculptures and architectural decorations. The monochrome sculptures of saints and Virtues for the S Domingo el Antiguo retable, and the later high altar in the Hospital Tavera, Toledo, were executed to his drawings and were in contrast to the Spanish polychrome tradition. Closer to this tradition is the polychrome wood group of the *Virgin Bestowing the Chasuble on St Ildefonsus* (1585–7) from the retable in the sacristy of Toledo Cathedral; the two other figures of *Pandora* and *Epimetheus* (both Madrid, Prado) have also been attributed to him. All these show the inevitable contradictions resulting from the application of El Greco's aesthetic approach to sculpture.

Of greater importance, though not directly influential, was El Greco's work as a designer of retables in an Italianate style. He introduced a type of retable in contrast to Spanish examples, based on models combining Palladian ideas with motifs derived from Michelangelo and Jacopo Vignola, in which the painted canvas is the focus of the composition, and the framework is only a complementary subordinate. The three retables (1577–9) in S Domingo el Antiguo exemplify this, while those in the S José Chapel (1597–8), the high altar (1603–7) in the hospital at Illescas and the side altars (1608) in the Hospital Tavera have a more complex composition, and that of the Ovalle Chapel in S Vicente Mártir (Toledo, Mus. Santa Cruz) makes richer use of the orders.

Although in the 19th century building designs were incorrectly attributed to El Greco, it is possible that his architectural ideas influenced the work of Nicolás de Vergara the younger and Juan Bautista de Monegro. His most important innovation in this area, however, is in the decorative compositions at Illescas and the Ovalle Chapel. There he produced a form of *Gesamtkunstwerk*, which combined the painted canvases and *quadri riportati* on the walls and vaults, the architecture of the brilliant gilded and painted niches, the monochrome and polychrome sculptures, and the decoration, in unpolished gold and limewash, of the backgrounds of the architectural framework, in which light becomes another element of the pictorial illusion.

2. WORKSHOP ORGANIZATION. El Greco's extensive production, particularly in Toledo, implies the existence of a large workshop, for which, however, there is little factual evidence. The Italian painter Francesco Prevoste (*c.* 1528–1607) worked with El Greco throughout his life, but this assistant's work cannot be identified, just as the work of Luis Tristán de Escamilla, El Greco's most important pupil, is only distinguishable from his master's once he had become independent. The engraver Diego de Astór was also a pupil, but his collaboration is only evident in the prints of the last period. From the 1590s El Greco's son, JORGE MANUEL THEOTOCOPOULOS, became an important assistant and continued to head the workshop after his father's death.

3. CHARACTER AND PERSONALITY. A member of a family of not overscrupulous officials and traders, El Greco appears from his youth to have been involved in disputes and lawsuits. A restless man, with professional, social and financial ambitions, he was proud and passionate, capable of whole-hearted admiration or contempt. Since his artistic vocation could not be satisfied in Crete, El Greco left his family and settled in Italy, where he learnt not only a new form but also a modern conception of artistic activity with its corresponding intellectual and social position. He probably moved to Spain in search, ultimately unsuccessfully, of royal commissions. Throughout, he enjoyed an extravagant lifestyle, taking legal action when it was necessary to defend the value he placed on his paintings, and he prided himself on his intransigence in the face of the demands of his clients and on his artistic freedom.

There is no evidence that he joined any of the innumerable religious confraternities or guilds in Toledo, a deduction that can be made from the instructions he left for his burial, and he seems to have had no interest in Spanish culture. He studied and meditated on his own work and theorized on art in general. His personal library reflects his intellectual interests, showing a preference for Greek, Latin and Italian authors and for Aristotelian rather than Neo-Platonic philosophy. His thoughts on art and his opinions on his contemporaries are conveyed in his annotations to his copy (Madrid, De Salas priv. col.) of Vasari's *Lives*, showing some similarities to those expressed by Federico Zuccaro and Agostino Carracci, and in his notes to his copy of the Italian edition (1556) of Vitruvius' *On Architecture*, translated and annotated by Daniele Barbaro (Madrid, Bib. N.).

4. CRITICAL RECEPTION AND POSTHUMOUS REPUTATION. In the 16th and 17th centuries El Greco was considered as an Italian, a philosopher given to aphorisms and a painter led to extravagance by an excessive desire for originality. His art was seen to combine the high qualities praised by such poets as Luis de Góngora and Hortensio Félix Paravicino and critics such as Giulio Mancini and Francisco Pacheco, together with a reprehensible contempt for the norms of decorum and religious devotion expected of painting (Fray José de Sigüenza). Antonio Palomino stressed the negative nature of this dual interpretation, and the 'Enlightened' critics of the 18th century explained his strangeness as madness. The revival of interest in El Greco's art was due to French and English Romantics (Théophile Gautier and William Stirling-Maxwell), but the idea persisted that his periods of lucidity alternated with phases of madness. In the 19th century, while such artists as Delacroix, Millet and Manet recognized his qualities and his genius, Charles Davilier, Gustave Doré and the historian Carl Justi (1867) postulated an unhealthy imagination, a notion against which only Paul Lefort (1869) spoke out.

The theory of mental infirmity was replaced by that of optical infirmity (astigmatism) in the 20th century, and the so-called 'El Greco fallacy' persisted. In Spain, artists such as Santiago Rusiñol and Martín Rico y Ortega, champions of Impressionism and Symbolism, revived interest in El Greco as a predecessor of Velázquez. This paved the way for an interpretation that was consonant with that of several historians who regarded El Greco and his paintings as the outstanding representatives of the temperament and religious art associated with the Counter-Reformation, and intimately linked with the spirit and writings of such mystics as St Teresa of Avila and St John of the Cross (Cossío, 1908; Camón Aznar, 1950; Wethey, 1962; Pita Andrade, 1981). This emphasis on El Greco as a Spanish artist is controversial, above all to Greek critics, who stress the importance of the Byzantine elements in his culture and painting. Other historians (Harris, 1938; Guinard, 1956; Davies, 1976) have introduced further factors in defining his personality, for instance his Italianized culture and Neo-Platonic ideology: this approach has been reinforced by linking El Greco's work and ideas with the Greek tradition and Hispanic interpretations of the philosophy of Erasmus (Davies, 1989).

Interpretations diverging from this have taken two directions. On the one hand, Brown (1982 and 1984) and Mann (1986) have placed El Greco's artistic production at the heart of the institutionalized revival in the age of Philip II of the Spanish Counter-Reformation, which he is seen as serving with an emotional and brilliant rhetorical style and the vital expression of a personal faith, providing religious consolation and inspiration to his viewers. On the other hand, Marías and Bustamante (1981), basing their views on the artist's writings, have outlined an Italianate painter–philosopher detached from the religious issues of the period, who was instead fundamentally concerned with artistic and intellectual problems and involved in the investigation of nature and the formal means of achieving a perceptive imitation of reality, visual beauty and vitality.

Stylistically, El Greco's art has been labelled as an expression of the Venetian school, and of the anti-naturalistic subjectivism of the international Mannerism of the second half of the 16th century. His distortion of reality is seen as a prefiguration of modern Expressionism and as an instrument by which he could express his visionary, mystical and religious personality. Despite these concepts, not devoid of historical anachronisms, El Greco's painting belongs to the framework of the general Italian tendency—demonstrated in writings from Federico Zuccaro to Agostino Carracci—to oppose the ideology represented by Vasari's categorization. Because of his late assimilation of a Western style, he tackled certain formal problems and, free from prejudice, rejected norms of proportion and geometrical perspective that he considered superfluous to his purposes, particularly in his search for personal originality. His use of Venetian colouring, appraisal of naturalism and taste for complexity and late Cinquecento aestheticism reveal his preference for naturalistic representation in terms that are strikingly visual; this is realized by highly original compositions of elegance and dynamism, executed in a vital style.

BIBLIOGRAPHY

EARLY SOURCES

Fray J. de Sigüenza: *Fundación del monasterio de El Escorial* (Madrid, 1605; rev. 1963)

G. Mancini: *Considerazioni sulla pittura* (1617–21); ed. A. Marucchi, 2 vols (Rome, 1956)

F. Pacheco: *Arte* (1649); ed. F. Sánchez Cantón (1956)

A. A. Palomino de Castro y Velasco: *Museo pictórico* (1715–24), iii

T. Gautier: *Voyage en Espagne* (Paris, 1845)
W. Stirling-Maxwell: *Annals of the Artists of Spain* (London, 1848, rev. 2/1891)
P. Lefort: 'Dominico Theotocopuli, surnommé le Greco', *Histoire de toutes les écoles: Ecole espagnole*, ed. C. Blanc and others (Paris, 1869)
C. Justi: 'Die Anfänge des Greco', *Z. Bild. Kst*, viii (1897), pp. 199–218

MONOGRAPHS

M. B. Cossío: *El Greco*, 2 vols (Madrid, 1908/*R* 1972; Eng. trans., 1972)
J. Meier-Graefe: *Spanische Reise* (Berlin, 1910)
H. Kehrer: *Die Kunst des Greco* (Munich, 1914)
A. L. Mayer: *Dominico Theotocopuli: El Greco* (Munich, 1926)
J. Camón Aznar: *Dominico Greco*, 2 vols (Madrid, 1950, rev. 2/1970)
P. Guinard: *El Greco: A Biographical and Critical Study* (Barcelona and New York, 1956)
A. Vallentin: *El Greco* (Buenos Aires, 1956)
P. Keleman: *El Greco Revisited: Candia, Venice and Toledo* (New York, 1961)
F. J. Sánchez Cantón: *El Greco* (Milan, 1961; Eng. trans., London, 1963)
H. E. Wethey: *El Greco and his School*, 2 vols (Princeton, 1962)
K. D. Mertzios: *Dominikos Theotokopoulos: O bios kai ta erga tou* [Dominikos Theotokopoulos: his life and works] (Athens, 1966)
L. Puppi: *El Greco* (Florence, 1967)
G. Manzini and T. Frati: *L'opera completa del Greco* (Milan, 1969)
J. Gudiol: *Doménikos Theotókopoulos: El Greco, 1541–1614* (Barcelona, 1973; Eng. trans., New York, 1973)
D. Davies: *El Greco* (Oxford and New York, 1976)
J. M. Pita Andrade: *El Greco* (Milan, 1981)
El Greco of Toledo (exh. cat., ed. J. Brown; Madrid, Prado; Washington, DC, N.G.A.; Toledo, OH, Mus. A.; Dallas, TX, Mus. A.; 1982–3)
El Greco Exhibition (exh. cat., ed. K. Kanki; Tokyo, N. Mus. W. A., 1986)
Domenikos Theotokopoulos Kres: El Greco of Crete (exh. cat., ed. N. Hadjinicolaou; Herakleion, Basilica of St Mark, 1990)
F. Marías: *El Greco* (Milan, 1991)

SPECIALIST STUDIES

M. Barrès: *Le Greco ou le secret de Tolède* (Paris, 1910/*R* 1966)
F. de B. San Román: *El Greco en Toledo* (Madrid, 1910); repr. in *El Greco en Toledo* (Toledo, 1982)
——: 'De la vida del Greco', *Archv Esp. A. & Arqueol.*, iii (1927), pp. 139–95, 275–339
E. Harris: 'A Decorative Scheme by El Greco', *Burl. Mag.*, lxxii (1938), pp. 154–64
N. Chadzidakis: 'O Dominikos Theotokopoulos kai e kretike zographike' [Dominikos Theotokopoulos and Cretan painting], *Kretika Chron.*, iv (1950), pp. 371–440
G. Marañón: *El Greco y Toledo* (Madrid, 1956, rev. 2/1973)
H. Sochner: 'Greco in Spanien', *Münchn. Jb. Bild. Kst*, n. s. 2, viii (1957), pp. 123–94; ix–x (1958–9), pp. 147–242; xi (1960), pp. 173–217
X. de Salas: 'Un Exemplaire des "Vies" de Vasari annoté par Le Greco', *Gaz. B.-A.*, n. s. 5, lxix (1967), pp. 177–80
——: *Miguel Ángel y El Greco* (Madrid, 1967)
E. Lafuente Ferrari and J. H. Pita Andrade: *El Greco di Toledo e il suo espressionismo estremo* (Milan, 1969; Eng. trans., New York, 1972)
M. Constantoudaki: 'Dominicos Théotocopoulos (El Greco) de Candie à Venise: Documents inédits (1566–1568)', *Thesaurismata*, xii (1975), pp. 292–308
S. Bettini: 'Maistro Menegos Theotocopulos sgurafos', *A. Ven.*, xxxii (1978), pp. 238–52
F. Marías and A. Bustamante: *Las ideas artísticas de El Greco: Comentarios a un texto inédito* (Madrid, 1981)
J. Brown: 'Figures of Thought: El Greco as Interpreter of History, Tradition and Ideas', *Stud. Hist. A.*, xi (1982)
J. Brown and J. M. Pita Andrade: 'El Greco: Italy and Spain', *Stud. Hist. A.*, xiii (1984)
R. G. Mann: *El Greco and his Patrons: Three Major Projects* (Cambridge, 1986)
N. Panagiotaki: *E kretike periodos tes zoes tou Domenikou Theotokopoulou* [Dominikos Theotokopoulos' Cretan period] (Athens, 1986)
C. L. Ragghianti: *Periplo del Greco* (Milan, 1987)
J.-L. Schefer: *Le Greco ou l'éveil des ressemblances* (Paris, 1988)
El Greco: Mystery and Illumination (exh. cat., ed. D. Davies; Edinburgh, N.G., 1989); review by E. Harris in *Burl. Mag.*, cxxxi (1989), p. 726
X. de Salas and F. Marías: *El Greco y el arte de su tiempo: Las notas de el Greco a Vasari* (Madrid, 1992)
F. Marías: *El Greco: Biographie d'un peintre extravagant* (Paris, in preparation)

FERNANDO MARÍAS

Greco, Emilio (*b* Catania, Sicily, 11 Oct 1913). Italian sculptor, draughtsman and printmaker. He was brought up in a working-class district; at the age of 10 he began work in a marble-cutter's workshop. He first discovered sculpture as a youth, in the archaeological museums of Syracuse and Palermo and became interested in Etruscan sculpture and Roman portraiture. He was later influenced by Francesco Laurana's bust of *Eleanor of Aragon*, by the works of Antonello and Domenico Gagini, Giacomo Serpotta and 15th-century Mannerists. In 1933 he was in Rome, where he made the acquaintance of Renato Guttuso, Leoncillo Leonardi (1915–68) and Marino Mazzacurati (*b* 1907). In 1948 he exhibited in the Galleria del Secolo, and in 1956 he won the sculpture prize in the Venice Biennale, gaining international recognition.

Greco's expressive line evolved from his study of Classical art and the work of the sculptors Arturo Martini, Marino Martini and Giacomo Manzù. With his *Omino* (1939; Rome, G.N.A. Mod.), Greco found his true sculptural direction; using the basic layout of Roman portraits he introduced a feeling of controlled sensuality. In his terracotta and bronze versions of *Female Cyclist* (1947–8; Rome, Répaci priv. col., see Sciascia, p. 21) and *Wrestler* (1947–8; Antwerp, Openluchtmus. Beeldhouwkst Middelheim), the gentle spread of light over the broad masses of blocked shapes induces a sense of calm and dignified composure. In his portraits of men from the same period (e.g. *Man's Head*, 1948; Rome, G.N.A. Mod.), the archaic flavour of the funerary mask is enlivened by a harmonious balance between profile and flattened areas; the shapes suggest spiritual tensions combating physical transience. In *Female Cyclist* the nervous play of light lends a romantic touch to certain details; in the naked body, constructed with sinuous contortions and deft spatial calculations, the contrast between three-dimensional volume and the outlines dissolving in light accentuates a carefree sensuality. *Woman's Head* (1957; Venice, Ca' Pesaro) absorbs and reinterprets these same elements.

Certain concessions to avant-garde sculpture can be detected in the *Monument to Pinocchio* (1953–6), created for the Parco di Collodi, Pistoia; this work contains echoes of the filled and empty spaces of Henry Moore and Ossip Zadkine but without dramatic movement. A metaphor for the garland and the dance, it is a plastic invention that involves both the surrounding space and the indefinable space of memory. In portraits of the same period Greco still displays, however, a debt to the most memorable Pompeian portraits as well as to the sculpture of Arturo Martini. Greco's *Large Nude* (1952; Zürich, Schrafl priv. col., see Sciascia, p. 39) and his *Large Seated Figure* (1945; London, Tate), in which he tackled the intimate structure of the female figure and created solid architectural compositions with an unusual sense of balance, show how he reconciled the Archaic with Mannerism, combining undulating with flattened areas and enlivening the nude. In his *Large Bather No. 1* (1956; Rome, N.G.A. Mod.; versions in London, Tate; Tokyo, Ginza and elsewhere), which he repeated on several occasions, Greco revived the Mannerist theme of the figure of a woman covering her nudity. His *Crouching Figure* (Verona, Gal. Civ. A. Mod. & Contemp.) also represents his return to a Mannerist prototype, as does the *Female Skater* (1947; London, Ashley Clarke priv. col., see Sciascia, p. 23). These works impress themselves on the viewer by the way they focus on a single gesture or movement to express sensuality and an intimate awareness of the body.

In his larger decorative undertakings Greco abandoned the overtones of melancholy, sensuality and pathos to create a plastic syntax that was more dramatic and more easily accessible. In his bronze panels for the church of S Giovanni Battista in Florence (1960–61), the alternation of empty and filled spaces, of light and shade, creates an extraordinary visionary violence. The bronze doors for Orvieto Cathedral (1961–2, installed 1970), in which episodes of the *Seven Works of Charity* emerge from a skilfully hammered background, are impressive in their dramatically conceived sense of dialogue, but they do not invade their architectural setting. Similarly, in his monument to *John XXIII* (1965–7) in St Peter's, Rome, Greco rejected monumentalism, affectedness and mannerism to build a monument to human suffering.

Greco's prints and drawings are characterized by a thin and highly sensitive line that freezes either moments from everyday existence, which are presented as events, or episodes from Classical literature. This type of line, along with a sporadic use of cross-hatching attracting attention to intimate details (as in the series of drawings of lovers, 1968–70; see Sciascia, pp. 212–30) reveals and exalts the idea of sculptural form.

BIBLIOGRAPHY

Emilio Greco (exh. cat. by C. L. Ragghianti, Florence, Pal. Strozzi, 1953)
C. L. Ragghianti: 'Emilio Greco', *Sele A.*, 24 (1956), pp. 45–7
J. P. Hodin: *Emilio Greco* (Oslo, 1958)
M. Seuphor: *La Sculpture de ce siècle* (Neuchâtel, 1959)
Emilio Greco (exh. cat. by B. Degenhart, Munich, Lenbachhaus, 1959)
F. Bellonzi: *Emilio Greco* (Rome, 1962)
W. Hofmann: *La scultura del XX secolo* (Rome, 1962)
G. Ballo: *La linea dell'arte italiana* (Rome, 1964)
P. Bucarelli: *Scultori italiani contemporanei* (Milan, 1967)
G. Fallani: *Papa Giovanni di Emilio Greco* (Rome, 1967)
J. P. Hodin: *Emilio Greco, Sculpture & Drawings* (Bath, 1971)
L. Sciascia: *Emilio Greco* (Rome, 1971)
C. L. Ragghianti: 'Emilio Greco, disegni e grafica', *Crit. A.*, 131–2 (1973), pp. 3–160

PIERO PACINI

Greco, Gennaro [il Mascacotta] (*b* Naples, 1663; *d* Nola, nr Naples, 2 May 1714). Italian painter. He started his career as a painter of ornament, but after studying Andrea Pozzo's treatise *Perspectiva pictorum et architectorum* (Rome, 1693–1700) he began to produce easel paintings of imaginary views (*vedute ideate*), referred to by his biographer de Dominici as 'crumbling architectural ruins . . . magnificent buildings . . . marvellous underground places . . . and wonderful bizarre prisons'. He may also have created temporary decorations for religious celebrations. The sources claim that he worked as a specialist in perspective with decorative artists such as Francesco Solimena and Paolo De Matteis. He is thought to have created the gilded surrounds of De Matteis's frescoes (1696–8) in S Francesco Saverio (now known as S Ferdinando) in Naples. Voss rediscovered Greco when he found his signature on an architectural view that, with its pendant, came on to the Berlin art market in 1923. To these Voss added two canvases that appeared in London, attributed to Giovanni Ghisolfi, and two tondi (ex-Messinger priv. col., Rome) attributed to Pannini. There are also two signed paintings (Rouen, Mus. B.-A.; Castenaso, Molinari Pradelli priv. col.; for illustration of these and above works see Voss, 1926). These few works suggest a gifted artist, who played a major role in the development of the Neapolitan *veduta ideata*: his airy and theatrical architectural scenes transformed the 17th-century tradition of Viviano Codazzi and Codazzi's pupil, Ascanio Luciani (*d* 1706). Often viewed from an angle and constructed with consummate perspective skill, Greco's works reflect his gifts as a stage designer; in their fluent and brilliant designs, and pale greens, greys and blues, they are truly akin to 18th-century capriccios. His art is close to that of Pietro Capelli (*d* 1724), whose style is only slightly more ornate and sumptuous. The quietly decorative tone of Greco's work contrasts with the visionary and dramatic art of Leonardo Coccorante (1680–1750). It has been suggested that the stylistically diverse figures in Greco's paintings were executed by collaborators. A spatially daring perspective decoration in S Pietro at Cava dei Tirreni is attributed to him and dated to 1709 by Borelli. Greco died from falling from the scaffolding while frescoing the vault of an unspecified church in Nola. One of his sons, Vincenzo (*d* 1737), became a painter.

BIBLIOGRAPHY

Thieme–Becker
B. de Dominici: *Vite* (1742–5), pp. 553–5
H. Voss: 'Panninesque Paintings before Pannini', *Apollo*, iii (1926), pp. 332–6
O. Giannone: *Giunte sulle vite de' pittori napoletani*, ed. O. Morisani (Naples, 1941), pp. 181–2
G. Borelli: 'Il rococo napoletano', *Napoli Nob.*, xviii (1979), pp. 201–19
La raccolta Molinari Pradelli: Dipinti del sei e settecento (exh. cat., ed. C. Volpe and E. Riccomini; Bologna, Pal. Re Enzo, 1984), p. 143, cat. no. 107 [entry by A. Brogi]

ALESSANDRO BROGI

Greco-Bactrians. *See* BACTRIAN AND INDO-GREEK MONARCHIES.

Grecolini, Giovanni Antonio. *See* CRECCOLINI, GIOVANNI ANTONIO.

Grècque, François. *See* ERNI, HANS.

Greece, Hellenic Democracy of [Elliniki Dimokratia]. Country in south-east Europe, comprising the southern part of the Balkan peninsula and bordering the former Yugoslav Republic of Macedonia and Bulgaria to the north, Albania and the Ionian Sea to the west, Turkey and the Aegean Sea to the east and the Mediterranean Sea to the south. The principal cities are the capital, Athens (including Peiraeus), Thessaloniki, Larisa, Volos, Patras and Herakleion. The country's area is 130,833 sq. km and includes hundreds of islands in the Aegean and the Ionian seas. The central region of Thessaly has large plains, but most of the country is mountainous, with such ranges as the Pindus in the west. The coastline is rocky and indented, and there are few navigable rivers. One of Greece's chief industries is agriculture, although only a third of its land is cultivable. Other industries include fishing, shipping and tourism. Greece was under Turkish rule from 1453 to 1821. During this long period of occupation, living and working conditions were arduous, and thus few artistic commissions were available. The arts, in particular the folk crafts, were able to flourish to some extent in remote mainland areas and on some of the islands. The following survey, while referring to production during Turkish occupation, concentrates on Greek art since 1830, the date when independence was achieved. For the earlier history of Greece *see* CYCLADIC; MINOAN; HELLADIC; CRETE; MYCENAE; GREECE, ANCIENT; EARLY CHRISTIAN AND BYZANTINE ART; POST-BYZANTINE ART and VENETIAN EMPIRE. Further information on 19th- and 20th-century Greece is found in this dictionary under ATHENS, §I, 5 and 6, and THESSALONIKI, §§I and II, and within the relevant articles on islands and on other Greek cities.

I. Introduction. II. Architecture. III. Painting. IV. Sculpture. V. Textiles. VI. Interior decoration and furniture. VII. Ceramics. VIII. Metalwork. IX. Patronage. X. Collecting and dealing. XI. Museums. XII. Art education. XIII. Art libraries and photographic collections.

I. Introduction.

During Turkish occupation (1453–1821) the Greek language and Orthodox Christianity were the most important elements of Hellenic culture that kept the Greek nation united. In the last decades of the 18th century substantial efforts were made by intellectuals in educational centres especially among the diaspora to increase interest in Greek philosophy, history and literature through systematic publication of the works of ancient Greek and western European writers. Ancient Greek became an important subject in schools and academies, while the principles and consequences of the Enlightenment also contributed to Greek nationalism. This prepared the ground for the War of Independence (1821–8) and directly influenced every aspect of cultural life during the 19th century. After the revolution and a short period of internal political changes (1828–32), Britain, Russia and France placed the new state, which gained independence in 1830, under their guarantee and appointed a monarch, Otto of Wittelsbach (*reg* 1832–62), son of Ludwig I, King of Bavaria. In 1834 Athens was chosen to be the capital, primarily because of its strong Classical heritage and the symbolic inspiration it offered to Greeks and philhellenes, who saw in the city's revival a resurrection of 'ancient Greek glory'. As political, social, administrative and cultural affairs became centred in Athens, construction activity steadily increased (*see* §II below).

The state initially comprised only the Peloponnese and the southern part of the mainland, as well as some Aegean islands. The culturally rich Ionian islands were united with Greece in 1864, soon after the appointment of the Danish Glücksburg king George I (*reg* 1863–1913) as head of the constitutional monarchy. Thessaly and south-eastern Epiros were added in 1881, Macedonia, Crete and the eastern Aegean islands in 1913 (after the Balkan Wars of 1912–13), and the Dodecanese islands were ceded by Italy after World War II. The territories comprising eastern Thrace to Constantinople (now Istanbul) and the area around Smyrna (now Izmir, Turkey) were ceded to Greece by the Treaty of Sèvres (1920), but this was not ratified. In 1922 the Greek army was defeated by the Turks in Smyrna, forcing 1,500,000 Greeks to seek refuge on the independent Greek mainland. This conflict and mass displacement had a profound impact on the development of modern Greek culture, as the visual arts, poetry and literature stirred nostalgic feelings for the Byzantine tradition. In the 20th century the consequences of political history, combined with the need to define aspects of Greek cultural identity, preoccupied most artists and architects; apart from references to heritage, iconography was also influenced by the heroic aspects of the Balkan Wars and the Greco-Italian War of 1940–41. The poverty that ensued during the German occupation (1941–4), the years of the Resistance, the political polarization with its deep and long-lasting social ramifications after the Civil War (1944–9) and the military dictatorship of 1967–74 all had an impact on the development of Greek culture. From the 1960s there has been extensive foreign contact and exploration of artistic ideas on the international scene through a significant increase in cultural exchanges, especially within Europe and with the USA. In 1981 Greece became a full member of the European Union.

BIBLIOGRAPHY

J. Campbell and P. Sherrard: *Modern Greece* (London, 1968)
C. M. Woodhouse: *The Story of Modern Greece* (London, 1968); rev. as *Modern Greece: A Short History* (London, 5/1991)
R. Clogg: *A Short History of Modern Greece* (Cambridge, 1980, rev. 1992)
R. Browning, ed.: *The Greek World* (London, 1986), pp. 263–321

EVITA ARAPOGLOU

II. Architecture.

1. *c.* 1830–1900: Neo-classicism and Eclecticism. 2. *c.* 1900–45: Critical regionalism and Modernism. 3. After 1945.

1. *c.* 1830–1900: NEO-CLASSICISM AND ECLECTICISM. The establishment of an independent Greek state in 1830 signified the need for a distinctive cultural identity that could express the aspirations of the young state. In architecture the development of this identity essentially took the form of a quest for a proper architectural style, which resulted in the import of Neo-classicism from western Europe. For Greece, Neo-classicism was seen not as the expression of absolutist rule but rather as the embodiment of independence from Turkish rule (Lefaivre and Tzonis, 1981). Neo-classical iconography came to represent freedom, order, justice and progressiveness. The majority of early public buildings, all in Athens, were commissioned by the royal court or the government and were designed in the Neo-classical style, mostly by foreign architects: the Royal Palace (1835–41; now the Parliament Building) by the German Friedrich von Gärtner; the National Capodistrian University (begun 1837) by the Dane Christian Hansen; and the Academy (1859–87) and the National Library (1859–91) by Theophilus Hansen. The last also designed the Dimitriou House (1842–3; now the Hotel Grande Bretagne), the first significant private building in Athens. Smaller private dwellings were built mainly for Greeks of the diaspora, foreign aristocrats and diplomats who gradually established themselves in Athens. The most eminent Greek architects of this period were the rival figures LYSANDROS KAFTANTZOGLOU and Stamatis Kleanthis (1802–62). Kaftantzoglou, an austere and fervent Neo-classicist, designed a number of major public

buildings, the most significant being the National Technical University of Athens (1861–76), which provided the strongest expression of the meaning of Neo-classicism for the young Greek state. Kleanthis, a student of Schinkel, was more eclectic in style. His works include such Neo-classical structures as the Skouzes House (1841) on Nikodimou Street and the Wertheim House (1843) on Panepistimiou and Trikoupi streets and such Renaissance Revival buildings as Ilissia (1840–48; now the Byzantine Museum), all in Athens. He also designed buildings influenced by vernacular form and construction, as in his own residence (1831) on Tholou Street, Athens.

Foreign and foreign-educated architects, despite their obvious preference for Neo-classicism as the appropriate style for the birthplace of Classical architecture, were seldom reluctant to include other influences in their designs. Characteristic examples are LEO VON KLENZE's Renaissance Revival Hagios Dionysios (1848–53), the Roman Catholic cathedral of Athens, and Kleanthis's Rododafni (1841–5), a Gothic Revival villa on Mount Penteli, near Athens. Another source of influence was from Byzantine architecture, which was promoted for both ecclesiastical and secular buildings in an attempt to stress the historical continuity of Greek civilization. Kaftantzoglou, for example, included Byzantine-style elements in the Eye Clinic (1844–54) in Athens at the explicit request of King Otto (*reg* 1832–62). The German-born ERNST ZILLER, the leading architect of the late 19th century and the early 20th in Greece, characteristically adopted a different design approach for various types of building. He employed Neo-classicism or Renaissance Revival for secular urban buildings, *Rundbogenstil* with Byzantine and Romanesque references for ecclesiastical buildings, and his 'Greco-helvetian' style, a picturesque fusion of Neo-classicism and Alpine vernacular, for country houses.

Historicism continued to dominate Greek architecture into the 20th century and extended to new styles, including Art Nouveau and Art Deco. In general, it provided such Greek urban centres as Athens and Ermoupolis, on Syros, which grew rapidly in the 19th century, with a uniform character based mainly on Neo-classical features. Historicist influences on vernacular architecture were generally restricted to the use of mass-produced decorative elements, while articulation of volumes and spaces remained faithful to traditional designs.

2. *c.* 1900–45: CRITICAL REGIONALISM AND MODERNISM. The first decades of the 20th century were marked by a reaction to established and imported cultural forms and a reappraisal of national traditions. This change resulted from the growth in power and consciousness of the middle class and was kindled by such major socio-political events as the territorial gains made in the Balkan Wars and World War I and the population exchange of 1922 between Greece and Turkey. Aristotelis Zahos (1872–1939) was the first architect who attempted to define a regional identity on the basis of vernacular elements. He sought the true character of Greek architecture in the anonymous buildings that had escaped Neo-classical and other recent stylistic influences. Although Zahos's influence on Greek architecture was deep and extensive, his achievements fell short of his intentions. His works include: Hagios Konstantinos (1933–5) in Volos and the rebuilding (1926–48) of Hagios Demetrios in Thessaloniki (*see* THESSALONIKI, §III, 3), two of the few successful Byzantine Revival buildings in Greece; the Hatzimihali House (1924–7), Ypereidou 18, Athens, where he combined elements from Byzantine and Macedonian models; and the Loverdos House (1928–30) in Tatoi, Attica, which is derived from the architecture of the north Aegean islands. Zahos also participated in the major urban planning project of the time, the reconstruction of Thessaloniki after a fire in 1917; he was responsible for the Byzantine influences evident in the new urban plan.

DIMITRIS PIKIONIS was more successful in establishing vernacular architecture as the source of 'Greekness'. Pikionis acknowledged and studied contemporary folk art and architecture as part of a living vernacular tradition. He considered that from antiquity to modern times there were transcendent forms, which he called 'transhellenic'. The acceptance and utilization of these forms were therefore not a matter of nostalgia, but rather they promoted the development of an architecture functionally and culturally fit for the Greek environment. Pikionis's approach brought him close to Modernism, as exemplified in his school building (1933) in Pefkakia, Athens, and encouraged early Greek Modernists, in particular NIKOLAOS MITSAKIS, to integrate traditional forms in their works. However, Pikionis's work remained primarily based on traditional forms, as in the Experimental School (1933) of the Aristotelian University of Thessaloniki and the block of flats (1936; with Mitsakis; destr.) at Heyden 37, Athens. (For further discussion of Greek vernacular architecture *see* VERNACULAR ARCHITECTURE, §II, 2 (v).)

In the 1930s a group of enthusiastic young architects introduced Modernism to Greece. Some of them had first-hand experience of contemporary European developments: IOANNIS DESPOTOPOULOS had studied at the Bauhaus, PATROKLOS KARANTINOS had worked for Auguste Perret, and Polyvios Mihailidis (1907–42) had worked for Le Corbusier. The majority of early Modernist works were blocks of flats in Athens, such as one (1933) by THOUKIDIDIS VALENTIS and Mihailidis on Zaimi and Stournara streets and another (1932–3) by KYRIAKOS F. PANAGIOTAKOS on Themistokleous and Arahovis streets, as well as projects for the Programme of New School Buildings for the Ministry of Education. This programme gave ample opportunity to many young architects to implement bold and ambitious Modernist designs, such as those of 1932 by Karantinos on Kalisperi Street and by Mitsakis on Koletti Street and of 1932–3 by Panagiotakos on Liossion and Voda streets, all in Athens. These projects illustrate a consistent development from simplified versions of Neo-classicism towards clear and mature Modernist compositions. This progression explains the surprisingly wide and quick adoption of Modernism in Greece as a rational approach to the fundamental problems of architecture that were left unaddressed by Electicism and also links Greek Modernism to the regionalist approach advocated by Zahos and Pikionis.

Several Greek architects developed their careers mainly outside their native country. THANOS TSINGOS, who later became a stage designer and painter, studied architecture in Greece in the 1930s but in the late 1940s worked in

1. Takis Ch. Zenetos: house at Xanthou 21, Glyfada, Athens (1961)

France and also in Brazil with Oscar Niemayer and Lúcio Costa.

3. AFTER 1945. World War II and the Civil War (1944–9) left Greece with a large deficit in housing. This led to a construction boom that was blown out of all proportion in terms of both bulk and duration due to the domination of the private sector. Post-war governments promoted the private sector in the construction market, and this, combined with the lack of effective control and planning, resulted in overbuilding and the degradation of the architectural and urban environment. CONSTANTINOS A. DOXIADIS attempted to rectify this through his various government positions immediately after World War II and through the promotion of his theory of ekistics. In spite of this urban decline, the quality of individual buildings improved considerably. Valentis, one of the Modernists active in the 1930s, made a major contribution to post-war architecture in Greece. His office buildings, together with the early urban projects of NIKOS VALSAMAKIS, represent the essentially Functionalist prototypes of urban residential and office buildings in the second half of the 1950s and after. Another significant contribution to the post-war design of blocks of flats was that of TAKIS CH. ZENETOS, who attempted, with significant success, to develop a unified formal approach, as well as an effective control of external climatic conditions. Unfortunately, his solutions, as well as those of Valsamakis and Valentis, were not adopted but merely imitated by speculative developers, and their elements turned into functionally meaningless and often aesthetically unsuccessful decoration. Parallel developments characterize another thriving part of the building industry in Greece, that of the private house in the country or suburbs. Here, too, the prototype was provided by Valsamakis's works in the early 1960s, the most daring application of Modernism in Greece. Similarly dramatic in form, although motivated by different considerations, the private houses by Zenetos of the same period, such as the one (1961) in Glyfada, Athens (see fig. 1), achieve a remarkably high degree of integration of the interior with the environment and also allow for innovative and effective control of climatic conditions.

Complementary to these efforts to adapt Modernism and technology to the physical and social environment were regionalist approaches, represented mainly by Pikionis, whose post-war projects include his masterpiece (with A. Papageorgiou), the landscaping, from 1951 to 1957, of the hills of the Acropolis and Philopappou, Athens, a remarkable series of places conceived as containers for a variety of human activities, linked by a network of pathways. A different interpretation of vernacular architecture is represented by the work of ARIS KONSTANTINIDIS, the most original and influential architect in post-war Greece, who, in such buildings as the Hotel Xenia (1960) in Mykonos (see fig. 2), combined Modernist and vernacular elements into a system of regular geometric forms and strict grids, consistent with his vision of Mediterranean architecture and in harmony with the character of the landscape. His approach profoundly influenced modern Greek architecture in that it established

2. Aris Konstantinidis: Hotel Xenia, Mykonos (1960)

new standards of sensitivity and restraint in construction and also established an effective manner of pursuing the development of a regional architectural identity by a rational interpretation of vernacular patterns. These varying approaches practised by Pikionis, Zenetos and Konstantinidis were catalytic in avoiding a polarization between Modernism and a vernacular revival, which at times had seemed inevitable during the 1950s. The tendency to fuse the two traditions is characteristic of a large part of modern Greek architecture. Two prime exponents are Dimitris Antonakakis and Suzana Antonakakis (*see* ANTONAKAKIS), who, in the block of flats (1972) at Benaki 118, Athens, and the vacation house (1973) at Spata, Attica, introduced into residential architecture innovative concepts of spatial organization. In their buildings the influence of Konstandinidis is evident, particularly his concern with geometry and structure, which is seen in the regular organization of structural elements and zoning of functions. A flexible and elaborate articulation of spaces and activities is thus developed, which reflects Pikionis's creative transformation of vernacular patterns.

Despite such concern for regional identity, post-war Greek architecture has not been insensitive to international tendencies. Unfortunately, most of these influences were misused and abused in the framework of consumerism that has dominated post-war Greece. One of the few exceptions is the work of Alexandros N. Tombazis (*b* 1939), whose Difros complex of residential buildings (1971–5) at Ethnikis Antistasseos 84, Neo Psychiko, Athens, and a country house (1968) at Kineta, Attica, are obvious Metabolist compositions (*see* METABOLISM). Another tendency that seems to originate from international developments is a return to historicist and vernacular styles, as in recent works by Valsamakis. The diversity of these tendencies and their common roots signify a period of both maturity and transition in Greek architecture. Post-war architecture has achieved surprisingly high accomplishments in politically and economically awkward times and despite the lack of planning and construction technology (Tzonis and Lefaivre, 1984). However, some successful individual buildings do not entirely compensate for the overall low quality of the environment. The key problems of poor infrastructure and ineffective planning and control continue to hamper the development of a public face and structure in Greek architecture.

BIBLIOGRAPHY

H. H. Russack: *Deutsche Bauen in Athen* (Berlin, 1942)

V. Scully jr: 'Kleanthes and the Duchess of Piacenza', *J. Soc. Archit. Historians*, xxii (1963), pp. 139–54

F. Loyer: *Architecture de la Grèce contemporaine* (diss., U. Paris III, 1966)

L. Lefaivre and A. Tzonis: 'The Grid and the Pathway', *Archit. Themata* [Archit. Greece], xv (1981), pp. 164–81; also in K. Frampton, ed.: *Atelier 66: The Architecture of Dimitris and Suzana Antonakakis* (New York, 1985), pp. 14–25

D. Philippides: 'Greece', *International Handbook of Contemporary Developments in Architecture*, ed. W. Sanderson (Westport, CT, 1981), pp. 331–40

A. Tzonis and L. Lefaivre: 'A Critical Introduction to Greek Architecture since the Second World War', *Post-war Architecture in Greece*, ed. O. B. Doumanis (Athens, 1984), pp. 16–23

A. Giacumakatos and E. Godoli: *L'architettura delle scuole e il razionalismo in Grecia* (Florence, 1985)

ALEXANDER KOUTAMANIS

III. Painting.

Most Greek paintings dating from the period of Turkish occupation are the works of mostly unknown, self-taught artists and are found in various small churches on the mainland and the Aegean islands. The only area of significant artistic activity before the War of Independence of 1821 was the Ionian islands. Eighteenth-century artists mostly painted religious subjects commissioned for local churches; their works, for example *Birth of the Virgin*

3. Nikolaos Gysis: *Engagement of the Children*, oil on canvas, 1.03×1.55 m, 1877 (Athens, National Gallery)

(Zakynthos, Zakynthos Mus.) by Nikolaos Doxaras (*see* DOXARAS, (2)), were strongly influenced by Venetian High Renaissance altarpieces. NIKOLAOS KOUTOUZIS and NIKOLAOS KANTOUNIS were the two most prominent painters of the 18th century and the early 19th. Artists in the Ionian islands, though, were also significantly involved with portraiture: their sitters were usually noblemen, intellectuals and members of the clergy, and the style of the portraits reveals a heavy influence from the nearby Italian schools. The Ionian islands—mainly Corfu, Zakynthos and Kephallinia—continued to be an active artistic centre throughout the 19th century; the most characteristic paintings of the later period were translucent watercolour seascapes, such as those by Angelos Giallinas (1857–1939) and Aimilios Prosalentis (1858–1926). The impact of the artistic tradition of the Ionian islands on the mainland was particularly prominent after 1864, when they were united with Greece.

The most important artistic centre in Greece throughout the 19th and 20th centuries was Athens. Chosen in 1834 as the new capital, the city was dominated by German artistic influence promoted by the appointed Bavarian court. Popular themes were philhellenic subjects and scenes from the War of Independence. THEODOROS VRYZAKES's works are perhaps the most characteristic; they consist of scenes from recent history, such as *Lord Byron in Messolonghi* (1862; Athens, N.G.), whose academic and romantic style is well shown in the rendering of the Greek landscape and the ruins of Classical monuments. The Royal School of Fine Arts was founded in Athens by the Germans in 1836, but the emphasis of its curriculum was initially on architectural studies. The political and social connection with Munich accounted for the significant tendency of young art students to pursue their studies at the Akademie der Bildenden Künste. NIKIFOROS LYTRAS and NIKOLAOS GYSIS are regarded as the two most prominent figures among the so-called School of Munich; they concentrated on portraits and genre paintings, such as Lytras's *The Kiss* and Gysis's *Engagement of the Children* (1877; both Athens, N.G.; see fig. 3), which retained the characteristic range of dark, earthy colours and the academic style prevailing in Munich. Both artists influenced a great number of painters, such as POLYCHRONIS LEMBESSIS, SYMEON SAVVIDIS and Georgios Iakovidis. Naval scenes and seascapes were another significant interest of 19th-century Greek painters, notably Konstantinos Volanakis (1837–1907) and IOANNIS ALTAMOURAS, who were inspired by historical or mythological themes, for example in Volanakis's *Sea Battle by Aktion* (1882; Athens, N.G.). There were a few exceptions to the established pattern of studying in Munich; PÉRICLÈS PANTAZIS's landscapes and still-lifes, such as *Vases, Plates and Umbrella* (*c.* 1876; Athens, Leventis Col.), show the influence of the Impressionist schools in Paris and Belgium.

In the first decades of the 20th century conservative artists such as GEORGIOS ROILOS and GEORGIOS IAKOVIDIS dominated the artistic scene in Athens. The latter was especially influential both through his teaching at the Royal School of Fine Arts and as the Director of the new

National Gallery in Athens after 1900. It was the work of KONSTANTINOS PARTHENIS and Konstantinos Maleas (1878–1928), both prominent founder-members of the progressive group Techni in 1917, which was particularly important in introducing the influence of the French school into Greek painting. It initiated a new painterly approach based on defining genuinely Greek qualities and the symbolic values of the surrounding world, for example in Parthenis's *The Hillside* (1908; Athens, N.G.). Artists derived their inspiration from the liveliness and variety found in the Greek countryside and in their depictions of it emphasized the intensity of colour, the boldness of shapes and, more strikingly, the luminosity of surfaces, as in Maleas's *Monemvasia* (Athens, N.G.). Nikolaos Lytras (1883–1927) and Pericles Byzantios (1893–1972) were important followers of this movement, while SPYROS PAPALOUKAS's landscapes and paintings of traditional houses show a parallel development.

Another form of breaking away from the German academicism of the previous century was effected through the work of the self-taught artist THEOPHILOS (ii). He sought to introduce an essentially Greek pictorial vocabulary by illustrating the continuity of the Greek world and tradition; his rather naive paintings, such as the *Symposium by Empress Eudoxia* (1932; Mytilene, Varia Mus.), spontaneously referred to the Classical, the Byzantine and the modern and had a profound impact on later artists' development. FOTIS KONTOGLOU's work was also overtly influential. He interpreted the visual sources of Byzantine tradition and iconography, to which he was devoted, and developed them in his portraits, landscapes and his numerous religious works, thereby influencing a significant number of followers to recreate a Byzantine ideology.

Just as most Greek artists of the 19th century pursued their studies in Munich, most 20th-century artists went to Paris (the Expressionist GIORGOS BOUZIANIS was perhaps the only major exception), a trend that continued until the early 1960s. NIKO GHIKA, GIORGOS GOUNAROPOULOS, NIKOS ENGONOPOULOS and YANNIS MORALIS are only a few of those who attended the Ecole des Beaux-Arts before eventually returning to Greece. Although inevitably they were all influenced by the prevailing atmosphere during their time abroad, it seemed that the endeavour of every Greek artist in the 20th century was a preoccupation with finding a Greek identity within their individual style: Ghika introduced Cubism and abstraction to Greek art, while his 'fragmented' landscapes, such as *Hydra* (Athens, N.G.), are reminiscent of Byzantine mosaics; Engonopoulos's surrealistic paintings are based on an iconography heavily inspired by Greek history and mythology; the linear works of Moralis, influenced by Matisse, reflect an austere perception of such Greek references as the static geometry of Classical funerary reliefs (e.g. *Composition*, 1958; Athens, N.G.).

There was, however, a stylistically detached group of artists, who, based on original Greek themes and tradition, formed a new Greek pictorial vocabulary. His painting based on Theophilos's and Kontoglou's re-evaluation of Byzantine and popular style and iconography, YANNIS TSAROUHIS—a major figure in 20th-century Greek art—developed this simplicity of drawing, the luminous flat surfaces and the representation of the Greek life and psyche, for example in *The Sailor* (1963; see fig. 4) and *The Coffee House* (1966; both Athens, N.G.). SPYROS VASSILIOU's works, although often leaning towards a decorative, folkloric interpretation, show a sensitive insight into the essential elements of the Greek pictorial environment. The 1960s to 1980s were characterized by extensive contact with international artistic movements as Greek artists lived and worked in European artistic centres and in the USA; this often lessened the tendency to interpret new trends through a 'national perception', as painters concentrated on exploring purely artistic concerns.

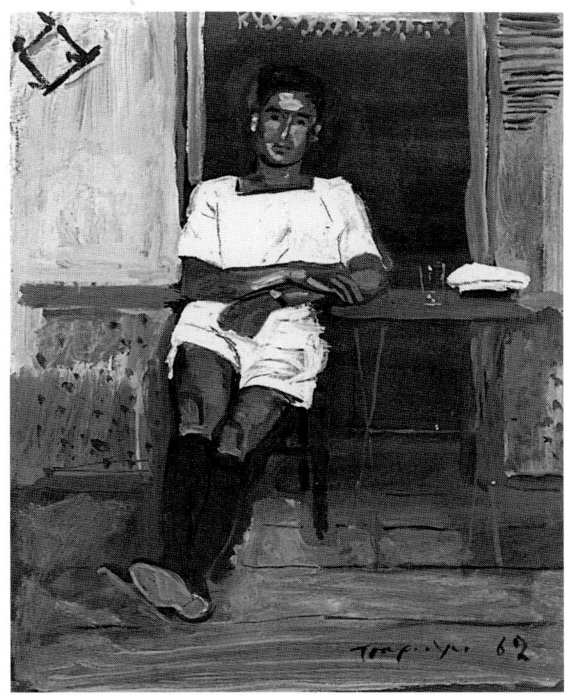

4. Yannis Tsarouhis: *The Sailor*, oil on cardboard, 320×240 mm, 1963 (Athens, National Gallery)

BIBLIOGRAPHY

S. Lydakis: *I istoria tis neoellinikis zographikis* [The history of modern Greek painting] (Athens, 1976)

C. Christou: *I elliniki zographiki, 1832–1922* [Greek painting, 1832–1922] (Athens, 1981)

E. Arapoglou: *The Leventis Collection: 19th and 20th Century Greek Paintings* (Athens, 1989)

C. Christou: *The National Gallery: 19th and 20th Century Greek Painting* (Athens, 1992)

A. Kotidis: *Nineteenth Century Painting* (1996), xiv of *Greek Art* (Athens, 1994–6)

C. Christou: *Twentieth Century Painting* (1996), xv of *Greek Art* (Athens, 1994–6)

EVITA ARAPOGLOU

IV. Sculpture.

Because of the absence of any significant non-decorative sculptural practice during the Byzantine period and the Turkish occupation, it is difficult to assess chronologically the beginnings of modern Greek sculpture. The first examples free from a decorative function were made in the Ionian islands by Pavlos Prosalentis the elder (1784–

1837), an academic sculptor from Corfu who, having studied in Rome in the circle of Canova, brought to Greece the Neo-classical principles of the latter's teachings. His bust of *Plato* (marble, 1815; Athens, N.G.) can be considered the first piece of modern Greek sculpture, although sculptures from the Ionian islands are quite separate in tradition from the culture of mainland Greece. In this respect, the starting point of Greek sculpture should be sought in the workshops on the Aegean islands, especially Tinos, where there was a long tradition of decorative sculptural work. In 1834 Athens became the capital, and the ensuing amount of construction attracted many artists from Tinos who worked on the new public buildings. In 1835 Jacob Malakate and Frangiskos Malakate (*see* MALAKATE) founded in Athens the first sculpture workshop, the Ermoglypheion, where many young artists were trained. The foundation of the Royal School of Fine Arts in 1836 and the instruction given by foreign sculptors there, particularly Christian Heinrich Siegel (1808–83), proved instrumental in the formation of the prevailing Neo-classical spirit, clearly expressed in the works of Demetrios Kossos (1819–72) and Ioannis Kossos (1822–73), Georgios Fitalis and Lazaros Fitalis (*see* FITALIS), as well as Leonidas Drossis (1834–82). These were mostly funerary monuments (e.g. Georgios and Lazaros Fitalis' tomb of *Michael Tositsas*, marble, 1856; Athens, First Cemetery) and busts (e.g. Ioannis Kossos's *Adelaide Ristori*, marble, 1867; Athens, N.G.), as well as such architectural decorations as those by Drossis for the Academy of Athens.

The Neo-classical tradition, strongly related to the architectural style dominant in Athens, influenced the work of the next generation of artists, such as GEORGIOS VROUTOS. At the same time a realist tendency was gradually introduced in the work of some artists, especially that of DEMETRIOS PHILIPPOTIS, who was the first in Greece to represent themes from everyday life in sculpture that was not necessarily the result of a commission nor part of architectural decoration. His *Reaper* (marble, 1870; Athens, Zappeion) and the *Little Fisherman* (marble, 1874; Athens, Zappeion Garden) are characteristic examples of this type of work, while the *Spirit of Copernicus* (marble, 1877; Athens, N.G.) by Vroutos was seen as an unorthodox sculpture that aroused controversy when exhibited. The most representative examples of late 19th-century sculpture are to be found in the First Cemetery of Athens. Such works include the *Papadakis* tomb (1881) by Vroutos, the *Sleeping Woman* (1883) by Ioannis Vitsaris and the Kouppa funerary monument (1902) by Philippotis. YANNOULIS HALEPAS, perhaps the most important figure in modern Greek sculpture, produced such marble works as the *Sleeping Girl* (tomb of Sophia Afantakis, 1878; Athens, First Cemetery) and *Satyr Playing with Eros* (marble, 1877; Athens, N.G.; plaster version, 1918; Tinos, Mus. Tinian Artists), as well as later expressionist plaster pieces (e.g. *Medea and her Children*, 1922–3; Tinos, Mus. Tinian Artists; version, 1934; Athens, N.G.; see fig. 5). The need for innovation became increasingly apparent towards the end of the 19th century. Paris became the centre where most young Greek sculptors went to study. The transitional period from Neo-classicism to Realism, with a more liberal perception of sculptural plasticity, is characterized

5. Yannoulis Halepas: *Medea and her Children*, plaster, 720×240×430 mm, 1934 (Athens, National Gallery)

by the works of such sculptors as Lazaros Sochos (1862–1911), who depicted the heroic figure *Kolokotronis* (bronze, 1894; Athens, Stadiou Street), and GEORGIOS BONANOS, who executed the Realistic and monumentalizing statue of *P. Vallianos* (1899; Athens, N. Lib.). KOSTAS DEMETRIADES's work shows the influence of Rodin's Romantic style and Symbolist tendencies (e.g. *The Dilemma*, marble, before 1905), as well as a distinct attempt at abstraction (e.g. *Woman Bathing*, marble, 1920; Athens, N.G.).

In the first half of the 20th century academic styles developed concurrently with modernist tendencies, while at the same time the ideas of Rodin, Aristide Maillol, Emile-Antoine Bourdelle and Charles Despiau continued to attract Greek sculptors. The work of ANTONES SOCHOS and MIKHAEL TOMBROS represents efforts to develop and adapt Greek sculpture to contemporary western European ideas. Some of the primitive elements in Sochos's sculptures can be related to works by his progressive contemporaries, but there are also references (e.g. in *Digenis*, wood; Athens, N.G.) to traditional wooden ships' figureheads (Gr. *akroproroi*). Tombros's sculpture parallels developments in western Europe. *Fat Seated Women* (bronze, 1926; Athens, N.G.) is completely innovative in its conception, while his *Mask* (bronze, 1929) is a purely Cubist work.

The work of THANASSIS APARTIS (e.g. *Adolescent*, bronze, 1939; Athens, Arditou Street), a student of

Bourdelle, shows a complete turn towards Realism, having strong references to Archaic art of the 6th century BC as well as to the Severe style in the early 5th century BC. Together with Tombros, he was the most significant sculptor of the period between World Wars I and II to follow western European ideals. The main characteristic of the first half of the 20th century, however, was the co-existence of conservative and liberal tendencies. There was a gradual distancing from a literal representation of the human form and a turn towards abstraction; this took place mainly after World War II and was directed towards such 20th-century styles as Constructivism. These trends are apparent in the works of GEORGE ZONGOLOPOULOS, such as the marble monument (12.5×17.6 m, 1954–61) above the monastery at Zalonga, Epiros, and the 18 m high bronze sculpture (1966) at the entrance to the Trade Fair ground, Thessaloniki; they are also reflected in the works of CLEARCHOS LOUKOPOULOS, such as the *Acrocorinth* (bronze, 1965; Athens, N.G.), or in ACHILLEAS APERGIS's compositions of small bronze rods done after 1961 (e.g. *Composition*, 1963; Athens, N.G.) and ladders after 1981, as well as in the Abstract Expressionist bronze figures by various sculptors, including those (1960–61) by CHRISTOS CAPRALOS.

Since the 1950s experimentation with new materials, as well as with light, movement and sound, has been the characteristic element in the works of Greek sculptors. TAKIS's *Signals Multiples* series (issued by Unlimited, Bath, 1966) and *Electromagnétiques* series (e.g. *Télé-lumière II*, 1963; Paris, Pompidou), as well as CHRYSSA's compositions made of plastic, glass and perspex pipes with neon light (e.g. *The Gates to Times Square*, 1964–6; Buffalo, NY, Albright–Knox A.G.), are examples of such sculptural explorations. YERASSIMOS SKLAVOS's monumental iron, cement and granite compositions are expressions of abstract Cubism, in which the strength of conveying the message dominates the construction itself. Besides Takis and Chryssa, LUCAS SAMARAS is a Greek-born artist who has made his career abroad. A painter, sculptor and photographer, he was one of the first to use his body as the subject for his art and was a key figure in Conceptual art circles in New York in the 1960s and 1970s. Since 1970 Greek sculpture has been characterized by variety and individual experimentation. Artists from the previous generation tended to consider aspects of figurative realism, while such younger sculptors as Georgios Lappas (*b* 1950) and Yiannis Bouteas (*b* 1941) explored combinations of materials, technology and space.

BIBLIOGRAPHY

S. Lydakis: *I ellines glyptes* [The Greek sculptors] (Athens, 1981)

C. Christou, M. Koumvakali and B. Anastassiadi: *Modern Greek Sculpture, 1800–1941* (Athens, 1982)

I. Myconiatis: *Modern Greek Sculpture* (1996), xii of *Greek Art* (Athens, 1994–6)

TONIA P. GIANNOUDAKI with EVITA ARAPOGLOU

V. Textiles.

Linen and cotton were cultivated locally in Greece and, together with wool in the northern mainland, they constituted the majority of commercial textile production. In the main textile centres, silk was used for decorated work. The silk industry was established between the 5th and the 9th centuries, and vast areas of the mainland, particularly the Peloponnese, were planted with mulberry trees to provide for the silkworms. Benjamin of Tudela (*d* 1173), writing of his travels between 1160 and 1173, referred to 2000 Jewish silk-workers in Thebes and a further 2500 in Pera (*Massa'ot: Itinerary of a Journey*; Eng. trans. by A. Asher, London, 1840–41). The islands also produced large quantities of silk, the most important centre being Chios, whose velvets and brocades vied with those of Bursa. The craft, which operated on a semi-industrial basis, was introduced to the island by the Genoese in the 15th century and reached its peak *c.* 1775. Greek silk was exported throughout the Ottoman empire and Europe as yarn, woven fabric and manufactured stockings, but in the 1830s a disease attacked the mulberry trees, and this, along with political instability and the growing availability of cheap mass-produced textiles from western Europe, virtually destroyed the trade.

1. ORTHODOX CHURCH EMBROIDERY AND WEAVING. The largely Byzantine tradition of ecclesiastical embroidery, which had reached its peak in the 14th century (*see* EARLY CHRISTIAN AND BYZANTINE ART, §VII, 8(ix)), continued in the Orthodox Church until the 19th century. Under Turkish occupation, however, the professional embroiderers who had been patronized by the aristocracy were largely replaced by amateur women and semi-professional workshops within the larger monasteries. Although the goldwork technique and strict conventions in subject-matter were retained, there was a marked decline in quality. An epigonation of 1587 (London, V&A) that depicts the *Washing of Feet*, for example, is poorly drawn and has a cluttered background, though the embroidery is well executed. This piece, which was commissioned by a metropolitan of Larissa, was possibly made by the monk Arsenios in a monstery of the Meteora. A welcome revival took place in the late 17th century. This can be seen especially in the work of Despoineta (*fl* 1682–1723), a Greek embroideress working in Constantinople (now Istanbul), who in simplifying the overcrowded images drew selectively on Italian ornament designs, iconography and techniques. She employed a wider range of couching patterns and used floss silk in long and short stitch to shade the faces (e.g. epitaphios for Ankara Cathedral, 1682; Athens, Benaki Mus.). Her influence survived well into the 18th century.

In addition to this ecclesiastical work, there were instances in which secular embroidery was reused in a religious context. Cretan skirt borders and Epirote embroideries, for example, were converted into copes and hymeneal veils. Also, some weaving took place in the larger monasteries. The table carpet (*peuki*) at Nea Moni on Chios was made from brocade woven by a monk, Antonios Pyrinos; it has an Ottoman pattern of pomegranates and an inscription with the date 1742. There are also traces of two painted dedicatory panels in the traditional Byzantine style. On other occasions the monks used precious fabrics that had been donated.

2. THE MAINLAND. During the Turkish occupation the native traditions of costume and textile production

were largely extinguished. There was, however, a continuing tradition of tailoring and gold embroidery, carried out by professionals in urban workshops. In the early 19th century, with the growing prosperity of the middle classes and the relaxation of Turkish rule, the demand for this work greatly increased, a trend that reached its height in Ioannina at the ostentatious court of Ali Pasha (*reg* 1788–1822). Ioannina exported costumes and uniforms, in local broadcloth heavily embroidered with gold thread and braid, to the Balkans, Egypt and North Africa; in the late 20th century it was still a centre of embroidery. Regional costume, with gold and silk embroidery, continued to be worn throughout the 19th century and, for special occasions, into the 20th.

The rural communities of the mainland have always worked mainly in wool, producing clothing and such utilitarian household items as blankets, cushion-covers and bags. These feature traditional, highly abstracted designs with birds, fishbone patterns, coffee pots etc. *Floccati* rugs, with a long, loose tufted pile, are also woven, as are kilims with geometric designs that are similar to their Thracian counterparts.

3. GREEK ISLAND EMBROIDERY. The Aegean islands, because of their number and inaccessibility, were largely left to govern themselves during the period of Turkish rule. This, together with the more independent spirit of the islander, allowed a great flowering of the textile arts. Whereas the embroidery of the mainland forms part of the Balkan tradition, that of the islands developed in isolation. It reflects in different degrees the complex political and economic history of the region: Mamluk motifs are mixed with geometric patterns from Classical Greece; Byzantine designs are set alongside Turkish ones, which in themselves reflect the Middle-Eastern world of the Turk; and the enduring influence of Italy can be seen in the use of Renaissance iconography. The embroideries are difficult to date because the designs, once established, were fossilized in the highly conservative communities. It is possible that the practice developed in the medieval period, with workers using silk left over from the woven silk industries. The earliest surviving examples date from the late 17th century (e.g. Cretan skirt border fragment, 1697; New York, Met.).

6. Bed curtain, silk embroidery on linen, cross stitch, side panels each 2.63×0.40 m, door panel 2.63×0.90 m, from Rhodes, *c.* 1720–50 (London, Victoria and Albert Museum)

Although the larger, more elaborate pieces were made by professionals, most Greek island embroidery was carried out by girls for their dowries. It was executed in polychrome silk, often restricted to red and blue, on a linen or sometimes cotton ground. Metal threads were less commonly used. Much of the work was domestic, intended largely for the bridal bed, which required sheets, pillows and hangings for privacy (see fig. 6). The bed was the only fixed furniture of the simple, single-roomed island houses, and its position, set either on a mezzanine floor or in an alcove, dictated the form of hangings that were used. In the Dodecanese a dramatic bed tent, the *sperveri*, evolved, whereas in the Cyclades multi-panelled curtains were standard.

Stylistically Greek island embroideries can be divided into three main groups: the Aegean, the Ionian, each with subsidiary groups, and the Cretan. In the areas of Italian influence—the Ionian, south Cycladic and Dodecanese islands—counted thread work was preferred, but in areas of Turkish influence—Samos, the north Sporades, Epiros and Crete—the designs were freely drawn. The embroideries of the Aegean are the most diverse and eclectic. A particularly lively group is attributed to Skyros. The colours are pale, and the freely drawn, open designs include wedding processions, sailing vessels derived from Iznik pottery, horsemen in Ottoman dress, cockerels and delicate scrolling foliage. In some the drawing is excellent, in others charmingly naive. Naxos embroidery has unmistakable geometric quatrefoil patterns based on paired serrated leaves. The surface stitching is densely worked in brick-red silk, occasionally with some blue or green, and the effect depends on the tracery of the reserved ground and the light reflected off the blocks of stitching that lie in different directions. Patmos work is also particularly fine. Bed curtains are worked in fine cross stitch, predominantly red with subtle additions of blue, green and yellow. The designs include a variety of tree of life motifs, animals, birds, figures and ships enclosed by geometric linear elements that border the curtains and form gables. Ionian embroidery is generally grouped with that of Epiros on the nearby mainland. Epirote work includes bridal cushion-covers with wedding scenes or embroidered borders whose flower and serrated leaf designs are Ottoman in origin. The colours are rather dark, though white embroideries were also common. Using cut work and drawn thread techniques, they are decorated with distorted, fanciful animals derived from those on Italian lacis and drawn thread work. (Needle and bobbin lace, also in the style of 16th- and 17th-century Italian work, were made on the Ionian islands into the early 19th century.) The embroideries of Crete are distinctive in their use on women's skirts rather than on furnishings, and in their powerful designs. Composed of scrolling foliage, double-tailed mermaids, vases and birds, they reflect the long period of Venetian rule (1204–1669). Whether in monochrome red or blue or in polychrome silks, they are worked largely in Cretan feather stitch.

See also CYPRUS, §V, 5.

BIBLIOGRAPHY

A. J. B. Wace and R. M. Dawkins: 'Greek Embroideries', *Burl. Mag.*, xxvi (1914), pp. 49–50, 99–107

Catalogue of a Collection of Old Embroideries of the Greek Islands and Turkey (exh. cat. by A. J. B. Wace, London, Burlington F.A. Club, 1914)

Mediterranean and Near Eastern Embroideries from the Collection of Mrs F. H. Cook (exh. cat. by A. J. B. Wace, London, Burlington F.A. Club, 1935)

P. P. Argenti: *The Costumes of Chios: Their Development from the 15th to the 20th Century* (London, 1953)

A. Chatzimichali: *Hellenic National Costumes*, 2 vols (Athens, 1954)

P. Johnstone: *Greek Island Embroidery* (London, 1961)

M. Gentles: *Turkish and Greek Island Embroideries from the Burton Yost Berry Collection in the Art Institute of Chicago* (Chicago, 1964)

P. Johnstone: *The Byzantine Tradition in Church Embroidery* (London, 1967)

'Greek Contemporary Handweaving', *Ciba Z.* (1969), pp. 2–44

P. Johnstone: *A Guide to Greek Island Embroidery*, London, V&A cat. (London, 1972)

Aegean Crossroads (exh. cat. by J. Trilling, Washington, DC, Textile Mus., 1983)

H. Polychroniadis: *Hellénika kentémata* [Greek Embroideries], Athens, Benaki Mus. cat. (Athens, 1980)

R. R. Taylor: 'The Early Collectors of Greek Embroidery', *Hali*, xxxvi (1987)

C. Van Steen and E. Lykiardopoulos: 'The Textiles of the Vlachs of Metsovo', *Hali*, lxiii (1992), pp. 90–95

R. R. Taylor: 'Greece, the Greek Islands and Albania', *5000 Years of Textiles*, ed. J. Harris (London, 1993), pp. 242–9

——: *Embroidery of the Greek Islands and Epirus* (in preparation)

RODERICK TAYLOR

VI. Interior decoration and furniture.

Features of the medieval Greek house, with single-room plan, division into ground and upper floors, a sleeping area and a hearth area, seen at Mystras and on Chios, survived the Ottoman conquest. The sleeping area was usually on a mezzanine floor, separated by an arch (as on Naxos), an embroidered curtain (as on Rhodes; see fig. 6 above) or a wooden screen carved with tendrils and tulip patterns; non-vegetable forms were rare. Ceramic and copper vessels were hung on the walls of the sleeping area. A chimney-piece dominated the remaining area, and the room had cupboards with carved wooden doors built into the walls. The space was sparsely furnished with a low, round table, stools, low chairs and chests: the furniture of Skyros and Crete in particular was renowned for the quality and imagination of its workmanship. Textiles, usually of wool on the mainland and cotton on the islands, were the main decoration, covering cupboard openings and low benches along the walls and stretching in bands on the walls themselves. Patterns varied according to region (*see* §V above).

Lavish building was exceptional and was found only in the capital, in Constantinople (now Istanbul), in territories held by Venice (e.g. Zante) or in areas favourably treated by the Turks (e.g. Chios). The emerging Greek merchant class in the 18th century built homes on a grander scale, for example at Siatista, Verroia and Kastoria in Macedonia; at Ioannina and Metsovo in Epiros; at Ambelakia, Tirnavos and Pelion in Thessaly; and on the islands.

During this period western Macedonia, Epiros and the Peloponnese became important centres of wood-carving. Skilled local craftsmen combined Western and local motifs in carved panelling that covered some of the rooms in wealthy households (see fig. 7). Such houses were on two or three floors. The ground floor was for storage and had no windows. The first floor had the winter quarters with a raised fireplace and a cooking area. There were small windows, a basin, cupboards and shelves. The second floor, which jutted out beyond the main walls of the house, contained the reception rooms and summer quarters. The staircase ended in a room with raised floor areas behind wooden arches. Next was the richly decorated reception room with carved woodwork and a painted ceiling. It contained chests, stools and low tables. The windows sometimes had coloured glass (Kastoria, Ambelakia); ceilings were sometimes gilded (Verroia). From the late 18th century the main room was sometimes decorated with wall paintings, commonly depicting such mercantile cities as Vienna, Trieste or Constantinople (e.g. the Triantaphyllou House at Drakia, Pelion).

With independence (1830) there emerged a Western-inspired Greek Revival style, initially for public buildings (*see* §II above). The superficial change is in decorative features derived from antiquity; the fundamental change

7. Wood-panelling by Macedonian wood-carvers, from a reception room in a wealthy house in Kozani, 18th century (Athens, Benaki Museum)

is a Western organization of the space, reflecting the progressive adoption of a European lifestyle. Notable exponents of this genre in the 19th century were Stamatis Kleanthis (1802–62), Schaubert, Lysandros Kaftantzoglou, Christian Hansen and Ernst Ziller. In the 20th century Aristotelis Zahos (1872–1939) produced houses with interior designs alluding directly to traditional decorative forms, particularly in the use of carved wood and textiles (e.g. the Hatzimihali House, 1924–7, Athens). Following the introduction of Modernism to Greece in the 1920s some architects, notably Dimitris Pikionis, assimilated traditional Greek features into modernist design. In the late 20th century designs in such international styles as Post-modernism have been produced.

BIBLIOGRAPHY

A. Hatzimihali: *Elliniki laiki techni* [Greek handicrafts] (Athens, 1925)

E. Leimona-Trempela: *To laiko Karpathiko spiti* [The folk house of Karpathos] (Thessaloniki, 1970)

K. Makris: *I laiki techni tou Piliou* [The popular arts of Pelion] (Athens, 1976)

D. Philippides, ed.: *Elliniki paradosiaki architektoniki* [Greek traditional architecture], 3 vols (Athens, 1982; Eng. trans., Athens, 1983)

D. Philippides: *Neoelliniki architektoniki* [New Greek architecture] (Athens, 1984)

VII. Ceramics.

Owing to its geographical position, Greece was exposed to influences both from the East and the West. Evidence from the early modern period suggests a continuation of Byzantine traditions both in the use of pottery, for example in the decoration of external church walls, and in the use of such manufacturing techniques as sgraffito and painting with translucent glazes. During the later periods incised decoration became coarser and painted decoration brighter. On the island of Rhodes the so-called 'Rhodian terracottas' have been well-known from the 14th and 15th centuries and are derived from Asia Minor prototypes. The traditional Rhodian forms are terracottas decorated with a white slip; a typical shape is a three-handled jar for food. The Asia Minor style was revived between World Wars I and II and was dominant in wares produced at the end of the 20th century; these feature vividly coloured flowers on a white ground, covered with a transparent glaze. On Samos simply shaped and decorated wares were produced. On the nearby island of Chios production is centred around the village of Armolia, which has a pottery tradition going back to antiquity. Terracottas covered with white slip and coloured glazes are made. The most important ceramic kilns in Crete are in Chania, Chalepa-Pelekopina, Margarites, Herakleion, Thrapsano, Kentri (nr Ierapetra) and Agios Nikolaos. Many traditional shapes, some recalling Minoan prototypes, are produced, including miniature incense-burners and vast storage jars (pitharia) made by coiling. On the island of Siphnos flame-proof, red terracotta pottery often decorated with white slip has been produced, although the number of active potters has markedly declined since World War II. On Aegina the popular Aeginetan water pitcher has been produced. The shape has two handles and is decorated with such simple designs as boats or the Greek flag. In the late 20th century these are produced only for decorative purposes. On the island of Skopelos production is dominated by reproduction antique shapes. On Skyros traditional shapes and decoration continue to be used. There are two styles: tin-glazed pitchers with trefoil spouts, decorated with flora, birds and two-headed eagles; and a local style with fish and fowl in white slip on red clay. On the mainland, in the region of Thessaly, utilitarian vessels in tin-glazed earthenware or terracotta are produced in Volos, while red jugs with delicate decoration in white slip have been made in Fanari Karditsas. Besides the continuing folk tradition, art pottery has been introduced that combines traditional Greek elements with influences from the West.

BIBLIOGRAPHY

A. Hatzimihali: *L'Art populaire grec* (Athens, 1937)

A. Kyriakidou-Nestoros and M. Avramidis: 'Mia kallitechniki physiognomia tis Thessalonikis' [An artistic physiognomy of Thessaloniki], *Makedoniki Zoi* (Aug 1966)

V. Kyriazopoulos: 'Minas kai Dimitris: Duo ellines laikoi keramistes' [Minas and Dimitris: two Greek folk potters], *Nea Estia*, 975 (1968), pp. 223–31

——: 'Pottery', *Greek Handicrafts* (Athens, 1969), pp. 88–120

A. Vavylopoulou-Kharitonidou: 'Neoelliniki kerameiki stin Arta epi Tourkokratias' [Modern Greek ceramics in Arta during the Turkish occupation], *Ethnographika*, iii (1981–2), pp. 5–22

VIII. Metalwork.

In the 16th century the skill of Greek gold- and silversmiths was renowned: the Ottoman sultan Süleyman I was taught metalworking by Constantine of Trebizond, while Evliya Celebi in the 17th century named Michael Simicioglu as the best contemporary enameller. They produced such secular objects as jewellery, dress accessories, armour and household wares, as well as ecclesiastical objects. In the early Ottoman period ecclesiastical work continued in the Byzantine tradition, particularly in iconography (e.g. the 16th-century reliquary of St Nephon; Mt Athos, monastery of Dionysiou), while secular work reflects the taste of patrons of the Ottoman ruling class.

Identification of local workshops by style is problematic because of the uniformity of work throughout the Balkans, with the exception of some island jewellery, which can be distinguished by the greater Western influence it shows. This uniformity and the anonymity of the craftsmen also makes dating difficult. A *firman* of 1592 made it obligatory to stamp silverwork with the sultan's *tugra*, after which there are more datable objects from Constantinople (e.g. ink holder, 1679; Athens, Mus. Gr. Flk A.); it is not known whether marking was practised by Greek goldsmiths elsewhere. The principal source of silver was the Mademochoria mines of Chalkidike and the techniques used include chasing, enamelling, filigree, repoussé, piercing, openwork and niello. The chief centres of production were Soufli in Thrace, Stemnitsa in the Peloponnese and Ioannina in Epiros, together with two Epirot villages, Kalarrytes and Syrrako.

By 1800 the silversmiths of Kalarrytes were the most famous in Greece. Until it was sacked in 1821 they worked there and in Ioannina; afterwards they migrated to the Ionian islands and later to Italy. Signed pieces by four silversmiths of Kalarrytes survive: gospel covers by the two Papageorgiou brothers (e.g. of 1792; monastery of Proussos) and Athanasios Tzimouris (e.g. of *c.* 1792; Ioannina Cathedral); and a wider variety of objects (e.g. gospel cover, icon cover, reliquary and sepulchral urn; Zante, St Dionysius) by Georgios Bafas (1784–1853). The

Papageorgiou brothers and Tzimouris retained elements of the Byzantine tradition in their work, whereas Bafas was wholly open to Western influence. In the 20th century Ioannina continued to be the leading centre of Greek silverwork, along with Corfu and Rhodes; traditional objects are made but for decorative use only.

Work in copper, brass and iron was produced in Thessaloniki, Larisa, Ioannina and Cyprus. Copper was mined on the southern coast of the Black Sea, in Thrace, on Thasos, at Domokos on the borders of Thessaly and on Euboea. The forms and decoration of Greek copperwork show heavy Ottoman influence. Most copperwork was for domestic use; the only ecclesiastical work in copper was for baptismal fonts. Other objects for church use (e.g. lecterns and candelabra) were of brass. A distinctive Greek style of architectural ironwork emerged in the 19th century as an integral part of the Neo-classicism that was adopted as a national urban architectural style after independence in 1830. As a result of post-World War II rebuilding, however, not much survives.

BIBLIOGRAPHY

K. Makris: *Neoklassikes sideries* [Neo-classical ironwork] (Athens, n.d.)

——: 'Metalwork', *Greek Handicrafts*, ed. S. A. Papadopoulos (Athens, 1969), pp. 221–40

P. Zora: 'Silverwork', *Greek Handicrafts*, ed. S. A. Papadopoulos (Athens, 1969), pp. 241–75

J. Raby: 'Silver and Gold', *Tulips, Arabesques and Turbans: Decorative Arts from the Ottoman Empire*, ed. Y. Petsopoulos (London, 1982), pp. 17–72

C. Christou: *Modern Greek Engraving* (1996), xiii of *Greek Art* (Athens, 1994–6)

NATASHA LEMOS

IX. Patronage.

Patronage in the 18th century was related mostly to ecclesiastical commissions for church decoration, mainly in the Ionian islands. After independence there was a tremendous demand for architectural and fine arts projects in Athens, and patronage developed accordingly. As there was a relative absence of experienced Greek artists, the court, as well as various government sectors, commissioned major public buildings from such foreign architects as the German Friedrich Gärtner, who designed the Royal Palace (now the Parliament Building; 1835–41), Athens, and the Dane Christian Hansen, who built the National Capodistrian University of Athens (1837–42; *see* §II above). Among the best-known Greeks who received important commissions were Stamatis Kleanthis (1802–62) and LYSANDROS KAFTANTZOGLOU. Perhaps the first occurrence of private patronage of painting was that by Gen. Yannis Makryiannis, who commissioned the self-taught painter Panagiotis Zographos (*fl* late 1830s–early 1840s) to illustrate, in a series of 26 watercolours, battles from the War of Independence (1836–9; four sets were made, one in Windsor Castle, Berks, Royal Lib.). Patrons in the 19th century showed interest in funding art competitions and providing scholarships for such Greek artists as Nikolaos Gysis to pursue their studies abroad. The most important aspect of 19th-century patronage, however, is that wealthy Greeks either directly commissioned paintings and funerary monuments or else made large donations to the state for the design and building of major public projects. Examples of such public patronage in Athens include the funding of the Academy of Athens by Simon Sinas, the National Library by the Vallianos brothers and the Zappeion exhibition buildings by Evangelos Zappas. Greek artists became increasingly involved in these projects, either exclusively or in collaboration with foreign artists or architects. By the end of the 19th century a considerable number of group exhibitions and artistic competitions had been organized, art criticism had become an essential feature in the contemporary press, and artists had far greater exposure to the general public than previously. Still centred in Athens, the arts became increasingly active as the city expanded in the 20th century, especially during the 1950s and 1960s; architects especially benefited from the post-war construction boom. Apart from a few exceptions—such as the art critic and publisher TÉRIADE's patronage of THEOPHILOS (ii) or Alexandros Iolas's promotion of 20th-century art—there was little direct patronage, since the prevailing style of art or architecture and the choice of artists were generally determined by a combination of political, social and economic factors.

X. Collecting and dealing.

The majority of collections formed during the 19th century, such as those of Spiridon Comnos and Nikolaos Saripolos, focused mostly on ancient art; the prevailing atmosphere of Neo-classicism in Athens prompted the collecting of ancient Greek coins, sculpture, pottery and bronzes. Most of the richest collections were formed during the second half of the century, and a number of them were later donated to the state. Similarly, archaeological collections were established in Syros, Naxos, Corinth and various Ionian islands, especially Corfu. In the early 20th century ANTHONY BENAKI assembled a collection of ancient Greek, Byzantine and Ottoman artefacts, which eventually comprised the Benaki Museum, opened to the public in 1931 in his former home in Athens (*see also* §XI below). Fine arts collections were initially fewer. One of the most important, the collection of Old Master and 19th-century paintings assembled by Alexandros Soutzos (1839–95), was donated to the state and formed the basis of the National Gallery, Athens (*see* §XI below). Important collections of 19th- and 20th-century Greek paintings include those owned by Euripides Koutlidis, whose works were donated to the state in 1977 (now in Athens, N.G.), and Evangelos Averoff (1910–89), now in the Averoff Gallery in Metsovo and the A. G. Leventis Collection in Athens. The Vorres Museum of Greek Art (founded 1982) in Paiania, Attica, and the Pierides Gallery in Glyfada are private collections of modern Greek art open to the public. In the late 20th century some Greek collectors have shown particular interest in specific fields; members of the Goulandris family, for example, have formed large and important collections of ancient Greek art (the Museum of Cycladic and Ancient Greek Art, Athens) and modern art (the Museum of Modern Art, B. & E. Goulandris Foundation, Andros). A great number of Greeks, including those living abroad, have important international collections, particularly of French Impressionist and 20th-century European art. One of the most important collectors was GEORGE COSTAKIS, of Greek origin but of Russian birth, who from the late 1940s in Moscow began to collect Russian avant-garde and modernist art. He left the USSR in 1978 and settled in Greece, where he continued to collect and to donate to museums until his death in 1990.

Dealing in the 19th century was largely limited to the organization of various group shows. Small-scale commercial exhibitions of paintings and sculptures began appearing towards the end of the 19th century and the beginning of the 20th, usually in association with cultural institutions. Official dealing developed concurrently with exhibitions held in private commercial galleries; although they began in the 1930s, these exhibitions started to make an impact only during the 1950s. The number of commercial galleries continuously increased, the Zygos Gallery (associated with the art journal *Zygos*), Desmos Gallery, Nees Morphes Gallery and Galerie Zoumboulakis, all in Athens, being among the most influential. During the 1980s art auctions were established by Stavros Mihalarias Art in Athens, concentrating on Greek icons and 19th- and 20th-century Greek paintings.

BIBLIOGRAPHY

S. Lydakis: *I istoria tis neoellinikis zographikis* [The history of modern Greek painting] (Athens, 1976)

XI. Museums.

Nineteenth-century concern for the preservation of ancient Greek monuments led to the establishment of two museums in Athens: the Acropolis Museum, housing sculpture taken from buildings on the Acropolis, was finished in 1874 and was designed in a style compatible with its Classical surroundings; the National Archaeological Museum, designed and built between 1834 and 1889 in Neo-classical style by Leo von Klenze, Ludwig Lange (1801–68) and Ernst Ziller, exhibits numerous collections of ancient Greek art (*see* GREECE, ANCIENT, §XI). In 1882 the Historical and Ethnological Association was founded—exclusively by Greek members—in Athens in order to 'collect and safeguard historical and ethnological material as well as any object which contributed to the understanding of modern Greek history and life, language and literature'; its museum, the National Historical Museum, was to promote these aims through its, now considerably large, collections of history paintings, marble busts, manuscripts and memorabilia from the War of Independence (1821–8). The study and preservation of Byzantine works of art were significantly increased during the later part of the 19th century. Various collections of icons, reliefs and religious objects were assembled and in 1930 were finally housed in the Ilissia mansion (now the Byzantine Museum) in Athens. The foundation of the National Gallery and Alexandros Soutzos Museum in Athens in 1900 was the first major official attempt to gather various public and private collections of paintings that had been assembled since the reign of King Otto (*reg* 1832–62). The Gallery's collections, consisting of paintings, modern Greek sculpture and graphic and decorative art, were housed in a number of locations until the Gallery's permanent home on Vassileos Konstantinou Avenue was inaugurated in 1976. The first organized efforts to exhibit vernacular applied art took place in the 1920s, when the Museum of Greek Folk Art opened in Athens. It displays important collections of Greek embroideries, costumes, ceramics, wood-carvings and metalwork in its new quarters, opened in 1973. The Benaki Museum, named after its founder and donor ANTHONY BENAKI, also in Athens, opened to the public in 1931 and includes collections of Classical art, Byzantine and post-Byzantine icons, applied arts, 19th-century paintings, prints and drawings, as well as historical documents, a photographic archive and important collections of Chinese ceramics and Ottoman and Coptic art. The Archaeological Museum (opened 1912) in Thessaloniki displays the notable collection of finds from Vergina. Smaller museums of archaeological collections and of folk art are found throughout Greece.

BIBLIOGRAPHY

A. Andronikos, M. Hadjidakis and V. Karagiorgis: *The Greek Museums* (Athens, 1974)

A. Kokkou: *I merimna yia tis ellinikes archaeotites kai ta prota mouseia* [The care of Greek antiquities and the first museums] (Athens, 1977)

M. Kontou: *Musea kai pinakothikes tis Elladas kai tou Kyprou* [Museums and galleries of Greece and Cyprus] (Athens, 1993)

XII. Art education.

The School of Fine Arts (now the Higher School of Fine Arts) was established in Athens in 1836 as the first school of its kind in Greece. Its primary emphasis was on the study of architecture and engineering, but its programme gradually increased to include painting and sculpture. An academic, Bavarian influence was initially present thanks to German teachers as Carl Heller (sculpture, 1838–40), Christian H. Siegel (sculpture, 1847–59) and Ludwig Thiersch (painting, 1852–5), although in the 1840s and 1850s the Frenchman Pierre Bonirote (1811–91) and the Italian Raffaello Ceccoli (*fl* 1839–52) introduced a freer approach to painting. Printmaking was introduced after 1843, resulting in a more comprehensive programme. From 1844 to 1862, under the direction of the architect LYSANDROS KAFTANTZOGLOU, there were signs of a clearer emphasis on the arts in comparison to engineering. NIKIFOROS LYTRAS's tenure from 1866 to 1904 as Professor of Painting also proved decisive for the development of studies in painting: it reflected a predominance of the principles of the School of Munich, especially in genre painting (*see* §III above). Vincenzo Lanza (1822–1902) taught drawing, focusing on landscapes with Classical monuments. In the 1880s and 1890s Konstantinos Volanakis (1837–1907) and GEORGIOS ROILOS were appointed to teach at the school; they followed a rather academic approach to the visual arts, which was to be pursued under GEORGIOS LAKOVIDIS's direction (1904–32). In 1894 women were first admitted to the school to study art. In 1909 the school became officially independent, while architecture and engineering became part of the National Technical University of Athens. Throughout the 20th century the Higher School of Fine Arts, the Department of Architecture at the National Technical University and the Department of Architecture (est. 1957) of the Aristotelian University of Thessaloniki have been the most important and prestigious educational establishments for the study of fine arts and architecture in Greece. Similar institutions of significance are the Department of Applied

Arts (est. 1987) at the Aristotelian University and various private schools, among the most important the Vakalo School and the Doxiadis Centre of Ekistics (est. 1958; *see* DOXIADIS, CONSTANTINOS A.), both in Athens.

BIBLIOGRAPHY

C. Biris: *Istoria tou Ethnikou Metsoviou Polytechneiou* [The history of the National Technical University] (Athens, 1956)

S. Lydakis: *I istoria tis neoellinikis zographikis* [The history of modern Greek painting] (Athens, 1976)

XIII. Art libraries and photographic collections.

The library of the National Gallery, Athens, has a comprehensive collection of reference books, monographs, 19th- and 20th-century art periodicals and exhibition catalogues, mainly on the history of modern Greek painting, sculpture and graphic arts. The photographic archive includes the National Gallery collection and the Koutlidis Collection. The National Library, Athens, has a major collection of Greek rare editions, fine illuminated manuscripts and illuminated New Testaments of the 10th to 14th centuries. Its extensive collection of books and research material covers mainly the Classical period, as well as the Byzantine era and the period of Turkish occupation. Based on the private collection of Joannes Gennadius, the Gennadius Library in Athens has a significant number of rare editions, as well as various research archives on antiquity, the Middle Ages, the Byzantine period and modern Greece. It also houses an important collection of drawings, prints and illustrated editions by 18th- and 19th-century European travellers to Greece. The library of the Benaki Museum, Athens, has an extensive selection of books on Greek decorative arts, Byzantine art, 19th-century Greek and European art, Ottoman art and Coptic art. The museum's photographic collection contains important documentation on Greek monuments and works of art (especially from the Early Christian, Byzantine and Post-Byzantine periods), as well as on traditional Greek architectural settlements and folklore. There is also a significant collection of 19th- and early 20th-century photographers' views of Greece. The Hellenic Literary and Historical Archives Society was founded in Athens in 1980 and contains a large collection of manuscripts and books on Greek political, literary and cultural history. It has *c.* 100,000 photographs and 180,000 postcards covering aspects of Greece from the 19th century to between World Wars I and II, and among the 500 Greek archives there are some on architecture and theatre design. Notable libraries outside Athens include the Reading Society of Corfu and the Korais Library in Chios.

EVITA ARAPOGLOU

Greece, ancient. Term referring to the lands and civilization of the ancient Greeks, a culture that represents a pinnacle of achievement in art and architecture, literature and philosophy. It had its origins in the Bronze Age cultures of the 2nd millennium BC and reached its peak between the 8th and 4th centuries BC with the flowering of the city states, especially Athens; it survived their loss of independence and continued to pervade the eastern Mediterranean long after the Roman Empire was established. It spread far beyond the Greek homeland (which was not quite as extensive as modern Greece), reaching Cyprus as early as *c.* 1200 BC and many parts of the Mediterranean and Black Sea littoral from the 8th century BC onwards (see fig. 1). Alexander's conquests extended it across the Middle East to India. Western Europe is its heir, indirectly through Rome and directly through the revival of Greek studies in the Renaissance and the rediscovery of Greek art by travellers and archaeologists from the 17th century AD onwards. The inexhaustible mythology of the gods and heroes of Greece remains influential in the art and poetry of a world that has long ceased to worship them.

I. Introduction. II. Architecture. III. Planning. IV. Monumental sculpture. V. Pottery. VI. Wall and panel painting. VII. Mosaics. VIII. Metalwork. IX. Terracotta. X. Other arts. XI. Collection and display.

DETAILED TABLE OF CONTENTS

I. Introduction 366
  1. History 366
    (i) Bronze Age (before *c.* 1050 BC) 366
    (ii) Dark Age (*c.* 1050–*c.* 700 BC) 366
    (iii) Archaic (*c.* 700–*c.* 480 BC) 368
    (iv) Classical (*c.* 480–323 BC) 368
    (v) Hellenistic (323–27 BC) 369
    (vi) Postscript: Imperial Roman rule and later 369
  2. Religion 369
    (i) Belief and practice 369
    (ii) Religious imagery 370
    (iii) Manufacture of offerings 371
  3. Trade 372
  4. Patronage 373
    (i) Architecture 373
    (ii) Sculpture, painting and other arts 374
II. Architecture 375
  1. Overview 376
    (i) Building types 376
      (a) Religious 376
        – Early temples 376
        – Temple plans and elevations 376
        – Doric temples 377
        – Ionic temples 379
        – Other sacred structures 380
      (b) Civic 380
      (c) Domestic 382
      (d) Funerary 383
      (e) Entertainment and recreation 384
        – Theatres 385
        – Odeia 385
        – Hotels and dining halls 386
        – Athletic and recreational facilities 386
    (ii) Materials and construction 386
      (a) Stone 386
        – Types 387
        – Preparation 387
        – Transport and manipulation 387
        – Assembly of blocks 388
        – Surfacing and finishing 389
      (b) Other materials 389
        – Mud-brick 389
        – Wood 389
        – Terracotta 390
        – Metals 391
    (iii) Decoration 391
      (a) Façade 391
      (b) Mouldings and motifs 391

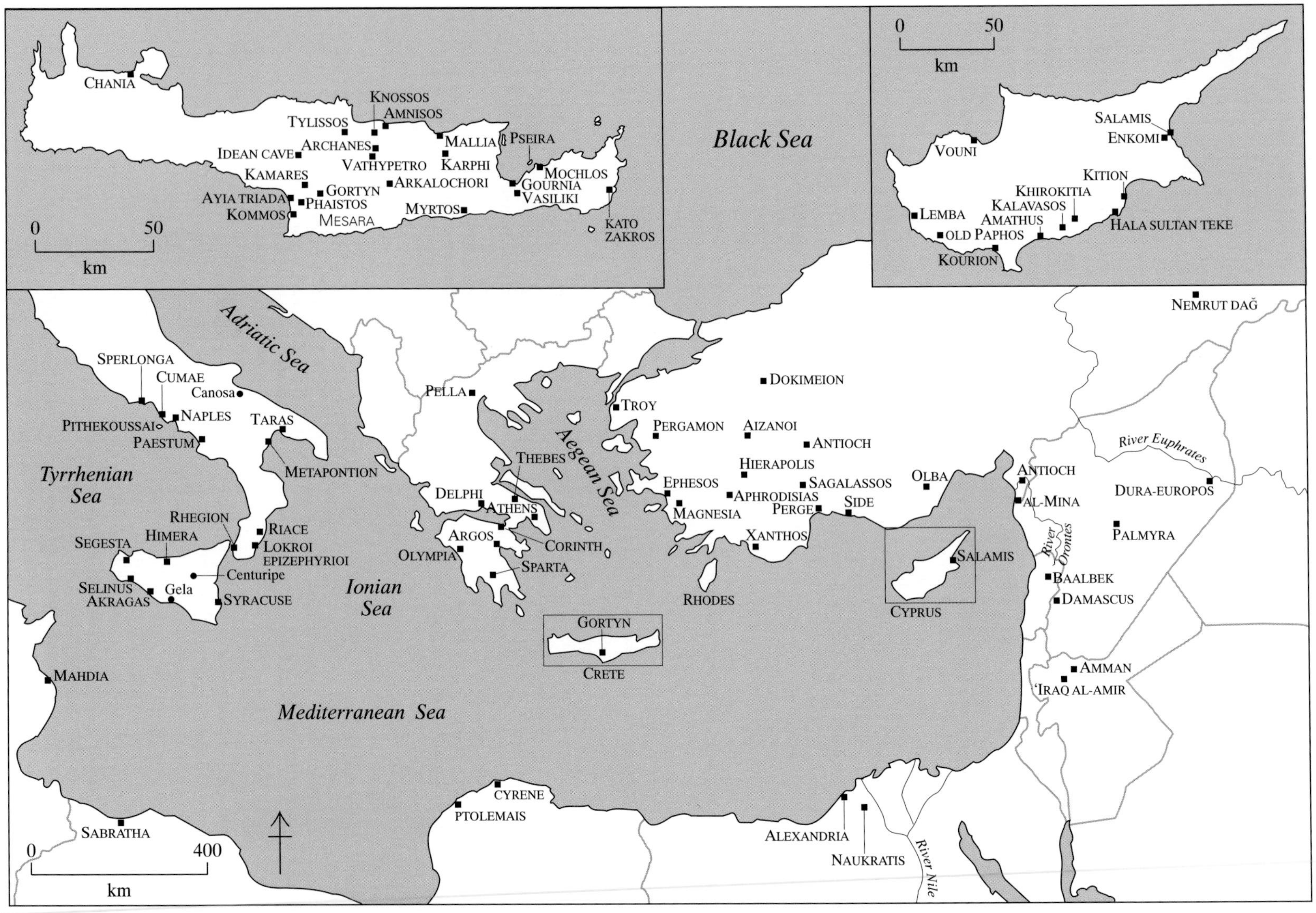

1. Map of the territories of the ancient Greek civilization; those areas with separate entries in this dictionary are distinguished by CROSS-REFERENCE TYPE

2. Map of ancient Greece and related Aegean sites; those areas with separate entries in this dictionary are distinguished by CROSS-REFERENCE TYPE

(c) Colour 392
(iv) Architects, masons and society 394
2. Historical survey 395
(i) Dark Age 396
(ii) Archaic 396
(a) Early Archaic temples 397
(b) Development of the architectural orders 398
– Doric 398
– Ionic 398
(iii) Classical 400
(a) Introduction 400
(b) Religious 400
(c) Secular 401
– Organization of cities 401
– Building types 402
(iv) Hellenistic 403
(a) Materials and techniques 403
(b) Regional styles 404
(c) Building types 405
– Temples and altars 405
– Stoas 406
– Theatres and stadia 406
– Gymnasia, palaestras and baths 406
– Tombs and commemorative monuments 407
– Halls and storehouses 407
– Domestic architecture 407
3. Theory and design 408
(i) Theorists 408
(ii) Drawings, models and specifications 409
(iii) Measurement 410
(iv) Module 412
(v) Proportion 412
(vi) Refinements 413
(vii) Symbolism 415

III. Planning 416
1. Sanctuaries 416
(i) Location 416
(ii) Organization 416
(iii) Landscaping 418
2. Towns 419
(i) Early urban development 419
(ii) The science of urban planning 419

IV. Monumental sculpture 421
1. Overview 421
(i) Forms and functions 421
(a) Free-standing 421
– Formal development 422
– Functions 424
(b) Architectural 424
– Pediments 424
– Metopes 425
– Friezes 426
– Acroteria and other forms 426
(c) Non-architectural reliefs 427
– Graves 427
– Votives 427
– Records 428
– Bases 428
(ii) Subject-matter 428
(a) Free-standing sculpture 428
– Divinities 428
– Other mythological figures 429
– Personified abstractions 429
– Generic figures 429
– Representations of individuals 429
– Groups 430
– Animals 430
– Plant life 430
(b) Free-standing reliefs 430
(c) Architectural sculpture 431
– Pediments 431
– Metopes 432
– Friezes 432
– Acroteria 432
(iii) Materials 433
(a) Introduction 433
(b) Terracotta 433
(c) Wood 433
(d) Limestone 434
(e) Marble 434
(f) Bronze 434
(g) Chryselephantine 435
(iv) Techniques 435
(a) Stoneworking 435
(b) Clay-modelling and moulding 436
(c) Bronze-casting 437
(d) Models and reproduction 437
(v) Craftsmen and society 439
(a) Professional skills and organization 439
(b) Working environment and conditions 440
(c) Status 440
2. Historical survey 441
(i) Antecedents 441
(a) Dark Age and Geometric (*c.* 1050–*c.* 700 BC) 441
(b) Proto-Daidalic (*c.* 700–*c.* 675 BC) 442
(c) Early Archaic Daidalic (*c.* 675–*c.* 600 BC) 442
(ii) Archaic (*c.* 700–*c.* 500/480 BC) 444
(a) Early (*c.* 700–*c.* 600 BC) 444
(b) Middle (*c.* 600–*c.* 550 BC) 445
(c) Late (*c.* 550–*c.* 500/480 BC) 447
(iii) Classical (*c.* 500/480–323 BC) 449
(a) Early (*c.* 500/480–*c.* 450 BC) 449
– Introduction 449
– Centres of production 450
– Types and subject-matter 451
(b) High (*c.* 450–*c.* 375 BC) 452
– Free-standing works 452
– Architectural and relief sculpture 455
(c) Late (*c.* 375–323 BC) 458
– Introduction 458
– Free-standing works 459
– Architectural sculpture 460
– Reliefs 461
(iv) Hellenistic (323–27 BC) 461
(a) Introduction 461
(b) Early (323–*c.* 220 BC) 462
(c) High (*c.* 220–*c.* 150 BC) 464
(d) Late (*c.* 150–27 BC) 465
3. Theory and criticism 467
(i) Ancient 467
(ii) Modern 468
4. Collections, museums and exhibitions 469
(i) History of collecting 469
(ii) Major collections and exhibitions 469

V. Pottery 470
1. Introduction 470
(i) Subject-matter 472
(ii) Shapes, uses and decoration 474
(a) Shapes and uses 474
– Storage and transport vessels 474
– Mixing vessels 476
– Jugs and cups 476
– Vases for cosmetics, oils and perfumes 477
– Vases associated with women 478

(b) Decoration 478
(iii) Materials and techniques 479
(a) Clay 479
(b) Forming the vase 479
(c) Decorative techniques 480
(d) Firing 482
(iv) Potters, painters and society 484
(v) Trade 486
(vi) Inscriptions 487
(a) Introduction 487
(b) Mythological names 487
(c) Names of contemporary persons 489
(d) Artists' signatures 489
(e) Other texts 489
(f) Scripts 490
2. Protogeometric 491
(i) Introduction 491
(ii) Attic 491
(iii) Other regional styles 492
3. Geometric 493
(i) Introduction 493
(ii) Attic 493
(iii) Other mainland styles 495
(iv) Island styles 496
4. Orientalizing 498
(i) Introduction 498
(ii) Proto-Corinthian 499
(iii) Proto-Attic 500
(iv) Other areas 502
5. Black-figure 504
(i) Corinthian 504
(a) Introduction 504
(b) Early 505
(c) Middle 505
(d) Late 505
(ii) Attic 506
(a) *c.* 625–*c.* 600 BC 506
(b) *c.* 600–*c.* 560 BC 507
(c) *c.* 560–*c.* 520 BC 508
(d) *c.* 520–*c.* 480 BC 510
(iii) Lakonian 512
(iv) Boiotian 513
(v) East Greek and islands 514
(vi) Chalcidian 515
(vii) Caeretan 516
(viii) Euboian 516
6. Red-figure 517
(i) Attic 517
(a) The first generation (*c.* 530–*c.* 500 BC) 517
– The Pioneer group 518
– Cup painters 518
(b) Late Archaic (*c.* 500–*c.* 480 BC) 519
– Pot painters 519
– Cup painters 520
(c) Early and High Classical (*c.*480–*c.*425 BC) 521
– Mannerists 521
– The tradition of the Berlin Painter 521
– The tradition of the Niobid Painter 522
– Cup painters 523
– Other painters 523
(d) Late 5th century BC 523
– The Meidias Painter 523
– Other painters 524
(e) 4th century BC 524
(ii) South Italian 525
(a) Lucanian 525
(b) Apulian 526
(c) Sicilian 530
(d) Campanian 531
(e) Paestan 532
(iii) Other areas 533
7. White-ground 535
8. Unpainted 536
(i) Black-glaze 536
(ii) Domestic wares 538
9. Hellenistic 538
10. Collecting and collections 540
VI. Wall and panel painting 543
1. Introduction 543
(i) Materials and techniques 543
(a) Supports 543
(b) Techniques 543
(c) Composition of paints 544
(ii) Subject-matter 544
(a) Geometric to Archaic (*c.* 900–*c.* 480 BC) 545
(b) Classical (*c.* 480–323 BC) 545
– Early mid-5th century BC 545
– Mid-5th century BC–late 4th 545
(c) Hellenistic (323–27 BC) 546
(iii) Painters and society 547
2. Historical survey 549
(i) Geometric to Archaic (*c.* 900–*c.* 480 BC) 549
(ii) Classical (*c.* 480–323 BC) 550
(a) 5th century BC 550
(b) 4th century BC 551
(iii) Hellenistic (323–27 BC) 551
3. Theory and criticism 553
(i) 5th century BC 553
(ii) 4th century BC 554
4. Collections and collectors 554
VII. Mosaics 556
1. Introduction 556
(i) Uses 556
(ii) Materials, techniques and form 556
(iii) Mosaicists 557
(iv) Motifs and subject-matter 558
(a) Patternwork 558
(b) Figural scenes 559
2. History and development 560
(i) Origins 560
(ii) Dating 562
(iii) Stylistic development 562
(a) Pebble 562
(b) Mixed and intermediate 565
(c) Tessera 566
VIII. Metalwork 568
1. Gold and silver 568
(i) Survival and evidence 568
(ii) Shapes and techniques 569
(iii) Craftsmen 570
(iv) Metrology 570
(v) Plate and pottery 570
2. Bronze 571
(i) Statuettes and figurines 571
(a) Introduction 571
(b) Geometric (*c.* 900–*c.* 700 BC) 572
(c) Archaic (*c.* 700–*c.* 480 BC) 572
(d) Classical (*c.* 480–323 BC) 573
(e) Hellenistic (323–27 BC) 573
(ii) Vessels and mirrors 574
(a) 9th–7th centuries BC 575
(b) 6th–1st centuries BC 575
– Cauldrons 575

– Other vessels 576
– Mirrors 577

IX. Terracotta 577
1. Introduction 577
2. Figurines and statuettes 578
(i) Before *c.* 700 BC 578
(ii) Archaic (*c.* 700–*c.* 480 BC) 578
(iii) Classical (*c.* 480–323 BC) 579
(iv) Hellenistic (323–27 BC) 581
3. Reliefs and plaques 582
4. Masks, protomes and busts 582

X. Other arts 583
1. Arms and armour 583
(i) Construction 583
(ii) Decoration 584
2. Coins 585
(i) Archaic (*c.* 700–*c.* 480 BC) 585
(a) The earliest coins 585
(b) Principal centres of production 585
(c) Conclusion 586
(ii) Classical (*c.* 480–323 BC) 586
(a) Techniques and materials 586
(b) Coin designs 586
(c) Individual die-engravers 587
(d) The political use of coinage 587
(iii) Hellenistic (323–27 BC) 588
(a) Ruler portraits 588
(b) General and stylistic development 588
(c) Coinages under Roman rule 589
3. Faience 589
4. Furniture 591
(i) Types 591
(a) Seats 591
(b) Couches 591
(c) Tables and chests 592
(ii) Materials and decoration 592
(iii) Evidence and development 592
5. Glass 593
(i) Core-formed bottles 593
(ii) Cast and polished glass 593
(iii) Ptolemaic plaques, canes and bars 595
6. Ivory and bone 595
(i) Seals, reliefs and statuettes 595
(ii) Composite works 596
(iii) Furniture 596
7. Jewellery 597
(i) Gold 597
(a) Sub-Mycenaean and Protogeometric (*c.* 1050–*c.* 900 BC) 597
(b) Geometric (*c.* 900–*c.* 700 BC) 597
(c) Archaic (*c.* 700–*c.* 480 BC) 597
(d) Classical (*c.* 480–323 BC) 598
(e) Hellenistic (323–27 BC) 599
(ii) Bronze 600
(a) Pins 600
(b) Fibulae 600
(c) Diadems 601
(d) Bracelets 601
(e) Rings 601
(f) Pendants 601
(g) Beads 602
8. Lamps 602
9. Stucco 602
10. Textiles 604
11. Wood 604

XI. Collection and display 604
1. Collectors, collections and museums 604
(i) Introduction 604
(ii) Development of collections after the mid-17th century 605
(a) Europe 605
(b) USA 606
2. Exhibitions 606

I. Introduction.

1. History. 2. Religion. 3. Trade. 4. Patronage.

1. HISTORY. In ancient times free Greece (Hellas) was never politically united. Divided by mountain and sea barriers, there were scores of independent city states (see fig. 2), without a common coinage or even calendar and each with its own (usually unstable) political system. Aristotle published accounts of 157 different Greek constitutions, and wars over disputed territory were endemic. What identified the Greeks was their language, divided into mutually intelligible dialects. By the 6th century BC they were calling themselves Hellenes by contrast with the barbarians who spoke foreign tongues. Barbarians were excluded from competing in the Panhellenic Games at the great religious centres of Delphi and Olympia (which housed dedications from almost every corner of the Greek world), the Corinthian Isthmus and Nemea. But the admission of Alexander I, King of Macedon (*reg* 495–450 BC), to the Olympic Games as a Hellene was a portent. Greeks shared a common religious tradition but did not sharply distinguish between their own and foreign gods.

Modern scholars divide Greek history into periods (see fig. 3), but these were not recognized in ancient times: the words 'Helladic' and 'Hellenistic' were coined only in the 19th century AD. The delimitations of these periods are arbitrary and vary from one modern work to the next.

(i) Bronze Age (before *c.* 1050 BC). (ii) Dark Age (*c.* 1050–*c.* 700 BC). (iii) Archiac (*c.* 700–*c.* 480 BC). (iv) Classical (*c.* 480–323 BC). (v) Hellenistic (323–27 BC). (vi) Postscript: Imperial Roman rule and later.

(i) Bronze Age (before c. *1050* BC*).* It is not certain whether the CYCLADIC civilization of the Aegean islands was Greek-speaking. Crete's MINOAN civilization was not. But the Mycenaean civilization (*c.* 1600 to *c.* 1050 BC) was Greek (*see* HELLADIC), as was confirmed by the decipherment in the 1950s of the syllabic script of palace inventories (Linear B). Poetic imagination, centuries later, transformed the age of palaces into the so-called Heroic Age. The Homeric epics (8th century BC) tell of the legendary ten-year war against Troy by a Greek alliance led by Agamemnon, King of Argos/Mycenae, and the homecoming of the victors, especially the much-travelled Odysseus. The mythology of the Heroic Age continued to loom large in the art and poetry of the Greeks of the Classical period and beyond. Their historians dated the Trojan War to the 13th century BC. Troy VIIa, one of the successive walled citadels of Troy unearthed by modern archaeologists, was indeed destroyed by fire *c.* 1250 BC.

*(ii) Dark Age (*c. *1050–*c. *700* BC*).* The destruction of the mainland palaces *c.* 1200 BC is connected by some scholars with invasions from the north of new Greek races,

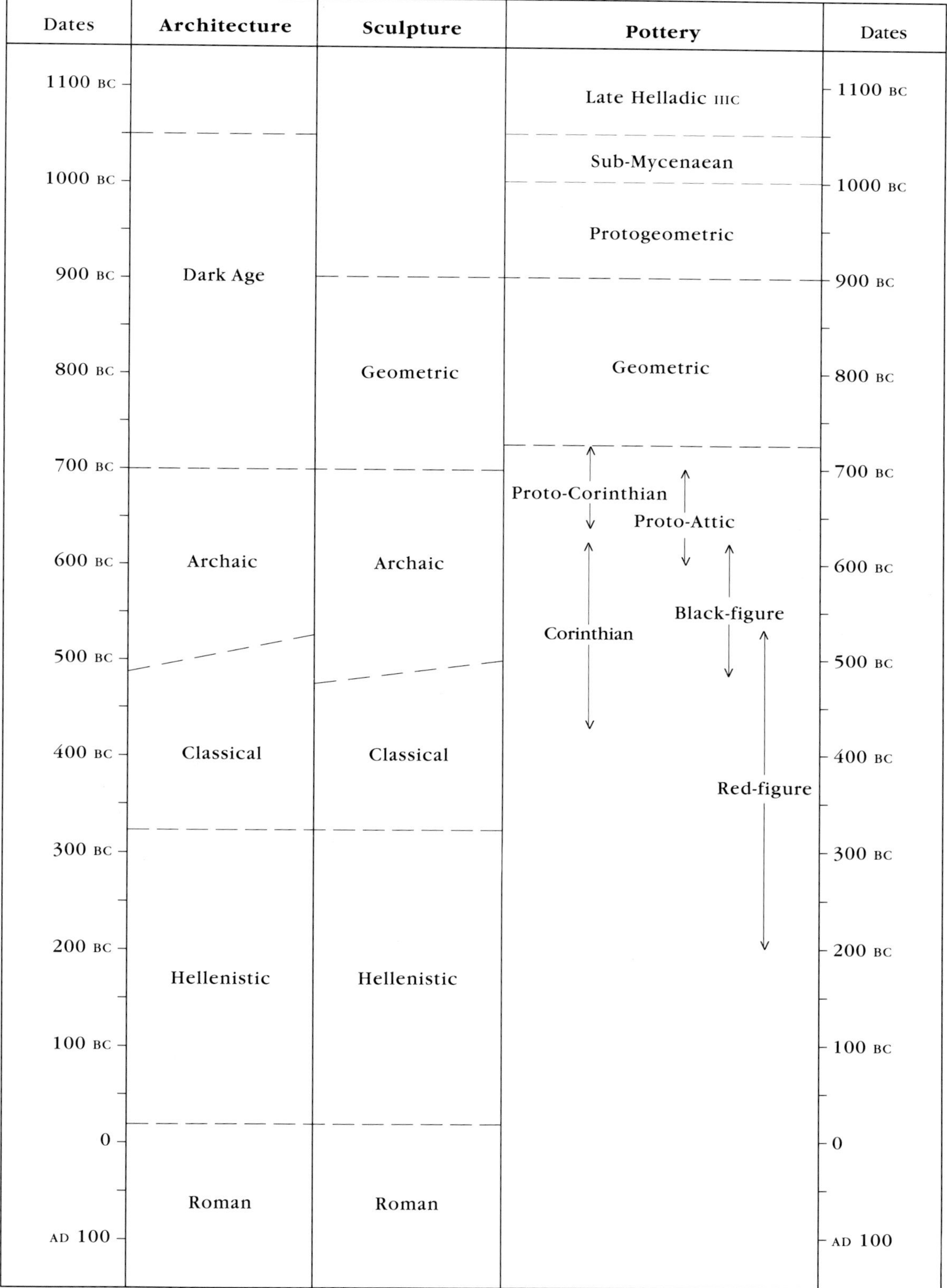

3. Chronological chart showing generally accepted dates for the development of Greek architecture, sculpture and pottery

especially the Dorians who occupied most of the Peloponnese. The population of mainland Greece declined, and material culture was impoverished. Fugitives founded the Ionian cities on the west coast of Asia Minor *c.* 1000 BC, flanked by outrunners of the invaders: Aiolians to the north, Dorians to the south and on the islands of Rhodes and Kos. The Athenians believed that in this period of migrations they had withstood the invaders and had always occupied the same territory. Finds in the Kerameikos cemetery, outside Athens' walls, indeed show continuity from Mycenaean times. The Dark Ages have left no trace of writing. The remains of simple wooden and mud-brick buildings have been uncovered (*see* §II, 2(i) below). As civilization revived on a modest scale, Protogeometric painted pottery was succeeded by the disciplined Geometric style at Athens and elsewhere (*see* §V, 3 below). Contacts with the Near East were resumed. Recent excavations at Lefkandi prove that Euboeans were trading with Syria from the 9th century BC and Phoenician goldsmiths are now known to have settled in Crete.

(iii) Archaic (c. *700*–c. *480* BC*)*. With the introduction of the alphabet from Phoenicia in the 8th century BC and the founding of the Olympic Games (traditionally in 776 BC), we begin to trace political history. Euboeans pushed out to the Bay of Naples *c.* 760 BC to trade and colonize, and from 734 BC Euboeans, Corinthians and other Greeks founded independent cities on the coasts of Sicily, South Italy and Thrace. In the 7th and 6th centuries BC there was further Greek colonization around the Black Sea and its approaches, in Cyrenaica and, despite Carthaginian and Etruscan hostility, in the western Mediterranean. Greeks ventured to North Africa and Spain and even explored beyond Gibraltar and into Central Asia. Greek mercenary soldiers and traders settled in Egypt. Greek literature begins with the Homeric epics, in a style and metre already perfect, and continues with a brilliant succession of poets including Hesiod, Archilochos, Tyrtaeus, Solon, Sappho, Alkaios, Anakreon and Pindar. Monumental architecture and sculpture, largely inspired by Egyptian models but transcending them, began in the 7th century BC. The stylized beasts and monsters of Orientalizing pottery (produced from *c.* 725 BC, especially at Corinth) gave way to the vivacious naturalism of Athenian Black-figure pottery in the 6th century BC, which was itself superseded in the last quarter of the century by the classic beauty of Athenian Red-figure. Though subject to social unrest and periods of tyranny, many Greek states evolved responsible government with codified laws. Solon's reforms in 594 BC made Athens a constitutional state, and after an interlude of tyranny, Athenian democracy was instituted in 508 BC. In wealth and political importance the Greek cities were dwarfed by the older civilizations of the Near East; but Greek culture—though Orientals and Greeks alike were slow to realize it—was already superior when the Near Eastern kingdoms were swallowed by the emerging Persian empire between *c.* 546 and 525 BC.

Hoping to increase his use of disciplined Greek soldiers, King Croesus of Lydia had invited Sparta, the foremost Greek military power, into alliance. But *c.* 546 BC he was overwhelmed by King Cyrus of Persia before he could call for Spartan help. Persia then conquered the Greek cities of western Asia Minor. After suppressing a revolt by their Ionian subjects in 493 BC, the Persians turned on mainland Greece. Athens repelled a Persian landing at Marathon in 490 BC, and an improvised coalition defeated King Xerxes' massive invasion in 480–479 BC—the Greeks' proudest achievement.

(iv) Classical (c. *480–323* BC*)*. Athens, at the head of a league of islanders and liberated coastal cities, continued to harass the Persian empire in the eastern Mediterranean until the peace of *c.* 449 BC. In 447 BC the Athenian democratic politician PERICLES initiated the finest building programme of ancient times. The Athenian Acropolis was adorned with a monumental entrance, the Propylaia, leading to the Parthenon, the goddess Athena's temple, adorned with Pheidias' sculptures, and the shrine to Athens' ancient king Erechtheus. Pericles saw Athens as the 'School of Hellas'. Here at the city festivals Aeschylus, Sophocles and Euripides produced their verse tragedies, complemented by the politically outspoken comedies of Aristophanes. Herodotus, the 'father of history', judged the Athenians to have saved Greece in the Persian wars, though he was no pro-Athenian propagandist and knew that this assessment would be unpopular. The Athenians incurred resentment by using their allies' money for their building programme and by turning their defensive maritime league into an empire. In the Peloponnesian War against the Spartan alliance (431–404 BC), recorded by Thucydides, the Athenians proved resilient, drawing on the loyalty of the democracies they had set up throughout their empire. But the war ended in Spartan victory, with the help of Persian subsidies.

During the 4th century BC Sparta's attempts to keep the Asian Greeks free of Persian domination were frustrated by the Corinthian War of 395–386 BC, when a recrudescent Athens joined Thebes, Argos and Corinth against Sparta. Persian diplomacy and money re-established Spartan ascendancy in mainland Greece in return for the surrender of the Asian Greek cities. Patriotic Greeks saw this as a humiliation, though Persia now ruled benignly and never repeated Xerxes' invasion. Athens organized a second maritime league on a modest scale in 377 BC, and Sparta's hegemony was finally broken in 371 BC by Thebes, which, however, was dominant for only a decade.

There was little poetry in the 4th century BC, but the philosophers Plato and Aristotle taught at Athens, and it was the golden age of Athenian oratory. Demosthenes' speeches roused Athens, though weakened by the near-collapse of her second league in 355 BC, to champion Greece against the expansion of Philip II of Macedon. Victorious at the Battle of Chaironeia in 338 BC, Philip spared Athens' democracy, though Greece was now under a single ruler for the first time. In 335 BC, Philip's son ALEXANDER THE GREAT destroyed Thebes, but he continued his father's magnanimity to Athens. He re-established Greek democracies in Asia Minor at the beginning of the crusade in which he conquered the entire Persian empire (334–323 BC), including Egypt, where he founded the Greek city of Alexandria. He penetrated as far as Samarkand and the Punjab.

(v) Hellenistic (323–27 BC). Alexander's empire did not long survive him. Huge tracts fell to competing Macedonian generals, the *diadochi* or 'successors', who proclaimed themselves kings and founded dynasties. Greek now became the language of government and of a superimposed universal culture throughout the Near East. A Macedonian ruler abolished Athens' democracy in 322 BC. In mainland Greece periodic efforts were made to shake off Macedonian rule; the Achaean and Aetolian leagues asserted themselves. Rhodes was an independent, prosperous naval state. The chief power, however, lay with the kings: those of Macedonia and Epiros in Europe, the Attalids of Pergamon in Asia Minor (*see* PERGAMON, §1), the Ptolemies of Egypt and SELEUCIDS of Syria, and the rulers of distant Bactria (Afghanistan). Hellenistic Athens was politically unimportant, though still a focus of civilization. As a university city, it housed not only the Platonic Academy and the Aristotelian Lyceum but also the new influential schools of Stoic and Epicurean philosophy. The Ptolemies endowed the 'Museum' of Alexandria, a centre for scholars, and the famous Library, whose librarians Kallimachos of Cyrene and Apollonios Rhodios wrote poetry competing in refinement with Theocritus' pastorals. The Seleucids, whose rule at times extended to the Indus, founded numerous Greek cities. Seleucia-on-Tigris, established *c.* 312 BC, remained Greek long after the Parthians had re-orientalized Mesopotamia and Iran, leaving Bactria isolated. Eumenes II of Pergamon (*reg* 197–159 BC) planned his capital with buildings impressively grouped to exploit the sloping hillside site—a 'baroque' development, as was the dramatic sculpture of the 'Great Altar' there.

The advancing power of Rome, supreme in the west after defeating Carthage in 202 BC, rapidly subdued the Greek world. But the Romans were always aware—sometimes uncomfortably—of Greek cultural superiority. Their general Titus Flamininus, victorious in his mission to help the mainland Greeks against Philip V of Macedonia, proclaimed the liberation of Greece at the Isthmian Games of 196 BC. But Rome's continuing involvement in local conflicts culminated in the destruction of Corinth and annexation of Greece in 146 BC. Pergamon was bequeathed to Rome by the will of its last king in 133 BC. Most Asian and mainland Greeks welcomed Mithradates VI of Pontus as liberator in 88 BC, but reconquest by the Roman general Sulla left many cities in ruins. The shrunken Seleucid domain was annexed in 64 BC and Ptolemaic Egypt in 30 BC. The Greek cities were looted by Roman magnates and suffered grievously in the Roman civil wars that ended with Augustus as emperor (27 BC–AD 14).

(vi) Postscript: Imperial Roman rule and later. Roman governors could be extortionate even during the succeeding imperial peace, but Greek city civilization flourished. Much ancient art was still visible in mainland Greece when Pausanias wrote his *Guide to Greece* in *c.* 150 AD. In Asia Minor and the Levant, Greek architecture was revived in innovative styles, and the Greek language continued to dominate the eastern Roman Empire. Ancient Greek literature was widely studied (many 20th-century discoveries of lost literature on papyrus derive from the rubbish-dumps of the provincial Egyptian town of Oxyrhynchus), and new Greek writings outdistanced Latin in most genres, from the squibs of Lucian to the romantic novel. The Jews Philo and Josephus wrote in Greek; the Christian Gospels were composed in the colloquial Greek common language. In AD 66–7 Nero toured Greece, winning prizes for music at all the Panhellenic Games and once again proclaiming Greek liberty at the Isthmus—a boon soon revoked. One can still see the nail-marks of the gold letters mounted on the Parthenon to welcome Nero. The emperor Hadrian adopted Greek fashions and added a suburb to Athens. Marcus Aurelius, emperor and philosopher, wrote his *Meditations* in Greek. Roman citizenship by AD 212 was extended to all free persons in the Empire. With the transference of the capital to the 'New Rome' of Byzantium (renamed Constantinople) in AD 324, Greek civilization received another lease of life. What survives of ancient Greek literature was largely preserved by the Byzantine empire, to be brought west when Constantinople fell to the Turks in 1453. The Greeks who remain there still call themselves *Romaioi*, 'Romans'.

BIBLIOGRAPHY

Herodotus: *Histories*
Thucydides: *History of the Peloponnesian War*
Strabo: *Geography*
Plutarch: *Lives*
Pausanias: *Guide to Greece*
J. Boardman: *The Greeks Overseas* (London, 1964, *R*/1973, rev. 1980)
J. B. Bury and R. Meiggs: *A History of Greece* (London, 1900, New York, 5/1978)
J. Boardman, J. Griffin and O. Murray, eds: *The Oxford History of the Classical World* (Oxford, 1986)

THOMAS BRAUN

2. RELIGION. Ancient Greek religion is a complex subject with many ramifications; this article focuses on the relationship between the Greeks' religious beliefs and practices and their art and architecture. This connection also is discussed in more specific contexts, both in the articles on individual art forms below and elsewhere in the *Dictionary* in such articles as SANCTUARY and TEMPLE.

(i) Belief and practice. Greek religion centred on the 12 major deities, known as the Olympian deities after their supposed home, Mt Olympos. These were Zeus, Hera, Poseidon, Athena, Apollo, Artemis, Aphrodite, Hermes, Demeter, Dionysos, Hephaistos and Ares. Many other deities were also worshipped, including the healing god Asklepios, whose cult became important in the 5th century BC. In the Classical and Hellenistic periods there was a growing interest in the cults of such personified abstractions as 'Peace' (e.g. see fig. 39 below) and 'Fortune'. Furthermore, many other figures, some legendary and some historical, were venerated as semi-divine heroes with cults and sacrifices. Some of the Greek gods were worshipped in the Bronze Age, but most information about their myths and festivals dates from the 8th century BC onwards, the earliest major record being the Homeric epics.

The Olympian deities were worshipped throughout Greece, but each city had a certain cult or cults to which it accorded particular importance, often using a distinctive cult title for the deity worshipped at a local sanctuary.

Worship in sanctuaries and religious festivals were regular and essential features of Greek society from at least the 8th century BC to the end of Greco-Roman

4. Attic Red-figure bell krater depicting a *lampadedromia* (torch race), possibly during the Panathenaic festival, in the manner of the Peleus Painter, h. 361 mm, *c*. 430–420 BC (Cambridge, MA, Arthur M. Sackler Museum)

antiquity. Greek religious ritual consisted typically of an open-air sacrifice performed on an altar within a sacred area (the temenos or sanctuary) in front of worshippers. A CULT STATUE representing the deity might also be set up, and it was from the 'houses' built for these statues that temples developed. It was customary for worshippers to make offerings to the deity, dedications ranging from simple terracotta figurines to costly works of art.

(ii) Religious imagery. The myths of the gods and heroes were transmitted in various ways, particularly through the poetry of the Homeric epics and Hesiod and through dramatic performances. Art was another important way in which these myths were made familiar to Greeks. Many recognizable mythological scenes appear on Greek painted pottery from the 7th century BC onwards. Deities and heroes are identifiable by their context in a scene or by distinctive attributes, such as Zeus' thunderbolt or Herakles' club. Mythological scenes were also used on embroidered textiles, wall paintings, bronze vessels and utensils, ivory seals and plaques, and in many other domestic or public contexts.

Statues of deities, especially the cult statues made for Greek temples, had more than decorative or narrative importance, and they often formed a major focus for ritual. Cult statues, made of wood, stone, gold or ivory, could create such a firm association between the work of art and the deity represented that there might even be some confusion as to whether the statue was an inanimate creation or in some way actually embodied the deity. Thus, though the philosopher Herakleitos (*fl c.* 500 BC) objected to confusing the statue with the god, many other ancient texts do not make such a clear distinction, referring to the statues in a way that is indistinguishable from that in which the gods were addressed. The gods were believed to travel and to lodge in local temples inside their cult statue. The statues were cleaned, dressed, bound and treated in various ways in rituals that also associated them directly with the deity.

Some Greek sculptors may thus have seen their work as performing a vital role in illuminating the religion of their people. One of the most famous cult statues of antiquity was PHEIDIAS' *Zeus* at Olympia (mid-5th century BC; destr. in antiquity), about which many ancient anecdotes survive. Quintilian commented that 'Pheidias added something to traditional religion' (*Institutio oratoria* XII.x.9). Pheidias himself is said to have stated that his work was based on a description of Zeus in the *Iliad* (I.528–30), acknowledging the special authority of the Homeric poems on religious matters (Strabo: *Geography* VIII.iii.30).

Important cult statues continued to be produced in the Hellenistic period (323–27 BC), but many of these later works reflect the changing philosophical and religious attitudes of the time. New cults centred on such personified abstractions as the Fortune (*tyche*) of a city were introduced. Eutychides' statue of the *Tyche of Antioch* shows the goddess as a seated woman with various suitable attributes (*see* ANTIOCH, fig. 1). By giving human form to such personifications, artists presented them in an immediate way to their worshippers.

Ancient works occasionally depict scenes of religious worship, for example festivals or sacrifices. Such representations, some of which show cult statues, occur on the richly decorated pottery of Attica and South Italy between the 6th and the 4th century BC (see fig. 4). Other classes of pottery were specially made, presumably locally, for certain cults and were sometimes decorated with scenes connected with the cult. Examples from the Archaic and Classical periods come from the Sanctuary of Artemis at Brauron (Brauron Mus.) and the Kabeirion near Thebes (Athens, N. Archaeol. Mus.; New York, Met.; Oxford, Ashmolean).

In the Archaic period (*c*. 650–*c*. 480 BC) terracotta votive plaques were decorated with figures of deities or scenes of worship (*see* §IX, 3 below). Large numbers have been found at the Pente Skouphia hill near Corinth (Corinth, Archaeol. Mus.), and wooden plaques are known from Pitsa (Athens, N. Archaeol. Mus.). Sculpted stone votive reliefs occur from the 6th century BC onwards. They often show worshippers paying homage to the god, and occasionally the worshipper and his family or attendants are shown approaching the seated deity, who is usually depicted on a much larger scale (see fig. 5). The most famous representation of a religious ritual is the Parthenon frieze (*c*. 442–438 BC; London, BM; Athens, Acropolis Mus., and elsewhere; for illustration *see* FRIEZE, fig. 1). It seems certain that this represents the procession in the Panathenaic festival, one of the most important celebrations in Athens, watched by all the Olympians. These are shown seated and may be identified by their size and attributes, though their facial types share the Classical smooth features of the human figures on the frieze.

(iii) Manufacture of offerings. The demand for dedications stimulated the manufacture of many works of art, including entire buildings, sculptures, bronzes and pottery. Sanctuaries provided an opportunity for conspicuous display, and cities or powerful individuals could advertise their prestige by building temples or treasuries, occasionally decorated with elaborate sculpture. From the Archaic to the Hellenistic periods, sanctuaries remained a major source of commissions for Greek architects, both in publicly funded projects and, especially in the Hellenistic period, in those carried out under the patronage of rulers (*see also* §III, 1 below).

Many other types of offering allowed individuals to vaunt wealth or commemorate military or athletic successes. Large bronze cauldrons were typical dedications in the 8th and 7th centuries BC, succeeded in the Archaic period by large, sometimes over life-size sculptures. The two main Archaic sculptural types, the nude male statue, or KOUROS, and the draped female figure, or KORE, were used both as funerary markers and as dedications. Many examples, including statues from Delos and Samos, are conspicuously inscribed with the dedicator's name. Ancient Greek literature provides many further instances of splendid dedications perpetuating the name of the dedicator. Indeed ancient inscriptions record regulations controlling the siting of particular offerings in the sanctuary, perhaps as a means to avoid cluttering the most prestigious areas.

There were other important motives for making dedications. Inscriptions and literary texts clearly show that many offerings were made in connection with a vow, in hope of (or in gratitude for) a divine favour. Such votive offerings often marked a special occasion in the life of the dedicator, such as marriage or childbirth, and thus were one way in which Greek society could mark important moments in life. The artists and craftsmen who made such artefacts were thus providing the essential equipment with which the community could carry out important rituals.

Dedications were made in many materials, some that rarely survive—gold, silver, wood, textile—and others that are found in great quantity in rich votive deposits within the temenos (the sacred area surrounding a shrine or temple), particularly bronze and terracotta. Some objects made sacred by dedication may originally have been manufactured for an everyday purpose. Many pieces of sanctuary jewellery were probably originally worn in daily life and only later dedicated. Other sanctuary finds, including musical instruments, vessels, knives and other utensils, may occasionally be identified as ritual equipment. Many offerings, however, were manufactured exclusively for dedication, for example pottery with painted dedicatory inscriptions added before firing. There is also considerable evidence for the manufacture of offerings within the sanctuary itself. Among such workshops a notable example is that used by Pheidias for the making of the cult statue of *Zeus* at Olympia.

Even if the actual workshop has not been found, local production in the sanctuary is often suggested by the presence of miscast or misfired items and other by-products of the process of manufacture. Thus, miscast bronze griffin protomes (Samos, Archaeol. Mus.) from the Sanctuary of Hera on Samos suggest that some of the numerous 7th-century BC griffin cauldrons dedicated there were made locally. Many other Archaic sanctuaries, including those at Olympia, Delphi, Sparta and Philia, have also produced evidence of metalworking. At some, it is possible that the sanctuary workshop made tools for use in the community as well as religious objects for dedication. At the sanctuaries of Hera at Perachora votive objects of coral, ivory and pottery were probably worked on the site. Such artefacts were presumably sold at the sanctuary or near by, though little is known about merchants or votive 'shops' in Greek sanctuaries.

5. Votive relief depicting a sacrifice in a rural sanctuary to two gods (? Asklepios and Hygieia), marble, h. 610 mm, said to be from Corinth, 3rd–1st century BC (Munich, Glyptothek)

Local manufacture need not imply that each sanctuary had resident craftsmen. Instead, itinerant artists and craftsmen may have travelled to different sanctuaries, and it has been possible to attribute bronzes, terracottas and ivories found in sanctuaries across a wide geographical area to the same original 'school'. The craftsmen themselves could also make offerings. Among the dedicatory epigrams, mostly of Hellenistic date, collected in the *Palatine Anthology* VI, there are many examples of craftsmen dedicating the tools of their trade on retirement. They might also dedicate their own work to a deity in gratitude for their skill. Thus bronzeworkers gave the first fruits of their work to Athena and other deities, for example a 6th-century BC miniature bronze chariot wheel (Rhodes, Archaeol. Mus.) dedicated to Apollo by a Rhodian bronzesmith, Onesos.

BIBLIOGRAPHY

W. H. D. Rouse: *Greek Votive Offerings* (Cambridge, 1902)
E. A. Gardner: *Religion and Art in Ancient Greece* (London and New York, 1910/*R* 1969)
A. Rumpf: *Die Religion der Griechen*, xiii and xiv of *Bilderatlas zur Religionsgeschichte* (Leipzig, 1928)
J. Boardman: 'Painted Votive Plaques and an Early Inscription from Aegina', *Annu. Brit. Sch. Athens*, xlix (1954), pp. 183–201
K. Schefold: *Griechische Kunst als religiöses Phänomen* (Hamburg, 1959)
U. Hausmann: *Griechische Weihreliefs* (Berlin, 1960)
T. J. Dunbabin: *Perachora*, ii (Oxford, 1962), pp. 528–30
T. B. L. Webster: *Potter and Patron in Classical Athens* (London, 1972), pp. 126–51, 250–69

W. F. M. Burkert: *Griechische Religion der archaischen und klassischen Epoche* (Stuttgart, 1977); Eng. trans. by J. Raffan (Oxford, 1985), pp. 4–7, 66–73, 84–95

U. Gehrig: 'Frühe griechische Bronzegusstechniken', *Archäol. Anz.*, 1979, pp. 547–58 (553–4)

R. L. Gordon: 'The Real and the Imaginary: Production and Religion in the Graeco-Roman World', *A. Hist.*, ii (1979), pp. 5–34

F. T. van Straten: 'Gifts for the Gods', *Faith, Hope and Worship*, ed. H. J. Versnel (Leiden, 1981), pp. 65–151

R. Hägg, ed.: *Greek Renaissance of the Eighth Century BC: Tradition and Innovation* (Stockholm, 1983), pp. 131–47, 162, 165

K. Schefold: *Die Bedeutung der griechischen Kunst für das Verständnis des Evangeliums* (Mainz, 1983)

E. Simon: *Festivals of Attica* (Madison, 1983)

M. Robertson: 'Greek Art and Religion', *Greek Religion and Society*, ed. P. E. Easterling and J. V. Muir (Cambridge, 1985), pp. 126–51

F. T. van Straten: 'The God's Portion in Greek Sacrificial Representations: Is the Tail Doing Nicely', *Early Greek Cult Practice. Proceedings of the 5th International Symposium at the Swedish Institute at Athens: Athens, 1986*, pp. 51–68

R. Hägg, ed.: *The Iconography of Greek Cult in the Archaic and Classical Periods* (Liège, 1992)

CHRISTOPHER G. SIMON

3. TRADE. Most long-distance trade in the Greek world was by sea. Literary texts rarely provide information about trade in art, being more concerned with the transport of staples and slaves. Nevertheless, Kritias, writing in Athens in the 5th century BC, drew attention to trade in Etruscan gold and bronzework that 'adorns the home' (Athenaeus: *Deipnosophists* I.xxviii.b–c). Hermippos, writing at roughly the same time, mentioned Libya as a source for ivory (Athenaeus: *Deipnosophists* I.xxvii.b–c). Sometimes ancient sources mention the movement of specific items: in the 6th century BC the Spartans sent by sea a large bronze krater as a present for King Croesus of Lydia, in Asia Minor, 'covered with small figures all around the rim'; it never arrived, ending up in the Sanctuary of Hera on Samos (Herodotus: *Histories* I.lxix–lxx).

A few Archaic (*c.* 700–*c.* 480 BC) and Classical (*c.* 480–323 BC) shipwrecks have been recognized and excavated. Most of the cargoes, such as that found in what appears to be an Etruscan shipwreck off the Italian island of Giglio (see Bound), seem to be linked to the carrying of staples, such as oil and wine, as well as metals. These mixed cargoes would have allowed shipowners, probably members of the social élite, to spread their risk. Commercial graffiti from pottery has identified the role of Phoenicians and Etruscans, among others, in the movement of Attic pottery, proof that the trade in Greek objects was not exclusively in the hands of Greek merchants. A commercial graffito on a piece of Greek silver plate from Dălboki in modern Bulgaria (Oxford, Ashmolean) suggests that trade in such luxury items was organized along similar lines.

It is hard to estimate the level of ancient Greek trade and the proportion of this traffic that contained materials for the production of art or the finished products themselves. Estimates derived from the slag heaps of the Classical period at Populonia in Etruria suggest that if the finished iron had been exported, it would represent the movement of some 10–20 ships per year, each carrying 120–160 tons of ore, over some four centuries. At Athens, estimates of grain consumption suggest that even in a non-famine year some 100–200 ships would have arrived at Peiraeus merely to feed the population of Attica; to these figures may be added ships carrying other materials, such as timber.

Some trade moved through such large emporia as the well-explored city of NAUKRATIS in the Nile Delta. Herodotus (II.clxxviii–clxxix) states that the city was established under Amasis (*reg* 570–526 BC) to allow the Greeks to trade with Egypt. One of the important inscriptions from the site, the Naukratis stele, records the tariffs on items, including gold and silver, passing through the town during the reign of Nektanebo II (*reg* 360–343 BC). Prominent traders included the Aeginetans, and it is perhaps noteworthy that the Archaic Temple of Aphaia on Aegina contained, according to an inscription, an ivory cult statue; ivory was in part obtained through Egypt. Other important centres of exchange include AL-MINA at the mouth of the Orontes River in modern Syria. This port may have been one of the key links in the movement of Eastern objects and influences to the Greek world. In the west, one of the earliest centres for trade was PITHEKOUSSAI, on the island of Ischia in the Bay of Naples.

The acquisition of raw materials for the production of luxury items was one aspect of ancient trade. The 4th-century BC geographic text of Pseudo-Scylax records that Phoenicians traded on the Atlantic coast of Africa, exchanging Attic pottery and glass for ivory tusks and hides (*Peripius* 112). Given the presence of Attic pottery in the exchange, it is reasonable to suppose that Athens was one of the places that received the items acquired in Africa. This may have been through the intermediary of some other port in the western Mediterranean, although the presence of Phoenician traders at Piraeus is recorded. The orator Isokrates (436–338 BC) saw Piraeus as a 'market in the centre of Hellas' where surpluses from the Greek world could be traded (*Panagyricus* xlii). Once at Athens or some other urban centre, these raw materials could be worked into luxury items. The painted ivory plaques from Kul Oba (near Kerch) in southern Russia (St Petersburg, Hermitage), with scenes such as the *Judgement of Paris*, were almost certainly made within the Greek world and exported to the region; they express the complex interplay between the non-Greek world (the ivory source, the initial exchange with traders and the final consumer) and the Greek cities where the objects were made. Parallel to this movement of painted ivory products is the appearance of silver plate with gold-figured decoration from graves at Chemyrev (ex-Hermitage, St Petersburg) and Semibratny, eastern Crimea (St Petersburg, Hermitage); these pieces are likely to have been made in a major Greek centre such as Athens.

Some primary materials for the creation of sculpture and other works of art were available within the Greek world: marble came from the Cyclades and from Attica, and silver was mined at Laurion in Attica. Bronze was made from an alloy of Cypriot copper and tin from Sardinia and other areas in the western Mediterranean. This trade with Cyprus is reflected in the quantity of Greek pottery on the island, probably brought in the ships coming to collect the ore. Tracing the movement of raw materials has been made easier with the use of scientific analysis; silver from Laurion has been recognized in the Porticello shipwreck, for example (see Eisman and Ridgway), and lead from the same source has been found in Archaic votive figurines in the Lakonian Sanctuary of Artemis Orthia.

Evidence for trade in finished art objects includes the numerous Egyptian bronzes found in the Sanctuary of Hera on Samos (Vathy, Archaeol. Mus.), which presumably had been dedicated there by Samians returning from Naukratis. Pieces of Greek gold and silver plate found in the tombs of Thracians, for example at Dălboki (Oxford, Ashmolean) and Duvanli (Plovdiv, Archaeol. Mus.), and Scythians, for example at Semibratny and Kul Oba (St Petersburg, Hermitage), are likely to have reached there via Greek trade. A large bronze krater with relief decoration, found in a grave at Vix in Burgundy, France (late 6th century BC; Châtillon-sur-Seine, Mus. Archéol.), is another example of the ancient trade in large pieces of metalwork; the krater appears to have been shipped in pieces and put together at its final destination (*see also* §VIII, 2(ii)(b) below; for illustration *see* VIX).

When considering sculpture, the art historian must consider if the piece was produced locally or imported, if the sculptor was local, itinerant or an emigrant, and if the materials had been imported. Ancient literary sources, and to a lesser degree epigraphy, have drawn attention to the movement of sculptors in the Greek world; Cretan craftsmen, for example, appear to have worked in Arcadia, the Argolid, at Sikyon and in Aetolia (see Snodgrass). Although the evidence for the movement of sculpture in the Greek world is small, there are pointers, such as the bronze statue of a philosopher from the Porticello shipwreck in the Straits of Messina (head in Reggio Calabria, Mus. N.), which probably dates to the 430s BC. The cargo, especially the amphorae, suggests that the ship set sail from the Greek mainland, implying that the statue had been commissioned from a sculptor there. Even in the Archaic period marble dedications from the Athenian Acropolis included pieces made from Cycladic marble. As some of these are similar in style to sculptures from Naxos, they may indicate that élite Athenians were commissioning island sculptors to create their dedications within the main civic sanctuary. As these sculptors would be familiar with Naxian marble, it is argued that this was the medium in which they would execute the work.

Although local buildings usually drew on local materials, sometimes imported stone was used. At the end of the 6th century BC the Alkmaionid family are said to have rebuilt the Temple of Apollo at Delphi (*see* DELPHI, §1) using marble brought from Paros (Herodotus V.lxii.3); the Treasury of the Siphnians in the same sanctuary was also said to have been built with island marble (Herodotus III.lvii.4). The Temple of Zeus at Olympia, although made from local stone, carried pedimental sculptures carved from Parian marble (*see* OLYMPIA, §§1(ii)(a) and 2(i)). The 4th-century BC building accounts from Epidauros, in the Argolid, even allow the ratio between the quarrying and transport costs of Corinthian limestone to be calculated, as between 2:1 and 3:1. The weight of a marble statue is considerable: a giant kouros from the island of Delos (*in situ*), dedicated by the Naxians and dating to *c.* 600 BC, weighed approximately 23 tons, with a further 34 tons for its inscribed base. The base (5.14×3.47×0.71 m) is too large to have fitted into a normal oared ship, and it has been suggested that the marble was brought to Delos either on a broader, cargo-carrying ship (although the evidence for these at this date is slight) or perhaps on a specially constructed raft (see Snodgrass). It has been estimated that in a single year during the Archaic period, some 270 tons of 'sculptural marble' (some 350 'kouros-units') would have been moved round the Aegean, in addition to marble that would have been used for architectural purposes.

BIBLIOGRAPHY

A. M. Burford: *The Greek Temple Builders at Epidauros* (Liverpool, 1969)

R. J. Hopper: *Trade and Industry in Classical Greece* (London, 1979)

J. Boardman: *The Greeks Overseas: Their Early Colonies and Trade* (London, 1980)

B. B. Shefton: 'Greeks and Greek Imports in the South of the Iberian Peninsula: The Archaeological Evidence', *Phönizier im Westen*, ed. H. G. Niemeyer, Madrider Beiträge, viii (Mainz, 1982), pp. 337–70

A. M. Snodgrass: 'Heavy Freight in Archaic Greece', *Trade in the Ancient Economy*, ed. P. Garnsey, K. Hopkins and C. R. Whittaker (London, 1983), pp. 16–26

M. Bound: 'Una nave mercantile di età arcaica all'Isola del Giglio', *Il commercio etrusco arcaico* (Rome, 1985), pp. 65–70

C. J. Eisman and B. S. Ridgway: *The Porticello Shipwreck: A Mediterranean Vessel of 415–385 BC* (College Station, TX, 1987)

D. W. J. Gill: 'Silver Anchors and Cargoes of Oil: Some Observations on Phoenician Trade in the Western Mediterranean', *Pap. Brit. Sch. Rome*, lvi (1988), pp. 1–12

A. J. Parker: 'Classical Antiquity: The Maritime Dimension', *Antiquity*, lxiv (1990), pp. 335–46

D. W. J. Gill: 'Pots and Trade: Spacefillers or *Objets d'art*', *J. Hell. Stud.*, cxi (1991), pp. 29–47

——: 'The Ivory Trade', *Ivory in Greece and the Eastern Mediterranean from the Bronze Age to the Hellenistic Period*, ed. J. L. Fitton, BM Occas. Pap., lxxxv (London, 1992), pp. 233–7

D. Ridgway: *The First Western Greeks* (Cambridge, 1992)

Greek Gold: Jewellery of the Classical World (exh. cat. by D. Williams and J. Ogden, London, BM, 1994)

DAVID W. J. GILL

4. PATRONAGE. Detailed information about architectural and artistic patronage in ancient Greece is scarce. However, monumental building projects are in general better documented than sculpture or other art forms, and it is on architectural patronage that this article mainly focusses.

(i) Architecture. Communities, not individuals, commissioned monumental buildings in the Greek world. Examples of personal patronage are virtually unknown before the Hellenistic period (323–27BC), apart from the Leonidaion (4th century BC), built by a rich Naxian, and the Philippeion (*c.* 338 BC) of Philip II of Macedon, both at Olympia. Powerful individuals such as tyrants sometimes provided impetus for particular building projects: tradition associates the large Temple of Olympian Zeus at Athens (begun mid-6th century BC; completed 2nd century AD) with Peisistratos and the gigantic Temple of Zeus at Akragas (early 5th century BC) with Theron. Tyrants, however, did no more than exploit an existing interest in public works: when Herodotus discussed 6th-century BC Samos, he attributed the public works of the period—the mile-long rock-cut tunnel, the harbour mole and the great Temple of Hera—not to the tyrant Polykrates but to 'the Samians: they are responsible for three of the greatest buildings and engineering feats in the Greek world' (*Histories* III.xxxix–lx).

Decisions to build were made in much the same way in every community, as shown by a decree from mid-5th-century BC Athens: 'It seemed good to the council and popular assembly.... Glaukos proposed: that a priestess of Athena Nike be appointed, and that her sacred place be closed by a door... and that a temple and a stone altar be constructed according to Kallikrates' designs' (*Inscr. Gr./2*, i, 24). The pan-Hellenic sanctuaries were also largely administered by their local communities: the city state of Elis oversaw the construction of the Temple of Zeus at Olympia (*c.* 470–457 BC); building at Delphi was supervised by a board of Delphic citizens and representatives from elsewhere; at Epidauros the city officials decided what should be built in the Sanctuary of Asklepios. The patriotic need to emulate or outdo a rival city state was often a major motive for building, as in the Sicilian cities of Selinus and Akragas, where at least seven large temples were built at both places within four generations. Once a temple had been built, however, it was not replaced by a new structure unless the existing building became unusable. This happened, for example, on Samos, where the earliest stone Temple of Hera (*c.* 650 BC) burnt down and was soon replaced by a new temple (*c.* 560 BC); and the magnificent Periclean building programme on the Athenian Acropolis (*see* PERICLES) might have been far less ambitious had the Persians not sacked the city in 480–479 BC. The communities responsible for the pan-Hellenic sanctuaries seem to have been under obligation to meet the needs of worshippers. Nevertheless, at Olympia, Zeus was accorded no more than an open-air altar and a share of the Temple of Hera until *c.* 470 BC, when the Eleans took charge of the sanctuary. The great Temple of Zeus built then thus marked Elis' new regional influence as much as it honoured the god. At Epidauros, by contrast, the wider following gained by the cult of Asklepios prompted the city to enhance its rural sanctuary; the buildings of the city itself remained modest.

Funds for building might come from war booty, as at Elis; loot from piracy, as in Polykrates' Samos; or reserves from the allies' tribute, as in 5th-century BC Athens. Often, however, the regular city revenues were all that could be used, and when these failed, contributions were called for from citizens. At Delphi, for example, contributions were solicited both from other cities and from private individuals, and personal patronage may often have gained public recognition by the inclusion of the donor's name in a published list of contributors. The total cost of only one temple is definitely known; the Asklepion of Epidauros cost something over 23 talents, or about 280 times the architect's annual salary. The Parthenon, by comparison, may have cost about 450 talents—equivalent to one year's tribute from Athens' allies. Shortage of money may have contributed to slow progress on the later Temple of Apollo at Delphi, or on the Temple of Zeus at Akragas, though delays could also be caused by such factors as war, political unrest or the need to import skills and materials, for example fine limestone or marble, not available in a particular city state.

The details of an architectural project seem to have been entrusted to a select few with the advice of an expert (*see also* §II, 1(iv) below). The Athenian decree quoted above continues: 'Hestiaios proposed: that three men are to be chosen... and they are to draw up specifications with the architect Kallikrates and demonstrate to the council [how the work] will be contracted out.' At most building sites, the project was divided into manageable sections, which were advertised and put out on contract to the best bid. Rich and influential men who wanted to take an active part could guarantee contracts, use their contacts to gain access to foreign quarries or craftsmen or even take up contracts themselves as entrepreneurs, at generously low prices. For example, in the 6th century BC the Alkmaeonids, exiled from Athens, gained renown for themselves as well as for the new Temple of Apollo at Delphi (*c.* 525–*c.* 500 BC) by using Parian marble for the pedimental sculptures, instead of the cheaper limestone specified in their contract.

It is not clear who ultimately determined the design of a building. Records of some architects' specifications, as presented to the deliberating body, suggest that the public took some interest in the technical detail of a proposed building. Presumably the building commissioners themselves were selected partly for their understanding of such matters, though they must have depended heavily on the architect's professional expertise. To what extent the public could appreciate such architectural refinements as the upward swell and taper of column shafts or the subtle divergences from strict vertical and horizontal lines incorporated into some buildings it is impossible to say. If they were readily apparent, as were the themes and designs of the architectural sculptures, which were probably widely debated, they no doubt attracted admiration, as did simple and satisfying proportional relationships throughout the building. But the introduction of Pythagorean mathematics into the measurements and proportions of a design, as in some 4th-century BC structures, seems unlikely to have been at the behest of an architect's patrons. Though arguments doubtless often arose concerning building schemes, the only evidence for outspoken opposition is the condemnatory reference in Plutarch's *Life of Pericles* (xii.1–2) to the 'thousand-talent temples' at Athens. This was, however, less an aesthetic or moral criticism of the Acropolis buildings themselves than a political judgement on the democratic government and its means of financing them.

(ii) Sculpture, painting and other arts. In many cases the purposes served by monumental sculpture imply the presence of a patron or patrons. Votive statues in sanctuaries, athlete statues commemorating victories in pan-Hellenic games, funerary sculptures and honorific public statues all come into this category. In some instances the names of statues' dedicators or donors survive, but there is little to indicate the exact relationship between sculptors and their patrons. The domain of public patronage included such works as the cult statues inside temples, among the most celebrated examples of which were Pheidias' colossal chryselephantine *Athena* at Athens and *Zeus* at Olympia (both destr. in antiquity). However, sculpture clearly provided more scope for private commissions than did monumental architecture. Occasionally there is a literary tradition linking an artist with an eminent patron, and among sculptors Pheidias has always been closely associated with Pericles (*see also* §IV, 1(v) below).

Literary sources suggest that painters, like sculptors, relied on several forms of patronage, including public commissions and competitions as well as privately commissioned work. Unlike sculpture, however, the record of ancient Greek painting is almost exclusively literary, since hardly any important original works survive. Panel painting was evidently highly regarded, and the names of several famous painters are associated with strong anecdotal traditions. Pliny's celebrated account of Apelles and Alexander the Great suggests an intimacy between artist and patron in which the painter's skill allowed him to transcend normal social barriers. The finest surviving Greek paintings, those from the tombs at Vergina, also represent Macedonian royal private patronage.

In other arts, the careers and even the names of the most accomplished artists are usually undocumented. The presence of the patron or buyer can be glimpsed, for example, in precious artefacts such as engraved gems, which sometimes bear their owner's name; and the everyday subjects depicted on painted vases include scenes of life in well-to-do households and of artists and craftsmen at work (*see also* §V, 1(iv) below).

BIBLIOGRAPHY

A. Burford: *The Greek Temple Builders at Epidauros* (Liverpool, 1969)

——: *Aspects of Greek and Roman Life: Craftsmen in Greek and Roman Society* (London, 1972)

J. J. Coulton: *Greek Architects at Work* (London, 1977); pubd in USA as *Ancient Greek Architects at Work* (Ithaca, NY, 1977)

ALISON BURFORD

II. Architecture.

The architecture of ancient Greece ranges from the remains of small Dark Age temples built of wood and mud-brick to the colossal marble Archaic and Classical temples (see fig. 6) and magnificent public buildings of the Hellenistic period. Even in the case of stone buildings, however, the effects of earthquakes and general neglect or abuse mean that these now survive only in more or less ruined states, and many aspects of their original appearance are thus conjectural.

In the Bronze Age Mediterranean civilizations of Crete and Mycenaean Greece the most important buildings had been royal palaces and tombs (*see* MINOAN, §II and HELLADIC, §II). By contrast, the history of Greek architecture before the Hellenistic period is dominated by the development of the temple. The political organization of Archaic and Classical Greece on the basis of the *polis* (city state) rather than the kingdom also meant that temples and other types of buildings, both sacred and secular, were state-financed and essentially public projects.

More than the architecture of any other ancient civilization, ancient Greek architecture has profoundly influenced later styles in the Western world. The elaborate aesthetic rules and the range of building types established by the Greeks were taken up by Roman architects and thus diffused throughout the Empire. Later still, the architects of the Renaissance and of the Neo-classical revival returned to Greek forms and concepts, which have continued to be adapted and used in buildings up to the present day.

BIBLIOGRAPHY

W. B. Dinsmoor: *The Architecture of Greece and Rome* (New York, 1902); rev. as *The Architecture of Ancient Greece* (New York, 1927, rev. 3/1950)

6. Acropolis at Athens, view from the south-west

D. S. Robertson: *A Handbook of Greek and Roman Architecture* (Cambridge, 1929, rev. 2/1943); repr. as *Greek and Roman Architecture* (London, 1969)

A. W. Lawrence: *Greek Architecture*, Pelican Hist. A. (Harmondsworth, 1957, rev. 4/1983, with additions by R. A. Tomlinson)

R. A. Tomlinson: *Greek Architecture* (Bristol, 1989)

1. Overview. 2. Historical survey. 3. Theory and design.

1. Overview.

(i) Building types. (ii) Materials and construction. (iii) Decoration. (iv) Architects, masons and society.

(i) Building types. In nearly every domain of religious, cultural and social life the Greeks developed distinctive building types, and these forms, once established, remained remarkably consistent. Characteristically, they combined functional elements with close attention to the overall aesthetic effect of a building.

a) Religious. (b) Civic. (c) Domestic. (d) Funerary. (e) Entertainment and recreational.

(a) Religious. Religious architecture was the first area in which the Greeks began to evolve distinctive building styles, and religious sites, either associated with cities or in isolated locations, continued to attract ambitious and costly projects throughout the history of ancient Greek architecture.

Early temples. The focal point of sacred precincts in ancient Greece was originally an outdoor altar, rather than a roofed temple (*see* Temple, §I, 4). It was around this altar that the worshippers gathered for prayers and sacrifices. By the 8th century BC, however, there is indirect evidence for sacred roofed structures, mainly in the form of terracotta votive models from Argos (8th or 7th century BC; Athens, N. Archaeol. Mus.) and Perachora (*c.* 750–*c.* 725 BC; Athens, N. Archaeol. Mus.; for illustration *see* Perachora). Existing remains of buildings of this date are ambiguous, since their sacred nature is not always certain. Early Greek temples initially resembled large houses (see fig. 20 below). They appear to have been rectangular or apsidal in plan, with a central row of supports, as at the Cretan sites of Prinias (7th or 6th century BC) and Dreros (8th century BC), or with more numerous axial columns, as in the first Temple of Hera on Samos (*c.* 800 BC). These temples were built of mud-brick on stone foundations or on orthostates (upright stone slabs), an element that survived even when temples were built entirely of stone. Vertical wooden planks at the projecting front ends of the walls protected the mud-brick. These were later imitated in stone structures by the antae (wall-end pilasters that usually had ornamental capitals and occasionally ornamental bases; see fig. 7a and fig. 17 below). The main room of the temple (cella) was fronted by a porch (pronaos), usually with two columns, as the terracotta models show, either prostyle or *in antis* (i.e. either in front of or between the antae). Wood was also used for the superstructure of these early buildings, as at Eretria, where the lower part of the apsidal Temple of Apollo (*c.* 750 BC) was of stone with wooden supports, and the upper part was probably of wood and thatch.

The internal columns in early temples were necessary to support the roof. An external colonnade, the peristyle, which was to become the most characteristic element in

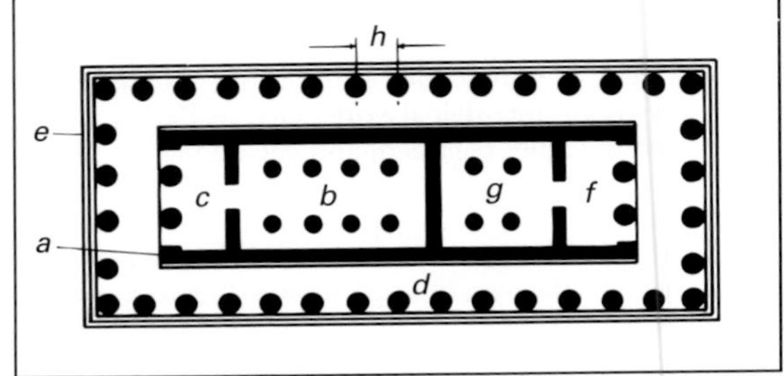

7. Greek temple components: (a) anta; (b) cella; (c) pronaos; (d) peristyle; (e) stylobate; (f) opisthodomos; (g) adyton; (h) intercolumniation

Greek temple architecture, was perhaps introduced in the late 8th century BC in Megaron B at Thermon in west Greece (see fig. 8a; *see also* Thermon), though some scholars date this building considerably earlier and its function as a temple is not undisputed. (For a different view of early peristyles *see* §2(ii)(a) below.) There a horseshoe-shaped peristyle was added so that the roof could be extended to provide shade and protect the mud-brick walls.

In the 7th century BC monumental stone temples began to be built in Greece, coinciding with the emergence of monumental stone sculpture. Temples, conceived as houses for divinities in the form of cult statues, could thus provide correspondingly lasting dwellings for the new stone images. The Temple of Poseidon at Isthmia (first half of the 7th century BC) had an old-fashioned elongated rectangular plan (*c.* 40.02×14.02 m) with a peristyle of 19 by 7 wooden columns (h. *c.* 4.25 m) standing on a continuous step (stylobate), and a row of internal columns. Both at Isthmia and in the contemporary early Temple of Apollo at Corinth, the walls are of poros limestone, an easily worked material. The details of the superstructure are uncertain, but the roofs of both temples were hipped and covered with sophisticated terracotta combination pan-and-cover tiles. An anomaly of the temple at Isthmia was that the outside walls were decorated with colour paintings in panel form on thin stucco. These temples both faced east, as do about 80% of ancient Greek temples.

Temple plans and elevations. By the end of the 7th century BC certain forms of both plan and elevation had been established, setting standards that were to be followed for several centuries in a highly conservative manner. The typical plan consisted of the cella fronted by a pronaos. For the sake of symmetry a back porch (opisthodomos) was added. These porches could be distyle (i.e. with two columns) *in antis* or prostyle. If the back porch also had a prostyle arrangement, the temple is termed amphiprostyle. These basic variants were especially common both in small temples and in the treasury buildings dedicated by city states in the great sanctuaries (see below). The most common plan for temples, however, was probably the peripteral one (i.e. with a peristyle or pteron). Occasionally, especially in large Ionic temples, the peristyle was doubled or even tripled, giving a dipteral or tripteral plan and creating a veritable forest of columns. Sometimes cult

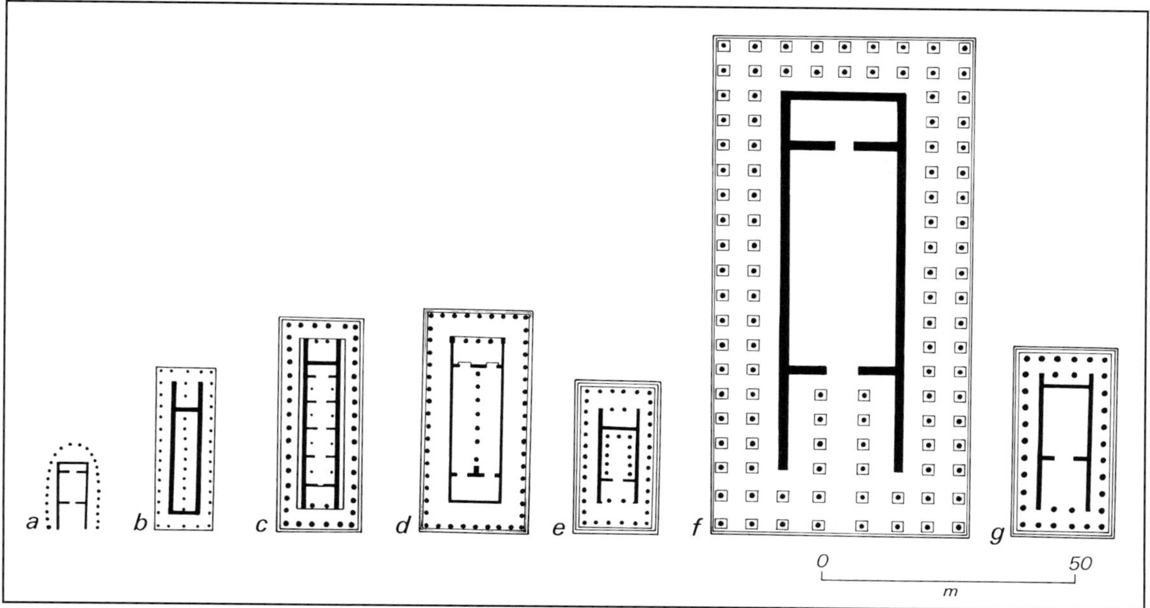

8. Greek temple plans: (a) Megaron B, Thermon, ?late 8th century BC; (b) second Temple of Apollo, Thermon, *c.* 620 BC; (c) Temple of Hera, Olympia, *c.* 590 BC; (d) first Temple of Hera, Paestum, mid-6th century BC; (e) Temple of Hephaistos (Hephaisteion), Athens, *c.* 450–*c.* 445 BC; (f) Temple of Artemis, Ephesos, *c.* 560–*c.* 460 BC; (g) Temple of Athena Polias, Priene, begun *c.* 340 BC

practices dictated double cellae or an inner sanctum (adyton). The peristyles of later, Classical temples eventually had a standard number of columns, usually 6 by 13 but sometimes 8 by 17, making the number of flank columns twice the number of columns at each end plus one. Indeed, the peristyle, which was functional as well as decorative, had a further importance in that it provided the basic units (e.g. column diameter and intercolumniation; *see also* §3(iv) below) for determining the overall proportions of a temple, and the external colonnade was thus apparently built before the inner walled structure it was meant to surround.

Again by the end of the 7th century BC, Greek temples had assumed standard forms of superstructure (see fig. 9). These are known as ARCHITECTURAL ORDERS, and the two principal types are termed Doric and Ionic. The earliest known Doric columns (e.g. those in the first Temple of Athena Pronaia at Delphi; 7th century BC) were slender, perhaps an imitation in stone of wooden prototypes. They soon, however, assumed the heavy proportions more characteristic of Doric buildings, especially at the beginning of the development, suggesting that the builders were still unsure of the structural properties of stone. Columns in large buildings were thus often only four lower diameters in height. Early columns were often monolithic and were grooved with between 16 and 36 flutes by sharp arrises. Doric columns have no base, and the capitals and architrave they support are simple (for further discussion *see* §2(ii) below). Along the top edge of the architrave runs a continuous projecting band (taenia) with shorter strips (regulae) decorated with 'drops' (guttae) projecting downwards at regular intervals. Above the architrave, the Doric frieze consists of alternating triglyphs and metopes; the latter can contain decoration, either carved or painted. Above this, the projecting cornice (geison) has slablike protrusions (mutules) on its underside, also decorated with guttae. The entablature is crowned by a triangular pediment (*see* PEDIMENT, §I). Colour played an important part in the decoration of Doric temples and was applied according to a generally consistent scheme (*see also* §(iii)(c) below). Thus the regulae, triglyphs, the horizontal fascia on the metopes, and the mutules were usually painted blue; the taenias and bed mouldings of the cornices were red; metopes and guttae were white.

The Ionic order developed in Asia Minor and the Aegean islands only slightly later than the Doric of the mainland. Its most distinctive features were the slender column shaft and the capital. The column had a base and generally more flutes than a Doric column, with flat fillets instead of sharp arrises, while the capital had volutes on either side. The architrave consisted of three projecting bands crowned with elaborate mouldings. In mainland Greece it carried a continuous frieze, occasionally carved, but in Asia Minor there were heavy, toothlike projections (dentils) instead, which were, in fact, part of the overhanging cornice.

Doric temples. One of the earliest Doric peripteral temples was the second Temple of Apollo at THERMON (*c.* 620 BC; see fig. 8b above). It was 38.1×12.2 m, with an opisthodomos but no pronaos, a peristyle of 5 by 15 columns and a central row of internal columns. Many terracotta revetments from its superstructure survive, including large painted metopes (Athens, N. Archaeol. Mus.), indicating that the entablature was Doric. The most notable early Doric temple is the Temple of Hera at

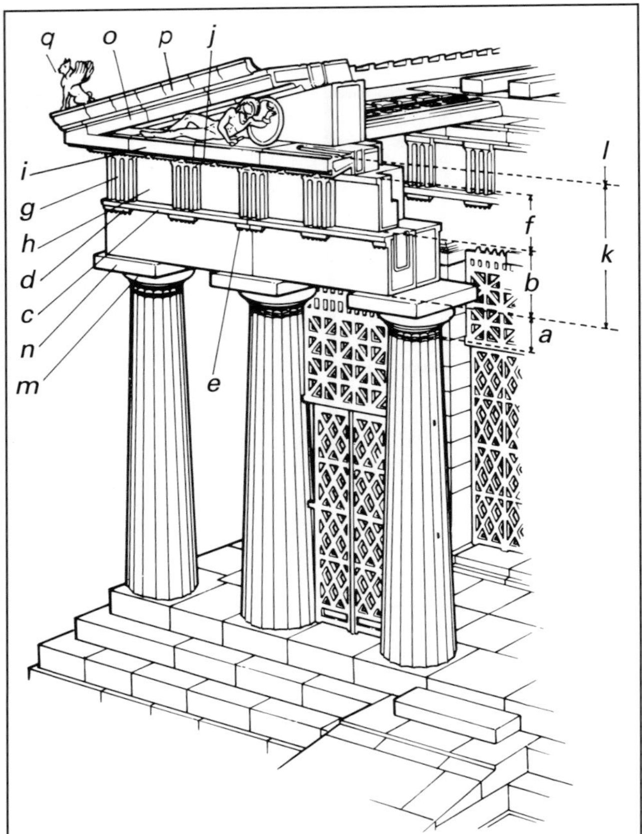

9. Temple elevation, sectional view of the front of the Temple of Aphaia, Aegina: (a) capital; (b) architrave; (c) taenia; (d) regula; (e) guttae; (f) frieze; (g) triglyph; (h) metope; (i) cornice; (j) mutule; (k) entablature; (l) pediment; (m) echinus; (n) abacus; (o) slanting cornice; (p) corona; (q) akroterion

Olympia (*c.* 590 BC; see fig. 8c above; *see also* §2(ii)(b) below). It had an elongated plan measuring 50.01×18.75 m, with both a pronaos and an opisthodomos, mud-brick walls on stone orthostates and a wooden superstructure. The peristyle had sixteen wooden columns (h. 5.22 m) on the flanks but six on the ends instead of the earlier five, since the cella now had two rows of internal columns, as in later buildings, rather than one. This was an important innovation, since it allowed the cult statue to be placed at the centre of the rear wall of the cella without being obscured by columns. Almost immediately after construction, the wooden columns began to be replaced with stone ones. This process spanned some 800 years, however, and the replacement columns vary.

The later Temple of Apollo at Corinth (*c.* 540 BC) measured 53.82×21.48 m overall, having two cellae placed back to back, both fronted by a pronaos. The peristyle of 6 by 15 columns reflects these proportions, and its monolithic columns were only 4.15 lower diameters in height (7.24 m). The Temple of Athena at Assos (*c.* 540 BC or later) was the only Doric temple built in Archaic times in the Ionic stronghold of Asia Minor. It had some abnormal features, such as a carved frieze on the architrave, under the metopes and triglyphs, but otherwise was already more Classical in feeling, with 6 by 13 columns, each 5.22 lower diameters high (4.78 m; for illustration *see* ASSOS).

Archaic Sicilian and South Italian Doric temples differed significantly in plan and elevation from their mainland Greek counterparts. In Sicilian temples the opisthodomos was replaced by an adyton and the internal columns eliminated, resulting in elongated cellae and wide peristyles. Other significant differences include the efforts made to dispense with porch columns, thus breaking the alignment between the cella and the external colonnade.

During the 6th century BC the Sicilians outbuilt the mainland Greeks in quantity and often size. One of their largest temples, Temple GT at Selinus (begun *c.* 500–480 BC, built over many decades and left unfinished), measured 110.36×50.10 m and had a peristyle of 8 by 17 columns (for plan *see* SELINUS, fig. 1). In the Sicilian tradition, it was pseudo-dipteral (i.e. there was room for a second peristyle inside the existing one) because of the relatively narrow proportions of the cella. Even so, the cella was too wide to be roofed completely, despite the provision, as in mainland temples, of two rows of internal columns. These were probably part of a later alteration and simply supported pentroofs over the aisles, leaving the nave uncovered. The immense tetrastyle (four-columned) prostyle porch was completely unroofed. This porch was a traditional Sicilian feature, but the inclusion of a distyle *in antis* opisthodomos, probably in the 5th century BC, was dictated by mainland models.

Archaic South Italian Doric temples were mainly influenced by Sicilian models. Many were 'experimental', however, and included mainland Doric and even Ionic features. Two good examples occur at PAESTUM. The mid-6th-century BC Temple of Hera (see fig. 8d above) was almost pseudo-dipteral, with an old-fashioned peristyle of 9 by 18 columns and a single row of internal columns. The flutes on the columns had semicircular Ionic tops beneath a unique moulding of outcurved leaves, while floral bands of varying design on the echinus (lower half or 'cushion' of the capital) replaced the usual Doric annulets. Similar features occur on the Doric columns of the Temple of Athena (*c.* 530 BC), but Ionic features are also found, including elaborate mouldings on the entablature and Ionic three-quarter columns that terminate the side walls, fronted by an Ionic tetrastyle prostyle porch, a Sicilian characteristic. However, the absence of either an adyton or an opisthodomos enabled the peristyle to be restricted to 6 by 13 columns, a formula that was gradually becoming canonical.

This reduction in the length of the peristyle is best attested on the Greek mainland. The Late Archaic second Temple of Aphaia on Aigina (*c.* 500–*c.* 490 BC; see fig. 21 below) had a peristyle of only 6 by 12 columns, and though later Classical architects apparently found these proportions too truncated, they were revived in the 4th century BC. As in most contemporary Archaic temples, the cella had internal columns in two storeys, with the taper of the lower columns prolonged by the upper ones. An entry ramp, a specifically Peloponnesian trait, was constructed at the east end.

A typical Early Classical Doric temple was the Temple of Zeus at Olympia (*c.* 470–*c.* 457 BC). It has a peristyle of

6 by 13 columns, each approximately 4.7 lower diameters high (*c.* 10.43 m), distyle *in antis* porches and internal columns in two storeys. It was built of shelly limestone coated in stucco, while the tiles, gutter and architectural sculptures were of marble.

The marble Temple of Hephaistos (Hephaisteion) in the Agora at Athens (*c.* 450–*c.* 445 BC; see fig. 8e above; for illustration *see also* TRABEATED CONSTRUCTION) was also a canonical Doric temple with 6 by 13 columns, each 5.6 lower diameters high (5.71 m). It also had Ionic features, however: a moulded wall-base and continuous Ionic frieze over the columns of the porches. For the first time here, the third flank columns from the front were aligned with the columns of the pronaos, allowing the heavy architrave over the latter to continue to the flank architrave, thus creating a separate compartment for the front exterior ceiling. This scheme was used extensively thereafter. The internal columns did not simply run from front to back of the cella as in earlier buildings but made a return at the rear to form a continuous ambulatory around the room. The Ionic elements in this building continued an Athenian tradition already attested by the Archaic Temple of Athena on the Acropolis (*c.* 515 BC) and perpetuated in the Parthenon. Built between 447 and 432 BC on the Athenian Acropolis by the architects Iktinos and Kallikrates, the Parthenon had an unusual inner plan (*see* ATHENS, fig. 10b), with a treasury behind the cella, approached through the opisthodomos, and hexastyle (six-columned) prostyle porches at both ends, necessitating a peristyle of 8×17 columns, each 5.5 lower diameters high (10.43 m). The cella had superimposed Doric columns framing the chryselephantine (gold and ivory) statue of *Athena* by Pheidias. In the treasury, in order to save floor space, the ceiling rested on four tall, slender Ionic columns. This was the first use of internal Ionic columns in a Doric temple, and it was to become the norm.

From the 4th century BC Greek temples tended to become shorter, while columns became thinner. The entablature became lighter, too, and two triglyphs instead of one appeared over each intercolumniation. There were temples with peristyles of 6 by 11 or even 6 by 10 columns, reflecting the gradual diminishing or even absence of the opisthodomos. Ornamentation also changed, with the use of novel elements such as the Corinthian order for internal columns, as in the Temple of Athena Alea at Tegea (*c.* 350 BC) and the Temple of Zeus at Nemea (*c.* 330 BC). In the later Hellenistic period Doric finally ceased to be used frequently in temples, largely because of the unsatisfactorily resolved problem of the corner triglyph (*see* ORDERS, ARCHITECTURAL, §I, 2(i)).

Ionic temples. A typical Archaic Ionic temple was the Temple of Artemis at Ephesos (*c.* 560–*c.* 460 BC; for illustration *see* EPHESOS fig. 5 and fig. 8f above). Its stylobate measured 115.14×55.10 m, and like other giant Ionic temples it was dipteral, with eight columns at the front, nine at the back and twenty-one on the flanks, each *c.* 12.08 m high. Its pronaos was deep, again an Ionic trait, with four rows of columns. The column bases varied but were mostly of standard Asiatic Ionic profile, with elaborate mouldings. Some columns had lower drums decorated with relief sculpture (*see also* §2(ii)(b) below and EPHESOS, §II).

10. Temple of Asklepios, Epidauros, *c.* 380–*c.* 375 BC; reconstruction after A. Defrasse and H. Lechat

After the Persian Wars (490–479 BC), temple construction in Ionia was on the wane until the Hellenistic period. Ionic temples continued to be constructed in mainland Greece, however. The Temple of Athena at Sounion (*c.* 450 BC) shows the mainland Ionic style, with a frieze instead of dentils. This strange building had colonnades on the front and south flank only (10 and 12 columns respectively). The columns were closely spaced and 10.4 lower diameters high (*c.* 6.22 m). The Erechtheion on the Athenian Acropolis (*c.* 421–405 BC) had a highly unusual plan, which allowed it to incorporate elements of both Asiatic and Attic Ionic. One of its four porches, the porch of the Caryatids, thus has Asiatic dentils, while the rest have a frieze. It is by far the most elaborate Ionic building on the Greek mainland, with richly decorated capitals, doorframes and wall crowns, and friezes of white marble figures set against a blue-grey limestone background.

The building of Ionic temples declined in mainland Greece after the 5th century BC, although at Epidauros the Temple of Asklepios (*c.* 380–*c.* 375 BC; see fig. 10) had 6 by 11 columns, with no internal colonnade and no opisthodomos. A second flowering took place in Asia Minor, however, from the mid-4th century BC, involving the construction of several large temples, including a new Temple of Artemis at Ephesos. This replaced the burnt Archaic temple but kept largely to its floor plan. The column bases were of Asiatic Ionic form, as was the entablature with dentils. At Priene the Temple of Athena Polias (begun *c.* 340 BC; see fig. 8g above) was designed with a careful scheme of proportions by the architect Pytheos, who also wrote a book about it. The peristyle had 6 by 11 columns set on plinths, as at Ephesos, and there was a shallow opisthodomos. A Temple of Aphrodite at Messa on the island of Lesbos (begun *c.* 280 BC) was pseudo-dipteral with a peristyle of 8 by 14 columns, and it had both a frieze and dentils (a popular combination from then on). The pseudo-dipteral plan was also used in the Temple of Artemis Leukophryene at Magnesia on the Maeander (2nd century BC). Its architect, Hermogenes, codified the Ionic order, and his writings later exerted a great influence on Roman architecture. The temple rests on a platform, a characteristic of large Ionic temples, and the peristyle was of 8 by 15 columns. The columns had Attic bases, again set on plinths, and capitals shaped in accordance with Hermogenes' theories.

The Corinthian capital was originally developed for internal columns, but it occurs on the exterior of buildings from the early 3rd century BC. Several large Hellenistic temples built in the Ionic style thus had Corinthian peristyles, such as the Temple of Olympian Zeus at Athens. It was not until Roman times, however, that Corinthian temples became a widespread standard form.

Other sacred structures. By *c.* 500 BC, monumental stone temples loomed as giants within sanctuaries throughout the Greek world. Conceptually and religiously these buildings functioned as public landmarks. Around them cult activity took place, and on or beside them, votive offerings were lodged. The need to provide a secure repository for valuable offerings resulted in the development of the TREASURY as a building separate from the temple itself. Among the earliest are those at Olympia and Delphi. Though they were not strictly sacred buildings, in plan a typical, non-peripteral treasury resembles a typical Greek temple, with a pronaos and an abbreviated cella. It is distyle *in antis* and, like the temple, is crowned by a triangular pediment at the end of a gabled roof. Occasionally the treasury has a pediment with sculptural decoration (e.g. the Megarian Treasury at Olympia and the Siphnian Treasury at Delphi; see fig. 22 below). The treasury has no opisthodomos, and there is an absence of a spreading, stepped platform. It may be that only a frontal set of steps distinguished the public civic treasury from its religious counterpart.

Before the Hellenistic period, the ancient Greek altar (*see* ALTAR, §I, 3) was not usually an elaborate structure. The series of altars in the Sanctuary of Hera on Samos, begun in the 10th century BC, were mostly long and narrow enclosures for sacrificial ashes; the 6th-century BC altar built by Rhoikos, the architect of the Temple of Hera, was pi-shaped on a rectangular podium 36×17 m long with a wide staircase. Altars could be crowned with decorative mouldings or have sides decorated with a triglyph and metope frieze. Some were huge, for example the Altar of Zeus Eleutherios at Syracuse (3rd century BC). The most elaborate of all was the Altar of Zeus (or 'Great Altar') at Pergamon (first half of 2nd century BC; *see* PERGAMON, fig. 2), which was situated in a rectangular court surrounded by double Ionic columns and raised on a high podium 36.44×34.20 m in plan. The podium itself had an Ionic external colonnade, which also flanked the monumental staircase on the west. Sculpted friezes adorned the walls of the podium and the inner face of the court walls.

Two other main types of sacred buildings are found in ancient Greek sanctuaries: the THOLOS (a distinctive round building) and various types of hall for mystery cults. The latter often resembled secular meeting halls. At Eleusis, for example, the Telesterion, or Hall of Mysteries (5th century BC and later), was an almost square building measuring 52×53 m with a two-storey grid of 6 by 7 internal columns. Eight tiers of seats lined the walls, and in the centre was a small room, the *anaktoron*, forming the focus of the mystery cult. By contrast, the Hieron on Samothrace (started *c.* 325–*c.* 300 BC, with later additions) was rectangular with a Doric porch at the north end, consisting of 6 by 2 columns each with a single column separating the rows at either side, as in some Archaic Sicilian temples. The interior had an apse at the south and benches along the walls.

The function of the few tholoi is uncertain, but some at least may have been heroa (centres for hero cults). The most elaborate is the Thymele at Epidauros (mid-4th century BC), with a peristyle of 26 limestone Doric columns and an internal colonnade of 14 marble Corinthian columns. There is much ornament, from the carved rosettes on the Doric frieze to the fine sculptural internal capitals and the carved mouldings of the Ionic entablature and the coffers (for illustration *see* COFFERING).

BIBLIOGRAPHY

W. B. Dinsmoor: *The Architecture of Greece and Rome* (New York, 1902); rev. as *The Architecture of Ancient Greece* (New York, 1927, rev. 3/1950)

A. W. Lawrence: *Greek Architecture*, Pelican Hist. A. (Harmondsworth, 1957, rev. 4/1983, with additions by R. A. Tomlinson)

H. Berve and G. Gruben: *Griechische Tempel und Heiligtümer* (Munich, 1961); Eng. trans. by R. Waterhouse as *Greek Temples, Theatres and Shrines* (London, 1963)

F. E. Winter: 'West Greek Temples', *Amer. J. Archaeol.*, lxxx (1975), pp. 139–45

J. J. Coulton: *Greek Architects at Work* (London, 1977); publ. in USA as *Ancient Greek Architects at Work* (Ithaca, NY, 1977)

F. E. Winter: 'Archaic and Classical Doric East of the Adriatic', *Amer. J. Archaeol.*, lxxxii (1978), pp. 151–61

——: 'The Work of Iktinos', *Amer. J. Archaeol.*, lxxxiv (1980), pp. 399–416

——: 'The Fourth Century', *Amer. J. Archaeol.*, lxxxvi (1982), pp. 387–400

(b) Civic. Greek public buildings of similar types occurred in both state-run religious sanctuaries and agoras. The latter were the civic and commercial centres of the *polis* (city state) and developed with the rise of the *polis* as a place of assembly for the people. Early agoras were little more than open areas, at most equipped with some seats. Rock-cut steps for seating or standing exist at Dreros (*c.* 725–*c.* 700 BC) and Lato (?7th century BC) on Crete. The agora remained important in the organization of cities throughout the history of ancient Greece, and the principal civic buildings were often sited around it (e.g. at Miletos; see fig. 11).

Among the most important civic building types was the BOULEUTERION (council house). This was an enclosed hall for meetings of city officials, and it often contained an altar of Hestia, goddess of the hearth, a religious aspect that reveals the original link between the bouleuterion and the PRYTANEION. The latter was used for entertaining city guests and traditionally contained the city's sacred hearth. The prytaneion, however, did not develop into an architecturally distinct type but instead resembled a private house with a dining-room. The bouleuterion, on the other hand, ultimately evolved into a theatre-type auditorium inside a characteristically square or rectangular building, often utilizing the natural slope of a hill. Its roof was usually carried by four internal supports, and its size varied

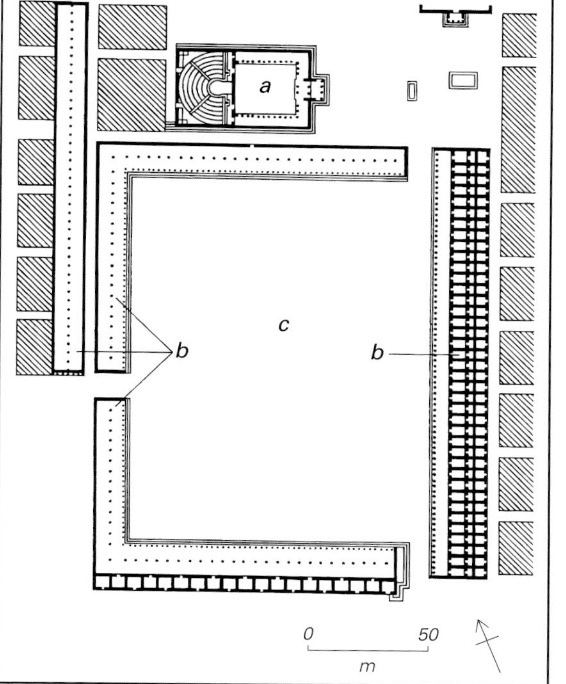

11. Plan of the agora at Miletos, *c.* 175–*c.* 165 BC: (a) bouleuterion; (b) stoas; (c) square

according to the needs of each *polis*. This general type was established by the 5th century BC, though the best examples are Hellenistic.

The early bouleuterion in the Sanctuary of Zeus at Olympia had an unusual plan. Two apsidal structures (6th and 5th centuries BC respectively) with central rows of roof supports were unified in the 3rd century BC by a square room inserted between them. The original apsidal plans were probably dictated by tradition, though the seating arrangement is uncertain, as in the function of the inner rooms with their curved end walls. The Old Bouleuterion in the Athenian Agora (early 5th century BC) was almost square (23.3×23.8 m) and probably had five internal supports. The New Bouleuterion (late 5th century BC) was built to the west and behind the old one, which eventually became the state archive. The new building was south-facing, rectangular and had four internal supports. Again, the seating arrangement is uncertain. The Thersilion at Megalopolis (*c.* 360 BC) was a much larger building (66.60×50.43 m) for the Arcadian state assembly of 10,000 delegates. Its many columns radiated from the centre to allow the audience a clear view of the speaker. Even so, councillors sometimes used for their meetings the large theatre that adjoined the Thersilion. By the 2nd century BC, perhaps due to the invention of the truss roof, greater roof spans were attainable, as in the bouleuteria at Priene and Miletos, thus keeping visual impediments to a minimum. At Priene the bouleuterion or ekklesiasterion (popular assembly hall; *c.* 200 BC) was built into a natural slope. It could seat over 600 people on three sides of a rectangular auditorium, while a rectangular niche, presumably for officials, occupied the fourth; the roof was supported by 14 pillars. The later bouleuterion at Miletos (*c.*175–*c.*165 BC; see fig. 28 below) had only four internal supports in a chamber for 1200 people. Its ornate exterior was adorned with engaged half columns and fronted by a colonnaded court.

Important as bouleuteria were, it was the stoa (*see* STOA, §1 and fig.) or colonnaded hall that became most typical of civic building types. Stoas were generally elongated buildings up to 200 m long, walled at the back and ends, with a colonnaded front, preferably facing south to exclude the winter north winds and admit warmth from the low winter sun. Many had rooms behind their porticos, and some were two-storey, with their lower and upper colonnades of different orders (usually Doric and Ionic respectively). Occasionally, on sloping sites, the chief floor was the upper one, with the lower one serving as a basement. Some stoas also had an inner row of columns, spaced twice as widely as the outer ones, to increase the depth of the portico. Stoas had multiple functions, serving as law courts, indoor running tracks (*see also* GYMNASIUM), dining halls, sleeping quarters in oracular sanctuaries, schools and shops, while all provided pleasant sheltered promenades as well. They are found in virtually every civic and religious centre of ancient Greece. In the cities of Asia Minor especially, stoas of various forms lined streets, defined enclosed areas and created vistas. Agoras often had stoas on three sides, with a major street running along the fourth, backed either by public buildings or another stoa, as at Miletos.

Though law courts were often housed in stoas or situated in open areas surrounded by stoas, a square peristyle building of the 4th century BC in the Athenian Agora may also have served this purpose. This interpretation is, however, based on the court furnishings associated with the building rather than on its architectural features. Similarly, administrative buildings tend to be identified by their furnishings rather than their forms. Arsenals (storage buildings), however, did have distinctive long, narrow plans, as attested by the specifications for the Arsenal of Philon at Peiraeus (*c.* 340 BC; destr. 86 BC). This measured 132.22×17.95 m and had three aisles. Similar buildings have been identified at Pergamon and Athens.

Water supply was especially important in the semi-arid climate of Greece. Individuals sunk private wells and stored water in cisterns, but public supply of clean water was the concern of the State, and its importance was underlined by the religious character attached to water sources. Supplies could be conveyed over long distances by concealed aqueducts, as at Samos (6th century BC) and Olynthos (?*c.* 420 BC), but it was obviously more practical to have a water supply in the immediate vicinity, and the existence of a source often determined the location both of a city and of the city's public areas, as was notably the case at Corinth.

Water was made available at fountain houses (*krenai*), and these show considerable architectural variety. Early fountains were simple: most stood above ground at the bases of cliffs and terraces, and while most had piped supplies, many were built against springs. The fountain of Glauke at Corinth (6th century BC) had rock-cut reservoirs, and the rock face was simply dressed smooth. Unusually, the fountain built in the late 7th century BC at Megara and traditionally associated with the tyrant Theagenes was built of masonry with the ceilings of the reservoirs supported by pillars. The late 6th-century BC south-east fountain house in the Athenian Agora (*see* ATHENS, fig. 16j) may have been the celebrated Enneakrounos ('nine-spouter'). It is rectangular (6.84×18.20 m), with a central entry fronted by three columns and a shallow basin at either end. Fountain houses are frequently represented in vase paintings from the 6th century BC onwards, shown as buildings with Doric porches and water running from spouts in the form of lions' heads. In the 4th century BC the south-west fountain house in the Athenian Agora (*see* ATHENS, fig. 16k) was built in an L-shape and with an outer colonnade and draw-basin against the walls. Between columns in front of the draw-basin, slabs were inserted to retain the water. Slanting grooves were cut on the top to facilitate raising the filled jars, and there were circular holes for women to rest their jars while conversing. From the 4th century BC onwards the addition of a porch in front of the draw-basin, either *in antis* or prostyle, became the norm. The draw-basin itself had a parapet with pillars; there were almost always lion-head spouts of stone or bronze, though occasionally the jars had to be dipped into the basin. In fountains with spouts, surplus water was collected in open basins, which in turn served another fountain lower down. The parapets were occasionally decorated, but otherwise façades generally remained simple until Roman times.

Another civic building connected with water was the water-clock. The earlier type, invented in the 4th century BC, was operated by water outflow. It consisted of a vertical shaft *c.* 2.5 m deep with an outlet pipe at the bottom. The shaft was filled with water and a graduated wooden rod floated in it, descending as the water escaped. Examples exist at the Sanctuary of Amphiaraios (Amphiaraion) at Oropos in northern Attica, in the Agora of Athens and probably at Stymphalos in the Peloponnese. The difficulties with this type of water-clock are that the water escapes more slowly as it is depleted and that it is not easy to allow for the differing length of hours in summer and winter. In the 3rd century BC a new type of clock, operated by water inflow, was invented in Alexandria. This consisted of two tanks: an upper one kept full of water with a faucet near the bottom, which controlled the flow of water into a lower tank in which the marked wooden rod rose. The best-known example was in the Tower of the Winds at Athens (2nd or 1st century BC).

BIBLIOGRAPHY

W. A. McDonald: *The Political Meeting Places of the Greeks* (Baltimore, 1943)

R. E. Wycherley: *How the Greeks Built Cities* (London, 1949, 3/1969)

H. A. Thompson and R. E. Wycherley: *The Agora of Athens* (1972), xiv of *The American Excavations in the Athenian Agora* (Cambridge, MA, 1933–)

J. J. Coulton: *The Architectural Development of the Greek Stoa* (Oxford, 1976)

John M. Camp: *The Athenian Agora* (London, 1986)

(c) Domestic. Standard house types evolved comparatively late in ancient Greek architecture. Dwellings with apsidal, round or rectangular plans existed in prehistoric times. Of these, the megaron type, rectangular in plan with a porch in front, survives from the 8th century BC at Zagora, and the apsidal plan is found at Emporio on Chios in houses of the 7th century BC. Here also square and rectangular forms occur (*see also* §2(i) below). From these rather hazy beginnings emerged two main types of house: the megaron or *prostas* type, typical of the houses in Priene; and the *pastas* type, best exemplified in the houses of Olynthos. Out of the latter evolved the most popular plan, the *pastas*-type house with a peristyle court, most characteristic of Hellenistic houses on Delos (for house plans see fig. 12).

The megaron (*prostas*) plan is named for its resemblance to the Mycenaean MEGARON and is characterized by a large main room (*oikos*) with a columned porch (*prostas*) facing south into a courtyard. A 6th-century BC example from Onythe on Crete even includes the four columns of Mycenaean palaces, adding to the evidence for a continuation of Mycenaean architectural traditions down to the 3rd century BC.

At Priene, the megaron type developed from 350 BC onwards, also becoming popular in other cities. Priene was laid out on a grid plan (*see* PRIENE, fig. 1), with blocks of houses built back to back. It utilized a house plan that could remain constant but in which the entrance could be at the north or south. This was accomplished by means of a hall along the east side of the building, which could have the front door at either end. A central court led off from this hall and gave access to the house proper. At the north end of the court was a complex of four rooms facing south: an *oikos* consisting of a colonnaded porch with

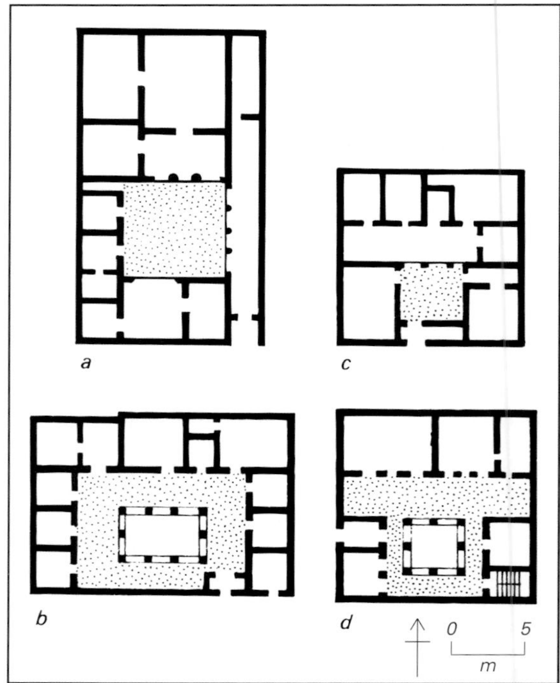

12. Greek domestic architecture, house types: (a) megaron or *prostas* type, Priene, *c.* 350 BC onwards; (b) *pastas* type with peristyle court, Olynthos isolated villa, 4th century BC; (c) *pastas* type, Olynthos, *c.* 432 BC; (d) *pastas* type with peristyle court, Delos, 2nd century BC

living-room behind and two bedrooms to the west. The other two sides of the court, to the west and south, had accommodations for servants and storerooms (see fig. 12a). In the 2nd century BC, under the strong commercial influence of Rhodes, some of the houses at Priene were altered to conform to what Vitruvius described as the 'Rhodian' type. This had large columns at the north of the court and a peristyle of smaller columns on the other three sides. Occasionally, two adjoining houses were combined, creating some of the few ancient Greek houses with two courts.

The *pastas*-type house derives its name from a broad verandah that opened into a courtyard to the south and was the main feature of the rooms to the north of this courtyard (see fig. 12c). The columns of the *pastas* itself later developed into a complete peristyle, as in 4th-century BC examples at Olynthos (see fig. 12b). It was this type of ancient Greek house that eventually outlived the *prostas* type. Some cities evolved distinctive house plans, but dwellings in Athens had no standard plan. Here the common trait was an open court surrounded by a single storey of rooms. On the north slope of the Areopagos are the remains of several 5th-century BC houses of different sizes, some with party walls. The largest had ten rooms, an entry hall off an alley and a colonnaded court with a cistern. A feature of these houses is the *andron* (dining-room) with a raised strip along the walls for couches. The central flooring often has a mosaic, plain or figured, which was wetted to cool the room through evaporation; otherwise these buildings were generally without decoration.

Olynthos (founded 432 BC, destr. 348 BC) had a grid plan with ten lots to a block (*see also* §III, 2(ii) below). The houses were one-storey with asymmetrical plans (see fig. 12c above). Most were *c.* 18.3 m square, bisected by a *pastas* running east–west. The south half comprised a court, sometimes paved with cobblestones and surrounded by a peristyle (*see* OLYNTHOS, fig. 1); the north half comprised the main room, often with a hearth, and the kitchen and bathroom. The *andron*, resembling those at Athens, was in the south-east corner, with a raised cement floor for couches and a central mosaic. At the end of the 4th century BC and the beginning of the 3rd, the Olynthos type of *pastas* house with a peristyle occurred in larger versions at Pella, again in Macedonia. The Olynthian tradition of pebble mosaic floors reached its highpoint with the large figure panels on the floors of *andrones* and anterooms of houses at Pella.

The houses of prosperous merchants, typical of Hellenistic domestic architecture, are best exemplified in 2nd-century BC Delos. This city was not organized on a systematic grid, and house plans were often irregular. Almost all, however, included a square peristyle court with a large family room on its north side, normally with a wide central doorway flanked by two windows. This room and others usually surrounded three sides of the court, the fourth being an exterior wall (see fig. 12d and DELOS, fig. 3). Staircases led to an upper storey. The richer homes had thresholds and moulded doorjambs and lintels of marble; those in the more modest houses were of gneiss. The columns were almost always Doric, slender and graceful; they were often of marble, with unfluted, smooth or faceted lower drums. Sometimes other types of stone were used and covered with stucco to give a marble-like finish. Some peristyles again displayed the Rhodian system of larger, taller columns at the north side of the court with brackets to receive the entablature over the lower ones. In the court itself the floor was lowered, forming a sunken *impluvium*, often with an elaborate mosaic of large tesserae. Beneath it was a cistern for rainwater, supplied by lead pipes from the roof. The family room was elaborately decorated, often with a figured mosaic floor, and walls were covered with coloured stucco that sometimes imitated masonry, a practice that anticipated the perspective architectural scenes in villas at Pompeii.

BIBLIOGRAPHY

D. M. Robinson and J. W. Graham: *The Hellenic House* (1938), viii of *Excavations at Olynthus* (Baltimore, 1929–52)

J. W. Graham: 'Origins and Interrelations of the Greek House and the Roman House', *Phoenix*, xx (1966), pp. 3–31

W. Hoepfner and E. L. Schwander: *Haus und Stadt im klassischen Griechenland* (1986), i of *Wohnen in der klassischen Polis* (Munich, 1986–)

ANASTASIA N. DINSMOOR, WILLIAM B. DINSMOOR JR

(d) Funerary. The origins of several types of Greek funerary monuments go back to Helladic times, and early forms were particularly persistent in the remoter areas. The earliest funerary structures were tumuli, which first appeared in the Middle Helladic period (*c.* 2050–*c.* 1600 BC). These were simply large-scale burial markers in the form of low conical earth or stone mounds (diam. 10–20 m; h. up to 5 m), usually encircled by a stone socle with retaining or marking function. Tumuli continued to be constructed into the Hellenistic period (323–27 BC), notably in northern Greece and Attica. They were used to cover many varieties of tombs, ranging from Mycenaean tholoi (*see* THOLOS TOMB) and chamber tombs to the much later tombs of Madeconian type (see below). Tumuli were, moreover, often erected over multiple burials in pithoi (storage jars) or dug graves (e.g. at Vergina; 10th–7th century BC). The most common type of tumulus-covered grave, surviving from Helladic times, was the cist burial (a rectangular pit lined with slabs or rubble walls and with cover slabs), though shaft graves, which originated as larger, royal versions of cist graves in the Helladic period at Mycenae, also occur.

Examples of the most famous Mycenaean form of tomb, the circular, corbel vaulted tholos, continued to be built in Thessaly in the Archaic and Classical periods (*c.* 700–323 BC) and perhaps even later in Thrace. Versions of the Mycenaean chamber tomb, which was also used for lavish burials, again continued to be employed in later periods. Rock-cut chamber tombs were used on Crete in Protogeometric and Geometric times, and built chamber tombs occurred on Aigina (6th century BC) and at Eretria (mid-3rd century BC) as well as in Macedonia and at Taras in Italy (see below).

From the Protogeometric to the Early Archaic period (10th–7th century BC) graves were sometimes grouped inside rectangular enclosures (e.g. at Nea Ionia in Attica). These were occasionally surrounded by a further rectangular wall, creating an outer area reserved for cult practice (e.g. at Tenos, Naxos, Megara, Brauron and Eretria). From the Protogeometric period onwards burials in Attica were laid in pits, cists, sarcophagi or tile graves (rows of tiles propped up to form a pointed cover over the body).

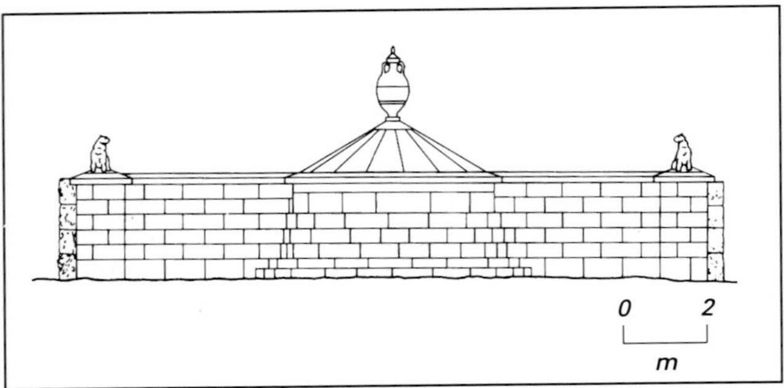

13. State burial chamber on the road to the Academy, Athens, late 5th century BC; reconstruction

Around 600 BC the small rectangular earth mounds erected over single graves in the Geometric and Early Archaic periods assumed a monumental form with walls of mud-brick protected by a jutting cornice of slabs and surmounted by a flat or shallow pitched roof. The whole structure was coated with mud and lime plaster bearing painted decoration (as on a grave in the Kerameikos, Athens; 6×3×2 m; *c*. 570–*c*. 560 BC).

During the late 5th century BC and the 4th this Attic type of funerary monument, also known from Samos, developed into the family peribolos tomb, consisting of a raised rectangular earth core surrounded with walls on one or more sides. The front had an ashlar or polygonal masonry façade. Peribolos tombs each covered several burials and were crowned along the top of the front wall by an assembly of different grave markers (e.g. stelai, statuary) for the individual burials. Examples of peribolos tombs have been found at Athens (Kerameikos), Rhamnous, Hellenikon and Rentis in Attica. The best-known peribolos tomb at Kerameikos is the one adorned with the Relief of Dexileos (early 4th century BC; see fig. 62 below).

Similarly, during the 6th century BC the traditional tumulus was transformed into a circular stone structure enclosing an earth core. The earliest example is the grave monument of Menekrates on Corfu (*c*. 600 BC), while a slightly later limestone monument (*c*. 560–*c*. 550 BC; partially reassembled in Athens, Kerameikos Mus.) has various Doric architectural features, foreshadowing those of the 4th-century BC tholos–heroon. The problem of combining the tumulus form with the Attic peribolos tomb was solved in the state burial monument on the road to the Academy at Athens (late 5th century BC; see fig. 13). Here a circular structure with a conical roof was set into the face of a rectangular structure.

The funerary monuments of the hellenized dynasts of Asia Minor consisted of a rectangular podium, derived from Lycian tombs, surmounted by a small Ionic temple-like structure. One of the earliest examples, the Nereid Monument from Xanthos in Lycia (*c*. 400 BC; reassembled in London, BM) has elaborate sculptural decoration and a peripteral superstructure (for illustration *see* XANTHOS). The Heroon at Limyra, also in Lycia (*c*. 380–*c*. 350 BC), has an amphiprostyle superstructure that recalls the Erechtheion on the Athenian Acropolis in its use of caryatids. Roofs in the form of stepped pyramids probably covered the Mausoleum at Halikarnassos (*c*. 365–*c*. 350 BC; *see* HALIKARNASSOS, fig. 2), the Lion Tomb at Knidos (mid-4th century BC) and the Mausoleum at Belevi (date disputed, ?3rd century BC; see fig. 30 below), which provided one of the first instances of the Corinthian order used externally. The roof of the Mausoleum at Halikarnassos was surmounted by a chariot group, as probably was that at Belevi, while the Lion Tomb at Knidos bore a sculpted lion. The influence of Asiatic monuments on Attic tombs is illustrated by a late 4th-century BC example from Kallithea in Athens (h. 8.5 m; partially reassembled in Peiraeus, Archaeol. Mus.), which consists of a high podium decorated with a relief frieze and topped by a naiskos (small shrine) containing statues.

Distinctive Macedonian tombs were used in the kingdom of Macedonia from around 350 to 150 BC for royal and aristocratic burials, the most characteristic being the groups in west and central Macedonia (e.g. at Vergina, Dion and Leukadia). They have a rectangular underground chamber, sometimes preceded by an antechamber, built of finely dressed ashlar masonry and adorned both inside and outside with architectural or figural decoration in painted stucco. The chambers are surmounted by vaults, which developed from the horizontal roofs of the smaller built chamber tombs also found in the region, at Vergina, Sedes and Katerine (early–mid-4th century BC), and which enabled larger spans of up to 7 m to be covered. The vaults are hidden by independent façade walls, which may have originated in the rock-cut façades of non-Greek tombs in Asia Minor but consist of free combinations of architectural elements in the Ionic or Doric orders, imitating the fronts of houses or temples. An exceptional two-storey façade tomb at LEUKADIA (*c*. 300–*c*. 250 BC) has false windows in its upper storey that are reminiscent of the windows of the palace at Vergina (*c*. 300 BC). The dead were laid on marble couches or in couch-shaped sarcophagi. After the funeral the tomb was covered by a tumulus. Akin to the Macedonian tombs are the 6th–2nd century BC underground chamber tombs with a stepped approach at Taras, which also bear painted decoration. (For further general discussion, *see also* HEROON and TOMB, §I.)

BIBLIOGRAPHY

Kerameikos: Ergebnisse der Ausgrabungen (Berlin, 1939–)
K. Kübler: 'Der attische Grabbau', *Mitt. Dt. Archäol. Inst.*, ii (1949), pp. 7–22
M. Andronikos: 'Ellenika epitaphia mnemeia' [Greek funerary monuments], *Archaiol. Deltion*, xvii/1 (1961–2), pp. 152–210
P. M. Petsas: *O taphos ton Leukadion* [The tomb at Leukadia] (Athens, 1966)
D. C. Kurtz and J. Boardman: *Greek Burial Customs* (London, 1971)
J. Borchhardt: *Die Bauskulptur des Heroons von Limyra: Das Grabmal des lykischen Königs Perikles* (Berlin, 1976)
P. G. Themelis: *Frühgriechische Grabbauten* (Mainz, 1976)
B. Gossel: *Makedonische Kammergräber* (Berlin, 1980)
M. Andronikos: *Vergina: The Royal Tombs and the Ancient City* (Athens, 1984)
J. Fedak: *Monumental Tombs of the Hellenistic Age: A Study of Selected Tombs from the Pre-Classical to the Early Imperial Era* (Toronto, 1990)

I. LEVENTI

(e) Entertainment and recreation. As in the domain of civic architecture (*see* §(b) above), the evolution of secular building types connected with public entertainment and recreation was associated with the development of the

Greek *polis* and the concept of providing good public facilities for its citizens.

Theatres. Although the theatre in ancient Greece is usually associated with dramatic performances, it was often built to accommodate other kinds of performance also, especially music and poetry. Greek theatres were ideal auditoria and were even used for political gatherings. The placing of a theatre was usually dictated by geographical features, ideally a sloping hillside that could accommodate spectators. Only if this was not possible were an auditorium and performing area constructed artificially by the costly and laborious process of excavating a level area and shoring up earthen banks.

Early Greek theatres consisted of two main parts, the *theatron* (auditorium) and the *orchestra* (circular performing area). These two parts were related increasingly closely as the *theatron* developed into an element enveloping the *orchestra* with retaining walls, which extended the seating on either side of the natural slope. The *theatron* was separated from the *orchestra* by a corridor incorporating a gutter to drain rainwater. At both ends, wide corridors (*parodoi*) gave access to the *orchestra* from outside. The *theatron* consisted of wedge-shaped segments of seats (*kerkides*) divided by stairs and varying in number. The staircases facilitated access by the audience. For the same purpose and to permit better viewing, later, larger theatres often had the end *kerkides* on either side set back slightly from the *orchestra*, changing the curvature of the *theatron* and widening the corridor around the *orchestra*. Many theatres extended the audience capacity by the addition of an extra tier of seats (*epitheatron*) separated from the lower seats by a wide corridor (*diazoma*). In its developed form the Greek theatre has a third element, in addition to the *orchestra* and *theatron*; this is the *skene* (stage building), which faces the *theatron* across the *orchestra* (see fig. 14). Originally a makeshift backdrop, it eventually became a permanent structure with side wings (*paraskenia*) and, later, a decorative façade (*proskenion*). Spectators in early Greek theatres sat on the ground or on wooden benches. Only important officials or priests had individual seats (*proedriai*), usually designated by inscriptions. These seats occasionally intruded into the *orchestra*.

Stone *theatra* were constructed from the 4th century BC onwards, and the *epitheatron* in these sometimes had a sharper slope, as in the theatre at Epidauros (*c.* 350–*c.* 330 BC; see fig. 26 below). Such *theatra* could accommodate up to 21,000 spectators. The round or semicircular *orchestra*, usually associated with the architectural form of the Greek theatre, especially after the discovery in the late 19th century of the beautifully preserved theatre at Epidauros, evolved only gradually. The remains of early theatres suggest that the *orchestra* was simply an amorphous open area, often rectilinear, as in the oldest extant theatre, at Thorikos in Attica (late 6th century BC). Also in Attica are the early rectilinear theatres in the Sanctuary of Dionysos at Ikaria (5th century BC), at Rhamnous (5th century BC) and at Trachones (4th century BC). The last is also important because of its capacity (*c.* 4750 spectators) and because it contained the earliest extant *proskenion*. Outside Attica there is evidence for early rectilinear theatres at Argos, Syracuse and elsewhere.

The earliest rounded *orchestra* may have been that of the Theatre of Dionysos at Athens. Its site on the south slope of the Acropolis may not have been the original one. It appears that wooden seating, possibly in the Athenian Agora, collapsed in the early 5th century BC, and there is archaeological evidence that the *theatron* of the Theatre of Dionysos was shored up at that time. It was therefore probably moved to its present location at the beginning of the 5th century BC, since a curved retaining wall of that date may have been part of it. If so, it was not, as originally thought, strictly circular, since the remains of the wall do not form a regular segment of a circle. The existing stone *theatron* was erected in the second half of the 4th century BC around an *orchestra* in the shape of an extended semicircle. This type of curved *orchestra* eventually became standard in Greek theatres, ranging from a semicircle to a complete circle, as at Epidauros.

Regardless of its shape, the *orchestra* remained throughout the Classical period the performing area for both actors and chorus. The *skene*, which provided accommodation for scenery, changing facilities and so on, did not intrude on the performance, except to provide a door or doors for entrances and, on occasion, a platform from which the figures of deities could deliver their speeches. This is the usual function assigned to 'platform T' in the Theatre of Dionysos, which projected from a long wall supporting a wooden *skene* or scenery and backed by a long colonnade to the south. The stone *skene* in this theatre was built in the second half of the 4th century BC, but at a later date the projecting *paraskenia* were cut back considerably to accommodate an ornamental Doric *proskenion*. Similar *proskenia*, sometimes wooden but (especially later) mostly of stone, became common from the end of the 4th century BC onwards. They provided projecting platforms ranging in height from 2.43 m to 3.96 m and in depth of projection from 1.92 m to 3.96 m. The colonnade of the *proskenion* could be closed off by scenery or ornamental panels.

Proskenia may originally have served only as backdrops for the performance in the *orchestra*, but at some date between the 3rd and 1st centuries BC the main stage area

14. Theatre at Oropos, 2nd century BC, showing (left to right) *skene* complex, *orchestra* and part of the *theatron*; reconstruction drawing from Ernst Robert Fiechter: *Das Theater in Oropos* (Stuttgart, 1930), pl. 8

moved to the flat roof of the *proskenion*, which provided an acting platform (*logeion*) suitable for small groups of actors though not for a chorus. This fundamental change can be understood in the context of the decrease in importance of the chorus. The action increasingly took place against the upper floor of the *skene* (*episkenion*), at first a wooden structure. The narrow *logeion* was widened in the theatre at Oropos (2nd century BC; see fig. 14) by the addition of a rear stage inside the *episkenion*, accessible and visible through five large openings (*thyromata*), which could also be ornamented with scenery. Ramps were built on either side of the *skene* to provide access to the upper level. This was the form the *skene* complex assumed during the Hellenistic period: a two-storey building abutting on the *orchestra* but not enclosed by the *theatron*. (*See also* THEATRE, §II, 2.)

Odeia. The ODEION was a roofed structure for musical performances. In the Classical period its architectural plan was based on that of religious or secular assembly halls. Accordingly, the earliest odeion for which conjectural reconstruction is possible, the Odeion of Pericles at Athens (mid-5th century BC), was a square hypostyle hall with sides of 62.4 m and nine rows of nine columns supporting a pyramidal roof. There were external colonnades on its east, west and, perhaps, south sides. Odeia did not become widespread until Roman times.

Hotels and dining halls. Accommodation for visitors to both cities and sanctuaries was provided in hotels (*katagogeia*). The *katagogeion* is a distinct architectural type, with a roughly square plan and one- or two-storey elevation. The rooms were arranged around a colonnaded court. Surviving examples all date from the 4th century BC. The Leonidaion at Olympia (*c.* 330 BC; 74.80×81.08 m), named after its donor and architect, Leonidas of Naxos, had an internal Doric peristyle court with 12 columns per side and an Ionic external peristyle of 34 columns on the east and west sides and 37 columns on the north and south. In Epidauros the *katagogeion* (76.3 m square) had four interior courtyards surrounded by Doric peristyles; its two storeys provided about 160 rooms. In the *katagogeion* of Kassope, Epiros, each room had a table and a hearth.

Dining halls (*andrones*) existed in both private houses and such public buildings as the stoa (*see* STOA, §1). They are characterized by the off-centre positioning of the doors, displaced to accommodate dining couches, which stood on raised platforms around the walls. The portion of the floor not occupied by couches was sometimes decorated with plain or figured mosaics.

Athletic and recreational facilities. Athletic shows usually took place in the open air, and like the theatre, the STADIUM originated as a simple adaptation of suitable terrain to provide a level running track with terraced seating for spectators. Some stadia had masonry retaining walls, but stone seating was rare, occurring only in later examples.

The GYMNASIUM was an integral part of the education of young men and boys; it was a place not only for athletic but also for intellectual training: philosophers frequented gymnasia and gave formal lectures in designated rooms. Early gymnasia (i.e. those dating from before *c.* 400 BC) were open areas with trees, water and shrines. Later, in the Hellenistic period, they developed into extensive architectural complexes with areas enclosed by colonnades. Some of these stoas were in fact running tracks for the use of the athletes in bad weather. They were based on the standard distance of one *stade* (600 Greek feet), from which the stadium was named. Large cities such as Athens had more than one gymnasium, and gymnasia existed naturally in sanctuaries, which organized athletic contests.

The PALAESTRA or wrestling ground was a smaller structure that was normally part of the gymnasium but might also exist as an independent structure. It developed into a peristyle courtyard lined by rooms of various sizes and functions, some of which were fronted by colonnaded porches.

Bathing establishments existed early in the Greek world (*see also* BATH (ii), §1). These were generally simple affairs, although there were also instances of hot baths, as at Sybaris (6th century BC). Gymnasium complexes at Delphi and Olympia provide the best examples. Next to the palaestra at Delphi (4th century BC) was a pentagonal court with showers arranged along a retaining wall and a circular plunge bath in front of them (diam. 10.05 m, depth 1.82 m). At Olympia, the plunge bath or swimming pool was rectangular (16×24 m, depth 1.6 m); it dates from the 5th century BC, as do the early phases of the baths, a rectangular building (21.32×5.33 m) equipped with a water spout. This was later enlarged by the addition of a room containing hip baths, and it was eventually equipped with hot water. Olympia may also have had a sauna (*laconicum*), if that was the original function of the round heroon.

The late 3rd-century BC baths at Oiniadai already included the triple sequence of rooms characteristic of Roman baths: a *frigidarium* with a cold plunge, a large circular *tepidarium* with eight warm-water basins sunk in the floor, and a circular *caldarium* with seventeen hot-water basins. These simple and utilitarian arrangements were later developed by the Romans, who turned the bath into a magnificent architectural form.

BIBLIOGRAPHY

M. Bieber: *The History of the Greek and Roman Theatre* (Princeton, 1939, rev. 2/1961)
R. E. Wycherley: *How the Greeks Built Cities* (London, 1949, 3/1969)
J. Delorme: *Gymnasion* (Paris, 1960)
R. Ginouvès: *Balaneutikè* (Paris, 1962)
A. L. Hawkins Robkin: *The Odeion of Perikles* (diss., Washington, DC, George Washington U., 1975)
R. Mienel: *Das Odeion, Untersuchungen an Überdachten antiken Theatergebäuden* (Frankfurt am Main, 1980)
C. Courtois: *Le Bâtiment de scène des théâtres de l'Italie et de Sicile*, Archaeol. Transatlant., viii (Louvain-la-Neuve, 1989)

ANASTASIA N. DINSMOOR, WILLIAM B. DINSMOOR JR

(ii) Materials and construction. Greek architecture was profoundly influenced by the natural resources of the area, and its very style was partly determined by the quality of the materials available, the most common of which were stone, clay or wood.

(a) Stone. (b) Other materials.

(a) Stone. The earliest stone temples were constructed during the 7th century BC (*see* §(i)(a) above); before this

time both sacred and secular buildings had been mainly of such perishable materials as mud-brick, wood and thatch.

Types. Roughly speaking, ancient Greece can be divided into those areas where the usual building stone was poros, a granular variety of calcareous tufa that need not necessarily be porous, and those areas that used marble. The former group (the Peloponnese, South Italy and Sicily) was inhabited mainly by the so-called Dorian Greeks, and it was here that the Doric order arose. The latter group (Attica, the Cyclades and Asia Minor) was the domain of the Ionians and the birthplace of the Ionic order. In a felicitous combination, the geology of these regions supplied each of these two peoples with the type of stone best suited to the expression of their own particular genius.

A particularly fine poros was quarried at Corinth and exported to the Peloponnese and Delphi. It was extremely soft and could be cut with an axe. It was vulnerable to frost and erosion and had to be coated with a layer of mortar made from lime and marble powder, which gave it the appearance of marble. Its fragility meant that it could not be used to produce projecting features, while the mortar coating would obscure any elaborate carving. It thus corresponded perfectly to the bare severity of the Doric order, in which mouldings were rare and adorned only with decorations painted on to the stucco.

The fragility of poros also explains the structure of the Doric doorway. This had no jambs; instead, the sill was merely slipped into grooves cut in the bases of the walls on either side, so that it could be removed and replaced when worn. Similarly, Peloponnesian temples were generally equipped with a special access stairway at the front, to prevent the wearing down of the stepped base and reduce the expense of repairs. However, such stairs were also sometimes needed because the steps of the base were too high to be used with ease, and they had the further aesthetic advantage of drawing attention to the temple's main façade. These access stairs became so typical a feature of Peloponnesian Doric that they were used even when a temple's base was constructed in a hard stone, for example marble at the Temple of Athena Alea, Tegea (*c.* 350 BC), or St Elias limestone at the Temple of Apollo, Delphi (rebuilt *c.* 366–*c.* 329 BC).

Being solid, compact and impermeable, marble was ideally suited to the Ionic order, with its slim, ornately profiled column bases, capitals with lavish volutes that overhung their shafts, and numerous finely carved mouldings on the entablatures. It was also the obvious choice for the even more ornate Corinthian capital. Since the marble sills of Ionic doorways were unlikely to be worn down quickly, they were fixed firmly in place, held down by heavy doorjambs. Similarly, distinct access stairways were not needed to protect the bases of marble Ionic temples.

Although at first marble was used exclusively for Ionic buildings and poros for Doric structures, later both materials were employed for both orders: poros for Ionic (and Corinthian) in the Peloponnese in the 4th century BC, particularly at Epidauros, and marble for the Doric order in Asia Minor, on the Aegean islands and in Attica. The Parthenon at Athens (447–432 BC) was the first great Doric temple built entirely of marble. The only Classical marble temple in the Peloponnese was that of Athena Alea, built at Tegea near the quarries of Doliana. Greek architects preferred pure white varieties of marble (from Paros, Naxos, Mt Pentelikon and Prokonnesos) to the tinted varieties (bluish from Tinos, grey-blue from Mt Hymettos) or the veined marbles favoured by the Romans.

Marble tiles, apparently invented by Byzes of Naxos (?late 7th century BC–early 6th; see Pausanias: *Guide to Greece* V.x.3.) and widely used where marble was plentiful, were a great luxury in areas where poros was the usual building stone. They were employed for the Temple of Zeus at Olympia (*c.* 470–*c.* 457 BC), the Temple of Apollo at Bassai (429–*c.* 400 BC), the tholos (thymele) at Epidauros (*c.* 360–*c.* 320 BC), the Treasury of the Athenians (*c.* 510 or *c.* 490 BC) and the tholos (*c.* 380 BC) at Delphi .

In addition to poros and marble, Greek architects also made occasional use of limestone. The varieties employed included fine St Elias limestone quarried near Delphi during the 4th century BC; Peiraeus stone; the dark limestones of Eleusis and Argos (used for flagstones and the bases of chryselephantine statues); the speckled limestone of Epidauros (used for flagstones); and gneiss and volcanic andesite, which were difficult to work but were employed for the earliest monuments at Pergamon.

Preparation. Blocks of stone were quarried using iron or wooden wedges; the latter were driven into the rock and soaked with water to make them swell and split the blocks away from their strata. The blocks were rough-hewn on the spot to the size specified by the architect before being sent to the building site. Inscribed accounts from Delphi, Miletos and Eleusis show that transportation by land and sea was extremely expensive, even when there was no need for the sophisticated equipment required to move the heaviest blocks of the giant temples in Sicily and Asia Minor.

Once they had arrived at their destination, the blocks were prepared for assembly. Ancient Greek buildings were constructed without any mortar to smooth out irregularities in the surfaces of the masonry, and imperfections in the joint faces of the blocks created a risk of cracking. To combat this, Greek masons did not attempt to make contiguous blocks fit snugly over their entire joint faces. Instead, they used the device of *anathyrosis*, whereby the centre of each joint face was hollowed out and the joint surface itself confined to a carefully smoothed strip around its border. The precision of the work was checked by placing a ruler covered in red lead on each strip to show up any irregularities by colouring them. The outer surfaces of the wall were only evened and finished, and the columns fluted, during the final stage of construction when the blocks no longer risked being exposed to blows and collisions during work on the building site.

Transport and manipulation. After being prepared by *anathyrosis* and sometimes numbered, the blocks were hoisted into place by means of lifting equipment mentioned in inscriptions and described by Vitruvius (*On Architecure* X.ii.1–10). These included a simple derrick, equipped with a pulley or a hoist at the top, the inclination of which could be controlled by a system of guy-ropes; another type of derrick formed by three poles attached together at the top; and gantries with two (*dikolos*) or four

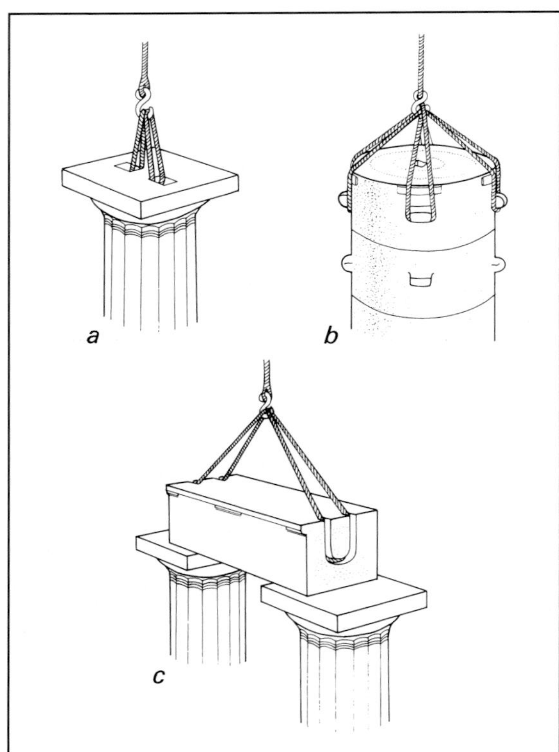

15. Types of lifting device: (a) handling boss; (b) closed U-shaped channel; (c) open U-shaped furrow

(*tetrakolos*) supports linked by horizontal beams from which hoists were suspended (*see also* CONSTRUCTION MACHINERY, §1). The blocks were sometimes raised with ropes that were prevented from slipping by temporary protuberances of undressed stone (handling bosses; see fig. 15b). Alternatively, in the case of poros blocks, they might be inserted into closed U-shaped channels bored into the thickness of the block or open U-shaped furrows cut into its ends (15a and c). Metal pincers were more often used, however, with their tips fitting into notches cut in the block's upper surface, and from the Hellenistic period onwards the lewis was used as a simple and convenient means of setting blocks in place.

Assembly of blocks. The blocks were generally either polygonal or rectangular. Polygonal masonry was mainly used for utilitarian construction, for example retaining walls, fortifications and the bases of mud-brick walls. This technique allowed the builders to economize on material, as the joint faces, of which there were always at least five, were cut to follow as closely as possible the contours of the original rough-hewn block. Polygonal masonry with straight joints was the most common form, particularly during the Hellenistic period (323–27 BC). During the Archaic period (*c.* 700–*c.* 525/480 BC), however, a method of polygonal masonry with curved joints was also used, as in the 6th-century BC great terrace wall below the Temple of Apollo at Delphi; this is the finest example of this method, known as 'Lesbian' masonry. The curvature of the joints gave the masonry greater cohesion and a highly decorative appearance.

Rectangular masonry was the favoured method for monumental architecture. The typical Greek wall stood on a plinth of orthostates (slabs placed on edge), which in turn rested on a low course (toichobate). This was decorated with mouldings in Ionic structures and occasionally in Doric ones (e.g. the Temple of Hephaistos at Athens, *c.* 450–*c.* 445 BC; the tholos and the Temple of Apollo at Delphi; and the tholos (thymele) at Epidauros). Similarly, in Ionic buildings the wall was crowned by a narrow course decorated with mouldings. The courses of the wall proper could be of varying height (broken ashlar), of the same height (isodomic bond) or of alternating heights (pseudo-isodomic), as was often used at Pergamon. The blocks used were either parpend stones (large stones passing through the whole thickness of the wall) or stretchers (thin blocks arranged back-to-back in two rows (three in larger buildings)), which alternated with headers placed transversely through the rows so as to hold the bond together. Poros walls consisted almost exclusively of parpend stones, while the structurally more solid marble walls, particularly in Ionic buildings, were built in a combination of the two techniques.

Blocks were manoeuvred tightly into place using levers and pincers. Levers fitted into notches cut in the lower edges of the block ends and in adjacent and underlying blocks. Joints alternated from one course to the next, and assembly might be facilitated by shallow marker lines cut into the faces of the blocks or by assembly lettering (as in the Stoa of Philip V on Delos, *c.* 216–*c.* 200 BC). Sometimes narrow strips were chiselled along the edges of the blocks to indicate the depth to which their unfinished surfaces must be cut back.

During the Archaic period the blocks were often simply held in place by their own weight. However, from the late 6th century BC onwards the masonry was bonded vertically by dowels and horizontally by clamps. These were usually of metal, either iron or bronze, sealed in lead. Wooden dowels of boxwood or cypress, which were reputed never to rot or swell, were used to link the column drums, but dowels in wall blocks generally took the form of thin metal plates. These were embedded into the join between adjacent blocks, but at corners dowels were also inserted into the main bodies of the blocks to be secured. As a consequence, special pour channels were provided for the molten lead, particularly from the Hellenistic period onwards.

The shape of the clamps used developed over the years, though this cannot always be used as a reliable guide to the date of a building. During the Archaic period clamps were shaped like dovetails either with or without masonry ties (see fig. 16a–c). At the end of the 6th century, double-gamma or double-T varieties appeared and were in use during the 5th–4th century BC (16d–f), and clamps in the form of a pi were used throughout the 4th century BC (16g). Nevertheless, some dovetail clamps were still used during the Hellenistic period, and several different types of clamp could also occur in the same building in cases where different materials were employed. Local traditions among craftsmen from different areas may also have influenced the choice of clamps: the accounts kept at

Delphi and Epidauros show that the craftsmen came from the regions that supplied the materials on which they worked (for the Temple of Asklepios, Epidauros, see Roux, pp. 131–70, 424–32).

Surfacing and finishing. The final stage of construction involved dressing the walls and fluting the columns, so that some unfinished buildings still have handling bosses and drafted edges on their masonry and protective carapaces of unworked stone around their column drums. Masonry was smoothed with fine-toothed chisels, while in the Classical period (*c.* 525/480–323 BC) walls built in poros received a coating of stucco, and those of marble were polished to conceal the lines of the joints. This gave the Classical buildings a monolithic appearance; their beauty lay in the continuity of the forms. From the early 4th century BC, however, and particularly in the Hellenistic period, architects tried to accentuate the structural elements of their buildings. A recessed band formed a dark line beneath each step of the base, while two underlined the stylobate. Similarly, each wall block was distinguished from the next by a relief panel surrounded by a chiselled band or by having a bossed surface with a convex or flattened profile. This novel use of architectural elements to create an interplay of light and shadow was imitated in the interiors of buildings, either in stucco or painted in *trompe l'oeil*, for example in the Hieron on Samothrace (begun *c.* 325–*c.* 300 BC, completed *c.* 150–*c.* 125 BC) and private houses on Delos (mainly 2nd century BC).

Finally, the fluting of the columns was carved out after the appropriate number of planes had already been roughly cut on the shafts. At the time of assembly, the flutes were carved only at the base of the bottom drum and the top of the highest drum (or on the neck of the capital) in order to serve as a guide for the workers. Fluting was an expensive, difficult and lengthy operation. The sharp arrises between the flutes on Doric columns were particularly fragile when the drums were cut in poros, and it cost roughly 4500 drachmas to flute each column at the Temple of Apollo at Didyma: six times the annual salary of the architect. The bases of Ionic columns and the mouldings on the toichobate were protected during construction by coffering of wood or unbaked brick, and when the other building work was complete they were given their final decorations. During the 3rd century BC an innovation probably introduced by Pergamene architects involved substituting facets for flutes on the lower third of column shafts to reduce the danger of damage. This device was particularly common in Hellenistic stoas, where large numbers of people were likely to pass through.

The bases of buildings, columns and walls were all either left as bare stone or covered in white stucco. The entablatures of Doric buildings were picked out in colour, however (*see* §(iii)(c) below), as were both carved and uncarved mouldings, which themselves received decorative features (*see* §(iii)(b) below).

(b) *Other materials.*

Mud-brick. Though stone was the material preferred by Greek architects, unbaked brick was also used. The bricks were made of clay and chopped straw, kneaded in water and then moulded and dried in the sun. They were easy to use, provided effective insulation and were extremely cheap, costing only 50 drachmas per 1000 on Delos in the 3rd century BC. Brick walls, however, had to be protected from the damp by being built on a stone plinth and coated with a regularly renewed layer of plaster. They were also sometimes reinforced by half-timbering. Mud-brick was the most common material for private houses, but it was also used, in conjunction with a plinth of stone orthostates or polygonal blocks, for public buildings such as the early Temple of Hera at Olympia (*c.* 590 BC) and various utilitarian buildings at Epidauros during the 4th and 3rd centuries BC. Even the palace of Mausolos (*reg* 377–353 BC) at Halikarnassos was of mud-brick, though it was faced in marble.

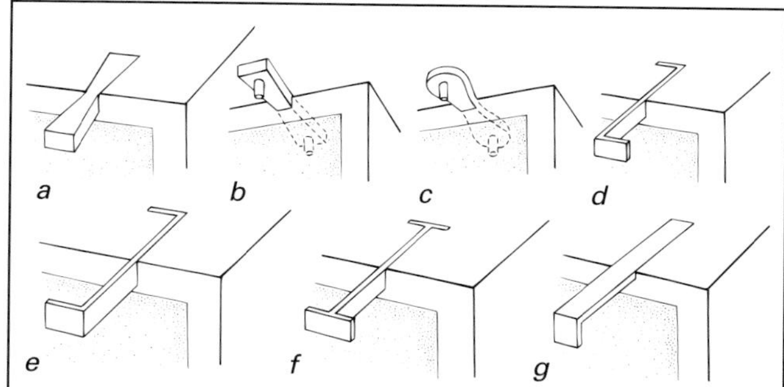

16. Types of clamp for bonding masonry blocks: (a)–(c) dovetail, 7th–6th century BC; (d)–(f) double-gamma and double-T, 5th–4th century BC; (g) pi-shaped, 4th century BC

Due to its low cost and its capacity for absorbing the shock of battering-ram attacks, mud-brick was widely used for city walls, including the particularly finely preserved example at Gela in Sicily (late 4th century BC).

Wood. In ancient times Greece was relatively thickly wooded, with great pine forests in Macedonia and Thrace, oak forests in Epeiros and Arcadia and cypress forests in the Peloponnese and Crete. Wood was of particular architectural importance in Archaic times, when it was used for columns, including those in the earliest version of the Temple of Hera at Olympia. Examples in the Archaic temples at the Argive Heraion (early 7th century BC) and at Orchomenos (late 6th century BC) were placed on stone discs to insulate them from the damp. The entablature of Doric buildings constructed in stone was apparently inspired by wooden prototypes, though their forms were modified for decorative purposes, and there is disagreement over the exact nature of the elements reproduced.

Even during Archaic times, wood was apparently rarely used for entire buildings. However, literary evidence concerning Delphi (e.g. Pausanias: *Guide to Greece* X.v.9) and excavations at Eretria indicate that early temples of Apollo at these sites took the form of laurel huts. Also according to Pausanias (VIII.x.2), the Temple of Poseidon Hippios, on the edge of the Arcadian forest near Mantinea, was built entirely of oak by Trophonios and Agamedes, the architects of the first stone Temple of Apollo at Delphi (7th century BC).

Later, wood was used essentially for fine furniture-making, doors, ceilings and structural frameworks. The only surviving evidence for these is in references in texts and inscriptions and the occasional traces left in stone surrounds. The doors of temples and treasuries were made of precious woods, particularly cypress from the Peloponnese and Crete. Inlaid with ivory and decorated with elements in gold, silver and bronze, these doors were expensive works of art. Thus Verres, Roman governor of Sicily in 73–71 BC, was accused of having removed ivory panels, gold nails and a bronze Gorgon's head from the doorway of the Temple of Athena at Syracuse. Lavish doors in temples and treasuries with distyle *in antis* porches were protected by grilles in the intercolumniations. Indeed, the necessity of taking such precautions may explain the preference for porches of this kind.

The accounts of the Erechtheion at Athens and the temples on Delos (see Stevens and Paton, and Davis respectively) give information on the use of ceilings in wood, consisting of beams decorated with astragal mouldings bearing coffers adorned with stars, acanthus motifs and figures of gods and heroes. From the 5th century BC onwards, wooden ceilings were progressively replaced by stone ceilings over the peristyles, which nevertheless continued to reproduce the shapes of the earlier wooden type. Those from the tholos (thymele) at Epidauros (Epidauros, Archaeol. Mus.; for illustration *see* COFFERING) are especially rich and refined. Although the ceilings over the peristyle, pronaos and opisthodomos of a temple were flat, interior ceilings usually followed the slope of the cella roof. Indeed, the coffers of the Neorion (Monument of the Bulls) at Delos (late 4th century BC–early 3rd) were carved out of the same marble slabs as the tiles of the roof: in this way the interior space was maximized and the roof's timber framework was left visible.

Most, if not all ancient Greek roofs were constructed on the post-and-lintel principle, merely by stacking elements one on top of another. In these, the lower ends of the principal rafters rested on the building's outer wall or the entablature of its colonnade, while their upper ends were supported by a ridge beam either resting directly on a central row of internal columns or carried by a vertical prop erected on a cross-beam between two internal colonnades. Large purlins held up in a similar way to the ridge beam provided additional support if needed. All the elements of such roofs were subject only to vertical pressures and held in place simply by means of superimposition. Truss roofs based on a series of triangular frames, formed by linking the outer ends of the rafters with a horizontal tie-beam, may have been employed to cover exceptional spans (e.g. 14.5 m in the bouleuterion at Miletos). In such roofs the weight acts outwards, stretching the tie-beam and exploiting wood's considerable tensile strength. Exceptional spans may, however, simply have been bridged by unusually large timbers, and the use of the truss roof is not definitely attested before Roman times (*see also* TIMBER STRUCTURE, §II, 2(i)). Continuous planking was used to support marble tiles, while terracotta tiles were simply laid on a base of reeds covered in clay, which improved their adhesion, compensated for any distortion caused by firing and insulated the roof timbers.

Circular buildings of tholos type had conical roofs formed by rafters with their converging upper ends secured by a metal element, for example a bronze poppy at the Philippeion at Olympia (*c.* 338 BC), while the foot of each beam rested on a circular wall plate, which resisted its outward thrust. On top of the principal rafters came varying numbers of subsidiary beams and battens.

Terracotta. During the Archaic period terracotta was occasionally employed for the metopes of Doric entablatures (e.g. at THERMON, *c.* 630 BC), for pedimental sculptures (e.g. the great Gorgoneion of Temple C at Selinus; Palermo, Mus. Reg.) and for acroteria (e.g. the Victories on the Temple of Athena Pronaia at Delphi; late 6th century BC). However, it was principally used for making roof tiles. These were much cheaper than their marble counterparts and, being much lighter, also permitted the use of substantial timbers. Consequently, they were used throughout the Greek world (*see also* TERRACOTTA, §II,1).

There were two types of tile in use. The Corinthian tiling system involved the use of flat rectangular pantiles with pointed cover tiles sealing their joints (*see* TERRACOTTA, fig. 1), whereas the Lakonian scheme employed semi-cylindrical tiles as both pantiles and cover tiles. Despite their regional epithets, both schemes were widely diffused. Only the rarer Aiolian system, which combined flat pantiles with semi-cylindrical cover tiles, was restricted to a particular geographical area: Ionia, Athens and the Aegean islands. There were also tiles made in special shapes designed for particular purposes. Tiles with a hole acted as chimneys above both the hearths of private houses and the altars of temples when located inside. Combinations of triangular and diamond-shaped tiles or tiles in the form of scales were used to create a handsome decorative effect on the roofs of circular monuments (e.g. the tholos at Athens, *c.* 470 BC; and the Arsinoeion at Samothrace, early 3rd century BC).

Roofs without gutters were decorated with antefixes at the ends of the cover tiles nearest the eaves. These were usually in the shape of palmettes but sometimes took more elaborate figural forms, particularly during the Archaic period (*see* ANTEFIX). The outer edges of the flat eaves tiles occasionally also bore painted decoration. Finally, the ridge tiles were surmounted by further palmettes, while acroteria sometimes crowned the gable ends (*see* ACROTERION). A terracotta gutter (sima) was frequently employed to channel rainwater to a series of waterspouts, thereby preventing damage to the buildings' walls. It too was lavishly decorated (*see* TERRACOTTA, fig. 2), sometimes even with figural friezes (e.g. chariot races at Larissa-on-Hermos, *c.* 540–*c.* 525 BC, Istanbul, Archaeol. Mus.; and hunting scenes at Thasos, *c.* 540–*c.* 525 BC, Thasos, Archaeol. Mus.). The waterspouts were usually painted tubes, though later they were sometimes made in the shape of lions' heads.

Roofs covered in terracotta tiles were occasionally surrounded by a marble gutter. At the beginning of the 4th century BC a new type of marble guttering appeared on the tholos of Delphi and the monuments of Epidauros. This 'Epidaurian' type consisted of a lion's-head gargoyle flanked on each side by a double foliated scroll of acanthus and underlined by a flat strip decorated with a Greek fret. It was immediately widely copied in terracotta.

Metals. The commonest use of metal in ancient Greek architecture was for producing clamps and dowels (see (a) above). Iron girders were used to strengthen the architraves of the Olympieion at Akragas (*c.* 500–*c.* 460 BC) and the Propylaia at Athens (*c.* 437–432 BC), the ceilings at Bassai and the horizontal cornice below the pediment of the Parthenon, but such sophisticated structural devices are rare. In general, ancient Greek buildings did not require reinforcement, as they were held in position by their own weight. Even when Alexander the Great introduced the use of the vault, it was only employed to cover underground chambers, such as Macedonian tombs and water tanks, or spaces enclosed by massive walls sufficiently heavy to counter the resultant thrusts.

According to legend, the third Temple of Apollo at Delphi was made of bronze (Pausanias: *Guide to Greece* X.v.11): what exactly is implied is unclear. In the 2nd century AD, however, the Archaic Temple of Athena Chalkioikos ('bronze house') at Sparta still had walls faced with bronze plaques bearing mythological scenes in low relief by Gitiadas, and in general the role played by metals in Greek architecture was ornamental. The steps of the Temple of Zeus at Stratos (4th century BC) and of the Arsinoeion on Samothrace were apparently underlined by an astragal in bronze. During the Archaic period bronze annulets decorated with palmettes were used to adorn the base of certain Doric capitals; in a similar fashion, during the Hellenistic period the Corinthian capitals of Delos and Alexandria had bronze volutes and acanthus leaves. Bronze and even gold and silver (as in the doors of the Parthenon) were sometimes used for the decorations on doors; for the accessories of architectural sculptures, particularly weapons; and for entire acroteria (e.g. the tripods on the Temple of Zeus at Olympia and the triton weather vane on the Tower of the Winds in Athens, *c.* 50–*c.* 37 BC).

BIBLIOGRAPHY

G. P. Stevens and J. M. Paton: *The Erechtheum* (Cambridge, MA, 1927)

P. Davis: 'The Porch Ceiling of the Temple of Apollo at Delos', *Amer. J. Archaeol.*, xxxviii (1938), pp. 71–80

A. K. Orlandos: *Ta ulika ton archaion Ellenon*, 2 vols (Athens, 1955–8); Fr. trans. as *Les Matériaux de construction et la technique architecturale des anciens Grecs*, 2 vols (Paris, 1966–8)

G. Roux: *Architecture de l'Argolide aux IVe et IIIe siècles* (Paris, 1961)

R. Martin: *Manuel d'architecture grecque*, i (Paris, 1965)

R. Ginouvès and R. Martin: *Dictionnaire méthodique de l'architecture grecque et romaine*, i, ii (Paris, 1985, 1990)

GEORGES ROUX

(iii) Decoration. Although most ancient Greek buildings survive in an undecorated state—indeed, traces of painted decoration are extremely rare—decoration played an important role, especially in the Greek temple, which was the first building type designed to be seen externally more than internally. (For architectural sculpture *see* §IV, 1(i)(b) below.)

(a) Façade. (b) Mouldings and motifs. (c) Colour.

(a) Façade. The development of façade architecture depended ultimately on overcoming the need for a building's appearance to be determined by its structural elements. This can first be seen in the interior of the Temple of Apollo at Bassai (429–*c.* 400 BC; see fig. 24 below). Here the internal colonnade was constructed close to the side walls of the cella, and the columns were engaged in short spur walls so that the illusion of an internal colonnade was created without the sacrifice of space usually necessary to achieve it. The façades of Greek temples and other buildings from the Archaic period (*c.* 700–*c.*525 BC) onwards usually consisted of a row of columns in either the Doric or the Ionic orders: good examples include the second Temple of Aphaia on Aigina (*c.* 500–*c.* 490 BC; *see* AIGINA, fig. 1) or the Propylaia on the Acropolis at Athens (437–432 BC). The columns were surmounted by an entablature and pediment. The triangular space of the pediment was usually filled with sculpture, forming the main purely decorative element in the façade: on the west pediment of the Temple of Zeus at Olympia (*c.* 470–*c.* 457 BC), for example, the *Battle of the Lapiths and the Centaurs* is represented. Pedimental sculpture does not usually survive *in situ* (*see also* PEDIMENT, §2(i)). The frieze directly below the pediment might also have sculptural decoration, as in the Parthenon at Athens (447–432 BC; *see* POLYCHROMY, colour pl. I, fig. 1) or the Temple of Zeus at Olympia, where the metopes were carved with figures in relief.

More elaborate schemes of façade architecture were developed with the invention of pilasters, which are in effect engaged rectangular-section columns with no structural function. Pilasters were apparently first used in the Temple of the Athenians on Delos (late 5th century BC), but they were not properly exploited decoratively before the Roman period, when they were used to decorate the façades of stage buildings in theatres and monumental gateways. It is, however, difficult to assess the part played by ancient Greek stage buildings in the development of façade architecture, since, although they could be decorated with engaged columns in two tiers, as at Sikyon (?*c.* 300 BC), the precise dates and arrangements of these buildings are disputed. It was only with the tombs of the early Hellenistic period that façade architecture was increasingly employed in the Greek world. Rows of columns were set one above the other for visual effect but without any structural necessity, as in the most famous example of this type, the tomb at LEUKADIA in Macedonia (early 3rd century BC). Here the lower part of the façade has engaged Doric columns, and the upper part has engaged Ionic columns. This type of architecture foreshadows much Roman decorative building, such as the Porta Aurea in Turin and the façades of stage buildings at Aspendos (2nd century AD) and Sabratha (3rd century AD).

BIBLIOGRAPHY

A. W. Lawrence: *Greek Architecture*, Pelican Hist. A. (Harmondsworth, 1957, rev. 4/1983, with additions by R. A. Tomlinson) [good illustrations of principal bldgs]

P. M. Petsas: *O taphos ton Lefkadion* [The tomb at Leukadia] (Athens, 1966)

(b) Mouldings and motifs. The earliest examples of mouldings come from Archaic Doric temples, and the patterns of some types (e.g. the MEANDER or Greek key design) apparently originated on painted vases. The Doric and Ionic orders each had their own distinctive set of decorated mouldings. Concave or flat surfaces in both orders were often carved with a meander, the difference being that those of the Ionic order were more elaborate

and more numerous than those of the Doric. Like the orders themselves (*see* ORDERS, ARCHITECTURAL, fig. 1), mouldings were standardized in Greek architecture, and it was not until the Roman period that they incorporated a rich variation of decoration. They followed the same pattern and sequence throughout the Greek world, rather than showing regional variations, and they evolved slowly.

Apart from the flat fillet, mouldings can be divided into those with a profile of single curvature and those of double curvature. Among those of single convex curvature, obvious examples are the egg and tongue (ovolo; *see* EGG AND DART) or BEAD AND REEL (astragal) moulding. The most common type of double curve is the CYMA reversa, as in leaf and dart mouldings. The cyma reversa usually has a concave lower part and a convex upper part; while the cyma recta has the upper part concave and the lower part convex. A cyma recta moulding was commonly used for the crowning member of the cornice from the 6th century BC onwards. The egg and tongue and leaf and dart mouldings probably originated in imitation of leaf patterns and doubtless evolved from more rudimentary Egyptian mouldings. They were used primarily as decoration on entablatures and column bases (see fig. 17). In the Doric order the hawksbeak moulding was considered particularly appropriate and was often used for gutters. In the Ionic order concave surfaces were decorated with leaf and dart, also known as Lesbian cymation. Convex surfaces were decorated with egg and tongue or bead and reel. The echinus of Ionic capitals was often carved with egg and tongue moulding, as can be seen in the Temple of Artemis at Ephesos (*c.* 560–*c.* 460 BC), and later in the columns of the Temple of Athena Polias at Priene (begun *c.* 340 BC; see fig. 18). GUILLOCHE mouldings were occasionally used for column bases, as can be seen relatively early in Sicilian temples and later in the Temple of Apollo at Didyma (3rd century BC and later).

Mouldings could equally well consist simply of an undecorated carved band, and they were then described as such, for example in the building accounts for the Erechtheion at Athens. Occasionally the pattern on, for example, egg and tongue might be painted rather than carved, as can be seen in the Khasne at Petra. Such painted mouldings have been reconstructed on a fragment of the Doric entablature of the Parthenon in the British Museum, London (*see* POLYCHROMY, colour pl. I, fig. 1).

Carved decorative motifs also used on ancient Greek buildings include rosettes (for example in ceiling coffers, metopes and the volutes of Ionic columns), bucrania (as on the exterior Ionic frieze of alternating bucrania and rosettes on the mid-3rd-century BC Ptolemaion at Samothrace), lions' heads (often forming waterspouts in the external decoration of the sima or gutter) and other vegetal or animal motifs.

BIBLIOGRAPHY

L. T. Shoe: *Profiles of Greek Mouldings* (Cambridge, MA, 1936)

A. W. Lawrence: *Greek Architecture*, Pelican Hist. A. (Harmondsworth, 1957, rev.4/1983, with additions by R. A. Tomlinson) [good illustrations]

MARGARET LYTTELTON

(c) Colour. Until the early 19th century scholars had generally believed that ancient Greek temples and Greek sculpture were originally white and unpainted (a concept fostered in particular by Winckelmann). It was Antoine Quatremère de Quincy who first aroused general interest in the use of colour in ancient Greek art with a paper given in 1806 on the chryselephantine statue of *Zeus* at Olympia, coining the term 'polychromy'. In the 1810s several architects who had travelled and excavated in Greece noted traces of colour on Greek temples, and

17. Mouldings, including leaf and dart and egg and tongue, on an anta capital from the north porch of the Erechtheion, Athens, 421–405 BC

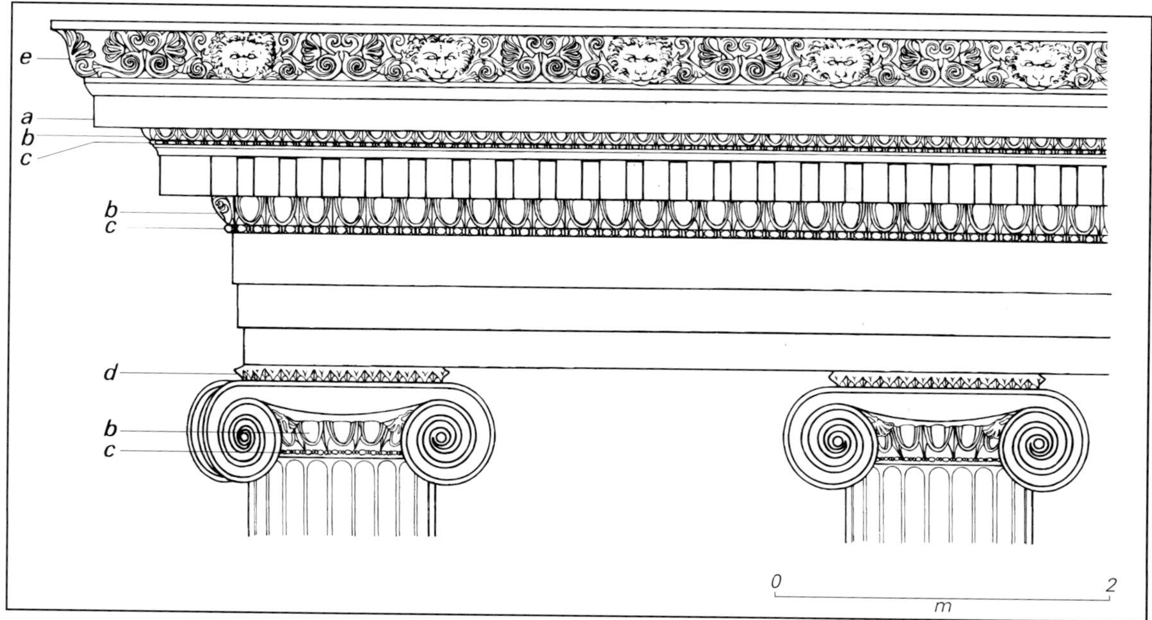

18. Mouldings and motifs on the entablature of the Temple of Athena Polias, Priene, begun *c.* 340 BC; restoration: (a) cornice crowned by small convex moulding and flat fillet; (b) egg and tongue; (c) bead and reel; (d) cyma reversa moulding on abacus, decorated with leaf and dart; (e) cyma recta moulding on gutter, decorated with lion-head spouts, palmettes and vegetal motifs

theories of its systematic use began to be put forward. At one extreme it was asserted that intense colour had been applied to virtually every surface of ancient Greek buildings (see Hittorff). By the mid-19th century the notion of systematic polychromy in Greek architecture was widely accepted, and the definitive approach was presented in F. C. Penrose's observations on material from the Athenian Acropolis (1851).

Colour in Greek temples was first provided by terracotta. By the end of the 6th century BC this was largely supplanted by colour applied directly to stone, although terracotta roof ornaments continued to be used into the Hellenistic period. Colour applied directly to stone appeared even on some of the earliest stone buildings (e.g. the Temple of Artemis, Corfu (Kerkyra), *c.* 590–*c.* 570 BC).

The usual technique was to apply colour after designs had been incised, sometimes over a coating of lime wash or marble stucco. In early Greek temples built of rough poros limestone the entire surface was generally stuccoed. Applied colour was then normally confined to architectural mouldings and sculpture. The techniques of application apparently included encaustic, tempera and fresco, though it is difficult to determine the exact technique in individual instances. It has been suggested that the entire surface of some marble buildings (e.g. the Parthenon) may have had a protective coating of oxides to reduce the glare of the sun or to consolidate the surface, but it is just as likely that these oxidized surfaces result from minerals leached out of the stone. Wall surfaces were otherwise uncoloured, except when mural paintings were applied, for example inside the Temple of Hephaistos and the Stoa Poikile (Painted Stoa) in Athens (*c.* 449 BC and *c.* 465–*c.* 460 BC respectively). Other colouristic effects were achieved through gilding, metal attachments (e.g. rosettes in the eyes of Ionic volutes) or inlaid glass beads or paste (e.g. Erechtheion, Athens, north porch capitals, 421–405 BC).

The system of applying different colours to different architectural elements was never entirely standardized. In the Doric order triglyphs were usually dark blue or black, as were regulae and mutules; the taeniae, and the fascia below the mutules and the scotia above were usually red. Taeniae could often be decorated with chevron patterns in the Early Archaic period and with gilded meanders and palmettes in the Classical period and later. The background of metopes and Ionic friezes was usually red or uncoloured, although sometimes blue. Doric hawksbeak mouldings were usually red and blue in alternation with rims and ribs in gold, green or white. In the Ionic order, egg and dart and leaf and dart mouldings usually had the same alternation of colours. The surface of the channel (*canalis*) of Ionic capitals was probably not painted except when decorated with floral motifs. The surfaces of column shafts, architraves and walls were uniformly left blank before the Hellenistic period. Stone cornices were usually painted. Decorative patterns were often simply painted rather than carved on mouldings.

Different coloured stones were also used for colouristic effects. Eleusinian limestone was frequently used in 5th-century BC Athenian architecture (e.g. the frieze of the Erechtheion). Coloured stone was also often used for pedestals (e.g. the blue limestone image base at Olympia) and altars (e.g. the black limestone altar of the Chians at Delphi). The Ionic Temple of Aphrodite on Lesbos had a red stone frieze course. Evidence for the deliberate use of naturally coloured materials before the widespread appearance of stone architecture in the late 7th century BC is rare, though the early 7th-century BC temple at Kalapodhi has courses of alternating colours of mud-brick.

Wall painting in monumental architecture was usually limited to pictorial scenes or cycles, as in the Lesche of the Knidians at Delphi or the Painted Stoa in Athens. Early examples include those on the walls of the 7th-century BC Temple of Poseidon at Isthmia. Otherwise, wall surfaces in monumental stone buildings seem to have been unpainted, except for mouldings. In non-monumental or domestic architecture, however, wall surfaces were commonly painted and sometimes relief moulded in imitation of masonry. Such surfaces may have occurred as early as the late 5th century BC in Athens (e.g. the rectangular Law Court in the Agora), and they are clearly attested in the 4th century BC at Olynthos and in the 3rd century and 2nd century BC on Delos. These in turn influenced the development of Roman painting of the Pompeian First Style.

BIBLIOGRAPHY

A.-C. Quatremère de Quincy: *Le Jupiter olympien, ou l'art de la sculpture antique considéré sous un nouveau point de vue* (Paris, 1815)

J. I. Hittorff: *Restitution du temple d'Empodocle à Selinonte, ou l'architecture polychrome chez les Grecs* (Paris, 1851)

F. C. Penrose: *An Investigation of the Principles of Athenian Architecture* (London, 1851, rev. 2/1888/*R* Washington, DC, 1973)

L. Fenger: *Die dorische Polychromie* (Berlin, 1886)

T. Wiegand: *Die archaische Poros-Architektur der Akropolis zu Athen* (Kassel, 1904)

L. T. Shoe: 'Dark Stone in Greek Architecture', *Hesperia*, suppl. viii (1949), pp. 341–52

A. K. Orlandos: *Ta ulika ton archaion Ellenon*, 2 vols (Athens, 1955–8), Fr. trans. as *Les Matériaux de construction et la technique architecturale des anciens Grecs*, 2 vols (Paris, 1966–8)

R. D. Middleton: 'Hittorff's Polychrome Campaign', *The Beaux-Arts and Nineteenth Century French Architecture*, ed. R. Middleton (Cambridge, MA, 1982)

Paris—Rome—Athens: Le Voyage en Grèce des architectes français aux XIXe et XXe siècles (exh. cat., Paris, Ecole N. Sup. B.-A.; Athens, N.G.; Houston, TX, Mus. F.A.; 1982–3)

THOMAS NOBLE HOWE

(iv) Architects, masons and society. Architects and masons provided the skills essential to a city state's religious and civic structures and to its fortifications, where these were considered strategically or financially viable. Yet most architects and masons remain anonymous: even the name of the designer of the Erechtheion in Athens is not preserved. Occasionally the names of masons and other craftsmen concerned in public works are known from official building records, and other rare exceptions include a mason's signature, 'Parmenon made me', on a stretch of city wall in Thasos and what is known of Socrates' career as a stone mason.

Monumental builders were public workers, and architects were public servants, paid by the city as technical advisers to the community (*see also* §I, 4(i) above). As to social background, some doubtless resembled Philon of Eleusis, who worked at Eleusis as well as designing the arsenal at Peiraeus (*c.* 350 BC) but who was also a man of wealth able to assume a trierarchy (the fitting out of a trireme for public service). Others followed their fathers as architects, for example Theodoros, who may have been the son of Rhoikos of Samos (*see* RHOIKOS AND THEODOROS), or Metagenes, the son of Chersiphron of Ephesos. In 4th-century BC Delphi official architects came from the same family for at least three generations. Others were born into craftsmen's families, for example POLYKLEITOS and SKOPAS, who was both a sculptor and an architect, and two Delian architects who were carpenters' sons.

Vitruvius pointed out that an architect needed to be well educated (*On Architecture* I.i), but this did not mean that aspiring architects born to craftsmen's families had to abandon practical skills and become theoretical 'gentleman designers'. On the contrary, such architects as Philon of Eleusis must have required practical experience on the site and in the workshop in order to acquire all the skills necessary for co-ordinating the work of temple building. Tradition attributes many practical skills, including structural engineering, bronzeworking and gem-cutting, to Rhoikos and Theodoros, who built the monumental stone third Temple of Hera or 'First Dipteros' on Samos. Nor was there any professional divide between architects and specialist masons or carpenters, for all good craftsmanship depended on an understanding of other techniques, especially in temple building.

The architect's training would also have involved careful review of existing buildings, study of treatises (now lost) by earlier architects, such as Theodoros' account of the Temple of Hera on Samos, that by Iktinos and Karpion on the Parthenon and Philon's account of his arsenal, and discussion with fellow craftsmen; indeed, communication between such mobile and highly motivated professionals as temple builders must have done much to spread new ideas and stimulate innovation. Moreover, such topics as harmony and proportion were surely also debated with the philosophers, despite their disdain for applied, as opposed to pure, mathematics. It is not clear quite how architects gained professional recognition: perhaps temple designs were put out to competition, as with some sculptural projects, allowing the winners to claim the status of *architekton* or master builder.

Some architects worked on more than one building. Of those active in mid-5th-century BC Athens, IKTINOS designed the Parthenon and directed work on the Telesterion at Eleusis as well as designing the Temple of Apollo at Bassai; KALLIKRATES worked on the Temple of Athena Nike and probably one other; MNESIKLES on the Propylaia and perhaps the Erechtheion; and the unknown architect of the Temple of Hephaistos has been ascribed three other temples. The work generated by the Periclean building programme meant that these men were more or less full-time architects; but few others would have found continuous employment on large structures, since monumental building projects were in most places not a regular occurrence. Architects and craftsmen were alike in that they needed to move from place to place for work or be content with less exciting jobs. When opportunities to build on a large scale were lacking, numerous small shrines, altars and other structures all over the Greek world would have required occasional repair or improvement. Mobility and versatility both ensured employment and countered local shortages of skilled labour. Records from Delos show that a versatile carpenter worked not only on temple roof timbers but also on house doors and roofs, and built in brick; another man who made wooden ceiling coffers for the Temple of Apollo also built and plastered a brick wall elsewhere.

As building commissions' advisers, architects helped to ensure the availability of workers and materials by specifying stone from active quarries in places where competent craftsmen were concentrated. In this way, though working at Delphi and Epidauros respectively, the Corinthian architects Spintharos and Theodotos used limestone and masons from Corinth; and when the Argive architect Polykleitos specified black limestone for the pavement of the tholos (thymele) at Epidauros, he must have known that a black Argive stone could be provided and worked by an Argive mason and his two sons, as the building's accounts show.

The builders took their instructions from the architect by various means: drawings, models, demonstration pieces and written specifications. One contract from Levadeia in Boiotia (*Inscr. Gr./1*, vii, 3073) contains directions of such minute detail that no further instructions need have been given. For example, a mason laying pavement blocks had, among other things, 'first [to] make the under-faces of all the stones true and without flaw . . . with a close-toothed chisel . . . making no larger a margin in the under cut along the upper foundation-course than a small inch . . .'. The masonry of the Temple of Apollo at Delphi provides a good example of such work (see fig. 19). Even so, the architect and, in this instance, the assistant architect had to inspect all sides of each block; for although accuracy was important, some flexibility of measurement had to be allowed within the set overall dimensions, not least because masons often had to dress off varying amounts of stone to remove flaws (*see also* §(ii)(a) above).

19. Masonry executed to precise specifications: foundation courses and pavement of the platform and columns of the east façade of the Temple of Apollo, Delphi, *c.* 366–*c.* 329 BC

The architect's task was complicated by the diversity of his workforce. Sometimes two or more architects designed a building, or the architect had an official assistant, so that differences over interpretation of the design might arise, exacerbated by experienced and opinionated older masons. Clashes could easily occur between workers from rival cities, locals and outsiders, free men and slaves or skilled men and labourers, especially when workers were crowded together, as when six teams of six or seven men cut the flutes of the six columns in the north porch of the Erechtheion. Building commissions attempted to reduce trouble through contractual regulations, and similar rules must have governed such projects as the Parthenon, where most labour was hired and materials purchased direct. Accordingly, the building commissions could intervene in quarrels between contractors before they went to court, and contractors received payment only when the completed work had been inspected by the commissioners and the architect. If contractors exceeded their time limit or reneged on their contracts, they were fined heavily. They had to replace damaged work at their own expense and might be expected to work 'every day and all day', with a fixed minimum of skilled assistants, or else pay a fine. In return, the builders may have earned little more than a living wage, and some contractors may even have lost money through penalties and miscalculations. Sculptors and decorators sometimes received large contract payments, but their work was probably slow and expensive, even when their materials were provided. Architects received salaries commensurate with the pay given to the armed forces, but they seem not to have received extra payment for their design work. They seem to have refrained from advertising themselves in dedicatory or funerary inscriptions, but they appear to have been men of professional integrity, and there is certainly no record of dishonest or incompetent practice.

BIBLIOGRAPHY

Plutarch: *Pericles*

A. Burford: *The Greek Temple Builders at Epidauros* (Liverpool, 1969)

——: *Aspects of Greek and Roman Life: Craftsmen in Greek and Roman Society* (London, 1972)

J. J. Coulton: *Greek Architects at Work* (London, 1977); publ. in USA as *Ancient Greek Architects at Work* (Ithaca, NY, 1977)

ALISON BURFORD

2. Historical survey. The chronology of ancient Greek architecture spans approximately 11 centuries, from the earliest Iron Age buildings *c.* 1050 BC to the inception of the Roman Imperial era in 27 BC. Within this timespan, a broad division into four main periods is generally accepted: Dark Age or early Greek architecture, Archaic, Classical and Hellenistic. The precise dating and characteristics of these periods are in some cases still a matter for discussion, given the difficulties in dating and reconstructing many architectural remains and the scarcity of documentary material. The relative importance assigned by scholars to different sites and buildings is often a question of interpretation, and excavations continue to reveal fresh evidence. Nevertheless, the combination of

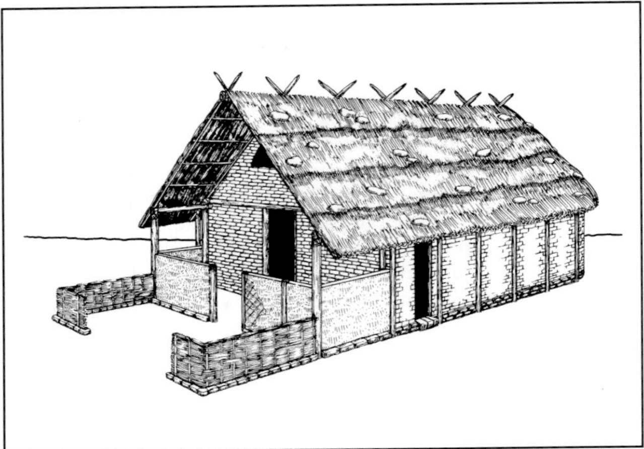

20. Dark Age architecture, phase 2 of House IV.1, Nichoria, 10th–9th century BC; reconstruction drawing

durable materials, widespread building programmes and the development of distinct architectural types and principles means that the history of Greek architecture from the Archaic period onwards can be traced in considerable detail.

(i) Dark Age. (ii) Archaic. (iii) Classical. (iv) Hellenistic.

(i) Dark Age. After the decline of the Late Bronze Age cultures of Greece during the first half of the 12th century BC there followed several centuries of lower material culture and, it seems, smaller population until a dramatic recovery began during the second half of the 8th century BC. During this Dark Age (sometimes also referred to as the Iron Age, the Protogeometric or simply the early Greek period) monumental architecture—the palaces and tombs of Mycenaean and Minoan society—disappeared, together with other prestige arts.

Most of the remains of Greek Dark Age architecture belong to houses. In Crete, where Bronze Age traditions were more lasting, settlements of Late Bronze Age type, with flat-roofed, rectangular houses set close against each other, remained normal. But in mainland Greece such settlements were soon replaced by loose groups of free-standing buildings, often with curved, particularly apsidal plans and steep thatched roofs. The reduced population and unsettled conditions at the start of the period may have favoured this change, rather than any influx of immigrants, for simple temporary structures often have curved plans, to which thatch adapts easily; and thatch can only be used on free-standing buildings.

Once adopted, however, these features remained characteristic until the 8th century BC, and may even appear in quite substantial buildings, such as the mid-10th-century BC Toumba building at LEFKANDI. This was over 45 m long and 10 m wide, but even in a building of this size the walls were of mud-brick on rubble socles, with wooden posts carrying a thatched roof. These materials were characteristic of Dark Age buildings generally, virtually none of which incorporated dressed stone or blocks bigger than a man could lift. No other surviving contemporary building is as large and complex as the Lefkandi building, but many houses have similar characteristics, comprising entry through a porch at one end into a main room, beyond which there may be a storage area, as in phase 2 of House IV.1 at Nichoria in south-west Greece (10th–9th century BC; see fig. 20). Smaller houses, however, sometimes consisted of a single room.

The few extant cult buildings from before the mid-8th century BC differ little in size, plan or construction from contemporary houses. Graves were generally simple pits or cists, except for some corbelled tombs in Thessaly and chamber tombs on Crete. Some cemetery sites, however, have associated buildings (e.g. Tsikalario on Naxos). Fortification walls reappeared in the late 9th century BC at Smyrna (*see* SMYRNA, §1) and ZAGORA, and they became more common in the 8th century BC.

In the denser settlements of the later 8th century BC closely packed houses with clay roofs reappeared, and larger houses, at least, received more complex plans. In the houses of this era at Zagora a clearer separation of storage and living space can be seen, and their rooms tend to open on to a court, like those of Classical houses, rather than directly to the outside. At about the same time the temple emerged as a clearly defined building type (*see also* §1(i)(a) above). Whether originally intended to provide ritual dining areas, to accommodate cult statues or to replace the houses of rulers as cult centres, temples became important foci of civic pride for the new city states. The form of the temple was similar to that of a large house (for an illustration *see* PERACHORA), but some were exceptionally long (e.g. the *hekatompedon* ('hundred footer') at ERETRIA and the first Temple of Hera on Samos (*see* SAMOS, §1(i)), both *c.* 30 m long). None, however, were as complex as later houses. Important temples also came to be given a portico round the main building. This feature occurred in the Toumba building at Lefkandi two centuries before its appearance on a temple, which suggests that it may have derived from the formal repertory of high-status houses of earlier times.

Some dressed stonework was used at Old Smyrna and Corinth before 700 BC, but building materials and techniques, even for temples, generally remained unchanged throughout the 8th century BC. Only in the succeeding Archaic period did carefully dressed stonework and tiled roofs, together with a clear system of architectural forms, revolutionize the appearance of Greek architecture.

BIBLIOGRAPHY

H. Drerup: *Griechische Baukunst in geometrischer Zeit* (Göttingen, 1969)

W. A. McDonald and others: *Dark Age and Byzantine Occupation* (1983), iii of *Excavations at Nichoria in Southwest Greece* (Minneapolis, 1978–)

A. Mazarakis Ainian: 'Early Greek Temples: Their Origin and Function', *Early Greek Cult Practice: Proceedings of the 5th International Symposium at the Swedish Institute at Athens: Athens, 1986*, pp. 105–19

K. Fagerström: *Greek Iron Age Architecture: Developments through Changing Times* (Göteborg, 1988)

J. J. COULTON

(ii) Archaic. The Archaic period generally designates the time from the start of the 7th century BC to the end of the Persian Wars in 479 BC. In the context of ancient Greek architecture, this is primarily the period of the emergence and development of the temple as an architectural form and of the concurrent evolution of the architectural orders. Most of the major Greek sanctuaries had been founded during the 9th–8th centuries BC, when they consisted

simply of an open area with an altar. Around 750–700 BC temples began to be constructed (see §(i) above), but it was during the 7th century BC that the more wealthy and cosmopolitan Greek city states began to finance the building of monumental temples. These prestigious structures incorporated many of the forms that were to establish the essential repertory of Greek architecture.

(a) Early Archaic temples. (b) Development of the architectural orders.

(a) Early Archaic temples. During the 7th century BC three characteristic features of Greek temple construction evolved: temple plans became rectangular, rather than apsidal; size increased, with the *hekatompedon* ('hundred footer') as the norm; and at this time or slightly later, the distinctive peripteral colonnade became an established feature (*see also* §1(i)(a) above). The weight of the roof and the lack of technology for supporting wide spans inhibited an increase in temple width commensurate with the enlarged length. A single row of posts running down the centreline gave vertical support to a ridge beam. By *c.* 600 BC (as in the Temple of Hera at Olympia) two parallel rows of internal columns ran either side of the temple axis and allowed the centrally placed cult image to be admired from a direct line of view. In some cases, though, the centreline internal colonnade persisted, as in the Temple of Hera (the 'Basilica') at PAESTUM (*c.* 550–*c.* 530 BC), but by the end of the 6th century BC the standard treatment was a double row stacked in two tiers. In this design the cella divides into a central aisle and two side aisles with the diameter of the internal columns kept to a minimum, as in the second Temple of Aphaia at Aigina (*c.* 500–*c.* 490 BC; see fig. 21; *see also* AIGINA, §2(i)).

It has long been believed that a colonnade appeared around a megaron-type building as early as the 8th century BC (e.g. the second Temple of Hera at Samos and Temple B at Thermon), and that such peristyle temples were fairly common in the 7th century BC. In fact, the restoration of these early examples into peristyle temples does not withstand close scrutiny of the archaeological evidence. The peripteral temple probably did not appear before 600 BC, thus coinciding with the invention of the Doric and Ionic capitals. In any case the adoption of the peristyle was gradual, taking nearly 75 years. For instance, as late as *c.* 570–*c.* 560 BC the first Temple of Aphaia on Aigina was non-peripteral. Even so the rich colours of the original decoration of the wonderfully preserved superstructure of this *hekatompedon* provide an idea of the lavish care bestowed even on non-peripteral designs.

Dressed and fitted stone gradually replaced the more perishable materials of rubble, mud-brick and wood. The terracotta roof system replaced thatch and comprised eaves tiles, pantiles, cover tiles and ridge tiles. Terracotta

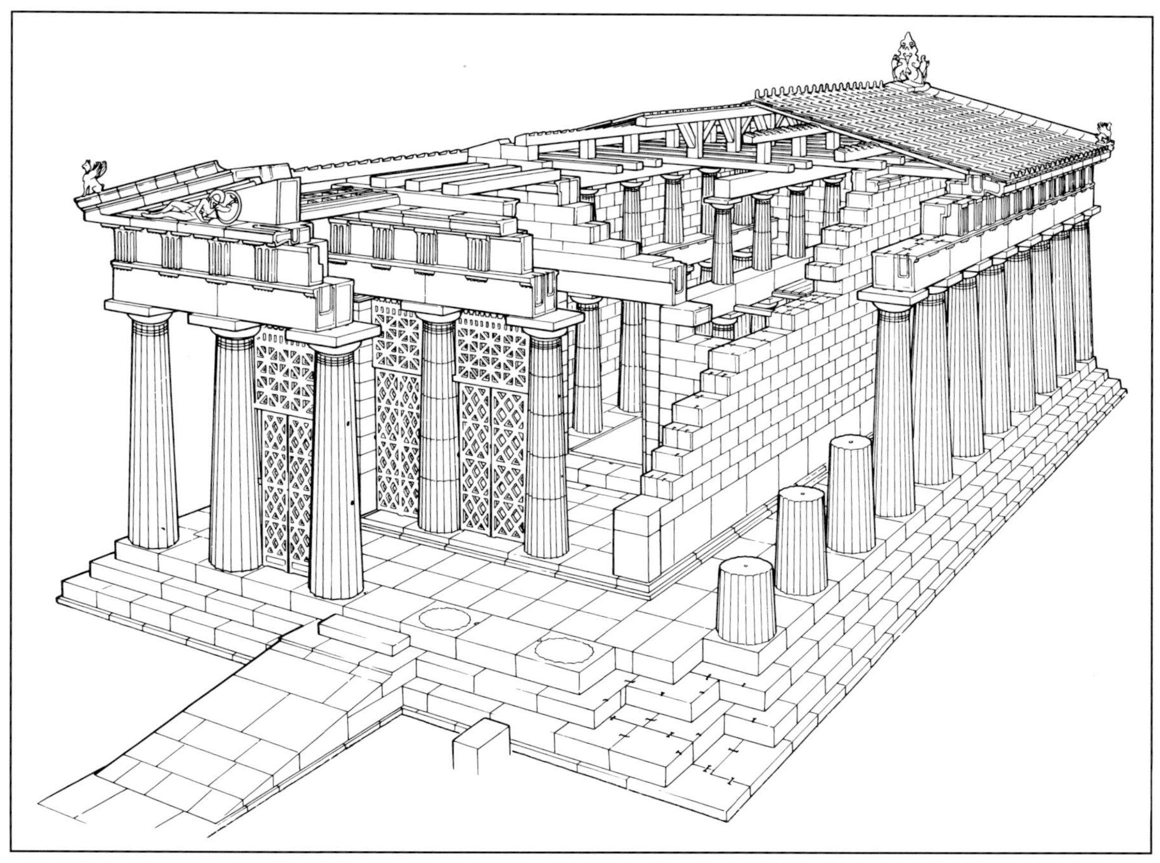

21. Archaic-period Temple of Aphaia, Aigina, *c.* 500–*c.* 490 BC; restored cutaway view

casings enlivened the gables and sometimes terracotta simas (gutters) trimmed the eaves. These elements were painted in rich, bold colours in a variety of geometric patterns, including chevrons, guilloches and meanders. Often a large, brightly patterned terracotta disc crowned the pinnacle of a gabled pediment, as on the Temple of Hera at Olympia (*c.* 590 BC; Olympia, Archaeol. Mus.; *see* OLYMPIA, fig. 3).

(b) Development of the architectural orders. Around 600 BC the two main Greek ARCHITECTURAL ORDERS can be discerned: the Doric in mainland Greece and the Ionic in coastal Asia Minor and the Aegean islands. A third order, the Aiolic, with a slender column and double-volute capital, clearly related to Ionic, derived from the Levant and was perhaps Phoenician in origin. The Aiolic is found in a region extending from Smyrna to Neandria in north-west Asia Minor but did not survive the Archaic period. All three orders were also employed as votive columns that supported a dedication (e.g. the Naxian column at Delphi; see below).

Doric. The Temple of Hera at Olympia is one of the earliest extant peripteral temples. Its plan (see fig. 8c above) exemplifies features that typify Doric temples for the following 250 years: it is hexastyle (i.e. with a row of six columns across front and back), with a peristyle and a cella. The flank walls of the cella extend beyond the entrance and the back wall to terminate in antae. The wall extensions create two porches, a pronaos at the front and an opisthodomos at the rear of the cella. The fronts to both porches embrace distyle *in antis* columns (i.e. a pair of columns between the antae). In the canonical hexastyle plan of the Doric order, therefore, the façade columns respond to the major components of the temple as taken across the porches: two flank columns, two antae and two columns *in antis.* The pronaos communicates directly with the main chamber through an entrance. The opisthodomos, by contrast, remains an independent chamber, often serving as a treasury. Sometimes, especially in Sicilian temples, an internal cross-wall creates a back chamber to the cella, and in most of these cases the opisthodomos is dropped from the plan. This extra and inner chamber is conventionally called an adyton.

In elevation the Temple of Hera at Olympia exemplifies the major features of the Doric order, its entablature consisting of architrave, frieze of alternating metopes and triglyphs, and cornice. The earliest known metopes are 7th-century BC terracotta examples from THERMON. The earliest surviving examples of metopes and triglyphs in stone date from the generation of buildings that followed the Temple of Hera at Olympia, namely the Sikyonian Treasury at Delphi (*c.* 570 BC) and Temple C at Selinus (*c.* 550–*c.* 525 BC). Doric columns are generally without bases. In Archaic times the Doric column shaft had between 16 and 32 flutes, though by the Classical period 20 had become standard. All Greek columns taper from the base and an additional refinement known as ENTASIS (a slight bulge in outline) was developed. Entasis may have been an invention of the colonial Greek cities in South Italy, where it is found in its most exaggerated form, as in the columns of the Temple of Hera at Paestum. At the top of the Doric column shaft, a set of incised rings (usually four in the Archaic period) disguises the necking or juncture between the shaft and the capital. In earlier Archaic examples the profile of the Doric echinus flares outwards in a flat, horizontally driven curve; it later becomes progressively steeper.

The orders appear not to have been entirely mutually exclusive: a large peripteral temple (55×20 m) was built *c.* 590–*c.* 570 BC on Corfu (Kerkyra; *see* CORFU, §1). The inhabitants were Dorian settlers from Corinth who constructed their temple in the Doric order. Yet this early temple embodies an octastyle (eight-columned) façade, a feature usually found only in the Ionic order. Perhaps also of Ionian inspiration is the deep relief sculpture in the pediment.

By the 560s BC the construction of large-scale Doric temples was being eagerly undertaken in South Italy. Around 565 BC at Syracuse the colossal Temple of Apollo (6 by 17 columns; 21.57×55.33 m) was begun. Physical remains of this temple are relatively complete and illustrate the experimental nature of the ambitious designs used in early Doric buildings during the first half of the 6th century BC. The double rank of columns before the pronaos is an abbreviation of the Ionic fully dipteral plan, and it is comparable to the earlier temple on Corfu. The columns themselves are tall monoliths and overall vary randomly in diameter by 20%. They are thoroughly Doric in spirit, with the stout Archaic proportions of 1:4 on the façades (compared with the much slimmer Classical ratio of 1:6, as on the Parthenon at Athens). The shafts were given 16 flutes, and the wide spread of the echinus extends beyond the base circumference of the columns. Terracotta revetments (Syracuse, Mus. Archeol. Reg.) sheathed the lateral cornices and pediments; a terracotta sima (Syracuse, Mus. Archeol. Reg.) with wildly projecting trumpet spouts thrust rain water away from the temple foundations.

During the Archaic period the main Sicilian cities might have one or more building projects simultaneously underway. Until the end of the 6th century BC, their temples were both more numerous and on a larger scale than those of mainland Greece. Within a decade at Syracuse, the even larger Temple of Zeus (Olympieion) was under construction (6 by 17 columns; 22.40×62.05 m), and by the mid-6th century BC the Syracusans were hard at work on an Ionic temple that competed in size with contemporary temples at Samos and Ephesos. At SELINUS a building programme launched around 550 BC continued for over a century, and as elsewhere in Sicily, construction periods overlap: Temple C was begun *c.* 550–*c.* 525 BC; Temple D ?*c.* 500 BC; and the Temple of Apollo (GT) by *c.* 500–*c.* 480 BC. Construction of the last two temples continued until the mid-5th century BC, when additional temples were started.

Ionic. Geographically Delphi is not an Ionian site, but it offers two of the most complete examples of Archaic Ionian architecture: the Naxian column (*c.* 560 BC) and the Siphnian Treasury (finished by *c.* 525 BC). The former is a tall, free-standing Ionic column (h. 9.9 m) surmounted by a sphinx and is one of the earliest known Ionic columns (*see* DELPHI, fig. 2a). The Ionic third Temple of Hera at Samos was also under construction around 560 BC, but

22. Archaic-period Siphnian Treasury, Delphi, *c.* 525 BC; restored view

because little of its superstructure survives, the elevation is difficult to reconstruct. Theodoros, one of the reputed architects of the third Temple of Hera, also contributed to the designs of the slightly later Temple of Artemis at Ephesos (*c.* 560–*c.* 460 BC; *see* EPHESOS, §I, 1(i)).

More than the Doric order the Ionic order offered opportunities for the carving of stone mouldings using a variety of concave and convex curves, projections or sunken planes, and patterns such as egg and dart, heart and dart, petals and dentils (*see* §1(iii)(b) above). Ionic column proportions are quite slender in comparison with the more massive proportions of the Doric order: this difference is apparent in the height to base ratio of 8:1 in the Ionic columns at Ephesos, compared with the Doric column ratio of 4:1 for the Temple of Apollo at Syracuse. The capitals from the Temple of Artemis at Ephesos are typical of the Archaic Ionic form: the band joining the volutes is convex, and the long, narrow abacus extends nearly the whole distance between volutes. As the Ionic order developed the volutes became concave, with the shallow curling channel (*canalis*) ending in a button-like eye (*oculus*) that filled the volute centre. Throughout the history of Greek architecture, Ionic columns were designed in sets, and the capitals varied according to their different positions within the building. The capitals at Ephesos form two distinct kinds: a normal capital and a second type with large, petalled rosettes replacing the volutes and eyes (e.g. rest. London, BM). Unlike the Doric, the Ionic column generally rises from a moulded base, and the column shaft typically has more flutes than does that of the Doric; during the Archaic period, Ionic flutes numbered from 18 to 48.

The third Temple of Hera at Samos and the Temple of Artemis at Ephesos were the first colossal Greek temples and were seldom surpassed even in later times. The Temple of Hera extended to *c.* 105 m in length and *c.* 52.5 m in width. The Temple of Artemis was slightly grander, having stylobate dimensions of 115.1×55.1 m. The outer colonnades of the two temples were dipteral (i.e. with double rows of columns). This scheme creates an octastyle façade and was employed in the design of other colossal Ionic temples. To this veritable forest of columns were added the columns that filled a deep and wide pronaos. A third rank of columns also went across the fronts. For the third Temple of Hera the total number of columns was 132; the number for the Temple of Artemis was 117.

Towards the end of the 6th century BC, throughout the 5th and most of the 4th century, Persian suzerainty or the threat of Persian domination combined with internal strife to restrain the grand, expensive building projects of the sort undertaken earlier in the Archaic period in Ionia and on the Aegean islands of coastal Asia Minor. This is one reason for the importance of the Siphnian Treasury at Delphi (see fig. 22; see also fig. 53 below). Built entirely of marble as a thank-offering, this building set the architectural trends for the first half of the Classical period, though during the 5th century BC it was the city of Athens, rather than the island sanctuaries or the cities of South

Italy, that increasingly took a leading role in the development of Greek architecture.

BIBLIOGRAPHY

E. Van Buren: *Greek Fictile Revetments in the Archaic Period* (London, 1926)

C. Anti: *Teatri greci arcaici* (Padua, 1947)

P. Amandry: '*La Colonne des Naxiens et le Portique des Athéniens*, Fouilles de Delphes (Paris, 1953)

T. E. Kalpaxis: *Früharchaische Baukunst in Griechenland und Kleinasien* (Athens, 1976)

P. Betancourt: *The Aeolic Capital* (Princeton, 1977)

J. J. Coulton: 'Doric Capitals: A Proportional Analysis', *Annu. Brit. Sch. Athens*, lxxiv (1979), pp. 81–153

A. Mallwitz: 'Kritisches zur Architektur Griechenlands im 8. und 7. Jahrhundert', *Archaol. Anz*, xcvi (1981), pp. 599–642

E. L. Schwander: *Der altere Porostempel der Aphaia auf Aegina*, Denkmäler Antiker Architektur, xvi (Berlin, 1985)

(iii) Classical.

(a) Introduction. (b) Religious. (c) Secular.

(a) Introduction. Although in some ways it might be more precise to limit the use of the term Classical to the art and architecture of the city of Athens during the two decades of Pericles' leadership (*c.* 450–429 BC), the Classical period is conventionally dated from the end of the Persian Wars (479 BC) to the death of Alexander the Great (323 BC). The stages in the development of ancient Greek architecture, however, do not neatly parallel those in the representational arts, and, indeed, the Persian Wars represent a hiatus in the development of architectural forms and techniques, rather than a division between two distinct periods or styles. For the inception of Classical architecture, therefore, it is necessary to look back to the last quarter of the 6th century BC and to such buildings as the Siphnian Treasury at Delphi (*c.* 525 BC; *see* §(ii)(b) above). At this time Greek architecture was undergoing a period of both consolidation and change, not only in the design of temples but also in the emergence of a diversity of secular building types. Broadly speaking, therefore, the two centuries between *c.* 525 BC and 323 BC can be taken as the timespan of Classical Greek architecture. The period divides into two halves, the mid-point being the revolutionary designs for the Temple of Apollo at Bassai (429–*c.* 400 BC) and the Erechtheion at Athens (421–405 BC).

A 'grammar' of architectural principles and forms became standardized during the last quarter of the 6th century BC as builders and architects concentrated on the invention of a host of architectural refinements and on improvements in building technology. In about 515 BC a type of crane employing compound pulleys and winches began to play an important role in the construction of buildings. This machinery placed limits on the weights of stones that could be hoisted and thus brought to a close the first age of colossal temples (the Late Archaic period) and normalized the size of new temples. More importantly, the crane sharply increased the precision by which building stone could be manoeuvred into place. By 500 BC Greek architects were experimenting with a variety of technical possibilities in the use of such tools as the claw chisel and the drill. The new crane and tool types provided the requisite precision for the development of architectural refinements, and during the Classical period buildings acquired a high degree of optical sophistication, with intentional variations from the vertical and the horizontal

23. Parthenon, Athens, showing upward curvature in the east krepidoma, 447–432 BC

(*see also* §3(vi) below). Moreover, these refinements are often composites, for example deflections from straight lines working in conjunction with arcs of wide radials in all three planes occupied by a building. Shortly after the introduction of entasis other refinements appeared, for example upward curvature to the stylobate, repeated in the entablature (e.g. the Temple of Apollo at Corinth, *c.* 540–*c.* 520 BC, and the Archaic Temple of Athena at Athens, *c.* 515 BC). The Temple of Aphaia at Aigina (*c.* 500–*c.* 490 BC) included the refinement of thickened corner columns. By the 470s BC double contraction of corner intercolumniations appeared in Sicily. These architectural sophistications reached a highpoint in the design of the Parthenon (447–432 BC; see fig. 23; *see also* ATHENS, §II, 1(i)), in which other refinements include a 'batter' or inward inclination to the exterior planes of walls, inward curvature of the stylobate in plan and a declination from the horizontal of the platform. Not all of these deflections are visible with the unaided eye, but they created a great escalation in building costs in the Classical period.

(b) Religious. The temple played a pivotal role in the development of Classical architecture because experiments in temple architecture were often incorporated into other types of buildings. Iktinos may have brought Greek architecture to its purest moment by designing the Parthenon, but the Temple of Apollo at BASSAI, also by Iktinos, and the Erechtheion at Athens, perhaps by Kallikrates, were revolutionary buildings that loosened the

bonds of standardized design at a time when Greek architecture was headed in the direction of tired and academic formulae characterized by touches of mannerism. The major turning point involved a fresh conception of the temple as a complete building. The Parthenon and earlier temples were essentially works of art, the exteriors of which were meant to please; conceptually they were closer to sculpture than to architecture. In contrast, the exterior of the Temple of Apollo at Bassai has the austerity of a Late Archaic version of the Doric. Ignoring precedent, Iktinos turned all the vitality of his genius towards the inside of the temple, where he employed the Corinthian order for the first time, designed a bizarre form of Ionic and, perhaps inspired by the Temple of Hera at Olympia (*c*. 590 BC), resurrected the Archaic use of engaged columns (see fig. 24). Furthermore, a continuous Ionic frieze (London, BM), previously only found on temple exteriors, was located inside. Although the Temple of Apollo does not include many of the oldest of architectural refinements, such as entasis, upward curvature and inclined columns, refinements are still present. Curvature and truncation are used in the temple plan, as is batter to the cella walls and other refinements.

The completion *c*. 405 BC of both the temple at Bassai and the Erechtheion at Athens initiated a period of architectural exuberance. The Corinthian capital, for example, quickly gained recognition, though at first it was used only in a secondary function as internal ornament, inside either tholoi or such temples as those at Tegea and Nemea. By 334 BC, however, external Corinthian capitals were being used, as in the choregic monument of Lysikrates at Athens.

It is fair to say that the volume of construction in Greece during the second phase of Classical architecture from *c*. 405 to 323 BC was equal to if not greater than the total of construction for the preceding 500 years. Athens ceased to dominate the architectural scene after 400 BC, and provincial Greek city states initiated vigorous and inventive building programmes. From *c*. 370 BC there was a general return to architecture on a colossal scale intended to impress by sheer size.

(c) Secular. The first phase of the Classical period was distinguished by the development of a number of diverse building types such as the stoa, theatre and gymnasium. It also coincided with the beginnings of the planned Greek city (*see also* §III, 2(ii) below).

Organization of cities. The grid-plan had long been in use in the Near East and Egypt, but ancient authors credited HIPPODAMOS of Miletos for its introduction into Greece and for planning new cities at Peiraeus, the port of Athens (after 479 BC; *see* PEIRAEUS, §1), Thurii (443 BC) and Rhodes (408 BC; *see* RHODES, §3(i)). Consequently, modern scholars have dated recognizably organized cities after the floruit of Hippodamos. It is more likely, however, that the grid or orthogonal plan was adopted earlier by colonies during the Archaic period, since these new settlements required a fair parcelling and distribution of land. Some system of equal land subdivision, therefore, dates to the last quarter of the 6th century BC and coincides with the emergence of Pythagorean mathematics and

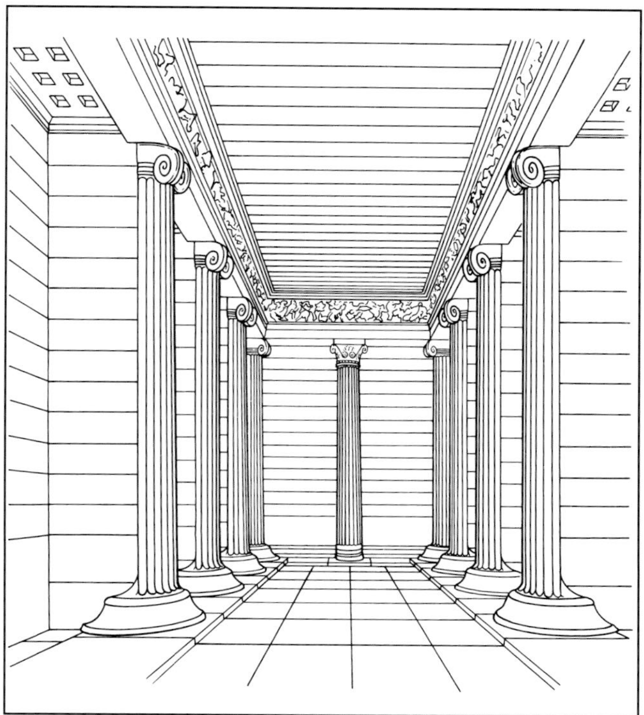

24. Temple of Apollo, Bassai, interior of cella, 429–*c*. 405 BC; reconstruction drawing

geometry. Aerial photography combined with systematic excavation at Syracuse, Metapontion, Halieis and elsewhere have confirmed this estimate of a Late Archaic or Early Classical date for the orthogonal Greek city plan. In the 4th century BC the planned city increasingly became the rule. The populations of a few sites such as Priene (*see* PRIENE, §1) abandoned their haphazard Archaic cities and moved to a planned and gridded *polis* near by. Whether Greek cities were planned or of unregulated growth, the building façades lining their narrow residential streets were merely drab and uninspired walls of rubble or mud-brick. (Selinus is an exception, where houses have façades of ashlar masonry.) Inside the house, though, spaces could be quite pleasant, with an entry porch leading to an ample peristyle courtyard with rooms opening off (*see also* §1(i)(c) above). Beyond this general layout, however, Greek domestic architecture was determined by the owner's individual needs.

It was, therefore, in the realm of public architecture that Classical Greece advanced far beyond anything previously attained. Market places, public squares, parks, educational establishments, athletic facilities and civic offices entailed the development of the rich variety of building types found in Classical Greek cities. The PRYTANEION (town hall), BOULEUTERION (council house), *katagogeion* (hotel) and *hestiatorion* (dining hall) are just several of the public building types that gained widespread usage during the Classical period. Their origins, however, are obscure, and there are relatively few certain identifications of archaeological remains until the second half of the 4th century BC. The idea of constructing an improved

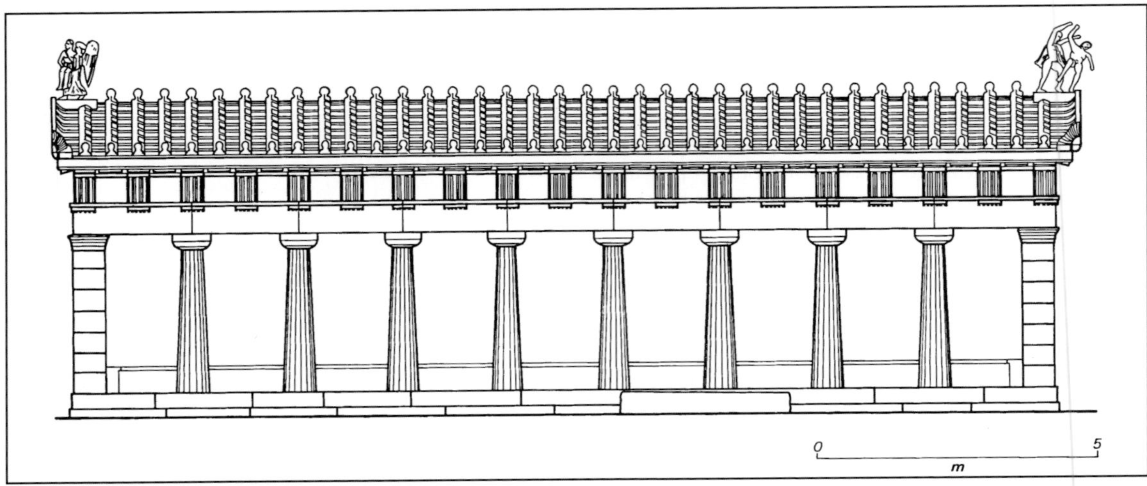

25. Stoa Basileios (Royal Stoa), Agora, Athens, late 6th century BC; restored elevation

city for the ordinary citizen lies at the heart of the Greek concept of the *polis* and coincides with the beginning of the Classical period. (Examples of several of the most important building types are discussed briefly below, but *see also* §1(i) above.)

Building types. The STOA, a free-standing, colonnaded portico, rivals the peristyle temple as one of the most characteristic architectural forms of ancient Greece. Although stoas are found in sanctuaries before the Classical period, the earliest civic application is perhaps the Stoa Basileios (Royal Stoa) in the Agora at Athens (late 6th century BC, extensively remodelled in the 5th century BC; see fig. 25; *see also* ATHENS, §II, 2(i)). It was the seat of the King Archon, a civic magistrate. Slightly later, *c.* 470 BC, Athens dedicated an Ionic stoa at Delphi (*see* DELPHI, §1). The building represents the beginning of the Attic version of the Ionic order, and its function was to display war trophies, as a sort of art gallery. Later still, the Stoa Poikile (Painted Stoa) at Athens displayed a set of commemorative wall paintings. Stoas continued to proliferate throughout

26. Theatre at Epidauros, *c.* 350–*c.* 330 BC

the Classical period, bounding public areas and sanctuaries and being attached to theatres. They also grew in size and incorporated such refinements as curvature and entasis.

Stone theatres were not constructed until the latter part of the Classical period. Thus the grand and imposing stone theatre at Epidauros (*c.* 350–*c.* 330 BC; see fig. 26; *see also* EPIDAUROS, §1) and the Theatre of Dionysos at Athens (rebuilt *c.* 338–*c.* 326 BC) were structures that set the pattern for Hellenistic times. They represented an architectural response to a demand for increased audience capacities that occurred in the second half of the 4th century BC with the revival of dramatic performances. During and after this time there were theatres that could seat 14,000 or more spectators, and most Greek cities and even some suburban communities eventually boasted their own theatres.

Although athletic competitions at first required not much more than a running track with a starting line and turning post and an arena for wrestling and other combat events, by the mid-5th century BC (e.g. at Olympia; *see* OLYMPIA, §1) but particularly in the 4th century BC (e.g. at Epidauros, *c.* 370 BC, and Nemea, *c.* 315 BC) the built STADIUM had become a necessity, if only for crowd control. In addition to the stadium, other building types associated with athletics include the GYMNASIUM, which by the second half of the 4th century BC incorporated changing rooms, baths, exercise rooms and practice tracks set within a walled building and arranged around an open courtyard (e.g. at Delphi).

Ancient Greek fortifications are still to be seen today, scattered throughout the countryside of South Italy, Sicily, Greece itself and western Turkey. Scholarly preoccupations with the military function of Greek fortifications or with the problems of chronology have obscured the architectonic aspects of these structures, which were not solely defensive in function but unequivocally marked the boundary of a city. Gleaming stone temples were, after all, only one way in which a Greek city could declare its importance and wealth, and a well-built fortification of large stone blocks also became a quantified means of glorification. Aristotle (*Politics* 1330a) endorsed this as the city wall's primary purpose, stating that it must first 'contribute to the embellishment of the city' and second 'suit military needs in general'. The construction methods employed in monumental stone fortifications do not, however, parallel those used in religious architecture, and the stonework in fortifications often displays styles of masonry generally in use at a date earlier than the walls themselves. The majestic fortifications at MESSENE were built around 368 BC, when the city was founded by the Theban general Epaminondas. These walls probably established the form followed by many later fortifications. (*See also* MILITARY ARCHITECTURE AND FORTIFICATIONS, §II, 4.)

BIBLIOGRAPHY

R. E. Wycherley: *How the Greeks Built Cities* (London, 1949, 3/1969)
H. Berve and G. Gruben: *Greek Temples, Theaters and Shrines* (New York, 1962)
G. Gruben: *Die Tempel der Griechen* (Munich, 1966)
J. J. Coulton: *The Architectural Developments of the Greek Stoa* (Oxford, 1976)
——: *Ancient Greek Architects at Work: Problems of Structure and Design* (London, 1977)
A. W. Lawrence: *Greek Aims in Fortification* (Oxford, 1979)
J. -P. Adam: *L'Architecture militaire grecque* (Paris, 1982)
R. Ginouvés and R. Martin: *Dictionnaire méthodique de l'architecture grecque et romaine I: Matériaux, techniques de construction*, Col. Ecole Fr. Rome, lxxxiv (Paris, 1985)
W. Hoepfner and E. L. Schwander: *Haus und Stadt im klassischen Griechenland* (1986), i of *Wohnen in der klassischen Polis* (Munich, 1986–)
F. A. Cooper, ed.: *The Temple of Apollo at Bassai*, 4 vols (Princeton, 1992–5)

FREDERICK COOPER

(iv) Hellenistic. The Hellenistic period is conventionally dated from the death of Alexander the Great in 323 BC to the foundation of the Roman Empire in 27 BC. Little building, however, was undertaken in Greek lands after the annexation of Achaia and Macedonia as provinces by Rome in 146 BC, and the period effectively began around 360 BC, when rulers such as Philip II of Macedon (*reg* 354–336 BC) and the Carian dynast Mausolos of Halikarnassos (*reg* 377–352 BC) became patrons of the arts on an international scale. Alexander's conquests subsequently spread Greek architectural concepts throughout the eastern Mediterranean and as far east as Afghanistan, and Greek cities west of the Adriatic, especially in South Italy and Sicily, long remained centres of Greek influence. In the Aegean basin particularly, Hellenistic architecture grew directly out of later Classical architecture. In predominantly non-Greek areas it was a blend of Greek and native forms, the character and significance of the synthesis varying from region to region. Hellenistic architects were more flexible, as well as more original, than their Classical predecessors, both in producing new designs and in adapting old ones to new needs. Except for temples and stoas, nearly all their building types were essentially new, and even their stoas and temples often broke new ground. Moreover, the Hellenistic period was a time of more significant technical progress than ever before in the history of Greek architecture. Yet the influence of Hellenistic architecture was not due merely to progress in design and techniques. Roman architects were also heavily indebted to the Hellenistic achievement in architectural theory, beginning *c.* 350–*c.* 340 BC with Philon of Eleusis and the Ionian PYTHEOS and continuing down to the later Hellenistic writers HERMOGENES and Arkesios (Vitruvius: VII.Pref.12, 14). The coherence of design and decoration in many Hellenistic buildings was certainly largely due to the success of Hellenistic writers in providing a sound theoretical basis for the architects' work (*see also* §3(i) below).

(a) Materials and techniques. (b) Regional styles. (c) Building types.

(a) Materials and techniques. New developments in materials and techniques between *c.* 350 and *c.* 300 BC seem to have resulted largely from the growth of Macedonian ambitions in the later years of Philip II, but perhaps even more from the eastern campaigns of Alexander, during which a large number of Greco-Macedonian engineers and architects had opportunities to appreciate the advantages of arch and vault construction, baked bricks, and mortar as a binding material. After *c.* 320 BC arches and vaults were frequently used in Greek gateways, substructures and tomb chambers. Although there is still no general agreement about the existence of earlier examples, the evidence points increasingly to the use of vaulting in Macedonia before the death of Philip II in 336 BC. Mortar

and baked bricks, however, were not traditional Greek materials and were never widely employed before Roman times.

Nevertheless, the Hellenistic period was the golden age of Greek engineering science, thanks largely to the work of specialists assembled by the Ptolemies at the famous Museum at Alexandria, though some discoveries probably derived from Seleucid Syria. The truss roof may have been invented to span the great halls of Ptolemaic palaces. Perhaps, too, the vaulted and domed ceilings of Alexandrian rock-cut tombs reproduced real Ptolemaic vaults and domes. The principles of radiating arch construction were certainly well understood by eastern Hellenistic architects and engineers, who sometimes used them with great sophistication, as in the 'tower-gate' at Sillyon (*c.* 200 BC). Even so, they failed to appreciate the potential of mortarwork, especially in vaulting, as their Italo-Hellenistic counterparts clearly did not. In the later 3rd century BC, Philon of Byzantium (V.lxxx.5–9) recommended mortar only for the faces of fortification walls and not for the central fill, though mortarwork foundations and cores were already extensively used in Italo-Hellenistic structures. Again, while the cement vault of the Upper Peirene fountain on Acrocorinth (*c.* 200–*c.* 150 BC) is almost unique outside Italy, Roman Republican builders of the mid-2nd century BC were already developing the mortarwork vaults that were to transform completely Greco-Roman architecture.

Roman architecture, however, retained a largely Hellenistic theoretical basis. This is true not only of arches and vaults, and perhaps truss roofs, but also of the hypocausts of Roman baths. The Romans probably used Greek-derived words, such as *hypocaustum* and *thermae*, to designate eastern Hellenistic inventions, employing Latin terms (e.g. *suspensurae*, *tubi*) only for Roman refinements. In architecture and engineering the Hellenistic period was often more important for its influence on Rome than for its own practical accomplishments.

(b) Regional styles. Hellenistic architecture was never in a real sense 'international'. Instead, distinctive regional features modified forms and ideas common to all schools. Projects sponsored by royal patrons outside their own domains might be designed by local architects in a local idiom; given the badly ruined state of most Hellenistic buildings, however, only vague outlines of major regional styles now remain.

The older centres of mainland Greece played little part in Hellenistic innovations, and their important new buildings were usually gifts from foreign patrons. In Macedonia, however, Philip II, Alexander and their early successors built the first Greek palaces since Mycenaean times and created a new type of monumental tomb. Macedonian architecture was eclectic, borrowing forms from both Ionia and mainland Greece. The result was a distinctively Macedonian decorative use of the architectural orders, so that the façades of Macedonian tombs (e.g. at LEUKADIA; *c.* 300–*c.* 250 BC) look quite different from any Classical design.

Pergamene architects had the major task of transforming the hilltop fortress of Pergamon into a royal capital (*see* PERGAMON, §2). They created vistas of architecture

27. Model of the Hellenistic Sanctuary of Athena Lindia, Rhodes, ?*c.* 330–*c.*150 BC (with minor Roman additions), view from the north (Copenhagen, Nationalmuseum)

28. Hellenistic bouleuterion, Miletos, *c.* 170 BC; reconstruction drawing from Hubert Knackfuss: *Das Rathaus von Milet* (Berlin, 1908), pl. 14

and landscape equalled only in Italo-Hellenistic projects. Similar groups of buildings are found at other Pergamene sites, such as ASSOS and Aigai (probably *c.* 200–*c.* 150 BC; *see* AIGAI (i)), and in late Hellenistic additions to the Sanctuary of Athena Lindia on Rhodes (see fig. 27) and the Sanctuary of Asklepios on Kos (*see* KOS, §2(i)). Furthermore, the numerous small Doric temples built at Pergamon and elsewhere gave Hellenistic Doric a new respectability, and the Pergamene leaf-capital long retarded the spread of the Corinthian capital in western Asia Minor.

The architects of Seleucid Syria were primarily responsible for the development of the 'orthodox' Corinthian capital later adopted by the Romans. The two earliest significant Corinthian temples, the Temple of Zeus at Uzuncaburç (*c.* 175–*c.* 150 BC) and the Temple of Olympian Zeus at Athens (*see* ATHENS, §II, 4), and a predecessor of the Roman temple of Jupiter at Baalbek, were probably all commissioned by Antiochos IV (*reg* 175–164 BC; *see also* SELEUCIDS). The bouleuterion (council house) at MILETOS (*c.* 170 BC; see fig. 28), which established the classic form for the bouleuterion, was a Seleucid gift. Hellenistic Syria's cultural pluralism seems to have generated exceptionally rich syntheses of Greek and non-Greek forms. The distinctive cella of Syrian temples (an adyton above a 'crypt') also seems Hellenistic in origin.

Much of the culture of Ptolemaic Egypt was essentially 'sub-Pharaonic'; nevertheless, Ptolemaic architects still made important contributions, including a rich series of religious and secular buildings in a polychrome Corinthian order. Moreover, the scale and magnificence of Ptolemaic palaces seem to have surpassed anything elsewhere, and their great 'royal halls' were direct ancestors of Roman basilicas and 'Egyptian' dining-rooms (Vitruvius: VI.iii.8–9). Even so, the Hellenistic world was soon eclipsed by Rome, so that the Italo-Hellenistic style influenced the history of architecture in the Western world much more directly than any eastern Hellenistic school.

(c) Building types.

Temples and altars. The principal Hellenistic temples are the small Ionic Temple of Athena at Priene, designed *c.* 350–*c.* 340 BC by Pytheos (*see* PRIENE, §1), and several giant structures: the Ionic temples of Artemis at Ephesos (*c.* 350–*c.* 220 BC), Sardis (*c.* 300 BC to Roman times) and Magnesia on the Maeander (*c.* 200–*c.* 135 BC); the Temple of Apollo at Didyma (late 4th century BC onwards); and the Corinthian Temple of Olympian Zeus at Athens. The most impressive of these is the Temple of Apollo at DIDYMA (see fig. 29); the most original in plan, however, are the temples at MAGNESIA ON THE MAEANDER and SARDIS, being respectively 'simple' and 'complex' versions of Hellenistic pseudo-dipteral buildings (i.e. there was room for a second peristyle inside the existing one). In the Hellenistic Hieron on Samothrace (*see* SAMOTHRACE, §1), a Doric temple façade fronted an apsidal hall used for congregations.

In Greek as well as non-Greek Asia Minor, Doric and Ionic were both widely employed. Thus, though one of the main temples of the Letoon near Xanthos (2nd century BC) was Doric, both have eastern Ionic peripteral plans (*see* XANTHOS, §1), and the Roman temple at Pessinous (first half of the 1st century AD) was perhaps influenced by the late Pergamene 'mixed' orders in combining Ionic columns with a plan derived from the Doric Temple of Asklepios at Epidauros. The early Hellenistic temple at Klaros in Ionia, now thought to post-date Lysimachos' death in 281 BC, and probably sponsored by the Seleucids, was Doric, like Lysimachos' Temple of Athena at Troy. Finally, Antiochos IV commissioned not only the Corinthian Temple of Olympian Zeus at Athens but also a large Doric Temple of Zeus at Lebadeia (*c.* 175–*c.* 171 BC); an enlarged copy (*c.* 175–*c.* 150 BC) of the Temple of Asklepios at Epidauros overshadowed the small Ionic temple in the Sanctuary of Asklepios on Kos (early 3rd century BC; for illustration *see* KOS, 2 (i)).

29. Hellenistic Temple of Apollo, Didyma, from late 4th century BC; view from the north-east

Monumental altars with columnar and sculptural ornament were a Hellenistic innovation, which began with the Altar of Artemis at Ephesos (*c.* 325 BC). The Altar of Hieron II at Syracuse (*c.* 225 BC) and the Altar of Zeus ('Great Altar') at Pergamon (*c.* 180–*c.* 170 BC) in effect served as both altar and temple.

Stoas. Hellenistic stoas were often much larger than earlier examples and sometimes had an upper storey. They frequently enclosed three or even four sides of a precinct or agora, though the basic design (single- or double-aisled hall with one or more rows of rooms behind) varied considerably. The Harbour Stoa at Perachora (*c.* 320 BC) was perhaps the first two-storey stoa to have a Doric lower and an Ionic upper order. The Harbour Stoa at Miletos (late 4th century BC) contains the earliest example of a Doric heart-shaped pier at an internal angle. Heart-shaped piers were also used around 300 BC at the corners of what is probably the earliest stoa with a pi-shaped plan, in the agora at Priene.

The South Stoa at Corinth (late 4th century BC) and the East Stoa of the South Agora at Miletos (*c.* 300–*c.* 280 BC) were enormous. The former had two storeys of rooms looking out on a single-storey promenade; the latter, a Seleucid gift, combined Greek colonnade and Oriental bazaar by having shops facing both the agora and a street outside. The columns of even the longest single-storey stoas rarely exceeded 7–8 m in height and must often have seemed disproportionately low. The addition of an upper storey thus improved the buildings' proportions as well as doubling the available floor space without increasing the ground area. Two-storey stoas were also skilfully employed by Pergamene designers to connect lower and upper terraces (e.g. between the precinct of Athena and the Library at Pergamon). The Pergamene stoas of Eumenes II and Attalos II at Athens (for illustration *see* STOA, §1) were architectural showpieces. Interesting multi-storey 'market stoas' occur at sites where the agora terrace rises well above a street (e.g. at Assos, Aigai (*c.* 150–*c.* 125 BC) and Carian Alinda (?late Hellenistic)). In such situations, additional costly terracing was avoided by placing two storeys beneath the covered promenade; these rooms were accessible only from the street outside.

Theatres and stadia. Before the later 4th century BC theatres and stadia were simple structures, and Hellenistic stadia generally remained so. From *c.* 325 BC onward, however, the Theatre of Dionysos at Athens began to assume a more monumental form, with both auditorium (*theatron*) and stage building (*skene*) of stone (*see also* §I, 1(i)(e) above). Most eastern Hellenistic theatres derived from the Athenian building. The new *skene* at Athens, designed for both tragedies (performed at or near ground level in the *orchestra*) and New Comedy (performed on a raised stage), had a two-aisled lower storey with a colonnade in front. The flat roof of the front aisle doubled as the New Comedy stage, with a wooden upper storey (*episkenion*) over the back aisle as the backdrop. For performances in the *orchestra*, the colonnaded lower storey was the backdrop, the action being framed on either side by projecting wings (*paraskenia*). Later, when single-storey stages (*proskenia*) became normal, the *paraskenia* were reduced, as at Epidauros and Athens, or eliminated, as in most Hellenistic *skenai*, for example at Priene (?late 3rd century BC) and Oropos (*c.* mid-2nd century BC; see fig. 14 above). While most *proskenia* were Doric, some were Ionic, as at Epidauros (?early Hellenistic) and Dodona (3rd century BC).

Western Greek cities had a long tradition of low wooden stages with elaborate backgrounds of wooden columns, often depicted on South Italian vases. These served as models for Roman stage buildings and thus influenced the history of theatre design more than the eastern Hellenistic *proskenion* stage, which became increasingly rare west of the Adriatic.

Gymnasia, palaestras and baths. The first buildings designed to a more or less standard plan for general education and athletic training seem to belong to late 4th-century BC Athens. All activities other than running were accommodated in a relatively small structure, the PALAESTRA, where rooms opened off a colonnaded court. For running, unless there was a stadium near by, there were full-length tracks (183 m), ideally one open-air, another covered by a colonnade, in a rectangular enclosure, the GYMNASIUM. Palaestras were far more common than complete gymnasium-palaestra complexes. Architectural embellishments were generally limited to modest entranceways, Doric colonnades around the court and perhaps colonnaded fronts to the main rooms.

Variations on this basic plan are found all over the Hellenistic world and as far east as Ai-Khanum in Afghanistan. Familiar Aegean examples include the gymnasium at Sikyon (early 3rd century BC), the gymnasia and palaestras at Olympia (early 2nd century BC and 3rd respectively), Delphi (*c.* 335–*c.* 326 BC) and Delos (early 3rd century BC and 2nd) and the Lower Gymnasium at Priene (mid-2nd century BC). The gymnasia in royal capitals were more extensive; the upper and middle terraces of the complex at Pergamon (early 2nd century BC), remodelled in Roman times, are extraordinarily impressive, while the gymnasium at Alexandria was the city's finest monument after the royal palace.

Bathing facilities in Greek gymnasia were always modest in scale and usually unheated, though an important heated bath of the mid-Hellenistic period in the Asklepieion at Gortys in Arcadia already used the hypocaust system of heating so integral to later Roman baths (*see also* BATH (ii), §1).

Tombs and commemorative monuments. The great Mausoleum at Halikarnassos (*c.* 365–*c.* 350 BC; *see* HALIKARNASSOS, §2) developed the scheme of the Nereid Monument at Xanthos (early 4th century BC) by adding a crowning stepped pyramid with a group of sculptures. The Lion Tomb at Knidos (*see* KNIDOS, §1) and the impressive Mausoleum of BELEVI (?*c.* 285–*c.* 280 BC; see fig. 30) are its earliest extant successors. Similar smaller tombs and commemorative structures range from the Monument of Lysikrates at Athens (334/3 BC) to the Augustan mausoleum at Aquileia. Related designs also occur in the Kidron Valley at Jerusalem (2nd–1st century BC) and in the Tomb of Hamrath at Suwayda in Syria (*c.* 50 BC). Mausoleum B at SABRATHA (2nd century BC) was a startlingly baroque Punic structure that incorporated Greek forms into a Semitic tower-tomb. Such monuments were probably designed to be impressive rather than orthodox, the most striking being the great 'temple-tomb' façades of PETRA (possibly later 1st century BC onwards).

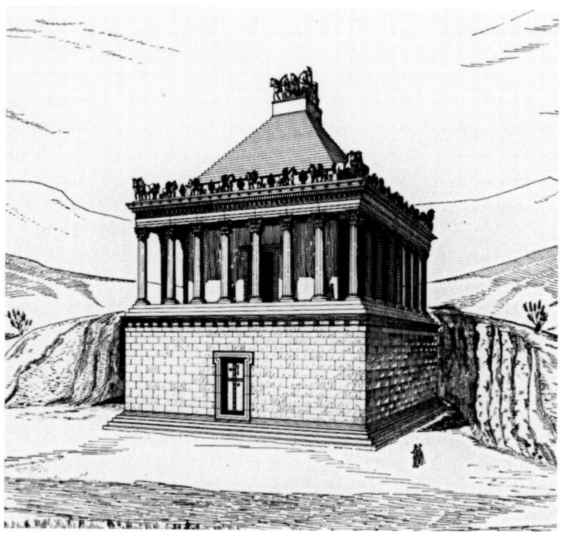

30. Hellenistic mausoleum, Belevi, ?*c.* 285–*c.* 280 BC; reconstruction drawing

Macedonian tumulus tombs, though less imposing on the outside, are important for the vaulted structure of the burial chambers. The earliest examples of such vaulting may belong to the latter years of Philip II; in any event the long series of tombs dating from the late 4th century to *c.* 150 BC certainly includes the earliest fairly closely dated examples of Hellenistic monumental vaulting. Moreover, the façades, whether in stone or stucco, are important illustrations of Hellenistic use of the architectural orders for decorative rather than structural purposes.

Halls and storehouses. For these buildings Hellenistic architects introduced lasting innovations in design and construction. In place of earlier forest-like rows of internal supports, as in the Odeion of Pericles at Athens (mid-5th century BC), they created much more open and spacious interiors, perhaps with the use of truss roofs. The audience halls of the Ptolemaic palaces must have been notable examples, though none now survive. The more modest Hypostyle Hall on Delos (*c.* 210 BC; *see* DELOS, §1(ii)) dimly suggests their scale and splendour. As already noted, the design of the bouleuterion at Miletos, with its curvilinear auditorium inside a rectangular chamber, became standard for such buildings; the plan was probably developed in Seleucid Syria. The bouleuteria at Carian Alabanda and Pisidian Termessos and the remodelled New Bouleuterion at Athens are probably all slightly later. Similar meeting halls at Priene and at HERAKLEIA UNDER LATMOS (*c.* 200 BC and *c.* 150 BC respectively) possessed simpler rectangular auditoria.

The arsenal at Peiraeus, designed *c.* 345 BC by Philon of Eleusis, had an elaborate exterior but rather primitive form of roof. By contrast, some of the granaries described by Philon of Byzantium (V.lxxxvii.10–18) were ingenious structures with wooden floors supported by transverse arches, like those in water cisterns on Delos (3rd century BC onwards). The storehouses on the acropolis at Pergamon (later 3rd century BC to early 2nd) had cellular stone basements to provide cross-ventilation.

Domestic architecture. Most Hellenistic houses followed Classical models but were larger and better built. Vitruvius' 'Rhodian peristyle', with higher columns on one side (VI.vii.3), and his four types of main rooms (Tetrastyle, Corinthian, Kyzikene and Egyptian; *On Architecture* VI.iii.8–10) were also of eastern Hellenistic origin. The most influential domestic structures of Hellenistic times, however, were urban palaces of the type found at Pella (*c.* 300 BC; *see* PELLA (ii), §1), multi-level structures such as the House of the Hermes on Delos (late Hellenistic) and the great royal palaces. The earliest of these was built by Mausolos at Halikarnassos and later admired by Vitruvius (II.viii.10–11). The enormous complex excavated at Pella in the late 20th century is at least a generation later. The 'summer palace' at VERGINA (*c.* 300–*c.* 275 BC), built on a terrace commanding magnificent views over the plain to the sea, is still the only completely excavated example. Most splendid of all was the Ptolemaic palace at Alexandria, covering, according to Strabo (*Geography* XVII.i.8), between a quarter and a third of the city area. The only hints of its magnificence come from the great monoliths of the Alabaster Tomb at Alexandria (?*c.* 275–*c.* 250 BC) and the account in Athenaeus (*Deipnosophists* 204d–206c) of polychrome masonry, exotic wooden panelling and gilded ivory carvings on the river barge of Ptolemy IV (*reg* 221–204 BC); but Ptolemaic palaces clearly remained unrivalled until the time of Nero and Domitian (later 1st century AD).

Also worth noting are forerunners of the Roman *insulae* (tenements), such as the houses of the Masks and the Comedians, and probably the Granite Building, on Delos (after the late 2nd century BC). These were clearly attempts to provide a variety of rented urban accommodation in an overcrowded late Hellenistic settlement.

BIBLIOGRAPHY

EWA: 'Hellenistic Architecture'

Philon of Byzantium: *Mechanics*

Vitruvius: *On Architecture*

R. Delbrück: *Hellenistische Bauten in Latium*, 2 vols (Strasbourg, 1907–12)

S. B. Murray: *Hellenistic Architecture in Syria* (Princeton, 1917)

T. Fyfe: *Hellenistic Architecture* (Cambridge, 1936)

A. von Szalay and E. Boehringer: *Die hellenistischen Arsenale* (1937), x of *Altertümer von Pergamon* (Berlin, 1885–)

G. Roux: *L'Architecture de l'Argolide aux IVe et IIIe siècles avant J-C* (Paris, 1961)

P. Bernard: 'Ai Khanum on the Oxus', *Proc. Brit. Acad.*, liii (1967), pp. 71–95

R. Martin: 'Architecture', *Grèce hellénistique: Univers des formes*, ed. J. Charbonneaux, R. Martin and F. Villard (Paris, 1970); Eng. trans. as *Hellenistic Art* (London, 1973), pp. 3–94

F. E. Winter: 'Building and Town Planning', *The Hellenistic World*, Cambridge Anc. Hist. (Cambridge, 1970, 2/1984), pp. 371–83

M. Lyttelton: *Baroque Architecture in Classical Antiquity* (London, 1974)

C. Williams: 'The Corinthian Temple of Zeus Olbios at Uzuncaburç: A Reconsideration of the Date', *Amer. J. Archaeol.*, lxxviii (1974), pp. 405–14

H. von Steuben: 'Seleukidische Kolossaltempel', *Ant. Welt*, xii (1981), pp. 3–12

H. Lauter: *Die Architektur des Hellenismus* (Darmstadt, 1986)

R. A. Tomlinson: 'The Architectural Context of the Macedonian Vaulted Tombs', *Annu. Brit. Sch. Athens*, lxxxii (1987), pp. 305–12

J. de la Genière: 'Le Sanctuaire d'Apollon à Claros: Nouvelles découvertes', *Rev. Etud. Grecques*, ciii (1990), pp. 95–110

F. E. WINTER

3. THEORY AND DESIGN.

The design of Greek buildings, especially those based on the orders, was highly standardized. The elaborate rules of procedure, intended above all to bring harmony and proportion to the buildings, were the subject of treatises by Greek authors, later recorded by the Roman theorist Vitruvius (*On Architecture*). They were not, however, applied with mechanical precision: indeed, intentional distortions from the norm, termed 'refinements', were introduced to the most important buildings to breathe life into the architecture.

(i) Theorists. (ii) Drawings, models and specifications. (iii) Measurement. (iv) Module. (v) Proportion. (vi) Refinements. (vii) Symbolism.

(i) Theorists. Our only sources for ancient Greek architectural theory are the writings of Roman authors, primarily the ten books *On Architecture* by Vitruvius (1st century BC) and the *Natural History* by Pliny (1st century AD). Vitruvius mentioned the names of Greek authors of architectural treatises and some of their contents, but how much practicing architects were aware of or followed these theoretical studies is a matter of controversy, as is the content of the Greek written accounts.

While most of the Greek accounts mentioned in Roman sources, such as the book by Theodoros (*fl c.* 550 BC) perhaps on the third Temple of Hera on Samos (*c.* 560 BC; Vitruvius: VII.Pref.12), appear to have contained descriptions of the buildings or accounts of the procedures of construction, some treatises were devoted to questions of theory, such as Silenos' study of Doric symmetries (VII.Pref.12), Arkesios' investigation of the Corinthian order (IV.iii.1; VII.Pref.12), and Pytheos' and Hermogenes' writings on the Ionic order (IV.iii.1; VII.Pref.12).

PYTHEOS and HERMOGENES are two major Greek theorists whose writings we know of only from Vitruvius' account. Pytheos, writing in the 4th century BC, discussed the use of systematic proportions as applied to the design of a temple; his book on the Temple of Athena Polias at PRIENE must have detailed his use of such proportions in the design of that temple. A close study of the remains of the temple reveals the consistent use of a module of 6 Ionic feet, making the building an embodiment of Pytheos' canon of proportions in much the same way that the statue of the *Doryphoros* embodied the canon of Polykleitos. Pytheos is also credited with being the first to assert the superiority of the Ionic order over the Doric; the virtual absence of Doric temples after the time of Pytheos may indicate the influence of his writings.

Vitruvius also noted that Hermogenes, who wrote in the 2nd century BC, was an important Greek theorist who invented a new system of ideal proportions for the Ionic order, thus continuing the theoretical considerations of Pytheos. A certain Hermogenes designed the altar of the Temple of Athena at Priene, and if this is the same Hermogenes as the theorist, then he may have learned about Pytheos' work from the temple itself as well as from Pytheos' book. Hermogenes followed Pytheos also in his favouring of the Ionic order over the Doric. Vitruvius is believed to have used Hermogenes' writings extensively, especially for his system of proportions for the height and spacing of columns. While the Temple of Artemis at Magnesia on the Maeander, which Hermogenes designed, still stands, it differs somewhat from Hermogenes' proportional system as laid out in Vitruvius. The difference between the proportions in the text and those used in the building may be due either to an error in the recording of Hermogenes' text or to the architect's manipulation of his own theories. If the latter is the case, then Greek architectural theories, like the Greek orders, were not hard and fast rules but guidelines that allowed for flexibility on the part of the builder.

A major interest for Pytheos, Hermogenes and other theorists was the achievement of harmony in the design of a building. They thought that harmony could be achieved by proper proportions or through the use of the order that best embodied the desired proportion. Vitruvius (III.i.1–9) likened the harmony that could be achieved by well proportioned architecture to good bodily health for a human body.

Although we can glean the ideas of these theorists from Vitruvius and from some of the buildings they designed, we are far less certain of the extent to which their work influenced other architects. Pytheos himself (Vitruvius: I.i.12) believed in an extensive education for architects, but whether such an education was a general practice in Pytheos' time, or a practice at all before the Hellenistic period, is unknown. Xenophon (*Memorabilia* IV.ii.8–10) related that Socrates asked one of his pupils if his interest in architectural treatises meant that he intended to study to become an architect; this suggests that such treatises were indeed studied by aspiring architects (*see also* §1(iv) above).

The writings of the ancient architects must be understood in their intellectual context. The earliest treatises, by such authors as Theodoros, and Chersiphron and Metagenes (both *fl* mid-6th century BC) on the Temple of Artemis at Ephesos, were produced in Ionia during the period in which the Ionian philosophers were writing about the natural world, and the architectural treatises may reflect the general intellectual explorations of the period. Likewise the writings of Pytheos and Hermogenes reflect the intellectual climate of the Hellenistic period, particularly the creative innovations of a writer such as Kallimachos. In certain aspects, the ideas of the Hellenistic architects are also akin to Plato's explorations of the Forms, embodiments of a perfect and immutable ideal.

The theories of the Greek architects were closely allied in their focus, if not also their form, with the ideas of other Greek thinkers, such as mathematicians and musicians. Such thinkers as Pythagoras (late 6th century BC) were profoundly interested in proportion and harmony (*see* §3(v) below). Pytheos and Hermogenes were both interested in the first, as a means of achieving the second.

Although architectural criticism was not an established literary genre in Greek times, criticism as well as theory is inherent in the writings of Pytheos and Hermogenes. By stating that the Ionic was the best order for temples and that Doric was the worst, the two architects were acting as architectural critics. Whether earlier writers had also made critical judgements is unknown.

BIBLIOGRAPHY

Vitruvius: *On Architecture*

F. W. Schlikker: *Hellenistiche Vorstellungen von der Schönheit des Bauwerks nach Vitruv* (Berlin, 1940)

R. A Tomlinson: 'The Doric Order: Hellenistic Critics and Criticism', *J. Hell. Stud.*, lxxxiii (1963), pp. 133–43

J. J. Pollitt: *The Ancient View of Greek Art: Criticism, History, and Terminology* (New Haven, 1974)

J. J. Coulton: *Ancient Greek Architects at Work: Problems of Structure and Design* (Ithaca, NY, 1977)

P. Gros: 'Le Dossier vitruvien d'Hermogènes', *Mél. Ecole Fr. Rome: Ant.*, xc (1978), pp. 687–703

B. Wesenberg: 'Zu den Schriften der griechischen Architekten', *Bauplanung und Bautheorie der Antike. Bericht über ein Kolloquium in Berlin vom 16.11–18.11: Berlin, 1983*

R. A. Tomlinson: 'Vitruvius and Hermogenes', *Munus non ingratum: Proceedings of the International Symposium on Vitruvius' 'De Architectura' and the Hellenistic and Republican Architecture: Leiden, 1989*, pp. 71–5

B. Wesenberg: 'Griechisches and Römisches in der vitruvianischen Architektur: Ein Beitrag zur Quellenfrage', *Munus non ingratum: Proceedings of the International Symposium on Vitruvius' 'De Architectura' and the Hellenistic and Republican Architecture: Leiden, 1989*, pp. 76–84

W. Hoepfner and E. L. Schwander, eds: *Hermogenes und die hochhellenistischen Architektur* (Mainz, 1990)

BARBARA TSAKIRGIS

(ii) Drawings, models and specifications. There can be little question of architectural drawings or models preceding the construction of the simple vernacular buildings of the Protogeometric and Geometric periods. Even the exceptionally large Toumba building at Lefkandi was quite simple in arrangement and built of traditional materials, so that its plan could be laid out directly on the ground and its construction could follow normal craft practices, without preliminary design. Building models from this period certainly exist, but they are votive offerings, rather than aids to design. Such models, of varying detail and accuracy, continued to be made into the Classical period.

With the introduction of monumental temple construction in the 7th century BC, questions of preliminary design arise more seriously, for plans were certainly used in Egypt and the Near East. Evidence for design procedures is virtually non-existent before the 5th century BC, however, and to get any coherent picture, the evidence from the 5th and 4th centuries BC must be taken together. It comes almost entirely from inscriptions relating to various public building projects, especially at Athens, and it is notable for the rarity, perhaps the total absence, of any mention of scale drawings of the kind we normally associate with architectural design. The most plausible reference to such a drawing is in a fragmentary inscription of about 420 BC relating to an Athenian sanctuary, which invites citizens to submit a design at least one cubit (*c.* 500 mm) high. The inscription seems to refer to a doorway rather than a complete building; a plan would be unnecessary, and the design could simply show the proposed ornament at full scale, like the specimens discussed below.

References to three other means of communicating a design are, by contrast, clear and repeated: the template (*anagrapheus*), the specimen (*paradeigma*) and the specification (*syngraphe*). Templates, used where a profile had to be specified (e.g. for a moulding), would inevitably be made at full scale. Specimens were used where the design was three-dimensional, for instance a wax specimen for carved wooden ornament on the ceiling of the Erechtheion at Athens. Again they are virtually all cases where full-size execution would be appropriate, and in one case the specimen was used in the finished building, so that it must have been both full-size and in the intended material. Although *paradeigma* is sometimes translated 'model', it did not have the implications of small scale that 'model' may carry, and there is little to suggest the use of small-scale building models in Archaic or Classical Greek architectural design.

The third means of communicating design, the specification, is purely verbal. It may be a technical description of work to be done, for instance supplying or finishing blocks of marble to given sizes and standards, as the basis for builders' contracts. But it may also be a more or less complete and detailed description of a proposed building. The most important such document is a virtually complete inscription recording the design of a naval storehouse at PEIRAEUS, prepared by Euthydomos and Philon *c.* 340 BC. Under the heading 'Specifications' it sets out the design of the building in sufficient detail to allow its size and general arrangement to be clearly understood. For the lower parts it contains enough detail on procedures, materials and block sizes for contracts to be written and agreed, but the description of the upper parts is more general; for instance, a Doric frieze is mentioned, but no details of its design are given. It is notable that this specification, which seems to present the design to the Athenian people as well as to potential builders, mentions no plans or elevations, and the only specimen (*paradeigma*) is for a tackle chest.

There is therefore a strong probability that Greek architects of the 5th and 4th centuries BC did not use scale drawings or models. They were able to manage without them because their buildings were generally simple and conventional in overall design, so that all parties would know broadly what was planned. Rules of proportion, although not formally attested before the writings of VITRUVIUS, are clearly suggested by the character of earlier Greek architecture, and they could encapsulate simply and accurately the essentials of a Doric or Ionic order, allowing it to be repeated or modified as required. The variations and subtleties of Classical architecture are too small to show clearly in scale drawings and are more easily expressed in words or in full-scale specimens. Since there was no major change in the character or methods of architecture between the Archaic and Classical periods, it is likely that much the same system, perhaps in simplified form, applied in the Archaic period also.

This system probably changed significantly in the Hellenistic period, for Vitruvius assumed the use of plans, elevations and perspectives and employed Greek terms for them (*On Architecture* I.ii.2). Scale models were certainly used in Hellenistic catapult design, although none survives. Hellenistic buildings, although sometimes less fine in detail than earlier ones, are often more varied and complex in general layout, so that plans and elevations would be more useful. One small-scale architectural drawing has in fact survived on the underside of a wall block of the 4th-century BC Temple of Athena at Priene. It apparently shows the entablature and pediment of a temple, perhaps that of Athena, in which case the scale is 1:48. It is more a diagram than an elevation and more of an explanatory sketch than an accurate preliminary design.

The most impressive surviving Greek architectural drawings are, however, largely at full scale. On the inner wall face of the sunken court of the Temple of Apollo at Didyma a number of drawings were incised in fine lines on the smooth but unfinished surface. The temple was probably begun in the late 4th century BC, but the drawings date to the 3rd. One drawing shows the heights and projections of the architrave, frieze and cornice of the little temple within the sunken court, all at full scale, but gives no continuous profile. The building width and column axes are indicated (again at full scale), but do not match those of the remains. The most interesting drawing relates to the column shafts of the main colonnade. It gives at full scale the profile of part of the column base (the existence of alternative lines shows that the design was still being worked out), and above that is a series of parallel lines spaced a dactyl ($\frac{1}{16}$ of a foot, 19 mm) apart, across which the arc of a large circle has been drawn, as a means of setting out the entasis (slightly curving taper) of the column shaft. The parallel lines correspond in number to the number of feet in the height of the column shaft, so that shaft height is represented at a scale of 1:16, but the varying radius is shown at full scale from a vertical line at the right, which represents the column axis. The distance between the vertical line and the circular arc along, say, the sixth parallel line is thus the exact radius required six feet up the shaft. The effect of this method is to stretch the conspicuous circular arc of the drawing into a barely perceptible elliptical one in the building.

The Priene and Didyma drawings show that the concept of scale drawing was understood, and it is quite possible that a small-scale plan was drawn of the temple at Didyma as a whole, since it is unusually complex. But no such plan has survived from the Hellenistic period, and full-scale drawing remained important, especially where detail and precision were required.

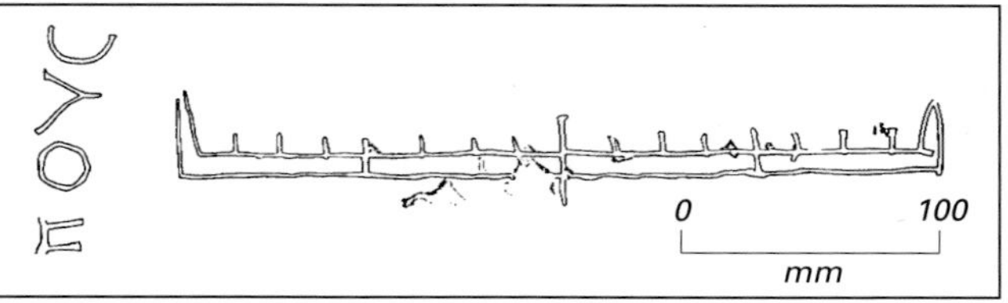

31. Incised stone measure representing Attic foot, inscribed '*pous*' (foot), from Gortyn, Crete, late Hellenistic–early Imperial; reconstruction drawing (original now lost)

BIBLIOGRAPHY

J. A. Bundgaard: *Mnesicles: A Greek Architect at Work* (Copenhagen, 1957), pp. 93–5, n. 217

J. J. Coulton: *Greek Architects at Work* (London, 1977), pp. 51–9; pubd in USA as *Ancient Greek Architects at Work* (Ithaca, NY, 1977)

L. Haselberger: 'Werkzeichnungen am jüngeren Didymeion: Vorbericht', *Istanbul. Mitt.*, xxx (1980), pp. 191–215

——: 'Bericht über die Arbeit am jüngeren Apollontempel von Didyma: Zwischenbericht', *Istanbul. Mitt.*, xxxiii (1983), pp. 90–104

——: 'The Construction Plans for the Temple of Apollo at Didyma', *Sci. Amer.*, ccliii/6 (Dec 1983), pp. 126–32

W. Koenigs: 'Der Athenatempel von Priene', *Istanbul. Mitt.*, xxxiii (1983), pp. 166–8

T. G. Schnatter: *Griechische Hausmodelle: Untersuchungen zur frühgriechischen Architektur* (Berlin, 1990)

J. J. COULTON

(iii) Measurement. The commonest ancient Greek units of measurement were the cubit (*pechus*) and the foot (*pous*). The foot was usually subdivided into half feet (*hemipodia*), hand-breadths (*palaistai*) and fingers (*daktyloi*). References to half cubits or 'spans' (*spithamai*) occur almost exclusively in relation to the construction of siege engines. The following scheme emerges: 1 foot=4 *palaistai*= 16 *daktyloi*; 1 cubit=2 *spithamai*=6 *palaistai*= 14 *daktyloi*. References to half *daktyloi* occur quite frequently in architectural sources, and the diameter of a column (?late Hellenistic) in the Temple of Apollo at Didyma was calculated to $\frac{1}{32}$ foot (=$\frac{1}{2}$ *daktylos*). Indeed, the calculation of the volumes of columns in Heron's *Stereometrica* (II.xi) includes fractions down to $\frac{1}{448}$ foot ($\frac{1}{28}$ *daktylos*).

Important larger measures were the fathom (*orguia*) (=4 cubits=6 feet), the *plethron* (=100 feet), and the stade (*stadion*) (=100 fathoms=600 feet). The units up to a fathom were derived from the human body (Vitruvius: *On Architecture* III.i.5; Heron: *Geometry* IV.i), and their simple ratios formed an integrated system of measurement. Area measures were expressed in square feet, square cubits and square *plethra*, while architectural volumes (though not necessarily other volumes) were measured in cubic feet or cubic cubits.

Three distinct Greek systems of measurement have been identified. Other, hypothetical systems (excluding the Alexandrian foot; see below), also referred to as 'local foot measures', are often explicable as modules (*see* §(iv) below). The Doric foot (*c.* 325–8 mm) was probably among the 'Pheidonian measurements' (Strabo: *Geography* VIII.iii.33) that Pheidon of Argos established before the mid-7th century BC 'for the Peloponnesians' (Herodotus: *Histories* VI.cxxvii.3) and that had been used in Attica for some time before the Solonian reforms of 594/3 BC (Aristotle: *Constitution of Athens* x). Later, it was certainly employed in the Erechtheion at Athens and possibly also in the Parthenon. Its metric value was first determined by W. Dörpfeld, who compared the precise measurements of the stones given in the Erechtheion building accounts of 409/8 BC with the extant blocks in the building itself, thus

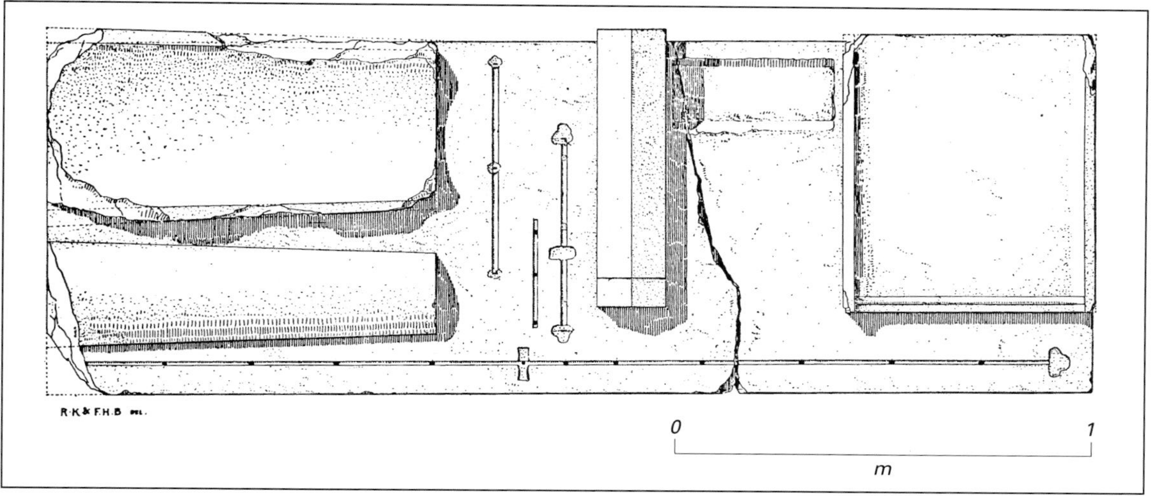

32. Measuring table in stone with standard tile sizes and measures of length, from Assos, ?Hellenistic; reconstruction drawing (original now lost)

establishing a recognized fixed point in Greek metrology (see Dörpfeld).

The Attic foot (*c*. 293–6 mm), sometimes also called the Ionian or Cycladic foot, was used on the Cyclades from the early 6th century BC. It bears the simple ratio of 9:10 to the Doric foot. It was probably not introduced into Attica during the Solonian reforms, as has been suggested, but was probably employed at Eleusis in Peisistratid times (*c*. 560–*c*. 530 BC). It may later have been used in the Parthenon and other Attic buildings, though not in the Erechtheion. The 5th-century BC Metrological Relief (Oxford, Ashmolean; Michaelis 83) may be related to an Athenian imposition of this system of measurement on the recently acquired island of Samos, and Athenian influence apparently made this the most widely used Hellenistic unit of measurement. Through methods analogous to those of Dörpfeld, its use has been detected at Eleusis in 329/8 BC, at Didyma from the 3rd century BC and at Gortyn, where an incised measure was found in a wall (see fig. 31). It is identical to the Roman foot and, as such, became universally recognized in Roman times.

The Samian or East Ionian foot (*c*. 348–50 mm) was apparently introduced from Egypt, since the Samian cubit was identical to the Egyptian Royal cubit (Herodotus: II.clxviii.1). It formed the basis for measurement in east Ionia from the Archaic period until at least the mid-5th century BC but was eventually ousted by the Attic foot, as attested by the Metrological Relief. However, the measure survived in Egypt until Roman Imperial times as the 'Ptolemaic foot' or as the 'Philetairian' or 'Royal' foot. Its metric value is known from that of the Egyptian Royal cubit (*c*. 523.5–525.0 mm).

The three systems of measurement detailed above are in a ratio of 30:27 (=10:9):32, probably representing the official conversion rate. The Alexandrian foot (*c*. 306–8 mm) was used in the calculations of the geographer Eratosthenes (*fl* 3rd century BC) and probably remained in use in the south-eastern Mediterranean until early Byzantine times. It bears a ratio of 25:24 to the Roman foot.

The amazing consistency of these systems of measurement over the centuries was due to standardization, as is clear from the use of standard measures in Attica. One set of standard measures (*symbola*) was guarded in the Tholos in the Athenian Agora, another in Peiraeus and another in Eleusis (*Inscr. Gr./2*, ii, 1013). These were used to make the only metal equivalents (*sekomata*) for use by tradesmen and officially sanctioned by Athens' 10 inspectors of weights and measures (*metronomoi*; Aristotle: *Constitution of Athens* li.2). On Delos a standard fathom measure was kept in the prytaneion (*Inscriptions de Délos*, Paris, 1929, 502, L. 24). A measuring table found at Assos bore standard tile sizes and measures of length (see fig. 32). The foot-measure from Gortyn was probably too inaccurate for use as an official standard.

For construction work the most important instruments were the straight-edge (*kanon*), compasses (*tornos*), rule (*diabetes*), plumbline (*stathme*) and square (*prosagogeion*). The invention of most of these instruments was ascribed by Pliny (*Natural History* VII.lvi.198) to Theodoros of Samos (*see* RHOIKOS AND THEODOROS), who must indeed have used remarkably accurate equipment for his huge temples on Samos and at Ephesos (*c*. 570–*c*. 550 BC). Even greater technical expertise was required in the construction of the 6th-century BC tunnel of Eupalinos of Megara on Samos (*see also* SURVEYOR).

Apart from a few compasses, no strictly ancient Greek measuring instruments survive. However, the multi-purpose measuring instrument of Hermias found near Tyre (Paris, Louvre) certainly belongs to the Hellenistic tradition. Straight-edges were often made either of stone or of good quality wood, with recommended minimum lengths of up to 20 feet (around 6 m; *Inscr. Gr.*, viii, 3073) and were probably calibrated. Direct measurement of longer distances was made with measuring cables and chains (Herodotus: I.lxvi.2; Heron: *Definitions* cxxxv.8). A simple gauge and level, the *chorobates*, can be reconstructed from information in Vitruvius (*On Architecture* VIII.v), while Heron gave a detailed description of precision instruments, called *dioptra*, made from the Hellenistic period onwards (*Dioptra* III–V).

Despite some setbacks due to the use of imprecise methods, the metrological analysis of buildings forms an important part of the study of ancient Greek architecture, since clear, rational measurements and combinations of measurements were fundamental to the Greek concept of aesthetics.

BIBLIOGRAPHY

F. Hultsch: *Metrologicorum scriptorum reliquiae*, i (Stuttgart, 1864/*R* 1971)
——: *Griechische und römische Metrologie* (Berlin, 1878, 2/1882/*R* Graz, 1971)
W. Dörpfeld: 'Metrologische Beiträge', *Mitt. Dt. Archäol. Inst.: Athen. Abt.*, xv (1890), pp. 167–87
M. Guarducci: *Inscriptiones Creticae*, iv (Rome, 1950), p. 384, no. 411
J. J. Coulton: 'Towards Understanding Greek Temple Design', *Annu. Brit. Sch. Athens*, lxx (1975), pp. 59–99
B. Wesenberg: 'Zum metrologischen Relief in Oxford', *Marburg. Winckelmann-Programm* (1975/6), pp. 15–22
K. Hecht: 'Zum römischen Fuss', *Abh. Braunschweig. Wiss. Ges.*, xxx (1979), pp. 1–31
E. Berger: 'Zum Mass- und Proportionssystem des Parthenon: Ein Nachwort zur Diskussion des Bauentwurfes', *Parthenon-Kongress: Basel, 1982*, pp. 119–74
H. Büsing: 'Metrologische Beiträge', *Jb. Dt. Archäol. Inst.*, xcvii (1982), pp. 1–45
H. Bankel: 'Zum Fussmass attischer Bauten des 5. Jahrhunderts v. Chr.', *Mitt. Dt. Archäol. Inst.: Athen. Abt.*, xcviii (1983), pp. 65–99
——: 'Moduli am den Tempeln von Tegea und Stratos? Grenzen Fussmassbestimmung', *Archäol. Anz.* (1984), pp. 413–30
B. Wesenberg: 'Der Fuss des Kallikrates', *Archäol. Anz.* (1984), pp. 547–54

(iv) Module [Lat. *modulus*; Gr. *embates*; *embater*]. A comparatively small unit of measurement used as a basis for determining the proportions of different elements of any structure, in relation both to each other and to the structure as a whole, which could be anything from a siege engine to a temple (Philon of Byzantium: *Mechanics* LIII.x.10–12; Vitruvius: *On Architecture* IV.iii.3; *see also* §(v) below). The module may be a unit, such as a quarter of a foot, in one of the standard systems of measurement, which themselves have a modular basis (*see* §(iii) above), or it may be an independent measure, perhaps laid down in drawings, as at the Temple of Apollo at Didyma. It is not, however, simply an abstract arithmetical lowest common denominator but a unit related directly to the work to which it is applied (Vitruvius: II.ii.2), just as the proportions of the human body depend on the relationship of one part to another. Thus the most important module determining the proportions of any structure in one of the architectural orders was the lower diameter of the column shaft. The Hellenistic architect HERMOGENES created an integrated system of proportions based on this module, which governed every type of temple and arrangement of columns and which was espoused by Roman architects until well into the Imperial period. Through the work of Vitruvius its influence even extended into 20th-century concepts of proportion, such as Le Corbusier's Modulor.

BIBLIOGRAPHY

H. Diels and E. Schramm, eds: 'Philon's Belopoiika', *Abh. Preuss. Akad. Wiss.*, Philol.-Hist. Kl., xvi (1918), pp. 1–68
L. Haselberger: 'Antike Planzeichnungen am Apollontempel von Didyma', *Spektrum der Wissenschaft* (Mainz, 1985), pp. 70–83
J. J. Coulton: 'Modules and Measurement in Ancient Design and Modern Scholarship', *Bull. Ver. Bevord. Kennis Ant. Besch.*, lxiii (1988), pp. 189–93

(v) Proportion. The Latin term *proportio* was used to render the Greek *analogia* (Vitruvius: III.i.1), and it described the numerical relationship of individual parts of a whole to each other and to the whole. Based on mathematical theory, proportion was central to ancient (especially Greek) aesthetics and related closely to the concepts of SYMMETRY and harmony on the one hand and of module on the other (*see* §(iv) above). Numbers and numerical relationships were already apparently fundamental to the philosophy of Pythagoras (*fl* second half of the 6th century BC), since they occurred in the teachings of the Pythagoreans (see Iamblichos: *De vita Pythagorica* xii.59). The application of numerical proportions to monuments and parts of buildings began around the mid-6th century BC, an example being the well-preserved Archilochos Capital from Paros (see fig. 33). Its main measurements (total length and diameter of echinus) give a ratio of 5:3, while the parts of its exposed side give a ratio of 3:4:3. Later, the practical use of mathematical proportions was given a theoretical basis, as in the 'Canon' of POLYKLEITOS.

Theories of proportion established relationships between individual, numerically expressible parts of a work based on fixed mathematical laws. For example the numbers 2, 4 and 8 are related to each other by the common proportion 1:2. According to Plato,

> The most beautiful of the bonds. . .is one that effects the closest possible unity between itself and the parts that it is combining, as can best be accomplished by proportion. . . . For when out of any three numbers. . .the middle is related to the last in the same way as the first is related to the middle, and the middle is related to the first in the same way as the last is to the middle, and when therefore the middle becomes the first and the last, and the last and the first for their part become the middle. . .then they will all be one (*Timaeus* 31c–32a).

Aristotle concluded that 'proportion is the equality of relationships and consists of at least four members' (*Nicomachaean Ethics* 1131a31).

While the module articulated the separate parts of a work, making them commensurable, proportion combined them into a unified whole, creating symmetry and the correct relationships between measurements. Vitruvius defined proportion as 'the harmonizing of the module of the members applied everywhere in the whole work' (III.i.1). The choice of proportions and their application to the parts of a work was not arbitrary. It was governed, to a greater or lesser extent, by logic, though still subject to changing ideas (Vitruvius: IV.i.6–8). The universally accepted model was the human body; hence Vitruvius' statement (III.i.1) that 'no temple can have a rational design without symmetry and proportion' because its parts must be 'in a definite relationship to each other like those of a well-formed person' (*see also* ORDERS, ARCHITECTURAL, §I, 2(i)(c), and VITRUVIUS, fig. 2).

Proportion in architecture was not solely an aesthetic concept; it was also inseparably linked to the practical function of every part of a building (Vitruvius: I.ii.3). The writings of Biton and Philon (*fl* late 3rd century BC–2nd)

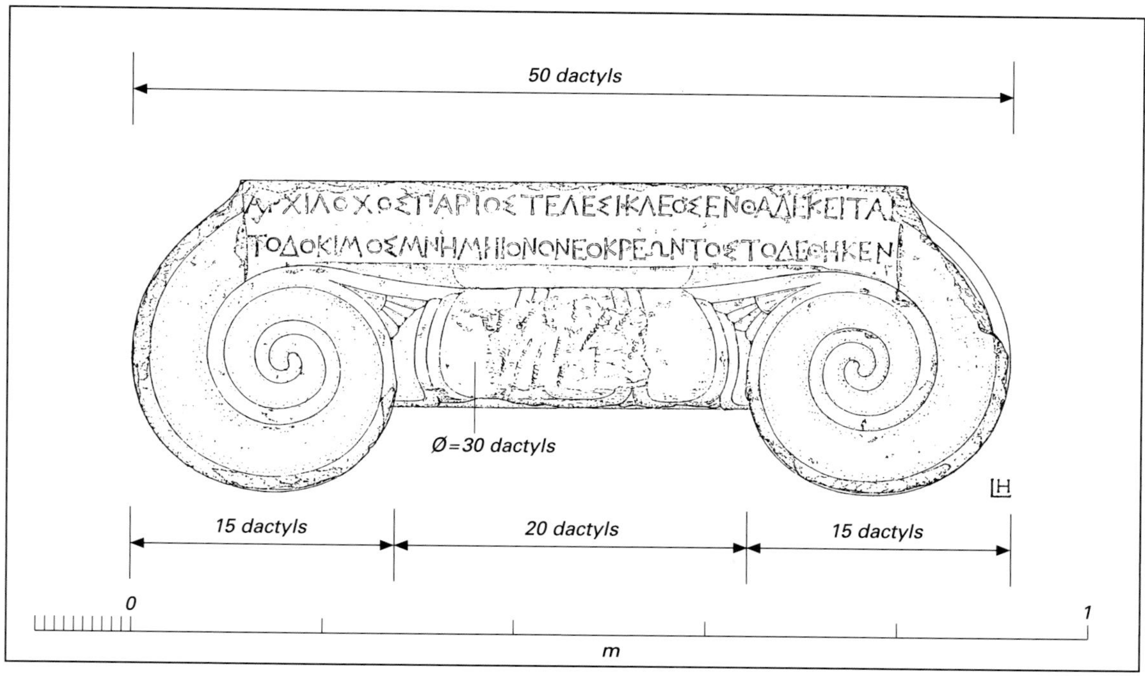

33. Proportional measurements illustrated by the Archilochos Capital from Paros, mid-6th century BC (inscription 4th century BC) (Paros, Archaeological Museum)

show that module and proportion were applied uniformly to all fields of architecture and engineering, including the construction of siege engines in the 3rd century BC. This applied equally to the Roman Imperial period, when temples were constructed on the same theoretical principles as catapults (Vitruvius: I.ii.4). Nonetheless, physical beauty was always regarded as a manifestation of spiritual beauty, as demonstrated by the single Greek concept of the *kalos kagathos* ('beautiful-and-good'). The use of fixed proportions had a further practical benefit, since it facilitated the scaling up or down of existing designs. Thus Biton emphasized that no one need adhere to the actual measurements specified by him, only to the proportions, and Philon explained how to make a pair of rules for scale enlargements (*Mechanics* IV.lv).

The underlying proportions of Greek buildings often cannot be determined simply by comprehensive surveys and analysis of their designs. Some scholars argue that only exact proportional relationships were acceptable, since they alone could unify a building's various parts. However, others argue that they were modified, as in the construction of siege engines (Philon: *Mechanics* IV.li), by rounding measurements up and down.

In mathematics the concept of the 'Golden Section', whereby a line is divided into two parts so that the ratio of the shorter section to the longer is the same as that of the longer section to the whole line (e.g. 1:1.618), was known from the 3rd century BC (Euclid: *Elements* VI.iii; VI.xxx; XIII.i–iv). Its use in ancient art, however, is disputed. Also relevant to proportion was the concept of the mean (arithmetic, geometric, harmonic etc), which was related to the early Greek philosophical doctrine of avoidance of excess and was certainly applied to music.

BIBLIOGRAPHY

Philon of Byzantium: *Mechanics*

Vitruvius: *On Architecture*

F. W. Schlikker: *Hellenistische Vorstellungen von der Schönheit des Bauwerks nach Vitruv* (Berlin, 1940), pp. 34–71

G. Gruben: 'Das archaische Didymaion', *Jb. Dt. Archäol. Inst.*, lxxviii (1963), pp. 78–182

J. J. Coulton: 'Towards Understanding Greek Temple Design', *Annu. Brit. Sch. Athens*, lxx (1975), pp. 59–99

L. Haselberger: 'Bericht über die Arbeit am jüngeren Apollontempel von Didyma', *Istan. Mitt.*, xxxiii (1983), pp. 90–123

Bauplanung und Bautheorie der Antike (1984), iv of *Diskussionen zur archäologischen Bauforschung* (Berlin), pp. 13–23, 33–8, 137–45, 159–66

W. Koenigs: *Masse und Proportionen in der griechischen Baukunst* (in preparation)

LOTHAR HASELBERGER

(vi) Refinements. The details later termed 'refinements' were observed on the Parthenon at Athens in the 19th century. One of the most remarkable and original features of ancient Greek architecture, the use of refinements essentially entailed the non-observance of strict geometric rules, so that on certain buildings apparently straight lines have a slight curvature, and verticals an imperceptibly oblique set (see fig. 34). Both the existence of these architectural features and the conclusion that they were deliberately designed have been questioned, the observed discrepancies being simply attributed to subsequent movement of the building, earthquakes or even the clumsiness of the builders. Numerous examinations using highly accurate measurements have, however, shown that these anomalies were intentional and have led to a better understanding of the methods used for calculating them.

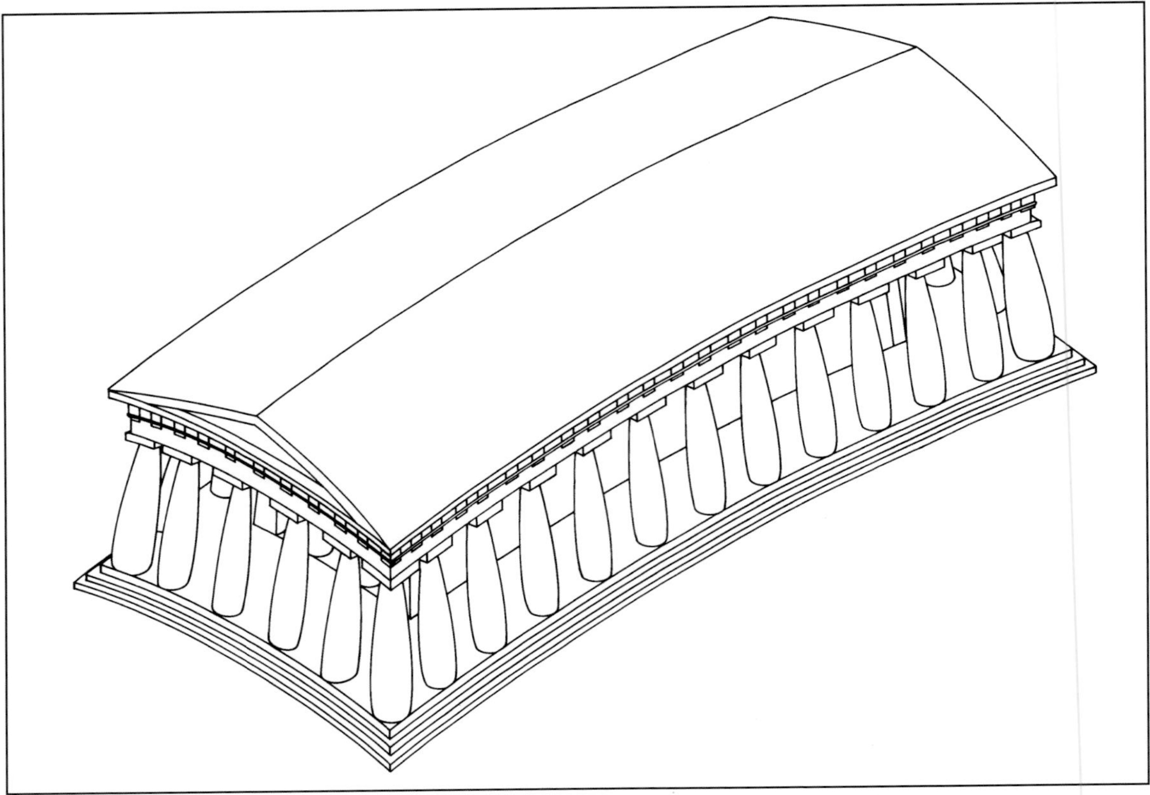

34. Refinements shown in exaggerated form on a Doric temple

The reasons for the use of refinements are, however, still disputed. All known refinements are clearly demonstrated on a single building, the Parthenon. If one considers the whole of ancient Greek architecture, however, they are far from universal, and most buildings appear either not to have had any, or only partial application of one type (e.g. curvature of the long sides or the short sides only). Overall, the existence of refinements appears to express a general rejection of inflexibility, of the absolutely uniform line and of all that might appear mechanical. Rather than representing optical corrections, they can be seen as stylistic effects, intended to breathe life and a sensual dimension into architecture.

The most common refinement is a slight, regular convexity in the horizontal lines of the building. The temple platform and stylobate formed a bulging curve, sometimes with a differential of as much as 110 mm, sometimes only 20–40 mm, and this might be repeated on the entablature and pediment. It was extremely expensive, since it meant that standard blocks of stone could not be used. Examples of this refinement occur as early as the 6th century BC on the Temple of Apollo at Corinth, then at the Archaic Temple of Athena on the Athenian Acropolis (*c.* 515 BC), the second Temple of Aphaia at Aigina (*c.* 500–*c.* 490 BC) and the unfinished predecessor of the Parthenon. Later examples include the Parthenon (447–432 BC; see fig. 23 above) and the Temple of Hephaistos (*c.* 449 BC) at Athens, the 'Temple of Poseidon' at Paestum, and later the Temple of Athena at Priene, the Temple of Apollo at Didyma and the Temple of Zeus at Labraunda. It occurred more rarely on secular buildings, though examples include stoas at Corinth, Oropos and Thasos, the Propylaia on the Athenian Acropolis and the Treasury of the Athenians at Delphi. Curvature applied to horizontal lines seems to have been particularly popular in the 5th century BC–4th, but it is also found on such Roman buildings as the Library of Celsius at Ephesos (2nd century AD) and on others at Rome itself. Vitruvius' discussion of this refinement as being a normal contemporary (i.e. 1st-century AD) building process (*On Architecture* III.iv.5–v.8) should not, therefore, be interpreted as a conservative adherence to outdated practices.

Studies of the incomplete temple at Segesta confirm that horizontal curvature may have been achieved empirically, without complex mathematical calculations. A piece of string was stretched from end to end of the face of the stylobate, and the downward curve, which was almost parabolic, was transferred into its mirror image by measuring upwards from a level horizontal axis. Marks were made at regular intervals, enabling the construction of a slope with a decreasing gradient towards the centre of the stylobate. Any irregularities in this can be explained as errors in the levelling process. The resulting curvature could have had both practical and aesthetic benefits. It would allow rainwater to run off the platform, and it would correct the optical illusion that makes straight parallel lines in perspective appear to curve inwards towards each other.

ENTASIS, an outward swelling of the vertical profile of column shafts, is generally considered a refinement of the same type as horizontal curvature. It may have been achieved in several ways, for example by stretching a length of string along the axis of the column as drawn on a wall of the building and adding a curve to this, which was then transferred to the column. Entasis was initially a characteristic feature of the 6th-century BC Doric temples of South Italy; it later occurred on both Doric and Ionic buildings, such as the second Temple of Aphaia on Aigina and the Propylaia on the Athenian Acropolis respectively. It cannot have been used simply to avoid the illusion of a straight-sided column shaft sagging and is better explained as a stylistic device to give the columns the appearance of straining under the weight of the entablature.

In addition to those involving curvature, other refinements were used. The axis of column shafts was sometimes tilted towards the centre of the building by an average maximum of 70 mm from the vertical. The corner columns were thus tilted towards the building's diagonal axis, and in the case of the Parthenon were made over 40 mm thicker than standard flank columns, in order not to appear spindly (Vitruvius: III.iii.11). The walls of the cella and porches were made thinner towards the top, with the outer side leaning inwards, and the doorjambs were tapered. The appearance of compactness and stability was thus enhanced. The upper sections could also be set back, adding to this impression, though Vitruvius preferred the entablature to slope outwards (III.v.13), avoiding the illusion caused when rainwater ran off that it was slipping into the building.

BIBLIOGRAPHY

W. H. Goodyear: *Greek Refinements: Studies in Temperamental Architecture* (New Haven, 1912)

G. P. Stevens: 'Concerning the Curvature of the Steps of the Parthenon', *Amer. J. Archaeol.*, xxxviii (1934), pp. 533–42

——: 'The Curves of the North Stylobate of the Parthenon', *Hesperia*, xii (1943), pp. 135–43

A. W. Lawrence: *Greek Architecture*, Pelican Hist. A. (Harmondsworth, 1957, rev. 4/1983, with additions by R. A. Tomlinson), pp. 222–7

D. Mertens: 'Zur Entstehung der Entasis griechischer Säulen', *Bathron: Festschrift H. Drerup* (Saarbrücken, 1988), pp. 307–18

MARIE-CHRISTINE HELLMANN

(vii) Symbolism. Though other cultures have similar concepts, it was the Greeks who first used the term 'symbol' (*symbolon*) to express the concept that one thing may be a token or sign, often secret or known only to a few, of something else. For them a *symbolon* might be intentional, as when a carved lion was described as a symbol of strength, or it might simply announce by association, as when clouds were described as symbols of rain. In all cases what makes something a symbol is that it is understood by a particular group or community to stand for or represent something else.

An early example of symbolism in Greek architecture is the use of the hundred-foot measure in the plans of *hekatompedon* or 'hundred-foot' temples from the 8th century BC onwards (*see also* §1(i)(a) above). This number made the building perfect, just as a perfect sacrifice consisted of 100 oxen (hecatomb). At a different level, the peripteral colonnades of early stone temples, unparalleled in other cultures, were probably designed, with their rigid geometry and uniformity of shape, to represent the properties required in the military formation of the phalanx. Such architectural symbolism is made explicit in Iphigeneia's comment in Euripides' *Iphigeneia in Tauris* (l. 57), that sons are 'the columns of a house', and underlies the use of male figures (*see also* ATLANTID) alternating with Doric columns in the Temple of Olympian Zeus (Olympieion) at Akragas (Agrigento), built to celebrate the defeat of the Carthaginians in the Battle of Himera in 480 BC (for illustration *see* AKRAGAS). These heroic nudes commemorate the column-like virtues of the Agrigentine warriors. Female figures (caryatids) were similarly substituted for columns in treasuries at Delphi and in the Athenian Erechtheion (421–405 BC; *see* CARYATID, fig. 1), where the correspondence between the folds of their dresses and the flutes of the adjoining columns ensures that women and columns harmonize.

Since the temple at Akragas was constructed in the Doric order and the Delphi treasuries and the Erechtheion in the Ionic order, it appears that by the Classical period these two orders were felt to embody male and female qualities respectively (*see also* ORDERS, ARCHITECTURAL, §I, 2(i)(c)). The surrender of the wealthy Ionians to the Persians around 500 BC and the opposition in the Peloponnesian War of 431–404 BC between the reputedly tough Dorian Spartans and the correspondingly refined Athenians, who were culturally related to the Ionians, encouraged the view, found in such writers as Thucydides, that Greek culture was dominated by two streams: the Dorian was simple, strong and manly; the Ionian was rich, refined and feminine. Pericles claimed that the Athenians possessed both qualities, and the combination of both Doric and Ionic orders in the Parthenon (447–432 BC) would have been seen to symbolize this. Recognition of this symbolic difference led to the formulation of the theory, recorded by Vitruvius but almost certainly developed in the late 5th century BC, that the Doric column was derived from the form of the naked male body and the Ionic from the clothed female body. If Doric was associated with men, whose qualities were most apparent out of doors, and Ionic with women, whose virtues were associated with interiors, it would also explain why, in the Propylaia (438–432 BC) on the Athenian Acropolis, for example, the Doric order is found outside and Ionic inside the building.

The use of such terms as 'head' (*kephale*) for the highest part of the column, 'step' (*basis*) for the lowest and 'distention' (*entasis*), as of the abdomen, for the swelling of the middle of the shaft shows how normal it was for the Greeks, unlike previous communities in Egypt, Mesopotamia or Crete, to think of the column as manlike. The Greeks had long worshipped different gods in the form of pillars, as evidenced by Dark Age aniconic statues, and it is possible that the single central column of the Temple of Apollo at Bassai (429–*c.* 400 BC; see fig. 24 above) also represented the divinity. The acanthus leaf decoration that appears on the capital of that column for the first time, and which becomes typical of the similar capitals later categorized as the Corinthian order, is almost certainly an allusion to Apollo as god of the seasons and of regeneration. The acanthus, with its spiny exterior containing milky juices, suggested recovery and resurrection. Similar reasons account for the frequent use, shortly afterwards, of Corinthian capitals at Epidauros, site of the Sanctuary of Asklepios, god of health.

The symbolism implied in the correspondence between the first peripteral temples and a protective military formation, and the association of the Corinthian capital with a symbolically protective plant, both developed out of relatively primitive fears as Greece emerged from poverty and illiteracy. With Alexander the Great's conquests, Greek culture as a whole entered a phase of wealthy urbanism and external peace, and the main anxieties now related to the internal stability of the social order. Planned cities such as Alexandria came to stand for the general coherence of Greek civilization, and the varied forms of architecture, such as the Doric, Ionic and Corinthian orders, were increasingly seen as giving visual expression to the categories on which people relied for ordering their lives. The differences between architectural forms could be related to other spheres of life: to regional cultural values, to social classes or to contrasts in life-styles. It was to help people to organize their lives using such categories that the different forms were variously combined in stoas, such as that of Attalos at Athens, and gymnasia, such as that at Miletos. Collectively and individually the buildings of the Hellenistic world symbolized the concerns of their users.

BIBLIOGRAPHY

Vitruvius: *On Architecture*

W. Andrae: *Die ionische Saüle: Bauform oder Symbol* (Berlin, 1933)

V. Scully: *The Earth, the Temple and the Gods* (New Haven, 1962, rev. 3/1979)

A. Schmidt-Colinet: *Antike Stützfiguren* (Cologne, 1977)

J. Rykwert: *The Necessity of Artifice* (Cambridge, 1980), pp. 33–43

G. Hersey: *The Lost Meaning of Classical Architecture* (Cambridge, MA, and London, 1988)

J. Onians: *Bearers of Meaning: The Classical Orders in Antiquity, the Middle Ages and the Renaissance* (Princeton, 1988)

JOHN ONIANS

III. Planning.

1. Sanctuaries. 2. Towns.

1. SANCTUARIES. These were originally simply areas set aside and recognized as the property of a particular deity. From the Archaic period onwards, however, many sanctuaries became the focus for major building projects, and these now form collectively by far the most important ancient Greek sites in terms of their architectural remains (*see also* SANCTUARY, §1).

(i) Location. (ii) Organization. (iii) Landscaping.

(i) Location. Sanctuaries could be situated either within a city boundary or in country districts. There are no obvious rules for the selection of particular localities, and various factors may be postulated. Several important sanctuaries are in places that appear to have been occupied in the Late Bronze Age, and in some instances these were already sacred sites, raising the question of continuity of worship through the Dark Age. This may have been the case in the important but comparatively remote sanctuaries at Delos and Delphi. However, the material evidence for such continuity is never strong, and any connection may be nothing more than the sense of atmosphere that resulted

35. Sanctuary at Akragas, view of the temple ridge

from the remains of earlier occupation. In other instances there may have been a change of function: in Bronze Age communities the focus of society was the ruler, and his palace was the architectural expression of this, often sited on a fortified hilltop. After the disintegration of Late Bronze Age society, the gods and the sites allocated to them emerged as the corresponding focus. (For a discussion of Minoan palaces as cult centres, *see* MINOAN, §II, 3.) Fortified sites might still defend the later community: an obvious example is the Sanctuary of Athena on the Athenian Acropolis. Elsewhere, the choice of site derived from natural features: springs in particular attracted religious usage. Sanctuaries are frequently sited in prominent places, such as the Acropolis at Athens (see fig. 6 above) or the long ridge crowned with a succession of temples at AKRAGAS (see fig. 35). Some important sanctuaries, however (e.g. those of Hera at Samos and Artemis at Ephesos), are in low-lying, marshy areas, while others are on the slopes of hills rather than the summits (e.g. that of Demeter at Corinth).

The extent of a sanctuary depended on the importance of its cult. Where sanctuaries were recognized as important throughout the Greek world, the area allocated to the gods was substantial (for example at Delphi, Delos and Olympia). The patron deity of a city would receive a major sanctuary, usually within the city itself, as at Athens, but at times outside (e.g. at Samos and Didyma). Lesser deities naturally had less prominent sanctuaries: some were restricted to a few devotees or were even small private places of worship.

(ii) Organization. The arrangements within each sanctuary varied according to usage, the numbers of worshippers

and the particular character of the cult. Sanctuaries were arranged primarily to accommodate the festivals of the resident deity. These normally occurred only once a year, though they might last for several days, and some particularly important festivals took place at four-yearly intervals. Thus a major sanctuary had to be able to receive large numbers of worshippers.

The climax of the festival was the offering of sacrifices. These were normally animals, brought to the sanctuary and ritually slaughtered, token parts of the animal being burnt on the altar as the god's portion. Consequently, the altar itself was always the central feature and marked the most sacred area. The worshippers assembled round it to watch the sacrifices, and there was thus generally no need for an enclosed, roofed building for worship. Thus the planning of sanctuaries is in principle external rather than internal, open rather than closed off, except in the case of mystery cults, which required a process of initiation, for example the cult of Demeter and Kore at Eleusis.

It was usual to mark off the sanctuary as the property of the god, but it was not necessary to enclose it within a wall, and simple marker stones were often used. Minor sanctuaries were often informally accessible from the street. Major festivals frequently included a formal procession to the sanctuary, and for this a particular street was designated as a 'sacred way'. The procession at Athens for the festival of Athena gathered at the Sacred Gate and made its way along the Sacred Way through the Agora up to the Acropolis. Similarly, the worship of Eleusinian Demeter required a procession from Athens to Eleusis, and the festival of Asklepios at Epidauros began with a procession to the rural sanctuary some 10 km distant. The entrance to the sanctuary might, therefore, be marked by a gateway or PROPYLON, which was as much symbolic as functional. The propylon to the Athenian Acropolis replaced a military gate and had doors that could be bolted. At Epidauros, on the other hand, the propylon had no doors and served a purely ritual function. The processions included sacrificial animals and thus eventually proceeded to the altar (*see* ALTAR, §I, 3). This could take many forms, ranging from a simple podium or even, as at Olympia, a pile of accumulated ashes to elaborate architectural structures.

The temple was the house of the god and as such provided shelter for the cult image. It was usually a prestigious building, intended to demonstrate both the piety and the wealth of the sanctuary authorities, and temples soon became the dominant, most splendid structures in most Greek sanctuaries. The temple's position within the sanctuary varied. In smaller sanctuaries it tended to be placed at one end, allowing a space in front for the altar and worshippers. The temple was, however, usually free-standing within the sanctuary and could thus be viewed from all directions. Some temples may have been placed to achieve a three-quarter view from the main approach. Most faced east towards the point at which the sun rose on the day of festival and sacrifice, so that the exact orientation of temples varied according to the local skyline and the time of the festival (and its position within the variable system of the Greek calendar). Exceptions to the eastwards alignment include the north-facing Temple of Apollo at Bassai (429–*c.* 400 BC) and the west-facing Temple of Artemis at Ephesos (*c.* 560–*c.* 460 BC). Ideally the door gave a direct view from the cult statue inside to the altar. Again there were exceptions: the altar of Athena on the Athenian Acropolis was in front of the position occupied by her original temple, but remained unchanged even when the final version of that temple was destroyed, and her cult image moved to a new building on the adjacent site; neither this (the Erechtheion) nor the Parthenon faced the altar. Where possible the approach from the sanctuary entrance was to the front of the temple, though the easiest access to the Athenian Acropolis was from the west, and all the temples, therefore, turn their backs on the sacred approach.

Other buildings served ancillary functions. Some provided shelter for worshippers and those dedicatory gifts that were not kept in the temple itself. Extended colonnades (*see* STOA) were normal for this and might be placed on the sanctuary boundary, facing inwards. Other buildings provided accommodation for privileged persons (e.g. priests, magistrates) to consume the sacrificial meat in formal dining-rooms (*hestiatoria*; examples at Perachora, Epidauros and Delos); these are often erroneously described as 'priests' houses'. Such buildings might be located in a secondary area of the sanctuary, away from the principal temple, as at Perachora and on the Athenian Acropolis, where it has been suggested that the north-west wing of the Propylaia was arranged for this purpose (see J. Travlos: *Pictorial Dictionary of Ancient Athens*, London, 1971, p. 482). Ordinary worshippers presumably ate their share of the meat alfresco.

Specialized cults required special buildings. There is no discernible regular plan for the sanctuaries of oracular cults, which varied considerably in their practice. Usually the plan of the temple was modified in some way, as at Delphi and probably Didyma, though the officials operating the oracle at Didyma also had a separate office. The healing cult of Asklepios required dormitories for the sick. This type of building (*abaton*) resembles the stoa, though *abata* are always close to the heart of the sanctuary. The initiatory cults needed enclosed buildings for the ritual of admission (e.g. at Eleusis and SAMOTHRACE), though these vary considerably both in form and in placing within the sanctuary.

Most sanctuaries required water supplies, which might receive architectural embellishment in the form of a fountain house, not necessarily within the sanctuary itself. All sanctuaries were adorned with free-standing statues and other monuments, which tended to be grouped around altar, temple and sacred way.

Thus the internal planning of sanctuaries varied considerably. With the development of planned cities in the Hellenistic period, the area set aside for a sanctuary often became more regular, giving rise to rectangular precincts bordered by continuous stoas, with the temple towards one end and the altar axially aligned in front of it (e.g. the Sanctuary of Artemis Leukophryene at Magnesia on the Maeander; 2nd century BC). Such sanctuaries are uncommon, though the loss of such important Hellenistic cities as Antioch and Alexandria doubtless contributes to this. Their influence can be seen, however, in the developed sanctuary arrangements of Roman architecture (*see* ROME, ANCIENT, §III, 1).

BIBLIOGRAPHY

Pausanias: *Guide to Greece*

R. D. Martienssen: *The Idea of Space in Greek Architecture* (Johannesburg, 1956, rev. 2/1964)

H. Berve, G. Gruben and M. Hirmer: *Griechische Tempel und Heiligtümer* (Munich, 1961); Eng. trans. as *Greek Temples, Theaters and Shrines* (New York, 1963)

H. F. Mussche, ed.: *Greek Architecture* (1963), ii/1 of *Monumenta Graeca et Romana* (Leiden, 1963–)

B. Bergquist: *The Archaic Greek Temenos* (Lund, 1967)

E. Melas, ed.: *Temples and Sanctuaries in Ancient Greece* (London, 1973)

R. A. Tomlinson: *Greek Sanctuaries* (London, 1976)

R. A. TOMLINSON

(iii) Landscaping. Whatever system (if any) was used for the internal planning of a sanctuary, individual constructions or an entire sanctuary complex, urban or rural, often required alteration of the terrain. Foundations in general offset the instability or irregularity of sacred terrain; but construction on uneven surfaces sometimes made it necessary to cut into bedrock (e.g. the Sanctuary of Asklepios, Corinth), build terraces (e.g. the Temple of Apollo, Delphi; Temple of Zeus, Stratos) or platforms (e.g. the later Temple of Artemis, Ephesos; Temple of Athena, Smyrna) and lay deep stone substructures (e.g. the earlier shrine on the site of the Parthenon on the Athenian Acropolis). In gently sloping areas, sanctuaries could be constructed on one or more large terraces (e.g. the Sanctuary of Asklepios, Kos); but sanctuaries on steep mountainsides required a series of smaller terraces, as at Delphi. Small terraces or outworks could also support single buildings in rocky locations (e.g. the Temple of Athena Nike on the Athenian Acropolis; the Athenian Treasury, Delphi). Larger terraces provided unity as much as stability for groups of buildings (e.g. the treasuries at Olympia). Different levels were linked by stairs or inclined paths, as at Delphi. Exigencies of the terrain may also have produced unusual temple orientation, as perhaps at the Temple of Apollo at Bassai, which is aligned north–south. The location of particular sacred spots apparently sometimes necessitated anomalous buildings, for example the Erechtheion on the Athenian Acropolis.

Temples were not the only large, important structures at sanctuaries. Long narrow stoas required careful siting and extra support in hilly terrain, as on the acropolis at Lindos (see fig. 27 above). Their back walls, however, could provide support for terraces, either above (e.g. the South Stoa, Sanctuary of Hera, Argos) or below (e.g. the Stoa of Apollo Maleatas, Epidauros). The seating in stadia and theatres also required structural support. The siting of a theatre could conform to a convenient hillside, minimally altering the landscape, as at Epidauros. On flat terrain, however, walls were needed, as at Dodona. Stadia could be built with one long side cut into a hillside, as at Delphi, supported by earth in a flat area, as at Olympia (*see* STADIUM, fig. 1), or at right angles to a slope, making use of both the natural hillside and earth fill, as at Nemea.

Simple rural shrines and sanctuaries, which might only contain trees, a rough altar and dedications overseen by a caretaker (Dio Chrysostom: *Orationes* i.52–4), required little alteration of the landscape. They were, nevertheless, influenced by physical features. Mountain ranges forming political boundaries, for instance, dictated the siting of border shrines. Other shrines, for instance those on mountain-tops or at springs, may reflect a particular aspect of the environment controlled by the patron deity. For instance, it was appropriate to worship Zeus the rain-giver on a mountain-top. Sanctuaries where springs were important range from the comparatively simple (e.g. the grove and spring of Apollo near Pharai in Messenia; Pausanias: IV.xxxi.1) to the extremely complex (e.g. the Hellenistic oracle of Apollo at Didyma). The realistic description of a spring and sanctuary of the nymphs of Ithaka (*Odyssey* XVII.205–11) shows how a simple rural shrine might integrate everyday practicality with worship.

The Greeks commonly used trees and bushes at shrines, probably to enhance an atmosphere of age, provide shade and demarcate sacred territory. No doubt they also intensified the sacredness of shrines founded in observation of some quality of nature. Few sites have, however, yielded any archaeological evidence for plantings. The best example is the Temple of Hephaistos at Athens; others include the Temple of Zeus at Nemea and traces of planting for a single tree at Dodona. The abbreviated, sometimes symbolic depiction of landscape in ancient Greek art is usually unhelpful, though written evidence shows that sacred groves were common at urban, suburban and rural shrines.

Every major deity possessed at least one sanctuary where there were trees, and numerous heroes and heroines had trees at their shrines. Particular species were not exclusive to one deity or hero (thus groves of wild olives

36. Planting pits on the south side of the Temple of Hephaistos, Athens, ?from early 3rd century BC

were sacred to Zeus, Poseidon and Apollo), while groves of a single deity could have different kinds of trees, so that not only laurels but also cypresses (Daphne in Syria) and myrtles (Delphi) are recorded in groves of Apollo. Some sacred groves were said to have been planted in legendary or mythical times; in other instances the deliberate planting of trees at sanctuaries in the recent historic past was recorded. Citizens were honoured for their donation and maintenance of trees, and laws against grazing and woodcutting at shrines were designed to keep groves intact. Many sanctuaries, therefore, must have had pleasant, parklike grounds (e.g. Olympia, see Pindar: *Olympian Odes* iii.17–24; Patrai, see Pausanias: VII.xxi.11). Descriptions of ancient Athens provide a good indication of how trees were used in a city: they grew, for instance, in the Agora (Plutarch: *Kimon* xiii.8; not necessarily sacred) and at various suburban shrines (e.g. Kolonos Hippios, see Pausanias: I.xxx.4; Sophocles: *Oedipus at Colonus*) and gymnasia (e.g. Plato's Academy, see Plutarch: *Kimon* xiii.8, *Sulla* xii.3). An olive tree on the Acropolis, burnt by the Persians, apparently miraculously recovered (Herodotus: *Histories* VIII.lv). Around the Temple of Hephaistos planting pits and terracotta pots for seedlings have been found, evincing an extensive planting programme (see fig. 36).

BIBLIOGRAPHY

Pausanias: *Guide to Greece*

C. A. Doxiadis: *Raumordnung im griechischen Städtebau* (Heidelberg, 1937); Eng. trans. as *Architectural Space in Ancient Greece* (Cambridge, MA, 1972)

D. B. Thompson: 'The Garden of Hephaistos', *Hesperia*, vi (1937), pp. 396–425

A. Philippson: *Die griechischen Landschaften* (Frankfurt am Main, 1950–59)

R. Stillwell: 'The Siting of Classical Greek Temples', *J. Soc. Archit. Hist.*, xiii (1954), pp. 3–8

S. I. Dakaris: 'To hierón tis Dodonis' [The sanctuary at Dodona], *Archaiol. Deltion*, xvi (1960), pp. 4–40

V. J. Scully: *The Earth, the Temple and the Gods* (New Haven, 1962, rev. 3/1979)

M. K. Langdon: 'A Sanctuary of Zeus on Mount Hymettos', *Hesperia*, suppl. xvi (1976)

D. Birge: *Sacred Groves in the Ancient Greek World* (diss., Berkeley, U. CA, 1982)

R. Osborne: *Classical Landscape with Figures: The Ancient Greek City and its Countryside* (London, 1987)

DARICE BIRGE

2. Towns.

(i) Early urban development. Many of the towns in mainland Greece developed from small settlements of the Geometric period (*c*. 900–*c*. 700 BC). These included widely scattered groups of farmsteads, as at Athens and Argos, as well as densely packed clusters of small houses. The plans of these settlements were not based on right angles but took shape in accordance with the natural terrain, so that they were characterized by crooked alleys, irregular terraces and squares and small houses of varied design.

Of decisive importance in the development of more sophisticated urban planning was the foundation of numerous Greek colonies from the 8th century BC onwards at sites on almost all Mediterranean coasts. These colonies were entirely new foundations, and they thus had to have a more imposing form that would maintain their identities and independence amid alien peoples. For example, Megara Hyblaea in Sicily was laid out in the 8th century BC with parallel streets. The marking out was so inaccurate, however, that the lengths of the blocks (*insulae*) varied considerably. All the early colonial strip cities had similar plans, with long rows of houses ranged along relatively narrow streets and hardly any transverse streets. The town walls were irregular and followed the most appropriate line of defence. Within the walls a fairly large site was reserved for sanctuaries, and an open space in the residential area formed the agora (market place), which was lined by public buildings. The strip layout was still usual in the Archaic period, though it was improved by the increased use of transverse streets.

In mainland Greece also new towns were constantly being founded. These generally developed from a *synoikismos* ('settling together'), when the inhabitants of several small villages jointly founded a town so that they could pursue a more organized way of life. The first generation of settlers must have supported extensive building programmes, but by the 6th century BC ordinary citizens throughout Greece became more prosperous, and the construction of towns expanded still further. Many had populations of more than 10,000, which necessitated major public works, notably the installation of piped water supplies, as at Athens and on Samos. Agoras began to develop into civic centres and were provided with public buildings (*see* §II, 1(i)(b) above).

(ii) The science of urban planning. Scientific urban planning developed at the beginning of the 5th century BC and was connected with political changes following the democratic reforms of Kleisthenes in 508/7 BC. Among the greatest building projects after the Persian Wars (490–479 BC) were the rebuilding of Miletos and the laying out of the port of Peiraeus. The new MILETOS may have been the first regularly planned city with a dense grid of streets. The width of these streets varied, with some genuine ceremonial ways 40 m wide. Large open spaces at the centre of the city were reserved for public buildings. House plots were of uniform size and united to form relatively small *insulae* (*see* INSULA).

The layout of Peiraeus (*see* PEIRAEUS, §1) was undoubtedly determined by the famous town planner HIPPODAMOS, who came from Miletos. It too was based on a closely knit, differentiated street system, and house plots and *insulae* were relatively small. The most important innovation, probably attributable to Hippodamos, was the introduction of standard housing units. These terraced houses, which were partly two-storey, were divided into three distinct areas to suit the needs of a large family and reflected the concept of the equality of all citizens in a democratic state. The agora in Peiraeus was called the 'Hippodamic Agora' (Suidas: *Hippodameia*). Its location and form are uncertain. Ancient sources suggest, however, that Hippodamos divided the town into separate districts according to function, as in modern urban planning. Characteristically, the planned Greek city employed an orthogonal grid centred on the agora, as at Dura Europos in Mesopotamia, founded *c*. 300 BC by Hellenistic Greeks (see fig. 37).

The port of Rhodes, laid out in 408/7 BC (*see* RHODES, §3), is the only Classical metropolis that has been systematically studied. It shows that 'building according to the

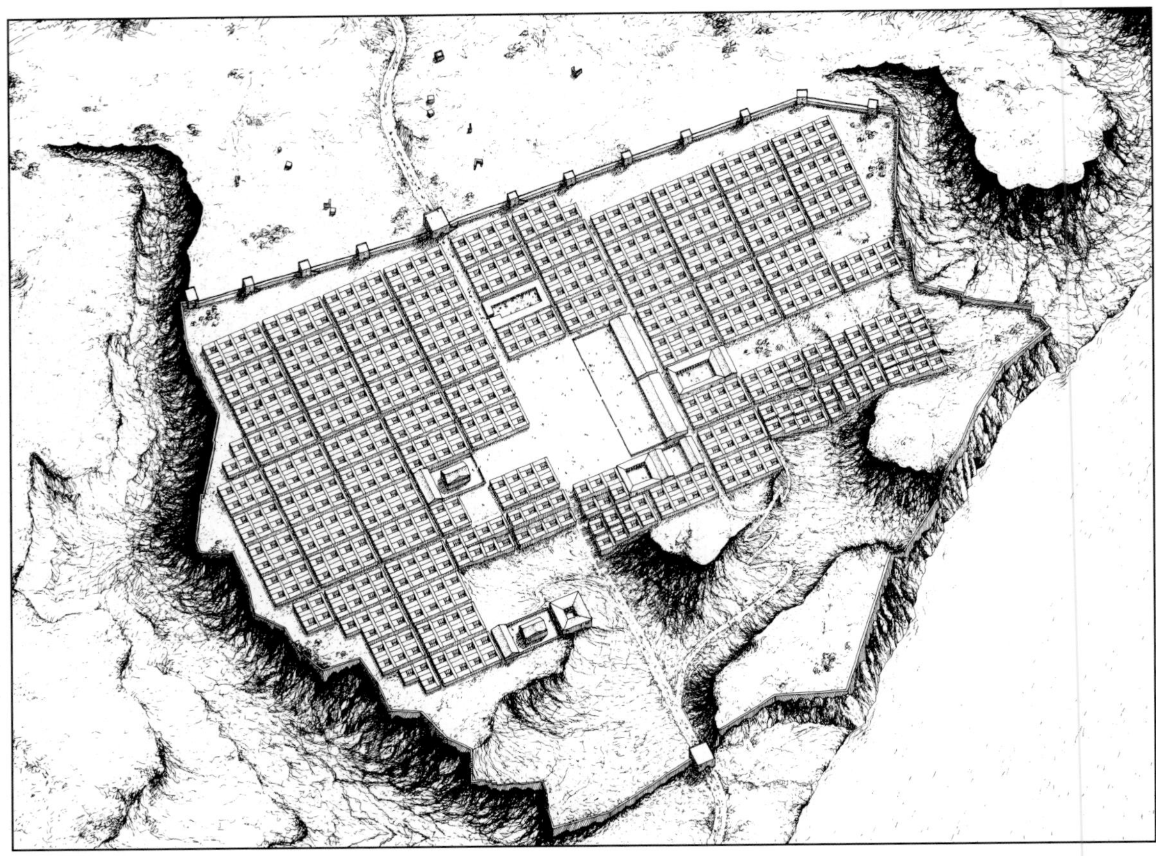

37. Dura Europos, plan of the city *c.* 300 BC; reconstruction drawing

Hippodamic method' (Aristotle: *Politics* IV.1330b24) meant using a consistent, close-knit street grid involving a hierarchy of rectangular blocks, with proportions determined by simple Pythagorean ratios. The basic unit was a standard house plot, of which the size and shape depended on the land available and the house type involved. Areas known vary from 207 sq. m at Priene (*see* PRIENE, §1(i)) to about 400 sq. m at Rhodes. Most plots were of about 250 sq. m. They were linked together in groups of three (Rhodes), six (Miletos), eight (Peiraeus, Priene, Dura Europos) and, exceptionally, sixteen houses (Abdera), to form *insulae.* Individual *insulae* were surrounded by relatively narrow residential streets, but at Rhodes, for example, wider streets were used to group the blocks into residential districts of equal size. Such a division, involving perhaps more than a thousand people, was of course feasible only in large cities.

Besides Hippodamian foundations there were also new settlements based on a development of the strip city scheme, which did not depend on carefully proportioned rectangular plots. These include Olynthos, founded in 432 BC and destroyed in 348 BC (*see* OLYNTHOS, §1), where *pastas*-type houses stood on almost square plots (360 sq. m) joined together in rows to form *insulae* of various lengths (*see also* §II, 1(i)(c) above). As in the Archaic strip cities, two rows of houses backed on to each other, giving an interval of 30–40 m between streets. Between the backs of the houses ran a narrow passage (0.8 m to 1.2 m wide) that served for drainage and light. At another Late Classical strip city, Kassope in Epeiros, the houses were again joined together to form long *insulae.* The rigid grid of the residential area did not, however, extend to the agora, situated on the edge of the city, and the public buildings around it. The prytaneion, market building and hall are aligned with the streets, but the bouleuterion (council house) and the great altars are completely off axis, presumably to counteract the geometric order.

From the mid-5th century BC onwards, newly founded cities nearly always had a precise southerly orientation to exploit sunlight, as advocated by Xenophon (*Memorabilia* III.viii.8–10). The high summer sun was excluded from the colonnaded areas of the houses (both *prostas* and *pastas* types), while the oblique winter sun penetrated deep into them, even warming rooms behind. Even so, the main orientation of Dura Europos was instead designed to exploit cooling breezes.

In the newly founded Classical cities the central sanctuary was erected on a dominant site (*see also* §1 above), as shown by the Temple of Athena at Priene, which stood on a high, specially reserved terrace in the middle of the residential city, near the agora. Similar schemes apparently existed at Rhodes and Olynthos. Hippodamos seems to have attached great importance to sanctuaries (Aristotle: *Politics* II.1267b33–5) and wanted to designate a third of the area of any city as 'sacred land'. Many cities also developed special ceremonial avenues or 'sacred ways', which were used in annual processions to important sanctuaries, though almost all were built over in Hellenistic times and reduced to narrow streets.

The most important act during the foundation of any new colonial city was probably the allocation of equal plots of agricultural land to the settlers. In addition, every family was presumably also allocated a plot for a garden. These were in the lowest and dampest areas of the city. Similarly, plots in the cemeteries flanking the main streets outside the city were probably also distributed among the citizens when the city was founded.

The newly founded Classical cities were based on strict geometric principles. In Hellenistic times, however, a more romantic approach to urban planning developed, employing parks, groups of trees and fountains. Again, whereas earlier domestic architecture had been modest, the elaborate architecture of royal palaces now became a prominent feature of many city centres.

BIBLIOGRAPHY

R. E. Wycherley: *How the Greeks Built Cities* (London, 1949, 3/1969)
R. Martin: *L'Urbanisme de la Grèce antique* (Paris, 1956, rev. 2/1974)
E. Greco and M. Torelli: *Storia dell'urbanistica: Il mondo greco* (Rome, 1983)
W. Hoepfner and E. L. Schwander: *Haus und Stadt im klassischen Griechenland* (Munich, 1986, 2/1993)

WOLFRAM HOEPFNER

IV. Monumental sculpture.

The Greeks produced sculpture in many different materials for display or use in various contexts. This article focuses mainly on the development of large-scale sculpture, while smaller-scale or mass-produced works, such as bronze statuettes or terracotta figurines, are discussed elsewhere (*see* §§VIII, 2(i) and IX, 2 below).

1. Overview. 2. Historical survey. 3. Theory and criticism. 4. Collections, museums and exhibitions.

1. OVERVIEW. Together with painting, monumental sculpture, particularly free-standing statues and prestigious architectural ensembles, was associated with the most accomplished Greek artists and was the medium in which new techniques and aesthetic trends first became manifest. While hardly any original ancient Greek paintings survive, however, numerous datable and (if not always securely) attributable sculptures are known, and the evidence they provide can be compared with descriptions by ancient writers. Particularly important early sources, constantly referred to in the survey that follows, are the works of the Roman writer Pliny (*see* PLINY, (1)) and the Greek traveller and geographer PAUSANIAS. Most large-scale Greek sculptures come from public and religious contexts—sanctuaries, agoras, cemeteries. Important categories include the gravestones of the Archaic period (*c.* 700–*c.* 500/480 BC) and the contemporary KORE and KOUROS statue types; the architectural sculptures associated with the great marble temples of the Archaic and Classical (*c.* 525/480–323 BC) periods; and the statues dedicated in sanctuaries.

In the 2nd and 1st centuries BC, as the Romans conquered the ancient Greek world, they looted the finest works of art, which often found their way to the private collections of wealthy individuals in Italy. The most famous statues of the Classical period, many of which were cast in bronze, were reproduced by Roman copyists in marble. Except for the chance survival of a few important works, such as the RIACE BRONZES or ARTEMISION BRONZES, the original bronzes—more easily destroyed than marble—are lost. It was Roman marble copies in papal and other collections, rather than authentic Greek sculptures, that inspired interest in ancient Greek art in Renaissance Europe and at the time of the Neo-classical movement of the later 18th century. Even today, these white marble copies continue to underlie the popular notion of the ancient Greeks' artistic achievements and ideal of beauty. To the Romans and later European collectors, such pieces represented desirable possessions and were acquired and displayed as works of art rather than as sacred objects. The attitude of the Greeks themselves to sculpture is harder to recapture; for example, deities were both represented by and embodied in their cult statues, and it would have been unimaginable to separate such works from the context of worship.

Because of its extraordinarily wide-reaching influence on the formation of Western aesthetics, Greek sculpture—hard as it is now to view it objectively—has been among the most intensively debated and researched subjects in art history, and the associated scholarly literature is immense. The consensus is still frequently revised on such matters as the date, attribution and meaning of specific works.

BIBLIOGRAPHY

G. M. A. Richter: *The Sculpture and Sculptors of the Greeks* (New Haven and London, 1929, 4/1970)
G. Lippold: *Griechische Plastik* (Munich, 1950)
R. Lullies and M. Hirmer: *Greek Sculpture* (New York, 1957/*R* London, 1960)
R. Carpenter: *Greek Sculpture: A Critical Review* (Chicago, 1960)
B. Rowlands: *The Classical Tradition of Western Art* (Cambridge, MA, 1963)
S. Adam: *The Technique of Greek Sculpture in the Archaic and Classical Periods* (London, 1966)
C. Blümel: *Greek Sculptors at Work* (London, 1969)
M. Robertson: *History of Greek Art*, 2 vols (Cambridge, 1975)
J. Barron: *Greek Sculpture* (London, 1982)
A. F. Stewart: *Greek Sculpture: An Exploration*, 2 vols (New Haven and London, 1990)
N. Yalouris: *Ancient Sculpture* (1994), iii of *Greek Art* (Athens, 1994–6)

□

(i) Forms and functions. (ii) Subject-matter. (iii) Materials. (iv) Techniques. (v) Craftsmen and society.

(i) Forms and functions.

(a) Free-standing. (b) Architectural. (c) Non-architectural reliefs.

(a) Free-standing. In the absence of any surviving works by the great ancient Greek panel painters, free-standing sculpture is the most sensitive indicator of the stylistic development of Greek art. It was the field in which the most important sculptors worked and from which innovations and new tendencies spread to other branches of sculpture. Again with the exception of panel painting, it was the art form that commanded the highest respect among contemporaries: architectural and relief sculpture, by contrast, are seldom mentioned in ancient literary

sources, though they now account for most of the surviving original large-scale Greek works. Most Greek sculpture is concerned with the human figure, though other subjects occur throughout its history. In free-standing sculpture, single figures are generally much commoner than group compositions (see below).

Formal development. By the mid-7th century BC at the latest, life-size and over life-size sculptures in stone were being produced. These works were not determined by the direct observation of nature, and there was no straightforward development towards an increasing naturalism. However, from the austere stylization of the figurines of the preceding Geometric period (*see* §2(i) below), the proportions of the human body were brought into a fixed, recognizable and measurable relation to each other. Firm rules were established, clearly influenced by the Egyptian canon of proportion, though, unlike it, they included the whole head, did not imply a back support and could be developed freely and continuously by individual artists. Even so, the mode of representation remained in principle two-dimensional, being applied to only two sides of the block, with mediation at the edges (*see* KORE, fig. 1). Later in the Archaic period there appeared a playful tendency to stylize certain motifs ornamentally, for example hair or parts of the body. Despite the unity that can be seen in the overall development of Archaic Greek sculpture, as in the KOUROS type (a striding nude male figure), regional styles occurred, particularly in the Late Archaic period, and these sometimes perpetuated technical and stylistic peculiarities. Though conforming to certain basic patterns, Late Archaic statues show a greater openness to every kind of variation and to increasingly rich adornment, as is seen most clearly in the kore statues (draped female figures; *see* KORE, fig. 2). At the same time, sharp transitions and stylization within the modelling of the body were reduced. For example, the musculature of the abdomen was treated more subtly, making it possible to show turning movements of the body. About the end of the 6th century BC a new stage was imperceptibly reached, even though the kouros pattern, as in the Aristodikos Kouros (*see* KOUROS, fig. 2), was still applied. Though at first sight this work is similar to the *Kritios Boy* from the Acropolis at Athens (see fig. 55 below), the latter marks the decisive transition from Late Archaic sculpture to the Severe style of the Early Classical period (*see also* §2(ii)(c)–(iii)(a) below). In the *Kritios Boy* the realization of the shifting of weight from one leg to another, distributed through all parts of the body, signals the end of the simple conventions of the Archaic portrayal of the human being. Body structure and movements had to be elaborated plausibly as a whole. Such careful analysis of the interrelatedness of all the details of the body presupposes a close observation of nature by the leading sculptors, who must have been responsible for the new direction. In keeping with this development there is, from the beginning of the Severe style, an increasing diversity of subjects and poses, elaborated especially with figures in motion: only slight gestures or changes of position were needed to convey a new interpretation of the human figure in the manner of a code.

These new possibilities were rapidly elaborated in the mid-5th century BC, with the dynamic potential of the human figure treated in such works as the Artemision *Zeus* (see fig. 43 below) and Myron's *Diskobolos* (see fig. 38). This formal development was also connected with advances in bronzeworking techniques. Bronze succeeded stone as the preferred medium for free-standing sculpture (though many of the most important works are known only from Roman copies in marble). The next decisive step was the perfection of the balanced asymmetrical type of pose known as Classical contrapposto, realized by Polykleitos in his 'Canon' (both a written treatise, now lost, and a statue, probably the *Doryphoros*; for illustration *see* POLYKLEITOS). This work set new standards for Greek sculpture, since Polykleitos' theoretical system, which he derived in a revolutionary way from the old canon of proportions, involved the precise harmonizing of proportions and symmetries. By comparison, other types of the balanced stance, such as the standing pose with the unweighted foot forward, found in Attica up to the late 5th century BC, were soon only marginal.

Of almost equal importance to Polykleitan contrapposto were the variations in the treatment of textiles in relation to the body in High Classical sculpture, so that a sense of movement in draped figures was clearly conveyed and even accentuated. At the same time, drapery folds were composed into complex figures that emphasized the underlying forms of the figure. Thus the High Classical form of the traditional *peplos*-wearing female figure was joined in the last quarter of the 5th century BC by other

38. *Diskobolos* by Myron, marble copy of bronze original of *c.* 450 BC, h. 1.55 m (Rome, Museo Nazionale Romano)

female statue types, for example those showing the garment adhering to the body as if wet, as in Paionios' *Nike* at Olympia (*see* OLYMPIA, fig. 5) and the Fréjus *Aphrodite* (see fig. 59 below).

The end of the 5th century BC and the early 4th thus brought a working-out of the possibilities discovered by High Classical sculpture and a continuation of its tradition, first in a mannered calligraphic form, then with greater reserve and severity. This transitional period is exemplified by such works as Kephisodotos' *Eirene and Ploutos* (see fig. 39). New tendencies gradually emerged within this framework in the mid-4th century BC, notably in the work of Praxiteles. He varied the standing figure by crossing the legs and using a leaning pose, already found in a late 5th-century BC *Aphrodite* from the circle of Pheidias (Naples, Mus. Archeol. N.), and he thus entirely reinterpreted contrapposto (for illustration of his *Apollo Sauroktonos see* PRAXITELES). The new nudity of the female figure in Praxiteles' statues of *Aphrodite* was accompanied by a continuation of the technique of contrasting drapery folds, as seen also in figures from Herculaneum. There was also a tendency to frame individual statues, such as cult statues or famous masterpieces, in small shrines (*naïskoi*) on a high pedestal. Some sought-after effects included equally the violent, sometimes opposed, turning poses exemplified by Skopas' *Maenad* (Dresden, Skulpsamml.); the over-emphatic representation of rest and weight, as in the figures of *Herakles* by Lysippos; the suggestion of actions extending out into space in a single figure; and the alteration of the canonical proportions to yield still slenderer forms with smaller heads—a tendency originated by Lysippos that remained influential in the Hellenistic period. However, around the mid-4th century BC there were also retrospective tendencies, especially in the field of sacred subjects, in which an Archaic structure might be combined with Late Classical drapery folds, in a way that may have been influenced by a restoration of old cult statues. Such tendencies could also take the form of an archaizing treatment of hair and folds, as practised occasionally by Alkamenes in the High Classical period. Though such experiments still adhered firmly to Classical assumptions, they also prepared for new developments in the late 4th century BC that diverged more sharply from the Late Classical style.

39. *Eirene and Ploutos* by Kephisodotos, marble copy of bronze original of *c.* 375–*c.* 370 BC, h. 2.01 m (Munich, Staatliche Antikensammlungen)

At this time the beginnings of Early Hellenistic sculpture emerged, discarding some of the Classical conventions and even in some respects running counter to Late Classicism. At first, a trend can be discerned towards terse, stiff figures that do not reach beyond themselves. The sculpture of the following High Hellenistic period of the later 2nd century BC is almost the converse of this, with the figures characterized by violent movements and twists. Entirely new subjects, poses and group arrangements were tried out in large sculptures, especially at Pergamon, in works commemorating victories over the Gauls (see fig. 67 below and PERGAMON, fig. 4). These played an important role in combining the Classical tradition with the latest tendencies.

In the mid-2nd century BC there was a gradual return to the forms and models of Classical sculpture, which might be used as a stimulus and developed in their own terms, taken further in the style of the time, or merely copied. Sculptors continued, especially on Rhodes, to develop the High Classical style, while works were produced elsewhere that were purely Hellenistic in conception. Characteristic of such Late Hellenistic works is the restriction to a single viewing side, determined by the original siting of the sculpture. This is particularly noticeable in group compositions, though some groups are exceptions. From the early 1st century BC an increasingly clear neo-Classicism emerged, with new works produced in an earlier style and a flourishing production of straightforward copies of famous Classical works. At this time the market for sculpture was increasingly dominated by rich Romans, whose preference for earlier masterpieces over contemporary art stimulated the making of copies. This phase of Greek sculpture thus passed seamlessly into the early Roman Empire, where there was no room for the unfettered formal developments of the Hellenistic period. The influence of Roman taste can also be seen in the verist emphasis in portraiture that spread from Hellenistic central Italy.

Group compositions occurred from the Archaic period onwards. To begin with, they were usually formed simply by lining up figures on an extended common base, and only in the Early Classical period was the row of figures given a clear group connection. Later in the Classical period the multi-figure offerings by Greek states at the large pan-Hellenic sanctuaries provided opportunities for many different solutions to this problem, and from the Late Classical to the Hellenistic period increasingly large and complex groups were constructed. A reaction to this is represented by some Late Hellenistic groups, which adopt symmetrical arrangements with only one possible viewing side.

Functions. The forms and subjects of free-standing sculpture were closely related to their functions, almost all of which must be understood, at least to begin with, in a religious context. They include the representation of deities as cult statues in sanctuaries and the decoration of religious sites, which included the votive offerings made there. An honorific statue was also primarily a votive offering, even if this is not immediately evident in a secular context. Such statues were usually only legitimate after the death of the person honoured, though this was less in deference to the deity than to protect the state from excessive self-display by an individual citizen using sacred means. Though tomb statues also served the purpose of commemorating the dead and their families, they arose from an Archaic practice of marking graves with a sculpted stele. Sanctioned by this tradition, they soon took over modes of representation from sacred sculpture, a pattern that was often to be repeated.

Not until the Hellenistic period were statues, rather than mere utensils, used to decorate the living areas of palaces and houses, a practice that constituted an extension of the domestic shrine. In the Late Hellenistic period the acquisition of works of art by private collectors sometimes led to separate displays of statues, for example in the palaces of kings such as the Attalids of Pergamon. This practice was widely imitated in the villas of wealthy Romans, though even then an attempt was usually made to retain the sacred context, for example by displaying the works in a gallery dedicated to a 'presiding deity' in imitation of the votive collection at a shrine, or in a section of a library laid out as a shrine.

By the Hellenistic period, sculptures with similar subjects served widely differing functions, and a clear division into distinct genres occurred, though outstanding individual works continued to transcend these categories.

BIBLIOGRAPHY

G. Krahmer: 'Stilphasen der hellenistischen Plastik', *Mitt. Dt. Archäol. Inst.: Röm. Abt.*, xxxviii–xxxix (1923–4), pp. 138–89

——: 'Die einansichtige Gruppe und die späthellenistische Kunst', *Nachrbl. Ges. Wiss. Göttingen, Philos.-Hist. Kl.* (1927), pp. 53–91

R. Horn: 'Stehende weibliche Gewandstatuen in der hellenistischen Plastik', *Mitt. Dt. Archäol. Inst.: Röm. Abt.*, suppl. 2 (1931)

G. Krahmer: *Figur und Raum in der ägyptischen und griechisch-archaischen Kunst* (Halle, 1931)

C. Karusos: *Aristodikos: Zur Geschichte der spätarchaisch-attischen Plastik der Grabstatue* (Stuttgart, 1961)

R. Kabus-Jahn: *Studien zu Frauenfiguren des vierten Jahrhunderts vor Christus* (Darmstadt, 1962)

U. Knigge: *Bewegte Figuren der Grossplastik im Strengen Stil* (diss., Munich, Ludwig-Maximilians U., 1965)

G. M. A. Richter: *The Portraits of the Greeks*, 3 vols (London, 1965; abridged and rev. by R. R. R. Smith (Oxford, 1984)

B. Fehr: *Bewegungsweisen und Verhaltensideale* (Bad Bramstedt, 1970)

B. S. Ridgway: *The Severe Style in Greek Sculpture* (Princeton, 1970)

P. Kranz: 'Frühe griechische Sitzfiguren: Zum Problem der Typenbildung und des orientalischen Einflusses in der frühen griechischen Rundplastik', *Mitt. Dt. Archäol. Inst.: Athen. Abt.*, lxxxvii (1972), pp. 1–55

A. H. Borbein: 'Die griechische Statue des 4. Jahrh. v. Chr.: Formalanalytische Untersuchungen zur Kunst der Nachklassik', *Jb. Dt. Archäol. Inst.*, lxxxviii (1973), pp. 43–212

H. von Steuben: *Der Kanon des Polyklet: Doryphoros und Amazone* (Tübingen, 1973)

R. R. Holloway: *Influences and Styles in the Late Archaic and Early Classical Greek Sculpture of Sicily and Magna Graecia* (Leuven, 1975)

H. L. Schanz: *Greek Sculptural Groups: Archaic and Classical* (New York and London, 1980)

R. Tölle-Kastenbein: *Frühklassische Peplosfiguren: Originale* (Mainz, 1980)

B. S. Ridgway: *Fifth-century Styles in Greek Sculpture* (Princeton, 1981)

H. Jung: *Thronende und sitzende Götter: Zum griechischen Götterbild und Menschenideal in geometrischer und früharchaische Zeit* (Bonn, 1982)

C. Vorster: *Griechische Kinderstatuen* (Cologne, 1983)

P. Karakatsanis: *Studien zu archaischen Kolossalwerken* (Frankfurt, 1986)

H.-H. von Prittwitz und Gaffron: *Der Wandel der Aphrodite: Archäologische Studien zu weiblichen halbbekleideten Statuetten des späten Hellenismus* (Bonn, 1988)

B. S. Ridgway: *The Styles of c. 331–200 BC* (1990), i of *Hellenistic Sculpture* (Bristol, 1990–)

A. F. Stewart: *Greek Sculpture: An Exploration*, 2 vols (New Haven and London, 1990)

L. Todisco: *Scultura greca del IV secolo: Maestri e scuole di statuaria tra classicità ed ellenismo* (Milan, 1993)

(b) Architectural. Greek architectural sculpture developed as decoration for stone temples in the Doric and Ionic orders, but it occurs on other imposing formal buildings and on smaller structures, often in temple form. Only certain parts of any building were adorned, typically the pediment, the frieze section of the entablature and, less often, columns, cella walls and other parts. Mythological battle scenes appear to have been subject-matter particularly well suited to architectural sculpture. Individual themes recur, particularly when there was concern to find a motif with local reference. In general, weight-bearing elements were decorated only with reluctance and particularly not in high relief. The most important decorated areas could be viewed as having a masking function: metope friezes and pediment fields cover the ends of ridge beams, for example.

Pediments. Pedimental sculpture occurs mainly in the Doric order and only exceptionally in the Ionic. The triangular field formed by the pediment (*see* PEDIMENT, §§1 and 2(i)) created particular compositional problems that were not satisfactorily solved until the end of the Archaic period (see below). The earliest temple pediments may simply have had a central terracotta revetment (a tradition that continued in Etruscan architecture until the Late Hellenistic period); the use of stone reliefs began in the late 7th century BC soon after the first stone temples were built.

The earliest large-scale ensemble, from the Temple of Artemis at Corfu (*c.* 600 BC; *see* CORFU, fig. 1), has three distinct figural groups on different scales. The running Gorgon at the centre is both fearsomely apotropaic and, with the smaller-scale figures on either side, part of a mythological narrative (Perseus and Medusa), while the recumbent lions flanking this group further suggest the motif of the Mistress of the Animals. The corners contain small three-figure scenes from a *Gigantomachy* and the *Trojan War*, both subjects that were later of great importance in architectural sculpture. Contemporary with the Kerkyra pediment are the symmetrical facing lions tearing apart a steer, which appear on a pediment on the Acropolis at Athens (Acropolis Mus.). Here fish were used to effect closure in the narrowing corners. In two later examples there the discontinuities between unrelated pictorial motifs were removed by the placing of figures of diminishing size within the pediment to form a unified thematic framework. By the mid-6th century BC sculpture in high relief or, for large pediments, in the round increasingly became the norm, as at the earlier Temple of Apollo at Aigina, where figures were not finished in detail on their backs. The tendency was towards thorough finishing, however, and in addition limestone was superseded by marble. In the older Temple of Apollo (*c.* 520–*c.*510 BC) at Delphi, for example, the west pediment was limestone, but the east was marble. The latter had rows of kouroi and korai either side of Apollo's chariot, a far more static composition than the *Gigantomachy* on the west pediment, with its battle scenes unfolding either side of a central figure. In the slightly later Temple of Apollo (*c.* 510–*c.*500 BC) at Eretria, chariot groups were used to make the transition from the central figures and the lateral groups, a device that often recurs in later pediments. The pediments of the Temple of Aphaia on Aigina demonstrate the transition from Archaic to Early Classical. Both have the same subject (Athena flanked by fighting warriors), but the east pediment, replaced in the early 5th century BC, shows a new, bravura approach to the overall composition in the foreshortening of the figures and other details (see fig. 54 below).

The two great pedimental ensembles of the 5th century BC come from the Temple of Zeus (*c.* 470–*c.* 457 BC) at Olympia and the Parthenon (447–432 BC) at Athens. In both sets, mythological subjects of local significance were used, and as at the Temple of Apollo, Delphi, there are clear differences between the relatively static compositions on the east sides (at Olympia, the *Preparations for the Chariot Race between Pelops and Oinomaus*, see fig. 45 below; at Athens, the *Birth of Athena*) and the stronger sense of movement in the west pediments (at Olympia, a *Centauromachy*; at Athens, the *Struggle between Athena and Poseidon for Possession of Attica*). In terms of composition, the central fighting pair, as originally in the Parthenon's west pediment, was to become a more important element than the quietly standing central figure. One of the last great sculptural pediments with subjects of local significance was created by Skopas, as architect–sculptor, on the Temple of Athena Alea at Tegea. Here the *Kalydonian Boar Hunt* and the *Legend of Telephos* were rendered with a strong, unquiet sense of movement quite different from High Classical sculpture.

Pedimental sculpture is rare in the Hellenistic period, the more so since the Doric order was steadily eclipsed by Ionic and Corinthian. An important exception is the pediment (first half 2nd century BC) of the Hieron of the Kabeiroi at Samothrace.

Metopes. This form belongs to temples in the Doric order. Sculpted metopes could be placed on the exterior entablature or inside, over the pronaos and opisthodomos, where they provided a series of rectangular fields separated by triglyphs, suitable for at most three figures. During the Archaic period a single scene was sometimes divided between two or three metopes, and this device developed into metopal cycles consisting of a series of related individual scenes.

Painted terracotta metopes were used on the late 7th-century BC Temple of Apollo at Thermon (for illustration *see* THERMON), and from the first half of the 6th century BC relief metopes in stone occur, for example on the Sikyonian Treasury at Delphi. The first extensive series comes from the Treasury (*c.* 530 BC) in the Sanctuary of Hera at Foce del Sele in South Italy. These are still relatively simple, in low relief and often with only one figure, but they are notable for their representation of the *Labours of Herakles*, which was to become one of the main subjects in the metopal repertory. The tendency towards thematic structuring is already evident in the Athenian Treasury (*c.* 510–*c.* 490 BC) at Delphi , with its parallel cycles of the *Labours of Herakles* and the *Exploits of Theseus.* Mostly two-figure groups, these metopes show an extensive mastery of physical perspective.

In the Temple of Zeus (*c.* 470–*c.* 457 BC) at Olympia the canonical cycle of the *Twelve Labours of Herakles* was divided between the pronaos and the opisthodomos. These two- or three-figure reliefs (*see*, for example, OLYMPIA, fig. 4) relate not only to each other, forming an integrated cycle, but also to their positions on the building itself. However, the high-point of metopal sculpture is undoubtedly the Parthenon (447–432 BC). Each of the temple's

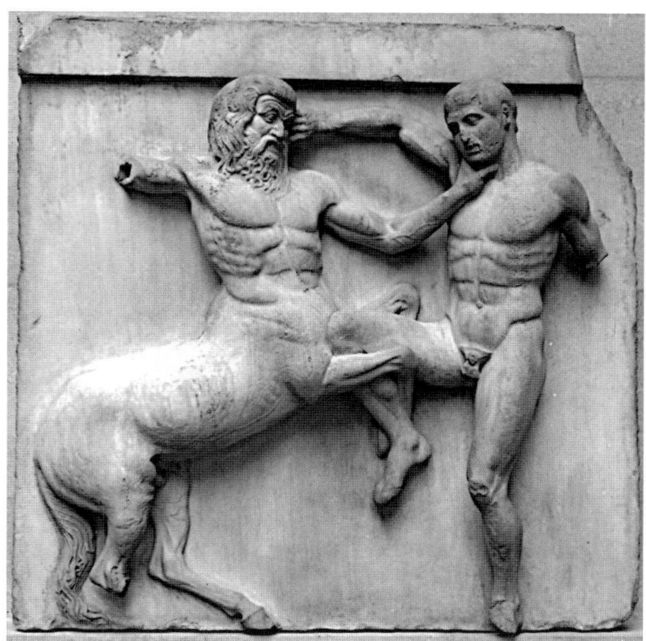

40. Metope showing a *Centauromachy*, marble, h. 1.2 m, from the south side of the Parthenon, Athens, High Classical, *c.* 447 BC (London, British Museum)

four sides had a different battle subject: a *Gigantomachy*, an *Amazonomachy*, a *Centauromachy* (see fig. 40) and *Trojan War* scenes. In the metopes of Skopas' Temple of Athena Alea at Tegea the form reached its technical limits, with figures carved almost fully in the round (as a result, only fragments now remain).

With the decline of the Doric order, the metope ceased to be an important form, though the concept of the metopal series was continued in figurative coffer reliefs (e.g. the Early Hellenistic *Centauromachy* from the heroon at Belevi).

Friezes. Unlike metopes, the frieze formed an uninterrupted horizontal field. The external frieze is an Ionic feature originating in the marble architecture of the Cyclades, but in the High Classical period friezes were even used to adorn Doric buildings, both on the inside of the peristyle and on the cella walls. Early Archaic frieze-like sculptures are known from Crete, but the first important Ionic frieze is that of the Late Archaic Siphnian Treasury (*c.* 525 BC) at Delphi. This may well represent the work of two sculptors, one more progressive than the other, and its subjects are the *Judgement of Paris*, the *?Abduction of Helen*, *Trojan War* scenes and a masterful *Gigantomachy*, densely composed, with bold overlappings (see fig. 53 below).

The high-point of frieze sculpture is again the Doric Parthenon, with its external cella frieze showing the *Panathenaic Festival* (*see* FRIEZE, fig. 1). This further provides the most comprehensive expression of the formal language of High Classical Attic sculpture, since it was produced by several sculptors collaborating under Pheidias' direction. Ionic friezes from the Acropolis include those of the Temple of Athena Nike (*c.* 425 BC), with battle scenes that probably depict a historical rather than mythological conflict and figures of the *Consulting Gods* over the entrance, and the Erechtheion (421–405 BC), where the relief figures were attached to slabs of black Eleusinian marble. Athenian sculptors were responsible for the internal cella frieze (*c.* 410 BC) of the High Classical Temple of Apollo at Bassai, which shows an *Amazonomachy* (see fig. 41) and a *Centauromachy*.

Between the end of the 5th century BC and the 2nd century BC (e.g. the Temple of Artemis at Magnesia on the Maeander), friezes generally ceased to be a feature of large temples, though the tradition was continued on other types of monument. These included altars, cult statue pedestals and tombs, most notably the Mausoleum (completed *c.* 349 BC) at Halikarnassos, the Nereid Monument at Xanthos (*c.* 425–400 BC; for illustration *see* XANTHOS, §1) and the Tomb of Pericles (mid-4th century BC) at Limyra. The Monument of Lysikrates (336/5 BC) at Athens has a circular frieze of *Dionysos Transforming the Pirates into Dolphins*, which neatly fits the architecture, though with its single plane of figures that do not overlap, it belongs rather to the genre of subsidiary ornamental friezes than to the temple frieze tradition. Among the most important Hellenistic friezes are those from the colossal altars at Ephesos, Magnesia on the Maeander and Pergamon. The Altar of Zeus at Pergamon had an extremely vivid *Gigantomachy* (the 'Great Frieze'; *see* PERGAMON, fig. 2) on the exterior of the socle and a series of scenes from the *Legend of Telephos* (*see* NARRATIVE ART, fig. 3) on the interior of the altar enclosure. The latter shows a development of illustrative technique that was important for Roman Imperial relief sculpture.

Acroteria and other forms. Acroteria (*see also* ACROTERION) ornamented the slanting cornices of pediments (one at the apex, one on each side). Favoured types of subject were figures that could leap or fly or move easily through water (e.g. winged *nikai*, riders, dolphins), or vegetal palmette-scroll forms. Groups were also sometimes used, as in *Boreas Abducting Oreithyia* from the Athenian Temple of Apollo on Delos.

The other special forms of architectural sculpture were mostly developed in the Archaic period by the more experimental East Greeks. Metopes might be combined

41. Frieze showing an *Amazonomachy*, marble, h. 640 mm, from the interior of the Temple of Apollo at Bassai, High Classical, *c.* 410 BC (London, British Museum)

with a frieze (e.g. the Doric Temple of Athena, Assos; *c.* 540 BC), columns were carved as figures (e.g. the Siphnian Treasury, Delphi, and the Erechtheion; *see also* ATLANTID and CARYATID) or given relief decoration on part of the shaft (e.g. the Temple of Apollo, Didyma, and the Temple of Artemis, Ephesos, 6th and 4th centuries BC). Wall reliefs, of which there are many 7th-century BC examples from the Sanctuary of Hera on Samos, perhaps developed out of the plastic enhancement of murals. They were later abandoned, but since the interiors of houses were a favourite location for wall paintings, the same interiors later offered a place for mural reliefs.

BIBLIOGRAPHY

P. Demangel: *La Frise ionique* (Paris, 1932)
W.-H. Schuchhardt: *Archaische Giebelkompositionen* (Freiburg, 1940)
E. Lapalus: *Le Fronton sculpté en Grèce des origines à la fin du quatrième siècle* (Paris, 1947)
B. S. Ridgway: 'Notes on the Development of the Greek Frieze', *Hesperia*, xxxv (1966), pp. 188–204
B. Ashmole: *Architect and Sculptor in Classical Greece* (London and New York, 1972)
A. Delivorrias: *Attische Giebelskulpturen und Akrotere des fünften Jahrhunderts* (Tübingen, 1974)
A. Schmidt-Colinet: *Antike Stützfiguren* (diss., U. Cologne, 1977)
N. Bookidis: *A Study of the Use and Geographical Distribution of Architectural Sculpture in the Archaic Period (Greece, East Greece and Magna Graeca)* (Ann Arbor, 1979)
E. Schmidt: *Geschichte der Karyatide* (Würzburg, 1982)
F. Felten: *Griechische tektonische Friese archaischer und klassischer Zeit* (Waldsassen, 1984)
P. Knell: *Mythos und Polis: Bildprogramme griechischer Bauskulptur* (Darmstadt, 1990)

REINHARD STUPPERICH

(c) Non-architectural reliefs. There are four main types of Greek non-architectural reliefs, distinguished by their forms and functions: grave reliefs, votive reliefs, record reliefs and base reliefs.

Graves. Funerary reliefs (stelai) form the largest and most widespread group. Their development can be traced from the late 7th century BC to the 2nd century AD. The earliest examples come from Athens and its surrounding countryside, where they appeared among other types of grave markers erected by wealthy families. Occasionally made of limestone but generally of marble, these reliefs bear a marked resemblance to grave statues of the period. The narrow slabs, often of monumental size, represent a single standing figure in profile. Initially only male figures occurred (*see also* KOUROS). Attributes such as swords, spears and flowers indicate upper-class status.

From the mid-6th century BC onwards, the images became more varied, highlighting aristocratic preoccupations by showing naked athletes, armed warriors or men wearing patterned cloaks and accompanied by dogs. The stelai frequently also included a small area at the bottom depicting animals or scenes from everyday life and a top section representing an animal, a palmette, or a mythical creature, such as a sphinx, gorgon or siren. The few reliefs made for women differ in shape and structure, showing the deceased enthroned. Rare in the Archaic period (*c.* 700–*c.* 500/480 BC), they were prevalent during the Classical period (*c.* 500/480–323 BC).

During the first half of the 5th century BC, sumptuary laws restricted the size and appearance of graves, but sepulchral reliefs were produced again in Attica from *c.* 440 BC (*see* STELE, fig. 3). These monuments were commonly erected for married women but also for unmarried young people and sometimes for adult men. The Stele of Hegeso (*see* CHAIR, fig. 1) exemplifies a widespread type of relief, depicting a deceased matron in the company of her servant. The servant is handing Hegeso a box from which the latter lifts an object that was once painted. Such gravestones were erected alongside other monuments to display the family group as an important unit in the community. Unity was also expressed by the motif of the handshake, which became increasingly popular in the 4th century BC. At the same time, the number of family members and servants represented increased, while the deceased were occasionally marked by their names. The representative character of such reliefs was accompanied by a stylistic development, with figures in the foreground positioned frontally, in high relief.

The production of grave reliefs ended in Attica after 317 BC with the introduction of laws restricting burial practices. Other Mediterranean regions, however, developed their own traditions, profiting from a favourable political and economic environment. The sepulchral reliefs of Samos and Smyrna (now Izmir) are examples of the many such idiosyncratic styles. On Samos, grave stelai (Pithagorio Mus.) borrowed the iconography of votive reliefs, depicting the deceased banqueting with relatives. Tombstones from Smyrna (e.g. Izmir, Kültürpark, 31, 164, 3277, 519; Oxford, Ashmolean, Michaelis 204), on the other hand, show single or paired figures, attended by their servants and among objects reflecting the values of a prosperous hellenized world. The architecturally shaped frames often carry inscriptions and a wreath symbolizing honours received by the citizens from their community (*demos*).

Votives. Early Greek votive reliefs of marble or limestone show the epiphany of the god or represent a shrine's donor. The first reliefs carved with what was to become the typical arrangement of divine or semi-divine beings and worshippers in a single scene were made shortly after 600 BC (e.g. *c.* 580–*c.* 570 BC, Athens, Acropolis Mus., 586–7, 622; *c.* 570–*c.* 560 BC, Munich, Glyp., 241). These are of various sizes, generally square or rectangular, and were set up in urban and rural sanctuaries. Reliefs dedicated to Hermes, Pan and the nymphs often take the shape of a cave. Lakonian hero reliefs are a special case; these were erected in sanctuaries as well as on grave tumuli. One of the best-known votive reliefs is the so-called Mourning Athena (see fig. 42).

Large numbers of votive reliefs were produced in Athens between the late 5th century BC and the 4th. Most show processions of men, women and children, some carrying offerings, others driving animals to be sacrificed. They approach a god or, more commonly, groups of deities represented on a considerably larger scale than the worshippers. Some reliefs represent the god or hero banqueting or show Dionysian and bucolic scenes. Changes in religious beliefs found expression in the range of deities addressed by humans in the Late Classical (*c.* 375–*c.* 323 BC) and Hellenistic (323–27 BC) periods. Healing deities, semi-divine beings connected with fertility and vegetation, oriental gods, heroes such as Herakles, and mythical founders of cities had replaced the Olympian

42. Votive relief showing the *Mourning Athena*, marble, 540×310 mm, from the Acropolis, Athens, *c.* 460 BC (Athens, Acropolis Museum)

gods as the focus of worship. From their predominantly humble size and quality and from occasional inscriptions it can be concluded that votive reliefs were mainly dedicated by the middle classes.

Records. Record reliefs were erected by decree to publish documents of private or public institutions. They were simple marble plates displaying the text of the decree. In some instances modestly sized, rectangular reliefs, paid for privately, were included above the inscription. Most of the numerous published documents were made in Athens (and set up mainly on the Acropolis) from *c.* 430 BC to the early 3rd century BC. They record, for example, treaties, accounts by treasurers and honours given to individuals in recognition of services to the city. Simple, often repeated representations reflect the content of the inscribed texts. For example, on some reliefs from the 5th century BC and early 4th, Athena, the patron goddess of Athens, is shown shaking hands (*dexiosis*) with another deity, thus expressing alliance between Athens and a foreign Greek state. On others, Athena or Demos (the personification of the Attic people) honours individuals with a wreath. Motifs similar to those on votive reliefs were also used, especially in decrees concerning religious matters. As a result of changed political and economic circumstances (including the rise of Macedonia), production of record reliefs almost completely ceased in the early 3rd century BC.

Bases. Attic sculptors of the Archaic period were the first to decorate the marble bases of stelai and statues. Depending on the character of the monument, the bases were adorned with reliefs showing animals, sports activities, mythical contests and heroic deeds. Several Archaic square bases of excellent quality display scenes reflecting the aristocratic lifestyle. A round base of the same period in Istanbul (Archaeol. Mus., 5370) shows young people dancing. Bases of commemorative votive monuments for athletic victories, mainly from the 4th century BC, often represent sports scenes on three sides with an explanatory inscription on the fourth. Another form of base relief comprises the plaques of *c.* 330/20 BC that once decorated the base of the cult group in the temple in Mantinea (Athens, N. Archaeol. Mus., 215–16), depicting the *Musical Contest between Apollo and Marsyas.*

BIBLIOGRAPHY

G. M. A. Richter: *The Archaic Gravestones of Attica* (London, 1961/*R* Bristol, 1988)

E. Mitropoulou: *Attic Votive Reliefs of the 6th and 5th Centuries BC* (1977), i of *Corpus* (Athens, 1977–)

E. Pfuhl and M. Möbius: *Die ostgriechischen Grabreliefs*, i–iii (Mainz, 1977–9)

G. Neumann: *Probleme des griechischen Weihreliefs* (Tübingen, 1979)

B. Schmaltz: *Griechische Grabreliefs* (Darmstadt, 1983)

M. Meyer: 'Die griechischen Urkundenreliefs', *Mitt. Dt. Archäol. Inst.: Athen. Abt.*, suppl. 13 (1989) [whole vol.]

C. W.Clairmont: *Classic Attic Tombstones* (Kilchberg, 1993)

KALINKA HUBER

(ii) Subject-matter. By far the most popular subject in monumental Greek sculpture was the human figure. It was used to represent a divinity, a mythological personage, an abstract concept, a particular individual or a typical mortal. Inscription, attribute or context was usually sufficient to make the intended meaning clear. Animals were also represented, occasionally in their own right but more usually in conjunction with the human figure. Monsters were sometimes depicted; plant life is rare and generally stylized; other subjects are exceptional.

(a) Free-standing sculpture. (b) Free-standing reliefs. (c) Architectural sculpture.

(a) Free-standing sculpture.

Divinities. The major divinities differed broadly in character—Apollo was always depicted as young, Zeus and Poseidon as mature—but their identities were usually specified by means of attributes. Thus Athena is recognized by her aegis (and often her helmet as well), Apollo by his bow or kithara, Hermes by his traveller's hat and winged shoes and Eros by his wings. Traces of Poseidon's trident or Zeus' thunderbolt would establish beyond dispute the identity of the bronze god (Athens, N. Archaeol. Mus., Br. 15161; see fig. 43) found in the sea off Cape Artemision. The characterization of some gods changed in the course of time; thus Dionysos and Hermes, generally bearded in the Archaic period, were usually represented as youths in the Hellenistic period, and Eros gradually changed from a youth to a baby. An image of a god could serve as a CULT STATUE or a dedication and could also appear in narrative contexts as a part of a mythological representation. Aniconic or roughly shaped images, despite their professed holiness, will not be treated here, but something of an intermediate form is represented by the herm, a pillar topped by a head of Hermes and graced with male genitals, which was popular from Archaic times and stood at entrances of houses and along roadsides, providing protection to residents and wayfarers. Eventually heads other than those of Hermes were placed on herms, sometimes even double heads (Janus-like) or portraits.

Other mythological figures. These are usually identified in one of four ways: first, by inscription, usually on the base; second, by attribute (e.g. Herakles' lionskin and club); third, by the use of a unique and characteristic type, for instance the seated figure of the mourning Penelope; and fourth, by means of particular features specific to the type (e.g. tails and horse-ears on satyrs, horse-bodies on centaurs, fish-tails on Tritons or monstrous visages on gorgons).

Monsters appeared in sculpture from the Archaic period onwards. Sphinxes frequently surmounted Archaic grave stelai or sometimes served as dedications in their own right (e.g. the *Crouching Sphinx* on the Naxian Column at Delphi; *see* DELPHI, fig. 4). Sirens are shown in funerary contexts in the 4th century BC, and centaurs, satyrs and figures of Pan, with his goat-legs and horns, became increasingly popular in the Hellenistic period, often interacting piquantly with human or divine figures. Other monsters, for example Skylla (e.g. London, BM), also occur occasionally in narrative contexts or in isolation.

Personified abstractions. It is not always easy to draw the line between genuine divinities and personified abstractions. Vividly anthropomorphic personifications exist in Homer and Hesiod; Nike (Victory) appears in sculpture already in the Archaic period (e.g. the *Nike of Archermos*; *see* DELOS, fig. 4) and is probably a *bona fide* goddess; Eirene (Peace) was accorded a cult and a statue, made by Kephisodotos, in Athens at the same time (*c.* 375 BC); but Kairos (Opportunity), an ingenious invention by Lysippos in the late 4th century BC (see Posidippos: *Greek Anthology* XVI.275), seems to be a fully-fledged personification of an abstract concept. Personified abstractions became increasingly popular in the Hellenistic period (e.g. the *Tyche of Antioch* by Eutychides; *see* ANTIOCH (i), fig. 1) and could be incorporated into complicated allegories.

Generic figures. Archaic standing nude male figures (kouroi; *see* KOUROS), which were neither placed on graves as memorials nor equipped with special attributes (e.g. a bow for Apollo), may simply have represented non-specific votaries of a god, particularly when they were found in a sanctuary, for instance the kouroi (Athens, N. Archaeol. Mus., and Thebes Mus.) found in the Ptoion sanctuary to Apollo in Boeotia. The same may apply to draped female figures (korai; *see* KORE), for example those found on the Athenian acropolis (*see* KORE, fig. 2). Most athlete statues, now known chiefly through Roman copies and literary references, were probably votive offerings

43. *Zeus* or *Poseidon*, bronze, h. 2.09 m, from Cape Artemision, High Classical, *c.* 450 BC (Athens, National Archaeological Museum)

placed in sanctuaries to commemorate victories. According to Pliny the elder (XXXIV.viii.16), it was customary for those who won a victory in a sacred contest, particularly at Olympia, to dedicate a statue of themselves, but only those who won three times were allowed to dedicate a statue that bore a physical resemblance to the dedicator. Some figures that appear generic may originally have been representations of mythological characters: for instance, the *Doryphoros* (*see* POLYKLEITOS, fig. 1) may have been a representation of Achilles and the *Discobolos* one of Hyacinthus.

During the Hellenistic period there was an immense expansion of the sculptor's repertory. Generic figures, which we might call 'ideal' or perhaps better 'non-specific', became rarer, and a wide variety of specific characterizations far more popular. Not only did portraiture of both real and imaginary sitters increase, but sympathetic and highly individualized representations were made of barbarians (Gauls, Africans, Scythians etc) and deformed people (grotesques), and even the extremes of age (chubby babies and desiccated elderly people) came in for artistic scrutiny. Along with representations of a wide range of humanity came representations of a wide range of activities: people were shown at work or at play, making war or making love; genre subjects became acceptable for major works of sculpture.

Representations of individuals. Individuals could be identified by inscriptions or by means of specific characterizations. Kouroi or korai placed as memorials on graves were identified as representations of the deceased by means of inscriptions (e.g. 'Kroisos', 'Aristodikos', 'Phrasiklea'; all Athens, N. Archaeol. Mus.). Portraits, which attempted to capture the physical appearance of an individual, may have begun as early as the 5th century BC; but characterization always remained more important, as is obvious from the imaginary portraits the Greeks felt free to create (e.g. of *Homer*) and the portraits of real people that they felt free to re-create (e.g. of *Socrates* or *Alexander the Great*). Greek portraits were full-length; a truncated or abbreviated image was not felt to be an adequate representation, except when portraits were made as herms. Portraits were normally either commemorative or honorary, with the result that most (though not all) were of the famous and powerful: poets, statesmen, orators, rulers or philosophers.

Groups. Free-standing statues could be grouped either as loose assemblages (e.g. the *Genelaos Group*; Berlin, Pergamonmus. and Samos, Archaeol. Mus.) or tightly knit entities (e.g. the *Gaul Killing Himself and his Wife*; Rome, Mus. N. Romano; *see* PERGAMON, fig. 4) or something in between, for example the *Tyrannicides* (Naples, Mus. Archaeol. N.). Groups could commemorate individuals (as seems to have been the case with the *Genelaos Group*, which consisted of several figures—standing, seated and reclining—lined up along a single base), a group (as in the case of the Messenian statues at Olympia in honour of 35 boys lost at sea along with their trainer and flautist; Pausanias, V.xxv.2–4), heroic action (e.g. the *Tyrannicides*; Pliny the elder, XXXIV.ix.17) or a victory (e.g. the *Gaul Killing Himself and his Wife*, a copy of part of an Attalid monument at Pergamon, of which this was the centrepiece). Not only were real people assembled in groups (as in the above examples) but mythological figures also—or even a mixture of the two, as in the Athenian dedication at Delphi, which included Athena, Apollo, a group of heroes and the general Miltiades (Pausanias, X.x.1) or the nearby Lacedaemonian dedication comprising the Dioskouroi, Zeus, Apollo, Artemis and Poseidon with Lysander accompanied by his soothsayer and helmsman (Pausanias, X.ix.7). From the 4th century BC groups were occasionally composed of a naturalistic figure combined with an archaistic image, for instance *Artemis* leaning on a statue of herself (Vienna, Ksthist. Mus.).

Myths could be represented by means of figures loosely assembled, as in Myron of Eleutherai's representation of *Athena and Marsyas* (Pliny the elder, XXXIV.xix.57; copy of *Athena*, Frankfurt am Main, Liebieghaus; copy of *Marsyas*, Rome, Vatican, Mus. Pio-Clementino), or in tighter groups where a hero is shown in conflict with his adversary, the adversary often serving to identify the hero (e.g. *Theseus and the Minotaur*). Lysippos is said to have sculpted a series of representations of the *Labours of Herakles* (Strabo: *Geography* X.459), which would have consisted of tightly-knit groups showing Herakles in combat with the lion or the deer or carrying the boar (compositions that seem to be reflected on many Roman sarcophagi). More complex groups were favoured in the Hellenistic period (e.g. *Menelaos with the Body of Patroklos* (Florence, Loggia Lanzi); *Artemis Rescuing Iphigeneia* (Copenhagen, Ny Carlsberg Glyp.); the *Laokoon* (Rome, Vatican, Mus. Pio-Clementino); the Farnese *Bull* (Naples, Mus. Archaeol. N.)).

Representations of men and horses were frequently grouped together to form equestrian statues, one of the earliest being the Rampin *Horseman* (Athens, Acropolis Mus., 590, and Paris, Louvre, 3104), or chariot groups (e.g. the one now lost to which the bronze *Charioteer* from Delphi (Delphi, Archaeol. Mus.) originally belonged). Men were shown carrying animals (e.g. the *Calf-bearer*, Athens, Acropolis Mus., 624; see fig. 52 below) or carried by them (e.g. *Odysseus under the Ram*; Rome, Gal. Doria-Pamphili) or sacrificing them (Pliny the elder, XXXIV.xix.79 and 80). Children were shown with pets—the representation of infants with various sorts of geese was particularly popular in the Hellenistic period—and those beloved of the gods with amorous divinities in animal disguise (e.g. *Leda and the Swan* (Boston, MA, Mus. F.A., 04.14) or the *Ganymede and the Eagle* (Pliny the elder, XXXIV.xix.79)).

Animals. As well as appearing in groups animals were occasionally shown on their own. Lions from early times were represented as guardians of the grave, for example the *Lion of Menekrates* (Corfu, Archaeol. Mus.), and probably continued to serve the same function, though in an attenuated form, on the Mausoleum at Halikarnassos (*see* HALIKARNASSOS, fig. 4). Sometimes the meaning imputed to a lion used as a commemorative image could be deeper, as with the lioness set up to commemorate Leaina, the mistress of Aristogeiton (Pausanias, I.xxiii.2 and Pliny the elder, XXXIV.xix.72) or the Lion of Chaironeia, which, according to Pausanias (IX.xl.10), alluded to the spirit of the men who died fighting Philip of Macedon. Under Oriental influence, a whole sequence of lions was erected to line the Sacred Way at Delos. Of domestic animals, the noble horse was always admired and occasionally represented without rider or chariot. Bulls were represented (Pausanias, X.ix.3), and a bronze *Heifer* by Myron was much admired (Pliny the elder, XXXIV.xix.57). Dogs became a subject of interest in their own right (Pliny the elder, XXXIV.xix.90), especially in the Hellenistic period. Even reptiles and insects were occasionally represented, for instance the lizard slain by Apollo in the *Apollo Sauroktonos* by Praxiteles (copy, Paris, Louvre; for illustration *see* PRAXITELES) or the tree-cricket and locust sculpted by Myron (Pliny the elder, XXXIV.xix.57).

Plant life. Flowers and trees are rare in Greek sculpture, though stylized plant forms were often used for architectural decoration, and 'palm trees' in sculptural form were set up at Delphi and on Delos and even within the Erechtheum in Athens (Pausanias, I.xxiv.7).

(b) Free-standing reliefs. Free-standing reliefs fall into three main categories: grave monuments, document reliefs and votive offerings. Grave stelai in their most elaborate form were topped by free-standing sphinxes, but in time a palmette finial was considered sufficient. Archaic grave stelai were usually carved with a single standing figure representing the deceased, who might be characterized as a boxer by a broken nose and a boxing glove on his upraised hand (Athens, Kerameikos Mus.), as a warrior in armour (Athens, N. Archaeol. Mus.) or as an athlete carrying an oil flask (New York, Met.), but neither at this time nor later is there any hint of real portraiture in grave reliefs. Occasionally two figures were shown: a brother and sister (New York, Met., 11.185; see fig. 44) or a mother and child (Athens, N. Archaeol. Mus., 3845). In the second half of the 5th century BC, with the introduction

44. Grave stele showing the deceased, Me[gakles], with his sister, restored h. 4.23 m, from Attica, Late Archaic, *c*. 540–*c*. 530 BC (New York, Metropolitan Museum of Art)

of more varied formats, seated figures gradually came to be preferred, often accompanied by standing ones, as on the Hegeso Stele (Athens, N. Archaeol. Mus.; *see* CHAIR, fig. 1). In the 4th century BC the number of figures increased; a seated figure often grasps the hand of a standing one in the presence of others (Athens, N. Archaeol. Mus.). Standing figures, alone or with others (e.g. the Ilissos Relief; Athens, N. Archaeol. Mus.), and commemorative scenes of battle (e.g. the Dexileos Stele; Athens, Kerameikos Mus.; see fig. 62 below) were also occasionally carved, until the production of Attic grave stelai came to an end *c*. 310 BC. Occasionally some hint was given as to the deceased's way of life but only in the most general way (e.g. huntsman, athlete etc).

Documents such as treaties that were carved on stone were frequently headed by a figured relief. The figures often represented the signing parties—for example a relief from the Acropolis shows *Athena Clasping the Hand of Hera* (Athens, Acropolis Mus., 1333), the two goddesses representing Athens and Samos respectively—or glossed the contents of the document with abstractions, as with *Democracy Crowning the Seated Demos* (Athens, Agora Mus., I.6524).

Votive reliefs usually show worshippers bringing homage to deities. The deities were carved on a large scale, which contrasts with their minute votaries (e.g. *Worshipper with (?)Triptolemos, Persephone, Demeter and a God*; Copenhagen, Ny Carlsberg Glyp., 197). Such reliefs sometimes hint at a landscape setting, such as a cave or a tree or a shrine (see fig. 5 above). Other miscellaneous reliefs can be religious (e.g. the Eleusis Relief; Athens, N. Archaeol. Mus.) or mythological. The Hellenistic period favoured elaborate allegories, such as the *Apotheosis of Homer* (London, BM) or simple slices of nature.

See also §(i)(c) above.

(c) Architectural sculpture. Temples, treasuries and other buildings were frequently decorated with sculptures, almost without exception illustrating myths. These can usually be identified by means of the attributes carried by the principal figures or by their characteristic opponents (Gorgon, Hydra, Minotaur etc). Sometimes, however, only a literary source can explain the subject as in the case of the east pediment of the Temple of Zeus at Olympia, which Pausanias' description (V.x.6–7) reveals as the *Preparation for the Chariot Race between Pelops and Oinomaos* (see fig. 45).

Pediments. The awkward triangular shape of the pediment made it difficult for artists to fill with a unified and coherent subject. In the first half of the 6th century BC and sometimes later, animals were used to cope with some of the problems presented by pediments, snakes filling the corners, lions devouring cattle in the centre (Athens, Acropolis Mus.) and reclining panthers (Corfu, Archaeol. Mus.) mediating the slope between the centre and the corners. Later this last role was taken over by horses, which could be integrated into the story being told, as on the east pediment of the Temple of Zeus at Olympia (Olympia, Archaeol. Mus.) and probably on the west pediment of the Parthenon (see the Carrey drawings of the Parthenon sculptures; Paris, Bib. N.). The pediment

45. *Preparation for the Chariot Race between Pelops and Oinomaos*, h. 3.3 m, l. 26.4 m, east pediment of the Temple of Zeus at Olympia, Early Classical, *c.* 470–457 BC; reconstruction

in the early Temple of Artemis at Corfu (Kerkyra; Corfu, Archaeol. Mus.; for illustration *see* CORFU) has the story of the Gorgon Medusa and her progeny told in the centre, but a *Gigantomachy* is squeezed into one (or both) of the corners. Later artists were usually able to fill the whole pediment with a single story. Scenes of action were most adaptable, and mythological battles were therefore popular, for instance the two Trojan wars depicted in the pediments of the Temple of Aphaia at Aigina (Munich, Glyp.) and the *Battle between the Lapiths and the Centaurs* in the west pediment of the Temple of Zeus at Olympia (Olympia, Archaeol. Mus.). But Classical sculptors could also effectively deploy subjects without overt conflict, for example the *Preparation for the Chariot Race between Pelops and Oinomaos* in the east pediment of the Temple of Zeus at Olympia or the *Birth of Athena* (central figures now lost) in the east pediment of the Parthenon (Pausanias, I.xxiv.5).

Metopes. Being nearly square in shape, metopes required stories to be condensed and usually illustrated by no more than two or three figures. The themes chosen for illustration could be loosely or tightly organized. A series of metopes could present either a miscellany of heroic deeds (e.g. *Perseus and Medusa* and *Herakles and the Kerkopes* among others on Temple C at Selinus (Palermo, Mus. Reg.; *see* SELINUS, fig. 2); the *Argonauts*, the *Kalydonian Boar Hunt* and *Europa and the Bull* on the Sikyonian Treasury at Delphi (Delphi, Archaeol. Mus.); *Herakles and the Amazon* and *Zeus and Hera* among others on Temple E at Selinus (Palermo, Mus. Reg.)), a sequence of related incidents pertaining to a single myth (e.g. the *Gigantomachy* on the east front of the Parthenon (Athens, *in situ*); various deeds of Herakles on the east front of the Temple of Hephaistos at Athens (*in situ*)) or a single theme embracing the whole metopal decoration (e.g. the *Labours of Herakles* on the east and west metopes of the Temple of Zeus at Olympia (Olympia, Archaeol. Mus.)).

Friezes. In contrast to metopes, friezes (or friezelike decoration) required subjects that could easily be extended by the addition of as many figures as were necessary to fill up the space available. For this reason battles were particularly popular; hunts, processions, revels and assemblies could also be used. Gigantomachies were used on one of the friezes on the Siphnian Treasury at Delphi (Delphi, Archaeol. Mus.) and on the 'Great Altar' at Pergamon (Berlin, Pergamonmus.; *see* PERGAMON, fig. 5), and amazonomachies and centauromachies at Bassai and on the mausoleum at Halikarnassos (both London, BM). A new style, continuous narration, was used to present the biographical cycle illustrating the *Legend of Telephos* on the small frieze from the 'Great Altar' at Pergamon (Berlin, Pergamonmus.). The Doric architrave of the temple at Assos (Paris, Louvre; Boston, MA, Mus. F.A.) was used to carry friezelike decoration illustrating *Herakles' Fight with the Centaurs.* Action, generally combat, was preferred for friezes, but occasionally peaceful assemblies were illustrated, as on the east frieze of the Temple of Athena Nike at Athens (*in situ*), or processions, as on the Parthenon (Athens, Acropolis Mus.; London, BM, and elsewhere).

Friezes may sometimes have been decorated with historical rather than mythological scenes; it has been suggested that the battle friezes on the Temple of Athena Nike in Athens (*in situ* and London, BM) reflect the Battle of Marathon and events in the Peloponnesian War, that the frieze on Aemilius Paulus' Monument (Delphi, Archaeol. Mus.) at Delphi reflects part of the Macedonian War, and that the Parthenon frieze is an idealized portrayal of the Panathenaic procession, perhaps the last before the Battle of Marathon in 490 BC.

Acroteria. These were usually graced with stylized floral decoration, but they could also carry winged figures, such as *nikai* or sphinxes. More elaborate ones could even portray abductions or other mythological scenes, for example *Theseus Throwing Skiron into the Sea* and *Hemera Carrying off Kephalos*, once on the Stoa Basileos (Royal Stoa) in Athens (Pausanias, I.iii.1).

BIBLIOGRAPHY

Pliny the elder: *Natural History*

Pausanias: *Guide to Greece*

G. Rodenwaldt: *Das Relief bei den Griechen* (Berlin, 1923)

H. Kähler: *Das griechische Metopenbild* (Munich, 1949)

K. F. Johansen: *The Attic Grave Reliefs of the Classical Period* (Copenhagen, 1951)

U. Hausmann: *Griechische Weihreliefs* (Berlin, 1960)
G. M. A. Richter: *The Archaic Gravestones of Attica* (London, 1961/*R* Bristol, 1988)
——: *The Portraits of the Greeks* (London, 1965); abridged and rev. by R. R. R. Smith (Oxford, 1984)
Å. Åkerström: *Die architektonischen Terracotten Kleinasiens* (1966)
M. Bieber: *The Sculpture of the Hellenistic Age* (New York, 1967)
G. M. A. Richter: *The Sculpture and Sculptors of the Greeks* (New Haven, 1970)
B. S. Ridgway: *The Severe Style in Greek Sculpture* (Princeton, 1970)
——: *The Archaic Style in Greek Sculpture* (Princeton, 1977, rev. Chicago, 1993)
J. Boardman: *Greek Sculpture: The Archaic Period* (London, 1978/*R* 1988)
G. Neumann: *Probleme des griechischen Weihreliefs* (Tübingen, 1979)
B. S. Ridgway: *Fifth Century Styles in Greek Sculpture* (Princeton, 1981)
B. Schmaltz: *Griechische Grabreliefs* (Darmstadt, 1983)
F. Felten: *Griechische tektonische Friese archaischer und klassischer Zeit* (Stiftland, 1984)
J. Boardman: *Greek Sculpture: The Classical Period* (London, 1985)
J. J. Pollitt: *Art in the Hellenistic Age* (Cambridge, 1986)
H. Wrede: *Die antike Herme* (Mainz, 1986)
M. Meyer: *Die griechischen Urkundenreliefs* (Berlin, 1989)
J. J. Pollitt: *The Art of Ancient Greece: Sources and Documents* (Cambridge, 1990)
A. F. Stewart: *Greek Sculpture: An Exploration*, 2 vols (New Haven and London, 1990)
R. R. R. Smith: *Hellenistic Sculpture* (London, 1991)
C. W. Clairmont: *Classical Attic Tombstones* (Kilchberg, 1993)
H. C. Ackermann and J. R. Gisler, eds: *Lexicon iconographicum mythologiae classicae* (Zurich, 1981–) [int. iconog. enc. with entries arranged alphabetically under the names of gods and other mythol. figures; vols 1–7 pubd]

SUSAN WOODFORD

(iii) Materials. In their choice of materials, Greek sculptors did not apparently feel bound by the Apolline law of moderation. Clay, wood, stone, bronze, iron, silver, gold and ivory were all employed, sometimes in combination, and, where appropriate, were painted or further embellished with precious stones, enamel, glass, copper and tin.

(a) Introduction. (b) Terracotta. (c) Wood. (d) Limestone. (e) Marble. (f) Bronze. (g) Chryselephantine.

(a) Introduction. The choice of materials for a given sculpture was conditioned by factors as diverse as skill, cost, availability, appropriateness to context or subject, and simple delight in experiment and variety. The nature of the materials themselves was also important. Clay, wood and limestone generally ceased to be used for major sculpture after *c.* 500 BC, for these materials are not only less durable but are also duller than the others, which are extolled in Homeric and later poetry as both long-lasting and visually exciting. All have 'radiance' or 'gleam' (Gr. *aigla*) and can 'flash' or 'sparkle' (*marmairein*; hence *marmaros*, marble). Not only do these materials fulfil the requirement of a monument to be lasting, but they also engage and delight the spectator.

From the sculptor's point of view, other considerations besides appropriateness to context or the material's effect may be more relevant, for example hardness or tensile strength. In addition, some sculptors worked in several media, while others specialized. Particularly after *c.* 500 BC, when bronze came to dominate large-scale, free-standing sculpture, a clear distinction emerged between sculptors in marble, who were often Athenians or islanders, and sculptors in bronze, often Peloponnesians. In part a matter of availability of materials in different regions, this distinction also corresponds to a practical difference between glyptic work, which involves direct carving of hard materials whose properties must be absolutely familiar to the sculptor, and fictile work, which involves the modelling of soft clay to produce hollow-cast bronzes. Yet it was only in the Hellenistic period that the forms attainable in freely modelled clay began to influence bronzes; earlier Greek sculpture in all media had remained glyptic throughout.

A Greek sculptor's relationship to his materials was complex and differed in several respects from that of medieval, Renaissance or modern sculptors. In particular, unlike Renaissance sculptors, the Greeks never regarded themselves as locked in hopeless combat with their materials. Nor, unlike modern sculptors, did they have the concept of 'truth to materials'. Rather, they viewed their materials as resources, to be exploited as fully and daringly as possible. Aristotle wrote of the way in which skill (*techne*) could allow the artist to transcend the limitations of nature (*Physics* ii.8, 199a15–20). More pragmatically, a 6th-century BC sculptor's dedication explains that 'skilled craftsmen do well to show their cunning in their *techne*, for whoso possesses *techne* has a better life' (*Inscr. Gr./2*, ii, 678): thus improved technical control brought both material and psychological rewards in the battle for commissions.

(b) Terracotta. Clay was the earliest sculptural material and was apparently the only one to continue in use throughout the Greek Dark Age. Its popularity, at least for small-scale work, continued into Roman times. Hundreds of thousands of terracotta figurines survive (*see* §IX, 2 below), ranging from cheap votive offerings to the high-quality 3rd-century BC figurines from Tanagra (examples in London, BM, and elsewhere) and the extraordinary grotesques of Hellenistic Alexandria. Most such figurines were painted in rather garish colours and were sometimes even gilded. In large-scale terracotta sculpture, Corinth and the Greek cities of Sicily and South Italy dominated production during the Archaic and Early Classical periods, principally because marble was not easily available in these areas. The making of hollow-cast bronzes, which utilized many of the same skills, supplanted this industry during the 5th century BC.

(c) Wood. Though hardly any wooden sculpture survives, ancient sources record that the earliest Greek cult images were wooden *xoana* ('scraped things'), some mere logs, others hewn roughly into human form. The existence of *xoana* has been challenged, but the literary references, chiefly in Pausanias' *Guide to Greece*, cannot be explained away. Some woods, such as Lebanese cedar, were chosen for their sculptural qualities and durability; others were selected for religious or patriotic reasons. Thus, the statue of *Athena Polias* (destr. in antiquity) on the Athenian Acropolis was made of olive wood, since she was said to have given the olive tree to Attica. Wood was also used for statuettes, at least in the Archaic period, though since most of the finds are due to the unique conditions for preservation at the Sanctuary of Hera on Samos, it is uncertain how widespread or long-lived this practice was. Like clay, wooden sculpture could be painted or gilded, and cult statues were often further adorned with real

jewellery and clothing. After the Archaic period wood all but disappeared in mainland Greece as a sculptural medium, though in such areas as Sicily or Egypt, where marble was scarce or had to be imported, acrolithic statues, consisting of wooden bodies with stone limbs and heads, were not uncommon. Wood-carving also survived as the basis for chryselephantine sculpture (*see* §(g) below), which succeeded the Archaic *sphyrelaton* technique, in which bronze plates were applied to a wooden core (*see* §(f) below).

(d) Limestone. The earliest limestone sculpture occurred on Crete around 700 BC, apparently stimulated by contact with the Neo-Hittite kingdoms of north Syria. Free-standing statues and architectural sculpture were both carved in this medium, knowledge of which soon spread to the rest of the Aegean, then to the Greek colonies of South Italy and Sicily. Yet by the time the Cretan tradition died out in the early 6th century BC, marble had supplanted limestone in mainland Greece for all but architectural sculpture. Attic limestones were the finest of the mainland varieties and were used for architectural sculpture until the late 6th century BC, when a general preference for marble emerged. In the western Greek world, limestone architectural sculpture is to be found until the mid-5th century BC, though the latest examples, from Temple E at Selinus (*c.* 470–*c.* 460 BC), often have limbs and heads of imported marble. This mixed technique, a variant of acrolithic sculpture (*see* §(c) above), was also used for a colossal statue of a goddess of *c.* 400 BC (Malibu, CA, Getty Mus., 88.AA.76). In the Late Classical and Hellenistic periods (mid-4th century BC–late 1st), limestone sculpture was popular both at Taranto (anc. Taras) and in Egypt. Tarentine grave shrines (*naïskoi*) were embellished with small reliefs in the local soft limestone (*pietra tenera*) from *c.* 330 BC to *c.* 250 BC, and in Egypt the local Pharaonic tradition of limestone-carving never died out but was simply applied to Greek genres and iconography.

(e) Marble. Marble was first used as a material for sculpture in Greece in the mid-7th century BC, and even though the earliest example is a statue of a woman, the Nikandre Kore dedicated on Delos (*see* KORE, fig. 1), its introduction was closely related to the development of the KOUROS statue-type, a striding nude male figure. This fact, coupled with the apparent use of a grid to lay out the proportions of the kouroi (*see also* §(iv)(a) below), suggests that the inspiration for using such a hard stone came not from the Near East but from Egypt, where grid-based statues in hard stones of striding, kilted males had been produced for centuries. The date of the Nikandre Kore (*c.* 660–*c.* 650 BC) coincides with the successful use of East Greek mercenaries by Psammetichus I (*reg* 664–610 BC) to establish himself on the throne of Egypt and with the subsequent founding of an East Greek trading colony at Naukratis in the Nile Delta. Sculptors on Naxos and Samos pioneered the technique of marble-carving, which soon spread throughout the Aegean. By the later 6th century BC Samian marble was no longer used, while Naxian had been largely supplanted by the sugary Parian marble and by the fine-grained stone from the Pentelic quarries just north of Athens. Local marbles, such as Thasian, Proconnesian, Ephesian and Doliana (from the Peloponnese), were also occasionally used, but only Parian and Pentelic were consistently and widely exported before Roman times. Piecing was common, at least for draped statues, as sculptors progressively attempted to transcend the limitations of the block, including making outstretched arms or heads separately. As with limestone, terracotta and wood, marble sculpture was usually at least partly painted: traces of paint have been found on hair, eyes and lips, and patterns and borders were painted on to clothes and armour (*see* STONE, colour pl. VIII, fig. 1). Earrings, bracelets and sandals were painted as appropriate. The background of relief sculpture was also coloured. Figures were further embellished with attributes, jewellery or other attachments in bronze and other metals. By the end of the 6th century BC marble dominated all forms of sculpture in the Aegean, yet within a few decades hollow-cast bronze, with its greater tensile strength, had virtually supplanted it for free-standing work. Though some Attic cult statues were still made of marble, it was otherwise restricted to architectural and funerary sculpture until Praxiteles initiated a revival around 350 BC with his marble *Aphrodite of Knidos* (copy, Rome, Vatican, Mus. Pio-Clementino; for illustration of copy in Paris, Louvre, *see* KNIDOS). The few large-scale, free-standing Classical works in marble, such as the *Nike of Paionios* (*see* OLYMPIA, fig. 5), show sculptors striving to overcome the limitations of their material and to rival bronze. Meanwhile, acrolithic statues continued to be produced in such areas as Sicily and South Italy, where marble was difficult to obtain.

The *Aphrodite of Knidos*, with its unrivalled surface finish, including a more subtle coloration invented by the painter Nikias, reawakened interest in free-standing marble sculpture. Though bronze was still regularly used for portraits and groups, Hellenistic marble sculptures of all sizes abound at such sites as Delos, Pergamon and Alexandria. Inscriptions reveal a distinction emerging between cult statues (*agalmata*), which were often of marble, and statues of mortals (*andrianta*), normally of bronze; the reasons for this distinction remain unclear.

(f) Bronze. Bronze is usually defined as an alloy of about nine or ten parts of copper to one part of tin. In antiquity, however, these proportions varied widely, and large admixtures of other elements, such as lead, were sometimes introduced. The Greek term *khalkos* covered all variations from pure copper to heavily leaded tin-bronze, and the range is demonstrated by the published analyses of surviving bronzes. Some 'bronze' statuettes, for example, contain almost no tin, while the arms of one of the RIACE BRONZES included up to 14.5% lead. The small number of surviving large-scale Greek bronzes (total *c.* 30) further complicates the issue. Though many seem to conform to the standard alloy, others do not. Two factors that undoubtedly influenced the sculptors' choice of alloy were ductability and ease of working when cold: alloys with large amounts of lead flow well into the mould but are hard to work cold, whereas alloys with much tin and little lead tend to be less ductile but take chiselled detail much better. The Greeks apparently preferred the latter formula for large-scale bronzes, which are characterized by a compelling attention to detail, while the Etruscans

and Romans, less concerned with detail, adopted the former.

Bronze statuettes, solid-cast using the lost-wax method (*see* §(iv)(b) below), occur from the 8th century BC (*see also* §VIII, 2(i) below), and large-scale bronzes from around 700 BC. The latter initially fall into two classes, both employing Near Eastern technology. The first are statues made using the *sphyrelaton* technique, which involved hammered and riveted bronze plates (for illustration *see* CULT STATUE); the second are griffin protomes of Near Eastern type attached to bronze cauldrons (examples in Olympia, Archaeol. Mus.). The earliest of these protomes were hammered, but hollow-casting soon became the norm. The technique of indirect casting via piece-moulds taken from a prototype in wood or clay may be Egyptian, since Samian bronze-casters are reputed to have visited Egypt, and many Egyptian bronzes were found in the Sanctuary of Hera on Samos, where the bronze industry flourished as almost nowhere else during the Archaic period. Indirect casting allowed the sculptor to produce several versions of a prototype without destroying the original, as the direct method necessitated, but the detailing, done cold after casting, was always individualized.

The advantages of indirect casting were soon applied to sculptures of the human figure. Already by 600 BC Samian merchants had dedicated a giant bronze griffin-cauldron supported by three bronze women, each over 3 m tall (lost in antiquity), at the Sanctuary of Hera, which has also yielded bronze statuettes with identical torsos and heads but with limbs in various poses (examples in Vathy, Archaeol. Mus.). By the mid-6th century BC the *sphyrelaton* technique, with its sharp transitions and doll-like articulation, was obsolete. At about this time the earliest life-size, indirect-cast bronzes also began to appear, and once established, the new technique soon became widely popular. Remains of statue bases from the Athenian Acropolis show that free-standing bronzes equalled marble works by *c.* 500 BC and far exceeded them by *c.* 480 BC. Novelty apart, the burgeoning demand for statues of victors in the Panhellenic games and other contests may have stimulated this change, for not only could polished and burnished bronze evoke a sense of the tanned, oiled body of the athlete, but its excellent tensile strength also made it the perfect medium for the action poses increasingly favoured for both statues of athletes and narrative groups. Eyes were usually inset in ivory and glass, teeth silvered, hair gilded and nipples coppered. Drapery and other attributes were inlaid with patterns in various metals, gilded or even painted. Sometimes whole statues were gilded, either using wafer-thin gold leaf applied over size or glue or, more expensively, using sheet-gold hammered into grooves cut into the bronze. Fire-gilding by a solution of gold in mercury is not attested before Roman Imperial times.

(g) Chryselephantine. Statues of cast silver or gold were always rare in antiquity. The preferred chryselephantine technique, which used much less metal, derived from the Near East, where it had been in use for centuries. The earliest remains of chryselephantine sculptures come from Delphi (6th century BC; Delphi, Archaeol. Mus.). They are about half life-size, technically all but identical to the colossal statues of *Athena Parthenos* at Athens and *Zeus* at Olympia by Pheidias, erected a century later (both destr. in antiquity). As in the *sphyrelaton* technique, gold sheets for the drapery were hammered over a wooden core, but exposed flesh surfaces were of ivory; solid in the examples from Delphi, applied in thin strips over wood on the Pheidian statues. Both gold and ivory often occur in ancient Greek poetry in metaphors for divine perfection, yet in the case of the *Athena Parthenos* a more prosaic motive for the choice of chryselephantine also applied: the one and a half tons of gold involved formed part of the State treasury and could be removed in an emergency and later replaced. In 295 BC, however, the tyrant Lachares permanently despoiled the statue, which Athens subsequently had only sufficient resources to cover with gold leaf. Further effects applied to chryselephantine works included rouging cheeks and lips, setting eyes in aquamarine and embellishing drapery with silver, copper and enamel inlay. The moulds found at Pheidias' workshop at Olympia, once thought to be for the golden drapery of his *Zeus*, were in fact for glass pieces set into the clothing of an over life-size goddess, perhaps his *Athena* or *Aphrodite* at Elis. Several versions of many of these moulds survive, in increasingly detailed series, showing that the glass was heated and then 'slumped' into them in stages to prevent cracking.

Normally used exclusively for statues of deities, and even then only rarely, chryselephantine was selected by Philip II of Macedonia (*reg* 359–336 BC) for the images of himself and his family in his Philippeion at Olympia, erected after his defeat of Athens and Thebes at Chaironeia in 338 BC. The intended message was clearly that his deeds approached divine status, and though few later monarchs followed his example directly, gilded cult statues of Hellenistic kings and eventually even of important benefactors were later commonly erected in sanctuaries and temples.

BIBLIOGRAPHY

C. Blümel: *Griechische Bildhauer an der Arbeit* (Berlin, 1927, 3/1934); Eng. trans. by L. Holland (London, 1955, 2/1969)

S. Adam: *The Technique of Greek Sculpture in the Archaic and Classical Periods* (London, 1966)

R. A. Higgins: *Greek Terracottas* (London, 1967)

J. J. Pollitt: *The Ancient View of Greek Art* (New Haven and London, 1974)

R. Meiggs: *Trees and Timber in the Ancient Mediterranean World* (Oxford, 1982)

L. Mannoni and T. Mannoni: *Il marmo: Materia e cultura* (Genoa, 1985); Eng. trans. by P. J. Hammond-Smith as *Marble: The History of a Culture* (New York, 1985)

C. Rolley: *Greek Bronzes* (London and New York, 1986)

A. Donohue: *Xoana and the Origins of Greek Sculpture* (Atlanta, 1988)

C. C. Mattusch: *Greek Bronze Statuary: From the Beginnings through the Fifth Century BC* (Ithaca, NY, 1988) [analyses of bronzes on pp. 14–15]

A. F. Stewart: *Greek Sculpture: An Exploration* (New Haven and London, 1990), i, pp. 36–40

D. Haynes: *The Technique of Greek Bronze Statuary* (Mainz, 1992)

ANDREW F. STEWART

(iv) Techniques.

(a) Stoneworking. (b) Clay-modelling and moulding. (c) Bronze-casting. (d) Models and reproduction.

(a) Stoneworking. Evidence for ancient Greek stoneworking methods and tools is abundant. Greek sculptors in marble are known, for example, to have used a range

of tools similar to those of a modern sculptor, comprising chisels, drills and abrasives. Even on such highly finished work as the Parthenon sculptures (mainly in London, BM) there are recesses where the marks of tools were not smoothed away, and the numerous carved grave stelai of the Archaic and Classical periods have many areas where the use of drills and chisels shows clearly. Similar methods appear to have been widely employed throughout the Aegean islands and mainland Greece, and the changes that occurred during the Archaic and Classical periods were also general rather than local.

Marble from the islands of Paros and Naxos was especially prized, and on Naxos there is good evidence of marble quarrying from early times. Instead of being cut from deep vertical faces, large blocks could be removed across the surface of the hills. Drills were used to cut vertically into the rock around a block, forming a row of perforations that could then be knocked into continuous channels to separate the block from the surrounding marble. Wedges were driven in underneath the block until they detached it from its bed.

As well as the quarry sites, a number of unfinished Archaic statues have been found on Naxos (*see* NAXOS, fig. 2). These are of the kouros type, which probably derived from Egyptian models. It seems clear that the Greeks also adopted Egyptian methods when they began to produce sculpture in stone. The Egyptians marked the block to be carved with a grid of equal squares, producing a canon of proportion (*see* EGYPT, ANCIENT, §VII, 1(ii)(c)). Thus the medial line was fixed, and the sculptor would be able to visualize the finished statue in terms of the grid, which could be continually renewed as the work progressed. The Archaic Greek kouroi from Naxos show, rather surprisingly, that a statue might be shaped almost down to its final surface while still at the quarry, possibly in order to reduce the weight for transportation. While the Egyptians produced over life-size statues to a similar design for centuries, the Greeks broke away from their original format in just over a hundred years to develop a wide formal repertory of smaller-scale sculpture, though there was little change to the sequence of tools employed.

First, a pointed chisel was used to shape the general outlines of the figure. Though a pointed chisel can remove large flakes of stone, evidence from Greek statues suggests that sculptors preferred to use short strokes, holding the chisel almost at a right angle to the block and removing only small flakes. The sculptor could finely control the contours he was shaping, because his attention at any one time was closely focused on a small area, which he worked slowly. The drill was also important from an early stage of the work. Drills were simply chisels that were whirled round while being pressed into the stone. The sculptor might have assistants to turn the drill by means of a thong round its shaft, or he might work single-handed with a bow drill. Drill holes can be seen between the arms and body of certain kouroi, in the ringlets of the hair of female statues, in drapery channels on statues of all periods and around heads in profile in relief sculptures. In the drapery channels of figures on the Parthenon frieze (*c.* 442–*c.* 438 BC) rows of holes made by repeated use of a small drill are visible in places. The use of a running drill, which could be moved along the surface to carve simplified lines and planes, does not appear until the 4th century BC. The flat chisel was used for more detailed shaping, to give crisp edges to eyelids, locks of hair and drapery channels and to prepare the surfaces for their final smoothing. There is a striking contrast between the short, careful strokes of the flat chisel in early work and the long, unsubtle strokes on some later pieces, where all the varied contours of an arm may be reduced to a few facets. Metal rasps were sometimes used next. The final smooth, burnished but not shining finish to the marble was given by emery blocks or powder.

BIBLIOGRAPHY

C. Blümel: *Griechische Bildhauer an der Arbeit* (Berlin, 1927, 3/1934); Eng. trans. by L. Holland (London, 1955, 2/1969)

S. Casson: *The Technique of Early Greek Sculpture* (Oxford, 1933)

S. Adam: *The Technique of Greek Sculpture in the Archaic and Classical Periods* (London, 1966)

B. Ashmole: *Architect and Sculptor in Classical Greece* (London and New York, 1972)

O. Palagia: 'Les Techniques de la sculpture grecque sur marbre', *Marbres helléniques* (Brussels, 1987)

SHEILA ADAM

(b) Clay-modelling and moulding. Free-standing terracotta sculpture could be either mould-made or handmade. It includes both statuettes, of which great numbers survive (*see* §IX, 2 below), and a few larger statues that range in height from under half life-size to approximately three-quarters life-size. In handmade statues the body was built up from coils of clay and modelled to give the figure its basic shape. Earlier statues sometimes had an internal clay support in the form of a solid wall dividing the statue from front to back, but in the Classical period only small clay

46. *Athena Modelling a Horse in Clay*, Attic Red-figure oinochoe, h. 215 mm, Early Classical, *c.* 460 BC (Berlin, Antikenmuseum)

supports might be used, or none at all. Once the body of the statue had dried, the separately modelled head, neck, arms, feet and plinth were added. Scoring marks made during attachment can often be seen. The face was sometimes made in piece-moulds. During the Archaic period, tempered clay was used to reduce the risks of cracking and shrinkage, but by the Classical period it was no longer needed for free-standing statues, though it was still used sparingly for architectural sculpture. The entire figure was covered with a layer of fine clay, in which details, such as of face, hair and drapery, were cut or modelled (see fig. 46). During the Archaic period, the figure was painted after drying, then fired at a low temperature. By the 5th century BC, however, a white slip was fired with the clay, and the more delicate colours were added after firing. Finally, vent holes left for the escape of gases were plugged, and the statue was burnished to produce the finished surface.

(c) Bronze-casting. Greek sculptors used the lost-wax technique for casting both large and small bronzes. Large-scale works were widely produced in this way from the 6th century BC onwards in a diversified industry, adapted to the idiosyncracies of individual artists and the requirements of specific commissions. Despite the development of techniques for duplicating or copying works (*see* §(d) below), bronze statues were generally unique works, produced in temporary workshops that were closed down after casting was completed. Small statuettes (*see* §VIII, 2(i) below) might be cast solid, but larger figures were always cast hollow and in pieces that were then fitted or soldered together.

Lost-wax casting in ancient Greece essentially differed little from the process used in modern foundries (*see* BRONZE, §II, 2). It involved the construction of a preliminary full-size model of the sculpture, probably usually of clay, though wax, wood or stone could also have been used. A clay master mould was taken from the model in separate but joining pieces, then dried. The pieces of the master mould were then reassembled in manageable groups: a nude figure might have as few as four major parts (e.g. head, arms, trunk and legs), but a draped statue might have many pieces, since it was easy to conceal joins within folds. Next, each of the master mould assemblages was lined with a beeswax layer, either poured in, brushed on or applied in slabs. A liquid clay core was then poured into the hollow wax model and sometimes reinforced with simple iron rods or armatures. After this, the master moulds were removed, and the wax model was worked over in what could be an extensive process, involving the addition of more wax for such features as locks of hair

47. Two workmen heating a metallurgical furnace, while a third pieces together a life-size bronze statue of an athlete, detail from the Berlin Foundry Cup, Attic Red-figure, diam. 305 mm, from Vulci, Late Archaic, *c.* 490–*c.* 480 BC (Berlin, Antikenmuseum)

and beard and the tooling of surface details, such as ears and eyebrows. The wax model was now ready for casting, and a wax 'gate' system was attached to it, comprising a pouring funnel and gates for admitting the molten bronze. In one-piece casting, vents were also needed for the escape of gases from within the core, though in piece-casting the core was partly exposed. To hold the core in position when the wax layer was melted out, pins or chaplets made of iron or bronze were driven through the wax into the core at several points, with their outer ends left exposed. A final investment mould was applied in two or more layers, covering the entire model and gate system but leaving the lip of the wax funnel and the tops of the vents exposed. Its innermost layer was fine enough to ensure that the wax was completely coated, while its outer layers were of coarser clay with rough sandy inclusions or 'temper' to prevent cracking and reduce shrinkage during drying and baking.

Next the mould was placed on a base inside a hole or casting pit, and a fire was built around it to melt out the wax and evaporate any moisture. The elimination of the wax left a moulded cavity for the bronze, and the wax gates, vents and funnel became channels for admitting the molten bronze and evacuating any gases. After cooling, the moulds were packed firmly in sand in the casting pit. Bronze was heated to 1000–1100°C, either in an adjacent shaft furnace or in a crucible furnace, and poured into the funnels. Once the bronze had cooled, the sand packing was removed and the investment moulds were broken away. The clay core was either left in place or removed as far as it could be reached inside the bronze statue. Inlays of other materials, such as copper, stone and silver, were set in the bronze to emphasize the eyes, eyelashes, eyebrows, teeth and nipples. Finally, the pieces of the statue were fitted together (see fig. 47) and sometimes soldered. Joins and imperfections were smoothed and patched, and the bronze was polished to a high gleam.

To produce a statue with many projecting parts would have required special procedures: for example, loose locks of hair would surely have been best produced by being individually modelled in wax, cast solid, then attached to the statue. Similarly, the model for a statue's head might be so rough as to provide only an indication of scale and general contours, with most of the detailing left until the wax layer with its clay core had been prepared. Thus irregularities in the thickness of the walls of some Greek bronzes testify to additions made to the wax model. Where the inner surface of a bronze is visible, the drips, brush-marks or seams resulting from the application of the wax to the master moulds are sometimes evident.

BIBLIOGRAPHY

P. C. Bol: *Antike Bronzetechnik* (Munich, 1985)

C. C. Mattusch: *Greek Bronze Statuary: From the Beginnings through the Fifth Century BC* (Ithaca, NY, 1988) [analyses of bronzes on pp. 14–15]

CAROL C. MATTUSCH

(d) Models and reproduction. The introduction of the use of full-scale models in clay or other materials was part of the technical and stylistic revolution that was responsible for the development of the Classical style of sculpture in the 5th century BC. Models are first attested for bronze statuary in the early 5th century BC, with the development of the indirect lost-wax technique, which involved the construction of a clay model on an iron armature from which clay piece-moulds were then taken (*see* §(c) above). The stage of fashioning this type of clay model for a bronze statue is illustrated on an Attic Red-figure oinochoe of *c.* 460 BC (Berlin, Antikenmus., F 2415; see fig. 46 above), showing *Athena Modelling a Horse in Clay.* A similar process employing piece-moulds may have been used to produce plaster models for marble sculptures from the 5th century BC onwards. The existence of full-scale models for marble statues of the Classical period is suggested by references to models in wax, wood and plaster for architectural members, such as lion-head spouts, ornaments for ceiling coffers and mouldings, in the building accounts of the Erechtheion at Athens (408–406 BC) and of the Temple of Asklepios and the Tholos at Epidauros (4th century BC; *Inscr. Gr./2*, i, 374; iv, 102a and 102b; iv, 103 respectively). The use of plaster in monumental sculpture was already known in the 5th century BC. Pausanias (*Guide to Greece* I.xl.4) described an unfinished chryselephantine statue of *Zeus* by Theokosmos of Megara, modelled in clay and plaster, over a wooden core, and in the 4th century BC Lysistratos, the brother of Lysippos, is credited with the invention of life masks in plaster, of which he took wax impressions. Further evidence for the use of models in marble sculpture is provided by traces of measuring points on unfinished pieces.

The earliest examples of the use of a copying device are the bosses and the grooves left by the removal of bosses on the foreheads of a few figures from the metopes and pediments of the Temple of Zeus at Olympia (*c.* 470–*c.*457 BC; Olympia, Archaeol. Mus.). These bosses may have served as fixed points for the attachment of plumb-lines for taking measurements both horizontally and vertically, so that the sculptor could determine the angles of his planes and the depth to which he had to cut. Another copying method perhaps employed in antiquity involves the use of three calipers. It is extremely precise and can also be employed for enlargement or reduction.

Copying methods made possible the production of more than one 'original' work at a time. Duplicate original sculptures of the 5th century BC include not only votive reliefs, which may have been duplicated freehand, but also free-standing marble statues. One example is the marble *Mourning Penelope* from the ruins of Persepolis (*c.* 460 BC; Tehran, Archaeol. Mus.). Persepolis was destroyed by Alexander the Great in 331 BC, but Roman copies of an identical work (Rome, Vatican, Mus. Pio-Clementino, 754; Copenhagen, Ny Carlsberg Glyp., 1944) imply the existence of a second original. Similar circumstances are also postulated for the bronze Peiraeus *Athena* (*c.* 350 BC; Peiraeus, Archaeol. Mus.; see fig. 65 below). The extant statue was buried in the 1st century BC, but copies of this type were still being made, presumably after a second original, in the 2nd century AD (e.g. the *Athena Mattei*; Paris, Louvre, MA 530).

The mechanical reproduction of marble statuary was facilitated by the introduction of an early form of pointing machine in the 1st century BC. This served to transfer measurements taken in three dimensions from the model to the marble block. It consisted of a movable needle calibrated on a fixed axis, which could bore a network of holes on the surface of the marble. The machine was hung from a hook mounted on a perforated boss on top of the figure and was also supported by a pair of symmetrical protrusions at its base. As the statue was carved, measuring points in the form of bosses punctuated its surface and were only removed on completion of the work. Unfinished pieces from Delos, sacked in 69 BC, have bosses that show they were carved with the aid of a primitive pointing machine. This device was, however, not strictly accurate and therefore required some freehand adjustment by the sculptor. On the other hand, it allowed a piecemeal approach, with parts of a statue being thoroughly finished while others were still roughly formed. However, it was never the only method in use for the reproduction of copies of Classical or contemporary works in the Hellenistic or Roman periods.

BIBLIOGRAPHY

C. Blümel: 'Griechische Bildhauerarbeit', *Jb. Dt. Archäol. Inst.* (1927), suppl. 11 [whole issue]

——: *Griechische Bildhauer an der Arbeit* (Berlin, 1927, 3/1934); Eng. trans. by L. Holland (London, 1955, 2/1969)

F. Brommer: 'Vorhellenistische Kopien und Wiederholungen von Statuen', *Studies in Honor of D. M. Robinson*, i (St Louis, 1951), pp. 674–82

J. J. Pollitt: *The Ancient View of Greek Art* (New Haven and London, 1974), pp. 204–15

V. M. Strocka: 'Variante, Wiederholung und Serie in der griechischen Bildhauerei', *Jb. Dt. Archäol. Inst.*, xciv (1979), pp. 143–73

M. Pfanner: 'Über das Herstellen von Porträts', *Jb. Dt. Archäol. Inst.*, civ (1989), pp. 157–257

B. S. Ridgway: 'Defining the Issue: The Greek Period', *Retaining the Original*, Stud. Hist. A., xx (Hannover and London, 1989), pp. 13–26

OLGA PALAGIA

(v) Craftsmen and society. Monumental stone sculpture first appeared in Greece in the first half of the 7th century BC, though it is not until some time thereafter that sculptors can be named with any assurance and related to extant statues, or that one can gain any real sense of their place in society. The sculptor's profession clearly had important links with earlier image-makers, who made not only figurines in ivory, terracotta and metal but also larger representations of deities in wood, and sculptors would have been credited, like their legendary forerunner DAIDALOS, with mysterious skills. The legend of Daidalos in fact reflects many aspects of the sculptors' real situation and may have owed much of its persistence to the sculptors themselves. Later literary sources preserve extensive information on attributions, individual sculptors' techniques and the judgements of connoisseurs, but they have little to say about other aspects of sculptors' lives, except when these are mentioned in anecdotes about famous patrons. Pheidias is thus less obscure than other sculptors because of his connection with Pericles, and Lysippos because he was Alexander the Great's favourite sculptor.

Despite sculpture's importance from its inception, little more can be said of the initiators of the craft than that they learnt it through contact with Egyptian sculpture. Naxian stoneworkers were among the first to exploit the new medium, and one of the first sculptors known by name from his 'signature' is the Naxian Euthykartides, who dedicated a statue he had made to Delian Apollo (feet and base in Delos, Archaeol. Mus.). The Naxians' role in the early development of sculpture, however, is scarcely remembered in literary sources. Instead sculptors from elsewhere—the Cretan Dipoinos and Skyllis (*see* DAIDALOS, §2), Smilis of Aigina, Klearchos of Rhegion or Rhoikos and Theodoros of Samos—are counted among the first great practitioners.

(a) Professional skills and organization. The versatility characteristic of the leading sculptors in every age is demonstrated by Rhoikos and Theodoros (*fl* early and mid-6th century BC). Their skills may have included bronze-casting, monumental temple architecture and jewellery. A similar versatility was shared by the Classical sculptors Pheidias of Athens and Polykleitos of Argos. Pheidias designed and worked on the Parthenon sculptures, and he made two colossal chryselephantine statues, of *Athena* at Athens and of *Zeus* at Olympia (destr. in antiquity). Polykleitos, most famous for his work on harmony in the sculpted figure, also probably made a chryselephantine statue of *Hera* and, like Pheidias, cast statues in bronze. Many other sculptors worked in bronze and may customarily have overseen the alloying of the metal itself, as the scene on the Berlin Foundry Cup (see fig. 47 above) indicates, together with the accounts for Pheidias' *Athena Promachos*, which include payments for tin, copper, fuel and a furnace.

Sculpture was both an art dependent on the inspiration of its leading exponents for its development and a craft held together by strength of tradition. There were many lesser sculptors whose competence was limited to one or two processes only, including assistants and apprentices in an established sculptor's workshop or sculptors who worked only on such small projects as grave reliefs or monuments for private dedication. Nevertheless, many such sculptures, especially of the 6th and 5th centuries BC, demonstrate an expertise that could only have existed within a tight-knit craft in which there was close communication between the various branches. For example, the sculptors brought together at Athens to work on the Parthenon, like those employed on the Erechtheion a generation later, no doubt included some who came from the more workaday section of the profession. Their workshop training and the cohesiveness of the craft as a whole enabled them to reach the same high standard of work, under proper direction.

The sculptural tradition was fostered in workshops, where masters and fathers taught apprentices and sons. Many sculptors were born to their craft, as the literary records together with many sculptors' signatures indicate: for example, when some Parian sculptors signed their work as 'the sons of Charopinos', they surely intended to acknowledge not their family descent but their professional indebtedness. In some instances the sculptor's craft was handed down through several generations: the late 6th-century BC Athenian Antenor was the son and nephew of sculptors, and Kritios and Nesiotes, who made the replacement for his *Tyrannicides* group, were probably younger relatives. Praxiteles, too, was the son and nephew of sculptors, whose descendants in the craft can be traced to *c.* 200 BC.

(b) Working environment and conditions. The most notable sculptors and the best examples of family descent are found in connection with places that could offer inducements to skilled workers to congregate and settle down. Prosperity of the kind that encouraged artistic activity was one factor and the availability of raw materials another. Athens in the 6th and 5th centuries BC was such a centre, and vase painters especially offered sculptors a challenge in dealing with perspective and the human body. This cross-professional competitiveness may be seen in the fine relief (Athens, N. Archaeol. Mus.) by the Naxian Alxenor, on which he experimented with foreshortening in much the same way as contemporary Athenian vase painters, and to which he appended the comment, 'You have only to look and see!' Athens could also offer good marble, as did Naxos and Paros. Sikyon in the 4th century BC was a centre for painters as well as sculptors, the most famous of whom was Alexander the Great's portraitist Lysippos (his brother was a painter, as was the brother of Pheidias).

But how had a sculptor like Paionios of Mende in Thrace entered the profession? There can usually have been little more than competent stone masonry called for in such a place. Yet he acquired the skill to win the competition for sculpting the acroteria on the Temple of Zeus at Olympia and to make the fine *Nike* for the Messenian and Naupaktian dedication there (*see* OLYMPIA, fig. 5). The fact that he included his home town in his signature to this piece, together with the information about the competition, suggests that he wished his rise from provincial obscurity to be advertised. He perhaps owed his opportunity to a chance encounter with an established sculptor temporarily working in Thrace, and at some point he came under Athenian influence, possibly that of Pheidias himself (both sculptors worked at Olympia).

Although there were times and places in which sculptors could find more or less continuous employment, for example Periclean Athens, 6th-century BC Samos and Olympia in the mid-5th century BC, they often had to travel to find work. No city remained permanently prosperous: for example, the defeat of Athens in 404 BC meant that a large nucleus of skilled labour was broken up. Moreover, few communities were ever prosperous enough to be regular bases for accomplished craftsmen. When the Epidaurians developed their Sanctuary of Asklepios during the 4th century BC, they had to call on imported skilled labour: architects and masons came in from Corinth and Argos, and among the sculptors were Timotheos of Athens and Thrasymedes of Paros.

Mobility was characteristic of good sculptors at all periods; for example, Myron of Eleutherai may have worked not only at Athens but also at Olympia, on Aigina and Samos, at Ephesos, Orchomenos and Akragas (now Agrigento). This mobility facilitated both the exchange of ideas and the influence of styles that had evolved in one centre on sculptors brought up in different traditions. The need to search out work would have enhanced competitiveness to the benefit of the craft, though it may often have kept prices, and thus earnings, down. Though some sculptors could doubtless command high prices, the scanty evidence (mainly from public works) suggests that a sculptor's earnings generally provided little more than a bare living. Sculptors were conceived of first and foremost as craftsmen; valuable for their skill and often hard to find when needed, but nonetheless not deserving of vast payments.

The sculptors of figures for the Erechtheion frieze were paid a standard rate of 60 drachmas per figure, which may have worked out at around 1 drachma a day, in other words, not much more than was earned by the masons who fluted the columns. At Epidauros the Athenian Timotheos provided reliefs for pronaos of the Temple of Asklepios at 150 drachmas apiece, but the cost of the marble and its transportation were included. Thrasymedes of Paros, on the other hand, received a large sum simply for decorating the temple ceiling, the materials being provided. Chryselephantine statue-making was probably well rewarded, but otherwise the only unequivocal indication that sculptors could do well is Pliny's reference (*Natural History* XXIV.xxxvii) to Lysippos' savings from his many sales. Nevertheless, competition among patrons for the services of famous sculptors may have allowed them to charge more than the usual rate for public projects.

(c) Status. Sculptors appear to have had much the same status as other manual workers, regardless of sculpture's cultural importance as Greek connoisseurs themselves saw it. Yet even though there was some intellectual sympathy between sculptors, who were concerned with the principles of harmony, and philosophers, who considered number and proportion in the abstract, it was not close enough to break down the prejudice against banausic occupations. The admirers of works of art did not value their makers equally, and sculptors were no less banausic than smiths, cobblers or potters, as the Berlin Foundry Cup suggests, with its portrayal of workers hunched over the furnace or swinging hammers at the bronze statue under construction.

There is little evidence that sculptors were ever rewarded for good work on a public monument, for example with political privileges (apart from those of the resident alien, a status enjoyed by numerous craftsmen in Greek cities), and no sculptor is known to have held political office. A few sculptors' dedications are known, showing entirely conventional religious observance, and many sculptors displayed a public personality by signing their works. A sculptor who, like Thrasymedes, could sign the chryselephantine statue of *Asklepios* and so have his name preserved in the god's temple, had no other need of public reward. A few signatures are accompanied by personal statements of pride in the work.

BIBLIOGRAPHY

J. Overbeck: *Die antiken Schriftquellen zur Geschichte der bildenden Künste bei den Griechen* (Leipzig, 1868)

G. M. A. Richter: *The Sculpture and Sculptors of the Greeks* (New Haven and London, 1929, 4/1970)

J. J. Pollitt: *The Art of Greece, 1400–31 BC: Sources and Documents* (Englewood Cliffs, 1965)

B. Ashmole: *Architect and Sculptor in Classical Greece* (London and New York, 1972)

A. Burford: *Craftsmen in Greek and Roman Society* (Ithaca, NY, 1972)

C. C. Mattusch: *Greek Bronze Statuary: From the Beginnings through the Fifth Century BC* (Ithaca, NY, 1988)

H.-P. Müller: *Die gesellschaftliche Stellung des griechischen bildenden Künstlers im 4. Jahrhundert v.u.Z.*, Ethnographisch-Archäologische Zeitschrift, xxix (1988), pp. 139–45

A. F. Stewart: *Greek Sculpture: An Exploration* (New Haven and London, 1990), i, pp. 19–99

ALISON BURFORD

2. HISTORICAL SURVEY. The following discussion traces the development of large-scale Greek sculpture from the 7th century BC, when during the Early Archaic period Greek sculptors began carving life-size and over life-size marble statues of nude male youths (*see* KOUROS) and draped female figures (*see* KORE), until the end of the Hellenistic period (27 BC). It begins, however, with a discussion of the small-scale precursors to these monumental sculptural forms. For further discussion of small-scale Greek sculpture of all periods *see* §§VIII, 2(i); IX, 2; and X, 3, 6 and 11 below.

(i) Antecedents. (ii) Archaic (*c.* 700–*c.* 500/480 BC). (iii) Classical (*c.* 500/480– 323 BC). (iv) Hellenistic (323–27 BC).

(i) Antecedents.

(a) Dark Age and Geometric (*c.* 1050–*c.* 700 BC). (b) Proto-Daidalic (*c.* 700–*c.* 675 BC). (c) Early Archaic Daidalic (*c.* 675–*c.* 600 BC).

*(a) Dark Age and Geometric (*c. *1050–*c. *700* BC*).* When the palatial civilization of the Bronze Age Aegean collapsed around 1200–1100 BC, the Minoan–Mycenaean traditions of creating figures and reliefs in stone, ivory and metals also collapsed (the Minoans of Crete are noted for their cast bronze figurines, but the Mycenaeans, though they used bronze for many other purposes, do not seem to have favoured it as a material for sculpture). Some Mycenaean cult statues may have retained their function after the end of the Bronze Age, and indeed the break with Minoan–Mycenaean traditions was otherwise not clean or absolute. From the ensuing 'Dark Age' (*c.* 1050–*c.* 725 BC) there are, for example, some relatively large terracotta idols found at Karphi on Crete (*c.* 1000 BC; Herakleion, Archaeol. Mus.) that are clearly indebted to Late Bronze Age religious imagery. The use of the potter's wheel to shape their cylindrical skirts was also a Bronze Age technological inheritance. Judging from the evidence, however, Greek sculptors worked at first only in baked clay and did not begin to cast bronze figurines, using the lost-wax technique, until at least the second half of the 9th century BC and possibly only in the early 8th.

Sculpture from the Geometric period (*c.* 900–*c.* 700 BC), named from the style of contemporary pottery decoration (*see* §V, 3 below), is limited to small-scale figures in bronze, terracotta and, exceptionally, ivory. The terracotta figures are mostly handmade animals, and a few combine a cylindrical wheelmade body with hand-formed head and limbs. A good example is the early terracotta centaur from Lefkandi on Euboia (*c.* 900 BC; Eretria, Archaeol. Mus.; see fig. 48). This remarkable work, both animal and human, is painted in the Geometric style and bears a gash intentionally made on the left knee, a wound that probably identifies it as the centaur Cheiron, struck by Herakles' arrow. Whatever the case, the Lefkandi centaur is a creature of the imagination and thus the earliest hint that Greek artists would in time become obsessed with the representation of myth.

Most Geometric sculpture is of bronze rather than terracotta. Bronze statuettes occur almost exclusively as votive gifts, and the pan-hellenic sanctuaries at Olympia,

48. Terracotta centaur, h. 360 mm, from Lefkandi on Euboia, Geometric period, *c.* 900 BC (Eretria, Archaeological Museum)

Delphi and Delos received bronze votives from many regions. The identification of regional styles is based on finds at such local shrines as the Athenian Acropolis, the Sanctuary of Hera at Argos, the Sanctuary of Artemis at Sparta and the Sanctuary of Hera at Perachora. The most important votive dedications were three-legged bronze cauldrons, sometimes 2 m high, with small figures of horses, men or birds placed on or beside the vertical ring-handles (e.g. bronze man, *c.* 750 BC; Olympia, Archaeol. Mus., B4600). Free-standing bronze votives include animals, chariots with drivers, hunters and their prey, goddesses standing nude or riding sidesaddle, circle-dancers, musicians and craftsmen (e.g. helmet-maker, early 7th century BC; New York, Met., 42.11.42). Mythological subjects are rare, though a group of a *Man Fighting a Centaur* (*c.* 750–*c.* 700 BC; New York, Met., 17.190.2072; see fig. 49), perhaps from Lakonia, may represent Herakles and Nessos. Bronze figures were solid-cast using the direct lost-wax technique, which was introduced into Greece from Syria–Palestine, along with such Near Eastern figure types as spear-brandishing warriors and nude females, derived respectively from Levantine weather gods and fertility goddesses. A group of apelike seated figures, probably Lakonian, was based on Phoenician ape figurines.

49. *Man Fighting a Centaur* (?Herakles and Nessos), bronze, h. 110 mm, Geometric period, *c.* 750–*c.* 700 BC (New York, Metropolitan Museum of Art)

Early human figurines in bronze (*c.* 800–750 BC) have triangular or lozenge-shaped torsos, elongated legs and fluidly curving arms. Their faces are flattened ovals with rudimentary features, attached to the head at a 45° angle as if tilted strongly upwards. In the second half of the 8th century BC, however, the torso gained depth and the waist thickened; shoulders and elbows were articulated as joints; and faces became convex and vertical, with more cleanly defined eyes, nose, lips and ears. The elongated proportions reached their extreme soon after 700 BC, especially in Athens.

There were clear regional variations in style and technique. Athenian bronzesmiths specialized in hammered tripod-cauldrons, and their attached figures of horses and humans have long limbs and slender bodies. By contrast, Argive bronzesmiths cast their tripod-cauldrons, and their men and horses have fuller, rounder forms. Lakonian figures tend to have short torsos and large heads, while Corinthian horses, which combine sharp angles with gracefully curved outlines and rounded volumes with sheet-thin extremities, are the most elegant of Geometric statuettes.

Other late 8th-century BC cult statues, such as the one that stood in the early Temple of Hera on Samos, were primarily wooden *xoana* ('scraped things'). Once routinely considered the 'source' of Archaic statuary (an assumption now challenged), these early wooden icons have in any case all disintegrated. However, the cedars and ebonies out of which many early cult statues were carved came, according to literary sources, from the East, as did many of the ideas that began to infiltrate Greek culture at this time.

Early and Middle Geometric sculpture is not abundant, but the number of terracottas and bronzes rapidly increases towards the mid-8th century BC and in the following Late Geometric period (*c.* 760–*c.* 700 BC), and this is one of several symptoms of the general recovery of 8th-century BC Greece, associated also with the consolidation of the city-state (*polis*) as a political entity and the construction of the first important temples, which were intended to house cult statues. Figurines in Near Eastern ivory also occur at this time. Though Geometric ivories are generally rare, a grave near the Dipylon Gate in Athens produced five nude female figurines, datable from pottery finds to *c.* 735–*c.* 720 BC (Athens, N. Archaeol. Mus., 776–9, 2602), the tallest being 240 mm high. The largest and among the latest of Geometric sculptures are three bronze figures from Dreros, Crete. These were made in the *sphyrelaton* technique using hammered bronze plates over a wooden core, and they probably represented Artemis, Apollo and Leto (h. 400 mm, 800 mm and 450 mm respectively, early 7th century BC; Herakleion, Archaeol. Mus., 2445–7; for illustration of 'Apollo' *see* CULT STATUE).

*(b) Proto-Daidalic (*c. *700–*c. *675* BC*).* The formative Geometric period of Greek sculpture may be said to have concluded with a bronze statuette, reportedly from Thebes, known as the *Mantiklos Apollo* (Boston, MA, Mus. F.A., 03.997; see fig. 50). Combined with its Geometric-style body are features usually associated with the ensuing Daidalic style, including prominent eyes, triangular face, low forehead and thick vertical locks of hair framing the face. But the face is shorter, with sharply slanted sides and a more pointed chin, than in Early Daidalic examples, and for this reason the piece has been assigned to the transitional Proto-Daidalic phase (*c.* 700–*c.* 675 BC). The identity of the figure is not certain: he represents either the god Apollo (if what his left hand held was a bow) or (if a spear) his mortal votary Mantiklos, whom two lines inscribed across the statuette's thighs name as dedicant, asking 'The Far Darter of the Silver Bow' for a favour in return. It is the earliest Greek sculpture to record the circumstances of its own creation and use, and in its expressiveness and pose, which is upright and rigidly frontal with the left leg slightly advanced, it seems to anticipate the birth, slightly later in the 7th century BC, of Greek monumental statuary.

*(c) Early Archaic Daidalic (*c. *675–*c. *600* BC*).* The term 'Daidalic' derives from the legendary sculptor DAIDALOS ('cunning worker'). Although the name itself is only a convenience (it eventually came to personify the concept of craftsmanship), it was in fact via Crete, Daidalos' legendary home, that the style—the earliest homogeneous style of Greek Archaic sculpture—seems to have been introduced to the Aegean, probably by *c.* 675 BC. It was an Orientalizing style that fused both Syro-Phoenician and native Geometric elements. The impact of Near Eastern imagery and techniques had often been felt in Greece before, but it was in the 7th century BC that Near Eastern

50. *Mantiklos Apollo*, bronze, h. 203 mm, from ?Thebes, Proto-Daidalic period, *c.* 700–*c.* 675 BC (Boston, MA, Museum of Fine Arts)

influences were strongest. Bronze protomes of griffins, lions and sirens, all based on foreign types, occur frequently on the rims of tripod-cauldrons, and the idea of supporting stone water basins (*perirrhanteria*) with statuettes of maidens standing beside or on the backs of lions was also suggested by Eastern practice (for illustration *see* ISTHMIA).

While not every 7th-century BC Greek sculpture belongs to the Daidalic style (the maidens of *perirrhanteria* do not), it was rapidly diffused throughout Greece, Ionia, South Italy and Sicily. The chief centres, however, were Dorian: Crete, Rhodes, Sparta and Corinth. The most common Daidalic products are mould-made and mass-produced clay reliefs, but the essentially two-dimensional and decorative character of the style is preserved wherever it occurs, not only in terracotta works but also in ivory, wood, gold jewellery, bronze and limestone. Numerous examples of the terracotta plaques were found at Cretan sites; with their representations of nude female figures, they show a close connection to terracotta plaques from Syria depicting the goddess Astarte (e.g. plaque in Oxford, Ashmolean, AE 403). The oriental technique of mould-made terracottas reached Greece around 700 BC, and the resulting proliferation helped to spread the Daidalic style.

Daidalic figures are characteristically frontal, with heads flattened on top and low foreheads defined by the straight horizontal line of the hair or headdress (e.g. terracotta bust from Gortyn; see fig. 51). The hair falls in front of the shoulders, framing the face, and may take the form either of solid triangular panels with horizontal divisions (the Egyptianizing stepped wig) or thick vertical locks. Both male and female figures often wear a wide belt, and Cretan female figures often have a short cape. Compared with Proto-Daidalic works, Early Daidalic faces (*c.* 670–*c.* 655 BC) were more elongated with U-shaped chins, as in the ivory group of two standing females (New York, Met., 17.190.70). In Middle Daidalic works (*c.* 655–*c.* 630 BC), the faces became shorter and wider. The earliest large-scale stone statues of the Archaic Greek world are soft limestone Middle Daidalic works from Crete. It was on Crete, too, that stone statues and reliefs may first have been incorporated into the architecture of temples, for example at Gortyn, where reliefs depicting *Apollo Striding between Two Goddesses* decorated a temple dado or orthostat course of *c.* 630 BC (Herakleion, Archaeol. Mus.); or at Prinias, where a combination of reliefs of felines, deer and riders with statues of seated goddesses decorated lintels or dadoes and a relieving space above the doorway

51. Terracotta bust of a woman, h. 160 mm, from Gortyn, Daidalic period, *c.* 650–*c.* 625 BC (Herakleion, Archaeological Museum)

of Temple A, variously dated between 650 and 620 BC (Herakleion, Archaeol. Mus.). To this phase also belong the marble Nikandre Kore from Delos (Athens, N. Archaeol. Mus., 1; *see* KORE, fig. 1) and the famous 'Auxerre Goddess' (Paris, Louvre, 3098). The limestone 'metope' from Mycenae (Athens, N. Archaeol. Mus., 2869), depicting a cloaked woman with the angular jaw and squared chin of later Middle Daidalic, illustrates the emergence of high-relief sculpture, and the famous bronze statuette from Delphi (Delphi, Archaeol. Mus., 2527) shows the pose of the kouros type fully developed by *c*. 630 BC. Hollow-casting was introduced before the mid-7th century BC and used for larger works, such as the head in Karlsruhe (Bad. Landesmus., F1890), probably once riveted to a hammered bronze body about 500 mm tall. Late Daidalic faces (*c*. 630–*c*. 615 BC) continued to become shorter until the length of the face equalled its width and the line of the chin became level, as in the life-size torso from Eleutherna, Crete (Herakleion, Archaeol. Mus., 47). In general, figures gained volume and plasticity during the 7th century BC. Heads gradually became deeper and foreheads higher, while ears, eyes and lips became smaller and better proportioned to the whole figure. Ears, which were regularly omitted in early phases, later appeared carved in relief against the hair at the sides.

In the late 7th century BC the Greek fascination with Orientalizing styles and motifs began to fade, and the Daidalic style also declined, essentially reaching the end of its development around 600 BC, though works displaying Daidalic features continued well into the 6th century BC. Before that, however, the Daidalic style was applied to two kinds of statues that Greek sculptors began to carve in emulation of works they saw or heard about in Egypt, the kouros type of striding nude male and the kore type of clothed female statue, as in the Nikandre Kore (*see also* §(ii)(a) below).

BIBLIOGRAPHY

R. J. H. Jenkins: *Daedalica* (Cambridge, 1936)
N. Himmelmann-Wildschütz: *Bemerkungen zur geometrischen Plastik* (Berlin, 1964)
R. M. Cook: 'Origins of Greek Sculpture', *J. Hell. Stud.*, lxxxvii (1967), pp. 24–32
B. Schweitzer: *Die geometrische Kunst auf Griechenland* (Cologne, 1969; Eng. trans. by P. Usborne and C. Usborne, London, 1971)
Dädalische Kunst auf Kreta im 7. Jahrhundert v. Chr. (exh. cat., Hamburg, Helms-Mus., 1970)
C. Davaras: 'Die Statue aus Astritsi: Ein Beitrag zur dädalische Kunst auf Kreta und in den Anfängen der griechischen Plastik', *Ant. Kst*, suppl. 8 (1972)
H. V. Hermann: 'Zum Problem der Entstehung der griechischen Grossplastik', *Wandlungen: Studien zur antiken und neueren Kunst Ernst Homann-Wedeking gewidmet* (Waldsassen, 1975), pp. 35–48
J. N. Coldstream: *Geometric Greece* (New York, 1977)
L. Adams: *Orientalizing Sculpture in Soft Limestone*, Brit. Archaeol. Rep., Suppl. Ser., 42 (Oxford, 1978)
A. C. Brookes: *The Chronology and Development of Dedalic Sculpture* (diss., Philadelphia, U. PA, 1978)
J. M. Hurwit: *The Art and Culture of Early Greece, 1100–480 BC* (Ithaca, NY, 1985)
J. Floren: *Die geometrische und archaische Plastik* (1987), i of *Die griechische Plastik*, ed. W. Fuchs and J. Floren (Munich, 1987–)
A. A. Donohue: *Xoana and the Origins of Greek Sculpture* (Atlanta, 1988)
S. Langdon: 'From Monkey to Man: The Evolution of a Geometric Sculptural Type', *Amer. J. Archaeol.*, xciv (1990), pp. 407–24
A. F. Stewart: *Greek Sculpture: An Exploration*, 2 vols (New Haven and London, 1990)

JANE BURR CARTER, JEFFREY M. HURWIT

*(ii) Archaic (*c. *700–*c. *500/480* BC). Whatever the subject, material, genre or scale, the sculpture of Archaic Greece was primarily religious in function. The typical work was made to be dedicated as a 'delight' or 'pleasing gift' (the basic meaning of *agalma*, one of several ancient Greek words for 'statue') in the sanctuary of a deity, to decorate a temple or other structure in the sanctuary or to be placed in or on a grave. Though decorative figurines were often attached as handles or supports to such objects as vessels or mirrors, the idea of 'private' sculpture as the prized possession of individuals was essentially foreign to early Greece.

There are basically three categories of Archaic sculpture: free-standing works; architectural sculpture, including pediments, metopes and friezes; and non-architectural reliefs, such as gravestones. The subject-matter is diverse, encompassing images of deities, heroes and mortals, and even, according to literary sources, portraiture. Animals and monsters, myths and everyday activities are also represented (*see* §1(ii) above). The range of material is wide, including terracotta, bronze (hammered or cast), various woods, gold, ivory, chryselephantine, silver and stone (primarily limestone and marble (*see* §1(iii) above)). Archaic sculptors were generally regarded as craftsmen rather than as 'artists', and they worked within accepted traditions of image-making, as skilled technicians, whose task was not to innovate but to produce well-made examples of established genres (*see* §1(v) above). The names of only a few dozen Archaic sculptors are known from inscribed signatures and ancient literary sources. Of these, a few, such as DAIDALOS, were less historical persons than personifications of early styles (*see* §(i)(c) above), and only a handful of sculptors' names (e.g. Aristion of Paros or Geneleos of Samos) can be plausibly associated with extant works. In some cases groups of unsigned works can be attributed to a single sculptor, who is then given an invented name (e.g. the Rampin Master).

The limits of the Archaic style in sculpture are difficult to define, and the generally accepted chronology has been fiercely, if inconclusively, disputed. The beginning of Archaic sculpture is conventionally placed in the middle of the 7th century BC, when the first large-scale marble statues appear, and there is general agreement that the style did not continue past the Persian destruction of the Athenian Acropolis in 480 BC.

(a) Early (*c*. 700–*c*. 600BC). (b) Middle (*c*. 600–*c*. 550 BC). (c) Late (*c*. 550–*c*. 500/480 BC).

*(a) Early (*c. *700–*c. *600* BC). The origins of the large statues of draped, standing maidens (korai) and nude youths in an upright pose with left leg advanced and arms held down (kouroi) are complex and controversial. The debate centres on whether they were the product of sudden foreign stimuli or rather of slow, internal development within the Aegean region itself. Most scholars would probably concede at least some degree of Egyptian technological influence, since this was the period of the 'opening up' of Egypt to Greeks during the reign of Psammetichus I (*reg* 664–610 BC). Nevertheless, a Greek kore or kouros can hardly be mistaken for an Egyptian work. Greek sculptors either did not adopt or consciously rejected the relative naturalism of contemporary Egyptian

works, and kouroi were not given the clothing and artificial screens and supports of the standard Egyptian prototype. The Greek image of the ideal male figure was balanced on his own two feet and free in space.

The earliest marble korai and kouroi are still Daidalic in style. Probably the earliest is the much-eroded but still impressive kore dedicated in the Sanctuary of Artemis on Delos by Nikandre of Naxos, *c.* 650 BC (*see* KORE, fig. 1). While the earliest kouroi are not even as well preserved as this, a belted figurine in bronze from Delphi, dated to *c.* 630 BC (*see also* §(i)(c) above) must surely reflect contemporary large-scale examples in marble. Though Crete had been the home of the Daidalic style, the kore and kouros types seem first to have appeared in the orbit of Naxos (the earliest figures are of Naxian marble) and then Samos, spreading from these islands to other, though by no means to all, parts of Greece. These statues were clearly prestige works, affordable primarily by members of Archaic élites, and were in some way emblematic of a 'youth-and-beauty' culture fundamental to Archaic society.

Korai and kouroi could be funerary as well as votive in function, and in some areas of Greece one use predominated over the other. The precise meaning of the types is, however, open to question. It is not clear, for example, whether the Nikandre Kore represents the goddess Artemis, the dedicant Nikandre or just a beautiful woman—a generic 'delight' for Artemis' sanctuary. The identity of the earliest kouroi is similarly uncertain. The scholarly consensus is that from the beginning the kouros was a generic representation of eternal 'handsome youth' that could be given a more specific identity only by inscriptions or attributes. However, some kouroi certainly represent Apollo (e.g. the four-times life-size kouros dedicated on Delos by the Naxians; *c.* 600 BC; fragments, Delos, Archaeol. Mus., and London, BM), and some scholars maintain that the kouros began as an image of Apollo, only later acquiring a generic character that fitted it for a range of purposes that included grave-marking and dedication in the sanctuaries of other gods (and even goddesses).

*(b) Middle (*c. *600–*c. *550* BC). By the beginning of the 6th century BC different regions of Greece were clearly developing local interpretations of the kouros and kore: Naxian kouroi are lean and relatively flat, with oval faces and grooves and ridges indicating anatomical details; Samian kouroi, which could be colossal, are rounded, with spherical heads and soft transitions between anatomical parts; Attic kouroi are angular yet muscular, revealing the sculptor's special interest in anatomical pattern and structure; Argive kouroi, represented by the statues identified as the legendary twins *Kleobis* and *Biton* by [?Poly]medes (*c.* 580 BC; Delphi, Archaeol. Mus.) are thick-set and massive, with short torsos and a suggestion of the Daidalic style about them. Though they differ widely, kouroi seem to illustrate a tendency towards ever-increasing representational accuracy in Greek sculpture in the course of the 6th century BC. The later a statue, the more anatomically 'correct' it appears. Yet it should not be assumed that Archaic sculptors were somehow striving for a lifelike ideal (much less trying to become Classical sculptors) or that each kouros was primarily an experiment in rendering anatomy. Archaic sculptors eschewed the naturalism of Egyptian prototypes and do not seem to have valued naturalism especially highly. Rather, it was the distillation of nature and the imposition of order and pattern (patterns of anatomy, patterns of cloth) that governed Archaic sculpture.

Though kouroi and korai dominate any discussion of Archaic sculpture, many other forms of large-scale sculpture in stone were developed in the first half of the 6th century BC. For example, a seated female and a reclining male figure appeared with a row of korai and a draped youth on a single base in the Geneleos group from Samos (*c.* 560–*c.* 550 BC; Berlin, Pergamonmus., and Vathy, Archaeol. Mus.). The kouros type itself could be adjusted for use in high-relief sculpture, as on the Egyptian-influenced limestone pillar-relief of *Dermys and Kittylos* from Tanagra in Boiotia (*c.* 580 BC; Athens, N. Archaeol. Mus.), or could be transformed into an offering-bearer by the addition of an animal in the arms or over the shoulders. On Thasos a colossal *Ram-bearer* was left unfinished around 580 BC, and the history of marble sculpture on the Athenian Acropolis essentially begins in the years before 560 BC with the dedication, by a certain [Rh]onbos, of the *Calf-bearer* (*Moschophoros*; Athens, Acropolis Mus.; see fig. 52). Major cult statues were also created at this time: the Temple of Hera at Olympia, built *c.* 590 BC, contained images of a standing *Zeus* and a seated *Hera*; a huge limestone head (Olympia, Archaeol. Mus.), often said to be from the statue of the goddess, is more likely to have come from a sphinx dedicated on a column outside the temple, like the gigantic *Crouching Sphinx* dedicated by the Naxians at Delphi *c.* 560 BC (Delphi, Archaeol. Mus.; *see* DELPHI, fig. 4). By the mid-6th century BC other important categories of Archaic free-standing and relief sculpture had become established: the earliest stone *nike*, the *Nike of Archermos*, was set up on Delos *c.* 550 BC (Athens, N. Archaeol. Mus.; *see* DELOS, fig. 4), while a little earlier a row of 16 lions was placed beside the precinct of Leto, in the Egyptian manner. A life-size *Bull*, made of silver plates in the *sphyrelaton* technique, was dedicated at Delphi in the mid-6th century BC (Delphi, Archaeol. Mus.), and equestrian statues began to occur in large numbers. This type was mainly Attic, and examples include the Rampin *Horseman* (Athens, Acropolis Mus., and Paris, Louvre). Grave stelai carved in low relief with images of the dead, for example a warrior carrying sword and spear (*c.* 560 BC; Athens, Kerameikos Mus.), began to fill Archaic cemeteries, especially those at Athens.

Equally significant were the emergence in the Middle Archaic period (*c.* 600–*c.* 550 BC) of large-scale stone architectural sculpture and its use for the representation of mythological narrative, in contrast to the earlier non-narrative Daidalic architectural reliefs from Crete. Large-scale stone architectural sculpture required massive stone architecture to carry it: thus the first stone pedimental sculptures, and possibly the first stone metopes, occur on the first all-stone Greek temple, the Temple of Artemis at Corfu (Kerkyra; *c.* 580 BC; for illustration of west pediment *see* CORFU, §1). Compositionally, the major problem presented by a pediment is how to fill its low triangular space with figures that must vary greatly in either scale or posture. In terms of subject-matter, the problem is one of

52. *Calf-bearer*, marble, restored, h. 1.65 m, Middle Archaic period, *c.* 560 BC (Athens, Acropolis Museum)

thematic unity. In the Temple of Artemis the solutions to both problems seem disjointed. At the centre of the west pediment stood a gigantic relief of the Gorgon Medusa, flanked by her children Pegasos and Chrysaor (since they were born only after Medusa's beheading by Perseus, a chronologically plausible narrative is immediately subverted). Two huge leopards flank this central image, offering a sinuous transition to the angles, where there are disconcertingly puny groups of Zeus hurling a thunderbolt at a giant or Titan and, on the other side, a spearman threatening a seated male figure (Priam or Kronos). Crammed into the corners and again on a different scale are two larger Titans or giants, lying dead on their backs. The precise relationship of these parts is unclear. The common theme is violence, which might relate to the ferocity of nature, Artemis' province; but the central group is easier to explain. The Gorgon often appeared in early Greek art as a version of the Near Eastern 'Mistress of the Animals', and she, in turn, was commonly identified with Artemis. Thus, the Gorgon and leopards must not only have been apotropaic temple guardians, transfixing the visitor with their masklike, demonic faces, but must also have been considered as expressions of Artemis and her wild power.

Though sculptural narrative first appeared on Corfu, there are numerous mid-6th century BC examples from the Athenian Acropolis, where brilliantly painted limestone pedimental reliefs and groups adorned a series of temples and small treasury-like buildings. The buildings have not been securely identified and located, and the relationship of the pedimental groups to each other is also controversial. One small building bore a pediment with an incised olive tree and high-relief building and figures (Athens, Acropolis Mus.), perhaps representing an early legend relating to the Acropolis itself. Another pediment, in low relief, depicted *Herakles Fighting the Hydra* (Athens, Acropolis Mus.). The pediments of a large temple of Athena built on the Acropolis *c.* 570–*c.* 550 BC were possibly filled with a Gorgon flanked by lions as at Kerkyra, lions savaging a bull, snakes, a narrative group of Herakles wrestling with a sea-god (Triton or Nereus) in one angle and, occupying the opposite angle, a problematic triple-bodied, snaky-tailed monster with bearded human heads (Athens, Acropolis. Mus.). No single reconstruction or interpretation of these large mythological groups has yet been agreed upon; one controversial theory is that the narratives dealing with Herakles were political allegories, with the hero standing for the Athenian tyrant Peisistratos, who seized power for the first time *c.* 560 BC. However, at least one, even more fundamental meaning is evident: the actions of such heroes as Herakles were considered appropriate expressions and reinforcements of the divine order, and Athena, goddess of the Acropolis and patron of Athens, would protect those who so honoured the gods with their might and courage.

The history of pedimental sculpture from the mid-6th century BC onwards reflects attempts to replace the narrative and proportional disjunction of the earliest compositions with a unity of theme and scale in which one myth rather than several forms the subject and in which all the figures are as close in scale as possible. The individually carved metopes that alternated with triglyphs in the entablatures of Doric buildings were more suitable fields for the display of mythological diversity, though the separate myths represented in a series of metopes often share thematic associations. Heroic combats filled at least some of the metopes of the Temple of Artemis at Kerkyra (a duel between Achilles and Memnon may have been divided by a triglyph), and a building at Delphi (probably an early treasury built by the city of Sikyon), dating from before the fire of 548 BC, was adorned with metopes representing the *Kalydonian Boar Hunt*, the *Dioskouroi Stealing Cattle*, the *Argo and the Argonauts* and other subjects (Delphi, Archaeol. Mus.). Though individually treated, these myths were not haphazardly chosen: for example, the presence of the Dioskouroi (who were worshipped at Sikyon) at least twice on the treasury was one unifying factor in the series.

The carved metope was, however, not a common feature of mainland Greek temples in the 6th century BC, and there are no certain examples from the Athenian Acropolis, so rich in other forms of architectural sculpture. Metopes seem instead to have been a major feature of Sicilian and South Italian Greek temples: a series of vigorously conceived high-relief panels decorated Temple C at Selinus (*c.* 550 BC; Palermo, Mus. Reg.; *see* SELINUS, fig. 2), and nearly 40 extant metopes, variously depicting the legend and labours of Herakles and the punishment of such impious figures as Sisyphos, filled the entablature of a treasury or temple of Hera at Foce del Sele (*c.* 530 BC). As a medium for narrative, the third main genre of architectural sculpture, the continuous 'Ionic' frieze characteristic of East Greek architecture, did not assume importance until the second half of the 6th century BC (ironically on the mainland, at Delphi).

*(c) Late (*c. *550–*c. *500/480* BC*).* In 546 BC Ionia became part of the expanding empire of Persia, and *c.* 540 BC workshops on Naxos, the probable birthplace of Greek marble statuary, essentially ceased production of kouroi. In the 530s BC the production of free-standing sculpture on Samos declined: Polykrates was tyrant, and kouroi and korai, the emblems of the rival aristocracy, went rapidly out of favour. Other cities and regions emerged as the sculptural centres of Greece: Paros, with its excellent local marble quarries, became a major centre, with accomplished artists and extensive influence. The most important centre of Archaic sculpture in the second half of the 6th century BC was Athens, which experienced a phenomenal burst of prosperity and cultural activity from 547/6–510 BC under the tyrant Peisistratos and his sons. By *c.* 550 BC even a Parian sculptor, Aristion, had journeyed to Attica to undertake, in a style at least as 'Attic' as 'Parian', such commissions as the brilliant Phrasikleia Kore (Athens, N. Archaeol. Mus.). Dressed in an elaborately incised and painted *peplos* and bedecked with jewellery and crown, this statue marked the grave of an unmarried girl. Athens, then, was the centre where, in the third quarter of the 6th century BC, many regional styles combined. Presumably introduced by artists attracted by the city's wealth, they seem to have fused into what has been termed an 'International style'.

With a few exceptions, however, korai were not common in Attic cemeteries, where relief stelai and kouroi predominated. The Anavysos Kouros (Athens, N. Archaeol. Mus.), bulgingly muscular and slightly smiling, which was placed over the grave of a certain Kroisos, killed in battle *c.* 530 BC, is an excellent example. Most 'Ripe Archaic' sculpture (*c.* 550–*c.* 510 BC), however, comes from the Athenian Acropolis, where korai were especially plentiful. They were among the earliest marble dedications on the site, but they proliferated after *c.* 550 BC, and 30 or more examples survive. Almost all wear the elaborate Ionian costume of *chiton* and *himation*, and many seem to vie with each other in brilliance of texture, colour and patterning of the dress. This competitive element possibly reflects social rivalry among either the dedicants (often male) or their families. Thus huge statues such as 'Antenor's Kore' (h. 2.15 m; Athens, Acropolis Mus.) claim higher status in terms of their great cost. Artistically, however, the contest between ornamentality and the surface led to a certain decorative unreality by the end of the 6th century BC. Such works as the small but fantastically variegated kore possibly imported from Chios (*c.* 510 BC; Athens, Acropolis Mus.; *see* KORE, fig. 2) seem remote from any concern with naturalism.

The Acropolis korai were far from the only free-standing marble statues on the site in the Late Archaic period. Statues of animals (including dogs), horsemen, warriors, draped youths, kouroi, *nikai*, seated figures of

53. *Gigantomachy*, marble, h. 640 mm, from the north frieze of the Siphnian Treasury at Delphi, Late Archaic period, *c.* 525 BC (Delphi, Archaeological Museum)

Athena, and officials also existed on the Acropolis, as did marble and terracotta reliefs and bronze statues and statuettes. Bronze, in fact, became a favoured medium there and elsewhere towards the end of the Archaic period. Knowledge of large-scale Archaic bronze statuary is derived from such fragments as the head of an under life-size *Zeus* from Olympia (Athens, N. Archaeol. Mus.), from smaller works and statuettes that presumably reflect larger works (for example the striding god (?Zeus) from Ugento in Italy (h. 718 mm, *c*. 525–*c*. 500 BC; Taranto, Mus. N.)) and from rare monumental bronzes, such as the life-size Peiraeus *Apollo* (h. 1.91 m, *c*. 530–*c*. 520 BC; Peiraeus, Archaeol. Mus.).

Independent narrative groups were also dedicated on the Acropolis, for example *Theseus Wrestling with Prorustes* (marble, *c*. 510–*c*. 500 BC; Athens, Acropolis Mus.). However, the mythological compositions that dominated the Late Archaic Acropolis occurred in the pediments of the Old Temple of Athena Polias (possibly as late as *c*. 510–*c*. 500 BC; Athens, Acropolis Mus.), which may have been among the earliest products of the period of Athenian democracy. One pediment was apparently filled with a scene of *Lions Attacking a Bull*, a rather conservative, if suitably apotropaic, way of filling the triangular field. The other pediment contained a single narrative scene, the *Battle between Gods and Giants*. Athena played a major role, with fighting and falling figures occupying the varying heights and angles of the field without violating the unity of scale. The main problems of pedimental sculpture have been solved here, and this temple may also have included a continuous interior frieze representing a divine procession. If so, the presence of an Ionic frieze on an otherwise Doric building anticipates the combination of architectural orders later seen on the Parthenon.

Mythological narrative also flourished at Delphi, where several richly adorned Ionic treasuries and a new Temple of Apollo were built in the last decades of the 6th century BC. The Siphnian Treasury can be dated on historical grounds to *c*. 525 BC, and this remains the first of the very few 'fixed points' in the chronology of Archaic sculpture. The treasury's abundant sculpture (Delphi, Archaeol. Mus.) included acroteria in the form of *nikai*; a pediment representing *Herakles and Apollo Struggling over the Delphic Tripod*; a frieze on all four sides of the building, representing a *Homeric Combat and Council of Gods*, the *Judgement of Paris*, an *Abduction Scene* and a *Gigantomachy* (see fig. 53); and two caryatids in the porch. It seems to have been produced by two distinct workshops, and there even exists the signature of the artist responsible for the north and east sides, carved into the shield of a giant, though the actual name of this master of narrative structure and foreshortening is lost. The Siphnian Treasury, standing as it did in a pan-hellenic sanctuary, constituted both a sculptural lesson and a challenge to the rest of Greece, answered near the end of the Archaic period by those most contentious of Greeks, the Athenians. Their treasury at Delphi was a Doric structure located along the Sacred Way above the Siphnian Treasury. It was adorned with metopes representing the *Exploits of Herakles and Theseus* and, across the entire east side, a *Battle between the Greeks and the Amazons*. The date of the Athenian Treasury is notoriously controversial, but scholars increasingly accept Pausanias' statement that it was built to commemorate the Athenian victory over the Persians at Marathon (490 BC). If so, the *Battle between the Greeks and the Amazons* would allude to the recent historical struggle between West and East.

The *Battle between the Gods and Giants* on the Siphnian Treasury, with its implicit moral theme of the defeat of *hubris* by wisdom and order, was repeated in the limestone

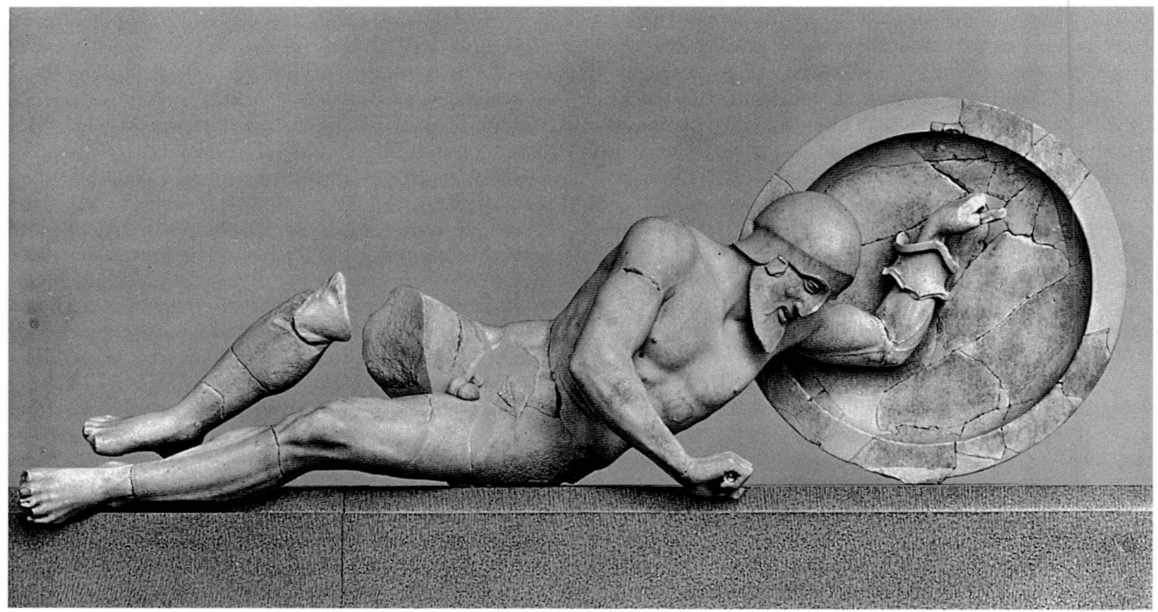

54. *Dying Warrior*, Parian marble, h. 640 mm, from the east pediment of the Temple of Aphaia at Aigina, Late Archaic period, *c*. 490–*c*. 480 BC (Munich, Glyptothek)

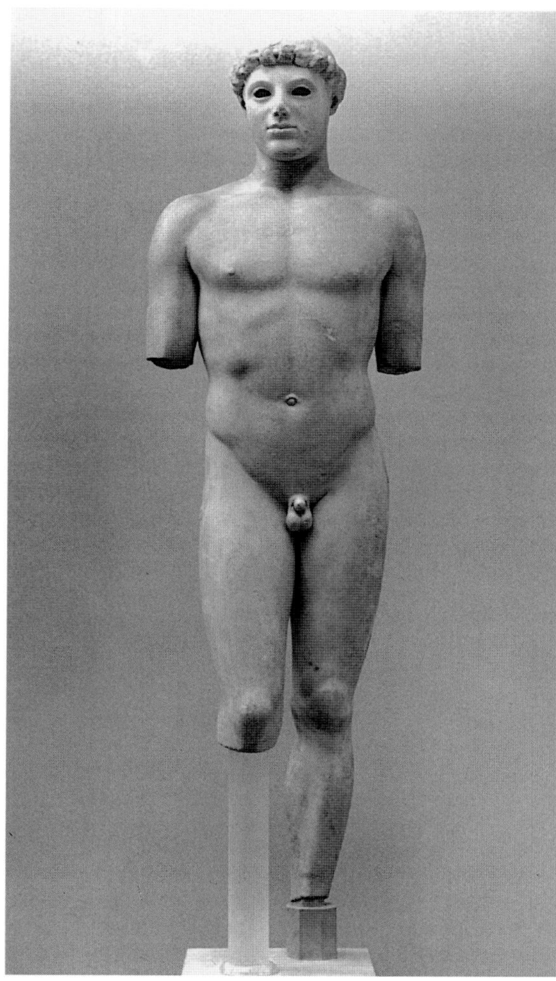

55. *Kritios Boy*, marble, h. 1.17 m, from the Acropolis, Athens, Late Archaic period, *c.* 480 BC (Athens, Acropolis Museum)

west pediment of the Archaic Temple of Apollo (*c.* 510 BC) at Delphi, though these sculptures are poorly preserved. The marble east pediment, commissioned by an important Athenian family *c.* 513 BC, depicted *Apollo in a Chariot* flanked by kouroi and korai (often stylistically linked to the Antenor Kore from the Acropolis) and, in the angles, by groups of lions attacking animals, apparently an old-fashioned compositional solution though perhaps also an intentional symbol of the suppression of the savage violence of nature to the corners of a pedimental cosmos dominated by the calm, civilizing power of Apollo.

Later still are the pedimental sculptures of the Temple of Apollo Daphnephoros at Eretria (*c.* 500 BC or later; Chalkis, Archaeol. Mus., and Rome, Mus. Conserv.), which depicted *Theseus Abducting Antiope under the Protection of Athena.* This alluded to the close political ties between Eretria and Athens, which together raided Persian Sardis in 498 BC. On Aigina, Athens' bitter foe, the Temple of Aphaia had its first set of pediments (*c.* 500–490 BC) replaced by a second set (*c.* 490–480 BC or later; Munich, Glyp.), depicting two legendary sacks of Troy (by Herakles and by Agamemnon). Even though these later pediments do not seem to differ appreciably in date (the east seems slightly later than the west), their radical differences of style and mood embody the transition from the Archaic to the Classical style. The west pediment is stylistically conservative: its *Dying Warrior* is essentially an awkwardly reclining, vacantly smiling kouros. The east pediment, however, is stylistically advanced: its *Dying Warrior* has drama and pathos, vainly struggling to support himself with his shield (see fig. 54). These qualities mark it as already essentially Early Classical in spirit.

The end of the Archaic style came quickly. Even by 500 BC such quintessentially Archaic types as the kouros must have seemed old-fashioned, especially when contrasted with vigorous and sophisticated relief scenes on their bases, in which twisting and foreshortened poses were used to create a sense of space (e.g. the *Ball-player* base, *c.* 510 BC; Athens, N. Archaeol. Mus.) or to manipulate perspective (on two sides of a base the same procession of warriors and chariot is depicted as if seen from different angles; *c.* 500 BC; Athens, N. Archaeol. Mus., 3477). Such juxtapositions of old schemata with bold experiments must have seemed increasingly incongruous. Even the elaborate ornamentality of Late Archaic korai no longer appealed: one of the latest Acropolis korai, dedicated by Euthydikos *c.* 490 BC, eschews the elaborate surfaces of earlier examples in favour of a simplicity that emphasizes the form of the body beneath the cloth; and it no longer has the Archaic smile. Perhaps by the same sculptor is the moody *Blond Boy* (Athens, Acropolis Mus., 689), which, like the *Kritios Boy* (see fig. 55), was dedicated on the Acropolis *c.* 480 BC, the year of the Persian sack of Athens. Though little remains of the *Blond Boy*, both figures originally stood with all their weight shifted on to one leg and with the other leg relaxed, thus assuming a pose suggestive of a spontaneous moment, rather than the traditional quadratic pose of the 'eternal' kouros. Both turn their heads to the right, breaking with the accustomed Archaic frontality, and both appear not to look out at the world like a kouros but inwards, in self-conscious contemplation. Whenever they were dedicated on the Acropolis, either just before 480 BC or just after, the Archaic style in sculpture ended with them.

BIBLIOGRAPHY

H. Schrader and others: *Die archaischen Marmorbildwerke der Akropolis* (Frankfurt am Main, 1939)

G. M. A. Richter: *Kouroi: Archaic Greek Youths* (London, 1942, 3/1970)

——: *The Archaic Gravestones of Attica* (London, 1961)

——: *Korai: Archaic Greek Maidens* (London, 1968)

J. Boardman: 'Herakles, Peisistratos, and Sons', *Rev. Archéol.* (1972), pp. 52–72

B. Freyer-Schauenburg: *Bildwerke der archaischen Zeit und des strengen Stils* (1974), xi of *Samos* (Bonn, 1961–)

L. Schneider: *Zur sozialen Bedeutung der archaischen Korenstatuen* (Hamburg, 1975)

J. G. Pedley: *Greek Sculpture of the Archaic Period: The Island Workshops* (Mainz, 1976)

B. S. Ridgway: *The Archaic Style in Greek Sculpture* (Princeton, 1977, rev. Chicago, 1993)

J. Boardman: *Greek Sculpture: The Archaic Period* (London, 1978/*R* 1988)

J. M. Hurwit: *The Art and Culture of Early Greece, 1100–480 BC* (Ithaca, NY, 1985)

Archaische und klassische griechische Plastik: Akten des internationalen Kolloquiums: Athen, 1985

J. Floren: *Die geometrische und archaische Plastik* (1987), i of *Die griechische Plastik*, ed. W. Fuchs and J. Floren (Munich, 1987–)
C. C. Mattusch: *Greek Bronze Statuary: From the Beginnings through the Fifth Century BC* (Ithaca, NY, 1988)
J. M. Hurwit: 'The Kritios Boy: Discovery, Reconstruction and Date', *Amer. J. Archaeol.*, xciii (1989), pp. 41–80
A. F. Stewart: *Greek Sculpture: An Exploration*, 2 vols (New Haven and London, 1990)

JEFFREY M. HURWIT

(iii) Classical (c. *500/480–323* BC).

(a) Early (*c.* 500/480–*c.* 450 BC). (b) High (*c.* 450–*c.* 375 BC). (c) Late (*c.* 375–323 BC).

(a) Early (c. *500/480*–c. *450* BC).

Introduction. Sculpture of this period is termed 'Severe style', being distinguished both from fully developed High Classical sculpture (*see* §(b) below) and from the mannerism of the Late Archaic period (*see* §(ii) above). It is characterized by new and effective means of representing the human form. Even before the early 5th century BC, there had been experiments in foreshortening, in three-dimensional representation of the human body and in balanced distribution of masses. Although in the few remains of Early Classical free-standing sculpture these attempts can no longer be clearly discerned, they are evident in reliefs and in contemporary vase paintings. Unfortunately, ANTENOR's first group of *Tyrannicides* does not survive, but the group of *Theseus Abducting Antiope*, from the pediment of the Temple of Apollo at Eretria (*see* §(ii)(c) above), can be adduced.

Antenor was probably among the important sculptors who brought about the shift from Late Archaic sculpture to the Severe style. About the end of the 5th century BC Antenor worked in Athens, where KRITIOS AND NESIOTES were later of special importance. They were commissioned to produce a new work (see fig. 56) to replace Antenor's *Tyrannicides* on the Agora, which had been removed by the Persian king Xerxes in 480/79 BC. Other famous sculptors of the early Severe style whose names are known but whose works do not survive include Kanachos of Sikyon (*see* KANACHOS (ii)) and PYTHAGORAS OF RHEGION. ONATAS' and KALAMIS' work is much disputed. MYRON OF ELEUTHERAI's *Diskobolos* (see fig. 38 above) and *Athena with Marsyas* have been identified, although these statues already demonstrate the transition to High Classical art, also marked by the works of younger sculptors such as POLYKLEITOS, PHEIDIAS or ALKAMENES.

In contrast to the situation with High and Late classical sculpture, the Romans left few copies of Severe style works. A few original bronzes have been preserved: works from the second quarter of the 5th century BC include the *Charioteer* from Delphi (*see* DELPHI, fig. 5), the ARTEMISION BRONZES, a *Youth* from Selinus (Palermo, Mus. Reg.) and a similar head from the Athenian Acropolis (Athens, N. Archaeol. Mus.), the head of the Chatsworth *Apollo* (London, BM), a bearded head with portrait-like features from Messina and, at the point of transition from Early to High Classical, the RIACE BRONZES (see fig. 58 below). The stylistic development of marble sculpture can be traced from architectural sculptures, grave and votive reliefs, bronze statuettes (e.g. of sportsmen or *peplos*-clad female figures), especially from the second quarter of the 5th century BC (*see* STATUETTE, fig. 1), and through figural

56. Kritios and Nesiotes: *Tyrannicides*, early 5th century BC, Roman copy (Naples, Museo Archeologico Nazionale)

bronzes ornamenting such objects as mirror handles. Few large votive statues of victors in pan-hellenic games are recorded before the end of the Early Classical period.

Sculpture in terracotta remained important. Large pieces frequently took the form of acroteria, still popular in South Italy and also represented at Olympia, including a group of *Zeus Abducting Ganymede* (*see* OLYMPIA, fig. 6) and an *Athena* (Olympia, Archaeol. Mus.). Smaller votive terracottas also provide important evidence, although the reuse of moulds creates problems of dating. Clay reliefs from Melos and Lokroi Epizephyrioi deserve special mention, even though many examples from earlier moulds were probably not cast until after the mid-5th century BC.

Centres of production. Despite the restrictions imposed by sumptuary laws and the effects of the Persian Wars, Athens was an important centre for sculpture in this period, and the destruction of the city by the Persians in 480/79 BC provides an invaluable chronological reference point. Also central to the development of marble sculpture in the first half of the 5th century BC was Paros, where there was an important statue of *Nike* (for illustration *see* PAROS). Ionian relief sculpture also includes a delicate depiction of a funerary banquet from Thasos (Istanbul, Archaeol. Mus.) and grave reliefs, proscribed in Attica at this time. Of these, the best-known type depicts a girl holding a bird. Ionian workshops produced large numbers of broad-format tomb stelai especially suited to family scenes, for example the grave relief from Ikaria. Sculptures from Paros were widely exported; Parian marble was of outstanding quality and, when exported for a temple pediment, might be accompanied by an entire workshop (one reason for the itinerant nature of sculptors and for the 'internationalization' of ancient Greek art; *see also* §1(v) above). Parian grave reliefs also inspired local imitation, such as the copious if partly provincial production of stelai in Thessaly.

Types and subject-matter. Kouroi (*see* KOUROS) and korai (*see* KORE) continued to be produced as votive offerings, even in Athens, but their character quickly changed, with details, gestures and shaping becoming freer and more individual and new basic types being added. The same applies to cult statues. An important turning point, marking the end of Late Archaic art (*see* §(ii)(c) above), is seen in a comparison of the *Aristodikos Kouros* (*see* KOUROS, fig. 2) or the *Antenor Kore* (Athens, Acropolis Mus.) with the *Kritios Boy* (see fig. 55 above), whose pose demonstrates a truly balanced distribution of masses, the *Blond Boy* or the closely-related *Euthydikos Kore.* A dating reference shortly after this is provided by the *Tyrannicides* group by Kritios and Nesiotes (477/6 BC; see fig. 56). The end of the Severe style is marked by a number of statues of Apollo that, despite a clearer distribution of body masses, have not yet mastered the contrapposto pattern perfected by Polykleitos at around the same time, still having both feet fully on the ground.

Female Severe style statues are usually masked by their garments, quite unlike Late Archaic korai, whose garments clearly reveal the forms of the female body. Examples include the Angelitos *Athena* by Euenor (Athens, Acropolis Mus.), the *Ludovisi Candia*, the so-called *Hestia Giustiniani* (Rome, Villa Albani) and, completely wrapped in her cloak, the *Aspasia* in Berlin (Pergamonmus.). The impression given by these works is governed by the play of folds: the contrast between the simple, ideally formed heads, with their partly veiled but delicate and animated hair styles, and the flat, almost unstructured surfaces of the garments. The same is true of the bronze *Charioteer* from Delphi dating from the same time. About the mid-5th century BC this stage, strict and yet rich in contrasts, is taken to its conclusion and transcended by the youthful *Athena* (copy; Frankfurt am Main, Liebieghaus) from Myron's *Athena with Marsyas* group.

Children are infrequent subjects in free-standing sculpture, although they appear as secondary figures in the pediments at Olympia and are sometimes accurately portrayed in Severe style reliefs. At the end of the Early Classical period, however, children begin to be shown in terms of their age, (e.g. in the family scenes on the stele in Ikaria).

The character of narrative reliefs and pedimental sculpture slowly changes; the emphasis shifts from pure action to the underlying situation as in the *Preparations for the Chariot Race between Pelops and Oinomaos* on the east pediment at Olympia (see fig. 45 above).

In terms of detail, the folds at the vertical edge of a garment, initially forming a schematic zigzag pattern, become larger and more individual; Archaic embossed locks of hair, still seen in Harmodios in the *Tyrannicides* group, give way to a plastic rendering of crescent locks. Formally, however, a conservative element persisted, evident in the old-fashioned folds with projecting zigzag edges in the *Nike* dedicated by Kallimachos, who died at Marathon in 490 BC (Athens, Acropolis Mus.). Such stylized, sub-Archaic features should not be confused, however, with the archaizing and archaistic tendencies that began somewhat later, around and after the turn of the century.

Although votive reliefs became less common in Athens, pieces of high quality were produced in other regions, for example Thasos and Paros. Two works in a category of their own are the Ludovisi Throne, originating in South Italy (see fig. 57), and the Boston Throne (Boston, MA, Mus. F.A.; *see also* LOKROI EPIZEPHYRIOI), perhaps sculptural elements of altars depicting central mythological scenes (the birth of Aphrodite, probably, and the weighing of souls by Hermes respectively) on the front side, accompanied by supplementary sitting figures on the small sides. The votive offerings at large shrines include various free-standing groups that mostly seem to have been conceived as accumulations of single figures. The two bronze warriors from Riace probably formed part of such a group produced shortly before the mid-5th century BC.

Two-figure groups begin to express an inner relation and a concrete event taking place between the figures; this is particularly true of combat groups—including those on temple pediments—and of figures facing each other, as in reliefs of this time and later. Two-figure grave reliefs also became more common. With regard to the group formation, the *Tyrannicides* of Kritios and Nesiotes are a special case: despite the simple axial symmetry of the concept, a wider context and a complex political statement are evoked. The Severe style also first made possible the depiction not only of figures in motion but of fighters in action on pediments and in groups, for example a torso from the Temple of Zeus at Akragas or the *Leonidas* from the acropolis at Sparta (Sparta, Archaeol. Mus.), with its unusual rotating movements.

Of special importance in the Severe style is the first development in Greece of genuine portrait sculpture, which strove for individual characterization, even emphasizing features that diverged from the ideal of beauty. The portrait of *Themistokles* (Ostia Antica, Mus. Ostiense) still shows a close proximity to the *Tyrannicides*, but the portrait of *Pindar* (Oslo, Nmus.; long mistakenly attributed to Pausanias of Sparta and dated too early) is part of the transition to High Classicism.

The overall contribution made by architectural, especially pedimental, sculpture to the dissemination and unification of Early Classical innovations must be emphasized. The sculpture of the Temple of Aphaia on AIGINA is of major importance (*see* §(ii)(c) above): the sculptures in the earlier west pediment are still in the Archaic style, whereas the later east pediment shows new features clearly belonging to the Severe style, as in the difference between the dying warriors in the corners (see fig. 54 above). Still more important are the large sculptural groups from the two pediments of the Temple of Zeus at OLYMPIA. While the traditional difference between the more static east

57. Ludovisi Throne, marble, h. at corner 840 mm, second quarter of 5th century BC (Rome, Museo Nazionale Romano)

pediment and the more animated west pediment is preserved, both show convincing new solutions in representing movement and depth, thus foreshadowing the sculptures of the Parthenon (*see* §(b) below). They offer the best examples of the attempt to resolve the spatial problems posed by fighting groups. In the treatment of the canonical Twelve Labours of Herakles, the metopes of Temple E at Selinus are close to those of the Temple of Zeus at Olympia. In both series a change in the choice of moment can be noted: instead of the dramatic climax of a struggle, a moment of rest after it is often shown.

BIBLIOGRAPHY

E. Langlotz: *Frühgriechische Bildhauerschulen* (Nuremberg, 1927)
P. Jacobsthal: *Die melischen Reliefs* (Berlin, 1931)
V. Poulsen: 'Der strenge Stil: Studien zur Geschichte der griechischen Plastik 480–450', *Acta Archaeol.* [Copenhagen], viii (1937), pp. 1–142
S. Brunnsaaker: *The Tyrant-slayers: A Critical Study of the Sources and Restorations* (Lund, 1955, rev. Stockholm, 1971)
W.-H. Schuchardt: *Die Epochen der griechischen Plastik* (Princeton, 1959)
H. Biesantz: *Die thessalischen Grabreliefs: Studien zur nordgriechischen Kunst* (Mainz, 1965)
U. Knigge: *Bewegte Figuren der Grossplastik im strengen Stil* (diss., U. Munich, 1965)
H. Prückner: *Die lokrischen Tonreliefs: Beitrag zur Kulturgeschichte von Lokroi Epizephyrioi* (Mainz, 1968)
E. Berger: *Das Basler Altzrelief: Studien zur griechischen Grab- und Votivrelief um 500 v. Chr. und zur vorhippokrateischen Medizin* (Basle, 1970)
B. S. Ridgway: *The Severe Style in Greek Sculpture* (Princeton, 1970)
D. Metzler: *Porträt und Gesellschaft: Über die Entstehung des griechischen Porträts in der Klassik* (Munster, 1971)
H. Hiller: *Ionische Grabreliefs der ersten Hälfte des 5. Jahrhunderts v. Chr.*, *Istanbul. Mitt.*, suppl. 12 (1975) [whole vol.]
D. Willers: *Zu den Anfängen der archaistischen Plastik in Griechenland*, *Dt. Archäol. Inst.: Athen. Abt. Mitt.*, suppl. 4 (1975) [whole vol.]
J. Dörig: *Onatas of Aegina*, Monumenta Graeca et Romana, i (Leiden, 1977)
R. Tölle-Kastenbein: *Frühklassische Peplosfiguren: Originale* (Mainz, 1980)
D. Haynes: *Greek Art and the Idea of Freedom* (London, 1981)
R. Tölle-Kastenbein: 'Frühklassische Peplosfiguren: Typen und Repliken', *Ant. Plast.*, xx (1981) [whole vol.]
B. Fehr: *Die Tyrannentöter oder: Kann man der Demokratie ein Denkmal setzen?* (Frankfurt am Main, 1984)
G. B. Triches: *Die bronzi da Riace: Rinvenimento, restauro, analisi ed ipotesi di interpretazione*, 2 vols (Rome, 1984)
J. Boardman: *Greek Sculpture: The Classical Period* (London, 1985/*R* 1991)
W. Fuchs: 'Die Eroberung der Freiheit in der griechischen Kunst', *Spiegelungen*, ed. W. Knopp (1986), pp. 1–20

(b) High (c. 450–c. 375 BC). Towards the mid-5th century BC a new phase of Classical Greek sculpture, different in character from the Severe style, was inaugurated with the discovery of new and even more striking possibilities for representing the human figure in three dimensions. This High Classical period can be subdivided into three phases, each corresponding roughly to a quarter of a century. High Classicism proper reached its peak in the third quarter of the 5th century BC, when the most important and innovative works were produced. Then came a phase in the last quarter of the century, known as the Rich style, during which the successful formulae were perfected, often being lavishly applied, occasionally to the point of mannered exaggeration, with strong graphic tendencies. The Rich style was followed by a late phase in the first quarter of the 4th century BC, when the repetition of these formulae became hackneyed and sometimes meaningless. Almost immediately a reaction set in, characterized by greater plasticity, simplification and hardening of forms, preparing the way for the Late Classical Plain style in the second quarter of the 4th century BC.

Free-standing works. Although most of the free-standing works by the celebrated masters of the High Classical period, which was regarded already by the Romans as the greatest age of Greek art, are now lost, some of them are known from descriptions in ancient sources, many of them Roman, and from Roman copies. The task of interpreting this evidence, which has occupied scholars since the Renaissance, has produced some convincing results, especially in the 19th and early 20th centuries, and, in some cases, more recently. It is thus possible to gain a vague impression of these lost masterpieces, though the quality of the evidence varies considerably from sculptor to sculptor, and the uncertain methodological basis for interpreting it has sometimes led to quite contradictory conclusions. Moreover, evaluation of copies and written sources can give only an imprecise outline of the lives or development of individual sculptors. Nevertheless, some idea can be formed of lost works by the sculptors Myron, Pheidias, Polykleitos, Alkamenes, Kresilas and Agorakritos and, less certainly, of those by Kalamis and Kallimachos. There is also some record of the early 4th-century BC sculptors Naukydes and Timotheos but almost none of others such as Kolotes and Strongylion.

The most important and versatile sculptor of the 5th century BC, and the most famous even in antiquity, was the Athenian PHEIDIAS, whose career extended from the late Severe style to the Peloponnesian War. However, the attribution of many of the works traditionally assigned to him is disputed, including the two RIACE BRONZES (*c.* 455–*c.* 450 BC; Reggio Calabria, Mus. N.; see fig. 58). These demonstrate the striving towards a clearer and more spatially convincing representation of the body in action, a quality shared by copies of other mid-5th century BC works attributed to Pheidias with greater certainty. Among these are the Kassel *Apollo* (*c.* 450 BC; copy, Kassel, Hess. Landesmus.), the *Anakreon* (*c.* 450–440 BC; best copy, Copenhagen, Ny Carlsberg Glyp.), in collaboration with Kolotes Theokosmos and the painter Panainos, and the *Hermes Ludovisi* (*c.* 450–440 BC; named after copy, Rome, Mus. N. Romano), with its Attic contrapposto (a balanced standing posture with the flexed leg set firmly in front). Pheidias' masterpieces were considered to be two colossal chryselephantine cult statues, which received the longest descriptions of any sculptures in ancient literature. One of these, the *Zeus* (*c.* 430 BC; remains of piece-moulds from Pheidias' workshop, Olympia, Archaeol. Mus.) at Olympia, is reproduced only on Roman Imperial coins. The other, the *Athena Parthenos* (*c.* 440 BC), survives in small-scale copies, the most important of which are the Varvakeion Statuette (h. 1.05 m) and the Lenormant Statuette (h. 420 mm; both Athens, N. Archaeol. Mus.).

On the other hand, the works of POLYKLEITOS of Argos, who is assumed to have been active from the middle to the end of the 5th century BC, present a unified picture. His representations of youths, with their rather uniformly schematized curly hair, reveal a clear pattern of development, especially in his late work. His treatise explaining in theoretical terms the ideal proportions displayed in a sample statue known as the Canon (both now lost) exemplified the Greek belief that the ideal proportions of the human figure were based on fixed mathematical relationships and that it was the artist's task to represent this. The Canon is probably represented by the *Doryphoros* (*c.* 440 BC; most complete copy with best copy of the head, Naples, Mus. Archeol. N.; for illustration of copy in Minneapolis, MN, Inst. A., *see* POLYKLEITOS). Developed here for the first time is the definitive Classical contrapposto, a standing posture with equilibrium based on reciprocal antithesis: the unengaged leg bears no weight and is set back, and the overall composition reveals the working of individual parts of the body by means of the clearly recognizable distribution of weight.

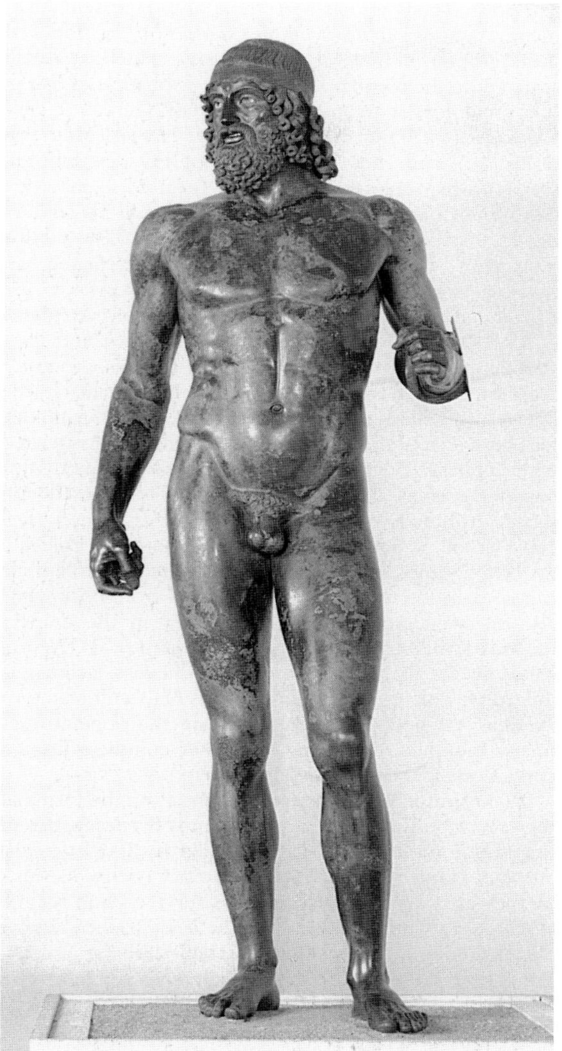

58. *Warrior* (Statue A), bronze, h. 1.98 m, from Riace, High Classical period, *c.* 455–*c.* 450 BC (Reggio Calabria, Museo Nazionale)

Pheidias' fellow sculptors and rivals in Athens, such as ALKAMENES, an exact contemporary who worked until the end of the 5th century BC, AGORAKRITOS and KRESILAS, were strongly influenced by him. Consequently, in several cases the attribution of works is disputed among them, for example two statue-types of Aphrodite from *c.* 420 BC: the Daphne type (copy, Naples Mus. Archeol. N.) and the Seated Olympias type (copy, Rome, Mus.

Torlonia). The latter has been thought to represent Alkamenes' famous *Aphrodite in the Gardens* on the slopes of the Acropolis. However, Polykleitos' influence is also apparent in the contrapposto and the formation of hair in other sculptors' work, particularly that of Kresilas (e.g. his *Diomedes*, *c.* 430 BC; full-length copy, Naples, Mus. Archeol. N.), and even in the work of Pheidias himself. Occasionally, sculptors deliberately reverted to the Attic contrapposto, which had been usual in the mid-5th century BC, as in Alkamenes' Borghese *Ares* (*c.* 420 BC; named after copy, Paris, Louvre). This sculptor retained, on purpose, some archaic elements in such works as the *Hecate* and *Hermes Propylaios* on the Acropolis at Athens (*c.* 430 BC; copies, Athens, Brit. Sch. Archaeol. and Panathenaic Stadium, respectively). The famous group of Amazons from Ephesos must all have been made shortly before the Peloponnesian War, though their chronology has been disputed. If the *Amazon* generally associated with Kresilas (Copenhagen–Sciarra type; named after copy, Copenhagen, Ny Carlsberg Glyp.) is compared with those attributed to Pheidias (Mattei type; named after copy, Rome, Vatican, Mus. Pio-Clementino) and Polykleitos (copy signed by Sosikles, Rome, Mus. Capitolino), it can be seen to have borrowed elements from both while also showing an exaggerated tendency in the drapery towards symmetrical and finely delineated folds. Agorakritos seems to have had more of Pheidias' genius, as indeed was his reputation in antiquity. His cult statue of *Nemesis* has been reconstructed from the original fragments found at Rhamnous (*c.* 430 BC; complete Roman copy, Copenhagen, Ny Carlsberg Glyp.).

The introduction of a clearer emphasis on the forms of the female body by means of apparently 'wet' transparent drapery seems to have been initiated by PAIONIOS OF MENDE, whose *Nike* (*c.* 420 BC; Olympia, Archaeol. Mus.; *see* OLYMPIA, fig. 5) at Olympia has survived, and KALLIMACHOS, to whom is attributed the Fréjus *Aphrodite* (or Venus Genetrix type, *c.* 420–*c.* 410 BC; named after copy, Paris, Louvre; see fig. 59). The preference for the lavish treatment of folds that became increasingly apparent in the 430s BC led in the last two decades of the 5th century BC to other mannered works. Many of these, typifying the early Rich style, cannot be securely attributed, for example the *Hera Borghese* (*c.* 410 BC; copy, Copenhagen, Ny Carlsberg Glyp.) and the *Athena Velletri* (*c.* 420–410 BC; copy, Paris, Louvre). By the beginning of the 4th century BC, however, a reaction is apparent in the works of Polykleitos' pupil NAUKYDES (e.g. his *Diskobolos* (*c.* 400 BC; copy, Rome, Pal. Conserv., Mus. Nuovo) and the *Hermes of Troizen* (*c.* 390 BC; copy, Athens, N. Hist. Mus.), though the Polykleitian tradition is still discernible in them, as in the works of TIMOTHEOS, to whom the *Hygieia* (*c.* 380 BC; copy, Athens, N. Archaeol. Mus.) at Epidauros can probably be attributed. New motifs were explored, with striding figures in vigorous action. The calligraphic treatment of both drapery folds and hair was disrupted though not rejected immediately.

To the Greeks the most important large free-standing sculptures were the cult statues in temples, representing single or paired gods either calmly standing or enthroned (e.g. Pheidias' *Athena* in Athens and *Zeus* at Olympia). Iconographically these were often indistinguishable from

59. Fréjus *Aphrodite*, h. 1.65 m, High Classical period, *c.* 420–*c.* 410 BC; marble copy (Paris, Musée du Louvre)

votive statues, but other types of sculptures set up in temples and sanctuaries included statues of animals, such as the famous *Heifer* by MYRON OF ELEUTHERAI on the Acropolis at Athens (Pliny: *Natural History* XXXIV. xix.57), and mythological figures and groups, such as the *Trojan Horse* by STRONGYLION, also on the Acropolis (now lost), as well as an increasing number of honorary portrait statues. The latter, which were generally posthumous, are of special historical value, since some can be dated by the names inscribed on copies. The first signs of a concern with the realistic depiction of age and with a subject's individuality are found at the beginning of the High Classical period, for example in a portrait of the poet *Pindar* (*c.* 440 BC; copy, Oslo, Nmus.), who died soon after 446 BC. This contrasts with idealized portraits, such as that of *Pericles* (*c.* 425 BC; copy, London, BM) by Kresilas.

Architectural and relief sculpture. A detailed picture of the stylistic developments of the Classical period is, however, derived less from surviving copies of important free-standing sculptures than from works of relief sculpture. Although often smaller and anonymous (but original), these are more numerous and provide more evidence for making comparisons and historical connections. They include architectural sculptures such as metopes and friezes, funerary and dedicatory reliefs and related works; particularly important among these are the so-called record reliefs.

During the mid-5th century BC important marble statues and reliefs were produced on the Aegean islands, especially Paros, with its supply of high-quality marble, and these were distributed throughout the Aegean. Typical Parian products of the early High Classical period are some children's grave stelai depicting birds, the best known being the Dove Stele (*c.* 440 BC; New York, Met., 27.45). Some of these pieces were found as far away as northern Greece, and they apparently influenced the production of reliefs in Thessaly. These were plentiful until the beginning of the 4th century BC, but they often appear stiff and coarse in their proportions and execution, as do reliefs from other regions. In some regions independent styles also developed. Thus in Boiotia around 430–420 BC, besides Ionian-influenced grave reliefs imported either directly or via Athens, a number of accomplished, finely incised local stelai occur. These were apparently intended to be painted and were clearly influenced by wall painting. In Lakonia, whose rich Archaic artistic tradition had long expired, a small workshop produced extremely provincial flat reliefs. However, most Rich style reliefs come from Athens, which at that time was the most important city state in Greece, both politically and artistically. During the Periclean building programme, Athens attracted many Ionian artists, above all the celebrated Agorakritos of Paros. Though individual, independent or regional groups existed, most of the works found outside Attica from the late 5th century BC already show the influence of developments in Athens. This influence even appears to have been stimulated by the collapse of Athens at the end of the Peloponnesian War (404 BC), since many artists were apparently forced to seek work and patrons in other Greek states from the Black Sea to Italy. They took with them not only models but also whole workshops with their accumulated expertise and in effect created a common school of Greek sculpture in the 4th century BC, which continued to be dominated by artistic practice in Athens.

For the High Classical period it is precisely the great Periclean religious buildings in Attica itself that provide the most exact sculptural record. The chronological sequence can sometimes be established from the surviving inscriptions of the annual building accounts, which were then customary only in the Attic democracy, though in the 4th century BC they also existed in other city states. Here the Parthenon on the Acropolis at Athens, the construction of which was in some way overseen by Pheidias, is of the greatest importance. The iconographic programme of its architectural sculpture was certainly conceived by Pheidias himself and became an influential model for all similar later projects. Its full extent was recorded in drawings made by Jacques Carrey shortly

60. *Hestia, Dione (or Themis) and Aphrodite*, marble, h. 1.3 m (highest fig.), from the east pediment of the Parthenon, Athens, High Classical period, *c.* 437–*c.* 432 BC (London, British Museum)

before the Parthenon was blown up in 1687. Enough is preserved (mostly London, BM; also Athens, Acropolis Mus., and elsewhere) to give an idea of the sequence of construction and the corresponding subtle stylistic changes in the 440s and 430s BC. The massive metopes, probably commissioned at the beginning of construction around 447 BC, show traditional mythological battle scenes, though some are imaginatively treated (see fig. 40 above). The earliest metopes only just begin to depart from the Severe style. By contrast, the great Panathenaic frieze, with the inexhaustible variety of its new subject-matter, is more softly modelled. It dates from *c*. 442–*c*. 438 BC, and parts of it were finished *in situ*. Finally, the free-standing sculpture in the two pediments belongs to *c*. 437–*c*. 432 BC. Here Pheidias, who has always been thought to have designed the works, gave a new form to a traditional theme (a divine birth among the Olympians; east pediment) and put a new theme (the quarrel of the gods over the land of Attica; west pediment) into visual form. Despite the loss of the central figures and much other damage, the better preserved east pediment remains a magnificent sculptural ensemble (for detail showing a group originally in the right-hand angle of the pediment, see fig. 60). The completion of Pheidias' chryselephantine statue of *Athena Parthenos* can be dated to 438 BC, when the cella was already roofed. Its sculpted and painted ornament, including the animals on the upper part of the helmet, the reliefs on the outside and the images on the inside of the shield, and the reliefs on the sandals and on the base, evidently reflected the iconographic programme of the temple itself. Small-scale reproductions of the statue and fairly accurate neo-Attic relief copies of the figures on the outside of the shield contribute to a clear overall idea of the High Classical style in sculpture. Despite the collaboration of many sculptors, the Parthenon is characterized by a varied but coherent style, presumably attributable to Pheidias' involvement (*see also* ATHENS, §II, 1(ii)).

61. Bridge-building Relief, marble, h. 830 mm, from Eleusis, High Classical period, 421/20 BC (Eleusis Museum)

Fragments of pedimental sculpture, acroteria, friezes and metopes survive from several slightly later Periclean temples. The best preserved are the friezes and metopes of the Temple of Hephaistos (Hephaisteion; *c*. 450–*c*. 430 BC; Athens, Agora Mus., and *in situ*). The east frieze, at least, should be dated to the end of the 430s BC, and the increasingly high relief of the friezes led to a denser calligraphic treatment of individual figures, a style subsequently perfected in the frieze of the small Temple of Athena Nike on the Acropolis (slabs *in situ*, Athens, Acropolis Mus., and London, BM). The latter must date from after a change in plan of the Propylaia during the Peloponnesian War, probably *c*. 425 BC. Though all its formulae are High Classical, the effect is sterile and crowded, so that it already represents the long 'mannered' final phase of High Classicism, the Rich style.

Two new developments in Attic sculpture ensure that the evolution of the Rich style is well-documented. One was the rescinding of the Kleisthenic prohibition of luxurious grave monuments, which had been in force from *c*. 500 BC. This meant a rapid increase in the number of Attic sculpture workshops returning to the tradition of funerary sculpture that had been continued since the Archaic period on the Aegean islands and in northern Greece. Instead of free-standing kouroi or korai, however, these now produced various types of funerary reliefs. Besides the traditional tall, narrow single-figure stelai there appeared increasing numbers of the broader stelai, usually with a pedimental top and several figures. This type of relief immediately became widespread, predominating until the end of the Classical period. It was characterized by increasingly high relief accompanied by a tendency to architecturalize the stelai to the point at which they suggest *naïskoi* (grave shrines). Ever more varied requirements led to the development of large grave temples, eventually constructed from several pieces, and small flat stelai with a simple painted frame, both types probably being produced in specialist workshops. The old custom of placing special funerary vases on graves led to the development of marble funerary lekythoi and loutrophoroi adorned with reliefs. Some stood on pedestals, which could have relief decoration, as could the 'funerary tables' on other graves. The production of votive reliefs also increased, but, though some display the architecturalizing tendency evident in grave reliefs, most are still in the form of framed oblong panels (*pinakes*), often placed on high pillars in sanctuaries. The reliefs depicting *Orpheus* and *Peliads* (*c*. 420 BC; copies, Naples, Mus. Archeol. N., 6729, and Berlin, Pergamonmus., 925) brilliantly encapsulate a whole myth in a single crucial scene, recalling the plays of Euripides. By contrast, a round base with *Dancing Maenads* (*c*. 410–400 BC; copy, Rome, Mus. Conserv., 1094) illustrates the Rich style sculptors' obsession with the abstract linear play of fluttering drapery.

The second important new development in sculpture was the use of reliefs to decorate public inscriptions in Athens (*see also* §1(i)(c) above). These record reliefs began to appear early in the Peloponnesian War (431–404 BC), and the series ends in the early 3rd century BC. As a source for the absolute dating of Greek sculpture, record reliefs carry risks, since they cannot be directly compared with large-scale architectural or free-standing sculpture. They usually depict only two figures, representing the partners concerned in the document, and though Late Classical record reliefs of the second half of the 4th century BC occasionally strive for more complex compositions, spatial depth and clearer perspective, reliefs in the Rich style use perspective only for the bodies of stationary figures. Moreover, the workmanship of some record reliefs makes a misleading basis for the stylistic analysis of drapery, which is usually particularly helpful for dating. They are thus best compared with technically similar works, particularly small funerary and votive reliefs or tectonic friezes, though even here slight differences of genre occur.

Early Rich style record reliefs from the 420s BC onwards show a preference for highly calligraphic drapery, sometimes swathing the whole figure with rippling tubular folds. Despite their relatively high quality, this remains an inadequate means of giving expression to the three-dimensional physicality of the figures, as demonstrated by the breasts of figures on the Eleusinian Bridge-building Relief (421/20 BC; Eleusis Mus.; see fig. 61) representing *Athena with the Eleusinian Triad.* The rippling folds of drapery on the upper bodies of the three female figures form almost symmetrical triangles. Smaller folds are gathered near the girdle in the female figures, with steep folds in front of the weight-bearing leg and taut, smooth folds over the relaxed leg. The frontally facing pose used for the figures of Demeter and Persephone became usual only at this time. Other record reliefs of before *c.* 410 BC display even more finely differentiated movement of the drapery, sometimes with larger smooth areas of cloth between the folds, which are otherwise still conceived as calligraphically as possible. In stark contrast to the figures on two documentary reliefs of 410/9 BC (Paris, Louvre, 83; Athens, Epig. Mus., 6598), which are particularly vital and delicate, are the figures on reliefs from the end of the Peloponnesian War, which are stiff and hard, with larger smooth areas of drapery. Nevertheless, the Rich style survived a long time. Both the unusual battle frieze from a State grave (Athens, N. Archaeol. Mus., 2744) and the funerary Dexileos Stele (Athens, Kerameikos Mus.; see fig. 62), dated by inscriptions to 394/3 BC, cling almost desperately to the calligraphic tendencies of the Rich style. Conversely, the figures of the city goddesses of Athens and Syracuse on the severely damaged record relief from the same year honouring Dionysios I of Syracuse (Athens, Epig. Mus., 6899) already show signs of stylistic changes. They have higher waists and almost conical bodies, and are generally stiff and lifeless. As part of a further reaction, the figures on the record relief for the treaty between Athens and Kerkyra (Corfu) of 376/5 BC (Athens, N. Archaeol. Mus., 1467) are no longer stiff but combine an elegance and ease of posture derived from the Rich style, with individual motifs and a new simplicity that announce the Late Classical Plain style (*see* §(c) below).

The Attic building documents are also useful for dating architectural sculptures, though often not with absolute certainty. Thus, though the frieze of the Temple of Athena Nike (see above) cannot be dated securely, the frieze on the Nike Balustrade (*c.* 415 BC; Athens, Acropolis Mus.), perhaps the purest embodiment of the Rich style, must be

62. Dexileos Stele, marble, h. 1.75 m, from the Kerameikos, Athens, High Classical period, 394/3 BC (Athens, Kerameikos Museum)

later than the long series of statues of Athena with trophies and *nikai* from the years shortly before Athens' catastrophic Sicilian campaign (415–413 BC). The Erechtheion is even more informative. Its relief frieze figures, attached by an unusual appliqué technique to a background of dark Eleusinian marble (Athens, Acropolis Mus.), are apparently mentioned in documents of *c.* 409 BC, which even make it possible to estimate the cost of the sculptors.

By contrast, the breaking down and hardening of Attic forms can be seen in the architecture and the frieze (*c.* 410 BC; London, BM, 540–42) of the Temple of Apollo at Bassai (see fig. 24 above). Though built in the middle of the Peloponnesian War, judged by Attic standards it can appear to be of a later date. And whereas the architectural sculpture of the rebuilt Temple of Hera (*c.* 400 BC; Athens, N. Archaeol. Mus., 1561) at Argos is only fragmentary, the more complete architectural sculpture from the Temple of Asklepios (*c.* 380 BC; Athens, N. Archaeol. Mus., and Epidauros, Archaeol. Mus.) at Epidauros provides examples of the final phase of the Rich style. Within this great ensemble, experiments in the construction of figures and depiction of action were clearly being attempted. This is especially apparent in the *Amazon on Horseback* (Athens, N. Archaeol. Mus.; see fig. 63) from the west front or the figure of a *Fallen Man* (Athens,

63. *Amazon on Horseback*, marble, h. 900 mm, from the west front of the Temple of Asklepios at Epidauros, High Classical period, *c.* 380 BC (Athens, National Archaeological Museum)

N. Hist. Mus.), which has a contorted pose that is far more vivid than that of any comparable earlier figure. The formation of the drapery folds also shows an acceptance and development of the conventions of the Rich style, while endowing them with a new animation. This contrasts with the simplifying and hardening tendencies of the Plain style and shows how the formal achievements of the High Classical period could be carried over into Late Classical sculpture.

Attic influence and also, to some extent, the presence of Attic craftsmen are behind much of the Rich style architectural and relief sculpture in East Greece. This includes funerary monuments in Lycia, for example the mythological friezes from the Heroon of Trysa (*c.* 410 BC; Vienna, Ksthist. Mus.), the battle reliefs and dancing girls of the Nereid Monument (*c.* 400 BC; London, BM) from Xanthos, the friezes and caryatids from the Heroon of Limyra (*c.* 390 BC) and the friezes on the higher-quality relief sarcophagi from the royal necropolis of Sidon (the Satraps Sarcophagus, *c.* 410 BC, and Lycian Sarcophagus, *c.* 390 BC; both Istanbul, Archaeol. Mus., 9(367) and 63(369)). In both areas Attic iconography combined with subject-matter commissioned by the local ruler to create something radically new in Greek sculpture, as shown by the inclusion of perspective and staggered architecture in continuous frieze narratives, an innovation based on oriental precedents and methods developed in wall painting.

BIBLIOGRAPHY

R. Carpenter: *The Sculpture of the Nike Temple Parapet* (Cambridge, MA, 1929)
G. M. A. Richter: *The Sculpture and Sculptors of the Greeks* (New Haven and London, 1929, 4/1970)
F. Brommer: *Die Skulpturen der Parthenon-Giebel* (Mainz, 1963)
B. Schlörb: *Untersuchungen zur Bildhauergeneration nach Phidias* (Waldsassen, 1964)
G. M. A. Richter: *The Portraits of the Greeks*, 3 vols (London, 1965); abridged and rev. by R. R. R. Smith (Oxford, 1984)
F. Brommer: *Die Metopen des Parthenon* (Mainz, 1967)
D. Arnold: 'Die Polykletnachfolge', *Jb. Dt. Archäol. Inst.*, suppl. 25 (1969)
P. N. Boulter: 'The Frieze of the Erechtheion', *Ant. Plast.*, x (1970), pp. 7–28
T. Bowie and D. Thimme: *The Carrey Drawings of the Parthenon Sculptures* (Bloomington, 1971)
G. Despinis: *Symboli sti meleti tou ergou to Agorakritou* [A contribution to the study of the work of Agorakritos] (Athens, 1971)
A. Delivorrias: *Attische Giebelskulpturen und Akrotere des 5. Jahrh. v. Chr.* (Tübingen, 1974)
D. Willers: 'Zu den Anfängen der archaistischen Plastik in Griechenland', *Mitt. Dt. Archäol. Inst.: Athen. Abt.*, suppl. 4 (1975)
F. Brommer: *Der Parthenonfries* (Mainz, 1977)
E. Mitropoulou: *Corpus of the Attic Votive Reliefs of the 6th and 5th Centuries BC*, i (Athens, 1977)
G. Despinis: 'Zum Hermes von Troizen', *Mitt. Dt. Archäol. Inst.: Athen. Abt.*, xcvi (1981), pp. 237–44
B. S. Ridgway: *Fifth-century Styles in Greek Sculpture* (Princeton, 1981)
L. Alscher: *Klassik* (1982), ii/2 of *Griechische Plastik* (Berlin, 1954–)
C. Houser: *Greek Monumental Bronze Sculpture* (New York and London, 1983)
B. Schmalz: *Griechische Grabreliefs* (Darmstadt, 1983)
J. Boardman: *Greek Sculpture: The Classical Period* (London, 1985/*R* 1991)
——: *The Parthenon and its Sculpture* (London, 1985)
Archaische und klassische griechische Plastik: Akten des internationalen Kolloquiums: Athen, 1985
M. Meyer: 'Die griechischen Urkundenreliefs', *Mitt. Dt. Archäol. Inst.: Athen. Abt.*, suppl. 13 (1988)
C. Höcker and L. Schneider: *Phidias* (Reinbek, 1993)

REINHARD STUPPERICH

*(c) Late (*c. *375–323* BC*).* Greek sculpture of the 4th century BC encompasses several styles, beginning with a straightforward continuation of the Rich style during the first quarter century. By *c.* 375 BC new trends were established, constituting what has come to be known as Late Classical sculpture. Though the inception of the Hellenistic period is conventionally set at the death of Alexander the Great in 323 BC, a Hellenistic idiom is in evidence by the 330s BC. A classicizing trend, the Plain style, apparent *c.* 330 BC, continued into the first decades of the 3rd century BC. Throughout the 4th century BC the character of Greek sculpture, previously produced exclusively for the city states of Greece, was transformed by its dissemination through the kingdoms of Asia Minor, where Greek forms were combined with Asiatic iconography.

Introduction. After its defeat in the Peloponnesian War in 404 BC, Athens was no longer the principal centre of sculptural production. Greek sculptors thus sought employment in the sanctuaries of the Peloponnese, Boiotia and Phokis and in the hellenized satrapal courts of the disintegrating Persian empire. The main representatives of the Attic school were KEPHISODOTOS, his son PRAXITELES, LEOCHARES, SILANION and EUPHRANOR. Its formal preoccupations include a more sentimental rendering of High Classical prototypes as well as a more intimate treatment of divine images: Kephisodotos was responsible for the first free-standing group of a divine mother and child, his *Eirene and Ploutos* (*c.* 360 BC; copy, Munich, Glyp.), and Praxiteles sculpted the first full-scale female nude in Western art, the *Aphrodite of Knidos* (*c.* 360–*c.* 340 BC; copy, 'Venus Colonna', Rome, Vatican, Mus. Pio-Clementino; for illustration of copy in Paris, Louvre, *see* KNIDOS). At the same time LYSIPPOS in Sikyon and the followers of Polykleitos (*see* POLYKLEITOS, §2) in Argos developed important workshops specializing in bronze statues, mainly of male athletes, with a market not only in the pan-hellenic sanctuaries of Greece but also in South Italy and Sicily. Itinerant artists of high calibre, such as SKOPAS and BRYAXIS, produced works throughout the Greek world. Other workshops making architectural sculptures in marble were active in local sanctuaries. Regional schools, however, are not readily distinguished, since new ideas travelled fast and styles could be mixed.

Late Classical sculptors considered themselves the direct successors of 5th-century BC masters, whose works they consciously adapted and emulated. A break with the High Classical period, however, was marked not only by differences in the treatment of draperies, which were given a thicker texture and an individuality of their own, and changes in hairstyles but also by a tendency towards mass production, more rapid working methods, the enhancement of the pictorial qualities of marble and a higher degree of subjectivity. A new awareness of viewing angles began to affect the proportions of figures: by the mid-4th century BC long legs, shorter torsos and smaller heads were common features, while Plato (*Sophist* 236a) complained of sculptors' predilection for 'apparent' as opposed to 'real' proportions. Adaptations by 4th-century BC sculptors of High Classical models can sometimes be distinguished only on grounds of proportions. Any experiments with new forms of expression were ultimately tempered by a streak of classicism, which appears to run through all schools of Late Classical sculpture. Portraiture also flourished, even though many surviving portraits are clearly imaginary, showing prominent men of earlier generations. The highest achievement of the period, however, was the popularization of High Classical art, and it was this new, more accessible version of the Classical that inspired later Greco-Roman art.

Free-standing works. Though many original Late Classical sculptures survive, most are anonymous, often second-rate works. The mutilated cult statue of *Apollo Patroos* by Euphranor (*c.* 330 BC; Athens, Agora Mus., S 2154; *see* ATHENS, fig. 17) is a rare example of a relatively secure attribution. The most outstanding of the anonymous original marble statues are the portraits traditionally identified as *Mausolos* from the Mausoleum at Halikarnassos (*c.* 360–*c.* 350 BC; London, BM, 1000), those of the ancestors and family of Daochos II at Delphi (*c.* 335 BC; Delphi, Archaeol. Mus.), the head of *Zeus Labrandeus* from Mylasa in Caria (*c.* 350 BC; Boston, MA, Mus. F.A., 04.12) and the Bartlett Head from Athens (*c.* 325 BC; Boston, MA, Mus. F.A., 03.743). The colossal *Mausolos* is a masterpiece of characterization of a hellenized Asiatic prince, while among the figures on Daochos' monument the statue of the Olympic victor *Agias* is a prime example of the 'pendulum' stance of a restive athlete (see fig. 64). The head of *Zeus Labrandeus* from hellenized Caria recalls images of Pheidias' majestic cult statue of *Zeus* at Olympia, though on a much smaller scale. The Bartlett Head, from a statue of Aphrodite, has blurred, luminous features contrasting with the roughly modelled hair, high triangular forehead, narrow eyes and dreamy expression associated with works by Praxiteles and his followers.

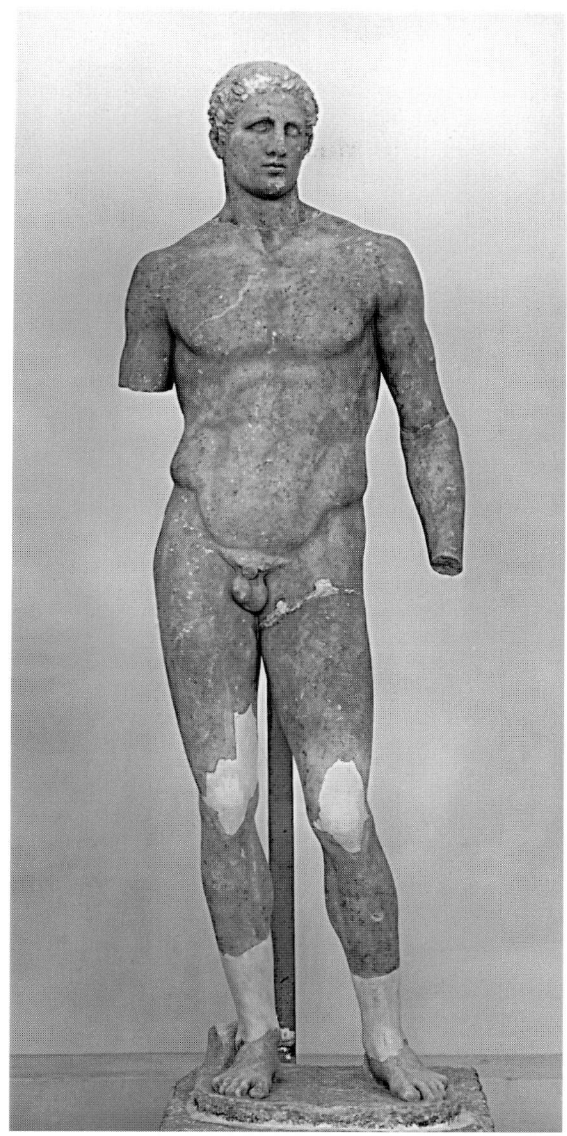

64. Lysippos (attrib.): *Agias*, marble, h. 1.97 m, from the monument of Daochos II at Delphi, Late Classical period, *c.* 335 BC (Delphi, Archaeological Museum)

Two of the most striking bronzes of the 4th century BC seem to be portrait heads: one, the *Boxer* from Olympia (*c.* 330 BC; Athens, N. Archaeol. Mus., 6439), is a superb characterization that may have come from the statue of *Satyros* by Silanion; the other, from the Porticello shipwreck, represents an elderly man with a long beard (*c.* 380 BC; Reggio Calabria, Mus. N.). The more conventional bronze *Youth* from the shipwreck at Antikythera (*c.* 340 BC; Athens, N. Archaeol. Mus., 13396) is based on Polykleitan models and probably represented Perseus triumphant, holding up the head of Medusa. Both the *Youth* and the Peiraeus *Athena* (*c.* 350 BC; Peiraeus, Archaeol. Mus.; see fig. 65), attributed to Euphranor, appear to have distorted proportions, corrected when the statues are viewed from a particular angle. The two statues of *Artemis* from the Peiraeus cache (both Peiraeus, Archaeol. Mus.) differ considerably in proportions and general appearance. The larger (*c.* 340 BC) is of uneven quality, with a squat body, large limbs and dull drapery but an exquisite head. The smaller (*c.* 325 BC) is elegant and well-proportioned, exuding Attic grace and charm. The *Boy* from the Bay of Marathon (?*c.* 340–*c.* 300 BC; Athens, N. Archaeol. Mus., 15118) is an enigmatic work. Sometimes associated with Praxiteles because of its lithe limbs and sinuous outline, it has an athlete's headband but apparently functioned as a lampholder and may in fact be of Roman date.

65. Euphranor (attrib.): *Athena*, bronze, h. 2.35 m, from the Peiraeus cache, Late Classical period, *c.* 350 BC (Peiraeus, Archaeological Museum)

Architectural sculpture. The fully-blown Late Classical style was anticipated by several important High Classical examples, including metopes from the Tholos at Delphi depicting an *Amazonomachy*, a *Centauromachy*, the *Labours of Herakles* and the *Exploits of Theseus*, and acroteria in the form of *nikai* (*c.* 390 BC; Delphi, Archaeol. Mus.). These represent a new approach to architectural sculpture, which was beginning to shed its formal character in favour of spontaneity. The Tholos workshops also produced sculpted pediments and acroteria for the Temple of Asklepios at Epidauros. The temple pediments depict an *Amazonomachy* and the *Fall of Troy* (or a *Centauromachy*), the latter represent the *Rape of Koronis*, *Nikai* and *Nereids* or *Aurai* ('breezes'; *c.* 380 BC; Athens, N. Archaeol. Mus.; *see* EPIDAUROS, fig. 2). This project is uniquely documented by detailed accounts, and the work of the four master sculptors involved—TIMOTHEOS, Hektoridas, Theo(?dotos) and one other—seems to blend into a harmonious whole. Although they are, strictly speaking, late High Classical, the Epidauros sculptures (see fig. 63 above) are distinguished by their technical virtuosity: their rotating poses, high-waisted figures and new density in the texture of draperies reveal a new approach to the depiction of both form and movement. The fragmentary remains of the Late Classical architectural sculptures showing battle and hunting scenes (*c.* 340 BC; Tegea, Archaeol. Mus., and Athens, N. Archaeol. Mus.) from the Temple of Athena Alea at Tegea are considered a landmark, with their particularly powerful heads in contorted poses. Their affinity with the earlier architectural sculptures of the Temple of Hera at Argos (early 4th century BC; Athens, N. Archaeol. Mus.) and the Temple of Athena at Mazi (early 4th century BC; Olympia, Archaeol. Mus.; Patras, Archaeol. Mus.; Athens, N. Archaeol. Mus.) testifies to the continuity in Peloponnesian workshops of the earlier High Classical tradition.

The large quantities of free-standing and architectural relief sculpture from the Mausoleum at Halikarnassos are notable for their uniformity of inspiration. The ensemble is attributed to the workshops of Skopas, Timotheos, Bryaxis, Leochares, PYTHEOS and Satyros (*see* HALIKARNASSOS, §2). The colossal portrait statues of Carian magnates, with their mixture of Carian and Greek dress and hairstyles, are particularly striking. Praxiteles is associated by literary sources with the Altar of Artemis at Ephesos, and the single extant *Horse's Head* (*c.* 330 BC; Selçuk, Ephesos Archaeol. Mus.) demonstrates a successful attempt to go beyond the Parthenon type of horse by exploiting a subtle interplay of light and shade. The colossal sculpted column drums from the Temple of Artemis (after 336 BC; London, BM) reproduce the iconography of their Archaic predecessors but in a style indebted to Attic grave reliefs.

Reliefs. The many grave, votive and record reliefs found in Attica are a testimony both to the taste of a flourishing society and to the techniques and practices of lesser 4th-century BC marble workshops. Grave reliefs were ready-made in a wide range of sizes, designed to stand on the edge of a grave plot. Within an architectural frame they depict single figures, family or battle scenes, none of which is individualized. The scenes are restrained in gesture, showing little emotion, and their quality is uneven. The general tendency is for both figural groups and the monuments themselves to become larger, developing into full-scale *naïskoi* (grave shrines) containing free-standing figures. A sumptuary decree ended the practice in Attica between 317 and 310 BC.

Votive reliefs also usually have an architectural frame in the form of a flat roof adorned with antefixes and supported by pilasters. The deities honoured tend to be in groups of three, approached by their votaries. Towards the end of the 4th century BC the gods were depicted frontally in order to establish a more intimate link with the spectator. Both votive reliefs and the more modest record reliefs provide invaluable evidence because, among other things, they reproduce statue types of the 5th and 4th centuries BC. Relief bases are less common and more original in conception. The best relief sculpture is directly indebted to painting in its atmospheric quality, its ingenious exploitation of space and use of perspective diminution of background figures. Pictorial qualities are especially apparent in the relief slabs depicting the *Contest of Apollo and Marsyas* from Mantinea (*c.* 325 BC; Athens, N. Archaeol. Mus., 215–17), where the outlines of the figures merge with the background, and in the relief dedicated by Neoptolemos to Apollo and the nymphs (*c.* 325 BC; Athens, Agora Mus., I 7154), in which the action is broken into small groups spread over different planes. Relief and architectural decoration also featured on certain oriental sarcophagi: thus the Sarcophagus of the Mourning Women from Sidon (late 4th century BC; Istanbul, Archaeol. Mus.) was treated as a miniature Ionic temple, with relief figures on the eaves and pediment and in the intercolumniations.

A revival of 4th-century BC styles and ideals towards the end of the 2nd century BC was to produce such outstanding works of the Hellenistic period as the *Venus de Milo* (*see* §(iv) below), paving the way for the assimilation of Late Classical art by the artists of the Roman Empire.

BIBLIOGRAPHY

B. R. Brown: *Anticlassicism in Greek Sculpture of the Fourth Century BC* (New York, 1973)
G. Neumann: *Probleme des griechischen Weihreliefs* (Tübingen, 1979), pp. 42–75
B. Vierneisel-Schlörb: *Glyptothek München: Katalog der Skulpturen*, ii (Munich, 1979), pp. 216–514
O. Palagia: 'An Attic Head in Oxford', *Boreas*, iii (1980), pp. 5–11
——: 'A Colossal Statue of a Personification from the Agora of Athens', *Hesperia*, li (1982), pp. 99–113
R. Fleischer: *Der Klagefrauensarkophag aus Sidon* (Tübingen, 1983)
C. Houser: *Greek Monumental Bronze Sculpture* (London, 1983)
B. S. Ridgway: 'Painterly and Pictorial in Greek Relief Sculpture', *Ancient Greek Art and Iconography*, ed. W. G. Moon (Madison, 1983), pp. 193–208
B. Schmalz: *Griechische Grabreliefs* (Darmstadt, 1983)
E. Paribeni: 'Le statue bronzee di Porticello', *Boll. A.*, xxiv (1984), pp. 1–14
J. P. Niemeier: *Kopien und Nachahmungen im Hellenismus* (Bonn, 1985)
C. J. Eiseman and B. S. Ridgway: *The Porticello Shipwreck: A Mediterranean Merchant Vessel of 415–385 BC* (College Station, TX, 1987)
M. Meyer: 'Die griechischen Urkundenreliefs', *Mitt. Dt. Archäol. Inst.: Athen. Abt.*, suppl. 13 (1988)

OLGA PALAGIA

(iv) Hellenistic (323–27 BC*).* Given the cultural, political and artistic diversity of the Greek world during the three centuries following the death of Alexander the Great in 323 BC, Hellenistic sculpture is particularly difficult to classify. This article follows a chronological scheme comprising Early, High and Late Hellenistic periods, though these relate far less clearly to corresponding stylistic developments than in the case of Greek sculpture of the Classical period, and apparently contradictory styles sometimes flourished simultaneously.

(a) Introduction. (b) Early (323–*c.* 220 BC). (c) High (*c.* 220–*c.* 150 BC). (d) Late (*c.* 150–27 BC).

(a) Introduction. After Alexander the Great died, his generals soon abandoned any pretence of unity, and the ensuing power struggle took some 40 years to resolve. It left three dominant empires: Ptolemaic Egypt, Seleucid Syria and Antigonid Macedonia. While these contended for hegemony, however, lesser states attempted to assert their independence. The most successful of these were Bactria (now Afghanistan), Pergamon, the Aitolian League and Achaian League in mainland Greece, and later the non-Greek states of Pontos and Hasmonean Israel. In the west, Syracuse and Taras (now Taranto), which had never come under Macedonian control, maintained their power until conquered by Rome in 211 BC and 209 BC respectively.

In a world unprecedented in Greek experience—rich, far-flung, and astonishingly diverse—it is hardly surprising that art, and in particular sculpture, should be characterized by contradiction and confusion. Late Classical Greek sculptors such as Lysippos and Praxiteles had achieved a daunting mastery of styles and techniques, and in the Hellenistic context, where earlier social or stylistic constraints had all but ceased to function, dogged conservatism, unbridled virtuosity, bombastic magniloquence, light-hearted playfulness and sheer bad taste all began to compete. The range of subjects as well as styles expanded. Allegories began to appear on temple pediments and friezes; portraits of the bourgeoisie exceeded those of great men; and contemporary foes took their place alongside, and sometimes replaced, the time-honoured enemies of myth. New subjects were also invented, of which the most radical were the numerous studies of satyrs molesting a variety of erotic partners, and a motley array of low-life characters such as fishermen and peasants. Drawing on pre-existing traditions in the minor arts, both genres seem to have begun *c.* 200 BC. This plurality of styles and types was encouraged by the demands of patrons as different as half-hellenized Levantines, Roman aesthetes, members of the Alexandrian bourgeoisie and Hellenistic monarchs (for illustration *see* SELEUCIDS).

Artistic presentation became more a matter of choice than of convention and was determined by a complex interrelationship of genre, patron, school and locale. Styles developed simultaneously, not successively. The task of providing a historical framework is complicated by the loss of all but a few of the thousands of Hellenistic monumental bronzes and an almost complete lack of context for those that survive and is further impeded by the abrupt ending of Pliny's list of famous sculptors. For him 'art' ceased in 292 BC, though he grudgingly recorded half a dozen names under a neo-Classical 'revival' in the year 156 BC. Roman collectors preferred Classical Greek works, and when they did want contemporary sculpture, they usually favoured busts of intellectuals for their libraries and villas and erotic and low-life subjects for their gardens. Original works were seldom copied exactly but were reproduced freehand in an endless series of variations, and novelty was valued more than fidelity to a type or style. This makes it almost impossible to determine what, if anything, is 'original' in much Hellenistic sculpture.

*(b) Early (323–*c. *220* BC*).* At Alexander's death, Athens and Sikyon dominated Greek sculpture. The Attic sculptors were the more diverse, cultivating styles that ranged from the somewhat conservative classicism of the carvers of grave monuments (whose staple product was banned by sumptuary legislation in 317 BC) to the extremely delicate manner of the sons of Praxiteles (*see* PRAXITELES, §2). The stilted *Themis* from Rhamnous by Chairestratos (*c.* 300–*c.* 250 BC; Athens, N. Archaeol. Mus.; *see* DRESS, fig. 3) exemplifies the former approach, while the famous *Hermes Carrying the Infant Dionysos* from Olympia (Olympia, Archaeol. Mus.) probably represents the latter, since its technique, drapery and footwear have no 4th-century BC parallels, though they are found in more developed form in 2nd-century BC monuments, such as the 'Great Altar' at Pergamon. Almost all of the most prominent sculptors made portraits, and by 300 BC this had become a leading genre. Surviving copies include representations of *Menander* (?early 3rd century BC; copy, Boston, MA, Mus. F.A.), *Demosthenes* (*c.* 280 BC; copy, Copenhagen, Ny Carlsberg Glyp.; see fig. 66) and the philosophers *Epicurus* and *Hermarchos* (first half of 3rd century BC; copy, New York, Met.; and early 3rd century BC; copy, Florence, Mus. Archeol. respectively). These testify to the rapid supersession of the Classical 'role portrait' by true character studies. Attic sculptors were in demand throughout the Aegean world and were increasingly encouraged to emigrate by Athens' accelerating economic and political decline. They established workshops in cities as far apart as Syracuse, Rhodes, Pergamon and Alexandria, exercising a profound influence on local tastes.

The Sikyonian school was founded by Alexander's court sculptor, LYSIPPOS. His three sons and numerous followers inherited his Peloponnesian and Macedonian clientele and were frequently commissioned to produce royal portraits and battle and hunt groups (genres pioneered by Lysippos himself) as well as private portraits and statues of athletes, all executed in bronze. The Getty Bronze (?late 4th century BC; Malibu, CA, Getty Mus.), found in the Adriatic Sea, gives a good idea of their approach, which sought to capture the sitter's actual appearance while also subtly idealizing it. With its commanding manner, slim, mobile body, portrait-like features and relatively small head (giving an impression of greater height), the Getty Bronze conforms in every way to Pliny's description of Lysippos' style (*Natural History* XXXIV.xix.65), probably quoted from a handbook by Lysippos' own follower XENOKRATES. The Lysippic school also occasionally made statues of the gods. In antiquity, the most famous of these was the colossal statue of *Helios* (the so-called Colossus of Rhodes; h. 32 m, *c.* 305 BC) by CHARES OF LINDOS. Poised much like the Getty Bronze, this work was a technical feat of the highest order, celebrating the deliverance of Rhodes from the siege of 305 BC. It did not stand astride the harbour, as medieval tradition alleged, but on a hill overlooking the town. It was felled by an earthquake in 224 BC. More innovative in terms of composition was the *Tyche of Antioch* by EUTYCHIDES, made just after the city's foundation in 301 BC (copy in Rome, Vatican, Gal. Candelabri; *see* ANTIOCH (i), fig. 1). This representation of Tyche (Fortune), the most characteristic of Hellenistic divinities, was seated in a pose of studied

66. Polyeuktos of Athens: *Demosthenes*, Hellenistic period, *c.* 280 BC; marble copy, h. 1.92 m (Copenhagen, Ny Carlsberg Glyptotek)

nonchalance on a rock symbolizing the nearby Mt Silpion, with the personified River Orontes swimming below, and it inaugurated a long tradition of similar images produced for eastern cities.

Though literary sources present a vivid picture of the wealth and beauty of ancient Antioch, almost nothing remains of the city. The great statue of *Apollo* made by BRYAXIS for its sanctuary at Daphne is lost, except for a series of miniature reproductions on later Seleucid coins (see Stewart, 1990, fig. 629), and the bronze portraits of the Seleucid kings have fared no better. Alexandrian sculpture is only slightly more accessible, chiefly through copies of Bryaxis' *Sarapis* (*c.* 280 BC; copies, Athens, N. Archaeol. Mus.; Rome, Villa Albani) and the numerous portraits of the Ptolemaic kings. The *Sarapis* was enthroned like Zeus and designed to appeal to both Greeks and Egyptians, for it combined the chthonic attributes of Hades with the Egyptian Osiris–Apis cult of death and rebirth. The styles of the portraits range from pure Greek to pure Egyptian, according to their intended context. Indeed, during the 3rd century BC even the Greek-style works began to take on much of the masklike character of Egyptian-style portraits, as the Ptolemaic monarchy sought to create a distinctive court style. Egyptian influence is also recognizable in the growing repertory of miniature grotesque and genre pieces in bronze and terracotta, presumably made for the Alexandrian bourgeoisie (bronzes, e.g. *Dancing Dwarf*, London, BM; *Street Boy*, Paris, Bib. N.; terracottas, e.g. *Hunchback*, New York, Met.). Their mixture of pathos and satire was echoed in contemporary Alexandrian poetry and by *c.* 200 BC also began to appear in monumental sculpture.

Though the Ptolemies and the Seleucids were at war for much of the 3rd century BC, the only evidence for early Hellenistic victory monuments comes from Roman copies of Pergamene dedications commemorating victories over invading Gauls. The most decisive of these occurred around 237 BC and prompted Attalos I (*reg* 241–197 BC) to assume the title of king and declare Pergamon's independence from Syria. Further successes over the Seleucid and Macedonian armies extended Pergamene influence over much of western Asia Minor and the Aegean and occasioned massive construction projects on the acropolis at PERGAMON, as the new monarchy sought to outdo its rivals in grandeur and present itself as the Athens of the East. The sculptural groups of Gauls, made *c.* 230–*c.* 220 BC by the local sculptor Epigonos (*see* ISIGONOS, EPIGONOS, STRATONIKOS AND ANTIGONOS), are extremely problematic, not least because copies of only a few figures survive, and none of these portray the victors. Though represented with an objectivity and sympathy unique in Greek art, the barbarians are nevertheless characterized as mortal threats to civilization. One figure, representing a trumpeter, accepts his fate with dignity (the *Dying Gaul*; copy, Rome, Mus. Capitolino; see fig. 67), while a group of two figures shows a *Gaul Killing Himself*

67. Epigonos of Pergamon: *Dying Gaul*, Hellenistic period, *c.* 230–*c.* 220 BC; marble copy, h. 930 mm (Rome, Museo Capitolino)

and his Wife (copy, Rome, Mus. N. Romano; *see* PERGAMON, fig. 4). The heightened pathos of the latter paralleled contemporary literary developments in 'tragic' history and rhetoric and anticipated the 'baroque' style of the Altar of Zeus at Pergamon. The first sculptor to imbue his works with such intense feeling was apparently the Athenian PHYROMACHOS, whose portrait of the philosopher *Antisthenes* (*c.* 200–*c.* 150 BC) is known from a copy (Rome, Vatican, Mus. Pio-Clementino). The trend may derive from late 4th-century BC paintings, such as the fresco of *Hades and Persephone* (*c.* 340–*c.* 330 BC) from Tomb I at Vergina in Macedonia. At Pergamon, Phyromachos' colossal *Asklepios* (Polybios: *Histories* XXXII.xv.4) may have pioneered the style.

*(c) High (*c. *220–*c. *150* BC*).* The acknowledged zenith of Hellenistic sculpture coincided with the outbreak of warfare on an unprecedented scale, as Macedonia and Syria each tried one last time for hegemony, and smaller states sought help from Pergamon and from Rome, now the dominant power in the western Mediterranean. Sucked into the conflict, the Romans defeated Macedonia (197 BC) and Syria (189 BC), and many plundered works were taken to Rome. From this point onwards, power and prosperity passed increasingly from the eastern Hellenistic kingdoms westwards to Rome. A final attempt by Macedonia to reassert its authority on a purely local level led to its defeat and dismemberment in 168 BC and its annexation as a Roman province in 146 BC. The immediate beneficiaries of these events, however, were Pergamon, Rhodes and the southern Greek cities that had sided with Rome. To advertise their success, all soon embarked on major sculptural and architectural programmes. The most spectacular of these was the Altar of Zeus at Pergamon (reconstr. in Berlin, Pergamonmus.; *see* PERGAMON, fig. 2), which, as research now suggests, may have been a hero-shrine for the city's legendary founder, Telephos. It dates from *c.* 170 BC, and its extensive podium was embellished with a large-scale frieze (h. 2.3 m) of a *Gigantomachy*, while inside the colonnaded court above ran another, somewhat smaller frieze representing the *Life of Telephos*. Sculptors were hired from throughout the Aegean world, and their signatures advertise the international character of the enterprise. Nevertheless, the style is remarkably uniform, testifying, like the complex iconography, to a meticulously conceived plan. The *Gigantomachy* is generally viewed as the apotheosis of the 'baroque' style in Greek sculpture, and it exploits every device available to drive home its vision of cosmic turmoil and irresistible power, with surfaces ripped open by the drill, muscles that appear to heave and pulsate and drapery that swirls and flares. Classical compositional patterns were rephrased here into a new emotive rhetoric of persuasion, while Stoic notions of a conflict between cosmic order and irrational impulse can be perceived in the carefully designed composition and the contrast between the cool, self-possessed figures of the gods and the wild, often grotesquely deformed giants. In contrast, the frieze depicting the *Life of Telephos* is more subdued and selfconsciously classicizing, though it also shows evidence of experiments with such pictorial devices as perspectival diminution. It charts the hero's life in a series of interconnected episodes that unfold from left to right, making it the earliest monumental example of continuous narration, a method that was to have considerable importance in Roman and medieval art (*see also* PERGAMON, §3).

From Pergamon, the 'baroque' style spread throughout Asia Minor, overriding both national boundaries and the conventions of genre. The NIKE OF SAMOTHRACE (Paris, Louvre; *see* SAMOTHRACE, fig. 2), possibly dedicated by the Rhodians to celebrate their part in the Syrian War of 192–188 BC, is an extraordinary *tour de force* of baroque rhetoric. The figure of the *Nike* stands on the prow of a warship, and her criss-crossing drapery evokes the turmoil of the wind and sea as she guides the victorious vessel safely into port with a hand outstretched in greeting. Other baroque compositions of the period include the originals of the LAOKOON (Rome, Vatican, Mus. Pio-Clementino; *see* ROME, ANCIENT, fig. 59) by HAGESANDROS, POLYDOROS AND ATHANODOROS of Rhodes, and of their Odysseus groups from Sperlonga (*see* SPERLONGA, §2). One of the latter, showing *Odysseus Dragging Achilles' Body out of Battle*, adapts a composition known from numerous other replicas, the Pasquino Group type (2nd century BC; copy, Florence, Loggia Lanzi). The original probably represented the rescue of the corpse of Patroklos by either Menelaos or Ajax. Despite its strongly articulated pathos, the Pasquino Group's pyramidal structure and strict emphasis on the frontal plane betray the growing influence of neo-Classicism.

Neo-Classical touches also appear in several contemporary studies in a lighter vein, showing satyrs grappling with nymphs, hermaphrodites and others, a 'rococo' genre that was evidently popular in Asia. Yet not all such erotica were so violent: one group composition particularly favoured by the Roman copyists featured a young satyr playing castanets and foot-clappers, jauntily inviting a half-naked nymph to dance. The originals apparently stood in Kyzikos (*c.* 200–*c.* 150 BC; copies, Florence, Uffizi). Meanwhile, a replica of Pheidias' *Athena Parthenos* erected in the library at Pergamon *c.* 190 BC inaugurated the neo-Classical movement proper. Soon other centres began to look to Athens' golden age for inspiration and support in the disintegrating Hellenistic world.

The Athenian sculptors themselves, nostalgic for their days of greatness and never particularly comfortable with the 'baroque', responded enthusiastically. Indeed, since the late 3rd century BC, the leading Attic exponents of the neo-Classical style, the POLYKLES family, had produced numerous cult statues for the powerful Aitolian confederacy. One of these, the *Athena* (excavated in the 19th century; untraced) at Elateia, even had a shield bearing a replica of the *Amazonomachy* on the shield of the *Athena Parthenos*, a subject that was later to become a staple product of Athenian neo-Classical decorative sculpture. When the Aitolians were defeated in the Syrian War, Attic sculptors began to work for the victors, the Achaian confederacy and the Romans. In Achaia, however, the leading exponent of the neo-Classical style was the local sculptor DAMOPHON of Messene, best known for his colossal cult group for the Temple of Despoina at Lykosoura in Arcadia (fragments of heads; *c.* 200–*c.* 150 BC, Athens, N. Archaeol. Mus.). At Rome from this period onwards, temples were increasingly embellished with specially commissioned cult statues in the neo-Classical style, designed to stand alongside the artworks looted from defeated Hellenistic kingdoms.

Neo-Classicism also became popular in the eastern Hellenistic world, particularly in Syria under the eccentric Antiochos IV (*reg* 175–164 BC). He sought to revive and unify his battered, truncated realm by adopting a policy of Roman efficiency combined with Attic culture, choosing a replica of Pheidias' *Zeus* at Olympia as his special symbol. Antiochos' attempt to impose the cult on the Jews led, however, to the Maccabean revolt, and his intended invasion of Egypt was repulsed by the threats of a single Roman envoy. Soon after his death, Babylonia fell to the Parthians, cutting off the Greek colonists in Bactria and India entirely. Such sculpture as survives from these areas is decidedly provincial, though a few pieces exhibit a novel blend of surface calligraphy and sensitivity to volume, anticipating the Gandhara style that is usually considered Greek art's greatest legacy to the East (*see also* INDIAN SUBCONTINENT, §IV, 5(ii)).

In Egypt, though High Hellenistic royal portraits were often rather more dramatic than before, it was on genre sculpture that the 'baroque' style made the greatest impact. The rhetoric of the low-life studies in bronze and terracotta intensified, perhaps as a response to increased racial tension as the kingdom declined further and the native population reasserted itself. Numerous marble replicas in the same vein show that by the early 2nd century BC monumental sculpture had responded to the challenge—though no single type can be confidently traced to Egypt. This unlovely array of characters includes virtuoso studies, such as the so-called *Seneca*, actually representing a rheumatic old man (black marble copy, Paris, Louvre), a *Drunken Old Woman* nursing her wine bottle (copy, Munich, Glyp.; see fig. 68); and the *Old Market Woman* (New York, Met.), whose ivy-leaf crown indicates that she is a participant in a rustic festival of Dionysos. All three may date to the 2nd century BC, though the *Old Market Woman* betrays a hint of neo-Classicism that suggests a slightly later date. These genre pieces may have embellished the gardens of the Alexandrian élite, even the royal parks of the Ptolemies, but the archaeological record is blank.

Ptolemaic court art proper is best exemplified by the *Apotheosis of Homer* relief by Archelaos of Priene, found in Italy but probably taken there from Alexandria as loot (London, BM). It celebrates the establishment of the cult of Homer by Ptolemy IV (*reg* 221–205 BC), and its inscribed lowest register shows Ptolemy and his wife crowning Homer while an array of figures representing the literary genres inspired by him perform sacrifices. Its three upper registers depict the Muses, Apollo and Zeus gathered on Mt Parnassos, accompanied by an unidentified poet. The composition emphasizes Homer's status as the central figure in Greek literature and thus, by association, Alexandria's status as the main Hellenistic literary centre. It also symbolically replicates the relationship between the institutions at the heart of Alexandrian intellectual life, with the upper levels representing the Mouseion (the world's first university) and the lowest one its incomparable resource, the great Library. A greater contrast to the thematic and stylistic concerns of Pergamene sculpture, exemplified by the huge *Gigantomachy*, could hardly be imagined.

68. *Drunken Old Woman*, Hellenistic period, 2nd century BC, marble, h. 920 mm (Munich, Glyptothek)

*(d) Late (*c. *150–27* BC*).* Rome's victories over Carthage, Macedonia and Achaia in the mid-2nd century BC greatly accelerated the decline of the Hellenistic world, while Egypt and Syria increasingly succumbed to civil war and the petty kingdoms of Asia Minor remained locked in local conflicts. Pergamon was bequeathed to Rome by its last king, Attalos III, in 133 BC, thus losing its role both as a stabilizing force in the region and as a flourishing sculptural centre. Thereafter the disintegration of the Hellenistic sculptural tradition was inevitable. Neo-Classicism could not substitute for the Hellenistic 'baroque' in every context, and the requirements of an increasingly splintered clientele led to a rapid proliferation of sculptural styles.

These developments are best illustrated by portraiture, always a barometer of political reality. The characteristics of individual works range from pseudo-Classical repose to 'baroque'-style histrionics and even hard-boiled realism, according to the image that each individual wished to project. On Delos, members of a colony of Italian slave-traders hired sculptors from Asia Minor and Athens to render their features in the grimly realistic 'verist' manner then in favour at Rome, where it suggested the traditional Roman virtues of self-discipline (*gravitas*) and resolution (*constantia*). These portraits were given idealized heroic bodies, and the combination must have looked almost as offensive to traditionally minded Greeks as the 'Slipper-slapper' group of *Aphrodite Defending Herself with her Sandal against the Amorous Advances of Pan* (Athens, N. Archaeol. Mus., 3335), dedicated by another foreign trader on Delos, Dionysios of Berytos (Beirut). The Delian workshops also met the needs of this heterogeneous, *nouveau-riche* clientele by producing vast quantities of decorative sculpture for houses and gardens. At Athens, too, this type of sculpture was turning into a major industry, chiefly devoted to copies of Classical masterpieces, either free-standing or in relief, which were shipped west to embellish Roman temples, public squares and buildings and private villas.

Neo-Classicism also significantly affected other sculptural genres. Thus two of the most famous masterpieces of Greek sculpture of any period, the VENUS DE MILO and the BORGHESE GLADIATOR (both Paris, Louvre), signed by sculptors from Asia Minor (Alexandros of Antioch on the Meander and Agasias of Ephesos respectively), are strongly classicizing. The *Venus* (or *Aphrodite of Melos*; see fig. 69) combines a Pheidian-style head with a Praxitelean body, Pergamene drapery and a highly contemporary Hellenistic 'sprung' rhythm (cf. the *Nike of Samothrace*). The *Borghese Gladiator* blends exaggerated Lysippic proportions and musculature with a dramatic 4th-century BC lunging pose. Other works in a similar vein include a *Sleeping Hermaphrodite* (2nd century BC; copy, Rome, Mus. N. Romano), often attributed to Polykles, and a bronze *Boxer* from Rome (2nd or early 1st century BC; copy, Rome, Mus. N. Romano). Numerous Greek sculptors had by now settled permanently in Rome, though few were as successful as the versatile PASITELES, whose works captivated the Roman upper classes and who wrote an influential five-volume guide to the 'classics' of Greek sculpture. Yet while sculpture at Rome flourished, its decline in the eastern Hellenistic world was hastened by the increasing impoverishment both of cities and of their ruling élites, as well as by the progressive annexation by Rome of almost all the surviving kingdoms, including Syria (64 BC). After the devastation of the Mithradatic Wars (88–66 BC), the Roman civil wars (49–30 BC) and a Parthian invasion of much of Asia Minor (41–39 BC), the combination of huge indemnities levied by the Romans on rebel states, pirate raids and the rapacity of tax-collectors reduced many cities to the last extremity. In portraiture, the prevailing manner became more introverted and morose. Against the assertive individuality of Roman taste, the portraits from Greek Asia Minor oppose a quasi-philosophical sense of introverted reflection, an awareness of the instability and illusoriness of human existence.

In the three main surviving kingdoms, however, conditions were somewhat different. Herodian Israel has yielded no sculpture, but both Commagene (now part of eastern Turkey) and Egypt experienced something of a revival in the mid-1st century BC. In Commagene, the eccentric Greco-Iranian monarch Antiochus I was obsessed with ideas of religious and racial unity between East and West, and his vast tomb on the summit of NEMRUT DAĞ was approached via terraces with massive reliefs of his ancestors and colossal statues of Antiochus and his

69. Alexandros of Antioch on the Meander: *Venus de Milo*, marble, h. 2.04 m, Hellenistic period, *c.* 150–*c.* 120 BC (Paris, Musée du Louvre)

gods, constructed in coursed masonry in a dignified, highly formalized Greco-Iranian style (*in situ*). In Egypt, Cleopatra (*reg* 51–30 BC) had taken advantage of the chaos of the Roman civil wars to secure the throne and used first Julius Caesar then Mark Antony to realize her dream of reviving the Ptolemaic empire. A superb portrait (*c.* 50–*c.* 30 BC; Berlin, Antikenmus.) gives expression to these ambitions; it shows her with a fresh, delicate complexion and a look of regal determination: a rival to the great Ptolemaic queens of the 3rd century BC and a virtual double of their common alter ego, Aphrodite. In 31 BC, however, the combined forces of Cleopatra and Mark Antony were defeated by Octavian at Actium. By 27 BC, when Octavian assumed the title Augustus, the power of Rome was supreme and the Hellenistic world effectively at an end. Yet in sculpture, the Hellenistic legacy was tenacious, informing almost every Roman Imperial style from the neo-Classicism of the Augustan 'Golden Age' to the 'baroque' revival exemplified by the Laokoon and the works produced by the school of Aphrodisias. It was in these forms that it was later rediscovered by the sculptors of the Renaissance, when Hellenistic art again influenced the mainstream Western sculptural tradition.

BIBLIOGRAPHY

W. Klein: *Vom antiken Rokoko* (Vienna, 1921)
E. Buschor: *Das hellenistische Bildnis* (Munich, 1949, 2/1971)
G. Lippold: *Die griechische Plastik* (1950), III/i of *Handbuch der Archäologie* (Munich, 1939–), pp. 293–387
A. Schober: *Die Kunst von Pergamon* (Vienna, 1951)
M. Bieber: *The Sculpture of the Hellenistic Age* (New York, 1955, rev. 1961)
P. H. von Blanckenhagen: 'Narration in Hellenistic and Roman Art', *Amer. J. Archaeol.*, lxi (1957), pp. 78–83
R. Carpenter: *Greek Sculpture: A Critical Review* (Chicago, 1960), pp. 180–254
T. Dohrn: *Die Tyche von Antiocheia* (Berlin, 1960)
A. Adriani: *Repertorio d'arte dell'Egitto greco-romano*, ser. a, i-ii (Palermo, 1961)
J. J. Pollitt: *The Art of Greece, 1400–31 BC: Sources and Documents* (Englewood Cliffs, 1965)
G. M. A. Richter: *The Portraits of the Greeks*, 3 vols (London, 1965); abridged and rev. by R. R. R. Smith (Oxford, 1984)
T. B. L. Webster: *The Art of Greece: The Hellenistic World* (New York, 1966)
E. Buschor: *Das hellenistische Bildnis* (Munich, 1971)
E. Künzl: *Die Kelten des Epigonos von Pergamon* (Würzberg, 1971)
C. M. Havelock: *Hellenistic Art* (London, 1972, rev. New York, 2/1981)
J. Charbonneaux, R. Martin and F. Villard: *Hellenistic Art* (New York, 1973)
G. S. Merker: *The Hellenistic Sculpture of Rhodes*, Stud. Medit. Archaeol., xl (Göteborg, 1973)
B. Andreae: 'Die römischen Repliken der Skulpturengruppen von Sperlonga', *Ant. Plast.*, xiv (1974), pp. 61–108
B. Conticello: 'I gruppi scultorei di soggetto mitologico a Sperlonga', *Ant. Plast.*, xiv (1974), pp. 7–58
H. Kyrieleis: *Die Bildnisse der Ptolemäer* (Berlin, 1975)
E. Simon: *Pergamon und Hesiod* (Mainz, 1975)
A. M. U. Linfert: *Kunstzentren hellenistischer Zeit: Studien an weiblichen Gewandfiguren* (Wiesbaden, 1976)
A. F. Stewart: 'To Entertain an Emperor: Laokoon, Sperlonga, and Tiberius at the Dinner Table', *J. Roman Stud.*, lxvii (1977), pp. 76–90
J. Frel: *The Getty Bronze* (Malibu, 1978)
J. Onians: *Art and Thought in the Hellenistic Age* (London, 1978)
R. Wenning: *Die Galateranatheme Attalos I* (Berlin, 1978)
A. F. Stewart: *Attika: Studies in Athenian Sculpture of the Hellenistic Age* (London, 1979)
B. Frischer: *The Sculpted Word* (Berkeley, 1982)
H. P. Laubscher: *Fischer und Landleute* (Mainz, 1982)
K. D. Morrow: *Greek Footwear and the Dating of Sculpture* (Madison, 1985)
A. Pasquier: *La Vénus de Milo et les Aphrodites du Louvre* (Paris, 1985)
J. J. Pollitt: *Art in the Hellenistic Age* (Cambridge, 1986)
M. Mattei: *Il Galata Capitolino* (Rome, 1987)
E. D. Reeder: *Hellenistic Art in the Walters Art Gallery* (Baltimore, 1988)
R. R. R. Smith: *Hellenistic Royal Portraits* (Oxford, 1988)
B. S. Ridgway: *The Styles of 331–200 BC* (1990), i of *Hellenistic Sculpture* (Madison, 1990–)
A. F. Stewart: *Greek Sculpture: An Exploration*, 2 vols (New Haven and London, 1990)
R. R. R. Smith: *Hellenistic Sculpture* (London, 1991)
A. F. Stewart: *Faces of Power: Alexander's Image and Hellenistic Politics*, ii of *Hellenistic Culture and Society* (Berkeley, CA and Oxford, 1993)
For further bibliography *see also* individual site entries.

ANDREW F. STEWART

3. THEORY AND CRITICISM.

(i) Ancient. The ancient Greeks did not distinguish between fine art and craftsmanship. Both were designated by the word *techne*. By the mid-5th century BC this had come to mean the rational and technical procedure for realizing a desired end result. Thus it could apply equally to carpentry or sculpture. During the 5th and 4th centuries BC, however, the term *sophia* (the 'skill' of the craftsman or artist) gradually acquired connotations of theoretical knowledge (Aristotle: *Metaphysics* 981a.24–982a.2). This distinction was retained by Roman writers on art, who translated *techne* with the Latin word *ars* ('art') but distinguished between *ratiocinatio* (the intellectual and theoretical foundation for art) and *opus* (the practical and technical side of production; see Vitruvius: *On Architecture* I.i.15). Treatises on ancient Greek sculptural theory were produced by several different categories of writers. Particularly during the Classical and Early Hellenistic periods (*c.* 450–*c.* 300 BC) artists themselves wrote books addressing the formal problems of their craft, such as proportion. No ancient sculptural treatises survive, though Pliny apparently summarized portions of a lost critical work by the Hellenistic sculptor Xenokrates, while fragments and paraphrases of a treatise by Polykleitos also survive in ancient authors (see Pollitt, pp. 14–22).

The two crucial artistic concepts, *rhythmos* and *symmetria*, were first formulated in the Early Classical period by Pythagoras of Rhegion (see Diogenes Laertius: VII.x/vii). *Rhythmos* (Lat. *numerus*), or 'form', referred to the way a statue's 'frozen' pose could convey a specific impression of action. Thus the *rhythmos* of Myron's *Diskobolos* (see fig. 38 above) captures the poised instant between the discus thrower's backswing and the forward-swinging release of the discus. *Eurhythmia* meant the successful achievement of *rhythmos*, while *symmetria* indicated the 'commensurability of parts' in a work of art, or proportion. Polykleitos wrote a sculptural treatise, the *Canon*, which he probably illustrated with his statue the *Doryphoros* (*see* POLYKLEITOS, fig. 1). He apparently described the theoretical ideal of 'the good' (*to eu*) or 'the beautiful' (*to kalon*). This was based on a carefully conceived system of *symmetria*, while the works themselves had to be executed with 'precision' (*akribeia*; Lat. *diligentia*). The sculptor aimed at 'the mean' (*to meson*) between excess and deficiency and thus came to a theoretical understanding of the true nature of his subject (*aletheia*; Lat. *veritas*), and his statues revealed the workings of nature to others. Varro called the works of Polykleitos *quadrata* (Gr. *tetragona*), referring either to their four-square composition or to the chiastic arrangement of their limbs (Pliny: *Natural History* XXXIV.xix.56).

In the Late Classical and Early Hellenistic periods (*c.* 375–*c.* 323 BC), such sculptors as Lysippos are said to have retained an interest in *symmetria* while experimenting with new systems of proportion and torsional compositions. Indeed, Lysippos appears to have addressed the optical problems that derive from the subjective way in which works of art are perceived. Pliny described his works as more 'slender' (*gracilis*) and 'drier' (*siccus*)—that is, leaner—than those of his predecessors (*Natural History* XXXIV.xix.65; for illustration of the *Apoxyomenos see* LYSIPPOS).

From the mid-5th century BC onwards Greek philosophers such as Plato and Aristotle wrote on artistic issues, though they were primarily concerned with art's moral, political and epistemological value. Art was an 'imitation' (*mimesis*) of the perceived world and had the power to affect man's 'character' (*ethos*). *Mimesis* involved not only the imitation of physical objects but also 'imitation by psychological association' (Pollitt). The latter was the way in which artists could evoke states of mind. Artists could thus communicate both good and bad character, as well as 'suffering' (*pathos*), through the features, poses and forms of their figures (Xenophon: *Memorabilia* III.x.1–8; Aristotle: *Politics* 1340a.30–38). Plato believed in a realm of immutable 'forms' (*eidos*; pl. *eide*) that underlay everything in the visible world and could be comprehended by the mind alone. These *eide* constituted the only 'true reality', and nature merely imitated them. Since art imitated nature, Plato regarded it as 'an imitation of an imitation' and condemned artists for being concerned with the merely illusory 'appearance' of objects, rather than their true essence (*Sophist* 235d–236c; *Republic* X.597a–e).

In the 2nd century BC Greek rhetoricians began to formulate analogies between rhetoric and art on the basis of style. Their works do not survive, but they are reproduced in passages by such Roman authors as Cicero and Quintilian that suggest a view of the history of Greek sculpture as an evolution from a 'stiff and undeveloped' (*durus* or *rigidus*) kind of work to that which was 'supple' (*mollis*). Excellence in sculpture involved 'fidelity to nature' (Gr. *aletheia*; Lat. *veritas*), 'beauty' (Gr. *to kallos*; Lat. *pulchritudo*), 'precision' (Gr. *akribeia*; Lat. *diligentia*) and 'appropriateness' (Gr. *to prepon*; Lat. *decor*). The culmination of this evolutionary scheme was seen in the works of Pheidias, who had suffused his creations with spiritual insight. For the Latin writers, the greatest works of Greek sculpture were characterized by their 'majesty' (*maiestas*), 'presence' (*auctoritas*) and 'grandeur' (*pondus*). The concept of 'intuitive insight' (*phantasia*) replaced the Classical idea of mere *mimesis* as a criterion for excellence, and with the advent of this theory, artists were no longer regarded as mere craftsmen but were thought to possess an inspired, spiritual awareness.

BIBLIOGRAPHY

J. A. Overbeck: *Die antiken Schriftquellen zur Geschichte der bildenden Künste bei den Griechen* (Leipzig, 1868)

E. Sellers and K. Jex-Blake: *The Elder Pliny's Chapters on the History of Art* (London, 1896/*R* Chicago, 1966)

B. Schweitzer: 'Xenokrates von Athen', *Schr. Königsberg. Gelehrten Ges.: Geistwiss. Klasse*, ix (1932), pp. 1–15

S. Ferri: 'Nuovi contributi esegetici al "canone" della scultura greca', *Riv. Reale Ist. Archeol. & Stor. A.*, vii (1940), pp. 117–52

J. J. Pollitt: *The Ancient View of Greek Art* (New Haven and London, 1974)

GREGORY V. LEFTWICH

(ii) Modern. It was between the late 17th century and the mid-18th that ancient Greek sculpture was first recognized as a discrete category of antique statuary, in the writings of ANDRÉ FÉLIBIEN, the Comte de CAYLUS and, most importantly, JOHANN JOACHIM WINCKELMANN. Although all of these authors characterized Greek sculpture as superior to Roman, Winckelmann went beyond his predecessors in offering aesthetic and historical grounds for distinguishing Greek from Roman in his monumental *Geschichte der Kunst des Alterthums* (1764), a chronological survey of ancient sculpture. Invoking the analogy of biological growth, Winckelmann charted the stylistic development of Greek art from its birth in the Archaic period to maturity in the High Classical period and subsequent decline in the Hellenistic and Roman periods, and his essential stylistic and chronological divisions are still accepted. Whereas his predecessors had championed ancient Greek sculpture as a whole, Winckelmann singled out works of the Classical period, especially idealized male nudes, for his highest praise. His theories were widely admired, by Goethe and Hegel among others, and the statues that he extolled became renowned works of art.

Winckelmann had never visited Greece, and he unwittingly based his history not on original statues by Classical Greek masters but on Roman copies, that he saw in Italy. His friend Anton Raphael Mengs (*see* MENGS, (2)) was among the first critics to recognize that many of the works celebrated by Winckelmann were not in fact Greek. Mengs initiated a critical evaluation that was ultimately to remove such sculptures as the APOLLO BELVEDERE from their exalted position as paradigms of Greek aesthetics. The arrival in England of the architectural sculptures from the Parthenon, brought to London by the 7th Earl of Elgin in the early 19th century, further eroded the reputation of the statues most admired by Winckelmann. Purchased by the British Museum in 1816, the Elgin Marbles (*c.* 442–*c.* 438 BC) set new standards for the evaluation of Greek art (for examples see figs 40, 41 and 60 above). Their weathered, ruined condition helped bring about a shift in popular taste away from the highly polished and restored statues of Winckelmann's day. At the same time, the Elgin Marbles confirmed Winckelmann's judgement that the second half of the 5th century BC was the highpoint of the Greek achievement in sculpture. Finds from excavations at other ancient Greek sites, however, soon caused that long-standing opinion to be challenged. The discovery of Severe style pedimental figures at Aigina (Munich, Staatl. Antikensamml.; see fig. 54 above) in 1811, of Archaic statuary on the Athenian Acropolis in the 1860s and 1870s and of the Hellenistic reliefs that once decorated the Altar of Zeus at Pergamon (Berlin, Pergamonmus.; *see* PERGAMON, fig. 2) in the 1870s combined to alert the European public to the range and quality of ancient Greek sculpture from outside the High Classical period.

The survival of many ancient literary references to Greek sculptors and their works has inspired scholars and antiquaries since the Renaissance to attempt to link extant statues with the names of artists known from texts and inscriptions. An early example is the 16th-century attribution of the LAOKOON to the Rhodian sculptors HAGESANDROS, POLYDOROS AND ATHENODOROS on the basis of Pliny's account (*Natural History* XXXVI.iv.37). This approach formed the basis of a highly influential work by ADOLF FURTWÄNGLER, *Meisterwerke der griechischen Plastik* (1893). Taking Roman copies to be accurate reflections of lost Greek masterpieces, Furtwängler attempted to reconstruct statues mentioned by the sources as works of the 5th or 4th century BC. On the basis of his reconstructions, he outlined the careers of individual sculptors as well as constructing a detailed stylistic history of Classical sculpture. His methodology has, however, been much criticized (see Zanker, Ridgway) for its assumptions both of the stylistic closeness of the copies to lost originals and of the correlation between extant works and ancient descriptions.

No single critic or methodology has dominated 20th-century investigations of Greek sculpture. Late 20th-century scholars have pursued two approaches initially suggested by Winckelmann: the formalist and the contextual. The formalist approach emphasizes style as the primary means for dating and interpreting a statue. Examining such details as drapery, musculature and pose, formalist scholars have devised developmental schemes that assume the ever-increasing attainment of naturalism (see Richter, 1942, 1968, and Carpenter). Their analyses often ignore the roles both of individual artists and of historical factors. The contextual approach was intended to remedy this deficiency by considering sculpture in a wider context embracing cultural history (Pollitt), the conditions of production (Stewart) or social function (Schneider). In particular, articles in the German periodical *Hephaistos* (1979–) exemplify the more theoretical dimension of this approach.

BIBLIOGRAPHY

A. Félibien: *Des Principes de l'architecture, de la sculpture, de la peinture* (Paris, 1697)

Comte de Caylus: *Recueil d'antiquités égyptiennes, étrusques, grecques et romaines*, 7 vols (Paris, 1752–67)

J. J. Winckelmann: *Geschichte der Kunst des Alterthums* (Dresden, 1764); Eng. trans. by G. H. Lodge as *The History of Ancient Art* (Boston, 1856)

A. Furtwängler: *Meisterwerke der griechischen Plastik* (Leipzig, 1893; Eng. trans. and rev., London, 1895)

G. M. A. Richter: *Kouroi: Archaic Greek Youths* (New York, 1942, rev. London, 3/1970)

R. Carpenter: *Greek Sculpture: A Critical Review* (Chicago, 1960)

G. M. A. Richter: *Korai: Archaic Greek Maidens* (London, 1968)

J. J. Pollitt: *Art and Experience in Classical Greece* (Cambridge, 1972)

P. Zanker: *Klassizistische Statuen* (Mainz, 1974)

L. A. Schneider: *Zur sozialen Bedeutung der archaischen Korenstatuen* (Hamburg, 1975)

J. Rothenberg: *'Descensus ad terram': The Acquisition and Reception of the Elgin Marbles* (New York, 1977)

A. D. Potts: 'Greek Sculpture and Roman Copies, I: Anton Raphael Mengs and the Eighteenth Century', *J. Warb. & Court. Inst.*, xliii (1980), pp. 150–73

F. Haskell and N. Penny: *Taste and the Antique* (New Haven and London, 1981)

A. D. Potts: 'Winckelmann's Construction of History', *A. Hist.*, v (1982), pp. 377–407

B. S. Ridgway: *Roman Copies of Greek Sculpture: The Problem of Originals* (Ann Arbor, 1984)

A. F. Stewart: *Greek Sculpture: An Exploration*, 2 vols (New Haven and London, 1990)

ELIZABETH BARTMAN

4. COLLECTIONS, MUSEUMS AND EXHIBITIONS. Ancient Greek architectural and funerary reliefs and free-standing sculptures can be seen in many museums and collections. Many of the extant sculptures are in a badly damaged or fragmentary state, and few are visible *in situ*. Though a high proportion of Greek sculpture has been destroyed, some of the sculptures most famous in antiquity are known today through Roman copies. Examples of Greek sculpture are held in major museums throughout the world, but the greatest concentration is in Greece itself. There are few important private collections of Greek sculpture, and temporary or travelling exhibitions are rare. This article necessarily covers only the most important works; fuller information can be obtained from the selection of museum catalogues listed in the bibliography below.

(i) History of collecting. The ancient Greeks themselves collected sculpture, but interest in the collecting of art did not really flourish until the Hellenistic period. The ruler of Pergamon, Attalos I (*reg* 241–197 BC), for instance, collected sculpture to adorn the city's acropolis, and his successor, Eumenes II (*reg* 197–160 BC), commissioned copies of works when he could not acquire originals. Roman interest in collecting developed following the importation of works of art as war trophies; Sulla, Lucullus and others displayed looted Greek antiquities both publicly and privately. When the desired Greek originals were unobtainable, Roman copies were made. In the late Roman Republic, the concept of the art collection as an investment gained popularity; thus Marcus Agrippa urged that works should be kept in the city and available for the public, instead of being removed to their owners' country villas. Christianity in the West later became a deterrent to the collection and preservation of 'pagan' Greek sculpture, but the humanism of the Renaissance brought about renewed interest in Greek antiquities. Before the 18th century, most collections were private and inaccessible to the public, though the Musei Capitolini, presented to the people of Rome in 1471, were a notable exception.

During the 18th century, popular interest in art became more widespread, and public museums were developed and expanded. The influence of Neo-classicism and the rediscovery of Pompeii and Herculaneum led to a renewed interest in Greek and Roman antiquity generally, and new discoveries and collecting both increased. Archaeology became fashionable, and wealthy Europeans excavated Greek and Roman sites, placing their finds in personal or public collections. Increasingly often, private collections were consolidated and opened to the public. American collectors began to be active in the 19th century, and after 1900 collection was increasingly dominated worldwide by the magnates of American industry. The public display of works of art was disrupted in Europe by World War II, with museums closed and sculptures placed in storage. The Glyptothek in Munich, for example, closed in 1939 and did not reopen until 1972 after its restoration. New directions in research and in the restoration and display of ancient Greek sculpture were stimulated by the discovery off the Italian coast of the RIACE BRONZES (see fig. 58 above), first exhibited in Florence in 1981.

(ii) Major collections and exhibitions. Unfortunately, no Greek temple complex survives with its architectural sculpture intact. The pediments, friezes and metopes of the Athenian Parthenon, the most extensive programme in all Greek architectural sculpture, survive in a fragmentary state, mostly in the British Museum in London, where they were placed after their removal from Athens by the 7th Earl of Elgin in the early 19th century. Other fragments are in the Acropolis Museum in Athens, the Louvre in Paris and the Kunsthistorisches Museum in Vienna. Fragments of pediments from other buildings on the Acropolis are also displayed in the Acropolis Museum. The magnificent pedimental figures and metopes from the Temple of Zeus at Olympia are in the museum on the site, and the pedimental figures from Aigina, which were severely damaged during restoration, are now in the Glyptothek in Munich. Other important architectural remains include

the pediment of the earlier Temple of Athena on the Acropolis (Athens, Acropolis Mus.); figures and friezes from the temple at Bassai (London, BM); the pediment from the Temple of Artemis on Corfu (Corfu, Archaeol. Mus.); the pediment, caryatids and frieze of the Siphnian Treasury at Delphi (Delphi, Archaeol. Mus.); a column base from the Temple of Artemis at Ephesos (London, BM); figures and frieze fragments from the Mausoleum of Halikarnassos (London, BM); the metopes from the Temple of Hera at the mouth of the River Sele (Paestum, Mus. Archeol. N.); and the metopes from the Temple of Hera at Selinus (Palermo, Mus. Reg.). More sculptures were once visible *in situ*, but many architectural or dedicatory sculptures, such as the caryatids of the Erechtheion in Athens and some grave stele in the Kerameikos Cemetery there, are gradually being removed to protect them from the effects of modern pollution.

Many of the most important examples of Greek sculpture of all types are in Athenian museums. The collections of the Acropolis Museum were begun during the cleaning of debris from the Turkish settlement on the Acropolis in 1834, when antique finds were amassed. The Acropolis Museum contains kouros and kore figures from the Acropolis, including the *Kritios Boy* (see fig. 55 above), the *Nike* parapet reliefs from the Temple of Athena Nike and caryatids from the Erechtheion. The National Archaeological Museum in Athens, established in Aigina in 1829 and moved to Athens in 1834, contains the colossal kouros from the Temple of Poseidon at Sounion, several later kouroi, the bronze *Boy* from Marathon, grave reliefs from the Kerameikos Cemetery, the *Dipylon Head* and the bronze *Zeus* (?or *Poseidon*), the most famous of the ARTEMISION BRONZES (see fig. 43 above). Museums at other ancient Greek sites also contain important finds. The Archaeological Museum at Olympia houses a colossal Archaic *Head of Hera*, the terracotta *Zeus Abducting Ganymede*, the *Nike of Paionios* and *Hermes Holding the Infant Dionysos*, perhaps by Praxiteles. The Archaeological Museum at Delphi has the bronze *Charioteer*, fragments of his quadriga and architectural sculpture from the treasuries of the Athenians and Siphnians. Other important site museums include those at Alexandria, Corfu, Corinth, Cyrene, Delos, Eleusis, Ephesos, Epidauros, Paestum, Pergamon, Priene, Rhodes and Thessaloniki.

In Italy, Rome and Naples contain major collections of Greek sculpture and Roman copies of Greek sculpture: the first because of ancient Roman interest in and copying of Greek antiquities, the second because of the discoveries near by at Pompeii and Herculaneum. These collections include many Hellenistic works and some of the finest Roman copies. Among the works in the Musei Vaticani are the APOLLO BELVEDERE, the LAOKOON and the BELVEDERE TORSO. The Museo Nazionale Romano includes the Ludovisi Throne (from the Ludovisi Collection), the *Venus of Cyrene*, the bronze *Boxer* by Apollonios, the best-preserved copy of Myron of Eleutherai's *Diskobolos* and the bronze *Hellenistic Prince*. The collections of the Musei Capitolini include Roman copies of figures of Gauls from Pergamon. The Museo Archeologico Nazionale in Naples houses the impressive ancient works from the Farnese collection. The Museo Civico Archeologico in Bologna has a copy of the head of Pheidias' *Athena Lemnia*, and the Museo Regionale di Palermo, established in 1866, when several local collections were consolidated, also houses important Greek sculptures.

Elsewhere in Europe, other museums with important collections include the Pergamonmuseum in Berlin, which contains the reconstructed frieze from the Altar of Zeus at Pergamon. Acquisitions for the ancient collection at the Glyptothek in Munich, founded by Ludwig I of Bavaria from his private collection, began as early as 1804. In addition to the sculptures from Aigina, which Ludwig purchased soon after they were excavated in 1812, the Greek collections include the Tenea Kouros, the Hellenistic *Drunken Old Woman* (see fig. 68 above) and the *Sleeping Satyr* (also called the Barberini *Faun*). The Department of Greek and Roman Antiquities at the Louvre in Paris was established in 1800, and its collection includes the *Auxerre Goddess*, the Cheramyes Kore, the Rampin Head, the *Apollo of Piombino*, a bronze head from Benevento, the VENUS DE MILO (see fig. 69 above) and the NIKE OF SAMOTHRACE. The Archaeological Museum at Istanbul has a group of sarcophagi found at Sidon in 1887. Other European collections include those of the National Museum in Belgrade, the Museum of Greek and Roman Antiquities in Berlin (Staatl. Museen), the Museum of Fine Arts in Budapest, the Prado in Madrid, the Ny Carlsberg Glyptotek in Copenhagen, the Staatliche Kunstsammlungen in Dresden (Albertinum), the Hermitage in St Petersburg, the British Museum in London and the Kunsthistorisches Museum in Vienna.

In the USA there are important collections at the Metropolitan Museum of Art in New York, the Museum of Fine Arts in Boston and the J. Paul Getty Museum in Malibu, CA. The Metropolitan Museum contains a 7th-century BC kouros, Classical grave stelai and the Hellenistic *Old Market Woman*. The Museum of Fine Arts collection began with the purchase of part of the collection of the excavator Luigi Palma di Cesnola (1832–1904) in 1872 and was increased from 1895 to 1905, primarily through the work of Edward Warren (1860–1928) and Samuel Warren (1851–1910). It includes the Boston Throne, a counterpart to the Ludovisi Throne, and many Greco-Roman portrait busts. The Getty Museum houses a collection of ancient works begun by J. Paul Getty in 1939. It includes a 4th-century BC bronze *Victorious Athlete*, acquired in 1977, which has been attributed to a sculptor influenced by Lysippos. Among other American collections with important works are the Walters Art Gallery in Baltimore, the Brooklyn Museum in New York, the Cleveland Museum of Art, the Fogg Art Museum of Harvard University in Cambridge, MA, the Art Institute of Chicago, the Detroit Institute of Arts, the Wadsworth Atheneum in Hartford, the Nelson–Atkins Museum of Art in Kansas City, MO, the Los Angeles County Museum of Art, the Minneapolis Institute of Arts, the Museum of Art of the Rhode Island School of Design in Providence, the Santa Barbara Museum of Art and the Worcester Art Museum. In Canada there is an important collection at the Royal Ontario Museum in Toronto.

There have been few important temporary or travelling exhibitions of ancient Greek sculpture, partly because of the difficulties in moving major works. Representative of such exhibitions have been *Ancient Greek Art* at the

Burlington Fine Arts Club in London in 1904, an exhibition of Greek art at the Royal Academy, London, in 1946, *Meisterwerke griechischer Kunst* at Basle in 1960 and *Ancient Art from New York Private Collections* at the Metropolitan Museum of Art in New York in 1959–60.

BIBLIOGRAPHY

W. Amelung and G. Lippold: *Die Skulpturen des Vaticanischen Museums*, i, ii (Berlin, 1903–8)

G. Mendel: *Istanbul, Musées impériaux ottomans: Catalogue des sculptures grecques, romaines et byzantines*, 3 vols (Athens, 1908)

H. Stuart Jones, ed.: *The Sculptures of the Museo Capitolino* (Oxford, 1912)

L. D. Caskey: *Catalogue of Greek and Roman Sculpture: Fogg Art Museum* (Cambridge, MA, 1925)

H. Stuart Jones, ed.: *The Sculptures of the Palazzo dei Conservatori*, 2 vols (Oxford, 1926)

C. Blümel: *Katalog der griechischen Skulpturen des fünften und vierten Jahrhunderts vor Christus* (1928), iii of *Berlin: Katalog der Sammlung antiker Skulpturen* (Berlin, 1928–38)

R. N. Pryce: *British Museum: Catalogue of Sculpture*, I/i (London, 1928)

A. Hekler: *Die Sammlung antiker Skulpturen in Budapest* (Budapest, 1929)

J. Charbonneaux: *La Sculpture grecque et romaine au Musée du Louvre* (Paris, 1936)

G. Lippold: *Die Skulpturen des Vaticanischen Museums*, iii/1–2 (Berlin, 1936–56)

Greek Art (exh. cat., ed. J. Chittenden and C. Seltman; London, RA, 1946)

D. B. Harden, ed.: *Summary Guide to the Department of Antiquities, Ashmolean Museum* (Oxford, 1951)

F. Poulen: *Catalogue of Ancient Sculpture in the Ny Carlsberg Glyptotek* (Copenhagen, 1951)

G. M. A. Richter: *Catalogue of Greek Sculptures in the Metropolitan Museum of Art* (Cambridge, MA, 1954)

Meisterwerke griechischer Kunst (exh. cat., ed. C. Schefold; Basle, Ksthalle, 1960)

Ancient Art in New York Private Collections (exh. cat., New York, Met., 1961)

M. A. del Chiaro: *The Collection of Greek and Roman Antiquities at the Santa Barbara Museum of Art* (Santa Barbara, 1962)

W. Helbig: *Führer durch die öffentlichen Sammlungen klassischer Altertümer in Rom*, 4 vols (Tübingen, 1963–72)

S. Karouzou: *National Archaeological Museum, Athens: Collection of Sculpture* (Athens, 1968)

E. Rohde: *Griechische und römische Kunst in den Staatlichen Museen zu Berlin* (Berlin, 1968)

M. B. Comstock and C. C. Vermeule: *Greek, Etruscan and Roman Bronzes in the Museum of Fine Arts, Boston* (Boston, 1971)

C. C. Vermeule and N. Neuerburg: *Catalogue of the Ancient Art in the J. Paul Getty Museum* (Malibu, 1973)

Greek and Roman Portraits in the J. Paul Getty Museum (exh. cat., Northridge, CA State U., 1975)

M. B. Comstock and C. C. Vermeule: *Sculpture in Stone: The Greek, Roman and Etruscan Collections of the Museum of Fine Arts* (Boston, 1977)

C. C. Vermeule and A. Brauer: *Stone Sculptures: The Greek, Roman, and Etruscan Collections of the Harvard University Art Museums* (Cambridge, MA, 1990)

ANN THOMAS WILKINS

V. Pottery.

Ancient Greek pottery was produced in most areas around the Mediterranean and is among the most distinctive in the history of the craft. The pots were intended for a wide variety of uses—domestic, funerary, commercial and ceremonial—and range from plain kitchenware to elaborately decorated cups and bowls. Thousands of specimens, many in excellent condition, have been recovered and are now eagerly sought by museums and private collectors as well as providing study material for both the archaeologist and the art historian. The archaeologist finds pottery remains helpful in reconstructing the histories of particular sites; such information does not depend on the quality of the pottery, though decorated ware is usually more closely datable than other types. Pottery can also provide information about social behaviour, customs, economic trends and trade connections and in some cases be connected with historical events. Art historians, by contrast, are concerned primarily with the development of manufacturing techniques, the aesthetics and uses of different shapes of the fine decorated wares and especially the stylistic development and subject-matter of their painted decoration. They have also sought to identify individual painters and workshops using Morellian techniques, first applied by J. D. Beazley to the study of Attic vase painting. Those individual vase painters distinguished by small capital letters throughout §IV have separate biographical entries under VASE PAINTERS, §II.

1. Introduction. 2. Protogeometric. 3. Geometric. 4. Orientalizing. 5. Black-figure. 6. Red-figure. 7. White-ground. 8. Unpainted. 9. Hellenistic. 10. Collecting and collections.

1. INTRODUCTION. A continuously developing tradition of Greek pottery-making can be traced from *c.* 1000 BC to the end of the 1st century BC, by which time Rome had taken over the Greek areas of the eastern Mediterranean and was already imposing her ceramic styles and techniques on the provinces of her empire. Excluding the Sub-Mycenaean phase, during which pottery styles were essentially debased versions of their Mycenaean precursors (*see* HELLADIC, §III, 2(iii)), Greek pottery spanned five historical periods: Protogeometric (*c.* 1000–*c.* 900 BC), Geometric (*c.* 900–*c.* 700 BC), Archaic (*c.* 700–*c.* 480 BC), Classical (*c.* 480–323 BC) and Hellenistic (323–27 BC). The extent to which the development of the pottery styles described below follows these conventional historical divisions is, however, debatable. While Protogeometric and Geometric pottery have provided the key datings and identity for the cultural periods they have been used to define (*see* §§2–3 below), the same cannot be said of the later periods. The development of the Orientalizing style (*see* §4 below) at the beginning of the Archaic period can be associated with the establishment of trade links with the Near East, but the emergence of the important Black-figure technique (*see* §5 below) in the same period seems unrelated to known historical events, as does the introduction of Red-figure and White-ground pottery (*see* §§6–7 below) at the end of the Archaic period. The Classical period was dominated by the Red-figure style, though there were also important examples of White-ground and Black-glaze (unpainted) pottery (*see* §8 below). The Hellenistic period is characterized by the continuation of unpainted pottery and the development of several new techniques (*see* §9 below). Although the evolution of pottery styles and techniques after the Geometric period was only marginally influenced by developments in Greek cultural and political history, production in certain regions does seem to have been affected by such events as the fall of cities, foreign invasions and the creation of new settlements, which in their turn provide some evidence for dating. The chronology of Greek pottery is thus firmer for some periods than for others, and it would be unwise to consider it finally established.

By the beginning of the 1st millennium BC the Greeks had colonized not only mainland Greece but also the Aegean islands and the west coast of Asia Minor: over the following five centuries they established settlements in South Italy, Sicily, southern France, Spain, coastal north Africa and the shores of the Black Sea. All these areas either produced their own distinctive range of pots or imported from other Greek areas what they themselves lacked. Local pottery shapes and decoration were often severely practical, tending towards heavy-duty, plain and coarse wares: but in some areas both the potting and decoration were of the highest quality. The decoration might simply be linear patterns, as on Geometric wares; though figured narrative scenes gradually became dominant, and it is these which are in a sense the hallmark of Greek ceramic decoration, allowing art historians to follow the development of figure drawing from early schematized renderings to the three-dimensional effects of 5th-century BC and later vase painters. This development cannot be traced in other media, since the panel and wall paintings that undoubtedly pioneered such effects as chiaroscuro and perspective are almost entirely lost.

BIBLIOGRAPHY

P. E. Arias and M. Hirmer: *Tausend Jahre griechischer Vasenkunst* (Munich, 1960); enlarged Eng. trans. by B. B. Shefton as *A History of Greek Vase Painting* (London, 1962)

R. M. Cook: *Greek Painted Pottery* (London, 1960/*R* 1972)

B. A. SPARKES

(i) Subject-matter. (ii) Shapes, uses and decoration. (iii) Materials and techniques. (iv) Potters, painters and society. (v) Trade. (vi) Inscriptions.

(i) Subject-matter. The exceptional interest in the human figure on ancient Greek, and especially Athenian, fine pottery grew gradually. The Protogeometric and earlier Geometric styles are concerned almost wholly with abstract ornamentation; animals made their first appearance in the early 8th century BC, at first singly and then in files of single species. In the 7th century BC the Orientalizing animal style dominated, where both real fauna such as the lion and fabulous beasts such as the griffin and siren are clearly borrowed from Near Eastern art, along with many floral ornaments. Corinth was the most creative, even playful, centre in depicting animals, inventing new hybrids such as the lion-siren and phallus-bird as well as new complex varieties of lotus and palmette (*see* §4(ii) below). Corinth is also important for the early development of scenes with human figures, but from *c.* 550 BC produced only pots with floral decoration or simple patterns. Similar unpretentious styles are found throughout the Greek world. Even more popular, from the later 6th century BC onwards, were the plain black wares (*see* §8 below). The finely drawn and complex figural compositions found on some Greek vases are the exception rather than the rule.

Human figural scenes first appeared at Athens around the mid-8th century BC. Many Geometric pots were intended for the grave or as grave-markers; consequently the depictions on them are frequently funerary in nature: figures in mourning around the bier, the transport of the dead to the cemetery, chariot processions at the funeral (see fig. 86 below). There are also scenes of warfare by land and at sea, and at Argos, another great centre of Geometric pottery, men 'taming' horses are a popular motif. The pure silhouette style of Geometric, however, made it difficult to tell visual stories of any complexity.

Although the appearance of mythological narrative after *c.* 700 BC has often been connected with the contemporary rise of literary epic, it is more likely that artists drew for inspiration on stories told informally. There are many scenes specifically connected with the *Iliad*, far fewer of the *Odyssey*, with the exception of Odysseus' escape from Polyphemos' cave, and some of the most frequently shown Trojan scenes, such as the Ambush of Troilos, are from non-Homeric parts of the epic cycle. Of Greek heroes Herakles is by far the most popular in all periods, and his fight with the Nemean lion is the most favoured scene of all. This is the first of his labours, but some of the most numerous episodes with Herakles are not the canonical labours but other incidents in his career such as his struggle with Apollo over the Delphic tripod or his confrontation with the centaur Nessos (see fig. 95 below). Among the gods all the Olympians get depicted to some degree, sometimes grouped together without narrative thrust as on Oltos' famous cup (late 6th century BC; Tarquinia, Pal. Vitelleschi, RC 6848), sometimes shown singly (Aphrodite on her goose (see fig. 125 below), Dionysos standing quietly with his son Oinopion, Artemis as Mistress of Beasts), more often interacting with other gods and mortals in narrative contexts (Athena helping various heroes in their tasks, Zeus' many and varied love affairs, Apollo and Artemis shooting down the children of Niobe.

Archaic vase painters preferred vigorous, even violent, scenes that emphasize the monstrous or bizarre, such as the Birth of Athena from the head of Zeus. In the Classical period the focus of attention was more on the psychology of the situation before the climax of the action or during its aftermath. True, there are many action stories, such as the Gigantomachy, that never went out of vogue, but some narratives undergo considerable modification of treatment. On Black-figure vases the Judgement of Paris is a scene of movement as the goddesses are brought in procession to the shepherd prince, who stands or makes to run away (see fig. 80 below). In the 5th century BC the atmosphere is quieter: Paris is calmly seated, the goddesses stand by. The more subtle, fluid drawing of Red-figure, and in particular the development of the profile eye in the human face, made it possible to convey dramatic interaction between even quietly posed figures, as in *Polyneikes Bribing Eriphyle with the Necklace of Harmonia* (Chicago Painter; Lecce, Mus. Prov. Sigismondo Castromediano) or *Odysseus with Elpenor's Shade* (Lykaon Painter; Boston, MA, Mus. F.A.). In Black-figure only a superlative artist such as Exekias could inject psychological power into his scenes by effectively transcending the Archaic conventions of his time.

Where a vase displays more than one scene they may be connected, especially obverses and reverses; but often they are not, in particular scenes set one above the other, although presumably at the subconscious level the juxtaposing of scenes was rarely arbitrary.

Vase painters employed various devices to make their story-telling clear to the viewer, of which the most important is the inclusion of attributes. Athena sported her spear and aegis, Zeus his sceptre and thunderbolt, Herakles his club, often in contexts in which they are not needed or where their presence is illogical, simply as a means of identification. Thus the necklace with which she has been secretly bribed may be carried as an attribute by Eriphyle in public. Another helpful device is the addition of painted inscriptions, though their use is by no means universal (*see* §(vi) below). It is presumably for clarity's sake too that artists made free play with time sequences. Whereas most scenes show only one moment of time, others imply different moments of the same story: so Polyphemos may carry the cup with which he has drunk himself into a stupor while the stake is being driven into his eye (see fig. 90 below). But rarely is the same character shown more than once to create a 'continuous' narrative, the exception being a series of Red-figure cups depicting on the exterior the adventures of Theseus. It is not always an easy matter to distinguish mythological from theatrical scenes, which figure most prominently on South Italian vases (*see* §6(ii) below), for often the same narratives are common to both. The problem is greatest with representations of tragedy, where props such as masks are rarely shown, and yet in scenes of comedy and farce not only are masks and the comic padded costume with phallus usually included but even details of the stage setting. The satyrs of satyr plays are shown sometimes as actors and sometimes as real satyrs; the most revealing illustration of the former is provided by the Attic Red-figure Pronomos vase (late 5th century BC; Naples, Mus. Archeol. N.), which shows a full satyr chorus warming up, complete with elaborate costumes, masks, musical accompaniment and dance movements. This whole aspect of vase painting is important for the illustration of plays for which only the title has otherwise survived.

70. Niobid Painter: kalyx krater depicting (top) *Gods Creating Pandora* and (bottom) a *Pan/Satyr Chorus*, Red-figure, h. 499 mm, 5th century BC (London, British Museum)

Scenes of everyday life are more common in the 5th century BC than the 6th, but the data offered is uneven in its scope. There are plentiful scenes of banqueting and drinking, of sexual encounters with *hetairai*, music (especially on flute and lyre), dance and other entertainments, as in *Pandora and Chorus* (Niobid Painter; see fig. 70). The vases are also a mine of information about homosexual courtship and copulation. Sporting activities are very common, and it may be that the opportunity to study nude male athletes in the palaistra inspired vase painters to experiment with and modify their renderings of poses and anatomy so rapidly in the Late Archaic period (see fig. 101 below). There are, however, few representations of hoplites in battle formation (most battles are split into individual duels in the heroic/epic manner) and of trade and industry, although pottery production—appropriately enough—is shown in some detail (see figs 74 and 76 below).

Most painters, however, showed little in the way of setting. A mirror or pot suspended in the background is enough to indicate an interior, a single stylized tree an exterior. Occasionally there is something more, as in the Priam Painter's scene of women swimming in a stretch of water fronted by large trees (*c.* 520 BC; Rome, Villa Giulia), but most of the numerous hunting sequences show no setting at all. Fuller treatment of landscape would involve more complex recession and spatial relationships that are unsuited to curving vase surfaces; the multiple hilly ground-lines favoured by some artists from the mid-5th century BC onwards are derived almost certainly from contemporary monumental painting.

In choosing a subject the vase painter took into account not only the shape of the field offered by the vase but also the function of the vessel. Many of the most popular vase shapes are connected with the drinking, serving or storage of wine; consequently Dionysos as wine-god features conspicuously, along with his entourage of satyrs and maenads (see fig. 100 below). So too, on the human level, are featured symposia, drinking parties organized by the wealthy young urban males, and the vases show all the stages of such an evening: the cavorting through the streets, the symposiasts drinking as they recline on their couches, the singing and dancing and party games, the effects of over-drinking (see fig. 111 below) and the sexual pleasures of the later evening. The only women shown participating are *hetairai* and prostitutes; other depictions of women occur on hydriai, pots specifically handled by women for carrying water. On these, scenes of fetching water from the fountain-house are often shown, as well as other female domestic activities: spinning, weaving, dealing with maidservants and children. The latter subject is also found on white lekythoi—tall flasks for oil that at Athens came to have an exclusively funerary use—where we are probably to imagine the deceased among the figures shown. But the funerary context of the painting on these is often made explicit: the tomb itself is depicted with mourners around it, or the dead person is taken by Hermes and Charon to the underworld. Where the close correspondence between shape and decoration is concerned, the Panathenaic amphora is a special case. On these prize vases it was traditional to place an armed Athena on one side and on the other a scene of the victor's sporting event.

The study of iconography is far less advanced than connoisseurship, and most studies are inevitably Athenocentric or based on South Italian Red-figure. Yet other regional schools are of considerable interest and may offer surprises. One of the most detailed versions of the Ambush of Troilos is on a Chiot chalice, while Lakonian Black-figure abounds with winged youths ('Boreads'), whose significance is obscure, and a late Black-figure workshop in Boiotia specialized in lively mythological and low-life burlesque. But wherever Greek pottery is produced it is astonishing how few scenes repeat each other precisely; there is endless variation of story and detail. The overwhelming impression is of artists working freehand, without any degree of mechanization or recourse to pattern books, and that they did so is proved by preliminary sketches on the pots themselves, together with details that have been erased. It is even true of stock scenes such as the draped youths that occur on the reverses of innumerable Red-figure kraters.

Late 20th-century studies have attempted to elucidate choice of decoration in terms of historical events, religious attitudes, political ideology and cultural values. Possible links between the images and the final destinations of the vases (tombs, sanctuaries, particular export localities) have begun to be explored. Scenes of actual historical figures and events are rare (for King Arkesilaos of Cyrene, see fig. 103 below); more often—as in architectural sculpture—historical events may be alluded to in mythological terms. A case has been made out for the popularity at Athens of Herakles and later of Theseus being fostered by different political regimes, and it is likely that the introduction of new cults may explain the sudden cultivation by vase painters of particular gods. These kinds of approaches are on the increase and have much to offer, although their conclusions are hardly susceptible to proof.

BIBLIOGRAPHY

K. Schefold: *Myth and Legend in Early Greek Art* (London, 1966)
T. B. L. Webster: *Potter and Patron in Classical Athens* (London, 1972)
Lexikon iconographicum mythologiae classicae (Zurich, 1981–)
W. G. Moon, ed.: *Ancient Greek Art and Iconography* (Wisconsin, 1983)
C. Bérard and others: *A City of Images* (Princeton, 1989)
T. H. Carpenter: *Art and Myth in Ancient Greece* (London, 1991)
T. Rasmussen and N. Spivey, eds: *Looking at Greek Vases* (Cambridge, 1991)
B. A. Sparkes: *Greek Pottery: An Introduction* (Manchester, 1991), chap. 5
K. Schefold: *Gods and Heroes in Late Archaic Greek Art* (Cambridge, 1992)

TOM RASMUSSEN

(ii) Shapes, uses and decoration. Almost all Greek pots were intended for specific practical uses, which in turn determined their form and decoration. The appearance of finer wares, however, was also influenced by current aesthetics or fashion. The names currently used to designate pottery shapes have developed largely through convention and are not always used consistently or with precision. Though some of the more firmly established terms have ancient Greek origins, few are used in their original sense. Some other names are those of modern forms of pots and vary from language to language; yet others are hybrid terms (e.g. neck amphora), and a few are pure inventions (e.g. bolsal, formed from *Bo*logna and *Sal*onica, where two examples of this type of low cup occur).

Knowledge of the uses to which particular shapes were put derives from several sources. The shapes themselves often declare their function: a spout and a single handle, for example, suggest that a vase was used for pouring liquids. Figural scenes on decorated pottery often show vases in use, and some vases are labelled with their original names, though the significance of these terms is not always clear. Literary sources are surprisingly unhelpful since they are rarely specific, and it is often uncertain whether a term in modern usage had the same connotations in ancient times. They do, however, show that the Greeks often used anatomical terms such as 'body', 'foot' and 'ears' (i.e. handles) to designate parts of vases, much as is done today. Moreover, since few potters signed their vases (*see also* §§(iv) and (vi) below), shapes can be useful in identifying the work of individual craftsmen; but this area remains to be researched more fully.

(a) Shapes and uses. (b) Decoration.

(a) Shapes and uses. Though they were a utilitarian product, not all pots were intended for uses that are currently familiar: for example, large Geometric amphorae served as grave markers, while Apulian kraters were produced specifically as tomb offerings. Other shapes were dedicated in sanctuaries and generally differed in size and elaboration from their more utilitarian counterparts, while others again were made in direct imitation of foreign pottery shapes (e.g. the kyathos and rhyton) or to reproduce the appearance of the non-ceramic item (metal container, basket, drinking-horn etc) they were designed to replace.

Nonetheless, the underlying emphasis on practicality of design probably helped to limit the number of shapes produced: a vase's function defined the essential features of its various components, while hygiene and durability were additional considerations. The skill of the Greek potters lay in their ability to produce vases that were clearly articulated and well-proportioned, with tight, lively contours; the relative emphasis given to practical sturdiness or elegance varied at different times and in different centres of production. Though a discussion of the shapes of Greek vases can be organized in various ways, the utilitarian emphasis noted above makes it most suitable to consider them in the context of their functions (see fig. 71). Since most research has centred on Attic pottery and, to a lesser extent, on Corinthian and South Italian, the shapes of these wares inevitably form the main basis for study.

Storage and transport vessels. One of the main functions of pottery was the bulk storage of liquids or solids (see fig. 71(i)). The heavy-duty pithos was the principal shape used for this purpose. Goods in transit, particularly wine, were usually carried in the transport amphora, which had a long body, small toe, narrow, offset neck and two vertical handles from shoulder to mouth. The mouth could be sealed, and the shape facilitated stacking during transit. The vase could also be handled easily by using the toe as an extra grip and could even be fixed in the ground. Smaller sizes of amphorae, with plumper bodies, wider mouths and more stable feet, were produced in various finishes for temporary storage (71(i)a–d).

For fetching and carrying water either a hydria (71(i)f) or a kados was used. The hydria was produced in metal and in both coarse and fine clays but invariably had a

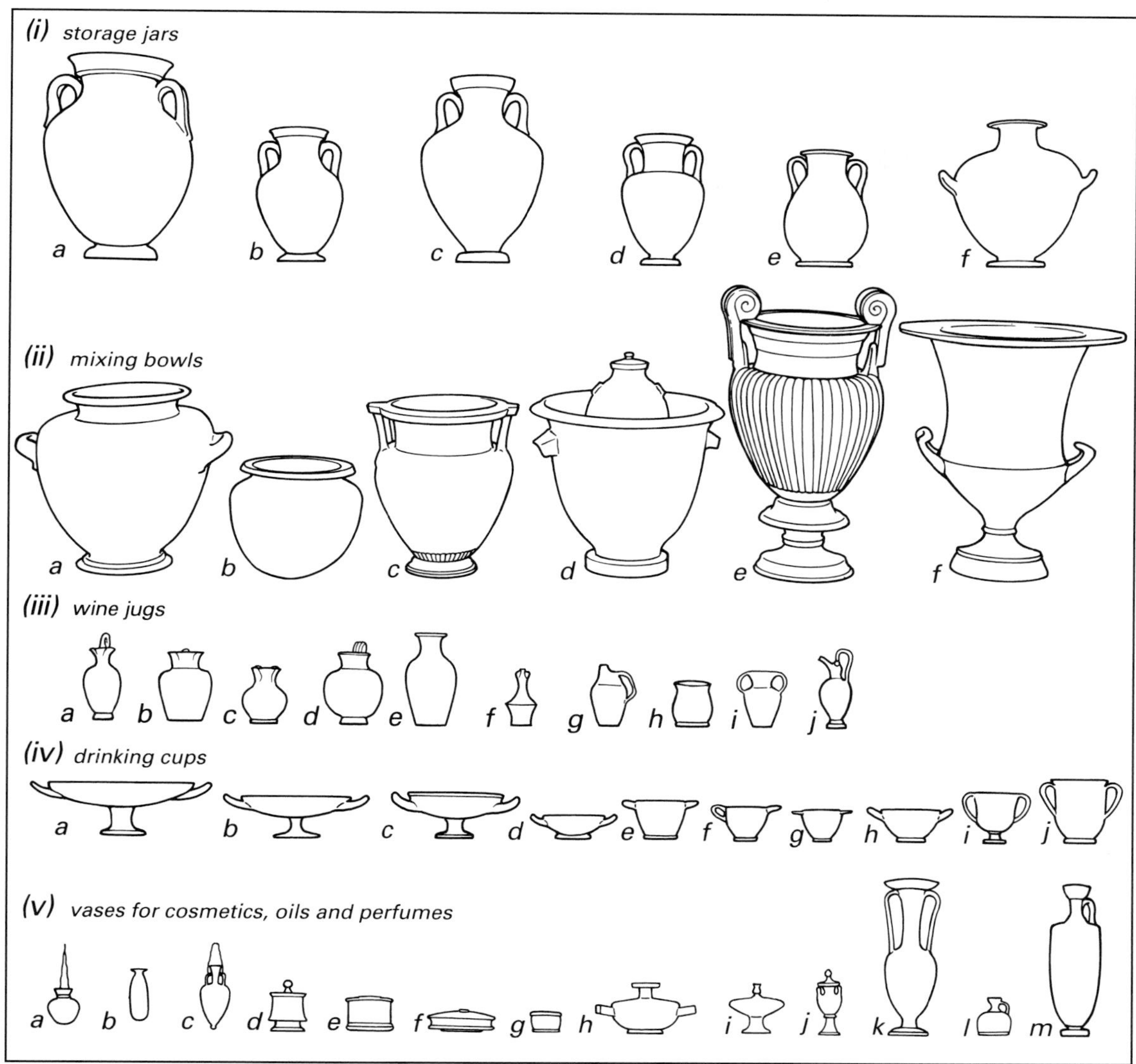

71. Vase shapes from Attica, 6th–4th centuries BC

capacious body, sturdy foot, wide mouth and three handles, one rising vertically from shoulder to neck for dipping, pouring and carrying when empty and two horizontal handles at the sides of the body for lifting when full. Illustrations of hydriai are common in fountain scenes on Attic Black-figure vases and in depictions of *Achilles' Ambush of Troilos*. The kados was a form of bucket used exclusively for drawing water from courtyard wells, and pottery versions were invariably of coarse clay. It had a broad body, wide mouth and plain foot, with two small vertical handles on its shoulder for attaching a rope when letting it down the well.

Among the finest examples of Greek pottery are the vessels used at aristocratic drinking parties. Since wine was mixed with water and drunk in large quantities, great mixing bowls (see below) were provided. The wine itself was stored in amphorae, which could double as mixing bowls and were varied in shape. The neck amphora, with a neck meeting the body at an abrupt angle (71(i)d), was popular in most areas from Protogeometric times onwards, with certain regional and chronological variations such as the Nolan amphora, named from its principal findspot in South Italy, which is small with a high neck. The one-piece or belly amphora, with a neck and body profile forming a continuous double curve (71(i)a–c), was mainly an Athenian shape of the 6th and 5th centuries BC. It is on examples of one-piece amphorae that some of the most outstanding Attic Black- and Red-figure painting occurs. An Attic and South Italian alternative to the wine amphora was the pelike (71(i)e), which closely resembles the one-piece amphora but has its broadest diameter near the base of the body. It was particularly popular in the 4th century BC and seems also to have served as a container for perfumed oil.

72. Cup-skyphos by Epiktetos: *Serving the Wine*, Attic Red-figure, h. 95 mm, late 6th century BC (Oxford, Ashmolean Museum)

Mixing vessels. The ancient Greek word for mixing bowl (*krater*) is now used to designate a group of large pots with mouths wide enough to admit jugs and ladles (see fig. 71(ii)). The earliest are Protogeometric plain open bowls, but the four best-known forms were produced by Archaic and Classical Athenian potters. The first of these was the column krater (71(ii)c and the large vessel depicted at the lower centre of fig. 72 below), apparently invented in Corinth and probably known in antiquity as the Corinthian krater. Its stepped foot is topped by a round body, steep neck and wide mouth, while two columnar handles stretch from the shoulder to the handle plates, which are extensions of the overhanging lip. In Attica this form attracted few first-rate artists. The volute krater, known also from bronze examples such as the 6th-century BC Vix Krater (Châtillon-sur-Seine, Mus. Archéol.; for illustration *see* VIX) and the 4th-century BC Derveni Krater (Thessaloniki, Archaeol. Mus.), is the most elaborate of the four and was sometimes furnished with a separate stand (71(ii)e above). Its neck was usually given figure decoration, as was the body, though the latter is sometimes covered with vertical ribs. Its most distinctive feature is its pair of handles, which were formed with increasingly tightly curled volutes overhanging the lip. The most elaborate decoration occurs on Red-figure funerary examples from Apulia, which sometimes have relief clay figures and mascaron handles. The kalyx krater (71(ii)f), which first appeared in the mid-6th century BC, had quite a different profile and an even wider mouth. On top of the foot a short stem opens out to form the lower body; above this is the splaying flower-like 'calyx', the transition being marked by two horizontal handles. Like other forms of krater, this type tended to become taller and narrower, and in the 4th century BC the best pieces were plain black with relief decoration added in gilt clay. The bell krater (71(ii)d) is the latest of the four types and consists simply of a sturdy foot and a body shaped like an inverted bell. Two horizontal handles or, more rarely, lugs are set near the top of the bell, and the shape may have been based on that of a wooden tub. It was popular in Athens during the later 5th century BC and the 4th, and it tended over the years to acquire a more strongly outcurved mouth and incurved lower body. Other shapes that served the same purpose as the kraters include the stamnos (71(ii)a), with a bulbous body, high shoulder and flaring mouth. Two horizontal handles were placed just below the shoulder, occasionally with small projections at either side as though they had been woven into the vase's wall. Another mixing bowl, the lebes (71(ii)b), consisted simply of an almost spherical body with short neck and wide mouth and was often produced in metal. It had no handle or foot and was placed on a separate round stand. In the late 6th century BC a wine cooler, the psykter, began to be used at Athens. It was a mushroom-shaped pot containing cold water that floated inside a krater (shown in the bell krater, 71(ii) d). One version had a lid and pierced tubes at the sides, which vase paintings show were used for attaching cord handles.

Jugs and cups. After mixing, wine was poured out using an oinochoe (such as that being dipped in the column krater in fig. 72). Many shapes and sizes of oinochoai were produced, as demonstrated by the range of Attic examples (see fig. 71(iii)a–j above). The basic form is a jug with one vertical (high or low) handle and a narrow neck (71(iii)a). Its mouth is often modelled into a trefoil shape to aid pouring; but round and beak-shaped examples also occur, and some of the more elaborate versions have animal heads as necks and mouths. Body shapes also vary: some are conical, others concave, but most are convex, either with a single curve from mouth to base or with the neck offset from the body. Some variants have their own specific names: the olpe (71(iii)e) was a slender form with an uninterrupted curve, and the mug (71(iii)h) may also have been used for drinking. The chous, with a plump body and trefoil mouth (71(iii)c), figured prominently in the Anthesteria festival at Athens, when miniature versions decorated with pictures of children's games were given to the young. Similar miniatures were also placed in the graves of children too young to have received them in the normal way. A popular shape in Hellenistic times was the lagynos (71(iii)j), with a bulbous body, low foot, tall narrow neck and tall vertical handle.

The most elegant of the many types of Greek cup (71(iv)) was the kylix (71(iv)a–d; *see also* MYTHOLOGICAL PAINTING AND SCULPTURE, fig. 1). Protogeometric examples tended to be deep with a high foot; in Geometric times they became squatter. The most exquisite forms, however, occurred in Athens in the 6th and 5th centuries BC and are designated by various names, such as komast cups, Siana cups, lip cups, band cups and eye cups, of which there are three further variants, Types A, B and C (71(iv)a–c). They consisted essentially of a wide low body with a high stem and thin footplate, and two spreading horizontal handles attached near the rim or lip. A less elegant stemless form had a ring foot attached directly to the body (71(iv)d). The skyphos, sometimes called the kotyle, is a smaller and deeper cup, with two handles attached just below the rim. Usually both of the latter are horizontal, but in one variant one of the handles is vertical (71(iv)f). The two main varieties of skyphos, called Corinthian (71(iv)g) and Attic (71(iv)e) after their places of origin, differ in the curvature of the wall and the shape

73. Kantharos by the Brygos Painter: *Zeus Pursuing Ganymede*, Attic Red-figure, h. 247 mm, *c.* 490–*c.* 480 BC (Boston, MA, Museum of Fine Arts)

of the foot, and the Corinthian type also has a thinner wall, finer rim and foot and daintier handles. There are also hybrid forms of the kylix and skyphos, such as the cup-skyphos (71(iv)h and fig. 72). A special form of cup, the kantharos, was closely associated with Dionysos; it consisted essentially of a deep bowl with two vertical handles. Some extravagant versions have a tall stem and high handles curving in a wide arc from the base of the body to the rim (see fig. 73), but others have low handles and stem (71(iv)i), and yet others low handles and no stem (71(iv)j). The shape was popular at Athens and in Boiotia. The kotyle krater was a deep, two-handled cup on a high, flaring pedestal, while a kotyle pyxis was a deep, two-handled cup with a lid (see fig. 93 below).

Less important varieties of drinking cup are the phiale, which was generally used in libation ceremonies; the different forms of rhyta, shaped as horns or animal heads; the sturdy one-handler; the delicate bolsal; and the breast-shaped mastos. In addition there are also various mugs moulded into the shape of human and animal heads. In Hellenistic times mould-made hemispherical bowls with relief patterns and figures, once called 'Megarian' bowls, replaced all other shapes in popularity.

Vases for cosmetics, oils and perfumes. Oil and perfume were stored in containers of various sizes (see fig. 71(v) above), the smallest of which had very narrow openings so that they could be sealed with a tiny stopper and used to pour out droplets or thin streams. The alabastron (71(v)b) was based on Oriental alabaster prototypes and developed in Corinth in the 7th century BC for use by women; it remained popular until the 4th century BC in South Italy and Sicily. It was a long, slender flask, usually with a round bottom and sometimes with two small lugs high up on the body. Though its top was flat and wide, its opening was only large enough for a dip-stick used to perfume the hair and body. A less widespread shape was the amphoriskos (71(v)c), a miniature version of the pointed amphora with a small toe, an egg-shaped body and two vertical handles running from shoulder to neck. Few examples have figural decoration, most being black with impressed or incised patterns. A larger container for perfume, or perhaps for perfumed water, is variously referred to as a kothon, exaleiptron, plemochoe or smegmatotheke (71(v)i). This is a stemmed and lidded bowl with a deep, downcurved mouth designed to prevent its contents from spilling. The small lydion may have been used as a container for the Lydian perfume *bakkaris*. The heavy, bulbous body, small foot and thick rim of the Lydian original were, however, frequently refined by Greek craftsmen. In the absence of soap, men used olive oil to cleanse themselves after exercise, carrying it with them in a small flask, the aryballos (71(v) a). It was usually ovoid or round and fitted easily into the palm of the hand. A cord attached to one or two small vertical handles was fastened around the wrist. Again, though its top is flat, the actual opening is narrow. The lekythos was a more important type of oil container. It usually had a small vertical handle from shoulder to neck, a narrow neck and wide mouth above a broader body. Early examples are ovoid, but later ones were increasingly elongated, culminating in the large cylindrical White-ground lekythoi used for funerary purposes in 5th-century BC Athens (71(v)m). A variant represented by both Black- and Red-figure specimens is the squat lekythos (71(v)l). Some aryballoi and lekythoi, mainly from Corinth, Athens and Greek Asia Minor, take the form of human or animal figures, human heads or other anatomical features such as feet, while others simply have mouths in the shape of human or animal heads. Small lekythoi, particularly from Attica, can also take the shape of such objects as acorns and cockleshells; larger examples sometimes bear relief figures or scenes or are treated as statuettes, for example of sphinxes or Erotes.

Vase paintings show that the large pelike, in addition to being used for wine, was employed for pouring oil into lekythoi and alabastra, while the Black-figure Attic amphorae presented to victors in the Panathenaic Games each contained a prize of almost 40 litres of oil. Since these had to be transported they had the same general shape as transport amphorae, with narrow, easily sealed mouths and small feet, rather than adhering to the conventional forms for other painted examples. Miniature Red-figure versions substituting for lekythoi were also produced as souvenirs.

Vases associated with women. The marriage gifts received by Greek women may traditionally have included a pyxis (see fig. 71(v)d–g), a round, lidded box without handles used to store cosmetics, trinkets and powder. Depending on date and place of manufacture, the precise form of pyxides varied. Attic Red-figure examples are small and often bear dainty scenes of weddings and home-life. A similar but larger shape is the lidded lekanis (71(v)h) with handles, usually ribbon-shaped. Such vases were also given as wedding presents, and Red-figure specimens bear similar scenes to those on pyxides and probably also contained trinkets or heirlooms. Both shapes occur among vases found as grave goods, and large Geometric pyxides may have been produced specifically for funerary use.

Two other shapes particularly associated with Athenian women were the loutrophoros and the lebes gamikos. The loutrophoros (71(v)k) is basically a thin neck amphora with an exaggeratedly elongated neck; some examples have two side handles and one long vertical handle in the manner of hydriai. Loutrophoroi were used to carry water for the bridal bath but were also buried with those who died unmarried, and the scenes painted on them reflect these two functions. Indeed, a few show battle scenes and presumably constituted funeral offerings for men who had died fighting. Those made specially for the grave often had no floor, perhaps to enable libations to enter the ground. In Apulian Red-figure examples the elaboration of the shape became extreme, with ribbed upper and lower bodies, concave sides, tendril-shaped handles and separate stands. The lebes gamikos (71(v)j) has a bulbous body, short neck, pointed lid and horizontal hooplike handles on its shoulders. It occurs in two forms, one with an attached stand, the other with a low foot. These vases carry wedding and domestic scenes and probably held the heated water for the bride's bath; they were also deposited in graves.

(b) Decoration. The production of high-quality Greek pottery involved maintaining a fine balance between shape and decoration. Floral and geometric designs, which continued to be used throughout the history of Greek pottery, were relatively easily accommodated to the various parts of the vases they adorned. By contrast, figural scenes, which began to be used to decorate pots towards the end of the Geometric period, posed greater challenges to the potter. Nonetheless, from their introduction in the 8th century BC until the later 5th century BC their disposition was also largely determined by a vase's form. However, when the influence of wall paintings led to a striving for three-dimensional effects and the abandonment of a single ground-line, figural scenes no longer reflected the physical shapes of their vases so precisely.

There were essentially three decorative fields available to the vase painter. One was the long horizontal band on the outside of cups and kraters, which suited figural friezes or repetitive floral patterns. Another was the large, squarish 'metope' shape provided, for example, by the body of an amphora and best suited to depictions of large single figures or small groups of large figures. The third was the circular tondo inside a cup or on the surface of a plate, which was treated differently in different regions. Lakonian Black-figure painters ignored the circular surround and treated the area as a 'porthole' for viewing a conventional, square-framed scene. By contrast, Attic cup painters fitted their compositions carefully into the circular field, producing designs of great subtlety. The most accomplished painters, however, invariably used their pictures to enhance the shapes that they were decorating, leaving their contours unbroken and adapting their compositions to the space available (e.g. a cup-skyphos by Epiktetos; late 6th century BC; see fig. 72 above). Indeed, when a vase was both made and painted by the same artist its shape and decoration may have been conceived as a unity from the outset.

It is often unclear why particular subjects from the wide repertory were associated with certain vase shapes. Some are clearly related to a shape's function (*see* §1(i) above). This is perhaps especially evident on funerary wares. Paintings on Geometric funerary vases usually depict the deceased lying in state or being taken away for burial, or allude to the circumstances of death with battle scenes. Similarly, 5th-century BC Attic White-ground lekythoi bear graveside scenes and depictions of such mythological characters associated with the dead as Hermes, Charon, Hypnos and Thanatos, as well as pictures of soldiers departing and quiet domestic activities designed to evoke a sense of pathos (*see* CERAMICS, colour pl. II, fig. 1). The relevance of scenes on certain other classes of pots is also readily apparent. Examples include the representations of weddings and home-life, both real and mythological, on pyxides and lebetes gamikoi; scenes of drinking, singing and lovemaking on cups and wine containers; the depictions of women at the fountain so frequent on hydriai; and the children's games shown on choes. More specific still are the scenes on the reverse sides of Panathenaic amphorae depicting the particular athletic event for which the vase was to serve as prize, though these are a special case. Finally, some fish plates have depictions of seafood arranged around a central dip for sauce.

Painted designs or figural scenes were not the only form of pottery decoration: incised decoration is found from Geometric times (*see* §3(iv) below), while plain Black-glaze ware (*see* §8 (i) below) probably constituted the most popular pottery type in Classical and Hellenistic times, partly because the glaze could make the pot look like patinated silver. These pots were decorated with vertical or horizontal ribbing, by incised or stamped patterns and by the addition of moulded reliefs representing persons, animals or plants or imitating the rivets seen on silverware. Moulded reliefs of heads or figurines were also a frequent aspect of Hellenistic pottery (*see* §9 below), either appliqued to wheelmade wares or moulded integrally with the vessel, while on painted vases three-dimensional pictures or designs were created by the application of a thick clay, which was subsequently gilded or painted, to the glazed surface.

BIBLIOGRAPHY

L. D. Caskey: *Geometry of Greek Vases* (Boston, 1922)
G. M. A. Richter and M. J. Milne: *Shapes and Names of Athenian Vases* (New York, 1935)
W. Schiering: *Griechische Tongefässe: Gestalt, Bestimmung und Formenwandel* (Berlin, 1967, rev. 2/1983)
M. G. Kanowski: *Containers of Classical Greece: A Handbook of Shapes* (St Lucia, Queensland, 1984)
M. Vickers, O. Impey and J. Allan: *From Silver to Ceramic* (Oxford, 1986)
B. A. Sparkes: *Greek Pottery: An Introduction* (Manchester, 1991)

B. A. SPARKES

(iii) Materials and techniques. The labours involved in the production of ancient Greek pottery included digging and purifying the clay, wedging it, throwing the vase on the potter's wheel, joining separately made sections, turning and finishing, decorating and firing. Fine wares were made from well-settled clays and generally turned on a fast wheel to ensure crispness of profile: their production and decoration are described in detail in §§(a)–(d) below, and further information can be found in the global survey of CERAMICS. Coarse wares used for cooking and other domestic purposes were made from fire-resistant clay and shaped on an anvil with a beater, possibly a stone, while heavy-duty storage vases such as pithoi were usually built up by hand: some other heavy-duty shapes such as mortars were made in moulds. In the smallest potteries a single potter and his wheel-turning apprentice probably performed all these tasks, but an average Athenian pottery employed four to six workers and the largest perhaps a dozen, permitting much greater specialization. In particular, though a potter sometimes decorated his own vases, the vase painter was usually a separate artist (*see also* §§(iv) and (vi) below).

(a) Clay. (b) Forming the vase. (c) Decorative techniques. (d) Firing.

(a) Clay. Fine pottery requires a large amount of fine clay, and Greece and its neighbouring Mediterranean regions had abundant deposits of good-quality secondary clay, which fired to an attractive reddish-orange colour due to its contamination by iron oxide. The clay that occurred around Corinth was purer and fired to a light creamy colour, but pure primary white clay was rare and was used sparingly as an accessory colour or on White-ground vases (*see* §7 below) as a coating applied in a thin, uniform layer as the vase rotated on the potter's wheel.

Before use the clay was purified through a process of sedimentation (*see* CERAMICS, §I, 1). This was particularly important, because the presence of such impurities as quartz or limestone might cause spalling or cracking during firing. This rarely happened in Attic pottery; in South Italian pottery, however, many spalls were caused by limestone pebbles. After sedimentation the purified clay was matured to improve its cohesion and finally wedged to make it suitable for working.

(b) Forming the vase. The earliest forming technique for pottery, practised in prehistoric times, was by pinching and shaping a lump of clay. This process eventually led to the development of the coil method, in which strands of clay were rolled out and coiled around a flat base disc of clay. They were pinched and smoothed to form a good joint, and additional strands were added to achieve the desired height and shape. This process could produce remarkably fine pottery with walls of uniform thickness, and even after the introduction of the potter's wheel the coil method continued to be used for the construction of extremely large plain ware such as storage jars and unglazed utilitarian pottery.

Wheelmade pottery dating to *c.* 2500 BC has been found at Troy, and the use of the potter's wheel subsequently spread throughout the Greek world. Most Classical Greek pottery was formed on the wheel, although some pieces were mould-made and a few decorative elements were hand-formed and then added to wheelmade vases. The Greek potter's wheel was a sturdy disc of wood, terracotta or stone about 600 mm in diameter, with a socket underneath that fitted over a low fixed pivot. The wheel was carefully balanced to run true without wobble or vibration. An apprentice boy turned it by hand and adjusted the speed at the command of the potter (see fig. 74). Once in motion its size and weight provided ample momentum to keep it running freely, and the potter was able to use both hands to form the vase and to give it his undivided attention. The vase shapes were based on the cylindrical or spherical forms most naturally produced on the wheel and were formed freehand using only a pair of dividers and a ruler as guides. There is no evidence that a template was used either to form the vases or even to check their measurements.

By these simple means the Greek potter achieved an elegant balance between utilitarianism and beauty. The emphasis was on perfecting existing designs and forms rather than exploring the development of radically new

74. *Apprentice Turning a Potter's Wheel*, detail from an Attic Black-figure hydria by the Leagros group, h. 440 mm, *c.* 510 BC (Munich, Staatliche Antikensammlungen)

shapes. This repetition of form could have encouraged mass production without artistic development; it was, however, the striving for perfection within a limited framework of shapes that caused Greek pottery to develop in such a splendid manner. The proportions of the vases are harmonious: the size of the mouth relates to the size of the neck, the neck to the body and the entire vase to its foot. Handles, which were modelled separately and added before firing, do not appear as mere appendages but as organic parts of the whole composition; for structural reasons they widen at the point where they join the vase, and this requirement for strength causes them to emerge gracefully. In some vases the contour is a single, unbroken curve; most, however, have their sections clearly articulated, and their beauty is based on the harmonious relationship between the various areas of the vase. This articulation enabled the potter to contrast a straight line with a strongly curved one and a swelling form with an incurving plane.

The production of wheelmade pottery required a high degree of manual dexterity and a continual application of artistic judgement. The shape of the vase had to evolve gradually; too slowly, however, and the damp clay slumped and the vase collapsed. A simple bowl or plate could therefore be formed in a single operation, but vases taller than about 300 mm were composed of several sections thrown separately on the wheel, left to dry a little, then joined together with wet clay slip. The joints were carefully smoothed and usually located at points where they could be concealed, such as the points of articulation between foot and body, body and neck, neck and mouth. In the case of some exceptionally large vases the bodies themselves had to be thrown in several sections, their joints being located on a continuous curved area where they were not hidden by articulation. They were turned and smoothed so skilfully that the joints are still invisible on the outside of the vase, though on the inside they can often be detected in the occasional crack or variation in thickness. Vases as tall as 1.5 m required four or five sections to be joined in this way.

Two techniques, though widely used in other parts of the world, were only occasionally employed by the Greeks: one was the freehand modelling of ornamental elements such as the snakes on certain ritual or funerary vases; the other was the cutting or carving of a vase before firing to create patterns, for example the Black-glaze Attic ware (*see* §5(ii) below) carved with flutes or ribs in imitation of metal vessels. A small quantity of Greek pottery, for instance the so-called 'plastic' vases, usually in the form of animals' heads, and a series of Hellenistic bowls (*see* §9 below), was produced using moulds. The first stage in this process involved the creation by a sculptor of a clay master model of the vase, which was then fired and used to form a two-part clay mould designed to separate on a line where there was no undercutting. After being dried and retouched the mould itself was fired. To form the pot a layer of soft clay was pressed into each section of the mould, its edges scored and coated with a clay slip, and the mould sections were bound together: within a few hours the new clay had dried and shrunk sufficiently for the mould to be removed. Most mould-made vases had separate mouths, and sometimes feet, that were made on the wheel and added prior to decoration and firing, using wet clay slip as an adhesive. The fingerprints of the potter can often be seen on the inside of such mould-made vases.

(c) Decorative techniques. A major feature of Greek pottery is the use of a black 'glaze' with a pronounced metallic lustre, quite different from conventional ceramic glazes in use today. Indeed, the substance was not a mixture of silica and mineral pigments but a fine solution of the same reddish clay that was used for the main body of the vase, with no additional colouring agents. The contrast between the black glazed and red unglazed areas was only achieved by means of a complex and ingenious method of firing, based on the fact that iron oxide present in the clay is red in colour if fired in an oxidizing atmosphere and black if fired in a reducing atmosphere (*see* §(d) below). The process was probably discovered by accident in the Bronze Age, when an observant potter noticed that a coating of purified clay over a coarse-bodied vase was susceptible to partial fusing or sintering and locking in streaks of black on a red background.

Only clays that possessed very small particles and platelets were suitable to produce the black glaze matter. The separation of these particles from the coarser materials in the clay was accomplished by sedimentation. A solution of clay and water mixed with potash to prevent flocculation was allowed to stand for 48 hours until it separated into three areas. The sediment of sand and coarse particles at the bottom was discarded; the middle zone of clay slip was used for the body of the vase; at the top the colloidal suspension of very fine particles was carefully removed and thickened by evaporation to form a brownish liquid slightly darker than the clay itself. When this was applied to the vase and allowed to dry before firing, it already had a slight metallic sheen caused by the horizontal alignment of the platelets; this could be enhanced by burnishing the surface with a smooth pebble or piece of bone and polishing it with a cloth. However, it was only after firing

75. Black-glaze relief lines and dots, detail from an Attic Red-figure amphora by the Kleophrades Painter, h. 473 mm, *c.* 490 BC (New York, Metropolitan Museum of Art)

that the glaze became black. The greater sheen of Attic black glaze helps to distinguish Attic vases from those of South Italy and perhaps reflects minor differences in the quality of the clay.

Black-glaze achieved particular prominence after the introduction of the Black-figure technique, when it was used to produce silhouette figures: when the glaze had dried, anatomical and other details were incised using a sharp point, revealing the red clay underneath. In the later and more realistic Red-figure technique, figures were drawn in outline and then left red, while the entire background was covered over with black glaze. Minor details and occasionally shading were painted in with a dilute black glaze solution that remained brown even after firing. However, outlines and more significant details were executed in relief lines of extremely concentrated black glaze, which projected appreciably from the vase's surface. These cannot have been painted with brushes in the usual way and must have been applied with a syringe, probably a tapered nozzle of bone or bronze pierced with a fine hole and attached to a piece of animal intestine filled with the glaze: this is most apparent where blobs were used to denote grapes or curly hair (see fig. 75). The two paint pots shown in certain depictions of vase painters (e.g. Milan, Torno Col.; see fig. 76) probably contained glazes of different consistencies. The blacking in of the background was usually done by apprentices, who sometimes carelessly painted over parts of figures and decorative borders. On some pots with entirely black grounds, pale lines formed by unglazed areas of the underlying clay were used to emphasize or clarify certain elements such as a black-glazed head of hair (see fig. 111 below) or to articulate the concentric panel-work on Geometric vases (fig. 84 below). This technique is called reservation.

During Classical and Hellenistic times many vases were coated entirely in a plain black glaze similar to that used on figured pots, and decorated with incised, stamped, moulded or impressed patterns, figures or scenes (*see* §8 below). Stamped or impressed designs were made with terracotta punches while the clay was still quite soft. As the vase rotated on the potter's wheel a vibrating tool was held against it, producing a series of uniform dots. Occasionally mould-made appliqué ornaments were also added: these were applied to the unfired vase while they were still moist, using clay slip as a binder, and when dry were covered with black glaze along with the rest of the vessel. From the 3rd to the 1st century BC floral patterns and other ornament such as decorative series of dots were produced in relief using a white or red clay slip, as on Attic West Slope ware (*see* §9 below).

The reddish clay of Black- and Red-figure vases was usually covered with a burnished coat of thin yellow ochre wash before the black glaze was applied, thereby accentuating the contrast, while both Red- and Black-figure artists also made sparing use of accessory colours. Added white was made from a pure white primary clay and used for details of clothing, architectural elements and statues; added red was made from red ochre and used for details of clothing or to depict blood. Both pigments were rather friable and have often flaked off, though their original presence on areas of black glaze is indicated by dull matt patches. For another important class of pottery known as

76. *Vase Painter with Two Paint Pots*, detail from an Attic Red-figure hydria by the Leningrad Painter, h. 100 mm, *c.* 480–*c.* 470 BC (Milan, Torno Collection)

White-ground (*see* §7 below) the part of the pot's surface to be painted on was given a preliminary coating of liquid clay containing kaolinite: Black- or Red-figure or in later times polychromatic scenes or decoration were then painted on to this prepared surface.

The method of decoration known as Six's Technique, used by some Black-figure artists on small vases, involved painting figures in added white or red on top of a black-glaze ground and incising details so that the black glaze showed through. The effect is similar to Red-figure, though less refined.

Small objects on later Red-figure vases were sometimes executed in relief lines made from a plain clay slip and covered with thin gold leaf. The gold was glued with egg white, pressed into shape with a brush and burnished with a small pointed instrument: it could be applied before the vase was fired because the melting-point of gold was well above the firing temperature. The restrained colour scheme on Greek vases was not by choice; these were the only colours available that would withstand firing. A wider palette of colours, such as pink, blue and green, made from vegetable and mineral pigments, was occasionally employed. However, these were too fragile to withstand high temperatures or daily use and so were painted on after firing and confined to funerary vases, notably Attic White-ground lekythoi and the elaborate Hellenistic pottery from Canosa in South Italy.

Before they began work on a vase, painters may well have made trial sketches, at least of their most complex compositions, though none has survived. Some were possibly based on sculptural groups or wall paintings. However, the vases' curved surfaces limited the usefulness of conventional drawings, and sketching must have been done directly on to the vases themselves with a stick of lead or charcoal. The resultant lines generally burnt away during the firing process, but when a vase was not as dry as it should have been, the stick left slight indentations, which have been preserved. Figures were usually first sketched nude to render their movement correctly, and the clothing added later. If a Red-figure artist made a mistake while executing the actual vase painting, he could easily erase it with a moist sponge. Such corrections have sometimes left telltale brown smudges, while slightly roughened patches show where dry glaze was removed by scraping. Although some scenes on different vases show a close similarity, they were always drawn freehand and never duplicated by tracing.

77. Modern plaques painted in the Black-figure (above) and Red-figure (below) techniques, shown before (left), and after (right) firing; reproduction by Joseph Veach Noble, each plaque *c.* 950 sq. mm, 1959

(d) Firing. Ancient Greek pottery was fired only once, partly to economize on fuel but principally because the black glaze so frequently used adhered better to an unfired surface. For decorated vases this single firing was accomplished in three phases. The first was an oxidizing phase during which the temperature reached about 900°C and air was allowed to enter the kiln freely, so that both the clay of the pot itself and the black glaze turned red. The second was a reducing phase during which the potter covered the air vent at the top of the kiln, threw in large quantities of green wood, leaves or dung and closed the stoking door. Because the kiln was deprived of oxygen from the outside, combustion was incomplete and a reducing process began, releasing carbon monoxide, which united with the oxygen in the clay and the glaze, turning both into black ferrous oxide. During this phase the temperature reached about 950°C, but before the start of the third phase it was allowed to decline to about 875°C. This final phase was a reoxidizing one, during which the potter opened both the air vent at the top of the kiln and the kiln door to allow oxygen free access. The oxygen readily entered the porous clay and turned its black ferrous oxide back into its red ferric form. However, because the glaze had sintered, its black ferrous oxide was sealed off from contact with the oxygen, and at this temperature it remained black. The kiln was allowed to cool down slowly, and the following day, when the vases were removed, they displayed their characteristic red and black colour combination. The dramatic transformation is illustrated by modern plaques painted in Black- and Red-figure techniques and shown before and after firing (see fig. 77).

In Athens in the 6th and 5th centuries BC a special red glaze was sometimes produced to be used in conjunction with the standard black glaze. It was achieved by creating a black-glaze mixture with such a high sintering-point that at the customary firing temperature it reoxidized and turned red during the final phase, while preserving the shiny surface quality of the glaze. At the same time, adjoining areas in the conventional black glaze with a lower sintering-point turned black. However, the process was very hard to control and was soon abandoned.

Funerary vases that were to be decorated only with delicate pigments were fired in a single oxidizing phase before painting but after receiving their white slip. This provided the artist with an excellent white background for painting.

The entire firing cycle probably lasted six to eight hours, though it must have taken at least a further twelve hours for the kiln to cool down to the point at which the fired pottery could be removed safely. The potter judged the temperature of the various phases by looking through a spy-hole and monitoring changes in the colour of the fire or by withdrawing small test-pieces. These were unfired plaques or fragments of vases coated with black glaze and equipped with holes so that they could be hooked out through the spy-hole using a wire or stick. They would indicate when the pottery had been correctly fired and had achieved a satisfactory black glaze.

Much ancient pottery was fired in the open by piling fuel under and around the vases to be fired. Greek pottery, however, had to be fired in a kiln in order to control the atmosphere for oxidation and reduction. Most of the essential features of an operating kiln are shown on a fragment of a Corinthian Black-figure pinax (Berlin, Antikenmus.; see fig. 78), which has been restored on the basis of similar ancient depictions. As a rule, the kiln was a domed structure about 1.8–2.4 m in diameter, fronted by a short stoking tunnel with a removable door. The lowest level was occupied by the firing chamber, separated from the main kiln chamber above by a perforated clay floor. The chamber was filled with pottery through a loading door incorporating the spy-hole (not illustrated) and surmounted by the small chimney or vent that was closed during the reducing phase of firing. In the painting two perforated test-pieces are shown near the chimney, and the boat-shaped vessel beneath the kiln chamber perhaps contained water to provide extra moisture during the reducing phase. The unfired vases themselves had to be thoroughly dry, as otherwise the steam released from their clay would have burst them. In the painting they are spaced out to display their shapes, but in practice they would have been tightly stacked to economize on fuel. Small bowls could even be nested inside larger ones, since the black glaze would not fuse to the glaze of other vases. Lidded pots were almost certainly dried and fired at the same time as their lids to ensure that they shrank by the same amount, while a temper of sand, crushed stone or terracotta was added to the clay of large storage jars to stiffen them during forming, so that they did not slump under their own weight, and to minimize shrinkage during drying and firing. The firing of elaborate monumental funerary vases required a large kiln doorway, which was presumably bricked up and sealed with wet clay. If the vase had a large mouth, it was fired upside down for greater stability or else propped up with fired terracotta struts. Perhaps also the kiln was not so tightly packed, allowing the heat to circulate freely around the huge vessel; and the libation openings in the feet of many funerary vases must also have helped ensure even firing. Because their size made them more prone to damage while being manoeuvred into and out of the kiln, some large South Italian pots had separately fired feet and decorative attachments, such as masks and figurines, which were glued on with a casein adhesive made from milk or with pine pitch or asphalt. The adhesives and the unfired colours made such vases impractical for daily use, but these gaudy assemblages were highly prized as offerings for the dead (*see* §(c) above) .

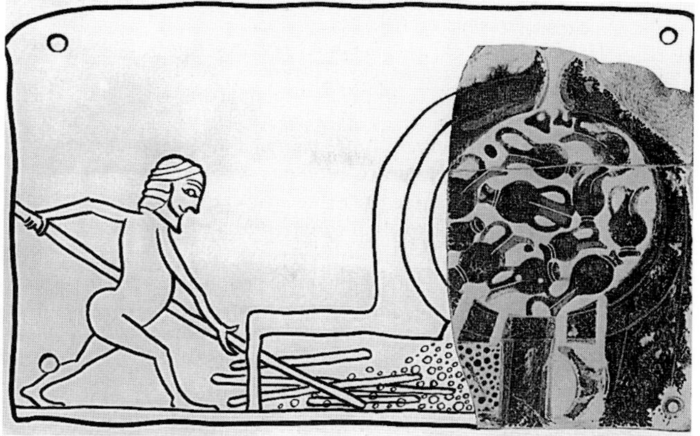

78. Modern reconstruction of a potter stoking a kiln, based on a Corinthian Black-figure pinax, h. 101 mm, 6th century BC (Berlin, Antikenmuseum)

Many mishaps could occur during firing. A stack of vases could topple and be broken. One part of the kiln might be at a higher or lower temperature than it should have been due to a draught, and this would result in red streaks and blemishes in the black glaze. Various Black-glaze batches had slightly different correct firing temperatures, and this could produce a dull black glaze rather than the metallic gloss of the best Greek pottery. Despite these pitfalls, the ancient potters normally achieved excellent results by controlling the firing temperatures.

Vases placed on funeral pyres as offerings were usually broken by the unequal expansion caused by rapid and uneven heating. Such fragments can be identified because they tend to have irregular wavy edges rather than the straight edges caused by normal impact breakage. They would be badly discoloured by carbon smudging from the smoke, and the iron in the clay body would have been reduced by the lack of oxygen, which also caused a change in colour, often to grey. Unless there has been permanent warpage or destruction of the glaze, it is possible to eliminate the disfiguring appearance of these fragments by reversing the chemical process through refiring. It is important for uniformity that all surviving fragments of the vase be refired at the same time, including those that do not show any discolouration. It is also possible to correct blemishes suffered at the time of production by using the three-stage firing process exactly as if the pieces had never been fired previously. Both under- and overfired vases can be restored to the original appearance of the black glaze as intended by the ancient vase painter. (For further information on the conservation and restoration of pottery *see* CERAMICS, §III.)

BIBLIOGRAPHY

G. M. A. Richter: *The Craft of Athenian Pottery* (New Haven, 1923)

C. F. Binns and A. D. Fraser: 'The Genesis of the Greek Black Glaze', *Amer. J. Archaeol.*, xxxiii (1929), pp. 1–9

T. Schumann: 'Oberflächenverzierung in der antiken Töpferkunst: Terra sigillata und griechische Schwarzrotmalerei', *Ber. Dt. Ker. Ges.*, xxiii (1942), pp. 408–26

J. D. Beazley: 'Potter and Painter in Ancient Athens', *Proc. Brit. Acad.*, xxx (1946), pp. 87–125

M. Farnsworth: 'Draw Pieces as Aids to Correct Firing', *Amer. J. Archaeol.*, lxiv (1960), pp. 72–5

J. V. Noble: *The Techniques of Painted Attic Pottery* (New York, 1965, rev. London, 1988)

H. A. G. Brijder, ed.: *Ancient Greek and Related Pottery: Proceedings of the International Vase Symposium: Amsterdam, 1984*

JOSEPH VEACH NOBLE

(iv) Potters, painters and society. The social position of pottery workers in any Greek city was complex and is now largely unclear, since the effects of various factors are hard to assess, and the available evidence is often meagre. While a little is known about some aspects of pottery production in Classical Athens (*c*. 480–323 BC), and there are occasional insights into conditions at other places and during other periods, conclusions are frequently hypothetical. Artisans seem likely to have been free men, working to order or developing their own styles and iconography; but the statutory distinction between slave and free man had only developed in the years between *c*. 600 and *c*. 450 BC, as had the use of official coinage for everyday transactions. Contemporary or later literary documentation, even of Classical Athenian pottery production, is scant, but the contrast with numerous references to work in other media during the same period probably indicates the low status of painted pottery.

Evidence for the social status of pottery workers is ambiguous and largely confined to Athens. Outside Attica a few potters and painters signed their vases between *c*. 700 and 580 BC, after which the practice began at Athens and ceased elsewhere except for Boiotia. However, the artists' names rarely give any indication of social status. Many appear to be slave names (e.g. Lydos 'the Lydian', or Thrax 'the Thracian'), and there is clear evidence in other areas of production of slaves working for citizen or resident alien shop-owners. One signature of *Lydos* has the added phrase *being a slave*, but the piece is too late to have been made by the famous Lydos, and the words could be jocular. The potter and painter Syriskos, the 'little Syrian', perhaps acquired the sobriquet Pistoxenos, 'trusty stranger', after displaying his loyalty to Athens during the Persian Wars (490 and 480–479 BC). Scenes of potters' shops on vases certainly appear to depict both slaves and free men, while two vases, one Boiotian and one Attic, show a woman at work, though female participation is not otherwise documented. That pottery production could be a family tradition is clear from a few signed Athenian vases on which the potter or painter mentions a father known from earlier signatures: TLESON, for example, succeeded his father NEARCHOS.

Evidence for the economics of the pottery industry is again confined largely to Athens. Overhead costs are uncertain. Smaller neighbouring potteries probably shared kilns that would have been used to fire all kinds of terracotta objects, including figurines and tiles as well as the plain or Black-glaze pots that must have been the staple of production even in 5th-century BC Athens. No information has come to light concerning the cost of clay and other materials, notably fuel. Inscriptions under the feet of 5th-century BC Attic vases record some 50 prices, probably wholesale. They range from $\frac{1}{20}$ obol for a small Black-glaze handleless bowl to 3 drachmas (18 obols) for a large Red-figure hydria with two rows of figures. The pricing is not entirely consistent, but there are no wild fluctuations during the century, throughout which a drachma represented a good day's wage. Two pairs of nearly identical vases indicate the relative price for Black-glaze and Red-figure wares, with a mark-up of 33% in one case and 100% in the second. This, however, is insufficient to build up a true picture of relative profits or of the additional labour required to produce a figured piece. Such prices as we know are those likely to have been paid by the 'shipper' at Athens. There is extremely little evidence for prices asked at the end of the many routes that Attic vases travelled.

Scale of production must be judged by a measure that converts the amount of preserved material into a percentage of the original total. The most plausible figure may come from counting preserved, if often fragmentary, prize Panathenaic amphorae and comparing them with the known production run. About the first half of the 4th century BC at least 1450 were awarded every four years at the greater Panathenaia. This would yield a preservation rate of about 0.25%, but this depends on two major assumptions: that all the amphorae were decorated and that the same number was awarded in earlier centuries. The first assumption is plausible, but the second is debatable. Another method of estimating production figures is to consider the debris from three potters' shops unearthed in Athens. The painters involved are in two cases known only from a few other works. If a 1% survival rate were hypothesized, the formula would mean that the debris from perhaps one firing would constitute up to a quarter of the painter's life-time output—an unlikely result. Here too 0.25% seems more reasonable.

Potters are rarely mentioned in contemporary documents. Inscriptions show that two 4th-century BC Athenian potters, Kittos and Bakchios, emigrated to Ephesos and received honours there, while earlier references occur on inscribed stone bases in the debris from the Persian sack of the Athenian Acropolis (480 BC). Thus a base for a large sculpted kore (Athens, Acropolis Mus., 681) apparently refers to its dedicator Nearchos as *kerameus* (Gr.: 'potter'), though the word is largely restored (see Raubitschek, pp. 232–3, no. 197). The word certainly does accompany the names of Euphronios, Peikon, Mnesiades and Andokides, who dedicated smaller marble or bronze offerings, implying that potters enjoyed a modicum of wealth.

Indeed, the larger Athenian potteries were probably run by men of substance, whose names may be preserved in the most frequently occurring signatures. However, wealth need not imply high social status. True, a figure in a (frequently aristocratic) symposium scene on a stamnos by Smikros (*c*. 515–*c*. 510 BC; Brussels, Musées Royaux A. & Hist., A 717; see fig. 79) is labelled with the artist's own name; but this may have been wishful thinking, and those making and painting pots would normally have been classed as artisans or tradesmen.

In addition to Kittos and Bakchios, other pottery workers are known to have worked abroad. While many were surely small-scale operators, some may have run more substantial establishments. An East Greek painter was active in Etruria *c*. 600 BC, while *c*. 525 BC the Athenian Teisias signed Boiotian pots, and *c*. 400 BC the Athenian Suessula Painter decorated some Corinthian Red-Figure before returning to Athens. Potters accompanied Greek

79. *The Vase Painter Smikros at a Symposium*, detail from a stamnos, h. 385 mm, *c.* 515–*c.* 510 BC (Brussels, Musées Royaux d'Art et d'Histoire)

colonists in the 8th and 7th centuries BC, while South Italian Red-figure production was started *c.* 430 BC, probably at Herakleia, by artists from the Attic workshop of POLYGNOTOS.

It is difficult to untangle the relationships between pottery producers and their clients and to distinguish between commissioned and uncommissioned works, despite the frequent implicit assumption that producers enjoyed 'artistic freedom'. Whether the greatest vase paintings were specially commissioned is disputed. Webster argued that vases with *kalos* inscriptions (*see* §(vi)(c) below) must have been made specifically for an admirer of that person to use in a symposium, and that many other pieces were commissioned. However, *kalos* names appear on several vases intended for traders, and while such names do appear on some masterpieces, these may not be unique works, since some have duplicates or near duplicates; for example, there are fragments of a piece close to the Chigi Vase (Rome, Villa Giulia), of a krater similar to the François Vase (Florence, Mus. Archeol.) and of doublets by the painter EXEKIAS.

In addition, although special types of pottery were used in a variety of cultic rites throughout Greece, not all scenes of cult appear to have been commissioned. Thus Attic White-ground funerary lekythoi often depict generic scenes, although the particular details on a few suggest individual orders, and a few vases with painted inscriptions, mostly dedications to a deity by a named individual, were clearly specifically commissioned. The most numerous are plain Chiot chalices from sanctuaries at Naukratis and on Aigina. However, even commissioned works sometimes ended up far from the homes of those who had ordered them. A dinos (a wide-mouthed vessel with no handle) with Exekias' signature on the rim, accompanied by a dedication in the distinctive Sikyonian script, ended up in Etruria. A similar route was taken by those prize Panathenaic amphorae found in Etruria, since they could be won only by Greeks. They were a particularly distinct class of commissioned work, and, significantly, none bears a 'trademark'.

Sets of vases used in funerary rites can sometimes be identified, though whether or not they were commissioned is hard to say. One example is provided by 7th-century BC White-ground vases from the Kerameikos at Athens, another by the sets of Red-figure vases painted by a single artist, which often accompanied 4th-century BC Athenian burials; such sets are rare elsewhere. Some paired vases also exist, each decorated with half a scene or even half a figure, and the Siren Painter appears to have decorated a whole set of stamnoi with *Adventures of Odysseus* but 'services' of vases for symposia comprising kraters, oinochoai and cups are conspicuously absent. In the later 5th century BC some merchants scratched identificatory marks and prices for batches of pots under the foot of one 'master' vase, but again these groups cohere into no recognizable set.

Finally, 4th-century BC Apulian vase painters specialized in producing a group of huge volute kraters without bottoms, depicting scenes from Greek tragedies and clearly intended exclusively for funerary use. One tomb of *c.* 400 BC at Herakleia, near Taranto, contained so many vases with theatrical scenes that they may well have been commissioned for the funeral of a playwrite or actor. Although most intact Greek vases come from burials, this is a rare example where it is possible with any confidence to suggest that the scenes on them reflected the interests and achievements of the occupant.

BIBLIOGRAPHY

J. D. Beazley: 'Potter and Painter in Ancient Athens', *Proc. Brit. Acad.*, xxx (1944), pp. 87–125

A. E. Raubitschek: *Dedications from the Athenian Akropolis* (Cambridge, MA, 1949)

C. M. Robertson: '"Epoiesen" on Greek Vases: Other Considerations', *J. Hell. Stud.*, xcii (1972), pp. 180–83

T. B. L. Webster: *Potter and Patron in Classical Athens* (London, 1972)

M. M. Eismann: 'A Further Note on "Epoiesen" Signatures', *J. Hell. Stud.*, xciv (1974), p. 172

J. Ziomecki: *Les Représentations d'artisans sur les vases attiques* (Warsaw, 1975)

A. W. Johnston: *Trademarks on Greek Vases* (Warminster, 1979)

Ancient Greek and Related Pottery. Proceedings of the International Vase Symposium: Amsterdam, 1984

R. M. Cook: 'Pots and Pisistratan Propaganda', *J. Hell. Stud.*, cvii (1987), pp. 167–9

J. H. Oakley: 'An Athenian Red-figure Workshop from the Time of the Peloponnesian War', *Les Ateliers de potiers dans le monde grec aux époques géométrique, archaique et classique*, ed. F. Blondé and J. Perreault, *Bull. Corr. Hell.*, suppl. xxiii (Paris and Athens, 1992), pp. 195–203

(v) Trade. Down to Hellenistic times all Greek cities used Greek pottery, as did many other peoples of the West and of Anatolia. From the 7th to the 4th century BC most of these places relied on imports for their fine wares and sometimes for their coarse wares as well. Corinth and Athens dominated the fine export trade from Late Geometric times (*c.* 760–*c.* 700 BC) until the end of the 5th century BC: thereafter the market fragmented, and in the following century there was a general decline in decorated pottery manufacture.

Little evidence is available for the mechanics of the pottery trade, whether internal or international, though the scope and, to a limited extent, the volume of the latter is indicated by the distribution of pottery find-spots. This article attempts merely to provide an overview of the principal trends in the trade in fine painted wares; for more detailed information on a particular centre or period the appropriate article in §§2–9 below should be consulted.

There is no evidence to suggest that potters themselves organized the export and sale of their wares in other markets, and the entrepreneurs who performed this function are shadowy figures indeed. A significant proportion of the Athenian and Corinthian exports may have been carried by foreigners, for the flow of vases suffered little interruption when the manufacturing state was at war, suggesting that the cartage was in neutral hands. As well as shiploads heading directly to a targeted market, it is clear from excavated wrecks that a large share of the trade was in the hands of general carriers plying a coastline with a mixed cargo that was partially sold off and replenished at each port of call. Merchants must have expected a retail profit that compared well with that derived from more easily shipped commodities such as corn or oil.

The principal evidence for the extent of the vase export trade is gained by plotting find maps for each style of pottery. Such evidence must be used with caution, especially when it is based only on a handful of items, since allowance must be made for the dissemination of heirlooms, gifts etc. The large numbers of Panathenaic amphorae (*see* §5(ii) below) in Etruscan tombs and, some have argued, the wide distribution of vases bearing *kalos* names also indicate the existence of a second-hand market. A city-state's colonies would often be a major market for its potteries, but export patterns were much broader, and decorated pottery formed only one part of any cargo. Traders were often residents of other states, supplying needed and coveted items throughout the Mediterranean. Nonetheless, the products of higher aesthetic quality did gain the largest share of the export trade. The corollary is that the originating workshops would also have produced much second- and third-rate material to satisfy the markets that they had created.

The percentage of pots that any given centre exported varied widely, from minimal to vast. During the 7th century BC Attic figured vases and Cycladic and Cretan relief pithoi, some with mythological scenes, travelled little, but these are rare exceptions, at least for comparatively productive centres. The Corinthian Thapsos cups, for example, are commonly found in the West from *c.* 730 BC onwards, and it has been suggested that they were produced specifically for the use of emigrating Greeks. Even earlier, the functionally similar Euboian skyphoi, decorated with sets of pendant semicircles, were used in many parts of the Mediterranean, not least the eastern seaboard. Later, Corinthian figured ware was extremely popular in Etruria (notably Caere), as, of course, was Attic ware. There is a little evidence for migrant potters working in foreign cities (*see* §(iv) above), and it would be natural for the most talented artists to gravitate towards the state whose mercantile expertise was currently generating the greatest wealth.

It is impossible to build up any coherent picture of the vase export trade in Protogeometric and Geometric times, but it is clear from the distribution of finds that with the recovery from the political chaos of the post-Mycenaean Dark Ages, vases were an element in cargoes on the newly opened trading routes around the Mediterranean. Thus in the 9th century BC the trading primacy enjoyed by the Euboian cities Chalkis and Eretria gained markets all round the Aegean and even in Cyprus and the Levant for an Euboian sub-Protogeometric ware that was by Athenian standards stuck in something of a rut. Middle Geometric ware (*c.* 850–*c.* 760 BC) from Athens achieved a high artistic standard and had an unusually wide distribution for the period, but in the Late Geometric period (*c.* 760–*c.* 700 BC) Attic ware was exported. Instead, Corinthian workshops, producing a range of very different shapes, provided an increasing percentage of Greek exported wares, and over the next two centuries Corinth's export trade continued to grow; she became the principal supplier of fine Black-figure vases to the whole Greek world.

By the beginning of the 6th century BC Attica was establishing a market for her Black-figure wares, which appear at the Greek trading post of Naukratis on the Nile delta, around the Black Sea coast and a little later in great numbers in the graves of Etruria. It is harder to explain

Athens' displacement of Corinth in the pottery export trade by the mid-6th century BC. Corinth had suffered no political or economic setback, and the early 6th-century Athenian product shows no manifest artistic superiority, though its orange clay (which the Corinthians came to imitate) may have made the wares visually more attractive, and there is some evidence that superior firing may have made Attic pottery more durable. Attic dominance of the market continued through the Red-figure period until her political decline at the end of the century. Competing Red-figure workshops had also been established in South Italy, a major export area for Attic products, between 440 BC and 400 BC. In the 4th century Athenian exports of figured pottery were concentrated more in the Black Sea and eastern Mediterranean areas; South Italian production expanded, with limited amounts of exports. The final period of Red-figure production at Athens persisted into the last quarter of the century.

Other centres gained significant secondary shares in the pottery export trade. Finds of Orientalizing Fikellura ware (*see* §4(iv) below) are plentiful at Naukratis, south Ionia and the Black Sea coast, while in the 6th century BC Lakonian ware led the smaller Black-figure producers, with especially strong trade to Sicily, South Italy and Etruria in the west and Samos, North Africa and Egypt in the east. Klazomenian ware (*see* §5(v) below) was plentiful in north Ionia and Egypt.

Although some Corinthian and Athenian vases bear trading marks that indicate their inclusion in specific bulk consignments (*see* §(vi)(a) below), there is only limited evidence that potters produced special shapes, scenes or decorative schemes to satisfy foreign demand. In the 6th century BC Athenian potters in the circle of NIKOSTHENES copied Etruscan shapes, and there are a few Athenian Red-figure copies of native South Italian shapes; but basically the same vases were sold abroad as at home. Individual vases probably were sometimes made to order for foreign clients: two Athenian examples have pre-fired painted inscriptions in Etruscan, one of them indicating that the vase was a gift.

BIBLIOGRAPHY

R. M. Cook: 'Die Bedeutung der bemalten Keramik für den griechischen Handel', *Jb. Dt. Archäol. Inst.*, lxxiv (1959), pp. 114–23

J. Boardman: 'The Athenian Pottery Trade: The Classical Period', *Expedition*, xxi/4 (1979), pp. 33–4

I. Scheibler: *Griechische Töpferkunst: Herstellung, Handel und Gebrauch der antiken Tongefässe* (Munich, 1983)

J. Boardman: *Athenian Red Figure Vases: The Classical Period* (London, 1989)

A. W. Johnston: 'Greek Vases in the Marketplace', *Looking into Greek Vases*, ed. T. Rasmussen and N. Spivey (Cambridge, 1991), pp. 203–31

M. Vickers and D. Gill: *Artful Crafts: Ancient Greek Silverware and Pottery* (Oxford, 1994)

ALAN JOHNSTON

(vi) Inscriptions. Incised (graffito) inscriptions occurred on Greek pottery from the time of the invention of the Greek alphabet in the 8th century BC, while painted (*dipinto*) inscriptions are found only from the 7th century BC; both types continued to be used on figured vases until the end of the Classical period in the late 4th century BC. In the Hellenistic period they were much rarer. The majority occurred on Attic pots, of which about one in ten was inscribed, giving a total of some 8000–10,000 extant examples. Their principal uses were to identify the characters or objects depicted or to record the names of persons involved in the commissioning or manufacture; some record remarks passed between the characters portrayed or the comments of the painter himself.

(a) Introduction. (b) Mythological names. (c) Names of contemporary persons. (d) Artists' signatures. (e) Other texts. (f) Scripts.

(a) Introduction. Like the adoption of the alphabet, the custom of incorporating inscriptions in works of art was a feature of the Orientalizing movement (*see* §4 below). In the art of the Near Eastern cultures, the inscribing of monuments (especially sculpted reliefs) was a long-standing tradition, but their syllabic writing systems are not directly comparable with the Greek. However, the Aramaic inscriptions on a relief from Zincirlı (*c.* 730–*c.* 700 BC; Berlin, Pergamonmus.) identifying King Barrakab and the god Baal of Harran provide a closer parallel: Aramaic script is sufficiently closely related to the Greek to have inspired Greeks to use a similar technique for naming figures. Whatever the inspiration, two elements indigenous to Greek culture greatly encouraged the use of such inscriptions: the development of mythology as transmitted in the early epic poems of Homer and Hesiod, and the rise of individualism as evidenced by the earliest lyric poetry. Inscriptions were used not only in vase painting: in early sculpture too, identifying labels or dedications were sometimes placed on the figures themselves or near them on the background.

The earliest surviving inscriptions (of *c.* 750 BC from Lefkandi on Euboia and the Euboian colony of Pithekoussai) are casual graffiti on the vase's shoulder; their content is unrelated to the pot's decoration. The message of those that can be interpreted is often of the 'I belong to X' type, leading scholars to suggest that those that consist merely of a couple of letters or of some non-alphabetic device may also be indications of ownership applied by the purchaser to safeguard his property; similar marks appear on the shoulders of a long series of Attic amphorae dating from *c.* 730 BC to *c.* 570 BC.

A second important class of non-artistic vase inscription is the trading mark that is sometimes found on the foot of a vase. Its exact purpose remains unclear: perhaps to identify the merchant to whose bulk order the vase was assigned or perhaps simply to serve as the potter's 'trademark' in the modern sense. The earliest examples are red *dipinti* on Corinthian vases of *c.* 625–*c.* 575 BC: they coincide with the foundation of the Greek trading post at Naukratis in Egypt (*c.* 620–*c.* 610 BC). While the use of painting or incision of trading marks was probably partly determined by which would show up better against the background of the pot, graffiti eventually became dominant, and *dipinti* are rare on Attic Red-figure vases. The most frequent incidence of trading marks is on Attic pottery of *c.* 550–*c.* 450 BC, and relatively few are found on Corinthian or East Greek vases or indeed on the earliest Attic Black-figure. Even on Attic Red-figure their incidence gradually declined after 450 BC, and by the end of the 5th century BC they were rare.

In the Archaic period inscriptions were used in several regional schools, such as Naxian, Rhodian, Lakonian, Boiotian and Chalkidian. Indeed, some of the earliest painted inscriptions are on pottery from Ithaka and include some hexameter lines of *c.* 700 BC and a potter's signature (*c.* 675–*c.* 650 BC; for a discussion of both items see Jeffery, pp. 230–31). Ithaka had close connections with Corinth, and it was in Corinth that the main types of inscriptions were developed in the 7th century BC, to be taken over by Attic artists in the following century when their pottery dominated the market.

The painted inscriptions on Attic Black-figure vases were usually executed in the same paint as the figures, although added red also occurs. In the later Red-figure style inscriptions were initially sometimes incised or even reserved, but later they were usually in added red (and even later, pink or white) painted on the black background, making them more evanescent and often hard to read. Red-figure artists used a soft brush, which allowed a more casual style, so that their letter forms are much more variable than those on stone inscriptions. Vase inscriptions were normally written by the painters in their own handwriting, although some may have been based on models of some kind or even be in the potter's hand; copybooks were probably not used at this early date. Several inscriptions refer to the projected use of the vases as dedications or gifts; more frequently they allude to the drinking parties for which the pots were intended, in the form of exhortations to drink and praise for handsome youths (*see* §(c) below). The idea that most of the finest vases were made for specific clients, however, has been overstated.

(b) Mythological names. These are perhaps the most common inscriptions in figural scenes. They first appeared *c.* 675 BC on Proto-Corinthian vases, and slightly later specimens include the famous Chigi Vase (*c.* 640–*c.* 630 BC; Rome, Villa Giulia, 22,697; see fig. 80), which has a subsidiary scene of the *Judgement of Paris* under its handle. Here the figures are named *Al*[exand]*ros* (Paris's other name), *Athanaia* and *Aphrod*[ite] in large letters (not in the Corinthian alphabet) aligned at their tops in the Early Archaic manner. Contemporary is a row of warriors on a stand from Aegina (*c.* 640 BC; destr.; for illustration see Jeffery, pp. 110 and 112) in a style related to Proto-Attic. One of the warriors is named *Menelas* in a non-Attic dialect and an alphabet that may not be Attic. Without the inscription there would be no way of identifying this figure, which is not the case in the *Judgement of Paris* scene or indeed in most mythological scenes: labels often appear in scenes where they are not needed and are frequently absent from scenes where they are. Their function is therefore not necessarily one of identification. One of the principal motives for adding inscriptions to such scenes may have been to connect the pictures with the world of the *logos*, the literary or oral stories told about gods and heroes. This is demonstrated by a famous lost monument, the gold and ivory chest dedicated by the Corinthian tyrant Kypselos (*c.* 657–*c.* 625 BC) at Olympia (Pausanias: *Description of Greece* V.xvii.5–xix.10). Here, in addition to the labels, were some explanatory inscriptions in verse, which gave the scene a certain 'literary' quality: it certainly did not need this explanation. Similar inscriptions inspired by epic poetry also occur on vases. There may also have been an ornamental function to this writing, for

80. Inscription on a Proto-Corinthian oinochoe (the Chigi Vase) showing the *Judgement of Paris* (detail), h. 262 mm, *c.* 640–*c.* 630 BC (Rome, Museo Nazionale di Villa Giulia e Soprintendenza alle Antichità per l'Etruria Meridionale)

Archaic artists did not favour large empty spaces, and inscriptions therefore doubled as filling ornaments.

(c) Names of contemporary persons. During the 6th century BC genre scenes became increasingly popular on Attic vases, especially those depicting symposia and athletics. A common practice was to add the word *kalos* ('handsome'), even where no such figure appeared in the scene, with or without reference to a specific person; in the former case the formula became 'So-and-so is handsome' or 'So-and-so appears handsome to So-and-so'. These *kalos* names (or love-names) mostly belong to aristocratic males, although female names, no doubt referring to courtesans, also occur; those that can be associated with known historical figures have played an important role in establishing the chronology of Attic vase painting, for they were presumably written when the named person was young, although some have questioned this. There are also large numbers of contemporary aristocratic names attached to figures in symposium and athletic scenes, and most of these must also be names of real people, since the same names sometimes appear elsewhere with *kalos*. Both categories include well-known figures: among the *kalos* names are the Athenian general Miltiades (*c.* 550–489 BC; Oxford, Ashmolean, 310) and Euaion, a son of the dramatist Aeschylos (525/4–456 BC) and himself a poet or actor, while labelled figures include the poet Anakreon (*c.* 570–after 514 BC; Copenhagen, Nmus., 13365) and Phayllos, a South Italian athlete who fought at Salamis (480 BC).

(d) Artists' signatures. The signatures of both potters and painters can be found in Beazley's *Black-figure, Red-figure* and *Paralipomena.* Additional signatures appear in T. H. Carpenter's *Beazley Addenda*, appendix 2. They are among the earliest painted inscriptions on vases, appearing soon after the beginning of the 7th century BC. Signatures are of three kinds: some are accompanied by *egraphsen* ('painted it'), indicating that the named person furnished the painted decoration; some are followed by *epoiesen* ('made it'), which may refer either to the potter or the owner of the workshop (it is probable, however, that the former is meant, even where the latter is also true: since they occur at random and are not easily interpreted as advertising a factory, they may indicate pride in individual achievement); third, some artists (e.g. EXEKIAS) sometimes signed as both potter and painter.

The tondo of a Red-figure cup by DOURIS depicting *Eos Carrying the Dead Memnon* (*c.* 490–*c.* 480 BC; Paris, Louvre, G 115; see fig. 81) illustrates most of the types of inscriptions mentioned above. The names of Eos and Memnon are written beside their heads; near the former is the painter's signature (*Doris egraphsen*); below the latter, that of the potter (*Kalliades epoiesen*); in the left part of the field is the praise of a youth (*Hermogenes kalos*); and along the left margin is an unintelligible inscription, perhaps some miswritten comment by the painter.

(e) Other texts. There are well over a hundred Attic vases bearing more unusual texts that show a close involvement of the painters or their clients with their work and the subjects represented, as well as a considerable

81. Inscription on the tondo of an Attic Red-figure cup by Douris: *Eos Carrying the Dead Memnon*, diam. 260 mm, *c.* 490–*c.* 480 BC (Paris, Musée du Louvre)

interest in the spoken and even the written word. Most examples date to the late 6th century BC and early 5th, but some are earlier. Already on the François Vase (*c.* 570 BC; Florence, Mus. Archaeol., 4209), objects are labelled 'altar', 'fountain', 'hydria' and 'seat'. On a Black-figure hydria (late 6th century BC; Münster, Westfäl. Wilhelms-U., 565) the winged figure of the dead Patroklos hovering over his tomb is named as his spirit, *psyche*. Several pots bear laudatory references to themselves, such as 'I am a fine drinking cup' (Rhodes, Archaeol. Mus., 10527) or 'Greetings and buy me' (Paris, Louvre, EL. 98). Vases by the Pioneer group (*see* §6(i)(a) below) often bear comments on the quality of their figures. The painter Euthymides placed along the margin of one of his amphorae (Munich, Staatl. Antikensamml., 2307) the bold 'Euphronios never did this', which is probably a taunt addressed to his famous rival.

Many of these inscriptions provide the remarks of the characters portrayed. On two vases courtesans playing the game of *kottabos*, in which wine dregs were hurled from the drinker's cup against a metal stand or basin, are made to say: 'I throw this for you'; one (a hydria by Phintias; Munich, Staatl. Antikensamml., 2421) bears the *kalos* name of Euthymides, the other (a psykter by Euphronios; St Petersburg, Hermitage, 644) that of Leagros; if the throws are successful, these are their predicted lovers. 'Dysniketos' horse has won', says a herald on a Black-figure Panathenaic amphora (London, BM, B 144). 'Zeus, make me rich' and 'It is full, full already, it has spilt', exclaims the oil-seller in two scenes on a Black-figure pelike (*c.* 530 BC; Rome, Vatican, Mus. Gregoriano Etrus., 413). On a Red-figure vase depicting *Oedipus and the Sphinx* (*c.* 470 BC; Rome, Vatican, Mus. Gregoriano Etrus.,

16541) the latter says 'and three' as part of her riddle. Snatches of song occur on early Red-figure vases, as on a fragmentary kalyx krater by the Kleophrades Painter (Copenhagen, Nmus., 13365) depicting a banqueter singing what was probably a drinking song of Theognis. Poetry appears on representations of book rolls, such as on the famous School cup by Douris (Berlin, Antikenmus., 2285), which has lines resembling the openings of Homeric hymns.

Sometimes characters engage in conversations. In two Black-figure scenes depicting *Achilles and Ajax Playing a Board Game* (lekythos, Boston, MA, Mus. F.A., 95.15; amphora, Rome, Vatican, Mus. Gregoriano Etrus., 344), each hero calls out his score, while a Red-figure pelike (St Petersburg, Hermitage, 615) related to works by the Pioneer group depicts the *Three Ages of Man*: a youth says 'Look, a swallow!', a man replies 'Yes, by Herakles!', and a boy says 'Spring has come'. On a slightly earlier oinochoe (Munich, Staatl. Antikensamml., 2447), which has no figural decoration, there is a rather inane conversation: 'Nikolas is handsome. Dorotheos is handsome. Yes, I think so too. That other boy, Memnon, is also handsome. He is a good friend of mine, too'.

Some everyday scenes are also identified by inscriptions. One Black-figure hydria (*c.* 550–*c.* 500 BC; London, BM, B 331) identifies a fountain as the famous Athenian fountain Kallirhoe, while on a late 5th-century BC Red-figure bell krater (New York, Met., 25.18.66), lyre-playing satyrs are identified as actors by the inscription 'Singers at the Panathenaic Festival'. Finally, an early Red-figure psykter by Oltos (Kings Point, NY, N. Schimmel priv. col.) has six warriors riding on dolphins (an early example of a comic chorus), each figure accompanied by the words 'on a dolphin', perhaps part of a song or a kind of title to the picture.

(f) Scripts. Attic vase inscriptions include specimens of individual handwriting closer to everyday script than are the more formal inscriptions on stone; they are therefore important evidence for the development of script as well as for attitudes towards ornamentation. In the 7th century BC inscriptions were usually integrated with the filling ornament, which may explain their large scale; it was not until *c.* 570 BC that the Attic script finally developed regular, more geometric letter forms and writing was organized into more consistent lines. Around 575–550 BC the alphabet was revised, perhaps in conjunction with the production of Homeric texts for recitation at Athens, and beautiful writing occurs on large vases by such painters as Kleitias and Nearchos. Such was the enthusiasm for writing in the Archaic period that meaningless inscriptions frequently occur, often written by vase painters who were otherwise perfectly literate but also by those who were wholly or partially illiterate.

On the 6th-century BC Little Master cups inscriptions are very much a part of the standard decoration. There are more signatures on these small vases than on any other class of pottery, as well as drinking inscriptions and meaningless strings of letters. Vase painters were prominent in developing the new script, and the most elegant lettering of the period, and perhaps of any period, is that of Exekias, who established a fine counterpoint between the varied poses of his figures and the margins of his scenes by carefully calibrated lines of inscriptions.

Towards the end of the 6th century BC, and perhaps reflecting the establishment of democracy at Athens, inscriptions came to be used more freely and the writing formed more casually, contrasting strongly with the elegance of the figures executed in the new Red-figure technique. This is particularly evident in the works of the Pioneer group, but such exuberance had already diminished by the early 5th century BC, as shown by the works of Douris, for example. Soon after the Persian Wars (490 and 480–479 BC) vase painters began to be influenced by the 'chancellary script' developed by the Athenian State for official use, but for the rest of the century there was a gradual decline in the number of inscriptions, and towards the end they were executed in small lettering running horizontally above the heads of the figures, sometimes

82. Inscriptions on fragments of an Attic Panathenaic prize amphora, 316 BC (Athens, Kerameikos Museum)

more as a symbol of erudition than for their decorative value. This style of inscription also occurs on some 4th-century BC Attic vases as well as on pottery from South Italy, especially Apulia and Paestum, where scenes were frequently influenced by the theatre.

Vase painters had turned to the Ionic alphabet several decades before it was adopted officially at Athens in 403 BC, replacing local Attic; but they participated little in the concurrent development of monumental, plain official and cursive scripts. However, some Panathenaic prize amphorae of the period bear inscriptions in a calligraphic script paralleled in the earliest papyri. Particularly noteworthy are the elegantly curved strokes and the thickening of the end points on a fragmentary specimen of 316 BC (Athens, Kerameikos Mus., PA 29; see fig. 82). Important 4th-century BC inscriptions also occur on South Italian vases and on Boiotian vases connected with the cult of the Kabeiroi. A class of Black-glaze drinking vessels also bears one-line inscriptions in a calligraphic style referring to divinities presiding over the symposium: 'Of Zeus the Saviour', 'Of Dionysos' etc; these were known as 'lettered drinking cups' by contemporary writers and were still produced in the Hellenistic period. A more informal style occurs in inscriptions on the numerous 3rd-century BC funerary vases from the cemetery of Hadra at Alexandria, while certain faience vases from Egypt bear inscriptions connected with the cult of Hellenistic queens. Finally, the so-called Megarian bowls, which were widely produced in the Hellenistic period and decorated in relief, sometimes carried scenes from the Homeric poems with copious inscriptions added in a bookish manner for didactic purposes. Generally, however, vase inscriptions were not of great importance in the Hellenistic period: most writing, both formal and informal, was now done on papyrus; inscriptions on stone were more common; and most pottery production had sunk to a lowly craft no longer at the centre of artistic creation.

BIBLIOGRAPHY

J. D. Beazley: *Red-figure* (1942, 2/1963)
——: *Black-figure* (1956)
A. G. Woodhead: *The Study of Greek Inscriptions* (Cambridge, 1959, rev. 1981)
L. H. Jeffery: *The Local Scripts of Archaic Greece* (Oxford, 1961, rev. 1990)
H. R. Immerwahr: 'Inscriptions on the Anacreon Krater in Copenhagen', *Amer. J. Archaeol.*, lxix (1965), p. 153 and no. 10
J. D. Beazley: *Paralipomena* (1971)
J. Boardman: *Athenian Black-figure Vases* (London, 1974)
M. Guarducci: *Epigrafia greca*, iii (Rome, 1974), pp. 456–95
M. A. Lang: *Graffiti and Dipinti* (1976), xxi of *The Athenian Agora* (Princeton, 1953–)
F. Lorber: 'Vaseninschriften', *Das Studium der griechischen Epigraphik*, ed. G. Pfohl (Darmstadt, 1977), pp. 97–115
A. W. Johnston: *Trademarks on Greek Vases* (Warminster, 1979)
F. Lorber: *Inschriften auf korinthischen Vasen* (Berlin, 1979)
L. Burn and R. Glynn: *Beazley Addenda* (Oxford, 1982); rev. by T. A. Carpenter and others (Oxford, 1989), appendix 2
H. R. Immerwahr: *Attic Script: A Survey* (Oxford, 1990)
B. Cohen: 'The Literate Potter: A Tradition of Incised Signatures on Attic Vases', *Met. Mus. J.*, xxvi (1991), pp. 49–95

HENRY R. IMMERWAHR

2. PROTOGEOMETRIC. The term derives from the abstract decorative designs on Greek pottery of the Early Iron Age (*c.* 1050–*c.* 900 BC), which precede the more fully developed and varied ornament of the Geometric style (*see* §3 below).

(i) Introduction. After the collapse of Mycenaean civilization in the 12th century BC, fine painted pottery was the only art form that maintained a continuous tradition throughout the ensuing Dark Age. The latest Mycenaean pottery had been decorated chiefly with highly stylized floral and marine motifs; in the intervening Sub-Mycenaean phase (*c.* 1050–*c.* 1000 BC) these motifs were further simplified to create abstract patterns of wavy lines, languettes and concentric arcs or semicircles. Without more sophisticated art forms for inspiration, Protogeometric (PG) vase painters still relied on these simple abstract motifs, carefully subordinated to the shapes of their vases. On this limited repertory, however, they imposed a geometrical precision by using a multiple brush attached to a compass, with which sets of concentric semicircles or circles could be executed with a deft flick of the wrist. At the same time standards of potting improved: a fast wheel fashioned the vessels in crisper contours and more harmonious proportions, and a higher firing temperature gave the paint—a fine solution of the clay—a more brilliant lustre.

After the severe disruption following the Mycenaean demise, the appearance of PG pottery indicates a return to more settled conditions of life and a recovery of ceramic finesse. One result of the Mycenaean collapse had been a decline in communications within the Aegean world. Thus a common Mycenaean idiom in pottery style (*koinē*) gave way to wide local variations. The Attic PG style, first to emerge, gradually influenced the output of most other Aegean areas through exported pottery, thereby restoring a limited *koinē*; but each regional style nevertheless retained its own character. Such styles evolved throughout the Greek world, including the seaboard of Asia Minor recently settled by Ionian Greeks; to the north, however, potters on Lesbos and in the Aeolian Greek coastal settlements produced instead grey Bucchero ware in a traditional Anatolian technique.

(ii) Attic. The finest PG pottery was produced for funerary use, and in Attica, where cremation had become the usual burial rite, exceptional care went into the making and decoration of ash urns. A continuous sequence of whole vessels offered in single cremations illustrates the development of the Attic PG style over *c.* 150 years. The shapes prefigure those of Archaic and Classical Athenian vases and are remarkable for their excellent proportions, which became progressively more refined. The larger closed forms have a taut ovoid body and a tall concave neck; open vessels are roughly hemispherical, often resting on a high and skilfully turned conical foot.

The chief closed shape is the amphora, designed as a cremation urn. Those for the ashes of men have vertical strap handles springing from the shoulder to the middle of the neck (neck-handled amphorae), as in an example from the Athenian Kerameikos (*c.* 980–*c.* 960 BC; Athens, Kerameikos Mus., 572; see fig. 83), while those for women have more globular bodies, initially with round horizontal handles attached to their bellies and later with vertical strap handles on their shoulders (shoulder-handled amphorae). Other common closed shapes are the oinochoe, trefoil-lipped to facilitate pouring; the narrow-necked lekythos, which replaced the Mycenaean stirrup jar as the

83. Protogeometric neck-handled amphora, h. 435 mm, from PG Grave no. 17, *c*. 980–*c*. 960 BC (Athens, Kerameikos Museum)

standard oil flask; and the globular pyxis with a short, everted lip and a fitted lid. The largest open shape is the krater, while the most common drinking vessels are the skyphos and a deep cup with one vertical handle; both rest on high conical feet, but the cup also occurs in a shallow flat-based variety. Less frequent is the kantharos; rarer shapes of special interest include clay miniatures of bronze tripod cauldrons and a lentoid pilgrim flask of Cypro-Levantine character. The conical foot was probably also of Cypriot origin; otherwise, apart from the pyxis and the kantharos, all the standard shapes were developments of the less sophisticated Attic Sub-Mycenaean forms.

The decoration gradually changed from light to dark ground during Attic PG. Except on the largest belly-handled amphorae, the ornament was usually confined to a single zone: the shoulder of a closed vessel or the area between the handles of an open one. A major role was played by compass-drawn sets of concentric circles and semicircles, the latter emphasizing the vigorous curve of a shoulder, the former employed on flatter areas such as the handle zone of a deep skyphos. The repertory adopted large wavy lines from the Sub-Mycenaean style and admitted some rectilinear patterns: latticed triangles provided an alternative to the semicircles, and rectangular panels of chequerboard or diagonal latticing were sometimes inserted between two sets of circles. Typical of the latest Attic PG were narrow horizontal strips of rectilinear ornament (e.g. dogtooth, single zigzag, oblique bars) reserved between large areas of shiny dark paint: other late vessels, near the change to Geometric, carried heavy accumulations of chequerboard and latticing to the exclusion of circular motifs. The few instances of figural designs among an otherwise wholly abstract repertory are sketchily rendered in silhouette: they are confined to four amphorae from the Kerameikos cemetery in Athens, on which horses make an unobtrusive appearance (e.g. Athens, Kerameikos Mus., 560T18 and 1260), and an Attic skyphos exported to Lefkandi with birds tucked under its handles (Eretria, Archaeol. Mus.).

(iii) Other regional styles. These arose at different times and display varying combinations of local and Attic elements. Closest to Attic are the PG wares of Boiotia, Corinth, the Cyclades (notably Naxos) and the newly established Ionian settlements in the east Aegean. The Argolid, once the heartland of Mycenaean civilization, developed a more individual PG style, sharing some features with Attic but also deriving much from the latest Mycenaean pottery, perhaps without any intervening Sub-Mycenaean phase: Argive decoration consists largely of rectilinear motifs, especially latticed triangles; the same is true of vases from the Dodecanese, which also have some links with contemporary pottery on Cyprus.

Furthest from the Attic style are the PG wares of Lakonia, the western Peloponnese, Achaia and Ithaka, which nevertheless share the common decorative principle of heavily latticed triangles and lozenges placed in square or rectangular panels. A distinctive Lakonian shape is a grooved and baggy skyphos, the ancestor of the Archaic lakaina; the most usual drinking vessel in Achaia and Ithaka was the tall kantharos. In Thessaly, Attic and Euboian features were grafted on to a local style derived from handmade pottery in the Macedonian tradition.

The Euboian PG style is well documented from numerous grave offerings at Lefkandi. It developed from a local Sub-Mycenaean tradition, displaying throughout some affinity with Attic, especially in its late phase. Almost all the Attic shapes are present, often furnished with high conical feet. Cremation, as in Attica, was the normal rite at Lefkandi, but not urn cremation; hence the rarity of large and elaborately decorated amphorae, and their relatively unpretentious ornament, characterized by the wavy line. Nevertheless, there were some adventurous experiments: a small hydria (early 10th century BC) bears the earliest post-Mycenaean figural Greek vase painting, comprising two archers crudely rendered in silhouette; under the handle of a vast krater, probably a marker for a royal grave, is depicted an oriental Tree of Life; and a ritual vessel takes the form of a centaur, with modelled limbs added to a wheelmade body (*c*. 900 BC; all Eretria, Archaeol. Mus.). The PG tradition enjoyed a long life in Euboia, persisting far into the period of Attic Geometric. During the 9th century BC and into the early 8th the Euboians took the initiative in maritime trade and established a common Sub-Protogeometric pottery style shared by parts of Thessaly, Boiotia and the northern Cyclades. Its most characteristic shape, the low-footed skyphos decorated with pendent concentric semicircles, was widely exported around the Aegean and even to Cyprus and the Levant.

Crete suffered less than the Greek mainland in the upheaval at the end of the Bronze Age; hence its pottery reveals an exceptionally smooth transition from the Minoan past. A Sub-Minoan phase throughout the island preserved many Minoan shapes decorated with spare curvilinear ornament on a light ground. Afterwards there was much local variation, but the subsequent PG style was most fully developed around Knossos, the area most open to outside influences. Knossian PG, well represented in collective chamber tombs, evolved in the early 10th century BC as a hybrid style, combining Sub-Minoan elements with Attic late PG: Attic types of amphora were common alongside the stirrup jar of Minoan origin; the local deep bell krater was decorated with Attic concentric circles; and globular pithoi, also decorated with circles, were designed as ash urns, cremation having by then become the rule. This style developed on its own lines until *c.* 850 BC when, before the arrival of true Geometric, there followed an interlude of florid and ebullient decoration known as Protogeometric B, unique in the Greek world: to the usual PG repertory was added a profusion of freehand curvilinear motifs—cables, spirals and massed arcs—probably derived from metalwork made by immigrant Levantine craftsmen. The chief shape of PG B is a straight-sided pithos used as an ash urn.

Knossian PG includes several experiments in figure drawing. Wild goats appear several times, once as prey in a hunting scene on a bell krater (*c.* 900 BC; Herakleion, Archaeol. Mus.); another bell krater (*c.* 850 BC; see Coldstream, p. 93) depicts a warrior struggling with two lions on one side and heraldic sphinxes on the other. The most outstanding example of PG B is a straight-sided pithos on which is boldly portrayed a nature goddess with trees, birds and fish (late 9th century BC; Knossos, Stratig. Mus., T.107.114).

BIBLIOGRAPHY

W. Kraiker and K. Kübler: *Die Nekropolen des 12. bis 10. Jahrhunderts* (1939), i of *Kerameikos: Ergebnisse der Ausgrabungen* (Berlin, 1939–)
K. Kübler: *Neufunde aus der Nekropole des 11. und 10. Jahrhunderts* (1943), iv of *Kerameikos: Ergebnisse der Ausgrabungen* (Berlin, 1939–)
V. R. d'A. Desborough: *Protogeometric Pottery* (Oxford, 1952)
J. K. Brock: *Fortetsa: Early Greek Tombs near Knossos* (Cambridge, 1957)
E. L. Smithson: 'The Protogeometric Cemetery at Nea Ionia, 1949', *Hesperia*, xxx (1961), pp. 147–78
V. R. d'A. Desborough: 'The Dark Age Pottery from Settlement and Cemeteries', *Lefkandi*, i, ed. M. R. Popham, L. H. Sackett and P. G. Themelis, Brit. Sch. Athens, Suppl. vol. xi (London, 1980), pp. 281–350
B. Wells: *The Protogeometric Period* (1983), iv/2–3 of *Results of the Excavations East of the Acropolis 1970–1974*, ii of *Asine* (Stockholm, 1938–)
J. N. Coldstream: 'A Protogeometric Nature Goddess from Knossos', *Bull. Inst. Class. Stud. U. London*, xxxi (1984), pp. 93–104
W. D. E. Coulson: 'The Dark Age Pottery of Sparta', *Annu. Brit. Sch. Athens*, lxxx (1985), pp. 29–84

3. GEOMETRIC. Geometric pottery (*c.* 900–*c.* 700 BC), a style characterized by abstract rectilinear designs, evolved in Attica from a Protogeometric (PG) phase in which the motifs were predominantly circular. It was always subject to wide regional variations, initially as a result of poor communications during the Dark Age, later reflecting the emergence and growth of the independent city state (*polis*) and its pride in local tradition. Of the many regional styles, Attic Geometric was the most fully developed and the most influential.

(i) Introduction. (ii) Attic. (iii) Other mainland styles. (iv) Island styles.

(i) Introduction. Painted Geometric pottery, almost always made on the wheel, is found in Greek settlements, sanctuaries and cemeteries. Its export outside the Aegean, eastwards to Cyprus and the Levant, westwards to the newly founded Greek colonies in Italy and Sicily, attests the expanding horizons of the Greek world, especially in the 8th century BC. The best-preserved specimens come from graves, and special care was often taken in the manufacture of vessels designed for funerary purposes. Groups of whole vessels offered in individual graves illustrate the development of local styles; but their absolute chronology is determined, however indirectly, by exported specimens found in datable contexts overseas.

Geometric pottery is divided into Early (EG; *c.* 900–*c.* 850 BC), Middle (MG; *c.* 850–*c.* 760 BC) and Late (LG; *c.* 760–*c.* 700 BC) phases; in the Attic and related styles, each phase is subdivisible into two further stages, thus EG I (*c.* 900–*c.* 875 BC) and EG II (*c.* 875–*c.* 850 BC), MG I (*c.* 850–*c.* 800 BC) and MG II (*c.* 800–*c.* 760 BC), LG I (*c.* 760–*c.* 735 BC) and LG II (*c.* 735–*c.* 700 BC). During EG and most of MG, ornament was almost always abstract, with a few cautious experiments in representational drawing. Then, from MG II onwards, Attic vase painters introduced extended scenes that constituted the first consistent figural style in Greek art. Funerals and battles were portrayed, notably on enormous vessels (LG I) designed as monuments to mark aristocratic graves. During LG figural scenes became quite common on Argive, Euboian and Boiotian pottery; but the preoccupation with elaborate funerary and warlike themes was peculiar to Attica. The battle scenes may reveal interest in a heroic past, though attempts to identify specific events in Homeric and other epic poetry remain inconclusive. In LG II, however, the introduction of centaurs and other supernatural creatures implies an awakening interest in the portrayal of myth. The rendering of human figures and animals, almost always drawn in full silhouette, was conceptual rather than representational; the artist drew not what he saw from any one viewpoint, but the sum of what he knew to be there. Despite their simplicity, minor variations in figure drawing have led to the identification of individual painters and workshops.

(ii) Attic. The EG and MG stages of the Attic styles are best represented in the Kerameikos cemeteries of Athens, where the vase forms evolved naturally from their Protogeometric precursors. The amphora cremation urn remained the leading closed shape, its proportions more attenuated than before, but the placing of its handles still varied according to the sex of the deceased (*see* §2(ii) above). The oinochoe developed a plumper body and a ring base. Pyxides were globular or pointed in EG, but a new broad and flat form appeared in MG I; the lips were inset to receive lids. The chief drinking vessels, the skyphos and the kantharos, were shallower than in PG, and a ring base replaced the PG conical foot; the kantharos with high-swung handles was introduced in MG II. The krater occurs only in the graves for male cremations and gradually developed a tall pedestal with a ribbed stem.

84. Attic Geometric shoulder-handled amphora, h. 515 mm, MG I, late 9th century BC (Eleusis, Eleusis Museum)

As in mature PG, decoration in EG and MG was still predominantly executed on a dark ground, but the motifs were new. Concentric circles were replaced by rectilinear designs applied in reserved panels and zones to emphasize the focal points of the vase. The principal motif was the key meander with diagonal hatching. Multiple zigzags and battlements were also frequent. Ornament in EG was usually simple and austere, small units of decoration being dominated by large expanses of dark paint. In MG I the decorated areas became larger, producing a fine balance between light and dark and emphasizing the form and articulation of the vase (see fig. 84), in which there is complete harmony between shape and decoration, with the reserved panels coinciding with the handle attachments. In MG II the decoration spread still further, covering the upper part of large vases and organized round a central meander panel.

Whereas representations of living creatures had previously been exceptional and confined to isolated figures inconspicuously placed, from late MG II to late LG I there was a sudden abundance of funerary and battle scenes painted on gigantic vessels up to 1.7 m high. They stood as markers over aristocratic graves in the Dipylon cemetery of Athens, enabling libations to be poured to the dead through holes pierced in their bases. For female graves these monuments took the form of especially large belly-handled amphorae with figured panels surrounded by geometric ornament, which depicted the deceased lying in state on a bier among mourners (*prothesis*). On the vast pedestalled kraters provided for men, the *prothesis* also included retinues of warriors and chariot teams; scenes of war on land or sea might be added on other parts of the vase. The figural decoration occasionally included depictions of deer and goats, often in continuous decorative friezes. The Dipylon cemetery gives its name to the leading vase painter of the LG I phase, the DIPYLON MASTER. Most of the monumental grave vases (e.g. Athens, N. Archaeol. Mus., 804; see fig. 85) are attributed to him, his younger contemporary the HIRSCHFELD PAINTER or their close associates. The human figures are stiff and static, hardly less abstract than the surrounding ornament, but these painters achieved clarity by avoiding overlapping bodies and representing every limb. To soften the contrast between the silhouettes and the hatched geometric motifs, light filling ornaments were inserted into the figured panels.

In LG I decoration covered virtually the entire surface of the vase. On the vessels without figures important zones were emphasized by large and complex meanders or by rows of square panels ('metopes'); usually containing

85. Attic Geometric belly-handled amphora by the Dipylon Master, h. 1.55 m, *c*. 760 BC (Athens, National Archaeological Museum)

86. Attic Geometric neck-handled amphora from the workshop of Athens 894, h. 600 mm, LG II, *c*. 720 BC (Athens, National Archaeological Museum)

quatrefoils, swastikas, lozenges, chequerboards or water-birds with hatched bodies. During the final phase, LG II, figure drawing became more fluid and more varied in theme, while the geometric ornament lost its discipline, both in execution and in its arrangement on the vase. The monumental Dipylon cemetery vases passed out of fashion, but much figured pottery was still made for funerary purposes. The chief shape was a neck-handled amphora of moderate size, its lip encrusted with freely modelled serpents, the guardians of the dead. The neck panel often contained a condensed *prothesis* scene, with female mourners distinguished by long hair and latticed skirts. Processions of chariots and foot soldiers filled the main body zones, conveying a greater sense of movement than their precursors on the Dipylon vases; narrower zones contained friezes of grazing deer, or hounds pursuing a hare. Towards the end of LG II the *prothesis* was sometimes replaced by a chain of female dancers, while lions, bulls, centaurs and winged goats joined the repertory of animals in subsidiary friezes. Other important shapes included the large round-mouthed pitcher and the shallow skyphos decorated inside with concentric figural bands in the manner of embossed metal bowls imported from the Levant.

The figure drawing on Attic LG II varies greatly in style and quality. Many different artists and workshops have been distinguished, but the most significant vase painters followed the tradition of the Dipylon Master. Humans and animals were still depicted conceptually and in silhouette but gradually became less rigid. This process began with the Sub-Dipylon group, which includes a krater (London, BM, 1899.2–19.1) showing an unusual scene of a man and a woman departing by ship, perhaps alluding to the legend of Theseus and Ariadne, an early experiment in mythological representation. The style was developed further by the Philadelphia Painter and led to the prolific output of the workshop that produced an amphora in Athens, NM 894 (N. Archaeol. Mus., St. 222; see fig. 86).

Attic Geometric vases were copiously exported during the two MG phases, influencing the pottery of almost every region, but the export and influence of Attic pottery declined sharply in LG, when the regional styles diverged most widely.

(iii) Other mainland styles. The best-known and most important Geometric styles in the Peloponnese were the Argive and Corinthian, which evolved from the local PG a little later than their Attic equivalent. Both displayed a close affinity with Attic shapes and decoration during their EG and MG I phases, but subsequently they developed on more original lines.

Argive LG is distinguished by both its linear ornament and its figural motifs. The best and most characteristic work occurs on large kraters and amphorae found in graves. Their purely geometric compositions, covering most of the vessel, are elaborate but less carefully structured than those of Attic: the result is often a patchwork of zones, long panels and metopes without the central emphasis of the Attic designs. The meander appears in a stepped form, giving the composition a diagonal thrust. Smaller motifs were mass-produced with a multiple brush; most typical are rows of leaf-shaped lozenges and small birds in silhouette. Figural scenes were not funerary but drawn from everyday life, the favourite subject being a man reining in one or two horses (e.g. Argos, Archaeol. Mus., C 201 and C 1). The field sometimes also contained small filling ornaments such as fish, large birds or T-shaped objects, perhaps representing mangers or tripods. Rows of female dancers entered the repertory in LG II, linking hands and carrying branches. The chief manufacturing centre was Argos, where many different artists and workshops have been distinguished. Asine, on the gulf of Argos, produced a slightly different style, still influenced to some degree by Attic. Unlike its Attic and Corinthian counterparts, Argive LG was not succeeded by any consistent Orientalizing style; deep kraters with Sub-Geometric decoration were made throughout the 7th century BC and even imitated at Syracuse (Syracuse, Mus. Archeol. Reg.).

Quite different was the character of Corinthian LG, which excelled in small shapes with simple and restrained decoration. Thin zones of vertical chevrons or sigmas were preferred to heavy motifs such as the meander, and much of the surface was covered with fine horizontal lines. Corinthian LG potters eschewed figure drawing almost entirely; the only living creature to appear regularly in the repertory is the marsh bird, at first drawn singly or in confronted pairs, and later mass-produced in miniature silhouette files using the multiple brush. An important innovation in shape was the kotyle, which at once became the favourite Corinthian drinking vessel.

Corinthian pottery of this phase was already remarkable for its well-levigated yellow clay, its precise potting and its thin walls; it was thus becoming the most widely and abundantly exported fine ware in the Greek world and often inspired local imitations elsewhere. Most exports went west to Delphi, Ithaka and to the new colonies of Magna Graecia, whose foundation dates—given by Thucydides and others—help to establish absolute dates for the Corinthian pottery found there and thence for all other LG schools.

During the last two decades of the 8th century BC Corinthian artists were the first to develop an Orientalizing style. Even so, the bulk of their output was still of Geometric character. The most important shapes of these years, both of outstandingly fine fabric, were the globular aryballos and a deeper version of the kotyle. In a grave group at the Euboian colony of Pithekoussai on Ischia, several globular aryballoi are accompanied by an Egyptian scarab of the pharaoh Bocchoris (*reg* 717–712 BC), thereby providing another dating point for Geometric pottery.

In Lakonia, finds of Geometric pottery are limited to fragments from sanctuaries at Sparta and Amyklai. Little is known of the Geometric sequence there before the rise of the distinctive LG style. It is characterized by tall and baggy shapes inherited from the local PG tradition, including the lakaina, the normal Lakonian drinking vessel. The decoration, usually applied over a creamy slip, was at first influenced by Argive LG, especially on large vases; subsequently delicate ornament of Corinthian character appeared on the smaller vessels. Figures were rare and confined to scenes of dancing and horse-taming. A Sub-Geometric or 'Transitional' phase persisted through the early 7th century BC until the appearance of the local Orientalizing style.

Like Lakonia, other parts of the Peloponnese show little sign of any settled EG or MG phase. Arcadian LG was strongly influenced by the pottery of the Argolid. The other regions—Achaia, Elis and Messenia—shared a West Greek LG style that lasted well into the 7th century BC and spread to Aetolia, Acarnania and Ithaka. There are local differences between the LG pottery of these regions, but all shared a preference for a tall kantharos and a common debt to Corinth in the decoration, consisting of small, widely spaced motifs in narrow zones encased between large numbers of fine horizontal lines.

The Boiotian style was closely related to that of its Attic neighbour until the outset of LG, when individual characteristics emerged. The most distinctive vessels were large oinochoai, their decoration becoming increasingly rich, with funerary serpents modelled on their handles; they were produced at Thebes, along with kraters, kantharoi and pyxides in a similar style. The linear ornament is compounded of Corinthian, Attic and Euboian elements; the wide range of figural themes includes warriors with horses, dancers, hunters, boxers and a nature goddess flanked by beasts and birds. From outside Thebes comes a very different Boiotian group of mainly Sub-Geometric pottery: high-footed burial amphorae with wide necks, coated with a thick white slip and decorated with a different repertory of motifs derived from Euboia.

Thessaly was the most northerly region to manufacture wheelmade Geometric pottery. Its local style was influenced from the south by Attica and Euboia and from the north by the handmade painted ware of Macedonia. The chief northern shapes adopted were the jug with cut-away neck, the high-handled kantharos and the trigger-handled cup. The profusion of densely packed rectilinear ornaments on 9th century BC vases was derived from the north, but from MG II onwards the new influences were from Attica and Euboia.

(iv) Island styles. In Euboia and the Cyclades the transition from PG to Geometric was very slow: throughout the 9th century BC and even in the early 8th both areas continued essentially in the local PG tradition, which Thessaly also shared to some extent. The chief drinking vessel in this Sub-Protogeometric style was the Euboian skyphos with pendent concentric semicircles; its wide Mediterranean distribution, from al-Mina in northern Syria to Veii in Etruria, attests the trading enterprise of the Euboians even before their foundation of the first western colonies.

Much Euboian Sub-Protogeometric pottery has been found in the graves and settlement at Lefkandi, where the usual shapes were amphorae, oinochoai, lekythoi, globular pyxides, kraters, skyphoi, kalathoi and cups. Apart from the rendering of ships on two 9th-century BC vessels (Eretria, Archaeol. Mus.), decoration was unadventurous. On a dark ground, concentric circular motifs still play a leading part, supplemented by groups of diagonal bars, silhouetted double-axes and hour-glasses, and latticed triangles. Occasional imitations of Attic Geometric appear from MG I onwards, while at Eretria (founded *c.* 800 BC) the earliest pottery echoes the Attic MG II phase, with little sign of Sub-Protogeometric features.

The change to Euboian LG is associated with the Cesnola Painter, who decorated a vast ovoid krater (New York, Met., 74.51.965; see fig. 87) found at Kourion in Cyprus, which is now generally thought to be Euboian rather than Naxian. Though much influenced in style by the Attic Dipylon Master, the Cesnola Painter evolved a typically Euboian repertory of figural themes, all of which appear on the Kourion Krater; the horse at the manger with a double-axe in the field, the frieze of grazing horses and the oriental Tree of Life flanked by deer or goats. Pottery by this painter or his workshop was widely exported and profoundly influenced a colonial Euboian school on Pithekoussai. The decoration of Euboian LG skyphoi and other small shapes was at first adapted from the Attic metopal friezes, with local variations; later miniature bird files were introduced from Corinth, and

87. Euboian Geometric ovoid krater with lid by the Cesnola Painter, h. 1.15 m, LG I, *c.* 750 BC (New York, Metropolitan Museum of Art)

some motifs were painted in added white. Towards the end of LG large high-footed amphorae were produced, with thick vertical wavy lines on their broad necks.

In the 9th century BC a Sub-Protogeometric style like that of Euboia flourished in the Cyclades, especially on the northern islands of Andros and Tenos, but influence from Attic MG gradually permeated the entire archipelago. The Attic connection persisted into the beginning of Cycladic LG with its metopal decoration on the smaller shapes; subsequently distinct schools on Naxos, Paros, Melos and Thera moved away from Attic. Naxos and Paros produced most of the pottery offered at the sanctuary on Delos: Naxian figural and linear decoration was close to that of Euboia, and the most individual shape was a very slim neck-handled amphora with bands on its body and birds on its neck (e.g. Mykonos, Archaeol. Mus.); Parian linear decoration was light and airy, often confined to sigmas, vertical dashes and dots floating in a wide field. A Melian workshop, specializing in kraters, amphorae and unusual fenestrated stands, rendered apparently tail-less birds, and animals in the manner of the Attic Hirschfeld Painter. On Thera a retarded LG style lasted through much of the 7th century BC. Its amphorae and neckless pithoi, made to contain cremations, were conservatively decorated with meanders, wheel motifs and other linear Geometric designs. Meanwhile artists on Tenos specialized in large amphorae made of coarse clay and decorated in relief with a wide variety of figural motifs.

The main Geometric style of Crete originated at Knossos, where copious offerings in family chamber tombs have been found. It again came to its fullest expression in the decoration of cremation urns, usually in the form of neckless ovoid pithoi with lids and two or four handles. A true Geometric style was not established until the end of the 9th century BC; instead of evolving directly from orthodox PG, it was preceded by an interlude of florid curvilinear decoration known as Protogeometric B (*see* §2(iii) above). During a fleeting EG phase, the PG B repertory was combined with meanders and other motifs borrowed from Attic Geometric, but the Attic element predominated in MG, and the decoration became more disciplined and rectilinear. In the LG period Attic influence waned, and though a dark ground was still used, it was often enlivened by ornament in white paint. Figural motifs were scarce, but there was a refreshing variety in the depiction of birds, including some with multiple heads (e.g. Herakleion, Archaeol. Mus., Fortetsa 1501). The influence of Cypriot imports can be seen in the globular lekythos with a ridge on the neck, which was often decorated with circles in the Cypriot manner.

The Knossian Geometric style spread over most of Crete but failed to reach either extremity. In the east an Eteocretan style, with wild curvilinear decoration, flourished throughout the 8th century BC, while the little-known Kydonian school in the far west seems to have been even further removed from the central Cretan style.

A fairly homogeneous East Greek Geometric style was shared by the Dodecanese, Samos, Chios and the Greek coastal settlements of Asia Minor. It even spread to the non-Greek inhabitants of Caria; further north, however, the Greeks of Lesbos and Asiatic Aiolis preferred to produce Greek vase shapes using the native Anatolian technique of a grey Bucchero fabric with incised decoration.

For EG and MG in East Greece the cemeteries of Kos and Rhodes provide the fullest sequence. On closed shapes, as in PG, the main decoration was confined to the shoulder with dark paint below. Concentric semicircles surviving from PG were supplemented by latticed or hatched rectilinear ornament: hour-glasses, lozenges and triangles in EG, followed in MG by battlements and nets of lozenges inside triangles. Attic influence was very slight, except on some MG wares from Samos and Miletos, and a few MG II vessels from Rhodes. From MG onwards, lekythoi acquired a ridge on the neck in imitation of Cypriot imports, but their decoration was still often in the local dark-ground Geometric manner.

The use of a dark ground persisted into East Greek LG, when the decoration was often broken up into metopal squares. Samos was unusual in maintaining links with Attic LG I: elsewhere a purely local stock of metopal motifs developed, including outlined and latticed lozenges, meander hooks, birds and the so-called 'Rhodian tree', composed of a latticed triangle with two square hooks attached to its apex. This repertory appeared on high-footed kraters, round-mouthed jugs and especially on the most popular drinking vessel, a local adaptation of the Corinthian hemispherical kotyle. Also typical of Dodecanesian LG are Geometric versions of the cable and the palm tree, adapted from Levantine ivories. Imitations of Cypriot unguent vessels continued, and Rhodian aryballoi of Oriental character, decorated with a spaghetti-like combination of concentric circles and wavy lines, were widely exported. Figure drawing is extremely rare, though a *prothesis* scene appears on a fragmentary Samian kantharos (Kolonna, Heraion Mus., K 76), and several vase fragments from Chios (Chios, Archaeol. Mus.) show scenes involving ships and human figures, including a warrior confronting a lion.

In the East Greek world a Sub-Geometric manner persisted well into the 7th century BC. Especially conservative was the shallow 'bird bowl', a descendant of the LG kotyle, which preserved the purely Geometric format of a latticed bird between lozenges until around 600 BC.

BIBLIOGRAPHY

C. Dugas and C. Rhomaios: *Les Vases préhelléniques et géométriques* (1934), xv of *Exploration archéologique de Délos* (Paris, 1909–)

S. S. Weinberg: *The Geometric and Orientalizing Pottery* (1943), vii/1 of *Corinth: Results of the Excavations Conducted by the American School of Classical Studies at Athens* (Princeton, 1932–)

K. Kübler: *Die Nekropole des 10. bis 8. Jahrhunderts* (1954), v/1 of *Kerameikos: Ergebnisse der Ausgrabungen* (Berlin, 1939–)

J. K. Brock: *Fortetsa: Early Greek Tombs near Knossos*, Brit. Sch. Athens, Suppl. Paper no. 2 (Cambridge, 1956)

K. F. Johansen: 'Exochi: Ein frührhodisches Gräberfeld', *Acta Archaeol.* [Copenhagen], xxviii (1958) [whole issue]

R. M. Cook: *Greek Painted Pottery* (London, 1960, rev. 1972), chap. 3

J. M. Davison: 'Attic Geometric Workshops', *Yale Class. Stud.*, xvi (1961) [whole issue]

E. T. H. Brann: *Late Geometric and Protoattic Pottery, Mid 8th to Late 7th Century BC* (1962), viii of *The Athenian Agora* (Princeton, 1953–)

P. Courbin: *La Céramique géométrique de l'Argolide* (Paris, 1966)

J. N. Coldstream: *Greek Geometric Pottery* (London, 1968)

B. Schweitzer: *Die geometrische Kunst Griechenlands* (Cologne, 1969); Eng. trans. by P. Usborne and C. Usborne as *Greek Geometric Art* (London, 1971), chaps 1–4

G. Ahlberg: *Prothesis and Ekphora in Greek Geometric Art* (Göteborg, 1971)

J. N. Coldstream: 'The Cesnola Painter: A Change of Address', *Bull. Inst. Class. Stud. U. London*, xviii (1971), pp. 1–15

A. Ruckert: 'Frühe Keramik Böotiens', *Ant. Kst*, x (1976) [suppl. issue]

J. N. Coldstream: *Geometric Greece* (London, 1977)

L. Morricone: 'Sepolture della prima età del ferro a Coo', *Annu. Scu. Archeol. Atene & Miss. It. Oriente*, lvi (1978), pp. 9–427

V. R. d'A. Desborough: 'The Dark Age Pottery from Settlement and Cemeteries', *Lefkandi*, i, ed. M. R. Popham, L. H. Sackett and P. G. Themelis, Brit. Sch. Athens, Suppl. vol. xi (London, 1980), pp. 281–350

J. Boardman with M. J. Price: 'The Late Geometric Pottery', *ibid.*, pp. 57–79

4. ORIENTALIZING. By the time Greece emerged from its Dark Age, significant trade links had been re-established between Greece and the eastern Mediterranean, and after the disintegration of the Geometric style in the late 8th century BC, Greek vase painters began to look to the Near East for fresh ideas, creating an Orientalizing movement. There was still little direct contact with the major artistic centres of Egypt and Assyria; the immediate sources of the new designs were chiefly the small-scale arts of the Neo-Hittite principalities of north Syria and the Phoenician trading cities, especially their ivories and metal bowls. Metalwork from the Anatolian kingdoms of Urartu and Phrygia also exercised some influence.

Curvilinear plant motifs, notably the lotus, palmette and rosette, formed striking contrasts with the predominantly abstract and rectilinear designs of the previous Geometric style. Animal friezes became more varied and naturalistic under eastern influences; the usual stock of Orientalizing animals, often varied within the same frieze, comprised lions, panthers, bulls, boars, birds, deer and goats, as well as fantastic creatures such as sphinxes, griffins and sirens. Human figures were affected too: facial features, hardly rendered at all in the simple Geometric silhouette technique, assumed exaggerated proportions, especially in the outline drawings on early Orientalizing vases.

(i) Introduction. (ii) Proto-Corinthian. (iii) Proto-Attic. (iv) Other areas.

(i) Introduction. As in the Geometric period, regional schools differed widely. Corinth and Athens produced the most ambitious Orientalizing styles, making much use of the human figure and thereby enabling the identification of individual painters and workshops. Since they anticipate the riper Archaic vase painting of the two cities (*see* §5(i) and (ii) below), these styles are called Proto-Corinthian and Proto-Attic. Other Orientalizing styles arose in Lakonia, on Crete, in the Cyclades, in various parts of the East Greek world and sporadically in the western colonies. In Boiotia and the Argolid, apart from a few Orientalizing experiments, a Sub-Geometric style prevailed; indeed, even at Corinth much Sub-Geometric pottery was contemporary with the masterpieces of Proto-Corinthian. There and elsewhere the Orientalizing style was initiated by a few innovative artists who tempered the local Geometric style with an eclectic repertory of oriental features always adapted to Greek taste.

In the rendering of figures, Orientalizing vase painters progressed from the plain silhouette of Geometric times towards outline drawing, silhouette with incised details, and the use of additional colours. Outline was suitable for large surfaces but not for the miniature unguent vessels in which the leading Proto-Corinthian artists specialized; here incision on silhouette achieved finer detail, and such was the origin of the incised Black-figure technique (*see* §5 below). The most frequently added colour was a purplish red, although Proto-Attic artists at first preferred white. During the mid-7th century BC polychrome vase painting was briefly attempted in Corinth, Athens and the Cyclades, perhaps prompted by the revival of large-scale wall painting in the first monumental temples. These technical innovations were skilfully exploited in the rendering of extended figural scenes; the incised silhouette technique in particular allowed the figures to overlap in tightly knit compositions without loss of clarity.

As Homeric and other epic poetry circulated around the Greek world, scenes of myth were more frequently attempted and are more recognizable than the tentative experiments of Attic LG vase painters. Many Orientalizing scenes portray violent conflicts between heroes and monsters: Herakles fighting Nessos or other centaurs, Perseus beheading Medusa, Bellerophon slaying the Chimaera, Odysseus and his companions blinding Polyphemos, or episodes from the Sack of Troy, as in the relief decoration on a coarse storage amphora found on Mykonos (Mykonos, Archaeol. Mus.). Sometimes personal attributes were added to identify individual deities or heroes, for example Apollo's lyre or Herakles' bow. In rare instances the artist painted names beside the figures, as on a Proto-Attic stand (*c.* mid-7th century BC; Berlin, Pergamonmus., A 42; destr.), on which the single word *Menela*[o]*s* identified a gathering of the Greek commanders at Troy. Another purpose of inscriptions was to identify the artist or potter (*see* §1(vi)(d) above).

The wide distribution of Orientalizing pottery outside the Aegean reflects the expansion of Greek trade and the establishment of more distant colonies, such as the shores of the north Aegean, the Sea of Marmara, the Black Sea and Libya. Corinth was the most prolific exporter to the western colonies, while from the late 7th century BC East Greek pottery predominated in the Black Sea, Cyprus, the Levantine coast and the Greek trading post of Naucratis in the Nile Delta. The absolute chronology of Orientalizing pottery is deduced from specimens found in datable contexts outside the Aegean. The foundations of Sicilian colonies from Gela (689 BC) to Selinus (*c.* 625 BC) supply clues for the dating of Proto-Corinthian, while for the East Greek styles a useful dating point is provided by finds from Meshad Hashavyahu in Palestine, occupied by Greek mercenaries only between 621 and 609 BC.

BIBLIOGRAPHY

R. M. Cook: *Greek Painted Pottery* (London, 1960, rev. 1972), pp. 41–160

K. Fittschen: *Untersuchungen zum Beginn der Sagendarstellungen bei den Griechen* (Berlin, 1969)

(ii) Proto-Corinthian. Corinth was the first centre to develop an Orientalizing style. Though its earliest products were the Cumae group of oinochoai (*c.* 720 BC), combining Late Geometric (LG) decoration on their necks with lotus and other bold floral designs on their bodies, the evolution of the style is best illustrated by the series of miniature aryballoi (h. seldom over 80 mm). The changes in their shape reflect the chronological subdivision of Proto-Corinthian into Early (EPC; *c.* 720–*c.* 690 BC), Middle (MPC; *c.* 690–*c.* 650 BC) and Late (LPC; *c.* 650–*c.* 640 BC): the aryballoi were globular in EPC; they became ovoid and increasingly attenuated in MPC; and they eventually assumed a slim piriform shape during LPC and the Transitional phase (*c.* 640–*c.* 625 BC) before Early Corinthian.

Figure drawing was very rare in Corinthian LG, but it often appeared on EPC globular aryballoi. Strutting cocks, grazing animals, fish and floral motifs were painted in an uneasy combination of silhouette, outline and reserve techniques, with occasional touches of incision. The limitations of this combination are apparent in the scene depicting a warrior and a mounted hunter on the only EPC aryballos to portray human figures (*c.* 700 BC; London, BM, 1969.12–15.1). In a scene only 35 mm high, even the finest painted line would be too heavy for anatomical details, especially of the human face.

Consequently the main figural zones on the bodies of the ovoid MPC aryballoi were rendered almost completely in the new Black-figure technique. Much finer detail could be obtained through incision on a full black silhouette, enlivened by touches of added red. Floral motifs, however, remained in outline and were relegated to the shoulder. Animal friezes often occupied the main zones, but the

88. Proto-Corinthian Orientalizing aryballos by the Ajax Painter with (top) a detail showing *?Herakles Attacking a Centaur*, First Black-figure style, h. 74 mm, MPC, *c.* 675 BC (Boston, MA, Museum of Fine Arts)

more ambitious hands began to experiment with mythical scenes. The most adventurous artist of the First Black-figure style (*c.* 690–*c.* 660 BC) was the Ajax Painter, named after an aryballos showing the hero falling on his sword (Berlin, Antikenmus., 3319). On another aryballos (Boston, MA, Mus. F.A., 95.12; see fig. 88) he depicted probably Herakles (or perhaps Zeus) using a firebrand to attack a centaur, while a puzzling scene on a third (Paris, Louvre, CA 617) is often explained as the rescue of the young Helen from Theseus and Peirithoos by her twin brothers Castor and Pollux. Although this painter's drawing is vigorous, his human figures are ill-proportioned, with arms and faces too large for the body; his compositions are episodic rather than unified, and the representation of movement is unconvincing.

The possibilities of Black-figure were also explored on larger MPC shapes, especially the oinochoe, the flat pyxis and the large kotyle. Three kotylai demonstrate growing mastery over the new technique. On the earliest, depicting a procession of horsemen (Aigina, Archaeol. Mus., 191), incision is virtually confined to the excessively large horses, but much more assured painting and incision distinguishes the 'Hound Kotyle' (London, BM, 1860.4–4.18) in the Second Black-figure style (*c.* 660–*c.* 650 BC): the animals are full of springy curves and latent energy, with touches of red on their necks. The third vessel is the finest example of the Second Black-figure style, the fragmentary 'Bellerophon Kotyle' (Aigina, Archaeol. Mus. 253), which depicts the Corinthian hero mounted on his winged horse Pegasus, confronting the fire-breathing Chimaera in a spacious and airy composition flanked by attendant sphinxes, all drawn with a graceful finesse of line never equalled in subsequent Corinthian vase painting.

The finest and most elaborately decorated aryballoi also belong to this decade, and despite their miniature scale some even incorporate subsidiary figural zones. The main

Black-figure scenes show a new mastery of movement and even give an impression of depth through the use of overlapping figures clearly separated by incision. The compositions are now much more unified, as though first sketched out on a flat surface; this, together with occasional experiments in polychromy, may imply that they were to some extent inspired by temple murals. Two masters of the Second Black-figure style were the Boston Painter and the MACMILLAN PAINTER. The Boston Painter's name-piece (Boston, MA, Mus. F.A., 95.11) shows a hero confronting an oriental lion-man, while a more mature work (Paris, Louvre, CA 931) has a grim hoplite duel as the main scene, and a mouth modelled as a human face in the Daidalic style of contemporary sculpture (*see* §IV, 2(i)(c) above). This painter achieves a monumental dignity on a miniature scale; his style is austere and restrained, with a minimum of incision and, unusually, no filling ornament. Very different was the approach of the Macmillan Painter, an exuberant virtuoso. His name vase, for example, the Macmillan Aryballos (London, BM, 1899.4–18.1; see fig. 89), has a Neo-Hittite lion-head mouth and three miniscule figural zones on its body, of which the main one depicts eighteen embattled hoplites bearing various blazons on their shields. The two tiny friezes below, a horse race and a fox hunt, are studies in rapid movement. On a larger scale, the LPC Chigi Jug (Rome, Villa Giulia, 22679) is a later work by the same hand, showing a scene of hoplites marching into battle, a second broad frieze combining a cavalcade, a lion hunt and a (fragmentary) representation of the Judgement of Paris, and another lively fox hunt below. The vase also displays the painter's experimental polychrome scheme: in addition to the usual black and red, two shades of brown were used for human flesh and body armour.

89. Proto-Corinthian Orientalizing aryballos by the Macmillan Painter, Second Black-figure style, h. 68 mm, MPC, *c.* 650 BC (London, British Museum)

The LPC phase was on the whole a time of consolidation rather than invention. New shapes included the baggy round-mouthed olpe and the drop-shaped alabastron; added white on black was used for some narrow animal zones, and a red-and-black scheme was used for incised tongue and scale patterns. Figural decoration rarely ventured beyond the animal frieze, which became increasingly stereotyped and perfunctory with the transition to Ripe Corinthian Black-figure style.

BIBLIOGRAPHY

H. G. G. Payne: *Protokorinthische Vasenmalerei* (1933), viii of *Bildergriechischer Vasen*, ed. J. D. Beazley and P. Jacobsthal (Berlin, 1930–)

T. J. Dunbabin and M. Robertson: 'Some Protocorinthian Vase-painters', *Annu. Brit. Sch. Athens*, xlviii (1953), pp. 172–81

T. J. Dunbabin: *Protocorinthian Pottery* (1962), ii of *Perachora*, ed. T. J. Dunbabin (Oxford, 1940–), pp. 4–132

J. L. Benson: 'Middle Protocorinthian Periodization', *Corinthiaca: Studies in Honour of D. A. Amyx* (Columbia, MO, 1986), pp. 97–106

D. A. Amyx: *Corinthian Vase-painting of the Archaic Period*, 3 vols (Berkeley, 1988)

(iii) Proto-Attic. Unlike Corinth, Athens had a firmly established Late Geometric (LG) figural style but little first-hand acquaintance with Near Eastern art. Consequently, the Proto-Attic style appeared later than the Proto-Corinthian and involved a gradual modification of the Geometric tradition, perhaps only under indirect oriental influence. It is divided into Early (EPA; *c.* 700–*c.* 670 BC), Middle (MPA; *c.* 670–*c.* 630 BC) and Late (LPA; *c.* 630–*c.* 600 BC) phases. The finest painting occurs on large vessels that seem to have been produced mainly for aristocratic burials. Outline drawing was introduced in EPA, chiefly for facial features; white was added to the usual colour scheme in MPA; little use was made of incision until LPA when, under Corinthian influence, a true Black-figure technique was developed.

The pioneer of Proto-Attic vase painting was the ANALATOS PAINTER, whose style was inspired by the latest products of the LG Athens 894 workshop (*see* §3(ii) above). The Analatos Painter's name vase is a hydria (*c.* 700 BC; Athens, N. Archaeol. Mus., 313) from Analatos, near Athens, which is decorated with Orientalizing plant motifs and heraldic lions; the dancing men and women on the neck are still in silhouette, but their features are accentuated in an un-Geometric manner. Throughout the next two decades the Analatos Painter experimented with outline faces and more fluent renderings of the human body than was achieved in Geometric vase painting. Typical of his mature style are squarish faces with over-emphasized features. Most EPA artists, however, clung more tenaciously to Geometric conventions. The Mesogeia Painter developed a lively if rough figural style derived from that of the Analatos Painter, but he crammed his backgrounds with Sub-Geometric filling ornament. Two other artists retained the angular contours of Geometric figure drawing: the N Painter, who introduced the cock into the repertory, is named after his preferred filling ornament, while the Passas Painter's best-known amphora (New York, Met., 21.88.18) shows a commanding figure with robe, sceptre and eagle, perhaps an early representation of Zeus. Around 680 BC the Passas Painter and the Analatos Painter collaborated in decorating two elaborate cauldrons with high stands for an aristocratic funeral (Mainz, Johannes Gutenberg-U., 153 and 156) which explored the possibilities of adding white and red to the colour scheme. White was preferred by these early artists and often used for subsidiary details on the latest EPA works of the 670s BC.

By MPA the Geometric heritage had been forgotten. The old themes of funerals, rows of dancers and chariot processions gave place to scenes of dynamic action, especially hoplite battles and mythical combats. White paint was used as much as black, and the combination—the Black-and-white style—could produce effective contrasts, as on a stand (Berlin, Antikenmus., A 40) with silhouetted warriors wearing white armour. Without incision, however, there could be confusion when bodies overlapped, as in two scenes showing Herakles rescuing Deianeira from the centaur Nessos, one on a stand (Athens, N. Archaeol. Mus.), the other on an amphora (New York, Met., 11.210.1). Both works are typical of a Wild style early in MPA, also remarkable for curious disparities in the scale of both figures and subsidiary motifs. Nevertheless, mastery of this new Black-and-white style was soon achieved by the POLYPHEMOS PAINTER and the RAM JUG PAINTER, though they were chary of overlapping figures and restrained in their choice of filling ornaments; the features of their outlined human faces assumed more naturalistic proportions. Rounded crowns, receding foreheads and bull necks are characteristic of the Polyphemos Painter, as in the eponymous scene on his amphora (Eleusis Mus.) showing the giant being blinded (see fig. 90, top register), whereas squarer faces, more in the tradition of the Analatos Painter, with long curved eyebrows and aquiline noses, were preferred by the Ram Jug Painter.

Soon after 650 BC a short-lived polychrome style using up to six colours was applied to some funerary vessels; but the main development in MPA was the gradual replacement of the Black-and-white style by an incised Black-figure technique derived from Proto-Corinthian pottery and accompanied by the use of red instead of white paint for subsidiary details. The fragmentary Kynosarges Amphora (*c.* 640 BC; Athens, N. Archaeol. Mus., 14497) combines Black-figure animal friezes, human scenes still in outline and luxuriant filling ornament everywhere; in the 630s BC the amphorae of the Pair Painter likewise combine opposed pairs of animal *protomes* in Black-figure with elaborate spirals of Cycladic origin.

Full Black-figure was achieved during LPA, and though the technique had first been perfected for miniature Corinthian work, it was now employed on grandiose Attic funerary vessels. Majestic lions and sirens were favourite subjects; filling ornament, sparser than before, was dominated by the Corinthian rosette, dotted or incised. Two important new shapes appeared: the kotyle krater, an

90. Proto-Attic Orientalizing amphora by the Polyphemos Painter, h. 1.42 m, MPA, *c.* 660 BC (Eleusis, Eleusis Museum)

enlargement of the lipless kotyle, and the one-piece amphora, often decorated with *protomes* of women or horses inside reserved panels. A Chimaera scene on a fragmentary kotyle krater (Athens, Kerameikos Mus., 154) may be an early work by the NETTOS PAINTER, the outstanding artist of this phase, who by the end of his career (*c.* 600 BC) had helped to lay the foundations of the Attic Black-figure style (*see* §5(ii) below).

Apart from some sparsely decorated wine amphorae, Proto-Attic pottery was rarely exported beyond immediate neighbours. The abundance of MPA finds on Aigina, together with the Aiginetan letter forms of the inscription *Menela*[o]*s* on a Proto-Attic stand (*see* §(i) above), have prompted the suggestion that Aigina, not Athens, was the chief centre for the MPA Black-and-white style.

BIBLIOGRAPHY

J. M. Cook: 'Protoattic Pottery', *Annu. Brit. Sch. Athens*, xxxv (1934–5), pp. 165–219

K. Kübler: *Altattische Malerei* (Tübingen, 1950)

J. D. Beazley: *The Development of Attic Black Figure* (Berkeley, 1951), pp. 1–16

K. Kübler: *Die Nekropole des späten 8. bis frühen 6. Jahrhunderts* (1959), vi/1 of *Kerameikos: Ergebnisse der Ausgrabungen* (Berlin, 1939–)

E. T. H. Brann: *Late Geometric and Protoattic Pottery* (1962), viii of *The Athenian Agora* (Princeton, 1953–)

S. Papaspyridi-Karouzou: *Angeia tes Anagyrountos* [Pottery from Anagyrous] (Athens, 1963)

S. P. Morris: *The Black and White Style: Athens and Aigina in the Orientalizing Period* (New Haven, 1984)

NICOLAS COLDSTREAM

(iv) Other areas. At Corinth the Orientalizing style had established itself by the end of the 8th century BC, and within a generation or two most other local schools were beginning to adopt it, though not regularly copying Corinthian models. Of these schools the Cretan was the earliest, indeed about as early as Corinthian; but though it lasted around a century it was more wayward than progressive, and invention was mainly restricted to forms of vegetable and abstract ornament. Birds occur fairly frequently, often in forms of pretty fantasy, notably with multiple heads. Animal and human figures are rare but may be adventurous. A spectacular early group of vases, perhaps peculiar to Knossos, is that of the so-called Polychrome pithoi, which have a white slip and bright red and indigo painted decoration; since both slip and paint wore badly, they were probably only for mortuary use.

In the Peloponnese, Argos had a robust Geometric school and admitted Orientalizing novelties reluctantly, but an impressive Orientalizing scene of the blinding of Polyphemos occurs on an exceptional polychrome krater (660s BC; Argos, Archaeol. Mus.). Presumably proximity to Corinth was fatal. There may, though, be Argive influence on the early 7th-century BC Fusco kraters of Syracuse, with their loose Orientalizing ornament and, in one instance, creditable animals; and a little later a more ambitious workshop, known from vases found at Megara Hyblaea, also in Sicily, attempted bolder figural scenes in a polychrome technique. However, in the Greek West as well, no independent new style took root.

In Lakonia, Orientalizing ornament became common early in the 7th century BC (Lakonian I): most was abstract, but some unpretentious little Lakonian I Fine ware pots (*c.* 650–*c.* 625 BC) bore rows of engagingly misshapen animals, and by the end of the century a Black-figure style had developed. Lakonian usually has a cream slip over a body fired pinkish to brown. Other finds suggest that some potters in the western Peloponnese experimented with the Orientalizing style but did not persevere.

Boiotian pottery was usually a debased version of that produced by its neighbours Athens, Corinth and Euboia. The first large group of Orientalizing vases, mainly big amphorae with tall conical feet, flaunt bands of thick zigzags, and their principal decoration, vegetable or animal, is often clumsily composed. This group may have continued throughout the 7th century BC or even longer. More remarkable is the 'Bird cup' group (*c.* 575–*c.* 500 BC), clumsy dishes, sometimes with a tall foot, and slightly less clumsy kantharoi; the decoration consists largely of flying birds and palmettes, generously coloured with red and later also yellow paint on a creamy (or later white) slip and drawn in a folksy style that is surprising for the period. In Euboia an Orientalizing group of big amphorae parallels those from Boiotia but are of better quality; and at Eretria a few artists towards the end of the 7th century BC misguidedly attempted human figures, though even these compare well with the ostensibly Black-figure work of the early 6th.

In the Cyclades the Orientalizing style was more welcomed, though only one school survived long. Lack of contextual information and close stylistic comparison makes dating and attribution to particular islands hazardous. The Ad group (?*c.* 700–*c.* 675 BC), now usually assigned to Paros, is a curious but enjoyable parody of Geometric. It is best represented by its broad amphorae, though other shapes occur. The neck usually depicts an elongated horse, which may be winged, the shoulder a tableau of animals, and the rest of the body carries bands of coarse ornament; often a creamy slip is used. Probably contemporary, but more innovative, is the Heraldic group, perhaps from Naxos. Its narrow amphorae have fronts bearing sinuous animals on the neck and below the shoulder, framed by ornament that is sometimes Orientalizing, while their backs are covered with rough scrawling, and the lower part of the body is banded; again a creamy slip is usual. Much more numerous is the Linear Island group (early to ?mid-7th century BC); these mostly largish amphorae are staider in style and less provincial than their counterparts in Euboia and Boiotia. Decoration is concentrated on the upper part and consists of a few bold ornaments and some occasionally imaginative Orientalizing birds and beasts in panels on the shoulder. Except for the Linear Island vases, these and other early Orientalizing groups seem to be the products of independent workshops rather than regional schools, too individual to consolidate into a tradition, unless 'Melian' vases were descendants of the Ad group. The 'Melian' group was the longest-lived and the most successful of the Cycladic ventures. The vases, usually assigned to Paros or Melos (or both) between the mid-7th century BC and the early 6th, usually took the form of amphorae, hydriai and plates. The staple decoration consists of female heads, animals and big volutes, with gaudily coarse ornaments covering the rest of the pot. There are also some big amphorae with high feet, which have ineptly ambitious figural scenes in a polychrome technique. 'Melian' works are generally dull and unoriginal, borrowing from the East Greek Wild Goat style (see below) and increasingly from Corinthian.

East Greek Orientalizing had a long and mainly undistinguished existence, and despite the extent of the region, comprising all the west coast of Turkey and the islands offshore, the style was remarkably uniform. Unluckily, though there has been much excavation, finds have been patchy and often inadequately published: little is known of important cities such as Miletos, Smyrna and Phokaia, and there is disagreement over local schools and dating. Producers on Lesbos and to some extent mainland Aeolis adhered to the traditional, usually undecorated, grey Bucchero ware, but elsewhere most larger pots were made of a coarsish clay with a whitish slip, while cups were of finer clay and, except on Chios, were unslipped, following normal Geometric practice. During the 7th century BC the favourite type of cup was the 'Bird bowl', a shallow, two-handled vessel with a low foot, decorated with a neat Geometric-style bird in a panel flanked by lozenges. About the end of the century this formula was replaced by a loose scatter of Orientalizing ornaments, most often dotted rosettes, and the execution became coarser. Clay analysis has revealed them to be mainly north Ionian, particularly from Klazomenai. A rarer form was the rather taller Vroulian cup, which was produced from *c.* 600 BC to after 550 BC, probably on Rhodes, and was among the most elegant of all Greek vases. Specimens were covered

91. East Greek Orientalizing oinochoe, Middle Wild Goat style, h. 360 mm, *c.* 625–*c.* 600 BC (London, British Museum)

inside and out with blackish paint and decorated with incised motifs, notably palmettes and lotuses, picked out in red paint. There are also innumerable cups decorated with simple bands of paint, which are used by the less wary as evidence of Ionian influence in Etruria.

The staple East Greek Orientalizing style has had various names, but now is most often known as the Wild Goat style. Graves on Rhodes have provided accurate dates for specimens from the last quarter of the 7th century BC, and judging by the extent of stylistic development and the paucity of earlier pieces that have been found, the style seems not to have arisen until *c.* 650 BC, being preceded by some Sub-Geometric and experimental Orientalizing, of which tantalizing scraps remain. After a little diversification the Wild Goat style settled into a routine—decorative but monotonous and increasingly arid. Largish oinochoai are the most frequent shape in the Rhodian burials, but dinoi, dishes and plates were also common, as, in the north, were amphorae. The principal decoration usually consists of animals, either filing round the body or grouped on the shoulders: goats occur most frequently, but the repertory includes spotted deer, geese, sphinxes, griffins and, less often, dogs and felines, all surrounded by well-spaced filling ornaments. On subordinate fields large versions of lotus flower and bud are characteristic. Heads and anatomical details are generally reserved; and purple was soon used to enliven the dark paint over the whitish slip. Typical of this Middle Wild Goat period is an oinochoe in London (*c.* 625–*c.* 600 BC; BM, 67.5–8.928; see fig. 91). Clay analyses suggest that early production was dominated by south Ionia and primarily by Miletos. But around 600 BC north Ionian workshops adopted from Corinth the Black-figure technique, with its animal forms and often its filling ornament, while retaining the old reserving technique, frequently using both—in different fields—on the same pot. Coarse though they were, vases in this Late Wild Goat style were exported in greater numbers than their south Ionian precursors, perhaps simply because there was a wider market. The Late style is usually said to have ended in the 570s BC, but that may be too early, since in its reserving version it survived with minor modifications on Klazomenian sarcophagi well into the 5th century BC.

Contemporary developments in south Ionia are obscure, but it seems unlikely that vase painters adopted the Black-figure technique, since around the 560s BC a new reserving style appeared there, again, according to clay analysis, at Miletos. This, usually called the Fikellura style (named after the site in Rhodes), is closer to the Middle Wild Goat style than to the Late, though its practitioners abandoned the outlining of heads and showed greater originality. The commonest shape is a squat amphora (e.g. London, BM, 61.4–25.47; see fig. 92); the decorative scheme ranges from close bands of ornament to a single figure in an empty field. Animals occur frequently, as do human figures, often revellers. Typical ornaments include crescents, simplified lotus flowers and buds and thick

92. South Ionian Orientalizing amphora, Fikellura style, h. 290 mm, from Rhodes, *c.* 540 BC (London, British Museum)

volutes, which may spread all round the body. The quality of workmanship is very uneven, even on the same pot, but Fikellura continued to be the liveliest of East Greek Orientalizing styles until the end of the 6th century BC, when it flagged and died out.

The pottery of Chios, recognizable by its very white slip, developed differently. Its best-known shape, the 'chalice', is a conical cup later supported on a conical or near-conical foot. In the 7th century BC a fairly orthodox if rather clumsy variant of the Wild Goat style was current. In the 6th century BC this reserving style continued, notably on chalices bearing a single sphinx or animal or occasionally a human figure, and no longer encumbered by filling ornaments. More elaborate scenes of human action, sometimes in a polychrome technique, are featured in the Grand style of *c.* 575–*c.* 550 BC; at about the same time and a little earlier a form of Black-figure became popular, with rows of lions, sphinxes or revellers, generally depicted in a perfunctory Corinthianizing style. There may have been Chian workshops at Naukratis (particularly since Grand style vases have been found there but not yet in Chios), though the clay seems to be uniform. Imitation, sometimes inventive, is more certain on Thasos.

Pottery in the East Greek style was also produced in the adjoining non-Greek areas of Caria and Lydia. Carian specimens exhibit only debasement of its models, but Lydia had its own ceramic traditions, and its style was more fanciful. Elsewhere East Greek pottery influenced only 'Melian' vases.

BIBLIOGRAPHY

E. Pfuhl: 'Der archaische Friedhof am Stadtberge von Thera', *Mitt: Dt. Archäol. Inst.: Athen. Abt.*, xxviii (1903), pp. 1–288, esp. pp. 183–93
H. G. G. Payne: 'Early Greek Vases from Knossos', *Annu. Brit. Sch. Athens*, xxix (1927–8), pp. 224–98, esp. pp. 277–98
R. M. Cook: 'Fikellura Pottery', *Annu. Brit. Sch. Athens*, xxxiv (1933–4), pp. 1–98
E. A. Lane: 'Lakonian Vase Painting', *Annu. Brit. Sch. Athens*, xxxiv (1933–4), pp. 99–189, esp. pp. 107–21
C. Dugas and C. Rhomaios: *Les Vases préhelléniques et géométriques* (1934), xv of *Exploration archéologique de Délos* (Paris, 1909–), pls 20–25
C. Dugas: *Les Vases orientalisants de style non mélien* (1935), xvii of *Exploration archéologique de Délos* (Paris, 1909–)
J. Boardman: 'Pottery from Eretria', *Annu. Brit. Sch. Athens*, xlvii (1952), pp. 1–48
J. K. Brock: *Fortetsa: Early Greek Tombs near Knossos*, Brit. Sch. Athens, Suppl. Paper no. 2 (Cambridge, 1956)
R. M. Cook: *Greek Painted Pottery* (London, 1960, rev. 1972)
C. Kardara: *Rhodiake angeiographia* [Rhodian vase painting] (Athens, 1963)
J. Boardman: *Excavations in Chios, 1952–1955: Greek Emporio* (London, 1967)
H. Walter: *Frühe samische Gefässe* (1968), v of *Samos* (Bonn, 1961–)
E. Walther-Karydi: *Samische Gefässe des 6. Jahrhunderts v. Chr.* (1973), vi/1 of *Samos* (Bonn, 1961–)
A. Ruckert: 'Frühe Keramik Boötiens, *Ant. Kst*, x (1976) [suppl. issue]
B. Schmalz: 'Zur Chronologie der böotischen Vogelschalen', *Marburger Winckelmann-Programm, 1977–8*, pp. 21–60
P. Dupont: 'Classification et détermination de provenance des céramiques grecques orientales archaïques d'Istros: Rapport préliminaire', *Dacia*, n. s., xxvii (1983), pp. 19–43
P. Zapheiropoulou: *Problemata tes Meliakes angeographias* [Problems relating to Melian vase painting] (Athens, 1985)
G. P. Schaus: 'Two Fikellura Vase Painters', *Annu. Brit. Sch. Athens*, lxxxi (1986), pp. 251–95
R. M. Cook: *East Greek Pottery* (London, 1996)

R. M. COOK

5. BLACK-FIGURE. Ancient Greek Black-figure vase painting is a silhouette technique in which black glaze is applied to the surface of the vase and enlivened by incision as well as accessory red and white. Vase painters at Corinth during the early 7th century BC were probably the first to incise lines through black glaze, a decorative approach very likely inspired by metalwork. From *c.* 620 to *c.* 480 BC, during the middle and late Archaic period, artists working there and in several other regions of the Greek world decorated vases in the Black-figure technique. Each of these fabrics takes its name from the region or city that produced it, with the exception of Chalcidian, which is named after inscriptions in the Chalcidian alphabet on many of the vases. The length of time these different fabrics were produced varied considerably, with Attic having the longest lifespan and the greatest quantity of surviving pieces.

(i) Corinthian. (ii) Attic. (iii) Lakonian. (iv) Boiotian. (v) East Greek and islands. (vi) Chalcidian. (vii) Caeretan. (viii) Euboian.

(i) Corinthian. During the 7th century Corinth was an especially active commercial centre, and from *c.* 625 to *c.* 580 BC it was the most productive ceramic centre in Greece. Corinthian vases are mostly small vessels, especially alabastra and aryballoi, and they are found in all areas of the Greek world. The figural decoration usually consists of animal friezes, horsemen or warriors. The rise of the rival Attic ceramic industry by *c.* 580 BC led Corinthian artists to produce larger shapes, especially column kraters and amphorae, which were often decorated with specific mythological themes. They also disguised the yellow Corinthian clay with a covering of red slip so that the finished products appeared to be direct imitations of Attic wares. Nevertheless, Attic vases soon dominated the market, and by *c.* 550 BC Corinthian Black-figure had declined steadily, although production of small vases, decorated just with ornament, continued.

□

(a) Introduction. Corinthian Black-figure vase painting is still usually classified in terms of the three stylistic periods defined by H. G. G. Payne: Early (EC; *c.* 625–*c.* 600 BC), Middle (MC; *c.* 600–*c.* 575 BC) and Late (LC; *c.* 575–*c.* 425 BC). Late Corinthian is subdivided by some scholars into two phases and by others into three: the stylistic characteristics of LC I (*c.* 575–*c.* 550 BC) are fairly well agreed on, but those distinguishing LC II and III (*c.* 550–*c.* 425 BC) are not. Since Payne's work scholars have concentrated primarily on identifying the hands of individual painters and workshops by tracing the influence of one painter on another. More than 190 painters have been distinguished, comprising around 60 EC, 95 MC and 60 LC artists; about 20% of these were active in more than one period. Only two painters, Chares of Lindos and Timonidas, signed their vases; the names of a few others are known from literary sources.

Transitions from one period to another were so gradual that many vases cannot be classified with certainty. Changes in style were accompanied by changes in vase shapes, and workshops usually specialized in manufacturing either small scent bottles or a selection of the larger vessels. Some painters seem to have decorated only one or two types of vase. The decoration is largely the same as that on Proto-Corinthian vases (*see* §4(ii) above).

(b) Early. Animal friezes developed from those of the Proto-Corinthian Transitional phase (*see* §4(ii) above). The new style is signalled by the widespread use of cross-incised rosette filling motifs, and its development is most easily followed by noting the evolution in the character and placement of these elements. Early forms are simply and neatly drawn and evenly but sparsely distributed in the field, as on several alabastra (St Petersburg, Hermitage; Brussels, Mus. Royaux A. & Hist., A51 and A52).

Soon the more innovative painters sought new effects and a new balance of proportions. They created new filling motifs, producing stronger contrasts between dark and light areas: some EC vases are quite baroque in this respect (e.g. an alabastron at U. Würzburg, Wagner-Mus., 254). Animals were made larger in relation to their friezes and friezes taller in relation to their vases. These changes probably reflect not only artistic but also economic factors, since vase paintings with larger animals and friezes could be made more quickly. But many painters resisted the pressure to sacrifice work of high quality and the pursuit of new interests to increased production. The variety of animals and filling ornaments was in fact greater than ever: the Dodwell Painter, for example, used at least 50 different filling ornaments. Panthers and goats became more numerous, lions and bulls rarer, and symmetrical compositions with pairs of animals flanking floral centrepieces occurred more frequently, as on the kotyle pyxis by the Royal Library Painter (*c.* 620–*c.* 600 BC; Brussels, Bib. Royale Albert 1er; see fig. 93). A hallmark of this painter is the form of the rosette just above the rear inner leg of the panther. The figures were also drawn in greater detail than before and embellished more often with touches of red and white. The decoration of different parts of vases became systematized, for example with petals on the mouthplates of aryballoi and rays at the bases of kotylai, though there were characteristic variations from workshop to workshop.

The Figure style of EC displays more naturalism than its Proto-Corinthian forerunner. Eyes and noses are smaller, rounder and more correctly related to each other and to the face; waves of hair are looser and less artificially arranged; figures are more slender. At the beginning of the period, although narrative scenes occur, human figures are usually merely elements in a frieze alongside the animals (e.g. aryballos; Rhodes, Archaeol. Mus., 13008). Increasingly, however, groups of human figures formed scenes in the centres of friezes, while the animals either appeared to be spectators or entirely disappeared. Towards the end of the period large narrative scenes appeared on column kraters, a new shape of vase (e.g. Paris, Louvre, E 635). The use of each side of a large vase for a single important figural composition was a momentous development in Greek vase painting. Most scholars look to Athens for the origins of monumental Black-figure painting, although the column krater is generally agreed to be a Corinthian invention. A significant consequence of this innovation was the relegation of the animal frieze to a subordinate position on these kraters.

(c) Middle. The period is one of transition for the Animal style. At first painters followed the trends of EC by continuing to invent new animal poses and combinations of animals and floral centrepieces, but there was less experimentation with the filling ornaments, which are usually either large and incised or small and unincised; the crowded fields and varied forms typical of some phases of EC are rarer. There was a growing tendency to use dots to echo the contours of animals; single rows of unincised dots along the backs of goats and deer are almost a trademark of the period. Painters yielded increasingly to the pressures of mass production and enlarged their animals to fill friezes more quickly; some succeeded with only two.

93. Corinthian Black-figure kotyle pyxis by the Royal Library Painter, h. 264 mm, EC, *c.* 620–*c.* 600 BC (Brussels, Bibliothèque Royale Albert 1er)

Later in the period painters showed interest in new effects that, fully developed, became characteristic of the LC I period. They favoured highly symmetrical compositions, choosing proportions and arrangements with a view to greater decorative effect. Their routine work shows that they had lost interest in the filling motifs and subsidiary ornamentation: the petals on the mouthplates of aryballoi, for example, were replaced by more quickly drawn groups of bands.

The greatest works of the period were those with human figures, skilfully creating exquisitely cadenced patterns of movement and serene figures of noble bearing and elegant proportions. Some painters sought greater naturalism in anatomical details and proportions, while others pursued elegance through attenuation of form and refinement of line, seen at its extreme in the long-legged horses on a krater by the Detroit Painter (New York, Met. 27.116). The repertory of narrative scenes was extended and improved by the use of inscriptions and props such as furniture, architecture and landscape elements. A red slip was usually applied to the background, and figures were often painted largely in white, creating a very colourful effect (e.g. krater; Paris, Louvre, E 629).

(d) Late. In LC I the Animal style friezes display, in fully realized form, the tendencies begun in MC. In their routine work, which was rather lifeless, painters neglected incision,

94. Corinthian Black-figure column krater showing the *Departure of a Warrior*, h. 267 mm, LC I, *c.* 575 BC (Berlin, Antikenmuseum)

often content to sketch or suggest details, and skimped or abandoned filling ornament. On their better work, however, which included some exquisite pieces, the more innovative artists cultivated a taste for large elaborate ornaments arranged in formal patterns, concentrating on the decorative, the symmetrical and the colourful at the expense of variety and animation. They drew animals with the attenuated proportions and elegant calligraphic lines developed for the human-figure scenes (e.g. Copenhagen, Nmus., 1630, 1631) and adopted from the Figure style the colourful scheme of red ground with large areas of white. Despite a general decline in ceramic production at Corinth after the mid-6th century BC, the Figure style continued to flourish. Painters developed greater facility in representing action, a good example being the figured frieze on a column krater showing the *Departure of a Warrior* (Berlin, Antikenmus., 1959.1; see fig. 94). They exploited the colourful combinations of the red ground, white figures and black silhouettes, with details picked out in red.

During LC II and III the production of Black-figure vases at Corinth declined. Those made are of two types. A number of vases from *c.* 525 to *c.* 475 BC were decorated in close imitation of Attic Black-figure ware, some of excellent quality. But some painters continued to decorate vases in a graceless Animal style with rough silhouettes and slapdash incision. The filling ornament, though meagre, is sometimes distinctive, and a few vases have an engaging charm, though most are routine works. Fragments from a well (*c.* 450–*c.* 410 BC) provide the latest evidence for Black-figure production at Corinth.

BIBLIOGRAPHY

H. G. G. Payne: *Necrocorinthia: A Study of Corinthian Art in the Archaic Period* (Oxford, 1931)

M. T. Campbell: 'A Well of the Black-figured Period at Corinth', *Hesperia*, vii (1938), pp. 557–611

D. A. Amyx: 'A Corinthian Kotyle in Mainz', *Jb. Ger. Zentmus. Mainz*, vi (1959), pp. 101–9

P. Lawrence: 'The Corinthian Chimaera Painter', *Amer. J. Archaeol.*, lxiii (1959), pp. 349–63

D. A. Amyx: 'The Medallion Painter', *Amer. J. Archaeol.*, lxv (1961), pp. 1–15

——: 'The Honolulu Painter and the "Delicate Style"', *Ant. Kst*, v (1962), pp. 3–8

T. J. Dunbabin, ed.: *Perachora: The Sanctuaries of Hera Akraia and Limenia*, ii (Oxford, 1962)

P. Lawrence: 'Notes on the Chimaera Group', *Amer. J. Archaeol.*, lxvi (1962), pp. 185–7

J. L. Benson: 'The Laurion Painter', *Oudhdknd. Meded. Rijksmus. Ouden Leiden*, xlvi (1965), pp. 76–86

D. A. Amyx: 'Observations on the Warrior Group', *CA Stud. Class. Ant.*, ii (1969), pp. 1–25

J. L. Benson: 'The Three Maidens Group', *Amer. J. Archaeol.*, lxxiii (1969), pp. 109–22

E. G. Pemberton: 'The Vrysoula Classical Deposit from Ancient Corinth', *Hesperia*, xxxix (1970), pp. 265–307

J. L. Benson: 'A Floral Master of the Chimaera Group: The Otterlo Painter', *Ant. Kst*, xiv (1971), pp. 13–24

D. A. Amyx and P. Lawrence: *Archaic Corinthian Pottery and the Anaploga Well* (1975), vii/2 of *Corinth: Results of the Excavations Conducted by the American School of Classical Studies at Athens* (Princeton, 1932–)

C. W. Neeft: 'The Dolphin Painter and his Workshop', *Bull. Ant. Besch.*, lii–liii (1977–8), pp. 133–58

M. Blomberg: *Observations on the Dodwell Painter* (Stockholm, 1983)

A. N. Stillwell, J. L. Benson and others: *The Potters Quarter: The Pottery* (1984), xv/3 of *Corinth: Results of the Excavations Conducted by the American School of Classical Studies at Athens* (Princeton, 1932–)

D. A. Amyx: *Corinthian Vase-painting of the Archaic Period*, 3 vols (Berkeley, 1991)

C. W. Neeft: *Addenda et corrigenda to D. A. Amyx, 'Corinthian Vase-painting in the Archaic Period*, Allard Pierson series (Scripta Minora), iii (Amsterdam, 1991)

MARY BLOMBERG

(ii) Attic. During the late 7th century BC Attic artists began to decorate vases in the incised Black-figure technique they had learnt from their Corinthian colleagues, and by the second quarter of the 6th century BC Attic Black-figure was the leading fabric in Greek ceramics. By *c.* 480 BC production of this technique had ceased, except for Panathenaic amphorae awarded as prizes in the Panathenaic games, which lasted until late in the Roman era. Many Attic vases are signed by potters and painters, and these provide the starting-points around which unsigned vases may be grouped. In turn, analysis of the drawing provides a chronological framework into which new finds may be fitted. Attic Black Figure is found in all areas of the Greek world, but the largest quantity comes from Etruscan tombs. Of all the Black-figure fabrics, Attic has the greatest variety of shapes and sizes, ranging from impressive monumental vases that marked tombs to miniature vessels that may have been toys for young children. Attic Black-figure exhibits for the most part a restrained effect, sometimes with drawing that is understated and sober, and in the case of true masterpieces the result is one of brilliant elegance. Almost from the beginning, the Attic Black-figure artist, more than any other, was interested in depicting mythological scenes from the various poems that comprised his literary heritage. The result is a rich and imaginative repertory of subjects.

(a) *c.* 625–*c.* 600 BC. (b) *c.* 600–*c.* 560 BC. (c) *c.* 560–*c.* 520 BC. (d) *c.* 520–*c.* 480 BC.

(a) c. *625*–c. *600* BC. Of the first generation of Attic Black-figure vase painters, the NETTOS PAINTER is the only one whose work has survived in sufficient quantity to reconstruct his artistic personality. He takes his name from the scene on a neck amphora (Athens, N. Archaeol. Mus., 1002; see fig. 95) showing *Herakles Slaying Nessos*. His contemporaries, such as the Painter of Berlin A 34 (formerly called the Woman Painter), the Piraeus Painter,

95. Attic Black-figure neck amphora by the Nettos Painter (detail): *Herakles Slaying Nessos*, h. 1.2 m, *c.* 625–*c.* 600 BC (Athens, National Archaeological Museum)

the Bellerophon Painter and the Lion Painter, have left far fewer vases, but, taken together, their works give a good idea of the activity in the Athenian Kerameikos (potters' quarter) during the last quarter of the 7th century BC. All of them preferred to decorate large funerary vessels (amphorae or kraters), allowing their figures to spread out over the surface as much as possible, containing them only with zones of ornament that articulated the various parts of the vase (neck, shoulder etc). The scenes themselves often depict monsters such as sirens and sphinxes, savage beasts such as lions, or occasionally mythological events, especially Bellerophon confronting the Chimaera and Perseus chased by the Gorgons, besides Herakles slaying Nessos.

(b) c. *600*–c. *560* BC. At the start of the 6th century BC there was a change in direction away from the large and monumental towards small shapes, especially oinochoai and lekythoi. Large vessels continued to be made, but their surfaces were divided into ornamental and figured friezes, a good example being the name-piece (dinos with stand; Paris, Louvre, E 874) of the GORGON PAINTER. He is the first known artist to take up the challenge of decorating smaller vessels, and he may have helped to initiate the splendid series of 'Horse-head amphorae' (*c.* 600–*c.* 550 BC). These are one-piece amphorae with a horse's head set in a panel on each side; they may have been intended for funerary use.

Contemporary with the later works of the Gorgon Painter are those of the Komast group, the KX Painter and the KY Painter (for Komast X and Komast Y respectively) as well as those painting in their manner. These were the first Attic painters to be influenced directly and primarily by Corinthian vase painting, which was still at its zenith. From Corinth they introduced the column krater and the komast cup and borrowed the komast dancer, a cheerful, bulky reveller that gives the group its name. Animal friezes, borrowed earlier from Corinth by the Nettos Painter for his lekanides, were also popular with painters of the Komast group. Occasionally a human figure or a mythological theme was inserted into the frieze, such as *Achilles Receiving his Armour*, which may be depicted on a lekanis (Rhodes, Archaeol. Mus., 5008).

SOPHILOS is the first Attic vase painter whose name is known from signatures; two vases may bear his potting signature as well. His colourful, exuberant style is demonstrated nowhere better than in the mythological scenes comprising his mature work (*c.* 580 BC). Sophilos continued the tradition of setting his human figures in friezes, and he painted many animal friezes, but his main contribution to Attic Black-figure was his imaginative treatment of mythological subjects, for he was the first Attic vase painter to be genuinely interested in narrative. He was also the first to identify his figures by inscription; at this early date most artists had not yet learnt how to distinguish their figures by visual attributes. A fragment of a dinos or lebes (Athens, N. Archaeol. Mus., 15499) illustrates both innovations: it depicts the *Funeral Games of Patroklos* (the scene is labelled on the vase) with its excited crowd cheering from the grandstand. Other good examples include the dignified procession of guests at the *Marriage of Peleus and Thetis* on a dinos (Athens, Acropolis Mus., 587; with stand, London, BM, 1971.11–1.1; see fig. 96) and the fierce fight between Herakles and the Centaurs on fragments of a krater or kettle (Athens, N. Archaeol. Mus., 15918, 15492). These are big, ambitious scenes that pave the way for the grand narratives of the second and third quarters of the 6th century BC.

Less able contemporaries of the Gorgon Painter, the Komast group and Sophilos include the Panther Painter, the Kerameikos Painter, painters from the Group of the Dresden Lekanis, and the Polos Painter, whose career may have extended beyond 550 BC. In the early years of the 6th century BC Attic pottery was exported for the first time, chiefly to Greek colonies such as Naukratis and later to Etruria. This is well demonstrated by the poorly painted and turned pots of the Polos Painter, which seem to turn up everywhere.

Sophilos' style was continued by KLEITIAS, who may have been his pupil. Kleitias, one of the undisputed masters of Attic Black-figure, always signed as painter in collaboration with the potter Ergotimos. He preferred to decorate

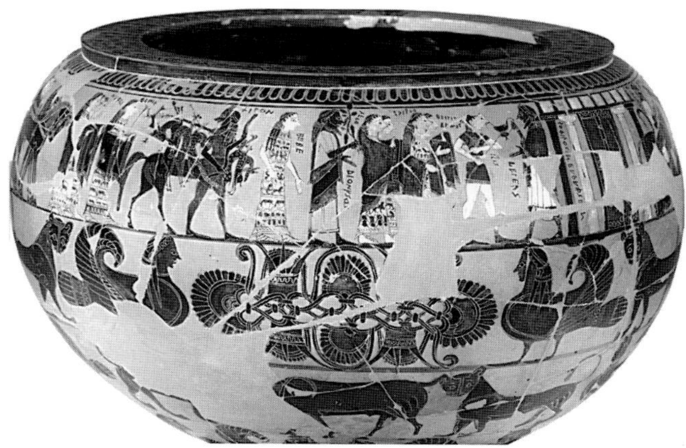

96. Attic Black-figure dinos by Sophilos (detail): *Marriage of Peleus and Thetis*, h. 710 mm, *c.* 600–*c.* 560 BC (London, British Museum)

97. Attic Black-figure volute krater (the François Vase) by Kleitias and Ergotimos, h. 660 mm, *c.* 600–*c.* 560 BC (Florence, Museo Archeologico di Firenze)

small shapes and divided large ones into friezes. His famous volute krater, the François Vase (Florence, Mus. Archeol., 4209; see fig. 97), is a good example. Kleitias had a precise, refined and delicate style that maintained a careful balance between the decorative and the plain. He was interested in mythological narrative and introduced many new themes into the Attic repertory. Nearly all his vases have inscriptions identifying the figures and enhancing the composition. His slightly younger contemporary NEARCHOS signed as both potter and painter. Like Kleitias, Nearchos preferred to decorate small vessels in a refined and precise drawing style, and he too was interested in narrative.

Around 560 BC the painters of Siana cups present the first evidence of Attic artists specializing in a particular shape. This sturdy, practical vessel with deep bowl, offset lip and echinus foot takes its name from the pair found at Siana in Rhodes (London, BM, B 379 and B 380). The best-known painters of these cups are the C PAINTER, who exhibits Corinthianizing elements in his work, and his more able contemporary the HEIDELBERG PAINTER. Lesser artists specializing in these cups include the Griffin Bird Painter.

Contemporary with these artists were the painters of the Tyrrhenian group who continued to be active until *c.* 550 BC. They decorated ovoid neck amphorae almost exclusively, and their products, judging from the known provenances, were intended for the Etruscan market. Among the painters belonging to this group were the Castellani Painter, the Kyllenios Painter and the Goltyr Painter. Human figures appear on the shoulder of their neck amphorae; below are animal friezes or ornament; on the neck there may be figures or patterns. The work of these painters is vivid and decorative, with abundant use of incision and accessory colour; their themes are most often mythological, frequently in unconventional compositions.

(c) c. 560–c. 520 BC. Whereas the earliest Attic painters decorated mostly small vessels or divided the format of large ones into friezes, by *c.* 560 BC a more monumental style began to develop. One of the first to display this trend was the PAINTER OF ACROPOLIS 606, whose name-piece (Athens, Acropolis Mus., 606; see fig. 98) is a large dinos depicting a battle scene in its main zone. Equally powerful, though more restrained, are the horsemen on each side of his two one-piece amphorae (Berlin, Antikenmus., 4823, and Tübingen, Eberhard-Karls-U., Antikensamml., S./10 1298).

The work of LYDOS 'the Lydian' also belongs to this period: he was active in the Athenian Kerameikos *c.* 570–*c.* 540 BC or even a little later. He signed as painter on an early amphora (Paris, Louvre, F 29) and on a dinos from his mature phase (Athens, Acropolis Mus., 607). He decorated a wide variety of shapes, from large ones such as dinoi, column kraters and amphorae to small ones such as lekythoi and cups, skilfully adapting figural compositions to varied formats. His earliest work, which overlaps with Kleitias and the Siana cup painters, is rather severe and restrained, exemplified by two hydriai (Munich, Staatl. Antikensamml., 1681, and Paris, Louvre, E 804), both demonstrating an economical use of incision. More mature works show a more decorative use of incision tempered by areas of plain black glaze. His best vases date from after 550 BC: these are ambitious compositions with densely overlapping figures, the groups rendered clear and legible through the juxtaposition of black glaze with areas of incision and accessory red and white. The effect resembles richly woven tapestry; a good example is a column krater depicting the *Return of Hephaistos* (New York, Met., 31.11.11; see fig. 99). Lydos had two companions of decidedly less talent, the Painter of Louvre F 6 and the Painter of Vatican 309, who produced a series of neck amphorae and column kraters, often decorated with pairs of opposed sphinxes or procession scenes.

The mature work of Lydos coincides with the output of the painters of GROUP E and the very early work of EXEKIAS, the greatest master of Attic Black-figure, from whom Group E takes its name (the 'E' stands for Exekianizing). Shapes preferred by the Group E painters are the Type B amphora with cylindrical handles, round foot and straight lip, the neck amphora and a precursor of the Type A amphora (which has a stepped foot and flaring lip) perfected by Exekias. They painted a variety of mythological subjects, especially the labours of Herakles, Theseus killing the Minotaur and scenes from the Trojan cycle. Their drawing style is generally sober and restrained, making economical use of incision and accessory colour. More colourful work was produced by the Towry Whyte Painter and the Painter of the Vatican Mourner on the periphery of Group E.

Like Sophilos and Kleitias, Exekias signed as both potter and painter. His perfection of the Black-figure technique and his sensitive approach to the subject-matter were unsurpassed and perhaps equalled only by his great contemporary, the AMASIS PAINTER (see below). Exekias preferred themes that depicted a broad range of human emotions, which he treated quietly and subtly. Good examples are the two scenes on a belly amphora (Rome, Vatican, Mus. Gregoriano Etrus., 344), one the intense concentration of *Achilles and Ajax Playing a Board Game* (for illustration *see* VASE PAINTERS, §II: EXEKIAS), and the other the *Homecoming of the Dioskouroi* with its exchange of glances between parents and sons. Occasionally he reworked well-known themes to give them new emphasis, as on two neck amphorae (Berlin, Pergamonmus., 1718; Munich, Staatl. Antikensamml., 1470) showing *Ajax Carrying the Body of Achilles.* Some of his subjects are rare, for example the archer grazing his horse (amphora; Philadelphia, U. PA, Mus., MS. 4873), and others unique, such as Dionysos sailing in his boat (cup; Munich, Staatl. Antikensamml., 2044). Exekias' tendency to depict the moment in a theme before its greatest action links him more with the narrative approach of artists of the high Classical period than it does with those of his own time.

Other good painters contemporary with those of the Group E workshop and Exekias include the Painter of Berlin 1686, whose name-piece (amphora; Berlin, Pergamonmus.) shows a procession in honour of Athena and who specialized in decorating amphorae. The Princeton Painter also preferred amphorae, and his most interesting piece is a Panathenaic amphora in New York (Met., 53. 11. 1) showing Athena in front of her altar and a flute-player behind it. More prolific than these two was the SWING PAINTER, whose work extended well into the 520s BC. His drawing is seldom first rate; his contribution to Attic Black-figure lies in his varied choice of subject-matter.

These painters represent a monumental aspect of Attic Black-figure, for they mostly decorated large vessels with amply proportioned figures. This tradition continued in the work of their successors, but a different approach is revealed by the Amasis Painter and other artists working during the mid-6th century BC. The Amasis Painter, who is named after several vases signed by the potter Amasis, is a true master of Black-figure, matched only by Exekias. His career spanned nearly five decades (*c.* 560–*c.* 515 BC), his earliest work being contemporary with that of Kleitias, Nearchos, the C Painter and the early Lydos and his latest overlapping with the early Red-figure vases decorated by the ANDOKIDES PAINTER, OLTOS, EPIKTETOS and the Pioneer group (*see* §6(i) below). The Amasis Painter decorated a wide variety of shapes, though usually preferring smaller vases. Like Kleitias, from whom he may have learnt some of his craft, he excelled at integrating ornamental patterns with friezes and inscriptions so that his vases exhibit perfect harmony between shape and decoration. This is particularly apparent on some larger vases, such as the neck amphora depicting *Dionysos and Maenads* (Paris, Bib. N., 222; see fig. 100), but also on exquisite smaller pieces, such as the Montclair Lekythos (Montclair, NJ, priv. col.; see D. von Bothmer: *The Amasis Painter and his World* (Malibu, 1985), pl. 50). Between them Exekias and the Amasis Painter exploited the decorative and narrative possibilities of Attic Black-figure technique almost to the full. Although good Black-figure continued to be produced until well into the 5th century BC, the Red-figure technique, invented *c.* 530 BC, increasingly attracted the more ambitious and talented artists.

98. Attic Black-figure dinos depicting a battle scene by the Painter of Acropolis 606, h. 460 mm, *c.* 560–*c.* 520 BC (Athens, Acropolis Museum)

99. Attic Black-figure column krater by Lydos: *Return of Hephaistos*, h. 565 mm, *c.* 560–*c.* 520 BC (New York, Metropolitan Museum of Art)

A vase painter active during this same period but whose style is highly distinctive was the AFFECTER, so called because his drawing style is affected, mannered and often old-fashioned. His career extended from *c.* 550 to *c.* 520 BC, but because his style remained relatively unchanged throughout it is difficult to place his vases chronologically. His favourite shape was the ovoid neck amphora, the type generally preferred in the second quarter of the 6th century but which went out of fashion by *c.* 550 BC. The Affecter's drawing style is precise, with liberal use of accessory colour, especially red. His figures have a delicate, fresh appearance; his ornamental patterns are tightly controlled and carefully related to the parts of the vase which they articulate. Associated with the Affecter is Elbows Out, named after the peculiar manner of depicting most of his figures with their arms akimbo. A

100. Attic Black-figure neck amphora by the Amasis Painter: *Dionysos and Maenads*, h. 330 mm, *c.* 560–*c.* 515 BC (Paris, Bibliothèque Nationale, Cabinet des Médailles)

colourful group of small vases, especially unusually shaped neck amphorae, come from the workshop of the potter Nikosthenes, whose signature is the most frequent in the history of Black-figure. He seems to have had a long career, for his latest vases date from *c.* 515 BC.

Just as in earlier times, there were workshops and painters in the third quarter of the 6th century BC who almost exclusively produced cups, in this case the 'Little Master' cup. These elegant cups are lightly made with crisply articulated profiles. Two systems of decoration prevail. The first, the lip cup, has figural decoration on the lip (one or two figures, not a frieze) and further figures in the tondo; since much of the exterior surface is unglazed, the visual effect is light and bright. The second, the band cup, has its figural decoration in the handle zone with the tondo left plain; since much of the outside is glazed, the appearance is dark. When signatures appear on these cups they are nearly always those of potters—the painter Sakonides being the exception—who thus lend their names to the painters. The former include Eucheiros (son of the Ergotimos who collaborated with Kleitias), Glaukytes, Hermogenes, Taleides, TLESON (the son of Nearchos) and Xenokles.

Besides cup specialists there were also painters during these years just before the invention of Red-figure who preferred to decorate lekythoi. These founded a long tradition of lekythos painting that reached its zenith during the Persian Wars (490–479 BC). The lekythoi are generally rather modest little vessels that stand in sharp contrast to the work of the masters. Their chief painters were from the Cock group and the Dolphin group.

(d) c. *520*–c. *480* BC. The Attic Black-figure produced during these decades overlaps with the more progressive and eventually more popular Red-figure, and a few painters tried their hands at both techniques, producing 'bilingual' vases (i.e. with Black-and Red-figure on a single vessel). The tradition of monumental compositions and heroic mythological subjects preferred by Exekias was continued by the LYSIPPIDES PAINTER, who may have been his pupil. Many vases attributed to the Lysippides Painter overlap with the mature and late work of Exekias, but the former continued to be active until *c.* 515–*c.* 510 BC. Like Exekias, he preferred one-piece amphorae (both types A and B), neck amphorae and hydriai. He has, however, also left the largest known Black-figure cup (London, BM, B 426). The drawing of the Lysippides Painter is looser and less precise than that of Exekias, but never is it slipshod.

Contemporary with the Lysippides Painter is the ANTIMENES PAINTER, who is called after a *kalos* name on a hydria in Leiden (Rijksmus. Oudhd., PC 63; see fig. 101) that shows *Youths in a Palaestra.* His early work seems to recall that of Lydos, who may have been his teacher. The Antimenes Painter decorated many standard neck amphorae, but one of his favourite shapes was the hydria, which offered him a variety of formats for his figural compositions (a frieze on the shoulder, a panel on the body and a narrow predella below). He often depicted rather well-known subjects, for example the exploits of Herakles (see fig. 164 below) or the departure of a warrior on a chariot,

101. Attic Black-figure hydria by the Antimenes Painter: *Youths in a Palaestra*, h. 440 mm, *c.* 515–*c.* 510 BC (Leiden, Rijksmuseum van Oudheden)

while his scenes of the harnessing of a war chariot, together with those by Psiax (see below), provided the model for those to come. But the Antimenes Painter is most memorable for some of his unusual themes, such as the full palaestra scene on the name-piece hydria in Leiden or the olive pickers on two neck amphorae (London, BM, B 226; Berlin, Pergamonmus., 1855). His drawing is crisp and sure, and his sparing use of accessory colour gives his vases a sober look.

Closely related to the Antimenes Painter, enough to be designated his 'brother' by Beazley, is PSIAX, an elegant, refined artist who also painted in Red-figure (as on his signed pieces, two alabastra: Karlsruhe, Bad. Landesmus., 242 (B120), and Odessa, A. Mus.); he also experimented with White-ground (*see* §7 below), Coral Red and Six's technique (*see* §1(iii)(c) above). Occasionally he decorated large vessels, such as the hydria formerly in Berlin (destr.; see Beazley, 1956, p. 293) showing the harnessing of a war chariot. But his best work appears on small vases such as the exquisite alabastron in St Petersburg (Hermitage, 381) or elegant kyathos in Würzburg (U. Würzburg, Wagner-Mus., 436). Two painters active in the last decade of the 6th century BC who may have been pupils of Psiax are the PRIAM PAINTER and the RYCROFT PAINTER. They preferred large vessels, chiefly amphorae and hydriai. Their incision is often quite fine with little accessory white or red added to the figures: the effect is one of sleek elegance.

The largest single group of good Black-figure pots that may be dated to the late 6th century BC comes from the workshop of the LEAGROS GROUP. These painters were contemporaries of the Red-figure artists known as the Pioneer group because of their innovative exploration of the new technique, and vases by painters of the Leagros group often reflect the boldness and spirit of their colleagues. Beazley (1956, pp. 354–9) identified several painters within the group, notably Painter A, Painter S and the painters of the Antiope group. The Leagros group preferred to decorate large vessels, in particular hydriai, amphorae (including neck amphorae and Panathenaics) and column kraters, but they also produced some splendid large lekythoi. Most of their subjects are drawn from myth, with episodes from the Trojan cycle and the exploits of Herakles being clear favourites. Often these are scenes of chilling violence, as on three hydriai depicting respectively *Achilles Hurling the Severed Head of Troilos at his Would-be Rescuers* (London, BM, B 326), *Herakles Stoning Kyknos to Death* (Munich, Staatl. Antikensamml., 1709) and *Neoptolemos Killing Priam* (U. Würzburg, Wagner-Mus., 311; see fig. 102). A good artist on the periphery of this group is the ACHELOOS PAINTER; two other contemporaries are the Nikoxenos Painter and his more able pupil, the Eucharides Painter. Both of the latter also worked in Red-figure, and their latest vases belong to the early years of the 5th century BC.

Other vase painters of this period specialized in small shapes; foremost among these artists is the Edinburgh Painter, whose style derives from the Leagros group. He perfected the White-ground cylindrical lekythos, and he also left a number of small neck amphorae; his drawing is simple and precise. Between *c.* 510 and *c.* 480 BC other painters also specialized in lekythoi, especially the Theseus Painter, the ATHENA PAINTER, the Sappho Painter and the Diosphos Painter. Most productive of all were the painters of the Haimon group, who decorated small mass-produced and rather hastily painted lekythoi, which were often used as humble furnishings for Athenian graves during the time of the Persian Wars.

102. Attic Black-figure hydria from the workshop of the Leagros group: *Neoptolemos Killing Priam*, h. 520 mm, *c.* 510–*c.* 500 BC (Würzburg, Universität Würzburg, Martin von Wagner-Museum)

A special class of Attic Black-figure vases are Panathenaic amphorae: large, handsome vessels filled with oil that were awarded as prizes in the games in honour of Athena that took place in Athens every four years. The earliest extant specimen dates from *c.* 560 BC, shortly after the games are said to have been reorganized by Peisistratos, but the series continued into the late Roman era. The vases have a set format: on one side Athena strides to her right from between columns surmounted by cocks, her spear poised and her shield at the ready, and in front of her is the prize inscription *ton athenethen athlon* ('a prize from the games at Athens'); on the other side is a representation of the contest for which the prize was awarded. The earliest Panathenaics are stylistically related to Lydos; the one surviving example by Exekias (*c.* 540 BC; Karlsruhe, Bad. Landesmus., 65.45) is slightly later. In *c.* 520 BC the Euphiletos Painter was commissioned to produce the amphorae; in the early 5th century BC the KLEOPHRADES PAINTER received the commission, which passed to the BERLIN PAINTER and some years later to his pupil the ACHILLES PAINTER (*see also* §6(i) below and CERAMICS, colour pl. II, fig. 1). During the first half of the 4th century BC the figure of Athena was reversed so that she is seen striding to her left, the name of the archon in power in the year that the oil was produced was inscribed next to the right-hand column, and often the columns themselves were surmounted by small figures, which were probably the insignia of the archon in office in the year that the vase was made.

BIBLIOGRAPHY

J. D. Beazley: *Development of Black-figure* (1951, 3/1986)

——: *Black-figure* (1956/*R* 1978)

——: *Paralipomena* (1971)

J. Boardman: *Athenian Black Figure Vases* (Oxford, 1974)

M. B. Moore and M. Z. P. Philippides: *Attic Black-figured Pottery* (1986), xxiii of *The Athenian Agora* (Princeton, 1953–)

□

(iii) Lakonian. The Black-figure technique was introduced to Lakonia around 620 BC, when it succeeded a short-lived Orientalizing style (Lakonian I; *see* §4(iv) above). Its experimental stage (Lakonian II; *c.* 620–*c.* 580 BC) is characterized by the production of small vases (lakainai, chalices, mugs, plates and bowls) with a few human figures, animals often in outline and primarily abstract subsidiary decoration. It is in this period that export began, particularly of cups. When a fully developed Black-figure style made its appearance (Lakonian III and IV; *c.* 580–*c.* 500 BC) the vases were widely exported: indeed, most extant specimens come from Samos, Olympia, Naukratis on the Nile delta, Cyrene, Etruria and South Italy (especially Taras and Sicily). The location of the Lakonian pottery workshops is problematic: some appear to have been located in Sparta itself, but most were in the surrounding towns, such as the port of Gytheion, since it was presumably their inhabitants (*perioikoi*) who had the major role in the practice of arts and running of commerce in Lakonia.

Decorated with a simple and lively figure style and rich floral ornament, Lakonian vases owed much to Corinthian Black-figure (*see* §(i) above) and were also influenced by East Greek (*see* §(v) below) and by Attic pottery (after *c.* 560 BC; *see* §(ii) above). However, they never lost their native character and strong originality. The clay is pink to light brown, the black glaze usually good, and much use was made of added purple. Until the middle of the 6th century BC a pale cream slip covered the surface as a background for the decoration, but its use declined thereafter. These vases used to be ascribed to the Theran colony of Cyrene in North Africa, mainly because of the subject-matter on some of them, for example *King Arkesilaos of Cyrene Supervising the Weighing and Packing of (?)Silphion* on a cup (Paris, Bib. N., Cab. Médailles, 189; see fig. 103) and the *Nymph Cyrene Struggling with a Lion* on another cup (Taranto, Mus. N., IG 4991). However, British excavations in Sparta at the beginning of the 20th century brought to light a large quantity of pottery that demonstrated a continuous ceramic production from Geometric times onwards, though with the degeneration of Lakonian Black-figure at the end of the 6th century BC Lakonian figured pottery as a whole fell into decline.

103. Lakonian Black-figure cup by the Arkesilaos Painter (interior): *King Arkesilaos of Cyrene Supervising the Weighing and Packing of (?)Silphion*, diam. 290 mm, *c.* 560 BC (Paris, Bibliothèque Nationale, Cabinet des Médailles)

Absolute dates for Lakonian Black-figure have been provided mainly by grave finds from Taras, where Lakonian vases have been discovered side by side with Corinthian examples adequately dated by other criteria, while development in the shape of the cup, its most characteristic vessel, has helped to establish a relative chronology: Lakonian cups of the late 7th century BC and the early 6th were small and footless or medium-sized with a short foot, but after *c.* 580 BC they acquired an elegant form with a higher stem, shallow bowl and high lip. A new type, the Lakonian 'Droop cup', appeared *c.* 550 BC, with thick walls, a concave lip, deep bowl and medium-high stem with horizontal grooves.

Unlike their Attic and Corinthian colleagues, Lakonian vase painters made the interior of the cup the main surface for their figural decoration, an odd choice since the circular tondo was not appropriate for the development of narrative. Under the main scene there is normally a narrow exergue filled with animal figures or floral patterns, recalling East Greek Orientalizing practice. The exterior of the cup carries characteristic decorative friezes—pomegranates, lotus buds, myrtle wreaths, tongues, rays or crescents—or sometimes animal friezes in the Corinthian manner. Horizontal palmettes normally flank the handles. Lakonian cups seem to have been made mainly for export, since few have been found in Sparta, where the usual drinking vessel was probably the lakaina. Other shapes of Lakonian Black-figure are the hydria, dinos, volute krater, amphora and oinochoe, apart from the smaller shapes mentioned above.

The scenes decorating Lakonian vases were taken both from myth and everyday life and generally from the stock Archaic repertory. Of the heroic scenes the most frequent are those featuring Herakles; other popular stories include Achilles' ambush of Troilos, the Boreads chasing the Harpies, Bellerophon and the Chimaera and perhaps the Kalydonian boar hunt. Gods are often shown alone (e.g. Zeus, Poseidon on a hippocampus, a nature goddess), but a characteristic scene is that of a seated deity (or deities) with worshippers approaching. Daemonic creatures such as Gorgons and Boreads are similar to those on Corinthian vases, but peculiar to Lakonia and difficult to interpret are the small winged daemons surrounding symposiasts, riders and a nature goddess. Everyday scenes include symposia, komasts, lyre-players, warriors fighting and the return from battle.

Apart from some minor artists with just a few vases attributed to each, five major Lakonian vase painters have been identified. Earliest are the NAUKRATIS PAINTER and the BOREADS PAINTER, who worked *c.* 575–*c.* 550 BC mainly under Corinthian influence and established the canonical Lakonian Black-figure style. The ARKESILAOS PAINTER was a younger contemporary influenced by them but with a strong originality. The HUNT PAINTER was a prolific artist who flourished *c.* 565–*c.* 530 BC and whose work exhibits Attic influence, while finally, the lesser RIDER PAINTER worked *c.* 570–*c.* 535 BC and imitated most of his predecessors. There are also works in the manner of these painters, particularly of the Naukratis Painter, who was imitated until the end of the 6th century BC. No signature of potter or painter has survived, but most of the major painters seem to have been literate, since there are inscriptions on some of their vases.

BIBLIOGRAPHY

J. P. Droop: 'The Laconian Pottery', *The Sanctuary of Artemis Orthia at Sparta*, ed. R. M. Dawkins (London, 1929), pp. 52–116

E. A. Lane: 'Lakonian Vase-painting', *Annu. Brit. Sch. Athens*, xxxiv (1933–4), pp. 99–189

B. B. Shefton: 'Three Laconian Vase-painters', *Annu. Brit. Sch. Athens*, xlix (1954), pp. 299–310

P. Pelagatti: 'La ceramica laconica del Museo di Taranto', *Annu. Scu. Archeol. Atene & Miss. It. Oriente*, xxxiii–xxxiv (1955–6), pp. 7–44

——: 'Laconici, vasi', *Enciclopedia dell'arte antica*, iv (Rome, 1961)

C. M. Stibbe: *Lakonische Vasenmaler des sechsten Jahrhunderts v.chr.*, 2 vols (Amsterdam and London, 1972)

Studi sulla ceramica laconica. Atti del seminario: Perugia, 1981

M. Pipili: *Laconian Iconography of the Sixth Century BC* (Oxford, 1987)

MARIA PIPILI

(iv) Boiotian. Boiotian Black-figure was produced at numerous local centres, and its study is therefore less a matter of tracing continuous lines of development than of identifying significant groups of pots, some of which can be attributed to specific painters and workshops. Little Boiotian pottery was exported, and there has been relatively little excavation in Boiotia itself, so that there is only a small amount of material involved.

Although Boiotian pottery is distinctive in both shape and decoration, proximity to Athens led to the continuous borrowing of Attic ideas, techniques and even subject-matter; some of the painters appear to have been Athenian immigrants. The influence of Corinthian pottery was strongest in the 7th century BC but continued in the 6th, transmitted both directly through trade and indirectly through Athenian borrowings. The commonest Corinthian exports found on Boiotian sites are aryballoi and piriform alabastra, which Boiotian artists were quick to copy; one of the earliest groups of Boiotian Black-figure vases, the Horse Bird group of alabastra (*c.* 600 BC), set the pattern for much that followed. Though very close to its Corinthian models, the group was produced by an immigrant Athenian painter whose work at Athens had also been Corinthianizing. The vases feature groups of animals, birds, hybrid monsters and the occasional human figure set amid rosettes and painted in rather thin black glaze; details are incised on the figures, less often on the florals.

The four distinguishable painters of the Boiotian Dancers group (*c.* 575–*c.* 550 BC), named after the frolicking komasts who appear in most of their scenes, were influenced strongly by the Athenian KY Painter, a decorator of cups and small vases in a miniaturizing style. The workshop of this group may have been near Tanagra, and their shapes, including tripod kothons (boxes with flared feet) with lion-paw feet and a kyathos (a small, single-handled type of kantharos) shaped like a ship and with a boar's-head spout (e.g. Paris, Louvre, CA 577; see fig. 104), suggest links with the local terracotta industry. The komasts—dancing, drinking and playing games—are sometimes accompanied by other scenes of drinking and

104. Boiotian Black-figure kyathos from the Boiotian Dancers group, h. 116 mm (incl. handle), *c.* 570–560 BC (Paris, Musée du Louvre)

sacrifice or by mythological subjects such as Perseus and the Gorgon (e.g. Berlin, Staatl. Mus., F 1727; see Kilinski, 1990, 7, 1–2), and by some Corinthianizing animals. Incision enhances what would otherwise be lively but undistinguished drawing. A number of these komast scenes appear on kantharoi, which remained a particularly popular shape in Boiotia, especially a type with a tall, deep lip and two high-swung handles with struts and thumb rests. The shape allowed for the occasional attempt at more complex mythological scenes such as the Kalydonian boar hunt (e.g. Athens, N. Archaeol. Mus., 432; see Kilinski, 1990, 18, 4 and 19, 1–2) or the ambush of Troilos (e.g. Berlin, Staatl. Mus., 3778; see Kilinski, 1990, 6.1), both popular in Athens and better executed there. In general, however, parades of humans and animals are more common; they are frequently used as friezes on lekanai, of which several groups survive from the mid- and late 6th century BC, such as those by the Protome Painter and the Triton Painter. These were produced near Tanagra, with incision and filling ornament influenced by East Greek fabrics, especially Fikellura (*see* §4(iv) above). Some contemporary groups of pots feature unincised Black-figure designs; these were quickly executed and more popular in Boiotia and Euboia (*see* §(viii) below) than at Athens.

Added red and white on a group of skyphoi testifies to the Boiotian love of colour. Vases of this shape were imported in quantity from Athens *c.* 500 BC and were imitated locally. The Athenian originals use red, white and even yellow; the Boiotian copies exhibit similar colourful effects, although their handling of mythology is inept but enthusiastic and their figure drawing sketchy. After Boiotian painters began to produce Red-figure pottery around 480 BC, they readily used both techniques on the same pot, so that Red-figure vases often have Black-figure lids. Black-figure was clearly the more popular, and towards 400 BC local production of Black-figure cups revived; they were often decorated in an unincised style and featured large palmettes with figures or groups between them.

The Kabeirion style, so called because most specimens were found at the Kabeirion sanctuary near Thebes, is notably different from normal Boiotian Black-figure. It was produced from the later 5th century BC until well into the 4th, and although it is a true Black-figure style, using incision and added white paint, it derives—and distorts—many features from contemporary Attic Red-figure. Its subjects are burlesque treatments of myths and scenes of everyday life; its figures have ill-proportioned bodies, circular heads and stick-like limbs. The most notable subjects include Kabeiros at the feast (e.g. Athens, N. Archaeol. Mus., 10426; see Sparkes, fig. 2)—heroes feasting are a popular Boiotian subject—and illustrations of the *Odyssey* (e.g. Oxford, Ashmolean, G 429; see Richter, fig. 477), especially those episodes that lend themselves to grotesque treatment; some of the scenes may have had connections with theatrical farce. Even in this style, however, vases with florals are more common than those with figures. The most usual shape is a deep kantharos with thumb and finger rests on its ring-handles. Some individual painters, including the Mystae Painter, can be distinguished.

BIBLIOGRAPHY

A. D. Ure and P. N. Ure: *Sixth and Fifth Century Pottery from Excavations at Rhitsona* (London, 1927)
A. D. Ure: 'Boeotian Geometricising Vases', *J. Hell. Stud.*, xlix (1929), pp. 160–71
A. D. Ure and P. N. Ure: 'Boeotian Vases in the Akademisches Kunstmuseum, Bonn', *Archäol. Anz.* (1933), pp. 1–42
A. D. Ure: 'More Boeotian Geometricising Vases', *J. Hell. Stud.*, lv (1935), pp. 227–8
P. Wolters: *Das Kabirenheiligtum bei Theben*, i (Berlin, 1940)
G. M. A. Richter: *A Handbook of Greek Art* (Cambridge, MA, 1953/*R* London, 1977)
K. Schauenburg: *Heidelberg I: Germany X*, Corp. Vasorum Ant. (Munich, 1954), p. 11, nos 24–30
A. D. Ure: 'Krokotos and White Heron', *J. Hell. Stud.*, lxxv (1955), pp. 90–103
B. A. Sparkes: 'The Taste of a Boeotian Pig', *J. Hell. Stud.*, lxxxvii (1967), pp. 116–30
K. Kilinski II: 'Boiotian Black Figure Lekanai by the Protome and Triton Painters', *Amer. J. Archaeol.*, lxxxi (1977), pp. 55–65
K. Kilinski II: 'The Boiotian Dancers Group', *Amer. J. Archaeol.*, lxxxii (1978), pp. 173–91
——: *Boiotian Black Figure Vase Painting of the Archaic Period* (1990)

ELIZABETH MOIGNARD

(v) East Greek and islands. In north Ionia the Late Wild Goat style (*see* §4(iv) above) had made much use of the Black-figure technique, and various experiments led to several genuine Black-figure styles *c.* 575–*c.* 550 BC. By this time a standard had been set by the Attic artists, whom the newcomers followed in rejecting slip, though not consistently in anything else. Because they were exported, and by the chances of discovery and publication are more available for study, the best-known vases are those of the so-called Klazomenian groups (*c.* 550–*c.* 525 BC), at least some of which seem from clay analysis to have been made at Klazomenai itself. Amphorae—one type abnormally narrow—and hydriai are frequent; also known are kraters and at the beginning an over-sized form of pyxis. The main decorative fields generally carried human figures, particularly files of women, as on an amphora at Tübingen (*c.* 550–*c.* 540 BC; Eberhard-Karls-U., Antikensamml., S 12.2656; see fig. 105), while sirens, sphinxes, animals and birds (notably feeding cranes) were relegated to subsidiary positions. Vegetable ornament lost the importance it had on Orientalizing vases; instead there was a preference for scales with white centres and initially for white or alternate white and red crescents. A row of white dots between incised lines was a favourite embellishment, and white was sometimes used for male as well as female flesh; inner details on white were more often painted than incised. The workmanship is inconsistent, even on the same pot, and does not display much concern for anatomical accuracy.

105. Klazomenian Black-figure amphora (detail) showing *Dancing Women*, h. *c.* 525 mm, *c.* 550–*c.*540 BC (Tübingen, Eberhard-Karls-Universität Tubingen, Antikensammlungen)

Two groups of vases tenuously related to Klazomenian were also exported. The Knipovitch class is notable for the forepart of a winged horse, which fills the decorative panels on many of its sloppy amphorae. The Enmann class is a looser group, consisting mostly of amphorae with one or two large figures in their panels, carelessly drawn and without merit. Its chief interest is its connection with the Campana group of dinoi and hydriai: from the distribution of finds the Campana painters should have been working in Etruria and the Enmann painters in Asia Minor, and if (as some maintain) pots from both groups were painted by the same hand, it implies that the artist emigrated from East Greece to Italy. Though much superior in technique and draughtsmanship, the Northampton group also has connections with the Campana group and was probably made in Etruria by an Ionian immigrant. These groups all date to *c.* 540–*c.* 520 BC: later evidence for the emigration of East Greek artists is hard to find, though one of the painters of Caeretan hydriai (the Busiris Painter: *see* §(vii) below) used Ionic script.

Other north-Ionian Black-figure vases occur in a range of styles; although a few are of high quality, only some column kraters from Old Smyrna have yet been classified into a fairly coherent group. Their effect is drab, though one more ambitious piece depicts a camel led by a man in Scythian dress (see J. M. Cook, 1965, pp. 123–4, no. 45

and fig. 6), suggesting a date after 546 BC, when Cyrus brought his camels from Persia to Sardis. There are also some poor late 6th-century BC imitations of Attic pottery, though there may be some earlier and better specimens. The general impression of all the north-Ionian groups is of a multiplicity of local workshops operating without discipline or much reference to each other.

Some Klazomenian clay sarcophagi were also decorated in a Black-figure style, though not the full technique, since the inner details were painted and not incised. The earliest examples (?530s BC) show some affinities with Klazomenian pottery, but the latest (early 5th century BC) conform to Attic principles in their depiction of anatomy, though some details are East Greek and their compositions tend to feature symmetrical and often meaningless arrangements of stock figures.

In the south a small number of cups of Attic shapes, which are given the mistranslated name of Ionian Little Masters, rivals Attic products in technical excellence and sureness of draughtsmanship. The inner details of their figures may be incised, sometimes with microscopically fine lines, or meticulously reserved in imitation of incision. Again, no coherent school developed. The date suggested by stylistic comparisons is *c.* 560–*c.* 525 BC, and they were perhaps produced on Samos. Some of these cups have close affinities with Fikellura vases (*see* §4(iv) above), where reserved detail is also sometimes as fine as incision.

Clay analysis assigns a final Black-figure group, the East Greek situlae (deep cylindrical vases), still further south to Rhodes. These tall, neckless jars were divided into three deep decorative zones: the lower two were separated by reserved lines and adorned with large pendent lotus flowers and palmettes, incised and picked out in purple on a black ground after the manner of Vroulian cups (*see* §4(iv) above), while the uppermost usually carried a Black-figure group or single figure in a panel on each side between the ring handles; the quality of the drawing ranges from good to bad. Discovery contexts and stylistic comparisons date the group to between 550 and 500 BC, though a few rather earlier situlae, sturdier and technically superior, are still Orientalizing in spirit.

BIBLIOGRAPHY

E. Kunze: 'Ionische Kleinmeister', *Mitt. Dt. Archäol. Inst.: Athen. Abt.*, lix (1934), pp. 81–122

R. M. Cook: 'A List of Clazomenian Pottery', *Annu. Brit. Sch. Athens*, xlvii (1952), pp. 123–52

CVA British Museum, viii (London, 1954)

J. M. Cook: *Greek Painted Pottery* (London, 1960, rev. 1972), pp. 134–41, 158

——: 'Old Smyrna: Ionic Black-figure and Other Sixth-century Figured Ware', *Annu. Brit. Sch. Athens*, lx (1965), pp. 114–42

——: *Clazomenian Sarcophagi* (1981)

R. M. COOK

(vi) Chalcidian. This name is given to the approximately 300 surviving vases produced *c.* 580–*c.* 510 BC by a Black-figure school, the exact site of which is disputed, and comes from the inscriptions in the Chalcidian alphabet on many of the vases. The vases have no visible predecessors, and this may indicate the work of a small group of painters. Chalcidian vases show a close awareness of developments in Attic Black-figure (*see* §(ii) above), although obvious borrowings are not constant, and dating depends on this close contact. Animal friezes, which appear on many vases and continue to do so later than in Athens, suggest the influence of Corinth, perhaps filtered through Athens. East Greek details also appear on some of the later vases.

The most usual shapes are short-necked amphorae, flat-shouldered hydriai very like the Attic shape, column kraters with distinctive kinked handles, and cups. The potting evidently imitated contemporary Attic models, and its quality is extremely high. The fine-textured clay varies in colour from pale pinkish-orange to reddish-brown. As in Attic practice, artists used added reddish-purple and white as well as dark brown paint, but the overall effect is perhaps more reminiscent of East Greek prototypes. A notable practice was dipping the necks of the vases in paint instead of painting them by hand.

The appearance of the vases resembles that of any other mature Black-figure works, with large figures in the main field framed by subsidiary decoration including animal friezes, fat interlaced buds, stepped, slanted zigzags, and square designs framed by interlaced lotuses and palmettes. The crisp, bright effect of the figures and patterns is often more striking than the scenes themselves. The Inscription Painter, conventionally regarded as the originator of the school, frequently adapted stock scenes to show specific mythological figures by using inscriptions. His figures are well separated from one another and delineated with flat areas of colour: there is little internal detail or clarity of outline (e.g. a krater, *c.* 540 BC; U. Würzburg, Wagner-Mus.; see fig. 106). The spacing of the figures and the balance of dark and light areas are characteristic and may

106. Chalcidian Black-figure krater near the Inscription Painter: *Hector's Farewell to Andromache, Paris and Helen*, h. 457 mm, *c.* 540 BC (Würzburg, Universität Würzburg, Martin von Wagner-Museum)

owe something to Corinthian influence. The figures of the Phineus Painter, who followed the Inscription Painter (later 6th century BC), are also solid and heavy, though he used much more linear detail, especially on cups. In general, even the figures on late Chalcidian vases tend to resemble those on earlier Attic examples of *c.* 565 BC. Some mythological scenes do appear, including Herakles, the Trojan War, Dionysos and even the occasional rarity such as Phineus and the Harpies, but the lack of internal detail prevents serious exploration of the subject-matter, and together with the use of colour, the style suggests a greater interest in decoration than in narrative art.

BIBLIOGRAPHY

A. Rumpf: *Chalkidische Vasen*, 3 vols (Berlin, 1927)
H. R. W. Smith: *The Origin of Chalcidian Ware* (Berkeley, 1932)
L. Banti: 'Calcidesi vasi', *Enciclopedia dell'arte antica*, ii (Rome, 1959), pp. 260–65
E. Simon, M. Hirmer and A. Hirmer: *Die griechischen Vasen* (Munich, 1976, rev. 1981), pp. 62–4

ELIZABETH MOIGNARD

(vii) Caeretan. The term is applied almost exclusively to a group of about 39 hydriai of markedly individual style (*c.* 530–*c.* 500 BC), all found in Etruria and very probably made at Caere. The same workshop produced other forms of vases, but with one exception these are hardly decorated and have nothing in common with the remarkably colourful style of painting of the hydriai. The form and decoration of the hydriai differ from contemporary examples produced elsewhere in the Greek world. The ornamentation comprises elaborate wreaths, generally of ivy, and polychrome lotus and palmette friezes. The figural scenes are mostly mythological and include no less than eleven depictions of Herakles and four of Dionysiac subjects; many are consciously humorous. The drawing is often exceptionally fine: the Eagle Painter used decoratively sweeping incised lines, and his younger colleague, the Busiris Painter, worked with swift sketchy strokes, as on his name piece depicting *Herakles Killing the Egyptian King Busiris* (*c.* 510 BC; Vienna, Ksthist. Mus., 3576; see fig. 107). In contrast, the pots themselves—most of which were apparently also potted by these artists—are often carelessly produced and ineptly fired.

Though working in Etruria, these two vase painters were clearly of East Greek origin, probably fugitives from the Persian conquest of Ionia (546 BC), since their paintings have definite East Greek features: male flesh may be white or even red, and reservation was often used instead of incision to separate the various elements of ornamental motifs. However, while the paintings have close stylistic affinities with East Greek sculpture, they bear surprisingly little detailed resemblance to any particular East Greek style of vase painting, prompting speculation that these vase painters came from a family of producers of architectural terracottas. During the 16 or so years between the fall of Ionia and the establishment of the Caeretan workshop they appear to have travelled widely, and paintings on a piece of wood from Saqqara in Egypt (see G. T. Martin: *The Tomb of Hetepka* (London, 1979), no. 289) closely resemble the style of the Eagle Painter. Once in Etruria the two artists seem to have worked mainly for the resident Greek community and remained uninfluenced by Etruscan art throughout their careers, in

107. Caeretan Black-figure hydria by the Busiris Painter: *Herakles Killing the Egyptian King Busiris*, h. 450 mm, *c.* 510 BC (Vienna, Kunsthistorisches Museum)

contrast to other immigrant artisans. However, the poor quality of some ornamental motifs suggests that they were executed by Etruscan assistants, who used templates. A more talented Etruscan pupil appears to have decorated an alabastron (New York, Met., 1981.11.7) with two tiny friezes, one in the style of the Eagle Painter, the other in the style of the Busiris Painter; certain peculiarities in each suggest a lack of understanding of Greek mythology. Other assistants may also have become vase painters in their own right, and these perhaps included the Painter of Munich 833; the Caeretan hydriai also influenced Etruscan La Tolfa pottery (*see* ETRUSCAN, §IV) and works by the Etruscan Tityos Painter. Those studying these vases should be aware of the production of fakes, some of which are quite skilful.

BIBLIOGRAPHY

J. M. Hemelrijk: *Caeretan Hydriai* (1984), v of *Kerameus* (Mainz, 1975–)
——: 'An Alabastron Produced by the Workshop of the Caeretan Hydriae', *Atti del Secondo Congresso Internazionale Etrusco: Firenze, 1985*, ii, pp. 729–32, pls I–IV

J. M. HEMELRIJK

(viii) Euboian. Knowledge of Euboian Black-figure is based on a small number of vases mainly, when their provenance can be traced, from Eretria. Earlier Euboian vases show links with the Cyclades, Attica and Corinth; the most characteristic shape is a large, krater-like amphora with a tall, conical foot and a wide neck, which had begun in the late 7th century BC to be decorated with figures and animals. Incision, the distinctive feature of the Black-figure technique, also began to appear on vases that continued to show outline drawing.

True Euboian Black-figure first appeared *c.* 540 BC on a group of amphorae whose shape owed something to the earlier krater-like Euboian vases and to the Attic lebes gamikos. The amphorae were found at Eretria and were decorated in a style so close to Attic that their painters must have trained in an Attic workshop. Two specimens (Athens, N. Archaeol. Mus., 1004 and 12076) carry wedding scenes, which are usual on the lebes gamikos, while a third (Athens, N. Archaeol. Mus., 12075) depicts *Herakles Fighting the Hydra.* Added red and white paint were used more freely than on Attic vases, especially for the subsidiary florals, and all of the vases have animal friezes, which continued to be fashionable in Euboia and Boiotia later than at Athens. The animals on the Herakles vase are unincised, as on the 7th-century BC vases and contemporary Euboian lekythoi and on the lekane, the most popular small shape. Lekanai of various forms continued to be produced in the Black-figure technique until the 4th century BC. The earlier ones carry depictions of animals and the occasional human figure, painted in much the same style as those on incised Black-figure pots; the later ones, and other small vases, have almost exclusively floral decoration, with large palmettes, honeysuckle and related designs.

BIBLIOGRAPHY

L. A. Amyx: 'The Gorgon Hydria from Eretria', *Amer. J. Archaeol.*, lxv (1941), pp. 64–9

J. Boardman: 'Pottery from Eretria', *Annu. Brit. Sch. Athens*, xlvii (1952), pp. 1–48

——: 'Early Euboean Pottery and History', *Annu. Brit. Sch. Athens*, lii (1957), pp. 1–29

A. D. Ure: 'Unincised Black Figure', *Bull. Inst. Class. Stud. U. London*, vi (1959), pp. 1–5

——: 'Euboean Floral Black Figured Vases', *Annu. Brit. Sch. Athens*, lv (1960), pp. 211–17

——: 'Euboean Lekanai', *J. Hell. Stud.*, lxxx (1960), pp. 160–67

——: 'Four Lekythoi in Chalcis', *J. Hell. Stud.*, lxxxii (1962), pp. 138–40

——: 'Small Vases from Euboean Workshops', *Annu. Brit. Sch. Athens*, lviii (1963), pp. 14–19

——: 'Euboean Floral Black Figured Vases: Additions and Corrections', *Annu. Brit. Sch. Athens*, lxv (1970), pp. 265–70

A. Andreiomenou: 'Archaïke kerameike ex Eretrias' [Archaic pottery from Eretria], *Archaiol. Chron.* (1976), pp. 1–7

ELIZABETH MOIGNARD

6. RED-FIGURE. In this painting technique, the visual antithesis of Black-figure, the figures were drawn in outline and the surrounding surface was blacked in. The less significant details of the figures were then painted with dilute glaze, and their more important features emphasized with relief lines, which also sometimes gave well-defined outer contours. Initially reddish-purple and white were used for some details, and later other colours were also employed. The technique was invented in Athens *c.* 530 BC, probably by the ANDOKIDES PAINTER. Many of its earliest exponents also worked in Black-figure, often using both techniques on the same ('bilingual') vase. After 500 BC, however, Red-figure became increasingly dominant, and, except for Panathenaic prize amphorae, little Black-figure was produced after *c.* 450 BC. During the 5th century BC Attic Red-figure was the most important fine ware in the Mediterranean region, where it was widely distributed (*see* §1(v) above). Production in Athens stopped *c.* 330–320 BC, possibly due to Macedonian control of the city. In South Italy there was significant production, with five recognized schools: Lucanian, Campanian, Apulian, Sicilian and Paestan. Etruria too became an active centre (*see* ETRUSCAN, §IV), especially its Faliscan school. Various other centres in Greece in the 5th and 4th centuries BC, including Boiotia, Corinth, Lakonia, the Chalcidici and Elis, made Red-figure pottery largely in imitation of Attic ware. Red-figure production ceased entirely at the beginning of the 3rd century BC.

(i) Attic. (ii) South Italian. (iii) Other areas.

(i) Attic. Attic Red-figure is regarded by many scholars as the highest achievement of Greek vase painting. Its earliest artists (late 6th century BC) used the revolutionary technique to break new ground in the depiction of anatomical detail and complex poses. Within 50 years of its inception Attic Red-figure had driven most other figured pottery from the market, and its artistic quality remained high throughout its history.

(a) The first generation (*c.* 530–*c.* 500 BC). (b) Late Archaic (*c.* 500–*c.* 480 BC). (c) Early and High Classical (*c.* 480–*c.* 425 BC). (d) Late 5th century BC. (e) 4th century BC.

*(a) The first generation (*c. *530*–c. *500* BC). The Red-figure technique was probably invented by the ANDOKIDES PAINTER, who is named from the potter with whom he worked. He decorated mainly amphorae and a few cups;

108. Attic Red-figure amphora by the Andokides Painter: *Ajax and Achilles Playing a Board Game*, h. 554 mm, *c.* 520 BC (Boston, MA, Museum of Fine Arts)

most of his later amphorae are bilingual, with the Black-figure side being decorated by the LYSIPPIDES PAINTER, who may have been the same person. The Andokides Painter's drawing style shows uncertainty with the new technique and clear vestiges of Black-figure. Thus he incised some details, especially the outer contour of the hair, and added purplish-red to colour parts of his figures. His subjects were also generally taken from Black-figure, as on his amphora depicting *Ajax and Achilles Playing a Board Game* (Boston, MA, Mus. F.A., 01.8037; see fig. 108). His richly dressed figures rarely overlap and have a statuesque dignity; most retain the standard Black-figure pose of chest frontal or in profile and legs and head in profile. Their anatomical details are stiffly rendered and recall those on relief sculpture, especially the frieze of the Siphnian Treasury in Delphi, with harsh relief lines used for details depicted by later artists in dilute glaze.

Similar features characterize the work of other early artists such as PSIAX, although he attempted more inventive poses and was a better draughtsman. A versatile artist who also worked in Black-figure, White-ground, Coral Red and Six's technique (*see* §1(iii)(c) above), he preferred to decorate a variety of such smaller shapes as alabastra and mastoi.

The Pioneer group. These were the first artists fully to explore the potential of the new technique. Their camaraderie suggests that they knew they were breaking new ground; theirs is the first identifiable movement in Western art. No longer do their figures stand isolated and stiff in profile; they overlap and entangle in a multiplicity of new poses: back views, frontal faces and twisted torsos. Earlier artists had experimented with foreshortening for drawing objects; now it was used for human figures, not always successfully but with increasing assurance. Even so, some Black-figure traits remained, including the selective use of incision, Black-figure subsidiary ornament and reserved lettering in early inscriptions. However, Red-figure floral bands became increasingly common, while later inscriptions began to be painted in added red or white, and the artists fully developed the use of dilute glaze to render details of anatomy.

109. Attic Red-figure kalyx krater by Euphronios: *Sleep and Death Lifting the Corpse of Sarpedon*, h. 457 mm, *c.* 515 BC (New York, Metropolitan Museum of Art)

The Pioneers preferred large vases such as kraters, stamnoi and amphorae, which provided large surfaces on which to experiment; they also decorated a few cups. They introduced new shapes, such as the psykter and pelike, and new versions of older shapes, such as neck amphorae with twisted handles. They were observant, depicting symposia, athletes, music lessons, jumping dancers and a youth pointing to a flying bird. The compositions are lively, and the poses allow the figures to interact more naturally: the dry repetitiveness of much Black-figure work is gone. The compositions are not arranged haphazardly, for there is a sense of balance and often symmetry. New mythological subjects appeared, and new compositions for older themes. The painters no longer looked to Black-figure models; rather, the Black-figure painters were influenced by them. Many of the vases have inscriptions, attesting to the painters' literacy. They labelled figures with their colleagues' names and challenged one another in friendly rivalry (*see* §1(vi)(e) above).

The greatest Pioneer was EUPHRONIOS, who signed as both painter and potter and continued to pot for other painters after abandoning painting. He preferred kraters but may also have invented the large neck amphora with twisted handles. More than any other Pioneer, he took delight in depicting anatomical detail: sometimes his figures almost seem flayed. His interest in mythology is evident in such masterpieces as a kalyx krater depicting *Sleep and Death Lifting the Corpse of Sarpedon* (*c.* 515 BC; New York, Met., 1972.11.10; see fig. 109). The balance and harmony of the scene is typical of Euphronios, with the majestic, fallen figure of Sarpedon raised on either side by Sleep and Death. Especially striking are the contrasts between the limp body and the taut limbs of its bearers, and between the moving figure of Hermes in the centre and the static warriors at either side.

EUTHYMIDES, Euphronios' younger rival and colleague, also signed as potter and painter. His father was Pollias, probably the sculptor of the same name who dedicated bases on the Acropolis in Athens, which indicates that he had some social standing. Euthymides preferred amphorae; his figures are more substantial than Euphronios' and his scenes more simply constructed.

PHINTIAS, probably the eldest member of the Pioneer group, also both potted and painted. His work retained more Black-figure features than that of his colleagues, and his figures are stiffer. Lesser members of the group include Smikros (see fig. 79 above), the Dikaios Painter and the Sosias Painter.

Cup painters. Nearly three-quarters of extant early Red-figure vases are cups, and many painters specialized in decorating them. The earliest specimens are normally bilingual. Type A cups have Red-figure exteriors consisting of a single figure on each side between palmettes and eyes, and a Black-figure tondo. Types B and C cups were introduced later; the most common scheme for the former is a Red-figure frieze between the handles on either side and a Red-figure tondo, for the latter simply a Red-figure tondo.

OLTOS, possibly a student of the Andokides Painter, worked with at least seven different potters. His best work is on the few large vases he decorated, including a psykter with *Dolphin-riders* (New York, Met., 1989.281.69) and a Type B cup with *The Assembled Gods* (Tarquinia, Pal. Vitelleschi, RC 6848). His figures are squat and drawn with an economy of line, but they are powerful and lively embodiments of the vitality offered by the new technique. He had an interest in scenes from epic and mythological subjects, including the exploits of Herakles and Theseus.

Oltos' younger contemporary EPIKTETOS also worked for several potters and painted a few large vases; in addition he decorated plates, including such masterpieces as the *Boy Riding a Cockerel* (New York, Met., 1981.11.10). Many of his cups are bilingual. He was the master of the circular format: his light and graceful figures elegantly fill the tondos of his cups and plates in new and varied poses. Everyday life inspired him, and he shared his contemporaries' interest in the rendering of action.

Several lesser artists specialized in cups, notably the Euergides Painter, the Nikosthenes Painter and Skythes, whose work is generally superior to most contemporary Black-figure. The names of many other potters survive too; Kachrylion, Nikosthenes and Pamphaios are among the most important.

*(b) Late Archaic (*c. *500–*c. *480* BC*).* The next generation of painters took the Red-figure technique to its highest artistic level. By *c.* 480 BC most of the problems of foreshortening had been successfully overcome: figures could now bend, twist, stoop or stretch successfully, and standing figures with one leg in profile and the other viewed frontally became the norm. There was less attention to detail and more selective use of relief lines, which are often replaced by lines in black glaze. Likewise, the amount of ornament decreased, and most was executed in Red-figure. Drapery is characterized by stacked folds arranged in a symmetrical, linear fashion, while depictions of muscles are also normally linear. The frontal eye on a profile head gradually changed to one truly viewed in profile; the process was completed by *c.* 460 BC in the Early Classical period, into which the careers of many Late Archaic painters extended.

A wider range of shapes was decorated, but only the askos, a wide flask with a small spout and a handle across its top, was new, the rest being new versions of old, such as Nolan amphorae, and shapes previously decorated only by Black-figure artists, such as the dinos and phiale. More artists specialized as painters either of pots or cups, and more worked exclusively with one potter. Production doubled, and many new genre and mythological subjects appeared, while the frequent depiction of Theseus may be connected with the founding of democracy.

Pot painters. The two greatest pot painters were the BERLIN PAINTER and the KLEOPHRADES PAINTER. The BERLIN PAINTER is named after a Type A amphora (Berlin, Antikenmus., F 2160; for illustration *see* VASE PAINTERS, §II). His long career (*c.* 500–*c.* 460 BC) began at the time of the Pioneers, and his style heavily influenced both contemporaries and students. He decorated a wide range of shapes; in 1976 a new shape was attributed to him, a pair of phialai (Malibu, CA, Getty Mus., 76.AE.16.1–2). His best work is on large vases from his early period; his late drawing is stiffer and mechanical and mainly confined to Nolan amphorae and lekythoi, the former shape possibly invented in his workshop. His charming, slender and graceful figures often stand isolated against a lustrous black background, frequently extending their arms to make them look broader and assert their forms. Subsidiary ornament is minimal or sometimes completely absent, so that his figures seem to float in space; the effect is powerful and immediate. One masterpiece, a Type A amphora (*c.* 490 BC; Basle, Antikenmus., BS 456; see fig. 110), shows Athena standing in profile, solemnly holding out an oinochoe to fill the kantharos of Herakles on the other side of the vase. Elsewhere too the figures on different

110. Attic Red-figure amphora by the Berlin Painter: *Athena*, h. 815 mm, *c.* 490 BC (Basle, Antikenmuseum Basel und Sammlung Ludwig)

sides of his vases work together to tell the story. Hair is sometimes rendered in clay relief, an early Red-figure technique; he also decorated Black-figure Panathenaic amphorae and a few White-ground vases.

The KLEOPHRADES PAINTER is named from the potter's signature on a large cup (Paris, Bib. N., 535, 699 and other fragments). However, he was primarily a pot painter, decorating the shapes favoured by the Pioneers. His style is closer to the Pioneers' than to the Berlin Painter's: indeed, he was a pupil of Euthymides, and some of his early work resembles that of his master. He was one of the last Red-figure artists to use incision for outlines of hair, and he used subsidiary Black-figure friezes on some Red-figure vases. He also produced Black-figure Panathenaic amphorae and neck amphorae. Though his compositions are generally more static than those of the Berlin Painter, the scale of the figures gives them considerable power. The outer figures often face outwards, drawing the focus away from the centre. Foreshortening is of less interest, and he was normally better at drawing figures in relaxed poses. The pathos common to many of his scenes is well illustrated by the Vivenzio Hydria (Naples, Mus. Archeol. N., 2422) with its moving depiction of the *Sack of Troy*. The artist apparently had a special interest in scenes from the Trojan War, but otherwise he painted many stock themes: Dionysiac revels, athletics, the exploits of Herakles and Theseus and scenes from everyday life. His late work declined sharply in quality.

There were many other competent pot painters, some of whom produced flashes of brilliance. MYSON, who specialized in column kraters, also painted a splendid amphora (Paris, Louvre, G 197) with the unusual subject of *King Kroisos on his Funeral Pyre*, while the Copenhagen Painter, Syriskos Painter and the Geras Painter produced some interesting mythological scenes. Artists specializing in particular shapes include the Tsyzkiewicz Painter (stamnoi and pelikai) and the Flying Angel Painter (pelikai).

Cup painters. These include some of the greatest Greek vase painters: Onesimos, Douris, the Brygos Painter and Makron. Most of their cups are Types B and C, which had virtually supplanted Type A. They regularly outlined the tondos with ornamental bands of meanders and patterned squares, which were also sometimes placed beneath the figures on the exterior. Some cups have White-ground interiors.

The early style of ONESIMOS was dependent on the Pioneers, especially Euphronios, who potted some of Onesimos' vases when he stopped painting. Onesimos' compositions are imaginative and harmonious, especially those in tondos with more than one figure. He was a master of the curved line, as exhibited in the expressive hands of his vigorous, thin-limbed figures. His early works show more interest in myth, such as his cup with *Theseus' Visit to Amphitrite* (Paris, Louvre, G 104), but he later favoured scenes of athletics, komos, symposia and youths with horses.

DOURIS signed over forty vases—more than any other painter—including two as potter. He began as a colleague of Onesimos and worked initially with the potters Kleophrades and Euphronios, and with Python throughout his career. Four phases in his work have been identified on the basis of drawing style, ornament and *kalos* names. Especially distinctive is the 'Dourian meander' of his third phase, with meander squares alternating with blackened cross squares. His figures were drawn with a fine line and are often charming, but there is an increasing dullness and repetitiveness in his late works. He painted several interesting Trojan War scenes but mostly favoured conventional scenes of everyday life. He decorated mainly cups but also a few other shapes, including some fine White-ground works such as a lekythos with *Atalanta and Erotes* (Cleveland, OH, Mus. A., 66.114).

The BRYGOS PAINTER is named after the potter of some of his cups. His style derives from the early work of Onesimos, and in addition to cups he decorated a variety of other, mostly small, shapes, including rhyta, skyphoi and lekythoi. Some cups have White-ground interiors. He was a masterly painter of action, and his revel scenes are unrivalled for excitement and movement. The artist could depict scenes of tenderness as well, however. One particular cup (*c*. 480 BC; U. Würzburg, Wagner-Mus., 479; see fig. 111) illustrates both aspects. The outside depicts wild revelry, while the inside shows a *Sick Reveller and Hetaira*, the young courtesan gently supporting the head of the vomiting youth. He excelled at rendering realistic gestures and poses and different human ages. His subjects include a good range of myth and genre; much of this vitality, however, is absent from his late work.

MAKRON was more prolific than any other Red-figure artist, with well over 400 vases attributed to him. However, he painted a more limited range of shapes than the other major Late Archaic vase painters: all are small, and almost all are cups. Mythological subjects occur, especially the Trojan War, but erotic scenes predominate. His figures are heavy; those of women are particularly well drawn. Though there is much repetition, the quality of his work remained consistently high.

111. Attic Red-figure cup by the Brygos Painter: *Sick Reveller and Hetaira*, diam. 323 mm, *c*. 480 BC (Würzburg, Universität Würzburg, Martin von Wagner-Museum)

These four major cup painters developed followings, and several major artists can be associated with each. Thus the style of the Antiphon Painter derives from the early style of Onesimos, while the Colmar Painter was also influenced by Onesimos and probably belonged to the same workshop. At least six painters worked in the 'Brygan Circle'. Some, such as the Foundry Painter, could equal the quality and mood of the master's work. Others, such as the Briseis Painter and Dokimasia Painter, were less intense. Similarly, the Triptolemos Painter (*fl c.* 480s–*c.* 470 BC) was linked to Douris by both potting and painting style: indeed, one of his cups (Berlin, Pergamonmus., F 2286) is even signed as if it were by Douris. He began as a cup painter but later decorated various large shapes, including stamnoi and kraters, with notable mythological scenes.

*(c) Early and High Classical (*c. *480–*c. *425* BC*).* The careers of many painters spanned the Early Classical (*c.* 480–*c.* 450 BC) and High Classical (*c.* 450–*c.* 425 BC) periods, and the major stylistic schools continued through both. In the Early Classical period figures became stockier and faces heavier, especially at the chin. The depiction of movement became less important than conveying a sense of seriousness and sometimes pathos; drapery became less linear and more plastic; tragedy began to have an important influence on the choice of scenes and their iconography.

In the High Classical period figures became slimmer, and pathos gave way to a godlike serenity. The draughtsmanship appeared more assured, and compositions became simpler and more symmetrical, giving a sense of balance and harmony. Drapery was more realistically drawn, hanging correctly on the body; its folds became increasingly varied and suggested greater depth. Although the artists did not gratuitously devise difficult poses, they could successfully render back views, frontal faces and so on as required. The influence of the Parthenon sculptures (*see* ATHENS, §II, 1(ii)) was the major impetus for these developments. Pots rather than cups were favoured, while White-ground vases, particularly lekythoi, grew increasingly popular; many artists worked in both techniques. Inscriptions occurred less frequently.

Mannerists. Not all Early Classical painters followed these trends; the MANNERIST WORKSHOP in particular retained many Archaic features in their work, including stacked, linear drapery folds and stiff poses. However, they combined these with various degrees of Early Classical innovation to produce a very distinctive style characterized by slim, small-headed figures with exaggerated gestures. The Mannerists originated from the workshop of Myson and apparently all worked together, mainly on column kraters, pelikai and hydriai, which they often adorned with old-fashioned Black-figure patterns. The first Mannerist was the Pig Painter, whose early works are particularly close to those of Myson. The Leningrad Painter and his younger contemporary the Agrigento Painter were also capable artists, but the consummate Mannerist was the PAN PAINTER, named after an unusual scene, *Pan Pursuing a Goatherd*, on a bell krater (Boston, MA, Mus. F.A., 10.185). Both the range of shapes he decorated and the variety of scenes are remarkable; he even worked in White-ground. Many of his subjects are original and some humorously lustful. They include such outdoor scenes as hunting and fishing as well as interesting scenes of sacrifice and sanctuary, all in well-ordered compositions. Many of his figures adopt somewhat affected but original poses, displaying a dramatic vitality. His followers never equalled this last successful use of the Archaic style in vase painting. Of the later Mannerists, the most important were the members of the Nausicaa and Hephaistos Painters' (or NH) group, who decorated the same shapes as their forebears. The Nausicaa Painter was the earliest: mythological scenes predominate in his work, many of them interesting and original, though his figures are awkward and affected. The latest Mannerists perpetuated the style until the end of the 5th century BC in a decadent form exemplified by the excessively linear work of their main artist, the Academy Painter.

The tradition of the Berlin Painter. The Providence Painter, Hermonax and the Achilles Painter were three important pupils of the Berlin Painter who used similar stylistic devices to those of their teacher and often similar iconography. The earliest was the Providence Painter (*fl c.* 480–*c.* 460s BC), who was a competent artist specializing in Nolan amphorae and lekythoi, shapes favoured by the Berlin Painter late in his career. The Providence Painter was fond of depicting moving figures and gods, as on his name piece showing *Apollo* (Providence, RI Sch. Des., Mus. A., 15.005).

Hermonax (*fl c.* 470s–*c.* 450s BC) signed ten vases. He painted Nolan amphorae and lekythoi, as well as several larger vases, especially stamnoi and pelikai. Some of his cups, mainly early works, recall Makron. Like other artists in the Berlin Painter's tradition he favoured pursuit scenes, while his rare mythological scenes can have unusual and interesting subject-matter, as on a hydria (Athens, Kyrou Col.) with *Hermes Bringing the Infant Dionysos to Athamas and Ino.*

The youngest pupil of the Berlin Painter was the ACHILLES PAINTER. Although his career began in the Early Classical period he became the Classical vase painter *par excellence*, reflecting the spirit of the Parthenon sculptures more than any other painter. Approximately half his extant vases are White-ground (*see* CERAMICS, colour pl. II, fig. 1), and he was the undisputed master of White-ground lekythoi, whose development he greatly influenced. He also apparently took over from the Berlin Painter the commission for producing Black-figure Panathenaic amphorae. His Red-figure, mainly on medium-sized vases, varies in quality, but his best is excellent. His name piece (*c.* 450–*c.* 440 BC; Rome, Vatican, Mus. Gregoriano Etrus., 16751; see fig. 112) depicts *Achilles* standing serenely in three-quarter view. The relaxed but commanding pose of the hero is reminiscent of the *Doryphoros* of Polykleitos (*see* POLYKLEITOS, §1), the canon of Classical Greek sculpture, while the solitary figure against a black background recalls the Berlin Painter.

The PHIALE PAINTER was the pupil of the Achilles Painter and the last major artist working in the Berlin Painter's tradition. Although he is credited with several

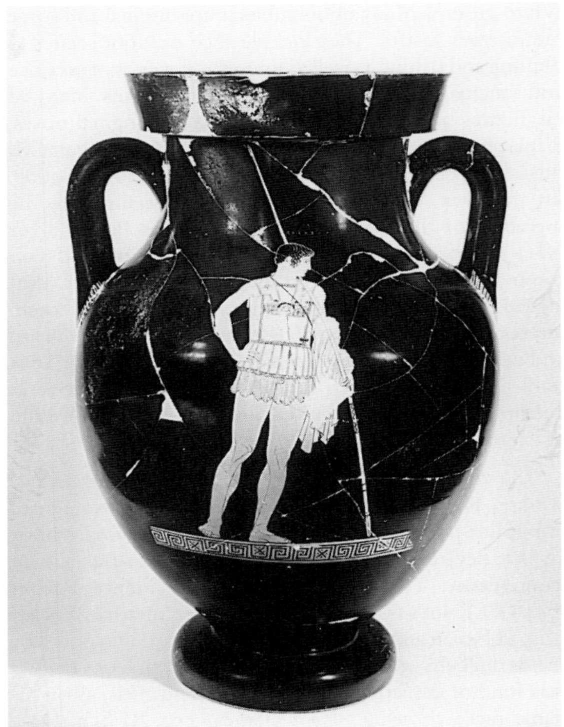

112. Attic Red-figure amphora by the Achilles Painter: *Achilles*, h. 596 mm, *c.* 450–*c.* 440 BC (Rome, Vatican, Museo Gregoriano Etrusco)

excellent White-ground vases, he worked primarily in Red-figure, decorating a wide range of shapes, but like his teacher favouring Nolan amphorae and lekythoi. He painted a wide variety of everyday and mythological scenes; many are rare and interesting, but his most memorable pictures feature young dancing girls and their mistresses (e.g. phiale; Boston, MA, Mus. F.A., 97.371).

The tradition of the Niobid Painter. The NIOBID PAINTER, his older colleague the Altamura painter (*fl c.* 470–*c.* 450s BC) and several followers, including the Painter of the Woolly Satyrs and the Painter of the Berlin Hydria, formed a school of artists whose scenes were often clearly influenced by contemporary wall painting. Thus the figures on the Niobid Painter's name piece, a kalyx krater (*c.* 460–*c.* 450 BC; Paris, Louvre, G 341; see fig. 113) showing *Apollo and Artemis Slaying the Niobids*, are dispersed on different levels in a rocky landscape, not on the normal single groundline. Other vases by the group portray grandiose, multi-figured scenes such as Amazonomachies, Gigantomachies, Centauromachies and the Sack of Troy. They exhibit bold attempts at foreshortening and monumental figures. Similar characteristics are ascribed by literary sources to such contemporary wall painters as POLYGNOTOS of Thasos and MIKON of Athens, although none of their work survives.

Both the Niobid Painter and the Altamura Painter favoured scenes involving myths and gods and preferred large vases, particularly kraters, though the latter specialized also in oinochoai. An innovation introduced by their workshop was the use of two registers of figures on kraters and hydriai. The Niobid Painter has often been underrated: although his figures are often stiff, their crisp lines and monumentality give them more solid substance than those of his contemporaries, and his work maintained a consistently high quality.

One of his younger pupils was POLYGNOTOS, who led the workshop during the next generation. His drawing is mellower and less stiff than the Niobid Painter's and betrays the influence of the Parthenon sculptures, but it still recalls the master's early work. He too preferred large shapes with combat scenes and other monumental subjects, such as the *Centauromachy* on a stamnos (Brussels, Musées Royaux A. & Hist., A 134). His large following included the Hector Painter, the Peleus Painter, the Lykaon Painter and the Christie Painter.

The KLEOPHON PAINTER was one of Polygnotos' younger followers. His work shows an even stronger influence of the Parthenon. His harmonious figures are full and fleshy, their heads often exquisite, as for example on a stamnos illustrating *A Warrior's Departure* (Munich, Staatl. Antikensamml., 2415). He continued the workshop's tradition of decorating large vases but favoured scenes from daily life, particularly those of sacrifice, procession and a warrior's departure. His pupil was the Dinos Painter (*fl c.* 420s–*c.* 410 BC), who maintained a monumental quality in his figures while adopting the elaborate and decorative style of his contemporaries; this he infused with greater excitement and movement, both trends being especially noticeable in the Dionysiac scenes he preferred. Kraters were his favourite shape; he did not continue his predecessors' interest in stamnoi.

113. Attic Red-figure kalyx krater by the Niobid Painter: *Apollo and Artemis Slaying the Niobids*, h. 540 mm, *c.* 460–*c.* 450 BC (Paris, Musée du Louvre)

Cup painters. After the Late Archaic period cups lost their popularity. However, some of the great Late Archaic cup painters created followings that persisted into the Classical period. Of the later followers of Douris, the Euaion Painter (*fl* mid-5th century BC) is the most important. His numerous but monotonous works exhibit well the Classical spirit. The Clinic Painter and the Telephos Painter, the principal followers of Makron, painted in a softer version of their master's style.

The most productive workshop was that of the Penthesilea Painter (*fl c.* 460s–*c.* 440s BC) and his followers, in which, most unusually, more than one artist often worked on the same vase. The Penthesilea Painter's work varies considerably in quality; his style is normally playful and sketchy, the bulbous heads of his figures contributing to this effect. His name piece depicting *Achilles and Penthesilea* (Munich, Staatl. Antikensamml., 2688) and a few other vases are more serious and monumental. He painted some mythological scenes, particularly pursuits involving Eos, but mostly he depicted youths, horses, athletes, women and satyrs with maenads. Some scholars have regarded the output of the Pistoxenos Painter (*fl c.* 475–*c.* 460 BC) as early works by the Penthesilea Painter, but the former's drawing is softer and more elegant; both produced notable White-ground vases. The Penthesilea Painter had numerous followers, including the Splanchnopt Painter and the Veii Painter: his workshop ceased production in the 420s BC.

Some later cup painters such as the Eretria Painter (*see* §(d) below), his colleague the Calliope Painter and the Codrus Painter are also notable: their output continued into the last quarter of the 5th century BC. The Codrus Painter was a particularly fine artist who painted several interesting scenes from Attic myth.

Other painters. Some other schools can be traced for more than one generation but had little influence. The VILLA GIULIA PAINTER was a repetitive artist, but his works are harmonious and tranquil. He decorated both large and small vases and sometimes worked in White-ground; his stamnoi with scenes of women before a rustic idol of Dionysos are his trademark. His main pupil, the CHICAGO PAINTER, continued his style in a less rigid manner. The Boreas Painter and the Florence Painter, the principal members of the Boreas–Florence group, produced mainly second-rate column kraters *c.* 475–*c.* 450 BC in a style continued by the Naples Painter. The Lewis Painter, an Early Classical specialist in skyphoi, was succeeded in the High Classical period by the Penelope Painter. The Sabouroff Painter specialized in cups, lekythoi and Nolan amphorae, an unusual combination. His better work is in White-ground; his cups recall the Brygos Painter, while some of his other works associate him with the Achilles Painter.

Other productive artists who specialized in particular shapes include the Painter of the Louvre Centauromachy (column kraters); the Bowdoin, Carlsruhe and Aischines painters (lekythoi); and the Shuvalov Painter (oinochoai), a transitional artist whose work continued into the last quarter of the 5th century BC. The workshop of the potter Sotades specialized in plastic (i.e. modelled) vases, many of which are strikingly beautiful.

(d) Late 5th century BC. Attic vase painting of this period reflected the developments of the Rich style in Attic sculpture exemplified by the Nike Balustrade (*see* ATHENS, §II, 1(ii)). There is a move toward the effeminate, with female figures modelled by elaborate, diaphanous drapery. Jewellery and other objects were commonly emphasized in relief and often gilded, while the use of added white and yellow became more frequent. Individual strands of hair were delineated, male bodies lost their muscular definition, and poses became more affected. Subject-matter was taken mainly from domestic life; Dionysos and Aphrodite were the preferred deities. These changes may be an attempt to escape from the horrors of the Peloponnesian War (431–404 BC) into a charming fantasy world.

Although no wall paintings survive from this period, literary sources attest major advances in shading and perspective, and both are evident on vases. Many have figures set on different levels and sometimes in different scales, giving a sense of spatial depth. Linear perspective was often applied to small objects (e.g. altars and stools), and some shading is evident, particularly on White-ground lekythoi.

Most of the best work of this period appears on smaller vases. Some of the smaller shapes used in the boudoir, such as the squat lekythos and the pyxis, became popular, as did lekanides, bell kraters, oinochoai and hydriai.

The Meidias Painter. The leading instigator of the new style was the MEIDIAS PAINTER, named after the potter of his magnificent hydria (*c.* 410 BC; London, BM, E 224; see fig. 114). His work recalls that of AISON and the ERETRIA

114. Attic Red-figure hydria by the Meidias Painter: *Rape of the Leucippidae* and *Herakles in the Garden of the Hesperides*, h. 521 mm, *c.* 410 BC (London, British Museum)

PAINTER; each has been proposed as his teacher. The Eretria Painter mainly painted cups with repetitive scenes of satyrs, maenads and athletes, but the elegant, miniature female figures on his many other small vases, such as an amphoriskos with a *Seated Woman* (Oxford, Ashmolean, 537), clearly foreshadow the Meidias Painter.

The Meidias Painter preferred smaller shapes—squat lekythoi, choes, pyxides and lekanides—but he also decorated hydriai, often with two registers of figures. His graceful figures are frequently set on several levels in landscape and are often arranged with a good sense of symmetry. Many scenes depict Aphrodite and her world, and the artist led the way in depicting personified abstractions, many of them named on the vases. Scenes of violence and physical exertion are rare and invariably softened when they could not be avoided. On his name piece (see fig. 114) depicting *Herakles in the Garden of the Hesperides* the hero obtains the apples with no apparent effort, while in the upper register the *Rape of the Leucippidae* seems a mere flirtatious encounter. The tilted heads and outstretched hands holding folds of drapery are typical of the artist's figures, as are the rich clothes and elaborate hairstyles.

Although fewer than 40 vases are ascribed to the Meidias Painter, he influenced numerous other artists, notably the Painter of the Carlsruhe *Paris* and Aristophanes. Many vases are assigned to his 'manner', some so close that they may indeed be his, others clearly poor imitations.

Other painters. The other major tradition in this period was that of the Dinos Painter, the last successor of the Niobid Painter. Other pot painters, such as POLION and the Painter of Munich 2335 (*fl c.* 430s–*c.* 410s BC), also favoured this more traditional style, although their works sometimes recall the Meidian school: many minor painters showed similar conservatism. The Painter of Munich 2335 was one of the last artists to work in both Red-figure and White-ground, and he had connections with several workshops, including those of the Achilles Painter and the Shuvalov Painter.

Painters who shared characteristics of both movements include the KADMOS PAINTER and the Pothos Painter: their large, statuesque, Polygnotan figures were often set in Meidian landscapes, while the NIKIAS PAINTER was conservative early in his career and Meidian later. Finally, the TALOS PAINTER and the PRONOMOS PAINTER produced several large, ornate vases at the end of the 5th century BC.

(e) 4th century BC. Vase painting of the 4th century has not been as well studied as that of earlier periods. At the start of the century two stylistic trends predominated, the Ornate style and the Plain style. The former derived from the Talos Painter, the Pronomos Painter and the Meidias Painter: its best exponents were the Meleager Painter (*fl c.* 400s–*c.* 380 BC) and the Painter of the New York *Centauromachy.* It is characterized by crowded, multi-level scenes, richly decorated drapery and coloured accessories, and more figures are shown in white than in earlier work. The Plain style developed from the Dinos Painter's tradition, its best exponents being the Jena Painter (*fl c.* 390s–*c.* 380s BC), who decorated some exquisite cups, and the Erbach Painter. Their uncrowded compositions lack depth, more heads are shown in profile, and fewer lines are used for drapery and anatomical details. Many other painters shared the characteristics of both schools.

The KERCH STYLE, named after the region where many of the vases were found, appeared *c.* 370 BC and reached its acme by *c.* 350 BC. In many ways it is an amalgamation of both earlier styles, but it owes more to the Ornate. Its compositions are still crowded, but there is more balance and harmony; the figures are statuesque, perhaps even influenced by the contemporary sculpture of Praxiteles and others, and complement the shapes of the pots so that each accentuates the other. The figures are drawn with many short, sketchy lines, with the occasional addition of wash to suggest volume and shadow. Accessory blue and green were also used, and some figures were rendered completely in relief with applied clay; towards the end of the 4th century BC some vases were produced with all their figures in relief.

The MARSYAS PAINTER was the best of the Kerch Painters. His pelike depicting *Peleus Abducting Thetis* (*c.* 340–*c.* 330 BC; London, BM, E 424; see fig. 115) epitomizes the style. The bodies of Thetis and Eros are white and placed centrally, as often with coloured figures; other areas are gilded or painted in blue and green. The elongated figure of the fleeing Nereid in three-quarter back view to the upper right blends with the lines of the vase, as do Aphrodite and her assistant on the left.

115. Attic Red-figure pelike by the Marsyas Painter: *Peleus Abducting Thetis*, h. 425 mm, *c.* 340–*c.* 330 BC (London, British Museum)

Far fewer shapes were decorated in this period, and cups of all types disappeared by *c.* 375 BC. Pelikai were the favourite, although hydriai, kalyx kraters, bell kraters, skyphoi, squat lekythoi and oinochoai were also common, and the lekanis was popular in the first half of the 4th century BC. Women remained the most common subject-matter, although there were several interesting cult scenes; Dionysos and Aphrodite were the most popular deities, Herakles the favourite hero. Oriental costumes and animals are often found, but inscriptions are rare.

It is unclear why Attic Red-figure production ceased *c.* 330–*c.* 320 BC. Perhaps the development of the technique had run its course, or the end may simply reflect a change in taste. Very likely it is connected in some way with the Macedonian domination of Greece.

BIBLIOGRAPHY

J. D. Beazley: *Red-figure* (1942, 2/1963)

G. M. A. Richter: *Attic Red-figured Vases* (New Haven, 1946, rev. 1958)

M. Robertson: *Greek Painting* (Geneva, 1959)

P. E. Arias and M. Hirmer: *Tausend Jahre griechischer Vasenkunst* (Munich, 1960); enlarged Eng. trans. by B. B. Shefton as *A History of Greek Vase Painting* (London, 1962)

J. D. Beazley: *Paralipomena* (1971)

J. Boardman: *Athenian Red Figure Vases: The Archaic Period* (London, 1975)

E. Simon, M. Hirmer and A. Hirmer: *Die griechischen Vasen* (Munich, 1976)

L. Burn and R. Glynn: *Beazley Addenda* (Oxford, 1982); rev. by T. A. Carpenter and others (Oxford, 1989), appendix 2

J. Boardman: *Athenian Red Figure Vases: The Classical Period* (London, 1989)

M. Robertson: *The Art of Vase-painting in Classical Athens* (Cambridge, 1992)

JOHN H. OAKLEY

(ii) South Italian. The Greek settlers who colonized South Italy and Sicily in the 8th century BC produced vases imitating the style prevalent in their mother-city, although they imported the finer vases from Greece, especially those made in Athens and Corinth. The situation changed in the second quarter of the 5th century BC, when Athenian potters and vase painters established workshops on the Gulf of Taranto, as first suggested by Adolf Furtwängler in 1893. His hypothesis associated the beginning of South Italian Red-figure vases with the foundation of Thurii by Athens in 443 BC. Eighty years after Furtwängler's hypothesis, two potter's kilns were discovered at Metapontion (now Metaponto), 80 km north-east of Thurii and 40 km west of Taras (now Taranto). Fragmentary vases have permitted the identification of one of them with the workshop of the Creusa Painter and Dolon Painter, two important Lucanian artists active in the first third of the 4th century BC. The second was used by the Amykos Painter, one of the first Lucanian vase painters, towards the end of his career late in the 5th century BC. The finds in Metapontion are of the utmost importance, since these are the earliest workshops involved in the production of Red-figure vases in South Italy to be discovered and scientifically studied. It is perhaps not surprising that the Red-figure technique appeared early at Metapontion, for the city was one of Athens' allies in the region. The new technique spread rapidly, and by the middle of the 4th century BC each hellenized region produced its own Red-figure vases. Hence we speak today of Lucanian, Apulian, Sicilian, Campanian and Paestan vases.

The great interest in such a production lies in the wide range of myths, sometimes inspired by the Athenian tragedies, that they depict. They also shed some light on the life of the native population and Greek colonists: warriors and banqueters are frequently depicted, and the private life of women and funerary subjects are favoured by many painters. Especially in late Apulian, the funerary scenes are omnipresent, perhaps reflecting the growing insecurity of the time as the natives contested the domination of Taras. The following description of the five fabrics owes much to the work of Dale Trendall, whose carefully annotated lists of vase painters provide the indispensable framework that has long been needed in this field.

(a) Lucanian. (b) Apulian. (c) Sicilian. (d) Campanian. (e) Paestan.

(a) Lucanian. The first Lucanian vase painters were active in the last third of the 5th century BC. These artists, namely the Pisticci Painter and the Amykos Painter, are very close to such contemporary Attic vase painters as the followers of the Achilles Painter and the members of the Polygnotan group. It is therefore possible that they were trained in Athens, although none of their vases has yet been found in Greece. The Pisticci Painter seldom departed from genre scenes, but some vases show that mythological subjects also appealed to him. The reverses of his vases are rather monotonous, and their draped youths are somewhat stiff when compared with Attic models. The Amykos Painter was keener on mythological subjects, and around the end of the 5th century BC he decorated monumental vases probably under the influence of the Tarentine school. Among the various shapes he used, there is one of Messapian (local) origin called a nestoris (see fig. 116).

A second workshop may have been located at Herakleia (now Policoro), a Tarentine colony near Metapontion. Three important artists worked there: the Palermo Painter, Karneia Painter and Policoro Painter, known as the PKP group. They produced vases of high quality with a predilection for mythological subjects on large vases. A pelike attributed to the Policoro Painter (Policoro, Mus. N. Siritide, 35297; see Trendall, 1967, pl. 27,4) and showing the *Punishment of Dirce* gives some idea of the painter's neat drawing, balanced composition and successful three-quarter views.

The second generation of Lucanian artists was led by the Creusa Painter and Dolon Painter working in Metapontion. The Creusa Painter was perhaps a pupil of the Amykos Painter, although he preferred genre scenes. The Dolon Painter was more original, treating mythology in an almost caricatural manner that perhaps reflects the work of the great painter Zeuxis, who worked in nearby Herakleia. His style was also influenced by the Tarporley Painter, an Apulian artist with whom he might have worked for a while. In a separate workshop, the Brooklyn–Budapest Painter was an artist of considerable importance. At the beginning of his career he remained close to the Amykos Painter, but he may have moved to Taras, since he shows considerable influence of the Iliupersis Painter in his work. Nevertheless, he used Lucanian patterns and decorated some nestorides, which distinguishes him from

116. Lucanian Red-figure nestoris (type I) by the Amykos Painter, depicting youths and women, h. 398 mm, *c.* 410–*c.* 400 BC (Richmond, VA, Virginia Museum of Fine Arts)

contemporary Apulian artists. He returned to Lucania *c.* 380 BC and started a workshop in northern Lucania, perhaps at Anzi.

Most Lucanian vase painters followed him, a migration that proved to be fatal since the artists lost contact with the major artistic developments of the time. Their repertory of subjects became more limited, and their stock figures were repeated without much variation. The most significant vase painter of this period is the Primato Painter, who directed a large workshop possibly located at Armento. He was probably trained in Taras by the Lycurgus Painter, since he liked to decorate large vases in the Apulian manner. His floral and ornamental patterns are finely drawn and show much originality for an isolated workshop; his choice of subjects is likewise remarkably large. One of his finest works is a large volute krater with *Herakles* (Paris, Louvre, K 518; see Trendall, 1967, pl. 73,3). His profile heads are rather squarish, while his three-quarter figures are well rendered. The Lucanian fabric died out early (*c.* 320 BC) because of the remote location of the workshops.

(b) Apulian. The Apulian fabric is by far the most important in South Italy, its production reflecting the level of wealth attained by the Tarentines during the 4th century BC, especially under the guidance of the philosopher Archytas (*fl* 367–361 BC). Red-figure vases began to be made in Taras in the last quarter of the 5th century BC, but no trace of the potters' quarter has yet been discovered. Since the cemetery of Taras lies under the modern city and has been only sporadically excavated, most Apulian vases have been discovered at other sites such as Ruvo and Canosa, where excavations have taken place since the early 19th century. Vases of the second half of the 4th century BC, especially those with funerary scenes, depict perhaps some of the products (weapons, bronze vessels, horses etc) that the Greek colonists were willing to trade with the native populations in exchange for wheat, wool and salt.

Two major trends are consistently discernible throughout the Apulian fabric, the Plain and Ornate styles. The Plain style includes most of the smaller vases, which present simple compositions involving a restricted number of figures and a limited choice of decorative patterns. The emblematic vase of this style is the bell krater. The subjects are limited to Dionysiac and genre scenes; many of the later vases are decorated solely with female heads. While myths are rarely depicted in the Plain style, they are very popular in the Ornate, together with funerary subjects. Vases are decorated with intricate floral and geometric patterns, which find an interesting parallel in the subsidiary decoration of temples and funerary monuments. The ornaments are enlivened by the use of added colours. The shapes favoured are the larger ones, such as volute kraters, amphorae and, from *c.* 350 BC, loutrophoroi.

The early vases are well-proportioned in the Attic tradition, but from *c.* 370–*c.* 360 BC much larger vases were produced, some of them over a metre in height. This phenomenon can perhaps be linked to changes observed in funeral practices, as wealthy families now occupied spacious chamber tombs. The increased size of vases allowed the painters to indulge in more complex multi-figural compositions. Although the Apulian artists were able to deal satisfactorily with problems of perspective and foreshortening, their ambitious compositions lack spatial unity: scenes are often divided into separate groups of figures that appear to float on the black background.

The Painter of the Berlin Dancing Girl and the Sisyphus Painter are the most important artists of the original Tarentine workshop. They worked in both Plain and Ornate styles and must be considered the pioneers of the Apulian fabric. They were fond of mythological subjects but decorated a sizeable number of their vases with Dionysiac or genre scenes. The influence of the Sisyphus Painter on later vase painters was substantial. On his name vase, a volute krater depicting a rare version of the myth of Sisyphus (see fig. 117), Ornate style characteristics such as the multi-figural composition, rich decorative patterns and monumental look of the vase are already evident.

For the next 50 years painters specialized: a large group, led by the Tarporley Painter, decorated vases in the Plain style, while a somewhat smaller group continued the tradition of the Ornate style. The Tarporley Painter preferred to decorate bell kraters with Dionysiac scenes or scenes from phlyax plays (farces); the reverses of his vases show two or three draped youths. Despite his association with the Plain style he occasionally depicted mythological scenes. The followers of the Tarporley Painter have been grouped around his three principal pupils: the Schiller Painter, the Hoppin Painter and the Painter of Karlsruhe B 9. These artists continued the tradition established by their master, bringing few novelties in subject-matter.

117. Apulian Red-figure volute krater by the Sisyphus Painter: *Aphrodite and Erotes* (neck), *Wedding of Sisyphus* (body, above) and *Jason Fighting the Dragon in the Presence of the Argonauts* (body, below), h. 730 mm, *c.* 420–*c.* 400 BC (Munich, Staatliche Antikensammlungen)

118. Apulian Red-figure volute krater attributed to the Iliupersis Painter, depicting a funerary scene with a youth inside a naiskos, h. 688 mm, *c.* 370–*c.* 360 BC (London, British Museum)

Evolving in parallel with the Tarporley school, the artists working in the Ornate style followed the Painter of the Birth of Dionysos. His favoured shape was the volute krater. Its increasing size allowed him to depict various mythological scenes in which the many figures are placed at different levels, sometimes giving the impression that the artist is afflicted by *horror vacui.* The greater surface available and the particular morphology of the volute krater called for an increased use of decorative patterns. In this Apulian artists followed Attic volute kraters, which were still exported to Apulia towards the end of the 5th century BC, although their fondness for decorative patterns led them to combine the Attic models in new ways and later to create their own. With added colours, these patterns gave a cheerful look to late Apulian vases.

Few immediate followers of the Painter of the Birth of Dionysos are well known. Their work has survived mainly in fragments from the occasional excavations of the cemetery under modern Taranto. These vases do, however, present perhaps some of the best drawn figures in Apulian ware, such as Priam on a large fragment of a kalyx krater attributed to the Black Fury group (New York, Met., 20.195; see Trendall and Cambitoglou, 1978, pl. 53,4). The richness of the patterns depicted on the clothes suggests some kind of stage performance. The whole vase must have been a masterpiece.

Around 360 BC a new decorative scheme was introduced by the Iliupersis Painter for the larger vases. The obverse is generally reserved for a mythological, bridal or funerary scene arranged on different levels. The reverse depicts a Dionysiac scene, but later this is replaced by a scene around a stele or naiskos (small shrine). The naiskos is a novelty, reflecting actual stone monuments, fragments of which have been retrieved from the Tarentine cemetery. A volute krater attributed to the Iliupersis Painter has one of the earliest depictions of one of these monuments (see fig. 118). Youthful visitors bringing various offerings are grouped around the naiskos in which the figure of the deceased stands. Both the naiskos and the deceased are in added white, perhaps to reflect the marble or stony look of the building. Usually two or four visitors, of both sexes, are grouped around the monument. These figures were repeated from vase to vase as stock figures with little variation. The Iliupersis Painter also modified the subsidiary decoration on the neck of volute kraters and amphorae by replacing the small figural or animal scenes by a head, usually female, in a floral setting. Likewise, the introduction of moulded frontal female heads on the volutes of kraters must be attributed to him or at least to his workshop. Finally, he made more extensive use of added colours in

119. Apulian Red-figure volute krater by the Darius Painter: *Funeral of Patroklos*, h. 1.45 m, *c.* 340–*c.* 320 BC (Naples, Museo Archeologico Nazionale)

conjunction with elaborate new patterns. His followers include the Lycurgus Painter, who showed improvements in foreshortenings and overlappings and who succeeded in rendering emotions on faces in three-quarter view.

Around the middle of the 4th century BC, the Varrese Painter and his followers were clearly at ease in both Plain and Ornate styles. They are, however, best known for their monumental vases in the Ornate style, which reveal an ever-increasing use of added colours and decorative patterns. Two new shapes were introduced: the loutrophoros and the situla. Curiously, they were made in two similar variants, the body being either concave or slightly convex. New myths were also introduced, such as the mourning Niobe or rare personifications. An excellent example is on a loutrophoros of type I (Malibu, CA, Getty Mus., 86.AE.680; see Jentoft-Nilsen and Trendall, pl. 186) attributed to the Painter of Louvre MNB 1148, a pupil of the Varrese Painter. The obverse shows the legend of Leda and the Swan with Hypnos ('Sleep'). Over them, Zeus and Aphrodite are depicted inside a palace. Astrape ('Lightning'), Eniautos ('Year') and the personification of Eleusis—the only certain representations of these figures in Greek art—stand slightly apart. All have their names inscribed. The Painter of Louvre MNB 1148 and his colleague, the Metope Painter, exhibit great care and refinement in their work, sometimes even surpassing their master.

These artists were succeeded by two groups of painters who began to specialize in particular subject-matter, some of them preferring funerary scenes, others myths. The first group is best represented by the Painter of Copenhagen 4223. He gave the funeral scene its canonical form by using a naiskos for the obverse and a stele for the reverse. Both are surrounded by visitors, and the deceased are almost exclusively youths, often with a horse or a dog. The second group is more complex, involving a growing number of artists of outstanding quality illustrated by a very limited number of surviving vases. They offer unusual myths or new renditions of popular ones. The reverses often show a funeral scene. Among these talented artists is the De Schulthess Painter, who was unknown until 1986. One of of his volute kraters (New York, Shelby White and Leon Levy Col., 381; see Trendall and Cambitoglou, 1991, pl. xxxiii, 1) shows a vivid *Gigantomachy*. The bending legs of the two giants are improperly rendered, indicating the limits attained in foreshortening. Of interest also are the dancing women on the vase's neck: their pose and the contrasting colours of their dresses recall the decoration on the walls of the 'Dancers' tomb' in Ruvo (Naples, Mus. Archeol. N., inv. 9355). These artists are very close in style to the Darius Painter and were either his immediate forerunners or colleagues at an early stage in his career.

The DARIUS PAINTER was the finest representative of the Ornate style. He preferred to decorate large vases that provided the appropriate space for his complex renditions of myths. His repertory seems to reflect in part a remarkable knowledge of the Classical Athenian tragedies, especially those of Euripides. One of his monumental volute kraters, which shows the *Funeral of Patroklos*, exemplifies the mature phase of the Ornate style (see fig. 119). The subsidiary decoration begins to invade such new areas as

120. Apulian Red-figure loutrophoros (type III) attributed to the White Saccos Painter, depicting a mistress with maids (above) and two women at a stele (below), h. 1.03 m, *c*. 320–*c*. 300 BC (London, Sotheby's, sale of 10 July 1989, no. 263)

the 'blinkers' of the volutes as well as the foot. The principal scene lies in the centre of the composition, around which the secondary scenes are clustered, providing clues to the myth depicted. Frequently, though, the Darius Painter felt it was necessary to clarify his subject by means of inscriptions identifying key figures or by giving a title, as on the Patroklos vase. His chief follower in the Ornate style was the UNDERWORLD PAINTER, a competent artist who followed his master closely. His inspiration was more limited, but he was still able to depict rare myths in a vivid manner, such as the unique representation of the story of Melanippe on a volute krater (Geneva, Pierre Sciclounoff Col.; see *Le Peintre de Darius et son milieu*, colour pl. p. 24).

Until the time of the Darius Painter, the major workshops were presumably located at Taras. In the later years of the fabric, however, a new centre, possibly located at Canosa (northern Apulia), supplied the rich local market. The artist responsible was perhaps the Patera Painter (*fl c.* 340–*c.* 320 BC), who may have been trained in Taras by the Painter of Copenhagen 4223 and who later moved to Canosa. His style and subjects were much influenced by those of the Painter of Copenhagen 4223. Like his master, he preferred funerary scenes to myths. On some of his vases the reverse is decorated solely with a large female head, which may be the work of an associate. The same is true for the GANYMEDE PAINTER, who is best known for the intricate and colourful floral patterns on the neck of his volute kraters and amphorae.

These artists were followed by a second workshop, in which the principal artist was the BALTIMORE PAINTER. His early works reflect the influence of the Patera Painter, whose pupil he must have been. Later on he was much closer to the Underworld Painter, his contemporary in Taras. He decorated large vases with mythological scenes, although his repertory lacks originality. His naiskoi tend to accommodate more figures, often three, with patterned clothes enlivened by added colours. When the deceased is a man, there is frequently a cuirass beside him or suspended from the ceiling. Such a practice is characteristic of the Canosan artists. The presence in the scene of M-handled hydriai is a characteristic of both the Baltimore Painter and his follower, the White Saccos Painter. They occur, for example, on a loutrophoros (type III) attributed to the White Saccos Painter (see fig. 120), a type of loutrophoros only decorated by Canosan artists. The upper register shows a toilet scene, while the lower depicts two women at a stele. The women of the upper register wear white *sakkoi*, hence the painter's name. It is a feature confined almost entirely to this painter.

Towards the end of the 4th century BC the Red-figure technique declined rapidly. Some artists tried to retain originality in their compositions or subject-matter, such as the Arpi Painter and the Virginia Exhibition Painter, but many confined themselves to funeral scenes and female heads until the whole fabric died out *c.* 300 BC.

121. Sicilian Red-figure skyphoid pyxis attributed to the Gibil Gabib group depicting a bridal scene, h. 292 mm, *c.* 340–*c.* 320 BC (Basle, Antikenmuseum Basel und Sammlung Ludwig)

(c) Sicilian. Despite the Athenian expedition against Syracuse in 415 BC, Sicilian production of Red-figure vases began towards the end of the 5th century BC with the help of Athenian artists. The first Sicilian Red-figure vase painter, the Chequer Painter (*fl c.* 410–*c.* 380 BC), remained very close to contemporary Athenian vase painters, especially to the Jena Painter. His name refers to his fondness for using chequer patterns. His subjects show a marked preference for Eros and genre scenes. The Dirce Painter, his immediate follower, introduced a number of typical Sicilian features, such as the wreath of ivy around the rim of kraters. He also depicted phlyax scenes and some rare myths in a colourful manner.

The death of Dionysios I, tyrant of Syracuse, in 367 BC opened a period of political turmoil in Sicily that might explain the significant diminution in production as well as a possible migration to Campania, where Sicilian vases have been found. This may have led to the foundation of local fabrics in Campania and at Paestum, hence explaining the many similarities between Sicilian, Campanian and Paestan vases. One of these migrants was the Locri Painter, who was previously thought to be Lucanian and working in Lokroi Epizephyrioi (now Locri). Recent discoveries of some of his vases in Sicily, however, suggest that he worked there before moving to Lokroi Epizephyrioi after Dionysios II's expulsion from Syracuse in 356 BC.

The arrival of Timoleon at Syracuse in 342 BC marked a return to stable government in Sicily and enabled an important revival of Red-figure vase painting. The workshops were apparently still concentrated in eastern Sicily, with the exception of one probably located on Lipari Island. Three main groups have been identified: the Lentini-Manfria group, the Etna group and the Lipari group. The Lentini-Manfria group (*c.* 340–*c.* 320 BC) produced some monumental vases that are among the best Sicilian vases. They show an unusual interest for mythological subjects treated in the grand manner with added colours, perhaps reflecting free painting. One of the masterpieces is a skyphoid pyxis attributed to the Gibil Gabib group and showing a bridal scene (see fig. 121). The figures are drawn with unusual care and delicacy, echoing the finest Attic vases of the KERCH STYLE. Further development of the Lentini-Mafria group may be seen in the Borelli group (*c.* 320–*c.* 300 BC), which exhibits some decline in the drawing of figures and decorative patterns but offers such examples of polychromy as the Falcone pyxis (Palermo, Mus. Reg., GE 4730; see Trendall, 1967, frontispiece to vol. I), on which Greek letters specifying the required colours are inscribed in order to help the painter. The vases of the Etna group are much smaller. The most popular shape is the lekanis, which accommodated only a limited choice of subjects, namely women, Nike, Eros and confronted female heads. The principal artist of the group was the Cefalù Painter. His delicate style and sense of composition permitted him some successful attempts at mythological subjects. His lekanis (Lipari, Mus. Archeol. Eoliano, 749 A; see Trendall, 1967, pl. 249,4–6), for example, shows Apollo and Artemis at Delphi.

The Lipari Painter (*fl c.* 320–*c.* 300 BC) stood at the head of a group whose vases are easily recognizable by the extensive use of added colours; not only the usual white, yellow and red, but also blue, pink and green. A skyphoid pyxis attributed to the Lipari Painter (Lipari, Mus. Archeol. Eoliano, 276 L; see Trendall, 1967, pl. 254,1) shows two naked women. The lid displays the usual decoration of laurel wreaths to which ovoid objects decorated with blue ribbons, recalling Easter eggs, are attached. The Lipari Painter had a fondness for three-quarter views and feminine subjects; the reverses of his vases often depict a large female head. His latest vases coincide with the end of the Sicilian Red-figure vases *c.* 300 BC.

(d) Campanian. The production of Red-figure vases in Campania started late in the second quarter of the 4th century BC. Three fabrics have been identified, two at Capua and one at Cumae. Campanian potters preferred smaller vases, and among the various shapes employed the most original is the bail amphora, which is restricted to Campanian. The body is close to a neck amphora, but the handles are replaced by a single one arched over the mouth. Mythological scenes were rare, while funerary scenes around a stele were quite popular. Women's flesh is often added in white. Native elements play an important part in the repertory, such as the cuirass with three metal discs and feathered helmets worn by Samnite warriors. Female heads were often used as subsidiary decoration on the necks of amphorae and below the handles of hydriai.

The first fabric in Capua was established by the followers of the Dirce Painter, who emigrated there from Sicily *c.* 370 BC. The Cassandra Painter owed much to their style but very soon departed from them and affirmed his originality. The ground on his vases is often enlivened by black and white spots perhaps representing the volcanic Campanian soil (e.g. Berlin, Antikenmus., 3238; see Trendall, 1967, pl. 89,1–3). His followers took separate paths. The Parrish Painter owed much to his master, although his drawing is less careful and his style much cruder. By contrast, the Laghetto Painter (*fl c.* 350–*c.* 320 BC) departed rapidly from the Cassandra Painter to develop a polychromatic style. His most important follower was the Caivano Painter, whose influence on contemporary Paestan vase painters is so clear that he perhaps worked at Paestum for a while; he was once thought to be Paestan himself. One of the distinctive features of his works is the depiction of what appears to be solidified lava. It is composed of parallel, slightly undulant black lines, as on a bell krater depicting the *Ambush of Dolon* (Naples, priv. col.; see Trendall, 1989, fig. 282). His choice of subjects is fairly extensive, with a good selection of myths, though some are difficult to recognize. He may well have been the first to include Samnite warriors in his repertory. This is perhaps a reflection of his clientele, which was part Greek colonists, part native.

The fabric is well represented in late Campanian by the Ixion Painter (*fl c.* 330–*c.* 300 BC), who favoured monumental vases with scenes treated in the grand manner, often with multi-level compositions comparable to contemporary Apulian. His mastery of the complex composition is exemplified by a bell krater showing *Boreas Ravishing Oreithyia* (Oxford, Ashmolean, 1894.5; see Trendall, 1967, pl. 133,5–6). The Ixion Painter offered an unusually wide choice of subjects for a Campanian artist. His warriors do not wear the typical Samnite armour and helmet. After him, vases declined drastically in quality.

The second Capuan fabric presents some interesting contrasts with the first; funerary scenes and native peoples are more frequently depicted, for example, which suggests that the vases might have been produced specifically for the Samnite market. There are also a greater number of phlyax vases. The first artist was the Capua Painter (*fl c.* 360–*c.* 330 BC), who decorated a large number of vases but whose subjects were restricted mainly to funerary and Dionysiac themes. He was followed by three groups of artists known collectively as the AV group. The Whiteface/Frignano Painter led the first group. He recalls the Capua Painter in his limited choice of subjects but is best known for the Praxitelean-like pose of his youths. In the second group, headed by the Libation Painter, a popular scene is the departure or arrival of a warrior to whom a woman makes a libation. A good example is represented on a bell krater attributed to the Libation Painter (see fig. 122). The warriors wear the characteristic feathered helmet of the Samnites, while the woman is

122. Campanian Red-figure bell krater attributed to the Libation Painter, depicting a libation to Samnite warriors, h. 360 mm, *c.* 340–*c.* 330 BC (Paris, Musée du Louvre)

represented in a native costume with a distinctive headdress. The painter seems equally at home with funerary and mythological subjects. The Danaid group (AV III) began its production a little later than the others (*c.* 340 BC). The choice of subjects shifted away from libation and stele scenes to Dionysiac, mythological and genre scenes. The influence of Paestan is important in composition, patternwork and the presence of a multiple lid on lebetes gamikoi, such as one attributed to the Danaid Painter and showing a naked mistress and her maid (London, BM, F 207; see Trendall, 1967, pl. 171,3). The female flesh is now rarely added in white. The AV group was succeeded by the Fillet group and an unusually swift barbarization of production.

In Cumae, the vases are classified in three succeeding groups known as Cumae A, B and C. The unity of style, patterns and subject-matter suggests a single large workshop (*c.* 350–*c.* 300 BC); the choice of subjects is even more restricted than on Capuan ware. The pioneer was the CA (= Cumae A) Painter (*fl c.* 350–*c.* 325 BC), who seemed to devote himself almost exclusively to funerary scenes showing women at a stele; these are occasionally accompanied by a Samnite warrior, as on a bell krater (Budapest, Mus. F.A., 51.41; see Trendall, 1967, pl. 175,5). Later in his career, during the Apulianizing phase, he depicted naiskoi and 'xylophones'. The 'xylophone' first appeared on Apulian vases. It is a musical instrument in the form of a small ladder which might be identified as the rattle of the philosopher Archytas.

The Apulianizing phase marked a turning-point in Cumaean ware. It has been suggested that the Tarentine embassy to Naples *c.* 330 BC might have brought Apulian artists, at least two of whom came to Cumae: the Ivo-leaf Painter and the APZ Painter. Vases by the Ivy-leaf Painter have been found at Canosa in Apulia, where he may have worked at the beginning of his career. The APZ Painter (*fl c.* 330–*c.* 320 BC) is the great figure of the Apulianizing phase, adding such Apulian features as the naiskos and 'xylophone' to the Campanian repertory. Nevertheless, he immersed himself quite rapidly in the local artistic environment, since he decorated neck and bail amphorae and used added white for women's flesh.

Cumae B ware (*c.* 330–*c.* 315 BC), the work of the second generation of vase painters, reflects a better understanding of the new Apulian elements present in Campanian. There was, however, a steady decline in its style, associated with a restricted use of added colours and a narrowing range of subject-matter, with monotonous repetition of figures from one vase to another. Some originality in style and subject-matter, however, is exhibited in the work of such artists as the Branicki Painter and the Painter of B.M. F 229 in the Rhomboid group. These vases are easily recognizable by the presence of rhomboids (lozenges) in the field. The female heads decorating the small vases of the Branicki Painter wear a unique headdress known as a 'tennis-racket' saccos, for example on a plate (Birmingham, Mus. & A.G., 1297.85; see Trendall, 1989, fig. 317/6). The fabric came to an end with the artists of Cumae C (*c.* 315–*c.* 295 BC). The influence of Sicilian is manifested by the introduction of a vase in the shape of a bottle, by subjects centred on women's daily life and by the return of polychromy. By this time, however, the drawing had declined irreversibly.

(e) Paestan. Most Paestan vases have been found in and around Paestum (anc. Poseidonia), hence indicating their probable production at that site. They present a remarkable unity of style, subject-matter and pattern-work. In fact, the canon established by the painters Asteas and Python was maintained throughout the life of the fabric, with the exception of the Apulianizing phase from *c.* 330 BC. The use of 'framing palmettes' is one of the characteristic features of the Paestan style: the palmette, to which a sinuous leaf is attached to each side, is placed below the handle and serves as a frame for the figural scenes on the vase. The so-called 'Asteas flower', restricted to the workshop of Asteas and Python, is also easily recognizable. The preferred shape was the bell krater, while the lebes gamikos, with its multiple lid, was the most original contribution of Paestan potters. Such lids are bold and complex creations composed of up to four elements, mainly miniature lekanides and lebetes gamikoi.

Scenes of women's daily life and Dionysiac subjects were favourite Paestan themes; mythology played a minor role, and funerary scenes and those involving native warriors are extremely rare. On larger vases a row of onlookers is often placed above the scene. These are represented as busts or heads looking down from a window. The reverses often show a pair of draped youths who may hold various objects. The drapery is patterned with a distinctive dot-stripe border going back to the Dirce Painter in Sicily, where Paestan ware must have originated.

The principal vase painter was Asteas (*fl c.* 360–*c.* 330 BC) who, along with his colleague Python, was the only South Italian vase painter to sign his products. Eleven of his surviving vases bear his name. His repertory is mostly confined to Dionysiac and phlyax scenes, but his larger vases present a good selection of myths. His most ambitious work may be a signed kalyx krater showing the *Rape of Europa* (see fig. 123). Although he took great care in the rendering of such complex mythological scenes, his best work is his simpler but vivid depiction of phlyax scenes. Like him, Python represented mythological scenes on his larger vases, and it is sometimes difficult to distinguish his works from those of Asteas. His signature appears on two vases.

There were a number of other vase painters in the same workshop. They show strong stylistic affinities with the two masters, while their subjects are restricted to Dionysiac and genre scenes. The Aphrodite Painter (*fl c.* 340–*c.* 320 BC), an outstanding figure among these artists, probably trained in Apulia before moving to Paestum, a situation recalling that of the APZ Painter in Cumae. The Aphrodite Painter brought elaborate floral ornaments and patternwork with him, as well as hollow rocks and 'xylophones'. He assimilated rapidly by decorating such non-Apulian shapes as the neck amphora and by using such Paestan features as the 'Asteas flower' and the dot-stripe border for his draped figures.

The Paestan style of the last quarter of the 4th century BC is best represented by the Painters of Naples 1778 and 2585. The production of their workshop reflects the swift decline of the Red-figure technique. Around 330 BC a group of Apulian vase painters came to Paestum, probably after its liberation from Lucanian domination by Alexander

123. Paestan Red-figure kalyx krater signed by Asteas: *Rape of Europa*, h. 710 mm, *c*. 360–*c*. 330 BC (Malibu, CA, J. Paul Getty Museum)

the Molossian. They used some local shapes and pattern-work but mostly remained apart, probably in a distinct workshop.

BIBLIOGRAPHY

P. Wuilleumier: *Tarente: Des origines à la conquête romaine* (Paris, 1939)

A. D. Trendall: 'Phlyax Vases', *Bull. Inst. Class. Stud. U. London*, suppl. 19 (London, 1959, rev. 2/1967)

A. G. Woodhead: *The Greeks in the West* (London, 1962)

A. D. Trendall: *The Red-figured Vases of Lucania, Campania and Sicily*, 2 vols (Oxford, 1967; 1st suppl., London, 1970; 2nd suppl., London, 1973; 3rd suppl., London, 1983)

A. Oliver jr: 'The Reconstruction of Two Apulian Tomb-groups', *Ant. Kst*, suppl. 5 (Berne, 1968)

H. R. W. Smith: *Funerary Symbolism in Apulian Vase-painting* (Berkeley, 1976)

A. Kossatz-Diessmann: *Dramen des Aischylos auf westgriechischen Vasen* (Mainz, 1978)

A. D. Trendall and A. Cambitoglou: *The Red-figured Vases of Apulia*, 3 vols (Oxford, 1978–82; 1st suppl., London, 1983; 2nd suppl., London, 1991–2)

H. Lohmann: *Grabmäler auf unteritalischen Vasen* (Berlin, 1979)

D. Adamesteanu, ed.: *Metaponto I* (Rome, 1980), pp. 355–452

G. Schneider-Herrmann: *Lucanian and Apulian Nestorides* (Amsterdam, 1980)

B. R. Macdonald: 'The Emigration of Potters from Athens in the Late Fifth Century BC', *Amer. J. Archaeol.*, lxxxv (1981), pp. 159–68

H. Lohmann: 'Zu technischen Besonderheiten apulischer Vasen', *Jb. Dt. Archäol. Inst.*, xcvii (1982), pp. 191–249

The Art of South Italy: Vases from Magna Graecia (exh. cat., ed. M. E. Mayo and K. Hamma; Richmond, VA Mus. F.A., 1982)

D. von Bothmer: 'Observations on the Subject Matter of South Italian Vases', *A. VA*, xxiii/3 (1983), pp. 28–41

M. W. Frederiksen: *Campania* (London, 1984)

R. Hurschmann: *Symposienszenen auf unteritalischen Vasen* (Würzburg, 1985)

A. D. Trendall: 'On the Divergence of South Italian from Attic Red-figured Vase-painting', *Greek Colonists and Native Populations. Proceedings of the First Australian Congress on Classical Archaeology: Sydney, 1985*, pp. 217–30

Napoli antica (exh. cat., ed. G. Macchiaroli; Naples, Mus. Archeol. N., 1985)

Le Peintre de Darius et son milieu (exh. cat. by A. Cambitoglou, C. Aellen and J. Chamay, Geneva, Mus. A. & Hist., 1986)

I. McPhee and A. D. Trendall: 'Greek Red-figured Fish-plates', *Ant. Kst*, suppl. 14 (Basle, 1987)

A. D. Trendall: *The Red-figured Vases of Paestum* (London, 1987)

F. Villard: 'L'Art: Céramique et peinture', *Un secolo di ricerche in Magna Grecia. Atti del ventottesimo convegno di studi Magna Grecia: Taranto, 1988*, pp. 177–97

A. D. Trendall: *Red Figure Vases of South Italy and Sicily*, World A. (London, 1989)

I. McPhee and A. D. Trendall: 'Addenda to *Greek Red-figured Fish-plates*', *Ant. Kst*, xxxiii (1990), pp. 31–51

M. R. Jentoft-Nilsen and A. D. Trendall: *The J. Paul Getty Museum, Malibu*, iii–iv, Corp. Vasorum Ant. USA, 26–7 (Malibu, CA, 1990–91)

A. D. Trendall: 'Farce and Tragedy in South Italian Vase-painting', *Looking at Greek Vases*, ed. T. Rasmussen and N. Spivey (Cambridge, 1991), pp. 151–82

A. D. Trendall and A. Cambitoglou: *Second Supplement to the Red-figure Vases of Apulia* (London, 1991)

E. Greco: *Archeologia della Magna Grecia* (Bari, 1992), pp. 321–40

Principi Imperator Vescovi: Duemila anni di storia a Canosa (exh. cat., ed. R. Cassano Marsilio; Bari, Monastery of Santa Scolastica, 1992)

PASCAL LEBLOND

(iii) Other areas. In the second half of the 5th century BC, particularly during the Peloponnesian War (431–404 BC), local Red-figure fabrics began to be produced in various areas of Greece, especially Boiotia, Corinth, Lakonia, Elis and the Chalcidice, in imitation of, and sometimes in competition with, Attic Red-figure vases. The earliest and most inventive workshop was in Boiotia. Its output apparently included an Early Classical pelike (*c*. 470–*c*. 460 BC; Munich, Staatl. Antikensamml., 2347) indebted to Athenian work by such artists as the Syleus Painter and the Geras Painter, but large-scale production is only attested to *c*. 430–*c*. 420 BC by the lekythoi and bell kraters from a mass burial at Thespiai. These vases still closely resembled their Athenian models—in the case of the lekythoi, works by the ACHILLES PAINTER—but contemporary or only slightly later kalyx kraters and skyphoi by the Painter of the Judgement of Paris exhibit pronounced non-Attic elements in shape, decoration and style. This local Red-figure style flowered *c*. 425–*c*. 375 BC, probably at Thebes. Though the vases were largely for local use, some were exported as far as Spina at the mouth of the Po. A wide variety of shapes occur, many derived from Attic, but some, such as the Kabeiric skyphos and the kantharos, took on popular local forms. The principal artists were the Argos Painter, the Painter of the Large Athens Kantharos, whose works include a kalyx krater depicting *Athena in a Quadriga* (*c*. 400 BC; London, BM; see fig. 124), and the Thetis Painter, who was unusual in being a bilingual artist. Subject-matter is varied, combining standard genre or mythological scenes with ones derived from local cults, such as those on the Kabeiric skyphoi; a large number of small bell kraters bear a head, usually female, on one side and a palmette on the other. Though many isolated Boiotian vases of the first half of the 4th century BC have been discovered, the later phase of the fabric is poorly understood and needs more research. Considerable production of local Red-figure is likely

14. Boiotian Red-figure kalyx krater by the Painter of the Large Athens Kantharos: *Athena in a Quadriga*, h. 279 mm, *c.* 400 BC (London, British Museum)

c. 375–*c.* 350 BC during the age of Boiotian military domination. Since the light brown colour of Boiotian clay is often indistinguishable from that of Attic, some vases now thought to be Attic may actually be Boiotian.

Corinth also produced considerable amounts of Red-figure pottery *c.* 440–*c.* 350 BC, mainly for local use, though some pieces reached Boiotia, Phokis, Olympia and perhaps even South Italy. The fabric is easily distinguished from Attic by the pale (cream to light brown) colour of the fired clay, the orange slip sometimes used and the flaking of the glaze. The most common shapes are the bell krater and kalyx krater, but the range is large, including pelikai, hydriai, oinochoai of various types, squat lekythoi, cups, stemless cups, skyphoi, lekanides and even plates. All these are derived from the Attic repertory of the late 5th century BC and early 4th; but one remarkable Corinthian form is the stemless bell krater, a shape adopted in Apulia and decorated in the Gnathia technique. The subject-matter of Corinthian Red-figure is similar to that found on contemporary Attic, though scenes involving torch racers are surprisingly common, and the influence of the theatre is evident in certain paintings depicting comic actors who resemble the *phlyakes* of South Italian vases. Stylistic resemblances between Corinthian and Attic works are very close: indeed, the Athenian Suessula Painter decorated at least one vase made of Corinthian clay and strongly influenced early Corinthian Red-figure works. Few individual artists have been identified due to the fragmentary nature of the evidence, apart from the Pelikai Painter (late 5th century BC) and the Dombrena Painter (early 4th century BC).

Lakonia also apparently produced Red-figure pottery *c.* 430–*c.* 375 BC, including colossal one-handled mugs, which must have served a cult function. Many fragments were unearthed at Sparta, and whole vases were found at Analipsis in Kynouria, including a colossal mug showing a traditional Spartan story, the *Birth of Helen* (*c.* 410–*c.* 390 BC; Athens, N. Archaeol. Mus., 19447). The fabric is coarser than Attic and fired light red to reddish brown, often with a grey core; its surface was sometimes coated with a light brown slip.

Production of Red-figure pottery in the vicinity of Elis from *c.* 430 BC was probably initiated by Athenian artisans working at Olympia during the construction of the cult statue for the Temple of Zeus. Many fragments have been found at Olympia and Ancient Elis, and a few at Elean Pylos and Mazi. The bell krater is the most common shape, and the fired clay is light brown to orange and easily mistaken for Attic: indeed, Elean pottery showed close stylistic links with Attic until *c.* 400 BC, when it began to look to Apulian Red-figure for inspiration. Whether the pottery was made in Olympia or Ancient Elis or both is not clear, but production apparently ceased by *c.* 350 BC.

The so-called 'Agrinion Group' of small squat lekythoi decorated with figures reserved and painted white occurs along the north-western coast of Greece and in Albania and the former Yugoslavia. To judge from the fabric, these vases may be imports from Elis rather than local productions, but some pottery in the museums at Agrinion, Arta and Ioannina may be local, and there is no doubt that many Red-figure vases were made in the Greek colonies at Dyrrhachion and/or Apollonia on the Adriatic coast of Albania, their style and iconography deriving from the pottery of South Italy.

In northern Greece, local Red-figure vases characterized by their micaceous, yellowish-brown clay were produced *c.* 425–*c.* 350 BC at Olynthos or another Greek settlement in the Chalcidice. Two main painters have been identified, the Painter of Olynthos 5.141 and the Painter of Olynthos 5.156, both of whom decorated various shapes but specialized in skyphoi and lebetes gamikoi. Finally, less significant Red-figure workshops seem to have existed also at Eretria (*c.* 430–*c.* 420 BC) and on Crete (*c.* 400 BC) as well as, perhaps, at Tegea and at Sikyon or Argos.

BIBLIOGRAPHY

R. Lullies: 'Zur boiotisch rotfigurigen Vasenmalerei', *Mitt. Dt. Archäol. Inst.: Athen. Abt.*, lxv (1940), pp. 1–27

A. D. Ure: 'Boeotian Vases with Women's Heads', *Amer. J. Archaeol.*, lvii (1953), pp. 245–9

——: 'The Argos Painter and the Painter of the Dancing Pan', *Amer. J. Archaeol.*, lxii (1958), pp. 389–95

B. A. Sparkes: 'The Taste of A Boeotian Pig', *J. Hell. Stud.*, lxxxvii (1967), pp. 116–30

S. Herbert: *The Red-Figure Pottery* (1977), vii/4 of *Corinth: Results of Excavations Conducted by the American School of Classical Studies at Athens* (Princeton, 1932–)

I. McPhee: 'The Agrinion Group', *Annu. Brit. Sch. Athens*, lxxiv (1979), pp. 159–62

K. Braun: *Bemalte Keramik und Glas aus dem Kabirenheiligtum bei Theben* (Berlin, 1981)

I. McPhee: 'Some Red-figure Vase-painters of the Chalcidice', *Annu. Brit. Sch. Athens*, lxxvi (1981), pp. 297–308

——: 'Local Red Figure from Corinth, 1973–1980', *Hesperia*, lii (1983), pp. 137–53

S. Karouzou: 'I Eleni tis Spartis' [Helen of Sparta], *Ephimeris Archaiol.* (1985), pp. 33–44

K. Gex-Morgenthaler: 'Der Berner Maler', *Ant. Kst.*, xxix (1986), pp. 115–25

I. McPhee: 'Laconian Red-figure from the British Excavations in Sparta', *Annu. Brit. Sch. Athens*, lxxxi (1986), pp. 153–65

I. McPhee and A. D. Trendall: 'Six Corinthian Red-figure Vases', *Corinthiaca, Studies in Honor of Darrell A. Amyx* (Columbia, 1986)

A. Eggebrecht: *Albanien, Schätze aus dem Land der Skipetaren* (Mainz, 1988)
B. Cook: 'Cretan Red-figured Lekythoi', *Annu. Brit. Sch. Athens*, lxxxv (1990), pp. 69–70
I. McPhee: 'Local Red-figured Pottery from Ancient Elis: The Austrian Excavations of 1910–1914', *Jhft. Österreich. Archäol. Inst. Wien*, lx (1990)
——: 'A Corinthian Red-figured Calyx-krater and the Dombrena Painter', *Oxford J. Archaeol.*, x (1991), pp. 325–34

IAN MCPHEE

7. WHITE-GROUND. Greek painted pottery with a light background produced by applying liquid clay containing kaolinite was made at various dates and in different regions. Only in Athens, however, did White-ground become a recognized class of pottery, equivalent to Black- and Red-figure, and associated with particular shapes of vessel, certain workshops, painters and techniques of painting. The White-ground technique relates, therefore, essentially to Attic pottery.

White-ground painting was not as durable in use as Red-figure or Black-figure work and was thus confined to funerary vessels and votive or possibly other special gifts, such as wedding presents. The vases' functions influenced the choice of subjects and motifs used. Only that part of the vase surface used for pictures or ornamentation had a white ground, and White-ground painting was often combined with Black- or Red-figure work. Athenian White-ground production started *c.* 530–*c.* 520 BC and continued uninterrupted until *c.* 400 BC. A series of different painting techniques developed in different workshops, though these overlapped to an extent, some being used only for specific shapes of vessel.

The use of Black-figure painting on a white ground was the earliest form of White-ground painting and was introduced to Athens by the potter NIKOSTHENES, presumably under the influence of Ionian models. It was adopted by other workshops and used mainly on small- and middle-sized vases, differing from normal Black-figure only in the changed background colour and the associated practice of not using white for women's skin. The ground was rarely pure white, tending to be yellowish or brownish. The oldest examples are two oinochoai (Paris, Louvre, F 116 and F 117) signed by Nikosthenes.

The technique of outline drawing was adapted from Red-figure painting for use on White-ground pottery towards the end of the 6th century BC and was applied particularly to cups and smallish ointment containers (alabastra and small lekythoi). The outer contours of a figure were first executed with relief lines similar to those used in Red-figure, an example being the *Dancing Maenad* on a cup by the BRYGOS PAINTER in Munich (Staatl. Antikensamml., 2645). From the start of the 5th century BC, however, outlines were increasingly drawn in the same diluted glaze as the subsidiary detail. Individual parts of the drawing were given a yellowish or brownish tone, also with diluted glaze, and red was occasionally used for minor details (e.g. hair ribbons). The so-called 'semi-outline technique' combined the outline technique with the Black-figure silhouette technique and was used only in the first half of the 5th century BC, almost exclusively on lekythoi and alabastra.

Four-colour painting using black and diluted glaze and earth colours was a technical development of *c.* 500–*c.* 475 BC, probably originating from the workshop of EUPHRONIOS, which specialized in cups. It combined pure outline drawing with areas of solid colour. Parts of the body and garments of thin material were drawn in outline, generally with diluted glaze, whereas garments of thick material were coloured in entirely. Details within the coloured areas such as patterns or folds were executed either in diluted glaze or in red or white paint as appropriate. Such objects as jewellery, fruit, parts of weapons and vessels or containers were often modelled in relief and gilded. Though the palette of colours was effectively reduced to shades of red by the exclusive use of earth colours, the painters could produce shades of black and yellow by varying the strength of the glaze. White was still largely reserved for the ground, though also employed for patterns on garments. Painting was completed before firing. Four-colour painting was used mainly on cups and pyxides. Even in the 5th century BC alabastra were generally decorated purely in outline, while special painting techniques were developed in the Classical period for lekythoi. White-ground was virtually confined to these four shapes, though it was used occasionally on others.

125. White-ground cup with four-colour painting by the Pistoxenos Painter: *Aphrodite*, h. 108 mm, *c.* 475–460 BC (London, British Museum)

The most beautiful four-colour cups were made *c.* 475–*c.* 460 BC and are attributed to the Pistoxenos Painter. They include a cup in Athens (N. Archaeol. Mus., Acropolis 439) depicting the *Death of Orpheus*, and one in London (BM, D2; see fig. 125) depicting *Aphrodite*. Most four-colour pyxides seem to have come from the workshop of the Penthesilea Painter, whose pyxis depicting the *Judgement of Paris* (New York, Met., 07.286.36) is a good example of the graphic potential of four-colour painting.

Early Classical lekythos painting using black and diluted glaze, earth colours and non-ceramic matt colours belongs to the second quarter of the 5th century BC. This technique was employed for painting large lekythoi used exclusively in burial rites, and it was the first to exploit non-earth colours such as cinnabar and 'Egyptian' blue, though glaze and earth colours still predominated. Compared with four-colour cup and pyxis painting, it made possible more marked colour contrasts and an altogether richer palette:

purely linear elements became subordinate to coloured surfaces. Flesh tints on female figures were painted over with a second white, and even thin garments were now rendered in colour. Other typical features include black robes with red folds and hemlines, and painters also strove for greater realism in reproducing the colours of objects: stones were painted white, wooden objects black or brown. Most of these Early Classical lekythoi paintings depict scenes in women's apartments, the best-known being by the ACHILLES PAINTER.

About the middle of the 5th century BC a new polychrome technique of lekythos painting using matt colours was introduced. The use of second white was abandoned as was that of large areas painted with glaze, while the use of non-ceramic colours increased. The ground was now usually chalky white, and large parts of the picture, including flesh and funerary stelai, were again drawn in pure outline. At the same time red or blackish-grey matt paint began to replace diluted glaze for outlines. The Sabouroff Painter was apparently the initiator of this new painting technique, though several painters, such as the Achilles Painter, still employed diluted glaze for contours, a practice that persisted until about 430 BC. Outlines in matt colours were still drawn before firing, but the rest of the painting was completed after firing, making it even less durable. The original colours on these lekythoi have now largely disappeared, and the scenes depicted can be recognized—if at all—only from their outlines, while a few painters (e.g. the Sabouroff Painter) no longer bothered to outline those parts of the picture that were to be coloured. Thus it is no longer easy to recapture the original colourful effect of these Classical lekythoi, which must in their day have been striking. The pigments used included cinnabar and haematite for red and malachite and copper hydroxide chloride for green, together with yellow ochre and 'Egyptian' blue. Other pigments, such as those used for pink and matt black, have not yet been identified. The most important painters of lekythoi during the Classical period were: the Achilles Painter, the Sabouroff Painter, the Thanatos Painter, the Triglyph Painter, the Bird Painter, the Quadrate Painter, the Woman Painter, the REED PAINTER, the PHIALE PAINTER and the painter of GROUP R. Towards the end of the 5th century BC the influence of contemporary panel painting on lekythos painting increased noticeably, with the first attempts at shading on human bodies (*see* GROUP OF THE HUGE LEKYTHOI).

In the second half of the 5th century BC White-ground was used exclusively in sepulchral contexts and was largely confined to lekythoi, generally with paintings of grave scenes. When the production of funerary lekythoi ceased *c.* 400 BC, Attic White-ground painting also came to an end.

BIBLIOGRAPHY

D. C. Kurtz: *Athenian White Lekythoi: Patterns and Painters* (Oxford, 1975)

J. R. Mertens: *Attic White-Ground: Its Development on Shapes other than Lekythoi* (New York, 1977)

I. Wehgartner: *Attische weissgrundige Keramik: Maltechniken, Werkstätten, Formen, Verwendung* (Mainz, 1983)

——: 'Neue Untersuchungen zur weissgrundigen Lekythenbemalung', *Ancient Greek and Related Pottery. Proceedings of the International Vase Symposium: Copenhagen, 1987*, pp. 640–51

IRMA WEHGARTNER

8. UNPAINTED. This section deals with pottery having no painted design or picture. Such pottery was, however, often painted or dipped in a single overall colour or decorated with bands of plain paint and might bear stamped, incised or moulded decoration.

(i) Black-glaze. Black-glazed (or, perhaps more accurately, black-glossed) pottery was one of the most popular forms of fine ceramics in the Classical and Hellenistic periods and was produced at various sites throughout the Mediterranean. In the eastern Mediterranean, workshops have been located at Athens, Corinth, Olynthos and Izmir, and in Boiotia and Lakonia; production centres in the west are being traced by scientific analysis. The vase shapes are often similar, possibly the result of the influence of a particular centre such as Athens or of another medium such as metalwork. That Athenians made Black-glaze pottery outside Attica is attested by an Ephesian decree bestowing temporary citizenship on two potters and by the appearance at Corinth of a series of Attic and Corinthian Black-glaze pots that share a common stamped design.

The popularity of Black-glaze pottery is demonstrable in several ways: for example, it accounts for some 99% of the imported Attic pottery at the north African port of Sabratha, and it is also the most frequently found ware at rural sites, such as the Classical and Hellenistic houses excavated at Dema and Vari in Attica. Indeed, many Classical and Hellenistic rural sites discovered by field surveys in Greece are characterized by the presence of Black-glaze wares. As for its market value, although Black-glaze Nolan amphorae may have cost half an obol less than Red-figure ones, a plain bell krater at nine obols cost twice as much as its Red-figure counterpart.

The shapes of Black-glaze vessels correspond closely to figure-painted ones. However, some of the larger shapes, such as amphorae, early hydriai, psykters and kraters, occur rarely, and often the examples are confined to Athens. Smaller shapes such as oinochoai, mugs, skyphoi and lekanides seem to have been made in roughly equal numbers of Black-glaze and figure-painted. In addition, Black-glaze vessels include many shapes that were rarely, if ever, figure-painted: bowls, one-handlers (a low cup with a single handle), stemmed plates, feeders, amphoriskoi, bolsals and Rheneia cups.

The glaze used on Attic Black-glaze pottery is generally similar to that used on figure-painted ware, although some shapes, such as the 'bare-bottom' lekanides, were simply dipped and were not of such high quality; these shapes seem to have been confined mostly to Attica. The use of reserving and added purple and white resembles that on figure-painted pottery. One of the most striking means of decoration was the use of large areas of 'coral red'. This technique is particularly common on stemless cups and phialai dating from after the Persian Wars (490–479 BC), on which the red body contrasts strikingly with the black lip and handles. These shapes may have been produced at Athens under the influence of Persian metalwork (see Shefton), and it is possible that the colour was intended to evoke gold. In a similar way, the 'metallic' finish of the black glaze itself may reflect a taste for patinated silver in different areas and periods. The use of 'glazes' to evoke metalwork is corroborated by one of the few ancient literary references to the decoration of pots, in which the potters of Naukratis are described as 'baptizing' their wares to make them appear like silver (Athenaeus: *Deipnosophists* XI.cdlxxx.e). Other decorative devices included garlands in added clay, which were frequently gilded (see Sparkes and Talcott, 1970, pl. 7).

The bodies of many Black-glaze shapes were also enhanced by ribbing. In the first half of the 5th century BC this was often horizontal, formed either by concave depressions or moulded rings. This technique is most commonly found on phialai (*ibid.*, pl. 23) and mugs. Later in the 5th century BC vertical ribbing became more popular, particularly on mugs, though it is also found on cups, stemless cups, squat lekythoi and amphoriskoi. This change may have been due to the appearance of a new type of vessel, the thericleian, which is attested in various literary and epigraphic sources, including a series of inscriptions on Black-glaze pottery from Kafizin on Cyprus (see T. B. Mitford: *The Nymphaeum of Kafizin: Kadmos* (New York, 1980), pp. 29–32, 35–6). Thericleians were also made in silver, terebinth wood and later in gold. One characteristic seems to have been their dark colour.

One of the main forms of decoration on unpainted pottery was the use of incised and stamped patterns. These techniques were used to decorate the insides of various shapes, such as stemless cups, bowls and plates, and the outsides of other vessels, including mugs, oinochoai, hydriai and amphoriskoi. The stamps were created from moulds and given convex faces, which allowed them to be applied with a rotary action to curved surfaces as well as flat. The patterns were impressed prior to glazing, while the clay was still moist.

Stamping and incision were not confined to unpainted wares but were also used in the decoration of Red-figure stemless cups and cup-skyphoi. Although it has been suggested that incised decoration preceded stamping in these workshops, the evidence from unpainted Attic wares from Stryme in Thrace shows that they were in fact introduced simultaneously. In the earliest designs, rays and arcs were used in conjunction with palmette stamps and sometimes in elaborate patterns, such as the ivy leaves on a stemless cup from Kameiros on Rhodes (*c*. 450–*c*. 440 BC; London, BM, 64.10–7.1591; see fig. 126). By far the commonest stamp was the palmette, although such other shapes as the meander, ovule and boxed triangle were also used (see Sparkes and Talcott, pl. 47). The complex stamped and incised patterns of the mid-5th century BC soon evolved into monotonous designs of enclosed ovules surrounded by, or enclosing, linked palmettes (*ibid.*, pl. 54). By the end of the 5th century BC even these patterns had degenerated into simple palmette crosses (*ibid.*, pl. 53). During the 4th century BC the technique known as 'rouletting' or 'chattering' was introduced, whereby a bent strip of metal left a series of indentations as the pot was turned on the wheel: this pattern was often combined with a zone of palmettes linked by short arcs.

Although much stamped decoration is repetitive, some designs are extremely attractive. The most unusual are found on two kantharoi (Boston, MA, Mus. F.A., 01.8023; Brussels, Musées Royaux A. & Hist., A741) and a mug

126. Attic Black-glaze stemless cup from Rhodes, diam. 254 mm, *c*. 450–*c*. 440 BC (London, British Museum)

127. Attic Black-glaze mug from Capua, depicting the *Slaying of Medusa*, h. 98 mm, *c*. 435–*c*. 430 BC (London, British Museum)

(*c*. 435–*c*. 430 BC; London, BM, G90; see fig. 127), which depict the *Slaying of Medusa*. On one side Hermes is shown leading Perseus, who clutches a sickle in his left hand and a bag containing the head in his right, to Athena; the other shows two gorgons in pursuit, Medusa sinking to the ground with Pegasus flying about her and the baby Chrysaor to her right. The scene is framed by Ionic columns surmounted by sphinxes. Related to these are two kantharoi (U. Newcastle upon Tyne, Gr. Mus., 58, and Naples, Mus. Archaeol. N., 166455; the latter found at Pithekoussai) decorated with horses and boxed triangles, and a fragment of another from Perachora (Athens, N. Archaeol. Mus.) stamped with lions.

A further type of decoration found on Black-glaze pottery consists of reliefs moulded to the upper surfaces of askoi and depicting various subjects, ranging from heads of Herakles, Helios, maenads or others, to actual scenes, such as a mounted Amazon (see Sparkes and

Talcott, 1970, pl. 46). Several of these rare pieces have been found at Marion on Cyprus. This decorative tradition continued into the Hellenistic period, when reliefs were applied to mould-made bowls.

The lack of painted decoration on Black-glaze pottery has led scholars to examine the relationships between different shapes in their potting technique and stamped decoration. Thus the carefully moulded feet of certain oinochoai (e.g. Leiden, Rijksmus. Oudhd., NL7) also occur on hydriai (e.g. Leiden, Rijksmus. Oudhd., GNV 57), and the heavy lips and reserved feet of Castulo cups (see Sparkes and Talcott, 1970, pl. 22) are also found on cup-skyphoi (*ibid.*, pl. 25), one-handlers, small bowls (*ibid.*, fig. 9) and askoi. These associations are sometimes strengthened by the use of common stamps on different shapes. Thus a swastika meander can link kantharoi, mugs and askoi, while a large, spindly palmette (which may represent a silphium plant, as on coins from Cyrene) is found on amphoriskoi, 'baby-feeders', bolsals and miniature kantharoi.

Black-glaze pottery was also produced in the same workshops as figure-painted wares. The Red-figure palmettes at the handles of otherwise plain bell kraters (e.g. Leiden, Rijksmus. Oudhd., NL1) associate them with kraters by the PHIALE PAINTER and the Cassel Painter. Some of the earliest plain-walled mugs (see Sparkes and Talcott, 1970, fig. 3 and pl. 11) were produced in the workshop of the Painter of Berlin F2268. Similarly, some fragments of Black-glaze mugs (*ibid.*, pl. 11) are attributable to the same workshop as Red-figure mugs decorated by a follower of Douris or by the Painter of Philadelphia 2449, a follower of Makron. The Black-glaze Castulo cup appears to have originated from the workshop of the Amphitrite Painter and the Carlsruhe Painter. Black-glaze stemless cups, many from Stryme, have a prominent moulded cone on the underside, which is also a feature of cups decorated by the Amphitrite Painter, while the concave moulded and reserved rings on the undersides of stemmed bowls are also found on products by the Dish Painter.

There can be little doubt that Black-glaze pottery was influenced by metalwork, especially given the availability of silver at Athens. A Black-glaze mug from Duvanli in Thrace was found in the same tomb as a silver one of the same shape; the tomb also contained a figure-decorated silver Rheneia cup, a shape frequently decorated in Black-glaze though not in Red-figure. Likewise, silver cups from Chemyrev parallel Black-glaze and Red-figure vessels, and a silver perfume pot from Selenskaya is identical to a series of Black-glaze vases.

(ii) Domestic wares. The domestic wares of antiquity were essentially utilitarian vessels used for cooking, the processing of foods, storage and transport. They occur in the archaeological record of most ancient dwellings. Among the mostly highly decorated pieces were louteria (washbasins on stands), a shape also represented in marble at sanctuaries. Their broad rims were often decorated with impressed mouldings, including tongues, ovules and wreaths; those made from the same material as Corinthian tiles could also be decorated with bands of red paint and black glaze. The pedestals of louteria were invariably fluted. Pithoi also carried some impressed decoration, though their motifs were generally quite different, including linked spirals, guilloches, concentric circles and lotus bands. Glazed lines were sometimes used to decorate table and storage amphorae, hydriai, jugs and lekanai; this simple decoration is also found on transport containers.

BIBLIOGRAPHY

B. A. Sparkes and L. Talcott: *Pots and Pans of Classical Athens* (1953), i of *The Athenian Agora* (Princeton, 1953–)

P. E. Corbett: 'Palmette Stamps from an Attic Black-glaze Workshop', *Hesperia*, xxiv (1955), pp. 172–86

B. A. Sparkes: 'Black Perseus', *Ant. Kst*, xi (1968), pp. 3–16

B. B. Shefton: 'Persian Gold and Attic Black Glaze: Achaemenid Influences on Attic Pottery of the 5th and 4th Centuries BC', *Proceedings of the IXth International Congress of Classical Archaeology: Damascus, 11–20 Oct 1969*, pp. 109–11

B. A. Sparkes and L. Talcott: *Black and Plain Pottery of the 6th, 5th and 4th Centuries BC* (1970), xii of *The Athenian Agora* (Princeton, 1953–)

S. I. Rotroff: *Hellenistic Pottery: Athenian and Imported Moldmade Bowls* (1982), xxii of *The Athenian Agora* (Princeton, 1953–)

D. W. J. Gill: 'The Workshops of the Attic Bolsal', *Ancient Greek and Related Pottery. Proceedings of the International Vase Symposium: Amsterdam, 1984*, pp. 102–6

A. J. N. W. Prag: 'Neutron Activation Analysis of Black-glazed Pottery: A Report on Work in Hand', ibid., pp. 54–8

S. I. Rotroff: 'Ceramic Workshops in Hellenistic Athens', ibid., pp. 173–7

D. W. J. Gill: 'Classical Greek Fictile Imitations of Precious Metal Vases', *Pots and Pans. A Colloquium on Precious Metals and Ceramics in the Muslim, Chinese and Graeco-Roman Worlds: Oxford, 1985*, pp. 9–30

—: 'Attic Black-glazed Pottery', *Excavations at Sabratha, 1948–1951*, ed. P. M. Kenrick (London, 1986), pp. 275–96

DAVID W. J. GILL

9. HELLENISTIC. Although early Hellenistic potters often imitated Athenian models, they soon developed their own diverse regional variations of shapes and decoration; in newly hellenized areas the local ceramic tradition often continued alongside the hellenizing one. Nonetheless, certain general characteristics are apparent: the pots developed from low, stable forms to tall, elegant ones, often imitated metal prototypes and shared ornamental motifs with works in other media such as glassware and wall painting.

Hellenistic pottery is difficult to date. Most is undecorated, much was carelessly made, and style is of little use in determining the date of mechanically reproduced mould-made products. There are a few archaeological contexts for which historical events can provide latest possible dates; for Attic pottery the most useful are the destruction of Olynthos (348 BC), the occupation of the Ptolemaic camp at Koroni in Attica (260s BC), the destruction of Corinth (146 BC) and the sack of Athens by Sulla (86 BC). Since Attic pottery was widely exported and imitated, at least in the early Hellenistic period, its dating has more than local importance: study of the material from Koroni caused a general downdating of some 35 years for early Hellenistic ceramics found throughout the eastern Mediterranean.

The most common Hellenistic tableware was Black-glazed (*see* §§1(iii)(c) and 8 above), with a gradual shift to Red-glazed beginning in the 2nd century BC, heralding the red wares of Roman times. The earliest well-defined Hellenistic red ware, Eastern Sigillata A (formerly called 'Pergamene'), probably originated in Syria or Palestine *c.* 150 BC. Grey wares, with black or dark grey glaze and grey fabric, were made in several centres, notably in Sicily (e.g. Campana C ware) and in Asia Minor.

Though Red-figure vase painting died out at the end of the 4th century BC, Black-figure continued to be used for Panathenaic amphorae, their depictions of Athena providing early evidence for the emergence of archaism in Greek art. The commonest type of painted pottery, however, was West Slope ware, named after finds from the west slope of the Athenian Acropolis. Its designs were executed in tan-coloured dilute clay and white paint on a Black-glaze background, sometimes with incised details. In Athens it evolved from 4th-century BC gold-decorated ware, with decoration painted on to the glazed surface in thick clay and gilded after firing. Increasingly gilding was omitted and designs enlivened with white paint. Local versions of West Slope ware were produced throughout the Hellenistic world from the early 3rd century BC to the 1st. Motifs are usually simple, consisting of wreaths, rosettes, leaping dolphins and charm bracelets, while figural scenes are rare. Occasionally there are painted inscriptions naming a divinity (e.g. Zeus Soter, Dionysos, Aphrodite) or a quality (e.g. friendship). Cretan West Slope ware is exceptionally fine, with a larger proportion of figural scenes and occasional use of pink and blue paint. Links between Crete, South Italy and Alexandria were strong enough for Cretan vase painters to have been influenced by the South Italian Gnathia ware produced at several centres in Apulia from the 360s to *c.* 250 BC; its designs are painted on a dark ground in red, white and 'gold'—a dilute clay wash on white—with more delicate, elaborate and carefully composed decoration than on most West Slope ware from the eastern Mediterranean.

Decoration in dark paint on a light background is restricted to only a few ceramic centres, several still unidentified. Hadra vases, hydriai used as cremation urns in 3rd- and 2nd-century BC Alexandria (*see* ALEXANDRIA, §2(iv)), are of two types. Those of coarse clay, with the surface whitewashed after firing to receive polychrome decoration, were probably made locally. Clay-ground Hadras, with glazed designs applied directly to the clay surface in silhouette or Black-figure technique, seem to have been produced on Crete, to judge from clay analyses and similarities with Cretan West Slope ware. Both floral and figural designs occur, the former probably being the earlier. The chronology is in part based on painted inscriptions giving the name of the deceased and a regnal year but omitting the name of the reigning monarch.

Another variety of dark-on-light ware was probably produced *c.* 200–*c.* 50 BC on the west coast of Asia Minor, to judge from its distribution. Its most common shape was the lagynos, though large pyxides and thymiateria (small incense altars) also occur. Glaze ranging from black to orange was applied either directly to the clay or over a white slip. Wreaths, garlands and musical instruments were the favourite motifs. The variety of fabrics and decorative schemes suggests the existence of several regional workshops.

Polychrome decoration was particularly common on South Italian pottery, such as the series of large vases, mostly lidded kraters and lekanides, from Centuripe in Sicily, many with moulded decoration (e.g. New York, Met., 53.11.5; see fig. 128). Against a pink (or, earlier, black) background appear scenes of marriages or Dionysiac ceremonies painted in tempera after firing in a figural style reminiscent of 1st-century BC wall painting. Their size, the placement of decoration on one side only and certain technical features (e.g. lids sometimes fired in one piece with bodies, fugitive paint) imply that they were grave goods. Stylistic and iconographic similarities suggest that Centuripe ware derived from late 4th-century BC Red-figure with polychrome details produced at Lipari off the coast of Sicily and that it dates to the 3rd century BC. A series of funerary vases produced at Canosa in northern Apulia from the late 4th century BC to the mid-2nd has painted decoration (floral designs, horses, chariots) on a pink background, sometimes combined with mould-made appliqués (often gorgoneia) and attached mould-made figurines (principally *nikai*, erotes, women and horse *protomes*).

128. Hellenistic bell krater with moulded decoration, h. 397 mm, probably from Centuripe, Sicily, mid-3rd century BC (New York, Metropolitan Museum of Art)

Large-scale use of moulds for pottery production began *c.* 225 BC with the emergence of the hemispherical relief bowl (formerly called the 'Megarian' bowl), a footless and handleless cup, developed in imitation of silverware and possibly invented at Athens, which became a standard drinking vessel. Floral and figural designs were the norm until *c.* 150 BC, the former derived from silverware, the latter mostly a ceramic development belonging to a repertory that spanned many centuries and media. The composition of the *Rape of Persephone* on an Attic example (Athens, Agora Mus., P 28545; see fig. 129) is paralleled in late 4th-century BC tomb painting (Vergina, Macedonia, Tomb I) and later on Roman sarcophagi and wall painting. Other specimens known as 'Homeric bowls' represent subjects from epic and tragedy, often with quotations or identifying labels; they were probably manufactured in

129. Hellenistic mould-made relief bowl showing the *Rape of Persephone*, h. 93 mm, from Athens, *c.* 225–*c.* 175 BC (Athens, Agora Museum)

Macedonia in the 2nd century BC and perhaps slightly earlier, their compositions possibly deriving from manuscript illumination. By 150 BC various linear schemes had become popular. 'Shield bowls' decorated with concentric semicircles imitated the traditional Macedonian shield also pictured on Macedonian coins; 'Long-petal' bowls, covered with tall, contiguous, rounded petals, derived ultimately from Achaemenid silver prototypes.

Mould-made appliqués were frequently added to wheel-made wares. Heads or busts in high relief, usually of mythological figures but sometimes portraits, were placed on the floors of hemispherical bowls, below the handle attachments of pitchers, on the covers of pyxides and in other appropriate places. Particularly fine is the Black-glaze 'Calenian' ware produced in Apulia, Campania and Etruria from the mid-4th century BC to the 3rd. Its most common shapes are *gutti* (oil jugs) with appliqué medallions on top and phialai with elaborate relief scenes on their interiors; exact parallels in metal have been found. Low-relief appliqués appear on fine, often red-fired ware from Pergamon (Pergamene appliqué ware; mid-2nd century BC to the 1st). The most common shape is a low skyphos; decoration includes ivy garlands, mythological figures and erotic scenes. Similar in technique are the Black-glaze *Plakettenvasen*, mostly bigger, closed shapes with large-scale reliefs of mythological figures on their reeded walls; they were probably made at several sites (Corinth, Taras, Crete) from the mid-4th century BC to the mid-3rd.

Relief-ware cups with a distinctive green, lead-based glaze were produced *c.* 50 BC–*c.* AD 50 in one- or two-piece moulds or on the wheel with added appliqué designs; floral decoration is more common than figural. This short-lived experiment with vitreous glaze probably began in the East, since several workshops have been identified in Asia Minor, but was imitated in the West; there are close parallels in silver.

Hellenistic kitchen ware has been little studied. While plain jugs and bowls were often locally made, there was considerable trade in vessels considered superior in material, method of manufacture or appearance: for example, elaborate braziers with figural appliqué decoration and mould-made lugs in the shape of bearded satyr heads were produced at several sites and widely exported.

BIBLIOGRAPHY

G. Leroux: *Lagynos* (Paris, 1913)

F. Courby: *Les Vases grecs à reliefs* (Paris, 1922)

G. Libertini: *Centuripe* (Catania, 1926)

H. A. Thompson: 'Two Centuries of Hellenistic Pottery', *Hesperia*, iii (1934), pp. 311–480

F. O. Waagé: 'Hellenistic and Roman Tableware of North Syria', *Ceramics and Islamic Coins* (1948), iv/1 of *Antioch-on-the-Orontes*, ed. G. W. Elderkin, J. Lassus and R. Stillwell (Princeton, 1934–)

F. F. Jones: 'The Pottery', *The Hellenistic and Roman Periods* (1950), i of *Excavations at Gözlü Kule, Tarsus*, ed. H. Goldman (Princeton, 1950–63), pp. 149–296

G. R. Edwards: 'Panathenaics of Hellenistic and Roman Times', *Hesperia*, xxvi (1957), pp. 320–49

U. Hausmann: *Hellenistische Reliefbecher aus attischen und böotischen Werkstätten* (Stuttgart, 1959)

P. W. Lapp: *Palestinian Ceramic Chronology, 200 BC–AD 70* (New Haven, 1961)

E. Vanderpool, J. R. McCredie and A. Steinberg: 'Koroni: The Date of the Camp and the Pottery', *Hesperia*, xxxiii (1964), pp. 69–75

L. Forti: *La ceramica di Gnathia* (Naples, [1965])

J. Schäfer: *Hellenistische Keramik aus Pergamon* (1968), ii of *Pergamenische Forschungen*, ed. E. Bochringer (Berlin, 1965–)

G. R. Edwards: *Corinthian Hellenistic Pottery* (1975), vii/3 of *Corinth: Results of Excavations Conducted by the American School of Classical Studies at Athens* (Princeton, 1932–)

U. Wintermeyer: 'Die polychrome Reliefkeramik aus Centuripe', *Jb. Dt. Archäol. Inst.*, xc (1975), pp. 136–241

A. Hochuli-Gysel: *Kleinasiatische glasierte Reliefkeramik (50 v. Chr. bis 50 n. Chr.) und ihre oberitalischen Nachahmungen* (Berne, 1977)

A. Laumonier: *La Céramique hellénistique à reliefs: Ateliers 'ioniens'* (1977), xxxi of *Exploration archéologique de Délos* (Paris, 1909–)

G. Siebert: *Recherches sur les ateliers de bols à reliefs du Péloponnèse à l'époque hellénistique* (Paris, 1978)

U. Sinn: *Die homerischen Becher: Hellenistische Reliefkeramik aus Makedonien* (Berlin, 1979)

J. P. Morel: *Céramique campanienne: Les Formes*, Bibliothèque des écoles françaises d'Athènes et de Rome (Rome, 1981)

S. I. Rotroff: *Hellenistic Pottery: Athenian and Imported Moldmade Bowls* (1982), xxii of *The Athenian Agora* (Princeton, 1953–)

L. Rossi and F. van der Wielen-van Ommeren: *Canosa*, ii (Bari, 1983)

P. J. Callaghan: 'Knossian Artists and Ptolemaic Alexandria', *Studi in onore di Achille Adriani*, iii (Rome, 1984), pp. 789–94

T. Dohrn: 'Schwarzgefirniste Plakettenvasen', *Mitt. Dt. Archäol. Inst.: Röm. Abt.*, xcii (1985), pp. 77–106

A. H. Enklaar: 'Chronologie et peintres des hydries de Hadra', *Bull. Ant. Besch.*, lx (1985), pp. 106–51

——: 'Les Hydries de Hadra, ii: Formes et ateliers', *Bull. Ant. Besch.*, lxi (1986), pp. 41–65

D. B. Thompson, H. A. Thompson and S. I. Rotroff: *Hellenistic Pottery and Terracottas*, 4 vols (Princeton, 1987)

G. Hübner: *Die Applikenkeramik von Pergamon* (1993), vii of *Pergamenische Forschungen*, ed. W. Radt (Berlin, 1965–)

SUSAN I. ROTROFF

10. COLLECTING AND COLLECTIONS. The ancient Greeks acquired painted pottery only for utilitarian purposes, and though the vast numbers of Greek vases imported into Etruria during the 6th and 5th centuries BC were prized items apparently displayed at parties, as shown in the paintings in the Tomb of the Ship at Tarquinii (end of 5th century BC), they too were put to practical use and were not mere collectors' items. Indeed, prior to the 17th century AD there is only sporadic evidence of interest in

Greek vases. A Tuscan altarpiece by Bonaventura Berlinghieri (13th century; Pescia, S Francesco) depicts buildings adorned with palmette scrolls remarkably similar to those on 4th-century BC Apulian vases, while later, another Tuscan artist, Antonio del Pollaiuolo, may have imitated lost works by the Niobid Painter or one of his followers in his frescoes of nude dancers at the Villa la Gallina, Arcetri, near Florence (1460s; *in situ*), or in his engraving of the *Battle of the Ten Nudes* (*c.* 1470–75; *see* POLLAIUOLO, (1), fig. 3). That Greek pottery was collected and studied at that time is confirmed by a letter of 1491 from Angelo Poliziano offering Lorenzo de' Medici a large vase and two smaller pots and implying that Lorenzo already had similar pieces: unfortunately, no further details are known. In his life of Battista Franco (*Vite* (1550, rev. 2/1568); ed. G. Milanesi (1878–85), vi, p. 571), Vasari referred to vases with Red- and Black-figure painting, though he mistook them for Roman works and commented that they were inferior to maiolica from Urbino. Around the same time Ulisse Aldrovandi recorded a few vases in the varied collection of Cardinal Rodolfo Pio da Carpi (1500–84) at Rome (*Delle statue antiche che per tutta Roma in diversi luoghi. . .si veggono*; Venice, 1556). Both Black- and Red-figure vases were excavated at Orbetello in 1565. The collection of Gerolamo Garimberto at Rome, inventoried in 1576, contained some 80 fictive vases.

In the 17th century Cassiano dal Pozzo included drawings of vases (five clearly Attic and five South Italian) in his vast *Museum chartaceum* (Lat.: 'Paper Museum'; now at Windsor Castle, Royal Lib., and London, BM), which was intended to be a comprehensive record of ancient sculpture and smaller antiquities known in his day. A few Attic, South Italian and Italo-Corinthian vases owned by G. P. Bellori and sold to Frederick III of Brandenburg were published along with other items from his collection by L. Beger (*Thesaurus regius et electoralis brandenburgensis*, iii (Berlin, 1701)). Soon afterwards Greek vases came to be of considerable interest to both collectors and scholars: Filippo Buonarroti's edition of Thomas Dempster's *De Etruria regali* (Florence, 1723–4) includes drawings of over 30 vases and a discussion of their origins, while his notes refer to several contemporary collections. A number of the vases mentioned were in the Medici collection, but the holding most frequently cited was that of the Orvietan cardinal F. A. Gualterio, containing 183 items from the Neapolitan collection of Giuseppe Valletta (*d* 1714) and from excavations at Chiusi and elsewhere; it passed to the Vatican after Gualterio's death in 1728, becoming the most substantial collection of Greek vases in the city of Rome. In Naples, the Marchese F. M. Mastrilli amassed a collection of nearly 400 vases between *c.* 1740 and 1755. Buonarroti's work had profound consequences. He argued that the vases could not be Roman, since they had never been discovered in Rome itself, and that they did not fit stylistically with either Greek or Roman art: he concluded that they must be Etruscan. This view was widely held for nearly a century, and Greek vases shared in the popularity of genuine Etruscan artefacts during the later 18th-century craze for all things Etruscan (*see* ETRUSCAN, §VIII). Thus Johann Wolfgang von Goethe recorded (*Italian Journey*, Naples, 9 March 1787) that every visitor to Italy wanted to acquire an Etruscan vase, for which extravagant prices were being paid. As a consequence, Giovanni Battista Passeri's *Picturae etruscorum in vasculis* (Rome, 1767–75) includes 300 plates illustrating specimens in some 40 collections in Italy and elsewhere.

The most famous collector of the period, Sir WILLIAM HAMILTON (i), amassed and disposed of two great collections and profoundly influenced contemporary attitudes. As British Plenipotentiary to the King of the Two Sicilies (1764–1800), Hamilton obtained his vases by excavation in southern Italy as well as by purchase; 65 specimens, for example, were selected from the Mastrilli collection. Unlike previous students of Greek vase painting, who had been interested primarily in the subjects depicted, he drew attention to the style of the paintings by publishing clear, attractive drawings to serve as models for contemporary designers. The publication of his first collection (P. F. Hugues [P. V. d'Hancarville]: *The Collection of Etruscan, Greek and Roman Antiquities from the Cabinet of the Honble Wm Hamilton*, 4 vols (1766–7)) was so successful that the British Parliament decided to purchase his pottery for £8400: thus in 1772 the British Museum, London, became the first public museum to display Greek vases. Hamilton's second collection had a much more eventful history. It, too, was published, in four lavish volumes edited by Wilhelm Tischbein (*Collection of Engravings from Ancient Vases . . .* (Naples, 1791–5)), but during shipment to England 8 of the 24 crates in which it was packed were lost when the *HMS Colossus* sank off the Scilly Isles. The remaining 16 crates were sold in London to the Amsterdam merchant Thomas Hope; their contents were dispersed throughout the world at the sale of the Hope collection in 1917. The wreck of the *Colossus* was rediscovered in 1975, and some 30,000 vase fragments were retrieved and deposited in the British Museum.

During the Neo-classical era motifs based on Greek vase paintings were incorporated in the designs of the Adam brothers and others for the décor of many 18th-century English country houses. In Johan Zoffany's painting of *Charles Towneley's Library in Park Street* (Burnley, Towneley Hall A.G. & Mus.; *see* ZOFFANY, JOHAN, fig. 2), a genuine Red-figure amphora may be seen, as well as copies of famous sculptures, while George Hammond Lucy placed a fine Black-figure hydria (*in situ*) on the cornice of the bookshelves in his antiquarian library at Charlecote House in Warwickshire (1820s), and Spencer Joshua Alwyne Compton, 2nd Marquess of Northampton (1790–1851), displayed his splendid collection of vases acquired in Rome (1820–30) along with other antiquities at Castle Ashby, Northants; vases were also acquired by collectors of more modest means, who could afford the price of what were then regarded as minor Classical items.

Although some 18th-century scholars had suspected that the so-called 'Etruscan' vases were really Greek, this was only widely accepted after the publication of Luigi Lanzi's *De' vasi antichi dipinti volgarmente chiamati etruschi* (Florence, 1806), which stresses that the vases' inscriptions, mythological subjects and representations of architecture are all Greek. By this time there was such great enthusiasm for these objects, as well as for all things Greek, that collectors continued to prize them. Soon afterwards, the excavations of Lucien Bonaparte, Prince of Canino, unearthed over 3000 specimens of decorated wares at the Etruscan cemeteries on his estates at Vulci (1828–9), while plain pottery was simply trampled underfoot on site; little record was kept of the vases' original contexts. Purchasers included Ludwig I of Bavaria and William I of the Netherlands (*reg* 1813–40); other specimens went to the Louvre, the British Museum and the Berlin Museum. O. Jahn's catalogue of Ludwig's vases (*Beschreibung der Vasensammlung König Ludwigs in der Pinakothek zu München* (Munich, 1854)) includes a detailed survey of other important European private and public collections of the period.

Among the most prominent 19th-century collectors was the archaeologist Giampietro Campana, Marchese di Cavelli, who amassed at Rome through excavation and purchase one of the most important private collections of vases and other antiquities. Unfortunately, his collecting activities were financed through embezzlement, and after his imprisonment his whole collection was sold. The catalogue prepared in 1857 includes 3791 vases, the largest number of which was purchased by Napoleon III and exhibited first in the Musée Napoleon III and then in the Louvre, where they now form the basis of one of the most important collections of Greek vases in the world.

Some ten years before its sale and dispersion the Campana collection was visited and described by George Dennis (*The Cities and Cemeteries of Etruria*, ii (London, 1848), pp. 528–31), whose account gives an impression of how a mid-19th-century private collection of Greek vases was displayed. Most of the selected specimens, which were predominantly Red-figure, were set up on shelves around a large room, while a few choice pieces stood on central pedestals that allowed a view from all sides. In the same volume (pp. 497–512) Dennis also gave an excellent description of the Museo Gregoriano Etrusco at the Vatican, despite an official ban on taking notes. Many of its specimens had been excavated by the Campanari family of Toscanella on papal estates at Vulci, Cerveteri, Tarquinii and elsewhere in Etruria, and four rooms were devoted exclusively to vases. The specimens were again mainly displayed on shelves, with a few special pieces on pedestals (e.g. the Black-figure amphora 344 depicting *Ajax and Achilles Playing a Board Game* by Exekias and the White-ground krater with *Hermes Bringing the Infant Dionysos to Papposilenos and the Nymphs of Nysa* by the Phiale Painter, both from Vulci). The organization of the display was based at least partly on vase shape: one room contained only kylikes, while another featured amphorae.

Numerous sales catalogues attest the heavy trade in Greek pottery during the 19th century, and Italian adventurers continued to excavate vases for sale to private collectors, especially in Paris. The most important Italian collectors after Campana were the members of the Castellani family, especially the brothers Alessandro and Augusto. The latter sold 250 vases to Vienna (now in the Kunsthistorisches Museum), while other parts of his collection ended up in the Museo dei Conservatori and the Museo Nazionale di Villa Giulia in Rome. Alessandro was active in Paris and London, but most of his collection was sold in lots in Rome after his death in 1883. After the unification of Italy in 1870 private excavation in Etruria was made illegal, limiting considerably the number of newly discovered vases entering the market; but pieces from existing collections continued to be traded, and items from clandestine digs still found their way on to the market.

Greek pottery from Greece itself was never traded in such vast quantities as that from Italy. Indeed, it excited little interest before excavators in the 1830s began to record it, and in any case, the export of Greek antiquities was forbidden by law from 1827. As a result many finds were put into the National Museum that was set up at Aegina in 1829 and subsequently moved to Athens. However, some vases, particularly those from outside the Greek mainland, did find their way into other European collections. For example, Red-figure vases from Kerch in south Russia were sent to the Hermitage in St Petersburg, pottery from Rhodes and Naukratis went to the British Museum, vases from Crete collected by Sir Arthur Evans went to the Ashmolean Museum in Oxford, and pieces from Cyprus went to the Kunsthistorisches Museum in Vienna and the Metropolitan Museum of Art in New York.

More sophisticated study of Greek vases in the late 19th century and the 20th inevitably influenced the market for antiquities. Following Jahn's emphasis in his Munich catalogue on the importance of provenance and his attempt to distinguish particular styles and schools, J. D. BEAZLEY began to identify individual hands and workshops. The publication in 1923 of the first fascicle of the *Corpus vasorum antiquorum* marked the start of an attempt to catalogue Greek vases in collections throughout the world. Well over 200 fascicles have been published, constituting a basic reference work for scholars, museums and indeed private collectors, who are not only more numerous than ever but also far more knowledgeable. Vases signed by important Attic artists now command extraordinary prices: in 1972 a krater by Euphronios purchased by the Metropolitan Museum of Art in New York became the first Greek pot to cost a million dollars. To discourage further price inflation, with its incentives to the illicit excavator, museums have tended since the 1970s to avoid making further purchases to complete their collections, collaborating instead to mount travelling loan exhibitions, which assemble items from a number of public and private collections to give a comprehensive view of the output of a particular period or area: an exhibition mounted at the Metropolitan Museum of Art in New York in 1985, for example, was able to concentrate exclusively on the works of a single ancient artist, the Amasis Painter. In modern displays the shelf-lined walls of 19th-century collections are usually replaced by free-standing glass cases that protect the pottery and allow it to be viewed from all sides. Labels supply information with varying degrees of precision, while the vases are carefully grouped by periods or schools, provenance, forms, subject-matter or manufacturing technique.

BIBLIOGRAPHY

E. M. W. Tillyard: *The Hope Vases: A Catalogue and a Discussion* (Cambridge, 1923)

P. Mingazzini: *Vasi della collezione Castellani*, 2 vols (Rome, 1930)

R. M. Cook: *Greek Painted Pottery* (London, 1960, rev. 1972)

Select Exhibition of Sir John and Lady Beazley's Gifts to the Ashmolean Museum, 1912–1966 (exh. cat., ed. R. W. Hamilton; Oxford, Ashmolean, 1967)

P. Mingazzini: *Catalogo dei vasi della collezione Augusto Castellani*, 2 vols (Rome, 1971)

M. Vickers: 'A Greek Source for Antonio Pollaiuolo's *Battle of the Nudes* and *Hercules and the Twelve Giants*', *A. Bull.*, lix (1977), pp. 182–7

D. von Bothmer: 'Notes on Collectors of Vases', *Wealth of the Ancient World* (exh. cat., ed. J. F. Tompkins; Fort Worth, Kimbell A. Mus., 1983), pp. 37–44

R. Morris: 'Ancient Pottery from the Scillonian Seabed', *Int. J. Naut. Archaeol. & Underwtr Explor.*, xiii (1984), pp. 156–63

M. Vickers: 'Value and Simplicity: Eighteenth-century Taste and the Study of Greek Vases', *Past & Present*, 116 (Aug 1987), pp. 98–137

N. H. Ramage: 'Sir William Hamilton as Collector, Exporter and Dealer: The Acquistion and Dispersal of his Collections', *Amer. J. Archaeol.*, xciv (1990), pp. 469–80

C. L. Lyons: 'The Museo Mastrilli and the Culture of Collecting in Naples, 1700–1755,' *J. Hist. Col.*, i/4 (1992), pp. 1–26

NANCY THOMSON DE GRUMMOND

VI. Wall and panel painting.

Painting was practised by Greek-speaking peoples first as wall painting and later also in the form of panel pictures. Other applications, discussed elsewhere, included architectural ornament, painting of statues and pottery decoration (*see* §§II, 1(iii)(c); IV, 1(iii) and (iv); V, 1(ii)(b) and (iii)(c) above). Very few Greek wall and panel paintings survive, and the works of most named painters, among them the most celebrated artists of their day in any media, are known only from literary sources. Nevertheless, the history of Greek painting can be inferred from developments in related arts, from large-scale sculpture to gem-carving, and from the Roman period survive hundreds of copies of Greek works, made as wall paintings or mosaics.

1. Introduction. 2. Historical survey. 3. Theory and criticism. 4. Collections and collectors.

1. Introduction.

(i) Materials and techniques. (ii) Subject-matter. (iii) Painters and society.

(i) Materials and techniques.

(a) Supports. Ancient literary sources and surviving fragments alike testify to the importance of painting as an art form in ancient Greece. All sorts of materials were painted, either in their natural state or specially prepared: wood, canvas, clay, marble and other stone, even leather, ivory and, in later periods, glass. Wall paintings were executed on specially prepared plaster, and the most important material for Greek easel painting was the wooden panel (*pinax*), either plain, framed or with protective folding doors. Sketchy comments in literary sources suggest that the lost great masterpieces of Greek painting were done on wooden surfaces, but the perishability of organic surfaces makes the reconstruction of the techniques and media used in such painting difficult. Only a few small examples of mediocre quality have been discovered: two panels at Saqqara, Egypt (one now in London, BM) and one whole panel and two fragments of a further three at Pitsa in Achaia (after *c.* 540 BC; Athens, N. Archaeol. Mus.). Wall paintings on stone, plaster and clay, however, may to some extent serve as a substitute. Stone, in particular, was much favoured in most periods, and many murals have been discovered, particularly in tombs. Ceramic painting (as on vases, architectural terracottas etc) constitutes a different category (the various techniques are discussed in §V above).

(b) Techniques. Apart from a few slight literary references, no ancient handbooks or instructions for painters have survived, and most material evidence comes from painted stone funerary stelai. For murals, the surface of plaster itself was an adequate ground, and it may reasonably be assumed that wooden panels were first given a ground. By contrast, stone was simply polished but does not appear to have been grounded. Surviving paintings on plaster, stone (including polychromy on marbles) and clay all show that the painter first scratched a rough design on the surface itself. Such sketches survive on large painted Archaic-period (*c.* 700–*c.*480 BC) marble funerary stelai (examples in Athens, Kerameikos Mus.) or Archaic clay metopes (e.g. from Thermon; Athens, N. Archaeol. Mus.). Similar preliminary sketches, invisible to the naked eye under the finished picture, have been detected under

130. Wall painting from the Tomb of the Diver, Paestum, plaster-coated limestone (Paestum, Museo Archeologico Nazionale)

131. Painting on stone grave stele showing preliminary design in black, 2nd–1st century BC (Volos, Athanassakeion Archaeological Museum)

murals from the early Classical period (*c.* 480–323 BC) onwards (e.g. the Tomb of the Diver, Paestum, see fig. 130; Persephone Tomb, Vergina). Preliminary designs were also done in red brushwork (e.g. the Lyseas Stele; Athens, N. Archaeol. Mus.).

Before the development of chiaroscuro in Greek painting (late 5th century BC), the final picture was composed of precise linear contours and areas of intense natural hues. By the Hellenistic period (323–27 BC) at the latest, technique and execution had become more complex. The rough preliminary design gave way to a detailed monochrome brush drawing, usually in black (as on a stele in Volos, Athanassakeion Archaeol. Mus.; see fig. 131). This preliminary drawing is more than a design: it predetermines the tonal effects of the finished picture. The next step was to apply successive washes of different hues and tones until the desired effect had been achieved, with a final layer of shading and lights. For the application of pastose paints, besides the brush, some sort of blunt tool was used for spreading. Once completed, easel paintings were given a coat of varnish: according to Pliny, Apelles invented a varnish that also intensified the colour effects. This careful method of building up a picture was not always used. An alternative, attested from the Late Classical period onwards, was to dispense with the preliminary drawing and paint the picture directly in its final form with quick brushwork, for example late Classical funerary stelai from Vergina (e.g. Thessaloniki, Archaeol. Mus.; Vergina, Archaeological Museum) and Hellenistic funerary stelai from Alexandria (e.g. Alexandria, Gr.–Roman Mus.; New York, Met.; Paris Louvre). Even unexceptional painters used this method for ordinary funerary stelai, though one may presume that it was originally developed in the more prestigious and advanced field of panel painting. Direct painting was also used for copying works from other sources.

Surviving literary sources on Greek painting deal almost exclusively with the encaustic technique. This involves mixing pigments with wax, either hot or cold, and fixing the mixture to the surface with a hot instrument. For centuries attempts have been made to revive it, with varying success. In the body of surviving Greek painting itself, examples of encaustic painting are extremely rare (e.g. the metopes from Cyrene; Paris, Louvre). However, given the overall evidence for the range of painted materials, it is clear that tempera was the normal medium, and the frequent mention of encaustic painting may simply represent the attention attracted by a special technique.

(c) Composition of paints. Scientific analyses have revealed that the emulsions used on surviving painted stelai consisted of either the egg-yolk or the white or both, as well as oils. Although the polychromy of marble statues has not yet been similarly analysed, it appears that the medium normally used here was tempera too, not wax. Chemical analyses will doubtless disclose many secrets of Greek tempera emulsions; contrary to modern assumptions, those used on both buildings and sculptures in the open were able to withstand the weather for many centuries.

The fullest list of pigments used in ancient painting is given by Pliny (*Natural History* XXXIII and XXXV). Chemical analyses of ancient Greek works have identified various pigments, of which the most common are Egyptian blue, a synthetic pigment made from lime, sand and copper ore; bone black (Pliny's *elephantinum*); lead white or ceruse; calcium carbonate, a white pigment; malachite, a copper carbonate, a green pigment; massicot, a synthetic monoxide, a yellow photosensitive pigment discolouring to reddish-brown; ochre, in yellow, brown and red varieties; red vegetable dye, probably lichen, used for pink; vegetable black (Gr. *tryginon*); lampblack; vermilion, both natural and synthetic mercury sulphide; and green earth, the most common green pigment in murals, though not found in paintings on stone.

BIBLIOGRAPHY

Pliny: *Natural History*
E. Berger: *Die Maltechnik des Altertums* (Leipzig, 1904)
S. Augusti: *I colori Pompeiani* (Rome, 1967)
M. Napoli: *La Tomba del Tuffatore* (Naples, 1970), pp. 167–71
R. Büll: *Das grosse Buch vom Wachs: Geschichte, Kultur, Technik*, 2 vols (Munich, 1977)
V. von Graeve and F. Preusser: 'Zur Technik griechischer Malerei auf Marmor', *Jb. Dt. Archäol. Inst.*, xcvi (1981), pp. 120–56
F. Preusser, V. von Graeve and C. Wolters: 'Malerei auf griechischen Grabsteinen: Technische und naturwissenschaftliche Aspekte eines archäologischen Materials', *Maltechnik, Rest.*, lxxxvii/1 (1981), pp. 11–34
M. Andronikos: *Vergina: The Royal Tombs* (Athens, 1984), pp. 86–95

V. VON GRAEVE

(ii) Subject-matter. As with other aspects of ancient Greek painting, the content and pictorial treatment of lost originals may often be inferred from literary sources, vase painting and other arts, and Roman wall paintings and mosaics reproducing Greek designs.

(a) Geometric to Archaic (*c.* 900–*c.* 480 BC). (b) Classical (*c.* 480–323 BC). (c) Hellenistic (323–27 BC).

*(a) Geometric to Archaic (*c. *900–*c. *480* BC*)* In the late 8th century BC in Ephesos, BOULARCHOS apparently painted the *Defeat of the Magnetes*; this must be associated with the battle scenes on Geometric pottery. An oinochoe in Munich (Staatl. Antikensamml.) bears a depiction of a shipwreck with a surviving sailor, which is either a primitive *ex voto* or a reference to the *Odyssey*. Mythological themes are clearly present on Orientalizing pottery (*see* §V, 4 above). The polychrome decoration on Corinthian wares shows parades of carts and cavalrymen, hunting and scenes of everday life. Dramatic tension informs a scene on a krater (Paris, Louvre) of the banquet held in the palace of Eurytos in Oechalia, with Herakles and Iole; a restless dog under the table is outlined in the Black-figure technique. The contest between Apollo and Herakles for the Delphic tripod, held before Artemis, is the subject of the oldest mythological panel painting still extant, which decorates the Archaic limestone slate of Persepolis (*see* §2 (i) below).

*(b) Classical (*c. *480–323* BC*).*

Early–mid-5th century BC. The cycle commissioned for the Sanctuary of Athena at Plataia, after the Athenian victory there over the Persians and Boiotians in 479 BC, revisited epic tradition in the light of history, with such subjects as *Odysseus Trapped by the Suitors* by POLYGNOTOS OF THASOS and the *Seven Against Thebes* by Onasias. Polygnotos also painted the *Greeks after the Sack of Troy* in the Stoa Poikile in the Agora at Athens, where MIKON painted the *Amazonomachy*. The portrayal of the *Battle of Marathon*, conceived by these two masters, was probably completed by PANAINOS when Pericles took power in 462–461 BC.

The panels painted by ZEUXIS were sometimes criticized by ancient writers for a concern with visual trickery, but his depictions of everyday life, conversation and games, for example, seem to have been innovative in their use of highlights rather than hatching or outline. *A Young Boy with Grapes* and an *Old Woman* are among titles that have survived; he is also known to have explored mythological and epic subjects such as *Eros*, *Pan*, a *Centaur Family* and a *Helen* perhaps painted for a Temple of Hera Lacinia at Akragas or at Kroton in southern Italy. Further works are attributed to him through later copies: the *Abduction of Helen* by Theseus represented in a mosaic in Pella (*c.* 325–*c.* 275 BC; Pella, Archaeol. Mus.; *see* PELLA (ii), §2) and the small scene on a marble slate from Herculaneum depicting *Women Playing Astragals* (*c.* 27 BC–AD 14; Naples, Mus. Archeol. N.).

PARRHASIOS produced small paintings with erotic subjects; feelings and pain he tended to express in his more monumental works, such as *Odysseus Feigning Madness*, *Prometheus in Chains* (tradition holds that a tortured slave was used as a model) and *Philoktetes on Lemnos*. He included such dramatic themes as the *Destruction of Troy* and the *Centauromachy* among the cartoons he was said to have prepared for engravings by the metalworker Mys; these works included acanthus racemes to emphasize the elegance of the line. The images of Silenus and a chariot race decorate the silver pieces inspired by Parrhasios' style found at Douvanli, Bulgaria.

TIMANTHES defeated *Parrhasios* in contest and painted the famous *Sacrifice of Iphigenia* for a competition against one Kolotes of Teos. He so exhausted all possible expressions of sorrow in his depiction of those attending the sacrifice of Agamemnon's daughter that he veiled the father's head rather than attempt to suggest his grief. Commissions for a portrait of the supreme priest were awarded to Zeuxis and Parrhasios by the Temple of Artemis in Ephesos.

The painting of *Scylla* by Androkydes of Kyzikos (*fl* early 4th century BC) reproduced a theme already widespread in Kyzicos coins, with the addition of space devoted to the representation of creatures (e.g. London, BM). This desire to explore natural subjects together with mythological ones brought to painting the knowledge of nature acquired through experiment and theoretical speculation in the East Greek context, particularly since the Archaic period.

Mid-5th century BC*–late 4th.* The next step was taken by Pauson (*fl c.* 425–*c.* 388 BC). In Athens, the advances in technique coincided with the breaking of the unity of form and content that had marked painting during the age of Pericles (*c.* 495–429 BC) and made alternatives to traditional themes possible. The description survives of a painting by Pauson of a galloping horse raising a cloud of dust (Aristotle: *Poetics* I, 2, *Politics* VIII, 5, 7; Aristophanes: *Archarnians* 354, *Thesmophoriazusae* 948, *Plutus* 602); if it was inverted, the animal seemed to be rolling on its back in the soil, exactly the image the patron had specified. The novelty lay not only in this exploitation of illusion but also in the autonomy of the animal subject, which existed irrespective of any link with a human being. Aristotle (384–322 BC) advised young people against looking at the works of Pauson, whom he used as a pretext to define the different modes of imitation: 'because those who represent, reproduce human beings in an action, such human beings have to be good or bad that is better or worse than us, as they are represented by painters. In fact Polygnotos represented them better than us, Pauson worse, Dionysios in a way similar to ours.' (*Politics* VIII, 5, 7) This preoccupation with representing the human being experimentally rather than morally constitutes the key to the new painting.

The incorporeal quality of the figures painted by NIKOMACHOS OF THEBES derives from their loss of weight and lack of apparent effort. This quality can be seen in *Cybele Riding on a Lion*, which is similar to *Dionysos Riding a (?)Cheetah* represented in a mosaic in Pella (*c.* 325–*c.* 275 BC; Pella, Archaeol. Mus.; see fig. 143 below); *Maenads Stalked by Satyrs*; *Victory Taking a Four-horse Chariot Heavenward*, a painting brought to Rome and reproduced on *denarii* under Julius Caesar; and the *Rape of Persephone*, the subject of a painting moved to Rome and of a fresco at VERGINA, which can be attributed to Nikomachos on the basis of the light handling of Hermes, who leads Hades' horses (*see* §2 (ii) (b) below).

Paintings of the 12 Olympian gods dominated the southern wing of the Stoa of Zeus in the Agora at Athens, painted *c.* 360 BC by EUPHRANOR; on the northern wing the Demos ('people') of Athens was represented as a person, crowned by Demokratia (the constitution) in Theseus' presence; a rendering of the cavalry clash that preceded the Second Battle of Mantinea in 362 BC occupied the central niche. The subject of Demos and Democracy is known from a record relief from the Agora (Athens, Agora Mus.), which conveys solemnity and strength. A man with a beard, seated in meditation next to a container of writing scrolls, appears on a marble slab, dated *c.* 340–338 BC, from the tomb of Hermon in the Kerameikos in Athens, the only original painting attributable to the circle of Euphranor.

NIKIAS projects a solid realism, whether in battle scenes or portraits, and a keen interest in animals; such realism was transmitted to him by his master Antidotos (*fl* late 4th century BC), who was in turn a pupil of Euphranor. Three of his mythological scenes of captivity and liberation are known through Roman and Pompeiian copies in several versions (e.g. *Perseus and Andromeda* from the House of the Dioscurides, Pompeii; Naples, Mus. Archeol. N.; see fig. 132); the other two subjects are *Seated Calypso* and *Io and Argus*. Descriptions survive of some of his other works, which have been used to argue for the attribution to him of the hunting scene painted on the tomb of Philip II in Vergina (336 BC). Different episodes of the hunt, involving stags, wild boar, lions and bears, are coerced into a temporal unity by means of a vigorous composition within a vast landscape.

PAMPHILOS compiled a catalogue of *Paintings in Alphabetical Order*, demonstrating his interest in their subject-matter. With the help of his followers, he painted the tyrant Aristratos (*fl* late 4th century BC) next to Nike on a chariot. Aratos (271–213 BC) furiously scratched out the image of Aristratos from the painting, suggesting that Nike's political significance was more important than her role as the symbol of victory. The emphasis was moving from private and municipal patronage of artists, commissioned to produce paintings of the best athletes, to the exploitation of artists as a means of strengthening the central power of the ruler.

132. Wall painting from the House of the Dioscurides, Pompeii, depicting *Perseus and Andromeda*, Roman version of a lost Greek original (by ?Nikias) (Naples, Museo Archeologico Nazionale)

A sizeable number of paintings has been attributed to APELLES on the evidence of copies and of elements in others' paintings borrowed from his known works; among his principal works mentioned by written sources, which would have inspired later paintings, are the *Heracules Aversus*, reproduced in a Herculaneum fresco, and *Alexander Holding the Thunderbolt* in the House of the Vettii in Pompeii. Many of those represented by Apelles belonged to the circle of Alexander the Great. Among his works produced after Alexander's death are some allegories, such as the *Charis* ('Grace') at Smyrna, reproduced in a mosaic from Byblos (Beirut, Mus. N.) and the *Calumny*, executed at the court of Ptolemy I (*reg* 305–283 BC), echoes of which can be found in the judicial scenes on a black background from the Villa Farnesina, Rome (40–20 BC; Rome, Mus. N. Romano). Apelles is the first painter for whom there is evidence of a self-portrait.

PROTOGENES' subjects included a portrait of *Aristotle's Mother*, allegories and minor gods set in a landscape. His *Ialysos*, a young hunter sitting with his dog, is reproduced in a cup by the Hesse Painter (London, BM). Protogenes was the author of a catalogue of 'schemes' (Pliny: *Natural History* XXXV.cii), which was of great importance in the dissemination of his iconographic creations. From a contest between Apelles and Protogenes, the Romans acquired the panel on which the two masters competed to draw the thinnest line. Pliny stated that it was burnt during the first fire on the Palatine (Pliny: *Natural History* XXXV.lxxxi–lxxxiii).

(c) Hellenistic (323–27 BC). During the Hellenistic period an interest in surroundings developed out of the mythological and historical genres and so gave rise to the landscape painting, either frankly naturalistic or with an idyllic and bucolic tone inspired by literature. The portrait acquired a more private character, as foreshadowed by Nikias, Apelles and Protogenes. A minor genre, in terms of picture size and character, depicting scenes from ordinary life, erotic groups, animals and still-lifes, became widespread.

In Macedonia, from the mythic and heroic themes of the earliest painted tombs evolved the illusionism of the Lyson and Kallicles tomb in Leukadia. Here the armour and weapons of the two commanders seem to hang within a bright pavilion, demonstrating the decorative solutions of the so-called Second Style of Roman mural painting (*c.* 90–*c.* 15 BC; *see* ROME, ANCIENT, §V, 2). In Athens the historical manner was perpetuated both by Hyppis, who painted an allegory in celebration of a naval victory (perhaps by the Macedonian Demetrios I Poliorketes, *reg* 294–288 BC) employing the images of Poseidon and Nike, and by Olbiades, who portrayed the strategy of Kalippos, leader of the Athenian army against the Galatians during their incursion in 279 BC. Kratinos, whose work exalted the glories of civilization, decorated the interior of

133. Wall painting, from a house on the Esquiline Rome, depicting *Odysseus in the Underworld*, h. 1.16 m, Roman version of a lost Greek original, *c.* 50–*c.* 40 BC (Rome, Vatican, Biblioteca Apostolica Vaticana)

the Pompeion in the Athenian Kerameikos with figures of playwrights; there is an inscription from Menander, possibly reproduced in the House of the Menander wall painting in Pompeii. Eirene, the daughter and pupil of Kratinos, painted a *Kore* in Eleusis, evidence of the growing interest in mystery cults. Realism, pioneered by Pauson, was adapted to the then prevailing taste in the simple *Scenes in a Shop* painted by PEIRAIKOS.

Theon of Samos (*fl* late 4th century BC), who painted a portrait of *Demetrios I Poliorketes*, was celebrated in eastern circles for a cycle on the Trojan War, later brought to Rome in the Portico di Filippo and frequently imitated in Pompeiian decoration. Timomachos of Byzantium (of uncertain date) painted not only the traditional mythological subjects, such as *Ajax*, *Medea*, *Orestes and Iphigenia among the Taurians* and the *Gorgon*, but also a portrait of the juggler *Lekythion* and family conversation groups. Frescoes in Delos and later mosaics in Lemnos reproduced scenes from a comedy in the Kalates style.

The adventures of Odysseus gave painters opportunities for grandiose landscapes, much as they were exploited for the large statuary groups of Rhodes and Pergamon, placed by the artists inside grottoes or in the middle of expanses of water. Vitruvius noted the success of these themes in Roman wall painting. Examples of it have been found in a house on the Esquiline, *c.* 50 BC, where *Polyphemos* (untraced), *Laestrygonians*, *Circe*, *Odysseus in the Underworld* (see fig. 133), *Sirens* (incomplete) and *Scylla* (untraced) appeared side by side.

In Alexandria, the versatile ANTIPHILOS explored both royal themes—for example, in *Ptolemy I of Egypt Hunting*, which can be reconstructed thanks to the consistency between a wall painting in Stabiae and a mosaic in Sétif—and subjects from everyday life. Hints of a realism that points towards *trompe l'oeil* can be found in the necklaces, shoes and other objects painted in polychrome technique on a light background on the Hadra vases. Caricature, already practised by Apelles, acquired a grotesque dimension, such pictures being known as *grylloi*. Dionysios of Alexandria (*c.* 170–90 BC), known as Thrax, was both a grammarian and a painter; he executed a portrait of the philologist Aristarchos (*c.* 215–143 BC) alongside a personification of Tragedy, an erudite use of allegory. Demetrios (*fl* mid-2nd century BC), known as Topographos, cultivated the art of landscape first at the court of Ptolemy VI Philometor (*reg* 181–145 BC) and later, *c.* 165 BC, in Rome. The *View of the Nile*, reproduced in the Palestrina mosaic (late 2nd century BC; Palestrina, Pal. Barberini; *see* PRAENESTE, fig. 2), was painted around this time. However, the fairy-tale expanse of water, populated by ducks, cranes, hippopotamuses, crocodiles and snakes among reeds, palm-trees and lotus flowers, is characteristic of the Alexandrian school, which derived the motifs from ancient Egyptian funerary iconography; the mosaic copy in Pompeii's House of the Faun (*c.* 100 BC; Naples, Mus. Archeol. N.; see POMPEII, fig. 7) is the earliest surviving example in a Roman context.

BIBLIOGRAPHY

K. Jex-Blake and E. Sellars: *The Elder Pliny's Chapters on the History of Art* (London, 1896)
C. M. Robertson: *Greek Painting* (Geneva, 1959)
T. Hölscher: *Griechische Historienbilder des 5. und 4. Jahrhunderts v. Chr.* (Würzburg, 1973)
P. H. von Blanckenhagen: 'Painting in the Time of Alexander and Later', *Macedonia and Greece in Late Classical and Early Hellenistic Times*, ed. B. Barr-Sharrar and E. N. Borza (Washington, DC, 1982)
A. Barbet: *La Peinture murale romaine* (Paris, 1985)
F. Ducatti: *Pittura antica* (Milan, 1987)

(iii) Painters and society. According to Pliny, monumental polychrome painting originated in Corinth, a centre of trade and a meeting-place *en route* from Syria and Phoenicia to the western Greek colonies. The splendid court of Kypselos (*reg c.* 657–*c.* 625 BC) and Periander (*reg c.* 625–*c.* 585 BC) attracted the first figurative artists as well as poets.

In 479 BC the paintings of Plataia (*see* §(ii) above) celebrated the unity of the Greeks, and in Athens the activity of POLYGNOTOS OF THASOS and his circle was favoured by the policy of Kimon (*c.* 512–449 BC). In 477 BC, when Lemnos entered the Athens-led Delian League, Polygnotos' brother Aristophon was commissioned to paint a picture representing the *Wounded Philoktetes.* Athens' annexation of Skyros led to Polygnotos' painting of the island's founder Achilles with the daughters of Lykomedes, its legendary sovereign. Kimon (*c.* 512–449 BC) claimed to have found the bones of Theseus, legendary king of Athens, at Skyros; these were taken as a symbol of Athenian power, and Theseus' exploits were represented in a frieze by MIKON that adorned the Sanctuary of Apollo showing battles against the Amazons and the Centaurs and Theseus' descent to the bottom of the sea for the miraculous recovery of a ring. Mikon later returned to the theme in painting the Stoa Poikile in the Athenian Agora during the last years of Kimon's regime. 'Polygnotos was not an artisan', declared Plutarch, and the poet Melanthios was the first among his contemporaries to understand that Polygnotos as a painter had a social role, illustrating the ideal of 'virtuous behaviour' (*ethos*) on the part of the heroes.

The arrival of ZEUXIS in Athens was as important for painting as the 427 BC visit of Gorgias of Leontini (*c.* 485–*c.* 380 BC) was for the birth of rhetoric. Like the Sophists, the new painters were attracted by Athens but remained essentially itinerant. In public they behaved with the pomp of 'masters of knowledge': Zeuxis displayed his name woven in his cloak in letters of gold; PARRHASIOS dressed in purple with gilt accessories. Like the Sophists, Zeuxis was accused of making too much money from his work, but he also gave away paintings declaring that no payment would be truly adequate. Socrates observed that the King of Macedonia had obtained Zeuxis' services at a very high price. APOLLODOROS scorned him for bringing with him the art 'stolen' from others and criticized him for treating his artistic experience as merchandise. Hence a painting that Zeuxis exhibited for a fee was called *Helen Hetaira.*

Plato compared the lesson to be learnt from Zeuxis with that imparted by the Sophists. And it was from the need to cultivate specific skills for each form of production, taught by the Sophists, that a system of education arose that addressed different areas of human activity. The dignity of Zeuxis and Parrhasios came from the new idea of the artist as a 'master'. While Socrates and the Sophists came into conflict in various ways with the city's constitution, painters came to depend less on social and political activity and public commissions. Zeuxis criticized the willingness of AGATHARCHOS to collaborate with the plans of Pericles, declaring that he preferred to work for posterity. Zeuxis had an idea of aristocratic perfection that ill accorded with Athenian democracy but found justification in the circle of the statesman Alcibiades (*c.* 450–404 BC).

The end of the Peloponnesian War in 404 BC marked a turning-point in painting; faith in the old institutions generally was weakened, and painters could no longer aspire to absolute truths in their work. From the beginning of the 4th century BC the Greeks in Asia Minor were particularly sensitive to the centralization of power that was taking place in the coastal satrapies of the Persian Empire. The naturalism introduced by Androkydes of Kyzikos (*fl* early 4th century BC) into mythological painting rested on the preferences of a nascent class that might be termed 'bourgeois': fish-plates with realistic reproductions of marine fauna have been found among the furnishings of a rich house in Olynthos, with numbers incised on the bottoms. Other pieces reached the flourishing mercantile cities on the Black Sea coast.

In Athens the comedies of Aristophanes (*c.* 448–*c.* 388 BC), with their numerous criticisms of Pauson (*fl c.* 425–*c.* 388 BC), denounce the production of pictures that do not celebrate the city: Pauson was considered a 'depraved' caricaturist, and in a climate of economic competition and social division, failure to appeal to wealthy patrons could condemn an artist to destitution. Nor did the social upheaval assure nobly born citizens the free practice of art: even Klisthenes of the Theopropides was a 'scenographer', a poor man. Around 340 BC Demosthenes (*c.* 383–322 BC) expressed a distinction between art and craft. He accused the painter Philochares of being a mere decorator of religious objects, although Pliny later attributed to him an 'immense artistic power'.

Painting of this period reflects the developments in the Athenian *polis*, whether it tends towards mystic and allegorical visions, in the tradition of ARISTEIDES, or accords with the general spirit of the expanding economy, with EUPHRANOR and his followers. The ideology of Isocrates (436–338 BC), master and political inspiration of the *strategos* ('general') Timotheos (*fl* early 4th century BC), can be discerned behind the decorative programme of the Stoa of Zeus in the Athenian Agora. He was responsible for the inscription that accompanied Euphranor's *Theseus*, presenting him as the founder of Athenian democracy. The Demokratia who crowned the Demos of Athens (*see* §(ii) above) in the presence of armed cavalry represented the moderate democracy of Isocrates, intended to recognize the merits of a privileged minority. The fallen warriors immortalized in the painting had not only redeemed the 'glory of their fathers' at the Battle of Mantinea, as Xenophon recounted, but had also defended the *patria politeia.* From this watershed in historical painting the greatest developments have come to light at sites within the empire of Alexander the Great. NIKOMACHOS OF THEBES, in a dialogue with the Macedonian regent Antipater (395–319 BC), advanced a sense of the dignity of the artist, which was of use in negotiating prices. His work on the Tomb of Persephone at Vergina and the fact that his pupil PHILOXENOS OF ERETRIA worked for Kassander (*reg* 305/4–297 BC), the son of Antipater, confirm the presence of Attic painters at the Macedonian court.

NIKIAS turned to the text of the *Odyssey*; to him, Homer was a part of cultural history, and the artist had no interest in bringing him up to date, as had been done in the time of Polygnotos. This explains Nikias' success in a cosmopolitan society that had no common goals: what had formerly been praised for giving a good example to the contemporary citizen now became important as a record of the past. Nikias was preoccupied with formal refinement, and with this aesthetic rather than moral ideal, he took the social role of the painter as far as it could go in the economic context of the Hellenistic realms. Ptolemy I (*reg* 306–284 BC) was said to have offered 60 talents for a picture of Odysseus descending into the underworld, the *Questioning of the Dead* (*nekromanteia*). But Nikias refused 'because he had abundant wealth' and donated the panel to Athens.

At Sikyon, the tradition of *Chrestographia* ('beautiful painting') expressed an aristocratic ideal. In harmony with Platonic principles, PAMPHILOS did not hide his élitist views of art. In his treatise *On Painting and the Illustrious Painters* he identifies his approach with the greatest achievements of Greek painting. Like the late Sophists, he was in sympathy with the oligarchic party and with Sparta; in 369 BC, with the arrival of the Thebans and the democratic regime of Euphron, he had to leave Sikyon. In exile he painted the *Victory of the Athenians at Phlious*, a reversal for the citizens of the town. After the demise of the Theban rule, Pamphilos returned to Sikyon. With MELANTHIOS, PAUSIAS and APELLES, who shared the aristocratic ideology of their master, he collaborated in celebrating the tyrant Aristratos (*fl* late 4th century BC), who upheld the policies of Philip II (*reg* 359–336 BC). The society that had supported the school of Sikyon was the largest to enter the union of the Greek states under monarchial rule; painting was in the service of political power, and the support Philip II gave to the aristocratic party was reflected in allegorical works of the kind already produced to exalt the local ruler.

In 343 BC Apelles was brought into the Macedonian court through the good offices of Aristratos and the relations Pamphilos maintained with his native city. The sovereign's goodwill towards the artist was matched by the latter's readiness to produce political propaganda, and Philip and Alexander discovered the Sikyonian organizational ability to produce paintings that could project the new image of the sovereign. The meeting between Apelles and PROTOGENES at Rhodes illustrates the opposing approaches prevalent in that period: Apelles, working in the context of monarchic power, requested payment in gold; Protogenes, originally an artisan, lived in the last Aegean city state to retain a certain independence, and he sold his paintings to the inhabitants of Rhodes at prices so modest as to worry Apelles.

During the Hellenistic period, the difference between the artisan and the successful artist grew more pronounced. The papyri archives of Zenon, an estate manager, established in 256 BC at Philadelphia in the Fayyum in Egypt, have revealed the modest financial position of Theophilos, a painter from Alexandria. He charged only 53 drachmai, of which 23 were spent on coloured paints, to decorate the walls of three rooms and a ceiling. On completing the work, Theophilos wrote to the buyer: 'If you require any further paintings, be so good as to commission me, so that I can earn a living. If you cannot do this, be so good as to send me a viaticum so that I can go back to my brothers in the city.' The Athenian painter and philosopher Metrodoros, by contrast, was invited by the consul Paullus Macedonicus in 168 BC to Rome, where he helped form the aristocratic circle of Attic artists. And DEMETRIOS OF ALEXANDRIA, who had come to Rome from Egypt, achieved such status at this period that he was able to shelter his own exiled king, Ptolemy VI Philometor (*reg* 181–145 BC). During the last century of the Republic, Iaia competed successfully against the noted portrait painters Sopolis and Dionysios for the best clientele between Naples and Rome.

BIBLIOGRAPHY

J. J. Pollitt: *The Art of Greece, 1400–31 BC: Sources and Documents* (Englewood Cliffs, NJ, 1965)
C. M. Robertson: *A History of Greek Art* (Cambridge, 1975)
J. J. Pollitt: *Art in the Hellenistic Age* (Cambridge, 1986)

2. HISTORICAL SURVEY.

(i) Geometric to Archaic (*c*. 900–*c*. 480 BC). (ii) Classical (*c*. 480–323 BC). (iii) Hellenistic (323–27 BC).

*(i) Geometric to Archaic (*c. *900*–c. *480* BC).* After the Mycenaean period (*c*. 1600–*c*. 1050 BC) and the so-called Dorian invasion (*see* HELLADIC, §§I, 4(iii)(a) and IV), the first artistic phase of historical Greece was defined by the taste for a wider use of pictorial decoration of pottery: the Protogeometric style (*c*. 1000– *c*. 900 BC) followed by the Geometric (*c*. 900–*c*. 725 BC) and the Orientalizing (*c*. 725–*c*. 600 BC) styles (*see* §V, 2, 3 and 4 above). According to tradition, the origin of figural painting lay in *skiagraphia* ('drawing the shadow'). Saurias of Samos was said by the 2nd-century AD philosopher Athenagoras to have drawn the contours of a horse's shadow; Pliny attributed a similar practice to the anonymous precursors of painting in Sikyon and Corinth. Literary references to this phase of Greek painting correlate the silhouette figures of men and animals on Geometric pottery (see fig. 86 above). The decoration on later Geometric pottery accords with the technique that Pliny attributed to the painters Aridikes of Corinth and Telephanes of Sikyon of giving more substance to the silhouette by adding internal lines within the outline (see fig. 134). Pliny (*Natural History*, VII.cxxvi, XXXV.lv) cites as belonging to this period a monumental painting (untraced) by BOULARCHOS. Fragments of mural decoration have been found in the first Poseidon Temple at Isthmia (*c*. 690–*c*. 650 BC).

The use of uniform colours is typical of the 7th century BC, inspired by Neo-Assyrian painted reliefs (*see* MESOPOTAMIA, §VI, 2). Links with Egypt can be discerned in the works of the painter Philokles from Naukratis. In Orientalizing pottery the figures are given more rounded profiles, coordinated movements and more complex narrative contexts. Polychrome painting originated in Corinth, in the works of Ekphantos. The Chigi Vase (*c*. 640–*c*. 630 BC; Rome, Villa Giulia, 22, 697; see fig. 80 above) decorated by the MACMILLAN PAINTER (*see* VASE PAINTERS, §II) represents the masterpiece of early polychrome Proto-Corinthian painted pottery (*see* §V, 4(ii) above). The palette was that used until the time of Apelles (late 4th–early 3rd century BC): white, black, red and yellow.

In Corinth at the beginning of the Archaic period, the use in pottery decoration of shapes outlined with black paint and with an engraved margin appears side by side with freely rendered outlines in brown lines. Vase painters from Corinth spread the new technique to Athens, where they became the basis of the Black-figure style of vase painting (*see* §V, 5 above). The François Vase (Florence, Mus. Archeol.; *c*. 570 BC) by KLEITIAS (*see* VASE PAINTERS, §II) displays all the characteristics that Pliny attributed to masters of the Archaic style: the clear distinction between

134. Painted clay plaque depicting mariners, from the Sanctuary of Athena, Sounion, Attica, l. 160 mm, *c.* 700 BC (Athens, National Archaeological Museum)

females and males, the representation of figures without stiffness and the ability to overlap and foreshorten. In the depiction on this vase of the *Kalydonian Boar-hunt*, for example, the heroes pursue the animal from both sides, so that the movement is placed in a tangible space: these are the 'slanting images' (*katagrapha*) introduced into large-scale painting by KIMON OF KLEONAI. A generation later, EXEKIAS (*see* VASE PAINTERS, §II) adapted to the needs of Athenian ceramics the resources of monumental painting, in which he was evidently skilled.

Cypress panels from Pitsa (*see* §1(i) above), dating from *c.* 525 BC and after, demonstrate the techniques of painting on wood and are comparable both with contemporary vase painting and with the limestone slate found in the Achaemenid Treasury, Persepolis, which depicts Greek myth. To the same period belong the wall paintings at GORDION and ELMALI, and the vivid Etruscan tomb paintings, which show Ionian influence (*see* ETRUSCAN, §V).

*(ii) Classical (*c. *480–323* BC). The Persian destruction of the Acropolis in Athens in 480 BC caused the loss of the legacy of the earlier tradition of Attic painting. It is clear, however, that Archaic painters had already given their figures a fluidity and a sensitivity to narrative context; these qualities are even more marked in the figures of the Classical period, which are part of, and are influenced by, a real environment.

(a) 5th century BC. The flowing graphics of the Red-figure style (*see* §V, 6 above) made it easier for vase painters to borrow themes from the great masters, so that the subject-matter, as described by Pausanias (IX.iv.1–2), of the cycle painted by Onasias (*fl* first half of 5th century BC) and POLYGNOTOS OF THASOS for the Sanctuary of Athena in Plataia can be identified in contemporary pottery. The vase painter who most closely follows the style of the masters is the Penthesilea Painter (*fl* 460s–440s BC): the face and the human body are arranged in a series of postures as if in accordance with a poetic code. The impression of monumentality stems from the rhythmic distribution of such schemes within geometric grids.

Stage sets for one of Aeschylus' tragedies (written *c.* 460 BC) were painted on wooden panels by AGATHARCHOS, who gave an impression of depth by his use of undulating ground, rocks and trees, among which figures were interspersed to suggest different planes, thus giving concreteness and credibility to the story. The plastic effect was enhanced by the handling of shadows. Polygnotos began with neutral shading, crosshatching and toning down, and PANAINOS added flesh-tints to the chromatic scale. APOLLODOROS varied the colour according to the intensity of the light, mixing different 'earths', from yellow to brown. He also studied the phenomenon of the *ombra portata* (chiaroscuro), which appears for the first time in ceramics just after 450 BC with the Chiusi Cup. This is how Apollodoros made his figures seem so realistic, a revolutionary quality found in his panel paintings even more than in his large wall paintings. He also developed, in his paintings on the cylindrical surfaces of lekythoi, the preference of the ACHILLES PAINTER (*see* VASE PAINTERS, §II) for a white ground, so creating easy and harmonious postures.

ZEUXIS, who arrived in Athens *c.* 430 BC and died in Macedonia, took the Classical style to its highest point.

The lightness of his draperies probably corresponded to the flowery style of the MEIDIAS PAINTER (*see* VASE PAINTERS, §II). The decorations engraved on the silver vases of Douvanli recall the Attic lekythoi of Group R with their white grounds, inspired by the perspective of PARRHASIOS' drawings: the line only suggests foreshortening, cancelling the solidity of background. TIMANTHES, a leading figure in the painting competitions that flourished among his generation of artists, on several occasions beat both Parrhasios and the otherwise unknown Kolotes of Teos.

(b) 4th century BC. At the end of the Peloponnesian War (404 BC), three distinct schools existed: one typical of East Greece, centred on Ephesos; an Attic school; and a particularly prestigious school at Sikyon in the Peloponnese. The 'Asian genre', as Pliny called it, was the oldest. Kolophon was the home town of Dionysios, contemporary and imitator of Polygnotos; in Ephesos, Euenor and his son Parrhasios were active; from Samos came Agatharchos. Androkydes was born in Kyzicos, a colony of Miletos; he was named by Pliny as a rival of Zeuxis but outlived him: a painting commissioned from Androkydes by the city of Thebes remained unfinished *c.* 180 BC. Aetion, active during the era of Alexander the Great (*reg* 336–323 BC), is reputed to have come from Miletos. APELLES, born in Kolophon *c.* 375, received his education in Ephesos under Ephoros, but as an artist he was pan-Hellenic. Through his longstanding contact with the most important schools of his time and his presence at the courts of Philip II (*reg* 359–336 BC), Alexander, and Alexander's warring successors, he absorbed the whole experience of Classical style, creating the vocabulary that became universal in Hellenistic art.

In Athens, the school was started by ARISTEIDES, a native of Thebes, who was trained *c.* 400 BC by Euxenidas. Two styles predominated: one, largely represented by his son Ariston and later descendants, featured allegorical subjects; the other, promoted by EUPHRANOR, is more natural, inspired by historical events. The first style can be regarded as of Theban origin, the second Athenian.

NIKOMACHOS OF THEBES, pupil of Ariston and creator of fantastic compositions, is one of the earliest Greek painters to whom a surviving original work can be attributed, the decoration of the Tomb of Persephone at Vergina. In *Hades and Persephone* (for illustration *see* VERGINA) Hades' hair—brown, yellow and purple—floats in the air; his facial features are delineated by hatching, in the same colours as the hair, with yellow used for highlights. The outline of the Hades group, with Persephone being dragged into the carriage, is repeated in the battle scene in the Alexander Mosaic at Pompeii (*see* POMPEII, fig. 7): this supports the attribution of the battle scene from which the mosaic was possibly copied to PHILOXENOS OF ERETRIA, who was a pupil of Nikomachos. Another piece by Philoxenos, the *Banquet of the Three Sileni*, known through its reproduction in an engraving on the back of an Etruscan mirror, indicates the painter's influence over neighbouring Thrace, where the Tomb of KAZANLUK bears a painting with a very similar perspective illustrating the offer of food to the dead.

Euphranor decorated the Stoa of Zeus in the Athenian Agora in 362 BC. Through his disciple Antidotos (*fl* late 4th century BC), his teaching was transmitted to NIKIAS, a versatile artist who flourished in the second half of the 4th century BC and may have painted the hunting scene on the façade of the Philip II's tomb in Vergina (336 BC). The hunters, with the dogs and the game, are set in a landscape punctuated by rocks and trees, with snow-covered mountains in the background. The palette is rich, from the white of the background and of the King's horse, through the warm tones of yellow–orange, red, brown, pale violet and purple, to the colder green and blue shades and the sombre tones of the rocks.

The founder of the Sikyonian school, Eupompos (*fl* early 4th century BC), argued *c.* 375 BC for the crowd scene as the natural subject, eschewing a moral selection based on the subject's heroic character. For his successors PAMPHILOS and MELANTHIOS, the objective was symmetry, founded on mathematical and geometric schemes; for PAUSIAS, realism was achieved by use of shading and foreshortening. The newly introduced encaustic painting had a parallel in the bright overpainting on West Slope ware and Gnathia vases.

Apelles arrived at Sikyon already possessing the powers of observation characteristic of Ionian art from the beginning. In his painting the Classical organic whole is broken up by the highlighting of peripheral detail. In addition to the plasticity achieved by the perspective, the colour and the light, interpreted in different ways by Melanthios and Pausias, there is what Pliny termed *splendor*: the representation of the source of light within the painting and the study of reflections on figures and objects. Novel but typical of the Sikyon school was a sparing use of shadow, limited to the four colours of the Archaic tradition (black, white, yellow and red). A remarkable technique was used for applying the colours, the 'glazing' sharply observed by Aristotle: 'colours show one through the other, an effect painters sometimes achieve by laying one colour on top of a brighter one'.

Invited by Philip, Apelles moved from Sikyon to Macedonia *c.* 343 BC. Later he returned to Ephesos, where he worked for Alexander; after the King's death, he worked at the court of Ptolemy I (*reg* 305–283 BC) in Egypt. He visited Rhodes, where he met PROTOGENES, then on his way back from Athens. Finally he established his residence in Kos, where he painted his unfinished masterpiece, the *Aphrodite Anadyomene*, between 306 and 301 BC.

(iii) Hellenistic (323–27 BC*).* During the Hellenistic period, the quest for space, colour and light was enriched by techniques comparable to those used in modern painting from the Baroque period to the Neo-classical and Impressionist. The kingdom of Macedonia continued to attract artists of different origins, as is shown by the commissioning of Philoxenos by Kassander (*reg* 305/4–297 BC) and of Theon of Samos by Demetrios I Poliorketes (*reg* 294–288 BC).

North of Vergina, on the Macedonian plain, a series of remarkable discoveries includes a tomb with a façade on two levels (?3rd century BC), found at LEUKADIA. The whole is designed like the gate of a city, denoting the entrance to the underworld. Two wall paintings depict the deceased as a military leader in armour together with Hermes, the guide of souls, and the infernal judges Aeacus and Rhadamanthys. Of slightly later date is the monument at Naousa, the interior decoration of which, now lost, was reproduced in watercolour at the time of its discovery; it represented a knight in combat against an Oriental. Another tomb, dated 250 BC, was explored there in 1971; this has beautiful floral motifs painted at the entrance and a married couple on the façade. The most recent work is painted on the tomb discovered in Leukadia in 1942 inscribed with the names of the brothers Lyson and Kallikles, officers of the Macedonian army; decorative panels depict armour, shields, helmets and swords in brilliant colours. Perhaps the two occupants had fallen at the Battle of Cynoscephalai (197 BC).

The Leukadia façade shows an artist working according to the internal demands of painting, no longer 'applying to each part the colour that suits it', as Plato recommended. The effect derives from the proximity of colours: employing a type of 'pointillist' technique, bodies and draperies are represented by the overlapping of small, differently coloured touches of the brush that are not mixed with one another but blend only when seen from a distance (see fig. 135). This technique was disseminated by a master active at the Macedonian court; he painted the original of the allegorical and dynastic cycle that was reproduced in the Boscoreale Villa (Naples, Mus. Archeol. N.; New York, Met.). Another native of Macedonia was Heraklides, who moved to Athens in 168 BC after the fall of the Macedonian king Perseus (*reg* 179–168 BC).

135. Wall painting from a tomb at Leukadia (detail), h. 420 mm, ?3rd century BC

In Athens, the investigation of light was further advanced by Hyppis, who painted the *Marriage of Pirotoo*, presenting an interior heavy with drapery and gold, lighted by a flaming chandelier.

In Sikyon, Timanthes the younger painted the vigorous *Victory of Aratos over the Aitolians at Pellene*; Leontiskos represented the general next to a trophy. Nealkes, who produced mythological and genre paintings, examined relations between Aratos (271–213 BC) and the Ptolemies, thus recalling the battle between Darius II Ochos (*reg* 423–404 BC) and the Egyptians a century before. His daughter Anaxandra and Erigonos, who in turn was master to Pasias, are mentioned as his disciples.

In Pergamon, the artist Pytheas, educated in Sikyon but a native of Bura in Arcadia, painted an elephant that is echoed in a fresco at the House of Sacello Iliaco in Pompeii, probably depicting the 'Battle of the Elephants', at which Antiochus I (323–261 BC) of Syria defeated the Galatians in 275 BC. Pausanias mentioned a painting in Pergamon, associated with the wars waged by the Pergameni in 238 BC, that celebrated a *Galatomachy*, later reflected in Roman sarcophagi, by artists from Asia Minor such as Milon of Solos. A plasticity derived from Pergamene painting, evident in the wide spaces and shading of atmospheric tones of the *Dionysos Discovering Ariadne*, in the House of Cithara Player in Pompeii, suggests that this work was modelled on a 3rd-century BC original. The neo-Classical taste became popular *c.* 140 BC, as is evidenced by the despatch of the painters Asklepiades (*fl c.* 100 BC), Gaudotos and Kalas to Delphi by Attalos II (*reg* 160–139 BC) to copy famous originals. When Pergamon became part of the Roman Empire in 133 BC, the painter Iaia of Kyzicos, a woman, went to Italy. Around 290 BC Artemon worked at the court of Seleukos of Antioch (*reg* 305–281 BC). His paintings depicting Herakles were moved to the Porticus of Octavia in Rome, where they are said to have inspired the decoration of the House of Octavius Quartone in Pompeii, which is dominated by an intense chiaroscuro, with a rich impasto of colours and specks of light. To the same milieu belongs the exuberant painting representing stories of Dyonisos and Herakles in the House of Marcus Lucretius Fronto.

In Rhodes, Protogenes developed the observation of social reality, a course followed by Philiskos (*fl ?c.* 100 BC), who portrayed a shop-boy blowing on a fire in the artist's studio, and by Simos, who painted a dyer's shop. The iridescent effect obtained in the theatrical scenes, as evidenced in mosaic copies signed by Dioskourides of Samos (Naples, Mus. Archeol. N.), derives from developments in technique in Asia Minor and the offshore islands during the 2nd century BC. In this case the technique is used to suggest the transparency of dresses made of Kos silk.

In Alexandria, ANTIPHILOS progressed from chromatic harmony to tonal painting, in the manner of Apelles. The elaboration of *splendor* enabled fire to operate as a source of light in an enclosed space. It seems to have been in Alexandria too, in a reaction against the neo-Attic fashion, that the *a macchia* style was born. There are several examples of this in wall paintings at Rome, including the yellow frieze in the House of Livia on the Palatine representing a scene on the Nile, as well as a nocturne in Pompeii relating to the cult of Isis, authentic *plein-air* paintings.

BIBLIOGRAPHY

J. Overbeck: *Die antiken Schriftquellen zur Geschichte der bildenden Künste bei den Griechen* (Leipzig, 1868/*R* Hildesheim, 1959)
K. Jex-Blake and E. Sellars: *The Elder Pliny's Chapters on the History of Art* (London, 1896)
E. Pfuhl: *Malerei und Zeichnung der Griechen* (Munich, 1923)
——: *Masterpieces of Greek Drawing and Painting* (Munich, 1926)
C. M. Robertson: *Greek Painting* (Geneva, 1959)
V. J. Bruno: *Form and Colour in Greek Painting* (London, 1977)

3. THEORY AND CRITICISM. For the Greeks, painting was perhaps the most highly regarded art form. Travellers, writers and poets from Simonides (*c.* 556–*c.* 468 BC) until the Byzantine age consistently rated painters higher than other artists.

(i) 5th century BC. Pausanias' description (X.xxv–xxxi) of the paintings by Polygnotos on the walls of the *lesche* (clubhouse) built by the Knidians *c.* 450 BC at Delphi helps explain why Simonides thought of Polygnotos when he declared, 'Painting, silent poetry; poetry, speaking painting'. The mastery of *techne* ('craft', 'skill') became the artistic equivalent of poetic *sophia* ('wisdom'). But Polygnotos' work was not seen simply as an illustration of a literary text: the artist was credited with the power to elaborate his material independently. Avoiding immediate realism and dramatic excess, painters treated myths and heroes with the detachment of the epic, and human sentiments with the sublimation of the lyric. The *ethos* or depiction of character attributed to Polignotos by his contemporaries represents the perfect balance between descriptive observation and formal perfection. Ancient critics connected the new expressive possibilities shown by Panainos in the physiognomies of the combatants in his *Battle of Marathon* (*see* §(ii) above) with the increased use of colours, which they thought had already created a 'perfect' art. Progress coincided with technical experimentation: Panainos had elsewhere used an original milk tempera and a yellow made from crocuses.

In the 5th century BC, among those who developed the perspective theories of Agatharcos, the sculptor Anaxagoras inspired Pheidias, who was originally a painter, and Demokritos was the theorist of painting as illusion, the adviser of Apollodoros. With his treatise on perspective, Anaxagoras, the teacher and friend of Pericles, taught artists a new visual language. He asserted that our weak senses cannot discern the truth but that we can understand it through experience, memory and art, since the world of appearances reflects invisible truths. His rational, scientific approach and faith in the intellect were expressed in the concept of perspective. Demokritos held that our senses perceive not real things but insubstantial images emanating from the atoms that compose matter. According to Pliny, Apollodoros was a painter of 'appearance' (*species*); indeed, Apollodoros had been called *skiagraphos* ('painter of shadows', i.e. phantoms or illusory figures). The term *skiagraphia* was also used to refer to primitive painters, a usage that persisted. Plato confirmed this in the famous myth of the cave in the *Republic*, where the ignorant inhabitants live in a world of 'shadows' thrown by a fire, which they believe to represent reality. For Plato, art was merely the shadow of shadows. In Demokritos space is conceived as a visual field, and Apollodoros was known for the execution of single pictures rather than large wall paintings. This marks the beginning of painting in the modern sense, as a view opening on the world; Pliny said that, among Greek paintings, Apollodoros' were the first from which the observer could not tear his gaze away.

Once they had liberated their art from the directives of civic morality and politics, Greek painters of the late 5th–early 4th century BC engaged in a refined skirmish over formal qualities: theirs was an art of perfection, intended to be understood by other artists. Apollodoros declared that his works were easier to criticize than to imitate. Parrhasios described himself as the 'holder of first place in art among the Hellenes'; Zeuxis retorted that he did not consider himself second; and, in a third epigram, Parrhasios declared that his own heights were 'insuperable'. The figurative artistic vocabularly of this period was so secure in its expressive means that painters were conscious of having reached full self-realization. The preference that Parrhasios gave to line and Zeuxis to chiaroscuro allowed them both to take one technique to its furthest point. Zeuxis' attentive study of proportions was paralleled by that of the sculptor Polykleitos in his Canon (*see* POLYKLEITOS, §1(i)). This could be seen as the fulfilment of Pythagorean numerical speculation. Following Apollodoros' lead, Zeuxis also developed a theory of shading, apparently making use of the 'superposition' of transparent colours (i.e. glazing).

Thus Zeuxis continued to feature at the forefront of innovation and controversy. He had lived through the highpoint of the Classical period (*c.* 475–323 BC), but he had also experienced the crisis of the Peloponnesian War (431–404 BC), the elegance of the Athenian nobility, the intolerance of the new intellectuals and the exhausting search for beauty. In the end he escaped into an extroverted kind of painting; his scenes of life, conversation and play were addressed to refined art lovers, and the artist's expertise was exhausted in a process that was increasingly pitched at a specialist level. Art for art's sake was born, and so was the figure of the misunderstood artist.

When the process of formation of strictly Classical iconography, begun by Polygnotos, had come to an end, Parrhasios was credited with the power of a 'lawgiver', because his images of the gods, which were not based solely on natural models, had prevailed for centuries. In Parrhasios, creation arose from imagination rather than observation, and this approach absorbed following generations: Theon became famous, according to Quintilian, 'for his faculty of conceiving visions, which are called *phantasiai*'.

With Timanthes the aesthetic of the *ethos* (portrayal of essential character) became an almost hermetic art. The gifts attributed to Zeuxis and Parrhasios had been technical experience, search for the ideal type, elegance of invention and sympathy for the different aspects of human emotion; the painters were associated with Timanthes, to create an artistic synthesis appropriate for the age of the Sophists. In his painting, for the first time, critics looked beyond formal structures, recognizing that a work's reality lies beyond its appearance and that 'genius goes beyond art'.

Hellenism marked the exploration of realism of Greek painting; it remained to Timanthes, in the allusive play he derived from the theatre, to situate the real in extreme situations.

(ii) 4th century BC. After the Peloponnesian War, this tradition was replaced by the schools that flourished particularly in the years of Alexander the Great (*reg* 336–323 BC) and his successors. The Theban–Attic school (*see* §2(ii)(b) above) seems to have been orientated towards mediating between a realistic portrayal or experience and the need to depict events outside human history. The lightness of Nikomachos of Thebes is countered by the realism of Euphranor: the Athenians said that their *Theseus* was fed on meat, while that of Parrhasios was fed on roses. On the Theban side, painting showed a taste for ideal constructions close to Plato's view of the world. In the Athenian tradition, art's profane context allowed the painter a freedom of choice, invention and aesthetic unknown in the earlier Classical world. Its rich possibilities were not to be fully realized until the Renaissance.

A treatise on eloquence saved the artistic vocation of Nikias. He declared that history was a 'grandiose subject. . .and that this subject was part of pictorial art like the myths of the poets'. This corresponds to Aristotle's opposition of history, which comments on real events, and poetry, which suggests the possible. Similarly, Nikias attributed to history a greatness that placed it between the painting of myths and that of 'little things like birds and flowers'.

The preference accorded in Asia Minor to Androkydes' realism explains why he was subjected to the general condemnation of 'passions' in terms of the residual Athenian aristocratic ethic. Following Plato's critique of the emotions, Androkydes was accused of 'having obeyed his passion [*pathos*] because by nature [*physis*] he was a lover of that food—fish—that he had skilfully introduced into his painting'.

When Eupompos, founder of the Sikyon school (*see* §2(ii)(b) above), was asked *c.* 375 BC which painters he followed, he pointed to the crowd in the road and answered that one should follow nature, not another artist. This assertion represented the mature development of the culture of the Sophists, who similarly resolved the relation between law (*nomos*) and nature (*physis*), that is to say between convention established by man and what the world offers in its native state: they were in favour of the *physis*, source of all good for mortals. The Sophists, like their antagonist Plato, were engaged in discovering the natural character of techniques (extended later by Pliny): they wanted man to model his own enterprises on the multiform life of plants and animals. Eupompos infused these values into the artistic production of Sikyon.

In his essay on the art of drawing, Pamphilos expressed the approach of one who was 'first among painters to be erudite in every discipline'. He maintained that it was necessary to study mathematics and geometry, to introduce drawing into the education of the young and to teach the encaustic technique. Quintilian praised him for the exactness of his proportional calculation (*ratio*). Plutarch spoke of the Sikyon artists' awareness in cultivating 'perfect painting' (*chrestographia*) and their desire to realize an unchangeable beauty.

According to ancient criticism the process of discovery embarked on by Classical painters culminated in the late 4th century BC–early 3rd with Apelles. It seems that he had not intended to break with the past; he expressed admiration for exponents of different schools and had reworked earlier experiences in a wider synthesis. But on the level of theory he had boldly advanced the innovations of the masters of Sikyon, reaching an awareness of the relativity and subjectivity of representation. From the surviving fragments of his theoretical writings, it seems that he believed 'genius' and 'grace' to be natural gifts of the artist. An epigram from a papyrus speaks of Apelles as a 'demon', whose force fascinates and ensnares the viewer. And he had personified *charis* (grace) in a painting at Smyrna; it was reproduced in a mosaic of the Imperial period (31 BC–AD 330) from Byblos (Beirut, Mus. N.), a composition of a girl exhibiting *kairos* (propitious moment) and *akme* (flowering). In his essay on painting Protogenes confessed his uneasiness about the technical expertise he had achieved: he 'did not like the art that could not be attenuated, and seemed excessive, and moved too far away from the truth'. Pliny attributed to Protogenes the assertion that in painting 'verisimilitude' is not enough: in the soul of the former artisan, still caught up in myth and Classical language, the morality of 'truth' was born.

(iii) 3rd century BC. During the first half of the 3rd century BC, the Athenian sculptor and writer Xenokrates introduced into art criticism both a parallel between painting and plastic art and the idea that the 'inventions' of the great masters had evolved out of the work of their predecessors. Thus Apollodoros' innovative use of chiaroscuro was developed by Zeuxis in his theory of shading and by Parrhasios' use of symmetry, and following Euphranor's study of colour, Apelles brought it to perfection. Xenokrates' work was continued in Pergamon by Antigonos of Karystos (*fl c.* 250–*c.* 200 BC), who extended art criticism to include terms more appropriate to rhetoric. Polemon in turn introduced the idea of scholarly description of paintings according to their arrangement. Pasiteles developed this a century later in a work of five volumes, one of which was devoted to painting. He took account of the new organization of masterpieces in Rome (*see* §4 below), paving the way for Varro. The legacy of Greek artists and theorists can be traced in the development of Roman painting, of which many more examples survive (*see* ROME, ANCIENT, §V).

BIBLIOGRAPHY

K. Jex-Blake and E. Sellars: *The Elder Pliny's Chapters on the History of Art* (London, 1896)

4. COLLECTIONS AND COLLECTORS. The idea of the picture gallery itself comes from the Classical Greek world. In the mid-5th century BC, at the time of Pericles, the first building expressly designed to contain paintings was constructed: Mnesikles planned the north wing of the Propylaia on the Acropolis (*see* ATHENS, §II, 1(i)) to house the collection of precious votive pictures. Good light was assured by south-facing windows, and a cornice of grey marble marked the lower limit of the surface designated for the paintings.

In the Hellenistic period (323–27 BC) collections of paintings of different periods were assembled in the courts of rulers at Pergamon (where specially made copies were also hung), in Antioch and in Alexandria. After their independence was ended in 31 BC by the Romans, the Greeks themselves saw the places of their history more as art museums than as religious and political centres. In Strabo's *Geography*, written in the time of Augustus (*reg* 27 BC–AD 14), a description of the Temple of Hera at Samos gives that site, which had been so lively in the Archaic period (*c.* 700–*c.* 480 BC), the atmosphere of an involuntary museum: 'an ancient sanctuary and a great temple, which today is an art gallery; apart from the quantity of little pictures inside the cella, there are other buildings for the collection of pictures and numerous shrines that are also full of ancient works of art'.

With the conquest of the western Greek cities in the 2nd century BC, the Romans obtained their first substantial collections of pictures, which, after adorning their triumphal processions, were placed in the temples and porticos of the city. Other masterpieces came from Corinth, sacked by Lucius Mummius in 146 BC. It was then that Polybius saw the paintings of the Athenian and Sikyonian masters scattered on the ground, while soldiers played dice on them. Pliny recounted an episode that illustrates the difficulty the Romans had in understanding the commercial value of Greek painting, which was already fuelling the Hellenistic princes' passion for collecting: part of the booty of Corinth was sold at auction, and the Consul was astonished that Attalos II of Pergamon (*reg* 160–139 BC) offered 600,000 *denarii* for the *Dionysus* of Aristeides; concluding that the painting had magic powers, he withdrew it from sale and had it placed in a temple in Rome.

At the end of the Republic, Rome was a precious public art gallery, though many works had ended in private hands. Hortensius, a lover of art and rival of Cicero, had a special shrine built to hold a painting by Cydias depicting the *Argonauts*: the structure adorned his park at Tusculum, near the present Frascati. Agrippa (64/63–12 BC), the son-in-law of Augustus, promoted a cultural policy that even today seems advanced: he held that the works of the greatest Greek artists should not be owned by private individuals but should be offered for the enjoyment of the public, because of their aesthetic and moral value. He was overruled by wealthy collectors, who liked to link their own prestige to the possession of famous works. In the same years Vitruvius recommended that special rooms should be reserved for displaying paintings in houses. He conceived these galleries as little salons with seats and loggias. Following a more advanced ideal than Mnesikles, he advised that sources of light be opened on the north side rather than the south, so that the sun's rays could not reach the paintings, which would have the benefit of constant moderate light.

Petronius (*fl* 1st century AD) reflected on the end of Greek painting, imagining that Eumolpus, the protagonist of his romance *Satyricon*, entered the art gallery of a city in Campania (identified as Naples or Pozzuoli), where one could admire originals of Zeuxis and drawings by Protogenes. In Naples, Philostratos Lemnios (*see* PHILOSTRATOS, (1)) (*b c.* AD 187–91) visited a large Greek gallery and left a detailed account: the paintings, by different artists, were divided according to great themes. The first hall was dedicated to the personifications of rivers, the second to Dionysus, the next to Aphrodite, the fourth to myths of the origin of the world and the last to Herakles.

The Imperial picture collection had a special position in Rome compared to the civic and private collections. It came from the collections of Hellenistic monarchs and may have maintained a certain continuity through the dynasties. Augustus preferred the paintings of Nikias. Attic vases painted in the Archaic Black-figure technique were collected in an immense museum in the 1st-century AD Grotto of Tiberius at Sperlonga. Philo Judaeus, an Alexandrian Jew who came to Rome in AD 40, described how Caligula (*reg* AD 37–41), reconstructing a villa on the Esquiline, personally studied the proper environment for displaying Greek paintings. A funerary inscription from the time of Antoninus Pius (*reg* 138–61 AD) gives the names of the Director of the Imperial gallery, Flavius Apollonius, and of his Vice-Director, Capito.

Numerous Greek pictures were held in Constantinople, as evidenced by descriptions in medieval epigrams, and these contributed to the continuity of Hellenistic features in Byzantine painting, a continuity now supported by technical evidence.

Turning to modern collections, a fragment of painted panel from the Hellenistic period, from Saqqara, is on display at the British Museum. The small Archaic panels from Pitsa (*see* §1(i) above) are at the Archaeological Museum of Sikyon, near their place of origin. In Italy, the decoration of the Tomb of the Diver at Paestum (see fig. 130 above) has been transferred to the Museo Archeologico Nazionale there, with the whole stone support represented by the large slabs that closed the sepulchre; these scenes, together with the numerous paintings on the tombs of the Lucan age, form a collection of 5th- and 4th-century BC painting. This is supplemented with examples from other sites in Campania and Apulia in the Museo Archeologico Nazionale at Naples. Painted stelai can be seen in Greece in the museums of Veria, Volos, Thebes and Athens, as well as in Istanbul and Alexandria. Original wall paintings usually remain *in situ*. Many museum collections contain indirect evidence of Greek painting in Greek ceramics and Etruscan and Roman painting (*see* §V, 10 above; ETRUSCAN, §V; and ROME, ANCIENT, §V, 3). Of particular importance for understanding the development of Greek monumental painting are the great collections of figured Attic and South Italian vases in New York (Met.), London (BM), Paris (Louvre), Munich (Staatl. Antikensamml.), Rome (Villa Giulia), the Vatican (Mus. Gregoriano Etrus.), Taranto (Mus. N.) and Athens (N. Archaeol. Mus.).

BIBLIOGRAPHY

Strabo: *Geography*

Pliny: *Natural History*

Philostratos Lemnios: *Imagines*

K. Jex-Blake and E. Sellars: *The Elder Pliny's Chapters on the History of Art* (London, 1896)

A. Andronikos, M. Hadjidakis and V. Karagiorgis: *The Greek Museums* (Athens, 1974)

A. Kokkou: *I Merimna ghia tis Ellinikes Archaeotites kai ta prota Mouseia* [The care for Greek antiquities and the first museums] (Athens, 1977)

PAOLO MORENO

VII. Mosaics.

The first figural mosaics in Western art appeared in Greece at the end of the 5th century BC or the beginning of the 4th, primarily at Olynthos (*see* OLYNTHOS, §2). They decorated floors, as did all subsequent Greek mosaics. Though earlier examples of patterned floors exist (*see* §2(i) below), the art of the mosaic, as Pliny noted (*Natural History* XXXVI.clxxxiv), was essentially a Greek development. There are three main types of Greek mosaic: pebble mosaics, which are made with unshaped natural pebbles; *opus tessellatum*, made with tesserae (small pieces of stone with squared edges); and a 'mixed' type made by combining pebbles with tesserae or with small pieces of lead or terracotta. The earliest mosaics were laid in pebbles, and this type reached a high degree of sophistication in the later 4th century BC before giving way in the decades around 100 BC to the elaborate tessellated floors of the High Hellenistic period. The time, place and exact nature of this transition are disputed; it may have been via the 'mixed' type of mosaic, though the evidence is inconclusive.

1. Introduction. 2. History and development.

1. INTRODUCTION.

(i) Uses. (ii) Materials, techniques and form. (iii) Mosaicists. (iv) Motifs and subject-matter.

(i) Uses. Although mosaic floors, both pebble and tessellated, were used in public contexts, including temples, other sacred buildings and especially baths, most were made for private dwellings. Early pebble floors (first half of the 4th century BC) are typically found in houses of the *pastas* type (i.e. with a pillared portico opening on to a courtyard), best represented at Olynthos (*see* OLYNTHOS, fig. 1; *see also* §II, 1(i)(c) above). Here 12 of the more than 50 houses excavated in the 'new city' were found to contain mosaic floors. Some were in the courtyard, one was in the *pastas*, but most were in the *andron* (dining-room) and its anteroom. The *andron* normally had a flat plaster platform along the walls, on which stood couches for the reclining diners or drinkers, and a pebbled area in the centre from which they were served. When the centre had a decorative mosaic, the threshold leading to the anteroom was normally given one also (see fig. 136 below). If the anteroom had a mosaic, the threshold mosaic joined the two. The two great houses at Pella (*see* PELLA (ii), §2), which have yielded the finest pebble mosaics from the later 4th century BC, have different plans, but most of their mosaics are from *andrones*. The only large number of tessellated floors preserved in private houses is on Delos (*see* DELOS, §3), where the houses, from the decades around 100 BC, are built around a central colonnaded court (see fig. 12 above). Mosaics are found in courtyards and in various rooms, including fragments from collapsed upper storeys, but again most are in *andrones*. As earlier at Olynthos, however, only a small proportion of houses excavated were so adorned.

(ii) Materials, techniques and form. In Greece and other eastern Mediterranean countries floors were generally laid by putting down plaster and packing it while wet with more or less closely set pebbles of roughly similar size, which were held firm when the plaster dried. The art of mosaic arose from arranging light and dark pebbles to make patterns in such floors. At first naturally rounded pebbles from river-beds or beaches were used. In early mosaics they were spaced loosely, with a good deal of plaster visible between them, and they were not graded by size. Later they were more closely set and more even in size; in the most accomplished examples there is evidence of careful grading, with small pebbles used for fine detail. One early looking pebble floor at Olynthos (Salzmann, no. 83) has casual patterns that were surely put in as the craftsman or craftsmen went along, without reference to a prepared design. Most patterns and designs, however, must have followed a detailed cartoon, referred to in the Zenon Papyrus (mid-2nd century BC; Cairo, Egyp. Mus., P. Zenon 59665; see S, p. 9) as *paradeigma* ('example'). Under some of the elaborate pebble floors at Pella, traces of a *sinopia* in red were found on the lower plaster layer. This process must have been similar to that of fresco painting, with the craftsman laying only as much of the upper plaster layer as he could cover with pebbles before it dried. Basically the same methods must have been used initially for tessellated floors. For repeated patterns, instead of a *sinopia*, the craftsman of both types of mosaic probably used leaden templates, such as that for a wave-crest found on Delos (Bruneau, 1972, fig. 6). In some pebble floors, from the second half of the 4th century BC onwards, strips of terracotta or lead were introduced in figures to outline forms or emphasize details. These are also found in early tessera mosaics but later were confined to pattern borders.

Almost all pebble floors have a dark ground, with the design in lighter coloured stones, although exactly symmetrical patterns, such as wave-crests and triangles, can be read either way. A fragmentary floor of high quality from Sikyon (second quarter of the 4th century BC; S 116) has the expected light design on a dark ground for the complex floral motif that occupies the central circle, but exceptionally the ground of the surrounding square is light, and the circle has no frame but is edged with wave-crests that rise straight out of the dark ground; the light corners of the square have swimming youths set in dark pebbles. The normal scheme from which this departs is illustrated by a floor of similar design and date from Corinth (S 64), where the whole ground is dark, the central floral motif is framed by a circle of light wave-crests, and the dark corners have groups of animals in light stones. A few other contemporary examples combine light on dark figural scenes with reversed (i.e. dark on light) ornament, but only on late pebble floors are figural elements sometimes dark on light.

In Greek mosaics dark and light approximate to black and white, but the 'black' is often bluish or brownish and the 'white' an off-white of varying shades. Even in very early examples, reddish and yellowish pebbles were used discretely for enlivenment, and later these four basic colours were employed in a much subtler, more pictorial way. With the greater polychromy and pictoriality achievable with the introduction of tessera, a light ground became more common, but a dark one was still often used.

Light on dark motifs in early pebble floors produce an effect similar to that of Red-figure vases (*see* §V, 6 above). In particular, the figural groups in tondi suggest the interiors of Red-figure cups. However, a theory that vase painting influenced the mosaicists directly (Robertson, 1965; Bruneau, 1969) is doubtful. The light-on-dark principle was widespread in Greek art, notably in relief sculpture, where the backgrounds were normally uniformly painted so that the figures stood out. The mosaicists may have worked on this principle without specific reference to either sculpture or vase painting, though a shared inspiration with the latter cannot be ruled out, since Red-figure has been argued to owe something to precious metal vessels, in which gold figures were laid on silver that was then allowed to darken.

Most mosaic floors have an outer patterned frame that runs parallel to the walls of the rectangular or square room. Often most of the area is covered with a series of decreasing borders around a fairly small central feature (emblema), but in other cases virtually the whole space is occupied by a large floral or figural design. A favourite form, scarcely ever found in other branches of Greek art, is the circle within a square, whether as a small centre piece or a large circle filling most of the space. A particular feature of pebble mosaics, the form reappeared on tessellated floors of *c.* 100 BC on Delos (*see* DELOS, fig. 7). An emblema from Egypt (middle or third quarter of the 2nd century BC; Daszewski, no. 39) is circular, but it may be from a circular room. Mosaics in circular rooms are known from references in the Zenon Papyrus, and a splendid pebble example has been found at Pella (end of 4th century BC; S 105). A small central circle in a square or rectangular pebble floor may have a wheel, star or flower (the Zenon Papyrus names a poppy) or a palmette design; a larger circle may contain concentric rings of animals or figures around a similar centre (S 117), or the whole area may be filled by a complex floral motif (S 130) or a figural scene (S 78). Both pebble and tessellated floors sometimes have an overall geometric pattern: lozenges were favoured in both, *trompe l'oeil* cubes in tessera. Many tessellated floors have concentric frames around a central emblema, in the earlier pebble tradition, but their frames are generally sparser, with a lot of the floor left plain white. Sometimes there are several emblemata.

If figural, the emblema on an *andron* floor is designed to be viewed from the doorway, as is usually the threshold design. If there is a figural design in the anteroom, it is orientated the other way, so as to be seen from the same door. When animals, or occasionally human figures, are placed in the surrounding pattern bands, they are orientated to be viewed from the couches along the parallel wall, as in one from House B.v.1 at Olynthos (*c.* 400 BC; S 84), with its double sphinxes in a palmette band (see fig. 136). A unique feature of this mosaic is the way the outermost pattern band, a meander, is extended to enclose the normally separate threshold design, which, unusually, is here orientated to be seen not on entering or leaving the room but obliquely from one side of the door.

(iii) Mosaicists. The only mosaicist known from literary records is SOSOS, who worked at Pergamon, almost certainly in the 2nd century BC and in tessera. A pebble floor at Pella from the later 4th century BC (S 103; see fig. 143 below) bears the name of GNOSIS as maker, and a contemporary fragment at Athens (S 20) preserves the last two letters (... *ōn*) of another maker's name. On Hellenistic tessera mosaics the name SOPHILOS occurs at Alexandria (? *c.* 200 BC; *see* ALEXANDRIA, fig. 2), HEPHAISTION at Pergamon (2nd century BC; see figs 137 and 138 below) and both ASKLEPIADES (*c.* 100 BC; B 210) and Antaios, son of Aischrion (*c.* 100 BC), on Delos (B 195). The name of Dioskourides of Samos appears as maker on two exquisite miniature mosaics that formed part of the decoration of the House of Cicero at Pompeii (second half of the 1st century BC). They are certainly copied from 3rd-century BC Greek paintings, and the letter forms have suggested a date of *c.* 100 BC. These pieces, however, like the mosaic of *Alexander the Great* from the House of the Faun at Pompeii (Naples, Mus. Archeol. N.; *see* POMPEII, fig. 7), belong to the beginnings of the fashion, common in Roman art, of copying Greek masterpieces for the Roman market, often in a different medium.

136. Pebble mosaic with concentric pattern bands in the *andron* (dining-room) and animals in the threshold, House B.v.1, Olynthos, *c.* 400 BC or slightly later (*in situ*)

On his mosaic, Gnosis wrote *epoiesen* ('made') in the past definite, as did Dioskourides. Sophilos, Hephaistion, (Askle)piades and Antaios used the imperfect tense, *epoiei* (see fig. 137), perhaps because it was thought more appropriate for the gradual process of laying tessera. There is no way of knowing what precisely is implied in such signatures. Did the named person design the floor, execute it to another's design or, as is most likely, supply the design as well as supervise the execution? Large mosaics were probably laid by a team: this is almost certainly the case with (Askle)piades', which is composed of repeated patterns, mainly of a traditional kind. Gnosis set his signature in light pebbles on the dark ground of an elaborate and highly pictorial figural scene, and in this case the equally elaborate and individual floral border is surely an integral part of the design (see fig. 142 below). The signature of '... *ōn*' is set within the simple circle that borders a figural scene of *Herakles Attacking a Centaur*; though at a much lower artistic level than Gnosis' work, both the design and the execution of the bird and floral motifs in the borders seem integral with the picture.

The use of terracotta and lead strips in some but not all of the floors in the two houses at Pella, known commonly as the House of Dionysos and the House of Helen but

137. Tessera mosaic by Hephaistion, detail showing cartellino with his signature, from Palace V, Pergamon, first half of the 2nd century BC (Berlin, Pergamonmuseum, Antikensammlung)

called by the excavators I 1 and I 5 (hereafter House 1 and House 5), suggests the differing practices of two workshops. One might have been responsible for the mosaics in House 1, where these other materials were used in the *Lion Hunt* (S 98), the *andron* floor (S 96; see fig. 143 below) and the threshold mosaic with the two centaurs and omitted only from the animal threshold. The other, to which Gnosis presumably belonged, was responsible for the *andron* mosaic in House 5, with the first workshop brought in to assist with the large floor showing the *Abduction of Helen*, where lead strips were used. Alternatively, it might be a question of different dates, with House 5 coming first and the new method introduced there at a late stage and employed regularly in House 1. However, Gnosis' lines of tiny, closely set black pebbles in the *andron* mosaic (see fig. 142 below) produce so nearly the same effect as the lead strips that they look like a deliberate reaction to the challenge of the other technique.

Of the mosaicists working in tessera, Sophilos signed in black tesserae on the white ground of the emblema. In this case the surround, outside the emblema frame of isometric meander, is simply a wide white area with a narrow crenellation at the edge, so that the question of whether the signature applies to the whole floor or only the emblema has little meaning. Hephaistion's case is different: his cartellino (see fig. 137) is placed at the bottom centre of an emblema surrounded by framing zones of pattern, including one with a complex floral scroll enlivened with insects and Erotes (see fig. 138 below), and another that was carefully removed in antiquity but probably contained figures. Hephaistion was almost certainly signing the whole floor, though it is remotely possible that he meant only the emblema.

Since (Askle)piades' floor is a single overall design, the signature must apply to the whole. It is set in dark tesserae on a strip of white background between circling pattern bands. Antaios is a peculiar case: his mosaic occupies an exedra in the Sanctuary of the Syrian Gods on Delos and consists only of patternwork, with an area of *trompe l'oeil* cubes surrounded by a meander between two bands of wave-crest. The cubes are interrupted in the middle by a framed white panel that contains an inscription naming the man who had the exedra built and giving other details that end with the name of Antaios, son of Aischrion. His signature thus seems to be part of the very full documentation of the gift, rather than a personal artistic claim.

(iv) Motifs and subject-matter.

(a) Patternwork. The repertory of abstract patterns used on mosaic floors is generally that shared by other Greek art forms, but with its own emphases. The universal meander appears as a border on both pebble and tessellated floors. In early tessera mosaics, including Sophilos' emblema, it is found also in an 'isometric' form, giving an illusion of three dimensions. This is rare in other surviving forms of Greek art but is found earlier, on 4th-century BC South Italian vases. The chequer-board patterns evolved into a field of *trompe l'oeil* cubes in tessera mosaics. The guilloche is not very common in pebble and always of simple form, but it was more frequent and varied in tessera (see fig. 144 below). Narrow bands of black and white triangles are found sparingly in both types of mosaic. Bead and reel is rather more frequent, while other architectural patterns, such as cymation and ovolo, are used occasionally. For fields, lozenges are found in both types, scales in tessera only.

The wave-crest deserves special mention because of the frequency of its appearance in both pebble and tessera mosaics (see fig. 136 above and figs 139, 140 and 142 below). It is found in other art forms, for instance Red-figure vase painting from the late 5th century BC or the early 4th, when pebble floors first appeared, but it is almost a hallmark of mosaic. It sometimes occurs in formalized representations of the sea, so the term is not purely arbitrary, but the Zenon Papyrus calls it *kochlos nautikos* ('spiral seashell'). Border patterns used exclusively in tessera include stepped triangles and the related crenellation, which appears, for example, on the floors signed by Sophilos, Hephaistion and (Askle)piades, where it is always an extreme outer frame.

Floral borders on early pebble mosaics are of the kind traditional in other forms of Greek art: palmette, palmette and lotus, and ivy. These continue throughout the pebble tradition but are rarely found in tessera. A floor from Alexandria showing *Three Erotes Hunting a Stag* (early 3rd century BC; see fig. 144 below) has a dark-on-light ivy frame around the emblema. Complexes of palmettes or palmettes and lotuses are used for the decoration of circular or rectangular fields in pebble but not in tessera. In the 4th century BC an elaborate system of 'naturalistic' floral scrolls was developed, a phenomenon known as the Floral style (*see* §2 below). Though the same style appeared in other art forms, pebble mosaicists were apparently among its most imaginative exploiters, both for frames and to cover large fields (see fig. 141 below). No surviving tessellated floor has floral motifs as field decoration, but the scroll-border on Hephaistion's floor at Pergamon (see

138. Tessera mosaic by Hephaistion, detail showing scroll-border with Erotes, from Palace V, Pergamon, first half of the 2nd century BC (Berlin, Pergamonmuseum, Antikensammlung)

fig. 138) is clearly a modified derivative of the earlier type, treated less calligraphically and enlivened by the introduction of insects and Erotes. This is an early example of the 'peopled scroll', which was later used to such splendid effect in Roman decorative sculpture. In tessera there also evolved a different type of garland, consisting of heavier swags of foliage, sometimes with birds and often hung with objects, in particular theatrical masks. There are fragments from Pergamon, and more complete examples are the two tall panels framing a *trompe l'oeil* cube floor (B 215) in the House of the Masks on Delos. Such garlands are found in similar form in Roman mosaics; a 1st-century BC floor in the House of the Faun at Pompeii had an emblema with fish, almost certainly of Greek derivation, framed in a border that is a coarser version of Hephaistion's scroll.

(b) Figural scenes. Another type of border in pebble mosaic consists of a frieze of animals, imaginary or real, occasionally confronted over or separated by palmettes. Examples include the *Amazonomachy* pebble mosaic in House 5 at Pella (S 104) and two floors dated after the mid-3rd century BC from Assos in Turkey and Ol'viya in southern Russia (S 17 and 73). The same scheme occurs in the two floors of mixed technique from Alexandria (S 134–5; D 1–2; see fig. 144 below) and in two early tessellated floors, both of the 3rd century BC, one in irregular tessera from Erythrai (S 154) and the other in regular tesserae from Klazomenai in Turkey (S, p. 76). Animal friezes are not, however, found in later tessera mosaics. Human figures are only rarely introduced in pebble borders (e.g. a *Hunter and a (?)Greek Fighting a Centaur* at Olynthos; S 86). Beasts like those found in borders are a favourite subject for *andron* thresholds in pebble, where they are shown singly or in fighting pairs or threes (see fig. 136 above). Exceptionally, a threshold in House 1 at Pella has a male and female centaur with wine vessels (S 97), and one from the Villa of Good Fortune at Olynthos shows two Pans confronted over a krater (S 12, part). There the *andron* floor (S 87) depicts *Dionysos in a Panther-drawn Chariot with Eros and (?)Pan* (second quarter of the 4th century BC; see fig. 139), with an unusual framing frieze, on an only slightly smaller scale, that continues the Dionysiac theme, with maenads, a satyr, a Pan and fawns.

Dionysiac subjects seem an obvious choice for the main scene in an *andron* mosaic and are found in several others, for example the *Dionysos Riding a (?)Cheetah* in pebble from House 1 at Pella (see fig. 143 below). From Delos there is a beautiful emblema from an upper floor representing *Lykourgos Offending Dionysos by Attacking the Nymph Ambrosia.* This mosaic is of special interest as the first known example of a composition that was later repeated in several Roman mosaics and paintings. Subjects in a similar vein include theatrical masks, either in garlands or by themselves (e.g. in the altar room at Pergamon), and the vessels on a pebble *andron* floor from Sikyon (S 119) and on a floor of mixed technique (dark-on-light) from Thasos (S 141). Wild beasts and vegetation also have a Dionysiac connotation.

Other mythological scenes appear to have been chosen arbitrarily. Those in pebble mosaics include *Herakles Attacking a Centaur* at Athens (S 20), the *Abduction of Helen* at Pella (S 101), *Bellerophon on Pegasos Attacking the Chimera* at Olynthos (S 78; *see* OLYNTHOS, fig. 2) and *Thetis Bringing Armour to Achilles* (second quarter of the 4th century BC) also at Olynthos (S 88; see fig. 140). Among the subjects on tessellated floors are the *Rape of Ganymede* from Morgantina, Sicily, and from Delos an uncertain scene showing Athena and Hermes with a figure seated between them.

Mythological figures not shown in specific scenes include numerous sea creatures, which may also have

139. Pebble mosaic with emblema depicting *Dionysos in a Panther-drawn Chariot with Eros and (?)Pan* surrounded by a frieze with a satyr and maenads and bands of palmettes and wave-crests, from the *andron* of the Villa of Good Fortune, Olynthos, second quarter of the 4th century BC (*in situ*)

140. Pebble mosaic with emblema depicting *Thetis Bringing Armour to Achilles*, surrounded by borders of scrolls, meander and wave-crests, from the anteroom of the *andron* in the Villa of Good Fortune, Olynthos, second quarter of the 4th century BC (*in situ*)

Dionysiac associations, as in a floor from Sparta in irregular tesserae (S 169), where the emblema depicting a *Triton* is surrounded by a frieze of sea creatures, inside another frieze with a Pan, satyrs, centaurs and a krater. Tritons or tritonesses are found also in pebble at Rhodes (S 112), in mixed technique in the porch of the Temple of Zeus at Olympia (S 138) and in tessera (apparently imitating pebble) at Delos (B 75). Scylla is depicted in pebble at Eretria (S 42), New Paphos on Cyprus (S suppl. 3) and at Peiraeus in a bathhouse (S 108). Dolphins, tridents and anchors in various combinations were popular subjects in tessera on Delos. The early tessellated floor from Klazomenai has *Amphitrite Riding a Sea Monster* and, on the *andron* threshold, *Eros and Psyche.*

Eros appears in several of these scenes, and on the pebble floor of a circular bath at Ambrakia (now Arta), Erotes are shown playing with water-birds and fish (S 6). He is depicted alone in a central tondo on a pebble floor at Chalcis (S 28), which also shows a dolphin (dark-on-light). The most remarkable scene of this type is that on the pebble floor from Assos (S 16), showing *Aphrodite and a Man Weighing Erotes.* The mixed technique floor from Alexandria with *Three Erotes Hunting a Stag* (see fig. 144 below) adapted its composition from earlier hunting scenes with mortals.

The female head shown growing from a calyx among flowers on a pebble floor (S 33) from Dyrrhacion in Epiros (now Albania) must have a religious or mythological significance, but the interpretation is not certain. This subject is frequent on South Italian vases, but the identity of the figure seems to vary. One is named Aura (personified 'Breeze'), and some (perhaps most) probably represent Aphrodite. The female half-figures depicted growing from florals at the corners of a mosaic floor at Vergina (S 130) must belong in the same category.

Other scenes, in pebble and tessera alike, are not mythological but generic or historical. The *Lion Hunt* in House 1 at Pella (S 98) is one of a group of lion hunts of the late 4th century BC, executed in various media, which are thought to have been inspired by a famous bronze statue group by Lysippos and Leochares, dedicated at Delphi by Alexander the Great's friend Krateros after he had saved the King's life in a hunt. However, it is doubtful that the hunters in the mosaic are specifically intended to portray Alexander and Krateros. The sudden popularity of hunting subjects probably owes more to Alexander's calculated espousal of the traditional sport of eastern kings; Gnosis' *Stag Hunt* in the other house at Pella (see fig. 142 below) no doubt reflects Macedonian aristocratic pursuits.

Subjects taken from everyday life include what are probably copies of a portrait of a Ptolemaic queen, most likely Berenike II (*reg* 246–221 BC), represented in two tessera emblemata from Thumis (now Tell Timay) near Alexandria (D 38–9; *see* ALEXANDRIA, fig. 2). Both were previously interpreted as personifications of Alexandria. The pebble floor of a bathhouse at Chersonesos in southern Russia (S 29) is appropriately adorned with a group of two naked women at a wash-basin. In the altar room at Pergamon the only survivor of three emblemata ranged side by side shows a parrot in bright colours on a dark ground, and at Delos there are several still-lifes with prizes, for example a bronze hydria or a Black-figure Panathenaic amphora with a palm and a wreath (B 25, 217 and 235).

2. HISTORY AND DEVELOPMENT. The early history of the craft is fragmentary and obscure, and evidence for dating is woefully inadequate, but since the 1970s important work has been done (notably Salzmann's book of 1982 on pebble mosaics), and it is now possible to give a rational outline of the development. Areas of great uncertainty remain, however, especially between the fully developed art of the pebble floor in the later 4th century BC and the established tessera style of a hundred years later.

(i) Origins. (ii) Dating. (iii) Stylistic development.

(i) Origins. Remains of a Bronze Age floor from Tiryns (14th century BC; S 129) show dark and light pebbles arranged in rows, but no direct connection can be postulated with later Greek mosaic developments. In some Near Eastern countries, there was a continuous tradition

of patterned pebble floors, such as those of *c.* 700 BC from palace buildings at Gordion in Phrygia, where one large, nearly square floor (*c.* 10×10 m) is covered with geometric patterns evidently laid as the craftsman went along without reference to a preliminary design. More regular strips of chequerboard pattern occur on a floor there from the first half of the 6th century, and a building in which five rooms have floors decorated with regular rows of meander squares dates to *c.* 500 BC. However, there is little formal resemblance between the decorative pebble floors from Gordion and those that first appeared in Greece, and it is now generally held that the idea developed independently in Greece.

Yet the sudden popularity of elaborate floor decoration in Greece in the late 5th century BC and the early 4th may have had some particular impulse behind it. While it is still highly conjectural, there is evidence to suggest that the use of fine floor mosaics was a fashion begun and elaborated in Macedonian and imitation-Macedonian palaces and later taken up for private dwellings. The Macedonian capital was moved from Aigai (probably Vergina) to Pella during the reign of Archelaos of Macedon (*reg* 413–399 BC). He built a new palace at Pella and had it decorated by the Greek painter Zeuxis. Nothing is said of mosaic floors, but given the importance of Pella in the later history of the craft, it seems plausible (though undemonstrable) to suppose that it was Archelaos and Zeuxis who, perhaps aware of a tradition of decorated palace floors in the Near East, evolved the notion of more elaborately patterned and figured pebblework. One of the earliest mosaic sites, Olynthos, is situated on the Chalcidian peninsula, which borders Macedonia, and it was due to Perdikkas II of Macedon (*reg c.* 452–*c.* 413 BC) that Olynthos was established in 432 BC as chief city of a Chalcidian League, which led to the building of the 'new city', in which so many mosaics were found. The sack of Olynthos in 348 BC by Philip II of Macedon (*reg* 359–336 BC) was part of the absorption of the whole area into Macedonia.

It has been suggested that the first mosaics owe much to imported eastern textiles, which the Greeks are known to have prized, but this is not borne out by the character of the textiles discovered since the theory was advanced. On the other hand, some of the mid- to late 4th-century BC pebble mosaics from Pella are extremely pictorial and seem to show strong connections with South Italian vase painting. The finest examples of the distinctive Floral style that characterized both vases and mosaics of that period are from Sikyon, Macedonia and Epiros. Epiros was ruled by members of the Macedonian royal house, and there is evidence of cultural and artistic contact in the 4th century BC between Macedonia and the cities of South Italy. There is also a link between Macedonia and Sikyon. During the reigns of Philip II and Alexander the Great (*reg* 336–323 BC), Sikyon was ruled by their ally, the tyrant Aristratos. A famous school of painting flourished there, patronized by Aristratos. The second and most celebrated head of the school, Pamphilos, came not from Sikyon but from Amphipolis, a Thracian city absorbed into Macedonia by Philip II in 357 BC. One of the greatest Sikyonian painters was Pausias, who alone among Greek artists was famed as a flower painter. It has been suggested (Robertson, 1982) that Pausias was the inventor of the Floral style, so important in the history of pebble mosaic. While this cannot be proved, Pausias's flower pictures and the Floral style found on the floors and vases surely belong to the same movement. It is significant that he worked in a city that was ruled by a monarch who had close ties with the rulers of Macedonia and in which outstanding mosaics in this style were also produced. The only contemporary reference to 4th-century BC decorated floors comes from Douris of Samos (cited by Athenaeus: *Deipnosophists* XII.542d). Writing in the early 3rd century BC about the ruler of Athens in the Macedonian interest, Demetrios of Phaleron (*reg* 317–307 BC), Douris referred to his outdoing the Macedonians themselves in expenditure on dinners and to many of the floors in his *andrones* being flowery with patterns made by craftsmen.

It is likely that the invention of tessera mosaic also took place in the ambience of Hellenistic courts. In the decades following Alexander the Great's death in 323 BC his generals, all Macedonian aristocrats, fought each other for his empire but finally settled down as kings of their separate provinces. The first tessera mosaics could well have been made at Pella or elsewhere in Macedonia, at the new capital, Kassandreia, or at Thessaloniki, both founded by Kassandros *c.* 315 BC, or at Antioch, founded by Seleukos and his son Antiochos in 300 BC as capital of the huge eastern kingdom known as Syria. None of these palaces has been excavated, but fine floors in royal dwellings of the 2nd century BC have been found in Pergamon, which was ruled from *c.* 200 BC by another Macedonian dynasty, the Attalids.

The theory that tessera was invented in Sicily and introduced from there to Alexandria is based primarily on the supposed early date (before the mid-3rd century BC) of the *Rape of Ganymede* mosaic from Morgantina (see Phillips), but this is doubtful (S, pp. 60–62). According to one story, Hieron II of Syracuse (*reg* 270–215 BC) sent as a present to a Ptolemaic king in Alexandria a luxury galley made under the supervision of Archimedes (*c.* 287–212 BC), which included among its lavish furnishings three dining-rooms with what are thought to have been tessera floor mosaics illustrating the *Iliad*. Even if both the story and the early date are accepted, it is still just as likely that the tessera technique had already been invented in the courts of Greece and the east and was simply being imitated in the west.

As with pebble mosaics, though the fashion for tesselated floors may have been set in palaces, it soon spread to private houses. The merchants' houses on Delos (2nd–1st century BC) are the most conspicuous surviving examples, and here a new influence is discernible. The Romans established a free port there in 166 BC as part of their takeover of the Hellenistic world. Macedonia and Greece were absorbed in the 140s BC, Pergamon and Asia Minor in 133 BC. Many of the merchants on Delos were Italian, and they, like the Romans at home, were beginning to be interested in Greek products. Mosaics in the Greek manner became increasingly popular at Pompeii in the later 2nd century BC and the 1st, and these were surely often the work of Greek craftsmen who adapted their tradition to houses of Roman design and to the artistic tastes of another culture.

(ii) Dating. As has become increasingly clear from the preceding discussion, there are few fixed points for the absolute dating of pebble mosaics. A floor with animals from Motya in western Sicily (S 72) was long thought to antedate the sack of the city by Dionysios I of Syracuse in 397 BC, but the architecture of the house has been shown to be later. The archaeological context of one fragment from Corinth (S 65) is not, as had been stated, late 5th century BC but late 4th, though another floor in a bath building from the same site (S 63) can be securely dated to the end of the 5th century. The large body of pebble mosaics from Olynthos (S 78–92) must have been laid between the founding of the 'new city' in 432 BC and its destruction in 348 BC, and floors found in the city of Rhodes cannot be earlier than its foundation in 408/7 BC. Another important series of more sophisticated floors (S 116–21) comes from the 'old city' of Sikyon, which was abandoned for a new site in 303 BC. The floors from the two great houses in Pella (S 94–104), which exemplify the art of pebble mosaic at its most masterly, are now shown to have been laid above a fill in which the latest pottery is of the third quarter of the 4th century BC. They cannot be earlier than that, and surely in fact belong to that time. At Eretria, pottery from the end of the 5th century BC was found under one floor (S 38), and the house containing it and two others (S 36–7), all with accomplished animal and patternwork, seems to have been built early in the 4th century BC and destroyed about a hundred years later. The city was sacked by the Romans in 198 BC, but habitation and building went on later. Of buildings with simple pattern floors, the Sanctuary of Isis (S 43) was put up before the sack, the gymnasium (S 44) and the baths (S 46) after.

Since technical and stylistic differences are clearly distinguishable in surviving pebble mosaics, these fixed points can be used as the basis for tracing a chronological development. The problem is complicated, however, by wide geographical distribution and by the differing character of the various classes of building with mosaic decoration, as well as by variations in their quality. Yet developments paralleled in other branches of art, for example the Floral style vases produced by Greeks in South Italy from the second quarter of the 4th century BC to the 3rd, the chronology of which is established with some degree of precision, can also help in the dating of mosaics.

(iii) Stylistic development.

(a) Pebble. (b) Mixed and intermediate. (c) Tessera.

(a) Pebble. There is no reason to think that any formally patterned or figural mosaic floor in Greece is earlier than the Corinth bath (S 63) dating from the end of the 5th century BC. It has a large wheel motif surrounded by narrow concentric pattern circles, with the corners of the square floor occupied by animals orientated to be seen from the centre. Fragmentary remains of an even cruder floor from Megara (S 71) and a rather better one from Sikyon (S 119) are similarly designed and probably also early. Another from Megara (S 70) has a similar design but is unique in having white pebbles used for the outlines of some figures; for this reason it is dated much later by Salzmann (second quarter of 3rd century BC), though this is inconclusive.

Similar to the Corinth bath is the large body of mosaics from Olynthos, which must belong in the first half of the

141. Pebble mosaic with floral complex in the *andron* and griffin in the threshold, from Sikyon, second quarter of or mid-4th century BC (Sikyon, Archaeological Museum)

142. Pebble mosaic by Gnosis depicting a *Stag Hunt* surrounded by a floral-style border and wave-crests, from the *andron* of House 5, Pella, last quarter of the 4th century BC (Pella, Archaeological Museum)

4th century BC, with the *andron* mosaic from House B.v.1 (S 84; see fig. 136 above) near the beginning of the series, and perhaps the casually patterned courtyard mosaic (S 83) even earlier. Most of the Olynthos mosaics consist of patternwork, some with beasts introduced in a floral border (S 84) or an animal border with a few human figures substituted for a pattern band (S 86), but there are five with mythological scenes. One of these, a fragment from a courtyard (S 79), has unusual dark-on-light borders, including a cymation of architectural character. The surviving figure, a warrior, recalls figures in 4th-century BC carved friezes. The style seems later than most of the Olynthian mosaics, but the technique is coarse, with ungraded stones set loosely. Two of the other mythological scenes (S 87–8; see figs 139 and 140 above) come from the *andron* and anteroom of a large free-standing house, known as the Villa of Good Fortune, which has a modified plan and was probably not an ordinary private house (it may have been a *pandokeion* or lodging-house). Both are rectangular designs framed in bands of geometrical and floral pattern. The florals in the *andron* (fig. 139) are traditional palmettes, but the anteroom has a scroll with flowers (fig. 140), and a similar scroll is found among traditional pattern bands encircling the tondo on another *andron* floor (S 78), showing *Bellerophon on Pegasos Attacking the Chimera.* The Villa of Good Fortune has two more mosaic floors (S 89–90) in adjoining rooms, evidently not an *andron* complex, since neither has a plaster surround. These floors are not figured but have simple patterns and dark and light strips with inscriptions in praise of 'Good fortune' and Aphrodite, picked out in pebbles of the opposite hue.

Floors of generally similar character to the Olynthian examples but often more neatly laid are found at Corinth (S 64–5), Sikyon (S 116, 118 and 120), Athens (S 19) and Eretria (S 36–8), and these are dated in the second and third quarters of the 4th century BC, overlapping the dates of the Olynthian floors and leading on to the sophisticated ones at Pella (S 94–104), which are dated to the third or last quarter of the 4th century BC.

Of the same character as the scrolls on two of the mosaics at Olynthos (S 78 and 88), but of far greater accomplishment and used in a new way, is the scrollwork on an *andron* floor from Sikyon (S 118; see fig. 141). On the threshold is a heraldic griffin, but the whole rectangle of the floor is covered with a floral complex. The effect is still basically two-dimensional: the central flower is flattened, as are the broad stalks that issue from under its petals and, by their scrollings, build up the design. The leaves in which they end, however, are no longer traditional palmettes; they create an effect of growth and show some foreshortening, as do four big bell-flowers that accent the centre of each side. Similarly foreshortened bells appear in the more conventional floral motif of another floor at Sikyon (S 116) and one from Eretria (S 36), as well as in rather summary form in the two Olynthos scrolls. This is the beginning of the distinctive Floral style so important for dating. Salzmann dated the two Olynthos scroll mosaics to 380/70 BC (S 78) and 370/60 BC (S 88), that at Sikyon (S 118) to 360/50 BC and that at Eretria (S 36) to 350/40 BC. However, it is unlikely that the mosaicists at Olynthos were pioneers: the primitive technique they used does not necessarily put their floors earlier than the beautiful one from Sikyon. A direct descendant of the latter is the magnificent floor from one of the huge *andrones* in the palace at Vergina (S 130). Here the complex occupies a circle in the square, with female half-figures rising from floral volutes in the corners. The big central flower has a pictorial chiaroscuro effect, the leaves between the petals being slightly darker in colour, and three-dimensionality is emphasized by corkscrew tendrils that proliferate from the stalks. The floor is dated to the end of the 4th century BC or after (thus later than those from the two big houses at Pella), and Salzmann gives the same date to the floor of a circular building in Pella (S 105). The omission of corkscrew tendrils there makes for a flat effect reminiscent of the Sikyon floor, but the virtuoso execution of the varied, foreshortened flowers supports the later date.

The Floral style is seen at its peak in these and the mosaics of the two main houses at Pella. Only one floor was found with overall floral decoration, and this in a much ruined state (House 5; S 102), but the style was developed with extraordinary skill and charm in the broad borders of two others: the badly damaged *Lion Hunt* (House 1, S 98) and the perfectly preserved *Stag Hunt* (House 5, S 103), signed by Gnosis (see fig. 142). There are also remains of a third such border in House 5 (S 100, from a destroyed floor). The border of Gnosis' *Stag Hunt* is formed of two 'plants' that spring from calyces of acanthus leaves at the bottom left and top right corners and meet at the other two in fans of leaves. Their twisting lengths are loaded with flowers of many kinds and innumerable tendrils that cover the dark ground with three-dimensional corkscrew curls. The naturalistic detail, however, is subdued to the strong formal decorative effect. Flowers and spiralling tendrils frame a female head rising from a calyx in the centre of the floor at Dyrrhacion (S 33), a motif common on the South Italian vases. The large floor (the head is 1 m high) is damaged, but the centre is intact. The room was not an *andron* (it had semicircular niches at either side), and its purpose is not known.

143. Pebble mosaic depicting *Dionysos Riding a (?)Cheetah*, with some details in terracotta or lead strips, from the *andron* of House I 1, Pella, last quarter of the 4th century BC (Pella, Archaeological Museum)

Gnosis' *Stag Hunt* is the most pictorial of all pebble mosaics. The pebbles are carefully graded and used to produce surprising nuances of chiaroscuro and colour. While one hunter is in profile, the other is almost frontal and set back behind the stag, one foot hidden by a rock. They stand on uneven ground, though the upper part of the background is dark in the traditional way. Whether the floral frame of the *Lion Hunt* was as fine as this one is hard to say. The figural element is simpler and less pictorial, and it also seems a little mechanical. From the waist down the two figures are almost identical, apparently taken from one cartoon. Another floor in the same house, however, is even simpler and of stunning quality: within a narrow border of white pebbles young Dionysos, naked, thyrsus in hand, rides across an undifferentiated dark ground on a feline, probably a cheetah (S 96; see fig. 143). The pictorialism of the *Stag Hunt* and the more relief-like character of the *Lion Hunt* are eschewed. There is some modelling with shadow, but it is very light, and colour is used discretely to pick out detail. This is traditional flat surface decoration, the beautiful effect achieved by the contour of the light figure against the dark ground. But if the design here was more traditional than that of the *Stag Hunt*, the technique, using other materials, was innovative: terracotta strips were added in the hair, beads of the same material (originally coloured) in the ivy wreath and strips of lead for some contours (e.g. the eyebrow and eyelid, and the fingers holding the thyrsus). Such lead and terracotta strips are also found in the *Lion Hunt* and in the much damaged *andron* threshold with two centaurs (S 97). The fourth mosaic from House 1, the smaller threshold of the *andron* with *Dionysos Riding a (?)Cheetah* shows a *Griffin Attacking a Stag* and is without lead or terracotta additions.

House 1 at Pella also has two large rooms floored from wall to wall with pebbles in simple geometric patterns (S 95 and 99), while in House 5 another very large room without a platform for couches has the largest of the figure mosaics: the *Abduction of Helen* (S 101). This has no floral border but instead a band of meander inside another of lozenges. The scene shows Theseus carrying off the girl Helen protesting from her distraught duenna Deianeira while Phorbas holds his chariot ready (the names are in white pebbles on the dark ground, like Gnosis' signature on the *Stag Hunt*). This is the only floor in House 5 with lead strips, which are used in the horses' contours and the figures' hands. The figures are arranged on relatively level ground, in a friezelike composition, but there is a striking pictorialism in Deianeira's windblown drapery. Much is now lost, especially in the group of Theseus and Helen, making the effect difficult to judge, but it seems less visually satisfying than either the *Stag Hunt* or *Dionysos Riding a (?)Cheetah*.

Also dated to the last quarter of the 4th century BC are several fragments from Athens: a splendid *andron* with patterns and a threshold with animals (S 21–2), which seem particularly like the Pella circular mosaic (S 105) though the only preserved florals are palmettes, and the much damaged fragment with traces of the signature of . . . *ōn* (S 20). The scroll with corkscrew tendrils is found again on a fine mosaic from Assos (S 16), now lost except for fragments but recorded in a drawing. The mosaic is a wide rectangle framed in a broad meander and divided into three fields: a central square with the circular scene of *Aphrodite and a Man Weighing Erotes* surrounded by the scroll and with Erotes filling in the corners; this is flanked by two outer rectangles, orientated on the short ends, at right angles to the central field, each showing two *nikai* (Victories) confronted over a tripod. Both the subject and the design are unparalleled on other pebble floors (this cannot have been an *andron*), but Salzmann must be right in dating it *c.* 300 BC.

The further history of the pebble floor is hard to trace with precision. Several carefully constructed floors have been found in Rhodes. One from an *andron* (S 112) has a *Triton* within a square frame and a floral motif with spiralling tendrils, which appears also on the threshold. The modelling of the figure is much more linear than at Pella, and the floral motif is simpler and, in spite of the corkscrews, creates a less three-dimensional effect. Comparison with vase painting suggests that these are early 3rd-century BC characteristics. Two other *andron* floors from Rhodes show similar linear modelling: one, with a centaur, has no floral (S 113); another, representing *Bellerophon Attacking the Chimera*, has a further simplified scroll without spiralling tendrils (S 114). The composition of the latter is rectangular, but the odd position of the chimera's hind legs suggests that it was adapted from a circular prototype (not, however, that represented earlier at Olynthos; S 78). Similar is the fragment from Chalcis (S 28) showing *Eros* within a circle framed in dark-on-light ivy, with light-on-dark palmettes in the corners. Also dated to the first half of the 3rd century BC are the bathhouse floor from Chersonesos (S 29), with two naked women at a wash-basin, and the patterned floor from Ol'viya (S 74). Four crude *andron* floors from Eretria with circle in square figural scenes (S 39–42) have been convincingly dated to the mid- and later 3rd century BC, while only the very simple patterned floors (S 44–5) can be dated after the sack of Eretria in 198 BC. A rather crude floor from Tarsus with floral motifs and animals (partly dark-on-light) is archaeologically dated to the late 3rd century BC or the early 2nd, and many other mosaics from various sites seem to go with it, including one from Ai Khanum, the Hellenistic city in Afghanistan on the Oxus, which Salzmann assigned to the mid-2nd century BC. There seem no grounds for dating any pebble floor later than that.

(b) Mixed and intermediate. The introduction of lead and terracotta elements in floors at Pella and elsewhere was already a modification of the pure technique of pebble laying. However, at Pella the basic unit remained the unshaped pebble, and the floors there are thus always classed as pebble mosaics, though they certainly point the way to change. Several other floors are borderline: they employ only pebbles, but some of these are cut to make them suitable for particular purposes. A tradition of laying undecorated floors in chips of stone and terracotta also existed in the 4th century BC, obviously a way of making use of waste material. 'Chip floors', as these are known, may have influenced the development of intermediate mosaic techniques. *Opus sectile*, in which compositions are built up from larger pieces of stone cut to shape, is a Roman development, but such pieces occur in some floors made up of mixed pebbles and tesserae. Such practices may derive partly from chip floors, as may also a type of floor laid in irregular and usually rather large tesserae (*see* §(c) below).

An example of a pebble floor in which cut stones were used for details is in the porch of the 5th-century BC Temple of Zeus at Olympia (S 138). This has now largely perished, but a corner showing this peculiarity survives *in situ*. A coin found underneath dates to after the mid-3rd century BC. Other floors elsewhere in Greece, often of poor quality, show the same mixture or a mix of pebbles and tesserae. They probably belong to the 3rd and 2nd centuries BC, but their dates are not fixed. One from Lebena in Crete (*c.* mid-3rd century BC; S 137) has an irregularly divided field, a larger rectangle framed in wave-crests with a hippocampus, and a narrower strip with two palmettes. The dark ground and the framing pattern are in pebbles, the palmettes and hippocampus in tesserae of marble and terracotta, some irregular and some regular.

Some scholars (e.g. Dunbabin and Salzmann) believe that there is no direct development from pebble mosaics to floors laid in regular tesserae. They suggest that figural floors in irregular tesserae were developed during the 3rd century BC, influencing some later pebble floors and encouraging the shaping of pebbles and mixing of techniques; the use of regular tesserae then developed only in the later 3rd century BC, virtually driving the other techniques out during the first half of the 2nd. This theory makes good sense and fits much of the evidence. However, there are other factors that point to a different conclusion.

Two well-known floors from Alexandria (*see* ALEXANDRIA, §2(iii)) combine pebbles and regular tesserae. One (S 134, D 1), a fragment, is composed principally of pebbles; the other (S 135, D 2), an almost complete *andron* floor, is composed largely of marble, limestone and terracotta tesserae, both regular and irregular. The fragment is the left-hand edge of a floor, trimmed off on the right and completed by a broad band of tesserae at some later date in antiquity; within a border of animals a man is shown beside a leafless tree, moving violently to the left, his shield out behind him, thrusting back with a spear, perhaps in the act of hunting rather than fighting. The other floor shows *Three Erotes Hunting a Stag* (see fig. 144), likewise within a frieze of animals (which has two leafless trees). The pose of the figure on the left wielding an axe resembles that of the spearman on the fragment. The second figure leans forward with a sword swung behind his head. These two figures are very similar in pose and action to the two hunters in the *Lion Hunt* at Pella. The third figure, largely

144. Tessera mosaic, with some parts in pebble, depicting *Three Erotes Hunting a Stag* surrounded by a border of ivy leaves, a frieze of animals and a double guilloche, from an *andron* and threshold, Shatby, Alexandria, early 3rd century BC (Alexandria, Graeco–Roman Museum)

lost, advances from the right with a spear. The picture is separated from the animal frieze by a narrow white band with a black ivy wreath; outside the frieze is a double guilloche and a narrow band of polychrome chequerboard. The last was also carried around the threshold, now largely lost, which had a frame of meander and bead and reel. The couch platform was made not of smooth plaster but of white tesserae. Lead strips were used in both floors for contours and details. In the fragment the background, figure and animals are almost entirely of unshaped pebbles, but the spear shaft and shield are in tesserae, which were also used alongside pebbles in the hair and in parts of the animals and background. The man's eye is a black pebble between two bits of shaped white stone, framed by a strip of lead. In the *andron* floor yellow pebbles were introduced alongside the tesserae for the Erotes' hair and for hair-tufts on some of the animals. The menagerie includes (besides the usual griffins, lions, panthers, boars, bull and deer) a hyena and a mythical monster in the form of a horned lion, like an Achaemenid Persian griffin without wings. The only other known appearance of this unusual monster is carved on a built tomb from Athens (Peiraeus, Archael. Mus.), dated to the later 4th century BC.

The various dates suggested for these two mosaic floors range over the whole Hellenistic age, starting from the foundation of Alexandria in 332/1 BC. The site of the house with the *Erotes* mosaic was allegedly occupied by a cemetery in the 3rd and 2nd centuries BC, so that the house could only have been built in the 1st century BC. On this basis, Brown argued that the style of the floor was neo-classical and that it should be dated between 50 BC and 50 AD. However, it now seems that the cemetery did not in fact extend so far. Robertson (1965) argued for an earlier date, owing to the resemblance, in both motif and composition, to the floors at Pella, a view subsequently supported by Daszewski, who dated the fragment to 320–300 BC and the *andron* floor to 290–260 BC. However, Salzmann, having concluded that the use of regular tesserae was not developed before the later 3rd century BC, put the fragment in the first third or middle of the 3rd century BC, the other at the end of the 3rd century BC or in the first half of the 2nd, judging the likenesses to Pella a matter of motif, not style. The question is open, but the present writer still favours an early date.

(c) Tessera. No example of a floor in regular tessera is proven to be earlier than the late 3rd century BC, and there are few for which it is possible even to argue an earlier date. The date of the much damaged *Rape of Ganymede* from Morgantina, originally published as mid-3rd century BC, is now disputed, and Salzmann has argued for a date near the end of the century (*see also* §(i) above). The finer of the two emblemata from Thmuis showing a bust of a woman wearing a headdress in the form of a ship's prow, now thought to portray Queen Berenike II, is rectangular and bears the signature *Sophilos epoiei* (D 38; *see* ALEXANDRIA, fig. 2). It is framed in isometric meander and guilloche and, at the outer edge of the white floor, crenellation, while the other, a circular fragment, is framed in scale pattern. The mosaics were probably copied from

a contemporary painted portrait of the Queen. Sophilos has been dated to just before *c.* 200 BC, the other *c.* 150 BC or later (Daszewski). Lead strips were used in the pattern border of the first and in the headdress. They occur regularly in pattern borders of later mosaics, but this seems to have been their last appearance in figural elements in tessera (unless the Alexandrian *Three Erotes Hunting a Stag* really is late). A third emblema from Thumis (mid- or late 2nd century BC; D 40), framed in guilloche and isometric meander with leaden strips, shows an erotic group of a satyr and a maenad, close in composition to a similar group in a later mosaic floor from Pompeii.

Securely dated to the first half of the 2nd century BC are remains of important floors from Pergamon, found in two buildings identified as parts of a royal quarter erected by Eumenes II (*reg* 197–159 BC). In Palace IV only fragments from the floor of one big room, with patterns and garlands, were discovered, but in Palace V the layout and some details of floors in two rooms were preserved. One, with an altar opposite the door, was evidently a shrine. It had a white floor with two panels depicting theatrical masks flanking the altar, but only that on the left, with a tragic mask, is substantially preserved. Between these and the door was a broad rectangle with a lozenge pattern frame enclosing three long panels, the upper and lower with garlands, the central one divided into three emblemata, with a parrot in the largely preserved left-hand one. This disposition is unique, while that of the other room, perhaps an *andron*, is more usual. Along the walls of this large square room (8.5×8.5 m) was a broad band of white tesserae, probably for couches; in the centre of the mosaic is an emblema, now almost totally destroyed, within concentric squares of pattern band on a white ground: these are, from the centre, a double isometric meander, small black-and-white triangles, wave-crests between coloured strips, a leaf-scroll on a dark ground, with insects among the leaves and an occasional Eros (see fig. 138 above), guilloche, a broader band (probably once containing figures) that was carefully and totally removed and, at the outer edge, a double crenellation between coloured strips. All that survives of the emblema is the remains of a myrtle-spray and, in the centre bottom, on a blue-grey ground, the vivid representation of a small cartellino with Hephaistion's signature (see fig. 137 above).

Of the large body of Hellenistic floors on Delos, one is in *opus signinum* (an Italian technique using large, widely spaced fragments of different coloured stone or clay set in coloured plaster). This must have been done by an Italian craftsman or to the specifications of an Italian owner, but the rest of the mosaics adhere to Greek traditions. Tessera floors are subdivided into the ordinary *opus tessellatum* and the more refined *opus vermiculatum*, in which the small and closely set tesserae are used to achieve extremely subtle pictorial and colouristic effects. *Opus vermiculatum* was often employed for special detail in floors mainly of *opus tessellatum* (as two centuries earlier Gnosis had used tiny pebbles). Most of the well-preserved floors at Delos are from ground-floors, in which *opus tessellatum* prevails; but the fragments from lost upper storeys are often in fine *opus vermiculatum*. Some floors have overall geometric patterns; more common are concentric squares or rectangles of pattern bands on a white ground with a framed emblema in the middle. Both the emblema and the threshold may have either geometric or floral patterns or a figural representation. Some unusual designs are found. On one *andron* floor from the House of the Masks (B 214) a large rectangular pattern frame on a white ground encloses a square emblema with *Dionysos Riding a (?)Cheetah*, flanked by two lozenge-shaped emblemata with centaurs (a layout faintly reminiscent of that of the altar room at Pergamon). The central emblema, in a Hellenistic 'baroque' style, is highly pictorial in treatment. The house was named after another unusual mosaic floor with an overall decoration of *trompe l'oeil* cubes and a garland hung with theatre masks down each side (B 215).

One of the finest of the Delian floors is that signed by (Askle)piades. The square floor (B 210) is in the courtyard, surrounded by the colonnade, and has a single overall design consisting of a large circle reaching almost to the square of black crenellation at the outer edges. The circle within a square design, so popular in pebble mosaics, is not found elsewhere in regular tessera and only once in irregular tessera at Maroneia in Thrace (mid- to second half of the 3rd century BC; S 164). Unlike earlier Floral style pebble mosaics, in which the whole circle is filled with an intricate floral motif, (Askle)piades' mosaic has a series of separate pattern circles of great variety and complexity, with the floral motif at the centre. One of the circles has horned griffin heads and horned lion heads rising from calyces of leaves set on an arcade pattern. Animal ornament of this kind is extremely rare in Greek art, but there is a curiously close parallel on an Orientalizing Cretan vase of the 7th century BC (Herakleion, Archaeol. Mus.). Each of the corners of the mosaic has a pair of dolphins, one ridden by an Eros who leads the other on a rein, exquisitely rendered in *opus vermiculatum*—a new and enchanting invention, very much of the Hellenistic age. The outer border of crenellation resembles that of earlier tessellated floors at Alexandria and Pergamon. Thus the floor demonstrates the interplay between tradition and invention in Greek mosaics at this time. The conventional colouring, disposition and treatment of the figures in some works, such as an emblema (B 75) on a dark ground with a tritoness carrying a rudder and an Eros flying above, suggests deliberate imitation of the pebble mosaic tradition. Elements in other floors at Delos, as well as at Pergamon and Alexandria, seem to anticipate developments at Pompeii and the beginning of the great Roman tradition of mosaic.

BIBLIOGRAPHY

Pliny: *Natural History* XXI.iii, XXX.xl, XXXVI.clxxxiv

J. Overbeck: *Die antiken Schriftquellen zur Geschichte der bildenden Künste bei den Griechen* (Leipzig, 1868/*R* Hildesheim, 1959)

G. Kawerau and T. Wiegand: *Die Paläste vom Hochburg* (1930), V/i of *Altertümer von Pergamon* (Berlin, 1885–)

B. Brown: *Ptolemaic Paintings and Mosaics and the Alexandrian Style* (Cambridge, MA, 1957)

K. M. Phillips jr: 'Subject and Technique in Hellenistic and Roman Mosaics from Sicily', *A. Bull.*, xlii (1960), pp. 244–62

M. Robertson: 'Greek Mosaics', *J. Hell. Stud.*, lxxxv (1965), pp. 72–89

——: 'Greek Mosaics: A Postscript', *J. Hell. Stud.*, lxxxvii (1967), pp. 133–6

P. Bruneau: 'Prolongement de la technique des mosaïques de galets en Grèce', *Bull. Corr. Hell.*, xciii (1969), pp. 308–32

——: *Les Mosaïques*, Explor. Archéol. Délos (Paris, 1972) [B]

K. M. Dunbabin: 'Technique and Materials of Hellenistic Mosaics', *Amer. J. Archaeol.*, lxxxiii (1979), pp. 265–77

M. Robertson: 'Early Greek Mosaic', *Macedonia and Greece in Late Classical and Early Hellenistic Times*, ed. B. Barr-Sharrar and E. N. Borza, Studies in the History of Art, x (Washington, DC, 1982), pp. 241–50
D. Salzmann: *Untersuchungen zu den Kieselmosaiken* (Berlin, 1982) [S]
W. A. Daszewski: *Hellenistic and Early Roman Period* (1985), i of *Corpus of Mosaics from Egypt* (Mainz, 1985–) [D]

MARTIN ROBERTSON

VIII. Metalwork.

Greek metalworkers were skilled in extracting gold, silver, copper, tin, lead and iron, and in forging, hammering and casting a wide variety of objects in these metals. There is abundant evidence for the extraction of silver, lead and iron in Greece. Siphnos was a rich source of silver, and Thasos yielded gold as well as silver and lead. The extensive ancient silver and lead mines at Laurion in Attica were in heavy use by the 6th century BC. There are remains of surface trenches, adits, galleries with lamp-blackened walls, deep shafts and abundant debris from the on-site removal of impurities. These activities included pounding, sifting, smelting and washing of the ore. Gold and silver were used primarily to make jewellery, coins and vessels. Lead was used to make various utilitarian objects, such as vessels and architectural clamps, as well as occasional votive plaques and statuettes. Ironworking was introduced to Greece from Anatolia. There were major sources of iron ore in Macedonia, Euboia, Attica, the Peloponnese, the Aegean islands and Crete. Objects such as tools, weapons, architectural clamps, pins and vessels were produced by smelting and hot-forging. There is evidence that in some places iron was worked together with bronze by the same craftsmen in the same workshops. The Greeks made a wide variety of bronze objects, including jewellery, mirrors, tripods, lamps, vessels, tools, coins, arms and armour, statuettes and figurines and large-scale statuary.

BIBLIOGRAPHY

P. T. Craddock: 'The Composition of the Copper Alloys Used by the Greek, Etruscan and Roman Civilisations, 2', *J. Archaeol. Sci.* (1977), pp. 103–23
C. C. Mattusch: 'Bronze- and Ironworking in the Area of the Athenian Agora', *Hesperia*, xlvi (1977), pp. 340–79
C. E. Conophagos: *Le Laurium antique* (Athens, 1980)
A. M. Snodgrass: 'Iron and Early Metallurgy in the Mediterranean', *The Coming of the Age of Iron*, ed. T. A. Wertime and J. D. Muhly (New Haven and London, 1980), pp. 335–74
K. D. White: *Greek and Roman Technology* (Ithaca, NY, 1984)
P. C. Bol: *Antike Bronzetechnik* (Munich, 1985)
G. Zimmer: *Antike Bronzegusswerkstätten* (Mainz, 1990)

CAROL C. MATTUSCH

1. Gold and silver. 2. Bronze.

1. Gold and silver.

This section discusses gold and silver plate. For gold coins and jewellery *see* §X, 2 and 7(i) below.

(i) Survival and evidence. (ii) Shapes and techniques. (iii) Craftsmen. (iv) Metrology. (v) Plate and pottery.

(i) Survival and evidence. Finds of hoards containing gold and silver plate, such as that discovered at Rogozen in Bulgaria (Sofia, N. Archaeol. Mus.), give some impression of the great quantities of precious metal objects that must have existed in antiquity but that no longer survive. This problem of survival has hindered attempts to understand the range and function of plate in the Greek world. Plate, unlike pottery, has an intrinsic material value and was not carelessly discarded. Instead, it was melted down to make new artefacts. Thus none of the hundreds of items known to have existed in Athens in the Classical and Hellenistic periods seems to have survived in its original form. Indeed, only two pieces from that period have been found anywhere. Much plate was stored in Greek sanctuaries, yet few pieces survive intact: one is a gold phiale from Olympia (*c.* 625-*c.* 550 BC; Boston, Mus. F.A., 21.1843), dedicated by the Kypselids of Corinth after the sack of Herakleia. Thousands of other precious objects were looted during antiquity from cities, sanctuaries and even tombs. Gold and silver formed part of the booty of victorious armies, and descriptions of triumphs after Roman victories in the Greek world record waggon loads of plate. A silver phiale (Kozani, Archaeol. Col., 589), probably of the early 5th century BC but found in a 4th-century BC grave at Kozani in northern Greece, carries an inscription that shows that it had originally been dedicated to Athena at Megara, and this might indicate that her sanctuary there had been sacked.

Important sources of Greek plate are the tombs of Macedonian, Thracian and Scythian aristocrats, who were buried under large mounds with a selection of their wealth alongside them. One series of tombs at Duvanli in Bulgaria yielded several items of Greek silver (mid-5th century BC onwards; Plovdiv, Reg. Archaeol. Mus.), and another tomb group at Semibratny in south Russia contained a series of 5th-century BC silver cups (St Petersburg, Hermitage; for both *see* §(ii) below). Hoards are another important source of plate, although their survival has depended on the person who buried them never recovering the items. Some of the most important include the Rogozen hoard (probably deposited in the late 4th century BC), which seems to have consisted of two bags of damaged silver plate, both local and imported, possibly intended for melting down; the Tuch el-Karamus hoard from Egypt (*c.* 300–*c.* 250 BC; mostly in Cairo, Egyp. Mus.), which seems to have come from the ruins of a small temple and was found with coins and other gold and silver items; and the Taranto hoard (Rothschild priv. col.), which serves to illustrate the range of South Italian plate available in the Hellenistic period.

The poet Pindar considered a gold phiale to be 'the peak of all possessions' (*Olympian Odes* vii.1–4), and other sources seem to indicate that plate was used only by the social élite: during his raid on the house of Anytos, Alcibiades (*c.* 450–404 BC) found a table groaning with plate (Plutarch: *Alcibiades* iv.5), and Socrates was said to have drunk from a cup known as a 'silver well' (Athenaeus: *Deipnosophists* v.192a; Plato: *Symposium* 223c). The Athenian delegation to Segesta in Sicily before the Sicilian expedition of 415–413 BC was, however, astonished by the quantity of plate (albeit borrowed) in use in private houses (Thucydides: VI. xlvi. 3–4).

Plate was also owned by the state. Athens is known to have possessed a set of gold plate at the Olympic Games, where it was misused by Alcibiades for his own entertainment (Plutarch: *Alcibiades* xiii). A set of state plate (a krater, stand and strainer) seems to have been given to Sigeion by Phonodikos, as recorded on a stele (London, BM, 1816.6–10.107). A much larger set of plate is recorded in an inventory from the prytaneion (public hall) on Delos.

145. Silver oinochoe, h. 180 mm, possibly from Asia Minor, 6th century BC (New York, Metropolitan Museum of Art)

(ii) Shapes and techniques. The growing number of finds of gold and silver plate in the later 20th century has led to a reappraisal of the shapes made in precious metal. Most of the extant pieces are phialai, a shape frequently cited in temple inventories. However, as their weights often correspond to a round number of units (e.g. 100 silver drachmae or 100 gold darics; *see* §(iv) below), and phialai could easily be stacked, they probably served as a convenient source of portable wealth. Oinochoai are also relatively common. They may be plain, or ornate with elaborately worked handles.

An attractive example (see fig. 145), perhaps from Greek Asia Minor, has a handle formed by a naked youth who stands on two rams and holds the tails of two lions mounted on the rim. Alabastra are often plain, though their lugs are frequently decorated with duck's heads. One example (see fig. 146) has four incised zones depicting (from top to bottom) confronted cocks, bulls attacked by lions and lionesses, a battle and a duel, and fallow deer. Similar incised decoration is found on a 6th-century BC silver skyphos (New York, Met., 1971.118). A further shape of note is a silver incense burner (6th century BC; New York, Met., 1980.11.12) with its owner's name inscribed in Lydian. Its ridged stand has two duck's-head lugs that recall those on the alabastra, while its conical top bears a statuette of a cock.

Gold and silver rhyta and vases shaped like heads also occur frequently. The Panagyurishte treasure from Bulgaria (?late 4th century BC or early 3rd; Plovdiv, Reg. Archaeol. Mus.) contained a gold amphora–rhyton with two naked armed men attacking a man standing behind a partially open door. Other pieces include goat-, stag- and sheep-headed rhyta with relief scenes on their necks (e.g. the *Judgement of Paris*) and jugs in the form of female heads; one with griffins on the helmet may recall the chryselephantine statue of *Athena Parthenos* at Athens (*see* PHEIDIAS). A silver vase in the form of a head with two faces, perhaps from the Pithom hoard in Egypt (*c.* 400–*c.* 350 BC; London, BM, 1962. 12-12.1), is also decorated with a relief scene of the *Judgement of Paris*; the figures are identified by Lycian inscriptions. Some mid-4th century BC silver rhyta from the Borovo treasure in Bulgaria (Ruse, Reg. Mus. Hist., II 357–9) are decorated with the foreparts of a galloping horse, bull or sphinx, and one from the Tuch el-Karamus hoard (Cairo, Egyp. Mus., JE 38093) is shaped like a griffin.

Some relief scenes appear on medallions attached to pieces of plate. One inside a silver kantharos from

146. Silver alabastron, h. 103 mm, from Asia Minor, 6th century BC (New York, Metropolitan Museum of Art)

147. Silver cup with gold-figure decoration, diam. 130 mm, from Semibratny, 5th century BC (St Petersburg, Hermitage Museum)

Roscigno in Italy (Salerno, Mus. Archeol. Prov.) depicts the Amazon *Andromache*, while a gold medallion in the silver acrocup from the Chemyrev mound in Russia (once in St Petersburg, Hermitage, now lost; see Vickers, 1985, pp. 11–13) depicted a *Nereid on a Hippocamp*. In the gold-figure technique, gold-leaf figures were superimposed on an incised and burnished silver vessel so that the incised detail showed through. An early example of the technique is found on a silver phiale from the so-called Kourion hoard (7th century BC; New York, Met., 74.51.4554). Later examples occur on the finds from the tumuli at Semibratny and the mounds at Duvanli (*see* §(i) above). The subjects on the silver cups from Semibratny include a *Nike*, *Maenads and Satyrs* and a scene perhaps from a Greek tragedy (see fig. 147). The kantharos from Duvanli depicts *Maenads and Satyrs*, and the phiale a chariot race. A stemless cup that shows *Selene on a Horse* may also have been decorated in this technique, but only the incised design remains.

(iii) Craftsmen. The literary sources suggest that precious metals were used by the social élite, and it is thus little surprise to find this group owning slaves who could work in these media; in Attica the same group may have derived some of their wealth from the silver mines at Laurion. Kallias Lakkoploutos (*c*. 450–*c*.370 BC), for instance, is said to have been worth 200 talents (or 5.2 tonnes of silver), some of which may have been obtained from his mining interests. In the confiscated property lists of the mutilators of the herms in late 5th-century BC Athens, one of the slaves is described as a goldsmith and valued at the substantial figure of 360 drachmae, while an enfranchisement decree (possibly of 404/403 BC) includes a goldsmith, which may indicate that such craftsmen were usually slaves.

A crude inscription found on a silver phiale from the Rogozen hoard shows that it belonged to Kotys from Beos and was made by Disloias. A list of metalworkers may be found in Athenaeus' discussion of objects used at a symposion (*Deipnosophists* xi.782b): in particular he noted a Herakleiot skyphos decorated in relief and bearing the epigram, 'The design (*gramma*) is by Parrhasios, the work (*techna*) by Mys. I am the representation of lofty Ilium, which the sons of Aeacus captured.' The pair are known for their work on the bronze statue of *Athena Promachos* on the Athenian Acropolis, and this combination of craftsmen finds a parallel in the signatures of potters and painters on Greek pottery (*see* §V, 1(vi)(d) above). The epigram implies that one craftsman worked from designs (*graphides*) prepared by the other. Pliny (*Natural History* XXXV.xxxvi.68) recorded that many of the designs of PARRHASIOS were still extant in his day (1st century AD).

A further insight into the position of metalworkers is found in the inventory lists of the Treasurers of Athena at Athens, in which objects inscribed with their makers' names are cited: particularly notable are some phialai signed by Nikokrates of Kolonos, who is known from seven inventory lists and was active for over twenty years. Some 26 vessels are linked to his name. His work seems to have included melting down dedications and reworking the precious metal: in 320/319 BC he made five hydriai from silver phialai dedicated by freedmen.

(iv) Metrology. Gold and silver plate was significant for its sheer intrinsic value. A gold phiale could be treasured precisely because it was worth its weight in gold. Temple inventories show that silver phialai regularly weighed exactly 100 drachmae, while gold objects were often equivalent to a round number of darics (though valued in silver drachmae). Many silver items in these lists were ascribed weights in Attic drachmae, though they were actually made to a weight standard based on the Persian coin called the siglos. Indeed, very little extant silver plate was made to an Attic standard, as there was a great diversity of areas that were producing plate. Some of the few pieces that do seem to have been made to an Attic standard were found at Duvanli, for example the gold-figure silver phiale weighing 100 drachmae and two silver kantharoi weighing 250 and 200 drachmae respectively. The daric seems to have been a common unit for weighing gold plate. A gold phiale (New York, Met., 62.11.1) carries the Phoenician numeral for 180 but actually weighs 90 darics, while the gold phiale from Panagyurishte (Plovdiv, Reg. Archaeol. Mus., 3204) carries two inscriptions, one giving its weight in darics (100), the other, probably, its weight in Attic drachmae.

(v) Plate and pottery. Although much ancient plate has been melted down, it is possible to obtain a glimpse of the range of objects from their pottery surrogates. It has long been noted that Greek pottery includes metallic features (*see also* §V, 8 above). Rivets adjoining handles are found on the rims of hydriai, while palmettes are painted under the handles of oinochoai in the same position as the moulded palmettes on their metal counterparts, and moulded rings emphasize different parts of the vessel. Similarly, an Attic Red-figure acrocup attributed to the

Diomed Painter (Boston, MA, Mus. F.A., 00.354) is clearly derived from a silver cup such as the one found in the Chemyrev mound: their profiles are similar, and the bowls of both are decorated with vertical ribbing. The gold tondo of the Chemyrev cup showing a *Nereid on a Hippocamp* may be paralleled by the Red-figure painting of *Sparte* in the Boston cup. There are also close correspondences between two vertically ribbed mugs from the same mound at Duvanli (5th century BC; Plovdiv, Reg. Archaeol. Mus., 1518 and 1530): one was of silver and the other of Attic clay. Horizontally ribbed Thracian beakers, such as that from Boukyovtsi (4th century BC; Sofia, N. Archaeol. Mus., 6694), are directly paralleled by Attic Black-glossed beakers. Other close parallels in shape are found for Rheneia cups, skyphoi and even perfume pots.

It is possible, too, that particular colours were chosen by potters to evoke specific materials. Thus the grey slips of Etruscan pottery (*see* ETRUSCAN, §IV) were perhaps imitating 'patinated' silver, and yellow slips evoked gold. Likewise, the grey appearance of Lesbian Bucchero may have been intended to suggest silver. Similarly, the 'metallic' nature of Attic and other black-glossed pottery may reflect the taste for patinated silver in some parts of the Mediterranean. 'Patination' certainly occurs on the silverware from Dalboki in Thrace, though that found at Vergina in Macedonia seems to have been more highly polished. The idea that potters deliberately imitated metal prototypes is supported by Athenaeus' statement (*Deipnosophists* xi. 480e) that they 'baptized' their vases to make them appear like silver. It has also been suggested that the purple added to such features as fillets and ridges on Greek pottery might be evoking copper seams in silver vessels, and there is a clear association between the Red-figure decoration on clay vessels and the gold-figure technique found on silver ones.

BIBLIOGRAPHY

D. E. Strong: *Greek and Roman Gold and Silver Plate* (London, 1966)

A. Oliver jr: *Silver for the Gods: 800 Years of Greek and Roman Silver* (Toledo, 1977)

D. von Bothmer: 'A Greek and Roman Treasury', *Bull. Met.*, xlii/1 (1984) [whole issue]

M. Vickers: 'Demus's Gold *Phiale* (Lysias 19.25)', *Amer. J. Anc. Hist.*, ix (1984), pp. 48–53

M. Vickers, ed.: *Pots and Pans: A Colloquium on Precious Metals and Ceramics in the Muslim, Chinese and Graeco-Roman Worlds: Oxford, 1985*, pp. 9–30, 71–81

M. Vickers, O. Impey and J. Allan: *From Silver to Ceramic: The Potter's Debt to Metalwork in the Graeco-Roman, Oriental and Islamic Worlds* (Oxford, 1986)

D. W. J. Gill: 'Two New Silver Shapes from Semibratny (Seven Brothers' Tumuli)', *Annu. Brit. Sch. Athens*, lxxxii (1987), pp. 47–53

——: 'Expressions of Wealth: Greek Art and Society', *Antiquity*, lxii (1988), pp. 735–43

D. Harris: 'Nikokrates of Kolonos: Metalworker to the Parthenon Treasurers', *Hesperia*, lvii (1988), pp. 329–37

M. Vickers and D. W. J. Gill: *Artful Crafts: Ancient Greek Silverware and Pottery* (Oxford, 1994)

Greek Gold: Jewellery of the Classical World (exh. cat. by D. Williams and J. Ogden, London, BM; St Petersburg, Hermitage; New York, Met.; 1994-5)

DAVID W. J. GILL

2. BRONZE. Our fairly extensive knowledge of ancient bronze technology is based on the evidence of ancient foundries and the bronzes themselves, as well as literary testimonia and vase paintings. Aside from the striking of coins, bronzes were hammered or cast. Analyses of bronzes from Greece reveal the use of copper–tin and copper–tin–lead alloys. Copper and tin were apparently not available in Greece itself but were imported from other parts of the Mediterranean and the Near East. Bronze-casting workshops ranging in date from the 10th century BC to the Hellenistic period have been excavated on mainland Greece and the islands; these were evidently temporary establishments. Finds from them include casting pits, simple pit and shaft furnaces and casting debris in the form of broken clay moulds, pumice for polishing the bronzes and spills or drips from the pouring of the bronze. A number of Greek vases depict metalworkers, such as the name-piece of the Foundry Painter, the outside of which shows workmen joining and polishing two bronze statues (see fig. 47 above).

For jewellery, coins, and arms and armour *see* §X below; for monumental sculpture *see* §IV above.

(i) Statuettes and figurines. (ii) Vessels and mirrors.

(i) Statuettes and figurines.

(a) Introduction. (b) Geometric (*c.* 900–*c.* 700 BC). (c) Archaic (*c.* 700–*c.* 480 BC). (d) Classical (*c.* 480–323 BC). (e) Hellenistic (323–27 BC).

(a) Introduction. Bronze figurines were already being cast in significant numbers in the Greek world during the 9th century BC. Most served as votive gifts and were dedicated in sanctuaries. Olympia has yielded many early figurines, as well as many failed castings, proving that at least some of the bronzes were made in the region of the sanctuary. Free-standing figurines were cast solid by the direct lost-wax process: the wax was cut, rolled, pinched and tooled, and the wax body parts were stuck together; the wax model was invested with a clay mould, which was baked to burn out the wax, and bronze was then poured into the mould to replace the wax. Often the base was cast with the figurine.

The artists who made statuettes and figurines were working in a tradition that included decorative attachments for utilitarian objects, such as standing figurines made as part of mirror-handles, and reclining banqueters or cavorting satyrs, made separately as if free-standing and attached to the rims of bronze vessels.

Like the utilitarian objects and protomes that were always produced serially as a matter of course, small Greek bronzes were not necessarily unique productions. A growing body of evidence indicates that replication was an established process as early as the Archaic period. Bronzes from the same moulds could turn out looking very much alike, or the waxes could be finished so that the final appearance of the bronzes was quite varied.

Statuettes and figurines dedicated as votive offerings have been found in all the major sanctuaries. They occur before the earliest life-size statues, for which they may have served as less expensive alternatives. Significant numbers of small bronzes have been found in Athens, Olympia, Delphi, the Argive Sanctuary of Hera, the Kabeirion in Boiotia, Tegea, Sparta, Thasos, Samos and elsewhere. Traditionally they have been grouped according to the theory that there were various centres of production and that these turned out stylistically similar bronzes. Bronze workshops certainly existed near many sanctuaries, but small bronzes could also easily have been carried into a particular sanctuary from an entirely different locale. The use of duplicative processes complicates the question of regional styles, since this type of production meant that the master moulds taken from the original model could also be transported elsewhere for casting and finishing.

It is clear that bronze statuettes and figurines were produced long before large-scale bronzes and that their makers were working in a different technical tradition; this gave them far greater freedom than the sculptors of monumental bronzes, who were limited by types that had been established for works in marble. It was not until the Archaic period that sculptors began to make large-scale images, and these followed the formulaic types established by Archaic marble sculpture. Naturalistic statues that exploited the tensile strength of bronze seem to have first appeared in the Early Classical period. Questions still to be addressed in the field of bronze statuettes and figurines include an investigation of the nature of the connections between large- and small-scale bronzes of similar types; and a study of workshop practices, to see if artists producing large-scale bronzes might also have produced statuettes. The authenticity of certain Classical and Hellenistic bronzes collected during the 19th century has also been questioned, because of their close similarity to Renaissance and Baroque statuettes and the need at that time to satisfy an eager market.

(b) Geometric (c. *900*–c. *700* BC). Geometric figurines represented birds, animals and men. Horses, cows and deer might be grouped with their young. The figurines of men had little detail beyond head, limbs, genitals and sometimes a hat or helmet, a shield and a sword. Simple standing or splay-legged figures are usually described as warriors, and early images of women can be distinguished by their long skirts. By the 8th century BC there were images of artisans and musicians (e.g. *Seated Flute-player*, see fig. 148), as well as chariot groups, fighting animals and even a man fighting a centaur, perhaps an early representation of Herakles and Nessos (see fig. 49 above).

148. Bronze figurine of a *Seated Flute-player*, h. 71 mm, perhaps from Sparta, late 8th century BC (Baltimore, MD, Walters Art Gallery)

(c) Archaic (c. *700*–c. *480* BC). During the 7th century BC generic standing men became more specific representations of ram- or calf-bearers, kouroi and striding, attacking gods—all types that continued through the 6th century BC. Korai, riders and runners were also among the types of small bronzes produced during the 6th century BC. By the Archaic period bronze sculptors enjoyed great freedom to represent a wide range of poses and movements on a small scale. By contrast, large-scale cast bronze statuary was not introduced until the 6th century BC and was evidently limited, during the Archaic period, by the types and poses that were current in Archaic stone sculpture.

Archaic bronze statuettes and figurines have been found in particularly large numbers in Olympia, Athens, Delphi, Dodona and Samos. Traditionally, they have been grouped according to the theory that there were various regional centres of production, in Attica, Aigina, Corinth, Sikyon, Argos, Sparta, Arcadia, Sicily and South Italy, and East Greece. These identifications are generally based on style rather than find-spots. However, some of the most sophisticated of small Archaic bronzes have been found at the Sanctuary of Hera on Samos and were probably made in the vicinity. They complement the literary sources that ascribe legendary skills and achievements in casting techniques to the Samian bronzeworkers RHOIKOS AND THEODOROS.

Hollow-cast figures could be produced by starting with a wax model on a clay core; but if the casting failed, the wax model was lost. To avoid this there developed, as early as the Archaic period, many variations on the processes of lost-wax casting, some of which were no doubt intended to impress potential buyers, whereas others were needed to meet the growing demand for bronzes. An unusually large statuette of a kore from the Sanctuary of Hera on Samos (h. 270 mm, Samos, Archaeol. Mus., B 1441) is one of an increasing number of Archaic bronzes now known to have been hollow-cast; it originally had inlaid eyes. By the 6th century BC statuettes were being made in separately moulded sections that were either joined together before casting or cast in separate pieces and then joined. A similar process was developed for large bronzes at the same time. One example of this is a statuette of *Hermes Carrying a Ram* (Boston, MA, Mus. F.A., Pierce Fund 04.6). The figure of Hermes has black rays painted on his brimmed hat (*petasos*). The use of a single model for more than one bronze is proven by the identical appearance and measurements of two Archaic bronze riders from Samos (Samos, Archaeol. Mus., B 97 and B 2608) and by two bronze kouroi, also from Samos (Berlin, Antikenmus., 31098; Samos, Archaeol. Mus., B 2605), the only real difference between the latter being that the left leg of one was inscribed by the dedicator, Smikros.

*(d) Classical (*c. *480–323* BC). The introduction of commemorative athletic statuary in the late 6th century BC led to an emphasis, during the Early Classical period (*c.* 480–*c.* 450 BC), on the direct imitation of the physical appearance of victors—their ages, stances, gestures and movements. The athletes that were represented might be engaged in sport or they might be shown victorious, perhaps crowning themselves or making offerings, or they were simply shown as generic standing youths in the tradition of kouroi. A concern with space, action and viewpoint is also evident in statuettes of Early Classical date. For example, a runner at Olympia tensed for the start was placed lengthwise on the base, because the anticipated action would proceed in a straight line (e.g. see fig. 149), but a discus thrower preparing to throw was attached diagonally to the base to emphasize his pivoting movement (e.g. Athens, N. Archaeol. Mus., 6615 and 6930). The trend towards naturalism continued throughout the Classical period, in both monumental and small bronze sculpture. Copper and silver inlays were commonly used for lips and nipples, and eyes might be inset in materials that increased the illusion of realism. There is also evidence that the surfaces of some bronze statuettes were painted or patinated.

149. Bronze figurine of a *Runner*, h. 102 mm, Early Classical period, from Olympia, *c.* 480–*c.* 450 BC (Olympia, Archaeological Museum)

In the 5th century BC statuettes of standing athletes, heroes and generals developed from the Archaic type of the kouros. A few statuette groups from this period also survive. For example, two nude athletes of about 460 BC from Delphi (Delphi, Archaeol. Mus., 7722) stand on one plinth and turn inwards, one gesturing towards the other, who is holding jumping weights. Gaze and gesture link the two figures, not their shared base. The Classical subject of Athena Promachos ('warlike Athena') was apparently a variation on the popular 6th-century BC type of the striding attacking god. Statuettes of Athena Promachos from Athens (e.g. Athens, N. Archaeol. Mus., 6447) may have echoed the colossal bronze *Athena* by Pheidias that stood, fully armed, on the Athenian Acropolis.

Fewer bronze statuettes survive from the Classical period than from the Archaic period, and fewer come from known contexts. As a result, scholars tend to associate them not so much with regional centres of production as with particular sculptors, such as Pythagoras of Rhegion, Myron, Kresilas, Polykleitos and Pheidias, whose most famous large-scale works the highly naturalistic and three-dimensional bronze statuettes are thought to echo. The influence of large-scale works by Praxiteles has been discerned in the statuettes of Aphrodite that began to appear in the 4th century BC. His most famous statue was the *Aphrodite of Knidos* (Roman copy; Rome, Vatican, Mus. Pio-Clementino; for illustration of copy in Paris, Louvre, *see* KNIDOS), which showed the goddess emerging from the bath. Bronze statuettes show her thus, or with a seashell, hiding her nudity, drying her hair, crouching, binding her sandal, draped or baring one leg. Lysippos' large bronze athletes are thought to have influenced the many statuettes of athletes that survive. Lysippos was the court portraitist for Alexander the Great, and his portrait of the ruler, though based on the tradition of heroic standing figures, is a distinctive variant of that type that continued to be popular during both the Hellenistic and Roman periods. The emphasis that Lysippos is said to have placed on the turn of Alexander's head, on the gaze and on the sense of power can be seen in statuettes of this type, standing with one hand outstretched and the other raised, probably holding a spear.

(e) Hellenistic (323–27 BC). Early in the Hellenistic period significant additions were made to the types of bronze statuettes, and changes occurred in their production and distribution. The Classical stylistic tradition was still important, and some statuettes certainly still echoed large bronzes, for example one type of popular small-scale personification of Tyche (Fortune), which was presumably based upon an early 3rd-century BC statue made by

Eutychides for the city of Antioch (*see* ANTIOCH, fig. 1). In fact, so few original Hellenistic monumental sculptures survive that bronze statuettes are often incorrectly treated as if they were, in general, copies of large-scale works. Even for those that are, consideration must be given to reduction in scale, change in function and variations made by the new artist, who may have significantly revised the original appearance.

Small bronzes were obviously appreciated and collected for their own sake. Certain popular types, such as that of the sleeping Eros, had such a wide appeal that they were reproduced in bronze, terracotta and marble, in all sizes, and were distributed all over the Mediterranean, Europe, Egypt and Asia Minor. Genre subjects in particular proliferated, and private ownership of works of sculpture greatly increased. Deities were still represented, with new ones introduced to accommodate new cults and a wider clientele. Common subjects were Aphrodite at her toilet, Eros with his mother or on his own, hermaphrodites, Isis and Harpokrates, Hypnos, Pan, satyrs and various other Dionysiac figures. The ordinary, the exotic and the grotesque seem to have been of particular interest: besides the traditional gods, athletes and portraits, large numbers of statuettes now represented foreigners, blacks, comic actors and street-people. There were small bronzes not only of famous philosophers but also of unknown people, shown dancing, crouching, wrestling and sleeping. The human figure was shown in youth, old age, sickness and deformity. Decorative details were emphasized, patination and painting were used, and such features as eyes, teeth, lips, nipples, fillets and drapery ornaments were often inlaid in copper, silver and niello.

In addition to Greece proper, major centres of production now included Egypt, Asia Minor and Syria. During the Hellenistic period, Rome became a major market and established its own workshops, which also produced the popular types of small bronzes, in the same styles as Greek workshops. Thus an extremely widespread koine grew up, with the result that it is difficult to establish a chronology and identify regional differences among Hellenistic small bronzes. Stylistic dating is impossible: Hellenistic bronzes may be adaptations or copies of Classical or even Archaic works or types.

Because so few Hellenistic bronzes can be dated securely or placed firmly in context, much importance has been attached to the so-called Mahdia shipwreck, which still contained its large cargo of marbles and bronzes when it was discovered off the coast of Tunisia in 1907. The ship is thought to have sailed from mainland Greece, perhaps Attica, during the early 1st century BC and to have been wrecked *en route* to North Africa, Rome or the western Mediterranean. Besides bronze lamps, candelabra, vessels and furniture attachments, the cargo contained a large bronze herm, a bronze statue and numerous bronze statuettes of Hermes, erotes (see fig. 150), hermaphrodites, satyrs, dancing dwarfs, actors and a dog. Despite much scholarly speculation, it has not been possible to ascertain exactly where this cargo originated or to assign the bronzes to a particular regional workshop, and it is perhaps best to see them as exemplifying the range of marketable types and styles that were being produced throughout the Mediterranean during the late Hellenistic period.

150. Bronze statuette of a *Dancing Eros*, h. 130 mm, from the Mahdia shipwreck, early 1st century BC (Tunis, Musée National du Bardo)

BIBLIOGRAPHY

E. Langlotz: *Frühgriechische Bildhauerschulen* (Nuremberg, 1927)
W. Lamb: *Ancient Greek and Roman Bronzes* (London, 1929/*R* Chicago, 1969)
U. Jantzen: *Bronzewerkstätten in Grossgriechenland und Sizilien* (Berlin, 1937)
J. Charbonneaux: *Les Bronzes grecs* (Paris, 1958); Eng. trans. by K. Watson as *Greek Bronzes* (London and New York, 1962)
W. Fuchs: *Der Schiffsfund von Mahdia* (Tübingen, 1963)
H. G. Niemeyer: 'Attische Bronzestatuetten der spätarchaischen und frühklassischen Zeit', *Ant. Plast.*, iii (1964), pp. 7–76
D. G. Mitten and S. F. Doeringer, eds: *Master Bronzes from the Classical World* (Mainz, 1967)
C. Rolley: *Greek Minor Arts: The Bronzes* (1967), v/1 of *Monumenta Graeca et Romana*, ed. H. F. Mussche (Leiden, 1963–)
R. Thomas: *Athletenstatuetten der Spätarchaik und des strengen Stils* (Rome, 1981)
C. Rolley: *Les Bronzes grecs* (Fribourg, 1983)
K. Gschwantler and others, eds: *Guss und Form: Bronzen aus der Antikensammlung* (Vienna, 1986)
A. P. Kozloff and D. G. Mitten, eds: *The Gods Delight: The Human Figure in Classical Bronze* (Cleveland, OH, 1988)
——: *Small Bronze Sculpture from the Ancient World* (Malibu, 1990)

(ii) Vessels and mirrors. During the Geometric period (*c.* 900–*c.* 700 BC), the Greeks used bronze vessels for

dedications and for funerary offerings; later, bronze vessels were prizes for athletic victories. By the Classical period (*c.* 480–323 BC) they were being sold throughout the Mediterranean world as luxury items. Greek bronze vessels have been found not only in Greece, South Italy, Sicily and Asia Minor but also in northern Europe, in North Africa and at sites along the Black Sea coast. Bronze vessels were usually made by hammering discs of sheet-bronze into hollow shapes, which might then be turned on a lathe for further shaping and detailing. Occasionally, bronze vessels were cast. Handles were separately cast and mass produced, as often were feet and sometimes the rims of vessels. Feet, rims and handles were soldered or riveted to the body of the vessel, which might be decorated by the addition of other cast features. Sometimes the walls of bronze vessels were given repoussé or engraved decoration.

(a) 9th–7th centuries BC. (b) 6th–1st centuries BC.

(a) 9th–7th centuries BC. During the 9th and 8th centuries BC Geometric bronze cauldrons (round vessels with wide mouths attached to tripod bases) were standard dedications in Greek sanctuaries. Particularly large numbers of tripod cauldrons come from Olympia (Olympia, Archaeol. Mus.), but examples survive from all major Greek sanctuaries. They range in height from less than 100 mm to several metres. The smallest were fully cast, but larger tripod cauldrons were hammered vessels on to which cast legs and vertical ring handles were attached with rivets. The wax models made for casting the legs and handles by the lost-wax process (*see* §IV, 1(iv)(c) above) were incised or stamped to reproduce ornaments like those on Geometric pottery: zigzags, chevrons, circles, running spirals, meanders. Sometimes small panels near the tops of the legs contain human or animal figures in Geometric style. The ring handles may be solid bronze, or they may have pierced openwork designs; three-dimensional cast birds or horses may be attached to the tops of the ring handles, or they may be cast along with them. Sometimes human figures stand on the rim of the cauldron, supporting the handles.

During the Orientalizing period of the 8th and 7th centuries BC, dedications included the phiale, a type of offering-bowl with a raised central boss and repoussé walls. Phialai were also produced in contemporary Near Eastern cultures. Also at that time a new type of tripod cauldron was introduced to Greece from the East. The legs were formed of groups of bronze rods, which were bent into arches on three sides. A bronze ring attached at the tops of these arches supported the circular base of the hammered sheet-bronze cauldron. Another support just above the feet was often used to stabilize the base. The Greeks produced such cauldrons in large numbers, with separately made decorative Orientalizing motifs attached around the rims (see fig. 151). These motifs included bulls' heads, sirens and, most frequently, the necks and heads of griffins. Groups of four to eight griffins were attached to the rims by rivets at the bases of their long necks. The earliest of these griffin protomes were hammered bronze; by the 7th century BC they were usually cast, though some particularly large cast heads were fitted to hammered necks. Herodotus (*Histories* IV.clii) describes a cauldron made on Samos during the 7th century BC for a cost of six talents, a tithe of the profit made on a trading expedition to Spain. The cauldron was decorated with griffins' heads and supported by three kneeling bronze figures, which alone were seven cubits high (*c.* 3.5 m). Of the tripod cauldrons dedicated on the Acropolis at Athens during the Orientalizing period, only fragmentary sheet-bronze decorations for the tripod legs survive (Athens, Acropolis Mus.); they are embossed with both heraldic and narrative figural decoration.

151. Bronze rod tripod with cauldron and griffin protomes, h. 570 mm, from 6th-century BC tumulus at Sainte-Colombe, France (Châtillon-sur-Seine, Musée Archéologique)

(b) 6th–1st centuries BC.

Cauldrons. The popularity of cauldrons on rod-tripod bases continued throughout the 6th century BC and beyond, the tripods becoming more and more richly decorated. The legs might have feet in the form of paws, claws or hooves, and terminations above in the form of ducks' or serpents' heads. Cast ornaments, such as palmettes and, later, plaques with animal or figural decoration, were affixed to the arches at the tops of the legs. A third bronze ring was sometimes added to accommodate further ornament, such as crouching lions, striding bulls, horses' heads or snakes. Diagonal supports were sometimes needed to strengthen and stabilize the base.

Some cauldrons were colossal. One reported by Herodotus (*Histories* I.lxx) as being made for King Croesus of Lydia by the Lakedaimonians had figures around the rim and held some 2700 gallons; this, however, was only about half the capacity of a vast cauldron allegedly made for Ariantes of Scythia (*Histories* IV.lxxxi). Part of one such huge dedication survives: it is a cast bronze column in the form of three entwined snakes that supported a golden tripod cauldron set up at Delphi to commemorate the Greeks' defeat of the Persians at Plataia in 479 BC (*Histories* IX.lxxxi; Pausanias: *Guide to Greece* X.xiii.9). The column, which has been in the Hippodrome at Istanbul since the 4th century AD, is *c.* 5.35 m high; the ensemble of tripod and cauldron must have approached 6 m in height.

Other vessels. Beginning in the 6th century BC, many of the finest bronze vessels appear to have been made in South Italy and Sicily. These workshops are often said to have been influenced by centres in mainland Greece. Both Lakonian and local workshops have been suggested for a magnificent group of six bronze hydriai and two bronze amphorae of the late 6th century BC from the underground shrine at Paestum (anc. Poseidonia) in South Italy (Paestum, Mus. Archeol. N.). When found, the vases were still filled with honey and sealed with wax.

Most extant bronze kraters range in height from *c.* 500 mm to *c.* 700 mm. However, a late 6th-century BC krater from a tomb at Vix in Burgundy, France, is unusually large, being 1.64 m high with a volume of some 315 gallons (Châtillon-sur-Seine, Mus. Archéol.; for illustration *see* VIX). Its workmanship and its elaborate decoration are also very unusual. The body and neck of the Vix krater were hammered from a single sheet of bronze, resulting in walls of 1.0–1.5 mm thick. The foot, perhaps cast, is soldered on; the two parts of the rim, the volute handles and the strainer covering the mouth were separately cast and attached with rivets. The handles are supported by Gorgons with serpents' heads for feet. The strainer-cover, typical of large wine containers, has for a handle a cast statuette of a veiled female in a belted *peplos* (h. 190 mm). Twenty-three separately cast figures attached to the neck represent a military procession. Letters on the backs of the figures corresponding to letters on the neck indicate their proper placement. Corinth, Lakonia and a colony in South Italy have all been suggested as origins for the Vix Krater.

In addition to elaborate tripod cauldrons, other types of vessel particularly suited to manufacture in bronze included double-handled situlae, plates, and the bowls with human- and animal-figure handles known as paterae. Even some of these shapes, however, also occur in pottery. Other bronze vessels fairly closely match contemporary pottery shapes, including kraters, hydriai, amphorae, oinochoai and basins (for illustration of common pottery shapes see fig. 71 above). In bronze, the range of plastic decoration is vast and is generally more fully exploited than in pottery. Vertical handles may have a Gorgon's head, a palmette, a scroll, or the bust of a woman, a siren or a Silenos mask at the base. The tops of handles, too, may be decorated with floral elements, with the foreparts of horses or with busts of women. Beginning in the 6th century BC, some handles take the form of rampant lions or of youths resembling kouroi, arching over backwards (see fig. 152). Hands may also be used as parts of handles, either clutching a vertical handle or extending from a horizontal handle as if to clasp the body of the vessel. Handles on a type of 4th-century BC hydria known as a kalpis have relief scenes at the base of the handle relating to Eros, Dionysos, and Boreas and Oritheia.

152. Bronze hydria with handle in the form of a kneeling kouros, h. 420 mm, from Thessaly, second half of the 6th century BC (Athens, National Archaeological Museum)

A fragmentary late 5th-century BC cast bronze krater, found in south Russia but evidently made in Attica (original h. *c.* 420–45 mm; Berlin, Pergamonmus., 30622), is decorated with an entire Dionysiac scene: maenads dance and kill animals, and heads of a bearded Dionysos adorn the bases of the handles.

Numerous bronze vessels have been found in Macedonian tombs. One of the finest is a late 4th-century BC krater from a tomb at Derveni near Thessaloniki, weighing *c.* 40 kg (see fig. 153). Its decoration is similar to that of the Berlin krater, but there is far greater detail, and the Derveni Krater was produced with a technical virtuosity that surpasses that of the Vix Krater. Because of its high tin content (*c.* 15%) and its excellent state of preservation, the Derveni Krater resembles gold. A silver inscription inlaid on the lip names the man whose ashes it contained: Asteiounios of Larisa. The body of the Derveni Krater seems to have been hammered in two parts that join halfway up the neck at a point that serves as a ground-line for an animal frieze. The base, handles and cover of the krater were cast, as were the four statuettes seated on its shoulder (Dionysos, two maenads and a satyr with a wineskin, each *c.* 300 mm high). The rich plastic ornament on the volute handles includes snakes twining along the volutes and masks of Herakles, Acheloos, Poseidon and

153. Derveni Krater, bronze, h. 900 mm, from the 4th-century BC tomb at Derveni, Macedonia (Thessaloniki, Archaeological Museum)

Hades within the volutes. Below the animal frieze on the shoulder is a vine; there is another silver grapevine on the body, in appliqué. Repoussé decoration on the belly of the vase shows the marriage of Dionysos and Ariadne; a panther; and an orgiastic scene, with a wildly dancing maenad holding a child by the ankle, slung over her shoulder upside down, five more frenzied maenads, two of them holding animals, a bearded man dancing and brandishing his sword (?Pentheus or Lykurgos) and a standing Silenos. The left hand of Dionysos is solid-cast and attached to the vessel. Below the main scene, griffins tear up a stag and lions fell a bull. The decoration of the Derveni Krater has been described as chthonic, relating to resurrection and eternal revelry.

During the Hellenistic period (323–27 BC), tastes tended towards expensive and elaborate vessels, whether in bronze or silver and gold. The elegant shapes from this period include long-stemmed krateriskoi, graceful kantharoi, animal-head rhyta, fancy pyxides standing on lions' paws, and spouted situlae. On Hellenistic hydriai, oinochoai and amphorae the decoration at the base of the handle is commonly a bust or a mask, and the handle itself takes the shape of a human or animal. Inlays may be found. Decorative bosses within cups or bowls sometimes show in relief a rosette or leaf decoration, a figural scene or a three-quarter view of the head of a bejewelled woman, a drunken satyr or Silenos. Because artists travelled between cities, it is difficult to distinguish regional styles, but major centres for the production of metal vessels were apparently located in Macedonia and Thessaly, South Italy and Asia Minor.

Mirrors. Both hand mirrors and standing mirrors were cast in Greece during the 6th and 5th centuries BC. The disc of the hand mirror, polished on the reflecting side, terminated in either a flat handle or a tang for insertion into a wood or bone handle. The handle might be decorated with a figure in relief or with a more elaborate figural scene in openwork relief that was included between the disc and the handle. The standing mirror was particularly popular during the 5th century BC. Its handle might take the form of a column or a statuette of a kore wearing a *chiton* or *peplos*. The base of the mirror could be a stool or an animal upon which the statuette stood. Decoration included such elements as palmettes, volutes, rosettes, birds and animals, and it could encircle the mirror's polished disc. By the 4th century BC both types had been largely replaced by the more compact round box-mirror, consisting of a cast disc polished on the front and hinged to a hammered or cast lid. A repoussé decoration might be soldered on to the lid with lead. Aphrodite and Eros are among the most common subjects for lid-decoration, and there are some erotic scenes and scenes involving Dionysos or Herakles, but there are also a few examples of lids decorated with battle scenes. The inside of cast lids was sometimes decorated with incised and silvered figure scenes.

BIBLIOGRAPHY

W. Lamb: *Ancient Greek and Roman Bronzes* (London, 1929/*R* Chicago, 1969)

W. Züchner: 'Der Berliner Mänadenkrater', *98. Winckelmannsprogramm der Archäologischen Gesellschaft zu Berlin* (Berlin, 1938)

J. Charbonneaux: *Les Bronzes grecs* (Paris, 1958); Eng. trans. by K. Watson as *Greek Bronzes* (London and New York, 1962)

C. Rolley: *Greek Minor Arts: The Bronzes* (1967), v/1 of *Monumenta Graeca et Romana*, ed. H. F. Mussche (Leiden, 1963–)

E. Yuri: *O krateras tou Derveniou* [The Derveni Krater] (Athens, 1978)

R. Joffroy: *Vix et ses trésors* (Paris, 1979)

B. Barr-Sharrar: 'Macedonian Metal Vases in Perspective: Some Observations on Context and Tradition', *Macedonia and Greece in Late Classical and Early Hellenistic Times*, ed. B. Barr-Sharrar and E. Borza, Studies in the History of Art, x (Washington, DC, 1982), pp. 123–39.

J. R. Mertens: 'Greek Bronzes in the Metropolitan Museum of Art', *Bull. Met.*, xliii (1985), pp. 3–65

——: 'The Human Figure in Classical Bronzeworking: Some Perspectives', *Small Bronze Sculpture from the Ancient World*, ed. M. True and J. Podany (Malibu, 1990), pp. 85–99

CAROL C. MATTUSCH

IX. *Terracotta.*

1. Introduction. 2. Figurines and statuettes. 3. Reliefs and plaques. 4. Masks, protomes and busts.

1. INTRODUCTION. In ancient Greece the maker of small sculpture or figurines in clay was known as a coroplast ('modeller of girls'), a term that probably evolved because of the predominance of the female image in clay (*see also* KORE). The word TERRACOTTA refers to the finished product, which was baked in a kiln. Good sources of clay were found throughout the Greek world, a fact that contributed to the development of a thriving terracotta industry at many centres over some 700 years, from the early 7th century BC to the end of the 1st century BC or

later. The manufacture of terracotta figurines was complicated but resulted in an inexpensive product. Clay was mined and then purified in settling basins. The purified, liquid clay was solidified to a workable consistency in order to be hand-modelled or pressed into a mould. To make a mould, a hand-modelled prototype was created and fired. Moist clay was pressed around the prototype and, when carefully removed, contained the impression or imprint of the original image. The use of plaster moulds, a technique introduced from Egypt, can be documented from the 3rd century BC onwards (Merker, pp. 57–8) but never replaced the standard technique of production from clay moulds.

The earliest mould-made figurines were solid-cast, using a front mould only. By the end of the 7th century BC hollow figurines produced from a double mould were made, although single-mould figurines with simple, hand-made backs were more common. Toward the end of the 4th century BC, Greek coroplasts began to use multiple moulds for figures in complicated poses. Separate moulds for heads, torsos, arms, legs, wings and attributes produced individual parts of figurines that could be combined, varied or interchanged by the coroplast (*see also* §IV, 1(iv)(b) above). After the figurine was cast, and assembled if necessary, hair and drapery were frequently retouched by hand to produce fine detail. Sometimes hand-modelled components, such as wreaths, flowers and leaves, or jewellery were applied, and in some cases the surface was burnished while in the leather-hard state. A vent hole was cut, usually in the back, and the figurine was fired. After firing, many figurines were decorated with bright colours, such as red, light blue, pink or magenta, as well as black, often over a chalky white coating; occasionally gilding was applied in order to imitate bronze.

2. FIGURINES AND STATUETTES.

(i) Before *c.* 700 BC. (ii) Archaic (*c.* 700–*c.* 480 BC). (iii) Classical (*c.* 480–323 BC). (iv) Hellenistic (323–27 BC).

(i) Before c. *700* BC. From the 10th to the 8th century BC in Greece, figurines were chiefly made by potters who also hand-modelled small images of animals or humans that were pinched or rolled into shape. Around 700 BC, mould-made faces began to appear on otherwise hand-modelled figurines. The use of the mould was a technique practised in Mesopotamia and Egypt from the 3rd millennium BC onwards. By the mid-7th century BC, particularly at Greek centres with strong trading contacts with the East, such as those on Rhodes, Samos or Crete, the use of a full mould for the figurine became standard. Thus from the mid-7th century BC onwards, nearly all terracottas were produced from moulds, even though the technique of hand-modelling the figure never died out. The earliest mass-produced, mould-made terracottas were small, solid-cast figurines and plaques, made in frontal moulds, in the Daidalic style (*see* §IV, 2(i) above). Most come from Crete and Lakonia, but sites on the Greek mainland, in the Aegean, East Greece and South Italy also have yielded Daidalic figurines.

*(ii) Archaic (*c. *700–*c. *480* BC). In the last quarter of the 7th century BC, koroplasts at Corinth, on Rhodes and at Miletos began to manufacture small vessels in human or animal form, fitted with an alabastron-type neck and mouth, to act as attractive containers for perfume. Because they were conceived as vessels, a double mould was used, and the resulting casts were thin-walled and pleasant to hold.

Such figural vases and related figurines made in a fine, dusty rose, micaceous clay dominated the market from the 2nd century BC to the last quarter of the 6th. Once widely believed to have originated on Rhodes, they now are scientifically confirmed as coming from Miletos (Uhlenbrock, 1988, p. 147). The types, which collectively make up the 'Aphrodite group' (Higgins, 1967, pp. 32–7), comprise figural vases in the form of a standing kore wearing *chiton* (light, baggy-sleeved linen tunic) and *himation* (pleated and buttoned mantle) and, less commonly, a draped KOUROS, a hieratic seated, veiled woman wearing a tall *polos* (cylindrical crown) or low *stephane* (diadem), seated couples, sirens and various animals, as well as small figurines of banqueters, crouching dwarfs and female protomes. The best of these Milesian figural vases and figurines show extraordinarily refined detail and comprise some of the finest examples of Archaic miniature sculpture.

Together with the perfume they contained, the terracottas of the Aphrodite group were traded throughout the Mediterranean and Black Sea areas, where, in the later 6th century BC, they became the basis for local production at many centres, from Cyrene in North Africa to Ol'viya on the Black Sea, as well as at many sites in South Italy and Sicily. On the Greek mainland, however, Milesian terracottas had little impact. Corinth, Athens, Argos and several sites in Boiotia were the most important Archaic terracotta-producing centres on the mainland, although local production also is evident at many other sites. At Corinth, a vigorous coroplastic industry developed towards the end of the 8th century BC and flourished until the destruction of the city in 146 BC. Corinthian coroplasts worked a fine-grained clay that fired to a cream, orange-buff or pale greenish colour with a smooth, almost soapy surface. Apart from a series of Daidalic plaques of the 7th century BC, in the later 7th and 6th centuries BC the figurines were simple and hand-modelled, although moulds often were used for the faces. Principal types included animals, horses and riders, and standing or seated females whose boardlike bodies, bent to approximate a seated position, were supported at the back with vertical struts; applied decoration in the form of pellets and bands imitated earrings, necklaces and pectorals. Corinthian terracottas were distributed throughout the mainland and furnished the prototypes for local production at Aigina, Delphi, Kirrha, Elatea, Kalydon, Corfu, Ithaka and elsewhere.

Terracotta production at Argos may have received its stimulus from Corinth, although Argive figurines in general appear more primitive in technique and in a taste for heavy applied decoration. Primitive, hand-modelled female types with flat bodies and, in the 6th century BC, mould-made heads, are either standing or seated, in the Corinthian manner described above. The upper bodies are ornamented with rows of alternating strips, pellets and braids, seemingly held at the shoulders by large applied rosettes, while elaborate, high hairstyles are held in place by twisted strips of clay.

At Athens, finds from the Agora, Kerameikos and Acropolis suggest that extensive local production began in the early 7th century BC, although terracotta figurines were made earlier. Most of the Attic types of the 7th and 6th centuries BC are hand-modelled, even though, as at Corinth and Argos, moulds were occasionally used for faces. The standing or seated female board-figurine predominates, but protomes, horses and riders, chariots and warriors also are known, as well as a fine series of Late Archaic reliefs. In the last quarter of the 6th century BC a new typology based on the use of a complete, frontal mould appeared. The most influential type was that of a woman with an unarticulated body seated on a wing-back throne; more elaborate versions have detailed garments, a *chiton* and transverse *himation*, while abbreviated varieties were made as protomes. These and other related types, cast solid in a fine, brown clay, were traded along with Attic pottery throughout the Greek world and provided the impetus for local imitations at many sites.

154. Terracotta figurine of Boiotian board-figure type, h. 230 mm, from Tanagra, Boiotia, early 6th century BC (London, British Museum)

Terracottas from Thebes, Tanagra, Halai, Rhitsona and elsewhere in Boiotia attest to a lively coroplastic industry that flourished from the end of the 7th century BC until the early 2nd. In the Archaic period, Corinthian influence was strong in the development of standing or seated board-figures, but these are more sober in form and in decoration than their Corinthian counterparts. The lustrous glaze and painted decorative motifs of these figures (see fig. 154) are identical to those on contemporary Boiotian pottery.

Many other cities of the Greek world in the Archaic period had local workshops producing terracotta figurines. In the west, at Taranto (ancient Taras), Metaponto (Metapontion), Lokroi Epizephyrioi (Locri), Medma and Paestum in South Italy, as well as at Naxos, Megara Hyblaia, Catania, Syracuse, Gela, Agrigento (Akragas) and Selinus in Sicily, coroplasts were adapting and reinterpreting imported East Greek, Corinthian or Attic types. Most distinctive among the original western Greek types of the Late Archaic period (*c.* 550–*c.* 480 BC) is a hieratic form of seated or standing goddess, perhaps distantly related to the Corinthian board-figure in its slablike body, although it is entirely mould-made. Best known from hundreds of examples at Selinus and Agrigento, where it probably originated in the last quarter of the 6th century BC, this type is distinguished by a rich series of pectorals that cross the upper body from neck to waist.

*(iii) Classical (*c. *480–323* BC). In East Greece new types appeared at the end of the 6th century BC but were more common in the early 5th. Believed to originate on Rhodes because of the large numbers found there, these East Greek figurines filled the void throughout the Mediterranean left by the decline of the Milesian workshops at the end of the 6th century BC. The types collectively belong to the 'post-Aphrodite group' and comprise hieratic seated and standing females wearing a *chiton* and *himation*; they are generally carefully executed using a double mould and a refined light brown clay. Local reproductions and imitations were made at Olynthos, Thasos, Halikarnassos, Larissa, Kos, Erythrai, Cyrene and other sites.

During the 5th century BC, Athens was the most important terracotta-producing centre, and its figurines were widely exported. New types of standing and seated women wearing a *peplos* instead of the *chiton* and *himation* were created in response to the sculptural developments of the Early Classical Severe style (*see* §IV, 2(iii)(a) above), although the older, hieratic type of seated goddess continued to be made in slightly updated variants. The most popular of the new types presents a tall, thin figure with square shoulders, a long neck and an oval face marked by a sombre expression (see fig. 155); the type also is known in a version truncated below the waist. In the 2nd half of the 5th century BC, more majestic female types wearing a *peplos* over a *chiton* and carrying a torch and piglet occur at Athens and Eleusis, as do types of *hydrophoroi* ('water-jar carriers') and dolls with articulated limbs.

Local imitations of 5th-century BC Attic figurines were made at most terracotta-producing centres. In Boiotia, the Attic *peplophoros* ('*peplos*-wearer') was modified to wear a

155. Terracotta figurine of Attic *peplophoros* type, h. 230 mm, from Lake Kopais, Boiotia, *c.* 450–*c.* 440 BC (London, British Museum)

tall *polos*. In later 5th-century BC Boiotian versions, the *polos* was substituted for an over-sized, elaborate, braided coiffure and low *kalathos* (basket-shaped hat), elements believed to derive from a local cult statue. Protomes and several standing types of nude youths were introduced from Athens, perhaps to serve the cult of the Kaberioi at Thebes, where most examples have been found; some of these also have elaborate coiffures. In addition to these sculptural types of standing *peplophoroi* and nude youths, Boiotian coroplasts hand-modelled complex scenes reflecting activities from everyday life, such as a woman baking bread, a man sawing wood or a man writing (Higgins, 1967, p. 32).

At the end of the 6th century BC new types appeared at Corinth, although the old hand-modelled figurines continued to be made. These new figurines, solid and made in a complete, frontal mould, reflected stylistic trends in Late Archaic sculpture. The principal type was flat, almost like a cut-out, and represented a standing kore in *chiton* and *himation*; her hand was occasionally pierced to carry an offering, or it held a flower. Slightly later, other types were introduced: more fully three-dimensional standing and seated females, dolls with articulated limbs, protomes and cut-out reliefs. These continued to be produced with little variation well into the 4th century BC.

The western Greek cities are noted for original contributions to the terracotta repertory of the 5th century BC. A local style and a unique local typology distinguishes the early 5th-century BC seated and standing women from Lokroi Epizephyrioi and Medma, with their squat, block-like proportions, precise linear detail, exaggerated Severe style characteristics and lingering archaisms; the reliefs are similar, if more decorative. The coroplasts at Taranto, aside from other terracottas, produced a type of reclining Dionysos throughout the 5th century BC and into the 4th. Perhaps originally inspired by 6th-century BC East Greek banqueter figurines, the type quickly acquired the locally specific features of the head of Dionysos with an elaborate *stephane* with a central lotus or rosette (Mollard-Besques, 1954–92, i, pls xliii–xlvi). In Sicily in the 5th century BC, the Attic *peplophoros* was transformed into a pig-bearer at Syracuse and elsewhere, although local types of pig-bearers were already current in the late 6th century BC at Gela. A type of torch-bearing female figure accompanied the pig-bearer types; both are generally associated with the worship of Persephone (Bell, 1981, pp. 82–3), yet both pig- and torch-bearers have been found at sanctuaries in Sicily belonging to other goddesses. Syracuse was the most important terracotta-producing centre in the 5th century BC, but many other sites in Sicily, such as Gela, Agrigento, Naxos, Francavilla, Morgantina and Catania, had a flourishing coroplastic industry.

At the end of the 5th century BC and in the first half of the 4th, coroplasts tempered the hieratic character of the standard seated and standing females with rich movement in drapery and elaborately detailed surfaces reminiscent of Attic sculpture of the Rich style. New types were created, first at Athens and then at many other centres from the Ionian coast to Sicily and from North Africa to the Black Sea. Figurines of veiled dancers provided the coroplasts with the opportunity to create twisting movement and swirling drapery (Higgins, 1954, nos 884–6), in contrast to the earlier static and hieratic images of goddesses. Small figurines of comic actors, modelled in the miniature style of bronzes and reflecting bronze technique in the use of a double mould, reflect the increased popularity of the theatre at Athens (Higgins, 1954, pl. 97:736–40, pls 98–9).

In East Greece in the 4th century BC few sites show evidence of terracotta production. Halikarnassos has yielded hundreds of mediocre figurines dating from the end of the Archaic period to the last third of the 4th century BC; types include *hydrophoroi* based on Attic models, protomes, and a long series of standing male figures (Higgins, 1954, p. 102, nos 301–522). In Sicily and South Italy, earlier 5th-century BC types of seated females and standing pig-bearers were brought up to date in the 4th century BC by more fussy drapery (Higgins, 1967, pl. 40:D, E). Dancers, loosely based on Attic models, were among the new types to appear. Syracuse and Taranto continued to be the main centres for terracotta production, but other centres, such as Morgantina, also were active.

(iv) Hellenistic (323–27 BC). At the beginning of the Hellenistic period terracotta production all over the Greek world was profoundly influenced by developments in Athens. Early in the third quarter of the 4th century BC Athenian coroplasts began to imitate in miniature the style of the Athenian sculptor PRAXITELES in figures of standing, draped women. A variety of graceful standing and sometimes seated poses, complemented by intricate drapery patterns, characterized a new type of female image that reflected a sophisticated secular ideal (see fig. 156). The use of the double mould and crisp, metallic detail derived from the slightly earlier theatrical figures. This new repertory was immensely popular and by the beginning of the 3rd century BC was imitated throughout the Greek world, with the exception of Corinth, where coroplasts preferred to revise their religious types with new arrangements of drapery in a more monumental style.

Boiotian coroplasts were among the first to take up this new style immediately after it appeared in Athens. So many of these figurines were recovered from graves during illicit excavations in the late 19th century at TANAGRA that early scholars believed the types to have originated there and referred to all such figurines as 'Tanagras', a name that is still used (Higgins, 1986, pp. 117–61). While the standing draped woman typified late 4th-century production in Athens and Boiotia, other 'Tanagra' types (e.g. young men, old nursemaids, standing and seated children, and erotes) were also made. These continued to be produced, with a gradual decline in quality at Athens and its environs and in Boiotia, throughout the 3rd century BC and, for some types, as late as the 1st century BC. In the 3rd century BC and into the 2nd, the Tanagra style exerted a strong influence on workshops in northern Greece, such as those in Thessaly, Macedonia and Thrace, as well as on centres in Hellenistic Asia Minor, such as Troy, Amisos, Myrina, Smyrna, Pergamon, Knidos and Priene (Uhlenbrock, 1990, pp. 72–80) and in Alexandria. Some products from these centres rival the best Tanagras from mainland Greece and may have been made by Attic coroplasts.

In the 2nd century BC new influences began to be manifest. From Pergamon came a taste for the grandiose, best represented by a number of female figurines from nearby Myrina (Mollard-Besques, 1954–92, ii, Myr.223, Myr.226). Larger terracotta statuettes replicating well-known monumental sculptures may have been a speciality of Smyrna (Mollard-Besques, 1954–92, iii, 1097–1112) but can also be documented at Pergamon, Myrina and elsewhere. From Alexandria, probably via the Pergamene court, came a new feminine ideal, characterized by plump faces and small, squinting eyes (Töpperwein, nos 267, 286–93). At Smyrna and Alexandria, coroplasts seemed particularly interested in chillingly realistic representations

156. Terracotta group of two women chatting, h. 204 mm, from Myrina, *c.* 100 BC (London, British Museum)

of pathology and disease (Mollard-Besques, 1954–92, iii, pls 231–47).

Myrina, Smyrna, Amisos, Priene and Alexandria are the best sources for terracotta production in the eastern Mediterranean in the 2nd and 1st centuries BC. At Myrina, alongside the standing draped female figure of Tanagran inspiration, occur many winged *Nike* and Eros ephebe (Eros as a young man) figures in flight, whose backs were provided with suspension holes (Mollard-Besques, 1954–92, ii, pls 39–48; 80–88). Other popular types included Aphrodites and various mythological personages, sirens, youths, children and genre groups, actors, grotesques and caricatures. Over 40 different coroplasts' signatures and 20 monograms marked many of the figurines from Myrina, in contrast to the mostly unsigned figurines from other Hellenistic sites.

In South Italy the influence of the Tanagra style was strong at Taranto, Paestum, Naples and other Greek cities, as well as in Samnite Pompeii, Latin Rome and other centres in central Italy. Tarantine coroplasts personalized the motif of the standing draped woman with characterful expressions and dynamic drapery; scores of handsome figurines have been found in Tarantine tombs. In addition, completely new types, such as acrobats or long-legged male dancers, entered the repertory, which collectively was the richest and most influential in outlying workshops, such as those at Canosa, Herakleia, Egnatia and Ruvo. In Sicily, the products of the Hellenistic workshops of Syracuse provided the dominant influence over the lesser centres at Morgantina, Centuripe, Lentini and Agrigento, until Syracuse itself was destroyed in 212 BC. Thereafter, the workshops at Centuripe provided the local markets with stiff and provincial figures in a diluted Tanagra style, as well as dancers, Aphrodites and erotes.

Terracotta production had generally ceased in the West by the end of the 2nd century BC, although workshops at Taranto continued to manufacture credible figurines well into the 1st century AD. On the Greek mainland and the islands, output at most centres had dwindled by the 1st century BC, if not earlier, except at Corinth, where the making of terracottas was revived in the 1st century AD after a hiatus of a century and a half. In East Greece, the industry continued unabated into the 2nd century AD or even later at some major centres, until natural disasters or political circumstances intervened.

3. RELIEFS AND PLAQUES. Greek terracotta reliefs can take the form of small, figurine-like objects, large decorative plaques, grave stelai, architectural decoration (see fig. 157) or revetment (*see* ANTEFIX), *oscilla* (objects to be hung in the breeze) or applied decoration on furniture, pottery, lamps or other portable objects. In the Archaic period at many sites in Sicily and South Italy, terracotta altars (*arulae*) had hand-modelled or mould-made relief decoration. In the 4th century BC, terracotta appliqués, sometimes gilded, ornamented coffins at Taranto and large, funerary urns at Canosa. Tiny terracotta reliefs, also gilded, and strung to imitate expensive jewellery, were recovered from tombs at Cyrene, Myrina, Taranto and elsewhere.

The earliest terracotta votive reliefs belong to the second half of the 7th century BC and were particularly numerous on Crete, although they also were made at sites on the Greek mainland, in the islands and in East Greece. Independent terracotta reliefs, however, were not particularly popular, and it was not until the 4th century BC that this genre began to be widely explored. At certain periods and at certain centres, however, particular types of reliefs were produced over a short period, evidently for specific purposes. Such was the case at Athens and Brauron from the late 6th century BC to the early 5th, at Corinth, Locri and Melos in the early 5th century BC, and at Taranto in the 4th (here votive reliefs in the form of shrine façades carried images of the Dioskouroi in various exploits).

157. Terracotta relief depicting Aphrodite with a goat, 288×229 mm, from Gela, Sicily, *c.* 510–*c.* 500 BC (Oxford, Ashmolean Museum)

The Melian reliefs, dating to *c.* 475–*c.* 450 BC, are thin slabs decorated with mythological scenes; the backgrounds were cut away, and small, discreetly placed holes suggest that they were attached to furniture. The scenes are rendered in a lively if somewhat provincial style, with elongated figures and much surface detail (Higgins, 1967, pl. 28a, b). Very different are the contemporary Locrian reliefs, which are always in a rectangular format with attachment holes at the corners. They depict scenes relating to Persephone, in whose sanctuary at Locri most were found. Their compositions conform to a strong gridlike pattern, within which quiet figures are rendered with quasi-metallic detail and delicate, linear ornamentation.

4. MASKS, PROTOMES AND BUSTS. Terracotta masks are most often votive objects but also occur as grave offerings; they were made continuously from the 6th century BC onwards. The most interesting Archaic examples are types of grotesque masks with the eyes and mouth cut out, found in the Sanctuary of Artemis Orthia at Sparta, among other places, and modelled on Phoenician grotesque masks. Terracotta versions of theatrical masks also are known from the 6th century BC to the Hellenistic period, both in miniature and life-size. Most were probably votive offerings to Dionysos, patron deity of the theatre, although some may have been purchased as souvenirs. A fine series of theatrical masks of the 4th century BC reflecting characters from Middle and New Comedy were found in tombs on Lipari (see Bernabò Brea).

Protomes (i.e. half-length or truncated figures) were primarily votive, although they also occur in graves and houses. In the early 6th century BC at Athens female protomes, representing the front of a head wearing a rayed crown or decorated with pendant ornaments over the forehead, were attached to a flat plaque perforated at the corners for suspension. In East Greece female protomes originating in Miletos *c.* 545 BC were modelled in the form of a semi-cylindrical sheath, rounded at the top and cut off horizontally below the neck. At Corinth and in Boiotia protomes comprised a female head, neck and upper, disclike chest. East Greek protomes showed a veiled female whose particular style of headdress probably reflected Cypriot or Egyptian prototypes. Belonging to the Aphrodite group of terracottas, these were by far the most popular and, exported throughout the Mediterranean and Black Sea regions, were widely imitated during the second half of the 6th century BC.

At the beginning of the 5th century BC protomes in East Greece and on the Greek mainland were enlarged to include the upper part of the chest of the image, and by *c.* 450 BC arms were incorporated, so that attributes could be held. Most represent a female image, but several fine 5th-century BC examples from Boiotia portray Dionysos (Mollard-Besques, 1963, pl. xii). Without attributes, it is likely that the protome served as a generic image suitable for any divinity, since protomes have been found in sanctuaries belonging to every goddess, as well as to the nymphs and Pan.

In Sicily, the protome was modified; by the end of the 6th century BC the fully modelled female bust was developed, the earliest examples of which came from Agrigento. These represent a female head and neck on unarticulated shoulders, modelled in the round, as if the arms were lowered (Kilmer). Versions from the late 5th and 4th century BC show dress, floral *poloi* and elaborate jewellery. On the Greek mainland and in East Greece, female busts were also made from the late 5th century BC to the Hellenistic period. They have been found in sanctuaries and graves at many sites and in houses at Priene.

BIBLIOGRAPHY

GENERAL

D. Brooke: 'Terracottas', *Catalogue of the Acropolis Museum*, ed. S. Casson, ii (Cambridge, 1921), pp. 345–425

C. Blinkenberg: *Les Petits Objets* (1931), i of *Lindos: Fouilles et recherches, 1902–1914: Fouilles de l'acropole, 1902* (Berlin, 1931–60)

E. Breccia: *Terracotte figurate greche e greco-egizie del Museo di Alessandria* (Bergamo, 1934)

R. V. Nicholls: 'Type, Group and Series: A Consideration of Some Coroplastic Fundamentals', *Annu. Rep. Brit. Sch. Archaeol. Athens*, xlvii (1952), pp. 217–26

A. N. Stillwell: *The Potters' Quarter: The Terracottas* (1952), xv/2 of *Corinth: Results of the Excavations Conducted by the American School of Classical Studies at Athens* (Princeton, 1932–)

R. A. Higgins: *Greek: 730–330 BC* (1954), i of *Catalogue of the Terracottas in the Department of Greek and Roman Antiquities, British Museum* (London, 1954–9)

S. Mollard-Besques: *Musée National du Louvre: Catalogue raisonné des figurines et reliefs en terre cuite grecs, étrusques, et romains*, 4 vols (Paris, 1954–92)

——: *Les Terres cuites grecques* (Paris, 1963)

R. A. Higgins: *Greek Terracottas* (London, 1967)

G. Rizza and V. Santa Maria Scrinari: *Il santuario sull'acropoli di Gortina*, i (Rome, 1968)

E. Töpperwein-Hoffmann: 'Terrakotten von Priene', *Istanbul. Mitt.*, xxi (1971), pp. 125–60

B. Schmalz: *Terrakotten aus dem Kabirenheiligtum bei Theben* (Berlin, 1974)

E. Töpperwein: *Terrakotten von Pergamon*, Pergamenische Forschungen, iii (Berlin, 1976)

M. Bell: *The Terracottas*, Morgantina Studies, i (Princeton, 1981)

L. Bernabò Brea: *Menandro e il teatro greco nelle terracotte liparese* (Genoa, 1982)

R. Miller: *The Terracotta Votives from Medma: Cult and Coroplastic Craft in Magna Graecia* (diss., Ann Arbor, U. MI, 1983)

M. Sguaitamatti: *L'Offrant de porcelet dans la coroplathie géléenne: Etude typologique* (Mainz, 1984)

D. B. Thompson, H. A. Thompson and S. I. Rotroff: *Hellenistic Pottery and Terracottas*, 4 vols (Princeton, 1987)

M. Bell: 'Hellenistic Terracottas of Southern Italy and Sicily', *The Coroplast's Art: Greek Terracottas of the Hellenistic World*, ed. J. P. Uhlenbrock (New Rochelle, 1990), pp. 64–70

FIGURINES AND STATUETTES

F. Winter: *Die Typen der figürlichen Terrakotten* (1903), iii of *Die antike Terrakotten* (Berlin, 1880–1911)

A. Laumonier: *Les Figurines de terre cuite* (1956), xxiii of *Exploration archéologique de Délos* (Paris, 1909–86)

G. Kleiner: *Tanagrafiguren: Untersuchungen zur hellenistischen Kunst und Geschichte* (Berlin, 1942, rev. 1984)

E. Paul: 'Die bötischen Brettidole', *Wiss. Z. Karl-Marx-U. Leipzig*, viii (1958–9), pp. 165–206

D. B. Thompson: *The Terracotta Figurines of the Hellenistic Period, Troy*, suppl. monograph 3 (Princeton, 1963)

W. D. Heilmeyer: *Frühe olympische Tonfiguren*, Olympische Forschungen, vii (Berlin, 1972)

G. Olbrich: *Archaische Statuetten eines Metapontiner Heiligtums* (Rome, 1979)

S. Mollard-Besques and others: 'Cinquante ans de découvertes et de travaux sur les figurines de terre cuite grecques et romaines', *Rev. Archéol.* (1985), pp. 77–114

R. A. Higgins: *Tanagra and the Figurines* (Princeton, 1986)

G. S. Merker: 'Corinthian Figurines of the Hellenistic Period', *The Coroplast's Art: Greek Terracottas of the Hellenistic World*, ed. J. P. Uhlenbrock (New Rochelle, 1990), pp. 54–62

M. DeWailly: *Les Statuettes aux parures du sanctuaire de la Malophoros à Sélinonte: Contexte, typologie et interprétation d'une catégorie d'offrandes* (Naples, 1992)

OTHER FORMS

P. Jacobsthal: *Die melischen Reliefs* (Berlin, 1931)

R. Lullies: *Vergoldete Terrakotta-Appliken aus Tarent* (Heidelberg, 1962)

H. Prückner: *Die lokrischen Tonreliefs* (Mainz, 1968)

M. Kilmer: *The Shoulder Bust in Sicily and South and Central Italy: A Catalogue and Materials for Dating* (Göteborg, 1977)

F. Croissant: *Les Protomés féminines archaïques* (Paris, 1983)

J. P. Uhlenbrock: *The Protomai from Gela: A Discussion of Local Style in Archaic Sicily* (Rome, 1988)

JAIMEE UHLENBROCK

X. Other arts.

1. Arms and armour. 2. Coins. 3. Faience. 4. Furniture. 5. Glass. 6. Ivory and bone. 7. Jewellery. 8. Lamps. 9. Stucco. 10. Textiles. 11. Wood.

1. ARMS AND ARMOUR. The Greeks shared with other cultures the idea that military equipment, especially defensive armour, should if possible possess beauty as well as effectiveness. Weapons were already lavishly decorated in prehistoric times, and descriptions of ornate pieces occur frequently in the Homeric poems (notably the shield of Achilles, in *Iliad* xviii.478–608). The production of armour as an artistic medium can, however, be considered under both the constructional aspects of the armourer's work and the deliberate application of surface decoration, which is borne out by the fact that the Greek word for 'craft' (*techne*) was also the word for 'art'. Though actual finds of armour provide the most direct and reliable evidence for Greek practices, they are not the richest and fullest source of information. Much indirect evidence is derived from representations, particularly from Athenian vase paintings. These often show the armour being put on or in actual use, and though some details are clearly fanciful, they provide vital information on features such as shield blazons, which were frequently executed in paint and so seldom survive.

(i) Construction. From the late 8th century BC Greece possessed enough bronze to support the production of large amounts of armour. Bronze remained the staple material of the armourer for several centuries, and workmanship reached a standard seldom matched later in history. The fundamental technique involved hammering the metal into thin sheets, which were then shaped to fit closely and sometimes simulate the actual appearance of the part of the body to be protected. Helmets presented the severest test of skills, especially since as early as *c.* 700 BC Greek armourers set themselves an aim never achieved before and seldom since: to protect the entire head and neck with one piece of bronze, leaving only small apertures for the eyes, nostrils and mouth. The resultant helmet was known as 'Corinthian', though its success was such that it was adopted by many other Greek cities. The earlier versions are impressive, and by about 500 BC the design was virtually perfected. Despite the incredulity of some scholars, there is little evidence for the use of a cast model, and an early statuette (late 8th or early 7th century BC; New York, Met., 42.11.42) actually portrays a smith hammering out a Corinthian helmet on an anvil. Shaping

breast- and back-plates to fit the human torso was a less arduous task, but in the 7th century BC a sophisticated form of greave was developed, made from metal beaten so thin that its own elasticity sufficed to hold it in place. However, the most important item of defensive equipment was also the easiest to make: this was the round shield or *hoplon*, from which Greek heavy infantry took the name 'hoplites'. It normally consisted of a stout wooden frame fitted with an outer bronze facing and an inner, centrally located bronze armband, both often decorated.

Such equipment was not the prerogative of a narrow élite. On the contrary, each leading city raised a citizen army whose main component was a phalanx of heavy infantry so armed. Membership of the hoplite class was demarcated at the lower end by an effective means test, defined by the ability to afford the cost of the armour. At the upper end there was no such obvious cut-off: in some cases the richest citizens might form a cavalry corps, but in general a wide range of wealth was represented within the phalanx. One way to reintroduce some kind of social differentiation on the battlefield was by commissioning specially decorated, 'personalized' armour.

(ii) Decoration. Decoration was sometimes executed in intrinsically valuable materials (as with silver inlays), but in general it was simply incised. Apart from the simulation of appropriate anatomical details (e.g. eyebrows on a helmet or muscles on a breastplate) the commonest decoration consisted of animal and human figures, and the latter were occasionally grouped into masterly scenes.

Helmets provided a rich field for decoration. Common features are: a beaded lower rim extending up the front edges of the cheekpieces and round the eyeholes and noseguard; a relief ridge round the crown of the head; eyebrows above the eyeholes and snake-heads at their outer corners. More elaborate decoration was usually executed on the cheekpiece, often taking the form of an incised passant animal or higher relief work executed in a combination of repoussé and incision. The few metal crests or crest-holders that survive sometimes also have elaborate animal forms. In addition to relief depictions of the musculature of the chest and shoulder blades, breast- and back-plates sometimes bore more elaborate designs. The back-plate known as the Crowe Corslet (Olympia, Archaeol, Mus.; see fig. 158) is a major work of art with a large-scale incised figure scene representing Apollo and other deities. Of similar date is a large collection of decorated armour from Crete (Hamburg, Mus. Kst & Gew.; Kings Point, NY, N. Schimmel priv. col.), consisting of helmets, cuirasses and the semicircular stomach guards, suspended by a row of rings from the lower edge of the breastplate, that were a Cretan speciality and that are now often (wrongly) referred to as *mitrai.* The incised and repoussé scenes on some of the pieces are of high quality, and several items bear inscriptions identifying them as war booty dedicated at a sanctuary.

In Greece itself the production of decorated armour had its heyday in the Archaic period (*c.* 700–*c.* 480 BC); thereafter a more egalitarian ethos prevailed upon the battlefield, and a tendency towards lightening infantry armour also led to a much reduced use of bronze plate. However, the use of decorated Greek-style armour had spread to the fringes of the Greek world and beyond, where the local élites were wealthier and more autocratic. Thus much extant 5th- and 4th-century BC decorated bronze armour comes from Greek colonies and native settlements in Italy. More striking, however, is the material from the regions to the north of Greece: Macedonia, Thrace, the central Balkans and Scythia. Here armour continued to be decorated even later than in Italy and is so lavish that much of it must have been designed for use only on parade: sometimes gilding takes the place of direct relief decoration, emphasizing the impracticality of the objects. As in Italy, the most spectacular finds come from tombs.

158. Crowe Corslet, incised back-plate showing Apollo and other deities, bronze, h. 410 mm, second half of the 7th century BC (Olympia, Archaeological Museum)

There is, in fact, controversy over whether *any* of the decorated armour discussed here was actually intended for warfare. Though the numerous specimens from sanctuaries (notably at Olympia) are often pierced by holes or violently disfigured, this probably represents not battle damage but deliberate incapacitation of the armour from both religious and practical motives, so as to preclude re-use after a period of display in a sanctuary. However, other finds, such as the Cretan war booty and a helmet decorated with incised lions found in the debris of the Persian siege of Paphos on Cyprus (498 BC; Nicosia, Cyprus Mus., KA 2269) and apparently worn by a Greek defender, show that at least in the Archaic period decorated armour was worn in battle.

Offensive weapons were rarely decorated during Greek times because from as early as *c.* 1000 BC they were made predominantly of iron, which is difficult to ornament. The few bronze spearheads and spear butts of Archaic and later date found at sanctuaries were probably showpieces, made specifically for dedication in a metal that allowed for some surface decoration.

BIBLIOGRAPHY

A. M. Snodgrass: *Arms and Armour of the Greeks* (London, 1967)

H. Hoffmann: *Early Cretan Armorers* (Mainz, 1972)

E. Erdmann: *Ausgrabungen in Alt-Paphos auf Cypern*, i (Konstanz, 1977)

A. Jackson: 'Some Deliberate Damage to Archaic Greek Helmets Dedicated at Olympia', *Liverpool Class. Mthly*, viii (1983), pp. 22–7

P. Ducrey: *Guerre et guerriers dans la Grèce antique* (Paris, 1985)

A. M. SNODGRASS

2. COINS. Most of the coinages of the ancient world in the period before the Roman Empire are classified under the general heading 'Greek', because the Greeks were largely responsible for the spread of coinage throughout the Mediterranean and beyond.

(i) Archaic (*c.* 700–*c.* 480 BC). (ii) Classical (*c.* 480–323 BC). (iii) Hellenistic (323–27 BC).

*(i) Archaic (*c. *700–*c. *480* BC*).*

(a) The earliest coins. Ephesos, on the Ionian coast of Asia Minor, was the find-spot of the earliest coins yet known, dating from *c.* 600 BC (London, BM). These coins were unevenly shaped blobs of metal marked with the impression of a punch on one side and sometimes a simple scratched design on the other. The marks distinguished the coin from its nearest monetary relation, the ingot of precious metal, since they identified the piece as having an acknowledged worth. The simple scratched lines soon evolved into recognizable patterns or figures. The technique of engraving dies for striking coins was similar to the much older art of sealstone cutting, and the function of the coin die was also similar to that of the seal, in that it acted as a mark of identity as well as of value. It is thus not surprising that the same types of images or devices were used for both seals and coins. Particularly common were standing or recumbent animals, or animal foreparts, clearly selected to fit the limited available space.

In the earliest phase of coinage only white gold (electrum) was used, and because of its high value, coinage was restricted to the smallest denominations. Around 550 BC, however, the first bimetallic coinage of silver and gold was introduced in Lydia. Silver coinage then spread rapidly across the Aegean to Greece, and by the end of the Archaic period (*c.* 480 BC) silver coins were being minted by Greek city-states throughout the Mediterranean world. Because silver was a less valuable metal than white gold, larger coins could now be issued, providing more scope for the die-engraver's art. The typical Greek coin of the Archaic period was a silver piece weighing 8–17 g, though smaller fractional pieces were also common. On the obverse was a design impressed in high relief; on the reverse there was at first only a deeply impressed punch mark, either lacking a design or, more usually, with just a simple geometric pattern. Later, many cities developed more sophisticated designs for the reverse punch, though some retained the simple punch throughout or even beyond the Archaic period. As marks of identification, coin designs were selected to symbolize the city-state that had produced the issue. Heads or figures of locally favoured deities or characters from local legends might be chosen, as might local produce advertising the wealth of the state, local topographical features, or even designs punning on the city's name (*see* §(b) below).

(b) Principal centres of production. In the Archaic period the major areas of coinage production were the Aegean region and the western Greek colonies in South Italy and Sicily, though Greek coins were also issued in Massalia (Marseille), the Black Sea region, Cyprus and Cyrenaica. In most of these regions only silver coins were issued in the later Archaic period, though in Asia Minor some cities continued to produce electrum issues. In Asia Minor, the Black Sea coasts, Cyprus and Cyrenaica the dumpy fabric of the earliest electrum coins was retained throughout the Archaic period. Obverse designs tended to be simple, primarily animals or animal parts, human heads or figures, and plants. Reverse designs were generally simple punch marks, with or without a basic geometric pattern. A dumpy fabric and a simple punch mark on the reverse also characterize Archaic silver coins of the Aegean islands and Aigina. Aigina was one of the greatest coin producers of the late 6th century BC and early 5th, and its silver coins, known as 'turtles' from the sea-turtle design on their obverse, circulated in abundance throughout the Aegean and east Mediterranean.

In mainland Greece and further north in Macedonia and Thrace most issuing cities produced only silver coins in the Archaic period. The earliest Athenian coins are dumpy pieces with designs, in high relief, on the obverse only. The many different designs used, which include an amphora, a gorgon head, a three-legged device (*triskele*) and a wheel, may have been the heraldic badges of the individuals responsible for their manufacture, hence the use of the German term *Wappenmünzen* ('heraldic coins') for this group. In the late 6th century BC these coins were replaced by new Athenian issues depicting on the obverse a helmeted head of Athena (see fig. 159 left) and on the reverse an owl, Athena's sacred bird. This combination of designs remained standard for centuries on the coins of Athens, which were thus known by the popular name 'owls'. Another important Greek coinage with a nickname derived from its design was that of Corinth, whose silver 'colts' depicted the winged horse Pegasos. Unusually, even the earliest Corinthian coins (*c.* 550–*c.* 525 BC) have a flat, not dumpy, fabric. A reverse design, featuring a head of Athena, first appeared around 500 BC, replacing the earlier punch mark.

Elsewhere in Greece the development of coin designs followed a similar pattern, with the earliest issues having

159. Archaic coins: (left) silver four-drachma piece, obverse showing the head of Athena, diam. 25 mm, from Athens, *c.* 510 BC; (right) silver stater, obverse showing a nymph and a satyr, diam. 21 mm, from Thasos, *c.* 500 BC (both London, British Museum)

designs on the obverse only, though the punch mark on the reverse sometimes formed a regular geometric pattern, such as the swastika on the coins of Corinth. Reverse designs in the proper sense tended to be introduced at most cities, as at Corinth, *c.* 500 BC. In central Greece substantial Archaic coinages were issued in Boiotia and Phokis, where independent cities cooperated to produce confederate coinages; in Euboia, where the cities of Khalkis, Eretria and Karystos issued their own coins; and on the island of Kerkyra (now Corfu).

To the north of Greece, the presence of large natural deposits of silver enabled various cities and tribes in Macedonia and Thrace to produce substantial silver coinages, with an emphasis on large-denomination coins. The flans of the biggest coins, including many four- and eight-drachma pieces and sometimes even twelve-drachma coins, allowed the die-engravers increased scope for developing their designs. The city of Akanthos in Macedonia issued coins depicting a lion attacking a bull in a composition perfectly designed to fit the round field, and the issues of neighbouring Macedonian cities bore similar scenes featuring a lion attacking a boar or a stag. Another group of designs common in the north was the orgiastic scene, depicting nymphs with satyrs or centaurs. These appear on the coins of some tribes and on the island of Thasos (see fig. 159 right). Animals were also widely depicted, either alone or, in the case of cattle or horses, in scenes with human figures. As in Greece itself and Asia Minor, such lavish designs were generally restricted to the obverse, while the reverse was usually marked only with a quartered square punch.

The western Greek colonies also began issuing coins in the second half of the 6th century BC. In South Italy an unusual technique of coin manufacture, known as the 'incuse' method, was adopted by the cities of Sybaris, Kroton, Metapontion, Kaulonia and Poseidonia (Lat. Paestum), all of which had originally been founded by Achaian Greeks. The early silver coins of these cities were all struck on very thin flans, with the same design appearing on both sides; in relief on the obverse and in intaglio on the reverse. A different design was chosen by each city: a bull at Sybaris, a tripod at Kroton, an ear of corn at Metapontion, and figures of gods at Kaulonia and Poseidonia, but in each case the design was enclosed within a patterned frame. Veleia on the west coast of Italy did not belong to the Achaian group: it was founded *c.* 540 BC by refugees from Phokaia in Asia Minor and issued early coins of East Greek type, as did another Phokaian colony, Massalia in southern France.

The 'incuse' method of striking coins was also employed briefly at Zankle in Sicily. However, the other Greek cities of Sicily and Rhegion (now Reggio di Calabria), in South Italy, issued early silver coins more in the mainstream Greek tradition, though true reverse designs were generally preferred to the plain punch marks more common in the east. Designs relevant to the individual cities were chosen: Dionysos and grapes at Naxos, a representation of the local sickle-shaped harbour at Zankle, and a leaf of wild parsley (Gr. *selinon*) at Selinus (examples of all in London, BM). Coins from Syracuse had a design of a racing chariot on the obverse and the head of the local water-nymph Arethusa on the reverse. On the earliest issues the nymph's head appears within a small round frame in the centre of a square punch mark, but later it took over the whole design.

(c) Conclusion. Greek coin designs of the Archaic period provide a miniature view of Greek art in general. Parallels can be drawn, for instance, with stone sculpture and vase painting. The style in which human figures and heads are engraved in coin dies resembles that of figures in contemporary vase painting. Similarly, the animals that appear so frequently on Archaic coins can also be seen on vases, though in this period they are usually relegated to subsidiary decoration. The small surface area of coins led to the repeated use of certain appropriate subjects. The best die-engravers were not restrained by this limitation, however, but developed a specialist sculptural art in miniature, and their advances in technique prepared for a full flowering of the art in the Classical period (*see* §(ii) below).

*(ii) Classical (*c. *480–323* BC*).* During this period the use of coinage spread, until virtually all Greek communities in the Mediterranean and Black Sea regions, as well as many non-Greek peoples, were issuing their own coins.

(a) Techniques and materials. The technique of stamping designs on both sides of the coin became standard, leading to a greater uniformity in fabric. In South Italy the 'incuse' technique was gradually abandoned. Only in Asia Minor did Archaic-type coinages continue, with the electrum issues of the cities of Kyzikos and Phokaia, and Mytilene on Lesbos, and the gold darics and silver sigloi of the Persians. All of these coins retained a dumpy fabric and a simple punch mark on the reverse, with representational designs confined to the obverse. Elsewhere, the typical Greek coin of the Classical period was rounder and flatter than Archaic examples, though still chunky by modern standards, and it now had designs on both sides in high relief.

Silver continued to be the dominant metal throughout the Classical period, with electrum or gold used regularly by only a few issuers, mainly in Asia Minor. Bronze coinage appeared for the first time in the later 5th century BC, its earliest regular issuers being the Greek cities of Sicily and South Italy, though there was also a separate tradition of cast bronze coinage in the Greek colony of Olbia (now Ol'viya) on the northern shore of the Black Sea. At the end of the 5th century BC and the beginning of the 4th, bronze coinage also began to appear in many Greek cities in the Aegean.

(b) Coin designs. Significant changes in coin designs included the choice of new subjects. Some common Archaic motifs continued, however—notably the 'civic badge' designs on coins of the great trading cities, such as the owls of Athens and the colts of Corinth (*see* §(i) above). Both sides of the coin were now generally used for designs, so that two subjects of local relevance could be chosen, as at Athens (Athena, owl) and Syracuse (racing chariot, Arethusa; see fig. 160). At some cities a civic badge design was used on one side, while the other side carried a design relating to the local official responsible for the issue. Thus on 5th-century BC coins of Abdera in Thrace, the griffin representing the city occupied the

160. Classical silver ten-drachma piece showing a racing chariot (obverse) and Arethusa (reverse), designed by Kimon, diam. 34 mm, from Syracuse, *c*. 400 BC (London, British Museum)

obverse, while the reverse could show a wide variety of designs, each accompanied by the name of the issuing magistrate to whom it referred. At some cities the civic badge that had formerly been the main coin design was relegated to a subordinate role, as a constant symbol in the field of the coin alongside a frequently changing main design. This was the case at the electrum-minting cities of Kyzikos, Phokaia and Lampsakos, all in Asia Minor. At Selinus in Sicily the old civic badge of a parsley leaf became a minor element in a new and more imaginative 'city' design featuring a sacrificial scene, while at Metapontion in South Italy the corn-ear civic badge was relegated to the reverse of the coin, and the obverse was occupied by the head of a deity or local hero.

The use of the head as a standard coin-design motif became prevalent in the Classical period, particularly in the 4th century BC. The round coin shape then in use almost everywhere provided an appropriate frame for a head, and the popularity and wide circulation of the Athenian silver tetradrachm (four-drachma piece), with its head of Athena in profile, may have promoted the spread of this fashion. As well as heads in profile, facing heads also began to appear, notable examples being the heads of Apollo used at Katane (now Catania) in Sicily, Amphipolis in Macedonia, on Rhodes, and at Klazomenai in Asia Minor. Most of the heads were those of deities or mythological figures, though portraits of men also began to appear. A head of Pythagoras, the 6th-century BC Greek philosopher, was used on 5th-century BC coins of Abdera issued by a local magistrate of the same name, and coins of Kyzikos depicted bearded heads of elderly men with facial characteristics so individual that they have been assumed to represent local personages, though their identities are unknown Portraits of rulers also began to appear in western Asia Minor in the 5th century BC, and examples from the 4th century BC (e.g. London, BM) even include a facing portrait of Perikles of Lycia. Figures, mainly standing, of deities and heroes also appeared more frequently than in the Archaic period, often in increasingly complex and detailed scenes.

It is generally agreed that Greek coins of the Classical period achieved a level of artistic excellence that has never since been surpassed in numismatic art. The heads and figures are more lifelike than on coins of the Archaic period, and compositions in general are more imaginative, complex and detailed, and are usually more aesthetically pleasing than before. The die-engravers had developed their technique to such a level that they could achieve as much formal mastery within the restricted scope of coin design as their contemporaries were displaying in such major arts as sculpture. Among the finest coins were the four- and ten-drachma pieces of Syracuse issued towards the end of the 5th century BC (see fig. 160). The four horses pulling the chariot on the obverse provided the die-engravers with an excellent subject for demonstrating their virtuosity, and the result is a series of highly accomplished miniature sculptures, combining action and excitement with perfect balance.

(c) Individual die-engravers. Some of the Syracusan coins were signed by the die-engravers. Their names—Euainetos (see fig. 160), Eukleidas, Kimon and others—are not mentioned in literary sources, but the many coins that survive displaying their beautiful designs reveal their extraordinary technical skills. The presence of signatures indicates that they must have been recognized as important artists of their day. Signatures also appear on coins from other cities in Sicily (Katane, Messene) and South Italy (Herakleia, Rhegion (now Reggio di Calabria), Taras (Taranto), Thurii, Veleia) in the west and as far east as Klazomenai in Asia Minor. The best coin designs were also widely copied, demonstrating that the Greeks themselves were aware of their beauty. Common coin designs may have been copied for no better reason than familiarity, but there are clear examples of the copying of rare and exceptionally attractive Syracusan designs. These include the facing head of Arethusa by Kimon, which was copied, directly or indirectly, at Larissa in Thessaly and Tarsus in Cilicia (Asia Minor), and the even rarer three-quarter-view bust of Athena by Eukleidas, which was copied at Antiphellos in Lycia (also in Asia Minor).

(d) The political use of coinage. The employment of the best artists for the engraving of coin dies is a sign of the competitive attitude of the separate city-states during the Classical period. Coinage was one of the means by which a city declared and advertised its independence, so the production of an outstanding coinage by one city-state would have provoked its rivals to upgrade theirs. Thus groups of cities in certain regions might all produce exceptional coinages at about the same time. This happened in Sicily in the middle and late 5th century BC and in the Peloponnese in the middle of the 4th century BC, when the cities of Argos, Messene, Pheneos, Stymphalos and the Achaian and Arcadian leagues (whose only previous coinages, if any, had been of small-denomination silver) produced notable issues of silver staters. These had beautiful designs, mainly following a similar pattern, with an obverse head and a standing or seated figure on the reverse.

The political make-up of the Greek world in the Archaic and Classical periods, with numerous independent city-states striving for local or regional supremacy, created the ideal conditions for the production of a great diversity of coinages. In the mid-4th century BC, however, the emergence of a powerful Macedonian kingdom under Philip II (*reg* 359–336 BC) and Alexander the Great (*reg* 336–323 BC) heralded far-reaching political changes that were to transform the character of Greek coinage. Both Philip and Alexander introduced major new coinages, issued in massive quantities, and as the influence of these spread, many of the existing Greek city coinages began to disappear.

The coins of Philip and Alexander had designs with broad appeal to all Greeks. Philip's silver coins had a head of Zeus, his gold coins a head of Apollo on the obverse, with a horseman and a chariot respectively on the reverse. Alexander used a head of Herakles and a seated Zeus for his silver coinage and a head of Athena and a standing Nike for his gold. Coins with these designs continued to be issued long after the deaths of Philip and Alexander, because of the wide acceptability they had achieved. They also provided the models for many different Greek and even Celtic coinages in the succeeding centuries.

In addition to these standard 'royal' coinages, which were produced by mints throughout his empire, Alexander the Great also sanctioned the issuing of local coinages, which in some eastern provinces used local non-Greek imagery. Alexander's conquest of the Persian Empire brought the Greek world into much closer contact with the East. There was an inevitable absorption of eastern influences, and this is reflected in coin designs, as in all Greek art of the Hellenistic period (*see* §(iii) below). At the same time, the presence of Greeks and Macedonians as far east as India was to bring Greek artistic influences, including Greek coinage traditions, to more distant regions than ever before. The further spread of Greek coinage and its artistic influence, not only to the east but also south into Africa and west and north into Europe, became an important feature of the Hellenistic period.

(iii) Hellenistic (323–27 BC).

(a) Ruler portraits. Alexander's early death led to the break up of his empire into separate smaller kingdoms, fought over by his leading generals, the 'Successors' (*diadochi*). At first the Successors all produced coins with the designs and name of Alexander, with whose memory they each wished to be closely associated. Before long, however, new coinages were also introduced, some with portraits of Alexander, others with portraits of the Successors themselves. Once the use of ruler portraits was established, it quickly became standard on coins of most of the Hellenistic dynasties.

Alexander's silver coins had used a head of Herakles, showing the characteristic lion-skin headdress. Herakles' head was replaced with the head of a particular king, but the change was made less marked by the frequent inclusion of divine attributes in such ruler portraits. Thus, Ptolemy I of Egypt (*reg* 304–283 BC) was depicted wearing the goatskin aegis of Zeus, and both Demetrios Poliorketes of the Antigonid dynasty of Macedonian kings (*reg* 294–283 BC) and Seleukos I of Syria (*reg* 312–281 BC) had the bull's horns of Poseidon. The head of Alexander on coins of Lysimachos of Thrace (*reg* 306–281 BC) had the ram's horns of Zeus Ammon (see fig. 161). The diadem, reputedly invented by Dionysos, was ever-present and quickly became symbolic of royal power. The portrait was not always that of the living ruler: in Ptolemaic Egypt and at Pergamon the portrait of the founder of the ruling dynasty

161. Hellenistic silver four-drachma piece of Lysimachos of Thrace, showing Alexander the Great (obverse) and a seated Athena (reverse), diam. 31 mm, from the mint of Pergamon, *c.* 287–*c.* 282 BC (London, British Museum)

was retained on the coinage of later rulers, continuing the tradition of posthumous portraiture begun with Alexander. Alexander himself had attracted divine worship in his own lifetime, and in the Hellenistic period ruler cults and belief in the divine nature of kingship became widespread, thus further blurring the distinction between deity and earthly ruler. The Hellenistic kings, either as individuals or as dynasties, tended to claim specific associations with Olympian deities or Greek heroes, which could be reinforced through their coinage. Thus the Ptolemies of Egypt, as well as being shown wearing the aegis of Zeus on their portraits, consistently used the eagle of Zeus on the reverses of their coins, and many of the Seleucid kings of Syria depicted their patron deity, Apollo, on their coins. Athena was favoured by the Antigonids of Macedonia and by Lysimachos of Thrace.

(b) General and stylistic development. In a Greek world now dominated by the Hellenistic kingdoms there were fewer civic coinages of a size to rival the regal issues. Only the most powerful independent city states, such as Rhodes, and leagues of cities (e.g. in Achaia, Aitolia and Thessaly) issued substantial precious-metal coinages. However, widespread production of fractional silver and bronze coinages continued at cities under the domination of the Hellenistic kingdoms. The civic coins had designs of local relevance, often employing themes already used in earlier periods.

Hellenistic coins are generally larger in diameter than earlier Greek coins. The smallest silver fractions were eliminated by increased use of bronze coinage for lower values, and in all metals there was a tendency for coins to become much thinner and flatter. Thus, the Athenian four-drachma piece, which in the Archaic and Classical periods had been a chunky silver coin with a diameter of *c.* 25 mm (see fig. 159 above), re-emerged in the 2nd century BC as a silver coin of similar weight but with a diameter of 30–35 mm.

The increased surface area of the coins permitted further elaboration of design schemes. Although there was a tendency towards standardization in the use of accepted formulae, stylistic developments typical of the period in general can also be traced through the coinage. In the earlier Hellenistic period the impact of Alexander's coin designs is clearly evident, with many coinages repeating the formula of a head of a ruler or a god on the obverse and a seated or standing figure on the reverse, with one- or two-word inscriptions, and symbols, letters or monograms in the field. In the later Hellenistic period the same designs continued to be used, but there was a growing tendency for all the available space, especially on the reverse, to be filled with images, decoration, symbols and, above all, inscriptions. Thus, for example, on coins of the later Seleucid kings, while the obverse simply retains a portrait of the king (though this is usually framed within a more elaborate circular border), the seated god on the reverse is surrounded by inscriptions, with royal names and titles often extending to five lines or more, as well as symbols, monograms and dates. The city coinages became similarly cluttered, sometimes with magistrates' names or with such titles as 'autonomous' and 'holy' added to the city's name. The 'new style' silver four-drachma pieces issued by Athens in the 2nd and 1st centuries BC are typical of the coinage of the later Hellenistic period. The head of Athena on the obverse is large, to fill the increased space made available by the flattened and spread coin flan, and her helmet is covered with ornament, producing an overall effect of elaboration and fussiness in contrast to the simplicity of the head on earlier Athenian coinage. On the reverse the owl is shown standing on an overturned amphora, and several lines of inscriptions naming magistrates occupy the field on either side of the main design. Any remaining space is filled with symbols and letters, and the whole design is surrounded by an intrusive olive wreath.

The use of a wreath to frame the reverse design is a characteristic feature of late Hellenistic coins. It was introduced on Macedonian coins by Philip V (*reg* 221–179 BC), and in the 2nd century BC it was adopted for the major coinages of Athens and the kingdom of Pergamon—whose coins were nicknamed *cistophori* ('chest bearers') after their design depicting a Dionysiac chest—as well as many cities in western Asia Minor. Its appearance has been linked with the arrival of the Romans in the region, but it can more easily be explained as a fashion.

(c) Coinages under Roman rule. The coming of the Romans had an impact on the coinages in the Greek East. The conquerors did not at first impose their own coins on the region; instead they made use of certain existing coinages, such as the 'new style' Athenian silver issue in Greece and the 'cistophoric' coinage of Pergamon in Asia Minor (the kingdom was bequeathed to Rome in 133 BC). Local bronze coinages continued to be common in areas dominated by the Romans, but many of the silver coinages that had existed earlier disappeared. The coinage of the Macedonian kingdom was ended by the defeat of its last king, Perseus, in 168 BC. The other regal Hellenistic coinages continued until, one by one, the kingdoms were absorbed into the Roman Empire. Many of the later Hellenistic regal coinages are characterized by poor style and workmanship, but some portraits nevertheless stand out, including those of Mithridates VI of Pontos (*reg* 121–63 BC). Mithridates led the resistance against Rome, and his coins portrayed an idealized image of him, which contrasts sharply with the realistic 'warts and all' Roman portraits of this period (*see* BRASS, fig. 8a). Even in advanced age, Mithridates was shown as youthful, dynamic and Dionysos-like, with long flowing hair and an upturned gaze that consciously recalled portraits of Alexander the Great. This was the archetypal idealized image of late Hellenistic royalty.

Hellenistic coin designs are important for a number of reasons. They reflect general artistic developments of the period, and their pattern of survival helps to illustrate the spread of Greek artistic influences. They also provide by far the most extensive series of identifiable ruler portraits, depicting both the famous and the obscure, thus constituting significant evidence for both historical and iconographic studies. Their greatest importance is, however, in their key place in the broader history of coinage. The Roman emperors inherited Greek coinage from the Hellenistic kingdoms, and it was, therefore, the Hellenistic version of the Greek coinage tradition that was taken over and developed, eventually influencing medieval and ultimately modern coinage (for general discussion, *see* COINS).

BIBLIOGRAPHY

C. M. Kraay: *Greek Coins* (London, 1966)
G. K. Jenkins: *Ancient Greek Coins* (London, 1972, 2/1990)
N. Davis and C. M. Kraay: *The Hellenistic Kingdoms: Portrait Coins and History* (London, 1973)
C. M. Kraay: *Archaic and Classical Greek Coins* (London, 1976)
O. Mørkholm: *Early Hellenistic Coinage* (Cambridge, 1991)

IAN CARRADICE

3. FAIENCE. One of the earliest synthetic, non-ceramic materials created by man, faience (glazed quartz frit, not the tin-glazed porcelain to which the term more properly belongs) was first developed as an artistic medium in ancient Mesopotamia and Egypt (*see* EGYPT, ANCIENT, §XVII, 5; and ANCIENT NEAR EAST, §II, 5). In the Greek world, faience amulets and beads occur first in the Protogeometric period (*c.* 1000–*c.* 900 BC) and were imported from Egypt, Cyprus and the Levant. Large quantities of disc beads were found in burials at certain sites, for example at Lefkandi on Euboia, where they are accompanied by glass beads and faience vessels, and at Knossos on Crete. Imports of faience amulets, scarabs and disc beads continued throughout the Geometric period (*c.* 900–*c.* 700 BC). However, recognizable and consistent factory production of faience goods did not begin until *c.* 650 BC, due to new contacts established between East Greece and Egypt (Herodotus: *Histories* II.clii–cliv). Evidence suggests that manufacture was based outside Egypt, probably on Rhodes, but no workshop sites have been found. Popular and attractive miniature containers for perfumed oils or unguents began to be produced (the detailed modelling of these vases suggests expensive and rare contents; see fig. 162a and e).

The first phase (*c.* 650–*c.* 600 BC) began with imitations found at Knossos and on Rhodes of small Egyptian oil flasks like those found at Cumae. Next came faience versions of the distinctive piriform Late Proto-Corinthian aryballoi, which were given animal and plant decoration closely modelled on popular Egyptian low-relief decorative schemes (162b). Similarly decorated pyxides and alabastra soon appeared and were manufactured in large numbers. However, the most impressive containers in this early group were modelled in the form of a kneeling figure holding a large jar (162e). These contained two interconnecting voids (one inside the figure and one inside the

162. Greek faience (left to right): (a) vase in the form of an Oriental lion, h. 71 mm, l. 90 mm, from Kameiros, Rhodes, *c.* 625–*c.* 600 BC; (b) aryballos with relief diamonds and incised pattern, h. 99 mm, from Kameiros, Rhodes, *c.* 575–*c.* 550 BC; (c) vase in the form of two heads opposed, of a Syrian and a Nubian (not visible), h. 53 mm, found at ?Vulci, Italy, *c.* 575–*c.* 550 BC; (d) thick-walled hemispherical dish, decorated with three modelled kneeling figures and low-relief animals, h. 53 mm, diam. 120 mm, from ?Kameiros, Rhodes, *c.* 610–*c.* 590 BC; (e) vase in the form of a figure holding a jar, h. 95 mm, from a tomb at Kameiros, Rhodes, *c.* 650–*c.* 625 BC (all London, British Museum)

jar), with different sizes of opening, which were intended to exploit the principle of the siphon. The details and sophistication of the design point to Egyptian sources, but there is confusion in the iconography, and the workshop manufacturing the vases was unable to sustain the high technical standards of its earliest products.

The second phase of production (*c.* 630–*c.* 570 BC) overlapped with the first and involved solid figurines of humans and animals, modelled on rectangular bases and imitating Egyptian conventions in pose and hairstyle. The human figures are represented naked, with pubic hair and nipples indicated in black; they squat, kneel or stand with one leg advanced. They apparently represent worshippers bringing offerings and are shown playing flutes or lyres and accompanied by falcons or quadrupeds. The animals, which are less common, clearly mimic Egyptian sacred animals. Most are small figurines with suspension holes, but larger figures intended to stand on a base were also made. Contact with Egypt during this phase is confirmed. Many of the figures were found in sanctuaries at the Greek trading post of Naukratis on the Nile Delta, as well as in East Greek sanctuaries and tombs and Greek colonies in the West and on the Black Sea. Early products are sometimes exceptionally fine, but in one late group the figures are reduced to a blocklike simplicity (see also fig. 162d).

During the third and final phase (*c.* 575–*c.* 525 BC) faience was again used for vessels for precious oils. These vases, however, were clearly intended for Greek use, since they have the broad, concave lip typical of the Corinthian spherical aryballos. As well as spherical forms, there were various animal and human shapes, derived from both East Greece and Egypt. Heads of Achelous (e.g. Oxford, Ashmolean) and Herakles (e.g. Copenhagen, Nmus.), horses and cocks (e.g. Brussels, Mus. Royaux A. & Hist.) occur alongside representations of the Egyptian hedgehog (e.g. Oxford, Ashmolean) and Tilapia fish (e.g. London, BM), locusts (e.g. Oxford, Ashmolean) and opposed heads of Syrians and Nubians (162c), traditional enemies of Egypt. The workmanship varies considerably in quality. The exquisite, almost sculptural features of the head of Achelous (?or Nile) from Kawa in Nubia (Oxford, Ashmolean) contrast strikingly with those of the commonplace versions of the same prototype found all over the Greek world. The last examples of Greek faience comprise a mass of poorly made spherical and hedgehog-shaped aryballoi, decorated crudely with crosshatching. These had a wide distribution throughout the Mediterranean littoral and the Black Sea, to the extent that they often serve to mark the limits of Greek influence, especially in Spain. The Persian invasion of Egypt (525 BC) may have put an end to the by then artistically bankrupt production of faience.

BIBLIOGRAPHY

C. Blinkenberg: *Les Petits Objets* (1931), i of *Lindos: Fouilles et recherches* (Berlin, 1931–)

W. F. von Bissing: *Zeit und Herkunft der in Cerveteri gefunden Gefässe aus ägyptischer und ägyptisierender Fayence und glasiertem Ton* (Munich, 1934)

V. Webb: 'A Faience Vase from the Bomford Collection', *Levant*, iv (1972), pp. 150–55

A. Rathje: 'A Group of Phoenician Faience Anthropomorphic Perfume Flasks', *Levant*, viii (1976), pp. 96–106

V. Webb: *Archaic Greek Faience: Miniature Scent Bottles and Related Objects from East Greece, 650–500 BC* (Warminster, 1978)

——: 'Phoenician Anthropomorphic Flasks: A Reply', *Levant*, xiii (1980), pp. 77–89

E. Simon: 'Aigyptos-Neilos', *Würzburg. Jb. Altertwiss.*, n. s., i (1985), pp. 95–105, pl. i–2

V. Webb: 'A Faience Hedgehog Vase', *Catalogue of the Material from Tharros*, ed. R. D. Barnett (London, 1987)

VIRGINIA WEBB

4. FURNITURE. Most ancient Greek furniture was made of wood, a perishable material that has seldom survived. However, despite the lack of substantial remains, a basic picture of Greek furniture can be pieced together from descriptions in literary sources, as well as from surviving pieces of stone furniture and from contemporary representations and imitations of furniture in other art forms.

(i) Types.

(a) Seats. Among the best-documented items of Greek furniture is the throne (*thronos*), which occurred in four distinctive forms (*see* THRONE, §I, 3). An early variety, typical of the 6th century BC, had a back-rest with a top that curved backwards, often terminating in the head of a goose or a duck, and front and back pairs of clawed feet, facing either in the same or in opposite directions. A second type, attested from the Archaic period onwards, had cylindrical legs, often made of several turned sections. Occasionally there were arm-rests supported by small sculpted figures, and the increasingly ornate Hellenistic examples sometimes had figured inlays. Another form, mainly used in the 6th century BC though again continuing into Hellenistic times, had sawn legs of rectangular section, sometimes decorated with cut-out designs, carved volutes and painted palmettes. The fourth type, represented by the stone seats for dignitaries in Hellenistic theatres (see fig. 14 above), consisted of a massive, blocklike substructure supporting a back-rest, which was sometimes curved. Some were decorated at the front with lion heads on the arm-rest ends and with pairs of clawed feet.

The *klismos* was another type of easy chair, with legs that curved outwards and a sweeping concave back-rest. It was a distinctively Greek form of furniture, known from the Late Archaic period onwards and particularly popular in the Classical period. The *diphros* was a simpler chair without a back-rest (for illustration *see* VASE PAINTERS, §II: KLEOPHRADES PAINTER). Its use was widespread from the Archaic period onwards, and its variants included *diphroi* with straight legs either of round or rectangular cross section, with more complex turned legs, or with sawn legs, often ending in clublike feet. The *diphros okladias* was a folding version with legs that crossed beneath the seat and were often curved. The legs might end in animal feet facing inwards or outwards. Known from the Minoan–Mycenaean era, the *diphros okladias* was widely used from the 6th century BC to the Hellenistic period. It later developed into the Roman official *sella curulis*. There were also simple seats in block form (for illustration *see* VASE PAINTERS, §II: EXEKIAS) and benches, which could be blocklike or have either curved supports or straight legs with animal feet. Footstools were mostly used under couches or thrones and took the same three basic forms.

(b) Couches. The Greeks used the couch (*kline*) chiefly for sleeping and dining but also for laying out the dead (prothesis) during ritual mourning and in their tombs. The earliest depictions of *klinai*, in funerary scenes on Geometric vases, are rather distorted by efforts to combine views from different angles. However, two forms of legs are already apparent: one with thickened jamb-capitals at the top (see fig. 85 above); another with a concave curved profile. From the 6th century BC onwards these were replaced by several other varieties, including a rare type with animal legs. A much more common form had turned, multi-member legs of circular cross-section, which were even decorated with figured inlays in the Hellenistic period. The raised head end of the couch often had a curved head-rest, which might be decorated with bronze *fulcra*. A further variety had sawn legs of rectangular cross-section. This form, particularly popular in the Archaic period, continued as late as the Hellenistic period. The legs generally had characteristic cut-out decoration, carved volutes (see fig. 163) and painted palmettes. Representations of couches with inlaid decoration or supports in the form of sculpted figures show that many had double frames. A simplified version (5th century BC onwards) had plain sawn legs that generally tapered towards the ground.

163. Greek couch (*kline*) with sawn legs and a rectangular three-legged table, from a scene of *Herakles Banqueting* on an Attic Black-figure amphora by the Antimenes Painter, h. 420 mm, second half of the 6th century BC (Tarquinia, Museo Nazionale Archeologico)

(c) Tables and chests. The standard ancient Greek form of table (*trapeza*) used for dining had a rectangular top and three legs, though versions with four legs are known. Depicted from the Archaic period onwards, it was generally shown in conjunction with couches (see fig. 163), laid out with food and drink. Circular tables with three legs, sometimes carved in animal form, are reproduced in small-scale Minoan–Mycenaean terracotta models, but this type was most widespread in Hellenistic and Roman times. Stone tables with rectangular tops supported by upright slabs, which might be decorated at the sides with carved animal protomes, were used in villas and gardens in Hellenistic and Roman times.

In the absence of cupboards or wardrobes, chests (*kibotoi*) served to store garments, toilet items and valuables. From the Archaic period onwards, chests can be divided into three main types, depending on whether the lid is flat or has a gabled or a semicircular end. Some had animal feet or intricate inlaid panels. The sideboards occasionally represented were mainly used to store vessels, tools and other utensils.

(ii) Materials and decoration. Although most furniture was wooden, especially precious pieces were sometimes decorated with animal feet or inlaid panels of ivory and bone, bronze and even precious metals. Painted decoration was common and frequently included palmettes, rosettes and stars. Stone, particularly marble, was used primarily for outdoor benches and thrones in theatres, sanctuaries and gardens. Wooden items were often sprung with wickerwork or leather and lavishly covered. The couches depicted in use at aristocratic banquets on Attic vases are frequently adorned with ornately decorated mattresses, coverlets and cushions (see fig. 79 above), though only occasional fragmentary remains of fabric have survived. There were clearly considerable differences in the quality of the material, the accessories and the workmanship, so that an intricate piece of furniture, particularly a throne or couch, could easily be a status symbol. The work of the specialized craftsmen who produced such pieces is documented only by workshop scenes on painted vases. The decorative components made of bronze and ivory, as well as the textiles, were, of course, produced by specialists in the appropriate craft.

(iii) Evidence and development. Evidence for the development of ancient Greek furniture-making techniques comes both from literary sources (from the Homeric epics onwards) and from original finds. Among the most detailed of the literary sources is Pausanias' description (*Guide to Greece* V.xvii.5–xix.10) of the famous 7th-century BC Chest of Kypselos (untraced). This was of cedar wood, with mythological scenes inlaid in gold and ivory, and it stood in the opisthodomos of the Temple of Hera at Olympia. It is archaeological records, however, that constitute our most important source of information. Surviving original pieces of furniture, mostly of stone, include thrones and, especially, couches from chamber tombs and heroa at such sites as Eretria (4th century BC; *in situ*), Belevi (3rd century BC; *in situ*), Taras (4th century BC and Hellenistic; Taranto, Mus. N.), Kalydon (2nd century BC; Corinth, Archaeol. Mus.) and Vergina (Hellenistic; *in situ*). There are seats and benches from sanctuaries and theatres (e.g. the Theatre of Dionysos at Athens), feet and supports for marble tables (Archaic and Classical examples in Delphi, Archaeol. Mus.; Hellenistic examples in Delos, Archaeol. Mus.), and numerous bronze fittings, especially from the head-rests of couches, and occasional fragments of ivory inlay. Remains of wooden furniture are sparse (Archaic examples from the Samian Sanctuary of Hera, Samos, Archaeol. Mus.; 5th-century BC examples from Olympia, Archaeol. Mus.), with the best-preserved examples coming from the peripheral areas of the Greek world, such as Alexandria, the Black Sea region and Thrace (now Bulgaria). For example, at Duvanlji in Thrace the turned wooden sections of a Greek-type *kline* have been found, in which the tenon joints are still clearly recognizable (Plovdiv, Reg. Archaeol. Mus.). Finds of associated textiles are even rarer, despite important discoveries at Korope in Attica (?late 5th century BC; London, V&A) and in the Crimea (St Petersburg, Hermitage).

Representations of Greek furniture appear on stone and terracotta reliefs, painted vases and other artefacts. Examples from the Geometric period (*c.* 900–*c.*700 BC) occur primarily on Attic vases. Hardly any representations of furniture from the 7th century BC are known, but there are many examples from the 6th century BC to Hellenistic times, depicted above all on vases but also in architectural sculpture (e.g. the Siphinian Treasury at Delphi; the Parthenon at Athens; sculptures mostly in London, BM), on funerary and votive reliefs (e.g. see fig. 5 above), on painted terracotta relief plaques and metopes (for illustration *see* THERMON), in Thracian tomb paintings and on metal vessels, coins and gems. Further evidence for the appearance of furniture is provided by small-scale sculptural imitations incorporated into bronze utensils, as well as statuettes in terracotta, bronze and stone (e.g. seated statues from the Geneleos group from Samos, at Vathy, Archaeol. Mus.; from Didmya, in London, BM).

All of this evidence—both direct and indirect—suggests that the forms of furniture that developed from the Archaic period onwards represent a fundamental departure from the Geometric types of the 8th and 9th centuries BC. In some cases they reveal Oriental influences variously adapted in Greece, such as the use of turned legs on couches, thrones and *diphroi* and of lion's feet on some thrones. Combinations of Persian and Greek forms occurred mainly in Asia Minor. On the other hand, the sawn type of furniture leg was apparently a Greek invention of the Archaic period, and the most significant changes in the forms of Greek furniture took place in the supports, that is the legs. Some basic types were either already established in the Bronze Age or can be traced from the Archaic to the Hellenistic period and indeed into Roman times. From the 6th century BC onwards, Greek furniture greatly influenced Etruscan, and, from the late Republican period onwards, Roman forms of furniture.

BIBLIOGRAPHY

D. Kent Hill: 'Ivory Ornaments of Hellenistic Couches', *Hesperia*, xxxii (1963), pp. 293–300

T. H. Robsjohn-Gibbings and C. W. Pullin: *Furniture of Classical Greece* (New York, 1963)

G. M. A. Richter: 'The Furnishings of Ancient Greek Houses', *Archaeology*, xviii (1965), pp. 26–33

——: *The Furniture of the Greeks, Etruscans and Romans* (London, 1966)

G. Kopcke: 'Neue Holzfunde aus dem Heraion von Samos', *Mitt. Dt. Archäol. Inst.: Athen. Abt.*, lxxxii (1967), pp. 100–48
S. Laser: *Hausrat* (1968), ii of *Archaeologia Homerica* (Göttingen, 1967–)
H. Kyrieleis: *Throne und Klinen: Studien zur Formgeschichte altorientalischer und griechischer Sitz- und Liegemöbel vorhellenistischer Zeit* (Berlin, 1969)
G. Siebert: 'Mobilier déliens en bronze', *Bull. Corr. Hell.*, suppl. 1 (1973), pp. 555–87
H. Kyrieleis: 'Archaische Holzfunde aus Samos', *Mitt. Dt. Archäol. Inst.: Athen. Abt.*, xcv (1980), pp. 87–147
G. Seiterle and A. Mutz: 'Ein hellenistisches Bronzebett im Basler Antikenmuseum', *Ant. Kst.*, xxv (1982), pp. 62–70
R. H. Cohon: *Greek and Roman Stone Table Supports with Decorative Reliefs* (1984)
E. Brümmer: 'Griechische Truhenbehälter', *Jb. Dt. Archäol. Inst.*, c (1985), pp. 1–168

STEPHAN STEINGRÄBER

5. GLASS. The glass of Greece and the Greek-speaking parts of the Mediterranean falls into three broad groups: bottles made by core-forming, a technique first used in Egypt and Mesopotamia in the 16th century BC; vessels and inlays made by casting and polishing; and mosaic glass plaques. The core-formed bottles were made between *c.* 550 BC and *c.* AD 10; the first cast and polished objects were made in the 5th century BC, although the techniques were not applied to the production of tableware until *c.* 250 BC; the mosaic glass plaques were made in Ptolemaic Egypt between the 3rd century BC and the 1st century AD.

(i) Core-formed bottles. The most frequent type of glass vessel between the 6th and 1st centuries BC comprised core-formed bottles for perfume, scented oil and other cosmetics. Most of these are dark blue, with white, yellow and pale blue decoration (*see* GLASS, colour pl. VII, fig. 1); purple, green and red also occur. They have been divided into three chronological groups—Mediterranean Groups I, II and III—and it has been suggested that each was made in a different region. The shared features are: the techniques of forming molten glass around a removable core and decorating it with applied trails, which were marvered and dragged into zigzag or feather-like patterns; formal derivation from contemporary ceramics and metalware; and a common function. The chronology of the three groups is based on finds in datable archaeological contexts (usually tombs), and the suggested locations of the workshops that produced them is based on the distribution of find-places. It is no accident that the abandonment of core-forming coincided with the spread of glass-blowing, a revolutionary new technique that allowed producers to make bottles and other objects quickly, cheaply and in virtually any shape that the customer required.

Group I is the largest and most homogeneous of the three groups. The most common forms are alabastra, amphoriskoi, oinochoai and aryballoi, ranging in height from around 50 to 150 mm. The handles of the alabastra and most of the aryballoi consist of applied rings with well-made tailpieces, a feature that also occurs on earlier core-formed containers made in Mesopotamia. Together with the occurrence of a large number of find-places on Rhodes, this suggests that the technique of making core-formed vessels may have been introduced to the eastern Mediterranean from Mesopotamia and adopted by Rhodians. The date of the earliest Group I vessels is uncertain, and estimates range between *c.* 600 and *c.* 500 BC. In any case, the group appears to have been most popular *c.* 530–*c.* 480 BC. The latest examples date from the end of the 5th century BC.

Although the earlier shapes continued to be made, Group II vessels differ in detail, and apart from the techniques used to form and decorate them, they have little in common with their predecessors. The most common form is the alabastron; oinochai are scarce, and amphoriskoi almost disappear. A few stamnoi, hydriskai and 'unguentaria' occur. The range of sizes is larger than in Group I, and alabastra sometimes exceed 200 mm in height. The earliest closely dated examples of Group II were buried around the mid-4th century BC (i.e. 50 years after the end of Group I). Group II remained popular (but never on the scale of Group I) until the first or second quarter of the 3rd century BC. Thereafter it declined, although production probably continued until *c.* 200 BC. Group II has a wide distribution, from the western Mediterranean (especially Italy) to the Black Sea, and several centres of production probably existed.

164. Glass core-formed amphoriskos with applied handles, h. 240 mm, from the eastern Mediterranean, 2nd–1st century BC (Corning, NY, Museum of Glass)

Group III vessels again differ significantly from those of the preceding group. They are restricted to alabastra and amphoriskoi, and these were reduced in size and given longer necks (see fig. 164). Although some vessels were carefully made, others are lopsided and have irregular, carelessly applied decoration. Group III may have come into production around the mid-2nd century BC and continued until the beginning of the 1st century AD. It is believed that many examples were made in Cyprus, with the adjacent coast of Syria as another possible place of manufacture.

(ii) Cast and polished glass. Core-formed vessels apart, the earliest glass objects made in Greece after the Mycenaean period (*c.* 1600–*c.* 1050 BC) are inlays used as architectural ornament and in sculpture. In the early 5th century BC Pheidias used glass in his sculpture, and clay moulds containing traces of colourless glass (Olympia, Archaeol. Mus.) were found during the excavation of his workshop at OLYMPIA. The moulds were used to form drapery and other elements, presumably destined for inclusion in his colossal statue of *Zeus* (*see also* §IV, 2(iii) above). The glass, which is thought to have been imported from overseas, was deliberately decolourized with antimony. At a slightly later date (*c.* 420–*c.* 405 BC), red, blue, yellow and purple glass inlays were used to enliven the capitals in the north portico of the Erechtheion at Athens. A third group of cast and polished inlays was found in Tomb II (probably the tomb of Philip II (*d* 336 BC)) at Vergina in Macedonia. Like the glass from Olympia, the inlays were decolourized, and some of them are decorated with gold or silver foil.

The earliest cast glass vessels of the Hellenistic period (323–27 BC) consist of luxury tableware of the 'Canosa group', so called because of the large number of examples reportedly found at Canosa in southern Italy. Objects in the Canosa group include monochrome dishes, hemispherical bowls, footed bowls or kraters, bowls with projecting bosses or 'fins', ring-handled skyphoi and a unique lidded amphora. Like the core-formed bottles, they imitate the forms of fine ceramics and metalware. All of these objects are of pale green, dark blue or purple glass. They were cast in multi-partite moulds and finished by grinding and polishing. Lathe-cut grooves and base-mouldings are common. A few objects have painted and/or gold-leaf decoration. Similar objects have also been found elsewhere in Italy, in Greece, Asia Minor, the Crimea and perhaps also at Benghazi in Cyrenaica. Few of these objects were found in controlled excavations, and consequently their dating is uncertain. While some scholars suggest that the earliest examples were made in the early or mid-3rd century BC, others prefer a starting-date closer to the end of the 3rd century. A bowl from a tomb at Naxos in Sicily (Syracuse, Mus. Archaeol. Reg.) confirms that at least part of the Canosa group was made in the third or fourth quarter of the 3rd century BC. All told, the available evidence suggests that the group was made *c.* 250–*c.* 175 BC. Uncertainty also surrounds the place or places of manufacture. Alexandria in Egypt is often mentioned as the most likely origin of these luxury objects, although the many finds from southern Italy suggest the existence of a workshop there.

165. Cast gold-glass, h. 110 mm, diam. 200 mm, from Canosa, Italy, *c.* 275–*c.* 250 BC (London, British Museum)

Two other types of luxury tableware associated with the Canosa group of monochrome vessels are gold-glasses and mosaic glass. Hellenistic gold-glasses are bowls with a layer of gold leaf cut into intricate designs and sandwiched between two layers of colourless glass, which were heated until they fused (see fig. 165). Two fragments of gold-glass were found among the debris from a glass bead-maker's workshop of the 3rd or early 2nd century BC in the city of Rhodes. Mosaic glass was made by assembling large numbers of lengths and slices of preformed multi-coloured canes, fusing them and (probably in a second operation) shaping the resultant 'blank' in or over a mould. The most popular varieties of cane were made either from twisted colourless and white or yellow rods, lengths of which were arranged in a spiral pattern extending from the rim of the vessel to the centre of the floor in a 'lacework' or *reticello* pattern; or from dark blue, green, purple, brown, white and yellow rods, which were put together in such a way that the cross-section has a star-shaped or spiral pattern. In both cases, the rim was made from a spirally twisted bichrome cane. Although the earliest Hellenistic mosaic glass is contemporary with the Canosa group, the technique continued to be used throughout the 2nd century BC, when new varieties (e.g. the 'onyx' pattern of large brown and white cane slices) were introduced.

The production of monochrome bowls increased significantly after *c.* 150 BC. Many of the new products are hemispherical or conical bowls made by sagging preformed, disc-shaped blanks over former moulds. This new technique eliminated the difficulty of filling the entire hollow space in multi-part moulds, and since only one side of the blank came into contact with the mould, it reduced the amount of polishing required to finish the vessel. Large numbers of bowls of this type were found at Tel Anafa, Israel, in contexts datable to *c.* 125–*c.* 80 BC, and on Delos in contexts datable to *c.* 125–*c.* 69 BC. Other, less frequent 2nd–1st-century BC bowls are decorated on the outside with moulded fluting, lathe-cut stripes or petals, or a combination of moulded and lathe-cut ornament.

The most closely dated group of late Hellenistic glass was recovered from the remains of an underwater shipwreck near the island of Antikythera, between Kythera and Crete. Finds from the wreck indicate that the ship foundered shortly after 80 BC. Among its cargo (which included bronze and marble statues; Athens, N. Archaeol. Mus.) were monochrome and polychrome glass vessels. The monochrome glass consists of skyphoi, a bowl decorated with alternating bosses and petals, a bowl with carved sprays of leaves and several other bowls. The polychrome objects are mosaic glass bowls made of slices of composite canes, spirally twisted 'lacework' canes or lengths of canes of various colours. They have distinctive base-rings, formed from trails of mixed colours, which were attached with an adhesive.

(iii) Ptolemaic plaques, canes and bars. In Egypt, the custom of decorating furniture, shrines and other objects with cast, cut and polished inlays of coloured glass (*see* EGYPT, ANCIENT, §XVI, 8) revived not later than the Saite–Persian period (*c.* 570–486 BC). Most of the inlays were monochrome; but by the reign of Ptolemy V (*reg* 205–180 BC) glassworkers were producing polychrome elements made from preformed canes and bars. In some cases, dozens of canes were fused to form bars with designs of astonishing complexity. These bars were reheated, stretched to reduce their thickness, then cut into numerous identical slices. Some of the slices or plaques have traditional Egyptian mythological figures and motifs, while others are decorated with Greek theatrical masks.

BIBLIOGRAPHY

G. D. Weinberg: 'The Glass Vessels from the Antikythera Wreck', *Trans. Amer. Philos. Soc.*, n. s., lv/3 (1965), pp. 30–39

D. B. Harden: 'The Canosa Group of Hellenistic Glasses in the British Museum', *J. Glass Stud.*, x (1968), pp. 21–47

G. D. Weinberg: 'Glass Manufacture in Hellenistic Rhodes', *Archaiol. Deltion*, xxiv (1969), pp. 143–51

G. D. Weinberg: 'Hellenistic Glass from Tel Anafa in Upper Galilee', *J. Glass Stud.*, xii (1970), pp. 17–27

S. M. Goldstein: *Pre-Roman and Early Roman Glass in the Corning Museum of Glass* (Corning, NY, 1979)

D. B. Harden: *Catalogue of Greek and Roman Glass in the British Museum*, i (London, 1981)

J. Letsch, W. Noll and W. Schiering: 'Glasformegung in Tonmatrizen: Eine meisterliche Technologie der Werkstatt des Phidias in Olympia', *Glastech. Ber.*, lvi/4 (1983), pp. 96–105

M. C. McClellan: *Core-formed Glass from Dated Contexts* (Ph.D. diss., Philadelphia, U. PA, 1984)

E. M. Stern: 'Die Kapitelle der Nordhalle des Erechtheions', *Mitt. Dt. Archäol. Inst.: Athen. Abt.*, c (1985), pp. 405–26

D. F. Grose: *The Toledo Museum of Art: Early Ancient Glass* (New York, 1989)

N. Yalouris: 'The Shipwreck of Antikythera: New Evidence of its Date after Supplementary Investigation', *EUMOSIA: Ceramic and Iconographic Studies in Honour of A. Cambitoglou*, ed. J.-P. Descourdes (Sydney, 1990), pp. 135–36

M.-D. Nenna: 'Eléments d'incrustation en verre des nécropoles alexandrines', *Annales du 12e Congrès de l'Association Internationale pour l'Histoire du Verre: Vienne, 1991*, pp. 45–52

G. D. Weinberg: *Glass Vessels in Ancient Greece: Their History Illustrated from the Collection of the National Archaeological Museum, Athens* (Athens, 1992)

M.-D. Nenna: 'La Verrerie d'époque hellénistique à Délos,' *J. Glass Stud.*, xxxv (1993), pp. 11–24

DAVID WHITEHOUSE

6. Ivory and bone.

(i) Seals, reliefs and statuettes. Ivory was imported to Greece from the Near East, and ivory-carvings from Syria and Phoenicia have been found on Samos and Crete and at other ancient Greek sites. The types and styles of early Greek ivory-carvings naturally reflect these oriental prototypes, and seals, which are characteristic Near Eastern artefacts, were among the first figured ivories carved by Greeks. Euboian–Cycladic examples of the late 8th century BC have small crouching lions on their backs and intaglio designs in a Syrianizing stick-figure style on the underside.

In the 7th century BC the production of ivory seals was centred in the Peloponnese. Disc-shaped seals of ivory and bone, with intaglios on both faces, have been found at Sparta, at the Argive Sanctuary of Hera and at Perachora. Seals with animal designs, larger and more numerous than the earlier lion seals, have lions, bulls or rams on their backs. Their prototypes are Phoenician bronze weights in the shape of animals. The most extensive finds of 7th-century BC Greek ivory- and bone-carvings come from the Sanctuary of Artemis Orthia at Sparta. They include rectangular ivory relief plaques, which decorated the backs of bronze fibulae (examples in Athens, N. Archaeol. Mus.). The earliest of these depict a winged goddess holding a bird in each hand. The style is a crude but vigorous Greek imitation of north Syrian ivory reliefs: the oversized heads have large noses, eyes and mouths, and the figures have short, thick proportions. The tendency to constrict figures tightly within a frame also follows Syrian practice. Spartan reliefs from the second half of the 7th century BC are often in the Daidalic style (*see* §IV, 2(i)(c) above), and the subjects include warriors, funerary scenes and mythological subjects. The largest Spartan relief depicts a man leading a woman aboard a warship (Athens, N. Archaeol. Mus., 15362) and may represent the abduction of Helen by Paris or Theseus leaving Crete with Ariadne. Ivory combs from Sparta (Athens, N. Archaeol. Mus.) are adaptations of a Phoenician type of comb that has been found on Samos, at Carthage and in Spain.

An important group of ivories was discovered in 1939 under the Sacred Way at Delphi (Delphi, Archaeol. Mus.). Among these were many small ivory openwork reliefs depicting battle scenes and mythological subjects. The style, which has been variously identified as Spartan, Corinthian or East Greek, suggests a date in the first quarter of the 6th century BC. Subject-matter and technique recall the Chest of Kypselos at Olympia, known from Pausanias' description (*Guide to Greece* V.xvii.5–xix.10).

The earliest Greek ivory statuettes in the round are five nude female figures from a grave near the Dipylon Gate in Athens (*c.* 735–*c.* 720 BC; Athens, N. Archaeol. Mus., 776–9, 2603). The largest of these is 240 mm high. The motif of a standing female nude derives from Syrian representations of Astarte, but the slender bodies and sharp articulation are in late Geometric Greek style. Another early work in the round is the male figure in Assyrian garb flanked by a small lion, found with the openwork reliefs at Delphi and probably datable to the first half of the 7th century BC (h. 240 mm; Delphi, Archaeol. Mus., 9912). This is non-Greek in style: the long curls falling on the chest, the incised eyebrows and eyeholes drilled for inlay are all Near Eastern features, though the abacus of the leaf capital on which the figure stands has a Greek meander. This statuette may have been by a Syrian carver working in Greece. Several small seated and standing figures, mostly of bone, were also found at

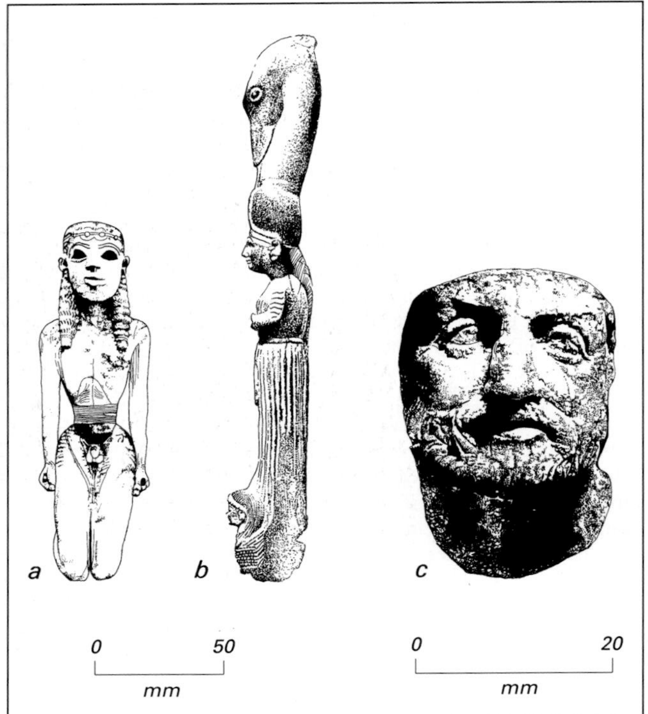

166. Ancient Greek ivory-carvings: (a) kneeling or leaping youth, probably the arm of a lyre, h. 145 mm, from the Sanctuary of Hera, Samos, *c.* 625 BC (Vathy, Archaeological Museum); (b) female figure, possibly the arm of a lyre, h. 225 mm, *c.* 600 BC (Berlin, Antikenmuseum); (c) head, possibly a portrait of *Philip II*, originally forming part of a couch (*kline*), from the Great Tumulus, Vergina, late 4th century BC–early 3rd (Thessaloniki, Archaeological Museum)

Sparta. Ivory-carvings found elsewhere, however, represent the best Peloponnesian workmanship, perhaps Spartan or Corinthian. One is a sphinx from Perachora, with the long face and flattened head typical of the early Daidalic style (h. 80 mm, *c.* 650 BC; Athens, N. Archaeol. Mus., 16519). Another is the figure of a youth found on Samos, his feet tucked under his buttocks as if kneeling or leaping in the air (*c.* 625 BC; Vathy, Archaeol. Mus., E.188; see fig. 166a). This probably formed one arm of a lyre, and it is arguably the most beautifully executed Greek ivory-carving to have survived.

The largest group of free-standing ivory statuettes comes from the Sanctuary of Artemis (Artemision) at Ephesos. Excavations in 1904 uncovered ten female statuettes, two fine lions and a sphinx. Several of the statuettes, among them the famous 'Hawk-priestess' (late 7th century BC; Istanbul, Archaeol. Mus.), have the cylindrical form and wear the *himation* outer garment common to contemporary Ionian marble statues. Later excavations (beginning in 1965) at the Artemision have produced several more ivory statuettes (Selçuk, Ephesos Archaeol. Mus.), which show that the cylindrical Ionian type with foot-length veil had developed by *c.* 600 BC. Two of the figures found in 1904–5, the 'Spinner' and the 'Megabyzos' (Istanbul, Archaeol. Mus., 2594, 2593), have incised eyes and tall round hats that are distinctly oriental in character. A stylistically similar female statuette (*c.* 600 BC; Berlin, Antikenmus.; fig. 166b) is of unknown provenance and may have been part of a lyre. The figure stands on what appears to be a sphinx and has a swan protome on its tall hat. Similar silver and ivory statuettes from a Phrygian tumulus in the Elmalı plain, Turkey, link the markedly oriental figures from Ephesos with the north Syrian, neo-Hittite empire (Antalya, Archaeol. Mus., 11.21.87 (silver), 2.21.87 (ivory)).

(ii) Composite works. Greek figures made partly of ivory and partly of other materials have prototypes in small composite figures from Nimrud and Urartu. An ivory head from Perachora (h. 38 mm, *c.* 700 BC; Athens, N. Archaeol. Mus., 16520) may have been imported from Syria: it is cut flat at the top, back and neck and must have been attached to a figure in another medium, probably wood. A similar head from Corfu (h. 63 mm; Corfu, Archaeol. Mus., MR 710) and one in Ionian style from Samos (h. 43 mm; Vathy, Archaeol. Mus., E.133) show that Greek sculptors had adopted the technique by the mid-6th century BC. These small works were the forerunners of life-size and larger composite figures. Literary sources record composite statues of ivory and ebony by Dipoinos and Skyllis, Cretan sculptors who worked at Sikyon in the 6th century BC, and chryselephantine statues, with ivory flesh and gold drapery, by their Lakonian pupils. The remains of three life-size chryselephantine statues were among the rich finds at Delphi in 1939 (Delphi, Archaeol. Mus.). In addition to heads, hands, arms and feet of ivory, there are gold diadems, gold hair and gold repoussé panels that may have decorated drapery. The style appears to be East Greek of *c.* 550 BC. Smaller heads, hands and feet of ivory, from the same deposit, belonged to smaller composite figures.

In the mid-5th century BC the scale of such works again increased dramatically with Pheidias' colossal chryselephantine statue of *Athena Parthenos* (h. *c.* 12.87 m) in the Parthenon at Athens and his even larger *Zeus* at Olympia (h. *c.* 12.38 m; both destr.). Many other Classical sculptors are known to have made chryselephantine statues, including Polykleitos, Theokosmos, Alkamenes, Kolotes, Naukydes, Leochares and Thrasymedes. The only extant example, however, is an almost life-size head (h. 142 mm) and arm (*c.* 425–*c.* 400 BC; Rome, Vatican, Mus. Gregoriano Profano).

(iii) Furniture. Luxurious furniture decorated with ivory inlays, veneer and reliefs had a long history in the Near East. The reference in the *Odyssey* (XXIII.199–200) to the bed of Odysseus represents the earliest Greek version of this type of work, though the earliest surviving example, from an Athenian grave of *c.* 550–*c.* 520 BC, is a couch (*kline*) with inlaid rosettes, stars and palmettes of ivory, bone and amber (Athens, Kerameikos Mus.). In the 4th century BC, the father of the orator Demosthenes apparently used ivory in the manufacture of couches (Demosthenes: *Against Aphobos* I.30–32), and an idea of such furniture may be gained from the ivory veneer with incised scenes and the ivory openwork inlays that decorated 4th-century BC wooden sarcophagi found in the Kerch peninsula, southern Russia (St Petersburg, Hermitage). Even more opulent furniture has come from Macedonian tombs.

The supposed tomb of Philip II, excavated at Vergina in 1977–8, contained a disintegrated *kline* decorated with ivory carvings (Thessaloniki, Archaeol. Mus.). Fourteen heads as well as hands and feet in high relief belonged to acro-elephantine figures (i.e. with exposed flesh of ivory). Among the heads may be portraits of *Philip II* (see fig. 166c) and *Alexander the Great*. Low reliefs from the same *kline* show a *Seated Muse*, *Dionysos Seated with a Silen* and two herm stelai. The nearby Prince's Tomb contained a similar couch decorated with Dionysiac scenes, including an ivory relief of a nude bearded man, clearly inebriated, supported by a woman and accompanied by Pan. Numerous ivory-carvings, including mythological reliefs, and 21 heads from acro-elephantine figures were found in a Macedonian tomb of the late 3rd or early 2nd century BC at Lefkadia. The Dionysiac imagery of the Macedonian examples continues with the ivory satyr heads that adorned the *fulcra* (head or foot boards) of couches throughout the Hellenistic period.

BIBLIOGRAPHY

D. G. Hogarth: *Excavations at Ephesus: The Archaic Artemisia* (London, 1908)

C. Albizzati: 'Two Ivory Fragments of a Statue of Athena', *J. Hell. Stud.*, xxxvi (1916), pp. 373–402

R. M. Dawkins: *The Sanctuary of Artemis Orthia at Sparta* (London, 1929)

P. Amandry: 'Rapport préliminaire sur les statues chryséléphantines de Delphes', *Bull. Corr. Hell.*, lxiii (1939), pp. 86–119

D. K. Hill: 'Ivory Ornaments of Hellenistic Couches', *Hesperia*, xxxii (1963), pp. 292–300

B. Freyer-Schauenburg: *Elfenbeine aus dem samischen Heraion* (Hamburg, 1966)

E. L. Marangou: *Lakonische Elfenbein- und Beinschnitzereien* (Tübingen, 1969)

M. Andronicos: *Vergina: The Royal Tombs and the Ancient City* (Athens, 1984)

A. Bammer: 'Neue weibliche Statuetten aus dem Artemision von Ephesos', *Jhft. Österreich. Archäol. Inst. Wien*, lvi (1985), pp. 39–58

J. B. Carter: *Greek Ivory-carving in the Orientalizing and Archaic Periods* (New York, 1985)

A. Bammer: 'Gold und Elfenbein von einer neuen Kultbasis in Ephesos', *Jhft. Österreich. Archäol. Inst. Wien*, lviii (1988), pp. 1–23

J. B. Carter: 'The Chests of Periander', *Amer. J. Archaeol.*, xciii (1989), pp. 355–78

JANE BURR CARTER

7. JEWELLERY. Although gold and silver have always been the pre-eminent materials for jewellery, bronze and other materials have also been used. Silver may well have been used to the same extent as gold, but owing to its perishable nature little silver jewellery has survived.

(i) Gold. (ii) Bronze.

(i) Gold. This section discusses gold jewellery of the Greek world after *c.* 1100 BC. For earlier jewellery *see* MINOAN, §IX, 1(i) and HELLADIC, §VIII.

(a) Sub-Mycenaean and Protogeometric (*c.* 1050–*c.* 900 BC). (b) Geometric (*c.* 900–*c.* 700 BC). (c) Archaic (*c.* 700–*c.* 480 BC). (d) Classical (*c.* 480–323 BC). (e) Hellenistic (323–27 BC).

(a) Sub-Mycenaean and Protogeometric (c. 1050–*c.* 900 BC). After the demise of the Minoan–Mycenaean world *c.* 1050 BC jewellery was very scarce for about two centuries. Most surviving Dark Age jewellery is of bronze; the old sources of gold were no longer available, and what little gold jewellery survives was no doubt made from recycled metal won by robbing Bronze Age tombs. The North Cemetery at Knossos in Crete has yielded two gold rosettes for attachment to clothing (London, BM), which follow on from the Minoan tradition. A few hair-spirals of Central European inspiration, made of double gold wire, were found in Athens, dating to *c.* 1050 BC. This meagre repertory has been greatly enriched by the discovery at Lefkandi in Euboia of a burial of a princess (*c.* 950 BC). The items uncovered (all Eretria Mus.) include gold-plated hair-spirals, two gold-plated iron dress-pins, an elaborate gold pectoral and a necklace of gold and faience beads with an exquisite pendant, richly granulated, which had probably been made in Babylonia some 500 years earlier.

*(b) Geometric (*c. *900–*c. *700* BC*).* From *c.* 900 BC contacts with western Asia were resumed, at first tentatively. During the Geometric period goldwork was still comparatively scarce, but jewellery of high quality was produced at certain important centres such as Knossos in Crete, Athens and Corinth. It was more plentiful, though not produced to such a high standard, at Lefkandi in Euboia. It is probable that immigrant goldsmiths from Phoenicia—famed at that time for its craftsmen—settled in these places, set up workshops and taught their trade to local apprentices. Much of this jewellery recalls that of the Mycenaean period, some five centuries earlier, in certain motifs and technical processes (*see* HELLADIC, §VIII, 2). Although the tradition had most certainly been lost in Greek lands, Mycenaean tastes and techniques found their way to the coasts of the Levant, where they were kept alive by the Phoenicians through the Dark Ages and then reintroduced to the Greek world when it was once more in a position to enjoy the luxuries of life.

A Phoenician workshop founded at Knossos in Crete shortly before 800 BC lasted for about a century. Its best products are the earliest, found in a tomb at Tekke, north of Knossos. Of these, two are outstanding: first, a half-moon of rock crystal set in gold, from which hang three crescent-and-disc ornaments inlaid with amber, which is suspended from two delicate gold chains ending in snakes' heads. The second masterpiece consists of a penannular pendant with figures of human heads and geese. Both ornaments are covered with minute granulation (both Herakleion, Archaeol. Mus.).

From a rich lady's grave in Athens (*c.* 850 BC) came a pair of unique earrings richly decorated with patterns in filigree and granulation and with finials in the shape of pomegranates (Athens, Agora Mus.); the work is Phoenician, but the patterns are Greek. More in the Phoenician style are a number of crescent-shaped earrings from the neighbourhood of Athens, decorated with extremely fine granulation and inlay and hung with gold chains (Athens, Agora Mus.).

*(c) Archaic (*c. *700–*c. *480* BC*).* In the 7th century BC the best jewellery came from the Aegean islands, especially Rhodes, Thera and Melos, and the Greek cities of western Asia Minor, Ephesos in particular. The best of the Rhodian jewellery consists of sets of rectangular gold plaques, worn either across the breast or attached to a high headdress (e.g. London, BM; Paris, Louvre). They were embossed by means of stamps, and the best of them were skilfully granulated. Favourite subjects were strongly Oriental and included a sphinx, a goddess with lions, a centaur, 'Astarte

at the window' (a common Phoenician motif of a woman wearing an Egyptian wig, looking over a balustrade out of a window) and a bee-goddess. The typical Rhodian earring was a spiral splayed out to form a letter W, rising higher in the centre; the ends are finished off with horizontal discs, and the apex is masked by an embossed rosette. The type lent itself to elaborate variations; one has griffins' heads, elaborately granulated, on the discs (see fig. 167).

Closely related to the Rhodian tradition is an exquisite class of rosettes made for attachment to diadems of cloth or leather. Most surviving examples were found on the island of Melos, and that is doubtless where they were made (now Athens, N. Archaeol. Mus.). They are decorated with human and animal heads, insects and flowers, in a sort of miniature sculpture, with granulated details of the highest quality.

The jewellery from Ephesos, made in the late 7th century BC and early 6th (now Istanbul, Archaeol. Mus. and London, BM), was mostly found on the site of the Temple of Artemis. The style has much in common with contemporary Rhodian jewellery, but given the Asiatic connections of the Ephesian Artemis, the Oriental element is more pronounced, and certain later motifs are included in the repertory. The earrings are of a boatlike shape of Syrian inspiration and continued to be produced in the Greek world from then on. There are gold beads of many simple shapes, including globular, melon, grain-of-wheat, biconical and segmented. The many gold clothing ornaments with somewhat unusual designs are inspired by Lydian or Phrygian examples. An Oriental tradition was probably also responsible for the numerous pins, fibulae and brooches in gold. The pin-heads, of great elaboration, are in the form of balls, eggs, pomegranates and drums.

167. Electrum griffin earring, h. 58 mm, from Kameiros, Rhodes, *c.* 650 BC (Boston, MA, Museum of Fine Arts)

In the later Archaic period, to judge by the scarcity of surviving examples, gold jewellery was very rare in Greece, although sculptures and vase paintings give plentiful evidence for its use. It may be that the Persians were denying the Greeks the gold they needed. A marble statue of a goddess from Athens (Berlin, Pergamonmus.) wears earrings in the shape of inverted cones and a plain necklace with a pendant to match the earrings. Later in the 6th century BC vase paintings and coins show more elaborate earrings based on the same simple forms. Most of the surviving jewellery of this period comes from the western colonies in South Italy and Sicily, from the Crimea and from marginal areas such as Macedonia and Thrace, where there were most probably skilled craftsmen who had emigrated from the commercial centres of Greece. A collection of gold jewellery from graves at Sindos in Macedonia (*c.* 550–*c.* 450 BC; Thessaloniki, Archaeol. Mus.) represents a Greco-Thracian style and is richly granulated. The women's graves contained earrings, necklaces, pins, fibulae, finger-rings etc, all of very high quality.

*(d) Classical (*c. *480–323* BC*).* After the final defeat of the Persians by the Greeks *c.* 450 BC, gold jewellery in Greece was somewhat less scarce and followed closely the style and technique of the little that remains from the previous period. The workmanship is fine but perhaps rather less fine than in the 7th century BC. In general the sculptural forms of the gold were unadorned, but filigree was used in decorative patterns, and enamel was becoming more popular. Granulation was rarely used; stone or glass inlays were even rarer. Towards the end of the Classical period, however, engraved stones were first used in the bezels of finger-rings.

The forms were very varied. Naturalistic wreaths developed in the 5th century BC and flourished in the 4th. They were worn by both sexes at parties and religious ceremonies, and by the dead. A superb gold oak-wreath comes from the burial of Philip II of Macedonia at Vergina in 336 BC. Diadems continued in many varieties; a magnificent example comes from the female burial in the tomb of Philip II, rich with openwork floral decoration and blue enamel (Thessaloniki, Archaeol. Mus.). Earrings took many forms. Ornamental spirals and embossed studs were common, but the most popular and enduring form was the boat-shape based on the half-moon. In one of the finest surviving examples (London, BM), the boat-shape hangs from a large enamelled rosette. A figure of a siren (a human-headed bird) sits on the boat-shaped element, and from it hang cockle-shell pendants on chains.

Beads and pendants of types already familiar are found in this period, altered to suit the taste of the new age. Elaborate necklaces were also made with interlocking beads, and acorns, buds and human heads were popular as pendants (e.g. London, BM, and Oxford, Ashmolean). Bracelets took the form of spirals or penannular hoops with elaborate finials. Finger-rings are found in several varieties: some engraved as signets, some set with sealstones, some purely decorative in purpose.

(e) Hellenistic (323–27 BC*).* As a result of the conquests of Alexander the Great between 333 and 323 BC, Greece was exposed to influences from Egypt and western Asia. There is a large quantity of material surviving from the Hellenistic period, thanks to the greater availability of gold. For the first time since the Bronze Age, gold was plentiful in Greece, partly because of the intensive mining operations in Thrace initiated by Philip II but mostly from the dissemination of the captured Persian treasures. The general appearance of the jewellery was at first much as before, but by the early 2nd century BC new forms took their place beside the old, and the system of decoration soon changed radically. Then, for about two centuries, there was little further change.

The principal innovations were in new decorative motifs, systems of decoration and forms. The so-called Herakles-knot (the reef-knot) was introduced at the beginning of the Hellenistic period and retained its popularity as an ornament for jewellery into Roman times. It probably came from Egypt, where it was used as an amulet from the beginning of the 2nd millennium BC. The crescent was another foreign import, from western Asia. Of purely Greek motifs, figures of Eros and Nike were among the most popular, as in all Hellenistic art, and were often incorporated into earrings or necklaces.

The most important innovation, which transformed the appearance of Greek jewellery, was the polychromy provided by the inlay of stones and coloured glass. Chalcedonies, cornelians and especially garnets (from India) were in use from 330 BC onwards. From the 2nd and 1st centuries BC are also found emeralds and amethysts from Egypt and small seed-pearls from the Red Sea.

Gold wreaths continued from the previous period in two principal forms. The naturalistic wreaths, too flimsy to have been worn by the living, are frequently found in tombs and must have been made for funerary use. Other, more substantial gold wreaths were probably worn by the living. They consist of a solid framework to which are attached leaves and flowers of sheet gold and berries of stone or glass. Rich filigree and enamel decoration were also used. Elaborate diadems come from rich 3rd- and 2nd-century BC tombs in northern Greece and southern Russia. These consist of a gold strap or a piece of sheet gold, with a centrepiece composed of a Herakles-knot of inlaid garnets set with tiny figures. From this would hang pendants of great complexity, set with quantities of garnets and other stones as in, for example, the diadem from Thessaly (see fig. 168).

Earrings from this period have been found in large quantities. The hoop-earring with animal or human head was introduced *c.* 330 BC from the repertory of Achaemenid Persian jewellery and remained popular in certain regions until the Roman period. In the later examples the hoop was threaded with coloured stones or glass. The wealthier Hellenistic lady might prefer to wear a pendant earring, of which many examples of great complexity have survived. The basic element is an ornamental disc with a hook behind for insertion in the ear. From it would hang an inverted cone or pyramid, a miniature amphora or the winged figure of a male or female deity such as Eros or Nike (examples in London, BM). A special variety of pendant consisted of a bird or other figure of dipped enamel.

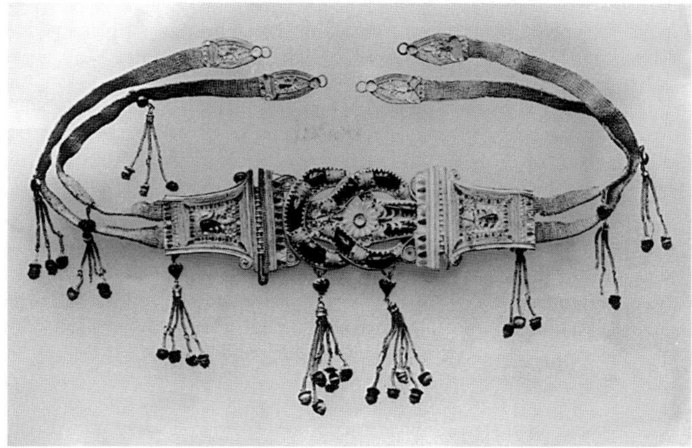

168. Gold diadem inlaid with cornelians and enamel, l. 510 mm, h. of knot 45 mm, from Thessaly, *c.* 2nd century BC (Athens, Benaki Museum)

Necklaces were as common as earrings. A new variety consisted of a strap with pendants of flasks or spearheads (for illustration *see* MACEDONIA (i)); joins were masked with ornamentation in filigree and enamel (e.g. London, BM). Such necklaces are mentioned in temple inventories from Delos of the 3rd century BC. Another popular type of necklace consisted of a chain or a string of beads (often gold-capped garnets) with animal-head finials that match and make a set with the hoop-earrings. Another common type, which was first made in the 2nd century BC and lasted well into the Roman period, was composed of linked bezel-set stones, terminating in animals' heads.

Large medallions, averaging *c.* 100 mm in diameter, were worn by the rich, either on their heads or as pectoral ornaments. They consisted of a central roundel with a bust of a goddess in high relief and a border of ornamental goldwork richly decorated with garnets, filigree, granulation and enamel (examples in Athens, Benaki Mus. and N. Archaeol. Mus.). Three principal varieties of bracelet were in use: animal-headed hoops (as also in the previous period; *see* JEWELLERY, colour pl. I), representations of a coiled snake (e.g. Berlin, Pergamonmus.) and a type consisting of a circlet of gold, often intricately worked, with a central Herakles-knot. Finger-rings were also popular. The gold ring with an engraved circular bezel continued into the 3rd century BC. Later, the typical ring was a plain or ornamental hoop with either a cabochon-cut stone (garnet or amethyst), an engraved stone or, rarely, a cameo. Coiled-snake rings were also worn, probably in combination with the bracelets.

BIBLIOGRAPHY

R. Higgins: *Greek and Roman Jewellery* (London, 1961, rev. 2/1980), pp. 88–172

H. Hoffman and P. F. Davidson: *Greek Gold: Jewellery from the Age of Alexander* (Brooklyn, 1965)

H. W. Catling: 'Knossos, 1978', *Archaeol. Rep.*, xxv (1978–9), pp. 43–58

M. Popham, E. Touloupa and L. H. Sackett: 'The Hero of Lefkandi', *Antiquity*, lvi (1982), pp. 169–74

M. Andronicos: *Vergina: The Royal Tombs and the Ancient City* (Athens, 1984)

B. Deppert-Lippitz: *Griechischer Goldschmuck* (Mainz, 1985)
A. Despini: *Gold Jewellery* (1994), vi of *Greek Art* (Athens, 1994–6)

REYNOLD HIGGINS

(ii) Bronze. Interest in ancient Greek bronze jewellery was aroused at the end of the 19th century by the discovery of vast amounts of small bronze objects in the course of the first systematic excavations at such sanctuaries as those at Olympia, the Argive Heraion, Aigina, Delphi, Ephesos, Lindos and Sparta. This gave rise to various attempts at classification according to function, form and date, including the first comprehensive study of a single type of artefact (Blinkenberg). However, there is still no general survey of Greek bronze jewellery as a whole.

(a) Pins. Morphologically, Greek Geometric pins are quite uniform. The commonest variety derives from the Sub-Mycenaean or Protogeometric type (*c.* 1000–*c.* 900 BC) with globe and disc. The upper part of the shaft above and some way below the globe became square in section, the globe was set off by a moulding on top and bottom, and the disc had a moulded, usually vase-shaped finial. A more elaborate version of this type appeared in the Middle Geometric period (*c.* 850–*c.* 760 BC). It has more than one globe and a long moulded finial above the disc. Oversized pins of this form, sometimes erroneously called spits, occur quite frequently as votive offerings in sanctuaries and occasionally in tombs. Together with numerous variants of this basic type there are a few rarer forms: pins ending with a cross bar (T-pins), a leaf-shaped head, or a conical head and no disc. Most Geometric pins were probably made in the Peloponnese, notably in the Argolid and around Corinth. Examples from Delphi and particularly from excavations at Kalapodi also provide evidence of flourishing local production in central Greece, and a regional Thessalian type of pin is distinguished by the less elegant proportion of the head. A separate class, comprising several types and variants, is the multi-globe pin with a series of superimposed beads, or alternating beads and reels, topped by a small disc (see fig. 169a). These pins were sometimes made in two pieces, with a cast bronze head and an iron shaft, and they are chronologically transitional between the Late Geometric and Early Archaic periods. Their distribution, and no doubt production too, is concentrated in the Peloponnese, with only a few examples from Delphi, Aigina, Ithaka and the Greek colonies in Sicily. In the Archaic period a new treatment of the elements of disc and globe developed, with the head consisting of a rimmed disc with a central projection, separated by heavy fillets from a globe with a smaller globe below it. There is great variety in the globes, which may be plain or melon-shaped and decorated with horizontal grooves or vertical strokes. Instead of the disc, a semicircular or lozenge-shaped loop may be placed on top of the upper globe.

During the Archaic period the Peloponnese remained the leading region of production, though the main types also occur in central Greece, Thessaly, Epiros, northern Macedonia, Sicily and North Africa. Towards the end of the Archaic period a further variety was developed. These pins are small, usually bipartite (with bronze heads and iron shafts) and have floral or animal heads. They occur as late as the 5th century BC. The two-shank pins that also

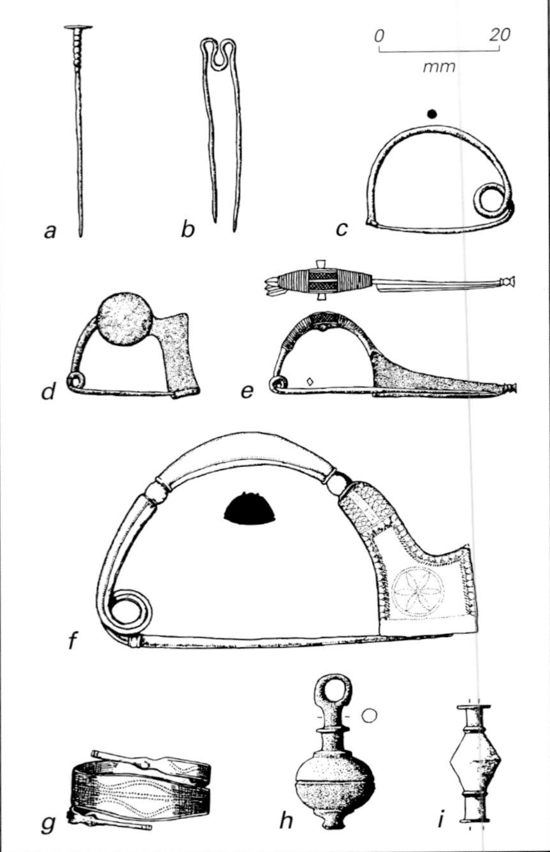

169. Bronze jewellery: (a) multi-globe pin, l. 84 mm, from the Heraion, Argos, *c.* 900–*c.* 700 BC (Athens, National Archaeological Museum); (b) Trebenishte type double-shank pin, l. 78 mm, from Olympia, 6th–5th century BC (Olympia, Archaeological Museum); (c) arched fibula, l. 57 mm, h. 43 mm, from Skoubris tomb 20, Lefkandi, *c.* 1050–*c.* 1000 BC (Eretria, Archaeological Museum); (d) Island-type fibula, l. 51 mm, from Ialysos, *c.* 750–*c.* 650 BC (Rhodes, Archaeological Museum); (e) Epirotic fibula, l. 95 mm, from Pherai, *c.* 700–*c.* 650 BC (Athens, National Archaeological Museum); (f) Attic–Boiotian fibula, l. 146 mm, h. 82 mm, from Skoubris tomb 59, Lefkandi, *c.* 850–*c.* 750 BC (Eretria, Archaeological Museum); (g) bracelet, diam. *c.* 52 mm, from Thebes, *c.* 700–*c.* 650 BC (Athens, National Archaeological Museum); (h) ball pendant, h. 67 mm, from Olynthos, *c.* 600 BC (Thessaloniki, Archaeological Museum); (i) bead, h. 46 mm, from Pherai, *c.* 750–*c.* 600 BC (Volos, Athanassakeion Archaeological Museum)

appeared in the Archaic period were a non-Greek invention: both the Glasinac type, with an upright arc between small lateral loops, and the Trebenishte type with three loops (169b) originated in Bosnia–Hercegovina. Around the mid-7th century BC their distribution ranges from the Balkans to Macedonia, southern Greece and even central Anatolia (Boğazköy). Late examples date from the 4th century BC.

(b) Fibulae. The earliest Greek fibulae date from the Late Bronze Age and are of violin-bow type, soon followed by simple arched fibulae with a plain or twisted bow and

a small catch plate (fig. 169c). The bow of Protogeometric fibulae may have a swelling at the centre or mouldings at the ends, but it was not until Middle Geometric times that the embellishment of the bow with globes, knobs, balls, beads and fillets and the enlargement of the catch plate resulted in many different types and variants.

The main categories (following Blinkenberg) are: Island types with a high, narrow catch plate and a high-stemmed bow consisting of one or more globes (169d); Epirotic types with a long, triangular catch plate and leech-shaped bow (169e); Thessalian types with a long rectangular catch plate and a bow with spherical globes between reels; Helladic types with square catch plate, a high moulded stem and bow with a cushion-shaped or spherical central element; Attic–Boiotian types with square catch plate, high stem and leaf-shaped bow (169f); crescent-shaped fibulae; types from Asia Minor with a T-shaped catch plate and a symmetrical bow; and spectacle fibulae. The distribution of fibulae of the Island types shows that they were produced on such Aegean islands as Rhodes, Paros and Crete. However, while the Thessalian, Helladic and Attic–Boiotian types were certainly produced in their respective regions, their distribution throughout Greece and the regional variations in their execution also suggest local manufacture elsewhere. It is on the engraved catch plates of Attic–Boiotian fibulae that some of the earliest mythological scenes in Greek art occur (see fig. 170). Virtually all the types of fibulae listed above evolved from the simple arched fibulae of Sub-Mycenaean times, but some foreign designs were also adopted. For example, the spectacle fibula was derived from northern precursors, the Epirotic or Navicella type shows Italic influence, and the Asiatic types are related to examples from western Anatolia.

(c) Diadems. From Early Geometric to Archaic times diadems intended exclusively for funerary purposes were made of thin sheet gold. By contrast, the contemporary bronze diadems that occur in female graves and in votive deposits from sanctuaries are usually sturdier and quite suitable for use by the living. Most take the form of simple bands with straight or rounded ends pierced for lacing together, but more elaborate versions have single or double spiral terminals. The decoration is restricted to rows of impressed dots and incised or dot-repoussé zigzags, and there are no figural motifs as on the gold diadems. The distribution of bronze diadems extends from Macedonia to Epiros, central Greece, the Peloponnese and the Ionian islands; evidence from the Aegean islands is still lacking.

(d) Bracelets. Bronze bracelets were never common during Mycenaean and Sub-Mycenaean times, but they occur sporadically in Protogeometric tombs, becoming more frequent in the Late Geometric and Archaic periods. They may be divided into four main classes: a solid hoop with plain terminals, a solid hoop with moulded terminals, flattened bands with moulded terminals and spiral bracelets. The fairly numerous bronze bracelets from the sanctuaries at Olympia and Pherai show that within these main classes there is considerable variety in execution and quality. There are slender wire hoops and heavy cast hoops of different sections; plain bracelets and those with incised

170. Bronze fibula depicting *Herakles Fighting the Moliones*, l. 250 mm, from Boiotia, 8th century BC (Heidelberg, Ruprecht-Karls-Universität, Sammlung Antiker Kleinkunst des Archäologischen Instituts)

or cast decoration; terminals with simple swellings, or globular or biconical bosses, or beads and fillets. The chronology and provenance of most types remain uncertain. The heavy cast bracelets of 7th-century BC date, with hoops of triangular section, thickened rectangular finials and fine incised decoration, are probably of a south Balkan or Macedonian origin. The distribution of the cast or hammered bronze bands with tapering ends, moulded finials and one, two or three coils, and the quality of their incised, sometimes figural, decoration (see fig. 169g above) suggest that they were manufactured in the same central Greek workshops as the arched fibulae of Attic–Boiotian type and belong to the Middle Geometric and Early Archaic periods. Bracelets occur all over the Greek world and range in date from Late Geometric to Hellenistic times. Snake-head bracelets are the most common type, and stylistic differences in the execution of the snake's head imply production in various regional workshops

(e) Rings. Bronze finger-rings with bezels disappear after Sub-Mycenaean times but occur again from the 6th century BC onwards. The simple circlets of Geometric and Archaic rings may be closed or open. They are cast or made of cylindrical wire or a band of sheet bronze, sometimes with incised or impressed decoration. The sections of cast examples vary from triangular to convex. Spiral finger-rings are less common. They consist of two or more coils of wire or sheet bronze, and a special type has spiral or double-spiral terminals. All types occur from the 10th to the 6th century BC and are found in tombs for both female and male burials.

Neck-rings (torques) do not occur in southern Greece. There are examples of 9th–7th-century BC date from Macedonia, Thessaly and Thera, which all take the form of a hoop of twisted bronze with the ends flattened and curled into small spirals.

Bronze earrings do not occur frequently in either tombs or sanctuary deposits. This may be because earrings were more usually made of precious metals, and bronze examples closely resemble types executed in gold, for which they were evidently cheaper substitutes.

(f) Pendants. In contrast to other types of bronze jewellery, especially those used to fasten clothing, the shapes of pendants were not determined by function and so were remarkably diverse. Together with abstract motifs,

such as rings, spoked wheels, discs or balls (see fig. 169h above), there are figures of birds, quadrupeds and humans. Though small and often of poor quality, these figural pendants show stylistic and technical features comparable with larger bronze figurines, especially of birds and horses, and regional workshops seem to have been active in Corinth, Lakonia, Argos, central Greece, Thessaly and Macedonia. Because they often occur in sanctuaries, pendants have been considered purely votive, though there is now clear evidence from excavated tombs that they were also worn as personal ornament. Most pendants date from the Late Geometric and Archaic periods, though in Macedonia simple ball pendants occur in tombs of the 5th century BC.

(g) Beads. Plain biconical bronze beads were first produced in Mycenaean times. More elaborate versions appeared in the Late Geometric period and continued into the 5th century BC. Some distinctive regional types include a biconical body with protruding rims and sharp ridges in Macedonia (see fig. 169i above); a cylindrical body with a sphere at the centre in Thessaly; and a shallow biconical body with a wide opening in southern Greece. Necklaces may consist of up to 20 such beads, sometimes of different kinds, or of only a few beads with one or two pendants. In Archaic times solid-cast beads with droplet-shaped bodies, cylindrical necks and discs with central knobs were common. The punched decoration on solid-cast bronze beads imitates the granulation on beads made of sheet gold, and the necklaces of the 'Berlin Kore' (*c.* 580–*c.* 570 BC; Berlin, Pergamonmus.) and the Acropolis Kore no. 593 (*c.* 580–*c.* 570 BC; Athens, Acropolis Mus.) probably represent beads of this type.

BIBLIOGRAPHY

C. Blinkenberg: *Fibules grecques et orientales* (Copenhagen, 1926)
P. Jacobsthal: *Greek Pins and their Connexions with Europe and Asia* (Oxford, 1956)
J. Alexander: 'The Spectacle Fibulae of Southern Europe', *Amer. J. Archaeol.*, lxix (1965), pp. 7–23
J. Bouzek: 'Die griechisch-geometrischen Bronzevögel', *Eirene*, vi (1967), pp. 115–39
E. Bielefeld: *Schmuck* (1968), ii of *Archaeologia homerica* (Göttingen, 1967–)
J. Boardman: *Greek Gems and Finger Rings: Early Bronze Age to Late Classical* (London, 1970)
K. De Vries: 'Incised Fibulae from Boeotia', *Forsch. & Ber.: Staatl. Mus. Berlin*, xiv (1972), pp. 111–27
I. Blanck: *Studien zum griechischen Halsschmuck der archaischen und klassischen Zeit* (diss., U. Mainz, 1974)
J. Bouzek: 'Die Armringe der Sammlung Bellos aus Theben', *Forsch. & Ber.: Staatl. Mus. Berlin*, xvi (1974), pp. 161–7
K. Kilian: *Fibeln in Thessalien von der mykenischen bis zur archaischen Zeit* (Munich, 1975)
E. Sapouna-Sakellarakis: *Die Fibeln der griechischen Inseln* (Munich, 1978)
I. Kilian-Dirlmeier: *Anhanger in Griechenland von der mykenischen bis zur spätgeometrischen Zeit* (Munich, 1979)
——: 'Bemerkungen zu den Fingerringen mit Spiralenden', *Jb. Röm.-Ger. Zentmus.*, xxvii (1980), pp. 249–69
H. Philipp: *Bronzeschmuck aus Olympia* (1981), xiii of *Olympische Forschungen* (Berlin, 1944–)
R. Vasić: 'Ein Beitrag zu den Doppelnadeln im Balkanraum', *Prähist. Z.*, lvii (1982), pp. 220–57
I. Kilian-Dirlmeier: *Nadeln der frühhelladischen bis archaischen Zeit von der Peloponnes* (Munich, 1984)

IMMA KILIAN-DIRLMEIER

8. LAMPS. Although lamps were used in Greek lands during the Bronze Age and are found on both Minoan and Mycenaean sites, the use of instruments designed for the production of artificial light has not yet been demonstrated for the early Aegean Iron Age. Only in the 7th century BC can lamps, represented by open examples similar to those from the Levant, be recognized, but thereafter terracotta lamps are frequently found on Greek sites throughout the Mediterranean. All early Greek lamps are wheelmade, with added features, such as nozzles and handles (see fig. 171a–f). Most were products of pottery workshops and often exhibit the black glaze found on Greek vases, decoration being largely confined to reserved bands left in the glaze, although appliqué designs and stamped patterns such as palmettes are occasionally found. The earlier wheelmade lamps have open reservoirs for the oil, but by the end of the 5th century BC the oil-chambers were partly enclosed, becoming more so with time. Multi-nozzled lamps, often for use in sanctuaries, were among the more sophisticated examples. The finest products of this period were made in Athens. Candelabra, more elaborate supports for several lights, might be made of metal, wood or marble (*see* CANDELABRUM).

During the 3rd century BC, wheelmade lamps, many of fairly poor quality, continued to be produced, and mould-made lamps were introduced (see fig. 171g–l), surprisingly late when one considers that Greek terracottas had been produced in two-piece moulds from at least the 6th century BC (*see* §IX above). Moulding made possible the easy manufacture of complete lamps in a single process; such lamps might be decorated with relief patterns or given plastic forms. Mould-made lamps were largely the products of specialist workshops. Like their immediate wheelmade predecessors, these Hellenistic mould-made lamps often had wide shoulders, on which bands of relief decoration, normally abstract patterns but occasionally including tiny figures, could be exhibited. The wide dished top, on which a whole scene could be shown, was a Roman invention of the Augustan period (27 BC–AD 14), sometimes reflecting late Hellenistic-type lamps. The Hellenistic shape, with a long nozzle and wide, sloping shoulders, persisted into early Imperial times but thereafter was superseded by the Roman shapes, mostly devised in Italy.

See also ROME, ANCIENT, §X, 6.

BIBLIOGRAPHY

O. Broneer: *Terracotta Lamps* (1930), iv of *Corinth: Results of Excavations Conducted by the American School of Classical Studies at Athens* (Cambridge, MA, and Princeton, 1929–)
R. H. Howland: *Greek Lamps and their Survivals* (1958), iv of *The Athenian Agora* (Princeton, NJ, 1953–)
G. M. A. Richter: *A Handbook of Greek Art* (Oxford, 1959, 9/1987), p. 369
P. Bruneau: *Les Lampes*, Explor. Archéol. Délos (Paris, 1965)
D. M. Bailey: *Greek, Roman and Early Roman Lamps*, i of *Catalogue of the Lamps in the British Museum* (London, 1975)
I. Scheibler: *Griechische Lampen* (1976), xi of *Kerameikos: Ergebnisse der Ausgrabungen* (Berlin, 1939–)
F. Blonde: *Greek Lamps from Thorikos* (Ghent, 1983)

DONALD BAILEY

9. STUCCO. Stucco was employed in both the art and the architecture of ancient Greece, and information about its application and composition is provided by archaeological remains and the accounts of the Roman authors Vitruvius (*On Architecture* VIII.i–iv) and Pliny (*Natural*

171. Greek terracotta lamps: (a) wheelmade lamp, l. 102 mm, from Samos, early 6th century BC; (b) wheelmade lamp, l. 116 mm, from Athens, 5th century BC; (c) wheelmade lamp, l. 105 mm, from Sicily, 5th century BC; (d) wheelmade lamp, l. 143 mm, from Athens, early 4th century BC; (e) wheelmade lamp, l. 130 mm, from Rhodes, 3rd century BC; (f) wheelmade lamp, l. 107 mm, from Knidos, 2nd–1st century BC; (g) mould-made lamp depicting kissing couple, l. 98 mm, from Cyprus, 3rd century BC; (h) mould-made lamp depicting erotes and hounds, l. 117 mm, East Greek origin, 2nd–1st century BC; (i) mould-made lamp with two nozzles and palmette handle, l. 176 mm, East Greek origin, 2nd–1st century BC; (j) mould-made lamp depicting head of a black, l. 113 mm, from Egypt, 1st century BC; (k) mould-made lamp, l. 151 mm, from Ephesos, 1st century BC; (l) mould-made lamp depicting Eros with torch, l. 158 mm, from Egypt, 1st century BC

History XXXVI.liii.174–lv.77; *see also* STUCCO AND PLASTERWORK). Its primary uses were to camouflage coarse stone or rubble masonry and to protect more perishable materials (e.g. wood), for relief decoration, and to form a base for wall painting. The earliest evidence for the use of stucco in the Aegean comes from Vasiliki on Crete, in buildings from the Early Minoan period (*c.* 3500/3000–*c.* 2050 BC). On mainland Greece the first lime stuccos are attested during the Middle Helladic period (*c.* 2050–*c.* 1600 BC) at palatial centres and other sites.

In the Archaic period (*c.* 700–*c.* 480 BC) evidence for the use of stucco comes mainly from temples and public buildings. It was applied to the surface of imperfect or poor-quality stone (especially the local limestones of Attica and the Peloponnese) to produce a white, marble-like appearance. On the Athenian Acropolis, for example, the '"H" Architecture' of porous limestone was coated with a fine layer of stucco to which marble dust had been added, so that when polished it would present an even surface. The existence of decorative stuccowork on Athenian grave monuments in the 6th century BC is implied by the legislation of Solon specifically prohibiting its use (Cicero: *De legibus* II.xxvi.64–5), but no examples have survived. Also from the 6th century BC there is evidence for the use of volcanic pumice from the island of Thera to make waterproof stucco for a basin and drain channel in the Sanctuary of Asklepios at Corinth. A similar mixture of volcanic powder with stucco is seen on monuments from the Classical period, when marble architectural members were coated with stucco as a basis for painting. The interior walls in the Temple of Hephaistos at Athens, for example, were covered with a stucco containing a mixture of volcanic powder and straw as a basis for elaborate wall paintings, which are now known only from ancient descriptions.

In the Hellenistic period stuccowork was found in private establishments as well as sanctuaries. The houses from Delos and Olynthos are among the finest preserved examples of private domestic architecture (*see* §II, 1(i)(c) above) and illustrate the range and technique of decoration. In addition to coating wall surfaces for protection or for painting, stucco was used to imitate such architectural features as panels, stone dado courses, ashlar masonry with drafted edges, and three-dimensional decorative mouldings. One of the more important examples of relief stucco decoration comes from a private Macedonian tomb at Leukadia, dated *c.* 300 BC. Its façade is made completely from stucco applied to stone and moulded to imitate Doric and Ionic elements.

Further artistic uses of stucco are now known only from ancient authors. Pliny (*Natural History* XXXV.xliv.153) recorded that the Sikyonian artist Lysistratos (*fl c.* 350–*c.* 300 BC) was the first to model a likeness in plaster from a living face. This has been understood by some scholars to indicate the beginnings of realistic portraiture in ancient Greece. Pausanias (*Guide to Greece* VIII.xxii.7) saw a temple in the Sanctuary of Artemis at Stymphalos with images of the Stymphalian birds on the roof (probably acroteria), which seemed to be made of either wood or plaster.

BIBLIOGRAPHY

R. Martin: *Matériaux et techniques* (1965), i of *Manuel d'architecture grecque* (Paris, 1965–)

A. Orlandos: *Les matériaux de construction et la technique architecturale des anciens grecs* (Paris, 1966)

P. Petsas: *Ho taphos ton Leukadion* [The grave at Leukadia] (Athens, 1966)

S. Hood: *The Arts in Prehistoric Greece*, Pelican Hist. A. (Harmondsworth, 1978)

NANCY L. KLEIN

10. TEXTILES. Few textiles have survived from ancient Greece. References in literature and evidence from vase painting and sculpture are, however, abundant. Wool was the most commonly used material, because of the plentiful supply of sheep. Linen was also popular but more expensive, because it had to be imported. Greece was not fertile enough for the growing of flax. Silk was also much prized but obtainable only from the East by those who could afford it. Cotton is mentioned by Herodotus in the 5th century BC as an exotic substance growing in India. The standard textile product was a rectangular piece of wool for use as a cloak or blanket, curtain or whatever was required. The weave and thickness of the material varied.

Wool-making was women's work. The wool was first washed and beaten in the courtyard of the Greek home. Then it was taken indoors and straightened into hanks. To do this, women sat on a chair and spread the wool across their knees, which they would protect with a special kind of leg-shield (*epinetron*). A number of these beautifully decorated objects made of terracotta have survived. They were probably often given to young women as wedding presents. For dyeing the wool, many colours were available, obtained from a variety of mineral and vegetable substances. The favourite, a purple dye, was extracted from the murex shellfish found along the shores of the eastern Mediterranean. After dyeing, the wool was spun with a distaff and spindle. The spindle, made of polished wood and *c.* 304 mm long, was weighted with whorls made of clay (these are often found in the excavation of ancient Greek homes).

After spinning, the wool became a fine yarn, suitable for weaving. The Greek loom was upright and made of wood; the warp hung from the crossbar of the loom with the lower end anchored with loom weights. Miniature looms also existed. These produced delicate patterns on small pieces of cloth, for use as borders and veils. The sprang process, involving the manipulation of a set of stretched threads, was widely used for patterned textiles.

BIBLIOGRAPHY

M. G. Houston: *Ancient Greek, Roman and Byzantine Costume and Decoration* (1931/*R* 1966), ii of *A Technical History of Costume* (London, 1920–39)

R. J. Forbes: *Studies in Ancient Technology*, iv (Leiden, 1956)

M. Hoffman: *The Warp-weighted Loom* (Oslo and Bergen, 1964)

G. M. A. Richter: 'The Furnishings of Ancient Greek Houses', *Archaeology*, xviii (1965), pp. 26–32

H. W. Parke: *Festivals of the Athenians* (London, 1977), pp. 38–9

ANNE PEARSON

11. WOOD. Timber was generally in far more plentiful supply in ancient Greece than the fairly treeless nature of much of modern Greece might suggest, and wood was used in many contexts including building construction, boat-building, furniture-making and sculpture. Literary sources record numerous famous objects made of wood, for example the Archaic statue of Athena on the Acropolis, so old it was believed to have fallen from the sky, or the chest in which Kypselos was hidden from the assassins sent to kill him. Poor conditions for preservation, however, have meant that few wooden artefacts survive, and much of what is known about Greek woodworking techniques has been deduced from such secondary sources as the many depictions of furniture in vase paintings (*see* §4 above).

Some notable exceptions include the objects discovered in the region of the BLACK SEA COLONIES or on the site of the Sanctuary of Hera (Heraion) on Samos (*see* SAMOS, §2), where the changing of the river's course resulted in areas of the sanctuary being buried in silt in which wood-destroying bacteria cannot live. Sculptures recovered from the silt were recorded photographically, but most no longer survive. They include a wooden footstool (?8th century BC; see Richter, p. 374, pl. 500), a plaque depicting a man and a woman embracing (possibly representing Zeus and Hera; *c.* 630–600 BC; Boardman, pl. 50) and a goddess (?Hera) wearing a *polos* (*c.* 630 BC; Boardman, pl. 49). The last two pieces are of iconographic interest in the early development of Greek sculpture, but hardly represent wood-carving as a high art form. Large-scale statues constructed as acroliths were evidently quite common: this technique involves making the figure's body out of wood, with only the head or extremities being carved from stone (*see also* §IV, 1(iii)(c) above).

Wood was also extensively used in building work, although again there are few physical remains. Wooden doors are shown in vase paintings and sometimes imitated in other media, for example the marble doors, probably from a heroon erected to Philip II of Macedon (*reg* 359–336 BC) by his son Alexander the Great, which may reproduce features of metal-covered wooden temple doors. While many monumental Greek temples and other buildings remain standing in some form, original roofs do not survive; the exact ways in which large timber members were used in their construction have been much discussed (*see also* §II, 1(ii)(b) above).

BIBLIOGRAPHY

G. M. A. Richter: *A Handbook of Greek Art* (London, 1959, Oxford, 9/1987)

J. Boardman: *Greek Sculpture: The Archaic Period* (London, 1978/*R* 1988)

R. Meiggs: *Trees and Timber in the Mediterranean World* (Oxford, 1986)

□

XI. Collection and display.

1. COLLECTORS, COLLECTIONS AND MUSEUMS.

(i) Introduction. Modern interest in Greek antiquities in Europe dates back to the Middle Ages. The fall of

Constantinople in 1453 and the subsequent dispersal of art works, texts and scholars themselves led to a renewed interest in the Classical world, with profound implications for the art of RENAISSANCE Europe. In 1415, when the popes returned to Rome after the schism, increased building activities in the prospering city led to the discovery of many pieces of ancient sculpture and other antiquities. Many of these works of art were acquired by wealthy individuals, among them noblemen and cardinals, who displayed them next to precious stones, minerals, coins and other curiosities (*see also* CONNOISSEURSHIP, §8). The foundations of today's impressive collections in Rome were laid by the popes, who acquired sculptures for their palaces. In 1506 Julius II (*reg* 1503–13) bought the *Laokoon*, discovered that year; this sculpture was to have a lasting effect on the appreciation of Greek art. Leo X (*reg* 1513–21) added to the papal collections in the Belvedere and in 1515 put RAPHAEL in charge of the sculptures in Rome. In other parts of Europe in the 17th century sovereigns and wealthy individuals also collected antiquities, initially mainly sculpture (the interest in pottery, especially Athenian ceramics, developed later), following a fashion set by the French court of Louis XIV. They were often assisted by professional agents. The increasing demand for objects of ancient art quickly exhausted existing stocks, and excavations were organized to replenish the dwindling supplies. During the century from *c.* 1750 to 1850 many ancient sites were turned over in the hunt for treasures.

(ii) Development of collections after the mid-17th century.

(a) Europe. From the end of the 17th century onwards important private collections increasingly were purchased by European sovereigns. GIOVANNI PIETRO BELLORI had accumulated an impressive number of sculptures and other antiquities. Parts of his collection were acquired by Frederick III, Elector of Brandenburg, with the help of his agent Lorenz Beger (1653–1705), and were the foundation of the Staatliche Museen in Berlin. The rest was bought by Johann Wilhelm von Berger (1665–1751) for the Dresden residence of Frederick-Augustus II, Elector of Saxony (*see* WETTIN, (8)), who also bought the collection of the Prince of Chigi (*c.* 1465–1520) and parts of the collection of Cardinal Albani (*see* ALBANI, (2)) in 1728. Cardinal Albani had organized excavations in the Villa of Hadrian at Tivoli (*see* TIVOLI, §2(iv)). The larger part of the Albani possessions was acquired by Pope Benedict XIII (*reg* 1724–29) and formed the basis for the Museo Capitolino. Pope CLEMENT XIV (*reg* 1769–74) laid the foundations for the Museo Pio Clementino, which was to house the Vatican and the Belvedere Collections. These hold the APOLLO BELVEDERE, the *Apoxyomenos* of Lysippos and the *Apollo Sauroktonos.* PIUS VI (*reg* 1775–1800) continued his work, and the Museo Pio Clementino became the first Roman collection to be opened to the public.

By the end of the 18th century the French government was considering admitting the public to the royal collections; these plans were again considered after the Revolution, and in 1803 the Louvre, which had been filled with the vast booty of Napoleon's Italian campaigns, was finally opened to the public (*see* BONAPARTE, (1)). Today it houses among other masterpieces the VENUS DE MILO and the NIKE OF SAMOTHRACE. From the late 18th century onwards the collections of other European sovereigns, princes and noblemen gradually became more accessible.

With the waning power of European monarchs and aristocrats during the 19th century, many royal collections became state possessions. The Museo Archeologico Nazionale in Naples has its roots in the collections of Charles III, King of Naples (*see* BOURBON, §II(4)), who owned sculptures from the Baths of Caracalla and the Palatine in Rome and who instigated excavations in Herculaneum and Pompeii. In 1822 the collection was moved into the old university building. Among the pieces in the Museo Nazionale are the Farnese *Bull*, found in 1456 in the Baths of Caracalla, Polykleitos' *Doryphoros*, found at Pompeii, and the Alexander Mosaic from the House of the Faun, Pompeii (*see* POMPEII, fig. 7). A more recent museum is the Villa Giulia in Rome, opened in 1955. It contains the Barberini collection, acquired in 1903, the collection of FRANCESCO DE FICORONI, among it the famous Ficoroni Cist purchased in 1912 (*see* ETRUSCAN, fig. 34), and the Castellani collection, bought in 1919. The Hermitage in St Petersburg, which originated in the private court museum of the Tsar, was erected in 1852 to house the imperial collections, to which the public had restricted access. Complete access was given at the end of the 19th century and after the Russian Revolution.

Many private collections were bequeathed or sold to public institutions, and a few formed the core of some of the finest museums in the world. The oldest public museum in Europe is the Ashmolean Museum, Oxford. John TRADESCANT, who published his accumulated antiquities in 1656 in *Musaeum Tradescantianum*, bequeathed his collection to another collector of his day, ELIAS ASHMOLE, who in turn made a gift of his collection—now enlarged—to the University of Oxford, on condition that it would be housed in a building of its own, the old Ashmolean Museum. A third collection that found its way into the Ashmolean was that of Thomas Howard, Earl of Arundel (*see* HOWARD (i), (1)), who discovered his love for antiquities on extensive journeys through Italy. He organized excavations in Rome and acquired other pieces, and after his return to England he employed agents to purchase antiquities all over Europe. In Smyrna (now Izmir) he bought the first Greek inscriptions to reach Britain. Sir HANS SLOANE, a doctor, collected Egyptian, Greek and Roman antiquities. On his death they were acquired by Parliament and formed the core of the British Museum. Sir William Hamilton (*see* HAMILTON, WILLIAM (i)) was the first to accumulate a great number of Greek vases. In 1772 he sold them to the British Museum, where they became the core of its collection of Greek pottery, soon added to by the purchase of Thomas Hope's vases in 1801 (*see* HOPE, (1)).

From the second half of the 19th century onwards the removal of antiquities from their places of origin was increasingly restricted. In some cases, however, where German, English or other archaeological institutions conducted excavations abroad, deals were struck that allowed the excavators to remove a percentage of the objects found to their own countries. In 1878 the German Institute of Archaeology began systematic excavations of PERGAMON in Turkey. Under the original contract they were allowed to keep one third of the finds, then two thirds. In the end the remaining third, which belonged to the Turkish government, was offered to the Germans as well. Thus the Altar of Zeus (the Great Altar) of Pergamon found its way into the Pergamonmuseum in Berlin. Around the same time, in 1875, German archaeologists began to excavate the site of OLYMPIA on the Peloponnese. They discovered among many other objects the architectural sculptures of the Temple of Zeus and a statue of *Hermes Holding the Infant Dionysos*, attributed to PRAXITELES, found in 1877 in the Temple of Hera. The finds were not shipped abroad but were housed in a museum in Olympia, built in 1886. The site museum at Delphi, built in 1902, houses the finds of the Ecole Française d'Athènes which started excavations in DELPHI in 1892. Other Greek collections, for example the National Archaeological Museum and the Acropolis Museum in Athens, are even older. From 1864 to 1874 the Acropolis Museum was erected to protect the votive offerings found on the Acropolis (*see* ATHENS, §II, 1(ii)), numerous statues, among them the *Kritios Boy* (see fig. 55 above), vases and bronzes. Funds for the building of the National Archaeological Museum in Athens were provided by Demetrios Bernardakis in 1866; it was completed in 1889. It houses the finds from Athens and surrounding areas, for example from the Temple of Hephaistos, the Varvakeion and the Stoa of Hadrian.

(b) USA. The American tradition of collecting is much more recent than that of Europe and different in nature. The American state did not have to take over the management of former royal collections, nor did it become involved in the organization of museums to the same degree. Some of the finest American museums are therefore private trusts. As in Europe, however, they often originate from the personal collections of private individuals, and the economic power of the New World soon made up for its relatively late entry into the world of collecting antiquities.

One of the most famous museums is the J. Paul Getty Museum in Malibu. J. PAUL GETTY started collecting antiquities in the 1930s. In 1950 a trust was created to look after his collection, which was opened to the public in 1954. In 1970 it moved into a building that replicates the Villa dei Papyri in Herculaneum. Among its famous exhibits is the Lansdown *Herakles.*

The Metropolitan Museum of Art in New York had until 1905 only few ancient pieces of importance, such as an Etruscan bronze chariot and frescoes from Boscotrecase. Bequests by private collectors and generous gifts, especially the Fletcher and Rogers funds, enabled the museum to acquire important objects. Among its exhibits are one of the most famous Greek vases, a kalyx krater signed by the painter Euphronios and the potter Euxitheos (New York, Met., 1972.11.10) with a rare scene from the Trojan War, *The Rescue of the Body of Sarpedon*; another well-known piece is the so-called New York Kouros.

The Museum of Fine Arts in Boston has its roots in the Library of the Anthology Society, which was instituted in 1805, and the Athenaeum. In 1827 it organized its first loan exhibition. Later, with the help of gifts and acquisitions, it assembled a collection of its own. In 1869 the Athenaeum received a collection of arms and funds for a room to exhibit them and purchased a collection of plaster casts. In 1871 a committee was founded to manage the collections and organize the display. The museum was opened in 1879 and had to be enlarged already by 1890.

2. EXHIBITIONS. Although there were earlier displays of Classical antiquities, a history of modern exhibitions may begin with the ELGIN MARBLES, the sculpted metopes, frieze and pedimental sculpture of the Parthenon, now in the British Museum. THOMAS BRUCE, 7th Earl of Elgin, became British ambassador to Turkey in 1799. He employed artists to record works of art, especially in Athens, then under Turkish rule. In 1801, after the Battle of Aboukir, the Turkish government, an ally in the war against Napoleon, gave Elgin greater access to the Athenian monuments. Elgin decided to transport the sculptures of the Parthenon to Britain. Shipments started in 1803, and the last transport reached England in 1812. There they went on exhibition in 1816 and were purchased for the British Museum by an Act of Parliament for £35,000 in 1816.

Since the 1960s exhibitions have increased enormously in number, not least because of improved methods of transport. They are considered by some to raise the profile of a museum and to attract visitors, but others regard them as costly detractions from the real task of museums—the preservation, publication and display of their own objects—and as a nuisance when the best exhibits of some collections are not accessible because they are lent to an exhibition. Often they are an additional source of income for institutions increasingly short of money. Sponsors are sought to assist in the not inconsiderable costs of display, insurance and publication, and in some cases sponsors have taken over the organization and design completely. In many respects taste has varied little. Gold, unique finds and the sensational contents of rich tombs still attract vast crowds, for example the RIACE BRONZES (see 1981 cat.), Thracian treasure from Bulgaria (see 1976 exh. cat.) and a splendid travelling exhibition of Tarentine goldwork (1984–89). Other exhibitions seem to be increasingly scholarly in focus. Some displays are designed to publicize collections of types of objects from certain areas, often including private collections, for example *Vase Painting in New England Collections* (Harvard, 1972), *Greek Vase Painting in Midwestern Collections* (Chicago, 1979–80) or *Gesichter, griechische und römische Bildnisse aus Schweizer Besitz* (Berne, 1982–83), or finds from a given area, for example *Veder greco* (Agrigento, 1988), an exhibition of objects found in and around Agrigento. In 1983–4 a cross-section of the Vatican collections was exhibited in New York, Chicago and San Francisco. Other exhibitions assemble material information about a particular era or artist, as in exhibitions devoted to single vase painters—*The Amasis Painter and his World* (see 1985–6 exh. cat.) and *Euphronios* (see 1990–91 exh. cat.)—or sculptors, for example *Polyklet: Der Bildhauer der griechischen Klassik* (Frankfurt am Main, 1990–91).

BIBLIOGRAPHY

F. Koepp: *Geschichte der Archäologie: Handbuch der Archäologie I* (Munich, 1939)
J. Evans: *A History of the Society of Antiquaries* (Oxford, 1956)
E. J. Sandys: *A History of Classical Scholarship* (New York, 1958)
G. Daniel: *A Hundred and Fifty Years of Archaeology* (London, 1975)
H. Lattimore and others: *J. Paul Getty Museum: Greek and Roman Antiquities* (London, 1975)
Thracian Treasure of Bulgaria (exh. cat. by I. Venedikov, London, BM, 1976)
L. Berge and W. G. Moon, eds: *Greek Vase Painting in Midwestern Collections* (Chicago, 1979)
H. Beck and others, eds: *Antikensammlungen im 18. Jahrhundert* (Berlin, 1981)
F. Haskell and N. Penny: *Taste and the Antique: The Lure of Classical Sculpture, 1500–1900* (London, 1981)
G. Forti and C. Sabbione: *I bronzi di Riace*, Novara, Inst. Geog. De Agostini cat. (Novara, 1981)
I bronzi di Riace: La Calabria fra leggenda e storia (Rome, 1981)
A. MacGregor: *Tredescant's Rarities: Essays on the Foundation of the Ashmolean Museum, 1683* (Oxford, 1983)
Gesichter, griechische und romische Bildnisse aus Schweizer Besitz (exh. cat., ed. H. Jucker and D. Willers; Berne, Hist. Mus., 1982–3)
Der Archäologe, Graphische Bildnisse aus dem Porträtarchiv Diepenbroich (Münster, 1983)
The Vatican Collections, the Papacy and Art (exh. cat. by H. N. Abrams, New York, Met.; Chicago, IL, A. Inst.; San Francisco, CA, F.A. Museums; 1983–4)
B. F. Cook: *The Elgin Marbles* (London, 1984/*R* 1993)
The Amasis Painter and his World: Vase Painting in 6th-century Athens (exh. cat. by D. von Bohmer, New York, Met.; Toledo, OH, Mus. A.; Los Angeles, CA, Co. Mus. A.; 1985–6)
Veder greco, le necropoli di Agrigento (exh. cat. by L. Franchi dell'Orto and R. Franchi, Agrigento, Mus. Civ., 1988)
E. Formigli and W.-D. Heilmeyer: *Tarentiner Goldschmuck in Berlin*, Winckelmannsprogram der archäologischen Gesellenschaft in Berlin, 130/131 (Berlin, 1990)
Euphronios: Peintre à Athènes au VIe siècle avant J.C. (exh. cat., Arezzo, Museo Archeologico Nazionale; Paris, Louvre; Berlin, Staatl. Museen Preuss. Kultbes.; Berlin, Antikenmus.; 1990–91)
Polyklet: Der Bildhauer der griechischen Klassik (exh. cat., ed. H. Beck, P. C. Bol and M. Bückling; Frankfurt am Main, Liebieghaus, 1990–91)
A. Pasquier: *The Louvre: Greek, Roman and Etruscan Antiquities* (London, 1991)

THOMAS MANNACK

Greef, Jan de (*b* Dordrecht, 2 July 1784: *d* Amsterdam, 2 Dec 1835). Dutch architect. He trained in Dordrecht with the marine painter Martinus Schouman (1770–1848) and the architect and carpenter Jacobus van Dalen before receiving a grant to study in Rome and Paris. In Paris de Greef met Charles Percier and was subsequently influenced by the Empire Style. In 1810 he returned to the Netherlands, where he was appointed supervisor of the Marine buildings in Rotterdam and shortly afterwards was appointed to the Water Board (established 1811). After the founding of the Kingdom of the Netherlands (1813), de Greef became architect of the Royal Palaces. In this capacity with the architect Zeger Reyers he rebuilt the Paleis Soestdijk (completed 1821). He extended the royal pleasure palace with two quadrant galleries and pavilions, both in Neo-classical style. He was also given the commission to complete the rebuilding of the Paleis Noordeinde in The Hague, which had been started (1814) by Barthold W. H. Ziesenis. De Greef's work includes the ballroom, the dining-room and the rear vestibule, which are rare Dutch examples of Empire Style.

While working on the royal palaces, de Greef was appointed (1818) professor of 'architecture and draughtsmanship' at the School of Artillery and Military Engineering in Delft. In 1820 he became director of city works and public buildings in Amsterdam, where building activities after the Napoleonic period had a slow and difficult start due to the economic recession. His first important work was the rebuilding (1823–6; with Tieleman Frans Suys) of the round 17th-century Nieuwe Luthersekerk on the Singel, which had burnt down in 1822. From 1825 to 1829 the 17th-century classical Almshouses on the Prinsengracht were rebuilt to his designs, with a soberly and severely classical façade. He enlarged the Entrepotdok on the Kadijksplein with a new main building (1827–30), also in a classical style.

In 1825 de Greef became a member of the certificate committee of the fourth class of the Royal Institute of Science, Literature and the Fine Arts in Amsterdam. The Institute's fourth class was concerned with arts policy, and as the only architect on the certificate committee, de Greef held a key position in the teaching of draughtsmanship and especially architectural drawing in the second quarter of the 19th century. From 1817 one was only allowed to teach draughtsmanship if one possessed a certificate as proof of competence in that field. It was due to de Greef that many important Dutch architects, such as J. F. Metzelaar and L. H. Eberson, were given qualifications to teach draughtsmanship. His son Ben de Greef (1818–98) also became city architect of Amsterdam.

BIBLIOGRAPHY

'De "Maatschappij tot aanmoediging der bouwkunde" en de toestand der bouwkunst in den aanvang der 19e eeuw' [The 'society for the encouragement of architecture' and the situation in architecture at the beginning of the 19th century], *Bouwknd. Tijdschr.*, xii (1892), p. 4
R. C. Hekker: 'De Nederlandse bouwkunst in het begin van de negentiende eeuw' [Dutch architecture at the beginning of the nineteenth century], *Kon. Ned. Oudhdknd. Bond: Bull. KNOB*, 1 (1951), pp. 1–29
H. J. F. Roy van Zuydenwijn: *Amsterdamse bouwkunst, 1815–1940* (Amsterdam, 1970), pp. 14–15
J. Immerzeel jr: *Levens en werken der Hollandsche en Vlaamsche beeldhouwers, graveurs en bouwmeesters* [Life and works of Dutch and Flemish sculptors, engravers and architects] (Amsterdam, 1974), p. 293
E. B. M. Lottman: 'Het Koninklijk Besluit van 13 April 1817 en de getuigschriften van bekwaamheid tot het geven van (bouwkundig) tekenonderwijs' [The Royal Decree of 13 April 1817 and the certificates of competence for teaching (architectural) draughtsmanship], *Kon. Ned. Oudhdknd. Bond: Bull. KNOB*, lxxxv (1986), pp. 3–20

DIANNE TIMMERMAN, FRANK VAN DEN HOEK

Greek key design. *See* MEANDER.

Greek Revival. Term used to describe a style inspired by the architecture of Classical Greece that was popular throughout Europe and the USA in the early 19th century, especially for the design of public buildings; it was also employed for furniture and interior design. Its gradual spread coincided with and was dependent on the growth of archaeology in Greece in the 18th and 19th centuries. Such archaeologist–architects as James Stuart (known as 'Athenian' Stuart in his lifetime) and Nicholas Revett, William Wilkins and C. R. Cockerell in England, Jacques-Ignace Hittorff and Henri Labrouste in France and Leo von Klenze in Germany were responsible for generating a remarkably self-conscious architectural revival; Cockerell used the term 'Greek revival' at least as early as 1842 in his lectures delivered as Professor of Architecture at the Royal Academy. The style was first used in mid-18th-century England for garden buildings in such houses as

Hagley Hall (Hereford & Worcs) and Shugborough (Staffs) by James Stuart. It later came to be seen as the most appropriate architectural style for the expression of civic virtues, and it was widely adopted for new urban-planning schemes and important public buildings during the first half of the 19th century.

1. Origins and development in France and England (*c.* 1670–*c.* 1800). 2. Early development in Germany (*c.* 1750–1800). 3. An international expression of public order (*c.* 1800–*c.* 1850). 4. The implications of polychromy (*c.* 1825–50). 5. After *c.* 1850.

1. ORIGINS AND DEVELOPMENT IN FRANCE AND ENGLAND (*c.* 1670–*c.* 1800). It is extraordinary that although theorists from the Renaissance onwards paid lip-service to the merits of Classical Greek architecture, no-one investigated surviving Greek buildings until the late 17th century, when a group of Frenchmen began to seek a new basis for French classicism. In 1674 the Marquis de Nointel, a French diplomat, explored Athens and several of the Greek islands. His party included the artist JACQUES CARREY who, in a series of not very alluring drawings (Paris, Bib. N.), was the first to record the sculptures of the Parthenon. Nointel sent back to France some notes by the Jesuit missionary J.-P. Babin, and these inspired Dr Jacob Spon, a French Classical scholar, to travel to Greece, financed by Jean-Baptiste Colbert, Louis XIV's chief adviser. He was accompanied by the English botanist George Wheler. On their return Spon published *Voyage d'Italie, de Dalmatie, de Grèce et du Levant* (1678), an influential work that remained for nearly 70 years the best account of the buildings of Athens, although it contained only one engraving of the Parthenon; despite its poor quality, this revealed the fluted Greek Doric column as heavy and baseless, attributes that seemed primitive to those accustomed only to the more elaborate Roman Doric. Wheler's *Journey into Greece* (London, 1682), dedicated to Charles II of England, gave further publicity to Spon's engraving of the Parthenon.

The next important development was the publication of drawings of some of the monuments of Athens in Richard Pococke's *Description of the East and Some Other Countries* (1743–5) and Richard Dalton's *Antiquities and Views in Greece and Egypt* (1751). The initiative then passed to England, where it was to remain for a century thanks largely to the SOCIETY OF DILETTANTI. Founded by a group of noblemen and gentlemen in 1732, this society institutionalized the obsession with the Antique that had previously been a private concern of Richard Boyle, 3rd Earl of Burlington, and his circle. In extending the Grand Tour from the familiar Italy to the unknown Greece, the wealthy members of the Society of Dilettanti were inspired by what they called 'Greek taste and Roman spirit'. By promoting and subsidizing the excavation and publication of numerous Classical sites, they made a profound architectural and archaeological impact on Europe. The most celebrated of the projects with which they were associated was the publication of *The Antiquities of Athens* by JAMES STUART and NICHOLAS REVETT, the first volume of which appeared in 1762; this publication and the *Ruines des plus beaux monuments de la Grèce* (1758) by JULIEN-DAVID LE ROY were the first attempts to provide full and accurate surveys of ancient Greek architecture.

When Stuart returned to London in 1755 from Athens, where he had spent four years measuring the Classical remains, he was much patronized by members of the Society of Dilettanti anxious to demonstrate their knowledge of the latest antique discoveries. As an architect, however, Stuart was essentially a miniaturist who excelled in the design of garden buildings, furniture and interior decoration. His chief contribution to the development of the Greek Revival style was to provide a decorative language based on the ornamental detailing of such Athenian buildings as the late 4th-century BC choregic monument of Lysikrates (see fig. 1) and the Erechtheion. Nevertheless, the Greek Doric portico with which he fronted a little temple (1758) in the park at Hagley Hall for George Lyttelton (1709–73), later 1st Earl of Lyttelton, set a pattern for countless Greek Revival buildings in which a simple box was lent spurious grandeur by an applied portico.

Architects who responded in the 1780s and 1790s with more vigour than Stuart to the expressive potential of Greek Doric included Joseph Bonomi, John Soane and Benjamin Henry Latrobe. Buildings inspired by the 'sublime' power of the primitive Doric found at Paestum (Poseidonia), South Italy, especially as captured in Piranesi's atmospheric engravings published in 1778, are Bonomi's church (1789–90) at Great Packington, Warwicks; Latrobe's Hammerwood Lodge (begun before 1792), East Grinstead, Sussex; and Soane's vestibules at Tyringham Hall (*c.* 1793), Bucks, and at Bentley Priory (1798), Stanmore, Middx. Similar buildings in Paris include Charles de Wailly's crypt at the church of St Leu-St Gilles (1773–80) and Claude-Nicholas Ledoux's Barrière des Bonshommes (1785–9). Such buildings were a rarity at the time, especially in France, where, inspired by the doctrines of Marc-Antoine Laugier, architects were more interested in understanding the supposed principles of Greek architecture than in imitating its accidental appearance.

2. EARLY DEVELOPMENT IN GERMANY (*c.* 1750–1800). German scholars and architects, after those of France and England, made the greatest contribution to the nascent Greek Revival style. Over them all towered the figure of JOHANN JOACHIM WINCKELMANN, whose books, beginning with *Gedanken über die Nachahmung der griechischen Werke in der Malerei und Bildhauerkunst* (1755), were important not only for promoting Greek art as an expression of 'noble simplicity and quiet grandeur' but also as the product of ideal men leading an ideal way of life. Ludicrously, Winckelmann had not even visited Rome, still less Athens, when he wrote his *Gedanken.* Although widely influential, his vision of Greek culture was charged by an obsession with the perfect male body and was expressed aesthetically in terms of his favourite artist, Raphael. Responding enthusiastically to the recent discovery of the primitive Doric temples of Sicily, he wrote in 1762 in *Anmerkungen über die Baukunst der Alten Tempel zu Girgenti in Sicilien*, his account of the temples at Akragas (Agrigento), that 'as elegance is added to architecture, beauty declines'.

Winckelmann's impact on architecture was evident in Germany as early as 1788–91 in the Brandenburg Gate, Berlin (*see* BERLIN, fig. 2). One of the earliest monuments

1. *Choregic Monument of Lysikrates*; from J. Stuart and N. Revett: *The Antiquities of Athens*, i (London, 1762), pl. I

of the Greek Revival in Europe, this was designed by Carl Gotthard Langhans, who modelled it on the Propylaia in Athens, or rather on Le Roy's ideal reconstruction of the building in his *Ruines*. The Brandenburg Gate was seen as embodying the heroic ideals with which Greek art was becoming identified in the German Romantic imagination. Langhans, moreover, was one of a number of German architects and artists whom Frederick William II, King of Prussia, had summoned to Berlin in 1787 in an attempt to turn a capital that had long been influenced culturally by France into a centre of German culture.

In 1796 the tenth anniversary of the death of Frederick the Great of Prussia prompted the Akademie in Berlin to announce a competition for a monument to his memory that would specifically promote 'morality and patriotism'. Greek Doric seemed the natural language with which to express this stern idealism, and the young architect Friedrich Gilly produced a design in 1797 that captivated the imaginations of Schinkel and Klenze, the leading German architects of the next generation. Gilly's unexecuted temple, intended to be raised high above its solemn precinct in the Leipziger Platz in Berlin, proclaimed a devotion to moral endeavour that, although deeply rooted in the Prussian national consciousness, had a timeless quality that was part of the appeal of Greek Doric (for illustration *see* GILLY, (2)).

3. AN INTERNATIONAL EXPRESSION OF PUBLIC ORDER (*c.* 1800–*c.* 1850). One of the first to develop the monumental manner that, implicit in the Brandenburg Gate, came to characterize the Greek Revival at its height was the English architect Thomas Harrison. He did so in his partially executed projects for Chester Castle (1788–1815), a combination of law courts, prison and barracks. His designs echoed the daunting scale of French Grand Prix designs, but they were handled with a new Greek austerity of detail. Working far from London, Harrison exercised little influence, however; instead it was William Wilkins, an architect of lesser ability but wider contacts, who, in the face of much professional controversy, produced the archetypal building of the early Greek Revival: Downing College (1804/5–22), Cambridge. This was a commission for which Wilkins was largely indebted to the connoisseur Thomas Hope, who combined first-hand knowledge of Greek architecture with enthusiasm for the doctrines of Marc-Antoine Laugier.

Wilkins was an archaeologist of some distinction who in 1807 published an important study of the monuments of the Greek world. The ambitious Greek Doric entrance gateway in the form of the Propylaia in Athens that he planned for Downing College was unfortunately never executed. All that was built were two long, low ranges in an architecturally subdued style characterized by plain wall surfaces, innocent of decorative pilasters and relieved only by chastely detailed porticos in the Erechtheion Ionic order (for illustration *see* WILKINS, WILLIAM). This understated sobriety, partly due to Laugier's rationalist influence, reappears in countless Greek Revival buildings, including

2. William Wilkins: east portico of Grange Park, Northington, Hampshire, *c.* 1808–9

3. Leo von Klenze: interior of the Walhalla, near Regensburg, 1830–42

Robert Smirke's Theatre Royal, Covent Garden (1808–9; destr. 1856; *see* SMIRKE, (2), fig. 1), General Post Office (1824–9; destr. 1912) and British Museum (1823–48; *see* ENGLAND, fig. 8), and Wilkins's University College (1826–30) and National Gallery (1832–8), all in London. A somewhat livelier design was developed for Grange Park (*c.* 1808–9; see fig. 2), the templar house that Wilkins built for the eccentric banker Henry Drummond. With its colossal portico modelled on the Hephaisteion (then known as the Theseion) and side elevations inspired by the choregic monument of Thrasyllus, both in Athens, this is probably the most grandiose if least convenient residence produced by a Greek Revival architect.

Early Greek Revival buildings in Scotland included William Stark's Glasgow Justiciary Court House (1809–11), while Edinburgh took to the style with such enthusiasm that, thanks to such talented local architects as THOMAS HAMILTON and William Henry Playfair (*see* PLAYFAIR, (2)), it became known as the 'Athens of the North'. Hamilton designed the Burns Monument (1820–23) and the Royal High School (1825–9), while Playfair provided the Royal Institution (now the Royal Scottish Academy; 1822–6 and 1832–5) and, with C. R. Cockerell, the National Monument (1824–9), a version of the Parthenon crowning Calton Hill that was left unfinished. A similar transformation occurred in Berlin during this period (*see* BERLIN, §I, 3): following its humiliating occupation by Napoleon from 1806 to 1813, the city was revitalized by KARL FRIEDRICH SCHINKEL with a new royal guardhouse (Neue Wache; 1816–18), theatre and museum (1823–30; now the Altes Museum; *see* GERMANY, fig. 9). These buildings were among the most imaginative monuments of the Greek Revival anywhere in Europe. In the Neue Wache (*see* BERLIN, fig. 3), which was influenced by Gilly, the Greek Doric order was used to symbolize the function of a public building dedicated to safe-guarding social order exactly as in Ledoux's Barrières and Salines de Chaux. Klenze left a similar impression on the city of Munich, where, with the active support of his patron, Ludwig I, King of Bavaria, he provided the Glyptothek (1816–30; *see* KLENZE, LEO VON, fig. 1) and two Greek Doric buildings, the Ruhmeshalle (1843) and Propyläen (1854–62). Klenze's Walhalla (1830–42; see fig. 3) is an imposing Greek Doric shrine for busts of great Germans; built above the Danube near Regensburg in Bavaria, it was inspired by Gilly's unexecuted monument to *Frederick the Great*.

The Greek Revival was enthusiastically adopted throughout Europe and the USA by architects who were anxious to express a growing sense of national identity. The forms of Greek architecture, unused from the ancient world to the 18th century, were free of all association with the aristocratically and ecclesiastically organized institutions of Europe before 1789. Nowhere was this freedom more appreciated than in the USA after the signing of the Declaration of Independence in 1776 and the close of the revolutionary war seven years later. The Greek Revival in the USA began in earnest with the Bank of Pennsylvania (1799–1801), built by BENJAMIN HENRY LATROBE in Philadelphia, the capital of the nation from 1790 to 1800. This austere Greek Ionic temple of commerce was effective as a durable symbol of the wealth and probity of the new democrats. At the Capitol in Washington, DC (*see* WASHINGTON, DC, fig. 5), Latrobe provided further poetic statements of the power of Greek architecture to express the freshness and gravity of the American experiment. As a result, Thomas Jefferson himself wrote to Latrobe in July 1812 (Washington, DC, Lib. Congr.) that the Capitol was 'the first temple dedicated to the sovereignty of the people, embellishing with Athenian taste the course of a nation looking far beyond the range of Athenian destinies'. Jefferson must have had in mind such interiors by Latrobe as the House of Representatives (completed 1811), with 24 columns inspired by those of the choregic monument of Lysikrates, and the Supreme Court Chamber (1809; rebuilt 1815–17; see fig. 4), where primitive Greek Doric columns support a trio of arches beneath a half umbrella-dome, a haunting disposition recalling the dreams of Ledoux, Soane and Gilly.

Although there were numerous skilled architects ready to follow Latrobe's path, especially his pupils Robert Mills and William Strickland, and Strickland's pupil Gideon Shryock, none had quite his ability. This resulted in the first half of the 19th century in an astonishing number of competent Greek Revival buildings expressing high ideals of civic order, which were supposedly in conformity with those of Athens in the 5th century BC. Mills made his name with the Washington Monument at Baltimore, MD (1813–42; *see* MILLS, ROBERT, fig. 2), an unfluted Greek Doric column of tremendous height. The most characteristic examples of the new style are the government buildings in Washington, DC, which include the Federal Treasury and Patent Office (both begun 1836) and Old Post Office (1839–42) by Mills. Scarcely less imposing was Strickland's contribution to Philadelphia, where his Second Bank of the United States (1818–24), built in marble, echoes the Parthenon, and his Philadelphia (or Merchants') Exchange (1832–4) boasts an elegant semicircular colonnade surmounted by a lantern based on the choregic monument of Lysikrates. A later work, the Tennessee State Capitol (1845–59), Nashville, had isolated picturesque elements hinting at the subsequent development of Greek Revival forms (*see* STRICKLAND, WILLIAM, fig. 2). Greek Revival was also widely popular for domestic architecture in the USA, as can be seen, for example, in Andalusia, a house near Philadelphia remodelled in 1831 for Nicholas Biddle. Here the architect THOMAS U. WALTER, who designed a wing in the form of the Hephaisteion, provided a worthy parallel to Wilkins's Grange Park for a remarkable patron who believed that 'there are but two truths in the world—the Bible and Greek architecture' (Crook, p. 41).

These buildings were designed in what became the international language of architecture, adopted in the early 19th century by countless architects for modernizing European cities with public buildings and urban-planning schemes. In addition to Schinkel in Berlin and Klenze in Munich, such architects included Andrey Voronkhin, Thomas-Jean de Thomon and Andreyan Zakharov in St Petersburg; I. D. Gilgardi, Afanasy Grigor'yev and Osip Bove in Moscow after the fire of 1812; Jakob Kubicki and Antoni Corazzi in Warsaw; C. F. Hansen and Gottlieb Bindesbøll in Copenhagen; Christian Henrich Grosch in Oslo; and Carl Ludwig Engel in Helsinki. The centre of Helsinki is one of the most harmonious and attractive of these Greek Revival ensembles. The city was established as the capital in 1812, following the incorporation of Finland into Russia as a Grand Duchy in 1809. Johan Albrecht Ehrenström (1762–1847) drew up the city plan, while Schinkel's disciple, Engel, provided a range of public buildings from 1818 to 1845; the climax is Senate Square, with an imposing domed Lutheran cathedral flanked by the Senate and the University (*see* ENGEL, CARL LUDWIG, figs 1 and 2), both boasting superb Greek Doric staircases.

Ironically the Greek Revival style was taken to Athens as a foreign importation following the liberation of Greece

4. Benjamin Henry Latrobe: interior of the Supreme Court Chamber (1809; rebuilt 1815–17), Capitol Building, Washington, DC

from Turkish rule in 1829. Otto von Wittelsbach, who became the first king of Greece (*reg* 1832–62), took to Athens from his native Bavaria two of its leading Neo-classical architects: Klenze, who drew up an urban plan for Athens in 1834, and Friedrich von Gärtner, from whose designs the Royal Palace (1836–41; now the Parliament; *see* ATHENS, fig. 8) was executed in a subdued Greek style. With the change in 1862 to a Danish dynasty in Greece, the Danish architects Christian Hansen and his brother Theophilus Hansen initiated a more comprehensive programme of Greek Revival public buildings in the centre of the new city of Athens. Their principal achievement is the imposing group of three adjacent buildings: the University (1837–49), Academy (1859–87) and National Library (1859, 1885–91).

4. THE IMPLICATIONS OF POLYCHROMY (*c.* 1825–50). A new phase of the Greek Revival style was stimulated by the discovery of polychromy in Greek architecture (*see* POLYCHROMY, §1 and colour pl. I, fig. 1). This had wider ramifications than might first appear: the discovery that Classical Greek buildings were brightly painted, and the fact that such decoration was essentially impermanent, immediately overthrew Winckelmann's image of the timeless purity of the Greek temple. From the time of Stuart and Revett, archaeologists had noticed traces of colour on Greek sculpture but had drawn no conclusions from this. Informal archaeological work at Aigina and Bassai in 1811–12 by an international group including Cockerell, Karl Haller von Hallerstein and Otto von Stackelberg (1787–1837) had resulted in the excavation of architectural fragments with colours that soon faded on exposure to the air. One of the earliest reconstructions of ancient polychromy was Klenze's painted plaster relief of a Doric temple front created in 1830 in the Aigina room of his Glyptothek in Munich. Here it formed a suitable backdrop to the pedimental sculpture from the Temple of Aphaia at Aigina, which had been restored and painted by Bertel Thorvaldsen.

In 1823 the English architect Samuel Angell (1800–66) discovered fully coloured metopes at Temple C at Selinus (Selinunte) in Sicily, which he published in 1826. The French architect Hittorff, who saw this sculpture in 1823, then discovered and excavated Temple B, the so-called Temple of Empedokles, at Selinus, and in 1824 he exhibited in Rome and Paris some drawings (Cologne, Wallraf-Richartz-Mus.) in which he restored this as a stuccoed and lavishly painted limestone temple combining Doric and Ionic orders. These and other imaginative restorations of the building were published in 1827 and 1851, but French architects in the 19th century were no more interested in attaching correctly detailed Greek porticos to otherwise conventional neo-Palladian buildings than architects had been in the 18th century. Just as Le Roy in his *Ruines* of 1758 had offered broad historical theory rather than the material for a stylistic revival, so in the 1820s and 1830s Hittorff and Henri Labrouste subjected ancient Greek architecture to a revolutionary new theoretical and practical analysis, sparked off by the discovery of polychromy.

In Paris in 1829–30 Hittorff delivered lectures and exhibited drawings in which he claimed that Greek temples had originally been painted yellow, with patterns, mouldings and sculptural details in bright red, blue, green and gold. His own use of colour, however, in his Rotonde des Panoramas (1838; destr. 1857) and Cirque National (1839–41), both in Paris, was not very successful. During his stay in Sicily in 1823–4 he had also made a detailed study of the Temple of Olympian Zeus at Akragas, 'the St Peter's of paganism' as he later called it, although it was generally known as the 'Temple of the Giants'. Klenze published a restoration of this massive and enigmatic temple in 1821 and Cockerell another in 1830. Its giant atlantids, polychromatic embellishment and concealed iron beams in the architraves were all an influence on Hittorff's masterpiece, the church of St Vincent-de-Paul (1832–44), Paris (for illustration *see* HITTORFF, JACQUES-IGNACE). The most striking polychromatic adornment of this church was the set of 13 enamel panels designed in 1844 to cover most of the west façade behind the portico. The nude figures depicted on them proved controversial, however, and they were removed in 1861.

In the meantime Henri Labrouste (*see* LABROUSTE, (2)) made drawings of a proposed restoration of the three temples at Paestum, which he submitted to the Académie des Beaux-Arts as his fourth-year *envoi* and exhibited in Paris in 1829. These and a series of cityscapes painted in the same year, for example one of Akragas, shocked the academicians for a range of reasons but especially because they seemed to rob Greek architecture of its mystique. Labrouste's emphatic polychromy resembled a kind of barbaric graffiti, while the first Temple of Hera at Paestum, shown in the restoration drawing by Labrouste as a secular basilica, was hung with notices and military trophies like a French provincial market hall. Labrouste's drawings, made just before the July Revolution of 1848 that finally deposed the French monarchy, interpreted Greek buildings as part of a historical process related to the development of societies. In the principal work of his career, the Bibliothèque Ste Geneviève (1839–51), Paris, he gave idiosyncratic but powerful expression to his new system of historical interpretation. In the library, as in his measured drawings of the basilica at Paestum, he separated the functional elements from the elements descriptive of function. Thus the wall panels on the library façade were carved with the names of 810 authors, suggesting the presence of the bookshelves immediately behind them. Bindesbøll, an admirer of Hittorff, provided a curious parallel to the essentially legible character of the Bibliothèque Sainte-Geneviève in his Thorvaldsens Museum (1839–47), Copenhagen (for illustration *see* BINDESBØLL, (1)). With its brightly painted architectural members, this partly Egyptian, partly Greek building is enlivened by an external painted frieze depicting the transport from Rome to Copenhagen of the works by Bertel Thorvaldsen that the museum was built to house.

Outside France, the response to Greek architecture of C. R. Cockerell was perhaps the most serious contemporary parallel to those of Hittorff and Labrouste. Although Cockerell played a significant role in the early investigation of polychromy, he was more influenced as an architect by his involvement in the discovery in 1811–12 of the pedimental sculpture at Aigina and of the figured frieze and uniquely curvilinear Ionic order at Bassai. Moreover, as a result of his exceptional sensitivity to the subtle lines of Greek architecture, he also seems to have been the first to notice the presence of entasis on the columns of the Parthenon, Erechtheion and Temple of Aphaia at Aigina. Stuart and Revett had shown such columns as completely straight, but in December 1814 Cockerell wrote to Robert Smirke from Athens enclosing a diagram in which he set out the curvature of the columns of the Parthenon (see Watkin, 1974, p. 17). These discoveries made Cockerell profoundly aware of the sculptural basis of Greek design. He was thus deeply hostile to the work of such contemporary Greek Revival architects as Smirke, Wilkins, George Dance (ii), William Inwood and Henry Inwood (*see* INWOOD), who, in his opinion, did not understand the spirit of Greek design. He was opposed to their attempt to restrict the stylistic range of modern buildings to a limited number of approved Greek sources. His belief in the orders as the basis of architecture in all periods was given triumphant expression in his masterpiece, the Ashmolean Museum and Taylorian Institution (1839–45; *see* COCKERELL, (2), fig. 2) in Oxford, a powerfully inventive sculptural combination of numerous historical references.

5. AFTER *c.* 1850. For a hundred years from the mid-18th century the study of ancient Greek architecture and the consideration of its application to contemporary architectural problems were pursued with a consistency that makes it possible to speak with confidence about a coherent Greek Revival. The impact of Greece did not end in 1850, however. In particular, German architecture in the first half of the 20th century was intimately bound up with a powerful image of Greek culture as a purifying force. German archaeologists of the later 19th century, such as Heinrich Schliemann, Theodor Wiegand and Adolf Furtwängler, had brought a fresh understanding to Classical and pre-Classical architecture. This found expression in the work of Peter Behrens, for example the Haus Wiegand (1911–12), Berlin, a convincing neo-antique house in the stern Doric style practised by Gilly, which was built for Dr Theodor Wiegand, an archaeologist who had excavated at Priene, Miletos and Samos, and who was Director of Antiquities of the Royal Prussian museums.

A similar mood in Scandinavia and Finland at this time produced a revival of interest in the masters of Nordic Neo-classicism of a century earlier. In their search for a national style, such architects as Carl Petersen, Hack Kampmann, Ivar Tengbom and Gunnar Asplund, working in the first 30 years of the 20th century, responded with a rare subtlety to the Nordic Doric sensibility that they found in the work of C. F. Harsdorff, C. F. Hansen and Bindesbøll. Indeed, it is improbable that Greece will ever cease to colour the imagination of architects. Such philosophers as Nietzsche and architects as varied as Adolf Loos, Le Corbusier and Albert Speer all devised a rhetorical language in which they could appeal to Greece as a source of inspiration.

See also ORDERS, ARCHITECTURAL, §I, 2(iii)(d).

BIBLIOGRAPHY

EARLY SOURCES

J. Spon: *Voyage d'Italie, de Dalmatie, de Grèce et du Levant*, 3 vols (Lyon, 1678)
G. Wheler: *Journey into Greece* (London, 1682)
R. Pococke: *A Description of the East and Some Other Countries*, 2 vols (London, 1743–5)
R. Dalton: *Antiquities and Views in Greece and Egypt* (London, 1751)
Comte de Caylus: *Recueil d'antiquités*, 7 vols (Paris, 1752–67)
M.-A. Laugier: *Essai sur l'architecture* (Paris, 1753)
J. J. Winckelmann: *Gedanken über die Nachahmung der griechischen Werke in der Malerei und Bildhauerkunst* (Dresden, 1755); Eng. trans. by H. Fuseli as *Reflections on the Painting and Sculpture of the Greeks* (London, 1765/*R* 1972)
J.-D. Le Roy: *Les Ruines des plus beaux monuments de la Grèce* (Paris, 1758)
J. Stuart and N. Revett: *The Antiquities of Athens*, 4 vols (London, 1762–1816)
J. J. Winckelmann: *Anmerkungen über die Baukunst der alten Tempel zu Girgenti in Sicilien* (Leipzig, 1762)
——: *Geschichte der Kunst des Alterthums* (Dresden, 1764); Eng. trans., ed. G. H. Lodge, 4 vols (London, 1849–72; rev. in 2 vols, 1881)
T. Major: *The Ruins of Paestum* (London, 1768)
S. Riou: *The Grecian Orders of Architecture* (London, 1768)
R. Chandler and others: *Ionian Antiquities*, 4 vols (London, 1769–1881)
G. B. Piranesi and F. Piranesi: *Différentes vues . . . de Pesto* (Rome, 1778/*R* Unterschneidheim, 1973)
J.-J. Barthélémy: *Voyage du jeune Anacharsis en Grèce dans le milieu du quatrième siècle avant l'ère vulgaire*, 5 vols (Paris, 1787); Eng. trans. by W. Beaumont as *Travels of Anacharsis the Younger in Greece* (London, 1791)
W. Wilkins: *The Antiquities of Magna Graecia* (Cambridge, 1807)
A.-C. Quatremère de Quincy: *Le Jupiter olympien, ou l'art de la sculpture considéré sous un nouveau point de vue* (Paris, 1815)
L. von Klenze: *Der Tempel des olympischen Jupiter zu Agrigent* (Stuttgart and Tübingen, 1821, rev. 1827)
S. Angell and T. Evans: *Sculptured Metopes Discovered among the Ruins of Selinus, 1823* (London, 1826)
P. H. Brøndsted: *Voyages et recherches dans la Grèce*, 2 vols (Paris, 1826–30)
O. M. von Stackelberg: *Der Apollotempel zu Bassae in Arcadien* (Rome, 1826)
J.-I. Hittorff and L. von Zanth: *Architecture antique de la Sicile* (Paris, 1827)
C. R. Cockerell and others: *Antiquities of Athens and other Places of Greece, Sicily, etc.* (London, 1830)
A. Blouet: *Expédition scientifique de Morée*, 4 vols (Paris, 1831–8)
F. Kugler: *Über die Polychromie der griechischen Architektur und Skulptur und ihre Grenzen* (Berlin, 1835)
J.-I. Hittorff: *Restitution du temple d'Empédocle à Sélinonte, ou l'architecture polychrome chez les grecs* (Paris, 1851)
C. R. Cockerell: *The Temples of Jupiter Panhellenius at Aegina, and of Apollo Epicurius at Bassae* (London, 1860)

GENERAL

L. Cust and S. Colvin: *History of the Society of Dilettanti* (London, 1898/*R* 1914)
E. M. Butler: *The Tyranny of Greece over Germany* (Cambridge, 1935)
T. Hamlin: *Greek Revival Architecture in America* (New York, 1944/*R* 1966)
N. Pevsner and S. Lang: 'Apollo or Baboon', *Archit. Rev.* [London], civ (1948), pp. 271–9
F. Saxl and R. Wittkower: *British Art and the Mediterranean* (Oxford, 1948)
T. Spencer: *Fair Greece, Sad Relic* (London, 1954)
W. St Clair: *Lord Elgin and the Marbles* (London, 1967)
D. Wiebenson: *Sources of Greek Revival Architecture* (London, 1969)
J. M. Crook: *The Greek Revival* (London, 1972)
The Age of Neo-classicism (exh. cat., Council of Europe exh., London, 1972)
D. Watkin: *The Life and Work of C. R. Cockerell, R.A.*, (London, 1974), p. 109
A. Drexler, ed.: *The Architecture of the Ecole des Beaux-Arts* (London, 1977)
D. Van Zanten: *The Architectural Polychromy of the 1830s* (New York, 1977)
R. Middleton, ed.: *The Beaux-Arts and Nineteenth-century French Architecture* (London, 1982)
Nordisk klassicism, 1910–1930 (exh. cat., Helsinki, Mus. Fin. Archit., 1982)
Paris, Rome, Athènes: Le Voyage en Grèce des architectes français aux XIXe et XXe siècles (exh. cat., Paris, Ecole N. Sup. B.-A., 1982)

D. Constantine: *Early Greek Travellers and the Hellenic Ideal* (Cambridge, 1984)
Paestum and the Doric Revival, 1750–1830 (exh. cat., Florence, 1986)
D. Watkin and T. Mellinghoff: *German Architecture and the Classical Ideal, 1740–1840* (London, 1987)
R. G. Kennedy and M. Bendtsen: *Greek Revival America* (New York, 1989)
M. Bendtsen: *Sketchings and Measurings: Danish Architects in Greece, 1818–1862* (Copenhagen, 1993)

DAVID WATKIN

Green, Anthony (*b* London, 30 Sept 1939). English painter. He trained from 1956 to 1959 at the Slade School of Fine Art, London, where he met Mary Cozens-Walker, a fellow student whom he married in 1961. Family biography is at the heart of Green's work, not only his marriage (a picture has celebrated each anniversary since 1973) but the wider project of affirming and reconstituting family life. The council flat in which he was brought up by his English father and French mother (divorced when he was 13) continued in his adult life to be his home and his studio.

Chaïm Soutine and Dubuffet were two early influences, particularly on Green's expressionistic handling of paint. The violently sexual imagery of *The Wedding* (1962; Lisbon, Mus. Gulbenkian) is bound within the structure of an Italian polyptych, but the stylistic conventions are borrowed from the children Green was then teaching. During his two-year Harkness Fellowship in the USA (1968–9) his pictures grew in scale and took on a new descriptive complexity, often re-creating a crowded interior from memory. Green stopped drawing from life in order to reach the most 'usual' view of things and in order to investigate the relation between memory and vision. In practice this meant use of a tilted space and a lucidity that could challenge the photograph. It also meant challenging rectangular formats because memory has an 'irrelevant perimeter' that may demand an eccentric shape.

The elaboration of this language, obvious enough to carry narrative force and sufficiently detailed to bear psychological complexity, was gradual. Whereas *Mr and Mrs Stanley Joscelyne/The Second Marriage* (1972; Belfast, Ulster Mus.) is still distanced by *faux-naïf* conventions, *My Mother Alone in her Dining Room* (1976; Norwich, U. E. Anglia, Sainsbury Cent.) is rendered much more compelling by a fetishized illusionism reminiscent of Neue Sachlichkeit artists such as Otto Dix. Green's procedures are relentless, each painting planned with a 'blueprint' and then worked on for two months; they yield ambitious and memorable images that form an unrivalled comedy of contemporary British middle-class manners.

WRITINGS

A Green Part of the World (London, 1984)

BIBLIOGRAPHY

Anthony Green Paintings (exh. cat., intro. B. Robertson; Rochdale, A.G., 1977)
Anthony Green (exh. cat. by T. Hyman and K. Hayashi, Tokyo, Setagaya Mus., 1978)

□

Green, Thomas (*b c.* 1659; *d c.* 1730). English sculptor. Like many minor English sculptors of the early 18th century, he possessed enough talent to enable him to rise above the artisan profession of mason. He also established a reputation as a fine carver of coats of arms on government buildings, such as his decorative stonework on the Royal Foundry at Woolwich (1717) and similar commissions at Chatham and Portsmouth. Green was apprenticed between 1673 and 1681 to John Fitch and later to William Hind and in 1694 served as journeyman to Thomas Cartwright the elder (*c.* 1617–1702), a leading Restoration sculptor. By 1697 Green was in independent practice at Camberwell, London. His best church monuments are impressive, although not always of the highest technical quality. In the tomb of *Lord Justice Sir John Holt* (*d c.* 1709; Redgrave, Suffolk, St Mary the Virgin) he used elaborate, large-scale architecture and monumental allegorical figures in the manner of Grinling Gibbons's tomb of *Henry Somerset, 1st Duke of Beaufort* (*d* 1700; Great Badminton, Glos, St Michael). However, the central seated contrapposto figure of the deceased was unusual for the time and foreshadowed the judicial type of *Sir William Blackstone* (1784; Oxford, All Souls College) by John Bacon (i). Green's magnum opus is the splendid monument to *Sir Henry Furnese* (*d* 1712; Waldershare, Kent, All Saints). The monument to *Richard Welby* (erected 1714; Denton, Lincs, St Andrew) shows his assured handling of a full-length, free-standing figure in contemporary dress, while that to *Robert Jennens* (*d* 1726; Acton, Suffolk, All Saints), which may be attributed to him on stylistic grounds, reveals the influence of the new architectural vocabulary of Palladianism as illustrated in James Gibbs's *A Book of Architecture* (1728), to which the family subscribed.

BIBLIOGRAPHY

Gunnis
K. A. Esdaile: *English Church Monuments, 1510–1840* (London, 1946), pp. 27–8, 65, 106, 128
N. Pevsner: *Suffolk*, Bldgs England (Harmondsworth, 1961), p. 59
M. Whinney: *Sculpture in Britain, 1530–1830*, Pelican Hist. A. (Harmondsworth, 1964), p. 66
T. Friedman: *James Gibbs* (New Haven, 1984), pp. 303, 323

TERRY FRIEDMAN

Green, Valentine (*b* Salford, Warwicks, 3 Oct 1739; *d* London, 29 June 1813). English engraver and draughtsman. He was educated by his father; in 1760 he apprenticed himself to Robert Hancock of Worcester and in 1764 combined his artistic and antiquarian skills in a *Survey of the City of Worcester*, with 15 illustrations drawn by him and engraved by Hancock. In 1765 Green moved to London, where he soon achieved fame and success, becoming mezzotint engraver to George III in 1773 and an associate engraver of the Royal Academy the following year. Although he was very prolific, his work is of the highest quality, delicate and precise. He is particularly associated with Benjamin West and Joshua Reynolds and largely established his reputation with his engravings *Regulus Returning to Carthage* (1771; e.g. London, BM) and *Hannibal Swearing Enmity to the Romans* (1773; e.g. London, BM), both after West.

In 1775 Green travelled in Europe and was appointed mezzotint engraver to Charles Theodore, the Elector Palatine. By 1778 he was sufficiently prosperous to move from his premises in Salisbury Street to a larger house off Oxford Street, from where he issued his prospectus for a series of six *Beauties of the Present Age* after Reynolds, at 12s. to subscribers and 15s. to the public. The series, which includes the splendid *The Ladies Waldegrave* (1791; e.g. London, BM), was successful enough to warrant the addition of three further plates. In 1788 Green, at the height of his powers and reputation, engraved his own portrait after Lemuel Francis Abbott (London, N.P.G.). In 1789 the Elector Palatine, now Elector of Bavaria, granted Green and his only son, Rupert Green, a monopoly to engrave and publish the paintings in the Düsseldorf Gallery. Green invested a large sum in the project, commissioning copies to be engraved in London; 72 of these copies and 14 engravings were exhibited in Spring Gardens in 1793. However, the scheme proved unprofitable and Green was in financial difficulties from 1796. His son's death in 1804 proved a further blow; and his appointment in 1805 as first Keeper of the British Institution was an act of kindness.

WRITINGS

A Survey of the City of Worcester etc. (Worcester, 1764)

A Review of the Polite Arts in France at the Time of their Establishment by Louis the Fourteenth Compared with their Present State in England (London, 1792)

BIBLIOGRAPHY

A. Whitman: *Valentine Green* (London, 1902)

DAVID RODGERS

Green, William Curtis (*b* Alton, Hants, 16 July 1875; *d* London, 26 March 1960). English architect and watercolourist. After studying engineering and architecture, he was articled to John Belcher. He then entered the Royal Academy schools in London and won the Bidlake Gold Medal and a travelling studentship. After extensive study tours of Spain and Italy developing his drawing skills, he returned to England in 1897. For a short period he was employed as draughtsman for *The Builder* before setting up his own practice in 1898. Initial commissions included a number of structures for power stations, for example Bristol Tramways Power Station (1898–9) and Chiswick (1904; destr.), which he designed in a classical style. He acquired a reputation for houses and contributed designs to Hampstead Garden Suburb (from 1905), Letchworth Garden City (from 1902) and municipal housing at Winchester (1919). In 1917 he became a partner in the firm of Dunn & Watson, and his work in the 1920s and 1930s was much concerned with large, mostly classically inspired office developments. He also designed a number of branches for Lloyds Bank and Barclays Bank (e.g. one in Piccadilly, London, 1922). His Wolseley House and showrooms (1921) for the Wolseley Motor Co. at 160 Piccadilly, London, won the first RIBA medal for street architecture in 1922. His largest project (1930) was the Dorchester Hotel, Park Lane, London, where he added coy Art Deco detail to the advanced reinforced-concrete structure designed by Owen Williams as well as radically altering the interior decoration. He was president of the Architectural Association (1913–14), vice-president of the RIBA (1923–4) and was elected a Royal Academician in 1933. An accomplished watercolourist, he exhibited repeatedly at the RA summer exhibitions and published collections of his drawings.

PRINTS

The Drawings of William Curtis Green (London, 1949)

BIBLIOGRAPHY

Obituary, *The Builder*, cxcviii (1960), p. 642; *RIBA J.* (1960), p. 307

J. S. Lloyd, ed.: *William Curtis Green RA: Architect and Draughtsman, 1875–1960* (London, 1978)

□

Greenaway, Kate (*b* Hoxton, London, 17 March 1846; *d* Hampstead, London, 6 Nov 1901). English painter, illustrator and writer. The daughter of a Fleet Street wood-engraver, John Greenaway (1818–90), she trained at Islington School of Art, Heatherleys Academy and the Slade School of Fine Art, all in London. In 1868 she did her first commercial work, producing Christmas and Valentine cards for Marcus Ward, Belfast. Greenaway wrote and illustrated children's books, usually depicting children dressed in Regency-style costume—her illustrations set a fashion in children's clothes—in idyllic rural locations. These were based on her memories of life at her great aunt's cottage in Rolleston, Notts.

Greenaway's first success, *Under the Window* (London, 1878), was the beginning of her collaboration with the publisher and colour printer Edmund Evans, who was a friend of her father. The book sold 70,000 copies in English and was translated into French and German. Greenaway's illustrations were exhibited at the Fine Arts Society, London, in 1879 to much critical acclaim. She assumed increasing financial control of her work as she became more successful and from the 1880s sold only the use of her paintings to her publishers.

Girl and Two Babies (1881; London, V&A), one of the illustrations from *Day in a Child's Life* (London, 1881), is typical of Greenaway's use of line drawing filled in with watercolour wash, as is the setting of a rose trellis as decorative background. Some of her most successful books include the *Birthday Book for Children* (London, 1880), *Mother Goose* (London, 1881) and *Kate Greenaway's Almanack* published in London in most years between 1888 and 1897. She exhibited widely as a member of the Royal Institute of Painters in Water-Colours and, apart from her illustrations, painted rural watercolours influenced by her friend Helen Allingham. She also painted portraits in oil and watercolour such as the full-length *Vera Evelyn Samuel* (watercolour, 1896; priv. col., see Spielmann and Layard, p. 206), daughter of Stuart M. Samuel, MP, for whom she designed a bookplate and a procession for the nursery. Her drawings of children were exhibited at the Royal Academy from 1877 to 1895. Greenaway sold work through the Dudley Gallery in London. John Ruskin admired her work, and they had a long correspondence, and in 1885 Richard Norman Shaw designed a house for her in Frognal, Hampstead, London.

BIBLIOGRAPHY

M. H. Spielmann and G. S. Layard: *Kate Greenaway* (London, 1905)

E. Ernest, ed.: *The Kate Greenaway Treasury* (London, 1968)

R. K. Engen: *Kate Greenaway* (London, 1976)

R. Engen, ed.: *Printed Kate Greenaway: A Catalogue Raisonné* (London, 1987)

EMMA M. ROUTH

Greenberg, Clement (*b* New York, 16 Jan 1909; *d* New York, 7 May 1994). American critic. He studied at the Art Students League in New York (1924–5) and obtained his BA from Syracuse University (1930). Working as a clerk for the US Customs, he began his writing career with frequent contributions to *Partisan Review* (1939–55) on politics, literature and art. Greenberg was an editor of *Partisan Review* (1940–42), regular art critic for *The Nation* (1942–9) and associate editor of *Commentary* (1945–57).

Until 1947 Greenberg was a Trotskyite Marxist, and at first his critical method took into account background factors in the genesis of art. Important social questions were considered in 'Avant-garde and Kitsch' (1939) as were personal factors in his book *Joan Miró* (1948). Thereafter, Greenberg adopted a more purely formal or modernist approach based on his understanding of Immanuel Kant's *Kritik der Urteilskraft* (1790), Hans Hofmann's theories of painting and the example of such critics as Walter Pater and Roger Fry.

Greenberg came to prominence as the most articulate early proponent of such Abstract Expressionist painters as Jackson Pollock, Adolph Gottlieb and Hans Hofmann, and of sculptor David Smith. In his exhibition *Post-painterly Abstraction* (1964) Greenberg championed a second generation of American and Canadian abstract painters such as Jack Bush, Helen Frankenthaler, Morris Louis, Kenneth Noland and Jules Olitski (*see* COLOUR FIELD PAINTING). He applied to their work Wölfflin's terms of 'openness' and linear clarity, attributing to it a freshness that he found lacking in Pop art. Greenberg was unusually influential in artists' studios. His encouragement and advice were important to Frankenthaler, Louis, Noland, Bush and the sculptor Anthony Caro; he gave them helpful suggestions for choosing an artistic direction and later increasingly emphasized questions of final adjustment in the work, such as cropping or changing the way it would hang.

Greenberg's concept of modernism was widely misinterpreted as prescriptive rather than descriptive and initiated a major debate. His article 'Modernist Painting' (1961) defined that phenomenon as a primarily 'artisanal' tendency towards the rejection of non-aesthetic aims, a heightened self-criticism of the medium in terms of itself, and a concomitant expulsion of both literary and sculptural values. 'Modernist' space was more 'optical' (i.e. indeterminate) than the 'tactile' (highly articulated) space of most older art. In 'Complaints of an Art Critic' (1967) Greenberg further argued that 'aesthetic judgements are involuntary' and intuitive rather than rational; they cannot be proven. Greenberg's judgements were often original and contentious: that Michelangelo's painting is superior to his sculpture; that Manet's *Déjeuner sur l'herbe* (1863; Paris, Mus. d'Orsay) would have benefited from cropping; that Picasso was not successful with large-scale painting even in *Guernica* (1937; Madrid, Prado); that Minimalist sculpture was vitiated by 'good safe taste' and 'remains too much a feat of ideation'. Greenberg consistently admired such formal properties as a 'hard-won' unity 'for the sake of feeling'. Nonetheless, he believed that 'content remains indefinable, unparaphrasable, undiscussable. . . . The unspecifiability of its content is what constitutes art as art.' He therefore aimed to work intuitively from the immediate experience of art and only then proceed towards understanding, without ever discussing 'content' as such. In one of his last important articles, 'Counter-avant-garde' (1971), Greenberg rejected much of the art since Post-painterly Abstraction, arguing that when Marcel Duchamp 'formalized' raw art by exhibiting his Ready-mades, he initiated 'vanguardism', an academy of newness for its own sake that aimed to avoid questions of aesthetic quality and resulted in developments such as Conceptual art.

Greenberg often lectured abroad on American art, served frequently as a juror and was a controversial executor for the estates of Smith and Bush. His polemical writings not only helped to establish the reputation of American abstract artists and the primacy of modernist interpretations of art in the 1960s and early 1970s but also had a profound impact on later criticism, as both a positive and a negative influence.

WRITINGS

'Avant-garde and Kitsch', *Partisan Rev.*, vi/5 (1939), pp. 34–49
Joan Miró (New York, 1948)
Matisse (New York, 1953)
Art and Culture (Boston, 1961)
Hofmann (Paris, 1961)
'Modernist Painting', *A. Yb.*, iv (1961), pp. 103–8
Three New American Painters (exh. cat., U. Regina, Mackenzie A.G., 1963)
Post-painterly Abstraction (exh. cat., Los Angeles, CA, Co. Mus. A., 1964)
'Complaints of an Art Critic', *Artforum*, vi/2 (1967), pp. 38–9
'Recentness of Sculpture', *American Sculpture of the Sixties* (exh. cat., Los Angeles, CA, Co. Mus. A., 1967) [Intro.]
'Counter-avant-garde', *A. Int.*, xv/5 (1971), pp. 16–19
J. O'Brien, ed.: *The Collected Essays and Criticism*, 4 vols (Chicago, 1986–93)

BIBLIOGRAPHY

H. Kramer: 'A Critic on the Side of History', *A. Mag.*, xxxvii/1 (1962), pp. 60–63
D. Kuspit: *Clement Greenberg: Art Critic* (Madison, 1979)
F. Orton and G. Pollock: '*Avant-gardes* and Partisans Reviewed', *A. Hist.*, iv/3 (1981), pp. 305–27
C. Harrison: 'Expression and Exhaustion: Art and Criticism in the Sixties: Part I', *Artscribe*, 56 (1986), pp. 44–9
S. Tillim: 'Criticism and Culture or Greenberg's Doubt', *A. America*, lxxv/5 (1987), pp. 122–7, 201
E. Frank: 'Farewell to Athene: The Collected Greenberg', *Salmagundi*, 80 (Autumn 1988), pp. 246–63

KEN CARPENTER

Greene, Belle da Costa (*b* Alexandria, VA, 13 Dec 1883; *d* New York, 10 May 1950). American librarian, curator and museum director. She began her career in the library of Princeton University, where she developed a particular interest in rare books. At the age of 21 she was appointed by J. Pierpont Morgan as curator of his collection of rare books and manuscripts in the library that he was founding in New York. She was initially responsible for organizing the books in the new premises, but came to play an increasingly influential role in the development of the library. She worked closely with Morgan and was entrusted by him to travel abroad in order to identify potential purchases; she developed increasing expertise in the identification of manuscripts through the contacts that she made with such specialists as Sydney Carlyle Cockerell, Director of the Fitzwilliam Museum, Cambridge, and Bernard Berenson. After Morgan's death, his son, J. P. Morgan (1867–1943), converted the library into an educational institution and museum, of which Greene was appointed the first director in 1924. Her work subsequently involved the organization of exhibitions, publications, lectures and seminars, as well as many trips to Europe to make further acquisitions. Under her guidance, the Library continued its founder's policy of supporting other institutions and scholars, to which her unique personality and capacity for friendship made a particular contribution. She retired in 1948, her career commemorated by an exhibition and a volume of collected studies.

BIBLIOGRAPHY

The First Quarter Century of the Pierpont Morgan Library: A Retrospective Exhibition in Honor of Belle da Costa Greene (exh. cat., New York, Pierpont Morgan Lib., 1949)

D. Miner, ed.: *Studies in Art and Literature for Belle da Costa Greene* (Princeton, 1954)

□

Greene, John Holden (*b* Warwick, RI, 2 Sept 1777; *d* Providence, RI, 6 Sept 1850). American architect–builder. He had little formal education and gained his architectural knowledge through apprenticeship, from British and American pattern books and from contemporary buildings in Boston, MA. In 1794 he went to Providence, RI, where he apprenticed himself to Caleb Ormsbee, then the city's principal architect–builder. He continued to work for Ormsbee after completing his training and was active independently from *c.* 1806 to 1835. His reputation as an innovative designer emerged in two early Providence commissions, St John's Episcopal Church (1809–10) and the Sullivan Dorr house (1810–11). St John's introduced a 'Gothick' vocabulary adapted from mid-18th-century English pattern books such as those by Batty Langley. Greene blended Gothick details with those probably derived from pattern books by William Pain (*c.* 1730–*c.* 1804), which were in turn reminiscent of Robert Adam's work. This amalgam appeared on the Dorr house, where he sited an L-shaped plan on a terrace on a steep slope. He repeated this striking formula on a number of occasions.

Greene built many three- and five-bay detached houses with hipped roofs between 1810 and 1830. The smaller ones were timber-framed; the larger ones, such as the Truman Beckwith House (1827–8), Providence, RI, were of brick. He apprenticed a considerable number of carpenters and builders during the course of his career. This, and his influential designs, ensured the proliferation of an identifiable local architecture during the first third of the 19th century in Providence. In addition to his work there, Greene was responsible for the Independent Presbyterian Church (1817–19; rebuilt 1891) in Savannah, GA, and he may have designed other buildings during his stay in the South.

BIBLIOGRAPHY

Macmillan Enc. Architects

F. D. Hurdis: *John Holden Greene: Carpenter–architect of Providence* (Providence, 1972)

——: *The Architecture of John Holden Greene* (diss., Ithaca, NY, Cornell U., 1973)

W. McKENZIE WOODWARD

Greene & Greene. American architectural partnership formed in 1893 by Charles (Sumner) Greene (*b* Brighton, OH, 12 Oct 1868; *d* Carmel, CA, 11 June 1957) and his brother Henry (Mather) Greene (*b* Brighton, OH, 23 Jan 1870; *d* Pasadena, CA, 2 Oct 1954). Both studied at the Manual Training School of George Washington University, Washington, DC, Charles entering in 1883 and Henry in 1884. There they were not only taught woodworking and carpentry but were introduced to the ideals of John Ruskin and William Morris, to which the school strongly adhered. In 1888 they entered the Massachusetts Institute of Technology, Cambridge. Upon completion of the two-year architectural course, Henry entered the office of Shepley, Rutan & Coolidge in Boston, MA, and Charles became a draughtsman with H. Langford Warren. Later Henry worked in the office of Chamberlin & Austin, and Charles with Winslow & Wetherell.

In the early 1890s the Greenes' parents moved to Pasadena, CA, and suggested that their sons join them in the new and developing city, which they did in 1893; *en route* they visited the World's Columbian Exposition at Chicago, where they saw the Ho-o-den, a traditional Japanese pavilion that later influenced their designs for the California bungalow and its garden. They opened a small architectural office in Pasadena in 1893 and slowly began to build up a clientele. Their work of the first ten years was professionally competent but not distinguished. Their designs ran the full gamut from Colonial Revival to Mission Revival to versions of the Shingle style and to what was referred to locally as the Rustic style. The strongest of these early designs was the Mission-style Hosmer House (1896) and the Colonial Revival Swan House (1895), both in Pasadena.

After 1900 striking changes took place in the Greenes' work. In part the brothers were responding, like a number of other southern Californian architects, to the developing American Arts and Crafts movement, coupled with a fascination with California's Hispanic architecture of the late 18th century and early 19th. In 1903 they brought together these elements in the Bandini House, Pasadena. The single-storey, U-shaped corridor house was clad in board-and-batten siding covered by a wood shingle roof and visually held to the ground by stout river-boulder fireplaces and chimneys. The concept of the Bandini House was Hispanic, but its rustic character was derived from the Arts and Crafts movement.

The Greenes continued to amalgamate these two sources into an informal Shingle-style dwelling that retained the indoor–outdoor relationship of the Hispanic house. This developed through the White House, the Sandborn House and the Claypole House, all built in Pasadena in 1903, the last in particular epitomizing the emerging bungalow type. The Greenes rapidly perfected their version of the California bungalow: an informal timber dwelling, in which the rustic was refined through impeccably crafted materials and details. Their interest in refinement led them to the traditional Japanese house with its meticulous wood detailing, and their next houses displayed timber jointing, panelling and cabinet work, often carried out by one of the brothers, which remain high points of wood construction. A series of what Randall Makinson called 'ultimate bungalows' followed in quick succession: the Tichenor House (1904), 582 East Ocean Boulevard, Long Beach, CA; the Blacker House, 1177 Hillcrest Avenue, Pasadena; the Gamble House (1908), 4 Westmoreland Place, Pasadena; and the Pratt House (1909; see fig.), Ojai, CA.

After 1910 the Greenes' commissions diminished. Although they continued to design timber bungalows, their strongest designs of this period turned towards Mediterranean and Hispanic traditions. The Culbertson House (1911), 1188 Hillcrest Avenue, Pasadena, not only has

Greene & Greene: Pratt House, North Foothill Road, Ojai, California, 1909

stucco walls and a tile roof but is set within a hillside Mediterranean-style garden. In 1917 Charles Greene moved to Carmel, CA, to join in the varied artistic and literary activities of this West Coast retreat. The partnership of the two brothers was formally dissolved in 1922, although they continued to collaborate on a few projects. Henry Greene's Arts-and-Crafts commitment to natural materials continued, as shown in his Richardson ranch house (1929), 27349 Avenue 138, near Portersville, CA. Its design made each element readable: a foundation of native stone, walls of adobe with intervening reinforced-concrete tie-beams, and a timber-framed roof hanging out over the walls to protect the building from the heat of the hot summer days of the San Joaquin Valley. Charles's designs reflected the new, openly expressed romanticism of the Mediterranean revivalism then flourishing, as in the stone James House (1918), Route 1, Carmel Highlands, CA, situated like a Mediterranean castle on a rocky cliff overlooking the Pacific, or in the Renaissance-inspired Fleishhacker water garden (1927), 329 Albion Avenue, Woodside, CA.

Although the Greenes did not invent the California bungalow, they transformed it into an acknowledged high-art product. Like other American adherents of the Arts and Crafts movement, they believed passionately in the ideal of democracy and had reservations about the uneven distribution of wealth within capitalism; they were also sceptical of the impact of the machine. In 1917 Charles Greene wrote:

> Whether or not we may find it possible to revise our present idea of democracy, to insure to the minority and to the weaker the privileges now only enjoyed by those most fitly equipped to secure them is a question that vitally concerns our national art progress. The insidious machine, from year to year has driven from the masses personal expression.

Ironically many of the brothers' designs were for wealthy clients. The garden settings of most were made feasible by the automobile, since bungalows with such areas of land were outside the city.

WRITINGS

C. S. Greene: 'Bungalows', *W. Architect*, xiii/1 (1908), pp. 3–5, pls 1–9
——: 'Impressions of Some Bungalows and Gardens', *Homes & Grounds*, 1 (1916), pp. 9–11
——: 'Architecture as a Fine Art', *The Architect*, xiii/4 (1917), pp. 217–22

BIBLIOGRAPHY

A. C. David: 'An Architect of Bungalows in California', *Archit. Rec.*, xx/4 (1906), pp. 306–15
'California's Contribution to a National Architecture: Its Significance and Beauty as Shown in the Work of Greene and Greene', *The Craftsman*, xxii/5 (1912), pp. 532–46
L. M. Yost: 'Greene and Greene of Pasadena', *J. Soc. Archit. Historians*, ix (1950), pp. 11–19
C. Lancaster: 'Some Sources of Greene and Greene', *J. Amer. Inst. Architects*, 34 (1960), pp. 34–46
R. Makinson: 'Greene and Greene', *Five California Architects*, ed. E. McCoy (New York, 1962), pp. 102–47
W. H. Jordy: *American Buildings and their Architects: Progressive and Academic Ideals at the Turn of the Twentieth Century* (New York, 1972), pp. 217–45
W. Current and K. Current: *Greene and Greene, Architects in the Residential Style* (Fort Worth, 1974)
J. Strand: *A Greene and Greene Guide* (Pasadena, 1974)
R. Makinson: *Greene and Greene*, 2 vols (Salt Lake City, 1977–9)

DAVID GEBHARD

Greenhill, John (*b* Orchardleigh, nr Frome, Somerset, 14 July 1642; *d* London, 19 May 1676). English painter and draughtsman. He was brought up in Salisbury but had joined Lely's studio in London by 1662. He was probably working independently soon afterwards. Mixing in theatrical circles, he drew crayon portraits of actors in character, such as *Thomas Betterton* (1663; Kingston Lacy, Dorset, NT) and *Henry Harris* (1664; Oxford, Magdalen Coll.). Both works were boldly executed but immaturely composed; his later pastel portraits show increasing mastery of the medium and a more painterly approach to it. A similar coarseness in drawing is evident in his solitary etching of his brother *Henry Greenhill* (1667; e.g. London, BM, and Oxford, Ashmolean). During the 1660s the actor William Cartwright commissioned from Greenhill six oil portraits, which he later bequeathed to Dulwich College. Apart from a more conventional portrait of *James, Duke of York* (*c.* 1663), these works are virtually devoid of Lely's influence and are closer to the native tradition. Greenhill's self-portrait is confidently exuberant, and Cartwright's 'First Wifes Pictur Like a Sheppardess' (see Waterhouse, 1978, pl. 94) is entirely individual.

Through family connections in Salisbury, Greenhill painted *John Locke* (London, N.P.G.), *Bishop Seth Ward* (commissioned 1673; Salisbury, Guildhall) and the distinctly hieratic full-length of *Anthony Ashley Cooper, 1st Earl of Shaftesbury* (1673; St Giles House, Dorset). By that date he had reverted to Lely's manner, but towards the end of his short career he was influenced by continental Baroque art, as in the identically posed pastel of *Philip Woolrich* (New Haven, CT, Yale Cent. Brit. A.) and oil portrait of *Thomas Herbert, 8th Earl of Pembroke* (London, N.P.G.), both probably of 1676.

Greenhill was regarded as the most talented of Lely's pupils, but he did not survive to fulfil his promise. Having acquired some reputation for profligacy, 'he fell in to a kennel [gutter] in Long Acre coming down from the Vine Tavern very drunk, was carried home and died in his bed in the night' at the house of the painter Parry Walton (*d* 1699) in Lincoln's Inn Fields. He was survived by his wife and at least one son. The writer Aphra Behn mourned and defended him in an extended elegy.

BIBLIOGRAPHY

DNB

B. Buckeridge: 'An Essay Towards an English School of Painters'; in 3rd edn (London, 1750) of *The Art of Painting*, pp. 378–81; Eng. trans. by J. Savage of R. de Piles: *De arte graphica: L'Art de peinture* (Paris, 1688)

H. Walpole: *Anecdotes of Painting in England* (1762–71); ed. R. N. Wornum (1849), ii, pp. 452–3

'The Notebooks of George Vertue', i–iv, *Walpole Soc.*, xviii (1930), xx (1932), xxii (1934), xxiv (1936)

E. K. Waterhouse: *Painting in Britain, 1530 to 1790*, Pelican Hist. A. (Harmondsworth, 1953, 4/1978), pp. 111–12

E. Croft-Murray and P. Hulton: *British Museum Catalogue of British Drawings*, i (London, 1960), pp. 338–40

J. S. Whittingham: 'John Greenhill, 1642–1676: Sir Peter Lely's Most Excellent Disciple', *Hatcher Rev.*, ii/12 (1981), pp. 58–69

RICHARD JEFFREE

Greenhouse [glasshouse]. Building for the protection, propagation and cultivation of plants. Greenhouses, probably roofed in mica, existed in Roman times. During the 16th century, the beginnings of the application of science to plant-growing, which led to the development of the BOTANIC GARDEN in Europe, encouraged the construction of greenhouses. In 'houses' formed of a 'hot bed' of such heat-generating substances as bark or dung, situated against a south wall and 'roofed' with straw, canvas matting or individual glass cones, tender plants could be encouraged to survive and prosper. Such 'houses' gradually became more substantial, with brick or masonry sides, and eventually incorporated small panes of expensive glass. One of the most dramatic uses of portable glass coverings for plants was at Sanssouci (*see* POTSDAM, §2), where from 1773 the vineyard terrace (1747; by Georg Wenceslaus von Knobelsdorff), which was also used for growing pomegranate and orange trees, was covered in glass in cold weather. The greenhouse was introduced on the east coast of America during the 18th century, an early example being the 'little greenhouse with two or three orange trees' that was on the estate of Colonel William Byrd (1674–1744) at Westover, VA, by 1740 (destr.). Later in the century, greenhouses for oranges and lemons were quite usual in and around Philadelphia.

The preoccupation with gaining maximum heat from the sun's rays by the optimum angling of glass in plant-houses continued until well into the 19th century. In a paper read to the Horticultural Society in London in 1815, JOHN CLAUDIUS LOUDON recommended the construction of half-dome glasshouses. He also approved spherical glasshouses with the tops pointed to deflect rain, such as at Bretton Hall, W. Yorks., constructed in 1827 to Loudon's design (destr. 1832). Loudon favoured a form of ridge-and-furrow roof construction, which he said achieved 'two daily meridians'. This style was adopted by JOSEPH PAXTON for his revolutionary Great Stove or Conservatory (1836–40; destr. 1920; *see* GLASS, fig. 7) at Chatsworth House, Derbys. In 1850 Paxton used flat ridge and furrow for the *Victoria regia* (*amazonica*) House (Lily House; destr.) at Chatsworth, patenting the design, which used prefabricated parts.

Throughout the 19th century there was controversy about the relative merits of constructing the framework for glasshouses of wrought and/or cast iron, or wood, and, later in the century, steel. The main frame of the Great Stove at Chatsworth was of wood, but prefabricated cast iron was first used with glass for the complete façade of a plant-house in 1823 at the Camellia House, Wollaton Hall, Notts. Subsequently it was often deployed in conjunction with wrought-iron and became the preferred material for such large, complex constructions as the Palm House (1845–8) of the Royal Botanic Gardens, designed by DECIMUS BURTON (for illustration *see* KEW, ROYAL BOTANIC GARDENS).

The repeal of the Glass Tax in Britain in 1845 and the implementation of a new manufacturing process to produce sheet glass two years later allowed the inexpensive construction of greenhouses with adequate light. Free-standing, clear-span greenhouses could now be built in addition to the lean-to version, and new types of putty, which allowed greater expansion and contraction without fracturing the glass, were an extra benefit.

Methods of heating hothouses also improved. Underfloor heating had been provided for the Society of Apothecaries' greenhouse in Chelsea, London, described by the diarist John Evelyn on 7 August 1685. Hot-water pipes gave a more even heat than smoke and steam, without the attendant fumes that could harm tender plants: hot-water boilers could heat the range of interconnected plant-houses in gardens, while domestic boilers could be used to provide warmth in glazed rooms attached to homes (*see* CONSERVATORY).

A miniature greenhouse, 'the Wardian Case', developed in 1833 by Nathaniel Bagshaw Ward (1791–1868), enabled plants to be transported over long distances in a protected environment and reach their destinations in good shape. The 19th-century boom in plant-collecting was in part incentive for, and part result of, improvements in glasshouse construction and temperature control. Whole houses were occupied by one or more types of plant requiring the same degree of hot, warm or cool air. These glasshouses were seen in the many public botanic gardens that came into existence during the 19th century and on private estates of all sizes.

Britain's lead in industrialization had made her preeminent in glasshouse building. During the 19th century, advances in technology, combined with improvements in design recommended by Loudon, Paxton and others, enabled mass ownership of glasshouses to become possible. The later success of firms that specialized in glasshouse construction (e.g. Messenger, Handyside, Macfarlane, and Boulton and Paul) was based on these discoveries, and British glasshouses were exported world-wide.

See also ORANGERY.

BIBLIOGRAPHY

J. C. Loudon: *Remarks on the Construction of Hothouses* (London, 1817)

S. Hibberd: *The Amateur's Greenhouse and Conservatory* (London, 1873, rev. T. W. Sanders, 1897)

M. Hadfield: *Gardening in Britain: An Historical Outline to 1939* (London, 1960); rev. as *A History of British Gardening* (Feltham, 1969)

S. Koppelkamm: *Gewächshäuser und Wintergärten im 19. Jahrhundert* (Stuttgart, 1981)
B. Elliot: *Victorian Gardens* (London, 1986)
M. Woods and A. Swartz Warren: *Glasshouses: A History of Greenhouses, Orangeries and Conservatories* (London, 1988)

PRISCILLA BONIFACE

Greenland [Green. Kalaallit Nunaat]. Island to the north-east of North America. Bordered by the North Atlantic and Arctic oceans, it is the second largest island in the world. Five-sixths of its area is covered by an ice cap, and much of its coastline is deeply indented by fjords and faced by mountains. Less than 5% of Greenland is habitable and most of the population (est. 1991 at 56,752) lives in the west of the island, where both the capital, Godthåb (Nuuk), and the northernmost settlement of Thule are situated. Greenland was settled by seal-hunting Inuits (Eskimos) from North America at least as early as 2500 BC. It was subsequently colonized by Vikings in the 10th century AD and came under the rule of Denmark in the 18th century. In 1979 Greenland was granted home rule as a self-governing province of Denmark and in 1985 the island left the European Economic Community.

Archaeological speculation continues as to the exact nature of prehistoric settlement and the relation of Greenlandic culture to both the Dorset people and the later Thule culture. The former came from Baffin Island to east Greenland. They invented both the igloo and the woman's crescent-shaped knife of later Inuit culture; many of their art forms survived until the 20th century, for example carvings of vertical rows of multiple faces or masks. In the 10th century AD the later Thule culture spread from south-west Alaska to Canada and to north, west and finally east Greenland, establishing its dominance by 1300. Thule culture developed the umiak and kayak (large and small skin boats), together with wooden figurines, decorated needlecases, ivory snow-goggles and papoose cradles, which are seen as typical of indigenous Inuit culture. Inuit decoration uses scrimshaw techniques of scraping or scratching patterns with a knife or employs light and dark animal skins to form often complex embroidery. Beadwork developed, particularly in western Greenland, progressing from simple bead chokers in the 17th century to capes rich in geometric pattern.

Dorset and Thule culture both contain significant evidence of aboriginal shamanistic practice. The fundamental animism of the Inuit found expression in the wearing of *aarnquaq* (amulets), especially by men. The *tupilak* figures from eastern Greenland were originally made from human or animal remains and later from wood; they may depict a malevolent spirit, half-man, half-raven, for example. Art was understood as a ritual and functional process rather than a product (Carpenter).

Greenland was discovered and colonized by the Viking leader Eric the Red in the late 10th century; some remains of buildings from this period survive (*see* VIKING ART, §III, 3). The south-west colonies were converted to Protestantism in 1721, coming under Danish administration in 1728. Since the end of the 18th century the Kongelige Danske Akademi for de Skønne Kunster and other schools of art in Copenhagen have continued to enrol a small number of pupils from Greenland. In the mid-19th century Lars Møller, for example, went to Copenhagen to learn lithography and then drew the illustrations for the paper that he founded.

Under the comparatively benevolent rule of Denmark, from the mid-19th century Greenland moved slowly towards autonomy. Greenlandic artists began to address the tensions between a renascent sense of tradition stretching back to Dorset culture and Western-style modernity. In the 20th century massive Danish investment created a social and cultural transformation whereby hunters became literate wage-earners; the resultant culture-clash was depicted in the lithographic work of Anne-Birth Hove (Kaalund, 1986, p. 21). Following the publicity that the small, walrus-ivory, *tupilak*-like fantasy figures of Otto Thomassen began to attract in the late 1950s, the east Greenland *tupilak* tradition helped to stimulate western Greenlandic artists in their search for a contemporary identity (Kaalund, 1986, p. 5). An important exhibition of Greenlandic art, *Grønlandsk Kunst*, took place at the Louisiana Museum in Humlebæk in 1969–70, to be followed by one in Århus, *Greenlandic Art from Aron till Today*, in 1970: at both of these, the surreally grotesque, split soapstone sculpture of Knud Petrussen was praised. The multimedia artist Hans Lynge attracted equal attention for his combination of Danish–European spatial devices with a deep sense of native mythical tradition, as in the imposing triptych the *Past of Nuuk* (1981–3; see fig.), the tapestry woven by Mette Rössing. Lynge, who studied at the Akademi in Copenhagen, wrote an important book about the inner life of Greenland, which revived the metamorphosing, animistic qualities that distinguish the flowing contemporary graphic forms of Aka Høegh and

Hans Lynge: *The Past of Nuuk*, tapestry, woven by Mette Rössing, 1981–3 (collection of the Municipality of Godthåb)

Jessie Kristensen, Principal of the School of Art in Greenland.

See also sections on Arctic peoples in NATIVE AMERICAN INDIAN ART.

BIBLIOGRAPHY

E. Carpenter: *Eskimo Realities* (New York, 1973)

M. Banks: *Greenland* (Newton Abbot, 1975)

C. I. A. Ritchie: *The Eskimo and his Art* (London, 1975)

W. Herbert: *Eskimos* (London, 1976) [good general bibliog.]

J. Malaurie: *The Last Kings of Thule* (London, 1982)

B. Kaalund: *The Art of Greenland* (Berkeley and London, 1983)

Inuit Eskimo: People of the North American Arctic (exh. cat., London, Mus. Mankind, 1984)

B. Kaalund: 'Greenland and Sapmi', *Northern Poles: Breakaways and Breakthroughs in Nordic Painting and Sculpture of the 1970s and 1980s*, ed. T. Bløndal (Copenhagen, 1986), pp. 2–28

B. Lopez: *Arctic Dreams: Imagination and Desire in a Northern Landscape* (London, 1987)

MICHAEL TUCKER

Greenough. American family of sculptors.

(1) Horatio Greenough (*b* Boston, MA, 6 Sept 1805; *d* Somerville, MA, 18 Dec 1852). Sculptor and writer. He was brought up in a wealthy, cultured home and was given a classical education. He drew and modelled from engravings and antique plaster casts in the Boston Athenaeum and studied with the French sculptor J. B. Binon (*fl* 1818–20) in Boston. After graduating from Harvard, he was encouraged by Washington Allston, his first mentor and life-long friend, to go to Italy in 1825 to study ancient and Renaissance art. Influenced by the Neo-classical aesthetic of the international art community in Rome and by his studies with Bertel Thorvaldsen, he aspired to create a truly American art. In 1826, illness forced him to return home.

Greenough's first extant bust, of the Mayor of Boston, *Josiah Quincy jr* (plaster, 1827; Boston, MA, Hist. Soc.), shows a rigorous application of Neo-classical ideals. The life-size bust of the President, *John Quincy Adams* (marble, 1828; Boston, MA, Athenaeum), modelled from life in Washington, achieved a stronger realism suited to the young American Republic. His portrait style was fully developed in the expressive life-size bust of *Samuel F. B. Morse* (1831; Washington, DC, N. Mus. Amer. A.), an artist who shared his devotion to the cause of a national art.

On his return to Italy in 1828, Greenough had workmen at Carrara carve his busts in marble, initiating the subsequent American practice of using the finest materials and inexpensive, highly skilled labour. He settled in Florence, seeking to learn greater naturalism in the studio of Lorenzo Bartolini, exponent of the theory 'all nature is beautiful'. With Hiram Powers and Thomas Crawford he formed a triumvirate who led the first of two generations of American Neo-classical sculptors, most of whom followed Greenough to live in Italy as expatriates. The two putti in his first important commission (from James Fenimore Cooper, 1789–1851), *Chanting Cherubs* (1828; untraced), a theme based on a painting by Raphael in the Palazzo Pitti, Florence, created a furore for their nudity when exhibited in Boston as the first sculptural group by an American. Two related compositions, *Child and Angel* (1833) and *Love Prisoner to Wisdom* (1834; both Boston, MA, Mus. F.A.) were more acceptable. They are particularly American in their use of children in a moralizing context. The new Romantic sensibility, demanding comprehensible themes and literary evocations, inspired Greenough's choice of the bride from Byron's poem *The Corsair* for the dead *Medora* (1832; Baltimore, MD, Mayor & City Council on loan to Baltimore, MD, Mus. A.). This was his first full-length ideal statue and was commissioned by Robert Gilmor jr. The majestic, striding, under life-size *Angel Abdiel* (1838; New Haven, CT, Yale U. A.G.) was inspired by Milton's *Paradise Lost*. Greenough's life-size homage to his bride, *Venus Victrix* (1839; Boston, MA, Athenaeum), popularized representations of the female nude in America.

Greenough's ambitions were fulfilled when he became the first American from whom Congress commissioned a major monumental sculpture: *George Washington* (marble, 3.37 m, 1832–41; Washington, DC, N. Mus. Amer. Hist.; *see* UNITED STATES OF AMERICA, fig. 20), intended for the Rotunda of the US Capitol. Convinced that this challenge would affect all future Americans, and that the form should follow the symbolic function, Greenough faced the dilemma of the American artist in reconciling the real and the ideal. Attempting a synthesis, he took the statue's enthroned, half-draped, god-like image from recent reconstructions of Pheidias' *Olympian Zeus* and its realistic, fleshy head from the terracotta bust of *Washington* that Jean-Antoine Houdon had made from life (1785; Mount Vernon, VA, Ladies' Ass. Union). The work attracted criticism for showing Washington as a semi-nude Classical deity. Before it was unveiled Greenough was already at work on a second major over life-size government commission for the east portico of the Capitol. *The Rescue* (marble, 1837; Washington, DC, US Capitol, in storage) is the most complex group attempted by an American at that date and was assembled only after his early demise at the height of his career as the first American sculptor of international renown.

During the last decade of his life, Greenough was chiefly occupied in producing influential theoretical writings. In a series of essays he expounded the dictum that 'form follows function', using architecture as his model. He wrote to Ralph Waldo Emerson:

> Here is my theory of structure: a scientific arrangement of spaces and forms to function and to site; an emphasis of features proportioned to their gradated importance in function; color and ornament to be decided and arranged and varied by strictly organic laws having a distinct reason for each decision; the entire and immediate banishment of all make-shift and make-believe.

Greenough was the first to formulate a theory of organic art, and he inspired American functionalist aesthetics in design and architecture, later developed by Louis Sullivan and Frank Lloyd Wright.

WRITINGS

H. Bender [H. Greenough]: *The Travels, Observations and Experience of a Yankee Stonecutter* (New York, 1852/*R* Gainsville, 1958)

F. B. Greenough, ed.: *Letters of Horatio Greenough to his Brother, Henry Greenough* (Boston, MA, 1887, rev. New York, 1970)

H. A. Small, ed.: *Form and Function* (Berkeley, 1947)

N. Wright, ed.: *Letters of Horatio Greenough, American Sculptor* (Madison, 1972)

——: *Miscellaneous Writings of Horatio Greenough* (Delmar, 1975)

BIBLIOGRAPHY

H. T. Tuckerman: *A Memorial of Horatio Greenough: Memorial Selections from Writings and Tribute* (New York, 1853)

T. B. Brumbaugh: *Horatio and Richard Greenough: A Critical Study with a Catalogue of their Sculpture* (PhD diss., Columbus, OH State U., 1955)

N. Wright: *Horatio Greenough: The First American Sculptor* (Philadelphia, 1963) [biog. and pls]

W. Craven: *Sculpture in America* (New York, 1968), pp. 100–11 [crit. appraisal and pls]

S. Crane: *White Silence: Greenough, Powers and Crawford, American Sculptors in Nineteenth-century Italy* (Coral Gables, 1972)

K. Greenthal, P. M. Kozol and J. S. Ramirez: *American Figurative Sculpture in the Museum of Fine Arts, Boston* (Boston, 1986)

(2) Richard Saltonstall Greenough (*b* Jamaica Plain, MA, 27 April 1819; *d* Rome, 4 April 1904). Brother of (1) Horatio Greenough. He studied with Horatio in Florence in 1837. After making portrait busts in Boston (1838–48), he settled in Rome. The marble life-size bust of *Cornelia Van Rensselaer* (1849; New York, NY Hist. Soc.) typifies his tempering of the Neo-classical with a Victorian love of surface patterning and details of dress. The under life-size *Shepherd Boy with an Eagle* (1853; Boston, MA, Athenaeum) amalgamates 'high art' with genre; exhibited at the Salon in 1853, it was one of the earliest bronzes cast in America and heralded an American vogue for bronze statuettes. Boston's first major commission to an American brought the sculptor's career to its climax: *Benjamin Franklin* (bronze, over life-size, 1855; Boston, MA, Old City Hall) won acclaim for its commonsense quality, witty expression and realistic detail. Richard Saltonstall Greenough was one of the first sculptors to live in Paris (1856–75), and he was in the vanguard of the expatriate Americans' shift of focus to that city. The Victorian fussiness of his style thereafter was typical of the decline of Neo-classical ideals in post-Civil War American art.

BIBLIOGRAPHY

T. B. Brumbaugh: 'The Art of Richard Greenough', *Old-Time New England*, liii/3 (1963), pp. 61–78

W. Craven: *Sculpture in America* (New York, 1968), pp. 269–74 [crit. appraisal and pls]

ETHELYN ADINA GORDON

Greenway, Francis (Howard) (*b* Mangotsfield, nr Bristol, 20 Nov 1777; *d* nr East Maitland, NSW, *bur* 26 Sept 1837). Australian architect of English birth. His architectural training included working for John Nash in London where he also submitted work to the Royal Academy. However, his architectural practice in the Bristol area ended when he was convicted of forgery and transported with his wife Mary in the *General Hewitt* to Australia in February 1814. As a result his standing was never secure, and his arrogant nature made him many enemies among those he criticized in colonial society in and around Sydney. His support and patronage in Sydney came from Governor Lachlan Macquarie (governor 1810–22), who has become a model in Australian culture of enlightened public support for architecture. Greenway's important surviving buildings include St Matthew (1817) and the Court House (1821), both in Windsor, NSW; St Luke (1818), Liverpool, NSW; and St James (1819), Queens Square, Sydney, the adjacent Hyde Park (Convicts) Barracks (1817; see fig.) and the Government House Stables (1817). His first government commission was the South Head lighthouse, named the Macquarie Tower (1816–18), which at the time of its demolition was replaced by a near replica honouring

Francis Greenway: Hyde Park (Convicts) Barracks, Sydney, 1817

Greenway. A small obelisk in Macquarie Place, Sydney, survives as an example of some ornamental structures he designed. The majority of his surviving buildings are in brick and of a chaste expression, which has led Greenway to be called a Georgian architect. Other demolished designs belie this narrow categorization and reveal his command of the many styles common to early 19th-century English architects. Notable examples were the house (*c.* 1822–8) for Robert Campbell jr in a polished and restrained Regency idiom; the barracks (for convicts) in the grounds of the Campbell house, which drew on Baroque techniques; a delightful Toll Gate in a free Tudor and Gothic manner; the Fort Macquarie, which was on the site of the present Opera House, in a castellated Tudor mode similar to the surviving Government House Stables (now the New South Wales Conservatorium of Music and much altered); and a water fountain in a free Doric manner suggestive of John Soane's work. Indeed the surviving bold but plain brick buildings, such as the Hyde Park (Convicts) Barracks, Sydney, and St Matthew, Windsor, are strongly suggestive of Soane's Chelsea Stables and Dulwich Picture Gallery. On the other hand, both Fort Macquarie and the Stables are believed to be derived from Thornbury Castle, Glos, restoration drawings of which Greenway exhibited at the Royal Academy in 1802 while working for Nash. The variety of Greenway's work and the affinity with Soane was first suggested (1959) by Franz Philipp (1914–70) but was not pursued thereafter.

An enquiry into the affairs of the Colony of New South Wales, made between 1819 and 1821 by J. T. Bigge on behalf of the British House of Commons, caused great strain among opposing factions and the recall of Governor Macquarie. Greenway's relations with the Governor before his departure soured to the former's detriment. With great effrontery he submitted an account for £11,000 covering fees for the government buildings he had designed while in government employment. Early in the administration of Governor Brisbane he designed more buildings, including the Supreme Court in Sydney (*c.* 1822; later enlarged and altered) and the Liverpool Hospital (*c.* 1822; later to become a technical college). He was dismissed from office in 1822 and struggled to maintain a practice, relying on support from his wife, who opened a small school. The major commission from these years was the Campbell house and barracks but after their completion his practice seems to have completely withered. He published reminiscences in the *Australian Almanac* in 1835. Macquarie had made a land grant to Greenway of 800 acres on the Hunter River to which the architect retreated and attempted to farm. Greenway was important as the first significant architect in Australia and the designer of the earliest public buildings of note.

BIBLIOGRAPHY

AUDB

M. H. Ellis: *Francis Greenway: His Life and Times* (Sydney, 1949, 2/1953)

M. Herman: *Early Australian Architects and their Work* (Sydney, 1954)

F. Philipp: 'Notes on the Study of Australian Architecture', *Hist. Stud.*, vii/32 (1959), pp. 405–21

J. Ritchie: 'The Architects', *The Evidence of the Bigge Reports*, ii (Melbourne, 1971), pp. 124–63

GEORGE TIBBITS

Greenwich. Former metropolitan borough of south-east London, England, and from 1965 a borough of Greater London, situated on the south bank of the River Thames, *c.* 7 km downstream from the City of London. In Greenwich Park is the original Royal Observatory (1675), designed by Christopher Wren, accepted internationally from 1884 as being on the prime meridian of longitude and the source of Greenwich Mean Time. The Royal Naval Hospital (begun 1696), also by Wren, stands on the site of Greenwich Palace (begun 1427), a former royal palace, birthplace of Henry VIII, Mary I (*reg* 1553–8) and Elizabeth I.

1. PALACE. The original palace, known as Bella Court, was built in 1427 by Humfrey, Duke of Gloucester, brother of Henry V. The estate became the property of the Crown in 1447 and was given to Margaret of Anjou, who renamed it Placentia ('pleasant place'). Substantial rebuilding took place under Henry VII, who laid out three successive courtyards along the Thames, and further improvements were made by Henry VIII. Lying between the royal shipyards of Deptford and Woolwich, it became a favourite palace of the Tudors. The extensive red-brick palace was largely demolished in 1661–9, when Charles II embarked on the construction of a new palace under the direction of JOHN WEBB (i). Only an early 17th-century undercroft survives from the earlier building.

On the boundary between the palace grounds and the royal park to the south, Inigo Jones built an Italian-style villa, the Queen's House, in two stages, beginning it for Anne of Denmark, wife of James I, in 1616–19 and completing it for Henrietta Maria in 1630–38 (*see* JONES, INIGO, §1(i); *see also* STUART, House of, (7), and VILLA, §II, 4). The building later proved frustrating to schemes for both the palace and the naval hospital, as it was too small to provide the necessary focus for a Baroque ensemble, but the possibility of its demolition was dismissed. Various schemes for enlarging the Queen's House were proposed in the 1660s, but little was built beyond the addition of further rooms spanning the Woolwich–Deptford road and connecting the two parallel ranges of the building.

In 1663 Webb prepared drawings for a palace of three ranges, built around an open-ended courtyard facing the Thames. Only the west range, the King Charles block, was built. It was begun in 1664 and was to be the King's side of the palace, but work on it was abandoned in 1669–70, its interior still incomplete and its windows boarded up. This block, Webb's masterpiece, is now regarded as the earliest Baroque building in England; it relies on large statements, which are emphasized to dramatic effect through the use of the giant order and overall rustication. It is a tribute to the balance of the composition that it survives without the proposed domed cross-range, which would have provided an appropriate, upward conclusion to the ensemble. Webb realized that this range was unlikely to be built, and, in 1665, he produced designs for a grotto in the park to the south of the Queen's House, which would have closed the vista from the river, but there is no evidence that this was begun.

2. ROYAL NAVAL HOSPITAL. In 1694 the site of Greenwich Palace, including the King Charles Block and adjoining lands but excluding the avenue leading from the Queen's House to the Thames, passed from royal ownership to that of trustees in order to be converted for use as the Royal Naval Hospital for seamen, on the pattern of Christopher Wren's Chelsea Hospital for soldiers. As Surveyor at Greenwich from 1696 to 1716, Wren was responsible for the general layout of the blocks, which were built over the next 50 years (*see* WREN, CHRISTOPHER, §I, 5). This included the construction of the Queen Anne Block (1699–1729) to match the King Charles Block, which was itself extended westwards (1696–8, with later additions); and, immediately to the south, the construction of the matching King William Block (1698–1723) and Queen Mary Block (1699–1752). The two southern blocks, each consisting of three ranges and a colonnade arranged around a quadrangle, contain the Painted Hall, decorated (1708–27) by JAMES THORNHILL, and the chapel (remodelled by James Stuart, 1779–89), both surmounted by Wren's impressive domes (see fig.).

Nicholas Hawksmoor acted as Wren's Clerk of Works at Greenwich and, from 1705, as Deputy Surveyor. In these capacities he was responsible for the east range (1700–03) of the Queen Anne Block, the west range (1701–2) of the King William Block and the designs for three extraordinary schemes for closing the vista from the river, which, if built, would have invited comparison with St Peter's, Rome, and Versailles. Samuel Johnson, visiting in 1763, found the buildings at Greenwich 'too magnificent for a place of charity' and 'too much detached to make one great whole'; nevertheless, they form the most magnificent architectural group in England.

The sumptuous interiors planned by John Webb (i) for the staterooms of the palace were not realized (*see* WEBB (i), JOHN) and such magnificence was not required after the building had been converted to hospital use. With the exception of three notable rooms—the Baroque Painted Hall, the Greek Revival chapel and the austere, apsed

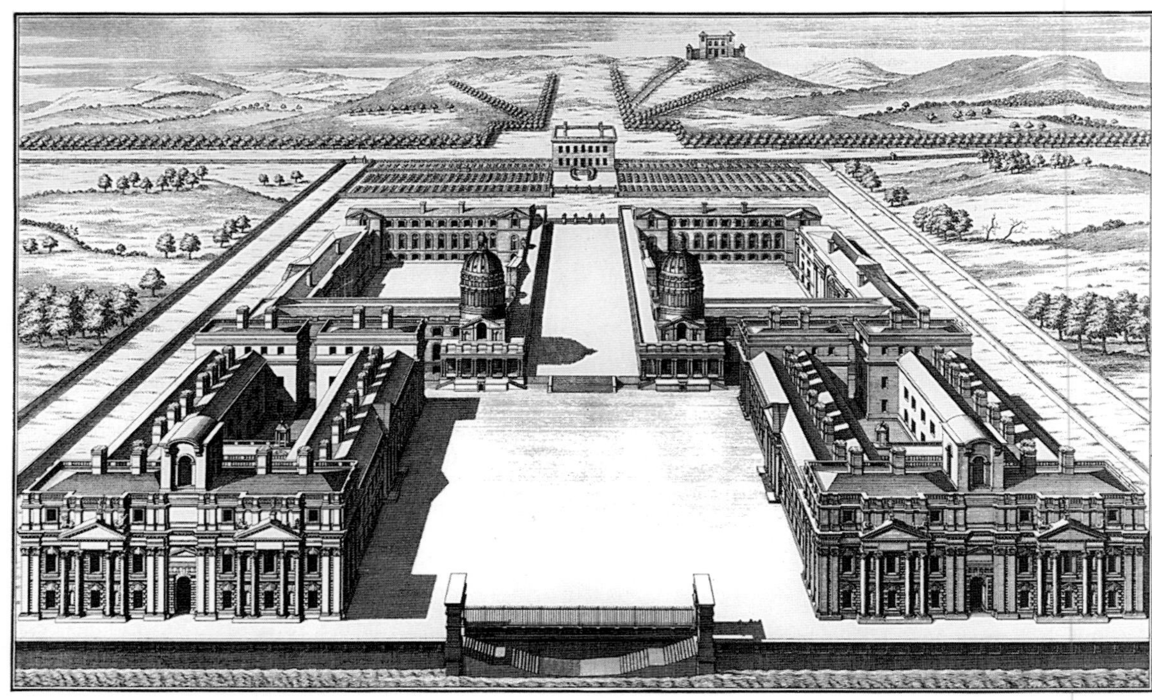

Greenwich, Royal Naval Hospital, 1696–1716; idealized perspective from Colen Campbell: *Vitruvius Britannicus*, iii (London, 1725), p. 3

entrance to the King Charles Block—the interiors of the hospital are entirely utilitarian.

The Hospital accepted its first pensioners in 1705 and continued in use until 1869. Four years later the buildings became the home of the Royal Naval College. In 1806 the Queen's House was sold to the hospital and became a school for sailors' orphans; colonnades and flanking wings were added to the Queen's House in 1809. The complex has been occupied by the National Maritime Museum since 1934.

BIBLIOGRAPHY

N. Hawksmoor: 'Remarks on the Founding and Carrying On the Buildings of the Royal Hospital at Greenwich, 1728', *Wren Soc.*, vi (1929), pp. 17–27

London, Royal Comm. Anc. & Hist. Mnmts & Constr. England, v (London, 1930)

J. H. V. Davies: 'The Dating of the Buildings of the Royal Hospital at Greenwich', *Archaeol. J.*, cxiii (1956), pp. 126–36

H. M. Colvin, ed.: *The History of the King's Works*, 6 vols (London, 1963–82), iv, pp. 96–123; v, pp. 140–52; vi, pp. 326–7

K. Downes: *English Baroque Architecture* (London, 1966)

J. Harris: *Inigo Jones and John Webb*, London, RIBA cat. (Farnborough, 1972)

J. Charlton: *The Queen's House* (London, 1976)

K. Downes: *Hawksmoor* (London, 1979)

J. Harris and A. A. Tait: *Catalogue of the Drawings by Inigo Jones, John Webb and Isaac de Caus at Worcester College, Oxford* (Oxford, 1979)

J. Bold: 'Greenwich: "The Grott & Ascent by Mr. Webb"', *Burl. Mag.*, cxxix (1982), pp. 149–50

B. Cherry and N. Pevsner: *London, 2: South*, Bldgs England (Harmondsworth, 1983)

J. Bold: *John Webb* (Oxford, 1989)

JOHN BOLD

Greenwood, John (*b* Boston, MA, 7 Dec 1727; *d* Margate, Kent, 16 Sept 1792). English painter, engraver and auctioneer of American birth. In 1742 he was apprenticed to the Boston engraver Thomas Johnston. He abandoned engraving for painting (e.g. the group portrait of his own family, the *Greenwood-Lee Family*, *c.* 1747; Boston, MA, Mus. F.A.). In 1752 he went to Paramaribo, Surinam, where, in the space of five years, he painted 113 portraits, which he recorded along with numerous other events and observations in a notebook. While there he painted his best-known work, *Sea Captains Carousing in Surinam* (*c.* 1752–8; St Louis, MO, A. Mus.). It is the only tavern scene conversation piece painted in colonial America and was most likely inspired by a print of William Hogarth's *Midnight Modern Conversation* (New Haven, CT, Yale Cent. Brit. A).

Greenwood remained in Surinam until May 1758, when he departed for Amsterdam, where he helped reopen the Amsterdam Art Academy, returned to engraving and produced numerous mezzotints. While in the Low Countries he began buying Dutch Old Masters for English collectors and moved to London by 1763. His letters to Sir Lawrence Dundas, with whom he was particularly associated, show how profitable the trade was. He also acted as agent for John Stuart, 3rd Earl of Bute. Although he became one of the most prominent auctioneers in late 18th-century London, with rooms in the Haymarket and from 1783 in Leicester Square, his connoisseurship was rudimentary: Titian's *Death of Actaeon* (*c.* 1559; London, N.G.) passed unrecognized through his hands.

BIBLIOGRAPHY

F. Weitenkampf: 'John Greenwood: An American-born Artist in Eighteenth-century Europe', *Bull. NY Pub. Lib.*, xxxi (1927), pp. 623–34 [cat. of his prts]

John Greenwood in America, 1745–1752 (exh. cat. by A. Burroughs, Andover, MA, Phillips Acad., Addison Gal., 1943)

D. Sutton: 'The Dundas Pictures', *Apollo*, lxxxvi (Sept 1967), pp. 204–13
Rembrandt in Eighteenth Century England (exh. cat. by C. White, D. Alexander and E. D'Oench, New Haven, CT, Yale Cent. Brit. A., 1983), pp. 58, 128–9

RICHARD H. SAUNDERS

Grégoire, Henri-Charles-Martin (*b* Maubeuge, 1791; *d* 1854). French architect. After studying at the Ecole Spéciale d'Architecture (1806–11), he was appointed architect to the département of Seine-Inférieure, in which capacity he directed the construction of the lunatic asylum (1821–30) at Saint-Yon. Consisting of several U-shaped buildings overlooking open countryside, each separate and devoted to single categories of patient, it was the first asylum in which the nosographic and architectural ideas of the psychiatrist Jean-Etienne-Dominique Esquirol (1772–1840) were put into practice. Little is known of Grégoire's other buildings, apart from the hospital and seminary (1837–9) at Yvetot (Seine-Maritime). He also restored the church of St Etienne at Fécamp. He was appointed by the Commission des Monuments Historiques to complete the façade of St Ouen, Rouen, for which funds were voted in the spring of 1845. Grégoire presented three alternative projects, one without towers, one with diagonal towers, and the third with frontal towers, which was accepted; building work began in November 1845. After the reorganization of the Service des Edifices Diocésains, he was offered the post of diocesan architect to Rouen and Amiens, but he refused it, believing it would be undiplomatic to replace Pinchon and Dubois as head of a project to complete the cast-iron spire of Rouen Cathedral. The spire had been conceived originally by Jean-Antoine Alavoine, who had been the teacher of Pinchon and Dubois. He also refused the proposed compromise of working on the main door and Cour des Libraires at Rouen Cathedral, his reason being, according to the archbishop, that 'he was accustomed to creating new and beautiful things and was little drawn to a work of mere maintenance'.

BIBLIOGRAPHY

J. M. Leniaud: 'Historicité ou perfectionnisme': Le Débat sur la façade de Saint-Ouen de Rouen', *Bull. Archéol. Cté Trav. Hist. & Sci.* (1978), pp. 141–62
——: 'Les Champs d'application du rationalisme architectural, les asiles d'aliénés', *Inf. Psych.*, lvi/6 (1980), pp. 747–61
——: 'Plaidoyer pour l'architecture psychiatrique', *Rev. Mnmts Hist.*, cxiv (1981), pp. 53–8
——: 'La Cité Utopie ou l'asile dans la première moitié du XIXe siècle', *Conf. Hist. Médec.* (1983), pp. 129–43

JEAN-MICHEL LENIAUD

Gregori. Italian family of engravers. Carlo Gregori (*b* Florence, 1719; *d* Florence, 1759) studied with Johann-Jakob Frey in Rome before pursuing his career in Florence. He made prints after Old Master paintings by, for example, Titian, Rubens and Correggio and also reproduced artists' portraits. His engravings illustrated some important 18th-century publications, including Ignazio Enrico Hugford's work (1762) on Anton Domenico Gabbiani. He primarily signed with his name in full, but also used an interwoven monogram of C and G.

Carlo's son Ferdinando Gregori (*b* Florence, 1743; *d* Florence, 1804) received his initial training from his father before journeying to Paris in 1761 to study with Jean-Georges Wille. He returned to Florence where, like Carlo, he produced numerous engravings after Old Master paintings, most notably his well-known depiction (inscribed and dated 1768; Florence, Bib. Marucelliana) of Raphael's *Madonna della sedia* (Florence, Pitti). His work, which often celebrated the art and artists of his native city, included prints after the sculpture of Baccio Bandinelli and Giambologna, and a large folio of 34 engravings, produced in collaboration with the English painter and engraver Thomas Patch, after Lorenzo Ghiberti's bronze doors (Florence, Baptistery of S Giovanni). His work was included in numerous contemporary publications, among the most important being M. Lastri's *L' Etruria pittrice.* He signed with an interwoven monogram of F and G.

PRINTS

A. F. Gori: *Museum Florentinum* (Florence, 1731–62) [engravings by both artists, Ferdinando's appearing only in vols dating after 1761]
Museum Capitolinum (Rome, 1750–83)
A. Gerini: *Raccolta di stampe rappresentanti i quadri più scelti dei signori marchesi Gerini* (Florence, 1759) [engravings by Carlo of paintings in the Gerini Col.]
I. E. Hugford: *A. D. Gabbiani: Raccolta di cento pensieri diversi fatti intagliare in rame da I. E. Hugford* (Florence, 1762); later pubd as: *Collection de cent pensées, gravées par J. B. Galli et autres* (Rome, 1786)
F. Gregori and T. Patch: *Porte del Battistero di Firenze* (Florence, 1774)
M. Lastri: *L'Etruria pittrice* (Florence, 1795) [incl. work by both artists, esp. Ferdinando]
P. Arrigoni and A. Bertarelli: *Ritratti di musicisti ed artisti di teatro conservati nella Raccolta delle Stampe e dei Disegni del Castello Sforzesco* (Milan, 1932), cat. nos 2041, 3693, 4800 [engraved portraits by Ferdinando]
C. A. Petrucci: *Catalogo generale delle stampe tratte dai rami incisi posseduti dalla Calcografia Nazionale* (Rome, 1953), n. 68 [prints by both artists in the col.]

BIBLIOGRAPHY

Bénézit; Bolaffi; Thieme–Becker
G. K. Nagler: *Neues allgemeines Künstler-Lexikon* (Munich, 1835–52), vi, pp. 94–5
C. Le Blanc: *Manuel de l'amateur d'estampes* (Paris, 1854–6), ii, pp. 317–18

□

Gregoriis, Gregorio de' (*b* Forlì; *fl* Venice, *c.* 1480–1528). Italian publisher, printer and woodcutter. He went to Venice *c.* 1480, where, with his brother Giovanni de' Gregoriis, he set up a press that produced many of the most admired illustrated books of the time (e.g. Boccaccio's *Decameron*, 1492; for illustration *see* BOCCACCIO, GIOVANNI). From 1505 to 1528 he ran the press on his own. In 1517 he published a five-block edition of Titian's *Triumph of Christ* (e.g. Bassano del Grappa, Mus. Civ.; and see 1976–7 exh. cat., no. 2) and two other woodcuts designed by Titian: the *Virgin and Child with SS John the Baptist and Gregory the Great* (see 1976–7 exh. cat., no. 13), which also bears the monogram of Lucantonio degli Uberti, and a *Martyrdom of St Cecilia*, which is signed and dated.

BIBLIOGRAPHY

F. Mauroner: *Le incisioni di Tiziano* (Venice, 1943/*R* 1982)
Tiziano e la silografia veneziana del cinquecento (exh. cat., ed. M. Muraro and D. Rosand; Venice, Fond. Cini; Washington, DC, N.G.A.; 1976–7), pp. 14, 17, 71, 74–8, 85, 91

FELICIANO BENVENUTI

Gregorini, Domenico (*b* Rome, 21 Aug 1692; *d* Rome, 2 Feb 1777). Italian architect. He trained under his father, Ludovico Gregorini (*c.* 1661–1723), also an architect; in the latter's workshop was a nephew of Filippo Juvarra,

Pietro Passalacqua (*fl* 1706–48), with whom Gregorini collaborated throughout his career. In 1713 he won first prize in a competition of the Accademia di S Luca, Rome, of which he later became a member, and in 1722 he joined the Congregazione dei Virtuosi al Pantheon. A year later he took over his father's workshop and in 1725 completed the restoration of the Palazzo Sforza-Cesarini in Genzano. In 1726, together with Passalacqua, he entered the service of Cardinal Pietro Ottoboni, for whom he may have enlarged the Palazzo Episcopale in Magliano Sabino (1726) and altered the church and convent of S Maria in Monterone. His work also included designs for festival architecture in the Piazza della Cancelleria (engraved by Filippo Vasconi (*c.* 1687–1730), e.g. Rome, Pal. Braschi). In 1727–30 he was commissioned by Ottoboni to erect the oratory of the SS Sacramento in S Maria in Via, Rome. Its ground-plan echoes Francesco Borromini's nearby chapel of the Collegio di Propaganda Fide, while Gregorini's interest in the effects of light shows the influence of Juvarra. In 1732 Gregorini took part in the competition for the façade of the basilica of S Giovanni in Laterano. In 1736 he became Ottoboni's court architect, and in 1737 he completed the rebuilding of the presbytery and confessional in S Lorenzo in Damaso (destr.; recorded in a painting by Giuseppe Valeriani (*d* 1761), Rome, Pal. Braschi).

Between 1740 and 1746 Gregorini and Passalacqua restored the basilica of Santa Croce in Gerusalemme, a commission from Pompeo Aldrovandi, governor of Rome, for whom Gregorini had already carried out a number of commissions including the restoration of the Teatro Tordinona (1734). The interior of the basilica was extensively altered, despite the retention of the original structure. Before the nave the architects placed an oval vestibule divided by pillars into an inner domed space and an outer ambulatory. This motif is reminiscent of Gregorini's work at S Lorenzo in Damaso. It allowed for the skilful incorporation of two chapels situated in front of the entrance wall. It also determined the plan of the convex three-bay façade, which faces the streets used by pilgrims that lead to S Giovanni in Laterano and the basilica of S Maria Maggiore. As a specialist in restoration, Gregorini was appointed to the commission set up by Benedict XIV in 1742 to evaluate damage to the dome of St Peter's.

BIBLIOGRAPHY

R. Besozzi: *La storia della basilica di Santa Croce in Gerusalemme* (Rome, 1750)

A. Schiavo: 'La veduta di Giuseppe Valeriani del S Lorenzo in Damaso', *Stud. Romani*, xx (1972), pp. 228–34

P. Mancini and G. Scarfone: *L'oratorio del SS Sacramento di S Maria in Via* (Rome, 1973)

N. A. Mallory: *Roman Rococo Architecture from Clement XI to Benedict XIV, 1700–1758* (New York, 1977), pp. 145–73

G. Scarfone: 'La "Legnara al Popolo": Un'opera inedita di Domenico Gregorini', *Strenna Romanisti* (1981), pp. 430–40

Fochi d'allegrezza a Roma dal cinquecento all'ottocento (exh. cat., ed. L. Cavazzi; Rome, Pal. Braschi, 1982), pp. 33–44

P. Mancini and G. Scarfone: 'Appunti per una scheda sulla vita e le opere di Domenico Gregorini', *Alma Roma*, xxvi (1985), pp. 3–19

C. Varagnoli: 'Ricerche sull'opera architettonica di Gregorini e Passalacqua', *Archit.: Stor. & Doc.*, 1–2 (1988), pp. 21–65

In urbe architectus: Modelli, disegni, misure: La professione dell'architetto: Roma, 1680–1750 (exh. cat. by T. Manfredi and D. Gregorini, Rome, 1991–2)

A. BUSCHOW OESCHLIN

Gregorio, Goro di. *See* GORO DI GREGORIO.

Gregorio di Cecco (di Luca) (*b* Siena, ?1390–95; *d* Siena, before 1 July 1424). Italian painter. He was first mentioned on 24 May 1418, when he was paid for painting book covers (untraced) for *biccherne* (Sienese official records). He was a pupil of Taddeo di Bartolo, with whom he jointly signed an altarpiece (1420; untraced) in the Marescotti chapel (Siena, S Agostino). He became Taddeo's partner on 25 October 1421 and was named in his will as his adoptive son and heir (Aug 1422). In 1422 he was one of the advisers on the construction of the church and loggia of S Paolo, Siena. On 11 April 1423 Gregorio married Jacopa, daughter of the Sienese sculptor Domenico di Niccolò dei Cori (1363–1453). The polyptych of the *Madonna of Humility with SS Augustine, John the Baptist, Peter and Paul* (Siena, Mus. Opera Duomo), signed and dated 1423, was made for Siena Cathedral and is Gregorio's only securely attributed work. Although the figure style and decorative elements owe much to Taddeo di Bartolo, Gregorio's style is more refined, brittle and elegant and his colour more delicate and clear than his master's. It has been suggested that he polychromed the wooden statue of the *Virgin and Child* (the '*Virgin of the Magnificat*'; Siena, S Agostino), attributed to Francesco di Valdambrino. Also attributed to Gregorio are a *Crucifixion* (Siena, Mus. Opera Duomo, 25), a *Birth of the Virgin* (Rome, Pin. Vaticana, 187), a *Marriage of the Virgin* (London, N.G., 1317), a *Crucifixion* (Avignon, Mus. Petit Pal., MI 368) and a *St Louis of Toulouse* (Siena, Pin. N.).

BIBLIOGRAPHY

G. Milanesi: *Documenti per la storia dell'arte senese*, i (1854), pp. 46–7

E. Carli: *Il Duomo di Siena* (Siena, 1979), p. 85

M. Boskovits: 'Su Niccolò di Buonaccorso, Benedetto di Bindo e la pittura senese del primo quattrocento', *Paragone*, xxxi/2 (1980), pp. 2–22

G. Corti: 'La compania di Taddeo di Bartolo e Gregoria di Cecco, con altri documenti inediti', *Mitt. Ksthist. Inst. Florenz*, xxv (1981), pp. 373–7

E. Neri Lusanna: 'Un episodio di collaborazione tra scultori e pittori nella Siena del primo quattrocento: La Madonna del Magnificat di Sant'Agostino', *Mitt. Ksthist. Inst. Florenz*, xxv (1981), pp. 325–40

L. Bellosi: 'Gregorio di Cecco', *Il gotico a Siena* (exh. cat., Siena, Pal. Pub., 1982), pp. 346–8

JACQUELINE MONGELLAZ

Gregory, Bishop of Tours (*b* Clermont-Ferrand, 30 Nov AD 538; *d* Tours, 17 Nov 594; *fd* 17 Nov). Gallo-Roman saint, bishop and writer. He was appointed Bishop of Tours in AD 573. He came from a distinguished family that played a pre-eminent role in Gaul. His writings, the *History of the Franks* and books of miracles of the saints, provide reliable evidence of 6th-century buildings and monuments, documenting, for example, the existence of 408 sanctuaries. A sanctuary would be built over the tomb of a saint at the same time that a bishop, in an attempt to institute a cult in that saint's honour, commissioned a life of the saint. As Gregory often had to decide questions concerning the construction or decoration of churches he must have looked closely at the buildings he visited. His accounts of Clermont-Ferrand Cathedral, St Martin, Tours, and Old St Peter's, Rome, with their measurements and details of the number of columns and windows, recall the dry listings of the *Liber pontificalis* and differ markedly from the poetic descriptions of his friend Venantius

Fortunatus. The sanctuaries Gregory mentioned, including St Symphorien, Autun, and the cathedrals of Lyon and Chalon-sur-Saône, must have been comparable to the contemporary Roman basilicas of S Maria Maggiore and S Sabina, with their colonnades, inlaid marbles and mosaics or paintings representing scenes from the Old and New Testaments. There were also sanctuaries with centralized plans, as at La Daurade, Toulouse, and with oval plans as at St Gereon, Cologne, where 'admirable mosaic work makes it shine as if it were truly made of gold, so that the residents have called it the House of the Golden Saints'. The Christian monuments of his day seemed to Gregory grander and more beautiful than those they replaced.

Gregory himself was a prominent builder, and he enumerated with pride the buildings he had erected in his diocese. He reconstructed the cathedral, burnt in his predecessor's time, on a much larger scale and decorated it with paintings. Venantius Fortunatus wrote a poem on the paintings that Gregory had had done in his cathedral, which, in his view, were not inferior to those of Justinian's Ravenna. Gregory also had the walls of St Martin repainted by his own craftsmen. He built a new baptistery near St Martin, but preserved the old one. In addition, he dedicated many churches and oratories in Touraine and presented them with relics.

BIBLIOGRAPHY

B. Krusch: *Gregorii episcopi Turonensis decem libri historiarum, scriptores rerum Merovingicarum*, Mnmt Ger. Hist. (1884/*R* Hannover, 1937–51)

——: *Gregorii episcopi Turonensis miracula et opera minora* (Hannover, 1885/*R* 1969)

O. M. Dalton: *The History of the Franks by Gregory of Tours*, 2 vols (Oxford, 1927)

M. Vieillard-Troïekouroff: *Les Monuments religieux de la Gaule d'après les oeuvres de Grégoire de Tours* (Paris, 1976)

MAY VIEILLARD-TROÏEKOUROFF

Gregory I [the Great], Pope (*b* Rome, *c*. 540; elected 590; *d* 12 March 604; *fd* 3 Sept). Italian saint, pope and writer. Born into a noble family, he received a broad cultural education that was later enriched by biblical and patristic studies. His activities as pope also indicate that he had a good grounding in law. After serving as Prefect of Rome (573), he retired from the world, devoting his wealth to the relief of poverty and the foundation of monasteries, one of which, St Andrew's in Rome, he entered as a monk; but *c*. 578 Pelagius II sent him to Constantinople as nuncio to Emperor Tiberios II (*reg* 579–85). After his return, six years later, he served as abbot at St Andrew's until his election to the papacy.

As pope he fervently believed in his mission to support the Church and devoted himself to improving the secular and religious situation in Rome, as well as throughout Europe. He made peace with the Lombards (592–3) and converted them from Arianism. He was unswerving in his aim of eliminating abuses and violence within the Church. He defended the Jews' right to worship and in 597 sent St Augustine, later first Archbishop of Canterbury (*d* 604/5), to convert the Anglo-Saxons. Gregory also demonstrated exceptional talents in the management of the property of the Church of Rome. Portraits show him wearing papal dress, carrying a crosier with a single or double cross and, as a Doctor of the Church, holding a book; in those from the 12th century he also wears the papal tiara. His attribute is the dove of the Holy Spirit dictating his writings: his output as a writer and liturgist was vast, and he had a significant influence on the standardization of the texts of the Western service-books and ecclesiastical music.

Gregory's views on art are particularly expressed in two letters written in 599 to St Serenus, Bishop of Marseilles, reprimanding him for having destroyed some images of saints and maintaining that, although images, as man-made objects, should not be worshipped, they could fulfil a didactic purpose, especially for illiterate people. Paintings, and especially narrative works, could also prompt religious feelings, just as the Scriptures did for the literate. This conviction was the directive behind Gregory's conversion of 'barbaric' peoples, for whom, he considered, pictures could serve as a substitute for books.

Despite Gregory's belief in the educative function of images, he was accused of the destruction of pagan literature and classical art in medieval times, particularly in the *Chronicon pontificum et imperatorum* by Martinus Polonus (*d* 1278), which was the most widely read historical work during the Middle Ages. This tradition was perpetuated by the *Chronicle* (1321) of Amalricus Augerius, who attributed the destruction of the pagan idols not to Pope Silvester I (*reg* 314–35) but to Gregory and who adopted the arguments, with few changes, from Polonus's work.

Doubts regarding the validity of the accusations against Gregory were later expressed by Sicco Poleton, Platina, Albrecht Dürer and Raphael, the last in a letter to Leo X. During the second half of the 16th century, as part of the Counter-Reformation, Gregory was praised for his destructive zeal. The only pictorial records of this period of Gregory as iconoclast are two paintings by Giulio Romano (Rome, Vatican, Sala di Costantino) that depict the workshop of a converted sculptor who is destroying pagan statues and Gregory engaged in writing under the inspiration of the Holy Spirit.

WRITINGS

U. Moricca, ed.: *Dialogues* (Rome, 1924); Eng. trans. as *Saint Gregory the Great: Dialogues* (New York, 1959)

M. Adriaen, ed.: *Magna moralia in Job* (Turnhout, 1979)

D. Norberg, ed.: *S Gregorii Magni registrum epistularum* (Turnhout, 1982)

BIBLIOGRAPHY

J. Endres: 'Die Darstellung der Gregormesse im Mittelalter', *Z. Christ. Kst.*, xxix (1917), pp. 146ff

T. Buddenseig: 'Gregory the Great: The Destroyer of Pagan Idols', *J. Warb. & Court. Inst.*, xxviii (1965), pp. 44–65

R. P. Lee: 'St Gregory the Great and the Santa Maria Maggiore Altarpiece', *Burl. Mag.*, cxxvii (1978), pp. 295–7

H. L. Kessler: 'Pictorial Narrative and Church Mission in Sixth-century Gaul', *Stud. Hist. A.*, xvi (1985), pp. 75–91

CHIARA STEFANI

Gregory XIII, Pope [Boncompagni, Ugo] (*b* Bologna, 1 Jan 1502; elected 1572; *d* Rome, 10 April 1585). Italian pope and patron. He received a doctorate in canon and civil law in 1530 from the University of Bologna, where he remained for eight years as Professor of Law. He moved to Rome in 1539 and held several important judicial posts under Paul III, Pius IV and Pius V until his election as their successor in 1572. His principal biographer, Marc Antonio Ciappi, states that the Pope was concerned to emulate 'in customs and actions' his namesake, Gregory the Great. His patronage reflected this concern. Near the provisional hostel set up in the Campo Santo beside St

Peter's, pilgrims were greeted with a cycle of the life of Gregory the Great painted by Lorenzo Sabatini; in the church of SS Cosma e Damiano the Pope ordered that the figure of S Felice in the apse mosaics be replaced with one of Gregory the Great. He also venerated Gregory of Nazianzus, whose relics he had transferred in a triumphal procession (1580) from S Maria di Campo Marzo to the new Cappella Gregoriana in St Peter's. He fostered the development of Greek Orthodox rite in Rome with the founding of S Atanasio, constructed by Giacomo della Porta. Like his predecessor, Gregory encouraged the cult of the early Christian saints, an interest that found expression in his art patronage when he commissioned Niccolò Circignani (called il Pomarancio) and Matteo da Siena (1533–88) to paint vivid scenes of martyrdom in S Stefano Rotondo in 1582. Among other painters who received support from Gregory XIII were Giorgio Vasari and Federico Zuccaro, who painted, respectively, the frescoes of the *Battle of Lepanto* and the *St Bartholomew's Day Massacre* (both 1572) in the Vatican's Sala Regia. Tommaso Laureti painted the vault of the Sala di Costantino with the *Triumph of Christian Faith*. Raffaellino da Reggio, Marco da Faenza (*d* 1588) and Antonio Tempesta worked on the vault frescoes of the Galleria delle Carte Geografiche, a gallery designed by Ottaviano Mascherino, papal architect, as a fourth storey to the west corridor of the Cortile del Belvedere. The 'carte' were topographical frescoes designed by the noted architect, astronomer and mathematician Ignazio Danti (who also enabled the Pope to achieve his reform of the Julian Calendar; *see* DANTI, (2)) and painted by his brother Antonio Danti (*c*. 1530–after1597). The observatory known as the Torre dei Venti was built at the northern end of the gallery and contained the Sala della Meridiana, which Pomarancio and Cristoforo Roncalli decorated with allegorical representations of the winds, while Matthijs Bril and Paul Bril frescoed imaginary *vedute* of Rome in the suite of rooms above. Under Gregory's benefaction, the Accademia di San Luca was accorded official statutes (1577) and Girolomo Muziano, who had urged this development, became its first president (*see* ROME, §VI).

Gregory was a notable patron of architecture and public works, described by the French writer Montaigne, on his visit to Rome in 1580, as 'très-magnifique en bastimans publiques et reformation des rues'. In preparation for the Holy Year of 1575, he reopened ancient roads, such as the Via Tuscolana, and laid new ones, most notably the Via Merulana, linking S Maria Maggiore with the Lateran and the Via Gregoriana, leading from the Monte Cavallo to Trinità dei Monti. The papal bull known as 'Quae publice utilia' (1574) was of importance in regulating the façades of private buildings along the city's main thoroughfares. The ancient Pons Senatorum (Ponte Rotto) was rebuilt by Matteo da Castello (*c*. 1525 - after 1604), and the architect Martino Longhi I converted the planetarium of the Baths of Diocletian into granaries. In 1574 the Acqua Vergine, supplying water to the most populated quarters of Rome, was renovated. Giacomo della Porta was commissioned to design four fountains: for the Piazza del Panteon, Piazza Colonna and two for the Piazza Navona (all 1574–5; *in situ*). He also designed the more fanciful Fontana delle Tartarughe in Piazzetta Mattei (1581–4; *in situ*). At S Giovanni in Laterano, Giacomo del Duca was commissioned to design a new rusticated portal leading through the Aurelian wall from the Via Latina. Restorations were made to the portico of the basilica and the Scala Santa was re-erected along the south side of the portico. Some work was also done to S Giovanni in Fonte, where the Boncompagni dragons appear on the coffered ceiling. The restoration of the portico at S Maria Maggiore, for which ancient columns were transported from old St Peter's, is generally ascribed to Martino Longhi I (Baglione). Other restorations were made to the medieval porch of S Maria in Trastevere; and under Gregory's patronage the painter Girolamo Sicciolante (1521–80) completed the gilt coffering over the nave of S Maria in Aracoeli, begun in Pius V's pontificate.

Gregory XIII was responsible for initiating the construction (1583) of the Palazzo del Quirinale, planned as a summer retreat and designed in its first stages by Mascherino. He also spent considerable sums on furthering work on St Peter's (*see also* ROME, §VI, 14(ii)(a)). He commissioned a fresco over the central portal of the façade (destr. 1605) depicting Christ bearing the message 'pasce oves meas' while the Pope kneels before him accompanied by a flock of sheep. Despite Gregory's support, work on Michelangelo's design (which was recorded on a papal medal of 1572) progressed slowly. The dome was still unfinished in June 1584, by which time della Porta had succeeded Jacopo Vignola as Maestro della Fabbrica. The Cappella Gregoriana, which in Michelangelo's Greek-cross plan would have stood just inside the narthex of the basilica, was consecrated in 1578. It housed the icon of the *Madonna del Soccorso* and had ceiling mosaics by Muziano and walls decorated by Cesare Nebbia and Paul Bril.

BIBLIOGRAPHY

M. A. Ciappi: *Compendio delle heroiche et gloriose attioni et santa di vita di Papa Gregorio XIII* (Rome, 1591)

G. Baglione: *Vite* (1642); ed. V. Mariani (1935), p. 68

L. von Pastor: *Geschichte der Päpste seit dem Ausgang des Mittelalters*, 24 vols (Freiburg, 1891–1924; Eng. trans. as *History of the Popes*, ed. R. F. Kerr, London, 1930), xx, pp. 560–630

H. Röttgen: 'Zeitgeschichtliche Bildprogramm der katholischen Restauration unter Gregor XIII (1572–85)', *Münchn. Jb. Bild. Kst.*, xxvi (1975), pp. 89–122

M. F. dell'Arco, ed.: *La Roma dei Longhi: Papi e architetti tra Manierismo e Barocco* (Rome, 1982)

A. Herz: 'Vasari's "Massacre" Series in the Sala Regia: The Political, Juristic and Religious', *Z. Kstgesch.*, xlix (1986), pp. 45-54

P. Jacks: 'A Sacred Meta for Pilgrims in the Holy Year 1575', *Architectura*, XIX (1989), pp. 42–72

PHILIP J. JACKS

Gregory XIV, Pope. *See under* SFONDRATO.

Gregory XV, Pope. *See* LUDOVISI, (1).

Gregory XVI, Pope [Cappellari, Bartolommeo Alberto] (*b* Belluno, 18 Sept 1765; elected 1831; *d* Rome, 1 June 1846). Italian pope and patron. The son of a lawyer, he entered the strict Camaldolese branch of the Benedictine Order. He became a professor of science and philosophy at the monastery of S Michele, on the island of Murano, Venice, in 1790 and was also noted for his knowledge of East Asian languages. In 1805 he became abbot of S Gregorio al Celio in Rome, in 1807 Procurator-General of the Camaldolese, in 1814 Vicar-General of the Camaldolese and in 1826 a cardinal. As a patron of art Gregory XVI made a significant contribution to the expansion and organization of the Vatican collections. He encouraged archaeological research and excavation in and around Rome and founded a museum at S Giovanni in Laterano to accommodate the new finds, although in 1963 these were transferred to the Museo Gregoriano Profano in the Vatican. In 1837 he founded the Museo Gregoriano Etrusco in the Vatican and in 1839 created the Museo Gregoriano Egizio, which was arranged for him by the Bolognese Barnabite friar and Egyptologist Luigi Maria Ungarelli (1779–1845). Gregory XVI was also responsible for the transfer in 1838 of the Roman wall painting known as the *Aldobrandini Wedding*, discovered on the Esquiline Hill in 1605, from the Villa Aldobrandini to its present location in the Vatican. He was buried in the 16th-century Cappella Gregoriana in St Peter's in a tomb designed in 1855 by Luigi Amici.

BIBLIOGRAPHY

Hoefer
J. N. D. Kelly: *The Oxford Dictionary of Popes* (Oxford, 1986), pp. 307–9

JANET SOUTHORN

Gregory, Eric (Craven) [Peter] (*b* Bradford, W. Yorks, 6 Oct 1887; *d* Lagos, Nigeria, 10 Feb 1959). English patron, collector and philanthropist. He was educated at Bradford Grammar School. He then began a successful career in the printing business, becoming Director and then Chairman of the printing and publishing firm of Percy Lund, Humphries & Co. Ltd, Bradford. In the 1920s he began to collect drawings, prints, paintings and sculpture, developing a rare appreciation for contemporary British art, especially sculpture. He became friends with several architects, artists, writers and musicians, and in 1923 met Henry Moore. Gregory is remembered as a philanthropist and as one of the earliest patrons of Moore, Barbara Hepworth, Graham Sutherland and Ben Nicholson, buying their work before World War II when they were little known (e.g. Henry Moore's *Woman's Head and Shoulders*, stone, 1932; now London, Tate). In 1947–8 he helped found the Institute of Contemporary Arts, London, and assumed the duties of Treasurer, maintaining this position for the rest of his life. In 1948 his company, known for their high-quality art books, took over the printing of the *Burlington Magazine*. Gregory joined the board of directors and thereafter took an active part in the magazine's affairs. As a collector, he continued to show his preference for avant-garde works, patronizing such young British sculptors as Kenneth Armitage, Reg Butler, Lynn Chadwick, Bernard Meadows and Eduardo Paolozzi. At the University of Leeds he established in 1943 the Gregory Fellowships for painters, sculptors, poets and musicians. He was involved in the Battersea Park Open-Air Sculpture Exhibition, London (1951), served as a member of the Arts Panel for the Arts Council of Great Britain (1954–6) and was on the government's Standing Commission on Museums and Galleries (from 1952). In later years, Gregory and Moore became close friends, visiting Greece and Italy together.

BIBLIOGRAPHY

H. Read: Obituary, *Burl. Mag.*, ci (1959), p. 149
The Gregory Collection (exh. cat., intro. H. Moore; London, ICA, 1959)

Gregotti, Vittorio (*b* Novara, 10 Aug 1927). Italian architect, urban planner, theorist, critic and teacher. He qualified at the architectural faculty of the Politecnico, Milan, in 1952 and a year later opened his first practice together with Lodovico Meneghetti (*b* 1926) and Giotto Stoppino. In the fervent architectural debates of the post-war period, he distanced himself from the prevailing theories and styles inherited from the Modern Movement and turned instead to local and regional cultures as a source of inspiration. In the block of workers' dwellings (1956) for the Bossi Company in Cameri, the brick and cement detailing around the doors and windows and the small front-entrance courtyard created by the U-shaped plan both recall local vernacular building forms. His early projects are also characterized by the introduction of elements taken from diverse architectural sources, a practice that for many years earned him an inaccurate and limiting reputation as an exponent of eclecticism. In the Teatro Civico (1959) for Alessandria, the decorative motif of the modulated façade pays tribute to Frank Lloyd Wright, while the structural hierarchy and articulation of the vertical circulation spaces of the residential blocks (1962–4), Via Palmanova, Milan, evoke the work of Louis I. Kahn. This allusive tendency is also visible in such later projects as the Rinascente store (1969) in Palermo, in which he makes clear reference to the Expressionist architecture of Erich Mendelsohn.

In 1964 Gregotti began an intense period of exhibition design, receiving immediate recognition by winning the International Gran Premio for the introductory section of the XIII Triennale in Milan. Based on the theme of free time, pictures, films and graphics were reflected infinitely in mirrored prisms, creating dynamic spatial effects in which the geometry and scale of the space were annulled. From the late 1960s he concentrated on large building developments, analysing their impact on the landscape and attempting to achieve a harmonious integration between built and natural form. His designs of this period adapt metaphorically some familiar building typologies, such as enclosures, squares, courtyards, axes, bridges and dams, taken from both architectural and civil engineering sources. In the Science Department Building (1969) for the Università degli Studi, Palermo, the three stepped enclosures on the gently sloping site recall closed monastic cloisters. The buildings (1971) for the Università degli Studi, Florence, consist of five long thin parallel blocks that stretch like dams across the valley between the lines of hills on each side. In the winning entry (1973) for the Università di Calabria, 21 university buildings (see fig.) are distributed along a bridge-like structure stretching for 3 km across undulating terrain.

In 1974 Gregotti Associati was formed with Pierluigi Cerri (*b* 1903), Hiromichi Matsui, Pierluigi Nicolin (*b* 1930) and Bruno Viganò. The group established an international reputation in 1980 by winning the competition for the Lutzowstrasse area in Berlin. Here Gregotti approached the complex problem of inserting a new building into a historically significant urban context by emphasizing rather than camouflaging this contrast. Throughout the 1980s Gregotti Associati continued to work on major architectural projects both within and outside Italy, including the Olympic Stadium (1983–5),

Vittorio Gregotti: Università di Calabria, near Cosenza, begun 1973

Barcelona. Gregotti held the post of Professor of Architectural Composition at the universities of Milan, Palermo and Venice, and from 1974 to 1976 he was Director of the architecture and visual arts section of the Venice Biennale.

WRITINGS

Utopia della realtà (Bari, 1965)
Il territorio dell'architettura (Milan, 1966)
Orientamenti nuovi nell'architettura italiana (Milan, 1967; Eng. trans., London, 1968)
Regular contributions to *Casabella* (from 1957) and *Rass. Archit. & Urb.*

BIBLIOGRAPHY

Il progetto per l'università della Calabria e altre architetture di V. Gregotti (exh. cat., ed. I. Rota; Rende, U. Calabria, 1979)
V. Gregotti (Tokyo, 1979)
M. Tafuri: *Vittorio Gregotti: Progetti e architetture* (Milan, 1982)
S. Crotti: *Vittorio Gregotti* (Bologna, 1986)

□

Greifen, House of. German family of patrons and collectors. Pomerania-Wolgast and Pomerania-Stettin (Szczecin) were the most important (and the only secular) domains of medieval Pomerania, ruled by the Greifen dynasty. Over the centuries its members founded, built and extended many towns, castles and palaces, some on a lavish scale, within the constantly moving borders of its territories; few remain. At the beginning of the 15th century Vratislav VIII, Duke of Pomerania-Wolgast (*reg* 1457–78), had the ambulatory of the Petrikirche in Wolgast decorated with murals (uncovered 1942). About 1490 Bogislav V, Duke of Pomerania-Stettin (*reg* 1474–1523; VIII, Duke of Pomerania-Wolgast, *reg* 1478–1523), settled in Stettin and extended its fortress (1368) in the style of his time; almost all subsequent rulers had the palace enlarged and modernized. His son Philip, Duke of Pomerania-Wolgast (*reg* 1531–60), also had the palace in Wolgast enlarged and built a luxurious hunting-lodge at Ückermünde. His brass epitaph (1560) by Wolf Hilger I (1511–76) is in the Petrikirche, Wolgast. The inventory of his estate lists paintings, armour, silverware, coins, books and an important collection of tapestries. His grandson (1) Philip, Duke of Pomerania-Stettin, became the most important collector and patron of art in the Greifen dynasty. In the year of his death (1618), the appearance of Pomeranian towns and residences was recorded in 49 engraved views in the margins of the large (1.25×2.21 m) map of the region (Amsterdam, 1618; Kiel, Stift. Pommern) designed by Eilhard Lübben (Lubinus) (*d* 1621). The dynasty became extinct at the death of Bogislav VII, Duke of Pomerania-Stettin, IX of Pomerania-Wolgast (1580–1637), and its art treasures were subsequently scattered and destroyed to an unusual extent (now primarily Greifswald, Ernst-Moritz-Arndt U.; Berlin, Staatl. Museen Preuss. Kultbes.; Szczecin, N. Mus.; Słupsk, Mus. Cent. Pomerania). After the Peace of Westphalia (1648) Pomerania was divided between Sweden and Brandenburg. West Pomerania is now in Germany and east Pomerania in Poland.

(1) Philip, Duke of Pomerania-Stettin (*b* Franzburg, 29 July 1573; *reg* 1606–18; *d* Stettin [Szczecin, Poland], 3 Feb 1618). The product of a careful humanistic education, at 17 he wrote a philosophical treatise, *Oratio de duarum naturarum necessitate* (Barth, 1590), and soon afterwards announced (again in Latin) his interest in books, art works and old coins. In 1595–7 he travelled in Italy and in 1599 visited Bohemia. The first work of art he donated is the epitaph (1603) of Barnim V, Duke of Pomerania-Wolgast (*reg* 1394–1405), in the Wallfahrtskirche, Kenz. In 1603 he moved to Stettin, where he established an ancestral portrait gallery and a scholarly library in the palace. Among the artists at his court was Johann Körver (*d* 1607), whom he commissioned to produce repoussé silver panels modelled on an engraved *Passion* (1596–8) by Hendrick Goltzius. However, Körver died before he could complete the series.

As he suffered from gout, the Duke was confined to his residence, but through connections already established he developed into an important art patron and collector. Of especial importance was his correspondence with Philipp Hainhofer, through whom he commissioned many works, including completion of Körver's silver reliefs by Christoph Lencker, Zacharias Lencker (*d* 1612) and Jan de Vos (1578–after 1626); the panels were later incorporated into the famous Silver Altar of Darłowa (1636; Darłowa, Schlosskirche). The most famous work produced for the Duke through Philipp Hainhofer's mediation is the Pomeranian Cabinet (1605–7; contents, Berlin, Tiergarten, Kstgewmus.; cabinet destr. 1945), worked on by more than 20 Augsburg artists. Among the albums compiled by the Duke, his *Neues Stammbuch* (dispersed; individual pictures in Berlin, Kupferstichkab. and Munich, Residenz) included works, received through Philipp Hainhofer in 1612, by Johann König, Paul Bril, Anton Mozart, Johann Mathias Kager, Lucas Kilian, Hans Bol, Jan Breughel I and Hans Rottenhammer I; inventories of the album were published in Latin (1615) and German (1617). Of his other albums, the only survivors are an *Emblem- und Impresenbuch* (1609; Berlin, Staatsbib. Preuss. Kultbesitz., MS. Boruss. 4° 141) and one (1617) of four *Visierungsbücher* (reduced format; Szczecin, N. Mus.).

In 1612 the Duke laid the foundation stone in Stettin for a pleasure house (completed 1617; destr. 1630) modelled on Heinrich Schickardt's Neuer Bau in Stuttgart. From 1616, also to house his collections, the Duke added a three-storey wing to the west side of the palace in Stettin for the armour cabinet, library and art cabinet; the latter was to be kept in the Meierhof (drawing in Munich, Bayer. Staatsbib.), commissioned by Philipp Hainhofer. The magnificent Renaissance fireplace with mythological depictions in Schloss Mellenthin was produced in 1613. On the Duke's initiative, works on the history, Church history and geography of Pomerania were produced, including the large map (Amsterdam, 1618; Kiel, Stift. Pommern) by Eilhard Lübben (Lubinus). He had portraits of himself and his wife painted (1612) by Sebastian Hepp (*d* ?1618), engraved in copper (1613; Wolfenbüttel, Herzog August Bib.) by Lucas Kilian and embossed in silver relief (1614; Brunswick, Herzog Anton Ulrich-Mus.) by Jan de Vos. Among works that Philip commissioned from local artists is the *Apotheosis of Philip II* (1608; Szczecin, N. Mus.), a small painted copper panel by Pancratius Reinicke (*fl* 1604–10) in the 'international' (i.e. mainly Florentine) court style.

BIBLIOGRAPHY

ADB

F. L. B. v[on] M[edem], ed.: 'Philipp Hainhofers Reise-Tagebuch, enthaltend Schilderungen aus Franken, Sachsen, der Mark Brandenberg und Pommern im Jahre 1617', *Balt. Stud.*, ii (1834), pp. I–XX, 1–180

F. Trautmann: 'Der Mayerhof, entworfen von Philipp Hainhofer: Ein Beitrag zur Geschichte der Kleinkunst im 17. Jahrhundert', Sber. Münchn. Altert.-Ver., iii (1871), pp. 26–30

D. von Schlegel: 'Die ersten 7 Briefe des Augsburger Patriziers Phil. Hainhofer an den Herzog Philipp von Pommern aus dem Jahre 1610, hrsg. von Dr. Schlegel', *Programm (Nr. 114) der städtischen Real-Lehranstalt zu Stettin* (Ostern and Stettin, 1877), pp. 1–28

O. Doering, ed.: *Des Augsburger Patriciers Philipp Hainhofer Beziehungen zum Herzog Philipp II. von Pommern-Stettin: Correspondenzen aus den Jahren 1610–1619 im Auszuge mitgeth. u. commentiert. . .*, n. s. 6 of *Quellenschriften für Kunstgeschichte und Kunsttechnik des Mittelalters und der Neuzeit* (Vienna, 1894)

J. Lessing and A. Brüning: *Der pommersche Kunstschrank* (Berlin, 1905) [with illustrations of the cab. and its contents]

A. Haas: *Die grosse lubinsche Karte von Pommern* (Stolp, 1926)

H. Bethe: *Die Kunst am Hofe der pommerschen Herzöge* (Berlin, 1937)

Z. (Krzymuska-) Fafius, M. Glińska and Z. Radacki: 'Mecenat książąt zachodniopomorskich w XVI i XVII wieku' [Patronage of West Pomeranian dukes in the 16th and 17th centuries], *Funkcja dzieła sztuki: Materiały sesji S(towarzyszenia) H(istoryków) S(ztuki), Szczecin, listopad 1970 (Widmungsschrift f. Mieczysław Gębarowicz)* [Function of works of art: material from the session of the Association of Art Historians, Szczecin, November 1970 (dedicated to Mieczysław Gębarowicz)] (Warsaw, 1972), pp. 135–84

D. Alfter: *Die Geschichte des Augsburger Kabinettschranks* (Augsburg, 1986), pp. 42–62

Sztuka na dworze książąt pomorza zachodniego w XVI–XVII wieku [Art at the court of the dukes of Western Pomerania in the 16th and 17th centuries] (exh. cat., Warsaw, Royal Castle, 1986; Szczecin, N. Mus.; 1986–7)

JÜRGEN ZIMMER

Greiffenklau, Karl Philipp von, Prince-Bishop of Würzburg (*b* Schloss Vollrads, Rheingau, 1 Dec 1690; *d* Würzburg, 25 Nov 1754). German ecclesiastic and patron. He was ordained a priest in 1715 and admitted to the Würzburg Cathedral chapter in 1728. He studied at the Johannes Gutenberg-Universität Mainz, where he later became Rector (1738–49). Although he reformed the Bayerische-Julius-Maximilians-Universität in Würzburg, he also tolerated the last witch-burning in Franconia. He made a long stay in Rome before his election as Prince-Bishop of Würzburg in 1749. He reappointed all the court artists dismissed by his apathetic predecessor, notably Balthasar Neumann, architect of the Residenz, whom he commissioned to remove the Romanesque high chancel in Würzburg Cathedral and enlarge his summer palace in Veitshöchheim (1749–53). Greiffenklau also summoned the fresco painter Matthäus Günther from south Germany to paint (1752) the Wallfahrtskapelle in Würzburg.

At the Residenz the central staterooms, vestibule, staircase and imperial hall and all the decoration were still lacking (*see* WÜRZBURG, §2). Greiffenklau began by having the garden hall (*sala terrena*) frescoed by Johann Zick but recognized the artist's weaknesses. After an episode with the incompetent painter Giovanni Visconti from Milan, Greiffenklau offered the commission to Giambattista Tiepolo (*see* TIEPOLO, (1), §I, 3), who accepted it in order to 'immortalize his name and art throughout Germany'. He arrived on 12 December 1750 and completed the work in the Kaisersaal in July 1752. The decorative programme, adapted for Tiepolo, stressed the special relationship between the prince-bishopric and the imperial house, and the artist depicted the historical bishops with Greiffenklau's features. To 'increase the splendour and embellishment', Tiepolo was induced to fresco the immense vault of the stairwell, for which Greiffenklau chose the subject. This shows on one side Apollo and on the other the portrait medallion of Greiffenklau above portraits of

Tiepolo and the court artists, including Neumann and the stuccoist Antonio Bossi.

In the winter intermissions Tiepolo painted two *Altarblätter* ('altar-leaves'; 1752; Würzburg, Palace chapel) for the Hofkirche, and, with his son Giandomenico Tiepolo, a number of history paintings (U. Würzburg, Wagner-Mus.; Würzburg, Residenz). On his departure (8 Nov 1753) Tiepolo expressed his thanks to Greiffenklau with a painting of the *Virgin*, and Giandomenico Tiepolo dedicated his series of etchings of the *Flight into Egypt* to the Prince-Bishop. Tiepolo's departure, Neumann's death in 1753 and Greiffenklau's death in 1754 brought to an end the brief but glorious flourishing of the 'Würzburg Rococo'.

BIBLIOGRAPHY

R. Sedlmaier and R. Pfister: *Die fürstbischöfliche Residenz zu Würzburg* (Munich, 1923)
M. H. von Freeden and C. Lamb: *Das Meisterwerk des Giovanni Battista Tiepolo: Die Fresken der Würzburger Residenz* (Munich, 1956)
F. Büttner: 'Die Sonne Frankens: Ikonographie der Fresken im Treppenhaus der Würzburger Residenz', *Münchn. Jb. Bild. Kst*, n. s. 2, xxx (1979), pp. 159–86
——: *Giovanni Battista Tiepolo: Die Fresken der Residenz zu Würzburg* (Würzburg, 1980)
E. Hubala and O. Mayer: *Die Residenz zu Würzburg* (Würzburg, 1984), pp. 192–221

TILMAN KOSSATZ

Greiner, Dick (*b* Amsterdam, 6 Nov 1891; *d* Amsterdam, 1964). Dutch architect. He worked in the Amsterdam offices of Eduard Cuypers, Filip Anne Warners (1888–1952), Jan Gratama and Gerardus Versteeg (1873–1938), and Gerrit Jan Rutgers (1877–1962), and from 1920 he had his own office. He completed the Higher Architecture course in the Academie van Bouwkunst, Amsterdam, in 1922. As a result of his experience in other offices, Greiner's work initially showed influences from H. P. Berlage and Frank Lloyd Wright as well as the AMSTERDAM SCHOOL. In addition to a number of traditional designs, such as the mansion block (1920) on the corner of Nicolaas Maasstraat and Banstraat, Amsterdam, he designed a residential block (1922) in Rijnstraat in the Amsterdam school style. The music school (1927; destr.), Albert Hahnstraat, Amsterdam, was much more influenced by Wright. However, Greiner became best known through his designs (1921–8) for the garden suburb Watergraafsmeer in Amsterdam, also known as Betondorp (Concrete Village), which were Functionalist in style. The high price of brick and the need to build quickly and flexibly explains why concrete was chosen for this garden suburb as an experiment in system building. Greiner was responsible for the multi-functional buildings around the square; these are characterized by cubic shapes, a strongly plastic treatment of volumes and horizontal articulation of the windows. Another notable work is the residential building (1922–6) at Javastraat-Gorontalostraat-Niasplein, Amsterdam. During and after World War II Greiner was involved with the reconstruction of Middelburg, Yrseke and Schore.

BIBLIOGRAPHY

P. K. A. Pennink: 'Het betondorp', *Forum*, 5–6 (1965), pp. 9–23 [Eng. text]
G. Fanelli: *Architettura moderna* (1968)
P. Groenendijk and P. Vollaard: *Guide to Modern Architecture in the Netherlands* (Rotterdam, 1987)
M. Casciato: *De Amsterdamse school* (Rotterdam, 1991)

E. MATTIE, M. DE MOOR

Greiner, Otto (*b* Leipzig, 16 Dec 1869; *d* Munich, 24 Sept 1916). German painter and printmaker. He started a lithography apprenticeship in Leipzig in 1884 and also took drawing lessons. Between 1888 and 1891 he studied at the Akademie der Bildenden Künste in Munich under Sándor Liezen-Mayer. In the autumn of 1891 he made his first journey to Italy, visiting Florence and Rome, where he met and befriended Max Klinger. From 1892 to 1898 he lived in Munich and Leipzig. In 1898 he moved to Rome, where he used Klinger's former studio, and where he remained until 1915, when he was forced to leave because of Italy's affiliation with the Allies. Greiner's work is based on careful graphic preparation and in particular on accurate life drawing. The nude was central to his interests: like Klinger he saw it as the epitome of beauty in nature and believed it should serve as a basis for all stylistic formation. This is apparent from such paintings as *Odysseus and the Sirens* (1902; Leipzig, Mus. Bild. Kst.) as well as from his prints. Among his recurrent interests, along with portraiture, were antique and fantastic subjects, which are represented in the majority of his 112 paintings. His only cycle, *On Woman* (1895), the eroticism of which is typical of the last decade of the 19th century, is his best-known work.

BIBLIOGRAPHY

J. Vogel: *Otto Greiner: Graphische Arbeiten in Lithographie, Stich und Radierung* (Dresden, 1917)
——: *Otto Greiner* (Bielefeld, 1925)

SEPP KERN

Greis, Otto (*b* Frankfurt am Main, 28 Sept 1913). German painter, also active in France. In 1933 he gave up studying mechanical engineering for painting. The development of his characteristic works began after World War II and his meeting with the painter Ernst Wilhelm Nay. Greis created his first paintings in the style of *Art informel* in 1951–2. As a member of QUADRIGA (1952), with Karl-Otto Götz, Heinz Kreutz and Bernard Schultze, he was a pioneer of this style of art. The influence of both Cézanne and Klee played a crucial role in Greis's approach to painting. From the outset he set himself the task of realizing an autonomous 'breathing spatial body' on the picture surface. Beginning in 1954 Greis gradually moved away from the *Art informel*, giving more emphasis to the deliberately applied stroke and the 'significant form'. The period from 1955 to 1958 is characterized by dark enigmatic pictures where paint is thickly applied, for example *Fetish* (1957; Kassel, Neue Gal.). From *c.* 1958 Greis brightened his colours and integrated a quality of internal illumination into his paintings, as in *Encircled Light* (1972; artist's col., see 1978 exh. cat. no. 13). He lived in France from 1956 to 1984.

WRITINGS

'Skizzen', *Bl. & Bild.*, 10 (1960), pp. 71–5
'Warum lebe ich in Paris?', *Kstwk*, xv/12 (June 1962), p. 13

BIBLIOGRAPHY

Otto Greis, Retrospective: Gemälde, Aquarelle, Handzeichnungen, 1946–1977 (exh. cat. by W. Haftmann and M. Seuphor, Bremen, Ksthalle, 1978)

K. O. Götz/Otto Greis (exh. cat. by O. Greis and A. Herbst, Wiesbaden, Mus. Wiesbaden, 1984)
Otto Greis: Bilder, Aquarelle und Zeichnungen aus den Jahren 1970–1985 (exh. cat. by G. Ladstetter, Mannheim, Städt. Ksthalle, 1985)
Otto Greis: Retrospective zum 75. Geburtstag (exh. cat. by K. Gabler and others, Mainz, Landesmus., 1988–9)

URSULA GEIGER

Greither [Greitter; Greitther; Greuter]**, Elias, I** (*b* 1565–70; *d* Weilheim, 9–11 Nov 1646). German painter and draughtsman. He is first mentioned in 1591, when he painted the Betbergkapelle of SS Salvator and Sebastian at Weilheim using the secco technique. A panel of the *Holy Family* (Weilheim, Stadtmus.) dates from 1604; he was in Augsburg, painting barrels and polychroming Hans Degler's three monumental wooden altars and pulpit at SS Ulrich and Afra between 1604 and 1608. He painted for the Benedictines at Andechs and Benediktbeuren (1610–11); worked under Peter Candid on the Munich Residenz (1614–16), painting frescoes on the vaulting of the Kaisertreppe and background painting for the Vierschäftesaal; and painted three altarpieces for the pilgrimage church at Hohenpeissenberg (*c*. 1618). He was back in Weilheim in 1627, assisted by his son Johann in frescoing *Mary Encircled by the Seven Angels* in the compartmented octagonal cupola of the parish church of Mariae Himmelfahrt. The Augustinians commissioned an altarpiece of the *Baptism of St Augustine* (1623) for the parish church at Polling, and a *Deposition* (*c*. 1630–35) for SS Peter and Paul, Beuerberg, near Wolfratshausen—the latter freely interpreted from a work by Daniele da Volterra.

Greither's drawings, some of which are distinguished, and the 'old-fashioned, provincial' look (Geissler) of his paintings seem to be at variance. The drawing of a *Frieze of Six Saints* (Munich, Staatl. Graph. Samml.) for the predella of the Frauenkirche in Munich is superbly individual, with a sure, finely modulated hand. The pen and wash drawing of the *Flagellation* (Munich, Staatl. Graph. Samml.) is an assured, powerfully expressive work, with the modelling of the body enhanced by graduated shading. South German Mannerism, familiar to Greither from Augsburg and Munich, is still clearly present, but the new figure compositions from the southern Netherlands as practised by Rubens are already beginning to prove influential.

BIBLIOGRAPHY

Thieme–Becker
L. Zottmann: 'Zur Kunst von Elias Greither dem Älteren, seinen Söhnen und Mitarbeitern', *Stud. Dt. Kstgesch.*, cxii (1909)
H. Geissler and R. Biedermann: 'Augsburger Handzeichnungen und Druckgraphik, 1620–1720', *Augsburger Barock* (exh. cat., Augsburg, Rathaus and Holbeinhaus, 1968), no. 225
H. Bauer and B. Rupprecht: *Corpus der barocken Deckenmalerei* (Munich, 1976), pp. 305, 553
Zeichnung in Deutschland: Deutsche Zeichner, 1540–1640, i (exh. cat. by H. Geissler, Stuttgart, Staatl. Ksthalle, 1979), no. 40

BERNT VON HAGEN

Greive, Johan Conrad (*b* Amsterdam, 2 April 1837; *d* Amsterdam, 14 May 1891). Dutch painter, draughtsman and printmaker. He initially wanted to be a musician like his father, but he decided to become a painter and studied with his uncle, the genre and figure painter P. F. Greive (1811–72). Thereafter he was taught by Cornelis Springer, and around 1861 he worked with L. Lingeman (1829–94) in the latter's studio.

Greive painted river and harbour scenes and townscapes, mainly in Amsterdam, but also in Gelderland and Zeeland, for example the *Shellproof Barracks in Flushing* (Amsterdam, Hist. Mus.). In 1860 he made a series of 12 lithographs showing types of ships, *Studies of Dutch Ships Drawn After the Original*. After the death of his father, Greive was for a time obliged to take on much illustration work for magazines at home and abroad to support his family, and he briefly abandoned painting. He remained, however, active within the Amsterdam artistic world and for three years was chairman of the society Arti et Amicitiae.

Although Greive was not an innovative painter, his work is striking for its fluent style. Important paintings include *Lunchbreak in a Shipbuilding Yard on the Maas* (1867; The Hague, State Col., on loan to Den Helder, Marmus.), *View of the Amstel from the Hoge Sluis* (1876) and the *Pipe Market in Amsterdam* (1882; both Amsterdam, Hist. Mus.). His watercolours and sketches show him in his best light.

BIBLIOGRAPHY

Scheen
D. van der Kellen jr: 'J. C. Greive jr', *Eigen haard* (1891), pp. 348–50

WIEPKE F. LOOS

Grekov, Mitrofan (Borisovich) [Martyshchenko, Mitrofan (Pavlovich)] (*b* Sharpayevka farm, nr Rostov-on-Don, 15 June 1882; *d* Sevastopol', 27 Nov 1934). Russian painter. He studied from 1899 to 1903 at the Odessa Art College under Kiriak Kostandi (1852–1921) and from 1903 to 1911 at the Academy of Arts, St Petersburg, under Il'ya Repin, but mainly under F. A. Frants Rubo (1856–1928), the leading Russian battle painter of the time. He adopted the name Grekov in 1911. As a soldier in World War I, he made many sketches at the front. He was an active member of the Association of Artists of Revolutionary Russia (AKhRR).

Grekov continued 19th-century traditions of battle painting, using subject-matter from the Civil War of 1918–20. He became a chronicler of this war and in particular of the campaigns of the First Cavalry Army. His most successful images are impressive fragments of academic history, faithful reproductions of environments and national types, as in *To the Budennyy Detachment* (1923; Moscow, Tret'yakov Gal.), in which a sullen Cossack rides across the scorched steppe in order to join the revolutionary troops, or *First Cavalry Army Trumpeters* (1934; Moscow, Tret'yakov Gal.), which depicts a dashing military band playing in clouds of dust whipped up by horses' hooves. However, many of Grekov's battle scenes, especially those with large numbers of 'reds' and 'whites', are much less spontaneous as, following the cultural policy of the Stalinist period, they express the systematic falsification of Civil War historiography and become fictional 'artistic documents'.

A Grekov Studio of Military Artists was set up in 1935 and later became the largest working collective of Russian battle-painters. The Grekov House-Museum was opened in 1957 as a branch of the Museum of the Don Cossacks in Novocherkassk.

BIBLIOGRAPHY
G. A. Timoshin: *M. B. Grekov* (Moscow, 1961)
M. B. Grekov v vospominaniyakh sovremennikov [M. B. Grekov in the reminiscences of his contemporaries] (Leningrad, 1966)
N. Lapunov: *M. B. Grekov* (Moscow, 1982)
S. N. Levandovsky: *M. B. Grekov* (Leningrad, 1982)
V. Zotov: *Povest' o M. Grekove* [The story of M. Grekov] (Moscow, 1982)

M. N. SOKOLOV

Gremiale. *See under* VESTMENTS, ECCLESIASTICAL, §1(iii).

Grenada [Grenadine Islands]. *See under* ANTILLES, LESSER.

Grendey, Giles (*b* Wotton-under-Edge, Glos, 1693; *d* Palmers Green, London, 3 March 1780). English cabinet-maker. He was the son of William Grendey, a farmer, and was apprenticed in London at the age of 16 to William Sherborne, a second-generation joiner. He became a freeman of the Joiners' Company in 1716 and was taking on apprentices by 1726. One such apprentice, Christopher Petfield, took him to court for making him spend all his time sawing planks and for beating him 'in a very barbarous manner'. This incident did not prevent Grendey from being elected to the Livery of the Joiners' Company in 1729. He rose steadily through the hierarchy to the post of Master in 1766. In 1731 a fire damaged his workshop in Aylesbury House, St John's Square, Clerkenwell, destroying furniture to the value of £1000, including an easy-chair 'to be purchas'd by a Person of Quality who design'd it as Present to a German Prince'.

Grendey was commercially successful, producing plain furniture of a somewhat conservative design with little decoration. Some of it was for export. In about 1738 the Duque de Mendoza-Infantado purchased over 70 pieces (some in Leeds, Temple Newsam House; London, V&A; New York, Met.), japanned in scarlet and gold, for his castle at Lazcano in northern Spain. A walnut and mahogany mirror bearing Grendey's label was found in Norway. An important English client was the Hoare family: he supplied pieces to Sir Richard Colt Hoare (i) at Barn Elms, Surrey, and to his brother, Henry II Hoare (i), at Stourhead, Wilts. Mentioned in Sir Richard's account-books are a chest-of-drawers, a 'Burow Table', dressing-glasses, chimney-glasses and a 'Wrighting Disk'. His work for Stourhead seems to have been mainly in the form of chairs. Grendey's trade label has been found on a variety of walnut, mahogany and japanned pieces dating from about 1735 to 1760 (London, V&A; Leeds, Temple Newsam House; Colonial Williamsburg, VA).

BIBLIOGRAPHY
R. W. Symonds: 'In Search of Giles Grendey', *Country Life*, cx (30 Nov 1951), pp. 1792–4
C. Gilbert: 'Furniture by Giles Grendey for the Spanish Trade', *Antiques*, xcix (1971), pp. 544–50
S. Jervis: 'A Great Dealer in the Cabinet Way', *Country Life*, clv (6 June 1974), pp. 1418–19
G. Beard and C. Gilbert, eds: *Dictionary of English Furniture Makers, 1660–1840* (Leeds, 1986)

JAMES YORKE

Grenier, Pasquier (*fl* Tournai, 1447–93). Burgundian tapestry merchant. He is one of the most important figures in the history of late medieval tapestry. Once considered a master weaver, he was subsequently revealed as the most influential 15th-century tapestry merchant. He dealt in many of the finest tapestries surviving from the second half of the 15th century. He secured his first payment for textiles from Philip II (the Good), Duke of Burgundy, in 1454–5 and subsequently supplied him with many magnificent and expensive hangings. In 1459 he sold tapestries of *Alexander the Great*, in 1461 the *Passion* and *Peasants and Woodcutters*, in 1462 *Esther and Ahasuerus* and the *Swan Knight* and in 1466 *Orange Pickers* and *Woodcutters*. Those of *Alexander* and the *Passion* were particularly splendid sets, being of huge dimensions and containing much gold and silver thread. In 1459 two members of Grenier's family were in Milan showing designs for tapestries of *Alexander* to Francesco Sforza, Duke of Milan, and in 1467–8 Grenier made a very large sale, including tapestries of *Nebuchadnezzar*, *Alexander* and the *Passion*, to Edward IV of England. Moreover, in 1471–6 he received payments for a set of 11 tapestries of the *Trojan War* for Charles the Bold, Duke of Burgundy; Grenier's son Jean (*d* Feb 1520) sold another set in 1475 to Federigo II da Montefeltro, Duke of Urbino. In 1486 both Pasquier and Jean were granted protection and licences to import various goods, including tapestries, into England by Henry VII; by 1488 Henry had also purchased tapestries of the *Trojan War*. Further sets were owned by Charles VIII of France, Don Iñigo López de Mendoza (1442–1515), 1st Marqués de Mondéjar, and Matthias Corvinus, King of Hungary.

Grenier was evidently a man of considerable wealth and status. The family chapel (1474) in his parish church of St Quentin, Tournai, was built at his expense and painted (before 1493) with symbols of the Holy Sacrament. Among his many benefactions to this church were tapestries of the *Seven Sacraments* for the choir (possible fragments, New York, Met.; Glasgow, Burrell Col.). Other examples of his goods include surviving pieces of the *Trojan War* tapestries (see Asselberghs, 1970), two tapestries of *Alexander the Great* (Rome, Pal. Doria-Pamphili), two of the *Swan Knight* (Kraków, St Catherine; Vienna, Mus. Angewandte Kst) and two of the *Passion* (Rome, Vatican, Mnmt., Musei & Gal. Pont.; Brussels, Mus. Royaux A. & Hist.). There is no evidence that Grenier's tapestries were woven only in Tournai or to designs by Tournai artists. Therefore, so-called 'Tournai style' tapestries need not have had any connection with Grenier.

In his will of 13 July 1493 Grenier divided his property, including his 'patrons' or cartoons, among his four sons Jean, Imbert, Colinet and Antoine. Of these, Jean and Antoine continued to sell tapestries of high quality to the nobility of Europe into the second decade of the 16th century. Among their clients were Philip IV (the Fair), Henry VII and George d'Amboise, Archbishop of Rouen.

BIBLIOGRAPHY
E. Soil: 'Les Tapisseries de Tournai, les tapissiers et les hautlisseurs de cette ville', *Mém. Soc. Hist. & Litt. Tournai*, xxii (Tournai, 1891)
P. Rolland, M. Crick-Kuntziger and M. Morelowski: 'Le Tapissier Pasquier Grenier et l'église Saint-Quentin à Tournai', *Rev. Belge Archéol. & Hist. A.*, vi (1936), pp. 203–21
La Tapisserie tournaisienne au XVe siècle (exh. cat., ed. J. P. Asselberghs; Tournai, Cathedral, 1967)
J. P. Asselberghs: 'Les Tapisseries tournaisiennes de la guerre de Troie', *Rev. Belge Archéol. & Hist. A.*, xxxix (1970), pp. 93–183

S. McKendrik: 'The *Great History of Troy*: A Reassessment of the Development of a Secular Theme in Late Medieval Art', *J. Warb. & Court. Inst.*, liv (1991), pp. 43–82

SCOT McKENDRICK

Grenoble [Lat. Cularo; Gratianopolis]. Capital city of Isère prefecture in south-east France. A university and industrial city, it is sited in the Alps at the junction of the Isère and Drac valleys. The tendency of both rivers to severe flooding has always forced the city to give a high priority to maintaining flood defences, and its closeness to Savoy made it a walled and fortified frontier town for much of its history. Most of the city lies south of the Isère, but on the north bank is the necropolis of St Laurent, the oldest tombs of which date from the 4th century AD (*see* §2 below).

1. HISTORY AND URBAN DEVELOPMENT. The original Celtic settlement of Cularo lay on the north bank of the Isère. The Roman settlement grew up on the south bank and in the late 3rd century AD was surrounded by a wall (remains survive near the present cathedral). Emperor Gratian (*reg* 367–83) raised it to the status of a town and renamed it Gratianopolis, whence the modern name derives. Christianity arrived before AD 381, when Gratianopolis sent its bishop to the Council of Aquileia. From about the 4th century a necropolis developed on the north bank of the Isère, around the present church of St Laurent, and the baptistery of the city's early cathedral complex, on the south bank, dates from the late 4th or early 5th century.

By the Middle Ages, Grenoble was the seat of the counts of Vienne, who later called themselves Dauphins. Under their rule the brick-towered cathedral was built in the 12th and 13th centuries, as was the 13th-century collegiate church of St André (formerly the chapel of the Palais des Dauphins). In the 1340s Comte Humbert II, lacking an heir, sold the Dauphiné to France, of which it became a province (and the inheritance of the heir to the throne), with Grenoble as its capital and, from 1451, the seat of its parliament. The present Palais de Justice was built in the 15th and 16th centuries as the parliament house and contains impressive work (1524) by the Swabian wood-carver Paul Jude. On the north bank of the Isère, beneath the hilltop Fort de la Bastille (see fig. 1), the cloister and Baroque chapel of the former Visitation convent of Ste Marie-d'en-haut (now the Musée Dauphinois) date from 1622. Suburbs had long since sprung up outside the Roman walls, and, after the late 16th-century Wars of Religion, François de Bonne, Duc de Lesdiguières (*see* LESDIGUIÈRES, (1)), whose palace is now the Musée Stendhal, built a new city wall encircling three times the former area. At the French Revolution the Dauphiné was split into three départmentes, one of them Isère. Subsequent industrial prosperity caused congestion within the 17th-century walls, with blocks rising three or four storeys

1. Grenoble, view from the north showing the bridge over the Isère and Fort de la Bastille (background); from a lithograph by Day and Haghe, *c.* 1850 (Grenoble, Musée Dauphinois)

high over narrow, winding streets and small squares. Another city wall was built (1835), which doubled the enclosed area, and a new industrial quarter developed outside the walls, around the railway station (1856). The fortifications were partly demolished to develop a new city centre designed around business and banking interests. The glove-making industry, which had for centuries been the foundation of Grenoble's wealth, eventually gave way to mechanical engineering, which was established in the city towards 1880 and was closely linked to the first attempts to harness the local waterfalls in order to control what was then a new source of energy—hydroelectric power. Since then Grenoble's scientific vocation has become increasingly well established, its success demonstrated by the growth of the university laboratories, the Centre d'Etudes Nucléaires and the European Synchrotron.

BIBLIOGRAPHY

R. Blanchard: *Grenoble: Etude de géographie urbaine* (Grenoble, 1935)
V. Chomel, ed.: *Histoire de Grenoble* (Toulouse, 1976)
J.-F. Parent: *Grenoble: Deux siècles d'urbanisation* (Grenoble, 1982)
Histoire des communes de l'Isère: Grenoble et son arrondissement (1988)

ANNIE BOSSO

2. ST LAURENT, ORATORY OF ST OYAND. The origins of the St Laurent religious complex on the north bank of the Isère go back to a suburban necropolis of the late Roman Empire. Here, in the 4th century AD, graves scattered along the road gave way to burials in open ground: in amphorae (for children) or cists of Roman tiles. In the foundations of the later church are several quadrangular mausolea of important people; two have been excavated, both barrel-vaulted, one decorated with painting in imitation of marble. A large, rectangular, half-underground structure containing at least two large sealed cellars with several coffins dates from the 5th century. Its north–south orientation and lack of an apse might argue against Christian use but could nevertheless be explicable as a *memoria* of the members of the first Christian community. In the late 6th century, or perhaps the 7th, this building became the narthex of a large church of unique plan: a cross with arms of equal length, each with trefoil apses. Two wooden lateral staircases led to a lower chapel—dedicated to a local saint, St Oyand—identical in plan to the choir above and forming its base. The apses provided spaces for interring notables, and burials were concentrated around the church and narthex, the earlier necropolis falling into disuse.

2. Grenoble, St Laurent, Oratory of St Oyand, crypt, interior looking west, begun late 6th century, altered 8th–9th centuries

The church seems to have reached the height of its splendour with a campaign of embellishment in Carolingian times, from the late 8th century. The plan was not changed but the narthex was given a double staircase for processional use, a reliquary and an axial altar with painted *canthari* (vases); the east end of the church was rebuilt to introduce supplementary trefoil crypts to the north and south. The crypt beneath the choir was lined by a wall colonnade; although it was built partly with re-used masonry, several of its capitals and most of the abaci were newly carved. The colonnade supports a barrel vault, and the apses have segmented half-domes decorated with stucco *rinceaux* (see fig. 2). The Corinthian capitals and, above all, the abaci display the Christian iconographic repertory of the period: lambs, monsters, chalices spouting leafy *rinceaux*, and crosses surrounded by doves with ears of wheat or bunches of grapes in their beaks.

Thereafter, liturgy and religious outlook moved on, martyrological cults faded, and economic and political decline set in at the end of the Carolingian period. St Laurent fell into disuse, and in 1012 the Bishop of Grenoble gave it to the Benedictines of Saint-Chaffre-en-Velay, who founded a priory there. The multiple-apse church was replaced by a building with a wide nave, suited to the parochial needs of the time, and a cloister was added. The complex was rebuilt and enlarged several times until the French Revolution, when it fell into temporary disuse and the cemetery was abandoned. The crypt of St Oyand was rediscovered in 1804, and extensive excavation and restoration has taken place.

BIBLIOGRAPHY

J. Hubert: 'La Crypte de Saint-Laurent de Grenoble et l'art du sud-est de la Gaule au début de l'époque carolingienne', *Atti del convegno per lo studio dell'arte dell'alto medio evo: Turin, 1953*, pp. 327–44
R. Girard: *L'Eglise et la crypte de Saint-Laurent de Grenoble* (Grenoble, 1977) [booklet]
M. Colardelle and R. Colardelle: 'La Nécropole paléochrétienne de Saint-Sixte et la topographie chrétienne de Grenoble', *Congrès national des sociétés savantes: Grenoble, 1983*, pp. 131–42
R. Colardelle: *Grenoble aux premier temps chrétiens: Saint-Laurent et ses nécropoles* (Paris, 1986)
J. F. Reynaud and others: 'Les Edifices funéraires et leurs nécropoles dans les Alpes de la vallée du Rhône: Origines et premiers développements', *Actes du XIe congrès international d'archéologie chrétienne: Grenoble, 1986*, pp. 1535–49

RENÉE COLARDELLE

Grenoble, Mathieu. *See* JACQUET, (1).

Grenville. English family of politicians, patrons and collectors.

(1) Richard Grenville, 2nd Earl Temple (*b* 26 Sept 1711; *d* Stowe, Bucks, 11 Sept 1779). He was brought up at STOWE and inherited the house and its celebrated garden from his uncle, RICHARD TEMPLE, 1st Viscount Cobham, in 1749. Although he took high office in William Pitt's ministry, with the outbreak of the Seven Years War in 1756, and was active in political life, he spent much of his time and money on improvements at Stowe. He set aside one room for portraits of his immediate family, mostly commissioned from William Hoare (ii) in the 1750s. Portraits of himself (1762; Melbourne, N.G. Victoria) and his wife (1760; Chevening, Kent) were painted by Allan Ramsay. His portrait by Sir Joshua Reynolds (destr. World War II) was painted in 1776. Sensitive to the new mood in garden design, he was responsible for gradually replacing Charles Bridgeman's geometrical layout with the more natural landscape garden. Temple was one of several scholarly amateur architects in the Society of Dilettanti and was determined to remodel Stowe House, already palatial, in a more splendid style. By 1752 Giovanni Battista Borra's alterations to state rooms in the west wing had started. From 1759 guide books to Stowe all included descriptions of the interiors. Designs for the south front supplied by Borra (1752), Jean-François Blondel (*c.* 1765) and Robert Adam (1770) were set aside in favour of a scheme derived by Temple and his cousin, the gentleman architect Thomas Pitt, 1st Baron Camelford, from Adam's drawings; the north front too was probably the result of their collaboration. Sculptural ornaments on the south front were made by James Lovell (*fl* 1746–77). The monumental oval saloon and the two adjoining state rooms were in progress from 1775. The harmonious concept of the house and its landscape setting were due to Temple alone.

BIBLIOGRAPHY

L. Whistler, M. Gibbon and G. Clarke: *Stowe: A Guide to the Gardens* (Buckingham, 1956, rev. 3/1974) [guidebk]

L. Whistler: 'Signor Borra at Stowe', *Country Life*, cxxii (29 Aug 1957), pp. 390–93

M. McCarthy: 'James Lovell and his Sculptures at Stowe', *Burl. Mag.*, cxv (1973), pp. 221–32

(2) George Temple-Nugent-Grenville, 1st Marquess of Buckingham (*b* 18 June 1753; *d* Stowe, Bucks, 11 Feb 1813). Nephew of (1) Richard Grenville, 2nd Earl Temple. Following family tradition, he was active in politics and twice, for brief periods, was Lord Lieutenant of Ireland. During his Grand Tour in 1774 he visited Pompeii and acquired furniture and antique sculptures in Rome. In 1779, on the death of his uncle, Richard Grenville, 2nd Earl Temple, he inherited Stowe, the family seat. Earl Temple had been engaged in rebuilding the house; Buckingham's immediate task was to complete the decoration and furnishing of its interiors. In the entrance hall he installed a marble alto relievo, *Caractacus Pleading before the Emperor Claudius in Rome* (exh. RA 1780; Stowe, Bucks), by Thomas Banks which he had commissioned while in Italy. The Italian painter–architect Vincenzo Valdré (1742–1814) decorated the music room in the Pompeian style and was kept continuously at work at Stowe until 1787. After employing John Soane to rebuild his London house (Buckingham House, 91 Pall Mall, 1790–94; destr.), Buckingham commissioned him to design the Gothic Library at Stowe (1805–7) for his newly acquired collections of Saxon and Irish manuscripts. The architectural details were inspired by Henry VII's Chapel in Westminster Abbey, London. Soane's immaculate Gothic Revival interior, in a small low-ceilinged basement room, is a delightful anomaly to find in a palatial Neo-classical house. In addition to commissioning family portraits from Reynolds and Gainsborough, Buckingham greatly increased the size and improved the overall quality of the family picture collection; his purchases included *Bellona* (1663; New York, Met.) by Rembrandt, *Virgin and Child with SS John the Baptist and Catherine* (1504; London, N. G.) by Andrea Previtali, *View of a Village with Three Peasants Talking in the Foreground* (*c.* 1645; London, N.G.) by David Teniers (ii) and *Titania and Bottom* (completed *c.* 1790; London, Tate; *see* FÜSSLI, (3), fig. 4) and *Oberon Wakes Titania* (*c.* 1790; Winterthur, Kstmus.) by Henry Fuseli.

BIBLIOGRAPHY

M. Gibbon: 'A Forgotten Italian at Stowe', *Country Life*, cxl (4 Aug 1966), pp. 260–63

M. McCarthy: 'Soane's Saxon Room at Stowe', *J. Soc. Archit. Hist.*, xliv (1985), pp. 129–46

(3) Richard Temple-Nugent-Brydges-Chandos-Grenville, 1st Duke of Buckingham and Chandos (*b* London, 20 Mar 1776; *d* Stowe, Bucks, 17 Jan 1839). Son of (2) George Temple-Nugent-Grenville, 1st Marquess of Buckingham. In 1796 he married Anna Eliza Brydges, sole heiress of the last Duke of Chandos. Through her he acquired an independent fortune and a collection of sculpture and paintings, notably the Chandos portrait of *William Shakespeare* (London, N.P.G.) and Orazio Gentileschi's *Rest on the Flight into Egypt* (Malibu, CA, Getty Mus.). He took advantage of increased opportunities in London's art market resulting from the upheaval of the French Revolution and its aftermath. In 1798 he acquired Albani's *Baptism* (untraced), Domenichino's *Persian Sibyl* (London, Wallace) and Poussin's *Exposition of Moses* (Oxford, Ashmolean) from the Orleans collection and in 1801 the Colonna *Finding of Moses* by Salvator Rosa (Detroit, MI, Inst. A.). In 1813, on the death of his father, he became the 2nd Marquess of Buckingham and took up residence at Stowe; he was elevated to ducal rank in 1822. To enrich the house and collection he had inherited, he spent lavishly on fine furniture and paintings. During a lengthy Mediterranean cruise (1827–9) he acquired antique sculptures in Rome and a collection of majolica in Florence. His diary of this journey, published posthumously, reveals his deep interest in both antiquity and geology. These enthusiasms had been united earlier when, in 1821, he had commissioned John Martin to paint the *Destruction of Pompeii and Herculaneum* (formerly London, Tate; destr. 1928). Buckingham's son, Richard Plantagenet-Temple-Nugent-Brydges-Chandos, 2nd Duke of Buckingham and Chandos (1797–1861), inherited a much encumbered estate which combined with his own extravagance led to his bankruptcy and the sale of the family collection in 1848.

WRITINGS

The Private Diaries, 3 vols (London, 1862)

BIBLIOGRAPHY

R. Chandler and J. Seeley: *Stowe: A Description of the House and Gardens* (Buckingham, 1832)

H. R. Forster: *The Stowe Catalogue, Priced and Annotated* (London, 1848)

For further bibliography *see* STOWE.

COLIN ANSON

Gresham group. Association of Hungarian artists who met regularly at the Gresham Café in Budapest from the mid-1920s to 1944. A loose and friendly association free from institutional constraints, they were united merely by the approximate similarity of their aesthetic thinking, rather than any particular style. Such leading members of the Hungarian avant-garde as Róbert Berény and Aurél Bernáth were, especially in their youth, among the artists at the Gresham. In the 1920s the group contained such representatives of the nascent Hungarian Expressionist movement as József Egry, István Szőnyi, Béni Ferenczy and Pál Pátzay (1896–1979). They are also often referred to as the 'post-Nagybánya school', which refers to the principles of the NAGYBÁNYA COLONY, active in the 1910s, and to their desire to uphold the artistic tradition and stance of the group represented primarily by Károly Ferenczy.

The avowed goal of the Gresham group was to align themselves with the internal development of Hungarian art, while emphasizing the importance of quality. They opposed the official art policy of the day and rejected the artistic establishment. They were generally against the avant-garde, but they equally repudiated the resurgence of Neo-classicism and distanced themselves from academic, nationalistic art. Their ideal was an art that drew on the resources embedded in tradition, while retaining qualities of abstraction and timelessness. Aurél Bernáth's *Self-portrait in a Yellow Coat* (1930; Budapest, N.G.) may be taken as a representative example of their work.

The Gresham group exerted a decisive influence on Hungarian art between the wars, and its influence was still felt after World War II. Several former members were among the most respected artists in the country between 1945 and 1949. The painters Géza Bornemisza (1884–1966), Béla Czóbel (*b* 1883), Jenő Elekfy (1895–1968), Imre Szobotka (1890–1961) and Elemér Vass (1887–1957) were also members, as was the tapestry designer Noémi Ferenczy. Others joined for various lengths of time and at different intervals. The group also contained critics such as Zoltán Farkas (1880–1969), István Genthon (1903–69), Simon Meller, Miklós Rózsa (1874–1945) and Arnold Schoen (1887–1973), and patrons, notably Lajos Fruchter (*d* 1953), Sándor Szilágyi and Béla Radnai. The economist and publisher Imre Oltványi Ártinger (1893–1963) was an outstanding promoter of the group, and he commissioned a number of monographs on members of the group for his series *Ars Hungarica.*

BIBLIOGRAPHY

P. Pátzay: *Alkotás és szemlélet* [Creation and perspective] (Budapest, 1967)

L. Németh: 'A Gresham—múlt és jelen' [The Gresham—past and present], *Művészet,* xvii/12 (1976), pp. 6–10

J. Szabó: 'A rajz és az akvarell a Gresham-kör művészetében' [Drawings and watercolours in the art of the Gresham circle], *Művészet,* xvii/12 (1976), pp. 20–22

L. Végvári and S. Kontha: 'A Gresham csoport kialakulása és esztétikája' [The formation and aesthetics of the Gresham group], *Magyar Művészet, 1919–1945* [Hungarian art, 1919–1945], ed. S. Kontha (Budapest, 1985), pp. 446–89

MÁRIA SZOBOR-BERNÁTH

Greuze, Jean-Baptiste (*b* Tournus, 21 Aug 1725; *d* Paris, 21 March 1805). French painter and draughtsman. He was named an associate member of the Académie Royale de Peinture et de Sculpture, Paris, in 1755 on the strength of a group of paintings that included genre scenes, portraits and studies of expressive heads (*têtes d'expression*). These remained the essential subjects of his art for the next 50 years, except for a brief, concentrated and unsuccessful experiment with history painting in the late 1760s, which was to affect his later genre painting deeply. Though his art has often been compared with that of Jean-Siméon Chardin in particular and interpreted within the context of NEO-CLASSICISM in general, it stands so strikingly apart from the currents of its time that Greuze's accomplishments are best described, as they often were by the artist's contemporaries, as unique. He was greatly admired by connoisseurs, critics and the general public throughout most of his life. His pictures were in the collections of such noted connoisseurs as Ange-Laurent de La Live de Jully, Claude-Henri Watelet and Etienne-François, Duc de Choiseul. For a long period he was in particular favour with the critic Denis Diderot, who wrote about him in the Salon reviews that he published in Melchior Grimm's privately circulated *Correspondance littéraire.* His reputation declined towards the end of his life and through the early part of the 19th century, to be revived after 1850, when 18th-century painting returned to favour, by such critics as Théophile Thoré, Arsène Houssaye and, most notably, Edmond and Jules de Goncourt in their book *L'Art du dix-huitième siècle.* By the end of the century Greuze's work, especially his many variations on the *Head of a Girl*, fetched record prices, and his *Broken Pitcher* (Paris, Louvre) was one of the most popular paintings in the Louvre. The advent of modernism in the early decades of the 20th century totally obliterated Greuze's reputation. It was only in the 1970s, with Brookner's monograph, Munhall's first comprehensive exhibition of the artist's work, increased sale prices, important museum acquisitions and fresh analyses of his art by young historians, that Greuze began to regain the important place that he merits in the history of French art of the 18th century.

1. Life and work. 2. Working methods and technique.

1. LIFE AND WORK.

(i) Training and early years, to 1755. (ii) The Italian journey, 1755–7. (iii) Success in France, 1757–65. (iv) The crisis of 1767–9. (v) Late years, after 1769.

(i) Training and early years, to 1755. Greuze was the sixth of nine children of a roofer (whom the artist would later describe as an architect and property developer) named Jean-Louis Greuze (1697–1769) and his wife, Claudine Roch. He was baptized Jean Greuze. Although he later signed his portrait of the model *Joseph* (Paris, Louvre) *J. Greuze* and affixed the initials *J. G.* to his *Filial Piety* (St Petersburg, Hermitage), in the mid-1750s he adopted the name Jean-Baptiste, by which he is generally known.

According to tradition, Greuze's talents were so developed by the age of eight that he was able to deceive his father into believing that the drawing he had executed for him after an engraving was a print. Surviving versions of a *Portrait of an Old Woman* (priv. col., see 1976–7 exh. cat., no. 1) and a canvas depicting *St Francis in Ecstasy* (Tournus, La Madeleine) suggest that Greuze had some sort of training in his home town and began painting there. In the late 1740s he went to Lyon, where he studied with Charles Grandon (*c.* 1691–1762), a successful portrait painter. Around 1750 the latter went to Paris to join his son-in-law, the composer André Grétry, and it was probably in his mentor's company that Greuze arrived in the capital. There he studied drawing at the Académie Royale with Charles-Joseph Natoire and, according to Melchior Grimm, painted small pictures to make a living. One of these may be a *Triumph of Galatea* (Aix-en-Provence, Mus. Granet) in the style of François Boucher. Greuze won the favour of the sculptor Jean-Baptiste Pigalle and of the painter Louis de Silvestre (i), who had been named director of the Académie in 1752. Supported by Pigalle, the young artist presented some of his work to the Académie, including the *Family Bible Reading* (Paris, Hottinguer priv. col., see 1976–7 exh. cat., no. 2), and executed in public a brilliant portrait of *Silvestre* (Munich, Alte Pin.) to dispel rumours that some of his work had been done by others. On the strength of what he showed, Greuze was named an associate member (*agréé*) of the Académie on 28 June 1755, in the category of 'peintre de genre particulier'. The records of the event noted that '... Greuze will go to the director, who will tell him what he should do for his reception piece'. He did not, however, present his *morceau de réception* for another 14 years.

Later in 1755 Greuze exhibited at the Salon for the first time. Critics, while remarking on the Dutch character of his art and of the resemblances to the paintings of Chardin, hailed 'the new athlete' with enthusiasm. But despite the acclaim, regrets were expressed over such a talented 'young man' (he was already 30 years old) devoting himself to lowly genre subjects. Nevertheless, the popular *Family Bible Reading* was acquired, along with two other canvases, by La Live de Jully.

(ii) The Italian journey, 1755–7. On 22 September 1755, not long after the closing of the Salon, Greuze left Paris for Italy as the guest of Louis Gougenot, Abbé de Chezal-Benôit, a historian, theorist and collector whose acquaintance Greuze had made probably through Pigalle. Greuze later claimed that he had paid his own expenses throughout the trip. However, Gougenot noted in his travel-journal—illustrated with watercolours by Greuze (Paris, Soucy priv. col.)—that after a friend had abruptly declined to travel with him 'I proposed to M. Greuze ... to accompany me, covering all his expenses throughout the trip. He accepted this offer as a piece of good luck.' Greuze painted a sympathetic portrait of *Gougenot* (Dijon, Mus. B.-A.) that was shown in 1757, but he had nothing to do with his patron following his return to Paris. After stopping to see his family in Tournus, where he would not return for many years, Greuze and Gougenot crossed the Alps in perilous conditions, visited monuments and collections in

1. Jean-Baptiste Greuze: *Broken Eggs*, oil on canvas, 730×940 mm, 1756 (New York, Metropolitan Museum of Art)

Turin, Genoa, Parma, Modena, Bologna and Florence, and arrived in Rome on 28 January 1756, having previously visited Naples. In Rome, Gougenot was at a loose end when Greuze threw himself into his work, but he patiently paid for the artist's materials as well as for the models whom Greuze hired and dismissed on erratic whims. Gougenot finally set off alone for Paris four months later, Greuze declaring that he wished to remain in Italy, in order—according to the Abbé Jean-Jacques Barthélémy—to profit from the 'piquant riches of the sites and ruins of Rome' and from the example of the paintings of Raphael, which 'might enable him to rise above himself'.

From Versailles, the Marquis de Marigny, Louis XV's Surintendant des Bâtiments, sent instructions that Greuze should be given lodgings and working space in the Palazzo Mancini, home of the Académie de France in Rome, and commissioned two paintings from him for the Marquise de Pompadour, his sister. Instead of responding to Marigny's generous and flattering offer, Greuze put off executing the commissions until long after his return to Paris; the works were *Simplicity* (1759; Fort Worth, TX, Kimbell A. Mus.) and *Young Shepherd Holding a Flower* (1761; Paris, Petit Pal.). Greuze was more concerned with completing the extraordinary set of paintings that he rushed back to Paris to exhibit at the Salon of 1757 as 'Four Pictures in Italian Costume': *Broken Eggs* (New York, Met.; see fig. 1), *Neapolitan Gesture* (Worcester, MA, A. Mus.), *Indolence* (Hartford, CT, Wadsworth Atheneum) and *The Fowler* (Warsaw, N. Mus.). Employing the highly finished, minutely detailed execution he had learnt from looking at works by the Dutch masters in Paris, Greuze presented in these two sets of pendants—the first horizontal, the second vertical—theatrical evocations of contemporary Italian life, fraught with moral undertones and sardonic wit. Innocence and naivety are contrasted with sin and deceit in the first pair; sloth and lust are memorably conjured up in the second. In addition to painting these four major canvases in a period of 15 months, Greuze executed portraits, including those of the French ambassador to the Holy See, the *Comte de Stainville* (later the Duc de Choiseul) and of the *Comtesse de Stainville* (both untraced), and some figural compositions such as the *Neapolitan Sailor* (London, Wallace) as well as a great many drawings, including an ensemble depicting regional costumes that were later engraved by the Moitte family. He even found time for a romantic involvement with a member of the noble Pignatelli family. Jean-Honoré Fragonard, who was at the Académie at that time, called Greuze 'an amorous cherub'.

The effect of the Italian sojourn on Greuze's development continues to be debated. Sauerländer saw reminiscences of Michelangelo's *Ignudi* (Rome, Vatican, Sistine

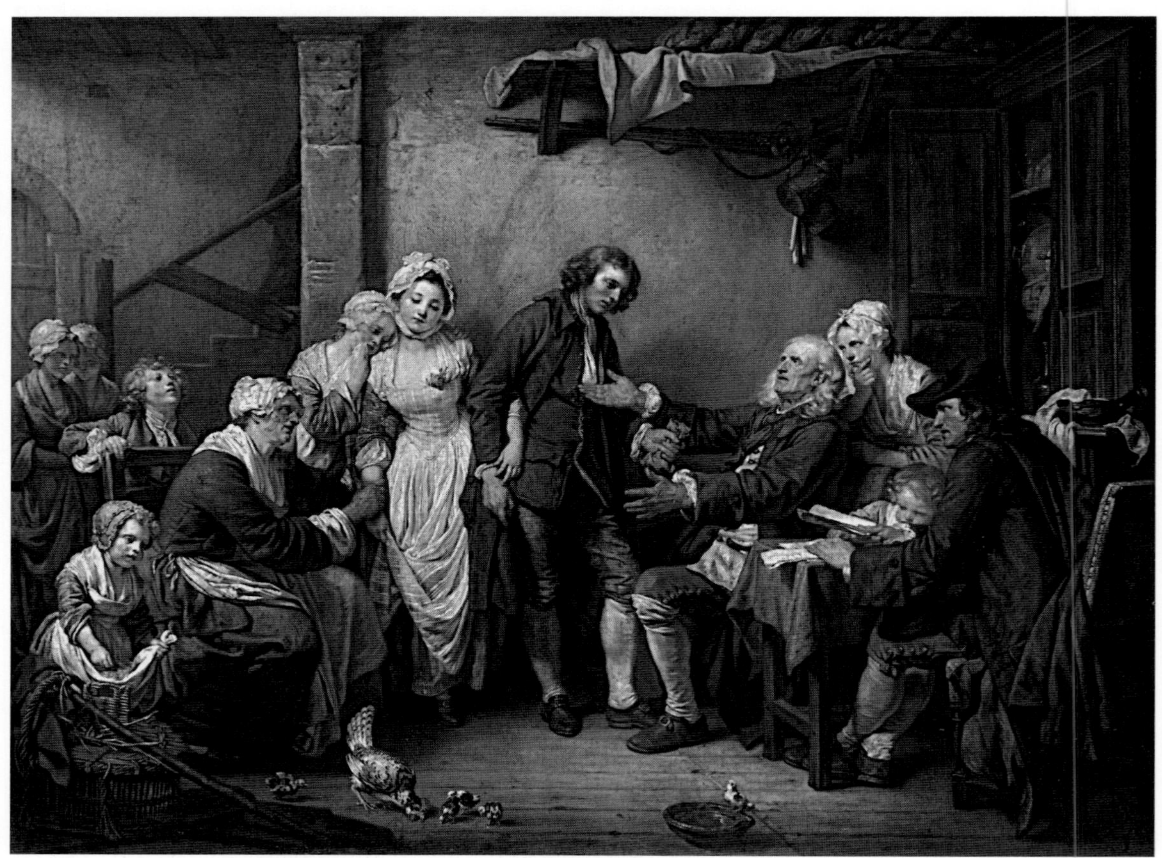

2. Jean-Baptiste Greuze: the *Marriage Contract*, oil on canvas, 0.92×1.17 m, 1761 (Paris, Musée du Louvre)

Chapel) in the pose of *The Fowler* and of the *Laokoon* (Rome, Vatican, Mus. Pio-Clementino) in the gesture of the son in the *Father's Curse* (Paris, Louvre); there is evidence that Greuze drew after antique sculpture (e.g. *Female Torso after the Antique*; U. Warsaw, Lib.), and a carefully depicted foliated capital appears in the foreground of *Neapolitan Gesture*. These amount, however, to no more than superficial ornaments on an artistic manner that Greuze had evolved earlier in France. Like his French contemporaries in Rome, Fragonard and Hubert Robert, Greuze was more interested in the picturesque details of contemporary life than in the august examples of the ancient past or the monuments of the Renaissance.

(iii) Success in France, 1757–65. On 27 April 1757 Natoire, then director of the Académie de France in Rome, informed Marigny that Greuze had left for Paris. His intention to visit Venice seems not to have been fulfilled. Always adept at self-promotion, Greuze must have felt that it was more important to show the products of his Italian trip at the Salon that summer than to study Titian or the work of his Venetian contemporaries. In Paris he exhibited over a dozen works, including the 'Four Pictures in Italian Costume', portraits of *Pigalle* (untraced) and of *Gougenot* (Dijon, Mus. B.-A.), and the Rembrandtesque and sombre *Boy with a Lessonbook* (Edinburgh, N.G.).

Soon after his return from Rome, Greuze became involved with Anne-Gabrielle Babuti (1732–after 1812), the beautiful and wealthy daughter of a Paris bookseller. After a tempestuous courtship they were married on 3 February 1759 at St Médard, the bride bringing Greuze a dowry of 10,000 livres. They had three daughters, one of whom died in infancy. Mme Greuze's flagrant infidelities and meddlings in her husband's affairs were to turn their marriage into a private nightmare and a public scandal. It was also in 1759 that Greuze befriended the German engraver and dealer Jean-Georges Wille, whose *Journal* provides valuable references to the artist. In 1763 he sat for one of Greuze's finest portraits (Paris, Mus. Jacquemart-André).

Denis Diderot spoke of Greuze for the first time, and with a certain familiarity, in his *Salon* of 1759. The critic saw in Greuze's genre scenes the visual equivalent of his own sentimental dramas, an embodiment of his call for a new seriousness in painting and the perfect occasion for his own idiosyncratic criticism, which depended to a large degree upon the emotive power of a painting's subject-matter. Relations between the *philosophe* and the artist developed over the ten years from 1759, culminating in a separation: Diderot spoke of 'my friend Greuze' in 1761; two years later he addressed him as 'tu' and in 1763 he opened his long article on *Filial Piety* with the exclamation, 'That is really my man, that Greuze!'. By 1767, when relations between Greuze and Diderot had deteriorated (the latter was then referring to the former as 'my late friend Greuze'), Diderot intervened with Catherine II to have her rescind her invitation to Greuze to come to Russia, using Mme Greuze as the reason.

If Greuze's showings at the Salon of 1759 appealed because of the exotic details of the Italian subjects, those of 1761 were devoted to themes of family life and depictions of idealized girls: *Silence!* (London, Buckingham Pal., Royal Col.), showing a nursing mother disciplining an unruly child, the *Wool Winder* (New York, Frick) and the *Sleeping Knitter* (San Marino, CA, Huntington Lib. & A.G.). Portrait subjects included several aristocrats, among them the artist's early patron, *Ange-Laurent de La Live de Jully* (Washington, DC, N.G.A.; for illustration *see* LA LIVE DE JULLY, ANGE-LAURENT DE), shown playing a harp and surrounded by his avant-garde Neo-classical furniture. Critical reactions to these works were muted, Diderot saying merely, 'the Greuzes are not marvellous this year'. Nevertheless, the Salon of 1761 brought Greuze phenomenal success with the *Marriage Contract* (Paris, Louvre; see fig. 2)—more familiarly known as *L'Accordée de village*—in which the artist alluded to a crucial detail of his own marriage two years earlier by showing an old father handing over a dowry to his timid son-in-law. Further portrait subjects among Greuze's 20 entries that year included the artist himself (untraced), his father-in-law *François Babuti* (Paris, David-Weill priv. col., see 1976–7 exh. cat., no. 26) and *Mme Greuze as a Vestal Virgin* (untraced). The *Marriage Contract*, painted on commission for Marigny, was the only work from the minister's collection to be acquired after his death by Louis XVI. It received a delirious popular and critical reception; even the demanding connoisseur Pierre-Jean Mariette pronounced it 'the painter's masterpiece'. Greuze's reputation had reached its zenith. At the Salon of 1763 he provided what was interpreted as a dramatic sequel to the *Marriage Contract*: *Filial Piety* (St Petersburg, Hermitage), in which a paralysed old man is shown being cared for by several generations of loving family members. The picture drove Diderot, in an exceptionally long article, to announce that with it Greuze had created a new genre of painting,

3. Jean-Baptiste Greuze: *Girl Weeping over her Dead Bird*, oil on canvas, 460×533 mm, 1765 (Edinburgh, National Gallery of Scotland)

what he called 'moral painting', that would finally replace the artificialities of Boucher's tradition. Despite the critical acclaim, the high price Greuze set on the painting and its depressing subject-matter held up its sale for some time, until Catherine II of Russia purchased it in 1765. In that same year Greuze exhibited at the Salon the *Girl Weeping over her Dead Bird* (Edinburgh, N.G.; see fig. 3), a pathetic subject inspired by Catullus that provoked from Diderot a celebrated text analysing it as a symbol of the loss of virginity. Portrait subjects included the collector *Claude-Henri Watelet* (Paris, Louvre), the sculptor *Jean-Jacques Caffiéri* (New York, Met.) and *Jean-Georges Wille* (Paris, Mus. Jacquemart-André).

(iv) The crisis of 1767–9. After several years of such professional success and relative happiness at home, Greuze's peace was disturbed in 1767 when he received a letter from Charles-Nicolas Cochin II, secretary of the Académie Royale, informing him that because he still had not presented his reception piece after 12 years (it was normally expected within six months after an artist was named an associate member), he would not be permitted to exhibit at the Salon that year. Cochin explained that his colleagues felt that such a highly regarded artist as Greuze ought to be an academician. Greuze's reply to Cochin's courteous letter was later described by Diderot as 'a model of vanity and impertinence'.

Privately Greuze made the decision at this time to abandon genre painting and to enter the grand arena of history painting. He perhaps thought that his skills were equal to those of any of his contemporaries working in that field, or he realized that he could reach the highest posts and honours of the Académie only as a history painter. He also perhaps relished the idea of surprising everyone when he finally presented the long-awaited *morceau de réception.* For the next two years Greuze doubled his efforts. He undertook an unusual variety of religious and historical subjects, including *Lot and his Daughters* (Paris, Louvre), *Cimon and Pero* (Paris, Louvre; Cambridge, MA, Fogg), *Aegina Visited by Jupiter* (New York, Met.), *Vespasian and Sabinus* (Chaumont, Mus. Mon.), the *Funeral of Patroclus* (Paris, priv. col., see 1976–7 exh. cat., no. 66) and the *Death of Brutus* (Bayonne, Mus. Bonnat), a subject that Diderot had suggested to him. He made fresh studies from ancient sculpture and casts, and he looked at the example of Nicolas Poussin's paintings for guidance—both for composition and for a new painterly manner, flatter and matt. By the summer of 1767 Greuze had chosen the subject for his Académie painting, Septimius Severus rebuking his son Caracalla for having attempted to assassinate him, and had painted the first version of it (untraced) that Grimm and Diderot saw and admired. Writing to the sculptor Etienne-Maurice Falconet, the latter extolled Greuze's *tour de force* in changing genres and lauded the composition, with its 'broad, naked background, with so great a silence that it seems the voice of Septimius Severus reverberates in the emptiness of the apartment'. Two years later, however, Diderot described the final version of the picture as 'worth nothing'.

Diderot's reaction was echoed by Greuze's fellow members of the Académie Royale when he presented *Septimius Severus Reproaching Caracalla* (Paris, Louvre; see fig. 4) to them on 23 July 1769. After examining the picture with its unexpected, and unannounced, historical subject, and keenly aware of the artist's acerbic attitude towards them, his colleagues first voted to elect Greuze as an academician but then voted separately on his classification. In a majority of twenty-one to nine they received him 'with the same rights as his associateship, that is to say as a genre painter'. To humiliate him further, Greuze was informed of this condition only after taking his oath of membership. Enraged, the artist initially sought to remove his painting but then left it there in the hope that he would be vindicated by the public who would view it shortly at the Salon. Unfortunately, his hopes were dashed, as *Septimius Severus* was greeted with an avalanche of negative criticism. The artist spoke back, in vain, in a letter published in the *Avant-Coureur* on 25 September. In vain, too, he attempted to resign from the Académie, but he did at least dissociate himself from the organization, not exhibiting at the Salon again until 1800. His only consolation lay in flight, so he returned to his native Tournus, where his father died on 10 October.

(v) Late years, after 1769. The remaining 36 years of Greuze's life were far from easy, but they saw a continual artistic growth, a deepening humanity in his outlook and a ceaseless daring in the face of adversity. While he did not exhibit at the Salons of the Académie, he occasionally attended its meetings when his vote could count, such as at that of 28 September 1770 concerning the admission of female members. His work appeared at the Salon de la Correspondance in 1779, 1782, 1783 and 1785, at the Salon de l'Encouragement des Arts in 1790, at the Société des Arts in Montpellier in 1779, and at the Salon des Arts in Lyon in 1786. More importantly, Greuze managed to embarrass the Académie and tease the critics by staging private exhibitions in his studio in the Louvre that coincided with the biennial Salons. Numerous distinguished foreigners made a point of visiting Greuze, including Gustav III of Sweden (1771), Joseph II of Austria (1777) and the Grand Duke Paul Petrovitch, son of Catherine II (1782). Greuze also publicized himself in the press, announcing the publications of the numerous reproductive engravings of his works by artists including Jean-Jacques Flipart, Carlo Antonio Porporati (1741–1816), Jean Massard, René Gaillard (*d* 1790) and Jean-Charles Le Vasseur. The sale of such prints brought the artist wealth, but his fortune was decimated by the onerous settlement he was obliged to give his wife at the time of their divorce in 1792.

In his late years Greuze executed a certain number of important works depicting scenes of contemporary life, in which he mixed realistic observation with the grand manner of history painting. These include the *Twelfth-night Cake* (1774; Montpellier, Mus. Fabre), the *Charitable Woman* (1775; Lyon, Mus. B.-A.) and the *Drunkard's Return* (*c.* 1780; Portland, OR, A. Mus.). The masterpieces of his old age, however, are the majestic pendants, the *Father's Curse* and the *Punished Son* (both Paris, Louvre). In these the family discords that Greuze had known all

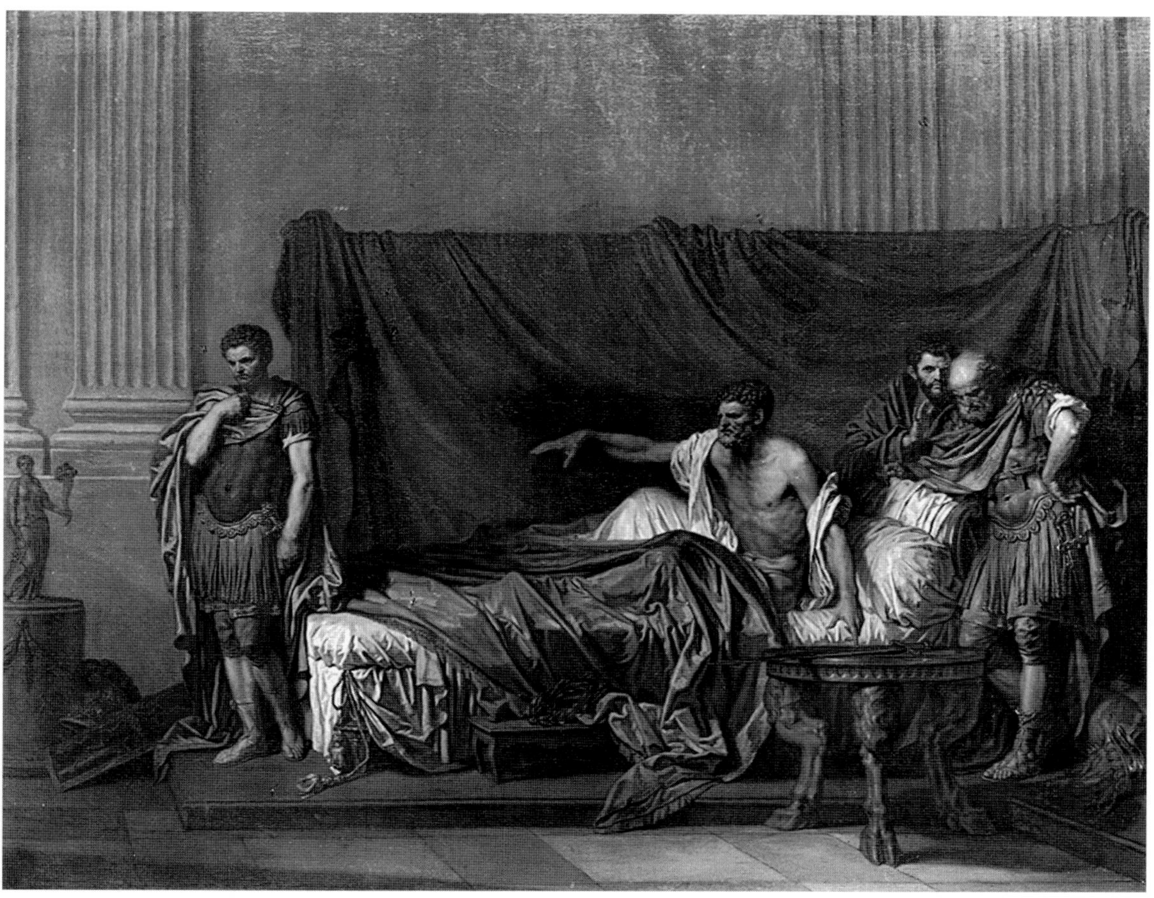

4. Jean-Baptiste Greuze: *Septimius Severus Reproaching Caracalla*, oil on canvas, 1.24×1.60 m, 1769 (Paris, Musée du Louvre)

his life are intensified to an expressionistic degree but at the same time elevated through the clarity and beauty of their formal presentation. Two important history paintings date from this period—*Innocence Carried Off by Cupid* (before 1786; Paris, Louvre) and *St Mary of Egypt* (*c.* 1800; Norfolk, VA, Chrysler Mus.)—as well as a great number of portraits and self-portraits (e.g. Paris, Louvre; Marseille, Mus. B.-A.), and many drawings.

Greuze's activities during the French Revolution remain obscure. He treated a very few Revolutionary subjects, but he did execute some notable portraits during those years, including that of *Jean-Nicolas Billaud-Varenne* (Dallas, TX, Mus. A.). During these difficult times the artist produced a quantity of versions of his ever-popular *Head of a Girl* and may even have sold some he knew he had never painted. These unfortunate productions continue to mar his reputation to this day. In 1793 he joined the Commune Générale des Arts, led by Jacques-Louis David and Jean-Bernard Restout. He certainly applauded the dissolution of the old Académie Royale, returning after its reorganization to exhibit at the Salons of 1800, 1801 and 1804. He died in his studio in the Louvre, still attended by his unmarried elder daughter, Anne-Geneviève (1762–1842), whom he called his Antigone. He is buried in the cemetery of Montmartre, Paris.

2. WORKING METHODS AND TECHNIQUE. From his early *Family Bible Reading* to his late *Drunkard's Return*, Greuze's programme in developing a multi-figured composition remained the same. He proceeded from rough compositional schemes to studies of individual figures, heads, hands and accessories. Few drawings for portraits are known, however, though the artist did execute some that were notable. He experimented only once with printmaking, preferring to turn over the production of reproductive engravings after his paintings to specialists. His earliest surviving works, such as the *Triumph of Galatea*, were painted in the manner of Boucher, with lush, fluid brushstrokes and a light palette. By 1755, when he dated his portrait of *Joseph* (Paris, Louvre), his debt to Rembrandt in his use of dark coloration and dramatic lighting was remarked upon by a contemporary. In his portraits Greuze continued to follow the manner of Rembrandt and of Anthony van Dyck, but many of his early figural compositions, such as the *Broken Eggs* or the *Wool Winder*, with their highly finished technique, recall the work of the popular 17th-century Dutch masters Gerrit Dou and Frans van Mieris (i). By the late 1760s, however, Greuze's study of Poussin led him to adopt a flatter, broader handling of form and a somewhat murky

palette. In the 1780s he was employing panel supports for his portraits, with brilliant translucent effects. Despite his disdain for the study of anatomy, Greuze had a perfect innate knowledge of it, and anatomical faults are to be weighed carefully in pondering any Greuze attribution. He rarely signed his paintings.

BIBLIOGRAPHY

D. Diderot: *Correspondance, 1741–84*; ed. G. Roth, 16 vols (Paris, 1955–70)
——: *Salons* (1759–81); ed. J. Adhémar and J. Seznec, 4 vols (Oxford, 1957–67, rev. 1983)
J.-G. Wille: *Journal* (1759–93); ed. G. Duplessis as part of *Mémoires et journal*, 2 vols (Paris, 1857)
E. de Goncourt and J. de Goncourt: *L'Art du dix-huitième siècle*, i (Paris, 1880), pp. 289–360
J. Martin and C. Masson: *Catalogue raisonné de l'oeuvre peint et dessiné de J.-B. Greuze* (Paris, 1908)
L. Hautecoeur: *Greuze* (Paris, 1913)
W. Sauerländer: 'Pathosfiguren im Oeuvre des Jean-Baptiste Greuze', *Walter Friedlaender zum 90. Geburtstag* (Berlin, 1965)
A. Brookner: *Greuze: The Rise and Fall of an Eighteenth-century Phenomenon* (London, 1972)
Jean-Baptiste Greuze, 1725–1805 (exh. cat. by E. Munhall, Hartford, CT, Wadsworth Atheneum; Dijon, Mus. B.-A.; 1976–7)
S. Laveissière: 'Jean-Baptiste Greuze', *Dictionnaire des artistes et ouvriers d'art de Bourgogne* (Paris, 1980)
E. Munhall: 'Jean-Baptiste Greuze', *Diderot et l'art de Boucher à David: Les Salons, 1759–1781* (exh. cat., ed. M.-C. Sahut and N. Volle; Paris, Hôtel de la Monnaie, 1984–5), pp. 217–67

EDGAR MUNHALL

Greville. English family of patrons and collectors. One of the earliest notable members of the family was the leading Renaissance poet, Fulke Greville, 1st Baron Brooke (1554–1628); from 1605 the family was established at Warwick Castle, Warwicks. Francis Greville, 1st Earl Brooke and 1st Earl of Warwick (1719–73), was a patron and collector on a considerable scale, acquiring Dutch pictures and commissioning a series of family portraits from Joshua Reynolds and views of *Warwick Castle* from Canaletto (*c.* 1748 and 1751; examples New Haven, CT, Yale Cent. Brit. A.; Birmingham, Mus. & A.G.). The Earl also engaged 'Capability' Brown to make improvements to Warwick Castle and its park during the 1750s. His eldest son, George Greville, 2nd Earl Brooke and 2nd Earl of Warwick (1746–1816), whose portrait was among those by Reynolds (1754; priv. col., see *Reynolds*, exh. cat., ed. N. Penny; London, RA, 1986, no. 22), was an active buyer of pictures in the London sale-rooms in the 1770s and had eclectic if conventional tastes. He also acquired the Warwick Vase (Glasgow, Burrell Col.), a colossal Roman marble excavated in Italy in 1771.

Charles Francis Greville (*b* 12 May 1749; *d* London, 23 April 1809), younger brother of the 2nd Earl, made the Grand Tour in 1768–9, studying at Rome with the dealer James Byres; there his interest in antiquities was aroused and encouraged by his maternal uncle, Sir William Hamilton (i). Greville was elected to the Society of Dilettanti in 1774 and returned to Italy the following year, where he built up a collection of antiquities—unsuccessfully offered to Charles Manners, 4th Duke of Rutland, in 1784 (Historic Manuscripts Commission, Rutland Papers, iii, p. 156)—and probably bought four of his five early Italian pictures. The fifth, the fresco fragment of *Two Haloed Mourners* (London, N.G.) by Spinello Aretino, was probably purchased in London from his friend and rival Charles Townley. In 1782 the young Emily Hart (who, later, as Lady Hamilton, was the mistress of Admiral Horatio Nelson) became his mistress, but the shortage of money that cramped Greville's style as a collector forced him to persuade Hamilton to take her on four years later. Greville's collection was one of the finest of the late 18th century, and he was widely regarded as one of the outstanding connoisseurs of the time. Although many of his pictures were of the fashionable schools of the period, he was a pioneer in his interest in early Italian painting. With the exception of the Spinello, the only such work from the collection that can be traced is Gherardo di Giovanni del Foro's *Madonna and Child* (Seattle, WA, A. Mus.), then attributed to Domenico Ghirlandaio. The fullest account of Greville's collection is the catalogue drawn up for the posthumous sale at Christie's, London, on 31 March 1810.

The 2nd Earl's third son, Major-General Sir Charles John Greville (1780–1836), was a notable collector of Old Master drawings, many of which were later sold anonymously at Christie's on 18 March 1831 and by Francis Greville, 5th Earl Brooke and 5th Earl of Warwick (1853–1924), at Christie's on 20–21 May 1896. Lugt (L 549) confuses Sir Charles with his kinsman Captain Charles Greville (1762–1832); the latter was presumably the 'C.G.' who bought back 23 pictures at the posthumous sale (Christie's, 18 Nov 1794) of works formerly owned by his father, Fulke Greville of Wilbery. In 1978 Warwick Castle and much of its contents were sold to Madame Tussaud's Ltd.

BIBLIOGRAPHY

DNB
A. Morrison: *The Hamilton and Nelson Papers*, 2 vols (London, 1893–4)
F. Lugt: *Marques* (1921)
D. Lygon and F. Russell: 'Tuscan Primitives in London Sales, 1801–1837', *Burl. Mag.*, cxxii (1980), pp. 113, 115
D. Buttery: 'Canaletto at Warwick', *Burl. Mag.*, cxxix (1987), pp. 437–45

FRANCIS RUSSELL

Grévin, Alfred (*b* Epineuil, nr Tonnerre, Yonne, Jan 1827; *d* Saint-Mandé, Seine, 5 May 1892). French printmaker and costume designer. After leaving school he became an apprentice draughtsman for the Paris-Lyon-Méditerranée railway company. While thus employed he also made his début as a caricaturist in the journal *Gaulois*, to which he contributed from 1858. In 1859 he had the first of many works published in the *Journal amusant*; his *At the Opéra Ball* (1860; Paris, Bib. N.) was for this publication. In 1860 he left the railway company and started to contribute to the *Petit journal pour rire* as well. He began working for *Le Charivari* in 1869, the year in which he co-founded, with Adrien Huart, the *Almanach des Parisiennes*, which published albums of prints for the next 19 years. It was about this time, when he began to concentrate on the manners and language of Parisian society, that Grévin established his mature style. Many of his designs, which were always accompanied by humorous captions, were inspired by the women of the demi-monde. Unlike many caricaturists of his age he avoided political topics.

Grévin also worked for many years as a costume designer for the popular theatres of Paris, collaborating on over 65 productions of operettas, comic operas and ballets. Several of his designs were published in albums, such as those for the comic opera *Fille de Mme Angot* (Paris, 1875). He also illustrated such books as Paul Véron's *Paris vicieux* (Paris, 1880) and *La Chaîne des dames* (Paris, 1881). In 1877 his drama *Le Bonhomme misère*, written in collaboration with Ernest d'Hervilly, was performed at the Odéon in Paris. He is perhaps best remembered today for the waxwork museum named after him, which he founded in 1882 in the Boulevard Montmartre, Paris.

BIBLIOGRAPHY

DBF

H. Béraldi: *Les Graveurs du XIXe siècle*, 12 vols (Paris, 1885–92), vii, pp. 238–60

Inventaire du fonds français après 1800, Paris, Bib. N., Dépt. Est. cat. (Paris, 1930–), ix, pp. 396–401

□

Grey [de Grey]. English family of architects, patrons and collectors. Principally noted for their interest in garden design and architecture as represented in the family estate at Wrest Park, Beds, many generations of the family were active as statesmen and parliamentarians. Among the important works of art once owned by the family are Claude Lorrain's *Coast View of the Embarkation of Carlo and Ubaldo* (Toronto, A. G. Ont.) and Anthony van Dyck's portrait of the *Balbi Children* (London, N.G.). In 1676 Anthony, 11th Earl Grey (*b* 1645; *d* 19 Aug 1702), designed and built a new north front for the Elizabethan house at Wrest; during the late 1680s he began making Baroque formal gardens to the south of it. His son, Henry Grey, 12th Earl of Kent (*b* 1671; *d* 5 June 1740), whose Grand Tour in 1690–91 had included a visit to Rome, inherited the estate on his father's death and resumed work on the gardens in 1703. Two pavilions were built to designs by Thomas Archer, one of which, the striking Banqueting House (1709–11), survives at the head of a long canal. Built in brick on a hexagonal plan, this example of Archer's enthusiasm for the 17th-century Italian architect Francesco Borromini consists of a domed circular drum moulded by a series of alternating rectangular and segmental projections. On completion, its interior was decorated with *trompe l'oeil* figures and grisaille by Louis Hauduroy (*fl c.* 1704–*c.* 1712). In 1710 Grey was created Duke of Kent; five years later he commissioned a new house for Wrest from the Italian architect James Leoni, who was then trying to establish himself in England, but his designs (Bedford, Rec. Office) were not executed. The Duke of Kent commissioned far more work than was executed: the family papers include designs by Filippo Juvarra, Nicholas Hawksmoor and William Kent. Works built at Wrest during this period include Batty Langley's remodelling (1729) of the Bowling Green House. The wooded gardens, by then cut through with grassed walks, were decorated with numerous terms and statues supplied by the workshop of John van Nost (i) and other sculptors and masons. In 1735 John Rocque published a plan of Wrest Park; as one in his established series of estate engravings, this includes perspective views of the buildings by then built or proposed.

In 1758–60 Jemima, Marchioness Grey (*b* 20 Oct 1722; *d* 11 Jan 1797), the Duke's granddaughter, and her husband Philip Yorke, 2nd Earl of Hardwicke (1720–90), employed 'Capability' Brown to improve the gardens at Wrest, and in 1763 the architect Henry Flitcroft built a new drawing-room. A chinoiserie pavilion, root-house and other garden structures date from the same period. The couple also employed Brown at another of their estates, Wimpole Hall, Cambs, where a ruinous Gothick castle (1774) was built to earlier designs by Sanderson Miller. Wrest subsequently passed to Amabel, Countess de Grey (*b* 22 Jan 1751; *d* 4 May 1833), and on her death to a nephew, Thomas Philip Robinson, 3rd Baron Grantham (*b* 8 Dec 1781; *d* 14 Nov 1859), who became 1st Earl de Grey in 1833. Son of the diplomat, patron and amateur architect THOMAS ROBINSON (ii), 2nd Baron Grantham, he was a talented draughtsman who won premiums at the Society of Arts in London. In 1835 he became the first president of the Institute of British Architects (later the RIBA), a post he held for 25 years. Jean-Auguste-Dominique Ingres drew his portrait in Rome in 1816. His early architectural works include sets of lodges at Wrest (1816, 1826) and the nearby Silsoe parish church (1830–31), designed and built in Perpendicular Gothic style. In 1834 he began his most ambitious work, rebuilding Wrest Park in the Louis XV style (*see* ENGLAND, fig. 43). This was a novel undertaking on an estate in England, for which he drew extensively upon such treatises as Jacques-François Blondel's *De la distribution des maisons de plaisance et de la décoration des édifices en général* (1737–8) and *L'Architecture française* (1752–6); the resultant 15-bay palace with mansard roofs, completed in 1839, was built adjacent to the demolished old house, whose site was turned into a French garden consisting of terraces, fountains and walks flanked with statues. The family's informed interest in architecture was maintained by de Grey's daughter, Lady Mary Vyner (1809–92), who lived at Newby Hall, N. Yorks. She commissioned two Gothic Revival churches from William Burges: St Mary's (1871–8), Studley Royal, N. Yorks; and Christ the Consoler (1871–6), Skelton, which is on the Newby estate. The family retained Wrest Park until after World War I, when it was sold; it is now the National Institute of Agricultural Engineering. The gardens are open to the public and maintained by English Heritage.

UNPUBLISHED SOURCES

Bedford, Rec. Office [Lucas Papers]

BIBLIOGRAPHY

Colvin; *DNB*

J. Godber: *Wrest Park and the Duke of Kent* (Bedford, 1963)

——: *The Marchioness Grey of Wrest Park* (Bedford, 1968)

S. Houfe: 'Wrest Park, Bedfordshire', *Country Life*, cxlvii (25 June 1970), pp. 1250–53; cxlvii (2 July 1970), pp. 18–21

T. Hudson: 'A Ducal Patron of Architects', *Country Life*, clv (17 Jan 1974), pp. 78–81

T. Friedman: 'Lord Harrold in Italy, 1715–16: Four Frustrated Commissions to Leoni, Juvarra, Chiari and Soldani', *Burl. Mag.*, v (1988), pp. 836–45

KIM SLOAN

Grey school. *See* HAGUE SCHOOL.

Gribelin, Simon, II (*b* Blois, 5 May 1661; *d* London, 18 Jan 1733). French engraver, active in England. He was a Huguenot from a family of engravers and watchmakers. By 1681 he had moved to London and was admitted to the Clockmakers Company in 1686, possibly because of work he did for them engraving watchcases. He engraved other silver objects such as salvers and snuff boxes (e.g. a silver-gilt comfit box, *c.* 1690; London, V&A). He published two books of prints intended as pattern books for his fellow craftsmen—*A Book of Severall Ornaments* (London, 1682; O'Connell, no. 1) and *A Book of Ornaments Usefull to Jewellers Watchmakers and All Other Artists* (London, 1697; O'C 2). These were derived from the work of earlier French designers, including Jean Berain I and Jean Vaquer (1621–1686). In 1707 Gribelin was the first engraver to reproduce the Raphael Cartoons (O'C 7), then on display at Hampton Court (British Royal Col., on loan to London, V&A). These prints had a significant influence on the development of printmaking in England. In response to them a group of noblemen brought Nicholas Dorigny to London from Rome to engrave the Cartoons on a larger scale. When Dorigny received a knighthood in 1720, Gribelin reissued his prints, adding a frontispiece showing the Cartoon Gallery. In 1712 he engraved six Italian Old Master paintings in the Royal collection (O'C 8) and in 1720 Rubens's ceiling at the Banqueting House, Whitehall (O'C 10). In addition, he engraved illustrations after his own or others' designs for John Dryden's translation of Charles Alphonse Du Fresnoy's *De Arte Graphica* (London, 1695 and 1716), Lord Shaftesbury's *Characteristics* (London, 1711 and 1714; O'C 11 and 12) and Alexander Pope's *Works* (London, 1717; O'C 13). In 1722 he compiled two albums of his prints and impressions on paper of engraved metalwork (London, BM and St Mary's Coll.). His designs were still being reprinted in the 1750s.

BIBLIOGRAPHY

C. Oman: *English Engraved Silver, 1150–1900* (London, 1978)

S. O'Connell: 'Simon Gribelin (1661–1733), Printmaker and Metal-engraver', *Prt Q.*, ii (1985), pp. 27–38 [with an oeuvre catalogue] [O'C]

The Quiet Conquest: The Huguenots, 1685–1985 (exh. cat., ed. T. Murdoch; London, Mus. London, 1985)

ELIZABETH MILLER

Gricci, Giuseppe (*b* Florence, *c.* 1700; *d* Madrid, 1770). Italian sculptor and modeller. He trained as a sculptor in Florence before moving in 1738 to Naples, where he was appointed chief modeller of the Capodimonte Porcelain Factory between 1743 and 1759. Most Capodimonte figures have been attributed to him. Factory records indicate that he originated a popular snuff-box moulded in relief with shells and marine life (1743–55; New York, Met.) as well as figures of peasants, street traders, characters from the *commedia dell'arte* and such religious figures as his only signed work, the *Mourning Virgin* (*c.* 1745; New York, Met.). He contributed to the creation of porcelain cabinets, including the Salottino di Porcellana (1757–9; now Naples, Capodimonte; *see* ITALY, fig. 71), from the Palazzo Reale in Portici near Naples, and the Gabinete de la Porcelana (1763–5; *in situ*) for the Aranjuez Palace, near Madrid, both of which comprised interlocking plates of porcelain decorated with chinoiseries. In 1759 he moved with other personnel to Madrid, where he held the same position of chief modeller until his death.

BIBLIOGRAPHY

F. Stazzi: *Capodimonte* (Milan, 1972)

A. Gonzales-Palacios: *The Golden Age of Naples: Art and Civilization under the Bourbons, 1734–1805* (exh. cat., ed. S. F. Rossen and S. L. Caroselli; Detroit, MI, Inst. A.; Chicago, IL, A. Inst.; 1981–2), pp. 385–7

CLARE LE CORBEILLER

Grice, Michael. *See under* ARCHITECTS' CO-PARTNERSHIP.

Grien, Hans Baldung. *See* BALDUNG, HANS.

Griesbeck von Griesbach [Gryspek z Gryspach]**, Florian** (*b* Innsbruck, 18 Dec 1509; *d* 29 March 1588). Austrian diplomat and patron, active in Bohemia. He was the second son of Georg Griesbeck, councillor to the Holy Roman Emperor Maximilian I. After studying in Paris he accompanied the Holy Roman Emperor Charles V to the Diet of Augsburg in 1530. Subsequently he entered the service of the future Holy Roman Emperor Ferdinand I, then King of Hungary and Bohemia, settled in Bohemia and in 1532 became secretary to the King and the Royal Chamber of Bohemia. As a councillor, he was several times entrusted with important diplomatic tasks. Although he was a Catholic, his numerous sons were Protestants, and he corresponded with the reformer Philipp Melanchthon (1497–1560). Among several castles that Griesbeck had built or restored is the four-winged Kaceřov Castle, which had the first Renaissance arcades (1540) in the classical style in Central Europe. At Nelahozeves Castle near Prague the court architect Bonifaz Wolmut enlarged the original east wing (1553) to produce a three-winged château with corner bastions, richly decorated with figural sgraffiti and with original, complicated arcades with Mannerist traits. Griesbeck also had a large palace with a garden constructed in Prague in 1568. Bonifaz Wolmut also added the first classicizing façade (1575–81) in church architecture north of the Alps to the Gothic church at Kralovice, near Kaceřov, and designed its burial chapel for the Griesbecks, which contains an elaborate memorial (1593) for Florian Griesbeck von Griesbach, with paintings by Hans Bulleus.

As well as being a controller of finances in the building office of the Royal Castle of Prague, in 1548 Griesbeck advised the government of the Tyrol about obtaining pieces of fine wood for Schloss Ambras, near Innsbruck, and in 1562 negotiated with the goldsmith Wenzel Jamnitzer for gilt statues of the *Four Evangelists* for Archduke Ferdinand of Austria, Count of Tyrol (*reg* 1564–95). He was also a patron of literature and science and wrote in Czech two books on progressive management and farming. He protected and supported the writer Matthew Collin, a former pupil of Melanchthon, and entertained him with other writers at Nelahozeves. In 1593 Salamon Frencelius composed an epitaph on Florian Griesbeck von Griesbach in his book *Epigrammatum silvula prima* (Wittenberg, 1593) and celebrated in verse the library at Nelahozeves, famous for its collections. After the Battle of the White Mountain (1620) the possessions of the Griesbecks were confiscated, and this Czech branch of the family died out by the end of the 17th century.

UNPUBLISHED SOURCES

Prague, Cent. State Archvs [Royal Registers of Missives xv, fols 146–7; xix, fols 44, 233; liii, fol. 183; lvii, fols 455–6, 541; lxx, fols 27–8]

BIBLIOGRAPHY

J. Dyk: *Rod rytířů Gryspeků z Gryspachu v Čechách* [The house of the knights of Griesbeck von Griesbach in Bohemia] (Kralovice, 1924)

O. Frejková: *Palladianismus v české renesanci* [Palladianism in Renaissance Bohemia] (Prague, 1941), pp. 29–34, 52–7, 70–76, 122–78

——: *Zámek Nelahozeves* [Nelahozeves Castle] (Prague, 1954)

E. Šamánková: *Architektura české renesance* [Architecture of Renaissance Bohemia] (Prague, 1961), pp. 29–32, 119, 121
Rukověť humanistického písemnictví v Čechách a na Moravě [Manual of humanistic literature in Bohemia and Moravia], ii (Prague, 1966), pp. 164–70, 229–30, 416–51
K. Merten: 'Die Pfarrkirche St. Peter und Paul in Kralowitz (Kralovice bei Plass)', *Bohemia-Jb. Coll. Carolinum*, viii (Munich, 1967), pp. 134–43
J. Krčálová: 'Kostel sv. Petra a Pavla v Kralovicích a Bonifác Wolmut' [The church of St Peter and Paul at Kralovice and Bonifaz Wolmut], *Umění*, xx (1972), pp. 297–317
M. Flegl: 'K významu osobnosti Floriana Gryspeka v předbělohorských Čechách' [Importance of Florian Griesbeck in Bohemia before the Battle of the White Mountain], *Středočeský Sborn. Hist.*, viii (1973), pp. 181–7
——: 'Florian Gryspek a česká předbělohorská společnost' [Florian Griesbeck and Bohemian society before the Battle of the White Mountain], *Křesťanská Rev.*, xliv (1977), pp. 169–74
——: 'Florián Gryspek, Matouš Collin a humanistické písemnictví' [Florian Griesbeck, Matthew Collin and humanistic literature], *Křesťanská Rev.*, xlvi (1979), pp. 25–31
J. Krčálová: 'Arts in the Renaissance and Mannerist Periods', *Renaissance Art in Bohemia* (London, New York, Sydney and Toronto, 1979), pp. 49–147 (53–5, 69–71)
Hrady, zámky a tvrze v Čechách, na Moravě a ve Slezsku [Fortified castles, châteaux and small castles in Bohemia, Moravia and Silesia], iv (Prague, 1985), pp. 96, 122–5, 146, 161, 212, 225

J. KRČÁLOVÁ

Griffier, Jan [John]**, I** (*b* Amsterdam, ?1645; *d* London, 1718). Dutch painter, active in England. He was a pupil of the landscape painter Roelant Roghman (*c*. 1620–86). About 1666 he moved to London, where he derived more instruction from the anglicized Dutch painter Jan Looten (1618–81). Both these painters employed an earthy tonality and frequently painted on a large scale. Only one painting by Griffier, an immense and spectacular *Noah's Ark* (ex-Nettlecombe Court, Somerset), illustrates these twin influences. Griffier's other paintings of his middle years are quite at variance with this style: he executed numerous small Rhineland views in a highly finished and refined technique reminiscent in both colour and subject-matter of the mature style of Herman Saftleven. Griffier was admitted to the Company of Painter-Stainers in London in 1677; he contributed a *Landscape with Ruins* to their hall. Griffier's work as a draughtsman reflects his training by Roghman; he was an expert etcher and produced an impressive series of plates of birds after Francis Barlow (e.g. *Group of Birds in a Garden*, Hollstein, nos 3–7), as well as a number of good mezzotint portraits after such London portrait painters as Peter Lely and Godfrey Kneller. Griffier seems to have been peripatetic (Horace Walpole suggested that he had his own yacht in which he travelled while sketching the scenery) and, to judge from his surviving views, was acquainted with many of the main British cities, including London, Windsor, Oxford and Gloucester. His English views provide valuable early evidence of British topography at a date when surprisingly little visual information survives. Their style is much broader and the brushwork more cursory than his Rhineland works. Griffier visited Holland *c*. 1695 and remained there for about ten years before returning to London. His later years saw a widening of his subject-matter, to include occasional imaginary landscapes with grottoes and fantastic figures, a *Turkey and other Fowl* (London, Tate) and occasional marine views. Jan Griffier's son Robert Griffier (1688–*c*. 1750) and grandson Jan Griffier II (*fl* 1738–73) continued the family landscape tradition. Robert's early work, where unsigned, is hard to distinguish from that of his father, by whom he was no doubt taught.

BIBLIOGRAPHY

Hollstein: *Dut. & Flem.*; Waterhouse: *18th C.*
H. Walpole: *Anecdotes of Painting in England*, iii (1763), pp. 46–8
H. V. S. Ogden and M. S. Ogden: *English Taste in Landscape in the Seventeenth Century* (Ann Arbor, 1955)
E. Croft-Murray and P. Hulton: *Catalogue of British Drawings in the British Museum* (London, 1960), p. 340

CHRISTOPHER FOLEY

Griffin. American architects and designers, also active in Australia and India. Marion Mahony Griffin (née Mahony) (*b* Chicago, 14 Feb 1871; *d* Chicago, 10 Aug 1961) worked together with her husband Walter Burley Griffin (*b* Maywood, IL, 24 Nov 1876; *d* Lucknow, 11 Feb 1937) after their marriage in 1911. She was the second woman to graduate in architecture (1894) from Massachusetts Institute of Technology, Cambridge, MA, and worked for Dwight Perkins (1867–1941) before joining Frank Lloyd Wright's studio in 1895. There she produced many of the

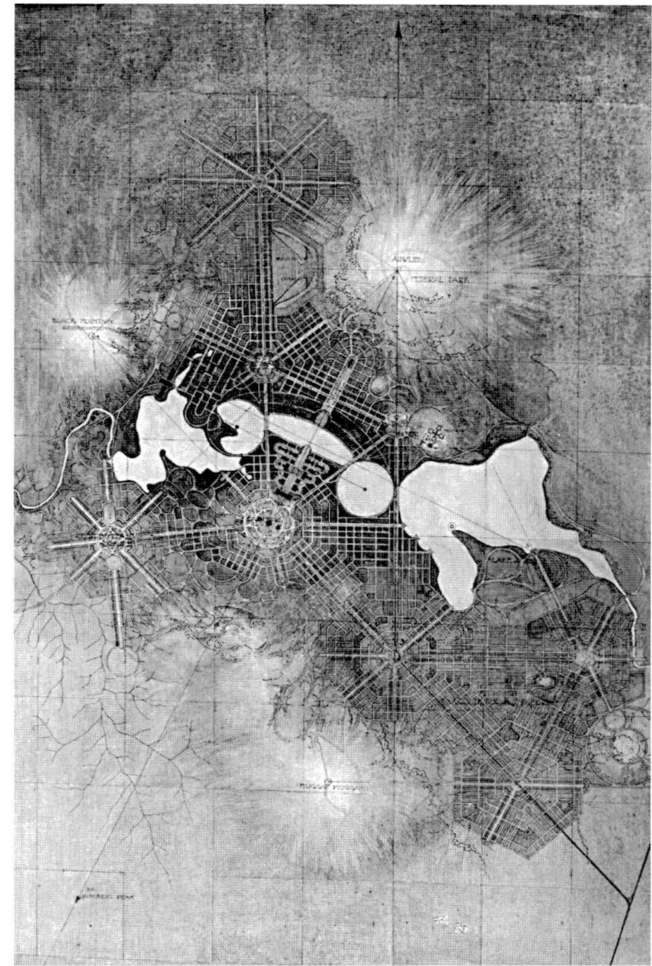

Walter Burley Griffin and Marion Mahony Griffin: rendered site-plan for the new capital city of Canberra; competition entry, 1912

perspective drawings for Wright's designs, including several of those used for the influential Wasmuth portfolio *Ausgeführte Bauten und Entwürfe von Frank Lloyd Wright* (Berlin, 1910), which are among the finest architectural drawings of the 20th century. After Wright's departure from Chicago in 1909, she assisted Hermann von Holst, who took over his practice. In Wright's studio she also met Walter Burley Griffin, who had studied architecture (1895–9) at the University of Illinois, Urbana, and was Wright's assistant from *c.* 1901 to 1906, when he established his own practice. Marion Mahony Griffin executed many of the drawings for Griffin's projects, including the competition drawings for Canberra (see below). In later years she sometimes managed his office and appears to have been responsible for much of the decorative work, although it is unclear what role she played in the overall design of the buildings.

Griffin's early domestic buildings, usually considered as part of the Midwest Prairie school, with which both Walter and Marion were associated, are reminiscent of Wright's, employing similar forms and open-plan living areas around massive central fireplaces; an example is his remarkably mature Emery House (1901–2), Elmhurst, IL, constructed while he was still in Wright's office. Griffin's split-level plans extended Wright's exploration of the inter-penetration of levels, notably in the Hurd Comstock House I (1912), Evanston, IL, which has a one-and-a-half-storey living room overlooked by a first-floor study. Griffin also favoured heavier forms, with less horizontal emphasis and more compact plans. His most striking early departure from Wright was the cubic, fortress-like Melson House (1912), Mason City, IA, with rock-faced stonework incorporating mannerist, oversized keystones that became a hallmark of his work, and the related Stinson Memorial Library (1913), Anna, IL, both of which recall the work of Henry Hobson Richardson.

In 1912 Griffin won the international competition to design an urban plan for CANBERRA, Australia's new capital city. The Griffins' scheme (see fig.), with a central people's 'Capitol' and symmetrical groups of subsidiary government buildings set out in a triangle overlooking a manmade lake, was intended to symbolize the democratic structure of Australian society, in harmony with the natural world. The plan was closely related to its site, with formal axes linking prominent hills on either side of the valley, involving a combination of Beaux-Arts ideas and a sensitive understanding of the topography. The Griffins moved to Australia in 1914 to work on the project, but by 1920 Walter had lost control and was forced to resign. The basic elements of the plan were eventually carried out, but the location of the major public buildings does not reflect the Griffins' ideas; in particular, the new Parliament House (1988) by Mitchell/Giurgola & Thorp was placed upon Capitol Hill rather than below and subordinate to it, as Griffin intended.

The Griffins remained in Australia, obtaining substantial commissions and developing a thriving practice. Notable buildings include Newman College (1915–17), University of Melbourne, in an abstracted medieval idiom; Leonard House (1921–4), an office building with one of the first glass curtain walls in Australia, and the Capitol Theatre (1921–4; altered), both in Melbourne; and a series of dramatic suburban incinerator buildings (1929–37; *see* AUSTRALIA, fig. 5), mostly in Sydney and Melbourne. In these works, and particularly in the ceiling for the Capitol Theatre, possibly designed by Marion, they developed some extraordinary, crystalline architectural and decorative forms with echoes of European Cubist and Expressionist architecture. Griffin also patented in 1917 an ingenious 'Knitlock' construction system of interlocking reinforced-concrete tiles, which anticipated Wright's heavier 'Textile Block' system. After 1920 the Griffins planned a model bushland suburb at Castlecrag, Sydney, where they lived, and built several individual houses there, some in 'Knitlock' and others continuing the rugged character of the earlier American work, but usually with more traditional, spatially distinct rooms. A similar character appears in their municipal incinerators of the early 1930s.

In 1935 Griffin was invited to India to develop a plan for the University of Lucknow Library (1935–6; unexecuted). In 1936 Marion joined him and they worked on several ambitious designs that sometimes incorporated abstracted Indian motifs. These included the Town Hall (1936; unexecuted), Ahmadabad; and, in Lucknow, the Shanti Devi Bahtia House (1936–7) and the Pioneer Press Building (1936–9). After Griffin's sudden illness and death in Lucknow in 1937, Marion spent one year in Australia before returning to the USA. Throughout their working life together the Griffins had attempted to create an organic architecture in which form was related to function in a manner analogous with natural processes. Like Wright, and particularly Louis Sullivan, they never abandoned the invention of new kinds of ornament derived from natural forms, in later years linked to their interest in theosophical and then anthroposophical ideas.

BIBLIOGRAPHY

J. Birrell: *Walter Burley Griffin* (Brisbane, 1964)

D. T. Van Zanten: *Walter Burley Griffin: Selected Designs* (Palos Park, IL, 1970)

D. L. Johnson: *The Architecture of Walter Burley Griffin* (Melbourne, 1977)

Walter Burley Griffin: A Re-View (exh. cat., ed. J. Duncan; Melbourne, Monash U., A.G., 1988) [with list of Australian works]

Transition [Austral.], 24 (1988) [issue dedicated to the Griffins]

J. Weirick: 'Marion Mahony at MIT', *Transition* [Austral.], 25 (1988), pp. 49–54

P. Proudfoot: *The Secret Plan of Canberra* (Kensington, NSW, 1994)

M. Walker, A. Kabos and J. Weirick: *Building for Nature: Walter Burley Griffin and Castlecrag* (Castlecrag, NSW, 1994)

J. Weirick: 'Griffin and Knitlock', *Content*, 1 (1995), pp. 102–17

RORY SPENCE

Griggs, F(rederick) L(andseer Maur) (*b* Hitchin, Herts, 30 Oct 1876; *d* Campden, Glos, 7 June 1938). English etcher, illustrator and designer. Originally trained as an architect, he remained fascinated by ruins, and these formed his principal subject-matter. His first exhibited work at the Royal Academy, in 1897, was an architectural perspective. His first illustrated book was an edition of Tennyson's *In Memoriam* (1900). From 1902 he worked for Macmillan Publishers, illustrating their Highways and Byways series, completing nine volumes and thirty-nine drawings for the Essex volume (on which he was working when he died).

Reception into the Roman Catholic church in 1912 (taking the baptismal name of Maur) had a profound influence on him and confirmed a nostalgic reverence for pre-Reformation England inherited from William Morris. This appears in his etchings in a preference for buildings in the Gothic style and a deliberately archaizing manner. He recognized the symbolic and emotive potential of architecture, which he used to express not only passionate devotion to the lost Gothic order, but also his sense that the modern world was fundamentally inferior to the past. This gives his work a curious hallucinatory quality: ruins are restored to completeness and inhabited by medieval figures, as though viewed in a timewarp (his etching, *The Barbican* (1916–20; priv. col., see Salaman, pl. x), includes tiny heads of executed prisoners set on spikes).

Technically, Griggs's etching was influenced by early encounters with the work of Samuel Palmer and of early German wood-engravers, which led to his use of fine lines densely hatched and carefully bitten to achieve rich texture and orchestrated massing of light and shadow. The juxtaposition of monumental forms gives his prints animation, while the austerity of his images does not diminish their expressive quality. His skies are usually blank, although certain plates, particularly those of contemporary subjects, such as *Maur's Farm* (1913–14; priv. col., see Salaman, pl. ii), show him capable of evocative meteorological effects.

From 1919 Griggs designed a series of memorial crosses for Cotswold villages, the best-known of which is probably that at Painswick. In 1922 he spent his only considerable period abroad, on his honeymoon in Avignon, and produced a series of exceptionally fine watercolours. In this medium, undertaken as a relaxation from etching, he achieved a picturesque poetry through the use of sensitive colour and broad, simplified masses in a manner similar to J. M. W. Turner and John Sell Cotman.

A fine and painstaking craftsman, in later years Griggs set up his own press at his home in Campden to ensure the quality of the prints from his etchings. He acquired fine-quality handmade papers, selecting colours and durability to suit individual plates. An interest in classic script led him to design two sets of Roman type, the Littleworth and the Leysbourne, cut by the Monotype Corp. in 1933–4. Always prepared to encourage young artists, Griggs was the first teacher of Graham Sutherland.

BIBLIOGRAPHY

M. Salaman: *Modern Masters of Etching*, xii: *F. L. Griggs* (London, 1921)
H. Wright: *The Etched Work of F. L. Griggs* (London, 1941)
F. A. Comstock: *A Gothic Vision: F. L. Griggs and his Work* (Boston, 1966)

JUSTINE HOPKINS

Grigi, de'. Italian family of architects and sculptors.

(1) Guglielmo [Vielmo] **de' Grigi** (*b* Alzano, Bergamo, *c.* 1480; *d* Venice, ?1550). Almost all of his recorded works are in Venice, the first being at the Procuratie Vecchie in Piazza S Marco, which were rebuilt after the fire of 1512. From 1517 he was chief assistant there to the *proto* (chief architect), Pietro Buon (ii), to whom he may have been related. The nickname of 'i Bergamaschi' by which the Buon family are sometimes known is also occasionally used more broadly to include Guglielmo, who shared the Buons' Lombard origins. Due to his subordinate position, Guglielmo would have had little influence on the basic design of the Procuratie Vecchie, which had already been established by Pietro Buon after an initial design by Mauro Codussi. Guglielmo was chiefly responsible for the top storey of the façade (*c.* 1517–20), with its decorative oculi and crenellation. Such decorative touches were to become Guglielmo's most clearly identifiable characteristic, and, although he has been cited as a follower of Codussi, he shows the greater influence of Pietro Lombardo in his light, decorative style. In particular, his delicate low relief mouldings are typically Lombard features. In 1519 he completed the Porta Portello, Padua, one of the city's gates, and even here, despite its military function, the gate is faced with a light screen of Istrian stone, with paired columns *in antis.* His next significant work was the altar (*c.* 1524) of Scaligera Verde, a member of the della Scala family, in SS Giovanni e Paolo, Venice, transferred there from the suppressed Servi church. In the same year he was also commissioned to build the high altar (completed 1534) at S Salvatore, where he also carved the altar of St Jerome.

Guglielmo de' Grigi: Palazzo dei Camerlenghi, Venice, 1525–8

Among many attributions to Guglielmo's later career, two are of particular importance. The first is the Palazzo dei Camerlenghi (1525–8; see fig.), now recognized as Guglielmo's work although it has also been attributed to Pietro Buon and to Antonio Scarpagnino. The original building's basic structure had survived the disastrous fire that destroyed the Rialto district of Venice in 1514 but was in poor condition, and Guglielmo was recommended to the Venetian government by Scarpagnino, who was responsible for replanning the whole zone. The building housed the city's treasurers' offices and was considered sufficiently prestigious to be faced entirely with stone. Guglielmo strengthened and refaced the surviving structure, and the work was completed within three years. The highly distinctive façades are typical of his work; they show the influence of Pietro Lombardo and have extensive low-relief carving and inset marble panels. A slightly later, fully documented work is the Miani (Emiliani) Chapel at S Michele in Isola, north of Venice. It is attached on one side to Codussi's slightly earlier church of S Michele and was begun to Guglielmo's design in 1527, although only completed in 1543. The site was a very difficult one, bounded on two sides by the open lagoon, and the hexagonal chapel was built of the white Istrian stone used in the façade of Codussi's church. The style of the chapel is sympathetic to the church but its unusual form renders it clearly distinct; indeed some of Guglielmo's richly detailed decorative work seems excessively fussy in contrast with Codussi's disciplined order. The chapel is crowned with a highly distinctive dome, again all of white stone.

Many other minor works are attributed to Guglielmo. Among the more likely are the side portal of S Francesco della Vigna and the fine portal of Palazzo Tasca near S Lio, the latter transferred from the Tasca palace at Portogruaro. As in so much of his work, columns predominate, with their flutes, pronounced entasis and sharply defined bases and capitals. Two other Venetian palaces are sometimes ascribed to Guglielmo: the Palazzo Cappello Trevisan 'in Canonica' incorporates many Lombard motifs and may be the product of a collaboration between Guglielmo and Pietro Buon, while the Palazzo Coccina Tiepolo is a stronger attribution, since the Coccina family came from Bergamo and the house was completed by Guglielmo's son Giovanni Giacomo (*see* (2) below). Guglielmo also worked for a time at the Scuola Grande di S Rocco, Venice. Other ecclesiastical works included a model (1534) for the lost church of S Antonio, and one of his last works was another lost church, S Maria delle Vergini, where he directed operations until his death.

(2) Giovanni Giacomo de' Grigi (*fl* 1549; *d* Venice, 1572). Son of (1) Guglielmo de' Grigi. He had a long association with the Scuola Grande di S Rocco. In 1549 he was appointed *proto* to the works on the death of Antonio Scarpagnino, although by the time of his appointment much of the main fabric was already complete, and his own works were chiefly confined to interior decorations. He remained there until 1560, when he left after one of the many notable disputes that characterized relations between the Scuola Grande and its architects. In the same period he completed the Palazzo Coccina Tiepolo, incorporating several elements traceable to other sources: the single lights, for example, recall Palladio, while the high-level oculi are characteristic of Jacopo Sansovino. The house was complete by *c*. 1560, and almost immediately afterwards Giovanni Giacomo was employed by Gerolamo Grimani II to complete his great palazzo begun in 1556 by Michele Sanmicheli. Here he continued the robust, powerful classicism of his predecessor with the addition of a second *piano nobile*, and he continued to work there intermittently until his death. One of his last recorded works dates from 1567, when he signed a contract with the monastery of S Giorgio Maggiore to assist Palladio in the reconstruction of the church (*see* VENICE, fig. 21). However, little had been completed at his death. Giovanni Giacomo remains a rather elusive figure, whose work lacks the characteristic lightness of detail of his father. It is instead more closely related to the work of Sanmicheli and Palladio, although lacking the clarity of purpose of either of these masters.

BIBLIOGRAPHY

Portoghesi
A. Venturi: *Storia* (1901–40)
A. Mazzucato: *La Scuola Grande e la chiesa di S Rocco in Venezia* (Venice, 1953)
L. Angelini: *Bartolomeo Bono e Guglielmo d'Alzano: Architetti bergamaschi in Venezia* (Venice, 1961)
E. Bassi: *Palazzi di Venezia* (Venice, 1976)
F. Forlati: *S Giorgio Maggiore* (Padua, 1977)
J. McAndrew: *Venetian Architecture of the Early Renaissance* (Cambridge, MA, and London, 1980)
M. Tafuri: *Venice and the Renaissance* (Cambridge, MA, and London, 1989)

RICHARD J. GOY

Grignion, Charles (*b* London, 1754; *d* Livorno, 4 Nov 1804). English painter and draughtsman. He was the nephew of the engraver Charles Grignion (1717–1810), and at the age of 11 he received a premium for drawing from the Society of Artists. He studied with Giovanni Battista Cipriani and was admitted to the Royal Academy Schools in 1769. He received the Gold Medal in 1776 for his *Judgement of Hercules* (untraced), and continued to exhibit portraits and mythological subjects until 1782, when he left for Rome on a Royal Academy travel scholarship. Grignion remained in Italy for the rest of his life, devoting himself to the study of the Antique and the production of large historical compositions, including the *Death of Captain Cook* (exh. RA 1784; untraced). While in Rome, Grignion collected drawings by his friends John Deare and Robert Fagan. He received several commissions from visiting Englishmen. Among these were an oil study of *Homer Reciting his Poems at the Tomb of Achilles* (untraced) for Lord Berwick, subsequently purchased in 1786 by Cardinal Doria, and two drawings entitled *Assassination near the Porta del Popolo* and *Peasants Dancing the Saltarella* (both untraced) completed in 1787 for Robert, 1st Baron Clive, and later engraved. In 1798 Grignion left Rome for Palermo where he met Lord Nelson and painted his portrait (untraced). His acquaintance with one of Nelson's captains led Grignion to assist in arranging safe passage to London for the Altieri Claudes (Anglesey Abbey, Cambs, NT; *see* ALTIERI) during the French invasion of Rome. One of the few extant works that can be ascribed to him with certainty is a portrait of the *Hon. Charlotte Clive* (Powis Castle, Powys, NT), which is signed and dated 1787.

UNPUBLISHED SOURCES

London, Brinsley Ford Archive

BIBLIOGRAPHY

DNB
S. Redgrave: *A Dictionary of Artists of the English School* (London, 1878/*R* Amsterdam, 1970)
W. Whitley: *Artists and their Friends in England 1700–1799*, 2 vols (London, 1928/*R* New York, 1968)

MARY ANN A. POWERS

Grigorescu, Lucian (*b* Medgidia, 1 Feb 1894; *d* Bucharest, 28 Oct 1965). Romanian painter. He studied from 1912 to 1915 at the Fine Arts School in Bucharest under G. D. Mirea (1852–1934), then at the Accademia di Belle Arti in Rome (1920); subsequently he went with a government scholarship to Paris, where he attended the Académie de la Grande Chaumière and the Académie Ranson in 1925. Between 1924 and 1939 he spent long periods at Cassis in the south of France, while also exhibiting in Bucharest at the official salon and with the artistic groups

Tinerimea Artistică (The young artists), Grupul Nostru (Our group) and Arta. After a short impressionist period, shared by many Romanian painters around 1920, Grigorescu began to show the influence of Derain and Cézanne, especially in the arid but poetic landscapes and the still-lifes he painted at Cassis, which are conspicuous for their dull tones of ochre, browns and cool greens (e.g. *Square in Cassis*, 1927; Bucharest, N. Mus. A.). Also notable is a poetic quality reminiscent of Pittura Metafisica, which he may have encountered in Rome. After 1930 he rediscovered richer pictorial values; his painting became characterized by a robust, spontaneous sensuality and an unbridled vitality in its evocation of nature. In his subsequent work he concentrated on landscapes painted with thick impasto and an almost abstract use of colour (e.g. *Park of the Casa de Creaţie at Mogoşoaia*, 1957; Braşov, Distr. Mus.).

BIBLIOGRAPHY

Lucian Grigorescu (1894–1965): Expoziţie retrospectivă (exh. cat. by P. Oprea, Bucharest, N. Mus. A., 1967)

N. Argintescu Amza: *Lucian Grigorescu* (Bucharest, 1969)

M. Cârneci: *Lucian Grigorescu* (Bucharest, 1989)

IOANA VLASIU

Grigorescu, Nicolae (*b* Pitaru, 15 May 1838; *d* Câmpina, 21 July 1907). Romanian painter. From 1848 he trained in Bucharest with various church painters, producing icons and religious mural decorations. These works, which soon attracted attention, were influenced in style by the Viennese classicism widespread in the Romanian principalities in the early 19th century and by the Italian academicism established there after 1850 by Gheorghe Tattarescu. The earliest of his known paintings are in the church of SS Constantin and Elena at Baicoi, where his signature can be seen beside that of Niţă Pîrîescu on the icon of *St George* (1853). He subsequently painted a series of icons (1854–5) at Căldăruşani Monastery. In the later ensembles he was assisted by his older brother Georghe Grigorescu, who participated under his direction in the decoration of churches, such as those of the Zamfira (1856–8) and Agapia (1858–60) monasteries. In Nicolae's paintings at Agapia, classicism in Romanian art reached its highest point. The royal icons are distinguished for the elegance of the figures, both in their attitudes and in their drapery. The murals include some portraits from life. In the compositions, Grigorescu used engravings after Western masters, but the colouring is entirely his own, as is the harmony created by his luminous tones and, in some places, their aerial transparency. In these early years he also painted some secular works, including a sensitive *Self-portrait* (*c.* 1856; Bucharest, N. Mus. A.).

In the autumn of 1861 Grigorescu was awarded a government grant to study abroad. In Paris he first frequented Charles Gleyre's studio, and in April 1862 was admitted at the Ecole des Beaux-Arts, where he was a pupil of Sébastien Cornu. In his formative years he made copies of some of the Old Masters in the Louvre, including works by Sebastiano del Piombo, Rubens, Nicolaes Berchem and Salvator Rosa. Among painters of his own century he was particularly attracted by Pierre-Paul Prud'hon and Gericault. From the same years (1863–4) dates a group of Romantic painted sketches representing a legendary episode inspired by Romanian history (*Dragoş and the Bison*; 2 variants, Bucharest, N. Mus. A.) and a Romanian rustic scene (*Country Dance*, 1864; Bucharest, N. Mus. A.). After leaving the Ecole des Beaux-Arts in the summer of 1863, Grigorescu established himself in Barbizon, where he became a friend of Millet and produced his first *plein-air* paintings (e.g. *Yard Interior*, 1866; Bucharest, N. Mus. A.), though most of his early landscapes were created in his studio. As a landscape painter, Grigorescu assimilated the influence of Corot, Courbet and the Barbizon school masters. During this period, some of his masterpieces were devoted to nature (e.g. *Landscape with Rocks at Fontainebleau*, 1864–7; Bucharest, N. Mus. A.). In the representation of French peasants he occasionally emulated Millet, but his figures generally suggest a more lyrical mood, as in *French Peasant Woman Carrying a Sack on her Back* (1867–9; Braşov, Mus. A.). The *Watchman from Chailly* (*c.* 1867; Bucharest, N. Mus. A.) is closer to Courbet. Grigorescu participated in the Exposition Universelle of 1867 and in the Paris Salon (1868, 1869).

After his return to Romania in June 1869 Grigorescu was commissioned by the Administration of Civil Hospitals to paint portraits of former benefactors in period costume (e.g. *Constantin Năsturel-Herescu*, 1870; Bucharest, N. Mus. A.). He painted portraits of Bucharest society ladies (e.g. *Speranţa Alexianu*, *c.* 1870; Bucharest, G. Oprescu Mus.), but he also chose models in the city's streets. The *Gypsy Woman of Ghergani* (Bucharest, N. Mus. A.) reveals a Flemish exuberance in the subject's elemental sensuality. A significant part of the artist's work between 1869 and 1873 was devoted to Romanian rural life. In a mobile studio, improvised in a coach, he undertook tours in the Prahova, Dimbovita and Muscel districts, where he painted landscapes, portraits of young peasant women, and also fairgrounds (e.g. the *Sinaia Fair*, 1873; Bucharest, N. Mus. A.). In spite of his success at the Exhibition of Living Artists (1870), he met with hostility from the partisans of academic taste, who criticized his broad and spontaneous brushwork (characteristic of this type of execution is *Hearth of Rucar*, 1870; Bucharest, N. Mus. A.). This animosity later led him to withdraw in 1872 from the official exhibition of living artists and to show two of the paintings destined for it in a shop in Bucharest. In the following year he contributed a large number of works to a great exhibition in Bucharest organized by the Society of the Friends of Fine Arts.

In 1873–4 Grigorescu visited Florence, Venice, Naples and Rome, and, during his return voyage, Athens and Constantinople. In Rome he drew costumed and nude models in a private academy (Bucharest, N. Mus. A.; Bucharest, Roman. Acad. Lib.). Some of the paintings dating from this trip have a Romantic character (e.g. *View of Naples*, 1873–4; Bucharest, N. Mus. A.). After returning to Romania he went to Moldavia (July–Dec 1874), where he executed landscapes showing, in the interpretation of their motifs, affinities with the art of the Impressionists (e.g. *On the Shore of the River Siret*; Bucharest, Zambaccian Mus.). He painted and drew the Jews of Bacău in dramatic contrasts of light and shadows, with a profound psychological penetration (e.g. *Jew with a Caftan*; Bucharest, N. Mus. A.). In the autumn of 1876 Grigorescu visited Vitré, Dinan and Mont Saint-Michel in Brittany, depicting on small-scale panels, in delicate greys, a provincial world still wedded to the past. In Paris he painted a portrait of his compatriot *Georges de Bellio* (Paris, Mus. Marmottan), in whose collection Grigorescu found many Impressionist masterpieces. One of Grigorescu's own paintings from de Bellio's collection was shown in the Salon of 1877.

Grigorescu witnessed the actions of the Romanian army during the Russo-Turkish war of 1877–8, sometimes from the front line. In hundreds of drawings (Bucharest, N. Mus. A.; Bucharest, Roman. Acad. Lib.; Bucharest, National Military Museum) he recorded the manoeuvres of the troops, the movement of camps and tragic episodes during the battles of Grivita and following the fall of Plevna. Among his canvases of the campaign, *Hunters on the Camp at Calafat* (Bucharest, Cent. Mil. Mus.) is a luminous *plein-air* study. Subsequently he executed a number of compositions inspired by the war. Some of them appeared in his first one-man exhibition (1881). The vast canvas the *Attack of Smardan* (1885; Bucharest, N. Hist. Mus. Romania) was preceded by masterly drawn and painted studies. From 1879 Grigorescu frequently visited France, where he resided in 1881–4. He exhibited at the Paris Salon (1880, 1882) and returned to Barbizon, to the Seine valley and to Brittany, where his calm contemplation and his sense of light reached their full maturity (e.g. *Beach on the Ocean*, 1883–4; Brașov, Mus. A.). Following the example of the Impressionists he used brighter tones and continued to produce *plein-air* paintings. In the *Old Woman from Brolle* (1883–4; Bucharest, N. Mus. A.), his technique, including the use of the palette knife, is particularly vigorous. A refined balance settled the structure of his painterly forms and the sketch, for which Grigorescu showed a special predilection, acquired the autonomy of a definitive work. Some of his paintings exhibited at Louis Martinet's (Feb 1887) were remarked upon by French critics.

In 1885 Grigorescu opened his second exhibition in Bucharest (8 others followed between 1887 and 1904). The artist had definitely settled in Romania but continued regularly to visit Paris, where he kept a studio until 1894. Besides his studio in Bucharest he had another in the region of his preferred motifs, Posada, and from 1890 at Câmpina. The *plein-air* sketch became, in the following decade, one of his fundamental modes of expression. Sometimes during a single session he painted slightly different variants of the same motif, such as *Landscape with Birches* (1899; Arad, Reg. Mus.; Cluj-Napoca, Mus. A.). He also made some graceful figure studies and portraits, with a fine understanding of form and of individual life (see fig.). Some of them represent Maria Danciu, his life-long companion, usually shown sewing in an interior (painting and drawings, *c.* 1885–90, Bucharest, N. Mus. A.; drawings, Bucharest, Roman. Acad. Lib.). In his final period Grigorescu also planned some large compositions inspired by village life, which he called 'syntheses' and which were preceded by many studies from nature and variants. In these thematic cycles the composition studies of middle size, maintaining the liberty of the sketch, are generally more personal than the definitive versions. Among these compositions are the *Return from the Fair* (most elaborate ver., *c.* 1900; Bucharest, N. Mus. A.), *Gypsy Band on the Road* (*c.* 1900; Constanța, Mus. A.) and *Peasant Wedding Procession* (*c.* 1900; a painted study, Râmnicu Vâlcii, Mus. A.). He

Nicolae Grigorescu: *Portrait of a Woman*, oil on canvas, 565×430 mm, *c.* 1890 (Bucharest, Zambaccian Museum)

also frequently painted carts with oxen on country roads and shepherds with their flocks in various landscape settings. Generally in his compositions and to a lesser degree in his sketches from nature, which he continued to paint during his late years (mainly around Câmpina, 1901–2 at Agapia, 1902 in the Buzău district), Grigorescu modified his palette, tending towards a harmony of bright greys, with subtle nuances of blue, violet-pink and pale green. The artist discovered affinities between the shapes of the landscape and those of its inhabitants, integrating them in a subtle unity. His ability to set his motifs in an ambient light contributed to this unity. The revelations of Grigorescu's art informed the early work of such masters as Ioan Andreescu, Ștefan Luchian and Gheorghe Petrașcu, who later participated in the creation of the modern Romanian school of painting.

BIBLIOGRAPHY

A. Vlahuta: *Pictorul N. I. Grigorescu* [The painter N. I. Grigorescu] (Bucharest, 1910)

V. Cioflec: *Grigorescu* (Bucharest, 1925)

F. Sirato: *Grigorescu* (Brussels, 1938)

G. Oprescu: *Grigorescu desinator* (Bucharest, 1941)

——: 'Corespondenta lui N. Grigorescu', *Analecta*, ii (1944), pp. 9–102

R. Niculescu: 'Grigorescu intre clasicism si romantism', *Stud. & Cerc. Istor. A.*, iii/3–4 (1956), pp. 127–72

Expoziția Grigorescu: Catalog (exh. cat. by R. Niculescu, Bucharest, N. Mus. A., 1957)

R. Niculescu: 'Grigorescu și primii săi critici', *Stud. & Cerc. Istor. A.*, v/1 (1958), pp. 139–82

G. Oprescu and R. Niculescu: *N. Grigorescu*, 2 vols (Bucharest, 1961–2)

R. Niculescu: 'William Ritter despre N. Grigorescu: Aspecte ale perioadei finale a pictorului' [William Ritter on N. Grigorescu: aspects of the final

period of the painter], *Stud. & Cerc. Istor. A.: Ser. A. Plast.*, xxxi (1984), pp. 31–65
Nicolae Grigorescu (exh. cat. by I. Beldiman and G. Cosma, Bucharest, N. Mus. A., 1984)

REMUS NICULESCU

Grigorescu, Octav (*b* Bucharest, 22 May 1933; *d* Bucharest, 3 Feb 1987). Romanian painter. In 1958 he graduated from the Institute of Plastic Arts 'Nicolae Grigorescu' in Bucharest, where he had studied painting with Rudolf Schweitzer-Cumpana (1886–1975), sculpture with Dimitrie Onofrei (1896–1980) and engraving with Vasile Kazar, and where he also taught (1958–87). Grigorescu developed his work through abstract drawings. His rigorous compositions and classical vision are reminiscent of the art of the Renaissance, although he selected forms and motifs from Classical art, Romanticism and Surrealism, and was influenced by the work of Paul Klee. His handling of watercolour to create the effect of weathered translucence, similar to that of medieval frescoes, is evident in such works as the *Death of Brâncoveanu* (1978; Hamburg, Winter). In the *Burning of Arhondology in 1848* (1978; Galaţi, Mus. Visual A.) Grigorescu used monochrome colours, which he built up to vibrant intensity with dramatic effect. Many of his drawings and paintings are in cycles, in which he attempted to 'reveal in images, events and people of great significance for the destiny of the Romanian people'. He also produced drawings for the Romanian editions of the poems of Rainer Maria Rilke (Bucharest, 1966) and Gérard de Nerval (Bucharest, 1979), and of the Abbé Prévost's *Manon Lescaut* (Bucharest, 1972).

BIBLIOGRAPHY

O. Busneag: 'Octav Grigorescu', *Arta*, x (1976), pp. 26–7
I. Vlasiu: 'Reflecţii asupra realului şi asupra limbajului plastic în desenul lui Octav Grigorescu' [Reflections on the real and on the language in the drawing of Octav Grigorescu], *Stud. & Cerc. Istor. A.*, xxiii (1976), pp. 157–69
D. Coşoveanu: *Octav Grigorescu (Monografy)* (Bucharest, 1985)

DORANA COŞOVEANU

Grigorovich-Barsky, Ivan (Grigor'yevich) (*b* Kiev, 1713; *d* Kiev, 1785). Ukrainian architect. He studied at the Kiev Academy. A brilliant designer in the Ukrainian version of the Baroque, his ecclesiastical works were either built with nave and aisles and one or three domes, such as the gate-church and bell-tower (1760) of the Kirillovsky Monastery and the church of the Virgin of the Protective Veil (1766), both Kiev, or were domed, tower-like buildings, such as the church (1761) in the village of Lemeshi, Chernihiv Region, which has a square plan and four attached apses, and the church of St Nicholas by the River (Nikolay Naberezhny; 1772), Kiev. Another notable work is the church of the Nativity of the Virgin (Rozhdestvo Bogoroditsy; 1764) at Kozelets, north-east of Kiev, built in conjunction with Aleksey Kvasov. Grigorovich's secular work included almost the whole of Podol, the commercial district of old Kiev, and regimental offices (1757) at Chernihiv. He aimed at using architectural forms to integrate the spaces of his buildings. Thus, his churches are cruciform, with short transepts and low apses, and often have a monolithic quality, which is particularly evident in the Kirillovsky gate-church and the church at Lemeshi. As a Baroque architect he used a great deal of decoration both inside and out, often an adapted version of the Corinthian order, but in his last buildings he almost completely renounced sculptural ornamentation, relying instead on the architectural mass of the buildings for the design.

BIBLIOGRAPHY

N. V. Kholostenko: 'Ivan Grigorovich-Barsky: Zodchiy Kiyeva XVIII stolittya' [Ivan Grigorovich-Barsky: 18th century Kievan architect], *Arkhit. Radyans'Koï Ukraïni*, xi (1940)
V. Zabolotny: 'Ukraïns'kiy arkhitektor XVIII stolittya Grigorovich-Bars'ky' [The 18th-century Ukrainian architect Grigorovich-Barsky], *Ukraïn. Literatura*, v–vi (1942)

L. I. POPOVA

Grigoryan, Mark (Vladimir) (*b* Nor-Nakhijevan [now in Rostov-on-Don], 29 April 1900; *d* Yerevan [now Erevan], 10 Jan 1978). Armenian architect of Russian birth. He studied from 1924 to 1928 in the architectural department of the State University, Yerevan. After graduating he worked in Yerevan with Alek'sandr T'amanyan, who had a decisive influence on him. Among his early projects is the house (*c.* 1930; altered), Yerevan, for the painter Martiros Saryan, its composition founded on the contrast of concise masses, and with natural stone walls. The design of the first Government Building of the Armenian SSR (1931–3) on Prospekt Lenina (now Messrop Mashtoc Avenue), Yerevan, with Nikolay Buniatyan (1884–1943), reflects the established classicist style of the period. It was remodelled by Grigoryan as a women's hospital in 1935. In 1936, following the death of T'amanyan, he took over the construction of the central square in Yerevan, where he designed the Hotel Armenia (1955), the Ministry of Post and Telecommunications (1956) and the Council of Trade Unions Building (early 1960s), all with E. A. Sarapyan (1917–84). The designs are all variations on the 'Neo-Armenian' style, largely the creation of T'amanyan, with pink Armenian tufa determining the general colour scheme.

Grigoryan's other works of the 1940s and 1950s come closer to an international classicism, with only the use of local stone giving them a specific character, as in the residential block (1943) on Prospekt Lenina, and the Central Committee of the Communist Party of Armenia Building (1950), both in Yerevan. His individuality is best expressed in the Matenadaran, the depository for medieval Armenian manuscripts (1949), Yerevan. The symmetrical stone parallelepiped, its centre emphasized by the tall arcade, unites, in its concise outlines, the characteristics of classicism and medieval Armenian architecture. From 1938 to 1950 he was the Chief Architect of Yerevan.

BIBLIOGRAPHY

Mark Grigoryan (Yerevan, 1976)
N. P. Bilinkin and A. V. Ryabushin: *Istoriya Sovetskoy arkhitektury* [The history of Soviet architecture] (Moscow, 1985), pp. 130, 133

A. V. IKONNIKOV

Grigor'yev, Afanasy (Grigor'yevich) (*b* Vasil'yevskaya settlement, Kozlov District, Tambov Province, 10 Jan 1782; *d* Moscow, 1 May 1868). Russian architect. He studied architecture in Moscow under Giovanni Battista Gillardi (1755–1819) and later at the Kremlin Architecture School under Francesco Camporese (1747–1831). Having been born a serf, he acquired his freedom in 1804 and in 1808 became assistant to Gillardi and, after his death in

1819, to his son Domenico Gillardi. Grigor'yev's life and work were inseparably linked to the Gillardi family and the Board of Guardians of the Foundling Hospital. When the younger Gillardi left for Italy, Grigor'yev succeeded him as architect to the Foundling Hospital (1832–47), which involved him in the repair and alteration of all almshouses, schools and institutes falling under the Board's jurisdiction. He played an important part in rebuilding Moscow after the fire of 1812, his principal legacy being in the design of detached houses, comfortable, classical buildings that typify the originality of the Russian version of the Empire style. One of the most important was the Tuchkov House (1818–19; now the Moscow Institute of International Affairs) on Ostozhenka Street, which incorporates elements of the richly decorated houses of Matvey Kazakov as well as elements of what was later regarded as the specifically Moscow version of Neo-classicism. Looking like a country house, it has a central block with lower wings and pavilions, a low dome and a hexastyle Doric portico of the Paestum type. The sparse external decoration contrasts with the smooth walls. The Khrushchov House (1815–17; now the Pushkin Museum) and the Lopukhin House (1822; now the Tolstoy Museum) on Prechistinka (now Kropotkin) Street are two of several built to a common plan. They were timber, stuccoed, single-storey buildings, with or without an attic, and with a tetrastyle or hexastyle Ionic or Doric portico. The plans incorporate large and small rooms, and the Lopukhin House has remarkable Neo-classical ceilings. Grigor'yev designed two identical architectural ensembles comprising a church, an almshouse and an inn in Moscow, the church of the Resurrection (1822) at the Vagan'kovskoye Cemetery and the church of the Trinity at the Pyatnitskoye Cemetery. His most famous country house and church were built on the Olsuf'v estate at Yershovo, near Moscow. The house was typical of his Moscow Empire style, but the church (destr. 1941–5) is reminiscent of the tower-like, tiered forms of 17th-century Russian churches. By the 1840s Grigor'yev reflected architectural fashion in using Gothic, Egyptian, Turkish and Old Russian elements in his work.

BIBLIOGRAPHY

V. V. Zgura: *Arkhitektor A. G. Grigor'yev* [The architect A. G. Grigor'yev] (exh. cat., Kazan', 1926)
S. A. Zombe and Y. A. Beletskaya: 'Afanasiy Grigor'yevich Grigor'yev', *Arkhit. SSSR*, v (1939)
A. G. Vvedenskaya: 'Arkhitektor A. G. Grigor'yev i yego graficheskoye naslediye' [The architect A. G. Grigor'yev and his graphic legacy], *Arkhit. Nasledstvo*, ix (1959)
N. Nezhina: 'Zhiloy dom v tvorchestve Grigor'yeva' [The residential house in Grigor'yev's work], *Stroitel'stvo & Arkhit. Moskvy* (1973)
Arkhitektor A. G. Grigor'yev [The architect A. G. Grigor'yev] (exh. cat. by Y. A. Beletskaya, Moscow, Shchusev Res. & Sci. Mus. Rus. Archit., 1976)
Y. A. Beletskaya: 'A. G. Grigor'yev', *Zodchiye Moskvy* [Moscow's architects], i (Moscow, 1981)
——: 'Master shkoly klassitsizma: K biografii A. G. Grigor'yeva' [A master of the classical school: towards a biography of A. G. Grigor'yev], *Stroitel'stvo & Arkhit. Moskvy*, vii (1982)

YE. I. KIRICHENKO

Grigor'yev, Boris (Dmitriyevich) (*b* Rybinsk, 11 July 1886; *d* Cagnes-sur-Mer, nr Nice, 7 Feb 1939). Russian painter and graphic artist. After attending the Stroganov School in Moscow from 1903 to 1907, Grigor'yev enrolled at the Academy of Arts in St Petersburg [later Petrograd], where he took lessons from Aleksandr Kiselyov (1838–1911) and Dmitry Kardovsky until 1912. At the Academy he gained his technical expertise as an illustrator, which is demonstrated in his caricatures for the satirical journals *Satirikon* and *Novy Satirikon* in 1912–14. During those years Grigor'yev lived mainly in Paris, where he attended the Académie de la Grande Chaumière, and he published some of his interpretations of Parisian street and café life in his collection of piquant bordello scenes, *Intimité* (1918). Just before the Revolution of 1917 Grigor'yev frequented the cabarets of Paris and Petrograd, and he helped Sergey Sudeykin and Aleksandr Yakovlev, for example, to decorate the interior of the Petrograd cellar known as Prival Komediantov (The Comedians' Halt) in 1915. A member of the Petrograd bohemia, Grigor'yev was close to many artists and writers of the time, such as Vasily Shukhayev, Velimir Khlebnikov and the poet Anna Akhmatova, and he often drew or painted their portraits. Grigor'yev was also fascinated by the Russian countryside, and his cycle of pictures *Raseya* (e.g. *The Countryside*, 1918; St Petersburg, Rus. Mus.) are startling expressions of the poverty, primitive strength and resentment of the Russian peasantry.

After a brief tenure as a professor at the Free Art Studios (Svomas) and as a designer for the Bol'shoy Theatre, both in Moscow, Grigor'yev emigrated in 1921 to France, where he later enjoyed a certain success as a landscape painter and salon portrait painter. During the 1920s he visited the USA several times, and in 1928 he became a professor at the Academia Chilena de Bellas Artes in Santiago, Chile. In 1930 he returned to France before becoming Dean of the School of Applied Arts in New York in 1935. Both before and during emigration, Grigor'yev maintained the traditions of the St Petersburg graphic school represented by artists such as Alexandre Benois, Mstislav Dobuzhinsky and Konstantin Somov. But in emotional intensity, Grigor'yev's expressive use of line recalls the graphic work of contemporary German artists such as Otto Dix and George Grosz, Neue Sachlichkeit rather than the Russian *fin de siècle* (see, for example, his portfolio of 12 drawings, *Russische Erotik*, Berlin, 1920).

BIBLIOGRAPHY

V. Dmitriyev and V. Voynov: *Boris Grigor'yev: Intimité* (Petrograd, 1918)
N. Tolstoy and others: *Boris Grigor'yev: Raseya* (Petrograd and Berlin, 1918; Potsdam, 1922)
C. Farrère and others: *Boris Grigoriew: Bouis Bouis* (Berlin, 1924)
L. Réau and others: *Boris Grigoriev: Faces of Russia* (Berlin and London, 1924)
Boris Grigoriev (exh. cat., Cagnes-sur-Mer, Château-Mus., 1978–9)
T. Galeyeva: 'Boris Grigor'yev', *Iskusstvo* (1986), no. 10, pp. 59–66
——: 'Risunki Borisa Grigor'yeva' [The drawings of Boris Grigor'yev], *Sov. Graf.* (1986), no. 10, pp. 251–62

JOHN E. BOWLT

Grillandai. *See* GHIRLANDAIO.

Grilo, Sarah (*b* Buenos Aires, 1920). Argentine painter. She studied painting in Buenos Aires under the Spanish Catalan painter Vicente Puig until 1943 and lived in Spain and France from 1948 to 1950, when she returned to Buenos Aires. She was a founder-member of the Grupo de Artistas Modernos de la Argentina in 1952 and in 1957 went on a study trip to Europe and the USA with her husband, the painter José Antonio Fernández Muro. Having worked briefly in a figurative idiom she adopted a lyrical style of abstraction, characterized by refined colour harmonies and thick impasto, that was in marked contrast to the Constructivist tendencies then prevalent in Argentina. Emphasizing emotive over rational qualities, she combined highly tactile surfaces with more ambiguously defined areas.

In 1962 Grilo again left Argentina, funded by a Guggenheim Fellowship, and settled in New York, where she began using letters and numbers reminiscent of the graffiti on city walls; these suggestive signs of contemporary urban life were superimposed over pale, delicate colours in horizontal rhythms or tightly interwoven into structures that sometimes covered the entire surface. After 1970 Grilo divided her time between Madrid and Paris.

BIBLIOGRAPHY

D. Bayón: *Aventura plástica de Hispano América* (Mexico City, 1974), p. 151

Sarah Grilo (exh. cat., intro. D. Bayón; Madrid, Mus. A. Contemp., 1985)

NELLY PERAZZO

Grimaldi, Fabrizio [Fra Francesco] (*b* Oppido Lucano, Calabria, 1543; *d* Naples, 1 Aug 1613). Italian architect. He joined the THEATINE ORDER in Naples in 1574. His first major building was the church of S Paolo Maggiore, Naples (1581–1603). Its nave arcades give a strong sense of movement, with arches of alternating height opening into domed or vaulted bays. In 1588, as presumably the most eminent Theatine architect, he was summoned to Rome to design the Order's new church of S Andrea della Valle. Because of the influence of Cardinal Alfonso Gesualdo (*d* 1603), he was obliged to submit his designs to Giacomo della Porta for approval; this leaves the evolution of the design uncertain, especially as della Porta left soon after the foundation stone was laid, while Grimaldi remained in Rome until 1598. During this time he also visited Lecce, where he worked on the church of S Irene (1588–1639). Grimaldi's first major commission on his return to Naples was to build S Maria degli Angeli (begun 1600). Each bay of the aisles is covered by a small dome lit by a lantern, with light flooding into the nave through widely spaced piers, uniting the parts into a continuous space. Three other commissions, all in Naples, followed in quick succession: the Cappella di S Gennaro (1608–after 1613), Naples Cathedral; SS Apostoli (1609–32); and S Maria della Sapienza (1614–1630s). Grimaldi approached his buildings with a strongly sculptural sense, using light and such architectural forms as clustered pilasters to produce an effect of richness and movement indicative of the arrival of a more Baroque style in Naples.

BIBLIOGRAPHY

H. Hibbard: 'The Early History of S Andrea della Valle', *A. Bull.*, xliii (1961), pp. 289–310

A. Blunt: *Neapolitan Baroque and Rococo Architecture and Decoration* (London, 1978)

ALICE DUGDALE

Grimaldi, Giacomo (*b* Bologna, 1560; *d* Rome, 7 Jan 1623). Italian writer, priest and, possibly, draughtsman. The first known document, dated 1581, records his official election as notary and archivist in St Peter's, Rome. He was the author of a great number of unpublished writings; his major undertaking, preserved in the Vatican Library, is a list of all Christian monuments in Rome, including those destroyed, rebuilt and changed. The compilation of this inventory is written in a clear, albeit dry, style, and it is illustrated by a large number of pen-and-ink drawings possibly by him, or perhaps after his original designs. The work forms a valuable source of information about the loss of paintings, mosaics and buildings of the period and influenced the works of such later writers as Giovanni Ciampini and L. A. Muratori.

UNPUBLISHED SOURCES

Instrumenta autentica translationum sanctorum corporum et sacrarum reliquiarum (1613; Rome, Vatican, Bib. Apostolica, MS. Barb. lat. 2733) [Grimaldi's earliest dated work]

Florence, Bib. Marucelliana

Milan, Bib. Ambrosiana and Castello Sforzesco

Paris, Bib. N.

Rome, Bib. Casanatense and Vatican, Bib. Apostolica, Archv Capitolare S Pietro

WRITINGS

R. Niggl, ed.: *Descrizione della basilica antica di S Pietro in Vaticano: Codice Barberini latino 2733* (Vatican City, 1972)

BIBLIOGRAPHY

E. Muntz: *Recherches sur l'oeuvre archéologique de Jacques Grimaldi* (Rome, 1887)

P. d'Archiardi: *Atti del congresso internazionale di scienze* (1903), vi, pp. 19–24

R. Niggl: *Untersuchungen zu Giacomo Grimaldi* (in preparation)

OLIMPIA THEODOLI

Grimaldi, Giovanni Francesco (*b* Bologna, 1606; *d* Rome, 28 Nov 1680). Italian painter, printmaker, draughtsman and architect. He was an accomplished fresco painter, whose decorative landscapes were popular with such leading Roman families as the Santacroce, the Pamphili and the Borghese; his many landscape etchings and drawings spread the influence of 17th-century Bolognese landscape throughout Europe. After studying in Bologna in the circle of the Carracci, he arrived in Rome *c.* 1626 and by 1635 was already a member of the Accademia di S Luca and associated with the circle of artists working with Pietro da Cortona. Sometime between 1635 and 1640 he collaborated with François Perrier and Giovanni Ruggieri on the decoration of the gallery in the Palazzo Peretti–Amalgia, Rome; the vault, which was probably designed by Grimaldi, was modelled on Cortona's gallery in the Villa Sacchetti at Castelfusano. In 1640–41, again inspired by the Villa Sacchetti, Grimaldi frescoed the vault of the great hall of the Palazzo Santacroce ai Catinari, Rome. The ceiling is framed with stucco cartouches, and the vault is decorated with five *quadri riportati*. At the centre, an allegorical composition, the *Triumph of Authority over Time*, celebrates the Santacroce family, and surrounding this are four compositions of Old Testament scenes set in landscapes deeply influenced by the Carracci tradition, in which trees form a natural frame for views across varied terrain with distant figures. Illusionism is limited to the allegorical figures set against the sky at the corners of the vault.

From 1645 to 1647 Grimaldi was involved in the building of the Villa Pamphili, Rome. It seems that, while Alessandro Algardi was responsible for the design, Grimaldi acted as site architect and may have contributed to

Giovanni Francesco Grimaldi: *Landscape*, pen and brown ink and brown wash, 237×341 mm (Windsor Castle, Berks, Royal Library)

the design of the garden; he also painted frescoes of episodes from the *Life of Hercules*, to accompany Algardi's stucco reliefs of the same theme. In 1647–8 Grimaldi worked with Gaspard Dughet on the decorations at S Martino ai Monti, Rome. From 1649 to 1651 he was in Paris, where he worked with Giovanni Francesco Romanelli in the palace of Cardinal Mazarin (now Bibliothèque Nationale) and at the Palais du Louvre. On his return to Rome, Grimaldi worked for Alexander VII on the decoration of the Sala Gialla in the Palazzo del Quirinale.

Between 1656 and 1659 Grimaldi was absent from Rome, and in this period he was probably employed by Cardinal Marcello Santacroce, Bishop of Tivoli, on the chapel of the Immaculate Conception in Tivoli Cathedral. A wash drawing of an architectural detail (London, BM) suggests that Grimaldi designed the chapel, as well as painting frescoes of scenes from the *Life of the Virgin*. In 1672 he painted wall frescoes of landscapes at the Villa Falconieri, Frascati, and between 1674 and 1676 he worked on the gallery of the Palazzo Borghese and decorated the end room, overlooking the port of Ripetta; from the end of 1674 he is documented as supervising the palace decoration. Between *c*. 1660 and 1680 he frescoed the gallery of the Palazzo Muti–Papazzurri, Rome, decorating the long walls with landscapes in fictive marble frames. The organization of the vault, decorated with mythological scenes, is similar to that of Grimaldi's earlier works, but the decorative motifs are more profuse and are painted rather than stuccoed.

Grimaldi made many drawings (e.g. Paris, Louvre; London, BM), mainly in pen and ink with brown wash, often on blue paper. His *Landscape* (Windsor Castle, Berks, Royal Col.; see fig.), where space is created by a clear sequence of planes leading into the distance, punctuated by travelling figures and geometric buildings, is a characteristically accomplished variation on a landscape formula developed by the Bolognese artists Annibale Carracci and Domenichino. Grimaldi's over 50 etchings are in a similar style, and his graphic work deeply influenced artists of the second half of the 17th century. His rare cabinet pictures include four paintings on copper (Rome, Gal. Borghese), acquired by the Borghese family in 1678.

BIBLIOGRAPHY

L. Pascoli: *Vite* (1730–36), i, pp. 45–51

A. Nava Cellini: 'Il Borromini, l'Algardi e il Grimaldi per Villa Pamphilj', *Paragone*, xiv/159 (1963), pp. 73–4

M. Roethlisberger: 'Drawings around Claude, Pt I: A Group of 60 Grimaldesque Drawings', *Master Drgs*, ix (1971), pp. 251–3

D. Batorska: 'Grimaldi and the Salone Santacroce', *Stor. A.*, 18 (1973), pp. 173–9

M. Lauvain-Portemer: 'Le Palais Mazarin à Paris et l'offensive baroque de 1645–50 d'après Romanelli, P. de Cortone et Grimaldi', *Gaz. B.-A.*, cxv/81 (1973), pp. 156–9

P. Bellini: 'Giovanni Francesco Grimaldi: Catalogo completo delle incisioni', *Quad. Conoscitore Stampe*, xxii (1974), pp. 6–27

D. Batorska: 'Grimaldi's Design of the Chapel of the Immaculate Conception at the Cathedral, Tivoli', *Master Drgs*, xiv/2 (1976), pp. 169–71

——: 'Grimaldi and the Galleria Muti–Papazzurri', *Antol. B.A.*, ii/7–8 (1978), pp. 204–15

——: 'Grimaldi's Frescoes in Palazzo del Quirinale', *Paragone*, xxxiii/387 (1982), pp. 3–12

□

Grimani. Italian family of statesmen, ecclesiastics, collectors and patrons. They had settled in Venice by the 10th century, and their wealth was derived from trade with the eastern Mediterranean; one branch of the family settled on Crete in the early 13th century. The Venetian Grimani emerged as prominent members of the hereditary nobility in the 13th and 14th centuries and advanced their influence through holding offices in the Republic and later in the Church. The most important branch was that of S Maria Formosa, notably the descendants of (1) Antonio Grimani, who became doge of Venice in 1521. Of his sons, (2) Domenico Grimani, the eldest, became a Cardinal Patriarch of Aquileia, while Gerolamo Grimani I's extensive family included (3) Marino Grimani, (4) Marco Grimani, (7) Giovanni Grimani, all of whom became Patriarch of Aquileia, and (5) Vettor Grimani. (6) Gerolamo Grimani II belonged to the S Luca branch of the family.

BIBLIOGRAPHY

O. Logan: *Culture and Society in Venice* (London, 1972)

(1) Antonio Grimani, Doge of Venice (*b* Venice, 28 Dec 1434; *reg* 1521–3; *d* Venice, 7 May 1523). A fortune amassed mostly through trade with the eastern Mediterranean made him one of the richest men in Venice, able to afford a cardinalate for his son (2) Domenico Grimani in 1493. Antonio began his political career relatively late but attained the high office of Procurator of S Marco. As commander of the naval forces of the Venetian Republic he captured the coastal cities of Apulia in 1495 but was disgraced in 1499 after his failure to destroy a Turkish armada at the Battle of Zonchio. He spent the following years in exile, largely in Rome, where he acquired a villa on the Quirinale; he was recalled to Venice in 1509 on account of his wealth, experience and family connections. He was restored to the procuratorship and in that capacity paid for the final stage of work on the campanile in the Piazza S Marco (1510–14), giving it its characteristic pyramidal roof, and urged repairs to the Procuratie Vecchie: the architects included Bartolomeo Buon (ii). On 6 July 1521 Antonio was elected doge and tried to exercise that office in ostentatious and princely style but at the age of 87 was too decrepit to make much impact on government. Titian painted his portrait (1523; destr. 1571), and likenesses of Antonio were produced in marble and bronze (all untraced). *Doge Antonio Grimani Adoring Faith and St Mark in Glory* by Titian in the Sala delle Quattro Porte of the Doge's Palace is a posthumous celebration, ordered by the Senate in 1555 and eventually completed by Marco Vecellio *c.* 1600. Four medals with Antonio's portrait were also cast, one by Vittore Gambello. A memorial to Antonio, as well as his tomb in S Antonio di Castello (destr. 1807), were never completed.

BIBLIOGRAPHY

A. Armand: *Les Médailleurs italiens* (2/1883–7)
T. Okey: *The Old Venetian Palaces* (London, 1907)
G. F. Hill: *Corpus* (1930)
A. Da Mosto: *I Dogi di Venezia* (Milan, 1939), pp. 153–8
J. McAndrew: *Venetian Architecture of the Early Renaissance* (Cambridge, MA, 1980), pp. 415–16
G. Benzoni, ed.: *I Dogi* (Milan, 1982)
D. S. Queller: *The Venetian Patriciate* (Urbana and Chicago, 1986), pp. 164–6, 233

(2) Domenico Grimani, Cardinal Patriarch of Aquileia (*b* Venice, Feb 1461; *d* Rome, 27 Aug 1523). Son of (1) Antonio Grimani. He graduated in arts from the university of Padua (1487), and an interest in philosophy brought him into contact with Lorenzo de' Medici, Giovanni Pico della Mirandola (1463–94) and Angelo Poliziano. Domenico eventually embarked on an ecclesiastical career, acquiring the offices of Protonotary and Apostolic Secretary in 1491. His father's wealth and influence secured him a cardinalate in 1493 and other high ecclesiastical benefices, notably the patriarchate of Aquileia in 1497, which he renounced in favour of his nephew (3) Marino Grimani in 1517. Although a pluralist and absentee bishop Domenico was sufficiently regarded as an ecclesiastic to participate in the condemnation for heresy of the German humanist and theologian Johannes Reuchlin (1455–1522).

Domenico's learning attracted the praise of such scholars as Erasmus, but he is best remembered as a lavish but discerning collector of books, Classical antiquities and contemporary works of art. Of his 15,000 volumes he left 8000 to found a public library in the Venetian monastery of S Antonio di Castello (destr. 1807). One of the few surviving works is the GRIMANI BREVIARY (*c.* 1510–20; Venice, Bib. N. Marciana, MS. lat. I.99). This lavishly illuminated liturgical text was acquired for 500 ducats *c.* 1520; it is regarded as a masterpiece of South Netherlandish manuscript painting. Its ornate binding has been attributed to Vittore Gambello and includes medallion portraits of the Cardinal Patriarch and his father. Although left by Domenico to the State, his nephews (3) Marino Grimani and (7) Giovanni Grimani retained its use until 1594. Domenico acquired most of his important collection of Classical antiquities, which included marbles, bronzes, gems and medallions, during his periods of residence in Rome; statues of *Marcus Agrippa* and *Augustus* (now Venice, Mus. Archeol.), for example, were removed from the Pantheon to the Palazzo Grimani near S Maria Formosa, Venice. He bequeathed the smaller items to Marino; the bronzes and marbles, including Hellenistic and Roman works, were left to the Venetian Republic, which began to exhibit them in the Doge's Palace from 1525. The bequest influenced such artists as Titian and, together with Giovanni's collection, constituted the foundation of the Museo Archeologico in Venice.

Domenico's taste also extended to contemporary artists. He possessed works by Raphael, including the cartoon (1515–16; destr.) for the tapestry of the *Conversion of St Paul* (Rome, Pin. Vaticana), and by Titian and Giorgione, and possibly drawings by Leonardo and Michelangelo. Northern painters represented in his collection included Dürer, Hans Memling, Joachim Patinir and five works by Bosch (the latter in Venice, Doge's Palace); other paintings were left to (4) Marco Grimani and Marino Grimani. In Venice, Domenico lived in the Palazzo Grimani and in a villa on Murano. In Rome the Grimani maintained their villa on the Quirinale, and from 1505 Domenico also resided in considerable splendour at the Palazzo di S Marco (now Palazzo di Venezia; from 1455). His likeness is preserved in several medals, including one by Gambello and two by Sperandio. A portrait (Windsor Castle, Berks, Royal Col.), possibly of Domenico, has been attributed to Domenico di Bernardino Capriolo. Domenico was buried, according to his wishes, in SS Giovanni e Paolo, Rome, but the Grimani secured permission to transfer his body to Venice, though his tomb in S Francesco della Vigna is lost.

BIBLIOGRAPHY

A. Armand: *Les Médailleurs italiens* (2/1883–7)

P. Paschini: 'Le collezioni archeologiche dei prelati Grimani del cinquecento', *Atti Pont. Accad. Romana Archeol.*, n. s. 2, v (1926–7), pp. 149–90
G. F. Hill: *Corpus* (1930)
C. H. Collins Baker: *Catalogue of the Principal Pictures in the Royal Collection at Windsor Castle* (London, 1937), p. 177
P. Paschini: *Domenico Grimani: Cardinale di San Marco* (Rome, 1943)
R. Gallo: 'Le donazioni alla Serenissima di Domenico e Giovanni Grimani', *Archv Ven.*, n. s. 4, l–li (1952), pp. 34–77
M. Perry: 'The *Statuario Pubblico* of the Venetian Republic', *Saggi & Mem. Stor. A.*, viii (1972), pp. 76–252
M. J. C. Lowry: 'Two Great Venetian Libraries', *Bull. John Rylands Lib.*, lvii (1974–5), pp. 128–66
P. Paschini: *Storia del Friuli* (Udine, 1975)
M. Perry: 'Cardinal Domenico Grimani's Legacy of Ancient Art to Venice', *J. Warb. & Court. Inst.*, xli (1978), pp. 215–44

(3) Marino Grimani, Cardinal Patriarch of Aquileia (*b* Venice, *c.* 1488; *d* Orvieto, 28 Sept 1546). Grandson of (1) Antonio Grimani. His ecclesiastical career was successful in terms of his accumulation of benefices, and he became Bishop of Ceneda (now Vittorio Veneto) in 1508, Patriarch of Aquileia (*reg* 1517–29, 1538–45) and a cardinal in 1527. Although ambitious and favoured by his family's wealth and influence, he was interested in theology and reform and defended the rights of his sees and of the papacy. He shared his family's luxurious lifestyle and cultural tastes. Much of his considerable library was inherited from (2) Domenico Grimani, from whom he probably also acquired some works by contemporary artists. In addition he owned a collection of antiquities largely comprised of medals and small pieces in marble and bronze. According to Vasari, Marino employed GIULIO CLOVIO and owned *Christ Carrying the Cross* (*c.* 1530; Madrid, Prado) by Sebastiano del Piombo.

In 1529 Marino recommended Jacopo Sansovino to carry out repairs to S Marco, and Marino and his brother (5) Vettor Grimani were also among the wealthy patrons who defrayed the cost of building Sansovino's S Francesco della Vigna (*c.* 1537), in which they acquired a family chapel. Together with Vettor and another brother, (7) Giovanni Grimani, Marino employed a number of Roman-influenced artists to decorate the interior of the family palace near S Maria Formosa (1537–40): Federico Zuccaro, Francesco Salviati, Giovanni da Udine, Giovanni Battista Franco and Camillo Capelli (Mantovano; *fl* 1514; *d* 1568). Marino employed Pordenone or, more probably, Pomponio Amalteo to fresco a celebration of *Justice* (1535–6) in the loggia of the council hall in Ceneda (1535–9); the loggia itself was possibly designed by Sansovino. Other architectural commissions assigned to Giovanni da Udine in Aquileia and Udine were never executed. Marino's tomb in S Francesco della Vigna has disappeared, but three portrait medals of the Cardinal survive, two attributed to Giovanni Cavino and one (*c.* 1535) to Niccolò Cavallerino della Mirandola (*fl* 1523). Marino died in debt, but much of his library and collection of antiquities was acquired by (7) Giovanni Grimani.

BIBLIOGRAPHY

G. Vasari: *Vite* (1550, rev. 2/1568); ed. G. Milanesi (1878–85), v, pp. 565–86; vii, pp. 73–134, 557
A. Armand: *Les Médailleurs italiens* (2/1883–7)
G. F. Hill: *Corpus* (1930)
P. Paschini: 'Il mecenatismo del Cardinale Marino Grimani', *Miscellanea in onore di Roberto Cessi*, ii (Rome, 1958), pp. 79–88
——: *Il Cardinale Marino Grimani ed i prelati della sua famiglia* (Rome, 1960)
——: *Storia del Friuli* (Udine, 1975)

(4) Marco Grimani, Patriarch of Aquileia (*b* Venice, *c.* 1494; *d* Rome, July 1544). Grandson of (1) Antonio Grimani. Family wealth and influence secured him the secular office of Procurator of S Marco in 1522. He entered the Church after the death of his wife in 1526 and succeeded his brother (3) Marino Grimani as Patriarch of Aquileia in 1529, although he probably never took holy orders. In 1538 he returned the see to Marino but retained the title of Patriarch, and in the same year was papal legate with a crusading fleet. In 1543–4 he was entrusted with a sensitive embassy to Scotland. Little is known concerning his collecting or patronage, although he is known to have acquired some items from the collection of paintings and antiquities of his uncle (2) Domenico Grimani. His tomb in S Francesco della Vigna in Venice is lost.

BIBLIOGRAPHY

P. Paschini: *Il Cardinale Marino Grimani ed i prelati della sua famiglia* (Rome, 1960)
——: *Storia del Friuli* (Udine, 1975), p. 799
C. Burns: 'Marco Grimani in Scotland', *Ren. Stud.*, ii (1988), pp. 299–311

JOHN LAW

(5) Vettor Grimani (*b* Venice, 1495–7; *d* Venice, 24 Aug 1558). Grandson of (1) Antonio Grimani. In 1521 he married Isabetta, daughter of the Procurator Girolamo Giustinian and Agnesina Badoer, builders of the Castello Giustinian at Roncade (1511–13). He was elected Procurator of S Marco in 1523. In 1527–8 he acquired the Cá del Duca, the basement of an unfinished palazzo on the Grand Canal, begun for Andrea Cornaro by Bartolomeo Buon (i). Grimani intended to build on its foundations a vast palace in the latest Tuscan–Roman style; only a wooden model (untraced) was made and a presentation drawing of the plan (Venice, Correr, no. III.6038), attributed to Michele Sanmicheli (Lewis, 1972) or Jacopo Sansovino (Foscari and Tafuri, 1981). Vettor was the moving force behind Sansovino's project for the rebuilding (1534–42) of S Francesco della Vigna, Venice: two large wooden models for this project (untraced) were inventoried in his estate. Four of Sansovino's civic works also owe their origin, character or completion to Grimani's efforts: the Marciana library, the Loggetta, S Geminiano and the Scala d'Oro in the Doge's Palace. With his brother (7) Giovanni Grimani, he played a leading role in commissioning the sumptuous decoration of the Palazzo Grimani at S Maria Formosa (rebuilding attributed to Sanmicheli, 1556), which included ceiling decorations by Francesco Salviati. Vettor served as ambassador to Emperor Charles V in 1543 and to Henry II of France in 1547. He was also knighted and was a candidate for Doge in 1553. A superb sculptured bust (terracotta, Providence, RI Sch. Des., Mus. A., no. 1954.167; marble, London, V&A, no. A.11–1970) has been identified tentatively as his likeness. A secure portrait is a fine uniface lead medal (London, BM) by the so-called 'Venetian medallist of 1550', perhaps Danese Cattaneo.

BIBLIOGRAPHY

G. F. Hill: 'Eight Italian Medals', *Burl. Mag.*, xiv (1908–9), p. 216

D. Lewis: 'Un disegno autografo del Sanmicheli e la notizia del committente del Sansovino per S Francesco della Vigna: Nuovi appunti per il mecenatismo artistico del Procuratore Vettor Grimani', *Boll. Civ. Mus. Ven. A. & Stor.*, xvii (1972), pp. 7–36
——: 'Proposals for the Grimani Tombs at S Francesco della Vigna, Venice', *The Drawings of Andrea Palladio* (exh. cat., Washington, DC, N.G.A., 1981), pp. 186–7, no. 111
A. Foscari and M. Tafuri: 'Un progetto irrealizzato di Jacopo Sansovino: Il palazzo di Vettor Grimani sul Canal Grande', *Boll. Civ. Mus. Ven. A. & Stor.*, xxvii (1981), pp. 71–87
D. Lewis: 'Patterns of Preference: Patronage of Sixteenth-century Architects by the Venetian Patriciate', *Patronage in the Renaissance*, ed. G. Lytle and S. Orgel (Princeton, 1981), pp. 354–80
A. Foscari and M. Tafuri: *L'armonia e i conflitti: La chiesa di San Francesco della Vigna nella Venezia del '500* (Venice, 1983)

DOUGLAS LEWIS

(6) Gerolamo Grimani II (*b* Venice, *c.* 1500; *d* Venice, 30 April 1570). Statesman and patron, from the S Luca branch of the family. He had a prominent political career, becoming Procurator of S Marco in 1560. He devoted considerable attention and money (40–50,000 ducats) to the building of an imposing palazzo on the Grand Canal, on a site he acquired from the Contarini in 1556. The palazzo was designed by Michele Sanmicheli, who supervised the construction of the first floor before his death in 1559. From *c.* 1560 to 1572 work was continued, and the design modified, by Giovanni Giacomo de' Grigi; it was completed *c.* 1575, after Grimani's death, by Giovanni Antonio Rusconi. The Palazzo Grimani is distinguished from its neighbours by its sheer scale, and by the bold forms of its classically inspired façade.

BIBLIOGRAPHY

L. Heydenreich and W. Lotz: *Architecture in Italy, 1400–1600*, Pelican Hist. A. (Harmondsworth, 1974), pp. 220–22
E. Bassi: *Palazzi di Venezia* (Venice, 1976), p. 146
D. Howard: *The Architectural History of Venice* (London, 1980), pp. 155ff

(7) Giovanni Grimani, Patriarch of Aquileia (*b* Venice, *c.* 1500; *d* Venice, 3 Oct 1593). Grandson of (1) Antonio Grimani. He entered the Church and acquired the benefices that the Grimani regarded as their own: the bishopric of Ceneda (1520) and the patriarchate of Aquileia (1545). The suspicion that he held unorthodox views on such central aspects of Catholic doctrine as Grace and Predestination, however, interrupted and curtailed his career, although he was cleared of heresy at the Council of Trent in 1563. He acquired a reputation as a man of learning and a collector. The historian Paolo Paruta (1540–98) chose him as an interlocutor in his *Della perfettione della vita politica* (Venice, 1579/*R* 1599). Giovanni acquired part of the collection of antiquities belonging to his brother (3) Marino Grimani and augmented it to create one of the largest collections of Greek and Roman marbles, bronzes, medals and cameos in 16th-century Venice. He also collected contemporary works, including paintings by South Netherlandish artists and Giorgione.

Giovanni took a leading role in remodelling the Palazzo Grimani near S Maria Formosa (completed 1569). The design of the entrance has been attributed to Michele Sanmicheli, while that of the building itself has been credited to the Patriarch. It is certain, however, that Giovanni played a leading role in commissioning the decoration of its interior (*see* (3) above). Giovanni was also responsible for commissioning the decoration (*c.* 1560) by Giovanni Battista Franco, Federico Zuccaro and the sculptor TIZIANO ASPETTI of the Grimani Chapel in S Francesco della Vigna; this, designed by Jacopo Sansovino, was the burial-place of several of the Grimani, and Giovanni himself was later buried there. Aspetti was particularly close to the Patriarch and was a member of his household; he also executed the bronze statues of *Moses* and *St Paul* that flank the principal entrance to S Francesco della Vigna. Giovanni commissioned Palladio to design the façade (1565) of this church and also persuaded the commune of S Daniele in Friuli, which was under his jurisdiction as Patriarch, to accept a design by Palladio for one of its gates (the Porta Palladio, 1579). Like his uncle (2) Domenico Grimani, Giovanni left most of his collection to the Venetian Republic, and a new site to display the Grimani bequests was begun next to the Libreria Marciana before his death.

BIBLIOGRAPHY

T. Okey: *The Old Venetian Palaces* (London, 1907), pp. 153–4
G. Zorzi: *Le opere pubbliche e i palazzi privati di Andrea Palladio* (Venice, 1965), pp. 87–8
J. S. Ackerman: *Palladio* (Harmondsworth, 1966), pp. 140–41, 143–4
P. Paschini: *Storia del Friuli* (Udine, 1975), pp. 811–14, 819–23
E. Bassi: *Palazzi di Venezia* (Venice, 1976), pp. 228–35
For further bibliography *see* §(2) above.

JOHN LAW

Grimani Breviary. Illuminated manuscript of the Ghent–Bruges school of book illustration, dating from *c.* 1510–20. The Breviary (Venice, Bib. N. Marciana, MS. lat. I. 99) follows the Franciscan Office of 1477 and consists of 831 parchment sheets (each 275×215 mm) with illuminations on 1280 pages. Most of the pages of text have illuminated border strips on the outer edges, while the 110 text incipits are distinguished by pictorial decoration that ranges from column-width miniatures and decorated or historiated borders to full-page miniatures.

The Breviary is first mentioned in the will of Cardinal Domenico Grimani of 2 October 1520, and it must have reached Italy before that date. According to Michiel, the Cardinal had purchased the 'famous office' for 500 ducats from Antonio Siciliano, whose coat of arms, known from a diptych attributed to Jan Gossart (Rome, Gal. Doria–Pamphili), appears in the border of fol. 81*r*. This is a relatively subordinate position, however, and it cannot be assumed that Siciliano was the original patron of the manuscript, even though Gossart seems also to have worked on the Breviary. The calendar miniatures are based on those in the Très Riches Heures (*c.* 1411/13–16; Chantilly, Mus. Condé, MS. 65) of Jean, Duc de Berry (*see* LIMBOURG, DE, fig. 2), which in the early 1500s was in the possession of Margaret of Austria in her castle chapel at Mechelen (Durrieu). It therefore seems likely that Margaret herself commissioned the Breviary, making the Très Riches Heures available to the copyists, but this hypothesis does not exclude the possibility that she always intended to present it to Siciliano or to his master, Massimiliano Sforza, Duke of Milan (*reg* 1512–15), on whose behalf Siciliano travelled to the Netherlands in 1513.

Michiel recorded that the Grimani Breviary was 'illuminated by many masters over a period of many years' and that it contained miniatures by 'Zuan Memelin, Girardo de Guant…, and Livieno da Anversa…'. The participation of different workshops is confirmed by the

Grimani Breviary, miniature introducing the Office of the Dead, showing a deathbed scene in the tondo and a *Dance of Death* in the lower border, 275×215 mm, *c.* 1510–20 (Venice, Biblioteca Nazionale Marciana, MS. lat. I. 99, fol. 449*v*)

extra contour lines in gold added to many of the miniatures to compensate for slight divergences in format and by variations in style, but these attributions are unreliable: Hans Memling had died in 1494, and his work shows no stylistic similarities to the Breviary, and 'Livieno da Anversa' cannot be identified. Michiel's 'Girardo da Guant [Ghent]', however, is undoubtedly Gerard Horenbout (*see* HORENBOUT, (1)), the probable MASTER OF JAMES IV OF SCOTLAND (*see* MASTERS, ANONYMOUS, AND MONOGRAMMISTS, §I), whose style can be seen in the fine calendar miniatures, as well as in the night scene of the *Nativity* (fol. 43*v*), the opening with the *Crucifixion* and the *Raising of the Brazen Serpent* (fols 138*v*–139*r*), the *Building of the Tower of Babel* (fol. 206*r*) and the miniature introducing the Office of the Dead (fol. 449*v*; see fig.).

A second artist, known as the Master of the David Scenes in the Grimani Breviary, who was also responsible for two Books of Hours (Oxford, Bodleian Lib., MSS Douce 112 and 256), employed a similar style, but his illuminations are more colourful and the brushwork is more fluid. Most of the other illuminations in the Breviary can be attributed to Simon Bening, who also drew on the calendar miniatures of the Très Riches Heures in his other works. The scenes with large figures, such as the *Ascension* (fol. 191*v*) and the pictures of Saints, are more archaic in style, however, and may be the work of Simon's father, Sanders Bening. Finally, the full-page miniature of *St Catherine of Siena Disputing with the Doctors* (fol. 824*v*) bears the inscription COSART on an architrave, probably the signature of JAN GOSSART.

BIBLIOGRAPHY

[M. Michiel]: *Notizia d'opere di disegno nella prima metà dell' secolo XVI* [MS.; 1521–43]; ed. J. Morelli (Bassano, 1800; rev. Bologna, 1884), pp. 201–5

P. Durrieu: 'Les Très Riches Heures du Duc de Berry conservées à Chantilly, au Musée Condé, et le bréviaire Grimani', *Bib. École Chartes*, lxiv (1903), pp. 321–8

S. De Vries and S. Morpurgo, eds: *Das Breviarium Grimani: Vollständige photographische Reproduktion* (Leiden and Leipzig, 1903–8) [complete facs.]

F. Winkler: 'Die Anfänge Jan Gossarts', *Jb. Preuss. Kstsamml.*, xlii (1921), pp. 5–19

J. Duverger: 'Nieuwe Gegevens betreffende het Breviarium Grimani', *Annu. Mus. Royaux B.-A. Belgique/Jb. Kon. Mus. S. Kst. België*, i (1938), pp. 19–30

A. Grote, ed.: *Breviarium Grimani: Faksimileausgabe der Miniaturen und Kommentar* (Berlin, 1973) [partial facs.]

BODO BRINKMANN

Grimm. Austrian family of architect-builders. They were active in Moravia in the 17th and 18th centuries.

(1) Mauriz [Mauritzius; Moritz; Mořic; Mořice] **Grimm** [Grimb; Grimma] (*b* Achdorf, nr Landshut, Germany, ?3 April 1669; *d* Brno [Ger. Brünn], 17 June 1757). He was registered in 1690 as a journeyman with the Prague Old Town masons' guild. After a reputed stay in Vienna, in 1704 he reached Brno, where he secured control over the masons' guild and established a prosperous building company, which, under his direction, determined the appearance of the capital city of Moravia in the early 18th century. Grimm's first known works are the completion of the manor house of Buchlovice (from 1706; architect unknown), the Dominican monastery (from 1706) and a number of other buildings in Brno. His mature style developed between 1714 and 1733. The Jesuit church of the Holy Cross (1714–15; destr.), which he built in Soběšice, near Brno, was a simplified variation of Johann Lukas von Hildebrandt's Peterskirche in Vienna. Among his most important works is the New Town Hall in Brno (originally the Regional Hall of the Estates), which he enlarged in 1717–19, creating a façade in 1726–33, and which contains a large conference hall reached by a monumental staircase. He also built several Franciscan structures noted for their double façades, for example the Loreto (1716–19), the Holy Staircase and the Loreto church (1722–6). Other important commissions included the reconstruction of the church of St John (1722; 1729–33) and the tower of the Jesuit church (1733), Brno. In their design these buildings all demonstrate Grimm's predilection for Viennese Baroque architecture of the late 17th century and the early 18th. He had close ties with the Danube school of Baroque architecture represented by the Viennese architect Christian Alexander Oedtl (1661–1737), to whose plans Grimm built the Schrattenbach Palace (from 1730) in Brno. Grimm's familiarity with Oedtl's work is also reflected in his own designs for urban palaces in Brno. From the 1730s Grimm was in charge of several projects for the monastery of the Austin Canons, including the monastery buildings (1732–55; from 1741 collab. (2) Franz Anton Grimm) and the choir of St Thomas's (1751–2). At the old Cistercian convent in Brno he built the abbey (*c*. 1737).

Mauriz Grimm was assisted from 1740 in the management of his building company by the master mason Bartoloměj Zintner (1711–73). At this period he also began building to the designs of his son (2) Franz Anton Grimm, and it is therefore difficult to determine the identity of the architect of some of the later works built by Mauriz Grimm's company. Outside Brno Grimm is known for his design of the 'Flora' wing of the manor house of Buchlovice (before 1738), the manor house of Hrotovice and above all the monumental centralized plan of the church at Střílky (1727, unexecuted). While most of Grimm's works were limited to reconstructions of churches and urban buildings, he was nevertheless responsible for developing the Baroque style in Brno and had an important influence on fellow architects in the city.

(2) Franz [Franciscus] **Anton Grimm** [Grime] (*b* Brno, *bapt* 2 Oct 1710; *d* Brno, 17 Jan 1784). Son of (1) Mauriz Grimm. He learnt the art of building from his father. He studied painting (1730–33) at the Akademie der Bildenden Künste, Vienna, and military engineering (1733–4) under Donato Felice Allio, becoming a member of the Imperial Royal Engineering Corps, where he achieved the rank of Captain. In 1735 and again in 1739–40 he made study tours of France, Germany and Italy, spending some time in Rome at the workshop of Nicola Salvi, and possibly even working there. Before his second journey to Italy, he may already have designed the Dietrichstein-Salm Palace (from 1739; destr.), Brno, and the manor house of Kupařovice (1739–48), near Pohořelice, two buildings that were among the first works in the French style to be built in the Habsburg empire outside Vienna. He may also have worked with the Allio studio in the design of the Klosterneuburg Monastery, near Vienna. From 1743 Grimm served as a court architect to the princely house of Dietrichstein. He designed Rococo villas, for example the summer-house at the Mikulov manor house (1743) and the villas at Leopoldsruhe (1743–8), near Pohořelice, Diváky (*c.* 1750), and Sokolnice (1750; later rebuilt). He also designed hospitals, agricultural estates and bridges.

Grimm's finest works were built in the late 1740s and the early 1750s. They include the chapel of the Židlochovice manor house (1746) and the churches of Drnholec, Pravlov, Hranice (1750), Soběchleby and Bělotín (1753). His ecclesiastical buildings all have façades with strongly classical features and a monumental centralized interior. He accentuated spatial unity by constructing a shallow dome over a circular or oval plan. Grimm created some of his most important secular works outside the Dietrichstein court. With his design of a manor house displaying a prominent central hall he created a personal version of Central European Neo-classicism, for example at Vizovice (1748–57; completed 1766–77), Bystřice pod Hostýnem (from 1763) and Napajedla (1764–72). In these schemes Grimm attempted to create an architecture built to the Parisian taste and in the Roman manner. He remained at the Dietrichstein court until *c.* 1769, when he collaborated with his father and Bartoloměj Zintner on several projects in Brno, including those for a barracks, the monastery, the hospital of the Brethren of Mercy (from 1747; only partly realized), the Elizabethan Convent (from 1751) and possibly other works as well.

In his last years Grimm was active mainly in the field of engineering and technical work, although he designed the great Neo-classical cathedral of the Austin Canons at Šternberk (1775–83) in Moravia. His works mark the end of the late Baroque period of architecture in Moravia. An outstanding draughtsman, his collection of approximately 2000 designs has survived complete (Brno, Morav. Mus.; manor house of Rájec nad Svitavou).

UNPUBLISHED SOURCES

Brno, State Archvs [MS. of A. Schweigl: *Bildende Künste in Mähren* (1795); MS. of J. P. Cerroni: *Skitze einer Geschichte der bildenden Künste in Mähren und österr. Schlesien*, i–iii (1807)]

BIBLIOGRAPHY

A. Prokop: *Die Markgrafschaft Mähren in kunstgeschichtlicher Beziehung*, iv (Brno, 1904)

V. Richter: 'K dílu architekta Mořice Grimma' [On the work of the architect Mauriz Grimm], *Roč. Kruhu Pěstování Dějin Umění* (1934)

H. Franz: *Studien zur Barockarchitektur in Böhmen und Mähren* (Brno, 1943)

V. Richter and Z. Kudělka: 'Die Architektur des 17. and 18. Jahrhunderts in Mähren', *Sborník Prac. Filoz. Fak. Brn. U.*, xvi (1972), pp. 91–130

H. Lorenz: 'Unbekannte Projekte für die Fassade von San Giovanni in Laterano', *Wien. Jb. Kstgesch.*, xxxiv (1981), pp. 183–7

J. Kroupa: *František Antonín Grimm: Architekt XVIII. století na Moravě* [Franz Anton Grimm: 18th-century architect in Moravia] (Brno and Kroměříž, 1982)

——: 'Materiály k brněnským stavebním dějinám 18. století' [Materials on the 18th-century architectural history of Brno], *Uměleckohist. Sborn.* [Art-historical journal], ed. J. Sedlář, i (Brno, 1985), pp. 260–64

J. Pernička: 'Brněnský architekt Mořic Grimm' [The Brno architect Mořic Grimm], *Uměleckohist. Sborn.* [Art-historical journal], ed. J. Sedlář, i (Brno, 1985), pp. 172–94

JIŘÍ KROUPA

Grimm, (Johann) Georg (*b* Immenstadt, 1846; *d* Palermo, 24 Dec 1887). German painter, active in Brazil. He entered the Akademie der Bildenden Künste in Munich in 1868 but interrupted his studies in 1870 to fight in the Franco-Prussian War. After travelling through Italy, Greece, Turkey, the Near East and North Africa, he left for Brazil from Lisbon, probably in 1878. He settled in Rio de Janeiro but also went to other parts of the country. The paintings resulting from these travels were exhibited in 1882 by the Sociedade Propagadora das Belas Artes in Rio de Janeiro. His work was well-received as an antidote to the lifeless conventionalism of Brazilian painting at the time, and he was invited by the Academia Imperial das Belas Artes to teach landscape painting. Although he was at the Academia only until 1884, he completely transformed its teaching methods by introducing *plein-air* painting. His best-known pupils were Giovanni Battista Castagneto and Antonio Parreiras. Suffering from tuberculosis, he left Brazil in the middle of 1887. *Rock of the Good Voyage* (1887; Niterói, Mus. Parreiras) typifies his landscapes, vibrating with their own light and combining realist precision with exotic fantasy.

BIBLIOGRAPHY

L. Gonzaga Duque: *A arte brasileira* (Rio de Janeiro, 1888)

A. Morales de los Rios Filho: *O ensino artístico* (Rio de Janeiro, 1942)

C. R. M. Levy: *O grupo Grimm: Paisagismo brasileiro no século XIX* (Rio de Janeiro, 1982)

ROBERTO PONTUAL

Grimm, Ludwig Emil (*b* Hanau, nr Frankfurt am Main, 14 March 1790; *d* Kassel, 4 April 1863). German draughtsman, engraver and painter. He was a brother of the philologists and fairy-tale collectors Jakob Grimm (1785–1863) and Wilhelm Grimm (1786–1859). He attended the Kunstakademie in Kassel from 1805 to 1807. He then moved to Munich to study with the engraver Carl Ernst Hess (1755–1828), and he became a student at the Akademie der Bildenden Künste there. He revealed a talent for portraiture in numerous sketches of his family and friends. In 1814 he served with the Prussian army in the military campaign against France, then completed his studies in Munich. In 1816 he visited Italy, where he made a large number of landscape and genre drawings.

At this period Grimm frequently attempted work in oils, producing both genre pictures and a number of works on religious themes in the poetic manner of the Nazarenes. However, his strength lay in drawing and etching his immediate environment and the people in it. He was able to etch his subjects directly on to the plate, which gave his portraits great spontaneity. He had a keen eye for the sitter's characteristic features; he made not only portraits of well-known contemporaries such as *Heinrich Heine* (etching, 1827), *Niccolò Paganini* (sketch, 1830; both Kassel, Brüder Grimm-Mus.), *Clemens Brentano* (sketch, 1837; priv. col.) and *Bettina von Arnim* (sketch, 1838; Hanau, Hist. Mus.), but also studies of ordinary people with striking or expressive features, which were very popular at the time, for example *Head of an Old Peasant Woman* (sketch, 1809; Hanau, Hist. Mus.). In 1832 Grimm became Professor of historical painting at the Kunstakademie in Kassel. Apart from the painting *Baptism of a Black African* (1841; Kassel, Brüder Grimm-Mus.), he did not produce any notable works during the following years. His work thus consists mainly of his pencil drawings and etchings, which finally numbered over 200.

WRITINGS

A. Stoll, ed.: *Lebenserinnerungen* (Leipzig, 1911)

BIBLIOGRAPHY

Thieme–Becker

J. Rowlands: 'A Gift for Goethe', *Connoisseur*, clxxxvii/754 (1974), pp. 264–7

Ludwig Emil Grimm, 1790–1863: Maler, Zeichner, Radierer (exh. cat., Kassel, Mus. Fridericianum, 1985)

I. Koszinowski and V. Leuschner: *Ludwig Emil Grimm, 1790–1863: Zeichnungen und Gemälde* (Marburg, 1990)

INGRID SATTEL BERNARDINI

Grimm, (Friedrich) Melchior, Baron von (*b* Regensburg, 26 Dec 1723; *d* Gotha, 19 Dec 1807). German writer, diplomat, critic and agent, active in France. He was the son of a Lutheran pastor and a graduate of the Universität Leipzig. By 1749 he was in Paris, where he was engaged as a personal secretary and tutor to members of the German nobility. In Paris his friends DENIS DIDEROT and Jean-Jacques Rousseau helped launch his journalistic career. He first attracted attention with *Le Petit Prophète de Boehmischbroda* (1753), a satire published during a heated debate raging between the champions of French music and those of Italian music. In 1753 he succeeded the Abbé Guillaume-Thomas-François Raynal (1736–96) as confidential correspondent on French literary and artistic matters to Augustus William (1722–58), Henry (1726–1802) and Ferdinand (1730–1813), brothers of Frederick II, King of Prussia. Grimm transformed Raynal's modest venture (begun in 1747) into Europe's premier privately circulated gazette. By the early 1770s the bimonthly manuscript *Correspondance littéraire, philosophique et critique*, as Grimm's cultural insider's newsletter came to be known, reached regal subscribers in Sweden, Poland and a dozen courts in Germany. (It was not formally published until 1812.) In 1755 he was appointed Secrétaire des Commandements to Louis-Philippe, Duc d'Orléans (1725–85). He assiduously cultivated the acquaintance of several German princes: for this he was awarded such posts in Paris as chargé d'affaires (1759–61) for the city of Frankfurt am Main. In 1772 he was created baron by Maria-Theresa, Empress of Austria. From 1768 to 1773 he travelled abroad frequently, and his increasing diplomatic duties forced him, starting in 1773, to cede direction of the *Correspondance* to the Swiss, Jakob Heinrich Meister (1744–1826). In 1773 he went with Diderot to Russia, where he remained a year. While there, Catherine II inducted him into the Imperial Academy of Sciences. In 1775 he became Minister Plenipotentiary for the duchy of Saxe-Gotha, and from 1793 until his death he resided at Gotha.

Over two decades Grimm's enduring monument, the *Correspondance*, was a redoubtable vehicle for European cultural cross-pollination. Grimm must also be credited with advancing the career of Diderot, whose landmark critical writings for the biennial Salons in Paris appeared in the clandestine periodical from 1759 to 1781. Diderot's reviews contained frequent comments and repartee by Grimm and were sometimes presented as dialogues or letters addressed to his editor friend. Grimm himself was a connoisseur of contemporary art. In 1753, 1755 and 1757, prior to Diderot's début in the Salons field but possibly with some assistance from him, Grimm reported on the Salons in the newsletter. In his criticism he echoed Diderot's distaste for the stilted work of Boucher and Jean-Marc Nattier and the sterile academic tendencies in the work of Carle Vanloo. He also shared Diderot's enthusiasm for artistic originality, for a measured return to nature and the Antique and for art attuned to the progressive ideals of the French *philosophes*.

As a non-native observer, Grimm was uncommonly open to talented outsiders, and he judged contemporary French intellectuals, writers and artists with lucidity. He used the *Correspondance* and his personal contacts with élite subscribers to promote select Parisian artists, notably Greuze and Jean-Antoine Houdon, and he favoured such foreigners or provincials as the Swiss artist Jean Huber (*see* HUBER, (1)), or Joseph Rosset (1706–86) from Saint-Claude in eastern France, who specialized in ivory busts, statuettes and reliefs of Voltaire. Grimm also exercised artistic influence at the court of Saxe-Gotha, an important source of early patronage for Houdon, and the court of Catherine II, serving as self-styled 'factotum' to the Empress for two decades. Like Grimm, Catherine II was a great admirer of Voltaire, and at his behest she acquired from Huber about a dozen paintings depicting scenes from Voltaire's private life, nine of which have survived (St Petersburg, Hermitage; e.g. the *Levée of the Patriarch*, *c.* 1775). Through Grimm's agency, Catherine also acquired Voltaire's large personal library (St Petersburg, Rus. N. Lib.) after his death, as well as two of Houdon's finest statues, *Diana* (1780; Lisbon, Mus. Gulbenkian) and a marble version of *Voltaire Seated* (1781; St Petersburg, Hermitage).

WRITINGS

Le Petit Prophète de Boehmischbroda (Paris, 1753; Eng. trans., 1950)

M. Tourneux, ed.: *Correspondance littéraire, philosophique et critique*, 16 vols (Paris, 1877–82)

J. Grot, ed.: 'Lettres de Grimm à Catherine II', *Imp. Rus. Ist. Obshchestvo Sborn.*, xliv (1885)

L. Réau, ed.: 'Correspondance artistique de Grimm avec Catherine II', *Archvs A. Fr.*, xvii/1 (1932)

BIBLIOGRAPHY

J. Grot, ed.: 'Pisma Imperatritsiy Ekateriniy II k Grimmu (1774–1796)' [Letters of Empress Catherine II to Grimm (1774–1796)], *Imp. Rus. Ist. Obshchestvo Sborn.*, xxiii (1878)

E. Schérer: *Melchior Grimm* (Paris, 1887)

A. Cazes: *Grimm et les Encyclopédistes* (Paris, 1933/*R* Geneva, 1970)

J. Monty: *La Critique littéraire de Melchior Grimm* (Geneva, 1961)

J. Chouillet: 'Grimm critique d'art, le Salon de 1757', *La Correspondance littéraire de Grimm et Meister (1754–1813): Saarbrücken, 1974*, pp. 191–9

J. Sgard: *Dictionnaire des journalistes (1600–1789)* (Grenoble, 1976) [good bibliog.]

E. M. Bukdahl: *Diderot critique d'art*, ii (Copenhagen, 1982), pp. 166–83

S. Karp and others, eds: 'Les Lettres inédites de Grimm à Catherine II', *Rech. Diderot & Enc.*, x (1991), pp. 41–55

GARRY APGAR

Grimm, Samuel Hieronymous (*b* Burgdorf, Switzerland, *bapt* 18 Jan 1733; *d* London, 14 April 1794). Swiss painter and draughtsman, active in England. He studied in Berne under Johann Ludwig Aberli and became established as a painter of topographical views in oil and watercolour. His early surviving works (e.g. *River Landscape* and *Landscape with Chasseurs*; Basle, priv. col.) are principally tinted drawings of landscapes and alpine scenery, with scenes of rustic life in the foreground; they display his characteristically charming and informal style. He also produced many decorative book illustrations: the frontispiece and plates to Friedrich von Hagedorn's *Poetische Werke* (1769–72) are among his finest. By 1764

Grimm had abandoned oils and was painting only in watercolour. From 1765 to 1768 he travelled and painted in France; he then moved to England, where he settled for the rest of his life.

Grimm became well known in England for his satirical and caricature drawings and illustrations to Shakespeare, as well as his topographical views, such as the *Queen's Head and Artichoke, Marylebone Turnpike* (see Mallalieu, vol. ii, p. 397). He showed four works at the first exhibition of the Royal Academy in 1768 and later exhibited with the Society of Artists and the Free Society. In 1776 he was employed by Gilbert White (1720–93) to make drawings for the *Natural History and Antiquities of Selborne* (London, 1789). Later he worked for a succession of patrons, including Richard Kaye (1736–1809), with whom he was most closely associated and with whom he travelled through England, making drawings of antiquities. From 1780 to 1791 Grimm and James Lambert (1725–88) were employed by the antiquary Sir William Burrell to make drawings of all antiquities and important houses in Sussex. Most of these drawings are now in the Burrell Collection of the British Library.

BIBLIOGRAPHY

Thieme–Becker
R. M. Clay: *Samuel Hieronymous Grimm in Burgdorf in Switzerland* (London, 1941)
H. L. Mallalieu: *The Dictionary of British Watercolour Artists up to 1920*, i (Woodbridge, 1976), p. 118; ii (1979), p. 397
English Watercolours and Other Drawings: The Helen Barlow Bequest (exh. cat., ed. K. Andrews; Edinburgh, N.G., 1979)

□

Grimmer [Grimer; Grimmaer; Grimmars; Grummaert; Grymer]. South Netherlandish family of painters and draughtsmen.

BIBLIOGRAPHY

R. de Berthier de Sauvigny: 'Les Grimmer', *A. & Curiosité*, xciv (1984), pp. 31–43

(1) Jacob Grimmer (*b* Antwerp, 1525–6; *d* Antwerp, before May 1590). In 1539 he was apprenticed in Antwerp to Gabriel Bauwens (*fl* 1536–9); later he also joined the workshops of Matthijs Cock and Kerstiaen van de Queckborne (1515–78). He became a member of the society of rhetoricians De Violieren in 1546, and a year later a master of the Guild of St Luke. In 1548 he married Lucia van de Wouwer, who bore him four children, including Abraham Grimmer (*b* 1570), who was active as a minor print publisher in Antwerp, and (2) Abel Grimmer, who became a painter.

As early as 1550 Jacob Grimmer was praised by Vasari as one of the best landscape painters of his time; Karel van Mander later claimed he knew of no other artist as 'outstandingly skilled in landscapes'. Grimmer, a contemporary of Pieter Bruegel I, was one of the first Netherlandish landscape painters to make a radical break with Joachim Patinir's tradition of the panoramic mountain landscape, with high horizons and a profusion of detail. This is apparent in his earliest landscape drawing (1573; Hamburg, Ksthalle) and in paintings such as the series of *Four Seasons* (1577; Budapest, Mus. F.A.) in which he represented flat Flemish landscapes dominated by villages and farmhouses and populated with country-folk. Hoogewerff dubbed him a 'minor' Pieter Bruegel. He fell short of Bruegel's great ability to capture a sense of atmosphere and grandeur, but his work is characterized by a simple and sincere grasp of everyday life. In his landscapes the scenery runs continuously from the foreground to the horizon. Large zones of uniform colour are juxtaposed and define the compositions. His trees are slimly silhouetted against the sky, with scanty crowns of foliage, each leaf of which is individually drawn.

Some of Grimmer's landscape designs were used for prints, including a series of 12 *Landscape Views in the Environs of Antwerp*, engraved by Adriaen Collaert (Hollstein: *Dut. & Flem.*, iv, nos 547–58). Philip Galle published a series of four circular engravings of *Landscapes with Cephalus and Procris* (Hollstein: *Dut. & Flem.*, vii, nos 291–4), the first two of which were based on the landscape backgrounds in two drawings with Hagar, Ishmael and the Angel (1586; Oxford, Ashmolean). By the end of Grimmer's career, anecdotal details—never abundant in his work—decreased markedly, and the artist apparently became more interested in representing an intimate view of the landscape, as in the brush drawing of a *Wooded Landscape* (1589; Vienna, Österreich. Nbib.). Late drawings such as this foreshadow the type of forest landscape that was to be developed by artists of the next generation, for example David Vinckboons and the artists of the Frankenthal school.

BIBLIOGRAPHY

G. Vasari: *Vite* (1550, rev. 2/1568); ed. G. Milanesi (1878–85), vii, p. 586
L. Guicciardini: *Descrittione di . . . tutti i Paesi Bassi* (1567), p. 99
K. van Mander: *Schilder-boeck* ([1603]–1604), ii, fol. 256*v*
G. J. Hoogewerff: *Het landscap van Bosch tot Rubens* (Antwerp, 1954), p. 69
H. G. Franz: *Niederländische Landschaftsmalerei im Zeitalter des Manierismus*, Forsch. & Ber. Ksthist. Inst. Graz, Karl-Franzens-U., ii (Graz, 1969), i, pp. 242–8; ii, pp. 177–89
——: 'Unbekannte Landschaftszeichnungen von Jacob Grimmer', *Pantheon*, xxvii (1969), pp. 213–23
E. Greindl: 'Jacob Grimmer', *Die Hals-Familie und ihre Zeit* (Vienna, 1972), pp. 13–46

(2) Abel Grimmer (*b* Antwerp, *c.* 1570; *d* Antwerp, 1618–19). Son of (1) Jacob Grimmer. He married Catharina Lescornet on 29 September 1591 and in 1592 became a master in the Antwerp Guild of St Luke. He is principally known for his numerous small paintings of country scenes, sometimes with a biblical theme, which often form part of a series of the Four Seasons or the Months of the Year. Some of these paintings were inspired by or even copied from prints by Pieter Bruegel I and Hans Bol, both of whose work strongly influenced Abel, even more so than did the example of his father's work, which was also an important source of inspiration. Abel's series of the *Twelve Months* (1592; Montfaucon-en-Velay, Haute-Loire, Chapelle Notre-Dame) are exact copies of Adriaen Collaert's prints after Hans Bol (Hollstein: *Dut. & Flem.*, iv, nos 523–34), published by Hans van Luyck (*fl c.* 1580–85) in 1585. *Spring* and *Summer* (Antwerp, Kon. Mus. S. Kst.) are almost exact copies of two prints by Pieter van der Heyden after designs by Pieter Bruegel (Hollstein: *Dut. & Flem.*, ix, nos 63–4; iii, nos 200 and 202).

The tendency to simplify and systemize both figures and landscapes is even stronger in Abel's work than in Jacob's. Abel's decorative landscapes are typified by splendid colour harmonies and a certain linearity, which is expressed in the slightly schematized compositions and the tendency to represent buildings as geometric shapes. This linear quality may reflect the artist's interest in architecture, which is also revealed in a number of paintings of church interiors by him. These works, for example *Interior of a Gothic Church with a Franciscan Monk Preaching* (sold London, Sotheby's, 9 March 1983, lot 3), are particularly successful; the interest in perspective and the use of a golden light anticipate the work of Pieter Saenredam. Two autograph architectural drawings (ex-Paul Saintenoy priv. col., Brussels, before 1900), an elevation of the gable of Antwerp Cathedral and a church gable with a Gothic spire, led earlier scholars to conclude that he was also an architect. In interior views, such as *A Ball* (Wrotham Park, Middx) and *Jesus in the House of Martha and Mary* (Brussels, Mus. A. Anc.), the artist's main preoccupation was portraying the interior space. He relied on other artists to paint the figures. In neither work, however, can he be described as original; both scenes are set in a Renaissance room, clearly inspired by Hans Vredeman de Vries's *Jesus in the House of Martha and Mary* (London, Hampton Court, Royal Col.).

BIBLIOGRAPHY

P. M. Auzas: 'Les Douze Mois de Grimmer', *Pro A. & Libris*, vii (1948), pp. 3–16

F. C. Legrand: 'Abel Grimmer, peintre d'architectures', *Rev. Belge Archéol. & Hist. A.*, xxvi (1957), pp. 163–7

HANS DEVISSCHER

Grimod, Pierre-Marie-Gaspard, Comte d'Orsay (*b* Paris, 14 Dec 1748; *d* Vienna, 1 Jan 1809). French collector. He was the nephew of Laurent Grimod de la Reynière. His father, Pierre Grimod du Fort (*d* 1748), brother of Laurent, commissioned the huge series of the *History of Don Quixote* (cartoons Compiègne, Château; tapestries, Aix-en-Provence, Mus. Tap.) from Charles-Joseph Natoire. In 1768, two years before Louis XV raised Pierre-Marie-Gaspard to the rank of comte, he bought the Hôtel de Chaulnes, otherwise known as Clermont (now 69 Rue de Varenne), in Paris, which he redecorated and furnished in the Neo-classical style (fragments of panelling in Washington, DC, Corcoran Gal. A.). Those involved in this project included the architect Jean-François-Thérèse Chalgrin and the *ébénistes* Jean-Henri Riesener, Jean-François Leleu and Louis Delanois (1731–92). Delanois supplied the first Neo-classical seat furniture (untraced) to come from his workshop, while Riesener made a magnificent inlaid secrétaire *à cylindre* with gilt-bronze mounts (London, Wallace). For d'Orsay, Philippe Caffiéri (ii) is known to have remounted as girandoles a set of four bronze groups of the *Seasons* (Windsor Castle, Berks, Royal Col.) attributed to Martin Desjardins. The decorative painting was, however, carried out by a more traditional artist, the painter Hugues Taraval. After the death of his first wife (for whom he commissioned a monument from Clodion), in 1775 d'Orsay undertook a trip to Italy. In Rome he was elected to the Accademia degli Arcadi, where he met many notable antiquaries, including the influential José Nicolás de Azara. There he began a collection of antique sculpture, much of it acquired from Bartolomeo Cavaceppi and extensively restored or of dubious provenance, as well as copies of such famous pieces as the Ludovisi *Mars*, the *Antinous* and the *Wounded Amazon* (all copies Paris, Louvre) as well as the Belvedere *Apollo* (copy Versailles, Château); he also collected a great many drawings (Paris, Louvre), some of which came from the collection of Charles-Joseph Natoire. D'Orsay was a generous patron of students at the Académie de France in Rome, and several of them, such as the architect Roussel and the painter Joseph-Benoît Suvée, accompanied him to southern Italy and on a pioneering journey (1776–7) to Sicily. In addition to passing on commissions to them, he commissioned from Joseph-Marie Vien, the Académie's director, a history painting of *Hector and Paris* (exh. Salon 1779; Fontainebleau, Château). Just before his departure from Rome, he was elected an honorary member of the Accademia di S Luca.

After his return to Paris in 1778, d'Orsay continued to enlarge his sizeable collection of Italian, French, Flemish and Dutch drawings (see 1983 exh. cat.), as well as to buy paintings, sculptures and *objets d'art*. He also patronized contemporary artists, including the sculptor François-Nicolas Delaistre, who carved the marble *Cupid and Psyche* (Paris, Louvre) for him. He endowed three places at the Ecole Gratuite de Dessin, directed by Jean-Jacques Bachelier, and supported publication of Pahin-Champlain de la Blancherie's *Nouvelles de la république des lettres et des arts* (Paris, 1779–88). His extensive library was in part inherited from his stepfather, the magistrate and poet Jean-Jacques Le Franc, Marquis de Pompignan, the known contents of which, derived from a contemporary inventory, provide evidence of his wide cultural interests. After his marriage in 1784 to Marie-Anne Hohenlohe-Waldenbourg-Bartenstein, and by then somewhat impoverished as a result of unsuccessful financial investments, d'Orsay settled in the German Rhineland; after 1789 this led French Revolutionary officials to consider him as an émigré, and the remainder of his property was expropriated by the State. D'Orsay's eventual death in Vienna thus came about in one of the city's general hospitals for the poor and destitute.

BIBLIOGRAPHY

F. Boyer: 'Les Hôtels parisiens et les châteaux des Grimod d'Orsay au XVIIIe siècle', *Bull. Soc. Hist. A. Fr.* (1951), pp. 107–17

——: 'La Collection d'antiques du Comte d'Orsay à la veille de la Révolution', *C. R. Séances Acad. Inscr. & B.-Lett.* (1953), pp. 439–43

S. Eriksen: *Early Neo-classicism in France* (London, 1974), p. 210

M. Le Moel: *L'Hôtel de Clermont* (Paris, 1978)

Le Faubourg Saint-Germain: La Rue de Varenne (exh. cat. by C. Baulez, Paris, Mus. Rodin, 1981)

Les Collections du Comte d'Orsay: Dessins du Musée du Louvre (exh. cat. by J.-F. Méjanès, Paris, Louvre, 1983)

□

Grimou, Alexis (*b* Argenteuil, nr Paris, 24 May 1678; *d* Paris, May 1733). French painter. In 1704 he married a niece of the tavern-keeper Procope, whose house in Paris was a meeting-place for artists and intellectuals. The following year Grimou was approved (*agréé*) by the Académie Royale de Peinture et de Sculpture. Although instructed by the Académie to paint as his *morceaux de réception* portraits of the sculptor Jean Raon (1630–1707) and the painter Antoine Coypel, he failed to present either picture and in 1709 the *agrément* was annulled. As a result he joined the Académie de St Luc.

Grimou was probably a pupil of François de Troy, from whom he learnt to use a palette of unusually warm colours and to work with uncomplicated pictorial formats (e.g. *Woman with a Fan*, 1711; see sale cat., Paris, Hôtel Drouot, 27 April 1983, no. 23). Certain audacities in his handling, however (e.g. *Man Wearing a Cuirasse*, 1728; Orléans, Mus. B.-A.), place him well into the 18th century. Grimou's portraits, often *intimiste* works, comprise his known oeuvre; their significance for the development of early 18th-century French art has hitherto not been fully appreciated. Many of them are half-lengths, and they clearly provoked the fantasy portraits later sketched by Jean-Honoré Fragonard, who, moreover, painted pastiches of Grimou's manner (e.g. *Portrait of a Girl*, London, Dulwich Pict. Gal.). Grimou's influence can also be discerned in the work of Charles Eisen, Joseph Ducreux and Jean-Baptiste Greuze. For this reason it can be said that by introducing into France northern formulae for improvised portraits, Grimou played a role not unlike that of Antoine Watteau, who was responsible for introducing the *fête galante* into French art. Grimou's success was such that he often repeated the same types, the best known being the *Young Male Pilgrim* and *Young Female Pilgrim* (both 1725; Florence, Uffizi), which he conceived as pendants—a successful commercial formula of that period. He introduced relaxed poses, informal costume and a light-hearted symbolism based on music and wine. Examples include the *Young Man Playing a Recorder* (1716), which appears on the cover of *Figaro illustré* (1906), the portrait of the *Marquis d'Artaquiette* (1720; Niort, Mus. B.-A.), the *Hurdy-Gurdy Player with a Boy Playing a Recorder* (1727; see sale cat., Paris, Hôtel Drouot, 25 March 1985, no. 25), the *Young Woman Playing a Hurdy-Gurdy* (1728; see *Art at Auction*, vii, March 1985, p. 7) and the *Happy Drinker* (1729; Paris, Louvre). Grimou also painted many self-portraits on the same themes: *Self-portrait as a Drinker* (1724; Paris, Louvre), *Self-portrait as Bacchus* (1728; Dijon, Mus. Magnin) and other personal likenesses that depended on the same symbolic references. Nevertheless he did not scorn to use more traditional formats from time to time, for example in his portrait of the *Marquis de Sourches* (1723; see Gabillot, p. 315), and occasionally he painted allegorical portraits, such as the *Woman and Child* (1727; Béziers, Mus. B.-A.).

In terms of style as well as iconography, Grimou was influenced by Dutch 17th-century masters, notably Rembrandt van Rijn, almost to the point of pastiche, and because of this he was often confused with his contemporaries Jean-Baptiste Santerre and Jean Raoux (e.g. his *Girl Reading*, 1731; Karlsruhe, Staatl. Ksthalle). The many anecdotes concerning Grimou, though distortions of the truth, reveal how, from a very early stage, critics felt the need to discuss a type of painting that was hard to praise but the success of which forced it to be noticed.

BIBLIOGRAPHY

C. Gabillot: 'Alexis Grimou, peintre français (1678–1733)', *Gaz. B.-A.* (1911), pp. 157–72, 309–23, 412–26

L. Réau: 'Grimou, 1678–1733', *Les Peintres français du XVIIIe siècle*, ed. L. Dimier (Paris, 1930), ii, pp. 195–216

G. Levitine: 'The Eighteenth-century Rediscovery of Alexis Grimou and the Emergence of the Proto-Bohemian Image of the French Artist', *18th C. Stud.*, ii (1968–9), pp. 58–76

C. Maisant and D. Brême: 'Alexis Grimou (1678–1733): Nouvelle attribution au Musée de Mulhouse', *Bull. Soc. Indust. Mulhouse*, iv (1987), pp. 15–21

CORINNE MAISANT

Grimshaw, (John) Atkinson (*b* Leeds, 6 Sept 1836; *d* Leeds, 31 Oct 1893). English painter. He had no formal art training but learnt from examples he saw in local art shops. The greatest influence on his early work was John William Inchbold, a Pre-Raphaelite landscape painter from Leeds. Grimshaw gave up his work as a clerk on the railways to take up painting full-time in 1861. His first pictures were of dead birds, blossom and fruit studies in the manner of William Henry Hunt. He accepted Ruskin's view of the world in his 'truth to nature' paintings of the woods around Adel and Meanwood in Leeds. Grimshaw's picture *A Mossy Glen* (1864; Brighouse, Smith A.G.) is close to Inchbold's technique and colour range. His first patrons were members of the Leeds Philosophical and Literary Society. Grimshaw began to exhibit from 1862, and he showed five paintings in all at the Royal Academy of Arts, London. Two works from this period show his Pre-Raphaelite interests: *Nab Scar* (1864; London, Christopher Wood Gal.) and the *Bowder Stone, Borrowdale* (*c.* 1864; London, Tate). Both are painted in a crisp, hard-edge manner in brilliantly fresh colours. *Nab Scar* is closely based on a photograph that Grimshaw used as an aide-mémoire. The culmination of this early period is *Autumn Glory: The Old Mill* (1869; Leeds, C.A.G.), in which all the detail of leaves, twigs, ivy and moss-covered stone is painstakingly shown. Moonlight scenes are Grimshaw's best-known subjects. The earliest is *Whitby Harbour by Moonlight* (1867; priv. col., see 1979 exh. cat., pl. 42), which shows the town in full colour, bathed in moonlight. This broader technique, often featuring the mysterious atmosphere of mist-laden horizons, was particularly appreciated by middle-class clients, often northern industrialists. Grimshaw's dock scenes of Liverpool, Hull and Glasgow, and the manor houses glimpsed down leafy, stone-walled suburban lanes, along which a single figure walks, were especially popular. The lonely houses are usually combinations of different buildings, often taken from architectural plates.

In the 1870s Grimshaw was at the peak of his success. He rented Knostrop Hall, a manor house in Leeds, and a seaside home, Castle-by-the-Sea, at Scarborough; he sold his work through William Agnew's galleries in London and the provinces. He extended his subject-matter to include re-creations of ancient Greece and Rome in the style of Lawrence Alma-Tadema, as well as producing paintings of fashionable modern women, imitating James Tissot. There were also literary subjects from Tennyson and Longfellow. However, Grimshaw's roots remained strongly in the north, and in 1880 he produced his masterpiece of townscape, *Leeds Bridge* (Leeds, C.A.G.). A financial crisis around this time forced him to vacate his Scarborough home, and in the 1880s he took a studio in Chelsea, London. His output increased, but often he painted over photographs, and, it has been claimed, developed a technique of projecting images on to a canvas, which could then be painted. Two of his sons, Arthur Grimshaw (1864–1913) and Louis H. Grimshaw (1870–?1944), imitated their father's style, as did Walter Meegan and Wilfred Jenkins. In his final years Grimshaw produced small riverscapes, in a two-tone colour range, very much in the mood of Whistler, whom Grimshaw is reputed to have known in London. During the last winter of his life he painted snow scenes. Today Grimshaw is seen as one of the minor Victorian masters, his place assured by his moonlights, evocative of Victorian life of the 1870s and 1880s.

BIBLIOGRAPHY

Atkinson Grimshaw (exh. cat., ed. J. Abdy; London, Ferrers Gal., 1970)
G. R. Phillips: *John Atkinson Grimshaw, 1836–1893* (Leeds, 1972)
Atkinson Grimshaw (exh. cat., ed. J. Abdy and C. Wood; London, Alexander Gal., 1976)
Atkinson Grimshaw (exh. cat., ed. A. Robertson; Leeds, C.A.G., 1979) [well illus., with crit. essay by D. Bromfield; 75 pls]
A. Robertson: *Atkinson Grimshaw* (Oxford, 1988)

ALEXANDER ROBERTSON

Grimshaw, Nicholas (*b* Hove, 9 Oct 1939). English architect. He studied at the Edinburgh College of Art and the Architectural Association, London. On graduating in 1965, he formed a partnership with Terry Farrell; their work included a refabricated plastic bathroom tower (1967; destr.) for a student hostel, and flats (1968) in Park Road, both London, and the Herman Miller Factory (1976), Bath. In 1980 Grimshaw split from Farrell and formed his own practice. His independent work is characterized by the almost exclusive use of industrialized components, especially glass curtain walling, and the use of prominent structures—usually steel—to achieve clear internal spans and open façades. His Oxford Ice Rink (1982–4) has a roof suspended from two masts; the Sainsbury Supermarket (1986–8), Camden Town, London, has a vaulted roof carried on cantilevers; and the Igus Factory (1990–92), Cologne, is clad in aluminium profiled sheeting, while the suspended roof contains shallow domical roof-lights. Two printing works, for the *Financial Times* in London (1987–8) and the *Western Morning News* in Plymouth (1990–92; with Peter Rice), show contrasting approaches: the former is a sober, glazed shed with a tubular steel structure and an entrance framed by two tall cylindrical elements clad in aluminium; the latter has nautical imagery, with outward curved glazed walls supported by curved external steel ribs and a 'bridge' accommodating the boardroom. His British Pavilion (1992; destr.), Seville, was a glass box with a roof of steel *brises-soleil*; it was ingeniously cooled by a combination of shading and water-cooled façades. One of Grimshaw's most prominent works is the Channel Tunnel Terminal (1989–92), Waterloo Station, London; it has a sinuous glazed roof formed by a vault of asymmetrical steel trusses. Other works of the 1990s include the Berlin Stock Exchange (begun 1991) and the RAC Control Centre (begun 1993), Bristol.

BIBLIOGRAPHY

Nicholas Grimshaw & Partners, 2 vols (exh. cat., London, RIBA, 1988)
C. Davies, ed.: *UK Pavilion, Seville Expo 1992: Nicholas Grimshaw & Partners*, Architecture in Detail (London, 1993)
R. Moore, ed.: *Structure, Space and Skin: The Work of Nicholas Grimshaw & Partners* (London, 1993)

□

Grīnbergs, Andris (*b* Riga, 3 March 1946). Latvian performance artist and teacher. As a central figure in Latvia's small hippy community of the 1960s, he declared his liberation from the cultural prescriptions of Soviet life. Though trained in clothing design at Riga's Applied Arts High School (1964–7), he was more profoundly shaped by the music, film and fashion innovations of Western counter-culture. In late August 1972, with his musician wife, Inta Grīnberga (*b* 1955), he staged the happening *Jesus Christ's Wedding*, notable not only as the début of performance art in Latvia but also as an expression of religious belief in violation equally of Soviet atheism and of conventional Christian doctrine. Considered subversive, a private photography exhibition in his apartment was raided by state security forces at this time. Grīnbergs's performances and body-art works during the 1970s and 1980s explored issues of free expression, sexual identity, politics of the body, human interaction with nature, ethnographic preservation (particularly of the Liv tribe) and the supposed boundaries separating art and life. His conclusions challenged Latvian mores as often as they refuted Soviet social theory, and in its sociopolitical trenchancy his work can be considered a precursor to the performance art of MIERVALDIS POLIS and the WORKSHOP FOR THE RESTORATION OF UNFELT SENSATIONS. With no chance of state support for his artistic activities (1976) Grīnbergs began a teaching career that has been equally revolutionary, achieving sensational results with marginalized youth, as celebrated in Lazima Žurgina's documentary film about his art-therapy methods, *The Ugly Duckling, Humanity's Child* (1985).

WRITINGS

Riga: Lettische Avantgarde (exh. cat., W. Berlin, Staatl. Ksthalle, 1988), pp. 42–3, 80
M. Svede: Latvian Non-conformist Art: Smaller Measures, to Equal Effect, *Non-Conformist Art: The Soviet Experience, 1956–1986* (London, 1995), pp. 323–5

MARK ALLEN SVEDE

Grīnbergs, Teodors. *See* ZAĻKALNS, TEODORS.

Grippo, Víctor (*b* Junín, Buenos Aires, 10 May 1936). Argentine sculptor. After studying chemistry and drawing at the Universidad Nacional de la Plata, he applied his scientific background from the early 1970s to a series of works entitled *Analogy*, in which he established correlations between scientific experiments and the poetry of artistic discourse. Concerned with emulating the processes of nature, he presented sculptural installations in the form of controlled investigations, for example using copper and zinc electrodes to measure the energy of potatoes as a means of demonstrating the parallel between the transformations in the tuber and the process of human perception. In another series, entitled *Crafts* (1976; see Glusberg, p. 171), he presented tools used for manual activities as a way of defending human dignity in an age in which any form of manual ability is considered archaic. Such themes were in line with those of the Grupo CAYC, of which he was a member.

BIBLIOGRAPHY

J. Glusberg: *Del Pop-art a la Nueva Imagen* (Buenos Aires, 1985), pp. 167–76

JORGE GLUSBERG

Gripsholm Castle. Swedish royal fortification and residence in Mariefred, near Stockholm, begun in 1537 by

King Gustav I. It is one of the finest remaining examples of Swedish architecture of the Vasa dynasty (1523–1600) founded by Gustav, and combines sophisticated Renaissance interiors with a form that remains essentially medieval. The site, strategic since Viking times, became more important during the Middle Ages when an estate and castle were erected in 1383 by Chancellor Bo Jonsson. In 1472 the property was purchased by Sten Sture the Elder (1440–1503), who donated it in 1498 to a Carthusian monastery. Gustav I seized the property in 1526, claiming the legal rights of inheritance through his kinship with Sten Sture. The existing medieval stone keep was inadequate for Gustav, who commissioned the architect Henrik Cöllen to design a new castle (begun 1537), a practical fortress-refuge for the king, his family and the royal chancery and treasury. Defensive in nature, the castle has a polygonal plan, with four massive circular towers at the angles. Built of brick, with 3–4 m thick walls surrounded by a moat, it retains a bold, severe appearance with few extraneous details, although a picturesque element is added by the irregular silhouette of towers and roofs (*see* SWEDEN, fig. 3). A painted ceiling in Halberdiers' Hall, attributed to Anders Larsson, survives from 1543. The year 1578 marked the completion of major restorations initiated by Duke Karl (later Karl IX), who wanted quarters to befit the position of a Renaissance king; and further alterations took place during the 1590s. The 16th-century interiors of Gripsholm are among Sweden's greatest Renaissance treasures (*see* SWEDEN, §V and fig. 15). In the 1690s Queen Hedvig Eleonora, a great patron of art and architecture, commissioned Nicodemus Tessin (ii) to change the building substantially with the addition of a queen's wing. Modernization of parts of the interior was initiated by Crown Princess Lovisa Ulrika in the 1740s, and a theatre in the former church was commissioned in 1781 by Gustav III from Eric Palmstedt, whose scheme was influenced by Andrea Palladio's Teatro Olimpico, Vicenza (1585).

Gripsholm is now a museum and houses the National Portrait Gallery of Sweden, which is under the auspices of the National Swedish Art Museum.

BIBLIOGRAPHY

Gripsholm Castle: Official Illustrated Guide (Stockholm, 1969)

KARIN M. E. ALEXIS

Gris, Juan [González Pérez, José Victoriano Carmelo Carlos] (*b* Madrid, 23 March 1887; *d* Boulogne-sur-Seine, 11 May 1927). Spanish painter, draughtsman, illustrator and writer, active in France. His artistic career was spent almost exclusively in France, where he was considered one of the leading Cubist painters from 1912 until his death. An artist valued for the depth and consistency of his approach rather than as an innovator, he is recognized for his independent and distinctive approach to Cubism and as one of its most influential later practitioners and theoreticians.

1. Training and work, to 1910. 2. First Cubist phase, 1911–14. 3. Wartime Cubism and maturity, 1914–22. 4. Career success and the question of compromise, 1922–4. 5. Last works, 1924–7.

1. TRAINING AND WORK, TO 1910. Gris specialized in mathematics, physics and engineering at the Escuela de Artes y Manufacturas in Madrid from 1902 to 1904; he later described this phase of his education as formative. His approach to Cubism, which has often been called scientific in its logic and precision, may well have been affected by his knowledge of technical drawings. He broke his scientific studies, however, to train briefly with the academic painter José Moreno Carbonero (1860–1942), and he decided to become an artist. From 1905 to 1906 he worked as an illustrator, producing pleasant drawings under the influence of Art Nouveau for the periodical *Renacimiento latino* and for a book of poems, *Alma América* (Madrid, 1906), by the Peruvian José Santo Chocano. In September 1906 he settled permanently in Paris; avoidance of military service made it impossible for him to return to Spain. He first signed himself Juan Gris, which was to become his professional name in France, in the illustrations of 1905 for *Renacimiento latino*. From 1907 to 1911, and occasionally until 1914, he continued his work as an illustrator, publishing satirical drawings in the Parisian periodicals *Le Témoin*, *Cri de Paris*, *Le Charivari* and *L'Assiette au Beurre*, and in the Barcelona periodicals *Papitú*, *Esquella de la Torratxa* and *Campagna de Gracia*.

On his arrival in Paris, Gris met Pablo Picasso, through whom he found a studio (by 1908) at the BATEAU-LAVOIR, where Picasso was also resident until 1909. By 1908, through Picasso, he knew Georges Braque and Guillaume Apollinaire, André Salmon and Max Jacob, and until 1910 he was witness to the formation of Cubism by Picasso and Braque. His paintings of this period have not survived, and it was only in 1910, determined to follow the example of Picasso and Braque, that Gris became a committed painter.

2. FIRST CUBIST PHASE, 1911–14. By 1910 Braque and Picasso had made sophisticated use of Cubist multiple perspective; they had so thoroughly broken apart the subjects represented, scattering their components in faceted form across the picture surface, that their very identity was threatened. Gris chose not to take Cubist methods to such an extreme conclusion. Instead he grouped objects and asked friends to pose so that he could paint still-lifes and portraits from direct observation, studying for himself the transformative effects of shifting viewpoints and of a flat planar treatment of light and dark contrasts. He worked from preparatory drawings for his first Cubist paintings in 1911–12, which included townscapes of Montmartre as well as portraits and still-lifes such as *Bottles and Knife* (1912; Otterlo, Kröller-Müller Sticht.). Fifteen of these paintings were shown by Clovis Sagot early in 1912, and three of them, including *Homage to Picasso* (1912; Chicago, IL, A. Inst.), reached a much wider public at the Salon des Indépendants that year.

In his first Cubist style Gris achieved a novel combination of flattened Cubist structure and a lucid depiction of objects. In paintings such as *Jar, Flask and Glass* (1911; New York, MOMA) he used linear grids both as a means of controlling the depiction of features from different vantage points and as a flat overall compositional structure. The often arbitrary pattern of light and shadow made the surface of the paintings look like a carved relief lit by raking light, giving equally clear emphasis to subject-matter and planar structure. Related drawings such as

Flowers in a Vase (charcoal drawing, 1912; Bloomington, IN U. A. Mus.) reveal an intuitive sensitivity as well as a determination to systematize the perceptual evidence, but it was the combination of control and lucidity characteristic of the paintings that effectively set Gris's work apart from that of other Cubists. Since still-life proved his predominant subject, his work was repeatedly compared by later critics to the calm orderliness yet crisply lit factuality of Spanish Baroque still-life painting, especially that of Francisco Zurbarán.

After participating in the Salon des Indépendants in 1912, Gris was introduced into the circle of the PUTEAUX GROUP, which included, besides Marcel Duchamp and his brother Jacques Villon, Francis Picabia, Albert Gleizes and Jean Metzinger. The combination by Gris of an urbane, man-about-town subject with a controlled Cubist technique in *The Man in the Café* (1912; Philadelphia, PA, Mus. A.) closely relates to Cubist works by Metzinger such as *The Yellow Feather* (1912; Mr and Mrs R. Stanley Johnson priv. col., see 1983 exh. cat., p. 439), and his introduction of proportional practices based on the golden section aligns him with the mathematical preoccupations of the Section d'Or (*see* SECTION D'OR (ii)), at whose Salon of October 1912 this painting and 11 other works by Gris were exhibited. Gris's participation in this exhibition and at the Salon d'Automne led to a contract late in 1912 with Daniel-Henry Kahnweiler, who also represented Picasso and Braque and who had followed his Cubism from the beginning. This gave him the opportunity to pursue his interests more intensively and privately and led both to a retreat from the Salons and to a strengthening of his ties with Picasso and Braque. During 1913 and 1914, a period of concentrated activity for the group of Cubists sponsored by Kahnweiler, Gris explored the potential of words in Cubist painting as introduced by Picasso and Braque by means of collage and papier collé. He was quick to exploit papier collé to achieve greater surface activity, clearer compositional structures and a more complex play between modes of descriptive and allusively verbal representation. At Céret in summer and autumn 1913 (including two weeks in the company of Picasso) he produced a series of monumental still-lifes such as *The Three Cards* (Berne, Kstmus.), a few amusingly abbreviated figure paintings and two dazzlingly coloured landscapes, one of which is *Landscape at Céret* (Stockholm, Mod. Mus.). They are again distinctive in their structural and representational clarity, but also in their rich and suggestive use of colour.

Gris had used papier collé in coloured drawings early in 1913, but it was only in 1914 that he allowed it to take over his painting in still-lifes such as *The Coffee Packet* (Ulm, Ulm Mus.), in which he superimposed a concise drawing of fragments of objects over intricate jigsaws of cut-out paper shapes. He always included enough information to enable the spectator to reconstruct the subject conceptually, but this lucidity was often offset by playful equivocation and obscured in complex, ambiguous arrangements of planes and materials. Interwoven with the material and representational fragments were witty verbal messages provided by newspaper items or labels: in one papier collé, *The Pedestal Table* (1914; Philadelphia, PA, Mus. A.; see fig. 1), in which objects are displayed on an

1. Juan Gris: *The Pedestal Table*, coloured papers, printed matter and charcoal on paper, mounted on canvas, 597×445 mm, 1914 (Philadelphia, PA, Museum of Art)

occasional table, the words 'le vrai et le faux' comment on the entire representational enterprise, as does the phrase 'contributions indirectes', a reference to tobacco tax, in *Tobacco, Newspaper and Bottle of Vin Rosé* (1914; Paris, priv. col.). Like Picasso and Braque, Gris was an avid reader of Mallarmé at this time, and the indirectness of his papiers collés of 1914 owes much to this example.

3. WARTIME CUBISM AND MATURITY, 1914–22. When World War I was declared in August 1914 Gris, as a foreigner, was one of the few Cubist painters able to continue with his work. He painted with undiminished energy throughout the war, never keeping to a single mode for longer than a few months, and produced an extraordinarily varied range of Cubist art. In early 1916 he painted brilliant pointillist still-lifes such as *Newspaper and Fruit Dish* (New Haven, CT, Yale U. A.G.); these were succeeded in the summer and autumn by paintings characterized by severely flattened contrasts of light and dark planes, for example *Fruit Dish, Glass and Lemon* (Aug 1916; Washington, DC, Phillips Col.). In the space of one year he veered between dynamic, diagonally structured pictures such as *Fruit Dish, Pipe and Newspaper* (Nov 1917; Basle, Kstmus.) and much more stable compositions such as *The Man from Touraine* (Sept 1918; Paris, Pompidou), in which verticals and horizontals predominate. Papier collé gave way to pictures that in their thick accumulations of oil paint are sometimes almost like shallow reliefs.

Although Picasso was also in Paris, Gris worked at first in relative isolation, enduring financial hardship induced by Kahnweiler's exile (as a German) and his refusal to allow him to break his contract. From early 1915, however, Gris was given support by Léonce Rosenberg, with whom a contract was signed in April 1916. Rosenberg also took up other Cubists who had not been mobilized, including new friends shared by Gris and Picasso such as Jacques Lipchitz and the former Futurist Gino Severini. Between 1916 and 1918 Gris took on a leading role within Cubism; he was also a respected friend of other artists who were to make a mark after the war, including Amédée Ozenfant. His clarity of purpose made him a model for the wartime avant-garde that gathered around Pierre Albert-Birot's periodical *S.I.C.* and Pierre Reverdy's *Nord-Sud.* Gris was especially close to Reverdy, who had been a friend and neighbour in Montmartre since 1910, and it was Gris's example most of all that guided Reverdy's influential theories concerning Cubism, which were launched in March 1917 with his article 'Sur le Cubisme' in *Nord-Sud.*

During World War I Gris concentrated on a limited range of subjects, to most of which he was to remain faithful. He continued to use musical instruments, music sheets, books and domestic paraphernalia, as in *The Violin* (1916; Basle, Kstmus.). He made direct allusion to other artists such as Jean-Baptiste-Camille Corot and especially Paul Cézanne, for example in a group of pencil drawings of 1916 such as *Man Resting on his Elbows, after Cézanne* (Mannheim, Städt. Ksthalle) and *Copy after a Self-portrait by Cézanne* (Chicago, IL, A. Inst). Associations with earlier artists were especially strong in the figure subjects that he introduced during this period, as in the two portraits of his wife Josette and *Woman with Mandolin, after Corot* (1916; Basle, Kstmus.); from 1917 he painted harlequins and pierrots reminiscent of Cézanne, of the early works of Picasso and of Antoine Watteau before them (e.g. *Pierrot*, 1919; Paris, Pompidou). The links with 'tradition', seen also in his portrayal of sturdy peasant figures with nationalist overtones, as in *The Man from Touraine*, were associated with a general sense of classical order in tune with a 'new Classical age', which by 1917 was being heralded by *Nord-Sud.* This has been related to nationalist themes that became dominant during the war in both literature and propaganda, above all the portrayal of France as essentially a Mediterranean culture, rational and orderly. By the end of the war Gris was at the centre of what Jean Cocteau called a 'rappel à l'ordre' in French culture.

The Cubist 'classicism' practised by Gris was associated between 1916 and 1920 with the development of an emphatically 'pure' Cubist practice. In 1921, writing in *L'Esprit nouveau*, the Purist magazine run by Ozenfant and Le Corbusier, he tried to formulate the essentials of this practice. He claimed to start with the manipulation of flat shapes, only afterwards 'qualifying' them so that they became identifiable in terms of subject-matter. He worked, he said, 'deductively' from the general to the particular, the abstract to the concrete, ensuring a basis for his art in conception rather than perception. He called this process 'synthetic' to distinguish it from the 'analysis' of things that he considered fundamental to his earlier Cubism. It is unlikely that he often worked in such a pure way, but he certainly aspired to it, and both the simplicity of his vocabulary of representational signs and the way it generated elaborate visual rhymes testifies to the priority he

2. Juan Gris: *The Cloud*, oil on canvas, 655×996 mm, 1921 (Hamburg, Hamburger Kunsthalle)

gave from 1917 to the manipulation of form. A comparable insistence on 'purity' of practice, found also in statements by or about Braque, Metzinger and Lipchitz between 1918 and 1920, was allied to the general claim that Cubist art was not so much an art of representation as one of 'creation', and that it transcended naturalism in such a way that the intellect and imagination could work freely on a 'poetic' level. Gris was presented as both one of the 'purest' and one of the most classical of the Cubists.

Gris's prominence among the avant-garde coincided with a solo exhibition of 50 works at Léonce Rosenberg's Galerie de l'Effort Moderne in Paris in April 1919, and with his inclusion early in 1920 in the Salon des Indépendants and the revived Salon de la Section d'Or. His production and his leading role as a painter were undermined, however, in May 1920 by the onset of illness, possibly undiagnosed pulmonary tuberculosis. He was hospitalized until August and was convalescent until 1921, though he began to work again from autumn 1920. In 1921–2, as he returned to better health at Bandol and Céret, he produced some of the most successful of his classical synthetic works, especially a series of open-window paintings in which still-lifes are placed before open windows so that they appear to merge into Mediterranean and mountain views, as in *The Cloud* (July 1921; Hamburg, Ksthalle; see fig. 2). However purely these works were synthesized, they convey an intense sensitivity to qualities of texture, light and atmosphere, to the things and places depicted.

4. CAREER SUCCESS AND THE QUESTION OF COMPROMISE, 1922–4. Between autumn 1922 and 1924 both Gris's career and his art went through a change that some have described as a period of crisis. His health was restored and he achieved prominence with both the public and the avant-garde. In November 1922 he was commissioned by Serge Diaghilev to design costumes and sets for a Ballets Russes production of the ballet, *Les Tentations de la bergère* (with music by the 18th-century composer Michel Pignolet Montéclair), and other commissions followed in 1923 and 1924. He had previously published illustrations for literary works: Pierre Dermée's *Beautés de 1918* (Paris, 1919), Vicente Huidobro's *Horizon carré* (Paris, 1918), Pierre Reverdy's *La Guitare endormie* (Paris, 1919) and Max Jacob's *Ne coupez pas mademoiselle, ou les erreurs des P.T.T.* (Paris, 1921). The commissions from Diaghilev, however, represented collaboration on a larger scale and exposure to a larger and more influential public.

Concurrent with these signs of his growing public success, Gris moved in his paintings towards a richer, more ingratiating range of colours and to subjects that seemed both more naturalistic and more anecdotal in treatment; such is the case with his images of clowns, sometimes in a drunken state, such as *Harlequin Leaning on a Table* (1924; Munich, Staatsgal. Mod. Kst). The appearance is of compromise in the face of severe criticisms of Cubism for its purity and austerity, encouraged by the ambience of the Ballets Russes.

In fact, Gris remained publicly committed to his advanced Cubist position, and in April 1924 he delivered a lecture at the Sorbonne, 'Sur les possibilités de la peinture', which was speedily published in English, Spanish and German and which was the most elaborate exposition of his ideas on synthesis and on art as creation. His exhibition at Kahnweiler's Galerie Simon in Paris in March–April 1923, while including the first of the more naturalistic works, was attacked by the critic Maurice Hiver as that of an uncompromising Cubist.

5. LAST WORKS, 1924–7. Kahnweiler, who had renewed his association with Gris in 1920, was among his closest friends in the 1920s; and it was he and his wife who found the flat and studio in Boulogne-sur-Seine to which Gris and Josette moved from the Bateau-Lavoir in spring 1922. The Kahnweilers, whom they now had as neighbours, were the centre of a social circle that brought Gris into contact with the fringes of the emergent Surrealist movement as early as 1924. He met Antonin Artaud, Michel Leiris and André Masson, and his synthetic practice of 'finding' subjects in 'abstract' arrangements of lines or shapes may well have helped Masson towards his early experiments with automatism in drawings of 1923–4. Gris was also close to Gertrude Stein, who had offered him financial support at the onset of World War I. It was, in fact, for one of her texts, *A Book Concluding with a Wife has a Cow. A Love Story* (Paris, 1926), that Gris made his last prints: four lithographs of which one was in two colours. Kahnweiler, under the imprint Editions de la Galerie Simon, was the publisher, as he was of all the books illustrated by Gris after 1920. Except for a group of lithographic portraits of friends, executed in 1921, and his early satirical drawings, all Gris's graphic work was produced either to accompany or to illustrate texts by writers whom he knew as friends.

Gris did not work for Diaghilev after May 1924, but from 1924 to his death he enjoyed increasing commercial and critical success; at the same time he had the confidence to return to what he regarded as a more uncompromising synthetic Cubism. The collector Alphonse Kahn began to buy works by Gris in 1925, and G. F. Reber bought 28 pictures. Gris felt sufficiently secure financially to decline a contract offered to him by the influential dealer Paul Rosenberg. In paintings such as *The Open Book* (1925; Berne, Kstmus.) the things represented are so completely interlocked with the composition that they become unimaginable outside their specific pictorial context, but the subject-matter remained knowingly suggestive. In particular, Gris produced a group of still-lifes, such as *The Painter's Window* (1925; Baltimore, MD, Mus. A.), that for the first time take as subject the attributes of the painter, the palette and brushes, both reviving a traditional still-life type associated with Chardin and giving expression to his conviction that the painter is the inventor of another world.

From October 1925 Gris's health was in decline. There were two periods of crisis, from October 1925 to spring 1926, and from October 1926 to his death. Uraemia and cardiac attacks preceded final renal failure. This fatal decline was probably related to his initial bout of serious illness in 1920, but no definitive diagnosis of his condition was made. The chief mourners at his funeral on 13 May 1927 were his son Georges González-Gris, Picasso, Lipchitz, Maurice Raynal and Kahnweiler.

The first retrospective devoted to Gris's work was held in 1933 at the Kunsthaus in Zurich, and three years later he was treated as a significant figure in the survey exhibition of *Cubism and Abstract Art* at MOMA in New York. His critical reputation, established by writers such as Apollinaire and Raynal, was sustained after his death above all by Kahnweiler.

WRITINGS

The writings listed below are published in D.-H. Kahnweiler: *Juan Gris: Sa vie, son oeuvre, ses écrits* (Paris, 1946), except for the letters.

Valori Plast. (Feb–March 1919), p. 2 [on elements]
'L'Art nègre', *Action*, 3 (1920), p. 24
Espr. Nouv., 5 (1921), pp. 533–4 [on aesthetics and methods]
'Notes sur ma peinture', *Der Querschnitt*, 1–2 (1923), pp. 77–8
'Sur les possibilités de la peinture', *Transatlantic Rev.* (1924), i/6, pp. 482–8; ii/1, pp. 75–9
'Réponse à l'enquête "chez les cubistes"', *Bull. Vie A.*, vi/1 (1925), pp. 15–17
M. Raynal, ed.: *Anthologie de la peinture en France de 1906 à nos jours* (Paris, 1927), p. 172 [on analysis and synthesis]
D. Cooper, ed.: *Letters of Juan Gris* (London, 1956) [based on D.-H. Kahnweiler's unpubd compilation]

BIBLIOGRAPHY

M. Raynal: 'Juan Gris', *Espr. Nouv.*, 5 (1921), pp. 531–54
W. George: 'Juan Gris', *Amour A.*, ii/11 (1921), pp. 351–2
M. Raynal: 'Juan Gris et la métaphore plastique', *Feuilles Libres*, 31 (1923), pp. 63–5
C. Zervos: 'Juan Gris et l'inquiétude d'aujourd'hui', *Cah. A.*, i/10 (1926), pp. 269–74
——: 'Juan Gris', *Cah. A.*, ii/4–5 (1927), pp. 170–72
D.-H. Kahnweiler: *Juan Gris* (Leipzig and Berlin, 1929)
G. Waldemar: *Juan Gris* (Paris, 1931)
D.-H. Kahnweiler: *Juan Gris: Sa vie, son oeuvre, ses écrits* (Paris, 1945); Eng. trans. and rev. D. Cooper as *Juan Gris: His Life and Work* (London, 1968–9)
W. A. Camfield: 'Juan Gris and the Golden Section', *A. Bull.*, xlvii (1965), pp. 128–34
J. A. Gaya-Nuño: *Juan Gris* (Barcelona, 1971)
Juan Gris (exh. cat., ed. D. Cooper and H. A. Peters; Baden-Baden, Staatl. Ksthalle, 1974)
Juan Gris (exh. cat., preface J. Leymarie; Paris, Mus. Orangerie, 1974)
E. A. Carmean jr: 'Juan Gris' *Fantômas*', *A. Mag.*, li/5 (1977), pp. 116–19
D. Cooper: *Juan Gris*, 2 vols (Paris, 1977) [cat. rai. of ptgs]
C. Green: 'Purity, Poetry and the Painting of Juan Gris', *A. Hist.*, v/2 (1982), pp. 180–204
——: 'Synthesis and the "Synthetic Process" in the Painting of Juan Gris, 1915–1919', *A. Hist.*, v/1 (1982), pp. 87–105
M. Rosenthal: *Juan Gris* (New York, 1983)
The Essential Cubism: Braque, Picasso & Their Friends, 1907–1920 (exh. cat. by D. Cooper and G. Tinterow, London, Tate, 1983), pp. 134–97
Juan Gris (1887–1927) (exh. cat., ed. G. Tinterow; Madrid, Salas Picasso, 1985)
Juan Gris (exh. cat. by C. Green, London, Whitechapel A. G.; Stuttgart, Staatsgal.; Otterlo, Rijksmus. Kröller-Müller; 1992–3)

CHRISTOPHER GREEN

Grisaille [Fr.: 'grey in grey painting']. Term applied to monochrome painting carried out mostly in shades of grey. The use of the French word can be traced only to 1625, since although grisaille painting was done in preceding centuries, it was not referred to as such. The alternative expression *peinture en camaïeu (gris)* is also documented only more recently. In the 16th century there are occasional references to 'dead colour', but this term is no longer used. At the time of its origin, in the medieval period, grisaille painting was simply called 'painting in black and white', as is clear, for example, from an entry in the inventories of Jean de France, Duc de Berry, of 1401, 1413 and 1416: 'Item, unes petites heures de Nostre Dame. . .enluminées de blanc et de noir'. However, this description is not very precise, as grisaille painting was never merely black and white at that time but was always combined with (more or less sparingly used) colours. The term grisaille, as commonly used today, itself only inadequately describes the various modes it subsumes. Their only common feature is the more or less exclusive use of non-coloured pigments, while they diverge technically and aesthetically to an often astonishing extent.

1. Before *c.* 1400. 2. From *c.* 1400.

1. Before *c.* 1400.

(i) Stained glass. (ii) Wall painting. (iii) Manuscript illumination. (iv) Other portable paintings.

(i) Stained glass. Probably the oldest form of grisaille in Western art appeared in stained-glass painting in the 12th century. Following the prohibition on colour issued by the Cistercian Order in 1134, artists in Cistercian monasteries were restricted exclusively to interlaced windows in clear glass with (black) lead stripes and black enamel drawing. Despite all the prohibitions, however, small amounts of coloured glass were soon introduced (e.g. in a window of *c.* 1210 in La Bénisson-Dieu, Loire). Perhaps as a result of this shift from rigorous severity to aesthetic charm, grisaille glass painting enriched with some colour also gained importance outside the Order in the course of the 13th century. In the third quarter of the century, grisaille windows were standard fittings in French churches, where they often alternated with polychrome figural panes (*see* STAINED GLASS, colour pl. VI, fig. 1). Occasionally the whole glazing of a church was done with grisaille windows, or they were given at least a prominent place in combination with figural depictions, as a contrasting frame. Among the earliest examples of this use of grisaille are the windows (*c.* 1270) of the church of St Urbain, Troyes (*see* GOTHIC, fig. 69). Hand in hand with the dominance of grisaille glass with coloured inserts went a change in the use of colour in figural glass painting. The strong reds and blues of the early 13th century were replaced by more delicate and transparent tones, but there were still no figural windows that even approached a monochrome treatment.

The preconditions for monochrome figural glass painting were created around 1300, with the development of the technique of silver stain painting (*see* STAINED GLASS, §I, 4), which made it possible to stain a pane in any colour, usually transparent and with a yellow tone. In this way a glass surface could be painted in two colours without the need for lead strips (to hold the different-coloured pieces together). This meant an enormous increase in the artistic qualities of a painted window, which also profited from new, more subtle black enamel techniques. This advance, however, was not adequately exploited either in France or in the neighbouring countries during the whole of the 14th century. While the white and silver-stained parts took an important place within figure depictions from the second quarter of the century, they seldom made up the whole painting. One of the few surviving exceptions is a strip in the lower part of an older window in Chartres Cathedral, donated by a Canon Thierry in 1327. The figures (the Virgin with saints and the donor), exclusively in white, grey and silvery yellow, are seen against an ornamental grisaille background, which (like all patterned grisaille windows painted with a silver-stain) no longer has an interlace pattern but one of irregularly strewn flowers and leaves. Because of their rarity, figural grisaille windows such as this one should be seen as reflecting developments in other genres. Not until the 15th and 16th centuries did they become established as the dominant element within their own medium, often in conjunction with a Renaissance treatment of figures and landscape, which thus shows them to be innovations drawn from other branches of art.

(ii) Wall painting. The origin of monochrome figure painting is to be found in Italian wall painting. Between 1303 and 1306 Giotto painted the stone-coloured allegories of the *Virtues* and *Vices*, conceived as statues facing each other in fictive niches on the walls of the nave, in the dado area of his fresco cycle in the Arena Chapel in Padua. Their monochrome, which can be referred to only in part as grey (apart from lime white and vegetable black, earth pigments such as terra verde and ochre were used), is the colour of the material of which they appear to consist. Though opinions differ slightly on this point, it seems most likely that neither a systematic abstraction of form from colour, nor an autonomous artistic method was intended, but that monochrome painting here is used just as a means of reproducing stone. The allegories, subordinated by their stone quality to the coloured (and therefore more lifelike) figures in the scenes from the *History of Salvation*, have nontheless the highest degree of reality within the picture programme because of their illusionistic presentation. They are linked to the reality of the beholder not only spatially through the niches seemingly a part of the beholder's world but also temporally through their stone colour. Their frozen movements are not seen as contradicting the incessant flux of earthly reality, since they are only stones, not living people.

Simultaneously with Giotto's illusionistic sculptures, painted statuettes appeared in the internal context of pictures, as in the images of the cycle of the *Legend of St Francis* (Assisi, Upper Church of S Francesco; *see* ASSISI, §II, 2) and in the scenes from the *History of Salvation* in the Arena Chapel; precedents of these internal grisailles can be found in Byzantine painting. They too are painted entirely in monochrome and thus, like the allegories, do not follow the usual polychrome appearance of contemporary sculpture. The stone colour clearly served to distinguish them from the painted living persons and to define them as of the same material as the painted architecture.

Surprisingly, few works produced in the following years of the fourteenth century have this sculptural character. The grisaille painted statues of prophets (?*c.* 1340) in the refectory of the abbey of Pomposa, near Ferrara, are an exception. Giotto's innovations were modififed in two ways: either figures presented in a sculptural manner were painted in colour, which made it unclear whether they were intended as painted statues or living beings, or the stone character of monochrome figures was relativized by showing them in non-sculptural and sometimes quite incongruous settings. Examples of the latter are Taddeo Gaddi's vault paintings (*c.* 1328) in the Baroncelli Chapel in Santa Croce, Florence, in which monochrome figures (also allegorical) float in fictitious openings in the ceiling in a quite unsculptural manner. Moreover, grisaille painting increasingly appeared only in thematically or formally subordinate areas and would thus have been considered inferior to polychrome painting, which was not true to the same extent of Giotto's relatively large allegories painted as a *trompe l'oeil*.

(iii) Manuscript illumination. French manuscript illumination established itself as another field for grisaille in the first half of the 14th century. The first surviving manuscript illuminated entirely in this technique is the Hours of Jeanne d'Evreux (New York, Cloisters, MS. 54.1.2; see fig. 1), attributed to the Paris illuminator Jean Pucelle (for further illustrations *see* GOTHIC, fig. 80, and PUCELLE, JEAN). The miniatures already show the distribution of colours that was to be adhered to in *camaïeu* painting throughout the 14th century: only the garments of the figures are monochrome grey, while the background and the (still relatively few) architectural and other backdrops have undergone varying degrees of colour treatment. Although the drawn architectural frames and the enamel-like backgrounds recall other genres (such as goldsmiths' work), suggesting a kind of media-specific context, the grisaille figures, unlike Italian monochrome paintings, were clearly intended from the outset not to seem made from a particular material such as marble or ivory. Rather, the many allusions to other, highly prized art forms lend the miniatures of this manuscript—and thus the technique of grisaille—an aura of extreme value and refinement. That grisaille retained this aura, so that the *camaïeu* technique became synonymous with something rare and precious, is shown by its further application in French manuscript painting: it was generally used only in first-class manuscripts often intended for the highest stratum of patrons, without any allusion to other media. The quality of its surface did not allow associations with particular materials. The modelling was produced solely by applying a more or less thinned black pigment with sparing white heightening.

Grisaille painting should not be confused with drawing: whereas drawings in the 14th century were either given a coloured wash or hatched, *camaïeu* modelling was applied with a fairly dry brush and rather dense pigment. Unlike drawing, which reproduces without colour a depiction that is in principle thought of as coloured as a kind of abbreviation or which unmistakably indicates the polychromy of the protagonists by delicate tinting, in the *camaïeu* image it is the figures that are in grisaille and are unavoidably seen in monochrome in contrast to their polychrome surroundings.

(iv) Other portable paintings. Grisaille was also used for 14th-century panel paintings, though far less frequently and only in special cases, as in two paintings with scenes from the *Apocalypse* produced in Naples (both *c.* 1340; Stuttgart, Staatsgal.). Although these works were not painted with grey, but rather with brownish pigments on white chalk priming, the manner of application and the effect are essentially the same as the techniques used for grisaille manuscript illumination. Although the monochrome protagonists and objects, enriched with gold and isolated coloured accents, are arranged in sculptural groups by small areas of ground before the deep-blue background, here too the aim was not to represent a particular material but to create a suggestion of preciousness and rarity *per se*.

1. Grisaille illustrations in the Hours of Jeanne d'Evreux, attributed to Jean Pucelle, folio size 90×60 mm, 1325–8 (New York, The Cloisters, MS. 54.1.2, fols 34*v*–35*r*)

Grisaille was given a somewhat different interpretation in works on cloth. Thus the *Parement de Narbonne* (*c.* 1375–80; Paris, Louvre; *see* GOTHIC, fig. 70), painted on silk exclusively in modulations of black, may have been a Lenten veil, so that its lack of colour is explained by its function. Here French *camaïeu* painting, usually regarded as having a positive value in itself, is reinterpreted as a deliberate renunciation of colour. However, merely the exquisite execution of such works suggests that grisaille was also chosen for aesthetic reasons and not only for ascetic ones.

2. FROM *c.* 1400. The 15th century, with its stylistic innovations, brought changed conditions for grisaille painting. This applies primarily to panel painting. In manuscript painting, despite the stylistic advances, the basic concept and meaning of grisaille were unchanged, though its status declined somewhat.

(i) Imitating stone and other materials. (ii) Other artistic aims.

(i) Imitating stone and other materials. In the Netherlands, in particular, the relatively new field of the winged altarpiece brought with it a reappraisal of monochrome in terms of form and content and an apparent return to Giotto's concept of 'stone painting'. Like the latter, Netherlandish grisaille appeared in two variants: as an autonomous sculptural image presented illusionistically on the outer faces of winged altars (i.e. in a similarly 'marginal' zone to the stone paintings of Italy) and as sculpture inserted into polychrome scenes. The so-called 'arch motif' has a special place: it is a painted architectural frame filled with statues, as in Rogier van der Weyden's altar of *St John* (after 1450; Berlin, Gemäldegal.), which was intended as an internal part of the picture but also had a mediating role with the beholder's reality and was thus brought closer to the autonomous sculptural image. The somewhat more illogical use of painted stone images on the outer sides of wooden altarpieces, as compared to their role in Giotto's frescoes, was counterbalanced by the perfect illusionistic rendering of their surface and their convincing presentation on socles and in niches. The earliest surviving examples are deliberately presented as statue images, as on the lower outer wings of Hubert and Jan van Eyck's Ghent Altarpiece (*c.* 1423–32; Ghent, St Bavo; see fig. 2); on the outer panel of the Master of Flémalle's *Marriage of the Virgin* (*c.* 1425; Madrid, Prado); on the outer wing of Jan van Eyck's triptych with the *Virgin and Child* (1437; Dresden, Gemäldegal. Alte Meister); and in his diptych with the *Annunciation* (*c.* 1435–40; Madrid, Mus. Thyssen-Bornemisza). Yet even in these cases—not unlike the situation in Italian monochrome painting—a disconcertingly living quality cannot be denied and has even given rise in the literature to the term 'living stones'; in extreme cases, this could entirely nullify the sculptural character of the grisaille figure.

As in the 14th century, two directions in the transformation of stone painting can be discerned: either the monochrome figures show a more or less unstatuesque agility in a context that is not expressly made for pieces of sculpture and may even be coloured; or (partly) coloured figures appear in monochrome surroundings or are presented in a deliberately sculptural way. One of the few examples of the last variant is the depiction of the prophet *Jeremiah* by the Master of the Aix Annunciation (1443–5; Brussels, Mus. A. Anc.), in which the fully coloured figure stands in a statuesque pose on a fictive stone plinth in a fictive stone niche (enriched with coloured objects), so that its sculptural quality is not quite lost despite its polychromy. Much more frequent, however, is the first variant; nearly monochrome figures were given a degree of life that blurred their character as creatures of stone. For example, in the *Annunciation* on the outer sides of the wings of the Bladelin Altarpiece (*c.* 1450; Berlin, Gemäldegal.) by Rogier van der Weyden, the frames have lost their character as niches and the figures their socles, so that there is no compelling association with sculpture, despite the stone-colour.

Between these two extremes there are various intermediate stages; monochrome figures presented in a sculptural context with only a hint of life are the most frequent. In addition, grisaille images with little resemblance to the appearance of stone and even somewhat reminiscent of the *peinture en camaïeu* of manuscript illumination were produced at a relatively early stage. Among the comparatively few examples of this variety are Rogier van der Weyden's *Crucifixion* diptych (*c.* 1450; Philadelphia, PA, Mus. A.) and the slightly later *Crucifixion* panel (*c.* 1455–6; Madrid, Escorial; *see* WEYDEN, VAN DER, (1), fig. 4). That it was themes of this kind that were painted *en camaïeu* appears to confirm the idea that the striking success achieved by grisaille in Netherlandish panel painting is to be explained at least in part by an almost liturgical use of 'ash colour', a use ultimately reserved for Lent. However, neither Italian stone painting nor French *camaïeu* painting admits such a negative interpretation, a fact that should be borne in mind in assessing Netherlandish statue images, and indeed recent scholarship has begun to distance itself from this somewhat one-sided view.

The Netherlandish variant of grisaille painting established itself in neighbouring France and Germany. French works tended towards a sculptural approach, as in the outer side of Simon Marmion's *St Bertin* altarpiece (*c.* 1454–9; Berlin, Gemäldegal.) or the outer sides of the wings of Nicolas Froment's triptych of *Moses* (1476; Aix-en-Provence Cathedral). In Germany examples of a fairly independent use of the technique appeared at an early stage, perhaps due to the hierarchy of genres prevalent there (real sculptures inside reliquaries, paintings on their outsides). The retable (*c.* 1450; Munich, Alte Pin.) by the Master of the Tegernsee Altar shows grisaille figures at the centre of the panel, flanked by monochrome saints presented in a sculptural manner and small grisaille-coloured statuettes in frames, the degree of life in the figures rising in inverse proportion to the use of colour. There were also in Germany, until well into the 16th century, depictions of statues on the outer sides of altarpiece wings. However, some of them are treated in an

2. Grisaille figures of *St John the Baptist* and *St John the Evangelist*, with the donors *Jodocus Vijd* and *Elisabeth Borluut*, detail of the lower outer wings of the Ghent Altarpiece by Hubert van Eyck, completed by Jan van Eyck, oil on panel, *c.* 1423–32 (Ghent, St Bavo)

extremely painterly and living manner, such as the saints in Matthias Grünewald's Heller Altarpiece (*c.* 1509; Frankfurt am Main, Städel. Kstinst. & Städt. Gal.), which are directly based on the Netherlandish tradition.

In Italy, too, the most diverse variants of monochrome painting can be traced in the 15th century. The primary opportunity for grisaille remained monumental wall painting. Grisaille is found in this medium and—though fairly infrequently—in paintings on panel and canvas. Examples of the use of grisaille to imitate sculpture are the painted monuments in Florence Cathedral showing *Sir John Hawkwood* and *Niccolò da Tolentino on Horseback*, executed by Paolo Uccello in 1436 and Andrea del Castagno in 1456 respectively (*see* UCCELLO, PAOLO, fig. 1, and CASTAGNO, ANDREA DEL, fig. 4) or Andrea Mantegna's fictive reliefs painted on small-format canvases, for example the *Sacrifice of Abraham* (*c.* 1490; Vienna, Ksthist. Mus.) or *Samson and Delilah* (late 1490s; London, N.G.; *see* MANTEGNA, ANDREA, fig. 6). In contrast, Parri Spinelli's *Crucifixion* fresco (1445) in the Palazzo Comunale at Arezzo or Andrea del Sarto's frescoes (*c.* 1523) in the Chiostro dello Scalzo in Florence show a purely painterly use of monochrome painting, as became more usual in the north, too, after 1500. Many of these works can no longer be read as depictions of statues, not only because the sculptural context, such as a niche, is lacking but because of the extreme spatial depth of their conception. In them, grisaille appears as a pure abstraction of form from colour, an autonomous artistic method without significance for the interpretation of the subject-matter.

Nevertheless, the explicit imitation of stone continued to play an important role, though one that was increasingly subordinate to polychrome painting. In the large fresco programmes of the 16th, 17th and 18th centuries it helped to spread illusionism to painting in colour; until that time it had essentially been confined to grisaille. Michelangelo's polychrome prophets and sibyls (1508–12) on the ceiling of the Sistine Chapel in Rome are placed between grisaille figures appearing like reliefs or caryatids on pilasters and are thrust by them into the beholder's space. The case is similar with Annibale Carracci's frescoes (1597–1600) of the Galleria of the Palazzo Farnese in Rome (*see* ITALY, fig. 36) or Paolo Veronese's wall paintings (1561–2) in the Villa Barbaro in Maser (*see* VERONESE, PAOLO, fig. 3, and ILLUSIONISM, colour pl. IV).

Even in easel paintings the imitation of sculpture enjoyed increasing popularity in the following centuries. It developed into a bravura piece with which artists—who often specialized in this kind of grisaille painting—achieved astonishing *trompe l'oeil* effects, as did Jacob de Wit in his oil painting of *Vertumnus and Pomona* (1752; Paris, Mus. A. Déc.) or Jean-Josèphe Delvigne (*fl c.* 1770) in his picture *The Bronze Serpent* (Paris, priv. col.). Grisaille was used not only to render stone illusionistically, it could even imitate other media such as prints, as in François-Xavier Vispré's *Wandering Musicians* (*c.* 1760–70; Dijon, Mus. B.-A.), which depicts a torn reproductive engraving under broken glass after a painting by Adriaen van Ostade. Despite their technical perfection, such works were mainly curiosities that could no longer match the astonishing prestige attained by grisaille painting in the 14th and 15th centuries.

(ii) Other artistic aims. Grisaille painting was also used for purposes other than imitating stone and other materials, though increasingly these were of a practical nature. For example, it was adopted for preparatory oil sketches that preceded finished (coloured) paintings by the same artist in order to clarify the distribution of light and shade, as in Federico Barocci's oil sketch (*c.* 1590; Oxford, Ashmolean) for the altarpiece of the *Virgin and Child with St Dominic* (the '*Madonna del Rosario*', finished *c.* 1593; Senigallia, Pal. Vescovile); it could also be used for the modello for a reproductive print to be executed by someone other than the author of the sketch: Rubens provided numerous such grisaille modelli, for instance the *Christ Carrying the Cross* (*c.* 1623; Berkeley, U. CA, A. Mus.). Acting as links between polychrome paintings and engravings, such monochrome oil sketches helped the engraver to translate the different colours into tonal values, as in Anthony van Dyck's oil sketch of *Carlo and Ubaldo See Rinaldo Conquered by Love for Armida* (*c.* 1634–5; London, N.G.; see fig. 3), with its squared grid for transfer clearly visible.

In the 19th century grisaille paintings were also used as preliminary studies for various book illustration techniques, such as photogravure and even photography, since it was recognized that coloured models did not produce the modulations of grey needed for black-and-white photography. An example is Thomas Eakins's oil painting of

3. Grisaille sketch by Anthony van Dyck: *Carlo and Ubaldo See Rinaldo Conquered by Love for Armida*, oil on panel, 572×416 mm, *c.* 1634–5 (London, National Gallery); modello for an engraving of 1644

the *Fairman Roger's Four-in-Hand* (1899; St Louis, MO, A. Mus.), which was intended to be photographed for a publication on carriage-driving. A similarly close connection with black-and-white photography, though of a quite different kind, is found in monochrome photorealistic paintings such as Chuck Close's monumental portrait of *Phil* (1969; New York, Whitney), which uses, and estranges, grisaille in an entirely new way as a media-orientated *trompe l'oeil*. Admittedly, such examples do not exhaust the important role played by monochrome painting in the 20th century. It is found in Picasso's key work *Guernica* (1937; Madrid, Cent. A. Reina Sofía; *see* HISTORY PAINTING, fig. 5) and in the works of the American post-war generation (e.g. Jasper Johns, Robert Rauschenberg and Frank Stella).

Used more than ever as an autonomous artistic method without any practical function, the technique of grisaille can throw light on the mental and spiritual state of the artist (not necessarily in a negative way) rather than on the qualities of the object depicted. It can no longer be described as the abstraction of form from colour, for often enough monochrome is at the same time abstract painting. It is thus a paradox: the abstraction of colour from colour and therefore the purest form of grisaille ever produced in Western art.

BIBLIOGRAPHY

L. de Laborde: *Glossaire français du moyen âge* (Paris, 1872), p. 191

N.-C. de Fabri de Peiresc: *Lettres à sa famille et principalement à son frère, 1602–1637*, vi (Paris, 1896), p. 173 [first known use of the term]

M. Teasdale Smith: 'The Use of Grisaille as Lenten Observance', *Marsyas*, viii (1959), pp. 43–54

S. Sulzberger: 'Notes sur la grisaille', *Gaz. B.-A.*, n. s. 5, lix (1962), pp. 119–20

K. Kraft: *Zum Problem der Grisaille-Malerei im italienischen trecento* (diss., Munich, Ludwig-Maximilians U., 1963)

M. Kozloff: 'The Many Colorations of Black and White', *Artforum*, xi (1964), pp. 22–5

P. Philippot: 'Les Grisailles et les "degrés de la réalité" de l'image dans la peinture flamande des 15e et 16e siècles', *Mus. Royaux B.-A. Belgique: Bull.*, xv (1966), pp. 225–42

D. Coekelberghs: 'Les Grisailles de van Eyck', *Gaz. B.-A.*, n. s. 5, lxxi (1968), pp. 79–92

——: 'Les Grisailles et le *trompe l'œil* dans l'œuvre de van Eyck et de van der Weyden', *Mélanges d'archéologie et d'histoire de l'art offert au professeur Jacques Lavalleye* (Leuven, 1970), pp. 21–34

A. Legner: *Polychrome und monochrome Skulptur in der Realität und im Abbild vor Stefan Lochner: Die Kölner Maler von 1300–1430. Ergebnisse des Kolloquiums und der Ausstellung* (Cologne, 1974), pp. 140–63

Gray is the Color: An Exhibition of Grisaille Painting, XIIIth–XXth Centuries (exh. cat., Houston, TX, Rice U. Inst. A., Rice Mus., 1974)

H. Jackson Zakin: *French Cistercian Grisaille Glass* (diss., New York, Syracuse U., 1977)

La Grisaille (exh. cat., Paris, Mus. A. & Ess., 1980)

M. Osterstrom Renger: 'The Netherlandish Grisaille Miniatures: Some Unexplored Aspects', *Wallraf-Richartz-Jb.*, xliv (1983), pp. 145–73

E. Ostländer: *Gemalte Plastik: Studien zur Rolle und Funktion der Skulptur in der französischen Malerei des 18. Jahrhunderts* (diss., U. Cologne, 1983)

M. Krieger: *Die Grisaillemalerei im Stundenbuch der Jeanne d'Evreux und ihre Bedeutung für das Entstehen der neuzeitlichen Kunstauffassung* (diss., U. Vienna, 1984)

M. Grams-Thieme: *Lebendige Steine: Studien zur niederländischen Grisaillemalerie des 15. und frühen 16. Jahrhunderts* (diss., U. Cologne, 1988)

R. Preimesberger: 'Zu Jan van Eycks Diptychon der Sammlung Thyssen-Bornemisza', *Z. Kstgesch.*, liv (1991), pp. 459–489

D. Täube: *Monochrom gemalte Plastik: Entwicklung, Verbreitung und Bedeutung eines Phänomens niederländischer Malerei der Gotik* (diss., Bonn, Rhein. Friedrich-Wilhelms-U., 1991)

T. Dittelbach: *Das monochrome Wandgemälde: Untersuchungen zum Kolorit des frühen 15. Jahrhunderts in Italien* (Hildesheim, Zürich and New York, 1993)

M. Krieger: *Grisaille als Metapher: Zum Entstehen der peinture en camaieu im frühen 14. Jahrhundert* (Vienna, 1995)

MICHAELA KRIEGER

Grisebach, Hans (*b* Göttingen, 26 June 1848; *d* Berlin, 11 May 1904). German architect. He started his architectural training at the Polytechnikum in Hannover in 1868. After the interruption of the Franco-Prussian War (1870–71) he completed his studies under the prominent Gothic Revival architects Conrad Wilhelm Hase in Hannover and Friedrich von Schmidt in Vienna before working (1876–9) under Johannes Otzen, another Gothic Revivalist, on his Bergkirche at Wiesbaden. In 1879 Grisebach embarked on tours of France, Spain and Italy, and on his return to Germany he settled in Berlin and set up his own practice, designing mainly private houses and commercial buildings. He received a number of commissions from the newly rich industrialists, for whom he designed large houses, for example the Villa Springmann (1890–91; destr.) at Elberfeld and the Villa Levin (1899–1900) at Michelstrasse 4, Göttingen. In these buildings he was influenced by English domestic design, the plan of Villa Springmann, for example, being an almost exact copy of an English country-house plan published in *Building News* in 1882. His commercial buildings, for example the rich Renaissance-style offices (1881–2) for the firm A. W. Faber on Friedrichstrasse, Berlin, and the Haus Fasskessel & Müntmann (1889–90) at Unter den Linden 12, Berlin, were seen by many as exemplary. Despite his Gothic Revival training, Grisebach's own style was mainly developed from German and Dutch Renaissance models. He used much sculpture and plastic ornament on his buildings in the manner of the Arts and Crafts Movement, often working with the sculptor Wilhelm Gieseke (1854–1917). Cornelius Gurlitt, the prominent 19th-century critic and art historian, saw Grisebach as a highly original designer who enlivened eclectic styles with his individual approach. From 1889 to 1901 Grisebach worked with the architect August Georg Dinklage (1844–1910). During his last years, he devoted himself to his book collection. The 2000 volumes, many of them source-books and illustrated books on architecture and architectural history, were acquired in 1908 for the library of the Kunstgewerbemuseum, Berlin.

BIBLIOGRAPHY

NDB; Thieme–Becker; Wasmuth

V. Hammerschmidt: *Anspruch und Ausdruck in der Architektur des späten Historismus in Deutschland, 1860–1914* (Frankfurt am Main, 1985)

B. Edle von Germersheim: *Unternehmervillen der Kaiserzeit, 1871–1914* (Munich, 1988)

□

Grisoni [Grifoni; Grison]**, Giuseppe** [Pierre Joseph] (*b* Mons; *bapt* 24 Oct 1699; *d* Rome, 1769). Italian painter and sculptor, of Flemish birth. He was first documented in Florence, where he studied under the painter Tommaso Redi. In 1715 he accompanied the amateur painter John Talmann (1677–1726) to London, where he became a portrait painter. Lacking success in London, he returned to Florence in 1728, became a teacher at the academy and remained there until 1740; after a short stay in Pisa he went to Rome. A great amount of his work can be found in Cambridge, London and Florence. Grisoni's *Self-portrait* (Florence, Uffizi) is realistic but fails creatively and is also badly designed. Grisoni's works are noted for the landscapes in the background of his portraits and historical subjects. His painting representing the *Death of St Romuald* (Florence, Uffizi) is a masterpiece of composition, design, colouring and painting, with a feeling for proportion. Grisoni abandoned his Flemish origins in favour of the Italian tradition, as is also shown in his statues, such as that of *St Joseph* (Florence, SS Anunziata).

BIBLIOGRAPHY

Thieme–Becker
P. Tonini: *Il Santuario della SS Annunziata di Firenze* (Florence, 1876)
F. R. Earp: *A Descriptive Catalogue of Pictures in the Fitzwilliam Museum* (Cambridge, 1902), pp. 83–4

IRIS KOCKELBERGH

Gritchenko, Alexis. *See* HRYSHCHENKO, OLEKSA.

Gritti, Andrea, Doge of Venice (*b* Bardolino, nr Verona, April 1455; *d* Venice, 28 Dec 1538). Italian statesman and patron. In his youth he accompanied his grandfather, Triadano Gritti, on journeys to England, France and Spain, and he studied in Padua. His first career was as a successful grain merchant based in Constantinople, where he also served as a diplomat and spy. In 1509 he led the Venetian forces in the recapture of Padua during the Wars of the League of Cambrai. Three years later he was imprisoned by the French at Brescia and taken to France, where he formed a friendship with Francis I. In 1517 he led the Venetians in their triumphal re-entry into Verona. Despite these wartime triumphs, Gritti's election as Doge of Venice on 20 May 1523 was not a popular one among the more powerful members of the patriciate. During his dogeship the Venetian constitution limited his personal power. Nevertheless, he was able to express his ambitious character through his imaginative patronage.

Titian, who recorded Gritti's likeness (*Andrea Gritti*, disputed date; Washington, DC, N.G.A.), first received his salary as official painter to the Venetian Republic in 1523. At the start of his reign Gritti also commissioned from Titian a fresco (*in situ*) of *St Christopher* with Venice in the background for the wall of the staircase to the ducal apartments in the Doge's Palace. In the same year Gritti witnessed the completion of the Doge's private chapel of S Nicolò rebuilt by Giorgio Spavento and decorated with a fresco (destr.) by Titian of the Doge himself as a donor figure before the Virgin and Child, St Nicholas and the four Evangelists (fragments, Venice, Doge's Palace, Sala della Quarantia Criminale). The chapel also housed a relief tabernacle by an unknown sculptor depicting *St Andrew Presenting Doge Gritti to SS Nicholas and Bernardino* (now Venice, S Marco, chapel of S Clemente).

Barbarigo claimed that Gritti had intended to extend the Doge's Palace on the far side of the Ponte della Paglia but was prevented by the outbreak of war against the Turks in 1537. Within the palace most of Gritti's efforts were concentrated on the part of the building where important visitors were received. In the anteroom between the staircase of the ducal apartments and the chapel of S Nicolò, Gritti installed the collection of antique sculpture bequeathed (1523) to the Republic by Cardinal Domenico Grimani. For the nearby Sala del Collegio, he commissioned an altarpiece (1531) by Titian, of the *Madonna and Child with SS Mark, Alvise (Louis), Marina and Bernardino* (destr. 1574, replaced with a new version by Tintoretto). For the large meeting-room (destr. 1577) in the wing over the Piazzetta, Gritti commissioned a coffered ceiling from Sebastiano Serlio in 1531, the compartments of which were painted (1532–8) by Pordenone.

In 1529 the Doge persuaded the Procurators of S Marco to employ Jacopo Sansovino as their *proto* (chief architect) and took a personal interest in his remodelling of the Piazza S Marco as a Roman-style forum from 1536 onwards. In 1534 Gritti laid the foundation stone of Sansovino's church of S Francesco della Vigna. The Gritti family palace was completely rebuilt during Gritti's reign. It consists of two corner blocks linked by an enclosed courtyard. The block opposite the church is dated 1525, while the block over the canal was begun about ten years later. The architect of this huge project is not known, but Antonio Scarpagnino may have been responsible.

Much of Gritti's personal wealth was spent on public projects. In 1525 he ordered a new ducal processional umbrella, and in 1532 he and his illegitimate son Alvise each anonymously donated the huge sum of 200,000 ducats towards the rebuilding of the Rialto Bridge. Such vast expenditure reduced his personal income to a mere $143\frac{1}{2}$ ducats at the time of his last tax return in 1537. Perhaps his most blatant attempt at self-glorification was the tapestry (Venice, Mus. S Marco) made in Flanders in 1532 for the high altar of S Marco, depicting the Lion of St Mark with Venice in the background and surrounded by trophies and symbols of his own achievements. Gritti presided over Venice's economic and political recovery after the Cambrai Wars, leaving potent symbols of the State's resurgence in the form of works of art.

BIBLIOGRAPHY

N. Barbarigo: *Vita di Andrea Gritti doge di Venezia* (Venice, 1793) [trans. by C. Volpi of 16th-century Latin text]
A. da Mosto: *I dogi di Venezia* (Venice, 1939), pp. 158–63
D. Howard: *Jacopo Sansovino: Architecture and Patronage in Renaissance Venice* (New Haven and London, 1975, rev. 1987)
S. Bettini and others: *Tiziano e Venezia: Convegno internazionale di studi: Venezia, 1976*
A. Olivieri: 'Capitale mercantile e commitenza nella Venezia del Sansovino', *Crit. Stor.*, xv/4 (1978), pp. 44–77
R. Finlay: *Politics in Renaissance Venice* (London and New Brunswick, 1980)
A. Foscari and M. Tafuri: *L'armonia e i conflitti: La chiesa di San Francesco della Vigna nella Venezia del '500* (Turin, 1983)
M. Tafuri, ed.: *'Renovatio urbis': Venezia nell'età di Andrea Gritti (1523–1538)* (Rome, 1984)

DEBORAH HOWARD

Grodno. *See* HORADNIA.

Groenesteyn, Anselm F(ranz) Ritter zu. *See* RITTER ZU GROENESTEYN, ANSELM F.

Groenewegen, Gerrit (*b* Rotterdam, 16 Dec 1754; *d* Rotterdam, 17 Aug 1826). Dutch printmaker, draughtsman, painter and wallpaper designer. Groenewegen spent nearly all his life near Rotterdam on the Westzee Dyke, which leads towards Delfshaven. Like his father he was a ship's carpenter, until he lost part of his right leg and was forced to take up another trade. He became an artist and began to make faithful representations of topographical subjects and shipping scenes. He found his subjects in Rotterdam as well as around Delfshaven, Schoonderloo,

Overschie and other neighbouring villages. Apart from paintings, he made wallpaper decorations, all with shipping as their subject-matter. From 1779 until his death he produced hundreds of drawings in gouache and watercolour or pen and ink, mostly of topographical subjects. For example, his prints comprise figures in traditional costume, a number of river and port views and the illustrations of ship types known as the *Collection of 84 Dutch Ships*, published in seven series between 1786 and 1801 by J. van den Brink in Rotterdam. The importance of these illustrations for Dutch maritime history is considerable, as they are faithful representations by an expert in shipping; moreover, captions on prints in their second state give the names by which the various types of ships were known. Most of Groenewegen's prints are etchings. He used the engraver's burin to strengthen shadows, while in a number of prints he successfully combined etching with aquatint. Seven paintings by him, including *View of the Marepoort, Leiden, from a Northerly Direction* (undated; Leiden, Stedelijk Mus. Lakenhal; related watercolour, Rotterdam, Boymans–van Beuningen), are known; these, like his wallpaper designs, all represent shipping scenes.

BIBLIOGRAPHY

Gerrit Groenewegen, tekenaar van Rotterdam, 1754–1626 (exh. cat., ed. P. Ratsma; Rotterdam, Gemeentelijke Archfdienst, 1976–7)

P. Ratsma: 'De Rotterdamse tekenaar Gerrit Groenewegen', *Rotterdam. Jb.*, xxxi (1977), pp. 153–80

——: 'Het topografische tekenwerk van Gerrit Groenewegen', *Holland* (Feb 1978), pp. 17–31

CHRISTIAAN SCHUCKMAN

Groenewegen, J. H. (*b* 24 June 1901; *d* Amsterdam, 7 March 1959). Dutch architect and writer. After studying at the School voor Bouwkunde in Haarlem, he worked in the office of Joseph Cuypers from 1924 to 1925 and thereafter independently. He was a founder-member of the Functionalist ARCHITECTENGROEP DE 8 in Amsterdam in 1927 and as such was one of the pioneers of *Nieuwe Bouwen* (Dut.: new building) in the Netherlands. From 1927 to *c.* 1935 he worked in the typical Functionalist idiom developed by such pioneers as Johannes Duiker and Brinkmann & vander Vlugt, producing concrete skeleton buildings with severe geometrical architectural spaces, white façades, much glass, particularly ribbon windows, and flat roofs. The influence of these architects appears in his most important works from this period, such as the competition design (1927; with Ben Merkelbach; unexecuted) for a water-tower in Wassenaar, the Montessori School (1930), Huizen, and the Quinine Factory (1931), Amsterdam. Functionalist concepts, such as the 'minimum' and terraced housing, also predominate in a winning competition design (1934; with Alexander Bodon, Charles Karsten and Merkelbach; unexecuted) for cheap housing for workers. Towards the end of this 'severe' period Groenewegen developed a more pragmatic Functionalism, in which there was room for some formal freedom, for example the rounded building forms in the extension (1932) of the Quinine Factory, Amsterdam. He also adopted a freer use of materials, particularly the use of more wood and brick, as in the country house (1934) in Huizen. In 1935 and 1938–42 he was an editor of the periodical *De 8 en Opbouw*. He continued building in a Functionalist style for the remainder of his career, completing a large number of commercial projects.

WRITINGS

Regular contributions to *De 8 & Opbouw* (1932–42)

BIBLIOGRAPHY

G. Fanelli: *Architettura moderna* (1968)

B. Rebel: *Het Nieuwe Bouwen* (Amsterdam, 1983)

Het Nieuwe Bouwen: Amsterdam, 1920–1960 (exh. cat., ed. K. Bosma and others; Amsterdam, Stedel. Mus., 1983)

J. P. BAETEN

Grof [Groff], **Guillielmus** [Wilhelm] **de** (*b* Antwerp, *bapt* 13 Nov 1676; *d* Munich, 16 Aug 1742). Flemish sculptor and draughtsman, active in France and Germany. He was first apprenticed to Frans Bedeloo (*fl* 1663–94) in Antwerp and continued his training in Paris, where he is believed to have entered the service of the French court around 1708. His first confirmed work is a lavish, small-scale equestrian statue of *Maximilian II Emanuel, Elector of Bavaria* (1714; Munich, Bayer. Nmus.), then living in exile in Paris. De Grof produced two drawings (*c.* 1713–14; Düsseldorf, Kstmus.) for another statue of *Maximilian II Emanuel*. In 1716, after the return to power of Maximilian Emanuel, he moved to Munich, where a foundry had already been fitted out for him; he became court sculptor, receiving a remarkably high wage. His chief duty was to produce garden sculptures in gilded lead (all untraced) for the gardens of Nymphenburg and Schleissheim palaces; among them were a *Flora* fountain and 16 large vases for the parterre at Nymphenburg (from 1717), as well as 14 groups of putti (allegorical representations of months and continents) for the waterfall there (before 1736–8). An impression of the highly plastic quality of de Grof's lead sculpture can be obtained from two fountain

Guillielmus de Grof: votive statue of *Maximilian Joseph*, silver, h. 940 mm, 1737 (Altötting, Heilige Kapelle)

groups (1722) in the hall of the Badenburg pavilion in the Nymphenburg gardens and the two wall fountains (1729), commissioned by Elector Clemens August of Cologne, in the dining hall of Schloss Augustusburg in Brühl.

Outstandingly fine among de Grof's works are the alcove fountain (gilded bronze and silver, 1717; Munich, Bayer. Nmus.) for the Elector's cabinet of the Residenz, Munich; the life-size votive statue of the Elector's heir *Maximilian Joseph* (silver, 1737; *in situ*; see fig.) for the Heilige Kapelle, Altötting; and the funerary monument for three bishops of the Schenk von Castell family, with one recumbent figure and two portrait busts in bronze (1731; Eichstätt Cathedral). De Grof also produced outstanding ornamental bronze objects, such as mounts for furniture, andirons and stoups. He occasionally produced sculptures in marble, such as the *Neptune* at Nymphenburg (1737), and even stucco ceilings (stair-well at Dachau, Schloss Dachau, 1716–17). He also worked in silver, and several drawings exist that are known to be by him. De Grof's manner combines the court style of Louis XIV with the Flemish Baroque tradition; this is particularly noticeable in his numerous putti. It was precisely with these that he influenced the development of sculpture in Bavaria. His lead sculpture provided a decisive stimulus for Georg Raphael Donner and consequently for the development of sculpture in Vienna also.

De Grof's son, Charles de Grof (1712/13–1774) was also a court sculptor in Munich.

BIBLIOGRAPHY

P. Volk: *Guillielmus de Grof (1676–1742): Studien zur Plastik am kurbayrischen Hof im 18. Jahrhundert* (Witterschlick, 1966)
——: 'Darstellungen Ludwigs XIV. auf steigendem Pferd', *Wallraf-Richartz-Jb.*, xxviii (1966), pp. 61–90
——: 'Zur Geschichte der Nymphenburger Gartenplastik, 1716–1770', *Münchn. Jb. Bild. Kst*, xviii (1967), pp. 211–40
——: 'Ein Wandbrunnen von Guillielmus de Grof im Badischen Landesmuseum Karlsruhe', *Jb. Staatl. Kstsamml. Baden-Württemberg*, vi (1969), pp. 147–60
——: 'Bronze- und Bleiplastik am Hof Max Emanuels', *Kurfürst Max Emanuel: Bayern und Europa um 1700* (exh. cat., ed. H. Glaser; Schleissheim, Neues Schloss, 1976), i, pp. 239–39
——: 'Georg Raphael Donner und München', *Akten des XXV. Internationalen Kongresses für Kunstgeschichte: Wien 1983*, vii, pp. 131–4

PETER VOLK

Grohar, Ivan (*b* Spodnja Sorica, 15 June 1867; *d* Ljubljana, 19 April 1911). Slovenian painter. He studied for three years at the Graz School of Painting under the Slovenian painter M. Bredaška and the Italian painter N. Milanesi. In 1896 he studied at the Ažbé School in Munich, where he was influenced by Franz von Defregger (1835–1921) and Arnold Böcklin. After 1902 he evolved towards Impressionism and with other Yugoslav painters tried to develop a distinctly Slovenian version of modern art. His first works in this period were in Late Romanesque and Secession style and were visibly influenced by the North Italian painter Giovanni Segantini, especially his pantheistic landscapes and firm brushwork.

Between 1905 and 1907 Grohar's Impressionism was at its height; he was engrossed in the study of the optical problems of light and colour, particularly under specific climatic conditions such as snow and mist, creating a few subjective, lyrically transformed images of the Slovenian landscape. After 1909 his brushstroke broadened again, his scenes acquiring a monumental structure that was most often achieved by triangular composition. He attempted to elevate peasant work to the level of a symbol signifying eternal glorification of human work on earth, as in the *Sower* (1907) or the *Shepherd* (1910–11; both Ljubljana, Gal. Mod. A.).

BIBLIOGRAPHY

A. Podbevšek: *Ivan Grohar* (Ljubljana, 1937)
F. Stele: *Ivan Grohar* (Ljubljana, 1960)
M. Stele-Možina: *Ivan Grohar* (Ljubljana, 1962)
J. Kajzer: *The Larch* (Ljubljana, 1978) [biog. novel on the artist]

JURE MIKUŽ

Grohé, Guillaume (*b* Wintersheim, Grand Duchy of Hesse-Darmstadt [now Hessen], 9 Feb 1808; *d* Neuilly-sur-Seine, 6 April 1885). German furniture-maker, active in France. He came to Paris *c.* 1827 with his older brother, Jean-Michel Grohé (*b* 1804), and became a journeyman. In 1829 the brothers started manufacturing and selling furniture. Their business developed rapidly as demonstrated by their success at the eighth Exposition de l'Industrie (Paris, 1834) where they showed Egyptian- and Gothic-style furniture. At the tenth Exposition de l'Industrie, in 1844, they won a gold medal with an octagonal ebony *dressoir* (design, Paris, Mus. A. Déc.), decorated with sculpted figures designed by Michel-Joseph-Napoléon Liénard (1810–*c.* 1875). In 1862 Guillaume Grohé showed at the International Exhibition, London, where he won a medal with a piece in the Louis XVI style, decorated with chased bronze sculpture by the brothers François-Auguste Fannière (1818–1900) and François-Joseph-Louis Fannière (1822–97). One of the principal furniture-makers of his period, he built a reputation as a specialist in high-quality, 18th-century French reproduction furniture (buffet, *c.* 1845; Chantilly, Mus. Condé) and supplied furniture to Queen Victoria, Louis-Philippe, Napoleon III and his wife, the Empress Eugénie. An article in *Le Figaro* (Jan 1884) deemed him a worthy successor to André-Charles Boulle, Pierre Gouthière and Jean-Henri Riesener.

BIBLIOGRAPHY

D. Ledoux-Lebard: *Le Mobilier français du XIXe siècle, 1795–1889: Dictionnaire des ébénistes et des menuisiers* (Paris, 1984, rev. 2/1989)

□

Grohmann, Will (*b* Bautzen, Saxony, 4 Dec 1887; *d* Berlin, 6 May 1968). German art historian. Although he had received a conventional classical education at the Kreuzschule in Dresden and was awarded a DPhil by the Universität Leipzig in 1913 for a dissertation on 18th-century German drama, he was drawn to the study of art by exhibitions of painting by Die Brücke in Dresden in 1907 and 1910. Personal contact with this group and, through his association with the Bauhaus, with Vasily Kandinsky, Paul Klee and Oskar Schlemmer led to early publications on Kandinsky (1924), Ernst Ludwig Kirchner (1925 and 1926) and Klee (1929). Identified as hostile to the Nazi regime, Grohmann was debarred from gainful employment in 1933, and the first volume of his major study of Paul Klee's drawings, published in 1934, was confiscated. His publications resumed only following his migration to West Germany after World War II and his appointment in 1948 as professor of the history of art at the Hochschule für Bildende Künste in Berlin. He then earned an international reputation with his definitive monographs on Kandinsky, Klee, Kirchner and Karl Schmidt-Rottluff and his support for the younger generation of German and Swiss artists. Grohmann played a major role, partly through his prefaces to catalogues of exhibitions at the Marlborough Galleries in London, in introducing some of the outstanding exponents of 20th-century art to a wider public.

WRITINGS

Wassily Kandinsky (Leipzig, 1924)
Zeichnungen von Ernst Ludwig Kirchner (Dresden, 1925)
Das Werk Ernst Ludwig Kirchners (Munich, 1926)
Paul Klee (Paris, 1929)
Paul Klee: Handzeichnungen, 1921–1930 (Berlin, 1934, 2/1949; Eng. trans., New York, 1944)
Paul Klee (Stuttgart, 1954, 4/1965; Eng. trans., London, 1958)
ed.: *Paul Klee, 1879–1940* (Munich, Vienna and Basel, 1955; Eng. trans., New York, 1957)
Wassily Kandinsky: Farben und Klänge, i: *Aquarelle* (Baden-Baden, 1955)
Expressionisten (Munich, Vienna and Basel, 1956)
Karl Schmidt-Rottluff (Stuttgart, 1956)
Paul Klee (1879–1940) (London, 1957)
E. L. Kirchner (Stuttgart, 1958; Eng. trans., London, 1961)
Wassily Kandinsky: Leben und Werk (Cologne, 1958; Eng. trans., London, 1959)
ed.: *Paul Klee: Handzeichnungen* (Cologne, 1959; Eng. trans., London, 1960)
ed.: *Painters of the Bauhaus* (exh. cat., London, Marlborough F.A., 1962)
Willi Baumeister: Leben und Werk (Cologne, 1963)
ed.: *Oskar Schlemmer: Zeichnungen und Graphik* (Stuttgart, 1965)
ed.: *Kandinsky and his Friends* (exh. cat., London, Marlborough F.A., 1966)
Der Maler Paul Klee (Cologne, 1966, Eng. trans., London, 1967)

BIBLIOGRAPHY

K. Gutbrod, ed.: *Lieber Freund: Künstler schreiben an Will Grohmann* (Cologne, 1968)
K. von Maur, ed.: *In memoriam Will Grohmann: Wegbereiter der Kunst, 1887–1968* (Stuttgart, 1988) [incl. comprehensive writings list and bibliog.]

N. A. FURNESS

Grolier [Grollier], **Jean**, Vicomte d'Agnisy (*b* Lyon, 1479; *d* Paris, 22 Oct 1565). French official and collector. After receiving a classical education in Paris, he was made a general by Francis I during the war against Milan. On his return to France he was appointed treasurer (from *c.* 1501) before returning to Italy as envoy to Pope Clement VII. During his time in Rome he surrounded himself with scholars and literary figures and acquired a vast number of bronzes, medals, illuminated manuscripts and books, forming the most important private collection in France. He had all his books given his own characteristic binding, which was extremely beautiful (*see* BOOKBINDING, fig. 5). The remains of his library, which was compared to that of the ancient Roman Gaius Asinius Pollio (76 BC–AD 4), were sold in 1675, while his collection of medals was acquired by Louis XIV. He was buried in the church of St Germain-des-Prés, Paris.

BIBLIOGRAPHY

Pernelti: *Les Lyonnais dignés de memoire*, 2 vols (1757)

□

Gromaire, Marcel (*b* Noyelles-sur-Sambre, Nord, 24 July 1892; *d*?Paris, 11 April 1971). French painter and designer. He was set to follow a legal career and received little formal artistic training. From 1910, however, he frequented the studios of Montparnasse, assimilating Matisse's style through tuition from Henri Le Fauconnier at the Académie de la Palette and from Félix Vallotton at the Académie Ranson. He exhibited six canvases at the Salon des Indépendants of 1911. He continued to draw while serving in the Army from 1913 to 1919 but was wounded on the Somme in 1916. From 1919 he devoted himself to painting and to writing about art and the cinema. His post-war paintings were marked by an admiration for the Flemish and to a lesser extent German Expressionists and for the work of Fernand Léger, although Gromaire later repudiated the Expressionist label. From 1920 he exhibited regularly at the Salon d'Automne and at the Salon des Indépendants and in 1921 held his first one-man show at the Galerie La Licorne in Paris; the gallery's owner, Maurice Girardin, to whom he was contracted between 1920 and 1932, later donated his collection of Gromaire's work to the Musée d'Art Moderne de la Ville de Paris. Wider recognition of his art was signalled in 1925 by the publication of the first monograph on him and by the controversy aroused by *War* (1925; Paris, Mus. A. Mod. Ville Paris) on its exhibition at the Salon des Indépendants.

Gromaire was particularly productive in the late 1920s, when he achieved a new sensuality in his work. In the 1930s he played an active part in the artistic and political struggles against Fascism. In 1937 he produced a frieze for the Sèvres Pavilion at the Exposition Universelle in Paris, the first of numerous public mural commissions, followed in 1938 by his first tapestry. In 1939, together with Jean Lurçat, he founded the Ecole d'Aubusson, dedicated to the teaching of tapestry technique and restoration, by means of which they helped to revitalize the tapestry industry. After World War II the forms in Gromaire's paintings became more splintered, partly as a result of his work in stained glass, and he was active in the debate between realism and abstraction.

Gromaire's characteristic subjects were landscapes, cityscapes, nudes and celebrations of peasant and urban working-class life; the latter became a particular interest after a visit to the USA in 1950, where he also produced city views such as *New York, Central Park* (1951; Paris, Pompidou). He was never an official member of the Communist party, but his mature work was fired by profound Socialist convictions and by an almost mystical belief in a truly humanist art in which aesthetics and ethics were inextricably linked. Using deep and rich colours in his paintings, he endowed the human form with considerable monumental dignity.

PUBLISHED WRITINGS

L'Art moderne (1919)
Notes sur l'art d'aujourd'hui (1919)

BIBLIOGRAPHY

J. Cassou: *Marcel Gromaire* (Paris, 1925)
W. George: *Gromaire* (Paris, 1928)
M. Zahar: *Gromaire* (Geneva, 1961)
Marcel Gromaire (exh. cat. by J. Cassou, Paris, Mus. A. Mod. Ville Paris, 1963)
Marcel Gromaire, 1892–1971 (exh. cat., ed. M.-O. Briot; Paris, Mus. A. Mod. Ville Paris, 1980)
L'Oeuvre gravé [de] Marcel Gromaire, 1892–1971 (exh. cat., Gravelines, Mus. Arsenale, 1980)

MONICA BOHM-DUCHEN

Grøningen, Gert [Giert] **van** (*fl* c. 1564–86). Danish sculptor of Dutch birth. His earliest activity as a sculptor is represented by a series of some 87 tomb slabs and funerary monuments produced for the North Jutland nobility by a workshop with which he was probably associated. Stylistic characteristics common to these are the use of hard grey or yellow limestone, and the precision of the chiselling and lettering. The tomb slab in the church at Aalsø, near Grenå, for *Nils Krabbe til Hessel* (*d* 1564) and his wife *Anne Urup* (*d* 1568) is the earliest tomb carving associated with Grøningen; in it the crisp chiselling of the figures, the symbols of the Evangelists and the coats of arms, as well as the female figure's distinctive pose with arms crossed, are the hallmarks of his work. They are evident also in the tomb of *Christen and Peder Skram* (1579) in the parish church of Østbirk, near Skandeborg; the sculptor introduced motifs from Northern Renaissance architectural designs into the frame around the figures. Grøningen's most classical tomb design is the epitaph and alcove tomb (Uth Church, nr Vejle) for *Holger Rosenkrantz* (*d* 1575) and his wives *Mette Krognos* (*d* 1558) and *Karin Gyldenstjerne*, in which he introduced Italianate architectural forms into the pedimented portal design of the tomb.

Documents show that around 1573–6 Grøningen was in the service of Frederick II of Denmark and Norway, working as a stone-carver under the direction of Hans Hendrik van Paesschen, on works for Kronborg Castle, Helsingør. His *Rosenkrantz* tomb design may have been the prototype for a portal commissioned by the King in 1573 for Skanderborg Castle near Århus and now in Kronborg Castle. In the same period Grøningen was paid 30 daler for the tomb of *Borge Skram* in the church of Frederiksborg Castle, Hillerød. He is last recorded in 1576. His influence in the Skåne region of Sweden is evident in the tomb (Helsingborg, St Maria), by a local stonemason, of *Sten Bille til Vanås* (*d* 1586) and his wife *Kristine Lindenow* (*d* 1612); its design and figure types refer to Grøningen's *Krabbe* tomb.

BIBLIOGRAPHY

Thieme–Becker

E. Lassen, ed.: *Dansk kunst historie billedkunst og skulptur: Rigets maend lader sig male 1500–1750* [History of Danish art, painting and sculpture: portraits of statesmen] (Copenhagen, 1973), pp. 54–61

ANTONIA BOSTRÖM

Groningen [Gronningen], **Johan van** [Johann von] [Snitker, Johan] (*fl* 1565; *d* Husum, Schleswig-Holstein, 5 July 1606). Sculptor and wood-carver, probably of Netherlandish origin, active in Germany. In 1565 and 1568 he made oak pulpits for the Gasthaus zum Ritter church of St Jürgen in Husum and for the church in Mildstedt. These pulpits are hexagonal in form and richly decorated with Renaissance motifs. The door that forms part of the pulpit in Husum is also lavishly decorated, having a wooden rail of pilasters with heads of children on the capitals and, on the frieze, mythical creatures with cartouches. In 1575 van Groningen made a decorative rail for an organ that Duke Adolf of Holstein-Gottorp (1526–82) and his wife had commissioned from the Schleswig organ builder Goos for the Marienkirche in Husum. Of this organ, four pilasters remain (Husum, Nissenhaus–Nordfries. Mus.). The church at Pellworm houses the epitaph that van Groningen made for *Thomas Elersen*: a panel depicting the *Crucifixion* is framed by wooden columns; God the Father is represented at the top of the frieze; fragments of polychrome painting are still visible. Van Groningen almost certainly had a hand in the decoration of the new castle that the Duke Adolf built between 1567 and 1582 on the site of the abbey at Husum; he probably entered the Duke's service in 1582, remaining in it for 22 years. It is not clear whether he was in any way related to Hendrik van Groningen (*fl* 1563), a sculptor of Netherlandish origin, about whom all that is known is that he probably worked in Hadersleben in Schleswig-Holstein *c.* 1563.

BIBLIOGRAPHY

E. Sauermann: *Handwerkliche Schnitzeren des 16. und 17. Jahrhundert aus Schleswig-Holstein* (Frankfurt am Main, 1910)

H. Brauer, W. Scheffler and H. Weber: *Die Kunstdenkmäler des Kreises Husum* (Berlin, 1939), pp. 127–36

G. Dehio: *Hamburg, Schleswig-Holstein*, Hb. Dt. Kstdkml. (1971), pp. 233, 251, 280, 466, 502, 508, 602

P. Hirschfeld: *Herrenhäuser und Schlösser in Schleswig-Holstein* (Horw, 1973)

M. J. T. M. STOMPE

Gröninger. German family of sculptors. They worked in Münster and Paderborn and were the leading Westphalian sculptors of the 17th century and the early 18th. The family was originally from Groningen in the Netherlands but settled in Paderborn after the sculptor Gerdt Gröninger (*d* before 1604) acquired citizenship there in 1578.

(1) Heinrich Gröninger (*b* Paderborn, *c.* 1578; *d* Paderborn, 6 Nov 1631). He lived in Paderborn, where he was probably apprenticed to his father, Gerdt Gröninger. Most of Heinrich's work consisted of stone monuments and religious statues for Paderborn Cathedral. These included the tomb of *Heinrich von Meschede* (*d* 1598), made in 1600; the Apostle statues (1608–9) in the nave; numerous monuments (1613–25) in the cloister; the monumental *St Christopher* (1619) in the transept; and a monument to *Anna Katharina von Nassau-Wiesbaden* (*d* 1622; untraced). His greatest work was the huge funerary monument to *Prince-Bishop Dietrich von Fürstenberg* (*d* 1618) in the transept. The life-size statue of the donor kneels in prayer on a ledge projecting from the wall monument and gazes upon a crucifix held aloft by an angel. Behind, dozens of figures and a wealth of armorial and ornamental carvings are set into a four-tiered architectural frame. The mannered profusion of decoration, the exaggerated poses and the overall design of the monument recall those of an earlier date in the Braunschweig–Hildesheim area. Some of his figures derive from Netherlandish prints.

(2) Gerhard Gröninger (*b* Paderborn, *c.* 1582; *d* ?Münster, 1652). Brother of (1) Heinrich Gröninger. He received some training from his father and brother before travelling to the southern Netherlands (?Antwerp). In 1609 he settled in Münster and married a daughter of the local sculptor Hans Lacke (*fl* 1569–1618). Gerhard enjoyed immediate success as he received numerous commissions for monuments and other religious carvings, mostly for Münster Cathedral. Between 1612 and 1618 he supplied statues for the octagonal Wasserschloss at Darfeld. Legal and financial problems resulted in his bankruptcy in 1636 and exile from Münster in 1639 together with his wife and their eight children. Gerhard was in

Gerhard Gröninger: *Stephanus* altar (monument to *Heidenreich von Lethmathe*), Baumberg sandstone, *c.* 1630 (Münster Cathedral)

Rheine in 1641–2 and, from 1645 to 1649, in Nijmegen in the Netherlands. While in Nijmegen he collaborated with Symon Bosboom (*fl* 1614–62), the German-born architect, on the orphanage; Gerhard carved the portal with sandstone statues of two orphans. The sculptor also made the large sandstone coat of arms on the *Nijmegen Belvedere* in 1647.

Gerhard's remarkable inventiveness was already evident in his sandstone monument to *Wennemar von Aschebrock* (1609; Münster Cathedral). A large *Flagellation of Christ* is represented above the imaginative reclining portrait of the donor, who appears to be transported heavenwards by the surrounding angels. The free-standing column projects both outwards and upwards so that, despite the other decorative features, the focus of the monument is clearly on the column and the athletic figure of Christ, who strains at the ropes that bind his arms. Although he based the poses of Christ, with its strong contrapposto, and the two flanking tormentors on an engraving by Marten van Heemskerck, the sculptor created his own highly charged composition.

Gerhard probably carved the sandstone *St Mauritius* (1613), a gift of deacon Heinrich von Galen, which was placed in the ambulatory of Münster Cathedral. As in his previous work, the sculptor exaggerated the pose and focused on both the classical armour and the colour contrasts of the saint's rich black skin with his golden armour. Gerhard's interest in exotic sensuality has parallels in the work of Hendrick Goltzius, Bartholomäus Spranger and other Netherlandish Mannerists.

In 1619 the cathedral chapter commissioned Gerhard to make a new high altar. His drawing shows an elaborate reliquary altar with the enthroned Virgin and Child surrounded by standing Apostles and, above, busts of saints. The wings were to have been painted by Rubens but were ultimately done by Adrian van den Bogart. Of Gerhard's carvings, which were finished in 1622, little remains other than the tall (1.95×1.30 m) limewood reliefs with scenes from the *Life of St Paul*, the patron of the cathedral.

Gerhard created the sandstone *Stephanus* altar (or monument to *Heidenreich von Lethmathe* (*d* 1625)), his best-known work, about 1630 (see fig.). The strong architectural frame controls the wealth of statues and reliefs that are spread over five vertically arranged zones. As in the monument to *Wennemar von Aschebrock*, the deceased donor lies immediately beneath the principal scene, which here is the *Ecce homo*. Gerhard's figures are slightly less elongated and physically more substantial than in the monument of 1609. By various devices Gerhard involved the spectator in the action of the scene. He restricted the number of figures to Christ, Pilate and three soldiers, two of whom direct our attention back to Christ. These near life-size, free-standing statues are positioned just above the viewer. Their physical presence and dramatic bearing, heightened by the polychromy, create an emotional situation in which the viewer suddenly finds himself among the audience Pilate asks to determine Christ's fate. In addition to numerous other sculptures that Gerhard made for Münster Cathedral, he carved various religious reliefs and statuettes for private patrons and for regional churches. Although little is known about his activities after 1636, he asserted a strong stylistic influence on later Westphalian sculptors.

(3) Dietrich (Theodor) Gröninger (*b* ?Münster, *c.* 1618; *d* Paderborn, *c.* 1667). Son of (2) Gerhard Gröninger. He trained with his father in Münster and moved *c.* 1650 to Paderborn. He worked primarily for the Jesuits in Paderborn and Cöesfeld. Johann Wilhelm von Sintzig, the provost of Paderborn Cathedral, commissioned the busts of *St Francis Xavier* (1660; destr.), *St Ignatius* (1660) and *St Francis Borgia* (1662) for the local Jesuit church of St Franz Xaver (both Paderborn, Diözmus. & Domschatzkam.). Using limewood, Dietrich subtly modelled each head by emphasizing the facial musculature and the fine detailing of the hair and beard. Originally these busts were covered with silver. A slightly earlier polychromed reliquary bust of *St Carlo Borromeo* can be seen in the Westfälisches Landesmuseum, Münster. Dietrich is also documented as having carved the high altar for the parish church at Brilon, south of Paderborn, in 1655. Besides his son (4) Johann Mauritz, Dietrich's daughter Gertrud Gröninger (*c.* 1650–1722) was active as a sculptor in Paderborn.

(4) Johann Mauritz Gröninger (*b* Paderborn, *c.* 1652; *d* Münster, 21 Sept 1707). Son of (3) Dietrich Gröninger. He attended the local Jesuit school between 1662 and

Johann Mauritz Gröninger: *Virgin and Child*, sandstone, 1675 (Münster Cathedral)

1667 and probably received his initial training as a sculptor from his father. The strong Netherlandish influence on his work suggests that he may have been associated with the Antwerp artist Ludovicus Willemsen, who, between 1655 and 1661/2, built the high altar and two choir altars in Paderborn Cathedral. He probably also went to the Low Countries and saw works by Jerome Duquesnoy and Artus Quellinus. From 1674 until his death, he served as court sculptor to Prince-Bishop Christoph Bernhard von Galen in Münster. Most of his sculptures were for Münster Cathedral or for such churches as the Jesuitenkirche (Gymnasialkirche), Cöesfeld, patronized by the Bishop von Galen and his successors. Johann Mauritz collaborated with the architect Ambrosius von Oelde on commissions for the Fürstenberg family at Adolfsburg, with the stone tomb of *Friedrich von Fürstenberg* (*c.* 1680) in St Laurentius, Arnsburg, and carvings for Schloss Herdringen (*c.* 1680) and Schloss Schellenberg (*c.* 1686). He also worked on a stone high altar (1695) for the monastery church of Lamspringe, a stone *Crucifixion* altar (1701–3) for Trier Cathedral and a stone monument for Mainz Cathedral.

In 1674 Johann Mauritz began the redecoration of the choir of Münster Cathedral in the Baroque style. His most striking contributions are the sandstone figures of *Joseph and the Christ Child* and the *Virgin and Child* (the *Vision of the Cross*) of 1675. Each group is set on a cartouche-decorated console within a shallow niche. Joseph gently holds Christ's hand as the Infant takes his first steps. The positioning of Christ between Joseph's legs stresses the latter's role as protector. Johann Mauritz created wonderful contrasts in form and texture between the billowing folds of Joseph's garment and Christ's nudity. A similar juxtaposition occurs in the *Virgin and Child* (see fig.), although Mary's more particularly rendered dress and cloak reveal more of the shape of her body. These early sculptures are typical of Johann Mauritz's finest work, for, as Jászai (1979) noted, he stressed the figure's natural physical plasticity together with the emotional content of the subject.

In spite of the richness of its trophies, arms and secondary decoration, the tomb of *Prince-Bishop Christoph Bernhard von Galen* (1674–8) in the Josephskapelle retains the same simple clarity of the choir statues. The donor, dressed in his episcopal robes, kneels in prayer before the crucifix held by a single angel. While this motif was used by other artists, including his great-uncle Heinrich Gröninger 60 years earlier at Paderborn, Johann Mauritz placed a new emphasis on the realistic portrayal of the bishop. The white alabaster carvings, highlighted with gold paint, stand out distinctly against the black stone frame of the tomb.

Johann Mauritz enjoyed success throughout his career. Between 1700 and his death he carved the *Crucifixion* altar (1701–3) in Trier Cathedral, the monument to *Heinrich Ferdinand von der Leyen* (*d* 1714) of 1706 in Mainz Cathedral and six monumental alabaster reliefs of *Christ's Passion* (1702–6) and the tomb of *Prince-Bishop Friedrich Christian von Plettenberg* (*d* 1706) of 1706 for the choir of Münster Cathedral.

(5) Johann Wilhelm Gröninger (*b c.* 1675; *d* Billerbeck, 1724). Son of (4) Johann Mauritz Gröninger. He was active in Münster and its diocese. Following his *Wanderjahre*, he returned to Münster in 1701 to assist his father, who was also his teacher. For Münster Cathedral he carved the sandstone statues of *St Apollonia* and *St Barbara* (1708–10), and a few years later the monument to *Ferdinand von Plettenberg* (*d* 1712). The latter, with its dramatic *Agony in the Garden*, which places three free-standing statues against a background relief, is based on a drawing (Münster, Westfäl. Landesmus.) by Gottfried Laurenz Pictorius. Perhaps as early as 1710 he moved to the nearby town of Billerbeck, where he carved and signed the *Pietà* (1715) and the *Paulus* altar (1719) for the Johanniskirche.

In addition to his numerous religious statues, Johann Wilhelm also sculpted portraits. The signed *Hüchtenbruch* monument (1716/17) in the Schlosskapelle, Hünxe, includes the sandstone busts of Albrecht Georg von Hüchtenbruch (*d* 1716) and his two deceased wives. Based on painted models, these three busts lack spontaneity; however, the sculptor has patiently emphasized the sitters' fine costumes and elaborate coiffures. Between 1721 and 1723, Johann Wilhelm created the much more lifelike alabaster portrait busts of Ferdinand Adolf, Count of Plettenberg-Nordkirchen, and his wife Bernhardine, and the full-length statue of their son Franz Joseph von Plettenberg (all Münster, Westfäl. Landesmus.). The poses, especially that of the young son who stands with his dog, are more individual, and each button or bit of lace is painstakingly replicated.

BIBLIOGRAPHY

NDB

F. Koch: *Die Gröninger: Ein Beitrag zur Geschichte der westfälischen Plastik in der Zeit der Spätrenaissance und des Barock* (Münster, 1905) [somewhat outdated but still the only comprehensive monograph on the family]

E. Franke: 'Der Bildhauer Heinrich Gröninger in Paderborn', *Westfäl. Z.*, xc (1934), pp. 1–69

A. Fuchs: 'Zur Forschung über die Paderborner Gröninger', *Westfalen: Hft. Gesch., Kst & Vlksknd.*, xxvii (1948), pp. 110–15

T. Rensing: 'Monumenta memoriae', *Westfalen: Hft. Gesch., Kst & Vlksknd.*, xxxvi (1958), pp. 60–90

A. Fuchs: 'Unbekannte Werke der Paderborner Gröninger', *Westfalen: Hft. Gesch., Kst & Vlksknd.*, xl (1962), pp. 169–79

W. Honselmann: 'Zur älteren Geschichte der Bildhauerfamilie Gröninger in Paderborn und Münster', *Westfäl. Z.*, cxv (1965), pp. 437–57

T. Rensing: 'Zur Genealogie der Gröninger', *Monasterium: Festschrift zum siebenhundertjährigen Weihegedächtnis des Paulus-Domes zu Münster* (Münster, 1966), pp. 137–48

Grupello und seine Zeit (exh. cat., Düsseldorf, Kstmus., 1971), pp. 224–9 [on Johann Wilhelm Gröninger]

R. Gunter: 'Neue Ergebnisse zum Werk des Johann Wilhelm Gröninger', *Westfalen: Hft. Gesch., Kst & Vlksknd.*, xlix (1971), pp. 138–40

G. T. M. Lemmens: 'Meester Gerhard Groninger: Een Westfaals beeldhouwer als balling in Nijmegen' [Master Gerhard Gröninger: A Westphalian sculptor in exile in Nijmegen], *Numaga*, xxiii/3 (1976), pp. 73–82

J. Rasmussen: *Barockplastik in Norddeutschland* (exh. cat., Hamburg, Mus. Kst & Gew., 1977)

Barockskulptur (exh. cat. by G. Jászai, Münster, Westfäl. Landesmus., 1979) [useful if brief comments on each family member]

G. Jászai: *Dom und Domkammer in Münster* (Königstein im Taunus, 1981)

C. Stiegemann: *Heinrich Gröninger um 1578–1631* (Paderborn, 1989)

Das Werk des Bildhauers Gerhard Gröninger (exh. cat. by G. Jászai, Münster, Westfäl. Landesmus., 1989)

U. Grote: *Johann Mauritz Gröninger* (Bonn, 1992)

JEFFREY CHIPPS SMITH

Groosman, E(rnestinus) F(lorimond) (*b* Ovezande, 21 July 1917). Dutch architect and theorist. After graduating from polytechnical school in 1936, Groosman continued his studies and obtained a master's degree in architecture in 1944. In 1948 he founded Groosman Partners in Rotterdam. In collaboration with Wilhelm van Tijen and Hugh Art Maaskant, Groosman was involved in the construction of council housing in the Zuidwijk district of Rotterdam; he was also part of a study group led by Jacob B. Bakema working on the development of the town of Nagele (from 1953) in the Noordoostpolder. These projects were, in fact, studies of how a housing programme designed by the Functionalist avant-garde of the 1930s could be executed using post-World War II technological achievements. Following discussions in DE OPBOUW, an association of modernist architects in the Netherlands, Groosman is chiefly credited with the 1960s revival of the arguments associated with CIAM debates. Writing in professional journals, he expressed the need for far-reaching standardization and rationalization of the building process as a logical consequence of the technical revolution and increasing prosperity. During this time he designed many houses based on various building systems, including flats (1958) in Den Helder and Schiedam using the Muwi system, and Rotterdam's first modular school (1960) and Rotterdam Lombardijen (1961) using the Dura-Coignet system. His concern for the social aspects of his work led him also to cultivate a sense of quality by formulating criteria for a good housing unit. He retired in 1981 but his firm continued to practise.

WRITINGS

'Industriele bouw Dura-Coignet' [Dura-Coignet industrial building], *Bouw*, xxiii (1960), pp. 670–77

'Schaalvergroting, ook in het bouwen' [Increasing scale, also in building], *Bouw*, xvii (1966), pp. 611–12

'Bouwen voor een veranderende samenleving' [Building for a changing society], *Stedebouw & Vlkshuisvest.*, iii (1966), pp. 323–7

BIBLIOGRAPHY

'Some New Housing Developments in the Netherlands', *Archit. Aujourd'hui*, xxv (Dec 1954), pp. 78–81

'Woningbouw te Amsterdam: Venoer polder blok II', *Bouw*, xli/26 (21 Dec 1985)

D'LAINE CAMP

Groot, Cornelis Hofstede de. *See* HOFSTEDE DE GROOT, CORNELIS.

Gropius, Martin (Philipp) (*b* Berlin, 11 Aug 1824; *d* Berlin, 13 Dec 1880). German architect. He attended the Gewerbeinstitut in Berlin (1843–6) and the Bauakademie until 1855. After qualifying as an architect, he stayed on as assistant to Karl Bötticher, teaching about ornamental drawing and building materials; he became a professor in 1866. At this stage his style was predominantly classical and influenced by Bötticher. He designed villas and houses in Berlin, for example Villa Bleichröder (1863–6; destr.) and Villa Warschauer (1870–71; destr.), altered mansions in the Prussian provinces (e.g. Zuchow, Gutshaus, 1866; Rosenfelde, Gutshaus, 1873) and devoted himself particularly to interior decoration and arts and crafts. He attracted attention in 1862 with his idiosyncratic competition design for the Thomaskirche in Berlin, and in the same year was awarded the contract for the lunatic asylum at Eberswalde (begun 1864); from then on he applied himself to the art of polychrome brickwork. He and Heino Schmieden (1835–1913) went into partnership in 1866. The first result of the collaboration was a prize-winning competition design (unexecuted) for a cathedral in Berlin, followed by the hospital (1867–74) at Friedrichshain, in which Gropius sought to give the *Rundbogenstil* greater tautness as the 'segmented arch'. In 1869 he was appointed Director of the Kunst- und Gewerbeschule, Berlin, and later of all the other art schools in Prussia. His failure in the competition (1872) for the Reichstag building brought a period of uncertainty and as a concession to the prevalent taste he designed buildings in the Renaissance Revival style, including the post office (1878–81; destr.) at Kassel and the unrealized plans (1878) for the Landesbibliothek (State Library) in Berlin. In his buildings for hospitals, however, he regained a clarity and economy of idiom, demonstrated by a strict articulation of façades and balanced proportions in his usually block-shaped buildings. He also continued to use systematically the polychrome brick style in the Schinkel tradition, for example the colourful brick buildings for Kiel University (1873–6) and the Kunstschule (1878–80) in Berlin. His principal works were the Kunstgewerbemuseum (1877–81; partly destr.; now the Martin-Gropius-Bau) in Berlin and the Gewandhaus (built posthumously, 1881–4; destr.) in Leipzig.

BIBLIOGRAPHY

E. Jacobsthal: Obituary, *Dt. Bauztg*, xv (1881), pp. 313–15 and 323–5

H. Schliepmann: *Martin Gropius in seiner Bedeutung für die Entwicklung von Architektur und Kunstgewerbe* (Berlin, 1892)

P. Wallé: 'Martin Gropius', *Der Baumeister*, ii (1904), pp. 49–55

M. Klinkott: *Martin Gropius und die Berliner Schule* (diss., Berlin, Tech. U., 1971)

——: *Die Backsteinbaukunst der Berliner Schule* (Berlin, 1988)

MANFRED KLINKOTT

Gropius, Walter (Adolf Georg) (*b* Berlin, 18 May 1883; *d* Boston, MA, 5 July 1969). American architect, industrial designer and teacher of German birth. He was one of the most influential figures in the development of the MODERN MOVEMENT, whose contribution lay as much in his work as theoretician and teacher as it did in his innovative architecture. The important buildings and projects in Gropius's career—the early factories, the Bauhaus complex at Dessau (1925–6), the Totaltheater project for Berlin, the housing estates and prefabricated dwellings—were all more than immediate answers to specific problems. Rather, they were a series of researches in which he sought prototypical solutions that would offer universal applicability. They were also didactic in purpose—concrete demonstrations, manifestos, of his theories and beliefs. His theories sought to integrate the individual and society, art and industry, form and function and the part with the whole. He left Germany for England in 1934; three years later he emigrated to the USA, where he continued to teach, write and design for the rest of his life.

1. The early years, 1903–18. 2. From Bauhaus to Berlin, 1918–34. 3. England and the USA, 1934–69.

1. THE EARLY YEARS, 1903–18. Gropius had only five terms of formal training as an architect. The first was in 1903 at the Technische Hochschule, Munich, which was followed by some practical experience in Berlin (1903–4) in the office of Solf & Wichards; the remainder were spent at the Technische Hochschule, Charlottenburg, in 1906–7 and were followed by a series of small independent commissions in Pomerania. In 1908 he entered the Berlin office of Peter Behrens, then acting as design consultant to the Allgemeine Elektrizitäts-Gesellschaft (AEG). Gropius had difficulty in holding a pencil, and he called himself Behrens's 'factotum' rather than architectural assistant. This difficulty in drawing, from which he suffered all his life, had two positive side-effects: a shift of interest from the drawing-board as an end in itself to the process of design and construction as one integrated activity, and a sharpening of his ability to define and analyse problems in architecture and prescribe solutions in principle, with greater clarity and precision than many of his contemporaries. In Behrens's office Gropius met fellow-assistants Adolf Meyer and Mies van der Rohe and perhaps Le Corbusier, who came to work there in 1910, at around the time that Gropius left.

One can see the effects of the years with Behrens not only through such contacts but also in Gropius's own realization of the powerful influence of industry, both for

1. Walter Gropius: model factory at the Werkbund Exhibition, Cologne, 1914

architectural patronage and in the building process, and in his appreciation of the architect's comprehensive role, from graphics and product design to building and urban planning. The synthesis of his enduring fascination with the industrial process and his holistic approach ('the scope of total architecture') was already apparent in his ideas for industrial housing outlined in a memorandum presented to the head of AEG in 1910. The following year he joined the DEUTSCHER WERKBUND; this was an organization dedicated to that synthesis of art and industry that Gropius himself so ardently advocated.

On leaving Behrens (1910), Gropius opened his own office in Berlin, with Adolf Meyer as his associate. Their practice flourished until interrupted by World War I. Two buildings of this period stand out: the Fagus Factory (1911–13) on the Leine at Alfeld and the model factory of 1914. The Fagus Factory was a striking example of early modernist architecture. The simplified modular treatment of the main façades, the extensive use of glass and the dramatic omission of piers at its corners—usually stressed as a visual point of stability—made this an innovative landmark in the evolution of the Modern Movement. At the same time Gropius retained an elemental classicism, not only in the ordered regularity of its columned façade, but in the nuances of design: the entasis-like treatment of the narrow brick piers, the correction of optical illusions in the graduated spacing of the glazing bars and the precision of detail of the metal profiles. The model factory built for the Werkbund Exhibition in Cologne (1914) was equally bold: while it retained a classical discipline in the axial symmetry of its plan, the façades of the administration block (see fig. 1) were entirely original—notwithstanding some very muted influences derived from the work of Frank Lloyd Wright. The glazed, circular stair-towers at the outside corners are lyrical, and the curtain-wall theme, tentative in the main Fagus building and explored further in the Fagus machine-house, was here taken to its logical and dramatic conclusion. The outbreak of World War I brought Gropius's career to a halt. He served as an officer on the Western Front and in 1915, while on leave, married Alma Mahler, the composer Gustav Mahler's widow.

2. FROM BAUHAUS TO BERLIN, 1918–34. At the end of World War I, Gropius returned to a chaotic, revolutionary Germany. He joined the newly formed ARBEITSRAT FÜR KUNST, becoming its director the same year. Soon afterwards he accepted an offer to head the Kunstschule and the Kunstgewerbeschule in Saxony, which he combined and renamed the Staatliches Bauhaus, Weimar. On assuming directorship of the BAUHAUS in April 1919, his main preoccupations became education and the establishment and consolidation of the institution. It was an idealistic institution, and his opening manifesto proclaimed a utopian vision of ways to build, 'which will embrace architecture and sculpture and painting in one unity, and which will rise one day towards heaven from the hands of a million workers'. The immediate reality of the Bauhaus was more modest, its goals more realistic and its scope restricted to the theory and practice of design. Within these parameters its achievements were notable (as demonstrated by the impressive Bauhaus exhibition of 1923). But the ultimate goal, the 'composite but inseparable work of art, the great building', remained elusive during the early 1920s: it was not achieved at the Bauhaus, nor in Gropius's office, which he had re-established with Meyer after the war. Up to 1922 Gropius's work was exploratory and indecisive, with no clear line of development. It reflected the uncertainties and tensions of a Germany in political and economic turmoil, but also perhaps the personal emotional stresses induced by his divorce in 1920.

Of all his early post-war work, only the house for Adolf Sommerfeld in Berlin, the so-called 'blockhouse' (1920–21), showed that integration of arts, crafts and architecture at which he aimed. If there was a regression, compared to the pre-war work, then it was not towards Expressionism (as is usually claimed), for his work of this period lacked the emotional intensity and overt symbolism of Expressionist architecture; rather, it was stamped by a pervading romanticism in which traditional forms, and, as at the 'blockhouse', traditional techniques, were reworked in a process of innovative conservatism. By 1922 a new clarity had appeared in his work, in his and Meyer's entry for the Chicago Tribune competition (see Nerdinger, p. 63) and their unrealized proposals two years later for a research and study centre, an academy of philosophy, which was to have been built at Erlangen-Spansdorf (see Nerdinger, p. 69). Gropius's romantic phase had ended, and the architecture as well as the designs produced in the Bauhaus itself were now uncompromisingly committed to the avant-garde and closer in spirit to Russian Constructivism and De Stijl. Gropius's private life at this time also became more stable, with his marriage to Ilse Frank in 1923.

In 1925 the Bauhaus moved from Weimar to Dessau, occupying temporary accommodation while the new school and staff housing were being built to designs by Gropius. The Bauhaus buildings (1925–6; *see* GERMANY, fig. 12) are his major works; his audacious use of glass as hanging, transparent planes, the clear spatial and functional organization of the whole and overall synthesis of architecture, interior design, furniture and equipment made these buildings a paradigm of the Modern Movement. They were not wholly a construction of machine-made parts, but they were totally expressive of the machine aesthetic—an appropriate symbol of the Bauhaus commitment to a unique synthesis of art and industry and of itself, as both educational institution and social microcosm. The first years in Dessau, when the Bauhaus reached its peak of international fame, were also a productive period for Gropius. His Törten housing estate (1926–8) for the city council, built in stages and comprising some 600 dwellings, made considerable advances in construction technology and site layout; his employment office (1927–9), also for the council, was a model of functional planning. For the Werkbund's Weissenhofsiedlung at Stuttgart in 1927, Gropius built two houses; he used prefabricated techniques, stressing technological advances in house design rather than the sociological dimensions of *l'habitation minimum* or Modernist aesthetics. His Totaltheater project (see Nerdinger, pp. 95, 97, 99) in Berlin for the theatre director Erwin Piscator the same year expressed his search for the *Gesamtkunstwerk* in its most comprehensive form, a desire to embrace architecture, theatre and cinema and unite performer and audience in a rich pluralistic synthesis.

In 1928 Gropius gave up his Bauhaus directorship and returned to private practice in Berlin; he also made an extended visit to the USA. His most significant achievements by this time were in the field of public housing: Karlsruhe (Dammerstock, 1928–9), Frankfurt am Main (Am Lindenbaum, 1929–30) and Berlin (Siemensstadt, 1929–30; see fig. 2). His typical approach to planning, with long parallel blocks of walk-up flats, efficiently planned and of a simple but pleasing appearance, provided the best possible orientation and use of space, but at the cost of an overall visual monotony and a lack of focus both in formal and social terms. He also advocated the high-rise slab building (in which he perceived a sociological validity, i.e. the 'big' family of cooperative dwellers replacing the individual family), for its economical construction through new building techniques and its preservation of open spaces. Examples include his project of 1929–30 for high-rise, steel-frame dwellings (see Nerdinger, pp. 137, 139, 141) and his luxury development on the Wannsee shore of Berlin's Lake Havel (1930–31; see Nerdinger, p. 157).

Housing apart, few of Gropius's projects were realized during this period. Two important ones were entries for international competitions: the Ukrainian State Theatre (1930–31; see Nerdinger, p. 155), Khar'kov (now Kharkiv), and the Palace of the Soviets (1931; see Nerdinger, pp. 161–3), Moscow. Both derived from his ideas for the Total Theatre, and the form of each was determined by its function; the boldly articulated, fan-shaped masses of both were perhaps less dramatic than Le Corbusier's proposals for the Palace of the Soviets, but probably much more workable. Along with many contemporary avant-garde architects Gropius had looked favourably on the USSR, but following a later visit to Leningrad (now St Petersburg) in 1933 he was left somewhat disillusioned with the harsh realities beyond the Socialist dream.

2. Walter Gropius: apartment buildings, view from courtyard, Siemensstadt, Berlin, 1929–30

3. ENGLAND AND THE USA, 1934–69. In the early 1930s economic depression caused a major recession in the building industry, and commissions were scarce. For architects, the rising power of Nazism in Germany was a further source of perturbation. DER RING, of which Gropius had been a leading member, was regarded as an organization of 'Jewish-Bolshevik' architects, and the Bauhaus was castigated in the Nazi press as a 'Cathedral of Marxism'. Confronted by growing professional impotence and political discomfort, in 1934 Gropius went voluntarily (and he hoped temporarily) into exile. He travelled to England and went into partnership with E. Maxwell Fry. Their patron and principal client was the enlightened industrialist J. C. Pritchard, head of the Isokon company. He not only gave opportunities to Gropius, who acted as a design consultant to Isokon in 1934–5, but also extended patronage to other émigrés, including Marcel Breuer, who had joined Gropius in London in 1935.

Hopes were high, but the climate in England was not propitious for a revolution in architecture. There were many ambitious projects, but few Gropius and Fry buildings, and these, though radical for England, were of no great architectural significance. Only one, the Impington Village College (1936–9), Cambs, was a work of distinction and quality. It retained the functional clarity of the best buildings by Gropius in Germany, but it was less austere, a reflection perhaps of its English context. Gropius was aware that, although his presence was appreciated by a small group of young architects, the MARS Group, he was making little impact on the broad and overwhelmingly conservative architectural scene. He had thus kept in touch with contacts in the USA throughout his stay in England. In 1937 he accepted a professorship at Harvard University.

On taking up his new position at Harvard's Graduate School of Design, Gropius was soon joined by several former colleagues, including Breuer and Martin Wagner, with whom he had worked closely in Berlin. The next few years were professionally rewarding, despite being personally distressing for Gropius (because of the difficulties of exile compounded with tensions generated by approaching war). He was appointed Chairman of the architectural department, and he established himself in the USA as an influential teacher, although he never really became reconciled to the divorce of theory and practice inherent in a university environment. When, in 1938, he built his own house at Lincoln, MA, it was more than a desire for stability; it was a proclamation of intent and a statement of faith. The house remains one of his best works, one which integrated modern European design with the traditional techniques of New England timber construction. The rectangular prism of its basic form was enriched by a projecting screen, overhanging canopies and free-standing posts, an outrigging which reduced the old Bauhaus dependence on mass and surface and related more closely to De Stijl Constructivism. The Lincoln house was undoubtedly designed by Gropius, although formally it represented a partnership between himself and Breuer. In other work by this partnership, which included several houses in the same genre, Breuer played a more incisive role. This is particularly evident in one major project, a competition entry of 1938 (see Nerdinger, p. 197) for Wheaton College Art Centre, Norton, MA, where Breuer's characteristic plan-forms are apparent. The only important executed project by this partnership was 'Aluminium City' (1941–2), a housing estate at New Kensington, Pittsburgh, PA. Designed for only 250 families in a loosely-knit group and adapted to its topography, this estate was very different in scale and character to the great *Siedlungen* of Gropius's period in Berlin.

In 1941 the partnership came to an end, following disagreements both in the architectural school and in the office. In September of that year Konrad Wachsmann came as a penniless refugee to live with Gropius and his family, and he began to work on some of the office projects, notably a recreation centre (1941–2; see Nerdinger, p. 203) for Key West, FL, which initially had also involved Breuer. This and many other projects were aborted in December 1941 when the USA entered World War II. The major result of the association between Gropius and Wachsmann was the development of a system of prefabrication, the Packaged House (1942–52), which, despite its technical ingenuity and the growing need for such houses, failed to reach full production; only a small number of these houses was actually sold. Although by 1944 Gropius had distanced himself from this particular project, its eventual failure was a sad climax to his lasting interest in the factory-made house. This had started with his memorandum to AEG in 1910 and later included the combinatory *Baukasten im Grossen* system of 1923 (with Meyer; see Nerdinger, p. 233), Muche and Paulick's steel house for the Bauhaus (1926–7), the Werkbund's prefabricated dwellings for the Weissenhofsiedlung (1927) and his involvement with the Hirsch houses made from copper (1931–2; see Herbert, 1984, pp. 109, 122, 126–7, 130–31). The practical results of this struggle to put housing on an industrialized basis, but controlled by architects, were minimal; but Gropius played a major role in defining the principles. When opportunities resumed after the war he united with a group of young architects to form TAC (The Architects Collaborative) in 1945, and he continued to practise until his death. The first major work of TAC, the Harvard University Graduate Centre (1948–50), Cambridge, MA, continued the forms and many of the details of Gropius's earlier work, a humanized international-style building related sympathetically to the *genius loci* of Harvard's campus. In many other buildings by TAC his role continued to be an important (sometimes dominant) one, but inevitably his personal imprint was less evident in later years. Such works included the neo-classical US Embassy in Athens (1956–61) and university buildings in Baghdad (from 1957; see Fitch, pls 129–35) as well as projects in the USA and Germany. As a result, his 32 years in the USA were rich in achievement and honour, but the greatest achievements lay in his early life and work in pre-Hitler Germany.

WRITINGS

The New Architecture and the Bauhaus (London, 1935)
Rebuilding our Communities (Chicago, 1945)
Architecture and Design in the Age of Science (New York, 1952)
I. Gropius, ed.: *Scope of Total Architecture* (New York, 1952)
with S. P. Harkness, eds: *Architects Collaborative: 1945–1965* (Tenfen, 1966)
Apollo in the Democracy: The Cultural Obligation of the Architect (New York, 1968)

BIBLIOGRAPHY

S. Giedion: *Walter Gropius* (Paris, 1931)
G. C. Argan: *Walter Gropius e la Bauhaus* (Turin, 1951)
S. Giedion: *Walter Gropius: Work and Teamwork* (New York, 1954)
C. Y. Kurata, Y. Nosu and M. Koyama: *Walter Gropius* (Tokyo, 1954)
S. Giedion, G. Argan and D. Haskell: *Walter Gropius* (Montevideo, 1955)
G. Herbert: *The Synthetic Vision of Walter Gropius* (Johannesburg, 1959)
J. M. Fitch: *Walter Gropius* (New York, 1960)
H. Weber: *Walter Gropius und das Faguswerk* (Munich, 1961)
H. M. Wingler: *Das Bauhaus, 1919–1933* (Bramsche, 1962; Eng. trans. with suppl. material, Cambridge, MA, 1969)
W. B. O'Neal, ed.: 'A Bibliography of Writings by and about Walter Gropius', *Amer. Assoc. Archit. Bibliog.: Pap.*, iii (1966); suppl., ix (1972), pp. 1–24
K. Wilhelm: *Walter Gropius: Industriearchitektur* (Brunswick, 1983)
R. Isaacs: *Walter Gropius: Der Mensch und sein Werk*, 2 vols (Berlin, 1983–4)
G. Herbert: *The Dream of the Factory-made House: Walter Gropius and Konrad Wachsmann* (Cambridge, MA, 1984)
W. Nerdinger: *Walter Gropius* (Berlin, 1985) [Eng. and Ger. texts]

GILBERT HERBERT

Gros, Antoine-Jean, Baron (*b* Paris, 16 March 1771; *d* Meudon, Hauts-de-Seine, 25 June 1835). French painter. He was one of the most honoured and respected painters during the reigns of Emperor Napoleon I, King Louis XVIII and King Charles X. For these monarchs he executed large paintings of contemporary history and allegory, although he was also known as a painter of mythological subjects and of portraits in a Romantic vein.

1. Paris and Italy, 1785–1800. 2. First Empire and Restoration commissions, 1801–20. 3. Mythological paintings and late works, 1821–35. 4. Influence.

1. PARIS AND ITALY, 1785–1800. He received his first lessons in drawing from his parents, the miniature painters Jean-Antoine Gros and Madeleine-Cécile Durand, who lived in the Rue Neuve-des-Petits Champs, in the commercial district of Paris popular with such painters. He also frequented the studio of Elisabeth-Louise Vigée Le Brun. However, his earliest paintings show no obvious trace of any influence prior to that of David, whose studio he entered as a pupil in 1785. At this time, inspired by his visits to the race-course in the Bois de Boulogne, he developed his lifelong passion for drawing horses. In 1787 he entered the Académie Royale de Peinture et de Sculpture and progressed steadily through the competitions, winning the Prix de Torse in 1791 and becoming a final competitor for the Prix de Rome in 1792 with *Antiochus Attempting to Prevent Eleazar from Eating an Impure Dish* (Saint-Lô, Mus. B.-A.). *Bather* (Besançon, Mus. B.-A. & Archéol.), executed as a pupil of David, is usually dated to this period as well because of the academic style of the figures, although there is a strong naturalism akin to Rubens that makes it unusual for its time. Gros's formal education ended in 1793, due to the bankruptcy and death of his father, and, like other artists in the tumult of the French Revolution, he turned to portrait painting for an income. In January 1793 he left for Italy, having obtained a passport issued at the request of David. Augustin Pajou, whom he had met through Vigée-Le Brun, accompanied

him part way and introduced him to contacts in Montpellier, where he paused long enough to paint two portraits (e.g. *Paul François des Hours de Calviac*, 1793; Lyon, priv. col., see G. Delestre, pl. 3) before continuing by way of Marseille and Genoa to Florence. Again Gros supported himself by painting portraits and by giving lessons to the writer Count Niemcewicz, who remained a lifelong friend and patron and through whom Gros met other Polish exiles. He probably intended to go to Rome, but with the uprising there in 1793 against the French and the closing of the Académie de France, it was not a secure city for French artists. He therefore returned to Genoa, where, for a time, he shared lodgings with Anne-Louis Girodet. Before Girodet left for France, the two artists painted portraits of each other (both Versailles, Château) and exchanged them as tokens of friendship. In 1796 in Genoa, Gros was introduced to Josephine, who had heard of his skill in painting horses and his desire to paint a portrait of Napoleon to commemorate his victories. That year he met Bonaparte in Milan and painted a lively head-and-shoulders study (Paris, Louvre), which was used as a model for his portrait of *Bonaparte on the Bridge at Arcole, 17 November 1796* (1801; Versailles, Château). The success of this work established his reputation among Napoleon's occupying forces in Italy, resulting in further commissions for portraits and a position on the committee set up to inspect works of art from the conquered cities of Italy and to remove them to the Musée du Louvre. This period of relative security ended abruptly when Napoleon left on his Egyptian campaign, and Gros was confined in Genoa for two months because of the Austrian siege. After the evacuation of the city, he returned to Paris in October 1800.

Even before the siege, Gros had been restless to return home. He was aware of the revival of painting in France after the disasters of the French Revolution and wanted to move away from portraits into more ambitious subject-matter. Turning to history painting, he looked to the Classical world for possible subjects. His interest in horses made him think of painting *Alexander Taming Bucephalus* (sketch, Paris, priv. col., see G. Delestre, pl. 21). He then considered a subject from the poetry of Ossian, sketched a composition from ancient Greek history (*Timoleon at Corinth*, 1798; Paris, Louvre, Cab. Dessins).

2. First Empire and Restoration commissions, 1801–20. On his return to Paris, Gros painted *Sappho at Leucadia* (Bayeux, Mus. Gérard). In this work, lit by eerie, greenish moonlight, he depicted Sappho throwing herself from the top of a cliff. Despite its bizarre colour, critics were impressed by the painting when it appeared at the Salon of 1801. Its strong light effects, sharp contours and the melancholy subject link it to paintings by Girodet and other pupils of David, and it would probably have been

1. Antoine-Jean Gros: *Bonaparte Visiting the Victims of the Plague at Jaffa, 11 March 1799*, oil on canvas, 5.23×7.15 m, 1804 (Paris, Musée du Louvre)

the type of picture that Gros would have continued to paint during the First Empire had he not been drawn into Napoleon's propagandist programme of painting contemporary events. On 25 April 1799 Napoleon had announced a competition for a painting to celebrate the victory of General Andoche Junot against the vastly superior forces of the Turks and Arabs 17 days earlier at Nazareth. In March 1801 the conditions for the competition were published, and in December a jury unanimously awarded the prize to Gros on the basis of his sketch (Nantes, Mus. B.-A.), a tumultuous panorama painted with lively brushstrokes that reminded some of his contemporaries of the Rococo style. The sketch was intended as a preliminary work for a large painting, over 8 m long, of the Battle of Nazareth, but the project was halted by Napoleon, who appeared to have had second thoughts about honouring Junot. By way of compensation, Gros received a commission to paint a picture recording the fearless encouragement given by Napoleon to his staff to assist the victims of the plague at Jaffa during the Syrian campaign in 1799. Using a fragment of the canvas intended for the *Battle of Nazareth*, Gros painted *Bonaparte Visiting the Victims of the Plague at Jaffa, 11 March 1799* (1804; Paris, Louvre; see fig. 1) in time for the Salon of 1804, where it had an overwhelming success with his fellow artists, the critics and the public. Unlike the episodic *Battle of Nazareth*, the painting is tightly organized in the manner of David's work, with Napoleon occupying the central position. Gros, however, added a vivacity of colour and a naturalism not commonly found in the work of other history painters at that time. In 1806 he received a commission from Joachim Murat, Napoleon's brother-in-law, to paint the *Battle of Aboukir* (Versailles, Château). For this work he used another portion of the canvas that had originally been intended for the *Battle of Nazareth*, and for the figure of Junot on a rearing horse he substituted that of Murat, swinging his sabre in the midst of the battle.

The Battle of Eylau, in Silesia, took place on 8 February 1807 between the combined forces of Russia and Prussia and those of France. Two months later, Napoleon, then Emperor, announced a competition to commemorate not the battle itself but the appalling aftermath when, lamenting the extent of the casualties, he brought medical aid to the wounded Russian soldiers. Gros won the competition with his painting *Napoleon on the Battlefield at Eylau, February 1807* (1808; Paris, Louvre), in which he emphasized the presence of the Emperor on the battlefield the day after the fighting and the role of the French in attending to the wounded Russians, who are prominently displayed in the foreground. The competition was intended to provide evidence of the French victory (which was not certain) and, as in *Bonaparte Visiting the Victims of the Plague at Jaffa*, to establish the reputation of the Emperor as a humane conqueror. Gros adapted a print of *Henry IV* by Gravelot for the central motif of his composition, linking the reputation of the Bourbon monarch as the father of his people with the myth of Napoleon (Herbert, pp. 52–75). When it appeared at the Salon of 1808, the painting confirmed Gros's reputation and led to a further series of paintings celebrating the Emperor's military career: the *Capture of Madrid*, the *Battle of the Pyramids*, both shown at the Salon of 1808, and the *Battle of Wagram* shown at the Salon of 1810 (all Versailles, Château). None of these quite equalled the huge successes of his earlier paintings, but they reinforced his position as the most effective painter of imperial propaganda and as one of the leading painters of the period.

2. Antoine-Jean Gros: *Christine Boyer*, oil on canvas, 2.14×1.34 m, 1800 (Paris, Musée du Louvre)

During the Empire, Gros was constantly employed in painting portraits of imperial society and, in particular, of the military. He was clearly familiar with the work of such 18th-century English portrait painters as Reynolds and Gainsborough, whose poses inspired that of *Lieutenant Legrand* (1810; Los Angeles, CA, Co. Mus. A.), in which the figure stands cross-legged beside his horse. The elegiac mood in the portrait of the first wife of Lucien Bonaparte, *Christine Boyer* (1800; Paris, Louvre; see fig. 2), also owes something to English portraiture: the woman gazes at a rose carried along by a stream through wild parkland. The painting has a literary and melancholic element, common to French painting of *c.* 1800–20.

Gros's role as Napoleon's propagandist brought him two commissions outside his normal range. Following the Concordat (1801), the Saint-Denis Abbey was refurbished, and there was to be a series of paintings for the reconsecrated sacristy. The restitution of the abbey, in which many of the kings of France were buried, marked an act of reconciliation between the Emperor and past and present royal dynasties, and this is depicted allusively in *Charles V Received by Francis I at the Abbey of Saint-Denis (1540)* (1811; Paris, Louvre). In the painting the two monarchs lay aside their former hostilities and visit the royal tombs at Saint-Denis.

This theme was treated more ambitiously in 1812, when Gros was commissioned to paint images of *Clovis*, *Charlemagne*, *Louix IX* and *Napoleon*, representing four dynasties, for the central cupola of the Panthéon. He worked on the frescoes (*in situ*) from 1814, when the Bourbons were restored to the throne. At this time he was ordered to substitute *Louis XVIII* in place of *Napoleon*. During the Hundred Days (1815), he restored the image of Napoleon to the cupola, but when the French leader was defeated at Waterloo, Gros was asked to reinstall the painting of *Louis XVIII*. Although his paintings celebrating the achievements of Napoleon were removed from public exhibition during the Restoration, he was nevertheless the most honoured painter in France. In 1814 he was appointed Portrait Painter to Louis XVIII, and in 1815 he was given a seat in the Institut de France. In 1819 he was made Chevalier of the Order of St Michel and later, in 1828, Officer of the Légion d'honneur. He received many commissions from Louis XVIII, among them the *Departure of Louis XVIII from the Tuileries on the Night of 19–20 March, 1815* (1816; Versailles, Château), painted to commemorate the King's flight from Paris. The *Embarkation of the Duchesse d'Angoulême at Pauillac* (1819; Bordeaux, Mus. B.-A.) was commissioned by the Chambre des Députés as a pendant to the *Departure of Louis XVIII*. Both were rare excursions by the artist after 1815 into the field of contemporary history.

3. MYTHOLOGICAL PAINTINGS AND LATE WORKS, 1821–35. David went into exile in 1816, and Gros subsequently taught many of his pupils and, like David, was successful in preparing them for the Prix de Rome. In his own work, the depiction of academic figures assumed renewed importance, and he rejected themes from modern life in favour of paintings based on ancient myths. He exhibited *Bacchus Consoling Ariadne on the Island of Naxos* (1821; Ottawa, N.G.) at the Salon of 1822, and *Cupid Stung by a Bee* (Toulouse, Mus. Augustins) at the Salon of 1833. In *Acis and Galatea* (Norfolk, VA, Chrysler Mus.), shown at the Salon of 1835, there is a strong debt to the academic figure painting he taught in his life classes: the figure of Acis is based on the antique statue of the *Crouching Venus* (Florence, Uffizi). In 1824 he finally completed the series of frescoes for the cupola of the Panthéon, for which he was made Baron by Charles X. In 1827 he painted the allegory *Charles X Presenting the New Museum to the Arts* (removed in 1830; Versailles, Château) on the ceiling of one of the rooms in the Musée Charles X, a recently completed part of the Louvre. He also executed a large painting for the ceiling of the Musée des Antiquités Egyptiennes depicting *Humanity Imploring Europe in Favour of the Greeks: The Genius of France Thrusting Forward to Protect them* (1830; *in situ*). This was a topical subject, referring to the Greek War of Independence (1821–9) and the wave of philhellenism that drew French sympathies to the Greek side.

Gros's contemporaries were generally disappointed with these late works. It is doubtful that they would have been admired at any time, but in the late 1820s and 1830s they were, in addition, unfashionable. His paintings of Napoleon, which were shown again to the public during the July Revolution of 1830, reminded critics of his earlier talent for evoking the heroism of modern times. Despite the fact that his paintings were given positions of honour at Versailles in the Musée Historique, established by Louis-Philippe, he was reluctant to return to his former subject-matter. In 1835 he agreed to add strips (Cleveland, OH, Mus. A.) to enlarge the *Battle of the Pyramids* but refused to paint a scene of the Battle of Iena for the new museum. Perhaps sensing that he had sacrificed too much of his natural talent in painting characterless depictions of the human figure, he composed *Hercules and Diomedes* (1835; Toulouse, Mus. Augustins), a large picture with a subject more in keeping with the Rubensian vigour of his earlier work and with the talent he had for painting horses. He sent it, along with *Acis and Galatea*, to the Salon of 1835. At best the critics were mildly appreciative. On 25 June 1835 he drowned himself in the River Seine. At the time, it was said that he did so because of his failure at the Salon, but contemporaries also hinted at domestic difficulties. His marriage in 1809 to the painter Augustine Dufresne (1789–1842), who was 18 years younger than he, had not been a happy one.

4. INFLUENCE. Although nothing Gros painted in the last 20 years of his life left any lasting mark on French art, he was one of the most influential artists of the 19th century, primarily for the Romantic tendencies in his work that inspired younger painters and sculptors. Apart from teaching a generation of pupils that included Richard Parkes Bonington, Paul Huet, Antoine-Louis Barye, Paul Delaroche and Thomas Couture, he was admired by many younger artists who worked in other studios. Delacroix was profoundly affected by Gros's early work, despite his belief that modern life offered little to inspire the artist. Géricault, however, who had made his public début ten years earlier than Delacroix, when the Empire was at its height, assimilated Gros's talent for endowing modern subjects with the timeless pathos of ancient drama, particularly when the subject-matter had as its main theme the power and passion of the horse in motion.

BIBLIOGRAPHY

J. B. Delestre: *Gros et ses ouvrages* (Paris, 1845); rev. as *Gros: Sa vie et ses ouvrages* (Paris, 1867)

E. Delacroix: 'Peintres et sculpteurs modernes, III: Gros', *Rev. Deux Mondes*, xxiii (1848), pp. 649–73; also in *Oeuvres littéraires*, 2 vols, ed. E. Fauré (Paris, 1923), pp. 163–200

E.-J. Delécluze: *David, son école et son temps* (Paris, 1855/*R* 1983)

C. Blanc: *Histoire des peintres: Ecole française*, iii (Paris, 1865), pp. 1–32

J. Tripier-Lefranc: *Histoire de la vie et de la mort du baron Gros* (Paris, 1880)

G. Dargenty: *Le Baron Gros*, Les Artistes célèbres (Paris and London, 1887) [trilingual text]

Gros, ses amis, ses élèves (exh. cat., intro. Duc de Trévise; Paris, Petit Pal., 1936)

G. Delestre: *Antoine-Jean Gros, 1771–1835*, Col. Maîtres A. (Paris, 1951)

R. Herbert: 'Baron Gros's *Napoleon* and Voltaire's *Henri IV*', *The Artist and the Book in France: Essays in Honour of Jean Seznec*, ed. F. Haskell, A. Levi and R. Shackleton (Oxford, 1974), pp. 52–75

C. Millard: 'Baron Gros's *Portrait of Lieutenant Legrand*', *Bull. LA Co. Mus. A.*, xx/2 (1974), pp. 36–45

C. Sells: 'The Death of Gros', *Burl. Mag.*, cxvi (1974), pp. 266–70

J. H. Rubin: 'La Sépulture romantique de Christine Boyer et son portrait par Antoine-Jean Gros', *Rev. Louvre* (1975), pp. 17–22
——: 'Gros and Girodet', *Burl. Mag.*, cxxi (1979), pp. 716–21
E. Lilley: 'Consular Portraits of Napoléon Bonaparte', *Gaz. B.-A.*, n. s. 5, cvi (1985), pp. 143–56
A. Boime: *Art in an Age of Bonapartism, 1800–1815*, A Social History of Modern Art, ii (Chicago, 1990), pp. 3–95, 300–02

JON WHITELEY

Grosch, Christian Heinrich (*b* Copenhagen, 21 Jan 1801; *d* Christiania [now Oslo], 4 March 1865). Norwegian architect of Danish birth. He was educated at the Royal School of Design in Christiania, where his father, Heinrich August Grosch (1763–1843), a landscape painter and engraver of German origin, worked as an instructor. From 1820 to 1824 Christian Heinrich studied at the Royal Danish Academy of Art under C. F. Hansen. On his return to Christiania, he worked as a draughtsman under Hans Ditlev Franciscus Linstow from 1824 to 1827, and in 1828 he was appointed City Architect of Christiania, where he also served as a teacher at the Royal School of Design. In 1814 Norway had been liberated from Danish rule, and although the country was still united with Sweden under a common king, its new political status created a need for public buildings. Grosch was therefore soon awarded important public commissions in Christiania, of which the first was the state hospital (1826–42; destr.). He demonstrated a secure grasp of the classical idiom in the Stock Exchange (1826–8), the Bank of Norway (1826–30) and the Immanuel Church (1827–33). The exchange and the bank, in plastered brick, both use a severe Doric order in keeping with the gravity of their functions. The former is dominated by a portico of six giant fluted, free-standing columns, and the latter by a portal with two giant columns *in antis*. This was a favourite motif of C. F. Hansen and one of the many traces of his influence on Grosch in this early period.

In 1838 Grosch visited Berlin to discuss his university project for Christiania with Karl Friedrich Schinkel, who played a decisive role in the development of the design, as has been proved by seven drawings by him in the University Archives in Oslo. The layout of the university (1838–54) consists of three main blocks symmetrically grouped around a square, as well as two smaller buildings at the back of an adjacent garden. The formal solution is a masterpiece of classical design, incorporating a variation of Schinkel's wall articulation from the Schauspielhaus in Berlin as well as repeating the open staircase from his Altes Museum on a smaller scale. In other works in Christiania, Grosch used medieval forms, for example at the fire station (1854–6) and the 'bazaar' market stalls for butchers (1843–54), curving around the portal of the Saviour Church (now the cathedral). The first project for the market stalls (1835) was in the plastered brick characteristic of Norwegian Neo-classicism, but they were eventually built in the red brick that came to distinguish the 'romantic historicism' that dominated architecture in Norway in the second half of the 19th century. Grosch also designed domestic buildings and numerous country churches using the 'Swiss style', introduced by Linstow, and was thus an important figure in the initiation and dissemination of the 'romantic historicist' style.

BIBLIOGRAPHY

NKL
A. Bugge: *Arkitekten, stadskonduktør Chr. H. Grosch* (Oslo, 1928)
U. Hamran: 'Schinkel og Norge', *St Hallvard*, xxxviii/1 (1960), pp. 1–36
T. Aslaksby: *Schinkels planer for Universitetet i Oslo* (Bergen, 1986)

CHRISTIAN NORBERG-SCHULZ

Grose, Francis (*b* Greenford, Middx, 1730; *d* Dublin, 12 May 1791). English antiquary and draughtsman. He studied at William Shipley's drawing school in London and became a member of the Society of British Artists in 1766. From 1769 he exhibited a series of tinted drawings, chiefly of architectural remains, at the Royal Academy. He was elected a Fellow of the Society of Antiquaries in 1757 and contributed to the journal *Archaeologia*. In 1755 he was made Richmond Herald but resigned the post in 1763.

Grose is chiefly remembered for his antiquarian interests; over a period of 20 years he produced works on a variety of scholarly subjects. The text of *The Antiquities of England and Wales* (1773–87) is accompanied by maps and over 300 engravings based on watercolours by himself and others, including Samuel Lysons and Paul Sandby. Most of the originals, in many cases the only record of buildings that have since been destroyed, are now owned by the Society of Antiquaries. In 1789 Grose undertook a tour of Scotland—during which he was entertained by the antiquary Robert Riddell (*d* 1794) and met the poet Robert Burns—resulting in the publication of *The Antiquities of Scotland* (1789–91). In 1791 he set out to tour Ireland but had got no further than Dublin when he suddenly died; *The Antiquities of Ireland* (1791–5) was completed by Edward Ledwich (1738–1823) and published posthumously; a third volume was prepared by his nephew Daniel Grose (*c.* 1766–1838) but was not published until 1991.

WRITINGS

The Antiquities of England and Wales, 4 vols, 2 suppls (London, 1773–87)
Rules for Drawing Caricaturas: With an Essay on Comic Painting (London, 1788)
The Antiquities of Scotland, 2 vols (London, 1789–91)
with E. Ledwich: *The Antiquities of Ireland*, 2 vols (London, 1791–5)

BIBLIOGRAPHY

J. H. Hopkins: 'Francis Grose FSA and the "Antiquities of England and Wales"', *Antiqua. J.*, lvi (1976), pp. 253–5
J. Holloway: 'A Travelling Antiquarian: Francis Grose in 18th-century Scotland', *Country Life*, clxxi (15 April 1982), pp. 1084–5
D. Grose: *The Antiquities of Ireland: A Supplement to Francis Grose*, ed. R. Stalley (Dublin, 1991)

NICHOLAS MARLOWE

Groslier, George (*b* 4 Feb 1887; *d* Phnom Penh, 17 June 1945). French art historian and museum curator. He was the Director of Arts and Curator of the National Museum of Phnom Penh in Cambodia and published several volumes on Khmer art, epigraphy and ethnography. He was killed by the invading Japanese forces in Phnom Penh in 1945. His son Bernard Philippe Groslier (1926–86) continued his work in Indo-China.

WRITINGS

A l'ombre d'Angkor: Notes et impressions sur les temples inconnus de l'ancien Cambodge (Paris, 1916)
Recherches sur les Cambodgiens d'après les textes et les monuments depuis les premiers siècles de notre ère (Paris, 1921)
Arts et archéologie khmers: Revue des recherches sur les arts, les monuments et l'ethnographie du Cambodge, depuis les origines jusqu'à nos jours, i (Paris, *c.* 1922)
Angkor (Paris, 1924, rev. 3/1933)

La Sculpture khmère ancienne (Paris, 1925)
Les Collections khmères du Musée Albert Sarraut à Phnom-Penh (Paris, 1931)
Les Arts indigènes au Cambodge (Hanoi, 1938)

BIBLIOGRAPHY

R. Fazy: Obituary, *Bull. Soc. Suisse Amis Extrême Orient*, viii (1946), pp. 100–01

□

Gross, Anthony (*b* London, 19 March 1905; *d* Boulvé, Lot, France, 8 Sept 1984). English painter and printmaker. He trained in London, Paris and Madrid from 1923 to 1925, specializing in etching. In 1926 he settled in France, where he created a number of animated films between 1931 and 1939; in 1936 the first of many books illustrated by him was published, an edition of Jean Cocteau's *Les Enfants terribles.* His oil paintings of this period are largely affectionate depictions of French and English life and leisure, as in *Place du Théâtre, Brive-la-Gaillarde* (1929; London, Tate). Gross returned to England in 1939 and from 1941 to 1946 served as an Official War Artist, covering campaigns in El Alamein, India, Burma, Iran and Normandy; among the works produced in this connection are three watercolours depicting episodes in the *Liberation and Battle of France* (1944; London, Tate). After World War II he divided his time between France and England, where in 1965 he became the first President of the Print Makers Council. From the 1950s he adopted an increasingly emphatic line and densely packed compositions, particularly in his etchings, for which he remained best known, and devoted much of his attention to landscape, as in *Wheatfield* (etching, 1966; London, Tate).

BIBLIOGRAPHY

The Etchings of Anthony Gross (exh. cat. by G. Reynolds, London, V&A, 1968)
Anthony Gross: Five Decades of Personal Vision (exh. cat. by J. Russell, London, New A. Cent., 1976)
Anthony Gross: Paintings, Drawings, Prints (exh. cat. by J. Lee, Oxford, Ashmolean, 1989)

MONICA BOHM-DUCHEN

Gross, Chaim (*b* Wolow, Austria-Hungary [now Poland], 17 March 1904; *d* 1991). American sculptor, draughtsman, painter and printmaker of Austro-Hungarian birth. After studying art in Budapest and Vienna, he settled in the USA in 1921, continuing his studies in New York at the Educational Alliance Art School and the Art Students League. He produced a large number of works in different media, including stone and bronze sculptures, pen-and-ink drawings and watercolours, but he was noted above all for sculptures in wood such as *Two Sisters* (1956; New York, Mr and Mrs Lewis Garlick priv. col., see 1977 exh. cat., p. 4). He never treated or disguised the surface of wood but respected its basic texture and grain; until the early 1960s he favoured the solid masses of direct carvings in which he exploited the qualities of rare tropical woods and colourful stones. Much of his subject-matter was derived from popular art forms, including the circus, Jewish traditions and holidays, which he recalled from his early years in the Austrian countryside. In later works such as *Happy Children No. 1* (1968; New York, Forum Gal.), sand-cast in bronze from maquettes modelled in plaster, he adopted light, airy forms.

BIBLIOGRAPHY

Chaim Gross: Sculpture and Drawings (exh. cat. by J. C. Taylor and J. A. Flint, Washington, DC, N. Col. F.A., 1974)
Chaim Gross: Retrospective Exhibition (exh. cat. by R. K. Tarbell, New York, Jew. Mus., 1977)

Gross, Michael (*b* Tiberias, Palestine [now Israel], 1920). Israeli painter and sculptor. After studying at the Teachers' Seminary in Jerusalem from 1936 to 1940, he studied architecture at the Technion Institute of Technology in Haifa (1943–5) and art at the Académie des Beaux-Arts in Paris (1951–4). In 1954 he returned to Israel and began working as a painter and sculptor in the artists' village of Ein Hod. In early paintings such as *A Roof and a Window* (1966–7; Jerusalem, Israel Mus.) Gross simplified form in order to concentrate on proportion, on boldly juxtaposed broad areas of colour and on the size and placement of each element; a similar reductive process was applied also to his early sculptures and to later pieces, whether in painted iron or in other materials such as white concrete (e.g. the monumental sculpture at Simon Bolivar Park in Jerusalem, 1974). In later paintings such as *Light of Jerusalem* (triptych, 1974; Jerusalem, Israel Mus.) he often juxtaposed large panels into polyptych formats to build bold shapes of empty off-white fields and broad tonal patches; occasionally these were supplemented by the textures of objects such as wooden beams, burlap and rope physically attached to the picture, as in *Female Nude and a Log of Wood II* (1981–2; Jerusalem, Israel Mus.). In spite of the extreme economy of his work, Gross's rough and freely-brushed surfaces and his consistent use of soft pastel colouring suggest a direct link with the Israeli landscape.

BIBLIOGRAPHY

Michael Gross: 1975–1977 (exh. cat. by M. Scheps, Y. Fischer and M. Gross, Tel Aviv, Mus. A., 1977)
Encounters with Jerusalem, 1968–1986 (exh. cat., intro. M. Omer; Ein Harod, Mus. A., 1980)
Michael Gross: Eight New Works (exh. cat. by M. Omer, Tel Aviv, Mus. A., 1983)
Michael Gross, Seeing Through and Beyond (exh. cat., Tel Aviv, Mus. A., 1985–7)
Michael Gross, Sculptures, Paintings, Drawings, Prints (exh. cat. by J. Nicolau, Haifa, MOMA, 1989)
Michael Gross: Mordechai Omer (exh. cat., Tel Aviv U., Genia Schreiber A.G.)

SUSAN T. GOODMAN

Grossberg, Yitzroch Loiza. *See* RIVERS, LARRY.

Grossheim, Karl von. *See under* KAYSER & VON GROSSHEIM.

Grossi, João [Giovanni] (*b* Milan, 1719; *d* Lisbon, 1781). Italian sculptor and stuccoist, active in Portugal. Sometime between 1740 and 1750 he served Ferdinand VI of Spain as a military designer but fled to Portugal after being involved in a murder. His first commission was for the plaster decoration (before 1755; destr. 1755) of the ceiling of the church of the Mártires (Martyrs), Lisbon, which involved using moulds for the Rococo motifs. He was skilled in modelling stucco, wax and clay, and his lively use of Rococo ornament includes shell forms, flowers and asymmetrical motifs.

Grossi benefited from the patronage of Sebastian Carvalho e Mello, 1st Marquês de Pombal, and among projects commissioned by the Marquês were the stucco ceilings of his palace at Oeiras (*c.* 1770), now the property of the Gulbenkian Foundation. In 1755 Grossi carried out decorative work in the houses of the Machadinho family in Lisbon, with the assistance of Pedro Chantoforo and of his cousin Agostinho de Guardi, who had learnt in central Europe to work stucco using a fresco technique that involved mixing sufficient glue to give the surfaces a high gloss. The earthquake in 1755 brought him many commissions including the ceilings of the Jesuit church of São Antão, Lisbon. An outstanding example of his work, carried out with his cousin Toscanelli, is the plaster ceiling of the 17th-century church of Sta Catarina or dos Paulistas (*c.* 1760), Lisbon. With its asymmetrical targes, foliage and flowers, and allegorical figures tinted to resemble marble, it is one of the finest schemes of Rococo decoration in Portugal.

BIBLIOGRAPHY

Machado
D. de Macedo: 'Notas de arte', *Ocidente*, l (1942), pp. 271–2
——: *A escultura portuguesa nos séculos XVII e XVIII* (Lisbon, 1945)
F. de Pamplona: *Dicionário de pintores e escultores* (Lisbon, 1955)

ANTÓNIO FILIPE PIMENTEL

Grossman, Nancy (*b* New York, 28 April 1940). American sculptor. She studied art at the Pratt Institute, New York (1958–62), and was subsequently awarded a Haskell Scholarship for Foreign Travel in 1962. Her early influences included the American painter Richard Lindner and sculptor David Smith. Grossman's work addresses both philosophical and physical aspects of sculpture. Her first assemblages in the early 1960s incorporated numerous items from an extensive gathering of used materials and found objects. Her works are identified particularly with feminist subjects and sexual themes; they frequently contain an element of repressed sensuality. During the 1970s she became known for her meticulously crafted, life-size male heads, swathed in leather. After an absence from exhibiting between 1977 and 1980, Grossman presented new sculptures that moved away from the obsessive object–totemic works formed from disparate elements bound together with cane and wire. Masks of studded brass and leatherwork nevertheless continued to suggest an undercurrent of sexual tension.

BIBLIOGRAPHY

B. Diamonstein: *Open Secrets* (New York, 1972)
D. Blau: 'Nancy Grossman', *A. Mag.*, lv/6 (Feb 1981), p. 3

□

Grosso, Giacomo (*b* Cambiano, nr Turin, 25 May 1860; *d* Turin, 15 Jan 1938). Italian painter. At the age of 14 he moved to Turin where he attended the Accademia Umbertina and studied under the history painter Andrea Gastaldi (1826–89). He had his first exhibition in 1881 in Turin. In 1883, already an accomplished and sought-after portrait painter, he moved to Rome. Grosso became famous when in 1884 he took part in the Promotrice delle Belle Arti in Turin where he exhibited the *Madwomen's Cell* (1884; Turin, Gal. Civ. A. Mod.), which was inspired by Giovanni Verga's novel *Storia di una capinera*, and which provoked much debate because of its emphatically anti-academic realism. From this time and throughout his long career Grosso continued to paint in a naturalistic idiom that owed much to contemporary French painting. In 1889 he was appointed professor of drawing at the Accademia Albertina, a post that he held for 45 years. A fashionable portrait painter, he tended towards naturalistic effects and theatrical compositions. He was famous for his idealized, voluptuous female nudes, set in turn-of-the-century interiors draped with silks and velvets. He came to be considered the chief exponent of a bourgeois and reactionary conservatism and as such acquired considerable notoriety. He lived for brief periods in Florence, Venice and Paris and maintained numerous contacts with South America. Grosso was a prolific artist. In addition to his activity as a portrait painter, he also executed landscapes, still-lifes, genre scenes, engravings and frescoes (e.g. for S Gioacchino, Turin, *Holy Women at the Sepulchre*, 1896; destr., see 1991 exh. cat., p. 146). His numerous exhibitions included participation at the Venice Biennale of 1895 where he showed the *Last Meeting* (1895; destr.), a painting that provoked much violent debate because of its expressive audacity, and for which he won the Premio del Pubblico.

BIBLIOGRAPHY

Giacomo Grosso nelle collezioni torinesi (Turin, 1960)
A. Fogliato and C. A. Fogliato: 'Il caso Grosso: Un artista "datato"', *Ottocento*, 16 (1987), pp. 92–3
Giacomo Grosso (exh. cat., Turin, Promot. B.A., 1991)

SILVIA LUCCHESI

Grosvalds, Jāzeps (*b* Riga, 24 April 1891; *d* Paris, 1 Feb 1920). Latvian painter, printmaker and diplomat. Raised in a family of patriots, he was naturally suited to become the founder and chief proponent of a modern national style in Latvian painting. His awareness of uniquely Latvian cultural traits grew apace with his dissatisfaction with the training he received from 1909 to 1914 in the studios of Simon Hollósy in Munich and Hermen-Anglada Camarasa, Charles Guérin and Kees van Dongen in Paris; concomitantly, Latvia's struggle for independence during World War I galvanized his devotion to nationalist art, and he was a member of both the Ekspresionisti and the RIGA ARTISTS' GROUP. For younger colleagues working in Riga before the War, Grosvalds was a conduit of information about French and German modernism, though much of it was cautionary. His period of military service inspired him to produce *Refugee* and *Riflemen*, an influential series of paintings and prints that demonstrated his preference for classical monumentality and communicated the epic forbearance of the Latvian peasantry and infantry in exile and in battle. As he had intended, the painting the *Old Refugee* (1917; Riga, Latv. Mus. F.A.) became a national icon. Its solemnity, integrity of form, absence of decoration and earthen palette is typical of his work, and such characteristics would later endear him to the Purists, particularly Amédée Ozenfant. Despite the sobriety of his pictorial means, Grosvalds was a deeply romantic painter, favouring vignettes filled with great pathos and treasuring even the most sombre colours as extractions from the Latvian landscape. His empathy for cultural singularities and mood resulted in his lyrical watercolour series *Persijas ainas* (Persian tableaux; from 1918; e.g. Stockholm, Nmus.; Karlstad, Värmlands Mus.), conceived while serving with a British Army expedition in Iraq and acclaimed by Ozenfant as '"psychogeographic" landscape'. Shortly after completing this series, Grosvalds died in Paris while serving as a diplomat, but his circumspection and restraint continued to affect the timbre of modernism in Latvia.

WRITINGS

Persijas ainas/Tableaux persans (Stockholm, 1978) [bilingual text]

BIBLIOGRAPHY

B. Vipers: *Jāzeps Grosvalds*, Latviešu māksla monografiju serija [Latvian art monograph series] (Riga, 1938)

MARK ALLEN SVEDE

Grosvenor. English family of patrons and collectors. The family, of Norman descent, settled in Eaton, Ches, in the 15th century. Eaton Hall (destr. 1963; rebuilt 1989) was built for Sir Thomas Grosvenor, 3rd Baronet (1656–1700), between 1675 and 1683 on designs by the architect William Samwell (1628–76). In 1677 Grosvenor married Mary Davis, the 11-year-old heiress of the manor of Ebury, and acquired the developing areas of Mayfair (100 acres) and Belgravia and Pimlico (*c*. 400 acres) in London (now borough of Westminster), on which the family's vast wealth was to be founded. The development of Mayfair began in 1720, and the centrepiece was Grosvenor Square (1725–31); work did not begin in Belgravia until 1820, when (2) Robert Grosvenor, 2nd Earl Grosvenor and 1st Marquess of Westminster, employed the architect THOMAS CUBITT to develop the area with residential properties, of which Belgrave Square (1826), laid out by GEORGE BASEVI, became the centrepiece. The family also acquired an outstanding collection of paintings, which was started by (1) Richard Grosvenor, 7th Baronet and 1st Earl Grosvenor. The family and the trustees of the estate have retained control of much of the area, selling only Pimlico (1950); the areas remain some of the most exclusive parts of London.

□

(1) Sir **Richard Grosvenor**, 7th Baronet and 1st Earl Grosvenor (*b* 18 June 1731; *d* London, 5 Aug 1802). He was the eldest son of Sir Robert Grosvenor, 6th Baronet, and Jane Warre of Swell Court. In 1755 he succeeded his father as 7th Baronet and in 1784 was created Earl Grosvenor. In 1758–9 Richard Dalton, librarian to the Prince of Wales (later George III), was sent to Italy to procure works of art for the Prince; at the same time he purchased 42 Old Masters for Grosvenor, which later formed the nucleus of the Grosvenor Gallery at Grosvenor House, London. A sum of £3 was paid by the Eaton agent in 1761 to John Leadbetter for 'painting a large tarpaulin for Eaton Hall Dining Room'. This was possibly a preparatory painting for *Mares and Foals under an Oak Tree*, the background landscape being recorded before 'Capability' Brown's rearrangement in 1764. George Stubbs's *Grosvenor Hunt* was painted in the Saloon (1762; Eaton Hall, Ches; *in situ*; *see* SPORTING SCENES, fig. 2). Other contemporary artists from whom Grosvenor purchased paintings were Benjamin West, Gainsborough, Hogarth and John Wilson.

BIBLIOGRAPHY

DNB

P. de Figueiredo and J. Treuherz: *Cheshire Country Houses* (Chichester, 1988)

IRENE MAY BAKER

(2) Robert Grosvenor, 2nd Earl Grosvenor and 1st Marquess of Westminster (*b* London, 22 March 1767; *d* Eaton, Ches, 17 Feb 1845). Son of (1) Sir Richard Grosvenor. He succeeded his father as 2nd Earl Grosvenor in 1802 and was created Marquess of Westminster in 1831, an honour he owed to his support of the Whig party. The heir to substantial property in Cheshire and to the Grosvenor Estate in London, he also inherited the collection formed by his father. The 2nd Earl's purchase in 1805 of Grosvenor House (now replaced by the Grosvenor House Hotel), Park Lane, London, was the catalyst for an extraordinary campaign of acquisition of works of art. The most important feature of the house, the picture gallery, was redecorated at a cost of £17,000 in 1807–8 by William Porden, surveyor of the Grosvenor Estate, who also was responsible for reconstructing Eaton Hall, Ches, in the Gothic style (1804–12).

In 1806 Grosvenor acquired *en bloc* the collection of Welbore Agar Ellis for 30,000 guineas. This included a celebrated group of landscapes by Claude, of which *Evening* and *Morning* (both Duke of Westminster priv. col.) were considered the most valuable. Other masterpieces from the Agar Ellis collection included *The Riding School* (Duke of Westminster priv. col.) by Velázquez. Another acquisition of 1806 was Rubens's altarpiece of the *Adoration of the Magi* (Cambridge, King's Coll.), bought at the sale of pictures acquired by William Petty, 2nd Earl of Shelburne and 1st Marquess of Lansdowne. Grosvenor was advised on his purchases by William Seguier, who from 1806 received a retainer of £100 a year to attend to the collection. Many pictures acquired by the 1st Earl were sold in 1807, but the 2nd Earl continued to buy individual masterpieces, including in 1809 Gainsborough's *Blue Boy* (San Marino, CA, Huntington Lib. & A.G.).

The acquisition in 1818 of four large tapestry designs by Rubens from the monastery of Loeches (Sarasota, FL, Ringling Mus. A.) was the cause of the extension of the gallery at Grosvenor House, undertaken by Thomas Cundy (i) and his son Thomas Cundy (ii) at a total cost of £23,000. This addition is seen in the conversation piece of the Grosvenor family commissioned in 1831 from C. R. Leslie (Duke of Westminster priv. col.). A catalogue of the collection was published by John Young in 1821, and of the great London galleries of the period only those of Cleveland (later Bridgewater) House, Stafford House and Apsley House were of comparable scale. Lord Grosvenor was not a pioneering connoisseur, but his resources—owed largely to the development of his London property—meant that he could buy works of the highest quality by fashionable artists; his collection was therefore a *locus classicus* of early 19th-century patrician taste.

BIBLIOGRAPHY

J. Young: *A Catalogue of the Pictures at Grosvenor House, London; with Etchings from the Whole Collection Executed by Permission of the Noble Proprietor, and Accompanied by Historical Notices of the Principal Works* (London, 1821)

G. F. Waagen: *Treasures of Art in Great Britain*, ii (London, 1854), pp. 161–74

G. Huxley: *Lady Elizabeth and the Grosvenors: Life in a Whig Family* (London, 1967)

G. Acloque and J. Cornforth: 'The Eternal Gothic of Eaton', *Country Life*, cxlix (11 Feb 1971), pp. 304–7; cxlix (18 Feb 1971), pp. 360–64

J. Cornforth: 'Old Grosvenor House', *Country Life*, cliv (15 Nov 1973), pp. 1538–41

The Grosvenor Treasures (exh. cat., Eaton Hall, Ches, 1984)

FRANCIS RUSSELL

(3) Hugh Lupus Grosvenor, 3rd Marquess and 1st Duke of Westminster (*b* Eaton Hall, Ches, 13 Oct 1825; *d* Dorset, 22 Dec 1889). Grandson of (2) Robert Grosvenor. He succeeded his father Richard Grosvenor, 2nd Marquess of Westminster (1795–1869). In 1868 he travelled to France and Italy to purchase furniture, marbles, mosaics, pictures, statuary and ceramics, which were used to furnish Eaton Hall, Cheshire. In 1870 Grosvenor employed ALFRED WATERHOUSE to reorganize completely and transform Eaton Hall. The work lasted 13 years and cost £600,000. Grosvenor's purchases of paintings included Turner's *Conway Castle* in 1876, the Magniac Miniatures and Dürer's *The Hare* in 1870; he also patronized contemporary artists, including Edward Burne-Jones, John Everett Millais, Edwin Lutyens and Frederick Goodall. Rodin visited nearby Saighton Grange as a guest of the Duke's previous daughter-in-law, Lady Sibell Grosvenor, and her second husband, George Wyndham. Grosvenor was a great philanthropist and spent large sums of money on rebuilding whole villages and building schools and churches on his estates.

BIBLIOGRAPHY

F. Herrmann: *The English as Collectors: A Documentary Chrestomathy* (London, 1972)

P. de Figueiredo and J. Treuherz: *Cheshire Country Houses* (Chichester, 1988)

IRENE MAY BAKER

Grosz, George [Georg] (*b* Berlin, 26 July 1893; *d* W. Berlin, 6 July 1959). German painter, draughtsman and illustrator. He is particularly valued for his caustic caricatures, in which he used the reed pen with notable success. Although his paintings are not quite as significant as his graphic art, a number of them are, nonetheless, major works. He grew up in the provincial town of Stolp, Pomerania (now Słupsk, Poland), where he attended the Oberrealschule, until he was expelled for disobedience. From 1909 to 1911 he attended the Akademie der Künste in Dresden, where he met Kurt Günther, Bernhard Kretschmar (1889–1972) and Franz Lenk (*b* 1898). Under his teacher Richard Müller (1874–1954), Grosz painted and drew from plaster casts. At this time he was unaware of such avant-garde movements as Die Brücke, also active in Dresden. In 1912 he studied with Emil Orlik at the Kunstgewerbeschule in Berlin. A year later he moved to the Académie Colarossi in Paris, where he learnt a free drawing style that swiftly reached the essence of a motif.

Before World War I, Grosz was completely apolitical. As a young man he sought refuge from the reality of his lower-middle-class circumstances in the fictitious world of cheap novelettes. He formed a predilection for modern adventures, assassinations, catastrophes, man-hunts and executions. In his early drawings Grosz rendered these subjects with a mixture of contradictory styles, which became a characteristic of his work. He was particularly influenced by the caricatures in satirical *Jugendstil* periodicals, copying their schematic, expressive gestures and hectic movements. Grosz was also impressed by the sublime gestures of historical academic painting, which he combined with exactly rendered elements from his immediate surroundings. His realism was also exemplified by his sensational reproductions of horrifying scenes.

In 1914 Grosz, like many of his generation, volunteered for service in World War I. Six months later he was back in Germany. Although he was called up again in 1917, he was finally discharged as unfit for service after an episode involving violence and a short compulsory spell in a mental hospital. With the war his artistic approach changed fundamentally, taking its starting-point from his own experience of battlefields, death and destruction. Grosz had learnt to hate war and German militarism, as can be seen in the drawing *Fit for Active Service* (1916–17; New York, MOMA; *see* SATIRE, fig. 3). Such feelings gave rise to his aversion for Germans, whom he saw as ugly, obese and degenerate: 'I drew and painted from a spirit of contradiction, and attempted in my work to convince the world that this world is ugly, sick and mendacious' (*Kunstblatt*, 1924). The war made Grosz into a misanthropist and a Utopian. In his art he fought against preoccupations of Wilhelmine society by uncovering their shadowy aspects of crime, murder and erotic licence. The sexual murder became a prominent motif, in which the combination of sexuality and violence was presented as a ritualization of the human quest for power, exemplified by political practice. Art became the vehicle of his pessimistic world view, reflecting a ruined world that manifested itself most trenchantly in the big city and its excesses.

In 1915 Grosz met Wieland Herzfelde (1896–1989) and Helmut Herzfelde (who soon after changed his name to John Heartfield) in Berlin. They became enthusiastic supporters of his uncompromising stance: a year later he changed his first name to George and began to work for Wieland Herzfelde's left-wing literary–political journal *Neue Jugend*, and began to share a studio with Heartfield. Grosz frequented the Alte Café des Westerns, where he became familiar with revolutionary ideas. Out of opposition to the military scare campaign against Britain and intellectual affinity to the USA, he anglicized his name, which confirmed his anti-nationalist attitude. By giving his art a strong moral purpose, he intended to become the German Hogarth. In 1918 he listed the qualities that he wished his art to possess: 'Hardness, brutality, clarity that hurts! There's enough soporific music.' In the same year he joined the German Communist Party.

The war experience influenced not only his work's content but also his style. In the painting *Dedication to Oskar Panizza* (1917–18; Stuttgart, Staatsgal.) he conveyed a hellish vision of the big city as a valediction to Wilhelmine society and its representatives: the composition is formed of simultaneous scenes overlapping in the painting and reproducing reality in a fragmentary form. In this aspect the influence of the Italian Futurists is clear; they had made a lasting impression on him through an exhibition held by Herwarth Walden in the Sturm-Galerie, Berlin, in 1913. An immense crowd of people—porcine grimacing faces, and stout citizens in bowler hats and pinstriped trousers between half-naked prostitutes, monarchists and clerics—flows between collapsing façades. They form a danse macabre against a blood-red background. 'That this epoch is heading downhill towards destruction is my unshakable conviction', he wrote to a friend in 1917.

George Grosz: *Max Herrmann-Neisse*, oil on canvas, 1.0×1.0 m, 1925 (Mannheim, Städtische Kunsthalle Mannheim)

Such a critical analysis of his time, together with its radical pictorial formulation, brought Grosz close to the Berlin Dada movement, which he joined in 1918 (*see* DADA, §4). In 1920, with Heartfield and Otto Dix, he took part in the Erste Internationale Dada-Messe. As well as developing the technique of PHOTOMONTAGE, Grosz and Heartfield criticized the contemporary art world and the elevation of the artist to quasi-divine status. In a letter of opposition to the 'Novembergruppe' (*Der Gegner* 2, no. 8–9, 1921), Grosz called on artists to 'collaborate in the building of a new human community, the community of working people'.

Grosz made his contribution towards realizing this goal by engaging with contemporary events through his works. For him Dada was the expression of a specific political stance. He remained politically committed even when he left Dada and turned to a realistic style of painting in the 1920s, in keeping with the spirit of the decade. During this period Grosz became internationally recognized as one of Germany's most significant critical artists. The antagonisms of artistic and political life in the Weimar Republic found an extreme form of expression in Grosz's work. Grosz himself was torn between a partisan, rationalist attitude and a passionate, reckless craving for the feverish pleasures of the 1920s, between basic Communist convictions and a longing for the USA. In his work he created a portrait, with acerbic cynicism, of the manners of the Weimar period, developing a new artistic idiom. He characterized the age in terms of the class society and invented specific figures who stood for the new classes and economic interests in German society. A few signs suffice to enable the artist to mark out a particular temporal and social context, and to indicate class and group affiliations: war cripples are depicted beside ragged soldiers, fat, cigar-smoking bourgeois figures and businessmen with monocles, suits and homburgs. In 1926 Grosz produced his major work, the *Pillars of Society* (Berlin, Neue N.G.; *see* GERMANY, fig. 25). He depicted the representatives of the ruling class—press publishers, nationalists, monarchists and clerics—as a class of brainless and amoral people and held them responsible for the reactionary spirit, the hypocrisy and the beginnings of renewed warmongering in Germany. Grosz launched his most vicious attacks on society after World War I in his drawings: in 1920 the first two collections were published by Wieland Herzfelde's Malik-Verlag. In 1928 the collection *Background*, which contained the drawing *Shut Your Mouth and Keep on Serving*, showing Christ on the cross wearing a gas-mask and soldiers' boots, brought an accusation of blasphemy: the case continued until 1933. As well as producing portfolios of drawings, Grosz also illustrated works by such writers as Alphonse Daudet.

Grosz's political commitment and increasing popularity brought him into lively contact with the cultural élite of the time, for example Kurt Tucholsky, Erwin Piscator, Josef von Sternberg and Bertolt Brecht. As conditions became more stable he gained a certain standing and was adopted by the gallery of Alfred Flechtheim in 1925. However, his attitude towards the class struggle was thereby blunted. He subsequently received portrait commissions from personages of the time (e.g. portrait of the poet *Max Herrmann-Neisse*; see fig.): he carried these out using a glazing technique borrowed from the Old Masters, which he had seen Dix using in Dresden. In these portraits Grosz neither caricatured nor poured scorn on his subjects. On the contrary, he rendered physiognomies marked by fate, displaying subtle psychological insight and employing a form of realism that placed him among the exponents of NEUE SACHLICHKEIT.

With the increasing strength of the Nazis, Grosz came under renewed outward pressure and considered, as he had done before, emigrating to the USA, the free land of his youthful dreams. He was encouraged in this by the early recognition accorded to his work there, and by a visiting professorship at the Art Students League, New York, in 1932. He continued to teach there until 1955. In 1933, shortly before Adolf Hitler's seizure of power, he left permanently for the USA. Under the influence of new, positive impressions, and because he had lost his faith in the strength of the masses, he turned away from political propaganda and lost his mordant style. Almost affectionately, he caricatured New York types and painted landscapes from nature. In 1958, with his collages that point in some ways towards Pop art, he reverted to Dada techniques. In 1959 he returned to West Berlin, where he died soon afterwards.

WRITINGS

Ein kleines Ja und ein grosses Nein (Hamburg, 1955)

BIBLIOGRAPHY

W. Wolfradt: *George Grosz* (Leipzig, 1921)

George Grosz: Frühe Druckgraphick, Sammelwerke, illustrierte Bücher, 1914–1923 (exh. cat. by A. Dückers, Berlin, Kupferstichkab., 1971)

U. M. Schneede: *George Grosz: Der Künstler in seiner Gesellschaft* (Cologne, 1975)

——: *George Grosz: Leben und Werk* (Hamburg and Frankfurt am Main, 1975)

L. Fischer: *George Grosz in Selbstzeugnissen und Bilddokumenten* (Reinbek, 1976)

H. Hess: *George Grosz* (Dresden, 1982)

K. M. Flavell: *George Grosz: A Biography* (New Haven and London, 1988)
George Grosz, die Berliner Jahre: Zeichnungen und Aquarelle (exh. cat., ed. S. Sabarsky; Passau, Mus. Mod. Kst, 1993)
George Grosz: Berlin–New York (exh. cat., ed. P.-K. Schuster; Berlin, Tiergarten, N.G., 1994)

URSULA ZELLER

Grotell, Maija (*b* Helsinki, 19 Aug 1899; *d* 1973). American potter and teacher of Finnish birth. She studied at the School of Industrial Art in Helsinki and then under Alfred William Finch (1854–1930), a Belgian potter working in Helsinki, for six years. She arrived in the USA in 1927 and studied with Charles Fergus Binns at Alfred University, Alfred, NY. She taught in several institutions including the Henry Street Settlement House, New York City, and Rutgers University, New Brunswick, NJ, before being invited in 1938 to teach at the Cranbrook Academy of Art, Bloomfield Hills, MI, one of the foremost art schools in America. At Cranbrook Grotell's work developed from low-fired figurative pots to simplified geometric forms in stoneware and porcelain. She experimented with glazes and glaze effects, especially those using ash, copper, chrome and iron; Albany slip (dark brown) and Bristol glaze (thick and white) were among her favourites. Grotell was in charge of the ceramic department at Cranbrook until she retired in 1966.

BIBLIOGRAPHY

Cranbrook Academy of Art: *Cranbrook Ceramics, 1950–1980* (Bloomfield Hills, 1983)

ELLEN PAUL DENKER

Grotesque. French term derived from the Italian *grottesco*, describing a type of European ornament composed of small, loosely connected motifs, including scrollwork, architectural elements, whimsical human figures and fantastic beasts, often organized vertically around a central axis.

1. Origins. 2. 1480–1529. 3. 1530–1600. 4. 1601–1752. 5. After 1752.

1. ORIGINS. Grotesque ornament was inspired by the archaeological discovery at the end of the 15th century, of the ancient Roman interiors of the Domus Aurea of Nero in Rome, and by subsequent finds of other palaces, tombs and villas in and around Rome and Naples. The interior walls and ceilings of these underground rooms, known as *grotte*, were painted in a light and playful manner previously unknown to those familiar only with the formal grammar of Classical ornament derived from more accessible antique ruins. A ceiling in such a room might be covered with an interlocking arrangement of compartments containing mythological or allegorical scenes depicted as *trompe l'oeil* cameos, or it might be subdivided into areas dominated by a single such compartment with the remaining space filled with a variety of motifs, symmetrically organized but otherwise unrelated either by scale or subject-matter. Vitruvius, in his treatise *On Architecture* (*c.* 15 BC), Book VII, had contemptuously described this kind of painting: 'Reeds are substituted for columns, fluted appendages with curly leaves and volutes take the place of pediments, candelabra support representation of shrines, and on top of their roofs grow slender stalks and volutes, with human figures senselessly seated upon them.' This play of fantasy and appeal to the realm of the senses, as opposed to the monumental solemnity of much rediscovered Roman architecture and sculpture, captured the imagination of Renaissance artists and revived the medieval predilection for the fanciful and the monstrous seen in

1. Grotesque design by Raphael's workshop for a pilaster in the Vatican Loggia, 1518–19; engraving by Giovanni Ottaviani after Gaetano Savorelli and Pietro Camporese from *Loggie di Raffaele nel Vaticano* (Rome, 1772)

the ornament in the margins of medieval manuscripts or the stone gargoyles of abbeys and cathedrals.

2. 1480–1529. Soon after its discovery at the end of the 15th century, Classical grotesque ornament was copied and disseminated by the drawings of Italian artists, mostly from Umbria and Florence. However, many artists were uncomfortable with the loose organization of unconnected elements and sought to impose a structure that would enable them to use the motifs in a more orderly manner. They therefore employed a vertical format based on the pilaster and traditional candelabrum type of framework, with individual motifs placed one above the other and connected by a central axis; the engravings of Giovanni Pietro da Birago (late 15th-century; London, V&A) are some of the earliest examples of this format. The decorative candelabrum also appeared in such frescoes as those (1489–93) by Filippino Lippi in the Carafa Chapel in S Maria sopra Minerva in Rome, in the Collegio del Cambio (1499), Perugia, by Perugino, in the chapel of the Assumption (1499–1503) at Orvieto Cathedral by Luca Signorelli, and in the fresco cycle (1492–4) of the Appartamento Borgia in the Vatican by Bernardino Pinturicchio. Engravings of grotesque designs were also circulated to craftsmen in other media: silversmiths, goldsmiths and sculptors adapted the designs engraved by Nicoletto da Modena, Giovanni Antonio da Brescia, Agostino dei Musi, Enea Vico and by Marcantonio Raimondi and his school. In Raphael's painted interiors in the Vatican, the *stufetta* (1516) of Cardinal Bernardo Bibbiena and the Vatican Loggia (1518–19), grotesque ornament was developed into complete decorative schemes. In the Loggia, the candelabrum motif was used extensively, dividing the entire surface of the wall into some 200 vertical strips within which a compendium of classical motifs mingled with fantastic birds and animals, fruit and foliage, scrollwork and abstract ornament (see fig. 1). A new element was also introduced in the irregularly shaped compartments of the vaulted ceiling by allowing sections of the bandwork border to penetrate the space of the design, producing a kind of internal scaffolding on which individual motifs could be supported. This innovation was developed further by Raphael's successors in bandwork and strapwork that firmly enclosed and anchored the whimsical grotesques. His style was immediately imitated by his assistants: Giovanni da Udine at the Villa Madama in Rome (1525), and Giulio Romano at the Palazzo del Te in Mantua (mid-1520s–*c.* 1535).

3. 1530–1600. In 1530 Francis I invited Rosso Fiorentino to decorate his new château at Fontainebleau. Rosso was joined in 1532 by Francesco Primaticcio, and together they created a new, more elaborate form of ornament and a richer variation on the grotesque theme for the decoration of the Galerie (*in situ*). The STRAPWORK or bandwork used by Rosso and Primaticcio at Fontainebleau enclosed a series of allegorical frescoes on the grandeur of royalty and the glory of the French king. This structure anchored the paintings within a framework of complex curling straps in high-relief stucco within which were imprisoned monumental figures, putti, hybrid monsters, garlands, swags and the king's emblem: the salamander. The ornament of Raphael and his followers had been small in scale, delicate, in low relief and classical. No precedent existed for the robust, twisted, bent, overlapping leather-like strapwork depicted at Fontainebleau. This transmutation of classical scrollwork into a richly hybrid type of ornament was Rosso's contribution to the contemporary Mannerist taste for the distorted, the twisted, the ambiguous and the strange.

Another significant contribution to the history of the grotesque in this period was the decorative tradition of Islam, which provided the inspiration for the stylized, interlaced complex patterns of foliage and abstract geometric shapes in an endlessly interlaced linear rhythm that were known in the West as ARABESQUES or Moresques after their Saracenic origins. Damascened and engraved metalwork produced in the Near East, and by Muslim craftsmen in Venice at the end of the 15th century, was decorated with sinuously interwoven lines that created a strong bandwork design, with ogival intersections enclosing variegated polygonal shapes in a repeated framework. Although the delicate scale of Arabesque ornament is very different from the three-dimensional solidity of the style of Rosso Fiorentino, it was Rosso's assistant, Francesco Pellegrino (*d* 1552), who produced one of the first books of Arabesque designs, *La Fleur de la science de pourtraicture* (Paris, 1530), and many artists working at Fontainebleau used Arabesque ornament in their own work, including André Boyvin (*c.* 1525–98), Léonard Thiry and Antonio Fantuzzi. The impact of Fontainebleau was immense: a union of classical grotesques and northern strapwork, enriched by Arabesque influence, had been forged there, and subsequently the two types of ornament developed together.

After the death of Rosso in 1540, Primaticcio became the overseer of the works at Fontainebleau. From 1540 to 1570 he decorated the Galerie d'Ulysse (destr.) with grotesques that were light and elegant, less naturalistic than those of Raphael and his school, and that also incorporated a strapwork structure. He continued to use this decorative scheme at the château of Ancy-le-Franc in Burgundy (1546; *in situ*), where the ceiling of the Chambre de Diane echoed the designs from the Domus Aurea and the Villa Madama in Rome. It also included new details that were to become an important part of 17th-century French ornamental vocabulary: the pelmet shape, the temple structure and graceful depictions of the Four Elements. Primaticcio's work was a significant influence upon Jacques Androuet Du Cerceau (i), who published engraved designs for furniture, silver and textiles in *Livre de grotesques* (*Petites grotesques*, Paris, 1562; *Grandes arabesques*, Paris, 1582). Inspired by such Italian designers as Agostino Veneziano and Enea Vico, Du Cerceau's work was particularly important for the development of furniture, providing a characteristically French alliance of classical form with voluminous carved imaginary motifs that was to influence the architect and designer Hugues Sambin.

During the second half of the 16th century the engraved designs of the Fontainebleau grotesque and strapwork decoration were disseminated throughout Europe. Such books as *Livre de la conqueste de la toison d'or* (1563),

2. Grotesque etching by Hans Vredeman de Vries; from his *Grottesco in diversche manieren* (Antwerp, *c.* 1565)

designed and drawn by Léonard Thiry and engraved by René Boyvin, or *Petit ornemens* (1560) by Etienne Delaune spread the fashion in the northern countries, and treatises proliferated to meet the demand of workshops and studios. *Veelderley veranderinghe van grotissen ende compatimenten* ('Grotesque ornaments and tomb designs'; Antwerp, 1556) by Cornelis Floris and *Grottesco in diversche manieren* (Antwerp, *c.* 1565; see fig. 2) by Hans Vredeman de Vries were published in the Low Countries. In Germany some outstanding designs for metalwork were produced by Georg Wechter I in *30 Stuck zum Verzachnen fur die Goldschmied Verfertigt Geörg Wecher 15 Maller 79 Nürmberg* (Nuremberg, 1579). A more tortured element was introduced to the grotesque by Wendel Dietterlin in *Architectura und Ausstheilung der V. Seulen* (Stuttgart and Strasbourg, 1593). Although the grotesque motif was then being used mainly on furniture and silverware, it was still employed in interior decoration, for example in the library (destr.), designed by Friedrich Sustris, of the apartments of Hans Fugger in the Fugger Palace in Augsburg (1568–75).

During the second half of the 16th century and the beginning of the 17th, the grotesque was a contributory factor to the development of the hybrid reptilian forms of the AURICULAR STYLE, of which Adam van Vianen from Utrecht was the main exponent.

4. 1601–1752. In the 17th century, while Germany and the Low Countries were absorbed in the extravagant Fontainebleau style, France returned to a sense of classical restraint and discipline. In 1627 Simon Vouet returned from Rome, where he had studied antique remains as well as Renaissance works. In 1644 he decorated the Cabinet des Bains (destr.) of Anne of Austria at the Palais-Royal in Paris with classical grotesques; the designs survive in *Livre de diverses grotesques peintes dans le cabinet des bains de la reine regente au palais royal* (Paris, 1647). The style was rather heavy, but harmonious, with landscapes and figures incorporated among the flat, ponderous acanthus scrollwork.

During the reign of Louis XIV (1643–1715) the whimsical grotesque had no part in the majestic court style that evolved under the direction of Charles Le Brun; the lighter spirit of classical ornament was, however, revived by the designer Jean Berain I. In 1671 he designed the painted stucco grotesques that decorate the Galerie d'Apollon at the Louvre. This light and airy style of decoration was developed simultaneously by several other ornamentalists: Claude Audran III (for illustration *see* AUDRAN, (3)), Claude Gillot and Antoine Watteau. Berain was among the first to use the interlaced bandwork and delicate tendrils reminiscent of the Muslim Arabesque in the frame surrounding a central design, usually a figure or group of figures standing under a fanciful architectural structure, with various animals, insects and hybrid creatures frolicking beneath swags, ribbons and trophies of all sorts. His work was an important influence on André-Charles Boulle, whose mirror (early 18th century; London, Wallace) for Charlotte de Saint-Simon, Princesse de Chimay, exhibits all these motifs together with lambrequins and SINGERIE. Textiles also employed the grotesque vocabulary: Audran's tapestry cartoons, the *Douze mois grotesques* (1699; published Paris, 1726), and Gillot's *Livre de portières*, published after his death (Paris, 1737), developed Berain's ornament further by softening the bandwork frame and introducing curves instead of angular lines. Bandwork was gradually reduced to the curving ribbons and tendrils important in the ROCOCO style, a particularly French version of grotesque ornament that spread to the whole of Europe. Designs by Juste-Aurèle Meissonnier and François de Cuvilliés I are triumphs of Rococo art, in which the Saracenic origins of the flowing, interlacing and interweaving bandwork are hardly recognizable.

5. AFTER 1752. The publication of the excavations of Pompeii and Herculaneum in 1752 renewed awareness of the Classical grotesque. Artists again sought inspiration in Rome, where they looked not only at the Classical examples but also at the work of Raphael. Engravings of the Vatican Loggia had been published in the 16th and 17th centuries, but a new publication in 1772 by Giovanni Battista Volpato was followed in 1776 by a set of engravings of the Domus Aurea itself by Lodovico Miri. Ornamentalists and artists throughout Europe took up the style again. In France Jules-Hughes Rousseau (1743–1806) and his brother Jean-Simeon Rousseau de La Rottière (1747–after 1781) adapted it for the Petits Appartements of Marie-Antoinette at Versailles in 1783 and at Fontainebleau in 1786, achieving ensembles of great elegance and refinement. In order to become acceptable to the Age of Reason, the grotesque had shed its earlier fantastic and monstrous qualities, although in doing so it had lost much of its previous vitality.

Grotesque ornament was a component of the Etruscan style, which Robert Adam used for the decoration of the Etruscan Dressing-room (1775) at Osterley Park House, Middx. Charles Percier and Pierre-François-Léonard Fontaine also created attenuated, graceful grotesque ornament interspersed with *trompe-l'oeil* cameo panels at the château of Malmaison in 1799. In these forms the style was gracious and elegant but deprived of its earlier robustness. In the 19th century grotesque ornament was often featured in such Renaissance Revival interiors as those at Chatsworth (1840s), Derbys, and Longleat, Wilts, by the Crace family of decorators.

The 20th-century ethos no longer favoured the elegant decorative qualities of the grotesque, the whimsical, fanciful motifs disciplined within a classical format. Yet there might be a distant reminiscence in the controlled designs of the fantastic and evocative curves and forms of Art Nouveau and Symbolist artists such as Aubrey Beardsley or Gustav Klimt, or in the Surrealist *frottages* of Max Ernst and the meandering line of Paul Klee.

BIBLIOGRAPHY

Vitruvius: *De architectura* (*c.* 15 BC); Eng. trans. by M. H. Morgan as *The Ten Books on Architecture* (Cambridge, MA, 1914/*R* New York, 1960)
D. Guilmard: *Les Maîtres ornemanistes* (Paris, 1880)
P. Jessen: *Der Ornamentstich* (Berlin, 1920)
——: *Meister des Ornamentstiches* (Berlin, 1923)
J. Baltrusaitis: *Réveils et prodiges* (Paris, 1960)
P. Ward-Jackson: 'Some Main Streams and Tributaries in European Ornament, 1500–1750', *V&A Mus. Bull.*, 3 (1967), pp. 58–70, 90–103
N. Dacos: *La Découverte de la Domus Aurea et la formation des grotesques à la Renaissance* (London and Leiden, 1969)
C. Ossola: *Autunno del rinascimento* (Florence, 1971)
A. Chastel: *La Grotesque* (Paris, 1988)

MONIQUE RICCARDI-CUBITT

Grotta. *See under* NAXOS, §1.

Grottes, Sebastian. *See* GÖTZ, SEBASTIAN.

Grottger, Artur (*b* Ottyniowice na Podolu, Eastern Galicia, 11 Nov 1837; *d* Amélie-les-Bains, Pyrénées-Orientales, 13 Dec 1867). Polish draughtsman and painter. He received his first drawing-lessons from his father Jan Józef Grottger (1799–1853), a talented amateur artist. From 1848 or 1850 he studied drawing and painting under Jan Kanty Maszkowski (1794–1865) and Juliusz Kossak in Lwów (now Lviv, Ukraine). His watercolour the *Entry of Francis Joseph into Lwów* (1851), brought Grottger an imperial scholarship in 1852, enabling him to continue his studies in the Kraków School of Fine Arts, under Władysław Łuszczkiewicz (1828–1900) and Wojciech Kornel Stattler (1800–75). During this period he met the Bavarian magnate Aleksander Pappenheim, who purchased his painting the *Recovery of the Tatars' Booty* (1854; Stuttgart, Roland Willer priv. col.) and remained his patron and benefactor until 1863. Early in his career Grottger painted numerous battle-scenes, in oil and watercolour, whose landscape sections are frequently inept, but whose horses, riders and fighting cavalry are depicted with great vitality and sense of movement. In 1854 he travelled to Vienna, where he studied at the Akademie der Bildenden Künste in 1855–9 under Karl von Blaas, Carl Wurzinger (1817–83) and Peter Geiger (1805–80). He lived in Vienna until 1865, working as an illustrator for various periodicals including *Mussestunden*, *Illustrierte Zeitung* and, from 1862, *Postęp*, whose editor he became in 1863. About 300 drawings are attributed to Grottger, and together these constitute a cohesive political, social, literary and satirical commentary on contemporary and historical events. In Vienna Grottger continued to produce watercolours but he also painted numerous oils, including a number of historical compositions (e.g. *Sigismund II Augustus and Barbara Radziwiłłówna*, two versions: 1859/60; ex-J. Radziwiłł priv. col., Tyczyn; and 1860; ex-Wodzicki priv. col., Kraków), works on themes from the January Uprising of 1863 (*In the Saski Gardens*, 1863; Warsaw, N. Mus.), some portraits (*Gräfin Thun with Roses*, 1860; Bytom, Mus. Upper Silesia), and a number of self-portraits. In several series of deeply patriotic drawings Grottger depicted events preceding the January Uprising (e.g. *Warsaw I*, 1861, Wrocław, N. Mus.; and *Warsaw II*, 1863, London, V&A). A further series, *Lithuania* (1864–6; Kraków, N. Mus.), was devoted to the Lithuanian peasant–partisan movement, while *War* (1867; Wroceław, N. Mus.) was a protest against the mutual destruction of nations. These series were popularized through albums published by the Viennese firm of F. Bodny. In 1865 Grottger returned to Poland, visiting Kraków and Lwów, but in 1866 he left for good. He travelled to Paris, and then, seriously ill, to the South of France, where he died. His last *Self-portrait* (1867; Warsaw, N. Mus.) was executed shortly before his death.

BIBLIOGRAPHY

PSB; *SAP*
W. Juszczak: *Artur Grottger: Pięć cyklow* [Artur Grottger: five series] (Warsaw, 1957)
M. Porebski: *Interregnum* (Warsaw, 1975), pp. 129–91
Polnische Malerei von 1830 bis 1914 (exh. cat., Kiel, Christian-Albrechts U., Ksthalle; Stuttgart, Württemberg. Kstver.; Wuppertal, von der Heydt-Mus.; 1978–9), pp. 43–62, 191–4
La Peinture polonaise du XVIe au début du XXe siècle, Warsaw, N. Mus. cat. (Warsaw, 1979), pp. 191–4

WANDA MAŁASZEWSKA

Grotto. Artificial cavern built above a spring or a fountain, usually in a private garden. In Classical times grottoes were widespread in Mediterranean countries, and after the Renaissance they became common throughout Europe. Used initially as a place in which to honour the Muses and to seek philosophical inspiration, the grotto could also form a pleasant summer retreat, the running water affording coolness and repose. It gradually acquired associations with magic and alchemy, and later with Christianity.

Natural rock grottoes were regarded by the ancient Greeks as the abode of nymphs and deities, and the water emerging within them was considered sacred. In some cases doorways were simulated at the entrances, and later fountain-houses were built, with a basin to hold the sacred water. Hellenistic fountain-grottoes of the 3rd century BC could be semicircular or of a tall fountain type later found at Pompeii, some decorated with shells, others with lion-headed waterspouts. Under the Romans, nymphaea became huge public buildings decorated with tufa, shells and innumerable statues, but those in private gardens, with rich statuary, preserved their traditional character as shrines and seats of the Muses. In Roman literature and painting the idea of the grotto was frequently used to emphasize the rustic atmosphere of a landscape or scene.

The nymphaeum at Hadrian's Villa (AD 118–34) at Tivoli is regarded as the most famous from Classical antiquity (*see* TIVOLI, §2(i)), and the grotto of the nymph Egeria in the villa of Herod Atticus (first half of the 2nd century AD), again on private land, was one of the most frequently visited fountain shrines in Rome. Owing to its good state of preservation and the figure of the sleeping nymph (*in situ*), it was an influential model during the Renaissance.

Excavations in the 15th and 16th centuries led to the revival and re-creation of the ancient form of building. The discovery of the 'grotesques' at the Domus Aurea in Rome about 1490 (*see* GROTESQUE), however, had less impact on the decoration of Renaissance grottoes than the word itself would suggest. It is more likely that a number of the grottoes and nymphaea from antiquity being rediscovered (e.g. a nyphaeum at Albano, now lost; see Neuerberg, p. 50) were recognized for what they were and copied. As in Classical antiquity there was a contrast between the 'natural grotto' and the 'architectural grotto'. Down to modern times the former continued to be decorated with pumice stone, tufa, moss and shells, rounded off with sculptures and small pools. On the latter type the walls were articulated and covered with a mosaic of coloured pebbles, shells and pieces of coral. Frescoes and marble figures completed the decoration. Before long there were Mannerist versions of the architectural grotto in particular: 'ruined grottoes' threatening to collapse on those entering them (e.g. at Schloss Hellbrunn, 1615, Salzburg, by Santino Solari); walls that were three-dimensional images of seas with mysterious and magical creatures (e.g. the Grotta Pavese at the Villa Doria alle Madre Franzoniane, *c.* 1594, Genoa); or arbours with tender tendrils of blossom and exotic birds (e.g. in the third room of the Grotta Grande, 1583–5, by Bernardo Buontalenti at the Boboli Gardens, Florence). In many grottoes, such as the Mirror Grotto at Schloss Hellbrunn, mirrors replaced the missing water. There were also experiments combining 'natural' and 'architectural' grottoes (e.g. the Grotticina di Madama, 1553–5, at the Boboli Gardens, Florence). Grottoes represented the reverse of rationally organized architecture, of which the formal garden also formed part. This was the irrational realm of the underworld, in which rules ceased to apply. In the Mannerist tension between 'nature' and 'art', 'constructed nature' really represented the apotheosis of the artificial.

The first centre of the rapidly spreading fashion for grottoes was Rome, where, from the beginning of the 16th century, partly in imitation of the Egeria grotto, ancient sculptures or architectural elements were placed in natural grottoes. As early as 1508–11 the nymphaeum found its first modern successor in the building in Genazzano (Lazio), which is attributed to Donato Bramante. The Fonte Basso at the Villa Giulia in Rome (1550–55; by Bartolomeo Ammanati) is also in the same tradition, which reached its peak at the beginning of the 18th century with the exedra-shaped 'water theatre' with fountains resembling waterfalls at the papal villas at Frascati (*see* FRASCATI, fig. 2). From the 1530s the emphasis shifted to Mannerist Florence, where several important grottoes were created, beginning with the Grotta degli Animali in the Medici villa at Castello (1538–75; by NICCOLÒ TRIBOLO and Giorgio Vasari). BERNARDO BUONTALENTI installed a grotto storey at the Medici villa of PRATOLINO, which became famous for its water-driven automata (1569–84). The *Slaves* (*c.* 1521–3; now Florence, Accad.) by Michelangelo were displayed from 1585 in the Grotto Grande, Boboli Gardens (for illustration of the façade of the Grotto Grande *see* BUONTALENTI, BERNARDO, fig. 1). At around the same time the architect Galeazzo Alessi and his followers in Genoa were producing grottoes of the classic architectural type, for example in the Villa Pallavicino delle Peschiere (after 1556), resolving the ground-plans in extraordinary ways that anticipated the spatial arrangements of the Baroque. The Grottenhof at the Residenz in Munich, where Friedrich Sustris designed a very Mannerist grotto wall (1581–6), was directly influenced by Italian models.

1. Entrance to the Appartamento della Grotta, attributed to Giulio Romano, Palazzo del Te, Mantua, *c.* 1530–35

In Italy no outer form peculiar to the grotto evolved. It was always integrated into an overall architectural framework: sometimes as a grotto in a revetment wall, a hollow dug out in the centre of terrace steps, the dark entrance of which served as an optical focal-point of the garden, as at the Villa d'Este, Tivoli (1550–69); or as part of a building, for example in the Appartamento della Grotta (*c.* 1530–35; see fig. 1) at the Palazzo del Te, Mantua, traditionally ascribed to Giulio Romano. Francesco Primaticcio's Grotte du Jardin des Pins (1541–3) at Fontainebleau reveals Italian Mannerist influence in its ashlar rustication and deliberately unfinished appearance (*non finito*); but in France there soon evolved an independent 'pavilion grotto', a detached building with a strictly articulated interior construction containing only a few of the distinguishing characteristics of the grotto (e.g. Wideville, 1630). This form was also adopted in German lands, for example for the Orpheus Grotto at Schloss Hellbrunn. The use of regularly hewn tufa for the interior and exterior of grotto pavilions (e.g. Noisy-le-Roy, 1582–99) remained confined to France. The Grotte de Thétis at Versailles

2. Grotte de Thétis, possibly by Charles Perrault, Versailles, 1664

(see fig. 2), designed in 1664 for Louis XIV, possibly by Charles Perrault, represented the epitome and culmination of French grotto architecture. There, each element of the expensive setting represented a tribute to the 'Roi soleil'. At the opposite pole to these architectural grottoes were the French grotto hills—artificial hills containing a grotto, which developed at the beginning of the 16th century from festive decorations—such as the hermitage at Gaillon (*c.* 1560; destr. 1798). The designs of the ceramicist BERNARD PALISSY acquired great fame; in three treatises he described grotto hills on artificially created lakes containing interior rooms lined with brightly coloured glazed terracotta. Although his aim was the complete imitation of nature, the ideas behind his works were religious and philosophical rather than artistic.

The large grotto sites laid out in the 16th century and early 17th, such as those at Pratolino, at Saint-Germain-en-Laye (1600; by Thomas Francini), in the Hortus Palatinus (1613–19, Heidelberg, by Salomon de Caus; *see* CAUS, (1)), and at Schloss Hellbrunn, Salzburg, were linked with their surrounding gardens by complicated iconographical programmes based on Neo-Platonic ideas. The antitheses of 'nature and art', 'heavenly and earthly love' and 'Dionysian and Apollonian music' were expressed visibly, in that the grottoes represented the mystic Dionysian realm while the gardens stood for the Apollonian domain of reason that produced artistic order. The automata that appeared in large grottoes after 1570 also belonged to the domain of nature as a creator. The translation of Heron of Alexandria's *Pneumatica* (1st century AD) made possible the reinvention of automata in use in ancient times. The fact that they could be driven by water-power made the grotto their ideal setting: they both represented the 'subterranean' forces of nature and demonstrated man's mastery of them. The only fully preserved example of such a water-garden is at Hellbrunn, where the automata range in complexity from the simple *Germaul* ('Big-mouth') in the Neptune Grotto to the intricate 'grotto theatre' (1750; by Lorenz Rosenegger and others) depicting daily life in a town.

Grottoes, mainly in their architectural form, were built in England from the 17th century, for example at Woburn Abbey (*c.* 1630), Beds. The start of a reappraisal of the grotto and its use as part of a landscaped garden coincided with the awakening of the 18th-century enthusiasm for Classical antiquity and Italy. The nostalgia for the Classical age evoked by Latin inscriptions was mixed with a tingle of fear as one entered the dark cave—both feelings were intended to heighten the poetic inspiration that was sought in grottoes. Tableaux depicting Classical landscapes enabled the visitor to settle his thoughts on ancient times, for example in Charles Bridgeman's Dido Grotto at Stowe (begun 1713, Bucks). In 1718 Alexander Pope built a grotto at his villa in Twickenham, near London, where, as a poet and philosopher, he could retreat from the world in surroundings that had been dedicated to the Muses since time immemorial. In Germany interest in the grotto increased with the Gothic revival, which, inspired by Romantic and religious ideas, linked Gothic architecture (perceived as 'natural') with naturally occurring caves in the rocks. The earliest example of this tendency is the Magdalenenklause (1725–8; by Joseph Effner) at Schloss Nymphenburg, Munich; outwardly it was made to appear a ruin, inside it combines religious and 'grotesque' motifs. Modelled on the Temple of the Sibyl (1st century BC) at Tivoli, which stands on a ledge of rock that is naturally mined with caves, a series of monopteral structures arose that combined 'antique' ruins with concealed basement rooms fitted out as grottoes, such as the Temple of Apollo (1762–76) by Nicolas de Pigage at Schloss Schwetzingen (Baden-Württemberg).

In the first half of the 18th century, while the impact of the Baroque could still be felt, an independent type of grotto architecture came into being in Germany associating the grotto with the garden room, open to nature. Shells and glittering minerals combined with frescoes and stucco rocaille indicated the owner's wealth and suggested his scientific scholarship and activity as a collector; thus Lothar Franz von Schönborn displayed part of his important collection of shells at Schloss Weissenstein (1723), Pommersfelden, as the décor of the SALA TERRENA. There was also in Germany a Rococo type of grotto architecture in the form of a grotto pavilion that went with the 'Romantic' garden; it differed from the earlier French pavilion grotto in being richly decorated with shells and pebbles outside as well as in, and in a tendency to free itself of the architectonic. Examples are found at the grotto pavilion in the garden at Falkenlust, the Great Grotto Hall (1763–9) in the Neues Palais at Potsdam, the Neptune Grotto (begun 1774) at Sanssouci, Potsdam, and the Belvedere grottoes (1772–3) at Veitshöchheim, Bavaria. Eighteenth-century French grottoes and nymphaea followed a variety of themes: some were linked with a dairy in a reference to Longus' *Daphnis and Chloë* (3rd century AD), such as the Queen's Dairy with grotto (1785–8) designed by Hubert Robert at Rambouillet; others were designed in the spirit of revolutionary architecture in huge cubic shapes using rusticated ashlars and heavy rocks, for example the nymphaeum at Chatou (*c.* 1774) by Jacques-Germain Soufflot, and the grotto of the Folie Saint-James (1780–85) at Neuilly-sur-Seine by François-Joseph Bélanger.

In 1876–7 King Ludwig II of Bavaria had a Venus grotto built at Schloss Linderhof; it was a mixture of the Blue Grotto in Capri and the abode of Venus in the Hörselberg from Richard Wagner's *Tannhäuser*. Showings of the relevant scenes gave the 'stage' in front of an artificial lake, on which Venus could be seen attended by nymphs and putti, an illusory reality that the King enjoyed from his seat in a shell boat. Newly developed electric spotlights could bathe the grotto in pink or blue light or produce a thunderstorm. This permanent stage-set brought the vogue for grottoes to a grandiose, if kitschy, conclusion.

See also HERMITAGE; FOLLY.

BIBLIOGRAPHY

S. de Caus: *Hortus Palatinus* (Frankfurt am Main, 1620/*R* Worms, 1980; Paris, 1981)
G. W. Elderkin: 'The Natural and the Artificial Grotto', *Hesperia*, x/2 (1941), pp. 125–37
N. Neuerburg: *L'architettura delle fontane e dei ninfei nell'Italia antica* (Naples, 1965)
E. MacDougall: 'The Sleeping Nymph: Origins of a Humanist Fountain Type', *A. Bull.*, lvii (1975), pp. 357–65
M. Fagiolo: *Natura e artificio: L'ordine rustico, le fontane, gli automi nella cultura del manierismo europeo* (Rome, 1979)
L. Zangheri: *Pratolino: Il giardino delle meraviglie*, 2 vols (Florence, 1979)
N. Miller: *Heavenly Caves: Reflections on the Garden Grotto* (London, 1982)
L. Magnani: *Tra magia, scienza e 'meraviglia': Le grotte artificiali dei giardini genovesi nei secoli XVI e XVII* (Genoa, 1984)
A. Vezzosi: *La fonte delle fonti: Iconologia degli artifizi d'acqua* (Florence, 1984)
Arte delle grotte: Per la conoscenza e la conservazione delle grotte artificiali: Atti del convegno: Firenze, 1985
B. Rietzsch: *Künstliche Grotten des 16. und 17. Jahrhunderts: Formen der Gestaltung von Aussenbau und Innenraum an Beispielen in Italien, Frankreich und Deutschland* (Munich, 1987)
M. Szafranska: 'The Philosophy of Nature and the Grotto in the Renaissance Garden', *J. Gdn Hist.*, ix (1989), pp. 76–85

BARBARA RIETZSCH

Groult, Camille (*b* Paris, 1837; *d* Paris, 13 Jan 1908). French collector. Heir of a rich flour-milling family, he was one of the most considerable and original figures in the world of Parisian art collecting at the end of the 19th century and the beginning of the 20th. He assembled an important collection of French paintings, drawings and pastels of the 18th century. Towards 1890 he almost completely abandoned this in favour of paintings of the 18th-century and early 19th-century English school, then relatively unknown in France, which he bought through London dealers. Groult was an ardent and sometimes eccentric enthusiast who was believed to have himself painted several of the 'Turners' in his collection. In addition to paintings, drawings and pastels by François Boucher, Jean-Marc Nattier, Maurice-Quentin de La Tour, George Romney, John Hoppner and Joshua Reynolds, his collection included J. M. W. Turner's *View of the Pont Neuf, Paris* and Thomas Gainsborough's *Conversation in a Park* (both Paris, Louvre). He also owned important paintings by Thomas Lawrence, including the *Portrait of Charles William Bell* (Paris, Louvre); by Antoine Watteau, including the *Portrait of a Gentleman* and the *Bath of Diana* (Paris, Louvre); by Jean-Honoré Fragonard, including *The Swing* and *Blind-man's Buff* (Washington, DC, N.G.A.) and *Don Quixote* (Chicago, IL, A. Inst.); and by Francisco de Goya, including *Bartolomeo Iriarte* (Strasbourg, Mus. B.-A.) and the *Marquesa de Santa Cruz* (Paris, Louvre).

BIBLIOGRAPHY

A. Dalligny: 'Camille Groult', *J.A.* [Paris], xxx/4 (1908), p. 1
A. Flament: 'La Collection Groult', *L'Illustration*, 18 Jan 1908, pp. 49–56

STÉPHANE LOIRE

Ground. Preparatory coating or foundation layer on a SUPPORT that renders it more suitable for the application of paint or other artists' media. The term is also used in a more general sense to refer to the background of a painting or drawing. Where no special preparation is required, the surface of the support may itself be regarded as the ground. In the term's historical usage the notion of the ground as a background or foundation is sometimes extended to incorporate underpainting and dead-colouring within its meaning; the term then refers to isolated areas of preparatory colouring, instead of the preliminary overall covering normally implied.

The term 'priming' is often interchanged with the term 'ground', though technically it is possible to differentiate between them. A priming is the material applied to create a ground and may also be a further preparatory layer on top of a ground, sometimes referred to as 'imprimatura'. Each of these terms can be applied with varying degrees of general or specific meaning, depending on whether they are used technically or as loose descriptions. In printmaking, the ground refers to the dark protective acid-resistant coating, which usually consists of wax, asphalt and resin, applied to the metal plate in the process of etching (*see* ETCHING, §I). A softer ground, including tallow, was also developed in the 18th century (*see* ETCHING, SOFT-GROUND, §1) and was widely used for the reproduction of drawings. The aquatint (*see* AQUATINT, §1) and mezzotint (*see* MEZZOTINT, §1) methods of intaglio printmaking also involve the use of stages described as grounds that produce overall areas of tone. The following sections primarily describe the use of grounds in Western easel painting. For information on the use of grounds in wall painting *see* WALL PAINTING, §I.

1. Function. 2. Types. 3. History and use.

1. FUNCTION. In painting the application of a ground performs several functions. Firstly, it stabilizes the support, by restricting its ability to move and/or by reducing the effect of environmental factors, chiefly changes in temperature and relative humidity, by acting as a sealant. Canvas (*see* CANVAS, §1), for example, is stretched across a frame and then fixed by a coating of SIZE, usually with further ground layers on top. The size layer may be regarded as a component part of the ground. The result is a semi-rigid surface in which individual threads in the canvas are no longer free to move separately. The inherent instability of the support material is thus much reduced. With canvas, the combination of a ground with a loose lining of cloth, especially if that is also prepared with a ground, reduces movement to a minimum. A secondary form of stabilization occurs coincidentally as a result of the sealant action of the ground; deterioration by the effect of environmental factors such as temperature changes can be reduced by an equivalent treatment of the rear of a support. With panels, for example, a coating applied to the back that balances the ground and paint layers on the front prevents warping. Jan van Eyck's double portrait of *Giovanni Arnolfini and Giovanna Cenami*, commonly known as the *Arnolfini Marriage* (1434; London, N.G.), has been treated in this way.

Secondly, the ground protects both the support and the superimposed painting by separating them from each other: a ground can act as a buffer between incompatible chemistries and may thus preserve a painting that might otherwise decay. For example, without a ground, oil would penetrate canvas or paper, and the acidity of the oil would accelerate the decay of the support. The third and, from the artist's standpoint, most important function of a ground is its modification of the support for its intended purpose: depending on the type of fibre and nature of weave, cloth may present a surface that is hostile to paint on; a ground, however, fills the pores of the cloth, flattening any surface roughness and smoothing out irregularities; it can also alter the colour. Although a tooth or surface texture conditioned by the weave is generally retained on canvas, the ground presents a smoother surface than would otherwise have been present.

Since the physical properties of the ground may be varied in order to make the support more receptive to a certain paint type or technique, the choice of ground may affect the evolution of the painting and the longevity of the completed work. Deliberate tailoring of the ground and the marrying of support, ground and manner of painting have been recurrent themes throughout the history of grounds and their use.

2. TYPES. There are at least two ways to categorize the different kinds of ground used in painting: the first is by reference to their composition and, in particular, to the binding medium employed. For example, 'oil ground' describes the general type of ground that contains a drying oil as a major ingredient. The second is by reference to the specific physical properties: a ground may be described as 'elastic and non-absorbent'. There is, however, often a close relationship between certain ground compositions and certain sets of characteristic properties: an oil ground is in fact usually non-absorbent and elastic. A full technical description of a given ground may often be complex, for example a smooth, white gesso ground, rendered non-absorbent by an oil priming applied as a honey-coloured glaze. The following categories of ground are not intended to be exhaustive, though they probably cover most commonly used types.

(i) Gesso or chalk. This type of ground consists of powdered gypsum or chalk, bound with animal glue size, likely to be hide glue, gelatin or a historical equivalent (*see also* GESSO). These ingredients produce a white ground that is inflexible and consequently best suited to panels; it is easily built into a thick application and readily worked to a smooth finish. Such grounds are also absorbent, making them suitable for water-based paints, e.g. tempera, but ideally need to be sealed or primed if they are to be worked on with oil colour. They are, however, compatible with all types of paint and, though susceptible to impact and stress, are the most stable and durable types of ground.

(ii) Emulsion or half-chalk. This type of ground is a modification of the basic gesso or chalk ground by the addition of an emulsified binding medium (*see* EMULSION), which also results in differing properties to those of a gesso ground. Emulsion grounds typically contain a small amount of oil, as well as animal glue size, but often also egg and resin. The oil gives the ground some elasticity and reduces its absorbency, though some drawing in of the paint medium remains a feature. Unless deliberately coloured, the colour of this type of ground is usually an off-white tending towards yellow. Emulsions of flour, starch and oil or of resin mixed with animal glue also occur in grounds of this type. They are better suited to use on canvas and to the use of oil paint than gesso or chalk grounds.

(iii) Oil. Oil grounds are bound either entirely or predominantly by a drying oil. Emulsion grounds with a very high oil content properly belong in this category, but a paint-like preparation of pigment and oil would be the more usual interpretation of this term, with solvents and resins and different types of oil preparation being incorporated into variant recipes. Oil grounds are comparatively flexible until they begin to age and are therefore well suited to canvas supports, even allowing them to be rolled while removed from their stretchers. Oil grounds are also less susceptible to temperature and humidity changes and to

microbiological attack than other traditional types of ground and are therefore, in theory, more durable; in practice this is not always the case.

Oil grounds are compatible only with oil paint, because they are usually non-absorbent and may present a slick surface with which it is difficult to form a permanent bond. Even oil paint might not always adhere well, were it not for the aid of the tooth derived from the canvas grain. In the long term, various complications can arise. The basically unsympathetic nature of an oil ground can create problems within the superimposed paint layers, as can latent faults in the ground itself. For example, oil grounds may take a long time to dry thoroughly and can develop faults as a result of being painted on too quickly. Paint can also crack or even flake off because it does not have a firm hold on the ground (*see* CRAQUELURE), and colours can be spoilt by an excessive use of oil encouraged, or at least aggravated, by the non-absorbent oil ground. The obvious advantages of oil grounds are thus accompanied by inherent risks, and many paintings on them are not preserved well.

(iv) Acrylic. This type of ground, sometimes known as acrylic gesso, together with the related 'universal primings' were introduced in the late 20th century (*see also* ACRYLIC PAINTING, §1). They use synthetic resins as binding media, with the apparent advantages of permanent elasticity, as well as a degree of stability that prevents deterioration. Although to date they have proved compatible with both acrylic and oil paint, it is argued that they are less suitable for oil colour in the long term, because of differentials in the way they age. Acrylic grounds are usually brilliant white. They can be quite absorbent but more often present a rather plastic surface. They are susceptible to extreme cold, and the wisdom of applying them directly on to cloth without preliminary sizing is disputed. However, it is not yet possible to assess in detail the advantages and disadvantages of acrylic grounds and universal primings.

(v) Bole and coloured. These terms refer to coloured grounds of any composition, but the techniques applied on them are different from those used on white or near white grounds and may relate closely to the colour. The term 'bole' originally referred only to Armenian bole, a natural red-brown clay used, usually on top of gesso, specifically as a ground for water gilding (*see* GILDING, §I, 1(i)). The hydroscopic nature of the clay assists the laying of the gold leaf, while its colour makes the translucent leaf appear redder and warmer in hue. If a cooler look is required, a green foundation layer, traditionally containing terra verde, is applied instead. In both cases, the effect of the underlying colour becomes even more apparent when the gold is distressed.

Coloured grounds can influence paint in the same way, though there are other potential advantages and methods of using them. The term bole ground has come to mean any relatively dark, solidly coloured ground or priming, including various shades of red, brown and grey. Much more luminous coloured grounds that behave rather differently are achieved by laying a thin, coloured priming, sometimes a tinted transparent glaze, over a lower white ground layer. For a double ground, a priming of one colour is laid in a half-covering fashion over a lower ground of another colour; double grounds usually present a colour value or optical quality that would be difficult to achieve by more direct means.

Coloured grounds are employed by painters to abbreviate their painting method, to establish a sense of atmosphere or to exert an overall influence on the colouring. Their use is chiefly associated with oil painting, though coloured paper beneath gouache or pastel can also be classified as a coloured ground. Colour-tinted grounds are also a feature of drawings in chalk, charcoal or crayon and in metalpoint.

(vi) Composite. In practice, many grounds are composite, i.e. multi-layer preparations that combine the properties of several different basic ground types, often in order to suit the materials being used. For example, a gesso ground is best suited to a panel and can present a superbly smooth surface ideal for fine detail, but its capacity to absorb medium restricts the artist's ability to manipulate oil paint; this can be corrected by coating it with a layer of oil ground, a process sometimes referred to as 'isolating' the gesso. An emulsion ground might be used to fill the pores of a loosely woven cloth, with an oil ground placed on top to coat the consolidated surface, covered perhaps with a layer of priming to modify the colour. Many coloured grounds can also be described as composite grounds.

3. HISTORY AND USE. Painting grounds have evolved through adaptation to suit changes in painting materials, the most significant being the introduction of oil paint and canvas, and the development of different techniques. The evolution of the manufacture and use of grounds may have been influenced by the availability of certain constituent materials and by locally established technical practices. There is evidence of alternative but essentially similar solutions to the same problems being found by different artistic communities, of the dissemination of different types of ground through trade, of certain grounds being associated with the work of particular painters and, in the 19th and 20th centuries, of the circumstantial influence of commercial availability.

With regard to technique, it is difficult to distinguish whether grounds have influenced painting methods or vice versa, but there has obviously been a close relationship between them. Colour and tone may oblige a painter to work away from shadow if the ground is dark or towards it if it is light and thus may affect the thickness or thinness with which the paint is applied. The colour of the ground may likewise affect the painter's palette, and its surface finish or degree of absorbency can also materially affect the methods used. The extent to which grounds may help or hinder attempts to paint in a certain manner is not instantly apparent to the observer of a finished work, but it can safely be assumed that, at least prior to the 19th century, most painters were aware of it; it might even be argued that ignorance of how best to employ grounds has since contributed to the development of different painting techniques, as less technically informed artists have sought refuge in simple and direct methods. The changing use of grounds is therefore an element of considerable importance in the development of painting.

Gesso, the oldest and most simple ground used in Western painting, probably has origins in antiquity and is paralleled by similar materials in the art of other cultures, for example the white foundation, known as *khadi*, of Indian miniature painting. From the full account given by Cennino Cennini in *Il libro dell'arte* (*c.* 1390) of the use of gesso in Italy at the beginning of the Renaissance it is evident that gesso was applied to both panels and cloth, though its shortcomings on the latter were known. A thick, multi-layered coating was applied to panels, but on cloth a variant recipe with starch or sugar added as a plasticizer was firmly pressed into the fabric, with the object of producing as thin a ground as possible.

As oil painting evolved in the medieval period, painters in northern Europe prepared panels as for tempera painting but with an additional priming. The unfinished *St Barbara* (1437; Antwerp, Kon. Mus. S. Kst; *see* EYCK, VAN, (2), fig. 6) by Jan van Eyck appears to be on gesso coated with a yellowish glaze, quite possibly a prepared oil or oil-and-resin varnish rubbed thinly over the ground, in a similar manner to the established practice of varnishing tempera paintings. The Florentine Filarete, referring in his *Trattato di architettura* (1461–4; see Eastlake) to oil painting as practised by Jan van Eyck and Rogier van der Weyden, specifically described an oil priming on top of gesso on panel. He recommended white but clearly acknowledged the use of tinted or coloured grounds. He also described the process of highlighting with white in the underpainting, a process greatly facilitated by the use of a coloured or toned ground. Coloured, tinted and glazed grounds may therefore have evolved from the introduction of colour to the primings applied to gesso in order to render them fit for painting on in oil.

Italian restorers at the beginning of the 19th century believed that Titian had painted on a gesso ground coated with glue size (Merryfield); modern scientific study tends to confirm this. The generation of painters that followed Titian, however, began to use grounds of oil paint applied on top of the thin filler coat of gesso. These were coloured imprimatura or *mestica* of a substantial thickness, compared with the transparent or translucent coatings of the Flemish tradition, described as '*primuersel*' by Karel van Mander I. Painters often favoured certain colours, for example a grey-green in the case of Veronese and much darker hues, sometimes in fact black, in that of Tintoretto. The influence of these primings and grounds is apparent in the colouring and tonal values of their respective works, but artistic preference was not the only important factor: Vasari described such primings as being made with siccative pigments that promoted a rapid and thorough drying of the oil; these included white lead and the earth colours, which either individually or in combination could explain many of the colours of grounds. There is some evidence of palette scrapings being added to such grounds or of their being boiled with oil to extract their siccative qualities. In the early 17th century Richard Symonds referred to *ogliaccio* ('dirty oil') being used as a priming, which could have been of this type and which may have influenced the often dull and indeterminate colouring of the grounds used at that time.

Vasari also described the use of a flour paste emulsified with oil and mixed with white lead, in place of the initial coating of gesso. This would have been more flexible and therefore better suited to canvas. According to Vasari, the coloured oil priming was beaten on with the palm of the hand, suggesting that it was a thick and sticky paste. Similar accounts of canvas preparation were given in 17th-century Spanish sources, though Francisco Pacheco recommended the use of clay mixed with oil, applied on to a canvas sized with weak glue. Pacheco also described the use of ashes in place of gesso and primings of red earth or of a mixture of white lead, red lead and charcoal black that must have produced a brown or dirty pink ground. El Greco, for example, used a dark red-brown 'bole' ground. Diego Velázquez also seems to have employed darkish brown, grey and red-brown grounds.

Although by the late 16th century and early 17th the use of panels was in decline in northern Europe, Henry Peacham, in *The Compleat Gentleman* (London, 1622), gave a method for preparing a ground for oil painting on panel that, for all practical purposes, is the same as Filarete's. He did however recommend a priming of red lead or another colour.

In the 17th century the use of solid, dull-coloured grounds influenced technique and encouraged the use of paint in variable thicknesses, with dense, opaque paint being massed in the highlights. The paintings of Rembrandt are an extreme example of this, though in addition to dark grounds he favoured double grounds, consisting of a coloured ground over which a priming of another colour is applied (*see* OIL PAINTING, colour pls I and II). The dark, vaporous voids in Rembrandt's paintings would have been easier to achieve on grounds of this type. Evidence of a selective use of grounds by Velázquez in his *Rokeby Venus* (*c.* 1648–9; London, N.G.) suggests that the potential of coloured grounds was being explored to its limits during the 17th century. The use of coloured grounds over a primary layer of white, providing luminosity, is often evident in the work of Peter Paul Rubens, where it tends to be of a distinctive form, consisting of a streaky or scrubbed-on colour through which a white base is visible. In his *Samson and Delilah* (*c.* 1609–10; London, N.G.; *see* BELGIUM, fig. 16), for example, a warm, honey-coloured priming is evident in many places and indeed is used quite deliberately to trick the viewer into perceiving areas of minimal painting as being complete. A similar streaky ground is visible in his portrait of *Susanna Fourment* (*c.* 1622–5; London, N.G.; *see* PORTRAITURE, fig. 16), and his use of coloured grounds is further and emphatically illustrated by his series of modelli (1636–7; London, N.G.) in which the grounds form the greater part of the work.

Prepared supports were already available in the 17th century, but in the 18th century there was increasing standardization and a progressive separation of the artist's craft and the colourman's trade. Eventually a simple preparation of white lead in oil became the typical commercially produced ground, probably representing the lowest common denominator of customers' requirements. J. M. W. Turner, who as a watercolourist was familiar with the use of a white ground (consisting of gouache), may have been the first major European painter to adopt this plain white ground for oil paintings. As with earlier painters, his choice of ground can be related to his methods, as can that of John Constable, who continued to use coloured grounds, favouring red-browns and a warm pink, probably made to order, which features his *Chain Pier, Brighton* (1827; London, Tate). Attempts to rediscover traditional painting practices during the 19th century did lead to some experimentation with differing ground types, a fascinating example being furnished by the portrait of *Carlo Pellegrini* (*c.* 1864; Bodelwyddan Castle) by Henry Thompson (1820–1904).

As the 19th century progressed, the continued simplification of painting methods, exemplified by the direct application of opaque paint by the Impressionists and their followers, made the colour of the ground increasingly irrelevant, and the skilful exploitation of coloured grounds was no longer prevalent. Relatively light grounds in pale grey, cream and buff feature in the work of Monet, Renoir and van Gogh, but the significance of their delicate colours is often marginal because of the heavy and unvarying method of applying paint and the concentration of all aspects of colour, design and form within the paint layer. Possibly nothing more than experimentation with various commercially available grounds is evident in these works. From the practical point of view, pale grounds are less challenging than starkly white ones and make the careful covering of every bit of support less necessary. This explains the common practice among painters of toning down white grounds with a wash of colour prior to painting.

In the 20th century white grounds continued to dominate, but preparations of white lead in oil were superseded during the last quarter of the century with alkyd primers, often containing titanium white. Even in that form, however, oil primers are no longer as important as commercially made acrylic primings, although a few technically minded painters have also continued to employ traditional materials, such as gesso, and various forms of coloured ground.

BIBLIOGRAPHY

C. Cennini: *Il libro dell'arte* (*c.* 1390); Eng. trans. and notes by D. V. Thompson jr (1933)

G. Vasari: *Vite* (1550, rev. 2/1568); ed. G. Milanesi (1878–85); intro. trans. by L. S. Maclehose as *Vasari on Technique* (London, 1907; rev. New York, 1960)

T. Bardwell: *The Practice of Painting and Perspective Made Easy* (London, 1756)

C. L. Eastlake: *Methods and Materials of the Great Schools and Masters*, 2 vols (London, 1847/*R* New York, 1960)

M. P. Merryfield: *Original Treatises Dating from the XIIth to XVIIIth Centuries on the Arts of Painting*, 2 vols (London, 1849)

R. J. Gettens and M. E. Morse: 'Calcium Sulphate Minerals in the Grounds of Italian Paintings', *Stud. Conserv.*, i (1954), pp. 174–89

P. Hendy, A. Lucas and J. Plesters: 'The Ground in Pictures', *Mus.: Rev. Trimest.*, lxxxiv (1968), pp. 245–76

G. Emile-Mâle: *The Restorers' Handbook of Easel Painting* (New York, 1976)

N.G. Tech. Bull. (1977–)

M. K. Talley: *Portrait Painting in England: Studies in the Technical Literature before 1700* (London, 1981)

Z. Veliz, ed. and trans.: *Artists' Techniques in Golden Age Spain* (Cambridge, 1987)

Art in the Making: Rembrandt (exh. cat. by D. Bomford, C. Brown and A. Roy, London, N.G., 1988)

J. Stephenson: *The Materials and Techniques of Painting* (London, 1989)

Art in the Making: Italian Painting before 1400 (exh. cat. by D. Bomford and others, London, N.G., 1989)

D. Bomford and others: *Art in the Making: Impressionism* (London, 1990)

J. Dunkerton and others: *Giotto to Dürer: Early Renaissance Painting in the National Gallery* (London, 1991)

J. Stephenson: *Paint with the Impressionists* (London, 1995)

JONATHAN STEPHENSON

Grounds, Sir **Roy (Burman)** (*b* Melbourne, 18 Dec 1905; *d* Melbourne, 7 March 1981). Australian architect and teacher. He was articled to Blackett & Forster, Melbourne, in 1924 and attended the Melbourne Technical School. After working for RKO and MGM studios in Hollywood (1930–32), he set up practice with Geoffrey Mewton (*b* 1905) in Melbourne until 1936. In 1938–9 he worked in England for Raymond McGrath, then returned to intermittent practice in Australia. Grounds was an early supporter of Modernism in Australia but soon developed a simple regional idiom using timber, brick or blockwork and glass, strongly reminiscent of the work of William Wilson Wurster in California, whom he admired, but also recalling the Georgian forms of Australian colonial architecture. His early domestic work is exquisitely understated, as seen in the fan-shaped 'Quamby' block of flats (1939–41), Toorak, Melbourne, his own house (1937), Mt Eliza, and the house 'Iluka' (1950), Mornington, both in Victoria. Grounds became a lecturer at the University of Melbourne in the late 1940s and in this role had a considerable influence on younger architects in Melbourne, notably Robin Boyd (*see* BOYD, (1)). From 1953 to 1962 he practised in partnership with Boyd and FREDERICK ROMBERG in the firm of Grounds, Romberg & Boyd. Around 1950 Grounds instigated a fashion in Melbourne for strong geometrical plan forms; he built triangular and circular houses and a house for himself (1953) at Toorak with a circular courtyard cut into the centre of a square plan. He also used primary geometrical forms in some of his larger buildings, for example the circular, dome-shaped Academy of Science (1957–9), Canberra, probably inspired by Eero Saarinen's Kresge Auditorium (1954) at Massachusetts Institute of Technology. Grounds's largest project was the Victorian Arts Centre (1959–84), Melbourne, with a triangular art school and an astonishing tall spire, circular in plan, over the auditoria (for illustration *see* MELBOURNE); only the rectilinear, fortress-like National Gallery of Victoria was completed before his death, and a subsequent extension of the brief resulted in substantial alterations to the other buildings of the project. Grounds was knighted in 1969.

BIBLIOGRAPHY

R. Boyd: *Australia's Home* (Melbourne, 1952, rev. 3/1987), pp. 190–93

C. Hamann: 'Roy Grounds, Frederick Romberg and Robin Boyd', *Architects of Australia*, ed. H. Tanner (South Melbourne and Artarmon, NSW, 1981), pp. 129–39

RORY SPENCE

Group E. *See* VASE PAINTERS, §II.

Groupe de Recherche d'Art Visuel [GRAV]. Group of artists active in Paris from 1960 to 1968. Eleven artists signed the original manifesto, but only six of them formed the core of the group: Horacio García Rossi (*b* 1929), Francisco Sobrino, François Morellet, Julio Le Parc, Joël Stein (*b* 1926) and Jean-Pierre Vasarely, known as Yvaral (*b* 1934). The group took its name from the Centre de Recherche d'Art Visuel, founded in Paris in July 1960. Following the belief of Victor Vasarely (father of Yvaral) that the concept of the artist as a solitary genius was outdated, the artists' main aim was to merge the individual identities of the members into a collective activity that would be more than the sum of its parts. They also believed that 'workers collaborating with the aid of scientific and technical disciplines [would] be the only true creators of the future'. The group exhibited in Europe within the framework of the NOUVELLE TENDANCE movement, and it successfully developed the logic of group activity through the strategy of anonymity and the holding of collective events called *Labyrinths*. From the outset, members of GRAV adopted the principle of submitting individual work to the consideration of the group as a whole, which would determine its relevance to the overall programme. In 1961 they felt confident enough to assert that 'plastic reality' was inherent in 'the constant relationship between the plastic object and the human eye'. This conviction led them to experiment with a wide spectrum of kinetic and optical effects, employing various types of artificial light and mechanical movement as well as optical or 'virtual' movement. In *Assez de mystifications!*, the text that they published on the occasion of the Paris Biennale in 1961, they sought to forge a connection between their efforts to engage the 'human eye' and their forthright denunciation of the élitism of traditional art, which appealed to 'the cultivated eye. . .the intellectual eye'.

The first *Labyrinth*, presented at the Paris Biennale of 1963, was the culmination of three years of joint research into optical and kinetic devices. It also, however, demonstrated the difficulties inherent in the group's position. The emphasis on the 'human eye' had shifted to a more general concern with 'spectator participation', and the new slogan became: 'It is forbidden not to touch'. No special privilege could be attached from then on to the purely visual stimuli of the earlier works, and on 19 April 1966 GRAV held a *Day in the Street* in central Paris, inviting passers-by to walk on uneven wooden blocks, or experience the deformation of their vision through elaborate distorting spectacles. Close as these events were to the Happenings being pioneered in the USA at the same time, they sprang from the rationalistic premises of the European kinetic movement. When the group members presented *Labyrinth 3* in New York in March 1965, they realized that their work, based as it was on research into optical and kinetic effect, had little relevance to the American context.

The agreed dissolution of the group in November 1968 sprang from the recognition that it was impossible to maintain the rigour of a joint programme. Morellet commented at the time that he had argued from the start for a suppression of individual signatures, and that the members who had hesitated to take this step had condemned the group to eventual disappearance. Stein, however, laid more emphasis on the inability of both commercial and public galleries to tolerate the group strategy and singled out the decision of the committee of the Venice Biennale in 1966 to give their major prize to Le Parc as one of the crucial factors in the group's decline (*see* RENÉ, DENISE). In discussing and publicizing the reasons for their failure, rather than just dissolving tacitly, the surviving members remained consistent with the scientific claims of their original programme.

PUBLISHED WRITINGS

Assez de mystifications! (Paris, 1961)
'The Texts of the Groupe Recherche d'Art Visuel, Paris: 1960–1965', ed. and trans. R. Gadney and S. Bann, *Image* (Winter 1966), pp. 13–30

BIBLIOGRAPHY

F. Popper: *Origins and Development of Kinetic Art* (London, 1968)
J. Stein: 'Dissolution du GRAV', Leonardo, ii (1969), pp. 295–7

STEPHEN BANN

Group f.64. American group of photographers, active 1932–5. It was a loose association of San Francisco Bay Area photographers who articulated and promoted a modern movement in photographic aesthetics. The group was formed in August 1932 by photographers who shared an interest in pure and unmanipulated photography as a means of creative expression. It derived its name from the smallest possible aperture setting on a camera, the use of which resulted in the greatest and sharpest depth of field, producing an image with foreground and background clearly focused. The original membership consisted of Ansel Adams, Imogen Cunningham, John Paul Edwards (1883–1958), Sonya Noskowiak (1900–75), Henry Swift (1891–1960), Willard Van Dyke (1906–86) and Edward Weston. The emphasis on clarity was partly a reaction against the lingering Pictorialism in West Coast photography, exemplified by the work of William Mortensen (1897–1965) and Anne Brigman (1869–1950), who achieved painterly effects through manipulation of the negative and print.

Group f.64's working technique demanded the use of a large-format view camera, and their pristine presentation of exhibition photographs required the dry-mounting of glossy contact prints to proportionally correct white boards. The collective imagery of the group incorporated a broad range of organic and industrial forms as well as occasional portraiture, but the common concern was for technical precision in rendering a formally well-defined image. This style of realism complemented contemporaneous American Precisionist painting (see PRECISIONISM) and paralleled similar photographic developments in European NEUE SACHLICHKEIT.

Group f.64 mounted only one exhibition, at San Francisco's M. H. de Young Memorial Museum in November 1932. Works shown included Cunningham's *Leaf Pattern* (*c.* 1929; Berkeley, CA, Imogen Cunningham Trust), Edwards's *Boats and Riggings* (*c.* 1930; Oakland, CA, Mus.), Adams's *Lakes and Cliffs, Sierra Nevada* (1927), Noskowiak's *Sand Pattern* (1932), Van Dyke's *Bone and Sky* (1932) and Weston's *Pepper No. 30* (1930, for illustration *see* WESTON, EDWARD; all San Francisco, CA, MOMA). The show also featured photographs by associate members Preston Holder (*b* 1907), Consuela Kanaga (1894–1978), Alma Lavenson (*b* 1897) and Brett Weston (*b* 1911). Although the group remained active for only a few years, its concept of 'straight' photography proved a viable photographic proposition for America in the 1930s and was influential as an approach for future generations of photographers.

BIBLIOGRAPHY

J. P. Edwards: 'Group f.64', *Camera Craft*, xvii/3 (1935), pp. 107–13
G. M. Craven: *The Group f.64 Controversy: An Introduction to the Henry F. Swift Memorial Collection of the San Francisco Museum of Art* (San Francisco, 1963)
Group f.64 (exh. cat. by J. S. Tucker, St Louis, U. MO, 1978)
K. Tsujimoto: *Images of America: Precisionist Painting and Modern Photography* (Seattle, 1982)

RICHARD LORENZ

Group of Plastic Artists [Czech: Skupina Výtvarných Umělců]. Bohemian avant-garde group, active 1911–17. In February 1911 a fundamental rift between the older and younger generations in the MÁNES UNION OF ARTISTS was occasioned by the fall in subscriptions to the union's journal *Volné směry* after its new editors, Emil Filla and Antonín Matějček, reproduced Picasso's work and published Filla's article on the virtues of the new primitivism. The majority of the young contributors to the journal pointedly withdrew from the Mánes Union. Towards the end of 1911 they established the Group of Plastic Artists, oriented towards Cubism; its members were Vincenc Beneš, V. H. Brunner, Josef Čapek, Emil Filla, Josef Gočár, Otto Gutfreund, Vlastislav Hofman (1884–1964), Josef Chochol, Pavel Janák, Zdeněk Kratochvíl, František Kysela, Antonín Procházka, Ladislav Šíma, Václav Špála, the writers Karel Čapek (1890–1938) and František Langer, and the art historian V. V. Štech. For personal reasons and differences of opinion, Bohumil Kubišta, Otokar Kubín and Matějček remained outside the group and soon returned to the Mánes Union. Gočár was elected the group's first president.

In the autumn the group began publishing its own journal, *Umělecký měsíčník*. The first editor was Josef Čapek and the editorial board consisted of Filla, Janák, Kysela, Langer, Štech and the composer Václav Štěpán (1889–1944); after April 1912 Čapek, Janák and Langer took turns as editor, and Hofman joined the editorial board. The group's first exhibition was organized as an independent part of the Exhibition of Art at the Community House (Obecný Dům) in Prague, in which the Mánes Union and the Union of Plastic Artists also took part. The architectonic arrangement of the room used for this purpose was designed by Janák; there were exhibits of furniture, ceramics, glass, architectonic models and photographs of buildings alongside Cubo-Expressionist pictures and sculptures (*see* CUBO-EXPRESSIONISM).

The group's second exhibition (Community House, Sept–Nov 1912) was considerably more representative and brought together almost 100 exhibits, including paintings by the guest artists Willy Nowak (1886–1977) and Friedrich Feigl (1884–1965) and 20 works by German Expressionists. Gočár was responsible for the general arrangement and Kysela for the poster, while Štech wrote the introduction to the catalogue. Within the group itself the tension between two camps gradually came to a head: one, led by Filla and Beneš, was in favour of orthodox Cubist methods, the other, led by the Čapek brothers, saw Cubism as an aesthetic system open to all but gave equal acceptance to Italian Futurist works. The dispute reached its climax in 1912 when the Čapek brothers, Brunner, Hofman, Chochol and Špála left the group (the last named artist had recently joined the Mánes Union).

The third exhibition took place in the Goltz Salon, Munich, in April 1913 and presented works by Beneš, Filla, Procházka, Gutfreund, Gočár and Janák. In May 1913 the group opened a fourth exhibition at the Community House, with eleven paintings by Braque, nine by Picasso, five by Derain and two by Gris. There were also works by Cézanne and Ardengo Soffici, as well as examples of folk art, exotic art and ancient art, to underline the group's relationship to these sources. In this respect the exhibition was reflecting ideas expressed in *Umělecký měsíčník*. In October 1913 the group's fifth exhibition took place at the Sturm-Galerie in Berlin. There were many works by Beneš and Filla from the years 1909–13, and exhibits by Gutfreund, Gočár, Janák and Procházka. The sixth and last exhibition was held in February 1914 at the Community House. Paintings and sculptures by members of the group were placed side by side with African statuettes; guest artists included Munch, Picasso, Max Pechstein, Braque and Derain. In 1914 *Umělecký měsíčník* ceased publication. During World War I the group disbanded, and in 1917 Beneš, Gočár, Janák, Kratochvíl and Kysela joined the Mánes Union. Filla followed them after his return from the Netherlands in 1920.

BIBLIOGRAPHY

M. Lamač: *Osma a Skupina výtvarných umělců* [The Eight and the Group of Plastic Artists] (Prague, 1988; Fr. trans., 1992)

Český kubismus (exh. cat., ed. A. von Vegesack; Weil am Rhein, Vitra Des. Mus., 1991; Ger. trans., 1991)

Kubismus in Prag (exh. cat., ed. J. Švestka and T. Vlček; Düsseldorf, Kstver., 1991)

LENKA BYDŽOVSKÁ

Group of Seven. Canadian group of painters. It was named in May 1920 on the occasion of an exhibition held in Toronto and was initially composed of Frank Carmichael (1890–1945), Lawren S. Harris, A. Y. Jackson, Franz Johnston (1888–1949), Arthur Lismer, J. E. H. MacDonald and Fred Varley. On Johnston's resignation in 1926, A. J. Casson (1898–1992) was invited to join. The group later expanded to include two members from outside Toronto, Edwin H. Holgate from Montreal (in 1930) and Lionel LeMoine FitzGerald from Winnipeg (in 1932). The essential character of the group's style and approach to landscape painting was in evidence well before their official formation in 1920, and some of their most important pictures also pre-date that first exhibition. Although they continued to show together officially only until December 1931 and disbanded in 1933, when former members helped establish a successor organization with a much larger membership drawn from all over the country (the Canadian Group of Painters), the term continued to be applied to the later works of the group's original members.

The Group of Seven had its origins in Toronto from 1910 to 1913, when a number of its future members, together with like-minded painters such as Tom Thomson, met while working as commercial artists in the studios of the company Grip Limited. The Toronto Arts & Letters Club, founded in 1908, also became a vital meeting point for them and other interested artists. They were united in their frustration at the conservative and limited character of art in Canada and by a belief in their capacity to give expression to a national and independent artistic image through the painting of the northern Canadian landscape, as in Jackson's *Terre Sauvage* (1913; Ottawa, N.G.; see fig.). There was early opposition to their style, not so much because of their debts to late 19th-century European art (Symbolism, with mystical overtones, and Post-Impressionism) but because of their simplification of form and boldness of colour, which seemed shocking in relation to more traditional approaches to landscape painting. There was also resentment towards their presumption of representing a national school. Nevertheless they received

A. Y. Jackson: *Terre Sauvage*, oil on canvas, 1.28x1.54 m, 1913 (Ottawa, National Gallery of Canada)

strong support from Eric Brown, Director of the National Gallery, and eventually broke down some of the resistance through their own aggressiveness in advocating their position. Controversy abounded after the official formation of the group, but the issue was forced by their successful participation in 1924 in the *British Empire Exhibition* in Wembley, England, from which the Tate Gallery in London purchased Jackson's *Entrance to Halifax Harbour* (1919). Through the later 1920s the group's pre-eminent position in Canadian art was established.

Although projected as a national school, the Group of Seven was essentially based in Ontario, which created resentment among artists in other parts of the country. Moreover, the ties among former members of the group gradually weakened through the 1930s, but their approach to landscape, increasingly resistant to change but secure in broad-based public support, became an oppressive restraint on succeeding generations of painters in Ontario. Their unassailable position was broken only in the 1950s with the emergence of Painters Eleven.

BIBLIOGRAPHY

F. B. Housser: *A Canadian Art Movement: The Story of the Group of Seven* (Toronto, 1926)
T. MacDonald: *The Group of Seven* (Toronto, 1944)
P. Duval: *Group of Seven Drawings* (Toronto, 1965)
P. Mellen: *The Group of Seven* (Toronto, 1970)
The Group of Seven (exh. cat. by D. Reid, Ottawa, N.G., 1970)
D. Reid: *A Bibliography of the Group of Seven* (Ottawa, 1971)
H. Hunkin: *The Group of Seven: Canada's Great Landscape Painters* (Edinburgh, 1979)
M. Tooby, ed.: *The True North: Canadian Landscape Painting, 1896–1939* (London, 1991)

DAVID BURNETT

Group of the Huge Lekythoi. *See* VASE PAINTERS, §II.

Group R. *See* VASE PAINTERS, §II.

Group X. Group of British artists formed in 1920. It exhibited at the Mansard Gallery, Heal's, in London, between 26 March and 24 April of that year. The nucleus of the group, whose name had no precise significance, was a regrouping of the Vorticists, comprising Wyndham Lewis, Jessica Dismorr, Frederick Etchells, Cuthbert Hamilton, William Roberts and Edward Wadsworth; these artists were joined by Frank Dobson, Charles Ginner, McKnight Kauffer and John Turnbull. Although the artists were united in a belief that 'the experiments undertaken all over Europe during the last ten years should be utilized directly and developed, and not be lightly abandoned or the effort allowed to relax' (Lewis, exh. cat., intro.), the works exhibited were characterized chiefly by a tendency to angular figuration; the critic Frank Rutter (1876–1937) wrote in the *Sunday Times* (28 March 1920) that 'the real tendency of the exhibition is towards a new sort of realism, evolved by artists who have passed through a phase of abstract experiment'.

Although the group had intended to exhibit together twice annually, the show of 1920 was their first and last. The short-lived and relatively conservative nature of Group X was indicative both of the disruption to British avant-garde activity caused by World War I, and of the more widespread cultural retrenchment, referred to as a 'rappel à l'ordre' in the post-war period.

BIBLIOGRAPHY

Group X (exh. cat. by W. Lewis, London, Mansard Gal., 1920)

MONICA BOHM-DUCHEN

Groux, De. *See* DE GROUX.

Gruamonte [Gruamons] (*fl* Pistoia, 1166). Italian sculptor. The inscription *Fecit hoc opus Gruamons magister bonus et Adeodatus frater eius* is carved on the lintel of the main doorway of S Andrea in Pistoia, with a date generally interpreted as 1166 and with scenes from the *Story of the Magi*. The jamb capitals represent, on the left, the *Annunciation to Zacharias* and the *Visitation*, and on the right the *Annunciation to Joachim and Anne*; the latter bears the inscription *Magister Enrigus me fecit*. Some of the capitals inside the church can be attributed to the same masters.

The signature *Gruamons magister bonus* reappears on a lintel with the *Last Supper* above the north portal of S Giovanni Fuorcivitas, Pistoia. Another lintel, with *Christ and the Apostles* (1167; Pistoia, S Bartolomeo in Pantano, main portal), is closely related to the carvings at S Andrea.

The sculptors working under Gruamonte were talented followers of Guglielmo; however, with the exception of the capital signed by Enrigus, it is not possible to attribute specific carvings to the named individuals.

BIBLIOGRAPHY

P. Bacci: 'Gruamonte ed altri maestri di pietra', *Riv. A.*, iii (1905), pp. 57–76

R. Salvini: 'La scultura romanica pistoiese', *Il romanico pistoiese nei suoi rapporti con l'arte romanica dell'occidente* (Pistoia, 1966)

ANTONIO CALECA

Grubenmann. Swiss family of architects and bridge builders. Ulrich Grubenmann (*b* Gstalden, Appenzell Ausserrhoden, 1668; *d* Gstalden, 27 June 1736) was probably an architect-builder or carpenter. His three sons, Jakob Grubenmann (*b* Gstalden, 10 Jan 1694; *d* Hombrechtikon, Zurich, 5 Oct 1758), Johannes Grubenmann (*b* Gstalden, 15 June 1707; *d* Teufen, 10 June 1771) and Hans Ulrich Grubenmann (*b* Gstalden, 23 March 1709; *d* Teufen, 22 Jan 1783), shared a building business that dominated the construction of timber bridges and village churches in eastern Switzerland.

Jakob trained locally as a carpenter, roofer and joiner, and he established himself as a building contractor and architect. He was responsible for 22 village churches, which typically comprise a single rectangular hall with a shallow barrel vault, a choir enclosed on three sides, a pitched roof and the tower positioned at the choir end. His Reformed churches, such as those at Steinach (Thurgau; 1743) and St Gallenkappel (St Gall; 1754), are topped by Gothic-style pointed caps, while his Catholic churches have Baroque cupolas and shallow domes. His church architecture served mainly as a vehicle for paintings, stuccowork and interior furnishings, although the sophisticated construction of the roof timbering is of special interest. Jakob also built timber bridges and large houses, of which the Kawatzen and Baumgarten houses in Lindau (1728–30) and two houses for the Wetter family in Herisau (Appenzell Ausserrhoden; 1737) are typical. The façades of his houses are notable for their individual ornamentation, which reflects the taste of the client rather than the architect's style. Johannes, the least prominent member of the family business, is known to have built the octagon at the entrance to the chapel on St Martinsberg in Oberwangen (Thurgau; 1728–30), after designs by Caspar Moosbrugger.

Hans Ulrich Grubenmann established an international reputation as a bridge builder. His advanced construction techniques, founded on experience and, especially, on accurate scale models, included allowances for variable loading, wind pressure, the stiffening of the structure and protection from weather. The most important of the 14 covered timber bridges he is known to have built were those over the River Rhine at Schaffhausen (1755–8; model, Schaffhausen, Mus. Allerheiligen) and over the River Limmat at Wettingen (1765–6; model, Aargau, Chief Engineer's office; both destr.). The former was an arch construction in which the individual elements were held together by the truss posts. Another original feature was the mansard roofing, which increased the height of the construction. The arch of interlocking beams at Wettingen was stiffened by a truss frame made up of many elements, which made possible completely new forms of loading (*see* BRIDGE, §2(ii)). His churches had similarly complex roof timbering. The most important, such as those in Wädenswil (Zurich; 1764–7), Teufen (1776–9) and Trogen (Appenzell Ausserrhoden; 1779–82), show him to have been a progressive engineer but traditional in his architectural forms.

BIBLIOGRAPHY

J. Killer: *Die Werke der Baumeister Grubenmann* (Zurich, 1941, rev.3/Basle, 1985)

E. Grubenmann: *Die Familien Grubenmann von Teufen (Appenzell A. Rh.)* (Berne, 1965)

J. G. James: 'The Evolution of Wooden Bridge Trusses to 1850', *J. Inst. Wood Sci.* ix (1982), pp. 116–35, 168–93

E. Steinmann: 'Der Kirchenbaumeister Jakob Grubenmann von Teufen (1694–1758)', *Appenzell. Jb.*, cxii (1984), pp. 3–72

——: *Hans Ulrich Grubenmann: Erbauer von Holzbrücken, Landkirchen und Herrschaftshäusen, 1709–1783* (Niederteufen, 1984)

E. Steinmann and P. Witschi: 'Johannes Grubenmann der Jüngere von Teufen und Appenzell: Brückenbauer und Klosterarchitect', *Appenzell. Jb.*, xi (1987), pp. 3–28

HEINZ HORAT

Gruber, Francis (*b* Nancy, 15 March 1912; *d* Paris, 1 Dec 1948). French painter. His father, Jacques Gruber (1870–1933), was a stained-glass artist of Alsatian origin. Francis moved with his family to Paris in 1916. Although ill-health during childhood led to the neglect of his formal education, he read widely and precociously and from the age of eight showed an eagerness to paint; even as a child he admired the work of Hieronymus Bosch, Matthias Grünewald and Albrecht Dürer, who were to prove important influences on his work of the 1930s and 1940s, and sought advice from Georges Braque and Roger Bissière, who were close neighbours. Between 1929 and 1932 he was taught at the Académie Scandinave by Charles Dufresne, Othon Friesz and Henry de Waroquier (1881–1970). He worked essentially from the imagination during these years, although he also produced a few still-lifes. From 1930 he exhibited regularly at the Salon d'Automne and the Salon des Tuileries.

In 1933 Gruber met Alberto and Diego Giacometti, who were to become close friends; Gruber's example may well have influenced Alberto's return to realism in sculpture. Between 1933 and 1936, in part because he was housebound by tuberculosis, he painted the view through his window, as well as working from the model in the studio. At the time that he painted *Homage to Work* (1936; see 1976 exh. cat., p. 19) he associated with politically involved artists such as Boris Taslitzky (*b* 1911) and took part in discussions about Socialist Realism. A mural, *Homage to Le Nôtre*, was commissioned by the State for the Lycée Lakanal de Sceaux in 1936, and a stained-glass window, *Sports and Pastimes* (exh. 1937, Paris, Exposition Universelle), by the City of Paris. In 1938 he executed another stained-glass window, *Homage to Sculpture*, for the Musée National d'Art Moderne in Paris (now Pal. Tokyo). In 1947 he was awarded the Prix National des Arts, shortly after he had joined the French Communist Party. Following his early death, the Musée National d'Art Moderne gave him a major retrospective exhibition in 1950.

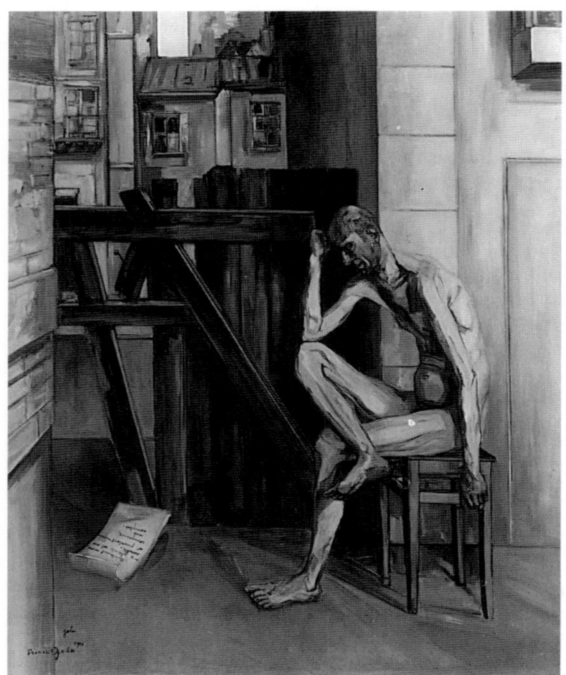

Francis Gruber: *Job*, oil on canvas, 1.62×1.30 m, 1944 (London, Tate Gallery)

Most of Gruber's work until the early 1940s could be described as Surrealist-influenced, with a strong vein of fantasy. During the Occupation, however, by which time he had begun to work in the open air, he often introduced hidden messages of direct political relevance to the plight of France, as in *Homage to Jacques Callot* (1942; Paris, J. Bazaine priv. col., see 1959 exh. cat., p. 6). *Job* (1944; London, Tate, see fig.), one of a series of biblical subjects initiated in 1942, carries a similar message of resistance and protest. Gruber's later images tend to be more straightforwardly realistic and comprise mainly nudes, portraits, still-lifes and views from and of his studio. The single figures in interiors which he painted in the mid-1940s form part of a current in post-war French art sometimes labelled *Misérabiliste*, which paralleled the Existentialist novel. After the war Gruber began to paint Breton landscapes in which he employed a clearer and more delicate palette while retaining the spiky, nervous linearity characteristic of all his work.

BIBLIOGRAPHY

T. Tzara: 'Francis Gruber', *Le Point*, 36 (1947), pp. 36–41

Francis Gruber (exh. cat. by B. Dorival, Paris, Mus. N. A. Mod., 1950)

Francis Gruber, 1912–1948 (exh. cat. by R. Huyghe, London, Tate, 1959)

Francis Gruber, 1912–1948 (exh. cat., ed. M. Schmidt and J. Gachnang; Berne, Ksthalle; Nancy, Mus. B.-A.; Paris, Mus. A. Mod. Ville Paris; 1976)

MONICA BOHM-DUCHEN

Grubicy [Grubicij] **(De Dragon), Vittore** (*b* Milan, 15 Oct 1851; *d* Milan, 4 Aug 1920). Italian painter, dealer, critic and collector of Hungarian origin. Around 1870 he frequented the circle of GLI SCAPIGLIATI and in 1870–71 visited London. Grubicy's acquaintance with the art galleries there inspired him to start his own gallery in Milan, specializing in the Scapigliati artists, particularly Tranquillo Cremona and later Daniele Ranzoni. After Cremona's death in 1878, Grubicy extended his interest to younger Lombard artists, primarily Giovanni Segantini (whose *Choir of S Antonio* impressed him at the 1879 annual exhibition at the Brera, Milan), Emilio Longoni (1859–1932) and later Angelo Morbelli. Grubicy became Segantini's dealer and they were in close collaboration from this time. Between 1882 and 1885 Grubicy was in the Low Countries and probably informed Segantini of Millet and The Hague school. During his visit Grubicy also began to draw (e.g. *Housemaid Washing*, 1884; Milan, Castello Sforzesco) and to paint (e.g. *The Hague: My First Work*, 1884) under the supervision of his friend Anton Mauve. On his return to Milan Grubicy became art critic for the newspaper *Riforma*.

In 1886 Grubicy expressed his interest in the divided brushstroke to Segantini. It is unlikely that he had seen pointillist works in the original; his source was almost certainly Rood's *Modern Chromatics* (London, 1879). Segantini subsequently painted the second version of *Ave Maria atrasbordo* (1886; St Gall, Kstmus.) under Grubicy's supervision and using the new technique. This enthusiasm for Divisionism was gradually communicated to other Italian artists and hence Grubicy is generally considered the founding father of the movement. In 1888 the Grubicy Gallery exhibited works by Segantini, Morbelli, Cremona, Ranzoni, Attilio Pusterla (*b* 1862) and others at the Italian

Exhibition held in Earl's Court, London; inevitably, Scapigliati and Divisionist works were described as impressionist and were neither understood nor appreciated. At the beginning of the 1890s Grubicy left the running of the gallery to his brother Alberto Grubicy (with whom he had entered into partnership *c.* 1880) and concentrated on writing for the new journal *Cronaca d'Arte.* Almost simultaneously, friction arose between Segantini and Grubicy, who did not approve of the new directions in Segantini's painting.

The Brera Triennale in 1891 marked the first public display of Divisionist works in Italy, provoking considerable criticism. Grubicy defended Segantini's *Two Mothers* (1889; Milan, Gal. A. Mod.) and Gaetano Previati's *Motherhood* (1891; Novara, Banca Pop., *see* PREVIATI, GAETANO) in *Riforma* and *Cronaca d'Arte.* Grubicy also showed works at the exhibition and his interpretation of the Divisionist technique is characterized by his constant elaboration of the surface with minute, brilliantly coloured, juxtaposed brushstrokes. The dense colour and intense concentration of texture thus produced are unlike the nebulous effects produced by the Scapigliati artists and are clearly distinguishable from the works of other Divisionists. Continual reworking makes Grubicy's paintings difficult to date precisely. They are generally quite small, and he concentrated almost exclusively on landscape, deriving his subject-matter largely from the area around Miazzina, Lake Maggiore, as in *The Mist Rises up from the Valley* (1895; Rome, G.N.A. Mod.). In some works, for example *Joyous Morning* (1895–1911; Milan, Gal. A. Mod.), a Japanese-like delicacy is evident, and in others, such as *Moonlit Night* (1895; Como, ex-W. Toscanini priv. col., see 1985 exh. cat., no. 21), strikingly dramatic juxtapositions of form can be seen. Grubicy also executed an impressive series of etchings *c.* 1893, using the Famiglia Artistica press. For these, he drew on his experiences in Italy and the Netherlands, for example *Evening on the Wyweberg at The Hague* (1893–4; Milan, Castello Sforzesco). Grubicy continued to write and paint, expounding ever more emphatically Scapigliati and Symbolist theories concerning the unification of all forms of artistic expression, in particular the 'musical harmonies' fundamental to them all. In 1920 he donated his collection of paintings, drawings and etchings to the recently formed Galleria d'Arte Moderna in Milan. These (mostly minor) works were largely the fruit of his travels abroad, those from The Hague school for example, and of his multifarious activities in Italy. Grubicy had been one of the strongest promoters of the gallery and his collection formed part of the core around which the municipal collection was later built up.

BIBLIOGRAPHY

Luciani
O. N. Rood: *Modern Chromatics* (London, 1879)
S. Pagani: *La pittura lombarda della scapigliatura* (Milan, 1955)
Mostra del divisionismo italiano (exh. cat., Milan, Pal. Permanente, 1970), pp. 81–4
M. Valsecchi and F. Vercellotti: *Vittore Grubicy De Dragon* (Milan, 1976)
Post-Impressionism: Cross-currents in European Painting (exh. cat., ed. J. House and M. A. Stevens; London, RA, 1979–80)
The Hague School: Dutch Masters of the 19th Century (exh. cat., ed. R. de Leeuw, J. Sillevis and C. Dumas; London, RA, 1983), pp. 94–102
A.-P. Quinsac: *Segantini: Trent'anni di vita artistica europea nei carteggi inediti dell'artista e dei suoi mecenati* (Oggiono, 1985)
Omaggio a Vittore Grubicy De Dragon (exh. cat., Como, Gal. Cavour, 1985)

CLARE HILLS-NOVA

Grue, Francesco Antonio Xaverio (*b* Castelli, 7 March, 1686; *d* Castelli, 1746). Italian potter. He came from an illustrious family of maiolica potters and painters from Castelli in Abruzzo. In 1716, after graduating in philosophy and theology in Urbino (1706) and travelling in Rome and L'Aquila, he arrived in Naples, where he concentrated on the production of ceramics; he decorated plates, albarelli and shields in the style of wares from his home town. His considerable output influenced contemporary Neapolitan production. Among his most notable works is the series of albarelli for the apothecaries of the sanctuary of the S Casa in Loreto and of the monastery of S Martino in Naples. Wares were often Baroque in style and included shields decorated with mythological themes, and plates decorated with landscapes or putti in the centre and tendril or festoon borders. Wares were also often signed and dated. In 1736 he returned to Castelli, where he continued to work until his death.

BIBLIOGRAPHY

C. Cherubini: *I Grue pittori in maiolica* (Teramo, 1857)
C. Rosa: *Notizie storiche delle maioliche di Castelli* (Naples, 1857)
G. C. Polidori: *Maiolica antica abruzzese* (Milan, 1949)
Mostra dell'antica maiolica di Castelli d'Abruzzo (exh. cat., Castelli, Mus. Cer., 1965)
L. Arbace: *Maioliche di Castelli la raccolta acerbo* (Ferrara, 1993)

LUCIANA ARBACE

Grueby, William Henry (*b* 1867; *d* 1925). American potter and ceramic manufacturer. He was apprenticed in 1882 to the J. and J. G. Low Art Tile Works, Chelsea, MA, where he remained for ten years. At the World's Columbian Exposition in Chicago in 1893, he was very impressed with the high-temperature flambé glazes of the French art pottery created by Auguste Delaherche and Ernest Chaplet, which encouraged Grueby's own experiments with matt, monochromatic glazes. In 1895 he set up his own factory, the Grueby Faience Co., in Boston, which produced tiles and architectural faience in Greek, Medieval and Hispano-Moresque styles, popularized by the Arts and Crafts Movement. From 1897–8 he manufactured a range of vases finished in soft, matt glazes in greens, yellows, ochres and browns, with the 'Grueby Green' predominating. Until 1902 the potter George Prentiss Kendrick was largely responsible for the designs, executed in heavily potted stoneware based on Delaherche's Art Nouveau shapes. Young women were employed to carry out the hand-moulded and incised surface decoration, which consisted mainly of vertical leaf-forms in shallow relief (e.g. stoneware vase, late 19th century; London, V&A). The work was enthusiastically received by the public and such designers as Tiffany ordered ceramic bases for their lamps. Many American workshops and factories quickly introduced matt glazes, but few could surpass the velvety perfection of Grueby's wares. Between 1900 and 1904 Grueby pottery won awards at a number of important international exhibitions, including a silver and two gold at the 1900 Exposition Universelle in Paris. Despite these successes, the firm was declared bankrupt in 1908. Grueby then opened the Grueby Faience & Tile Co., which was taken over in 1919 by the C. Pardee Works of Perth Amboy, NJ. The firm continued in the production of Grueby-style wares until the late 1920s.

BIBLIOGRAPHY

E. Cooper: *History of World Pottery* (London, 1972/*R* 1988), p. 171

G. Clark: *American Ceramics: 1876 to the Present* (New York, *c.* 1979/*R* London, 1987)

□

Gruen, Victor (David) [Grünbaum, Viktor] (*b* Vienna, 18 July 1903; *d* Vienna, 14 Feb 1980). American architect of Austrian birth. He received his architectural training at the Akademie der Bildenden Künste, Vienna. He maintained a practice there until Adolf Hitler annexed Austria. In 1938 he went to New York where he worked in the office of the Ivels Corporation and for Norman Bel Geddes. An early commission in New York was for the Ledererd Shop (1939) on Fifth Avenue. He formed a partnership with Elsie Krummeck (1940–48) and then moved to Los Angeles where he established the office of Victor Gruen Associates in 1951.

Gruen gradually specialized in commercial architecture and in his Northland Center (1954), Detroit, MI, he developed the basic organization of the modern suburban shopping centre. This was followed by other similar developments such as Southdale Shopping Center (1956), Minneapolis, MI; Cherry Hill Center (1960), Camden, NJ; Midtown Plaza (1962), Rochester, NY; Randhurst Shopping Center (1962), Mount Prospect, Chicago, IL; and The Mall (1968), Fresno, CA. Other major public buildings by him include the Museum of Arts and Sciences (1960), Evansville, IN, and Sea World (1966), San Diego, CA.

See also SHOPPING MALL.

WRITINGS

'Typical Downtown Transformed [Ft. Worth]', *Archit. Forum*, civ/5 (1956), pp. 146–55

with L. Smith: *Shopping Towns USA* (New York, 1960)

'Approaches to Urban Revitalization in the United States', *J. AA.*, lxxviii (Dec 1962), pp. 178–94

Centers for the Urban Environment (New York, 1973)

BIBLIOGRAPHY

Contemp. Architects

T. F. Hamlin: *Forms and Function of 20th Century Architecture* (New York, 1952)

J. M. Fitch: *Architecture and the Aesthetics of Plenty* (New York, 1961)

G. Eckbo: *Urban Landscape Design* (New York, 1964)

LELAND M. ROTH

Gruenwald, Alfred Emanuel Ferdinand. *See* BAARGELD, JOHANNES THEODOR.

Grumbach, Antoine (*b* Oran, Algeria, 24 Jan 1942). French writer, teacher and architect. He graduated in architecture (1967) from the Ecole des Beaux-Arts, Paris, where he was introduced to urban design practice and theory by Eugène Beaudouin. At the same time, he attended Roland Barthes's courses in linguistics at the Ecole Pratique des Hautes Etudes. During the 1970s Grumbach, who was influenced by the historian Joseph Ryckwert (*b* 1926), devoted most of his time to theory and criticism. He published extensively in specialized reviews in France, exhibited and sold his drawings and taught at the Unité Pédagogique d'Architecture 6 in Paris, the University of Toronto and Princeton University, NJ; he also lectured throughout the world. From his typological studies of the traditional urban fabric in Paris and his participation in Rome in the international exhibition *Roma Interrota* (1977), he became convinced that the integration of new architectural projects within the existing urban fabric was an essential prerequisite for high-quality urban design, and he adopted a polemical and theoretical approach to architectural competitions he entered at the time, such as those for the systematization of the Place Napoléon (1975), La Roche-sur-Yon, and the development of Les Halles (1978), Paris.

From 1975 to 1978 Grumbach worked on the landscaping of public spaces in the Val Maubuée district of the new town of Marne-la-Vallée (with Christian de Portzamparc), and in 1980 his career became more practice-orientated when he won the competition for the Direction Départementale de l'Equipement in Poitiers, an administrative complex completed in 1987. Later projects included a multi-purpose community centre and residential complex (1980–86) on Quai de Jemmapes, Paris; several designs for infill blocks of flats, in Paris on the Place Brancusi (1981–6) and in Berlin-Tiergarten at the intersection of Kluchstrasse and Lützowstrasse (1983–5). These buildings express Grumbach's interest in an 'impure' and 'cumulative' approach to design, which, though relying on a modern vocabulary, played on ambiguity rather than on straightforwardness, on complexity rather than on unity, echoing some aspects of Post-modernism and the work of Robert Venturi. They are composed of horizontal or vertical layers, which emphasize contrasts in materials, textures and colours.

The interweaving of the old and the new is also a recurrent theme in Grumbach's work. For example, instead of erecting a single structure for an archaeological museum in Arles, as was indicated in the brief for the competition he entered with the historian Bruno Fortier in 1984, he proposed a 'museographic promenade' throughout the oldest part of the city. He also included a number of renovated structures in his housing project Cascades et Industrie (1982–6) in the 20e arrondissement of Paris. Another example concerns the Hôtel de Région (1983–6), the headquarters of the regional assembly of Poitou-Charente, located in the grounds of a former Catholic boarding school in the historic centre of Poitiers; the chapel, which was threatened with demolition, was the object of a daring operation of adaptive reuse, with new additions successfully integrated into the existing fabric. Through this work, his teaching and writings, Grumbach became one of the most influential architects of his generation in France.

WRITINGS

'Les Promenades de Paris', *Archit. Aujourd'hui*, 185 (1976), pp. 97–106

'Les Promenades de Rome', *Archit. Aujourd'hui*, 198 (1978), pp. 20–23

'The Art of Completing the City', *Lotus Int.*, 1 (1984), pp. 94–103

BIBLIOGRAPHY

'Rétrospective Antoine Grumbach', *Archit., Movt, Cont.*, 16 (1987), pp. 38–59

ISABELLE GOURNAY

Grummaert. *See* GRIMMER.

Grünbaum, Viktor. *See* GRUEN, VICTOR.

Grund, Norbert (*b* Prague, *bapt* 4 Dec 1717; *d* Prague, 17 June 1767). Bohemian painter. He was the son of the painter Kristián Grund (*c.* 1686–1751) and brother to the painters František Karel Grund (1721–43), Petr Pavel Christian Grund (1722–84)—also a violin virtuoso—and the harpist Jan Eustach Grund. He learnt painting with his father, who released him from his apprenticeship in 1737. Subsequently he lived in Vienna and then perhaps in Germany; he probably knew his great models, Watteau, Nicolas Lancret and Francesco Guardi, only from engravings.

Grund's work consists of a rather confused range of small pictures, embodying almost all genres in which landscapes or dwellings include figures. He painted scenes from myths, the Bible, legends and battles; he depicted love scenes, the theatre, storms at sea, visits to ruins, studios etc. Although the human figures always endow his pictures with a light touch, often there is an implicitly deeper allegorical meaning. His paintings from the 1740s are marked by a heavy Late Baroque colour scheme, in the 1750s by fragile Rococo shades; later he accomplished a smooth transition to a classicist realism. The popularity of his works in aristocratic and bourgeois circles is underlined by reproductions by Jan Balzer (1710–99) existing in over 200 prints. In the context of Czech Baroque painting his only predecessors were Jan Jakob Hartmann (1660–1745), František Antonin Hartmann (1694–1728) and Václav Jan Hartmann (1700–45) in Kutná Hora; thus it was his work that set the trend for bourgeois paintings.

BIBLIOGRAPHY

Thieme–Becker
P. Toman: *Nový slovník československých výtvarných umělců* [New dictionary of Czechoslovak fine artists], i (Prague, 1947), pp. 274–6
Norbert Grund (exh. cat. by J. Kříž, Vienna, Belvedere, 1967)
P. Preiss: 'Malířství vrcholného baroka v Čechách' [Painting at the height of the Baroque in the Czech lands], *Dějiny českého výtvarného umění* [History of Czech fine arts], ii/2 (Prague, 1989), pp. 781–2

IVO KOŘÁN

Gründerzeit [Ger.: 'foundation time']. Term that refers to the burst of artistic activity and optimism that occurred in Germany after the establishment of the German Empire in 1871. In its narrower sense, this is taken to mean the period from 1871 to 1873, while a wider definition extends this to about 1888, the year of Emperor William I's death. Following the defeat of France in the Franco-Prussian War (1870–71), the millions of marks of war reparations that were paid to Germany fuelled reckless financial speculation that came to an end in the crash of 1873. Nevertheless, over the longer time span a self-confident optimism founded on rapid industrial and scientific development came to be a guiding force. As the rapidly expanding capital of the new nation, Berlin was the place where the effects of these phenomena were most evident. Building speculation particularly flourished there (*see* BERLIN, §I, 3), while the splendid road network helped to give the city the character of a metropolis. In the extended period of the *Gründerzeit* art came to be seen no longer as it had been *c.* 1800 as 'the noblest means of educating humanity' but rather as an expression of power and wealth. This resulted in the emergence of such prominent and influential 'painter-princes' as Franz von Lenbach in Munich and of a form of historicism that was supposed to reflect a flowering comparable to that of the Renaissance in Italy. In the 1870s architecture in Berlin was adapted to its new status through a measured style in which the idiom of Karl Friedrich Schinkel and his successors was heightened by Renaissance elements. This is seen in such buildings as the Deutsche Reichsbank (1869–76; destr. 1945), the Technische Hochschule (begun 1878), both by Friedrich Hitzig, the Foreign Office (1873–7) by Wilhelm Neumann (1826–1907) and the Kunstgewerbemuseum (1877–81) by Martin Gropius. Soon afterwards, and initially in private houses and commercial buildings, the more costly, primarily neo-Baroque style of the Ecole des Beaux-Arts in Paris became the model. After protracted competitions, this tendency culminated in the Reichstag building (1884–94; *see* GERMANY, fig. 10) by Paul Wallot and the Protestant Cathedral (1888–1905) by Julius Raschdorff.

BIBLIOGRAPHY

Berlin und seine Bauten, Architekten- und Ingenieurverein Berlin, i (Berlin, 1877/*R* 1984, rev. 2/1896 as 2 vols) and iv–xi (Berlin, 1970–74)
W. Hegemann: *Das steinerne Berlin* (Lugano, 1930/*R* Berlin, Frankfurt am Main and Vienna, 1963)
W. Bussmann: *Das Zeitalter Bismarcks, Handbuch der deutschen Geschichte*, iii/II (Konstanz, 1956/*R* Frankfurt am Main, 4/1968)
R. Hamann and J. Hermand: *Gründerzeit* (Berlin, 1965)

EVA BÖRSCH-SUPAN

Grundig. German artists.

BIBLIOGRAPHY

Hans Grundig—Lea Grundig. Malerei und Graphik (exh. cat. by E. Frommhold, Dresden, Gemäldegal. Neue Meister, 1958)

(1) Hans Grundig (*b* Dresden, 19 Feb 1901; *d* Dresden, 11 Sept 1958). Painter, etcher and draughtsman. He studied at the Kunstgewerbeschule in Dresden (1920–21), then until 1926 at the Akademie der Bildenden Künste in Dresden, where he was influenced by the Neue Sachlichkeit of Otto Dix. In 1926 he joined the Communist Party with his future wife, Lea Langer. He was arrested several times during the Third Reich because of his political beliefs and imprisoned in the concentration camp at Sachsenhausen from 1940 to 1944. From 1946 to 1948 Grundig was rector of the Hochschule für Bildende Künste in Dresden, but he had to wait for recognition until 1958, when the Albertinum in Dresden mounted the first large exhibition of his work and that of his wife.

Grundig's artistic career was strongly influenced by the socially critical views expounded by the circle around Dix. He was initially an Expressionist, but in paintings such as *Unemployed Cigarette Worker* (1925; see 1962 exh. cat.) and *Loving Couple* (1925; see 1962 exh. cat.) he was more lyrical than Dix and less cynical about society. His favourite subjects were the proletariat and petty bourgeoisie, whom he depicted sympathetically in *Hunger March* (1932; Dresden, Gemäldegal. Neue Meister). Around 1930 his work showed a tendency towards Pittura Metafisica, and later in the 1930s his tendency to lyricism and romanticism became stronger.

When Hitler came to power in 1933, Grundig, like other artists who opposed the Nazis, had to find new ways of taking issue with the regime, particularly as he was forbidden to exhibit by the Ministry of Culture. In 1937 his painting *Mother and Children* was shown at the *Entartete*

Kunst exhibition in Munich, and in the following year he completed the large-scale triptych of the *Reich of a Thousand Years* (1935–8; Dresden, Gemäldegal. Alte Meister), which is visionary in its portrayal of the violence and sacrifice taking place in macabre nightmare townscapes. The image of the burning town in the central panel is a prophetic warning of the forthcoming World War, as were the *Hunted Horse* (1937) and *Fight of the Bears and Wolves* (1938; see 1962 exh. cat.). The longing for peace and freedom is expressed in the picture *Tessin Landscape II* (*c.* 1938).

After World War II Grundig planned a series of concentration-camp pictures; only the triptych of the *Victims of Fascism* (1946–8; Dresden, Gemäldegal. Neue Meister) was completed, because he felt that it was not possible to depict the tremendous horror of the subject-matter. He remained committed to expressing his political stance in his paintings, however, though not always with convincing results, for example in *Youth Demonstration II* (1951; see 1962 exh. cat.). In 1953, the year of the workers' revolt in the German Democratic Republic (East Germany), he painted *Carnation Picture.* A planned triptych *Beware of the Atom Bomb* (see 1962 exh. cat.) had only one panel completed, an image of beautiful strange colours and forms.

BIBLIOGRAPHY

Hans Grundig: Malerei, Zeichnungen, Druckgraphik (exh. cat. by L. Zinserling, E. Berlin, Alte N.G., 1962)
Hans Grundig: Malerei, Graphik (exh. cat. by G. Feist, East Berlin, Gal. Fernsehturm; Leipzig, Mus. Bild. Kst.; 1973)
L. Zinserling: *Hans Grundig* (Moscow, 1974)
Hans Grundig: Un artista tedesco tra le due guerre (exh. cat. by M. de Micheli and G. Feist, Lecco, Villa Manzoni, 1976)
G. Feist: *Hans Grundig* (Dresden, 1979)

(2) Lea Grundig [née Langer] (*b* Dresden, 23 March 1906; *d* Dresden, 10 Oct 1977). Printmaker, wife of (1) Hans Grundig. She studied at the Kunstgewerbeschule (1922–3) and then at the Akademie der Bildenden Künste (1923), both in Dresden. However, the painting of Otto Dix influenced her more than her teachers, as did Dix's associate Hans Grundig, to whom she was married in 1928 and who encouraged her sharp social criticism and her enthusiasm for Communism. She was arrested twice during the Third Reich because of her party membership and her Jewish background, and because she was producing etchings with anti-Nazi themes, such as *Under the Swastika* (1933–7; Berlin, Ladengal.) and the 12-plate series *War Is Threatened* (1935–7; see 1975–6 exh. cat., pp. 63–5).

In 1939 Grundig had to flee to Palestine, where in the internment camp she produced 15 drawings entitled *Anti-Fascist Primer* (1941) and 14 drawings entitled *In the Valley of the Dead* (1942–4), which portrayed the annihilation of the Jews. On her return to Germany in 1948 she concentrated on prints with a humanitarian message, as in *Fight the Atom Death* (1958; see 1975–6 exh. cat., p. 79) and *Proletarians of Every Country Unite!* (1969; see 1975–6 exh. cat., p. 87). She played a leading role in the Verband Bildender Künstler der DDR from its inception in 1950, and from 1964 to 1970 she was its president.

BIBLIOGRAPHY

G. Feist: *Lea Grundig: Zeitgenossen* (Dresden, 1963)
W. Hütt: *Lea Grundig* (Dresden, 1969)
Lea Grundig: Zeichnungen, Graphik (exh. cat. by E. Bartke, E. Berlin, Akad. Kst. DDR, 1975–6)

VOLKER HELAS

Grundy [née Ullmann]**, Anne Hull** (*b* Nuremberg, 1927; *d* ?Chilbolton, Hants, 9 Aug 1984). English collector. She was born into a family of wealthy German bankers and came to live in England as a small child. A strong-willed young woman with a generous allowance, she became a familiar figure among London dealers, who respected her sharp eye and considerable self-taught expertise. She ascribed her lifelong passion for collecting to her background among the objects acquired by generations of her forebears. With the help of her husband, Professor John Hull Grundy (1907–84), an artist and entomologist, she amassed her vast and varied collections over many decades. She bought hundreds of signed and dated pieces of jewellery, often in their original presentation cases stamped with the retail source. Her fondness for art in miniature and animals inspired a fascination for wood and ivory *netsuke* carved into images of rabbits, deer, birds, fish, cats and dogs. She bought ahead of ascending market prices and gathered together one of the best collections of its type in private hands, part of which she sold in later years to fund additions to her already prodigious collection of antique jewellery.

Anne Hull Grundy was the benefactress of museums and public collections throughout the British Isles; the Fitzwilliam Museum, Cambridge, and the British Museum, London, received major gifts. In 1975–6 she donated a collection of paste, Berlin iron and cut-steel jewellery, cameos and mosaic-set pieces to the Iveagh Bequest, Kenwood, London. The British Museum received over 1000 pieces of jewellery and objects of vertu, dating from *c.* 1700 to the 1930s. Among the jewellery were rare 17th-century Spanish gem-set gold pendants and crosses, 17th-century German and Netherlandish engraved gold lockets, French and English Gothic Revival and Art Nouveau pieces and 19th-century Italian 'architectural' jewellery. Among the objects were over 600 pieces of 18th- and 19th-century Japanese *netsuke* and *inro*, a large collection of Martinware (*see* MARTIN (ii)), 17th- and 18th-century ivory and tortoiseshell boxes inlaid with gold, and glass by René Lalique.

BIBLIOGRAPHY

H. Tait and C. Gere: *The Jeweller's Art: An Introduction to the Hull Grundy Gift to the British Museum* (London, 1978)
H. Tait, ed.: *The Art of the Jeweller: A Catalogue of the Hull Grundy Gift to the British Museum*, 2 vols (London, 1984)
G. Munn: 'Mrs Anne Hull Grundy', *Ant. Colr*, lvii/2 (Feb 1986), pp. 42–7
V. Harris: *Netsuke: The Hull Grundy Collection in the British Museum* (London, 1987)

□

Gruner, Elioth (Lauritz Leganyer) (*b* Gisborne, New Zealand, 16 Dec 1882; *d* Sydney, 17 Oct 1939). Australian painter. The son of a Norwegian father and Irish mother, he came to Sydney from New Zealand with his family in 1883. He received his first art lessons from Julian Rossi Ashton, although for many years he had little time for painting, instead working to support his family. He finally achieved recognition as an artist around the beginning of

World War I. Following successful sales he became a full-time painter, championed in Sydney as the exemplary heir to the impressionist pastoral tradition of Australian art, which had been established in the late 19th century. Between 1915 and 1920, under the influence of Max Meldrum, he focused on the landscape as seen against the light. Painting *en plein air* he specialized in effects of early morning, for example *Morning Light* (1916; Sydney, A.G. NSW), one of a series painted at Emu Plains (1915–19), employing a broken brushwork style typical of painting in Sydney of the period.

After two years in Europe (1923–5), Gruner tried to accommodate aspects of modernist painting by making his pictures flatter, and with harder shapes, for example *Weetangera, Canberra* (1939; Sydney, A.G. NSW). Although he continued to be regarded as one of Australia's foremost painters of light and landscape, he became increasingly lonely in the 1930s until in 1939, during one of many bouts of severe depression, he drank himself to death.

BIBLIOGRAPHY

J. Ashton and N. Lindsay: *The Art of Elioth Gruner* (Sydney, 1923)
Elioth Gruner Memorial Loan Exhibition (exh. cat., intro. B. J. Waterhouse; Sydney, A.G. NSW, 1940)
N. Lindsay: *Elioth Gruner* (Sydney, 1947)
Elioth Gruner, 1882–1939 (exh. cat. by B. Pearce, Sydney, A.G. NSW, 1984)

BARRY PEARCE

Grünewald, Isaac (Hirsche) (*b* Stockholm, 2 Sept 1888; *d* nr Oslo, 22 May 1946). Swedish painter, stage designer and teacher. He studied at the Konstnärförbund school in Stockholm (1905–8), then travelled to Paris and studied at Matisse's school (1908–11). He was a member of the Young Ones group. In 1911 he married SIGRID HJERTÉN. Grünewald was greatly influenced by Matisse between 1910 and 1920, and Fauvism was generally important to him. His prize-winning design (1912–14) for decorating the Register Office of Stockholm Town Hall was purely Fauvist, and he was forbidden to execute the project. This French influence can be seen in *Ivan in the Armchair* (1915; Stockholm, Mod. Mus.). Cézanne's paintings also had an early significance for him. In 1915 he exhibited together with his wife at the Sturm-Galerie in Berlin. Grünewald carried out the first of many stage designs for a production of *Samson and Delilah* at the Kungliga Teater, Stockholm, in 1921. He was a sought-after decorator during the 1920s and worked in a classical spirit. He was also an able portrait painter and illustrator, e.g. *Bullfighting* (1917; Norrköping, Kstmus.). Grünewald taught at the Konsthögskolan in Stockholm from 1932 to 1942, and from 1942 he ran his own painting school, also in Stockholm.

BIBLIOGRAPHY

J. P. Hodin: *Isaac Grünewald* (Stockholm, 1949)
K. A. Arvidsson, ed.: *Isaac har ordet* [Isaac has the word] (Stockholm, 1959)
E. Sundler: *Isaac Grünewalds scenografi, 1920–1930: Vision och verklighet* [Isaac Grünewald's stage designs, 1920–1930: vision and reality] (Uppsala, 1975)
'Det sjungande trädet'. Grünewald, 1889–1989 [*The Singing Tree.* Grünewald, 1889–1989] (exh. cat., Stockholm, Liljevalchs Ksthall, 1989)

JACQUELINE STARE

Grünewald, Matthias [Gothart Nithart, Mathis; Gothardt-Neithardt, Matthis] (*b* ?Würzburg, *c.* 1475–80; *d* Halle, 30 or 31 Aug 1528). German painter, draughtsman, hydraulic engineer and architect. He is generally regarded as the greatest painter of the German Renaissance and certainly its greatest colourist. His paintings are unparalleled in their extraordinary beauty and expressive force. He was a man of profound religious beliefs whose vision transcended the visible world and led him to paint some of the most moving and memorable images of Christ's Passion in Western art. His pictorial language is rooted in the symbolic imagery of the Middle Ages, especially the mysticism of the 14th century, but is at the same time proto-Baroque in its dramatic movement, in the highly expressive language of drapery forms and gestures and in the strong contrasts of light and shadow. Unlike Dürer, he did not make prints; the linear techniques of printmaking were foreign to this quintessentially painterly artist. Even his drawings are consistently rendered in the painterly medium of black chalk rather than pen and ink.

1. Biographical sources. 2. Works. 3. Working methods and technique.

1. BIOGRAPHICAL SOURCES. The circumstances of Grünewald's life slipped soon after his death into oblivion until a slow rediscovery began in the late 19th century, given momentum especially by German Expressionism, which saw a kindred spirit in Grünewald and his pictorial language. In his biography of Grünewald (1675–9), Sandrart decried the dearth of knowledge about the artist. He was the first to introduce the nickname Grünewald, still used today, but the origin of this name remains obscure; evidently the artist was known as such as early as the 1630s. It was only in 1938 (see Zülch) that the artist's real name, cited in 1528 in the posthumous inventory of his possessions as 'Meister Mathis Maler Nithart oder Gothart', came to light. Zülch's discovery explained the monogram the artist used, consisting of either two initials, MG, for instance on a drawing of the *Trias Romana* (Berlin, Kupferstichkab.), or three initials with an added N, as on the *St Lawrence* panel (Frankfurt am Main, Städel. Kstinst. & Städt. Gal.) and the frame (1519; Aschaffenburg, SS Peter und Alexander) of the dismembered *Virgin of the Snow* altarpiece. The documents published by Zülch often refer to Grünewald only as 'Meister Mathis' or 'Mathis of Aschaffenburg'. Other contemporary sources are not more informative: in 1531 Philipp Melanchthon, writing on the great artists of his time, mentioned Dürer, Lucas [Cranach] and 'Mathias'; here the context verifies that Grünewald was meant.

Since Zülch's publication, the artist's biography has been intermittently expanded and confused but not substantially changed. Assembling the basic information has been immensely complicated by the destruction of archives in Frankfurt, Aschaffenburg and Mainz and by the fact that Meister Mathis was a very common name in the middle Rhenish area where Grünewald worked. The literature must be consulted with caution. Scholars often indiscriminately applied almost any archival reference to a 'Meister Mathis' to Grünewald's biography. Even Zülch occasionally fell into this trap. Sandrart's early biography, which was in some details obviously incorrect, was called into question whenever his information did not correspond with new archival discoveries. The historian H. J. Rieckenberg confused matters further in the early 1970s by proposing quite a different biography, according to which Grünewald did not die in Halle in 1528 but lived longer, but his ideas have not generally found favour among specialists. It is now known that Grünewald had no connection with Seligenstadt, as Zülch believed, other than as the city in which his adopted (or perhaps illegitimate) son Endres was apprenticed to the organ-builder Arnold Rücker in 1526. In particular, Grünewald is not identical with 'Mathis der Bildschnitzer', a sculptor active in Seligenstadt, as Schädler demonstrated in 1962. The confusion originated in the fact that both Grünewald and Mathis the sculptor worked for the same patron, the wealthy canon Heinrich Reitzmann, in Aschaffenburg. The biographical data assembled in this article are based on archival documents now generally agreed to refer to Grünewald. The chronology of the paintings, however, has not been studied since the early 1970s and as presented here reflects the opinion of the author.

2. Works.

(i) To mid-1516. Grünewald's recently discovered (1968) earliest extant paintings, the *Last Supper* and *SS Dorothy and Agnes* (both Georg Schäfer priv. col., on loan to Coburg, Veste Coburg), originally the predella wings of an unknown altarpiece of *c.* 1500, show unequivocally the stylistic influence of Hans Holbein the elder, the most important painter in Augsburg at the end of the 15th century. Whether or not Grünewald was actually apprenticed to Holbein is unknown. The connection could have been established either in Augsburg or in Frankfurt, where Holbein and two assistants painted the high altarpiece for the Dominican church in 1500–02. Grünewald's earliest firmly datable works, the panels of the *Fourteen Auxiliary Saints* and the *Man of Sorrows* on the altarpiece in the parish church in Lindenhardt, near Bayreuth, were originally painted for the parish church in neighbouring Bindlach and are dated 1503 on the frame housing the sculpture; despite their poor condition, they also display stylistic affinities with Holbein the elder. Soon thereafter Grünewald painted the *Mocking of Christ* (Munich, Alte Pin.), an epitaph commissioned by Johann Schweikard von Kronberg in Aschaffenburg for his sister Apollonia, deceased on 23 December 1503. The panel can be dated between 1504, the presumed date of the commission given soon after her death, and 1506, the date of Kronberg's death. It remained *in situ* in the former Collegiate Church in Aschaffenburg (now SS Peter und Alexander) until 1613. This commission is the first to localize Grünewald in the city in which he spent much of his career. In late 1504 or early 1505 he is documented as working on another epitaph (untraced) for Johann Reitzmann, the vicar of the same church in Aschaffenburg, deceased 13 September 1504.

Grünewald's seven different renderings of the *Crucifixion* are among the most powerful and most memorable religious images in the history of Western art. The earliest was created *c.* 1505–8 (Basle, Kstmus.) and is thought to have been either part of an altarpiece consisting of several other panels (untraced) or a small autonomous devotional picture. For whom and where it was painted are not known. A document of 1510, however, locates the artist again in Aschaffenburg, working as a master mason for Archbishop Ulrich von Gemmingen. The Archbishop recommended his employee to the cathedral chapter in Mainz to repair a well at Burg Klopp near Bingen on the Rhine. Gemmingen was the Archbishop of Mainz but resided in the archepiscopal palace in Aschaffenburg, which explains Grünewald's activity in both places. The well repair is the first mention of Grünewald's expertise as a hydraulic engineer, an activity in which he is documented as having engaged again in 1517 in Aschaffenburg and later in Halle. His technical skills also included a knowledge of mining, as materials listed in the posthumous inventory of his possessions testify.

The second extant *Crucifixion*, the so-called *Small Crucifixion* (Washington, DC, N.G.A.), was painted *c.* 1510–12. The depiction of a solar eclipse, such as that which occurred on 1 October 1502, led to an earlier dating of *c.* 1502 for the panel; this, however, is not convincing either on stylistic grounds or in its plausibility, since the awesome experience of observing an eclipse of the sun could have been depicted in Grünewald's work much later as well. The painting displays a greater simplicity and fewer figures than the earlier panel in Basle and an astonishing intensity of emotion.

It is disputed whether the *Small Crucifixion* was executed before or directly after Grünewald's four saints painted in grisaille as the fixed wings of the Heller Altarpiece and attached subsequently to Dürer's central panel showing the *Assumption and Coronation of the Virgin* (1508–9; ex-Residenz, Munich, destr. 1729; known from a copy). One of the major monuments of German Renaissance art in that it combined paintings by these great masters, the Heller Altarpiece was evidently assembled in two stages. Jakob Heller, a wealthy merchant, commissioned Dürer's central panel in 1507 for the Dominican church in Frankfurt; it was installed in 1509. Grünewald must have created his wings with *St Lawrence* and *St Cyriacus* (both Frankfurt am Main, Städel. Kstinst. & Städt. Gal). and *St Elizabeth* and *St ?Lucy* (both Karlsruhe, Staatl. Ksthalle; see fig. 1) towards the end of 1511. The date is revealed in the transcripts of a trial (*Kemenatenprozess*) held in 1515, where it is stated that after designing and overseeing the construction of a large chimney in the archepiscopal palace in Aschaffenburg, the artist moved to Frankfurt to work for the Dominicans. The male saints were originally located over the female ones and subsequently sawn apart, as the configuration of the grisaille columns on the backs of the panels demonstrates. The subtlety of modelling, the spectrum of colour gradations within the grisaille, the extraordinary liveliness of the drapery forms and the painstaking realism of the plants place these panels among Grünewald's most beautiful and unusual pictures. Sandrart reported on another work by Grünewald for the same church, the *Transfiguration*, which was executed in *Wasserfarben*, meaning perhaps in fresco or as a mural; nothing is known about this composition other than the evidence of two preparatory drawings (both Dresden, Kupferstichkab.).

1. Matthias Grünewald: *St Elizabeth* and *St ?Lucy*, oil on panel, 950×420 mm and 1010×430 mm, *c.* 1511 (Karlsruhe, Staatliche Kunsthalle); two panels from the wings of the Heller Altarpiece

Grünewald's Isenheim Altarpiece (Colmar, Mus. Unterlinden) is the single most important work of German Renaissance painting. Executed soon after the completion of the altarpiece for the Dominicans in Frankfurt, the large panels, added on to the existing sculptural parts of the altar by Nikolaus Hagenauer and Desiderius Beichel, must have been painted between 1512–13 and 1515. The date 1515, assumed to designate the completion of the panels, appears on the Magdalene's ointment jar in the *Crucifixion.* Contracts with a carpenter in Altkirch, near Isenheim, dated 1513 and 1515, indicate that Grünewald was in Alsace at those dates, and the trial transcripts prove that he was not available at home to testify between September 1514 and February 1516. Thus he must have spent about three years in Isenheim. His patron, Guido Guersi (*d* 1516), the learned Italian preceptor of the monastery belonging to the hospital order of St Anthony at Isenheim, surely had a considerable role in determining the imagery of the famous panels, but very little is known about him. His coat of arms and perhaps a portrait in the

2. Matthias Grünewald: *Angels' Concert* and the *Incarnation*, outer wing panels from the Isenheim Altarpiece, oil on panel, 2.69×3.07 m (closed), 1512/13–1515 (Colmar, Musée d'Unterlinden)

guise of St Anthony appear in the *Meeting of SS Anthony and Paul*. On his death, Guersi was buried before Grünewald's *Magdalene* altarpiece (untraced), which he perhaps also commissioned but which is known only from a poor copy (Donaueschingen, Fürstenberg-Samml.). The monumental Isenheim panels have produced as much profound admiration as puzzlement regarding their meaning, primarily the *Angels' Concert* and the *Incarnation* panels (see fig. 2), which generations of art historians have attempted to interpret within the theological programme of the altarpiece as a whole, without a completely convincing result having yet been found. The Antonite monks' care for the sick and dying in the Isenheim monastery has offered the most generally plausible explanation of the 'hospital context' (Hayum) for numerous details of Grünewald's imagery thus far.

(ii) Late 1516 and after. By August 1516 Grünewald had returned from Alsace, since the cathedral chapter in Mainz made a salary payment, meaning either that he received back pay or that he was once again employed by the Archbishop. In October 1517 he was working as a hydraulic engineer for the former Collegiate Church in Aschaffenburg (now SS Peter und Alexander). Heinrich Reitzmann commissioned the *Virgin of the Snow* altarpiece, the frame of which is dated 1519. The *Virgin and Child* in the parish church at Stuppach, near Würzburg, and the *Miracle of the Snow* (Freiburg im Breisgau, Augustinmus.) appear to belong to this project, though the arrangement of panels is a matter of conjecture. Sandrart reported that three altarpieces by Grünewald, among them the *Martyrdom of St Alban* dated 1520, were stolen as war booty by Swedish troops in 1632 and perished with the ship transporting them.

Grünewald's major work of the late period is the remarkable *Meeting of SS Erasmus and Maurice* (Munich, Alte Pin.; see fig. 3), painted *c.* 1520–25 for Cardinal Albrecht of Brandenburg, Archbishop of Mainz and Halle, as part of an anti-Lutheran campaign in the Collegiate Church in Halle. The nearly life-size figure of St Erasmus is a portrait of the patron, a major figure in the religious strife of his era. He also commissioned the very moving panel with the *Lamentation* (*c.* 1525; Aschaffenburg, SS Peter und Alexander), which bears his coat of arms. This most unusual composition, presumably originally a predella but with areas painted over later, shows only the hands of the grieving Virgin but not her torso; it does not seem, however, to have been cut down, since the paint edge is reportedly intact along all four sides. Today it is Grünewald's only painting remaining in Aschaffenburg. Typical of his late work are the dark colours, also found in his *Crucifixion* and *Christ Carrying the Cross* (both Karlsruhe, Staatl. Ksthalle), which were originally two sides of the same panel created for the parish church of Tauberbischofsheim. The inscription *Er ist umb unser sund gesc[h]lagen* underscores the sufferings of Christ inflicted by sinful mankind. Both pictures are poorly preserved.

Grünewald's religious sympathies may be assumed from the Lutheran tracts listed in the posthumous inventory of 1528. Grünewald left the employ of the Archbishop, whose palace in Aschaffenburg was besieged during the Peasants' War, and moved to Frankfurt. There he made technical drawings of the water mills in May 1527 for the city of Magdeburg. In Halle he worked again as a hydraulic engineer for the city council. On 1 September 1528 the council was notified of his death, presumably a day or two earlier, with the remark that he 'hadn't achieved very much' during his stay, perhaps due to illness or to personal turmoil over religious beliefs, which also for a time sapped Dürer's creative energy.

4. Matthias Grünewald: *St Mary Magdalene under the Cross*, black chalk, 400×300 mm, *c.* 1515 (Winterthur, Sammlung Oskar Reinhart am Rümeraolz)

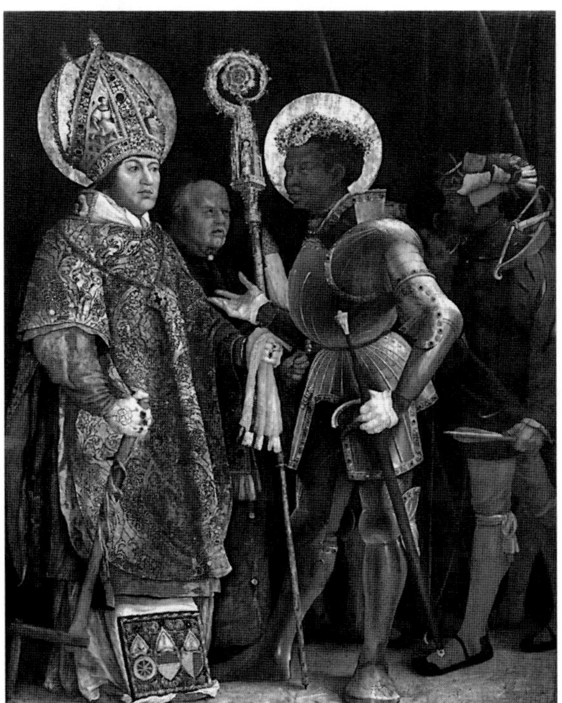

3. Matthias Grünewald: *Meeting of SS Erasmus and Maurice*, oil on panel, 2.26×1.76 m, *c.* 1520–25 (Munich, Alte Pinakothek)

3. Working methods and technique. Grünewald's *alla prima* technique of painting is evident in the many changes made during the execution of the Isenheim panels, most obviously in the *Angels' Concert* and in the *Incarnation.* No underdrawings have yet been found under the paint layers. An exceptionally gifted draughtsman, he employed drawings in the traditional manner to make preparatory studies for paintings rather than as autonomous works of art in their own right, as Hans Baldung and Urs Graf were doing soon after 1500. About 35 drawings by Grünewald have been preserved, all of them in black chalk (see fig. 4).

BIBLIOGRAPHY

H. A. Schmid: *Die Gemälde und Zeichnungen von Matthias Grünewald*, 2 vols (Strasbourg, 1911)
M. Escherich: *Grünewald-Bibliographie, 1489–1914* (Strasbourg, 1914)
M. Hausenberg: *Matthias Grünewald im Wandel der Kunstanschauung* (Leipzig, 1927)
W. K. Zülch: *Der historische Grünewald* (Munich, 1938)
L. Behling: *Die Handzeichnungen des Mathis Gothart Nithart genannt Grünewald* (Weimar, 1955)
E. Ruhmer: *Grünewald: The Paintings, Complete Edition* (London, 1958)
A. Schädler: 'Zu den Urkunden über Mathis Gothart Neithart', *Münchn. Jb. Bild. Kst*, n. s. 2, xiii (1962), pp. 69–74
A. Weixlgärtner: *Grünewald* (Vienna and Munich, 1962)
G. Scheja: *Der Isenheimer Altar des Matthias Grünewald* (Cologne, 1969)
E. Ruhmer: *Grünewald Drawings: Complete Edition* (London, 1970)
H. Geissler, B. Saran, J. Harnest and A. Mischlewski: *Mathis Gothart Nithart, Grünewald: Der Isenheimer Altar* (Stuttgart, 1973)
H. J. Rieckenberg: 'Matthias Grünewald: Name und Leben neu betrachtet', *Jb. Staatl. Kstsamml. Baden-Württemberg*, xi (1974), pp. 47–120; review of Rieckenberg's opinions by P. Strieder in *Pantheon*, xxx (1972), p. 520

P. Schmitt: *Matthias Gothart Nithart Grünewald: Essai d'une bibliographie, 1924–1974* (Colmar, 1974)
A. Châtelet, ed.: *Grünewald et son oeuvre: Actes de la table ronde à Strasbourg et Colmar, 1974* (Strasbourg, 1976)
H. J. Rieckenberg: *Matthias Grünewald* (Herrsching, 1976)
E. Ruhmer: *Matthias Grünewald: Der Isenheimer Altar* (Munich and Zurich, 1979)
L. Behling: *Matthias Grünewald* (Strasbourg, 1981)
W. Lükking: *Mathis: Nachforschungen über Grünewald* (Berlin, 1983)
W. Fraenger: *Matthias Grünewald* (Munich, 1985)
P. Vaisse and P. Bianconi, eds: *Tout l'oeuvre peint de Grünewald* (Paris, 1984)
A. Hayum: *The Isenheim Altarpiece: God's Medicine and the Painter's Vision* (Princeton, 1989)
C. Heck: 'Le Retable d'Issenheim et la sculpture au nord des Alpes à la fin du moyen âge', *Actes du colloque de Colmar: Colmar, 1989*
A. Stieglitz: 'The Reproduction of Agony: Toward a Reception-History of Grünewald's Isenheim Altar after the First World War', *Oxford A. J.*, xii/2 (1989), pp. 87–103
K. Arndt: 'Der historische Grünewald, Anmerkungen zum Forschungsstand', *Kirche und Gesellschaft im Heiligen Römischen Reich des 15. und 16. Jahrhunderts*, ed. H. Brookmann (Göttingen, 1994), pp. 116–47

CHRISTIANE ANDERSSON

Grünstein [Grünestein]**, Anselm F(ranz) Ritter zu.** *See* RITTER ZU GROENESTEYN, ANSELM F.

Grünwald, Béla Iványi. *See* IVÁNYI GRÜNWALD, BÉLA.

Grunwald, Henryk (*b* Łany, nr Warsaw, 14 Jan 1904, *d* Warsaw, 21 March 1958). Polish painter, illustrator, metalworker, designer and writer. From 1924 to 1929 he studied at the Warsaw School of Fine Arts, where he was later an assistant professor (1927–30, 1933–5). From 1929 to 1930 he studied in France. He exhibited his works from 1928 until his death. At the beginning of his career he concentrated on painting, to which he later returned. He became a popular cartoon artist while working for the satirical weekly *Szpilki* from 1935 to 1939 and from 1946 to 1958. His illustrations to the works of N. V. Gogol and Fyodor Dostoyevsky were highly acclaimed. Grunwald mastered various techniques in metalworking, until 1939 concentrating on jewellery and promoting abstract forms; he also made lighting equipment, particularly lamps, sconces and chandeliers. During this period he introduced avant-garde features into traditional Polish metalwork. In the post-war period he accepted commissions for monumental works, for example gates, screens, mantelpiece designs and lighting units. In Warsaw he designed the decorative elements for the *Tomb of the Unknown Soldier* between Liberty Square and the Saxonian Garden, and for many public buildings, for example interior features such as lamps and chandeliers, as well as iron gates and balustrades, for the Office of the Council of Ministers, and the Belvedere Palace. He also designed the gates of the Polish embassies in Berlin and Beijing and wrote poetry and articles on art issues.

WRITINGS

'"Wielka" i "mala" sztuka' ['Great' and 'small' art], *Problemy* (1948), no. 11, pp. 665–70
'Na podróznej palacie' [The traveller's finger], *Problemy* (1950), no. 12, pp. 79–84
'O rysunkach' [On drawing], *Przegląd A.*, 5/6 (1955), pp. 124–6
'Swierszcz na kościele kapucynów' [The cricket at the Capuchin church], *Przegląd Kult.*, 33 (1959), p. 4; 34 (1959), p. 4

BIBLIOGRAPHY

M. Rogoyska: *Polski Słownik Biograficzny* [Polish biographical dictionary], ix (Wrocław, 1960)
I. Witz: *Obszary malarskiej wyobraźni* [The spaces of the artistic imagination] (Kraków and Warsaw, 1967), pp. 83–93
H. Kubaszewska and E. Szańkowska: *Słownik artystów polskich i obcych w Polsce dziakajacych* [The dictionary of Polish artists], ii (Wrocław, 1975)

TADEUSZ CHRZANOWSKI

Grünwedel, Albert (*b* Munich, 31 July 1886; *d* Lenggries, near Tölz, 7 Nov 1935). German explorer, archaeologist and art historian. He started his Asian studies in 1876 and obtained a doctorate in 1881 from the Technische Universität, Munich. In the same year, on the recommendation of his teacher Ernst Kuhn, he became an assistant in the Museum für Völkerkunde (Museum of Ethnology) in Berlin, where in 1883 he was made Assistant Director. In the following years his most important publications were written: *Buddhistische Kunst in Indien*, *Buddhistische Studien* and *Mythologie des Buddhismus in Tibet und der Mongolei.* Entrusted with the running of the first and third German expeditions to East Turkestan (now Xinjiang Autonomous Region, China) in 1902 and 1905–7 (ALBERT VON LE COQ led the second and fourth expeditions), a new phase of life began for Grünwedel. His report on the archaeological excavations in Idikutshahri and the surrounding area (*see* KHOCHO) during the winter of 1902–3 was published in 1905; in 1912 a study appeared of the ancient Buddhist cult places in East Turkestan; in 1920 his great tabular work was published on ancient KUCHA, dealing with archaeological, religious and historical researches on wall paintings from Buddhist caves. In 1904 he became Director of the Indian Art Department in the Museum für Völkerkunde, Berlin, and contributed considerably to its collection through his finds (*see* CENTRAL ASIA, §II, 7). Until he retired in 1921 he dedicated himself to a reappraisal of the Turkestan finds.

Despite his great scientific successes he became increasingly lonely and embittered. Within the museum he was exposed to harsh attacks. After retirement he devoted himself almost exclusively to Tibetan Buddhism. It became almost impossible to follow his mystic and speculative theories and the publications appearing at this time were scientifically untenable.

WRITINGS

A Róng-English Glossary (Leiden, 1892)
Buddhistische Kunst in Indien (Berlin, 1893)
Buddhistische Studien (Berlin, 1897)
ed. and rev.: G. B. Mainwaring: *Dictionary of the Lepcha-Language* (Berlin, 1898)
Zur buddhistischen Ikonographie (Braunschweig, 1899)
Mythologie des Buddhismus in Tibet und der Mongolei (Leipzig, 1900)
Die Kunst im alten Indien (Berlin, 1903)
'Einige praktische Bemerkungen über archäologische Arbeiten in Chinesisch-Turkestan', *Bull. Assoc. Int. Explor. Hist. Asie Cent. & Extrême-Orient*, ii (Oct 1903), pp. 1–16
'Bericht über archäologische Forschungen in Turfan und Umgebung (Nov 1902–Feb 1903)', *Bull. Assoc. Int. Explor. Hist. Asie Cent. & Extrême-Orient*, iii (April 1904), pp. 18–25
Bericht über archäologische Arbeiten in Idikutschari und Umgebung im Winter, 1902–1903 (Munich, 1905)
Die archäologischen Ergebnisse der dritten Turfan-Expedition (Berlin, 1909)
'Buddhistisches Wandgemälde aus Qyzyl bei Kutscha', *Amtl. Ber. Kön. Kstsamml.*, xxx (1908–9), pp. 171–6
Altbuddhistische Kultstätten in Chinesisch-Turkistan (Berlin, 1912)
Alt-Kutscha: Archäologische und religionsgeschichtliche Forschungen an Tempera-Gemälden aus buddhistischen Höhlen der ersten acht Jahrhunderte nach Christi Geburt (Berlin, 1920)

BIBLIOGRAPHY

E. Waldschmidt: 'Albert Grünwedel', *Ostasiat. Z.*, n. s., xi (1935), pp. 215–19

J. Schubert: 'Albert Grünwedel und sein Werk', *Artibus Asiae*, vi (1936), pp. 124–42

P. Hopkirk: *Foreign Devils on the Silk Road* (London, 1980/*R* Oxford, 1984)

M. YALDIZ

Grupello, Gabriel (*b* Grammont, 22 May 1644; *d* Ehrenstein, nr Aachen, 20 June 1730). Flemish sculptor, active in Germany. He was the son of a Milanese cavalry captain and a Flemish mother. He trained in Antwerp with the sculptor Artus Quellinus I from 1658 and probably took part in the sculptural decoration of the Stadhuis in Amsterdam. He was in France before 1670; there he would have seen the sculptural work at the château of Versailles, executed under the direction of Charles Le Brun and François Girardon. In 1673 he was a master in the guild of the Four Crowned Heads in Brussels. He became municipal sculptor and, in 1688, court sculptor to Charles II of Spain. Among his works dating from this period are the classicizing garden statues of *Diana* and *Narcissus* (marble, *c.* 1670–75; Brussels, Mus. A. Anc.) and the elaborate Rubensian wall fountain with marine gods (marble, 1675; Brussels, Mus. A. Anc.), made for the fishmongers' guild of Brussels.

From 1695 Grupello worked in Düsseldorf as court sculptor to John William, Elector Palatine. He was awarded numerous commissions for monumental and decorative work, as well as portraits, up to the Elector's death in 1716. Grupello's most important work in Düsseldorf is his marble equestrian statue of *John William* in the Marktplatz; completed in 1711, it is one of the best Baroque statues of its kind. Other works of note are marble garden statues of *Mercury*, *Minerva Pictura*, *Galatea*, *Justice* and *Minerva in the Temple* and a marble statue of *Electress Mary Anne Louise of Tuscany as Minerva*, all originally at Schloss Bensberg but moved to the Schlosspark in Schwetzingen after 1720. Grupello's bronze Pyramid Fountain (1722), an ambitious programmatic composition of the four cardinal virtues and other allegorical figures, originally erected in Schwetzingen, has stood in the Paradeplatz, Mannheim, since 1741. Its Baroque base is by Alessandro Galli-Bibiena. Many of the models recorded in the inventory (Brussels, Bib. Royale Albert 1er) drawn up by Grupello's daughter on the eve of his departure from Düsseldorf to Brussels in 1716, after John William's death, were never executed in permanent materials, being designs for the decoration of the projected Neues Residenzschloss at Düsseldorf, a gigantic palace complex that was supposed to surpass Versailles.

Following his return to Brussels, in 1719 Grupello became court sculptor to the Holy Roman Emperor Charles VI. Among his surviving works of that period are an ivory Crucifix (*c.* 1720; St Truiden, Redemptorist monastery) and a wood Crucifix (*c.* 1720–25; Aachen Cathedral). In 1725 he moved to Ehrenstein, where he spent his last years.

While Grupello's early works have a classicist flavour, perhaps derived from his contacts with French sculpture, by the time of his residence in Düsseldorf, under the dominant influence of Rubens, he had developed a style reminiscent of Flemish Baroque. Although attributions to him are not always unambiguous, owing to the size of his workshop and to later alterations to his marbles, he shows himself in his main works to be one of the virtuoso sculptors of the Baroque in western Europe.

BIBLIOGRAPHY

Thieme–Becker

U. Kultermann: *Gabriel Grupello* (Berlin, 1968)

La Sculpture au siècle de Rubens (exh. cat., Brussels, Mus. A. Anc., 1977), pp. 118–25, 369–71 [with bibliog. to 1976]

KAI BUDDE

Grupo CAYC. Argentine group of artists. It was founded in Buenos Aires in 1971 as the Grupo de los Trece by the critic Jorge Glusberg (*b* 1938) and renamed Grupo CAYC because of its close association with the Centro de Arte y Comunicación. The group held its first public show in 1972 in the exhibition *Hacia un perfil del arte latino americano* at the third Bienal Coltejer, Medellín, Colombia. The group's chief members were Jacques Bedel, Luis Benedit, Jorge Glusberg, Víctor Grippo, the sculptor Leopoldo Maler (*b* 1937), the sculptor Alfredo Portillos (*b* 1928) and Clorindo Testa. Treating the visual aspect of works of art as just one element in order to demonstrate the complexity and richness of the creative process, they took a wide view of Latin American culture that spanned the cosmogony of Pre-Columbian societies to the technological and scientific concepts of the late 20th century. In 1977 they won the Gran Premio Itamaraty at the 14th São Paulo Biennale with their collective work *Signs of Artificial Eco-systems.*

BIBLIOGRAPHY

J. Glusberg: *El Grupo CAYC* (Buenos Aires, 1979)

H. Safons: *A Sense for History: CAYC Group* (Buenos Aires, 1980)

J. Glusberg: *Del Pop-art a la Nueva Imagen* (Buenos Aires, 1985), pp. 127–32, 483–8

HORACIO SAFONS

Grupo de Artistas y Técnicos Españoles para el Progreso de la Arquitectura. *See* GATEPAC.

Grupo Hondo. Spanish group of painters. It was formed in Madrid in 1961 by Juan Genovés, José Paredes Jardiel (*b* 1928), Fernando Mignoni (*b* 1929) and Chilean Gastón Orellana (*b* 1933) and was active until 1964. They first exhibited together in 1961 at the Galería Nebli, Madrid, reacting against the total abstraction of *Art informel* but applying its free, automatic, rapid and uninhibited techniques to a socially committed and Expressionist 'neo-figurative' style. They acquired two new members, José Vento (*b* 1925) and Carlos Sansegundo (*b* 1930), for their second exhibition in 1963, at the Sociedad de Amigos de Arte in Madrid, but they went their separate ways a year later.

BIBLIOGRAPHY

Grupo Hondo (exh. cat., intro. M. Conde; Madrid, Gal. Nebli, 1961)

Grupo Hondo (exh. cat., Madrid, Soc. Amigos A., 1963) [incl. group statement]

V. Sánchez Marín: 'Pop-art y Nueva Figuración: Las tendencias más recientes en el arte español', *Artes* (Dec 1964) [special issue], pp. 33–8

Grupo R. Catalan group of architects. They were active in Barcelona from 1951 to 1959. Their aim was the renewal of Catalan architecture. The group, which included Oriol Bohigas, Joaquim Gili Moros (*b* 1916), Josep Martorell,

Antoni de Moragas Gallissa (*b* 1913), José Pratmarsó Parera (*b* 1913), José María Sostres Maluquer and Manuel eq Valls Verges (*b* 1912), was formed through a competition organized by the Colegio de Arquitectos de Cataluña y Baleares in January 1949 to solve housing problems in Barcelona. They were later joined by Pau Montguró and Francesc Vayreda. For them the development of architecture and urban planning was based not only on technical, but also on economic and social considerations. Outstanding among their activities were the exhibitions held in the Galerias Layeyanas in Barcelona (1952, 1954 and 1958) and courses that they organized including 'Economics and Urban Development' and 'Sociology and Urban Development'.

BIBLIOGRAPHY

A. Fernandez Alba: *La crisis de la arquitectura española, 1939–1972* (Madrid, 1972)

PILAR BENITO

Gruppe 5 [Nor.: 'Group 5']. Norwegian group of artists active from 1961. It has had a decisive influence on the recognition of abstract art in Norway. The group was founded in 1961 by the Spanish-born Ramon Isern (Solé) (*b* 1914; *d* 1989), together with Håkon Bleken (*b* 1929), Halvdan Ljøsne (*b* 1929), Lars Tiller (1924–94) and Roar Wold (*b* 1926). They were all teachers in the architectural department (Institutt for form og farge) of the Norges Tekniske Høgskole in Trondheim. They wished to define their shared opposition to the traditional and conventional Trondheim art world and to break Oslo's dominance of Norwegian art. Without any agreed ideological platform, they examined, in non-representational paintings, the relationship between plane, form, colour, space, the process of abstraction and the legacy of Constructivism, as they had in their teaching. In their abstract paintings the Constructivist stamp was rhythmically enlivened by the materiality of colours and such evocative spatially expansive subjects as that of Wold's *At the Edge of the Beach* (1963; Oslo, Mus. Samtidskst). Isern made geometrically defined and totem-like sculptures in different materials, as well as tapestries with similar forms. Most of the group's members also executed charcoal drawings, graphics and collages, such as Ljøsne's oil painting *Accumulation* (1965; Oslo, Mus. Samtidskst) with glued-on newspaper clippings and disturbing spatial effects, and wrote articles about art theory (see Bleken).

In general the group's exhibitions were well received in Norway and abroad; the response to their only show in Oslo, in 1966, emphasized their academic background. The twelfth Gruppe 5 exhibition, in Odense, Denmark, in 1970, made it clear that the original shared ethos had become channelled into quite different, personal expressions: Bleken drew socially critical and universal figurative visions with an advanced charcoal technique, for example *The Judges* (1970; Oslo, Norsk Kulturåd) from the series of 12 charcoal drawings entitled *Fragments of a Dictatorship*; Ljøsne painted expressive, relief-like, symbol-laden signs on the border of figuration; Wold's Abstract Expressionism also approached the figurative; Tiller alternated between irregular and strictly geometric forms with strong colour contrasts; while Isern created non-figurative collage variations, often with political titles. During the period of the group's activity its individual members executed such large decorative commissions as Isern's monumental concrete sculpture *Tetrahedon* (h. 12 m, 1969), placed in front of the Board of Health Building in Oslo. The group was never formally dissolved but held its farewell exhibition in 1980, only to arise again at the same place, Trondhjems Kunstforening (Trondheim Art Association), in 1994.

WRITINGS

H. Bleken: 'Kunst-Kunstner', *Samtiden*, 10 (1964), pp. 620–29

BIBLIOGRAPHY

Gruppe 5 (exh. cat., foreword A. Holm; Trondheim, Kstforen., 1961)
Gruppe 5 (exh. cat., foreword and commentary O. Thue; Odense, Fyns Stiftsmus., 1970)
J. Brockmann: 'Fem kunstnere tar felles avskjed med "Gruppe 5"' [Five artists take their leave of Gruppe 5], *Årsberetning, Trondhjems Kstforening: Trondhjem, 1980*
——: *Malerne på Gløshaugen* (Trondheim, 1985), pp. 4–6 [with Eng. trans.]
T. Nergaard: *Håkon Bleken* (Oslo, 1986), pp. 26–39
Gruppe 5 (exh. cat.; Trondheim, Kstforen.; Reykjavik, Hafnarfjørdur Cult. & A. Fund.; Tampere, Tammerfoshuset; 1994)
S. Aamold: *Ramon Isern* (diss., U. Oslo, in preparation)

SUSANNE RAJKA

Gruppe 33 [Künstlervereinigung Gruppe 1933]. Swiss group of artists. It was founded in Basle in 1933 by the painters Otto Abt (1903–82), Walter Bodmer, Paul Camenisch (1893–1970), Theo Eble (1899–1974), Max Haufler, Charles Hindenlang (1894–1960), Carlo König (1900–70), Rudolf Maeglin (1892–1971), Ernst Max Musfeld (1900–64), Otto Staiger (1894–1967), Max Sulzbachner (*b* 1904) and Walter Kurt Wiemken (1907–40), the sculptors Daniel Hummel and Louis Weber (*b* 1891) and the architect Paul Artaria. Camenisch was effectively leader of the group, which arose in opposition to the conservatism of the Gesellschaft Schweizerischer Maler, Bildhauer und Architekten (GSMBA) and also to the rising tide of hostility to modern art engendered by the Nazis in neighbouring Germany. Soon after its foundation a programme propagated by the members claimed their aim to be 'the active participation in the development of the plastic arts without ignoring the phenomena and expression of our time'. Left-wing and anti-fascist politically, the members of the group worked within various modern currents such as Surrealism, Constructivism and abstract art. With the expansion of its membership, however, it soon attracted artists from less modern tendencies as well as photographers, film makers, graphic designers and stage designers. There also arose a significant grouping of socially engaged architects.

The first Gruppe 33 exhibition took place on the ground floor of a scarcely finished building in Basle in December 1933. A larger and more significant show took place in Basle in October 1934, arousing fierce opposition in the press. Unable to obtain any official recognition and exhibiting space, in November 1934 Club 33 was opened in Basle as a place for the group to meet and exhibit. Gruppe 33 continued to organize exhibitions there into World War II, and a large show was held at the Kunsthalle in Basle in 1943 to celebrate their tenth anniversary; this also marked the beginning of their cultural integration. Another anniversary exhibition was held at the same location in 1953, but, with the change in political climate caused by the Cold War, Camenisch was excluded, as he was a member of the left-wing political party, the Partei der Arbeit. This brought to a close the oppositional role that had previously characterized the group, although it continued to function in this tamer form.

BIBLIOGRAPHY

50 Jahre 'Gruppe 33': Der Mitglieder der ersten Zehn Jahre (exh. cat. by Y. Höflinger, Basle, Ksthalle; Chur, Bündner Kstmus.; Lugano, Villa Malpensata; Lausanne, Pal. Rumine; 1983–4)

□

Gruppe 53. German group of painters founded in Düsseldorf in 1953 and active until 1959. In 1953 some young Düsseldorf artists banded together to form an association known as the Künstlergruppe Niederrhein, with a shared interest in *art informel* and the intention of mounting exhibitions, in opposition to the established artists' association, the Rheinische Secession. From 1954 the group emerged as Gruppe 53, with joint exhibitions held primarily in buildings owned by the Kunstverein für die Rheinlande und Westfalen, and every second year at the Städtische Kunsthalle in Düsseldorf. The members included Peter Brüning, Winfried Gaul (*b* 1928), Gerhard Hoehme, Horst Egon Kalinowski, Herbert Kaufman (*b* 1924), Peter Royen (*b* 1923), Rolf Sackenheim (*b* 1921) and Friedrich Wertmann (*b* 1927). Abstract artists from outside Düsseldorf, such as Karl Fred Dahmen (1917–81), Bernard Schultze and Emil Schumacher, were also invited to exhibit with them, as were other Düsseldorf artists representing various developing trends in painting. Thus Konrad Klapheck, who worked figuratively, and members of the Zero group, including Heinz Mack, Otto Piene and Günther Uecker, exhibited with Gruppe 53. There was no common aesthetic programming policy, although representative works include Brüning's *Bild 2/63* (1963; Bonn, Städt. Kstmus.), Gaul's *Good-bye to Rembrandt* (1956–7; Saarbrücken, Saarland Mus.) and Hoehme's *Black Spring* (1956; priv. col.). Economic and organizational interests formed the basis of their joint action, along with the desire to establish abstract art. All those involved painted in an abstract way and rejected geometrically inspired 'cold abstraction'. The group received considerable support from the collector, art historian and later gallery owner Jean-Pierre Wilhelm (1912–68). He made contacts with gallery owners, especially in Paris, and with artists from abroad. When the opportunities for exhibiting abstract work by young artists in Düsseldorf had improved as a result of Gruppe 53's commitment, and when other commercial galleries opened in addition to Wilhelm's Galerie 22, the reasons motivating the group disappeared, and it was consequently disbanded in 1959.

BIBLIOGRAPHY

H. Schubert: 'Ausstellungen, S. 34/39', *Kstwk*, xi/10 (April 1958)

CLAUDIA BÜTTNER

Gruppe der Ungegenständlichen. *See* ZEN 49.

Gruppe G. *See* SCHOLLE, DIE.

Gruppe Progressiver Künstler [Gruppe der Progressiven]. German group of artists. It was founded in Cologne in 1925 by Franz Seiwert (1894–1933) and Heinrich Hoerle (1895–1936), with Otto Freundlich, Gerd Arntz (*b* 1900), Hans Schmitz (1896–1977), Augustin Tschinkel (*b* 1905) and the photographer August Sander. The group extended the programme of a 'proletarian' art that had characterized Seiwert and Hoerle's STUPID GROUP and their intervening work to include artists from other centres in the Rhineland and throughout Germany. They supported the revolutionary opposition to the ineffectual Weimar Republic, which they saw as a tool of repressive right-wing elements in the establishment. Following collaborations with the idealist and pacifist Berlin periodical *Die Aktion*, Seiwert and Hoerle started their own artistic publication, *A bis Z*, in October 1929, beginning the group's most fertile period. While the periodical attracted contributions from a broad cross-section of artists (including Raoul Haussmann, Jean Hélion and László Moholy-Nagy), the group favoured a stripped-down figurative style, whose schematized forms and abstract elements drew attention to the mechanization of contemporary existence. With echoes of Oskar Schlemmer's work and of Parisian Purism, some compositions also tended towards the coldness of Neue Sachlichkeit. Their critical political stance made them an immediate target for Nazi opposition. The group and periodical were ended in 1933, Seiwert died the same year, and Hoerle and Freundlich's work was subsequently designated as *entartete Kunst*.

BIBLIOGRAPHY

A bis Z: Organ der Gruppe Progressiver Künstler, Koln, 1929–33 (*R* Cologne, New York, Munich, 1969)

Vom Dadamax bis zum Grüngürtel: Köln in den zwanziger Jahren (exh. cat., ed. W. Herzogenrath; Cologne, Kstver., 1975), pp. 78–130

U. Bohnen: *Das Gesetz der Welt ist die Änderung der Welt: Die rheinische Gruppe Progressiver Künstler, 1918–1933* (Berlin, 1976)

Franz W. Seiwert (1894–1933); Leben und Werk (exh. cat. by U. Bohnen, Cologne, Kstver.; Münster, Westfäl. Kstver.; W. Berlin, Kstamt Kreuzberg; Ludwigshafen, Städt. Kstsamm., 1978), pp. 28–63

Heinrich Hoerle; Leben und Werk (1895–1936) (exh. cat. by D. Backes, Cologne, Kstver., 1981–2), pp. 30–52

MATTHEW GALE

Gruppe Spur. *See* SPUR.

Gruppo degli Otto Pittori Italiani. Italian group of eight painters. It was formed in 1952 after the disintegration of FRONTE NUOVO DELLE ARTI. Six of them had belonged to the earlier group: Renato Birolli, Antonio Corpora, Ennio Morlotti, Emilio Vedova, Giuseppe Santomaso and Giulio Turcato; the other founder-members were Afro and Mattia Moreni (*b* 1920). The group, which exhibited at the Venice Biennale of 1952, was coordinated by Lionello Venturi, who described its style as 'abstract-concrete . . . born of a tradition that began around 1910 and that includes Cubism, Expressionism and Abstraction'. Geometric or post-Cubist forms dominate these artists' work; however, the naturalistic colour and atmospheric luminosity of such paintings as Vedova's *Cosmic Vision* (1952; New York, MOMA) and Birolli's *Brambles and Paths* (1953; Brescia, Cavellini priv. col., see Venturi, 1959, pl. 14, p. 47) typify this group's leanings towards expressive abstraction. During the 1950s Birolli, Corpora and Morlotti became more involved with Informalism and Tachism, and Santomaso and Vedova were significantly inspired by Hans Hartung and Wols respectively. Of the eight, Afro was the most outstanding exponent of lyrical expressionism, largely achieved through his use of vibrant and transparent colour in works such as *Underwater Fishing* (1955; Pittsburgh, PA, Carnegie).

BIBLIOGRAPHY

L. Venturi: *Otto pittori italiani* (Milan, 1952)
——: *Italian Painters of Today* (Rome, 1959)

□

Gruppo N. Italian group of artists. It was formed in Padua in 1959. It included Alberto Biasi (*b* 1937), Ennio Chiggio (*b* 1937), Giovanni Antonio Costa (*b* 1935), Edoardo N. Landi (*b* 1937) and Manfredo Massironi (*b* 1937). The group gained notoriety in 1959 when Massironi competed unsuccessfully for the Premio San Fedele, for which he submitted a piece of cardboard that he had selected because of the interesting optical qualities of its surface. During the 1960s Gruppo N played an important part in the development of Op art in Italy. The work of Biasi, for example, included geometric abstract reliefs with striking optical effects, such as the *Optical-dynamic Relief (Drops)* (painted iron and card, 1962; Padua, priv. col., see exh. cat., p. 37); this attempted to create an effect analogous to the patterns caused by drops of water falling on a liquid surface. The group's gallery, Studio N, which opened in Padua in November 1960, rapidly became an important centre for experimental art, music and poetry. The group had its own room at the Venice Biennale of 1964 and also participated in various exhibitions of *Arte programmata* in Italy, as well as showing work at Studio F in Ulm (1963) and the Museum Sztuki, Łódź (1967).

BIBLIOGRAPHY

I. Mussa: *Il gruppo enne: La situazione dei gruppi in Europa negli anni 60* (Rome, 1976)
Antologia Alberto Biasi (exh. cat. by D. Banzato and others, Padua, Mus. Civ., 1988)

Gruppo 7. Italian group of architects. It was formed in 1926 by seven students from the Scuola Superiore di Architettura del Politecnico, Milan: GIUSEPPE TERRAGNI, Guido Frette, Ubaldo Castagnoli, Sebastiano Larco, Carlo Enrico Rava, Luigi Figini and Gino Pollini (*see* FIGINI AND POLLINI). Castagnoli was replaced in 1927 by Adalberto Libera.

The avant-garde group was the first to be formed in support of modern architecture in Italy, and its four-part manifesto, published in *Rassegna italiana* (Dec 1926 to May 1927), laid the foundations for Italian *Rationalismo* (*see* RATIONALISM (ii)). Seeking to distance itself equally from the Futurists and their 'destructive fury' as well as from the blandly classicizing work of contemporary *novecento* architects such as Giovanni Muzio, Gruppo 7 called for sincerity, logic and order in architecture. Echoing Le Corbusier, their manifesto announced the advent in Europe of the *esprit nouveau*, already manifest in literature, art and music as well as in architecture; it was distinguished by strict adherence to logic and rationality, a concern for rhythm and classical proportions and a sense of history as faith in the spirit of the age. The second and third parts of the manifesto discussed the architectural scene in Europe, particularly in Italy, deploring the poor quality of architectural education and the general public's lack of comprehension, while the last part characterized that period as 'a new archaic era' in which architects were confronted with the promising beginnings of a new style.

Central to the writings of Gruppo 7 was the belief that the 'universal' achievements of the Modern Movement were not incompatible with a national character. Indeed, the manifesto embraced a nationalist programme consistent with the cultural policies of the fascist regime. Equally significant was the insistence on the need to develop a few fundamental building types by concentrating on essential problems of architecture and by renouncing individualism. Immediately after the publication of its manifesto, Gruppo 7 mounted an exhibition at the 3rd Biennale in Monza (1927), showing renderings and models of unexecuted projects in which a concern for structural clarity and abstract rhythms combined with an impersonal, perhaps even metaphysical, style of presentation. Terragni's gas factory referred to a wide range of modernist sources, from Erich Mendelsohn to El Lissitzky, while Figini and Pollini's more restrained garage project anticipated the 'Mediterranean' purism of their later work. Some of the Monza material was included in the Italian section of the Weissenhofsiedlung exhibition organized by the Deutscher Werkbund in Stuttgart later that year (1927) and it was here that Gruppo 7 was able to witness at first hand the achievements of the European masters.

The critical success of the group's initiatives and encouragement from political circles led to a larger exhibition the following year in Rome: in the first Esposizione dell'Architettura Razionale (1928), organized by Adalberto Libera and the critic Gaetano Minnucci, Gruppo 7 found itself in the company of about 40 other Rationalists from various parts of Italy. Soon after this a larger organization was formed under the name of Movimento Italiano per l'Architettura Razionale (*see* MIAR), with Libera as its secretary. MIAR itself was dissolved in 1931 following reactions to its second Esposizione dell'Architettura Razionale in Rome, which included a photomontage attacking respected members of the profession. By this time, however, Terragni, Figini and Pollini had produced some seminal works and the group had achieved its prime objective: that of provoking a wide-ranging public debate on many issues central to the development of modern architecture in Italy.

WRITINGS

'Architettura', *Rass. It.*, xviii (Dec 1926), pp. 849–54
'Architettura (II): Gli stranieri', *Rass. It.*, xix (Feb 1927), pp. 129–37
'Architettura (III): Impreparazione, incomprensione, pregiudizi', *Rass. It.*, xix (March 1927), pp. 247–52
'Architettura (IV): Una nuova epoca arcaica', *Rass. It.*, xix (May 1927), pp. 467–72

BIBLIOGRAPHY

C. Belli: 'Origini e sviluppi del Gruppo 7', *La Casa*, 6 (1959), p. 177
E. Shapiro: 'Gruppo 7', *Oppositions*, 6 (1976), pp. 86–102 [contains Eng. trans. of parts 1 and 2 of manifesto]
——: 'Gruppo 7', *Oppositions*, 12 (1978), pp. 88–104 [contains Eng. trans. of parts 3 and 4 of manifesto]
D. P. Doordan: *Building Modern Italy: Italian Architecture, 1914–1936* (New York, 1988)
R. Etlin: *Modernism in Italian Architecture, 1890–1940* (Cambridge, MA, 1991)

LIBERO ANDREOTTI

Gruppo T. Italian group of artists. It was founded in Milan in 1959 and active until 1962. The founders were Giovanni Anceschi (*b* 1939), Davide Boriani (*b* 1936), Gianni Colombo (*b* 1937) and Gabriele de Vecchi (*b* 1938). These artists, who were primarily interested in kinetic art, first exhibited as a group in 1960 in the Galleria Pater in Milan, where they held six exhibitions entitled *Miriorama 1–6*, none lasting more than a few days. In the last of these shows the four founder-members were joined by Grazia Varisco (*b* 1937). Gruppo T's works frequently invited the participation of the exhibition visitor: for example, Boriani's *Magnetic Surfaces* contained patterns of iron dust that changed as the objects were handled. By contrast the exhibits of a show held at the Galleria Danese in December 1960 were powered by electric motors (e.g. *Rotoplastik* by Colombo). The group cooperated with other artists with similar aims, including Gruppo N, at whose gallery, Studio N, in Padua they exhibited in 1962. They also were supported by Lucio Fontana, who presented an exhibition of their work at the Galleria La Salita in Rome in 1961. Gruppo T's last exhibition was at the Galleria del Cavallino in 1962.

BIBLIOGRAPHY

I. Mussa: *Il gruppo enne: La situazione dei gruppi in Europa negli anni 60* (Rome, 1976)

CHRISTOPHER MASTERS

Grützke, Johannes (*b* Berlin, 30 Sept 1937). German painter and stage designer. From 1957 to 1964 he studied under the German painter Peter Janssen (*b* 1906) at the Hochschule für Bildende Künste in West Berlin. At first he painted figurative works influenced by Baroque models and by 19th-century history painting. In aligning himself with the great tradition and the values of figurative painting in the idiom of Rubens or Hans Makart, he deliberately set himself apart from all the artistic tendencies predominant in West Germany in the 1950s and 1960s. Characteristic of his painting is a theatrical element that in the 1960s occasionally took on a quality of caricature. This is in keeping with his interest in the theatre, in which he also worked as an actor, musician, playwright and scene painter (particularly in the 1980s, when he was associated with the director Peter Zadeck in Berlin and Hamburg). As a 20th-century artist who thought in historical terms, Grützke played on the contradiction between the traditional form of figure painting and its contemporary content. In some works, such as *Bach Being Disturbed by his Children* (1975; Berlin, Berlin Gal., see 1977 exh. cat., pl. 179), historical figures are shown in casual, even slightly absurd activities. In others he filled the stylistic shell of great Baroque figural compositions with mundane contents: these included scenes of direct personal contact and immediate experience, without any historical dimension, such as the depiction of three men saying goodbye to a friend, with handshaking and back-slapping, in *When you Come Back it'll Start All Over Again* (1972; Berlin, priv. col., see 1977 exh. cat., pl. 147), the ordinariness of which parodies Baroque history painting. In 1973 Grützke, with the Berlin painters Manfred Bluth (*b* 1926), Matthias Koepell (*b* 1937) and Karlheinz Ziegler (*b* 1935), founded the Gruppe der Neuen Prächtigkeit, whose aim was to enliven art by harking back to tradition. The group was dissolved after a few years. In the mid-1970s Grützke continued to parody Baroque art in a series of paintings of improbably athletic nudes (e.g. *Five Naked Women*, 1973; see 1977 exh. cat., pl. 157), although in the 1980s his style became looser. From 1987 to 1991 Grützke worked on a mural for the Pauluskirche in Frankfurt am Main (where the first German parliament met in 1848), showing 200 deputies entering the building.

BIBLIOGRAPHY

B. Holeczek and P. O. Krückmann: *Johannes Grützke: Werkverzeichnis der Druchgraphik, 1964–1975* (Freiburg im Breisgau, 1975)
Johannes Grützke: Gemälde, 1964–77 (exh. cat. by E. Schenk zu Schweinsberg, Brunswick, Kstver., 1977)
Johannes Grützke: Neue Bilder, 1988–1990. Gemälde und Pastelle (exh. cat., ed. J. C. Jensen; Kiel, Christian Albrechts-U., Ksthalle, 1990)

LUCIUS GRISEBACH

Gruuthuse, Louis de [Lodewijk van]. *See* LOUIS DE GRUUTHUSE.

Grymbault, Paoul. *See* GOYBAULT, PAOUL.

Grymer. *See* GRIMMER.

Gryspek z Gryspach, Florian. *See* GRIESBECK VON GRIESBACH, FLORIAN.

Grzimek, Sabine (*b* Rome, 12 Nov 1942). German sculptor and printmaker. She was the daughter of the sculptor Waldemar Grzimek (1918–84). From 1962 to 1968 she studied at the Hochschule für Bildende und Angewandte Kunst at Weissensee, Berlin, under Heinrich Drake and Ludwig Engelhardt, and from 1969 to 1972 she was a graduate student at the Akademie der Künste of the DDR under Fritz Cremer. Grzimek worked in bronze, treating the surface in a rough, expressive but realist style; her sculptures reveal a strictness of form. She invariably represented the human figure and sought to express human vulnerability and spiritual values, as well as sensitivity and power, as in *Mother and Child* (bronze, 1976–81; Berlin, Alte N.G.).

BIBLIOGRAPHY

Bildhauerkunst der DDR (exh. cat., Bonn, Rhein. Landesmus.; Munich, Staatsgal. Mod. Kst; Mannheim, Städt. Ksthalle; 1987–8), pp. 86–7, 216

BARBARA BARSCH

Gsell [Gesell; Xell; Xsell], **Georg** (*b* St Gall, 28 Jan 1673; *d* St Petersburg, 22 Nov 1740). Swiss painter. He trained in Vienna from 1690 to 1695 with the painter Anton Schoonjans (1655–1726). He lived in St Gall from 1697 to 1704. He moved subsequently to Amsterdam, where Tsar Peter I noticed him during his visit to the Netherlands in 1717 and took him into his service, initially as director of his galleries. From 1727 Gsell held classes in painting and drawing at the Imperial Academy of Sciences in St Petersburg, and illustrated various Academy publications. He painted a series of icons for the cathedral of SS Peter and Paul in St Petersburg (1730–32) as well as portraits, genre scenes, still-lifes, and religious and mythological subjects, such as *Venus and Cupid* (1722; Solothurn, Kstmus.). Most of his works are in Russia.

BIBLIOGRAPHY

SKL
Schweizer Stilleben im Barock (exh. cat., Zurich, Schweizer. Inst. Kstwiss., 1973)

MATTHIAS FREHNER

Guacialoti [Guacialotti; Guazzalotti], **Andrea** (*b* Prato, 1435; *d* Prato, 9 Nov 1495). Italian medallist. Working for a series of papal and ecclesiastical patrons in Rome, Guacialoti, who was himself a member of the clergy, seems to have maintained his residence primarily in Prato, where his family, of distinguished Florentine origins, had settled. Besides being a medallist and bronze-founder, he became a papal scriptor, a canon of Prato and priest of Ajolo (Iolo), near Prato. He established a foundry in Prato, where he accepted commissions to cast the works of other artists as well as producing a series of medals. He cast Bertoldo di Giovanni's medal commemorating the *Pazzi Conspiracy* (26 April 1478), which had been made at the request of Lorenzo the Magnificent de' Medici (Hill, no. 915). On 11 September 1478, Guacialoti sent four examples of the medal to Lorenzo, accompanied by a letter referring to Bertoldo.

Guacialoti's own medals are grouped around three signed pieces with their variants. The first of these is a medal of *Pope Nicholas V* (H 740–41), which is crude in comparison with Guacialoti's other work, itself not notably refined. The second signed medal, of *Niccolo Palmieri, Bishop of Orte* (H 742–4), is one of Guacialoti's finest portraits, and the inscription on some variants indicates that the artist was a member of the Bishop's household around 1467, when the medal was cast. The third signed medal is Guacialoti's most interesting and daring; it commemorates the *Recovery by Alfonso of Aragon, Duke of Calabria, of Otranto from the Turks in 1481* (H 745–6). Alfonso is shown on the obverse in three-quarter view, a departure from the normal profile portrait that is not entirely successful.

Guacialoti's portrait style is distinctive enough to allow the secure attribution to him of a group of medals. Some of the portraits verge on caricature, for example those of *Calixtus III* (H 747) and *Pius II* (H 749). In some pieces, notably those of *Niccolo Palmieri, Alfonso of Aragon* and *Sixtus IV* (H 751), details of the reverse scenes and parts of the inscriptions are crudely engraved. In contrast to the appealing and strongly characterized portraits, the subjects of Guacialoti's reverses were often lifted bodily from the works of other artists. For a medal of *Sixtus IV* he used the Pelican in her Piety from Pisanello's medal of *Vittorino da Feltre* (H 38), and he relied on groups or individual figures found in the medals of Cristoforo di Geremia: part of the crowd on the reverse of the *Alfonso of Aragon* medal is drawn from Cristoforo's medal of *Lodovico Scarampi* (H 756), and the reverses of two medals of *Sixtus IV* are copied from Cristoforo's medals of *Paolo Dotti* (H 758; the figure of Constantia) and *Constantine* (H 755).

Guadalajara, Teatro Degollado by José Jacobo Gálvez, mid-19th century

BIBLIOGRAPHY

Forrer

J. Friedländer: *Die italienische Schaumünzen des fünfzehnten Jahrhunderts* (Berlin, 1880/*R* Bologna, 1976), pp. 130–38

G. F. Hill: *Corpus*, i (1930), pp. 191–5 [H]

G. Pollard: *Italian Renaissance Medals in the Museo Nazionale of Bargello*, i (Florence, 1984), pp. 305–13

STEPHEN K. SCHER

Guadalajara. Mexican city, capital of the state of Jalisco, in western Mexico, *c.* 200 km from the Pacific coast. It features some notable examples of colonial architecture. A point of convergence of transport routes, which has helped the development of its industry, commerce and agricultural production, it has a population of *c.* 1.6 million. It was founded on its present site in the Valley of Atemajac in 1542, and in 1560 it was declared capital of the kingdom of Nueva Galicia, entailing the transfer of the tribunal and royal treasury from Compostela (now Tepic). When New Spain was divided into 12 *intendencias*, the city became the capital of the *intendencia* of Guadalajara, which comprised the present state of Jalisco, part of Aguascalientes and Zacatecas.

Guadalajara contains examples of all the artistic and architectural styles imported from Europe by the Spanish colonists, from the Gothic to Neo-classicism. The Cathedral (1561–1618) was planned as a basilica and begun by Martín Casillas. It is the only one in Mexico to have an interior in the Gothic style. It contains oil paintings by such renowned artists as José de Alcibar and Miguel Cabrera, and, in the sacristy, there is a painting attributed to Bartolomé Esteban Murillo and a large canvas by Cristobal de Villalpando. Other religious edifices of note are the former monastery of S Monica, which has a magnificent Baroque façade with solomonic columns (1773), the church of S Francisco (16th century; altered in the 17th), a Baroque work of fine quality, and the Capilla de Nuestra Señora de Aránzazu, a Churrigueresque construction that retains its original altarpieces.

The 18th-century Palacio de Gobierno has an austere Baroque façade, while the wall paintings in its main stairwell, representing *Father Hidalgo and National Independence*, were executed in 1937 by José Clemente Orozco and are among his greatest works (for further discussion and illustration *see* OROZCO, JOSÉ CLEMENTE). The Neo-classical Teatro Degollado (mid-19th century; see fig.), by José Jacobo Gálvez, is fronted by a portico with 16 Corinthian columns in imitation of the Pantheon in Rome. The auditorium is semicircular, and the dome is decorated with a painting based on Canto IV of Dante's *Divina Commedia.*

The Neo-classical Hospicio Cabañas (1805; now Instituto Cultural Cabañas) on Plaza Tapatía was built by José Gutiérrez to a design by Manuel Tolsá. Its chapel contains murals (1938–9) by José Clemente Orozco depicting the conquest of Mexico, with the extraordinary *Man of Fire* in the dome. Orozco's colours are vibrant and his painting shows his mastery of perspective.

The bandstand in Plaze de Armas, cast in Paris in the early 20th century, is a magnificent example of Art Nouveau. Notable modern buildings in the city include the series of houses (1927) by Luis Barrágan, the IBM building (1975) by Ricardo Legorreta and the Banco Refaccionario de Jalisco (1973) and the Archivo del Estado de Jalisco (1989), both by ALEJANDRO ZOHN. The Museo de Arqueología del Occidente de México (1960) houses pre-Columbian artefacts, including anthropomorphic receptacles and figurines.

BIBLIOGRAPHY

B. Luis Pérez: *Guadalajara de Indias* (Guadalajara, 1932)
J. Cornejo Franco: *Guadalajara colonial* (Guadalajara, 1939)

S. LETICIA TALAVERA, P. MARTANO MONTERROSA

Guadalajara, Palacio del Infantado. Former aristocratic residence in the town of Guadalajara in Castile, Spain. The Palacio del Infantado is a fine example of the HISPANO-FLEMISH ('Isabelline') STYLE, showing a harmonious blend of *Mudéjar* and Flamboyant Gothic forms. It belonged to the House of Mendoza, the most influential family in Castile at the time of Queen Isabella (*reg* 1474–1504). The family had settled in Guadalajara in the 14th century, and it is recorded that Pedro González de Mendoza (*d* 1385) finished building his houses there in 1376. The old palace was renovated by the humanist Don Iñigo Lopez de Mendoza, Marques de Santillana, and was decorated with works of art imported from the Netherlands; travellers such as Baron Rosmital (1466) recorded that it was magnificently furnished. This palace was demolished by the 2nd Duque del Infantado, Don Iñigo Lopez de Mendoza, and construction of the present building was begun in 1480. The façade and courtyard were finished in 1483 under the direction of Juan Guas, who had previously worked for the Mendoza family on the construction of the Castillo del Real, Manzanares, and the sculptor Egas Cueman. Master Lorenzo de Trillo, a wood-carver and master mason, worked on the building from 1484 to 1497, as did many other Christian and Moorish craftsmen. It was completed *c.* 1500.

The plaster rendering of the façade has been lost, but the original decoration consisted of an incised lozenge pattern punctuated by projecting, faceted stones. This arrangement, which is similar to that still to be seen on one of the towers of the Castillo del Real, Manzanares, is derived from Islamic architectural decoration. The main entrance of the façade (for illustration *see* GUAS, JUAN), set off-centre, is flanked by large columns decorated with lozenges. The inscription on the archivolt alludes to its construction, and mill-hoppers, the Duke's emblem, appear in the spandrels. The elaborate tracery of the tympanum is composed of ogees and ogees with broken profiles. Above the door two 'wild men' support the family coat of arms. The façade is crowned by a richly ornamented loggia with small curved balconies and ogee arcading. The broad stalactite cornice was inspired by a ceiling frieze in one of the rooms of the palace, a transposition into stone of a *Mudéjar* timber ceiling. The rectangular windows were inserted into the façade in the 16th century, when some of the rooms of the palace were decorated; Diego de Romulo Cincinato was employed on this work from 1578 to 1580.

The magnificent two-storey courtyard (see fig.) was altered under the 5th Duke in 1570. The original spiral columns with foliate decoration on the ground-floor were replaced with Tuscan columns, but the double ogee arcading was retained. Above, mill-hoppers again appear, supported by lions, and in the spandrels are the coats of arms of the Infantado family. An inscription in Latin and Spanish (as in the throne room in the Aljaferia, Saragossa) runs above this decoration, bearing the names of the patron and the architects (the 'Master Anri' mentioned must refer to Egas Cueman). It ends with a short text from Ecclesiastes 1:2 ('Vanity of vanities; all is vanity'), in an arrangement that recalls Islamic work. The upper arcade, still supported by spiral columns, has broken ogees surmounted by fleurons framed by griffins; some of the elements are related to decorative motifs of the MANUELINE STYLE and appear at the Colegio de S Gregorio, Valladolid. On one side of the palace a large gallery with round-headed arches opens on to the remains of some of the gardens; it was built by Lorenzo di Trillo in 1496.

The palace was severely damaged during the Civil War of 1936–9. The magnificent ceilings with their arabesque decoration and rich friezes were burnt, but old photographs and descriptions show that the finest were in the

Guadalajara, Palacio del Infantado, view of courtyard, 1480–83; altered 1570

Salon de los Salvajes and the Salon de los Cazedores. Restorations on the façade began in 1942. The Palacio del Infantado now houses the Museo de Bellas Artes and is the headquarters of other cultural institutions.

BIBLIOGRAPHY

F. Layna Serrano: *El palacio del Infantado de Guadalajara* (Madrid, 1941)

——: *Historia de Guadalajara y los Mendoza en los siglos XV y XVI* (Madrid, 1942)

——: 'La desdichada reforma del palacio del Infantado hecha por el quinto duque en el siglo XVI', *Bol. Soc. Esp. Excurs.* (1946)

J. M. Azcárate Ristori: 'La fachada del Infantado y el estilo de Juan Guas', *Archv. Esp. A.*, xxiv (1951), pp. 307–19

A. Herrera Casado: *El palacio del Infantado* (Guadalajara, 1975)

JOSÉ MARIA AZCÁRATE RISTORI

Guadalquivir, Marqués de **Las Marismas del.** *See* LAS MARISMAS DEL GUADALQUIVIR, Marqués de.

Guadalupe. Hieronymite monastery in Cáceres Province, Estremadura, Spain. The monastery of Nuestra Señora de Guadelupe was founded to house an ancient image of the Virgin on the site of a small *Mudéjar* chapel of the type characteristic of Toledo (for a long time Guadalupe belonged to the archbishopric of Toledo). In 1325 the original building was enlarged by Alfonso XI of Castile and León (*reg* 1313–50), and, following the foundation of the monastery on 29 October 1340, the date of the Battle of Salado, the dependent buildings gradually rose around the church. In 1389 the Hieronymite monks were installed under their first prior, Fray Fernand Yáñez of Cáceres. The monastery was sacked by the French in 1809 and abandoned in 1835 but in 1908 it was occupied by Franciscans.

Most of the building was constructed using brick, which was dressed and then plastered. The parts built in this way include the late 15th-century Gothic façade; the towers of the Reloj and the Mayordomía (both 14th century); the square *Mudéjar* cloister (1402–12) of two storeys, which has horseshoe arches framed in *alfiz* (rectangular) moulding; the 'Templete' (or Glorieta) Fountain (1405), which is located in the centre of the *Mudéjar* cloister and is surmounted by a pavilion covered with an octagonal spire rising in three stages, each with gables, blind arcading and decorated with alabaster and glazed tiles (*azulejos*); and the second Gothic cloister (1516–24), which now forms part of the hostel. The extensive use of brick has often led to the monastery being described as 'Gothic-*Mudéjar*', despite the fact that the style of the buildings is Western.

The old church, with its highly decorated façade (1389–1412), built by Juan Alfonso and completed during the lifetime of Fray Yáñez, has a nave, two aisles, a transept and a polygonal apse. It also has cross-vaulting, except for the crossing, which is covered by a dome supported on pendentives. The nave is closed by a fine wrought-iron grille or *reja* (1510–14) by Fray Francisco de Salamanca (*fl* 1493–1547). The classical principal retable (1615–18) has paintings by Vicente Carducho and Eugenio Cajés and statues by Giraldo de Merlo. Above the high altar is the venerated image of Nuestra Señora de Guadalupe, enthroned in the *camarín*, which is built on a quatrefoil plan and decorated with paintings of the *Life of the Virgin* (1697) by LUCA GIORDANO. The chancel contains the tombs of *Henry IV of Castile and León* (*reg* 1454–74) and of his mother, *Doña María*, both also by Giraldo de Merlo; and at the east end are the Panteón Real and chapels of S Gregorio and S Catalina, with the tombs (1461) of *Prince Denis of Portugal* and his wife, *Juana*. The sacristy (1638–47) contains an important series of paintings by Francisco de Zurbarán (*see* ZURBARÁN, (1)), depicting scenes from the lives of many leading figures connected with the foundation (1638–9; for illustration *see* HIERONYMITES), and three others illustrating the *Life of St Jerome*, all characteristic of the artist's tenebrist and naturalistic style. The sacristy is remarkable for its unity of design, with the paintings, wardrobes and window- and mirror-frames all forming part of the scheme.

Several of the monastic buildings are now used as museums. The former refectory contains the Museo de Bordados, with a fine collection of embroidered church vestments and altar frontals (14th–17th centuries), that of Enrique IV of Castile and León being outstanding among the latter. In the former chapter house is the Museo de Cantorales, housing a collection of choir-books, some with fine miniatures, missals and bindings. The Antesacrestia contains paintings by JUAN CARREÑO DE MIRANDA. The octagonal Relicario (1595) is by Nicolás Vergara the younger, and among the finest reliquaries there is the Gothic, engraved silver box by Juan de Segovia (mid-15th century) with earlier enamels. The new church (1730) is derelict.

BIBLIOGRAPHY

Fray G. Rubio: *Historia de Nuestra Señora de Guadalupe* (Barcelona, 1926)

I. Acemel and G. Rubio: *Guía ilustrada de Santa María de Guadalupe* (Barcelona, 1927)

Fray D. de Ecija: *Libro de la invención de esta Santa Imagen de Guadalupe* (Cáceres, 1953)

Fray A. Alvarez: *Guadalupe: Arte, historia y devoción mariana* (Madrid, 1964)

M. C. Pescador del Hoyo: 'La hospedería real de Guadalupe', *Rev. Estud. Extrem.*, xxi (1965); xxiv (1968)

H. Zamora: 'La primitiva iglesia de Guadalupe', *Rev. Guadalupe*, 582 (1971)

S. Garcia and F. Trenado: *Guadalupe: Historia, devoción y arte* (Seville, 1978)

A. C. Floriano: *El monasterio de Santa María de Guadalupe* (León, 1984)

CONCEPCIÓN ABAD CASTRO

Guadeloupe. *See under* ANTILLES, LESSER.

Guadet, Julien Azais (*b* Paris, 25 Dec 1834; *d* Paris, 17 May 1908). French architect and teacher. He was an outstanding student for 11 years at the Ecole des Beaux-Arts in Paris (1853–64), where he was taught by Henri Labrouste and Jules André (1819–90). While there he amassed awards and in 1864 won the Grand-Prix de Rome with a project for a hospice in the Alps. The previous year he had found himself at the head of the huge majority of students at the school who opposed the attempt at reform made by Napoleon III's government. In 1871 he began teaching architecture at the Ecole des Beaux-Arts, and from 1894 until his death he taught theory there. Although he agreed with Viollet-le-Duc on the principles of a reasoned and analytical study of architecture, Guadet's vision of architectural education was founded on the relationship of mutual trust between master and pupil within an independent study-group. He believed that 'in all things the first studies must be classical' and rejected the idea that the teaching of aesthetics should be obligatory and founded exclusively on the study of medieval architecture. He was also opposed to the exercises in restoration that were imposed on the *pensionnaires* at the Academy, although he recognized the supple and fertile imagination that his predecessors had shown. As a teacher of theory Guadet adopted a liberal attitude, encouraging a modernist approach derived from the free study of form in ancient architecture, and during his 37 years of teaching he turned the Ecole des Beaux-Arts into a training centre for numerous French and foreign architects. He was also involved in the planning and setting up of regional schools of architecture in France in 1903.

Guadet's architectural projects include a design submitted in the competition of 1873 for a new town hall in Paris and, most importantly, the building of the central post office (1878–84) in the Rue du Louvre in Paris, which he provided with vast work-spaces furnished with movable partitions and sophisticated mechanical equipment. After the fire at the Comédie Française in 1900, Guadet and his son Paul Guadet (1873–1931) rebuilt the theatre, following exactly the plans of Victor Louis. Paul Guadet followed his father's principles in his career as an independent architect. Notable among his buildings was his own home, in reinforced concrete, at 95, Boulevard Murat in Paris, which he built in 1912 with the Perret brothers.

WRITINGS

'Etude sur la disposition et la construction du Colisée', *Moniteur Architectes* (1879), no. 1, col. 7–9; no. 3, col. 36–42

A propos du nouvel hôtel des postes (Paris)

Eléments et théorie de l'architecture (Paris, 1901)

'A l'Ecole des beaux-arts, souvenirs de 1863', *Recueil du millième de la société des architectes diplômés par le gouvernement* (Paris, 1911)

BIBLIOGRAPHY

E. Paulin: 'Julien Guadet: Sa vie et ses oeuvres', *L'Architecte* (June 1908), pp. 41–3

S. Kuthy: *Julien Guadet* (diss., U. Paris IV, 1968)

D. Van Zanten: 'Architectural Composition at the Ecole des Beaux-Arts from Charles Percier to Charles Garnier', *The Architecture of the Ecole des Beaux-Arts* (exh. cat., ed. A. Drexler; New York, MOMA, 1975–6)

S. Kuthy: 'L'Académie des beaux-arts et Guadet contre Viollet-le-Duc', *Gaz. B.-A.* (October 1983), pp. 134–8

JEAN-PAUL MIDANT

Gualandi, Michelangelo (*b* Bologna, 13 March 1793; *d* ?Bologna, after *c.* 1860). Italian art historian. From his home (2, Via Manzoni) in the Palazzo Fava, Bologna, a 16th-century building with frescoes by the Carracci family on the *piano nobile*, he edited, annotated and organized the publication (1840–56) of almost 200 hitherto unpublished documents (the *Memorie originale italiane*) and letters (the *Nuova raccolta*) relating to art. In 1850 he published his guidebook, *Tre giorni in Bologna*. He was a member of many Italian academies, including those of Florence (where Grand-Duke Leopold II in 1841 granted him permission to publish material from the Medici archives) and Naples, and an honorary associate of the Accademia dei Virtuosi al Pantheon in Rome.

WRITINGS

ed.: *Memorie originale italiane risguardanti le belle arti*, 2 vols (Bologna, 1840–45)

Le porrettane di Michelangelo Gualandi: Lettere artistiche ad un amico (Bologna, 1841)

ed.: *Nuova raccolta di lettere sulla pittura, scultura ed architettura scritte da' più celebri personaggi dei secoli XV a XIX con note ed illustrazioni . . . in aggiunta a quella data in luce da Mons. Bottari e dal Ticozzi*, 3 vols (Bologna, 1844–56/*R* Olms, 1975)

Lettera di Michelangelo Gualandi e risposta di Andrea Tessier intorno agli artisti Gio. Gherardini, Ugo da Carpi e Francesco Marcolini (Venice, 1855)

BIBLIOGRAPHY

Nouvelle Biographie générale, xxii (Paris, 1858), pp. 302–3

JANET SOUTHORN

Gualdo, Matteo da. *See* MATTEO DA GUALDO.

Gualdorp, Gortzius. *See* GELDORP, (1).

Gualtieri di Giovanni (da Pisa) (*b* Pisa, ?1370; *d* Siena, after 1445). Italian painter. He had settled in Siena by 1409. He may be the Gualtieri di Giovanni documented in Pisa in 1400–06 (Tanfani Centofanti). Between 1409 and 1411 he frescoed the vaults of the sacristy chapels of Siena Cathedral. Subsequently he did further decorative work in the cathedral (1414, 1415, 1424) and in the canon's house (1416), where he was helped by his son Giovanni. Previously known as one of the Masters of the Sacristy of Siena Cathedral and credited with a major part in the fresco decoration there, it is now evident that his role was very minor (Mongellaz, 1985).

In October 1432 Gualtieri and Cecchino da Verona (?1370–1450) assessed Sassetta's altarpiece of the *Virgin and Child with Saints* (the '*Madonna of the Snow*'; Florence, Pitti), painted for Siena Cathedral. In 1439 he painted the vault of the Pellegrinaio of the hospital of S Maria della Scala, Siena. Boskovits suggested that a group of works given to the Master of San Davino should be attributed to Gualtieri. This anonymous Master probably trained in Pisa and was named after the *Burial of St Davino* (Florence, Acton priv. col.); his later works have strong affinities with those of Taddeo di Bartolo.

BIBLIOGRAPHY

L. Tanfani Centofanti: *Notizie di artisti tratte dei documenti pisani* (Pisa, 1897), p. 283

M. Boskovits: 'Su Niccolo di Buonaccorso, Benedetto di Bindo e la pittura senese del primo quattrocento', *Paragone*, xxxi/2 (1980), pp. 2–22 (18–19, n. 31)

J. Mongellaz: 'A propos d'une fresque peu connue de la cathédrale de Sienne', *Fond. Stud. Stor. A. Roberto Longhi, Firenze: An.*, i (1984), pp. 27–34

——: 'Reconsidération de la distribution des rôles à l'intérieur du groupe des Maîtres de la Sacristie de la Cathédrale de Sienne', *Paragone*, xxxvi/2 (1985), pp. 73–89

JACQUELINE MONGELLAZ

Guan. Chinese family of painters. Based in Guangzhou (Canton) in the late 18th century and the 19th, they are best known for their production of Western-style paintings created for the export market. (1) Guan Zuolin, known by his Western name, Spoilum, was the first identifiable artist of the Cantonese export school (*see also* CHINA, §I, 4(ii)(c)). He was probably the father, uncle or grandfather of (2) Guan Qiaochang, known as Lamqua (Lamqua (i)), and Lamqua's younger brother, (3) Guan Lianchang, known as Tingqua. (4) Guan Shicun, also known as Lamqua (Lamqua (ii)), may have been the son or nephew of (2) Lamqua (i), although the relationship is not certain. All four artists painted portraits using Western techniques, and all except the younger Lamqua were known for their landscapes and views of Guangzhou. It is possible that other members of the family also painted under the title of 'Lamqua'.

(1) Spoilum [Guan Zuolin; Kuan Tso-lin; Spilem; Spillem] (*b* Nanhai, Guangzhou, Guangdong Province; *fl* 1770–1810). According to a gazetteer of the district (*Nanhai xian zhi*, 1910 edn, *juan* 21, p. 8a), he travelled in Europe and America, where he was impressed by the realism of Western oil painting; his travels no doubt explain the similarities of his style to that of contemporary North American portrait painters. On his return to Guangzhou, he opened a studio, which probably grew into a family business maintained in the second and third generations by (2) Lamqua (i) and (4) Lamqua (ii).

Spoilum was engaged in glass painting in the 1770s, and in the following decade he painted portraits in oils. Oil paint was an unfamiliar medium in the context of the Chinese pictorial tradition, and its use stemmed from Western influences. However, the Cantonese export painters of the late 18th century rapidly acquired a facility in this medium and, in the case of Spoilum, an individuality that could be regarded, in Western terms, as evidence of original genius.

Spoilum's portraits, of Chinese and Western sitters alike, share certain idiosyncrasies: a sharply defined outline, a direct, almost quizzical expression, carefully observed costume details and, in the background, a markedly pale passage above the right shoulder. Typical examples are the portraits of the Cantonese silk merchant *Eshing* (before 1809; Salem, MA, Peabody Mus.) and *Captain John Watts, R.N.* (ex-Martyn Gregory, London; see 1986 exh. cat., p. 51). Watts, one of Captain Cook's officers, put in at Guangzhou in the course of Cook's last voyage. These portraits represent an intermediate stage between the traditional conventions of Chinese portraiture and the more thorough assimilation of Western artistic principles that is to be seen in the work of Lamqua (i). That Spoilum had several Chinese followers is clear from a number of portraits painted in Guangzhou in the years 1800–25, many of them now in American collections. They share the format and mode of presentation exhibited in Spoilum's work but lack the latter's subtlety and sympathy of treatment. One of these followers has been called the Carwick Painter on the basis of a Cantonese portrait, *Henry Carwick* (*c*. 1819; Salem, MA, Peabody Mus.). The Carwick group of portraits is characterized by a somewhat crude chiaroscuro in the faces, by backgrounds sketchily handled and by severe expressions on the sitters' faces.

(2) Lamqua (i) [Guan Qiaochang; Kuan Ch'iao-ch'ang] (*b* Guangzhou, Guangdong Province, 1801; *d* 1860). Perhaps the son of (1) Spoilum. He was the leading export artist of his generation, painting in the Western tradition for Western markets. According to several reports by Westerners who visited his studio in China Street, Guangzhou, Lamqua had worked as assistant to GEORGE CHINNERY in the early years of that artist's residence in Macao. Chinnery is said to have denied this. In any event, Lamqua became an oil painter in a manner very similar to Chinnery's, sharing much of the English artist's fluency of handling and adopting his mannerism of adding touches of strong colour at the final stage. As a portrait artist painting both Chinese and Western merchants, Lamqua was able to undercut Chinnery's fees. Lamqua's sitters, like Chinnery's, are usually positioned not quite full-face to the spectator and are often seated by a window, allowing a glimpse of landscape beyond. He also painted landscapes and made copies in oils of engravings that Westerners brought to his studio.

Many of Lamqua's compositions were produced in more than one version. An example is his seated portrait of the leading hong merchant Howqua (Wu Bingjian); one of several recorded versions of the painting is in the collection of Matheson & Co. Lamqua's portrait is based on a portrait of *Howqua* executed by Chinnery in the years 1825–32 (Hong Kong, Hongkong & Shanghai Bank. Corp.; see 1986 exh. cat., p. 54). A *Self-portrait* (Hong Kong, Mus. A.) is inscribed at the back of the frame in Chinese characters, 'Lamqua, age at [sic] 52, painted by himself, Guangzhou, 1853'. Some of Lamqua's pictures, for example his version of Ingres's *Grande Odalisque* (London, priv. col., see 1986 exh. cat., p. 56), are signed in both Chinese and Roman script. Of those that are unsigned, many may easily be mistaken for the work of Chinnery or other Western artists.

Lamqua is not known to have travelled beyond the Chinese coast, but his paintings were exhibited at the Royal Academy in London (1835, 1845) and in New York (Apollo Club, 1841), in Philadelphia (Acad. F.A., 1851, 1860) and in Boston (Athenaeum, 1851). Of considerable medical interest is a large series of portraits executed by Lamqua free of charge, depicting the Chinese patients of the American missionary Dr Peter Parker, whose chief Chinese assistant was Lamqua's nephew, Guan A-to. These pictures record the variety of disfiguring tumours that Parker was in many cases able to cure.

(3) Tingqua [Guan Lianchang; Kuan Lien-ch'ang; Tinqua] (*b c*. 1809; *fl* 1840–70). Brother of (2) Lamqua (i) and probably a close relation of (1) Spoilum. Tingqua's studio at 16 China Street, Guangzhou, was perhaps the most prolific source of Chinese export paintings of its time. Working in a manner influenced by Western artistic traditions, Tingqua and the painters of his studio restricted themselves to gouache and watercolours, perhaps to avoid rivalry with Lamqua's oil paintings. Their pictures, which were often sold in sets, represent manufacturing processes (of tea, cotton etc.), deities, ceremonies, gardens, boats, decorative objects and specimens of natural history, as well as views of Guangzhou, the Pearl River at Huangbu (Whampoa), Macao and Shanghai. Tingqua's landscapes (e.g. *Houqua's Garden*, gouache, 267×349 mm; Salem, MA, Peabody Mus.) are generally sunlit, with little gradation of shadowing. Characteristic mannerisms are trees represented with thick clusters of yellow-green leaves and seas denoted by regular parallel lines, sometimes with ripples in the foreground. Tingqua and his studio also redrew works brought in to them. The substantial collection of Tingqua pictures (*c*. 1855) brought back by the American China trader Augustine Heard (Salem, MA, Peabody Mus.) includes Tingqua's version of a country-house view by an American amateur artist and a series of watercolours depicting Filipino men and women, based on originals by the Filipino artist Justiniano Asunción (see Crossman, 1991, pls 93–5).

Of particular historical interest (although no doubt idealized) is Tingqua's view of his own studio workshop,

Studio of Tingqua (priv. col., see *Tingqua's China*, p. 9), which exists in several versions. It shows his associates at work, with stock paintings for sale on the walls: portraits of Westerners and Chinese, and topographical scenes. A signed portrait by Tingqua entitled *Portrait of Howqua* (*c.* 1840; New York, Met.), a representation of Wu Bingjian, the leading Cantonese merchant of his day, is characterized, as is all the work of Tingqua and his studio (the two are scarcely separable), by sharp outline, precise detail and vivid colouring.

(4) Lamqua (ii) [Guan Shicun; Kuan Shih-ts'un] (*fl c.* 1840–70). Probably the son or nephew of (2) Lamqua (i). He was identified by the Chinese inscriptions on the stretchers of two portraits (1864; Brighton, A.G. & Mus.; see 1986 exh. cat., p. 56). Of these, perhaps only the male portrait, *Hexing of Hong Kong* (785×620 mm), can be regarded as his work. The female figure (841×660 mm) was reproduced in several other very similar versions, and in this instance she was allocated a false identity—the *Fourth Concubine of Hexing of Hong Kong*—in order to satisfy Western demand for paired portraits representing husband and wife.

BIBLIOGRAPHY

C. Toogood Downing: *The Fan-qui in China in 1836–7*, 3 vols (London, 1838/*R* Shannon and New York, 1972)

C. L. Crossman: *The China Trade: Export Paintings, Furniture, Silver and Other Objects* (London and Princeton, 1972); repr. as *The Decorative Arts of the China Trade: Paintings, Furnishings and Exotic Curiosities* (Woodbridge, 1991)

E. V. Gulick: *Peter Parker and the Opening of China* (Cambridge, MA, 1973)

Tingqua: Paintings from his Studio (exh. cat., ed. J. Warner; Hong Kong, Mus. A., 1976)

C. Clunas: *Chinese Export Watercolours* (London, 1984)

Tingqua's China (exh. cat., London, Martyn Gregory, 1986)

The China Trade, 1600–1860 (exh. cat., ed. P. Conner; Brighton, Royal Pav., 1986)

PATRICK CONNER

Guangala. Pre-Columbian culture of coastal Ecuador, which flourished *c.* 500 BC–*c.* AD 500. Archaeological research initiated by Geoffrey Bushnell in 1951 has shown that the Guangala people occupied the forest of the Santa Elena Peninsula from the Chongón-Colonche Cordillera to the sea, extending north through the narrow coastal strip of southern Manabí Province. Like their predecessors, who made Engoroy style pottery, the Guangala people were experts at farming dry land, mostly using condensed fog for irrigation, as well as being accomplished sailors. Ceramic wares similar to those of Engoroy and Guangala have been found in Guatemala, suggesting that a long-distance trade network between Ecuador and Mesoamerica already existed at this period. Studies of settlement patterns in the Chanduy Valley show that Guangala people established permanent hamlets in diverse micro-environments, as well as larger sites, which served as centres of economic, religious and political power, and regional and long-distance trade. Guangala houses were built on a rectangular plan and had wooden frames and wattle-and-daub construction, with ornate baked clay eaves, window and door frames.

At the end of the Engoroy phase in the region, several distinct ceramic types appeared. These included globular vessels incised with fine lines or having stamped, applied or modelled decoration (nicked appliqué fillets and small nubs), as well as positive-painted white-on-red ware and ceramic seats (*compoteras*). Associated thin cups and bowls, decorated inside with burnished line designs and with iridescent painted motifs on the outside, also claim Engoroy descent. This transitional style was followed sequentially by red- or brown-on-buff Bichrome ware, Polychrome ware, Thin Orange ware with fugitive black resist decoration, Somber ware, and Frog ware; the latter examples mark a transition towards the MANTEÑO style. Guangala pottery is thin and well-fired. The ceramic figurines found in Guangala are thin and finished to a well-polished orange surface; decorated by fine incised linear designs with occasional red-slipped highlights, they have resonance chambers to function as one- or two-tone flutes.

Other Guangala crafts included shellwork, stonework and metalwork. Typical shell products include mother-of-pearl fish-hooks, pendants and carved plaques depicting animals and humans; red *Spondylus* shell end hooks for spear throwers, labrets (lip ornaments) and lime box plugs; and scrimshaw lime containers, made of *Conus* conch shell. Small greenstone pebbles with carved monkey faces, beautifully carved mortars and milling stones, highly polished celts and chert projectile points are characteristic examples of the stonework. The Guangala contribution to ancient Ecuadorian metallurgy comprises ornate gold beads, and small zoomorphic copper pins, cast in the lost-wax technique.

For discussion of Pre-Columbian Ecuador *see also* PRE-COLUMBIAN SOUTH AMERICA, §II.

BIBLIOGRAPHY

G. H. S. Bushnell: *The Archaeology of the Santa Elena Peninsula in Southwest Ecuador*, Cambridge University Museum of Archaeology and Ethnology occasional papers, i (Cambridge, 1951)

M. D. Coe: 'Archaeological Linkages with North America and South America at La Victoria, Guatemala', *Amer. Anthropologist*, xlii (1960), pp. 363–93

C. Evans and B. J. Meggers: 'Mesoamerica and Ecuador', *Hb. Mid. Amer. Ind.*, iv (1966), pp. 243–64

B. J. Meggers: *Ecuador* (London, 1966)

J. G. Marcos: 'Puntas de proyectil bifaciales en la cultura Guangala', *Cuad. Hist. & Arqueol.*, xx (1970), pp. 57–115

A. C. Paulsen: *A Chronology of Guangala and Libertad Ceramics of the Santa Elena Peninsula, South Coastal Ecuador* (diss., New York, Columbia U., 1970)

H. Bischof: 'La fase Engoroy: Periodos, cronologia y relaciones', *Estudios sobre la arqueología del Ecuador*, ed. U. Oberem (Bonn, 1975), pp. 132–58

A. Lapiner: *Pre-Columbian Art of South America* (New York, 1976)

JORGE G. MARCOS

Guanghan [Kuang-han]. County in Sichuan Province, China, near Chengdu. The remains of a city dating from the Shang period (*c.* 1600–*c.* 1050 BC) were found there. Jades of archaic type were unearthed in Guanghan County as early as the 1920s, but it was only in the 1980s that archaeologists established the presence there of a major city site by showing that a number of mounds near the modern village of Sanxingdui are, in fact, remnants of a rammed-earth city wall that once enclosed an area of more than 100 ha. In 1986 the discovery just outside the city wall of two pits filled with extraordinary artefacts (most Chengdu, Sichuan Prov. Mus.) attracted worldwide attention.

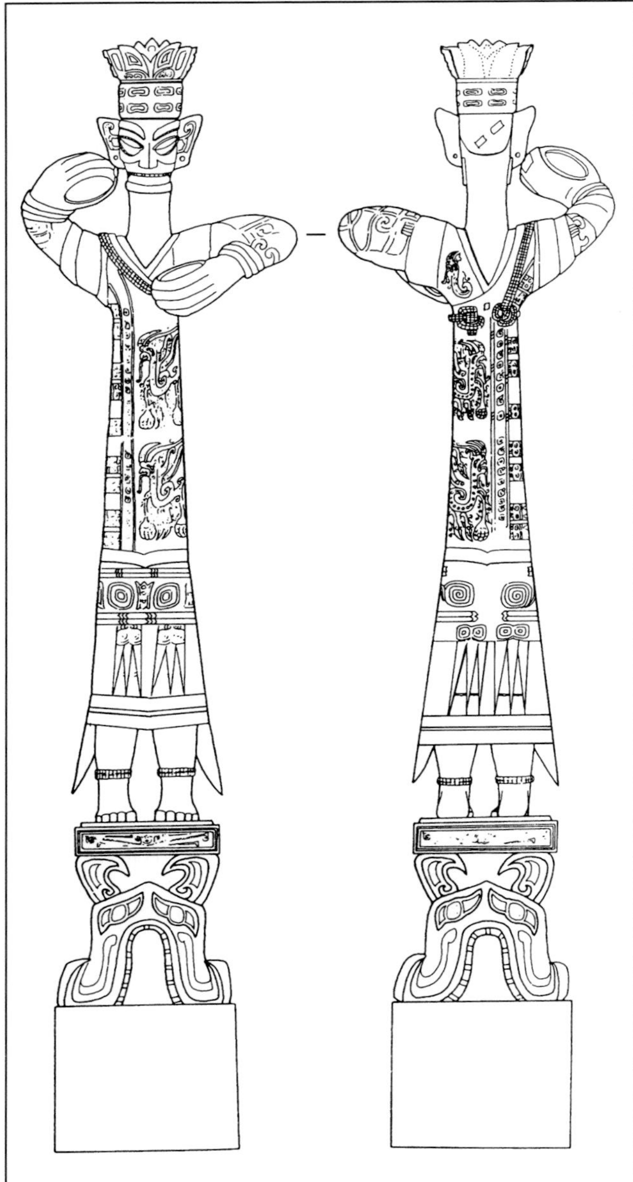

Guanghan County, Sanxingdui, bronze statue (front and back views), overall h. 2.62 m (figure h. 1.82 m), excavated from Pit 2, 13th–12th centuries BC (Chengdu, Sichuan Provincial Museum)

On the evidence of potsherds found within it, the city wall is believed to have been constructed before the Anyang phase (before *c.* 1300 BC). The two pits are somewhat later; they seem to represent large-scale sacrificial offerings made on two different occasions, a few decades apart, in the 13th or 12th century BC. The artefacts buried in the second pit are more numerous and more spectacular than those in the first, but the form of the offering ceremony was the same on both occasions: large numbers of animals were killed and burnt, jades and bronzes were broken and burnt, and then everything was buried. Following excavation, both pits were filled in once more.

Pit 1 (4.6×3.5×1.6 m deep) was the earlier of the two. It contained about 300 objects in gold, bronze, jade, stone and pottery, as well as cowrie shells, 13 elephant tusks and more than 3 cubic m of burnt and broken animal bones. The jades are for the most part familiar Shang types, but some are eccentric in design, and the sheer quantity of large blades is unmatched. The bronzes are extraordinary. A few ritual vessels, the artefacts that normally dominate early Chinese Bronze Age assemblages, are quite overshadowed by objects of a type never discovered elsewhere: life-size bronze heads with angular facial features and enormous eyes. Clay core material is thought to show that the heads were locally cast.

Pit 2 was about the same size as Pit 1 but was more lavishly filled. Bronzes included 41 heads of varying size, some with gold face covers, 15 bizarre faces, the largest 1.38 m across, a dozen *zun* and *lei* vessels (for illustrations of these types *see* CHINA, fig. 138), whose distinctive style suggests that they are imports from the middle Yangzi region, some wheel-like objects, two or three puzzling and badly broken objects, which the excavators call 'spirit-trees', and one life-size statue of a robed figure with large cupped hands standing on a pedestal (see fig.). The pit also contained many jades and a layer of more than 60 charred elephant tusks strewn over the other offerings.

The Guanghan finds established that the Chengdu plain of Sichuan Province was the home of a sophisticated Bronze Age civilization far earlier than had previously been supposed. They showed that the Shang civilization extended beyond the middle reaches of the Yellow River valley, to which scholars had tended to assume that it was confined, and that it varied greatly from one region to another. The bronze- and jade-using culture represented by the two sacrificial pits at Guanghan had much in common with, but also differed from, the Shang culture known from such sites as ANYANG, and this raises questions about political and historical connections with the Anyang culture and indeed about the definition of 'Shang civilization'. Like other less spectacular finds in outlying areas at Ningxiang and Shilou, the city at Sanxingdui suggests that the historical geography of the early Chinese Bronze Age is due for thorough revision.

BIBLIOGRAPHY

Chen Dean and Chen Xiandan: 'Guanghan Sanxingdui yizhi yi hao jisikeng fajue jianbao' [Brief report on the excavation of sacrificial pit 1 at the Guanghan Sanxingdui site], *Wenwu* (1987), no. 10, pp. 1–15

R. W. Bagley: 'Sacrificial Pits of the Shang Period at Sanxingdui in Guanghan County, Sichuan Province', *A. Asiat.*, xviii (1988), pp. 78–86

Chen Dean and Chen Xiandan: 'Guanghan Sanxingdui yizhi er hao jisikeng fajue jianbao' [Brief report on the excavation of sacrificial pit 2 at the Guanghan Sanxingdui site], *Wenwu* (1989), no. 5, pp. 1–20

R. W. Bagley: 'A Shang City in Sichuan Province', *Orientations*, xxi/11 (Nov 1990), pp. 52–67

ROBERT W. BAGLEY

Guangzhou [Canton; Kuang-chou]. City situated in the delta of the Pearl River (Zhu jiang) in the eastern part of Guangdong Province, China. It has been the provincial capital since the Han period (206 BC–AD 220). The history of Guangzhou can be traced back to the early part of the Western Zhou period (*c.* 1050–771 BC), when the Bai tribe occupied a walled town called Nanwu cheng on Mt Yuexiu; the site has been identified in the northern part of the modern city. Around 887 BC Nanwu cheng came under the control of the Chu state and was renamed Wuyang cheng (Five Goats Town). When China was unified under the Qin dynasty (221–206 BC), the town became the capital of the Nanhai Prefecture. It later became the capital of a small independent state ruled by the Nanyue until it finally fell to the Han in 111 BC. During this time the town underwent a cultural transition under Han Chinese influence and became the main bastion of the expanding Chinese civilization in the south.

Guangzhou continued to thrive during the Six Dynasties period (AD 222–589) and had attained the status of an international port by the beginning of the Tang period (AD 618–907), when merchants from South-east Asia, India and Persia traded in the city. By the middle of the Tang period the city had a large community of Arabs, who lived in their own quarter and had their own mosque. Guangzhou was also the main entry port for Buddhist missionaries and pilgrims from India and Indonesia, who introduced the newest scriptures and doctrinal developments. At the close of the Tang, Guangzhou became the capital of the Southern Han dynasty (AD 907–71) under the name of Da Guang fu. It continued to flourish as a city of commerce and culture.

The first Europeans to trade in Guangzhou were the Portuguese, who travelled there during the first half of the 16th century. The Dutch and the British, who arrived in 1685, set up a trading station or 'factory'. In the course of the 17th century, 13 such trading stations were established by the Americans and Europeans under the auspices of their respective East India companies.

In the 18th and early 19th centuries Guangzhou reached its height as China's main port for trade with the West. The major European companies had their trading stations on Whampoa and the neighbouring islands in the Pearl River, downstream from the city. The major export commodities were tea and porcelain, some of which was made locally but most of which came from provinces further north. The city was the scene of major battles between the Chinese and the British in the First and Second Opium Wars in 1839–42 and 1856–60 respectively, and it remained occupied until 1861. With the new concessions granted to the Western powers after the war of 1860–61 against the British and French, Guangzhou lost some of its importance, as foreign trade was permitted in cities further up the coast such as Xiamen (Amoy) and Shanghai. There was an intellectual ferment in the city during the 1920s, when Sun Yat-sen revitalized the Guomindang (or KMT), the Chinese Nationalist Party.

During the Ming (1368–1644) and Qing (1644–1911) periods, a wide range of artistic goods, chiefly for export, were produced in Guangzhou and its vicinity. These included SHIWAN ceramics, enamelware, silverware and painted glassware. During the 19th century the city developed its own schools of oil painting based on Western techniques (*see* CHINA, §I, 4(ii)).

Originally there were many Buddhist temples in the city, but by the late 20th century only two remained. The largest is the Guangxiao si (Temple of Bright Filial Piety), associated with Bodhidharma (*d c.* AD 530) and Huineng (AD 638–713), two of the most celebrated figures in Chinese Chan Buddhism. The temple has several large halls, stupas, pagodas and stelae. The Liurongsi (Temple of the Six Banyan Trees) is characterized by the Hua ta (Flower Pagoda), a nine-storey brick structure commanding a fine view of the city. This temple also houses a large bronze image of Huineng (late 10th century), modelled on the lacquered clay image kept in the Nanhua Temple in Shaoguan (also in Guandong Province). The Haitong Temple (first half of the 18th century; destr.) was situated on the Pearl River and featured a hall with a painting of *Five Hundred Luohan.*

The large Huaisheng si (Cherish the Sage Mosque), situated centrally in the city, probably dates to the Tang period; it has undergone many repairs. The tall, conical minaret, which rises to a height of over 30 m, dominates the edifice. The inside of the mosque is lavishly decorated with gilded wooden panels and red lacquered beams, as well as large displays of Arabic calligraphy on the wall (*see also* CHINA, §II, 4(iv)).

Among the important secular architectural monuments of the city is the ancestral temple of the Chen family (1840s). It consists of several high-ceilinged, interconnected halls with thousands of ancestral tablets set in the back walls behind richly carved altar tables. The roofs are covered with multicoloured tiles and on the ridges are finely detailed ceramic models of animals and protecting deities.

Located within the old city wall on North Hill stands the Zhenhai lou (Tower Guarding the Sea), a large, rectangular, five-storey brick building that faces south over the city. It was built in the Qing dynasty during the Kangxi reign (1662–1722). Below and outside the city is a small mosque surrounded by graves. On Mt Baiyun, also outside the city, are numerous small shrines, a huge cemetery and a few Buddhist temples, including the Nengren Temple, located on the summit of the mountain. The factories south of the city are no longer extant, but the remains of some of the forts guarding the Pearl River can still be seen.

BIBLIOGRAPHY

Guangzhou Guangxiao si [Guangxiao Temple, Guangzhou] (Guangzhou, n.d.)

Guangzhou Liurong si Hua ta [Guangzhou Six Banyan Pagoda] (Guangzhou, n.d.)

J. H. Gray: *Walks in the City of Canton* (Hong Kong, 1875)

C. L. Crossman: *The China Trade: Export Paintings, Furniture, Silver and Other Objects* (Princeton, 1972)

Guangzhou Han mu [The Han Tombs of Guangzhou], 2 vols (Beijing, 1981)

Guangdong chutu Wu dai zhi Qing wenwu/Archaeological Finds from the Five Dynasties to the Qing Periods in Guangdong (exh. cat., Hong Kong, China U., A.G., 1989)

J. D. Spence: *The Search for Modern China* (London, Sydney, Auckland, Johannesburg, 1990), pp. 119–23, 147–8

HENRIK H. SØRENSEN

Guan Lianchang. *See* GUAN, (3).

Guan Qiaochang. *See* GUAN, (2).

Guan Shicun. *See* GUAN, (4).

Guan Tong [Kuan T'ung] (*b* Chang'an [now Xi'an], Shaanxi Province; *fl* AD 907–23). Chinese painter. He was active at the court of the Later Liang dynasty (907–23) at Nanjing. Guo Ruoxu (*see* CHINA, §V, 5(i)) placed him in the highest category of painters, equated with Li Cheng and Fan Kuan: 'These three masters stand like the legs of a tripod, and they will serve as models for a hundred generations' (Soper, p. 19). Such esteem is substantiated by the relatively large number of paintings attributed (Chang Chao and others, Shih-ch'ü pao-chi, 1745) to Guan in the imperial collection of Huizong, of which only three remained later (Chang Chao and others, *Shih-ch'ü pao-chi*, 1745) (*Xuanhe huapu*). His work did not receive unqualified approval, however. Mi Fu wrote that he had seen 20 of his paintings and 'the human figures in them are vulgar' (Sirén, p. 191).

No details of Guan's life are known, but his stylistic development is divided into three stages. In his youth he studied the work of JING HAO. Liu Daochun (late 11th century) reported that he concentrated so hard upon his studies, in an effort to surpass Jing Hao, that he neglected to eat or sleep. Elements can also be related to the slightly younger FAN KUAN. In maturity, the second stage of his development, Guan is supposed to have been influenced by WANG WEI and a lesser known, late 8th-century AD painter, Bi Hong from the district of Yanshi in Henan Province, who specialized in rocks and trees. Guan's later work in his own personal style has been described as freer and more expressive.

Guan left no writings or commentaries of his own, but others have described his distinctive qualities. Guo Ruoxu wrote that

> his rock-style formations seem hard and solid ("a crystalline hardness"). The [clumps] of mixed trees are luxuriant and dense.... When he painted trees, he made the foliage of some as drenched in ink, and let a withered branch stick out here and there ... an antique elegance in his terraces and pavilions; and a lonely peacefulness in his human figures (Soper trans., p. 19).

The *Xuanhe huapu* ('Xuanhe collection of painting'; preface 1120) notes that 'T'ung's [Guan Tong's] pictures were done in a fluent fashion with a soft brush, and the more sketchy the brushwork, the stronger was the life-breath; the simpler the scenery, the deeper seemed the thoughts. His pictures had a profound meaning; they were noble and pure like Tao Yuanming's poetry and He Ruo's music. No ordinary painter could do such things' (Sirén, p. 191). The preface to the collection by the emperor Huizong (*reg* 1101–26) comments, 'Most of all it delighted him to paint autumn hills and winter forests, with groups of cottages, river-crossings, hermits, recluses, fishermen selling their catch, mountain hostelries.' In short, Guan's subjects were rustic genre scenes showing country folk engaged in their daily activities.

Because of the range of Guan's sources of inspiration and style, and in the absence of signed paintings, attribution of his work is extremely difficult. Certain qualities are generally accepted as his, however. Guan's treatment of trees and foliage, for example, reflects a much greater diversity of perception than that expressed by earlier masters. His motif of withered branches or dead trees clustered together with other deciduous trees in full foliage represents a realism that could only have been based on direct observation of nature; it became part of the general vocabulary of landscape painters. The development of mountain forms built up in terms of repeated masses also seems to have been introduced by Guan. He may have been less accomplished in figure drawing, since it is

Guan Tong (attrib.): *Travellers at a Mountain Pass*, hanging scroll, ink and some light colour on silk, 1.44×0.57 m, 10th century (Taipei, National Palace Museum)

recorded that an artist by the name of Hu Yi added figures to landscape at Guan's request, though the documentation or extent of such a practice can not be verified.

No fully documented paintings by Guan Tong survive. One work to be tentatively attributed to him is the hanging scroll *Ford Across the Mountain Stream* (ink and slight colours on silk, 1.56×0.99 m; Taipei, N. Pal. Mus.). Another painting that has been attributed to him is the hanging scroll *Travellers at a Mountain Pass* (see fig.). This is seen as a Song painting but preserves certain important earlier traditions. A sharply tilted ground plane makes a somewhat unresolved transition from a river valley to a slightly asymmetrical, mushrooming, background mountain mass built up from repeated superimposed forms in the style identified with Guan Tong. Visual entry into the landscape is at the lower left-hand corner, opening into a small village set along the river bank and peopled with small figures performing various carefully detailed activities. Genre elements constitute only a small portion of the painting. The minuteness of the human figures in proportion to the landscape enhances a sense of the overwhelming domination of nature. A path leads from the village across a bridge and into the mountain range, where small structures can be detected. The foreground area provides ample room for movement through the landscape, but depth is limited by mountainous obstruction. Mid-ground mists at the base of the mountain serve as a transitional area and enhance the silhouette of skeletal and leafy tree forms. Other indications of vegetation are sparse. The painting is rendered with variable calligraphic brushstrokes with relatively strong contrasts of light and shade. The work is not signed and is only attributed to Guan Tong or a follower, but does appear consistent with Chinese 10th-century painting traditions.

BIBLIOGRAPHY

FrankeGuo Ruoxu: *Tuhua jianwen zhi*, 6 *juan* (preface 1075); *R* in Huashu congshu (Taipei, 1974); Eng. trans. by A. C. Soper as *Kuo Jo-hsü's 'Experiences in Painting' (T'u-hua chien-wen chih): An Eleventh Century History of Chinese Painting* (Washington, DC, 1951/*R* 1971)

Xuanhe huapu [Xuanhe collection of painting] (preface 1120); in Shanpen tsung-shu (Beijing, 1971), 10 *juan*, p. 9

O. Sirén: *Chinese Painting: Leading Masters and Principles* (London, 1956–8), i, pp. 191–3

Chinese Art Treasures: A Selected Group of Objects from the Chinese National Palace Museum and the Chinese National Central Museum (exh. cat., New York, Met., Boston, MA, Mus. F.A., Chicago, IL, A. Inst. and elsewhere; 1961–2)

M. Loehr: *The Great Painters of China* (New York, 1980), pp. 85–7, 92–8

T. Miyagawa, ed.: *Chinese Painting* (Tokyo, 1983), pp. 173, 121

MARY S. LAWTON

Guanxiu [Kuan-hsiu; original family name Jiang; *zi* Deyin; *hao* Chanyue] (*b* Lanxi, Zhejiang Province, AD 832; *d* Chengdu, Sichuan Province, 912). Chinese painter, calligrapher, poet and Buddhist monk. During the reign (AD 901–3) of the Tang emperor Zhaozong (*reg* AD 888–904), he visited Sichuan Province and was honoured by the King of Shu, who bestowed on him the title of Master. At that time, Daoism and Buddhism flourished in Sichuan, prompting many temple-building projects and giving an unprecedented impetus to the liturgical arts and figurative painting. Of the 50 or more painters recorded as then working in Sichuan, most were producing Daoist and Buddhist figure paintings.

According to contemporary sources, Guanxiu deviated from current fashions in depicting the Buddhist *luohan* (Skt *arhats*; enlightened beings) in his paintings with Tatar features and Indian faces. Like those of his predecessor, YAN LIBEN, these ascetics had long, trailing eyebrows, enormous, deep-set eyes, huge ears and bulbous noses. Guanxiu said that his inspiration 'came from dreams'. Although he is said to have used only ink wash, his dexterity in that medium produced the effect of a full-colour spectrum. He reputedly sat in meditation in a room perfumed by incense and, when a genuine vision of the Buddha came to him, leapt up and rapidly depicted two or three *luohan*. The surreal quality of his paintings was described by the poet Ouyang Jiong of the Northern Song period (960–1127). The foreign-looking figures sat in the lotus position, resembling 'emaciated cranes of robust spirit, with their skulls thick and bones strong as an earth-ploughing rhinoceros'. They were shown dressed in thread-sewn garments, the hemp sashes opening to reveal Indian lining.

> One of them leans against a pine root which emerges from a rocky crevice, his torso is crooked and his waist tall as if about to sway. A *sūtra*-reading disciple attempts to harmonize the spirit, as his youthful attendant drops off into dreamland... An ancient gibbon dangles obliquely with arm outstretched, as in the woods the leaves fall and the incense dies out.

Towards the end of the 10th century, when the second Song emperor, Taizong (*reg* 976–97), sought ancient paintings for his court, the newly subjugated Shu submitted Guanxiu's *luohan* paintings that had been worshipped in the Shu palace. They exuded a 'wild and antique look, unlike the usual kind'. By then his calligraphy and paintings had already become scarce. The *Xuanhe huapu* ('Xuanhe collection of painting', preface 1120) listed 30 of his paintings, including portraits of Vimalakirti (the lay disciple of Buddha), Indian and Chinese monks and 26 *luohan*. Extant paintings of the Song (960–1279) and Yuan (1279–1368) periods that bear a hint of Guanxiu's style are mainly in the Imperial Household Collection, Tokyo, the Asano Collection, and some temple collections, all in Japan. In his calligraphy Guanxiu developed a distinctive variant of the draft cursive script (*zhangcaoshu*), which became known as the Jiang style (after his surname) and was compared to that of the great Tang-period (AD 618–907) master of the draft script, Huaisu.

BIBLIOGRAPHY

Franke: 'Kuan-hsiu'

Huang Xiufu: *Yizhou minghua lu* [Record of famous painters of Yizhou], 3 *juan* (preface 1006), *juan* 3

Guo Ruoxu: *Tuhua jianwen zhi* [Experiences in painting] (preface 1075), ed. Huan Miaozi (Shanghai, 1963); Eng. trans. in A. C. Soper: *Kuo Jo-hsü's 'Experiences in Painting' (T'u-hua chien-wen chih): An Eleventh Century History of Chinese Painting* (Washington, DC, 1951/*R* 1971)

Xuanhe huapu [Xuanhe collection of paintings], 23 *juan* (preface 1120); ed. Yu Jianhua (Beijing, 1964), *juan* 2

Zhou Bida: *Zhou Yiguo wenzhong gongji erbaijuan* [Collected writings of Zhou Bida], 200 *juan* (*c.* late 12th century), *juan* 169

Tang Hou: *Hua jian* [Mirror of Painting] (late 12th century/*R* ed. Ma Cai, Beijing 1959; ed. Ma Cai and Deng Yizhe, 1962; Taipei, 1963)

Chen Si: *Shu xiaoshi* [A brief history of calligraphy], 10 *juan* (1225–64/*R* Taipei, 1983), *juan* 10

Xia Wenyan: *Tuhui baojian* [Precious mirror for examining painting], 5 *juan* (1365), *juan* 3

O. Sirén: *Chinese Painting: Leading Masters and Principles* (London and New York, 1956–8), i, pp. 154–7
J. Cahill: *An Index of Early Chinese Painters and Paintings* (Berkeley, 1980), pp. 38–9
Zhongguo meishujia renming cidian [Dictionary of Chinese artists], ed. Yu Jianhua (Shanghai, 1981)

JOAN STANLEY-BAKER

Guan Zuolin. *See* GUAN, (1).

Guarana. Italian family of painters.

(1) Jacopo Guarana (*b* Venice, 28 Oct 1720; *d* Venice, 18 April 1808). He first studied the work of Sebastiano Ricci and then that of Giambattista Tiepolo. Throughout his career Jacopo faithfully followed the great Venetian decorative artists of the 18th century. He was resident in Venice for the whole of his life and is documented as travelling to Ravenna, where in 1751 he decorated the dome of S Vitale, taking over from Ubaldo Gandolfi. He also worked at Valnogaredo (1763) and Stra (1770). His early works in Venice are painted in the style of Tiepolo but with a lighter palette. Examples include the *Martyrdom of St Thomas* (1755) on the ceiling of S Tomà; and the ceiling (1753–8) for the room now known as the Sala degli Arazzi in the Ca' Rezzonico. He became a member of the Accademia in Venice in 1756. In 1758 he was decorating the ceiling of S Teonisto at Treviso, where, with the assistance of the *quadratura* painter Domenico Fossati (1743–84), he executed the *Assumption of the Virgin* (destr.).

Guarana's most ambitious work is the ceiling canvas depicting the *Sacrifice of Iphigenia* (1760; St Petersburg, Hermitage), commissioned by Catherine II, Empress of Russia, for the saloon of the Winter Palace in St Petersburg. From the same year is the ceiling for the main *salone* of the Scuola di S Giovanni Evangelista in Venice. After the departure of Tiepolo for Madrid (1762), Guarana became the painter most in demand for the decoration of Venetian *palazzi*. He worked on the Palazzo Donà dalle Rose in the parish of S Stin, on the Palazzo Tron near S Stae, on the Palazzo Zen near the Frari, and on the Palazzo Nani near S Trovaso. The frescoes in the central *salone* of the Villa Contarini-Rota at Valnogaredo, near Padua, which are based on subjects from the *Pastor fido* (1590) by Battista Guarini, were executed in 1763. In 1767 he painted the ceiling of the chapel in the Palazzo Ducale with the *Apotheosis of St Mark*. About 1770 Guarana was at Stra, where he painted frescoes in the Sala di Bacco at the Villa Pisani. It is also probable that he was responsible for the ornamental decoration there, which is among the finest produced in Venice during the period. His last major work was the decoration (1776) of the music room at the Ospedaletto in Venice, executed in collaboration with the Ferrarese *quadratura* painter Girolamo Mengozzi, called Colonna (*c.* 1688–*c.* 1766). In all these works Guarana reacted against the reigning academic Neo-classicism by imitating the compositional structure and palette of the great Venetian decorators working in the Rococo style. However, his paintings, and in particular the late works, lack luminosity and are often repetitive and rhetorical.

(2) Vincenzo Guarana (*b* Venice, 1753; *d* Venice, 1815). Son of (1) Jacopo Guarana. After studying with his father, he specialized in religious and historical subjects. His devotional works, such as the *Virgin and Saints* in S Tomà, are characterized by a mannered elegance reminiscent of the style of Jacopo Amigoni, while his historical subjects, such as *Massinissa Sending the Poison to Sophonisba* (1777; Parma, G. N.), are rhetorical and empty. Vincenzo subsequently abandoned the Rococo tradition in favour of a rather trite academic style. This can be observed in the two signed historical scenes of the *Deeds of Doge Agostino Barbarigo*, which are still in the Palazzo Barbarigo in Venice. Towards the end of his life Vincenzo also turned to portraiture, but his work in this field is known only through engraved copies, which would seem to suggest that his style developed in the direction of that of Alessandro Longhi.

BIBLIOGRAPHY

R. Pallucchini: *La pittura veneziana del settecento* (Venice and Rome, 1960), pp. 170–71, 237–8
E. Martini: *La pittura veneziana del settecento* (Venice, 1964), pp. 126–8
B. Scott: 'Jacopo Guarana: An Eighteenth-century Venetian History Painter', *Apollo*, lxxxiii (1966), pp. 364–71
K. Garas: 'Appunti per Jacopo Amigoni e Jacopo Guarana', *A. Ven.*, xxvi (1978), pp. 383–9
E. Martini: *La pittura del settecento veneto* (Udine, 1982), pp. 110, 556
E. Manzato: 'Guarana, Jacopo', *La pittura in Italia: Il settecento*, ed. G. Briganti (Milan, 1990), ii, pp. 745–6 [with bibliog.]

FILIPPO PEDROCCO

Guardi. Italian family of painters and draughtsmen. Although generally thought of as Venetian, the family had its origin, at least as far back as the early 16th century, in the Val di Sole in the Trentino, the mountainous district that is now the most northern part of Italy. They were of some distinction and were granted a patent of nobility by Emperor Ferdinand III in 1643. Domenico Guardi (1678–1716), the father of the best-known members of the family, (1) Giovanni Antonio Guardi and (2) Francesco Guardi, learnt to paint in Vienna, but nothing is known of his artistic production. He married there before removing to Venice about the turn of the century. His eldest child, Giovanni Antonio, was baptized in Vienna in 1699; but a daughter Cecilia was born in Venice in 1702. Francesco was also born in Venice, as was a third son, Nicolò Guardi (1715–1786), who also became a painter. Attributions to Nicolò have been suggested; but that is all speculation. In 1719 Cecilia married Giambattista Tiepolo, later reckoned one of the most celebrated painters of his time. On the death of Francesco, the studio was inherited by his son Giacomo Guardi (1764–1835).

(1) Giovanni Antonio [Gianantonio; Antonio] **Guardi** (*b* Vienna, *bapt* 1699; *d* Venice, 22 Jan 1760).

1. LIFE AND WORK. Gianantonio (as he is usually called) presumably took over the studio in Venice at the age of 17, on his father's death. Various documents relating to him have been published (Fogolari, De Maffei, Ciccolini): he was elected a founder-member of the Venetian Accademia in 1756 (whereas his brother Francesco was elected only in 1784); he inherited an estate in the Val di Sole in 1737 from his father's brother; in 1739 another

1. Giovanni Antonio Guardi: *Death of St Joseph*, oil on canvas, 1690×755 mm, *c.* 1730 (Berlin, Bodemuseum, Gemäldegalerie)

member of the family, the priest Pietro Antonio Guardi, obtained from the family studio in Venice three lunettes—depicting the *Sacrilegious Communion*, the *Washing of the Disciples' Feet* and the *Vision of St Francis*—for his parish church in Vigo d'Anaunia, near Trento, and (probably a little later) the small altarpiece of the *Virgin and Child and Four Saints* (all still *in situ*). From 1730 for the next 15 years Gianantonio was much employed by the German Graf Johann Matthias von der Schulenburg, Field Marshal of the Venetian armies, to paint for him numerous copies of Venetian masters (Titian, Tintoretto, Sebastiano Ricci and others) and of portraits of the ruling families of Europe. There are records, too, relating to altarpieces of the *Virgin and Child with Saints* at Belvedere (1746) between Aquileia and Grado, near Trieste, and Cerete Basso (1754) in the Bergamasque Alps (both *in situ*), which are now attributed to Gianantonio, as head of the studio.

Only two signed paintings by Gianantonio are known: a poor little half-length of *St John Nepomuk* (1717; Treviso, priv. col., see 1965 exh. cat., no. 1), signed and dated when the artist was 18, and an altarpiece of the *Death of St Joseph* (Berlin, Bodemus.; see fig. 1). There are also one or two signed or credibly inscribed drawings. Besides the lunettes at Vigo d'Anaunia and the altarpieces at Belvedere di Grado and Cerete Basso, certain other works are connected by document with the Guardi studio and generally agreed to be (mainly) by Gianantonio. Payment is recorded in 1750 for an altarpiece of the *Vision of St Giovanni di Matha*, still in the parish church at Pasiano di Pordenone, near Udine, as the work of 'Sig. Antonio Guardi di Venezia della scuola di Bastiano Rizzi' (Querini). And to these may be added most of the long series of small scenes of *Turkish Life*, commissioned by von der Schulenburg and said in his inventory of 1741 to be 43 in number, although only 21 are now known. The von der Schulenburg archives also show that in 1738 Gianantonio copied for him a *Last Supper* (Halle, Staatl. Gal. Moritzburg) by Sebastiano Ricci (untraced).

2. STUDIO PRACTICE. It was the practice of the Guardi studio to borrow compositions from earlier sources. The greater part of the small altarpiece at Vigo d'Anaunia is copied from Solimena; the Cerete Basso altarpiece depends on Paolo Veronese; one of the Vigo d'Anaunia lunettes is from a print after Tintoretto; and there are many other instances. Evidently most of the Guardi production in history or religious painting, up to the death of Gianantonio, was studio work, involving no doubt also the third brother, Nicolò. Nevertheless a few of the 'histories' were attributed to Gianantonio by Fiocco, who gave the best to Francesco; and these included the charming and now famous *Story of Tobias* paintings that adorn the organ-loft of the church of the Angelo Raffaele in Venice (see fig. 2), the *Aurora* ceiling now in Palazzo Cini, Venice, the six scenes from the *Story of Joseph* (all Milan, Lutomirski priv. col., see 1965 exh. cat., nos 50–51) and the series of seven of the *Triumph of Venus* (five now in the Italian Embassy, Paris). Two other series of large paintings from the Guardi studio were discovered in time to be shown at the Venice exhibition of 1965: the five scenes based on engravings in the 1745 Albrizzi edition of Torquato Tasso's *Gerusalemme liberata* (dispersed; two in Washington, DC, N.G.A.); and four scenes from *Roman History* (Oslo, Villa Bogstad).

3. PROBLEMS OF ATTRIBUTION AND COLLABORATION. The attribution of all these 'history' series to one or other of the brothers has been much disputed: whereas Fiocco and Pallucchini were both inclined to credit Francesco with the best, the reputation of Gianantonio, after meagre beginnings, has been enhanced in the second half of the 20th century, by some documentary evidence and

2. Giovanni Antonio Guardi: *Marriage of Tobias* (detail), oil and tempera on canvas, 0.80×3.42 m, *c.* 1750 (Venice, Church of the Angelo Raffaele)

by recent opinion; Morassi (1974), writing of four little Turkish scenes that were discovered too late for inclusion in his corpus of Guardi's paintings of 1973, went so far as to call Gianantonio 'this great painter, one of the most important innovators of the Venetian Settecento'. This high praise is not undeserved by the painter of the *Tobias* series. Technically, these frescoes are a surprise and a delight; the flickering brushwork and the light, gay colours (no doubt largely due to the fresco technique) are signs of a move towards full Rococo, an advance on anything in Gianantonio's paintings in oil. Since the whole decoration of the organ-loft may be dated *c.* 1750, thus excluding the possibility of extensive collaboration with Francesco, they can perhaps best be described as 'Francesco *avant la lettre*', anticipating the style and technique developed by the younger brother long after Gianantonio's death.

The great Guardi exhibition at Palazzo Grassi in 1965, despite its excellent catalogue, did not succeed in solving some important problems: the final distinction of the styles of Gianantonio and Francesco as 'history' painters; the extent to which collaboration took place in the studio; and the chronology. The subsequent publication *Problemi Guardeschi* still contained many conflicting contributions, made at a conference on the spot in 1965, which did not help in this respect. A valuable essay by Mahon developed his own careful conclusions in much the longest of these; but again, they were often at variance with those of others included in the book. On the division of work between the brothers, to judge from the evidence presented so far, the views of Morassi (1973 and 1975) are probably the most acceptable; and they are supported in the main by Pignatti (1967).

As for the problem of collaboration in the Guardi studio, it is surely wrong to dismiss it as though it implied the absurdity of one brother snatching the brush from the other and continuing where he left off; collaboration was in the tradition of the Venetian family studios, characteristic of the Vivarini and the Bellini, of Jacopo Bassano with his sons, of Tintoretto with his son, daughter and son-in-law, and of Paolo Veronese with his heirs, down to the Guardi's own time in the studio of their famous brother-in-law, Giambattista Tiepolo, with his sons Giandomenico and Lorenzo Tiepolo.

(2) Francesco Guardi (*b* Venice, 5 Oct 1712; *d* Venice, 1 Jan 1793). Brother of (1) Giovanni Antonio Guardi.

1. Life and work. 2. Studio practice. 3. Forgeries.

1. LIFE AND WORK. If Morassi's distinction of the hands is accepted, there is some justification for considering Gianantonio a better figure painter than Francesco. Those religious subjects that are signed or now generally agreed to be Francesco's—the small bust-length representations of the *Virgin and Child*, various versions of the *Pietà*, even the altarpiece of *SS Peter and Paul* (late 1770s) in the parish church of the remote mountain village of Roncegno, near Trent—are no masterpieces; they show

undeniable weakness of drawing, wavering contours, distorted anatomy. The verdict of his own time, and of the succeeding 150 years or so, was surely the right one: that Francesco came into his own as a VEDUTA painter, after his brother's death or only shortly before. Suggestions that he began to paint views of Venice as early as 1730 have been shown to be based on invalid evidence; there is no reason to suppose that any of his *vedute* can be dated earlier than the later 1750s. And here again he followed the studio practice of borrowing compositions from others: he borrowed, for instance, from the etchings of his near-contemporary Michele Giovanni Marieschi, as in the *Grand Canal with the Palazzo Pesaro* (London, N.G.); but his main source of inspiration at this time was certainly Canaletto. A group of large drawings of familiar Venetian views by Francesco (London, BM; New York, Met.; Berlin, Kupferstichkab.; Bayonne, Mus. Bonnat and elsewhere) are much closer to Canaletto in style, especially in the little figures, and also more accurate in their topography, than the more typical productions of Francesco's pen (see fig. 1) or brush; some of them have been doubted for that reason, wrongly, for most of them relate to paintings that are certainly by him (some signed), but of his earliest phase as a *vedutista.*

A sidelight on this Canalettesque phase is provided by an entry in the diary of a contemporary Venetian, the Procurator Pietro Gradenigo, who recorded that on 25 April 1764 Francesco Guardi 'buon scolaro del rinomato Canaletto' exhibited in the Piazza S Marco two Venetian views that he had painted for a 'forestiere inglese' and was much applauded. He added that they were painted with the aid of the 'camera ottica' or camera obscura, which was certainly used by Canaletto. Fiocco, though he quoted this contemporary evidence, treated it too slightly while drawing attention so emphatically to Francesco's activity as a figure painter; and other authorities have followed him in this respect. But if Francesco really worked for a time in Canaletto's studio, that is only likely to have happened after Canaletto returned to Venice, probably in 1756, having spent nearly ten years (with two short breaks) in England; and by then Francesco was in his 40s. It may be significant that he seems to have moved out of the family studio before Gianantonio's death in 1760. In fact, according to the 19th-century Venetian critic Missaglia, who remarked on the 'magia d'effetto' in Guardi's views when contrasted with those of Canaletto, Francesco was sometimes required by Canaletto to execute a picture that he (Canaletto) had designed or laid in, to which Francesco then added some finishing touches himself. Perhaps the most instructive example of Guardi adapting Canaletto's designs is offered by his 12 canvases representing *Ceremonies at the Installation of the Doge*, which were seized by the French Revolutionary government in 1797, when they were attributed to Canaletto himself (11 now in Paris, Louvre; the other in Brussels, Mus. A. Anc., where it was deposited by the French, when the others were allotted to

1. Francesco Guardi: *Gondola Race on the Grand Canal, Venice*, pen and brown ink and brown wash over black chalk, 240×351 mm, *c.* 1770 (London, British Museum)

various museums in France). These are copied, with many variations, from the set of engravings (Venice, Correr) after Canaletto by Giambattista Brustolon, which was published between 1763 and 1766. No such paintings by Canaletto are known, but ten of the drawings, probably done expressly for the engraver, once belonged to Sir Richard Colt Hoare in England, and are now scattered in various collections (e.g. London, BM). The variations introduced by Guardi in his 12 paintings show that some of them, at least, are considerably later in date than their models: the *Doge in the Bucintoro on his Way to the Lido for the Ceremony of Wedding the Adriatic* (ex-Mus. Augustins, Toulouse; now Paris, Louvre) may be one of the earliest, while the *Doge Giving Audience to the Ambassadors in the Sala del Collegio* (Paris, Louvre) may be as late as 1780, judging by the coiffure of the lady in the right-hand corner.

These adaptations of Canaletto's *Ceremonies*, produced probably between 1770 and 1780, illustrate the gradual development of the most admired Guardi style: the brushwork becomes looser and freer, the colour lighter, the 'magical effects' more and more apparent. And as Francesco's mannerisms in the little figures increased, his respect for the topography of Venice declined. Working probably in his studio, often from some earlier model, he would take liberties with the actual scene; and topographical evidence, as a means of dating his views of Venice, is no longer reliable. A painting by Francesco showing an architectural feature that disappeared at a known date—the campanile of the church of the Carità, for instance, which collapsed in 1741—may derive from an earlier painting or print and need not have been done before that date; on the other hand, the presence of a datable feature in a painting does, of course, provide an indisputable *terminus post quem*. Thus his view of the *Grand Canal Looking towards the Rialto*, one of the series belonging to the Duke of Buccleuch which some scholars have dated *c*. 1730, cannot be earlier than 1754, since it shows the Baroque campanile of the church of S Bartolomeo, which was finished only in that year.

With small figures in contemporary dress—the staffage, particularly of his paintings of ceremonies and festivals—Guardi was much more successful than with larger figures in his religious subjects. Nothing could be more charming, conveying both the grandeur and the gaiety of the scene, than the *Concert of Girl Musicians in the Sala dei Filarmonici* (Munich, Alte Pin.) with innumerable figures, painted to commemorate a performance by 80 orphan girls in honour of the so-called Conti del Nord, the Russian Grand Duke Paul Petrovich and his consort, on 20 January 1782. This is one of several paintings by Francesco recording the visit of the Russian prince and princess; they were probably a commission from the Venetian state, his first, at a late stage of his career. Later in the same year he received a state commission that is actually documented, for four paintings to record the visit of Pope Pius VI to his native city; and it is evident that Francesco took extra care in these cases, for several preliminary drawings exist for both series, including a nearly full-size modello (Canterbury, Royal Mus. & A.G.) for the *Concert of Girl Musicians*. Dress and hairstyle, particularly of the ladies, provide a valuable indication of date. In paintings of the early,

2. Francesco Guardi: *View of the Piazza S Marco, Venice*, oil on canvas, 552×854 mm, *c*. 1775–80 (Edinburgh, National Gallery of Scotland)

Canalettesque phase of Guardi as a *vedutista*, ladies of the upper class have their hair dressed low—as in works by Canaletto or in Marieschi's etchings (published in 1741) or Pietro Longhi's drawing-room pieces of the mid-century. But in the 1770s French and English fashions had reached Venice, and the ladies' coiffure went up—first piled in a narrow shape, with a feather or small tricorne perched on top, and finally, in the 1780s, dressed high and wide with feathers or flowers. So the fashionable ladies appear in the *View of the Piazza S Marco, Venice* (Edinburgh, N.G.; see fig. 2), one of the finest of that favourite subject; or in paintings of the ceremonies and festivals in honour of some distinguished visitor; or of life in the grand villas of the Venetian mainland.

Francesco Guardi occasionally found a place, too, for elegant figures in those imaginary compositions called capricci (*see* CAPRICCIO), which he produced apparently to suit the taste of his compatriots—for Venetian patrons evidently preferred them, as displaying the artist's power of *invenzione*, to those straightforward views of Venice aimed at the foreign tourists. Canaletto had turned to this mode, and Guardi again followed him, perhaps with greater success. The motifs are many: ruined Classical arches or colonnades, sometimes complete settings in Classical style (see Morassi, 1973, nos 752–8); Gothic arches on the shore of the lagoon, by a dilapidated bridge; fantastic harbours with towers, or sometimes a surprising obelisk. There is much repetition, both of the principal motif and of the little figures—peasants, fishermen, washerwomen and, more rarely, the elegant couple seen from the back. There are at least four versions, all by Francesco, of the *Lagoon Landscape with an Obelisk* (see Morassi, 1973, nos 911–14), with only slight variations. Then there are many with isolated motifs derived from the actual architecture of Venice—the clock-tower arch (Morassi, nos 784–6) or the colonnade or courtyard of the Doge's Palace (Morassi, nos 774–8 and 788–91). It is clear from the number that have survived that these capricci, mostly small, had a considerable vogue; and the best of them are indeed charming in conception and exquisitely painted.

Francesco Guardi was over 80 when he died, and perhaps, in his old age, a trembling hand was to some extent responsible for the peculiar idiom of his latest drawings. The contours of figures and buildings became more and more tremulous and broken; and this is especially noticeable in drawings that can be dated to his last years on certain grounds: for instance, the drawing used for the painting of the *Ascent of Count Iambeccari's Balloon in Venice, 14 April 1784* (ex-Altmann priv. col., London) or for the *Fire at S Marcuola, 28 December 1789* (New York, Met.); or for the Polignac wedding of September 1790, of which only drawings (Venice, Correr) have survived.

2. STUDIO PRACTICE. It is a difficult task to distinguish the hand of the master from those of his own studio assistants, especially when more than one hand might have been at work on the same picture. Francesco Guardi was no doubt assisted in producing the favourite views of Venice, in the latter part of his career, both by his younger brother Nicolò and by his son Giacomo. While attributions to Nicolò remain speculative, of Giacomo a good deal is known. Hundreds of little Venetian views by him exist, drawn in plain black and white or coloured in gouache, signed on the back: *Giacomo de' Guardis* (he was evidently proud of the patent of nobility), with the address: *all'Ospedaletto in Calle del Peruchier al No 5245*, or in some cases *a S: Canciano in Campiello della Madonna.* Twenty of those in black and white are in the Lehman Collection (New York, Met.), having come from albums brought to England or Ireland in the early 19th century; some are copied from his father's work. No-one could mistake these for Francesco's; but there are earlier drawings by Giacomo, done when his father was still alive or only lately dead; and at that time his drawings (and presumably his paintings) were more like his father's. He seems to have busied himself for some years after his father's death in selling the remains of the studio to foreign visitors or (for very small sums) to Teodoro Correr; himself finishing some that were left unfinished, and copying others in drawings that he sometimes signed with Francesco's name (e.g. Byam Shaw, 1951, pl. 78). Paintings no doubt went out from the studio simply as by 'Guardi', to less demanding clients. But studio remains are likely to contain scribbles and doodles that may not reflect credit on the deceased artist, but are nevertheless by his hand. Pallucchini (1943) published many such examples from the Museo Correr in Venice; and it is surely a mistake to dismiss these, as some more recent writers have done, as the work of Giacomo (whose style is not apparent there) or of some nameless imitator. At his best, Francesco Guardi was inimitable, but occasionally, like Homer, he could be said to nod.

3. FORGERIES. It was perhaps inevitable, once Francesco's fame was established at the beginning of the 20th century, and his mannerisms were recognized, that imitations, especially of his drawings, should come on to the market; and clever forgeries, produced about the second or third decade of the 1900s (the drawings generally on 18th-century paper, which was easily obtained), are dangerous to the hopeful collector. Some have even passed as originals into the great museums and remained for a time undetected. Exhibitions at the British Museum in 1961 (*Forgeries and Deceptive Copies*) and 1990 (*Fake? The Art of Deception*) and at the Minneapolis Institute of Arts in 1971 (*Fakes and Forgeries*) all contained imitations of Guardi drawings (see also Byam Shaw, 1977). It is generally easier to detect a forgery in a drawing than in a painting, where dark varnish and false craquelure may facilitate the deception.

BIBLIOGRAPHY

L. Lanzi: *Storia pittorica della Italia*, 2 vols (Bassano, 1795–6); rev. and expanded edn (Bassano, 1809), iii, pp. 289–90

V. Missaglia: *Bibliografia*, xxvi (Venice, 1826)

G. Simonson: *Francesco Guardi* (London, 1904) [valuable appendices]

G. Fogolari: 'L'Accademia veneziana di pittura e scultura nel settecento', *L'Arte*, xvi (1913), pp. 241–72 and 364–94

G. Fiocco: *Francesco Guardi* (Florence, 1923)

L. Livan, ed.: *Notizie d'arte tratte dai notatori e dagli annali di Pietro Gradenigo* (Padua, 1942)

R. Pallucchini: *I disegni del Guardi al Museo Correr di Venezia* (Venice, 1943)

M. Goering: *Francesco Guardi* (Venice, 1944)

J. Byam Shaw: *The Drawings of Francesco Guardi* (London, 1951)

F. De Maffei: *Gian Antonio Guardi: Pittore di figura* (Verona, 1951)

V. Moschini: *Francesco Guardi* (London, 1952)

G. Ciccolini: 'La patria e la famiglia di Francesco Guardi', *Stud. Trentini Sci. Stor.* (1953–4)
I disegni veneti della Coll. Scholz (exh. cat. by M. Muraro, Venice, Fond. Cini, 1957), no. 92 A, B and C
M. Levey: *Painting in Eighteenth-century Venice* (London, 1959, rev. 1980)
A. Morassi: 'Antonio Guardi ai servigi del feldmareschallo Schulenburg', *Emporium* (April 1960), pp. 147–63; (May 1960), pp. 199–212
——: 'Le cinque storie della *Gerusalemme liberata*', *Emporium* (June 1960), pp. 247–56
R. Pallucchini: *La pittura veneziana del settecento* (Venice, 1960)
S. Sinding-Larsen: 'Recently Discovered Paintings by Guardi and Other Italian Artists in a Norwegian Collection', *Connoisseur* (1961)
Canaletto e Guardi (exh. cat. by K. T. Parker and J. Byam Shaw, Venice, Fond. Cini, 1962)
Querini: *Messagero di Venezia* (21 Nov 1963)
Guardi (exh. cat., ed. P. Zampetti; Venice, Pal. Grassi, 1965) [excellent documentation and bibliog.]
Problemi Guardeschi: Atti del convegno di studi promosso dalla mostra dei Guardi: Venezia, 1965
D. Mahon: 'The Brothers at the Mostra dei Guardi: Some Impressions of a Neophyte', *Problemi Guardeschi* (Venice, 1967), pp. 66–155
T. Pignatti: *Disegni dei Guardi* (Florence, 1967) [excellent large pls]
A. Morassi: *I Guardi: L'opera completa di Antonio e Francesco Guardi*, 2 vols (Venice, 1973)
——: 'Four Newly Discovered Turkish Scenes by Antonio Guardi', *Apollo*, xcix (April 1974), pp. 274–8
——: *Guardi: Tutti i disegni* (Venice, 1975)
J. Byam Shaw: 'Some Guardi Drawings Re-discovered', *Master Drgs*, xv/1 (1977), pp. 3–15
T. Pignatti and A. Dorigato: *Disegni antichi del Museo Correr di Venezia*, iii (Venice, 1983)
Francesco Guardi: Vedute, caprice, teste (exh. cat. by A. Bettagno, Venice, Fond. Cini, 1993)
Guardi: Quadri turcheschi (exh. cat. by A. Bettagno, Venice, Fond. Cini, 1993)

JAMES BYAM SHAW

Guarienti, Pietro Maria (*b* Verona, *c.* 1700; *d* Dresden, 27 May 1753). Italian painter, writer and connoisseur. Orphaned at the age of 11, he trained for three years with the Veronese painter Biagio Falcieri (1628–1703). With the help of a member of the Bolognese Albergati family, he then moved to Bologna, where for the next seven years he studied with Giuseppe Maria Crespi. In 1725 he became a member of the Bolognese Accademia Clementina. For the next 20 years he worked in Venice, more as a connoisseur than as a painter. By his own account, his chief wish had always been to make himself expert in connoisseurship and he had accordingly read widely, studied works of art with care (copying sections in order to understand better the styles of different artists) and travelled throughout Italy and in England, Germany and Spain, taking every opportunity to see the works of Old Masters. He thus developed an intimate knowledge of artistic style, which, as he observed in 1753, was all the more valuable because art dealers were not always trustworthy. In Venice he joined the circle of art agents and connoisseurs that included Anton Maria Zanetti the elder who, in a letter to his fellow collector F. M. Gabburri in Florence, refers to Guarienti as early as April 1723.

In 1744 Guarienti was involved with Zanetti in negotiations for the purchase of 100 pictures from the gallery of Francesco III d'Este, Duke of Modena (*d* 1780), for the gallery that Frederick-Augustus III, Elector of Saxony and King of Poland, was then establishing. Guarienti acted as intermediary in dealings between Augustus' court painter, Bonaventura Rossi, and the curator of the ducal collection in Modena, Abbate Pietro Gherardi. In January 1746 Guarienti was himself in Dresden and, following the arrival in September of the paintings, which included such celebrated masterpieces as the *Adoration of the Shepherds* (known as *La Notte*) by Correggio (Dresden, Gemäldegal.), he was appointed inspector of the gallery, in collaboration with the German artist Johann Gottfried Riedel (1691–1755). In this capacity Guarienti began (1747) an inventory of the elector's Italian pictures and in 1748 visited Prague in connection with the acquisition of more pictures for the Dresden gallery from the imperial collection.

At the same time Guarienti was also preparing a revised edition of the celebrated *Abecedario pittorico* (1704) by PELLEGRINO ANTONIO ORLANDI. Guarienti's new edition, published in the year of his death, incorporated corrections and additions which brought the book up to date for a new generation of artists and connoisseurs. Much of the information available on his early life and career is derived from the book's prefatory address to the reader, '*Al lettore*'.

WRITINGS

ed.: *Abecedario pittorico del M. R. P. Pellegrino Antonio Orlandi bolognese . . . in questa edizione corretto e notabilimente di nuove notizie accresciuto da Pietro Guarienti, Accademico Clementino, ed Inspettore della Regia Galleria di SM Federic Augusto III* (Venice, 1753)

BIBLIOGRAPHY

G. Bottari and S. Ticozzi: *Raccolta di lettere sulla pittura, scultura ed architettura scritte da più celebri personaggi dei secoli XV, XVI e XVII, 8 vols* (Milan, 1822–5), ii, pp. 130–33; iv, pp. 107–8, 108–9
D. Zannandreis: *Le vite dei pittori, scultori e architetti veronesi*, ed. G. Biadego (Verona, 1891/*R* Bologna, 1971), p. 372
J. Winkler, ed.: *La vendita di Dresda* (Modena, 1989), pp. 27–57, 59–60

JANET SOUTHORN

Guariento (di Arpo) (*fl* Padua, 1338; *d* 1367–70). Italian painter. He was the leading painter of his time in Padua and is first recorded there as a master in 1338. The origin of his eclectic but highly distinctive style is not to be explained in terms of the influence of an ill-defined regional Byzantinism, as posited in older accounts, but rather as an alert and discriminating synthesis of trends current in the Veneto following visits to the area by such artists as Giotto and Giovanni Pisano. Guariento's style combines elements obviously drawn from Giotto's work in Padua and elsewhere with a more overtly Gothic sense of line and rhythm and a dramatic approach to narrative, occasionally verging on caricature.

Guariento's only extant signed work is a *Crucifix* (Bassano del Grappa, Mus. Civ.; see fig.) from S Francesco in Bassano del Grappa. In general terms this is closely modelled on the *Crucifix* by Giotto in the Arena Chapel in Padua and must be dated early in Guariento's career. Analogies between this panel and the *Crucifixion* scenes from a small triptych of the *Crucifixion with Saints* (Bergamo, priv. col.) and the fragmentary polyptych of the *Coronation of the Virgin with Scenes from the Life of Christ* (1344; Los Angeles, CA, Norton Simon Found.) support the attribution of these works on stylistic grounds. The distinctive facial features of the *Virgin* and *Christ the Redeemer* in the Bassano terminals—straight nose, square mouth and exaggeratedly large, staring eyes with a pronounced lower lid—find clear echoes in both altarpieces and the other works commonly ascribed to Guariento. The surviving narrative scenes of the *Coronation* polyptych, though largely based on Giottesque models, reveal a more

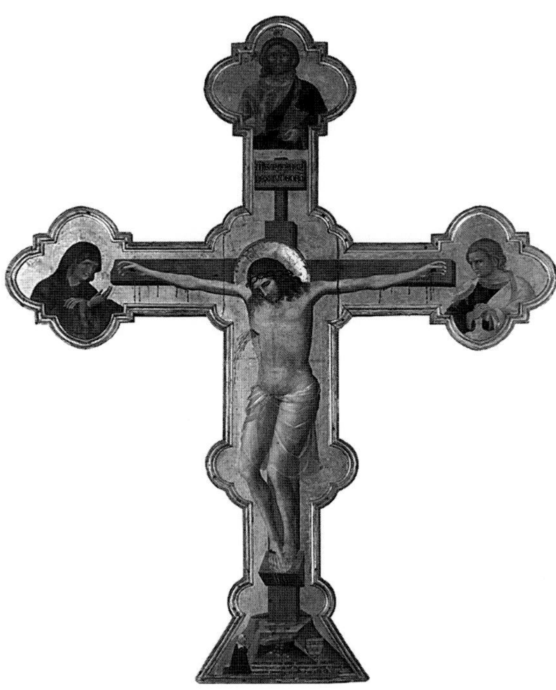

Guariento: *Crucifix*, tempera on panel, 366×275 mm, ?1340s (Bassano del Grappa, Museo Civico)

emotive and agitated style reminiscent of Riminese painting. Guariento had immediate access to Riminese models through the altarpiece (untraced) made in 1324 for the Eremitani in Padua by Giuliano and Pietruccio da Rimini and the surviving, though ruinous, frescoes of the *Life of Christ* (*c.* 1320–30; Padua, Mus. Civ.), usually attributed to Pietro da Rimini.

Guariento must have begun to work for the da Carrara, Lords of Padua, by the early 1350s, when he painted the (now fragmentary) fresco of the *Coronation of the Virgin* above the tomb of *Giacomo II da Carrara* in S Agostino, Padua (both Padua, Eremitani). The sculptor, Andriolo de' Santi, was paid for the tomb in 1351, and the fresco, distinguished by an extremely elaborate architectural throne and associated with two smaller fragments with sharply characterized portraits of kneeling male *Donors*, may be dated to the same year. Guariento's major work for the da Carrara family certainly post-dates the completion of their palace in Padua (1345) and can probably be assigned to the mid-1350s. It consists of the decoration of the private chapel (now Sala dell'Accademia) and comprised an extensive fresco cycle of *Old Testament* subjects (fragmentary; *in situ*) and 29 variously shaped panels, which decorated the ceiling. These panels include *Virgin and Child*, a *St Matthew* and a series devoted to the *Heavenly Hierarchies* (all Padua, Mus. Civ.) and show Guariento's style at its most consciously courtly and elegant. The variety of postures within the basic format of the standing *Angels*, or those weighing souls, testifies to considerable powers of invention and draughtsmanship. The associated fresco cycle is laid out in two continuous bands above a fictive arcade. It combines Guariento's taste for architectural intricacy with a vivid portrayal of biblical events. Three panels of the *Virgin and Child* (U. London, Courtauld Inst. Gals; ex-Weizner Col., London; Berlin, Bodemus.) were probably painted in this period: the analogies between them and the *Thrones* of the chapel ceiling are very close.

The date of Guariento's other major fresco cycle (partially destr. 1944), a *Last Judgement* and scenes from the *Lives of SS Augustine, James and Philip* in the presbytery and main apse of the Eremitani in Padua, is uncertain, but the maturity of illusionistic spatial invention in such a fresco as the *Ordination of St Augustine* (*in situ*) suggests that they were painted late in Guariento's career, probably in the 1360s. The wall between the main frescoes and the dado is decorated with a series of iconographically interesting grisaille *Astrological Figures* in fictive marble surrounds. One of the side chapels contains another, badly abraded set of frescoes attributable to Guariento on the basis of the more legible figures of *Saints* on the soffit of the chapel's entrance arch.

Although Guariento was recorded in Padua on many occasions throughout his life and especially in the 1350s and 1360s, a document of March 1366 records him living in Venice 'at present'. This coincides with the execution of the work that brought him most fame in the region after his lifetime, the huge fresco of *Paradise* (1365–8; Venice, Doge's Pal., Sala dell'Armamento), formerly in the Sala del Maggior Consiglio and commissioned, as the inscription records, by Doge Marco Cornaro in 1365–8. No documentary evidence links Guariento's name with this commission, but the attribution is quite secure on grounds of style and is supported by 15th- and 16th-century accounts. The fresco was damaged by fire in 1577 and the charred but extensive fragments were discovered (1903) under Jacopo Tintoretto's canvas painting (1588–94; *in situ*) of the same subject. The central element was a *Coronation of the Virgin* on an immense and complex throne, surrounded by a host of *Angels* and seated *Saints*. Vestiges of the original colour suggest that the chromatic range was as distinctive and rich as that of the Carrarese *Angels*, and the variety of the large number of individual figures confirms the fertility of Guariento's imagination. The specific iconography of the scene, with ranks of seated and conversing *Patriarchs* and *Prophets*, can be read as an enormous expansion of the type of teaching scene common throughout north Italy on the tombs of doctors of law and other masters. The relevance of this adaptation in the context of the central debating chamber of the Venetian Republic is clear. Guariento was again recorded in Padua in December 1367, but he had died by 22 September 1370. He left no significant school, but aspects of his painting find echoes in the work of his presumed pupil, Nicoletto Semitecolo, and, more significantly, in the later Paduan frescoes of Altichiero and Giusto de' Menabuoi.

BIBLIOGRAPHY

F. D'Arcais: *Guariento* (Venice, 1965, rev. 1975) [pls and comprehensive bibliog.]

S. Bettini and L. Puppi: *La chiesa degli Eremitani di Padova* (Vicenza, 1970)

F. D'Arcais: 'La personalità del Guariento nella cultura figurativa del trecento padovano', *Da Giotto al Mantegna* (exh. cat., ed. L. Grossato; Padua, Pal. Ragione, 1974), pp. 46–50

Da Giotto al Mantegna (exh. cat., ed. L. Grossato; Padua, Pal. Ragione, 1974), nos 12–35

J. White: 'The Reconstruction of the Polyptych Ascribed to Guariento in the Collection of the Norton Simon Foundation', *Burl. Mag.*, cxvii (1975), pp. 517–26

E. Cozzi: 'Gli affreschi della "Cappella Angelorum" agli Eremitani di Padova', *A. Ven.*, xxxv (1981), pp. 27–40

JOHN RICHARDS

Guarini, Guarino (*b* Modena, 17 Jan 1624; *d* Milan, 6 March 1683). Italian architect, mathematician, astronomer, theorist, writer and priest. Together with Francesco Borromini, he is the most renowned exponent of the anti-classical, anti-Vitruvian trend that dominated Italian architecture after Michelangelo but increasingly lost ground from the late 17th century. His subtly designed buildings, crowned with daring and complex domes, were ignored in Italy outside Piedmont, but illustrations published in 1686 and again in Guarini's treatise *Architettura civile* (1737) proved a fruitful source of inspiration in the development of south German and Austrian late Baroque and Rococo architecture.

1. Life and architectural work. 2. Theory and writings. 3. Critical reception and posthumous reputation.

1. Life and architectural work.

(i) Early career, before 1666. (ii) Mature and late work, 1666 and after.

(i) Early career, before 1666. Guarini came from a deeply religious family; he and his four brothers all joined the Theatine Order. At the age of 15 he became a novice and was sent to Rome (1639–48), where he was able to study High Baroque architecture, in particular the work of Borromini, Gianlorenzo Bernini and Pietro da Cortona. The details of Guarini's architectural training are not known, but in the excellently equipped libraries of his Order he presumably studied such well-known treatises as those of Serlio and Jacopo Vignola. In 1648 he returned to Modena as an ordained priest and two years later was appointed lecturer in philosophy at the Theatine College there. His career as an architect for the Order, which had a tradition of using its own members as architects, began in 1649 with the reconstruction of S Vincenzo, Modena, in collaboration with Bartolomeo Avanzini. In 1655 Guarini was elected Provost (*preposito*) of the Theatine house in Modena against the wishes of Alfonso IV d'Este, who was acting as Viceroy for his father, Francesco I d'Este, Duke of Modena: he forbade the appointment and banished Guarini from the city. After short sojourns in Parma and Guastalla (1656), Guarini's movements are unknown until his arrival in Messina in 1660. Claims are often made that he travelled in Spain and Portugal during this period in connection with a scheme to build a church in Lisbon, but this cannot be proved. In Messina, in addition to teaching activities, Guarini built the façade of S Maria Annunziata (destr. 1908) for his Order, placing it diagonally to the nave to conform with the building line of the street. The adjoining Theatine College is also attributed to him. A scheme for a church for the Somasian Fathers in Messina is illustrated in *Architettura civile*, but there is no indication of its date, nor if it was ever built. If contemporary with the Annunziata, it already announced a number of themes that characterize his style, such as centrality, telescoped space and the idiosyncratic treatment of vaulting.

In November 1662 Guarini travelled to Paris at the invitation of his Order to design the church of Ste Anne-la-Royale (destr. 1823). Although he incorporated the existing foundations of an oval church by the engineer Antonio Maurizio Valperga (*fl* 1626–67), he developed a completely independent design, again illustrated in *Architettura civile*. This had a Greek-cross plan extended by a polygonal choir chapel on the far side of the east arm. The central square bay of the plan was defined by four piers set at a diagonal of 45°, which supported a high drum with an arcaded walk lit by small lanterns. Above the drum was a double dome, the soffit of the lower one decorated with an interlace of flat ribs springing in pairs from plinths in a way that recalled the vaulting in Borromini's chapel of the Re Magi (1660–64) at the Collegio di Propaganda Fide, Rome. At Ste Anne, however, the wide central octagon produced by the interlaced ribs was left open, enabling a smaller, truncated dome capped by a lantern to be seen through the oculus thus created. The façade, with its three-part curvature, was reminiscent of Borromini's for S Carlo alle Quattro Fontane, Rome, although as this was not begun until 1665 (and with Borromini's well-known fear of competitors it is unlikely that Guarini would have seen drawings) Guarini may well have devised the curved façade of Ste Anne-la-Royale independently. The church, his first ecclesiastical masterpiece, incorporated all the essential elements of his style: the geometric patterning of the dome, the autonomy of the volumetric components, openness to Gothic principles of construction, and receptivity to contemporary architecture in Rome. When funds for its completion ran low in 1666, he accused the head of the Chapter of falsifying the accounts; his own position became untenable and he was glad to accept an invitation from the Theatines of Turin to take charge of the work on their church of S Lorenzo.

(ii) Mature and late work, 1666 and after.

(a) Ecclesiastical buildings. (b) Secular buildings.

(a) Ecclesiastical buildings. When Guarini arrived in Turin towards the end of 1666 he submitted a completely new design for S Lorenzo, the first stone of which had been laid in 1634. It originally had a Latin-cross plan, variously attributed to Ascanio Vitozzi, Carlo di Castellamonte and Carlo Morello (*fl c.* 1630–60). Progress was slow, and there are records of payments for work on it as late as 1661. Work was begun on Guarini's scheme in 1668, when he was appointed the architect. Except for remnants of the outer walls, he had the body of the previous structure destroyed to make way for his own design, planned as a centralized nave set in a square frame, with a small presbytery to the east backed by a retrochoir. Into the central space intrude eight convex wall elements, pierced at ground level by large Serlianas framing altars. Four of these convex elements, on the cardinal points, are smoothly curved; the other four, located diagonally, have flat faces and sweep up, like huge chamfered piers, to form concave pendentives. They appear to support a cornice ring (itself pierced by eight oval openings) and drum, from the lower level of which springs a network of hyperbolic vaulting ribs, criss-crossing to create a diaphanous dome and rosette-like geometric mesh (see fig. 1). The cupola

of the lantern, also embellished with a network of ribs, is visible through an octagonal opening at the top. The surfaces between the ribs of the dome are broken up with windows of different shapes and sizes, creating a mysterious fusion of light and abstract linear grid. The small dome over the high altar has a similar, simplified structure.

Guarini's surface modelling gives the impression that the enormous thrusts of the superstructure are ultimately being channelled to earth via the slender columns of the diagonal Serlianas at ground-level. The real task of load-bearing, however, is sustained by an unseen deep structure of massive brick arches, buttressed by equally massive squinches, that spring at high level from points within the chamfered protrusions. The inspiration for this extraordinary design seems to be twofold: Gothic and Islamic. In *Architettura civile* Guarini referred to the contrast between Gothic and Classical art, the aim of the former being 'to erect buildings that were in fact very strong, but would seem weak and as though they needed a miracle to keep them standing'. The Islamic influence is seen in Guarini's diaphanous dome, where the parabolic ribs create a pattern similar to that of the domes over the mihrab in the Great Mosque at Córdoba (*see* CÓRDOBA, fig. 2), albeit on a much larger scale; Guarini also cut out some of the infill web and placed a lantern on the ribwork of the open central octagon. Some scholars have seen in his legerdemain a late instance of Mannerism; others have suggested that Guarini intended that the building should appear to be held together not by the laws of nature but by transcendental powers, while the construction of the dome, with its endlessly leaping parabolic arches, was meant to manifest God's infinity and the perfection and harmony of his creation (see Wittkower).

1. Guarino Guarini: S Lorenzo, Turin, interior of the dome, begun 1668; pre-World War II photograph (paintings in pendentives were subsequently restored)

The design skills evinced by Guarini at S Lorenzo prompted Charles-Emanuel II, Duke of Savoy, to appoint him, by a patent dated 19 May 1668, engineer for the chapel of the Holy Shroud (Santa Sindone), Turin. Work on the project had been under way intermittently since 1607 to a design by Carlo di Castellamonte, superseded in 1657 by one from Bernardino Quadri (*fl c.* 1647–60). The location chosen for this reliquary chapel, joined both to the west wing of the new Palazzo Reale and to the east end of the cathedral, was meant to symbolize the unity of Church and State, or the divine favour and recognition bestowed on the House of Savoy. When Guarini took over as head of works, the circular structure of the chapel, elevated high above the cathedral floor, had been completed up to the entablature of a giant order. It was faced with black marble, and its three portals, one leading to the palace, the other two leading to the stairs from the cathedral aisles, were already in place, as was the huge window to the central nave through which the relic of the Holy Shroud could be seen. The appointment of a new architect at this advanced stage of construction was due to major structural problems, which Guarini solved by taking the chapel walls down to the lower orders and superimposing a curved intermediate zone articulated by three flat, two-dimensional arches spanning between the portals (see fig. 2). The abstract Trinitarian symbolism of the equilateral triangle inscribed by these arches is reflected in the three circular vestibules he introduced in front of the portals, projecting into the central circular space. These vestibules were each designed like a small monopteros, with shallow triangular vaulting supported by three groups of three free-standing black marble columns. The vestibule leading from the palace is only partially visible, because it is sunk into the wall. Guarini's design for the capitals of the giant order incorporates thorns and nails, symbols of the Passion.

The dark, windowless cylinder of this lower zone creates a grave-like atmosphere that contrasts intensely with the conical dome above: made of light-coloured stone, it is pierced by a filigree of windows admitting a flood of light—an overwhelming symbolism for death vanquished (*see* ITALY, fig. 20). The dome is formed by a series of segmental ribs. At the lowest level these spring from the heads of six large arched windows that light the drum. From the crowns of the first row of ribs the next row springs, spanning between the crowns. This sequence is repeated six times, creating tiers of arches of diminishing height and, in plan, a series of staggered hexagons. With an impression of height increased by the diminishing perspective in the dome, the overall effect is of strong upward movement, as if following the path of Resurrection towards a seemingly free-floating 12-pointed star at the apex, with the dove of the Holy Spirit. From the outside only the upper parts of the chapel are visible, and there Guarini introduced a further element: a tall, pointed three-tiered lantern on a stepped base. The oval windows of this

2. Guarino Guarini: chapel of the Holy Shroud (Santa Sindone), Turin Cathedral, begun 1668; section

pagoda-like construction serve to provide a halo of light for the dove of the Holy Spirit, the culmination of the bright celestial zone above presiding over the dark, restless zones below. At Santa Sindone, Guarini once more displayed his propensity for concealing the structural bases of his design. The bird's nest of ascending ribs that constitutes the dome is in fact supported by powerful buttresses, visible as such externally but read within only as the vertical spines that bisect the openings created by the superimposed segmental ribs.

Guarini also designed a number of longitudinal churches, including the Immacolata Concezione, Turin (begun 1673), which was first attributed to Guarini by Onorato Derossi in *Nuova guida per la città di Torino* (Turin, 1781), and others known only from engravings. These include designs for S Filippo Neri, Turin (unexecuted; the church of this name that collapsed in 1714 was to a substitute plan of 1683 by Michelangelo Garove), and another for S Maria della Divina Provvidenza, Lisbon (destr. 1755), intended for the Theatines. The latter's date is uncertain, but the engravings of it in *Disegni d'architettura* (Turin, 1686) are dedicated to Fra Antonio Ardizone Spinola (1609–97), who established the Order in Lisbon in the early 1650s.

The design of S Maria della Divina Provvidenza epitomized Guarini's dynamic reinterpretation of the Counter-Reformation church type, which was primarily responsible for his high standing with Baroque and Rococo architects north of the Alps. The Roman model for this type, Il Gesù (*see* ROME, §V, 16), has a Latin-cross plan, a dome over the crossing and wide nave with side chapels, interconnected by narrow passages, the nave walls being composed of wide arches and pilaster-faced piers. All these elements were present in the Divina Provvidenza, but Guarini transformed the schema by substituting spaces defined by ovals and circles for those previously defined by straight lines (see fig. 3). The two bays of the nave were intersecting ovals, each capped by a quadripartite dome with a lantern above. The presbytery was two-thirds of a circle in plan; and the crossing, between two elongated ellipses that served as transepts, was roofed by a huge dome and an octagonal lantern. The piers between each bay, from the entrance end to the presbytery, were canted outwards to induce a continuous undulation in the walls; the ceiling also undulated, as the bay vaults interpenetrated with soft curves at the lines of intersection; and the giant pilasters, their trabeation articulating the nave walls, undulated as well. They were components of what Guarini termed in his architectural treatise 'the Supreme Corinthian order, which I make undulating' (*see* ORDERS, ARCHITECTURAL, fig. 7). The all-pervading sinuosity of the order is extrapolated from the corkscrew columns found in Old St Peter's, Rome, which were believed to be relics of Solomon's Temple in Jerusalem. A 'complete Salomonic Order' had in fact been pioneered, on paper at least, by an older contemporary of Guarini's, Fra Juan Rizi, a Spanish Benedictine monk whom he may have met on his travels. These peculiarities were not intended to be capricious but were the logical outcome of Guarini's basic conception of the interpenetration and fusion of bodies. The dissolution of prismatic mass in Guarini's designs is perhaps his most important contribution to architectural history.

(b) Secular buildings. Guarini's most renowned achievement in secular architecture is the Palazzo Carignano in Turin. His patron was the deaf-mute Prince Emanuele Filiberto Amedeo of Savoy-Carignano (1628–1709), descendant of a cadet branch of the ruling dynasty but at that time heir to Victor Amadeus II, Duke of Savoy. This position obliged Emanuele to have a suitable residence, and in 1679 Guarini was commissioned to build on a site outside the medieval walls of Turin. The palace was originally designed to have four wings around a large courtyard, but it was completed in 1683 as an open three-winged composition; decorating and finishing continued well into the 18th century. Four stages in the planning of the Palazzo Carignano exist in draft form (Turin, Archv Stato) and have often been published. The final scheme, which was the one built, shows a layout with a central

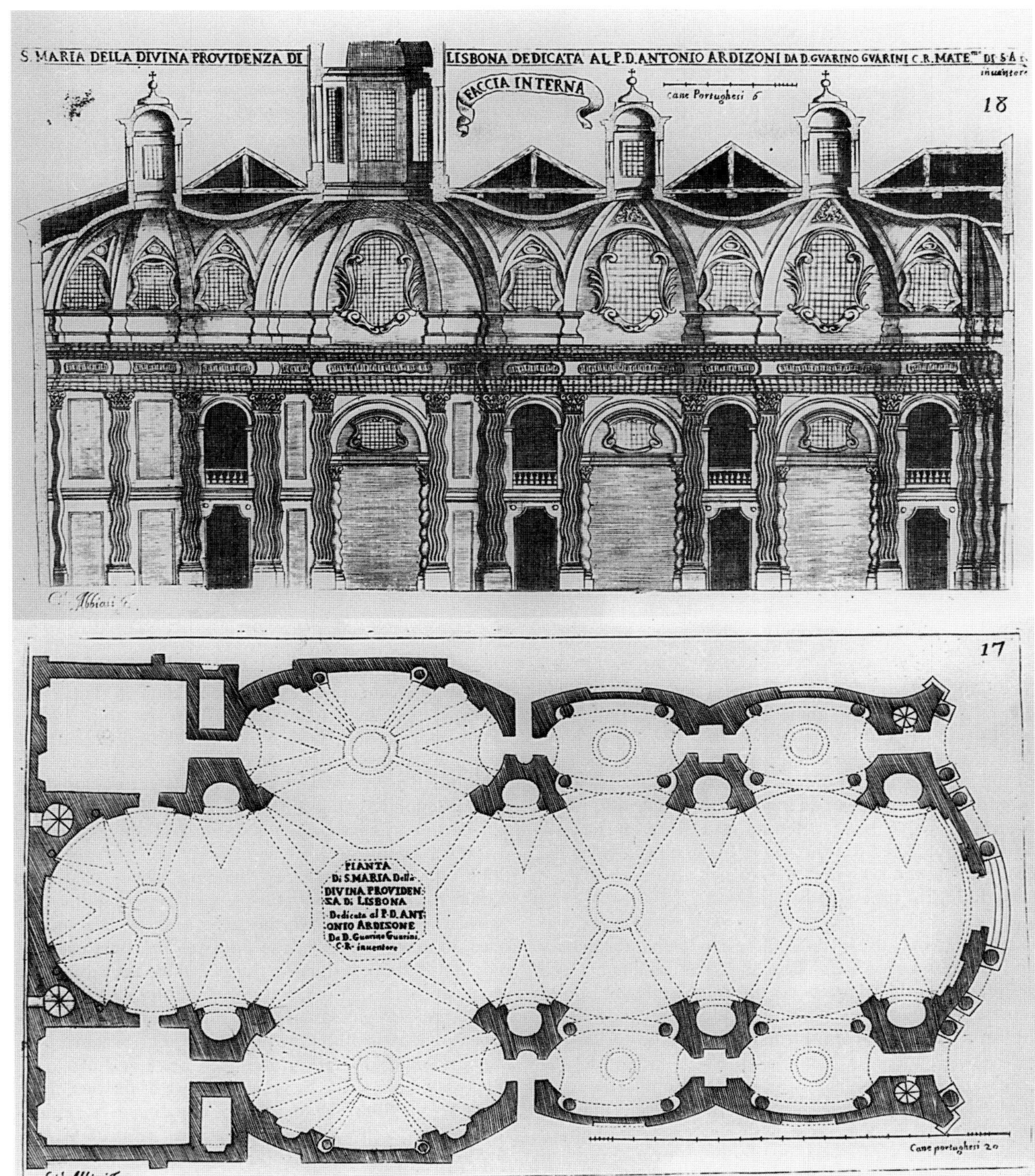

3. Guarino Guarini: S Maria della Divina Provvidenza, Lisbon (destr. 1755); plan and section from his *Disegni d'architettura civile et ecclesiastica* (Turin, 1686)

block facing a piazza and set between two straight side wings running back. The façade of the central block is formed with two sinuous S-curves. In the middle is a tall, oval cylinder, which is joined by sweeping counter-curves to the rectilinear end bays of the wings (see fig. 4). Two great staircases wind around the central oval pavilion like arms. They connect to a hexagonal salon on the *piano nobile*, which in turn leads to the oval grand *salone*, with a magnificent balcony over the main entrance. This design gives the impression of dramatic conflict between the architectural masses: the central block, wedged between the two side blocks, seems to undulate in slow motion.

4. Guarino Guarini: façade of Palazzo Carignano, Turin, 1679–83

The uniformity of the brick façade is interrupted by the central portal and the grand balcony above, which are both made from brilliant white stone and seem to burst from the centre impelled by a force exerted from the core of the building at the point of greatest tension. This type of curved inflection was an innovation in Italian Baroque palace design, although Bernini had featured an oval pavilion connected to side bays in his first project for the east front of the Louvre (1664), which Guarini may have seen during his time in Paris.

At the Palazzo Carignano the medium of brick was exploited to the utmost, both in the handling of the masses and in the extraordinary detailing. The pediments and architraves of the windows on the *piano nobile* are said to represent the face and feathered headdress of an Iroquois Indian, in celebration of the feats of arms of the Carignano-Salières Regiment in Canada (1665–8), while on the courtyard side every bay is articulated by pilaster-strips studded all the way along with eight-pointed stars in brick, crowded tip to tip. Various metaphysical explanations have been suggested for this feature, but in his treatise Guarini simply said 'they make a marvellous show'. During the 19th-century Risorgimento—the struggle for Italy's national unity—the palace served as the provisional seat of the first Italian parliament. Carlo Ceppi added a crowning feature to the central balconied niche of the main façade in 1880 and placed a monumental memorial plaque to *Victor Emmanuel II, King of Italy and Sardinia* over the cornice of the entrance bay. In the execution of these additions Ceppi was guided by an engraving from *Architettura civile* showing the details of the (then incomplete) façade.

Guarini's other major secular building in Turin, the Collegio dei Nobili (begun 1679; now the Palazzo dell'Accademia delle Scienze), is very different in character from the Palazzo Carignano. It was commissioned by the Dowager Duchess Mary Joanna of Savoy, to be used for the education of young aristocrats by Jesuits. The building was never completed, but a Neo-classical wing was added *c.* 1800: Guarini's touch may now be seen on two elevations only of the U-shaped building. The Collegio dei Nobili has three floors with pairs of large windows set between pilasters. Above the large windows are smaller ones, to enable intermediate floors to be constructed, if required, without disturbing the elevation. The storeys are separated by broad entablatures. Like the Palazzo Carignano, the Collegio is built of brick, but the corner pilasters are emphasized with stone rustication. The ornaments of the window-frames are in moulded brick and cast deep shadows on the wall. The large windows of the two upper levels are very unusual in being placed directly above the cornices without balustrades. As the purpose of the building was to house a school, not a prince, no storey is marked out as the *piano nobile.*

2. THEORY AND WRITINGS. Throughout his working life Guarini kept up a steady output of literature at the rate of a book every other year. His *Placita philosophica* (1665), which contains a long excursus on the nature of art, influenced by the philosophy of occasionalism, is an attempt to digest all philosophical knowledge in a single work. He did the same for mathematics in *Euclides adauctus* (1671), which reveals him as a keen student of the descriptive geometry of Gérard Desargues; in the 32nd

treatise of this book Guarini expounded the theoretical bases of the effects achieved in practice by his vaults. His *Coelestis mathematicae* (1683) is a summa of astronomy, albeit on a geocentric basis; he was correcting the proofs of it when he died. Three years later, the Theatines released for publication a collection of his architectural designs, engraved by various hands, under the title *Dissegni d'architettura civile et ecclesiastica.* It had no accompanying text but included 33 plates illustrating Guarini's schemes, which helped to spread the knowledge of his architectural style abroad. In the 1730s the Theatines invoked the help of the architect Bernardo Antonio Vittone to reissue these plates and several more, together with Guarini's unpublished manuscripts for a treatise on architecture, surveying and drawing. It came out under the title of *Architettura civile* (1737). Much of the book is highly technical in character, although even here Guarini's characteristic preoccupations are evident, as in his declaration that 'vaults are the main thing in architecture'. One of the most interesting aspects of the work is the insight it affords into Guarini's views on aesthetics, for example: 'Architecture has as its purpose the gratification of the senses' (I.iii.7). He went on to say that those people whose senses were to be thus gratified must be free of prejudice and artistically sophisticated. He noted that taste varied from age to age: 'Roman architecture formerly displeased the Goths, and Gothic architecture displeases us' (III.iii), but he could not repress his admiration for the skills of medieval architects in dissimulating the statical bases of their structures. The ultimate implication is that the rules could be changed and the orders were simply handy components, not the basic modules of proportion.

3. CRITICAL RECEPTION AND POSTHUMOUS REPUTATION. Guarini's diaphanous domes, his superimposition of apparently unrelated units in his centralized churches and the interpenetration of spaces in his longitudinal ones, together with his manipulation of statical forces in overt and deep structures, found no imitators among his contemporaries in Italy. The publication of *Architettura civile* inspired a modest Guarini revival in Piedmont (most notable in the work of Vittone), but later in the 18th century the rise of Neo-classicism in Italy led to the revilement of Guarini's architecture. This attitude is apparent in Francesco Milizia's scornful attack on Guarini in *Le vite de' più celebri architetti* (Rome, 1768). The reaction in the German lands was different: Johann Bernhard Fischer von Erlach's Trinity Church (1694–1707), Salzburg, has a façade that distinctly recalls the massing of the Palazzo Carignano. What began in Austria continued in Bohemia with Christoph Dientzenhofer (Obořiště, Pauline Abbey, 1699–1712) and culminated in Franconia, where Balthasar Neumann's pilgrimage church of the Assumption, VIERZEHNHEILIGEN (1740s), would have been unthinkable without the precedent of the splayed piers and interpenetrating spaces of Guarini's longitudinal churches. A new appreciation of Baroque architecture, which began in the late 19th century, has led to a re-evaluation of Guarini's work, which included a week-long conference on his life, work and influence held at Turin in 1968.

WRITINGS

Placita philosophica (Paris, 1665)
Euclides adauctus et methodicus mathematicaque universalis (Turin, 1671)
Modo di misurare le fabbriche (Turin, 1674)
Trattato di fortificatione, che hora si usa in Fiandra, Francia & Italia (Turin, 1676)
Leges temporum, et planetarum quibus civilis (Turin, 1678/*R* Milan, 1683)
Coelestis mathematicae (Milan, 1683)
Disegni d'architettura civile et ecclesiastica (Turin, 1686/*R* Milan, 1966)
B. Vittone, ed.: *Architettura civile* (Turin, 1737/*R* Farnborough, 1964); ed. B. Tavassi La Greca (Milan, 1968)

BIBLIOGRAPHY

Macmillan Enc. Architects
T. Sandonnini: 'Il padre Guarino Guarini modenese', *Atti & Mem. RR. Deput. Stor. Patria Prov. Moden. & Parm.*, n. s. 2, v (1888), pp. 483–534
E. Olivero: 'La vita e l'arte del P. Guarino Guarini', *Duomo Torino*, ii/5 (1928), pp. 7–14
——: 'Gli scritti del P. Guarino Guarini', *Duomo Torino*, ii/6 (1928), pp. 5–9
G. Rigotti: 'La chiesa dell'Immacolata Concezione ora Cappella Arcivescovile in Torino', *Boll. Soc. Piemont. Archeol. & B.A.*, xvi (1932), pp. 56–73
A. E. Brinckmann: 'La grandezza di Guarino Guarini e la sua influenza sull'architettura in Germania nell '700', *Atti Soc. Piemont. Archeol. & B.A.*, xv (1933), pp. 348–74
D. Coffin: 'Padre Guarino Guarini in Paris', *J. Soc. Archit. Historians*, xv/2 (1956), pp. 3–11
R. Wittkower: *Art and Architecture in Italy, 1600–1750*, Pelican Hist. A. (Harmondsworth, 1958, rev. 4/1980), pp. 108–10, 271, 403–13
G. M. Crepaldi: *La real chiesa di San Lorenzo in Torino* (Turin, 1963)
M. Passanti: *Nel mondo magico di Guarino Guarini* (Turin, 1963)
H. Millon: *Guarino Guarini and the Palazzo Carignano in Turin* (diss., Cambridge, MA, Harvard U., 1964)
R. Pommer: *Eighteenth Century Architecture in Piedmont: The Open Structures of Juvarra, Alfieri and Vittone* (New York, 1967)
L. Tamburini: *Le chiese di Torino dal rinascimento al barocco* (Turin, 1968)
Guarino Guarini e l'internazionalità del barocco: Atti del convegno internazionale promosso dall'Accademia delle scienze di Torino: Torino, 1968 [with important articles by C. G. Argan, A. Lange, W. Müller, H. Millon, N. Carboneri, F. Tricomi and R. Wittkower]
E. C. Robison: *Guarino Guarini's Church of San Lorenzo in Turin* (diss., Ithaca, NY, Cornell U., 1985)
C. Müller: *Unendlichkeit und Transzendenz in der Sakralarchitektur Guarinis* (Hildeshiem, 1986)
H. A. Meek: *Guarino Guarini and his Architecture* (New Haven and London, 1988)

PETER STEIN

Guarino [Guarini]**, Francesco** (*b* Sant'Agata Irpina, nr Solofra, 1611; *d* Gravina di Puglia, 13 July 1654). Italian painter. He was first taught by his father, Giovanni Tommaso Guarino (*d* 1637), and then trained in the studio of Massimo Stanzione, during that painter's brief Caravaggesque phase, and responded to the naturalism of Giovanni Battisti Caracciolo, Filippo Vitale and the Roman Caravaggisti of the 1620s. Between *c.* 1630 and 1635 he painted his first important works, a series of canvases for the ceiling of the collegiate church of S Michele Arcangelo, Solofra. The earliest are the *Agony in the Garden* (in collaboration with his father), the *Liberation of St Peter*, a highly individual response to Caravaggio, *Joseph's Dream* and *Joseph Warned by the Angel*. In the same church the more richly composed *Christ among the Doctors* and *Circumcision*, distinguished by the weightier realism of the figures, reveal the influence of Jusepe de Ribera and Francesco Fracanzano. A little later, in the damaged *Annunciation to the Shepherds*, also in S Michele, the grave naturalism of the humble figures suggests the impact of Velázquez, who had been working in Italy between 1629 and 1631. Two paintings of the *Martyrdom of St Agatha*

(Sant'Agata Irpina, parish church) showing her tortured, one with burning coals and the other by having her breasts cut off, are from the same period; the figure types and the composition of the second seem to be directly inspired by Velázquez's *Bacchus and his Companions* (*c.* 1628; Madrid, Prado). In his later paintings of *St Agatha* (Moscow, Pushkin Mus. F.A.; *c.* 1637, Naples, Capodimonte; see fig.) Guarino explored the type of female half-length study introduced by Simon Vouet and Massimo Stanzione, focusing on the refined sensuality of the subject, whom he portrayed with one shoulder bare, languidly holding a blood-stained cloth to her mutilated breasts.

Later Guarino, in such works as the *Immaculate Conception* (1637; Solofra, S Michele) and the elegant *Annunciation* (1642; Solofra, S Michele), developed, like many Neapolitan painters of the 1630s, a brighter, warmer palette, indebted to Venetian colour. He also painted small pictures, such as the nine scenes from the *Life of St Anthony Abbot* (1642; Campobasso, Sant'Antonio Abate). The altarpiece in this church, the *Miracle of St Benedict*, with, above it, the *Pietà* (1643) and the pair of pictures *Esau Selling his Birthright* and *Isaac Blessing Jacob* (1640–42; Pommersfelden, Schloss Weissenstein), bear a complex relationship to Stanzione and Ribera. The two stories of Jacob, with three-quarter-length figures, unite a powerful naturalism with a new formal clarity. The paintings are richly decorative and sumptuous fabrics are rendered in brilliant blues, bright reds and yellows.

The increasing influence on Guarino of the more elegant, academic style of Stanzione is apparent in the two versions of the *Madonna of the Rosary* (1644, retouched by the artist in 1649, Solofra, S Domenico; and 1645, Nocera Inferiore, S Maria di Materdomini) and in the *Madonna del Suffragio* (*c.* 1649; Gravina di Puglia, Chiesa del Suffragio). The more classical style of his last works for S Michele at Solofra, the *Baptism*, the *Assumption* and *Christ among the Angels*, show the increasing influence of Poussin, Domenichino and Francesco Cozza. Guarino's most important patrons were the Orsini family of Gravina and Solofra, and many of his paintings remain in their Neapolitan palace. He died at their court, involved, according to de Dominici, in a crime of passion.

Francesco Guarino: *St Agatha*, oil on canvas, 870×715 mm, *c.* 1637 (Naples, Museo e Gallerie Nazionali di Capodimonte)

BIBLIOGRAPHY

Thieme–Becker
B. de Dominici: *Vite* (1742–3), iii, pp. 104–6
R. Causa: *La pittura del seicento a Napoli dal naturalismo al barocco*, v/2 of *Storia di Napoli* (Cava dei Tirreni, 1972), pp. 931–2, 933–41, passim
G. Rubsamen: *The Orsini Inventories* (Malibu, 1980)
R. Lattuada: 'Problemi di filologia e di committenza nelle opere di Francesco Guarino alla Collegiata di San Michele Arcangelo a Solofra', *An. Fac. Lett. & Filos. U. Napoli*, n. s. 11, xxiii (1980–81), pp. 115–46
——: 'Opere di Francesco Guarino a Campobasso', *Prospettiva*, xxxi (Oct 1982), pp. 50–69
V. de Martini: 'A Solofra: F. Guarino', *Restauri a Solofra: La Collegiata di San Michele* (Rome, 1982), pp. 46–71
Painting in Naples, 1606–1705: From Caravaggio to Giordano (exh. cat., ed. C. Whitfield and J. Martineau; London, RA; Washington, DC, N.G.A.; Paris, Grand Pal.; 1982–3), pp. 181–6
V. Pugliese: *Pittura napoletana in Puglia*, i of *Seicento napoletano: Arte–Costume–Ambiente* (Milan, 1984), pp. 198, 220, 235–9, passim
Civiltà del seicento a Napoli (exh. cat., Naples, 1984), i, pp. 154–5, 324–32
V. Pacelli, ed.: *I dipinti del Guarino e le arti decorative nella Collegiata di Solofra* (Naples, 1987)
Escales du Baroque (exh. cat., Marseille; Paris; 1988)

RICCARDO LATTUADA

Guarino da Verona (*b* Verona, 1374; *d* Ferrara, 4 Dec 1460). Italian humanist and educator. He was one of the great humanist teachers of the 15th century. Having studied in Verona, Padua and Venice, Guarino was among the first Italian scholars to visit Constantinople, where he studied Greek from 1403 to 1408, living part of the time in the household of the neo-Platonic philosopher Manuel Chrysoloras (1350–1415). Laden with Greek manuscripts, Guarino returned to Italy via Rhodes and Chios in 1409, stayed in Venice for a short period, moved to Verona (1409–10) and finally settled in Florence, where he was employed as a Greek tutor (1410–14). Between 1414 and 1419 he was teaching in Venice and in 1419 he opened a private school in Verona. In 1429 Guarino was summoned to Ferrara by Niccolò III d'Este as tutor for his son Leonello. He remained there until his death.

Guarino was the author of numerous translations from the Greek, commentaries on both Greek and Latin authors and the biographies of Homer and Plato. His Latin translation of Lucian's *Calumny*, with its ekphrasis of Apelles' painting of the subject, served as the model for Alberti's account in *De pictura* (1435). He also wrote a very influential Latin grammar, the *Regulae grammaticae.* Under Guarino's aegis, Ferrara became an active centre for humanist study and learning. Pope Pius II described him as '. . . the teacher of almost all who have attained distinction in the humanities in our day'.

There are two slightly varying accounts of Guarino's response to the visual arts. The persona given Guarino in his pupil Angelo Decembrio's *De politia litteraria*, much of which is corroborated by opinions set forth by Guarino himself in his correspondence, shows him to be dismissive of the expressive potential of the visual arts. In a *paragone* between the visual arts and literature, the latter is clearly superior in every way. In Bartolommeo Fazio's *De viris illustribus*, however, Guarino is credited with favourable views concerning the *ars*, *varietas* and *expressio* of such painters as Rogier van der Weyden, Jan van Eyck, Lorenzo Ghiberti, Donatello, Pisanello and Gentile da Fabriano. Guarino may have considered the visual arts inferior to literature; nevertheless, at a practical level he seems to have played an active part in the promotion of all aspects of the visual arts in Ferrara. He supplied iconographic formulae for Leonello's artistic commissions, such as the *studiolo* at Belfiore (destr.) painted by Cosimo Tura and Angelo del Maccagnino, wrote prose and verse panegyrics in praise of contemporary artists (most notably, a poem extolling Pisanello's skill), seems to have played a major role in the development of the humanist portrait-medal (Lippincott, 1990) and may have been the intellectual impetus behind much of Alberti's writings on art. Baxandall (1965) has suggested that Guarino's model of ekphrasis, based on Philostratos the younger's *Eikones*, as the appropriate form in which to discuss Renaissance works of art may have played a significant role in setting the stylistic criteria for much of northern Italian art of the 15th century. There are also indications that certain aspects of the iconographic programmes of Ferrarese decorative cycles, such as the Salone dei Mesi in the Palazzo Schifanoia, may have been constructed in accordance with Guarino's pedagogical methods.

Guarino was depicted on a medal by Matteo de' Pasti (Washington, DC, N.G.A.) and in a manuscript of Guarino's Latin translation of Strabo's *Geographia* (Albi, Bib. Rochegude, MS. 4).

WRITINGS

R. Sabbadini, ed.: *Epistolario* (Venice, 1915–19)

A. Manetti, ed.: *Carmina* (Bergamo, 1985)

BIBLIOGRAPHY

B. Fazio: *De viris illustribus* (MS., 1456; Florence, 1745)

A. Decembrio: *De politia litteraria* (MS., 1462; Augsburg, 1540; Basle, 2/1562)

A. S. Piccolomini (Pius II): *Commentarii* (MS. before 1464); ed. and It. trans. by L. Totaro, i (Milan, 1984), pp. 408–9; selected Eng. trans. by F. A. Gragg as *Memoirs of a Renaissance Pope: The Commentaries of Pius II* (New York, 1959; London, 1960)

C. de' Rosmini: *Vita e disciplina di Guarino Veronese e de' suoi discepoli* (Brescia, 1805–6)

R. Sabbadini: *Vita di Guarino Veronese* (Genoa, 1891/*R* Turin, 1964)

——: *La scuola e gli studi de Guarino Guarini Veronese* (Catania, 1896/*R* Turin, 1964)

W. H. Woodward: *Studies in Education during the Age of the Renaissance, 1400–1600* (Cambridge, 1906/*R* New York, 1965), pp. 26–47

G. Bertoni: *Guarino da Verona. Fra letterati e cortigiani a Ferrara (1429–1460)* (Geneva, 1921)

R. Sabbadini: *Il metodo degli umanisti* (Florence, 1922)

M. Baxandall: 'A Dialogue on Art from the Court of Leonello d'Este: Angelo Decembrio's *De politia litteraria* Pars LXVIII', *J. Warb. & Court. Inst.*, xxvi (1963), pp. 304–26

——: 'Guarino, Pisanello and Manuel Chrysoloras', *J. Warb. & Court. Inst.*, xxviii (1965), pp. 183–204

——: *Giotto and the Orators: Humanist Observers of Painting in Italy and the Discovery of Pictorial Composition, 1350–1450* (Oxford, 1971, rev. 2/1986), pp. 39–41, 87–96, 138–9, 154–60

R. Schwegen: *Guarino Veronese. Philosophie und humanistische Pädagogik* (Munich, 1973)

A. K. Eörsi: 'Lo studiolo di Lionello d'Este e il programma di Guarino da Verona', *Acta Hist. A. Acad. Sci. Hung.*, xxi (1975), pp. 15–52

A. T. Grafton and L. Jardine: 'Humanism and the School of Guarino: A Problem of Evaluation', *Past & Present*, xcvi (1982), pp. 51–80; also in A. Grafton and L. Jardine: *From Humanism to the Humanities: Education and the Liberal Arts in Fifteenth- and Sixteenth-century Europe* (Cambridge, MA, 1986), pp. 1–28

K. Lippincott: 'The Genesis and Significance of the Fifteenth-century Italian *Impresa*', *Chivalry in the Renaissance*, ed. S. Anglo (Woodbridge, 1990), pp. 49–76

——: 'The Iconography of the *Salone dei Mesi* and the Study of Latin Grammar in Fifteenth-century Ferrara', *La corte di Ferrara e il suo mecenatismo, 1441–1598*, ed. M. Pade and others (Modena, 1990), pp. 93–109

KRISTEN LIPPINCOTT

Guarinoni, Hyppolytus [Guarinonius, Hippolytus] (*b* Trent, Tyrol, 18 Nov 1571; *d* Hall in Tyrol, 31 May 1654). Austrian doctor, theologian and amateur architect-builder. He wrote prolifically about living habits and health: his main work, *Die Grewel der Verwüstung des menschlichen Geschlechts*, was printed in Ingolstadt in 1610.

Documentary sources indicate that Guarinoni originated the design for the Karl-Borromäuskirche (1620–54) at Volders in the Tyrol; he supervised the construction himself, worked on the site as a mason and in other ways, and invested the whole of his considerable fortune in the building. The squat, centrally planned building with its original, imaginative, picturesquely evocative style has a wealth of odd design details that give it a peculiar, exotic charm.

Guarinoni based his church on the symbolic concept of the Trinity: to the circular central space he adjoined three semicircular domed spaces to incorporate chapels and a choir, and to the west a projecting bay, on to which dome-covered chapels were later built. The tower to the east with its circular core and semicircular projections repeats the pattern of this ground-plan on a reduced scale. The inspiration for this building can be found not only in Rome, in the works of Francesco Borromini (although Guarinoni's forms are simpler), but principally in the Bohemian Mannerism of Carlo Lurago (ii) in Prague (where Guarinoni had spent several years) or in the mausoleum of Emperor Ferdinand II at Graz. The Karl-Borromäuskirche was not, however, based directly on one model. As a dilettante, Guarinoni could ignore the normal rules of architecture and give his imagination free rein. The Volders church may, in its turn, have provided the inspiration for the design by Konstantin Pader (1610–81) of the brilliantly original pilgrimage church of Maria Birnbaum (1661–5) near Aichach, likewise centralized, and even for the Dreifaltigkeitkirche (begun 1684) by Georg Dientzenhofer (1643–89) at Kappel, Upper Palatinate.

Two other chapels, one in Volderwildbad (founded 1625, ded. SS Cosmas and Damian) and another in Baumkirchen (*c*. 1650, ded. St Anne), are attributed to Guarinoni, though there is no proof of his involvement, despite the manifest similarities between these chapels and the Karl-Borromäuskirche, especially as regards the characteristic coursework, structure and the highly original curving of the walls.

BIBLIOGRAPHY

K. Koch: *Hippolytus Guarinoni* (diss., Innsbruck, Leopold-Franzens U., 1925)

H. Hammer: 'Ein Baudilettant des 17. Jahrhunderts in Tirol', *Innsbruck. Nachr.* (1928) [jubilee issue]

R. Klebelberg, ed.: 'Hippolytus Guarinonius (1571–1654)', *Schlern Schr.*, cxxvi (1954) [whole issue]

BRIGITTE SCHNEIDER

Juan Guas: façade of the Palacio del Infantado, Guadalajara, 1480–83; from an engraving by Jenaro Pérez Villaamil in *España artística y monumental* (Paris, 1842–3)

Guas, Juan [Jean] (*b* Saint Pol de Léon, Finistère, *c*. 1430; *d* Toledo, April 1496). French architect and possibly sculptor, active in Spain. He was the most prominent exponent of the Hispano-Flemish or Isabelline style. Guas was the son of the mason Pedro Guas, who arrived in Toledo from Brittany *c*. 1440 with the group of masons led by Hanequin de Bruselas, in whose workshop Juan Guas probably trained. His supposed brothers Enrique and Bonifacio, cited as assistants through the mistaken interpretation of an inscription and a document, never existed. In 1453 he was named as an assistant in the building of the Puerta de los Leones in Toledo Cathedral. In 1458 he was listed as a master mason in the cathedral accounts, and in the following year he married Marina Álvarez.

In 1471 Guas was appointed master mason of Ávila Cathedral, where his contribution to the porch is evident in the remaining inner side. The outer part was modified when it was moved to the north transept. In 1472 Juan Pacheco, Marqués de Villena (*d* 1474), the Grand Master of the Order of St James, summoned him to continue work on the capilla mayor of the monastery of El Parral in Segovia, which had been begun by Juan Gallego (*fl* 1459–72) in 1459. Guas was master mason of the old cathedral of Segovia from 1473 to 1491. The Flamboyant cloister was transferred to the present cathedral in the 16th century (*see* SEGOVIA, §2). Guas probably also worked on the monastery of El Paular (Madrid) at this time: his style is recognizable in the porch and cloister, with ogee arches and stalactite decoration, as well as the rich ornamentation, which is reminiscent of its Toledan models.

At about this time Guas must also have begun work on the Palacio del Infantado in Guadalajara, belonging to the powerful Mendoza–Infantado family. Previously he had worked for them at the castle of Manzanares el Real (from 1475), one of the most sumptuous palaces of this period. The contribution of Guas is of key importance, as Manzanares el Real is closely linked to the Palacio del Infantado (see fig.; *see also* GUADALAJARA, PALACIO DEL INFANTADO). The Palacio was badly damaged during the Civil War, although the restored façade survives, as well as the series of arches in the courtyard; the rich *Mudéjar* ceilings of its reception rooms have disappeared. The unparalleled richness and magnificence of the Palacio del Infantado is described in the reports of the astonished travellers who visited it. Lost inscriptions dated the building to 1480–83, but work was still in progress in the 1490s.

Between 1483 and 1487 Guas was also in charge of work on the Hospedería Real in Guadalupe (destr.), the favourite retreat of Isabella, Queen of Castile and León. This perhaps ensured his appointment as Master of the

Royal Works, which title was included in the inscription on his funeral chapel in SS Justo y Pastor, Toledo. Examples of Guas's civil architecture include his contribution to the palace of the Duke of Alba in Tormes (Salamanca) in 1493, of which traces remain. His most important work, however, was undoubtedly the monastery of S Juan de los Reyes in Toledo (*see* GOTHIC, fig. 26), which was commissioned by the Queen in 1476. It is a fundamental representative of the Hispano-Flemish style, its extraordinary sculptural richness contributed by Egas Cueman. The church has an aisleless, rib-vaulted nave with side chapels located between interior buttresses. Over the crossing is an octagonal *cimborio* with parallel ribs, as in the domes of the new Maqṣūra of the Mosque at Córdoba. The cloisters are in two storeys (*see* TOLEDO, fig. 3). Guas's carved decoration covers the piers and arcades like filigree work in stone. The style is a harmonious fusion of the Baroque forms of Flamboyant Gothic with the decorative style of *Mudéjar* art.

From 1475 Guas is referred to as a master at Toledo Cathedral, and in 1484 he was appointed warden (deputy) to the master mason Martín Sánchez Bonifacio. The decoration of the *trascoro* was begun in 1483 but completed only in 1493, with the collaboration of, among others, Egas Cueman. In 1487 Guas and his assistant Juan de Talavera (*fl* 1487–1520) built the chapel in the Colegio de S Gregorio in Valladolid (for illustration *see* HISPANO-FLEMISH STYLE). The founder of the College, Fray Alonso de Burgos, was dissatisfied with the building, but it introduced the Toledan style to Old Castile. Although Guas made his will on 11 October 1490, he was appointed master mason of Toledo Cathedral in 1491 or 1492, and in 1494 he took part in a masonic Expertise on El Parral in Segovia, as well as work on S Juan de los Reyes, which was to be evaluated later by Simón de Colonia. His last documented work, early in 1495, was his design for the staircase of Don Pedro Tenorio in the cloister of Toledo Cathedral, and that year he acquired the funeral chapel for his burial in SS Justo y Pastor.

Although firm evidence is lacking, Guas may also have been a sculptor, as in 1492 he was mentioned in connection with sculptures that he failed to execute for the monastery of S Agustin in Seville, and his daughters received requests for sculptures that he failed to execute for Valladolid. Certain tombs in Ávila Cathedral are attributed to him. His constant sculptural collaborators were Egas Cueman and Sebastián de Toledo. Guas produced the most interesting architecture in late medieval Spain, fusing Gothic and *Mudéjar* forms typical of Castilian culture in the Late Gothic period. In spite of their profuse decoration, the form and strength of his architectural designs are always clearly visible. As master mason of the three important cathedrals and architect to the house of Mendoza–Infantado and to Ferdinand II, King of Sicily and Aragón, and Queen Isabella, he was able to influence stylistically the whole of Castile, forming the link between Hanequín de Bruselas, Antón Egas and Enrique Egas.

BIBLIOGRAPHY

Macmillan Enc. Architects

G. Weise: *Studien zur spanischen Architektur der Spätgotik* (Reutlingen, 1933)

F. Layna Serrano: *El palacio del Infantado en Guadalajara* (Madrid, 1941)

J. M. Azcárate: 'El supuesto Bonifacio Guas', *Archv Esp. A.*, xxii (1949), pp. 83–4

——: 'El origen de Juan Guas', *Archv Esp. A.*, xxiii (1950), pp. 255–6

——: 'La fachada del Infantado y el estilo de Juan Guas', *Archv Esp. A.*, xxiv (1951), pp. 307–19

——: 'La obra toledana de Juan Guas', *Archv Esp. A.*, xxix (1956), pp. 9–42

——: *La arquitectura gótica toledana del siglo XV* (Madrid, 1958)

F. Arribas: 'Noticias sobre San Juan de los Reyes', *Bol. Semin. Estud. A. & Arqueol.*, xxix (1963)

A. Herrera Casado: *El palacio del Infantado* (Guadalajara, 1975)

J. M. Azcárate: *Datos histórico-artísticos de fines del siglo XV y principios del XVI*, Colección de documentos para la historia del arte en España, ii (Zaragoza and Madrid, 1982)

J. M. AZCÁRATE RISTORI

Guasparri di Spinello. *See* SPINELLI, (2).

Guaspre, Le. *See* DUGHET, GASPARD.

Guastavino (y Moreno), Rafael (*b* Valencia, 1842; *d* Asheville, NC, 2 Feb 1908). Spanish architect and engineer, active in the USA. After winning a medal for design at the Philadelphia Centennial (1876), he settled in the USA in 1881 to develop his system of vault construction. In 1888 he was awarded the contract for the vaulting of McKim, Mead & White's Boston Public Library, which proved a great success and launched his business. In 1899 he established the Guastavino Fireproof Construction Company. The Guastavino vault perfected the Catalan system of *bovedas tabicadas* or tile vaults, the kind used extensively by Antoni Gaudí. These vaults are made of highly fired tiles laid in a herringbone pattern in a tenacious mortar; three or four layers are applied over each other, with the pattern staggered so that no joint lies over another. The strength of the Guastavino vault arises from its curvature of surface and stiffness, not from its mass as in traditional vaulting; high-quality standardized tiles were combined with very strong Portland cement mortar. The rise of Guastavino's company was closely linked with that of McKim, Mead & White, and domes with Guastavino vaults were used in that firm's New York University Library (1897), the restoration (1898–9) of Thomas Jefferson's Rotunda at the University of Virginia, the Brooklyn Museum (1903–4), New York, the Bank of Montreal (1904), New York, and the Madison Square Presbyterian Church (1905–6; destr.), New York. Guastavino's son Rafael Guastavino y Esposito (1872–1950) continued to develop the technique, as in the vast dome for the crossing of the Cathedral of St John the Divine (1908–11), New York, the largest dome ever built without scaffolding. He also worked closely with Wallace Clement Sabine (1868–1919) to develop a patented sound-absorbing masonry tile, 'Akoustolith', which was used in many churches in the 1920s.

WRITINGS

Essay on the Theory and History of Cohesive Construction (Boston, 1893)

BIBLIOGRAPHY

P. B. Wight: 'The Life and Works of Rafael Guastavino', *Brickbuilder*, x (1901), pp. 79–81, 100–02, 184–8, 211–14

G. R. Collins: 'The Transfer of Thin Masonry Vaulting from Spain to America', *J. Soc. Archit. Hist.*, xxvii (1968), pp. 176–201

LELAND M. ROTH

Guatemala, Republic of. Central American country, bordered on the north and west by Mexico, on the north-east by Belize and on the south-east by El Salvador and Honduras. The Pacific Ocean forms a coastline 250 km long to the south-west and the Caribbean Sea a shorter coast to the north-east (see fig. 1). The capital is GUATEMALA CITY (formerly Nueva Guatemala or Guatemala de la Asunción), although before its foundation in 1776 the capital was Santiago de Guatemala (founded 1527), which, following a landslide in 1541, was relocated (1543) several kilometres away on the site of present-day ANTIGUA. Despite the country's relatively small size, it can be divided into three distinct geographical areas: the lowlands in the north (comprising about a third of the country's territory); the central, mountainous highlands; and the southern coastal plain. The lowlands contain notable classic Maya

1. Map of Guatemala; those areas with separate entries in this dictionary are distinguished by CROSS-REFERENCE TYPE

archaeological sites (*see* MAYA, §1). The highlands include two more or less parallel mountain ranges: to the north the Sierra de los Cuchumatanes and to the south the Sierra Madre. A chain of *c.* 30 volcanoes runs across the latter, some still active. The southern part of the country is subject to earthquakes, which have influenced its architecture (*see* §III below). The abundant stone in Guatemala is not of a quality sufficient for building, although in the late 20th century marble was found in the middle valley of the River Motagua. There is a good supply of clay, which is used for domestic utensils, brick and tile. The highlands are fertile in conifers and the lowlands in precious woods, such as mahogany, which have been used for building and for furniture.

I. Introduction. II. Indigenous culture. III. Architecture. IV. Painting, graphic arts and sculpture. V. Textiles. VI. Gold and silver. VII. Ceramics. VIII. Furniture. IX. Patronage, collecting and dealing. X. Museums, art libraries and photographic collections. XI. Art education.

I. Introduction.

The region was part of the Maya civilization until the Spanish conquest (1524–35; for a discussion of the art and architecture of Pre-Columbian Guatemala, *see* MAYA, §§1 and 2). Under the Spanish it formed part of the Kingdom of Guatemala or Audencia de Guatemala, which included the modern Mexican state of Chiapas, together with the territories now occupied by Costa Rica, Nicaragua, El Salvador and Honduras. The economy was largely based on agriculture, with limited mining resources. The population included Spanish, mestizo (mixed race), black, and indigenous Indian people, this last group forming the majority. Independence was achieved in 1821 without great military campaigns. From 1823 to 1838 the former colonial region (without Chiapas) operated as the Federación de Central América and then separated definitively into the five Central American Republics. Guatemalan independence was formally declared in 1847. The 19th century was marked by long-term administrations, first a conservative, pro-Catholic one (1838–71), then for the rest of the century a liberal, progressive and anti-clerical regime. Until 1944 the government was dominated by the heirs of liberalism, with continued anti-clericalism and restrictions on democracy. From 1945, with varying success, efforts were made to modernize the country and to make it more democratic. Under populist governments (1945–54) a new, democratic constitution was introduced, together with legislation affecting the distribution of land and working conditions. Thereafter these efforts were compromised by periods of great violence, including guerrilla and counter-guerrilla warfare. In the late 20th century the country underwent a difficult period in pursuit of socio-economic development in the face of an enormous demographic growth, from an estimated 2.7 million in 1950 to *c.* 9.5 million in 1990. There was also a significant growth in Protestantism, and Guatemala became the Latin American country with the largest proportion (30%) of non-Catholics in its population.

BIBLIOGRAPHY

E. Chinchilla Aguilar: *Historia del arte en Guatemala: Arquitectura, pintura y escultura* (Guatemala City, 1963, rev. 1965)

H. Berlin: 'Artistas y artesanos coloniales de Guatemala: Notas para un catálogo', *Cuad. Antropol.*, v (1965), pp. 5–35

J. Alonso de Rodríguez, ed.: *Arte contemporáneo occidente Guatemala* (Guatemala City, 1966)

L. Luján Muñoz: *Síntesis de la arquitectura en Guatemala* (Guatemala City, 1968, rev. 1972)

P. Gerhard: 'Colonial New Spain, 1519–1786: Historical Notes on the Evolution of Minor Political Jurisdictions, XVI. Guatemala', *Hb. Mid. Amer. Ind.*, xii, pt 1 (1972), pp. 129–32

M. J. MacLeod: *Spanish Central America: A Socioeconomic History, 1520–1720* (Berkeley and Los Angeles, CA, 1973)

J. A. Móbil: *Historia del arte guatemalteco* (Guatemala City, 1974/*R* 1977)

J. Alonso de Rodríguez: *Plateros y batihojas* (1981), ii of *El arte de la platería en la Capitanía General de Guatemala* (Guatemala City, 1980–81) [specialist discussion of silverwork]

JORGE LUJÁN-MUÑOZ

II. Indigenous culture.

About 42% of Guatemala's inhabitants are Indian descendants of the builders of the Maya civilization, which was at its peak *c.* AD 250–*c.* 900. On the arrival of the Spanish, the Maya kingdoms were gradually conquered. Nevertheless certain indigenous traditions remained, including an architectural one. Despite suffering through the import of diseases during the 16th and 17th centuries, the indigenous population grew again slowly following independence. By the late 20th century there was an increase in the number of Indians entering non-agricultural occupations and the emergence of an Indian intellectual sector, with massive migration to cities.

In the first recognizable period of indigenous artistic production following the Spanish conquest (*c.* 1524–1600), the long Maya pictorial tradition came close to a dramatic termination with the population being forced into *reducciones* (settlements) for easier religious and tax control. The Catholic Church's zeal for massive indoctrination into the new faith led to a systematic destruction of pagan sculptural and architectural works, murals, codices and pictorial books. Ancient cities that had been abandoned began to decay, and palaces and temples were robbed of their valuable art objects. Art in the pre-conquest Maya tradition continued only in remote places away from the Spanish. Notable examples of this include the large pictorial polychromatic wall paintings in some huts in Chajul in the department of Quiche.

By the second period (*c.* 1600–*c.* 1773) the Indians had been christianized, resettled and protected by laws that diminished abuse and interference from the Spaniards. A new form of community organization developed around a patron saint that first complemented but later obliterated Pre-Columbian organizations. The *cofradías*, hierarchically organized religious associations, paralleled and complemented the political–administrative organization. Their devoted members clothed and decorated the saints' images and celebrated their holy days with processions and theatrical dances, for which they produced elaborate masks representing animals, Spaniards or other themes and other paraphernalia. Women's artistic contributions were considerable, since the decorations for these festivities depended heavily on textile-making and sewing, although women did not participate in dancing or other public representations. Indian men could engage in the making of religious ornamentation as carpenters, sculptors and painters, but fine imagery and painting were usually executed by licensed members of the trade unions of European origin. Earthquakes have destroyed most of the evidence of native contributions. However, the Indian influence in the Baroque church of S Andres Semetabaj with its superb polychrome façade is one of the best surviving examples.

After *c.* 1773 there was a consolidation of the Indian *municipio* (county), a social organization that developed from the *reducciones*, the protected and secluded *pueblos de Indios* and the parochial administration. The Indian *municipio* gradually acquired the characteristics of a little government. It gave the individual a self-identity, which had to be expressed by symbols easily recognizable by other Indians as well as by the rest of the population. Dress became in this way a very important and distinctive feature of each *municipio* (*see also* §V below). While differences in dress had been promoted by the Spaniards for easy identification, its cultural and socio-psychological relevance grew as the *municipio* developed as the first and often the only fatherland for its people. Dress was simple and of the dull colour of unpainted native fibres during the previous centuries. Increasing availability of new materials and vividly coloured threads coincided with the growing importance of the *municipio*. This was crucial for artistic development, because it made possible the casting of old mythological–religious themes and old and new designs into a semi-pictorial utilitarian art. At this late point in history the painting abilities of Pre-Columbian times were transferred from stone to cloth and dress, and from the hands of men to women.

However, after 1934 there was a progressive deterioration of the Indian *municipio* as a self-contained entity and a growing consciousness of national identity. The loosening of the *municipio* organization had a greater liberating effect on men. In 1930 Andres Curuchich (*b* 1891), an Indian from the town of Comalapa in the central highlands, rose to international fame by initiating a pictorial Primitivist tradition, which attracted many followers. Two aspects of this tradition are particularly interesting: for the first time in centuries the work was individually conceived, yet the painter used traditional themes, such as the landscape around the village, its streets, groups of people in the *municipio*'s costume, festivities or other collective social affairs, without emphasizing individual features. The artist had, therefore, become sufficiently free from *municipio* tradition, which blurred individuality, to be able to objectivize its powerful binding force. Improvements in communication made it possible for *Ladinos* (non-Indians) to settle in increasing numbers among Indians. The *Ladinos* brought new technology, information, forms of production and commercial activity. The national revolution and the changes it brought allowed the Indians to participate in the national political life and establish the basis for a significant improvement of their education and the expansion of a national network of telecommunications and transportation. Most men adopted European dress, and women, more traditionally bound and less educated, used dress from other *municipios* as well as from their own, following fashion and personal taste rather than tradition.

A. MÉNDEZ

III. Architecture.

1. 1524–1821. 2. After 1821.

1. 1524–1821. During the period of Spanish rule in Guatemala most building was religious. A cathedral was completed in the first capital of Santiago de Guatemala by 1539 but lost when the settlement was carried away in a landslide in 1541. The wattle and adobe structures of early colonial buildings had roofs supported on timber and covered in thatch or palm leaves. Traditional skills in burnished plasterwork were applied to the stucco surfacing of the retable façades of numerous Catholic churches. Though often reinforced with brick or stone, the rubble structures were unfortunately too fragile to withstand earthquakes, and little has survived from the 16th and 17th centuries. Stucco surfaces and thatched roofs could be quickly restored as the occasion arose, however, and designers soon began to adapt practice to local conditions. The unique transition of Spanish styles was superimposed on the simple local techniques of building. In the mid-16th century, for example, there were still references to the Romanesque, as in the cloisters of the church of S Cristóbal Totonicapán; Gothic details can be found alongside early Renaissance forms, often with Plateresque surface treatment and *Mudéjar* elements in both interior and exterior design. In spite of frequent rebuilding, the standard Spanish grid-iron town plan, centred on a main square, has survived in the towns and cities of the earthquake zone as elsewhere. Antigua is said to have been laid out by an architect of Italian origin, Juan Bautista Antonelli the elder (*d* 1588), on a grand scale with fountains supplied from nearby mineral springs.

A characteristic example of mid-17th-century buildings for the religious orders in the capital was the Hospital de S Pedro Apóstol (1645–65), begun by Juan Pasqual (1628–*c.* 1660) and continued by Joseph de Porres (*see* PORRES), the Guatemalan architect who dominated the last third of the 17th century. He built the first vaulted cathedral in Guatemala (1666–9). During the 17th century there was also a zeal for renovation and replacement of earlier, less substantial buildings. Brickwork replaced adobe, naves were wider and higher, and façades more imposing in scale. The cathedral of Santiago de Guatemala (now Antigua) was rebuilt as a vaulted three-naved church with a dome at the crossing (1663–80). Joseph de Porres worked on it from 1670 until its completion (damaged in earthquake, 1717; restored by Diego de Porres, 1721; severely damaged and abandoned, 1773). Only the bases of the towers remain, but the classically composed Renaissance façade, said to be based on a model by Sebastiano Serlio, also displays a certain Baroque exuberance in the multiplicity of niches between each of four pairs of coupled giant-order columns, which rise through two-storeys and continue above the entablature to enclose a boldly voluted top storey. Joseph de Porres, appointed Arquitecto Mayor by the city fathers in 1687, moved slowly away from classical models towards early Baroque forms: features such as salomonic columns appear only in later buildings such as the church of S Francisco (completed 1698), Antigua, on which Ramón de Autillo had worked in the 1670s. Porres was also responsible for the church of Belén

(1678), the church and monastery of S Teresa (1683–7) and the church of La Compañía de Jesús (1698), all in Antigua. The church of La Merced (1650–90), Antigua, is perhaps the most characteristic example of the city's architecture. Parts of the rubble walls of this three-naved, vaulted and domed church are 3 m thick and survived well in the earthquake of 1773. Sturdy columns with Baroque spiral decoration to the lower (Tuscan) order frame the niches of a two-storey classical façade. The third (octagonal) storeys of the massive towers show examples of the new bolster (*almobadillado*) pilasters, and the second-storey pilasters simulate inverted lyres. The invention of new forms of pilaster was one of the hallmarks of 17th–18th-century Guatemalan architecture. The bolster pilasters of El Calvario (1655; destr. 1717; reconstructed 1720), Antigua, were among the first. Other buildings in Antigua of that period that incorporated pilasters were S Clara, Santa Cruz, San José, S Rosa de Lima and S Ana. The range came to include inverted urns and back-to-back volutes among other decorative forms.

The individual development of Baroque is associated with Diego de Porres in the first half of the 18th century and José Manuel Ramírez (*see* RAMÍREZ, (1)) in the second. The former became Arquitecto Mayor on his father Joseph's death, and he was himself succeeded in the post by Ramírez in 1743. In 1717, the year of a major earthquake, Porres completed one of the largest convents in Antigua, the Colegio de Cristo Crucificado or La Recolección, begun by his father in 1693. He was appointed also to assess the damage in the city and to repair many of the buildings, including the cathedral. Important commissions over the succeeding decades included the oratory of S Felipe Neri (1720–30), the Real Casa de Moneda (1734–8), and convents and churches for the Capuchins (1731–6), all in Antigua. His work culminated in the largest building of 18th-century Guatemala, the sanctuary at Esquipulas, in the east near the borders with El Salvador and Honduras (see fig. 2). Like Guadalupe in Mexico and Copacabana in Bolivia, Esquipulas was probably a popular place of pilgrimage before the Spanish arrival. A small church was built there to house the *Christ of Esquipulas* (1595) by Quirio Cataño (*fl* 1594–1617), and it was the growing popularity of the pilgrimage to Esquipulas that necessitated so vast a building in so remote a place. Completed (1759) by Diego's son Felipe, who supervised the work after 1740, the church is raised on a mighty podium with a squat four-storey tower at each of its four corners and has a narrow three-storey façade, the cornices of which are out of line with those on the towers. A flat dome, finials at each level of the towers and a large multi-foil arch above the portal are expressions of continuing *Mudéjar* influence. *Mudéjar* influence is also apparent in the work of José Manuel Ramírez in the new building for the Universidad de S Carlos (licensed to grant degrees, 1676), previously housed in the Dominican college of St Thomas Aquinas. The new buildings (1763–73), adjacent to the Seminario Tridentino (*c.* 1758; designed by Ramírez), were restored in the late 19th century. Other mid-18th-century civil buildings in Antigua include the Real Cabildo (1740–43) and the later Real Palacio (1758–68), probably the work of the military engineer Luis Díez Navarro, who came to Guatemala from Mexico in 1741.

2. Sanctuary at Esquipulas, probably by Diego de Porres, completed 1759

The buildings face each other across the Plaza Mayor. Both reflect the style adopted for government buildings in the Spanish colonies: both have two-storey arcades facing the square. The former is constructed in stone and has a sober air; an Italianate cupola was added to the tower in the 19th century. Private dwellings in Antigua include the well-known Casa de los Leones (architect unknown), with its massive stone portal flanked by salomonic columns and high-relief rampant lions, and the Casa de Chamorro (1762; also by Díez Navarro), a more typical urban Baroque house with an arcaded patio.

Of the many churches of this period in Antigua, El Carmen (1728; rebuilt after 1717 earthquake; now in ruins) is unusual for the in-depth arrangement of many columns on both storeys of the façade and the Plateresque patterning around the portal and on upper-storey columns: the Hermitage church of Santa Cruz (rebuilt 1731–45) has 18th-century overall stucco decoration but combines a Renaissance style with Baroque features such as the bolster pilasters of the upper storey. An interesting example outside Antigua is the church at Jocotenango, which has a two-storey, classically arranged façade with a polygonal window flanked by bolster pilasters above the portal; elsewhere coupled salomonic columns frame the niches. The church was designed by Bernardo Ramírez (*see* RAMÍREZ, (2)), son of José Manuel, and was in process of construction at the time of the severe earthquake of 1773.

Guatemala City was begun in 1776, and the Neo-classical style was introduced almost immediately by the Spanish architect Marcos Ibañez (assisted by Antonio Bernasconi) in the design for the new cathedral. The execution of the work was taken over by PEDRO GARCI-AGUIRRE in 1802 and Santiago Marquí after 1805, and the cathedral (though uncompleted) was dedicated on 16 January 1813. However, Neo-classicism was slow to displace the local Baroque. Political unrest and economic difficulties slowed down the process of building a new city for over 30,000 displaced inhabitants of Antigua. Many buildings remained unfinished when Guatemala achieved independence in 1821.

2. AFTER 1821. The development of Guatemala City, the capital of the new independent Republic of Central America, and later of the Republic of Guatemala, was considerably delayed by political events in the 1830s and 1840s. Neo-classical buildings such as the cathedral and the church of S Francisco, however, were finally completed in the 1850s, the latter already beginning to show the influence of European academic classicism in its vast Corinthian portico. Few new buildings were begun during this period, though the Teatro Nacional, by Miguel Rivera-Maestre, begun in the 1830s, was completed in 1859 in modified form by an immigrant architect of German origin, José Beckers, in the classical style with a Tuscan order supporting a pediment on the main façade. Other important buildings in Guatemala City in the 1860s were the Mercado Central and the headquarters of the Sociedad Económica de Amigos de Guatemala, both by Julián Rivera.

When a new liberal regime acceded to power in 1871, it expropriated monasteries and put them to use as offices and schools, thus reducing the need for new buildings. Coffee was the main export crop, and new building was focused on roads and railways with their associated stations. The west of the country in particular benefited from the coffee industry: in Quetzaltenango the surge of construction of both public and private buildings was notable. There was a vigorously classical trend in designs based on Jacopo Vignola's treatise *Regola delli cinque ordini d'architettura* (Rome, 1562), using cut stones from nearby quarries and stonecutters brought over from Italy: outstanding examples were the Palacio Municipal, the Pasaje Henríquez, the Banco de Occidente and theatres in both Quetzaltenango and nearby Totonicapán. In the last decade of the century, building in Guatemala City included the Registro de la Propiedad Inmueble, and, as a result of the international fair held in 1897, a new boulevard, Avenida de la Reforma, was opened up and pavilions were built with roofs of imported steel and glass. The city was embellished in French taste—even sculptures imported from Europe were erected. Development continued beyond the turn of the century, after Quetzaltenango was partially destroyed by earthquakes in 1902.

The first two decades of the 20th century began (1901–2) and drew to an end (1917–18) with major earthquakes. Schools and hospitals were built after the first but did not

3. Skidmore, Owings & Merrill: Banco Occidente, Guatemala City, 1980

survive the second. More characteristic of the presidency (1898–1920) of Manuel Estrada Cabrera perhaps were the temples of Minerva, ostensibly built to honour the 'studious youth' of the country, and in which were held politically orientated fiestas to the goddess of learning and the arts. That in the capital (1901; destr. 1953), in the form of a Greco-Roman temple, boasted high-relief decoration by the Venezuelan sculptor Santiago González (*d* 1909), who was brought over expressly from Paris. After the presidency of Estrada Cabrera, there was a tendency to distance new designs from both the colonial tradition and the dominant classicism of the 19th century. In the decade of democratic government that followed, a number of astylar buildings emulated contemporary European rationalist trends: these included buildings for the Facultad de Medicina, the Corte Suprema de Justicia and the Edificio Sanidad Pública in Guatemala City and the Edificio Rivera in Quetzaltenango. During the government of Jorge Ubico(1931–44) there was a Spanish colonial revival. Important buildings of the period were the Central de Correos (1938), the Terminal Aérea (1942), the Palacio Nacional (1943) and the Policía Nacional (1944).

Thereafter, Guatemalan architecture gradually returned to Modernist lines. The so-called Olympic City (1950), a highly successful sports facility built in a ravine area, was a landmark in the urban development of the capital. In the 1950s and 1960s there followed a number of interesting buildings that subscribed to an experimental movement to integrate painting, sculpture and other art forms such as mosaics with architecture. Among these were the Palacio Municipal (1958), the Seguro Social building (1959), the Banco de Guatemala (1964) and the new Terminal Aérea (1969), all in Guatemala City. The Crédito Hipotecario Nacional (1964) and the Biblioteca Nacional (1965) are especially notable for concrete relief sculptures by the Guatemalan artist–engineer EFRAÍN RECINOS. His Gran Teatro (completed 1978) best demonstrates his originality and vigour in bringing together architecture and the other arts. Situated on a hilltop site in the middle of the city, it is conceived as a large-scale sculptural work in its own right, employing very original forms and decorated externally with mosaic.

The threat of earthquakes became less significant as anti-seismic building techniques in steel and reinforced concrete developed. Among the varied buildings using these new structural methods is the Hospital Nacional (1979), serving a rural area in western Guatemala. Consisting of 142 factory-built, steel-framed modules, it was designed by Mariani Associates of Washington, DC, and Robert Ziegelman of Birmingham, MI; the units were shipped from the USA ready for crane-assembly into a two- and three-storey 200-bed general hospital, the cold-rolled steel modules of which can readily articulate one with the other under seismic action. The urban Banco Occidente (1980) by Skidmore, Owings & Merrill (see fig. 3) is a simple three-storey rectilinear exposed reinforced concrete office building, its face set back from a sturdy street grid-façade reminiscent of Aldo Rossi's Gallaretese 2, Milan. A galleried patio, here rethought as an enclosed atrium, is part of the strategy of a building requiring no energy inputs for full operation in a city under reconstruction. Both buildings exemplify the significance of building regulations enacted to limit building heights, as well as a determination in both public and private sectors to make a virtue out of the necessity of appropriate technology against recurrent earthquakes.

BIBLIOGRAPHY

V. M. Díaz: *Las bellas artes en Guatemala* (Guatemala City, 1934)
P. Kelemen: 'Some Church Façades of Colonial Guatemala', *Gaz. B.-A.*, n. s. 5, xxvi/924 (1944), pp. 113–26
Catálogo del Museo Colonial de Antigua, Guatemala, Instituto de Antropología e Historia (Guatemala City, 1950)
P. Kelemen: *Baroque and Rococo in Latin America* (New York, 1951), pp. 39–40, 122–9, 133
D. Angulo Iñiguez, E. Marco Dorta and M. J. Buschiazzo: *Historia del arte hispano-americano*, 3 vols (Barcelona, 1945–56), iii (1956), pp. 1–17
E. Chinchilla Aguilar: *Historia del arte en Guatamala: Arquitectura, pintura y escultura* (Guatemala City, 1963, rev. 1965)
S. D. Markman: *Colonial Architecture of Antigua Guatemala* (Philadelphia, 1966)
V. L. Annis: *La arquitectura de Antigua Guatemala, 1543–1773* (Guatemala City, 1968)
L. Luján Muñoz: *Síntesis de la arquitectura en Guatemala* (Guatemala City, 1969)
B. Gauria: 'Prefabricated Modules Speed Hospital Construction', *Archit. Rec.*, clxv/4 (1979), pp. 141–3
'Banco de Occidente: SOM, Chicago', *Space Des.*, 221 (Feb 1983), pp. 52–3
T. Frisch: 'Reconstruction in Guatemala', *Archithèse*, xiv/5 (1984), pp. 10–12

IV. Painting, graphic arts and sculpture.

1. 1524–1821. 2. After 1821.

1. 1524–1821. The numerous churches built in the 16th century for both the Spanish and indigenous communities in Guatemala created an overwhelming demand for religious works of art executed in the approved manner. The first works arrived with the Spanish, who brought with them small-scale religious paintings and sculptures. They were followed by artists of mediocre ability who came over from Spain. In the principal Guatemalan cities these artists and artisans reproduced the guild organization of the Spanish mainland, especially of Castile and Andalusia, where most originated. Gradually the membership of these changed from being composed of artists of Spanish origin to include artists of mestizo, indigenous or African descent, no doubt the result of the continuing shortage of skilled artists and the indifference manifested by the Spanish for manual work, when more prestigious posts in colonial society were available to them. By 1600 Indian artists were also beginning to recover a sense of purpose after the systematic disparagement of their art by Roman Catholic missionaries (*see also* §II above).

The arts that thrived best were painting and sculpture, which were in continuous demand. Every new church required several altars and retables, each of which was adorned with paintings and sculptures. In an environment of mass production, only a few painters and sculptors maintained high standards. Of these, one of the earliest known painters was Pedro de Liendo y Salazar (*fl* 1615–26), active in Santiago de Guatemala (now Antigua). Other painters included Francisco Montúfar (*fl* 1611–50) and, later in the century, members of the de Merlo family, and Blas de Mesa (*fl* late 17th century), who worked in the Comayagua region of Honduras. Guatemalan painters generally followed Spanish and European trends, which they absorbed through engravings, books or through Mexican painters, such as CRISTÓBAL DE VILLALPANDO who painted a cycle of the *Life of St Francis* for the Franciscan convent at Santiago de Guatemala (1691; now at Antigua, Mus. Colon.). Although there was some wall painting in the 16th century, this soon diminished, and works were done in oils on canvas, or less frequently on panel or copper. Guatemalan sculptors received more attention, examples of their work being exported to Mexico and even Spain. These were religious effigies carved from wood and elaborately covered with gold (*dorado*) and colours to produce a vivid effect of reality, including the prized *encarnado* (Sp. flesh-colour); comparatively few sculptures were of plaster or stone. Among the recorded names of sculptors are Juan de Aguirre (*fl* mid-16th century); Quirio Cataño (*fl* 1594–1617), whose *Christ of Esquipulas* (1594–5; Esquipulas Church) is a celebrated example; Pedro de Brizuela (*fl* 1600); and later Alonso de la Paz (*fl* mid-17th century) and MATEO DE ZÚÑIGA. Painters, sculptors, carpenters (*ensambladores*) and decorators (*estofadores*) collaborated on the production of retables, for which Guatemala was a regional centre throughout the colonial period (*see* RETABLE, §2). Among the leading 18th-century practitioners were members of the GÁLVEZ family.

The centre of artistic life in Guatemala was initially at Santiago de Guatemala (now ANTIGUA) and then, after the capital's transfer, at Nueva Guatemala (now GUATEMALA CITY). All the important art commissions were executed by artists from the capital, either in the city itself or at the place where the work was to be installed. In the last quarter of the 18th century, the impact of Neo-classicism led to important changes in artistic production, especially in the capital. In painting there was a certain amount of secularization, which took the form of portraiture, particularly miniatures. In sculpture new materials were tried, but the lack of known marble deposits in the country until the 1950s—discovered at Zacapa in the Motagua Valley—prevented the disappearance of the popular polychromed wood sculpture. In the late 18th century and early 19th the quality of execution improved due to new art teaching (*see* §XI below).

The development of the graphic arts in Guatemala was comparatively slow, since printing presses were established only in 1660. The first prints were exclusively woodcuts, then around the beginning of the 18th century artists began engraving on copper; it was not until *c*. 1800 that etchings and aquatints were introduced. The subjects were mainly religious and published in the form of prayers, books containing prayers for novenas, and pious prints, for which plates were made locally, although they were also imported. Another important source of commissions were books commemorating royal funeral rites, for which large engravings were required to reproduce the catafalque made for the occasion. The development of engraving was also associated with the engravers of the Real Casa de Moneda, founded in Santiago de Guatemala in 1733, who also executed printing commissions and taught. This was especially true in the last part of the colonial period, when they excelled in engraving on copper (*see* GARCI-AGUIRRE, PEDRO). The capital was the main source of prints for the whole kingdom, since, for most of the colonial period, it had the only printing presses in the region.

2. AFTER 1821. Guatemala's independence had little direct effect on artistic activity, although the socio-political instability of the following decades meant that there were few commissions. Secularization continued, resulting in a slow decrease in the importance of religious art. Moreover, at times (1829–38; after 1871) the Roman Catholic Church was persecuted, thus ceasing to be the main patron of the arts. Attempts to institutionalize art education in schools or academies failed, and the guild-based training system of apprentice, artisan and master craftsman continued. There was little significant improvement in artistic standards in the course of the 19th century. Practice remained more or less at a competent level, concentrated in the capital. Unlike other Latin-American countries, where foreign artists were encouraged to settle and domestic artists helped to study abroad, Guatemala remained largely isolated. Nevertheless, direct artistic dependence on Spain was broken as influences were received from other European countries, especially France and Britain. With the diminishing role of the Church, the only remaining opportunities left to painters were portraits of politicians and the bourgeoisie. Guatemala's only outstanding 19th-century artist, the miniaturist and engraver FRANCISCO CABRERA, worked in this field, producing intense portraits of exquisite Neo-classical sensibility. Although he had pupils, none managed to equal his achievement. In sculpture the religious image in polychromed wood was dislodged from its dominant role only slowly, secular sculpture in marble and bronze being introduced only in the last quarter of the 19th century. Etching and lithography were practised for the first time in this period, notably in the work of Julián Falla.

When the government of José María Reyna Barrios (President, 1892–8) initiated a French-influenced plan for Guatemala City, which included the placing of several bronze monuments on newly made boulevards, foreign sculptors were invited to contribute. Together with earlier arrivals, these formed a largely Italian community and included Andrea Galeotti, Giovanni Esposito, Francesco Durini, Achille Borghi, Adriatico Froli, Desiderio Scotti and Carlo Nicoli; as well as the Spaniards Justo de Gandarias (1848–1933) and Tomás Mur. Notable examples of their work include bronze statues of *Fray Bartolomé de las Casas* (1897; Guatemala City) by Mur and of *Miguel García Granados* (1897; Guatemala City, Boulevard 30 de Junio) by Durini. Stylistically they are representative of late 19th-century academic sculpture. Engraving was usually associated with the mint, where the work of the Swiss-born Johann Baptist Frener (1821–98) was outstanding, particularly as a teacher. He also designed coinage and a series of medals commemorating presidents of the Republic. The government of Manuel Estrada Cabrera (President, 1898–1920) continued the policies of its predecessors on a reduced scale. The arrival from Paris of the Venezuelan sculptor Santiago González (*d* 1909) was important in introducing Impressionism and subsequent developments to Guatemala. He was initially commissioned to carve reliefs for the Templo de Minerva (1901; destr. 1953) and the Teatro Nacional (*c*. 1830–59), both in Guatemala City.

His real accomplishment, however, was in the training of Guatemalan artists and encouraging them to study abroad, which ended the country's artistic isolation. The Spanish painter Jaime Sabartés y Gual also visited Guatemala (1904–28) and was similarly influential. Consequently the painters Rafael Iriarte (1876–1962), Carlos Valenti (1884–1910) and CARLOS MÉRIDA went overseas, as did the sculptor Rafael Rodríguez Padilla (1890–1929). Later, in the 1920s, the painters HUMBERTO GARAVITO and ALFREDO GÁLVEZ SUÁREZ and the sculptor RAFAEL YELA GÜNTHER also studied abroad.

For the rest of the period artistic activity remained at a standstill in Guatemala, although in 1920 the Escuela de Artes Plásticas, Guatemala City, was established under the direction of Rodríguez Padilla. With no art market, galleries or regular source of commissions, artists had to engage in public or private teaching or resign themselves to living modestly. Governments barely concerned themselves with supporting the arts. Those artists who remained out of the country continued their development in milieus more attuned to internationally recognized movements, for example Carlos Mérida in Mexico, while those who did return tended to focus their activities on provincial themes, either in Impressionist-style landscapes (Garavito) or scenes of Indian life (Gálvez Suárez). The culture of the indigenous people was also expressed in the Primitivist paintings of Andrés Curruchic (1891–1969) (*see* §II above). These marked part of the movement for a rediscovery of national identity.

Optimism rose with the change of administration in 1944–5, on the presumption that a democratic government would be favourable to art. A process of artistic modernization began, as European movements of the last few decades, none of which had been adopted by local artists, started to be discussed and supported. Government support began in 1945, and gradually public taste broadened. Realism, dominated by landscape art, was replaced, at first timidly, by other trends more directly related to Latin-American art, especially Mexican, and to those of the USA and Europe. Again some artists went abroad on fellowships: GUILLERMO GRAJEDA MENA and DAGOBERTO VÁSQUEZ to Chile; ROBERTO OSSAYE and ROBERTO GONZÁLEZ GOYRI to the USA; and Adalberto de León (1919–57) to France. Both democratic governments (1945–51; 1951–4) sought, for the first time in Guatemalan history, to mobilize art for their cause, not always with positive results. In the process of political polarization, which culminated with the counter-revolution in 1954, some artists played an outstanding role, both in groups and individually. Nevertheless, in spite of the triumph then of anti-democratic forces, there was no return to the previous situation in the arts. Development, increasingly linked to international movements, continued, in particular towards a 'Guatemalan' style inspired by Pre-Columbian and vernacular arts.

Between 1955 and 1980 there were very interesting experiments in the integration of the fine arts with architecture. Several young architects called on sculptors and painters to decorate their buildings (*see also* §III above). Sculptors executed works of large dimensions, generally in concrete. During the 1960s the first commercial art galleries appeared in Guatemala City, and there was an economic upgrading of works of art and institutions that supported the arts. The number and quality of artists increased, as did the prices fetched by works of art; the latter made it possible for the first time in many decades for artists to live exclusively on the proceeds of their profession.

From the 1960s Guatemala experienced varied, even conflicting, currents of artistic style. Although predominantly expressionistic, there were also examples of abstract painting (*see* DÍAZ, LUIS) and realism, especially the landscape-oriented type. Of ever-growing importance was a 'school' of indigenous painters practising naive art in various communities in the western part of the country, especially Comalapa, Patzicía and Santiago Atitlán. Professional artists also played an important role in protests against the repression and violence that afflicted Guatemala after 1965. Enhanced confidence among artists led to the formation, in the mid-1960s, of the group Vértebra, comprising the painters ELMAR ROJAS, MARCO AUGUSTO QUIROA and ROBERTO CABRERA, whose work is characterized by a figurative expressionism with deliberately disconcerting overtones (see fig. 4). In spite of the fact that painting was the most popular art form, there were interesting developments in sculpture, although commissions were scarce, and many sculptors took up painting (e.g. Grajeda Mena, Vásquez and González-Goyri). The talents of the few artists of high quality in the graphic arts were not fully exploited. Generally, art with aspirations to the experimental and to novelty became more evident, with limited public and private support. Having shaken

4. Elmar Rojas: *Drowned Physiognomy of Reality*, oil on hardboard, 1.22×0.98 m, 1970 (Washington, DC, Museum of Modern Art of Latin America)

off its isolation and modernized the tastes of educated Guatemalans, art in Guatemala has risen above socio-political difficulties to reflect international movements. At the same time influences of the rich popular artistic tradition have emerged, both native and non-native.

BIBLIOGRAPHY

V. M. Díaz: *Las bellas artes en Guatemala* (Guatemala City, 1934)

G. Valenzuela: *La imprenta en Guatemala* (Guatemala City, 1934)

S. Toscano: 'La escultura colonial en Guatemala', *An. Inst. Invest. Estét.*, ii/5 (1940), pp. 45–53

C. A. Ward: 'The Guatemalan Art Renaissance', *Bull. Pan Amer. Un.*, lxxv (1941), pp. 282–90

E. Fernando Granell: *Arte y artistas en Guatemala* (Guatemala City, 1949)

H. Berlin: *Historia de la imaginería colonial en Guatemala* (Guatemala City, 1952)

J. L. Cifuentes: *Pintores y escultores guatemaltecos* (Guatemala City, 1956)

L. Méndez Dávila: *Art in Latin America Today: Guatemala* (Washington, DC, 1966)

——: *Arte de vanguardia: Guatemala* (Guatemala City, 1969)

E. I. Núñez de Rodas: *El grabado en Guatemala* (Guatemala City, 1970)

G. Grajeda Mena: *Los Cristos tratados por los escultores de Guatemala* (Guatemala City, 1972)

El grabado guatemalteco, Dirección General de Cultura y Bellas Artes y Estudio-Taller Cabrera (Guatemala City, 1973)

L. Luján Muñoz: 'Notas sobre la pintura mural en Guatemala', *Antropol. & Hist. Guatemala*, ii (1980), pp. 197–213

J. B. Juárez: *Pintura viva de Guatemala* (Guatemala City, 1984)

B. La Duke: *Compañéras: Women, Art and Social Change in Latin America* (San Francisco, 1985), pp. 47–52

I. Lorenzana de Luján and L. Luján Muñoz: 'Apuntes sobre la pintura popular en Guatemala', *La pintura popular en Guatemala* (Guatemala City, 1987), pp. 1–11

L. Castedo: *Precolombino: El arte colonial*, i of *Historia del arte iberoamericano* (Madrid, 1988), pp. 271–6

JORGE LUJÁN-MUÑOZ

5. Guatemalan Maya Indians wearing cotton and wool clothes, from a late 19th-century photograph (Cambridge, MA, Harvard University, Peabody Museum); blouses woven on backstrap looms, skirts and jackets on treadle looms

V. Textiles.

On the arrival of the Spanish conquistadores in Guatemala in 1524, the Highland Maya possessed a textile tradition similar to that of other ethnic groups in Mesoamerica. This tradition comprised a technology based on cotton and agave fibres, natural dyes (e.g. indigo and purple) and hand-weaving on a backstrap loom. In addition to brocade (supplementary weft weaving), the decorative techniques included embroidery, featherwork and printing with ceramic or wooden stamps (*see* MESOAMERICA, PRE-COLUMBIAN, §IX, 10). Weaving was a women's domain. Textiles were used for family clothing, as an exchange medium and for the payment of taxes to the rulers.

The Spaniards introduced European textile technology, which included new materials and instruments such as wool, silk, carding-boards, the spinning-wheel and the treadle loom. In the largest urban centres of the Audiencia de Guatemala, notably Santiago de los Caballeros (now Antigua), Quetzaltenango, Ciudad Real and San Salvador (now in El Salvador), treadle-loom weaving was practised through the guild system. This European system of production operated until the end of the Colonial period (1524–1821), when economic liberalism replaced the mercantilism that protected the guilds. In the 'Indian towns', the settlements set up by the colonizers to control the Maya population, weaving in the pre-Hispanic tradition produced cotton textiles for family clothing (*see also* §II above), exchange and the payment of taxes to the colonial authorities. In some of these towns treadle looms were introduced to manufacture cloth for local and regional consumption.

Guild weaving was affected by the earthquake of 1773, which destroyed the city of Santiago, and by economic changes that put an end to the guilds. Despite these transformations urban treadle-loom weaving survived in Guatemala City, Antigua and Quetzaltenango during the 19th century and the beginning of the 20th. With competition from factories producing cotton yarn and cloth, such as that founded in Cantel in 1876, treadle-loom weaving in these cities began to die out. However, it continued to be important in several Maya communities (see fig. 5), and after World War II tourist demand for Maya textiles increased treadle-loom production in their workshops.

The advent of synthetic dyes during the second half of the 19th century and the establishment of textile factories affected the materials used in Maya weaving on both backstrap and treadle looms. By the mid-20th century synthetic dyes had replaced natural ones, and factory-spun cotton thread had, with some exceptions, replaced hand-spun thread. Imported rayon and fine cotton yarns rivalled silk as the most prestigious materials for brocade and embroidery. Acrylic thread was introduced in the 1960s, and in the following decades it largely displaced cotton and rayon. This was due, among other factors, to the political and economic crises that afflicted the country, especially the Maya population. The designs of contemporary Maya ethnographic textiles reflect Guatemalan history. Some geometric motifs are pre-Hispanic; other motifs, introduced during the Colonial period, are related to the Spanish and Arabic repertories. The most modern brocaded designs, representing flowers, fruit and birds, have been copied from cross-stitch magazines.

BIBLIOGRAPHY

C. M. Pancake: *The Costumes of Rural Guatemala* (Guatemala City, 1976)
M. Anderson: *Guatemalan Textiles Today* (New York, 1978)
M. B. Schevill: *Evolution in Textile Design from the Highlands of Guatemala* (Berkeley, 1985)
O. Arriola de Geng: *Los tejedores en Guatemala y la influencia española en el traje indígena* (Guatemala City, 1991)
M. B. Schevill: *Maya Textiles of Guatemala: The Gustavus A. Eisen Collection, 1902* (Austin, 1993)

LINDA ASTURIAS DE BARRIOS

VI. Gold and silver.

Documentary sources show that there were workers in precious metals in the settlement of Santiago de los Caballeros (now Antigua) from its foundation in 1524, while an attempt was made to regulate their activities as early as 1540. Antonio de Rodas, described as '*maestro platero, pintor y escultur*', and Juan de Salazar, a Sevillian first recorded in 1604 who served as an assaymaster, were prolific craftsmen, but, due to the disastrous earthquake of 1773, virtually no pieces survive from the 16th and 17th centuries. A rare survival, the silver antependium of the church of Jerez de la Frontera in Spain, made in Guatemala in 1730 by Manuel Quesada (*fl* 1721–48), is in the typical Baroque style.

The establishment of the new capital, Guatemala City, after the earthquake of 1773 and the building of new churches there resulted in numerous ecclesiastical commissions for Guatemalan silversmiths, who were more adept than their South American counterparts at assimilating Rococo decorative elements into their work (see fig. 6). The silver tabernacle of the church of S Augustín Acasaguastlán successfully incorporates rocaille motifs and foliate scrolls into a Baroque form; similarly, the antependium of S Antonio, Retalhuleu, is decorated with distinctive heavy gadrooning, which, like cast and applied stylized leaves, is a constant feature of Guatemalan silver dating from the last quarter of the 18th century. Ornament consisting of grapes and European flowers was preferred to the more exotic, native vegetal motifs employed by South American silversmiths.

The work of Miguel Guerra (*fl* 1774–1802), a prolific maker of domestic articles, shows a decided French influence, for example in his use of moulded borders and cast, applied decoration. Fine engraving of foliage and animals appears on many of his trays and dishes. Cast cagework formed of rocaille motifs and foliate scrolls superimposed over plain forms was popular and was used for such domestic items as table braziers, as well as ecclesiastical silver, for example a ciborium by Patricio Girón (Guatemala City, Nuestra Señora de las Mercedes). Typical Guatemalan silver items from the end of the 18th century include signs, usually embossed with the figure of a saint, that were made for the *cofradías* (exclusively male religious organizations) and large, two-handled bowls with lobed decoration and handles elaborately cast as foliage or crowned lions that were popular for domestic use. One of the few surviving Neo-classical works is the great tabernacle in the sanctuary of Guatemala Cathedral, formed of four Ionic columns and executed in 1813 by Francisco Alvarez (*fl* 1785–1813). A *quinto* (tax) mark of a closed crown appears on some pieces from the 18th century, often in conjunction with a maker's mark and a town mark depicting either St James over the mountains of Guatemala

6. Silver and mahogany *Virgin and Child*, h. 400 mm (with pedestal), figure from Guatemala City, 18th century; pedestal from Santiago de Guatemala, 19th century (private collection)

(for Antigua, the former capital), the initials SS flanking a mountain (for San Salvador) or a bird (possibly for Quetzaltenango).

BIBLIOGRAPHY

H. U. Samoyoa Guevara: 'El gremio de plateros de la ciudad de Guatemala y sus ordenanzas (1524–1821)', *Antropol. & Hist. Guatemala*, ix/1 (Jan 1957), pp. 16–24

Platería de Guatemala (exh. cat., Antigua, Mus. Colon., 1975)

J. Alonso de Rodríguez: *El arte de la platería en la Capitanía General de Guatemala* (Guatemala, 1981)

CHRISTOPHER HARTOP

VII. Ceramics.

There are two clearly distinguishable ceramic traditions in Guatemala: the indigenous and the Spanish. The former derives from Pre-Columbian, utilitarian ceramics; wares are created manually and 'baked' by covering them with burning straw. There are many centres of production, among the most notable being Chinautla, Santa Apolonia, San Luis Jilotepeque and San Cristóbal Totonicapán. The most common items are *tinajas* (large earthenware jars for water), *apastes* (earthenware tubs for corn), *comales* (flat clay dishes for making tortillas), *batidores* and *jarros* (pots and jars for drinking coffee and chocolate) and *ollas* (pots or saucepans). A reddish clay is used, which can be buffed, burnished or painted with black-and-white designs. Small pottery figures of humans and animals are made in the town of Rabinal (Baja Verapaz) and decorated with aniline paint. The ceramics inspired by the Spanish wares and made since the Conquest were produced on a potter's wheel and fired in a kiln. Most notable in this range are the maiolica wares, which in the late 20th century were manufactured only in the town of Antigua, although until the beginning of the 20th century they were also made in Guatemala City. A glazed pottery, which is not maiolica, is made in San Miguel Totonicapán and Jalapa. Common wares include tablewares, kitchen wares, flowerpots, gargoyles and glazed tiles. In Antigua fruit-shaped money-boxes and shepherd figures for Nativity scenes are also made.

BIBLIOGRAPHY

L. Luján Muñoz: *Historia de la mayólica en Guatemala* (Guatemala City, 1975)

R. E. Reina and R. M. Hill: *The Traditional Pottery of Guatemala* (Austin, 1978)

I. Morales Hidalgo: *Cerámica tradicional del Oriente de Guatemala* (Guatemala City, 1980)

C. A. Lara Figueroa: *Síntesis histórica de las cerámicas populares de Guatemala* (Guatemala City, 1981)

VIII. Furniture.

In the majority of regional towns simple, traditional Spanish-style furniture is produced for local consumption. The furniture industry, which began early in the Colonial period, is mainly concentrated in Guatemala City, where pieces in wood, metal and other materials are produced. In some cases traditional Spanish or other European designs are imitated; in others modern international designs, especially those of Scandinavia, are copied. Another important centre of production is Totonicapán, where chairs, tables, cupboards, sideboards and chests of pine, in some cases painted with aniline, are made; only recently has carved cedar furniture begun to be produced. In San Juan Ostuncalco (Quetzaltenango) furniture in pine and knotted maguey is produced, while in Antigua large numbers of pieces of furniture carved from cedar, mahogany and other woods are manufactured by craftsmen such as Joaquín Gaytán and Florencio Ruíz. The quality of Guatemalan cabinetwork has improved in the late 20th century, and some pieces are now exported.

BIBLIOGRAPHY

B. de Santos: *Artesanías de Guatemala* (Guatemala City, 1971)

A. Ortíz Domingo: *Artesanías de madera en Totonicapán* (Guatemala City, 1986)

JORGE LUJÁN-MUÑOZ

IX. Patronage, collecting and dealing.

During the colonial period the Roman Catholic Church was by far the largest patron of art in Guatemala. It was followed in size by the colonial administration, which employed artists either through agencies, such as the Real Casa de Moneda, or in such projects as the building (after 1776) of Guatemala City, the new capital. Private patrons began to make an impact only at the turn of the 18th century, for example commissioning portrait miniatures. A flow of mainly religious art continued in and out of Guatemala throughout the period. Destinations included other parts of the kingdom of Guatemala, New Spain (now Mexico) and Spain itself, where Guatemalan religious statues were highly appreciated. From the existence from the 16th century of collections of Pre-Columbian objects in Europe, a modest trade in these must also be supposed (*see* MESOAMERICA, PRE-COLUMBIAN, §X, 2). During the 19th century the role of the Church as the main patron declined, virtually ending with the anti-clerical laws passed in 1871. The state assumed this role, which reached a highpoint in the late 19th century and the early 20th in connection with the embellishment of cities. Private patronage tended to focus on works of art imported from France, Britain or, in the case of marble statues for cemeteries, from Italy. This trend declined in the 20th century, but mediocre genre paintings, still-lifes and landscapes continued to be imported from Europe for the homes of the Guatemalan bourgeoisie.

Generally during the 20th century there has been a growth in patronage of the arts in Guatemala. The state, through the Ministry of Culture and Sports (before 1986 through the Ministry of Education), provided artists with tuition that was either free or greatly reduced. Some artists were given positions in teaching and administration in the public sector, while others sporadically received fellowships for study abroad. The ministry also organized competitions, prizes, exhibitions and publications. From *c.* 1970 private patronage began to take shape. This was initially in the form of foreign corporate support (e.g. Esso Central America) and later by domestic firms, both sources of funding occasionally sponsoring valuable competitions. The first permanent organization in this field was the Patronato de Bellas Artes (founded 1971), which has sponsored exhibitions and publications. In 1978 the Programa Permanente de Cultura was established by Organización Paiz, an important commercial group, which began with a biennial exhibition of contemporary fine arts that became the most important show in the country and, arguably, in Central America. As the result of the Biennale, a collection gradually took shape, forming the basis of the

Museo de Arte Contemporáneo. In 1983 the Organización para las Artes Francisco Marroquín was founded. A filiation of the university of the same name, it has organized exhibitions, courses and performances. In the mid-20th century a valuable role was played by the foreign cultural institutes in Guatemala City, notably those of France, the USA, Italy, former West Germany and Spain, which organized exhibitions, courses and travel fellowships. Later their importance was reduced, but they have continued to function as exhibition venues for Guatemalan and other artists.

A market in contemporary art developed in Guatemala from the 1960s, with commercial galleries opening in Guatemala City. Guatemala has not played any significant role in the international art market, except in the case of antiquities. Since these are prohibited by law from leaving the country, illegal dealing occurs. The greatest demand, especially from museums and collectors in Europe and the USA, is for Pre-Columbian items (jade and ceramics), which has encouraged unauthorized excavations, especially at Maya sites in Petén. The number of Maya items appearing in foreign auctions also rose in the late 20th century, a significant proportion believed to have been plundered from sites in Guatemala. The illegal export of items from the colonial period, such as paintings, sculpture, engravings and gold and silver work, also increased.

ROSSINA CAZALI DE BARRIOS,
JORGE LUJÁN-MUÑOZ

X. *Museums, art libraries and photographic collections.*

Short-lived attempts were made to found the first museums at the end of the colonial period and the beginning of independence. It was not until the 1930s, however, that they existed with any degree of continuity, most being state institutions. The Museo Nacional de Arqueología y Etnología, Guatemala City, established in 1931, has a copious collection of Pre-Columbian, especially Maya, objects. The Museo Nacional de Historia, Guatemala City, with displays of 18th- and 19th-century religious art and a collection of prints, was established in 1976, when the former Museo Nacional de Historia y Bellas Artes (founded 1934) was divided into two separate institutions. At the same time the Museo Nacional de Arte Moderno, Guatemala City, was created, with a collection of late 19th-century and 20th-century painting, sculpture and graphic arts, including an important collection of paintings of the first period of Carlos Mérida. The Museo Nacional de Artes e Industrias Populares, Guatemala City, was founded in 1959 in a private residence that unfortunately lacked adequate facilities; it also has a specialized library.

Museums in Antigua include the Museo Colonial (founded 1936) and the Museo de Santiago (founded 1957). The former is located in a building once used by the University of S Carlos. It has the best public collection of colonial paintings in Guatemala, including works by Tomás de Merlo and Cristóbal de Villalpando, as well as religious statues and fragments of retables. The Museo de Santiago, occupying a part of the town hall, has some colonial silverwork, pottery and other crafts, as well as paintings and religious items. The Museo del Libro Antiguo, Antigua, was founded in 1960 on the occasion of the tricentenary of the arrival of the printing press in Antigua, then the capital of the kingdom of Guatemala. It exhibits books, pamphlets and leaflets from the colonial period and has a library of antiquarian books. Also run by the state are regional archaeological museums, located at important sites. Among these are the Museo Arqueológico-Sylvanus G. Morley, in Tikal Park, Petén (*see* TIKAL); Museo Arqueológico de Zaculeu, near Huehuetenango (*see* ZACULEU); and IXIMCHÉ, in Tecpán Guatemala. State museums are generally modest institutions with few activities, due to their limited resources. Most lack restoration workshops, and they are not yet up to date with modern museographic trends, in either the presentation of their objects or their relations with the visiting public.

There are also several important private museums. The first, the Museo Ixchel del Traje Indígena, Guatemala City, was founded in 1977 and is devoted to the collection, preservation, exhibition and investigation of textiles and native costumes of Guatemala. Besides a collection of *c.* 5000 items, it has an extensive specialized library. There is also the Museo Popol Vuh, Universidad Francisco Marroquín, Guatemala City, with Pre-Columbian items, especially pottery, and religious statues from the colonial period. Both museums operate in the sphere of activities of the privately run Francisco Marroquín University and have their own education, publication and research programmes. The Museo de Arte Contemporáneo was founded in 1989 by the Programa Permanente de Cultura de la Organización Paiz, in Guatemala City, making use of the collection of the Paiz Biennale. It has organized exhibitions of national and foreign artists, lectures and short courses.

In the provinces there are also private and municipal museums, among them the Museo de la Democracia, Escuintla, founded in 1966, devoted to the OLMEC culture; the Museo Regional Verapacense in Cobán and the museum at San Pedro Carchá, both in Alta Verapaz, with archaeological and ethnic materials of the area; the Museo Municipal at Amatitlán, with archaeological objects drawn from Lake Amatitlán and environs; and the Museo Regional in Chichicastenango, with objects found in the province of that name. The Catholic Church also plays an important role in the conservation of collections and objects from the colonial period. In the Archbishop's Palace next to Guatemala City Cathedral is the Museo Cafarnaum, containing historical documents as well as paintings, objects and religious statues of different epochs. The Museo Fray Francisco Vázquez, attached to the church of S Francisco, Guatemala City, has a small collection of statues and furniture of the 18th and 19th centuries.

In both state and private museums and other institutions specialized libraries of modest proportions have been taking shape. The Instituto de Antropología e Historia, Guatemala City, has a centralized library that includes Pre-Columbian, colonial and modern art. The Academia de Geografía e Historia, Guatemala City, has a library with material on art history, as does the Centro de Investigaciones de Mesoamérica (CIRMA) in Antigua. The former is in the process of organizing its store of photographs into a genuine collection, with emphasis on national historical themes, while the latter has the only well-organized photographic collection in Guatemala, with photographs dating from 1880 and works by the photographers Juan J. Yas, Domingo Noriega, Valdeavellano and others. Founded in the 1980s, it has gradually developed its collection.

BIBLIOGRAPHY

L. Luján Muñoz: *Guía de los museos de Guatemala* (Guatemala City, 1971)

——: 'Museums in Latin America: Guatemala', *Museum* [Paris], xxv (1973), pp. 187–9

——: *El primer museo nacional de Guatemala, 1866–81* (Guatemala City, 1979)

ROSSINA CAZALI DE BARRIOS

XI. Art education.

For most of the colonial period, art education in Guatemala was in the hands of the guilds, which faithfully reproduced European patterns of organization. The Real Casa de Moneda, after its foundation in 1733, played a leading role until the late 19th century in training artists and employing them, mainly in engraving. The first attempt to establish formal art education in Guatemala occurred in 1795, when the newly founded Real Sociedad Económica de Amigos del País de Guatemala asked King Charles IV of Spain (*reg* 1788–1808) to establish an Academia de Bellas Artes in Guatemala. When this proposal was unsuccessful, the Sociedad Económica itself founded an Escuela de Dibujo, in Guatemala City in 1797, under the direction of PEDRO GARCÍ-AGUIRRE, a senior engraver at the Casa de Moneda and original instigator of the plan for an Academia de Bellas Artes. The Escuela de Dibujo offered courses in sculpture and painting, as well as draughtsmanship and engraving, and continued a precarious existence well into the 19th century. There was little advance in art education in the 19th century apart from isolated efforts, such as an attempt in 1834 to establish a collection of graphic and sculptural reproductions for teaching purposes. Hence, much of the art training of the second half of the 19th century and the first two decades of the 20th was carried on in short-lived private schools. Among these, that of the Venezuelan sculptor Santiago González (*d* 1909), active between 1904 and 1909, is particularly noteworthy. In 1920 the government-sponsored Academia de Bellas Artes was finally founded in Guatemala City. Despite changes of curriculum and, in 1947, a change of name to Escuela Nacional de Artes Plásticas, it has been in continuous existence since as the main art training centre in Guatemala.

In the second half of the 20th century other developments in art education were largely tied to the universities. In the 1940s courses were added to the curriculum of the Universidad Popular in drawing, painting and sculpture, all at an intermediate, non-professional level. The first school of architecture in Guatemala was established at the University of S Carlos de Guatemala, Guatemala City, in 1960. Towards the end of the 1970s, schools of architecture also opened in three private universities. In 1969 for the first time studies in the fine arts were established at university level in the Escuela de Arte, University of S Carlos, which later offered courses in restoration, museum administration and the teaching of art in schools, both BA and MA. The Rafael Landívar University (founded in 1961) and Mariano Gálvez de Guatemala University (founded in 1966) both instituted teacher-training courses in fine arts and graphic design, while the Instituto Femenino de Estudios Superiores included courses in art education and fashion design.

BIBLIOGRAPHY

E. I. Núñez de Rodas: *Reseña histórica de la escuela de artes plásticas* (Guatemala City, 1970)

ROSSINA CAZALI DE BARRIOS,
JORGE LUJÁN-MUÑOZ

Guatemala City [formerly Guatemala de la Asunción]. Capital of Guatemala. It is situated 1492 m above sea-level in a broad, elongated valley running from north to south. It was founded on 2 January 1776 following the transfer of the capital from Antigua (*see* ANTIGUA (i)), which had been largely destroyed by an earthquake in 1773. The problems of housing *c.* 30,000 inhabitants were compounded by an ensuing economic recession, which slowed the construction process. The grid-plan urban design of Antigua was reproduced (although with broader streets), orientated to the cardinal points and focusing on a central main square. The major buildings were not generally completed until the mid-19th century. Those in the main square include the cathedral: its Neo-classical design was drawn up by the Spanish architect Marcos Ibañez with the help of Antonio Bernasconi, although the building's execution was taken over by Bernasconi, José de Sierra and PEDRO GARCÍ-AGUIRRE from 1783 and Santiago Marqui from 1803 to *c.* 1835. It was dedicated in an incomplete state in 1813 and eventually finished in 1865. The church of S Francisco, completed in 1851, showed the influence of European academic classicism.

The city underwent expansion towards the end of the 19th century, notably to the south (1896–7), with the opening up of the Avenida de la Reforma and the grounds of an international fair. By *c.* 1900 the city had a population of 100,000. Artistic activity in the city was stimulated by the establishment in 1920 of the government-funded Academia de Bellas Artes (later Escuela Nacional de Artes Plásticas), which quickly became the focal point of art education in Guatemala. Developments in architecture mid-century were demonstrated by the Palacio Nacional (1939–43), designed by Enrique Pérez de León (1896–1958) to simulate a Spanish Renaissance-style stone construction, and the so-called 'Centro Cívico', with the Palacio Municipal (1958), the Seguro Social building (1959) and the Banco de Guatemala (1964); the last three all showed the attempt to integrate the visual arts with architecture. The Teatro Nacional (completed 1978) by EFRAÍN RECINOS is possibly the most original and successful 20th-century building in the city, having been conceived effectively as a large-scale sculptural work on its hilltop site in the city centre.

Repeated earthquakes throughout the 20th century (notably in 1917–18 and 1976) led to the destruction of many buildings, and in general the fear of earthquakes has caused few tall buildings to be put up, although anti-seismic techniques using steel and reinforced concrete have improved safety.

The population of Guatemala City had reached 2 million in 1990, and the cultural life of the city was enriched by the fine arts and architectural courses at the Universidad de S Carlos and other universities and by various museums and art galleries, as well as by an active art market.

BIBLIOGRAPHY

L. Luján Muñoz: *Síntesis de la arquitectura en Guatemala* (Guatemala City, 2/1969)

R. Aycinena E.: 'Algunas consideraciones sobre el valle de La Ermita y la fundación de la ciudad de Guatemala y su desarrollo', *An. Acad. Geog. & Hist. Guatemala*, lxi (1987), pp. 245–80

G. Gellert: *Ciudad de Guatemala: Dos estudios sobre su evolución urbana* (Guatemala City, 1992)

JORGE LUJÁN MUÑOZ

Guay, Jacques (*b* Marseille, 26 Sept 1711; *d* Barre, nr Senlis, 8 Feb 1797). French gem-engraver. He abandoned his apprenticeship to a goldsmith and moved to Paris, where he entered the workshop of François Boucher to study drawing and engraving. His acquaintance with the collector Pierre Crozat, who owned a collection of almost 1500 ancient and Renaissance engraved gems (St Petersburg, Hermitage), induced him to take up gem-engraving. It is not known where Guay learnt the craft, but the pale sard intaglio the *Muse of Poetry* (*c*. 1735–40; Paris, Bib. N., Cab. Médailles), which he described as his earliest figure subject, already shows his mastery of technique. It is based on a design by Edmé Bouchardon, whose drawings of Louis XV's gems were published by Pierre-Jean Mariette, an intimate of Crozat's. Guay journeyed to Italy (1742–4) to study the collections of gems and other antiquities in Florence and Rome. He returned with gems engraved with antique subjects, notably his cornelian intaglio of the head of *Antinous* (Paris, Bib. N., Cab. Médailles). He now essayed himself in a new genre, that of historical allegory. Deriving this approach from medallic art, especially as practised in France in the series glorifying Louis XIV, Guay made this subject peculiarly his own in the medium of engraved gems. For the *Triumph of Fontenay* (cornelian, 1745; Paris, Bib. N., Cab. Médailles), Guay drew on Bouchardon's design for the medal celebrating the French victory in the War of the Austrian Succession (*see also* GEM-ENGRAVING, fig. 14). This work procured him the title of Graveur du Roi en Pierres Fines and a lodging in the Louvre. Two years later he became an associate at the Académie Royale and began to show at the Paris Salon; he became a member in 1748. Tradition has it that it is Guay who is depicted in Mariette's treatise, as a gem-engraver in his workshop, presided over by a bust of Louis XV (pl. opp. p. 208).

The Marquise de Pompadour had lodged Guay at Versailles, and from 1759, when he ceased to exhibit, he worked primarily for her. She wore his gems set in rings, a seal and bracelet-clasps. Among them were further allegories glorifying the reign of Louis XV; tiny emblematic scenes, some after designs by Boucher, figuring personifications of Friendship and Love (e.g. *Cupid as Gardener*; St Petersburg, Hermitage); and a range of brilliant portraits from life, among them the large sardonyx cameo bust of *Louis XV* (1753; Paris, Bib. N., Cab. Médailles), laureate and in antique armour, which Babelon called the finest cameo of modern times. The Marquise de Pompadour further expressed her appreciation of Guay by etching a set of 63 plates after his works (Paris, Bib. N., Cab. Est.), and she even became his pupil in gem-engraving, producing, for example, the *Muse of Music* (agate, 1752; Paris, Bib. N., Cab. Médailles).

BIBLIOGRAPHY

P.-J. Mariette: *Traité des pierres gravées*, i (Paris, 1750)

J.-F. Leturcq: *Notice sur Jacques Guay, graveur sur pierres fines du roi Louis XV* (Paris, 1873)

E. Babelon: *Histoire de la gravure sur gemmes en France* (Paris, 1902), pp. 159–208, pls xiv–xvi

J. Jacquiot: 'Les Camées et les intailles', *Louis XV: Un Moment de perfection dans l'art français* (exh. cat., Paris, Admin. Monnaies & Médailles, 1974), pp. 617–49

GERTRUD SEIDMANN

Guayabo de Turrialba. Pre-Columbian site in Costa Rica, in the Línea Vieja central highlands of Cartago Province. It flourished *c*. AD 1000–*c*. 1500, but with earlier occupation. Guayabo de Turrialba lies near the Reventazon River on the slope of Turrialba volcano, *c*. 1000 m above sea-level. Its location in a tropical region of dense forest and fertile soil contributed to its growth and importance as a political and religious ceremonial centre. It is also known for its stone cist tombs, containing such lavish burial goods as carved stone objects and several varieties of ceramics. The site's late 19th-century owner, Don Ramon Rojas Troyo, collected hundreds of artefacts, which later became a major part of the collection of the Museo Nacional de Costa Rica, San José. At the same time the first archaeological investigations, of several burials, were undertaken by Anastasio Alfaro. A number of the objects recovered by Troyo and Alfaro were first exhibited in the Americas section of the 1893 Historical Exposition in Madrid. Among these were objects carved on local volcanic stone: pedestal-based circular tables with quadrupeds or human and feline faces sculpted on the rims; human heads; standing human images; and large, thin slabs (probably grave markers) with free-standing and relief-sculptured decoration (*see* SOUTH AMERICA, PRE-COLUMBIAN, §II, 3). Similar objects have been recovered from nearby sites, particularly Las Mercedes. In 1968 more scientific excavations were undertaken by Carlos Aguilar of the Universidad de Costa Rica. Unfortunately, the site had previously been consistently looted, but in 1973 it was declared a national park, thus protecting it from further vandalism. From 1978 further study and excavation were supervised by Carlos Fonseca Zamora of the Universidad de Costa Rica.

The Guayabo de Turrialba architectural complex comprises over 50 features including 43 mounds, 3 aqueducts, 2 plazas, an enclosure and a causeway. While they vary in size (from 4.2 sq. m to 888 sq. m) and in form (from circular to rectangular), all are connected by paved walkways, steps and bridges. The layout is orientated on a north-east–south-west axis, with an eastern entrance along an 8 m-wide causeway extending 150 m to the principal, central plaza. Narrower paved walkways or roads continue through the site, linking other structures and areas. The full extent of the site has not yet been determined, but it is thought to cover almost 33 ha, making it the largest site of this type in Costa Rica. Several other sites of similar plan and arrangement in the Línea Vieja region include Las Mercedes, Anita Grande and LA CABAÑA. Ceramics from Guayabo de Turrialba include modelled and fine-line incised monochrome vessels, painted bichromes and polychromes imported from Guanacaste Province on the Pacific side of the isthmus. While the ceramics indicate a lengthy site occupation from *c.* 500 BC to *c.* AD 1500, the only radiocarbon dates yet obtained have been AD 980±258 and AD 953±241.

For further discussion of Pre-Columbian Costa Rica *see* SOUTH AMERICA, PRE-COLUMBIAN, §II.

BIBLIOGRAPHY

C. H. Aguilar: *Guayabo de Turrialba* (San José, 1972)
——: *Un monolito zoomorfo en el parque arqueológico de Guayabo de Turrialba* (San José, 1975)
O. Fonseca Zamora: 'Informe de la primera temporada de reexcavación de Guayabo de Turrialba', *Vínculos*, v (1979), pp. 35–52
——: 'Guayabo de Turrialba and its Significance', *Between Continents, between Seas: Precolumbian Art of Costa Rica*, ed. E. P. Benson (New York, 1981), pp. 104–11

JOAN K. LINGEN

Guayasamín, Oswaldo (*b* Quito, 1919). Ecuadorean painter. He studied at the Escuela de Bellas Artes in Quito. He worked first in an Indigenist style: influenced by Mexican muralism, he painted village scenes, notably in the fresco *The Incas and the Conquest* (1948; Quito, Mus. A. Mod.; *see* ECUADOR, fig. 3) and in the series of 100 paintings *Road of Sorrow* (Quito, Mus. Fond. Guayasamín), exhibited for the first time in 1952. He adopted a more universal approach in *Age of Anger* (Quito, Mus. Fond. Guayasamín), first exhibited in 1966, in which he depicted the disasters of World War II in 220 paintings.

Guayasamín's work is characterized by geometric composition, fine draughtsmanship, thick lines and vigorous brushwork; his central theme was the human condition afflicted by the evils of war and injustice. He also painted portraits, still-lifes, landscapes and nudes. Guayasamín exhibited internationally and was also patron of the Fundación Guayasamín in Quito.

BIBLIOGRAPHY

J. Camón Asnar: *Guayasamín* (Barcelona, 1973)
J. Lassaigne: *Oswaldo Guayasamín* (Barcelona, 1977)

CECILIA SUÁREZ

Guayde, Jehan. *See* GAILDE, JEAN.

Gubba, Tell. *See under* HAMRIN REGION.

Gubbio [Lat. Igurium]. Italian city on the south-western slope of Mt Ingino in Umbria, with a population of *c.* 32,000.

1. HISTORY AND URBAN DEVELOPMENT. Traces of human settlements dating back *c.* 130,000 years have been found in the area. The character of the oldest centres of population can be reconstructed with the aid of seven bronze tablets (Gubbio, Mus. & Pin. Com.), four of which were written before the 11th century BC. It is thought that the settlement preceding Gubbio was situated on the slope of Mt Ingino above the Camignano River, and surrounded by a wall with three gates. It was probably divided north–south by the Via Augurale, on which were the *comitium* and the forum. The ruins of a castle (*c.* 1000 BC) on the peak of Mt Ingino and part of a polygonal wall on the opposite slope are all that survives from this early phase.

In the Roman period, Gubbio, mentioned by Pliny the elder among the *municipia* in the *Natural History*, spread to the more level area below the earlier settlement and continued to grow until the 4th century AD; the remains of a theatre and a mausoleum have been discovered. The town ceased to thrive during the 5th and 6th centuries AD especially after its destruction by the Goths in 542.

Gubbio was probably occupied by the Lombards in the 7th and 8th centuries. It was reconstructed on the slopes of Mt Ingino, while the disused Roman theatre was transformed into a fortress. In the 10th and 11th centuries a new nucleus developed, separated from the old centre by the Camignano River. A disastrous fire in 1127 was followed by a reconstruction mainly concentrated north-east of the town on land obtained through a papal and imperial grant. There is documentary evidence that the first communal organization dates from that period, and the first public square was constructed there at the end of the 12th century, with a town hall and cathedral.

Gubbio was continually at war with Perugia. In the 13th century a new ring of walls (partly extant) was built, and a new nucleus was formed some way downhill, with the rebuilt church of S Giovanni and the Bargello Palace. Still further downhill was the church of S Francesco, facing the market square. The district of S Pietro was extended on a regular plan from 1234, and in the 1260s and 1270s the city was subdivided into quarters (S Pietro, S Andrea, S Giuliano and S Martino). It was undoubtedly in connection with this development that in 1321 the Guelph commune decided to construct a new city centre below the original one, at the point where the four quarters met. It consisted of the rectangular Piazza della Signoria (begun 1322) projecting from the mountainside and supported on arches, facing the valley on one side and flanked on its two short sides by two tall public buildings: the Palazzo dei Consoli (or del Popolo; 1332–41; see fig.) and the Palazzo Pretorio (completed 1348–9). The complex was designed by ANGELO DA ORVIETO. The piazza was given its present size and form only after 1480, when the commune decided to extend it on new arches constructed between the two palaces.

From 1384 Gubbio was ruled by the Montefeltro family, and in that year Antonio Montefeltro set about reinforcing the existing castle (destr.) and the walls. In 1480 the commune presented Federigo II Montefeltro with a new Palazzo Ducale (begun *c.* 1476) built in the old cathedral square. The medieval Palazzo della Guardia formed its nucleus, the cathedral square became the courtyard, and a water-tank and service areas were located in Corte Vecchia. The design of the courtyard and the interiors recalls the Palazzo Ducale in Urbino, supporting the attribution of the plan to Francesco di Giorgio Martini (*see* FRANCESCO DI GIORGIO MARTINI, §1), who is named in a document as having designed at least one room, perhaps the *studiolo*. Francesco di Giorgio Martini is named again in contracts of 1481 and 1486 for new ravelins to protect the city gates. Gubbio subsequently enjoyed a long period of peace, with only a few interruptions. During this time most construction work within the walls involved the enlargement of buildings and remodelling of façades, but a few new public buildings and churches were added. In the 18th century the church of the Madonna del Prato was built just outside

Gubbio, Palazzo dei Consoli, by Angelo da Orvieto, 1332–41

the walls; it is similar to Francesco Borromini's church of S Carlo alle Quattro Fontane in Rome and may be the work of the same architect. Among Gubbio's important later transformations is the Neo-classical façade (1812–30) of the Palazzo Ranghiasci in Piazza Grande.

BIBLIOGRAPHY

R. Paci: *Politica ed economia in un comune del ducato di Urbino: Gubbio tra '500 e '600* (Urbino, 1966)

C. Spaziani: *La chiesa e l'abbazia di S Pietro in Gubbio* (Gubbio, 1966)

I. Moretti: *Architettura romanica religiosa a Gubbio e nel territorio della sua antica diocesi* (Florence, 1973)

G. Martines: 'Il Palazzo Ducale di Gubbio', *Ric. Stor. A.*, vi (1977), pp. 89–110

A. L. Prosdocimi: *Le tavole di Gubbio* (Padua, 1978)

D. Whitehouse and B. Graeme: 'La rocca posteriore di Gubbio: Secondo rapporto preliminare', *Archeol. Med.*, (1978), pp. 461–74

G. Venturini: 'Il Palazzo Ducale di Gubbio, riscoperta di antiche strutture urbane', *Ric. Stor. A.*, xi (1980), pp. 70–74

P. Micalizzi: 'Gubbio, l'architettura delle piazze comunali', *Stor. Città*, 18 (1981), pp. 77–116

G. Cerboni Baiardi, G. Chittolini and P. Floriani, eds: *Le arti* (1986), ii of *Federico di Montefeltro: Lo stato, le arti, la cultura* (Rome, 1986), pp. 151–85

P. L. Menichetti: *Storia di Gubbio dalle origini all'unità d'Italia*, 2 vols (Città di Castello, 1987)

O. Lucarelli: *Memorie e guida storica di Gubbio* (Città di Castello, 1988)

P. Micalizzi: *Storia dell'architettura e dell'urbanistica di Gubbio* (Rome, 1988)

FRANCESCO PAOLO FIORE

2. CENTRE OF MAIOLICA PRODUCTION. This small Umbrian town owes much of its fame during the Renaissance to the work of GIORGIO ANDREOLI, known as 'Mastro Giorgio'. Andreoli was a very competent potter who was respected by both clientele and colleagues, who sent their most important works to him to be finished with a brilliant, metallic lustre (a thin film of metal deposited over the tin glaze during a third firing). Lustres applied in Gubbio included gold and ruby (e.g. two-handled vase, *c.* 1500–25; London, Wallace). During the 19th century, lustrewares were revived in Gubbio by Giovanni Spinacci (*fl* 1853–76), who successfully produced reproductions of 16th-century wares.

BIBLIOGRAPHY

G. Mazzatinti: 'Mastro Giorgio', *Il Vasari*, iv (1931), pp. 1–16, 105–22

F. Filippini: 'Nuovi documenti intorno a Mastro Giorgio e alla sua bottega (1515–1517)', *Faenza*, xxx (1942), pp. 76–7

G. Polidori: 'Errori e pregiudizi su Mastro Giorgio', *Stud. A. Urbin.*, ii (1953), pp. 13–29

CARMEN RAVANELLI GUIDOTTI

Gubitz, Friedrich Wilhelm (*b* Leipzig, 27 Feb 1786; *d* Berlin, 5 June 1870). German woodcutter, draughtsman, writer and publisher. He was taught the technique of woodcutting by his father, Johann Christoph Gubitz (1754–1826), and first exhibited prints in 1800 at an exhibition of the Akademie der Künste in Berlin. He became a member of the Akademie in 1805 and succeeded Johann Friedrich Gottlieb Unger (1753–1804) as a teacher of woodcutting and block-cutting, becoming Professor in 1812. He published several periodicals, including *Der Gesellschafter* (1817–1848), *Das Jahrbuch der deutschen Bühnenspiele* (1822–65) and the *Deutscher Volkskalender* (1835–69). He produced many commissioned pieces for these journals and did numerous woodcuts. Until 1829 he principally used the grain from the length of the block to produce designs in the manner of Thomas Bewick's wood-engravings. Many of his early woodcuts look like copper engravings. From 1829 he preferred the grain from the end of the block. He also printed coloured woodcuts: one of his best-known is the portrait of *Gräfin Voss* (1812; Nuremberg, Ger. Nmus.; after Anton Graff) printed from eight plates. He tinted some of his woodcuts and employed crayon in others to give an appearance of drawing or watercolour. Gubitz's interest in the medium of woodcut helped to revive the technique in Germany in the 19th century. He also wrote plays and poems and published various essays as well as his memoirs, *Erlebnisse* (Berlin, 1868–9). His son Anton Gubitz (1821–57) was his pupil and assistant.

WRITINGS

Erlebnisse, 3 vols (Berlin, 1868–9)

BIBLIOGRAPHY

E. Marx: *Fr. W. Gubitz und die Wiederbelebung des deutschen Holzschnitts im 19. Jh.* (diss., Berlin, 1955)

E.-M. Hanebutt-Benz: 'Studien zum deutschen Holzstich im 19. Jahrhundert', *Archiv für Geschichte des Buchwesens*, ed. M. Estermann, R. Wittmann and M. Kleiss, xxiv (Frankfurt am Main, 1983), cols 644–51

VERONIKA BRAUNFELS

Gucci, Santi (*b* Florence, *c.* 1530; *d* Pińczów, nr Kielce, 1599–1600). Italian sculptor and architect, active in Poland. He was the son of Giovanni Gucci (Giovanni della Camilla; *d* 1566), who had worked on the restoration of Florence Cathedral, and was the step-brother of Francesco Camilliani (*d* 1586), a sculptor and Baccio Bandinelli's disciple. He was trained at his father's workshop and probably also at that of Bandinelli. After 1550 he went to Poland and settled in Kraków, where he initially represented the *all'antica* Italian Renaissance style. From 1558 he was the architect to the Polish monarchs Sigismund II Augustus, Anna Jagiellon and Stephen Bathory (*reg* 1576–86). He also worked for the noble families of the Firlejs and Myszkowskis: for example he designed the layout of the private town of Pińczów for the latter family. He was simultaneously a citizen of Kraków and of Pińczów, where he leased a quarry from the Myszkowskis. The Pińczów sandstone served him as material for numerous tombs, fonts, portals and fountains.

In his early tombs Gucci placed medallion portraits against a pyramidal obelisk (e.g. the monument to *Galeazzo Guicciardini* (*d* 1557); Kraków, Dominican Monastery). The pyramid was combined with a triumphal arch in the two-figure infant tomb of the *Tęczyńskis* (before 1579) in Kraśnik, near Lublin. This two-tier composition was also employed in the family tombs of *Andrzej Firlej and Barbara Firlej* (*c.* 1586; Janowiec parish church) and *Arnulf Uchański and Stanisław Uchański* (*c.* 1590; Uchanie, parish church of the Assumption). From *c.* 1575 Gucci's style slowly evolved into Mannerism, intentionally anti-classical, probably under the influence of the style developed in Bandinelli's studio or 'Academy'. His work was characterized by an irrational transformation of the architectural vocabulary of tombs and portals, and by an unnatural arrangement of figures consisting of simplified forms. The influence of Michelangelo is apparent in the three-figure tomb of the *Kryskis* (1569–76) at Drobin and in the seven-figure tomb of the *Jordans* (1569–before 1584) in St Catherine's Church in Kraków, both with seated figures. An outstanding example of Gucci's later style is the tomb of *Stephen Bathory* (1594–5; see fig.), his only signed work, one of three royal monuments executed on Anna Jagiellon's commission in Wawel Cathedral, Kraków; the others, located in the Sigismund Chapel of the cathedral, are the figure of *Sigismund II Augustus* (1574–5), based on a model (1571) by Giovanni Maria Mosca Padovano and placed below the tomb of *Sigismund I the Old*, and the monument to *Anna Jagiellon* of 1583–4 and 1592 (*see* KRAKÓW, fig. 5). Gucci's royal tombs and the majority of his tombs of the nobility follow the 'Sansovino type' with a sleeping figure reclining on its side, as also in the tomb of *Sigismund I*.

Gucci also designed many buildings. The earliest of those in Kraków were the attic of the Cloth Hall (the model dating from 1557), the Boners' house (with its attic) at 6 Market Square (*c.* 1560) and the chapter house at 21 Kanonicza Street (after 1582). He also worked on castles and palaces, for example for Sigismund II Augustus in Niepołomice (where he built portals in 1568; destr.), and for Stephen Bathory, for whom he worked in Łobzów, near Kraków (1583; destr.), Grodno (where he remodelled the palace, after 1580; partly destr.) and Riga (unidentified works, *c.* 1580). He also enlarged the residence of Andrzej Firlej (1565–95) in Janowiec, near Poznań, and built palaces for Bishop Piotr Myszkowski in Książ Wielki (1585–95) and for Rafał Leszczyński in Baranów (1591–1606). His palaces are generally axial, with two linear suites of apartments, and the façades and portals are rusticated. His work also includes two domed chapels: the Branicki Chapel (1595–6) in Niepołomice, and St Anne's Chapel (1600) in Pińczów. He also created a monument in Niepołomice to *Katarzyna and Grzegorz Branicki* (1595–9), with kneeling figures. Gucci elaborated an individual

Santi Gucci: tomb of *Stephen Bathory*, 1594–5, Lady Chapel, Wawel Cathedral, Kraków

repertory of ornamentation, creating a peculiar Polish variant of Mannerism. Through his sculptor–mason workshop at Pińczów, where he employed apprentices from such countries as Italy, Germany and Poland, he strongly influenced Polish art. His most illustrious follower was Tomasz Nikiel (*d* 1605).

SAP

BIBLIOGRAPHY

K. Sinko: *Santi Gucci Fiorentino i jego szkoła* [Santi Gucci Fiorentino and his school] (Kraków, 1933)

W. Kieszkowski: 'Santi Gucci Fiorentino', *Biul. Hist. Sztuki & Kult.*, iii (1934–5), pp. 134–52

A. Fischinger: *Santi Gucci, architekt i rzeźbiarz królewski XVI wieku* [Santi Gucci, royal architect and sculptor of the 16th century] (Kraków, 1969)

H. Kozakiewiczowa: *Rzeźba XVI wieku w Polsce* [16th-century sculpture in Poland] (Warsaw, 1984), pp. 153–76

J. Kowalczyk: 'Nagrobek królowej Anny Jagiellonki w Kaplicy Zygmuntowskiej' [The tomb of Queen Anna Jagiellon at the Sigismund Chapel], *Fol. Hist. A.*, xxxiii (1987), pp. 5–22

JERZY KOWALCZYK

Guccio di Mannaia [Malnaia; Malnaggia; Manaie; Mannaie] (*fl* 1288–1318). Italian goldsmith. One of the most important goldsmiths of the period, he is first documented on 5 July 1292 in a payment for a seal, in which he is referred to as 'Guccio Mannaie aurifici'. A further three payments for seals are recorded on 1 January 1294, 4 September 1298 and 7 July 1318. In 1311 he enrolled in the Sienese goldsmiths' guild. His only signed work is the chalice (silver gilt and translucent enamel; h. 220 mm; Assisi, Tesoro Mus. Basilica S Francesco) made in 1288–92 for Pope Nicholas IV and donated to S Francesco, Assisi. The stem is inscribed GUCCIUS MANAIE DE SENIS FECIT and NICCHO[L]AUS PAPA QUARTUS. The chalice is first described in an inventory of 1370 and is mentioned in successive inventories: that of 1430 refers to a paten (lost) decorated with an enamel of the *Last Supper*. The chalice is the earliest dated example of *basse taille* or translucent enamel in Europe, preceding the first known French example by *c.* 30 years. It is decorated with 96 enamels, arranged from the base to the stem to form a unified iconographic programme related to the Eucharist. The base is decorated with 32 plaques, each framed by a beaded band between which are finely wrought repoussé leaves. The larger quadrilobe plaques depict the *Crucifixion* and half-length busts of the *Virgin*, *St John*, *St Francis*, *St Claire* and *St Anthony of Padua*, the *Virgin and Child* and a *Pope* (?Nicholas IV; *see* GOTHIC, fig. 90). In between, smaller plaques depict the *Evangelist Symbols* and various animals. The eight-faceted knop has circular enamel medallions of *Christ the Redeemer* and seven half-length *Apostles*. The chalice was without immediate precedent; its form was highly influential, and it was never technically superseded. It has been suggested that the fluid lines of the enamels on the chalice reflect contemporary French manuscript illuminations by Master Honoré and his workshop.

A number of other objects have been attributed to Guccio on the basis of this chalice. Although none of the documented seals has survived, the possible appearance of one of his seals, produced for the Siena Nove, is preserved in the border decoration beneath Simone Martini's *Maestà* fresco (completed 1315–16) in the Palazzo Pubblico, Siena. Attempts have been made to attribute, on the basis of stylistic similarities, three extant seals to Guccio: the seal of a Sienese confraternity, the Società dei Raccomandati al Santissimo Crocifisso (*c.* 60×36 mm; Rome, Pal. Venezia, 177), and those for Cardinal Matteo d'Acquasparta (55×40 mm; Rome, Vatican, Archv Capitolare S Pietro, AA, Arm. I–XVIII, 2178) and for Cardinal Teodorico da Orvieto (*c.* 1299; Paris, Archvs N., DD 6173).

An incised marble slab of the *Crucifixion* (Carrara marble, 448×280×32 mm; Siena, S Pellegrino alla Sapienza) is also attributed to Guccio and dated 1310–15. It is one of the earliest examples of a new iconography for the Crucifixion with the Virgin and St John seated beside the Cross. The fine quality of the incised lines and the use of polychromy have been compared to contemporary enamel work, although there is no evidence that Guccio ever worked in marble, and the attribution is based purely on the close stylistic similarity between the figure of *Christ* and that on the chalice. A silver processional cross (max. dimensions 448×325 mm; Florence, Bargello, 685 C) is also attributed to Guccio by De Castris.

The existence of Guccio's workshop is speculative: Gauthier attributed to Guccio or his workshop a medallion of *St Elizabeth of Hungary* (diam. 74 mm; Paris, Louvre, OA 2011) and one of *St Anthony* (diam. 90 mm; Berlin, Tiergarten, Kstgewmus., 97,5) and also associated with this artist an enamel plaque of the *Virgin and Child Enthroned with SS Peter and Paul* (120×90 mm; Florence, Bargello, collection Carrand, 678 C). This plaque has also been tentatively attributed to Tondino di Guerrino, possibly a pupil of Guccio's, and dated *c.* 1310.

The goldsmiths Gheri di Mannaia and Pino di Mannaia referred to in documents dating 1311–12 were possibly Guccio's brothers. The artist had three sons, Montigiano, Mannaia and Giacomo, who were also goldsmiths and are mentioned in a document of 31 May 1329 as 'aurifices cives senenses'.

BIBLIOGRAPHY

A. Lisini: 'Notizie di orafi e di oggetti di oreficeria senese', *Bull. Sen. Stor. Patria*, xi/3 (1904), pp. 649–54 [docs]

I. Machetti: 'Orafi senesi', *La Diana*, iv (1929), pp. 14, 18

I. Hueck: 'Una crocifissione su marmo del primo trecento e alcuni smalti senesi', *Ant. Viva*, viii/1 (1969), pp. 22–34

M. M. Gauthier: *Emaux du moyen âge occidental* (Fribourg, 1972), pp. 387–8

E. Cioni Liserani: 'Alcune ipotesi per Guccio di Mannaia', *Prospettiva*, xvii (April 1979), pp. 47–58

P. Leone De Castris: 'Smalti e oreficerie di Guccio di Mannaia al museo del Bargello', *Prospettiva*, xvii (April 1979), pp. 58–64

R. Bonito Fanelli, ed.: *Il tesoro della basilica di San Francesco ad Assisi* (Assisi, 1980), pp. 123–5, figs 57–63

Il gotico a Siena: Miniature, pitture, oreficerie, oggetti d'arte (exh. cat., Siena, Pal. Pub., 1982), nos. 27–8, 30–31, 35

□

Gucewicz, Wawrzyniec [Stuoka Gucevicius, Laurynas] (*b* Migańce (now Lithuania), before 5 Aug 1753; *d* Wilno (now Vilnius), 21 Dec 1798). Polish architect. He was the son of a peasant, and in order to obtain a higher education he chose a career in the church, studying at the Seminary in Vilnius (1773) and at the Vilnius Academy, where he attended lectures on architecture given by Marcin Knakfus (1742–*c.* 1821). In 1776–7 he studied in Rome on a scholarship funded by Ignacy Massalski, Bishop of Vilnius. After his return to Vilnius he taught mathematics at the Seminary and left the Church. In 1778 he travelled abroad with Massalski to various cities including Gdańsk, Berlin and Hamburg. They also stayed in Denmark and Sweden for a short while before going to Paris, where Gucewicz stayed for 18 months, studying under Jacques-Germain Soufflot, Jean-Baptiste Rondelet and Claude-Nicolas Ledoux, as well as at the Académie d'Architecture and at Jacques-François Blondel's school of architecture. Gucewicz returned to Poland at the end of 1780. In early 1781 he worked on Bishop Massalski's residence (completed 1792) in Werki, near Vilnius, which was built to designs by Knakfus.

In 1781-6 Gucewicz worked on plans for Vilnius Town Hall (completed 1789), which he designed as a peripteral temple articulated by a colossal order of Tuscan columns, with a prostyle portico and, at the rear, a tower in the form of a Tuscan column surmounted by a statue. In 1783 he took on the supervision of the rebuilding of Vilnius Cathedral, giving it a new, monumental Neo-classical form, for which he received the 'Merentibus' medal from King Stanislav II Poniatowski. In 1790 Gucewicz was elevated to noble rank and in February 1794 he was appointed professor of civil architecture at Vilnius Academy. Gucewicz had a strong impact on the architecture of Vilnius and its surroundings during the latter years of the 18th century and in the early 19th. His studies in

Paris influenced the distinct nature of Vilnius's Neo-classical architecture, which broke away from the current trends in Warsaw.

BIBLIOGRAPHY

PSB

E. Budreika: *Architektas Laurynas Stuoka Gucevicius* [The architect Laurynas Stuoka Gucevicius] (Vilnius, 1954)

ANDRZEJ ROTTERMUND

Gucht, van der. *See* VANDERGUCHT.

Guckeisen, Jakob (*b* Cologne; *fl* Strasbourg, 1590s). German cabinetmaker, writer and engraver. He is recorded as a cabinetmaker and citizen of Strasbourg from 1596. He appears to have been a pupil of the architect Johann Schoch, who designed Schloss Gottesau, near Karlsruhe (*c.* 1587), and the Friedrichsbau of the Heidelberg Schloss (*c.* 1601–7). Guckeisen, in collaboration with Veit Eck (*fl* Strasbourg, 1587), wrote a *Kunstbüchlein* (Strasbourg, 1596) dedicated to masons and cabinetmakers. He also wrote a similar work, *Etlicher Architectischer Portalen, Epitapien, Caminen Und Schweyffen*, published in the same year in Cologne. They were followed in 1599 by a series of engraved designs for six chests, also published in Cologne. In collaboration with the cabinetmaker and etcher Hans Jakob Ebelmann, Guckeisen also produced the *Schränke* (1598), *Seilenbuch* (1598), *Architectura Kunstbuch Darinnen Alerhand Portalen Reisbetten Undt Epitaphien* (1599) and *Schweyfbuch* (1599), the last dedicated to the cabinetmaker Jacob Riedel in Strasbourg. As a designer of ornament, Guckeisen was familiar with the whole repertory of Renaissance decoration, using it in varied combinations.

BIBLIOGRAPHY

Thieme–Becker

H. Kreisel: *Die Kunst des deutschen Möbels*, i (Munich, 1968)

F. Lévy-Coblentz: *L'Art du meuble en Alsace du gothique au baroque, 1480–1698*, i (Strasbourg, 1975)

Die Renaissance im deutschen Südwesten (exh. cat., ed. H. Geissler and others; Karlsruhe, Bad. Landesmus., 1986)

KAI BUDDE

Gude, Hans Fredrik (*b* Christiania [now Oslo], 13 March 1825; *d* Berlin, 17 Aug 1903). Norwegian painter. He was the most renowned Norwegian landscape painter of his time. At the age of 12 he was enrolled as a pupil of Johannes Flintoe (1787–1880). After attending evening classes at the Kongelige Tegneskole in Christiania, he went to Düsseldorf in 1841 to study privately with the landscape painter Andreas Achenbach (1815–1910). In 1842 Gude was admitted to the landscape class at the Akademie under Johann Wilhelm Schirmer. He was later appointed an assistant teacher at Schirmer's private studio, and he succeeded his master as Professor of landscape painting both at the Düsseldorf Akademie (1854–62) and at the Karlsruhe Akademie (1864–80). In the 1840s Gude established his reputation in Norway and on the Continent with powerful images of the Norwegian mountains. These were shown in the Kunstforening galleries in Düsseldorf and Christiania and at the Berliner Akademische Kunstausstellung, where Gude exhibited throughout his life. Adolph Tidemand and Gude dominated the colony of Norwegian artists who studied in Düsseldorf in the mid-19th century. The two artists worked together on five paintings, all representing people in boats; Gude painted the landscape, Tidemand the figures. The *Bridal Procession at Hardanger* (1848; Oslo, N.G.) celebrates a ceremony of country life and is the most famous work of Norwegian National Romanticism. In a sunny western Norwegian landscape with snow on the high mountains, the bridal couple and wedding guests in national costume are shown rowing across the water from a medieval stave church on the headland in the background. Gude revealed greater maturity in *High Mountain* (1857; Oslo, N.G.). The disposition of mountains massed on the high plateau around a little lake produces an effect of monumentality. The predominant colours shade from grey to blue, concentrated in the cloud cover. The influence of Schirmer's tranquil landscapes is apparent, while the rhythmic arrangement of light and shadow is reminiscent of Achenbach.

In 1861–2 Gude stayed at Betws-y-Coed, Wales, where the mild climate enabled him to work out of doors all year and thereby to develop a greater fidelity to nature. The *Efeu Bridge* (1863; Oslo, N.G.) exemplifies Gude's creative innovations during this period, with its rich nuances, intimate charm and misty aerial perspective. After the Royal Academy, London, rejected his submissions to the exhibition of 1863, Gude realized he could not gain entry to the British market, and in 1864 he accepted the chair of landscape painting at Karlsruhe, where he was also Director of the Akademie for several years.

During the 1860s and 1870s Gude was particularly concerned with studying the reflection of light on water. He painted pictures of the Austrian lakes and small boats and sailing ships on the Christiania fjord in a light breeze, with the sun hidden behind light summer clouds (e.g. *Approaching Christiania*, 1874; Oslo, N.G.). He gradually gained confidence as a figure painter, although his human figures are never more than staffage. In 1880 Gude became Professor of the Akademie in Berlin and Director of the landscape-painting class. In the same year he completed the huge *Port of Refuge* (Oslo, Norwegian Shipowners' Association), which depicts a ship sinking in the breakers of a dramatic storm, in colours harmonized with the blue-grey and beige tones of the sea. Gude remained active as a painter until his death. The numbers of his pupils declined towards the end of the 19th century, when his style became increasingly outmoded, but throughout his 50 years of teaching he assisted a long succession of Norwegian and other artists, including Frits Thaulow and August Cappelen. Gude's son Nils (1859–1908) was also a painter.

WRITINGS

L. Dietrichson, ed.: *Af Hans Gudes liv og vaerker: Kunstnerens livserindringer* [Hans Gude's life and works: the artist's memoirs] (Christiania, 1899)

BIBLIOGRAPHY

NKL

T. Kjerulf: 'Gudes atelier i Wales', *Ved lovfaldstider* (1867), pp. 148–61

F. E. Haverkamp: *Hans Gude i Düsseldorf: Oeuvrekatalog*, 2 vols (Oslo, 1982)

Tidemand og Gude (exh. cat. by F. E. Haverkamp, Åmot, Stift. Modums Blaafarveværk, 1984)

ERNST HAVERKAMP

Gudewerdt [Guthwerdt; Gutwerth; Gudewirth]. German family of wood-carvers. In the 17th century three generations contributed to their family workshop in Eckernförde, Holstein, though the sons of (2) Hans Gudewerdt (ii) left no distinct body of work.

(1) Hans Gudewerdt (i) (*b* Eckernförde, second half of the 16th century; *d* Eckernförde, before 1642). He is first documented in 1596; by 1605 he was an alderman of the wood-carvers' guild, retiring from office in 1635. His most representative works are bride-chests, found in numerous German and Danish museum collections. These are more richly decorated than was common at that period, with wide cartouches, framed by elaborate scrollwork, enclosing carvings of animals and mythical creatures. Gudewerdt's bride-chests often represented a young couple in contemporary dress above a hare blowing a flute, an emblem of fertility; this has caused the artist to be referred to in literature as the Master of the Flute-blowing Hare. He often used as a subject the narrative of the Book of Esther. Also attributed to him has been the decoration of the chancel of the church at Gettorf, in the form of carved panels (dated 1598), which display other biblical narratives.

(2) Hans Gudewerdt (ii) (*b* Eckernförde, *c.* 1600; *d* Eckernförde, 12 Feb 1671). Son of (1) Hans Gudewerdt (i). He contributed significantly to the development of Baroque sculpture in the Holstein region, surpassing his father in the art of wood-carving. In 1634 he was already well established as a master wood-carver; in 1635 he succeeded his father as head of the family workshop. His work for Frederick III, Duke of Holstein-Gottorp (*reg* 1616–59), included decorations for ducal residences at Gottorp and Husum; between 1649 and 1654 he is known to have received commissions for four bridal carriages. However, his most notable work was on religious commissions. He decorated a number of church interiors in the region, most notably that of the Nikolaikirche in his native Eckernförde, to which he contributed some important pieces. The earliest known is the *Sleeping Death-watch* (1632), a naked putto resting on a skull, while holding an hour-glass. This was a popular motif in northern European art, especially in Schleswig-Holstein, and may have derived from a design by Dürer. Another early example, dated 1636, is a relief carving of a coat of arms, which formerly was part of an elaborate tomb decoration.

Gudewerdt's most important works were his huge high altars. The first was commissioned in 1640, also for the Nikolaikirche in Eckernförde, and is signed HANS+GVDEWERDT+INVENTER+ET+VECTZIT. The second, for the church of St Nikolai in Kappeln, followed in 1641. They are both particularly fine examples of his early Baroque style. They served as models for the other two high altars, at Schönkirchen (1653) and Dänischenhagen (1656; Preetz, Benedictine Klosterkirche), which were, however, heavier in design and with less well-proportioned figures. Most of the figures were carved in the round. The artist paid great attention to the finer detail, such as the eyes; the dark-brown oak was generally left unpainted, except for some restrained gilding on the frame and background. However, the high altar in Kappeln was fully polychromed.

The three-storey high altar at Eckernförde (*in situ*) departs from traditional altar design. Its height from the altar table to the vaulted ceiling of the choir is 6.58 m; at its widest it measures 4.15 m. The central panels, 2 m high, contain an elaborately framed *Crucifixion*, showing a living Christ. This feature, extremely rare in northern Europe, was not repeated in the other three high altars, for which Gudewerdt chose the traditional figure of a dead Christ. Two small praying angels hover on either side of the Christ figure. At the foot of the cross stand the figures of St John, a seated Mary Magdalene and the Virgin Mary, whose impassive upright pose is in contrast to the rest of the tableau; the angels and Mary Magdalene were added later, for an additional fee. Niches at the sides of the altar contain figures of the Evangelists *St John* and *St Mark* (see fig.). The church at Kappeln was renovated in 1790, at which time the high altar was disassembled: only the central portion, a *Crucifixion* and a *Resurrection*, was replaced in its original position. The seated figures of Moses and St John the Evangelist were transferred to the chancel, while the remaining parts of the altar were rearranged into a separate panel and hung on the north wall of the church. The high altar of Dänischenhagen, similar to the one at Kappeln but larger, already points the way to Rococo in its rich and fully developed ornamentation.

Between 1648 and 1661 Gudewerdt carved a number of epitaphs, which were polychromed. Only the *Hacke* epitaph (1648) at the Marienkirche in Flensburg has retained its original colours, while the epitaphs at Eckernförde, that of *Heinrich Ripenau* (3.40×1.75 m; 1650) and

Hans Gudewerdt (ii): *St Mark*, wood, from the high altar, Nikolaikirche, Eckernförde, 1640

the *Börnsen* epitaph (1661), the largest and most daring in concept, were at some stage toned down to match the colour of the oak used in the interior decoration. The chancel at Sörup (1663) is unusual in that Gudewerdt decorated the panels with relief carvings; he generally preferred figures carved in the round. He made a unique contribution to wood sculpture in Schleswig-Holstein and northern Europe. His compositional and figurative style bridged the High Renaissance and Early Baroque, while his later ornamental mode is Rococo-like in spirit.

BIBLIOGRAPHY

Thieme–Becker

E. Hempel: *Baroque Art and Architecture in Central Europe*, Pelican Hist. A. (Harmondsworth, 1965), p. 81, pls 39(B), 40(B), 41(A)

Barockplastik in Norddeutschland (exh. cat., ed. J. Rasmussen; Hamburg, Mus. Kst & Gew., 1977)

HANNELORE HÄGELE

Gudiashvili, Lado [Vladimir] **(Davidovich)** (*b* Tiflis [now Tbilisi], 30 March 1896; *d* Tbilisi, 20 July 1980). Georgian painter, draughtsman, illustrator and stage designer. From 1910 to 1914 he trained at the Tiflis School of Painting and Sculpture and from 1919 to 1926 at the Académie Ronson in Paris. While in Paris he became closely acquainted with Modigliani, Ignacio Zuloaga, Nata'ya Goncharova and Mikhail Larionov. His early works, with their theatrically romantic depictions of Georgian national life, fantastic and Symbolist motifs and surreal effects of colour, combine elements of the grotesque with a charming poetic mystery (e.g. the *'Tsotskhali' Fish*, 1920; Tbilisi, Mus. A. Georg.). His affinity with ancient Georgian and Persian art, of which he was a connoisseur, intensified on his return to Georgia in 1926; his colours became shimmering and tinged with gold, and, at the same time, the visual link with theatre became even stronger (many of his paintings have opera or ballet performances as their subjects or portray actresses in costume). He frequently depicted fantastic and mythological subjects (e.g. *Serafita's Outing*, 1940; Tbilisi, Mus. A. Georgia). Usually the central figure is a gracefully majestic and beautiful Georgian woman representing a mysterious earth goddess. His vast anti-totalitarian series of ink drawings (1942; e.g. Tbilisi, Mus. A. Georgia) recall the images in Goya's work: the chimerical visions that he evoked embody in equal measure Nazism and the tragedy of Georgian history during the years of Stalin's rule. Gudiashvili also painted frescoes, including one (1946) for the Kashveti Church in Tbilisi, a choice of commission for which he was expelled from the Communist Party and dismissed from the Tbilisi Academy of Arts, where he had taught. He illustrated many books, among them Sulkan Saba Orbeliani's *Mudrost' lzhi* ('The wisdom of falsehood'; 1939), and worked as a set designer for the theatre.

WRITINGS

Lado Gudiashvili: Kniga vospominaniy [Lado Gudiashvili: a book of reminiscenses], ed. I. Sh. Gagua (Moscow, 1987)

BIBLIOGRAPHY

A. I. Mikhaylov: *Lado Gudiashvili* (Moscow, 1968)

V. Beridze: *Lado Gudiashvili* (Tbilisi and Budapest, 1975)

M. N. SOKOLOV

Gudimallam [anc. Tiruvippirambedu]. Village and temple site in south-eastern Andhra Pradesh, India. The oldest and most important feature of the site is a *liṅga* (h. 0.8 m; *see* INDIAN SUBCONTINENT, fig. 150) in the form of a naturalistically rendered phallus with a figure of Shiva carved on one side. Shiva holds a spear, a water pot and an antelope skin and stands on a dwarfish earth spirit (*yakṣa*) symbolizing fertility and abundance. Stylistically, the figure represents a stage between the sculptures of Bharhut and Bodhgaya and is therefore the earliest extant *liṅga* erected for worship in a temple. Recent excavations have shown that the *liṅga* was originally surrounded by a stone railing similar to that shown in a relief of *liṅga* worship from Mathura (*c.* 2nd century AD; Mathura, Govt Mus., see Chandra, 1975, pls 2, 3). It has been restored to this original format. The *liṅga* was originally housed in an apsidal brick temple; the present temple, also apsidal, is of late Chola date (*see* INDIAN SUBCONTINENT, §III, 6(i)(g)). An inscription of AD 1127 on a loose slab found near by refers to a stone temple built for the god Parasurameshvara, the name by which the temple and its deity are currently known.

Another image at the site is of the sun god, Surya, and has been dated to the late 7th century. Like the *liṅga*, it is housed within a temple of much later date. Other shrines within the Parasurameshvara complex include temples to Surya, Karttikeya and the Goddess dating from the 12th to 13th centuries. A gateway (*gopura*) dates to *c.* 1200. Numerous inscriptions found at the site date from the times of the Pallava, Bana and early Chola dynasties (9th–13th century), with inscriptions of local rulers dating as late as 1801.

BIBLIOGRAPHY

T. A. G. Rao: *Elements of Hindu Iconography* (Madras, 1914–16)

P. Chandra, ed.: *Studies in Indian Temple Architecture* (New Delhi, 1975)

I.K. Sharma: *The Development of Early Saiva Art and Architecture* (Delhi, 1982)

G. von Mitterwallner: 'Evolution of the Linga', *Discourses on Siva*, ed. M. Meister (Philadelphia, 1985), pp. 12–31

WALTER SMITH

Gudin, (Jean-Antoine-)Théodore, Baron (*b* Paris, 15 Aug 1802; *d* Boulogne-sur-Seine, 12 April 1880). French painter and printmaker. He studied under Anne-Louis Girodet and Antoine-Jean Gros at the Ecole des Beaux-Arts in Paris, which he entered on 30 January 1817. With the emergence of the Romantic movement he interrupted his Neo-classical training to become a disciple and friend of Delacroix and Gericault. Like Delacroix, he first exhibited at the Salon in 1822, and his submission included the depiction of an eminently Romantic subject, *Episodes from a Shipwreck* (sold, Paris, 7 Dec 1973). However, his greatest success of the 1820s, which established him as a marine painter, was the *Fire on the Kent*, which he exhibited at the Salon of 1827. Following this direction he cultivated his talent for historical naval subjects on a large scale, becoming France's leading painter of sea battles. His style is characterized by the faithful rendering of water, the use of impasto and the careful execution of motifs.

From the beginning of his career Gudin's work was appreciated by both the public and the critics, and he received numerous state, royal and private commissions, becoming a baron under Louis-Philippe. He sold his paintings to the most eminent members of French society, such as the Baron de Rothschild, as well as to such foreign sovereigns as King Leopold I of Belgium and the Tsar. Gudin participated in many military expeditions. He was appointed an official artist to the Algerian expedition in 1830 and returned with many paintings that he exhibited at the Salon from 1831 onwards, such as *Hurricane at the Roadstead of Algiers, 7 January 1831* (1835; Paris, Louvre). He also painted other military subjects that glorified French valour, particularly French naval victories over the British. During the 1830s Louis-Philippe commissioned Gudin to paint 97 large scenes illustrating the most glorious episodes of French naval history to decorate the galleries at Versailles, 41 of which were shown at the Salon between 1839 and 1848. To this commission belong such works as *Capture of the English Corvette 'Le Vimiejo' by a Section of the Imperial Flotilla, 8 May 1804* and *Battle of Chio in 1681* (both Versailles, Château). This project seems to have drained his inspiration as from then on his work became very repetitive. In 1841 Gudin was commissioned by Tsar Nicholas I (*reg* 1825–55) to paint the ports of Russia and visited Warsaw and St Petersburg.

From the late 1840s into the 1860s Gudin continued to paint historical subjects while also producing some genre scenes, such as a *Scottish Hunting Party* (exh. Salon 1849). He also enjoyed the patronage of Napoleon III whom he joined on his campaigns to Italy and Algeria. Among the commissions from Napoleon III was the *Arrival of the Queen of England at Cherbourg* (exh. Salon 1861). After the Franco-Prussian War of 1870–71 Gudin retired to Scotland, where he raised money to support his wounded compatriots. As well as Paris, Gudin exhibited his work in London, and his paintings appeared intermittently at the Royal Academy between 1837 and 1873 and at the British Institution. In London he understandably showed his coastal scenes (e.g. *Dutch Coastal Scene*, 1846; London, Wallace) rather than his historical paintings. He also produced illustrations for such books as Eugène Sue's *Histoire de la marine française* (1835) and Mme de Staël's *Corinne ou l'Italie* (1841–2).

WRITINGS

E. Beraud, ed.: *Baron Gudin: Souvenirs, 1820–70* (Paris, 1921)

BIBLIOGRAPHY

Bellier de La Chavignerie–Auvray; *DBF*
Inventaire du fonds français après 1800, Paris, Bib. N., Dépt. Est. cat., ix (Paris, 1960), pp. 442–4
E. H. H. Archibald: *Dictionary of Sea Painters* (Woodbridge, 1980, 2/1989)

ATHENA S. E. LEOUSSI

Gudiol i Cunill, Josep (*b* Vic, 1872; *d* Vic, 1931). Spanish art historian, archaeologist and museum curator. He was deeply involved in the nationalist cultural renaissance that took place in Catalonia at the end of the 19th century. His publications include a monograph on 14th-century Catalan art, a companion to an earlier study by S. Sanpere i Miquel on 15th-century Catalan art. Much of the work of Gudiol i Cunill was, however, centred on the Museu Arqueologic Artistic Episcopal, Vic, founded in 1889 and inaugurated in 1891 with a superb collection of 1300 objects, most of which are examples of medieval Catalan art. Appointed curator in 1898, Gudiol i Cunill worked there until his death. He wrote extensively about the museum, as well as producing various guides to the collection.

WRITINGS

Arqueología sagrada catalana (Barcelona, 1902)
El Museu Episcopal de Vich (Vic, 1918)
Els trecentistes Catalans (Barcelona, 1924)
Memories del Museu Episcopal de Vich, 1895–1930 (Vic, 1930)

BIBLIOGRAPHY

E. Junyent: *Galería de vicenses ilustres: Mn. José Gudiol y Cunill* (Vic, 1948)

Gudiol i Ricart, Josep (*b* Vic, 1904; *d* 1985). Spanish art historian. After studying architecture he devoted himself to art history, concentrating at first on the Catalan artistic tradition. His most important book was *L'Art de la Catalogne*; he also produced books on medieval Catalan painting, as well as specialized works on such Catalan Gothic painters as Jaime Huguet, Luís Borrasá and Bernardo Martorell, and on Catalan stained-glass windows. Gudiol i Ricart also studied medieval art from other regions in Spain, particularly Castilian and Navarrese artists, and produced a work on Spanish Gothic painting. He published monographs, including detailed catalogues, on Velázquez and Goya. His main contribution to art history has been to continue the work of Josep Gudiol i Cunill, Chandler R. Post and Manuel Gómez Moreno in establishing a scientific inventory of Spanish art.

WRITINGS

L'Art de la Catalogne (Paris, 1937; Ger. trans., 1937)
La pintura gótica a Catalunya (Barcelona, 1938)
Pintura e imaginería románicas, A. Hisp., vi (Madrid, 1954)
Pintura gótica, A. Hisp., ix (Madrid, 1955)
Goya (Barcelona, 1970)
Velázquez (London, 1974)
Zurbarán (Barcelona, 1976)

BIBLIOGRAPHY

J. A. Gaya Nuño: *Historia de la crítica de arte en España* (Madrid, 1975)

FRANCISCO CALVO SERRALLER

Guðmundsson [Gudmundsson]. Icelandic family of conceptual artists.

(1) Kristján Guðmundsson (*b* Snœfellsnes, West Iceland, 1 June 1941). He trained as a pilot and was self-taught as an artist. In the 1960s and 1970s he lived in the Netherlands, the USA and Spain. He had his first one-man show in Reykjavík in 1968. He was introduced to Concrete poetry and the Fluxus movement by Dieter Roth, and by 1969 he had evolved a version of Arte Povera, which he showed at the first exhibitions of the avant-garde group SÚM. After moving to Amsterdam in 1970 he renewed his acquaintance with the minimalist art of Malevich, Lucio Fontana, Piero Manzoni and the De Stijl group and began to take an interest in Dutch conceptual art, which was generally more lyrical and less dogmatic. Throughout the 1970s Guðmundsson created minimal works embodying abstract or unfathomable concepts such as time, space, sound and energy. Typical of his early conceptual works are the *Supersonic Drawings* (1972; artist's col.), made by shooting bullets from a rifle across sheets of paper, each drawing taking approximately $\frac{1}{1500}$ of a second to produce. Among other notable works from this period are his *Once around the Sun* (1977), which consists of two volumes containing a continuous line of the distance referred to in the title, and the *Triangle in a Square* (exh. SÚM, 1972), where a square of ordinary earth contains a triangle of consecrated earth. Other bookworks include *Niður/Down* (Amsterdam and Reykjavík, 1972), *Circles* (Amsterdam, 1973) and *Drawings to Waterfalls* (Lucerne, 1975). In later years Guðmundsson's work became more formalist and free in interpretation, as in his installations of the raw materials of drawing—rolls of paper and blocks of graphite—which the artist regarded as 'a bank of material lying either side of zero', presumably awaiting the moment of creation (e.g. *Untitled*, 1988; Stockholm, Mod. Mus.).

BIBLIOGRAPHY

E. Pétursson and G. Harðarson: 'Kristján Guðmundsson', *Teningur*, 4 (1987), pp. 48–60 [interview]

Kristján Guðmundsson: Teikningar/Drawings 1972–88 (exh. cat., ed. G. B. Kvaran; Reykjavík, Kjarvalsstaðir, 1989) [Icel. and Eng. text]

AÐALSTEINN INGÓLFSSON

(2) Sigurður Guðmundsson (*b* Reykjavík, 20 Sept 1942). Brother of (1) Kristján Guðmundsson. He studied at the Icelandic College of Arts and Crafts from 1960 until 1963. Between 1963 and 1964 he was a student at the Academie 63 in Haarlem, the Netherlands. In 1965 he returned to Iceland, where he took part in the activities of the SÚM group. He was given his first one-man exhibition in 1969 at the SÚM Gallery, Reykjavík. In 1970 he settled in Amsterdam, and he trained at the Ateliers 63 in Haarlem (1970–71). After 1974 he made photographs of situations in landscapes or interiors, in which he featured himself, for example *Statement* (1977; Amsterdam, Stedel. Mus.). He also gave performances and published artists' books. In 1980–81 he worked at P.S.1, a gallery specializing in new art, in New York. After his return to Amsterdam, he started to construct three-dimensional installations from organic materials, for example *Het grote gedicht* ('The great poem'; 1981; Amsterdam, Stedel. Mus.).

BIBLIOGRAPHY

Sigurður Guðmundsson: Situaties/Situations (exh. cat., Amsterdam, Stedel. Mus., 1980)

M. Levels: *Sigurður Guðmundsson* (Amsterdam, 1982)

Z.-Z. Eyck, ed.: *Sigurður Guðmundsson* (Venlo, 1992) [Eng./Dutch; cat. rai.]

JOHN STEEN

Guðmundsson, Guðmundur. *See* ERRÓ.

Guðnason, Svavar (*b* Höfn, Hornafjörður, 18 Nov 1909; *d* Reykjavík, 25 June 1988). Icelandic painter. He was mostly self-taught, apart from a brief period at the Kunstakademi in Copenhagen (1935–6). In 1936–7 he abandoned figurative art by breaking up the motif into simple, fluid supporting structures. In Paris, where he studied for one week with Léger in 1938, he met the painter Asger Jorn and the sculptor Sonja Ferlov Mancoba and strengthened his connections with the Scandinavian avant-garde. His paintings up to 1940 betray a short-lived influence from Miró. Guðnason first achieved public attention at the exhibition *Skandinaverne* ('Scandinavians') at Charlottenborg in Copenhagen in 1939, where he was one of the representatives of Iceland.

In 1939–41 Guðnason developed a free but complex abstract style that he called 'fugue-style'. Many paintings of this period were shown at the 'Tent Exhibition', a collaborative effort by a group of Danish artists associated with the periodical *Helhesten*, who later became leading members of COBRA, at Bellevue in Copenhagen in 1941, and they displayed his spontaneous skill in interpreting complicated forms and in combining strong colours. After 1942 Guðnason's style became free and flowing and finally turned into expressive abstract painting. He used the palette knife in a broad and harsh manner, applying the colour thickly and abruptly or scraping it into waves across the canvas. This free style reached its height in 1945, when Guðnason settled in Iceland and held the first exhibition there of this kind of abstract art. In 1946–50 his paintings became more regular. The clear Icelandic light and the nature of the country had a direct influence on his choice of colour and his technique. With a spatula and brushes he built up powerful pattern blocks reminiscent of basalt columns and held together by straight connecting lines. Colours were overlaid and various coatings, surface textures and methods of painting were juxtaposed or superimposed. After 1950 his style became calmer and in 1952–8 it became geometric. From 1960 to 1980 Guðnason made daring syntheses of all his former styles, using horizontal emphases without a direct centre of gravity on tall, narrow canvases.

BIBLIOGRAPHY

B. Th. Björnsson: *Íslensk myndlist á 19. og 20. öld* [Icelandic art in the 19th and 20th centuries], 2 vols (Reykjavík, 1964–73)

H. Laxness: *Svavar Guðnason* (Copenhagen, 1968)

Svavar Guðnason (exh. cat., ed Ó. Kvaran, texts P. Hovdenakk and R. Dahlmann Olsen; Reykjavík, Nordic House, 1986)

HALLDÓR BJÖRN RUNÓLFSSON

Guedes, Amancio (d'Alpoim Miranda) [Pancho] (*b* Lisbon, 13 May 1925). Portuguese architect, sculptor and painter, active in Africa. His childhood was spent in Mozambique and its offshore islands. From the age of 14 he was educated in Johannesburg, first at Maritz Brothers' School and then at the University of the Witwatersrand School of Architecture, from which he graduated in 1949. After a brief period working as a draughtsman, he set up his own practice in Lourenço Marques (now Maputo), Mozambique, in 1950. His timing was fortunate: shortly afterwards a construction boom began that was to continue until the fall of the colonial government in 1974, and the bulk of his work was carried out during the 25 years preceding independence. He completed approximately 500 buildings, including churches, schools, houses, flats, restaurants and office buildings, in all parts of the country. The best of these rank among the finest post-war architecture in Southern Africa. In 1975 Guedes left Mozambique to take up the Chair in Architecture at the University of the Witwatersrand, Johannesburg. With the pressure to build now greatly reduced, Guedes was able to treat later projects in Portugal and South Africa as labours of love.

Guedes was known as an instinctive architect and a determined individualist. His working methods were inextricably linked to his charismatic personality. This he used as a powerful tool, whether for the purpose of charming clients into accepting his proposals, negotiating with officialdom or persuading builders to construct his often outlandish ideas. His most characteristic idiom is strongly influenced by the materials and trade skills that were at his disposal in Mozambique. Good quality softwood was scarce: shuttering tended to be of very poor quality, making a plaster covering necessary on all external walls, whether built of monolithic concrete or of clay or cement blocks. For this reason, Guedes's underlying theme is one of plasticity. Even where forms are geometric, there

Amancio Guedes: Smiling Lion Apartments, Maputo, Mozambique, 1956–8

is always a suggestion that the building might have been modelled in clay. This quality is found even in Guedes's work in South Africa, with its markedly different constructional tradition. Not until 1983, in the Cohen House in Johannesburg, did he design a house in load-bearing brick.

Also a painter and sculptor, Guedes developed a philosophy that was deeply influenced by student encounters with Dada, and he remained resolutely opposed to the idea of chronological development in an artist's work. Seeing a selection of his buildings for the first time, one is struck by what appear to be wild stylistic variations, chosen almost at random from a wide repertory of available models; examples include Sorgentini House, Maputo (1955–6; Frank Lloyd Wright); the Desirello House, Johannesburg (1965–8; Palladio); Smiling Lion Apartments, Maputo (1956–8; see fig.; Gaudí); Yes House Offices, Maputo (1961–2; Louis I. Kahn) and Cohen House, Johannesburg (1983–4; Le Corbusier). Mozambique's colonial architecture, into which Guedes researched extensively, also fired his imagination. In spite of frequent references to buildings by other architects, Guedes's work is not 'architects' architecture'. The development of a wider reputation has been hampered by the inaccessibility, for geographical and political reasons, of much of his work and the deceptive simplicity of a style that displays little concern for precise photogenic detailing or for an explicit theoretical rationale.

WRITINGS

'Vitruvius Moçambicanus', *Arquit. Port.*, i/2 (1985), pp. 12–62 [Eng. trans., pp. 67–78]

BIBLIOGRAPHY

S. Tavares: 'Pancho Amancio d'Alpoim Miranda Guedes: Arquitecto escultor, escultor arquitecto', *Colóq. A.*, xxxii (1977), pp. 14–23

T. Ostler: *Pancho Guedes: The Collective Unconsciousness of Architecture* (diss., U. Sheffield, 1978)

T. Tzara, A. Smithson and A. Berman: 'Amancio d'Alpoim Guedes', *A + U*, xciii (1978), pp. 3–52

Amancio Guedes (exh. cat., ed. D. Crompton; London, Archit. Assoc., 1980)

T. Ostler and others: 'Pancho Guedes', *Archit. SA*, xix (1982), pp. 19–34

C. A. Marques: 'A arte de Amancio de Alpoim Miranda Guedes', *Arquit. Port.*, i/2 (1985), pp. 64–6

TIMOTHY OSTLER

Guedes, Joaquim (*b* São Paulo, 18 June 1932). Brazilian architect, urban planner, teacher and writer. He graduated in architecture from the University of São Paulo (1954) and went into private practice (1955). Rejecting prevailing trends and influences, Guedes engaged in a constant search for new technical solutions, regarding each project as an opportunity to experiment with new ideas. His architecture can be divided into three groups: the first is characterized by the importance of structure as a means of defining space and volume, as in the church of Vila Madalena (1955) and the Cunha Lima House (1958), São Paulo; the industrial school (1966) at Campinas and one of his own houses (1973), São Paulo. The latter (see fig.), set below street level, has a modular, rectangular plan with roof and floor planes in exposed reinforced concrete, supported on four columns; thin concrete overhangs protect the glazed wall at first floor level, which slides back to turn the living room into a terrace. The second group exhibits a greater complexity of form in which the structure no longer determines the spatial result; examples include the forum of Itapira (1959), the Institute of Mathematics (1965) and the Pereira House (1968), all in São Paulo; the central library of Bahia (1968), Salvador, and the Dourado House (1974), São Paulo.

In the third group a concern for designing in accordance with Brazilian conditions, both environmental and economic, is evident, using simpler construction methods and incorporating traditional architectural elements to modify the climate. Examples include the Landi House (1967), Butantan, São Paulo, a basic, functional design using corrugated asbestos, brick and concrete, and his designs for houses in the new town of Caraíba (1976–80), incorporating internal patios and constructed of local clay bricks for thermal insulation. Some buildings combine several of these themes, though in a more compact and simple form, for example the Toledo House (1963), Piracicaba, São Paulo, a brick and concrete design reminiscent of Le Corbusier's Maisons Jaoul (1951–5), Paris, and the Beer House (1976), São Paulo, a severe composition in brick. Guedes's equally important activities as an urban planner began in 1957 when he took part in the national competition for the master-plan for the new national capital, Brasília. He went on to produce urban plans for São Paulo (1967), Campinas (1969), Porto Velho (1971), the new towns of Carajás and Marabá (1972), Piracicaba (1974), Campo Grande (1985) and Moji Guaçu (1971 and 1987), among others. He received particular recognition for his skill in the complex planning of new towns, his best-known works in this field being plans for the cities of Caraíba (1976–80), Bahia and Barcarena (1979–82), Amazonia. For Caraíba, located in a semi-arid area and planned to house a population of 13,000 workers from the copper mines, Guedes carried out extremely thorough analyses

Joaquim Guedes: Guedes House, São Paulo, 1973

that included not only the eco-geological systems of the region, urban hierarchy and future use of the town but also social organizations and local building materials and techniques. Inspired by the local tradition of grid-like village patterns, with plazas as focus points, his plan avoided social stratification by mixing dwelling types and creating spaces for future growth, both of individual houses and of the city. The orientation of the streets and houses, the architectural design and the construction methods were all planned to combat the harsh climatic conditions. His success as an urban planner resulted in Guedes being the only Brazilian invited to take part in the 1986 competition for the replanning of 70 ha of Bicocca Park in Milan, Italy, sponsored by Pirelli and the Prefecture of Milan. Guedes was also an influential teacher, encouraging philosophical reflection and technical innovation; he became Professor of Planning in the Faculty of Architecture and Urban Planning at the University of São Paulo in 1969, and he also taught at the Ecole d'Architecture de Strasbourg, France.

WRITINGS

'The Private House in Brazilian Tradition and the Problem of the New Generation', *Global Interiors*, 2 (1972)

'Obras y proyectos del studio de J. Guedes e Associados', *Rev. Summa*, 6 (1979)

'Caraíba New Town and Other Works', *Spazio & Soc.* (July 1979)

BIBLIOGRAPHY

P. M. Bardi: *Profile of New Brazilian Art* (São Paulo, 1969)

F. Bullrich: *New Directions in Latin American Architecture* (London and New York, 1969)

D. Bayón and P. Gasparini: *Panorámica de la arquitectura latino-americana* (Barcelona, 1977; Eng. trans., New York, 1979)

'Modern Brazilian Architecture', *Process: Archit.*, 17 (1980), pp. 71–81 [special issue]

REGINA MARIA PROSPERI MEYER

Guelfi [Guelphi]**, Giovanni Battista** (*fl* 1714–34). Italian sculptor, active in England. According to Vertue, he trained in Rome under Camillo Rusconi, a leading practitioner of late Baroque sculpture, before coming to England *c.* 1714 to work for Richard Boyle, 3rd Earl of Burlington and 4th Earl of Cork, for whom he may have executed garden statuary at Chiswick House, London. Shortly after his arrival he restored the Arundel Marbles (Oxford, Ashmolean), the collection of antique marbles assembled by Thomas Howard, 2nd (14th) Earl of Arundel, and then in the possession of Thomas Fermor, 1st Earl of Pomfret (1698–1753), at Easton Neston. He may have been responsible for the busts of the *Earl and Countess of Pomfret* (marble; Oxford, Ashmolean); if so, they are his finest works. Guelfi's known work is distinguished in design, perhaps owing to his association with such architects as James Gibbs and William Kent, but dull in execution. He carved a number of funerary monuments, among which that to *James Craggs* (terracotta model, 1724, London, Soane Mus.; marble, erected 1727, London, Westminster Abbey), designed by Gibbs, was very influential; the cross-legged stance of the standing effigy of the deceased, which leans on an urn, was adapted by other sculptors in 18th-century England, most notably by Michael Rysbrack. Guelfi himself used the composition again for his monument to *Thomas Watson Wentworth* (*d* 1723) (marble, *c.* 1731; York Minster), having already employed a variant of it in 1730 for that to *Edward Greville, 7th Earl of Warwick* (*d* 1727) (marble; London, St Mary Abbot's, Kensington). He also produced portrait busts for smaller monuments, including that to *Anne, Duchess of Richmond* (marble, 1734; Deene Park, Northants), also designed by Kent. The terracotta model (London, V&A) for this bust has the elongated form, blandly modelled features and vacuous expression common to all Guelfi's portraits. Around 1732 he was commissioned to carve a series of portrait busts of eminent Englishmen for Queen Caroline's Hermitage at Richmond Palace; the authorship of the surviving busts is debated, but those of *Sir Isaac Newton*, *John Locke*, *Samuel Clarke* and *William Wollaston* (all stone; London, Kensington Pal., Royal Col.) have been attributed to Guelfi on stylistic grounds. By 1734 he had fallen out of favour with Lord Burlington and his circle and returned to Italy, settling in Bologna.

BIBLIOGRAPHY

R. Gunnis: 'George Vertue's Notebooks', *Walpole Soc.*, xxii (1934) [Notebooks III]

K. A. Esdaile: 'Signor Guelfi, an Italian', *Burl. Mag.*, xc (1948), pp. 317–21

M. I. Webb: 'Giovanni Battista Guelfi, an Italian Sculptor Working in England', *Burl. Mag.*, xcvii (1955), pp. 139–45

M. Whinney: *Sculpture in Britain, 1530–1830*, Pelican Hist. A. (Harmondsworth, 1964); rev. J. Physick (Harmondsworth, 1988)

J. Physick: *Designs for English Sculpture, 1680–1860* (London, 1969)

M. Whinney: *English Sculpture, 1720–1830* (London, 1971)

T. Friedman: *James Gibbs* (New Haven, 1985)

KATHARINE EUSTACE

Güell (i Bacigalupi), Eusebi, Baron (*b* Barcelona, 15 Dec 1847; *d* Barcelona, 9 July 1918). Catalan industrialist and patron. After completing his studies in England, he returned to Barcelona to head the textile manufacturing company founded by his father, Joan Güell i Ferrer. He strongly supported Catalan nationalism and used his patronage of such Catalan Renaixença figures as the poet Ramón Picó i Campamar, the novelist Robles i Rodríguez Alcántara, the painter Alexis Clapés (1850–1920) and especially the architect ANTONI GAUDÍ, whom he met in 1878, to promote his progressive and paternalist visions of society. The first work by Gaudí for Güell was the gatehouse of his *finca* at Pedralbes, outside Barcelona (1884); the turrets covered with coloured ceramics show Gaudí's interest in Islamic architecture. The Palau Güell, Güell's residence in Barcelona (1886–91), is an extraordinary neo-Gothic palace, which contains some of Gaudí's most innovative interiors. The elaborate wrought-iron ornament of the entrance arches and bay windows is one of the earliest examples of the Catalan *modernisme*, a regional style related to Art Nouveau. The palace became a centre for Catalan intellectuals. The Park Güell, Barcelona (1900–14; *see* MOSAIC, colour pl. IV, fig. 2), reflecting Güell's reformist aims, was intended to be a garden suburb, containing a covered market and plaza, as well as individual houses, all brilliantly landscaped by Gaudí on a steep site overlooking the city; only two of the houses, one eventually owned by Gaudí and the other by Güell, were built. The warehouses and chapel at the Bodegas Güell, Garraf (1895–1905), were modest in scope and relatively restrained in manner. Gaudí's last work for Güell, the unfinished chapel at the Colonia Güell (1908–15), a model industrial village at his textile factory at Santa Coloma de Cervelló, is considered a masterpiece of neo-Gothic structural ingenuity.

BIBLIOGRAPHY

R. Descharnes and C. Prévost: *Gaudí the Visionary* (London, 1971)
J. de Puig: *El Palau Güell* (Barcelona, 1990)
C. Kent and D. J. Pringle: *Hacia la arquitectura de un paraíso: Park Güell* (Madrid, 1992)

□

Guelph [Guelf], House of. *See* WELF, House of.

Guénégaud, Henri de [Du Plessis-Guénégaud, Henri] (*b* 1609; *d* Paris, 16 March 1676). French administrator and patron. In 1638 he inherited from his father the office of Trésorier de l'Epargne and from 1643–69 he held other high offices including that of Secrétaire d'Etat for the Maison du Roi. In Paris, on the site of the Hôtel de Nevers on what is now the Quai de Conti, he built an hôtel to the designs of François Mansart. This he sold to the Princesse de Conti in 1670 and in 1771–5 it was rebuilt as the Hôtel de la Monnaie. Mansart also built the château of Fresnes-sur-Marne for Guénégaud. This has a highly original domed chapel that was probably designed not long after Mansart's Val-de-Grace, Paris (1645). In 1659 Mansart built a second Paris mansion for Guénégaud, next to the first (now the Hôtel Guénégaud-Sillery, 13 Quai de Conti). It was probably on this latter building that Guénégaud employed Etienne Le Hongre to provide architectural sculpture and Jean Jouvenet to paint the library. François Perrier painted an *Assumption* on the dome of the chapel at Fresnes.

Henri de Guénégaud's brother Claude de Guénégaud (*c.* 1610–86) succeeded his brother as Trésorier de l'Epargne in 1643. He is known to have employed Eustache Le Sueur and Nicolas-Pierre Loir at his Paris house in the Rue St Louis in the Marais, and Loir and Michel Anguier at his château of Le Plessis-Belleville near Dammartin. His career was ruined with the disgrace of the finance minister Nicolas Fouquet in 1661.

BIBLIOGRAPHY

DBF
F.-N. Baudot du Buisson-Aubenay: *Journal des guerres civiles* [MS. 1643–52], 2 vols (Paris, 1883–5)

PATRICK LE CHANU

Guérard, Eugene [Eugen; Eugène] **von** (*b* Vienna, 7 Nov 1811; *d* London, 17 April 1901). Austrian painter, draughtsman and lithographer, active in Australia. He was the son of Bernhard von Guérard (*d* 1836), a miniaturist who was court painter in Vienna to Francis II (*reg* 1792–1806). In 1826 he left with his father for Italy, and from 1830 he studied for a period in Rome. In 1832 they went to Naples and travelled extensively in southern Italy. After his father's death, he returned to Germany in 1838 and studied at the Staatliche Kunstakademie in Düsseldorf from 1839/40 to 1845/6, including landscape classes under Johan Wilhelm Schirmer. Sometime before 1852 he travelled to London; while there he succumbed to the lure of the Victorian Gold Rush, the subject of much excitement in England, and in 1852 he emigrated to Australia. He recorded his goldfield experiences of 1853–4 in a series of sketches (Ballarat, F.A.Gal.) and years later produced an important painting, *Ballarat in the Early Times, 1853–4* (1884; Ballarat, F.A.Gal.), based on them. By 1854 he had gained enough from gold prospecting to settle in Melbourne and to resume his career as a painter. He travelled extensively in the state of Victoria, making sketching expeditions from 1855 almost every year until 1864. He also sketched twice in Tasmania (1855 and 1875) and he made one visit each to South Australia (1855) and to New South Wales (1859).

Although he had been a landscape painter in Europe, in Australia von Guérard experimented briefly with figure painting before returning to landscape. Such painters as John Glover had found that a limited demand existed in England for depictions of the Australian landscape as an Aboriginal Arcadia, and von Guérard did two paintings in this manner: *Tower Hill* (1855; Melbourne, Min. A., Sport, Envmt & Terr.) and *Stony Rises, Lake Corangamite* (1857; Adelaide, A.G. S. Australia). Some sympathy for the aborigines is evident in his diaries, kept while exploring the interior, and in such paintings as *Warrenheip Hills near Ballarat* (1854; Melbourne, N.G. Victoria). His contact with aborigines was, in fact, minimal: he simply transferred his own experience of Arcadian bliss to the native figures depicted in his paintings. In 1857 he executed *Ferntree Gully in the Dandenong Ranges* (Canberra, N.G.), a work that contemporaries considered also to be valuable as an accurate botanical study of the area. On his various expeditions in Victoria he visited homesteads, which often resulted in commissions. His first paintings of homesteads, executed in November 1857, depict the cattle station of Purrumbete, on the lake of the same name, near Camperdown in the Western District of Victoria. In 1858 he was commissioned by the landowners of the station, John Manifold and Peter Manifold, to paint two additional views, *From the Verandah of Purrumbete* and *Purrumbete from across the Lake* (both Canberra, N.G.). In 1858 Sir Henry Barkly (1815–98), Governor of Victoria, commissioned from him a series of pen-and-ink drawings (Melbourne, State Lib. Victoria) of places of topographical interest. Having a genuine interest in the discovery of new regions, von Guérard also travelled into the bush to explore wilder areas. He accompanied the explorer William Howitt to the Australian Alps in 1860 and in 1862 joined the German scientist Georg Neumayer's expedition to Cape Otway on the south coast of Victoria. In the same

Eugene von Guérard: *North-east View from the Northern Top of Mt Kosciusko*, oil on canvas, 665×117 mm 1863 (Canberra, Australian National Gallery)

year he went with Neumayer to the North-East territories of Victoria and to Mt Kosciusko. *North-east View from the Northern Top of Mt Kosciusko* (Canberra, N.G.; see fig.) is possibly his finest topographical study and is an accurate observation of nature, painted following his return to Melbourne in 1863 from Neumayer's expedition. Von Guérard depicted not only Australia's highest peak but also the expedition party and even his dog, so lending the work a personal significance. In 1865 he sent *Fall of the Wetterboro Creek . . . in the Blue Mountains* (Melbourne, ANZ Bank Archvs) to the exhibition of the Royal Academy in London, and in 1867 he exhibited at the Exposition in Paris. He published a series of lithographs, *Eugène von Guérard's Australian Landscapes*, in Melbourne in 1866–8, and over the following decade continued to travel extensively in Australia. In 1870 he was appointed Head of the School of Art in Melbourne and Curator of the National Gallery of Victoria and in 1881–2, obliged to resign from these positions on account of ill-health, he returned to Düsseldorf. In 1891 Von Guérard and his wife moved to London, to be with their daughter.

For further illustration *see* AUSTRALIA, fig. 8.

WRITINGS

M. Tipping, ed.: *An Artist on the Goldfields: The Diary of Eugene von Guérard* (Melbourne, 1982)

PRINTS

Eugène von Guérard's Australian Landscapes (Melbourne, 1866–8)

BIBLIOGRAPHY

D. Thomas: *Outlines of Australian Art: The Joseph Brown Collection* (South Melbourne, 1973, rev. 3/1989), pp. 16–18

M. T. Lansdowne: *Eugene von Guérard's Australian Landscapes* (Melbourne, 1975)

Eugen von Guérard (exh. cat. by C. Bruce, Sydney, Austral. Gal. Directors Council, 1980)

T. Bonyhady: *Images in Opposition: Australian Landscape Painting, 1801–90* (Melbourne, 1985)

JANET SPENS

Guercia, Jacopo della. *See* JACOPO DELLA QUERCIA.

Guercino [Barbieri, Giovanni Francesco] (*b* Cento, ?2 Feb 1591; *d* Bologna, 22 Dec 1666). Italian painter and draughtsman. He was one of the leading painters of the Bolognese school and one of the most accomplished draughtsmen of the Italian Baroque. His paintings show a command of subtle effects of light and dark, with the figures revealing a wide variety of gesture and facial expression, the result of the artist's good grasp of human psychology. Guercino's style changed dramatically during his long career. His early works are robust in handling, rich in muted colour and dramatic in lighting and composition. But after a short visit to Rome in 1621–3, his painting began slowly to alter as he came under the influence of a more classical style of painting, then so popular in official circles. He was deeply affected by the austere classicism of one of his greatest rivals, Guido Reni. Following Reni's death in 1642, Guercino moved from his native Cento, where he had previously spent almost the whole of his career, to Bologna, and assumed the position of the city's principal painter. His activity as a painter is particularly well documented, thanks to the extensive list of his commissions in Malvasia's biography (based on documentation to which he had access in Guercino's house), together with the *Libro dei conti* (account book) recording payments for his commissions, which was kept in Guercino's studio from 1629 until his death by his younger brother, PAOLO ANTONIO BARBIERI, with whom he occasionally collaborated.

1. Life and painted work. 2. Drawings. 3. Critical reception and posthumous reputation.

1. Life and painted work.

(i) Training and early work in Cento and Bologna, before 1621. (ii) Rome and Cento, 1621–42. (iii) Bologna, 1642–66.

(i) Training and early work in Cento and Bologna, before 1621. Guercino (It.: 'squinter') was given his nickname at an early age because of the squint he is said to have developed as a result of a childhood accident. Although he received some form of basic training in his native Cento, a small town near Ferrara, in Emilia, he seems to have been largely self-taught. In 1607, however, the 16-year-old youth was sent by his father to be apprenticed to the Centese painter Benedetto Gennari the elder (*d* 1610), an arrangement that lasted until the latter's death. Through the marriage in 1628 of Guercino's sister Lucia Barbieri to Ercole Gennari (1597–1658), a younger member of the same family, Guercino continued his close association with the Gennari. Indeed, in his later years Guercino was assisted by his nephews, Benedetto Gennari the younger and Cesare Gennari, to both of whom his entire estate passed at his death, as he himself never married.

The main influences on the development of the young Guercino came from the nearby centres of Ferrara and Bologna. The work of two Ferrarese painters, Scarsellino and Carlo Bononi, at first affected him deeply. At the same time the Bolognese painter Ludovico Carracci, whose *Holy Family with St Francis and Donors* (1591; Cento, Pin. Civ.) decorated the altar of the church of the Cappuccini in Cento (where it was much admired by Guercino), also provided a strong exemplar. Ludovico's younger cousin Annibale Carracci, who was by far the most influential Bolognese painter of the period, also strongly inspired Guercino's work in its plasticity and rugged naturalism.

1. Guercino: *St William Receiving the Monastic Habit*, oil on canvas, 3.45×2.31 m, 1620 (Bologna, Pinacoteca Nazionale)

The first person to appreciate fully the young Guercino's prodigious talents was Padre Antonio Mirandola, canon of S Salvatore in Bologna and later president of the monastery of Santo Spirito in Cento. Mirandola became Guercino's promoter and lifelong friend. Through his agency, the artist received his first important public commission, the altarpiece of *All Saints in Glory* (untraced), painted in 1613 for the church of Santo Spirito in Cento. Other commissions followed quickly, including wall decorations for some of the private residences in the town, such as the Casa Provenzale (now Benazzi), which he painted in 1614, and the Casa Pannini, which he painted with the help of assistants in 1615. The following year Guercino opened an academy for life drawing in the house of one of his Centese patrons, Bartolomeo Fabbri, an unusual enterprise that lasted only two years. He must have found the task of running the academy too great a drain on his time, for from 1617 onwards the painter was increasingly in demand from patrons in Cento and elsewhere. One of the more important official Centese commissions from this period was for the altarpiece of *Christ Handing the Keys to St Peter and Pointing to the Papal Chair* (the '*Cattedra di San Pietro*', 1618; Cento, Pin. Civ.), for the Collegiata di S Biagio (the cathedral) there.

Among Guercino's more influential early patrons from outside his native town were Cosimo II, Grand Duke of Tuscany; Cardinal Alessandro Ludovisi, Archbishop of Bologna and later Pope Gregory XV; Cardinal Jacopo Serra, papal legate of Ferrara; and Ferdinando Gonzaga, Duke of Mantua. What seems to have attracted these discerning collectors to Guercino's pictures was their bold naturalism, broad brushwork, powerful chiaroscuro and daring compositional inventiveness. The crowning moment of his early career, also the most prestigious ecclesiastical commission he had received to that date (once more through the agency of Mirandola), was the *St William Receiving the Monastic Habit* (1620; Bologna, Pin. N.; see fig. 1), painted for the church of S Gregorio in Bologna. The picture was an immediate success and secured the painter's growing reputation in Bologna.

(ii) Rome and Cento, 1621–42. A fundamental turning-point in Guercino's career occurred soon afterwards in 1621, when his early patron, Cardinal Alessandro Ludovisi, was elected pope as Gregory XV (*reg* 1621–3). According to Malvasia, Guercino was at once summoned to Rome by the Pope to decorate the Loggia delle Benedizioni in St Peter's, a vast undertaking that in the end came to nothing because of the premature death of the Pope. Nevertheless, Guercino did complete one prominent papal commission, the *Burial and Reception into Heaven of St Petronilla* (Rome, Pal. Conserv., Pin.), painted for one of the altars in St Peter's and completed shortly before the artist's departure

from the Holy City in 1623. While in Rome, Guercino received other important commissions, both private and ecclesiastical, mainly from the Ludovisi and their entourage. One of these was the decoration of a ceiling in the Ludovisi villa on the Pincio, known as the Casino Ludovisi, with a fresco of *Aurora* (1621; *in situ*; see fig. 2). Guercino's Roman period (1621–3), short in span though it was, exerted a lasting impact on his subsequent development. His early naturalistic chiaroscuro style, so successfully practised in Emilia, was not highly regarded in the sophisticated Roman court milieu in which he then found himself. His subsequent attempts to modify his style, acknowledging the more fashionable classical language of form made popular by the work of such painters as Guido Reni, heralded a fundamental change in his work. Henceforth there was a lightening of his palette and a tendency to make the spatial setting of his figures more lucid.

With the death of Gregory XV, Guercino returned to Cento, where he remained, with only brief interruptions, until 1642. For the rest of the 1620s he was again much occupied with ecclesiastical commissions for key churches in Emilia. These include the altarpiece of the *Virgin and Child Appearing to St Laurence*, painted for the church of the Seminario Arcivescovile at Finale nell'Emilia (1624; *in situ*); the famous altarpiece of the *Crucifixion, with the Virgin, the Magdalene, St John the Evangelist and St Prosper, Bishop of Reggio*, painted for the church of the Madonna della Ghiara in Reggio Emilia (1624; *in situ*); and the fresco decoration (1626–7) of *Prophets* and *Stories from the New Testament* in the cupola and drum of Piacenza Cathedral.

Guercino's steady rate of work throughout the 1630s continued unabated. Especially fine are the two pendant pictures (both 1632) painted for the walls of the Giroldo Chapel in the cathedral at Reggio Emilia, the *Visitation* (Rouen, Mus. B.-A.) and the *Martyrdom of SS John and Paul, with the Virgin and Child above* (Toulouse, Mus. Augustins). Guercino's refined classical manner, in which the strong forms, stately movements and preference for light midtones recall the work of Guido Reni, may be seen at its best at this point in his career. Although he was back in provincial Emilia, Guercino's fame was growing abroad. In 1632 Maria de' Medici, Queen Mother of France, was on the point of inviting him to the French court when the idea had to be abandoned because of political troubles that occasioned her hasty departure from Paris in July of that year. Guercino's red chalk study of *St Geneviève* (*c.* 1630; Windsor Castle, Royal Lib.), the patron saint of Paris, may be connected with a commission planned to encourage him to work in France. Another French patron who employed the painter in both the 1630s and 1640s was Louis Phélypeaux de La Vrillière, secretary of state to Louis XIII, who commissioned several large paintings of ancient historical subjects to decorate the gallery of his

2. Guercino: *Aurora* (1621), fresco, Casino Ludovisi, Rome

3. Guercino: *Abraham Expelling Hagar and Ishmael*, oil on canvas, 1.15×1.54 m, 1657–8 (Milan, Pinacoteca di Brera)

mansion in Paris, including Guercino's *Cato at Utica Saying Farewell to his Son* (1635–7; Marseille, Mus. B.-A.), *Coriolanus Entreated by his Mother* (1643; Caen, Mus. B.-A.) and *Hersilia Separating Romulus and Tatius* (1645; Paris, Louvre). Guercino painted a fourth, the *Mucius Scaevola Plunging his Right Hand into the Flames* (Genoa, Pal. Durazzo Pallavicini), the precise date of which is unknown, but it was not delivered and remained in the artist's house, where it was recorded on his death.

(iii) Bologna, 1642–66. With Guercino's move to Bologna in 1642 to take up the mantle as the city's leading painter, his work entered its final phase. At first he lived in the palace of Conte Filippo Aldrovandi; then in 1644 he moved his studio to the house he bought that later came to be known as the Casa Gennari (from the name of his heirs). His first picture to decorate a church in Bologna following his transfer there was the *St Francis Meditating in a Landscape*, painted for the church of S Giovanni in Monte (1645; *in situ*), one of several such pictures that he continued to supply with impressive regularity. Another was the *Circumcision* (1646; Lyon, Mus. B.-A.), painted for the high altar of the church of Gesù e Maria in Bologna. Guercino also continued to paint easel pictures of secular subjects for private patrons, such as the *Atlas* (1646; Florence, Mus. Bardini) for Don Lorenzo de' Medici. In the 1640s his painted work continued to develop along the lines set for it in the previous decade, although his drawings became less inhibited compared with the careful finish of the paintings for which they are preparatory.

The activity of Guercino's last years, from 1650 until his death, remains hard to assess. Although he was acclaimed more than ever—one such moment of recognition was the visit of Queen Christina of Sweden in 1655 on her way to Rome—he was beset by ill health and seems to have depended more and more on the help of his nephews, Benedetto and Cesare. As a draughtsman, his work undoubtedly lacks some of its former breadth and vigour. In a letter written in 1650 to one of his patrons, Guercino explained that his doctors had forbidden him to draw, owing to a pain in his chest, and that as a consequence he was resorting to sketching out his ideas directly on to canvas with a piece of chalk attached to the end of a cane. Guercino continued, nevertheless, to produce numerous paintings, such as the *Abraham Expelling Hagar and Ishmael* (1657–8; Milan, Brera; see fig. 3) and, more importantly, the *St Thomas Aquinas Writing the Hymn in Honour of the Holy Sacrament*, painted for the church of S Domenico in Bologna (1662–3; *in situ*).

2. Drawings. Guercino was a natural, unselfconscious draughtsman. For most of his life he maintained an extraordinarily prolific output in the medium, faltering only towards the end, probably as the result of failing

health. The largest surviving group, some 350 sheets, is preserved in the Royal Library, Windsor Castle, together with a further 450 or more that can be attributed to him or to members of his school. Their freshness and vitality remain undiminished to this day. The directness of their touch, their feeling for dramatic effects of light and space (*see* INK, fig. 3), and the energy of the figures make them among the most accessible of all Old Master drawings.

Most of Guercino's drawings were working studies made to prepare the compositions of his paintings or the prints after his designs. From the very beginning, he worked out his compositions by means of an often extensive series of studies on paper. These comprised rapid studies in pen or in pen and wash for the whole composition, in which the artist attempted to place the figure within a setting, or, if more than one figure was involved, in relationship with its companion or companions. Another type of compositional study is the small group of designs for prints, which, by their very nature, are more finished in execution. When he had reached the stage of making careful studies of the individual figures or groups of figures, Guercino then used pen, pen and brown wash, and red chalk, probably using the latter when he wished to make a more detailed rendering of the light and shade. Finally, towards the end of the preparatory process, he would often make detailed studies of the heads and draperies of the figures (a sizeable group of which has survived in Koenig-Fachsenfeld Col., on dep. Stuttgart, Staatsgal.), a further indication of the extraordinary care that went into the planning of his pictures.

Guercino's working studies serve to document the remarkable fecundity of his ideas, showing how he was prepared to revise his thoughts radically as he went along. One common trait of this phase of gestation was the frequent reversal of all or some of the figures within a given composition. Such a profound adjustment of the whole seems to have enabled the artist to refresh his ideas and to work out his preferences more fully. The complex evolution of his thoughts for a given composition may be glimpsed in the groups of preparatory studies at Windsor for the *Burial and Reception into Heaven of St Petronilla* (5), the *Assassination of Amnon* (2), the *Visitation* (5) and *The Atlas* (5). Essential to this reversal of his compositions, while the idea of them was still only a germ in his mind and a few sketches on paper, was the process of making what is known as an offset or counterproof. By this means a drawing, usually in red chalk, was reproduced by damping it and then pressing or 'squeezing' it on to another sheet of paper; the image obtained thereby is reversed from that of the drawing. Guercino used the device to allow him to judge whether or not the pose of a figure or of a group of figures was more successful in the sense in which he had first drawn it or reversed (for illustration *see* COUNTERPROOF).

In addition to his working studies, in his spare time and for his own amusement Guercino made numerous drawings of landscape, genre subjects, capriccios and caricatures. Since these informal categories of drawing were made very much for their own ends (unlike the working studies), they give an especially sympathetic insight into the painter's character, revealing his keen interest in his surroundings and in the antics of his fellow men. The landscape drawings bear no direct preparatory relationship to his paintings (even though in the backgrounds of some there are distant vistas of countryside). As a result, these drawings (with only rare exceptions) can be dated only from their style. They are almost invariably drawn in pen and brown ink and have a finished appearance, as if each were conceived as a set piece. Their well-ordered compositions suggest that they were not made on the spot but in the studio, with the artist working from his imagination, creating motifs inspired by real life. A notable characteristic of these landscape drawings is a sense of airiness and vast space; another is a feeling of the brilliance of sunlight, implied by the many areas of untouched white paper. The appearance of tiny figures dotted about the scene, busily engaged in various occupations, also provides points of focus on which the eye happily dwells.

The other independent categories of drawing—the genre subjects, capriccios and caricatures—are among his most popular. They are executed with great freedom and vitality and usually show the draughtsman's comical intent as well as his humanity; they continue to attract particular admiration because of their great immediacy. The *Street Scene with a Vendor* and *Three Peasants Picnicking* (both Windsor Castle, Royal Lib.) are of everyday scenes that caught the artist's eye, which he has treated in his characteristically teasing way. The *Standing Beggar* (Windsor Castle, Royal Lib.; see fig. 4) shows a poor man who wandered in the

4. Guercino: *Standing Beggar*, pen and brown ink and brown wash, 267×192 mm, mid- to late 1620s (Windsor, Windsor Castle, Royal Library)

artist's direction, his hat held at his side but looking rather as if it is about to be proffered in expectation of money.

The bizarre also provided inspiration for Guercino's drawings. The *Three Bathers Surprised by a Monster* and the *Symbolic or Magical Subject* (Windsor Castle, Royal Lib.) fall within the category of capriccios or drawings of fanciful subjects: both are esoteric, their precise significance now hard to determine. The caricatures also form a large group within the informal studies, often made in series. They are full of fun and were drawn deliberately to amuse the artist and his friends. No social rank escaped the satirizing powers of his pen, although the poor peasant folk of Emilia seem to have been his favourite subjects. The sort of facial distortions represented, for example, in the *Grotesque Head* (Windsor Castle, Royal Lib.) shows how Guercino continued a manner of caricature drawing that goes back to Leonardo da Vinci.

For further illustration *see* WASH.

3. CRITICAL RECEPTION AND POSTHUMOUS REPUTATION. Guercino's posthumous success was considerable and lasted until well into the beginning of the 19th century. His reputation was especially hallowed in Cento and Bologna. The Casa Gennari, the painter's house in Bologna that was maintained as a studio by the family of his nephews, Benedetto and Cesare Gennari, preserved until at least 1719 (the date of the famous inventory of its contents) a number of Guercino's pictures, as well as an immense quantity of his drawings.

Guercino's popularity outside Italy reached its height in England during the later 18th century. The first of his great altarpieces to reach Britain was the *St Luke Painting the Virgin* (1653; Kansas City, MO, Nelson–Atkins Mus.), which is recorded in the collection of the Earls of Spencer in 1750 and was soon to be followed by many others. Guercino's drawings enjoyed an even wider vogue with the English, prompting the great French connoisseur P.-J. Mariette to observe that 'les anglois sont passionés pour le Guerchin'. From about 1760 until well after the beginning of the 19th century, the greater part of the painter's entire surviving output of drawings was in collections in England. A large number had been purchased *c.* 1745 by John Bouverie and another, even bigger group *c.* 1758 by Richard Dalton, the future librarian to King George III; the engravings of several of these latter by Francesco Bartolozzi, Basire, and some even by Dalton himself, ensured their fame among a cultivated circle of collectors and amateurs.

From the mid- to late 19th century Guercino's work fell out of favour, along with that of other Italian Baroque painters. In England the Victorians had no sympathy for either the sentiment or the artistic language of his works, and this neglect continued well into the 20th century. The first to champion a reappraisal of his position as an artist was Denis Mahon, whose *Studies in Seicento Art and Theory* (1947) contained an illuminating investigation into the causes of Guercino's change of style. The passionate assumption that lay behind the essay was the importance of Guercino's place in the history of Italian painting. Mahon also organized and wrote the catalogues for the exhibitions of Guercino's paintings and drawings held in Bologna in 1967, on the occasion of the third centenary of the artist's death, as well as those for the exhibitions in 1991 celebrating the fourth centenary of Guercino's birth. With publications accompanying the celebrations elsewhere of this latter event, Guercino is now well served by exhibition catalogues and monographs of his work, to such an extent that his paintings and drawings are now probably better published than those of any other Italian Baroque painter.

BIBLIOGRAPHY

C. C. Malvasia: *Felsina pittrice* (1678), ii, pp. 358–86; ed. P. Zanotti (1841), ii, pp. 255–74, pp. 307–44 [the latter repr. in full the contents of the *Libro dei conti*]

J. A. Calvi: *Notizie della vita, e delle opere del Cavaliere Giovan Francesco Barbieri detto il Guercino da Cento* (Bologna, 1808) [pp. 59–160 for the full *Libro dei conti*]

D. Mahon: *Studies in Seicento Art and Theory* (London, 1947)

Il Guercino (Giovanni Francesco Barbieri, 1591–1666): Catalogo critico dei dipinti (exh. cat. by D. Mahon, Bologna, Pal. Archiginnasio, 1968)

Il Guercino (Giovanni Francesco Barbieri, 1591–1666): Catalogo critico dei disegni (exh. cat. by D. Mahon, Bologna, Pal. Archiginnasio, 1968, rev. 1969)

P. Bagni: *Guercino a Piacenza: Gli affreschi nella cupola della cattedrale* (Bologna, 1983)

——: *Guercino a Cento: Le decorazioni di Casa Pannini* (Bologna, 1984)

Guercino Drawings from the Collections of Denis Mahon and the Ashmolean Museum (exh. cat. by D. Mahon and D. Ekserdjian, Oxford, Ashmolean; London, Hazlitt, Gooden & Fox; 1986); repr. in *Burl. Mag.* (March 1986) [suppl.]

P. Bagni: *Il Guercino e suoi incisori* (Bologna, 1988)

L. Salerno: *I dipinti del Guercino* (Rome, 1988) [cat. rais.]

D. Mahon and N. Turner: *The Drawings of Guercino in the Collection of Her Majesty the Queen at Windsor Castle* (Cambridge, 1989)

Le Guerchin en France (exh. cat. by S. Loire, Paris, Louvre, 1990)

Drawings by Guercino from British Collections (exh. cat. by N. Turner and C. Plazzotta, London, BM, 1991)

Giovanni Francesco Barbieri, il Guercino (1591–1666): Dipinti (exh. cat. by D. Mahon, Bologna, Mus. Civ. Archeol.; Cento, Pin. Civ. and the church of the Rosario; 1991); rev. as *Giovanni Francesco Barbieri, il Guercino (1591–1666)* (exh. cat. by D. Mahon and others, ed. S. Ebert-Schifferer; Frankfurt, Ksthalle, 1991–2); rev. as *Guercino: Master Painter of the Baroque* (exh. cat. by D. Mahon, Washington, DC, N.G.A., 1992)

Giovanni Francesco Barbieri, il Guercino (1591–1666): Disegni (exh. cat. by D. Mahon, Bologna, Mus. Civ. Archeol., 1991)

Guercino in Britain: Paintings from British Collections (exh. cat. by M. Helston and T. Henry, London, N.G., 1991)

Guercino, Master Draftsman: Works from North American Collections (exh. cat. by D. Stone, Cambridge, MA, Sackler Mus.; Ottawa, N.G.; Cleveland, OH, Mus. A.; 1991)

Guercino (1591–1666): Drawings from Dutch Collections (exh. cat. by C. van Tuyll van Serooskerken, Haarlem, Teylers Mus., 1991)

Guercino: Drawings from Windsor Castle (exh. cat. by N. Turner, Fort Worth, TX, Kimbell A. Mus.; Washington, DC, N.G.A.; New York, Drg Cent.; 1991–2)

Genova e Guercino: Dipinti e disegni delle civiche collezioni (exh. cat. by P. Boccardo, Genoa, Pal. Rosso, 1992)

NICHOLAS TURNER

Guérin, Charles(-François-Prosper) (*b* Sens, Yonne, 21 Feb 1875; *d* Paris, 19 March 1939). French painter and illustrator. He trained at the Ecole des Beaux-Arts in Paris in the studio of Gustave Moreau and first exhibited in Paris at the Salon de la Société Nationale in 1897, also showing at the Salon des Indépendants from 1901, at the Salon d'Automne from 1903 and from 1923 at the Salon des Tuileries. In addition to portraits and still-lifes he painted nudes, such as *The Partition* (1906; Caen, Mus. B.-A.). In his still-lifes he often included musical instruments, as in *Still-life with Lute* (1910; Paris, Pompidou). His most striking works, however, included a number of imaginary romantic pictures in which the figures, often elongated, were given mid-19th-century dress, as in *Colombine* (1920; see Klingsor, p. 61). While most of his works were executed in an undistinguished realist style, these romantic paintings bear the influence of Impressionism and of Cézanne's geometrical brushstrokes.

Guérin also contributed illustrations to *L'Artiste*, *Byblis* and the *Gazette des beaux-arts* and illustrated a number of books including Paul Verlaine's *Fêtes galantes* (Paris, 1919), Colette's *Le Voyage égoïste* (Paris, 1922), Alfred de Musset's *Un Caprice* (Paris, 1930) and Gustave Flaubert's *Madame Bovary* (Paris, 1932). He also produced scenery for a production of Claudio Monteverdi's opera *L'incoronazione di Poppea* performed at the Théâtre des Arts in Paris in 1911. Later in life Guérin was appointed a professor at the Ecole des Beaux-Arts in Paris. His pupils included André Dunoyer de Segonzac, Luc-Albert Moreau and Jean-Louis Boussingault.

BIBLIOGRAPHY

T. L. Klingsor: *Charles Guérin* (Paris, 1920)
R. Escholier: *La Peinture française, XXe siècle* (Paris, 1937), pp. 59–60

□

Guérin, Gilles (*b* Paris, 1611–12; *d* Paris, 26 Feb 1678). French sculptor. He was trained by the sculptor Nicolas Le Brun (*d* 1648), father of the painter Charles Le Brun. In the 1640s Guérin worked under Jacques Sarazin on the royal works at the Louvre and at Fontainebleau as well as for such wealthy private clients as René de Longueil, for whom he carved two monumental chimney-pieces in wood and stucco at the château of Maisons (1645–51), now known as the château of Maisons-Lafitte. In 1648 he was the first sculptor to be elected to the newly founded Académie Royale de Peinture et de Sculpture. By 1654 his eminent status was reflected in commissions for a marble statue of *Louis XIV* for the Hôtel de Ville in Paris (Chantilly, Château; bronze reduction, Paris, Carnavalet) and, under the direction of the architect Louis Le Vau, for the innovative wood and stucco sculptural decoration of the King's bedchamber in the Louvre.

Guérin carried out numerous works for churches: the retable (1651) of the chapel of Notre-Dame de Bethléem in Ferrières-en-Gâtinais (*in situ*); the rood loft of Soissons Cathedral, of which the statues of *St Rufinus* and *St Valerius* (both 1662–4) survive; and the statues of the *Virgin and Child* (Paris, St Thomas d'Aquin) and *St Francis of Paola* (Paris, St Joseph des Carmes; both 1668–70) for the retable of the Minims of Paris. The sculptor executed little work for funerary art, but what he did was always for major works: the tomb of *Charles de La Vieuville and Marie Boulvier de Beaumarchais* (Paris, Louvre) and that of *Henri II, Prince de Condé* erected in the church in Vallery, Yonne (1646–51, *in situ*; terracotta model, Paris, Louvre).

Guérin's work belongs to the great tradition of French classicism but shows an attraction to Italian art that is demonstrated by his taste for deep, undulating drapery rather than by the use of tormented poses. At the end of his career he took part in the campaign of sculptural decoration at Versailles, producing a group of *Tritons Leading the Horses of Apollo to Drink* (1666–74; marble) and an allegorical marble statue of *America* (1674–8).

BIBLIOGRAPHY

G. de Saint-Georges: 'Mémoire historique des principaux ouvrages de sculpture de M. Guérin lu à l'Académie le 7 juillet 1691', *Mémoires inédits*, ed. J. Dumoulin, i (Paris, 1854), pp. 259–68
E. Chartraire: 'Le Tombeau de Henri II de Bourbon-Condé par Gilles Guérin', *Arts* [Paris], cl (1914), pp. 25–30
M.-T. Forest: 'Gilles Guérin et les commandes royales', *Provence Hist.*, xxii/88 (1972), pp. 145–52
——: 'Les Sculptures de Gilles Guérin au couvent des Minimes à Paris', *Bull. Soc. Hist. A. Fr.* (1973), pp. 121–9
——: 'Un Don de la Société des amis du Louvre: Le Modèle de la statue funéraire d'Henri II de Bourbon-Condé (1588–1646) par Gilles Guérin (1611/12–1678)', *Rev. Louvre* (April, 1993), pp. 27–51

MARIE-THERESE GLASS-FOREST

Guérin, Gustave (*b* 1814; *d* 1881). French architect. From 1850 he was architect for the Département of Indre-et-Loire and the city of Tours, for which he carried out most of his work; during the same period he was also the conservator for diocesan buildings in Tours. His best-known secular works there are the extensions that he designed for the Musée des Beaux-Arts; the covered markets (1869); and the extension to the Lycée. He is best remembered, however, for his many religious buildings. In Tours he restored the cathedral, repaired the portals of Notre-Dame-la-Riche (1852), and built the churches of Ste Anne (1857), St Pierre-des-Corps (1866) and St Etienne (1873–4) and the chapel of the Petit Séminaire (1849) and the Chapelle des Lazaristes (1861). St Etienne and the Chapelle des Lazaristes are generally considered to be among the best provincial examples of churches of the Romanesque Revival, a style that became fashionable throughout France in the second half of the 19th century. The solid, severe walls of these buildings, their steeply pitched roofs and bold semicircular chancels are reminiscent of 12th-century churches.

BIBLIOGRAPHY

L. Hautecoeur: *Architecture classique en France* (1943–57), vii, pp. 14, 86

□

Guérin, (Jean-Baptiste-)Paulin (*b* Toulon, 24 March 1783; *d* Paris, 16 Jan 1855). French painter. He was the son of a locksmith who fled from Toulon, which was in revolt against Jacobin rule, to Marseille in 1793. Although intended to follow his father, Guérin decided at 13 to study drawing, attending the Ecole des Bernardines, which had opened in Marseille in 1793. There he met Augustin Aubert (1781–1857), who became his adviser and lifelong friend. Guérin went to Paris in October 1802 and for about ten years lived in poverty and isolation, executing a number of self-portraits as he could not afford models (e.g. *Self-portrait*, 1804; Toulon, Mus. Toulon). In 1805 he was admitted as an apprentice to the studio of François-André Vincent where he met Auguste Heim and Horace Vernet. Although his studies under Vincent were free, he had to leave in order to provide money for his family in Marseille. He became a full-time assistant to François Gérard, painting accessories and drapery in his portraits.

In 1810 Guérin exhibited his first portraits at the Salon in Paris, and in 1812 he showed his first large composition there, *Cain after the Death of Abel* (Toulon, Mus. Toulon), which was critically acclaimed. Auguste, Comte de Forbin, became a friend and protector, obtaining portrait commissions for Guérin and employing him at Versailles. Guérin married his niece Maria, and, financially secure at last, began a series of history paintings and portraits, including *Louis XVIII* (1819) and *Charles X* (1827; Toulon, Mus. Toulon); his depictions of *Caroline, Duchesse de Berry* and *Félicité de Lamennais* were particularly well received. His mythological paintings, such as *Anchises and Venus* (1822; Toulon, Mus. Toulon), were strongly influenced by Jacques-Louis David and the cult of languid beauty espoused by Johann Joachim Winckelmann, and derived from antique vases and bas-reliefs. Although he employed colour, light and composition to give his pictures a strongly linear quality, Guérin's brand of Neo-classicism is tempered by the use of *sfumato*, which also distinguishes the increasingly Romantic atmosphere of Pierre-Paul Prud'hon's and Anne-Louis Girodet's paintings. A symbolic luminism suffuses many of his religious paintings, as in the *Holy Family* (exh. 1833; Paris, priv. col.). Other religious works include *St Anne* (exh. 1833; Le Castellet, church) and *St Catherine of Alexandria* (exh. 1833; Paris, St Roch).

In 1828 Guérin was appointed director of drawing and painting at the Maison Royale de St Denis, Paris. Remaining loyal to the Bourbons, he had little contact with Louis-Philippe and continued painting portraits of Parisian society. In 1836 he opened a studio in the Quai Malaquais where Vincent Courdouan (1810–93) was among his pupils. Guérin trained his daughter Isabelle, son Félix (1825–65) and nephew Jean-Pierre Philibert (1805–46), all of whom became painters. Praised by Théodore Géricault, François-Marius Granet and Jean-Auguste-Dominique Ingres, Guérin was the official painter to the royal family and aristocracy during the reigns of Louis XVIII and Charles X. Following in the 18th-century French tradition of Jean-Baptiste Greuze in particular, and influenced by the great English portrait painters Joshua Reynolds and Thomas Gainsborough, Guérin inherited a mild version of the Neo-classical aesthetic yet achieved a distinctly personal style that made him one of the most prominent portrait painters of the Restoration.

BIBLIOGRAPHY

A. Alauzen: *La Peinture en Provence du XIVe siècle à nos jours* (Lausanne, 1962)

La Peinture en Provence dans les collections du Musée de Toulon du XVIIe au début du XXe siècle (exh. cat. by J. Forneris and others, Toulon, Mus. Toulon, 1985)

JEAN-ROGER SOUBIRAN

Guérin, Pierre(-Narcisse), Baron (*b* Paris, 13 March 1774; *d* Rome, 16 July 1833). French painter, draughtsman and teacher. He was one of the most successful French painters working in the Neo-classical style at the end of the 18th century and the beginning of the 19th. He especially admired the art of Poussin and David, and derived inspiration from Greek mythology and from the Classical themes of the plays of Jean Racine. At the Salons in Paris he exhibited elegant compositions painted in a carefully controlled manner and with arresting chiaroscuro. He was never a prolific artist and, owing to ill-health, painted even less in his later years, devoting himself instead to teaching and to the directorship (1822–8) of the Académie de France in Rome.

1. Early years and Salon success, 1774–1805. 2. Later years: painting and teaching, 1806–33.

1. Early years and Salon success, 1774–1805. His talent for drawing was apparent at an early age and his father, an ironmonger with a shop on the Pont-au-Change, enrolled him at the Académie Royale de Peinture et de Sculpture in Paris in 1785. As required, his application was supported by a member of the Académie, in this case Hugues Taraval, who would have become his first master had he not died that year. Guérin then transferred to the studio of Nicolas-Guy Brenet and remained with him for five years before becoming a pupil of Jean-Baptiste Regnault, with whom he appears to have had a close and influential relationship. Guérin's lively manner of drawing, in which he combined a chalky *sfumato* with sharp contours, is similar to that of Regnault. His choice of subjects—sometimes dramatic or violent, sometimes graceful or erotic—is also reminiscent of Regnault. He made his début at the Salon of 1795 with a large wash drawing, *Coriolanus Pleading his Cause before the Roman People is Condemned to Death by a Tribune of the People and Defended by the Young Men of Rome who Drive Back the Aediles Sent to Arrest him*, and a painting, *Geta Assassinated on the Orders of Caracalla* (both destr.). The title of the drawing gives a clear idea of Guérin's complex and violent contrasts of pose and gesture that are frequently seen in the works of other late 18th-century artists. The painting, which depicts a scene of horrific violence, survives only as a preparatory drawing (Cambridge, Fitzwilliam). Such subjects as these were not favoured by David, who preferred to represent the drama either before or after the principal action, but they were encouraged by the academic tradition in other studios and in the Académie, where themes of violence allowed young artists to demonstrate their skills in composition, chiaroscuro, figure painting and the recording of gesture and physiognomy.

During the 1790s Guérin progressed through the system at the Académie, which was transformed into a state institution in 1793. He was briefly conscripted into the army but through the intervention of Regnault was released from duty after four months, which enabled him to return to Paris to participate in the competitions that were an important part of the curriculum. In 1796 he won the prize for painting the best half-length figure and graduated to the competition for the Prix de Rome, reintroduced in 1797 after an interval of four years. As no awards had been made during that time, the prize was given to Guérin, Pierre Bouillon (1776–1831) and Louis André Gabriel Bouchet (1759–1842). The subject set, the *Death of Cato*, was chosen to give them ample opportunity to demonstrate the skills they had developed as painters of dramatic narrative. In Guérin's painting of the theme (Paris, Ecole B.-A.) he shows his mastery of academic art in his portrayal of the reactions registered on the faces of the spectators, in the rendering of eloquent gestures and in the forceful treatment of light and shade falling on the half-nude figure of Cato. The geometry of parallel lines and the frieze-like arrangement of the figures are also clear evidence of the artist's interest in Poussin and David. Lack of public funds and unrest in Rome prevented Guérin from leaving for

Italy, and in the interim he followed the stipulated coursework in Paris, completing, as his final submission, the *Return of Marcus Sextus* (Paris, Louvre; see fig. 1), which he sent to the Salon of 1799. The composition originally began as a picture of the blind Belisarius returning home to find his wife dead and his daughter in mourning. One of Guérin's fellow artists, however, advised him to select another character, as Belisarius had already appeared in works by David (*Belisarius Receiving Alms*, 1781; Lille, Mus. B.-A.) and Francois Gérard (*Belisarius*, 1795; ex-Duke of Leuchtenberg; Munich, priv. col.; for illustration see *A.Q.* [Detroit], xxxvi/3 (Autumn 1973), p. 162, fig. 14). Guérin then painted the grief-stricken hero's eyes as open, gave him an invented name and recast him as one of the Romans sent into exile by Lucius Cornelius Sulla (*reg* 82–81 BC). The painting was outstandingly successful, and his contemporaries were quick to draw a comparison between the fate of émigrés during the Reign of Terror (1793–4) and Guérin's imaginary victim of civil war in ancient Rome. At a time when Robespierre and Sulla were often compared, it is difficult to believe that Guérin did not intend the allusion. Some saw the success of the painting as an attempt by Guérin to diminish David's reputation, although the influence of David's *Andromache Mourning Hector* (exh. Salon 1783; Paris, Ecole N. Sup. B.-A., on dep. Paris, Louvre) is very pronounced, not only in the relationship of the figures but also in the smoking candelabrum, an emblem of recent death, which gives a particular significance to the dramatic contrasts of light and shade in both pictures.

Guérin was a theatre enthusiast, and although his paintings have often been described as theatrical, they are not actual depictions of scenes from plays as such. His interest in the plays of Jean Racine was probably inspired, in the first instance, not by seeing them performed but rather by Pierre Didot's well-known illustrated edition of them (Paris, 1801). *Phaedra and Hippolytus* (1802; Paris, Louvre), Guérin's earliest major composition that reflected his love of the theatre, ostensibly illustrates a passage from Racine's *Phèdre* (1677). He painted it to be shown as part of an exhibition for which there was to be an admission charge, a scheme that he devised with three of David's

1. Pierre Guérin: *Return of Marcus Sextus*, oil on canvas, 2.17×2.43 m, 1799 (Paris, Musée du Louvre)

pupils—Gérard, Anne-Louis Girodet and Gioacchino Giuseppe Serangeli (1768–1852)—in imitation of the profitable exhibition of David's *Intervention of the Sabine Women* (1799; Paris, Louvre). Their show, advertised to open in 1801, was never held, probably because the artists, aware of a recent number of similar failed exhibitions, realized that the French public was reluctant to pay to see works of art when entrance to the Salon and the Musée du Louvre was free. Guérin, however, completed his painting and sent it to the Salon of 1802, where it was received as successfully as was the *Return of Marcus Sextus*. The composition is derived from a well-known Roman fresco (Naples, Mus. Archaeol. N.) from Herculaneum showing Phaedra and Hippolytus, although Guérin painted his in a more contemporary, academic manner. The telling use of light and shade conveying contrast of character, the effective repertory of gestures and the elegant figure-drawing all forcefully combine to represent the elements of guilt, vengeance and innocence that are expressed throughout Racine's play in a series of dramatic confrontations. Critics were puzzled by the moment depicted in the painting, which was at variance with the incidents in Act IV of the play that were actually cited in the catalogue. Guérin, though, was aware that the concerns of art and literature were not identical. In order to overcome the difficulty confronting artists when they had to deal with a sequence of events or with scenes that depended on the written or the spoken word, Guérin encapsulated time by combining several themes and characters into a single dramatic instance.

With the reopening in 1801 of the Académie de France in Rome, Guérin was given permission to take up his position as a student at the Villa Medici. While there his situation was unusual, for by now he was one of the most well-known artists in France. In 1803, shortly before his departure for Italy, he had been made a member of the Légion d'honneur and when he arrived he was allowed an independence that was not permitted the other students. Partly because of ill-health, he spent much of his time in Naples, going there for the first time in the spring of 1804, and visiting Herculaneum, Pompeii, Paestum and other Classical sites on a romantic voyage of exploration that confirmed his taste for the Antique without noticeably affecting the direction of his art. When he returned to Rome he continued to work on a composition begun before leaving Paris, *Shepherds at the Tomb of Amyntas* (1805; Paris, Louvre), an elegiac painting inspired by one of Salomon Gessner's *Idyllen* (1756). In February 1805 he returned to Naples for one month, where he completed the painting and met Mme de Staël, who was keenly interested in his use of literary themes.

2. LATER YEARS: PAINTING AND TEACHING, 1806–33. On his return to Paris in November 1805 after only 22 months in Italy, Guérin, along with other successful French artists, painted themes of propaganda glorifying the regime as part of the programme set up by Emperor Napoleon I. *Bonaparte Pardoning the Rebels at Cairo* (Versailles, Château), which appeared at the Salon of 1808, is a well-ordered recollection of his friend Antoine-Jean Gros's painting of *Bonaparte Visiting the Victims of the Plague at Jaffa*, on 11 March 1799 (1804; Paris, Louvre; *see* GROS, ANTOINE-JEAN, fig. 1). Guérin received one further commission for a painting of this type: the *Death of Marshal Lannes* (Valenciennes, Mus. B.-A.), but he did not complete it. His work did not have the elements of realism that were present in the paintings of Gros and David. The subjects of Gessner's *Idyllen*, which inspired *Offering to Aesculapius* (Paris, Louvre), exhibited in 1804, and *Shepherds at the Tomb of Amyntas*, better suited his talent for painting elegant, idealized figure compositions with pathetic or dramatic themes. In 1810 he exhibited *Andromache and Pyrrhus* (Paris, Louvre), another painting inspired by Racine's work. It followed the same elegant, schematized formula used in *Phaedra and Hippolytus*, where strong yet simple gestures and clear-cut expressions convey the sense of the spoken word. He also exhibited *Aurora and Cephalus* (Paris, Louvre), a new type of picture, the themes of which derived from ancient mythology. In the painting the subject of Dawn permitted him to introduce an extreme contrast of light and shade, an effect inspired by Girodet's *Sleep of Endymion* (exh. Salon 1793; Paris, Louvre; *see* GIRODET, ANNE-LOUIS, fig. 1), in which the male figure was the model for Guérin's sleeping Cephalus. Works of this type, illustrating ancient myths and painted with strong chiaroscuro, were fashionable among David's pupils in the first two decades of the 19th century and were popular with collectors. Guérin's *Aurora and Cephalus* originally belonged to the Italian collector Giovanni Battista Sommariva, and a replica of it was painted in 1811 for Prince Nikolay Yusupov (1794–1849), along with a pendant, *Iris and Morpheus* (both St Petersburg, Hermitage).

The two aspects of Guérin's art, the dramatic and the charming, were again evident in the paintings he sent to the Salon of 1817: the sinister, emotionally charged *Clytemnestra Hesitating before Stabbing the Sleeping Agamemnon* (see fig. 2) and the immensely popular *Aeneas Recounting the Misfortunes of Troy in the Presence of Dido* (both Paris, Louvre), the latter inspired by Virgil's *Aeneid*. He also exhibited a posthumous portrait of *Henri de la Rochejaquelein* (Cholet, Mus. A.), Commander-in-Chief of the Royalist army in the Vendée during the French Revolution. Although portraits are comparatively rare in his oeuvre, this was one of several of Vendéen generals that were commissioned by Louis XVIII for an antechamber of the château of Saint-Cloud. By depicting Rochejaquelin in a moment of dramatic action as he fires his pistol in the face of the Republican bayonettes, Guérin blurred the distinction between history painting and portraiture. In the early 1820s he briefly became interested in lithography, a process that was suited to his talent for drawing in black chalks, but he produced only four prints: *Le Paresseux* (1820), *Le Vigilant* (1821), *Qui trop embrasse mal étreint* and *Le Repos du monde*.

After 1817 he never again showed at the Salons, as teaching had become increasingly important to him. In 1815 he had been elected to the Institut de France and in 1816 was appointed Director of the Académie de France in Rome. Ill-health prevented him from taking up the directorship but he was reappointed in 1822. When he left for Rome he took with him a sketch (Angers, Mus. B.-A.) for his most ambitious composition so far, a scene in which the violent death of Priam at the hands of Pyrrhus is set against a background of lurid flames. The demands

2. Pierre Guérin: *Clytemnestra Hesitating before Stabbing the Sleeping Agamemnon*, oil on canvas, 342×325 mm, 1817 (Paris, Musée du Louvre)

of his position at the Académie prevented him from making progress with the huge composition, and he could only resume work on it in earnest after he returned to Paris in late 1828. He was awarded a baronetcy by Charles X and became an Officer of the Légion d'honneur, but his health deteriorated and, without informing his friends, he accompanied Horace Vernet back to Rome, where he died in 1833. He was buried in Trinità dei Monti, near the Villa Medici. Although he painted very little in his last 15 years, the unfinished *Death of Priam* (Angers, Mus. B.-A.) indicates a direction in his work that was taken up in the 1820s by those who had been his pupils. Many notable painters who worked during the Restoration (1814–30) and the reign of Louis-Philippe (1830–48) were trained in his studio, among them Gericault, Delacroix, Ary Scheffer, Léon Cogniet and Xavier Sigalon, all associated with the Romantic movement. They belonged to a generation that was not as exclusively devoted to subjects from the Antique as Guérin's had been but they learnt from him ways of transforming other non-Classical literary subjects into their own particular forms of expression.

BIBLIOGRAPHY

E. Delécluze: *Louis David: Son école et son temps* (Paris, 1855)

A. Soubies: *Membres de l'Académie des beaux-arts depuis la fondation de l'Institut*, i (Paris, 1909), pp. 128–33

H. Lapauze: *Histoire de l'Académie de France à Rome*, ii (Paris, 1924), pp. 155–83

J. Bottineau: '*Les Bergers au tombeau d'Amyntas* par Pierre Guérin', *Rev. Louvre*, xxiii (1973), pp. 355–60

J. Rubin: 'Guérin's Painting of *Phèdre* and the Post-Revolutionary Revival of Racine', *A. Bull.*, lix (1977), pp. 601–18
J. Bottineau: 'La Jeunesse de Pierre Guérin: Etude de quelques dessins', *Rev. Louvre*, xxxix (1989), pp. 300–09
S. Ginzburg: 'Sulla fortuna di Pierre-Narcisse Guérin come "peintre d'expression"', *Ric. Stor. A.*, xl (1990), pp. 5–22

JON WHITELEY

Guerini, Rochus, Graf zu Lynar. *See* LYNAR, ROCHUS QUIRINUS.

Guerra, Alfonso (*b* Naples, 24 Jan 1845; *d* Naples, 1920). Italian architect. He was the son of the painter Camillo Guerra (1797–1874) and studied at the Istituto di Belle Arti, Naples, graduating in literature and mathematics (1863) and later in engineering (1867). His interests lay in formal and decorative problems, but also in those of a technical and structural nature. He expressed the contemporary aesthetic preference for the eclectic style based on Renaissance examples. He received a large number of commissions for public and private buildings, but is best known for the Schilizzi Mausoleum (1881–9) at Posillipo and the Palazzo della Borsa (1890–98) in Naples. The austere exterior of the funerary chapel, with its Egyptian Revival forms, contrasts with the splendid interiors in an Arab style. The building is two storeys high and entered from an atrium; the nave comprises three bays with small transepts, a square apse and an imposing dome above the crossing. The Palazzo della Borsa in the Piazza Bovio was built in collaboration with the structural engineer Luigi Ferrara (1810–94), and the lengthy and complex design stage was preceded by study trips to central Europe. In plan it is almost square and at its centre is the two-storey trading hall. The general proportions of the exterior and the repeated Gerlian motif were inspired, as the designers themselves declared, by Veneto architecture of the late Cinquecento. The lower part of the exterior is heavily rusticated; above it, the smooth ashlar is regularly punctuated with elegant arches. The Ionic order of the ground and first floors is succeeded by the Corinthian order on the second floor, and crowning the whole is an attic storey with caryatids.

WRITINGS

with L. Ferrara: 'Il nuovo palazzo della Borsa in Napoli', *Boll. Coll. Ingeg. & Architetti Napoli* (1899)

BIBLIOGRAPHY

C. Guerra: *Opere e progetti di Alfonso Guerra, architetto ed ingegnere napoletano* (Milan, 1924)
——: 'Il mausoleo di Posillipo', *Quaderni di architettura e di urbanistica napoletana*, i (Naples, 1932)
G. Guerra: 'Il rivestimento in rame della cupola del mausoleo di Posillipo', *Questioni tecniche di architettura* (Naples, 1962)
G. Russo: *La Camera di Commercio di Napoli dal 1808 al 1978* (Naples, 1985)

ISABELLA DI RESTA

Guerra, Gabriel (*b* Unión de San Antonio, near Guadalajara, Jalisco, 1847; *d* Mexico City, 3 Nov 1893). Mexican sculptor. He entered the Escuela Nacional de Bellas Artes in Mexico City in 1873, with Miguel Noreña as his sculpture instructor. His outstanding student works include *Fisher Boy*, *Cupid Deceived*, also known as *Nymph and Cupid* (plaster, 1877), a sculptural group on the theme of the punishment of Cupid, and *Charity* (clay, 1881), a small sentimental group redeemed by the realistic observation of the protagonist and the use of modern dress; all three in Mexico City, Mus. N.A. The subject-matter of these academic works indicates the markedly secular tendency that took hold in the 1870s, replacing the Biblical iconography preponderant around the middle of the century; this development paralleled the coming to power of the liberals after the defeat of the conservative party. Moreover, the delicate sensuality and attenuated neo-Rococo style of *Cupid Deceived* is an important link in the transition to the frank eroticism of turn-of-century modernism.

Guerra profited from the incipient, but already growing, patronage of monumental sculpture. He created the *Torture of Cuauhtémoc* (plaster, exh. 1886; Mexico City, Mus. Ciudad), one of a group of great bronze reliefs made for the base of the monument to *Cuauhtémoc* designed in 1877 by the civil engineer Francisco M. Jiménez (*d* 1884). As a totality this monument, to which other sculptors also contributed between 1884 and 1887, was one of the most successful examples in Mexico of the revival of pre-Hispanic styles.

Guerra's most notable monumental work was a statue of *Gen. Carlos Pacheco* (plaster, exh. 1892; Mexico City, Mus. N.A.; bronze, 1894; Cuernavaca) commissioned by the state of Morelos. Although the posthumously cast bronze did not capture its full vigour, it achieves both grandeur and realism in depicting the figure of a man who had lost his left arm and leg in the struggle against the empire of Maximilian. Both iconographically and stylistically, Guerra's work helped prepare the way for other Mexican sculptors working at the end of the 19th century.

BIBLIOGRAPHY

Gabriel Guerra (1847–1893): Una voluntad escultórica (exh. cat. by M. Díaz, Mexico City, Mus. N.A., 1986)

FAUSTO RAMÍREZ

Guerra, Giovanni (*b* Modena, 1544; *d* Rome, 29 Aug 1618). Italian painter and draughtsman. Having arrived in Rome in 1562, he joined the Accademia di S Luca and the Virtuosi al Pantheon and set up in business with the painter Cesare Nebbia. Together they undertook important commissions from Sixtus V and Clement VIII, for which Guerra 'invented' the stories and Cesare Nebbia executed designs that were then frescoed by a large team of painters. Their projects in Rome included the decoration of the Salone Sisto of the Vatican Library (1585–9) and of the Scala Santa at Porta S Giovanni. Guerra's only documented autograph paintings are frescoes in the Palazzo Cenci (1590; *in situ*). He was a keen exponent of late Roman Mannerism and partly also of Lombard Mannerism. Many of his drawings have survived and include his scenes from the *Lives of the Seven Legendary Kings of Rome* (Paris, Louvre); scenes from the *Life of St Paul* (Paris, Ecole N. Sup. B.-A.); a substantial series of drawings of *Allegories* and *Signs of the Zodiac* (1593–1603; Paris, Ecole N. Sup. B.-A.); the *Book of Judith* (*c.* 1606; New York, Columbia U., Avery Archit. & F.A. Lib.); a series of drawings of villas, gardens and fountains (1601–4; Vienna, Albertina); and the *Libro di immagini con storie di San Geminiano* (Modena, Archv Stor.). His brother Gaspare Guerra (1560–1622) was also a painter. Giovanni Battista Guerra (*fl* 1586–after 1634), another brother, was an architect and gilder.

BIBLIOGRAPHY

G. Baglione: *Vite* (1642)

Libri di immagini, disegni, e incisioni di Giovanni Guerra (Modena 1544–Roma 1618) (exh. cat. by E. Cecchi Gattolin and E. Parma Armani, Modena, Pal. Musei, 1978) [complete bibliog.]

E. Cecchi Gattolin: 'Precisioni e aggiunte per Giovanni Guerra', *Ant. Viva*, xviii/4 (1979), pp. 16–27

G. Briganti, ed.: *La pittura in Italia: Il cinquecento* (Milan, 1987, rev. 2/1988), p. 738

FIORENZA RANGONI

Guerrero, José (*b* Granada, 29 Oct 1914; *d* 1991). Spanish painter. He trained at the Escuela de Artes y Oficios in Granada from 1930 to 1934 and in 1940, following the earlier advice of the poet Federico García Lorca (1898–1936), he moved to Madrid, where he studied until 1944 at the Escuela de Bellas Artes de San Fernando. In 1945 he obtained a grant from the French government to study fresco painting for one year at the Ecole des Beaux-Arts in Paris; there he gained direct knowledge of the French avant-garde and of the work of Juan Gris and Picasso. From 1945 to 1950 he travelled through Europe, staying in Berne, Paris, Rome, London and Brussels. In Rome he met an American, Roxanne Whittier, whom he later married, and in 1949 he visited Philadelphia. A year later he settled in New York, where he abandoned his earlier figurative style and came under the influence of Abstract Expressionism and action painting; among the friends he made there were Franz Kline, Mark Rothko, Willem de Kooning and Robert Motherwell. In works such as *Red and Black* (oil on canvas, 1.32×2.24 m, 1964; Barcelona, Cent. Cult. Fund. Caixa Pensions) he remained faithful to the Abstract Expressionist aesthetic. He exhibited widely in the USA but maintained his links with Spain through regular visits that became increasingly frequent after 1965. He established contact, in particular, with abstract painters in Cuenca such as Fernando Zóbel, Gustavo Torner and Gerardo Rueda (*b* 1926). In later years Guerrero's work continued to evolve, particularly in its use of brilliant colour, and to synthesize elements from Abstract Expressionism and *Art informel*.

BIBLIOGRAPHY

José Guerrero (exh. cat. by M. Pleynet, J. M. Bouet and J. J. Sweeney, Madrid, Min. Cult., 1980)

Pintura española: Aspectos de una década, 1955–1965 (exh. cat. by C. Bernárdez, Madrid, Fund. Caja Pensiones, 1988), pp. 62–5, 114–15

M. DOLORES JIMÉNEZ-BLANCO

Guerrero, Juan Agustín (*b* ?Quito, 1818; *d* ?Quito, 1880). Ecuadorean painter and musician. He was involved in the foundation of the Escuela Miguel de Santiago in Quito in 1849 (transformed in 1852 into the Escuela Democratica Miguel de Santiago), and he won third prize for his painting *Modesty* (Quito, Mus. Fund. Hallo) when the school held the first public art exhibition in Ecuador. He criticized the dependence of Ecuadorean art on Spanish and other European models, and he fought for the liberation of oppressed social classes and particularly of the indigenous people, as well as for individual creativity and the autonomy of the artist from the ecclesiastical powers that remained dominant in Ecuador at that time. Stylistically, Guerrero represented the transition from Quito's colonial Baroque style to Romanticism. He introduced watercolour painting into Ecuador and used the medium to illustrate, criticize and satirize leading figures of the time. His album of drawings and watercolours of landscapes, personalities and customs of the period (*c*. 1860–70; Quito, Mus. Fund. Hallo) constitutes an important document: the portrayal of regional customs and people (*Costumbrismo*) occurred rather late in Ecuador and was a product of the contact between Ecuadorean intellectuals and foreign travellers and scientists interested in the ethnography of indigenous groups in the mountains and jungle.

BIBLIOGRAPHY

J. Castro y Velázquez: *La colección Castro: Evaluación histórico-etnográfica de una serie de pintura costumbrista ecuatoriana del siglo XIX* (MA thesis, Bonn, Rhein. Friedrich-Wilhelms-U., 1976)

W. Hallo, ed.: *Imágenes del Ecuador del siglo XIX: Juan Agustín Guerrero* (Quito and Madrid, 1981)

J. Castro y Velázquez: 'Pintura costumbrista ecuatoriana del siglo XIX', *Cuad. Cult. Pop.*, xvi (1990)

J. G. Navarro: *La pintura en el Ecuador del siglo XVI al XIX* (Quito, 1991), pp. 179–80

ALEXANDRA KENNEDY TROYA

Guerrero, Xavier (*b* San Pedro de las Colonias, Coahuila, 3 Dec 1896; *d* Mexico City, 29 June 1974). Mexican painter, draughtsman and engraver. He was taught the basics of painting by his father, a painter and decorator, and the outstanding characteristic of his stylized realism was its decorative beauty. At the age of 16 Guerrero began to work as a house and church decorator in Guadalajara; there he joined the Centro Bohemio, an avant-garde group led by the painter and politician José Guadalupe Zuno (1891–1980), whose house Guerrero decorated in 1925. He was DIEGO RIVERA's assistant from 1922 to 1924 and joined the Mexican Communist Party with Rivera in 1922. Both became members of its executive committee, Rivera in 1923, Guerrero in 1925, when with DAVID ALFARO SIQUEIROS they founded the periodical *El machete* as the organ of the Sindicato de Obreros Técnicos, Pintores y Escultores. Guerrero had a relationship with Tina Modotti from 1924 until 1928, when he left for Moscow to study at the Leninist School, centre for political instruction, until 1932. He had one-man exhibitions at M. Knoedler & Co. in New York (1943) and at the Museo de Arte Moderno in Mexico City (1972). Some of his major works, such as *Self-portrait* (1947), *Man Making Paper* and *Landscape with Shacks*, are in the Instituto Nacional de Bellas Artes in Mexico City.

BIBLIOGRAPHY

J. Charlot: *The Mexican Mural Renaissance* (New Haven and London, 1963), pp. 241–51, 257–9, 269–79, *passim*

M. Constantine: *Tina Modotti: A Fragile Life* (New York, 1975, rev. 1983), pp. 64, 66, 82, *passim*

Xavier Guerrero y su obra (exh. cat., Mexico City, Mus. A. Mod., 1978)

RAQUEL TIBOL

Guerrero Galván, Jesús (*b* Tonila, Jalisco, 1 June 1910; *d* Cuernavaca, 11 May 1973). Mexican painter. He moved in the 1930s to Mexico City, where he became involved with the muralist movement, avoiding socio-political, folkloric and historical subjects in favour of poetic metaphor, as in *Fertility* (1931), painted in the former church of S Tomás in Guadalajara. Although he continued to paint murals, such as *Earth* (1958; Guadalajara, Mus. A. Mod.), his lyrical sensitivity was most suited to easel paintings, especially portraits and studies of women and children. His figures are shown in a dream-like state, absorbed in daily tasks or surrounded by symbols, as in *Woman with Birds* (1956; Mexico City, Mus. A. Mod.), in which a woman in profile is shown surrounded by hens and doves against the luminosity of the sky.

BIBLIOGRAPHY

Jesús Guerrero Galván (exh. cat., Mexico City, Pal. B.A., 1952)

Visión poética de un gran pintor, Jesús Guerrero Galván (exh. cat., Mexico City, Mus. A. Mod., 1977)

MARGARITA GONZÁLEZ ARREDONDO

Guerrero y Torres, Francisco Antonio de (*b* Villa de Guadalupe [now Guadalupe], *c.* 1727; *d* Mexico City, 1792). Mexican architect. He is first documented as carrying out various repairs and inspecting the work of others in Guadalupe. By 1767 he had been appointed Maestro de Arquitectura by the municipality of Mexico City. Between 1770 and 1774, as Maestro Mayor, he worked in Mexico City on the estate of the Marqués of Oaxaca, the royal palace, the cathedral and the Inquisition Tribunal, the Santo Tribunal de la Fe. His most important ecclesiastical commission was the Capilla del Pocito (1779–91) in Guadalupe. Its unconventional plan is derived from Sebastiano Serlio's interpretation of a Roman temple, with an oval central space (rather than Serlio's circular chamber) surrounded by rectangular chapels and an octagonal sacristy; the building is approached by a small circular vestibule. The exterior shows this juxtaposition of spaces thanks to a large central dome with smaller domes set over the vestibule and the sacristy. The traditional polychromy of Mexican Baroque architecture is achieved here, as in his other work, through the use of white Chiluca stone, red *tezontle* and Puebla glazed tiles, with the tiles covering the lanterns and parapets as well as the domes. In Mexico City he worked on numerous churches and convents, carrying out both renovations and new commissions. Among the latter is the church of La Enseñanza (1772–8), which has a rectangular plan; its aisleless nave is chamfered at the angles and divided into three sections by means of different roof heights.

In secular architecture Guerrero y Torres won great prestige with his numerous commissions from the nobility of Mexico for their private residences in Mexico City. In 1769 he began the house of the Marqués de Xaral de Berrio (now the Palacio Iturbide). The four-storey façade stresses its verticality by the use of a giant order of pilasters on the lower two floors, while a minor order flanks all the fenestration. The house (1769) he built for the Marqués de San Mateo de Valparaíso (now the Banco Nacional de México) has a courtyard where huge intersecting arches frame the corners and windows display concave sills. In 1778 Guerrero y Torres was working on the palace for the Condes de Santiago de Calimaya. In his domestic as in his ecclesiastical work, he used polychrome materials, reserving white stone to emphasize doorways, windows and ornamental features, such as the gargoyles in the form of cannon, which were intended as allusions to the posts of governor and captain-general that several of his patrons had held.

BIBLIOGRAPHY

A. Iñiguez, D.-M. Dorta and J. E. y Buschiazzo: *Historia del arte hispanoamericano*, 3 vols (Barcelona, 1945–56)

H. Berlin: 'Three Master Architects in New Spain', *Hisp. Amer. Hist. Rev.*, xxvii (1947)

G. N. Patton: *Antonio Guerrero y Torres and the Baroque Architecture of Mexico City in the Eighteenth Century* (Ann Arbor, 1958)

M. Toussaint: *Arte colonial en México* (Mexico City, 1962)

G. Gasparini: *América, barroco y arquitectura* (Caracas, 1972)

G. Tovar de Teresa: *El barroco en México* (Mexico City, 1981)

G. Loera Fernández: 'Francisco Antonio Guerrero y Torres: Arquitecto y empresario del siglo XVIII', *Bol. Mnmts Hist.*, 8 (1982), pp. 61–84

R. Gutíerrez: *Arquitectura y urbanismo en Iberoamérica* (Madrid, 1983)

MARIA CONCEPCIÓN GARCÍA SÁIZ

Guerrieri [Guerini; Guerreri]**, Giovan** [Giovanni] **Francesco** (*b* Fossombrone, 1589; *d* Pesaro, 1655–9). Italian painter. Apparently self-taught, he made copies after Federico Barocci. In 1606 he went to Rome and came under the influence of Caravaggio and his followers, above all of Orazio Gentileschi. He returned home, probably in 1614, and at this time produced his most important works, two paintings of the *Miracles of St Nicholas of Tolentino* (Sassoferrato, S Maria del Piano), in which the interpretation is realistic and the figures are monumental and strongly lit. During Guerrieri's second visit to Rome, between 1615 and 1618, he worked for Marcantonio Borghese on the decoration of the newly built Palazzo Borghese on the Campo Marzo. Here he created a series of decorative frescoes and various overdoor paintings. The frescoes, eclectic and compositionally hesitant, reflect the growing influence of the Bolognese school, which by this time had begun to replace that of Caravaggio in Roman painting. After returning to the Marches, Guerrieri worked mainly on religious commissions. His last known work was a signed *St Victor* (1654; Urbino, Pal. Ducale). There are some surviving examples of his work as a portrait painter, for example *Livia Feltro della Rovere* (Urbino, Pal. Ducale). After an accident in which his wife and daughter were killed, he moved to Pesaro to live with his other daughter, Camilla Guerrieri (1628–64), who was also a painter.

BIBLIOGRAPHY

P. della Pergola: 'Giovan Francesco Guerrieri a Roma', *Boll. A.*, xli (1956), pp. 214–37

A. Emiliani: *Giovan Francesco Guerrieri da Fossombrone* (Urbino, 1958)

Giovan Francesco Guerrieri, dipinti e disegni: Un accostamento all'opera (exh. cat. by S. Anselmi, A. Emiliani and G. Sapori, San Severino Marche, Pal. di Città; Bologna, S Giorgio in Poggiale; 1988) [illus., with bibliog.]

RENATE MÖLLER

Guerrino, Tondino di. *See* TONDINO DI GUERRINO.

Guespierre, Pierre Louis-Philippe de. *See* LA GUÉPIÈRE, PHILIPPE DE.

Guest, (Thomas) Douglas (*b* ?1781; *d* ?1839). English painter and theorist. He studied at the Royal Academy Schools, London, and specialized in mythological and historical subjects. His first publicly exhibited work appeared at the Royal Academy in 1803, and in 1805 he won a gold medal for an ambitious work, *Bearing the Dead Body of Patroclus to the Camp: Achilles's Grief* (exh. London, Brit. Inst., 1807; untraced). He competed unsuccessfully in the British Institution competition of 1816 for battle paintings to commemorate the end of the Napoleonic wars. Guest painted a large-scale *Transfiguration* altarpiece for the church of St Thomas in Salisbury (1810), possibly an indication of the preference for public rather than private patronage that he later expressed in his book, *An Inquiry into the Causes of the Decline of Historical Painting* (1829). In this book he bemoaned the low standard of artistic taste in England and the lack of patronage for the 'elevated' genre of history painting. Guest's complaint was articulated by many painters at this time, the most influential of whom were Martin Archer Shee and B. R. Haydon. Guest exhibited regularly at the British Institution and the Royal Academy, his last work appearing in 1839.

WRITINGS

An Inquiry into the Causes of the Decline of Historical Painting (London, 1829)

BIBLIOGRAPHY

DNB; Redgrave

JOAN HICHBERGER

Guevara, Fernando Niño de. *See* NIÑO DE GUEVARA, FERNANDO.

Guevara, Juan Niño de. *See* NIÑO DE GUEVARA, JUAN.

Guevara Moreno, Luis (*b* Valencia, 21 June 1926). Venezuelan painter and engraver. He studied at the Escuela de Artes Plásticas, Caracas, subsequently becoming an illustrator and cartoonist on various publications in Caracas. He went to Paris in 1949, where he attended André Lhote's studio and later the Atelier d'Art Abstrait, when it was directed by Jean Dewasne. In Paris he took part in the activities of the groups Los Disidentes and Madi. His work in this period was clearly Constructivist, and it attracted considerable critical attention in Paris. In 1954 he returned to figurative painting, partly with political motives and partly in response to the figurative and abstract–lyrical European trends of the time. His work was subsequently influenced by critical realism. Guevara Moreno represented Venezuela in the biennales of São Paulo and Venice and was awarded several important national prizes, including the National Award for Painting and the National Award for Drawing and Graphic Arts.

BIBLIOGRAPHY

F. Paz Castillo and P. Rojas Guardia, eds: *Diccionario de las artes visuales en Venezuela*, ii (Caracas, 1982), p. 113

C. Barceló: *De la abstracción a la figuración: El cambio de tendencia en cuatro pintores venezolanos* (diss., Caracas, U. Cent. de Venezuela, 1988)

CRUZ BARCELÓ CEDEÑO

Guevara y Tassis, Iñigo Vélez de. *See* OÑATE Y DE VILLAMEDIANA, Conde de.

Guévrékian, Gabriel (*b* Istanbul, 21 Nov 1900; *d* Antibes, 29 Oct 1970). American architect of Armenian birth. After studying at the Kunstgewerbeschule in Vienna, he worked for a time with Josef Hoffmann and Oskar Strnad. He went to live in Paris in 1920 and became an important colleague of Robert Mallet-Stevens. His first projects included a design for a concrete villa on pilotis, which Siegfried Giedion considered a forerunner of Le Corbusier's Villa Laroche, and which confirmed him to be an exponent of functionalism, favouring concrete, geometric volumes and smooth walls. He gained public recognition with his designs for Sonia Delaunay's Boutique Simultanée and the Cubist garden at the Exposition Internationale des Arts Décoratifs et Industriels Modernes in Paris in 1925. This led to the commission for the garden of the villa for Vicomte Charles de Noailles at Hyères. In 1926, while working on Robert Mallet-Stevens's Rue Mallet-Stevens in Paris, he set up his own firm and worked on a variety of projects for villas and large houses in the Paris area and on the Côte d'Azur. The widely publicized villa that he built for the couturier Jacques Heim at Neuilly (1927) marked him as one of the most notable architect-designers in Paris. Although far from being a theorist, he was associated with the Union des Artistes Modernes and with CIAM, and Le Corbusier appointed him Secretary-General of CIAM at the La Sarraz Congress in 1928 (*see* CIAM, fig. 1). He built two houses at the Deutscher Werkbund exhibition in Vienna in 1932. In 1933 he went to live in Teheran where the Shah appointed him City Architect and Planner. With *c.* 20 private villas and important public projects, he contributed to Teheran's image as a modern capital without giving up his traditional practice. Personal reasons led him to move to London in 1937 where he worked with Connell, Ward and Lucas, but World War II prevented their projects being realized, and he returned to Paris. At the Liberation he worked on the reconstruction of Saarbrücken with Georges-Henri Pingusson and taught at the school of architecture there. Through his former fellow-students from Vienna who were by this time expatriates in the USA, he became a professor at the Alabama Polytechnic Institute in 1948 and from 1949 to 1969 at the University of Illinois, Urbana-Champaign. Thereafter, apart from several competition entries, he gave up practising as an architect.

BIBLIOGRAPHY

E. Vitou: *Gabriel Guévrékian, une autre architecture moderne* (Paris, 1987)

ELISABETH VITOU

Gugel, Eugen (*b* Bergzabern, Bavaria, 26 March 1832; *d* The Hague, 21 May 1905). German architect and teacher, active in the Netherlands. He trained as an architect (1850–56) at the Polytechnischeschule and the Academie der Bildenden Künste in Munich. After working briefly for the National Bavarian Railway Company, he was commissioned to design the summer palace at Feldaffing on the Starnberger See for King Maximilian II of Bavaria (*reg* 1848–64). Work on the palace was, however, suspended in 1864 on the King's death. In the same year Gugel was appointed Professor of Fine Architecture at the Delft Polytechnic, where he was the first teacher of the history of architecture. He designed in an international Renaissance Revival style, and on moving to Holland he became increasingly interested in the Dutch Renaissance. He trained many architects who later worked in this style, among them Edouard Jean Niermans, who later worked successfully in France; Jacob F. Klinkhamer (later professor at the Delft Polytechnic); and W. C. Metzelaar (Government Architect for the Department of Justice). Due to his many administrative activities such as his membership (1874–9) of the committee that advised the government on art and historical monuments, he designed very few buildings himself. His most important achievements include the building (1875; destr.) for the students' society Minerva, at 5 Breestraat in Leiden; a new spire (1875; with P. J. H. Cuypers) for the Nieuwe Kerk in Delft; the Agneta Park (1884) in Delft; and the University Building (1894) at 29 Domplein in Utrecht. In 1902 Gugel retired as professor and was succeeded by Henri Evers.

WRITINGS

Geschiedenis van de bouwstijlen in de hoofdtijdperken der architectuur [Stylistic history of the main periods of architecture] (Arnhem, 1871)
Architectonische vormleer [Elementary geometry of architecture], 5 vols (The Hague, 1880–90)

BIBLIOGRAPHY

NNBW
Bouwknd. Wkbld, xxii (1902), pp. 121–4
Levensberichten der afgestorven medeleden van de maatschappij der Nederlandse letterkunde te Leiden: Bijlage tot de handelingen van 1906–1907 [Obituaries of deceased members of the Dutch literary society in Leiden: supplement to the proceedings of 1906–7]

DIANNE TIMMERMAN, FRANK VAN DEN HOEK

Guggenbichler, (Johann) Meinrad (*bapt* Einsiedeln, Switzerland, 17 April 1649; *d* Mondsee, Austria, 10 May 1723). Swiss sculptor, active in Austria. One of the foremost Baroque artists producing carved wood altars in the alpine area of Upper Austria, he was the son of Georg Guggenbichler, who worked for Einsiedeln Monastery as a sculptor and master builder. Meinrad Guggenbichler's works suggest that his travels as a young journeyman included areas of northern Italy. By 1670 he was working as an assistant to a woodcarver at the monastery of St Florian, near Linz, in Upper Austria. The greatest impact on the young artist came, however, from the local wood carving traditions of the Innviertel and the Salzburg Flachgau areas, where he had relations, a style reflected in such early works as the high altar (1675) in Strasswalchen Parish Church (extant, but no longer in original setting). In 1679 he settled at Mondsee, to the east of Salzburg, where he worked principally for the monastery, creating polychromed wood sculpture.

Guggenbichler's first works for Mondsee's monastery church are four carved wood altars: the Holy Ghost altar (1679–81), the *Speisealtar* (Corpus Christi altar; 1682–4), the Poor Souls altar (1682–4) and the Plague altar (1686). His sculptures at Mondsee of *St Benedict* and *St Bernard* in particular show the influence of works by Thomas Schwantaler, the region's leading sculptor during this period. Guggenbichler's own notable skills as a wood carver derive in part from his deep understanding of human anatomy, as can be seen, for example, in his *St Benedict*, the folded drapery of which is more finely modelled and more plausible than draperies by Schwantaler. In addition, Guggenbichler's emphatic modelling of the faces of his saints results in more striking expressions of soulfulness. His figures (1682–4) on the high altar of the pilgrimage church of Irrsdorf reveal the same characteristics. Once again Guggenbichler determined to make his saints stand out from the formal structure of the altarpiece itself, with the supporting figures of *St Martin* and *St Virgil* appearing above the altar, as if in conversation.

The first completely satisfactory integration of the architectural, sculptural and painted elements of an altarpiece in Guggenbichler's oeuvre is the one he produced in 1690–91 for Michaelbeuern Monastery Church, Salzburg, which may also have been designed as well as carved by him. The life-size, cloud-borne statues of bishops *Ulrich* and *Rupert* (see fig.) are not dominated by the architecture but seem to move freely in space, while to some extent taking up the theme of Johann Michael Rottmayr's contributions to the ensemble—his altarpiece paintings of the *Resurrection* and *St Michael*. One crucial aspect of the overall effect is the light that plays upon Guggenbichler's figures from a concealed source.

Meinrad Guggenbichler: *Bishop Rupert* from the high altar of Michaelbeuern Monastery Church, Salzburg, polychromed and gilded wood, life-size, 1690–91

At the end of the 1690s Guggenbichler received a number of commissions for parish churches in which, drawing on the Gothic tradition of the carved altarpiece, he used scenes with groups in high relief as the central feature of each altarpiece. They include *St Lawrence* (1699) at Abtsdorf, the *Stoning of St Stephen* (1699–1701) at Schleedorf and the *Martyrdom of St Kilian* at Oberwang. His finest works are the sculptures of 1706 for the altarpieces of St Anthony, of the Cross and of the Rosary for the pilgrimage church of St Wolfgang. His peripheral groups of *Abraham and Isaac* and *Tobias and the Angel* are fully free-standing in front of the retable. Guggenbichler's *Ecce homo* (1706) in the same church, which in its expressive power is akin to Spanish examples, is particularly affecting, making the beholder sense that Christ's suffering derives more from an inner sorrow than from his visible wounds. Guggenbichler's last works show that he continued in this emotive vein, forming the faces of his figures into expressive masks of mystical profundity but neglecting their draperies, which appear stylized and unconvincing. They include the altar to *St Sebastian* (1714) at the collegiate church at Mondsee, the altar to *St Leonhard* (1716) at Irrsdorf Pilgrimage Church—where his figure of *St Sebastian* is strikingly androgynous—the altar to *Our Lady* (1717) at Palting Parish Church and the four statues (1721–2) carved for the collegiate church, Salzburg.

Guggenbichler's workshop maintained a large output, and the many repetitions by assistants of favourite themes often fall below the high standard of those made by Guggenbichler himself. One example of this is the carved figure of the *Good Shepherd*, which appears in numerous versions (*c.* 1706)—St Wolfgang at Mondsee, Mariahilf near Mondsee, St Gilgen and Vöklabruck.

BIBLIOGRAPHY

H. Decker: *Meinrad Guggenbichler* (Vienna, 1949)
W. Lipp: 'Kunstregion Mondseeland', *Das Mondseeland: Geschichte und Kultur* (exh. cat., Mondsee, Stift, 1981), pp. 109–28

JOHANNES RAMHARTER

Guggenheim. American family of collectors. In the late 19th century Meyer Guggenheim (1828–1905), an immigrant Swiss Jew, established with seven of his sons a family fortune based on the mining and smelting of ore (particularly copper). Two of the sons were involved in the arts: (1) Solomon R. Guggenheim and Simon Guggenheim (1867–1941). The latter, a senator from 1907 to 1913, founded in 1925 the John Simon Memorial Foundation with an endowment of £3,000,000 to help young scholars, scientists and artists; from 1939 his wife, Olga Guggenheim, gave MOMA, New York, a renewable purchase fund of £50,000 (gradually increased to £150,000 by the 1960s) for the purchase of major works of art, such as Henri Rousseau's *Sleeping Gypsy* (1897). A third brother, Benjamin Guggenheim (1865–1912), was the father of (2) Peggy Guggenheim.

BIBLIOGRAPHY

P. Cabanne: *The Great Collectors* (New York, 1963)
A. Saarinen: *The Proud Possessors* (New York, 1968)
J. H. Davis: *The Guggenheims: An American Epic* (New York, 1978)

(1) Solomon R(obert) Guggenheim (*b* Philadelphia, PA, 2 Feb 1861; *d* Port Washington, NY, 3 Nov 1949). Initially he and his wife, Irene Guggenheim, collected Italian and French Primitive art and 19th-century French and American paintings. In the late 1920s, however, the Baroness Hilla von Rebay persuaded him to build a collection of modern art. Its focus was to be abstract painting, which Rebay considered to be the culmination of modern art, but works by such early 20th-century painters as Marc Chagall and Amedeo Modigliani were also acquired. In 1929 he bought his first modern painting, Vasily Kandinsky's *Composition 8* (1923). By the end of 1930, after a trip to Europe with Rebay, the collection also included works by Rudolf Bauer, Chagall, Robert Delaunay, Albert Gleizes, Modigliani and László Moholy-Nagy.

Guggenheim always intended that his collection would serve as a memorial to his patronage, and, although Rebay made the initial selections, he always reserved the final decision about acquisitions for himself. He had planned to donate the collection to an existing museum, such as the Metropolitan Museum in New York, but by 1936 he had decided to found his own. The Solomon R. Guggenheim Foundation was organized in 1937 with an endowment of £3,000,000. Over the next few years its collection grew rapidly, particularly in 1938, when *c.* 400 paintings were added. By 1939 it contained nearly 800 works, including *c.* 200 by Rudolf Bauer and 100 by Kandinsky. The growing collection was exhibited four times at various East Coast museums between 1936 and 1938, but in 1939 the Museum of Non-Objective Painting was opened in New York to show the abstract works in the Foundation's collection; the other works were kept in Guggenheim's private apartment, where they could be viewed on request. The Foundation's collection grew by only *c.* 100 works between 1940 and 1947, but in 1948, 550 paintings by such artists as Paul Klee and Kandinsky were acquired from the estate of Karl Nierendorf. Upon his death, together with the remainder of his private collection Guggenheim left the Foundation a further £8,000,000, a portion of which was reserved for building the museum a permanent home, designed by Frank Lloyd Wright. Over the years a number of works were sold and are no longer in the Guggenheim.

BIBLIOGRAPHY

Solomon R. Guggenheim Collection of Non-objective Paintings (exh. cat., Charleston, SC, Gibbes A.G., 1936)
Art of Tomorrow: Solomon R. Guggenheim Collection of Non-objective Paintings (exh. cat., New York, Mus. Non-obj. Ptg, 1939)
Guggenheim Museum: The Building, the Collection, Solomon R. Guggenheim Museum (New York, 1980)
The Benefactors: Three Twentieth Century Patrons of the Arts—Solomon R. Guggenheim, Joseph H. Hirshhorn and Roy R. Neuberger (exh. cat., Potsdam, NY, State U., Brainerd A.G., 1980)

A. DEIRDRE ROBSON

(2) Peggy [Marguerite] Guggenheim (*b* New York, 26 Aug 1898; *d* Venice, 23 Dec 1979). Niece of (1) Solomon R. Guggenheim. Her early years in New York were highlighted by frequent trips abroad, through which she became acquainted with European culture. After the death of her father, Benjamin Guggenheim, aboard the *Titanic*, she came into her inheritance and moved to France the following year. Her early taste in art was directed towards paintings by the Old Masters. In 1922, however, she married the avant-garde writer Laurence Vail (1891–1968), an American living in the bohemian quarters of Paris. In this milieu she grew increasingly interested in modern art and literature.

In 1932, after her divorce from Vail, Guggenheim moved to London, where in 1938 she opened Guggenheim Jeune, a modern art gallery, despite her limited knowledge of modernism. She relied on Marcel Duchamp, whom she had known in Paris, for her education in 20th-century art. He served as an informal adviser for her London gallery, which earned a reputation as a centre of avant-garde activity. She was also inspired to start her own collection.

Although Guggenheim Jeune was a commercial failure, it sparked off Guggenheim's enthusiasm for modern art. She decided to add extensively to her collection of paintings and sculpture with the aim of opening a new museum. Herbert Read became the museum's director and advised Guggenheim on acquisitions that would form a systematic survey of 20th-century art. Plans for the museum were cut short by World War II, but Read's list of artists and movements provided a solid basis for the rapidly growing collection. Howard Putzel (1898–1945), an art dealer from California, also advised Guggenheim on acquisitions in Europe, which included such works as Constantin Brancusi's *Bird in Space* (1940), Fernand Léger's *Men in the City* (1919) and Alberto Giacometti's *Woman with her Throat Cut* (1932–3); all of these are now in the Peggy Guggenheim Foundation, Venice.

In 1941 Guggenheim returned to the USA, where in December she married Max Ernst, who had accompanied her from Europe. She decided upon New York as the location for her new gallery, Art of This Century, which opened in October 1942. The gallery's interior was designed by Frederick Kiesler, who transformed an ordinary exhibition space into an abstract and Surrealist environment (*see* NEW YORK, fig. 8). In the Cubist gallery, paintings seemed to float, suspended on strings; in the Surrealist space, the pictures projected from concave walls. Guggenheim showed not only European modern art here but also the work of promising new American artists. By 1947, when the gallery closed, Guggenheim had introduced works by William Baziotes, David Hare, Hans Hofmann, Robert Motherwell, Jackson Pollock, Mark Rothko and Clyfford Still, which marked the beginning of American Abstract Expressionism.

After World War II Guggenheim settled in Venice, where she continued to promote modern art by exhibiting her collection, which then included many Abstract Expressionist canvases, for example *Moon-woman Cuts the Circle* (1942) by Pollock. She also patronized two new Italian painters, Parmeggiani Tancredi (*b* 1927) and Edmondo Bacci (*b* 1913). On her death the Guggenheim Foundation in Venice came under the auspices of the Solomon R. Guggenheim Museum of New York.

WRITINGS

ed.: *Art of This Century* (New York, 1942)

Out of This Century: Confessions of an Art Addict (New York, 1979) [reprint of texts originally pubd separately in 1946 and 1960, with add. essay 'Venice']

BIBLIOGRAPHY

M. P. Lader: *Peggy Guggenheim's Art of This Century: The Surrealist Milieu and the American Avant-garde, 1942–47* (diss., Newark, U. DE, 1981)

A. Rudenstine: *The Peggy Guggenheim Collection, Venice* (New York, 1985)

MELVIN P. LADER

Guggenheim, Willy. *See* VARLIN.

Guggiari, Hermann (*b* Asunción, 1924). Paraguayan sculptor. He studied sculpture under Vicente Pollarollo in Asunción and from 1943 at the Escuela Superior de Bellas Artes Ernesto de la Cárcova in Buenos Aires. In the late 1940s and early 1950s, he dealt with local political and social themes, but his style became progressively simplified and centred on the significant properties of materials and the sculptural possibilities of form, until he reached a strongly expressive abstraction that confirmed him as the central figure of modern sculpture in Paraguay. His principal materials were iron and steel, which were torn apart in dramatic gestures to suggest that man's existence is a search for liberty. This poetic of breaking and rending was a constant element in Guggiari's work throughout his career. It appears, for example, in *Christ* (steel, h. 4 m, 1969; Asunción, Santa Cruz) and in *Kansas* (iron and stone, 1980; Hays, KS, Fort Hays State U.).

BIBLIOGRAPHY

Guggiari, Blinder, Colombino (exh. cat. by L. Abramo, Asunción, Misión Cult. Bras., 1969)

T. Escobar: *Una interpretación de las artes visuales en el Paraguay* (Asunción, 1984)

TICIO ESCOBAR

Guglielmelli. Italian family of architects.

(1) Arcangelo Guglielmelli (*fl* Naples, 1674–1722). He was of sufficient professional standing in 1674 to help the young Francesco Solimena to gain a commission. His first important work, however, was the façade of S Maria in Portico, Naples, which dates from as late as 1682. It is a richly orchestrated version of the traditional Neapolitan open façade, which has a vestibule in the lower storey and a loggia above. The complex arrangement gives the building a highly decorative appearance, but it fails to blend the various compositional elements. In 1684 Arcangelo designed the architectural setting for Luca Giordano's frescoes in the church of the Gerolamini in Naples. Several of his most important commissions followed the devastation caused by the earthquake of 1688, such as the rebuilding of Salerno Cathedral (1691–8) and, in Naples, the reconstruction of the dome of Gesù Nuovo (1688–92) and the restoration of the chapel of S Restituta (completed 1692), attached to the cathedral. He redecorated the interior of the church of Gesù delle Monache, Naples, *c.* 1692. The plan of the church of Rosario al largo delle Pigne (1692–1700), built to his design, is an elongated Greek cross, an idea introduced to Naples by Cosimo Fanzago. Arcangelo's interpretation of the plan is interesting and scenographic: the bays of the longitudinal arms are staggered and the columns are recessed. This solution doubtless followed such Roman prototypes as Carlo Rainaldi's S Maria in Campitelli (1656–65). The later façade also adopts a theme formulated by Fanzago: the *doppia facciata* (a two-storey portico façade) with staircase vestibule. From 1695 to 1717 Arcangelo was engaged in building S Maria Egiziaca a Pizzofalcone (begun 1650) to the designs of Fanzago and Francesco Picchiatti. From 1697 to 1699 he worked for the Benedictines of Montecassino.

During the first two decades of the 18th century Arcangelo remained one of the most sought-after Neapolitan architects, especially by the Church. Until 1709 he supervised the redecoration of S Angelo a Nilo, the exterior design of which is dominated by delicately graded stuccowork. Its richly curved details anticipate the characteristic features of Neapolitan Rococo. In 1712 he designed a church for the house of the Jesuit novices of the Nunziatella but was ousted from this commission by

Ferdinando Sanfelice in the following year. At the same time he probably designed a plan (unexecuted) for the Jesuit church of Sulmona. In 1715 work began on S Maria delle Grazie a Mondragone, Naples, which was formerly attributed to Giambattista Nauclerio (*fl* 1705–37) but is now recognized as Arcangelo's main work. The plan is again based on a Greek cross, extended along the longitudinal axis, with an octagonal crossing. The rounded corners of the arms and the position of the columns at the key points of the building were presumably suggested by Roman buildings, such as Pietro da Cortona's SS Luca e Martina. Arcangelo is last recorded in 1722. His later work is not easily differentiated from that of his son (2) Marcello Guglielmelli.

(2) Marcello Guglielmelli (*fl* Naples, *c.* 1715–30). Son of (1) Arcangelo Guglielmelli. Between *c.* 1715 and 1720 he succeeded his father on projects that the latter had previously supervised. From 1723 until 1727 he acted as official architect for the Oratorian Order in Naples. During this period he drew up designs for the grand Biblioteca dei Gerolamini, one of the city's most beautiful Baroque interiors; its rich decoration, however, was started as late as 1732 and could not have been based on Marcello's designs. It is clear that he was responsible for the building (*c.* 1715–25) of the façade of S Giuseppe dei Ruffo, Naples, where the Neapolitan staircase vestibule, in which the portico is combined with a double flight of interior stairs, received its most impressive interpretation, although contemporary Roman influences are also recognizable.

BIBLIOGRAPHY

R. Pane: *L'architettura dell'età barocca in Napoli* (Naples, 1939), pp. 135–5

R. Mormone: 'Architettura a Napoli, 1650–1734', *Storia di Napoli*, vi/2 (Naples, 1970), pp. 1097–1153 (1117–20)

A. Blunt: *Neapolitan Baroque and Rococo Architecture* (London, 1975), pp. 103–5

G. Amirante: 'Arcangelo Guglielmelli e la chiesa del Gesù delle Monache', *Napoli Nob.*, n. s. 2, xvi (1976), pp. 170–84

——: 'La chiesa del Rosario al largo delle Pigne', *Napoli Nob.*, n. s. 2, xvii (1978), pp. 139–50

R. Bösel: 'Freitreppen und Treppenvorhallen im barocken Sakralbau Neapels', *Röm. Hist. Mitt.*, xx (1978), pp. 123–42

G. Amirante: 'Arcangelo Guglielmelli e l'architettura a Napoli tra la fine del '600 e l'inizio del '700', *Napoli Nob.*, n. s. 2, xviii (1979), pp. 88–104

R. Bösel: *Die Baudenkmäler der römischen und der neapolitanischen Ordensprovinz* (1985), i of *Jesuitenarchitektur in Italien, 1540–1773* (Vienna, 1985–), pp. 407, 462–7, 492

RICHARD BÖSEL

Guglielmi, Gregorio (*b* Rome, 13 Dec 1714; *d* St Petersburg, 2 Feb 1773). Italian painter, active also in Germany and Central Europe. He trained either with Francesco Trevisani (Pascoli; Mariette) or with Sebastiano Conca (von Stetten). He was a protégé of Cardinal Alessandro Albani, and his early activity was centred in Rome, where he executed three canvases for St Catherine, Prague (one, *St Augustine*, *in situ*; two untraced), and the main altarpiece for S Apollonia, Rome (untraced). His *Canonization of St Camillo de Lellis* (Rome, Pin. Vaticana) dates from 1746. His frescoes included those in the hospital of the Santo Spirito in Sassia (1742; destr.); *History Commands Time to Reveal the Truth* (1746; Rome, Pal. Corsini; see fig.), commissioned by Cardinal Neri Corsini to decorate the history section of the Biblioteca Corsiniana in the Palazzo Corsini, Rome; the vault fresco, *St Giovanni de Matha in Glory* (1744–8), in Santa Trinità degli Spagnoli, Rome, and frescoes in the refectory of S Agostino, Rome (1750–51; *in situ*). In these first documented works the use of warm, luminous colours and strongly modelled figures within a naturalistic composition demonstrates the artist's desire to unite the late Baroque of Conca with the developing classicism of Pierre Subleyras and Marco Benefial.

Guglielmi was a member of the Congregazione dei Virtuosi al Pantheon from 1741 and in 1748 was elected to the Accademia di S Luca. He remained in Rome till 1750, then, after a brief sojourn in Naples, he went to Dresden, where he was commissioned by the Elector Frederick-Augustus III to decorate the ceiling of the chapel of St John Nepomuk in the Hofkirche (1753). This work, however, failed to please and was later replaced. A religious image painted for the Gräfin von Brühl suffered a similar reception, as did the works planned for the castles of the Graf von Brühl at Pforten and Nischwitz. In 1754 Guglielmi painted the portrait of *Johann Georg, Chevalier de Saxe* (Dresden, Inst. Dkmlpf.). Possibly it was his bold and unusual style and his own character that provoked the aversion to his art and caused his failure in Saxony. In Dresden, Guglielmi met the court poet, Pietro Metastasio (1698–1782), and through him was invited to decorate the ceiling of the auditorium of Vienna University (1755) with an *Allegory of the Arts and Sciences*; Metastasio himself worked on the iconographic programme. Guglielmi was the dominant partner in this project (Garas), which was realized with the collaboration of the painter and architect Domenico Francia (1702–58). Other commissions included the frescoes in the palace of the wine merchant Edlinger at Odenburg (now Sopron) in Hungary (1756–7; destr.), known through descriptions. Other important Viennese commissions came through Luigi Malabaila, Conte di Canale (1704–73), who was responsible for the theme of the frescoes (1759–62) in the great gallery in the Schönbrunn Palace, Vienna. This work, which glorifies the ruling house of Austria, is the culmination of a tradition of Baroque ceiling painting that had been most brilliantly practised in that region by Giambattista Tiepolo and Franz Anton Maulbertsch. An inscription '*Guglielmi a Roma nel 1762*' on a ceiling sketch (St Petersburg, Hermitage) suggests that, after working at Schönbrunn, Guglielmi returned to Rome to execute an unspecified commission. Probably dating from this period is a portrait of one *Monsignore di Foligno* (Rome, ex-Massimo priv. col., see Griseri, 1956, pl. 40).

Guglielmi then accompanied Sophonias de Derich (1712–73) and his wife to Stuttgart; from there they travelled to Brussels, and after two and a half years Guglielmi went on to Berlin. Here, in 1764, he decorated two great ceilings in the palace of Prince Heinrich Hohenzollern (built 1748–64; now Humboldt University), representing an *Assembly of the Gods* and the *Four Parts of the World*. The first deteriorated almost immediately but was restored by Christian Bernhard Rode and today is in the auditorium of the University. The second, divided into two sectors, was destroyed when the palace was rebuilt in 1811. Fortunately, from earlier descriptions it is possible to recognize the structure of the decorations in two preparatory sketches: one represents the *Allegory of the Hero Led by Virtue to Olympus* (Vienna, Albertina), and

Gregorio Guglielmi: *History Commands Time to Reveal the Truth* (1746), fresco, Biblioteca Corsiniana, Palazzo Corsini, Rome

the second the *Four Parts of the World* (1768; Warsaw, N. Mus.).

After Berlin, Guglielmi returned to Italy, where he worked in Turin for the court of Savoy from 1765 to 1766, decorating the vault of a study in the Palazzo Reale with a fresco of the *Four Continents.* In the Palazzo Chiablese, Turin, he painted four overdoor allegories of *Peace, War, Autumn* and *Summer* (all *in situ*). While in Turin he executed the *Virgin in Glory, Surrounded by the Holy Martyrs Solutore, Avventore and Ottavio* (1759–60), the main altarpiece for SS Avventore Solutore e Ottavio (sketch, Salzburg, Barockmus.). The works of this period are characterized by their strongly decorative character and festive gaiety, inspired both by Venetian painting and by French Rococo art in Turin. He also painted at this time two canvases for the Colleoni Chapel at Bergamo, depicting *Jacob Wrestling with the Angel* and *Job and his Wife* (both 1765; *in situ*; drawings, Vienna, Albertina). Following his interlude in Italy, Guglielmi went to Augsburg in Bavaria, where he decorated the Schaezlerpalais of Baron Benedikt Adam von Liebert. On the ceiling of the main hall he executed an *Allegory of the Four Parts of the World*, drawing inspiration from the commercial and financial activity of his patron (preparatory drawing, Vienna, Albertina); on the small vault of the stairway he painted the *Allegory of Art.* During his stay in Berlin, Guglielmi had sent to the King of Poland, Stanisław II Augustus, through the court painter Marcello Bacciarelli, some studies and sketches as evidence of his artistic abilities. The Polish king wished to found an Academy of Fine Arts, and Guglielmi hoped to become its director, but the project did not materialize due to lack of funds. Guglielmi was, however, summoned to decorate the royal castle at Ujazdow, a work that he never completed, though several preparatory sketches remain (1768–9; Vienna, Albertina; Brno, Morav. Mus.; Nancy, Mus. B.-A.). His contacts with the Russian court are documented from 1767, the year in which he sent to St Petersburg from Augsburg a drawing for a decoration planned for the Imperial Palace at Tsarkoye Selo (Moscow, Pushkin Mus.

F.A.). The drawing was greatly admired and Guglielmi duly arrived in St Petersburg after visiting several European capitals: first Paris, in 1770, where he met Pierre-Jean Mariette, then Rome. In 1772 he went on to Munich and finally to St Petersburg, where he died.

UNPUBLISHED SOURCES

Perugia, Bib. Augusta, MSS n. 1383, fols 88–95 [L. Pascoli's second version of the life of Francesco Trevisani]

BIBLIOGRAPHY

Mariette, ii, p. 339; iv, p. 70; Thieme–Becker
P. von Stetten: *Erläuterungen der gestochenen Vorstellungen* (Augsburg, 1765), p. 247
——: *Kunst- Gewerb- und Handwerk- Geschichte der Reichs-Stadt Augsburg*, ii (Augsburg, 1788), p. 207
R. Longhi: 'Il Goya romano e la "cultura di via Condotti"', *Paragone*, v/53 (1954), pp. 28–39
A. Griseri: 'Guglielmo a Torino', *Paragone*, vi/69 (1955), pp. 29–38
——: 'Due "ritratti" romani: Un Giaquinto e un Guglielmi', *Paragone*, vii/83 (1956)
K. Garas: 'Gregorio Guglielmi (1714–1773), *Acta Hist. A. Acad. Sci. Hung.*, ix (1963), pp. 269–94 [fundamental study; with bibliography]
W. Witzthum: 'Guglielmi e Metastasio', *Paragone*, xiv/165 (1963), pp. 65–71
E. Borsellino: 'Il cardinale Neri Corsini mecenate e committente. Guglielmi, Parrocel, Conca e Meucci nella Biblioteca Corsiniana', *Boll. A.*, lxvi/10 (1981), pp. 49–66
G. Sestieri: *La pittura del settecento* (Turin, 1988), pp. 50–51
V. Casale: 'Quadri di canonizzazione', *La pittura in Italia: Il settecento*, ed. G. Briganti (Milan, 1990), p. 576, no. 15, pl. 821

ENZO BORSELLINO

Guglielmo [Guillielmus] (*fl* 1158–65). Italian sculptor. An inscription on the façade of Pisa Cathedral marks the *Sepultura Guillielmi magistri qui fecit perg[am]um Sancte Marie.* That pulpit (moved to Cagliari Cathedral in 1312), was originally signed *Hoc Guillielmus opus prestantior arte modernis quatuor annorum spatio, sed domini centum decies sex mille duobus* ('This work was created by Guglielmo, excellent among the modern masters, finished in 1162 after four years of work'). It is the oldest surviving example of a type made in Tuscany for many years. It comprises eight panels, each with two scenes from the *Life of Christ*, and has supporting columns resting on lions. Stylistically, decorative motifs relate to the carvings on the lower part of Pisa Cathedral façade and to some panels (Pisa, Mus. Opera Duomo) attributed to Rainaldo and his shop. Other panels in the same museum, from the wall adjacent to the pulpit, have been attributed (Baracchini) to Guglielmo. Strong stylistic affinities link Guglielmo's pulpit with cycles by Provençal sculptors (e.g. SAINT-GILLES-DU-GARD ABBEY, façade). Like the Pisans, they drew heavily on late Roman sarcophagi and statues, and evidence exists for cultural contacts between Provence and Pisa.

A detailed agreement, signed 1 January 1165, in which masters Guillielmus and Riccius undertook to work for the Opera del Duomo, Pisa, is the last record of Guglielmo's activity. There are, however, several decorative bands and two panels with New Testament scenes, now set into the floor of Pistoia Cathedral and probably from its pulpit, that are closely related in iconography and style to the Pisan pulpit and can be firmly attributed to Guglielmo. On the other hand, another pulpit (Volterra Cathedral) seems to be by a master related to both Guglielmo and to Biduino, while a stoup attributed to Guglielmo, with scenes from the *Life of St Ranierus* (New York, Cloisters), raises questions of attribution and authenticity.

BIBLIOGRAPHY

R. Zech: *Meister Wilhelm von Innsbruck und die Pisaner Kanzel in Dome zu Cagliari* (Bottrop, 1935)
G. De Angelis d'Ossat, ed.: *Il Museo dell'Opera del Duomo a Pisa* (Milan, 1986) [section by C. Baracchini]
R. Serra: *Pittura e scultura dall'età romanica alla fine del '500*, Storia dell'arte in Sardegna (Nuoro, 1990)

Guglielmo da Modena. *See* WILIGELMO.

Guglielmo da Pisa, Fra (*b* before ?1239; *d c.* 1312–13). Italian sculptor. He assisted Nicola Pisano on the tomb of *St Dominic* for S Domenico in Bologna (dispersed; sarcophagus, *in situ*). Gnudi distinguishes his contribution from that of Nicola and the other assistants and also attributes to Fra Guglielmo two groups of deacons (Boston, MA, Mus. F.A.; Florence, Bargello) from the tomb.

The reconstruction of Fra Guglielmo's artistic personality must be based on the remarkable pulpit in S Giovanni Fuorcivitas, Pistoia. A lost inscription bore the name *Guglielmo* and the date 1270. In this work he reverted to the traditional Tuscan rectangular plan, with two tiers of narrative reliefs. The carvings show a rigorous interpretation of Nicola's vocabulary, particularly in the rendering of drapery and in the late Classical borrowings.

Guglielmo was recorded in 1292 and 1298 in documents concerning the convent of S Caterina, Pisa, where he was a lay brother, and he may be the Frater Guiglielmus who in 1301 supplied Cimabue with tesserae for the apse mosaic in Pisa Cathedral. He may also be the subject of a lost inscription that declared *Guiglielmus pisanus* as the *operis factor, caput. . . et ordinis actor* of the façade decoration at S Michele in Borgo, Pisa. Comparison with the Pistoia pulpit suggests he carved several of the human and animal reliefs of the lower storey, including lions flanking the door lunettes. The style of Nicola is still recognizable, but ideas derived from the work of Giovanni Pisano are also present. The architecture of the upper storeys may have been conceived by Fra Guglielmo, but it was executed by others. Stylistic comparison suggests he may also have designed at least the lower storey of the apparently contemporary façade of S Caterina, Pisa.

BIBLIOGRAPHY

DBI
C. Gnudi: *Nicola, Arnolfo, Lapo: L'arca di San Domenico in Bologna* (Florence, 1948)
P. Toesca: *Il trecento* (Turin, 1951)

ANTONIO CALECA

Guglielmo del Magro. *See* GIRALDI, GUGLIELMO.

Guglielmo de Marcillat. *See* GUILLAUME DE MARCILLAT.

Guglielmus [Guglielmo] (*fl c.* 1138). Italian sculptor. He is known only from an inscription on the New Testament reliefs that were carved *c.* 1138 on the north side of the main portal of S Zeno Maggiore, Verona. Guglielmus was at one time mistakenly identified as Wiligelmo of Modena, but his style is very close to that of his collaborator at Verona, NICHOLAUS.

BIBLIOGRAPHY

A. K. Porter: *Lombard Architecture*, iii (New Haven, 1917), pp. 526–7

CHRISTINE VERZAR

Guiana, British. *See* GUYANA.

Guiard, Laurent (*b* Chaumont-en-Bassigny, Haute-Marne, 22 July 1723; *d* Carrara, 31 May 1788). French sculptor. After his early training at Chaumont, where the dominant artistic personality and his first professor was the architect and sculptor Jean-Baptiste Bouchardon (1667–1742), he entered the Paris studio of Bouchardon's son, Edme Bouchardon. In 1749 he won the Prix de Rome and entered the Ecole Royale des Elèves Protégés. While at the Ecole he exhibited several works at Versailles (e.g. *Hercules Resting*, terracotta, 1752; Parma, Mus. Lombardi) as well as a plaster model of *Louis XV on Horseback* (untraced), which found favour with Louis XV but caused a permanent breach between Guiard and Bouchardon, who was himself working on a commission from the City of Paris for an equestrian statue of the King. It was probably before his departure for Italy in 1755 that Guiard conceived the model for the Pendule de l'Etude ('à la Geoffrin'; Langres, Mus. Du Breuil de St-Germain), which was commissioned by Marie-Thérèse Rodet Geoffrin. From 1755 to 1758 Guiard completed his education at the Académie de France in Rome, remaining in the city at his own expense until 1767. Among works executed there was a reduced copy in bronze (*c.* 1756; untraced) of the equestrian statue of the *Younger Balbus* (Naples, Mus. Archeol. N.) discovered at Herculaneum in 1746, which was bought by the French ambassador in Rome, Etienne-François, Comte de Stainville (later Duc de Choiseul), as well as other copies after antique statues, executed for notable French collectors such as Etienne-Michel Bouret (e.g. *Gladiator*, marble, 1765; ex-Luxembourg Gardens, Paris). He also executed a group of *Aeneas and Anchises* (plaster, 1766; Aix-en-Provence, Mus. Granet). On Guiard's return to Paris, in 1767, he submitted the statuette *Mars Resting* (untraced) in order to gain admission to the Académie Royale, but it was refused, and in 1769 he contracted to enter the service of the Bourbon Duke Ferdinand of Parma. Before leaving for Parma he was commissioned to design an ambitious Neo-classical tomb for Louise-Dorothea, Duchess of Saxe-Gotha (plaster model, *c.* 1770; formerly Gotha, Schloss Friedenstein, a large drawing of which can still be found at the Castle Museum), which remained unbuilt. In 1772 Guiard was named Premier Sculpteur to the Duke of Parma. He was also director of the Accademia in Parma and a member of the Bologna and Padua academies. Few traces remain of the output of his 12 years in northern Italy, although, among others, he is known to have produced models for statues of *Christ* and *Flora* (both 1772; untraced) and a copy (marble, before 1786; Parma, Accad. B.A.) of Edme Bouchardon's statue *Cupid Carving his Bow from the Club of Hercules*, as well as a profile relief of a *Nude Youth* (plaster, 1772; Parma, Accad. B.A.). His last years were spent working on a marble monument to *St Bernard* for the monks of Clairvaux Abbey, commissioned in 1782 but left unfinished at Guiard's death (destr.).

BIBLIOGRAPHY

Lami

A. Roserot: *Laurent Guiard, premier sculpteur du Duc de Parme, 1723–1788* (Paris, 1901)

T. de Bogyag: 'Nouveaux documents relatifs aux rapports de la cour de Gotha avec les artistes français', *Bull. Soc. Hist. A. Fr.* (1933), pp. 246–57

F. Boyer: 'Une Lettre de Laurent Guiard, premier sculpteur du Duc de Parme', *Bull. Soc. Hist. A. Fr.* (1968), pp. 201–7

Nouvelles acquisitions du département des sculptures, 1984–1987 (exh. cat., ed. J.-R. Gaborit; Paris, Louvre), pp. 74–7 (entry by G. Bresc-Bautier)

C. Baulez: 'La Pendule à la Geoffrin', *L'Estampille*, 224 (1989)

H. Ronot: 'Oeuvres inédites et documents inexploités du sculpteur Laurent Guiard, 1723–1788', *Bull. Soc. Hist. A. Fr.* (1992), pp. 153–64

GUILHEM SCHERF

Guibal. French family of artists.

(1) Barthélemy Guibal (*b* Nîmes, 3 Feb 1699; *d* Lunéville, 5 April 1757). Sculptor. He was a pupil of François Dumont in Paris and accompanied him to the court of Léopold, Duke of Lorraine, at Lunéville, where in 1724 he was engaged on the decoration of the château. On Dumont's death (1726) Guibal became the Duke's principal sculptor, a position in which he was confirmed in 1738 by Stanislav, Duke of Lorraine. He collaborated with the architect Emmanuel Héré on the execution of colossal statues of *St Peter* and *St Paul* (stone, *c.* 1745) for St Jacques, Lunéville (*in situ*), as well as on numerous stone statues for the châteaux of Einville, Haroué and Lunéville (*in situ*); the latter depict mythological subjects in a rather insipid imitation of the style evolved at Versailles. His most successful works were those executed during Stanislav's rebuilding of Nancy. For the Place de la Carrière he sculpted the busts for the hemicycle (destr. 1792) and the four seated allegorical statues (stone, *c.* 1755) for the Palais du Gouvernement (Palais d'Intendance, *in situ*; *see* NANCY, fig. 1), while for the Arc de Triomphe he provided decorative sculpture in stone and lead (1750–55, altered 1790s; *in situ*). His masterpieces, in an animated Rococo style recalling the sculpture of the Adam (ii) family and the designs of François Boucher, are the gilt-lead fountains of *Amphitrite* and *Neptune* (both *c.* 1750–55) in the Place Stanislas (*in situ*). Among his pupils were Johann Joseph Söntgen (*d* 1788) and Jean-Baptiste Walnaeffer (*fl* 1751–9), both of whom assisted him at Nancy, and Paul-Louis Cyfflé (1724–1806), with whom he made the statue of *Louis XV* (bronze, 1755, destr. 1792; bronze reduction, Nancy, Mus. Hist. Lorrain), formerly on the Place Royale.

BIBLIOGRAPHY

Lami

P. Boyé: *Les Châteaux du roi Stanislas en Lorraine* (Nancy, 1910/*R* 1980)

P. Marot: *La Place Royale de Nancy* (Nancy, 1966)

FRANÇOIS PUPIL

(2) Nicolas [Nicholas] **Guibal** (*b* Lunéville, 29 Nov 1725; *d* Stuttgart, 3 Nov 1784). Painter, son of (1) Barthélemy Guibal. He began as a pupil of his father but soon turned from sculpture to painting. In 1738 he studied under Claude Charles (*c.* 1661–1747) in Nancy and in 1740 entered Charles-Joseph Natoire's studio in Paris. Natoire's polished mythological paintings and portraits exercised considerable influence on Guibal. In 1749 he went to Stuttgart and gained the protection of Charles Eugene, Duke of Württemberg, who sent him to Rome. While there in 1750–54 he spent two years in the studio of Anton Raphael Mengs, with whom he established a lasting friendship and from whom he acquired the skills of large-scale decorative painting. In 1755 he was appointed First Painter to the Court of Württemberg. Many of his works were allegories celebrating the glorious achievements of his patrons, as in the *Rise of the Württembergs under the Influence of the Arts and Sciences* (1754–6, destr.), painted with the help of Mengs for the Ducal Palace in Stuttgart. Guibal painted a great number of Rococo ceilings for the Württembergs and for the Elector Palatine, but almost all of these have been destroyed. He was also active as a designer of stage sets and other ephemeral decorations, and as a portrait painter. His portraits range from the stiff and artificial *Graf Leopold von Neipperg and his Family* (priv. col.) to the direct and relaxed *Franziska von Hohenheim* (untraced). He had academic and intellectual pretensions and wrote eulogies of Mengs (1778) and Nicolas Poussin, the latter being awarded a prize by the Rouen Académie in 1783. In 1784 he was made an honorary member of the Académie Royale in Paris and promised as a *morceau de réception* a ceiling painting for the Galerie d'Apollon in the Louvre representing *Aurora in her Chariot* (unexecuted).

BIBLIOGRAPHY

Thieme–Becker

A. J. H. Nast: *Programma in obitum N. Guibali* (Stuttgart, 1784)

B. Pfeiffer: *Herzog Karl Eugen und seine Zeit* (Esslingen, 1905)

SIMON LEE

Guicciardini, Lodovico [Lodovico di Jacopo di Piero Guicciardini] (*b* Florence, 19 Aug 1521; *d* Antwerp, 22 March 1589). Italian merchant and writer, active in the southern Netherlands. He was the son of Jacopo Guicciardini (*d* 1552) and Camilla d'Agnolo des Bardi (*d* 1557) and nephew of the historian Francesco Guicciardini (1483–1540); as a member of a patrician family, he received a good education and learnt to read Latin and a little Greek. He spent most of his adult life in Antwerp, where he is first documented in 1542. He was briefly imprisoned in 1567 and his house confiscated for his criticism of the regime of the Duque de Alba, Governor of the Netherlands. He published a number of works, including collections of anecdotes and maxims, but the most celebrated is his account of the Low Countries, the *Descrittione di. . .tutti i Paesi Bassi*, first published in Antwerp in 1567 and dedicated to Philip II, King of Spain; a French edition, dedicated to Margaret of Austria, Queen of Spain, appeared later in the same year. The volume is one of the most valuable sources of information for the country in the 16th century, describing the geographical, social and political aspects of the region and referring to notable Netherlandish artists.

Guicciardini stated that he was assisted in his work by the artists Lucas de Heere and Dominicus Lampsonius (1532–99) of Bruges. He also took certain passages directly from the first edition of Vasari's *Vite* (1550): for example, Vasari's assertion that Jan van Eyck discovered the technique of oil painting and that there was a very beautiful painting by 'Ugo d'Anversa' in S Maria Nuova, Florence, which is taken to refer to the Portinari Altarpiece by Hugo van der Goes (*see* GOES, HUGO VAN DER, fig. 1). Vasari in turn appears to have employed Guicciardini's account, since in his second edition of the *Vite* (1568) he included Hubert van Eyck, Jan's brother, who is in Guicciardini's work but not in the earlier *Vite*. In May 1569 Lodovico was denounced for his alleged relationship with Protestants and imprisoned in Brussels. He was arrested again in 1582, in connection with the attempt on the life of William the Silent, Prince of Orange. In 1588, during the final years of the war against the Protestants, he was arrested once more but freed because of his age. In the last years of his life, Lodovico received an annual pension of 50 livres d'artois from the city of Antwerp. He died at the age of 68 and was buried in Antwerp Cathedral.

WRITINGS

Descrittione di Lodovico Guicciardini patritio fiorentino di tutti i Paesi Bassi altrimenti detti Germania inferiore (Antwerp, 1567)

BIBLIOGRAPHY

M. Van Even: 'Lodovico Guicciardini', *An. Acad. Royale Archéol. Belgique*, n. s. 2, iii (1876), pp. 249–324

R. H. Touwaide: *Les Editions belges de la Description des Pays-Bas par Lodovico Guicciardini* (Brussels, 1973)

——: *La Description de tous les Pays-Bas par Lodovico Guicciardini* (Brussels, 1974)

□

Guichard, Joseph(-Benoît) (*b* Lyon, 14 Nov 1806; *d* Lyon, 31 May 1880). French painter. He was a close friend of Paul Chenavard, both at school and at the Ecole des Beaux-Arts, Lyon, where he trained (from 1819) as a designer. He was taught painting by Pierre Révoil and drawing by the sculptor Jean-François Legendre-Héral (1796–1851), in whose atelier he met Paul and Hippolyte Flandrin. In 1827 he went to Paris and entered Ingres's studio where he was joined by the Flandrin brothers in 1829. He also attended the Ecole des Beaux-Arts and copied exhibits in the Louvre. In 1833 he exhibited at the Salon with the huge *Dream of Love* (Lyon, Mus. B.-A.). It was praised by the critics, but its debt to Delacroix, whose work Guichard had been studying surreptitiously, infuriated Ingres, and Guichard was obliged to leave his studio. In November 1833 he travelled to Italy, where he copied Daniele da Volterra's *Deposition* (Rome, Trinità dei Monte) and frequented the salon of Horace Vernet. He left Italy for Paris in 1835, the year of Ingres's arrival there.

For the next 30 years Guichard received regular commissions from the state. In 1845 he painted the *Adoration of the Shepherds* and the *Deposition* for the chapel of St Landrin, St Germain l'Auxerrois, Paris; in 1848 *Moses Making Water Spring from the Rock* for the chapel of St Joseph, SS Gervais and Protais, Paris; and the *Dead Christ Surrounded by the Holy Women* for Notre-Dame de Passy (untraced). In 1849 he worked beside Delacroix in the Galerie d'Apollon in the Louvre, where he painted the voussoir with the *Awakening of the Earth* (*in situ*) after a drawing by Charles Le Brun. His studio was frequented by Félix Bracquemond, Henri Fantin-Latour and Berthe Morisot. Guichard's career in Paris was wrecked by financial and domestic problems and in 1862 he returned to Lyon where he succeeded Michel Génod (1796–1862) as a teacher of the painting class at the Ecole des Beaux-Arts, although he resigned after quarrelling with the staff in 1871. In 1879 he was made Director of the Musées de Peinture et Sculpture in Lyon, and he also acted as art critic for the *Courrier de Lyon*. Towards the end of his life he turned to Impressionism, producing a series of small paintings that are marked by a loose painterly style, delicate colour and a control of light and shade (e.g. *Dance at the Préfecture* and *Young Girl at her Mirror*; both Lyon, Mus. B.-A.).

WRITINGS

Les Doctrines de Mr Gustave Courbet, maître peintre (Paris, 1862)

BIBLIOGRAPHY

R. Chazelle: *Joseph Guichard: Peintre lyonnais* (diss., U. Lyon, 1956)

MADELEINE ROCHER-JAUNEAU

Guidebook. Compilation of information in printed form for the purpose of guiding travellers to places of interest. The travel book is one of the oldest forms of art historiography; it predates both the workshop manual and the artist's biography, genres usually acknowledged as older forms. The literature of travel is vast and defies easy classification; however, two main types of travel literature can be distinguished. One is the travel book written in a retrospective, narrative style, which seeks to entertain as well as instruct, linking descriptions of places and people to personal experiences and enriching them with economic facts and statistical data and with historical or artistic observations; the result is a book that can be appreciated as literature in its own right. In contrast, the guidebook proper is prescriptive and prospective, written either for a general audience travelling for pleasure or for a specialized audience travelling for a purpose (e.g. pilgrims, diplomats, scholars etc), and it presents all the factual information the would-be traveller might require. It is often difficult to make a clear distinction between the two types because a narrative travel report, or even the official topographical and statistical handbook of a country or region, can also be used to plan for future travel, thereby fulfilling the function of a guidebook. Thus the travel books of Classical antiquity, the written accounts of such early medieval travellers as Marco Polo (*Travels of Marco Polo*, *c*. 1300) and the narratives of 15th- and 16th-century explorers of distant continents during the age of discovery also function as guidebooks. Travel literature and autobiographical writing often overlap, and many famous autobiographies include diaries and lengthy accounts of 'voyages of self-discovery'. For instance, Johann Wolfgang von Goethe's famous *Italienische Reise* (1816–17; pubd Stuttgart, 1862), so rich in descriptions of works of art, is considered part of his autobiographical writings. *Viaggio in Italia* (1740; pubd Rome, 1932–3) by his father, Johann Caspar Goethe (1710–82), is a travelogue in book form, carefully composed in Italian. Anecdotal accounts of journeys by a variety of travellers co-exist alongside numerous travel guides, some of the more popular series being the *Berlitz* books published by the Société Internationale des Ecoles Berlitz, the *Michelin Guides de pneu* and *Travel Guides*, the *Penguin Guides* and *Travel Books*, *Touring Club Italiano* (TCI) guides to Italy and *Nagel's Encyclopedia Guides.* Travel guides have been published by popular writers, for example *Fodor's Modern Guide* (Litchfield, CT, 1964) by Eugene Fodor (1905–91), *The Fielding's Low Cost Guide to Europe* (New York, 1967) by Temple Fielding (1913–83) and *Europe on £20 a Day* (New York, 1981) by Arthur Frommer.

For further information on travel books and travellers' accounts *see* TRAVEL MANUSCRIPTS.

1. Ancient Greece and Rome. 2. Byzantine empire and Western world. 3. Latin America, Asia and Africa.

1. ANCIENT GREECE AND ROME. In the Western world the earliest guidebooks were produced for seafaring Greek merchants of Asia Minor, whose commercial interests also extended overland deep into the Persian empire. Books that described travel by land were called *ges peripatos* and included crude maps of roads linking major cities; those that described travel by sea, *ges periplous*, included tables on which distances between principal harbours were measured. *Periegesis* (Gr.: 'to lead') became the general term for guidebooks used by travellers in the Classical period. Hecataeus of Miletus (*fl* late 6th century BC), Scylax of Caryanda (*fl* early 6th century BC), Pasiteles and Gaius Licinius Mucianus (*fl c*. AD 65–77) appear to have been among the first authors of guidebooks, but their works are known to us only through Pliny, who mentions them in his *Natural History*. Fragments exist of similar works by Diodorus of Athens (*fl* 1st century BC) and by Polemon (*fl c*. 190 BC). The geographer PAUSANIAS, a native of Magnesia in Asia Minor, travelled extensively through the mainland of Greece. His *Description of Greece* (AD 150–80) is the only work from this early period to survive intact. It is important as a guidebook prototype not only because its author took pains to describe the topographical features of the places he visited, including Athens and other major Greek cities and the sanctuaries of Olympia and Delphi, but also, and more importantly, because he described in some detail individual buildings and even individual works of art. His description of the Acropolis in Athens (I.xxii.4–xxviii.2) is fairly complete. For example, he marvelled at its construction and noted as a curiosity that it had only one entrance. He was also deeply impressed with the age and superb state of preservation of the Propylaia (*c*. 437–432 BC), built 500 years earlier (I.xxii.4). Pausanias is also noteworthy because his work was aimed at the same type of reader whom the authors of many later guidebooks had in mind: the religious traveller. With his book he established a model for a rich literature of guides to the Roman Empire and *itineraria* (Lat.: 'accounts of journeys') to the Holy Land and other places of pilgrimage that became important in medieval times and continued to flourish during the Renaissance period. The question of just how much of Pausanias' information is based on personal observation, and to what extent he simply retold what he learnt from local custodians, has been the subject of much speculation.

The development of a voluminous literature on guidebooks in Imperial Roman times is linked to the emergence of a small class of connoisseurs and a larger class of wealthy collectors whose ambition it was to amass as many copies of Greek works as was possible. Although Egypt attracted much interest, it was Greece that became the increasingly popular destination for the Roman tourist because it was recognized as the cradle of a common civilization, and the Romans took more interest in the past than in the present, as do many modern travellers. The guidebooks of this period listed sculptures, wall paintings and buildings (chiefly temples) that were obligatory sights for any Roman traveller. A variant of the guidebook, the *ekphrasis*, emerged at this time. It featured a museographic description of individual works of art in the context of a sometimes real, and sometimes imagined, tour of a collection. Typical of this genre are the descriptions of 64 paintings in a villa at Naples that Philostratos Lemnios (*see* PHILOSTRATOS, (1)) gave in the *Eikones* and that Lucian of Samosata included in his satirical *Dialogues of the Gods* and *Dialogues of the Dead.*

2. BYZANTINE EMPIRE AND WESTERN WORLD.

(i) Before *c.* 1700. (ii) *c.* 1700–*c.* 1870. (iii) After *c.* 1870.

(i) Before c. *1700.* The first guide to Christian pilgrims, the *Itinerarium burdigalense* by an anonymous author known as the Bordeaux Pilgrim, was known in AD 333, during the reign of Emperor Constantine the Great. It gives detailed instructions on how to travel from Bordeaux to Jerusalem and was patterned on the travel customs of pagan tourists and their taste for 'curiosities', which included buildings and other works of art. In the Byzantine Empire, travel literature continued to flourish through the writings of Procopius of Caesarea (*c.* 499–565), Nicetas Choniates (*d* 1216) and Georgius Codinus (*fl* 1453). Descriptions of works of art continued to develop into a separate genre.

During the Middle Ages and well into the early Renaissance, the *itineraria*, or guides for pilgrims, from which guidebook literature in the West continued to develop, remained focused on the two principal destinations for the Christian pilgrim: the Holy Land and Rome. During the reign of Justinian I, Emperor of Byzantium, Jerusalem reached its zenith as a destination for pilgrims shortly before it was occupied, first by Persians (AD 614–28) and then by Muslims under their second caliph, 'Umar (*reg* 634–44). In spite of these events, initially the flow of Christian pilgrims was not seriously interrupted. Later, Charlemagne and the Abbasid caliph Harun al-Rashid (*reg* 786–809) came to an agreement that allowed Christian pilgrims free and unobstructed access to Jerusalem. The third most popular pilgrimage site was Santiago de Compostela in northern Spain, to which one of the earliest guidebooks for pilgrims, *Codex calixtinus* (*c.* 1160; Santiago de Compostela, Archvs Catedral, Cod. Calixt. Liber 5), is devoted, but soon there was a proliferation of holy places and eventually every region had its pilgrimage centre that could be classified according to its curative power—both spiritual and physical—and ranked according to its local, regional or supraregional importance. It is important to realize that up to the 18th century the ostensible reason for making a pilgrimage was religious, although other factors, such as the thrill of visiting a new place and enjoying oneself, figured prominently. After pilgrims had completed the religious requirements, they became tourists and sightseers, with a local priest, or the priest who had organized the pilgrimage, as guide. For example, the Scottish abbot St Adamnan (*c.* 628–704) in *De locis sanctis* (*c.* 670) not only narrated the pilgrimage to Palestine of the 7th-century Frankish bishop Arculf but was also careful to supplement verbal descriptions of buildings with schematic plans. His cataloguing of six gates and 84 towers and his recording of houses and churches is the first description of buildings there as they appeared shortly after the Islamic conquest. He also described several individual works of art, such as the chalice supposed to have been used at the Last Supper. It would be wrong, however, to credit St Adamnan with any real connoisseurship. The medieval traveller was, after all, preoccupied with the health of his soul rather than with aesthetic considerations. In later medieval travel accounts, there are more frequent and more obvious expressions of pure aesthetic delight in objects, even though they were introduced for their spiritual significance.

More has been written about Rome than almost any other city. In its earliest form, the *Mirabilia urbis Romae*, the prototype of the Roman guidebook, dates from the 12th century. Books about the 'marvels' of Rome began as guides for the pilgrim to the holy places within the city, but in later texts increasingly more space was devoted to descriptions of pagan antiquities; this format survived into the Renaissance period. The booklet *Opusculum de mirabilibus novae et veteris urbis Romae* (Rome, 1510) by FRANCESCO ALBERTINI, in which a clear distinction is made between the marvels of the new city and those of the Classical one, represents the turning-point in the historical emphasis in guidebooks.

During the Renaissance there were agencies in Venice that organized group trips to the Holy Land. They procured travel documents, booked passages and lodgings and provided tour guides to accompany the pilgrims. The invention of printing accelerated the production and dissemination of guidebooks. Although the account by Bernhard von Breydenbach (*c.* 1440–97) of his journey to the Holy Land in 1483–4, which was published as *Peregrinationes in terram sanctam* in Mainz in 1486 by Peter Schöffer (*c.* 1425–1502), with woodcuts by ERHARD REUWICH, could still be considered a travel history, it was used as a guidebook and was soon translated into Dutch and German and other vernacular languages (*see also* TRAVEL MANUSCRIPTS). On the other hand, the guide written by the monk Hermannus Künig von Vach for pilgrims to Santiago de Compostela (printed in Strasbourg in 1495 from an older manuscript copy) contains so much practical advice for pilgrims that it can be justly called the first printed travel guide. The oldest guidebook for Italy is perhaps *La Totale et Vraie Description de tous les passages, lieux et destroictz: Par les quelz on peut passer et entrer des Gaules es Ytalies* (Paris, 1518) by the Frenchman Jacques Signot. One of the best guidebooks of the 16th century is *Itinerarium per nonnullas Galliae, Belgiae partes* (Antwerp, 1584), in which the author, the celebrated geographer and archaeologist Abraham Ortelius, concentrates on the Classical antiquities and inscriptions to be found in what is present-day Belgium. Soon, other guidebooks began to include extensive lists of artists and their pictures and sculptures *in situ* in palaces and churches, and of public monuments, sometimes accompanied by illustrations interspersed with condensed narratives of historical events. Descriptions of local customs and costumes became standard features, and among the more noteworthy general guidebooks for Italy in the 16th and 17th centuries are *Descrittione di tutta l'Italia* (Bologna, 1550) by LEANDRO ALBERTI, *Ritratto delle più nobili e famose città d'Italia* (Venice, 1576) by Francesco Sansovino, *Il passagio per l'Italia* (Bologna, 1608) by Federico Zuccaro, and the *Itinerarium Italiae* (Antwerp, 1600) by Franz Schott (1549–1622). Schott's book became the most popular guide used by travellers to Italy. It remained popular for over a century and became the standard against which all other *itineraria* were measured, went through numerous editions and—especially in the English-speaking world—was rivalled only by the work of Giacomo Barri (*c.* 1632–90), *Viaggio pittoresco in cui si notano distintamente tutte le pitture famose* (Venice, 1671), a translation of which was published in London in 1679. *Newes itinerarium Italiae* (Ulm, 1627), by JOSEF FURTTENBACH the elder, is based on his first-hand experience; it contains a map and several realistic views and plans of buildings.

Venice, long the principal port of embarkation for pilgrims to Palestine, is the birthplace of the modern tourist industry. It was here that many of the first practical guidebooks, published in a variety of languages, were sold. The new typographical standardization that came with the invention of printing was an impetus for experimentation in the design of guidebooks; for example, information was arranged in alphabetical and tabular formats for easier access. As pilgrimages to the Holy Land often lasted seven or eight months, pilgrims were frequently kept waiting in Venice until a party had been assembled that was large enough to make the enterprise profitable for the entrepreneur. During this interval the entrepreneur's bureau offered sightseeing excursions into the Venetian hinterland. These trips soon extended further afield to such other Italian cities as Rome, Florence, Milan, Genoa, Lucca and Loreto, and increasingly the religious motif began to be replaced by purely touristic interests. The amount of time to be spent in the *loca sancta* steadily decreased, while travel to other locations in Italy steadily increased; eventually these side-trips were no longer thought of as mere stop-overs on the way to Jerusalem. By 1600 Milan had become an important junction of passenger- and mail-coach traffic by land. The *Compendio delle poste* (Milan, 1623), compiled by the postmaster Ottavio Cotogno (*fl* 1570–1620s), lists not only 'packaged' guided tours but also 18 'standard' pilgrimages, the itineraries of which could be 'customized' to fit an individual's needs. The *Compendio* is also important because the information it contains is not limited to pilgrimages; it contains dates of important trade fairs and details of hundreds of postal routes, including the one from Antwerp to London with information on the 'ferry' across the English Channel.

From the 17th century the guidebook for travellers developed further towards its late 20th-century format. A practical and immensely popular travel-book format was invented by the German topographer Martin Zeiller (1589–1661), who also wrote the captions and explanatory texts for *Topographia Germaniae* (21 vols, Frankfurt am Main, 1642–88) by Matthäus Merian (i) (*see* MERIAN, (1)). Zeiller combined distance-tables, timetables and road maps (all features of the postal directory) with aspects of the apodemic—'how to travel'—book. He also added descriptive notes on the political and social situation in each country. In 1632 he published a two-volume *Reissbuch und Beschreibung Deutschlands und angrenzender Länder* (Strasbourg), to which he soon added similar guidebooks for the traveller visiting France and Britain (both Strasbourg, 1634), Spain (Ulm, 1637) and Italy (Frankfurt am Main, 1640). Although he packed an enormous amount of disparate information into his books, obviously catering to the fashionable tastes of his contemporaries for all sorts of 'curiosities', he was careful to include much solid and reliable information about passports, tolls and duties, hostelries and costs of lodgings and meals. However, he paid little attention to the natural beauty of the countryside and in the Italian guide gave little or no information about art or artists.

(ii) c. *1700*–c. *1870.* Although there were antecedents in the 16th and 17th centuries, it was during the 18th century that a travel literature of another sort became popular. A flood of treatises in all major European languages began to appear that dealt primarily with the methodology of travel. These writings were aimed at a student about to attend a foreign university or a young nobleman ready to embark on what became known as the GRAND TOUR. For 300 years the Grand Tour (also called the *peregrinatio academica* or the *Kavaliersreise*) was a phenomenon that was popular in most European countries, although the bulk of the literature on it was produced by British authors during the 18th century. Their prominence was such that one of the contemporary bibliographies, *An Essay to Direct and Extend the Inquiries of Patriotic Travellers* (2 vols, London, 1789), was written in English by a German, Leopold Graf Berchtold (1759–1809). This genre of guidebook is also instructive and prescriptive but the emphasis is not so much on topography as on methodology, with information on transportation, personal safety, lodgings, currency, language, government, social life, etiquette and local customs. The character of these works, many of which took the form of letters to young, prospective travellers, is perhaps best exemplified by the admonitions for travel contained in the *Letters* (1774) of Lord Chesterfield to his son. The French Revolution (1789–99) brought to an end the concept of the Grand Tour and its concomitant literature.

The romantic sensibility of the 18th century transformed public attitudes towards untamed nature—what had been seen as threatening now became 'sublime'—and instilled a love of ruins and antiquities. *Geschichte der Kunst des Alterthums* (Dresden, 1764) by JOHANN JOACHIM WINCKELMANN, soon after translated into French (1766) and Italian (1779) but not until 1849 into English, changed contemporary attitudes towards works of Classical antiquity and stimulated in the educated a strong desire to see the objects and sites about which Winckelmann had written. The standard guidebook for travellers to Italy during the third quarter of the 18th century (it had, for example, been used by Goethe) was *Historisch-kritische Nachrichten von Italien* (3 vols, Leipzig, 1770) by Johann Jakob Volkmann (1732–1803) from Hamburg. *Der Passagier auf der Reise in Deutschland, in der Schweiz, zu Paris und Petersburg* by Heinrich August Ottokar Reichard (1751–1828) was printed in Berlin in no fewer than 19 editions between 1801 and 1861. A French edition became the *vade-mecum* (Lat.: 'go with me') of officers during the Napoleonic Wars (1803–15).

Until the coming of the Industrial Revolution, the discomforts associated with travelling prevented many people from undertaking long journeys. However, with the arrival of the railway after 1840 and the steel-built, ocean-going steamship in the 1880s, transportation became faster, safer and more comfortable. Reichard's guidebooks impressed the Scottish publisher John Murray II (1778–1843) so much that he suggested to one of his authors, Mariana Starke (?1762–1838), that she write her second book on Italy, *Travels on the Continent* (London, 1820), in the form of a guidebook; however, it was not a success. Murray's son JOHN MURRAY issued *A Handbook for Travellers on the Continent: Being a Guide through Holland, Belgium, Prussia, and Northern Germany, and along the Rhine, from Holland to Switzerland* (London, 1836). It was written by the younger Murray himself and was based on his many years of travel and exploration of northern and central Europe. It became an immediate success and served as a prototype for other guidebooks on France, southern Germany and Switzerland, also written by Murray. Later volumes in the series were written on contract by carefully chosen specialists on other regions, such as RICHARD FORD on Spain, John Gardner Wilkinson (1787–1875) on Egypt and FRANCIS PALGRAVE on northern Italy.

Karl Baedeker (1801–59), from Koblenz, became a formidable competitor. In 1832 he purchased the firm of the publisher Karl Röhling, whose list of titles included *Rheinreise von Mainz bis Köln*, a guide to the River Rhine by Johann August Klein (1778–1831) that had originally appeared in 1828. Baedeker issued an enlarged, improved edition of this work (*Rheinreise von Strassburg bis Rotterdam*; Koblenz, 1835), and in each of the following editions the original information was updated. By the time of the sixth edition in 1849, Baedeker's name was listed as editor and compiler. Prior to this, he had compiled and published four other handbooks, on Belgium and Holland (both Koblenz, 1839), Germany (Koblenz, 1842) and Switzerland (Koblenz, 1844), none of which had yet attained the characteristic format associated with him. He frequently and openly acknowledged Murray's pioneering efforts in developing the format of the modern guidebook, and in the 1850s he paid his British competitor the ultimate, albeit somewhat questionable, compliment of adopting the red cover that hitherto had been the hallmark of the Murray guides but subsequently became that of the Baedeker guides. Consequently, Murray was forced to change the colour of his books to blue. Baedeker's sons and grandchildren continued to expand the collection, often with the collaboration of outstanding experts. Parallel English and French editions appeared together with the German ones and soon reached the same edition size. The name Baedeker became synonymous with guidebook. The Murray–Baedeker success formula was based on carefully checked and verified facts and precise guidance about such aspects of travel as transportation, hotels and tipping. Where art is concerned, although the guides contain such practical information as descriptions of the arrangement of pictures in galleries or museums or advice on how to find the sacristan of a church or the custodian of a castle in order to get access, there is a noticeable reluctance to engage in any form of interpretation, as if the writer were wary of letting aesthetic values currently in vogue influence the traveller–sightseer's impressions.

The development of the specialized art-historical guidebook owes much to JACOB BURCKHARDT, the eminent Swiss historian, who produced prototypes for both the guide to a whole region or country and the art-historical guide to a city, the latter exemplified by *Les Villes d'art célèbres* (Paris, 1900–05), a series of more than 50 monographs by various authors on the art and architecture of European cities. Even before completing his doctoral studies at the Universität Basel, Burckhardt had published a small volume, *Die Kunstwerke der belgischen Städte* (Düsseldorf, 1842). His next work became the best-known title in the whole literature of guidebooks: *Der Cicerone: Eine Anleitung zum Genuss der Kunstwerke Italiens* (Basle, 1855; Eng. trans. by A. H. Clough as *The Cicerone, or Art Guide to Painting in Italy*, London, 1873, 2/1908/*R* New York, 1979). The 1000-page guidebook, filled with information on Italy's art treasures, was written almost entirely *in situ* during a one-year stay in Italy. During his travels Burckhardt had developed a technique of immediately recording in the afternoon his impressions of the art works he had seen that morning. This resulted in a freshness and directness of observation that has never been surpassed. *Der Cicerone* is an example of a guidebook for art-loving travellers that had developed over the centuries from the dual roots of the *periegesis* and the *ekphrasis* of Classical times. *The Treasures of Art in Great Britain* (4 vols, London, 1854–7) by GUSTAV FRIEDRICH WAAGEN is another such example. A slightly later guidebook in this tradition, *Handbuch der deutschen Kunstdenkmäler* (5 vols, Berlin, 1905–12, rev. 3/1925–38) by GEORG GOTTFRIED DEHIO, was also intended to be used as a field guide by the serious art historian.

(iii) After c. *1870.* At the end of the 19th century, topographical inventories or handbooks became important as sources for the popular guidebook. Without their copious information, the production of guidebooks could not have kept pace with the rapid proliferation of art tourism in the 20th century. The inventories were produced in ambitious multi-volume sets and were either directly sponsored by national or provincial government agencies responsible for their country's or region's patrimony of historic and artistic monuments, for example the Rijkscommissie voor de Monumentenbeschrijving (National Committee for the Cataloguing of Monuments) in the Netherlands, the Landesamt für Denkmalpflege in Bavaria or the Commission des Monuments Historiques de la France, or by equally enterprising non-governmental civic bodies dedicated to creating definitive, systematic surveys of the art of countries by region, province, district and place, such as the Schweizerische Gesellschaft für Erhaltung historischer Kunstdenkmäler.

Topographical handbook series seem typical products of the documentation-conscious 19th century, with its ambition to create the definitive work, the corpus. Among the earliest of these were the *Inventaire général des richesses d'art de la France*, of which the first was published in Paris in 22 volumes between 1876 and 1913 under the auspices of the Ministère de l'Instruction Publique et des Beaux-Arts, and *Die Bau- und Kunstdenkmäler der Provinz Sachsen* (Halle, 1879–1911), the official 29-volume inventory of the art and architecture of what was at that time the Prussian province of Saxony. However, most of these topographical series appeared during the first quarter of the 20th century and are constantly being reissued in revised editions. Ongoing revision became necessary because of the territorial changes caused by world wars I and II and because of the destruction of historic buildings and art treasures wrought by war, natural catastrophe and ill-conceived efforts in urban planning and restoration. Topographical handbooks exist for most western European countries and some eastern European ones, with official surveys of the monuments of Austria, France, Germany (including former East Germany), Switzerland, Great Britain, Ireland, the Netherlands, Spain and Sweden, and semi-official ones for Belgium, Denmark, Iceland, Norway, Portugal, Hungary, Bulgaria, Romania, Poland and Russia. They are all structured similarly: an introductory general historical sketch, followed by a general survey of the art and architectural history of the region or district, and then a detailed description of major buildings by place and location that includes their exterior and interior decoration and the works of art they contain. This is accompanied by a collection of plates, diagrams, plans and notes providing further historical data, maps indicating the locations of places and of monuments and works of architecture and art *in situ*, and extensive footnotes and bibliographies with references to specialized literature. Although the USA has not produced such systematic official inventories of monuments and works of art, a similar concept is realized in the *American Guide Series* (Washington, DC, 1937–49). Begun in the 1930s under the auspices of the Federal Writers' Project and with the art historian Harold Rosenberg as editor, the series includes guides to 48 states and many cities and regions. Some volumes in the series on individual states are still useful as sources of information about art, architectural monuments, museums and collections, although coverage of art and architecture is very uneven. Some of the guides have been revised and published in new editions by various publishers.

In the 20th century, increasing opportunities for travel and the more demanding needs of travellers led to many variations of the formula successfully devised by Murray and Baedeker in the 19th century. Among the more popular guidebooks have been the *Blue Guides* published in London by Ernest Benn and later by Macmillan and in Paris by Hachette as *Les Guides bleus*; the *Polyglott-Reiseführer* guides published by Polyglott-Verlag in Munich; the *Encyclopedia-Guides* by Louis Nagel (*b* 1908) published in Paris and Geneva; the series *Hur man reser* ('How to travel') published in Sweden, edited by Alva Övden Strömberg (*b* 1920); the *Companion Guides*, edited by Vincent Cronin, published from 1963 by Harper & Row in New York (from 1983 Prentice Hall, Englewood, NJ) and by Collins in London (e.g. Hugh Honour: *Companion Guide to Venice*, 1966; Eve Borsook: *Companion Guide to Florence*, 1966); and publications in the USA such as the *Penguin Guides* series and the *Penguin Travel Books*, published in New York by Penguin/Viking, and others by such writers as Terry T. Philip (*d* 1945), Eugene Fodor and Arthur Frommer.

Guidebooks based on the format of the topographical inventory and on prototypes created by Burckhardt and Waagen include the scholarly illustrated series *Bildhandbuch der Kunstdenkmäler* (1966–), edited by Reinhardt Hootz for Deutscher Verlag in Munich; the *Kleine Kunstführer* series (1949–), edited and published in Munich by Hugo Schnell, and the parallel *Grosse Kunstführer* (1960–), published in Munich and Zurich by Schnell & Steiner; *Reclams Kunstführer* (1961–), published in Stuttgart by Philipp Reclam; McGraw-Hill's series of *Art Treasures* of various European countries (New York, 1965–); and the unnumbered series, *Guida artistica d'Italia* (1981–), that Electa Editrice, Milan, is publishing on the art of selected Italian cities and regions. About 500 new guidebook titles each year are announced in the American booktrade magazine *Publisher's Weekly*, and virtually all large mass-market publishing houses regularly publish guidebooks. Tyre manufacturers and oil companies have also entered the market, with Michelin publishing its *Guides de pneu* and *Travel Guides* and Shell UK Ltd publishing its own series in London (e.g. *Shell Illustrated Guides to the Counties of England*). Such travel companies as Thomas Cook and American Express have for many years produced guidebooks for their customers and members, as have such automobile clubs as the AA, with their *Automobile Association Pocket Guides*.

3. LATIN AMERICA, ASIA AND AFRICA. In Latin America 19th-century travellers wrote accounts of their visits that functioned as the first guidebooks of the area. Such examples are *Incidents of Travel in Central America, Chiapas and Yucatán* (2 vols, New York, 1841) by John Lloyd Stephens (1805–52) and FREDERICK CATHERWOOD, and *Peru: Incidents of Travel and Exploration in the Land of the Incas* (New York, 1877) by Ephraim George Squier (1821–88). More recently, the governments of several Latin American countries have published series of guides to their archaeological and art-historical legacies. These include the series *Artes de México*, dealing with archaeology, ethnography and the fine and decorative arts, and the *Guías oficiales*, written by a variety of respected authorities on archaeological sites in Mexico and published by the Instituto Nacional de Antropología e Historia (INAH).

As in Europe, the archetype of travel in Asian countries is the pilgrimage, for example the religious command for Islamic peoples to make the pilgrimage to Mecca. Many travellers journeyed through the Islamic lands and recorded their impressions. For example, in *Kitāb al-Buldān* ('The countries'; AD 891), the geographer al-Ya'qūbī (*d* 897) describes the Abbasid capital at Samarra in great detail, and al-Muqaddasi (*c.* 946–88) discusses architecture in the central Islamic lands in *Kitab ahsan al-tagasim fi marifat al-agalim* (Leiden, 1877), published in French as *La Meilleure Répartition pour la connaissance des provinces* (Damascus, 1963). *'Al-Masalik wa 'l-Mamalik* ('Of ways and provinces'; 977) by Ibn Haukal (943–77) gives the first account of western Sudan and describes other areas of northern Africa. The Persian poet, moralist and theologian Naser-e Khosraw (1004–*c.* 1088) not only went to Mecca three times between 1046 and 1052–3 but also visited Azerbaijan, Armenia, Anatolia, Syria and most of Arabia and Egypt. The *Safarnāma* ('Book of travels'), a record of this journey (probably written after 1073), contains descriptions of many monuments and public buildings written in an abbreviated guidebook-like style.

Kitab nushat al-mushtāk fi 'khtirāk al-āfāk ('The book of the promenade of one who is yearning to penetrate the horizons') is a comprehensive guide to Asia Minor and north-western Europe, written by the Moroccan Il Idrīsī (1100–*c.* 1165) in the 12th century. Al-Harawi (*d* 1215) wrote a guidebook for Muslim pilgrims to Jerusalem and other cities, translated and edited by J. Sourdel-Thomine as *Guide des lieux de pèlerinage* (Damascus, 1952–7).

Guides to particular cities of the Islamic world include an account of Baghdad by al-Khatīb al-Baghdadi (1002–71), translated and edited by J. Lassner as *The Topography of Baghdad in the Early Middle Ages* (Detroit, 1970), and *Kitāb akhbār makka*, a description of Mecca by al-Azraqi (*c.* 1189) edited by Ferdinand Wüstenfeld in Leipzig in 1858 as *Die Chroniken der Stadt Mekka*. The medieval writer who travelled most extensively through the Islamic lands and beyond was the Berber Ibn Battuta (1304–77). Over a period of 25 years he journeyed from Morocco and the Near East to the Indian subcontinent and further to China, and on his return to Morocco he elaborated the manuscript notes of his travels, which give detailed accounts of Islamic architecture in India and discuss Islamic blue-and-white pottery. The Turkish dervish Ewliya Celebi (1611–84) wrote *Seyahatname* ('Travels'; cited in *Enc. Islam/2*; see also U. Haarmann: 'Eliya Celebis Bericht über die Altertümer von Gize', *Turcica*, viii (1976), pp. 157–230), in ten volumes, the last of which concerns Egypt, the Sudan and Ethiopia. It includes a rich historical section and perceptive descriptions of the monuments at Giza, notably the Pyramids and the Sphinx, which he visited after 1670.

In the 19th century, a *Personal Narrative of a Pilgrimage to El-Medinah and Meccah* (3 vols, London, 1855–6) was written by the Englishman Richard Burton (1821–90), who travelled there in 1853. *Description de l'Egypte* is a multi-volume guidebook that recounts the French expedition to Egypt, while valuable information on the monuments of Iraq and Persia is provided by Marcel Auguste Dieulafoy (1844–1920) in his several books, including *L'Acropole de Suse, d'après les fouilles exécutées en 1884, 1885, et 1886 sous les auspices du musée du Louvre* (Paris, 1890–92). For South-east Asia, such publications as *History of Java* (London, 1817) by Thomas Stamford Raffles (1781–1826) contain detailed descriptions of important monuments, often accompanied by illustrations. In the 20th century, *The Archaeological Survey of India*, a series published in New Delhi in the 1960s and written by experts on such topics as the Ajanta murals, is an invaluable guide to important archaeological sites and art-historical monuments.

In East Asia, the search for sacred texts was often a pretext for travel. For example, Xuanzang (*c.* AD 596–664) and Yijing (635–717), two Chinese Buddhist monks, made extensive tours through India in 629 and 671 respectively, ostensibly to find and bring back Buddhist texts but also to find out about the wealth and wisdom of lands to the west of China. Xuanzang's 15-year journey was recorded in *Da tang xiyou ji* ('Memories on west countries'). In the mid-19th century the French Lazarist missionary Father Evariste Régis Huc (1813–60) informed prospective visitors about parts of the Orient in his narrative guide *Souvenirs d'un voyage dans la Tatares, le Thibet et la Chine pendant les années 1844, 1845, et 1846* (2 vols, Paris, 1850), translated into English by William Hazlitt in 1852. The Japanese also loved to travel, and this is reflected in the copious literature of a genre that has flourished since the Nara period (AD 710–94) and Heian period (794–1185): *nikki*, objectively written travel diaries, and *kikō*, brief and often poetic travel accounts, the latter type compiled by some of the greatest poets, for example Karasumaru Mitsuhiro, Matsuo Bashō (1644–94) and Tachibana Nankei (1753–1805). The first significant Japanese literary work that could be called a true travel diary is the *Tosa nikki* (935) by Ki no Tsurayuki (?875–945). During the Edo period (1600–1868), many travel accounts were written either by government officials, who included detailed geographical and historical information, or by amateur scholars motivated by an interest in botany, medicine and, increasingly, art. Also, from the mid-17th century, gazetteers (*meisho-ki*; 'records of famous places') were produced commercially for pilgrims and travellers.

BIBLIOGRAPHY

TRAVELLERS' ACCOUNTS

F. Zuccaro: *Il passagio per l'Italia* (Bologna, 1608)

N. Trigault: *De Christiana expeditione apud Sinas* (Leiden, 1615); Eng. trans. by L. J. Gallagher as *The China that Was: China Discovered by the Jesuits at the Close of the Sixteenth Century* (Milwaukee, 1942)

G. Brice: *Description nouvelle de ce qu'il y a de plus remarquable dans la ville de Paris* (Paris, 1687)

F. K. G. Hirsching: *Nachrichten von sehenswürdigen Gemälde- und Kupferstichsammlungen . . . in Teutschland nach alphabetischer Anordnung der Städte*, 6 vols (Erlangen, 1786–92)

H. W. Davies: *Bernhard von Breydenbach and his 'Journey to the Holy Land', 1483–4: A Bibliography* (London, 1911)

HISTORY OF TRAVEL

R. Heberdey: *Die Reisen des Pausanias in Griechenland* (Prague, 1894)

J. von Schlosser, ed.: *Quellenbuch zur Kunstgeschichte des abendländischen Mittelalters: Ausgewählte Texte des vierten bis fünfzehnten Jahrhunderts* (Vienna, 1896/*R* Hildesheim, 1976)

C. von Klenze: *The Interpretation of Italy during the Last Two Centuries: A Contribution to the Study of Goethe's 'Italienische Reise'* (Chicago, 1907)

E. S. Bates: *Touring in 1600: A Study in the Development of Travel as a Means of Education* (Boston, 1911)

C. Howard: *English Travellers of the Renaissance* (London, 1914)

W. E. Mead: *The Grand Tour in the Eighteenth Century* (Boston, 1914)

A. P. Newton, ed.: *Travel and Travellers in the Middle Ages* (London, 1926)

B. Penrose: *Urbane Travelers, 1591–1635* (Philadelphia, 1942)

K. Wilhelm: *Roads to Zion: Four Centuries of Travelers' Reports* (New York, 1946)

R. S. Lambert: *The Fortunate Traveller: A Short History of Touring and of Travel for Pleasure* (London, 1950)

L. Schudt: *Italienreisen im 17. und 18. Jahrhundert*, Röm. Forsch. Bib. Hertziana, xv (Vienna, 1959)

B. Penrose: *Travel and Discovery in the Renaissance* (New York, 1962)

M. Link: *Der Reisebericht als literarische Kunstform von Goethe bis Heine* (diss., U. Cologne, 1963)

J. Carter, P. H. Muir and N. Barker, eds: *Printing and the Mind of Man* (London, 1967, rev. and enlarged Munich, 2/1983) [with new intro. by P. H. Muir and add. bibliog. by P. Amelung]

E. N. Borza: *Travel and Communications in Classical Times: A Guide to the Evidence* (University Park, PA, 1969)

R. Krautheimer: 'The Beginnings of Art Historical Writing in Italy', *Studies in Early Christian, Medieval and Renaissance Art*, ed. R. Krautheimer (New York, 1969), pp. 257–75

L. Casson: *Travel in the Ancient World* (London, 1974)

R. S. Pine-Coffin: *Bibliography of British and American Travel in Italy to 1860*, Biblioteca di bibliografia italiana, 76 (Florence, 1974)

E. L. Eisenstein: *The Printing Press as an Agent of Change: Communications and Cultural Transformations in Early-modern Europe* (Cambridge, 1979)

C. Small: *The Printed Word, an Instrument of Popularity* (Aberdeen, 1982)

Souvenirs of the Grand Tour (exh. cat., ed. D. Sutton; London, Wildenstein & Co. Ltd, 1982)

J. Stagl: *Apodemiken: Eine räsonierte Bibliographie der reisetheoretischen Literatur des 16., 17., und 18. Jahrhunderts* (Paderborn, 1983)
F. E. Peters: *Jerusalem: The Holy City in the Eyes of Chroniclers, Visitors, Pilgrims, and Prophets from the Days of Abraham to the Beginnings of Modern Times* (Princeton, 1985)
J. E. Vance: *Capturing the Horizon: The Historical Geography of Transportation since the Transportation Revolution of the Sixteenth Century* (New York, 1986)
P. G. Adams, comp. and ed.: *Travel Literature through the Ages: An Anthology* (New York, 1988)
H. Bausinger, K. Beyrer and G. Korff, eds: *Reisekultur: Von der Pilgerfahrt zum modernen Tourismus* (Munich, 1991)

GUIDEBOOK PUBLISHING

S. Smiles: *A Publisher and his Friends: Memoirs and Correspondence of the Late John Murray, with an Account of the Origin and Progress of the House, 1768–1843*, 2 vols (London, 1891)
R. Schmidt: 'Die Baedeker: Zum hundertsten Geburtstag Karl Baedekers', *Z. Bfreunde*, v (1901–2), pp. 398–402
D. Baedeker: 'Zur Geschichte des Reisehandbuchs', *Geographische Ausstellung des deutschen Buchgewerbevereins, den Mitgliedern des deutschen Geographentages gewidmet* (exh. cat., Leipzig, Mus. Bild. Kst, 1921), pp. 15–24
Avec les 'Guides bleus' à travers la France et le monde, Bibliothèque des voyages (Paris, 1959, rev. with suppl./1962)
J. Mangione: *The Dream and the Deal: The Federal Writers' Project, 1935–1943* (Boston, 1972)
J. O. Heise, ed.: *Travel Guidebooks in Review* (Syracuse, NY, 1974, 2/1975, rev. 3/1978)
D. L. Ehresmann: *Fine Arts: A Bibliographic Guide to Basic Reference Works, Histories and Handbooks* (Littleton, CO, 1975, 2/1979) [incl. the best lists of the official topographical inventories, by country]
Baedeker's Handbooks for Travellers: A Bibliography of English Editions Published Prior to World War II (Westport, CT, and London, 1975)
B. Lerivray: *Guides bleus, guides verts et lunettes roses* (Paris, 1975)
A. Hinrichsen: *Baedeker's Reisehandbücher, 1832–1944: Bibliographie der deutschen, französischen und englischen Ausgaben* (Holzminden, 1981)
J. A. Post and J. B. Post: *Travel in the United States: A Guide to Information Sources*, Geography and Travel Information Guide Series, iii (1981)
N. L. Edgar and W. Y. Ma: *Travel in Asia: A Guide to Information Sources*, Geography and Travel Information Guide Series, vi (1983)
W. Melczer: *The Pilgrim's Guide to Santiago de Compostela* (New York, 1993)

For further bibliography *see* TRAVEL MANUSCRIPTS.

WOLFGANG M. FREITAG

Guidetti, Guidetto (*b* ?1495; *d* Rome, before 20 Nov 1564). Italian architect. He was of Florentine origin and trained there as an architect, later settling in Rome. He is first mentioned there as being among the contributors to the expenses of the church of S Giovanni dei Fiorentini, in 1520. His first important patron in Rome was Cardinal Federico Cesi, for whom his first work was at the Giardino dei Cesi (1545–50), a sculpture garden at his palace near the Vatican (*see* ROME, fig. 65). Guidetti designed several garden structures, the most prominent of which was the Antiquarium, a sculpture museum in the form of a Greek cross (destr. 1940). He later worked at the Cesi palaces at Acquasparta (1562) and Cantalupo in Umbria. The Cardinal also commissioned the church of S Caterina dei Funari (1559–64), Rome. Guidetti's design was based on Il Gesù, but the rather flat pilastered façade was derived from Santo Spirito (1538–45) in Sassia by Antonio da Sangallo (ii). The Cesi Chapel in S Maria Maggiore, Rome, a severe Mannerist Greek-cross composition, is also attributed to Guidetti. Of his extensive works (1559–64) at the convent of S Maria sopra Minerva, only the cloister remains. This was a modest design: two identical storeys of five bays of open arcades on each side of a rectangular plan resulted in stretched bays on one pair of sides. In 1563 Guidetti was commissioned by Pope Pius IV to produce working drawings for the Palazzo dei Conservatori at the Piazza del Campidoglio in Rome, 'in accordance with Michelangelo's instructions', which are shown in various sketches by Michelangelo (London, BM; Oxford, Ashmolean; Vienna, Albertina; Florence, Casa Buonarroti). Work began in June 1563; Giacomo della Porta continued the works after Guidetti's death until their completion in 1584.

BIBLIOGRAPHY

P. Tomei: 'Guidetto Guidetti', *Riv. Reale Ist. Archeol. & Stor. A.*, viii (1940), pp. 62–83
P. Pecchiai: 'L'architetto Guidetto Guidetti aiuto de Michelangelo nella fabbrica del Campidoglio', *Riv. Reale Ist. Archeol. & Stor. A.*, ix (1942), pp. 253–9
——: *Il Campidoglio nel cinquecento sulla scorta dei documenti* (Rome, 1950), pp. 21–5
G. de Angelis d'Ossat and C. Pietrangeli: *Il Campidoglio di Michelangelo* (Milan, 1965)
L. H. Heydenreich and W. Lotz: *Architecture in Italy, 1400–1600*, Pelican Hist. A. (Harmondsworth, 1974), p. 250
A. Melogrami: 'Il cantiere cinquecentesco di S Caterina dei Funari e le pitture della cappella Cesi', *Stor. A.*, lxvi (1989), pp. 219–39
S. Benedetti and G. Zander: *L'arte in Roma nel secolo XVI*, Storia di Roma, xxix/1 (Bologna, 1990)

ZILAH QUEZADO DECKKER

Guidetto [Guidectus; Guido] (*fl* 1187–1211). Italian sculptor. His identification with *Guido magister lapidum*, noted in Lucca in 1183, is not entirely certain, but he can be identified with one *Guido magister* who appears in an inscription of 1187 concerning work (untraced) in S Maria Corteorlandini, Lucca. Various inscriptions and references link him with the cathedral of S Martino, Lucca, in 1191 and 1193, when he was also described as *magister petrarum quondam Aaroti* (*see* LUCCA, §3). In 1203 he was referred to as 'Master Guido who is working in the cloister' in S Ponziano, Lucca, but scarce traces of his work survive. Guidetto is credited with the upper loggia section of the façade of S Martino, Lucca, comprising ledges, bundles of columns, capitals, and cornices decorated with human figures and animal and vegetal motifs, as well as with a series of inlaid panels also with human, animal, vegetal and geometric designs. In 1204 he inscribed *condidit electi tam pulcras dextra Guidecti* on the scroll borne by a column figure at the extreme left of the first order of small loggias on the façade. In 1211, describing himself as 'magister marmolarius S Martini', Guidetto undertook to work for S Stefano in Prato, where the façade and cloister retain some of the colonnettes and carved capitals.

Various works have been attributed to Guidetto on stylistic grounds, including the decoration of the portal (*c.* 1185) and capitals of SS Giovanni e Reparata, Lucca; the façade of S Michele in Foro, Lucca, which is very similar in structure and decoration to that of S Martino; the capitals of the interior colonnade and the vault corbels at Pisa Baptistery (1180s or 1190s); late 12th-century portal decorations of S Cristoforo and S Giusto (both in Lucca) and S Leonardo in Treponzio (near Lucca). Although Guidetto's work displays similarities with that of north Italian artists (e.g. Anselmus, Benedetto Antelami), his exact origins are unknown. It is clear, however, that he was at the head of a large workshop active in western Tuscany, from which such artists as Lanfranco, Guido da Corno and other anonymous masters emerged.

BIBLIOGRAPHY

C. Barracchini and A. Caleca: *Il duomo di Lucca* (Lucca, 1973)

G. Kopp: *Die Skulpturen der Fassade von San Martino in Lucca* (Worms, 1981)

G. Dalli Regoli: *Dai maestri senza nome all'impresa dei Guidi* (Lucca, 1986)

A. Caleca: *La dotta mano: Il battistero di Pisa* (Bergamo, 1991)

ANTONIO CALECA

Guidi, Domenico (*b* Torano, nr Carrara, 6 June 1625; *d* Rome, 28 March 1701). Italian sculptor. He went to Naples in 1639 to assist his uncle, Giuliano Finelli, in the execution of a series of 13 statues (1646; Naples Cathedral, chapel of S Januarius) representing the patron saints of Naples. He remained under Finelli's tutelage for the next decade, during which time he was involved in the popular revolt led by Masaniello against the Spanish in 1647–8. In 1648 he arrived in Rome where he entered the studio of Alessandro Algardi. He remained there until Algardi's death in 1654 when he established himself as an independent sculptor. He assisted Algardi on many different projects, including the gigantic marble relief *Encounter of Leo the Great and Attila* (1646–53; Rome, St Peter's). He also collaborated with Ercole Ferrata and Francesco Baratta on the execution, from Algardi's design, of the marble high altar (1653–4) of S Nicola da Tolentino in Rome. His first major independent commission was for the large marble relief of the *Lamentation* (1659–76; Rome, Chapel of Monte di Pietà), a work that reveals his debt to Algardi and Finelli. The compactness and cohesiveness recall Algardi's *Leo and Attila* but Guidi's figures are crowded together into a single shallow plane with little attempt at spatial illusion. The sharply cut and jagged folds of drapery, characteristic of all his work, emulate Finelli's method of carving.

In 1676 Guidi was commissioned to carve an immense marble relief altarpiece, traditionally called the *Holy Family* (1676–83; Rome, S Agnese in Agone; see fig.), but in fact depicting a scene described by the Pseudo-Bonaventura in which the infant St John the Baptist approaches the infant Jesus, as the Holy Family is returning from Egypt, and refers to the latter's destiny as saviour of the world. The composition is similar to the *Lamentation.* However, the lack of spatial illusion is even stronger: rather than overlapping to create a sense of depth, the figures are placed above and beside one another. The detailing, the full, loose drapery and the equal emphasis on all the figures indicate an even more pictorial approach.

Guidi's approach to sculpture appears to have been that of mass-production. He worked as quickly as possible, according to a predetermined set of criteria, and was thus able to execute many works within a relatively short period. This formulaic approach allowed for little stylistic development, and an examination of one piece can provide an account of Guidi's style for nearly half a century. In the life-size bust of *Alexander VIII* (bronze, *c.* 1691; London, V&A) Guidi used a typical arrangement of drapery forms, with complex polymorphic folds forming the projecting cape and zig-zag folds on the chest. This composition is echoed with very little alteration in other sculptures attributed to or documented as by Guidi. His studio produced a vast amount of statuary, including monumental reliefs and centrepieces, papal tombs such as that of *Clement IX* (marble, 1671; Rome, S Maria Maggiore) and papal busts such as that of *Alexander VII* (marble, *c.* 1661; Rome, Bib. Alessandrina) as well as funerary monuments for *Cardinal Lorenzo Imperiale* (marble, *c.* 1675; Rome, S Agostino) and *Cardinal Friedrich von Hessen* (marble, *c.* 1684; Wrocław Cathedral), among others.

From early in his career Guidi had an important relationship with French artists. This began in the mid-1650s, when he was asked by Nicolas Poussin to execute three herms (*c.* 1661; Versailles, Château, Quinconces du Midi) after wax models that were provided for him by the painter. In 1675 Guidi invited Charles Le Brun, then Director of the Académie Royale de Peinture et de Sculpture in Paris, to become head of the Accademia di S Luca in Rome for 1676–7. When Le Brun was unable to leave his French position, Guidi suggested that Charles Errard *le fils*, Director of the Académie de France in Rome (and godfather to Guidi's daughter), could serve in his place. This proposal strengthened the position of French artists in Rome. Guidi was often asked to view and comment on the work of French students in Rome. He was also commissioned to execute a large marble sculpture of *Fame Writing the History of Louis XIV* (Versailles, Château, Bassin de Neptune) and an over life-size marble statue of *Louis XIV* (1697–9; Rome, Villa Medici). His style was not overtly classical, but his work, his intellectual tastes and his friends all indicate a preference for the academicism of the French.

Guidi's treatment of form was particularly influential on the French sculptors Jean Théodon, who worked under him in 1692–4, and Pierre (ii) Legros, as is attested by the marble reliefs, *Joseph Distributing Grain* by Théodon and *Tobias and the Tax Collector* by Legros (both 1705; Rome, Chapel of Monte di Pietà). Pierre-Etienne Monnot was also in contact with Guidi when he was commissioned to make the lateral reliefs of the Capocaccia chapel, S Maria della Vittoria, in Rome, while Guidi was executing the centrepiece of *Dream of St Joseph* (marble, *c.* 1694). Although his studio produced no notable followers, Guidi was one of the most important sculptors in Rome after the death of Bernini in 1680. He provided a link between Roman and French sculptors of the late 17th century and the early 18th, and his work helped to transform the style of the late Baroque and encouraged the spread of the classical style in Rome.

BIBLIOGRAPHY

Thieme–Becker

L. Pascoli: *Vite* (1730–36), i, pp. 252–6

E. Wind: 'Shaftesbury as a Patron of Art', *J. Warb. & Court. Inst.*, ii (1938), pp. 185–8 [Guidi's only documented drgs are repr.]

R. Wittkower: 'Domenico Guidi and French Classicism', *J. Warb. & Court. Inst.*, ii (1938), pp. 188–90

A. Riccoboni: *Roma nell'arte: La scultura nell'evo moderno dal quattrocento ad oggi* (Rome, 1942), p. 207–13

A. Nava-Cellini: 'Per Alessandro Algardi e Domenico Guidi', *Paragone*, cxxi (1960), pp. 61–8

D. Bershad: 'A Series of Papal Busts by Domenico Guidi' *Burl. Mag.*, cxii (1970), pp. 805–8

——: 'Domenico Guidi and Nicolas Poussin', *Burl. Mag.*, cxiii (1971), pp. 544–7

——: 'Two Additional Papal Busts by Domenico Guidi', *Burl. Mag.*, cxv (1973), pp. 736–9

——: 'Un bozzetto di Domenico Guidi a Palazzo Venezia', *A. Illus.*, vi (1973), pp. 384–6

M. Weil: *The History and Decoration of the Ponte S Angelo* (University Park, 1974), pp. 148–51 [oeuvre list and basic bibliog.]

Domenico Guidi: *Holy Family*, marble relief altarpiece, 1676–83 (Rome, S Agnese in Agone)

F. Den Broeder: 'A Drawing by Domenico Guidi for a Monument to Innocent XII', *Burl. Mag.*, cxvii (1975), pp. 110–13

D. Bershad: 'Some New Documents on the Statues of Domenico Guidi and Ercole Ferrata in the Elizabeth Chapel in the Cathedral of Breslau (now Wrocław)', *Burl. Mag.*, cxix (1977), pp. 700–03

——: 'Domenico Guidi: Some New Attributions', *Antol. B.A.*, i (1977), pp. 17–25

U. Schlegel: 'Il ritratto di Felice Zacchia Rondinini di Domenico Guidi', *Paragone*, cxxi (1977), pp. 26–8

DAVID L. BERSHAD

Guidi, Giovanni di ser Giovanni. *See* SCHEGGIA.

Guidi, Virgilio (*b* Rome, 4 April 1891; *d* Venice, 7 Jan 1984). Italian painter and writer. He was born into a family of artists and artisans and began his training at the Scuola Libera di Pittura in Rome and later in the workshop of the Italian painter and restorer Giovanni Capranesi (1852–1921). During this period he also cultivated his personal interests, studying above all the work of Correggio, Giotto, Piero della Francesca and Cézanne. These influences are apparent in early works such as *Self-portrait with Hat* (1914; Verona, Pal. Forti). In 1915 he showed his work at the third exhibition of the Rome Secession. His first important success, after several years of financial difficulty, came in 1924 when he exhibited *The Tram* (1923; Rome, G.N.A. Mod.), a masterpiece of this first Roman period, at the Venice Biennale. He participated in *La prima mostra del novecento italiano* at the Palazzo della Permanente in Milan in 1926, also contributing to the second exhibition there in 1929. In 1927 he moved to Venice to take up a teaching post at the Accademia di Belle Arti.

Guidi met with much resistance as a teacher in Venice and thus moved to Bologna, where he lived from 1935 to 1944. During the 1930s he held his first one-man shows, in Florence in 1932 and Milan in 1933 and 1936. He enjoyed considerable success as far as exhibitions were concerned; at the second Quadriennale in Rome in 1935 he showed 34 works and won an award. During the 1930s he was intensely involved with theoretical reflections on the problems of light and space, and his work of this time shows less concentration on the figurative aspects of painting than on the investigation of compositional and light-induced rhythms.

In the catalogue of the first Quadriennale (Rome, 1931, p. 102), Guidi had declared that he felt himself to be 'as far removed from the effects of physical light as from the mistiness of romanticism', and this fundamentally metaphysical outlook explains the facility with which, after the war, he turned to abstraction. In the early 1950s he was associated with LUCIO FONTANA and his concept of SPAZIALISMO. From this time until his death he worked on a few large painting cycles: *The Island of San Giorgio*, *Abstract Seascapes*, *Cosmic Constructions*, *Large Eyes*, *Meetings* and *Restless Figures* (e.g. *Restless Woman*, 1951; Florence, Rac. della Ragione). Parallel to his activity as a painter, and gaining in importance, was his work as a poet, beginning with the collection *Spazi dell'esistenza* (Padua, 1959).

WRITINGS

Riflessioni sul tema (Lugano, 1977)

BIBLIOGRAPHY

Virgilio Guidi (exh. cat., ed. F. Arcangeli and T. Toniato; Bologna, Pal. Archiginnasio, 1972)

P. G. Castagnoli and T. Toniato: *Guidi* (Venice, 1977) [text in It. and Eng.]

Guidi 1912–1948: Mostra antologica (exh. cat., ed. V. Sgarbi, F. Benzi and T. Toniato; Mésola, Castello Estense, 1987)

VALERIO RIVOSECCHI

Guidobono. *See under* GUIDO DA COMO.

Guidobono, Bartolomeo [il Prete Savonese] (*b* Savona, 1654; *d* Turin, 24 Jan 1709). Italian painter. His father, Giovanni Antonio Guidobono (*d* 1685), was a maiolica painter and his brother Domenico Guidobono (1668–1746) a decorative fresco painter. Bartolomeo Guidobono worked in Savona, Genoa and Turin, and his art brought an elegant, graceful spirit to late Baroque painting in Genoa, offering an alternative to the robustness of his friend and mentor, Domenico Piola, and to the flamboyance of Gregorio de' Ferrari. The small, multiple drapery folds, soft lighting and sweet-faced figures inspired by Correggio made his work irresistible to the public, invaluable to the Casa Piola, and influential on Daniel Seiter and, later, Stefano Maria Legnani (1660–1715) in Turin.

After studying literature and theology (1674–9) and training as a maiolica painter, Guidobono painted his first frescoes, in the small Crocetta Chapel completed in 1680 next to the Santuario della Misericordia at Savona. Study trips to Parma, Venice and perhaps Bologna, made after finishing the Crocetta Chapel frescoes, inspired the vault fresco depicting the the *Chariot of the Sun* (Savona, Pal. Gavotti), which is indebted to Correggio and Pellegrino Tibaldi, the *Ecstasy of St Francis* (Savona, Convento dei Cappuccini, Refectory) and the frescoed medallions (Genoa, Pal. Rosso) paid for in 1680. Characteristic of his work in the 1680s are the sweet-faced figures, soft smoky modelling and small drapery folds seen in the *Annunciation* (Savona, Pin. Civ.), in which the overlapping layers of colour produced subtle tonalities that contrast with the more energetic brushwork of Piola, with whom he maintained close ties throughout his career. The painting is thought to have been sent from Turin, where Guidobono's other activities included frescoing a vault and walls in the Palazzo Reale, an octagonal cupola in Nostra Signora del Pilone, and scenes of the *History of Savoy* (1685) in the Santuario di S Maria di Casanova in Carmagnola.

Guidobono's frescoes in SS Giacomo e Filippo and in the Palazzo Centurione mark his return to Genoa *c.* 1690. The rich decoration of two vaults in the Palazzo Centurione with the *Triumph of Juno* and scenes from Ovid's *Metamorphoses* elaborates on the array of vases, garlands, putti and medallions that he used in his frescoes in the Palazzo Reale in Turin. The rounded, full figures with broad, curved drapery contours also appear on the frescoed walls and were possibly also on the vault of a room (paid for 1691–2; Genoa, Pal. Rosso; repainted by Domenico Parodi (ii) in 1736). In 1692 Guidobono worked again in the Palazzo Rosso, painting scenes from the *Life of Daniel* (destr.) in a chapel and decorating a small passageway: the latter frescoes survive and include rosy-cheeked putti. This kind of picture, indebted to Giovanni Benedetto Castiglione and featuring figures framed by animals and still-lifes, was popular and adorned many canvases (e.g. mythological scenes in the Palazzo Reale; four Old Testament scenes of *c.* 1694–6 in the Palazzo

Rosso). Guidobono's late style is often characterized by smaller-proportioned figures, extremely refined lighting effects and broad draperies, as in the *Virgin and Souls in Purgatory* (1697–8; Montoggio, Parish Church) and the *Circumcision* (1699; Moneglia, S Giorgio); and frescoes in the Santuario della Madonnetta, Genoa (after 1696; vault and side walls in the crypt, three frescoes in the adjacent Fratini Chapel). The small-scale figures are similar to those painted by Piola and Gregorio de' Ferrari at the turn of the century. These were Guidobono's last works in Genoa and were probably done before his trip in 1705 to Turin, where he painted frescoes and an altarpiece, *Patron Saints of Turin* (1706), with his brother in S Francesco da Paola.

BIBLIOGRAPHY

R. Soprani: *Vite* (1674); enlarged, ed. C. G. Ratti (1768–9)
L. Puccio: 'Frescanti genovesi a Palazzo Centurione in Fossatello', *Boll. Ligustico Stor. & Cult. Reg.*, xxi/1–4 (1969), pp. 113–30
E. Gavazza: 'Il momento della grande decorazione', *La pittura in Genova e in Liguria*, ii/2 (Genoa, 1971), pp. 244–52, 290–01
R. A. Tardito: 'Alcune opere sconosciute di Bartolomeo Guidobono', *A. Lombarda*, 40 (1974), pp. 181–8
E. Gavazza: 'Problemi iconografici per Bartolomeo Guidobono', *Atti & Mem. Soc. Savon. Stor. Patria*, xii (1978), pp. 105–25
G. V. Castelnovi: 'Guidobono, Haffner e Piola nella Cappella della Crocetta al Santuario di Savona', *Atti & Mem. Soc. Savon. Stor. Patria*, xii (Savona, 1978), pp. 131–48
M. Newcome Schleier: 'Notes on Guidobono', *Ant. Viva*, xx/6 (1981), pp. 27–36
Kunst in der Republik Genua (exh. cat., Frankfurt am Main, 1992) [for recent bibliog.]

M. NEWCOME

Guido [di Bonagiunta Bigarelli] **da Como** (*b* ?Aragno, nr Lugano; *fl* ?1238; *d* 1257). Italian sculptor. His father, Bonagiunta, may have been a marblecutter working alongside Guidetto in 1203 at Ponziano, Lucca. Guido may be identified with a 'Magister Guidus de Como', one of many sculptors of that name, noted in Barga, near Lucca, in 1238. The earliest secure reference to him is in 1244 in Lucca. Two years later he signed the octagonal font in Pisa Baptistery (*in situ*) *Guido Bigarelli de Cumo fecit opus hoc*. It consists of panels in which geometrically patterned, polychrome marble inlay is combined with foliate bands and human and animal motifs. In 1248 Guido was again noted in Lucca, but he was in Pistoia by 1250, when he signed and dated the pulpit in S Bartolomeo in Pantano (*in situ*). The pulpit (partly dismantled on the basis of a mistaken hypothesis) is stylistically and functionally homogeneous, and it consists of four framed panels, each with two New Testament scenes, two lecterns with supporting figures, and supporting lions below. The design follows a type formulated by Guglielmo in his pulpit (Cagliari Cathedral) for Pisa Cathedral.

In October 1252 a 'Magister Guido de Como' was recorded working with assistants Giannino and Lucano on the north door of Pistoia Cathedral and on the water pipes for the nearby baptistery. Among other works to be attributed to Guido is the *Angel* that once crowned the façade of S Giuseppe in Pistoia, which is comparable with the most accomplished parts of Guido's pulpit. Furthermore, there is a clear link between the decoration of a series of carved and inlaid panels (Pistoia, S Andrea) and that of the Pisa font. Documents monitor Guido's presence in Lucca in 1252–4, and stylistic evidence indicates that he must have worked there. In particular, reliefs of an *Eagle* and *Angel* flanking the lunette above the central doorway of Lucca Cathedral appear to be his work. Indeed, a document of 1257 shows that he was in a specific workshop, probably that of Lucca Cathedral, where Master Guidobono (*fl* 1246–58), his half-brother with whom he is sometimes confused, was working.

BIBLIOGRAPHY

M. T. Olivari: 'Ancora su Guido Bigarelli', *A. Lombarda*, xi (1966), pp. 31–8
C. Baracchini and A. Caleca: *Il duomo di Lucca* (Lucca, 1973)
G. Dalli Regoli: *Dai maestri senza nome all'impresa dei Guidi* (Lucca, 1986)
A. Caleca: *La dotta mano: Il battistero di Pisa* (Bergamo, 1991)

ANTONIO CALECA

Guido da Siena (*fl* ?1262–127(?)). Italian painter. Although he was once seen as the founder of Sienese painting, responsible for the city's artistic primacy over Florence, Guido's achievements may have owed a considerable debt to painting outside Siena, and even the importance of his contribution to Sienese images of the Virgin and Child has been questioned. Whatever his personal role in the establishment of panel painting workshops in Siena may have been, the quality, variety and inventiveness of the anonymous painters associated with his style provided an essential and characteristic foundation for subsequent Sienese artists.

1. Palazzo Pubblico *Madonna* and Dossal no. 7. 2. Origins of Guido's style and Sienese painting before *c.* 1270. 3. Related works. 4. Influence.

1. PALAZZO PUBBLICO 'MADONNA' AND DOSSAL NO. 7. All interpretations of the artist are based on the slender foundation of the inscription on a large panel of the *Madonna and Child Enthroned* from S Domenico, Siena (2.83×1.94 m; Siena, Pal. Pub.; see fig. 1). The inscription reads ME GUIDO DE SENIS DIEBUS DEPINXIT AMENIS: QUEM XR[ISTU]S LENIS NULLIS VELIT A[N]GERE PENIS A[N]NO.D[OMINI].M[ILLESIMO].CCXXI ('Guido da Siena painted me in the pleasant days, whom may gentle Christ afflict with no sufferings, AD 1221'). A truncated dossal of the *Virgin and Child Flanked by SS John the Baptist, John the Evangelist, Mary Magdalene and Francis* (0.96 [max]×1.86 m; ex-S Francesco, Colle di Val d'Elsa; Siena, Pin. N., Dossal no. 7; see detail in fig. 2) bears an inscription, damaged at beginning and end, that repeats the formula employed on the Palazzo Pubblico *Madonna* and is thus universally assumed also to have begun ME GUIDO DE SENIS. The connection is reinforced by a stylistic comparison between the two works. The date on the dossal, however, reads ANNO.D[OMI]NI MILLESIMO.DUCENTESIMO.SEPTUAGESIMO . . . , and this disparity in dating, 1221 and 127..., has provoked considerable controversy. While Mancini, and many after him, took the Palazzo Pubblico *Madonna* as proof of Guido's precocity in relation to Florentine painting, the size, style, content and panel type find no dated comparisons in Tuscan painting of the 1220s, whereas they fit convincingly with works of the 1270s. This case has been most fully argued by Offner and is now generally accepted, although not universally (e.g. Brandi), and various explanations have been given for the puzzling use of an early date (Offner, Garrison, Carli (1955), Stubblebine, Gardner).

1. Guido da Siena: *Madonna and Child Enthroned*, tempera on panel, 2.83×1.94 m, ?1270s (Siena, Palazzo Pubblico)

2. Guido da Siena: *Head of the Virgin*, detail from the *Virgin and Child Flanked by SS John the Baptist, John the Evangelist, Mary Magdalene and Francis*, tempera on panel, 0.96×1.86 m, 1270s (Siena, Pinacoteca Nazionale, Dossal no. 7)

Parts of the Palazzo Pubblico *Madonna*, notably the faces of the Virgin and Child and the throne base, were repainted by a follower of Duccio, indicating the devotion the work must have been accorded. The rectangular panel is now displayed with a pediment panel of the *Redeemer Flanked by Two Angels*, which may have formed part of the original ensemble. Twelve small rectangular panels (360 [max]×470 mm) with scenes from the *Nativity* and *Passion*, dispersed from the Badia Ardegna in the 19th century (Altenburg, Staatl. Lindenau-Mus.; Siena, Pin. N.; Paris, Louvre; Princeton U., NJ, A. Mus.; Utrecht, Catharijneconvent), have also been associated with the Palazzo Pubblico *Madonna*. The reconstruction of a cumbersome, fixed-wing tabernacle (proposed by Weigelt and Stubblebine), however, would be unprecedented, and Oertel suggested that the Badia Ardegna panels could be arranged more convincingly flanking a standing figure on a simple retable.

The Palazzo Pubblico *Madonna* indicates a taste in Tuscany for large-scale panels of the Virgin and Child enthroned where the relationships between the protagonists, the spectator and illusory space are all explored. The unprecedented height of the panel ensures the dominance of the Virgin looking directly at the spectator, visible above the head of the officiating priest. Her gesturing hand, remarkably long fingers extended, leads the eye to the Child, who leans back, cradled in her arms; the six adoring angels in the spandrels prompt the onlooker's response. The impression of three-dimensionality is reinforced by the receding side of the throne and the twist of the Virgin's body, showing the position of her right leg in relation to the throne. Drapery folds are described by a formalized network of fine gold lines formed by mordant gilding.

As the original faces on the Palazzo Pubblico *Madonna* have been scraped away and repainted, Dossal no. 7 now provides the best indication of the original appearance of the Virgin's face. On a dark green ground the artist built up numerous fine lines of lighter tones, white and pale pink, reserving the ground to indicate shadows. The relatively subtle treatment of flesh contrasts with the stronger tones and schematic shapes used for features such as the bridge and tip of the nose. The darkly-outlined eyes are arresting, and the curving edges of the lips give some animation to the face.

2. ORIGINS OF GUIDO'S STYLE AND SIENESE PAINTING BEFORE *c.* 1270. There is no consensus on the origins of Guido's style and the place of his training. The few examples of panel painting in Siena before the middle of the 13th century (e.g. *Christ in Majesty with Six Scenes from the Legend of the True Cross*, 1215; Siena, Pin. N., no. 1; a depiction of the Virgin and Child known as the *Madonna degli occhi grossi*, Siena, Mus. Opera Duomo) are modest works, quite different from Guido's manner. The flourishing centres of the period, Lucca and Pisa, presumably influenced Guido (Stubblebine proposed a period of training in Bonaventura Berlinghieri's workshop in Lucca in the 1250s), but his debt to Byzantium, either through intermediaries such as artists returning from the Crusader Kingdoms (Weitzmann), or by direct contact, has been only partially explored (Derbes).

Stubblebine considered a pair of trapezoidal panels, with scenes from the life or passion of *SS Bartholomew, Catherine of Alexandria, Francis* and *Clare*, which presumably served as reliquary shutters (1215 [max]×710 mm; Siena, Pin. N., no. 4) to be Guido's earliest surviving works, painted *c.* 1260. Another work generally attributed to Guido's early career is the *Virgin and Child* from S Bernardino in Siena (1.42 [max]×1.00 m; Siena, Pin. N., no. 16) dated by a lost inscription to 1262. The panel has been severely cut down on all sides, but a painting thought to be by one of Guido's assistants (1.98×1.22 m; Arezzo, Gal. & Mus. Med. & Mod., no. 2) appears to be based on the composition type of the S Bernardino *Virgin* and presumably indicates its original form. The *Virgin and Child Enthroned* in Arezzo is a less developed version of the Palazzo Pubblico *Madonna*: the recession of the throne is less successfully planned, the Child is more upright and less relaxed, and the drapery is handled less ebulliently.

The date 1262 for the S Bernardino *Virgin and Child* leads directly to the issue of the relationship of Sienese painting with Florence, for 1261 is the date inscribed on Coppo di Marcovaldo's panel of the *Virgin and Child Enthroned* in S Maria dei Servi, Siena. The extent of Coppo's influence on Sienese paintings of the Virgin and the proficiency of local painters before his arrival are open questions. But the coincidence of these two dates invites the theory that the patrons of the S Bernardino panel, the Franciscan Confraternità di S Maria degli Angeli, required a rapid response to the innovations seen in the Servite work and that a Sienese artist was available with sufficient skill both to take account of these new ideas and to express them in his own distinctive style.

Both Stubblebine and White have drawn attention to the substantial differences between the styles of the *Virgin and Child* from S Bernardino and Dossal no. 7, notably variations in colour, facial proportions and treatment of forms. Stubblebine considered the *Virgin and Child* to be by an assistant of Guido whom he called the 'San Bernardino Master' and, discounting the lost inscription, dated the work to the 1270s. White also considered that the work was not by Guido, but he stressed its high quality, at the same time accepting the 1262 date. He thus saw the San Bernardino Master as an independent contemporary of Guido's, whose ideas Guido developed in his Palazzo Pubblico *Madonna*. White's radical proposal implies that Guido was only one among several gifted Sienese artists and probably not the originator of their manner of painting.

3. RELATED WORKS. The Palazzo Pubblico *Madonna* and Dossal no. 7 provide the basis for linking some two dozen works more or less closely with Guido's name. Stubblebine arranged Sienese painters of the generation before Duccio into a precise chronological and stylistic framework, with Guido as the dominant figure. In addition to the two paintings just mentioned he attributed three works to Guido himself: the panels of the *Nativity* and *Passion* from the Badia Ardegna which, despite their poor condition, indicate the artist's skill as a narrative painter; the *Lenten Hanging* (900×1860 mm; Siena, Pin. N., no. 8), a work of high quality painted, unusually, on linen and showing the Transfiguration, Entry into Jerusalem and Raising of Lazarus, which may have functioned as a cover for an altarpiece during Lent; and the reliquary shutters (Siena, Pin. N., no. 4).

Stubblebine divided the remaining works into three categories: assistants of the 1270s, assistants of the 1280s, later assistants and followers. These works range from the Galli-Dunn *Madonna and Child* (Siena, Pin. N., no. 587), a careful but lifeless imitation of the Palazzo Pubblico *Madonna*, to such accomplished, distinctive and iconographically inventive works as *Christ and the Virgin Enthroned* (Siena, Convent of S Chiara) and *St Peter Enthroned* (Siena, Pin. N., no. 15). All except the *Lenten Hanging* and the murals of the *Washing of the Feet*, the *Betrayal* and the *Virgin and Child* in the crypt of Siena Cathedral (Carli, 1977) are panels. The majority represent the Virgin and Child enthroned, on a gabled or rectangular panel, but the variety of other panel types and subjects belies the notion that these artists were mere Madonna painters. When expanding their repertory, they were prepared to look to diverse sources of inspiration. For example Cimabue's fresco of the *Crucifixion* in the left transept of the Upper Church of S Francesco, Assisi, appears to be the source for the principal figures in the *Crucifixion* in the Badia Ardegna panels, while Nicola Pisano's pulpit in Siena Cathedral supplied several motifs for the *Adoration of the Magi*. The iconography of the Virgin was expanded by the use of the hitherto exclusively northern subject of the Coronation of the Virgin in a gable-shaped painting in the Lee Collection (560 [restored max]×1640 mm; U. London, Courtauld Inst. Gals.). Presumably this originally surmounted a larger rectangular panel (Coor suggested the *Assumption of the Virgin*, Stubblebine the *Dormition of the Virgin*) and would have been an innovative combination. Another development in panel types, also used elsewhere in Tuscany, was the dossal with the image of the Virgin and Child supplemented by saints appropriate to church, altar or patron.

4. INFLUENCE. Guido's direct influence was limited. By 1285 Duccio's independent career was already well established, and the styles of the two painters presumably functioned concurrently for some time, making their relationship hard for us to chart. For example *St Peter Enthroned with Six Scenes* (the *Annunciation*, the *Nativity* and four scenes from his life) has a softer palette and modelling than the Badia Ardegna panels. This could be the result of Duccio's influence, but on the other hand Duccio may himself have learnt from this painter, who was either an independent-minded artist in Guido's circle or possibly Guido himself, modifying his style towards the end of his career. There is some indication that in the 1280s painters who had trained in the earlier style began to work in minor centres such as Montaione and San Gimignano. The more general legacy of Guido and his contemporaries was longer lived: Siena was established as a centre of excellence for panel painting, especially for panels of the Virgin, and was still regarded as such in Sassetta's time.

BIBLIOGRAPHY

G. Mancini: *Considerazioni sulla pittura* (*c.* 1625); ed. A. Marucchi and L. Salerno (Rome, 1956–7), i, pp. 166–7

C. Weigelt: 'Guido da Siena's Great Ancona: A Reconstruction', *Burl. Mag.*, lix (1931), pp. 15–22, 23–4

E. B. Garrison: *Italian Romanesque Panel Painting: An Illustrated Index* (Florence, 1949), pp. 20–21, 116

R. Offner: 'Guido da Siena and A.D. 1221', *Gaz. B.-A.*, n. s. 6, xxxvii (1950), pp. 61–90

C. Brandi: *Duccio* (Florence, 1951), pp. 94–120

C. Brandi and E. Carli: 'Relazione sul restauro della Madonna di Guido da Siena del 1221', *Boll. A.*, xxxvi (1951), pp. 248–60

E. Carli: *Dipinti senesi del contado e della Maremma* (Milan, 1955), pp. 15–33

G. Coor: 'The Earliest Representation of the Coronation of the Virgin', *Burl. Mag.*, xcix (1957), pp. 328–30

R. Oertel: *Frühe italienische Malerei in Altenburg* (Berlin, 1961), pp. 57–67

H. Hager: 'Die Anfänge des italienischen Altarbildes', *Röm. Forsch. Bib. Hertz.*, xvii (1962) [whole issue]

J. H. Stubblebine: *Guido da Siena* (Princeton, 1964) [with extensive bibliography]; review by H.-W. Kruft in *Kunstchronik*, xviii (1965), pp. 274–83

E. Carli: 'Affreschi senesi del duecento', *Scritti di storia dell'arte in onore di Ugo Procacci*, i (Milan, 1977), pp. 82–93

P. Torriti: *La Pinacoteca nazionale di Siena* (Genoa, 1977), pp. 30–43

J. Gardner: 'Guido da Siena, 1221, and Tommaso da Modena', *Burl. Mag.*, cxxi (1979), pp. 107–08

J. White: *Duccio* (London, 1979), pp. 25–32

E. Carli: *La pittura senese del trecento* (Milan, 1981), pp. 7–22

H. van Os: *Sienese Altarpieces, 1215–1460*, i (Groningen, 1984), pp. 11–30

K. Weitzmann: 'Crusader Icons and Maniera Greca', *Byzanz und der Westen*, ed. I. Hutter (Vienna, 1984), pp. 143–70

A. Derbes: 'Siena and the Levant in the Later Duecento', *Gesta*, xxviii (1989), pp. 190–204

JOANNA CANNON

Guido di Piero da Mugello. *See* ANGELICO, FRA.

Guidon. *See under* FLAGS AND STANDARDS.

Guiffrey, Jules(-Marie-Joseph) (*b* Paris, 29 Nov 1840; *d* Paris, 29 Nov 1918). French administrator and art historian. After a training in law and palaeography he was appointed a keeper at the Archives Nationales in 1866 and remained at the Archives until his appointment as director of the Mobilier National in 1893. He held this post until 1908. From 1866 he was also editor of the publications of the Société de l'Art Français, which he revived under the title of *Nouvelles archives de l'art français*, and in 1874 he was the founder of the Société de l'Histoire de Paris et de l'Ile-de-France. He was a regular contributor to the *Gazette des beaux-arts*, the *Bulletin de la Société des antiquaires* and other scholarly journals. His interests were wide-ranging and he published books on the Caffiéri family (1877), Delacroix (1877) and van Dyck (1882), among other artists. But his lasting contribution to art-historical studies lies in his works on tapestry and the series of publications of documents relating to French art of the 17th and 18th centuries. Such collections as the *Comptes des Bâtiments du roi sous le règne de Louis XIV*, the *Inventaire général du mobilier de la couronne sous Louis XIV* and his compilation of the *livrets* (catalogues) of the Paris Salon exhibitions are still fundamental tools of scholarship.

WRITINGS

Collections des livrets des anciennes expositions depuis 1673 jusqu'en 1800, 42 vols (Paris, 1869–73)
Les Caffiéri: Sculpteurs et fondeurs-ciseleurs (Paris, 1877)
Histoire générale de la tapisserie, 3 vols (Paris, 1880) [with E. Müntz and A. Pinchart]
Comptes des Bâtiments du roi sous le règne de Louis XIV, 5 vols (Paris, 1881–1901)
Scellés et inventaires d'artistes, 3 vols (Paris, 1883–5)
Inventaire général du mobilier de la couronne sous Louis XIV, 2 vols (Paris, 1885–6)
Histoire de la tapisserie depuis le moyen âge jusqu'à nos jours (Tours, 1886)
Les Manufactures parisiennes de tapisseries au XVIIe siècle (Nogent-le-Rotrou, 1892)
Correspondance des directeurs de l'Académie de France à Rome avec les surintendants des bâtiments, 13 vols (Paris, 1896–1908)
Tables des peintures, sculptures et gravures exposées aux salons du XVIIIe siècle (Paris, 1910)

BIBLIOGRAPHY

DBF
'Mélanges offerts à Jules Guiffrey', *Nouv. Archvs A. Fr.*, viii (1916) [whole vol.; with complete list of writings, pp. xvii–cxlv]
H. Stein: 'Jules Guiffrey', *Bib. Ecole Chartes*, lxxix (1918), pp. 242–4
M. Fenaille: 'Note sur la vie et les travaux de M. Jules Guiffrey', *Acad. B.-A.: C.R. Séances* (24 March 1923) [whole issue]

FRANÇOIS FOSSIER

Guignard, Alberto da Veiga (*b* Nova Friburgo, Brazil, 25 Feb 1896; *d* Belo Horizonte, 25 June 1962). Brazilian painter and draughtsman. As an adolescent he lived in Switzerland, France and Germany. He studied at the Akademie der Bildenden Künste in Munich from 1916 and completed his studies informally in Florence between 1925 and 1928, visiting museums. Throughout this period he absorbed a wide variety of influences, including Neue Sachlichkeit, Expressionism and Surrealism. He returned to Brazil in 1929, settling initially in Rio de Janeiro and expressing his enthusiasm for Brazil in a personal language derived from European modernism, for example in the *Newly Weds* (1937; Rio de Janeiro, Fund. Ottoni de Castro Maya). In 1944 he was invited to Belo Horizonte by the city's Prefect, Juscelino Kubitschek (later President of Brazil), to teach an open drawing course. His long teaching career had a profound influence on more than one generation of artists in Minas Gerais. His work was deeply affected by the mountainous landscape of the interior of this state, with its gentle slopes and vast misty panoramas reflected in works such as the *Landscape in Ouro Preto* (1950; São Paulo, Mus. A.). His spontaneous, lively powers of observation were likewise applied to his many portraits and still-lifes, for example the *Twin Sisters* (1940; Rio de Janeiro, Pal. Cult.). He also explored religious themes, as in the painting of *St Sebastian* (1960; Rio de Janeiro, Banco do Estado) and especially the figure of the suffering Christ.

BIBLIOGRAPHY

M. Leão: *Guignard* (São Paulo, 1963)
R. M. F. de Andrade: *Guignard* (Rio de Janeiro, 1967)
Guignard (exh. cat. by F. Morais, São Paulo, Cent. A. Novo Mundo, 1974)
F. Morais: *Alberto da Veiga Guignard* (Rio de Janeiro, 1979)
C. Zílio, ed.: *A modernidade em Guignard* (Rio de Janeiro, 1979)
R. Pontual: *Entre dois séculos: Arte brasileira do século XX na Coleção Gilberto Chateaubriand* (Rio de Janeiro, 1987)

ROBERTO PONTUAL

Guigou, Paul(-Camille) (*b* Villars, nr Apt, Vaucluse, 15 Feb 1834; *d* Paris, 21 Dec 1871). French painter. Born into a family of landowners, he became a notary's clerk at Apt in 1851 and then in 1854 at Marseille. He learnt to paint with Camp, a teacher at the school in Apt, and then at Marseille with Emile Loubon (1809–63), director of the local Ecole des Beaux-Arts, who urged him (according to Guigou's biographers) to paint directly from nature. Guigou settled in Marseille in 1854, where he participated regularly in the annual Salon of the Société Artistique des Bouches-du-Rhône. Guigou painted almost exclusively Provençal landscapes, which were influenced by the works of the Barbizon painters, who exhibited in Marseille, and by the brownish tones and picturesque figures of Loubon's paintings. *The Road to Gineste* (1859) and *The Washerwoman* (1860; both Paris, Mus. d'Orsay) reflect the independent tradition of Provençal painting during the Second Empire, which was characterized by warm colouring and precise lighting used to separate and distinguish forms. His knowledge of the works of Gustave Courbet, acquired during a visit to Paris in 1859, doubtless increased his liking for broad technique and sincere vision, articulated in a strong and ordered construction of space: for example, *The Gorges of the Lubéron* (*c.* 1861; Amiens, Mus. Picardie).

In 1862 Guigou gave up his notarial work to concentrate on painting. He moved to Paris and from 1863 exhibited every year in the Salon. In *The Hills of Allauch* (1862; exh. Salon, 1863; Marseille, Mus. B.-A.), he showed a more independent style, free of picturesque or romantic inspiration. In 1864 he painted at Saint-Paul-lès-Durance with Adolphe Monticelli. In his large landscapes such as *The Village of Saint-Paul-lès-Durance* (1865; Pasadena, CA, Norton Simon Mus.), the warm colours are heightened in a luminous brilliance that accentuates the rigorous construction of the composition. In 1866 he produced several views in the Ile de France, at Moret and Triel, such as *The Village of Triel* (Marseille, Mus. Cantini). He visited Algeria, but avoided picturesque orientalism by painting *The Gorges at Chiffa* (1868; untraced) as though it were a Provençal landscape.

Guigou met Théodore Duret in 1868 and frequented the Café Guerbois in Paris, where he probably met the future Impressionists. Although he shared their interests in realism and liking for broad handling, he was not a precursor of Impressionism. In his work the harsh southern light separated objects without relating them, picking out details and conferring on the arid, bare masses of the Provençal hills a sense of equilibrium and solidity. He often chose the motif of a road vanishing into the distance, as in his *View of Saint-Saturnin-d'Apt* (1867; Paris, Petit Pal.), or an elevated viewpoint (*Provençal Landscape*, *c.* 1869; Montpellier, Mus. Fabre), to create a spreading landscape and an impression of space. In 1871 he became the drawing teacher of Baroness Rothschild, but he died a few weeks later of a stroke. His works went unnoticed at the Salon; his talent was not recognized until Duret wrote an article in the *Electeur libre* on the Salon of 1870. At the Exposition Universelle of 1900 he was well represented thanks to Claude Roger-Marx.

BIBLIOGRAPHY

T. Duret: 'Un Grand Peintre de la Provence: Paul Guigou', *A. & Artistes*, xv/87 (1912), pp. 97–103
H. Simonnot: 'Centenaire de Paul Guigou', *Bull. Officiel Vieux-Marseille* (March–April 1934)
Guigou (exh. cat., Paris, Gal. Daber, 1950)
K. Scholtz: *Paul Guigou und die provenzalische Landschaft Malerei des 19. Jahrhunderts* (diss., U. Hamburg, 1954)
Paul Guigou (exh. cat., Marseille, Mus. Cantini, 1959)
F. Daulte: 'Un Provençal pur: Paul Guigou', *Conn. A.*, 98 (April 1960), pp. 70–77
Paul Guigou, 1834–1871 (exh. cat., Paris, Gal. Daber, 1970)

VALÉRIE M. C. BAJOU

Guijano, Jerónimo. *See* QUIJANO, JERÓNIMO.

Guild [Gild]. Sworn association, typically of merchants, craftsmen or tradesmen. Most guilds were associated with a particular town or city. They flourished in Europe in the medieval period and had considerable social, political, economic and religious power. Additionally, craft guilds often monitored training, standards of production and the welfare of their members. Significant patronage was provided by religious, social and commercial confraternities. Information on the activity of specific guilds is given in this dictionary within the relevant articles on cities and on countries (in the latter, especially under 'Painting and graphic arts' or 'Art education').

1. History. 2. Function. 3. Patronage.

1. HISTORY. The origins of guilds remain obscure, as in their medieval form they appeared to combine characteristics that recall both the social solidarity of the Roman *collegium* and a concern for skilful craftsmanship that is more easily identified with Germanic societies in the early Christian centuries. Following the expansion of towns and trade after *c.* AD 1000, the social strata of the commune—a sworn association of equals—developed into subgroups of people who practised a common trade. This was particularly true in Europe's towns and cities, although it must be seen in the context of an overwhelmingly rural society. From the 13th century guilds became essential to most aspects of civic life and reflected the advance of the division of labour. They were responsible for, among other trades, the production of leather and textiles (e.g. cloth merchants, dyers, stretchers, fullers, weavers, tailors, tanners and cobblers) and for building (e.g. masons, tilers, plasterers, carpenters and blacksmiths). In Nuremberg in the 13th century, for instance, there were craft organizations for goldsmiths, cutlers, furriers, beltmakers, clothweavers, armourers, swordsmiths, scythesmiths, pewterers and mirrormakers. Shortly after 1300, papermakers, wiresmiths, bottlemakers, brass-smiths, parchmentmakers and bell-founders also formed guilds. Gunsmiths, glaziers, saddlers and carpenters soon followed, and in 1400 the city council listed 141 separate crafts. Demarcation was strictly enforced: for example, Veit Stoss had great difficulty obtaining permission to cast a statue in bronze because the brass-smiths complained that this was not his trade. Approval for the project was eventually obtained through pressure from Stoss's patron, the Emperor Maximilian.

To protect their members, guilds tended to resist the dependence of large numbers of artisans on a single entrepreneur. In London from 1271 no cordwainer was allowed to employ more than eight journeymen. In Venice in 1457 the number of looms for silk-weaving that any individual producer was permitted to own was limited to six. Merchants themselves, however, also formed guilds to manage the local staple, sometimes providing insurance schemes to cover members engaged in long-distance trade. Guild membership was often a prerequisite for involvement in city government. The role of guilds in public life was celebrated in such processions as that of the Lord Mayor in London. The different interests represented by craft and merchant guilds were sometimes institutionalized, as in the major and minor guilds of Florence and the livery companies and trade guilds of London. The conflict of interest between different guilds frequently erupted in dispute: for example, around 1300 textile workers in the South Netherlands were denied the right to form guilds and expressed their solidarity through strikes; the revolt of the Ciompi in Florence in 1378 was partly a popular reaction to the efforts of merchants to reduce the number of guilds and thereby restrict the franchise. A similar conflict in Nuremberg at about the same time resulted in the suppression of guilds as political organizations.

Trade guilds were also religious organizations, and many guilds met only as devotional confraternities (*see* §2 below). In England such devotional confraternities were often parish-based. A small town such as Bodmin, for instance, had *c.* 40 such organizations in the 14th century. At Stratford-upon-Avon the guild of the Holy Cross was in existence by 1269. It employed four chaplains to say mass for the souls of all members in the Guild chapel (founded 1269) and at altars that it maintained in the Holy Trinity Church. It later built almshouses (*c.* 1427; partly rebuilt) and the Guildhall (1417; now the Grammar School). A Florentine observer in 15th-century Venice recorded that there were 200 such confraternities in the city, and records show that membership of each, which included men and women, may sometimes have run into hundreds.

In the 16th century the traditional economic and religious functions of guilds were subjected to new pressures. The conventional view is that the rise of merchant capitalism in cities that were rapidly expanding beyond the old limits marked by medieval walls, broke down guild privileges by operating in suburbs where guild jurisdiction did not apply; this was compounded in the 17th century by the increasing practice of putting out work to rural areas. At the same time, religious reformers criticized the confraternities. Martin Luther himself attacked them for having devoted themselves to the 'collecting of money for beer': 'if a sow were made the patron saint of such a brotherhood she would not accept' ('The Blessed Sacrament of the Holy and True Body of Christ, and the Brotherhoods', *Works*, ed. J. Pelikan and H. T. Lehmann, xxxv (Philadelphia, 1955–), p. 68). The perceived decline of religious sodalities into *Trinkstuben*, or drinking clubs, along with their reorganization did not necessarily indicate the demise of all the guild systems of Europe, however. In some towns in Germany medieval corporatism flourished during the Reformation. In the Roman Catholic world guilds remained essential components of the urban economy and adapted to the new religious climate. Confraternities were of enormous importance in the promotion of post-Tridentine Catholicism, and in many ways were among the most powerful expressions of a 'Counter-Reformation'. They opposed iconoclasm with the splendour of holiness, they defended the veneration of the Virgin Mary and they gave new life to the cult of the saints. Most important, perhaps, brotherhoods of the Holy Sacrament gave special prominence to the eucharistic cult.

Guilds were closely involved in the production and patronage of art (*see* §3 below). The artistic importance of guilds, however, waned with the rise in status of the individual artist and the quest for princely patronage. Under Pope Urban VIII (*reg* 1623–44), for example, the Accademia di S Luca, Rome, was allowed 'to establish its absolute authority in the art world of Rome and finally crush any opposition from the guilds' (F. Haskell: *Patrons and Painters: Art and Society in Baroque Italy* (New Haven, 1980), p. 17), which gave its members a new status and dignity (*see* ROME, §VI). Courts and academies were far removed from medieval workshops. Guilds survived, however: in the 17th century in the Dutch Republic painters in Utrecht and Leiden, for example, formed guilds. Elsewhere, too, while courts and academies commissioned paintings, sculptures and architecture, the luxury market was still dominated by the high-quality, expensive products of the traditional workshop, which were much in demand among wealthy visitors in the age of the Grand Tour. In the 19th century the Industrial Revolution swept aside the patterns of production that had allowed guilds to flourish. Factories that employed vast numbers of people on production lines (which turned out thousands of identical objects) were alien to the guilds' traditions of small-scale enterprise, a highly trained workforce and individually crafted products. Some guild traditions survived only as ceremonies (such as the Lord Mayor's Show in London), while the guild ethos of solidarity within a specific trade proved influential in the formation of trade unions.

2. FUNCTION. As Christian confraternities under the protection of a patron saint, guilds met regularly for Mass, for the celebration of a saint's day and for an annual feast. They also played an important role in ensuring the burial of members and occasionally provided a member's surviving dependants with material help. Guild statutes make it plain that practical work and religious devotion were never clearly distinguishable. Attendance on the dead and provision for the washing of bodies were among the most significant responsibilities of guild officers, and occasionally there are macabre references in the documents to the need to empty a guild tomb.

Craft guilds ensured the maintenance of standards of production and of wage levels through their elected officers: a warden, a secretary, a treasurer and perhaps a committee. The guild was also responsible for the training that took the apprentice to the status of journeyman and then master; work produced by the trainee in the workshop was submitted to a board of examiners, which consisted of qualified guild masters (see fig.; *see also* ART EDUCATION). Craft traditions were essential to the training of the artist; to become a master involved the production of a MASTERPIECE. The place of training and production for painters and for sculptors not working on site was the workshop (*see* STUDIO, §II, 1).

Masons' lodges (*see* MASON (i), §§II, 3; III; and IV, 2) were the administrative centre of that craft. They often controlled large areas; the master of the Strasbourg lodge, for instance, held jurisdiction over a number of subordinate regions in the 14th and 15th centuries. At the Expertises of masons held at this time (*see* MASON (i), §IV, 3), the masters present represented an area *c.* 800 km across. Masons' lodges were places where technical problems were discussed, as well as being storehouses. An inventory at York Minster in 1399 recorded the contents

Craftsmen Demonstrating their Skill in Working Stone and Wood to the Consul of the Guild, Florence, miniature, 14th century (London, British Library)

of the lodge as including 69 stone-axes, 96 chisels, 24 mallets, an iron compass, two drawing-boards, a wheel-barrow, buckets and ropes. Guilds also monitored competition; the cloth guild at Ypres imposed strict limitations on competition, and cloth was stamped with a seal of approval only after careful inspection.

3. PATRONAGE. Merchant guilds were often patrons of great civic monuments. Their buildings often defined the urban space, for example the Guildhall (*see* LONDON, fig. 3) and various livery halls (*see* LIVERY HALL) in the City of London. On a grander scale, members often contributed to such projects as the great Cloth Hall in Ypres, which was built between 1200 and 1304. It was a vast, communal warehouse, with most of the space given over to textiles. In Chartres a variety of guilds sponsored many of the cathedral's stained-glass windows (*see* CHARTRES, fig. 6). At Orsanmichele in Florence the city's guilds sought to outdo each other in their sponsorship of sculptures for the niches in the walls of the church (*see* GHIBERTI, (1), fig. 2; FLORENCE, §IV, 2 and fig. 17). The Wool Guild commissioned Ghiberti to cast a bronze statue of *St Stephen* (1425–9): 'it shall be done in whatever mode or form seems most honourable. . .provided that the said niche exceeds or at least equals in beauty and adornment the more beautiful of the others' (D. S. Chambers, ed.: *Patrons and Artists in the Italian Renaissance* (London, 1970), p. 46). The patronage of religious brotherhoods often operated at a comparatively modest level, maintaining a chapel or altar. Such organizations as the *scuole* in Venice (*see* VENICE, §V) sponsored more celebrated projects. For example, the Scuola di S Orsola (founded 1300) agreed at a meeting in 1488 to commission a cycle of paintings depicting the *Life and Martyrdom of St Ursula* (1490–95; Venice, Accad.) from Vittore Carpaccio (*see* CARPACCIO, (1), fig. 4), who also executed comparable cycles for other *scuole*.

The Counter-Reformation gave enormous impetus to Catholic patronage of the arts by religious confraternities, which commissioned works to celebrate the cults of the Virgin and the saints, and the doctrine of transubstantiation. In a great assertion of the importance of the splendour of holiness as an essential accompaniment to good works, the Scuola Grande di S Rocco in Venice spent large sums on its building projects and on Jacopo Tintoretto's great cycle of paintings (from 1565; *see* VENICE, fig. 28). Tintoretto also painted many versions of the Last Supper, often for *scuole del sacramento* (e.g. *see* TINTORETTO, (1), fig. 4). Outside Venice the idea of good works beyond the membership of the confraternity was emphasized in Federico Barocci's *Madonna del popolo* (1579; Florence, Uffizi; *see* BAROCCI, FEDERICO, fig. 3) for the confraternity of S Maria della Misericordia in Arezzo. Caravaggio's two altarpieces (Naples, Monte della Misericordia, and S Domenico Maggiore, on dep. at Capodimonte), which he produced for the Neapolitan confraternity Pio Monte della Misericordia in 1607, are more powerful as pieces of propaganda. However, as the economic importance of guilds declined, so did their ability to finance great artistic projects. In the Netherlands, Calvinism restricted the artistic interpretation of religious subject-matter, which, together with the absence of a court, increased the importance of commissions by wealthy corporations. Rembrandt's *Syndics of the Amsterdam Drapers' Guild* (1662; Amsterdam, Rijksmus.; *see* REMBRANDT VAN RIJN, fig. 11) commemorates the wealth of the company, and Frans Hals's *Banquet of the Officers of the St George Civic Guard Company* (1616; Haarlem, Frans Halsmus.; *see* HAARLEM, fig. 2) illustrates the continuance of ritual feasting and a confraternal solidarity that seem to hark back to the Middle Ages.

BIBLIOGRAPHY

J. Ruskin: *The Stones of Venice*, 3 vols (London, 1851–3)
G. Unwin: *The Gilds and Companies of London* (London, 1908, rev. 4/1963)
S. Kramer: *The English Craft Gilds* (1927/*R* 1976)
N. Pevsner: *Academies of Art Past and Present* (London, 1940, rev. New York, 1973)
G. Clune: *The Medieval Gild System* (1943)
S. C. Thrupp: 'The Gilds', *Cambridge Economic History of Europe*, iii (1963)
T. S. R. Boase: *Death in the Middle Ages* (London, 1972)
K. H. O. Haley: *The Dutch in the Seventeenth Century* (London, 1972)
J. Harvey: *The Master Builders* (London, 1972)
J. Martindale: *The Rise of the Artist* (London, 1972)
J. Harvey: *Medieval Craftsmen* (London, 1975)
G. Strauss: *Nuremberg in the Sixteenth Century* (Bloomington, 1976)
R. Goldthwaite: *The Building of Renaissance Florence* (Baltimore, 1981)
P. Humphrey and R. Mackenney: 'The Venetian Trade Guilds as Patrons of Art in the Renaissance', *Burl. Mag.*, cxxviii/998 (1986), pp. 317–30
R. Mackenney: *Tradesmen and Traders: The World of the Guilds in Venice and Europe, c. 1250–c. 1650* (London, 1987)
C. Black: *Italian Confraternities in the Sixteenth Century* (Cambridge, 1989)
R. Goy: *The House of Gold: Building a Palace in Medieval Venice* (Cambridge, 1992)

RICHARD MACKENNEY

Guilford, 5th Earl of. *See* NORTH, FREDERICK.

Guilhermy, (Roch François) Ferdinand (Marie Nolasque), Baron **de** (*b* London, 1808; *d* Paris, 27 April 1878). French archaeologist and architectural historian. He came from a noble family of royalist, Catholic lawyers, and studied law himself before embarking on a career in the civil service. At the same time he followed courses at the Sorbonne and Bibliothèque Royale and pursued a career as a scholar and archaeologist. He submitted reports to the Comité des Arts et Monuments, which was drawing up an inventory of French monuments. In 1855 he was asked to record inscriptions in France dating after the 5th century AD, and he spent the rest of his life on this work, which was published from 1873. Guilhermy also published numerous articles dealing mainly with the iconography of medieval historical and literary figures; in other articles he discussed the dispersed collections of the old Musée des Monuments Français (Petits-Augustins).

Guilhermy was admitted to the Commission des Monuments Historiques only in 1860, but very soon he became associated with a number of major restoration workshops. At Saint-Denis Abbey he advised Eugène Viollet-le-Duc on the restoration of the crypts, having joined Charles Lenormant, Prosper Mérimée and Louis Vitet in deploring the anachronisms and incorrect restorations of François Debret. At the Sainte-Chapelle he collaborated with Jean-Baptiste Lassus in restoring the iconographic programme, particularly of the windows. Guilhermy published a monograph on each of the buildings, and his studies were models of a critical method based on texts. His attitude towards the restoration of monuments was that of an archaeologist: he believed that intervention, whether repair or innovation, should be minimal. He challenged the idea of stylistic unity and stressed the respect due to later additions but also defended medieval architecture against the supporters of classicism, and deplored pastiche in the creations of his own century. He campaigned for a museum of casts to benefit the study of medieval art. Guilhermy bequeathed his notes, totalling 20,000 pages in 41 volumes, and including detailed dossiers on individual buildings, to the Bibliothèque Nationale.

WRITINGS

Monographie de l'église royale de Saint-Denis (Paris, 1848)
Itinéraire archéologique de Paris (Paris, 1855)
La Sainte Chapelle de Paris (Paris, 1857)
Inscriptions de la France du Vème au XVIIIème siècle, 5 vols (Paris, 1873–83)
L'Abbaye de Saint-Denis, tombeaux et figures historiques des rois de France (Paris, 1882)

BIBLIOGRAPHY

A. Darcel: 'Le Baron de Guilhermy, membre du Comité des travaux historiques', *Rev. Soc. Sav.*, viii (1878), pp. 3–12
J. G. Mozziconacci: Un Archéologue parisien, le baron de Guilhermy', *Bull. Soc. Hist. Paris & Ile-de-France* (1980), pp. 105–34

FRANÇOISE BERCÉ

Guillain. French family of sculptors.

(1) Nicolas Guillain [de Cambrai] (*b* Cambrai, *c.* 1560; *d* Paris, 20 May 1639). He is first recorded in 1597 in Paris, where he worked as a wood-carver (e.g. *Crucifixion with the Virgin and St John*, 1598; Yèbles-en-Brie, St Martin) and as a monumental mason specializing in incised tomb slabs and epitaphs. In 1597 he worked with Mathieu Jacquet, whose influence may have led him subsequently to produce more sophisticated funerary monuments, such as that of 1607 to *Claude de Villequier* in the church at Giseux, Indre-et-Loire, with two marble weeping figures. He is particularly noted for producing large tombs of black and white marble in which the decorative setting served as a counterfoil to the white marble effigies of the deceased in prayer. Among his surviving tombs of this type is that of *Martin du Bellay and Louise de Sapvenières*, also in the church at Giseux (erected after 1627). A number of fragments also exist, such as the impressive effigy of *Claude de l'Aubespine* (marble, 1614; Poitiers, Mus. B.-A.). They share the slight rigidity of composition, realistic but expressionless faces and minute attention to draperies and accessories typical of the craftsmanlike but unimaginative funerary sculpture of the reign of Louis XIII.

Guillain's most supple and successful sculptures belong to the period of his collaboration with his son, (2) Simon Guillain; they include, most notably, the tomb of *Catherine de Clèves, Duchesse de Guise* (marble, 1627–31) in the Lycée Chapel (formerly the Jesuit church) at Eu, Seine-Maritime, based on a model by Barthélémy Tremblay. His pupils included two of the foremost French sculptors of the next generation, his own son and Jacques Sarazin.

(2) Simon Guillain (*bapt* Paris, 15 June 1589; *d* Paris, 26 Dec 1658). Son of (1) Nicolas Guillain. He was trained by his father and studied with Alessandro Algardi in Rome, returning to France in 1612; he went on to become one of the leading sculptors of the reign of Louis XIII, rivalled only by Jacques Sarazin. Brought up in the craftsmanlike and realist traditions of late 16th-century French sculpture, he absorbed the influences of the Italian Baroque and through his pupils François Anguier and Michel Anguier helped to form the French classical style in sculpture. He collaborated with his father on a number of works, including a fountain (1613; destr.) for the château of Coulommiers, Seine-et-Marne, and the praying figures of *Président Jeannin* and his wife *Anne Guéniot* (marble, 1626–7; Autun Cathedral). His early independent works include the praying funerary effigy of *Henri de Montpensier* (marble, 1624–6) in the Sainte-Chapelle at Champigny-sur-Veude, Indre-et-Loire; the praying figures of *Charles Bailly* (reduced bust, marble, 1628; Versailles, Château), Bailly's widow *Chrétienne Leclerc* (marble, 1628; Paris, Louvre) and *Charlotte-Catherine de la Tremoïlle, Princesse de Condé* (marble, 1629; Paris, Louvre) reveal the development of a more fluid technique, broader composition and suppler gestures. He also produced at this time a number of tombs decorated with busts of the deceased, surviving examples including those of *François de Montholon* (marble, 1623; Versailles, Château) and *Robert le Roux de Tilly* (marble, 1639; Acquigny, Château), which is decorated with three funerary genii, evoking the art of François Du Quesnoy.

Guillain's secular monumental work has almost all disappeared. He provided decorative sculpture (1629–33; untraced) for the park of the château of Bagnolet, near Paris, and is known to have worked at the château of Caves, near Langres. His statues of *Louis XIII* for the portal of the Juges-Consuls at St Merry, Paris, and of *Hercules* and *Minerva* for the doorway of the Hôtel de Longueville, Paris, have similarly disappeared. Surviving works include the sumptuous ceiling (stucco, 1638) of the grand staircase in the wing added to the château of Blois by François Mansart, with monumental trophies and putti, as well as substantial fragments of the *Monument in Honour of the Bourbon Monarchy* for the Pont au Change, Paris, erected *c.* 1647. The exactly rendered classicizing stone relief carved with captives and trophies and the bronze statues of *Louis XIII*, *Anne of Austria* and the young *Louis XIV* are in the Louvre, Paris. Much of the best of Simon Guillain's quite considerable output of religious sculpture has also been destroyed, including his most important ecclesiastical commission, which he shared with Guillaume Berthelot, for the sculptural decoration of the church of the Sorbonne, Paris (1635–40). For this project Guillain executed half the stone statues on the exterior, the marble statues of *St Denis* and *St Louis* on the façade and eight stone statues of the *Apostles* in the interior.

Simon Guillain was a Sculpteur Ordinaire du Roi from 1627 and was one of the twelve original Anciens (professors) of the Académie Royale de Peinture et Sculpture from its foundation in 1648, acting as treasurer from 1651 and as rector from 1657.

BIBLIOGRAPHY

P. Vitry: 'Le Sculpteur Nicolas Guillain dit Cambray', *Rev. Archéol.*, i (1849), pp. 188–204
Guillet de Saint Georges: 'Simon Guillain', *Mémoires inédits . . . des membres de l'Académie Royale*, ed. L. Dussieux and others (Paris, 1854), pp. 184–94
E. Coyecque: 'Les Sculpteurs Nicolas et Simon Guillain: Contribution à leur biographie', *Bull. Soc. Hist. A. Fr.* (1925), pp. 247–71
——: 'Une Addition aux oeuvres de Simon Guillain', *Bull. Soc. Hist. A. Fr.* (1939), pp. 201–3
J. Coural: 'Addition aux oeuvres des Guillain', *Archvs A. Fr.*, xxii (1950–57), pp. 65–8

——: 'Les Tombeaux du Duc et de la Duchesse de Guise à Eu', *Bull. Soc. Hist. A. Fr.* (1957), pp. 251–5
——: 'Oeuvres inédites des Guillain', *Rev. des A.* (1959), pp. 181–6
J. Ciprut, ed.: 'Additions à l'oeuvre de Simon Guillain', *Bull. Soc. Hist. A. Fr.* (1967), pp. 173–83
R. Leblant: 'Sculpteurs du temps d'Henri IV d'après les documents du Minutier Central à Paris', *96e Congrès National des Sociétés Savantes: Archéologie: Toulouse 1971*, i, pp. 399–413

GENEVIÈVE BRESC-BAUTIER

Guillaume, Jean-Baptiste-Claude-Eugène (*b* Montbard, Côte d'Or, 4 July 1822; *d* Rome, 1 March 1905). French sculptor and writer. Having attended drawing school in Dijon, he entered the Ecole des Beaux Arts, Paris, in 1841. He won the Prix de Rome in 1845 and during his stay in Rome produced several works that were enthusiastically received by the Académie. These included the marble statue of *Anacreon* (exh. Salon 1852; Paris, Mus. d'Orsay), the hedonistic Classical subject and precise execution of which betray Guillaume's debt to his master, James Pradier. Another piece from his years in Rome, *The Reaper* (bronze, 1849; Paris, Mus. d'Orsay), while not going so far as to infringe Classical conventions, frees the representation of labour from traditional poetics.

Guillaume returned to Paris to pursue a successful career as an official sculptor. His identification with the regime of Napoleon III was confirmed by his series of five marble portrait busts and a marble statue of *Napoleon I* (some at Arenenberg, Napoleonmus.), destined for the Pompeian villa of Prince Napoléon-Jérôme Bonaparte. He was involved in virtually every major scheme of sculptural decoration for the public buildings of the Second Empire (1851–70), including the Paris Opéra, to which he contributed one of the façade groups, *Instrumental Music* (Echaillon stone, 1865–9). Guillaume was Director of the Ecole des Beaux Arts (1864–78) and played a prominent part in public life, becoming a member of the Commission on Public Instruction in 1866 and Inspector General of Drawing Instruction in 1872.

WRITINGS

Discours et allocutions (Paris, n. d.)
Essai sur la théorie du dessin et de quelques parties des arts (Paris, 1896)

BIBLIOGRAPHY

Lami
A. M. Wagner: *Jean-Baptiste Carpeaux, Sculptor of the Second Empire* (New Haven, 1986)

PHILIP WARD-JACKSON

Guillaume, Paul (*b* Paris, 1891; *d* Paris, 1934). French dealer. He began selling African sculpture *c.* 1911, before opening his gallery in Paris. He was one of the first art dealers in France to promote it, and this was probably how he met Guillaume Apollinaire, who provided him with important contacts in the art community. In 1914 he opened a small gallery and acquired, through Apollinaire, an important group of paintings by Giorgio de Chirico. In 1916 he held an exhibition of André Derain's work and became his principal dealer in 1923. He also bought numerous paintings by Modigliani, who described him as his *'novo pilota'* [sic] in a dedication on his portrait of *Paul Guillaume* (Paris, Mus. Orangerie). During the 1920s Paul Guillaume's gallery was one of the best known commercial outlets for modern art in Paris, and he represented many of the most accessible and fashionable artists of the Ecole de Paris. In 1918–19 Guillaume held a Matisse and Picasso exhibition, put on a Fête nègre (a bohemian *soirée* with an African theme) and bought up a stock of paintings by Utrillo. By 1920 he was able to move his gallery to the prestigious Rue La Boétie. In 1922–3 Albert C. Barnes, the founder of the Barnes Foundation in Merion, PA, made Guillaume his principal Parisian art supplier. After 1925 Guillaume appeared increasingly to be an establishment figure. After his early death his widow married the architect Jean Walter. The joint Walter–Guillaume collection was bequeathed to the nation and is now housed in the Musée de l'Orangerie in Paris. It includes works by Cézanne, Renoir, Picasso, Matisse, Modigliani, Utrillo, Derain, Soutine, Henri Rousseau and others.

WRITINGS

ed.: *Les Arts à Paris* (Paris, 1918–34)
with T. Munro: *Primitive Negro Sculpture* (London, 1926)
Cah. A. (1927) [supernumerary issue: *Les Feuilles volantes*, i: 'Nos enquêtes—entretien avec Paul Guillaume']

BIBLIOGRAPHY

W. George: 'La Grande Peinture contemporaine', *La Collection Paul Guillaume* (Paris, 1929)
P. Cabanne: 'Paul Guillaume', *L'Avant-garde au XXe siècle*, ed. P. Cabanne and P. Restany (Paris, 1969)
J. Bouret: 'Une Amitié esthétique au début du siècle: Apollinaire et Paul Guillaume', *Gaz. B.-A.*, lxxvi (1970), pp. 373–99
M. Gee: *Dealers, Critics and Collectors of Modern Painting* (New York, 1981)
Catalogue de la collection Jean Walter et Paul Guillaume (Paris, Mus. Orangerie, 1984)

MALCOLM GEE

Guillaume de Machaut (*b* ?Reims, *c.* 1300; *d* ?13 April 1377). French composer and poet. He was the most prolific and inventive poet and composer of his day. His texts and manuscripts characterize the taste of the royal court in mid-14th-century France. From *c.* 1323 to 1346 he was in the service of John of Luxembourg, King of Bohemia, after which he served members of the French royal family, among them Jean, Duc de Berry. Despite a peripatetic career, Machaut's chief home was in Reims, where he finally became a canon in 1337, and where the Dauphin, the future Charles V, had him sought from his house during a visit to the city in 1361.

Machaut's autobiographical poem *Voir-dit* (1362–5) shows his working methods. In his mature years at least, he dictated work to a secretary and could call on the services of copyists. Mention of Machaut's *Livre où je met toutes mes choses* in the poem appears to refer to a personal copy of his works, possibly partly in his own hand, that was unbound to facilitate copying, re-ordering and further additions. Miniatures showing the poet writing upon a roll refer to another means by which he transmitted texts, particularly suited for performance or reading aloud.

Seventeen 14th- and 15th-century manuscripts containing Machaut's works are known, of which seven contain his compositions alone. Three of these manuscripts were illuminated during Machaut's lifetime; the poet is presumed to have had some role in devising the sequence of illustrations for them. They are mostly the work of illuminators active in Paris, but one (Paris, Bib. N., MS. Fr. 1584) contains illuminations in a provincial style, possibly that of Reims, together with work by the hand of the Parisian illuminator the Master of the Boqueteaux; a rubric in the manuscript suggests that Machaut's instructions for its execution were being followed.

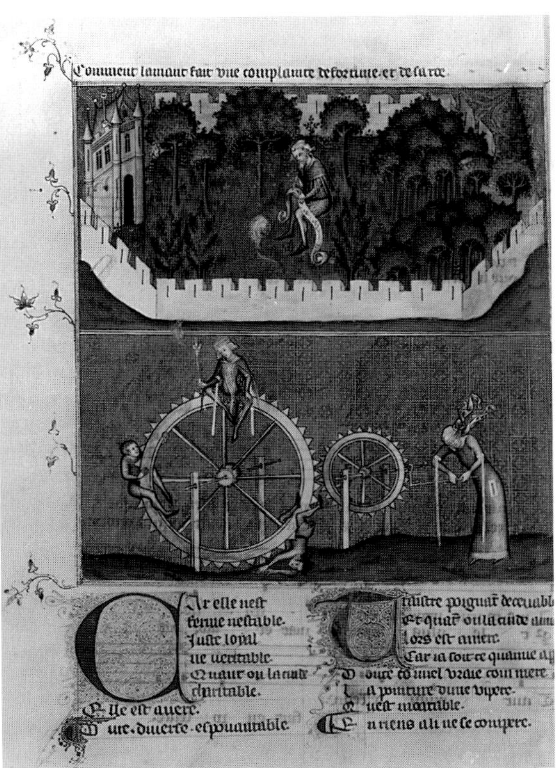

Manuscript by Guillaume de Machaut; *Poet in a Garden* and the *Wheel of Fortune* illuminations by the Remède de Fortune Master, *c.* 1350 (Paris, Bibliothèque Nationale, MS. Fr. 1586, fol. 30*v*)

The outstanding illuminated manuscript of Machaut's work (Paris, Bib. N., MS. Fr. 1586; *see* GOTHIC, fig. 84) is datable to *c.* 1350. The gatherings were distributed separately to three illuminators, the chief of whom is known as the Remède de Fortune Master, from the Machaut text he illustrated. The Remède de Fortune Master developed Jean Pucelle's interest in depicting spatial depth on the page, was notable for giving individual expressions to figures, here shown in outlandishly fashionable clothes carefully depicted (*see* DRESS, fig. 29), and promoted an empirically observed naturalism (see fig.). The Master was among the artists who illustrated the *Bible moralisée* of King John II, finished *c.* 1353 (Paris, Bib. N., MS. Fr. 167), and was responsible for the main illustrations in the St Denis Missal (1350; London, V&A, MS. 1346–1891). The second artist who worked on MS. Fr. 1586 can be identified as the Master of the Coronation Book of Charles V of *c.* 1365. He was also one of the five artists responsible for the other illuminated text of Machaut's works produced before the poet's death, the Voguë manuscript (New York, priv. col.), for which the Master of the Boquetaux and the Master of Charles V's Grandes Chroniques de France (named from the manuscript of *c.* 1380, Paris, Bib. N., MS. Fr. 2813) also provided miniatures.

WRITINGS

P. Paris, ed.: *Le Livre du voir-dit de Guillaume de Machaut* (Paris, 1875/*R* Geneva, 1969)

BIBLIOGRAPHY

A. Machabey: *Guillaume de Machaut, 130?–1377: La Vie et l'oeuvre musical*, 2 vols (Paris, 1955)
S. J. Williams: 'An Author's Role in Fourteenth Century Book Production: Guillaume de Machaut's *Livre où je met toutes mes choses*', *Romania*, xc (1969), pp. 433–54
F. Avril: *Manuscript Painting at the Court of France (1310–1380)* (London, 1978)
——: 'Les Manuscrits enluminés de Guillaume de Machaut', *Guillaume de Machaut. Colloque, table ronde: Reims, 1978* (Paris, 1982), pp. 117–83
E. Keitel: 'La Tradition manuscrite de Guillaume de Machaut', *Guillaume de Machaut. Colloque, table ronde: Reims, 1978* (Paris, 1982), pp. 75–94

ROWAN WATSON

Guillaume [Guglielmo] **de Marcillat** [Guillaume de Pierre] (*b* La Châtre, nr Bourges, 1467–70; *d* Arezzo, 30 July 1529). French stained-glass maker and painter, active in Italy. He was called to Rome before 1509, perhaps by Donato Bramante. Marcillat was employed by the popes Julius II and Leo X in the Vatican and at S Maria del Popolo, where the two Serlian windows in the choir are his earliest surviving works (1509; heavily rest.). Summoned to Cortona in 1515 by Cardinal Silvio Passerini, he established a workshop and began keeping a detailed account-book, which has survived; his prolific output there included a two-part window for the chancel of Cortona Cathedral, comprising the *Nativity* (1516; Detroit, MI, Inst. A., no. 37.138; *see* STAINED GLASS, fig. 5) and the *Adoration of the Magi* (London, V&A, no. 634.1902). Based in Arezzo by 1519, he produced the most skilfully executed windows of his age, notably the five splendidly illusionistic Gospel scenes, including the *Expulsion from the Temple* and the *Raising of Lazarus*, in Arezzo Cathedral (1519–24), a dramatic *Assumption* in SS Annunziata (1520) and an oculus in S Francesco (1524; all *in situ*). Traces of interior decoration remain (Cherici). His biblical frescoes in the vault of Arezzo Cathedral (1521–6) reflect the latest works in the Vatican by Michelangelo and Raphael and are painted in a style that Marcillat passed on to his pupil Giorgio Vasari. His panel paintings include an extraordinary *Disputation on Original Sin* (Berlin, Bodemus.) from S Francesco, Arezzo, and an *Annunciation and Four Saints* (Arezzo, Convent of Sargiano), originally from S Margherita.

By breaking the traditional division between design and glazing, Marcillat revitalized the production of stained glass and the status of its painters in 16th-century Italy, while his use of French glass enabled him to convey an unusual degree of nuance to his vivid figures.

BIBLIOGRAPHY

G. Vasari: *Vite* (1550, rev. 2/1568); ed. G. Milanesi (1878–85), iv, pp. 417–30
G. Mancini: *Guglielmo de Marcillat* (Florence, 1909) [fundamental documentary monograph]
S. Atherly: 'Marcillat's Cortona *Nativity*', *Bull. Detroit Inst. A.*, lviii (1980), pp. 72–82
——: *Studien zu den Glasfenstern Guillaume de Marcillat (1470?–1529)* (diss., U. Vienna, 1981) [stylistic analysis of windows; in Eng.]
Giorgio Vasari (exh. cat. by A. M. Maetzke, Arezzo, S Francesco, 1981), pp. 321–2; pls 225–7
A. Luchs: 'Stained Glass above Renaissance Altars: Figural Windows in Italian Church Architecture from Brunelleschi to Bramante', *Z. Kstgesch.*, xlviii (1985), pp. 177–224 (205–18)
N. Dacos: 'Un "Romaniste" français méconnu: Guillaume de Marcillat', *'Il se rendit en Italie': Etudes offertes à André Chastel* (Rome and Paris, 1987), pp. 135–47

A. Tafi: *Il sole racchiuso nei vetri: Guglielmo de Marcillat e le sue vetrate istoriate di Arezzo* (Arezzo, 1988) [good for colour illus.]
T. Henry: *'Il priore depentore': Guillaume de Marcillat at the Cathedral, Arezzo* (MA diss., U. London, Courtauld Inst., 1989)
A. Cherici: *Dalla Compagnia della Trinità all'Arciconfraternita della Misericordia* (Arezzo, 1990), pp. 7, 10–12
G. Virde: 'Le vetrate della chiesa della SS Annunziata in Arezzo', *Atti del convegno di studi su la chiesa della SS Annunziata di Arezzo nel 500° della sua costruzione: Arezzo, 1990*, pp. 169–223
T. Henry: ' "Centro e periferia": Guillaume de Marcillat and the Modernisation of Taste in the Cathedral of Arezzo', *Artibus & Hist.* (1994), no. 29, pp. 55–83

FRANK DABELL

Guillaume Julien (*fl* Paris, 1298; *d* ?Paris, *c.* 1316). French goldsmith. He is documented principally in the royal accounts of Philip IV, but no authenticated work by him survives. His atelier was on the Grand Pont in Paris, and his sons may also have been active there because they became proprietors after his death. In 1298 he was paid for a reliquary of St Louis (destr. after 1392) for the Sainte-Chapelle, Paris. Payments for the head reliquary of St Louis (destr. 1791) began the following year. The frontispiece engraving to Du Cange's edition of Jean de Joinville's *Histoire de S Louys IX* (1688), the only visual record of a work by Guillaume Julien to survive, shows the crowned and jewelled bust of repoussé gold only to the shoulders. Inventory descriptions show, however, that it was supported by four silver-gilt angels, holding attributes and standing on a base decorated with rosettes framing images of the 32 kings of France from Clovis to Philip IV. Champlevé inscriptions recorded their names at the top and Philip's gift and Julien's work at the bottom. The orphrey of the Saint was embellished with flowers formed of gems and *émaux de plique*. Guillaume Julien also restored objects at the Sainte-Chapelle and created many luxury items for Philip IV, including 28 fruit plates, spice and sauce dishes and other unspecified objects.

The most plausible attribution to Guillaume Julien is the *émail de plique* petal (Paris, Bib. N. Cab. Médailles) thought to have decorated the orphrey of the bust reliquary of St Denis. Two triangular pieces (Paris, Bib. N. Cab. Médailles) are also attributed to him; their shape corresponds to inventory descriptions of the altar frontal of the Sainte-Chapelle, which must have been made during the time that Guillaume Julien was active. Enlart proposed that the most prominent *émaux de plique* produced *c.* 1300 should also be attributed to him, including a hanap cover (Oxford, All Soul's Coll.), which may have been a wedding gift from the King. Enlart hypothesized that the high sums paid by Philip IV to Guillaume Julien from 1308 corresponded to commissions for the marriage of his daughter to Edward I of England in 1308; this may be supported by Philip's documented gift of a reliquary of the Cross to Notre-Dame, Boulogne, and the survival there of a reliquary of the Holy Blood with *émail de plique* similar to the medallions in the Cabinet des Médailles. Although Guillaume Julien's name has become almost synonymous with *émail de plique*, he was only one of several contemporary goldsmiths who created these precious enamels.

BIBLIOGRAPHY

A. Vidier: 'Le Trésor de la Sainte-Chapelle', *Mém. Soc. Hist. Paris & Ile-de-France*, xxxiv, pp. 199–324; xxxv, pp. 189–339; xxxvi, pp. 245–395 (276–81); xxxvii, pp. 185–369
C. Enlart: 'L'Emaillerie cloisonnée à Paris sous Philippe le Bel et le maître Guillaume Julien', *Mnmts Piot*, xxix (1927–8), pp. 1–97
B. de Montesquiou-Fezensac and D. Gaborit-Chopin: *Le Trésor de Saint-Denis*, iii (Paris, 1977), pp. 16–17, 108–11

BARBARA DRAKE BOEHM

Guillaumet, Gustave(-Achille) (*b* Paris, 25 March 1840; *d* Paris, 14 March 1887). French painter and writer. He was a student of François-Edouard Picot, Alexandre Abel de Pujol and Félix Barrias. After failing to win the Prix de Rome in historical landscape in 1861, he impulsively visited Algeria the following year; this journey, which he repeated ten times, determined his development as an Orientalist painter. He was a regular exhibitor at the Salon from 1861 where his combination of picturesque realism and academic composition was positively received by the State as illustrative of its Algerian policies (e.g. *Evening Prayer in the Sahara*, 1863; Paris, Mus. d'Orsay).

The Sahara (1867; Paris, Mus. d'Orsay), which depicts a camel skeleton in a desolate desert landscape, is an important 19th-century example of *vanitas* painting and evinces a philosophical strain in Guillaumet's work. In the *Labours* series (1869–76) he brought out the poetic quality of the remote duars of Algeria and imbued his Orientalism with unusual naturalistic touches. After 1878 his incisive social observations (e.g. the *'Seguia', Biskra*, 1884; Paris, Mus. d'Orsay) and careful study of the Saharan light placed him with Léon Belly among the most authentic Orientalist painters of their generation. Guillaumet's writings, notably *Tableaux algériens* (1888), belong to the travel-writing tradition of Eugène Fromentin. He was also a sensitive pastellist. He exerted a considerable posthumous influence over members of the Société des Peintres Orientalistes Français, which was formed in 1893.

WRITINGS

Tableaux algériens (Paris, 1888)

BIBLIOGRAPHY

A. Badin: 'Gustave Guillaumet', *L'Art*, xliv (1888), pp. 3–13, 39–45, 53–60
L. Bénédite: 'La Peinture orientaliste et Gustave Guillaumet', *Nouv. Rev.*, l (1888), pp. 326–42
Gustave Guillaumet (exh. cat., Paris, Ecole N. Sup. B.-A., 1888)
Gustave Guillaumet (exh. cat., Paris, Gal. Durand-Ruel, 1899)
L. Thornton: *Les Orientalistes: Peintres voyageurs, 1828–1908* (Paris, 1983), pp. 146–9

ANNE-MARIE DELAGE

Guillaumin, (Jean-Baptiste-)Armand (*b* Paris, 16 Feb 1841; *d* Paris, 26 June 1927). French painter and lithographer. He grew up in Moulins, but at 16 he returned to Paris to find work. Despite the opposition of his working-class family, he prepared for an artistic career while he supported himself in municipal jobs. He started drawing classes and then enrolled in the Académie Suisse, where he met Cézanne and Camille Pissarro. Guillaumin began his career as an avant-garde artist by exhibiting with them at the Salon des Refusés in 1863. He was also active in the Manet circle at the Café Guerbois, from which Impressionism developed.

Guillaumin developed his landscape style painting outdoors in the environs of Paris while employed on the Paris–Orléans railway. He frequently painted labourers and barges along the quays of the Seine, for example *Quai de la Rapée* (1879; Paris, priv. col.). Like Pissarro he empathized with the working-classes, and he influenced Seurat, Signac and their Neo-Impressionist followers towards depicting industrial settings. Guillaumin's painting style of the 1860s, like Cézanne's, was inspired by the naturalism and materiality of Courbet's paintings. Dense paint applied in thick strokes, sombre colours and heavy outlines are seen in his *Sunset at Ivry* (1869; Paris, Mus. d'Orsay). The works of the following decade, mostly landscapes, show a lightened palette and small touches of the brush. In the early 1870s Guillaumin worked with Pissarro at Pontoise and also with Cézanne and Dr Gachet at Auvers, where Daubigny also lived and worked. Guillaumin's mature Impressionist style, combining pictorial structure and shimmering light, evolved from his contacts with these artists and their shared aesthetic premises. His extensive work in pastel also contributed to the development of the spontaneous brushstroke which builds form as it captures light. The *Reclining Nude* (1876; Paris, Mus. d'Orsay) and the *Seine at Paris* (1871; Houston, TX, Mus. F.A.) exemplify Guillaumin's use of the constructive brushstroke. The artist's expressive use of colour, which transcends nature in its vibrant harmonies, is also characteristic of his style in the 1870s. He contributed to all but two of the Impressionist exhibitions, showing in 1874, 1877, 1880, 1881, 1882 and 1886.

In the 1880s, like his Impressionist colleagues, Guillaumin experimented with new pictorial techniques to convey a more personal expression of mood and feeling. He used heightened colour, favouring the effects of early morning light or the drama of sunset skies, composing harmonies from complementaries of orange-red and blue-green, purple and green or mauve and yellow. The *Road in the Valley* (1885; Paris, Mus. A. Mod. Ville Paris) and *Twilight at Damiette* (1885; Geneva, Petit Pal.) are typical paintings of this period which inspired critics such as J.-K. Huysmans to call Guillaumin a 'furious colourist', and Félix Fénéon to remark on his 'super-heated skies'.

Guillaumin's passionate response to nature impressed Vincent van Gogh who became his friend in Paris in 1886–7, while Theo van Gogh assisted Guillaumin with sales of his works. Guillaumin's personal fortunes improved with his marriage to a professor in a prestigious school for young women. He expanded his travels from the Ile de France to the central regions and Provence. In 1891 he won a state lottery of 100,000 francs, which allowed him to retire from government service and to devote himself wholly to painting. His extensive travels are reflected in landscapes of France and the Netherlands. Such paintings as *Rocks at Agay* (1893; Paris, priv. col., see Serret and Fabiani, pl. 233) are emblematic of rugged aspects of nature in their bold simplification and strong colour contrasts. They share the primitive spirit of Gauguin and his Pont Aven followers and directly prefigure the intensity of Fauvism. Guillaumin's work continued to show strength and individual character, developing the innovations of Impressionism in a modernist spirit. In 1896 Ambroise Vollard published a suite of his lithographs.

BIBLIOGRAPHY

Exposition Armand Guillaumin (exh. cat., pref. A. Alexandre; Paris, Gal. Durand-Ruel, 1924)

G. Lecomte: *Guillaumin* (Paris, 1926)

P. Gachet: *Lettres impressionnistes au Dr Gachet et à Murer* (Paris, 1957), pp. 63–78

G. Serret and D. Fabiani: *Armand Guillaumin: Catalogue raisonné de l'oeuvre peint* (Paris, 1971)

C. Gray: *Armand Guillaumin* (Chester, CT, 1972)

J. Rewald: *The History of Impressionism* (New York, rev. 4/1973)

Centenaire de l'impressionnisme et hommage à Guillaumin (exh. cat., Geneva, Petit Pal., 1974)

The New Painting: Impressionism, 1874–1886 (exh. cat., ed. C. Moffatt; Washington, DC, N.G.A.; San Francisco, F.A. Museums; 1986), pp. 128, 365, 400, 459

TAUBE G. GREENSPAN

Guillemer, Jean. *See under* JEAN DE LAVAL.

Guillemet, (Jean-Baptiste-)Antoine (*b* Chantilly, 30 June 1841; *d* Dordogne, 19 May 1918). French painter. He came from a wealthy family of ship-owners and ship-chandlers based in Rouen. His boyhood wish to become a sailor was opposed by his parents in favour of law studies, which Guillemet soon abandoned to take up painting full-time in Paris. After meeting Corot through the Morisot sisters in 1861–2, he remained throughout his career a devoted friend and admirer of the artist. During the early 1860s he made sketching trips with Charles-François Daubigny and Daubigny's son Karl Pierre, and he began a lifelong friendship with Manet, who immortalized Guillemet's tall, handsome figure in *The Balcony* (1869; Paris, Mus. d'Orsay). Guillemet also studied at the Académie Suisse, where he met Pissarro, Cézanne and, through the latter, Zola. Although Guillemet made his début at the Salon in 1865 with the *Pond at Bât (Isère)* (untraced), the 1860s were, in general, an unsettled time of experiment and travel. He lived and worked with Pissarro, Courbet and Cézanne and became the intimate friend and correspondent of Zola. Their correspondence gives fascinating insights into the interaction of influences between writer and painter.

In 1872, after serving in the Gardes Mobiles during the Siege of Paris, Guillemet exhibited *Low Tide at Villerville* (Grenoble, Mus. Peint. & Sculp.), which depicts a Normandy coastal village near the mouth of the Seine. It was purchased by Charles Blanc, director of the *Gazette des beaux-arts*. With this painting, Guillemet had reached his maturity and settled successfully to the style and subject-matter to which he devoted the remainder of his energetic and productive life. His favourite motifs were drawn from the beaches and countryside of Normandy, especially the Cotentin, riverside villages, usually along the Seine, and, less frequently, Paris. The capital was, however, the subject of a remarkable series of large-scale canvases, beginning with *Bercy in December* (exh. Salon 1874; Paris, Pal.-Bourbon), which was purchased by the Musée du Luxembourg. In a letter to Zola in 1896, relating to a now lost panorama of Paris, Guillemet explained how he had been inspired by the writer's description of Paris in *Une Page d'amour* (Paris, 1871). Although Guillemet gave encouragement to the Impressionists in 1874, the year of their first group exhibition, he preferred success in the Salon and fidelity to the teachings of Corot. The pattern of his life was established with sociable winters in Paris and summers in Normandy. His work sold well, although his independent means had always freed him from reliance on sales. Salon exhibits continued to attract critical acclaim, and he served as a member of the Salon jury. In 1882 he used the jury members' privilege of having their pupils admitted to the Salon to enable Cézanne to exhibit his work there. Cézanne's name subsequently appeared in the Salon catalogue with the description 'pupil of Guillemet'.

In 1910 Guillemet became a commandant of the Légion d'honneur, a very rare instance of a landscape painter reaching this rank. The purchase *c.* 1883 of a property at Moret-sur-Loing, near the junction of the Loing and the Seine, afforded the artist many tranquil river landscapes, of which one of the first exhibited examples was the *Loing, at Moret* (exh. Salon 1891; untraced). From about 1912 until the end of his life he lived and worked in the Dordogne, finding refuge there during World War I. Guillemet was largely forgotten within a decade of his death, and his work was not re-examined until the 1970s. He was a minor master of traditional landscape painting, with an individual style and a sound painterly technique. His work is uneven but, at its best, atmospheric and highly competent.

UNPUBLISHED SOURCES

Paris, Bib. N. [corr. between Guillemet and Zola]

WRITINGS

Notes, Paris, Bib. N.

R. Baligand, ed.: 'Lettres inédites d'Antoine Guillemet à Emile Zola (1870–1886)', *Cah. Naturalistes*, 52 (1978), pp. 173–205

Désir de rivage: De Granville à Dieppe (exh. cat., Caen, Mus. B.-A., 1994)

Landscapes of France: Impressionism and its Rivals (exh. cat., London, Hayward Gal., 1994)

Monet to Matisse: Landscape Painting in France, 1874–1914 (exh. cat., Edinburgh, N.G., 1994)

BIBLIOGRAPHY

P. Mitchell: *Jean Baptiste Antoine Guillemet* (London, 1981) [with complete bibliog.]

PETER MITCHELL

Guillén, Asilia (*b* Granada, Nicaragua, 1887; *d* Granada, 1964). Nicaraguan painter and embroiderer. Born to a prominent family in the old city of Granada, she was given a patrician education that emphasized embroidery and music as the arts proper to her station. For several decades she practised embroidery, gradually replacing the traditional formal elements and conventional subjects such as decorative floral motifs with landscapes and scenes from Nicaraguan history conveyed in a broad range of colour.

The growing national fame of Guillén's embroidery led her to take up oil painting in 1951 at the suggestion of a friend, the poet Enrique Fernández Morales. She studied under Rodrigo Peñalba at the Escuela Nacional de Bellas Artes in Managua but quickly arrived at a distinctive style of naive art by transposing the style and subject-matter of her embroidery to brightly coloured and richly detailed oil paintings that won the admiration of leading literary figures such as Ernesto Cardenal and Pablo Antonio Cuadra, for example *Rafaela Herrera Defends the Castle Against the Pirates* (1962; Washington, DC, MOMA Latin America). Typical of her mixture of fact and fantasy, of epic vision and modest scale, is *Heroes and Artists Come to the Pan-American Union to be Consecrated* (1962; Washington, DC, MOMA Latin America; *see* NICARAGUA, fig. 3), painted to commemorate her successful exhibition of 1962 at the gallery of the Pan American Union in Washington, DC. Her art was a significant precedent for the Solentiname primitivist painting, which flourished in Nicaragua after the Sandinista Revolution in 1979.

BIBLIOGRAPHY

E. Fernández Morales: 'Doña Asilia, pintora primitivista', *Pez & Serpiente*, 2 (Aug 1961), pp. 89–95

J. Gómez-Sicre: 'Embroidery in Oils: Asilia Guillén of Nicaragua', *Américas*, xiv/10 (1962), pp. 17–20

J. Valle-Castillo: 'El inventario del paraíso: Los primitivistas de Nicaragua', *Nicaráuac*, 12 (April 1986), pp. 161–75

DAVID CRAVEN

Guillet de Saint-Georges [Guillet, Georges] (*b* Thiers, Puy-de-Dôme, *c.* 1624; *d* Paris, 16 April 1705). French writer and stage designer. He began his career as a stage designer for the actors at the Hôtel de Bourgogne, Paris. His first important work was *Athènes ancienne et nouvelle* (1675), an account of the history and customs of Athens. Although he claimed that this work was an account of the travels of his brother La Guilletière, in fact it relied on missionaries' letters and a large measure of the author's imagination, and it brought furious criticism from the antiquary Jacob Spon. However, although often inaccurate, the work contains interesting material on social institutions. The sequel, *Lacédémone ancienne et nouvelle* (1676), is even more fantastic. He followed this success with *Les Arts de l'homme d'épée, ou: Dictionnaire du gentil'homme* (1676), a manual of the manners of polite society, which reached its definitive form in the fifth edition (1686) and was also successful. In 1682, in unknown circumstances, Guillet de Saint-Georges was appointed historiographer of the Académie Royale de Peinture, his duties being to record speeches and to describe the works of art submitted for approval, particularly to elucidate the more obscure points of allegory. Towards the end of 1689 he began to write the eulogies, which he called 'mémoires historiques', of deceased members. Among the artists whose obituaries he wrote were Jacques Sarrazin, Eustache Le Sueur, Charles Errard *le fils*, Claude Vignon, Sébastien Bourdon, Philippe de Champaigne and Jean-Baptiste de Champaigne, Nicolas-Pierre Loir, Laurent de La Hyre and finally Charles Le Brun. These notices were compiled from documentation supplied by the artists' families and from the archives of the Académie, and thus provide the most valuable and reliable source for many of the painters who died in the 1690s.

WRITINGS

La Guilletière [Guillet de Saint-Georges]: *Athènes ancienne et nouvelle* (Paris, 1675, rev. 3/1676)

Les Arts de l'homme d'épée, ou: Dictionnaire du gentil'homme, 3 vols (Paris, 1676, rev. The Hague, 5/1686)

Lacédémone ancienne et nouvelle (Paris, 1676)

L. Dussieux, ed.: *Mémoires inédits sur la vie et les ouvrages des membres de l'Académie Royale de Peinture et de Sculpture*, 2 vols (Paris, 1854)

BIBLIOGRAPHY

Michaud

□

Guillielmus. *See* GUGLIELMO.

Guilloche. Plait-like ornament. There are several variants; for example the spaces between the bands may be blank or may contain flower motifs (see fig.). It occurs often in Greek and Roman art: in particular, convex mouldings decorated with this pattern are found in all periods on Greek and Roman architecture and in the borders of

Types of guilloche

Roman mosaics. Guilloche decoration was revived in the Renaissance and from then onwards occurs in different media, notably in art and architecture of the Neo-classical revival.

MARGARET LYTTELTON

Guilmard, Désiré (*fl* 1839; *d* Paris, *c.* 1889). French publisher and furniture designer. He was an important disseminator of historical and contemporary designs in 19th-century France. After 1839 he published a constant stream of lithograph designs for furniture, both his own designs and illustrations of the products of commercial firms, which provide an important source for the study of furniture of the period. His chief work was the journal *Le Garde-meuble ancien et moderne*, which he edited from 1844 to 1882. After 1846 he also published a supplement, *L'Ameublement et l'utilité*, which soon merged with the parent publication: lithographic designs of seat furniture, case furniture and hangings were reproduced, aimed at both tradesmen and clients. The plates also include general views of interiors and plans of furniture layouts, which give a comprehensive view of the development of styles. Guilmard produced albums recording the furniture shown at the Expositions Universelles of 1844, 1849 and 1855 in Paris and a long series of albums showing designs for particular types of furniture, woodwork fittings or upholstery. He was an important figure in the developing study of historical ornament and design: as early as 1848 he published *Connaissance du style de l'ornementation depuis l'ère chrétienne jusqu'à nos jours*, but his best-known work, *Les Maîtres ornemanistes*, a collection of French, Italian, German and Netherlandish engravings for design, was published in 1880.

BIBLIOGRAPHY

J. Adhémar: *Inventaire du fonds français après 1800*, Paris. Bib. N., Cab. Est. cat. (Paris, 1958)

S. Jervis: *Dictionary of Design and Designers* (London, 1984)

SARAH MEDLAM

Guimarães. Portuguese town, with a population in the late 20th century of *c.* 12,000. It was founded in the 10th century by the Countess Mumadona and became the capital of Portucale, which formed the nucleus of the kingdom of Portugal when it won independence from Castile and León in the 12th century. Most of the art, architecture and layout of Guimarães date from the medieval period. Its most important buildings are the castle and the Romanesque church of S Miguel (both 12th century). Examples of Gothic conventual architecture include the collegiate church of Nossa Senhora da Oliveira (1387–93; Romanesque cloister and chapterhouse now Mus. Alberto Sampaio), which was the first Gothic building in the Minho; S Domingos (late 14th century; now Mus. Arqueol. Martins Sarmento); and S Francisco (1400; mostly rebuilt). Near the castle is the palace of the dukes of Braganza (begun *c.* 1400), which shows Italian and French influences. Several 14th- and 15th-century houses are found along the Rua de S Maria. The Renaissance Casa da Torre (mid-16th century) and Misericórdia Church (from 1588) define the space of the Largo João Franco Castelo-Branco amid the medieval network of streets; this leads to the Largo do Toural with several striking 17th-century houses and some 18th-century houses with porches. In the Baroque period a number of churches, convents and mansions were built or rebuilt: S Clara (1746); Domínicas (1725); Casa dos Lobos Machados (1750–60); Santos Passos Church (from 1769; altered 19th century), by André Ribeiro Soares da Silva; and Vila Flor. New interiors of *talha* (carved and polychromed wood) and *azulejos* (glazed tiles) were added to medieval churches, of which the most notable example is S Francisco. There was also considerable urban development, with expansion and the creation of new axial roads. The Pombaline architecture in the Largo do Toural was influenced by that of Oporto and Lisbon.

BIBLIOGRAPHY

A. Guimarães: *Azulejos artísticos de Guimarães* (Guimarães, n.d.)

S. Viterbo: *Artistas e artífices de Guimarães* (Oporto, 1807)

A. J. Ferreira Caldas: *Guimarães: Apontamentos para a sua história* (Porto, 1881)

A. Belino: *Archeologia cristã: Descripção histórica de todas as igrejas, capellas, oratórios, cruzeiros e outros monumentos de Braga e Guimarães* (Lisbon, 1900)

A. Guimarães: *Guimarães monumental*, A Arte em Portugal, xi (Oporto, 1930)

J. M. Gomes Alves: *Património artístico e cultural de Guimarães*, 2 vols (Guimarães, 1981–6)

F. Gonçalves: *A talha na arte religiosa de Guimarães* (Guimarães, 1982)

F. Távora: *Guimarães do passado e do presente* (Guimarães, 1985)

EDUARDO DUARTE

Guimard, (Gilles) Barnabé (*b c.* 1734; *d* Paris, 1792). French architect and urban planner, active in the southern Netherlands. He trained under Jacques-François Blondel and Anges-Jacques Gabriel and worked as a draughtsman for JEAN FAULTE. His major work was carried out in Brussels, where he was commissioned to execute a scheme drawn up in 1775 by Jean-Benoît-Vincent Barré for laying out a square, the Place Royale, on the site of the old ducal palace (destr. 1731). It is not known to what extent Guimard amended Barré's proposals, but the Neo-classical scheme resembles the Place Royale (1755) in Reims designed by Nicolas Legendre, which was itself based on the Place Royale, Nancy. The houses surrounding the symmetrical square are designed as an ensemble with rusticated arcades surmounted by two storeys articulated by pilaster-strips. Side streets enter on three of the four sides, with an attempt made to maintain the sense of enclosure by closing them off with gates in the style of a triumphal arch. Inserted in the centre of the uniform façades of the south-east side of the square is the church of St Jacques-sur-Coudenberg, built by Louis-Joseph Montoyer in 1785–6 to Barré's and Guimard's designs. It is faced with a hexastyle Corinthian portico, and the Neo-classical theme is continued inside with the use of Ionic and Corinthian columns; the nave is barrel-vaulted. The heavy domed lantern is an addition of 1847. An equestrian statue of the Governor of the Netherlands, *Prince Charles of Lorraine* (destr. 1794), by Peter Anton von Verschaffelt was placed in the centre of the square.

From 1773 Guimard cooperated with the Austrian architect Bartholomäus Zinner (*fl* 1720–74) on designs for the adjoining Parc de Bruxelles (the former hunting-ground of the dukes of Brabant). The park has a rectangular plan and long perspectives; one of its diagonals is a continuation of the central axis of the Place Royale. Guimard built a palace for the Council of Brabant (1778–83; now the Palais de la Nation) on the short north side of the park, with a modest Corinthian portico. The long sides of the park are lined with subtly modulated terraces of houses designed by Guimard. The orderly layout of his urban planning was highly influential in Brussels, serving as a continuing example for future expansion schemes, particularly in the 19th century.

Among Guimard's most highly acclaimed buildings is the castle of Wannegem-Lede (1783–6), near Oudenaarde, which was strongly influenced by the Petit Trianon, Versailles. Other works include a castle near Laeken and, in Ghent, a fountain in the Hoogstraat and a side portal (1782) for the cathedral.

BIBLIOGRAPHY

R. van Luttervelt: 'De bouwkunst in de zuidelijke Nederlanden in de 17e en 18e eeuw', *Kunstgeschiedenis der Nederlanden*, ed. J. Duverger (Utrecht, 1956)

H. Gerson and E. H. Ter Kuile: *Art and Architecture in Belgium, 1600–1800*, Pelican Hist. A. (London, 1960)

J. van Ackere: *Baroque and Classic Art in Belgium* (Brussels, 1972)

Le Patrimoine monumental de la Belgique, Ministère de la Culture Française (in preparation) [vol. i to contain details of the Place Royale, Brussels]

RENÉE VAN DER VLOODT

Guimard, Hector(-Germain) (*b* Lyon, 1867; *d* New York, 20 May 1942). French architect, furniture designer and writer. After attending the Ecole Nationale des Arts Décoratifs in Paris, in 1885 he entered the Ecole des Beaux-Arts; he left four years later without a diploma, however, to work for a builder as both architect and site craftsman. The influence of Eugène-Emmanuel Viollet-le-Duc is evident in his early works, particularly the Ecole du Sacré-Coeur (1895), in which the exposed cast-iron structure of V-shaped columns is an adaptation of a drawing taken from Viollet-le-Duc's *Entretiens sur l'architecture* (1863–72). These early commissions, built in a picturesque and eclectic manner, culminated in the Castel Béranger block of flats, Paris, where his first use of the ART NOUVEAU style appeared in its decorative elements. He visited Brussels in 1895, where he met Victor Horta, whose Maison du Peuple was then under construction. After seeing Horta's work Guimard made changes to the original neo-Gothic decorative elements of the Castel Béranger, introducing a colourful mixture of facing materials and organically derived embellishments, based on his belief that decoration is the more effective for being non-representational. Between 1899 and 1914 Guimard's style matured to a full-blooded Art Nouveau, although he also continued his picturesque manner in suburban villas, such as the Castel Henriette (1899), Sèvres, and the chalet La Surprise (1903), Cabourg, in which boldly projecting eaves protect large areas of fenestration, and solid walls consist of random rubble and ornate half-timbering.

In 1896 Guimard entered the competition to design Paris Métro stations, failing to win but getting the job because the railway company's president was attracted to the Art Nouveau style. He designed three types of station: a basic open one with steps and railings; another with enclosed and covered steps; and a third with complete pavilions. The first type, of which *c.* 90 survive, was fashioned in various forms, the most interesting of which consists of railings with decorated 'shields' incorporating the letter M and an iron arch over the entrance which supports an enamelled sign flanked by 'stalks' blossoming into lamps (e.g. Cité, 1898–1901; for illustration *see* METRO STATION). The second type, for example Abbesses in Montmartre, consists of an iron frame with decorated enamelled lava panels and translucent wired glass; a 'butterfly' glass roof, supported from a central girder, oversails the enclosure. The third type, of which only Porte Dauphine survives, provides waiting-rooms and has an enclosure like the second type but with more ample entrance arches and a roof consisting of tiered pyramidal sections reminiscent of covered market structures. The stations, which were modular and conceived for mass-production, were in production until 1913. Together with the Humbert de Romans auditorium (1897–1901; destr. 1905), an enormous concert hall and chapel with elaborate decorations and fittings, they represented the most complete architectural expression of Art Nouveau in France.

During this period Guimard also designed a number of town houses and blocks of flats. At his own house, 122, Avenue Mozart, Paris, which he built and furnished after marrying the American painter Adeline Oppenheim (*b* ?1872) in 1909, he achieved a synthesis in its furnishings and décor which he was never to surpass (examples New York, MOMA). The first-floor plan, with its delightful relationship of two ovals, harks back to the French Rococo tradition. The Jassedé flats (1905) at 142 Avenue de Versailles, Paris, with their free but vigorous corner treatment, were also the occasion for Guimard to launch into the design of standardized cast-iron fittings, such as guttering and garden seats (examples Paris, Mus. d'Orsay), later advertised in a catalogue (*Fontes artistiques*, 1907) as standard and available to order. His work from 1919 to 1929 marked his decline as an architect and furniture designer. After World War I he found it difficult to associate himself with the new Rationalism, even though his housing projects were based on a standardized system of dry concrete block construction and prefabricated elements. The apartment block (1925) at 18 Rue Henri

Heine, Paris, his best post-war work, became his own last home in Paris. He appears to have built nothing after 1929 and in 1939 he and his wife moved to New York.

WRITINGS

Le Castel Béranger: L'Art dans l'habitation moderne (Paris, 1898)
'An Architect's Opinion of "l'Art Nouveau"', *Archit. Rec.*, xii (1902), pp. 127–33
Fontes artistiques pour constructions, fumisterie, articles de jardins et sépultures, style Guimard (Paris, 1907)

BIBLIOGRAPHY

Hector Guimard (exh. cat. by F. Lanier Graham, New York, MOMA, 1970)
S. Cantacuzino: 'Hector Guimard', *The Anti-Rationalists*, ed. J. M. Richards and N. Pevsner (London, 1973)
G. Naylor and Y. Brunhammer: *Hector Guimard* (London, 1978)

SHERBAN CANTACUZINO

Guimerá, Conde de. *See* GURREA Y ARAGÓN, (2).

Guimet, Emile (*b* Lyon, 2 June 1836; *d* Fleurieu, Rhône, 12 Oct 1918). French industrialist, collector, museum founder and writer. He was the son of Jean-Baptiste Guimet (*d* 1871), the inventor of artificial ultramarine blue, and he worked in his father's factory from the age of 23. Spurred by his interest in theatre, dance and Asian religions, Guimet began to travel widely, publishing accounts of his journeys, and in 1876 he undertook a research mission sponsored by the Ministère de l'Instruction Publique to study world religions. For six months he travelled in Japan, China, Ceylon (now Sri Lanka) and India, bringing back silk paintings, engravings, sculpture in wood and stone, books and illuminated manuscripts. On his return to France he formed a plan, probably inspired by the principles of the Smithsonian Institution in Washington, DC, to create an institution devoted to Asian arts and culture comprising a museum, a library and a public lecture hall, together with a programme of regular publication of both scholarly and popular works on related topics. The Musée Guimet opened in Lyon in 1879.

In 1884, Guimet decided to donate his collections and his personal library to the French State, and when a new Musée Guimet opened, in the Place d'Iéna, Paris, in 1888, it was an instant popular success. Guimet's library of around 13,000 volumes was increased by many publications commissioned by the museum under the generic heading of 'Annales du Musée Guimet', including the series Bibliothèque d'études and Bibliothèque de vulgarisation, as well as the journal *Revue des arts asiatiques.* The Musée Guimet in Paris became one of the Musées Nationaux in 1928 and in 1945, with the transfer of the national collection of East Asian art from the Louvre, became the Musée National des Arts Asiatiques, one of the most important museums of its kind in the world, with, among other items, sculpture from India and Gandhara, Pakistan, and from South-East Asia (including a very fine Khmer collection from Cambodia); bronzes and paintings from Nepal and Tibet; sculpture stuccoes, ivories and glassware from pre-Islamic Afghanistan; and archaic bronzes, sculptures, paintings, lacquerware and ceramics from Sino-Central Asia, China and Japan.

Guimet's role, typical of his time, was that of an energetic and imaginative collector and cultural enabler rather than that of a scholar and professional curator.

WRITINGS

Croquis égyptiens: Journal d'un touriste (Paris, 1867)
Bonjour Kanagawa, illus. F. Régamey (Paris, 1876); Jap. trans. (Tokyo, 1977)
Rapport au Ministre de l'Instruction Publique et des Beaux-Arts sur la mission scientifique de M. Emile Guimet dans l'Extrême-Orient (Lyon, 1878)
Promenades japonaises, illus. F. Régamey, 2 vols (Paris, 1878–80); Jap. trans. (Tokyo, 1982)
Le Jubilé du Musée Guimet: 25ème anniversaire de sa fondation, 1879–1904 (Paris, 1904)
Cinquantenaire: 1er janvier 1860–1er janvier 1910 (Paris, 1910)

JEANNINE AUBOYER

Guindaleri, Pietro (*b* Cremona; *fl* 1464–1506). Italian illuminator. There is no evidence for his activity in Cremona, but like his almost exact contemporary, the Paduan painter Andrea Mantegna, Guindaleri was a lifelong court artist of the Gonzaga at Mantua. In a letter of 30 November 1489 to Francesco II Gonzaga, the artist stated that he had entered the service of the Marquis's grandfather, Ludovico, 25 years earlier, in 1464. Probably one of the first books that he decorated for the Gonzaga is the copy of Boccaccio's *Il filocolo* (Oxford, Bodleian Lib., MS. Canon. Italiani 85), the text of which was scheduled to be completed for Marquis Ludovico at the beginning of 1464. Its miniature of *Horsemen in a Piazza* (fol. 114*v*) includes foreshortened horses of a type that derives ultimately from the work of Pisanello, Mantegna's predecessor as court painter to the Gonzaga. Comparisons have also been drawn between the miniatures in the Oxford Boccaccio and the frescoes painted around 1470 in the Palazzo Schifanoia at Ferrara.

The miniatures by Guindaleri in the copy of Petrarch's *Canzoniere* and *Trionfi* (London, BL, Harley MS. 3567) are probably close in date to those in the Oxford Boccaccio. This manuscript, executed for Ludovico's son, Cardinal Francesco Gonzaga, was written by the scribe Matteo Contugi of Volterra, who in 1463–8 also wrote the text of the Turin Pliny, decorated years later by Guindaleri (see below). Its white-vine leaf and latticework borders are much more sober than the rich woven decoration on gold that frames the decorated pages of the Oxford manuscript. This suggests that the borders of one, or possibly both, books are not by Guindaleri. In the miniature of the *Triumph of Time* (fol. 184*r*) of the London Petrarch (see fig.), the rendering of the edge of the tiled piazza, which emphasizes the termination of pictorial space, recalls the practice of Jacopo Bellini in two of his Paris drawings (Paris, Louvre, fols 28*r* and 41*r*). Similarly, the archway in the miniature of the *Triumph of Cupid* (fol. 149*r*) is reminiscent of that in Bellini's drawing of the *Flagellation of Christ* (fol. 8*r*).

Papers in the Gonzaga archives indicate that in 1469 Guindaleri was designing patterns for brocade and between 1479 and 1484 decorated a large Book of Hours (untraced) for Francesco's brother Sigismondo (1469–1525). The copy of Pliny's *Natural History* (Turin, Bib. N.U., MSS. I-I, 22–3), on which Guindaleri was engaged between 1489 and 1506, includes several 'architectural text pages' of the type favoured by Paduan and Venetian illuminators. In these folios, the traditional relationship of decoration and script is abandoned and the text depicted as though it were inscribed on a placard fixed to a massive triumphal arch or similar antique monument. Even here,

Pietro Guindaleri: *Triumph of Time*, miniature from Petrarch: *Canzoniere* and *Trionfi* (London, British Library, Harley MS. 3567, fol. 184*r*)

towards the end of Guindaleri's career, the influence of Bellini recurred in the archway on folio 22*r*; its keystone carved in the form of a cupid is a device that occurs in the Paris drawings (fols 8*r* and 35*r*). In 1506, at the time of his death, Guindaleri was engaged on the decoration of a Pliny manuscript (untraced) for Francesco Gonzaga's wife, Isabella d'Este.

Mantegna's support of his follower, the illuminator Girolamo da Cremona, at the Mantuan court in 1461 is well known and it is probable that Mantegna was also involved in manuscript illumination. He doubtless found Guindaleri's classicizing miniatures congenial, but it would be incorrect to characterize the latter's style as 'Mantegnesque'. Guindaleri's general preference for monumental architectural settings peopled by tiny figures, as well as the derivation of spatial devices and specific motifs in the London Petrarch and the Turin Pliny, imply that he was a student of Bellini and a contemporary, rather than a follower, of Mantegna.

BIBLIOGRAPHY

A. Luzio: 'Isabella d'Este e Francesco Gonzaga promessi sposi', *Archv Stor. Lombardo*, ix (1908), pp. 59–60

U. Meroni: *Mostra dei codici gonzagheschi: La Biblioteca dei Gonzaga da Luigi I ad Isabella, 1328–1520* (Mantua, 1966), pp. 56–7, 80–81, pls 105–8

O. Pächt and J. J. G. Alexander: *Illuminated Manuscripts in the Bodleian Library, Oxford* (Oxford, 1966–73), ii, p. 40

G. M. Canova: *La miniatura veneta del rinascimento* (Venice, 1969), p. 147

Splendours of the Gonzaga (exh. cat., ed. D. S. Chambers and J. T. Martineau; London, V&A, 1981–2), pp. 112, 114–15

T. Kren, ed.: *Renaissance Painting in Manuscripts* (New York and London, 1983), pp. 96–8

B. Degenhart and A. Schmitt: *Jacopo Bellini: The Louvre Album of Drawings* (New York, 1984), pls 4, 31, 40, 48

MARK L. EVANS

Guinea, Republic of [République de Guinée]. Country in West Africa on the Atlantic coast, bordered by Guinea-Bissau and Senegal to the north, Mali to the north and east, Côte d'Ivoire to the east and south and Liberia and Sierra Leone to the south. The capital is Conakry. A French colony from 1891, Guinea became independent in 1958. A Marxist government subsequently came to power but was overthrown in a military coup in 1984. The population of 6,706,000 (UN estimate, 1989) comprises mainly Fula, Malinke and Susu peoples. The language of government is French. The country covers 245,857 sq. km, and the geography is varied and includes coastal marshlands, savannah, high mountains and forests. Guinea is rich in mineral resources, and this has encouraged industrial development; agriculturally, the country is less developed.

The area was settled early and became the political centre of the Mali Empire of the Malinke (Manding; 13th–15th centuries), with its capital at Niani. The Kissi, in the forest area, together with their Mel-speaking relatives found throughout southern Sierra Leone developed an important art-producing culture by the 14th century. By the 18th century the Fula of the Futa Jalou highlands had established a powerful Islamic theocratic hegemony while, from the 15th century, Portuguese and other Europeans working on the coast began to introduce Christianity along with new economic and cultural alliances. This entry covers the art produced in the area since colonial times. For art of the region in earlier periods *see* AFRICA, §VII, 3. *See also* BAGA, FULANI and KISSI.

Artistic activity in 20th-century Guinea can be divided into three regions: the savannah, the forest and the Atlantic coast. Throughout the savannah, dominated by the Islamic Fula, Malinke, Jalonke and Susu, the outstanding art forms are architecture, music, dance and body arts. The Fula of Guinea are noted for their huge, domed, fibre architecture and for their elaborate hairstyles. Susu dwellings often have wall paintings. The Malinke and Jalonke are well respected for their decorative leather work and their textiles. In the narrow forest region, the central organizing body is the men's Poro association. Poro masquerades involve a number of spirit representations incorporating small, wooden face masks, raffia costumes with cloth elaboration and a wealth of other items of regalia and costume. These masking traditions are part of a wider complex found also in Liberia and Côte d'Ivoire (*see* DAN, §2). The traditions of the Baga and other peoples of the Atlantic coastal area include large-scale wooden figurative sculpture, including drums, as well as horizontal animal masks, vertical superstructures and female bust headdresses, often painted in brightly coloured patterns. A fourth, isolated, artistic tradition, consisting of elaborate body ornamentation including impressive fibre costumes and dance superstructures, is found in the north-west among the Bassari and Coniagui.

During the French colonial period cultural change was rapid. The major artistic impact was the export of Guinean art objects to satisfy a burgeoning market in Paris. This resulted in a reduction in the number of objects for indigenous use and an increase in artistic forgery. A more dramatic change occurred between independence and the military coup of 1984. At this time Islam was established as the state religion, and the indigenous ritual power base was systematically destroyed by such means as forced conversion and the near-total confiscation of ritual objects. In 1959–60 the totalitarian Marxist state formalized a programme of 'demystification', decimating ritual art over the next three decades. Ironically, a concurrent policy to encourage 'folkloric' traditions contributed to the formation of other such cultural institutions as the Ballets Africains, the Musée National de Sandervalia, Conakry (founded 1960 and housing examples of traditional arts), and Guinea Radio-Television. There are also regional and local museums with ethnographic and contemporary art collections in Beyla, Boké, Kizsidougou, Koundara and N'Zerekore. In 1984 the regime was overthrown and the restrictions on indigenous religion lifted. Some artistic practices were revived, and ethnic groups began to re-evaluate the cultural heritage that had been interrupted for so long. The Musée National, though its collections were drastically diminished, became a focal point for the small community of people in the arts, and with new freedom under the government of the early 1990s it sponsored intellectual conferences of keen interest to a growing number of culturally concerned citizens.

BIBLIOGRAPHY

B. Appia: 'Masques de Guinée Française et de Casamance', *J. Africanistes*, xiii (1943), pp. 153–82

M. de Lestrange: *Les Coniagui et les Bassari* (Paris, 1955)

M. de Lestrange and M. Gessain: *Collections Bassari du Musée de l'Homme*, Paris, Mus. Homme cat. (Paris, 1976)

C. Rivière: *Guinea: The Mobilization of a People* (Ithaca, NY, 1977)

M. Renaudeau: *La République de Guinée* (Conakry, 1978)

L. Prussin: *Hatumere: Islamic Design in West Africa* (Berkeley, 1986)

FREDERICK LAMP

Guinea, Republic of **Equatorial.** *See* EQUATORIAL GUINEA.

Guinea-Bissau, Republic of [Repûblica da Guiné-Bissau; formerly Portuguese Guinea]. Country in West Africa. It is bordered by Senegal to the north, Guinea on the east and south and the Atlantic Ocean on the west. The capital is Bissau and the national language Portuguese. It includes within its territory of only 36,125 sq. km the Bijagós Archipelago and a string of coastal islands. The mainland territory comprises coastal swamps and rain-forests that slope upward to become heavily forested interior plains and then typical savannah. The hot climate receives all of its annual rainfall between December and May and supports the largely agricultural economy.

Although the Portuguese arrived in the mid-15th century and, because of the slave trade, maintained colonies thereafter, Guinea-Bissau did not formally become a Portuguese colony until 1879. In 1951 it was declared an overseas colony of Portugal, becoming independent in 1974. Major ethnic groups include coastal Balanta, Manjaco, Bijago (Bijogo), Diola and Beafada-Nalu; Mande and Fulbe (Fulani) in the savannah; and urban populations of Cape Verdean and mixed descent. Of the 966,000 inhabitants (UN estimate 1989), over 80% speak Western Atlantic languages; 35% are Muslim and 60%, mostly coastal groups, follow traditional religions. This entry covers the art produced in the area since colonial times. For art in the region in earlier periods, *see* AFRICA, §VII, 4(ii). *See also* BAGA and BIJOGO.

Although colonial art was of little significance, many European themes and materials have been incorporated into modern renditions of traditional sculpture, textiles, ceramics, basketry, leather- and metalwork and silver filigree jewellery. No significant colonial or post-colonial architecture has been built. Traditional dwellings include indigenous mud and thatch structures and the insular Manjaco houses, with living compartments forming a rectangle around an interior patio (15–30 sq. m) and tower-like cupolas over the corners. Naive oil paintings depicting daily life are produced for tourists but bear no resemblance to the dramatic red, black and white animal, human and geometric forms sometimes painted on hut walls. Stories from oral history and the trickster figure Nturi Palan are subjects of popular graphic art and comic strips.

Manjaco cotton textiles composed of six narrow, tightly woven strips (20×1800 mm) and incorporating brocade, inlay and plain-weave techniques were once used as a standard medium of exchange and continue to be an important form of wealth. These cloths are decorated with Arab geometric figures, Portuguese crosses, lettering and patterns from industrial fabrics, worked in black on white, or in vibrant combinations of blues, reds and yellows, shot with gold or silk thread. Strip cloth is used as clothing and burial shrouds. It may also be wrapped around wooden biers or ship forms and combined with mirrors, coloured braided cords and tassels to form oracles and funeral effigies that are interrogated to diagnose the causes of death and misfortune.

Balanta and Manjaco coiled earthenware water vessels are moulded into elaborate doubled, multiple-mouthed and rounded octahedron shapes, and then polished after firing. Sculpted clay also forms the moulds for papier-mâché masks painted in brilliant enamels that are made for the urban Portuguese-inspired pre-Lenten carnival. The artist's imagination, comic books and films, as well as such official annual themes as 'health' or 'production', are the inspirations for masks portraying monstrous sea and forest creatures, diseases and hypodermic syringes, and agricultural tools.

The Museo Etnográfico Nacional, Bissau (inaugurated 1988), displays a cross-section of indigenous arts, and the National Institute of Art, which also provides education in the plastic arts, has a small permanent exhibition of carnival masks. The Ministry of Tourism, the State Secretariat for War Veterans, the Italian Fathers and some private enterprises support artisan training and craft shops.

BIBLIOGRAPHY

H. A. Bernatzik: *Aethiopen des Westens: Forschungsreise in Portugiesisch Guinea*, 2 vols (Vienna, 1933) [excellent pls]

F. R. Quintino: 'A pintura e a escultura na Guiné Portuguesa', *Bol. Cult. Guiné Port.*, xix/75 (1964), pp. 277–88

F. Galhano: *Esculturas e objectos decorados da Guiné Portuguesa* (Lisbon, 1971)
D. Błażejewicz and others: *Arquitectura tradicional: Guiné-Bissau* (Uppsala, 1981/*R* 1983)
R. Quintino: 'Cestaria na Guiné Portuguesa', *Cestaria tradicional em Africa*, i, Publicações do Centro de Estudos Africanos, 9 (Coimbra, 1988), pp. 35–41
E. L. Crowley: *Contracts with the Spirits: Religion, Asylum, and Ethnic Identity in the Cacheu Region of Guinea-Bissau* (diss., New Haven, CT, Yale U., 1990)

EVE L. CROWLEY

Guinness, Edward (Cecil), 1st Earl of Iveagh (*b* Clontarf, Co. Dublin, 10 Nov 1847; *d* London, 8 Oct 1927). Irish collector, resident in England. A great-grandson of Arthur Guinness, founder of the family brewery in Ireland, Lord Iveagh was responsible for the collection of paintings still displayed at Kenwood House, an 18th-century villa by Robert Adam (i) in Hampstead, London, which he purchased in 1925. The Iveagh Bequest, Kenwood, opened as a public museum in 1928, two years after Lord Iveagh's death, and contains many celebrated British portraits of the late 18th century and the early 19th, including works by Joshua Reynolds, George Romney, Thomas Gainsborough, Thomas Lawrence and others. The Old Master paintings at Kenwood, collected by Lord Iveagh, are dominated by the Dutch and Flemish schools. These include *Self-portrait* by Rembrandt (*c.* 1665) and Johannes Vermeer's *Guitar Player* (*c.* 1672), with other works by Aelbert Cuyp, Frans Hals, Adriaen van Ostade, Anthony van Dyck and Frans Snyders. Lord Iveagh's Protestant merchant taste extended to include paintings by François Boucher and Jean-Baptiste Pater; examples of their work are also at Kenwood.

A collection that typifies the taste of the late 19th century, the Iveagh Bequest was largely formed between 1887 and 1891 through the London dealers Thomas Agnew & Sons; close parallels can be drawn with contemporaneous American collections, such as the Huntington collection at San Marino, CA, or the Frick Collection in New York. Portraits of society beauties and children predominate at Kenwood, with few history or sporting paintings or conversation pieces included among the original 64 bequeathed works.

For nearly 40 years Lord Iveagh's collection of paintings hung in his town house in Grosvenor Place, London, as part of the equipment he believed was necessary if his social aspirations in England were to be realized. The founding of the Guinness Housing Trust for the working poor and a donation to the Lister Institute of Preventive Medicine also contributed to his rise—from a baronetcy in 1885 to an earldom in 1919. Unfortunately, between his purchase of Kenwood in 1925 (by which time it had been stripped of its original furnishings) and his death two years later there was little time for him to furnish the house: he is not noted as a distinguished collector of furniture, sculpture or the decorative arts.

BIBLIOGRAPHY

C. Holmes: *Pictures from the Iveagh Bequest and Collections* (London, 1928)
P. Murray and A. Blunt: *The Iveagh Bequest, Kenwood: Catalogue of Paintings* (London, 1930, rev. 3/1964)
F. Mullaly: *The Silver Salver* (London, 1981)

JULIUS BRYANT

Guinness, May [Mary Catherine] (*b* Dublin, 11 March 1863; *d* Dublin, 16 July 1955). Irish painter. She was educated mainly at home, where she drew, painted and copied the family portraits. Although she exhibited *Turkeys* at the Royal Hibernian Academy in 1897, family obligations prevented her from studying art until *c.* 1910; she was taught in Paris by Kees van Dongen and later by Hermenegildo Anglada-Camarasa, and she spent each of the 15 subsequent winters in the city. She joined the French army as a nurse during World War I and received the Croix de Guerre in September 1915. From 1922 to 1925 she worked with André Lhôte, in the latter year holding her first solo exhibition in Paris, which helped to establish her as one of the first Irish artists associated with the Ecole de Paris. In 1925, having absorbed aspects of the work of Matisse, of Cubism and finally of the work of Marie Laurençin and Raoul Dufy, still maintaining Anglada-Camarasa's rather hot colouring, she achieved a free, decorative manner of her own. She said in 1925 that she had been 'through all the phases, and had now settled down to "stylisation", the flat and rhythmic arrangements of line and colour'. *A Russian Cossack* (Dublin, Represent. Ch. Body Lib.) and *A Religious Procession in Brittany* (Dublin, N.G.), which like her other paintings defy accurate dating, display her characteristic fusion of geometric structure and decorative lyricism. She was a strong influence on younger Irish artists, such as Evie Hone and Mainie Jellett.

BIBLIOGRAPHY

'Silhouettes in the Mirror', *Sphere Mag.*, ciii/1343 (1925), pp. 84–6
Irish Art, 1900–1950 (exh. cat. by H. Pyle, Cork, Crawford Mun. A.G., 1975)
Irish Women Artists from the Eighteenth Century to the Present Day (exh. cat., Dublin, N.G., 1987)

HILARY PYLE

Guinovart, Josep (*b* Barcelona, 20 March 1927). Spanish Catalan painter. He studied briefly at the Escuela de Artes y Oficios in Barcelona in 1941 while working as a painter-decorator and from 1945 painted Expressionist-influenced rural landscapes, urban scenes, figures and even work tools. For a period of about five years from 1958 he adopted procedures from *Art informel*, such as his use of wooden supports partly destroyed by fire. His paintings of this period pay direct tribute to the chiaroscuro contrasts typical of Spanish Baroque art. In the mid-1960s Guinovart produced a series of very inventive paintings with collage elements indebted to Pop art, including mixed medium works such as *Untitled* (500×600 mm, 1964; Madrid, Fund. Juan March) and a series interpreting Picasso's *Guernica*. In his subsequent work he systematically explored different aspects of representation while continuing to use diverse and unconventional materials such as wheat, maize, stones, sand and glass.

BIBLIOGRAPHY

C. Rodríguez-Aguilera: *Guinovart* (Madrid, 1959)
Guinovart: Obras desde 1946 (exh. cat. by C. Rodríguez-Aguilera, J. Benet Aurell and C.-A. Arean, Madrid, Ateneo, 1965)
C. Rodríguez-Aguilera: *Guinovart* (Madrid, 1971)
D. Giralt-Miracle: *Guinovart* (Barcelona, 1979)

LOURDES CIRLOT

Guiot de Beaugrant. *See* BEAUGRANT, GUYOT DE.

Guise, John (*b* 1682 or 1683; *d* London, 12 June 1765). English collector. He studied at Christ Church, Oxford (BA 1701), and afterwards undertook military service in the Low Countries. However, he devoted most of his time to amassing an impressive collection of over 2000 Old Master paintings and drawings. He attended picture sales in England and purchased works through agents in Italy, gradually accumulating a representative sample of the Italian schools of art. His collection included both copies and originals of Roman, Florentine, Venetian, Lombard and Bolognese paintings and drawings, especially of the High Renaissance and Seicento. The large number of copies in Guise's collection suggests a concern for comprehensiveness, even at the expense of quality. Some of the more striking works, such as a drawing of a grotesque head by Leonardo and Annibale Carracci's *Butcher Shop* (both Oxford, Christ Church, Pict. Gal.), reveal his personal fascination with unusual images. Although Guise also owned some Netherlandish paintings, he did not share the contemporary enthusiasm for such works. He also showed an intelligent interest in problems of technique and attribution. He assisted with research into the provenance of the *Massacre of the Innocents* (fragment, London, Foundling Hosp.), a cartoon attributed to Raphael. He also acted as an art adviser to Frederick, Prince of Wales, and in 1720 he became an enthusiastic patron of Jacob Christoph Le Blon, a German artist resident in London in 1718–34 who invented a new method for printing coloured mezzotints. In his will, Guise left his substantial collection to Christ Church, where inept 'repairs' were made, resulting in irreparable damage to many of the works.

BIBLIOGRAPHY

'The Guise Collection', *Lib. F.A.*, iv (1832), pp. 116–23

'The Note-books of George Vertue', *Walpole Soc.*, xxii (1934) [indexed in xxix (1947)]

J. Byam Shaw: *Paintings by Old Masters at Christ Church, Oxford* (Oxford, 1967)

——: *Drawings by Old Masters at Christ Church, Oxford* (Oxford, 1976)

SHEARER WEST

Guittonis, Johannes. *See under* RAINERIUS.

Guizot, François(-Pierre-Guillaume) (*b* Nîmes, 4 Oct 1787; *d* Val Richer, Calvados, 12 Sept 1874). French statesman, historian and writer. During the monarchy (1830–48) of Louis-Philippe, he was the dominant figure of the conservative party; his political career was marked by a passion for compromise. At a very young age he embarked on a career in journalism, before entering politics. During the years following the French Revolution he wrote for the *Publiciste.* His first independent publication on the arts was a review on the Salon of 1810, entitled: *De l'état des beaux-arts en France et du Salon de 1810*, in which he expressed his preference for modern history painting, especially that portraying the epic of Napoleon: the *Capture of Madrid* by Antoine-Jean Gros (1809; Versailles, Château); the *Revolt at Cairo* by Anne-Louis Girodet (1810; Versailles, Château). Of the Classical subjects, he was attracted by works such as *Andromache and Pyrrhus* (1810; Paris, Louvre) by Pierre Guérin. As a writer, he had a preference for historical and literary subjects.

Guizot showed himself to be more of a philosopher than an artist. His comments on works of art served as a pretext for general disquisitions on art. His aesthetic judgement lacked originality, being characterized, like his politics, by a desire for compromise. He was not in favour of realism but wished to see classical beauty transposed into modern subjects. As a devoted reader of Gotthold Ephraim Lessing's *Laokoon*, he similarly emphasized the distinct nature of the different media of artistic expression, sculpture, painting, architecture. He believed that the painter should not borrow from sculpture, because the latter can do what painting is unable to do. Guizot also wrote some reviews of paintings and sculpture for two publications that described the collections of the Louvre: *Le Musée français* (1803–9) and *Le Musée royal* (1816–18).

WRITINGS

S.-C. Croze-Magnan, E. Q. Visconti and T.-B. Emeric-David, eds: *Le Musée français*, 4 vols (Paris, 1803–9)

De l'état des beaux-arts en France et du Salon de 1810 (Paris, 1810)

'Essai sur les limites qui séparent et les liens qui unissent les beaux-arts', *Le Musée royal*, eds E. Q. Visconti, F.-P.-G. Guizot and C.-O.-F.-J.-B. de Clarac, 2 vols (Paris, 1816–18)

Etudes sur les beaux-arts en général (Paris, 1852) [Guizot's collected writings on art]

BIBLIOGRAPHY

H. Pouthas: *Guizot pendant la Restauration* (Paris, 1923)

——: *La Jeunesse de Guizot* (Paris, 1936)

D. Johnson: *Guizot: Aspects of French History* (London, 1963)

PASCAL GRIENER

Gujral, Satish (*b* Jhelum, West Punjab [now in Pakistan], 25 Dec 1925). Indian painter, sculptor, printmaker and architect. Totally deaf from the age of 13, he studied painting at the Mayo School of Art, Lahore, from 1939 to 1944, and then at the Sir Jamshetjee Jeejebhoy School of Art, Bombay, from 1944 to 1947. After independence and the partition of India and Pakistan in 1947, he pursued his artistic career in India and for several years expressed in his work the anguish of the partition. From 1952 to 1954 he studied at the Palacio de Bellas Artes, Mexico City, and from 1953 to 1954 worked under David Alfaro Siqueiros on murals in University City, MI. He was also influenced by the work of the Mexican artist José Clemente Orozco, especially by his use of large forms and his treatment of human anatomy. In his paintings of this period, such as *Despair* (1954; oil, 0.9×0.9 m; New Delhi, N.G. Mod. A.) and *Desolation* (1956; oil, 0.89×1.19 m; New Delhi, N.G. Mod. A.), Gujral worked in a powerful expressionist idiom inspired by his studies in Mexico. While retaining this idiom into the 1960s he also derived inspiration from other sources, including Surrealism. From 1961 a greater calm entered his work. He began to be inspired by Indian folk motifs and worked increasingly on murals for national and international institutions, including the World Trade Center, New York. For his sculptures, and for some murals, he employed a range of materials including ceramics, glass, wood and assorted metals; an example of his wooden sculpture is *Crucifixion* (1979; *see* INDIA, fig. 3). He also designed furniture. As an architect, his work included the design of buildings for the Belgian Embassy in New Delhi and the University of Goa at Panjim (formerly Panaji). He held solo exhibitions of his paintings and sculptures in India and abroad and participated in numerous group exhibitions. His honours include National Awards from the Lalit Kala Akademi, New Delhi (1956, 1957 and 1973), and the Order of the Crown from the Belgian Government. His works are in private and public collections, including the National Gallery of Modern Art, New Delhi, the Museum of Modern Art, New York, and the National Gallery, Washington, DC. His murals can be found in Ahmadabad (Roopali Cinema, Handloom House), Bombay (First National City Bank), Chandigarh (Punjab Museum, Punjab University), Hissar (Agricultural College), Ludhiana (Agricultural University), Madras (Handloom House), New Delhi (East India Hotels, 1965, ceramic, 2.0×7.0×13.7 m; Hotel Rajdoot, 1967, painted wood, 2.7×7.6 m; Ministry of Education, 1968, ceramic, 3.0×21.0 m (two works); Ministry of Works, 1976, ceramic, 7.6×4.8 m; and Palam Airport, Odeon Cinema, First National City Bank, Indian Medical Association) and New York (New York Port Authority, 1975, moulded metal 3.0×7.6 m).

BIBLIOGRAPHY

U. Vasudev: *Satish Gujral* (New Delhi, 1970)

Modern Indian Paintings: From the Collection of the National Gallery of Modern Art, New Delhi (exh. cat., New Delhi, N.G. Mod. A., 1982)

R. Bartholomew: *Gujral, Satish: Four Decades* (New Delhi, 1986)

The Sculpted Image: A Panorama of Contemporary Indian Sculpture (exh. cat. by N. Malani and R. Shahani, Bombay, Nehru Cent., 1987)

ANIS FAROOQI

Gu Kaizhi [Ku K'ai-chih; *zi* Changkang, *hao* Hutou] (*b* Wuxi, Jiangsu Province, AD 344; *d* 407). Chinese painter. According to his official biography in the *Jin shu* ('History of the Jin dynasty'; compiled Tang period (AD 618–907)), he held office at the Eastern Jin (AD 317–420) court at Jiangkang (Nanjing). The biography also records the opinion of his contemporary Xie An that he was an artist unexcelled in all time. In the history of Chinese painting his name remains a byword as one of the foremost figure painters, whose style was influential throughout the centuries. Some extremely well-known themes are associated with him, while literary records, particularly Zhang Yanyuan's *Lidai minghua ji* ('Record of famous painters of all periods'; AD 847), preserve Gu's own writings as well as many references to his paintings. By the late Tang period, paintings by Gu Kaizhi were among those that Zhang Yanyuan's grandfather had to surrender to the throne. Emperor Xianzong (*reg* 805–20) himself acknowledged them, professing to honour and treasure them. Zhang Yanyuan's judgement on Gu Kaizhi's brushwork is one of the cornerstones of Gu's reputation:

> In the works of Ku K'ai-chih [the strokes] are firm and tense and connect with one another uninterruptedly; they circle back upon themselves in sudden rushes. His tone and style are evanescent and variable, his atmosphere and interest lightning and sudden. His conception was kept whole [in his mind] before [he used] his brush, so that when the painting was all finished the conception was [embodied] in it, and therefore it was all divine breath (trans. Acker, pp. 177–9).

Zhang also praised the divine quality of Gu's 'thorough and exact brushwork', in which the ends of the strokes were not visible, although he was still more appreciative of the brushwork of the Tang-period master WU DAOZI, who seemed able to reflect an image with just one or two strokes and in whose work, though the strokes might be incomplete, the intention was fully realized.

About Gu Kaizhi's figure painting, however, Zhang was unreservedly enthusiastic, paying tribute to its subtlety, insight and enduring interest. As an example he cited Gu's painting of the Buddhist sage *Vimalakirti*, which was the first to depict the well-defined and emaciated features that revealed the subject's illness; the sage was shown leaning on a table, having forgotten how to speak. Other painters tried and, in Zhang's view, failed to equal this portrait. Zhang Yanyuan recorded that Gu's portrait of *Vimalakirti*, originally painted for the Waguan Temple (Waguan si) in Jiankang in 363–5, was saved from destruction in the reign of Emperor Wuzong (*reg* 840–46) and moved to the Ganlu Temple (Ganlu si) in modern Zhenjiang Jiangsu Province. Nevertheless, few of Gu's works had been preserved by Zhang's time, and it was therefore difficult to give an exhaustive and detailed account of them. Zhang's list of artists who worked in the tradition of Gu Kaizhi, including Zhan Zhiqian, Yan Lide and Yan Liben, the latter among the most distinguished of Tang-period figure painters, as well as Gu Kaizhi's own observations on the art of painting, are the most potent indicators of the extent of Gu's influence. Indeed, Zhang frequently used Gu as a yardstick by which to measure the achievements of other painters.

Foremost among the paintings associated with Gu Kaizhi's name are the *Admonitions of the Instructress to the Court Ladies* (*Nüshi jian tu*) and *Nymph of the Luo River* (*Luoshen tu*). *Biographies of Famous Women* (*Lienü zhuan*; handscroll; Beijing, Pal. Mus.), sometimes attributed to Gu, is of Song or later date. The *Admonitions* scroll, acquired by Laurence Binyon for the British Museum in

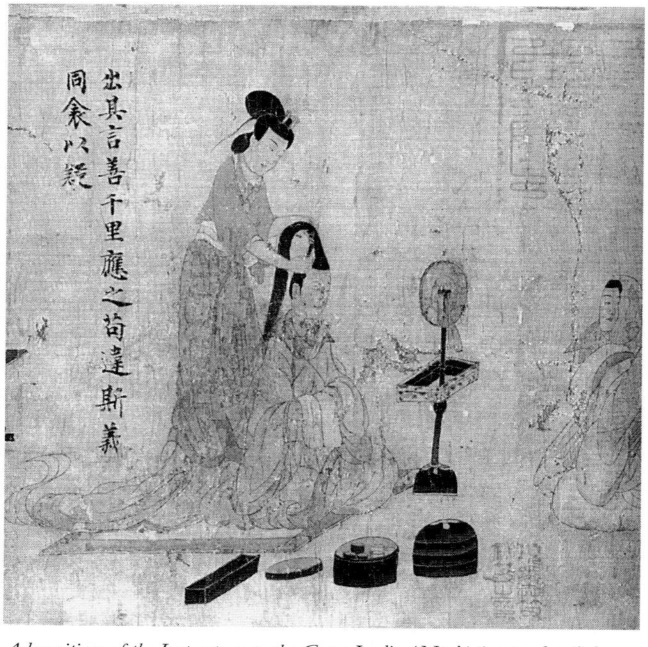

Admonitions of the Instructress to the Court Ladies (*Nüshi jian tu*; detail) by an anonymous artist in the style of Gu Kaizhi, handscroll, ink and colours on silk, 0.25×3.47 m, probably Tang period, AD 618–907 (London, British Museum)

1903, was formerly in the Qing imperial collections: indeed, it had been singled out for special treatment by the Qianlong emperor (*reg* 1736–96), who added the title, a flower sketch from his own hand and a colophon, and who commissioned the court artist Zou Yigui (1686–1772) to add a further ink painting as a graceful gesture of admiration at the end of the scroll. The *Admonitions* illustrates a text written in the 3rd century AD by Zhang Hua; nine of the original eleven scenes survive (for examples see fig. and CHINA, fig. 263), the first two having been lost. Each of the surviving scenes, except for the first, is accompanied by an appropriate excerpt from Zhang's text and illustrates either a story of wifely duty or a moral precept. The special distinction of the painting lies in the fine draughtsmanship and especially in the keen interplay of gesture and regard between the persons represented in each scene. While it is generally agreed to be a copy, of a date that has been the subject of much debate, the style and costume of the figures and of incidental elements suggest that it faithfully transmits a composition of Gu's time. The discovery of similar scenes, including one (AD 484) on a lacquered screen in the tomb of a Northern Wei (AD 386–534) general, very close in its iconography to the second scene in the present scroll, has lent strength to the argument for the veracity of the painting, which could have been executed in the Tang period, although the earliest seal impressions on it, of the Ruisi Hall, date to the Northern Song (1127–1279); in literary records Mi Fu was the first to attribute the *Admonitions* to Gu Kaizhi. Unfortunately, as all the original colophons on the scroll had been lost by the time it was recorded in the Qing imperial collections in the 18th century, little can be learnt of its history after the Song period.

Several versions exist of the *Luoshen tu*. Unlike the *Admonitions* scroll, the composition of the *Luoshen tu* is set in a continuous landscape. The story illustrates the prose poem (*fu*) by Cao Zhi (AD 192–232), written in memory of his first love and later addressed to the Nymph of the River Luo, describing his meeting with the deity, their parting and his subsequent heartbreaking and fruitless search for her. Most of the extant versions (Beijing, Pal. Mus.; Jinzhou, Liaoning Prov. Mus.; Washington, DC, Freer; *see* CONFUCIANISM, fig. 1) display archaistic landscape elements, small in comparison with the figures of the Nymph and her companions and those of the poet and his retinue. Two other scrolls, however (Beijing, Pal. Mus. and London, BM), display the same iconographical figure groups but in a fairyland setting, with lush vegetation, clouds and *lingzhi* fungus, and with a backdrop of ink landscape: they probably date no later than the 13th century.

The extant paintings associated with Gu Kaizhi are complemented by his writings, which include *Painting the Cloud Terrace Mountain* (see Bush and Shih, pp. 34–6, and Sullivan, pp. 94–100), a detailed description of a handscroll portraying the Daoist master Zhang Daoling in a complex landscape. Other writings by Gu include the *Prose Poem on Thunder and Lightning* (see Shih) and *Essay on Painting* (*Lunhua*; extracts in Bush and Shih, p. 24). Gu identifies human figures as being most difficult to accomplish, followed by landscapes, then dogs and horses. The inclusion of landscapes here is perhaps the first critical mention of the genre and an indication that in Gu's time landscape was already valued for its own sake, not merely as a setting for narrative.

BIBLIOGRAPHY

Fang Xuanling and others: *Jin shu* [History of the Jin dynasty] (Tang period, AD 618–907/*R* Beijing, 1974), lxxxixii, p. 2405

Zhang Yanyuan: *Lidai minghua ji* [Record of famous painters of all periods] (AD 847); Eng. trans. and annotation by W. R. B. Acker as *Some T'ang and Pre-T'ang Texts on Chinese Painting* (Leiden, 1954), i

M. Sullivan: *The Birth of Landscape Painting in China* (Berkeley, 1962), pp. 88–103

H. Kohara: 'Joshi zō zukan' [On the picture scroll *Admonitions of the Court Instructress to the Palace Ladies*], *Kokka*, 908 (Nov 1967), pp. 17–31; 909 (Dec 1967), pp. 13–27

Hsio-yen Shih: 'Poetry Illustration and the Works of Ku K'ai-chih', *Renditions*, 6 (Spring 1976), pp. 6–29

S. Bush and Hsio-yen Shih: *Early Chinese Texts on Painting* (Cambridge, MA, 1985)

RODERICK WHITFIELD

Gukei. *See* SUMIYOSHI, (2).

Gulácsy, Lajos (*b* Budapest, 12 Oct 1882; *d* Budapest, 2 Feb 1932). Hungarian painter, draughtsman, stage designer and writer. He studied at the School of Crafts and Design in Budapest (1900–01); in 1902 he registered at the Accademia di Belle Arti in Florence and in 1903 at the Accademia in Rome. From 1902 his work was regularly included in the exhibitions of the Budapest National Salon. In 1906 he went to Paris and from there travelled extensively. His work was inspired variously by small Italian towns, by Giotto, Botticelli and Alessandro Magnasco; in his early work the influence of the Pre-Raphaelites is also noticeable, as is that of the Viennese Secessionist style (e.g. *Paolo and Francesca*, 1903; Budapest, N.G.). In 1907 he exhibited with Ödön Márffy at the Uránia bookshop in Budapest, and the following year he took part in an international exhibition in London. In 1909 he took part in a travelling exhibition of Neo-Impressionist painters and literary figures. He sought to express himself through the themes and forms of the past: his 'Rococo' period was directly inspired by Italian and French art, and is characterized by its finesse, as well as by the use of the grotesque and the tragi-comic. The work of Toulouse-Lautrec was also influential on Gulácsy's style. He called his Rococo works 'Biedermeier frolics', and he professed to live in a world of 'noble dreams'. His work as a whole expresses raw feelings with soft lyricism, as in *Magician's Garden* (1906–7; Budapest, N.G.), sometimes even turning to wild fury (e.g. *Ecstasy*, 1908–10; Pécs, Pannonius Mus.).

The stories of E. T. A. Hoffmann and the dramas of Oscar Wilde and Gabriele d'Annunzio (1863–1938) also inspired Gulácsy (e.g. *Slav Fortune Teller*, 1910; Budapest, N.G.), and he himself wrote stories, plays and fantastic fables. His pictures of Don Juan mark a return to the figurative, and in general the titles of his works refer to his enthusiasm for literature. He was concerned with youth, the passage of time and questions of human fate, as in *Bier* (*c*. 1912; Budapest, N.G.). In such pictures he used pastels, opaline colours and an evocative, ethereal atmosphere. His interest in colour was further stimulated by his stage designs for the Thalia Theatre (1905) and the

Hungarian Theatre (1912) in Budapest. In 1914 he went to Venice, but developed severe mental problems due to his fear of war. This fear saturated his work; he broke away from a logical pictorial form, and replaced his earlier motifs with strange forms. His works were composed in free association concerned with his visions and paranoia (e.g. *Querra*, 1914–15; Budapest, N.G.). At this time his favourite Italian motifs of cypress trees became much more dramatic, and cemeteries, solitary people and houses were increasingly present. In a number of his works the motif of a burning candle became a symbol of the tragic present. As images of paranoia stemming from the subconscious, these works can be seen as surrealistic.

In 1916 Gulácsy exhibited with The Young (*Fiatalok*) and Seven (*Hetek*) groups. For a short time he associated with the Activists and was a member of MA group, taking part in their show of 1918. His monumental portraits after 1910 are typical of his experiments of this period (e.g. *Woman's Head*, 1916–17; untraced, see Szij, no. 113). The expressive force was influenced by the work of Oskar Kokoschka. In his last works Gulácsy returned to antiquity for inspiration. From 1919, however, he lived in mental institutions, and although in 1922 an exhibition of his work was organized in Budapest, during the last decade of his life he was practically forgotten, and incapable of working because of his mental ill-health.

WRITINGS

J. Szabadi, ed.: *A virágünnep vége* [The end of the flower festival] (Budapest, 1989) [collected writings]

BIBLIOGRAPHY

F. Lehel: *Gulácsy Lajos* (Budapest, 1922)
J. Szabadi: *Gulácsy Lajos* (Budapest, 1969)
——: 'The Life and Art of Lajos Gulácsy', *Acta Hist. A. Acad. Sci. Hung.*, xvi (1970), 3–4, p. 293–316
B. Szij: *Gulácsy* (Budapest, 1979)

ÉVA BAJKAY

Gulbarga [Gulbargā]. Town in Karnataka State, India. It was the capital of the BAHMANI dynasty from 1347 until 1424 (when it was superseded by BIDAR). As Gulbarga was the first urban centre of Islamic power in the Deccan, it was the starting-point of raids against the VIJAYANAGARA dynasty in an attempt to expand Muslim territories southwards. At the core of the city is the approximately circular fort, its double walls buttressed with semicircular bastions and protected by a moat. Inside the fort stands the Jamiʿ Masjid (*c.* 1367), built during the reign of Muhammad I (*reg c.* 1358–75). This unique structure has no courtyard, being roofed entirely with domes and vaults. A formidable and solid keep, the Bala Hisar, stands north-east of the mosque. A bazaar street lined with small vaulted chambers leads to the main entrance to the fort; this projects outwards from the walls at the north-west corner. Mounds of rubble inside the fort probably conceal the ruins of the Bahmani palace.

Other religious monuments are situated outside the fort. To the north, the Shah Bazar mosque dating from the period of Muhammad I has a large courtyard entered through a domed gateway. Nearby is the shrine (*dargāh*) of Shaykh Siraj al-Din Junaydi, with a monumental entrance portico flanked by tall minarets. The tombs of the early Bahmani sultans, in a severe, simple style, are located to the south-west. East of the fort, a crossing of arcaded streets in the middle of the modern city marks the original Bahmani-period bazaar.

Outside the city to the east is the Haft Gunbad complex, with funerary monuments of the later sultans, the most important being the finely decorated double tomb of Taj al-Din Firuz (*reg c.* 1397–1422). Further east is the shrine of Hazrat Gisu Daraz (*d* 1422), a celebrated Sufi saint, still attracting crowds of pilgrims. The main tomb dates from the Bahmani period but additions, including a monumental archway, were made up until the 16th century, when the city came under the sway of the ʿADIL SHAHI dynasty. Nearby is the shrine of Shah Kamal Mujarrad; a mosque and tomb are combined with a small caravanserai, or rest-house, and a line of domed stables. The mosque is notable for its elaborate stucco ornamentation.

See also INDIAN SUBCONTINENT, §III, 6(ii)(f).

BIBLIOGRAPHY

Enc. Islam/2: 'Gulbargā'; 'Bahmanīs: Monuments'
S. Toy: *The Fortified Cities of India* (London, 1965)
Z. A. Desai: 'Architecture: The Bahmanis', *History of Medieval Deccan (1295–1724)*, ed. H. K. Sherwani and P. M. Joshi (Hyderabad, 1974), pp. 229–52
E. Merklinger: 'Gulbarga', *Islamic Heritage of the Deccan*, ed. G. Michell (Bombay, 1986), pp. 26–41

GEORGE MICHELL

Gulbenkian, Calouste Sarkis (*b* Istanbul, 23 March 1869; *d* Lisbon, 20 July 1955). Iranian oil magnate and collector of Armenian descent. He studied at King's College, London, where he gained a diploma in engineering in 1887. He then embarked on travels that led to the publication of *La Transcaucasie et la Péninsule d'Apcheron—Souvenirs de voyage* (Paris, 1891), a work that showed his considerable interest in economics and his passion for art, which were also apparent in his diaries and letters. He was a pioneer in the development of the Middle Eastern oil fields as an energy source, and from the end of the 19th century he was closely involved in the growth of the oil industry, beginning with the formation of Royal Dutch Shell and the Turkish Petroleum Co. The income derived from these sources enabled him to become a collector of art. In 1902 he became a British citizen and in 1926 Persian.

Gulbenkian was a true connoisseur, highly knowledgeable and perceptive, and carried out extensive research in his own library and in museums before acquiring a work. The collection he formed is considered one of the most remarkable made in the 20th century. It comprises European paintings, Italian medals and coins, Egyptian sculpture, Islamic, Persian and Indian art, East Asian ceramics, illuminated manuscripts, book bindings, French furniture, sculpture, bronzes, silver, textiles, Roman glass, Greek coins and jewellery. The only contemporary artist he commissioned was René Lalique, who became a friend and from whom he acquired a fine collection of jewellery and many related designs. He bought sculpture directly from Auguste Rodin (e.g. *Head of Legros*, bronze, 1882; Lisbon, Mus. Gulbenkian) and owned five of his works. Between 1928 and 1930 he bought major works of art from the Russian Government; among these were French silver, furniture (for example a secrétaire by Jean-Henri Riesener that had once belonged to Marie-Antoinette), the full-length portrait of *Hélène Fourment* (1630–32) by

Rubens that had belonged to Catherine the Great, two works by Rembrandt (*Portrait of an Old Man* (1645), and *Pallas Athene* (1655), or *Alexander*) and the marble statue of *Diana* (1780) by Jean-Antoine Houdon (all ex-Hermitage, St Petersburg; Lisbon, Mus. Gulbenkian). From 1929 he also bought important works of art from the Rothschild family. From 1924 the collection was displayed in Gulbenkian's home at 51 Avenue d'Iéna, Paris, though works from the collection were also sent on long-term loan to the British Museum and the National Gallery, London, and then transferred to the National Gallery of Art, Washington, DC, in 1948 and 1950. In 1940 Gulbenkian moved to Vichy as economic councillor to the Persian legation in France, and in 1942 he settled in Lisbon, where he lived until his death. Portugal became the seat of the Foundation he created and the considerable work of philanthropy he had begun. After his death, part of the art collection was displayed at the Palácio Pombal at Oeiras until the Museu Calouste Gulbenkian (inaugurated 1969) was built in Lisbon to house the entire collection (*see* PORTUGAL, §XIII). Under the terms of Gulbenkian's will, the Foundation is dedicated to the promotion of education, science, culture, music, dance and the arts; there is also some emphasis on Armenian projects.

BIBLIOGRAPHY

J. de Azeredo Perdigão: *Calouste Gulbenkian coleccionador* (Lisbon, 1979)
Calouste Gulbenkian Museum Catalogue, Lisbon, Fund. Gulbenkian (Lisbon, 1982)

ANGELA DELAFORCE

Gulbransson, Olaf (*b* Oslo, 26 Nov 1873; *d* Tegernsee, W. Germany, 18 Sept 1958). Norwegian draughtsman, caricaturist and painter. He studied first at the School of Applied Arts in Oslo, entering there in 1892, and later at the Académie Colarossi in Paris in 1900. However, from an early age he had worked as a caricaturist for newspapers and magazines. From 1889 to 1898 he worked for the newspaper *Pejk* and from 1889 to 1902 for *Tyrihaus*; he also contributed to *Paletten*, *Flusoppen* and other periodicals. In 1901 his *24 Karikaturer af Olaf Gulbransson* (Oslo), a collection of caricatures of famous Norwegians, was published and this established his reputation. In 1902 Albert Langen invited Gulbransson to work for the periodical *Simplicissimus* in Munich and he soon became one of its foremost contributors, producing social and political caricatures. He was elected to the Akademie der Künste in Berlin in 1916 and in 1923 returned to Oslo, where he worked for the daily paper *Tidens Tegn* until 1927. After moving back to Munich he was appointed professor of drawing and painting at the Akademie der Bildenden Künste in 1929, while continuing to work for *Simplicissimus* until 1949.

In addition to his illustrations and caricatures Gulbransson also produced pastels and watercolours of landscapes and portraits, such as the pastel *Freiherr von Mumm* (1927; Munich, Lenbachhaus). He also illustrated books such as Hans Christian Andersen's *Däumelischen und andere Märchen* (Munich, 1927). In 1951 he was elected to the Bayerische Akademie der Schönen Künste and in 1956 won the Art Prize of the city of Munich.

BIBLIOGRAPHY

Olaf Gulbransson (exh. cat. by J. Askeland, Oslo, N.G., 1962)
Olaf Gulbransson (exh. cat. by E. Steingräber, Hagen, Osthaus Mus., 1970)

□

Guldara [Guldarra; Musa-i Logar]. Gandharan Buddhist site in Afghanistan, in a defile adjoining the Logar Valley, 22 km south-east of Kabul. Located on a rocky spur, the site has massive revetment walls, with a stairway to a levelled platform containing a main stupa courtyard and a monastery. On the lower slopes to the south there is a smaller stupa, perhaps another monastery and other unidentified remains. In 1833 Martin Honigberger tunnelled into the podium of the main stupa in an unsuccessful search for relics. The following year Charles Masson discovered the central relic chamber at the junction between the stupa dome and the podium. In the 1960s UNESCO provided funding for conservation and a survey of the site by Lézine, while the monastery was excavated by the Délégation Archéologique Française en Afghanistan. A second programme of conservation was carried out by the British Institute of Afghan Studies in 1977–9.

The main stupa has a socle and high, square podium supporting two drums and the dome (*see* AFGHANISTAN, fig. 4). The upper drum has a blind arcade of pilasters alternating with ogee and trapezoidal arches. The lower drum, podium and socle are decorated with pilasters. The centre of the north-east face of the podium contains a large niche, probably for a cult image. A flight of steps on the south-east side leads to the top of the podium. The relic deposit contained ashes, bones, 96 gold buttons (London, BM) and Kushana gold coins (London, BM) of Vima Kadphises and Huvishka, which date the foundation of the stupa to *c.* 2nd century AD (*see also* INDIAN SUBCONTINENT, §IV, 5(ii)(b)). The paved stupa courtyard had traces of structural remains, probably shrines and votive stupas. The monastery to the north-east was built of rubble with a diaper masonry facing and was fortified with bastions at each corner. The complex comprised an interior courtyard, enclosed on four sides by a corridor with adjoining cells and a stairway to an upper floor. Vaulting and mud-brick domes on stepped squinches were used for roofing. Coins, pottery and fragmentary stucco and clay sculptures from the vestibule, chapel and corridor niches (Kabul Mus.) suggest that the site flourished during the Kushano-Sasanian period (*c.* 3rd–4th centuries AD).

See also AFGHANISTAN, §II, 1(i)(c).

BIBLIOGRAPHY

C. Masson: 'Second Memoir on the Ancient Coins Found at Beghrām, in the Kohistān of Kabul', *J. Asiat. Soc. Bengal*, v (1836), p. 27, pl. III.1–3
H. H. Wilson: *Ariana Antiqua: A Descriptive Account of the Antiquities and Coins of Afghanistan, with a Memoir on the Buildings Called Topes, by C. Masson* (London, 1841/*R* Delhi, 1971), pp. 53, 115, 354–5, 375; antiquities pl. III.3–4, coins pls X.7–8, 10–11, 13, XIV.1–2
J. Hackin, J. Carl and J. Meunié: *Diverses recherches archéologiques en Afghanistan (1933–1940)*, Mém.: Dél. Archéol. Fr. Afghanistan, viii (Paris, 1959), p. 13, figs 38–42
A. Lézine: 'Trois stupa de la région de Caboul', *Artibus Asiae*, xxvii/1–2 (1964), pp. 5–18, 22–4, figs 1–7, 10–39
G. Fussman and M. Le Berre: *Monuments bouddhiques de la région de Caboul, I: Le Monastère de Gul Dara*, Mém.: Dél. Archéol. Fr. Afghanistan, xxii (Paris, 1976)

G. K. Rao, R. Pinder-Wilson and W. Ball: 'The Stupa and Monastery at Guldarra: Report on the British Institute's Preservation Programme', *S. Asian Stud.*, i (1985), pp. 79–88

E. ERRINGTON

Gulgee, Ismail (*b* Peshawar, 25 Oct 1926). Pakistani painter and sculptor. He began painting while training as an engineer in the USA (Columbia and Harvard universities) and held his first exhibition in 1950. He continued to paint while secretary at the Pakistan embassy at Ottawa during the 1950s, developing a reputation for portraiture. In 1957 he was commissioned to paint the portrait of King Zahir Shah of Afghanistan, and in 1959 he held an exhibition of 151 paintings and sketches in Kabul. He also painted portraits of Prince Karim Aga Khan (1961), Zhou Enlai (1964), Queen Farah Diba of Iran (1965) and President Ayub Khan of Pakistan (1968). He then turned to making portraits from marble mosaic and semi-precious stones, a technique that he had developed in Kabul in 1959. His abstract paintings, produced since the 1960s, incorporate ornamental calligraphy (*see* PAKISTAN, fig. 4), coloured beads, small pieces of mirror, and gold and silver leaf. These works include a large abstract mural painted in 1965 for the British engineering firm Wates Ltd of London. In 1967 he began to make calligraphic sculptures in bronze, based on verses of the Koran, which were first exhibited in Tokyo in 1970. He made a large crescent and star in copper plate for the Faisal Mosque in Islamabad in 1986, and produced calligraphy in stone inside the mosque.

BIBLIOGRAPHY

A Portfolio of Pakistani Paintings (Karachi, n.d.)
S. Amjad 'Ali: *Gulgee: Versatile Artist* (Islamabad, 1984)
Paintings from Pakistan, intro. A. Naqvi (Islamabad, 1988)
I. ul-Hasan: *Painting in Pakistan* (Lahore, 1991)
M. Nesom-Sirhandi: *Contemporary Painting in Pakistan* (Lahore, 1992)

□

Gulielmo da Modena. *See* WILIGELMO.

Gull, Gustav (*b* Zurich, 7 Dec 1858; *d* Zurich, 10 June 1942). Swiss architect and teacher. He studied at the Eidgenössische Technische Hochschule, Zurich (1876–9), under Julius Jakob Stadler (1828–1904) and Georg Lasius (*b* 1835), and in 1879–80 he attended courses on stone sculpture at the Ecole des Arts Décoratifs, Geneva. He completed his practical experience in architecture in 1880–82 under Benjamin Recordon (1845–90) and then travelled in Italy (1883–4). From 1895 to 1900 Gull was chief architect to the city of Zurich. His first public buildings were designed in a neo-Renaissance style; examples include the post office (1886–8), Lucerne, and the Lavater school (1896–7), Zurich. In his most important work, the Schweizerisches Landesmuseum (1893–8) in Zurich, he set aside symmetry and stylistic unity to produce a free grouping of individual buildings in a castle-like complex, using a style derived from Late Gothic and early Renaissance models. This delight in picturesque silhouettes is also seen in his private houses, for example the Villa Schindler-Huber (1899–1901), Zurich. He rebuilt the extremely slender spires of the Predigerkirche, Zurich (1899–1900), and the church at Turbenthal (1903–4), and he remodelled the façade and cloister of the Fraumünsterkirche in Gothic Revival style (1900–01 and 1911–12). Gull made generous use of statuary in his buildings: for example there are small half-figures on the window jambs of the Stadthaus (1898–1900) and crowning elements on the Urania observatory (1911), both in Zurich. From 1900 to 1929 Gull was a professor at the Eidgenössische Technische Hochschule in Zurich; he became President of the Eidgenössische Kunstkommission (1903–6) and was a founder-member of the Kunstgesellschaft, Zurich. Later work included an urban plan (1902–10) for the centre of Zurich, which incorporated Renaissance-style squares and public buildings with terraces and stairs down to arcades beside the river; only a small part of the plan was executed (1903–4 and 1917–19). He also extended (1914–25) Gottfried Semper's building for the Eidgenössische Technische Hochschule, Zurich, with wings and an oval dome in a neo-Renaissance style. Gull's public buildings made him one of the most important exponents of late historicism in Switzerland.

BIBLIOGRAPHY

SKL
A. Meyer: 'Museale Architektur am Beispiel des Schweizerischen Landesmuseum in Zürich', *Festschrift Walter Drack zu seinem 60. Geburtstag* (Stäfa, 1977), pp. 211–23
W. Fischer: 'Gustav Gull', *Jb. Ges. Schweiz. Famforsch.* (1983), pp. 192–204

CORNELIA BAUER

Gullager [Guldager]**, (Amandus) Christian** (*b* Copenhagen, 1 March 1759; *d* Philadelphia, PA, 12 Nov 1826). American painter of Danish birth. Gullager studied at the Royal Academy of Fine Arts in Copenhagen, where he was awarded a silver medal in 1780. His earliest known portrait, of his great aunt or grandmother, *Mrs Bodel Saugaard Acke* (Denmark, priv. col.), is dated 1782. He is next recorded on 9 May 1786, when he married Mary Selman in Newburyport, MA. The portraits he painted in 1787 portray Newburyport residents and, like *Mrs Acke*, are rendered in a Danish provincial style that suggests he rejected the Neo-classical manner current in his homeland. Gullager moved to Boston by 1789, when he advertised his Hanover Street portrait studio, and worked diligently to establish a local reputation.

Gullager's most important early portrait was of *George Washington* (Boston, MA Hist. Soc.), who sat for the artist in Boston in October 1789 and again in Portsmouth, NH, that November. His portraits in the Rococo style from the 1790s suggest the influence of the Swedish painter Carl Gustav Pilo, whose work had been popular in Denmark during Gullager's student days. Gullager opened a studio in New York in the autumn of 1797 but moved the following year to Philadelphia, where he remained until at least 1805. After that he apparently lived in New York and may have tried his hand at scene painting.

BIBLIOGRAPHY

L. Dresser: 'Christian Gullager: An Introduction to his Life and Some Representative Examples of his Work', *A. America*, xxxvii (July 1949), pp. 105–19
Christian Gullager: Portrait Painter to Federal America (exh. cat. by M. Sadik, Washington, DC, N.P.G., 1976)

CARRIE REBORA

Gullichsen, Kristian (*b* Helsinki, 29 Sep 1932). Finnish architect. He graduated from the Helsinki University of Technology in 1960, first working as an assistant architect in the office of Alvar Aalto and then directing his own practice from 1961. He was Head of the Exhibitions Office of the Museum of Finnish Architecture, Helsinki, in 1965–7 and later became State Artist Professor of Finland (1988–93). Gullichsen was a leading innovator in modern Finnish architecture; his style of design represents an assimilation of a broad variety of 20th-century sources, implemented with sensitivity to local requirements and with typical Nordic restraint. His mentors included, in addition to Aalto, such major mid-century Finnish architects and theorists as Aulis Blomstedt and Reima Pietilä. Noted projects by Gullichsen include the Suutarila housing complex (1977; with Timo Vormala), which was commissioned by the City of Helsinki Housing Production Office; and the Parish Centre (1983), Kauniamen, which emphasized his preference for an architecture of walls; the building was placed on stepped levels with subtle curved forms, discreet openings and light inlets which ingeniously balanced aspects of austerity and radiance. His interest in modular, prefabricated structures can be seen in 'Moduli' (1974; with Judani Palaasma), a system for low-cost standardized holiday homes designed around an open-plan living area of 15 cubes, which allow interchangeable use. This design typified his aptitude for thoughtful, compact and integrated schemes to withstand the variations of the Finnish climate.

BIBLIOGRAPHY

C. Page: 'Houses: Unit Planning', *House and Garden*, xxix/4 (1974), pp. 110–13

M. Seppanen: 'Housing Competition, Finland', *Arkhitehti*, lxxiv/7 (1977), pp. 47–8

A. C. Antoniades: *On the Work of Kristian Gullichsen* (Tokyo, 1988)

R. Connah: *Writing Architecture* (Cambridge, MA, 1989)

S. Poole: *The New Finnish Architecture* (New York, 1992)

□

Gully, John (*b* Bath, *bapt* 21 March 1819; *d* Nelson, NZ, 1 Nov 1888). New Zealand painter of English birth. He arrived in New Plymouth in 1852, first working as a shopkeeper, teaching privately and advertising for commissions. On the outbreak of the Taranaki land wars, Gully moved to Nelson where he again struggled to establish himself as an artist and art teacher, eventually finding full-time work as a draughtsman in the provincial Survey Office. Specializing in lake and mountain views in the style of J. M. W. Turner (e.g. *In the Southern Alps*, 1881; Wellington, Mus. NZ, Te Papa Tongarewa), and frequently working on a very grand scale, Gully exhibited regularly in New Zealand and Australia, and in Europe. A portfolio of chromolithographs based on his watercolours, *New Zealand Scenery*, was published in London in 1877. The vast number of works he exhibited, and the high prices he asked for them, indicate that Gully was one of the more successful New Zealand artists of the period.

BIBLIOGRAPHY

J. S. Gully: *New Zealand's Romantic Landscape: Paintings by John Gully* (Wellington, 1984)

ROGER BLACKLEY

Gulshanābād. *See* NASIK.

Gum. Water-soluble or water-dispersible carbohydrate of vegetable origin. (For proteinaceous animal glues *see* ADHESIVES, §1(i).) Gums have been the principal binding medium for watercolour paints as used for watercolours, miniatures and, to some extent, manuscript illumination. They have also found uses as adhesives.

Gums are polysaccharides, that is to say polymers formed by the linking together of monosaccharides—the sugars—through glycoside linkages. Sugar molecules have many free hydroxyl groups on them, and many of these are still free in the polysaccharides: it is this that gives them their water solubility. The particular components present in individual gums and their proportions have in many cases been identified, though the order in which the various sugars and uronic acids (sugar derivatives containing carboxylic acid groups) are linked together is not known exactly.

The most important gum is gum arabic or gum acacia, a product of the tree *Acacia senegal* and other species. Its main source has always been the Sudan and neighbouring parts of Africa, and it was therefore well known to the ancient Egyptians, though speculation that it formed the medium of Egyptian painting has never been confirmed experimentally (*see* EGYPT, ANCIENT, §X, 1). It is still collected in large amounts as it is important in the food industry. Compounded principally of arabinose, galactose and a lesser amount of rhamnose together with galacturonic acid, it is in consequence acidic and actually exists as a salt with calcium, magnesium and potassium cations. Solutions of gum arabic become less viscous with heating due to breakdown of the polymer chains, but it is not known how stable the dried material may be. When it is used as the medium for watercolours, it is usual to add sugar, honey or glycerol to improve its mixing qualities with water and the flexibility of the medium when dry.

Gum tragacanth, another widely used gum, is obtained from *Astragalus* species (Leguminosae family). It is more troublesome to collect than gum arabic and consequently more expensive. As it is of higher molecular weight than gum arabic, it produces more viscous solutions (or rather dispersions, since it is not wholly water-soluble), but it shares the same uses.

Cherry gum, as well as gums from related *Prunus* species such as plum, peach and almond, has found some use in painting practice. Cherry gum is mentioned in manuscript treatises such as that of Theophilus. It has also been detected by analysis in Central Asian wall paintings. Other gums of some economic importance, which may also have been used in artistic practice, are locust gum (from the carob or locust tree, *Ceratonia siliqua*), tamarind seed mucilage (*Tamarindus indica*), guar gum (*Cyanaposis tetragonolobus*) and ghatti gum (*Anogeissus latifolia*). In Japan a mucilage obtained from seaweed is sometimes employed, the main source being the marine alga *Gloiopeltis furcata*. It is used in *kirikane*, a cut gold- or silver-leaf decorative technique.

BIBLIOGRAPHY

F. N. Howes: *Vegetable Gums and Resins* (Waltham, MA, 1949)

F. Smith and R. Montgomery: *Chemistry of Plant Gums and Mucilages* (New York, 1959)

J. W. Twilley: 'The Analysis of Gums in their Artistic Applications: An Interim Report', *Archaeol. Chem. III*, ccv (1984), pp. 357–94

J. S. Mills and R. White: *The Organic Chemistry of Museum Objects* (London, 1987)

JOHN S. MILLS

Gum bichromate. *See under* PHOTOGRAPHY, §I.

Gumiel, Pedro (*b* Alcalá de Henares, *c.* 1460; *d* after 14 July 1518). Spanish painter and architect. He is first documented as the painter of the retable for the tomb of *Alvaro de Luna* (1388–1453) in the Santiago Chapel, Toledo Cathedral (1488), and for the library paintings in the Colegio de Santa Cruz, Valladolid (1492). Later, as alderman of Alcalá de Henares, he is recorded as the painter and donor of a private retable (1492; destr.), which included a self-portrait, at the Hermitage of Veracruz de Alcalá la Vieja, Madrid. He entered the service of Cardinal Francisco Jiménez de Cisneros *c.* 1495, and was appointed Maestro de Obras in 1498. He inspected, valued, and advised on a vast number of paintings and sculptures in Toledo Cathedral, working with Enrique Egas, who was Maestro Mayor of the cathedral from 1500 to 1517. From 1498 he also inspected various works financed by the Cardinal, such as the monastery of Madre de Dios, Torrelaguna, near Madrid (1495–1529; designed by Juan Guas), and he submitted a project with Egas for the cloister.

From 1495 Gumiel appears to have designed the street layout around the university at Alcalá de Henares (drawing, 1506; Madrid, U. Complutense). Also at ALCALÁ DE HENARES he designed the Colegio Mayor de S Ildefonso (1501–13), including its chapel (1501–13) and retables (1513), and the Colegio Nuevo Trilingüe (1506–20). Of the latter only the theatre remains, the interior of which is elaborately decorated with a mixture of Gothic and Italian motifs. Grotesques frame the windows and doors, and halfway up the walls pilasters rest on brackets. The precise nature of Gumiel's contribution as designer or as surveyor for many of these projects continues to be unclear. His participation in the design and decoration of the chapter house of Toledo Cathedral (1508–14), or in the design of S Juan de la Penitencia, Toledo (1519–23; destr. 1936), is also not proven. Even the university theatre in Alcalá could have been designed by Francisco de Carabaña, Gumiel's successor as college architect. What is particularly disputed is his role in the introduction of the Plateresque style, found in his economical, functional and ornamental designs in both stone and wood, since it appears that Egas was also capable of designing similar works.

BIBLIOGRAPHY

M. R. Zarco del Valle: *Datos documentales para la historia del arte español: Documentos de la catedral de Toledo*, 2 vols (Madrid, 1916)

F. Chueca Goitia: *Arquitectura del siglo XVI*, A. Hisp., xi (Madrid, 1953), pp. 135, 139

M. A. Castillo Oreja: *Colegio Mayor de San Ildefonso de Alcalá de Henares: Génesis y desarrollo de su construcción, siglos XV–XVIII* (Alcalá de Henares, 1980)

F. Marías: 'De Pedro de Gumiel a Francisco de Carabaña: El mito del estilo cisneros', *Bol. Mus. & Inst. 'Camón Aznar'*, lviii (1994), pp. 21–49

FERNANDO MARÍAS

Gummer, William Henry (*b* Auckland, 7 Dec 1884; *d* Auckland, 13 Dec 1966). New Zealand architect. After training under W. A. Holman (1864–1949) in Auckland from 1900 to 1907 and then at the Royal Academy School of Architecture, London, from 1909 to 1910, he worked for Sir Edwin Lutyens and in Chicago for Daniel Burnham and Co. Gummer returned to New Zealand in 1913. Although he designed relatively few houses, he was one of the most original New Zealand domestic architects of his generation. His most striking house is Tauroa (1916), Havelock North—a large, axially planned country house that freely combines classical forms with a picturesque quality derived from the Arts and Crafts Movement.

In partnership with C. R. Ford (1880–1972) from 1923, Gummer was, along with Cecil Walter Wood, the leading New Zealand architect of his generation, winning many architectural competitions and executing major commissions for public and commercial buildings. These included the Auckland Railway Station (1930) and the Dominion Museum and National Art Gallery (1936), Wellington, both designed in a stripped classical idiom derived from American sources. The free-style classicism and boldly modelled forms of his large office buildings—the New Zealand Insurance Building (1918), Auckland, State Insurance Building (1919), Wellington, and Dilworth Building (1927), Auckland—set new standards for commercial architecture in New Zealand. With the second State Insurance Building (1940), Wellington, Gummer adopted European modernism, the first occasion this style was used for a large office building in New Zealand.

BIBLIOGRAPHY

'William Henry Gummer', *NZ Inst. Architects J.*, xx (March, 1967), pp. 86–90

K. J. Shanahan: *The Work of William H. Gummer, Architect* (diss., U. Auckland, 1983)

M. Kelly: 'Four Splendid Houses', *NZ Hist. Places*, xxxvi (March, 1992), pp. 4–7

IAN J. LOCHHEAD

Gumpp. Austrian family of artists. They were active in the Tyrol, especially Innsbruck, and in Bavaria from the 16th to the 18th century. The architect (1) Christoph Gumpp the younger had five sons who became artists: Michael (*b* Innsbruck, 8 Sep 1636; *d* Munich, 1679) trained with Hans Schor and was active as court painter in Munich; (2) Johann Martin Gumpp the elder followed in his father's profession; Franz Gumpp (*b* Innsbruck, 5 Feb 1649; *d* Florence, *c.* 1663) was active as a painter in Italy; Johann Baptist Gumpp (*b* Innsbruck, 14 Aug 1651; *d* Innsbruck, 24 Nov 1728) remained in Austria, where he was active as a printmaker and military engineer; and (3) Johann Anton Gumpp was a painter. The most important member of the family, (4) Georg Anton Gumpp, was an architect, like his father (2) Johann Martin the elder. He is best known for his work on the Cistercian abbey at Stams and for his design of the Landhaus in Innsbruck.

BIBLIOGRAPHY

Macmillan Enc. Architects; Thieme–Becker

H. Hammer: *Die Paläste und Bürgerbauten Innsbrucks* (Vienna, 1923)

E. Hempel: *Baroque Art and Architecture in Central Europe*, Pelican Hist. A. (Harmondsworth, 1965)

F. Felmayer: *Die profanen Kunstdenkmäler der Stadt Innsbruck* (1972), xxxviii of *Österreichische Kunsttopographie* (Vienna, 1972)

G. Amman: *Das Tiroler Oberland*, ix of *Österreichische Kunstmonographie* (Salzburg, 1978)

M. Krapf: *Die Baumeister Gumpp* (Vienna and Munich, 1979)

Die Baumeister Gumpp: Eine Künstlerdynastie des Barock in Tirol (exh. cat., Vienna, Belvedere, 1980)

B. Schneider: *Die Innsbrucker Jesuitenkirche* (diss., Innsbruck, Leopold-Franzens U., 1985)

(1) Christoph Gumpp [the younger] (*b* Innsbruck, 28 May 1600; *d* Innsbruck, 2 March 1672). Architect. He trained as a cabinetmaker and is recorded from 1626 as Court Joiner to Leopold V, Count of Tyrol (*reg* 1625–32), then from 1633 as Court Architect. Between 1626 and 1630 he made the confessional boxes and other wooden furnishings for the Jesuitenkirche (1627–46) in Innsbruck; the façade (1635) is also attributed to him. In 1628 Leopold V sent Gumpp to Italy to study theatre buildings in Parma, Florence and possibly Rome. When Leopold's court architect Giovanni Sperandio died in 1629, Gumpp took charge of the building of the Comödienhaus at Innsbruck (begun 1628; destr. except for its outer walls 1944; reroofed 1973, when a congress centre was built on to it). In 1647–9 Gumpp built the Mariahilfkirche in Innsbruck, an early Baroque, centrally planned church surmounted by a circular dome and lantern. Six arched openings around the nave lead to the vestibule, four semicircular chapels and the choir, all with domed roofs. The square portico is articulated with huge pilasters. One of Sebastiano Serlio's designs for a temple in the third book of *Tutte l'opere d'architettura* (1619) has been suggested as a source. Between 1649 and 1665 Gumpp was engaged on alterations to the abbey church of St Laurentius in Wilten, a typical 17th-century south German wall-pillar church (*Wandpfeilerkirche*). During this period, he also built the Hoftheater (1653–5; destr. 1844) in Innsbruck, acting more in the capacity of clerk of works than of architect and planner.

Together with his brother, the engineer Elias Gumpp (1609–76), Christoph Gumpp also designed and wrote about fortifications, but the schemes for fortifying Ehrenberg, Leutasch-Scharnitz, Kufstein, Sill-Eisacktal and Pustertal in the East Tyrol were only partially executed. Between 1646 and 1665 Christoph produced a series of *castra doloris* for members of the Tyrolese ruling family, including Leopold V, Claudia de' Medici, Ferdinand-Charles (*reg* 1632–62) and Sigismund-Francis (*reg* 1662–5).

UNPUBLISHED SOURCES

Innsbruck, Tirol. Landesmus., MS. FB32 011 [with E. Gumpp: *Kurzer Tractat aller Schanz und Fortifikationsgebeuen* (1632)]

(2) Johann Martin Gumpp [the elder] (*b* Innsbruck, 7 Nov 1643; *d* Innsbruck, 3 July 1729). Architect, engineer and cartographer, son of (1) Christoph Gumpp. In 1672 Leopold I, Holy Roman Emperor, appointed Johann Martin Gumpp to succeed his father as director of the Court Architects' Office in Innsbruck. Besides his architectural work, early in his career Gumpp also worked as a cartographer (e.g. map of imperial Tyrol, 1674; Innsbruck, Landesmus., FB. 6336), designed catafalques (that of Archduchess Claudia Felicitas in 1676) and was involved in military fortifications, on which he wrote a treatise.

Gumpp's architectural work, carried out mainly in Innsbruck, consists of huge, but clearly and simply articulated structures, whose main function is to provide a base for heavily moulded stucco decoration. In 1677–8 he collaborated with Giovanni Battista Sperandio on the church of the Holy Sepulchre in Innsbruck and between 1672 and 1680 altered and lengthened the Jesuit College, an elongated building complex that is clearly articulated both externally and internally. In 1679–80 he built the Palais Fugger (now Palais Taxis) in Innsbruck. Although there is little manipulation of architectural elements, his interest in surface treatment is evident in the coarse foliage used to decorate the window hoods and in other sculptural devices. He is also credited with altering the Palais Troyer and creating its Baroque façade, with its high-relief stuccowork, and with building the Palais Ferrari, both in Innsbruck. Documentary evidence confirms that he altered, or built a new over-elaborate façade for, the Altes Regierungsgebäude (Old Government Building; 1690–92) in the city.

Following his promotion to Court Architect in 1692, Gumpp was commissioned to build the new Cistercian abbey at Stams (for further discussion *see* (4) below). The Spitalskirche in Innsbruck was built to his plans in 1700–01 after the old one had been enlarged. It is a wide hall church with a south tower, its long east side merging with the housing in Maria Theresienstrasse. A recurring feature of Gumpp's work, evident in the Spitalskirche, is his way of forming a doorway so that the window situated above it becomes part of it. Between 1700 and 1705 he collaborated with his sons (4) Georg Anton Gumpp and Johann Martin Gumpp the younger (1686–1765) in building the Ursulinenkirche. Like the Spitalskirche, the building is a simple hall church, originally richly decorated with stucco.

WRITINGS

Relation über Befestigungen im Achental und in Kufstein (1675; Innsbruck, Tiroler Landesarchv)

(3) Johann Anton Gumpp (*b* Innsbruck, 27 April 1654; *d* Munich, 28 March 1719). Painter, son of (1) Christoph Gumpp. His teacher (later his brother-in-law) Egid Schor introduced him to the Rome school of *quadratura* painters, whose influence remained in his works for a long time. By 1675 he was working in Munich where he painted the *Putti with the Gifts of Ceres* (Munich, Schloss Nymphenburg) and in 1677 provided theatre sets for court operas. His *Holy Sepulchre* (1675; Munich, Theatinerkirche) is an interesting example of 'ephemeral' architecture, in which he attempted a very progressive, strongly spatial illusionism. In 1678 he became a Bavarian citizen, received his trade licence and on 23 May married Magdalena de Pay (*b* 1654), daughter of the Munich court painter Johann de Pay. After his own appointment as court painter to Maximilian II Emmanuel, Elector of Bavaria, in the 1680s he worked with Andreas Wolff on the decoration of some of the rooms of the Residenz (1729, largely destr.).

After his trip to Italy *c.* 1682 with Egid Quirin and Cosmas Damian Asam, the influence of Veronese became noticeable, in particular in a ceiling painting portraying scenes from the *Diana* cycle (1687) in Jagdschloss Lustheim near Schloss Schleissheim. With Melchior Steidl, he painted frescoes (1690–95) in St Florian Abbey, near Linz. He also produced designs for ceremonial architecture, such as the triumphal arch of the Electress Maria Antonia (1685) and the arch of honour (1701) for the return of Max Emanuel from the Netherlands, altarpieces (e.g. Dingolfing, Franziskanerkirche, Siebenkapellenkirche [Innsbruck]) and drawings (Innsbruck, Ubib., Roschmannsche Samml., Bd Tirol, Zeichner, f. 55; Munich, Staatl. Graph. Samml.). Gumpp turned to ornament, with a significant French influence, in his later works, for example in a closet ceiling (1702; Schleissheim, Altes Schloss), frescoes (1716; Dachau, Schloss) and ceiling paintings (1717–19) in the 'Saletl' of the Padogenburg wing of Schloss Nymphenburg, Munich.

BIBLIOGRAPHY

J. Lemmen: *Tirolisches Künstlerlexikon* (Innsbruck, 1830), p. 82

H. Tinkhauser: *Beschreibung der Diöcese Brixen*, 2 vols (Brixen, 1879), ii, p. 150

H. Hammer: *Die Entwicklung der barocken Deckenmalerei in Tirol* (Strasbourg, 1912), p. 314

Barock in Innsbruck (exh. cat. by E. Egg and G. Ammann, Innsbruck, Tirol. Landesmus., 1980), p. 71

Die Johannes von Nepomukkirche und die Baumeisterfamilie Gumpp (exh. cat., Innsbruck, 1985)

(4) Georg Anton Gumpp (*b* Innsbruck, 22 Oct 1682; *d* Innsbruck, 19 Dec 1754). Architect, engineer and cartographer, son of (2) Johann Martin Gumpp. Apart from a period in Stams, he worked exclusively in Innsbruck. He may have trained in Rome, but *c.* 1700 was posted to work with his father in the Court Architects' Office in Innsbruck. He was appointed Court Architect in 1711, with additional duties as an engineer. The influence of Roman High Baroque architecture, particularly that of Francesco Borromini, is evident in his first projects, for example the addition of a portico (1713–14) to the façade of the abbey church at Stams, the alterations and new façade for the Franciscan monastery (1718) and in the design of the Palais Pfeiffersberg (1721–9; both in Innsbruck), where the window heads on the *piano nobile* are decorated with masks. The authorities rejected his model (1714) for the construction of a parish church at Innsbruck as too lavish and costly, but Gumpp's ideas were probably incorporated into the plan that was executed.

In 1715–17 Gumpp took over the restoration in Baroque style of the chapel of the Holy Blood at the Cistercian abbey in Stams, where the medieval building was still partly extant. Using the old nave walls, he constructed a two-bay nave that opens on to a square altar room that is roofed by a lanterned dome resting on a drum. Georg Anton Gumpp had already been involved in alterations at Stams with his father in 1700–05 and between 1719 and 1724 he completed the Bernardisaal there, which juts out as a central projection. A balustrade supported by herms fronts a rectangular gallery revealed through an opening in the ceiling. Gumpp built the Altes Gymnasium (now the Alte Universität) in Innsbruck in 1722–4; a group of buildings laid out in a horseshoe shape, it is clearly articulated both internally and externally.

Georg Anton Gumpp: Landhaus of the Tyrolean Estates, Innsbruck, 1725–8

Gumpp made a significant contribution to the secular architecture of Innsbruck when he created the Landhaus in 1725–8 (see fig.), a solid, imposing building on a monumental scale with 11 bays. In the centre, four immense piers at ground-floor level support a giant order of pilasters that rise above the roof-level of the main range. The Festsaal (banqueting hall) was located on the second floor, and not, as was customary, on the first. The vestibule has three bays and a generously proportioned, richly ornamented *Treppenhaus* ('stairhouse'). The Georgkapelle or chapel of St George at the Landhaus, a five-bay barrel-vaulted building with a semicircular apse, is one of Gumpp's finest works. St Johann Nepomuk (1729–35) displays a marked tendency to break up wall surfaces by means of chapels and windows or pilasters and buttresses. In Gumpp's work columns, pilasters, deeply projecting cornices and exuberant window frames are set off against each other in dynamic tension, with the main components building up to a climax at the centre, where additional surface decoration is judiciously applied to heighten the effect.

BIBLIOGRAPHY

L. Achatz: *Der Architekt Georg Anton Gumpp und seine stilgeschichtliche Stellung* (coursework, U. Vienna, 1962)

BRIGITTE SCHNEIDER

Gum Vihara. *See under* SANKHU.

Gun, Karl (Fyodorovich). *See* HŪNS, KĀRLIS.

Gunbad-i Qabus [Gombad-e Qabus; Gunbad-i Kabus; Gunbad-i Kavus; Gunbad-i Qābūs]. Town in north-east Iran. Set in the fork of the Qareh Su and Gurgan rivers, 5 km west of the ruins of medieval Gurgan (Arab. Jurjan), the town takes its name from the tomb of the Ziyarid ruler Qabus ibn Wushmgir (*reg* 978–1012), which stands at the north end of the main street (*see* ISLAMIC ART, fig. 28). The baked brick tower (h. 52 m) is raised on a 10 m artificial hill and dominates the surrounding plain. A slightly truncated cylinder (int. diam. 9.67 m) with ten buttressing flanges, it has a plain exterior relieved only by two identical inscription bands that encircle the tower between the buttresses, one 8 m above the ground and the other below the corbel. The text in kufic script states that Qabus ordered the tomb in the lunar year 397 and the solar year 375 (Sept 1006–March 1007). The stunning composition, soaring verticality and solid construction in baked brick make the tower a masterpiece of medieval Iranian architecture.

BIBLIOGRAPHY

Enc. Islam/2: 'Gunbad-i Ḳābūs'

E. Diez: *Churasanische Baudenkmäler* (Berlin, 1918), pp. 39–43, 100–06

A. U. Pope and P. Ackerman, eds: *Survey of Persian Art* (London, 1938–9, 3/1977), pp. 970–79

S. S. Blair: *The Monumental Inscriptions of Early Islamic Iran and Transoxiana* (Leiden, 1991), pp. 63–5

ABBAS DANESHVARI

Gundelach, Franz. *See* GONDELACH, FRANZ.

Gundelach [Gindelach; Gondelach; Gondolach], **Matthäus** [Matthias] (*b* Hessen [?Kassel], *c.* 1566; *d* Augsburg, between Oct 1653 and Feb 1654). German painter and draughtsman. The son of the painter Hans Gundelach, he was living in Prague by 1593. He worked in the sphere of Bartholomäus Spranger, Hans von Aachen and Joseph Heintz (i), whom he succeeded as court painter and whose widow he married, thereby acquiring citizenship of Augsburg. His son, Hans Wilhelm Gundelach, became his pupil, as did his stepsons Joseph Heintz (ii) and Ferdinand Heintz (*fl* 1609–21), in 1617 and 1621 respectively.

After the death of Emperor Rudolf II in 1612, Gundelach at first remained in Prague in the service of Emperor Matthias, but he left the court *c.* 1615. In 1616–17 he was employed by the Duke of Württemberg in Stuttgart, and in 1617 he finally settled in Augsburg. In 1622–3 he provided paintings for the Rathaus and decorated several churches. He was a member of the city's Great Council (1632–49) and remained until his death esteemed for his paintings and for his designs for engravings, mostly executed by Wolfgang and Lucas Kilian.

Gundelach always adhered to the themes of Rudolfine art, being particularly influenced by the delicate work of Heintz; *Cupid and Psyche* (1613; Augsburg, Schaezlerpal., on loan from Munich, Bayer. Staatsgemäldesammlungen) exemplifies these factors. He frequently made copies after his contemporaries' work, such as the *Adoration of the Shepherds* (Prague, N.G.), after an engraving (1606) by Jan Muller after Spranger. In the *Mystic Marriage of St Catherine* (1614; Vienna, Ksthist. Mus.; see fig.) Gundelach gave the Emperor Matthias's features to the apostle Matthew, while the Empress, Anne of Austria (*d* 1618), is portrayed as St Helena. He maintained the spirit of Rudolfine allegory in paintings such as the *Allegory of Mining or of the Earth* (*c.* 1620; Dortmund, Mus. Kst & Kultgesch.), with its reflections on treasure-seeking and the capriciousness of earthly fortune, and the *Allegory of Fishing or of Water* (Friedrichshafen, Städt. Bodensee-Mus.), with its nude figure of Fortuna, seen from behind, in the tradition of Rudolfine sensuality. Possibly both paintings were part of a cycle allegorizing the four elements.

In Augsburg, Gundelach produced numerous paintings of a religious nature as well as mythological and allegorical subjects. He worked for Catholic patrons, although himself a Protestant; one of his last works was designing the engravings for a small Protestant devotional book, *Die geistliche Uhr* (1651; Berlin, Kupferstichkab.). Here again Gundelach, aged over 80, though influenced by a wide range of other Augsburg artists (such as Johann Mathias Kager and Johann Heinrich Schönfeld), was still evidently closely attached to the ideal of Rudolfine art, transmitting it beyond the Thirty Years War to the period of the Baroque.

BIBLIOGRAPHY

Thieme–Becker

P. Bergner: 'Matthias Gundelach, Kammermaler Rudolfs II', *Jb. Ksthist. Inst. Ksr.-Kön. Zent.-Komm. Dkmlpf.*, v (1911), pp. 183–7

H. Möhle: 'Neue Beiträge zu Matthaeus Gundelach', *Festschrift F. Winkler* (Berlin, 1959), pp. 268–79

Zeichnung in Deutschland: Deutsche Zeichner, 1540–1640, i (exh. cat., Stuttgart, Staatsgal., 1979–80), nos F13–F16

Matthäus Gundelach: *Mystic Marriage of St Catherine*, oil on copper, 400×310 mm, 1614 (Vienna, Kunsthistorisches Museum)

E. Bender: *Matthäus Gundelach—Leben und Werk* (diss., U. Frankfurt am Main, 1981)

T. D. Kaufmann: *L'Ecole de Prague: La Peinture à la cour de Rodolphe II* (Paris, 1985; rev. and trans. Chicago and London, 1988)

Prag um 1600. Kunst und Kultur am Hofe Rudolfs II (exh. cat., Vienna Ksthist. Mus., 1988), i, nos 120–25, 199–203; ii, nos 557, 617

C. HÖPER

Gundersen, Gunnar S(igmund) (*b* Førde, Sunnfjord, 25 Dec 1921; *d* Baerum, 16 Jan 1983). Norwegian painter and printmaker. He was one of the pioneers of Norwegian non-figurative art. As a child he was absorbed by drawing and geometry and was impressed by the emotional force of nature. He studied in Oslo, at the Statens Håndverks- og Kunstindustriskole (1947–8) and the Kunstakademi (1949), where he was already noted for his intellectual and analytical approach. After finishing his formal education he independently studied the psychology of perception and the Constructivism of De Stijl, the Bauhaus and the work of Kazimir Malevich. He made his début at the *Høstutstilling* ('Autumn exhibition') in Oslo in 1947 with paintings and prints of landscapes tending towards abstraction. Three years later he participated in the first showing of concrete art in Norway, at the Kunstnerforbund (Artists' League) in Oslo, and explained in an interview that 'part of the meaning of art is to give the observer a sense of freedom through clarity in rhythm and form'. He interpreted this clarity with sharply delineated squares and rectangles, trapezoids and rhomboids, in soft or else strongly contrasting colours, as in *Painting* (1958; Oslo, Mus. Samtidskst), reminiscent of work shown at the Galerie Denise René in Paris, especially that of Victor

Vasarely and Auguste Herbin (1882–1960). Critics generally dismissed the work as 'decorative', but he gained many large decorative commissions, for example for the façade of the Kunstnerforbund's building (1950; with Ludvig Eikaas, *b* 1920) and for Høyenhall School (1972) in Oslo, where he decorated three large wall panels in the assembly hall. The panels and the wall surface between them offer strong contrasts of form and colour, today considered one of the masterpieces of Norwegian art. He worked with like-minded architects as well as other non-figurative painters, who, in protest against the critics' negativity, formed the group Terningen (The Dice), in which Gundersen was a leading figure; its members exhibited together from 1956 to 1960. Some of his own work from this period reveals an interest in the work of Serge Poliakoff and Nicolas de Staël.

During the 1960s Gundersen's articulated constructions became more analytical; the subtle displacements of the coloured planes and the finely-honed, irregular forms induce a constantly changing character, as in *Composition* (1963; Oslo, Mus. Samtidskst). Somewhat later his paintings show contradictory reflections on space and plane and the abstract and materially tangible. Large and exciting, rounded and rectangular, intricately-grouped forms are shown in continuously altered encounters in indefinable, timeless landscapes. Gundersen's point of departure was still the psychological process of sight; his earlier use of colour was enriched with metallic gleaming black while the compositions began to convey anxiety provoking moods (e.g. *Black Sun*, 1967; see Johansen, p. 47). Gundersen's gift for experimentation developed freely in the course of his teaching duties at the Norges Tekniske Høgskole (1958–66) in Trondheim. His unconventional method was based on a theory of unified elements in pictorial art based on intuition and its dynamic and psychological effects. Towards the 1970s his colours became more modulated, with an expanded register of grey tones. In *Dance* (1968; Høvikodden, Henies–Onstads Kstsent.), a powerful floating, ellipse-and-ribbon formation is mirrored in a gleaming, cold, imagined space.

From the beginning of the 1960s, Gundersen chose screenprinting as a form of expression to parallel his acrylic painting. His screenprints resemble the paintings with their balanced forms and smooth, coated surfaces, as in *Day of Champagne* (before 1973; Oslo, N.G.). Naturalistic watercolours of landscapes from the same period bear witness to his poetic sense and artistic range. His few sculptures, on the other hand, are distinctly architectonic: these are of wood and occasionally of perspex. Gundersen's paintings of his last years demonstrated a virtuoso handling of colour and of evocative spatial effects; his forms, mostly confined to the red–blue scale, became less strict (e.g. *Composition*, 1982; see Johansen, p. 77). Gundersen represented his country at three Biennales, in São Paulo (1955, 1959) and Venice (1968). An unconventional attitude and an understanding of the Constructivist tradition and the psychology of perception united with a lively imagination lie behind Gundersen's evocative and emotionally powerful paintings. Their unique formal, spatial and colouristic effects are visual and emotional challenges.

BIBLIOGRAPHY

M. Malmanger: 'Gunnar S. Gundersens malerier', *Paletten*, xxiv (1963), pp. 152–3

Gunnar S. Gundersen (exh. cat. by M. Malmanger, Venice Biennale, 1968) [Eng., It. and Ger. texts]

J. O. Johansen: *Gunnar S. Gundersen* (Oslo, 1982)

K. Berg and others, eds: *Inn i en ny tid* [Into a new era] (1983), vii of *Norges kunsthistorie* (Oslo, 1981–3), pp. 138, 150–52, 157, 196, 215, 268–9

Gunnar S. Gundersens offentlige utsmykninger 1949–1980 [Gunnar S. Gundersen's public decorative projects, 1949–80] (exh. cat., ed. T. Huse, foreword O. H. Moe; Høvikodden, Henies–Onstads Kstsent., 1983) [contains interview with artist and Eng. summary]

SUSANNE RAJKA

Gundestrup Cauldron. Silver vessel of the 2nd–1st centuries BC, found in 1891 in a peat bog at Gundestrup, Jutland, Denmark. The Gundestrup Cauldron (Copenhagen, Nmus.; see fig. and MUSICAL INSTRUMENTS, fig. 2) is arguably the finest and most fascinating example of toreutic (chased or repoussé) silverwork in the THRACIAN AND DACIAN ART tradition. A large, partly gilded silver vessel measuring 400 mm high×690 mm in diameter, the cauldron comprises a hemispherical bowl with vertical sides constructed from 13 plates covered with detailed figural scenes executed in the Thracian 'Animal style', its surfaces densely packed with representations of elephants, lions, dolphins, stags, snakes, griffins, hunters and deities. There are five long rectangular inner plates with inward-facing scenes and seven squarer outer plates; these do not enclose the entire circumference, and a missing eighth plate is presumed. A circular plate generally known as the base plate was probably once part of a lid.

When discovered, the cauldron was in a dismantled state, with the plates stacked together inside the bowl, and it was ascertained that it had been left on solid ground and that the bog had grown over it. These two observations suggest that, rather than having been a ritual or votive deposit in the manner of much prehistoric Scandinavian metalwork, the cauldron had been hidden, perhaps in long grass, by someone who intended to return for it. The cauldron has been the subject of controversy since the time of its discovery, although its date of manufacture is generally agreed to lie within the period *c*. 150 BC–AD 150. Three places of origin have been suggested: northern or southern Gaul, Scandinavia and south-eastern Europe. As early as 1915, Friedrich Drexel put forward arguments for a south-eastern European origin on the basis of comparison with contemporary toreutic metalwork of the region. This view seems to have been confirmed by subsequent discoveries and has gained the support of most scholars, although Erik Nylén has argued that it may have been produced in Scandinavia by immigrant Thracian silversmiths. The principal argument against Gaulish manufacture is the lack of any known tradition of repoussé silverworking in the region, while the main argument for a western provenance relies on the presence of Celtic elements in the iconography, particularly the claimed identification of the antlered god Cernunnos and the representation of warriors with Celtic helmets and weaponry. However, the appearance of the warriors is more consistent with a south-eastern European origin, and most of the types of artefact actually shown on the cauldron are known exclusively from south-eastern European archaeological contexts.

From a technical point of view, the cauldron is unambiguously a product of the Thracian toreutic tradition. All the metalworking techniques documented in material from AGIGHIOL, Romania, and in Thracian work of the 4th century BC were employed, but in a more sophisticated fashion: higher repoussé and more extensive pattern punching, partial gilding and insetting make it closer to the later corpus of Thracian and Dacian sheet silverwork. The absence of Roman stylistic influence suggests a date in the 2nd century BC. Scanning electron microscopy of the punch marks in the pattern has determined that at least three silversmiths worked on the plates.

The Gundestrup Cauldron's iconography is typically Thracian in its layout, employing closely packed yet discrete fields of representations, as in the material from Rogozen (*see* ROGOZEN TREASURE). The meticulous execution of such details as animal pelts and shoe fastenings, and the eclecticism of imagery, also point to a Thracian origin. One figure on the cauldron, a woman with her hair in tresses and flanked by birds, can be identified as a type of the western Asiatic goddess Hārītī, who also occurs on *phalerae* (horse ornaments) from Kuşana, in Sarmatian silverwork (*see* SCYTHIAN AND SARMATIAN ART) and on a silver-gilt *phalera* from Galiche in northern Bulgaria. Closely similar in all respects to Thracian *phalerae*, the base plate is a masterly and powerful accomplishment. It is decorated with a forest scene in which an androgynous human with animal fur on its shoulders—an image conceptually similar to earlier Thracian composite figures—attacks a massive wild ox, whose fully three-dimensional head rears out of the surface plane. Much of the meaning of the iconography is obscure and may well remain so. Nevertheless, the proposed dating and the presence of at least some Celtic elements make it plausible that the cauldron was made by local silversmiths for an intrusive Celtic élite. On this basis, one explanation for the cauldron's presence in Jutland is that it was among the booty taken by Teutonic Cimbri people during raids on the Celtic Scordisci of south-eastern Europe between 118 and 113 BC. Other explanations, however, remain possible.

BIBLIOGRAPHY

S. Müller: 'Det store sølvkar fra Gundestrup i Jylland', *Nord. Fortidsminder*, i (1892), pp. 35–68

F. Drexel: 'Über den Silberkessel von Gundestrup', *Jb. Ksr. Dt. Archäol. Inst.*, xxx (1915), pp. 1–36

O. Klindt-Jensen: *Gundestrupkedelen* (Copenhagen, 1961) [summary in Eng.]

E. Nylén: 'Gundestrup och den trakiska konsten', *Tor*, xii (1968), pp. 133–73

T. G. E. Powell: 'From Urartu to Gundestrup: The Agency of Thracian Metalwork', *The European Community in Later Prehistory*, ed. J. Boardman and others (London, 1971), pp. 181–210

N. K. Sandars: 'Orient and Orientalising: Recent Thoughts Reviewed', *Celtic Art in Ancient Europe: Five Protohistoric Centuries*, ed. C. F. C. Hawkes and P. M. Duval (London, 1976), pp. 41–57

R. Pittioni: *Wer hat wann und wo den Silberkessel von Gundestrup angefertigt?*, Veröffentlichungen der keltischen Kommission der österreichischen Akademie der Wissenschaften (Vienna, 1984) [good pls]

E. Benner Larsen: 'The Gundestrup Cauldron: Identification of Tool Traces', *Iskos*, v (1985), pp. 561–74

A. Bergquist and T. Taylor: 'The Origin of the Gundestrup Cauldron', *Antiquity*, lxi (1987), pp. 10–24

Gundestrup Cauldron, silver, h. 400 mm, diam. 690 mm, 2nd–1st centuries BC (Copenhagen, Nationalmuseum)

J. V. S. Megaw and M. R. Megaw: *Celtic Art from its Beginnings to the Book of Kells* (London, 1989)

TIMOTHY TAYLOR

Gundlach, F. C. (*b* Heinebach, Hessen, 1926). German photographer. After studying from 1947 to 1949 at the Höhere Lehranstalt für Photographie in Kassel, he began work as a photographer in 1952. In 1954 he started his own studio in Stuttgart and in 1956 settled in Hamburg. His work for women's magazines such as *Film und Frau*, *Elegante Welt* and *Annabelle* established him as one of Germany's most important fashion photographers. Until 1968 he reported on the *haute couture* collections in Paris. His archive contains a compendium of fashion of the 1950s and 1960s. He also specialized in portraits of film stars in those years, for example *Simone Signoret and Yves Montand, Paris 1953* (see Honnef, p. 43). In 1975 he founded the PPS-Galerie in Hamburg, through which he sought to ensure the propagation and recognition of photography as both an art object and a collector's item.

BIBLIOGRAPHY

K. Honnef: *Modewelten F. C. Gundlach: Photographien 1950 bis heute* (Berlin, 1985)

ERIKA BILLETER

Gundulf, Bishop of Rochester (*b* nr Rouen, France, ?1025; *d* Rochester, England, March 1108). French bishop and patron. He was a student and clerk at Rouen Cathedral, entering Bec Abbey *c.* 1059. There he began his lifelong association with Lanfranc and Anselm. In 1063 Gundulf accompanied Lanfranc to St Etienne, Caen, as his prior. Upon Lanfranc's elevation to the See of Canterbury in 1070 Gundulf again followed him, this time as proctor and estate manager. In 1076 he was appointed Bishop of Rochester. His appointment established a special relationship between Rochester and Canterbury, Gundulf relieving Lanfranc of many of his diocesan duties. During Archbishop Anselm's exile he took charge of the administration, both spiritual and temporal, of the Canterbury archbishopric.

Undoubtedly it was Gundulf's excellent abilities as a builder, attested to in contemporary documents, as well as his shrewd business sense, that prompted William the Conqueror to put him in charge of building the White Tower in London. He also built a castle at Rochester for William II. At Rochester Gundulf refounded the cathedral as a Benedictine community and rebuilt the church and monastic buildings. He founded a nunnery at West Malling (*c.* 1100), Kent, where he built a substantial church as well as domestic buildings. His usual residence seems to have been near by in another of his structures, St Leonard's Tower. Although mostly either replaced or altered, Gundulf's buildings were prime examples of the solid Norman style that spread across England in the years after the Conquest.

BIBLIOGRAPHY

The Life of Gundulf, Bishop of Rochester (n.d.); ed. R. Thomson (Toronto, 1977)

R. A. L. Smith: 'The Place of Gundulf in the Anglo-Norman Church', *Eng. Hist. Rev.*, ccxxxi (July 1943), pp. 257–72

LISA A. REILLY

Gunnlögsson, Halldor (*b* Copenhagen, 23 Jan 1918; *d* Rungsted, 12 April 1985). Danish architect. He won a large number of commissions through competition entries in which his analytical capacity was revealed in clear spatial ordering of functional programmes. The executed projects were worked out with a discipline consistent down to every detail. Nevertheless, his buildings do not attempt to advance any architectural philosophy, but rather manifest his receptiveness to contemporary trends. Characteristic in this respect are his own houses: the first (1951), in Vedbæk, is informal, like a Frank Lloyd Wright prairie house, while the second (1958), in Rungsted, is a Japanese-inspired wooden house articulated with window bays, simplified to the point of abstraction. Other important works include the town halls of Tårnby (1959) and Fredericia (1964), the Fiskeri-og Søfartsmuseet (1968) in Esbjerg, and the block of service flats and nursing home Hellebo (1970) in Elsinore. His office was also responsible for a number of schools, blocks of flats and smaller town halls in Bov, Nordborg and Tønder, Jutland, and it also supervised the construction of the Ministry for Foreign Affairs building (1977–80), Copenhagen. Gunnlögsson entered partnership with Jørn Nielsen (*b* 1919) in 1952 and from 1959 until his death was a professor at the Arkitektskole of the Kunstakademiet. His teaching was marked by an uncompromising demand for quality combined with an open-mindedness to different forms of expression.

BIBLIOGRAPHY

P. E. Skriver: 'H.G.'s own house', *Arkitektur DK*, iii/3 (1959), pp. 92–9

——: 'Tårnby Rådhus', *Arkitektur DK*, iv (1960), pp. 121–31

——: 'Fiskeri- og Sofartsmuseet i Esbjerg', *Arkitektur DK*, xii/5 (1968), pp. 209–16

——: Udenrigsministeriets nye bygninger i København', *Arkitektur DK*, 1 (1983), pp. 22–9

JØRGEN SESTOFT

Günther, (Franz) Ignaz (*b* Altmannstein, Oberpfalz, 22 Nov 1725; *d* Munich, 26 June 1775). German sculptor. He first trained with his father, Johann Georg Günther (1704–83), a cabinetmaker who produced occasional wood sculptures. In 1743 he travelled to Munich, where he is thought to have worked for seven years with Johann Baptist Straub, whose sculpture workshop was the leading one in the region. Günther's earliest known works are study drawings of historical monuments and sculptures that he made while apprenticed to Straub, and exercises in technical drawing that were mainly variations on material in Andrea Pozzo's *Perspectiva pictorum et architectorum* (Rome, 1693–1702). Probably *c.* 1750 he set off on his journeyman's travels and is documented in Salzburg in that year. In 1751–2 he was in Mannheim, in Paul Egell's workshop, where he drew works by Egell and made a copy in lime-wood (1751; Munich, Bayer. Nmus.) of Egell's relief of *St John the Baptist.*

Günther then travelled to Moravia, where, probably working in the workshop of Joseph Zahner (*d* 1752) in Olomouc, he executed his first independent sculptures. For the small parish church of Kopřivná (Geppersdorf) near the Silesian border he produced a statue of *The Virgin* on a globe, three large and several small angels, and statues of *St Peter* and *St Paul*. These sculptures show his style to be already fully developed; it displays the influence both of Straub and of Egell, particularly in the figure of *The Virgin*, with its closed body volume and the elongated folds of the robe broken in obtuse angles. From May to November 1753 Günther studied at the imperial Kunsta-

1. Ignaz Günther: high altar (1759–62), SS Marinus und Anianus, Rott am Inn

kademie in Vienna, where he won first prize for a terracotta group (untraced) of *Aeneas Carrying his Father Anchises from Burning Troy*. From this period there survive small-scale copies in wood of the *Venus de' Medici* and the Borghese *Gladiator* (1753; Munich, Bayer. Nmus.).

Günther then returned to Munich, settling there for the rest of his life; in June 1754 Maximilian III Joseph, Elector of Bavaria, appointed him Hofbefreiter Bildhauer. His first securely attributed work in Munich is a statuette of *Christ at the Column* (wood, h. 745 mm, 1754; Detroit, MI, Inst. A.), modelled on the miraculous image in the Wallfartskirche of Wies, near Steingaden. One year later he completed the kneeling figure (now severely damaged) of a saint (1755; Starnberg, Heimatmus.), which has a vivid sense of movement and space (two *bozzetti* related to it are in Munich, Bayer. Nmus. and priv. col.). At that period monasteries and churches were being built throughout the country and commissions were plentiful. For St Peter, Munich, Günther designed the funerary monument to the *Stadtkommandant Johann Egid de Courcelles von Wachsenstein* (1755) and the Mariahilf and Corpus Christi altars (1755–8). In 1755 he first worked for the Augustinian Canons of Weyarn, executing for the Stiftskirche (now Pfarrkirche) SS Peter und Paul a free-standing reliquary with two life-size angels. In 1758 he sculpted the first of his three life-size *Pietà* groups for the Pfarrkirche St Rupertus in Kircheiselfing; it is signed both by him and by the painter Mignolin Demuel (1724–89) who polychromed it. Subsequently he produced two side altars (1758–9) for the Anastasiakapelle adjacent to the Klosterkirche St Benedikt at Benediktbeuern, and a high altar for the Pfarr- und Wallfahrtskirche Mariae Himmelfahrt at Munich-Thalkirchen, which integrated existing Late Gothic figures.

In the 1760s Günther produced an impressive series of major works, beginning with a commission (1759–62) from Graf Joseph Franz von Seinsheim for a high altar with a white-painted relief of the *Assumption* in the chapel of his ancestral castle at Sünching, near Ratisbone, and also for allegorical reliefs in the banqueting hall, depicting *Fame* with putti. The high point of his oeuvre is represented by his works (1759–62) for the Benedictine Klosterkirche St Marinus und Anianus at Rott am Inn, built by Johann Michael Fischer. Günther's high altar is perfectly integrated with the Romanesque-style chancel wall and with his monumental statues of *St Corbinian* and *St Ulric*, and of the *Emperor Henry II* and his wife *Kunigunde* (see fig. 1). In this work the sculptor achieved a particularly harmonious balance between the demands of the individual figure and of the altar as an ornamental structure in an integrated ensemble. The plain side altars, with their pairs of statues of *St Peter Damian* and *Leo IV* and of the peasant saints *St Isidore (the Farm Servant)* and *Notburga* also rank among his most impressive achievements. Around 1761 he also made three altars for the Klosterkirche St Peter und Paul of the Dominican convent of Altenhohenau near Rott am Inn.

Between 1763 and 1764 Günther executed for the Augustinian Canons at Weyarn a tabernacle for the high altar and some more sculptures, including an *Annunciation* group (see fig. 2) and a *Pietà*. During the same period he also produced two oak doors with relief decorations (1763) for the Neues Schloss at Schleissheim, near Munich. The commission that he carried out (*c*. 1764–5) for the Augustinian Canons of Freising-Neustift, which comprised the high altar, two side altars, the abbot's chair and the choir-stalls, was comparable in size and importance to the work for Rott am Inn. The high altar of the Alte Pfarrkirche of Starnberg (*c*. 1765–8), with its group of the *Holy Family* over the tabernacle, points, in its simplicity and its closed formal structure, beyond the Rococo style. About 1768 Günther produced, for the Benedictine Klosterkirche St Johannes Evangelist at Mallersdorf, a large high altar with four statues, which is similar to those in Rott am Inn and Neustift but surmounted by a representation of the *Woman Clothed with the Sun* of the Apocalypse.

2. Ignaz Günther: *Annunciation*, lime-wood, h. 1.60 m, 1764 (Weyarn, SS Peter und Paul)

From the late 1760s Günther's commissions became less plentiful. They included two side altars (1773–4) in the Pfarrkirche St Georg in Munich-Bogenhausen. From 1770 his contribution to the modernization of the Frauenkirche in Munich included five oak portals with rich relief decoration, and a cycle of sixteen reliefs with scenes from the *Life of the Virgin* for the choir-stalls. The end of his career is marked by the expressive *Pietà* group (1774), a timeless monument to human suffering, in the small cemetery chapel at Nenningen in the Swabian Jura (models Munich, Bayer. Nmus., and Stuttgart, Württemberg. Landesmus.).

Günther was a virtuoso wood-carver (the complex polychromy of his sculptures was the work of other hands). He also occasionally produced works in other materials, such as two fountains in lead with gilt putti and swans (1758; untraced) for Ismaning, the summer palace of the prince-bishops of Freising, and a polychromed lead statuette of *The Virgin* (*c.* 1770–72; Augsburg, Maximilianmus.). The only stone sculptures that he is known to have executed were the figures of *Mars* and *Bellona* (1769–70; destr.) in the Hauptwache in Munich. He occasionally designed medals, and his workshop produced numerous models for the relief decoration of bells. He frequently made sculptural models for goldsmiths, chiefly for Joseph Friedrich Canzler (*fl c.* 1743–56), a master goldsmith in Munich (e.g. silver statuette of *The Virgin*, 1760; Ingolstadt, St Moritz).

Günther contributed several designs to the unfinished *Ecole de l'architecture bavaroise* by François de Cuvilliés II (1731–77); they include his only etching, *Pygmalion* (1769). His surviving drawings and watercolours, of which there are more than 80, show Günther to have been a gifted draughtsman and designer. His sculptural designs, in the form of sketches and models in wood and terracotta, give equal evidence of his talents; and all of them reveal an exact knowledge of current developments in ornamentation. Thus his designs from the 1770s for the Bürgersaalkirche and the doors of the Frauenkirche (both Munich) are in pure Louis XVI idiom, while his figural and altar compositions continued to be in the Rococo style, probably in accord with his patrons' preferences. Günther's most important patrons were ecclesiastical rather than secular, being chiefly prominent monasteries; his work displays the tension, characteristic of the period, between the demands of his craft and the higher ones of art. His work marks the high point of south German Rococo sculpture; he was the most important figural sculptor of his age, next to Egell and Georg Raphael Donner, and he continued the tradition of Munich sculpture that had been brought to a high artistic level by Egid Quirin Asam and Straub. Günther gave greater weight to the individual figure and endowed his figures with a more intensely spiritual expression than Straub, who concentrated on the overall decorative effect. Günther's sacred figures, with their haughty grandeur that is heightened to the point of Mannerism, are distanced, in their theatrical presentation, from everyday concerns; while emotion, heralding the age of sensibility, carries his work beyond the Rococo.

A portrait of Günther (1774) by Martin Knoller exists in two identical versions (Munich, Bayer. Nmus. and priv. col.). A self-portrait, probably an oval medallion in wood, is known only from a drawn copy (1806; Munich, Staatl. Graph. Samml.) by Ferdinand Piloty (1786–1844).

BIBLIOGRAPHY

A. Feulner: *Ignaz Günther: Kurfürstlich bayerischer Hofbildhauer (1725–1775)* (Vienna, 1920)

——: *Ignaz Günther: Der grosse Bildhauer des bayerischen Rokoko* (Munich, 1947)

Ignaz Günther (exh. cat. by A. Schönberger and G. Woeckel, Munich, Bayer. Nmus., 1951)

A. Schönberger: *Ignaz Günther* (Munich, 1954) [catalogue of sculptures]

G. Woeckel: *Ignaz Günther: Die Handzeichnungen* (Weissenhorn, 1975)

Bayerische Rokokoplastik: Vom Entwurf zur Ausführung (exh. cat., ed. P. Volk; Munich, Bayer. Nmus., 1985)

P. Volk: *Ignaz Günther* (Regensburg, 1991)

PETER VOLK

Günther, (Johann) Joachim (*b* Tritschengreith [now Trischenreuth], Bavaria, 3 March 1720; *d* Bruchsal, 2 July 1789). German sculptor and stuccoist. He may have trained with his uncle, the sculptor Ignaz Langelacher, in Moravia; the quality of his work suggests that he had some academic training, possibly in Munich, perhaps in the studio of Johann Baptist Straub. He worked in stone and in wood, as well as in stucco. In 1749–50 he produced statues of the *Twelve Apostles* for the church of Horgauergreuth, near Augsburg. In 1752 he carried out his first work at the Residenzschloss in Bruchsal for Franz Christoph von Hutten, Bishop of Speyer (1706–70); in 1755 the Bishop granted him protection. Apart from a short period spent working in Vienna, where he was summoned in 1773 to produce the group *Ceres and Bacchus* for the gardens at Schönbrunn, Günther continued to live in Bruchsal, working chiefly in the residences of the Bishops of Speyer in Bruchsal and Kislau; he also received commissions for churches of the region. Much of his work has been destroyed; what survives is difficult to characterize because of its uneven quality. Thus he is now thought to have contributed to the sandstone statues of the *Seasons* and the *Elements* (1759–61; Bruchsal, Schlosspark) formerly ascribed to Adolf Gnauth (see Zimmermann, exh. cat.); but these sophisticated inventions differ greatly from his substantiated works. His sculpture shows the influence of Paul Egell, and his stucco work that of Johann Michael Feichtmayer.

BIBLIOGRAPHY

A. Siegel: 'Johann Joachim Günther', *Oberrhein. Kst*, vii (1936), pp. 197–208

G. Poensgen: 'Beiträge zum Werk des Johann Joachim Günther', *Mitt. Hist. Ver. Pfalz*, lviii (1960), pp. 303–7

F. Gehrig: 'Der Bruchsaler Hofbildhauer Joachim Günther', *Freiburg. Diöz.-Archv*, lxxxix (1969), pp. 374–88

K. Jäckel: 'Forschungsergebnisse zum Leben des Bruchsaler Hofbildhauers und Stuckkateurs Joachim Günther', *Z. Gesch. Oberrheins*, cxxvii (1979), pp. 319–42

——: 'Die Sandsteinplastiken im Bruchsaler Schlosspark: Ein Werk des Bildhauers Joachim Günther (1720–1789)', *Pfälz. Heimat*, xxx (1979), pp. 90–100

E. Zimmermann: 'Joachim Günther', *Barock in Baden Württemberg: Vom Ende des dreissigjährigen Krieges bis zur französischen Revolution* (exh. cat., Bruchsal, Schloss, 1981), i, pp. 21–4

BERND WOLFGANG LINDEMANN

Günther, Matthäus (*b* Tritschengreith [now Trischenreuth], Bavaria, 7 Sept 1705; *d* Haid, Bavaria, 30 Sept 1788). German painter and etcher. He completed his apprenticeship in Murnau with Simon Bernhardt and subsequently worked under the leading south German painter Cosmas Damian Asam from 1723 to 1728. In 1730 Günther moved to Augsburg, and a year later, after marrying the widow of the fresco painter Ferdinand Magg (*b* 1679), he obtained his master's licence. From this point onwards Günther's work developed swiftly in both style and range, and records exist of his activity far beyond the frontiers of Bavaria. Günther generally spent the winter months in Augsburg, painting panel pictures and etching. In 1740 he acquired the artistic estate of the deceased Johann Evangelist Holzer, a prodigiously gifted rival, and this material became of great artistic importance to him as a source of motifs and ideas. The 1750s were very prolific years for Günther, with secular commissions through the Duke of Württemberg and religious commissions in

Würzburg, Wilten or Indersdorf. In 1762 Günther succeeded Johann Georg Bergmüller as director of the Kunstakademie in Augsburg. Günther's wife died in 1761, and in 1763 he married the widow of the well-known Wessobrunn stucco artist Johann Georg Uebelherr (1700–63), with whom he had previously collaborated. In 1765 Günther acquired a house in what was then Schonemergasse in Augsburg. At 79 he retired to his estate in Haid, and he thenceforth accepted commissions only occasionally.

Günther completed his earliest recorded frescoes in 1732 for the choir and nave of the parish church of Druisheim, near Donauwörth. These showed the *Story of St Vitus*. In painting the cupola, for which he was soon noted, Günther used *trompe l'oeil* architecture to divide the vault into two zones, and he arranged the main figures in a spiral pattern. He used this arrangement in subsequent frescoes, for example in the parish church of Sterzing (now Vipiteno, Italy) in the southern Tyrol in 1733. As he progressed with commissions, in the parish church of St Martin in Garmisch in 1732, or in the castle of Wolfsthurn in Mareit in 1735, Günther overcame the difficulties with perspective inherited from his early experience of panel painting, and he sought to merge the levels of reality separating real architecture from ceiling painting. He also began to draw from a wider range of sources: these included not only Hans Georg Asam, Cosmas Damian Asam and the Roman Baroque school, especially Andrea Pozzo's architectural illusionism, but also the techniques used by Pietro da Cortona to subject architectural space to painted space. Günther's first really major commission was to decorate the nave and side aisles of the Augustinian collegiate church at Neustift (now Novacella, near Bressanone, Italy), in 1736. The ceiling sections, which are reminiscent of stage sets, reinterpreted the originally Gothic space in rhythmically colourful Baroque decoration. In the parish church at Rattenberg, where Günther worked in 1737, his more restrained colours reveal the influence of Roman and Venetian examples (respectively Andrea del Pozzo's cupola painting and the figure types of Veronese). Günther subsequently completed other commissions for frescoes in Bavaria, such as those in the Maria-Hilf-Kirche in Bad Tölz (1737) and the parish church in Mittenwald (1740).

Günther's mature style may be seen in the ceiling frescoes of the Chorherrenstiftskirche in Rottenbuch, completed in 1742, where the painted surfaces are emphasized in cool, silvery colours. Günther continued in this style in the high-spirited, energetic frescoes at the eastern end of the church at Novacella, completed in 1743. With his 22 frescoes (1745–7) in the Benedictine abbey church at Amorbach, Günther achieved the quintessence of south German Rococo decoration. After several other commissions in 1747 and 1748, Günther produced the first purely 'terrestrial' decoration, without any figures in the central area, in his fresco of *David and Abigail* (1749) for the church at Herrgottsruh, near Friedberg. Thanks to his inspiring encounter with Giambattista Tiepolo in Würzburg in 1751–2, Günther's work was enlivened with new Italian ideas. He directly incorporated some of these into the frescoes of the Käppele in Würzburg on the theme of the *Virgin Mary as Protectress of Franconia* (completed in 1752). In the following years Günther worked at the parish church of Wilten (1754–5) and the Augustinerchorherren-Kirche at Indersdorf (1755 and 1758). In 1757 he completed his largest secular commission for Duke Charles-Eugen of Württemberg, for whom he undertook several projects between 1753 and 1760. The Aeneas Gallery (1756–7; destr.) in the Stuttgart Schloss again reflected Günther's encounter with Tiepolo but also showed Günther turning to the example of Pietro da Cortona's *Aeneas* cycle (1651–4) in the Palazzo Pamphili in Rome, Antoine Coypel's frescoes in the Palais Royal in Paris and other Italian sources such as Agostino Carracci and Federico Barocci.

After several further projects carried out in this style, most notably the frescoes in the main cupola of the Benedictine monastery church at Rott am Inn, *Apotheosis of the Benedictine Order* (1763), Günther noticeably adopted a style influenced by the spirit of Neo-classicism. The change may be seen, for example, in the frescoes (1770) in the chapel of Schloss Mentelberg in Gallwiese, near Innsbruck. In his seventies Günther continued to work in widely separated locations: in 1776 he carried out fresco commissions in Messbach (Württemberg), in Steinheim (in Swabia) and in Abtei (now Badia, Italy). It is clear, however, that Günther resorted increasingly to solutions devised in earlier work. This is especially clear in his last commission, the frescoes for the choir and nave of the parish church of Waalhaupten, finished a year before his death.

BIBLIOGRAPHY

H. Gundersheimer: *Matthäus Günther: Die Freskomalerei im süddeutschen Kirchenbau des 18. Jahrhunderts* (Augsburg, 1930)

B. Bushart: 'Augsburg und die Wende der deutschen Kunst um 1750', *Amici amico: Essays in Honour of Werner Gross* (Munich, 1968), pp. 261–304

J. Zahlten: 'Das zerstörte Aeneas-Fresko Matthäus Günthers im Stuttgarter Neuen Schloss', *Pantheon*, ii/xxxvii (1979), pp. 150–63

Barock in Baden-Württemberg (exh. cat., Bruchsal, Städt. Mus. Schloss, 1981), pp. 107–29

H. Bauer and R. Stalla: 'Die Deckenbilder Matthäus Günthers in Rott am Inn', *Rott am Inn: Beiträge zur Kunst und Geschichte der ehem. Benediktinerabtei* (Weissenhorn, 1983), pp. 113–27

B. Hamacher: *Arbeitssituation und Werkprozess in der Freskomalerei von Matthäus Günther* (Munich, 1988)

Matthäus Günther: Festliches Rokoko für Kirchen, Klöster, Residenzen (exh. cat., Augsburg, Zeughaus, 1988)

WOLFGANG HOLLER

Günther, Rafael Yela. *See* YELA GÜNTHER, RAFAEL.

Gunzo, Abbot of Baume (*fl c.* 1083–8). Monk. Apart from two versions of the *Life of St Hugh*, Abbot of Cluny (1049–1109), no document records Gunzo's abbacy of Baume-les-Messieurs (Jura), but there is a suitable gap in the list of its abbots between 1083 and 1089. Of the extant versions of the *Life*, five give differing accounts of a vision or dream recounted by Gunzo when he was elderly and sick; in the dream the project for the great church of Cluny III (*see* CLUNIAC ORDER, §III, 1(ii)) was revealed to him by St Peter. Building began shortly afterwards, in 1088. None of the sources dates from before 1120–21. The most elaborate account of Gunzo's dream survives in a late 12th-century manuscript from St-Martin-des-Champs, the *Anonymus secundus*, in which the sick monk, lying paralysed in the infirmary in Cluny, is given detailed instructions as to the plan and dimensions of the building. An illumination shows SS Peter, Paul and Stephen laying out the church with a grid of ropes, an image that has influenced the way in which architectural historians envisage the medieval architect's method of proportional construction (*see* ARCHITECTURAL PROPORTION, §I). There has been dispute as to whether Gunzo or Hezelo was the architect of Cluny III. The story of Gunzo's dream, written against a political background of financial crisis over funding the huge church, falls within a literary tradition of medieval dream miracles and is probably no more than a 'pious legend' (Salet).

BIBLIOGRAPHY

Anonymus secundus (late 12th century; Paris, Bib. N., MS. lat. 17716, fol. 43); ed. M. Marrier and A. Quercetanus in *Bibliotheca Cluniacensis* (Paris, 1614), cols 457–9 [primary source]

Hildebert: *Life of St Hugh* (probably 1121); ed. in *PL*, clix (1854), cols 857–94 (esp. cols 884–5) [primary source]

Raynald: *Life of St Hugh* (*c.* 1122, before 1128); ed. in *PL*, clix (1854), cols 893–905 (esp. cols 898–9) [primary source]

F. Salet: 'Cluny III', *Bull. Mnmtl*, cxxvi/3 (1968), pp. 235–92 (esp. p. 291)

H. E. J. Cowdrey: 'Two Studies in Cluniac History, 1049–1126', *Stud. Gregoriani*, xi (1978), pp. 26–7, 90–91 [primary source]

F. Barlow: 'The Canonization and the Early Lives of Hugh I, Abbot of Cluny', *Anlct. Bolland.*, xcviii (1980), pp. 321–3

C. M. Carty: 'The Role of Gunzo's Dream in the Building of Cluny III', *Gesta*, xxvii/1–2 (1988), pp. 113–23

For further bibliography *see* CLUNIAC ORDER, §III, 1 and HEZELO.

NEIL STRATFORD

Guo Xi [Kuo Hsi; *zi* Shunfu] (*b* Wen xian, Henan Province, *c.* 1020; *d c.* 1090). Chinese painter and theorist. He is considered one of the most important of the late 11th-century masters. Guo Ruoxu (*fl* 11th century), a minor official at the court of Bianliang (modern Kaifeng), in the *Tuhua jianwen zhi* ('Experiences in painting'; 1075) described Guo as supreme among the landscape painters of his generation. Other contemporary critics acclaimed his creativity, the spontaneity of his composition and the dexterity and versatility of his brushwork. Guo's ideas on the principles of landscape painting, as recorded by his son Guo Si (*fl c.* 1070–1123) are also important.

Very few details of Guo's life are known. In 1068 he was summoned to paint a screen for the imperial palace. He received special recognition from the emperor Shenzong (*reg* 1068–85) for his introduction of an innovative way of painting. He also served other emperors but was not equally honoured. Nevertheless, he remained at court, becoming an assistant teacher (yixue) and Scholar of Arts at the Hanlin Painting Academy. According to Huang Tingjian, writing in the *Shangu tiba* (Huang Tingjian's annotations), Guo was serving as painter-in-attendance (*daizhao*) to the Emperor when he was given the task of painting all the murals in the Forbidden City. In 1082 he also painted four murals described as landscapes and eroded rocks for the Confucian temple at Wen xian. In addition, about 1085 he painted 12 screen panels of unknown subjects for a monk of the Xiansheng si, one of the most important Buddhist monasteries in the capital. All of these murals are lost, but they have been described as having been executed with spontaneity and vigour.

Guo is recorded as having been extremely productive, but the number of extant paintings attributed to him is small. This can be partly explained by the fact that he painted some landscapes directly on the plastered walls of buildings, structures prone to destruction. According to tradition, he kept the plaster of such walls rough, even tossing on more plaster to achieve an irregular surface; when the plaster was dry he applied ink following the irregular contours to create abstract landscapes, thus obtaining a three-dimensional effect. If this information is correct, such landscapes must have relied less on the careful observation of nature and more on the spontaneously created image, despite Guo's philosophical statements to the contrary.

Guo Xi originally received his court appointment because he was recognized as the leading exponent of the style of LI CHENG. He also worked in the style of Fan Kuan. Out of this early dependence, however, he developed his own distinctive style. Both Li and Fan utilized strong, centrally-located, vertical masses as barriers to depth. Mists clustered at the base of mountains functioned as transitional areas and served to silhouette foreground elements (for illustration *see* FAN KUAN). Guo initiated a more irregular style of composition, which balanced contorted and irregular mountain forms against valleys that opened out into the distance. The vertical axis of Fan and Li was replaced by an arrangement of convoluting curves. A balance between immediate forms and distant views appears to have been a consistent compositional device in Guo's paintings. It is integral to both his horizontal handscroll *Pure and Remote Views of Streams and Hills* (Washington, DC, Freer), generally accepted as an example of his early style, and the large hanging scroll *Early Spring* (see fig.), an example of his mature style.

Early Spring is a visual representation of the ideal landscape described in Guo's commentaries. It continues the early Northern Song (960–1127) theme of the domination of landscape over human activity, but also exemplifies Guo's individual manner of modifying the heroic images of that period. Rock and mountain masses coil and twist and set up surface tensions throughout the composition. The limited depth to the right is countered on the left by an angled, but level, view of a valley disappearing towards an undefined horizon. The foreground is placed at the level of the observer. As a whole, the landscape represents the technique, new to the mid-11th century, of juxtaposing the 'three distances' (*sanyuan*): high (*gao*), deep (*shen*) and level (*ping*). The scroll is executed in a painterly style, with broad, wet outlines, varied textural strokes and misty transitional areas rendered in sensitive washes.

Other works by Guo include the handscroll *River and Mountains after a Snowfall* (Toledo, OH, Mus. A.), identified as approximating his late style, and *Plain with Eroded Rocks* (1078; see *Wenwu jinghua* [Best of artefacts], iii (1964), p. 14), his latest known dated work.

Guo's aesthetic precepts as regards rules of landscape painting make up part of the *Linquan gaozhi* ('Lofty message of forests and streams'), which was compiled by his son, Guo Si, the earliest known edition dating to 1271. The work is considered one of the most important early publications on landscape theory and the clearest expression of the fundamental principles involving the use of traditional forms, compositions and techniques. It also praises the arts as a means of ennobling the mind, a

Guo Xi: *Early Spring*, hanging scroll, ink and light colours on silk, 1.58×1.08 m, 1072 (Taipei, National Palace Museum)

Confucian and traditional approach that makes an association between philosophical and aesthetic concerns. Guo suggests that 'among landscapes there are those fit to walk through, those fit to contemplate, those fit to ramble in and those fit to live in. All pictures may reach these standards and enter the category of the wonderful; but those fit to walk through or to contemplate are not equal to those fit to ramble in or to live in' (Sirén, 1963, p. 44). For a more detailed discussion of the *Linquan gaozhi see* CHINA, §V, 3(iv)(b).

Guo had no immediate follower, but the work of later generations of artists reflects his importance. Painters of the Jin period (1115–1234) continued using the artistic grammar he perfected, and it came to be identified with the stylistic classification of northern traditions regardless of actual locality. In the Yuan period (1279–1368) there was a revival of the ideas of both Guo and Li Cheng. Guo was an inspiration for Wu Zhen and others, such as Cao Zhibai and Zhu Derun. His conception of barren skeletal branches clustered with other mixed varieties of trees was carried to its ultimate refinement in the paintings of Ni Zan. Guo's style has been identified in the early, detailed, archaistic paintings of Wen Zhengming in the Ming period (1368–1644). He also appears to have been studied by eclectics such as Zhou Chen. Even Chen Hongshou adopted certain aspects of his style. His reputation probably extended as far as Japan: Li Zai is recorded as having followed Guo's tradition, and the Japanese monk Tōyō Sesshū, who visited China in 1467–9, named Li as the most important master of the period.

WRITINGS

Linquan gaozhi [Lofty message of forests and streams] (*c.* 1170s); ed. Yu Haiyan: Hua lun congkan [Collected historical works on painting theory], i (Beijing, 1937)

BIBLIOGRAPHY

Guo Ruoxu: *Tuhua jianwen zhi* [Experiences in painting] (1075); ed. Huang Miaozi (Shanghai, 1963); Eng. trans. in A. C. Soper: *Kuo Jo-hsü's 'Experiences in Painting' (T'u-hua chien-wen chih)* (Washington, DC, 1951/*R* 1971)

Xuanhe huapu [Xuanhe collection of painting] (preface dated 1120); ed. Yu Jianhua (Beijing, 1964)

A. G. Wenley: '"Clearing Autumn Skies over Mountains and Valleys" Attributed to Kuo Hsi', *Archv. Chin. A. Soc. America*, x (1956), pp. 30–41

O. Sirén: *Chinese Painting: Leading Masters and Principles* (London, 1956–8), i, pp. 215–30

Chang An-shih: *Kuo Hsi* (Shanghai, 1959)

Chinese Art Treasures: A Selected Group of Objects from the Chinese National Palace Museum and the Chinese National Central Museum, Taichung (exh. cat., Washington, DC, N.G.A.; New York, Met.; Boston, MA, Mus. F.A.; and elsewhere; 1961–2), no. 13

O. Sirén: *The Chinese on the Art of Painting* (New York, 1963)

M. Loehr: *The Great Painters of China* (New York, 1980), pp. 144–51

Eight Dynasties of Chinese Painting: The Collections of the Nelson Gallery–Atkins Museum, Kansas City, and the Cleveland Museum of Art (exh. cat., Cleveland, OH, Mus. A., 1980)

T. Miyagawa, ed.: *Chūgoku no bijutsu: kaiga* [Chinese painting] (Tokyo, 1982), pp. 177–8

MARY S. LAWTON

Gupta. Dynasty that ruled most of northern India from the mid-4th century to the late 5th century AD. The Gupta dynasty had its origin in eastern India and first appeared as a significant power under Chandragupta I (*reg c.* 319–35). He probably established the Gupta era, a calendar that began in AD 319–20 and was used until the 7th century. The Guptas conquered the greater part of northern India during the reigns of Samudragupta (*reg c.* 335–76) and Chandragupta II (*reg c.* 380–415). The high-point of Gupta power is often placed in the long reign of Kumaragupta I (*reg c.* 415–55). By the third quarter of the 5th century, the Gupta realm was beginning to crumble. Considerable instability is suggested by the near simultaneous appearance of Govindagupta, Purugupta and Kumaragupta II between 467 and 477. Budhagupta (*reg c.* 477–500) checked the decline of the house, but he was the last of the 'imperial Guptas', and after his death most of northern India was overrun by the Huna people. A Varaha image at Eran is dated in the first year of the Huna king Toramana (*c.* 500).

During the 5th century, the rule of the Guptas coincided with remarkable achievements in sculpture and architecture. Inscriptional evidence, however, provides no clear indication that the Gupta monarchs were direct patrons of art. Surviving temples and images were mostly set up by a subordinate aristocracy and their subjects. In the 6th century there is evidence for a minor house using the Gupta name; by the 7th century this house was ruling parts of Magadha in eastern India. The genealogies of these later Gupta rulers do not trace their ancestry to the imperial Guptas of the 5th century.

See also INDIAN SUBCONTINENT, §§III, 4(i); IV, 5 and XI, 1.

BIBLIOGRAPHY

J. F. Fleet: *Inscriptions of the Early Gupta Kings and their Successors*, Corp. Inscr. Indic., iii (Calcutta, 1888); rev. by D. K. Bhandarkar, ed. B. Chhabra and G. S. Gai (New Delhi, 1981)

D. C. Sircar: 'The Maukharis and Later Guptas', *Journal of the Royal Asiatic Society of Bengal: Letters*, xi (1945), pp. 69–74

——: *Select Inscriptions Bearing on Indian History and Civilization* (Calcutta, 1965)

R. Gobl: *Dokumente zur Geschichte der iranischen Hunnen in Baktrien und Indien*, 4 vols (Wiesbaden, 1967)

R. S. Mishra: *Supplement to Fleet's Corpus Inscriptionum Indicarum, Vol. III (1888), Inscriptions of the Early Gupta Kings and their Successors*, ed. A. K. Narain; Monographs Dept Anc. Ind. Hist., Cult. & Archaeol., Banaras Hindu U., vi (Varanasi, 1971)

A. Biswas: *The Political History of the Hunas in India* (New Delhi, 1973)

R. Salomon: 'New Inscriptional Evidence for the History of the Aulikaras of Mandasor', *Indo-Iran J.*, xxxii (1989), pp. 1–36

MICHAEL D. WILLIS

Güran, Nazmi Ziya [Ziya] (*b* Istanbul, 1881; *d* Istanbul, 1937). Turkish painter. After studying for a career in government, he turned to painting and entered the Fine Arts Academy in Istanbul, where he studied under Joseph Warnia-Zarzecki (*b* 1850) and Salvator Valéri (1857–1946). His interest in Impressionism and painting *en plein air*, however, especially after 1905 when he observed Paul Signac working in Istanbul, led to quarrels with Warnia-Zarzecki and Valéri, and with Osman Hamdi, the Director of the Academy. As a result his graduation diploma was refused in 1907, and he did not graduate until 1908. Güran then went to Paris and studied at the Académie Julian, and under Marcel Bachet and Fernand Cormon. In 1913 he visited Germany and Austria. Upon his return to Istanbul he took up government employment and joined the Çallı Group, led by the painter Ibrahim Çallı. He was later assigned a teaching post at the Fine Arts Academy and became its director. Influenced by Impressionism, he strove in his paintings to capture the reflection of light on objects and painted some scenes many times to explore the changes of light. He was also a follower of Kemal Atatürk's cultural reforms, and one of the finest portraits of the leader, *Mustafa Kemal Atatürk in Military Uniform* (Istanbul, Mimar Sinan U., Mus. Ptg & Sculp.), was painted by him in the mid-1920s. Güran's later landscapes included *Landscape from the Bosporus* (1933; Istanbul, Mimar Sinan U., Mus. Ptg & Sculp.).

BIBLIOGRAPHY

Z. Güvemli: *The Sabancı Collection of Paintings* (Istanbul, 1984) [Eng. and Turk. texts]

S. Tansuğ: *Çağdaş Türk sanatı* [Contemporary Turkish art] (Istanbul, 1986)

G. Renda and others: *A History of Turkish Painting* (Geneva, Seattle and London, 1988)

□

Gure, Desmond (*b* London, 1906; *d* 30 April 1970). English collector. He graduated from Brighton College and qualified as a dental surgeon at Guy's Hospital in London. For 44 years he worked as a dentist in his own practice in the City of London. Gure's interest in Chinese art was aroused during World War II, and his great knowledge of the subject was acquired through reading during long hours of fire-watching. He became especially interested in jades and started what was to become a fine collection of early Chinese jade objects. Gure became noted for his scholarly articles, which mainly deal with the dating of jades. Apart from comparison with datable analogues in other materials such as pottery and metal, Gure based his attributions primarily on stylistic and technical factors. He classified jades into chronological groups that correspond roughly to dynastic eras. His interest in this respect was essentially focused on the periods following the Han (206 BC–AD 220) up to early Ming (1368–1611). His treatment of jade figures from the post-Han era is perceptive and original. Gure produced a handful of articles that are valuable contributions to the study of Chinese jades. Between 1956 and 1968 he served on three occasions on the Council of the Oriental Ceramic Society in London.

WRITINGS

'Notes on the Identification of Jade', *Orient. A.*, iii/3 (1951), pp. 115–20

'Jades of the Sung Group', *Trans. Orient. Cer. Soc.*, xxxii (1959–60), pp. 39–50

'Some Unusual Early Jades and their Dating', *Trans. Orient. Cer. Soc.*, xxxiii (1960–62), pp. 41–59

'Selected Examples from the Jade Exhibition at Stockholm, 1963: A Comparative Study', *Bull. Mus. Far E. Ant.*, xxxvi (1964), pp. 117–58

BIBLIOGRAPHY

H. Shire: 'Desmond Gure', *Trans. Orient. Cer. Soc.*, xxxviii (1969–71), p. xxiv

BENT NIELSEN

Gurganj. *See* KUNYA-URGENCH.

Gurjara-Pratihara [Gurjara-Pratīhāra]. Dynasty that ruled parts of northern India from the mid-8th century to the mid-11th century AD. The Gurjaras established power in the Malwa region under Nagabhatta I in the mid-8th century. However, under pressure from the neighbouring Rashtrakuta dynasty, Vatsaraja (*reg c.* 777–808) was defeated and forced to withdraw to Rajasthan. Later Gurjara-Pratihara rulers maintained that area as a power base. Nagabhatta II (*reg c.* 810–33) expanded the kingdom to the west and east, taking KANNAUJ, the ancient capital of the Gangetic heartland. The long reign of Mihira Bhoja (*reg c.* 836–85) marked the high-point of Gurjara-Pratihara power. The eastern frontier was pushed into Bihar, and military campaigns carried out in Malwa and Saurashtra. Centres of power included GWALIOR. Mahendrapala I (*reg c.* 885–910) over-extended the kingdom by pushing deep into eastern India; internal conflicts became evident during and after his reign. Devapala (*reg c.* 948–59) was able to maintain the dynasty as a major power in the Gangetic Plain, but the provinces south of the Yamuna River came under the sway of strong regional dynasties, including the Chandellas, Paramaras and Kacchapaghatas. The Gurjara-Pratiharas lingered as a power until the final defeat of Trilochanapala by Mahmud of Ghazna in 1019.

The Gurjara-Pratiharas ruled northern India during a period of considerable architectural activity and probably built temples and palaces. However, no surviving monument bears an inscription naming these monarchs as patrons.

See also INDIAN SUBCONTINENT, §§III, 5(i)(c), 5(i)(e) and IV, 7(iii)(a)).

BIBLIOGRAPHY

R. S. Tripathi: *History of Kanauj to the Moslem Conquest* (Varanasi, 1937)

R. C. Majumdar, ed.: *The History and Culture of the Indian People: The Age of Imperial Kanauj* (Bombay, 1955)

B. N. Puri: *The History of the Gurjara-Pratihāras* (Bombay, 1957)

MICHAEL D. WILLIS

Gurk Cathedral. Romanesque cathedral dedicated to the Assumption of the Virgin, located in a market town *c.* 30 km north of Klagenfurt, Austria. According to tradition, Gräfin Hemma von Zeltschach-Gurk (beatified 1287; *can* 1938) founded a convent between 1043 and 1045 in the remote valley of Gurk. In 1072, after its dissolution, Archbishop Gebhard of Salzburg declared the site the seat of a suffragan bishop. The diocese was tightly controlled from Salzburg. The cathedral was begun under Bishop Roman I (1131–67), and in 1174 the relics of Hemma were translated to the crypt. A violent dispute between the Archbishop of Salzburg and the Bishop of Gurk over Gurk's independent status resulted in a break in the building campaign from 1179 to 1180; the dedication of the main altar and the subsequent construction of the transept brought the second campaign to an end in 1200. The conversion of the western gallery into a richly decorated 'Bishop's Chapel' was planned by Bishop Walther (1200–12).

1. Architecture. The harmonious Romanesque cathedral, a three-aisled basilica of 66.2 m internal length, with transept, three parallel eastern apses and a massive pair of western towers, is especially impressive for its outstanding state of preservation (see fig.); the limited importance of the diocese and the remote site have prevented significant alterations and restorations. Before 1287 the transept galleries were removed; *c.* 1446 and 1500 transept and choir vaults were built. In 1591 the nave was net-vaulted in an archaic manner. Except for the furnishings the Baroque period has left few traces. In 1778–9 the apse of the Bishop's Chapel, which projected into the nave, was destroyed to make room for an organ loft.

The exterior is built of limestone on clean lines with well-cut ashlar. The two-tower arrangement of the west end is directly borrowed from Salzburg Cathedral, where Archbishop Konrad I built a pair of western towers after 1127 to demonstrate the restoration of the Church's authority after the Investiture Contest; this motif was adopted relatively quickly in many places within Salzburg's sphere of influence.

The decoration of the western portions of the building is very restrained, and decorative blank arches cap the south aisle and transept walls, continuing round the entire transept at a low level. The simple forms of the stepped south portal of the nave correspond to the earliest building campaign. The upper half of the south transept façade is articulated by rounded pilasters, while the eastern apses have massive socles and blind arcading; the liturgical pre-eminence of the central apse is emphasized by a relief of lions over the arcade.

The five-and-a-half-bay nave (including the inner narthex) leads to a choir raised by nine steps over the crypt. The strict proportional relationships of the architecture of the Salzburg reform movement, as seen at Seckau (*c.* 1147–90) or St Paul (second half of the 12th century), Lavanttal, are not followed, for the bays are strictly rectangular and the nave is narrower than the two aisles combined. Sturdy piers with moulded imposts support the nave arcade of round arches, which, with the windows, provide the only articulation. Identical pilasters mark both the division of

Gurk Cathedral, begun mid-12th century; view from the south-east

the nave from the two-bay choir and the east crossing piers. The spatial sequence and arrangement up to the transept follow the Bavarian-Alpine architectural tradition. The transept, which was not part of the original plan, is foreign to local architectural forms and can be explained in two possible ways: most critics argue that after 1179 the Bishop of Gurk wished to express his independence by constructing a transept; but since 12th-century church architecture associated with the Archbishop of Salzburg shows a preference for predominant structures at the east end, such as the transept of St Peter's (1130–43), Salzburg, and the triconch east end (from 1181) of Salzburg Cathedral, it is likely that at Gurk there was some influence, perhaps political, from the Archbishop.

Despite the powerful effect of the new transept when seen from the exterior, the cathedral interior is dominated by local tradition: door openings and holes intended to receive beams indicate the presence in both transept arms of galleries supported by paired columns, which corresponded to the engaged half columns with cushion capitals on neighbouring piers. Although the appearance of the gallery cannot be reconstructed in detail, in this respect it reflected the nave. The spaces flanking the transepts had the effect of *pastophoria*. The Gurk arrangement is similar to that at St Zeno (1136–1208), Reichenhall, near Salzburg.

The square hall crypt, half below ground-level, is reached by parallel stairways in the aisles. Six rectangular piers support the choir, and 96 regularly placed columns with cushion capitals and two paired columns in the eastern apse carry groin vaults of uniform size. The vast scale of the crypt shows that the builders intended to produce a monumental burial area where the relics could be venerated. Of the original furnishings only the funerary monument of Hemma, a sarcophagus resting on short columns ornamented with heads, and a 12th-century altar remain. The crypt, which is a deliberate development of northern Italian hall crypts such as those in the cathedrals of Modena (*c.* 1106), Nonantola (after 1120) or Piacenza (after 1120), is also perhaps indebted to Islamic multi-columnar structures such as the Mezquita in Córdoba, Spain.

The Bishop's Chapel above the narthex is rectangular, with domed groin vaults, and is divided into two bays by a rough transverse arch resting on engaged half columns. A stepped portal, now walled up, with a pair of engaged columns with crocket capitals led to the apse. On either side there are triforia with double columns open to the nave. The eastern structure of the chapel forms, in the floor below, a kind of triumphal arch reaching into the nave as an inner narthex. The engaged capitals, with their foliate and abstract geometric motifs, are *c.* 1200. The combination of the apotropaic function, seen in the dedication to St Michael, with the emphasis on the throne of a prince of the Church (here, the bishop) is the apogee of a development originating in the Carolingian westwork. The chapel is particularly famous for its wall paintings (*see* §(ii) below).

Stylistically, Gurk Cathedral is a mixture of regional influences, but it is also a well-preserved testimony to the quality of High Romanesque architecture in the central Alps. The indigenous tradition of the basilica with parallel eastern apses is combined with the new architectural developments of the reformed orders (twin towers and transept) and with northern Italian influences, apparent in the arrangement of the crypt and the exterior decoration of the apses.

See DOOR, fig. 2 for an illustration of the wooden doors of the cathedral.

BIBLIOGRAPHY

G. F. von Ankershofen: 'Die Baugeschichte des Domes zu Gurk', *Archv Vaterländ. Gesch. & Top.*, xiii (1876), pp. 1–34
F. G. Hann: *Der Gurker Dom* (Klagenfurt, 1910)
A. Schnerich: *Der Dom zu Gurk* (Vienna, 1919, 2/1925)
J. Löw: *Kleiner Gurker Domführer* (Klagenfurt, 1925, 3/1930)
K. Ginhart and B. Grimschitz: *Der Dom zu Gurk* (Vienna, 1930)
R. Pühringer: *Denkmäler der früh- und hochromanischen Baukunst in Österreich* (Vienna, 1931), pp. 22–31
H. Schnell: *Der Dom zu Gurk* (Munich, 1940)
H. Riehl: *Der Dom zu Gurk* (Königstein, [1944])
P. W. Posch: *Der Dom zu Gurk* (Gurk, 1952, 10/1991)
W. Buchowiecki: 'Die Baukunst', *Romanische Kunst in Österreich* (Vienna, 1962, 3/1974), pp. 28–9
S. Hartwagner: *Der Dom zu Gurk* (Klagenfurt, 1962, 2/1969)
Kärnten, Dehio-Handbuch (Vienna, 1976, 2/1981), pp. 97–206
W. Deuer: 'Die romanische Sakralarchitektur Kärntens unter besonderer Berücksichtigung des Gurker Domes', *Hemma von Gurk* (exh. cat., Strasbourg, Schlossmus., 1988)
G. Biedermann: *Romanik in Kärnten* (Klagenfurt, 1994), p. 54
W. v. d. Kallen and W. Deuer: *Der Dom zu Gurk* (Gurk, 1995)

WILHELM DEUER

2. PAINTING. The dating of the painting in the western gallery (the Bishop's Chapel) is controversial. This part of the building was completed soon after 1200 and the altar in the chapel was probably consecrated in 1214. A fire in the mid-13th century necessitated restoration and a second dedication in 1264. The ruling bishops of both periods, Otto I and Dietrich II, are represented in the paintings. The style of the work suggests it was done after the fire, *c.* 1260. Both bays of the chapel are covered in paintings representing, in the two vaults, *Adam and Eve in the Earthly Paradise* and the *Heavenly Jerusalem.* Scenes of the *Life of Christ* are on the walls and the *Throne of Solomon* (*see* AUSTRIA, fig. 12) on the upper east wall. The two artists' work shows the late phase of the *Zackenstil*, which had spread to Austria from Germany around 1250. The violent, jagged fold forms resemble the wall paintings (*c.* 1240) of St Gereon, Cologne, and, more closely, the illumination of the Aschaffenburg (or Mainz) Golden Gospels (1250s; Aschaffenburg, Schloss Johannisburg, Hof- & Stiftsbib., MS. 13; for illustration *see* ZACKENSTIL).

The paintings (*c.* 1340) in the west porch are of mediocre quality in a fully developed Gothic style. They form four registers on the facing walls with the Old Testament opposite the New, which shows links with the programme of the *Biblia pauperum.* The Lenten veil (1458) also has Old and New Testament scenes, 50 of each, set as square fields on the huge linen cloth that completely covers the view of the high altar during Lent.

BIBLIOGRAPHY

W. Frodl: *Die romanische Wandmalerei in Kärnten* (Klagenfurt, 1942)
——: *Die gotische Wandmalerei in Kärnten* (Klagenfurt, 1944)
K. Ginhart: 'Die Datierung der Fresken in der Gurker Westempore', *Gedenkbuch Bruno Grimschitz* (Klagenfurt, 1967), pp. 9–174
O. Demus: *Romanesque Mural Painting* (London, 1970), pp. 150–51, 634–6; pls 298–305 and on p. 39

For further bibliography *see* §(i) above.

NIGEL J. MORGAN

Gurlitt, Cornelius (*b* Nischwitz, Saxony, 1 Jan 1850; *d* Dresden, 25 March 1938). German architect, teacher and writer. He was originally apprenticed to a carpenter before studying architecture in Berlin and Stuttgart, and he entered private practice in 1871. In 1879 he joined the staff of the Dresden Kunstgewerbemuseum, where he wrote his monumental study *Geschichte des Barockstiles, des Rococo und des Klassicismus* (1887–9), a study of post-Renaissance architecture in Italy, Belgium, Holland, France, England and Germany. It was a remarkable rehabilitation of a period then generally regarded as one of decline. As a result of the success of this work, he was appointed to a chair in architecture at the Technische Hochschule, Dresden, where he remained until his retirement in 1920. Gurlitt's enthusiasm for the Baroque led him to reject the ideas of Karl Friedrich Schinkel and his followers as intellectually barren. He felt that the future of architecture lay in the hands of such architects as Paul Wallot and Alfred Messel, and by 1900, showing his sympathy for new developments, he was supporting Art Nouveau design, as seen, for example, in the work of Henry Van de Velde. In 1920 he used his position as an editor of *Stadtbaukunst alter und neuer Zeit* to help Bruno Taut publish his *Frühlicht.* Gurlitt was a prolific writer, producing 97 books and over 400 articles on subjects ranging from the history of architecture, painting, sculpture and urban planning to contemporary politics.

WRITINGS

Geschichte des Barockstiles, des Rococo und des Klassizismus, 3 vols (Stuttgart, 1887–9)
Die Kunst unter Kurfürst Friedrich dem Weisen (Dresden, 1897)
Die deutsche Kunst des neunzehnten Jahrhunderts (Berlin, 1899)
Die Kultur (Berlin, 1905)
Dresden (Dresden, 1907)

BIBLIOGRAPHY

A. Schlüter: *Cornelius Gurlitt* (Berlin, 1891)
D. Watkin: *The Rise of Architectural History* (London, 1980), pp. 11–12, 17, 120

NICHOLAS BULLOCK

Gurlitt, (Heinrich) Louis (Theodor) (*b* Altona, 8 March 1812; *d* Naundorf, Saxony, 19 Sept 1897). German painter. He studied with Siegfried Bendixen (1786–after 1864) in Hamburg from 1828. His early landscapes already showed the influence of Christian Morgenstern and Johann Christian Dahl. In 1832 he studied under C. W. Eckersberg at the Akademi for de Skønne Kunster in Copenhagen. He deepened his impressions of northern landscapes on trips to Norway and Sweden. In 1835 he moved to Munich and joined the circle of Carl Rottmann and Peter Cornelius, before returning to Copenhagen for three years, where he became a member of the Akademi. He was in central Italy between 1843 and 1847, then in Berlin and other places in Germany and Vienna from 1851 to 1859. He also made numerous visits to Italy, the Balkans, Spain and Portugal, returning to Rome in 1877.

Gurlitt's work balances the different influences of Munich and Denmark. Typically his works are atmospheric yet unsentimental landscapes, characterized by wide vistas over still plains, and light skies with warm colours, as in *Village Street* (Berlin, Alte N.G.). His most successful works are those drawn from nature, compared to which the somewhat sweeter Italian paintings are inferior. His reproduction of natural daylight was particularly significant, only gradually being replaced by the tones of chiaroscuro in later years. He aspired to achieve both truth and beauty through a mixture of naturalism and stylization. The importance of Gurlitt's work lay in his role as an intermediary between Nordic and German painting. He was a professor and member of the academies in Copenhagen, Munich and Madrid.

BIBLIOGRAPHY

Thieme–Becker

L. Gurlitt: *Louis Gurlitt: Ein Künstlerleben des 19. Jahrhunderts* (Berlin, 1912)

L. Martius: *Die Schleswig-holsteinische Malerei im 19. Jahrhundert* (Neumünster, 1956), pp. 235–45

SEPP KERN

Guro. Mande-speaking agricultural people, numbering *c.* 250,000, living in an area of central Côte d'Ivoire where the savannah merges with the dense tropical forest. The Guro are part of the 'peripheral Mande' and are linguistically related to the DAN. Three Guro cultural regions may be distinguished. In the north they have round houses, wood-carving is highly developed, and weaving and pottery are produced. In the west they have rectangular houses with wooden shingled roofs, weaving is practised, but no pottery is produced and little wood-carving. In the densely forested southern region they have rectangular thatched houses and only wood- and ivory-carving are practised.

Traditionally, the Guro did not recognize any centralized political authority but lived in independent villages that formed war alliances when necessary, while powerful patrilineages owned valuable ritual objects and associated paraphernalia. Of special importance in Guro society is the *trezan*, the 'master of the earth', regarded as the direct descendant of the village founder, who has the right to distribute land for cultivation. Another important personality in village life is the diviner, whose diagnostic interpretations are based mainly on a mouse oracle (*see* AFRICA, §VI, 7), an instrument probably developed by the Guro and from whom it spread throughout central Côte d'Ivoire.

The major artistic forms of the Guro are masks and masquerades, wooden figures, heddle pulleys, spoons and small chairs (for illustrations see 1986 exh. cat.). All of them are produced by specialists whose creativity has led in some cases to local fame.

1. Masks and masquerades. 2. Wood-carving. 3. Artists.

1. MASKS AND MASQUERADES. Guro masks belong to the category of sacred objects and extraordinary manifestations known as *yu*. The masks are considered to be the visible forms of 'prehistoric', animal-like creatures who lived in the forests or the mountains before being captured by hunters and dragged to the village, where they performed for the Guro ancestors. Just as domesticated animals once lived in the wilderness but now serve the villagers, so these creatures are said to have developed over the centuries into a new category of beings, who appear in raffia costumes and wooden face-masks with additional paraphernalia, dancing in well-defined styles. The manifestation of a specific mask type belongs to a lineage and is venerated as their *yu*, a cult-object of repute; its spirit becomes active through public performance.

In the north, the Guro recognize two major 'families' of masks. Gye is the most important sacred masker, which may never be seen by women. Its face depicts an animal with large buffalo horns and a wide, open mouth, sometimes featuring elements of elephant, crocodile or wild hog. It wears a closely knit, fibre overall costume and a collar of fresh oil-palm twigs, carries a metal bell and a whip and is accompanied by the sound of a bull-roarer.

The second mask family, exclusive to the northern region, includes Zamble, Gu and Zauli. These masks perform as a trio in the villages and may be seen by local women, though with caution. Although they are considered *yu*, sacred objects and ancient beings, they frighten their audience far less than the Gye masks. Zamble has a fine face-mask, painted black, red, yellow and white, with the snout of a crocodile, the eyes of a leopard and the horns of an antelope. It wears a costume of short raffia fibres, fresh oil-palm twigs, a fine cotton cloth around the neck, knitted textiles on the arms and legs, iron rattles and a leopard skin on the back. This magnificent masker, usually the best young dancer of the mask-owning lineage, performs with great vitality to the music of large drums, flutes and whips. Zamble performances are very stylized and acrobatic, yet they are the most elegant of Guro dances, executed with rapid footwork, high jumps and whirls.

Zauli, often considered a brother of Zamble, is more grotesque in appearance, with a similar mask but bulging cheeks and eyes, a long snout and curved horns with rills, a rough textile around the neck and an antelope skin on the back. Zauli jokes with the women, plays the buffoon, behaves in a rough and wild manner and is the opposite of the 'cultured' Zamble. It seems, however, that Zauli is considered the stronger and older of the two male maskers and therefore receives most of the offerings, and its help is often recommended by diviners.

Gu is classified as female and is the wife of Zamble or Zauli. Gu has a beautiful face-mask with all the desirable Guro feminine features: slit eyes, a bulging forehead with scarification marks, a small nose, a tiny mouth with thin lips, a rather heavy chin, small ears and an interesting, variegated hairstyle (see fig.). Such masks are carved with great virtuosity and reveal the carver's personal idea of beauty. The hairstyles depict the fashions of particular periods and regions and offer great scope for individual inventiveness. Gu wears a blue-and-white cotton textile around the shoulders, a knitted costume, iron rings with rattles and an antelope skin on the back. When a Gu dances, to the music of flutes alone, a companion holds the antelope's tail and strikes the masker if he stops.

Guro Gu mask carved by the Master of the Yasua, wood, black soot patination, h. 360 mm, central Côte d'Ivoire, *c.* 1915–20 (Switzerland, private collection)

The third group of maskers perform for entertainment only, to the accompaniment of fashionable music, while demonstrating the most modern dance steps. The masks are worn by the most distinguished dancer of a lineage or village, who may acquire fame by dancing with them. Some, called Sauli, Flali and Wali, have animal forms and features appropriate to the type of dance being performed (e.g. elephant, antelope, monkey or goat). Made of hardwood, they have only thin cotton cloths fixed around their rims to cover the dancers' necks and shoulders.

In the 1930s entertainment masks produced by the Master of Duonu (*fl c.* 1920–35) and his workshop displayed the peculiar features of the Kpelie masks of the neighbouring SENUFO and Mande of the Kong region. In further developments a figure was mounted on the forehead of horned masks, and later pairs and groups of figures were added, including boxers and jugglers, as well as Mamy Wata, the snake-charmer (*see* IBIBIO). Under BAULE influence, masquerade ensembles became common, with maskers performing in sequence up to the final dance of the most distinguished performer.

In the western and southern Guro regions there is a masquerade ensemble known as Dye. The maskers, equivalent to the Gye, are clad in large raffia attire and wear brightly coloured wooden masks. They are very powerful *yu*-cult manifestations: women are never allowed to see their day-long performances, otherwise, according to traditional belief, they would die immediately. The ensemble, usually more than seven maskers, consists of 'the tribunal of Dye', who are major maskers with human face-masks and feather crowns, wearing animal furs at the back and sometimes carrying wooden weapons. Kyesä, with a dark face, Lä, with a red face and a white beard, and Zahure, an older, white-skinned mask, have human features, whereas the magnificent Zäwi has four long horns on top of his dark animal face. He is the most powerful dancer, usually accompanied by a horde of antelope, elephant and buffalo maskers, who appear together but dance individually to the beat of large drums. Traditionally, this ensemble was probably involved in legal arbitration, or at least in supporting and enforcing the judgements of the village elders. Fine complete sets of Dye masks are in the Museum für Völkerkunde und Schweizerisches Museum für Volkskunde, Basle, and the Musée d'Ethnographie, Geneva.

The other mask traditions of the western and southern Guro, many of which seem to share traits with the neighbouring We, Bete and Kuya, are little known. Entertainment masks with beautiful faces and rich hairstyles were apparently once very common. All were carved from softwood and tend to have features similar to Gu, and thus also correspond to the general Guro ideal of female beauty.

2. WOOD-CARVING. On the advice of diviners, wooden figures are placed in the *zu-zu* shrines of helper spirits. They are ritual objects yet do not represent anything invisible or supernatural, nor are they direct manifestations of a spirit (such as the spirit spouses of the neighbouring BAULE). Rather they are parts of shrine ensembles, representing the wishes of spirits. It seems that most Guro figures are found in the north, bordering Mwa and Baule territory, and may well have been adopted from these peoples.

Guro heddle pulleys (*kono*) are among the most refined art objects from West Africa. Traditionally, they were used on looms to hold bobbins of string rotating over vertical iron pins fixed in a loom's stirrup. The stirrup terminates in a neck at the vertex, the top often being decorated with a small head. Often beautifully carved, their sole function was to provide the weaver with aesthetic pleasure while working. They were produced in a wide variety of shapes from triangular to horseshoe, and with rounded or angular contours. The necks are rarely stiff cylinders but display the typical scarification mark on the back, often a rather heavy bulge. The heads are carved in three dimensions, emphasizing the profile, in contrast to Baule works, the faces of which are flat and intended to be seen only from the front. The faces are delicate, with curved jaw lines, long chins, lipless mouths and high noses, often without nostrils. They have bulging foreheads, a zigzag hairline and a hairstyle with many plaits, sometimes held together over the parting by a leather band with square amulets and bags containing pages from the Koran. Many are simply decorated or carved with miniature utensils, pots, animal heads, masks or even figures. The figurative heddle pulleys probably were a genuinely old 'peripheral Mande' product, later adopted from the Guro ancestors by the neighbouring workshops of the Baule, Senufo and others.

Wooden spoons were used by the elderly for eating. They appear to have been common, especially in the north, but little is known about the meaning of their iconography. Many have buffalo horns carved at the ends of straight handles, often decorated with knobs and rims. Others have carved animal heads, but human heads are rare. The scoops are usually oval or even round, sometimes displaying the influence of a European prototype. There are examples of long-handled spoons, comparable with those from some Dan (*see* DAN, §4) workshops, but nothing is known about their function.

Chairs (h. *c.* 600 mm) are commonly used by elders in the north. They consist of a wooden board as a seat, four short legs and a rounded, wooden back-strip extending on both sides as arm rests that terminate with animal heads. Similar chairs have been produced by the BAULE and SENUFO, and smaller ones among the We, where they are of ritual significance.

3. ARTISTS. Guro wood-carvers choose their profession freely; all are farmers and produce objects at leisure. Sons often learn carving techniques from their fathers, thus taking over their repertory as well as their style. Famous wood-carvers were commissioned from near and far. Their work was considered important and prestigious, being more highly esteemed than the work of weavers or blacksmiths. They never worked in public, but usually in the sacred grove, since women were forbidden to watch the production of sacred objects. None of the early Guro masters is known by name, but the work of five major sculptors is easily distinguishable and can be associated with the places where, in all likelihood, they were working.

The most prolific and possibly the most famous carver of the 1920s was the Master of Buafle (*fl c.* 1900–25). He worked near the colonial headquarters, and many of his masks were exported. They display an innovative and witty style and have expressive profiles (e.g. New Haven, CT, Yale U. A.G.; Paris, Mus. A. Afr. & Océan.; Philadelphia, PA, Mus. A.; Zurich, Mus. Rietberg). His masks are characterized by prominently bulging foreheads; a deeply indented, zigzag hairline; diagonally placed and very thin eyelids with similarly elongated, thin eyebrows; long, slightly upturned noses without nostrils; and tiny vertical slits indicating a lipless mouth. Often, an indented line surrounds the mask's face, and on the hairstyle there are such unusual images as a carving of a ram or of an embracing couple.

Various works by the Master of the Yasua (*fl c.* 1915–35), from the northern region, have been identified (e.g. Stuttgart, Linden-Mus.; Zurich, priv. col.), while others have been attributed to his workshop (Tervuren, Kon. Mus. Mid. Afrika; Zurich, Mus. Rietberg). He is known to have produced large masks as well as outstanding Gu and entertainment masks typified by a relatively flat forehead with a shallowly indented hairline, finely rilled hair strands, prominent eyebrows and slightly encircled or bulging eyelids (see fig.). All his works have a slim nose with an edged bridge, clear-cut nostrils and a prominent nasal bone, his 'trademark'. The mouth forms are V-shaped, with very fine open lips and serrated teeth, and the chins are always heavy and round.

The most important artist practising in 1990 was Master Boti (*b c.* 1920), son of Sabu. Though residing in Tibeita, he had produced masks for clients from all over the Guro region, as well as for Baule dance groups, and specialized in sets of entertainment masks. He was already active in the early 1960s and produced hundreds of traditional masks. He is known especially for groups of figures cut from solid wooden blocks that surmount face-masks as head crests. All his masks have vivid decoration in oil paint (see 1994 exh. cat.). Another carver of repute in the 1990s, Tra bi Tra (*b c.* 1935), worked in the tradition of his grandfather, an influential carver in the northern region responsible for many beautiful Gu masks. Another, younger sculptor, Tra bi Ta (*b c.* 1950), produced gaudy masks and witty figures. His creations are much liked by the young mask dancers of the northern region.

Apart from those masters who cater to local needs, several commercial sculptors produce copies of various mask types (not only of the Guro tradition) for export worldwide. The most famous of these is Beli bi Ta, known as Descar, who comes from a lineage that has owned and produced masks for generations. This intelligent, talented and excellent craftsman is able to adopt any given style and form.

BIBLIOGRAPHY

L. Tauxier: *Nègres Gouro et Gagou* (Paris, 1924)

H. Himmelheber: *Negerkünstler: Ethnographische Studien über die Schnitzkünstler bei den Stämmen der Atutu und Guro im Innern der Elfenbeinküste* (Stuttgart, 1935)

——: *Negerkunst und Negerkünstler* (Brunswick, 1960)
A. Deluz: *Organisation sociale et tradition orale: Les Gouro de Côte d'Ivoire* (Paris and The Hague, 1964)
V. Kacou: 'Les Masques et leur fonction sociale chez les Gouro', *An. U. Abidjan*, Ser. F, vii (1978), pp. 77–84
Die Kunst der Guro: Elfenbeinküste (exh. cat. by E. Fischer and L. Homberger, Zurich, Mus. Rietberg, 1986)
Boti: Ein Maskenschnitzer der Guro, Elfenbeinküste (exh. cat. by E. Fischer and H. Himmelheber, Zurich, Mus. Rietberg, 1994)

FILM
H. Himmelheber: *Djé-Maskentanz der Guro* (Göttingen, 1966) [film, 16 mm; held Göttingen, Inst. Wiss. Film]

EBERHARD FISCHER

Guro, Yelena (Genrikhovna) [Notenberg, Eleanora] (*b* St Petersburg, 10 Jan 1877; *d* Uusikirkko, Finland [now in Russia], 6 May 1913). Russian painter and poet. She has an important place in the development of Russian modernism, as one of its founders and inspirations, and as an artist of independent and original vision. She studied at the drawing school of the Society for the Encouragement of the Arts, St Petersburg (1890–93), in Yan Tsionglinsky's private studio (1903–5) and at the Zvantseva School (1906–7) under Mstislav Dobuzhinsky and Léon Bakst. She was attracted to Symbolist literature and her visual art was characterized by a psychological impressionism that first appeared in the work she showed in exhibitions organized by Nikolay Kul'bin in 1908–10. Guro concentrated on elements of the Finnish landscape near her *dacha*, be that a leaf or the seashore, on her cats, her husband (the painter and musician MIKHAIL MATYUSHIN) or on items such as a drainpipe or the cobbles of a street. Using watercolour and ink, she moved away from visual mimesis towards a Japanese-style response to nature and an empathy with her surroundings, as in *The Shore* (*c.* 1909) and *Pines* (*c.* 1912; both Moscow, Cent. Archvs Lit. & A.). She was also affected by the Neo-primitivist movement that began in Russia *c.* 1908. Closely associated with the Burlyuk brothers and their Wreath group (Venok), she began to use Primitivist techniques derived from signboards and folk art, particularly in oil paintings such as *Morning of the Giant* (1910; St Petersburg, Rus. Mus.) and *Tea-drinking* (*c.* 1910; Orel, A.G.). In 1912, together with the Burlyuks and Futurist poets, including Aleksey Kruchonykh, Guro and Matyushin organized the group Hylaea, the literary counterpart of the UNION OF YOUTH, the leading St Petersburg avant-garde art society, originally founded by Guro and Matyushin in 1909. Guro's poetry and prose, like her visual art, was less iconoclastic than that of her colleagues. All forms of her creative output, which are cohesively integrated with one another, reflect her spiritual relationship with nature, a child-like perception and openness to fantasy, and a delicate, primeval freshness.

WRITINGS
Sharmanka [Hurdy-gurdy] (St Petersburg, 1909)
Osenniy son [Autumn dream] (St Petersburg, 1912)
Nebesnyye verblyuzhata [Little camels of the sky] (Petrograd, 1914)
A. Ljunggren and N. Nilsson, eds: *Elena Guro: Selected Prose and Poetry* (Stockholm, 1988)

BIBLIOGRAPHY
K. Jensen: *Russian Futurism, Urbanism and Elena Guro* (Aarhus, 1977)
Ye. Kovtun, 'Yelena Guro: Poet i khudozhnik' [Yelena Guro: poet and artist], *Pamyatniki kul'tury: Novyye otkrytiya, yezhegodnik 1976* [Monuments of culture: new discoveries, 1976 annual] (Moscow, 1977), pp. 317–26
A. Sarab'yanov: *Neizvestnyy russkiy avangard v muzeyakh i chastnykh sobraniyakh* [The unknown Russian avant-garde in museums and private collections] (Moscow, 1992), pp. 80–85
Yelena Guro: Poet, Khudozhnik, 1877–1913. Zhivopis', grafika, rukopisi, knigi [Yelena Guro: poet and artist, 1877–1913: paintings, drawings, manuscripts, books] (St Petersburg, 1994)

JEREMY HOWARD

Gurrea y Aragón. Spanish family of patrons, collectors and antiquarians.

(1) Martín Gurrea y Aragón, Duque de Villahermosa [Conde de Ribagorza] (*b* Pedrola, Aragon, 17 March 1526; *d* Pedrola, 9 or 19 April 1581). He was taught by his uncle, Cardinal Pedro Sarmiento, Archbishop of Santiago de Compostela, and became an expert on medals and their interpretation; he was also interested in painting. His diplomatic and military activities included missions to England, Flanders, France and Italy, where he visited the ancient monuments of Rome. On his travels he acquired art objects, medals and paintings on religious and secular subjects, including Titian's *Rape of Europa* (Boston, MA, Isabella Stewart Gardner Mus.), which was given to Gurrea y Aragón by the artist and mentioned in the former's *Memorias históricas*.... In 1558 he was made Duque de Villahermosa for his services to the Crown. He was deeply involved with the arts: he built a palace at Pedrola and a country house at Bonavia and founded the monastery of the Padres Predicadores in Saragossa. The painter Jerónimo Cosida y Ballejo (*fl* 1530–72) worked for him in the parish church of Pedrola. Rolan Mois (*d* 1590) painted for him a series of portraits of famous people and of his family (untraced), and copies of Titian's series of mythological paintings, the *Poesie*, in the royal collection of the Alcázar in Madrid were made and added to by Paul Scheppers (*d* 1579). Gurrea y Aragón continued to expand his collection and was in touch with such other leading antiquarians as Archbishop Antonio Agustín and Cardinal Antoine Perrinot de Granvelle. His cabinet of antiquities at Pedrola held the finest of his collection of Greek, Roman and medieval coins, some inherited, others given to him by Philip II and Granvelle, as were some pieces of Classical sculpture, marbles and bronzes from Italy and Spain. Both collections were the basis for his unpublished (and undated) writings on numismatics and antiques. In the 17th century the collections passed to his grandson, (2) Gasper Galcerán de Gurrea Aragón y Pino, Conde de Guimerá, but are untraced.

UNPUBLISHED SOURCES
Madrid, Bib. N. [various writings, incl.: *Memorias históricas de los Condes de Aragón, adornadas de sus blasones y retratos*, MS. 2.070; *Noticia del museo de medallas y de otras preciosas y rares antiguedades del Duque de Villahermosa*; *Diálogos de medallas antiguas españolas, de inscripciones, y de otros monumentos raros* (possibly the same as the *Libro de antigüedades, estatuas, monedas y medallas*...), MSS 7.534 and 8.509, fols 176–275]

BIBLIOGRAPHY
J. R. Mélida: *Discurso de las medallas y antiguedades que compuso el muy ilustre señor D. Martín Gurrea y Aragón, Duque de Villahermosa, Conde de Ribagorza*... (Madrid, 1903)
G. García Ciprés: 'Ricos hombres de Aragón, Condado de Ribagorza', *Lin. Aragón*, i (1910), pp. 54–5, 72–4
——: 'Ricos hombres de Aragón, Ducado de Villahermosa', *Lin. Aragón*, i (1910), pp. 87–90
F. Checa and M. Morán: *El coleccionismo en España* (Madrid, 1985)
F. Marías: *El largo siglo XVI: Los usos artísticos del renacimiento español* (Madrid, 1989)

NATIVIDAD SÁNCHEZ ESTEBAN

(2) Gasper Galcerán de Gurrea Aragón y Pino, Conde de Guimerá (*b* Saragossa, 1584; *d* 1638). Grandson of (1) Martín Gurrea y Aragón. His earliest interest was in medals, and he formed great collections of Roman and Imperial coins and medals and Aragonese coins, as well as cameos, early pottery, casts and models of ancient sculptures and fragments of mosaic. He was a significant pioneer in the study of Classical and Iberian antiquities and of medieval Aragonese history, notably in deciphering Iberian inscriptions, and his collection enabled him to further his researches. He employed the painters Jusepe Martínez and Pedro Orfelin of Saragossa to make drawings of Aragonese antiquities and monuments, and he collected paintings and sculptures. Like other Spanish virtuosi he was a deviser of emblems, and he composed *Emblemas Morales*. He was influential in forming the tastes of Vincencio Juan de Lastanosa and was the outstanding figure in the circle of antiquaries who led the cultural life of Aragon in the Baroque age.

BIBLIOGRAPHY

R. del Arco y Geray in *Rev. Hist. & Geneal. Esp.* (1913)

R. W. Lightbown: 'Some Notes on Spanish Baroque Collectors', *The Origins of Museums*, ed. O. Impey and A. Macgregor (Oxford, 1985), pp. 139–40

R. W. LIGHTBOWN

Gurría, Angela (*b* Mexico City, 24 March 1929). Mexican sculptor. She received some useful tuition from Germán Cueto but was otherwise self-taught, specializing in monumental works that explore volume and space and that exist somewhere between the real world and a language of abstract forms derived from it. Her materials for such works included concrete, as in *Station One* (1968) on the Ruta de la Amistad in Mexico City, and wrought iron, as in *The Papaloapán River* (1970; Mexico City, Mus. A. Mod.). She also produced works as integral to architectural settings, for example *Homage to the Ceiba Tree* (1977) for the Hotel Presidente Chapultepec in Mexico City. The sometimes sombre nature of her work came to the fore in a one-woman exhibition held in 1983 on the subject of death.

BIBLIOGRAPHY

L. Kassner: *Diccionario de escultura mexicana del siglo XX* (Mexico City, 1983), pp. 158–9

X. Moyssén: 'Angela Gurría', *Doce expresiones plásticas de hoy* (Mexico City, 1988)

XAVIER MOYSSÉN

Gurruwiwi, Mandjuwi [Manjuwi] (*b* Galiwin'ku, Elcho Island, 1 Jan 1935). Australian Aboriginal painter. As a leader of the Gälpu clan of the Dhuwa moiety of north-east Arnhem Land in the Northern Territory he alternated residence between Elcho and his homeland at Gekal on the mainland. He learnt the artistic and sculptural forms and meanings of Yolngu art from his father, Murupula Gurruwiwi. He used a combination of figurative and geometric designs in his bark paintings to represent sacred ancestral law. Figurative elements include animals, objects, plants, ancestral beings or Yolngu connected with the Gälpu clan; the geometric patterns locate these elements at specific sacred sites. One notable painting, *Sacred Wurrkadi*, purchased by the Australian National Gallery at Canberra in 1980, depicts the larvae of the horned beetle representing the children of the clan against a background of cross-hatching. The Northern Territory Museum of Arts and Sciences at Darwin also houses some of his works, notably a painting (purchased 1981) of the *Sacred Morning Star Ceremony*, depicting the Morning Star attached to a pole as a symbol of connectivity linking the Gälpu clan to other Dhuwa clans related by the ceremony.

BIBLIOGRAPHY

The Inspired Dream (exh. cat., Brisbane, Queensland A.G. and elsewhere, 1988–91)

W. Caruana, ed.: *Windows on the Dreaming: Aboriginal Paintings in the Australian National Gallery* (Canberra, 1989)

H. Morphy: *Ancestral Connections* (Chicago, 1991)

FIONA MAGOWAN

Gurunsi. *See* BWA AND GURUNSI.

Gūsho. *See under* MASUDA.

Gusmin of Cologne (*d c*. 1417–20). Goldsmith, sculptor and painter, probably of German origin. None of his works is known to have survived, but he is mentioned twice in mid-15th-century texts: in the second book of Lorenzo Ghiberti's *Commentarii* and in the manuscript of the Anonimo Magliabecchiano. Both texts relate that Gusmin died during the reign of Pope Martin (i.e. Martin V, *reg* 1417–31), in the year of the 438th Olympiad (i.e. between 1415 and 1420). He worked in the service of the Duke of Anjou, who was forced to destroy Gusmin's greatest work, a golden altar, in order to provide cash for his 'public needs'. Gusmin consequently retired to a hermitage where he led a saintly life, painting and teaching young artists. Although it is clear from his account that Ghiberti never knew the master or saw any of his original works, he stated that he had seen casts of his sculptures, which, he said, were as fine as the work of the ancient Greeks, although the figures were rather short. There have been numerous attempts to identify Gusmin with artists, both German and Italian, fitting the account of Ghiberti and the Anonimo Magliabecchiano. Swarzenski first named Gusmin as the author of the alabaster Rimini altar (Frankfurt am Main, Liebieghaus), but this has now been demonstrated to be of Netherlandish workmanship. Krautheimer proposed a convincing reconstruction of Gusmin's career, suggesting that his Angevin patron was Louis I, Duke of Anjou (*see* ANJOU, §II(1)), son of King John II. Gusmin probably worked for two decades in the Duke's service, up to the time when Louis needed money for his conquest of Naples (1381–2) and most of his riches were pawned or sent to the mint.

BIBLIOGRAPHY

Thieme–Becker

C. Frey, ed.: *Il codice Magliabechiano* (Berlin, 1892), pp. 87–8, 328–9

J. van Schlosser: *Lorenzo Ghibertis Denwürdigkeiten (I Commentari)*, 2 vols (Berlin, 1912); i, pp. 42–3; ii, p. 19

G. Swarzenski: 'Der Kölner Meister bei Ghiberti', *Vorträge der Bibliothek Warburg, 1926–27* (Leipzig, 1930), pp. 22–42

R. Krautheimer: 'Ghiberti and Master Gusmin', *A. Bull.*, xxix (1947), pp. 25–35

□

Gustav III, King of Sweden. *See* HOLSTEIN-GOTTORP, (2).

Gustav VI Adolf [Oscar Fredrik Wilhelm Olaf Gustaf Adolf], King of Sweden (*b* Stockholm, 11 Nov 1882; *reg* 1950–73; *d* Hälsingborg, 15 Sept 1973). Swedish ruler, collector and archaeologist. He was educated at Uppsala University, where he studied history, Nordic archaeology and Egyptology, and in his youth assisted in archaeological expeditions in Sweden, Greece, Italy and Cyprus. In 1907 he began to collect Chinese art and was soon attracted to the early periods, the area in which his collection eventually became pre-eminent. In 1908 he met the foremost scholars and collectors of Chinese art in London and then helped to plan a large exhibition of Chinese art at the Kungliga Akademien för de Fria Konsterna (Royal Academy of Fine Arts), Stockholm, in 1914. The following year he met Erik Nyström, Professor of natural history at Taiyuan University, who purchased items for him in China. His collection was also enriched from 1916 with the help of Orvar Karlbeck, the Swedish railway engineer active in China. Other Chinese pieces were purchased or presented to his collection during his journey to East Asia in 1926, and he also visited Korea and Japan, where he acquired other items. In 1948 his Chinese collection was published under the editorship of Nils Palmgren, Keeper of the collection from 1930 to 1955. It comprised about 1600 items, including bronzes, stonewares and porcelains, and was located in the Crown Prince's apartment at the Royal Palace in Stockholm. During the 1950s a new aspect of Chinese art—jades from the Han (206 BC–AD 220) to the Song (AD 960–1279) periods—took his interest, and during the last 15 years of his life he also collected Chinese rhinoceros-horn carvings. By 1967 his entire collection consisted of about 2500 objects. Apart from artefacts, he built up a library of books and periodicals on Chinese art and archaeology. As well as being a collector of renown, he was also an active patron and supporter of Swedish cultural and archaeological activities abroad. From 1921 to 1950 he was the Chairman of the China Committee, which had been founded in Stockholm in 1919, and later Grand Patron of the Association of Friends of the Östasiatiska Museet (Museum of Far Eastern Antiquities), Stockholm. He gave objects to the museum, lent his own items to exhibitions and allowed his collection to be visited by scholars and connoisseurs. Exhibitions of large portions of his collection were held in the USA in 1966–7 and at the British Museum, London, in 1972. His collection was bequeathed to the Swedish nation.

BIBLIOGRAPHY

N. Palmgren, ed.: *Selected Chinese Antiquities from the Collection of Gustaf Adolf, Crown Prince of Sweden* (Stockholm, 1948)

Chinese Art from the Collection of H. M. King Gustaf VI Adolf of Sweden (exh. cat. by B. Gyllensvärd, Stockholm, Östasiat. Mus., 1967)

H. M. Garner: Obituary, *Trans. Orient. Cer. Soc.*, xxxix (1971–3), p. x

B. W. Robinson: Obituary, *J. Royal Asiat. Soc. GB & Ireland* (1974), p. 98

B. Gyllensvärd: 'King Gustaf VI Adolf's Approach to Chinese Art', *Trans. Orient. Cer. Soc.*, xliv (1979–80), pp. 31–46

S. J. VERNOIT

Gustavian style. Expression of 18th-century Swedish Neo-classicism during the reign of Gustav III (*reg* 1771–92; *see* HOLSTEIN-GOTTORP, (2)). As a cultured man and an advocate of the European Enlightenment, the King's patronage of the visual arts was linked with patriotic ambition and an admiration for the French courtly life at Versailles. He spent part of 1770–71 in France, where he acquired a passion for the Neo-classical style. During his reign numerous palaces and country houses were built or refurbished in the Neo-classical style, either for himself or for members of his family and court. Early Gustavian interiors (*c.* 1770–85) were light and elegant interpretations of the Louis XVI style, with echoes of English, German and Dutch influences. Rooms were decorated with pilasters and columns; walls were applied with rich silk damasks or rectangular panels with painted designs framed in carved, gilded linear ornament and laurel festoons. Damask, usually crimson, blue or green, was used to upholster benches, sofas and chairs. Other rooms were panelled in wood, painted light-grey, blue or pale-green; the dominant feature was a columnar faience-tiled stove, decorated with sprigged floral patterns. Klismos-style chairs upholstered in silk were very popular, as were oval-backed chairs with straight, fluted legs, and bateau-shaped sofas were common. Rooms were embellished with long, giltwood-framed mirrors, crystal chandeliers, gilt *torchères* and Classical-style vases and urns of Swedish porphyry. Wooden floors were laid with Swedish carpets inspired by those of Savonnerie.

Swedish painters, architects, cabinetmakers and carvers were encouraged by Gustav to train in France and Italy and to return to Stockholm to assist in the realization of the King's vision of a Swedish golden age. Two prominent Swedish architects who received important commissions were JEAN ERIC REHN, whose work at the Royal Palace, Stockholm, and Drottningholm Palace on Lake Mälan introduced the Neo-classical style to Sweden, and C. F. Adelcrantz, who was responsible for designing the Royal Opera House (1775–82; destr. 1892), Stockholm, and the splendid Gustavian interiors at Sturehof (1778–81), outside Stockholm. The most important cabinetmaker of the period was GEORG HAUPT, who produced furniture inlaid with exotic woods for the royal family, including a mineral-cabinet (1773–4; Chantilly, Mus. Condé) presented by Gustav to Louis-Joseph, Prince de Condé (1736–1818). Notable contributors to the late Gustavian style (*c.* 1785–1810) were the French architect Louis-Jean Desprez and the designer Louis-Adrien Masreliez, both of whom worked on the interiors of the Pavilion at Haga Palace (*c.* 1790), which was constructed by the Swedish architect Olof Tempelman (1745–1816) after the Petit Trianon at Versailles. Masreliez covered the walls at Haga with Classical muses and grotesques derived from decoration at Pompeii, Herculaneum and the works of Raphael and Giulio Romano; it was the first decoration of this kind in Sweden. Late Gustavian furniture was rectilinear and austere, and there was a new accuracy in copying from antique models. Secrétaires, commodes, cupboards and desks were decorated with figured veneers and gilded mounts, or were sparsely inlaid with different woods, as seen in the secrétaire (*c.* 1790; Stockholm, Nordiska Mus.) by Gustav Adolf Ditzinger (1760–1800).

In the fine arts the Gustavian style was mainly concentrated in the medium of sculpture, especially in the work of Johan Tobias Sergel. He was recalled to court from Italy in 1779 and was best known for such Classical figures in a flowing, Baroque manner as the marble *Faun* (1774; Stockholm, Nmus.). Among the many painters at court was Carl Gustaf Pilo, who had spent the early part of his career in Denmark. His most famous work was the *Coronation of Gustav III* (1783; Stockholm, Nmus.), executed in silvery, Rococo colours. Despite political problems, Gustav continued to make expansive building plans prior to his assassination in 1792. Neo-classicism continued in Sweden in the form of the later Empire and Biedermeier styles.

BIBLIOGRAPHY

H. Groth and F. von der Schulenburg: *Neo-classicism in the North: Swedish Furniture and Interiors, 1770–1850* (London, 1990)

□

Guston, Philip (*b* Montreal, 27 June 1913; *d* Woodstock, NY, 7 June 1980). American painter. He moved to Los Angeles with his family in 1919. He began to paint and draw in 1927 and attended the Otis Art Institute for three months (1930). At this stage he based his technique on a close study of the art of Giorgio de Chirico and painters of the Italian Renaissance such as Paolo Uccello, Andrea Mantegna and Piero della Francesca. He was attempting to integrate the modelled architectural space of Renaissance art with the contracted, reassembled space of Cubism, for example in paintings of sinister hooded figures reminiscent of the Ku Klux Klan such as *Conspirators* (*c.* 1930; untraced, see Ashton, 1976, p. 10).

In the 1930s Guston became involved with the mural movement and the work of Mexican artists such as Diego Rivera. On his arrival in New York in 1935–6 he joined the group of artists that included Burgoyne Diller and James Brooks (ii) who worked for the Works Progress Administration's Federal Arts Project (WPA/FAP). Among the murals on which he worked are *Maintaining America's Skills* (destr.; see 1982 exh. cat., p. 59) on the façade of the WPA Building at the World's Fair of 1939, the Queensbridge Housing Project (1940) in New York and the Social Security Building (1942) in Washington, DC. The style of his mural work, particularly the organization of figures in space in the Queensbridge commission, owed much to Uccello, of whose *Rout of San Romano* he owned large colour reproductions. Another key influence was Picasso, whose major exhibition at MOMA in 1939 was an outstanding event for American painters. In 1940 Guston left the project and from autumn 1941 to 1945 was artist-in-residence at the State University of Iowa in Iowa City, before moving to St Louis, MO, as artist-in-residence at the School of Fine Arts, Washington University, a post that he left in 1947 when he was awarded a Guggenheim Fellowship. He continued to teach (mainly drawing) at New York University and at the Pratt Institute. He was awarded a grant from the Ford Foundation in 1959.

Like many of his contemporaries, Guston spent the years after World War II developing a personal style and vision out of the diverse range of realist and abstract influences that challenged American artists of his era. In the 1940s he constructed a private mythological world in paintings such as *Martial Memory* (1945; St Louis, MO, A. Mus.) and *If this Be Not I* (1945; St Louis, MO, Washington U., Gal. A.); in the latter a crowd of children, some masked or with faces partially covered, fill the columned porch of an old dilapidated Midwestern house. It is a night scene, predominantly blue in colour, richly and heavily painted. By 1947–8, when he painted *The Tormentors* (San Francisco, CA, MOMA), figures have almost disappeared, leaving behind only traces of floorboards, furniture and architecture. In the early 1950s he developed a lyrical abstract style in works such as *Dial* (1956; New York, Whitney), which towards the end of the decade evolved into single dark images embedded in a morass of grey paint, for example *Painter I* (1959;

Philip Guston: *Painter in Bed*, oil on canvas, 0.60×1.04 m, 1973 (London, Saatchi Collection)

Atlanta, GA, High Mus. A.) and *New Place* (1964; San Francisco, CA, MOMA). His most radical shift came in the late 1960s with works such as *Evidence* (1970; San Francisco, CA, MOMA), when he confounded the art world with a new figurative style in which blunt cartoon shapes are used to create a personal iconography. Certain images recur in these paintings, such as the soles of shoes (as in *Back View*, 1977; San Francisco, CA, MOMA) and people's heads (e.g. *Painter in Bed*, 1973; London, Saatchi Col.; see fig.), inhabiting a sort of spare parts world in which the disembodied, separate items have a unique and surrealistic life of their own.

BIBLIOGRAPHY

D. Ashton: *Philip Guston* (New York, 1959)
Philip Guston (exh. cat., Amsterdam, Stedel. Mus., 1962)
Philip Guston: Recent Paintings and Drawings (exh. cat., intro. S. Hunter; New York, Jew. Mus., 1966) [incl. dialogue between artist and H. Rosenberg]
D. Ashton: *Yes, but... A Critical Study of Philip Guston* (New York, 1976)
P. Brach: 'Looking at Guston', *A. America*, lxviii/9 (1980), pp. 96–101
Philip Guston (exh. cat., essays H. T. Hopkins and R. Feld; San Francisco, MOMA, 1980)
Philip Guston, 1980: The Last Works (exh. cat. by M. Feldman, Washington, DC, Phillips Col., 1981)
Philip Guston: Paintings, 1969–1980 (exh. cat., intro. N. Lynton; London, Whitechapel A.G.; Amsterdam, Stedel. Mus.; Basle, Ksthalle; 1982) [incl. lecture by Guston]
R. Storr: *Guston* (New York, 1986)

CHRISTOPHER BROOKEMAN

Gutai [Gutai Bijutsu Kyōkai; Jap.: Concrete Art Association]. Japanese group of artists, active between 1954 and 1972. It was formed by 18 young avant-garde artists, led by JIRŌ YOSHIHARA, one of the founders of Japanese abstract painting. Following Yoshihara's guidance in creating an anti-individualistic form of expression, the group started by holding an open-air exhibition at the Ashiyagawa riverside. The members began experimenting in performance art, for example breaking through single-leaf paper screens and creating other staged pieces such as *San basō ultra-moderne* by Kazuo Shiraga (*b* 1924). This consisted of archers firing at a theatrical set and was performed in Osaka in 1957 (see 1986 exh. cat., p. 298). The group also practised kinetic art, for example in *Work: Water* by Sadamasa Motonaga, in which water was filtered through suspended fabrics at the Second Open-air Exhibition in Ashiya in 1956 (see 1986 exh. cat., p. 319).

The members of Gutai (Jap.: embodiment) also continued to create many paintings that were related to European *Art informel* (e.g. Motonaga's *Painting, No. 7*, 1960; Kobe, Hyōgo Prefect., MOMA) and became closely associated with the French critic Michel Tapié, a champion of *Art informel*, when he visited Japan in 1957 on the occasion of an exhibition by Georges Mathieu. In 1958 Gutai, *Art informel* and the Abstract Expressionists Jackson Pollock and Franz Kline were the subjects of a large exhibition entitled the *International Art of a New Era*.

Although Gutai was based in Osaka, through its periodical, *Gutai*, the group became known internationally, in particular for its performance art, whose importance was recognized by Allan Kaprow in 1966. The bulletin was sent to many artists and critics including Jackson Pollock and Michel Tapié. In the early 1960s members of the group experimented with correspondence art, but the radical character of the early period was gradually diluted, and the group entered the mainstream of international painting: in particular Jirō Yoshihara, Kazuo Shiraga and Atsuko Tanaka (*b* 1932) displayed many works in international exhibitions. Important work was also produced by Motonaga, Shōzō Shimamoto, Saburō Murakami, Akira Kanayama and Toshio Yoshida. Although in the late 1960s Gutai expanded its activities in such areas as kinetic art and light art, the group disbanded in 1972 with the sudden death of Jirō Yoshihara. Although the artistic reputation of Gutai fell into decline during the 1970s, in the 1980s major exhibitions caused a re-evaluation of its achievements.

BIBLIOGRAPHY

J. Yoshihara: 'Sur l'art Gutai: L'Avenir du nouvel art', *Notizie*, viii (April 1959) [issue ded. to Gutai]
A. Kaprow: *Assemblage, Environments and Happenings* (New York, 1966), pp. 211–26
J. Love: 'The Group in Contemporary Japanese Art: Gutai and Jiro Yoshihara', *A. Int.*, xvi/6–7 (1972), pp. 123–7, 143
P. Restany: 'Le Groupe Gutai ou le Japon précurseur', *XXe siècle*, 46 (1976), pp. 96–103
F. Naujo and Y. Yurugi: 'Gutai, Informel and Abstract Art', *Reconstructions: Avant-garde Art in Japan, 1945–1965* (exh. cat., ed. D. Elliott and K. Kaido; Oxford, MOMA, 1985), pp. 49–65
A. Pacquement: 'Gutai: L'Extraordinaire Intuition', *Japon des avant-gardes, 1910–70* (exh. cat., ed. G. Viatte and T. Shūji; Paris, Pompidou, 1986), pp. 284–319
Kazuo Shiraga: Gutai, 1954–1972 (exh. cat. by C. Lonzi, M. Tapié and J. Yoshihara, Milan, Gal. Milano, 1987)
S. Osaki: *Gutai: Action on Painting* (Rome, 1991) [It.-Eng. text]

SHIN'ICHIRO OSAKI

Gutenberg [Gensfleisch zur Laden]**, Johann** [Johannes] (*b* Mainz, *c.* 1394–99; *d* Mainz, 1468). German printer. Trained as a goldsmith, he left Mainz for Strasbourg *c.* 1428 as a political exile. A lawsuit of 1439 indicates that while in Strasbourg he began experimenting with printing techniques. Gutenberg was back in Mainz on 17 October 1448 and by 1450 had begun a commercial printing venture employing his inventions of movable metal type cast in separate letters and a type-casting machine (*see* PRINTING). He was financed by a lawyer, Johannes Fust (*d* 1466), who also became his partner. Gutenberg's principal developments were the use of individual letters in raised type, which were manufactured in metal instead of wood, thus increasing the durability and clarity of the printed image, and the employment of a pressure press in the printing process. His 42-line Bible, set up during 1452–3, was published before 24 August 1456 (*see* BIBLE, fig. 6). It was a lectern book, in two volumes, comprising 1286 pages and was the first full-length book ever printed. The Bible was so named from the number of lines in each column of its double-column pages, though it is also known as the Mazarin Bible from a copy (Paris, Bib. Mazarine) in the library of Cardinal Mazarin. It is the one major work that can confidently be regarded as a product of Gutenberg's own workshop. Copies were sold across northern Europe and, when illuminated, could be mistaken for manuscripts: over 40 still exist.

In 1455 Fust foreclosed on the business and began legal proceedings to reclaim his loan to Gutenberg. As a result of this litigation, Gutenberg lost most of his property, including nearly all his types and presses. The one other certain product of his printing activities is the *Catholicon* (pubd Mainz, 1460; London, BM, IC.302), a 13th-century Latin encyclopedia and dictionary by Johannes Balbus (*d* 1298). After 1460 Gutenberg seems to have abandoned printing altogether, possibly because of failing eyesight.

BIBLIOGRAPHY

A. Ruppel: *Johannes Gutenberg: Sein Leben und sein Werk* (Berlin, 1939/*R* Nieuwkoop, 1967)

V. Scholderer: *Johann Gutenberg: The Inventor of Printing* (London, 1963)

Johannes Gutenbergs 42-zeilige Bibel, 2 vols (Munich, 1979) [facs]

□

Gütersloh, Albert Paris von [Kiehtreiber, Albert Conrad] (*b* Vienna, 5 Feb 1887; *d* Baden, nr Vienna, 16 May 1973). Austrian painter and writer. He began as an actor and taught himself to paint, joining the NEUKUNSTGRUPPE in 1909. In 1911 he published *Die tanzende Törin*, under the pseudonym 'Paris von Gütersloh', which established his reputation as a writer. His painting and writing are both marked by a lyrical Expressionism which has its roots in the Austrian Baroque: spiritual strength is combined with self-irony, sophistic brilliance with hedonistic joie de vivre, moral sincerity with wild fantasy. His opulent style was influenced by Cézanne, Cubism, Surrealism and Neue Sachlichkeit. In addition to still-lifes, portraits and landscapes he produced fairy-tale scenes, parables and allegories of an idyllic and endearing nature, rather than a sinister one, as in a *Little Night Music* (1938; Vienna, Albertina) and *In the Maze of Love* (1960; Vienna, priv. col.). In the later stages of his career he also made tapestries, mosaics and windows, for example the tapestry the *Writer at the Market* (1947; Vienna, Bundesmin. Unterricht & Kst), as well as paintings such as *Still-life with Barometer* (1947; Vienna, Hist. Mus.), and book illustrations.

In 1921 Gütersloh adopted as his official name the pseudonym he had been using. He began teaching at the Kunstgewerbeschule in Vienna in 1930 until he was dismissed by the National Socialists in 1938 and blacklisted in 1940. In 1945 he was made a professor at the Akademie der Bildenden Künste in Vienna and in 1946 was elected President of the Art Club. In this way he was closely involved in the artistic recovery of Austria after World War II and he became a mentor of PHANTASTISCHER REALISMUS, whose main exponents included the Austrian painter Wolfgang Hutter (*b* 1928), Gütersloh's illegitimate son.

WRITINGS

Die tanzende Törin (Berlin, 1911/*R* Munich, 1979)

BIBLIOGRAPHY

H. Hutter: *A. P. Gütersloh: Beispiele* (Vienna, 1977)

J. Adler, ed.: *Allegorie und Eros: Texte von und über Albert Paris Gütersloh* (Munich, 1986)

A. P. Gütersloh: Zum 100. Geburtstag (exh. cat., ed. H. Hutter; Vienna, Sezession, 1987)

EDWIN LACHNIT

Gutfreund, Otto (*b* Dvůr Králové, 3 Aug 1889; *d* Prague, 2 June 1927). Czech sculptor and draughtsman. One of the outstanding Czech sculptors of the early 20th century, he had a considerable influence both during his lifetime and subsequently. He studied at the Central School of Ceramics at Bechyně from 1903 and then under Professor J. Drahoňovský at the School of Applied Arts in Prague (1905–9) where his exceptional plastic sensibility became apparent. He then spent a year in Paris at the atelier of Emile-Antoine Bourdelle. Gutfreund's work can be divided into two contrasting periods: the first, beginning in 1910, is largely Cubist while the second, beginning *c.* 1919, shows a move to realistic sculpture. (Unless otherwise stated, all sculptures by Gutfreund mentioned below are in Prague, National Gallery.) His early work was influenced by Michelangelo's *Slaves* (*c.* 1514; Paris, Louvre) and by Honoré Daumier's modelling and treatment of light, which jointly inspired *Anguish* (1911) and *Hamlet* (1911–12). From the Cubistic *Anguish* he made the transition to a luminous shedding of form as he parted company with traditional realistic sculpture. This progression can be followed in four portraits of his father. The first takes the form of a traditional bust while the subsequent portraits are conceived in relief, which was already a departure from realistic portraiture.

Gutfreund incorporated impulses from both Expressionism and Cubism in his work: on the one hand he created sculptures that can be considered major works of Czech Expressionism (e.g. his reliefs *Concert*, *The Cellist*, *Don Quixote*), on the other he rid himself of content and strove for a purely plastic modelling, as in the Cubist *Bust* (1913–14). At this time he was a member of the Group of Plastic Artists and published some important theoretical reflections in its monthly journal, *Umělecký měsíčník*. In 1914 he left for Paris, anticipating a long stay, but his plans, like those of other Czech artists then living in France, such as Emil Filla, were upset by the outbreak of war. Although he enlisted in the Foreign Legion, he was instead interned for a number of years in a prisoner-of-war camp. Only two wooden sculptures have survived from this time. Many important autonomous drawings are extant from his first period. They are magnificent examples of CUBO-EXPRESSIONISM, revealing his interest in elementary forms such as crystals and in collage, the development of which was sporadic in Czech Cubism.

In his second period Gutfreund moved from Cubist principles to realistic modelling in a number of coloured wooden sculptures. His new orientation is to be seen in his terracotta *Self-portrait* (1919), which initiated the so-called non-combatant period in Czech art that was associated with democratic principles and the foundation of the Czechoslovak Republic. The majority of his sculptures of the 1920s are in coloured terracotta. His work in the second period has two strands: he entered all the prestigious state commissions such as the portrait of *T. G. Masaryk* and the *Smetana* monument (both 1926), but he also modelled small realistic groups of figures that typified the development of democratic post-war society, for example *Industry* (wood; 1923) and *Commerce* (plaster; 1923; *see* CZECH REPUBLIC, fig. 12).

The *Family* (1925), with its recumbent figures, can be considered the culmination of Gutfreund's sculpture in that it constitutes a synthesis of all the motifs in circulation since 1918 on this theme. The period around 1925 is, however, thought to have been the weakest in his development as a sculptor. Although the *Family* can be seen as representative of this period, just as *Anguish* is representative of the pre-war period, Gutfreund seems to have been unable to rise to the aesthetic of the non-combativism that he had helped to initiate. In his last sculptures, however, he again incorporated current trends in European sculpture, as in *Sitting* and *Woman with Arms Akimbo* (both 1927). In both these works he returned to autonomous plastic form, free from any narrative or episodic elements.

BIBLIOGRAPHY

J. Cícařovský: *Otto Gutfreund* (Prague, 1962)
Otto Gutfreund (exh. cat., Vienna, Mus. 20. Jhts, 1969)
Otto Gutfreund (exh. cat., Bochum, Mus. Bochum, Kstsamml., 1970)
J. Šetlík, ed.: *Otto Gutfreund: Zázemí tvorby* [Otto Gutfreund: background to creation] (Prague, 1989)

KAREL SRP

Guthrie, Sir **James** (*b* Greenock, 10 June 1859; *d* Rhu, Strathclyde, 6 Sept 1930). Scottish painter. He originally enrolled at Glasgow University to study law but in 1877 his father, a member of the Scottish clergy, allowed him to train as a painter under James Drummond (1816–77). In 1878 he began work in John Pettie's studio in London where he was encouraged to produce academic history and genre paintings. Every summer from 1878 to 1881, however, Guthrie returned to Scotland to paint landscapes alongside Joseph Crawhall and E. A. Walton. He was influenced by the work of Jean-François Millet and the Barbizon school and in the spring of 1882 completed his first major realist painting, *Funeral Service in the Highlands* (Glasgow, A.G. & Mus.).

In 1882 Guthrie encountered the naturalist paintings of Jules Bastien-Lepage in London and that summer at Crowland, Lincs, he began his first naturalist painting, *To Pastures New* (Aberdeen, A.G.). Guthrie adapted Bastien-Lepage's style, introducing more colour and direct sunlight, and over the next four years produced the most important naturalist paintings of the Glasgow school, becoming an important member of the GLASGOW BOYS. These paintings were produced at Cockburnspath, Berwicks, where, following Bastien-Lepage's example, Guthrie established a studio to form a closer relationship with the people of the village who became his subject-matter.

The most important works of this period include a *Hind's Daughter* (1883; Edinburgh, N.G.) and *Schoolmates* (1884–5; Ghent, Mus. S. Kst.). As his compositions became more complicated, however, developing from the single full-length figures that were a feature of Glasgow school paintings, Guthrie encountered such difficulties that he turned to portrait painting. Beginning with the portrait of *The Rev. Dr Andrew Gardiner* (1885; Edinburgh, N.G.), Guthrie became the leading portrait painter of his generation in Scotland. Influenced by Velázquez and Whistler, his practice ranged from informal studies of young women, such as *Miss Wilson* (1890; priv. col., see Billcliffe, p. 264), to the large and elaborate, as in *Some Statesmen of the Great War* (1919–30; London, N.P.G.).

With the exception of *Midsummer* (1892; Edinburgh, Royal Scot. Acad.), a group of realist pastels produced from 1888 to 1890 and a few small paintings from the early 1890s, Guthrie concentrated almost entirely on portraiture for the rest of his life. In 1888 he was the first member of the Glasgow school to join the Royal Scottish Academy, of which he was president from 1902 to 1919.

BIBLIOGRAPHY

J. L. Caw: *Sir James Guthrie PRSA LL.D: A Biography* (London, 1932)
D. Irwin and F. Irwin: *Scottish Painters at Home and Abroad, 1700–1900* (London, 1975), pp. 370–94 [with excellent bibliog.]
Guthrie and the Scottish Realists (exh. cat., ed. R. Billcliffe; Glasgow, F. A. Soc., 1981)
R. Billcliffe: *The Glasgow Boys: The Glasgow School of Painting, 1875–1895* (London, 1985) [most comprehensive account and selection of pls]

ROGER BILLCLIFFE

Guthwerdt. *See* GUDEWERDT.

Gutiéra, Antonio Mohedano de la. *See* MOHEDANO, ANTONIO.

Gutiérrez, Felipe S(antiago) (*b* Texcoco, nr Mexico City, 20 May 1824; *d* Texcoco, 4 April 1904). Mexican painter and writer. He entered the Academia de San Carlos in Mexico City in 1836, studying under Miguel Mata (1814–76) and subsequently with Pelegrín Clavé; the preponderance of biblical themes in his student production can be attributed to the emphasis on such subject-matter both in Clavé's work and among the conservative group that dominated the Academia in the mid-19th century. Gutiérrez's ideological sympathies with the liberal faction, however, soon led him to produce paintings such as the *Judgement of Brutus* (1857; Mexico City, Mus. N.A.), republican in theme and markedly influenced in style by David, although falling far short of the latter's technical perfection.

Unlike most of his fellow students at the Academia, Gutiérrez did not begin to teach until after he had completed many years of travelling; from 1862 he lived in various cities in Mexico, then in San Francisco, Paris, Rome, Madrid, New York and finally in Bogotá, where he achieved considerable renown as a teacher of painting. While travelling he supported himself by painting portraits, for example the particularly outstanding one of *Señora Sánchez Solís* (Toluca, Mus. B.A.), the wife of his patron Felipe Sánchez Solís, a Mexican lawyer and liberal intellectual for whom he also painted an interesting regional scene with autobiographical overtones, the *Indian Boy's Farewell* (1876; see 1990/91 exh. cat., p. 514). In Europe he embraced the contemporary revaluation of Spanish Baroque painting, later making it known in Mexico through works such as *St Bartholomew* and *St Jerome* (both exh. 1886; Mexico City, Mus. N.A.), directly influenced by Jusepe de Ribera. The rich blending of colours and boldness of execution of his works of this period, for example the *Andean Huntress* (exh. 1891; Mexico City, Mus. N.A.), also suggest affinities with Spanish artists such as Eduardo Rosales Martines and Mariano José Bernardo Fortuny y Marsal (both of whom had become his friends in Rome), and also with the work of Courbet; while in Europe he appears to have met Courbet's champion, Jules-Antoine Castagnary. Gutiérrez also wrote some art criticism, including articles on exhibitions held in 1875, 1877 and 1881 at the Escuela Nacional de Bellas Artes. He also published a long and interesting account of his travels and a treatise on drawing and painting.

WRITINGS

Viaje de F.S.G. por México, los Estados Unidos, Europa y Sudamérica, 2 vols (Mexico City, 1882–3)
Tratado de dibujo y pintura (Colima, 1864/*R* Mexico City, 1895)

BIBLIOGRAPHY

I. Rodríguez Prampolini, ed.: *La crítica de arte en México en el siglo XIX* (Mexico City, 1964), ii, pp. 366–82, 417–37; iii, pp. 81–125

J. M. Caballero-Barnard: 'Felipe S. Gutiérrez, pintor de Academia', *A. México*, 171 (1973) [whole issue]

Mexico: Splendors of Thirty Centuries (exh. cat., New York, MOMA, 1990–91), pp. 513–14

FAUSTO RAMÍREZ

Gutiérrez, Juan Simón (*b* Medina Sidonia, Cádiz, 1643; *d* Seville, 1718). Spanish painter. He was trained in Seville around 1660 in a milieu dominated by the painting style of Bartolomé Esteban Murillo. His membership of the Academia de Pintura in Seville is recorded from 1664 to 1672, as is his marriage in 1677. Although Gutiérrez worked as a painter in Seville for half a century, few of his paintings are known. The earliest, signed and dated 1698, is the *Virgin and Child with Augustinian Saints*, representing St Augustine, St Nicholas of Tolentino, St Monica and St Rita of Cascia (Carmona, La Trinidad). *St Dominic Comforted by the Virgin and Martyr Saints* (Seville, Mus. B.A.) is also signed. Against a background of golden clouds, the red and blue of the Virgin's mantle contrasts with the black-and-white habit of St Dominic. The tunics of the surrounding child martyrs blend harmoniously into the whole, and the sweet, contemplative faces of these young female saints are clearly influenced by Murillo. The *Assumption of the Virgin* (London, Wallace), attributed to Gutiérrez and almost certainly by him, is based on an engraving by Schelte à Bolswert inspired by two versions of the theme painted by Peter Paul Rubens (*c.* 1611–15; The Hague, Mauritshuis; Vienna, Ksthist. Mus.).

BIBLIOGRAPHY

D. Angulo Iñíguez: *Pintura del siglo XVII*, A. Hisp. (Madrid, 1971), p. 366

——: *Murillo y su escuela* (Seville, 1975), p. 7

E. Valdivieso: *Historia de la pintura sevillana* (Seville, 1986), p. 243

A. E. Pérez Sánchez: *Pintura barroca española* (Madrid, 1992), p. 365

ENRIQUE VALDIVIESO

Gutiérrez, Rodrigo (*b* San Luis Potosí, 1848; *d* Mexico City, 1903). Mexican painter. He studied at the Academia de San Carlos in Mexico City (1865–71) and was an outstanding pupil of the painter Pelegrín Clavé. He was considered one of the finest portrait painters of his time, but like the rest of his fellow-pupils Gutiérrez also practised history painting. One of his most remarkable group portraits was a key work in the development of national subject-matter in Mexican painting, *The Tlaxcala Senate* (oil on canvas, 1874; Mexico City, Mus. N.A.). This is a large canvas with many almost life-size figures, and, unlike other paintings of Mexican subjects, it shows well executed realism in the treatment of the individual figures despite the classicizing style of the poses and composition. Gutiérrez taught painting at the Instituto de Zacatecas, Mexico City, but his career ended abruptly in 1884, when he suffered brain damage in a fall from his horse.

BIBLIOGRAPHY

J. Fernández: *El arte del siglo XIX en México* (Mexico City, 1967, rev. 1983), pp. 64, 112

F. Ramírez: 'Arte del siglo XIX en la ciudad de México', *Historia del arte mexicano* (Madrid, 1982), p. 50

ESPERANZA GARRIDO

Gutiérrez Alarcón, Sérvulo (*b* Ica, 1914; *d* Lima, 21 July 1961). Peruvian painter, potter and sculptor. He had little formal education, but after training as a boxer in Lima he settled in Buenos Aires, where his interest in pottery led him to set up a workshop for the conservation of Pre-Columbian pottery and for the manufacture of pottery in the style of this period. He learnt to sculpt and studied painting under Emilio Pettoruti (1892–1971). In 1938 he went to Paris, where he studied the work of the French masters and relaxed his style, rejecting academic canons. Returning to Peru in 1942, he adopted a rather Expressionist style of painting, with clear lines, suggestive of sculpted forms. He avoided the other avant-garde European styles of the period, opting for a while for elements of the Indigenist style (*see* PERU, §IV, 2). Under Pettoruti he developed a great interest in sculpture. His activity in this field was limited to a few works, culminating in 1942 when he won first prize in a competition for his sculpture *Amazonía* (1942). He went on to develop a rather violent approach, including scoring paint to heighten textural qualities and using bold strokes of red, blue, green and black, and by the early 1950s his painting was truly Expressionist, as in *Don Juan* (1952; Lima, Mus. Banco Cent. Reserva). After the mid-1950s, his painting tended towards mystical themes, such as *St Rosa de Lima* (*c.* 1960–61), and became increasingly aggressive and violent, somewhat reminiscent of Fauvism.

BIBLIOGRAPHY

J. Villacorta Paredes: *Pintores peruanos de la República* (Lima, 1971), pp. 99–101

J. A. de Lavalle and W. Lang: *Pintura contemporánea: Segunda parte, 1920–1960*; Arte y tesoros del Perú (Lima, 1976), pp. 126–35

G. Banks: 'Authenticity and Restoration in the American Collections at the Manchester Museum', *Bull. Mus. Royaux A. and Hist.*, 63 (1992), pp. 145–54

W. IAIN MACKAY

Gutiérrez Cabello, Francisco (*b* Bárcenas, Burgos, *c.* 1616; *d* Madrid, *c.* 1669). Spanish painter. It is not known when he moved to Madrid, where he resided for the greater part of his life, nor under whom he trained. He was of noble background, and documents record that he always used the title of 'Don'. In 1639 he acquired a piece of sculpture in the public auction of the works of Vicente Carducho, and in 1658 he is recorded as testifying on behalf of Velázquez in evidence submitted before the Sevillian painter was awarded the Order of Santiago in 1659.

Gutiérrez Cabello specialized in paintings of architectural perspective, full of small-scale figures and depicting scenes from the Old and New Testaments and from Classical history and mythology. His work is characterized by a fine technical ability, a refined use of colours and a notable decorative sense. He frequently depended on engravings, in particular those by Hans Vredeman de Vries, for the composition of his architectural settings, and on at least two occasions in his groups of figures he made use of engravings after Lodovico Cigoli. His paintings were often grouped in series of the same size, using biblical themes (e.g. 1667; Serradilla, Cáceres, monastery of El Cristo de la Victoria) and evangelical ones (e.g. 1662; Villagarcía de Campos, Valladolid, collegiate church).

BIBLIOGRAPHY
D. Angulo Iñíguez and A. E. Pérez Sánchez: *Pintura madrileña del segundo tercio del siglo XVII* (Madrid, 1983)

JESUS URREA

Gutiérrez de la Vega, José (*b* Seville, 6 Dec 1791; *d* Madrid, Dec 1865). Spanish painter. His training at the Escuela de Bellas Artes in Seville was based on the cult and imitation of the art of Murillo, which deeply influenced his style, especially in his early years. Though otherwise in Seville at this time, he spent 1829 in Cádiz, where he became a friend of the English consul John Brackembury, and painted portraits of him, his wife Catherine and their children (Madrid, Delgado Brackembury priv. col.). Cádiz was then influenced by English art and culture, and Gutiérrez de la Vega assimilated something of the elegance and aristocratic manner characteristic of 19th-century English painting. His style corresponds perfectly to the Spanish Romantic spirit, and its refinement is especially evident in his portraits, many of which reflect the art of Murillo. This can be seen in *Richard Ford* and *Harriet Ford* (both 1831; London, priv. col.), in which both figures are dressed in 17th-century Spanish costume. The influence of Murillo in this period is even more marked in such religious works as *Christ and the Woman of Samaria* (Seville, S Pedro) and *St Clement* (Seville, Sagrario).

In 1831 Gutiérrez de la Vega, having refused an offer from Brackembury to travel to England, left Seville for Madrid. Here his portraits were favourably received, and he soon acquired a large bourgeois and aristocratic clientele. His technique greatly improved as he added elements of Goya's portrait style to his own. Important works of this period include the *Portrait of a Young Woman* (Havana, Mus. N. B.A.) and that of *Queen María Cristina* (Madrid, priv. col.), while the most important of his excellent nude studies is the *Naked Maja* (Madrid, Casón Buen Retiro), inspired by Titian. Gutiérrez de la Vega's portraits of children capture the charm and tenderness of infancy, the most successful being that of *Isabella II* and her sister, *Luisa Fernanda* (untraced). Significant among the numerous religious subjects he painted in Madrid is the *Last Communion of St Ferdinand* (1832; Madrid, Real Acad. S Fernando, Mus.), which appears to be set in the Arab Alcázar of Seville. This painting, which led to his appointment as a 'miembro de mérito' of the Real Academia de S Fernando, Madrid, shows the continued influence of Murillo. Gutiérrez de la Vega often chose religious subjects, generally of saints and martyrs, in which he could justifiably include beautiful and partially unclothed females, as in the *Martyrdom of St Catherine* (Madrid, Casón Buen Retiro). In 1840 he was made *Pintor honorario de Cámara*, but he failed to become a *Pintor numerario de la Corona* and so became embittered in his late years.

BIBLIOGRAPHY
J. A. Gaya Nuño: *Arte del siglo XIX*, A. Hisp., xix (Madrid, 1966)
A. M. de Cossío: *José Gutiérrez de la Vega* (Madrid, 1978)
E. Valdivieso: *Pintura sevillana del siglo XIX* (Seville, 1981)
——: *Historia de la pintura sevillana* (Seville, 1986), p. 371

ENRIQUE VALDIVIESO

Gutiérrez de los Ríos, Gaspar (*b* ?Salamanca; *d* ?1602). Spanish writer and theorist. Almost all the information on his life is given on the title-page of his *Noticia general para la estimación de las artes* (Madrid, 1600). He was the son of a tapestry maker, Pedro Gutiérrez (*fl* 1578–1601), and was a professor of law and literature in Salamanca. He seems to have been one of the first writers to argue on behalf of the rights of Spanish artists against the fiscal demands of the Spanish state. The *Noticia general* also includes a lengthy theoretical discussion on the nature of painting, developed, as was customary in Spanish Baroque theoretical treatises, using the moral and religious ideologies of the Counter-Reformation, as well as political ideas in defence of the value of the artist's work, the significance of which should not, it was claimed, be scorned in the rigid, autocratic Spanish society of his time.

BIBLIOGRAPHY
J. A. de Butrón: *Discursos apologéticos . . . todos los derechos* (Madrid, 1626)
V. Carducho: *Diálogos de la pintura* (Madrid, 1633)
F. J. Sánchez Cantón: *Fuentes literarias para la historia del arte español*, i (Madrid, 1923), pp. 307–18
P. Ballesteros: *Los pintores ante el fisco* (Madrid, 1942)
E. Lafuente Ferrari: 'Borrascas de la pintura y triunfo de su excelencia', *Archv Esp. A.*, lxi (1944), pp. 77–103
J. A. Gaya Nuño: *Historia de la crítica de arte en España* (Madrid, 1975)
J. Gállego: *El pintor de artesano a artista* (Granada, 1976)
F. Calvo Serraller: *Teoría de la pintura del siglo de oro* (Madrid, 1981)

FRANCISCO CALVO SERRALLER

Gutiérrez Solana, José. *See* SOLANA, JOSÉ.

Gutmann, John (*b* Breslau, Silesia [now Wrocław, Poland], 28 May 1905). American photographer and painter. He studied painting at the Staatliche Akademie für Kunst und Kunstgewerbe in Breslau during the mid-1920s with Otto Mueller and from 1927 to 1930 carried out graduate and post-graduate work in Berlin at Humboldt Universität and the Akademie der Künste. Between 1929 and 1932 he taught art at various schools in Berlin and Brandenburg. He began photographing in 1933 and was hired as a photojournalist by Presse-Foto in Berlin. That same year he travelled to San Francisco, which became his permanent home in 1937.

Gutmann viewed America with a fresh and sophisticated photojournalistic style that synthesized social and aesthetic concerns in daringly cropped compositions and juxtaposed forms. His painterly sensibilities drew him to visually stimulating subjects such as graffiti, quirkily painted signs, costumed Mardi Gras revellers and car-bonnet ornaments. He devoted much of his life to teaching at San Francisco State University, where he developed the graduate photography department in 1949.

BIBLIOGRAPHY
M. Kozloff: *The Restless Decade: John Gutmann's Photographs of the Thirties* (New York, 1976)
as i saw it: Photographs by John Gutmann (exh. cat. by J. Humphrey, San Francisco, CA, MOMA, 1976)
Gutmann (exh. cat. by M.-M. Sutnik, Toronto, A.G. Ont., 1985)

RICHARD LORENZ

Gutt, Romuald (*b* Warsaw, 6 Feb 1888; *d* Warsaw, 3 Sept 1974). Polish architect and teacher. He studied architecture in Winterthur until 1908, before returning to Warsaw. From 1910, when he made his début with the design for the Polish Pavilion at an exhibition in Rome, until *c.* 1920 his work adopted the '*styl dworkowy*' ('mansion house' style), influenced by local traditions. His projects included country houses, smaller houses and cottages, schools and local government offices, several of which were prepared during World War I as references for future use. He also designed military cemeteries and tombstones, work that he repeated after 1945. In his work of the early 1920s, including the Girls' Vocational Training School (1919–26), Górnośląska Street, and residential buildings (1922–5) in Słoneczny Square, both in Warsaw, he used simplified cubist forms and became fascinated with exposed, fair-faced brickwork using different types of bonds. This new, personal style was further developed after 1925 in his own house (1926–8), Wrońskiego Street, School for Nurses (1927–8), School for Political Sciences (1926–33) and ZUPU Building (1927–31), all in Warsaw, and the Post Office (1925–6) in Ciechocinek. In cooperation with the landscape architects Franciszek Krzywda-Polkowski (1881–1949) and later Alina Scholtz (*b* 1908), Gutt worked on several landscaping projects, including the house and park (1935–8) of Józef Piłsudski (1867–1935), at Żulów, and the Piłsudski memorial mound (1936–9), Kraków. He also designed a series of villas in Warsaw that were carefully integrated with surrounding gardens, for example at 33a Kielecka Street (1934), 2 Flory Street (1934–5) and 39a Łowicka Street (1936). The best example of Gutt's rationalist style of architecture is the GUS Building (1948–54), the main statistical office in Warsaw, which is based on a plan shaped like a three-bladed propellor. Also notable is his Chinese Embassy complex (1956–69; with Michal Gutt, his son, and others), Warsaw. Gutt was a professor at the Technical University (1946–60) and the Academy of Fine Arts (1957–65), both in Warsaw.

UNPUBLISHED SOURCES

Wrocław, Mus. Archit. [pre-1939 projects]

BIBLIOGRAPHY

'Centre des statistiques, Varsovie', *Archit. Aujourd'hui*, 62 (1955), p. 16 [on the GUS Bldg]

J. Strachocki: 'Budynki mieszkalne Ambasady Chińskiej w Warszawie' [Residential buildings of the Chinese Embassy in Warsaw], *Projekt*, 1 (1959), pp. 9–12

H. Buszko, G. Jonkajtys-Luba and T. Zielinski: *Romuald Gutt* (Warsaw, 1968)

Z. Gunaris: 'Biography of Romuald Gutt', *Avant-garde polonaise: Urbanisme, architecture/Awangarda polska: Urbanistyka, architektura/The Polish Avant-garde: Architecture, Town-planning, 1918–1939* (exh. cat., ed. O. Czerner and H. Listowski; Paris, Ecole Spéciale Archit.; Warsaw, Mus. Archit.; 1981–3), pp. 261–2

OLGIERD CZERNER

Gutta [Lat.: 'drop'] **(i).** Conical architectural ornament, sometimes cylindrical. Guttae usually occur on the underside of the mutules and under the triglyphs of a frieze in Doric architecture (*see* GREECE, ANCIENT, fig. 9e and ORDERS, ARCHITECTURAL, fig. 1xiii; *see also* POLYCHROMY, colour pl. I, fig. 1).

Gutta (ii). Small, teardrop-shaped vessel.

□

Guttenberg [Guttenberger]. German family of engravers and draughtsmen. Carl (Gottlieb; Gottfried) Guttenberg (*b* Wöhrd, nr Nuremberg, 21 Aug 1743; *d* Paris, 20 May 1790) attended the Zeichenschule in Nuremberg under Johann Justin Preissler, and for three years studied calligraphic engraving under Daniel Adam Hauer (1734–?89). In 1765 he worked in Berne as an etcher and engraver for Johann Ludwig Aberli, the architect Erasmus Ritter (1726–1805) and the publisher Beat Ludwig Walthard. In 1767 he went to Paris to train with the engraver Jean Georges Wille, who greatly encouraged him. From 1771, if not before, he apparently shared a studio in Paris with his brother Heinrich Guttenberg (*b* Wöhrd, 29 April 1749; *d* Nuremberg, 16 Jan 1818), who also trained as an engraver with Preissler and Wille. Carl Guttenberg worked as an engraver for Christian von Mechel in Basle from 1772–3, but thereafter worked in Paris as a draughtsman and engraver of calligraphy, portraits and illustrations. He engraved his own designs, such as *Views of Münchenstein and Angenstein* and *Harbours of Bruges and Ostend*, and those of other artists, including Greuze, Pierre Alexandre Wille and Henry Fuseli.

The French Revolution forced Heinrich Guttenberg to leave Paris for Italy in 1789; he finally settled in Nuremberg in 1816 after frequent visits to Paris. He made engravings after old and contemporary masters, for example after Antoine Borel, Greuze, Christian Wilhelm Ernst Dietrich and Jean-Michel Moreau the younger. He engraved illustrations for Saint-Non's *Voyage à Naples* and for Delaborde and Zurlauben's *Description de la Suisse*.

PRINTS

Die nürnbergischen Künstler: Geschildert nach ihrem Leben und ihren Werken, ii (1823) [cat. of the brothers' works]

BIBLIOGRAPHY

Thieme–Becker

J. G. Wille: *Mémoires et journal de J.-G. Wille*, ed. G. Duplessis (Paris, 1857)

Zeichnungen des 18. Jahrhunderts aus dem Basler Kupferstichkabinett (exh. cat. by Y. Boerlin-Brodbeck, Basle, Kstmus., 1978), pp. 23–4

CHRISTINA FREHNER-BÜHLER

Guttmann, Alfred. *See* HAJÓS, ALFRÉD.

Guttuso, Renato (*b* Bagheria, nr Palermo, 2 Jan 1912; *d* Rome, 18 Jan 1987). Italian painter. He gained his first practical experience of art in the form of Sicilian cart-painting in the bottega of a family friend Emilio Murdolo. The images of the exploits of the Normans in Sicily that adorned these carts instilled in Guttuso a strong and lasting preference for epic stories and vivacity of colour; similarly, the knowledge that he gained of the Sicilian countryside and peasantry through his father, a land-surveyor and committed socialist, had a marked effect on his work as a mature artist. While still at school in Palermo, he began to study painting in 1928 under Pippo Rizzo (*b* 1898), a minor Futurist who had extensive contacts with mainland Italy. He began studying law in 1930 at the University of Palermo but left the course soon after exhibiting at the Quadriennale in Rome in 1931.

Guttuso worked at first in a style influenced by the Novecento Italiano, but from 1933 he was drawn to the Pittura Metafisica of Carlo Carrà and Giorgio de Chirico. The influence in particular of Carrà, evident in paintings such as *Girl on the Gulf* (1933; see Cortenova, p. 19), remained a force even in a late work such as *Boy Greeting the Sea* (1978; Rome, priv. col., see Cortenova, p. 108) in its use of the heavy blues and exuberant whites so typical of Carrà's works of the early 1930s. Between 1932 and 1934 Guttuso completed his military service in Milan and participated in two exhibitions of work by Sicilian painters

Renato Guttuso: *Crucifixion*, oil on canvas, 2.0×2.0 m, 1941 (Rome, Galleria Nazionale d'Arte Moderna)

at the Galleria Il Milione. From then until 1937, when he settled in Rome, he divided his time between Palermo, Milan and Rome; in Milan he met Renato Birolli, Ernesto Trecanni (*b* 1920), Giacomo Manzù and Aligi Sassu (*b* 1912), who were among the founder-members of CORRENTE, an anti-Fascist association of artists with whom he exhibited in 1939. In Milan he also met Elio Vittorini (1908–66), a writer and editor working at that time as a courier for the Italian Communist party. During the same period that Vittorini was writing *Conversazione in Sicilia* (Milan, 1941) in response to the Spanish Civil War, Guttuso dealt with these events, and in particular the death of the Spanish poet Federico García Lorca, in his painting *Execution in the Countryside* (1939; Rome, G.N.A. Mod.), drawing his iconography from Francisco de Goya's *Third of May 1808* (1814; Madrid, Prado). This work marked Guttuso's first clear declaration as an artist of his political principles; in 1940 he joined the Communist party, to which he maintained a lifelong commitment, gaining a seat as a senator in 1976. A series of drawings produced by Guttuso as illustrations for Vittorini's novel was eventually published in 1986 (Milan).

Guttuso's formative influences included the work of artists such as James Ensor, Oskar Kokoschka, Vincent van Gogh, Gustave Courbet, Pablo Picasso and Franz Marc, and of writers such as Lorca, William Faulkner, F. Scott Fitzgerald and John Dos Passos. One of his major early paintings, *Flight from Etna* (1940; Rome, G.N.A. Mod.), for which he made oil sketches in 1938, was directly influenced in its format and imagery by Picasso's *Guernica* (1937; Madrid, Prado), which Guttuso had seen only in postcard reproduction. Both visionary and commemorative, Guttuso's painting refers not only to World War II but also to the heroic and desperate history of the Sicilian people, as it derives partly from his childhood memory of a peasant revolt that took place shortly after World War I. The awarding of a prize in 1942 for his *Crucifixion* (1941; Rome, G.N.A. Mod.; see fig.) at the officially sponsored Premio Bergamo resulted in a public outcry. Although members of the Catholic Church attacked the work for its female nudity, it was its contemporaneity and the directness of its denunciation of the forces of oppression that made it particularly controversial. It is rich in its references not only to works by van Gogh and Picasso but also to the strident reds of late works by Rosso Fiorentino.

During World War II Guttuso painted many emblematic still-lifes, for example *Chair with Skull* (1942; see Longhi and others, p. 29), one of a series of works in which red drapery alludes to the red flag of international Communism. In the same year he published an essay, 'Paura della pittura', in which he declared his belief in the validity of depicting objects from the real world. Based in Rome throughout World War II, Guttuso was obliged to paint secretly after joining the Resistance in 1943. He remained committed to political subject-matter, as in a series of drawings, *Gott mit Uns* (1944; Rome, G.N.A. Mod.), which he entitled after the words inscribed on the belt buckles of German soldiers. These drawings, which form part of a loose series named *Modern Myths*, refer to a massacre perpetrated by the Germans in the Ardeatine caves outside Rome in retribution for a Resistance attack on a German column entering Rome. The brutality depicted in them is shown as both specifically modern and timeless; in later years he continued to examine human violence in the context of major conflicts of the 1950s and 1960s, in Korea, Algeria and Vietnam.

Guttuso became a central figure in the cultural transformation of Italy in the years immediately after World War II, when lively discussions were taking place on the relationship between art and politics. From 1947 to 1952 Guttuso appears to have channelled the ideological demands of his political convictions into a post-Cubist structure, leading to a certain stylization. Concentrating on images of ordinary working life in Italy, he took as his subject-matter woodcutters, fishermen, seamstresses, weavers and rice-pickers. The easing of the Communist party's orthodoxy following its Congress of 1952–3 was paralleled by a considerable loosening of Guttuso's style of painting, for example in such images of the workers in the sulphur mines as *Injured Sulphur Miner* (1952; Rome, G.N.A. Mod.).

In 1952 Guttuso returned to monumental history painting with his *Battle at Ammiraglio Bridge* (Rome, Ist. Togliatti), which depicts a scene from Garibaldi's liberation of Palermo as a veiled reference to the contribution of the Resistance to the liberation of Italy at the end of World War II; he included portraits of several of his friends as a means of highlighting the contemporaneity of a picture that might otherwise have been taken simply as a reworking of a 19th-century subject. From the end of the war Guttuso was firmly established as Italy's most popular living artist. His growing international reputation, especially in England, the USA and Germany, was also reflected in the subject-matter of paintings such as *Boogie-woogie* (1953; Milan, priv. col., see Crispolti, 1987, p. 112) and *The Beach* (1956; Parma, G.N.). He was particularly influential in

Eastern European countries, to which he was a frequent visitor, and he enjoyed a privileged status in the USSR as an officially acceptable foreign artist, a situation that led to him being regarded as a reactionary by Soviet avant-garde artists.

Although Guttuso earned his reputation with large and complex paintings that dealt overtly with political issues and social comment, he also produced accomplished still-life paintings on a small scale, for example *Tomatoes* (1961; Verona, priv. col., see Cortenova, p. 94). In the late 1970s he paid homage to works by Gustave Courbet, Francisco de Zurbarán, van Gogh, Picasso, Lucas Cranach I and Albrecht Dürer in often highly complex allegories in which images derived from these artists mingle with his personal memories and experiences. *Allegories: Saint Jerome, or the Three Ages* (1978; Rome, priv. col., see Longhi and others, pp. 104–5), which forms part of this series, is a typical example. Guttuso's persistent concern with the metaphysical also re-emerged in late works such as *Self-portrait* (1980; Rome, priv. col., see Longhi and others, p. 93), in which a figure climbs the walls of the Villa Palagonia, near Guttuso's childhood home in Sicily, the parapets of which are surmounted by monstrous imaginary figures. Although he continued to favour strongly Italian settings for his representations of objects and people, Guttuso transcended, as always, the limitations both of geography and of realism to enter into a realm of speculative thought.

WRITINGS

'Paura della pittura', *Prospettive* [Rome] (15 Jan 1942)
Contadini di Sicilia (Rome, 1951)
Mestiere di pittore: Scritti sull'arte e la società (Bari, 1972)

BIBLIOGRAPHY

R. Longhi and others: *Hommage à Guttuso* (Paris, 1981)
Guttuso: Opere dal 1931 al 1981 (exh. cat., essays C. Brandi, A. Codognato and V. Rubiu; Venice, Pal. Grassi, 1982)
E. Crispolti: *Guttuso nel disegno: Anni venti/ottanta* (Rome, 1983)
E. Costantini: *Ritratto di Renato Guttuso* (Milan, 1985)
G. Cortenova, E. Mascelloni and A. Mercadente: *Guttuso: 50 anni di pittura* (Verona, Pal. Forti, 1987)
E. Crispolti: *Leggere Guttuso* (Milan, 1987)
A. Monferini, ed.: *La Donazione Guttuso*, Rome, G.N.A. Mod. cat. (Rome, 1987) [contains essays by A. Gulloti and E. Gaudioso]
Renato Guttuso dagli esordi al Gott mit uns, 1924–1944 (exh. cat., ed. A. Rais; Bagheria, Gal. Com. A. Mod. & Contemp., 1987)

DEMELZA SPARGO

Guy, Francis (*b* Burton in Kendall or Lorton, Cumbria, 1760; *d* Brooklyn, NY, 12 Aug 1820). American painter of English birth. In England he was apprenticed to a tailor and then worked in the textile trade. A business failure prompted him to leave London for New York in 1795. By early 1798 he was settled in Baltimore, MD, where he lived for the next 20 years. Having unsuccessfully attempted to establish a dyeing operation, he took up painting as a livelihood. Basically self-taught, Guy specialized in American views, especially cityscapes, although he occasionally painted English landscapes and treated more exotic places, undoubtedly using prints as sources of inspiration. *The Tontine Coffee House of New York* (New York, NY Hist. Soc.), one of his first major paintings, was probably executed in the early 1800s, although it has frequently been dated 1797. Guy is especially known for his panoramas of Baltimore (*Large View of Baltimore from Chapel Hill*, 1803; New York, Brooklyn Mus.) and for his meticulous renderings of various sites in and around his adopted city. He executed numerous views of country estates, some of which decorated painted chairs and tables made by the Finlay Brothers (Baltimore, MD, Mus. A.). Many of his paintings are preserved in the Maryland Historical Society, Baltimore. With their crisply drawn forms, strolling couples and atmospheric clarity his compositions have a charming naive quality, reflective of Guy's limited training but innate artistic ability; they also project an idyllic view of the young republic, its cultural development and natural potential.

In 1817 Guy returned to Brooklyn, where he produced some of his finest works, including several views of that city in winter (New York, Brooklyn Mus.) and *Carter's Tavern, Head of Lake George* (*c.* 1817; Detroit, MI, Inst. A.). His work was exhibited in Baltimore and at the Pennsylvania Academy of the Fine Arts, Philadelphia, in the early 1800s as well as in Brooklyn and New York around the time of his death.

BIBLIOGRAPHY

J. H. Pleasants: *Four Late Eighteenth-century Anglo-American Landscape Painters* (Worcester, MA, 1943/*R* Freeport, NY, 1970), pp. 55–116
S. T. Colwill: *Francis Guy (1760–1820)* (Baltimore, 1981)

EDWARD J. NYGREN

Guyana, Cooperative Republic of [formerly British Guiana]. South American country, bordered by Venezuela on the west, Brazil on the south, Surinam on the east, and the

1. Map of Guyana

Atlantic Ocean on the north (see fig. 1). It includes the counties of Demerara, Essequibo and Berbice. The capital is Georgetown in Demerara. Its terrain consists of a highly cultivated coastal region, an interior of rain-forest, and open savannah in the south-west. Initially colonized by the Dutch in the early 17th century, it came under British rule in the early 18th, gaining independence in 1966.

For the history and art of Guyana before colonization *see* SOUTH AMERICA, PRE-COLUMBIAN, §VII, 1.

I. Introduction. II. Indigenous culture. III. Architecture. IV. Painting, graphic arts and sculpture. V. Patronage and institutions.

I. Introduction.

The Dutch began to settle Guyana in 1616, and in 1621 the Dutch Chartered West India Company was given a monopoly in trade with the region. Failed attempts to settle the Pomeroon River were made by English colonists in 1639 and 1642. However, the Dutch created three colonies along the Essequibo, Demerara and Berbice rivers, trading with the various tribal groups, in particular the Caribs. The settlers also cultivated sugar cane from the end of the 17th century, which led to the organized importation of African slaves. Following a slave insurrection in 1763, the British conquered the three Dutch colonies in 1781, founding Georgetown (originally Fort St George) at the mouth of the Demerara River. After brief occupations by the French (1782) and the Dutch (1784), the territory, reconquered by the British in 1796, was ceded to Britain in 1803. This cession was formally confirmed by the Treaty of Paris in 1814, and in 1831 the three colonies were united as the colony of British Guiana. British rule resulted in considerable civic building, but during the 19th century fine art was limited to a few depictions of local life by visitors and amateurs (*see* §§III and IV below).

Initially British occupation led to a steep acceleration in imports of slaves and new capital. However, the slave trade was abolished in 1807, and evangelization among the slaves began in 1808. In the two decades following emancipation (1838), communities of freed slaves purchased sugar estates in the coastal region. This so-called Village Movement preserved areas of traditional Afro-Guyanese culture during a period of traumatic social change and mass influx of immigrants of different racial and linguistic affiliations. In the 80 years after emancipation, imported and indentured labour came to work in the European-owned sugar plantations, primarily from India, China and Madeira. During the final two decades of the 19th century a severe recession in the sugar industry led to the amalgamation of some estates and diversification of the economy. Through the Reform Movement, the rising Creole middle class began to challenge the constitutional power of the planters. The late 19th and early 20th centuries were also marked by the emergence of Afro-Guyanese art and architecture. Mass political action finally culminated in independence in 1966. In the 1970s the government of Forbes Burnham attempted to reorganize the economy along socialist lines.

BIBLIOGRAPHY

P. M. Netscher: *Gescheideinis van de koloniën Essequebo, Demerary en Berbice, van de vestiging der Nederlanders aldaar tot op onzen tijd* [History of the colonies Essequibo, Demerary and Berbice from the Dutch establishment to the present day] (The Hague, 1888)

V. T. Daly: *A Short History of the Guyanese People* (London, 1980)

II. Indigenous culture.

The indigenous population comprises a number of ethnic groups: *c.* 6300 Arawak (Lokono), *c.* 5200 Warao, *c.* 4500 Karinya (Carib), *c.* 4200 Kapon (Akawaio), *c.* 5000 Kapon (Patamona), and *c.* 500 Pemon (Arekuna), all occupying the north-west and the coastal region between the Demerara and Corentyne rivers. The south is occupied by *c.* 7800 Carib-speaking Makusi, *c.* 5600 Wapisiana and *c.* 200 Waiwai. The economy of all the groups is based primarily on manioc horticulture, supplemented by hunting and fishing. Manioc-based subsistence has guaranteed the survival of key traditional arts and industries, notably architecture, ceramics, basketry, featherwork, beadwork and weaving. The raw materials employed in the manufacture of all artefacts originally came mainly from the forests. Many materials were seasonal, for example the seeds of the crab-nut tree, used for body paint. Particular inorganic raw materials, such as pottery clay, tempering materials used in pottery manufacture such as sand, decomposed granite, mica etc, or a particular kind of stone suitable for the manufacture of grater chips, may be rare or unobtainable in a given area, and this placed specific values on the associated products.

Trade, based on the barter of such artefacts as Karinya pottery, Wapisiana cotton hammocks or Warao canoes and fibre hammocks, survived into the middle of the 20th century. Two ceramic traditions, both originating from the north-west, have characterized the indigenous groups, other styles of pottery in the south being of only local importance. The pottery tradition from the north-west known as the Mabaruma style is characterized by incision, punctation and low- and high-relief modelling. Red painting or white slip is occasionally used. Certain of its decorative motifs are specifically associated with rituals appertaining to manioc processing. Brewing manioc beer required chewing quantities of cassava bread by way of promoting fermentation. The process was thought to be facilitated by magical observances involving mouth and tongue tattooing. The representative pottery decoration features a two- or three-dimensional human head with a characteristically distended mouth representing the chewing process, which served to induce potency in the drink. Belief in the efficacy of these magical practices in due course crossed tribal frontiers, generating new motifs in incised and painted pottery decoration. The other tradition is represented by Karinya pottery, which survives to the present on the Pomeroon River. The inception of this polychrome Horizon style of the Karinya Caribs of the Moruka and Pomeroon rivers has been dated to *c.* 200 BC. It may have existed there much earlier. Decoration is by red or black geometric bands on a white slip, sometimes embellished with serial dots.

Surviving forms of basketware include the remarkable tubular manioc press, whose constricting action is believed to have derived from the ingesting motions of the anaconda snake. A miniature version is used for extracting oil from the crab-nut seed. Basketry fish-traps are still made by the Akawaio (*see* BASKETWORK, fig. 2). Basketry is also combined with featherwork to produce the magnificent feather crowns still used by the Waiwai, but which until the mid-20th century constituted distinguishing insignia among many of the other tribal groups. Made of parrot and macaw feathers, they were used on ceremonial or festive occasions in combination with a wide range of other decorations fashioned from such materials as seeds, bone, teeth, insect cocoons and beetles' wings. Feather ornaments are woven into the hair of Waiwai males, and feathers are also used to adorn such simple manufactured objects as cosmetic boxes, combs, fans and bone flutes. The ornate women's bead apron, originally made up from chains of grass or other seeds attached to a square of bark cloth, was later manufactured from European trade beads. Fabrics are woven with fibres from such plants as silk grass, moriche or other palm leaves. The Warao hammocks are of a sturdy rope made from moriche fibre. The finest specimens exhibit the texture of silk. Cotton thread spun on the traditional spindle-whorl is woven into baby slings, calf-bands and hammocks. They are usually characterized by a total absence of decoration.

Indigenous architectural traditions are continued by the peoples in the hinterland of the tropical forests, who build large, circular dwellings that symbolize aspects of their cosmological beliefs. Successive horizontal planes in the cone-shaped dwellings of the Warao and Waiwai serve to conceptualize specific areas of the universe. In the Waiwai buildings, apertures in the roof represent passageways to the cosmos. Around the central pole that supports the structure is a sacred space, the various Waiwai households being distributed around its periphery. The positions of the rafters and intermediate purlins also coincide with specific cosmological spaces. Such dwellings continue in use among the Waiwai and, until the early 20th century, were also characteristic of the Wapisiana, Makusi and Arecuna. The dwellings of certain coastal groups were of wattle and daub on square plans, roofed with dhalebana (*geonoma*) palm leaves.

BIBLIOGRAPHY

E. Im Thurn: *Among the Indians of Guiana* (London, 1883/*R* 1967), p. 269

W. Roth: *An Introductory Study of the Arts, Crafts and Customs of the Guiana Indians* (Washington, DC, 1924)

III. Architecture.

Transient European trading posts in the 16th century preceded the establishment by the Dutch West India Company of the first permanent settlement at Kijkoveral (1616–21), a small island at the confluence of the Cuyuni and Mazaruni rivers near present-day Bartica. The early Dutch settlements were protected by fortresses such as Fort Nassau on the Berbice River, founded in 1627 and rebuilt in brick during the 1720s (mostly destr.; see Hartsinck, pp. 284 and 299). The moated brick Fort Zeelandia on the Essequibo, designed by the Dutch governor Laurens Storm van 's Gravesande (1704–75), was built in 1744 on the site of earlier timber forts (1687 and 1739) and is relatively well preserved. The British conquest and foundation of Georgetown in 1781 led to a growth in civil architecture. The first building to use classical orders was an armoury in Georgetown (probably before 1800; destr.; anon. drawing, London, PRO). From 1808 London Missionary Society churches were built for the slaves. Both the churches and town houses were built in clapboarding imported from the USA, but most did not survive major fires in the 19th century. The unremarkable steepled Gothic Revival Presbyterian church of St Andrew (consecrated 1818), Stabroek, was built by Joseph Hadfield (*fl* 1818–34), as was the neighbouring brick and stucco Neo-classical parliament building (1829–34) with a central dome and Doric columns. The timber Smith Congregational Church (1841), still well preserved in Brickdam, Georgetown's oldest street, is also in the Gothic Revival style.

Labour shortages, particularly after the emancipation of the slaves, affected the quality of such buildings as the Seaman's Hospital (1838), the timber and metal railway station (1848), and the governor's residence, State House (1854), all in Georgetown. However, the development of infrastructure included a stuccoed brick prison (1841) at the penal settlement on the Mazaruni River. With an increased flow of immigrants and better economic conditions in the 1860s and 1870s, the quality of buildings improved, for example in the Renaissance-style church of the Sacred Heart (1861), Georgetown, built for Portuguese indentured immigrants from Madeira by the Italian Jesuit priest Benedict Schembri (*fl* 1860–75) and later much extended by Father Joseph Baldini (*d* 1883), also Italian. In 1881 Stabroek Market, an important iron building incorporating Tudor and Gothic motifs, was built by the American railway engineer Nathaniel Kay (1831–1902). Civic architecture in Georgetown flourished in the last two decades of the century, for example the Victoria Law Courts (1884) by Baron Hora Siccama (1842–1921), a civil engineer, the timber Gothic Revival City Hall of 1888 by the Jesuit priest Ignatius Scoles (1839–96) and, in the same style, the neighbouring City Engineer's Office (*c*. 1890), also by Scoles. A Magistrates Court (1890) was built by the Colonial Civil Engineer's Office. St George's Cathedral (1889–92), one of the world's tallest timber buildings (43.5 m), is reputedly by REGINALD BLOMFIELD. The indentured Muslims and Hindus on the sugar plantations built mosques and sivalas in traditional forms, first in wattle and daub and then in permanent materials. Towards the end of the century, as the older generation died out, such 'India style' buildings came under the influence of the Creole style developed by such Afro-Guyanese architects as James Sharples (1845–1913). This style was characterized by houses with steeply pitched roofs, raised on platforms above the swampy ground, with fretted bargeboards, decorative cast-iron balcony rails and jalousies. The use of platforms probably originated on sugar plantations as early as the 1830s. It was later extended to grand town houses and the cottages of the rising Creole middle class. Traditional Western styles were practised by LEONARD STOKES, who was chosen to design the Gothic and Romanesque-style Roman Catholic cathedral of the Immaculate Conception, Georgetown (1914–25; see fig. 2).

Little of the European Modern Movement reached Georgetown until rebuilding after a major fire in 1945. Because there were few locally based practices, until the late 1960s most major commissions went to expatriate British architects: for example the University of Guyana

2. Leonard Stokes: Roman Catholic cathedral of the Immaculate Conception, Georgetown, Guyana, 1914–25

(completed 1963), a tasteful series of lightweight framed buildings, was designed by the British architect Frank Mowbray Rutter (1911–89). In 1966 George Henry (*b* 1930), a Guyanese who had worked in Britain and Pakistan, started what is now the largest local practice with such Brutalist buildings as those for the National Insurance Scheme in Georgetown (1967) and New Amsterdam (1968). Another Guyanese, Norris Mitchell (*b* 1938), designed the colourful National Cultural Centre (1976), Georgetown. In 1984 Albert Rodrigues (*b* 1941), the local head of the major Caribbean practice Gillespie & Steel, went into partnership with Michael Cox (*b* 1945): both produced distinguished houses in the mid-1970s.

BIBLIOGRAPHY

J. J. Hartsinck: *Beschryving van Guiana of de wilde kunst in Zuid America* [Description from Guyana of the wild art in South America] (Amsterdam, 1770)

'Ignatius Scoles: Obituary', *Lett. & Not.: Inter. J. Eng. Prov. SJ*, xxxiii (1895–6), pp. 551–61

A. Leechman: 'Notes on Ancient Sites and Historical Monuments Now Existing in the Colony of British Guiana', *Official Gaz.* (12 July 1913), pp. 1–14

A. Crossthwaite: 'Trollope's Prepossessing City: Architecture of Georgetown, Guyana', *Country Life*, cxliii (28 March 1968), pp. 718–20

R. Westmaas: 'Building under our Sun: An Essay on the Development of Guyanese Architecture', *Cooperative Republic of Guyana, 1970*, ed. L. Searwar (Georgetown, 1970), pp. 129–58

'Wooden Wonder: Wooden Cathedral in Georgetown, Guyana', *Architects' J.*, clxxxii/28 (1985), pp. 16–17

L. Bosman: 'Een onbekend ontwerp van Abraham van der Hart: Het gouvernementsgebouw in Demerary' [An unknown design by Abraham van der Hart: The government building in Demerary], *Kon. Ned. Oudhdknd. Bond: Bull.*, xc/4 (1991), pp. 135–9

IV. Painting, graphic arts and sculpture.

A few map-illustrations and sketches in travel records are all that survive of the period before 1800. It is unlikely that painting or sculpture were practised by the Dutch. After the colonies were reoccupied by the British in 1796, officers and amateurs began almost at once to produce records of local scenery and events. The earliest recorded watercolour sketches, those of Lt Staunton St Clair (*fl* 1806–8), were executed during the first decade of the 19th century. The 1820s and 1830s were marked by the work of Joshua Bryant (*fl* 1810–36), whose watercolours of official ceremonies and public buildings suggest that he may have been an official colonial artist. The painter CHARLES BENTLEY, official artist to the expedition of Robert Hermann Schomburgk in Guiana and the Orinoco (1835–9), was the first to record scenes of Amerindian life in the interior, for example lithographs published in Schomburgk's *Twelve Views of the Interior of British Guiana* (1841). A contemporary, William Hedges (*fl* 1831–6), carefully executed several local landscapes in oil. The official artist to Schomburgk's second expedition (1841–3) was Edward Alfred Goodall (1819–1908), son of Turner's engraver, Edward Goodall. Working in the English topographical tradition, he executed watercolours of Georgetown and particularly of Kingston, as well as hundreds of ethnographical, topographical and botanical sketches (Berlin, Botan. Mus., and London, BL, Add. MSS 16936–9). A few mainly architectural pictures were executed by Goodall's predecessor on the Schomburgk expedition, W. L. Walton (*fl* 1840) (London, BL, Add. MSS 66939, nos 55–7). Photographs of undistinguished 19th-century paintings and a few originals from 1836 to 1882 have survived in the University of Guyana Caribbean Research Library in Georgetown: pictorial journalism included genre scenes submitted to the *Illustrated London News* (31 March and 28 April 1888) by M. Prior and A. Forestier; the drawings in the collection include one attributed to a Chinese immigrant working in 1886 and a portrait copy of the black Haitian general Toussaint L'Ouverture, probably by a Creole.

In the first half of the 20th century the first native Guyanese artist, Samuel Horace Broodhagen (1883–1950), a portrait sculptor, also produced some landscapes in oil. In 1931 the first exhibition of art in Georgetown was organized by a group of expatriate amateur painters who, in 1929, had formed the Arts and Crafts Society as a popular movement for stimulating the visual arts. Like the more economically orientated Self-Help Movement, it had a far-reaching influence. It served as the model for the Guyanese Art Group, founded in 1944 by a handful of native-born artists led by the watercolourist Guy Sharples (1906–56), son of the architect James Sharples (1845–1913). The Guyanese Art Group's exhibition became an annual national event.

Other important figures included Edward Rupert Burrowes (1903–66), born in Barbados, and his pioneering associate Hubert Moshett (*b* 1901), both sign-painters. Burrowes's pedantic work was inspired by late Victorian painting. He was most important as a teacher (*see* §V below), notably of such painters as Stanley Greaves (*b* 1934) and Emerson Samuels (*b* 1928), who also became involved in art education. During the 1940s and 1950s a small group of Guyanese painters attracted limited recognition in metropolitan centres: they included Denis Williams (*b* 1923), who came to the notice of Wyndham Lewis in the early 1950s, Frank Bowling (*b* 1936), now represented in the Tate Gallery, London, and Aubrey Williams (1926–90), who worked in an Abstract Expressionist style characterized by a tropical intensity of colour somewhat reminiscent of the later palette of Paul Gauguin. However, these artists had only partial success in creating an identifiable national form of art. The period was marked by the emergence of the outstanding painter Marjorie Broodhagen (*b* 1912).

Other artists, for example from Arawak and Makusi backgrounds, introduced elements of traditional arts and industries into contemporary art. The superimposed circular planes of traditional architecture were employed by the terracotta muralist Stephanie Correia (*b* 1930) in low reliefs articulated by such materials as feathers, seeds, shell, bone and fibre. Paintings of the Arawak artist George Simon (*b* 1947) translated the reticulations of thatching into serial units of light. Less ambitiously, the Makusi artist Guy Marco (b 1961) translated basketry weave into colour patterns. Forest woods were carefully selected by Oswald Hussein (*b* 1954) for sculpture inspired by Arawak myth. Dudley Charles (*b* 1945), Donald Locke (*b* 1930) and Ronald Savory (*b* 1933) all incorporated Amerindian petroglyph motifs in their early paintings.

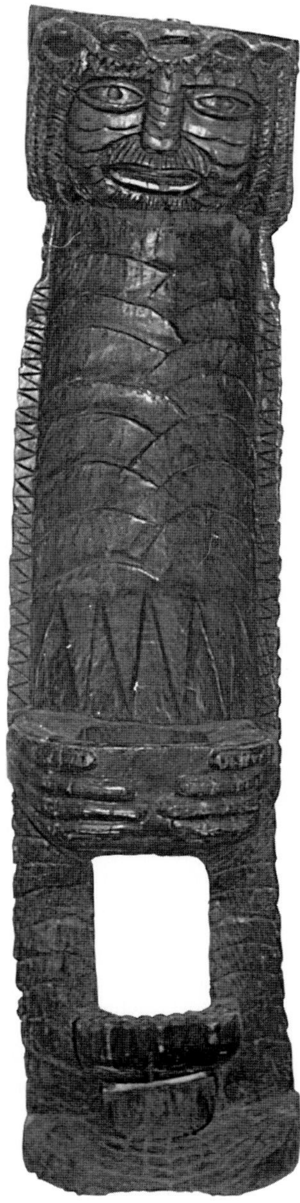

3. Philip Moore: *Stool of Resistance*, painted wood, h. 2.15 m, 1978 (Georgetown, National Art Collection)

During the early 1970s Expressionova was founded by a group of radical artists and writers, some still at school, in order to create a national artistic idiom. Its name came from the title of a contemporary literary journal edited by the writer Noel Williams. The catalogue cover of the short-lived movement's only exhibition, *Expressionova 1974*, held in Georgetown, consisted of a concrete poem by Terrence Roberts (*b* 1949) in the shape of the national flag of Guyana. Members included Roberts, the founder, Keith Khan (*b* 1949), and Carl Martin (*b* 1951). Their surrealistic art received little popular attention. Images drawn from the Guyanese landscape were juxtaposed with such universally known 'cultural sites' as the Taj Mahal in Agra. References to English poetry added to the works' ambiguity. Examples of Expressionova in the National Art Collection include the *Birth of Roraima* by Roberts and *Cloves* and *The Jungle* by Martin.

Important sculpture and painting was produced by Philip Moore (*b* 1921). Born into the Jordanites, a syncretic religious movement, Moore drew upon Afro-Guyanese history and forms (see fig. 3). His 5 m-high bronze memorial to *Cuffy*, the leader of the Slave Revolution of 1763 on the Berbice River, cast by the British Morris Singer Foundry, was installed in Georgetown in 1975. The sculptor Ivor Thom (*b* 1954) produced two bronze high reliefs (1986) on a heroic scale for the Burnham mausoleum in Georgetown, and a figurative bronze memorial (1.8×3.0 m) to the slave martyr *Damon* (1988) in Essequibo (both cast by the local firm BACIF). The Rastafarian musician and patron of the arts Compton ('Camo') Williams (*b* 1949) displayed his collection of painting and sculpture in his private Roots and Culture Gallery to serve as a focus for a new generation of wood-carvers led by Gary Thomas (*b* 1954). Outstanding were Omowale Lumumba (*b* 1952) and Ernest Van Dyke (*b* 1951). These artists expressed an unstudied Afro-Guyanese aesthetic drawn from the spirituality of their people, which was diametrically opposed to the intellectual concerns or 'book art' of Expressionova or the expatriate Guyanese artists.

BIBLIOGRAPHY

E. Goodall: 'The Diary of Edward Goodall, esq., during his Sojourn in Georgetown from 28 July to 11 September 1841', *J. Brit. Guiana Mus. & Zoo*, 35 (1962), pp. 39–53

W. Lewis: 'A Negro Artist', *The Listener* (7 Dec 1950), pp. 423–4

Guyana: Colonial Art to Revolutionary Art, 1966–1976 (Georgetown, *c.* 1976)

V. Patronage and institutions.

From *c.* 1620 to *c.* 1790 significant patronage of architecture and the decorative arts was concentrated in the Dutch fortresses. Shortly after the British took final control in 1796, the official posts of Colonial Artist and Colonial Architect were instituted. During the 19th century the British continued to develop civic architecture, although largely ignoring the fine arts (*see* §III above). From the first decade of the 19th century, the different religious groups, in particular the Roman Catholic Church, commissioned buildings, while neglecting painting and sculpture. The mercantile classes became significant patrons of architects, painters and draughtsmen during the second half of the 19th century, in particular in the town houses of absentee landlords. However, following the severe recession in the sugar industry in the late 19th century, the demand for domestic architecture passed to the rising Creole middle class.

Art education remained restricted until the late 1920s, when certain expatriate amateurs volunteered as art teachers in their own homes. In 1931 the first exhibition of art in Georgetown was organized by the Arts and Crafts Society (*see* §IV above). With the continuing growth of the Creole middle class, some Guyanese artists started working in advertising and sign-painting. Afro-Guyanese art was encouraged by the development in the 1930s and 1940s of a cultural identity among the middle class, inspired by international movements or associations such as the League of Coloured Peoples. From 1945 to 1956 the Working People's Art Class transmitted traditional Western artistic practices to a wider public. It was founded by the painter and sculptor Edward Rupert Burrowes and funded by businesses and institutions, including the British Council. Drawing and painting were taught solely by Burrowes in whatever building could be made available and to whoever attended. The Working People's Art Class democratized the art scene. It was not until 1975 that the Burrowes School of Art, Georgetown, only the second in the British Caribbean, was founded by the government. The University of Guyana has a small faculty of architecture. From the 1970s the newly independent state emerged as the most important patron of both art and architecture.

BIBLIOGRAPHY

A. J. Seymour: *Cultural Policy in Guyana*, UNESCO (Paris, 1977)
D. Williams: *From the National Collection, Guyana* ([Georgetown], 1987)

DENIS WILLIAMS

Guyane, La. *See* FRENCH GUIANA.

Guyot, Laurent (*b c.* 1575; *d* after 1644). French painter. He was mentioned in 1602 as being a Peintre Ordinaire du Roi. In 1607 he was one of the painters of cartoons for a series of tapestries commissioned by Henry IV; they represented the *History of Artemisia*, after drawings by Antoine Caron. Guyot worked with Henri Lerambert (*d* 1609), who directed the royal tapestry painters; when he died, a competitive examination in 1610 to decide his successor was won by Guyot and Guillaume Dumée. Guyot is recorded as a painter of cartoons for the Gobelins in 1618, 1625 and 1636. Towards the end of his life (1640–42) he collaborated with Noël Quillerier (1594–1669) on paintings for Michel Particelli, Sieur d'Emery (*c.* 1595-1650). Of his works, only the tapestries are known (Chambord, Château; Gien, Mus. Int. Chasse; Paris, Gobelins Mobilier N.). He mostly treated pastoral subjects, drawn from romances such as *Il Pastor Fido*, *L'Astrée* and *Gombault et Macée*: they reflect the taste prevailing during the regency of Marie de' Medici and reveal the knowledge of Antonio Tempesta's engravings in *Les Chasses de François Ier*. Guyot's style, solid and direct, is in contrast to the Mannerism of Ambroise Dubois or Martin Fréminet; it has affinities with that of Dumée, of Nicolas Bollery (*c.* 1560–1630) or of Louis Beaubrun (*fl* 1609–27). A drawing, *Les Noces de Gombault et Macée* (untraced), said to be by Guyot and published by Guiffrey in 1919, suggests that some of the illustrations in Blaise de Vigenère's (1523–96) *Images de Platte-Peinture* (pubd 1614) could be attributed to him. Jean Cotelle is said to have been his pupil (probably *c.* 1625–30).

BIBLIOGRAPHY

Jal; Thieme–Becker
A. Félibien: *Entretiens sur la vie et les ouvrages des plus excellens peintres anciens et modernes*, ii (Paris, 1668), p. 126
A.-L. Larcordaire: *Notice historique sur les Manufactures impériales de tapisseries des Gobelins* (Paris, 1853), p. 48
J. Guiffrey: *Les Amours de Gombault et Macée: Etude sur une tapisserie française du musée de Saint-Lô* (Paris, 1882)
——: 'Une Idylle champêtre: La Tapisserie de Gombault et Macée', *Gaz. B.-A.*, n. s. 3, xv (1919), pp. 352–68
Succession Gaston Menier (sale cat., Paris, Gal. Charpentier, 24 Nov 1936), nos 98–103
Chefs d'oeuvre de la tapisserie parisienne, 1597–1662 (exh. cat., Versailles, Château, Orangerie, 1967), pp. 16, 21–2
N. Sainte-Fare-Garnot: 'Noël Quillerier, peintre...', *Actes du colloque international Galeries nationales du Grand Palais. Simon Vouet: Paris, 1991*, pp. 473–97
La Chasse au vol du fil du temps (exh. cat. by I. Denis, Gien, Mus. Int. Chasse, 1994), pp. 255–8

SYLVAIN KERSPERN

Guyot de Beaugrant. *See* BEAUGRANT, GUYOT DE.

Guys, (Ernst-Adolphe-Hyacinthe-) Constantin (*b* Flushing, the Netherlands, 1802; *d* Paris, 13 March 1892). French draughtsman. His father was chief administrator of the merchant navy in the northern Netherlands, but Guys lived for most of his life in France; from 1848 he also spent some time in England. He belonged to the first generation of illustrators to be employed by the earliest of the great illustrated journals. As a correspondent for the *Illustrated London News* (after 1838) and for *Punch* in 1842, he was able to travel widely, visiting Bulgaria, Spain, Italy and Egypt and sending back sketches to be engraved as magazine illustrations. He recorded the *Memorial Service for Greek Independence* in Athens and *The Sultan at the Bairam Festival* in Constantinople. In 1855 he was sent to cover the Crimean War and witnessed the battles of Inkerman and Balaclava.

Guys settled in Paris in the late 1850s, and it was his sketches of society life that made him famous (see fig.). The compositions, taken from life, of women in crinolines, horse-drawn carriages in the Bois de Boulogne and ball and carnival scenes, were caught with rapid strokes in vigorous wash drawings (very solidly constructed in order to indicate the tonal values to the engravers). They earned him the respect of the most celebrated critics of his time. In 1863 Charles Baudelaire published a long study of him in *Le Figaro*, which achieved lasting fame. He singled out Guys as the quintessential 'painter of modern life' and gave an illuminating description of his working methods (*The Painter of Modern Life*, trans. Mayne, p. 17):

> [Guys] starts with a few slight indications in pencil which hardly do more than mark the position which objects are to occupy in space. The principal planes are then sketched in

tinted wash, vaguely and lightly coloured masses to start with, but taken up again later and successively charged with a greater intensity of colour. At the last minute the outline of the objects is once and for all outlined in ink.

Théophile Gautier, Philippe Burty, Champfleury, the Goncourts and, among artists, Delacroix, Manet and Nadar, admired the way he depicted his harshly lit subjects in a forthright style. Guys prefigured the flat tints and shadows found in the work of Manet—who owned some of his drawings—as well as that of Toulouse-Lautrec, Forain and Picasso, and was far more closely related to them than to the other Parisian society illustrators such as Marcelin (Emile Planat), or graphic journalists such as Paul Renouard. Without trying to be anything more than a reporter, Guys adopted the techniques of foreshortening and contrast, which were of concern to the Realist painters of the time. He avoided the complacent staginess and anecdotal detail of the Romantic illustrators and sacrificed description of setting to a stark presentation of his characters which had great expressive and dramatic force.

Guys was shy of publicity (he insisted that Baudelaire's *Le Figaro* article should refer to him only by his initials), and his personal life remained private, although he was a member of the Café Guerbois circle in the 1870s and enjoyed going to parties and receptions. On a carnival night in 1885 he was knocked down by a cab but survived for several years, eking out a living from the sale of the occasional drawing; he died aged 89. His reputation was kept alive by his few admirers, who put on an exhibition of his work at the Galerie Georges Petit in 1895. There is a fine collection of his wash drawings in the Musée Carnavalet, Paris.

BIBLIOGRAPHY

C. Baudelaire: 'Un Peintre de la vie moderne', *Le Figaro* (26, 28 Nov, 3 Dec 1863); also in *Oeuvres complètes* (Paris, 1976); also in *The Painter of Modern Life and Other Essays*; Eng. trans. and selection by J. Mayne (London, 1965)
G. Geffroy: *Constantin Guys* (Paris, 1920)
L. Jamar-Rolin: 'La Vie de Guys et la chronologie de son oeuvre: Faits et propositions', *Gaz. B.-A.*, xliii (1956), pp. 69–112
Inventaire du fonds français après 1800, Paris, Bibl. N. Dépt. Est. cat., x (Paris, 1958), pp. 79–83
The Crimean War Drawings of Constantin Guys (exh. cat. by K. W. Smith, Cleveland, OH, Mus. A., 1978)
P. Duflo: *Constantin Guys, fou de dessin, grand reporter, 1802–1892* (Paris, 1988)

MICHEL MELOT

Guzana. *See* HALAF, TELL.

Güzel sanatlar birliği. *See* ASSOCIATION OF OTTOMAN PAINTERS.

Guzmán. Spanish family of patrons and collectors.

(1) Leganés, 1st Marqués de [Diego [Messia, Mexia] Felípez de Guzmán] (*b c.* 1585; *d* Madrid, 1655). He was the fourth son of the Conde de Uceda. A cousin and close confidant of Gaspar de Guzmán y Pimentel, Conde Duque de OLIVARES, he was appointed Gentleman of the Chamber in 1624, Councillor of State in 1626 and created Marqués de Leganés in 1627. In 1628 he married Doña Policena Spinola (*c.* 1600–37), daughter of Ambrosio Spinola, the Genoese commander. Leganés appears on horseback beside Spinola in the event of 1622 depicted in Jusepe Leonardo's *Surrender of Julich* (1633–4; Madrid,

Constantin Guys: *Conversation*, pen and ink and wash, 185×180 mm, *c.* 1860–62 (Paris, Musée Carnavalet)

Prado), painted for the Palacio del Buen Retiro, Madrid. Leganés developed a taste for Flemish art during his service as a soldier in the Netherlands (1634–5). There he became a patron of Rubens (e.g. *Immaculate Conception*; Madrid, Prado) and van Dyck (e.g. the *Marqués de Leganés*; Madrid, Banco Hisp.-Amer.; the *Marquésa de Leganés*; Madrid, Prado). Rubens also made a fine drawing of the *Marqués de Leganés* (Vienna, Albertina).

Leganés's interest in Italian painting was initially spurred by Philip IV's gift of two portraits by Titian: *Federico Gonzaga, 1st Duke of Mantua* (1529; Madrid, Prado), and *Johann Friedrich, Elector of Saxony* (1550–51; Vienna, Ksthist. Mus.). A subsequent tenure as Governor of Milan (1635–41) provided him with access to the works of northern Italian artists, including Correggio, Parmigianino, the Bassano family, Scipione Pulzone and Francesco Cairo. Leganés was unusual among Spanish collectors in the 17th century in acquiring the works of contemporary Spanish, as well as foreign, masters. At the time of his death he had amassed over 1300 paintings.

Like the Condes de Benavente and the Marqueses del Carpio, Leganés sought to incorporate his picture collection into the *mayorazgo*, or entailed estate, attached to his title. In spite of this precaution, conflicting claims of inheritance led to the dispersal of his collection within a few decades of his death.

BIBLIOGRAPHY

V. Carducho: *Diálogos de la pintura* (Madrid, 1633), fol. 155*v*; repr. in F. J. Sánchez Cantón: *Fuentes literarias para la historia del arte español*, ii (Madrid, 1933), p. 109
J. López Navio: 'La gran colección de pinturas del Marqués de Leganés', *Anlct. Calasanct.*, viii (1962), pp. 261–330
M. C. Volk: 'New Light on a 17th-century Collector: The Marquis of Leganés', *A. Bull.*, lxii (1980), pp. 56–68 [further bibliog.]

M. Burke: *Private Collections of Italian Art in Seventeenth-century Spain* (diss., New York U., 1984; microfilm, Ann Arbor, 1986), i, pp. 75–83; Docs 2.6a–h

MARCUS BURKE

(2) Ambrosio Ignacio Spínola y Guzmán, Archbishop of Seville (*bapt* Madrid, 7 Jan 1632; *d* Seville, 13 May 1684). Son of (1) the 1st Marqués de Leganés. He was renowned for his piety and charity and had a clear understanding of the value of art in religion. He grew up surrounded by the art collection of his father. When Ambrosio Spínola arrived in Seville in 1669 as Archbishop-elect, he brought with him paintings by Jacopo Bassano, Giacinto Brandi, Lodovico Cigoli, Anthony van Dyck and Titian. His first important undertaking was the celebration in Seville Cathedral in honour of the canonization of Ferdinand III of Castile in 1671. Murillo, Juan de Valdés Leal, Pedro Roldán and Bernardo Simón de Pineda oversaw the extensive decoration of the cathedral. These ephemeral creations were recorded in a richly illustrated book with etchings by Valdés Leal, Arteaga and Francisco de Herrera (ii). At the same time the saint's silver-gilt reliquary urn (*in situ*) was designed by Herrera the younger. In 1673 Murillo and Valdés Leal painted altarpieces for the oratory in the archepiscopal palace, and in his testament of 1679 Spínola willed that these works remain in place. Murillo also painted a portrait of Spínola (untraced). Spínola left a large bequest of books to Seville Cathedral, including works on art.

BIBLIOGRAPHY

F. de la Torre y Farfán: *Fiestas de la S iglesia metropolitana y patriarcal de Sevilla al nuevo culto del señor Rey S Fernando* (Seville, 1671)
J. Loaysa: *Pénsame á la S metropolitana y patriarcal iglesia de Sevilla, en la reciente muerte de su venerable prelado señor el señor D. Ambrosio Spínola y Guzmán* (Seville, 1684)
D. Angulo Iñiguez: *Murillo: Su vida, su arte, su obra*, ii (Madrid, 1981), p. 150
D. Kinkead: 'The Altarpiece of the Life of Saint Ambrose by Juan de Valdés Leal', *A. Bull.*, lxiv (1982), pp. 472–81

DUNCAN KINKEAD

Guzmán, Alberto (*b* Talera, 4 Sept 1927). Peruvian sculptor. He studied at the Escuela Nacional Superior de Bellas Artes in Lima, graduating in 1958 with a gold medal. In 1959 he won the Premio Nacional de Escultura and settled in Paris. His sculptures, based on articulated structures, are made of bronze, stainless steel, wire and marble. In the late 1960s the aggressively spiky forms of his early Parisian works became enclosed in hemispherical forms, given a contrastingly high polish, as in *Large White Tension* (welded steel, 2.20×1.25 m, 1968; Paris, Mus. N.A. Mod.).

BIBLIOGRAPHY

J. M. Ugarte Eléspuru: *Pintura y escultura en el Perú contemporáneo* (Lima, 1970)
Exposition Guzmán (exh. cat. by J. Lassaigne, Paris, Mus. Bourdelle, 1972–3)

LUIS ENRIQUE TORD

Guzmán, Gaspar de Bracamonte y. *See* BRACAMONTE Y GUZMÁN, GASPAR DE.

Guzmán, Haro y. *See* CARPIO, Marqueses del.

Guzmán, Osorio Moscoso y. *See under* ALTAMIRA, Condes de.

Guzman, Pedro Tellez Girón y, Duque de Osuna. *See* OSUNA, (1).

Guzmán, Ramiro Nuñez de. *See* MEDINA DE LAS TORRES, Duque de.

Guzmán de Rojas, Cecilio (*b* Potosí, 1899; *d* La Paz, 1950). Bolivian painter. He studied painting in Potosí under Avelino Nogales. In 1920 he left for Spain, where he studied at the Escuela de Bellas Artes de San Fernando in Madrid, in the studio of Julio Romero de Torres (1880–1930); later he also studied at the Ecole des Beaux-Arts in Paris. He remained in Europe until 1929, travelling around several countries, and living in Paris and Rome. Although he initially had a provincial mentality, he benefited from his exposure to European artistic trends, and his work began to show the influence of Art Nouveau and Art Deco. On his return to Bolivia he settled in La Paz. There he became Director of the Escuela de Bellas Artes and Director General of the Fine Arts in the Ministry of Education, where he propagated a style and concept of native art that he called 'Indo-American'. In 1945 he was in London, with a grant from the British Council, to study restoration. Following this visit abroad he developed what he called the 'coagulatory' technique of painting, based on formulas developed from ancient treatises on painting. As a painter his output was prolific. It can be divided into several phases. The first of these began in Madrid, with such works as the *Triumph of Nature* (1928; La Paz, Mus. N. A.), executed with the technique of *calidadismo.* A second phase depicted the drama of soldiers during the Chaco War (1932–5), in an expressionistic style, as in *T. B. Can Be Evacuated* (1934; La Paz, Mus. N. A.). A third stage centred around the human figure, as in *Aymara Christ* (1939; La Paz, priv. col.) and numerous portraits. From 1940 he produced a large series of landscapes of Machu-Picchu and Lake Titicaca, and from 1947 until his death he worked on the coagulatory technique, both in landscapes and in semi-abstract works such as *Profundity* (1948; La Paz, priv. col.). As a restorer of paintings Guzmán de Rojas was the discoverer of Bolivian colonial art, particularly of the Baroque painter Melchor Perez de Holguín. He founded the first Pinacoteca Nacional in La Paz, now known as the Museo Nacional de Arte, and assembled the first collection of colonial paintings in the Museo Nacional de la Casa de Moneda in Potosí.

BIBLIOGRAPHY

Art of Latin America since Independence (exh. cat., New Haven, Yale U. A.G.; Austin, U. TX, A. Mus.; 1966)
L. Castedo: *Historia del arte ibero-americano*, ii (Madrid, 1988)
P. Querejazu: *La pintura boliviana del siglo XX* (Milan, 1989)

PEDRO QUEREJAZU

Guzmán y Pimentel, Gaspar de. *See* OLIVARES, Conde-Duque de.

Gwalior [Gvāliyar; anc. Gopagiri; Gopādri: 'Mountain of the cowherd']. City in Madhya Pradesh, India, situated around a rocky plateau known as Gwalior Fort. The site's strategic importance accounts for its central role in the region's history and thus its succession of important monuments. Sandstone quarries in the environs are the source of virtually all material used for the city's buildings and sculpture.

According to local lore, Gwalior was founded by a king who received a blessing from a sage named Gvalipa. Its oldest known artefact, however, is a small standing Buddha (3rd century AD; Gwalior, Archaeol. Mus.) made from the mottled red sandstone of Mathura and evidently imported from that city. This type of work was copied in local sandstone, as is shown by a damaged seated Buddha (Gwalior, Maharaja Jiwaji Rao Scindia Mus.). The earliest inscription (6th century AD) comes from the Suraj Kund (Hindi: 'sun tank') in the Fort. It records the establishment of a Sun temple (destr.) in the time of King Mihirakula, the son of the Huna king Toramana (*reg c.* 500), thus indicating that Gwalior was included in the north Indian conquests of the Hunas. Little is known about Gwalior in the following century except that it was probably an independent principality at the time of King Harsha (*reg c.* 606–47). In the 8th century Yashovarman (*reg c.* 720–50) incorporated it within his domain. Substantial remains from the 8th century onwards have been preserved. The earliest extant temple, the Teli ka Mandir ('oil-pressers' temple'), located on the Fort, is probably from the second half of the 8th century. Over 24 m high, it is unusual, being rectangular in plan and covered by a barrel-vaulted superstructure (Skt *valabhī*). The walls have large niches (*rathikā*) echoing the form of curvilinear spires (*laṭina*). The inscriptions and iconography of the sculptures indicate that the Teli temple was originally dedicated to some aspect of the Mother goddess.

Two inscriptions from the 9th century provide evidence that Gwalior was an important centre of the GURJARA-PRATIHARA dynasty. The most important 9th-century monument is the Chaturbhuja temple. According to the inscriptions, this monolithic building, originally known as the Vaillabhattasvamin temple, was carved out of the rock under the patronage of an officer of the Gurjara-Pratihara monarch in Vikrama year 932 (AD 875–6). The temple has a porch (*prāggrīva*) with a rudimentary tiered roof (*phaṁsanā*) and a sanctum crowned by the standard curvilinear superstructure. The wall section (*jaṅghā*) bears images of Vishnu's incarnations and guardians of the regions, now damaged. The upper portions of the spire are a modern restoration. The Chaturbhuja temple is on a roadway cut into the cliff-face of the Fort; the Chaturbhuja inscription describes the road (*pratoli*) as belonging to the monarch Mihira Bhoja (*reg c.* 836–85). The road is lined with a number of reliefs and shrine-niches ranging in date from the 9th to the 16th centuries. Pillars and fragments incorporated in the Fort's 15th-century palace, the Man Mandir (see below), are probably vestiges of a 9th-century Gurjara-Pratihara palace that stood in the vicinity of the Man Mandir.

In the late 9th century and the early 10th a number of elaborate rock-cut shrines dedicated to Jaina divinities were carved near the Fort's Urwahi Gate. Part of a female figure (New Delhi, N. Mus.), one of Gwalior's best-known sculptures, is from this period. In the 10th century, with the decline of the Gurjara-Pratiharas, the Kachchhapaghatas, a regional dynasty, began to assert their independence. The Kachchhapaghatas were responsible for many monuments, including two temples known as Sas-Bahu (Hindi: 'mother-in-law' and 'daughter-in-law'). The larger (see fig. 1) was originally sacred to Padmanatha and carries an inscription recording its construction in Vikrama year 1150 (1093–4). Only the entrance hall (Skt *maṇḍapa*) remains. It has a large and elaborate tiered roof (*phaṁsanā*), intricate domical ceilings and four small shrines inside at the corners. This was an arrangement favoured in the Gwalior region and shows an internalization of the five-shrine (*pañcāyatana*) plan, in which four small shrines were located outside the main temple, usually at the corners of the plinth. The entire building is covered with relief sculptures and stencil-like vegetal patterns. The Kachchhapaghatas seem subsequently to have lost power to the Parihars, who in turn were ousted by the sultans of Delhi in the early 13th century. Muslim rule brought Indo-Islamic building styles to Gwalior. An inscription of the Delhi sultan Iltutmish (*reg* 1211–36) at Gwalior records the construction of a mosque, no longer extant.

In the late 14th century the Tomara Rajputs, keen patrons of music, painting and architecture, were able to assert their independence. The most splendid reminder of Tomara rule is the palace of Raja Man Singh (*reg* 1486–1516), known as the Man Mandir. The palace is a multi-storey structure dramatically situated at the edge of the

1. Gwalior, larger Sas-Bahu, entrance, 1093–4

2. Gwalior, Man Mandir, courtyard arcade, late 15th century

Fort overlooking the city. The Hathi Por (Hindi: 'elephant gate') is richly carved and flanked by semicircular towers rising the full height of the building. Much of the exterior is covered with ceramic tiles (*see* INDIAN SUBCONTINENT, fig. 330), giving the palace the appearance of an enamelled jewel-box. The dome above the entrance passage carries floral and geometric paintings of the 15th century. The royal apartments (see fig. 2) are notable for their richly worked arcades and pierced screens. The sandstone panels used to face the walls were often selected for their swirling marble-like patterns. The rest of the palace, consisting mainly of rooms around large open courtyards, was evidently for courtiers and attendants and was executed in a plain style. A few fragments of wall painting have survived in the Man Mandir. They are similar to the *Caurapañcāśikā* group of manuscripts (*see* INDIAN SUBCONTINENT, §VI, 3(ii)(e)) and show that Gwalior was a centre of the innovative painting styles that were developing at this time.

In addition to the Man Mandir, the Tomaras built a number of gates, tanks and other buildings. Particularly unusual is the circular Ras Lila Ghar at Barai village, which was used for dance performances. One of the finest palace-residences, the Gujari Mahal, was built by Raja Man for his consort. The decorative carvings and ceramic tiles are close in style to those of the Man Mandir. The building was restored in the early 20th century as the Archaeological Museum.

A more conservative current of 15th-century art is found in the large-scale Jaina images cut into caves around the base of the Fort. This extensive series consists mainly of Jaina *tīrthaṅkara*s (Skt: 'ford-makers', the 24 teachers of Jainaism); many are dated and carry detailed dedicatory inscriptions. A Jaina manuscript, known to have been painted in Gwalior (see Doshi), shows traditional painters were also active in the city at this time.

A large building known as Assi Khambha, adjacent to the Man Mandir, consists of a hypostyle hall of massive post-and-lintel construction. Next to the hall is a circular stepwell surrounded by a covered walkway. The building was converted into a madrasa *c.* 1528, when an arched entrance recalling work at Chanderi was added on the north side. Also closely allied to the architecture of Chanderi is the free-standing gateway at Ladheri, on the outskirts of Gwalior north of the Fort, which has two tapering towers joined by an arch and decorative panels. It may have been built in 1518 to celebrate the submission of Gwalior to the Lodi sultans of Delhi. Although the city was brought under Delhi's rule at this time, any instability at the centre resulted in local powers asserting greater independence. Gwalior was finally brought firmly under Muslim rule in 1588 by the Mughal emperor Akbar (*reg* 1556–1605), ending the city's 'golden age'.

The last monument with a distinct local flavour is the tomb of the famous saint *Sayyid Muhammad Ghauth Shattari*, remarkable for its intricate and varied carved stone screens. It is possible that the craftsmen from Gwalior who produced this work travelled to the imperial capital to carve stone screens for Mughal buildings. The export of talent from Gwalior to the Mughal court is documented in the careers of the musician Tansen and the painter Nand Gvaliyari.

A number of monuments in Gwalior date to the Mughal period. Palaces were added adjacent to the Man Mandir and other Tomara buildings on the Fort. Gwalior's Jami' Mosque was begun by Jahangir (*reg* 1605–27), and a gate was added to the eastern entrance of the Fort in the time of Aurangzeb (*reg* 1658–1707). Gwalior has several tombs from the Mughal period; the most impressive is that of *Mu'tamid Khan*. An elegant 16th-century gate-house at Ladheri may have been the entrance to a now-vanished tomb. There are a number of ruined mosques and tombs near by and a 15th- or early 16th-century tomb at Sagar Tal, a short distance away. Two bridges (one at Ladheri, the other at more distant Nurabad) are also products of the Mughal period.

Gwalior Fort was captured by the Marathas in 1784. The Scindia rulers, who took control in the 19th century, made Gwalior one of the leading states of British India. A number of important monuments were added to the city in an area known as Lashkar (Pers.: 'camp'), where the Maratha armies camped. Lashkar's most famous building is the Jai Vilas Palace, built in an eclectic Indo-Classical style. The spacious audience hall has a chandelier that is reputedly the largest in the world. The Scindias built fine memorials to eminent members of their house as well as a number of public buildings, including Victoria College, which is in a revival style inspired by the tomb of *Muhammad Ghauth*. Homes of the well-to-do in Lashkar, little touched by Neo-classicism or conscious revivalism, are noted for their balconies and finely carved screens.

The British contributed little to Gwalior. The barracks on the Fort are unpretentious and utilitarian, as is the church built amid the Mughal palace complex. It has a simple Neo-classical façade and is now falling to ruins. The cantonment at Morar has the usual colonial bungalows, Gothic style church and cemeteries.

See also INDIAN SUBCONTINENT, §§III, 5(i)(g), and IV, 7(iv).

BIBLIOGRAPHY

A. Cunningham: 'Gwāliār or Gwalior', *Archaeol. Surv. India Rep.*, ii (1864–5), pp. 330–96
J. Keith: *Preservation of National Monuments: Gwalior Fortress* (Calcutta, 1883)
Gwal. State Archaeol. Dept Annu. Rep. (1925–6) to (1940–41)
M. Garde: *Archaeology in Gwalior* (Gwalior, 1934)
Quinquennial Administrative Report for Samvats, 1998–2002, Years 1942–46, Gwalior State Archaeological Department (Gwalior, 1949)
D. Patil: *The Descriptive and Classified List of Archaeological Monuments in Madhya Bharat* (Gwalior, 1952)
H. N. Dvivedi: *Gvaliyar ke Tomara* [Gwalior's Tomaras] (Gwalior, 1975)
S. Doshi: 'A Fifteenth Century Jaina Manuscript from Gwalior and Some Thoughts on the Caurapancasika Style', *J. Ind. Soc. Orient. A.*, x (1978–9), pp. 30–40
H. N. Dvivedi, ed.: *Gvāliyar Darśan* [Vision of Gwalior] (Gwalior, 1981)
Z. A. Desai: 'A Note on the Nagari Inscriptions of Mughal Emperor Babar from Gwalior Fort', *Sri Dinesacandrika: Studies in Indology*, ed. B. N. Mukherjee and others (Delhi, 1983), pp. 67–71
K. Chakravarty: *The Gwalior Fort* (New Delhi, 1984)
K. Deva: 'Teli-ka-mandir, Gwalior', *Indian Epigraphy: Its Bearing on the History of Art*, ed. F. M. Asher and G. S. Gai (New Delhi, 1985), pp. 161–3
M. Willis: 'An Eighth Century Miḥrāb in Gwalior', *Artibus Asiae*, xlvi (1985), pp. 227–46
G. K. Gori: *Gvāliyar kā rājanaitika evam saṁskṛtika* [Political and cultural history of Gwalior] (Dehli, 1986)
G. H. R. Tillotson: *The Rajput Palaces: The Development of an Architectural Style, 1450–1750* (New Haven and London, 1987), pp. 56–70
S. N. Caturvedī: Sūryopāsana aur Gvāliyar kā Vivasvān mandir [Sūrya worship and Gwalior's sun temple] (Delhi, 1990)
S. Majūpuriyā: *Gvāliyar kā itihāsa aur uske darśanīya sthāna* [Gwalior's history and notable places] (Gwalior, 1991)

MICHAEL D. WILLIS

Gwathmey, Charles (*b* Charlotte, NC, 19 June 1938). American architect and teacher. He studied at the University of Pennsylvania, Philadelphia (1956–9), and Yale University, New Haven, CT (1959–62), and he taught architecture at several universities in the USA from 1964. He was a member of the NEW YORK FIVE in the late 1960s and early 1970s, and his work strongly adheres to the tenets of early 20th-century Modernism as seen in Le Corbusier's buildings of the 1920s and 1930s; this he

Charles Gwathmey: Gwathmey Residence, Amagansett, Long Island, New York, 1966

tempered with pragmatism and an almost playfully experimental approach to design. In the Gwathmey Residence and Studio (1966; see fig.), Long Island, NY, for example, the whole complex, built in a large field, was sited so as to be seen in a continuing series of oblique views. The vertically orientated structures are strongly cubistic; the planar walls and cylindrical stairwell exteriors seem to shift and almost collide with one another. Unity and stability are maintained by the unpainted cedar panels, which adhere to the surface like an encasement, and by horizontal slots and windows that tie the various spaces together. In 1971 Gwathmey established a practice with Robert Siegel (*b* 1939) in New York, which completed a large number of public and private buildings. Typical examples include the Thomas & Betz Corporation Office Building (1976), Raritan, NJ, which is pervaded by geometric clarity, particularly in the creation of flowing, interconnected spaces. In the Menil House (1979), East Hampton, Long Island, the square is the basic module for complex grids that frame and define a variety of interpenetrating spaces. Gwathmey also redesigned existing structures. In the Spielberg House (1988), for example, he reassembled an 18th-century New Jersey barn in East Hampton, sheathing the exterior in new wooden shingles; a 'silo', creating a play of cylinder against cube that recalled the Gwathmey Residence, is actually a new addition. The interior combines the original exposed oak frame with walls of smooth white gypsum board. As in his other works, this house demonstrates the unique inventiveness that Gwathmey brought to Corbusian Modernism.

BIBLIOGRAPHY

Contemp. Architects

K. Frampton and C. Rowe: *Five Architects: Eisenman, Graves, Gwathmey, Hejduk, Meier* (New York, 1972, rev. 1975)

W. Martin: 'Taking a Section Through the Thinking of Gwathmey Siegel Architects', *Archit. Rec.*, clxvi/9 (1979), pp. 91–102

P. Arnell and T. Bickford, eds: *Charles Gwathmey and Robert Siegel: Buildings and Projects, 1964–1984* (New York, 1984)

C. Jenks: *Architecture Today* (New York, 1988)

'Sogno tra Country e Tudor', *Abitare*, n. s., 278 (1989), pp. 204–11

WALTER SMITH

Gwynn, John (*b* Shrewsbury, Nov 1713; *d* Worcester, 27 Feb 1786). English architect and writer. In his first pamphlet, *An Essay on Design* (1749), he stated themes that he often repeated: he urged the establishment of a 'public academy' of art and lamented the lack of encouragement given to artists in England. With the draughtsman Samuel Wale, he published in 1749 a copy of Wren's plan of 1666 for London, in 1755 a section of St Paul's Cathedral, London, drawn from personal survey and 'decorated according to the original intention of Sir Christopher Wren', and in 1758 a plan with dimensions. He was briefly prominent in 1759–60 when his design for Blackfriars Bridge, London, gained public support in three letters by Dr Samuel Johnson to a newspaper. In his important book *London & Westminster Improved*... (1766) Gwynn urged that the cause of 'public magnificence', including broad, healthy streets on a regular plan and elegant public buildings, must not be frustrated by private interests and that all building be made to conform to a 'general plan', of which he gave a detailed draft. Many of his suggestions for London were carried out during the next century; but he himself had opportunities much sooner to direct improvements in street widths and layouts adjacent to the new bridge in Worcester and in Oxford as surveyor to the commissioners of the Oxford Paving Act. His largest commissions as an architect were for bridges at Shrewsbury (the English Bridge, 1769–74), Atcham (1768–76), Worcester (1770–81) and Oxford (Magdalen Bridge, 1772–7); all except Atcham have been altered or rebuilt. They had studiously correct classical geometry and competent structural design. Their richness and correctness of architectural detail, in a rather Baroque idiom, were unrivalled, but unsatisfactory gradients resulted from the grandeur of the elevations at Shrewsbury and Atcham. Gwynn became the executive contractor for these two bridges when the first builder failed. His only other known commissions were for a workhouse and a market in Oxford and elsewhere a few houses and an altarpiece. His early ambition was satisfied when the Royal Academy of Arts was created in London in 1768, and he was one of only five architects named among the forty academicians. Being respected by leading intellectuals, he was more influential in architectural discourse than his small output of buildings suggests.

WRITINGS

An Essay on Design, Including Proposals for Erecting a Public Academy to be Supported by Voluntary Subscription... (London, 1749)

A Plan for Rebuilding the City of London after the Great Fire in 1666, Designed by that Great Architect Sir Christopher Wren (London, 1749)

Transverse Section of St. Paul's Cathedral, Decorated According to the Original Intention of Sir Christopher Wren (London, 1755)

London & Westminster Improved, to which is Prefixed a Discourse on Public Magnificence (London, 1766)

BIBLIOGRAPHY

Colvin

T. Ruddock: *Arch Bridges and their Builders, 1735–1835* (Cambridge, 1979)

TED RUDDOCK

Gyantse [rgyal rtse; Gyangzê]. Fourth largest city in Tibet, strategically located between Lhasa and Shigatse along the caravan route to India, Nepal, Sikkim and Bhutan. Gyantse is most famous for its fortress citadel, or Dzong, and its lamasery. The 15th-century fortress, situated on a hill overlooking the town, served as an effective buffer against invasions from the south for centuries until 1904, when it was partially destroyed and conquered by British forces led by Francis Younghusband. It suffered further damage by the Chinese in the 1960s. Although in poor condition, the fort still has significant traces of ancient wall paintings.

The complex of buildings within the old walls at Gyantse, often referred to as the Palkhor Choide or Pelkor Chode (dpal 'khor chos sde) Lamasery, was founded in 1418 by Rabten Kunsang (1389–1442), a follower of Khedrup Je (1385–1438), himself a disciple of Tsong Khapa (1357–1419), the founder of the Gelugpa sect. The monastic complex was formerly much more extensive, but a number of buildings were dismantled during the 1960s. The main buildings have survived relatively intact, however. Chief among these and one of the most impressive buildings in all of Tibet is the Kumbum Stupa or Pango Chorten (see fig.) built by Newari craftsmen from Nepal's Kathmandu Valley under the supervision of Rabten Kunsang. Newari artisans were honoured and much sought after in Tibet for their exquisite and intricate workmanship, and the Kumbum is one of their finest

Gyantse, Kumbum Stupa, completed *c.* 1439

architectural accomplishments. This stupa (h. *c.* 30 m) has 108 doors (a sacred number in Buddhism), 77 chapels and niches, and 20 corners and sides. An aerial perspective would reveal that the stupa is shaped like a *maṇḍala*, the embodiment of the Tibetan Buddhist universe. The shape was based on the schematic designs of the scholar and artist Buton Rinpoche (1290–1364) for the monastery of SHALU.

The stupa is virtually a museum with thousands of religious artefacts, each chapel having numerous colourful stucco statues and wall paintings. The inscriptions on the structure list the names of some of the artists, the first time this occurred in Tibet, where artists usually remained anonymous. The first storey of the stupa has four lofty chapels with one entrance at each of the four cardinal points. The first chapel through the main doorway is the Shakyamuni Chapel, which houses a large statue of Shakyamuni, the historical Buddha, seated in the posture of 'turning the wheel of *dharma*' and flanked by his disciples Shariputra and Maudgalyayana. The base of the stupa, subdivided into four successive terraces of chapels, is ascended by keeping the core of the structure to the right, thus identifying it with the world axis. The stepped terraces culminate with a shrine at the top in a circular dome, which has four doors at the cardinal points, framed by a highly decorative arch known as the 'arch of glory'; the arch includes a *garuda* (Skt: 'half-human, half-bird') grasping a snake at the top and a sea-monster (Skt *makara*) on either side below it. The square section above the circular dome has a large pair of eyes of the Adi Buddha (the supreme or primordial Buddha) painted on each side. This section is surmounted by a conical shaft of 13 tapering rings, which represent the 13 steps to enlightenment. The shaft is topped by an elaborate parasol and a small stupa-shaped spire.

The Assembly Hall of the lamasery has few artefacts of note, but it is connected to a number of important chapels with large statues and impressive murals. These include the Protector Chapel, containing three huge protector figures of Guru Gonpo (the principal guardian of the Sakya sect), Ekajati (the goddess of concentration) and Pelden Lhamo (the principal protectress of Tibet, especially of the Gelugpa sect); the Vairochana Chapel (noteworthy for the old lacquered clay figures of the Five Dhyani Buddhas); the Maitreya Chapel; the Samvara Chapel, which contains an important three-dimensional *maṇḍala* of gold and bronze said to have been erected by Khedrup Je; and the Main Chapel, with a central figure of Shakyamuni Buddha flanked by the *bodhisattva*s Avalokiteshvara and Manjushri. Behind the monastery, high on the hill and incorporated into the outer wall, is a large wall where giant Buddhist *tangka*s (scrolls) are unrolled during special religious festivals.

See also STUPA, §5.

BIBLIOGRAPHY

S. C. Das: 'The Monasteries of Tibet', *J. & Proc. Asiat. Soc. Bengal*, i/4 (1905), pp. 106–16

Li An-che: 'A Lamasery in Outline', *J. W. China Border Res. Soc.*, series A, xiv (1942), pp. 35–68

A. K. Gordon: *Tibetan Religious Art* (New York, 1952)

D. L. Snellgrove and H. E. Richardson: *A Cultural History of Tibet* (London, 1968, rev. London and Boulder, 1980)

The Art of Tibet (exh. cat. by P. Pal, New York, Asia Soc. Gals, 1969)

B. C. Olschak and G. T. Wangyal: *Mystic Art of Ancient Tibet* (London, 1973)

L. S. Dagyab: *Tibetan Religious Art*, Asiatische Forschungen, LII/i and ii (Wiesbaden, 1977)

M. Henss: *Tibet: Die Kulturdenkmäler* (Zurich, 1981)

M. Buckley and R. Strauss: *Tibet* (Berkeley, 1986), pp. 157–62

Zhongguo mingsheng cidian [Dictionary of Chinese historical sites] (Shanghai, 1986)

S. Batchelor: *The Tibet Guide* (London, 1987), pp. 279–83, 285–95

F. Ricca and E. Lo Bue: *The Great Stupa of Gyantse: A Tibetan Pantheon of the 15th Century* (London, 1992)

BARRY TILL

Gyaraspur [Gyāraspur]. Temple site in Vidisha district, Madhya Pradesh, India. Of the many ruins at Gyaraspur, the most complete is the Mala Devi temple, originally a Jaina dedication. Situated on a large platform cut into a hillside, it is the best-preserved 9th-century AD temple in the Vidisha region. The superstructure is an early example of the multi-spired (Skt *śekharī*) form. To the north, near the Mansarovar tank, are the ruins of two rare and important examples of 7th-century temple architecture. One is a dilapidated shrine of the *maṇḍapikā* type, with walls constructed of pillars and richly carved slabs; only the door is left of the second. A 7th-century image of *Ambika* (Gwalior, Archaeol. Mus.) is probably from this location.

To the west of Gyaraspur is a stupa faced with hammer-dressed masonry and raised on a platform. It has Buddha stelae assignable to the 10th century. Near Gyaraspur village are further remains. A large temple, the site of which is marked by fragments and four standing pillars, can be associated with an inscription (Gwalior, Archaeol. Mus.) dated AD 879–80 (Vikrama year 936). The temple's elegant free-standing gate, called Hindola Torana, is one of the few remaining examples of this period in northern India. Another ruin consisting of eight pillars (thus called Atha Khambha) is the vestige of a 10th-century temple hall. It carries a pilgrim record dated 982–3 (Vikrama year 1039). A large slab (London, BM, 1983.4–23.1) with a 33-line inscription recording the dedication of a temple is known to have been collected at Gyaraspur in the early 19th century and could have been taken from the Atha Kambha ruin. The more complete Bajra Math to the south is an unusual structure with three sanctums. Its elaborately carved doors are in the 10th-century style.

BIBLIOGRAPHY

D. R. Patil: *The Descriptive and Classified List of Archaeological Monuments in Madhya Bharat* (Gwalior, 1952)

S. R. Thakore: *Catalogue of Sculptures in the Archaeological Museum, Gwalior, M. B.* (Lashkar, n. d.)

Krishna Dev: 'Mālā Devī Temple at Gyāraspur', *Śrī Mahāvīra Jaina Vidyālaya Golden Jubilee Volume*, i (Bombay, 1968), pp. 260–69

O. Viennot: 'The Mahiṣāsuramardinī from Siddhi-Ki-Guphā at Deogarh', *J. Ind. Soc. Orient. A.*, iv (1971–2), pp. 66–77; pl. XI–6 [7th-century image from Gyaraspur]

M. Meister: 'Construction and Conception: Maṇḍapikā Shrines of Central India', *E. & W.*, xxvi (1976), pp. 409–18

A. C. Mittal: *The Inscriptions of the Imperial Paramāras* (Ahmadabad, 1979), p. 207

J. Williams: *The Art of Gupta India: Empire and Province* (Princeton, 1982)

R. D. Trivedi: *Temples of the Pratīhāra Period in Central India* (New Delhi, 1989)

MICHAEL D. WILLIS

Gyárfás, Jenő (*b* Sepsiszentgyörgy, Transylvania [now Sfîntu Gheorghe, Romania], 6 April 1857; *d* Sepsiszentgyörgy, 13 Dec 1925). Hungarian painter and illustrator. From 1873 he studied at the school for design drawing, Mintarajziskola, Budapest, under Bertalan Székely, and he attended the Akademie der Bildenden Künste in Munich (1877–80). He exhibited genre paintings in Budapest, Munich and Brussels, with considerable success. In 1880 he returned to Hungary, but he could find no buyers for his work. After a study trip to Italy (1882) he withdrew to his birthplace and thereafter played little part in public artistic life.

Gyárfás's first important work, *Testifying before the Corpse* (1881; Budapest, N.G.), is based on a poem by János Arany and employs strong chiaroscuro. His paintings couple the depiction of character with an intense sense of drama, the subjects often derived from literature. In his later historical pictures he was unable to repeat his early success. Among his portraits, which display strong realism and concentrated detail, a major work is that of *Bertalan Karlovszky* (1879–1880; Budapest, N.G.). Gyárfás did a great number of illustrations, primarily for the poems and tales he wrote himself. In 1907 he wrote a fairy tale, *Varázsfátyol* ('Magic veil'; unpublished), illustrated with pen-and-ink drawings.

BIBLIOGRAPHY

B. Lázár: *Gyárfás Jenő* (Budapest, 1921)

KATALIN GELLÉR

Gymnasium [Gr. *gymnasion*]. Ancient Greek and Roman sports and educational establishment. The barbarian prince Anacharsis, one of the seven sages of the ancient world, described the gymnasium as the place 'in every Greek city where the populace go mad daily' (Dio Chrysostom: *Discourses* xxxii.44), and it was certainly central to Greek urban life. It was conceived primarily as a public institution for the military and athletic training of young male citizens and for their intellectual and spiritual education. By *c.* 400 BC these combined activities had become formally integrated into the official system of ephebic (youth) education. Gymnasia also acquired various secondary civic and cultural functions. They attracted itinerant lecturers, philosophers, doctors and musicians, and their association with the patron deities Hermes and Herakles made them natural centres for religious uses, including the observance of Hellenistic ruler cults and, later, the worship of Roman emperors. A number of civic organizations, such as the association of youths (*neoi*) and the council of elders (*gerousia*), also had links with gymnasia as well as simply using their buildings. The chief administrator of the gymnasium, the *gymnasiarch*, was a distinguished official who presided over all aspects of the educational programme, employed professional teachers and trainers (*paidotribai*), organized games and competitions and performed religious rites.

Plato imagined ideal gymnasia as parklike areas outside the city (*Laws* VI.761c–d; *Critias* 112c); in Athens, all three of the pre-Classical and Classical gymnasia (the Academy, the Lykeion and the Cynosarges) occupied large sites on the city outskirts and had apparently no consistent architectural form. Their principal shared features were level, wooded sites, a convenient source of water, a hero shrine and perhaps a stoa. With the development of Hippodamian town planning, however, the scattered architectural elements characteristic of suburban gymnasia were made to cohere and to fit into one or more standard city blocks.

Although not sited in cities, the gymnasia at Delphi (see fig.) and Olympia had already developed a standard architectural form by the late 4th century BC. This comprised two basic elements: the PALAESTRA, usually squarish in plan with rooms around a peristyle courtyard; and the dromos, a range of sports grounds and running tracks, including the *xystos* (covered colonnade) and the *paradromis* (open track). Comparable 3rd-century BC establishments are the lower gymnasium at Priene, the gymnasium on Delos and the gymnasium at Eretria. The most impressive and, probably, the largest Hellenistic gymnasium was constructed on the steep hillside at Pergamon, and each of its three terraces was intended for a different age group.

Vitruvius (*On Architecture* V.xi) provides the most authoritative ancient description of the Greek gymnasium, though this 1st-century BC account is relatively late in terms of the development of gymnasia and is primarily theoretical. He referred to rooms under the colonnades of the palaestra as exedrae for informal discussion (*see* EXEDRA) and located the main room, the classroom (*ephebeum*), at the centre of one side. Rooms to either side of the *ephebeum* included the *coryceum*, which contained the boxers' punch-bag, the *conisterium*, where the wrestlers dusted their bodies, the *elaeothesium*, where athletes oiled themselves, and the *loutron* (cold-water washroom).

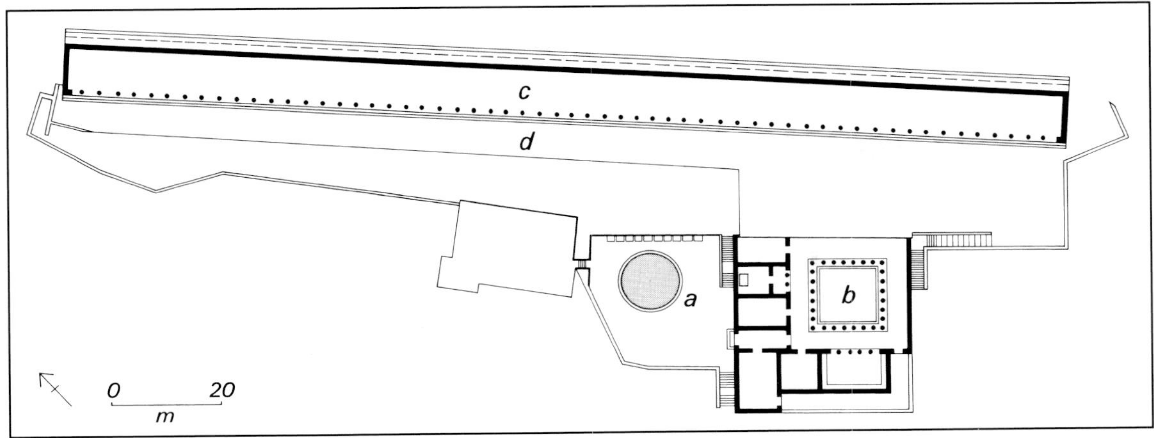

Gymnasium at Delphi, 4th century BC, plan: (a) *loutron*; (b) palaestra; (c) *xystos*; (d) *paradromis*

By the 1st century BC many existing gymnasia were being renovated by the addition of elaborate hot-water supply systems, while new ones were built to combine gymnasia and hot baths (Gr. *balaneutike*). This undoubtedly reflected both the growing taste for material luxury and the increased popularity of hot-water bathing in the period after the Peloponnesian War (431–404 BC), but it also undermined the gymnasium's original function as a place for the harmonious development of mind and body. The evolution in Asia Minor during the later 1st and 2nd centuries AD of the Roman bath-gymnasium represented the final fusion of the Hellenistic gymnasium and the Roman type of bath (*see also* BATH (ii), §1).

Except in the Greek colonies of southern Italy and Sicily, gymnasia were seldom built in western Europe, and Vitruvius considered the palaestra to be alien to Italian culture. The demise of the authentic gymnasium, the focal point of Hellenism, can be ascribed to the growing influence of Christianity, and the last references to gymnasia or gymnastic training in the East date from the 4th century AD, marking a wider shift in European culture from Classical to medieval.

BIBLIOGRAPHY

Pauly–Wissowa

E. N. Gardiner: *Athletics of the Ancient World* (Oxford, 1930)

C. A. Forbes: 'Expanded Uses of the Greek Gymnasium', *Class. Philol.*, xl (1945), pp. 32–42

H. I. Marrou: *Histoire de l'éducation dans l'antiquité* (Paris, 1948); Eng. trans. by G. Lamb (London, 1956)

R. E. Wycherley: *How the Greeks Built Cities* (London, 1949, rev. 2/1962/*R* 1976)

J. Delorme: *Gymnasion* (Paris, 1960)

FIKRET K. YEGÜL

Gyokudō. *See* URAGAMI GYOKUDŌ.

Gyokuen Bonpō [Gyokukei] (1348–*c.* 1420). Japanese Zen monk, scholar, calligrapher, poet and painter. He began his training as a monk at Nanzenji in Kyoto, under Shun'oku Myōha, the nephew and disciple of Musō Sōseki, one of the leading Zen prelates of the Muromachi period (1333–1568). His other teachers included the Zen recluse Shakushitsu Genkō and Gidō Shūshin, under whom he studied literature. A trusted adviser of the fourth Ashikaga shogun, Yoshimochi, Gyokuen was appointed to the prestigious abbacies of Kenninji (*c.* 1409) and Nanzenji (1413) in Kyoto. His true wish, however, was to retire from the world, and in 1420, after a disagreement with Yoshimochi, he left Kyoto to lead a life of seclusion. An accomplished poet, Gyokuen also brushed colophons on many *shigajiku* (poem-painting scrolls) of the period, including Josetsu's *Catching a Catfish with a Gourd* (c. 1413–15; Kyoto, Myōshinji; *see* JAPAN, fig. 92). His own painting, which shows the influence of the mid-14th-century Chinese priest–painter Xue Chuang and of Tesshū Tokusai, strongly reflects his literary disposition. He is especially well known for his subdued monochrome ink paintings of orchids (emblems of moral virtue), 30 of which have survived. A particularly fine example is the hanging scroll *Orchids and Rocks* (Tokyo, N. Mus.; see fig. on next page).

BIBLIOGRAPHY

H. Kanazawa: *Shoki suibokuga* [Early ink painting], Nihon no bijutsu [Arts of Japan], lxix (Tokyo, 1972); Eng. trans. by B. Ford as *Japanese Ink Painting: Early Zen Masterpieces*, Japanese Arts Library, viii (Tokyo and New York, 1979)

I. Tanaka: *Kaō, Mokuan, Minchō* (1974), v of *Suiboku bijutsu taikei* [Chinese and Japanese ink painting through the centuries], 15 vols (Tokyo, 1974–8)

Japanese Ink Paintings from American Collections: The Muromachi Period (exh. cat., ed. Y. Shimizu and C. Wheelwright; Princeton, NJ, Princeton U., 1976)

MASAMOTO KAWAI

Gyokuran. *See* IKE, (2).

Gyokusen. *See* ODANO NAOTAKE.

Gyokushū. *See* KUWAYAMA GYOKUSHŪ.

Győr [formerly Lat. Arrabona; Ger. Raab]. City in Győr–Sopron County in north-west Hungary at the junction of the rivers Rába and Rábca and a branch of the Danube. It is the major industrial town of western Hungary, noted especially for its engineering works. In the 11th century St Stephen (*reg* 1000–38) founded a bishop's seat there on the site of the Roman town. Its principal buildings include the Citadel and the Bishop's Castle on Chapter Hill, developed in stages over several centuries, the oldest section of the castle being the tower in the north-east

Gyokuen Bonpō: *Orchids and Rocks* (*Rankei dōhōzu*), hanging scroll, ink on paper, 1068×346 mm, late 14th century–early 15th (Tokyo, National Museum)

wing. Today, only its stair-well, containing the so-called 'escape corridor', and the Gothic sedilia have retained their designs from the 14th century. Above the sedilia a tall tower (*in situ*) was erected in the 15th century; at the end of the same century Bishop Orbán Dóczy built a dome with ribbed net vaulting in the south wing. The larger part of the castle complex was built between 1537 and 1554; its walls and bastions facing the River Rába in the south were built in 1664. The greater part of the Bishop's Castle was rebuilt in the 18th century in the Baroque style.

The earliest parts of the cathedral date from the 12th to the 14th century, with 17th-century Baroque additions. Its present Neo-classical form dates from 1823. The wide façade has a cast-iron gate (1938) and three large Palladian windows topped by circular ones. A single tower (destr. 1944; rebuilt) on the façade incorporates two red marble gates (1774) on its north and south sides. The interior, consisting of a nave and aisles, has remains of Gothic vaulting. The chancel (12th century) has three apses and includes an organ-loft (early 1760s) ornamented with garlands and having seven openings. In front of the chancel there is a triumphal arch. Melchior Hefele designed the high altar, supported by columns, and Franz Anton Maulbertsch painted the altarpiece of the *Assumption of the Virgin*. Maulbertsch also painted frescoes of the *Ascension* (1781) in the nave and images of Hungarian saints (1772–81) in the chancel. There are also two grisaille paintings in the chancel: *St Stephen Founding the Bishop's Seat* and *St Ladislas Striking Water out of a Rock*, the latter on the ceiling of the north aisle. The chancel also contains a bishop's throne, prepared for the coronation of Maria-Theresa and bought by Bishop Ferenc Zichy. From the south aisle there is access to the Hédérváry Chapel (now St Ladislas Chapel), which János Hédervári, Bishop of Győr, erected *c.* 1400. Its interior has a triumphal arch with lancet openings and a vaulted chancel with a crested keystone, all of which were renovated in 1861 by Jósef Lippert (1826–1902). The chapel's most valuable possession is the reliquary bust of *St Ladislas* (*c.* 1400), a significant example of medieval goldsmiths' work.

The former Benedictine monastery and church of St Ignatius (1636–42) was originally used by the Jesuit Order. The Baroque church has two towers. In 1738 the nave was reconstructed, and in 1744 Paul Troger painted its ceiling frescoes, including the *Apotheosis of St Ignatius*. Rich 17th-century stuccowork covers the stairway and the pantry of the monastery. Other important ecclesiastical buildings include the former priest's seminary (1686–8); the Renaissance-inspired Hungarian hospice, founded in 1666 as a home for the aged and indigent; and the Carmelite church (1722–5), built by the lay brother Márton Wittwer and containing altarpieces by Martino Altomonte and wooden altar frames, pulpits and pews by Franz Richter (1784–1841). Significant secular buildings are the neo-Baroque town hall (1896–8) by Jenő Huber; the 17th-century 'Napoleon House' (now the Picture Gallery of the János Xantus Museum); the 17th-century Széchény Pharmacy, a working pharmacy as well as a museum; and the Kisfaludy Theatre (1978), with ceramic decoration on the exterior by Victor Vasarely. Among the various public monuments is the late Baroque *Ark of the Covenant* in Gutenberg Square, erected in 1731 after a design by Joseph Emanuel Fischer von Erlach, with sculptures by Antonio Corradini. Győr is also the birthplace of the ceramicist Margit Kovács; a museum of her work is open to the public.

BIBLIOGRAPHY

J. Ranos: *Magyar oltárok* [Hungarian altars] (Budapest, 1938)

V. Borbíró and I. Valló: *Győr várospépitéstörténete* [The history of the buildings of the town of Győr] (Budapest, 1956)

F. Jenei: *Régi Győriházak* [Old Győr houses] (Budapest, 1959)

P. Granasztói: *Szép Magyar városok egy építész szemével* [Beautiful Hungarian towns through the eyes of an architect] (Budapest, 1978)

BARBRA RUCKRIEGEL EGERVÁRY

Györgyi, Dénes (*b* Budapest, 25 April 1886; *d* Balatonalmádi, 21 Nov 1961). Hungarian architect, writer and teacher. He came from a family of artists: his grandfather Alajos Györgyi (1821–63) was a painter and his father, Géza Györgyi (1851–1934), also an architect, was the Director of the Society of Applied Arts. Dénes studied architecture at the Hungarian Palatine Joseph Technical University, Budapest, between 1903 and 1909, where he joined *Fiatalok* (Hung.: 'the young'), the group that formed around Károly Kós and was influenced by the architecture of the Arts and Crafts Movement and Finnish National Romanticism. Györgyi's Elementary School (1911–12; with Kós), Városmajor Street, Budapest, exemplifies the trend, with a framed gate and steep saddle roof. These recur in Györgyi's red-brick school building (1913), Kiskunhalas, where the protruding symmetrical entrance block ends in a façade with a gable and turrets at each corner, decorated with tall, narrow windows and covered by pyramid roofs. His seven-storey office headquarters for the 'Hangya Cooperative' (1917–20), Budapest, shows a divergence from National Romanticist tendencies, and in the 1920s he accommodated himself to the conservative official cultural policy: the Déri Museum (1923–9; with Aladár Münnich, 1890–1975), Debrecen, is among the most significant works of Hungarian neo-Baroque. Györgyi's later works, such as his designs (1926–31), in collaboration with Ernő Román (1883–1959), of a residential block, Honvéd Street, and an office building, Markó Street, for the Electricity Board, both in Budapest, show the influence of German Expressionism in their distinctively layered brick architecture. He also designed pavilions for exhibitions at Barcelona (1929; with Miklós Menyhért, *b* 1878; see Merényi, p. 73), Brussels (1935; see Kubinszky, pls 40–42) and Paris (1937; see Kubinszky, pl. 39), while his school (1948), Balatonalmádi, with its restrained composition fitting perfectly into its environment, became the pattern for the elementary school system in Hungary after World War II. Between 1910 and 1946 he was a professor at the National Industrial Design School, Budapest.

WRITINGS

ed., with D. Hültl and L. Kozma: *Uj magyar építőművészet* [New Hungarian architecture], 2 vols (Budapest, 1935–8)

BIBLIOGRAPHY

F. Merényi: *A Magyar epiteszet, 1867–1967* [Hungarian architecture, 1867–1967] (Budapest, 1970)

M. Kubinszky: *Györgyi Dénes* (Budapest, 1974)

Györgyi Dénes, 1886–1961 (exh. cat., ed. C. Fülöp, A. Hadik and L. Pusztai; Budapest, Hung. Mus. Archit., 1986)

ÁKOS MORAVÁNSZKY,
KATALIN MORAVÁNSZKY-GYÖNGY

Gyōsai. *See* KAWANABE KYŌSAI.

Gyosha. *See* NAGASAWA ROSETSU.

Gyoshū Hayami. *See* HAYAMI, GYOSHŪ.

Gysels, Pieter (*bapt* Antwerp, 3 Dec 1621; *d* Antwerp, 1690). Flemish painter. He began his training in 1641, when he was already 20, with Antwerp painter Jan Boots. Houbraken assumed he was also apprenticed to Jan Breughel II, whose diary describes a painting completed in 1638 as a 'small wild boar somewhat touched up by Gys' ('een klein wilt verxken voor Gys wat geretosieert'). But it seems highly doubtful that, as van der Sanden claimed (Denucé, p. 155), 'Gys' refers to Pieter Gysels. In 1649 or 1650 he became a master in Antwerp's Guild of St Luke. It is not known whether he took on any pupils. On 13 November 1650 he married Joanna Huybrecht, who bore him six children.

Gysels is primarily known as a landscape painter, but he also made several pictures of village fairs in the style of David Vinckboons. His landscapes, which are usually small in format and depict rural subjects, are clearly influenced by Jan Breughel I, who had been dead 25 years before Gysels became a master. Breughel the elder's influence can be seen in the composition, the colour (although Gysels used slightly paler tones), the choice of motifs and the meticulous technique. He also painted a number of still-lifes in the style of Jan Weenix, Jan Fyt and Pieter Boel. Tradition has it that at the time of his death he was working on his canvas *Game with Fruit and Vegetables* (Antwerp, Kon. Mus. S. Kst.), which is sometimes referred to as 'Gysels's coffin' in older literature.

BIBLIOGRAPHY

A. Houbraken: *De groote schouburgh* (1718–21), iii, p. 53

A. Michiels: *Histoire de la peinture flamande*, 10 vols (Paris, 1865–76), v, p. 378

F. J. van den Branden: *Geschiedenis der Antwerpsche schilderschool* (Antwerp, 1883), pp. 1019–22

J. Denucé: *Brieven en documenten betreffende Jan Breughel I en II: Bronnen voor de geschiedenis van de vlaamse kunst*, iii (Antwerp, 1934), p. 155

Y. Thiéry: *Le Paysage flamand au XVIIe siècle* (Paris and Brussels, 1953), pp. 80–81

Y. Thiéry and M. Kervyn de Meerendré: *Les Peintres flamands de paysage au XVIIe siècle: Le Baroque anversios et l'école bruxelloise* (Brussels, 1987), pp. 4–11, 238

HANS DEVISSCHER

Gysin, Brion (*b* Taplow, Bucks, 19 Jan 1916; *d* Paris, 13 July 1986). American painter and writer of English birth. He grew up in Kansas City, MO, and Edmonton, Alberta, and briefly attended Downside College in England before studying painting at the Sorbonne in Paris (1933–5). In 1934 his drawings were to have been exhibited at the Galerie aux Quatre Chemins in Paris alongside works by Dadaists and Surrealists, but they were removed by Paul Eluard on André Breton's orders at the last moment. The incident left a permanent psychological scar, although his first one-man show of paintings at the same gallery was well received four years later.

Gysin returned to New York in 1940 and worked on costumes in Broadway musicals, then as a welder until he was drafted into the American Army. There, and after 1943 in Vancouver, as an intelligence analyst in the Canadian Army, he studied Japanese language and in particular the traditions of Japanese calligraphy, which had a profound influence on his painting.

In 1949 Gysin received a Fulbright fellowship to study slavery in Marseille but a year later abandoned the research and moved to Tangier. He soon introduced elements of the Moroccan landscape and the forms of Arabic calligraphy into his increasingly abstract 'desert paintings' and developed his theory of the primordial unity of painting and writing. At an exhibition of his paintings in Tangier in 1953, Gysin met the American writer William S. Burroughs (*b* 1914), and they became close friends. Six years later in Paris they invented the 'cut-up' technique, a post-Dada concept of text-collage as chance operation, which Burroughs brought to prominence in several of his novels. In Paris in the early 1960s Gysin co-founded, with Bernard Heidsieck and Henri Chopin, the Domaine Poétique, which promoted sound-poetry, and had contact with the American artist George Maciunas (1931–78) and the Fluxus group. His paintings were exhibited 1958–64 in New York, Rome, Paris and London, but their reception was marred by the mistaken idea that he was part of the movement known as Lettrisme. He turned to writing during the late 1960s, collaborating with Burroughs on several books. During 1970–73 he moved between Tangier, London, Cannes, Venice and New York, working on a script for an unsuccessful film project based on Burroughs's novel *Naked Lunch*.

In 1974 Gysin returned to Paris, where he spent the rest of his life. He continued to exhibit his paintings and in the late 1970s and early 1980s gave live performances accompanied by rock musicians; several recordings of his songs were released. Although he began to gain wider recognition, the diversity of his work and his long association with Burroughs (whose fame far overshadowed his own) combined to diminish his success as a painter. Nevertheless in 1985 he was named a Chevalier de l'Ordre des Arts et des Lettres by the French Ministry of Culture. Gysin bequeathed the majority of his paintings and drawings to the Musée d'Art Moderne de la Ville de Paris.

WRITINGS

The Process (New York, 1969)
with W. S. Burroughs: *Oeuvre croisée* (Paris, 1976)
with T. Wilson: *Here to Go: Planet R-101* (San Francisco, 1982)
Légendes de Brion Gysin (Montpellier, 1983)
The Last Museum (London, 1986)

BIBLIOGRAPHY

I Am that Am I?: Entre cristal et fumée (exh. cat., essay G. C. Fabre; Paris, Gal. de France, 1986)
William Burroughs: Painting (exh. cat., essay J. W. Grauerholz; London, Oct Gal., 1988)

JAMES W. GRAUERHOLZ

Gysis [Gyzes], **Nikolaos** [Nicolas] (*b* Tinos, 1 March 1842; *d* Munich, 4 Jan 1901). Greek painter, active in Germany. He studied at the School of Arts in Athens (1853–64) and at the Akademie der Bildenden Künste in Munich (1865–71), where he later became a professor (1882). Despite his great love for Greece and his desire to return there, he lived and worked in Munich, perhaps fearing that he might not find the same suitable conditions in Greece as in the Bavarian capital. He attracted many of the young Greek artists who went to study in Munich. Gysis worked on almost all types of subjects, and many of his paintings were inspired by Greek life. His primary failing was that he never really managed to free himself from the academicism of Munich, despite the revolutionary changes then taking place in art. Typical examples of this type of work are: the *Secret School* (1876), *The Betrothal* (1877; *see* GREECE, fig. 3) and *The Ex-voto* (1886; all Athens, N.G.). Also of interest are his portraits, especially the *Artist's Wife*, the *Artist's Son* and the *Artist's Daughter* (all Athens, E. Koutlides priv. col., on loan to Athens, N.G.). Influenced by the prevailing *fin de siècle* mood, for about the last 20 years of his life Gysis turned to both mythological and religious allegorical subjects with an intense mystical and Symbolist flavour. Representative works of this period are: *Art and its Geniuses* (*c.* 1876), *Eros and Psyche* (both Athens, E. Koutlides priv. col., on loan to Athens, N.G.), *Spring Symphony* (1886) and *'Behold the Bridegroom Cometh . . .'* (*c.* 1895; both Athens, N.G.).

BIBLIOGRAPHY

M. Montandon: *Gysis* (Bielefeld and Leipzig, 1902)
Y. Papaioannou: 'Nikolaos Gysis', *Oi ellenes zographoi* [The Greek painters], ed. S. Lydakes and A. Karakatsane, i (Athens, 1974), pp. 138–87
C. Christou: *Greek Painting, 1832–1922* (Athens, 1981), pp. 52–7
N. Misirli: *Elleneke zographike. 18os–19os aionas* [Greek painting, 18th–19th centuries] (Athens, 1993), pp. 86–121, 197–9

ALKIS CHARALAMPIDIS

Gyulafehérvár. *See* ALBA IULIA.

Gyzes, Nikolaos. *See* GYSIS, NIKOLAOS.

H

Haacke, Hans (*b* Cologne, 12 Aug 1936). German painter and conceptual artist, active in the USA. He studied at the Staatliche Hochschule für Bildende Künste in Kassel from 1956 to 1960, and during this period he painted pictures in a style close to Tachism, working on the visualization of movement. He also worked on examinations of colour fields, and in 1960–61 he spent a year in S. W. Hayter's Atelier 17 in Paris. While there he was brought into contact with the work of Yves Klein and the Zero group. He stayed in touch with Zero until 1965, and this was revealed in his work through a demonstration of optical phenomena that is more objective than romantic. In 1961–2 he received a Fulbright Scholarship and studied at Temple University in Philadelphia, PA, spending the remainder of 1962 in New York. From 1963 to 1965 he had a number of teaching posts in Germany, first at Kettwig, then at Düsseldorf, but he returned to the USA in 1965 to live in New York and to take up a visiting lectureship at the University of Washington, Seattle, WA.

With his mirrorworks of 1961, *Mirror Relief* (1961; artist's col.) and the *Battle of Reichenfels* (1961; Paris, Bernard Aubertin priv. col.), Haacke freed himself from the object, and the water-containers done after 1962 are determined by technical factors, only formally recalling minimal art. The *Rain Tower* (1962; New York, Wilfried P. Cohen priv. col.) is the artist's first object that not only is a sensory and optical stimulation for the viewer but also has a practical use. He followed it with other 'real time systems', such as the condensation containers of 1963, which address themselves to natural laws and phenomena, not on a metaphorical or literary level but by causing them to occur in real time. At the beginning of the 1960s he made the acquaintance of the American artist and theorist J. W. Burnham, exchanging ideas with him about the 'systematic comprehension' of art.

In the second half of the 1960s Haacke added new components to his physical systems in real time. Biological phenomena, as in *Grass Cube* (1967; see Haacke, 1972, pl. 57) and *Chicks Hatching* (1969; see Haacke, 1972, pl. 62), became 'unassisted ready-mades'. But unlike Duchamp's ready-mades, which lose their original function, Haacke's works were isolated phenomena which, although signed by the artist as works of art, still showed the real phenomenon in real time. In his political works after the late 1960s, Haacke transferred the principle of the real-time system to the analysis and exposure of social structures, as in *Isolation of News Broadcasting Systems* (1969). With the help of statistical investigations, questionnaires and his own research, he constructed 'social' systems in real time. The spectrum of the works extended from research into property relations in Manhattan, New York (leading to the cancellation of an exhibition by the Guggenheim Museum in 1971), to the exposure of interconnections in artistic and cultural politics within the museum world: the exhibition of his *Manet Project '74* was prevented by the Wallraf-Richartz-Museum in Cologne.

In his work Haacke touched on taboos in the social system, using his art to aim for the nerve-centre of the establishment. He cannot be bracketed in any artistic trend; his works from the 1960s consist, in a conceptual way, of text and photograph (for illustration *see* CONCEPTUAL ART), while towards the end of the 1970s he painted large pictures, as did many contemporaries. After 1967 he taught in New York at Cooper Union, which gave him a full professorship in 1979. He was guest professor at the Hochschule für Bildende Künste in Hamburg in 1973 and at the Gesamthochschule in Essen in 1979.

WRITINGS

Hans Haacke—Werkmonographie (Cologne, 1972) [intro. E. F. Fry]
A Breed Apart (Oxford, 1978)

BIBLIOGRAPHY

Hans Haacke: Recent Work (exh. cat. by J. Burnham, U. Chicago, Ren. Soc. Gal., 1979)
Hans Haacke (exh. cat., intro. D. Maticevic; Zagreb, Gal. Contemp. A., 1980)
Hans Haacke: Volume II, Works 1978–1983 (exh. cat. by T. Brown and W. Grasskamp, London, Tate, 1984)
Hans Haacke: Nach allen Regeln der Kunst (exh. cat. by U. Giersch and others, Berlin, Neue Ges. Bild. Kst, 1984)
Hans Haacke: Unfinished Business (exh. cat., ed. B. Wallis; New York, New Mus. Contemp. A., 1986)

EVA MEYER-HERMANN

Haag, Carl (*b* Erlangen, 20 April 1820; *d* Oberwesel, 24 Jan 1915). German painter, active in Britain. After studying in Nuremberg, he painted miniature portraits in Munich and Brussels. In 1847 he went to London to study English techniques of watercolour painting and evolved a method that he claimed achieved the 'brilliancy of oil painting, combined with the tender-sweetness of water-colours' (Millar, p. 144). From 1850 he exhibited at the Society of Painters in Water-Colours and was elected a full member in 1853. That year he was commissioned by Queen Victoria and Prince Albert to paint two large and elaborate watercolours commemorating deerstalking expeditions at Balmoral in Scotland (British Royal Col.); he returned to Balmoral in 1863 and 1864.

Between 1847 and 1858 Haag made painting excursions to Rome, Venice, the Tyrol, Montenegro, Dalmatia and Munich. A more ambitious expedition to Egypt, Palestine and Syria in 1858–60 provided subjects on which much of his subsequent fame and prosperity rested. He spent the first winter in Cairo sharing a house with Frederick Goodall and making sketching trips to Giza and Suez. The following Easter he went to Jerusalem, Palmyra and Baalbek. Haag returned to Egypt in 1873. His watercolours of the East, with their portrayal of bedouin life, deserts, camels, ruins and religious ceremonies, owed their popularity to the combination of ethnic detail and idealization. Works such as *The Swooping Terror of the Desert* (1873; sold London, Sotheby's, 13 March 1980) contained both a narrative and the idea of moral virtue. Haag retired to Oberwesel on the Rhine in 1903.

BIBLIOGRAPHY

M. Phipps-Jackson: 'Cairo in London: Carl Haag's Studio', *A. J.* [London] (1883), pp. 71–5

The Works of Mr. Carl Haag (exh. cat., London, Goupil Gals, 1885)

J. L. Roget: *A History of the 'Old Water-Colour' Society* (London, 1891)

D. Millar: *Queen Victoria's Life in the Scottish Highlands Depicted by her Watercolour Artists* (London, 1985)

BRIONY LLEWELLYN

Haag, Den. *See* HAGUE, THE.

Haagen, Joris van der (*b* ?Arnhem, *c.* 1615; *d* The Hague, *bur* 23 May 1669). Dutch painter and draughtsman. He was probably the son and pupil of the Arnhem painter Abraham van der Haagen. Sometime after 1640 he settled in The Hague, where he lived for the rest of his life; he entered the Guild in 1643 and became its dean in 1653. Van der Haagen painted landscapes, which are formally composed and often heavily wooded and dark. His colour scheme of muted greens and yellows creates a sombre but naturalistic effect. In these respects his paintings resemble those of Jacob van Ruisdael, but they tend to lack van Ruisdael's dramatic sense. Van der Haagen's paintings reflect his preference for the hillier countryside of the eastern part of the Netherlands (e.g. *Extensive Wooded Landscape*, The Hague, Mus. Bredius), and he painted a number of panoramic landscapes in the area of Arnhem and Cleve and in the extreme south of the country near Maastricht. This preference is also seen in numerous drawings that he made during sketching expeditions to the wooded area of the Hoge Veluwe, where he took advantage of the high ground to record the extensive views over the Rhine Valley. He was one of the few Dutch landscape artists to draw panoramas, typically in grey wash and black chalk on several sheets of white or blue paper (e.g. *View near Elten*, 1660; Berlin, Kupferstichkab.). He also employed this technique, often with white chalk heightening, for studies of groups of trees, which he made in the same region and in the woodland near The Hague (e.g. *View in the Haagse Bos*, 164(?4); Paris, Fond. Custodia, Inst. Néer.). These, and his more finished studies of towns, are frequently confused with the drawings of Antoni Waterlo and Simon de Vlieger.

Van der Haagen's two sons, Cornelis van der Haagen (1651–*c.* 1689) and Jacobus van der Haagen (1657–1715), and his grandson Joris Cornelisz. van der Haagen (1676–*c.* 1745), were also artists: Jacobus was a still-life painter, and Joris Cornelisz. painted landscapes and seems to have worked in Ireland. The latter has been confused with WILLEM VAN DER HAGEN, who was probably a member of the same family.

BIBLIOGRAPHY

J. K. van der Haagen: *De schilders van der Haagen en hun werk* [The van der Haagen painters and their work] (Voorburg, 1932)

W. W. Robinson: 'Early Drawings by Joris van der Haagen', *Master Drgs*, xxviii/3 (1990), pp. 303–9

GEORGE GORDON

Haan, Hermann. *See* HAHN, HERMAN.

Haan, Jacob Meyer de. *See* MEYER DE HAAN, JACOB.

Haanen, Remigius (Adrianus) van [Haan, Remy van] (*b* Oosterhout, 5 Jan 1812; *d* Aussee, Austria, 13 Aug 1894). Dutch painter. He learnt the theory of painting from his father, the painter Casparis Haanen (1778–1849), but he was largely self-taught. He began his career in Utrecht, where he made drawings and etchings, as well as painting land- and townscapes. From there he moved to Hilversum, then Amsterdam. *Landscape with Cottages on the Heath* (Amsterdam, Rijksmus.) is typical of his work at this period. Van Haanen was a keen traveller, visiting much of Germany and southern Europe between 1834 and 1841. He stayed in Frankfurt am Main in 1834–5, and based himself in Vienna from 1836. Here he changed his name to Remy van Haan and became famous for his Austrian summer landscapes. In 1850 van Haanen travelled to Russia, visiting St Petersburg, where his winter scenes were successful. He exhibited in Amsterdam and The Hague between 1832 and 1863, occasionally showing work in Antwerp after this time.

BIBLIOGRAPHY

Scheen

WIEPKE F. LOOS

Haarlem. Capital city of the province of North Holland, the Netherlands.

1. History and urban development. 2. Art life and organization. 3. St Bavo.

1. HISTORY AND URBAN DEVELOPMENT. Haarlem came into being during the 9th century in the narrow strip of land in North Holland between the coastal dunes, the Haarlemmermeer and Lake IJ. In 1245 it was granted a charter by William II, Count of Holland, who resided there. The Count's residence later became the town hall. Haarlem was the second city in the county and the centre of Kennemerland. The provincial government is housed in the Welgelegen Palace (1788; *see* NETHERLANDS, THE, fig. 9), which once belonged to the banker Henry Hope.

Haarlem's prosperity was originally based on brewing, textiles, shipbuilding and the shipping trade. By *c.* 1430 it had as many as 100 breweries, largely distributing to towns and cities outside Haarlem. Around 1500 there were 25 churches and abbeys. The main church is dedicated to the city's patron saint, St Bavo, and was built between 1370 and 1538. Within the Begijnhof there were 54 dwellings as well as Haarlem's oldest ecclesiastical building (1348–98), which is now used by the Walloon Church. Haarlem also had numerous almshouses for old women, 17 of which survive, the earliest being the Bakenessekamers (1395). The city shared in the general economic depression

1. *View of the Stadhuis and the Grote Market, Haarlem*, engraving by Jan van de Velde after Pieter Saenredam, 163×248 mm, *c.* 1627–8 (Amsterdam, Rijksprentenkabinet)

that struck the country *c.* 1500. It was spared the devastations of the iconoclasts but suffered severe damage at the beginning of the Eighty Years' War, when it was besieged by Spanish troops (1572–3). After seven months, the city was forced to surrender, losing its treasures and privileges, and was finally partly destroyed by fire (1576). Haarlem's motto *Vicit vim virtus* ('Virtue conquers strength') dates from this time.

After the pacification of Ghent (1576) and the fall of Antwerp (1585), Haarlem began its period of greatest prosperity. Thousands of people from Flanders and Brabant came to the city to establish their traditional industries. Linen and yarn were bleached in Haarlem for the whole of Europe, and the town became famous for its damask. The population grew from 18,000 in 1572 to 40,000 in 1622. By 1578 the Reformed Church had become prevalent; Catholic buildings either disappeared or were put to other uses. Some of the paintings that belonged to former abbeys were sold abroad.

Architectural commissions were issued for building the St Jorisdoelen (1590), the Waag (Weighhouse; 1595) by Willem Thybault (*d* 1599) and Cornelis Cornelisz., the Vleeshal (Meat Hall; 1603) by Lieven de Key, the tower of the Nieuwe Kerk (1613) by Lieven de Key and the Nieuwe Kerk itself (remodelled from 1645 by Jacob van Campen), and the Oudemannenhuis (Old Men's Home; 1609) by Pieter van Campen (1568–1615) and Lieven de Key, a building now used as the Frans Halsmuseum. The Stadhuis was modernized and enlarged (1620–30) by Lieven de Key (see fig. 1). Other artists were asked to embellish these buildings with paintings, tapestries and stained-glass windows. In many Dutch and Frisian churches stained-glass windows with scenes of Haarlem's legendary conquest of Damietta [now Dumyât] in Egypt during the Fifth Crusade were installed at the expense of the city.

Towards the end of the 17th century Haarlem expanded considerably with new classical architecture, although by then the city's prosperity had already reached its peak. Haarlem became the residence of wealthy people from Amsterdam and elsewhere, who bought houses in the city or had their mansions built in the surrounding countryside.

BIBLIOGRAPHY

C. Ekama: *Catalogus van boeken, pamfletten enz. over de geschiedenis van Haarlem*, 3 vols (Haarlem, 1874–5)
F. Allan: *Geschiedenis en beschrijving van Haarlem van de vroegste tijden tot op onze dagen*, 4 vols (Haarlem, 1874–8)
J. A. G. van der Steur: *Oude gebouwen in Haarlem* (Haarlem, 1907)
C. W. Royaards, P. Jongens and H. E. Phaff: *Het stadhuis van Haarlem* (Haarlem, 1961)
G. Ratelband: *Bijdrage tot een bibliografie van Haarlem, 1876–1960* (Haarlem, 1968)
S. Koster: *Van schavot tot schouwburg: Vijfhonderd jaar toneel in Haarlem* (Haarlem, 1970)
E. Taverne: *In 't land van belofte: In de nieuwe stadt* (Maarssen, 1978)
J. J. Temminck: *Haarlem door de eeuwen heen* (Haarlem, 1982)
P. T. A. Sormani: *Bijdrage tot een bibliografie van Haarlem, 1961–1980* (Haarlem, 1983)

2. Art life and organization.

(i) Guilds and other institutions. The activities of both entrepreneurs and artisans in Haarlem were regulated by *c.* 60 guilds, which occasionally merged or split up. All artistic and semi-artistic professionals were assembled in the Guild of St Luke (founded ?1496), which, after the Reformation, served two purposes: to maintain a high

level of craftsmanship and to bar foreigners with their goods and products. Especially after the fall of Antwerp in 1585, many traders and artists moved to the northern Netherlands. The members of the Haarlem guild feared this competition and introduced strict regulations barring anyone who did not meet certain requirements or had not paid his annual membership dues. Sometimes the guild also supported old and sick members without income.

The Guild of St Luke, which was reorganized in 1631, regulated the activities of a wide variety of professions: painters, sculptors and carvers, gold- and silversmiths, glaziers, embroiderers, jar-makers, tinkers, potters, brass-founders, pewterers, plumbers, organ-makers, slaters, tin-platers, lantern-makers and second-hand dealers. Little unites the members of these different professions, except for the fact that they all worked with paint, brush, graver, heating iron, candle or copper. The Guild was divided into two categories, with painters, engravers, etchers, glass-writers, sculptors, architects and surveyors in the first group, gold- and silversmiths and all the others in the second. The administration of the Guild was dominated by painters (*see* §(ii) below), and this caused other groups, especially the gold- and silversmiths, to make frequent attempts to create guilds of their own. Petitions with this aim, however, were usually rejected by the town government, though in 1639 the metalworkers finally succeeded.

In the 18th century there was a growing interest in the arts and sciences in Haarlem, in particular among members of the Mennonite church. Numerous scientific and learned societies came into being, among them the Hollandsche Maatschappij der Wetenschappen (Dutch Society of Sciences) in 1777, the first scientific academy in the Netherlands. One year later the Teylers Stichting was established from the estate of PIETER TEYLER. The foundation was given responsibility for both Teyler's scientific objects and his art collection. Opened to the public from 1784, it is the oldest museum in the country. Teyler was also the founder of two scientific societies. The municipal art collections were gathered in 1860 in the Stedelijk Museum, housed in the Stadhuis; from there they were transferred in 1913 to the former Oudemannenhuis, which opened as the Frans Halsmuseum. The collection has been growing ever since; a new wing for modern art was added in 1981. In 1940 a workshop for the conservation of antique textiles was established in Haarlem, and in 1986 the city opened the Stichting Foto- en Grafisch Centrum (with 2,500,000 press photos). In 1989 the ABC (Architectuur-Bouwhistorisch Centrum) was opened, and in 1994 a regional historical museum, Historisch Museum Zuid-Kennemeland, was established.

BIBLIOGRAPHY

G. J. Hoogewerff: *De geschiedenis van de St Lucasgilden in Nederland* (Amsterdam, 1947)

E. Taverne: 'Salomon de Bray and the Reorganization of the Haarlem Guild of St Luke in 1631', *Simiolus*, vi (1972–3), pp. 58–61

Teyler, 1778–1978: Studies en bijdragen over Teylers Stichting naar aanleiding van het tweede eeuwfeest (Haarlem, 1978)

H. Miedema: *De archiefbescheiden van het St Lucasgilde te Haarlem, 1497–1798*, 2 vols (Alphen aan de Rijn, 1980)

J. J. Temminck: 'The Saint Luke's Guild and the Painters', *Haarlem: The Seventeenth Century* (exh. cat. by F. Fox Hofrichter and others, New Brunswick, NJ, Rutgers U., Zimmerli A. Mus., 1983), pp. 24–7

K. A. Citroen: *Haarlemse zilversmeden en hun merken* (Haarlem, 1988)

G. F. van de Ree: *Een geschiedenis van Haarlem, 1245–1945* (Hilversum, 1995)

J. J. TEMMINCK

(ii) Artistic community. The art life of Haarlem reached a peak in the 17th century, when local historians, such as Samuel Ampzing (*c.* 1591–1632) and Theodore Schrevel (1572–1649), extolled the virtues of the city and its contemporary artists. By reminding readers of Haarlem's artistic legacy from Geertgen tot Sint Jans, Dieric Bouts and Aelbert van Ouwater in the 15th century to Maarten van Heemskerck in the 16th, these writers placed the proliferation of art in their own time in the context of an eminent, historic tradition.

Haarlem artists have never been completely unified by style, medium or subject, but there seems always to have been a strong sense of community—never more so than in the 17th century, the period of the city's greatest prosperity. The dynamic interrelationship of artists, media, workshops and ideas fostered artistic growth and change. Haarlem artists were linked by their membership of the guild and of the local *rederijkerskamer* (rhetoricians' chamber) and by teacher–pupil and family relationships, which were often extensive due to intermarriage. Furthermore, they often lived near each other, either in the area of the Bakenesserkerk or near the Grote Markt: Hendrick Vroom, for instance, was a neighbour of Hendrick Goltzius, and Jan Steen, the son-in-law of Jan van Goyen, was a neighbour of Adriaen van Ostade. It is also known from inventories that Haarlem artists owned each other's work.

The city itself became an important patron, especially after the fire of 1576 and the political and economic devastation of that period. It commissioned the building and decoration of the new Stadhuis (1620–30), as well as portraits of the trustees of its charitable institutions and large group portraits of its militia companies, most notably the majestic portraits by Frans Hals (see fig. 2). It also became a familiar subject in painting, prints and drawings by numerous artists during the 17th century, easily recognizable by the silhouette of St Bavo's dominating the surrounding landscape (e.g. Rembrandt's etching of the *Goldweigher's Field*) and its famous bleaching fields (e.g. Jacob van Ruisdael's painting of the *Bleaching Fields near Harlem*, *c.* 1670; Montreal, Mus. F.A.). Since the 19th century it is Hals who has probably been the artist most closely associated with Haarlem, but the 18th century ranked Philips Wouwerman at the top; moreover, the 17th century had several other champions besides Hals to meet the artistic challenges of its great diversity.

History, genre, portrait, still-life, landscape, townscape and marine painting were the innovative and often revolutionary concerns of 17th-century Haarlem artists. Half-length views of lone musicians set against a blank wall and colourful scenes of outdoor parties (for illustration *see* HALS, (2)) thrived there; monochromatic breakfast-pieces of herrings, rolls and goblets were developed by Haarlem still-life painters Pieter Claesz and Willem Heda (for illustrations *see* CLAESZ, PIETER, and HEDA, WILLEM), while land and sea painting with an even, low horizon line engaged Hendrick Vroom, Jan Porcellis and Salomon van Ruysdael (for illustrations *see* VROOM, (1), fig. 1; PORCELLIS, JAN; and RUYSDAEL, SALOMON VAN, figs 1 and 2).

2. Frans Hals: *Banquet of the Officers of the St George Civic Guard Company, Haarlem*, oil on canvas, 1.75 × 3.24 m, 1616 (Haarlem, Frans Halsmuseum)

The development of naturalism in Haarlem at the turn of the 17th century and the artificial, contrived images of Haarlem Mannerism in the late 16th century appear to have sprouted from a common source: the so-called Haarlem Academy of the 1580s, established jointly by Hendrick Goltzius, Cornelis Cornelisz. van Haarlem and Karel van Mander, all of whom had arrived in or returned to Haarlem by 1583. The Haarlem Academy, based on a tradition of drawing 'from life' ('*naer het leven*'), provided the nucleus of a vital artistic community. This community attracted international attention, among others from Peter Paul Rubens, Bartholomeus Spranger, Adriaen Brouwer, Johann Liss and even René Descartes. Other artists to spend time in Haarlem included Jacques de Gheyn II and Gerrit Pietersz. from Amsterdam; Willem Buytewech from Rotterdam; Jan van Goven, Rembrandt and Jan Steen from Leiden; and Caesar and Allart van Everdingen from Alkmaar. Each exerted an influence on contemporary local art and, in turn, was influenced by it.

Goltzius, the focal-point of the late 16th-century artistic community, was renowned for his teaching and his wit; he was a prolific and virtuoso engraver and draughtsman, later a painter. Cornelisz. van Haarlem, considered at the turn of the 17th century to be the greatest living Dutch painter, was viewed as the successor to van Heemskerck; he was even called on to replace the destroyed central panel of van Heemskerck's Clothmakers' Altarpiece, to which he contributed the *Massacre of the Innocents* (The Hague, Mauritshuis, on loan to Haarlem, Frans Halsmus.). Cornelisz.'s involvement in the reorganization of the Guild of St Luke of Haarlem in 1631 reveals a continued participation in the art life of the city. The third member of the group, the poet, writer, painter and raconteur Karel van Mander, is best known for his *Schilder-boeck* of 1603–4, which included biographies of the most famous artists of his day. It is an unashamed celebration of the city of Haarlem and of his colleagues, Goltzius and Cornelisz. van Haarlem in particular.

Many Haarlem artists were members of De Wijngaartrancken (The Vine Branch), one of the city's three *rederijkerskamers*. The relationship between painting and poetry was promoted, among others, by van Mander, and the artist members of De Wijngaartrancken, such as Gerrit and Job Berckheyde, Richard Brakenburg, Salomon de Bray, Adriaen Brouwer, Dirck and Frans Hals, Esaias van de Velde, Jan Vermeer van Haarlem and Jan Wijnants, may have written poetry, performed in plays or painted scenery. Other artists, including Jan Steen, Judith Leyster and Jan Miense Molenaer, were influenced by them; many of their costumed figures and subjects are derived from the theatre.

The interrelationship of media was critical for the development of art in Haarlem. Painters, engravers, sculptors, architects, glass painters and silversmiths, even lantern-makers, were all members of the Guild of St Luke. One possible reason for the scope of this guild umbrella is that so many of Haarlem's painters were also printmakers and its architects and draughtsmen were also painters. The diversity and breadth of Haarlem art are reflected in the varied, seemingly unlikely combinations of guild leadership in the 17th century. Among the artists who served in the important positions of dean (*deken*) and commissioner (*vinder*) were: Nicolaes Berchem, Gerrit Berckheyde, Job Berckheyde, Jan van Bouckhorst (*c.* 1548–1631), Jan de Bray, Salomon de Bray, Cornelis Dusart, Floris van Dyck, Frans de Grebber (1573–1649), Frans Hals, Willem Heda, Jacob Matham, Pieter Molyn, Adriaen van Ostade, Frans Post, Hendrick Pot, Salomon van Ruysdael, Pieter Saenredam, Floris van Schooten, Jan van de Velde II, Cornelis Claesz. van Wieringen and Philips Wouwerman.

The development of Dutch drawing and printmaking as well as the interdependence of media reached new heights in Haarlem. For example the term 'engraving style' applied to Goltzius's *Federkunststücke* refers to drawings done in imitation of engravings (*see* GOLTZIUS, HENDRICK, figs 1 and 2), and his three-block chiaroscuro woodcuts (*see* GOLTZIUS, HENDRICK, fig. 3) imitate the effects of broad areas of tone in wash drawings; both are *trompes l'oeil* of technique. Reproductive printmaking as well as book publishing was a crucial part of Haarlem's reputation: Rubens went to Haarlem in 1613 to employ an engraver to record his paintings; he chose Goltzius's stepson Jacob Matham. And Matham, Jacques de Gheyn II, Goltzius, Jan Saenredam and Jan van de Velde II all engraved works after the paintings and drawings of their fellow Haarlemers. The variety, depth, quality and multiplicity of talent were Haarlem's artistic bounty, the fulfilment of its distinguished tradition.

BIBLIOGRAPHY

K. van Mander: *Schilder-boeck* (Haarlem, [1603–]1604)
S. Ampzing: *Beschryvinge ende lof der stad Haerlem in Holland* (Haarlem, 1628)
T. Schrevel: *Harlemum* (Haarlem, 1647)
A. van der Willigen: *Geschiedkundige aanteekeningen over Haarlemsche Schilders* (Haarlem, 1866); Fr. trans. as *Les Artistes de Harlem* (The Hague, 1870)
F. Allen: *Geschiedenis en beschrijving van Haarlem*, 4 vols (Haarlem, 1874–88)
C. J. Gonnet: 'Sint Lucas Gilde te Haarlem in 1631', *Obreen's Arch. Ned. Kstgesch.*, i (1877–8), pp. 237–8
A. .J. Rieyl: *Das holländische Gruppenportret*, 2 vols (Vienna, 1931)
A. Heppner: 'The Popular Theatre of the Rederijkers in the Work of Jan Steen and his Contemporaries', *J. Warb. & Court. Inst.*, iii (1940), pp. 22–48
J. E. Snyders: 'The Early Haarlem School of Painting', *A. Bull.*, xlii (1960), pp. 39–55; 113–32
P. J. J. van Thiel: 'Frans Hals' portret van de Leidse rederijkersnar *Pieter Cornelisz. van der Morsch, alias Piero (1543–1628)*', *Oud-Holland*, lxxvi (1961), pp. 153–71
Seventeenth-century Painters of Haarlem (exh. cat., Allentown, PA, A. Mus., 1965)
J. J. Temminck: *Haarlem vroeger en nu* (Bassum, 1971)
Hendrick Goltzius and the Printmakers of Haarlem (exh. cat. by F. den Broeder, Storrs, U. CT, Benton Mus. A., 1972)
H. Miedema: 'Karel van Mander's *Grondt der edel vry schilderconst* ('Foundations of the Noble and Free Art of Painting')', *J. Hist. Ideas*, xxxiv (1973), pp. 653–68
S. J. Gudlaugsson: *The Comedians in the Work of Jan Steen and his Contemporaries* (Soest, 1975)
N. B. A. Vroom: *A Modest Message as Intimated by the Painters of the 'Monochrome Banketje'* (Schiedam, 1980)
Haarlem: The Seventeenth Century (exh. cat. by F. Fox Hofrichter and others, New Brunswick, NJ, Rutgers U., Zimmerli Art Mus., 1983)
Masters of Seventeenth-century Dutch Genre Painting (exh. cat., ed. P. C. Sutton; Philadelphia, PA, Mus. A.; W. Berlin, Gemäldegal.; London, RA; 1984)
Dutch Landscape: The Early Years, Haarlem and Amsterdam, 1590–1650 (exh. cat. by C. Brown, London, N.G., 1986)
Masters of 17th-century Dutch Landscape Painting (exh. cat., ed. P. C. Sutton; Amsterdam, Rijksmus.; Boston, MA, Mus. F.A.; Philadelphia, PA, Mus. A.; 1987–8)
Dawn of the Golden Age: Northern Netherlandish Art, 1580–1620 (exh. cat., ed. G. Luijten and others; Amsterdam, Rijksmus.; 1993–4)

FRIMA FOX HOFRICHTER

3. ST BAVO. The Late Gothic church of St Bavo, also known as the Grote Kerk, was briefly a cathedral between 1561 and 1578, before becoming a Protestant church. It is a cruciform basilica, measuring 108.44×31.37 m internally. The nave is *c.* 41 m high. The lower walls are brick; the buttresses, the west façade and the clerestory are all faced with stone, mainly from Gobertange, Lede and Bentheim. There is a wooden spire faced with lead over the crossing.

Stylistically the church is one of the group of Late Gothic churches from the provinces of Holland influenced by the architecture of Brabant, including the Oude Kerk, Amsterdam (*see* AMSTERDAM, §V, 1), and the Grote Kerk (St Jacobskerk) in The Hague (*see* THE HAGUE, §V, 1). These churches are characterized by their basilical construction, a polygonal choir with a gallery but without radiating chapels, a narrow transept, much brickwork, flat buttresses and the absence of a west tower. They have wooden vaulting, broad arcades with cabbage-like foliage on the capitals, and a second storey with (in St Bavo) a pseudo-triforium. St Bavo has a massive, rather squat character, which comes from the deep, blank walls between the pseudo-triforium and the windows and from the thick, squat columns (diam. 1.85 m). In the exceptionally deep choir (54 m) the arcades have continuous mouldings, a feature unique in north Netherlandish architecture.

The existing building is not the first on the site. An earlier parish church, which had presumably been founded by the Counts of Holland, was already dedicated to St Bavo in 1313. There was a fire in 1328 and the present choir was added to this older church from 1370 to 1390. The architect was probably Engelbrecht van Nijvel (*fl* 1392–1422). The lower parts of the transept were added between 1445 and 1455, then the west façade (1460–62) and the nave (aisles, 1456–70; clerestory, 1470–78). The old church was destroyed in 1470. The architects involved in the new building were: Evert Spoorwater from Antwerp, until his death in 1474–5; then presumably Cornelis de Wael from Utrecht (*d* 1505); and Anthonis Keldermans I (*see* KELDERMANS, (3)) in 1502–7. After the addition of the aisle vaults (1481–5) and the completion of the transept (1481–90), a star vault was built in the crossing in 1500. The stone crossing tower added in 1502 seems to have been too heavy, and it was removed in 1514–15 to be replaced by the present spire of 1519–20. In 1529 a large stained-glass window was installed in the west front (bricked up 1737). The church was completed in 1529–38 with wooden star vaults over choir and nave.

In 1593 the baptistery was modernized by Lieven de Key. Salomon de Bray (*see* BRAY, DE, (1)) designed the vestry (added in 1659). During restorations carried out between 1875 and 1920 a stone vault in the transept (1891–2) and a parapet round the roof were added. The restoration of 1981–5 revealed fragments of the original wall paintings.

BIBLIOGRAPHY

De Bavo te boek: Bij het gereedkomen van de restauatie van de Grote of St-Bavo kerk te Haarlem [The Bavo recorded: on the occasion of the completion of the restoration of the Grote Kerk (St Bavo) in Haarlem] (exh. cat., ed. J. N. de Boer and others; Haarlem, Frans Halsmus., 1985)
C. F. Janssen: *De grote- of St Bavokerk te Haarlem: De geschiedenis van haar bouw en inrichting tot de Reformatie* [The Great or St Bavokerk in Haarlem: the history of its building and interior decoration up to the Reformation] (Haarlem, 1985)

INGEBORG WORM

Haarlem, Cornelis Cornelisz. van. *See* CORNELISZ. VAN HAARLEM, CORNELIS.

Haas, Georg (*b* ?Flensburg, *c.* 1523; *d* Vienna, 1596–1603). German joiner and etcher, active in Austria. In 1571 he was commissioned to make the doors and magnificent inlaid ceiling of the Landhaus, Vienna. The ceiling in the Verordnetenstube, which was completed in 1572, demonstrates great artistic ability with its combination of delicate inlay, carving and applied decoration. The heraldic programme of the ceiling was very rich, featuring the coats of arms of Old Austria, New Austria, the imperial arms and those of Bohemia and Hungary; the armorials of the other ten hereditary states formed a border. According to the accounts of the city treasurer's office, he received 40 florins for his work on the Ehrenpforte, which was constructed by the Viennese city council on the occasion of the entry of Rudolf II into Vienna. In 1583 *Künstlicher und zierlicher Newer vor nie gesehener: Fünfftzig perspectifischer Stück . . . allen Malern Tischlern und denen sich des Bawens gebrauchen sehr nützlich und dienstlich mit sonderem Fleiss gestelt und in Kupffer gesetzt durch Georgen Hasen Hoff Tischler und Burger in Wienn*—his renowned series of etchings, with 48 designs for ceilings—was published in Vienna. A wooden coffered ceiling (*c.* 1600), originally installed in Burg Rapottenstein, lower Austria, now in the Franzensburg at Laxenburg near Vienna, has been attributed to Haas (*see* AUSTRIA, §V, 1(i)).

For an illustration of Haas's work *see* AUSTRIA, fig. 24.

BIBLIOGRAPHY

Thieme–Becker

E. Schaffran: 'Georg Haas, Hoftischler in Wien und sein Masterbuch', *Unsere Heimat*, vii (Vienna, 1934)

GABRIELE RAMSAUER

Habana, La. *See* HAVANA.

Haberle, John (*b* New Haven, CT, 1856; *d* New Haven, 1 Feb 1933). American painter and lithographer. The son of German immigrants, he displayed an early talent for drawing. At 14 he was apprenticed to a lithographer in New Haven and subsequently earned his living in that field. His only formal training was at the New York National Academy of Design in 1884. Haberle spent most of his life in New Haven, where he was a founder of the New Haven Sketch Club (1884), gave art lessons and was active in art circles until about 1910. In the 1880s he also worked for the Peabody Museum at Yale University, drawing illustrations for its publications.

Haberle began to practise *trompe l'oeil* painting, a popular art form in America after the Civil War. Although often employing the same subject-matter as William Michael Harnett and John F. Peto, Haberle was unique in the precision of his *trompe l'oeil* paintings and in their subtle irony and wit. His humour appears in the *Bachelor's Drawer* (1890–94; New York, Met.), which contains a conglomeration of brightly coloured playing cards, ticket stubs, photographs, letters, a cigar box top, currency and newspaper clippings, all representing aspects of a bachelor's life. They are set against the front of a bureau drawer, defying gravity, and are rendered to exact scale in realistic colours.

The *Bachelor's Drawer* provoked one Chicago art critic to accuse Haberle of deception—of gluing objects to the canvas instead of painting them. The technical expertise that made such illusion possible was perhaps due to Haberle's early career as an engraver; the surface of his work is smooth, without a trace of brushwork. His *Japanese Corner* (1898; Springfield, MA, Mus. F.A.) is one of the largest *trompe l'oeil* paintings in American art (0.91×1.83 m). With dazzling verisimilitude it presents a collection of Japanese furniture, scrolls and bibelots, which were popular at the time. Haberle signed the work with an envelope stuck into the edge of the frame. Written over the typed address is 'Do Not Touch!'

Despite their apparent detachment, Haberle's paintings are highly personal, replete with subtle meanings and visual puns. They are also autobiographical, including a painted tintype photograph as a signature, letters addressed to him and readable newspaper clippings reporting on his artistic importance (e.g. *Can You Break a Five?*, *c.* 1888; Fort Worth, TX, Amon Carter Mus.).

Haberle's work attracted considerable attention in the 1880s and 1890s and was exhibited widely in America. He fetched high prices from businessmen and saloon-keepers but was ignored by the artistic establishment who thought his subject-matter too commonplace. Due to failing eyesight, Haberle abandoned his career as a *trompe l'oeil* painter about 1900 and turned to undistinguished impressionistic still-lifes of flowers and animals, clay models and plaster reliefs. He died in obscurity. His work was rediscovered by A. Frankenstein in the 1950s, but in the late 20th century only about half of his known production of about 50 *trompe l'oeil* paintings had been traced; he also left quantities of small pencil sketches, some in the *trompe l'oeil* manner.

BIBLIOGRAPHY

A. Frankenstein: *After the Hunt: William Michael Harnett and other American Still-life Painters, 1870–1900* (Berkeley, 1953, rev. 2/1969)

Haberle Retrospective Exhibition (exh. cat., foreword by A. Frankenstein; New Britain, CT, Mus. Amer. A., 1962)

John Haberle: Master of Illusion (exh. cat. by G. G. Sill, Springfield, MA, Mus. F.A., 1985)

GERTRUDE GRACE SILL

Habermann, Franz Xaver (*b* Habelschwerdt, Silesia [now Bystryca Kłodzka, nr Wrocław, Poland], 1721; *d* Augsburg, 1796). German draughtsman, engraver and sculptor. After an apprenticeship as a sculptor and a journey to Italy in 1746, he obtained rights of citizenship and the right to practise as a sculptor in Augsburg by marrying Maria Catharina Wörle, widow of the miniature painter. He was president of the guild of sculptors and painters from 1756–7 and was a drawing tutor at the Kunstakademie in Augsburg from 1781 until his death. Although he generally signed himself *statuarius*, his only known surviving sculptural work (until its destruction in the Second World War) was the front of the organ by the instrument maker Johann Andreas Stein in the Barfüsserkirche in Augsburg (1755–7; destr. 1944). The dearth of commissions for sculptors in Augsburg in the mid-18th century led him to turn to ornamental engraving. The *c.* 600 surviving engravings by him cover a wide range of ornamental subject-matter. Their success probably depended primarily, despite Habermann's effervescent imagination, on their practical applicability by any artistic craftsman of the period. The engravings were published, mostly in series of four sheets, by the Augsburg publishers Martin Engelbrecht (*c.* 1684–1756) and Johann Georg

Hertel (*c.* 1700/01–76), and later by Habermann himself. According to contemporary accounts, Habermann also completed numerous designs for goldsmiths; of these, only his design for a table centrepiece has survived (Augsburg, Städt. Kstsammlungen, G. 24912). In the 1770s and 1780s he also engraved prints for peepshow boxes.

Habermann made a decisive contribution to disseminating contemporary style through the quality, quantity and variety of his ornamental designs. Objects after his engravings, such as furniture inlays, wall coverings, porcelain and ceramics, have been found all over Europe. His oeuvre reflected the stylistic development of the whole of Rococo as far as early classicism.

BIBLIOGRAPHY

Katalog der Ornamentstichsammlung der staatlichen Kunstbibliothek Berlin (Berlin and Leipzig, 1939)

E. Krull: *Franz Xaver Habermann: Ein Augsburger Ornamentist des Rokoko* (Augsburg, 1977)

Meisterzeichnungen des deutschen Barock (exh. cat. by R. Biedermann, Augsburg, Städt. Kstsammlungen, 1987), pp. 284–7

EBBA KRULL

Habert, Nicolas (*b* Paris, *c.* 1650; *d* Paris, *c.* 1715). French engraver, draughtsman and print publisher. The first prints he executed were vignettes for *L'Esope du temps* by M. L. S. Desmay, published in 1677. His last piece was a portrait of *Thomas (Old) Parr*, engraved in 1715. Habert was an engraver of average talent who produced almost exclusively portraits, mostly after painters, such as Philippe de Champaigne, Charles Le Brun, Nicolas de Largillierre, Pierre Mignard and Hyacinthe Rigaud; he did, however, occasionally execute portraits from his own drawings from life, such as *Elisabeth-Charlotte d'Orléans, Duchesse de Guise* (1678; see Weigert, no. 109). In all, he engraved nearly 200 pieces. His wife, Madeleine Masson (*c.* 1646–1713), was herself an engraver; she was the sister or some other relation of Antoine Masson, whom Habert greatly admired, and who published some of his portraits. Habert also engaged in publishing, but he seems to have published mainly his own works.

BIBLIOGRAPHY

Thieme–Becker

R.-A. Weigert: *Inventaire du fonds français: Graveurs du dix-septième siècle*, Paris, Bib. N., Cab. Est. cat., v (Paris, 1968), pp. 152–97

Y. Bruand, M. Hébert and Y. Sjöberg: *Inventaire du fonds français: Graveurs du dix-huitième siècle*, Paris, Bib. N., Cab. Est. cat., xi (Paris, 1970), pp. 189–93

MAXIME PRÉAUD

Habraken, Nicolaas (John) (*b* Bandung, West Java, 29 Oct 1928). Dutch architect and theorist. He came to the Netherlands in 1946 and studied architecture at the Technische Universiteit, Delft (1948–55). After two years in the Netherlands Air Force he returned to the university as an instructor (1958–60), and at the same time worked in the office of Johannes Berghoef. He practised independently (1960–62) and as a job captain for the office of Lucas & Niemeyer in Voorburg (1962–5). In 1961 he published *De dragers en de mensen.* In 1964 architects from ten offices in the Netherlands formed the Stichting Architecten Research ('Architecture Research Foundation'; SAR); Habraken was their first director. In 1967 the foundation relocated in Eindhoven, as did Habraken. There he worked as chairman (1967–70) and as professor (1967–75) of the new architecture department at the Technische Universiteit. From 1975 he was professor and head of department in the architecture department at the Massachusetts Institute of Technology, Cambridge, MA, although he retained close ties with SAR. He was the architect of a few individual buildings but most of his career was devoted to the development and promotion of the supports theory.

In reaction to the anonymous effects of mass housing, which followed World War II, architects, including members of TEAM TEN, sought means for occupants to identify and even participate in the building process, although still retaining the architect's traditional control over it. Habraken went one step further and worked out in detail an idea already implicit in traditional village construction, loft dwellings and do-it-yourself modification of suburban houses, and which Le Corbusier had presented in a high-density form in his *Plan Obus* drawings of 1932 for Algiers. Habraken began from the premise that a home cannot be provided by means of design alone but only by physical interaction between person and material, that is through direct intervention by the occupant. In order to guarantee this participation, the buildings were to be separated into two elements, one to be realized by the community and one by individuals. The first element is the *drager* (support), a construction in which a number of dwellings can be placed together, but in which each can be individually and independently constructed, altered or demolished. The other element is the *dragerswoning* (dwelling within the support), made of standard parts from which any number of variations may be formed according to the requirements and taste of the occupants. The support is built on the site as a complete unit, by either conventional or industrialized methods; it is a fixed infrastructure with utility connections for each dwelling, financed and governed, like a street, by public authorities. The individual dwelling is owned, financed and built by the occupants to their own standards using the appropriate mix of their own and paid labour.

Several advantages are promised by this system. The first is avoidance of the uniformity that characterized mass housing. The second is a faster and more flexible response by component manufacturers answering directly to consumers. The third is a better demarcation of the responsibilities of urban planner and architect; the former can concentrate on the best urban design arrangements for the support structures, and the latter on the technical execution of the support structures and, as the tenants' adviser, of the individual dwellings.

The basic premise of the supports theory, that a set of dwellings will not be 'designed' but rather 'evolved', entailed a deliberate avoidance of statements or drawn images establishing in advance the finished appearance of the buildings. While this made promoting and publicizing the supports theory more difficult, it had a slow growth and some success in the Netherlands. From 1971 to 1982 a neighbourhood of 5600 dwellings near Utrecht was built by 9 housing associations in consultation with SAR and the eventual occupants. Its external forms are indistinguishable from any other well-designed housing complex, illustrating one of the dilemmas confronting the theory: as density increases, fire and safety considerations impose more restrictions on tenants' freedom to personalize their units. The range of variation in interior layouts is considerable, however, and the projects are generally considered successful in social terms. Through Habraken's dedicated efforts, the supports theory continued to be developed and tested; it was widely examined by students and architects after Habraken and continued to yield results.

WRITINGS

De dragers en de mensen (Amsterdam, 1961); Eng. trans. as *Supports: An Alternative to Mass Housing* (London and New York, 1972)
3 R's for Housing (Amsterdam, 1970)
'You Can't Design the Ordinary', *Archit. Des.*, no. 4 (April 1971), pp. 230–31
'Involving People in the Housing Process', *J. RIBA*, 11 (1972)
with others: *Variations: The Systematic Design of Supports* (Alphen, 1974, Cambridge, MA, 1976)
General Principles about the Way the Built Environment Exists (Eindhoven, 1978)
The Appearance of Form (Cambridge, MA, 1985)

BIBLIOGRAPHY

Contemp. Architects
E. Dluhosch: 'Involving People in the Housing Process: The Story of Habraken's Supports and Detachables', *Industrialization Forum*, 1 (1976)
——: *John Habraken* (Amsterdam, 1979)
C. R. Hatch, ed.: *The Scope of Social Architecture* (Newark, 1988), pp. 22–93

MARLOES KLEIJN

Habsburg [Habspurg, Hapsburg], House of. Dynasty of Austrian and Spanish rulers, patrons and collectors. The Austrian branch of the family (*see* §I) ruled Austria from 1278 to 1918 and were Holy Roman Emperors from 1452 to 1806. The Spanish branch (*see* §II) was established in 1516, when the future Holy Roman Emperor Charles V succeeded to the Spanish throne as Charles I of Spain, and members of the Habsburg dynasty occupied the Spanish throne until 1700.

BIBLIOGRAPHY

R. Kann: *A History of the Habsburg Empire* (Berkeley, CA, 1977)
B. Hamann, ed.: *Die Habsburger: Ein biographisches Lexicon* (Vienna, 1988)

□

I. Austrian branch. II. Spanish branch.

I. Austrian branch (see figs 1 and 2).

Guntram the Rich (*b c.* 950; *fl* 973) founded the dynasty in the mid-10th century, but his great-grandson, Otto II, was the first to call himself Count of Habsburg, after the family castle the Habsburg or Habichtsburg [Eng. Hawk's Castle] in Aargau. Austria was the family's power base from 1276, and they entered national politics with the election of Rudolf I, Duke of Austria (1218–91; *reg* 1276–82), as King of Germany (*reg* 1273–91). (2) Frederick III was the founder of the dynasty's lasting power, and through the marriage alliances contracted by his son (3) Maximilian I with Spain (*see* §II below) and Bohemia-Hungary (*see* (6) below), the Habsburgs under (5) Charles V, who founded the Spanish Habsburg dynasty as Charles I of Spain, acquired immense world power and became active patrons of the arts. After Charles's abdication in 1556, the territories were divided between the two branches of the family. (6) Ferdinand I received the German and eastern Habsburg lands and continued the active patronage of his ancestors. Among the most notable of the Habsburg collectors were (9) Ferdinand, Archduke of Austria, whose collection at Schloss Ambras drew visitors from all over Europe, and (10) Rudolf II, who accumulated one of the greatest art collections ever assembled, containing over 2000 paintings, among them many masterpieces, as well as sculpture and decorative arts. He also drew to his court in Prague a variety of artists from all over Europe. Subsequent generations of collectors, connoisseurs and patrons added to the Habsburg collection. The male Austrian Habsburg line died out in 1740 with (20) Charles VI, but the marriage of his daughter (21) Maria-Theresa to Francis, Duke of Lorraine (1708–65), later Holy Roman Emperor (*reg* 1745–65), secured the continuation of the dynasty in creating the imperial line of HABSBURG-LORRAINE.

See also AUSTRIA, §§XII to XIV.

BIBLIOGRAPHY

A. Wandruska: *Die Habsburgermonarchie, 1848–1918* (Vienna, 1973)
K. Vocelka: *Habsburgische Hochzeiten, 1550–1600* (Vienna, Cologne and Graz, 1976)
A. Wandruska: *Das Haus Habsburg: Die Geschichte einer europäischen Dynastie* (Vienna, 1978)
E. Scheicher: *Die Kunst- und Wunderkammer der Habsburger* (Vienna and Munich, 1979)
T. DaCosta Kaufman: *L'Ecole de Prague; La Peinture à la cour de Rodolphe II* (Paris, 1985), rev. as *The School of Prague: Painting at the Court of Rudolf II* (Chicago and London, 1988)
——: *Art and Architecture in Central Europe, 1550–1620: An Annotated Bibliography* (Boston, MA, 1988)
B. Hamann, ed.: *Die Habsburger: Ein biographisches Lexikon* (Vienna, 1988)
A. Sked: *The Decline and Fall of the Habsburg Empire, 1815–1918* (London and New York, 1989)

HANS J. VAN MIEGROET

(1) Rudolf IV [Rudolf the Founder], Duke of Austria (*b* Vienna, 1 Nov 1339; *reg* 1358–65; *d* Milan, 27 July 1365). Despite poor health he proved, in his short rule, a far-sighted administrator of the Habsburg territories and acquired the Tyrol (1363–4). He founded the University of Vienna (1365) and during his reign Vienna developed into the cultural and intellectual centre of the Habsburg empire. Eager to enhance his personal status and the position of his family, he forged documents and invented fictitious titles and privileges; likewise most of his artistic enterprises aimed at exalting the House of Habsburg. Thus his two equestrian seals (1360, 1362) are the finest and largest surviving from the 14th century, and his anonymous, and possibly posthumous, portrait (*c.* 1365; Vienna, Dom- & Diözmus.) is among the earliest examples of the independent realistic portrait in medieval art.

The Duke's most notable achievements, however, were the new nave and the south tower of the Stephanskirche (from 1469 Stephansdom), Vienna, planned and partly constructed during his reign (*see* VIENNA, §V, 1(i) and fig. 14). By preserving the entire west front of the older church (*c.* 1240–63) and integrating it within the new structure, he showed his sensibility to the symbolic purport of ancient styles, whereas the new statuary and his tomb (originally placed near the main altar) demonstrate the most progressive trends in contemporary sculpture (*see* VIENNA, §III, 1 and fig. 7 and §V, 1(ii)). There are indications that the sculptors came not only from Austria but also from southern Germany, northern France and possibly even England. Highlights in their work are the statues (originals, Vienna, Hist. Mus.) from the west front and the lower storeys of the south tower, representing the

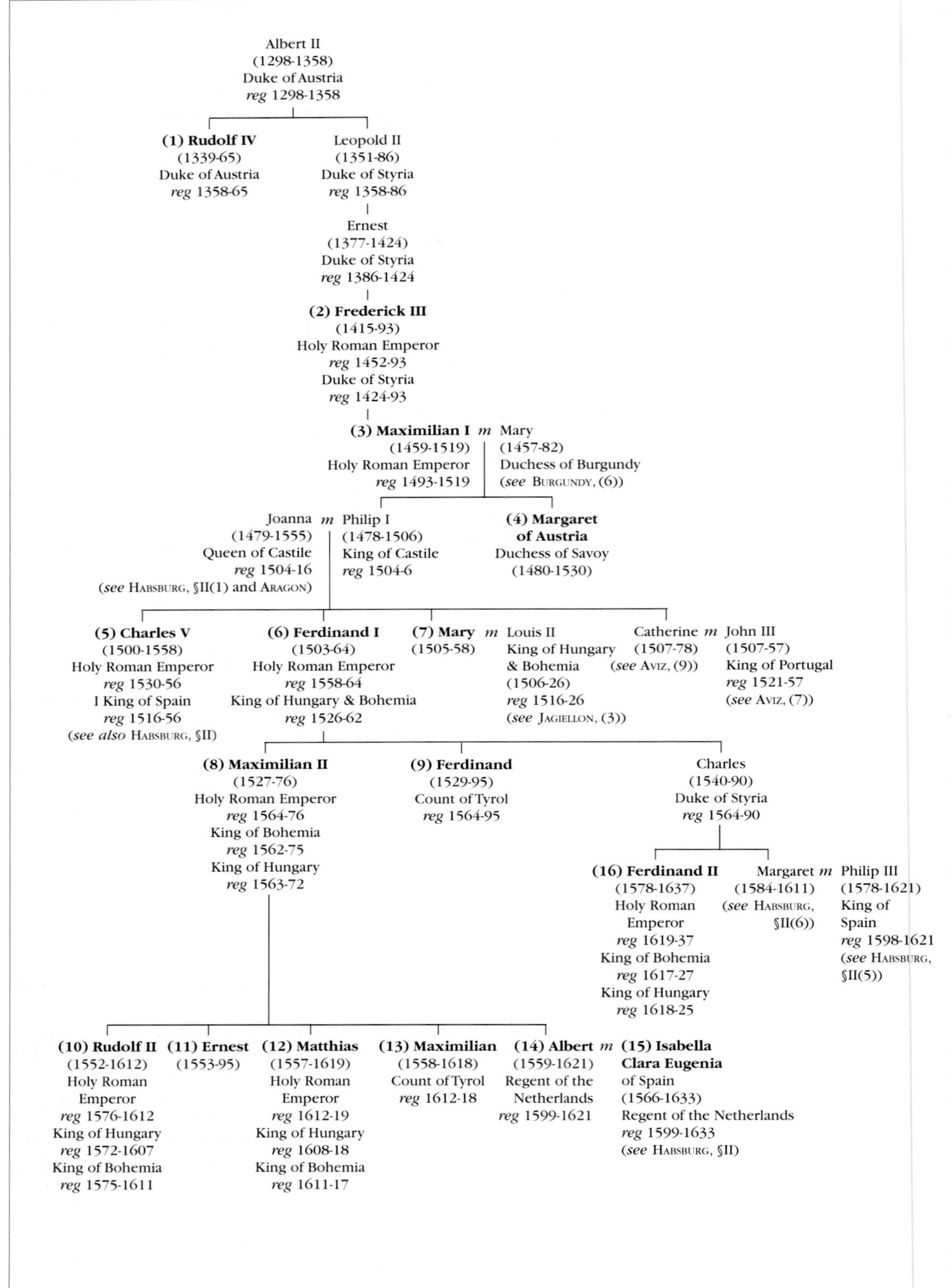

1. Family tree of the Austrian branch of the Habsburg dynasty

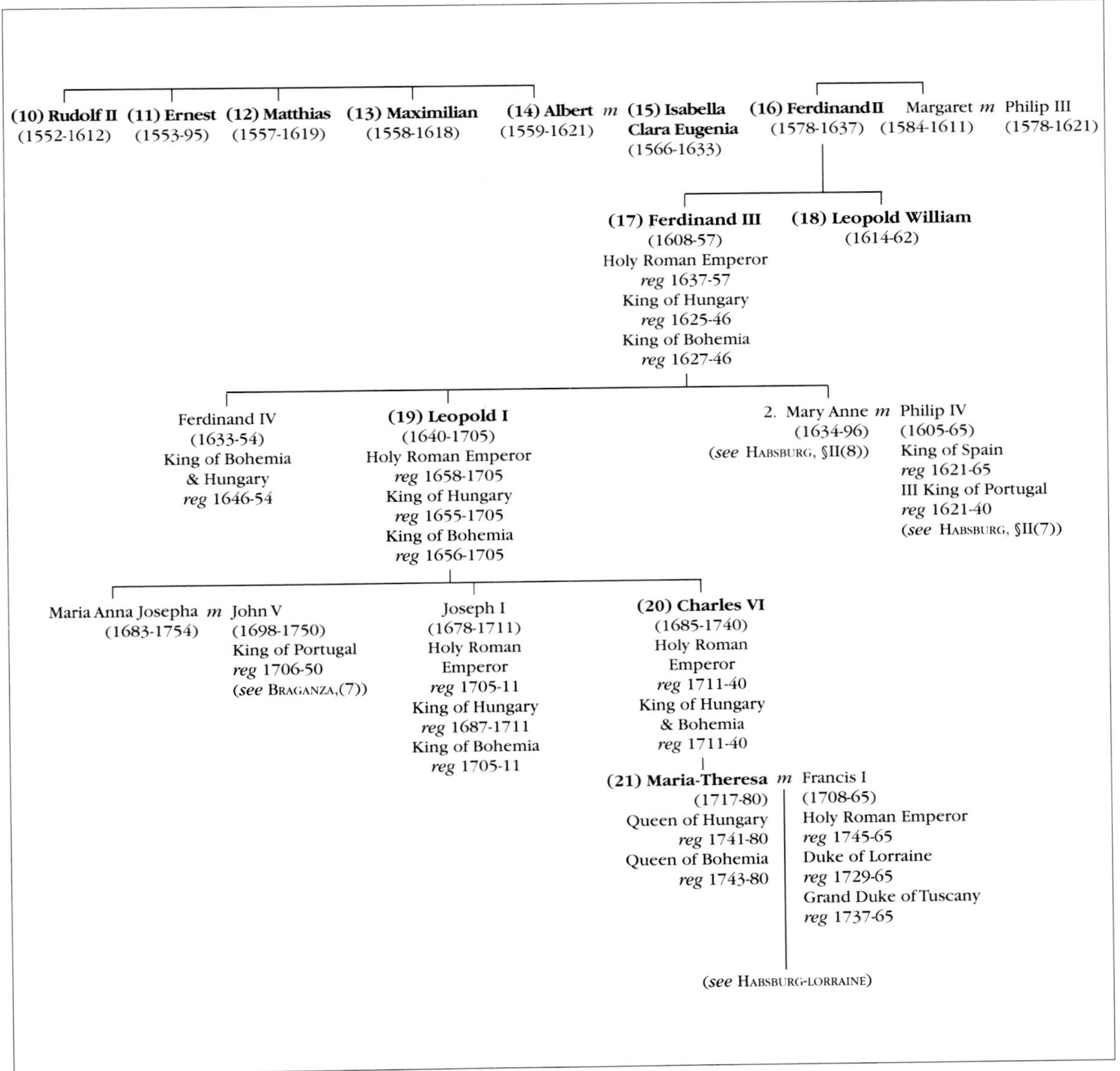

2. Continuation of the family tree of the Austrian branch of the Habsburg dynasty

Duke, his wife, Catherine of Bohemia (1342–95), and their respective parents and the sculptural decoration of the two lateral entrances of the nave, in particular the tympanum relief of the southern door. The only surviving item of goldsmith's work made for Rudolf is the *Melk Cross* (1363), produced as a reliquary of the True Cross, which he donated to Melk Abbey. His insignia are lost, as are the reliquary of the Holy Lance (destr. 1810) and the canopied tomb of St Coloman (destr. early 18th century; both ex-Melk Abbey).

BIBLIOGRAPHY

E. K. Winter: *Rudolf IV. von Österreich*, 2 vols (Vienna, 1934–6)

H. Fillitz: 'Das Kunstgewerbe', *Die Gotik in Niederösterreich*, ed. F. Dworschak and H. Kühnel (Vienna, 1963), pp. 194–213 [Melk reliquary of the True Cross]

U. Begrich: *Die fürstliche 'Majestät' Herzog Rudolfs IV. von Österreich* (Vienna, 1965) [insignia]

A. Kosegarten: 'Zur Plastik der Fürstenportale am Wiener Stephansdom', *Wiener Jb. Kstgesch.*, xx (1965), pp. 74–96

G. Schmidt: 'Johann von Troppau und die vorromanische Buchmalerei', *Festschrift K. H. Usener* (Marburg, 1967), pp. 275–92

A. Lhotsky: *Aufsätze und Vorträge*, i (Vienna, 1970), pp. 265–82; ii (Vienna, 1971), pp. 106–18; v (Vienna, 1976), pp. 127–42 [character and patronage]

G. Schmidt: 'Die Wiener Herzogswerkstatt und die Kunst Nordwesteuropas', *Wiener Jb. Kstgesch.*, xxx/xxxi (1977/8), pp. 179–206

R. Feuchtmüller: *Der Wiener Stephansdom* (Vienna, 1978), pp. 109–42 [good plates]

H. Fillitz: 'Zum Porträt Herzog Rudolfs IV. von Österreich', *Festschrift M. Stettler* (Berne, 1983), pp. 99–103

GERHARD SCHMIDT

(2) Frederick III [Frederick the Pacific], Holy Roman Emperor [Duke of Styria] (*b* Innsbruck, 21 Sept 1415; *reg* Styria 1440–93, Holy Roman Emperor 1452–93; *d* Linz, 19 Aug 1493). Great-nephew of (1) Rudolph IV. He became Duke of Styria on the death of his father, Duke Ernest, in 1424. The aggrandisement of the House of Habsburg influenced his interests as a builder and collector as they had those of Rudolf IV, whom he closely imitated. He had the letters AEIOU (generally interpreted as 'Austriae est imperare orbi universo') inscribed on the buildings he had constructed or renovated, on his silver dishes (e.g. goblet made in Burgundy, late 15th century; Vienna, Ksthist. Mus.) and on other precious objects. His sword (1440–52; Vienna, Ksthist. Mus.) is a rare surviving example of a richly decorated 15th-century edged weapon, and his horse armour (1477; Vienna, Ksthist. Mus.) is the first surviving example of etching on armour. In Graz he built the Burg (from 1438) beneath the old castle (*see* GRAZ) and during his reign initiated several important building projects in his favourite place of residence, WIENER NEUSTADT. PETER VON PUSICA converted the basilican nave of the Neukloster into a hall church in 1444 and made alterations (1450–75) to St Peter an der Sperr. He was also commissioned to build the Georgskapelle (1449–60) in the western tract of the castle at Wiener Neustadt. The outside of its middle window was framed by coats of arms, some of them imaginary; his statue is among them, surrounded by 14 coats of arms from the Habsburg lands. In Vienna he sponsored the building (begun *c.* 1450; not completed) of the north tower (Adlerturm) of the Stephanskirche (from 1469 Stephansdom; *see* VIENNA, §V, 1(i)) and commissioned the rebuilding of the Burgkapelle (1447–9) (*see* VIENNA, §V, 5(i)) in the Hofburg.

He was crowned Holy Roman Emperor in 1452, having been elected King of Germany in 1440. War with Hungary caused him, *c.* 1480, to equip his castles (including Wiener Neustadt, Linz and Krems) with modern fortifications. He spent the last years of his life in Linz, where he substantially decorated the castle. The most important work that he commissioned was his marble tomb begun (*c.* 1467) by NICOLAUS GERHAERT but finished only in 1513 by Michael Tichter, in the south choir in the Stephanskirche, Vienna (*see* VIENNA, §V, 1(ii)).

BIBLIOGRAPHY

A. Lhotsky: *Aufsätze und Vorträge*, ii (Vienna, 1971), pp. 239–63

R. Wagner-Rieger: 'Die Bautätigkeit Kaiser Friedrichs III.', *Wien. Jb. Kstgesch.*, xxv (1972), pp. 128–53

E. Hertlein: 'Das Grabmonument Kaiser Friedrichs III. (1415–1493) als habsburgisches Denkmal', *Pantheon*, xxxv (1977), pp. 294–305

E. Steingräber: 'Kunsthandwerk', *Spätmittelalter und beginnende Neuzeit*, ed. J. Bialostoki and others, Propyläen-Kstgesch., vii (Berlin, 1984), pp. 311–69

ULRICH KUDER

(3) Maximilian I, Holy Roman Emperor (*b* Wiener Neustadt, 22 March 1459; *reg* 1493–1519; *d* Wels, 12 Jan 1519). Son of (2) Frederick III. Through his marriage and those of his children and grandchildren, he contributed substantially to the territorial aggrandisement of the Habsburgs in the Netherlands, Spain and eastern Europe. His patronage tended largely to the glorification of the dynasty, notably in portraiture and in the large statues of his family and ancestors he commissioned for his tomb in Innsbruck. His autobiographical literary works reflect his medieval courtly ideals and were illustrated by major contemporary artists. He was also probably the greatest patron of armourers in the late 15th century (*see* ARMS AND ARMOUR, §II, 3).

1. Life and reign. 2. Patronage.

1. LIFE AND REIGN. In 1477 he married Mary, Duchess of Burgundy, daughter of Charles the Bold, from whom she inherited Burgundy and the Netherlands. After Mary's untimely death in 1482 Maximilian defended the Burgundian inheritance against French claims and the rebellious Netherlanders. From 1493 he ruled the Habsburg dominions and began constitutional and administrative reforms. His marriage (1494) to Bianca Maria Sforza (1472–1510) strengthened his position in Italy politically and financially. To counter French expansion threats, he joined the League of Venice and arranged Spanish marriages for his two children by Mary: Philip the Fair (1478–1506) to Joanna, Queen of Castile (*see* §II(1) below), and Margaret of Austria (*see* (4) below). With limited support from the German princes, changing European alliances and constant wars that he could ill afford, he pursued his dream of 'universal' monarchy. In 1515 he negotiated the betrothal of two of his grandchildren with members of the HOUSE OF JAGIELLON of Hungary and Bohemia to regain influence in eastern Europe. Despite numerous setbacks and failures Maximilian's reign is of the greatest cultural significance, not least through his creative patronage of the arts. Known as 'the Last Knight', he represented late-medieval ideals together with those of the Renaissance. He summoned to the University of Vienna prominent humanists who also advised him on artistic projects designed to ensure his own lasting fame and that of his dynasty according to his maxim: 'He who does not provide for his memory during his life will be forgotten with the sound of his death knell.'

2. PATRONAGE.

(i) Woodcuts and portraits. One of the most ambitious commissions was the *Triumphal Arch* (B. 138), an assemblage (3.41×2.92 mm) of 192 large woodcuts that were printed in 1517–18 (*see* REGALIA, fig. 3), imitating Roman structures that the Emperor could not afford. Its programme and explanatory text were devised by the court historiographer Johannes Stabius (*fl* 1498; *d* 1522); the court painter and architect Jörg Kölderer (*fl* 1512; *d* 1540) worked out the architectural framework and overall design, and Albrecht Dürer contributed woodcuts (*see* DÜRER, (1)). The complex iconography glorifies the Emperor through a family tree, much of which was provided by HANS SPRINGINKLEE, framed by the crests of all Habsburg dominions (central portal); of the 24 panels above the side doors recording historical events, 12 were provided by Wolf Traut. Scenes from his private life, characterizing him as virtuous and valiant, were provided largely by Albrecht Altdorfer (*see* ALTDORFER, (1)) and are depicted in the outer turrets. The adjoining vertical strips carry half-figure portraits of his ancestors and past Holy Roman Emperors. In the aedicula of the cupola, Maximilian is seated amid animals and attributes, chosen from Willibald Pirckheimer's Latin translation of Horapollon's *Hieroglyphica* (5th century) and decoded in a panegyric by Stabius

on the tablet below. They reappear in the opulent decoration of the arch, which was almost entirely created by Dürer. Also by Dürer are the crowned Emperor, the crown-bearing angel over the central door, some historical scenes and most column statues.

The *Triumphal Arch* is complemented by another memorial project, the *Triumphal Procession* (*c.* 1516–18; B. 81; *see* HARNESS AND TRAPPINGS, fig. 4). Planned with the Emperor's written instructions by Stabius and his secretary Marx Treitzsauerwein (1450–1527) and with preparatory designs (*c.* 1507–11; Vienna, Albrertina) by Jörg Kölderer, it was largely the work of Hans Burgkmair I (*see* BURGKMAIR, (2)). The long cortège comprises the imperial household, including musicians and jesters, banners of all Habsburg territories, royal weddings, effigies of Maximilian's great predecessors, even a group of elephants and parrots. Dürer was entrusted with the Emperor's chariot. A preliminary sketch was revised by Pirckheimer and elaborated into a complex allegory, in fact an apotheosis of the Emperor. The final coloured drawing (1518; Vienna, Albertina) was published separately by Dürer as an eight-sheet *Large Triumphal Chariot* (1522; B. 139), in contradistinction to the single woodcut of the *Small Triumphal Chariot* (*c.* 1518; B. vii, 229) or *Burgundian Wedding*, which is part of the *Triumphal Procession.* The ensemble, comprising 137 woodcuts, 54 m long, remained incomplete and was published in 1526; 63 designs were contributed by Hans Burgkmair I, the others by Springinklee, Hans Schäufelein (i), Leonhard Beck and Altdorfer. The last also executed the *Triumphal Procession* in the form of miniatures on parchment (*c.* 1514; 57, Vienna, Albertina) and contributed marginal pen drawings (Besançon, Bib. Mun.) to the incomplete *Prayerbook* (1513; Munich, Bayer. Staatsbib.) printed in a tiny edition by Johannes Schönsperger (*d* 1520) in Augsburg in a Gothic script specially designed to imitate manuscript. The content was determined by the Emperor, and the project was supervised by his adviser on legal, economic and historiographic questions, the humanist Conrad Peutinger. Dürer provided 45 marginal drawings in pen and coloured inks; others were executed by Burgkmair, Jörg Breu the elder, Hans Baldung and Lucas Cranach the elder. Another illuminated prayerbook (after 1486; Vienna, Österreich. Nbib., Cod. 1907, 20 L. impr. membr. 64) was made for Maximilian (*see* MASTERS, ANONYMOUS, AND MONOGRAMMISTS, §I: MASTER OF THE OLDER PRAYERBOOK OF MAXIMILIAN).

While the Emperor engaged Kölderer for work 'which is not so precious', he entrusted the woodcuts for his literary works to major artists. He and his advisers wrote to them, personally correcting both texts and images. His three autobiographical works are rooted in late medieval courtly literature. *Freydal* (1515–16; Vienna, Österreich. Nbib., Cod. 2831, 2835) recounting the chivalric occupations of a carefree youth, is a book on tournaments and festivals; it was never printed but five woodcut illustrations (1516; Vienna, Ksthist. Mus.) attributed to Dürer are extant, of which only one (B. app. 36), however, can be ascribed to him with certainty. *Theuerdank* (1510–17; Vienna, Österreich. Nbib., Cod. 2867, 2806, 2009, 2883), a verse epic written with Melchior Pfinzing (1481–1535) and others, tells the story of Maximilian's courtship of his

Maximilian I as Weisskunig in a Painter's Studio, by Hans Burgkmair I, woodcut, 1512 (Vienna, Österreichische Nationalbibliothek)

first wife. The 116 woodcut illustrations were designed by Beck, Schäufelein, Burgkmair and others. The *Weisskunig* (Vienna, Österreich. Nbib., Cod. 2834; 2892, 3032, 8145; 2832, 3034, 7326), denoting a white and/or wise king, comes closest to genuine, albeit allegorized autobiography. Begun in 1505 with the collaboration of Conrad Celtis (1459–1508), it was never completed and was not published until 1775. Of the 251 woodcut illustrations, Burgkmair provided *c.* 118 (see fig. and *see* BURGKMAIR, (2), fig. 1); others were supplied by Beck, Springinklee and Schäufelein. In *Weisskunig*, Maximilian writes of his role as patron: 'He [Weisskunig] has likewise supported the great artists of painting and sculpture to make many ingenious works which will remain in the world as lasting memory of him.' Another quasi-autobiographical project, the *Historia Friderici et Maximiliani* (1514–15; Vienna, Haus-, Hof- & Staatsarchv, MS. Böhm 4), was written from Maximilian's dictation, with the Emperor's written-in corrections, by his erstwhile secretary Joseph Grünpeck (1473–after 1540) for his grandson, the future Holy Roman Emperor Charles V (*see* (5) below). It is illustrated with 46 tinted pen drawings by an anonymous master.

The Emperor's foremost portrait-painter was Bernhard Strigel. In a half-figure portrait of *Maximilian I* (1499; Schweinfurt, Samml. Schäfer) he depicted him with crown, sceptre and sword, his gilt armour covered by a pearl- and gem-encrusted mantle, wearing the collar of the Golden Fleece. Many replicas exist, some with a window opening into a landscape (e.g. Vienna, Ksthist. Mus.). Similar portraits after 1508 show the winged imperial crown against a blank red background. In contrast, Strigel's *Maximilian I as Private Man* (*c.* 1510; Kreuzlingen, Heinz

Kisters), in bust form and in profile, depicts the Emperor wearing a fur over a brocade gown, the collar of the Golden Fleece and a large beret; he holds rolled-up papers in his left hand and lifts the other in a speaking gesture. This more intimate image was used for Strigel's *Family of Maximilian* (1515; Vienna, Ksthist. Mus.), in which the Emperor is depicted with his first wife, his son Philip the Fair, his grandsons the future Holy Roman Emperors Charles V and Ferdinand I and the future Louis II, King of Bohemia and Hungary. This is the first true group portrait in Germany.

The Milanese painter Giovanni Ambrogio de Predis, who, in 1493, arrived in Innsbruck, following the retinue of Bianca Maria Sforza, painted a profile portrait of *Maximilian I as King* (1502; Vienna, Ksthist. Mus.). In 1494 he was appointed by Maximilian to design portrait medals that popularized the image of the ruler. Dürer owned a drawing after the Ambrogio de Predis portrait of 1502 and used it in his *Virgin of the Rose Garlands* (1506; Prague, N.G., Šternberk Pal.). At the Diet of Augsburg (1518) he drew the Emperor from life 'high up in the castle in his small room'. After the Emperor's death this superb charcoal drawing (Vienna, Albertina) was employed for two painted portraits, one in tempera on canvas (1519; Nuremberg, Ger. Nmus.), the other in oil on panel (1519; Vienna, Ksthist. Mus.). It combines the private with the official image through the orb-like pomegranate, the Habsburg shield, surrounded by the Golden Fleece and surmounted by the imperial crown, and a Latin commemorative inscription. But it is the large-size woodcut (B. 154), also derived from the drawing and Dürer's first printed portrait, that keeps Maximilian's memory alive.

(ii) Building projects and memorials. As the Emperor constantly moved between his residences in Innsbruck, Augsburg, Vienna and Linz, his impact on contemporary architecture was negligible. The Neuer Hof in Innsbruck, known through Dürer's two watercolours (1494–5; Vienna, Albertina), was enlarged by his master-builder and mason Nikolaus Türing (*fl* 1488; *d* 1517), who was also responsible for the Goldenes Dachl (1494–6), in honour of the Emperor's second wedding, and its stone reliefs, depicting Maximilian with his two wives, flanked by Moorish dancers; the arms of his territories underneath embody once more the concept of universal rule (*see* INNSBRUCK, §1(ii)). This is true also for the planned life-size equestrian statue in stone for the church of SS Ulrich and Afra, Augsburg. Burgkmair's preparatory tinted pen drawing (1509; Vienna, Albertina) and a small model of a horse (1509; Brunswick, Herzog Anton Ulrich-Mus.) by Gregor Erhart are the only remains of the project. Maximilian's greatest monument to Habsburg glory was his tomb in the Innsbruck Hofkirche (*see* INNSBRUCK, §3(i)). Begun in 1508 under the supervision of GILG SESSELSCHREIBER, who was also involved in the casting, and completed between 1562 and 1583 by ALEXANDER COLIN, it too remained fragmentary. Paralleling the programme of the *Triumphal Arch*, it envisaged 40 over-life-size bronze statues of his ancestors, beginning with (Gaius) Julius Caesar and ending with his children, 34 busts of Roman emperors and 100 statuettes of the Habsburg family saints. The monumental ensemble reflects both Roman cult ceremonies and Burgundian tomb representations. Of the 28 ancestors now surrounding the cenotaph, only 11 were produced in Maximilian's lifetime. Two of them, the kings *Arthur* and *Theodoric*, were cast in 1513 by Peter Vischer the elder. *Duke Albert IV Habsburg*, cast by STEFAN GODL, is based on a wooden model (1514) by Hans Leinberger after a design by Dürer (Liverpool, Walker A.G.); *Zimburgis of Masovia* is after a design by Veit Stoss I. The busts are by Jörg Muscat (1474–1527) and the figures of the Habsburg family saints were cast by Godl (1514–18) from designs by Leonhard Magt. Although a torso, the Innsbruck tomb announces the Renaissance spirit in German sculpture and is a grandiose monument to Maximilian I's patronage (*see* AUSTRIA, §IV, 2, and fig. 20).

WRITINGS

Weisskunig (MS.; 1505; Vienna, Österreich. Nbib., Cod. 2834; 2892, 3032, 8145; 2832, 3034, 7326) (Vienna, 1775)

Theuerdank (MS.; 1510–17; Vienna, Österreich. Nbib., Cod. 2867, 2806, 2009, 2883); ed. H. Appuhn (Dortmund, 1979)

Die Historia Friderici et Maximiliani (MS.; 1514–15; Vienna, Haus-, Hof- & Staatsarchv, MS. Böhm 4); ed. O. von Benesch and E. M. Auer (Berlin, 1957)

BIBLIOGRAPHY

A. von Bartsch: *Le Peintre-graveur*, vii (Vienna, 1808) [B.]

H. T. Musper, ed.: *Maximilian I: Der Weisskunig*, 2 vols (Stuttgart, 1956)

Maximilian I, 1459–1519 (exh. cat., ed. F. Unterkircher; Vienna, Ksthist. Mus., 1959)

S. Applebaum: *The Triumph of Maximilian I* (New York, 1964)

H. C. von Tavell: 'Die Randzeichnungen Albrecht Dürers zum Gebetbuch Maximilians I', *Münch. Jb. Bild. Kst*, n. s. 2, xvi (1965), pp. 55–120

E. Egg: *Zur maximilianischen Kunst in Innsbruck* (Innsbruck, 1966)

K. Oettinger: *Die Bildhauer Maximilians am Innsbrucker Kaisergrabmal* (Nuremberg, 1966)

Maximilian I (exh. cat., ed. E. Egg; Innsbruck, Zeughaus, 1969)

V. Oberhammer: 'Die vier Bildnisse Kaiser Maximilians I von Albrecht Dürer', *Alte & Mod. Kst*, xiv (1969), pp. 2–14

——: *Das goldene Dachl zu Innsbruck* (Innsbruck, 1970)

W. Hilger, ed.: *Das ältere Gebetbuch Maximilians I* (Graz, 1973)

E. Egg: *Die Hofkirche in Innsbruck: Das Grabmal Kaiser Maximilians I und die silberne Kapelle* (Innsbruck, 1974)

W. Strauss: *The Book of Hours of the Emperor Maximilian I* (New York, 1974)

S. K. Rudolph: 'Illustration und Historiographie bei Maximilian I: Der "Weisse Kunig"', *Röm. Hist. Mitt.*, xxv (1983), pp. 35–108

F. Unterkircher: *Maximilian I: Ein kaiserlicher Auftraggeber illustrierter Handschriften* (Hamburg, 1983)

L. Silver: 'Prints for a Prince: Maximilian, Nuremberg, and the Woodcut', *New Perspectives on the Art of the Renaissance*, ed. J. C. Smith (Nuremberg, 1985), pp. 7–21

H. Wiesflecker: *Der Kaiser und seine Umwelt: Hof, Staat, Wirtschaft und Kultur* (Munich, 1986)

ROSEMARIE BERGMANN

(4) Margaret of Austria, Duchess of Savoy, Regent of the Netherlands (*b* Brussels, 10 Jan 1480; Regent of the Netherlands 1507–15, 1518–30; *d* Mechelen, 1 Dec 1530). Daughter of (3) Maximilian I. Her marriage as an infant to the future Charles VIII, King of France, in June 1483 was annulled. Charles refused to return Margaret's territories, which were part of her dowry, while keeping her imprisoned. Her release, as well as the return of some of the Burgundian territories (except the old duchy of Burgundy), was settled with the Peace Treaty of Senlis (12 June 1493). On 5 November 1495 she married by proxy John, heir of Castile and Aragon (1478–98). On 5 October 1497 the marriage was celebrated in Burgos, but five months later her husband suddenly died. On 26 July 1501 she married Philibert II, Duke of Savoy (1480–1504), by proxy and on 1 December 1501 in person. The marriage was childless. During her regency of the Netherlands, she resided in Mechelen, where she established a small but impressive court at the Hof van Kamerrijk, where she gathered together painters, poets and musicians.

Inventories (17 July 1516, 1523–4, 1530) provide an accurate understanding of her impressive collection, which included numerous paintings, sculptures and tapestries and an outstanding group of manuscripts (including some from the DE CRÖY collection) and incunabula. Jan van Eyck's double portrait of *Giovanni Arnolfini and Giovanna Cenami* (1434; London, N.G.), traditionally known as the '*Arnolfini Marriage*', was among the works itemized, as well as paintings by Hieronymus Bosch, Juan de Flandes and Michel Sittow. Among the most spectacular of her illuminated manuscripts were the Très Riches Heures of Jean, Duc de Berry (*c.* 1411–16, *c.* 1485; Chantilly, Mus. Condé, MS. 65), and the Hours of Bona Sforza (*c.* 1490; London, BL, Add. MS. 34294), gifts from Bianca Maria Sforza (1472–1510), second wife of the Holy Roman Emperor Maximilian I. In 1517 the Duchess commissioned Etienne de Lale to rewrite some missing leaves and have the book rebound (Lille, Archivs Dépt. Nord; nos 44065–44064); 16 miniatures (1519–21) were added by Gerard Horenbout (*see* HORENBOUT, (1)) who represented her twice in the manuscript, as the Virgin in the *Visitation*, and as the lady holding the candle in the *Presentation in the Temple.* Documents indicate that among the plethora of artists she employed were the sculptors Jean Mone and Conrat Meit, who sculpted her portrait bust (1523; Munich, Bayer. Nmus.), and the painters Jan Gossart, Jan Mostaert, Bernard van Orley, Jan Cornelisz. Vermeyen, Pieter van Coninxloo, Jan van Roome, Jacob van Lathem (*fl* 1493–1522) and Jacopo de' Barbari. The last remained in her service for an extended period from August 1510 until his death in the summer of 1516. During his journey to the Netherlands (1520–21) Albrecht Dürer went to see the Duchess's collection and gave her costly presents, but his request for Jacopo de' Barbari's painting box in the form of a book was rejected, perhaps because the Duchess, according to Jean Lemaire, her historiographer, occasionally painted herself. She also played music and wrote poems and literary dedications.

According to a document of 1 April 1515, Horenbout was appointed court painter; unlike Barbari, he stipulated that he would stay in Ghent. Barbari's production for the Duchess has been preserved only in documents, and it is not entirely clear what Horenbout painted in addition to the miniatures in the Sforza Book of Hours. Jan Mostaert is recorded as being active at Margaret's court in 1519 and 1521 and made copies for her after original court portraits (*see* MOSTAERT, (1)). Bernard van Orley was court painter from 1518 until 1530; his best-known work is the altarpiece depicting the *Ordeals of Job* (1521; Antwerp, Kon. Mus. S. Kst.; *see* ORLEY, VAN (i), (2) and fig. 1), commissioned by the Duchess as a gift for Antoine de Lalaing, Count of Hoogstraeten and Stadholder of Holland, Zeeland and Utrecht. As an artist affiliated to the court, van Orley depended on his workshop to fulfil such commissions as portraits of *Margaret of Austria* and the *Holy Roman Emperor Charles V*, for these exist in numerous replicas.

In 1507 Margaret of Austria was personally involved in commissioning funerary monuments for herself and Philibert II, Duke of Savoy, to be erected in the church of St Nicholas, Brou, near Bourg-en-Bresse. She consulted Pietro Torrigiano, Jean Perréal and Michel Colombe, but supervision of the works was eventually entrusted to her master builder, Lodewijk van Boghen (Louis van Bodeghem; *c.* 1470–1540), and they were executed by Jan van Roome and CONRAT MEIT.

BIBLIOGRAPHY

NBW

J. De Jongh: *Margaretha van Oostenrijk* (Amsterdam and Antwerp, 1946)

E. Winker: *Margarete von Österreich, Grande Dame der Renaissance* (Munich, 1966)

J. Duverger: 'Margareta van Oostenrijk (1480–1530) en de italiaanse Renaissance', *Relations artistiques entre les Pays-Bas et l'Italie à la Renaissance: Etudes dédiées à Suzanne Sulzberger* (Brussels and Rome, 1988), pp. 127–42

B. Hamann, ed.: *Die Habsburger: Ein biographisches Lexikon* (Vienna, 1988), pp. 272–5

M. Hörsch: 'Architektur unter Margarethe von Österreich, Regentin der Niederlande (1507–1530)', *Acad. Anlct.: Kl. S. Kst.*, lvi/58 (1994)

D. Eichberger and L. Beaven: 'Family Members and Political Allies: The Portrait Collection of Margaret of Austria', *A. Bull.*, lxxvii/2 (1995), pp. 225–48

HANS J. VAN MIEGROET

(5) Charles V, Holy Roman Emperor, Duke of Burgundy and Brabant [Charles I, King of Spain] (*b* Ghent, 24 Feb 1500; *reg* Spain 1516–56, Holy Roman Emperor 1530–56; *d* Yuste, Spain, 9 Sept 1558). Grandson of (3) Maximilian I. From his maternal grandfather, Ferdinand II, King of Aragon, he acquired Naples, Sardinia and Aragon; from his maternal grandmother, Queen Isabella, he acquired Castile, together with its New World possessions, Grenada and the West Indies (*see* ARAGON); on the death of Ferdinand in 1516, Charles became Charles I of Spain and thus founded the Spanish branch of the Habsburg dynasty (*see* §II below). He was responsible for important artistic and architectural commissions as well as for the creation of a significant collection.

1. Introduction. 2. Early reign, 1519–28. 3. Middle years, 1529–44. 4. Council of Trent to abdication, 1545–56.

1. INTRODUCTION. The paintings, sculpture, tapestries and other works with which Charles V was most closely associated emphasize directness and historical veracity rather than allegory; allegorical works were generally promoted and supervised by others on his behalf. He had a strong interest in mathematics, science and technology and collected splendid globes and maps, scientific instruments and beautifully illustrated books on astronomy and anatomy. The imperial inventories also list a rich and varied collection of tapestries, arms and armour (e.g. pistol by Peter Peck, *c.* 1540; New York, Met.; *see* ARMS AND ARMOUR, fig. 6), jewellery, rock-crystal medallions, medals and coins, hundreds of works of art in precious metals and featherwork obtained from Mexico and Peru, as well as manuscripts with depictions of animals and plants from the New World. Some of these objects formed the basis of the Spanish royal collection. Initially he preferred Late Gothic forms in architecture but increasingly accepted the classicizing Renaissance style, and his practical, technical frame of mind was exhibited in the many fortifications that he built throughout the Low Countries, Spain, Italy

and North Africa, all erected in accordance with the latest developments in bastion design.

2. EARLY REIGN, 1519–28. During these years, in which Charles lived principally in the Netherlands and Spain, a number of major architectural works were erected under imperial patronage. One of the most important was the Gothic ducal chapel in Brussels (1522–53; destr. 1731) by Rombout Keldermans II. The rounded arches of its nave arcade resembled those of St Eustache in Paris. In Granada the revised plan (1528) by Diego Siloe of the Cathedral and the Italianate palace (begun 1533) designed by PEDRO MACHUCA beginning in 1527 (*see* GRANADA, fig. 2) constituted important examples of an imported Renaissance style. Both plans were accepted with reservations: in the case of the cathedral, the dignity of the historically important Capilla Real (1506–21) had to be respected, whereas the palace could not be an isolated, representational structure but had to provide adequate facilities for an extensive court.

3. MIDDLE YEARS, 1529–44. After initial visits to Italy (1529–30, 1532–3, 1535–6), Charles seems to have become even more receptive to Italian Renaissance art and architecture. Important architectural commissions of the 1530s included the gallery of the Palais du Roi (destr.) at Brussels with its Italianate arcade (1533–7), the interior of which was decorated with putti and busts of emperors *all'antica*. In Spain work continued on the palace in Granada and its sculptural decorations by Niccolò da Corte from the della Porta workshop in Genoa. At the same time the Emperor initiated a massive project, the reconstruction of the alcázares of Seville (from 1540; *see* SEVILLE, §IV, 2 and GARDEN, §VIII, 3(iii)), Toledo (1538; *see* TOLEDO, §I, 2) and Madrid (from 1540s, destr. 1734; *see* MADRID, §§I, 1 and IV, 2). In Italy the innovative, star-shaped Castel Sant' Elmo in Naples, built by Pedro Scrivá, was inspected by the Emperor in 1535.

Works by important Italian masters began to enter the imperial collection after 1529. In addition to paintings by Titian there were works by Correggio (*Loves of Jupiter*; *c.* 1530; including *Danaë*, Rome, Gal. Borghese, and *Leda*, Berlin, Bodemus.), Alfonso Lombardi (portrait medal; 1533), who produced four marble busts of *Charles V*, only one of which has been identified (Paris, Mus. Jacquemart André), and Baccio Bandinelli (bronze relief of the *Deposition*, untraced, but known from a later cast by Antonio Susini; Paris, Louvre); rock crystal by Giovanni Bernardi da Castelbolognese (*Battle of Pavia*, *c.* 1532; Vienna, Ksthist. Mus.), who in 1530 presented the Emperor with a gold portrait medal (silver version, Vienna, Ksthist. Mus.); and helmets and shields by Filippo Negroli (*fl* 1534–45), the creator of the *all'antica* style in armour (e.g. Medusa shield and morion, 1541; Vienna, Ksthist. Mus.). Working in a comparable idiom in Augsburg under the protection of the Emperor was Christoph Weiditz I, who executed numerous medallic images of members of the court. In the Low Countries the noted poet Janus Secundus produced medals of Charles (*Charles V*, 1531; Brussels, Penningkab.) and his entourage, and large-scale sculptural commissions were given to another master working in an Italianate mode, Jean Mone, who executed altars in St Martin, Halle (1533; for illustration *see* MONE, JEAN) and the Ducal Chapel (1537; now in Brussels Cathedral) in the Palace, Brussels.

Titian's relationship with Charles V began *c.* 1532 in Bologna (*see* TITIAN, §1(vi)). The only surviving imperial commission from this period is *Charles V with his Hunting Dog* (?1532; Madrid, Prado), which appears to be a copy after a work by Jakob Seisenegger (1532; Vienna, Ksthist. Mus.; for illustration *see* SEISENEGGER, JAKOB), which may have been considered as a type of *prova*, testing the painter's ability to re-create portraits in his own style. The documentary evidence indicates that Titian was asked to supply only portraits during this period. These included *Charles V with Baton* and *Charles V with Drawn Sword* (both untraced but known through copies). The only painting by Titian in Charles's collection dating from this period that was not a portrait was the *Annunciation* (untraced), presented to Empress Isabella by the artist in 1537. In addition to those by Titian and Seisenegger, portraits of the Emperor were executed during the early 1530s by Lucas Cranach the elder (probably identical to a painting in a Brussels inventory of 1536), Jan Cornelisz. Vermeyen and Christoph Amberger (*Emperor Charles V*, 1532; Berlin, Gemäldegal.); Anton Woensam also produced a woodcut of *Charles V Seated on his Throne* (1538; for illustration *see* WOENSAM, ANTON). The major pictorial works from this period that were produced for Charles were tapestries after Bernard van Orley's designs: the *Battle of Pavia* (1531; Paris, Louvre), the most important battle tapestries produced up until that time, and the so-called *Hunts of Maximilian* (1528–33; Paris, Louvre), the first great topographic series, depicting the park at Brussels in extraordinary detail (*see* ORLEY (i), VAN, (2), fig. 2).

During the late 1530s and early 1540s the major court commission was the set of stained-glass windows that decorated the transept and the newly erected chapel of Saint-Sacrement du Miracle in Brussels Cathedral. In the windows of the chapel monumental figures of the imperial family and their spouses are represented beneath scenes from a legend of a miraculous Host. The designs for this important project were executed by van Orley in a Romanist style and completed after his death by MICHIEL COXCIE in a strikingly different manner, clearly influenced by Michelangelo's Sistine ceiling and the works of Sebastiano Serlio.

4. COUNCIL OF TRENT TO ABDICATION, 1545–56. The period between the opening of the Council of Trent in 1545 and the Emperor's abdication was especially important for imperial commissions. His great triumph over Protestant forces at Mühlberg (1547) was followed by his decisive defeat at the hands of the French at Metz (1553) and his abdication and retirement to Spain (1556). Architectural commissions included massive fortifications in Ghent, Cambrai, Antwerp, Charleville, Milan and elsewhere, erected by Italian engineers. During the final years of his life the Emperor commissioned relatively modest structures for himself and a small court: a residence on the grounds of the Brussels complex designed by JACQUES DU BROEUCQ and rooms for his retirement within YUSTE MONASTERY, near Plasencia in Spain.

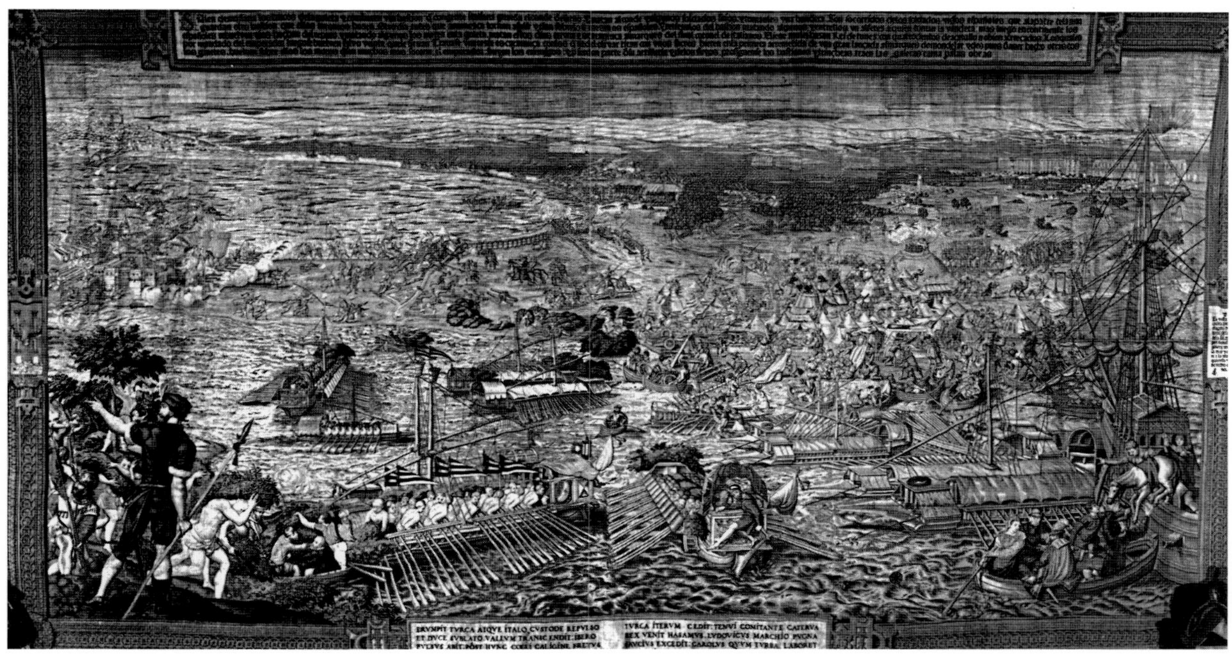

A naval victory depicted on a tapestry from the series the *Campaign of Charles V against Tunis* designed by Jan Cornelisz. Vermeyen, 1546–54 (Madrid, Palacio Real de Madrid)

The majority of Titian's works for Charles V were executed during these latter years and when the artist lived at the imperial residence in Augsburg (1547–8), when he was especially prolific. During this period he painted *Emperor Charles V at the Battle of Mühlberg*, *Charles V Seated*, and the *Empress Isabella* (1548; all Madrid, Prado), the *Empress Isabella Seated, Dressed in Black* (1545; untraced) and *Charles V and Empress Isabella* (1548; untraced but known from a copy by Rubens, 1636; Madrid, Col. Duque de Alba). In *Emperor Charles V at the Battle of Mühlberg*, the first great equestrian state portrait, two important traditions are merged: the Roman prototype (the Capitoline *Marcus Aurelius*) and the image of the Christian knight derived from Dürer's engraving of the *Knight, Death and the Devil* (1513) (*see* (3), §2 above). Also belonging to this period are a *Venus* (probably identical to *Venus with an Organ Player*, 1545; Madrid, Prado), for the Emperor, referred to in a letter (1545) from Titian to Charles, and the *Ecce homo* (1547; Madrid, Prado). *Philip II in Armour* (1550–51; Madrid, Prado) created the archetype for the image of Charles's son and successor as king of Spain (*see* HABSBURG, §II(2)). The artist's final work for his great patron, '*La Gloria*' (1551–4; Madrid, Prado), depicts the imperial family in adoration of the Holy Trinity, composed of identical figures of the Son and the Father, according to a medieval tradition favoured by Charles and his theologians.

The imperial commissions of the sculptor and medallist Leone Leoni were also executed during this period. The Emperor was impressed by Leone's project, inspired by that of Leonardo da Vinci, to erect an equestrian monument in Milan (unexecuted) and with the artist's proven abilities as a medallist. Leone arrived in Brussels in 1549 to work on a series of full-length sculptures as well as busts, medals and cameos. Leone's bronze figures of *Philip II* (1553; Madrid, Prado), *Mary of Hungary* (1555; Vienna, Ksthist. Mus.) and *Empress Isabella* (1555; Madrid, Prado) are perfect amalgams of northern European realism and Italian classicism, which must have appealed to the international court of the Emperor. The most extraordinary of these works is the over life-size bronze *Charles V and Fury Restrained* (1549–55; Madrid, Prado; for discussion and illustration *see* LEONI, (1), fig. 1), in which Charles is represented nude in a detachable suit of armour. Whereas the nude figure of the Emperor derives from the portraits of Charles's ally the Admiral *Andrea Doria* (1528; London, BM) by Bandinelli and Agnolo Bronzino (Rome, Gal. Doria-Pamphili), its removable bronze cuirass *all'antica* recalls the armour of Negroli executed for the Emperor in Milan.

The masterpiece of Jan Cornelisz. Vermeyen also dates from these years. The *Campaign of Charles V against Tunis* (or the *Conquest of Tunis*), a series of tapestries (see fig.) after Vermeyen's cartoons (1546–54; Madrid, Pal. Real; for further discussion and illustration *see* VERMEYEN, JAN CORNELISZ.), presents in minute detail, based on first-hand sketches, every incident in the campaign from the mustering of the troops in Barcelona to the final embarkation from Tunis. The work is the perfect embodiment of Charles's strong interest in cartography and detailed images of physical terrain (mentioned by Ludovico Dolce, 1561) as well as his desire to present precise images of his actions, unadorned by allegory. Before his death Charles V left the final decision regarding his burial to his son Philip II, who eventually resolved the matter through the creation of a royal mausoleum within the Escorial (*see* §II(2) below) from 1559 (*see* ESCORIAL and figs 1–4).

BIBLIOGRAPHY

L. Dolce: *Vita di Carlo V*, i (Venice, 1561), p. 172
H. E. Wethey: *The Paintings of Titian*, 3 vols (London, 1971–5)
M. Mezzatesta: *Imperial Themes in the Sculpture of Leone Leoni* (diss., New York U., 1980)
W. Eisler: *The Impact of the Emperor Charles V upon the Visual Arts* (diss., University Park, PA State U., 1983)
E. Rosenthal: *The Palace of Charles V in Granada* (Princeton, NJ, 1985)
F. Checa Cremades: *Carlos V y la imagen del héroe en el renacimiento* (Madrid, 1987)
H. J. Horn: *Jan Cornelisz. Vermeyen: Painter of Charles V and his Conquest of Tunis*, 2 vols (Doornspijk, 1989)

WILLIAM EISLER

(6) Ferdinand I, Holy Roman Emperor [King of Bohemia and Hungary] (*b* Alcalá de Henares, 10 March 1503; *reg* Bohemia and Hungary 1526–62, Holy Roman Emperor 1558–64; *d* Vienna, 25 July 1564). Brother of (5) Charles V. He was brought up and educated at the court of his maternal grandfather, Ferdinand II, King of Sicily and Aragon, and (from 1518) in the Netherlands under the supervision of his aunt, Margaret of Austria (*see* (4) above). In 1521 he married Anne of Hungary (1503–47) and was invested with Upper and Lower Austria, Styria, Carinthia and Carniola; by 1522 he was regent of all hereditary Habsburg lands. Following the death of his brother-in-law Louis II, King of Bohemia and Hungary, he became King of Bohemia and Hungary and, in 1531, King of the Romans. During his short reign as Holy Roman Emperor (1558–64) he continued the war against the Turks and consolidated his realm through centralization of government and monetary reform.

Ferdinand patronized the arts for the glorification of Habsburg rule and was the first to keep his collections in specially designed rooms which he called *Kunstkammer*. Family portraits, coins and medals held a place of honour. Ferdinand appears as a youth in the *Triumphal Arch* and *Triumphal Procession* of Maximilian I (*see* (3) above), in Bernhard Strigel's *Family of Maximilian I* (1515; Vienna, Ksthist. Mus.) and in works commissioned by Margaret of Austria, including a choir window in Brussels Cathedral (*c*. 1520) and the Notre-Dame-du-Sablon tapestry (1518; Brussels, Musées Royaux A. & Hist.), also in Brussels. Hans Maler was commissioned by the Emperor for portraits of *Anne of Hungary* (1520; Madrid, Thyssen-Bornemisza Mus.; 1521; Innsbruck, Tirol Landesmus.) as well as of the Archduke himself (1525; Vienna, Ksthist. Mus. and Florence, Uffizi). Erhard Schön created a large anamorphic print (1531; destr. 1945) of the then King Ferdinand with Charles V, Francis I, King of France, and Pope Clement VII. The Diet of Augsburg in 1530 occasioned many documentary images of Ferdinand and his brother Charles V. Hans Daucher is attributed with the *Meeting of Charles V and Ferdinand I* in a stone relief (1527 [?1530]; New York, Pierpont Morgan Lib.) and Jörg Breu the elder captured their festive entry in a ten-sheet series of woodcuts (1530; Hollstein, nos 172–3). Among portraits by Jan Cornelisz. Vermeyen several show Ferdinand as a lively, gesturing half-figure (1530; notably Paris, Col. Wilkinson). Barthel Beham sketched Charles V and Ferdinand for engravings (1531; B. 60, 61), of which there are also painted versions that may, however, be copies (e.g. on dep. Munich, Alte Pin.). In 1537 Hans Kels I created fine boxwood medallions of Ferdinand and his wife (Hamburg, Mus. Kst & Gew.) and a splendid gameboard (Vienna, Ksthist. Mus.) featuring central equestrian images of Ferdinand and Charles V surrounded by allegorical decorations. Jakob Seisenegger, court painter from 1531, was noted for his full-length portraits of Ferdinand and his family (e.g. *Anne of Hungary and her Children*; untraced) that may have influenced the ancestral portraits for Prague Castle commissioned from Hans Bocksberger. In 1548 Titian painted his portrait (untraced; copy, Naples, Capodimonte) and Lucas Cranach the elder executed a woodcut and a fine half-figure painted portrait (Schwerin, Staatl. Mus.) which shows Ferdinand bearded and in mourning for his late wife. An engraving (1556; Vienna, Albertina) representing the aging ruler before his city of Vienna, framed by an elaborate decorated arch, is by Hanns Lautensack, who was probably engaged in 1554 to portray Ferdinand's large collection of Classical coins. The catalogue of the collection was written by Ferdinand's historiographer Wolfgang Lazius (1514–65), but it was criticized by Jacopo Strada (*see* STRADA, (1)), who served as Imperial Antiquarius from 1554. Alexander Colin, Martino Ferrabosco, Wenzel Jamnitzer and Giuseppe Arcimboldo, like Strada, first found employment with Ferdinand.

Ferdinand's major architectural project was the Belvedere (1538–63; *see* PRAGUE, §I, 2), a garden villa for his wife. Its elegant High Renaissance design, partly relying on Sebastiano Serlio's treatise, is the work of PAOLO STELLA, who finished only the ground floor with its arcaded loggia; the upper part is by Bonifaz Wolmut, court architect from 1559. Ferdinand also commissioned Italian designers to lay out the gardens at Prague Castle in the Italian Renaissance style (*see* GARDEN, §VIII, 3(iii)). He was also instrumental in the urban development of Vienna as the residence of the Holy Roman Emperor (*see* VIENNA, §II, 2).

BIBLIOGRAPHY

Hollstein: *Dut. & Flem.*
W. Bauer, R. Lacroix, eds: *Die Korrespondenz Ferdinands I.*, 2 vols (Vienna, 1912–30)
A. Lhotsky: *Die Geschichte der Sammlungen* (1941–5), i/2 of *Festschrift des kunsthistorischen Museums zur Feier des fünfzigjährigen Bestandes* (Vienna, 1941–5)
E. Egg: 'Der deutsche König und die neue Kunst: Ferdinand I., der Begründer der österreichischen Kultur', *Alte & Mod. Kst*, xlvi (1961), pp. 16–20
K. Löcher: *Jacob Seisenegger Hofmaler Kaiser Ferdinands I* (Munich, 1962)
J. Krčálová: 'Il palladianesimo in Cecoslovacchia e l'influenza del Veneto sull'architettura ceca', *Boll. Cent. Int. Stud. Archit. Andrea Palladio*, vi (1964), pp. 89–110
W. Hilger: *Die Ikonographie Kaiser Ferdinands I.* (Vienna, 1969)
P. Sutter-Fichtner: *Ferdinand I* (Vienna, 1986)

ROSEMARIE BERGMANN

(7) Mary, Queen of Hungary [Regent of the Netherlands] (*b* Brussels, 15 Sept 1505; Regent 1530–56; *d* Cigalés, 18 Oct 1558). Sister of (5) Charles V and (6) Ferdinand I. She was the daughter of Philip, King of Castile (*b* 1478; *reg* 1504–6; *d* 1506), and Joanna, Queen of Castile (*see* §II(1) below). Until 2 May 1514 she lived in Mechelen at the court of her aunt Margaret of Austria, Duchess of Savoy, Regent of the Netherlands (*see* (4) above); she was then sent to Vienna to the court of her grandfather Maximilian I (*see* (3) above). She was destined to marry Louis II, King of Bohemia and Hungary (*see* JAGIELLON, (3)). After their marriage at Innsbruck, Austria, on 19 December 1520, Mary joined her husband in Buda (now Budapest). She was widowed in 1526, when Louis died at the Battle of Mohács. She never married again.

In the 16th century Buda was an important cultural centre, Matthias Corvinus, King of Hungary, having, during his reign (1468–90), promoted through his patronage the Italian Renaissance style in Hungary. Mary, who had received a Classical education in Vienna, chose her officers from among the Hungarian humanists, one of whom was Nicolas Olahus, appointed her secretary. Under the advancing threat of the Turks, Mary's household was forced to flee, first to Innsbruck and then to Vienna. There she occupied herself with hunting and the study of the Classics and the teachings of Erasmus. In 1530 Erasmus dedicated *De vidua Christiana* (*Concerning the Christian Widow*) to her. When Margaret of Austria died in 1530, Charles V named Mary her successor as Regent of the Netherlands. In the spring of 1531 she moved into the Palais du Roi (destr.), Brussels, which she furnished with her inheritance from the Hof van Kamerrijk in Mechelen, which had belonged to her aunt.

Of the painters employed by Mary, one of the most notable was Bernard van Orley (*see* ORLEY, VAN (i), (2)). He had been in the service of Margaret of Austria and had fallen from favour on suspicion of having Protestant sympathies. He was pardoned by Mary, who wished to avail herself of his knowledge for the acquisition of 18 works that had been donated to the church of St Nicholas, Brou, by Margaret of Austria. On 13 October 1532 he was appointed court painter and between 1533 and 1535 carried out several portrait commissions. Orley worked as a designer for the tapestry factories in Brussels and, at Mary's instigation, designed a series of 12 tapestries of the *Hunts of Maximilian* (1528–33; Paris, Louvre; *see* ORLEY, VAN (i), (2), fig. 2), for Charles V, of which several copies were made. He also designed stained-glass windows (1530–32) for the transept of Brussels Cathedral, one of which represents *Louis II, King of Hungary, and his Wife Mary, Queen of Hungary, Kneeling before the Holy Trinity* (see fig.). In the chapel of Saint-Sacrement du Miracle in the cathedral Mary is represented as one of the donors in a set of stained-glass windows by Orley, completed after his death by MICHIEL COXCIE. A follower of Orley, Coxcie succeeded him as court painter. He was known primarily as a copyist, and he earned the name the 'Flemish Raphael'. Another artist employed by Mary was PIETER COECKE VAN AELST, who was probably a pupil of Orley. In 1539 Frans Borreman is recorded as having carried out work for the palace in Brussels under the supervision of the master 'Petren van Aelst'.

Mary was little interested in contemporary painting, preferring the works of the early Netherlandish school. Her favourite paintings were both by Jan van Eyck: the double portrait of *Giovanni Arnolfini and Giovanna Cenami* (popularly known as the '*Arnolfini Marriage*', 1434; London, N.G.; *see* EYCK, VAN, (2) fig. 3), which passed to her from Margaret of Austria, and the *Virgin and Child* commissioned by Georg van der Paele (1436; Bruges,

4. *Mary, Queen of Hungary*, detail of a stained-glass window designed by Bernard van Orley, 1530–32 (Brussels, Cathedral)

Groeningemus.), then in the church of St Donatian, Bruges (*see* EYCK, VAN, (2), fig. 4). The *Descent from the Cross* by Rogier van der Weyden (Madrid, Prado; *see* WEYDEN, VAN DER, (1), fig. 2) was first recorded in 1549 in the château of Binche (destr.), Hainaut. It was later presented to her nephew Philip II, and Coxcie was commissioned to make a copy.

TITIAN was another painter whose work Mary admired. While on his first visit to Augsburg, summoned by Charles V, Titian was commissioned by Mary to paint four large pictures of the Furies for Binche, of which only *Tityus* and *Sisyphus* (both 1548–9; Madrid, Prado) survive. She had Titian's paintings copied by JAN CORNELISZ. VERMEYEN, who entered Mary's service on 5 July 1531. A document of 1556 reads, 'A maistre Jehan Vermeiyan . . . pour avoir faict un pourtrait d'un Dieu de pitié semblable à autre faict de la main de Tisian, painctre de Venise'. In 1556 she took 20 of the copies with her to Spain.

On 20 February 1546 Mary took possession of the château of Binche, which had belonged to Charles V. Almost at once plans were made to rebuild it. These were supplied by JACQUES DU BROEUCQ, who had entered Mary's service in 1540. Working with him were Philippe Lammekens (1493–1547) and Pierre Teels (1467–1543). Du Broeucq was also responsible for the château of Mariemont (destr.), Hainaut. Work at Binche was completed within four years but the château was destroyed in 1554 by the French. While work was in progress, Mary was in regular contact with her sister Eleanor, widow of Francis I, King of France, and sent her a wooden model of the building. The architecture of Binche was probably influenced by that of the château of Fontainebleau in France.

Mary's interest in Italian art developed mainly after 1540, when she began to employ Italian sculptors. The first of these was LUCA LANCIA, who came from Naples and was a disciple of Jacopo Sansovino. For Binche he made two garden sculptures, one representing the *Nile*, the other *Cleopatra*; he also made four stucco reliefs for the triumphal arch at the entrance to Binche. For Mariemont he made 13 statues, among them a *Venus* intended for the apartment of Eleanor of France.

A second Italian artist in Mary's employ was Leone Leoni (*see* LEONI, (1)), who in 1546 had entered the service of Charles V as a sculptor; on 21 March 1549 he arrived at Binche. Mary ordered 10 bronzes from him. Work progressed slowly, however, especially after he was granted a house in Milan by Charles V. After several urgent requests, he finally appeared at the court of Charles V with nine sculptures in cases. These were taken by Mary and Charles V to Spain in 1556, accompanied by Pompeo Leoni. Mary also took with her a marble bust by Du Broeucq of *Eleanor of France* (Madrid, Prado).

For Binche, Mary ordered several series of tapestries with religious and mythological themes: the *Story of Tobias* for the chapel and the apartment of Eleanor of France, the *Story of Psyche* (probably after a design by Coxcie), the *Story of Venus* and the *Story of Callisto*. She also commissioned from Orley the series of the *Battle of Pavia* (1531; Paris, Louvre) to commemorate Charles V's victory over Francis I.

In 1524 Marc de Glasere (*fl* 1516–36) was appointed court goldsmith, making mainly tableware. In 1538 he was succeeded by Pierre le Comte and Peter Wolfganck.

BIBLIOGRAPHY

T. Lejeune: 'Le Palais de Marie de Hongrie à Binche', *Doc. & Rap. Soc. Paléontol. & Archéol.*, ix (1878), pp. 415–46

R. Hedicke: *Jacques Dubroeucq de Mons* (Brussels, 1911)

G. Glück: 'Bildnisse aus dem Hause Habsburg, II: Köningen Maria von Ungarn', *Jb.Ksthist. Inst. Wien*, viii (1934), pp. 173–96

J. de Iongh: *Maria van Hongarije*, 2 vols (Amsterdam, 1946–51; Eng. trans., London, 1959)

G. de Boom: *Marie de Hongrie* (Brussels, 1956)

R. Wellens: *Jacques du Broeucq* (Brussels, 1962)

M. Binamé: 'Trois châteaux construits par Jacques Dubroecq: Boissu, Binche, Mariemont', *Rev. Archéologues & Historiens A. Louvain*, ii (1969), p. 105

J. Duverger: 'Marie de Hongrie, Gouvernante des Pays-Bas et la Renaissance', *Actes du XXIIe congrès international d'histoire de l'art: Budapest, 1969*; also in *Evolution générale et développements régionaux en histoire de l'art*, i (Budapest, 1972), pp. 715–26

M. J. T. M. STOMPÉ

(8) Maximilian II, Holy Roman Emperor [King of Bohemia; King of Hungary] (*b* Vienna, 31 July 1527; *reg* Bohemia 1562–75, Hungary 1563–72, Holy Roman Emperor 1564–76; *d* Regensburg, 12 Oct 1576). Son of (6) Ferdinand I. In 1548 he married his cousin, Mary of Spain (1528–1603), daughter of Charles V (*see* (5) above), as whose regent in Spain he acted from 1548 to 1550. As Emperor he resided in Vienna, governing his Austrian dominions and defending them against the Turks. His religious attitudes appear ambiguous: although he remained a Catholic, on his deathbed he refused the sacraments; he was demonstrably sympathetic to Protestantism and attempted to reunite the confessions. He ruled with tolerance and moderation and strove to establish a humanistic court that might reduce growing political and religious tensions. A cultured man with considerable linguistic ability and wide-ranging interests, he engaged some of the more notable intellectuals of his time: Joannes Sambucus (1531–84) was his official court historiographer, Hugo Blotius (1533–1608) his court librarian and Justus Lipsius advised him on Roman literature and stoic philosophy. Maximilian's antiquarian and bibliophilic concerns were matched by a profound interest in the natural sciences. He gathered a number of famous botanists, astronomers and alchemists at his court, among them Ghislain de Busbecq (1522–92), first purveyor of the tulip to western Europe, Charles de l'Ecluse (Clusius; 1524/6–1609), who introduced the water chestnut in Vienna, and Tadeas Hajek (1525–1600) and Leonhard Thurneysser (1530–96), who were instrumental in establishing the imperial collections of artefacts, naturalia and exotica. He also loved music and, in 1568, secured the services of Philippe de Monte (1521–1603) as *Kapellmeister*.

The study of Maximilian's role as collector and patron has been neglected, due in part to the significant activities of his brother Archduke Ferdinand of Austria (*see* (9) below) and his son Rudolf II (*see* (10) below) and also because no complete inventory of his collections exists. However, among the gifts he received are some of the finest examples of ceremonial weapons in the world (e.g. gold rapier, before 1550; Vienna, Ksthist. Mus.; *see* ARMS AND ARMOUR, §II, 1 and fig. 3). He built for his collections a pleasure palace, the Neugebäude (begun 1568, partially destr. 1775; *see* VIENNA, §II, 2 and AUSTRIA, §II, 2 and fig. 4), in the style of an Italian Renaissance villa. Pietro Ferabosco, who may have built the Stallburg (1558–69), and who later remodelled the Amalienburg (1575–7; *see* VIENNA, §V, 5(i)), was not employed on the project. Instead, Maximilian sought, unsuccessfully, the services of Andrea Palladio. However, the belvedere-like structure with galleries and towers, large walled and partly terraced gardens with stables, ball-park, waterworks and a number of fountains was a major undertaking to which several artists contributed. Jacopo Strada, who had served the court since 1558 as architect and from 1564 as Imperial Antiquarius, was adviser on all artistic matters, especially the acquisition of antiquities, and is generally acknowledged to have been involved in the design of the Neugebäude. Three fountains (commissioned 1570 and 1575; destr.) were executed by the sculptor Alexander Colin, who also worked on the imperial tombs in Prague, including that of the Emperor (*see* COLIN, ALEXANDER). Another fountain (1570–75) was commissioned by the Emperor in 1568, executed by the Nuremberg goldsmith Wenzel Jamnitzer in collaboration with Johann Gregor von der Schardt (*c.* 1530–85) and delivered to Rudolf II (*see* (10) below) in 1578. It was over 3 m high and represented the universe; surmounted by the imperial crown and statues of Habsburg emperors, it was an allegory of imperial power and universal Habsburg rule. Only the four gilt-bronze statuettes of *Flora*, *Ceres*, *Bacchus* and *Vulcan*, representing the seasons, survive (Vienna, Ksthist. Mus.). A bronze *Mercury* (Stockholm, Nmus.) with von der Schardt's initials in Maximilian's collection may have been connected with this project. For the decoration of the Neugebäude the Emperor engaged in 1575, on the recommendation of Giambologna, the sculptor and architect Hans Mont from Ghent and the Antwerp painter Bartholomeus Spranger, who had been working in Rome for Cardinal Alessandro Farnese. In 1565 Maximilian received three major works by Giambologna from Cosimo I de' Medici, Grand Duke of Tuscany: a *Flying Mercury*

(1565), a bronze relief of an *Allegory on Francesco de' Medici* and a 'figurina di metallo', which may be the small bronze of a *Bathing Woman* (both 1561–5; all Vienna, Ksthist. Mus.). The model for the *Mercury* came from the reverse of a medal (1555) of Maximilian by Leone Leoni who, however, was not regularly employed at court, unlike Antonio Abondio, who from 1566 served the Emperor as medallist and portrait-painter. Among his best work is a silver-mounted coloured wax relief portrait of *Maximilian II* (1575; Vienna, Ksthist. Mus.; see fig.).

The Emperor's official portrait-painter was Giuseppe Arcimboldo, who entered imperial service in 1564. No surviving painted portraits can be convincingly attributed to him, however, and his real fame rests on his studies of heads, ingeniously constructed from flowers, fruit, vegetables and animals. One set each of the *Four Seasons* (1563; Vienna, Ksthist. Mus.) and the *Four Elements* (1566; *Fire* and *Water*, Vienna, Ksthist. Mus.; *Earth* and *Air*, priv. col.) were presented to the Emperor in 1569 with an interpretative poem by an associate of Arcimboldo that clearly shows them to be imperial allegories rather than bizarre fancies. They contain Habsburg devices such as the Golden Fleece and are systematic elaborations of and allusions to the Habsburgs' universal rule (Kaufmann).

The themes of the frequent court festivals followed the same intellectual conceits for imperial imagery. During the Emperor's reign three major ones were staged: the Prague Tournament (1570), celebrating the betrothal of his daughter Anne of Austria to Philip II, King of Spain; the Vienna Festival (1571) for the wedding of his brother Archduke Charles of Austria and the Bratislava Festival (1572), celebrating the coronation of his son Rudolf as king of Hungary. Arcimboldo's designs for them are included in a volume of drawings (Florence, Uffizi), and Jacopo Strada produced costume designs (Vienna, Österreich. Nbib.) for the Vienna Festival.

BIBLIOGRAPHY

V. Bibl: *Maximilian II, der rätselhafte Kaiser* (Vienna, 1929)

A. Lhotsky: *Die Geschichte der Sammlungen (1941–5)*, ii/1 of *Festschrift des kunsthistorischen Museums zur Feier des fünfzigjährigen Bestandes* (Vienna, 1945)

G. Heinz: 'Studien zur Porträtmalerei an den Höfen der österreichischen Erblande', *Jb. Ksthist. Samml. Wien*, lix (1963), pp. 99–224

K. Vocelka: *Habsburgische Hochzeiten, 1550–1600: Kulturgeschichtliche Studien zum manieristischen Repräsentationsfest* (Vienna, 1976)

T. DaCosta Kaufmann: *The Imperial Theme in the Age of Maximilian II and Rudolf II* (New York, 1978)

E. Scheicher: *Die Kunst- und Wunderkammern der Habsburger* (Vienna, 1979)

R. Feuchtmüller: *Das Neugebäude* (Vienna, 1979)

D. J. Jansen: 'Jacopo Strada (1515–88): Antiquario della Sacra Cesarea Maesta', *Leids Ksthist. Jb.* (1982), pp. 57–69

M. Leithe-Jasper: *Renaissance Master Bronzes from the Collection of the Kunsthistorisches Museum, Vienna* (London, 1986)

H. Lietzmann: *Das Neugebäude in Wien* (Munich, 1987)

E. Edelmayer and A. Kohler, eds: *Maximilian II, Kultur und Politik im 16. Jahrhundert* (Munich, 1992)

ROSEMARIE BERGMANN

(9) Ferdinand, Archduke of Austria, Count of Tyrol (*b* Linz, 14 June 1529; *d* Innsbruck, 24 Jan 1595). Son of (6) Ferdinand I and brother of (8) Maximilian II. He was educated by outstanding humanists from the University of Vienna, including the mathematician Colimitus (Georg Tannstetter; 1482–1535) and the classical scholar and poet Caspar Ursinus Velius (Caspar Vel; 1493–1538). In 1544

Maximilian II, by Antonio Abondio, wax relief with pearls and obsidian, set in a silver frame, diam. 128 mm, 1575 (Vienna, Kunsthistorisches Museum)

he was given his own household and travelled to the Netherlands to the court of his uncle Charles V (*see* (5) above); he also took part in the ceremonies in Brussels in 1555 when Charles abdicated. His time at the court, his contact with royalty from all over Europe, especially Spain and the Netherlands, and his participation in tournaments and ceremonial occasions influenced his later activities as a collector and patron. In 1547 he was appointed governor of Bohemia and held court in Prague on a magnificent scale, instituting and organizing masked tournaments and festivities, in connection with which he established his own court armoury. Initially he advised on the completion and decoration of various buildings connected with Hradčany, including the Belvedere (*see* PRAGUE, §§I, 2 and IV, 1); in 1555–6 he himself designed Hvězda, a star-shaped summer-house in the Neuer Tiergarten, which derived its name from its ground-plan, unique for its time.

In 1556 Ferdinand led an Austro-Bohemian expedition against the Turks, for which Pope Paul IV awarded him a consecrated shield and sword (Vienna, Ksthist. Mus.). In 1557 he secretly married Philippine Welser (1527–80); since she was a commoner, their sons were not accorded imperial status, and the Archduke's attempt to gain the throne of Poland foundered because of his marriage. As count of the Tyrol, his official residence was the Hofburg in Innsbruck; in 1563 he bought for his family the medieval Schloss Ambras (*see* INNSBRUCK, §3 (ii) and fig. 3) and while still in Prague directed work on alterations to it and some new building. From 1567, when he settled in the

Tyrol, his court in Innsbruck and Schloss Ambras became a brilliant centre of European culture, in which his Ambras collection played a crucial role. Ferdinand had laid the foundations of the collection in Bohemia, though it is not possible to identify which items he acquired there.

In his collecting the main emphasis was on weapons (examples in Vienna, Ksthist. Mus.; Innsbruck, Schloss Ambras), and he corresponded with princes throughout Europe in order to acquire them. He was especially interested in items with a historical connection and displayed them according to the principles of historical scholarship, laid out chronologically and by the rank of the bearer of the weapon, whose *virtus* was to be handed down to the *memoria* of later generations. The collection of over 1000 mainly small-sized portraits (Vienna, Ksthist. Mus.) had the same objective. The Ambras collection of art and curiosities drew visitors from all over Europe because of its wide diversity and the high artistic and historical merit of individual items and groups of items. It was logically arranged according to similarity of material, with due regard to aesthetic quality, and it is assumed that the programme, content and display stemmed from the Archduke himself. Jakob Schrenck von Notzing (1530–1612) wrote the *Armentarium Heroicum* (Innsbruck, 1601–4), a picture catalogue of the fourth Ambras collection of arms, and acted as the Archduke's adviser on weapons, as did Gerard de Roo (*d* 1589), who became curator of the art collection in 1580.

One of Ferdinand's most important undertakings not relating to his collection was the completion of the tomb of his great-grandfather, Maximilian I (*see* (3) above), in the Hofkirche at Innsbruck. The familiarity he acquired with the history of the House of Habsburg led him to commission Francesco Terzio to produce a corpus of drawings for *Imagines gentis Austriacae*, a five-volume collection of engravings executed by Gaspare de Avibus containing portraits of the Habsburgs and related families; here too the main emphasis was on the historical and genealogical aspect. In 1570 Ferdinand founded the Hofglashütte in Innsbruck, where Venetian glassblowers were employed mainly to produce the glass needed for the court (*see* AUSTRIA, §VIII). There had been a court armoury in Innsbruck since the 15th century, and the Archduke kept it well supplied with work in connection with family festivities involving allegorical tournaments, for which he himself devised programmes. The tournament cavalcades at the Kolowrat-Payrsberg wedding (1580) and at the Archduke's own second marriage in 1582 to his niece Anna Katharina Gonzaga (1566–1621) were recorded with a commentary in series of tinted engravings (Innsbruck, Schloss Ambras; Munich, Bayer. Staatsbib.; New York, Pub. Lib.) by the court painter Sigmund Elsässen (*fl* 1579; *d* 1587). The founding of a court orchestra in Innsbruck was also linked to such festivities. The Archduke wrote the comedy *Speculum vitae humanae, auff Teutsch ein Spiegel des Menschlichen Lebens genandt* (Innsbruck, 1584), one of the earliest examples of German prose drama.

BIBLIOGRAPHY

J. Hirn: *Erzherzog Ferdinand II. von Tirol: Geschichte seiner Regierung und seiner Länder*, 2 vols (Innsbruck, 1885, 1888)

D. Schönherr: 'Ein fürstlicher Architekt und Bauherr', *D. Schönherr, Gesammelte Schriften* (Innsbruck, 1900), pp. 455–83

W. Senn: *Musik und Theater am Hof zu Innsbruck* (Innsbruck, 1953), pp. 63–186

O. Gamber: 'Erzherzog Ferdinand und die Ambraser Rüstkammern', *Die Rüstkammern, Führer durch das kunsthistorische Museum*, xxx (Vienna, 1981), pp. 24–33

E. Scheicher: 'Ein Fest am Hofe Erzherzog Ferdinands II.', *Jb. Ksthist. Samml. Wien*, lxxvii (1981), pp. 119–54

Zur Selbstdarstellung des Renaissancefürsten (exh. cat., ed. A. Auer; Innsbruck, Schloss Ambras, 1988)

ELISABETH SCHEICHER

(10) Rudolf II, Holy Roman Emperor [King of Hungary; King of Bohemia] (*b* Vienna, 18 July 1552; *reg* Hungary 1572–1607, Bohemia 1575–1611, Holy Roman Emperor 1576–1612; *d* Prague, 20 Jan 1612). Son of (8) Maximilian II. He was one of the greatest patrons and collectors in the history of Europe and used the resources available to him as ruler over his share of the Habsburg domains to commission paintings, sculpture, works of applied art (*see* CZECH REPUBLIC, §§VIII and IX), gardens and architecture, to establish a collection of several thousand paintings, the outstanding *Kunstkammer* of his time, and to support the sciences. His interest in the arts may be regarded not only as the outcome of family traditions but also as the culmination of a late Renaissance princely custom, which his own activities further encouraged.

1. Artistic influences. 2. Patronage. 3. Collections. 4. Posthumous reputation.

1. ARTISTIC INFLUENCES. His father, Maximilian II (*see* (8) above), was a major patron of the arts and learning and gathered at his court a group of scholars, anticipating his heir's support for humanism and astronomy, and numerous artists, of whom several, including Giuseppe Arcimboldo, Jacopo Strada, Martino Rota and Antonio Abbondio, remained in Rudolf's service. From 1563 to 1571 he was educated in Spain at the Habsburg court of his uncle, Philip II, King of Spain (*see* §II(2) below), which possessed Netherlandish paintings and masterworks of the Italian Renaissance. The impressions made by Italian paintings at the Spanish court may have been reinforced by his journeys through Italy on his way to and from Spain. His experiences as a youth at the Habsburg courts would also have made him familiar with his Burgundian heritage, including Burgundian ceremonial and elaborate tournaments with allegorical subjects, and in general the use of the visual arts to represent majesty.

2. PATRONAGE. After the first few years of his reign as emperor, during which he relied on the entourage he had inherited and when his major efforts at patronage involved the completion of architectural projects such as the Neugebäude and Amalienburg in Vienna (*see* VIENNA, §V, 5(i)), Rudolf II transferred the imperial court to Prague. From *c.* 1583, when his residence was firmly established in Prague, he called into his service artists, alchemists, astronomers, philosophers and other humanists to make Prague into what Joachim von Sandrart called 'a Parnassus of the arts' (*Teutsche Academie*, 1675 and 1679; *see* PRAGUE, §§I, 2; II, 2 and fig. 8).

Starting in the 1580s painters such as Bartholomäus Spranger, Hans von Aachen, Joseph Heintz (i) and Matthäus Gundelach came to the imperial court. They were

Rudolf II and the Electors of the Holy Roman Empire, by Joris Hoefnagel, woodcut, 180×132 mm, from the *Bocskay Schriftmusterbuch*, 1591–4 (Vienna, Kunsthistorisches Museum, Bocskay Codex, fol. 2*r*)

later joined by such artists as the miniaturists Joris Hoefnagel and his son Jacob Hoefnagel (1575–*c.* 1630) and Daniel Fröschl, who also succeeded Jacopo Strada and Ottavio Strada (1550–1607) as Imperial Antiquarius. Pieter Stevens and Roelandt Savery, Netherlandish specialists in genre, landscape, animal and still-life painting, expanded the complement of imperial painters, although many lesser-known artists also worked in that capacity for the court. In 1597 Aegidius Sadeler II was installed as imperial printmaker, and he disseminated knowledge of their works.

Among the sculptors and masters of the applied arts who gathered in Prague were the sculptor Adriaen de Vries, many of whose most important works were made for the Emperor, for example two bronze portrait busts (1603; Vienna, Ksthist. Mus.; 1607; Vienna, Schatzkam.), and the goldsmiths Paulus van Vianen, whose work for the Emperor included the mounting of a jasper pitcher (1608; Vienna, Ksthist. Mus.), and Wenzel Jamnitzer (*see* JAMNITZER, (1) and fig. 1). Erasmus Habermel (*d* 1606) supplied the Emperor and his astronomers Tycho Brahe and Johann Kepler (1571–1630) with exquisite scientific instruments. Jobst Burgi (?1552–1620) and Christoph Margraf (1584–*c.* 1604), among others, provided sophisticated clocks and automata. The Miseroni workshop relocated from Milan to Prague where its members celebrated 20 years of imperial patronage with a bloodstone bowl (1608; Paris, Louvre), while Cosimo Castrucci (*fl* in Prague ?1598–1615) and Giovanni Castrucci from Florence (*fl* in Prague *c.* 1596), specialist hardstone-cutters, worked on a number of commissions (*see* CZECH REPUBLIC, §§V, 2 and IX) producing, for example, a view of the Hradčany (after 1606; Vienna, Ksthist. Mus.). Other masters who worked for Rudolf II include Anton Schweinberger (*fl* 1587–*c.* 1603), Jan Vermeyen, maker of the magnificent imperial crown (1602; Vienna, Schatzkam.; *see* VIENNA, §V, 5(ii)), Nikolas Pfaff (*b* ?1556; *d* before 1612), master of the art of turning ivory, and Caspar Lehmann, who introduced the technique of wheel-engraving on glass (e.g. glass plaque engraved with portrait of *Rudolf II*, probably before 1606; Vienna, Ksthist. Mus.; *see also* CZECH REPUBLIC, §VII, 1).

The Emperor often visited his artists in their workshops, supervising their work, inventing subjects and even participating himself. Although it has often been emphasized that Rudolf's taste and influence were for the outstandingly erotic and the Mannerist style, he in fact possessed an almost universal interest that encouraged a wide variety of artistic production. Like other Renaissance rulers, he commissioned portraits and sponsored many, often learned, allegories on his own glory, but he also sent Savery to the Alps *c.* 1606–7 to sketch 'rare wonders of nature' (according to Karel van Mander I) and patronized the naturalistic illuminations of Joris Hoefnagel (e.g. *Rudolf II and the Electors of the Holy Roman Empire* from the *Bocskay Schriftmusterbuch*; 1591–4; Vienna, Ksthist. Mus., Bocskay Codex, fol. 2; see fig.), for example paying a high price for his *Four Elements* (1579; ex-Rosenwald priv. col.; Washington, DC, N.G.A.; *see* HOEFNAGEL, JORIS, fig. 2). Thus under the imperial aegis there originated not only some of the first painted landscapes based on actual motifs observed in nature (e.g. *Cascade* by Savery, *c.* 1608; Ghent, Mus. S. Kst.), but also some of the first surviving independent easel still-life and animal paintings by a Netherlandish artist (examples by Savery, 1603; Utrecht, Cent. Mus. and 1605; the Netherlands, priv. col.). These activities parallel the Emperor's support of the sciences: the astronomers Tycho Brahe and Johann Kepler, the inventor of logarithms, Jobst Burgi and the gemologist, Anselm de Boethius de Boodt, all worked for him. Even the 'mannered' mythologies with an erotic charge painted for the Emperor can be reconsidered: besides being typical of a kind of work cherished by many rulers throughout Europe, they often possess a humorous, epigrammatic edge and can be better described as *poesie*. Such a description is justified by the use of this and related terms in a variety of languages by contemporaries; it also indicates that many of the court artists collaborated with or were befriended by contemporary poets, musicians and humanists. Besides such painters as Hoefnagel who were humanists and poets themselves, many others collaborated with scholars: Giuseppe Arcimboldo (for his allegorical portrait of Rudolph II *see* ARCIMBOLDO, GIUSEPPE, fig. 2) with Giovanni Battista Fonteo (*fl* *c.* 1560–80) and Gregorio Comanini (*d* 1608), Bartholomäus Spranger with Paul Fabritius (*fl* *c.* 1577), Hans von Aachen with Jiří Barthold Pontanus (?1550–1614). As many highly intellectual allegories, often emphasizing the status of the arts, and comments by contemporary court painters suggest, Rudolf II seems thus to have sponsored the creation of an atmosphere that Sandrart could justly characterize as an 'academy', even though no formal academy was established in Prague.

3. COLLECTIONS. Many of the works made by the court artists were consolidated into the extensive imperial collections that contained masterpieces of both northern and Italian painting. Among the most outstanding were Albrecht Dürer's watercolours the *Large Piece of Turf* (1503; Vienna, Albertina; *see* DÜRER, (1), fig. 7) and *Hare* (1502; Vienna, Albertina), most of the pictures of Pieter Bruegel the elder, paintings from Correggio's *Loves of Jupiter* acquired by Charles V (*see* (5), §3 above), Parmigianino's *Self-portrait* (1524; Vienna, Ksthist. Mus.) and Leonardo da Vinci's *Lady with an Ermine* (1484/5; Kraków, Czartoryski Col.; *see* LEONARDO DA VINCI, fig. 3). The Emperor also acquired famous manuscripts, such as the *Codex Gigas* (Uppsala, Ubib.), and antiquities, including the *Gemma Augustea* (after AD 10; Vienna, Ksthist. Mus.; *see* GEM-ENGRAVING, §I, 4) and so-called *Ilioneus* (Munich, Glyp.).

The paintings and sculpture in the imperial collection complemented the *Kunstkammer* proper, which contained smaller bronzes, works in cut stone, medallions and ivories, coins, scientific instruments, books and drawings, natural objects and some paintings. The imperial *Kunstkammer* was the most impressive of its time (*see* KUNSTKAMMER, §2) and was mentioned, along with other local collections, by Karel van Mander I as one of the reasons to visit Prague. Formerly dismissed as an unsystematic curiosity cabinet, the collections are now believed to have served as a place of contemplation and refuge for the Emperor and as a resource that aided the scientific and artistic explorations of his court scholars and artists, stimulating the creation of works of art by inspiring emulation. As a universal collection that mirrored in microcosm the macrocosm of the world and the body politic over which the Emperor claimed to hold sway, they also symbolically represented his imperial majesty.

The way in which some parts of the collections were housed highlighted this last function. Recent scholarship has contradicted earlier interpretations and emphasized the stately manner in which at least some of the collections were displayed in the castle and in the Prague Belvedere (see Kaufmann, 1978 and 1993, and 1988 exh. cat.). The Emperor had parts of Hradčany Castle in Prague rebuilt, with new rooms, including the Gallery (1590–96) and the Spanish Hall (1604–6), created for the exhibition of paintings and sculpture (*see* PRAGUE, §IV, 1). Bartholomäus Spranger, Hans Vredeman de Vries and Paul Vredeman de Vries (*b* 1567; *d* after 1630) painted decorations with appropriate subjects, some playing on the macrocosm–microcosm analogy that glorified the Emperor, for some of the rooms in the castle. The *Kunstkammer* was shown to visiting dignitaries, and court artists probably had regular access to the collections, as the impact of older works on theirs suggests; documented visits by commoners, early copies after paintings in the collections and van Mander's recommendation to visit Prague indicate that artists' friends or associates also probably saw the collections. Works by the court artists were, however, also readily visible in churches in Prague and elsewhere in Bohemia and were sent as gifts to other courts, thereby prompting rulers such as Henry Julius, Duke of Brunswick-Wolfenbüttel, and Christian II, Elector of Saxony, to commission other works from Prague.

The dispersal of Rudolf II's court entourage and of his collections soon after his death in 1612 left few lasting traces *in situ*. The Holy Roman Emperor Matthias (see (12) below) moved the court and imperial collections back to Vienna; other paintings went to Archduke Albrecht in the Netherlands. During the 1620s and 1630s some works were sold and what remained in Prague became booty to the Swedish troops who sacked Hradčany in 1648, leading eventually to the further dispersal of works from Rudolf's collections throughout the world (though much of it passed to Queen Christina of Sweden). The disorder in Bohemia in that period made it difficult until recently to gain an accurate perception and appreciation of the character and importance of Rudolf II's patronage and collecting.

4. POSTHUMOUS REPUTATION. Though the Emperor's passion for the arts was long regarded as an eccentric idiosyncrasy, many contemporary rulers of Europe also dabbled in the arts. It may even be argued that by amassing the greatest collection of his time, Rudolf II was not avoiding affairs of state (as unsympathetic observers have long claimed) but making a political statement. In a world of rulers who were collectors, the arts could become a locus for diplomatic activity, in which the exchange and commissioning of works of art played a role. The Emperor accordingly had an impact not only on contemporary rulers, for whom collections were necessary signs of status, but on noblemen, and his collections were also known to commoners (see Kaufmann, 1993, for a review of the political and scientific significance of the collections and see Krčálová, 1975, and Hořejší and Neumann, 1979).

The redesign of Hradčany Castle exemplifies Rudolf II's support of building and garden construction. Recent research has disproved older theses that he lacked interest in architecture, demonstrating that GIOVANNI GARGIOLLI, PIETRO FERABOSCO and GIOVANNI MARIA FILIPPI, among others, were involved in a broad range of architectural commissions (*see* CZECH REPUBLIC, §II); these included the imperial mill (*c*. 1586), the castles and gardens at Brandýs-nad-Laben (1588–93) and Lysa (1600–07) and the so-called Matthias Gate at Hradčany Castle, Prague.

BIBLIOGRAPHY

R. J. W. Evans: *Rudolf II and his World: A Study in Intellectual History, 1576–1612* (Oxford, 1973)

J. Krčálová: 'Poznámky k rudolfínské architektuře' [Notes on Rudolphine architecture], *Umění*, xxiii (1975), pp. 499–526

J. Neumann: 'Rudolfínské umění I' [Rudolphine art I], *Umění*, xxv (1977), pp. 400–44

T. DaCosta Kaufmann: *Variations on the Imperial Theme in the Age of Maximilian II and Rudolf II* (New York and London, 1978)

Rudolfínská kresba [Rudolphine drawing] (exh. cat. by E. Fučíková, Prague, N.G., 1978)

J. Neumann: 'Rudolfínské umění II' [Rudolphine art II], *Umění*, xxvi (1978), pp. 303–75

J. Hořejší and J. Neumann, eds: *Die Kunst der Renaissance und des Manierismus in Böhmen* (Hanau, 1979), pp. 134–47, 159–217

E. Scheicher: *Die Kunst- und Wunderkammer der Habsburger* (Vienna and Munich, 1979), pp. 142–78

R. J. W. Evans: *The Making of the Habsburg Monarchy, 1550–1700: An Interpretation* (Oxford, 1979)

Zeichnung in Deutschland: Deutsche Zeichner, 1540–1640 (exh. cat., ed. H. Geissler; Stuttgart, Staatsgal., 1979–80), pp. 52–8, 187–92 [essay by E. Fučíková]

K. Vocelka: *Die politische Propaganda Kaiser Rudolfs II (1576–1612)* (Vienna, 1980)

Drawings from the Holy Roman Empire, 1540–1680; A Selection from North American Collections (exh. cat. by T. DaCosta Kaufmann, Princeton U., NJ, A. Mus., 1982), pp. 133–76

K.. Vocelka: *Rudolf II und seine Zeit* (Vienna, Cologne and Graz, 1985)

F. Seibt, ed.: *Renaissance in Böhmen* (Munich, 1985), pp. 185–93, 204–5, 275–314, 316–29

T. DaCosta Kaufmann: *L'Ecole de Prague: La Peinture à la cour de Rodolphe II* (Paris, 1985); rev. as *The School of Prague: Painting at the Court of Rudolf II* (Chicago and London, 1988)

E. Fučíková: *Rudolfinská kresba* [Rudolphine drawing] (Prague, 1986), rev. as *Die rudolphinische Zeichnung* (Hanau, 1987)

Meisterzeichnungen des Kunstlerkreises um Kaiser Rudolf II aus dem Szépművészeti Múzeum in Budapest (exh. cat. by T. Gerszi, Salzburg, Barockmus., 1987)

J. Dvorský, ed.: *Die Kunst am Hofe Rudolfs II* (Hanau, 1988)

T. DaCosta Kaufmann: 'Astronomy, Art and Humanism at the Entry of Rudolf II into Vienna', *Jb.Ksthist. Samml. Wien* (1988)

E. Fučíková, ed.: *Prag um 1600: Kunst und Kultur am Hofe Rudolfs II. (Beitrage)* (Freren, 1988)

Prag um 1600: Kunst und Kultur am Hofe Rudolfs II., 2 vols (exh. cat., Essen, Villa Hügel; Vienna, Ksthist. Mus., 1988–9)

'Umění na dvoře Rudolfa II v Praze', *Dějiny Českého Umění*, ii/1 (1989), pp. 159-247

The Stylish Image: Printmakers to the Court of Rudolf II (exh. cat. by M. Campbell, Edinburgh, 1991) [essays by R. J. W. Evans and E. Fučíková]

F. Antonovich: *L'Art à la cour de Rudolphe II empereur du Saint-Empire romain germanique: Prague et son rayonnement* (Paris, 1992)

T. DaCosta Kaufmann: *The Mastery of Nature: Aspects of Art, Science and Humanism in the Renaissance* (Princeton, 1993)——: *Court, Cloister and City: The Art and Culture of Central Europe, 1450–1800* (London and Chicago, 1995), pp. 184–203

THOMAS DACOSTA KAUFMANN

(11) Ernest [Ernst], Archduke of Austria (*b* Vienna, 15 July 1553; *d* Brussels, 12 Feb 1595). Son of (8) Maximilian II. From 1563 to 1571 he and his brother

Rudolf II were educated at the court of their uncle, Philip II, King of Spain (*see* §II(2) below). After an unsuccessful candidacy for the Polish crown, in 1576 he was appointed Regent of Lower Austria, in 1580 Governor of Inner Austria and in 1593 Governor of the Spanish Netherlands; he was constantly involved with the religious struggles in those lands. He was keenly interested in the arts. In 1594 the citizens of Antwerp presented him with six paintings of the *Seasons* (1565; three, Vienna, Ksthist. Mus.; New York, Met.; Prague, N.G., Šternberk Pal.; one untr.; *see* BRUEGEL, (1), fig. 5) by Pieter Bruegel the elder, originally from the collection of Nicolaas Jonghelinck, and the Archduke bought at least two more Bruegel paintings, the *Conversion of Saul* (1567) and the *Peasant Wedding* (1567; both Vienna, Ksthist. Mus.; *see* BREUGEL, (1), fig. 7). Martino Rota painted a fine three-quarter-length portrait of the *Archduke in Armour* (*c.* 1580; New York, Hisp. Soc. America) and a reduced bust-length version (*c.* 1580; Vienna, Ksthist. Mus.). A portrait by Otto van Veen (?1593–5; Vienna, Belvedere) was probably painted in the Netherlands. His court painters included Hendrik de Clerck and Tobias Verhaeght (*see* BELGIUM, §XII).

BIBLIOGRAPHY

C. Coremans: *L'Archiduc Ernest, sa cour, ses dépenses: Détails sur son voyage de Prague à Bruxelles (1593–95)* (Brussels, 1847)

A. Lhotsky: *Die Geschichte der Sammlungen (1941–5)*, i/2 of *Festschrift des kunsthistorischen Museums zur Feier des fünfzigjährigen Bestandes* (Vienna, 1941–5)

A. Doutrepont: 'L'Archiduc Ernest d'Autriche', *Miscellanea L. van der Essen*, ii (Brussels, 1947)

G. Heinz: 'Studien zur Portraitmalerei an den Höfen der österreichischen Erblande', *Jb. Ksthist. Samml. Wien*, lix (1963), pp. 99–224

(12) Matthias, Holy Roman Emperor [King of Hungary; King of Bohemia] (*b* Vienna, 24 Feb 1557; *reg* Hungary 1608–18, Bohemia 1611–17, Holy Roman Emperor 1612–19; *d* Vienna, 20 March 1619). Son of (8) Maximilian II. In 1577 the Catholic nobility of the Netherlands invited him to assume the regency, but he proved ineffective, and in 1581 he left Brussels and settled in Linz. In 1593 he was appointed Governor of Lower Austria by Rudolf, and in 1606 he negotiated peace treaties with the rebellious Hungarians and with the Turks. This resulted in a fierce power struggle with his brother Rudolf in which the Habsburgs acknowledged Matthias as their head and future emperor. In 1608 Rudolf granted him the kingdom of Hungary and duchy of Austria and Moravia, in return for the concession of considerable religious freedom for the Protestants there. In 1611 he was also crowned King of Bohemia, and in 1612 he became Holy Roman Emperor. He was an indecisive politician, and his short reign was dominated by his adviser, Cardinal Melchior Khlesel (1552–1630). He was unable to reconcile Catholic and Protestant forces in the Empire, and the Bohemian uprising (1618) triggered the Thirty Years War (1618–48).

Matthias kept a modest court. His court painter was Lucas van Valckenborch I who painted two youthful full-length portraits of the then *Archduke Matthias of Austria* (both 1579; Vienna, Ksthist. Mus.). One shows him bareheaded, wearing German armour and a baton; in the other he wears a blue Spanish court costume with black cape and Italian hat. Naturalness and bright local colours distinguish these images from the standard Spanish court portraits. An allegorical portrait by the same painter of *Archduke Matthias in Roman Armour with Small Shield-bearer* (1580; Vienna, Ksthist. Mus.) represents him as Publius Cornelius Scipio Africanus, and in the background landscape of the portrait Scipio/Matthias is depicted freeing two prisoners; this reference to his magnanimity and the *Liberation of Andromeda* on the shield clearly allude to his purported role in the Netherlands. Valckenborch also painted a three-quarter-length portrait of his patron wearing knee-length trousers and a sash (1582–5; Vienna, Ksthist. Mus.). A series of the *Labours of the Months*, of which seven survive (1585–7; five in Vienna, Ksthist. Mus.; two in Brno, Morav. Gal.), and a *View of Linz* by Valckenborch (1593; Frankfurt am Main, Städel. Kstinst. & Städt. Gal.) suggest that Matthias shared Rudolf's fondness for Bruegelian landscapes. Indeed, after Rudolf's death, several artists from his court joined that of Matthias in Vienna: Jeremias Günther (*fl* 1614–34), imperial court painter (1612–19), painted portraits of *Emperor Matthias* and his wife, *Anne of Austria* (1613; Florence, Uffizi; Vienna, Ksthist. Mus.); Hans von Aachen portrayed him twice as King of Bohemia (1612; Prague, Hradčany Castle; *c.* 1613–15; Vienna, Ksthist. Mus.); and Matthäus Gundelach and Roelandt Savery are also listed as court painters.

BIBLIOGRAPHY

A. Lhotsky: *Die Geschichte der Sammlungen (1941–5)*, i/2 of *Festschrift des kunsthistorischen Museums zur Feier des fünfzigjährigen Bestandes* (Vienna, 1941–5)

G. Heinz: 'Studien zur Portraitmalerei an den Höfen der österreichischen Erblande', *Jb. Ksthist. Samml. Wien*, lix (1963), pp. 99–224

W. Hummelberger: 'Erzherzog Matthias in den Niederlanden (1577–1581)', *Jb. Ksthist. Samml. Wien*, lxi (1965), pp. 91–118

A. Wied: 'Lucas van Valckenborch', *Jb. Ksthist. Samml. Wien*, lxvii (1971), pp. 119–231 [with cat. of works]

T. DaCosta Kaufmann: *The School of Prague* (Chicago and London, 1988)

A. Wied: *Lucas und Marten van Valckenborch* (Freren, 1990)

ROSEMARIE BERGMANN

(13) Maximilian, Archduke of Austria, Count of Tyrol (*b* Wiener Neustadt, 12 Oct 1558; *d* Vienna, 2 Nov 1618). Son of (8) Maximilian II. He became co-adjutor of the Teutonic Order in 1585 and High Master in 1590. In 1587–8 he made an unsuccessful attempt to gain the crown of Poland. He was commander-in-chief of the imperial army against the Turks in Hungary in 1596–7 and governor for his brother Emperor Rudolf II (*see* (10) above) in 1602. After the latter's death he became ruler of the Tyrol in 1612. His interests were primarily historical: as a preserver of monuments he had a highly developed sense of responsibility, and as a patron of historiography he commissioned works relating to the history of the House of Habsburg, such as the Austrian ducal crown (1616; Klosterneuburg, Stift Lapidarium) and a series of statuettes (Innsbruck, Schloss Ambras) depicting his ancestors since Emperor Rudolf I (1218–91). Although an inventory of his bequest shows that he had his own *Kunstkammer*, its contents cannot now be identified. His free-standing bronze tomb was begun in 1608 by HUBERT GERHARD and completed and set up (1615–19) in St Jacobskirche, Innsbruck, by Caspar Gras (*see* INNSBRUCK, §1(ii)).

BIBLIOGRAPHY

B. Dudik: 'Des Hoch- und Deutschmeisters Erzherzogs Maximilians Testament und Verlassenschaft vom Jahr 1619', *Archv Knd. Österreich. Gesch.-Quellen*, xxxiii (1865), pp. 235–43

J. Hirn: *Erzherzog Maximilian der Deutschmeister. Regent von Tirol*, 2 vols (Innsbruck, 1915, 1936, *R* 1981)
A. Lhotsky: *Die Geschichte der Sammlungen* (1941–5), ii/1 of *Festschrift des kunsthistorischen Museums zur Feier des fünfzigjährigen Bestandes* (Vienna, 1941–5), pp. 223–31
F. Caramelle: 'Die Einsiedelei Maximilians des Deutschmeisters in Innsbruck', *Tirol*, xxi (1982/3), pp. 39–50
H. Noflatscher: *Maximilian der Deutschmeister, 1558–1618*, Quellen Stud. Dt. Ordens ix (Marburg, 1987)

ELISABETH SCHEICHER

(14) Albert, Archduke of Austria, ruler of the Netherlands (*b* Neustadt, 13 Nov 1559; *reg* 1599–1621; *d* Brussels, 16 July 1621). Son of (8) Maximilian II. He was brought up in Spain and created Cardinal (1577) and Archbishop of Toledo (1595), Grand Inquisitor and Viceroy of Portugal and Viceroy of Spain.

(15) Isabella Clara Eugenia, Archduchess of Austria (*b* Segovia, 12 Aug 1566; *d* Brussels, 1 Dec 1633). Wife of (14) Albert, Archduke of Austria. She was the daughter of Philip II, King of Spain (*see* §II(2) below). In 1599 Albert received a papal dispensation and married Isabella. On their marriage, Philip granted the couple and their heirs sovereignty of the Netherlands and the title of Archdukes; this was intended to confer a measure of independence on the Netherlands, which had been in a state of civil war throughout Philip's reign. Albert's early years were devoted to arranging a cessation of hostilities, which he achieved in 1609 with the Twelve-year Truce, the signing of which ushered in a period of peace that enabled the southern Netherlands to regain their prosperity and during which the arts flourished.

The Archdukes' direct patronage was largely confined to commissions conforming to the Church's edicts resulting from the Council of Trent and Counter-Reformation propaganda; they were both devout Catholics and saw Spanish rule and Catholicism as inseparable and supported the work of the Jesuits and other new or reformed orders. The court architect was Wenceslaus Coebergher, who had returned to the Netherlands in 1604 after 25 years in Italy; he was joined by his brother-in-law Jacques Francart in 1608. Coebergher built the pilgrimage church of Onze-Lieve-Vrouwe at Scherpenheuvel, Brabant (1609–14), for the Archdukes and oversaw the designs for the charitable pawnbrokers' shops set up by them in many towns.

The Archdukes were both collectors and patrons—Albert favoured the Mannerism of Otto van Veen and Denijs van Alsloot—but Jan Breughel the elder was appointed to the court in 1609, and he was one of the 12 artists commissioned to execute a series of paintings depicting the *Five Senses* (1615–18; destr. 1731; copies of *Sight and Smell* and *Hearing, Touch and Taste*, by Breughel, Madrid, Prado), which also include paintings and objects belonging to the rulers. A work such as Willem van Haecht's *Gallery of Cornelis van der Geest* (Antwerp, Rubenshuis; *see* COLLECTING, fig. 1), although an imaginary gathering, gives some indication of the regeneration of the arts in the southern Netherlands under the auspices of Albert and Isabella.

Albert had commissioned work from PETER PAUL RUBENS while the artist was in Italy, and as soon as the artist returned to Antwerp in 1609 he entered their service and was granted the considerable favour of being able to remain in Antwerp and accept commissions other than theirs. Although he executed a few small works and some portraits for the Archdukes, to begin with most of Rubens's work was for the Jesuits. However, after the end of the Truce and the death of Albert in the same year, Isabella not only commissioned work from Rubens but also employed him as her ambassador to the courts of Europe. The designs for a tapestry series intended for the Order of the Descalzas Reales, or Poor Clares, in Madrid were commissioned in 1625; Isabella had lived with the nuns in her youth, and she intended to retire to the convent in old age; as a widow, she always wore the habit of the Order, as shown in van Dyck's portrait of the *Archduchess Isabella* (Turin, Gal. Sabauda). Rubens's 20 designs (examples in Cambridge, Fitzwilliam) are the apogee of Counter-Reformation imagery and represent the *Triumph of the Eucharist* (tapestries 1628; *in situ*). Isabella also commissioned an altarpiece from Rubens for St-Jacques-sur-Coudenberg, Brussels, the chapel of the Fraternity of S Ildefonso, founded by Albert. This triptych, the *Virgin Appearing to St Ildefonso* (1630; Vienna, Ksthistmus.), therefore commemorates the Archduke, and he is depicted on the left-hand panel, while the Archduchess kneels on the right. Rubens's work as an ambassador for Isabella was unsuccessful in obtaining the desired treaty between Spain and England, but it took him to England and Spain in 1629–30 and, although his international fame and connections with the Habsburgs had already brought him commissions from European rulers in London and Madrid, he again saw the great works of Titian, which influenced his last works, and he also met and profoundly influenced Velázquez.

A number of portraits of the Archdukes exist (for illustration of Isabella *see* PANTOJA DE LA CRUZ), including the pendants painted by Rubens and Jan Breughel the younger, which show them with the châteaux of Tervuren and Mariemont in the background (Madrid, Prado). After the death of Albert, and because the couple had no children, the sovereignty of the Netherlands returned to Spain and the Cardinal-Infante Ferdinand (*see* §II(9) below) was appointed governor. Ferdinand inherited many of the Archdukes' paintings and a considerable number are now in the Prado, Madrid.

BIBLIOGRAPHY

BNB
P. Saintenoy: 'Les Arts et les artistes à la cour de Bruxelles, III. Le Palais royal du Coudenberg du règne d'Albert et Isabelle à celui d'Albert Ier, Roi des Belges', *Bull. Cl. B.-A., Acad. Royale Sci., Lett. & B.-A. Belgique*, n. s. 1, vi/2 (1934–5), pp. 1–95
C. Terlinden: 'Le Mécénat de l'Archiduchess Infante Isabelle-Claire-Eugénie dans les Pays-Bas', *Rev. Belge Archéol. & Hist. A./Belge Tijdschr. Oudhdknde & Kstgesch*, iv (1934), pp. 211–23
M. de Maeyer: 'Albrecht en Isabella en de schilderkunst: Bijdrage tot de geschiedenis van de XVIIIe eeuwse schilderkunst in de Zuidelijke Nederlanden', *Acad. Anlct.: Kl. S. Kst.* (1955)
N. de Poorter: *The Eucharist Series*, 2 vols (1978), xi of *Corpus Rubenianum Ludwig Burchard* (Brussels, London and Philadelphia, 1968–)
Splendeurs d'Espagne et les villes belges, 1500–1700 (exh. cat., ed. J. M. Duvosquel and I. Vandevivere; Brussels, Pal. B.-A., 1985)

□

(16) Ferdinand II, Holy Roman Emperor [King of Bohemia; King of Hungary] (*b* Graz, 9 July 1578; *reg* Bohemia 1617–27, Hungary 1618–25, Holy Roman Emperor 1619–37; *d* Vienna, 15 Feb 1637). Grandson of (6) Ferdinand I. He was influenced by a strict Jesuit upbringing and became a loyal representative of the Counter-Reformation and used drastic measures to enforce it in Inner Austria (Styria, Carinthia, Carniola, Gorizia, Trieste), persecuting and proscribing Protestants and promoting the Jesuit order. He encountered Baroque art on his journey to Italy in 1598 and subsequently contributed to reinforcing the Italian influence in Austrian art in the transition from Mannerism to Baroque by engaging Italian artists.

As archduke he initially devoted himself more to founding Capuchin monasteries, promoting Jesuit establishments and building his mausoleum at Graz (1614–38) rather than to the government affairs that Emperor Matthias (*see* (12) above) entrusted to him. The foundation stone of the Capuchin church dedicated to St Antony of Padua was laid in 1600 at the spot on which Protestant books found in Graz had been ceremoniously burnt. Under the patronage of Ferdinand or his wives, Capuchin monasteries (architecturally very plain) were founded at Bruck an der Mur (1608), Cilli (1615) and the former Protestant stronghold of Radkersburg (1618), with the object of providing spiritual care, looking after the poor and generally reinforcing the Catholic faith. Medals commemorating these occasions were generally struck and buried when the foundation stone was laid; these medals were the work of PIETRO DE POMIS, the most important of the many court artists employed by Ferdinand.

During the years in which Pomis worked at the court in Graz, he gave the Archduke's Counter-Reformation endeavours a lasting pictorial expression, for example in the design for a ceiling painting that portrays Ferdinand as a Counter-Reformer (1614; Graz, Steiermark. Landesmus.), a motif that is repeated in the Graz Mausoleum (completed 1638), and in the *Apotheosis of the Counter-Reformation* (1602; Graz, St Anton von Padua). His painting of the *Virgin and Child* (1611) on the high altar of the Maria-Hilf-Kirche, for which Pomis also designed the façade (1611) and the interior (both altered 18th century), became the most famous miraculous image of the Baroque period in Styria. Pomis's masterpiece is Ferdinand's mausoleum (for illustration *see* GRAZ) on the south side of the present cathedral in Graz, on which building work started in 1614; for financial reasons it was not completed (by Pietro Valnegro) until 1638 and was subsequently restored and completed by Johann Bernhard Fischer von Erlach, who designed the stuccowork (1687) on the burial chapel and created the *St Catherine* altar (1697).

Ferdinand was elected King of Bohemia in 1617 and King of Hungary in 1618, and in 1619 managed to secure his own succession to the Habsburg hereditary lands and his election as Holy Roman Emperor, despite powerful opposition from the (predominantly Protestant) diet. After quashing widespread rebellion he implemented strong Counter-Reformation measures and established absolute rule based on religious belief. The main determining factor in Ferdinand II's reign was the Thirty Years War (1618–48), which originated in religious disputes and the confrontation of the Emperor by the imperial diets but later became a struggle about who should control Europe.

When he was elected emperor, Ferdinand moved his court to Vienna, where he began to promote Jesuit buildings, such as the university church of Maria Himmelfahrt (1627–31) and the Professhaus (1624) on the Platz am Hof. He also supported plans for a new Dominican monastery (1622), the rebuilding of the Dominican church (1631–4), and the building of the Carmelite church (1623–7), renovated the dilapidated fortifications of his chosen capital and completed several of his predecessors' projects, such as the imperial burial vault (Kaisergruft) beneath the Capuchin church.

Ferdinand II's reign marked a turning-point in the Habsburg collecting tradition. The collections of the *Kunst- und Wunderkammern* in Vienna, Prague and Ambras became organized treasuries; he tried to preserve what was already in the family's possession and to recover items that had been stolen or sold, but financial problems constrained him to reward his generals with objects from the collections, which resulted in some pieces going to Maximilian I, King of Bavaria, in Munich (see Lhotsky, pp. 316–7).

Ferdinand II has been portrayed both as an ideal Catholic prince and as a narrow-minded fanatic. There is no disputing his conscientiousness as a ruler, his zeal for duty, his piety, bigotry even, and his dogged determination in pursuing his goals, but invasions, war, rebellion and adverse commercial developments caused the financial strength of Inner Austria to decline. Nonetheless Ferdinand, as its ruler and in his role of emperor, continued to be a patron of the arts, even when on several occasions his closest adviser, Ulrich von Eggenberg (1568–1634), had to provide the financial backing to enable him to carry out his building plans. Ferdinand's Jesuit upbringing caused him to see art as an instrument of Catholic propaganda and a medium for glorifying the authority of the ruler, which is why as a patron he fostered those arts that work most powerfully on the senses: architecture, decorative arts and music (*see* AUSTRIA, §XII).

BIBLIOGRAPHY

ADB; *NDB*; Thieme–Becker
F. C. Khevenhüller: *Annales Ferdinandei*, i–xii (Leipzig, 1721–6)
F. von Hurter: *Geschichte Ferdinands II. . . .*, i–xi (Schaffhausen, 1850–64)
J. Wastler: *Das Kunstleben am Hofe zu Graz unter den Herzogen von Steiermark, der Erzherzogen Karl und Ferdinand* (Graz, 1897)
A. Lhotsky: *Die Geschichte der Sammlungen* (1941–5), ii/1 of *Festschrift des kunsthistorischen museums zur Feier des fünfzigjährigen Bestandes* (Vienna, 1941–5), pp. 313–34
H. Sturmberger: *Kaiser Ferdinand II. und das Problem des Absolutismus* (Vienna, 1957)
F. Popelka: *Geschichte der Stadt Graz*, i (Graz, Vienna, Cologne, 1959/*R* 1984), pp. 88–115
H. Haan: 'Kaiser Ferdinand II. und das Problem Reichsabsolutismus', *Hist. Z.*, ccvii (1968), pp. 297ff
K. Woisetschläger, ed.: *Der innerösterreichische Hofkünstler Giovanni Pietro de Pomis 1569 bis 1633* (Graz, Vienna, Cologne, 1974)
R. List: *Kunst und Künstler in der Steiermark* (Ried, 1978), pp. 788–9
J. Franzl: *Ferdinand II. Kaiser im Zwiespalt der Zeit* (Graz, Vienna, Cologne, 1978/*R* 1989)
G. Brucher: *Barockarchitektur in Österreich* (Cologne, 1983)
H. Ernst: *Madrid und Wien, 1632–1637. Politik und Finanzen in den Beziehungen zwischen Philipp IV. und Ferdinand II.* (Münster, 1991)

INGONDA HANNESSCHLÄGER

(17) Ferdinand III, Holy Roman Emperor [King of Hungary; King of Bohemia] (*b* Graz, 13 July 1608; *reg* Hungary 1625–46, Bohemia 1627–46, Holy Roman Emperor 1637–57; *d* Vienna, 2 April 1657). Son of (16) Ferdinand II. His reign was shaped by the Thirty Years

War (1618–48) and the threat of the Ottoman empire. In 1642 and 1644 Swedish troops invaded Lower Austria, and in 1648 they occupied Prague. The Peace of Westphalia (1648) gave the eastern part of the Holy Roman Empire to France, and Ferdinand III no longer had direct power. Thus his attention was transferred to the inherited Habsburg domains, in which he sought to secure and extend his power largely through the Counter-Reformation: religious commissions (1652, 1657) were successful in either converting or deporting Protestants, and as the majority of the nobles were Protestant, their power was weakened. Both the Ottoman Empire and Austria were too weak to embark on large-scale conflict, but there was intermittent fighting along the frontiers, despite the Peace of Zsitvatorok, renewed for 20 years in 1649.

The Emperor had been educated by Jesuits, and his deep piety was reflected in his personal devotion to the Virgin, to whom he had monuments erected in Vienna, for example the Mariensäule am Hof (1647; now in Wernstein am Inn) sculpted in marble by Johann Jakob Pock (1604–51). A bronze copy (1664–7) stands in the square. The Emperor spoke seven languages, wrote poems in Italian and had a special interest in the natural sciences, literature and art. In his youth he made some skilful pieces of woodwork. His musical compositions included masses, four motets, ten hymns, a *Stabat Mater*, a *Miserere* and a composition for the stage, *Drama Musicum* (1649). Giovanni Burnacini (*fl* 1650; *d* 1655), first documented as imperial architect in 1652, created a huge collapsible theatre for the Emperor in Regensburg in 1653. In 1655 his son Ludovico Ottavio Burnacini succeeded him. The imperial court painter Frans Luyckx, who had been taught in Rubens's studio in Antwerp, painted mainly portraits. The Emperor also collected pictures (Titian, Veronese, Rubens) and in 1657 arranged for the purchase of the library of Albrecht, Graf von Fugger (now in Vienna, Österreich. Nbib.). In 1657 he founded the Italian literary academy. Rather than commissioning sacred and secular pieces from an imperial goldsmith according to his own taste, he bought readymade jewellery and had pieces already in the treasury vault refashioned by Dionysio Miseroni (*d* 1661), keeper of the royal treasures and from 1650 to 1651 the Emperor's art dealer, together with Joachim von Sandrart. Textiles were also an item of expenditure, particularly for interior decoration. As war continually strained imperial finances, Ferdinand III commissioned no major construction work, but the imperial engineer, Filiberto Luchese, and other architects extended fortifications (*see* PRAGUE, §I, 2 and fig. 3) and after the end of the Thirty Years War converted or rebuilt imperial buildings which had been destroyed. The Emperor was also financially involved in the building or rebuilding of churches and chapels. For example in 1652 he gave a new set of bells to the Hofpfarrkirche (Augustinerkirche) in Vienna, and in 1653 the tower in which they were kept was rebuilt.

BIBLIOGRAPHY

M. Koch: *Geschichte des deutschen Reiches unter der Regierung Ferdinands III* (Vienna, 1865)

E. Ebenstein: 'Der Hofmaler Franz Luycz', *Jb. Ksthist. Samml. Allhöch. Ksrhaus* (1906/7), pp. 183–254

H. Haupt: 'Archivalien zur Kulturgeschichte des Wiener Hofes, Kaiser Ferdinand III, 1646–56', *Jb. Ksthist. Samml. Wien* (1975), pp. 1–120

A. GERHARDT

(18) Leopold William [Willem], Archduke of Austria (*b* Vienna, 6 Jan 1614; *d* Vienna, 20 Nov 1662). Son of (16) Ferdinand II. Destined for an ecclesiastical career from his youth, he became Bishop of Passau and Strasbourg in 1625, titular Bishop of Halberstadt in 1626, of Olmütz in 1637 and of Breslau in 1655. In 1642 he was made High Master of the Teutonic Order. Appointed commander-in-chief of the imperial army in the Thirty Years War in 1639, he held the post with varying strategic success until 1642, when he was defeated at Breitenfeld, Saxony, and again in 1645. In 1646 he was made Governor of the Spanish Netherlands by Philip IV, King of Spain (*see* §II (7) below) and in 1656 returned to Vienna, where he acted as adviser to his nephew Emperor Leopold I (*see* (19) below).

Archduke Leopold William was one of the outstanding collectors of the House of Habsburg, and he is regarded as the founder of the Gemäldegalerie of the Kunsthistorisches Museum in Vienna (*see* AUSTRIA, §XIV). Favoured by the political events at the end of the Thirty Years War, and by the sale of the collection of Charles I, King of England and Scotland (*see* STUART, House of, (6)), he was able to build up his collection by judicious purchases at auctions (*see* AUSTRIA, §XIII) during his governorship of the Netherlands. Apart from his own collection, transferred from Brussels to Vienna in 1656 and later set up in the Stallburg (*see* VIENNA, §V, 5(ii)), he also acquired paintings in the Netherlands for his brother, Ferdinand III (*see* (17) above), to replace the stock of the castle at Hradčany, Prague, plundered by the Swedes during the Thirty Years War. In the 18th century some of these paintings were moved to Vienna, where they were placed in the imperial picture gallery, the director of which from 1656 was Jan Anthonie van der Baren, who made an inventory of the collection in 1659. This inventory and the paintings of David Teniers II (e.g. *Archduke Leopold William Inspecting Pictures in his Gallery in Brussels*, 1651–6; Vienna, Ksthist. Mus.; see fig.) reveal that the Archduke's interest focused on Netherlandish and Italian (especially Venetian) paintings of the 15th and 16th centuries. Among *c.* 1500 works in the collection were several paintings by Giorgione, Palma Vecchio, Titian, Veronese, Tintoretto, Jacopo Bassano and Francesco Bassano. The majority of the Venetian paintings, including Giorgione's *Three Philosophers* (*c.* 1508–9; Vienna, Ksthist. Mus.; *see* GIORGIONE, fig. 4), came originally from the collection of BARTOLOMEO DELLA NAVE in Venice, the greatest part of which was eventually acquired (*c.* 1650) by the Archduke. Among his Netherlandish works were paintings of the 15th century and others by van Dyck, Hugo van der Goes and Geertgen tot Sint Jans. Two paintings by the last, on the right panel of the altarpiece for the Commandery church, the *Lamentation* (inner side) and the *Burning of the Bones of St John the Baptist* (outer side; both *c.* 1484–94; Vienna, Ksthist. Mus.; *see* GEERTGEN TOT SINT JANS, fig. 1), came from the collection of Charles I. Archduke Leopold William also collected the

Archduke Leopold William Inspecting Pictures in his Gallery in Brussels, by David Teniers II, oil on panel, 698×863 mm, 1651–6 (Vienna, Kunsthistorisches Museum)

works of his Netherlandish contemporaries: David Teniers II was his court painter from 1651 (*see* TENIERS, (2) and fig. 3), and he acquired directly paintings by Jacob Jordaens, such as the *Feast of the Bean King* (before 1656; Vienna, Ksthist. Mus.), and numerous paintings of the Rubens school, which show his preference for calmly composed small-figure paintings giving a close-up view. He owned Rubens's *Lamentation* (1614) and *Stormy Landscape with Philemon and Baucis* (1620–25; both Vienna, Ksthist. Mus.) but no large-format allegories, which suggests that he preferred an intimate dialogue with his pictures to the ostentation afforded by room-dominating Baroque works. This preference is also seen in his paintings by the 17th-century Italian artists Domenico Fetti, Bernardo Strozzi, Girolamo Forabosco and Guido Cagnacci. He also owned a jewel room and a separate art cabinet, both well documented by inventories. The jewel room, in the Amalia wing of the Hofburg in Vienna, contained precious objects, vessels of rock crystal and above all reliquaries and church plate. The art cabinet, in the Stallburg, contained mainly sculptures of stone, wood and bronze, including works (now in Vienna, Ksthist. Mus.) by Antico, which were originally owned by Isabella d'Este and came to the Archduke via the collection of Charles I. Apart from such first-rate works, the cabinet contained curiosities such as a 'Devil in Glass' and various horns. The Archduke bequeathed his collection of paintings and the art cabinet to his nephew, Leopold I (see (19) below), and the jewel room and tapestries to the latter's younger brother, Archduke Charles Joseph of Austria (1649–64), although after his early death they reverted to the main line of the family.

BIBLIOGRAPHY

A. Berger, ed.: 'Inventar der Kunstsammlung des Erzherzogs Leopold Wilhelm von Österreich', *Jb. Ksthist. Samml. Allhöch. Ksrhaus.*, i (1883), document 495; vii (1888), document 4717

A. Lhotsky: *Die Geschichte der Sammlungen* (1941–5), ii/1 of *Festschrift des kunsthistorischen Museums zur Feier des fünfzigjährigen Bestandes* (Vienna, 1941–5), pp. 55–360, 369–71

K. Garas: 'Die Entstehung der Galerie des Erzherzog Leopold Wilhelm', *Jb. Ksthist. Samml. Wien*, lxiii (1967), pp. 39–80

—: 'Das Schicksal der Sammlung des Erzherzog Leopold Wilhelm', *Jb. Ksthist. Samml. Wien*, lxiv (1968), pp. 181–278

A. A. Strnad: 'Wahl und Informativprozess Erzherzog Leopold Wilhelms', *Archv Schles. Kirchgesch.*, xxvi (1968), pp. 153–90

(19) Leopold I, Holy Roman Emperor [King of Hungary; King of Bohemia] (*b* Vienna, 9 June 1640; *reg* Hungary 1655–1705, Bohemia 1656–1705, Holy Roman

Emperor 1658–1705; *d* Vienna, 5 May 1705). Son of (17) Ferdinand III. His reign was marked by almost uninterrupted war against France and the Ottoman empire. After the relief of the second Ottoman siege of Vienna in 1683, the defence was transformed into a successful war offensive, which ended in 1699. The conflict with France continued, and although the peace treaties of Nymwegen (1679) and Ryswijk (1697) resulted in a territorial loss on the part of Spain and the Empire, Austria emerged as Europe's leading power.

Leopold I was the first Habsburg whose patronage carries the stamp of the High Baroque (*see* VIENNA, §§II, 2 and III, 2). He commissioned the building of the Leopoldinischer Trakt of the Hofburg (1660–67; *see* VIENNA, §V, 5(i)) and, in 1688–90, from Johann Bernhard Fischer von Erlach, plans for the Schloss Schönbrunn (1696–1700; *see* VIENNA, §V, 7(i)). During his reign the dispersed art treasures of the Habsburgs were assembled in the imperial art collection in the Hofburg in Vienna, including (1622) works owned by Archduke Leopold William (*see* (18) above) and (1644) the *Kunstkammer* of Archduke Charles Joseph of Austria. Leopold also inherited (1649–64) the Ambras collection of Cardinal-Archduke Sigismund Francis of Austria (1630–65), although, with the exception of the library, this remained in Innsbruck. Emphasis on the representative self-presentation of the House of Habsburg effected the transformation of the Schatzkammer in accordance with the new power politics of Austria (*see* VIENNA, §V, 5(ii)). The Emperor took a particular interest in the court library in Vienna, but his personal preference was primarily for music: he played several instruments and his remaining compositions (79 religious and 102 secular pieces) are evidence of his talent. He brought to Vienna the Italian opera and founded the musical equestrian performances still featured at the Spanish Riding School in Vienna. Notable artists he employed at court included the members of the STRUDEL family (*see* VIENNA, §III, 2 and fig. 8).

BIBLIOGRAPHY

A. Lhotsky: *Die Geschichte der Sammlungen* (1941–5), ii/1 of *Festschrift des kunsthistorischen Museums zur Feier des fünfzigjährigen Bestandes* (Vienna, 1941–5), pp. 361–82

O. Redlich: *Weltmacht des Barock. Österreich in der Zeit Kaiser Leopolds I.* (Vienna, 1961)

J. P. Spielman: *Leopold I. Zur Macht nicht geboren* (Graz, Vienna and Cologne, 1981)

T. M. Barker: *Doppeladler und Halbmond. Entscheidungsjahr 1683* (Graz, Vienna and Cologne, 1982)

R. Distelberger: 'The Habsburg Collections in Vienna during the Seventeenth Century', *The Origins of Museums* (Oxford, 1985), pp. 39–46

ELISABETH SCHEICHER

(20) Charles VI, Holy Roman Emperor [King of Hungary and Bohemia] (*b* Vienna, 1 Oct 1685; *reg* 1711–40; *d* Vienna, 20 Oct 1740). Son of (19) Leopold I. He was one of the claimants in the War of the Spanish Succession from 1700 until 1711, when he inherited the Austrian hereditary and crown territories and became Holy Roman Emperor. His primary artistic and aesthetic interest was music, which he himself played and also composed. He also received lessons in civilian and military architecture. When campaigning in Spain he took with him his collection of ancient coins and medals that was to form the basis of the collection of coins and antiquities opened in Vienna in 1717. His appointed Inspector of Medals and Antiquities, KARL GUSTAV HERAEUS, designed a series of medals *Historia metallica . . . seu numismatica* (Vienna, Ksthist. Mus.; designs published in *Inscriptiones et symbola*, Nuremberg, 1721), glorifying the political, cultural and military events of Charles's reign. His aesthetic discernment was praised by Gottfried Wilhelm Leibniz (1646–1716), who noted that the Emperor chose Johann Bernhard Fischer von Erlach's design in the competition for the Karlskirche in Vienna, despite the adverse opinion of many others. He should also be given personal credit for the quality and quantity of works in all fields of architecture, the fine and applied arts commissioned in his name as he created the necessary conditions by appointing a number of outstanding artists and reorganizing the business of art (*see* VIENNA, §§II, 2 and III, 2). In addition he originated the post of Generalbaudirektor, to which in 1716 he appointed Graf GUNDACKER LUDWIG VON ALTHANN, who was subsequently responsible for all court projects for the arts. In 1726 the count was also appointed Honorary President of the Akademie der Maler, Bildhauer und Baukünstler, which had been revived in 1725 after the closure in 1714 of the Kaiserliche Akademie, founded in 1692 by Peter Strudel (*see* STRUDEL, (2)). Charles initiated a gallery (completed 1728) in the Hofburg in which to show selected paintings from the Habsburg collection (*see* VIENNA, §III, 2), and the Schatzkammer was also displayed in its own rooms at the Hofburg. His role in commissioning buildings, monuments and other works of fine and applied art was reflected in the vocabulary of form and iconography of the so-called 'Kaiserstil' or 'Reichsstil'. The intention was to demonstrate the pre-eminence and claim to universal power of the Habsburg emperors as heirs to the ancient Imperium Romanum by imitating the models of classical Rome.

Charles did not only use architecture and fine art as propaganda, however, and soon after his accession he and his advisers worked out a wide-ranging programme of works, the practical purpose and pictorial decoration of which demonstrated his concern for public welfare, his aptitude as a ruler and provided proof of his 'good government'. These ranged from engineering projects and utilitarian buildings (roads, bridges, canals, warehouses, barracks, poorhouses and hospitals) to lavish show buildings. The last category included churches such as the Karlskirche (1716–37), designed by Fischer von Erlach but completed by his son Joseph Emanuel Fischer von Erlach (*see* FISCHER VON ERLACH and AUSTRIA, §V, 2 and fig. 6), and palace-style buildings, which Charles had built for the administrative institutions associated with his various functions as emperor and ruler, such as the Reichshofkanzlei (1723–30) and the Geheime Hofkanzlei (1717–19) in Vienna.

Other projects were also created as grand governmental buildings to illustrate the importance the emperor attached to them: the Hofbibliothek (from 1722; *see* VIENNA, §V, 5(i) and fig. 16) as a public educational institution, the Ritterakademie for the education of the nobility at Liegnitz (1726–35; now Legnica, Poland) and the Lanständische Akademie in Vienna (1731; destr. 1751) and hospitals for disabled servicemen in Prague (1731–7) and Budapest (begun 1727). In its geographical distribution the programme took account of the various crown territories, as did the siting of the religious monuments erected by the Emperor: the *Josephsäule* (1729–32) in Vienna, the *Bundesladendenkmal* (1731) in Györ, Hungary, and the silver funerary monument of *St John of Nepomuk* (1733–6) by Joseph Emmanuel Fischer von Erlach in St Vitus Cathedral in Prague.

BIBLIOGRAPHY

F. W. Riedel: *Kirchenmusik am Hofe Karls VI (1711–1740): Untersuchungen zum Verhältnis von Zeremoniell und musikalischem Stil im Barockzeitalter* (Munich and Salzburg, 1977)

F. Matsche: *Die Kunst im Dienst der Staatsidee Kaiser Karls VI. Ikonographie, Ikonologie und Programmatik des 'Kaiserstils'* (Berlin and New York, 1981)

F. Matsche: 'Die Verherrlichung der kaiserlichen Majestät Karls VI im Kunstwerk', *Prinz Eugen und das barocke Österreich*, ed. K. Gutkas (Salzburg, 1985), pp. 383–90

——: 'Die Hofbibliothek in Wien als Denkmal kaiserlicher Kulturpolitik', *Ikonographie der Bibliotheken*, ed. C-P. Warncke (Wiesbaden, 1992), pp. 199–233

FRANZ MATSCHE

(21) Maria-Theresa, Queen of Hungary and Queen of Bohemia [Holy Roman Empress] (*b* Vienna, 13 May 1717; *reg* Hungary 1741–80, Bohemia 1743–80, Holy Roman Empress 1745–65; *d* Vienna, 28 Nov 1780). Daughter of (20) Charles VI. She became Queen of Hungary (1741) and Queen of Bohemia (1743) under the terms of her father's Pragmatic Sanction (1713), which declared the possessions of the House of Habsburg inseparable and indivisible and ensured the right of daughters (in the absence of sons) to inherit property. In 1736 she married Francis, Duke of Lorraine, later the Holy Roman Emperor Francis I (*reg* 1745–65), by whom she had 16 children (*see* HABSBURG-LORRAINE). Her right to succeed did not go unchallenged: the War of the Austrian Succession, the outcome of which was a general acceptance of the Pragmatic Sanction under the Treaty of Aix-la-Chapelle, did not end until 1748. The main political task of her reign was to defend and maintain territorial possessions, with Frederick II, King of Prussia, as her principal adversary; as a result of the two Silesian wars (1740–42, 1744–5) and of the Seven Years War (1756–63) Silesia was lost to Prussia. The dispute with Prussia led to a rapprochement with France, culminating in the marriage of Maria-Theresa's daughter Marie-Antoinette to the future Louis XVI of France.

The Queen's reform programme still affects the internal structure of the Austrian hereditary lands today. It included the modernization of the penal process, the development of trade and industry, the abolition of customs tariffs, the improvement of transport links, reorganization of the universities and the introduction of compulsory education. An increasing preference for French cultural ideas replaced the Spanish and Italian influence prevalent in the reign of Charles VI (*see* VIENNA, §III, 2). This new emphasis was expressed in the employment of such French artists and scholars as Jean-Nicolas Jadot de Ville-Issey, who was appointed chief court architect in 1750 and whose designs included that for the Alte Universität (1753; now Akademie der Wissenschaften) in Vienna. Despite straitened financial circumstances, which restricted Maria-Theresa's personal role as a patron of the arts, she commissioned some notable metalwork, including a gold breakfast service (*see* AUSTRIA, §IX, 1(ii) and fig. 37), and the existing imperial collections were reorganized and new collections established in the field of the natural sciences, including a cabinet of natural history and a cabinet of physical science. The imperial Schatzkammer was rearranged under Joseph Angelo de France (*fl* 1752), and Valentin Jameray Duval (1695–1775) expanded the coin collection. The official residences in Prague and Innsbruck were rationalized to form large complexes of buildings, and alterations were carried out at Schloss Schönbrunn (*see* VIENNA, §V, 7(i) and AUSTRIA, §V, 2 and fig. 25) and Schloss Hetzendorf. The Queen is buried in the magnificent Rococo double sarcophagus for *Francis I of Lorraine and Maria-Theresa* (1753–4; Vienna, Kapuzinerkirche) by Balthasar Ferdinand Moll (*see* MOLL, (1)). There are also sculptures of *Empress Maria-Theresa* and *Emperor Francis I* (1764–6) by Franz Xaver Messerschmidt in the Belvedere, Vienna.

BIBLIOGRAPHY

A. von Arneth: *Geschichte Maria Theresias*, 10 vols (Vienna, 1863–79)

A. Lhotsky: *Die Geschichte der Sammlungen* (1941–5), ii/2 of *Festschrift des kunsthistorischen Museums* (Vienna, 1941–5), pp. 413–57

E. Guglia: *Maria Theresia. Ihr Leben und Wirken*, 2 vols (Vienna, 1979)

G. Mraz and G. Mraz: *Maria Theresia* (Munich, 1979)

P. Reinhold: *Maria Theresia* (Frankfurt am Main, 1979)

ELISABETH SCHEICHER

The survey of the **Habsburg** family (§II: Spanish branch) continues in vol. 14.

Illustration Acknowledgements

We are grateful to those listed below for permission to reproduce copyright illustrative material and to those contributors who supplied photographs or helped us to obtain them. The word 'Photo:' precedes the names of large commercial or archival sources who have provided us with photographs, as well as the names of individual photographers (where known). It has generally not been used before the names of owners of works of art, such as museums and civic bodies. Every effort has been made to contact copyright holders and to credit them appropriately; we apologize to anyone who may have been omitted from the acknowledgements or cited incorrectly. Any error brought to our attention will be corrected in subsequent editions. Where illustrations have been taken from books, publication details are provided in the acknowledgements below.

Line drawings, maps, plans, chronological tables and family trees commissioned by the *Dictionary of Art* are not included in the list below. All of the maps in the dictionary were produced by Oxford Illustrators Ltd, who were also responsible for some of the line drawings. Most of the line drawings and plans, however, were drawn by the following artists: Diane Fortenberry, Lorraine Hodghton, Chris Miners, Amanda Patton, Mike Pringle, Jo Richards, Miranda Schofield, John Tiernan, John Wilson and Philip Winton. The chronological tables and family trees were prepared initially by Kate Boatfield and finalized by John Johnson.

Gopura Photo: © American Institute of Indian Studies, Varanasi
Gordillo, Luis Photo: © DACS, 1996
Gordion *1* University of Pennsylvania Museum, Philadelphia, PA (neg. no. S4-101008); *2* University of Pennsylvania Museum, Philadelphia, PA (neg. no. Gordion Roll 329-20)
Gorky, Arshile *1* Whitney Museum of American Art, New York (Gift of Gertrude Vanderbilt Whitney; no. 31.95)/© ADAGP, Paris, and DACS, London, 1996; *2* Albright–Knox Art Gallery, Buffalo, NY (Gift of Seymour H. Knox, 1956)/© ADAGP, Paris, and DACS, London, 1996
Gorodets Photo: VAAP, Moscow
Gortyn From J.W. Myers, E.E. Myers and G. Cadogan, eds: *The Aerial Atlas of Ancient Crete* (Berkeley, Los Angeles and Oxford, 1992)
Gorze, Order of Bayerische Staatsbibliothek, Munich
Gospel book British Library, London (MS. 2788, fol. 109*r*)
Gossart, Jan *1* Trustees of the National Gallery, London; *2* National Gallery, Prague; *3–4* Photo: © ACL Brussels
Gothic *2–6, 28, 61, 69, 101–3* Photo: Arch. Phot. Paris/© DACS, 1996; *7–8, 33* Photo: Anthony Kersting, London; *9* Dean and Chapter of Westminster, London; *10–12, 17, 35, 37, 56, 75, 95* Photo: Bildarchiv Foto Marburg; *13, 23, 40,* 42, *60, 77, 113* Photo: Archivi Alinari, Florence; *14* Robert Harding Picture Library, London/Photo: © Walter Rawlings; *15–16, 18–20, 24, 26, 31–2, 45, 62, 67, 71* Photo: Conway Library, Courtauld Institute of Art, London; *21* Photo: Jan Derwig, Architectuur Fotografie, Amsterdam; *22* Photo: Osvaldo Böhm, Venice; *25, 47–50, 111* Photo: Ampliaciones y Reproducciones MAS, Barcelona; *27, 29, 70, 85, 87* Photo: Giraudon, Paris; *30, 66, 86, 97* Photo: © RMN, Paris; *34* Photo: Hirmer Fotoarchiv, Munich; *36* Photo: Bildarchiv, Österreichische Nationalbibliothek, Vienna; *38* Photo: Foto Zwicker-Berberich, Gerchsheim; *39, 112* Photo: Fotografia Lensini Fabio, Siena; *41* Museo Civico Medievale, Bologna (neg. no. AE100/10; inv. no. 1662)/Photo: C.N.B; *43–4, 52, 104* Photo: © ACL Brussels; *46* Antikvarisk–Topografiska Arkivet, Stockholm; *51* Musée des Beaux-Arts, Dijon; *53* Detroit Institute of Arts, Detroit, MI (Founders Society Purchase; Miscellaneous Memorials Fund); *54–5* Rijksmuseum, Amsterdam; *57* Stadshus, Stockholm; *58* Museum of Natural History and Archaeology, University of Trondheim; *59* Photo: Angela Franco Mata; *63* Photo: Scala, Florence; *64* British Library, London (Add. MS. 49999); *65* Master and Fellows of Corpus Christi College, Cambridge; *68* Dean and Chapter of Canterbury; *72* Pierpont Morgan Library, New York; *73* Bodleian Library, Oxford; *74* British Library, London (Yates Thompson MS. 8, fol. 7*r*); *76* Universitetets Oldsaksamlingen, Oslo; *78* Soprintendenza per i Beni Artistici e Storici, Naples; *79* British Library, London (Add. MS. 49622); *80* Metropolitan Museum of Art, New York (Cloisters Collection, 1954; MS. 54.1.2, fol. 102*v*–103*r*); *81* Museo de Navarra, Pamplona; *82* Museum des Chorherrenstiftes, Klosterneuburg; *83* State Institute for the Conservation of Historical Monuments and Nature, Prague; *84* Bibliothèque Nationale de France, Paris; *88* Germanisches Nationalmuseum, Nuremberg; *89* Photo: Judit Kolba; *90* Sacro Convento di San Francesco, Assisi/Photo: P. Gerhard Ruf; *91, 99* Board of Trustees of the Victoria and Albert Museum, London; *92* Museo Arqueológico Nacional, Madrid; *93* Metropolitan Museum of Art, New York (Gift of J. Pierpont Morgan, 1917); *94* Metropolitan Museum of Art, New York (Cloisters Collection; Purchase, 1962); *96* Nationalmuseum, Copenhagen; *98* Musées d'Angers; *100* Staatliche Museen zu Berlin, Preussischer Kulturbesitz/Skulpturengalerie/Photo: Hilda Deeke, Berlin; *105* © Sonia Halliday and Laura Lushington, Weston Turville, Bucks; *106* Rheinische Bildarchiv, Cologne; *107–8* Hessisches Landesmuseum, Darmstadt; *109* National Museum, Kraków/Photo: Pracownia Fotograficzna MNK; *110* Zornsamlingarna, Mora; *114* Metropolitan Museum of Art, New York (Cloisters Collection; Mensey Fund, 1932; no. 32.130.3a); *115* Cleveland Museum of Art, Cleveland, OH
Gothic Revival *1–4* Photo: Georg Germann; *5* British Library, London (no. C.119, fol. 1); *6* Ministerie van de Vlaamse Gemeenschap, Monumenten en Landschappen, Brussels/Photo: O. Pauwels
Gothic survival Photo: Bildarchiv Foto Marburg
Gottlieb, Adolph Museum of Modern Art, New York (Philip Johnson Fund)
Gouache manner Bibliothèque Nationale de France, Paris
Goudt, Hendrik Trustees of the British Museum, London
Goujon, Jean *1* Photo: Arch. Phot. Paris/© SPADEM; *2* Photo: © RMN, Paris
Gourd Trustees of the British Museum, London
Gourmont: (1) Jean de Gourmont (i) Bibliothèque Nationale de France, Paris
Govardhan Trustees of the Chester Beatty Library, Dublin
Government building *1* Photo: Conway Library, Courtauld Institute of Art, London; *2* Photo: British Architectural Library, RIBA, London
Gower, George Tate Gallery, London
Goya, Francisco de *1* Courtauld Institute of Art, London; *2–6* Museo del Prado, Madrid
Goyen, Jan van *1* National Gallery of Art, Washington, DC; *2* Art Institute of Chicago, Chicago, IL/© 1996. All rights reserved
Gozzoli, Benozzo *1* Trustees of the National Gallery, London; *2* Photo: Archivi Alinari, Florence
Gračanica Photo: J. Powell, Rome
Grado Photo: Osvaldo Böhm, Venice
Graf, Urs Öffentliche Kunstsammlung Basel, Kunstmuseum, Basle/Photo: Martin Bühler
Graffiti Photo: Susan A. Phillips
Gramatica, Antiveduto Photo: Arquivo Nacional de Fotografia, Lisbon
Gran, Daniel Bildarchiv, Österreichische Nationalbibliothek, Vienna
Granacci, Francesco Photo: Giraudon, Paris
Granada *1–2, 4* Photo: Conway Library, Courtauld Institute of Art, London

Gran Chiriquí Photo: National Museum of the American Indian, Smithsonian Institution, Washington, DC
Grandi, Ercole Photo: Archivi Alinari, Florence
Grandi, Giuseppe Photo: Conway Library, Courtauld Institute of Art, London
Grandjean de Montigny, Auguste-Henri-Victor Banco Chase Manhattan/Photo: Sergio Pagano
Grand Tour *1* Trustees of the British Museum, London; *2* British Library, London (no. Tab.435.a.15)
Grandville, J.J. Bibliothèque Nationale de France, Paris
Granet, François-Marius Metropolitan Museum of Art, New York
Gran Nicoya *1–2* Photo: Irene Pena
Grasser, Erasmus Münchner Stadtmuseum, Munich
Grassi, de: (3) Salomone de Grassi Biblioteca Trivulziana, Milan
Gravelot English Heritage, London
Graves, Michael Museum of Modern Art, New York (Lily Auchinloss Fund)
Graz Photo: Anthony Kersting, London
Great Coxwell Barn Photo: RCHME/© Crown Copyright
Great Gallery, Barrier Canyon Museum of Natural History, University of Utah, Salt Lake City, UT/Photo: Laurel Casjens
Great Zimbabwe National Museum and Monuments of Zimbabwe, Harare/Photo: Peter Chèze-Brown
Greco, El *1* Minneapolis Institute of Arts, Minneapolis, MN; *2* Photo: Archivi Alinari, Florence; *3* Museo del Prado, Madrid; *4* Metropolitan Museum of Art, New York (Bequest of Mrs H.O. Havemeyer, 1929, H.O. Havemeyer Collection; no. 29.100.5); *5* Metropolitan Museum of Art, New York
Greece *1* Photo: Orestis B. Doumanis; *2* Photo: Agra Publications (from A. Konstantinidis: *Projects and Buildings* (Athens, 1981)); *3–5* National Picture Gallery (Pinakothiki), Athens; *6* Board of Trustees of the Victoria and Albert Museum, London; *7* Benaki Museum, Athens
Greece, ancient *4* Arthur M. Sackler Museum, Harvard University Art Museums, Cambridge, MA (Bequest of David M. Robinson); *5, 39, 54, 68, 74, 117* Staatliche Antikensammlungen und Glyptothek, Munich; *6* Photo: James Austin, Cambridge; *10* British Library, London (no. L.R.4054.1.6); *14* British Library, London (no. AC.9830.c); *17* Photo: Archives, American School of Classical Studies at Athens; *19* Photo: Alison Burford; *20* Photo: University of Minnesota Press, Minneapolis, MN; *22* Photo: Ecole Française d'Archéologie, Athens; *23* Architectural Association, London/Photo: D. Grey; *26* Yale University Press Photo Library, London/Photo: © Sonia Halliday, Weston Turville, Bucks; *27* Nationalmuseum, Copenhagen (Department of Near Eastern and Classical Art); *28* British Library, London (no. 1829.k); *29* Photo: Fototeca Unione, American Academy in Rome; *30* Photo: Österreichisches Archäologisches Institut, Vienna; *32* From J. T. Clarke, F. H. Bacon and R. Koldewey: *Investigations at Assos* (Boston, 1902); *33* Drawing by L. Haselberger (from H. Bankel: *Haller von Hallerstein in Griechenland, 1810–1817*, Berlin, 1986); *35* Photo: Deutsches Archäologisches Institut, Rome (Inst. neg. no. 68.2917); *36, 129* Photo: American School of Classical Studies at Athens: Agora Excavations; *38, 97* Photo: Archivi Alinari, Florence; *40–41, 60, 70, 89, 91–2, 96, 114–15, 118, 124–7, 154–6, 159–62, 165, 171* Trustees of the British Museum, London; *42, 132–3* Photo: Scala, Florence; *43, 48, 51, 63, 85–6, 95, 98, 152* National Archaeological Museum, Athens (Archaeological Receipts Fund); *44* Metropolitan Museum of Art, New York (Rogers Fund, 1921; Munsey Fund, 1936 and 1938; Anonymous gift, 1951; no. H.185.a-d); *46–7, 78, 94, 137–8* Staatliche Museen zu Berlin, Preussischer Kulturbesitz; *49* Metropolitan Museum of Art, New York (Gift of J. Pierpont Morgan, 1917; no. 17.190.2072); *50* Museum of Fine Arts, Boston, MA (Francis Bartlett Collection); *52–3, 55* National Archaeological Museum, Athens (Archaeological Receipts Fund)/ Photo: Hirmer Fotoarchiv, Munich; *56, 119* Museo Archeologico Nazionale, Naples/Photo: Soprintendenza Archaeologica della Provincia di Napoli e Caserta; *57* Museo Nazionale Romano delle Terme, Rome/Photo: AKG Ltd, London; *58, 106* Photo: Hirmer Fotoarchiv, Munich; *59, 69, 81, 104, 113, 122* Photo: © RMN, Paris; *61, 65, 82–3* Photo: Deutsches Archäologisches Institut, Athens; *62* Kerameikos Museum, Athens (Archaeological Receipts Fund); *64* Archaeological Museum, Delphi (Archaeological Receipts Fund)/Photo: Deutsches Archäologisches Institut, Athens; *66* Ny Carlsberg Glyptotek, Copenhagen; *67* Archivio Fotografico dei Musei Capitolini, Rome; *72, 157* Ashmolean Museum, Oxford; *73* Museum of Fine Arts, Boston, MA (Catharine Perkins Collection); *75* Metropolitan Museum of Art, New York; *76–7* Photo: Prof. Joseph Veach Noble; *79* Photo: © ACL Brussels; *80* Photo: Deutsches Archäologisches Institut, Rome (Inst. neg. no. 59.1649); *84, 90* Eleusis Archaeological Museum/Photo: Deutsches Archäologisches Institut, Athens; *87* Metropolitan Museum of Art, New York (Cesnola Collection; purchased by subscription, 1874-6; no. 74.51.965); *88* Museum of Fine Arts, Boston, MA (Catharine Page Perkins Fund); *93* Bibliothèque Royale Albert 1er, Brussels; *99* Metropolitan Museum of Art, New York (Fletcher Fund, 1931); *100, 103* Bibliothèque Nationale de France, Paris; *101* Rijksmuseum van Oudheden, Leiden; *102, 111* Martin-von-Wagner-Museum, Universität Würzburg/Photo: K. Oehrlein; *105* Archäologisches Institut, Universität Tübingen; *107* Kunsthistorisches Museum, Vienna; *108* Museum of Fine Arts, Boston, MA (H.L. Pierce Fund); *109* Metropolitan Museum of Art, New York (Purchase, Bequest of Joseph H. Durkee, Gift of Darius Ogden Mills and Gift of C. Ruxton Love, by exchange, 1972; no. 1972.11.10); *110, 121* Antikenmuseum Basel und Sammlung Ludwig, Basle; *112* Vatican Museums, Vatican City, Rome; *116* Virginia Museum of Fine Arts, Richmond, VA; *120* Photo: Sotheby's, London; *123* J. Paul Getty Museum, Malibu, CA; *128* Metropolitan Museum of Art, New York (Purchase, Joseph Pulitzer Bequest, 1953; no. 53.11.5); *130* AKG Ltd, London/Photo: Erich Lessing; *131* Athanassakeion Archaeological Museum, Volos (Archaeological Receipts Fund); *132–3* Photo: Scala, Florence; *134* Photo: Deutsches Archäologisches Institut, Athens (no. NM 3588); *135* Photo: P.H. Petsas, Athens; *136* British Library, London (no. AC.2689/7); *139–40* British Library, London (no. P.P.1925.m); *141* Archaeological Museum, Sikyon/Photo: Deutsches Archäologisches Institut, Athens; *142–3* Photo: Martin Robertson; *144* Photo: Deutsches Archäologisches Institut, Cairo; *145* Metropolitan Museum of Art, New York (Rogers Fund, 1966; no. 66.11.23); *146* Metropolitan Museum of Art, New York (Rogers Fund, 1966; no. 66.11.27); *147* Hermitage Museum, St Petersburg; *148* Walters Art Gallery, Baltimore, MD; *149* Archaeological Museum, Olympia (Archaeological Receipts Fund); *150* Photothèque du Musée du Bardo; *151* Photo: Giraudon, Paris; *153* Archaeological Museum, Thessaloniki (Archaeological Receipts Fund); *158* Archaeological Museum, Olympia (Archaeological Receipts Fund)/Photo: Dietrich Widmer; *163* Photo: Deutsches Archäologisches Institut, Rome (Inst. neg. no. 80.1901); *164* Corning Museum of Glass, Corning, NY; *167* Museum of Fine Arts, Boston, MA (H.L. Pierce Fund, Purchase of E.P. Warren); *168* Benaki Museum, Athens (inv. no. 1548); *170* Antikenmuseum, Archäologisches Institut, Universität Heidelberg
Greek Revival *1* London Library, London; *2* Photo: RCHME/© Crown Copyright; *3* Photo: Bildarchiv Foto Marburg; *4* Library of Congress, Washington, DC
Greene & Greene Photo: David Gebhard
Greenland Photo: Lil-FOTO
Greenway, Francis Photo: Valerie Clack
Greenwich Photo: RCHME/© Crown Copyright
Gregotti, Vittorio Photo: Mimmo Jodice
Grenoble *1* Musée Dauphinois, Grenoble; *2* Musée Archéologique, Grenoble
Greuze, Jean-Baptiste *1* Fine Arts Museums of San Francisco, CA (Gift of Mark Adams); *2, 4* Photo: © RMN, Paris; *3* National Gallery of Scotland, Edinburgh
Griffin Photo: Australian Archives, Canberra
Grigi, de': (1) Guglielmo de' Grigi Gabinetto Fotografico, Soprintendenza ai Beni Artistici e Storici, Venice/Photo: Reale Fotografia Giacomelli, Venice
Grigorescu, Nicolae National Museum of Art of Romania, Bucharest
Grimaldi, Giovanni Francesco Royal Collection, Windsor Castle/© Her Majesty Queen Elizabeth II
Grimani Breviary Biblioteca Nazionale Marciana, Venice
Gris, Juan *1* Philadelphia Museum of Art, Philadelphia, PA (A.E. Gallatin Collection)/© DACS, 1996; *2* Hamburger Kunsthalle, Hamburg
Grisaille *1* Metropolitan Museum of Art, New York (Cloisters Collection, 1954; no. 54.1.2); *2* Photo: Scala, Florence; *3* Trustees of the National Gallery, London
Grof, Guillielmus de Bayerisches Nationalmuseum, Munich
Gröninger: (2) Gerhard Gröninger Photo: Bildarchiv Foto Marburg
Gröninger: (4) Johann Mauritz Gröninger Photo: Bildarchiv Foto Marburg
Gropius, Walter *1–2* Harvard University Art Museums, Cambridge, MA
Gros, Antoine-Jean *1–2* Photo: © RMN, Paris
Grosz, George Kunsthalle, Mannheim
Grotesque *1–2* Board of Trustees of the Victoria and Albert Museum, London
Grotto *1* Photo: Archivi Alinari, Florence; *2* Photo: © RMN, Paris
Group of Seven National Gallery of Canada, Ottawa/Photo: © Dr Naomi Jackson Groves
Gruber, Francis Tate Gallery, London/© ADAGP, Paris, and DACS, London, 1996

Grünewald, Matthias *1* Staatliche Kunsthalle, Karlsruhe; *2* Photo: Giraudon, Paris; *3* Bayerische Staatsgemäldesammlungen, Munich; *4* Sammlung Oskar Reinhart am Römerholz, Winterthur
Guadalajara Photo: Robert Harding Picture Library, London
Guadalajara, Palacio del Infantado Photo: Ampliaciones y Reproducciones MAS, Barcelona
Guanghan From *Wenwu*, v (1989), p. 4
Guan Tong National Palace Museum, Taipei
Guardi: (1) Giovanni Antonio Guardi *1* Staatliche Museen zu Berlin, Preussischer Kulturbesitz; *2* Photo: Scala, Florence
Guardi: (2) Francesco Guardi *1* Trustees of the British Museum, London; *2* National Gallery of Scotland, Edinburgh
Guariento Museo Biblioteca Archivio, Bassano del Grappa
Guarini, Guarino *1, 4* Photo: Archivi Alinari, Florence; *3* Syndics of Cambridge University Library, Cambridge
Guarino, Francesco Soprintendenza per i Beni Artistici e Storici, Naples
Guas, Juan Bibliothèque Nationale de France, Paris
Guatemala *2* Photo: Jorge Luján-Munoz; *3* Photo: Wheeler Photographics, Weston, MA/© Nick Wheeler; *4* Art Museum of the Americas (OAS), Washington, DC; *5* Peabody Museum, Harvard University, Cambridge, MA; *6* Photo: Christie's, New York
Gubbio Photo: Archivi Alinari, Florence
Gucci, Santi Andrzej Voellnagel, Warsaw/Photo: Edmund Kupiecki
Gudewerdt: (2) Hans Gudewerdt (ii) Eikenfude Church
Guedes, Amancio Photo: Tim Ostler
Guedes, Joaquim Photo: Joaquim Guedes, São Paulo
Guérard, Eugene von National Gallery of Australia, Canberra
Guercino *1–3* Photo: Scala, Florence; *4* Royal Collection, Windsor Castle/© Her Majesty Queen Elizabeth II
Guérin, Pierre *1–2* Photo: © RMN, Paris
Guggenbichler, Meinrad Photo: Bildarchiv Foto Marburg
Guglielmi, Gregorio Photo: Gabinetto Fotografico Nazionale, Istituto Centrale per il Catalogo e la Documentazione, Rome
Guidi, Domenico Photo: Archivi Alinari, Florence
Guido da Siena *1–2* Soprintendenza per i Beni Artistici e Storici, Siena/Photo: Fotografia Lensini Fabio, Siena
Guild British Library, London (MS. 07703, fol. 47/2)
Guillaume de Machaut Bibliothèque Nationale de France, Paris
Guindaleri, Pietro British Library (Harley MS. 3567)
Gu Kaizhi Trustees of the British Museum, London
Gumpp Photo: Bundesdenkmalamt, Vienna
Gundelach, Matthäus Kunsthistorisches Museum, Vienna
Gundestrup Cauldron Nationalmuseum, Copenhagen
Günther, Ignaz *1–2* Photo: Hirmer Fotoarchiv, Munich
Guo Xi National Palace Museum, Taipei
Gurk Cathedral Photo: Bundesdenkmalamt, Klagenfurt
Guro Museum Rietberg, Zurich/Photo: Eberhard Fischer
Guston, Philip Mr and Mrs Robert Lehrman, Washington, DC
Guttuso, Renato © DACS, 1996
Guyana *2* Photo: Denis Williams; *3* National Art Collection of Guyana/Photo: Winston Kendall
Guys, Constantin Musées de la Ville de Paris/© DACS, 1996
Gwalior *1–2* Photo: Michael D. Willis
Gwathmey, Charles Architectural Association, London/Photo: S. Groak
Gyantse Photo: Barry Till
Gyokuen Bonpō National Museum, Tokyo
Haarlem *1* Rijksmuseum, Amsterdam; *2* Frans Halsmuseum, Haarlem/Photo: Tom Haartsen
Habsburg, §I: (3) Maximilian I Bildarchiv, Österreichische Nationalbibliothek, Vienna
Habsburg, §I: (5) Charles V Photo: Patrimonio Nacional Archivo Fotografico, Madrid
Habsburg, §I: (7) Mary Photo: © ACL Brussels
Habsburg, §I: (8) Maximilian II Kunsthistorisches Museum, Vienna
Habsburg, §I: (10) Rudolf II Kunsthistorisches Museum, Vienna
Habsburg, §I: (18) Leopold William Kunsthistorisches Museum, Vienna